An Exceptional Rendez-vous

From February 8 to 15, 1987, Québec City will host one of the largest, most impressive sports events in America, as the world's best hockey players battle for the Rendez-Vous 87 Cup.

This match pitting the Soviet National Team against the National Hockey League's allstar players will give rise to grandiose celebrations where for seven days, galas, shows and popular festivities will light up the heart of Québec City.

This magnificent sports and arts event, which is associated with one of the world's largest Carnivals, promises to be filled with memorable moments in the fairy-tale surroundings of Québec City in the winter.

A MANDATE OF CONFIDENCE

January 1984 saw the governors of the National Hockey League entrust the Québec Nordiques with the mandate of presenting the 39th Allstar Game planned for Winter 1987.

From that time on, the project of making this sports bout an event of international caliber, bringing together the greatest names in the world of sports and the arts, began to take shape in the minds of its promoters.

And so was born the concept of RENDEZ-VOUS 87, launched officially in February 1986 in Hartford, Connecticut the day after the Allstar Game.

In accepting Québec City's project, the National League agreed to modify its regular schedule and bring its activities to a complete halt for five days, enabling the 1987 Allstar Game to become a genuine celebration of hockey at its best.

In doing so, the League showed its confidence in Rendez-Vous 87's president, Marcel Aubut, and in all Quebecers, who will be hosting this splendid event.

HOCKEY AT ITS BEST

The competition between the Soviet National Team and the National League's allstar players will take the form of a two-game series at the end of which there should be a winner. Should the teams be tied after the second game, overtime play will determine the winner.

The winning team will be presented the Rendez-Vous 87 Cup, a symbol of excellence and fraternity.

This great moment in sports history will not be celebrated on the ice of Québec City's Colisée alone. Throughout the streets of the city, events honoring hockey will be occurring.

Spectators will be offered a magnificent night parade of floats bearing the colors of the League's various hockey clubs. For the occasion, the NHL Hall of Fame will be moved to Quebec featuring hockey's greatest moments. Also, you may attend snow sculpture contests based on the theme of sports and hockey.

A GREAT CELEBRATION

This hockey extravaganza will be a great sports celebration but also a celebration of the world of arts where the greats of song will rub shoulders with painters, artists and musicians in a multitude of high-caliber activities.

Fashion, gastronomy, exhibitions and entertainment extravaganzas will mix with the festivities of the Québec City Winter Carnival to make this Rendez-vous a prestigious event.

This extraordinary combination of sports and cultural activities in North America's oldest French city will lend the event a unique character whose charm promises to be beyond compare.

A GROUP PROJECT

A non-profit Corporation is responsible for organizing Rendez-Vous 87 and will ensure the setting up and coordination of all Rendez-Vous 87 activities. Furthermore, this Corporation will see to it that all profits from Rendez-Vous 87 are donated to charitable organizations.

All public and private partners will contribute to ensure the success of this wide-ranging event, which will once again reflect Quebecers' hospitality and savoir-faire.

Finally, Rendez-Vous 87's festivities will have the great honor of being presided over by the Prime Minister of Canada, the Right Honorable Brian Mulroney.

Come share a great moment in sports history, an unforgettably charming, magnificent celebration, further proof of Québec's and Canada's dynamic character, in short, a special moment where the all eyes will be on Québec City.

1987, it's a Rendez-Vous!

The National Hockey League

Official Guide & Record Book

1986-87

Published by the National Hockey League.
Compiled by the NHL Communications Department
and the 21 NHL club Public Relations Directors.
Copyright © 1986 by the National Hockey League

The National Hockey League
Official Guide & Record Book/1986-87

Staff:
Senior editor: Gary Meagher; Executive editors: Benny Ercolani, Dan Leary; Associate editors: Steve Charendoff, Belinda Lerner; Editorial assistants: Jane Freer, Dave Roussy; Player Updates: Alison McLaughlin.

Consulting publishers: Dan Diamond, Peter McGoey.

Trade and retail distribution:
Cannon Book Distribution Ltd., Toronto 416/252-5207

Front cover photo: Bruce Bennett
Typesetting: Q Composition Inc., Toronto
Printing: The Alger Press Limited, Oshawa and Toronto

Printed in Canada
10 9 8 7 6 5 4 3 2 1

ISBN 0-920445-01-2

The National Hockey League
1155 Metcalfe Street, suite 960, Montreal, Quebec H3B 2W2
500 Fifth Avenue, 34th floor, New York, New York 10110
1 Greensboro Drive, suite 200, Toronto, Ontario M9W 1C8

Photo Credits

Special thanks to the Hockey Hall of Fame and Museum, Toronto and to the New York Rangers.

Historical photos: Bruce Bennett, Joe Bereswill, David Bier, Fran Byrne, Melchior Di Giacomo, Jerry Liebman, Rice Studio, Robert Shaver, Barton Silverman, Bruce Stotesbury, John Tremmel, Imperial Oil — Turofsky Collection, Hockey Hall of Fame.

Current photos: Graig Abel, Toronto; Bruce Bennett, NY Islanders, pgs. 150, 168, 169; George Kalinsky, NY Rangers; D. King, J. Henson Photographics, Washington; Jim Mackey, Detroit; Bob Mummery, Edmonton; Andre Pichette, Quebec; Richard Pilling, New Jersey; David W. Preston, St. Louis; Photography, Minnesota; Al Ruelle, Boston; Diane Sobolewski, Hartford; Brad Watson, Calgary; Bill Wippert, Buffalo.

Front cover photo: Bruce Bennett

Table of Contents

continued

Table of Contents continued

 **Introduction**

New features for 1986-87

Welcome to the 1986-87 edition of the *NHL Official Guide & Record Book.* This book continues the National Hockey League's commitment to produce the finest and most comprehensive publication in professional sports. No other book about hockey combines current and historical information in a manner that allows fans to do detailed research or read and browse for pleasure.

There are **many new features** in the 1986-87 *NHL Official Guide & Record Book:*

1. **Histories of the League**, its presidents and rules have been greatly expanded (pages 8, 114-116).

2. **Club information** now includes individual team home/road schedules, year-by-year draft selections, and a listing of team captains (pages 9 to 92).

3. **Player and Goaltender Registers** feature 400 new entries, reflecting increased coverage of junior, college, minor professional and European hockey (pages 195 to 348).

4. **NHL Record Book** has grown with the addition of several new individual records including career scoring by position and regular season overtime results (pages 143-163; overtime records: page 100).

5. **Biographies of Referees and Linesmen** (page 6-7).

6. **1986 All-Star Game Summary** and information on **Rendez-Vous '87**, a two-game series featuring the NHL's best and the stars of the Soviet Union (pages 157 and 162).

7. **1985-86 Transaction List** details every trade made by NHL clubs from October, 1985 to June, 1986 (page 351).

Enthusiastic response to the *NHL Official Guide & Record Book* has resulted in greatly increased availability of the book in the United States and Scandinavia this year.

Much of this success is due to continued improvements that are initiated by readers' comments. We welcome your suggestions.

Best wishes for an enjoyable NHL season in 1986-87.

National Hockey League

Organized November 22, 1917

Board of Governors

BOARD OF GOVERNORS — Officers
Chairman — William W. Wirtz
Vice-Chairman — Frank A. Griffiths
Secretary — Robert O. Swados

Boston Bruins
(Boston Professional Hockey Association, Inc.)
Paul A. Mooney — Governor
Harry Sinden — Alternate Governor

Buffalo Sabres
(Niagara Frontier Hockey Corporation)
Seymour H. Knox III — Governor
Northrup R. Knox — Alternate Governor
Robert O. Swados — Alternate Governor
W. Scott Bowman — Alternate Governor

Calgary Flames
(Calgary Flames Hockey Club)
Cliff Fletcher — Governor
Norman N. Green — Alternate Governor
Doug Mitchell — Alternate Governor

Chicago Black Hawks
(Chicago Blackhawk Hockey Team, Inc.)
William W. Wirtz — Governor
Thomas N. Ivan — Alternate Governor
Arthur M. Wirtz — Alternate Governor

Detroit Red Wings
(Detroit Red Wings, Inc.)
Michael Ilitch — Governor
James Devellano — Alternate Governor
James Lites — Alternate Governor

Edmonton Oilers
(Pocklington Amalgamated Sports Corp.)
Peter Pocklington — Governor
Glen Sather — Alternate Governor

Hartford Whalers
(Hartford Whalers Hockey Club)
Howard L. Baldwin — Governor
Emile Francis — Alternate Governor
Donald G. Conrad — Alternate Governor

Los Angeles Kings
(Los Angeles Kings, Inc.)
Jerry Buss — Governor
Ken Doi — Alternate Governor
Rogatien Vachon — Alternate Governor

Minnesota North Stars
(Northstar Hockey Partnership)
George Gund III — Governor
Gordon Gund — Alternate Governor
John F. Karr — Alternate Governor
Lou Nanne — Alternate Governor

Montreal Canadiens
(Le Club de Hockey Canadien Inc.)
Ronald Corey — Governor
Morgan McCammon — Alternate Governor
Serge Savard — Alternate Governor

New Jersey Devils
(Meadowlanders, Inc.)
John J. McMullen — Governor
Robert J. Butera — Alternate Governor
John C. Whitehead — Alternate Governor

New York Islanders
(Nassau Sports)
John O. Pickett, Jr. — Governor
William Torrey — Alternate Governor
William Skehan — Alternate Governor

New York Rangers
(New York Rangers Hockey Club — a division of Madison Square Garden Center, Inc.)
John H. Krumpe — Governor
Mel Lowell — Alternate Governor

Philadelphia Flyers
(Philadelphia Hockey Club, Inc.)
Jay T. Snider — Governor
Edward M. Snider — Alternate Governor
Ronald Rutenberg — Alternate Governor
Keith Allen — Alternate Governor

Pittsburgh Penguins
(Pittsburgh Penguins, Inc.)
J. Paul Martha — Governor
Eddie Johnston — Alternate Governor

Quebec Nordiques
(Le Club de Hockey Les Nordiques (1979) Société en commandite)
Marcel Aubut — Governor
Maurice Filion — Alternate Governor
Gilles Leger — Alternate Governor

St. Louis Blues
(St. Louis Blues Hockey Club, Inc.)
Harry Ornest — Governor
Mike Ornest — Alternate Governor
Jack Quinn — Alternate Governor
Maury Ornest — Alternate Governor
Ruth Ornest — Alternate Governor

Toronto Maple Leafs
(Maple Leafs Gardens Limited)
Harold E. Ballard — Governor
Arthur Gans — Alternate Governor

Vancouver Canucks
(Vancouver Hockey Club, Limited)
Frank A. Griffiths — Governor
Frank W. Griffiths — Alternate Governor
Arthur R. Griffiths — Alternate Governor

Washington Capitals
(Washington Hockey Limited Partnership)
Abe Pollin — Governor
Richard M. Patrick — Alternate Governor
David Poile — Alternate Governor

Winnipeg Jets
(8 Hockey Ventures, Inc.)
Barry L. Shenkarow — Governor
John B. Ferguson — Alternate Governor
Bill Davis — Alternate Governor

Referees and Linesmen

Ron Asselstine ... Linesman ... Joined NHL in 1979 ... 567 career NHL games ... Born November 6, 1946 in Toronto, Ont. ... Resides in Guelph, Ont. ... Chairman of "Make a Wish Foundation" in Guelph, a charity which grants wishes to terminally ill children ... Executive with Guelph City Fastball League and Ball Hockey League ... Married, two children.

Wayne Bonney ... Linesman ... Joined NHL in 1979 ... 521 career NHL games ... Born May 27, 1953 in Ottawa, Ont. ... Resides in Kirkland, Que. ... Coaches minor league soccer team in off-season ... Runs hockey school in off-season ... Married, one child.

Ryan Bozak ... Linesman ... Joined NHL in 1972 ... 1,032 career NHL games ... Born January 3, 1947 in Swift Current, Sask. ... Resides in San Diego, California ... Enjoys golf and tennis during off-season ... Has two children.

Gord Broseker ... Linesman ... Joined NHL in 1973 ... 821 career NHL games ... Born August 7, 1950 in Baltimore, Maryland ... Resides in Richmond, Virginia ... Played in the Texas Rangers baseball organization ... Married, one child.

Jim Christison ... Linesman ... Joined NHL in 1970 ... 1,122 career NHL games ... Born September 13, 1946 in Vancouver, B.C. ... Resides in Lake Oswego, Oregon ... Spends off-season doing community work with Forest Hills Elementary School ... Married, three children.

Kevin Collins ... Linesman ... Joined NHL in 1977 ... 726 career NHL games ... Born December 15, 1950 in Springfield, Mass. ... Resides in Springfield ... Owns and operates "Kevin Collins School of Officiating" ... Married, three children.

John D'Amico ... Linesman ... Joined NHL in 1964 ... 1,576 (21 as referee) career NHL games ... Born September 21, 1937 in Toronto, Ont. ... Resides in Rexdale, Ont. ... Co-Chairman of the Easter Seals Foundation ... involved with Villa Colombo Senior Citizens home ... Enjoys golf during off-season ... Married, four children.

Pat Dapuzzo ... Linesman ... Joined NHL in 1984 ... 93 career NHL games ... Born December 29, 1958 in Hoboken, New Jersey ... Resides in North Bergen, NJ. ... An avid weightlifter ... Single.

Mark Faucette ... Referee ... Joined NHL in 1985 ... Born June 9, 1958 in Springfield, Mass. ... Resides in Agawam, Mass. ... Organizes softball tournaments to raise funds for Boston Children's Hospital's "Jimmy Fund" ... Instructor at Western New England and Tom Berry Schools of Officiating during off-season ... Married.

Ron Finn ... Linesman ... Joined NHL staff in 1969 ... 1,327 career NHL games ... Born December 1, 1940 in Toronto, Ont. ... Resides in Brampton, Ont. ... Active in Canadian Special Olympics ... Enjoys gardening ... Married, four children.

Wayne Forsey ... Linesman ... Joined NHL in 1979 ... 549 career NHL games ... Born July 26, 1951 in Kamloops, B.C. ... Resides in Winnipeg, Man. ... Involved with Canadian Special Olympics and Big Brothers of Manitoba ... Married, two children.

Ron Fournier ... Referee ... Joined NHL in 1973 ... 390 career NHL games ... Born August 3, 1949 in Montreal, Que. ... Resides in St. Sauveur, Que. ... Owns "Ron Fournier Referee School" ... Active with several charitable societies and institutions ... Enjoys golf and fishing ... Single.

Kerry Fraser ... Referee ... Joined NHL in 1974 ... 357 career NHL games ... Born May 30, 1952 in Sarnia, Ont. ... Resides in Sarnia ... Instructor at referee's school during off-season ... Enjoys golf and racquetball ... Married, four children.

Gerard Gauthier ... Linesman ... Joined NHL in 1971 ... 1,142 career NHL games ... Born September 5, 1948 in Montreal, Que. ... Resides in Dollard-des-Ormeaux, Que. ... Instructor at officiating school during off-season ... An avid golfer ... Married, two children.

Terry Gregson ... Referee ... Joined NHL in 1979 ... 227 career NHL games ... Born November 7, 1953 in Guelph, Ont. ... Resides in Barrie, Ont. ... Active in Children's "Make a Wish Foundation" ... Speaks at athletic banquets and service club meetings ... Conducted officiating schools in Italy, France and the Netherlands during off-season ... Married.

Bob Hall ... Referee ... Joined NHL in 1981 ... 162 career NHL games ... Born September 8, 1952 in Penticton, B.C. ... Resides in Guelph, Ont. ... Teaches at officiating school run by B.C. government in off-season ... Married, three children.

Bob Hodges ... Linesman ... Joined NHL in 1972 ... 994 career NHL games ... Born August 16, 1944 in Hespeler, Ont. ... Resides in Hespeler ... Works at officiating school in off-season ... An avid outdoorsman and marksman ... Married, two children.

Ron Hoggarth ... Referee ... Joined NHL in 1971 ... 617 (50 as linesman) career NHL games ... Born April 2, 1948 in Barrie, Ont. ... Resides in Barrie ... Works with Children's "Make a Wish Foundation" in spare time ... Owns construction company ... Active in Special Olympics, Muscular Dystrophy and Canadian Cancer Society ... Married, two children.

League Offices

MONTREAL
960 Sun Life Building,
1155 Metcalfe Street,
Montreal, Que. H3B 2W2
Phone: 514/871-9220
Executive TWX: 610-421-3260
Central Registry TWX: 610-421-3188

ENVOY ID
Data Processing	NHLMTL.MIS
Administration	NHLMTL.ADM
Public Relations	NHLMTL.PR

NEW YORK
34th Floor, 500 Fifth Avenue,
New York, N.Y., 10110
Phone: 212/398-1100.
TWX: 710-581-2736

ENVOY ID
Administration	NHLNY.ADM
Public Relations	NHLNY.PR

TORONTO
Suite 200, 1 Greensboro Drive,
Rexdale, Ont., M9W 1C8
(Officiating) 416/245-2926.
(Central Scouting) 416/ 245-1813; 245-2926
TWX: 610-492-2703

ENVOY ID
Administration	NHLTOR.ADM
Central Scouting	NHLTOR.SCTG

Hockey Hall of Fame
Exhibition Place
Toronto, Ont. M6K 3C3
Phone: 416/595-1345
M.H. (Lefty) Reid — Director and Curator
Joseph Romain — Archivist/Administration
Esther Richards — Secretary
Ray Paquet — Display and Audio-Visual
Ray Bruce — Custodian
Kim Lennox — Library/Admissions

**National Hockey League
Players' Association**
65 Queen Street West
Suite 210
Toronto, Ont. M5H 2M5 Phone: 416/868-6574
Alan Eagleson — Executive Director
Sam Simpson — Director of Operations

League Departments

OFFICERS
President — John A. Ziegler, Jr.
Executive Vice-President — Brian F. O'Neill
Vice-President/General Counsel — Gilbert Stein
Vice-President of Finance and Treasurer — Kenneth G. Sawyer
Vice-President, NHL Project Development — Ian Morrison
Vice-President, Broadcasting — Joel Nixon
Vice-President, Marketing/Public Relations — Steve Ryan

MONTREAL

Administration
Brian O'Neill — Executive Vice President
Madeleine Supino — Secretary
Phil Scheuer — Director of Administration
Nancy Starnino — Secretary

Central Registry
Garry Lovegrove — Director of Central Registry
Madeleine Supino — Assistant Director

Communications
Gary Meagher — Director of Information Campbell Conference
Benny Ercolani — Associate Director of Information/Statistician
Steve Charendoff — Assistant Director of information, Campbell Conference

Computer Operations
Mario Carangi — Director of Data Processing/MIS
Miranda Ishak — Analyst/Programmer
Sharon Jardine — Programmer
Johanne Hinds — Operations

Finance
Kenneth G. Sawyer — Vice-President of Finance and Treasurer
Donald P. Grinton — Director of Accounting
Mary Skiadopoulos — Accounting Supervisor
John Leyland — Accountant
Doris Long — Secretary
Lynne Blagrave — Pension Supervisor
Vivianne Chen — Secretary
Jocelyne Comeau — Accounting Clerk
Mike Humes — Assistant Accountant

Office Services
Jeff Boyle — Administrative Assistant
Jean Huard — Printer
Robert Bouchard — Office Assistant
Linda Rotaple — Secretary
Marcia Golding — Receptionist

NEW YORK

Broadcasting
Joel Nixon — Vice-President, Broadcasting
Lois Cutler — Secretary

Finance
Patricia Cassell-Cooper — Controller
Theresa Baione — Assistant Controller
Ivonne Merchant — Secretary

Legal Department
Gilbert Stein — Vice-President/General Counsel
Pat Honig — Assistant

Marketing and Communications
Steve Ryan — Vice-President, Marketing and Public Relations
Lucia Ripi — Secretary
Steve Flatow — Director of Marketing/Sales
Maria Pace — Secretary
Dan Leary — Director of Information, Wales Conference
Linda Bair — Meetings and Special Events Manager
Maureen Brady — Marketing Services Manager
Belinda Lerner — Associate Manager, Public Relations
Stu Hackel — Editor, Goal Magazine
John Sohigian — Associate Manager, Marketing Services

Office Administration
Mike Rosenblum — Administrative Assistant
Lola Skaro — Receptionist

President's Staff
Susan Rudin — Assistant to the President

Security
Frank Torpey — Director of Security

TORONTO
Ian Morrison — Vice President, NHL Project Development
Jim Gregory — Executive Director of Hockey Operations
John McCauley — Director of Officiating
Bryan Lewis — Coordinator of Development/Supervisor of Officials
Pierre Dorion — Central Scouting
Kevin Prendergast — Central Scouting
Al Wiseman — Assistant Director of Security

Secretarial Staff
Irene Puddester, Dorothy Reeves, Mary Keenan

Officiating Supervisory Staff
John Ashley, Matt Pavelich, Lou Maschio

Central Scouting Staff
John Andersen, Mike Antonovich, Jack Barzee, Mike Donaldson, Gary Eggleston, Laurence Ferguson, Michel Georges, Doug Hinton, Tom Martin, David Prior, Marcel Pronovost, Jack Timmins, Barry Trapp

---

Swede Knox ... Linesman ... Joined NHL in 1971 ... 1,106 career NHL games ... Born March 2, 1948 in Edmonton, Alta. ... Resides in Edmonton ... Instructor at Western Pro-Am School of Officiating during off-season ... Enjoys carpentry ... Married, two children.

Don Koharski ... Referee ... Joined NHL in 1977 ... 370 (163 as linesman) career NHL games ... Born December 2, 1955 in Halifax, N.S. ... Resides in Burlington, Ont. ... Operates a referee's school in off-season ... An avid golfer ... Married, two children.

Brad Lazarowich ... Linesman ... In his first season as an NHL official ... Born August 4, 1962 in Vancouver, B.C. ... Resides in Vancouver ... Married.

Dan Marouelli ... Referee ... Joined NHL in 1982 ... 85 career NHL games ... Born July 16, 1955 in Edmonton, Alta. ... Resides in Barrie, Ont. ... Coaches minor league soccer team in off-season ... Worked as a firefighter at Canadian Forces Base (Borden) during off-season ... Married, three children.

Dan McCourt ... Linesman ... Joined NHL in 1981 ... 544 career NHL games ... Born August 14, 1954 in Sudbury, Ont. ... Resides in Falconbridge, Ont. ... Enjoys hunting and fishing during off-season ... Single.

Bill McCreary ... Referee ... Joined NHL in 1982 ... 48 career NHL games ... Born November 17, 1955 in Guelph, Ont. ... Employed by a roofing company during the off-season ... Enjoys golf and baseball ... Married, two children.

Randy Mitton ... Linesman ... Joined NHL in 1972 ... 907 career NHL games ... Born September 22, 1950 in Fredericton, N.B. ... Resides in LeDuc, Alta. ... Involved with the Elks Club and minor league softball during the off-season ... Instructor at the Western Pro-Am School of Officiating ... Married, two children.

Denis Morel ... Referee ... Joined NHL in 1972 ... 585 career NHL games ... Born December 13, 1948 in Quebec City, Que. ... Resides in Trois Rivieres, Que. ... Involved in fund-raising for handicapped persons through the Rotary Club ... Operates "Ron Fournier" Referee School ... Married, two children.

Bob Myers ... Referee ... Joined NHL in 1967 ... 1,110 (137 as linesman) career NHL games ... Born October 5, 1940 in Ancaster, Ont. ... Resides in Copetown, Ont.. ... Raises prize sheep and operates large apple orchard in off-season ... Coaches minor league baseball ... Married, four children.

Dave Newell ... Referee ... Joined NHL in 1967 ... 960 career NHL games ... Born February 25, 1945 in Sudbury, Ont. ... Resides in Copper Cliff, Ont. ... President of NHL Officials Association ... Involved in the community with Ronald McDonald House (for parents with sick children), minor hockey and a figure skating club ... Married, three children.

Mike Noeth ... Referee ... Joined NHL in 1979 ... 72 career NHL games ... Born December 27, 1958 in Boston, Mass. ... Resides in Shrewsbury, Mass. ... Studying financial planning and stock market during the off-season ... Enjoys cooking and gardening ... Married, one child.

Mark Pare ... Linesman ... Joined NHL in 1979 ... 551 career NHL games ... Born August 26, 1957 in Windsor, Ont. ... Resides in Windsor ... Enjoys gardening and golf during off-season ... Married, one child.

Jerry Pateman ... Linesman ... Joined NHL in 1982 ... 97 career NHL games ... Born January 12, 1958 in The Hague, Netherlands ... Resides in Tecumseh, Ont. ... Plays golf and baseball during the off-season ... Married, two children.

Dan Schachte ... Linesman ... Joined NHL in 1982 ... 246 career NHL games ... Born July 13, 1958 in Madison, Wisconsin ... Resides in Madison ... Completing Engineering Degree in off-season ... An avid golfer ... Single.

Ray Scapinello ... Linesman ... Joined NHL in 1971 ... 1,222 career NHL games ... Born November 5, 1946 in Guelph, Ont. ... Resides in Guelph ... Works with an industrial sales company in off-season ... Also coaches children's softball team ... Married, one child.

Rob Shick ... Referee ... Joined NHL in 1984 ... Three career NHL games ... Born December 4, 1957 in Port Alberni, B.C. ... Resides in Port Alberni ... Studied retail management in off-season ... Conducted officiating school during off-season ... Avid baseball player ... Single.

Paul Stewart ... Referee ... Joined NHL in 1985 ... Born March 21, 1955 in Boston, Mass. ... Resides in Jamaica Plain, Mass. ... A former police officer in Yarmouth, Mass. ... Attended real estate school in off-season ... Also umpires baseball during off-season ... Single.

Leon Stickle ... Linesman ... Joined NHL in 1970 ... 1,251 career NHL games ... Born April 20, 1948 in Toronto, Ont. ... Resides in Mount Forest, Ont. ... Involved with "Meals on Wheels", Special Olympics and minor league baseball ... Assisted in golf tournaments to raise money for Heart Foundation, Muscular Dystrophy and Ronald McDonald House during off-season ... Married, three children.

Andy vanHellemond ... Referee ... Joined NHL in 1971 ... 863 career NHL games ... Born February 16, 1948 in Winnipeg, Man. ... Resides in Guelph, Ont. ... Instructor at the Western Pro-Am School of Officiating during off-season ... Married, three children.

Mark Vines ... Linesman ... Joined NHL in 1984 ... 166 career NHL games ... Born December 3, 1960 in Kitchener, Ont. ... Resides in Elmira, Ont. ... Attends university during the off-season ... Single.

League Presidents

Top: The NHL's first president, Frank Calder, at left, presents the Calder trophy to Boston goaltender Frank Brimsek as the outstanding rookie of 1938-39. Middle: Mervyn "Red" Dutton, president from 1943-46, at right, congratulates Clarence S. Campbell who served as NHL president from 1946 to 1977. Bottom: John A. Ziegler, Jr., president from 1977 to date.

Frank Calder
President, 1917-1943

After an illustrious tenure as secretary of the National Hockey Association, Frank Calder was elected as the first president of the National Hockey League when the League was formed in 1917. He served in this capacity until his death on February 4, 1943.

Born in England in 1877, Calder came to Canada at the turn of the century as a school teacher, but turned to sports writing in 1909. His forthright writing style won him the attention and respect of Montreal Canadiens' owner George Kennedy whose support helped Calder to the position of NHL president.

For nearly 26 years, Calder worked hard to change the League from a small-time circuit to a grand international sports organization. Among his many achievements, Calder guided the NHL through its first expansion into the U.S., including the addition of the Boston Bruins in 1924 and the Chicago Blackhawks, Detroit Cougars and New York Rangers in 1926.

To commemorate his years of service, the League established the Calder Memorial Trophy to honor the rookie of the year at the conclusion of each season. Additionally, Calder was elected to the Hockey Hall of Fame in 1945 as one of its first inductees.

Mervyn "Red" Dutton
President, 1943-46

Born on July 23, 1898 in Russell, Manitoba, Mervyn "Red" Dutton succeeded Frank Calder as the second president of the NHL. For two seasons, 1943-44 and 1944-45, Dutton remained at the head of the League before resuming his career in private business. Most remembered for his rugged playing style, Dutton overcame severe war injuries to skate as a professional for over a decade. After anchoring the defense for Calgary in the Western Hockey League from 1921 to 1925, Dutton signed with the NHL's Montreal Maroons. He stayed with the Maroons through 1930 when he joined the New York Americans. In 1936, he took over coaching and managing that club and remained there until 1942 when the team disbanded.

Upon Frank Calder's death in 1943, Dutton became president of the NHL, a position he maintained until Clarence Campbell assumed the role in 1946. Dutton was elected to the Hockey Hall of Fame in 1958. Currently, the 88-year-old Dutton resides in Calgary, Alberta.

Clarence Campbell
President, 1946-77

Clarence Campbell was a Rhodes Scholar who was born July 9, 1905 in Fleming, Saskatchewan. In 1926, a 20-year-old Campbell graduated from the University of Alberta with bachelor of arts and bachelor of law degrees.

Following his studies at Oxford, England, Campbell returned to Canada to begin his law practise. Forever active in sports, he also became an NHL referee, working 155 regular-season games and twelve Stanley Cup playoff contests through 1939 when he joined the Canadian Armed Forces for the duration of World War II.

On September 5, 1946, Campbell became the NHL's third president succeeding Mervyn "Red" Dutton. Within a year of his appointment, he established the NHL Players' Pension Plan which has since become the prototype for other professional sports leagues.

Campbell led the League through its greatest era of expansion in 1967 when the NHL doubled in size from six to twelve teams. In 1972, he also succeeded in breaking ground in a new era of international competition, when, for the first time in hockey history, Canada's finest NHL talent faced-off against the Soviet Union's elite in an eight-game challenge series.

Elected to the Hockey Hall of Fame in 1966, Campbell also received the Lester Patrick Trophy for "outstanding service to hockey in the United States" in 1972. He retired from the NHL in 1977, but continued to stay close to the League until his death in 1984.

John A. Ziegler, Jr.
President, 1977 to date

John A. Ziegler, Jr., President and Chief Executive Officer of the National Hockey League, was born in Grosse Pointe,, Michigan on February 9, 1934.

He graduated from the University of Michigan in 1957, earning a bachelor of arts and *juris doctor* degrees. Upon graduation he joined the Detroit law firm of Dickinson, Wright, McKean and Cudlip and became a partner in the firm in 1964. In 1969 he left the firm and in September of 1970 he set up his own firm, Ziegler, Dykhouse & Wise. He continued as senior partner in the firm until assuming his present position in September, 1977.

In 1959 he began to do legal work for Olympia Stadium, the Detroit Red Wings and Mr. Bruce Norris. He continued to serve these clients in various capacities until his election as president of the National Hockey League. In 1966 he joined the NHL Board of Governors as an alternate Governor for the Detroit Red Wings and, as such, worked on many of the NHL's committees and was involved in various aspects of the League's litigation as well as relations and negotiations with the Players' Association.

In June of 1976, he succeeded William Wirtz as Chairman of the National Hockey League Board of Governors.

An ardent sports fan, Ziegler played amateur hockey in the Detroit area from 1949 to 1969. He has continued to make his home in the Detroit area (Ortonville, Michigan) while maintaining offices in Montreal and New York.

Boston Bruins
1985-86 Results: 37w-31L-12T 86 PTS. Third, Adams Division

Ray Bourque

Schedule

	Home		Away
Oct. Thur. 9 Calgary		**Oct.** Sat. 11 New Jersey	
Sun. 12 Hartford		Tue. 14 Winnipeg	
Thur. 30 Montreal		Thur. 16 Minnesota	
Nov. Sun. 2 Buffalo		Sat. 18 Los Angeles	
Thur. 13 Edmonton		Wed. 22 Vancouver	
Sat. 15 New Jersey		Fri. 24 Edmonton	
Thur. 20 Montreal		Sun. 26 Calgary	
Sat. 22 St. Louis		**Nov.** Sat. 1 Philadelphia	
Sat. 29 Buffalo		Wed. 5 Buffalo	
Dec. Thur. 4 Quebec		Sat. 8 Quebec	
Sat. 6 Philadelphia*		Wed. 12 Pittsburgh	
Sun. 7 NY Islanders		Mon. 17 Montreal	
Thur. 11 Vancouver		Wed. 19 Buffalo	
Thur. 18 Hartford		Mon. 24 Toronto	
Sat. 20 Chicago		Wed. 26 Washington	
Jan. Mon. 5 Montreal		Fri. 28 Buffalo	
Thur. 8 Detroit		**Dec.** Sat. 13 Montreal	
Sat. 10 Philadelphia*		Sun. 14 Quebec	
Mon. 12 NY Rangers		Tue. 23 Hartford	
Thur. 15 Hartford		Sat. 27 Los Angeles	
Sat. 17 Pittsburgh*		Tue. 30 St. Louis	
Thur. 22 Montreal		**Jan.** Fri. 2 New Jersey	
Sat. 24 Calgary*		Sat. 3 NY Islanders	
Mon. 26 Buffalo		Wed. 14 Hartford	
Thur. 29 Hartford		Tue. 20 Quebec	
Sat. 31 Winnipeg		**Feb.** Sun. 1 NY Rangers	
Feb. Thur. 5 Pittsburgh		Sat. 14 Toronto	
Sat. 7 Toronto*		Mon. 16 Montreal	
Sun. 8 Quebec*		Wed. 18 Buffalo	
Thur. 26 Quebec		Fri. 20 Winnipeg	
Sat. 28 Buffalo*		Sat. 21 Minnesota	
Mar. Mon. 2 Detroit		Wed. 25 Hartford	
Sat. 7 Washington*		**Mar.** Tue. 3 NY Islanders	
Thur. 12 St. Louis		Thur. 5 Hartford	
Sat. 14 Chicago*		Wed. 11 NY Rangers	
Thur. 19 Minnesota		Tue. 17 Detroit	
Sat. 21 Los Angeles*		Sun. 22 Washington*	
Thur. 26 Edmonton		Sun. 29 Chicago	
Sat. 28 Vancouver*		Tue. 31 Quebec	
April Sun. 5 Quebec		**April** Sat. 4 Montreal	

*Denotes afternoon game.

Home Starting Times:
Weeknights . . . . 7:35 p.m.
Saturdays & Sundays . . . . 7:05 p.m.
Matinees . . . . 1:15 p.m.

Franchise date: November 1, 1924

 63rd NHL Season

Year-by-Year Record

Season	GP	Home W	L	T	Road W	L	T	Overall W	L	T	GF	GA	Pts.	Finished	Playoff Result
1985-86	80	24	9	7	13	22	5	37	31	12	311	288	86	3rd, Adams Div.	Lost Div. Semi-Final
1984-85	80	21	15	4	15	19	6	36	34	10	303	287	82	4th, Adams Div.	Lost Div. Semi-Final
1983-84	80	25	12	3	24	13	3	49	25	6	336	261	104	1st, Adams Div.	Lost Div. Semi-Final
1982-83	80	28	6	6	22	14	4	50	20	10	327	228	110	1st, Adams Div.	Lost Conf. Championship
1981-82	80	24	12	4	19	15	6	43	27	10	323	285	96	2nd, Adams Div.	Lost Div. Final
1980-81	80	26	10	4	11	20	9	37	30	13	316	272	87	2nd, Adams Div.	Lost Prelim. Round
1979-80	80	27	9	4	19	12	9	46	21	13	310	234	105	2nd, Adams Div.	Lost Quarter-Final
1978-79	80	25	10	5	18	13	9	43	23	14	316	270	100	1st, Adams Div.	Lost Semi-Final
1977-78	80	29	6	5	22	12	6	51	18	11	333	218	113	1st, Adams Div.	Lost Final
1976-77	80	27	7	6	22	16	2	49	23	8	312	240	106	1st, Adams Div.	Lost Final
1975-76	80	27	5	8	21	10	9	48	15	17	313	237	113	1st, Adams Div.	Lost Semi-Final
1974-75	80	29	5	6	11	21	8	40	26	14	345	245	94	2nd, Adams Div.	Lost Prelim. Round
1973-74	78	33	4	2	19	13	7	52	17	9	349	221	113	1st, East Div.	Lost Final
1972-73	78	27	10	2	24	12	3	51	22	5	330	235	107	2nd, East Div.	Lost Quarter-Final
1971-72	**78**	**28**	**4**	**7**	**26**	**9**	**4**	**54**	**13**	**11**	**330**	**204**	**119**	**1st, East Div.**	**Won Stanley Cup**
1970-71	78	33	4	2	24	10	5	57	14	7	399	207	121	1st, East Div.	Lost Quarter-Final
1969-70	**76**	**27**	**3**	**8**	**13**	**14**	**11**	**40**	**17**	**19**	**277**	**216**	**99 2nd,**	**East Div.**	**Won Stanley Cup**
1968-69	76	29	3	6	13	15	10	42	18	16	303	221	100	2nd, East Div.	Lost Semi-Final
1967-68	74	22	9	6	15	18	4	37	27	10	259	216	84	3rd, East Div.	Lost Quarter-Final
1966-67	70	10	21	4	7	22	6	17	43	10	182	253	44	6th,	Out of Playoffs
1965-66	70	15	17	3	6	26	3	21	43	6	174	275	48	5th,	Out of Playoffs
1964-65	70	12	17	6	9	26	0	21	43	6	166	253	48	6th,	Out of Playoffs
1963-64	70	13	15	7	5	25	5	18	40	12	170	212	48	6th,	Out of Playoffs
1962-63	70	7	18	10	7	21	7	14	39	17	198	281	45	6th,	Out of Playoffs
1961-62	70	9	22	4	6	25	4	15	47	8	177	306	38	6th,	Out of Playoffs
1960-61	70	13	17	5	2	25	8	15	42	13	176	254	43	6th,	Out of Playoffs
1959-60	70	21	11	3	7	23	5	28	34	8	220	241	64	5th,	Out of Playoffs
1958-59	70	21	11	3	11	18	6	32	29	9	205	215	73	2nd,	Lost Semi-Final
1957-58	70	15	14	6	12	14	9	27	28	15	199	194	69	4th,	Lost Final
1956-57	70	20	9	6	14	15	6	34	24	12	195	174	80	3rd,	Lost Final
1955-56	70	14	14	7	9	20	6	23	34	13	147	185	59	5th,	Out of Playoffs
1954-55	70	16	10	9	7	16	12	23	26	21	169	188	67	4th,	Lost Semi-Final
1953-54	70	22	8	5	10	20	5	32	28	10	177	181	74	4th,	Lost Semi-Final
1952-53	70	19	10	6	9	19	7	28	29	13	152	172	69	3rd,	Lost Final
1951-52	70	15	12	8	10	17	8	25	29	16	162	176	66	4th,	Lost Semi-Final
1950-51	70	13	12	10	9	18	8	22	30	18	178	197	62	4th,	Lost Semi-Final
1949-50	70	15	12	8	7	20	8	22	32	16	198	228	60	5th,	Out of Playoffs
1948-49	60	18	10	2	11	13	6	29	23	8	178	163	66	2nd,	Lost Semi-Final
1947-48	60	12	8	10	11	16	3	23	24	13	167	168	59	3rd,	Lost Semi-Final
1946-47	60	18	7	5	8	16	6	26	23	11	190	175	63	3rd,	Lost Semi-Final
1945-46	50	11	5	4	13	13	4	24	18	8	167	156	56	2nd,	Lost Final
1944-45	50	11	12	2	5	18	2	16	30	4	179	219	36	4th,	Lost Semi-Final
1943-44	50	15	8	2	4	18	3	19	26	5	223	268	43	5th,	Out of Playoffs
1942-43	50	17	3	5	7	14	4	24	17	9	195	176	57	2nd,	Lost Final
1941-42	48	17	4	3	8	13	3	25	17	6	160	118	56	3rd,	Lost Semi-Final
1940-41	**48**	**15**	**4**	**5**	**12**	**4**	**8**	**27**	**8**	**13**	**168**	**102**	**67 1st,**		**Won Stanley Cup**
1939-40	48	20	3	1	11	9	4	31	12	5	170	98	67	1st,	Lost Semi-Final
1938-39	**48**	**20**	**2**	**2**	**16**	**8**	**0**	**36**	**10**	**2**	**156**	**76**	**74 1st,**		**Won Stanley Cup**
1937-38	48	18	3	3	12	8	4	30	11	7	142	89	67	1st, Amn. Div.	Lost Semi-Final
1936-37	48	9	11	4	14	7	3	23	18	7	120	110	53	2nd, Amn. Div.	Lost Quarter-Final
1935-36	48	15	8	1	7	12	5	22	20	6	92	83	50	2nd, Amn. Div.	Lost Quarter-Final
1934-35	48	17	7	0	9	9	6	26	16	6	129	112	58	1st, Amn. Div.	Lost Semi-Final
1933-34	48	11	11	2	7	14	3	18	25	5	111	130	41	4th, Amn. Div.	Out of Playoffs
1932-33	48	20	2	3	5	13	5	25	15	8	124	88	58	1st, Amn. Div.	Lost Semi-Final
1931-32	48	11	10	3	4	11	9	15	21	12	122	117	42	4th, Amn. Div.	Out of Playoffs
1930-31	44	17	1	5	11	9	1	28	10	6	143	90	62	1st, Amn. Div.	Lost Semi-Final
1929-30	44	23	1	0	15	4	1	38	5	1	179	98	77	1st, Amn. Div.	Lost Final
1928-29	**44**	**16**	**6**	**1**	**10**	**7**	**4**	**26**	**13**	**5**	**89**	**52**	**57 1st,**	**Amn. Div.**	**Won Stanley Cup**
1927-28	44	13	4	5	7	9	6	20	13	11	77	70	51	1st, Amn. Div.	Lost Semi-Final
1926-27	44	15	7	0	6	13	3	21	20	3	97	89	45	2nd, Amn. Div.	Lost final
1925-26	36	10	7	1	7	10	1	17	15	4	92	85	38	4th,	Out of Playoffs
1924-25	30	3	12	0	3	12	0	6	24	0	49	119	12	6th,	Out of Playoffs

1986-87 Player Personnel

FORWARDS

	Ht.	Wt.	Place of Birth	Date	1985-86 Club
BERALDO, Paul	5-11	175	Hamilton, Ont.	10/5/67	Sault Ste. Marie
BURRIDGE, Randy	5-9	180	Fort Erie, Ont.	1/7/66	Peterborough-Boston
BYERS, Lyndon	6-1	190	Nipawin, Sask.	2/29/64	Milwaukee-Moncton-Boston
CARTER, John	5-10	175	Winchester, Mass.	5/3/63	RPI-Boston
COURTNALL, Geoff	6-0	185	Victoria, B.C.	8/18/62	Moncton-Boston
CROWDER, Keith	6-0	195	Windsor, Ont.	1/6/59	Boston
FOSTER, Dwight	5-11	190	Toronto, Ont.	4/2/57	Detroit-Boston
GRADIN, Thomas	5-11	170	Solleftea, Sweden	2/18/56	Vancouver
JOHNSTON, Greg	6-1	190	Barrie, Ont.	1/14/65	Moncton-Boston
KASPER, Steve	5-8	170	Montreal, Que.	9/28/61	Boston
KOSTYNSKI, Doug	6-1	170	Castlegar, B.C.	2/23/63	Moncton
LINSEMAN, Ken	5-11	175	Kingston, Ont.	8/11/58	Boston
MARKWART, Nevin	5-10	185	Toronto, Ont.	12/9/64	Boston
McCARTHY, Tom	6-2	200	Toronto, Ont.	7/31/60	Minnesota
MIDDLETON, Rick	5-11	175	Toronto, Ont.	12/4/53	Boston
MILLER, Jay	6-2	205	Wellesley, Mass.	7/16/60	Moncton-Boston
NEELY, Cam	6-1	205	Comox, B.C.	6/6/65	Vancouver
NIENHUIS, Kraig	6-2	205	Sarnia, Ont.	5/9/61	Boston
PASIN, Dave	6-1	205	Edmonton, Alta.	7/8/66	Boston
PODLOSKI, Ray	6-2	210	Edmonton, Alta.	1/5/66	Portland
REID, Dave	6-0	215	Toronto, Ont.	5/15/64	Moncton-Boston
SIMMER, Charlie	6-3	205	Terrace Bay, Ont.	3/20/54	Boston
SLEIGHER, Louis	5-11	200	Nouvelle, Que.	10/23/58	Boston
SWEENEY, Bob	6-3	210	Concord, Mass.	1/25/64	Boston College

DEFENSEMEN

BLUM, John	6-3	205	Detroit, Mich.	10/8/59	Moncton-Boston
BOURQUE, Ray	5-11	210	Montreal, Que.	12/28/60	Boston
CAMPBELL, Wade	6-4	220	Peace River, Alta.	1/2/61	Sherbrooke-Winnipeg-Moncton-Boston
COTE, Alain	6-0	200	Montmagny, Que.	4/4/67	Granby-Moncton-Boston
CURRAN, Brian	6-5	215	Toronto, Ont.	11/5/63	Boston
FITZSIMMONS, Paul	6-2	205	Wethersfield, Conn.	8/25/63	Northeastern
HAWGOOD, Greg	5-8	175	Edmonton, Alta.	8/10/68	Kamloops
HYNES, Gord	6-1	165	Montreal, Que.	7/22/66	Medicine Hat
KLUZAK, Gord	6-4	210	Climax, Sask.	3/4/64	Boston
LARSON, Reed	6-0	195	Minneapolis, Minn.	7/30/56	Detroit-Boston
PEDERSEN, Allen	6-3	180	Edmonton, Alta.	1/13/65	Moncton
PREMAK, Garth	6-1	185	Ituna, Sask.	3/15/68	New Westminster
SIMONETTI, Frank	6-1	185	Melrose, Mass.	9/11/62	Moncton-Boston
THELIN, Mats	5-10	185	Stockholm, Sweden	3/30/61	Moncton-Boston
THELVEN, Michael	5-11	180	Stockholm, Sweden	1/7/61	Boston

GOALTENDERS

DASKALAKIS, Cleon	5-9	175	Boston, Mass.	9/29/62	Moncton-Boston
KEANS, Doug	5-7	190	Pembroke, Ont.	1/7/58	Boston
LAROCHELLE, Allan	5-9	185	Pontiez, Sask.	10/27/64	Milwaukee-Moncton
RANFORD, Bill	5-10	170	Brandon, Man.	12/12/66	New Westminster-Boston
RIGGIN, Pat	5-9	175	Kincardine, Ont.	5/26/59	Washington-Boston

Coach and General Manager

GORING, ROBERT THOMAS (BUTCH)
Coach, Boston Bruins. Born in St. Boniface, Man., October 22, 1949.
A disciple of such noteworthy NHL coaches as Al Arbour and Bob Pulford, Butch Goring took over the Boston coaching job on May 6, 1985. In his new role, Goring earned the same kind of respect around the NHL as he did during his illustrious playing days, which were highlighted by four Stanley Cup championships with the New York Islanders and the Conn Smythe Trophy as playoff MVP in 1981. During the 1984-85 campaign, Goring assumed the role of player-assistant coach with the Islanders and continued in the dual role after being traded to Boston. In 1107 NHL games, Goring amassed 375 goals and 513 assists for 888 career points.

SINDEN, HARRY JAMES
General Manager, Boston Bruins. Born in Collins Bay, Ont., September 14, 1932.
Harry Sinden never played a game in the NHL but stepped into the Bruins' organization with an impressive coaching background in minor professional hockey and his continued excellence has earned him a place in the Hockey Hall of Fame as one of the true builders in hockey history. In 1965-66 as playing-coach of Oklahoma City Blazers in the CPHL, Sinden led the club to second place in the regular standings and then to eight straight playoff victories for the Jack Adams Trophy. After five years in OHA Senior hockey — including 1958 with the World Amateur Champion Whitby Dunlops — Sinden was named playing-coach in the old Eastern Professional League and its successor, the Central Professional League. Under his guidance, the Bruins of 1967-68 made the playoffs for the first time in nine seasons, finishing third in the East Division, and were nosed out of first place in 1968-69 by Montreal. In 1969-70, Sinden led the Bruins to their first Stanley Cup win since 1940-41. The following season he went into private business but returned to the hockey scene in the summer of 1972 when he was appointed coach of Team Canada. He moulded that group of NHL stars into a powerful unit and led them into an exciting eight-game series against the Soviet national team in September of 1972. Team Canada emerged the winner by a narrow margin with a record of four wins, three losses and one tie. Sinden then returned to the Bruins organization early in the 1972-73 season. Sinden took over as the Bruins' coach in February, after replacing Gerry Cheevers. Boston finished 11-10-3 with Sinden behind the bench before being defeated by Montreal in five games in the Adams Division semi-finals.

Rick Middleton checked by Tomas Jonsson of the New York Islanders.

1985-86 Scoring
Regular Season

*—rookie

Pos	#	Player	Team	GP	G	A	Pts	+/−	PIM	PP	SH	GW	OT	S	%
F	18	Keith Crowder	BOS	78	38	46	84	14	177	20	0	4	1	184	20.7
F	13	Ken Linseman	BOS	64	23	58	81	15	97	8	0	3	0	132	17.4
F	10	Barry Pederson	BOS	79	29	47	76	19	60	12	0	6	0	192	15.1
D	7	Ray Bourque	BOS	74	19	57	76	17	68	11	0	3	0	289	6.6
D	28	Reed Larson	DET	67	19	41	60	36−	109	11	0	0	1	205	9.3
			BOS	13	3	4	7	5	8	1	0	0	0	41	7.3
			Total	80	22	45	67	31−	117	12	0	0	1	246	8.9
F	23	Charlie Simmer	BOS	55	36	24	60	12	42	14	0	5	1	141	25.5
F	16	Rick Middleton	BOS	49	14	30	44	17	10	4	2	0	0	100	14.0
F	12	*Randy Burridge	BOS	52	17	25	42	17	28	1	0	2	0	90	18.9
F	11	Steve Kasper	BOS	80	17	23	40	10−	73	1	3	1	1	149	11.4
D	6	Gord Kluzak	BOS	70	8	31	39	3	155	3	0	0	0	114	7.0
F	32	Geoff Courtnall	BOS	64	21	16	37	1	61	2	0	4	0	161	13.0
F	37	*Dave Pasin	BOS	71	18	19	37	1−	50	4	0	3	0	116	15.5
F	38	*Kraig Nienhuis	BOS	70	16	14	30	10−	37	3	0	2	1	120	13.3
D	22	*Michael Thelven	BOS	60	6	20	26	7	48	1	0	0	0	108	5.6
F	17	Nevin Markwart	BOS	65	7	15	22	2−	207	0	0	1	0	42	16.7
F	36	Dave Reid	BOS	37	10	10	20	2	10	4	0	1	1	53	18.9
F	20	Dwight Foster	DET	55	6	12	18	13−	48	1	1	0	0	41	14.6
			BOS	13	0	0	0	5−	4	0	0	0	0	8	.0
			Total	68	6	12	18	18−	52	1	1	0	0	49	12.2
D	33	John Blum	BOS	61	1	7	8	8	80	0	0	0	0	34	2.9
D	26	Mike Milbury	BOS	22	3	5	7	1	102	0	0	0	0	20	15.0
D	34	Brian Curran	BOS	43	2	5	7	6	192	0	0	0	0	23	8.7
D	25	Louis Sleigher	BOS	13	4	2	6	4−	20	0	0	1	0	18	22.2
D	26	*Alain Cote	BOS	32	0	6	6	5	14	0	0	0	0	15	.0
D	27	Mats Thelin	BOS	31	2	3	5	3	29	1	0	0	0	29	6.9
F	29	*Jay Miller	BOS	46	3	0	3	3−	178	0	0	0	1	21	14.3
F	8	Lyndon Byers	BOS	5	0	2	2	1	9	0	0	0	0	1	.0
F	39	Greg Johnston	BOS	20	0	2	2	1−	0	0	0	0	0	11	.0
D	21	Frank Simonetti	BOS	17	1	0	1	1−	14	0	0	0	0	8	12.5
G	31	Doug Keans	BOS	30	0	1	1	0	12	0	0	0	0	0	.0
D	28	Wade Campbell	WPG	24	0	1	1	12−	27	0	0	0	0	13	.0
			BOS	8	0	0	0	1	15	0	0	0	0	0	.0
			Total	32	0	1	1	11−	42	0	0	0	0	13	.0
G	35	*Cleon Daskalakis	BOS	2	0	0	0		0	0	0	0	0	0	.0
F	8	*John Carter	BOS	3	0	0	0		0	0	0	0	0	0	.0
G	30	*Bill Ranford	BOS	4	0	0	0		0	0	0	0	0	0	.0
F	29	Dave Donnelly	BOS	8	0	0	0	3	17	0	0	0	0	8	.0
G	1	Pat Riggin	WSH	7	0	0	0		2	0	0	0	0	0	.0
			BOS	39	0	0	0		4	0	0	0	0	0	.0
			Total	46	0	0	0		6	0	0	0	0	0	.0

Playoffs

* rookie

Pos	#	Player	Team	GP	G	A	Pts	+/−	PIM	PP	SH	GW	OT	S	%
F	12	*Randy Burridge	BOS	3	0	4	4	2	12	0	0	0	0	3	.0
F	18	Keith Crowder	BOS	3	2	0	2	1	21	0	0	0	0	10	20.0
D	6	Gord Kluzak	BOS	3	1	1	2	0	16	1	0	0	0	5	20.0
F	20	Dwight Foster	BOS	3	0	2	2	1	2	0	0	0	0	1	.0
F	11	Steve Kasper	BOS	3	1	0	1	4−	0	0	0	0	0	1	100.0
D	28	Reed Larson	BOS	3	1	0	1	2−	6	1	0	0	0	11	9.1
F	10	Barry Pederson	BOS	3	1	0	1	0	0	0	0	0	0	8	12.5
F	13	Ken Linseman	BOS	3	0	1	1	0	17	0	0	0	0	5	.0
F	37	*Dave Pasin	BOS	3	0	1	1	1	0	0	0	0	0	10	.0
D	26	Mike Milbury	BOS	1	0	0	0	2−	17	0	0	0	0	1	.0
G	1	Pat Riggin	BOS	3	0	0	0		0	0	0	0	0	0	.0
F	25	Louis Sleigher	BOS	1	0	0	0	1−	14	0	0	0	0	1	.0
D	34	Brian Curran	BOS	2	0	0	0	1−	0	0	0	0	0	1	.0
F	29	*Jay Miller	BOS	1	0	0	0	1−	17	0	0	0	0	0	.0
F	38	*Kraig Nienhuis	BOS	2	0	0	0	4−	14	0	0	0	0	2	.0
G	30	*Bill Ranford	BOS	2	0	0	0		0	0	0	0	0	0	.0
D	33	John Blum	BOS	3	0	0	0	6	0	0	0	0	0	0	.0
D	7	Ray Bourque	BOS	3	0	0	0	0	0	0	0	0	0	7	.0
F	32	Geoff Courtnall	BOS	3	0	0	0	4−	2	0	0	0	0	3	.0
F	23	Charlie Simmer	BOS	3	0	0	0	1−	0	0	0	0	0	4	.0
D	21	Frank Simonetti	BOS	3	0	0	0	0	0	0	0	0	0	1	.0
D	22	*Michael Thelven	BOS	3	0	0	0	2−	0	0	0	0	0	5	.0

Club Records

Team

(Figures in brackets for season records are games played; records for fewest points, wins, ties, losses, goals, goals against are for 70 or more games)

Most Points	121	1970-71 (78)
Most Wins	57	1970-71 (78)
Most Ties	21	1954-55 (70)
Most Losses	47	1961-62 (70)
Most Goals	399	1970-71 (78)
Most Goals Against	306	1961-62 (70)
Fewest Points	38	1961-62 (70)
Fewest Wins	14	1962-63 (70)
Fewest Ties	5	1972-73 (78)
Fewest Losses	13	1971-72 (78)
Fewest Goals	147	1955-56 (70)
Fewest Goals Against	172	1952-53 (70)

Longest Winning Streak
Over-all .... 14 Dec. 3/29-
Jan. 9/30

Home .... *20 Dec. 3/29-
Mar. 18/30

Away .... 8 Feb. 17-
Mar. 8/72

Longest Undefeated Streak
Over-all .... 23 Dec. 22/40-
Feb. 23/41
(15 wins, 8 ties)

Home .... 27 Nov. 22/70-
Mar. 20/71
(26 wins, 1 tie)

Away .... 15 Dec. 22/40-
Mar. 16/41
(9 wins, 6 ties)

Longest Losing Streak
Over-all .... 11 Dec. 3/24-
Jan. 5/25

Home .... *11 Dec. 8/24-
Feb. 17/25

Away .... 14 Dec. 27/64-
Feb. 21/65

Longest Winless Streak
Over-all .... 20 Jan. 28-
Mar. 11/62
(16 losses, 4 ties)

Home .... 11 Dec. 8/24-
Feb. 17/25
(11 losses)

Away .... 14 Three times
Most Shutouts, Season .. 15 1927-28 (44)
Most Pen. Mins.,
Season 1,921 1985-86 (80)
Most Goals, Game .... 14 Jan. 21/45
(NYR at Bos. 14)

Individual

Most Seasons	21	John Bucyk
Most Games	1,436	John Bucyk
Most Goals, Career	545	John Bucyk
Most Assists, Career	794	John Bucyk
Most Points, Career	1,339	John Bucyk
		(545 goals, 794 assists)
Most Pen. Mins., Career	2,095	Terry O'Reilly
Most Shutouts, Career	74	Tiny Thompson

Longest Consecutive
Games Streak .... 418 John Bucyk
(Jan. 23/69-Mar. 2/75)

Most Goals, Season ...... 76 Phil Esposito
(1970-71)

Most Assists, Season ..... 102 Bobby Orr
(1970-71)

Most Points, Season ..... 152 Phil Esposito
(1970-71)
(76 goals, 76 assists)

Most Pen. Mins., Season ... 265 Terry O'Reilly
(1979-80)

Most Points, Defenseman
Season .... *139 Bobby Orr
(1970-71)
(37 goals, 102 assists)

Most Points, Center
Season .... 152 Phil Esposito
(1970-71)
(76 goals, 76 assists)

Most Points, Right Wing
Season .... 105 Ken Hodge
(1970-71)
(43 goals, 62 assists)
Ken Hodge
(1973-74)
(50 goals, 55 assists)
Rick Middleton
(1983-84)
(47 goals, 58 assists)

Most Points, Left Wing
Season .... 116 John Bucyk
(1970-71)
(51 goals, 65 assists)

Most Points, Rookie
Season .... 92 Barry Pederson
(1981-82)
(44 goals, 48 assists)

Most Shutouts, Season ... 15 Hal Winkler
(1927-28)

Most Goals, Game .... 4 Several players

Most Assists, Game ...... 6 Ken Hodge
(Feb. 9/71)
Bobby Orr
(Jan. 1/73)

Most Points, Game .... 7 Bobby Orr
(Nov. 15/73)
Phil Esposito
(Dec. 19/74)
Barry Pederson
(Apr. 4/82)

* NHL Record.

All-time Record vs. Other Clubs

Regular Season

	GP	At Home						GP	On Road						GP	Total					
	GP	W	L	T	GF	GA	PTS	GP	W	L	T	GF	GA	PTS	GP	W	L	T	GF	GA	PTS
Buffalo	52	35	15	5	221	154	72	51	18	24	9	172	198	45	103	52	38	13	393	352	117
**Calgary	27	19	5	3	96	64	41	28	14	12	2	99	106	30	55	33	17	5	195	170	71
Chicago	265	153	81	31	955	740	337	267	85	138	44	694	858	214	532	238	219	75	1649	1598	551
Detroit	268	148	79	41	943	696	337	268	71	145	52	679	902	194	536	219	224	93	1622	1598	531
Edmonton	11	8	2	1	55	31	17	12	5	5	2	39	42	12	23	13	7	3	94	73	29
Hartford	24	17	3	4	103	59	38	24	9	12	3	91	96	21	48	26	15	7	194	155	59
Los Angeles	43	33	8	2	207	112	68	42	24	13	5	165	142	53	85	57	21	7	372	254	121
Minnesota	43	32	4	7	195	96	71	42	24	10	8	164	110	56	85	56	14	15	359	206	127
Montreal	278	127	102	49	820	743	303	277	77	159	41	630	944	195	555	204	261	90	1450	1687	498
*New Jersey	22	16	6	0	99	63	32	21	13	1	7	81	53	33	43	29	7	7	180	116	65
NY Islanders	28	15	5	8	110	79	38	27	14	12	1	92	86	29	55	29	17	9	202	165	67
NY Rangers	267	147	83	37	982	745	331	268	101	115	52	748	809	254	535	248	198	89	1730	1554	585
Philadelphia	41	28	7	6	177	122	62	41	18	17	6	130	142	42	82	46	24	12	307	264	104
Pittsburgh	42	33	5	4	201	113	70	43	23	11	9	173	130	55	85	56	16	13	374	243	125
Quebec	24	9	12	3	97	101	21	24	12	10	2	111	122	26	48	21	22	5	208	204	47
St. Louis	40	27	7	6	181	95	60	41	17	15	9	149	128	43	81	44	22	15	330	223	103
Toronto	269	143	79	47	880	717	333	269	80	143	46	684	916	206	538	223	222	93	1564	1633	539
Vancouver	32	27	2	3	153	68	57	33	19	7	7	147	104	45	65	46	9	10	300	172	102
Washington	24	16	5	3	108	56	35	23	13	5	5	98	69	31	47	29	10	8	206	125	66
Winnipeg	12	9	1	2	63	41	20	11	5	5	1	43	41	11	23	14	6	3	106	82	31
Defunct Clubs	164	112	39	13	525	306	237	164	79	67	18	496	440	176	328	191	106	31	1021	746	413
Totals	**1976**	**1153**	**549**	**274**	**7171**	**5201**	**2580**	**1976**	**721**	**926**	**329**	**5685**	**6419**	**1771**	**3952**	**1874**	**1475**	**603**	**12856**	**11620**	**4351**

* Totals include those of Kansas City (1974-75, 1975-76) and Colorado (1976-77 through 1981-82)
** Totals include those of Atlanta (1972-73 through 1979-80)

Playoffs

	Series	W	L	GP	W	L	T	GF	GA	Last Mtg.	Round	Result
Buffalo	2	2	0	11	7	4	0	49	34	1983	DF	W 4-3
Chicago	6	5	1	22	16	5	1	97	63	1978	QF	W 4-0
Detroit	7	4	3	33	19	14	0	96	98	1957	SF	W 4-1
Los Angeles	2	2	0	13	8	5	0	56	38	1977	QF	W 4-2
Minnesota	1	0	1	3	0	3	0	13	20	1981	P	L 0-3
Montreal	21	2	19	102	31	71	0	230	327	1986	DSF	L 0-3
NY Islanders	2	0	2	11	3	8	0	35	49	1983	CF	L 2-4
NY Rangers	9	6	3	42	22	18	2	114	104	1973	QF	W 4-1
Philadelphia	4	2	2	20	11	9	0	60	57	1978	QF	W 4-1
Pittsburgh	2	2	0	9	7	2	0	37	21	1980	P	W 3-2
Quebec	2	1	1	11	6	5	0	37	35	1983	DSF	W 3-1
St. Louis	2	2	0	8	8	0	0	48	15	1972	SF	W 4-0
Toronto	13	5	8	62	30	31	1	153	150	1974	QF	W 4-0
Defunct Clubs	3	1	2	11	4	5	2	20	20			
Totals	**76**	**34**	**44**	**358**	**172**	**180**	**6**	**1045**	**1031**			

Boston Bruins

Playoff Results 1986-82

Year	Round	Opponent	Result	GF	GA
1986	DSF	Montreal	L 0-3	6	10
1985	DSF	Montreal	L 2-3	2	10
1984	DSF	Montreal	L 0-3	17	19
1983	CF	NY Islanders	L 2-4	21	30
	DF	Buffalo	W 4-3	32	23
1982	DF	Quebec	L 3-4	26	28
	DSF	Buffalo	W 3-1	17	11

Abbreviations: Round: F – Final; **CF** – conference final; **DF** – division final; **DSF** – division semi-final; **SF** – semi-final; **QF** – quarter-final; **P** – preliminary round. **GA** – goals against; **GF** – goals for.

Coaching History

Arthur H. Ross, 1924-25 to 1927-28; Cy Denneny, 1928-29; Arthur H. Ross, 1929-30 to 1933-34; Frank Patrick, 1934-35 to 1935-36; Arthur H. Ross, 1936-37 to 1938-39; Ralph (Cooney) Weiland, 1939-40 to 1940-41; Arthur H. Ross, 1941-42 to 1944-45; Aubrey V. (Dit) Clapper, 1945-46 to 1948-49; George (Buck) Boucher, 1949-50; Lynn Patrick, 1950-51 to 1953-54; Lynn Patrick and Milt Schmidt, 1954-55; Milt Schmidt, 1955-56 to 1960-61; Phil Watson, 1961-62; Phil Watson and Milt Schmidt, 1962-63; Milt Schmidt, 1963-64 to 1965-66; Harry Sinden, 1966-67 to 1969-70; Tom Johnson, 1970-71 to 1971-72; Tom Johnson and Bep Guidolin, 1972-73; Bep Guidolin, 1973-74; Don Cherry, 1974-75 to 1978-79; Fred Creighton and Harry Sinden, 1979-80; Gerry Cheevers, 1980-81 to 1983-84; Gerry Cheevers and Harry Sinden, 1984-85; Butch Goring, 1985-86, to date.

Captains' History

No Captain, 1924-25 to 1926-27; Lionel Hitchman, 1927-28 to 1930-31; George Owen, 1931-32; Dit Clapper, 1932-33 to 1937-38; Cooney Weiland, 1938-39; Dit Clapper, 1939-40 to 1945-46; Dit Clapper, John Crawford, 1946-47; John Crawford 1947-48 to 1949-50; Milt Schmidt, 1950-51 to 1953-54; Milt Schmidt, Ed Sanford, 1954-55; Fern Flaman, 1955-56 to 1960-61; Don McKenney, 1961-62, 1962-63; Leo Boivin, 1963-64 to 1965-66; John Bucyk, 1966-67; no captain, 1967-68 to 1972-73; John Bucyk, 1973-74 to 1976-77; Wayne Cashman, 1977-78 to 1982-83; Terry O'Reilly, 1983-84, 1984-85; Ray Bourque, Rick Middleton (co-captains) 1985-86.

Retired Numbers

2	Eddie Shore	1926-1940
3	Lionel Hitchman	1925-1934
4	Bobby Orr	1966-1976
5	Dit Clapper	1927-1947
9	John Bucyk	1957-1978
15	Milt Schmidt	1936-1955

Entry Draft Selections 1986-72

1986
Pick
- 13 Craig Janney
- 34 Pekka Tirkkonen
- 76 Dean Hall
- 97 Matt Pesklewis
- 118 Garth Premak
- 139 Paul Beraldo
- 160 Brian Ferreira
- 181 Jeff Flaherty
- 202 Greg Hawgood
- 223 Steffan Malmquist
- 244 Joel Gardner

1985
Pick
- 31 Alain Cote
- 52 Bill Ranford
- 73 Jaime Kelly
- 94 Steve Moore
- 115 Gord Hynes
- 136 Per Martinele
- 157 Randy Burridge
- 178 Gord Cruickshank
- 199 Dave Buda
- 210 Bob Beers
- 220 John Byce
- 241 Marc West

1984
Pick
- 19 Dave Pasin
- 40 Ray Podloski
- 61 Jeff Cornelius
- 82 Robert Joyce
- 103 Mike Bishop
- 124 Randy Oswald
- 145 Mark Thietke
- 166 Don Sweeney
- 186 Kevin Heffernan
- 207 J.D. Urbanic
- 227 Bill Kopecky
- 248 Jim Newhouse

1983
Pick
- 21 Nevin Markwart
- 42 Greg Johnston
- 62 Greg Puhalski
- 82 Alain Larochelle
- 102 Allen Pederson
- 122 Terry Taillefor
- 142 Ian Armstrong
- 162 Francois Olivier
- 182 Harri Laurilla
- 202 Paul Fitzsimmons
- 222 Norm Foster
- 242 Greg Murphy

1982
Pick
- 1 Gord Kluzak
- 22 Brian Curran
- 39 Lyndon Byers
- 60 Dave Reid
- 102 Bob Nicholson
- 123 Bob Sweeney
- 144 John Meulenbrooks
- 165 Tony Fiore
- 186 Doug Kostynski
- 207 Tony Gilliard
- 228 Tommy Ichman
- 249 Bruno Campese

1981
Pick
- 14 Normand Leveille
- 35 Luc Dufour
- 77 Scott McLellan
- 98 Joe Mantione
- 119 Bruce Milton
- 140 Mats Thelin
- 161 Armel Parisee
- 182 Don Sylvester
- 203 Richard Bourque

1980
Pick
- 18 Barry Pederson
- 60 Tom Fergus
- 81 Steve Kasper
- 102 Randy Hillier
- 123 Steve Lyons
- 144 Tony McMurchy
- 165 Mike Moffat
- 186 Michael Thelven
- 207 Jens Ohling

1979
Pick
- 8 Ray Bourque
- 15 Brad McCrimmon
- 36 Doug Morrison
- 57 Keith Crowder
- 78 Larry Melnyk
- 99 Marco Baron
- 120 Mike Krushelnyski

1978
Pick
- 16 Al Secord
- 35 Graeme Nicolson
- 52 Brad Knelson
- 68 George Buat
- 85 Darryl MacLeod
- 102 Jeff Brubaker
- 119 Murray Skinner
- 136 Robert Hehir
- 153 Craig MacTavish

1977
Pick
- 16 Dwight Foster
- 34 Dave Parro
- 52 Mike Forbes
- 70 Brian McGregor
- 88 Doug Butler
- 106 Keith Johnson
- 122 Ralph Cox
- 138 Mario Claude

1976
Pick
- 16 Clayton Pachal
- 34 Larry Gloeckner
- 70 Bob Miller
- 88 Peter Vandermark
- 106 Ted Olson

1975
Pick
- 14 Doug Halward
- 32 Barry Smith
- 60 Rick Adduono
- 68 Denis Daigle
- 86 Stan Jonathan
- 104 Matti Hagman
- 122 Gary Carr
- 140 Bo Berglund
- 156 Joe Rando
- 171 Kevin Nugent

1974
Pick
- 18 Don Larway
- 25 Mark Howe
- 36 Peter Sturgeon
- 54 Tom Edur
- 72 Bill Reed
- 90 Jamie Bateman
- 108 Bill Best
- 126 Ray Maluta
- 143 Darryl Drader
- 160 Peter Roberts
- 175 Peter Waselovich

1973
Pick
- 6 Andre Savard
- 31 Jim Jones
- 36 Doug Gibson
- 47 Al Sims
- 63 Steve Langdon
- 79 Peter Crosbie
- 95 J.P. Bourgouyne
- 111 Walter Johnson
- 127 Virgil Gates
- 142 Jim Pettie
- 157 Yvan Bouillon

1972
Pick
- 16 Mike Bloom
- 32 Wayne Elder
- 48 Michel Boudreau
- 64 Les Jackson
- 80 Brian Coates
- 96 Peter Gaw
- 112 Gordie Clark
- 128 Roy Carmichael

Club Directory

Boston Garden
150 Causeway Street
Boston, Massachusetts 02114
Phone 617/227-3206
TWX 710-321-6863
ENVOY ID   TM.BOS
Capacity: 14,451

Board of Directors

William D. Hassett (Chairman)	Paul A. Mooney
Forrester A. Clark	Joshua M. Berman
Donald S. Carmichael	William A. Wolbach

President and Governor . . . . Paul A. Mooney
General Manager and Alternate Governor . . . . . Harry Sinden
Assistant General Manager . . . . Tom Johnson
Coach . . . . Butch Goring
Director of Public Relations . . . . Nate Greenberg
Coordinator of Minor League Player Personnel/
Scouting . . . . Bob Tindall
Director of Player Evaluation . . . . Bart Bradley
Special Assignment Scout . . . . Jean Ratelle
Scouting Staff . . . . Jim Morrison (Ontario),
                                                   Andre Lachapelle (Quebec),
                                                   Joe Lyons (New England),
                                                   Don Saatzer (Minnesota),
                                                   Lars Waldner (Europe)
Controller . . . . John J. Dionne
Trainers . . . . Jim Narrigan, Larry Ness
Physical Therapist . . . . Don Worden
Equipment Manager . . . . Bob Crocker, Jr.
Medical Coordinator . . . . Dr. Richard Weiss
Club Doctors . . . . Dr. Earle Wilkins, Dr. Ashby Moncure,
                                                   Dr. Bertram Zarins
Club Dentists . . . . Dr. Robert Thomas and Dr. Richard Miner
Sales and Marketing . . . . Steve Nazro
Public Relations Assistant . . . . Heidi Holland
Corporate Season Tickets Sales . . . . Milt Schmidt
Administrative Assistant . . . . John Bucyk
Dimensions of Rink . . . . 191 feet by 83 feet
Club colors . . . . Gold, Black and White
Training Camp Site . . . . Danvers, Mass.
Broadcasters (TV-38/NESN) . . . . Fred Cusick and Dave Shea
Broadcasters (Radio) . . . . Bob Wilson and John Bucyk
TV Channels . . . . WSBK-TV (UHF-38) and New England Sports
                                                   Network (NESN)
Radio Station . . . . WPLM (99.1 FM, 1390 AM) and Bruins Radio
                                                   Network

Steve Kasper in on goal.

Buffalo Sabres
1985-86 Results: 37w-37L-6t 80 pts. Fifth, Adams Division

Year-by-Year Record

Season	GP	Home W	Home L	Home T	Road W	Road L	Road T	Overall W	Overall L	Overall T	GF	GA	Pts.	Finished		Playoff Result
1985-86	80	23	16	1	14	21	5	37	37	6	296	291	80	5th,	Adams Div.	Out of Playoffs
1984-85	80	23	10	7	15	18	7	38	28	14	290	237	90	3rd,	Adams Div.	Lost Div. Semi-Final
1983-84	80	25	9	6	23	16	1	48	25	7	315	257	103	2nd,	Adams Div.	Lost Div. Semi-Final
1982-83	80	25	7	8	13	22	5	38	29	13	318	285	89	3rd,	Adams Div.	Lost Div. Final
1981-82	80	23	8	9	16	18	6	39	26	15	307	273	93	3rd,	Adams Div.	Lost Div. Semi-Final
1980-81	80	21	7	12	18	13	9	39	20	21	327	250	99	1st,	Adams Div.	Lost Quarter-Final
1979-80	80	27	5	8	20	12	8	47	17	16	318	201	110	1st,	Adams Div.	Lost Semi-Final
1978-79	80	19	13	8	17	15	8	36	28	16	280	263	88	2nd,	Adams Div.	Lost Prelim. Round
1977-78	80	25	7	8	19	12	9	44	19	17	288	215	105	2nd,	Adams Div.	Lost Quarter-Final
1976-77	80	27	8	5	21	16	3	48	24	8	301	220	104	2nd,	Adams Div.	Lost Quarter-Final
1975-76	80	28	7	5	18	14	8	46	21	13	339	240	105	2nd,	Adams Div.	Lost Quarter-Final
1974-75	80	28	6	6	21	10	9	49	16	15	354	240	113	1st,	Adams Div.	Lost Final
1973-74	78	23	10	6	9	24	6	32	34	12	242	250	76	5th,	East Div.	Out of Playoffs
1972-73	78	30	6	3	7	21	11	37	27	14	257	219	88	4th,	East Div.	Lost Quarter-Final
1971-72	78	11	19	9	5	24	10	16	43	19	203	289	51	6th,	East Div.	Out of Playoffs
1970-71	78	16	13	10	8	26	5	24	39	15	217	291	63	5th,	East Div.	Out of Playoffs

Schedule

	Home			Away
Oct.	Sun. 12 Calgary	Oct.	Thur. 9 Winnipeg
	Wed. 15 Montreal		Sat. 11 Toronto
	Fri. 17 Pittsburgh		Sat. 18 Washington
	Fri. 24 Hartford		Wed. 22 Pittsburgh
Nov.	Wed. 5 Boston		Sat. 25 Hartford
	Fri. 7 Vancouver		Wed. 29 Montreal
	Sun. 9 NY Islanders	Nov.	Sat. 1 New Jersey
	Wed. 19 Boston		Sun. 2 Boston
	Fri. 21 Quebec		Wed. 12 NY Rangers
	Fri. 28 Boston		Sat. 15 Montreal
Dec.	Tue. 2 Minnesota		Sat. 22 Quebec
	Fri. 5 St. Louis		Wed. 26 Hartford
	Sun. 14 Hartford		Sat. 29 Boston
	Fri. 19 Montreal	Dec.	Sat. 6 New Jersey
	Tue. 23 Philadelphia		Tue. 9 Detroit
	Fri. 26 Pittsburgh		Wed. 10 Chicago
	Sun. 28 Calgary		Sat. 13 Quebec
	Wed. 31 Chicago		Wed. 17 Hartford
Jan.	Fri. 2 Winnipeg		Sat. 20 Toronto
	Sun. 4 Quebec	Jan.	Wed. 7 Winnipeg
	Wed. 14 Montreal		Thur. 8 Minnesota
	Sun. 18 Edmonton		Sat. 10 Los Angeles
	Fri. 23 Washington		Sat. 17 Montreal
	Wed. 28 Philadelphia		Tue. 20 Minnesota
	Fri. 30 Quebec		Sat. 24 Washington
Feb.	Sun. 1 Detroit		Mon. 26 Boston
	Sun. 8 Chicago	Feb.	Wed. 4 Hartford
	Wed. 18 Boston		Sat. 7 Quebec*
	Sun. 22 Hartford		Sat. 14 NY Islanders
	Tue. 24 NY Rangers		Fri. 20 NY Rangers
	Thur. 26 St. Louis		Sat. 28 Boston*
Mar.	Sun. 1 Vancouver	Mar.	Tue. 3 Philadelphia
	Thur. 5 New Jersey		Sat. 7 Quebec
	Sun. 8 Quebec		Wed. 11 Los Angeles
	Fri. 20 Montreal		Fri. 13 Vancouver
	Sun. 22 Detroit		Sat. 14 Edmonton
	Tue. 24 Toronto		Tue. 17 Calgary
	Thur. 26 Los Angeles		Sat. 28 Montreal
	Sun. 29 Edmonton	April	Thur. 2 St. Louis
April	Sun. 5 Hartford		Sat. 4 NY Islanders

*Denotes afternoon game.

Home Starting Times:
All Games .... 7:35 p.m.
Except Sundays .... 7:05 p.m.

Franchise date: May 22, 1970

 **17th NHL Season**

Lindy Ruff

1986-87 Player Personnel

FORWARDS

	Ht.	Wt.	Place of Birth	Date	1985-86 Club
ANDERSSON, Bo Mikael	5-11	187	Malmo, Sweden	5/10/66	Buffalo-Rochester
ANDREYCHUK, Dave	6-3	200	Hamilton, Ont.	9/29/63	Buffalo
ARNIEL, Scott	6-1	170	Cornwall, Ont.	9/17/62	Winnipeg
BRYDGES, Paul	5-11	180	Guelph, Ont.	6/21/65	Guelph
CREIGHTON, Adam	6-5	205	Burlington, Ont.	6/2/65	Buffalo-Rochester
CYR, Paul	5-10	185	Port Alberni, B.C.	10/31/63	Buffalo
FOLIGNO, Mike	6-2	195	Sudbury, Ont.	1/29/59	Buffalo
FORTIER, Marc	6-0	190	Sherbrooke, Que.	2/26/66	Chicoutimi
FRASER, Jay	6-1	200	Ottawa, Ont.	10/26/61	Carolina-Rochester
GAGE, Jody	6-0	185	Toronto, Ont.	11/29/59	Buffalo-Rochester
GARDNER, Paul	6-0	195	Fort Erie, Ont.	3/5/56	Buffalo-Rochester
GRETZKY, Keith	5-9	157	Brantford, Ont.	2/16/67	Windsor
GUAY, Francois	6-0	183	Gatineau, Que.	6/8/68	Laval
HAJDU, Richard	6-0	170	Victoria, B.C.	4/10/65	Buffalo-Rochester
HARPER, Warren	6-0	175	Prince Albert, Sask.	5/10/63	Rochester
HARTMAN, Mike	6-0	180	Detroit, Mich.	2/7/67	North Bay
HOGUE, Benoit	5-10	180	Repentigny, Que.	10/28/66	St. Jean
HOUSLEY, Phil	5-10	180	St. Paul, Minn.	3/9/64	Buffalo
HUGHES, Pat	6-0	180	Calgary, Alta.	3/25/55	Buffalo-Rochester
JACKSON, Jim	5-8	181	Oshawa, Ont.	2/1/60	Rochester
KAESE, Trent	5-11	205	Nanaimo, B.C.	9/9/67	Lethbridge
KERR, Kevin	5-10	172	North Bay, Ont.	9/18/67	Windsor
LACOMBE, Normand	5-11	205	Pierrefonds, Que.	10/18/64	Buffalo-Rochester
LANGEVIN, Chris	6-0	190	Montreal, Que.	11/27/59	Buffalo
LAROSE, Guy	5-9	172	Hull, Que.	7/31/67	Guelph-Ottawa
LEVER, Don	5-11	185	South Porcupine, Ont.	11/14/52	Buffalo-Rochester
LOGAN, Robert	6-0	190	Montreal, Que.	2/22/64	Yale
McFEE, Dale	5-11	190	Edmonton, Alta.	2/11/65	Prince Albert
NYSTROM, Murray	5-11	180	Thunder Bay, Ont.	7/2/66	London
ORLANDO, Gaetano	5-8	175	Montreal, Que.	11/16/62	Buffalo-Rochester
PARKER, Jeff	6-3	198	St. Paul, Minn.	9/7/64	Michigan State
PRIESTLAY, Ken	5-10	172	Vancouver, B.C.	8/24/67	Rochester
RISTAU, Andrew	6-5	230	Winnipeg, Man.	1/28/61	Carolina-Rochester
RUFF, Lindy	6-2	190	Warburg, Alta.	2/17/60	Buffalo
SEILING, Ric	6-1	180	Elmira, Ont.	12/15/57	Buffalo
SHEPPARD, Ray	6-1	196	Pembroke, Ont.	5/27/66	Cornwall
SMITH, Doug	5-11	180	Ottawa, Ont.	5/17/63	Buffalo-Los Angeles
TRAPP, Doug	6-0	182	Balcarres, Sask.	11/28/65	Rochester
TUCKER, John	6-0	185	Windsor, Ont.	9/29/64	Buffalo
VERRET, Claude	5-9	165	Lachine, Que.	4/20/63	Rochester

DEFENSEMEN

ANDERSON, Shawn	6-1	191	Montreal, Que.	2/7/68	Team Canada
ARNDT, Troy	6-0	195	Regina, Sask.	4/30/68	Portland
BALDRIS, Miguel	6-0	192	Montreal, Que.	1/30/68	Shawinigan
BURTON, James	6-1	187	Brantford, Ont.	11/13/61	Ft. Wayne
DUNN, Richie	6-0	195	Boston, Mass.	5/12/57	Buffalo-Rochester
DYKSTRA, Steve	6-2	190	Edmonton, Alberta	2/3/62	Rochester (AHL)-Flint
ENGBLOM, Brian	6-2	190	Winnipeg, Man.	1/27/55	Buffalo-Los Angeles
FENYVES, Dave	5-11	190	Dunnville, Ont.	4/29/60	Buffalo
FERNER, Mark	6-0	180	Regina, Sask.	9/5/65	Rochester
GASSEAU, James	6-2	205	Carleton, Que.	5/4/66	Drummondville
HAJT, Bill	6-3	205	Radisson, Sask.	11/18/51	Buffalo
HALKIDIS, Bob	5-11	196	Toronto, Ont.	3/5/66	Buffalo
HOFFORD, James	6-0	188	Sudbury, Ont.	10/4/64	Buffalo-Rochester
HOOVER, Tim	5-10	175	North Bay, Ont.	1/9/65	Rochester
HOUSLEY, Phil	5-10	180	St. Paul, Minn.	3/9/64	Buffalo
MATIKAINEN, Petri	6-0	185	Savonlinna, Finland	1/7/67	Oshawa
MEYER, Jason	5-10	185	Regina, Sask.	2/21/65	Rochester
MOYLAN, Dave	6-2	194	Tillsonburg, Ont.	8/13/67	Sudbury
RAMSEY, Mike	6-3	190	Minneapolis, Minn.	12/3/60	Buffalo
REEKIE, Joe	6-3	195	Petawawa, Ont.	2/22/65	Buffalo-Rochester
RUSSELL, Phil	6-2	200	Edmonton, Alt.	7/21/52	Buffalo-New Jersey

GOALTENDERS

BARRASSO, Tom	6-3	195	Boston, Mass.	3/31/65	Buffalo
CLOUTIER, Jacques	5-7	155	Noranda, Que.	1/3/60	Buffalo-Rochester
CRAIG, Mike	6-0	165	Calgary, Alta.	11/1/62	Buffalo-Rochester

Coach and General Manager

BOWMAN, WILLIAM SCOTT
Alternate Governor, General Manager, Director of Hockey Operations and Coach, Buffalo Sabres. Born in Montreal, Que., September 18, 1933.

Scott Bowman joined the Buffalo Sabres on June 11, 1979 after guiding Montreal to four consecutive Stanley Cup championships. Bowman, who had a promising hockey career ended by a head injury during the 1951-52 season, began his coaching career in the Canadiens' organization in 1954. In 1957, Bowman assisted Sam Pollock as manager and coach of the Hull-Ottawa Junior Canadiens and until 1966, served in several capacities for Montreal. He joined the St. Louis Blues for the 1966-67 season and guided the Blues through four successful seasons before joining the Canadiens in 1971. During his eight seasons with Montreal, the Canadiens won the Stanley Cup five times and the final four were won in consecutive seasons. Bowman, Al Arbour of the New York Islanders and former Montreal great Hector "Toe" Blake are the only coaches in NHL history to have guided their teams to at least four straight Stanley Cups. During the 1981-82 season, Bowman began as coach of the Sabres but relinquished the duties to Jim Roberts in December, 1981. He returned to the coaching helm on March 19, 1982 and in 1983-84 finished runner-up to Washington's Bryan Murray for the Jack Adams Award (Coach of the Year).

1985-86 Scoring

Regular Season

*–rookie

Pos	#	Player	Team	GP	G	A	Pts	+/-	PIM	PP	SH	GW	OT	S	%
F	25	Dave Andreychuk	BUF	80	36	51	87	3	61	12	0	3	0	225	16.0
F	17	Mike Foligno	BUF	79	41	39	80	25	168	7	1	4	0	223	18.4
F	7	John Tucker	BUF	75	31	34	65	0	39	8	0	3	0	146	21.2
D	6	Phil Housley	BUF	79	15	47	62	9–	54	7	0	2	0	180	8.3
F	11	Gilbert Perreault	BUF	72	21	39	60	10–	28	5	1	3	0	164	12.8
F	18	Paul Cyr	BUF	71	20	31	51	4	120	4	1	2	0	151	13.2
F	9	Gilles Hamel	BUF	77	19	25	44	27–	61	4	3	4	0	158	12.0
F	15	Doug Smith	L.A	48	8	9	17	29–	56	1	1	0	0	115	7.0
			BUF	30	10	11	21	2	73	3	1	3	0	72	13.9
			Total	78	18	20	38	27–	129	4	2	3	0	187	9.6
F	22	Lindy Ruff	BUF	54	20	12	32	8	158	5	1	4	0	131	15.3
D	5	Mike Ramsey	BUF	76	7	21	28	1	117	1	0	1	0	154	4.5
D	3	Hannu Virta	BUF	47	5	23	28	2	16	1	0	0	0	81	6.2
F	23	*Gates Orlando	BUF	60	13	12	25	7–	29	1	2	1	0	70	18.6
F	16	Ric Seiling	BUF	69	12	13	25	5–	74	0	0	1	0	85	14.1
D	4	*Steve Dykstra	BUF	64	4	21	25	1	108	1	1	0	0	70	5.7
D	28	Brian Engblom	L.A	49	3	13	16	13–	61	0	0	0	0	53	5.7
			BUF	30	1	4	5	3	16	0	0	0	0	24	4.2
			Total	79	4	17	21	10–	77	0	0	0	0	77	5.2
D	24	Bill Hajt	BUF	58	1	16	17	17	25	0	0	0	0	42	2.4
F	32	Normand Lacombe	BUF	25	6	7	13	9	13	3	0	2	0	38	15.8
F	26	Pat Hughes	BUF	50	4	9	13	6–	25	0	0	0	0	51	7.8
D	26	Phil Russell	N.J	30	2	3	5	17–	51	0	0	0	0	22	9.1
			BUF	12	2	3	5	8–	12	0	0	0	0	15	13.3
			Total	42	4	6	10	25–	63	0	0	0	0	37	10.8
F	14	*Mikael Anderson	BUF	32	1	9	10	0	4	0	0	0	0	13	7.7
D	19	*Bob Halkidis	BUF	37	1	9	10	3–	115	0	0	0	0	19	5.3
F	21	Richie Dunn	BUF	29	4	5	9	5–	25	4	0	0	0	55	7.3
F	20	Don Lever	BUF	29	7	1	8	5–	6	1	1	0	0	31	22.6
D	31	Dave Fenyves	BUF	47	0	7	7	12	37	0	0	0	0	31	.0
F	12	Jody Gage	BUF	7	3	2	5	3–	0	3	0	0	0	18	16.7
G	30	Tom Barrasso	BUF	60	0	4	4	0	28	0	0	0	0	0	.0
F	15	*Chris Langevin	BUF	16	2	1	3	3	20	0	0	1	0	10	20.0
F	29	Mal Davis	BUF	7	2	0	2	1–	4	2	0	0	0	5	40.0
F	34	Adam Creighton	BUF	19	1	1	2	2–	2	0	0	1	0	9	11.1
G	1	Jacques Cloutier	BUF	15	0	2	2	0	2	0	0	0	0	0	.0
F	28	Paul Gardner	BUF	2	0	0	0	3–	0	0	0	0	0	4	.0
F	3	*Richard Hajdu	BUF	3	0	0	0	1	0	0	0	0	0	4	.0
F	31	*Joe Reekie	BUF	3	0	0	0	2–	14	0	0	0	0	1	.0
D	33	*Jim Hofford	BUF	5	0	0	0	1–	5	0	0	0	0	3	.0
G	35	*Daren Puppa	BUF	7	0	0	0	0	0	0	0	0	0	0	.0

Paul Cyr had 20 goals for the Sabres in 1985-86.

Club Records

Team

(Figures in brackets for season records are games played; records for fewest points, wins, ties, losses, goals, goals against are for 70 or more games)

Most Points	113	1974-75 (80)
Most Wins	49	1974-75 (80)
Most Ties	21	1980-81 (80)
Most Losses	43	1971-72 (78)
Most Goals	354	1974-75 (80)
Most Goals Against	291	1970-71 (78)
		1985-86 (80)
Fewest Points	51	1971-72 (78)
Fewest Wins	16	1971-72 (78)
Fewest Ties	6	1985-86 (80)
Fewest Losses	16	1974-75 (80)
Fewest Goals	203	1971-72 (78)
Fewest Goals Against	201	1979-80 (80)

Longest Winning Streak

Over-all . . . . 10 — Jan. 4-23/84
Home . . . . 12 — Nov. 12/72-Jan. 7/73
Away . . . . 8 — Feb. 17-Mar. 8/72

Longest Undefeated Streak

Over-all . . . . 14 — March 6-April 6/80
Home . . . . 21 — Oct. 8/72-Jan. 7/73
Away . . . . 10 — Dec. 10/83-Jan. 23/84 (10 wins)

Longest Losing Streak

Over-all . . . . 7 — Oct. 25-Nov. 8/70
Home . . . . 5 — Feb. 15-Mar. 3/85
Away . . . . 7 — Oct. 14-Nov. 7/70 Feb. 6-27/71

Longest Winless Streak

Over-all . . . . 10 — Nov. 7-Dec. 1/71 (8 losses, 2 ties)
Home . . . . 6 — Feb. 27-Mar. 26/72 (3 losses, 3 ties)

Away . . . . 23 — Oct. 30/71-Feb. 19/72 (15 losses, 8 ties)
Most Shutouts, Season . . . . . 7 — 1974-75 (80)
Most. Pen. Mins., Season . . . . . 1,591 — 1985-86 (80)
Most Goals, Game . . . . . . 14 — Jan. 21/75 (Wash. 2 at Buf. 14) Mar. 19/81 (Tor. 4 at Buf. 14)

Individual

Most Seasons	16	Gilbert Perreault
Most Games	1,171	Gilbert Perreault
Most Goals, Career	503	Gilbert Perreault
Most Assists, Career	807	Gilbert Perreault
Most Points, Career	1,310	Gilbert Perreault
Most Pen. Mins., Career	1,278	Larry Playfair
Most Shutouts, Career	14	Don Edwards

Longest Consecutive Games Streak . . . . . 776 — Craig Ramsay (Mar. 27/73-Feb. 10/83)

Most Goals, Season . . . . 56 — Danny Gare (1979-80)

Most Assists, Season . . . . 69 — Gilbert Perreault (1975-76)

Most Points, Season . . . . 113 — Gilbert Perreault (1975-76) (44 goals, 69 assists)

Most Pen. Mins., Season . . . 258 — Larry Playfair (1981-82)

Most Points, Defenseman Seasons . . . . 77 — Phil Housley (1983-84) (31 goals, 46 assists)

Most Points, Center Season . . . . 113 — Gilbert Perreault (1975-76) (44 goals, 69 assists)

Most Points, Right Wing Season . . . . 100 — René Robert (1974-765) (40 goals, 60 assists)

Most Points, Left Wing Season . . . . 95 — Richard Martin (1974-75) (52 goals, 43 assists)

Most Points, Rookie Season . . . . 74 — Richard Martin (1971-72) (44 goals, 30 assists)

Most Shutouts, Season . . . . 5 — Don Edwards (1977-78) Tom Barrasso (1984-85)

Most Goals, Game . . . . . . 5 — Dave Andreychuk (Feb. 6/86)

Most Assists, Game . . . . . . 5 — Gilbert Perreault (Feb. 1/76; Mar. 9/80) Gilbert Perreault (Jan. 4/84)

Most Points, Game . . . . . . 7 — Gilbert Perreault (Feb. 1/76)

Coaching History

"Punch" Imlach, 1970-71; "Punch" Imlach, Floyd Smith and Joe Crozier, 1971-72; Joe Crozier, 1972-73 to 1973-74; Floyd Smith, 1974-75 to 1976-77; Marcel Pronovost, 1977-78; Marcel Pronovost and Bill Inglis, 1978-79; Scott Bowman, 1979-80; Roger Neilson, 1980-81; Jim Roberts and Scott Bowman, 1981-82; Scott Bowman 1981-82 to 1984-85; Jim Schoenfeld, and Scott Bowman, 1985-86; Scott Bowman, 1986-87 to date.

Captains' History

Floyd Smith, 1970-71; Gerry Meehan, 1971-72 to 1973-74; Jim Schoenfeld, 1974-75 to 1976-77; Danny Gare, 1977-78 to 1980-81; Gil Perreault, 1981-82 to 1985-86.

All-time Record vs. Other Clubs

Regular Season

			At Home							On Road							Total			
	GP	W	L	T	GF	GA	PTS	GP	W	L	T	GF	GA	PTS	GP	W	L	T	GF	GA	PTS
Boston	51	24	18	9	198	172	57	52	14	34	4	154	221	32	103	38	52	13	352	393	89
**Calgary	27	16	7	4	126	77	36	27	10	9	8	93	85	28	54	26	16	12	219	162	64
Chicago	33	20	7	6	128	82	46	33	9	18	6	80	105	24	66	29	25	12	208	187	70
Detroit	34	24	4	6	153	80	54	36	14	19	3	105	128	31	70	38	23	9	258	208	85
Edmonton	11	5	4	2	48	45	12	12	3	7	2	34	49	8	23	8	11	4	82	94	20
Hartford	24	12	7	5	105	80	29	24	14	7	3	78	65	31	48	26	14	8	173	145	60
Los Angeles	35	19	9	7	144	100	45	34	15	12	7	114	114	37	69	34	21	14	258	214	82
Minnesota	35	22	7	6	137	88	50	34	17	12	5	114	102	39	69	39	19	11	251	190	89
Montreal	47	20	16	11	146	148	51	47	14	25	8	150	192	36	94	34	41	19	296	340	87
*New Jersey	22	18	2	2	110	58	38	21	16	1	4	92	57	36	43	34	3	6	204	115	74
New Islanders	28	16	8	4	97	74	36	28	13	11	4	81	81	30	55	29	19	8	178	155	66
NY Rangers	35	21	9	5	159	112	47	33	10	14	9	96	122	29	68	31	23	14	255	234	76
Philadelphia	32	15	11	6	110	93	36	34	7	21	6	85	126	20	66	22	32	12	195	219	56
Pittsburgh	34	19	4	11	156	83	49	35	12	11	12	128	125	36	69	31	15	23	284	208	85
Québec	24	14	6	4	100	80	32	24	7	15	2	70	94	16	48	21	21	6	170	174	48
St. Louis	32	22	6	4	137	93	48	33	9	19	5	85	126	23	65	31	25	9	222	219	71
Toronto	40	25	13	2	170	110	52	38	16	16	6	130	123	38	78	41	29	8	300	233	90
Vancouver	33	19	6	8	121	83	46	34	10	17	7	107	128	27	67	29	23	15	228	211	73
Washington	24	19	2	3	110	56	41	23	17	2	4	107	58	38	47	36	4	7	217	114	79
Winnipeg	12	11	0	1	63	28	23	11	5	4	2	40	39	12	23	16	4	3	103	67	35
Defunct Clubs	23	13	5	5	94	63	31	23	12	8	3	97	76	27	46	25	13	8	191	139	58
Totals	636	374	151	111	2612	1805	859	636	244	282	110	2040	2216	598	1272	618	433	221	4644	4021	1457

* Totals include those of Kansas City (1974-75, 1975-76) and Colorado (1976-77 through 1981-82)
** Totals include those of Atlanta (1972-73 through 1979-80)

Playoffs

	Series	W	L	GP	W	L	T	GF	GA	Last Mtg.	Round	Result
Boston	2	0	2	11	4	7	0	34	49	1983	DF	L 3-4
Chicago	2	2	0	9	8	1	0	36	17	1980	QF	W 4-0
Minnesota	2	1	1	7	3	4	0	28	26	1981	QF	L 1-4
Montreal	3	2	1	15	9	6	0	45	52	1983	DSF	W 3-0
NY Islanders	3	0	3	16	4	12	0	45	59	1980	SF	L 2-4
NY Rangers	1	1	0	3	2	1	0	11	6	1978	P	W 2-1
Philadelphia	2	0	2	11	3	8	0	23	35	1978	QF	L 1-4
Pittsburgh	1	0	1	3	1	2	0	9	9	1979	P	L 1-2
Quebec	2	0	2	8	2	6	0	28	34	1985	DSF	L 2-3
St. Louis	1	1	0	3	2	1	0	8	8	1876	P	W 2-1
Vancouver	2	2	0	7	6	1	0	28	14	1981	P	W 3-0
Totals	21	9	12	93	44	49	0	294	309			

Playoff Results 1986-82

Year	Round	Opponent	Result	GF	GA
1985	DSF	Quebec	L 0-3	5	13
1984	DSF	Quebec	L 2-3	22	22
1983	DF	Boston	L 3-4	23	32
	DSF	Montreal	W 3-0	8	2
1982	DSF	Boston	L 1-3	11	17

Abbreviations: Round: F – Final; **CF** – conference final; **DF** – division final; **DSF** – division semi-final; **SF** – semi-final; **QF** – quarter-final; **P** – preliminary round. **GA** – goals against; **GF** – goals for.

Entry Draft Selections 1986-72

1986
Pick
5	Shawn Anderson
26	Greg Brown
47	Bob Corkum
56	Kevin Kerr
68	David Baseggio
89	Larry Rooney
110	Miguel Baldris
131	Mike Hartman
152	Francois Guay
173	Shawn Whitham
194	Kenton Rein
215	Troy Arndt

1985
Pick
14	Carl Johansson
35	Benoit Hogue
56	Keith Gretzky
77	Dave Moylan
98	Ken Priestlay
119	Joe Reekie
140	Petri Matikainen
161	Trent Kaese
182	Jiri Sejba
203	Boyd Sutton
224	Guy Larose
245	Ken Baumgartner

1984
Pick
18	Mikael Andersson
39	Doug Trapp
60	Ray Sheppard
81	Bob Halkidis
102	Joey Rampton
123	James Gasseau
144	Darcy Wakaluk
165	Orwar Stambert
207	Brian McKinnon
228	Grant Delcourt
249	Sean Baker

1983
Pick
5	Tom Barrasso
10	Normand Lacombe
11	Adam Creighton
31	John Tucker
34	Richard Hajdu
74	Daren Puppa
94	Jayson Meyer
114	Jim Hofford
134	Christian Ruuttu
154	Don McSween
174	Tim Hoover
194	Mark Ferner
214	Uwe Krupp
234	Marc Hamelin
235	Kermit Salfi

1982
Pick
6	Phil Housley
9	Paul Cyr
16	Dave Andreychuk
26	Mike Anderson
30	Jens Johansson
68	Timo Jutila
79	Jeff Hamilton
100	Bob Logan
111	Jeff Parker
121	Jacob Gustavsson
142	Allen Bishop
163	Claude Verrett
184	Rob Norman
205	Mike Craig
226	Jim Plankers

1981
Pick
17	Jiri Dudacek
38	Hannu Virta
59	Jim Aldred
60	Colin Chisholm
80	Jeff Eatough
83	Anders Wikberg
101	Mauri Eivola
122	Ali Butorac
143	Heikki Leime
164	Gates Orlando
185	Venci Sebeck
206	Warren Harper

1980
Pick
20	Steve Patrick
41	Mike Moller
56	Sean McKenna
62	Jay North
83	Jim Wiemer
104	Dirk Reuter
125	Daniel Naud
146	Jari Paavola
167	Randy Cunneyworth
188	Dave Beckon
209	John Bader

1979
Pick
11	Mike Ramsey
32	Lindy Ruff
53	Mark Robinson
55	Jacques Cloutier
74	Gilles Hamel
95	Alan Haworth
116	Rick Knickle

1978
Pick
13	Larry Playfair
32	Tony McKegney
49	Rob McClanahan
66	Mike Gazdic
82	Randy Ireland
99	Cam MacGregor
116	Dan Eastman
133	Eric Strobel
150	Eugene O'Sullivan

1977
Pick
14	Ric Seiling
32	Ron Areshenkoff
68	Bill Stewart
86	Richard Sirois
104	Wayne Ramsey

1976
Pick
33	Joe Kowal
69	Henry Maze
87	Ron Roscoe
105	Don Lemieux

1975
Pick
17	Bob Sauve
35	Ken Breitenbach
44	Terry Martin
53	Gary McAdam
71	Greg Neeld
89	Don Edwards
107	Jim Minor
125	Grant Rowe
143	Alex Tidey
159	Andy Whitby
174	Len Moher

1974
Pick
11	Lee Fogolin
29	Danny Gare
47	Michel Deziel
65	Paul McIntosh
83	Gary Lariviere
101	Dave Given
119	Bernard Noreau
136	Charles Constantin
153	Rick Jodzio
168	Derek Smith
183	Taro Tsujimoto
196	Bob Geoffrion

1973
Pick
12	Morris Titanic
28	Jean Landry
44	Andre Deschamps
60	Yvon Dupuis
76	Bob Smulders
92	Neil Korzack
108	Bob Young
124	Tim O'Connell

1972
Pick
5	Jim Schoenfeld
25	Larry Carriere
37	Jim McMasters
53	Richard Campeau
69	Gilles Gratton
85	Peter McNab

Club Directory

Memorial Auditorium
Buffalo, N.Y. 14202
Phone 716/856-7300
TWX 710-522-1153
ENVOY ID   TM.BUF
Capacity: 16,433

Board of Directors
Edwin C. Andrews	John E. Houghton	Paul A. Schoellkopf
Peter C. Andrews	Seymour H. Knox III	Joseph T.J. Stewart
George L. Collins Jr., M.D.	Northrup R. Knox	George Strawbridge Jr.
John B. Fisher	Robert E. Rich Jr.	Robert O. Swados
David G. Forman	Howard T. Saperston Jr.	Arthur Victor Jr.

Chairman of the Board and Chief Executive Officer	Seymour H. Knox III
President	Northrup R. Knox
Vice-Chairman of the Board	David G. Forman
Vice-Chairman of the Board	Robert E. Rich, Jr.
Vice-President and Counsel	Robert O. Swados
Administrative Vice-President	Mitchell Owen
Vice President/Finance	Robert W. Pickel
Treasurer	Joseph T.J. Stewart
Secretary	James E. Rolls
Director of Hockey Operations, General Manager and Coach	William Scott Bowman
Assistant General Manager	Gerry Meehan
Assistant Coaches	Craig Ramsay, Don Luce, Barry Smith
Scouting Staff	Don Barrie, Jack Bowman, Frank Deegan, Andy Fila, Paul Goulet, Dennis McIvor, Rudy Migay, Mike Racicot, Frank Zywiec
Executive Trainer and Co-ordinator of Team Travel	Frank Christie
Athletic Trainers	Jim Pizzutelli, Rip Simonick
Director of Communications	Paul Wieland
Director of Public Relations	John Gurtler
Director of Ticket Operations	Jeff Pickel
Merchandise Manager	Scott Ross
Director of Advertising and Group Sales	Steve Donner
Director of Merchandising and Promotions	Jeffrey Pokerwinski
Communications/Public Relations Assistant	Jeanne Golanka
Sales Representatives	Paul D'Aiuto, Doug McKay, John Newhouse
Club Doctors	John L. Butsch, M.D., Joseph E. Buran, M.D.
Club Dentist	Donald R. DeRose, D.D.S.
Location of Press Box	Suspended from ceiling on West Side
Dimensions of Rink	196 feet by 85 feet
Ends of Rink	Plexi-glass above boards
Club Colors	Blue, Gold, White
Training Camp Site	Sabreland, Wheatfield, NY, Memorial Auditorium
Public Address Announcer	Milt Ellis, Joe Amorosi
Organist	Joe Mankowski
Anthem Singer	Sue Brittain
Play-by-Play Announcers	Ted Darling, Rick Jeanneret
Television Outlets	WGRZ-TV (2), Cable 10
Radio Station	WBEN (930) AM

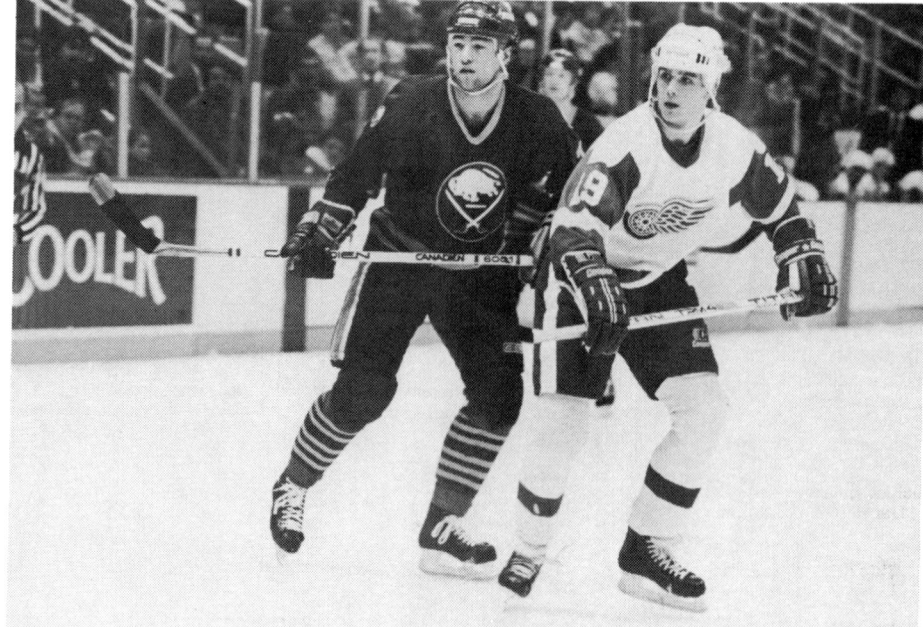

John Tucker, here checking Steve Yzerman of the Red Wings, had a 31-goal season in 1985-86.

Calgary Flames

1985-86 Results: 40w-31L-9T 89 PTS. Second, Smythe Division

Year-by-Year Record

		Home			Road			Overall							
Season	GP	W	L	T	W	L	T	W	L	T	GF	GA	Pts.	Finished	Playoff Result
1985-86	80	23	11	6	17	20	3	40	31	9	354	315	89	2nd, Smythe Div.	Lost Final
1984-85	80	23	11	6	18	16	6	41	27	12	363	302	94	3rd, Smythe Div.	Lost Div. Final
1983-84	80	22	11	7	12	21	7	34	32	14	311	314	82	2nd, Smythe Div.	Lost Div. Final
1982-83	80	21	12	7	11	22	7	32	34	14	321	317	78	2nd, Smythe Div.	Lost Div. Final
1981-82	80	20	11	9	9	23	8	29	34	17	334	345	75	3rd, Smythe Div.	Lost Div. Semi-Final
1980-81	80	25	5	10	14	22	4	39	27	14	329	298	92	3rd, Patrick Div.	Lost Semi-Final
1979-80	80	18	15	7	17	17	6	35	32	13	282	269	83	4th, Patrick Div.	Lost Prelim. Round
1978-79	80	25	11	4	16	20	4	41	31	8	327	280	90	4th, Patrick Div.	Lost Prelim. Round
1977-78	80	20	13	7	14	14	12	34	27	19	274	252	87	3rd, Patrick Div.	Lost Prelim. Round
1976-77	80	22	11	7	12	23	5	34	34	12	264	265	80	3rd, Patrick Div.	Lost Prelim. Round
1975-76	80	19	14	7	16	19	5	35	33	12	262	237	82	3rd, Patrick Div.	Lost Prelim. Round
1974-75	80	24	9	7	10	22	8	34	31	15	243	233	83	4th, Patrick Div.	Out of Playoffs
1973-74	78	17	15	7	13	19	7	30	34	14	214	238	74	4th, West Div.	Lost Quarter-Final
1972-73	78	16	16	7	9	22	8	25	38	15	191	239	65	7th, West Div.	Out of Playoffs

Schedule

Home

Oct.
Thur. 16 Quebec
Sat. 18 Detroit
Wed. 22 Edmonton
Sun. 26 Boston

Nov.
Sat. 1 Washington
Mon. 3 Los Angeles
Fri. 7 Edmonton
Sun. 9 Montreal
Tue. 11 Vancouver
Thur. 13 Hartford
Thur. 20 Pittsburgh
Sat. 22 NY Rangers
Mon. 24 Edmonton
Thur. 27 Winnipeg
Sat. 29 Chicago

Dec.
Tue. 2 NY Islanders
Thur. 4 Chicago
Tue. 16 Detroit
Thur. 18 Quebec
Mon. 22 Los Angeles

Jan.
Thur. 8 Los Angeles
Sat. 10 St. Louis
Wed. 14 NY Rangers
Sat. 17 Vancouver
Thur. 29 Minnesota
Sat. 31 New Jersey

Feb.
Tue. 3 Vancouver
Thur. 5 St. Louis
Sat. 7 NY Islanders
Fri. 20 Toronto
Sun. 22 Washington
Tue. 24 Vancouver
Thur. 26 Philadelphia
Sat. 28 Winnipeg

Mar.
Tue. 3 Montreal
Thur. 5 Los Angeles
Tue. 17 Buffalo
Thur. 19 Edmonton
Thur. 26 Winnipeg

April Sun. 5 Winnipeg *

Away

Oct.
Thur. 9 Boston
Sat. 11 Hartford
Sun. 12 Buffalo
Fri. 24 Winnipeg
Tue. 28 Minnesota
Wed. 29 Winnipeg

Nov.
Wed. 5 Edmonton
Sat. 15 Los Angeles
Tue. 18 Vancouver

Dec.
Sat. 6 Quebec
Mon. 8 Montreal
Wed. 10 Pittsburgh
Thur. 11 Philadelphia
Sat. 13 Los Angeles
Sat. 20 Vancouver
Sun. 28 Buffalo
Tue. 30 New Jersey
Wed. 31 Detroit

Jan.
Sat. 3 St. Louis
Sun. 4 Chicago
Sun. 11 Edmonton
Fri. 16 Vancouver
Tue. 20 NY Islanders
Thur. 22 New Jersey
Sat. 24 Boston *
Mon. 26 Toronto

Feb.
Sun. 8 Vancouver
Sat. 14 Minnesota
Mon. 16 Philadelphia *
Tue. 17 Pittsburgh

Mar.
Sun. 1 Winnipeg
Sun. 8 NY Rangers
Tue. 10 Washington
Wed. 11 Hartford
Sat. 14 Toronto
Fri. 20 Edmonton
Wed. 25 Winnipeg
Sat. 28 Los Angeles
Mon. 30 Los Angeles

April Thur. 2 Edmonton

Denotes afternoon game.

Home Starting Times:
Mondays through Fridays . . . . 7:35 p.m.
Saturdays & Sundays . . . . 6:05 p.m.
Except Apr. 5 . . . . 1:35 p.m.

Franchise date: June 24, 1980.
Transferred from Atlanta.

15th NHL Season

Hakan Loob had 67 points in the regular season and 14 in the playoffs for Calgary.

1986-87 Player Personnel

FORWARDS	Ht.	Wt.	Place of Birth	Date	1985-86 Club
BAKOVIC, Peter	6-1	190	Thunder Bay, Ont.	1/31//65	Moncton
BEREZAN, Perry	6-2	192	Edmonton, Alta.	12/5/64	Calgary
BODAK, Bob	6-2	190	Thunder Bay, Ont.	5/28/61	Moncton
BOZEK, Steve	5-11	175	Kelowna, B.C.	11/26/60	Calgary
BRADLEY, Brian	5-10	170	Kitchener, Ont.	1/21/65	Calgary-Moncton
COURTEAU, Yves	6-0	194	Montreal, Que.	4/25/64	Calgary-Moncton
DOUCET, Benoit	5-10	180	Montreal, Que.	4/23/63	Moncton
FOTIU, Nick	6-2	210	Staten Island, N.Y.	5/25/52	Calgary-New Haven
HULL, Brett	5-11	195	Belleville, Ont.	8/9/64	U. of Minnesota-Duluth
HUNTER, Tim	6-2	202	Calgary, Alta.	9/10/59	Calgary (NHL)
LOOB, Hakan	5-9	175	Karlstad, Sweden	7/3/60	Calgary
McDONALD, Lanny	6-0	190	Hanna, Alta.	2/16/53	Calgary
MULLEN, Joe	5-9	180	New York, N.Y.	2/26/57	Calgary-St. Louis
OTTO, Joel	6-4	220	St. Cloud, Minn.	10/29/61	Calgary
PATTERSON, Colin	6-2	195	Rexdale, Ont.	5/11/60	Calgary
PEPLINSKI, Jim	6-3	209	Renfrew, Ont.	10/24/60	Calgary
PICKELL, Doug	6-1	185	London, Ont.	5/7/68	Kamloops
QUINN, Dan	5-11	175	Ottawa, Ont.	6/1/65	Calgary
RISEBROUGH, Doug	5-11	183	Kitchener, Ont.	1/29/54	Calgary
ROBERTS, Gary	6-1	190	North York, Ont.	5/23/66	Guelph-Ottawa
TONELLI, John	6-1	200	Milton, Ont.	3/23/57	Calgary-NY Islanders
WENAAS, Jeff	6-0	185	Eastend, Sask.	9/1/67	Medicine Hat
WILSON, Carey	6-0	185	Winnipeg, Man.	5/9/62	Calgary
DEFENSEMEN					
BAXTER, Paul	5-11	189	Winnipeg, Man.	10/25/55	Calgary
DEGRAY, Dale	6-0	201	Oshawa, Ont.	9/3/63	Moncton
GLYNN, Brian	6-4	224	Iserlohn, W. Germany	11/23/67	Saskatoon
GREGOIRE, Bill	6-0	175	Victoria, B.C.	4/9/67	Victoria
GUY, Kevan	6-3	202	Edmonton, Alta.	7/16/65	Moncton
JOHNSON, Terry	6-3	210	Calgary, Alta.	11/28/58	Calgary-St. Louis
KIVELL, Rob	6-2	200	North Bay, Ont.	1/14/65	Moncton
LESSARD, Rick	6-2	198	Timmins, Ont.	1/9/68	Ottawa
MacDONALD, Chris	6-1	175	Barrie, Ont.	7/9/63	Western Michigan
MacINNIS, Al	6-2	193	Inverness, N.S.	7/11/63	Calgary
MACOUN, Jamie	6-2	197	Newmarket, Ont.	8/17/61	Calgary
McCUTCHEON, Darwin	6-5	210	Listowel, Ont.	4/19/62	Moncton
MELROSE, Kevan	5-10	180	Calgary, Alta.	3/28/66	Penticton
MERCIER, Don	6-4	210	Grimshaw, Alta.	1/21/63	U. of Denver
MERSCH, Mike	6-2	210	Skokie, Ill.	9/29/64	U. of Illinois at Chicago
REIERSON, Dave	6-0	185	Bashaw, Ont.	8/30/64	Michigan Tech.
REINHART, Paul	5-11	195	Kitchener, Ont.	1/8/60	Calgary
RIVINGTON, Dale	6-1	193	Ottawa, Ont.	3/7/64	Rochester Tech.
SABOURIN, Ken	6-4	204	Scarborough, Ont.	4/28/66	Cornwall
SHEEHY, Neil	6-2	215	Fort Francis, Ont.	2/9/60	Calgary-Moncton
SUTER, Gary	6-0	199	Madison, Wis.	6/24/64	Calgary
GOALTENDERS					
BLAIR, Grant	6-0	160	Ancaster, Ont.	8/15/64	Harvard
DADSWELL, Doug	5-10	175	Scarborough, Ont.	2/7/64	Cornell
D'AMOUR, Marc	5-10	165	Sudbury, Ont.	4/29/61	Calgary-Moncton
KOSTI, Rick	5-10	185	Kincaid, Sask.	9/13/63	Moncton-Salt Lake City
LEMELIN, Rejean	5-11	170	Quebec City, Que.	11/19/54	Calgary
VERNON, Mike	5-9	155	Calgary, Alta.	2/24/63	Salt Lake City-Moncton-Calgary

Coach and General Manager

JOHNSON, ROBERT (BOB)

Coach, Calgary Flames. Born in Minneapolis, Minn., March 4, 1931.

Bob Johnson was named coach of the Calgary Flames on June 2, 1982 after an outstanding coaching career at the collegiate and international levels in the United States. His coaching career began in 1956 at Warroad High School in Minnesota, and he moved on to become coach of Colorado College in 1963 and was named coach of the year in 1964 and 1965 while at Colorado. In 1967, Johnson was named coach at the University of Wisconsin where he guided the Badgers to three national titles and a record of 367 wins, 175 losses and 23 ties. Johnson also has been involved with U.S. national teams on several occasions, including World Championships in 1973, 1974, 1975 and 1981 and was also head coach of Team USA in the 1976 Winter Olympics and the 1981 and 1984 Canada Cup tournaments. Entering his fifth NHL season, Johnson guided the Flames to their first-ever Stanley Cup Finals appearance last year.

NHL Coaching Record

		Regular Season					Playoffs			
Team		Games	W	L	T	%	Games	W	L	%
Calgary	1982-83	80	32	34	14	.488	9	4	5	.444
Calgary	1983-84	80	34	32	14	.513	11	6	5	.545
Calgary	1984-85	80	41	27	12	.588	4	1	3	.250
Calgary	1985-86	80	40	31	9	.556	22	12	10	.545
NHL Totals		**320**	**147**	**124**	**49**	**.536**	**46**	**23**	**23**	**.500**

FLETCHER, GEORGE CLIFFORD (CLIFF)

General Manager, Calgary Flames. Born in Montreal, Que., August 16, 1935.

Cliff Fletcher's career in professional hockey began in 1956 when he joined the Montreal Canadiens' organization as manager of the Junior "B" Verdun Blues. For the next 10 years, working closely with former Canadien manager Sam Pollock, Fletcher carried out a variety of functions, including coaching and managing the Junior Canadiens and scouting for the parent team. In May, 1966, he joined the St. Louis Blues as Chief Scout for Eastern Canada and remained in that post until June, 1969, when he was appointed Assistant General Manager, a position he held until the end of the 1970-71 season. During his four full seasons with St. Louis, the Blues never failed to reach the playoffs; were Stanley Cup finalists three years in a row and captured two West Division titles. He was named General Manager of the Atlanta Flames, January 10, 1972, and retained the position when the franchise was transferred to Calgary in 1980.

1985-86 Scoring

Regular Season

*–rookie

Pos	#	Player	Team	GP	G	A	Pts	+/–	PIM	PP	SH	GW	OT	S	%
F	7	Joe Mullen	STL	48	28	24	52	7–	10	9	0	4	0	142	19.7
			CGY	29	16	22	38	3	11	5	0	4	0	61	26.2
			Total	77	44	46	90	4–	21	14	0	8	0	203	21.7
F	10	Dan Quinn	CGY	78	30	42	72	12–	44	17	3	3	1	191	15.7
F	9	Lanny McDonald	CGY	80	28	43	71	3–	44	11	0	3	1	227	12.3
F	27	John Tonelli	NYI	65	20	41	61	22	50	3	0	1	0	139	14.4
			CGY	9	3	4	7	0	10	1	0	1	0	18	16.7
			Total	74	23	45	68	22	60	4	0	2	0	157	14.6
D	20	*Gary Suter	CGY	80	18	50	68	11	141	9	0	4	0	195	9.2
D	2	Al MacInnis	CGY	77	11	57	68	39	76	4	0	0	0	241	4.6
F	12	Hakan Loob	CGY	68	31	36	67	22	36	10	0	1	1	174	17.8
F	29	*Joel Otto	CGY	79	25	34	59	22	188	9	0	2	1	147	17.0
F	24	Jim Peplinski	CGY	77	24	35	59	32	214	0	1	3	0	161	14.9
F	33	Carey Wilson	CGY	76	29	29	58	1	24	5	0	2	1	150	19.3
F	26	Steve Bozek	CGY	64	21	22	43	24	24	5	4	3	0	146	14.4
F	8	Doug Risebrough	CGY	62	15	28	43	22	169	0	3	1	0	92	16.3
F	21	*Perry Berezan	CGY	55	12	21	33	19	39	0	2	3	0	117	10.3
D	23	Paul Reinhart	CGY	32	8	25	33	4	15	4	0	2	0	58	13.8
D	34	Jamie Macoun	CGY	77	11	21	32	14	81	0	2	1	0	133	8.3
F	11	Colin Patterson	CGY	61	14	13	27	8	22	0	0	1	0	84	16.7
D	5	Neil Sheehy	CGY	65	2	16	18	1–	271	1	0	0	0	59	3.4
F	19	Tim Hunter	CGY	66	8	7	15	9–	291	2	0	2	0	65	12.3
D	6	Terry Johnson	STL	49	0	4	4	6–	87	0	0	0	0	21	.0
			CGY	24	1	4	5	3–	71	0	0	0	0	11	9.1
			Total	73	1	8	9	9–	158	0	0	0	0	32	3.1
D	4	Paul Baxter	CGY	47	4	3	7	5	194	0	1	0	0	41	9.8
D	32	Rik Wilson	STL	32	0	4	4	9–	48	0	0	0	0	45	.0
			CGY	2	0	0	0	2	0	0	0	0	0	3	.0
			Total	34	0	4	4	7–	48	0	0	0	0	48	.0
G	31	Rejean Lemelin	CGY	60	0	4	4	0	10	0	0	0	0	0	.0
F	25	*Yves Courteau	CGY	4	1	1	2	1	0	0	0	0	0	7	14.3
F	14	*Brian Bradley	CGY	5	0	1	1	3–	0	0	0	0	0	4	.0
F	22	Nick Fotiu	CGY	9	0	1	1	3–	21	0	0	0	0	7	.0
G	30	*Mike Vernon	CGY	18	0	1	1	0	4	0	0	0	0	0	.0
D	15	*Robin Bartel	CGY	1	0	0	0	1–	0	0	0	0	0	0	.0
D	28	*Dale Degray	CGY	1	0	0	0	1–	0	0	0	0	0	1	.0
F	16	*Mark Lamb	CGY	1	0	0	0	0	0	0	0	0	0	0	.0
G	1	*Marc d'Amour	CGY	15	0	0	0	0	22	0	0	0	0	0	.0

Playoffs

* rookie

Pos	#	Player	Team	GP	G	A	Pts	+/–	PIM	PP	SH	GW	OT	S	%
F	7	Joe Mullen	CGY	21	12	7	19	3–	4	4	0	2	0	53	22.6
D	2	Al MacInnis	CGY	21	4	15	19	11	30	2	0	0	0	79	5.1
F	9	Lanny McDonald	CGY	22	11	7	18	5	30	4	0	2	1	70	15.7
D	23	Paul Reinhart	CGY	21	5	13	18	2–	4	4	0	0	0	34	14.7
F	8	Doug Risebrough	CGY	22	7	9	16	9	38	0	1	1	0	38	18.4
F	27	John Tonelli	CGY	22	7	9	16	3	49	1	0	1	0	44	15.9
F	10	Dan Quinn	CGY	18	8	7	15	0	10	5	1	2	0	34	23.5
F	29	*Joel Otto	CGY	22	5	10	15	5–	80	3	0	1	0	41	12.2
F	24	Jim Peplinski	CGY	22	5	9	14	1	107	0	0	0	0	28	17.9
F	12	Hakan Loob	CGY	22	4	10	14	4–	6	1	2	0	0	56	7.1
D	20	*Gary Suter	CGY	10	2	8	10	1	8	0	0	1	0	17	11.8
F	11	Colin Patterson	CGY	19	6	3	9	0	10	1	1	1	0	36	16.7
F	26	Steve Bozek	CGY	14	2	6	8	1	32	0	0	0	0	28	7.1
D	34	Jamie Macoun	CGY	22	1	6	7	8	23	0	0	0	0	42	2.4
D	6	Terry Johnson	CGY	17	0	3	3	2–	64	0	0	0	0	5	.0
F	19	Tim Hunter	CGY	19	0	3	3	1	108	0	0	0	0	7	.0
F	21	*Perry Berezan	CGY	8	1	1	2	9–	6	0	0	1	0	6	16.7
F	17	Mike Eaves	CGY	8	1	1	2	5–	8	0	0	0	0	9	11.1
F	33	Carey Wilson	CGY	9	0	2	2	1	2	0	0	0	0	22	.0
D	5	Neil Sheehy	CGY	22	0	2	2	2–	79	0	0	0	0	11	.0
G	31	Rejean Lemelin	CGY	3	0	1	1	0	0	0	0	0	0	0	.0
F	22	Nick Fotiu	CGY	11	0	1	1	1	34	0	0	0	0	12	.0
D	4	Paul Baxter	CGY	13	0	1	1	4–	55	0	0	0	0	7	.0
G	30	*Mike Vernon	CGY	21	0	1	1	2–	0	0	0	0	0	0	.0
F	14	*Brian Bradley	CGY	1	0	0	0	0	0	0	0	0	0	2	.0
F	25	*Yves Courteau	CGY	1	0	0	0	1–	0	0	0	0	0	1	.0
F	16	*Brett Hull	CGY	2	0	0	0	0	0	0	0	0	0	1	.0
D	3	*Robin Bartel	CGY	6	0	0	0	0	16	0	0	0	0	2	.0

Doug Risebrough

Club Records

Team

(Figures in brackets for season records are games played; records for fewest points, wins, ties, losses, goals, goals against are for 70 or more games)

Most Points	94	1984-85 (80)
Most Wins	41	1978-79, 1984-85 (80)
Most Ties	19	1977-78 (80)
Most Losses	38	1972-73 (78)
Most Goals	363	1984-85 (80)
Most Goals Against	345	1981-82 (80)
Fewest Points	65	1972-73 (78)
Fewest Wins	25	1972-73 (78)
Fewest Ties	8	1978-79 (80)
Fewest Losses	27	1977-78 (80) 1980-81 (80)
Fewest Goals	191	1972-73 (78)
Fewest Goals Against	233	1974-75 (80)

Longest Winning Streak
- Overall . . . . 10 Oct. 14-Nov. 3/78
- Home . . . . 9 Oct. 17-Nov. 15/78
- Away . . . . 4 Six times

Longest Undefeated Streak
- Over-all . . . . 12 Oct. 11-Nov. 3/78 (10 wins, 2 ties)
- Home . . . . 18 Mar. 4/78-Nov. 15/78 (12 wins, 6 ties)
- Away . . . . 7 Mar. 13-Apr. 5/85 (4 wins, 3 ties)

Longest Losing Streak
- Over-all . . . . 11 Dec. 14/85 Jan. 7/86
- Home . . . . 4 Four times
- Away . . . . 9 Dec. 1/85 Jan. 12/86

Longest Winless Streak
- Over-all . . . . 11 Dec. 14/85 Jan. 7/86
- Home . . . . 6 Nov. 25/82-Dec. 18/82
- Away . . . . 13 Feb. 3-Mar. 29/73 (10 losses, 3 ties)

Most Shutouts, Season 8 1974-75 (80)
Most. Pen. Mins.,
Season 2,279 1985-86 (80)
Most Goals, Game . . . . 12 Mar. 21/75 (Van. 4 at Atl. 12)

Individual

Most Seasons	9	Dan Bouchard
Most Games	559	Eric Vail
Most Goals, Career	229	Kent Nilsson
Most Assists, Career	336	Guy Chouinard
Most Points, Career	562	Kent Nilsson (229 goals, 333 assists)
Most Pen. Mins., Career	1,267	Willi Plett
Most Shutouts, Career	20	Dan Bouchard

Longest Consecutive
- Games Streak . . . . 257 Brad Marsh (Oct. 11/78-Nov. 10/81)
- Most Goals, Season . . . . . 66 Lanny McDonald (1982-83)
- Most Assists, Season . . . . . 82 Kent Nilsson (1980-81)
- Most Points, Season . . . . . 131 Kent Nilsson (1980-81) (49 goals, 82 assists)
- Most Pen. Mins., Season . . . 291 Tim Hunter (1985-86)

Most Points, Defenseman
- Season . . . . 75 Paul Reinhart (1982-83) (17 goals, 58 assists)

Most Points, Center
- Season . . . . 131 Kent Nilsson (1980-81) (49 goals, 82 assists)

Most Points, Right Wing
- Season . . . . 108 Bob MacMillan (1978-79) (37 goals, 71 assists)

Most Points, Left Wing
- Season . . . . 83 Eric Vail (1978-79) (35 goals, 48 assists)

Most Points, Rookie
- Season . . . . 72 Carey Wilson (1984-85) (24 goals, 48 assists)

Most Shutouts, Season . . . . . 5 Dan Bouchard (1973-74) Phil Myre (1974-75)

Most Goals, Game . . . . 4 Keith McCreary (Mar. 21/75) Garry Unger (Jan. 11/80) Jim Peplinski (Nov. 17/81) Kent Nilsson (Feb. 27/82) Kent Nilsson (Dec. 20/84)

Most Points, Game . . . . 6 Guy Chouinard (Feb. 25/81) Gary Suter (Apr. 4/86)

Coaching History

Bernie Geoffrion, 1972-73 to 1973-74; Bernie Geoffrion and Fred Creighton, 1974-75; Fred Creighton, 1975-76 to 1978-79; Al MacNeil, 1979-80 (Atlanta); 1980-81 to 1981-82 (Calgary); Bob Johnson, 1982-83 to date.

Captains' History

Keith McCreary, 1972-73 to 1974-75; Pat Quinn, 1975-76, 1976-77; Tom Lysiak, 1977-78, 1978-79; Jean Pronovost, 1979-80; Brad Marsh, 1980-81; Phil Russell, 1981-82, 1982-83; Lanny McDonald, Doug Risebrough (co-captains), 1983-84; Lanny McDonald, Doug Risebrough, Jim Peplinski (co-captains), 1984-85 to 1985-86.

All-time Record vs. Other Clubs

Regular Season

	At Home							On Road							Total						
	GP	W	L	T	GF	GA	PTS	GP	W	L	T	GF	GA	PTS	GP	W	L	T	GF	GA	PTS
Boston	28	12	14	2	106	99	26	27	5	19	3	64	96	13	55	17	33	5	170	195	39
Buffalo	27	9	10	8	85	93	26	27	7	16	4	77	126	18	54	16	26	12	162	219	44
Chicago	30	14	10	6	98	91	34	29	5	17	7	76	113	17	59	19	27	13	174	204	51
Detroit	26	16	6	4	114	77	36	27	10	13	4	87	105	24	53	26	19	8	201	182	60
Edmonton	24	7	14	3	104	109	17	24	3	16	5	95	131	10	48	10	30	8	199	240	27
Hartford	12	8	3	1	67	45	17	11	5	4	2	40	38	11	23	13	7	3	107	83	28
Los Angeles	40	24	8	8	180	122	56	39	13	23	3	128	157	29	79	37	31	11	308	279	85
Minnesota	29	17	4	8	123	82	42	29	10	15	4	96	112	25	58	27	19	12	219	194	67
Montreal	26	4	17	5	76	104	13	27	7	16	4	63	100	19	53	11	33	9	139	204	32
*New Jersey	26	20	2	4	125	61	44	26	17	6	3	101	69	37	52	37	8	7	226	130	81
NY Islanders	32	13	10	9	113	104	35	33	6	18	9	83	133	21	65	19	28	18	196	237	56
NY Rangers	32	17	9	6	138	93	40	33	15	14	4	118	117	34	65	32	23	10	256	210	74
Philadelphia	33	15	11	7	135	114	37	33	5	27	1	75	149	11	66	20	38	8	210	263	48
Pittsburgh	27	16	5	6	109	71	38	27	7	12	8	94	97	22	54	23	17	14	203	168	60
Quebec	11	5	2	4	42	35	14	12	5	6	1	41	49	11	23	10	8	5	83	84	25
St. Louis	29	13	13	3	95	88	29	30	14	12	4	91	104	32	59	27	25	7	186	192	61
Toronto	29	16	10	3	122	103	35	27	10	12	5	94	110	25	56	26	22	8	216	213	60
Vancouver	41	28	7	6	194	115	62	41	17	16	8	135	144	42	82	45	23	14	329	259	104
Washington	21	16	4	1	90	47	33	22	9	10	3	84	85	21	43	25	14	4	174	132	54
Winnipeg	22	17	2	3	123	67	37	21	11	5	5	94	82	27	43	28	7	8	217	149	64
Defunct Clubs	13	8	4	1	51	34	17	13	7	3	3	43	33	17	26	15	7	4	94	67	34
Totals	558	295	165	98	2290	1754	688	558	188	280	90	1779	2150	466	1116	483	445	188	4069	3904	1154

* Totals include those of Kansas City (1974-75, 1975-76) and Colorado (1976-77 through 1981-82)

Playoffs

	Series	W	L	GP	W	L	T	GF	GA	Last Mtg.	Round	Result
Chicago	1	1	0	3	3	0	0	15	9	1981	P	W 3-0
Detroit	1	0	1	2	0	2	0	5	8	1978	P	L 2-0
Edmonton	3	1	2	19	8	11	0	75	90	1986	DF	W 4-3
Los Angeles	2	0	2	5	1	4	0	8	14	1977	P	L 1-2
Minnesota	1	0	1	6	2	4	0	18	25	1981	SF	L 2-4
Montreal	1	0	1	5	1	4	0	13	15	1986	F	L 1-4
NY Rangers	1	0	1	4	1	3	0	14	14	1980	P	L 1-3
Philadelphia	2	1	1	11	4	7	0	28	43	1981	QF	W 4-3
St. Louis	1	1	0	7	4	3	0	28	22	1986	CF	W 4-3
Vancouver	3	2	1	11	6	5	0	36	35	1984	DSF	W 3-1
Winnipeg	2	1	1	10	7	3	0	28	23	1986	DSF	W 3-0
Totals	18	7	11	83	37	46	0	262	298			

Playoff Results 1986-82

Year	Round	Opponent	Result	GF	GA
1986	F	Montreal	L 1-4	13	15
	CF	St. Louis	W 4-3	28	22
	DF	Edmonton	W 4-3	25	24
	DSF	Winnipeg	W 3-0	15	8
1985	DSF	Winnipeg	L 1-3	13	15
1984	DS	Edmonton	L 3-4	27	31
		Vancouver	W 3-1	14	13
1983	DF	Edmonton	L 1-4	13	35
	DSF	Vancouver	W 3-1	17	14
1982	DSF	Vancouver	L 0-3	5	8

Abbreviations: Round: F – Final; CF – conference final; DF – division final; DSF – division semi-final; SF – semi-final; QF – quarter-final; P – preliminary round. GA – goals against; GF – goals for.

Entry Draft Selections 1986-72

1986
Pick
- 16 George Pelawa
- 37 Brian Glynn
- 79 Tom Quinlan
- 100 Scott Bloom
- 121 John Parker
- 142 Rick Lessard
- 163 Mark Olsen
- 184 Warren Sharples
- 205 Doug Pickell
- 226 Anders Lindstrom
- 247 Antonin Stavjana

1985
Pick
- 17 Chris Biotti
- 27 Joe Nieuwendyk
- 38 Jeff Wenaas
- 59 Lane MacDonald
- 80 Roger Johansson
- 101 Esa Keskinen
- 122 Tim Sweeney
- 143 Stu Grimson
- 164 Nate Smith
- 185 Darryl Olsen
- 206 Peter Romberg
- 227 Alexandr Koznevnikov
- 248 Bill Gregoire

1984
Pick
- 12 Gary Roberts
- 33 Ken Sabourin
- 38 Paul Ranheim
- 75 Peter Rosol
- 96 Joel Paunio
- 117 Brett Hull
- 138 Kevan Melrose
- 159 Jiri Hrdina
- 180 Gary Suter
- 200 Peter Rucka
- 221 Stefan Jonsson
- 241 Rudolf Suchanek

1983
Pick
- 13 Dan Quinn
- 51 Brian Bradley
- 55 Perry Berezan
- 66 John Bekkers
- 71 Kevan Guy
- 77 Bill Claviter
- 91 Igor Liba
- 111 Grant Blair
- 131 Jeff Hogg
- 151 Chris MacDonald
- 171 Rob Kivell
- 191 Tom Pratt
- 211 Jaroslav Benak
- 231 Sergei Makarov

1982
Pick
- 29 Dave Reierson
- 37 Richard Kromm
- 51 Jim Laing
- 65 Dave Meszaros
- 72 Mark Lamb
- 93 Lou Kiriakou
- 114 Jeff Vaive
- 118 Mats Kihlstrom
- 135 Brad Ramsden
- 156 Roy Myllari
- 177 Ted Pearson
- 198 Jim Uens
- 219 Rick Erdall
- 240 Dale Thompson

1981
Pick
- 15 Allan MacInnis
- 56 Mike Vernon
- 78 Peter Madach
- 99 Mario Simioni
- 120 Todd Hooey
- 141 Rick Heppner
- 162 Dale Degray
- 183 George Boudreau
- 204 Bruce Eakin

1980
Pick
- 13 Denis Cyr
- 31 Tony Curtale
- 32 Kevin LaVallee
- 39 Steve Konroyd
- 76 Marc Roy
- 97 Randy Turnbull
- 118 John Multan
- 139 Dave Newsom
- 160 Claude Drouin
- 181 Hakan Loob
- 202 Steve Fletcher

1979
Pick
- 12 Paul Reinhart
- 23 Mike Perovich
- 33 Pat Riggin
- 54 Tim Hunter
- 75 Jim Peplinski
- 96 Brad Kempthorne
- 117 Glenn Johnson

1978
Pick
- 11 Brad Marsh
- 47 Tim Bernhardt
- 64 Jim MacRae
- 80 Gord Wappel
- 97 Greg Meredith
- 114 Dave Hindmarch
- 131 Dave Morrison
- 148 Doug Todd
- 165 Mark Green
- 180 Robert Sullivan
- 196 Berhn Engelbeckt

1977
Pick
- 20 Miles Zaharko
- 28 Red Laurence
- 31 Brian Hill
- 72 Jim Craig
- 82 Curt Christofferson
- 100 Bernard Harbec
- 118 Bob Gould
- 133 Jim Bennett
- 148 Tim Harrer

1976
Pick
- 8 David Shand
- 10 Harold Phillipoff
- 28 Bob Simpson
- 46 Richard Hodgson
- 64 Kent Nilsson
- 82 Mark Earp

1975
Pick
- 8 Richard Mulhern
- 26 Rick Bowness
- 62 Dave Ross
- 80 Willi Plett
- 98 Paul Heaver
- 116 Dale McMullin
- 134 Rick Piche
- 150 Nick Sanza
- 167 Brian O'Connell
- 181 Joe Augustine
- 192 Torbjorn Nilsson
- 216 Gary Gill

1974
Pick
- 28 Guy Chouinard
- 46 Dick Spannbauer
- 58 Pat Ribble
- 64 Cam Botting
- 82 Jerry Badiuk
- 100 Bill Moen
- 118 Peter Brown
- 135 Tom Lindskog
- 152 Larry Hopkins
- 167 Louis Loranger
- 182 Randy Montgomery

1973
Pick
- 2 Tom Lysiak
- 16 Vic Mercredi
- 21 Eric Vail
- 53 Dean Talafous
- 69 John Flesch
- 85 Ken Houston
- 102 Tom Machowski
- 117 Bob Law
- 133 Bob Bilodeau
- 148 Glen Surbey
- 149 Guy Ross
- 162 Greg Fox

1972
Pick
- 2 Jacques Richard
- 18 Dwight Bialowas
- 34 Jean Lemieux
- 50 Don Martineau
- 78 John Martin
- 82 Frank Blum
- 98 Scott Smith
- 114 Dave Murphy
- 130 Pierre Roy
- 132 Jean Lamarre

Club Directory

Saddledome
P.O. Box 1540 Station M
Calgary, Alberta T2P 3B9
Phone 403/261-0475
Telecopier 403/261-0470
TWX 610-821-0965
ENVOY ID TM.CGY
Capacity: 16,762

Owners
Norman N. Green
Harley N. Hotchkiss
Norman L. Kwong
Mrs. Ralph T. Scurfield
Byron J. Seaman
Daryl K. Seaman

President, General Manager, Governor	Cliff Fletcher
Vice President of Business and Finance	Clare Rhyasen
Assistant to the President	Al Coates
Assistant General Manager	Al MacNeil
General Counsellors	Howard Mackie & Company
Controller	Lynne Tosh
Vice-President of Sales & Broadcasting	Leo Ornest
Director of Public Relations	Rick Skaggs
Coach	Bob Johnson
Assistant Coaches	Bob Murdoch, Pierre Pagé
Goaltending Consultant	Glenn Hall
Development Club General Manager & Coach	Terry Crisp
Assistant Coach	Dan Bolduc
Chief Scout	Gerry Blair
Co-ordinator of Scouting	Ian McKenzie
Scouting Staff	Al Godfrey, Ben Hayes, Larry McNab, Garth Malarchuk, Lars Norrman, Larry Popein, Tom Thompson, Bill White
Executive Secretaries	June Yeates, Brenda Koyich
Assistant Controller	Dorothy Stuart
Marketing Assistant	Judy Shupe
Advertising Sales	Pat Halls
Assistant Public Relations Director	Mike Burke
Ticket Manager	Ann Marie Malarchuk
Assistant Ticket Manager	Avis Hunt
Receptionists	Robbie Forand, Sandy Hafichuk
Trainer	Jim "Bearcat" Murray
Equipment Manager	Bobby Stewart
Assistant Trainer	Al Murray
Team Physician	Dr. Pete McMurtry, Dr. Don Dinwoodie
Team Dentist	Dr. Tom Dunphy
Consulting Psychologist	Hap Davis and Robert Offenberger, Ph.D.
Location of Press Box	Print/TV—North side; Radio—South Side
Dimensions of Rink	200 feet by 85 feet
Ends of Rink	Plexiglass
Club Colours	White, Red, Gold
Club Trains at	Olympic Saddledome
TV Channels	CFAC-TV (Channels 2 & 7) CBC-TV (Channels 6 & 9)
Radio	QR-77 Radio (770 AM)

Goaltender Reggie Lemelin and Lanny McDonald

Chicago Blackhawks

1985-86 Results: 39w-33L-8T 86 PTS. First, Norris Division

Schedule

		Home				Away
Oct.	Thur.	9 NY Islanders	Oct.	Sat.	11	Detroit
	Sun.	12 Pittsburgh		Sat.	18	Toronto
	Wed.	15 NY Rangers		Tue.	21	Edmonton
	Sun.	19 Minnesota		Fri.	24	Vancouver
Nov.	Wed.	5 Minnesota		Sun.	26	Winnipeg
	Sun.	9 St. Louis		Tue.	28	Toronto
	Wed.	12 Washington		Wed.	29	Detroit
	Sun.	16 Toronto	Nov.	Sat.	1	Minnesota
	Wed.	19 Los Angeles		Sun.	2	St. Louis
	Sun.	23 New Jersey		Sat.	8	Washington
Dec.	Wed.	10 Buffalo		Sat.	15	St. Louis
	Sun.	14 Vancouver		Thur.	20	Philadelphia
	Wed.	17 Winnipeg		Wed.	26	Minnesota
	Sun.	21 Detroit		Fri.	28	Edmonton
	Fri.	26 St. Louis		Sat.	29	Calgary
	Sun.	28 Washington	Dec.	Tue.	2	Vancouver
Jan.	Sun.	4 Calgary		Thur.	4	Calgary
	Wed.	7 Toronto		Sat.	6	Los Angeles
	Sun.	11 Detroit		Sat.	13	St. Louis
	Wed.	14 New Jersey		Sat.	20	Boston
	Sun.	18 Quebec		Tue.	23	Detroit
	Wed.	21 Philadelphia		Tue.	30	NY Islanders
	Mon.	26 Montreal		Wed.	31	Buffalo
	Wed.	28 Toronto	Jan.	Sat.	3	Hartford*
Feb.	Sun.	1 Edmonton		Sat.	17	Minnesota
	Wed.	4 Detroit		Fri.	23	Philadelphia
	Sun.	15 Quebec*		Sat.	24	Montreal
	Tue.	17 Hartford		Sat.	31	St. Louis
	Thur.	19 NY Rangers	Feb.	Sat.	7	Pittsburgh
	Sun.	22 Detroit		Sun.	8	Buffalo
	Wed.	25 Montreal		Sat.	21	Hartford
Mar.	Sun.	1 Los Angeles		Sat.	28	Pittsburgh
	Wed.	4 Winnipeg	Mar.	Sat.	7	New Jersey
	Sun.	8 NY Islanders		Sat.	14	Boston*
	Wed.	11 St. Louis		Tue.	17	Minnesota
	Sun.	15 Minnesota*		Wed.	18	Toronto
	Wed.	25 St. Louis		Sat.	21	Detroit
	Sun.	29 Boston		Sun.	22	NY Rangers
April	Wed.	1 Minnesota		Sat.	28	Quebec
	Sun.	5 Toronto	April	Sat.	4	Toronto

*Denotes afternoon game.

Home Starting Times:
All Games . . . . 7:35 p.m.
Except Matinees . . . . 1:35 p.m.

Franchise date: September 25, 1926

Campbell Conference

61st NHL Season

Troy Murray, right, was selected the top defensive forward in the NHL in 1985-86.

Year-by-Year Record

		Home			Road			Overall							
Season	GP	W	L	T	W	L	T	W	L	T	GF	GA	Pts.	Finished	Playoff Result
1985-86	80	23	12	5	16	21	3	39	33	8	351	350	86	1st, Norris Div.	Lost Div. Semi Final
1984-85	80	22	16	2	16	19	5	38	35	7	309	299	83	2nd, Norris Div.	Lost Conf. Final
1983-84	80	25	13	2	5	29	6	30	42	8	277	311	68	4th, Norris Div.	Lost Div. Semi-Final
1982-83	80	29	8	3	18	15	7	47	23	10	338	268	104	1st, Norris Div.	Lost Conf. Championship
1981-82	80	20	13	7	10	25	5	30	38	12	332	363	72	4th, Norris Div.	Lost Conf. Championship
1980-81	80	21	11	8	10	22	8	31	33	16	304	315	78	2nd, Smythe Div.	Lost Prelim. Round
1979-80	80	21	12	7	13	15	12	34	27	19	241	250	87	1st, Smythe Div.	Lost Quarter-Final
1978-79	80	18	12	10	11	24	5	29	36	15	244	277	73	1st, Smythe Div.	Lost Quarter-Final
1977-78	80	20	9	11	12	20	8	32	29	19	230	220	83	1st, Smythe Div.	Lost Quarter-Final
1976-77	80	19	16	5	7	27	6	26	43	11	240	298	63	3rd, Smythe Div.	Lost Prelim. Round
1975-76	80	17	15	8	15	15	10	32	30	18	254	261	82	1st, Smythe Div.	Lost Quarter-Final
1974-75	80	24	12	4	13	23	4	37	35	8	268	241	82	3rd, Smythe Div.	Lost Semi-Final
1973-74	78	20	6	13	21	8	10	41	14	23	272	164	105	2nd, West Div.	Lost Final
1972-73	78	26	9	4	16	18	5	42	27	9	284	225	93	1st, West Div.	Lost Final
1971-72	78	28	3	8	18	14	7	46	17	15	256	166	107	1st, West Div.	Lost Semi-Final
1970-71	78	30	6	3	19	14	6	49	20	9	277	184	107	1st, West Div.	Lost Final
1969-70	76	26	7	5	19	15	4	45	22	9	250	170	99	1st, East Div.	Lost Semi-Final
1968-69	76	20	14	4	14	19	5	34	33	9	280	246	77	6th, East Div.	Out of Playoffs
1967-68	74	20	13	4	12	13	12	32	26	16	212	222	80	4th, East Div.	Lost Semi-Final
1966-67	70	24	5	6	17	12	6	41	17	12	264	170	94	1st,	Lost Semi-Final
1965-66	70	21	8	6	16	17	2	37	25	8	240	187	82	2nd,	Lost Final
1964-65	70	20	13	2	14	15	6	34	28	8	224	176	76	3rd,	Lost Final
1963-64	70	26	4	5	10	18	7	36	22	12	218	169	84	2nd,	Lost Semi-Final
1962-63	70	17	9	9	15	12	8	32	21	17	194	178	81	2nd,	Lost Semi-Final
1961-62	70	20	10	5	11	16	8	31	26	13	217	186	75	3rd,	Lost Final
1960-61	70	20	6	9	9	18	8	29	24	17	198	180	75	3rd,	Won Stanley Cup
1959-60	70	18	11	6	10	18	7	28	29	13	191	180	69	3rd,	Lost Semi-Final
1958-59	70	14	12	9	14	17	4	28	29	13	197	208	69	3rd,	Lost Semi-Final
1957-58	70	15	17	3	9	22	4	24	39	7	163	202	55	5th,	Out of Playoffs
1956-57	70	12	15	8	4	24	7	16	39	15	169	225	47	6th,	Out of Playoffs
1955-56	70	9	19	7	10	20	5	19	39	12	155	216	50	6th,	Out of Playoffs
1954-55	70	6	21	8	7	19	9	13	40	17	161	235	43	6th,	Out of Playoffs
1953-54	70	8	21	6	4	30	1	12	51	7	133	242	31	6th,	Out of Playoffs
1952-53	70	14	11	10	13	17	5	27	28	15	169	175	69	4th,	Lost Semi-Final
1951-52	70	9	19	7	8	25	2	17	44	9	158	241	43	6th,	Out of Playoffs
1950-51	70	8	22	5	5	25	5	13	47	10	171	280	36	6th,	Out of Playoffs
1949-50	70	13	18	4	9	20	6	22	38	10	203	244	54	6th,	Out of Playoffs
1948-49	60	13	12	5	8	19	3	21	31	8	173	211	50	5th,	Out of Playoffs
1947-48	60	10	17	3	10	17	3	20	34	6	195	225	46	6th,	Out of Playoffs
1946-47	60	10	17	3	9	20	1	19	37	4	193	274	42	6th,	Out of Playoffs
1945-46	50	15	5	5	8	15	2	23	20	7	200	178	53	3rd,	Lost Semi-Final
1944-45	50	9	14	2	4	16	5	13	30	7	141	194	33	5th,	Out of Playoffs
1943-44	50	15	6	4	7	17	1	22	23	5	178	187	49	4th,	Lost Final
1942-43	50	14	3	8	3	15	7	17	18	15	179	180	49	5th,	Out of Playoffs
1941-42	48	15	8	1	7	15	2	22	23	3	145	155	47	4th,	Lost Semi-Final
1940-41	48	11	10	3	5	15	4	16	25	7	112	139	39	5th,	Lost Semi-Final
1939-40	48	15	7	2	8	12	4	23	19	6	112	120	52	4th,	Lost Quarter-Final
1938-39	48	5	13	6	7	15	2	12	28	8	91	132	32	7th,	Out of Playoffs
1937-38	48	10	10	4	4	15	5	14	25	9	97	139	37	3rd, Amn. Div.	Won Stanley Cup
1936-37	48	8	13	3	6	14	4	14	27	7	99	131	35	4th, Amn. Div.	Out of Playoffs
1935-36	48	15	7	2	6	12	6	21	19	8	93	92	50	3rd, Amn. Div.	Lost Quarter-Final
1934-35	48	12	9	3	14	8	2	26	17	5	118	88	57	2nd, Amn. Div.	Lost Quarter-Final
1933-34	48	13	4	7	7	13	4	20	17	11	88	83	51	2nd, Amn. Div.	Won Stanley Cup
1932-33	48	12	7	5	4	13	7	16	20	12	88	101	44	4th,	Out of Playoffs
1931-32	48	13	5	6	5	14	5	18	19	11	86	101	47	2nd,	Lost Quarter-Final
1930-31	44	14	7	1	10	10	2	24	17	3	108	78	51	2nd,	Lost Final
1929-30	44	12	9	1	9	9	4	21	18	5	117	111	47	2nd,	Lost Quarter-Final
1928-29	44	3	13	6	4	16	2	7	29	8	33	85	22	5th, Amn. Div.	Out of Playoffs
1927-28	44	2	18	2	5	16	1	7	34	3	68	134	17	5th, Amn. Div.	Out of Playoffs
1926-27	44	12	8	2	7	14	1	19	22	3	115	116	41	3rd, Amn. Div.	Lost Quarter-Final

1986-87 Player Personnel

	Ht.	Wt.	Place of Birth	Date	1985-86 Club
FORWARDS					
BELLAND, Brad	6-0	180	Windsor, Ont.	1/4/67	Sudbury-Hamilton
BENIC, Geoff	6-2	198	Toronto, Ont.	9/1/68	Windsor
BOUDREAU, Bruce	5-10	170	Toronto, Ont.	1/9/55	Nova Scotia-Chicago
BRACCIA, Rick	6-0	195	Revere, Mass.	9/5/67	Boston College
BROWN, Bill	6-1	170	Dayton, Ohio	10/9/66	Ohio State
CAMAZZOLA, Jim	5-11	190	Vancouver, B.C.	1/5/64	Nova Scotia-Saginaw
ERIKSSON, Tom	5-11	183	Umea, Sweden	5/3/66	Modo Division 1 (Sweden)
FRASER, Curt	6-0	200	Cincinnati, Ohio	1/12/58	Chicago
GREENOUGH, Glenn	5-11	198	Sudbury, Ont.	7/20/66	Sudbury
HUDSON, Mike	6-1	185	Guelph, Ont.	2/6/67	Sudbury
LAPLANTE, Richard	5-11	175	Boucherville, Que.	3/15/67	U. of Vermont
LARMER, Steve	5-10	189	Peterborough, Ont.	6/16/61	Chicago
LAVARRE, Mark	5-11	170	Evanston, Ill.	2/21/65	Nova Scotia-Chicago
LOACH, Lonnie	5-10	181	New Liskeard, Ont.	4/14/68	Guelph
LOWES, Glenn	6-0	184	Burlington, Ont.	1/17/68	Toronto (OHL)
LUDZIK, Steve	5-11	186	Toronto, Ont.	4/3/62	Chicago
LYSIAK, Tom	6-1	204	High Prairie, Alta.	4/22/53	Chicago
MACKEY, David	6-3	190	N. Westminster, B.C.	7/24/66	Medicine Hat
MURRAY, Troy	6-1	195	Calgary, Alta.	7/31/62	Chicago
NANNE, Marty	6-0	180	Edina, Minnesota	7/21/67	U. of Minnesota
NOONAN, Brian	6-1	180	Boston, Mass.	5/29/65	Saginaw
OLCZYK, Ed	6-1	195	Chicago, Ill.	8/16/66	Chicago
PATERSON, Rick	5-9	187	Kingston, Ont.	2/10/58	Chicago
PERSSON, Joakim	5-8	163	Gavle, Sweden	5/15/66	Gavle Division 1 (Sweden)
POSA, Victor	6-0	193	Bari, Italy	11/5/66	Toronto (OHL)-Chicago
PRESLEY, Wayne	5-11	172	Detroit, Mich.	3/23/65	Chicago-Nova Scotia
SANIPASS, Everett	6-1	192	Big Cove, N.B.	2/13/68	Verdun
SAVARD, Denis	5-10	167	Pt. Gatineau, Que.	2/4/61	Chicago
SCEVIOUR, Darin	5-10	185	Lacombe, Alta.	11/30/65	Nova Scotia-Saginaw
SECORD, Al	6-1	212	Sudbury, Ont.	3/3/58	Chicago
STAPLETON, Mike	5-10	163	Sarnia, Ont.	5/5/66	Cornwall
SUTTER, Darryl	5-11	176	Viking, Alta.	8/19/58	Chicago
THAYER, Chris	6-2	190	Exeter, N.H.	11/9/67	Kent High School
TORKKI, Jari	6-0	163	Finland	8/11/65	Lukko (Finland)
VINCELLETTE, Dan	6-1	202	Verdun, Que.	8/1/67	Drummondville
WATSON, Bill	6-1	190	Pine Falls, Man.	3/30/64	Chicago
WILLIAMS, Sean	6-1	182	Oshawa, Ont.	1/28/68	Oshawa
YAREMCHUK, Ken	5-11	187	Edmonton, Alta.	1/1/64	Chicago
DEFENSEMEN					
BADEAU, Rene	6-0	190	Trois Rivieres, Que.	1/31/64	DID NOT PLAY
BECK, Brad	5-11	185	Vancouver, B.C.	2/10/64	Michigan St.
BERGEVIN, Marc	5-11	178	Montreal, Que.	8/11/65	Chicago
BROWN, Keith	6-1	191	Cornerbrook, Nfld.	5/6/60	Chicago
CASSIDY, Bruce	5-11	176	Ottawa, Ont.	5/20/65	Nova Scotia-Chicago
DIFIORE, Ralph	6-1	181	Montreal, Que.	4/20/66	Trois Rivieres
DOYON, Mario	6-0	174	Quebec City, Que.	8/27/68	Drummondville
DUPONT, Jerome	6-3	201	Ottawa, Ont.	2/21/62	Chicago
HAMILTON, Brad	6-0	175	Calgary, Alta.	3/30/67	Michigan St.
HEED, Jonas	6-0	174	Sodertalje, Sweden	1/3/67	Sodertalje (Sweden)
HERBERT, Rick	6-1	180	Toronto, Ont.	7/10/67	Portland-Spokane
HOWARD, Tarek	6-1	185	Tucson, Arizona	2/6/65	U. of North Dakota
KUCERA, Frantisek	6-1	180	Stibrova, Czech.	2/3/68	Sparta Praha (Czech.)
KURZAWSKI, Mark	6-3	199	Chicago, Ill.	2/25/68	Windsor
MANSON, Dave	6-2	190	Prince Albert, Sask.	1/27/67	Prince Albert
MURRAY, Bob	5-10	186	Kingston, Ont.	11/24/54	Chicago
O'CALLAHAN, Jack	6-1	189	Charleston, Mass.	7/24/57	Chicago
PAYNTER, Kent	6-0	186	Summerside, P.E.I.	4/27/65	Nova Scotia
POUND, Ian	6-1	183	Brockville, Ont.	1/22/67	Kitchener
WILLIAMS, Dan	6-2	180	Oak Park, Ill.	4/15/66	Elmira
WILSON, Behn	6-3	210	Toronto, Ont.	12/19/58	Chicago
WILSON, Doug	6-1	187	Ottawa, Ont.	7/5/57	Chicago
YAWNEY, Trent	6-3	183	Hudson Bay, Sask.	9/29/65	Team Canada
GOALTENDERS					
BANNERMAN, Murray	5-11	185	Ft. Francis, Ont.	4/27/57	Chicago
CLIFFORD, Chris	5-9	140	Kingston, Ont.	5/26/66	Kingston
HELMUTH, Andy	5-10	170	Detroit, Mich.	3/19/67	Ottawa
LEHKONEN, Timo	5-11	165	Helsinki, Finland	1/8/66	Finnish National Team
PANG, Darren	5-5	155	Medford, Ont.	2/17/64	Saginaw
RALPH, Jim	5-11	165	S.S. Marie, Ont.	5/13/62	Nova Scotia-Saginaw
REID, John	5-11	200	Windsor, Ont.	2/18/67	Belleville-North Bay
SAUVE, Bob	5-8	165	Ste. Genevieve, Que.	6/17/55	Chicago
SKORODENSKI, Warren	5-8	165	Winnipeg, Man.	3/22/60	Chicago-Nova Scotia

1985-86 Scoring

Regular Season

*–rookie

Pos	#	Player	Team	GP	G	A	Pts	+/–	PIM	PP	SH	GW	OT	S	%
F	18	Denis Savard	CHI	80	47	69	116	7	111	14	1	8	2	279	16.8
F	19	Troy Murray	CHI	80	45	54	99	32	94	9	5	7	0	197	22.8
F	16	Ed Olczyk	CHI	79	29	50	79	2	47	8	1	2	0	218	13.3
F	20	Al Secord	CHI	80	40	36	76	8	201	12	0	3	1	210	19.0
F	28	Steve Larmer	CHI	80	31	45	76	9	47	13	1	3	0	184	16.8
F	8	Curt Fraser	CHI	61	29	39	68	11	84	7	0	1	0	144	20.1
D	24	Doug Wilson	CHI	79	17	47	64	24	80	3	0	2	1	243	7.0
D	23	Behn Wilson	CHI	69	13	38	51	11–	113	10	0	6	0	138	9.4
D	4	Keith Brown	CHI	70	11	29	40	6–	87	1	1	0	0	151	7.3
D	6	Bob Murray	CHI	80	9	29	38	6	75	3	0	1	0	139	6.5
F	15	Ken Yaremchuk	CHI	78	14	20	34	17–	43	0	0	2	0	82	17.1
F	27	Darryl Sutter	CHI	50	17	10	27	15–	44	3	0	2	0	89	19.1
F	11	*Bill Watson	CHI	52	8	16	24	4–	2	2	0	0	0	67	11.9
D	5	Jack O'Callahan	CHI	80	4	19	23	5	116	0	0	0	0	86	4.7
F	12	Tom Lysiak	CHI	51	2	19	21	19–	14	0	0	0	0	77	2.6
F	17	*Wayne Presley	CHI	38	7	8	15	6–	38	0	0	1	0	56	12.5
D	25	Jerome Dupont	CHI	75	2	13	15	17–	173	0	0	0	0	69	2.9
D	2	Marc Bergevin	CHI	71	7	7	14	0	60	0	0	1	0	50	14.0
F	26	Rick Patterson	CHI	70	9	3	12	1–	24	0	5	0	0	36	25.0
F	29	Steve Ludzik	CHI	49	6	5	11	2–	21	0	1	0	0	41	14.6
G	30	Murray Bannerman	CHI	48	0	2	2	0	6	0	0	0	0	0	.0
F	32	Bruce Boudreau	CHI	7	1	0	1	1	2	0	0	0	0	3	33.3
G	31	Bob Sauve	CHI	38	0	1	1	0	27	0	0	0	0	0	.0
D	3	*Bruce Cassidy	CHI	1	0	0	0	0	0	0	0	0	0	2	.0
G	1	Warren Skorodenski	CHI	1	0	0	0	0	0	0	0	0	0	0	.0
F	10	Jeff Larmer	CHI	2	0	0	0	1	0	0	0	0	0	1	.0
F	7	*Mark Lavarre	CHI	2	0	0	0	2–	0	0	0	0	0	2	.0
F	34	*Victor Posa	CHI	2	0	0	0	0	2	0	0	0	0	1	.0
F	22	Tom McMurchy	CHI	4	0	0	0	1–	2	0	0	0	0	2	.0

Playoffs

* rookie

Pos	#	Player	Team	GP	G	A	Pts	+/–	PIM	PP	SH	GW	OT	S	%
F	18	Denis Savard	CHI	3	4	1	5	1–	6	2	0	0	0	16	25.0
F	12	Tom Lysiak	CHI	3	2	1	3	1–	2	0	0	0	0	6	33.3
F	27	Darryl Sutter	CHI	3	1	2	3	4–	0	1	0	0	0	7	14.3
F	28	Steve Larmer	CHI	3	0	3	3	1–	4	0	0	0	0	13	.0
D	24	Doug Wilson	CHI	3	1	1	2	5–	2	0	0	0	0	14	7.1
F	15	Ken Yaremchuk	CHI	3	1	1	2	2	2	0	0	0	0	2	50.0
F	20	Al Secord	CHI	2	0	2	2	1–	26	0	0	0	0	2	.0
D	6	Bob Murray	CHI	3	0	2	2	4–	0	0	0	0	0	6	.0
F	11	*Bill Watson	CHI	2	0	1	1	1–	0	0	0	0	0	1	.0
D	4	Keith Brown	CHI	3	0	1	1	1–	9	0	0	0	0	5	.0
F	8	Curt Fraser	CHI	3	0	1	1	4–	12	0	0	0	0	4	.0
D	5	Jack O'Callahan	CHI	3	0	1	1	3–	4	0	0	0	0	3	.0
D	25	Jerome Dupont	CHI	1	0	0	0	1	0	0	0	0	0	0	.0
G	30	Murray Bannerman	CHI	2	0	0	0	0	4	0	0	0	0	0	.0
F	19	Troy Murray	CHI	2	0	0	0	3–	2	0	0	0	0	1	.0
G	31	Bob Sauve	CHI	2	0	0	0	0	0	0	0	0	0	0	.0
D	23	Behn Wilson	CHI	2	0	0	0	1–	2	0	0	0	0	3	.0
D	2	Marc Bergevin	CHI	3	0	0	0	1–	0	0	0	0	0	5	.0
F	29	Steve Ludzik	CHI	3	0	0	0	1–	12	0	0	0	0	10	.0
F	16	Ed Olczyk	CHI	3	0	0	0	6–	0	0	0	0	0	10	.0
F	26	Rick Paterson	CHI	3	0	0	0	0	0	0	0	0	0	0	.0
F	17	*Wayne Presley	CHI	3	0	0	0	0	0	0	0	0	0	0	.0

Coach and General Manager

PULFORD, ROBERT JESSE (BOB)
General Manager and Coach, Chicago Blackhawks.
Born in Newton Robinson, Ont., March 31, 1936.

Bob Pulford was named general-manager and coach of Chicago, July 6, 1977, after five successful seasons as head coach of the Los Angeles Kings. He relinquished the coaching duties to Eddie Johnston prior to the start of the 1979-80 season, but returned behind the bench on February 3, 1982, replacing Keith Magnuson. At the conclusion of the 1981-82 season Pulford stepped down as coach of the Blackhawks and on June 16, 1982 named Orval Tessier as his successor. After 16 playing seasons in the NHL, Pulford began his coaching career with the Kings in 1972-73. For 14 of those seasons, Pulford was an industrious player with the Toronto Maple Leafs before being traded to Los Angeles where he finished his active career as captain of the Kings. Although he never won an individual award nor was ever selected to an All-Star team, Pulford was recognized as one of the hardest-working centers during the era in which he played. His all-round ability enabled him to be rated one of the League's outstanding penalty-killers. Pulford was named NHL coach-of-the-year in 1974-75 by the NHL Broadcasters' Association. Pulford replaced Orval Tessier in February, 1985, and coached the Hawks during the remainder of the season. In 27 games under Pulford, Chicago was one of the hottest teams in hockey down the stretch, finishing 16-7-4. In the playoffs, they forced Edmonton to six games before being defeated in the Conference Championship.

NHL Coaching Record

			Regular Season				Playoffs			
Team	Season	Games	W	L	T	%	Games	W	L	%
Los Angeles	1972-73	78	31	36	11	.468	....	....	....	....
Los Angeles	1973-74	78	33	33	12	.500	5	1	4	.200
Los Angeles	1974-75	80	42	17	21	.656	3	1	2	.333
Los Angeles	1975-76	80	38	33	9	.531	9	5	4	.556
Los Angeles	1976-77	80	34	31	15	.519	9	4	5	.444
Chicago	1977-78	80	32	29	19	.519	4	0	4	.000
Chicago	1978-79	80	29	36	15	.456	4	0	4	.000
Chicago	1981-82	28	13	13	2	.500	15	8	7	.533
Chicago	1984-85	27	16	7	4	.666	15	9	6	.600
Chicago	1985-86	80	39	33	8	.538	3	0	3	.000
NHL Totals		**691**	**307**	**268**	**116**	**.528**	**67**	**28**	**39**	**.418**

Club Records

Team

(Figures in brackets for season records are games played; records for fewest points, wins, ties, losses, goals, goals against are for 70 or more games)

Most Points	107	1970-71 (78)
		1971-72 (78)
Most Wins	49	1970-71 (78)
Most Ties	23	1973-74 (78)
Most Losses	51	1953-54 (70)
Most Goals	351	1985-86 (80)
Most Goals Against	363	1981-82 (80)
Fewest Points	31	1953-54 (70)
Fewest Wins	12	1953-54 (70)
Fewest Ties	7	1953-54 (70)
		1957-58 (70)
Fewest Losses	14	1973-74 (78)
Fewest Goals	*133	1953-54 (70)
Fewest Goals Against	164	1973-74 (78)

Longest Winning Streak

Over-all	8	Dec. 9-26/71
		Jan. 4-21/81
Home	13	Nov. 11-Dec. 20/70
Away	7	Dec. 9-29/64

Longest Undefeated Streak

Over-all	15	Jan. 14-Feb. 16/67 (12 wins, 3 ties)
Home	18	Oct. 11-Dec. 20/70 (16 wins, 2 ties)
Away	10	Nov. 2-Dec. 16/67 (8 wins, 2 ties)

Longest Losing Streak

Over-all	13	Feb. 25-Oct. 11/51
Home	11	Feb. 8-Nov. 22/28
Away	17	Jan. 2-Oct. 7/54

Longest Winless Streak

Over-all	21	Dec. 17/50-Jan. 28/51 (18 losses, 3 ties)
Home	*15	Dec. 16/28-Feb. 28/29 (11 Losses, 4 ties)
Away	23	Dec. 19/50-Oct. 11/51 (15 losses, 8 ties)

Most Shutouts, Season	15	1969-70 (76)
Most Pen. Mins., Season	1,775	1981-82 (80)
Most Goals, Game	12	Jan. 30/69 (Chi. 12 at Phil. 0)

Individual

Most Seasons	21	Stan Mikita
Most Games	1,394	Stan Mikita
Most Goals, Career	604	Bobby Hull
Most Assists, Career	926	Stan Mikita
Most Points, Career	1,467	Stan Mikita (541 goals, 926 assists)
Most Pen. Mins., Career	1,442	Keith Magnuson
Most Shutouts, Career	74	Tony Esposito
Longest Consecutive Games Streak	509	John Marks (Oct. 27/73-Jan. 2/80)
Most Goals, Season	58	Bobby Hull (1968-69)
Most Assists, Season	87	Denis Savard (1981-82)
Most Points, Season	121	Denis Savard (1982-83) (35 goals, 86 assists)
Most Pen. Mins., Season	303	Al Secord (1981-82)
Most Points, Defenseman Season	85	Doug Wilson (1981-82) (39 goals, 46 assists)

Most Points, Center, Season	121	Denis Savard (1982-83) (35 goals, 86 assists)
Most Points, Right Wing, Season	92	Jim Pappin (1972-73) (41 goals, 51 assists)
Most Points, Left Wing, Season	107	Bobby Hull (1968-9) (58 goals, 49 assists)
Most Points, Rookie, Season	90	Steve Larmer (1982-83) (43 goals, 47 assists)
Most Shutouts, Season	15	Tony Esposito (1969-70)
Most Goals, Game	5	Grant Mulvey (Feb. 3/82)
Most Assists, Game	6	Pat Stapleton (Mar. 30/69)
Most Points, Game	7	Max Bentley (Nan. 28/43)
		Grant Mulvey (Feb. 3/82)

* NHL Record.

Coaching History

Pete Muldoon, 1926-27; Barney Stanley and Hugh Lehman, 1927-28; Herb Gardiner, 1928-29; Tom Shaughnessy and Bill Tobin, 1929-30; Dick Irvin, 1930-31; Dick Irvin and Bill Tobin, 1931-32; Godfrey Matheson, Emil Iverson and Tommy Gorman, 1932-33; Tommy Gorman, 1933-34; Clem Loughlin, 1934-35 to 1936-37; Bill Stewart, 1937-38; Bill Stewart and Paul Thompson, 1938-39; Paul Thompson, 1939-40 to 1943-44; Paul Thompson and Johnny Gottselig, 1944-45; Johnny Gottselig, 1945-46 to 1946-47; Johnny Gottselig and Charlie Conacher, 1947-48; Charlie Conacher, 1948-49 to 1949-50; Ebbie Goodfellow, 1950-51 to 1951-52; Sid Abel, 1952-53 to 1953-54; Frank Eddolls, 1954-55; Dick Irvin, 1955-56; Tommy Ivan, 1956-57; Tommy Ivan and Rudy Pilous, 1957-58; Rudy Pilous, 1958-59 to 1962-63; Billy Reay, 1963-64 to 1975-76; Billy Reay and Bill White, 1976-77; Bob Pulford, 1977-78 to 1978-79; Eddie Johnston, 1979-80; Keith Magnuson, 1980-81; Keith Magnuson and Bob Pulford, 1981-82; Orval Tessier, 1982-83 to 1983-84; Orval Tessier and Bob Pulford, 1984-85; Bob Pulford, 1985-86.

Captains' History

Dick Irvin, 1926-27 to 1928-29; Duke Dutkowski, 1929-30; Ty Arbour, 1930-31; Cy Wentworth, 1931-32; Helge Bostrom, 1932-33; Chuck Gardiner, 1933-34; no captain, 1934-35; Johnny Gottselig, 1935-36 to 1939-40; Earl Seibert, 1940-41, 1941-42; Doug Bentley, 1942-43, 1943-44; Clint Smith 1944-45; John Mariucci, 1945-46; Red Hamill, 1946-47; John Mariucci, 1947-48; Gaye Stewart, 1948-49; Doug Bentley, 1949-50; Jack Stewart, 1950-51, 1951-52; Bill Gadsby, 1952-53, 1953-54; Gus Mortson, 1954-55 to 1956-57; no captain, 1957-58; Eddie Litzenberger, 1958-59 to 1960-61; Pierre Pilote, 1961-62 to 1967-68, no captain, 1968-69; Pat Stapleton, 1969-70; no captain, 1970-71 to 1974-75; Stan Mikita, Pit Martin, 1975-76; Stan Mikita, Pit Martin, Keith Magnuson, 1976-77; Keith Magnuson, 1977-78, 1978-79; Keith Magnuson, Terry Ruskowski, 1979-80; Terry Ruskowski, 1980-81, 1981-82; Darryl Sutter, 1982-83 to 1985-86.

All-time Record vs. Other Clubs

Regular Season

		At Home						On Road						Total					
	GP	W	L	T	GF	GA	PTS	GP	W	L	T	GF	GA	PTS	GP	W	L	T	GF	GA	Pts
Boston	267	138	85	44	861	694	320	265	81	153	31	740	955	193	532	219	238	75	1601	1649	513
Buffalo	33	18	9	6	105	80	42	33	7	20	6	82	128	20	66	25	29	12	187	208	62
**Calgary	29	17	5	7	113	76	41	30	10	14	6	91	98	26	59	27	19	13	204	174	67
Detroit	278	131	105	42	826	756	304	277	79	171	27	671	941	185	555	210	276	69	1497	1697	489
Edmonton	12	4	7	1	53	64	9	11	6	4	1	41	39	13	23	12	7	4	104	78	28
Hartford	12	6	3	3	63	39	15	11	6	4	1	41	39	13	23	12	7	4	104	78	28
Los Angeles	40	22	13	5	159	120	49	42	21	16	5	143	132	47	82	43	29	10	302	252	96
Minnesota	57	37	14	6	236	135	80	57	26	24	7	202	200	59	114	63	38	13	438	335	139
Montreal	256	87	119	50	680	709	224	257	49	160	48	605	801	146	513	136	279	98	1285	1510	370
NY Islanders	29	12	13	4	90	107	28	29	4	16	9	79	117	17	58	16	29	13	169	224	45
NY Rangers	267	122	105	40	812	735	284	268	105	112	51	761	787	261	535	227	217	91	1573	1522	545
Philadelphia	43	20	8	15	143	106	55	42	12	22	8	115	136	32	85	32	30	23	258	242	87
Pittsburgh	42	29	4	9	177	106	67	40	18	18	4	130	136	40	82	47	22	13	307	242	107
Quebec	11	7	4	0	51	36	14	12	3	6	3	41	55	9	23	10	10	3	92	91	23
St. Louis	60	40	13	7	241	163	87	58	22	26	10	194	200	54	118	62	39	17	435	363	141
Toronto	268	128	102	38	789	693	294	269	76	146	47	665	929	199	537	204	248	85	1454	1622	493
Vancouver	39	24	10	5	136	86	53	38	12	16	10	115	115	34	77	36	26	15	251	201	87
Washington	21	12	5	4	90	64	28	22	7	12	3	74	89	17	43	19	17	7	164	153	45
Winnipeg	13	8	4	1	68	46	17	14	5	7	2	55	61	12	27	13	11	3	123	107	29
Defunct Clubs	139	79	40	20	408	267	178	140	52	67	21	316	345	125	279	131	107	41	724	612	303
Totals	1943	961	671	311	6222	5149	2233	1943	608	1030	305	5251	6471	1521	3886	1569	1701	616	11473	11775	3754

* Totals include those of Kansas City (1974-75, 1975-76) and Colorado (1976-77 through 1981-82)

** Totals include those of Atlanta (1972-73 through 1979-80)

Playoffs

	Series	W	L	GP	W	L	T	GF	GA	Last Mtg.	Round	Result
Boston	6	1	5	22	5	16	1	63	97	1978	QF	L 0-4
Buffalo	2	0	2	9	1	8	0	17	36	1980	QF	L 0-4
Calgary	1	0	1	3	0	3	0	9	15	1981	P	L 0-3
Detroit	10	5	5	50	26	24	0	156	138	1985	DSF	W 3-0
Edmonton	2	0	2	10	2	8	0	36	69	1985	CF	L 2-4
Los Angeles	1	1	0	5	4	1	0	10	7	1974	QF	W 4-1
Minnesota	4	3	1	20	13	7	0	79	80	1985	DF	W 4-2
Montreal	17	5	12	81	29	50	2	185	261	1976	QF	L 0-4
NY Islanders	2	0	2	6	0	6	0	6	21	1979	QF	L 0-4
NY Rangers	5	4	1	24	14	10	0	66	54	1973	SF	W 4-1
Philadelphia	1	1	0	4	4	0	0	20	8	1971	QF	W 4-0
Pittsburgh	1	1	0	4	4	0	0	14	8	1972	QF	W 4-0
St. Louis	4	4	0	18	14	4	0	73	42	1983	DSF	W 3-1
Toronto	7	2	5	25	9	15	1	57	76	1986	DSF	L 0-3
Vancouver	1	0	1	5	1	4	0	13	18	1982	CF	W 4-1
Defunct Clubs	4	2	2	9	5	3	1	16	15			
Totals	68	29	39	295	131	159	5	720	945			

Playoff Results 1985-81

Year	Round	Opponent	Result	GF	GA
1986	DSF	Toronto	L 0-3	9	18
1985	CF	Edmonton	L 2-4	25	44
	DF	Minnesota	W 4-2	31	29
	DSF	Detroit	W 3-0	23	8
1984	DSF	Minnesota	L 2-3	14	18
1983	CF	Edmonton	L 0-4	11	25
	DF	Minnesota	W 4-1	22	17
	DSF	St. Louis	W 3-1	16	10
1982	CF	Vancouver	L 1-4	13	18
	DF	St. Louis	W 4-2	23	19
	DSF	Minnesota	W 3-1	14	14

Abbreviations: Round: F – Final; **CF** – conference final; **DF** – division final; **DSF** – division semi-final; **SF** – semi-final; **QF** – quarter-final; **P** – preliminary round. **GA** – goals against; **GF** – goals for.

Retired Numbers

9	Bobby Hull	1957-1972
21	Stan Mikita	1958-1980

Entry Draft Selections 1986-72

1986
Pick
14	Everett Sanipass
35	Mark Kurzawski
77	Kucera Frantisek
98	Lonnie Loach
119	Mario Doyon
140	Mike Hudson
161	Marty Nanne
182	Geoff Benic
203	Glen Lowes
224	Chris Thayer
245	Sean Williams

1985
Pick
11	Dave Manson
53	Andy Helmuth
74	Dan Vincellette
87	Rick Herbert
95	Brad Belland
116	Jonas Heed
137	Victor Posa
158	John Reid
179	Richard LaPlante
200	Brad Hamilton
221	Ian Pound
237	Rick Braccia

1984
Pick
3	Ed Olczyk
45	Trent Yawney
66	Tommy Eriksson
90	Timo Lehkonen
101	Darin Sceviour
111	Chris Clifford
132	Mike Stapleton
153	Glen Greenough
174	Ralph Di Fiorie
195	Joakim Persson
216	Bill Brown
224	David Mackey
237	Dan Williams

1983
Pick
18	Bruce Cassidy
39	Wayne Presley
59	Marc Bergevin
79	Tarek Howard
99	Kevin Robinson
115	Jari Torkki
119	Mark Lavarre
139	Scott Birnie
159	Kevin Paynter
179	Brian Noonan
199	Domenic Hasek
219	Steve Pepin

1982
Pick
7	Ken Yaremchuk
28	Rene Badeau
49	Tom McMurchy
70	Bill Watson
91	Brad Beck
112	Mark Hatcher
133	Jay Ness
154	Jeff Smith
175	Phil Patterson
196	Jim Camazzola
217	Mike James
238	Bob Andrea

1981
Pick
12	Tony Tanti
25	Kevin Griffin
54	Darrell Anholt
75	Perry Pelensky
96	Doug Chessell
117	Bill Schafhauser
138	Marc Centrone
159	Johan Mellstrom
180	John Benns
201	Sylvain Roy

1980
Pick
3	Denis Savard
15	Jerome Dupont
28	Steve Ludzik
30	Ken Solheim
36	Len Dawes
57	Troy Murray
58	Marcel Frere
67	Carey Wilson
78	Brian Shaw
99	Kevin Ginnell
120	Steve Larmer
141	Sean Simpson
162	Jim Ralph
183	Don Dietrich
204	Dan Frawley

1979
Pick
7	Keith Brown
28	Tim Trimper
49	Bill Gardner
70	Louis Begin
91	Lowell Loveday
112	Doug Crossman

1978
Pick
10	Tim Higgins
29	Doug Lecuyer
46	Rick Paterson
63	Brian Young
79	Mark Murphy
96	Dave Feamster
113	Dave Mancuso
130	Sandy Ross
147	Mark Locken
164	Glenn Van
179	Darryl Sutter

1977
Pick
6	Doug Wilson
19	Jean Savard
60	Randy Ireland
78	Gary Platt
96	Jack O'Callahan
114	Floyd Lahache
129	Jeff Geiger
144	Stephen Ough

1976
Pick
9	Real Cloutier
27	Jeff McDill
45	Thomas Gradin
63	Dave Debol
81	Terry McDonald
99	John Peterson
115	John Rothstein

1975
Pick
7	Greg Vaydik
25	Daniel Arndt
43	Mike O'Connell
61	Pierre Giroux
79	Bob Hoffmeyer
97	Tom Ulseth
115	Ted Bulley
133	Paul Jensen

1974
Pick
16	Grant Mulvey
34	Alain Daigle
52	Bob Murray
70	Terry Ruskowski
88	Dave Logan
106	Bob Volpe
124	Ed Mio
141	Mike St. Cyr
158	Stephen Colp
173	Rick Fraser
188	Jean Bernier
200	Dwayne Byers
210	Glen Ing

1973
Pick
13	Darcy Rota
29	Reg Thomas
45	Randy Holt
61	Dave Elliott
77	Dan Hinton
93	Gary Doerksen
109	Wayne Dye
125	Jim Koleff
140	Jack Johnson
141	Steve Alley
156	Rick Clubbe
165	Gene Strate

1972
Pick
13	Phil Russell
29	Brian Ogilvie
45	Mike Veisor
61	Tom Peluso
77	Rejean Giroux
93	Rob Palmer
109	Terry Smith
125	Billy Reay Jr.
141	Gary Donaldson

Club Directory

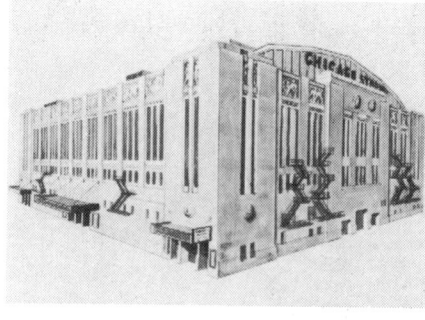

Chicago Stadium
1800 W. Madison St.
Chicago, Ill. 60612
Phone 312/733-5300
TWX 910-221-5676
ENVOY ID   TM.CHI
Capacity: 17,317

President	William W. Wirtz
Vice President	Arthur Michael Wirtz, Jr.
Vice President & Assistant to the President	Thomas N. Ivan
General Manager and Coach	Robert J. Pulford
Assistant G.M. & Director of Player Personnel	Jack Davison
Co-Coach	Roger Neilson
Assistant Coach	Cliff Koroll
Scouts	Jim Walker, Don Smith, Dave Lucas, Michel Dumas, Jan Spieczny, Jim Pappin
Secretary to the General Manager	Dorothy Folsom
Public Relations Director	Jim DeMaria
Assistant P.R. & Director of Community Relations	Susan Ocasek
Season Reservations	Mildred Hornik
Club Doctors	Dr. Louis W. Kolb, M.D./F.C.A.S, Howard Baim, M.D./E.E.N.T.
Club Dentist	Robert Duresa, DDS
Trainers	Charles "Skip" Thayer, Lou Varga, Randy Lacey
Executive Offices	Chicago Stadium
Largest Hockey Crowd	20,960 on April 10, 1982 vs Minnesota
Location of Press Box	West side of the Stadium
Dimension of Rink	185 feet by 85 feet
Ends of Rink	Plexi-glass extends above boards all around the rink
Club Colors	Red, Black and White
Radio Station	WBBM (AM)
Television Station	SportsVision (Subscription)
Broadcasters	Pat Foley, Dale Tallon

At left, Al Secord (20) and Jack O'Callahan played in all 80 games for the Blackhawks in 1985-86. Denis Savard, below had a career-high 47 goals and 69 assists for 116 points last season.

Detroit Red Wings

1985-86 Results: 17w-57l-6t 40 pts. Fifth, Norris Division

Peter Klima

Schedule

	Home			Away	
Oct.	Sat.	11 Chicago	**Oct.**	Thur.	9 Quebec
	Wed.	15 Los Angeles		Fri.	17 Edmonton
	Wed.	22 Montreal		Sat.	18 Calgary
	Fri.	24 St. Louis		Sat.	25 St. Louis
	Wed.	29 Chicago		Thur.	30 Minnesota
Nov.	Wed.	5 NY Rangers	**Nov.**	Sat.	1 Toronto
	Sun.	9 Pittsburgh		Sat.	8 NY Islanders
	Wed.	19 New Jersey		Wed.	12 New Jersey
	Fri.	21 Washington		Thur.	13 Philadelphia
	Wed.	26 Toronto		Sat.	15 Toronto
	Fri.	28 St. Louis		Sat.	22 Montreal
Dec.	Fri.	5 Montreal		Sat.	29 St. Louis
	Tue.	9 Buffalo	**Dec.**	Tue.	2 Los Angeles
	Thur.	11 Minnesota		Sat.	6 Hartford
	Sat.	20 Hartford		Tue.	16 Calgary
	Tue.	23 Chicago		Wed.	17 Vancouver
	Fri.	26 Toronto		Sun.	21 Chicago
	Wed.	31 Calgary		Sat.	27 Toronto
Jan.	Fri.	2 Minnesota	**Jan.**	Sat.	3 Minnesota
	Tue.	6 Toronto		Thur.	8 Boston
	Sat.	10 Winnipeg		Sun.	11 Chicago
	Tue.	13 Edmonton		Sun.	18 Pittsburgh
	Thur.	15 Toronto		Sat.	24 St. Louis
	Sat.	17 Quebec		Sat.	31 Toronto
	Wed.	21 NY Islanders	**Feb.**	Sun.	1 Buffalo
	Fri.	23 St. Louis		Wed.	4 Chicago
	Wed.	28 Washington		Sat.	7 Minnesota
Feb.	Fri.	6 Minnesota		Tue.	17 NY Rangers
	Sat.	14 New Jersey*		Sun.	22 Chicago
	Wed.	18 Winnipeg		Tue.	24 Washington
	Fri.	20 Quebec	**Mar.**	Mon.	2 Boston
	Thur.	26 Vancouver		Tue.	3 Hartford
	Sat.	28 NY Rangers*		Sat.	7 St. Louis
Mar.	Thur.	5 Minnesota		Tue.	10 Vancouver
	Tue.	17 Boston		Wed.	11 Edmonton
	Thur.	19 NY Islanders		Sat.	14 Minnesota*
	Sat.	21 Chicago		Sun.	15 Winnipeg*
	Wed.	25 Los Angeles		Sun.	22 Buffalo
April	Wed.	1 Philadelphia		Sat.	28 Philadelphia*
	Sun.	5 St. Louis	**April**	Sat.	4 Pittsburgh

*Denotes afternoon game.

Home Starting Times:
Weeknights & Saturdays .... 7:35 p.m.
Sundays .... 7:05 p.m.
Matinees .... 2:05 p.m.

Franchise date: September 25, 1926

 61st NHL Season

Year-by-Year Record

Season	Home W	L	T	Road W	L	T	W	L	T	GF	GA	Pts.	Finished	Playoff Result
1985-86	80	10	26	4	7	31	2	17	57	6	266	415	40	5th, Norris Div.	Out of Playoffs
1984-85	80	19	14	7	8	27	5	27	41	12	313	357	66	3rd, Norris Div.	Lost Div. Semi-Final
1983-84	80	18	20	2	13	22	5	31	42	7	298	323	69	3rd, Norris Div.	Lost Div. Semi-Final
1982-83	80	14	19	7	7	25	8	21	44	15	263	344	57	5th, Norris Div.	Out of Playoffs
1981-82	80	15	19	6	6	28	6	21	47	12	270	351	54	6th, Norris Div.	Out of Playoffs
1980-81	80	16	15	9	3	28	9	19	43	18	252	339	56	5th, Norris Div.	Out of Playoffs
1979-80	80	14	21	5	12	22	6	26	43	11	268	306	63	5th, Norris Div.	Out of Playoffs
1978-79	80	15	17	8	8	24	8	23	41	16	252	295	62	5th, Norris Div.	Out of Playoffs
1977-78	80	22	11	7	10	23	7	32	34	14	252	266	78	2nd, Norris Div.	Lost Quarter-Final
1976-77	80	12	22	6	4	33	3	16	55	9	183	309	41	5th, Norris Div.	Out of Playoffs
1975-76	80	17	15	8	9	29	2	26	44	10	226	300	62	4th, Norris Div.	Out of Playoffs
1974-75	80	17	17	6	6	28	6	23	45	12	259	335	58	4th, Norris Div.	Out of Playoffs
1973-74	78	21	12	6	8	27	4	29	39	10	255	319	68	6th, East Div.	Out of Playoffs
1972-73	78	22	12	5	15	17	7	37	29	12	265	243	86	5th, East Div.	Out of Playoffs
1971-72	78	25	11	3	8	24	7	33	35	10	261	262	76	5th, East Div.	Out of Playoffs
1970-71	78	17	15	7	5	30	4	22	45	11	209	308	55	7th, East Div.	Out of Playoffs
1969-70	76	20	11	7	20	10	8	40	21	15	246	199	95	3rd, East Div.	Lost Quarter-Final
1968-69	76	23	8	7	10	23	5	33	31	12	239	221	78	5th, East Div.	Out of Playoffs
1967-68	74	18	15	4	9	20	8	27	35	12	245	257	66	6th, East Div.	Out of Playoffs
1966-67	70	21	11	3	6	28	1	27	39	4	212	241	58	5th,	Out of Playoffs
1965-66	70	20	8	7	11	19	5	31	27	12	221	194	74	4th,	Lost Final
1964-65	70	25	7	3	15	16	4	40	23	7	224	175	87	1st,	Lost Semi-Final
1963-64	70	23	9	3	7	20	8	30	29	11	191	204	71	4th,	Lost Final
1962-63	70	19	10	6	13	15	7	32	25	13	200	194	77	4th,	Lost Final
1961-62	70	17	11	7	6	22	7	23	33	14	184	219	60	5th,	Out of Playoffs
1960-61	70	15	13	7	10	16	9	25	29	16	195	215	66	4th,	Lost Final
1959-60	70	18	14	3	8	15	12	26	29	15	186	197	67	4th,	Lost Semi-Final
1958-59	70	13	17	5	12	20	3	25	37	8	167	218	58	6th,	Out of Playoffs
1957-58	70	16	11	8	13	18	4	29	29	12	176	207	70	3rd,	Lost Semi-Final
1956-57	70	23	7	5	15	13	7	38	20	12	198	157	88	1st,	Lost Semi-Final
1955-56	70	21	6	8	9	18	8	30	24	16	183	148	76	2nd,	Lost Final
1954-55	**70**	**25**	**5**	**5**	**17**	**12**	**6**	**42**	**17**	**11**	**204**	**134**	**95**	**1st,**	**Won Stanley Cup**
1953-54	**70**	**24**	**4**	**7**	**13**	**15**	**7**	**37**	**19**	**14**	**191**	**132**	**88**	**1st,**	**Won Stanley Cup**
1952-53	70	20	5	10	16	11	8	36	16	18	222	133	90	1st,	Lost Semi-Final
1951-52	**70**	**24**	**7**	**4**	**20**	**7**	**8**	**44**	**14**	**12**	**215**	**133**	**100**	**1st,**	**Won Stanley Cup**
1950-51	70	25	3	7	19	10	6	44	13	13	236	139	101	1st,	Lost Semi-Final
1949-50	**70**	**19**	**9**	**7**	**18**	**10**	**7**	**37**	**19**	**14**	**229**	**164**	**88**	**1st,**	**Won Stanley Cup**
1948-49	60	21	6	3	13	13	4	34	19	7	195	145	75	1st,	Lost Final
1947-48	60	16	9	5	14	9	7	30	18	12	187	148	72	2nd,	Lost Final
1946-47	60	14	10	6	8	17	5	22	27	11	190	193	55	4th,	Lost Semi-Final
1945-46	50	16	5	4	4	15	6	20	20	10	146	159	50	4th,	Lost Final
1944-45	50	19	5	1	12	9	4	31	14	5	218	161	67	2nd,	Lost Final
1943-44	50	18	6	1	8	13	4	26	18	6	214	177	58	2nd,	Lost Final
1942-43	**50**	**16**	**4**	**5**	**9**	**10**	**6**	**25**	**14**	**11**	**169**	**124**	**61**	**1st,**	**Won Stanley Cup**
1941-42	48	14	7	3	5	18	1	19	25	4	140	147	42	5th,	Lost Final
1940-41	48	14	5	5	7	11	6	21	16	11	112	102	53	3rd,	Lost Final
1939-40	48	11	10	3	5	16	3	16	26	6	90	126	38	5th,	Lost Semi-Final
1938-39	48	14	8	2	4	16	4	18	24	6	107	128	42	5th,	Lost Semi-Final
1937-38	48	8	10	6	4	15	5	12	25	11	99	133	35	4th, Amn. Div.	Out of Playoffs
1936-37	**48**	**14**	**5**	**5**	**11**	**9**	**4**	**25**	**14**	**9**	**128**	**102**	**59**	**1st, Amn. Div.**	**Won Stanley Cup**
1935-36	**48**	**14**	**5**	**5**	**10**	**11**	**3**	**24**	**16**	**8**	**124**	**103**	**56**	**1st, Amn. Div.**	**Won Stanley Cup**
1934-35	48	11	8	5	8	14	2	19	22	7	127	114	45	4th, Amn. Div.	Out of Playoffs
1933-34*	48	15	5	4	9	9	6	24	14	10	113	98	58	1st,	Lost Final
1932-33	48	17	3	4	8	12	4	25	15	8	111	93	58	2nd,	Lost Semi-Final
1931-32	48	13	6	5	5	12	7	18	20	10	95	108	46	3rd,	Lost Quarter-Final
1930-31**	44	10	7	5	6	14	2	16	21	7	102	105	39	4th,	Out of Playoffs
1929-30	44	9	10	3	5	14	3	14	24	6	117	133	34	4th,	Out of Playoffs
1928-29	44	11	6	5	8	10	4	19	16	9	72	63	47	3rd,	Lost Quarter-Final
1927-28	44	14	7	1	5	12	5	19	19	6	88	79	44	4th, Amn. Div.	Out of Playoffs
1926-27***	44	6	15	1	6	13	3	12	28	4	76	105	28	5th, Amn. Div.	Out of Playoffs

* Team name changed to Red Wings.
** Team name changed to Falcons.
*** Team named Cougars.

1986-87 Player Personnel

FORWARDS

Player	Ht.	Wt.	Place of Birth	Date	1985-86 Club
BURR, Shawn	6-0	180	Sarnia, Ont.	7/1/66	Kitchener-Detroit-Adirondack
CARROLL, Bill	5-10	190	Toronto, Ont.	1/19/59	Edmonton-Nova Scotia-Detroit
CICHOCKI, Chris	5-10	185	Detroit, Mich.	9/17/63	Detroit-Adirondack
DONNELLY, Dave	5-11	185	Edmonton, Alta.	2/2/62	Boston-Moncton
FEDYK, Brent	6-0	180	Yorkton, Sask.	3/8/67	Regina
GALLANT, Gerard	5-10	168	Summerside, P.E.I.	9/2/63	Detroit
GRAVES, Adam	5-11	185	Toronto, Ont.	4/12/68	Windsor
HIGGINS, Tim	6-1	185	Ottawa, Ont.	2/7/58	New Jersey
KLIMA, Petr	6-0	190	Chaomutov, Czech.	12/23/64	Detroit
KOCUR, Joey	6-1	204	Calgary, Alta.	12/21/64	Detroit-Adirondack
KRENTZ, Dale	5-11	187	Steinbach, Man.	12/19/61	Adirondack
McRAE, Basil	6-2	205	Beaverton, Ont.	1/5/61	Detroit-Adirondack
MERKOSKY, Glenn	5-10	176	Edmonton, Alta.	4/8/60	Detroit-Adirondack
MURPHY, Joe	6-1	190	London, Ont.	10/16/67	Michigan Tech
OATES, Adam	5-11	190	Weston, Ont.	8/27/62	Detroit
OGRODNICK, John	6-0	189	Ottawa, Ont.	6/20/59	Detroit
PROBERT, Bob	6-3	208	Windsor, Ont.	6/5/65	Detroit-Adirondack
ROBERTSON, Geordie	6-0	165	Victoria, B.C.	8/1/59	Adirondack
SHEDDON, Doug	6-0	185	Wallaceburg, Ont.	4/29/61	Pittsburgh-Detroit
SPEERS, Ted	5-11	190	Ann Arbor, Mich.	1/21/61	Detroit-Adirondack
STASZAK, Ray	6-0	200	Philadelphia, Pa.	12/1/62	Detroit-Adirondack
YOUNG, Warren	6-3	195	Toronto, Ont.	1/11/56	Detroit
YZERMAN, Steve	5-11	175	Cranbrook, B.C.	5/9/65	Detroit

DEFENSEMEN

Player	Ht.	Wt.	Place of Birth	Date	1985-86 Club
CHIASSON, Steve	6-0	210	Barrie, Ont.	4/14/67	Guelph
DE GAETANO, Phil	6-1	203	Roslyn, N.Y.	8/9/63	Indianapolis
FRIDAY, Tim	6-0	190	Burbank, Ca.	3/5/61	Detroit-Adirondack
HOUDA, Doug	6-2	190	Blairmore, Alta.	6/3/66	Medicine Hat-Detroit
KOROL, David	6-0	175	Winnipeg, Man.	3/1/65	Adirondack
LADOUCEUR, Randy	6-2	200	Brockville, Ont.	6/10/60	Detroit
MELROSE, Barry	6-0	205	Kelvington, Sask.	7/15/56	Detroit-Adirondack
O'CONNELL, Mike	5-9	185	Chicago, Ill.	11/25/55	Boston-Detroit
SHARPLES, Jeff	6-1	185	Terrace, B.C.	7/28/67	Portland
SNEPSTS, Harold	6-3	215	Edmonton, Alta.	10/24/54	Detroit
TRADER, Larry	6-1	178	Barry's Bay, Ont.	7/7/63	Adirondack
VEITCH, Darren	6-0	195	Saskatoon, Sask.	4/24/60	Washington-Detroit
ZOMBO, Rick	6-1	195	DesPlaines, Ill.	5/8/63	Detroit-Adirondack

GOALTENDERS

Player	Ht.	Wt.	Place of Birth	Date	1985-86 Club
GOWANS, Mark	5-11	160	Bay City, Mich.	3/26/67	Oshawa
HANSCH, Randy	5-11	157	Edmonton, Alta.	2/8/66	Nosedo
HANLON, Glenn	6-0	185	Brandon, Man.	2/20/57	NY Rangers-Adirondack-New Haven
LAFOREST, Mark	5-10	178	Welland, Ont.	7/10/62	Detroit-Adirondack
ST. LAURENT, Sam	5-10	190	Arvida, Que.	2/16/59	New Jersey-Maine
MICALEF, Corrado	5-8	172	Montreal, Que.	4/20/61	Detroit-Adirondack-Kalamazoo
PUSEY, Chris	6-0	180	Brantford, Ont.	6/20/65	Detroit-Adirondack
STEFAN, Greg	5-11	178	Brantford, Ont.	2/11/61	Detroit

1985-86 Scoring

Regular Season

*–rookie

Pos	#	Player	Team	GP	G	A	Pts	+/–	PIM	PP	SH	GW	OT	S	%
F	14	Doug Shedden	PIT	67	32	34	66	7 –	32	19	0	5	0	179	17.9
			DET	11	2	3	5	1 –	2	2	0	0	0	33	6.1
			Total	78	34	37	71	8 –	34	21	0	5	0	212	16.0
F	25	John Ogrodnick	DET	76	38	32	70	30 –	18	15	1	2	0	208	18.3
F	16	Kelly Kisio	DET	76	21	48	69	21 –	85	7	3	0	1	140	15.0
F	85	*Peter Klima	DET	74	32	24	56	39 –	16	8	0	4	0	174	18.4
F	35	Warren Young	DET	79	22	24	46	34 –	161	9	0	1	0	95	23.2
F	19	Steve Yzerman	DET	51	14	28	42	24 –	16	3	0	3	0	132	10.6
F	17	Gerard Gallant	DET	52	20	19	39	10 –	106	3	1	2	0	116	17.2
D	2	Mike O'Connell	BOS	63	8	21	29	8 –	47	4	1	0	0	174	4.6
			DET	13	1	7	8	6 –	16	0	1	0	0	38	2.6
			Total	76	9	28	37	14 –	63	4	2	0	0	212	4.2
F	21	Claude Loiselle	DET	48	7	15	22	27 –	142	2	0	1	0	83	8.4
F	15	*Chris Cichocki	DET	59	10	11	21	8 –	21	1	1	0	0	76	13.2
F	24	*Bob Probert	DET	44	8	13	21	14 –	186	3	0	0	0	46	17.4
F	34	*Adam Oates	DET	38	9	11	20	24 –	10	1	0	1	0	49	18.4
D	29	Randy Ladouceur	DET	78	5	13	18	54 –	196	0	0	1	1	92	5.4
D	5	Darren Veitch	WSH	62	3	9	12	21	27	0	0	0	0	82	3.7
			DET	13	0	5	5	9 –	2	0	0	0	0	22	.0
			Total	75	3	14	17	12	29	0	0	0	0	104	2.9
F	18	Danny Gare	DET	57	7	9	16	19 –	102	1	0	0	0	108	6.5
F	26	*Joey Kocur	DET	59	9	6	15	24 –	377	2	0	1	0	65	13.8
D	4	*Jim Leavins	DET	37	2	11	13	23 –	26	1	0	0	0	63	3.2
F	12	Billy Carroll	EDM	5	0	2	2	2 –	0	0	0	0	0	0	.0
			DET	21	2	4	6	8 –	11	0	0	0	0	13	15.4
			Total	26	2	6	8	6 –	11	0	0	0	0	13	15.4
D	27	Harold Snepsts	DET	35	0	6	6	7 –	75		0	0	0	12	.0
D	14	Lane Lambert	DET	34	2	3	5	11 –	130		0	0	0	32	6.3
D	7	Steve Richmond	NYR	17	0	2	2	2	63	0	0	0	0	8	.0
			DET	29	1	2	3	18 –	82	0	0	0	0	18	5.6
			Total	46	1	4	5	16 –	145	0	0	0	0	26	3.8
D	4	*Tim Friday	DET	23	0	3	3	9 –	6	0	0	0	0	13	.0
F	11	*Ted Speers	DET	4	1	1	2	2	0	0	0	0	0	6	16.7
F	22	Glenn Merkosky	DET	17	0	2	2	12 –	0	0	0	0	0	18	.0
G	30	Greg Stefan	DET	37	0	2	2	0	23	0	0	0	0	0	.0
F	34	*Ed Johnstone	DET	3	1	0	1	0	2	0	0	0	0	3	33.3
F	11	*Shawn Burr	DET	5	1	0	1	1	4	0	0	0	0	6	16.7
F	32	Bruce Eakin	DET	4	0	1	1	4 –	0	0	0	0	0	5	.0
F	8	*Ray Staszak	DET	4	0	1	1	3 –	7	0	0	0	0	5	.0
D	34	*Rick Zombo	DET	14	0	1	1	10 –	16	0	0	0	0	8	.0
G	41	Ed Mio	DET	18	0	1	1	0	17	0	0	0	0	0	.0
G	31	*Chris Pusey	DET	1	0	0	0	0	0	0	0	0	0	0	.0
F	23	Basil McRae	DET	4	0	0	0	4 –	5	0	0	0	0	0	.0
D	22	*Doug Houda	DET	6	0	0	0	7 –	4	0	0	0	0	5	.0
G	1	Corrado Micalef	DET	11	0	0	0	0	8	0	0	0	0	0	.0
D	2	Barry Melrose	DET	14	0	0	0	6 –	70	0	0	0	0	2	.0
G	31	*Mark Laforest	DET	28	0	0	0	0	23	0	0	0	0	0	.0

Greg Stefan

Coach and General Manager

DEMERS, JACQUES
Coach, Detroit Red Wings. Born in Montreal, Que., August 25, 1944

After three successful seasons as coach of the St. Louis Blues, Jacques Demers was named head coach of the Detroit Red Wings on June 13, 1986. In 1985-86, he guided the Blues to the Campbell Conference Championship before losing to the Calgary Flames in a dramatic seven-game series. In addition, he finished runner-up to Edmonton's Glen Sather for Coach of the Year honors. A native Montrealer, Demers' coaching career began in the junior ranks close to his hometown in 1967-68. Later, he was appointed Director of Player Personnel of the Chicago Cougars of the World Hockey Association in 1972-73, and took on the Cougars' coaching duties in 1973-74. Demers eventually went on to coach the Cincinnati Stingers in the WHA and the Quebec Nordiques in both the WHA and NHL (1979-80). Because of his adept coaching of young talent, Demers moved to the Quebec farm system where, in 1982-83, he piloted the Fredericton Express of the American Hockey League to a 45-27-8 record and a first-place finish. The same year, he was named AHL Coach of the Year as well as Coach and Executive of the Year by the *Hockey News*.

NHL Coaching Record

Team	Season	Games	Regular Season				Playoffs			
			W	L	T	%	Games	W	L	%
Quebec	1979-80	80	25	44	11	.381	...	...	...	...
St. Louis	1983-84	80	32	41	7	.444	11	6	5	.545
St. Louis	1984-85	80	37	31	12	.538	3	0	3	.000
St. Louis	1985-86	80	37	34	9	.519	19	10	9	.526
NHL Totals		**320**	**131**	**150**	**39**	**.470**	**33**	**16**	**17**	**.485**

DEVELLANO, JAMES (JIM)
General Manager, Detroit Red Wings. Born in Toronto, Ont., January 18, 1943.

Jim Devellano was appointed general manager of the Red Wings on July 12, 1982 after spending several seasons with the New York Islanders. He began his career as a scout for the St. Louis Blues in 1967 and from there moved to join New York in 1972. In his first two years he acted as a scout for the organization and in 1974 was promoted to head scout. In 1979, Devellano held the dual capacities of head scout for the Islanders and general manager for their CHL affiliate Indianapolis Checkers. His results were impressive, and following the 1979-80 season he was named "*Hockey News* Minor League Executive of the Year". In 1981, Devellano was appointed assistant general manager of the Islanders and held that position until joining the Red Wings.

Club Records

Team

(Figures in brackets for season records are games played; records for fewest points, wins, ties, losses, goals, goals against are for 70 or more games)

Most Points	101	1950-51 (70)
Most Wins	44	1950-51 (70)
		1951-52 (70)
Most Ties	18	1952-53 (70)
		1980-81 (80)
Most Losses	57	1985-86 (80)
Most Goals	313	1984-85 (80)
Most Goals Against	415	1985-86 (80)
Fewest Points	40	1985-86 (80)
Fewest Wins	16	1976-77 (80)
Fewest Ties	*4	1966-67 (70)
Fewest Losses	13	1950-51 (70)
Fewest Goals	167	1958-59 (70)
Fewest Goals Against	132	1953-54 (70)

Longest Winning Streak
Over-all 9 1950-51; 1954-55

Home . . . . .14 Jan. 21-Mar. 20/65

Away. . . . . 5 Three times

Longest Undefeated Streak
Over-all . . . . .15 Nov. 27-Dec. 28/52 (8 wins, 7 ties)

Home . . . . .18 Dec. 26/54-Mar. 20/55 (13 wins, 5 ties)

Away. . . . . .15 Oct. 18-Dec. 26/51 (10 wins, 5 ties)

Longest Losing Streak
Over-all . . . . .14 Feb. 24-Mar. 25/82

Home . . . . 7 Feb. 20-Mar. 25/82

Away. . . . . .14 Dec. 21/66

Longest Winless Streak
Over-all . . . . .19 Feb. 26-Apr. 3/77 (18 losses, 1 tie)

Home . . . . .10 Dec. 11-Jan. 18/86 (9 losses, 1 tie)

Away. . . . . .26 Dec. 15/76-Apr. 3/77 (23 losses, 3 ties)

Most Shutouts, Season 13 1953-54 (70)
Most. Pen. Mins.,
Season. 2,393 1985-86 (80)
Most Goals, Game . . . . . . .15 Jan. 23/44 (NYR at Det. 15)

Individual

Most Seasons	*25	Gordie Howe
Most Games	*1,687	Gordie Howe
Most Goals, Career	*786	Gordie Howe
Most Assists, Career	*1,023	Gordie Howe
Most Points, Career	*1,809	Gordie Howe
		(786 goals, 1,023 assists)
Most Pen. Mins., Career	1,643	Gordie Howe
Most Shutouts, Career	85	Terry Sawchuk

Longest Consecutive
Games Streak . . . . . . .548 Alex Delvecchio (Dec. 13/56-Nov. 11/64)

Most Goals, Season . . . . . .55 John Ogrodnick (1984-85)

Most Assists, Season . . . . .74 Marcel Dionne (1974-75)

Most Points, Season . . . . .121 Marcel Dionne (1974-75) (47 goals, 74 assists)

Most Pen. Mins., Season . . .377 Joey Kocur (1985-86)

Most Points, Defenseman
Season . . . . .74 Reed Larson (1982-83) (22 goals, 52 assists)

Most Points, Center,
Season . . . . 121 Marcel Dionne (1974-75) (47 goals, 74 assists)

Most Points, Right Wing,
Season . . . . 103 Gordie Howe (1968-69) (44 goals, 58 assists)

Most Points, Left Wing,
Season . . . . 105 John Ogrodnick (1984-85) (55 goals, 50 assists)

Most Points, Rookie,
Season . . . . .87 Steve Yzerman (1983-84) (39 goals, 48 assists)

Most Shutouts, Season . . . . .12 Terry Sawchuk (1951-52; 1953-54; 1954-55) Glenn Hall (1955-56)

Most Goals, Game . . . . .6 Syd Howe (Feb. 3/44)

Most Assists, Game . . . . . . *7 Billy Taylor (Mar. 16/47)

Most Points, Game . . . . 7 Carl Liscombe (Nov. 5/42) Don Grosso (Feb. 3/44) Billy Taylor (Mar. 16/47)

* NHL Record

Coaching History

Art Duncan, 1926-27; Jack Adams, 1927-28 to 1946-47; Tommy Ivan, 1947-48 to 1953-54; Jimmy Skinner, 1954-55 to 1956-57; Jimmy Skinner and Sid Abel, 1957-58; Sid Abel, 1958-59 to 1967-68; Bill Gadsby, 1968-69; Bill Gadsby and Sid Abel, 1969-70; Ned Harkness and Doug Barkley, 1970-71; Doug Barkley and John Wilson, 1971-72; John Wilson, 1972-73; Ted Garvin and Alex Delvecchio, 1973-74; Alex Delvecchio, 1974-75; Doug Barkley and Alex Delvecchio, 1975-76; Alex Delvecchio and Larry Wilson, 1976-77; Bobby Kromm, 1977-78 to 1978-79; Bobby Kromm and Ted Lindsay, 1979-80; Ted Lindsay and Wayne Maxner, 1980-81; Wayne Maxner and Billy Dea, 1981-82; Nick Polano, 1982-83 to 1984-85; Harry Neale, 1985-86; Jacques Demers, 1986-87.

Captains' History

Art Duncan, 1926-27; Reg Noble, 1927-28 to 1929-30; George Hay, 1930-31; Carson Cooper, 1931-32; Larry Aurie, 1932-33; Herbie Lewis, 1933-34; Ebbie Goodfellow, 1934-35; Doug Young, 1935-36 to 1937-38; Ebbie Goodfellow, 1938-39 to 1941-42; Sid Abel, 1942-43; Mud Bruneteau, Bill Hollett (co-captains), 1943-44; Bill Hollett, 1944-45; Bill Hollett, Sid Abel, 1945-46; Sid Abel, 1946-47 to 1951-52; Ted Lindsay, 1952-53 to 1955-56; Red Kelly, 1956-57, 1957-58; Gordie Howe, 1958-59 to 1961-62; Alex Delvecchio, 1962-63 to 1973-74; Marcel Dionne, 1974-75; Danny Grant, Terry Harper, 1975-76; Danny Grant, Dennis Polonich, 1976-77; Dan Maloney, Dennis Hextall, 1977-78; Dennis Hextall, Nick Libett, Paul Woods, 1978-79; Dale McCourt, 1979-80; Errol Thompson, Reed Larson, 1980-81; Reed Larson, 1981-82; Danny Gare, 1982-83 to 1985-86.

All-time Record vs. Other Clubs

Regular Season

			At Home						On Road						Total					
	GP	W	L	T	GF	GA	PTS	GP	W	L	T	GF	GA	PTS	GP	W	L	T	GF	GA	PTS
Boston	268	145	71	52	902	679	342	268	79	148	41	696	943	199	536	224	219	93	1598	1622	541
Buffalo	36	19	14	3	128	105	41	34	4	24	6	80	153	14	70	23	38	9	208	258	55
**Calgary	27	13	10	4	105	87	30	26	6	16	4	77	114	16	53	19	26	8	182	201	46
Chicago	277	171	79	27	941	666	369	278	105	131	42	756	826	252	555	276	210	69	1697	1497	621
Edmonton	12	2	9	1	40	63	5	11	2	7	2	45	69	6	23	4	16	3	85	132	11
Hartford	12	4	3	5	50	41	13	11	3	6	2	29	52	6	23	7	11	5	79	93	19
Los Angeles	46	20	19	7	187	159	47	47	11	26	10	136	193	32	93	31	45	17	323	352	79
Minnesota	52	19	23	10	194	190	48	53	12	30	11	144	217	35	105	31	53	21	338	407	83
Montreal	263	120	92	51	737	669	291	263	60	161	42	582	927	162	526	180	253	93	1319	1596	453
*New Jersey	21	14	6	1	98	63	29	22	6	11	5	62	82	17	43	20	17	6	160	145	46
NY Islanders	26	11	13	2	85	89	24	27	10	17	0	74	114	20	53	21	30	2	159	203	44
NY Rangers	266	150	73	43	926	648	343	266	83	122	56	672	812	222	532	233	200	99	1598	1460	565
Philadelphia	41	19	15	7	137	128	45	40	6	25	9	104	1564	21	81	25	40	16	241	292	66
Pittsburgh	47	31	8	8	184	123	70	46	12	31	3	136	200	27	93	43	39	11	320	323	97
Quebec	11	5	5	1	44	47	11	12	3	7	2	34	53	8	23	8	12	3	78	100	19
St. Louis	53	20	26	7	180	168	47	52	11	34	7	129	200	29	105	31	60	14	309	368	76
Toronto	271	139	90	42	784	653	320	271	87	144	40	681	877	214	542	226	234	82	1465	1530	534
Vancouver	33	19	10	4	145	104	42	33	10	19	4	102	139	24	66	29	29	8	247	243	66
Washington	27	13	6	8	106	80	34	28	10	15	3	87	107	23	55	23	21	11	193	182	57
Winnipeg	13	6	5	2	47	55	14	14	4	6	4	40	53	12	27	9	12	6	87	108	24
Defunct Clubs	141	76	40	25	429	307	177	141	49	63	29	363	375	127	282	125	103	54	792	682	304
Totals	**1943**	**1015**	**618**	**310**	**6449**	**5124**	**2340**	**1943**	**573**	**1050**	**320**	**5029**	**6670**	**1466**	**3886**	**1588**	**1668**	**630**	**11478**	**11794**	**3806**

* Totals include those of Kansas City (1974-75, 1975-76) and Colorado (1976-77 through 1981-82)
** Totals include those of Atlanta (1972-73 through 1979-80)

Playoffs

	Series	W	L	GP	W	L	T	GF	GA	Last Mtg.	Round	Result
Boston	7	3	4	33	14	19	0	98	96	1957	SF	L 1-4
Calgary	1	1	0	2	2	0	0	8	5	1978	P	W 2-0
Chicago	10	4	6	50	21	29	0	138	156	1985	DSF	L 0-3
Montreal	12	7	5	62	29	33	0	149	161	1978	QF	L 1-4
NY Rangers	5	4	1	23	13	10	0	57	49	1950	F	W 4-3
St. Louis	1	0	1	4	1	3	0	12	13	1984	DSF	L 1-3
Toronto	20	9	11	97	48	49	0	239	249	1964	F	L 3-4
Defunct Clubs	4	3	1	10	7	2	1	21	13			
Totals	**60**	**31**	**29**	**281**	**135**	**145**	**1**	**722**	**742**			

Playoff Results 1986-82

Year	Round	Opponent	Result	GF	GA
1985	DSF	Chicago	L 0-3	8	23
1984	DSF	St. Louis	L 1-3	12	13

Abbreviations: Round: F – Final; CF – conference final; DF – division final; DSF – division semi-final; SF – semi-final; QF – quarter-final; P – preliminary round. GA – goals against; GF – goals for.

Retired Numbers

6	Larry Aurie	1927-1939
9	Gordie Howe	1946-1971

Entry Draft Selections 1986-72

1986
Pick
1	Joe Murphy
22	Adam Graves
43	Derek Mayer
64	Tim Cheveldae
85	Johan Garpenlov
106	Jay Stark
127	Per Djoos
148	Dean Morton
169	Marc Potvin
190	Scott King
211	Tom Bissett
232	Peter Ekroth

1985
Pick
8	Brent Fedyk
29	Jeff Sharples
50	Steve Chiasson
71	Mark Gowans
92	Chris Luongo
113	Randy McKay
134	Thomas Bjur
155	Mike Luckraft
176	Rob Schenna
197	Eerik Hamalainen
218	Bo Svanberg
239	Mikael Lindman

1984
Pick
7	Shawn Burr
28	Doug Houda
49	Milan Chalupa
91	Mats Lundstrom
112	Randy Hansch
133	Stefan Larsson
152	Lars Karlsson
154	Urban Nordin
175	Bill Shibicky
195	Jay Rose
216	Tim Kaiser
236	Tom Nickolau

1983
Pick
4	Steve Yzerman
25	Lane Lambert
46	Bob Probert
68	David Korol
86	Petr Klima
88	Joey Kocur
106	Chris Pusey
126	Bob Pierson
146	Craig Butz
166	Dave Sikorski
186	Stuart Grimson
206	Jeff Frank
226	Charles Chiatto

1982
Pick
17	Murray Craven
23	Yves Courteau
44	Carmine Vani
66	Craig Coxe
86	Brad Shaw
107	Claude Vilgrain
128	Greg Hudas
149	Pat Lahey
170	Gary Cullen
191	Brent Meckling
212	Mike Stern
233	Shaun Reagan

1981
Pick
23	Claude Loiselle
44	Corrado Micalef
86	Larry Trader
107	Gerard Gallant
128	Greg Stefan
149	Rick Zombo
170	Don Leblanc
191	Robert Nordmark

1980
Pick
11	Mike Blaisdell
46	Mark Osborne
88	Mike Corrigan
109	Wayne Crawford
130	Mike Braun
151	John Beukeboom
172	Dave Miles
193	Brian Rorabeck

1979
Pick
3	Mike Foligno
45	Jody Gage
46	Boris Fistric
66	John Ogrodnick
87	Joe Paterson
108	Carmen Cirella

1978
Pick
9	Willie Huber
12	Brent Peterson
28	Glenn Hicks
31	Al Jensen
53	Doug Derkson
62	Bjorn Skaare
78	Ted Nolan
95	Sylvain Locas
112	Wes George
129	John Barrett
146	Jim Malazdrewicz
163	Goeff Shaw
178	Carl Van Harrewyn
194	Ladislav Svozil
208	Tom Bailey
219	Larry Lozinski
224	Randy Betty
226	Brian Crawley
228	Doug Feasby

1977
Pick
1	Dale McCourt
37	Rick Vasko
55	John Hilworth
73	Jim Korn
91	Jim Baxter
109	Randy Wilson
125	Raymond Roy
141	Kip Churchill
155	Lance Gatoni
163	Robert Plumb
170	Alain Belanger
175	Dean Willers
178	Roland Cloutier
181	Edward Hill
184	Val James
185	Grant Morin

1976
Pick
4	Fred Williams
22	Reed Larson
40	Fred Berry
58	Kevin Schamehorn
76	Dwight Schofield
94	Tony Horvath
111	Fernand Leblanc
120	Claude Legris

1975
Pick
5	Rick Lapointe
23	Jerry Rollins
37	Alan Cameron
45	Blair Davidson
50	Clarke Hamilton
59	Mike Wirachowsky
77	Mike Wong
95	Mike Harazny
113	Jean-Luc Phaneuf
131	Steve Carlson
148	Gary Vaughn
164	Jean Thibodeau
176	Dave Hanson
178	Robin Larson

1974
Pick
9	Bill Lochead
44	Dan Mandryk
45	Bill Evo
63	Michel Bergeron
81	John Taft
99	Don Dufek
117	Jack Carlson
134	Greg Steele
151	Glenn McLeod

1973
Pick
11	Terry Richardson
39	Nelson Pyatt
43	Robbie Neale
59	Mike Korney
75	Blair Stewart
91	Glenn Cickello
107	Brian Middleton
118	Dennis Polonich
123	George Lyle
135	Dennis O'Brien
138	Tom Newman
139	Ray Bibeau
151	Kevin Neville
154	Ken Gibb
155	Mitch Brandt

1972
Pick
26	Pierre Guite
42	Bob Krieger
58	Dan Gruen
74	Dennis Johnson
90	Bill Miller
106	Glenn Seperich
122	Mike Ford
138	George Kuzmicz
150	Dave Arundel

Club Directory

Joe Louis Sports Arena
600 Civic Center Drive
Detroit, Michigan 48226
Phone: (313) 567-3900
TWX 810-221-5033
ENVOY ID   TM.DET
Capacity: 19,275

Owner and President	Michael Ilitch
Executive Vice-President	James Lites
Secretary-Treasurer	Marian Ilitch
General Counsel	Denise Ilitch-Lites
General Manager and Vice President	Jim Devellano
Asst. General Manager/Director of Player Development	Nick Polano
Head Coach	Jacques Demers
Director of Scouting/Player Procurement	Neil Smith
Assistant Coaches	Danny Belisle, Colin Campbell, Dave Dryden, Don MacAdam
Director of Public Relations	Bill Jamieson
Assistant Director of Public Relations	Russ Gregory
Director of Marketing	Rosanne Kozerski-Brown
Director of Advertising Sales/Promotions	Terry Murphy
Assistant Director of Advertising Sales	Gary Vitto
Director Business/Administration	Ruth Hoffman
Director of Finance	Dave Agius
Director of Broadcasting/Community Affairs	Dave Strader
Marketing Coordinator	Dan Belisle Jr.
Director of Season Tickets Sales	Gino D'Ambrosio
Director of Group Sales	Patty Ward
Box Office Manager	Bob Kerlin
Asst. to Exec. Vice-President	Paula Mikola
Special Projects	Budd Lynch
Eastern Canada Scout	Alex Davidson
Western Canada Scout	Ken Holland
USA College & High School Scout	Billy Dea
Minor League Scout	Chris Coury
Eastern USA Scout	Jerry Moschella
Michigan Scout	Frank Michalek
Northern Ontario Scout	Dave Polano
Sweden Scout	Christer Rockstrom
Germany Scout	Mike Daski
Physical Therapist	Jim Pengelly
Trainer	Mark Brennan
Assistant Trainer	TBD
Team Physicians	Robert Teitge, M.D.; John Finley, D.O.
Team Dentists	C.J. Regula, D.M.D., Midwestern Dental Centers
Public Relations Coordinator	Kathy Best
Public Relations Secretary	Marilyn Rowe
Graphic Designer	Beverly Romanchuk
Director of Merchandising Sales	Mike Gasser
Telemarketing Supervisor	Keith Maas
Director of Arena Operations	Steve Facione
Arena Building Manager	Al Sobatka
Home-Ice	Joe Louis Arena
Largest regular-season Pro crowd	21,019*Nov. 25, 1983; Detroit 5, Pittsburgh 2
Largest Pro Play-off crowd	20,090 Apr. 7, 1984; St. Louis 4, Detroit 3 — 2 OTS
Largest NHL All-Star game crowd	21,002*Feb. 5, 1980; Wales Conf. 6 Campbell Conf. 3
Location of Press Box, Radio-TV Booths	Jefferson Ave. side of Arena, top of seats (Row 42)
Location of Media Hospitality Lounge	First floor, in hallway, near Red Wings' dressing room, Atwater St. side of Arena.
Dimensions of Rink	200 feet by 85 feet; S.A.R. Plastic extends above boards all around rink
Club Colors	Red and White
Radio Flagship Station	WJR-AM, 760
TV Station	TBD
Radio Announcers	Bruce Martyn, TBD
TV Announcers	Dave Strader, Mickey Redmond

*NHL RECORD

Edmonton Oilers

1985-86 Results: 56w-17L-7T 119 PTS. First, Smythe Division

Year-by-Year Record

		Home			Road			Overall						
Season	GP	W	L	T	W	L	T	W	L	T	GF	GA	Pts.	Finished	Playoff Result
1985-86	80	32	6	2	24	11	5	56	17	7	426	310	119	1st, Smythe Div.	Lost Div. Final
1984-85	80	26	7	7	23	13	4	49	20	11	401	298	109	1st, Smythe Div.	Won Stanley Cup
1983-84	80	31	5	4	26	13	1	57	18	5	446	314	119	1st, Smythe Div.	Won Stanley Cup
1982-83	80	25	9	6	22	12	6	47	21	12	424	315	106	1st, Smythe Div.	Lost Final
1981-82	80	31	5	4	17	12	11	48	17	15	417	295	111	1st, Smythe Div.	Lost Div. Semi-Final
1980-81	80	17	13	10	12	22	6	29	35	16	328	327	74	4th, Smythe Div.	Lost Quarter-Final
1979-80	80	17	14	9	11	25	4	28	39	13	301	322	69	4th, Smythe Div.	Lost Prelim. Round

Schedule

Home				Away		
Oct.	Wed.	15	Quebec	Oct.	Thur.	9	Philadelphia
	Fri.	17	Detroit		Sat.	11	Montreal
	Tue.	21	Chicago		Sun.	12	Winnipeg
	Fri.	24	Boston		Sun.	19	Los Angeles
	Sun.	26	Vancouver		Wed.	22	Calgary
	Wed.	29	Washington		Fri.	31	Vancouver
Nov.	Sun.	2	Los Angeles	Nov.	Fri.	7	Calgary
	Wed.	5	Calgary		Tue.	11	NY Islanders
	Sat.	8	Montreal		Thur.	13	Boston
	Wed.	19	NY Rangers		Sat.	15	Hartford
	Sat.	22	Vancouver		Sun.	16	NY Rangers
	Wed.	26	Winnipeg		Mon.	24	Calgary
	Fri.	28	Chicago	Dec.	Fri.	5	Pittsburgh
Dec.	Wed.	3	NY Islanders		Sun.	7	Philadelphia
	Fri.	12	Winnipeg		Tue.	9	Minnesota
	Wed.	17	Quebec		Wed.	10	Winnipeg
	Fri.	19	Vancouver		Sun.	14	Los Angeles
	Sat.	20	Los Angeles		Tue.	30	Vancouver
	Tue.	23	Winnipeg	Jan.	Sat.	3	Los Angeles
	Sun.	28	Philadelphia		Tue.	13	Detroit
Jan.	Wed.	7	Los Angeles		Thur.	15	Quebec
	Fri.	9	St. Louis		Sat.	17	Toronto
	Sun.	11	Calgary		Sun.	18	Buffalo
	Fri.	23	NY Rangers		Wed.	21	Winnipeg
	Sat.	24	Pittsburgh		Tue.	27	Vancouver
	Wed.	28	Vancouver	Feb.	Sun.	1	Chicago
	Fri.	30	Minnesota		Tue.	3	St. Louis
Feb.	Fri.	6	NY Islanders		Wed.	4	Minnesota
	Sun.	8	St. Louis		Sun.	22	Winnipeg*
	Sun.	15	Washington		Tue.	24	Pittsburgh
	Wed.	18	Toronto		Wed.	25	New Jersey
Mar.	Fri.	6	Los Angeles		Fri.	27	Washington
	Sat.	7	Montreal	Mar.	Wed.	4	Vancouver
	Wed.	11	Detroit		Thur.	19	Calgary
	Sat.	14	Buffalo		Mon.	23	New Jersey
	Sun.	15	Hartford		Wed.	25	Hartford
	Tue.	17	New Jersey		Thur.	26	Boston
	Fri.	20	Calgary		Sat.	28	Toronto
	Tue.	31	Winnipeg		Sun.	29	Buffalo
April	Thur.	2	Calgary	April	Sat.	4	Los Angeles

*Denotes afternoon game.

Home Starting Times:
Mondays through Fridays . . . . 7:35 p.m.
Saturdays & Sundays . . . . 6:05 p.m.

Franchise date: June 22, 1979

8th
NHL
Season

Grant Fuhr

1986-87 Player Personnel

FORWARDS

	Ht.	Wt.	Place of Birth	Date	1985-86 Club
ANDERSON, Glenn	5-11	185	Vancouver, B.C.	10/2/60	Edmonton
BIGGS, Don	5-8	175	Mississauga, Ont.	4/7/65	Springfield-Nova Scotia
BRUBAKER, Jeff	6-2	210	Frederick, Md.	2/24/58	Toronto-Edmonton-Nova Scotia
CRAWFORD, Louis	6-0	185	Belleville, Ont.	11/5/62	Nova Scotia
EAVES, Murray	5-10	185	Calgary, Alta.	5/10/60	Sherbrooke
GRAVES, Steve	5-10	190	Trenton, Ont.	4/7/64	Nova Scotia
GRETZKY, Wayne	6-0	170	Brantford, Ont.	1/26/61	Edmonton
HOPKINS, Dean	6-1	210	Cobourg, Ont.	6/6/59	Nova Scotia
HUNTER, Dave	5-11	200	Petrolia, Ont.	1/1/58	Edmonton
JALO, Risto	5-11	185	Humppila, Finland	7/18/62	Edmonton
KRUSHELNYSKI, Mike	6-2	200	Montreal, Que.	4/27/60	Edmonton
KURRI, Jari	6-0	190	Helsinki, Finland	5/18/60	Edmonton
MacTAVISH, Craig	6-0	190	London, Ont.	8/15/58	Edmonton
McCLELLAND, Kevin	6-0	200	Oshawa, Ont.	7/4/62	Edmonton
McMURCHY, Tom	5-9	165	New Westminster, B.C.	12/2/63	Chicago-Moncton-Nova Scotia
McSORLEY, Marty	6-1	210	Hamilton, Ont.	5/18/63	Edmonton-Nova Scotia
MESSIER, Mark	6-1	205	Edmonton, Alta.	1/18/61	Edmonton
MOLLER, Mike	6-0	190	Calgary, Alta.	6/16/62	Nova Scotia
NAPIER, Mark	5-10	185	Toronto, Ont.	1/28/57	Edmonton
SEMENKO, Dave	6-3	215	Winnipeg, Man.	7/12/57	Edmonton
SHERVEN, Gord	6-0	185	Gravelbourg, Sask.	8/21/63	Minnesota-Edmonton-Springfield-Nova Scotia
SUMMANEN, Raimo	5-11	185	Jyvaskyla, Finland	3/2/62	Edmonton
TIKKANEN, Esa	5-11	185	Helsinki, Finland	1/25/65	Edmonton-Nova Scotia
TURCOTTE, Alfie	5-9	170	Gary, Ind.	6/5/65	Sherbrooke-Montreal

DEFENSEMEN

	Ht.	Wt.	Place of Birth	Date	1985-86 Club
BEUKEBOOM, Jeff	6-4	210	Ajax, Ont.	3/28/65	Nova Scotia
COFFEY, Paul	6-0	200	Weston, Ont.	6/1/61	Edmonton
FOGOLIN, Lee	6-0	200	Chicago, Ill.	2/7/55	Edmonton
GREGG, Randy	6-4	205	Edmonton, Alta.	2/19/56	Edmonton
HUDDY, Charlie	6-0	200	Oshawa, Ont.	6/2/59	Edmonton
JACKSON, Don	6-3	210	Minneapolis, Minn.	9/2/56	Edmonton
LOWE, Kevin	6-2	195	Lachute, Que.	4/15/59	Edmonton
MINER, John	5-10	190	Moose Jaw, Sask.	8/28/65	Nova Scotia
MUNI, Craig	6-2	200	Toronto, Ont.	7/19/62	Toronto-St. Catharines
PLAYFAIR, Jim	6-3	205	Vanderhoof, B.C.	5/22/64	Nova Scotia
SMITH, Steve	6-2	210	Glasgow, Scotland	4/30/63	Edmonton-Nova Scotia
TUER, Al	6-0	175	N. Battleford, Sask.	7/19/63	Los Angeles-New Haven

GOALTENDERS

	Ht.	Wt.	Place of Birth	Date	1985-86 Club
FUHR, Grant	5-10	185	Spruce Grove, Alta.	9/28/62	Edmonton
MOOG, Andy	5-9	170	Penticton, B.C.	2/18/60	Edmonton
REAUGH, Daryl	6-4	200	Prince George, B.C.	2/13/65	Nova Scotia

Coach and General Manager

SATHER, GLEN CAMERON
President, General Manager and Coach, Edmonton Oilers.
Born in High River, Alta., September 2, 1943.

In the first seven years of his NHL coaching career, Glen Sather has won two Stanley Cup titles and amassed 314 wins in only 560 games. In addition, he captured the Jack Adams Award in 1985-86 as Coach of the Year. He was named coach of the Oilers on January 27, 1977 when the Oilers were still members of the WHA. After they completed their first year in the NHL, Sather was given the additional duties of President and General Manager. Before joining the Oilers, Sather played in the NHL for nine years with Boston, Pittsburgh, New York Rangers, St. Louis, Montreal, and Minnesota.

NHL Coaching Record

Team	Season	Games	Regular Season				Playoffs			
			W	L	T	%	Games	W	L	%
Edmonton	1979-80	80	28	39	13	.431	3	0	3	.000
Edmonton	1980-81	80	29	35	16	.463	9	5	4	.555
Edmonton	1981-82	80	48	17	15	.694	5	2	3	.400
Edmonton	1982-83	80	47	21	12	.663	16	11	5	.687
Edmonton	1983-84	80	57	18	5	.744	19	15	4	.789*
Edmonton	1984-85	80	49	20	11	.681	18	15	3	.833*
Edmonton	1985-86	80	56	17	7	.744	10	6	4	.600
NHL Totals		**560**	**314**	**167**	**79**	**.631**	**80**	**54**	**26**	**.675**

* Stanley Cup win

1985-86 Scoring

Regular Season

*–rookie

Pos	#	Player	Team	GP	G	A	Pts	+/−	PIM	PP	SH	GW	OT	S	%
F	99	Wayne Gretzky	EDM	80	52	163	215	71	46	11	3	6	1	350	14.9
D	7	Paul Coffey	EDM	79	48	90	138	61	120	9	9	3	1	307	15.6
F	17	Jari Kurri	EDM	78	68	63	131	45	22	16	6	9	1	236	28.8
F	9	Glenn Anderson	EDM	72	54	48	102	38	90	18	2	9	0	243	22.2
F	11	Mark Messier	EDM	63	35	49	84	36	68	10	5	7	0	201	17.4
F	18	Mark Napier	EDM	80	24	32	56	13	14	3	1	4	1	117	20.5
F	14	Craig MacTavish	EDM	74	23	24	47	17	70	4	1	5	0	121	19.0
D	22	Charlie Huddy	EDM	76	6	35	41	30	55	1	0	0	0	151	4.0
F	26	Mike Krushelnyski	EDM	54	16	24	40	11	22	3	0	1	1	98	16.3
F	25	*Raimo Summanen	EDM	73	19	18	37	7	16	1	0	4	0	83	22.9
F	12	Dave Hunter	EDM	62	15	22	37	37	77	0	0	1	0	110	13.6
F	24	Kevin McClelland	EDM	79	11	25	36	9	266	0	0	1	0	104	10.6
D	21	Randy Gregg	EDM	64	2	26	28	30	47	0	0	0	0	55	3.6
D	2	Lee Fogolin	EDM	80	4	22	26	47	129	0	0	0	0	71	5.6
D	5	*Steve Smith	EDM	55	4	20	24	30	166	1	0	1	0	74	5.4
F	33	Marty McSorley	EDM	59	11	12	23	9	265	0	0	2	0	72	15.3
F	20	Dave Lumley	EDM	46	11	9	20	13	35	1	0	1	0	33	33.3
F	27	Dave Semenko	EDM	69	6	12	18	1−	141	0	0	0	0	51	11.8
D	4	Kevin Lowe	EDM	74	2	16	18	24	90	0	0	0	0	57	3.5
F	10	*Esa Tikkanen	EDM	35	7	6	13	5	28	0	0	2	0	44	15.9
D	29	Don Jackson	EDM	45	2	8	10	2	93	0	0	0	0	34	5.9
F	19	Mike Rogers	NYR	9	1	3	4	2	2	1	0	1	0	20	5.0
			EDM	8	1	0	1	2−	0	0	0	0	0	6	16.7
			Total	17	2	3	5	0	2	1	0	1	0	26	7.7
F	8	Gord Sherven	MIN	13	1	2	2	1	11	0	0	0	0	8	.0
			EDM	5	1	2	2	0	4	0	0	0	0	6	16.7
			Total	18	1	3	4	1	15	0	0	0	0	14	7.1
F	13	*Risto Jalo	EDM	3	0	3	3	2	0	0	0	0	0	3	.0
G	31	Grant Fuhr	EDM	40	0	2	2	0	4	0	0	0	0		
G	35	Andy Moog	EDM	47	0	2	2	0	8	0	0	0	0		
F	28	Ken Solheim	EDM	6	1	0	1	2−	0	0	0	0	0	8	12.5
F	15	Jeff Brubaker	TOR	21	0	0	0	0	67	0	0	0	0	8	.0
			EDM	4	1	0	1	1	12	0	0	0	0	4	25.0
			Total	25	1	0	1	1	79	0	0	0	0	12	8.3
F	34	Dean Hopkins	EDM	1	0	0	0	0	0	0	0	0	0	0	.0
F	15	Mike Moller	EDM	1	0	0	0	0	0	0	0	0	0	2	.0
D	16	*Selmar Odelein	EDM	4	0	0	0	1	0	0	0	0	0	2	.0

Playoffs

* rookie

Pos	#	Player	Team	GP	G	A	Pts	+/−	PIM	PP	SH	GW	OT	S	%
F	99	Wayne Gretzky	EDM	10	8	11	19	0	2	4	1	2	0	42	19.0
F	17	Jari Kurri	EDM	10	2	10	12	1	4	0	1	0	0	25	8.0
F	9	Glenn Anderson	EDM	10	8	3	11	2	14	1	0	2	1	38	21.1
F	11	Mark Messier	EDM	10	4	6	10	1	18	0	2	0	0	23	17.4
D	7	Paul Coffey	EDM	10	1	9	10	0	30	1	0	0	0	33	3.0
F	26	Mike Krushelnyski	EDM	10	4	5	9	3	16	1	0	2	0	15	26.7
F	14	Craig MacTavish	EDM	10	4	4	8	6	11	1	0	0	0	17	23.5
F	10	*Esa Tikkanen	EDM	8	3	2	5	1	7	0	0	0	0	19	15.8
F	12	Dave Hunter	EDM	10	2	3	5	7	23	0	0	0	0	18	11.1
F	18	Mark Napier	EDM	10	1	4	5	6	0	0	0	0	0	14	7.1
D	4	Kevin Lowe	EDM	10	1	3	4	6	15	0	0	0	0	16	6.3
F	25	*Raimo Summanen	EDM	5	1	1	2	2	0	0	0	0	0	6	16.7
F	20	Dave Lumley	EDM	3	0	2	2	0	2	0	0	0	0	1	.0
D	22	Charlie Huddy	EDM	7	0	2	2	3	10	0	0	0	0	5	.0
D	2	Lee Fogolin	EDM	8	0	2	2	3	4	0	0	0	0	5	.0
F	33	Marty McSorley	EDM	8	0	2	2	2	50	0	0	0	0	4	.0
D	21	Randy Gregg	EDM	10	1	0	1	3	12	0	0	0	0	6	16.7
F	24	Kevin McClelland	EDM	10	1	0	1	1−	32	0	0	0	0	7	14.3
D	5	*Steve Smith	EDM	6	0	1	1	4	14	0	0	0	0	5	.0
G	31	Grant Fuhr	EDM	9	0	1	1	0	0	0	0	0	0		
D	6	*Jeff Beukeboom	EDM	1	0	0	0	1	4	0	0	0	0	1	.0
G	35	Andy Moog	EDM	1	0	0	0	0	0	0	0	0	0		
F	27	Dave Semenko	EDM	6	0	0	0	0	32	0	0	0	0	1	.0
D	29	Don Jackson	EDM	8	0	0	0	3	21	0	0	0	0	7	.0

Club Records

Team

(Figures in brackets for season records are games played; records for fewest points, wins, ties, losses, goals, goals against are for 70 or more

Most Points	119	1983-84 (80)
		1985-86 (80)
Most Wins	57	1983-84 (80)
Most Ties	16	1980-81 (80)
Most Losses	39	1979-80 (80)
Most Goals	*446	1983-84 (80)
Most Goals Against	327	1980-81 (80)
Fewest Points	69	1979-80 (80)
Fewest Wins	28	1979-80 (80)
Fewest Ties	5	1983-84 (80)
Fewest Losses	17	1981-82 (80)
		1985-86 (80)
Fewest Goals	301	1979-80 (80)
Fewest Goals Against	295	1981-82 (80)

Longest Winning Streak
Over-all ... 8 Several times
Home ... 8 Jan. 19/85-
Feb. 22/85
Away ... 7 Dec. 14/83-
Jan. 11/84

Longest Undefeated Streak
Over-all ... 15 Oct. 11/84-
Nov. 9/84
(12 wins, 3 ties)
Home ... 12 Oct. 5-
Dec. 3/83
(10 wins, 2 ties)
Away ... 9 Jan. 17-
Mar. 2/82
(6 wins, 3 ties)

Longest Losing Streak
Over-all ... 6 Feb. 29-
Mar. 9/80
Home ... 3 Feb. 24-
Mar. 1/80
Away ... 9 Nov. 25-
Dec. 30/80

Longest Winless Streak
Over-all ... 6 Four times
Home ... 7 Oct. 24-
Nov. 19/80
(3 losses, 4 ties)
Away ... 9 Nov. 25-
Dec. 30/80
(9 losses)

Most Shutouts, Season ... 3 1984-85 (80)
Most Pen. Mins.,
Season ... 1,928 1985-86 (80)
Most Goals, Game ... 13 Nov. 19/83
(NJ 4 at Edm. 13)

Individual

Most Seasons	7	Several players
Most Games	553	Wayne Gretzky
Most Goals, Career	481	Wayne Gretzky
Most Assists, Career	856	Wayne Gretzky
Most Points, Career	1337	Wayne Gretzky
		(481 goals, 856 assists)
Most Pen. Mins., Career	981	Dave Semenko
Most Shutouts, Career	4	Andy Moog

Longest Consecutive
Games Streak ... 362 Wayne Gretzky
(Nov. 2/79-Feb. 3/84)
Most Goals, Season ... *92 Wayne Gretzky
(1981-82)
Most Assists, Season ... *163 Wayne Gretzky
(1985-86)
Most Points, Season ... *215 Wayne Gretzky
(1985-86)
(52 goals, 163 assists)
Most Pen. Mins., Season ... 266 Kevin McClelland
(1985-86)
Most Points, Defenseman,
Season ... 138 Paul Coffey
(1985-86)
(48 goals, 90 assists)

Most Points, Center,
Season ... *215 Wayne Gretzky
(1985-86)
(52 goals, 163 assists)
Most Points, Right Wing,
Season ... 135 Jari Kurri
(1984-85)
(71 goals, 64 assists)
Most Points, Left Wing,
Season ... 102 Glen Anderson
(1985-86)
(54 goals, 48 assists)
Most Points, Rookie,
Season ... 75 Jari Kurri
(1980-81)
(32 goals, 43 assists)
Most Shutouts, Season ... 1 by 3 goaltenders
Most Goals, Game ... 5 Wayne Gretzky
(Feb. 18/81, Dec. 30/81,
Dec. 20/84)
Jari Kurri (Nov. 19/83)
Pat Hughes (Feb. 3/84)
Most Assists, Game ... *7 Wayne Gretzky
(Feb. 15/80; Dec. 11/85;
Feb. 14/86)
Most Points, Game ... 8 Wayne Gretzky
(Nov. 19/83)
Paul Coffey
(Mar. 14/86)
Wayne Gretzky
(Jan. 4/84)

* NHL Record.

Coaching History
Glen Sather, 1979-80 to date.

Captains' History
Ron Chipperfield, 1979-80; Lee Fogolin, 1980-81 to 1982-83; Wayne Gretzky, 1983-84 to 1985-86.

All-time Record vs. Other Clubs

Regular Season

			At Home							On Road							Total					
	GP	W	L	T	GF	GA	PTS	GP	W	L	T	GF	GA	PTS	GP	W	L	T	GF	GA	PTS
Boston	12	5	5	2	42	39	12	11	2	8	1	31	55	5	23	7	13	3	73	94	17
Buffalo	12	7	3	2	49	34	16	11	4	5	2	45	48	10	23	11	8	4	94	82	26
**Calgary	24	16	3	5	131	95	37	24	14	7	3	109	104	31	48	30	10	8	240	199	68
Chicago	11	9	1	1	63	37	19	12	7	2	3	64	53	15	23	16	3	4	127	90	34
Detroit	11	7	2	2	69	45	16	12	9	2	1	63	40	19	23	16	4	3	132	85	35
Hartford	12	10	0	2	62	38	22	11	4	5	2	45	52	10	23	14	5	4	107	90	32
Los Angeles	24	16	3	5	152	93	37	24	12	7	5	118	97	29	48	28	10	10	270	190	66
Minnesota	12	8	1	3	68	45	19	11	5	4	2	42	43	12	23	13	5	5	110	88	31
Montreal	11	7	4	0	48	36	14	12	4	6	2	37	41	10	23	11	10	2	85	77	24
*New Jersey	14	10	2	2	79	49	22	14	7	6	1	52	50	15	28	17	8	3	131	99	37
NY Islanders	11	5	5	1	41	44	11	12	1	5	6	53	61	8	23	6	10	7	94	105	19
NY Rangers	11	5	5	1	41	38	11	12	7	4	1	55	51	15	23	12	9	2	96	89	26
Philadelphia	12	5	5	2	42	41	12	11	2	9	0	36	60	4	23	7	14	2	78	101	16
Pittsburgh	12	10	1	1	78	43	21	11	6	4	1	59	40	13	23	16	5	2	137	83	34
Quebec	11	7	4	0	69	40	14	12	6	5	1	61	53	13	23	13	9	1	130	93	27
St. Louis	11	6	3	2	56	49	14	12	5	5	2	58	52	12	23	11	8	4	114	101	26
Toronto	11	8	1	3	68	41	19	11	6	4	1	60	52	13	23	14	5	4	128	93	32
Vancouver	24	16	4	4	141	75	36	24	13	8	3	107	88	29	48	29	12	7	248	163	65
Washington	11	5	2	4	53	36	14	12	6	5	1	54	55	13	23	11	7	5	107	91	27
Winnipeg	22	17	5	0	123	76	34	21	15	5	1	119	92	31	43	32	10	1	242	168	65
Totals	280	179	59	42	1475	994	400	280	135	108	37	1268	1187	307	560	314	167	79	2743	2181	707

* Totals include those of Colorado (1979-80, 1980-81, 1981-82)
** Totals include those of Atlanta (1979-80)

Playoffs

	Series	W	L	GP	W	L	T	GF	GA	Last Mtg.	Round	Result
Calgary	3	2	1	19	11	8	0	92	65	1986	DF	L 4-3
Chicago	2	2	0	10	8	2	0	69	36	1985	CF	W 4-2
Los Angeles	2	1	1	8	5	3	0	34	34	1985	DSF	L 0-3
Minnesota	1	1	0	4	4	0	0	22	10	1984	CF	W 4-0
Montreal	1	1	0	3	3	0	0	15	6	1981	P	W 3-0
NY Islanders	3	1	2	15	6	9	0	47	58	1984	F	W 4-1
Philadelphia	2	1	1	8	4	4	0	27	26	1985	F	W 4-1
Vancouver	1	1	0	3	3	0	0	17	5	1986	DSF	W 3-0
Winnipeg	3	3	0	10	10	0	0	54	25	1985	DF	W 4-0
Totals	18	13	5	80	54	26	0	377	265			

Playoff Results 1986-82

Year	Round	Opponent	Result	GF	GA
1986	DF	Calgary	L 4-3	24	25
	DSF	Vancouver	W 3-0	17	5
1985	F	**Philadelphia**	W 4-1	21	14
	CF	Chicago	W 4-2	44	25
	DF	Winnipeg	W 4-0	22	11
	DSF	Los Angeles	W 3-0	11	7
1984	F	**NY Islanders**	W 4-1	21	12
	CF	Minnesota	W 4-0	22	10
	DF	Calgary	W 4-3	33	27
	DSF	Winnipeg	W 3-0	18	7
1983	F	NY Islanders	L 0-4	6	17
	CF	Chicago	W 4-0	25	11
	DF	Calgary	W 4-1	35	13
	DSF	Winnipeg	W 3-0	14	9
1982	DSF	Los Angeles	L 2-3	23	27

Abbreviations: Round: F – Final; CF – conference final; DF – division final; DSF – division semi-final; SF – semi-final; QF – quarter-final; P – preliminary round. **GA –** goals against; **GF –** goals for.

Retired Numbers
3 Al Hamilton 1972-1980

Entry Draft Selections 1986-79

1986
Pick
21	Kim Issel
42	Jamie Nichols
63	Ron Shudra
84	Dan Currie
105	David Haas
126	Jim Ennis
147	Ivan Matulik
168	Nicolas Beaulieu
189	Mike Greenlay
210	Matt Lanza
231	Mojmir Bozik
252	Tony Hand

1985
Pick
20	Scott Metcalfe
41	Todd Carnelley
62	Mike Ware
104	Thomas Kapusta
125	Brian Tessier
146	Shawn Tyers
167	Tony Fairfield
188	Kelly Buchberger
209	Mario Barbe
230	Peter Headon
251	John Haley

1984
Pick
21	Selmar Odelein
42	Daryl Reaugh
63	Todd Norman
84	Rich Novak
105	Richard Lambert
106	Emanuel Viveiros
126	Ivan Dornic
147	Heikki Riihijarvi
168	Todd Ewen
209	Joel Curtis
229	Simon Wheeldon
250	Darren Gani

1983
Pick
19	Jeff Beukeboom
40	Mike Golden
60	Mike Flanagan
80	Esa Tikkanen
120	Don Barber
140	Dale Derkatch
160	Ralph Vos
180	Dave Roach
200	Warren Yadlowski
220	John Miner
240	Steve Woodburn

1982
Pick
20	Jim Playfair
41	Steve Graves
62	Brent Loney
83	Jaroslav Pouzar
104	Dwayne Boettger
125	Raimo Summanen
146	Brian Small
167	Dean Clark
188	Ian Wood
209	Grant Dion
230	Chris Smith
251	Jeff Crawford

1981
Pick
8	Grant Fuhr
29	Todd Strueby
71	Paul Houck
92	Phil Drouillard
111	Steve Smith
113	Marc Habscheid
155	Mike Sturgeon
176	Miloslav Horava
197	Gord Sherven

1980
Pick
6	Paul Coffey
48	Shawn Babcock
69	Jari Kurri
90	Walt Poddubny
111	Mike Winther
132	Andy Moog
153	Rob Polmantuin
174	Lars-Gunnar Petersson

1979
Pick
21	Kevin Lowe
48	Mark Messier
69	Glenn Anderson
84	Max Kostovich
105	Mike Toal
126	Blair Barnes

Oiler record setters: Paul Coffey, left, set an NHL record for the most goals in a single season by a defenseman with 48. Wayne Gretzky, right, had 163 assists and 215 points, both all-time single-season records.

Club Directory

Northlands Coliseum
Edmonton, Alberta T5B 4M9
TWX 610-831-1711
Phone 403/474-8561
Ticketing 403/471-2191
Telecopier 403/471-2329
ENVOY ID TM.EDM
Capacity: 17,308 (standing 190)

Owner/Governor	Peter Pocklington
Alternate Governor	Glen Sather
General Counsel	Gary Frohlich, Bob Lloyd
President/General Manager/Coach	Glen Sather
Co-Coach	John Muckler
Assistant General Manager	Bruce MacGregor
Assistant Coach	Ted Green
Director of Player Personnel/Chief Scout	Barry Fraser
Director of Player Development	Bob McCammon
Scouting Staff	Lorne Davis, Ace Bailey, Bob Freeman, Ed Chadwick, Curly Reeves, Matti Vaisanen
General Manager/Coach (A.H.L.)	
Nova Scotia Oilers	Larry Kish
Director of Operations (A.H.L.)	
Nova Scotia Oilers	John Blackwell
Controller	Werner Baum
Accountants	Lori Padlewski, Ellie Merrick, Tracey Hillis
Executive Secretary	Diana Hrynchuk
Director of Public Relations	Bill Tuele
Co-ordinator of Publications and Statistics	Steve Knowles
Community Relations/Advertising	Trish Wilson
Promotions Manager	Mike Brennan
Director of Marketing	Mark Hall
Director of Properties	Barb Nickel
Assistant Director of Properties	Darrell Holowaychuk
Director of Ticketing Operations	Sheila Steil
Ticketing Operations	Sheila McCaskill, Brenda Osborne
Receptionist/Secretary	Debbie VanOs
Secretary	Elaine McBride
Athletic Therapist	Peter Millar
Trainer	Barrie Stafford
Assistant Trainer	Lyle Kulchisky
Team Physician	Dr. Gordon Cameron
Team Dentist	Dr. W.M. (Mel) Taskey
Fitness Consultant	Dr. Art Quinney
Team Administrative Offices	Northlands Coliseum Edmonton, Alberta Canada, T5B 4M9
Location of Press Box	East Side at top (Radio/TV) West Side at top (Media)
Dimensions of Rink	200 feet by 85 feet
Ends of Rink	Herculite extends above boards around rink
Club Colours	Blue, Orange, White
Training Camp Site	Northlands Coliseum, Edmonton, Alberta
Television Channel	CITV (Channel 13) (Cable 8) CBXT TV (Channel 5) (Cable 4)
Radio Station	CFRN (1260 AM)
Play-By-Play	Rod Phillips
Color	Ken Brown
Official Photographer	Bob Mummery

Hartford Whalers

1985-86 Results: 40w-36l-4t 84 pts. Fourth, Adams Division

Year-by-Year Record

Season	GP	Home W	L	T	Road W	L	T	Overall W	L	T	GF	GA	Pts.	Finished	Playoff Result
1985-86	80	21	17	2	19	19	2	40	36	4	332	302	84	4th, Adams Div.	Lost Div. Final
1984-85	80	17	18	5	13	23	4	30	41	9	268	318	69	5th, Adams Div.	Out of Playoffs
1983-84	80	19	16	5	9	26	5	28	42	10	288	320	66	5th, Adams Div.	Out of Playoffs
1982-83	80	13	22	5	6	32	2	19	54	7	261	403	45	5th, Adams Div.	Out of Playoffs
1981-82	80	13	17	10	8	24	8	21	41	18	264	351	60	5th, Adams Div.	Out of Playoffs
1980-81	80	14	17	9	7	24	9	21	41	18	292	372	60	4th, Norris Div.	Out of Playoffs
1979-80	80	22	12	6	5	22	13	27	34	19	303	312	73	4th, Norris Div.	Lost Prelim. Round

Schedule

	Home				Away
Oct.	Sat.	11	Calgary	Oct.	Sun. 12 Boston
	Thur.	16	Winnipeg		Fri. 24 Buffalo
	Sat.	18	Philadelphia		Thur. 30 Toronto
	Sat.	25	Buffalo	Nov.	Sun. 2 Quebec
	Tue.	28	Pittsburgh		Sat. 8 Los Angeles
Nov.	Sat.	1	Quebec		Wed. 12 Vancouver
	Wed.	5	NY Islanders		Thur. 13 Calgary
	Sat.	15	Edmonton		Sat. 22 NY Islanders
	Wed.	19	Montreal		Sat. 29 Montreal
	Fri.	21	St. Louis	Dec.	Mon. 1 Quebec
	Wed.	26	Buffalo		Thur. 4 Philadelphia
Dec.	Wed.	3	Quebec		Sun. 14 Buffalo
	Sat.	6	Detroit		Thur. 18 Boston
	Wed.	10	St. Louis		Sat. 20 Detroit
	Sat.	13	Vancouver		Sun. 21 NY Rangers
	Wed.	17	Buffalo		Sat. 27 Montreal
	Tue.	23	Boston		Tue. 30 Washington
	Fri.	26	Montreal		Wed. 31 Minnesota
Jan.	Sat.	3	Chicago*	Jan.	Wed. 7 St. Louis
	Sun.	4	Toronto		Fri. 9 Winnipeg
	Wed.	14	Boston		Sat. 10 Minnesota
	Sat.	17	Washington		Mon. 12 New Jersey
	Wed.	21	Montreal		Thur. 15 Boston
	Fri.	23	Quebec		Mon. 19 Montreal
Feb.	Wed.	4	Buffalo		Sat. 24 Toronto
	Sat.	7	Montreal		Tue. 27 Quebec
	Sat.	21	Chicago		Thur. 29 Boston
	Wed.	25	Boston		Sat. 31 NY Islanders
	Sat.	28	Quebec	Feb.	Sun. 1 Pittsburgh
Mar.	Sun.	1	New Jersey*		Fri. 6 Washington
	Tue.	3	Detroit		Sat. 14 Los Angeles
	Thur.	5	Boston		Tue. 17 Chicago
	Sat.	7	Philadelphia		Wed. 18 New Jersey
	Wed.	11	Calgary		Sun. 22 Buffalo
	Sat.	21	Minnesota	Mar.	Tue. 10 Quebec
	Sun.	22	Los Angeles*		Fri. 13 Winnipeg
	Wed.	25	Edmonton		Sun. 15 Edmonton
	Sat.	28	Pittsburgh		Wed. 18 NY Rangers
	Sun.	29	Vancouver*	April	Wed. 1 Montreal
April	Sat.	4	NY Rangers		Sun. 5 Buffalo

*Denotes afternoon game.

Home Starting Times:
All Games . . . . 7:35 p.m.
Except Jan. 1, Mar. 1,
  Mar. 22, Mar. 29 . . . . 2:05 p.m.
  Jan. 4 . . . . 7:05 p.m.

Franchise date: June 22, 1979

 8th NHL Season

Mike Liut recorded a goals-against-average of 1.90 in the 1986 Stanley Cup Playoffs.

1986-87 Player Personnel

FORWARDS	Ht.	Wt.	Place of Birth	Date	1985-86 Club
ANDERSON, John	5-11	190	Toronto, Ont.	3/23/57	Quebec-Hartford
BABYCH, Wayne	5-11	195	Edmonton, Alta.	6/6/58	Pittsburgh-Quebec
BRANT, Chris	6-1	180	Belleville, Ont.	8/26/65	Binghamton
BURKHOLDER, Barrie	5-9	160	Mississauga, Ont.	3/4/66	Kingston
CALLAGHAN, Gary	5-11	175	Oshawa, Ont.	8/12/67	Belleville
CHANNELL, Todd	5-10	165	Chicago, Ill.	10/8/63	Miami-Ohio
CHURLA, Shane	6-1	200	Fernie, B.C.	6/24/65	Binghamton
DINEEN, Kevin	5-10	180	Quebec, Que.	10/28/63	Hartford
EVASON, Dean	5-10	180	Flin Flon, Man.	8/22/64	Hartford-Binghamton
FERRARO, Ray	5-11	185	Trail, B.C.	8/23/64	Hartford
FRANCIS, Ron	6-2	200	Sault Ste. Marie, Ont.	3/1/63	Hartford
GARDNER, Bill	5-10	170	Toronto, Ont.	3/19/60	Chicago-Hartford
GAUME, Dallas	5-10	180	Innisfal, Alta.	8/27/63	U. of Denver
GAVIN, Stewart	5-11	185	Ottawa, Ont.	3/15/60	Hartford
GENDRON, Mark	5-10	175	Prince Albert, Sask.	10/22/62	Minnesota-Duluth
HAMILTON, Geordie	6-0	180	Hershey, Pa.	8/22/66	Michigan Tech.
HOFFMAN, Mike	5-11	190	Cambridge, Ont.	2/26/63	Binghamton
JARVIS, Doug	5-9	175	Brantford, Ont.	3/24/55	Washington-Hartford
JOHANSSON, Jim	6-1	175	Rochester, Minn.	3/10/64	U. of Wisconsin
LATOS, James	6-1	190	Wakaw, Sask.	1/4/66	Portland-Saskatoon
LAWLESS, Paul	5-11	185	Scarborough, Ont.	7/2/64	Hartford
MacDERMID, Paul	6-1	200	Chester, Ont.	4/14/63	Hartford
MacLEAN, Dave	6-0	195	Newmarket, Ont.	1/22/66	Binghamton-Salt Lake City
MILLAR, Mike	5-10	170	St. Catharines, Ont.	4/28/65	Team Canada
ROBERTSON, Torrie	5-11	200	Victoria, B.C.	8/2/61	Hartford
TIPPETT, Dave	5-10	180	Moosomin, Sask.	8/25/61	Hartford
TURGEON, Sylvain	6-0	195	Noranda, Que.	1/17/65	Hartford
VERBEEK, Brian	5-9	195	Wyoming, Ont.	10/22/66	Kingston
WALDIE, David	6-0	180	Roseneath, Ont.	4/8/65	Portland
YOUNG, Scott	6-0	185	Clinton, Mass.	10/1/67	Boston U.
DEFENSEMEN					
BABYCH, Dave	6-2	215	Edmonton, Alta.	3/23/61	Winnipeg-Hartford
BOTHWELL, Tim	6-3	190	Vancouver, B.C.	3/6/55	Hartford
BROWNSCHIDLE, Jack	6-2	195	Buffalo, N.Y.	10/2/55	Hartford-Binghamton
CHAPMAN, Brian	6-0	185	Brockville, Ont.	2/10/68	Belleville
COTE, Sylvain	5-11	175	Quebec City, Que.	1/19/66	Hartford-Hull
CAGNIN, Shawn	6-1	205	Melrose, Mass.	9/9/60	U. of Illinois-Chicago
KLEINENDORST, Scot	6-3	215	Grand Rapids, Mich.	1/16/60	Hartford
LAFORGE, Marc	6-2	200	Sudbury, Ont.	1/3/68	Kingston
McEWEN, Mike	6-1	185	Hornepayne, Ont.	8/10/56	Detroit-NY Rangers-New Haven-Hartford
MOKOSAK, John	5-11	200	Edmonton, Alta.	9/7/63	Binghamton
MURZYN, Dana	6-2	200	Regina, Sask.	10/9/66	Hartford
PATERSON, Mark	5-11	180	Ottawa, Ont.	2/22/64	Hartford-Binghamton
QUENNEVILLE, Joel	6-1	200	Windsor, Ont.	9/15/58	Hartford
SAMUELLSON, Ulf	6-1	195	Fagursta, Swe.	3/26/64	Hartford
SHAW, Brad	5-11	190	Cambridge, Ont.	4/28/64	Binghamton
VELLUCCI, Mike	6-1	180	Farmington, Mich.	8/11/65	Belleville
VICHOREK, Mark	6-2	200		5/1/63	Lake Superior State
GOALTENDERS					
EVOY, Sean	6-0	190	Sudbury, Ont.	2/21/66	Cornwall
FALLE, Jamie	5-11	190	Montreal, Que	8/26/64	Clarkson
HEINZ, Rick	5-10	165	Essex, Ont.	8/23/62	Salt Lake City-Binghamton
LIUT, Mike	6-2	195	Weston, Ont.	1/7/56	Hartford
SIDORKIEWICZ, Peter	5-9	180	Poland	6/29/63	Binghamton
WEEKS, Steve	5-11	165	Scarborough, Ont.	6/30/58	Hartford
WHITMORE, Kay	5-11	165	Sudbury, Ont.	4/10/67	Peterborough

Coach and General Manager

EVANS, WILLIAM JOHN (JACK)
Coach, Hartford Whalers. Born in Morriston, South Wales, April 21, 1928.

In 1985-86, Jack Evans led the Hartford Whalers to the strongest season in the club's history. The Whalers not only finished the season with their best record ever, 40-36-4, but also skated to their first playoff appearance since 1979-80, including a dramatic seven-game series with the eventual Stanley Cup champion Montreal Canadiens. Evans was named coach of the Whalers on July 7, 1983 after spending the previous five seasons as head coach of St. Louis' top minor league affiliate at Salt Lake. Evans guided the Eagles to a 230-143-23 record, three first place finishes and two Central Hockey League Championships during that time and was named CHL Coach of the Year in 1975, 1980 and 1981. Evans previously coached in the NHL with California and Cleveland from 1975-76 to 1977-78. His coaching career began with the San Diego Gulls of the Western Hockey League and his professional playing career as a defenseman spanned 22 seasons, including 12 years in the NHL with the New York Rangers and Chicago Black Hawks.

NHL Coaching Record

		Regular Season					Playoffs			
Team	Season	Games	W	L	T	%	Games	W	L	%
California	1975-76	80	27	42	11	.406	....	....	....	....
Cleveland	1976-77	80	25	42	13	.394	....	....	....	....
Cleveland	1977-78	80	22	45	13	.356	....	....	....	....
Hartford	1983-84	80	28	42	10	.412	....	....	....	....
Hartford	1984-85	80	30	41	9	.431	....	....	....	....
Hartford	1985-86	80	40	36	4	.525	10	6	4	.600
NHL Totals		**480**	**172**	**248**	**60**	**.421**	**10**	**6**	**4**	**.600**

1985-86 Scoring

Regular Season

*–rookie

Pos	#	Player	Team	GP	G	A	Pts	+/–	PIM	PP	SH	GW	OT	S	%
F	16	Sylvain Turgeon	HFD	76	45	34	79	1	88	13	0	5	0	249	18.1
F	26	Ray Ferraro	HFD	76	30	47	77	10	57	14	0	0	0	132	22.7
F	10	Ron Francis	HFD	53	24	53	77	8	24	7	1	4	1	120	20.0
F	20	John Anderson	QUE	65	21	28	49	1–	26	8	3	5	1	190	11.1
			HFD	14	8	17	25	18	2	1	0	1	0	50	16.0
			Total	79	29	45	74	17	28	9	3	6	1	240	12.1
D	44	Dave Babych	WPG	19	4	12	16	1–	14	2	0	0	0	53	7.5
			HFD	62	10	43	53	2	36	7	1	2	0	152	6.6
			Total	81	14	55	69	1	50	9	1	2	0	205	6.8
F	11	Kevin Dineen	HFD	57	33	35	68	16	124	6	0	8	0	167	19.8
F	7	Stewart Gavin	HFD	76	26	29	55	12	51	3	3	4	1	161	16.1
F	12	*Dean Evason	HFD	55	20	28	48	3	65	5	2	4	0	101	19.8
F	17	Wayne Babych	PIT	2	0	0	0	1–	0	0	0	0	0	0	.0
			QUE	15	6	5	11	0	18	1	0	0	0	32	18.8
			HFD	37	11	17	28	6	59	2	0	2	0	63	17.5
			Total	54	17	22	39	5	77	3	0	2	0	95	17.9
F	28	Paul Lawless	HFD	64	17	21	38	3–	20	5	0	1	0	139	12.2
F	32	Torrie Robertson	HFD	76	13	24	37	11–	358	3	0	0	0	89	14.6
F	15	Dave Tippett	HFD	80	14	20	34	9	18	0	2	1	0	118	11.9
F	27	Doug Jarvis	WSH	25	1	2	3	5–	16	0	0	0	0	19	5.3
			HFD	57	8	16	24	7	20	0	3	0	0	55	14.5
			Total	82	9	18	27	2	36	0	3	0	0	74	12.2
D	4	*Dana Murzyn	HFD	78	3	23	26	1	125	0	0	1	1	79	3.8
D	3	Joel Quenneville	HFD	71	5	20	25	21	83	1	0	1	0	49	10.2
D	5	Ulf Samuelsson	HFD	80	5	19	24	7	174	0	1	1	0	72	6.9
F	23	Paul MacDermid	HFD	74	13	10	23	1	160	0	0	2	0	88	14.8
D	25	Mike McEwen	DET	29	0	10	10	8–	16	0	0	0	0	82	.0
			NYR	16	2	5	7	4–	8	0	0	1	0	36	5.6
			HFD	10	3	2	5	5	6	0	0	0	0	18	16.7
			Total	55	5	17	22	7–	30	0	0	1	0	136	3.7
F	14	Bill Gardner	CHI	46	3	10	13	8–	6	0	0	0	0	29	10.3
			HFD	18	1	8	9	6–	4	0	0	0	0	12	8.3
			Total	64	4	18	22	14–	10	0	0	0	0	41	9.8
D	24	Tim Bothwell	HFD	62	2	8	10	13	53	0	0	0	0	50	4.0
D	18	Scot Kleinendorst	HFD	41	2	7	9	8	62	0	0	0	0	26	7.7
F	20	*Mike Hoffman	HFD	6	1	2	3	2–	2	0	0	0	0	7	14.3
D	38	*Brad Shaw	HFD	8	0	2	2	1–	4	0	0	0	0	17	.0
F	20	Mike Zuke	HFD	17	0	2	2	2–	12	0	0	0	0	2	.0
G	1	Mike Liut	HFD	57	0	2	2	0	0	0	0	0	0	0	.0
G	31	Steve Weeks	HFD	27	0	1	1	0	9	0	0	0	0	0	.0
F	29	Paul Fenton	HFD	1	0	0	0	1	0	0	0	0	0	3	.0
D	21	Sylvain Cote	HFD	2	0	0	0	1	0	0	0	0	0	0	.0
F	33	*John Newberry	HFD	3	0	0	0	4–	0	0	0	0	0	4	.0
D	6	Mark Paterson	HFD	5	0	0	0	5–	5	0	0	0	0	0	.0
D	34	Jack Brownschidle	HFD	9	0	0	0	4–	4	0	0	0	0	7	.0

Playoffs

* rookie

Pos	#	Player	Team	GP	G	A	Pts	+/–	PIM	PP	SH	GW	OT	S	%
F	11	Kevin Dineen	HFD	10	6	7	13	2	18	1	0	2	1	28	21.4
F	20	John Anderson	HFD	10	5	8	13	3	0	3	0	0	0	32	15.6
F	26	Ray Ferraro	HFD	10	3	6	9	1–	4	3	0	0	0	14	21.4
F	7	Stewart Gavin	HFD	10	4	1	5	6	13	0	0	0	0	19	21.1
F	16	Sylvain Turgeon	HFD	9	2	3	5	2	4	0	0	2	1	22	9.1
F	12	*Dean Evason	HFD	10	1	4	5	4	10	0	0	0	0	11	9.1
F	15	Dave Tippett	HFD	10	2	2	4	3	4	0	1	0	0	18	11.1
D	44	Dave Babych	HFD	8	1	3	4	0	14	0	0	0	0	18	5.6
D	25	Mike McEwen	HFD	8	0	4	4	0	6	0	0	0	0	9	.0
F	23	Paul MacDermid	HFD	10	2	1	3	1	20	0	0	1	0	8	25.0
F	10	Ron Francis	HFD	10	1	2	3	1–	4	0	0	0	0	27	3.7
D	5	Ulf Samuelsson	HFD	10	1	2	3	5	38	0	0	1	0	13	7.7
F	27	Doug Jarvis	HFD	10	0	3	3	1	4	0	0	0	0	7	.0
D	3	Joel Quenneville	HFD	10	0	2	2	6	12	0	0	0	0	3	.0
F	32	Torrie Robertson	HFD	10	1	0	1	1–	67	0	0	0	0	7	14.3
F	17	Wayne Babych	HFD	10	0	1	1	2–	2	0	0	0	0	10	.0
D	18	Scot Kleinendorst	HFD	10	0	1	1	6	18	0	0	0	0	6	.0
F	28	Paul Lawless	HFD	1	0	0	0	0	0	0	0	0	0	5	.0
G	31	Steve Weeks	HFD	3	0	0	0	0	0	0	0	0	0	0	.0
D	4	*Dana Murzyn	HFD	4	0	0	0	2	10	0	0	0	0	2	.0
G	1	Mike Liut	HFD	8	0	0	0	0	0	0	0	0	0	0	.0
D	24	Tim Bothwell	HFD	10	0	0	0	2	8	0	0	0	0	2	.0

FRANCIS, EMILE PERCY
President and General Manager, Hartford Whalers. Born in North Battleford, Sask., September 13, 1926.

Emile Francis was named President and General Manager of the Hartford Whalers on May 2, 1983 after seven seasons with the St. Louis Blues and a 15-year association with the New York Rangers. In July of 1977 he was named president of the Blues and at the same time relinquished his coaching duties to Leo Boivin. He concentrated solely on front office duties with the Blues until March 9, 1982 when he replaced Red Berenson behind the bench. Francis played professionally for 14 seasons as a goaltender which included parts of six years in the NHL with Chicago and New York. His retirement as a player came at the end of the 1959-60 season and he quickly joined the Rangers' organization. Francis served first as coach of the Rangers' sponsored junior team in Guelph, Ont., and then moved on to coach and general manager duties with New York.

Club Records

Team

(Figures in brackets for season records are games played; records for fewest points, wins, ties, losses, goals, goals against are for 70 or more games)

Most Points	.84	1985-86 (80)
Most Wins	.40	1985-86 (80)
Most Ties	.19	1979-80 (80)
Most Losses	.54	1982-83 (80)
Most Goals	.332	1985-86 (80)
Most Goals Against	.403	1982-83 (80)
Fewest Points	.45	1982-83 (80)
Fewest Wins	.19	1982-83 (80)
Fewest Ties	.4	1985-86 (80)
Fewest Losses	.34	1979-80 (80)
Fewest Goals	.261	1982-83 (80)
Fewest Goals Against	.302	1985-86 (80)

Longest Winning Streak
- Over-all ....7 Mar. 16-29/85
- Home ....5 Mar. 17-29/85
- Away ....4 Mar. 7-19/86

Longest Undefeated Streak
- Over-all ....10 Jan. 20-Feb. 10/82 (6 wins, 4 ties)
- Home ....7 Mar. 15-Apr. 15/86 (5 wins, 2 ties)
- Away ....6 Jan. 23-Feb. 10/82 (3 wins, 3 ties)

Longest Losing Streak
- Over-all ....9 Feb. 19/83-Mar. 8/83
- Home ....6 Feb. 19/83-Mar. 12/83 / Feb. 10-Mar. 3/85
- Away ....13 Dec. 8/82-Feb. 5/83

Longest Winless Streak
- Over-all ....12 Dec. 18/82-Jan. 11/83 (11 losses, 1 tie)
- Home ....13 Jan. 15-Mar. 10/85 (11 losses, 2 ties)
- Away ....15 Nov. 11/79-Jan. 9/80 (11 losses, 4 ties)

Most Shutouts, Season 4 1984-85 (80)
Most Pen. Mins., Season 1,759 1985-86 (80)
Most Goals, Game ....11 Feb. 12/84 (Edm. 0 at Hfd. 11)

Individual

Most Seasons	.6	Ray Neufeld
Most Games	.559	Rick Ley
Most Goals, Career	.228	Blaine Stoughton
Most Assists, Career	.285	Mike Rogers
Most Points, Career	.467	Mike Rogers (182 goals, 285 assists)
Most Pen. Mins., Career	.828	Rick Ley
Most Shutouts, Career	.4	Greg Millen

Longest Consecutive
Games Streak ....160 Mike Rogers (Oct. 11/79-Apr. 5/81)

Most Goals, Season ......56 Blaine Stoughton (1979-80)

Most Assists, Season ......65 Mike Rogers (1980-81)

Most Points, Season ......105 Mike Rogers (1979-80) (44 goals, 61 assists) (1980-81) (40 goals, 65 assists)

Most Pen. Mins., Season ...358 Torrie Robertson (1985-86)

Most Points, Defenseman Season ......65 Mark Howe (1980-81) (19 goals, 46 assists)

Most Points, Center, Season ......105 Mike Rogers (1979-80) (44 goals, 61 assists) Mike Rogers (1980-81) (40 goals, 65 assists)

Most Points, Right Wing, Season ......100 Blaine Stoughton (1979-80) (56 goals, 44 assists)

Most Points, Left Wing, Season ......80 Pat Boutette (1980-81) (28 goals, 52 assists)

Most Points, Rookie, Season ......72 Sylvain Turgeon (1983-84) (40 goals, 32 assists)

Most Shutouts, Season ......2 Al Smith (1979-80) Greg Millen (1983-84) Steve Weeks (1984-85) Mike Liut (1985-86)

Most Goals, Game ....5 Jordy Douglas (Feb. 3/80)

Most Assists, Game ....5 Mark Howe (Jan. 30/80) Ron Francis (Oct. 16/82) Ray Neufeld (Oct. 19/84)

Most Points, Game ....5 Seven players

Coaching History

Don Blackburn, 1979-80; Don Blackburn and Larry Pleau, 1980-81; Larry Pleau, 1981-82; Larry Kish and Larry Pleau, 1982-83; Jack "Tex" Evans, 1983-84 to date.

Captains' History

Rick Ley, 1979-80; Mike Rogers, 1980-81, 1981-82; Russ Anderson, 1982-83; Mark Johnson, 1983-84; Ron Francis, 1984-85, 1985-86.

Whaler captain Ron Francis

All-time Record vs. Other Clubs

Regular Season

		At Home							On Road							Total					
	GP	W	L	T	GF	GA	PTS	GP	W	L	T	GF	GA	PTS	GP	W	L	T	GF	GA	Pts
Boston	24	12	9	3	96	91	27	24	3	17	4	59	103	10	48	15	26	7	155	194	37
Buffalo	24	7	14	3	65	78	17	24	7	12	5	80	105	19	48	14	26	8	145	183	36
**Calgary	11	4	5	2	38	40	10	12	3	8	1	45	67	7	23	7	13	3	83	107	17
Chicago	11	4	6	1	39	41	9	12	3	6	3	39	63	9	23	7	12	4	78	104	18
Detroit	11	8	3	0	52	29	16	12	3	4	5	41	50	11	23	11	7	5	93	79	27
Edmonton	11	5	4	2	52	145	12	12	0	10	2	38	62	2	23	5	14	4	90	107	14
Los Angeles	12	5	5	2	49	55	12	11	4	5	2	47	42	10	23	9	10	4	96	97	22
Minnesota	12	5	7	0	39	51	10	11	2	8	1	38	59	5	23	7	15	1	77	110	15
Montreal	24	8	14	2	83	105	18	24	1	18	5	74	136	7	48	9	32	7	157	241	25
*New Jersey	12	7	3	2	47	39	16	11	5	4	2	47	35	12	23	12	7	4	94	74	28
NY Islanders	12	3	6	4	37	47	9	11	3	7	1	29	53	7	23	6	13	4	66	100	16
NY Rangers	12	6	4	2	50	43	14	11	3	6	2	31	49	8	23	9	10	4	81	92	22
Philadelphia	11	2	6	2	44	53	7	12	1	10	1	30	61	3	23	3	16	4	74	114	10
Pittsburgh	11	6	5	0	55	48	12	12	3	7	2	37	52	8	23	9	12	2	92	100	20
Quebec	24	10	7	7	105	98	27	24	5	17	2	73	126	12	48	15	24	9	178	224	39
St. Louis	11	5	5	1	41	40	11	12	5	6	1	43	46	11	23	10	11	2	84	86	22
Toronto	12	7	3	2	63	45	16	11	7	4	0	55	45	14	23	14	7	2	118	90	30
Vancouver	11	5	4	2	43	47	12	12	3	7	1	32	51	7	23	7	11	5	75	98	19
Washington	12	4	6	2	42	48	10	11	2	8	1	31	48	5	23	6	14	3	73	96	15
Winnipeg	12	6	3	3	56	39	15	11	5	6	0	43	43	10	23	11	9	3	99	82	25
Totals	280	119	119	42	1096	1082	280	280	67	170	43	912	1296	177	560	186	289	85	2008	2378	457

* Totals include those of Colorado (1979-80, 1980-81, 1981-82)
** Totals include those of Atlanta (1979-80)

Playoffs

	Series	W	L	GP	W	L	T	GF	GA	Last Mtg.	Round	Result
Montreal	2	0	2	10	3	7	0	21	34	1986	DF	L 3-4
Quebec	1	1	0	3	3	0	0	16	7	1986	DSF	W 3-0
Totals	3	1	2	13	6	7	0	37	41			

Playoff Results 1986-82

Year	Round	Opponent	Result	GF	GA
1986	DF	Montreal	L 3-4	13	16
	DSF	Quebec	W 3-0	16	7

Abbreviations: Round: F – Final; CF – conference final; DF – division final; DSF – division semi-final; SF – semi-final; QF – quarter-final; P – preliminary round. GA – goals against; GF – goals for.

Retired Numbers

2	Rick Ley	1979-1981
9	Gordie Howe	1979-1980
19	John McKenzie	1976-1979

Entry Draft Selections 1986-79

1986
Pick
11	Scott Young
32	Marc Laforge
74	Brian Chapman
95	Bill Horn
116	Joe Quinn
137	Steve Torrel
158	Ron Hoover
179	Robert Glasgow
200	Sean Evoy
221	Cal Brown
242	Brian Verbeek

1985
Pick
5	Dana Murzyn
26	Kay Whitmore
68	Gary Callaghan
110	Shane Churla
131	Brian Puhalsky
152	Brian Puhalsky
173	Greg Dornbach
194	Paul Tory
215	Jerry Pawlowski
236	Bruce Hill

1984
Pick
11	Sylvain Cote
110	Mike Millar
131	Mike Vellucci
173	John Devereaux
194	Brent Regan
215	Jim Culhane
236	Pete Abric

1983
Pick
2	Sylvain Turgeon
20	David Jensen
23	Ville Siren
61	Leif Karlsson
64	Dave MacLean
72	Ron Chyzowski
104	Brian Johnson
124	Joe Reekie
143	Chris Duperron
144	James Falle
164	Bill Fordy
193	Reine Karlsson
204	Allan Acton
224	Darcy Kaminski

1982
Pick
14	Paul Lawless
35	Mark Paterson
56	Kevin Dineen
67	Ulf Samuelsson
88	Ray Ferraro
109	Randy Gilhen
130	Jim Johannson
151	Mickey Kramptoich
172	Kevin Skilliter
214	Martin Linse
235	Randy Cameron

1981
Pick
4	Ron Francis
61	Paul MacDermid
67	Michael Hoffman
93	Bill Maguire
103	Dan Bourbonnais
130	John Mokosak
151	Denis Dore
172	Jeff Poeschl
193	Larry Power

1980
Pick
8	Fred Arthur
29	Michel Galarneau
50	Mickey Volcan
71	Kevin McClelland
100	Darren Jensen
113	Mario Cerri
134	Mike Martin
155	Brent Denat
176	Paul Fricker
197	Lorne Bokshowan

1979
Pick
18	Ray Allison
39	Stuart Smith
60	Don Nachbaur
81	Ray Neufeld
102	Mark Renaud
123	Dave McDonald

Club Directory

Hartford Civic Center Coliseum
One Civic Center Plaza
Hartford, Connecticut 06103
Phone 203/728-3366
TWX 710-425-8732
ENVOY ID   TM.HFD
Capacity: 15,126

Chairman/Managing General Partner/Governor	Howard L. Baldwin
President/General Manager/Alternate Governor	Emile Francis
Alternate Governor	Donald G. Conrad
Assistant General Manager	Robert W. Crocker
Head Coach	Jack Evans
Assistant Coach	Claude Larose
Special Assistant to the Chairman	Gordie Howe
Director of Player Personnel	Steve Brklacich
Scouting Staff	Leo Boivin, David McNab, John Cunniff
Head Trainer	Tom Woodcock
Assistant Trainer & Equipment Manager	Skip Cunningham
Vice President of Marketing & Public Relations	William E. Barnes
Vice President of Finance & Development	W. David Andrews III
Controller	Michael J. Amendola
Assistant to the Chairman	Camille Beck
Director of Public Relations	Phil Langan
Assistant Director of Public Relations	Dennis Buden
Chief Statistician	Frank Polnaszek
Ticket Office Supervisor	Dana Weybrew
Advertising Sales Manager	Jay Woods
Merchandise Manager	Mike Reddy
Club Doctor	Dr. Vincent Turco
Club Dentist	TBD
Radio Play-By-Play	Chuck Kaiton
TV/Cable Play-By-Play	Rick Peckham
Dimensions of Rink	200 feet by 85 feet
Location of Press Box	Center ice, Upper Level, Asylum Street
Location of Broadcast Booth	Center ice, Upper Level, Asylum Street
Location of Press Room	Adjacent to press box, Upper Level, Asylum Street
TV Outlet	WHCT (Channel 18)
Cable TV Outlet	SportsChannel
Radio Outlet	WTIC-AM (1080)
Team Colors	Green/Blue/White

Hartford's Torrie Robertson with Denis Potvin of the Islanders.

Los Angeles Kings

1985-86 Results: 23w-49L-8T 54 PTS. Fifth, Smythe Division

Year-by-Year Record

Season	GP	Home W	Home L	Home T	Road W	Road L	Road T	Overall W	Overall L	Overall T	GF	GA	Pts.	Finished	Playoff Result
1985-86	80	9	27	4	14	22	4	23	49	8	284	389	54	5th, Smythe Div.	Out of Playoffs
1984-85	80	20	14	6	14	18	8	34	32	14	339	326	82	4th, Smythe Div.	Lost Div. Semi-Final
1983-84	80	13	19	8	10	25	5	23	44	13	309	376	59	5th, Smythe Div.	Out of Playoffs
1982-83	80	20	13	7	7	28	5	27	41	12	308	365	66	5th, Smythe Div.	Out of Playoffs
1981-82	80	19	15	6	5	26	9	24	41	15	314	369	63	4th, Smythe Div.	Lost Div. Final
1980-81	80	22	11	7	21	13	6	43	24	13	337	290	99	2nd, Norris Div.	Lost Prelim. Round
1979-80	80	18	13	9	12	23	5	30	36	14	290	313	74	2nd, Norris Div.	Lost Prelim. Round
1978-79	80	20	13	7	14	21	5	34	34	12	292	286	80	3rd, Norris Div.	Lost Prelim. Round
1977-78	80	18	16	6	13	18	9	31	34	15	243	245	77	3rd, Norris Div.	Lost Quarter-Final
1976-77	80	20	13	7	14	18	8	34	31	15	271	241	83	2nd, Norris Div.	Lost Quarter-Final
1975-76	80	22	13	5	16	20	4	38	33	9	263	265	85	2nd, Norris Div.	Lost Quarter-Final
1974-75	80	22	7	11	20	10	10	42	17	21	269	185	105	2nd, Norris Div.	Lost Prelim. Round
1973-74	78	22	13	4	11	20	8	33	33	12	233	231	78	3rd, West Div.	Lost Quarter-Final
1972-73	78	21	11	7	10	25	4	31	36	11	232	245	73	6th, West Div.	Out of Playoffs
1971-72	78	14	23	2	6	26	7	20	49	9	206	305	49	7th, West Div.	Out of Playoffs
1970-71	78	17	14	8	8	26	5	25	40	13	239	303	63	5th, West Div.	Out of Playoffs
1969-70	76	12	22	4	2	30	6	14	52	10	168	290	38	6th, West Div.	Out of Playoffs
1968-69	76	19	14	5	5	28	5	24	42	10	185	260	58	4th, West Div.	Lost Semi-Final
1967-68	74	20	13	4	11	20	6	31	33	10	200	224	72	2nd, West Div.	Lost Quarter-Final

Schedule

Home				Away			
Oct.	Thur.	9	St. Louis	**Oct.**	Tue.	14	Pittsburgh
	Sat.	11	NY Islanders		Wed.	15	Detroit
	Sat.	18	Boston		Wed.	22	NY Rangers
	Sun.	19	Edmonton		Thur.	23	New Jersey
Nov.	Thur.	6	Montreal		Sat.	25	NY Islanders
	Sat.	8	Hartford		Mon.	27	Montreal
	Tue.	11	Winnipeg		Tue.	28	Quebec
	Thur.	13	Winnipeg	**Nov.**	Sun.	2	Edmonton
	Sat.	15	Calgary		Mon.	3	Calgary
	Wed.	26	Vancouver		Tue.	18	Washington
	Sat.	29	New Jersey		Wed.	19	Chicago
Dec.	Tue.	2	Detroit		Fri.	21	Winnipeg
	Thur.	4	Toronto		Sun.	23	Winnipeg
	Sat.	6	Chicago		Tue.	25	Vancouver
	Sat.	13	Calgary	**Dec.**	Tue.	9	NY Islanders
	Sun.	14	Edmonton		Wed.	10	NY Rangers
	Wed.	17	Pittsburgh		Sat.	20	Edmonton
	Sat.	27	Boston		Mon.	22	Calgary
	Tue.	30	Philadelphia		Tue.	23	Vancouver
Jan.	Sat.	3	Edmonton	**Jan.**	Fri.	2	Vancouver
	Sat.	10	Buffalo		Wed.	7	Edmonton
	Wed.	14	Vancouver		Thur.	8	Calgary
	Mon.	19	NY Rangers		Fri.	16	St. Louis
	Wed.	21	Pittsburgh		Sat.	17	St. Louis
	Fri.	23	Minnesota		Sat.	31	Montreal
	Wed.	28	New Jersey	**Feb.**	Sun.	1	Quebec
Feb.	Sat.	14	Hartford		Wed.	4	Toronto
	Mon.	16	Toronto*		Fri.	6	Winnipeg
	Wed.	18	Washington		Sun.	8	Winnipeg*
	Sat.	21	Philadelphia		Sat.	28	Minnesota*
	Tue.	24	Winnipeg	**Mar.**	Sun.	1	Chicago
	Thur.	26	Winnipeg		Thur.	5	Calgary
Mar.	Tue.	3	Minnesota		Fri.	6	Edmonton
	Sun.	8	Vancouver*		Tue.	17	Washington
	Wed.	11	Buffalo		Thur.	19	Philadelphia
	Sat.	14	Quebec		Sat.	21	Boston*
	Sat.	28	Calgary		Sun.	22	Hartford*
	Mon.	30	Calgary		Wed.	25	Detroit
April	Wed.	1	Vancouver		Thur.	26	Buffalo
	Sat.	4	Edmonton	**April**	Sun.	5	Vancouver

*Denotes afternoon game.

Home Starting Times:
All Games . . . . 7:35 p.m.
Except Feb. 16, Mar. 8 . . . . 1:05 p.m.

Franchise date: June 5, 1967

20th
NHL
Season

Marcel Dionne and Dave Taylor

1986-87 Player Personnel

FORWARDS

	Ht.	Wt.	Place of Birth	Date	1985-86 Club
BENOIT, Guy	5-10	187	St. Hyacinthe, Que.	3/8/59	New Haven-Toledo-Muskegon
CARSON, Jim	6-0	185	Southfield, Mich.	7/20/68	Verdun
CIPRICK, Trent	6-1	176	Russell, Man.	7/21/67	Brandon
COUTURIER, Sylvain	6-1	200	Greenfield Pk., Que.	4/23/68	Laval
CURRIE, Glen	6-2	180	Montreal, Que.	7/18/58	New Haven-Los Angeles
CROSSMAN, Jeff	6-0	200	Toronto, Ont.	12/3/64	West Michigan
DIONNE, Marcel	5-8	185	Drummondville, Que.	8/3/51	Los Angeles
DUNCANSON, Craig	6-0	190	Naughton, Ont.	3/17/67	Cornwall-Sudbury-Los Angeles
ERICKSON, Bryan	5-9	170	Roseau, Minn.	3/7/60	Binghamton-New Haven-Los Angeles
FLANAGAN, Tim	6-0	185	Red Deer, Alta.	3/6/67	Penticton-Michigan Tech.
FOX, Jim	5-8	175	Coniston, Ont.	5/18/60	Los Angeles
GANS, Dave	5-11	185	Brantford, Ont.	12/7/66	Los Angeles-New Haven-Hershey
GRATTON, Dan	6-0	185	Brantford, Ont.	12/7/66	Oshawa-Ottawa-Belleville
GUAY, Paul	6-0	193	North Smithfield, R.I.	9/2/63	Hershey-Los-Angeles-New Haven
KELLY, Paul	6-0	187	Hamilton, Ont.	4/17/67	Guelph
KRAKIWSKY, Sean	6-0	175	Calgary, Alta.	12/29/67	Calgary (WHL)
LOFTHOUSE, Mark	6-1	185	New Westminster, B.C.	4/21/57	New Haven
LUKOWICH, Morris	5-9	170	Speers, Sask.	6/1/56	Boston-Los Angeles
MARTIN, Brian	6-0	195	St. Catharines, Ont.	3/27/66	Windsor
McKENNA, Sean	6-0	190	Asbestos, Que.	3/7/62	Buffalo-Los Angeles
McSORLEY, Chris	5-11	185	Hamilton, Ont.	3/22/62	Toledo
NICHOLLS, Bernie	6-0	185	Haliburton, Ont.	6/24/61	Los Angeles
PATERSON, Joe	6-2	205	Toronto, Ont.	6/25/60	Philadelphia-Hershey-Los Angeles
PHAIR, Lyle	6-1	195	Pilot Mound, Man.	3/8/61	Los Angeles-New Haven
ROBITAILLE, Luc	6-1	190	Montreal, Que.	2/17/66	Hull
SYKES, Phil	5-10	175	Dawson Creek, B.C.	3/18/59	Los Angeles
TAYLOR, Dave	6-0	195	Levack, Ont.	12/4/55	Los Angeles
WILKS, Brian	5-11	175	North York, Ont.	2/27/66	Los Angeles
WILLIAMS, Dave	5-11	190	Weyburn, Sask.	2/3/54	Los Angeles

DEFENSEMEN

	Ht.	Wt.	Place of Birth	Date	1985-86 Club
BAUMGARTNER, Ken	6-1	200	Flin Flon, Man.	3/11/66	Prince Albert
DINEEN, Peter	5-11	180	Kingston, Ont.	11/19/56	Binghamton-Moncton
DUCHESNE, Steve	6-0	190	Sept-Iles, Que.	6/30/65	New Haven
ENGLISH, John	6-2	190	Toronto, Ont.	5/13/66	Hamilton-Ottawa
GALLEY, Garry	5-11	190	Montreal, Que.	4/16/63	Los Angeles-New Haven
GERMAIN, Eric	6-1	195	Quebec City, Que.	6/26/66	St. Jean
HAMMOND, Ken	6-1	190	Pt. Credit, Ont.	8/22/63	Los Angeles-New Haven
HARDY, Mark	5-11	187	Semanden, Switz.	2/1/59	Los Angeles
HAYTON, Brian	5-11	200	Peterborough, Ont.	1/22/68	Guelph
KENNEDY, Dean	6-2	200	Redvers, Sask.	1/18/63	Los Angeles
LAROCQUE, Denis	6-1	190	Hawkesbury, Ont.	10/5/67	Guelph
LEDYARD, Grant	6-2	190	Winnipeg, Man.	11/19/61	NY Rangers-Los Angeles
PLAYFAIR, Larry	6-4	220	Fort St. James, B.C.	6/23/58	Buffalo-Los Angeles
REDMOND, Craig	5-10	187	Dawson Creek, B.C.	9/22/65	Los Angeles
SAWKINS, Peter	6-3	190	Skagen, Denmark	8/29/63	New Haven-Toledo
TUITE, Steve	6-1	195	Brockton, Mass.	1/14/62	New Haven-Toledo
WELLS, Jay	6-1	205	Paris, Ont.	5/18/59	Los Angeles

GOALTENDERS

	Ht.	Wt.	Place of Birth	Date	1985-86 Club
ELIOT, Darren	6-1	175	Milton, Ont.	11/26/61	Los Angeles-New Haven
FRANZOSA, John	5-7	175	Reading, Mass.	3/3/63	Toledo-New Haven
HEALY, Glen	5-9	183	Pickering, Ont.	8/23/62	Toledo-Los Angeles-New Haven
HUBERT, Greg	6-1	160	Vancouver, B.C.	8/30/66	Regina
JANECYK, Bob	6-1	180	Chicago, Ill.	5/18/57	Los Angeles
MELANSON, Roland	5-10	178	Moncton, N.B.	6/28/60	Minnesota-New Haven-Los Angeles

Coach and General Manager

QUINN, PAT
Coach, Los Angeles Kings. Born in Hamilton, Ont., January 29, 1943.

Pat Quinn enters his third season as coach of the Kings after coaching Philadelphia from 1978-79 to 1981-82. In Philadelphia, Quinn was awarded the Jack Adams award for leading the Flyers to the Stanley Cup finals in 1979-80. He started his coaching career with the Maine Mariners of the AHL and eventually was promoted to the head coaching job with Philadelphia. An NHL defenseman himself, Quinn played in over 600 games over nine years.

NHL Coaching Record

Team	Seasons	Games	Regular Season				Playoffs			
			W	L	T	%	Games	W	L	%
Philadelphia	1978-79	30	18	8	4	.667	8	3	5	.375
Philadelphia	1979-80	80	48	12	20	.725	19	13	6	.684
Philadelphia	1980-81	80	41	24	15	.606	12	6	6	.500
Philadelphia	1981-82	72	34	29	9	.535	....	....	....	....
Los Angeles	1984-85	80	34	32	14	.513	3	0	3	.000
Los Angeles	1985-86	80	23	49	8	.338	....	....	....	....
NHL Totals		**422**	**198**	**154**	**70**	**.552**	**42**	**22**	**20**	**.524**

1985-86 Scoring
Regular Season

*—rookie

Pos	#	Player	Team	GP	G	A	Pts	+/−	PIM	PP	SH	GW	OT	S	%
F	9	Bernie Nicholls	L.A	80	36	61	97	5 −	78	10	4	0	0	281	12.8
F	16	Marcel Dionne	L.A	80	36	58	94	22 −	42	11	0	4	1	284	12.7
F	18	Dave Taylor	L.A	76	33	38	71	16 −	110	11	0	1	0	203	16.3
F	22	Dave Williams	L.A	72	20	29	49	6 −	320	5	0	1	0	138	14.5
F	7	Phil Sykes	L.A	76	20	24	44	6 −	97	1	2	4	1	132	15.2
F	15	Bryan Erickson	L.A	55	20	23	43	1	36	6	0	4	0	108	18.5
D	24	Jay Wells	L.A	79	11	31	42	7	226	4	0	2	1	113	9.7
D	4	Grant Ledyard	NYR	27	2	9	11	7 −	20	0	0	0	0	57	3.5
			L.A	52	7	18	25	22 −	78	4	0	2	0	113	6.2
			Total	79	9	27	36	29 −	98	4	0	2	0	170	5.3
F	19	Jim Fox	L.A	39	14	17	31	9 −	2	2	0	0	0	81	17.3
F	27	Joe Paterson	PHI	5	0	0	0	1	12	0	0	0	0	4	.0
			L.A	47	9	18	27	7 −	153	2	0	1	0	75	12.0
			Total	52	9	18	27	6 −	165	2	0	1	0	79	11.4
D	5	Mark Hardy	L.A	55	6	21	27	11 −	71	2	1	1	0	113	5.3
F	12	Morris Lukowich	BOS	14	1	4	5	2	10	0	0	0	0	25	4.0
			L.A	55	11	9	20	19 −	51	0	0	0	0	85	12.9
			Total	69	12	13	25	17 −	61	0	0	0	0	110	10.9
D	2	Craig Redmond	L.A	73	6	18	24	34 −	57	3	0	0	0	116	5.2
F	10	Sean McKenna	BUF	45	6	12	18	8 −	28	1	0	2	0	83	7.2
			L.A	30	4	0	4	15 −	7	0	1	0	0	47	8.5
			Total	75	10	12	22	23 −	35	1	1	2	0	130	7.7
D	3	Garry Galley	L.A	49	9	13	22	9 −	46	1	0	1	0	57	15.8
F	17	John Paul Kelly	L.A	61	6	9	15	17 −	50	0	0	0	0	38	15.8
F	8	*Brian Wilks	L.A	43	4	8	12	7 −	25	0	0	0	0	31	12.9
D	6	Dean Kennedy	L.A	78	2	10	12	10 −	132	0	0	0	0	59	3.4
F	12	*Paul Guay	L.A	23	3	3	6	6 −	18	0	0	0	0	18	16.7
F	14	Len Hachborn	L.A	24	4	1	5	9 −	2	1	0	0	0	14	28.6
F	21	Anders Hakansson	L.A	38	4	1	5	8 −	8	0	0	2	0	27	14.8
F	23	Bob Mongrain	L.A	11	2	3	5	3 −	2	0	0	0	0	10	20.0
D	20	Larry Playfair	BUF	47	1	2	3	8 −	100	0	0	0	0	35	2.9
			L.A	14	0	1	1	14 −	28	0	0	0	0	6	.0
			Total	61	1	3	4	22 −	128	0	0	0	0	41	2.4
D	28	Rick LaPointe	L.A	20	0	4	4	13 −	18	0	0	0	0	7	.0
F	23	Glen Currie	L.A	12	1	2	3	5 −	9	1	0	0	0	11	9.1
G	1	Bob Janecyk	L.A	38	0	2	2	0	11	0	0	0	0	0	.0
F	25	*Craig Duncanson	L.A	2	0	1	1	1 −	0	0	0	0	0	0	.0
D	4	*Ken Hammond	L.A	3	0	1	1	1 −	2	0	0	0	0	0	.0
F	25	*Dan Brennan	L.A	6	0	1	1	1 −	9	0	0	0	0	6	.0
F	11	*Lyle Phair	L.A	15	0	1	1	12 −	2	0	0	0	0	11	.0
G	35	Darren Eliot	L.A	27	0	1	1	0	0	0	0	0	0	0	.0
G	31	Roland Melanson	MIN	6	0	0	0	0	0	0	0	0	0	0	.0
			L.A	22	0	1	1	0	8	0	0	0	0	0	.0
			Total	28	0	1	1	0	8	0	0	0	0	0	.0
D	26	*Allan Tuer	L.A	45	0	1	1	16 −	150	0	0	0	0	14	.0
G	29	*Glenn Healy	L.A	1	0	0	0	0	0	0	0	0	0	0	.0
F	15	*Dave Gans	L.A	3	0	0	0	0	0	0	0	0	0	3	.0

Bob Janecyk

VACHON, ROGATIEN
General Manager, Los Angeles Kings. Born in Palmorelle, Que., September 8, 1945.

Rogie Vachon was named General Manager of the Kings on Jan. 30, 1984 after spending the first half of the 1983-84 season as an assistant coach to Don Perry. In his first year as GM of the club, Los Angeles improved from 59 points in 1983-84 to 82 points in 1984-85. A veteran of 16 NHL seasons, Vachon spent seven years in a Los Angeles uniform, in addition to Montreal, Detroit and Boston. While with the Canadiens in 1967-68, Vachon shared the Vezina Trophy with Lorne "Gump" Worsley. During his seven-year stint in Los Angeles from 1971 to 1978, Vachon helped the club emerge as one of the NHL's top defensive teams. In 1974-75, his finest season, Vachon was named *Hockey News'* Player of the Year after compiling a 2.24 average and a 27-14-13 record while leading the Kings to their highest point total in team history (105). Following his retirement in 1982, he returned to Los Angeles to instruct the Kings' young goaltenders.

Club Records

Team

(Figures in brackets for season records are games played; records for fewest points, wins, ties, losses, goals, goals against are for 70 or more games)

Most Points	.105	1974-75 (80)
Most Wins	.43	1980-81 (80)
Most Ties	.21	1974-75 (80)
Most Losses	.52	1969-70 (76)
Most Goals	.339	1984-85 (80)
Most Goals Against	.389	1985-86 (80)
Fewest Points	.38	1969-70 (76)
Fewest Wins	.14	1969-70 (76)
Fewest Ties	.8	1985-86 (80)
Fewest Losses	.17	1974-75 (80)
Fewest Goals	.168	1969-70 (76)
Fewest Goals Against	.185	1974-75 (80)

Longest Winning Streak
Over-all 8   Oct. 21-Nov. 7/72
Home 7   Four times
Away. 8   Dec. 18/74-Jan. 16/75

Longest Undefeated Streak
Over-all 11   Feb. 28-Mar. 24/74 (9 wins, 2 ties)
Home 10   Oct. 21-Nov. 18/72 (8 wins, 2 ties) Mar. 2-28/74 (8 wins, 2 ties)
Away. 11   Oct. 10-Dec. 11/74 (6 wins, 5 ties)

Longest Losing Streak
Over-all 10   Feb. 22-Mar. 9/84
Home 9   Feb. 8-Mar. 12/86
Away. 12   Jan. 11-Feb. 15/70

Longest Winless Streak
Over-all 17   Jan. 29-Mar. 5/70 (13 losses, 4 ties)
Home 9   Jan. 29-Mar. 5/70
Away. 21   Jan. 11-Apr. 3/70
Most Shutouts, Season 9   1974-75 (80)
Most Pen. Mins., Season 2,004   1985-86 (80)
Most Goals, Game 12   Nov. 28/84 (Van. 1 at L.A. 12)

Individual

Most Seasons	.11	Butch Goring / Marcel Dionne
Most Games	.854	Marcel Dionne
Most Goals, Career	.526	Marcel Dionne
Most Assists, Career	.707	Marcel Dionne
Most Points Career	.1,233	Marcel Dionne
Most Pen. Mins., Career	.1,132	Jay Wells
Most Shutouts, Career	.32	Rogie Vachon

Longest Consecutive Games Streak 324   Marcel Dionne (Jan. 7/78-Jan. 9/82)
Most Goals, Season 59   Marcel Dionne (1978-79)
Most Assists, Season 84   Marcel Dionne (1979-80)
Most Points, Season 137   Marcel Dionne (1979-80) (53 goals, 84 assists)
Most Pen. Min., Season 320   Dave Williams (1985-86)
Most Points, Defenseman Season 76   Larry Murphy (1980-81) (16 goals, 60 assists)

Most Points, Center, Season 137   Marcel Dionne (1979-80) (53 goal, 84 assists)
Most Points, Right Wing, Season 112   Dave Taylor (1980-81) (47 goals, 65 assists)
Most Points, Left Wing, Season 105   Charlie Simmer (1980-81) (56 goals, 49 assists)
Most Points, Rookie, Season 76   Larry Murphy (1980-81) (16 goals, 60 assists)
Most Shutouts, Season 8   Rogie Vachon (1976-77)
Most Goals, Game 4   Several players
Most Assists, Game 5   Marcel Dionne (Jan. 22/76) Danny Grant (Jan. 14/78) Dave Taylor (Nov. 4/79)
Most Points, Game 6   Butch Goring (Feb. 5/72) Syl Apps (Dec. 21/77) Marcel Dionne (Mar. 14/81) Bernie Nicholls (Oct. 20/83)

Coaching History

Leonard "Red" Kelly, 1967-68 to 1968-69; Hal Laycoe and John Wilson, 1969-70; Larry Regan, 1970-71; Larry Regan and Fred Glover, 1971-72; Bob Pulford, 1972-73 to 1976-77; Ron Stewart, 1977-78; Bob Berry, 1978-79 to 1980-81; Parker MacDonald and Don Perry, 1981-82; Don Perry, 1982-83; Don Perry, Rogatien Vachon and Roger Neilson, 1983-84; Pat Quinn, 1984-85 to date.

Captains' History

Bob Wall, 1967-68, 1968-69; Larry Cahan, 1969-70, 1970-71; Bob Pulford, 1971-72, 1972-73; Terry Harper, 1973-74, 1974-75; Mike Murphy, 1975-76 to 1980-81; Dave Lewis, 1981-82, 1982-83; Terry Ruskowski, 1983-84, 1984-85; Dave Taylor, 1985-86.

All-time Record vs. Other Clubs

Regular Season

	At Home							On Road							Total						
	GP	W	L	T	GF	GA	PTS	GP	W	L	T	GF	GA	PTS	GP	W	L	T	GF	GA	Pts
Boston	42	13	24	5	142	165	31	43	8	33	2	112	207	18	85	21	57	7	254	372	49
Buffalo	34	12	15	7	114	114	31	35	9	19	7	100	144	25	69	21	34	14	214	258	56
**Calgary	39	23	13	3	157	128	49	40	8	24	8	122	180	24	79	31	37	11	279	308	73
Chicago	42	16	21	5	132	143	37	40	13	22	5	120	159	31	82	29	43	10	252	302	68
Detroit	47	26	11	10	193	136	62	46	19	20	7	159	187	45	93	45	31	17	352	323	107
Edmonton	24	7	12	5	97	118	19	24	3	16	5	93	152	11	48	10	28	10	190	270	30
Hartford	11	5	4	2	42	47	12	12	5	5	2	55	49	12	23	10	9	4	97	96	24
Minnesota	45	19	13	13	161	138	51	47	11	29	7	119	188	29	92	30	42	20	280	326	80
Montreal	47	12	29	6	134	188	30	46	6	31	9	116	214	21	93	18	60	15	250	402	51
*New Jersey	24	19	1	4	136	70	42	24	12	8	4	96	78	28	48	31	9	8	232	148	70
NY Islanders	27	10	10	7	92	86	27	26	7	15	4	68	102	18	53	17	25	11	160	188	45
NY Rangers	41	16	17	8	131	145	40	40	12	23	5	111	157	29	81	28	40	13	242	302	69
Philadelphia	46	12	27	7	122	154	31	46	11	28	7	112	178	29	92	23	55	14	234	332	60
Pittsburgh	51	30	13	8	181	131	68	53	16	31	6	158	199	38	104	46	44	14	339	330	106
Quebec	12	5	6	1	43	47	11	11	5	4	2	49	53	12	23	10	10	3	92	100	23
St. Louis	46	22	17	7	154	131	51	45	11	30	4	109	166	26	91	33	47	11	263	297	77
Toronto	42	24	14	4	148	117	52	43	11	24	8	135	179	30	85	35	38	12	283	296	82
Vancouver	45	26	11	8	186	124	60	45	17	19	9	160	168	43	90	43	30	17	346	292	103
Washington	28	17	8	3	118	73	37	27	11	12	4	92	106	26	55	28	20	7	210	179	63
Winnipeg	21	7	12	2	88	96	16	22	7	10	5	93	106	19	43	14	22	7	181	202	35
Defunct Clubs	35	27	6	2	141	76	56	34	11	14	9	91	109	31	69	38	20	11	232	185	87
Totals	749	348	284	117	2712	2427	813	749	213	417	119	2270	3081	545	1498	561	701	236	4982	5508	1358

* Totals include those of Kansas City (1974-75, 1975-76) and Colorado (1976-77 through 1981-82)
** Totals include those of Atlanta (1972-73 through 1979-80)

Playoffs

	Series	W	L	GP	W	L	T	GF	GA	Last Mtg.	Round	Result
Boston	2	0	2	13	5	8	0	38	56	1977	QF	L 2-4
Calgary	2	2	0	5	4	1	0	14	8	1977	P	W 2-1
Chicago	1	0	1	5	1	4	0	7	10	1974	QF	L 1-4
Edmonton	2	1	1	8	6	2	0	38	30	1985	DSF	L 0-3
Minnesota	1	0	1	7	3	4	0	21	26	1968	QF	L 3-4
NY Islanders	1	0	1	4	1	3	0	10	21	1980	P	L 1-3
NY Rangers	2	0	2	6	1	5	0	14	32	1981	P	L 1-3
St. Louis	1	0	1	4	0	4	0	5	16	1969	SF	L 0-4
Toronto	2	0	2	5	1	4	0	9	18	1978	P	L 0-2
Vancouver	1	0	1	5	1	4	0	14	19	1982	DF	L 1-4
Defunct Clubs	1	1	0	7	4	3	0	25				
Totals	16	4	12	69	27	42	0	193	261			

Abbreviations: Round: F – Final; **CF** – conference final; **DF** – division final; **DSF** – division semi-final; **SF** – semi-final; **QF** – quarter-final; **P** – preliminary round. **GA** – goals against; **GF** – goals for.

Playoff Results 1986-82

Year	Round	Opponent	Result	GF	GA
1985	DSF	Edmonton	W 3-0	7	11
1982	DF	Vancouver	L 1-4	14	19
	DSF	Edmonton	W 3-2	27	23

Retired Numbers

| 30 | Rogatien Vachon | 1971-1978 |

Entry Draft Selections 1986-72

1986
Pick
2	Jimmy Carson
44	Denis Larocque
65	Sylvain Couturier
86	Dave Guden
107	Robb Stauber
128	Sean Krakiwsky
149	Rene Chapdelaine
170	Trevor Pochipinski
191	Paul Kelly
212	Russ Mann
233	Brian Hayton

1985
Pick
9	Craig Duncanson
10	Dan Gratton
30	Par Edlund
72	Perry Florio
93	Petr Prajzler
135	Tim Flannigan
156	John Hyduke
177	Steve Horner
219	Trent Ciprick
240	Marion Howarth

1984
Pick
6	Craig Redmond
24	Brian Wilks
48	John English
69	Tom Glavine
87	Dave Grannis
108	Greg Strome
129	Tim Hanley
150	Shannon Deegan
171	Luc Robitaille
192	Jeff Crossman
213	Paul Kenny
234	Brian Martin

1983
Pick
47	Bruce Shoebottom
67	Guy Benoit
87	Bob LaForest
100	Garry Galley
107	Dave Lundmark
108	Kevin Stevens
127	Tim Burgess
147	Ken Hammond
167	Bruce Fishback
187	Thomas Ahlen
207	Jan Blaha
227	Chad Johnson

1982
Pick
27	Mike Heidt
48	Steve Seguin
64	Dave Gans
82	Dave Ross
90	Darcy Roy
95	Ulf Issakson
132	Victor Nechaev
153	Peter Helander
174	Dave Chartier
195	John Franzosa
216	Ray Shero
237	Mats Ulander

1981
Pick
2	Doug Smith
39	Dean Kennedy
81	Marty Dallman
123	Brad Thompson
134	Craig Hurley
144	Peter Sawkins
165	Dan Brennan
186	Allan Tuer
207	Jeff Baikie

1980
Pick
4	Larry Murphy
10	Jim Fox
33	Greg Terrion
34	Dave Morrison
52	Steve Bozek
73	Bernie Nicholls
94	Alan Graves
115	Darren Eliot
136	Mike O'Connor
157	Bill O'Dwyer
178	Daryl Evans
199	Kim Collins

1979
Pick
16	Jay Wells
29	Dean Hopkins
30	Mark Hardy
50	J.P. Kelly
71	John Gibson
92	Jim Brown
113	Jay MacFarlane

1978
Pick
77	Paul Mancini
94	Doug Keans
111	Don Waddell
128	Rob Mierkains
145	Ric Scully
162	Brad Thiessen
177	Jim Armstrong
193	Claude Larochelle

1977
Pick
84	Julian Baretta
85	Warren Holmes
103	Randy Rudnyk
121	Bob Suter

1976
Pick
21	Steve Clippingdale
49	Don Moores
67	Bob Mears
85	Rob Palmer
103	Larry McRae

1975
Pick
16	Tim Young
33	Terry Bucyk
69	Andre Leduc
87	Dave Miglia
105	Bob Russell
123	Dave Faulkner
141	Bill Reber
157	Sean Sullivan
172	Brian Petrovek
186	Tom Goddard
197	Mario Viens
203	Chuck Carpenter
207	Bob Fish
210	Dave Taylor
213	Robert Shaw

1974
Pick
48	Gary Sargent
66	Brad Winton
84	Paul Evans
102	Marty Mathews
120	Harvey Stewart
137	John Held
154	Mario Lessard
169	Derrick Emerson
184	Jacques Locas
197	Lindsay Thompson
207	Craig Brickley
217	Brad Kuglin

1973
Pick
38	Russ Walker
54	Jim McCrimmon
70	Dennis Abgrall
86	Blair McDonald
102	Roly Kimble

1972
Pick
20	Don Kozak
36	Dave Hutchison
52	John Dobie
68	Bernie Germaine
84	Mike Usitalo
100	Glen Toner

Club Directory

The Forum
3900 West Manchester Blvd.
Box 10
Inglewood, California 90306
Phone 213/674-6000
TWX 910-328-6133
ENVOY ID   TM.LA
Capacity: 16,005

California Sports Directory

Owner	Dr. Jerry Buss
President	Lou Baumeister
Executive Vice-President	Ken Doi
Vice-Presidents	Dr. Dick Gold, Larry Noble
Vice-President, Advertising	Jim Harkins
Vice-President, Sales	Jim Hunkins
Vice-President, Booking & General Manager	Claire Rothman
Vice-President, Finance	Patrick Harris
Assistant to the Owner	John Jackson
Assistant General Manager	Rob Collins
Controller	Ross Cote
Personnel Director	Joan McLaughlin
Director of Marketing	Steve Chase
Director of Public Relations	Bob Steiner
Director of Promotions	Lon Rosen
Director of Public Relations, Special Events	John Black
Director of Broadcasting	Keith Harris
Director of Special Projects	Sharon Tol
Director of Computer Operations	Tommy Yamada
Director of Season Seat Sales	John Roth
Director, Senate Program	Steve Chase
Director of Group Sales	Lee Kessler
Assistant General Manager	Rob Collins
Director of Operations	Fred Corsi
Director of Advertising Sales	Steve Hohensee
Box Office Director	Vern Ausmus
Director of Forum Entertainment Network	Brent Imai

Kings Directory

Governor	Dr. Jerry Buss
Alternate Governors	Ken Doi, Rogatien Vachon
Head Coach	Pat Quinn
General Manager	Rogatien Vachon
Assistant Coaches	Mike Murphy, Phil Myre
Assistant to General Manager	Don Perry
Administrative Assistant	John Wolf
Trainers	Pete Demers, Mark O'Neill
Director of Public Relations	David Courtney
Assistant Director of Public Relations	Diane Reesman
Video Coordinator	Bob Borgen
Director of Travel	Ron Muniz
Hockey Office Secretary	Marcia Galloway
Head Amateur Scout	Ted O'Connor
Scouting Staff	Jim Anderson, Bob Owen, Skip Schamehorn, Alex Smart, Ross Tyrell, Nick Beverley, Serge Blanchard, Gary Sargent
Supervisor of Off-Ice Officials	Bill Meuris
Public Address Announcer	Dennis Packer
Team Physicians	Dr. Steve Lombardo, Dr. James Tibone
Internist	Dr. Michael Mellman
Team Dentist	Dr. Gordon Knuth
Broadcasters	Bob Miller, Nick Nickson
Team Hospital	Centinela Hospital Medical Center
Dimension of Rink	200 feet by 85 feet
Colors	Purple and Gold
Training Camp	Victoria, B.C. and The Forum
Location of Press Box	West Side Colonnade, Section 28, Rows 1-9
Radio Station	KLAC (570), KGIL (1260)
TV Station	Prime Ticket Network

Bernie Nicholls led the Kings with 97 points in 1985-86.

Minnesota North Stars

1985-86 Results: 38w-33L-9T 85 PTS. Second, Norris Division

Schedule

	Home			Away
Oct.	Thur. 16 Boston	**Oct.**	Sat. 11 Quebec
	Sat. 18 Vancouver		Mon. 13 Montreal
	Tue. 28 Calgary		Sun. 19 Chicago
	Thur. 30 Detroit		Wed. 22 St. Louis
Nov.	Sat. 1 Chicago		Fri. 24 Washington
	Thur. 6 Toronto		Sun. 26 Philadelphia
	Sat. 8 Pittsburgh	**Nov.**	Wed. 5 Chicago
	Tue. 11 Washington		Wed. 19 St. Louis
	Sat. 15 NY Islanders		Sat. 29 Toronto
	Tue. 18 St. Louis	**Dec.**	Tue. 2 Buffalo
	Sat. 22 New Jersey		Thur. 4 New Jersey
	Wed. 26 Chicago		Sat. 6 Pittsburgh
	Fri. 28 Toronto		Thur. 11 Detroit
Dec.	Tue. 9 Edmonton		Mon. 15 NY Rangers
	Sat. 13 Philadelphia		Tue. 16 NY Islanders
	Sat. 20 Quebec		Thur. 18 Toronto
	Tue. 23 Toronto		Sat. 28 Winnipeg
	Fri. 26 Winnipeg	**Jan.**	Fri. 2 Detroit
	Wed. 31 Hartford		Mon. 5 NY Rangers
Jan.	Sat. 3 Detroit		Tue. 6 NY Islanders
	Thur. 8 Buffalo		Wed. 14 Toronto
	Sat. 10 Hartford		Sun. 18 Winnipeg
	Mon. 12 St. Louis		Fri. 23 Los Angeles
	Sat. 17 Chicago		Thur. 29 Calgary
	Tue. 20 Buffalo		Fri. 30 Edmonton
Feb.	Wed. 4 Edmonton	**Feb.**	Sun. 1 Vancouver
	Sat. 7 Detroit		Fri. 6 Detroit
	Sat. 14 Calgary		Thur. 19 St. Louis
	Sun. 15 St. Louis		Mon. 23 Montreal
	Wed. 18 Vancouver		Tue. 24 Quebec
	Sat. 21 Boston	**Mar.**	Tue. 3 Los Angeles
	Sat. 28 Los Angeles*		Thur. 5 Detroit
Mar.	Sun. 1 Philadelphia		Sun. 15 Chicago*
	Sat. 7 Pittsburgh		Thur. 19 Boston
	Mon. 9 Montreal		Sat. 21 Hartford
	Wed. 11 Toronto		Wed. 25 Toronto
	Sat. 14 Detroit*		Fri. 27 New Jersey
	Tue. 17 Chicago		Sun. 29 Washington*
	Mon. 23 St. Louis	**April**	Wed. 1 Chicago
	Mon. 30 NY Rangers		Sat. 4 St. Louis

*Denotes afternoon game.

Home Starting Times:

All Games	7:35 p.m.
Except Matinees	1:35 p.m.
Except Nov. 18, Dec. 9	7:05 p.m.

Franchise date: June 5, 1967

20th NHL Season

Neil Broten became the first American-born NHL player to record more than 100 points in one regular season with 29 goals and 76 assists for 105 points in 1985-86.

Minnesota North Star's Year-by-Year Record

Season	GP	Home			Road			Overall						Finished		Playoff Result
		W	L	T	W	L	T	W	L	T	GF	GA	Pts.			
1985-86	80	21	15	4	17	18	5	38	33	9	327	305	85	2nd,	Norris Div.	Lost Div. Semi-Final
1984-85	80	14	19	7	11	24	5	25	43	12	268	321	62	4th,	Norris Div.	Lost Div. Final
1983-84	80	22	14	4	17	17	6	39	31	10	345	344	88	1st,	Norris Div.	Lost Conf. Championship
1982-83	80	23	6	11	17	18	5	40	24	16	321	290	96	2nd,	Norris Div.	Lost Div. Final
1981-82	80	21	7	12	16	16	8	37	23	20	346	288	94	1st,	Norris Div.	Lost Div. Semi-Final
1980-81	80	23	10	7	12	18	10	35	28	17	291	263	87	3rd,	Adams Div.	Lost Final
1979-80	80	25	8	7	11	20	9	36	28	16	311	253	88	3rd,	Adams Div.	Lost Semi-Final
1978-79	80	19	15	6	9	25	6	28	40	12	257	289	68	4th,	Adams Div.	Out Of Playoffs
1977-78	80	12	24	4	6	29	5	18	53	9	218	325	45	5th,	Smythe Div.	Out of Playoffs
1976-77	80	17	14	9	6	25	9	23	39	18	240	310	64	2nd,	Smythe Div.	Lost Prelim. Round
1975-76	80	15	22	3	5	31	4	20	53	7	195	303	47	4th,	Smythe Div.	Out of Playoffs
1974-75	80	17	20	3	6	30	4	23	50	7	221	341	53	4th,	Smythe Div.	Out of Playoffs
1973-74	78	18	15	6	5	23	11	23	38	17	235	275	63	7th,	West Div.	Out of Playoffs
1972-73	78	26	8	5	11	22	6	37	30	11	254	230	85	3rd,	West Div.	Lost Quarter-Final
1971-72	78	22	11	6	15	18	6	37	29	12	212	191	86	2nd,	West Div.	Lost Quarter-Final
1970-71	78	16	15	8	12	19	8	28	34	16	191	223	72	4th,	West Div.	Lost Semi-Final
1969-70	76	11	16	11	8	19	11	19	35	22	224	257	60	3rd,	West Div.	Lost Quarter-Final
1968-69	76	11	21	6	7	22	9	18	43	15	189	270	51	6th,	West Div.	Out of Playoffs
1967-68	74	17	12	8	10	20	7	27	32	15	191	226	69	4th,	West Div.	Lost Semi-Final

1986-87 Player Personnel

FORWARDS	Ht.	Wt.	Place of Birth	Date	1985-86 Club
ACTON, Keith	5-9	172	Stouffville, Ont.	4/15/58	Minnesota
ARCHIBALD, Jim	5-11	180	Craik, Sask.	6/6/61	Springfield-Minnesota
BELLOWS, Brian	5-11	195	St. Catharines, Ont.	9/1/64	Minnesota
BERGEN, Todd	6-3	185	Prince Albert, Sask.	7/11/63	Minnesota
BJUGSTAD, Scott	6-1	175	St. Paul, Minn.	6/2/61	Minnesota
BROTEN, Neal	5-9	169	Roseau, Minn.	11/29/59	Minnesota
CICCARELLI, Dino	5-10	180	Sarnia, Ont.	2/8/60	Minnesota
COULIS, Tim	6-0	200	Kenora, Ont.	2/24/58	Springfield-Minnesota
DePALMA, Larry	6-0	180	Trenton, Mich.	10/27/65	Saskatoon-Minnesota
GRAHAM, Dirk	5-11	190	Regina, Sask.	7/29/59	Minnesota
HABSCHEID, Marc	6-0	180	Swift Current, Sask.	3/1/63	Minnesota
HALLIN, Mats	6-2	202	Eskilstuna, Sweden	3/19/58	Minnesota-Springfield
HELMER, Tim	6-0	185	Woodstock, Ont.	11/6/66	Ottawa
HOUCK, Paul	5-11	185	N. Vancouver, B.C.	8/12/63	Springfield-Minnesota
LAWTON, Brian	6-0	173	New Brunswick, N.J.	6/29/65	Minnesota
LOMOW, Byron	5-11	180	Sherwood Park, Alta.	4/27/65	Brandon
MARUK, Dennis	5-8	174	Toronto, Ont.	11/17/55	Minnesota
McCOLGAN, Gary	6-0	192	Scarborough, Ont.	3/27/66	Oshawa
McKEGNEY, Tony	6-1	200	Montreal, Que.	2/15/58	Minnesota
MICHELETTI, Pat	5-10	175	Hibbing, Minn.	12/11/63	U. of Minnesota-Springfield
NILSSON, Kent	6-1	195	Nynashamn, Sweden	8/31/56	Minnesota
PAYNE, Steve	6-2	215	Toronto, Ont.	8/16/58	Minnesota
PLETT, Willi	6-3	220	Paraguay, S. America	6/7/55	Minnesota
PONER, Jiri	6-2	175	Pardubice, Czech.	2/9/64	Indianapolis-Muskegon
ROY, Stephane	5-11	181	Ste. Foy, Que.	6/29/67	Grandby
SERVINIS, George	5-11	175	Willowdale, Ont.	4/29/62	Springfield
SMITH, Randy	6-3	180	Saskatoon, Sask.	7/15/65	Saskatoon-Minnesota
DEFENSEMEN					
BERGER, Mike	5-11	193	Edmonton, Alta.	6/2/67	Lethbridge
GILES, Curt	5-8	179	The Pas, Man.	11/30/58	Minnesota
GRONSTRAND, Jari	6-3	197	Tampere, Finland	11/14/62	Tappara (Finland)
HARTSBURG, Craig	6-1	195	Stratford, Ont.	6/29/59	Minnesota
HIRSCH, Tom	6-4	211	Minneapolis, Minn.	1/27/63	Minnesota
JENSEN, David	6-1	190	Minneapolis, Minn.	5/3/61	Springfield-Minnesota
LANGEVIN, Dave	6-2	215	St. Paul, Minn.	5/15/54	Minnesota
LUCYK, Carey	6-1	195	Winnipeg, Man.	3/8/62	U. of Manitoba
MUSIL, Frantisek	6-3	205	Pardubice, Czech.	12/17/64	Dukla Jihlava (Czech.)
PRYOR, Chris	6-0	200	St. Paul, Minn.	1/23/61	Springfield-Minnesota
ROBERTS, Gordie	6-0	193	Detroit, Mich.	10/2/57	Minnesota
ROUSE, Bob	6-2	215	Surrey, B.C.	6/18/64	Minnesota
VIVEIROS, Emanuel	5-11	160	St. Albert, Alta.	1/8/66	Prince Albert-Minnesota
WILSON, Ron	5-10	170	Windsor, Ont.	5/28/55	Davos-Minnesota
GOALTENDERS					
BEAUPRE, Don	5-8	162	Kitchener, Ont.	9/19/61	Minnesota
CASEY, Jon	5-10	155	Grand Rapids, Mich.	3/29/62	Springfield-Minnesota
SANDS, Mike	5-9	146	Sudbury, Ont.	4/6/63	Springfield
TAKKO, Kari	6-2	182	Kaupunki, Finland	6/23/63	Springfield-Minnesota

Coach and General Manager

HENNING, LORNE EDWARD
Coach, Minnesota North Stars. Born in Melfort, Sask., Feb. 22, 1952.

Lorne Henning was seen fit to be named coach of the North Stars on June 21, 1985, following the valuable experience of playing on two New York Islander championship teams and working as an assistant coach to Al Arbour on two others. In 1985-86, he guided the North Stars to a second place finish in the Norris Division and placed third in voting for the Jack Adams Award. Henning played 543 games over nine seasons with the Islanders, and coached the Springfield Indians of the AHL during the 1984-85 season.

NHL Coaching Record

Team	Season	Games	Regular Season				Playoffs			
			W	L	T	%	Games	W	L	%
Minnesota	1985-86	80	38	33	9	.531	5	2	3	.400
NHL Totals		80	38	33	9	.531	5	2	3	.400

NANNE, LOUIS VINCENT (LOU)
Vice President and General Manager, Minnesota North Stars. Born in Sault Ste. Marie, Ont., June 2, 1941.

Lou Nanne was appointed coach and general manager of the North Stars on February 10, 1978 and served in the dual capacities until July 5, 1978 when he named Harry Howell as his coaching successor and concentrated his full-time duties in the North Stars' front office. Nanne has been associated with the North Stars since the club's entrance into the NHL. From 1967-68 through the first half of the 1977-78 season he played defense and right wing for the club. During his early playing days, Nanne, a naturalized American citizen, captained the 1968 U.S. Olympic team. He also played for the University of Minnesota where, as a defenseman, he captured the WCHA scoring title.

1985-86 Scoring
Regular Season

*—rookie

Pos	#	Player	Team	GP	G	A	Pts	+/−	PIM	PP	SH	GW	OT	S	%
F	7	Neal Broten	MIN	80	29	76	105	14	47	6	0	0	0	193	15.0
F	20	Dino Ciccarelli	MIN	75	44	45	89	12	51	19	0	5	1	262	16.8
F	23	Brian Bellows	MIN	77	31	48	79	16	46	11	2	2	2	256	12.1
F	14	Scott Bjugstad	MIN	80	43	33	76	5	24	14	1	6	0	217	19.8
F	15	Kent Nilsson	MIN	61	16	44	60	4	10	8	0	2	0	122	13.1
F	12	Keith Acton	MIN	79	26	32	58	11−	100	5	2	2	0	169	15.4
F	9	Dennis Maruk	MIN	70	21	37	58	13	67	1	0	2	0	135	15.6
D	4	Craig Hartsburg	MIN	75	10	47	57	7	127	4	0	2	0	185	5.4
F	21	Dirk Graham	MIN	80	22	33	55	6−	87	0	4	3	0	173	12.7
F	25	Tony McKegney	MIN	70	15	25	40	5−	48	3	1	0	0	141	10.6
F	8	Brian Lawton	MIN	65	18	17	35	10	36	4	0	7	0	98	18.4
D	2	Curt Giles	MIN	69	6	21	27	19	30	0	1	0	0	59	10.2
F	11	Tom McCarthy	MIN	25	12	12	24	3−	12	4	0	2	0	45	26.7
D	10	Gordie Roberts	MIN	76	2	21	23	14	101	0	0	0	0	66	3.0
F	24	Willi Plett	MIN	59	10	7	17	20−	231	4	0	0	0	72	13.9
D	3	Bob Rouse	MIN	75	1	14	15	15	151	0	0	1	0	91	1.1
F	44	Steve Payne	MIN	22	8	4	12	0	8	3	0	2	0	60	13.3
D	26	Dave Langevin	MIN	80	0	8	8	17−	58	0	0	0	0	54	.0
D	17	Ed Hospodar	PHI	17	3	1	4	0	55	1	0	0	0	11	27.3
			MIN	43	0	2	2	8	91	0	0	0	0	33	.0
			Total	60	3	3	6	8	146	0	1	0	0	44	6.8
F	28	Mats Hallin	MIN	38	3	2	5	3−	86	0	0	1	0	29	10.3
F	16	Marc Habscheid	MIN	6	2	3	5	2−	0	1	0	0	0	8	25.0
D	34	Craig Levie	MIN	14	2	2	4	5−	8	0	0	0	0	22	9.1
F	29	Tim Coulis	MIN	19	2	2	4	5	73	0	0	0	0	13	15.4
D	34	Ron Wilson	MIN	11	1	3	4	2	2	0	0	0	0	21	4.8
F	13	*Bill Stewart	MIN	8	0	2	2	2	13	0	0	0	0	0	.0
F	37	*Paul Houck	MIN	3	0	1	1	1	0	0	0	0	0	3	33.3
D	18	*Emanuel Viveiros	MIN	4	0	1	1	2	0	0	0	0	0	8	.0
D	36	*Chris Pryor	MIN	7	0	1	1	0	16	0	0	0	0	8	.0
F	6	*Larry Depalma	MIN	1	0	0	0	0	0	0	0	0	0	0	.0
F	32	*Randy Smith	MIN	1	0	0	0	0	0	0	0	0	0	0	.0
G	1	*Kari Takko	MIN	1	0	0	0	0	0	0	0	0	0	0	.0
D	32	Dan Mandich	MIN	3	0	0	0	0	25	0	0	0	0	0	.0
D	18	*Dave Jensen	MIN	5	0	0	0	2−	7	0	0	0	0	1	.0
F	31	*Jim Archibald	MIN	11	0	0	0	3−	32	0	0	0	0	7	.0
G	30	*Jon Casey	MIN	26	0	0	0	0	6	0	0	0	0	0	.0
G	33	Don Beaupre	MIN	52	0	0	0	0	34	0	0	0	0	0	.0

Playoffs

* rookie

Pos	#	Player	Team	GP	G	A	Pts	+/−	PIM	PP	SH	GW	OT	S	%
F	9	Dennis Maruk	MIN	5	4	9	13	5	4	1	0	0	0	14	28.6
D	34	Ron Wilson	MIN	5	2	4	6	4	4	1	0	0	0	15	13.3
F	23	Brian Bellows	MIN	5	5	0	5	1	16	3	0	0	0	16	31.3
F	7	Neal Broten	MIN	5	3	2	5	5−	2	1	0	0	0	16	18.8
F	15	Kent Nilsson	MIN	5	1	4	5	2	0	1	0	0	0	10	10.0
F	21	Dirk Graham	MIN	5	3	1	4	3	2	0	1	2	0	23	13.0
D	10	Gordie Roberts	MIN	5	0	4	4	3	8	0	0	0	0	2	.0
F	25	Tony McKegney	MIN	5	2	1	3	1−	22	0	0	0	0	12	16.7
F	12	Keith Acton	MIN	5	0	3	3	1−	6	0	0	0	0	9	.0
F	8	Brian Lawton	MIN	3	0	1	1	3−	0	0	0	0	0	4	.0
F	14	Scott Bjugstad	MIN	5	0	1	1	3−	0	0	0	0	0	9	.0
F	20	Dino Ciccarelli	MIN	5	0	1	1	6−	6	0	0	0	0	8	.0
D	2	Curt Giles	MIN	5	0	1	1	3−	10	0	0	0	0	3	.0
D	4	Craig Hartsburg	MIN	5	0	1	1	5−	2	0	0	0	0	15	.0
D	26	Dave Langevin	MIN	5	0	1	1	3−	0	0	0	0	0	5	.0
F	24	Willi Plett	MIN	5	0	1	1	1−	45	0	0	0	0	4	.0
F	28	Mats Hallin	MIN	1	0	0	0	0	0	0	0	0	0	0	.0
F	16	Marc Habscheid	MIN	2	0	0	0	1−	0	0	0	0	0	1	.0
D	17	Ed Hospodar	MIN	2	0	0	0	0	0	0	0	0	0	0	.0
D	3	Bob Rouse	MIN	3	0	0	0	2	0	0	0	0	0	3	.0
G	33	Don Beaupre	MIN	5	0	0	0	0	0	0	0	0	0	0	.0

Dennis Maruk

Club Records

Team

(Figures in brackets for season records are games played; records for fewest points, wins, ties, losses, goals, goals against are for 70 or more games)

Most Points	96	1982-83 (80)
Most Wins	40	1982-83 (80)
Most Ties	22	1969-70 (76)
Most Losses	53	1975-76 (80)
Most Goals	346	1981-82 (80)
Most Goals Against	344	1983-84 (80)
Fewest Points	45	1977-78 (80)
Fewest Wins	18	1968-69 (76)
		1977-78 (80)
Fewest Ties	7	1974-75 (80)
		1975-76 (80)
Fewest Losses	24	1982-83 (80)
Fewest Goals	189	1968-69 (76)
Fewest Goals Against	191	1971-72 (78)

Longest Winning Streak

Over-all	7	Mar. 16-28/80
Home	11	Nov. 4-Dec. 27/72
Away	5	Dec. 2-16/67 Feb. 5-Mar. 5/83

Longest Undefeated Streak

Over-all	12	Feb. 18-Mar. 15/82 (9 wins, 3 ties)
Home	13	Oct. 28-Dec. 27/72 (12 wins, 1 tie) Nov. 21-Jan. 9/80 (10 wins, 3 ties)
Away	6	Nov. 30-Dec. 16/67 (5 wins, 1 tie) Nov. 7-27/71 (5 wins, 1 tie) Nov. 9-Dec. 3/83 (5 wins, 1 tie)

Longest Losing Streak

Over-all	10	Feb. 1-20/76
Home	6	Jan. 17-Feb. 4/70
Away	8	Oct. 19-Nov. 13/75

Longest Winless Streak

Over-all	20	Jan. 15-Feb. 28/70 (15 losses, 5 ties)
Home	12	Jan. 17-Feb. 25/70 (8 losses, 4 ties)
Away	23	Oct. 25/74-Jan. 28/75 (19 losses, 4 ties)

Most Shutouts, Season	7	1972-73 (78) 1984-85 (80)
Most Pen. Mins., Season	1,735	
Most Goals, Game	15	Nov. 11/81 (Wpg. 2 at Minn. 15)

Individual

Most Seasons	12	Fred Barrett
Most Games	730	Fred Barrett
Most Goals, Career	267	Bill Goldsworthy
Most Assists, Career	316	Tim Young
Most Points Career	506	Bill Goldsworthy (267 goals, 239 assists)
Most Pen. Mins., Career	1,000	Brad Maxwell
Most Shutouts, Career	26	Cesare Maniago
Longest Consecutive Games Streak	442	Danny Grant (Dec. 4/68-Apr. 7/74
Most Goals, Season	55	Dino Ciccarelli (1981-82)
Most Assists, Season	76	Neal Broten (1985-86)
Most Point, Season	114	Bobby Smith (1981-82) (43 goals, 71 assists)

Most Pen. Mins., Season	316	Willi Plett (1983-84)
Most Points, Defenseman Season	77	Craig Hartsburg (1981-82) (17 goals, 60 assists)
Most Points, Center, Season	114	Bobby Smith (1981-82) (43 goals, 71 assists)
Most Points, Right Wing, Season	107	Dino Ciccarelli (1981-82) (55 goals, 52 assists)
Most Point, Left Wing, Season	85	Steve Payne (1979-80) (42 goals, 43 assists)
Most Points, Rookie, Season	97	Neal Broten (1981-82) (38 goals, 59 assists)
Most Shutouts, Season	6	Cesare Maniago (1967-68)
Most Goals, Game	5	Tim Young (Jan. 15/79)
Most Assists, Game	5	Murray Oliver (Oct. 24/71)
Most Points, Game	7	Bobby Smith (Nov. 11/81)

Coaching History

Wren Blair, 1967-68; John Muckler and Wren Blair, 1968-69; Wren Blair and Charlie Bruns, 1969-70; Jackie Gordon, 1970-71 to 1972-73; Jackie Gordon and Parker MacDonald, 1973-74; Jackie Gordon and Charlie Burns, 1974-75; Ted Harris, 1975-76 to 1976-77; Ted Harris, André Beaulieu, Lou Nanne, 1977-78; Harry Howell and Glen Sonmor, 1978-79; Glen Sonmor, 1979-80 to 1981-82; Glen Sonmor and Murray Oliver, 1982-83; Bill Mahoney, 1983-84 to 1984-85; Lorne Henning, 1985-86 to date.

Captains' History

Bob Woytowich, 1967-68; Elmer Vasko, 1968-69; Claude Larose, 1969-70; Ted Harris, 1970-71 to 1973-74; Bill Goldsworthy, 1974-75, 1975-76; Bill Hogaboam, 1976-77; Nick Beverly, 1977-78; J.P. Parise, 1978-79; Paul Shmyr, 1979-80, 1980-81; Tim Young, 1981-82; Craig Hartsburg, 1982-83; Brian Bellows, Craig Hartsburg, 1983-84; Craig Hartsburg, 1984-85, 1985-86.

All-time Record vs. Other Clubs

Regular Season

		At Home							On Road							Total					
	GP	W	L	T	GF	GA	PTS	GP	W	L	T	GF	GA	PTS	GP	W	L	T	GF	GA	PTS
Boston	42	10	24	8	110	164	28	43	4	32	7	96	195	15	85	14	56	15	206	359	43
Buffalo	34	12	17	5	102	114	29	35	7	22	6	88	137	20	69	19	39	11	190	251	49
**Calgary	29	15	10	4	112	96	34	29	4	17	8	82	123	16	58	19	27	12	194	219	50
Chicago	57	24	26	7	200	202	55	57	14	37	6	144	236	34	114	38	63	13	344	438	89
Detroit	53	30	12	11	217	144	71	52	23	19	10	190	194	56	105	53	31	21	407	338	127
Edmonton	11	4	5	2	43	42	10	12	1	9	2	45	68	5	23	5	13	5	88	110	15
Hartford	11	8	2	1	59	38	17	12	7	5	0	51	39	14	23	15	7	1	110	77	31
Los Angeles	47	29	11	7	188	119	65	45	13	19	13	138	161	39	92	42	30	20	326	280	104
Montreal	41	10	23	8	106	153	28	40	8	27	5	101	179	21	81	18	50	13	207	332	49
*New Jersey	27	18	4	5	115	62	41	26	11	12	3	84	86	25	53	29	16	8	199	148	66
NY Islanders	29	9	15	5	81	108	23	28	7	14	7	79	113	21	57	16	29	12	160	221	44
NY Rangers	43	13	24	6	129	172	32	42	8	26	8	115	153	24	85	21	50	14	244	325	56
Philadelphia	47	17	18	12	142	156	46	49	7	32	10	103	189	24	96	24	50	22	245	345	70
Pittsburgh	45	27	14	4	176	145	58	46	13	28	5	120	173	31	91	40	42	9	296	318	89
Quebec	12	7	3	2	54	35	16	11	1	7	3	24	59	3	23	8	12	3	78	94	19
St. Louis	61	28	19	14	217	181	70	63	20	32	11	176	214	51	124	48	51	25	393	395	121
Toronto	54	27	20	7	215	186	61	55	16	28	11	177	211	43	109	43	48	18	392	397	104
Vancouver	37	23	7	7	158	99	53	39	21	8	7	69	62	22	43	20	12	11	161	125	51
Washington	22	12	5	5	92	63	29	29	8	21	0	49	46	17	27	16	9	2	112	86	34
Winnipeg	14	8	5	1	63	40	17	13	8	4	1	49	65	17	27	14	9	2	207	191	70
Defunct Clubs	33	19	8	6	123	86	44	32	10	16	6	84	105	26	65	29	24	12	207	191	70
Totals	749	350	272	127	2702	2405	827	749	201	414	134	2134	2899	536	1498	551	686	261	4836	5304	1363

* Totals include those of Kansas City (1974-75, 1975-76) and Colorado (1976-77 through 1981-82)
** Totals include those of Atlanta (1972-73 through 1979-80)

Playoffs

	Series	W	L	GP	W	L	T	GF	GA	Last Mtg.	Round	Result
Boston	1	1	0	3	0	0	0	20	13	1981	P	W 3-0
Buffalo	2	1	1	7	4	3	0	26	28	1981	QF	W 4-1
**Calgary	1	1	0	6	4	2	0	25	18	1981	SF	W 4-2
Chicago	4	1	3	20	7	13	0	78	83	1985	DF	L 2-4
Edmonton	1	0	1	4	0	4	0	10	22	1984	CF	L 0-4
Los Angeles	1	1	0	4	3	0	0	26	21	1968	QF	W 4-3
Montreal	2	1	1	13	6	7	0	37	48	1980	QF	W 4-3
NY Islanders	1	0	1	5	1	4	0	16	26	1981	F	L 1-4
Philadelphia	2	0	2	11	3	8	0	24	41	1980	SF	L 1-4
St. Louis	7	3	4	41	21	20	0	121	112	1986	DSF	L 2-3
Toronto	2	2	0	7	4	3	0	35	26	1983	P	W 3-1
Totals	24	11	13	124	57	62	0	400	426			

Abbreviations: Round: F — Final; **CF** — conference final; **DF** — division final; **DSF** — division semi-final; **SF** — semi-final; **QF** — quarter-final; **P** — preliminary round. **GA** – goals against; **GF** – goals for.

Playoff Results 1986-82

Year	Round	Opponent	Result	GF	GA
1986	DSF	St. Louis	L 2-3	20	18
1985	DF	Chicago	L 2-4	29	33
	DSF	St. Louis	W 3-0	9	5
1984	CF	Edmonton	L 0-4	10	22
	DF	St. Louis	W 4-3	19	17
	DSF	Chicago	W 3-2	18	14
1983	DF	Chicago	L 1-4	17	22
	DSF	Toronto	W 3	18	18
1982	DSF	Chicago	L 1-3	14	14

Retired Numbers

19	Bill Masterton	1967-1968

Entry Draft Selections 1986-72

1986
Pick
12	Warren Babe
30	Neil Wilkinson
33	Dean Kolstad
54	Eric Bennett
55	Rob Zettler
58	Brad Turner
75	Kirk Tomlinson
96	Jari Gronstand
159	Scott Mathias
180	Lance Pitlick
201	Dan Keczmer
222	Garth Joy
243	Kurt Stahura

1985
Pick
51	Stephane Roy
69	Mike Berger
90	Dwight Mullins
111	Mike Mullowney
132	Mike Kelfer
153	Ross Johnson
174	Tim Helmer
195	Gordon Ernst
216	Ladislav Lubina
237	Tommy Sjodin

1984
Pick
13	David Quinn
46	Ken Hodge
76	Miroslav Maly
89	Jiri Poner
97	Kari Takko
118	Gary McColgan
139	Vladimir Kyhos
160	Darin MacInnis
181	Duane Wahlin
201	Mike Orn
222	Tom Terwilliger
242	Mike Nightengale

1983
Pick
1	Brian Lawton
36	Malcolm Parks
38	Frantisek Musil
56	Mitch Messier
76	Brian Durand
96	Rich Geist
116	Tom McComb
136	Sean Toomey
156	Don Biggs
176	Paul Pulis
196	Milos Riha
212	Oldrich Valek
236	Paul Roff

1982
Pick
2	Brian Bellows
59	Wally Chapman
80	Rob Rouse
81	Dusan Pasek
101	Marty Wiitala
122	Todd Carlile
143	Victor Zhluktov
164	Paul Miller
185	Pat Micheletti
206	Arnold Kadlec
227	Scott Knutson

1981
Pick
13	Ron Meighan
27	Dave Donnelly
31	Mike Sands
33	Tom Hirsch
34	Dave Preuss
41	Jali Wahlsten
69	Terry Tait
76	Jim Malwitz
97	Kelly Hubbard
118	Paul Guay
139	Jim Archibald
160	Kari Kanervo
181	Scott Bjugstad
202	Steve Kudebeh

1980
Pick
16	Brad Palmer
32	Don Beaupre
53	Randy Velischek
79	Mark Huglen
100	Dave Jensen
121	Dan Zavarise
142	Bill Stewart
163	Jeff Walters
184	Bob Lakso
205	Dave Richter

1979
Pick
6	Craig Hartsburg
10	Tom McCarthy
42	Neal Broten
63	Kevin Maxwell
90	Jim Dobson
111	Brian Gualazzi

1978
Pick
1	Bobby Smith
19	Steve Payne
24	Steve Christoff
54	Curt Giles
70	Roy Kerling
87	Bob Bergloff
104	Kim Spencer
121	Mike Cotter
138	Brent Gogol
155	Mike Seide

1977
Pick
7	Brad Maxwell
25	Dave Semenko
61	Kevin McCloskey
79	Bob Parent
97	Jamie Gallimore
115	J.P. Sanvido
133	Greg Tebbutt
151	Keith Hanson

1976
Pick
3	Glen Sharpley
31	Jim Roberts
39	Don Jackson
51	Ron Zanussi
75	Mike Federko
93	Phil Verchota
111	Dave Delich
129	Jeff Barr

1975
Pick
4	Bryan Maxwell
40	Paul Harrison
41	Alex Pirus
58	Steve Jensen
76	David Norris
94	Greg Clause
112	Francois Robert
130	Dean Magee
148	Terry Angel
164	Michel Blais
188	Earl Sargent
201	Gilles Cloutier

1974
Pick
6	Doug Hicks
24	Richard Nantais
42	Pete LoPresti
60	Kim MacDougall
78	Ron Ahston
96	John Sheriden
114	Dave Heitz
131	Roland Eriksson
148	Dave Staffen
164	Brian Anderson
179	Duane Bray
193	Don Hay
205	Brian Holderness
215	Frank Taylor
222	Jeff Hymanson

1973
Pick
18	Blake Dunlop
25	Johnny Rogers
41	Rick Chinnick
57	Tom Colley
73	Lowell Ostlund
89	David Lee
105	Lou Nistico
121	George Beveridge
136	Jim Johnston
152	Sam Clegg
161	Russ Wiechnik

1972
Pick
12	Jerry Byers
44	Terry Ryan
60	Tom Thomson
76	Chris Ahrens
92	Steve West
108	Chris Meloff
116	Scott MacPhail
124	Bob Lundeen
140	Glen Mikkelson
145	Steve Lyon
147	Jari Kudrasov
148	Marcel Comeau

Club Directory

Metropolitan Sports Center
7901 Cedar Avenue South
Bloomington, Minnesota 55420
Phone 612/853-9333
TWX 910-576-2853
ENVOY ID   TM.MIN
Capacity: 15,499

Co-Chairman of the Board	George Gund III
Co-Chairman of the Board	Gordon Gund
President	John Karr
Vice President/General Manager	Lou Nanne
Assistant General Manager	John Mariucci
Vice President, Marketing	Dave Jones
Vice President, Communications	Dick Arneson
Vice President, Met Center	Frank Jirik
Vice President of Finance	George Wettstaedt
Director of Player Development	Glen Sonmor
Coach	Lorne Henning
Assistant Coach	J.P. Parise
Assistant Coach	Les Jackson
Administrative Assistant	Murray Oliver
Chief Scout	Harry Howell
Special Assignment Scout	Dick Bouchard
Scouts	George Agar, Gump Worsley, Smoky Cerrone
Public Relations Director	Dick Dillman
Publications Manager	Joe Janasz
Marketing Manager	Peter Jocketty
Sales Manager	Wally Shaver
Community Relations Director	Patty Connolly
Ticket Manager	Rick Olson
Team Physicians	Dr. John Cragg, Dr. Charles Kelly, Dr. Don Miller, Dr. George Nagabods, Dr. Frank Sidell
Physical Therapist	Tom Coplin
Team Dentist	Dr. Paul Belvedere
Trainer	Dick Rose
Assistant Trainer	Dave Smith
Equipment Manager	Mark Baribeau
Location of Press Boxes	North Side — Press and Radio South Side — TV
Dimensions of Rink	200 feet by 85 feet
Ends of Rink	Unbreakable glass extends above boards all around rink
Club Colors	Green, White, Gold and Black
Club Trains at	Met Center and Eden Prairie Community Center
Radio Play-by-Play	Al Shaver (KSTP-AM, 1500)
TV Play-by-Play	Frank Mazzocco KITN-TV (Channel 29)

Dino Ciccarelli

Montreal Canadiens

1985-86 Results: 40W-33L-7T 87 PTS. Second, Adams Division

Captain Bob Gainey led a young Montreal team to the 1986 Stanley Cup.

Schedule

Home

Month	Day	Date	Opponent
Oct.	Sat.	11	Edmonton
	Mon.	13	Minnesota
	Sat.	18	Winnipeg
	Mon.	20	Washington
	Sat.	25	NY Rangers
	Mon.	27	Los Angeles
	Wed.	29	Buffalo
Nov.	Wed.	12	Quebec
	Sat.	15	Buffalo
	Mon.	17	Boston
	Sat.	22	Detroit
	Sat.	29	Hartford
Dec.	Mon.	1	Washington
	Wed.	3	St. Louis
	Mon.	8	Calgary
	Thur.	11	NY Rangers
	Sat.	13	Boston
	Sat.	20	New Jersey
	Mon.	22	Pittsburgh
	Sat.	27	Hartford
	Wed.	31	Quebec
Jan.	Wed.	7	Vancouver
	Sat.	10	Quebec
	Mon.	12	Toronto
	Sat.	17	Buffalo
	Mon.	19	Hartford
	Sat.	24	Chicago
	Sat.	31	Los Angeles
Feb.	Wed.	4	Quebec
	Sat.	14	Winnipeg
	Mon.	16	Boston
	Wed.	18	NY Islanders
	Mon.	23	Minnesota
	Sat.	28	New Jersey
Mar.	Sat.	14	Philadelphia
	Mon.	16	NY Islanders
	Sat.	21	Toronto
	Sat.	28	Buffalo
April	Wed.	1	Hartford
	Sat.	4	Boston

Away

Month	Day	Date	Opponent
Oct.	Thur.	9	Toronto
	Wed.	15	Buffalo
	Wed.	22	Detroit
	Thur.	30	Boston
Nov.	Sun.	2	Vancouver
	Thur.	6	Los Angeles
	Sat.	8	Edmonton
	Sun.	9	Calgary
	Wed.	19	Hartford
	Thur.	20	Boston
	Tue.	25	Quebec
	Wed.	26	Philadelphia
Dec.	Fri.	5	Detroit
	Sat.	6	Washington
	Sun.	14	New Jersey
	Tue.	16	St. Louis
	Fri.	19	Buffalo
	Fri.	26	Hartford
	Tue.	30	Quebec
Jan.	Sat.	3	Pittsburgh
	Mon.	5	Boston
	Wed.	14	Buffalo
	Thur.	15	Philadelphia
	Wed.	21	Hartford
	Thur.	22	Boston
	Mon.	26	Chicago
	Tue.	27	St. Louis
Feb.	Tue.	3	Quebec
	Sat.	7	Hartford
	Sat.	21	NY Islanders
	Wed.	25	Chicago
Mar.	Tue.	3	Calgary
	Fri.	6	Vancouver
	Sat.	7	Edmonton
	Mon.	9	Minnesota
	Wed.	11	Winnipeg
	Fri.	20	Buffalo
	Tue.	24	Quebec
	Sun.	29	Pittsburgh
April	Sun.	5	NY Rangers

*Denotes afternoon game.

Home Starting Times:

Weeknights & Sundays .... 7:35 p.m.

Saturdays .... 8:05 p.m.

Franchise date: November 22, 1917

WALES CONFERENCE 70th NHL Season

Year-by-Year Record

Season	GP	Home W	Home L	Home T	Road W	Road L	Road T	Overall W	Overall L	Overall T	GF	GA	Pts.	Finished	Playoff Result
1985-86	80	25	11	4	15	22	3	40	33	7	330	280	87	2nd, Adams Div.	**Won Stanley Cup**
1984-85	80	24	10	6	17	17	6	41	27	12	309	262	94	1st, Adams Div.	Lost Div. Final
1983-84	80	19	19	2	16	21	3	35	40	5	286	295	75	4th, Adams Div.	Lost Conf. Championship
1982-83	80	25	6	9	17	18	5	42	24	14	350	286	98	2nd, Adams Div.	Lost Div. Semi-Final
1981-82	80	25	6	9	21	11	8	46	17	17	360	223	109	1st, Adams Div.	Lost Div. Semi-Final
1980-81	80	31	7	2	14	15	11	45	22	13	332	232	103	1st, Norris Div.	Lost Prelim. Round
1979-80	80	30	7	3	17	13	10	47	20	13	328	240	107	1st, Norris Div.	Lost Quarter-Final
1978-79	80	29	6	5	23	11	6	52	17	11	337	204	115	1st, Norris Div.	**Won Stanley Cup**
1977-78	80	32	4	4	27	6	7	59	10	11	359	183	129	1st, Norris Div.	**Won Stanley Cup**
1976-77	80	33	1	6	27	7	6	60	8	12	387	171	132	1st, Norris Div.	**Won Stanley Cup**
1975-76	80	32	3	5	26	8	6	58	11	11	337	174	127	1st, Norris Div.	**Won Stanley Cup**
1974-75	80	27	8	5	20	6	14	47	14	19	374	225	113	1st, Norris Div.	Lost Semi-Final
1973-74	78	24	12	3	21	12	6	45	24	9	293	240	99	2nd, East Div.	Lost Quarter-Final
1972-73	78	29	4	6	23	6	10	52	10	16	329	184	120	1st, East Div.	**Won Stanley Cup**
1971-72	78	29	3	7	17	13	9	46	16	16	307	205	108	3rd, East Div.	Lost Quarter-Final
1970-71	78	29	7	3	13	16	10	42	23	13	291	216	97	3rd, East Div.	**Won Stanley Cup**
1969-70	76	21	9	8	17	13	8	38	22	16	244	201	92	5th, East Div.	Out of Playoffs
1968-69	76	26	7	5	20	12	6	46	19	11	271	202	103	1st, East Div.	**Won Stanley Cup**
1967-68	74	26	5	6	16	17	4	42	22	10	236	167	94	1st, East Div.	**Won Stanley Cup**
1966-67	70	19	9	7	13	16	6	32	25	13	202	188	77	2nd,	Lost Final
1965-66	70	23	11	1	18	10	7	41	21	8	239	173	90	1st,	**Won Stanley Cup**
1964-65	70	20	8	7	16	15	4	36	23	11	211	185	83	2nd,	**Won Stanley Cup**
1963-64	70	22	7	6	14	14	7	36	21	13	209	167	85	1st,	Lost Semi-Final
1962-63	70	15	10	10	13	9	13	28	19	23	225	183	79	3rd,	Lost Semi-Final
1961-62	70	26	2	7	16	12	7	42	14	14	259	166	98	1st,	Lost Semi-Final
1960-61	70	24	6	5	17	13	5	41	19	10	254	188	92	1st,	Lost Semi-Final
1959-60	70	23	4	8	17	14	4	40	18	12	255	178	92	1st,	**Won Stanley Cup**
1958-59	70	21	8	6	18	10	7	39	18	13	258	158	91	1st,	**Won Stanley Cup**
1957-58	70	23	8	4	20	9	6	43	17	10	250	158	96	1st,	**Won Stanley Cup**
1956-57	70	23	6	6	12	17	6	35	23	12	210	155	82	2nd,	**Won Stanley Cup**
1955-56	70	29	5	1	16	10	9	45	15	10	222	131	100	1st,	**Won Stanley Cup**
1954-55	70	26	5	4	15	13	7	41	18	11	228	157	93	2nd,	Lost Final
1953-54	70	27	5	3	8	19	8	35	24	11	195	141	81	2nd,	Lost Final
1952-53	70	18	12	5	10	11	14	28	23	19	155	148	75	2nd,	**Won Stanley Cup**
1951-52	70	22	8	5	12	18	5	34	26	10	195	164	78	2nd,	Lost Final
1950-51	70	17	10	8	8	20	7	25	30	15	173	184	65	3rd,	Lost Final
1949-50	70	17	8	10	12	14	9	29	22	19	172	150	77	2nd,	Lost Semi-Final
1948-49	60	19	8	3	9	15	6	28	23	9	152	126	65	3rd,	Lost Semi-Final
1947-48	60	13	13	4	7	16	7	20	29	11	147	169	51	5th,	Out of Playoffs
1946-47	60	19	6	5	15	10	5	34	16	10	189	138	78	1st,	Lost Final
1945-46	50	16	6	3	12	11	2	28	17	5	172	134	61	1st,	**Won Stanley Cup**
1944-45	50	21	2	2	17	6	2	38	8	4	228	121	80	1st,	Lost Semi-Final
1943-44	50	22	0	3	16	5	4	38	5	7	234	109	83	1st,	**Won Stanley Cup**
1942-43	60	14	4	7	5	15	5	19	19	12	181	191	50	4th,	Lost Semi-Final
1941-42	48	12	10	2	6	17	1	18	27	3	134	173	39	6th,	Lost Quarter-Final
1940-41	48	11	9	4	5	17	2	16	26	6	121	147	38	6th,	Lost Quarter-Final
1939-40	48	5	14	5	5	19	0	10	33	5	90	167	25	7th,	Out of Playoffs
1938-39	48	8	11	5	7	13	4	15	24	9	115	146	39	6th,	Lost Quarter-Final
1937-38	48	13	4	7	5	13	6	18	17	13	123	128	49	3rd, Cdn. Div.	Lost Quarter-Final
1936-37	48	16	8	0	8	10	6	24	18	6	115	111	54	1st, Cdn. Div.	Lost Semi-Final
1935-36	48	5	11	8	6	15	3	11	26	11	82	123	33	4th, Cdn. Div.	Out of Playoffs
1934-35	48	11	11	2	8	12	4	19	23	6	110	145	44	3rd, Cdn. Div.	Lost Quarter-Final
1933-34	48	16	6	2	6	14	4	22	20	6	99	101	50	2nd, Cdn. Div.	Lost Quarter-Final
1932-33	48	15	5	4	3	20	1	18	25	5	92	115	41	3rd, Cdn. Div.	Lost Quarter-Final
1931-32	48	18	3	3	7	13	4	25	16	7	128	111	57	1st, Cdn. Div.	Lost Semi-Final
1930-31	44	15	3	4	11	7	4	26	10	8	129	89	60	1st, Cdn. Div.	**Won Stanley Cup**
1929-30	44	13	5	4	8	9	5	21	14	9	142	114	51	2nd, Cdn. Div.	**Won Stanley Cup**
1928-29	44	12	4	6	10	3	9	22	7	15	71	43	59	1st, Cdn. Div.	Lost Semi-Final
1927-28	44	12	7	3	14	4	4	26	11	7	116	48	59	1st, Cdn. Div.	Lost Semi-Final
1926-27	44	15	5	2	13	9	0	28	14	2	99	67	58	2nd, Cdn. Div.	Lost Final
1925-26	36	5	12	1	6	12	0	11	24	1	79	108	23	7th,	Out of Playoffs
1924-25	30	10	5	0	7	6	2	17	11	2	93	56	36	3rd,	Lost Cup Playoff
1923-24	24	10	2	0	3	9	0	13	11	0	59	48	26	2nd,	**Won Stanley Cup**
1922-23	24	10	2	0	3	7	2	13	9	2	73	61	28	2nd,	Lost NHL Playoff
1921-22	24	8	3	1	4	8	0	12	11	1	88	94	25	3rd,	Out of Playoffs
1920-21	24	9	3	0	4	8	0	13	11	0	112	99	26	3rd,	Out of Playoffs
1919-20	24	8	4	0	5	7	0	13	11	0	129	113	26	2nd,	Out of Playoffs
1918-19	18	7	2	0	3	6	0	10	8	0	88	78	20	2nd,	Cup Final but no Decision
1917-18	22	8	3	0	5	6	0	13	9	0	115	84	26	1st and 3rd*	Lost NHL Final

* Season played in two halves with no combined standing at end.
From 1917-18 through 1925-26, NHL champions played against PCHL champions for Stanley Cup.

1986-87 Player Personnel

FORWARDS	Ht.	Wt.	Place of Birth	Date	1985-86 Club
ANASTOS, Tom	6-0	185	Dearborn, Mich.	7/5/63	Sherbrooke
BOISVERT, Serge	5-9	170	Drummondville, Que.	6/1/59	Sherbrooke-Montreal
BONAR, Graeme	6-3	208	Toronto, Ont.	1/21/66	Peterborough
BUCYK, Randy	6-0	183	Edmonton, Alta.	11/9/62	Sherbrooke-Montreal
CARBONNEAU, Guy	5-11	180	Sept-Iles, Que.	3/18/60	Montreal
CHARBONNEAU, José	6-0	190	Ferme-Neuve, Que.	11/2/66	Drummondville
CORSON, Shayne	6-0	175	Barrie, Ont.	8/13/66	Hamilton
DAHLIN, Kjell	6-0	175	Timra, Sweden	2/2/63	Montreal
DEBLOIS, Lucien	5-11	200	St-Thomas-de-Joliette, Que.	6/21/57	Montreal
DEMERS, Eric	6-3	192	Montreal, Que.	3/1/66	Drummondville
DESJARDINS, Martin	5-11	165	Ste-Rose, Que.	1/28/67	Trois Rivieres
DUFRESNE, Donald	6-1	190	Rimouski, Que.	4/10/67	Trois Rivieres
DUNDAS, Rocky	6-0	200	Edmonton, Alta.	1/30/67	Spokane
FLETCHER, Steven	6-3	205	Montreal, Que.	3/31/62	Sherbrooke
GAINEY, Bob	6-2	200	Peterborough, Ont.	12/13/53	Montreal
GANCHAR, Perry	5-9	175	Saskatoon, Sask.	10/28/63	Sherbrooke
GILCHRIST, Brent	5-11	175	Moose Jaw, Sask.	4/3/67	Spokane
HARLOW, Scott	6-0	190	E. Bridgewater, Mass.	10/11/63	Boston College
HOULE, Kevin	6-3	213	Acton, Mass.	4/21/64	Boston College
KEANE, Mike	5-10	175	Winnipeg, Man.	5/28/67	Moose Jaw
LEMIEUX, Claude	6-1	206	Buckingham, Que.	7/16/65	Sherbrooke-Montreal
MALEY, David	6-2	205	Beaver Dam, Wis.	4/24/63	Wisconsin
McPHEE, Mike	6-1	200	Riviere-Bourgeois, N.S.	7/14/60	Montreal
MOORE, Charlie	6-2	219	Ottawa, Ont.	3/27/66	Belleville
MOMESSO, Sergio	6-3	203	Montreal, Que.	9/4/65	Montreal
NASLUND, Mats	5-7	160	Timra, Sweden	10/31/59	Montreal
NESICH, Jim	5-11	170	Dearborn, Mich.	2/22/66	Verdun
NILAN, Chris	6-0	200	Boston, Mass.	2/9/58	Montreal
RICHER, Stephane	6-2	200	Ripon, Que.	6/7/66	Montreal
ROONEY, Steve	6-2	200	Canton, Mass.	6/28/62	Montreal
ROULEAU, Guy	5-9	174	Beloeil, Que.	2/16/65	Hull
SKRUDLAND, Brian	6-0	188	Peace River, Alta.	7/31/63	Montreal
SMITH, Bobby	6-4	210	North Sydney, N.S.	2/12/58	Montreal
SVOBODA, Karel	6-1	192	Most, Czech.	12/2/60	DNP
THIBAUDEAU, Gilles	5-10	165	Montreal, Que.	3/4/63	Sherbrooke
TREMBLAY, Mario	6-0	190	Alma, Que.	9/2/56	Montreal
VARGAS, Ernie	6-2	195	St. Paul, Minn.	3/1/64	Wisconsin
WALTER, Ryan	6-0	195	New Westminster, B.C.	4/23/58	Montreal
WILLIAMS, Brian	5-9	172	Fargo, N.D.	6/27/63	North Dakota
DEFENSEMEN					
CAMPEDELLI, Dominic	6-1	205	Boston, Mass.	3/4/64	Sherbrooke-Montreal
CHELIOS, Chris	6-1	186	Chicago, Ill.	1/25/62	Montreal
CLOUTIER, Rejean	6-1	187	Windsor, Que.	2/15/60	Sherbrooke-Saginaw
GINGRAS, Gaston	6-0	185	Temiscamingue, Que.	2/13/59	Sherbrooke-Montreal
GREEN, Rick	6-3	210	Belleville, Ont.	2/20/56	Montreal
HAYWARD, Rick	6-0	173	Toledo, Ohio	2/25/66	Hull
HERRING, Graham	6-1	170	Montreal, Que.	10/27/65	Shawinigan-Peoria-Sherbrooke
KORDIC, John	6-1	200	Edmonton, Alta.	3/22/65	Sherbrooke-Montreal
KURVERS, Tom	6-0	190	Minneapolis, Minn.	9/14/62	Montreal
LALOR, Mike	6-3	200	Buffalo, N.Y.	3/8/63	Montreal
LUDWIG, Craig	6-3	217	Eagle River, Wis.	3/3/61	Montreal
MACTAVISH, Scott	6-3	204	Fredericton, N.B.	1/25/66	Verdun
ROBINSON, Larry	6-3	217	Winchester, Ont.	6/2/51	Montreal
SANDELIN, Scott	6-0	191	Hibbing, Minn.	8/8/64	North Dakota-Sherbrooke
SVOBODA, Petr	6-1	170	Most, Czech.	2/14/66	Montreal
GOALTENDERS					
HAYWARD, Brian	5-10	175	Georgetown, Ont.	6/25/60	Winnipeg
KNICKLE, Rick	5-10	170	Chatham, N.B.	2/26/60	Saginaw
RIENDEAU, Vincent	5-9	173	St-Hyacinthe, Que.	4/20/66	Drummondville
ROY, Patrick	6-0	174	Quebec, Que.	10/5/65	Montreal

1985-86 Scoring

Regular Season

*–rookie

Pos	#	Player	Team	GP	G	A	Pts	+/–	PIM	PP	SH	GW	OT	S	%
F	26	Mats Naslund	MTL	80	43	67	110	11	16	19	0	7	1	223	19.3
F	15	Bobby Smith	MTL	79	31	55	86	10	55	5	0	7	1	202	15.3
D	19	Larry Robinson	MTL	78	19	63	82	29	39	10	0	1	0	167	11.4
F	20	*Kjell Dahlin	MTL	77	32	39	71	10	4	14	0	3	0	172	18.6
F	21	Guy Carbonneau	MTL	80	20	36	56	18	57	1	2	3	0	147	13.6
F	11	Ryan Walter	MTL	69	15	34	49	9–	45	9	0	1	0	115	13.0
F	23	Bob Gainey	MTL	80	20	23	43	10	20	0	2	4	1	135	14.8
F	35	Mike McPhee	MTL	70	19	21	40	8	69	0	2	3	0	103	18.4
F	14	Mario Tremblay	MTL	56	19	20	39	4	55	3	0	3	0	119	16.0
F	44	*Stephane Richer	MTL	65	21	16	37	1	50	5	0	2	1	112	18.8
F	30	Chris Nilan	MTL	72	19	15	34	10	274	2	0	1	0	120	15.8
D	24	Chris Chelios	MTL	41	8	26	34	4	67	2	0	0	0	101	7.9
F	27	Lucien DeBlois	MTL	61	14	17	31	3	48	2	0	1	0	102	13.7
D	18	Tom Kurvers	MTL	62	7	23	30	9	36	3	0	1	1	69	10.1
D	29	Gaston Gingras	MTL	34	8	18	26	10–	12	7	0	0	0	77	10.4
F	39	*Brian Skrudland	MTL	65	9	13	22	3	57	0	2	0	0	62	14.5
D	25	Petr Svoboda	MTL	73	1	18	19	24	93	0	0	0	0	63	1.6
F	36	*Sergio Momesso	MTL	24	8	7	15	4–	46	3	0	3	0	37	21.6
D	38	*Mike Lalor	MTL	62	3	5	8	4–	56	0	0	0	0	44	6.8
F	22	*Randy Bucyk	MTL	17	4	2	6	5	8	0	0	0	0	21	19.0
D	17	Craig Ludwig	MTL	69	2	4	6	7	63	0	0	0	0	58	3.4
D	5	Rick Green	MTL	46	3	2	5	9–	20	0	0	0	0	45	6.7
F	28	*Steve Rooney	MTL	38	2	3	5	4–	114	1	0	0	0	24	8.3
F	12	Serge Boisvert	MTL	9	2	2	4	1	2	0	0	0	0	18	11.1
F	32	*Claude Lemieux	MTL	10	1	2	3	6–	22	1	0	0	0	16	6.3
G	33	*Patrick Roy	MTL	47	0	3	3	0	4	0	0	0	0	0	.0
D	31	*John Kordic	MTL	5	0	1	1	1	12	0	0	0	0	0	.0
D	40	*Dom Campedelli	MTL	2	0	0	0	2–	0	0	0	0	0	1	.0
F	8	Alfie Turcotte	MTL	2	0	0	0	0	2	0	0	0	0	0	.0
F	34	*Shayne Corson	MTL	3	0	0	0	3–	2	0	0	0	0	1	.0
F	8	*David Maley	MTL	3	0	0	0	0	0	0	0	0	0	0	.0
G	37	Steve Penney	MTL	18	0	0	0	0	0	0	0	0	0	0	.0
G	1	Doug Soetaert	MTL	23	0	0	0	0	6	0	0	0	0	0	.0

Playoffs

* rookie

Pos	#	Player	Team	GP	G	A	Pts	+/–	PIM	PP	SH	GW	OT	S	%
F	26	Mats Naslund	MTL	20	8	11	19	1–	4	4	0	0	0	43	18.6
F	32	*Claude Lemieux	MTL	20	10	5	15	1	68	4	0	4	2	51	19.6
F	15	Bobby Smith	MTL	20	7	8	15	2–	22	3	0	3	0	44	15.9
D	19	Larry Robinson	MTL	20	0	13	13	4	22	0	0	0	0	42	.0
F	21	Guy Carbonneau	MTL	20	7	5	12	9	35	0	2	1	0	42	16.7
D	24	Chris Chelios	MTL	20	2	9	11	3	49	1	0	0	0	57	3.5
F	23	Bob Gainey	MTL	20	5	5	10	3	12	0	1	3	0	36	13.9
F	35	Mike McPhee	MTL	20	3	4	7	6	45	0	1	1	0	22	13.6
F	39	*Brian Skrudland	MTL	20	2	4	6	8	76	0	0	1	1	21	9.5
F	44	*Stephane Richer	MTL	16	4	1	5	3–	23	3	0	1	0	22	18.2
D	29	Gaston Gingras	MTL	11	2	3	5	1	4	1	0	0	0	37	5.4
F	20	*Kjell Dahlin	MTL	16	2	3	5	1	4	0	0	0	0	20	10.0
D	5	Rick Green	MTL	18	1	4	5	4–	8	0	0	0	0	18	5.6
F	8	*David Maley	MTL	7	1	3	4	4	2	0	0	0	0	5	20.0
F	30	Chris Nilan	MTL	18	1	2	3	6	141	1	0	0	0	32	3.1
D	38	*Mike Lalor	MTL	17	1	2	3	6	29	0	0	1	0	13	7.7
F	11	Ryan Walter	MTL	5	0	1	1	2–	2	0	0	0	0	8	.0
F	12	Serge Boisvert	MTL	8	0	1	1	1	0	0	0	0	0	7	.0
D	17	Craig Ludwig	MTL	20	0	1	1	3	48	0	0	0	0	13	.0
F	28	*Steve Rooney	MTL	1	0	0	0	1–	0	0	0	0	0	0	.0
F	22	*Randy Bucyk	MTL	2	0	0	0	1–	0	0	0	0	0	1	.0
D	25	Petr Svoboda	MTL	8	0	0	0	2	21	0	0	0	0	3	.0
F	27	Lucien DeBlois	MTL	11	0	0	0	4–	7	0	0	0	0	11	.0
D	31	*John Kordic	MTL	18	0	0	0	2–	53	0	0	0	0	5	.0
G	33	*Patrick Roy	MTL	20	0	0	0	0	10	0	0	0	0	0	.0

Coach and General Manager

PERRON, JEAN
Coach, Montreal Canadiens. Born in St. Isidore d'Auckland, Que., October 5, 1946

After succeeding Jacques Lemaire to become the 20th head coach of the Montreal Canadiens on July 29, 1985, Jean Perron achieved what few other rookie coaches in NHL history have ever done — he won the Stanley Cup. After having played for the University of Sherbrooke, he coached Junior B at the College de Matane. During his studies at Michigan State University, he served as assistant coach for that school's hockey team. In 1973, he became coach of the Blue Eagles of Moncton University. In the ensuing ten years, he coached the team to four regional and two Canadian championships. In 1983, he became assistant coach for the Canadian team at the World Championship in Munich and, in 1983 and 1984, he occupied the same position for the Canadian Olympic Team.

NHL Coaching Record

		Regular Season					Playoffs			
Team	Season	Games	W	L	T	%	Games	W	L	%
Montreal	1985-86	80	40	33	7	.544	20	15	5	.750
NHL Totals		**80**	**40**	**33**	**7**	**.544**	**20**	**15**	**5**	**.750**

SAVARD, SERGE A.
Managing Director, Montreal Canadiens. Born in Montreal, Que., January 22, 1946.

When Serge Savard was named Managing Director of the Montreal Canadiens on April 28, 1983, he took over a club that finished in fourth place with 75 points. In 1984-85, the Canadiens were vastly improved, finishing first with 94 points. Evidence of Savard's front office efforts were visible throughout the organization where he spent 14 of his 16 NHL seasons as a standout defenseman and an important part of eight Stanley Cup winning teams. As a player, Savard captured the Conn Smythe Trophy as the most valuable player in the 1969 Stanley Cup playoffs and was recipient of the Bill Masterton Trophy in 1978-79 for his dedication, perserverance and sportsmanship to the game of hockey. He was acquired by the Winnipeg Jets in the 1981 Waiver Draft and closed out his playing career with two seasons as a leader and teacher to the young Jets' team which showed remarkable improvement during Savard's term. In the 1960's, Savard twice suffered multiple leg fractures and most experts doubted he would ever play again. He was named to the NHL's Second All-Star Team in 1978-79.

Club Records

Team

(Figures in brackets for season records are games played; records for fewest points, wins, ties, losses, goals, goals against are for 70 or more games)

Most Points	*132	1976-77 (80)
Most Wins	*60	1976-77 (80)
Most Ties	23	1962-63 (70)
Most Losses	40	1983-84 (80)
Most Goals	387	1976-77 (80)
Most Goals Against	295	1983-84 (80)
Fewest Points	65	1950-51 (70)
Fewest Wins	25	1950-51 (70)
Fewest Ties	5	1983-84 (80)
Fewest Losses	*8	1976-77 (80)
Fewest Goals	155	1952-53 (70)
Fewest Goals Against	*131	1955-56 (70)

Longest Winning Streak
Over-all .... 12 Jan. 6-Feb. 3/68
Home .... 13 Nov. 2/43-Jan. 8/44 Jan. 30-Mar. 26/77
Away .... 8 Dec. 18/77-Jan. 18/78 Jan. 21-Feb. 21/82

Longest Undefeated Streak
Over-all .... 28 Dec. 18/77-Feb. 23/78 (23 wins, 5 ties)
Home .... *34 Nov. 1/76-Apr. 3/77 (28 wins, 6 ties)
Away .... *23 Nov. 27/74-Mar. 12/75 (14 wins, 9 ties)

Longest Losing Streak
Over-all .... 12 Feb. 13/26-Mar. 13/26
Home .... 7 Dec. 16/39-Jan. 18/40
Away .... 10 Dec. 1/25-Feb. 2/26

Longest Winless Streak
Over-all .... 12 Feb. 13-Mar. 13/26 (12 losses) Nov. 28-Dec. 29/35 (8 losses, 4 ties)
Home .... *15 Dec. 16/39-Mar. 7/40 (12 losses, 3 ties)
Away .... 12 Oct. 20-Dec. 13/51 (8 losses, 4 ties)

Most Shutouts, Season *22 1928-29 (44)
Most Pen. Mins., Season 1,464 1984-85 (80)
Most Goals, Game .... *16 Mar. 3/20 (Mtl. 16 at Que. 3)

Individual

Most Seasons	20	Henri Richard
Most Games	1,256	Henri Richard
Most Goals Career	544	Maurice Richard
Most Assists, Career	728	Guy Lafleur
Most Points Career	1,246	Guy Lafleur (518 goals, 728 assists)
Most Pen. Mins., Career	1,699	Chris Nilan
Most Shutouts, Career	75	George Hainsworth

Longest Consecutive Games Streak .... 560 Doug Jarvis (Oct. 8/75-Apr. 4/82)
Most Goals, Season .... 60 Steve Shutt (1976-77) Guy Lafleur (1977-78)
Most Assists, Season .... 82 Peter Mahovlich (1974-75)
Most Points, Season .... 136 Guy Lafleur (1976-77) (56 goals, 80 assists)
Most Pen. Mins., Season .... 358 Chris Nilan (1984-85)
Most Points, Defenseman Season .... 85 Larry Robinson (1976?-77) (19 goals, 66 assists)
Most Points, Center, Season .... 117 Peter Mahovlich (1974-75) (35 goals, 82 assists)
Most Points, Right Wing, Season .... *136 Guy Lafleur (1976-77) (56 goals, 80 assists)
Most Points, Left Wing, Season .... 110 Mats Naslund (1985-86) (43 goals, 67 assists)
Most Points, Rookie, Season .... 71 Mats Naslund (1982-83) (26 goals, 45 assists) Kjell Dahlin (1985-86) (32 goals, 39 assists)
Most Shutouts, Season .... *22 George Hainsworth (1982-29)
Most Goals, Game .... 6 Newsy Lalonde (Jan. 10/20)
Most Assists, Game .... 6 Elmer Lach (Feb. 6/43)
Most Points, Game .... 8 Maurice Richard (Dec. 28/44) Bert Olmstead (Jan. 9/54)

* NHL Record.

Coaching History

George Kennedy, 1917-18 to 1919-20; Léo Dandurand, 1920-21 to 1924-25; Cecil Hart, 1925-26 to 1931-32; Newsy Lalonde, 1932-33 to 1933-34; Newsy Lalonde and Léo Dandurand, 1934-35; Sylvio Mantha, 1935-36; Cecil Hart, 1936-37 to 1937-38; Cecil Hart and Jules Dugal, 1938-39; "Babe" Siebert, 1939*; Pit Lepine, 1939-40; Dick Irvin 1940-41 to 1954-55; Toe Blake, 1955-56 to 1967-68; Claude Ruel, 1968-69 to 1969-70; Claude Ruel and Al MacNeil, 1970-71; Scott Bowman, 1971-72 to 1978-79; Bernie Geoffrion and Claude Ruel, 1979-80; Claude Ruel, 1980-81; Bob Berry, 1981-82 to 1982-83; Bob Berry and Jacques Lemaire, 1983-84; Jacques Lemaire, 1984-85; Jean Perron, 1985-86 to date.

* Named coach in summer but died before 1939-40 season began.

Captains' History

Newsy Lalonde, 1917-18 to 1920-21; Sprague Cleghorn, 1921-22 to 1924-25; Bill Couture, 1925-26; Sylvio Mantha, 1926-27 to 1931-32; George Hainsworth, 1931-32; Sylvio Mantha, 1932-33 to 1935-36; Babe Seibert, 1936-37 to 1938-39; Walter Buswell, 1939-40; Toe Blake, 1940-41 to 1946-47; Toe Blake, Bill Durnan (co-captains) 1947-48; Emile Bouchard, 1948-49 to 1955-56; Maurice Richard, 1956-57 to 1959-60; Doug Harvey, 1960-61; Jean Beliveau, 1961-62 to 1970-71; Henri Richard, 1971-72 to 1974-75; Yvan Cournoyer, 1975-76 to 1978-79; Serge Savard, 1979-80, 1980-81; Bob Gainey, 1981-82 to 1985-86.

Retired Numbers

2	Doug Harvey	1947-1961
4	Jean Béliveau	1950-1971
7	Howie Morenz	1923-1937
9	Maurice Richard	1942-1960
10	Guy Lafleur	1971-1984
16	Henri Richard	1955-1975

All-time Record vs. Other Clubs

Regular Season

			At Home								On Road								Total				
	GP	W	L	T	GF	GA	PTS	GP	W	L	T	GF	GA	PTS	GP	W	L	T	GF	GA	PTS		
Boston	277	159	77	41	944	630	359	278	102	127	49	743	820	253	555	261	204	90	1687	1450	612		
Buffalo	47	25	14	8	192	150	58	47	16	20	11	148	146	43	94	41	34	19	340	296	101		
**Calgary	27	16	7	4	100	63	36	26	17	4	5	104	76	39	53	33	11	9	204	139	75		
Chicago	257	160	49	48	1001	605	368	256	119	87	50	709	680	288	513	279	136	98	1710	1285	656		
Detroit	263	161	60	42	927	582	364	263	92	120	51	669	737	235	526	253	180	93	1596	1319	599		
Edmonton	12	6	4	2	41	37	14	11	4	7	0	36	48	8	23	10	11	2	77	85	22		
Hartford	24	18	1	5	136	74	41	24	14	8	2	105	83	30	48	32	9	7	241	157	71		
Los Angeles	46	31	6	9	214	116	71	47	29	12	6	168	134	64	93	60	18	15	402	250	135		
Minnesota	40	27	8	5	179	101	59	41	23	10	8	153	106	54	81	50	18	13	322	207	113		
*New Jersey	21	15	3	3	101	56	33	22	19	3	0	117	51	38	43	34	6	3	218	107	71		
NY Islanders	26	15	6	5	101	81	35	28	11	14	3	81	100	25	54	26	20	8	182	181	60		
NY Rangers	257	170	54	33	1013	590	373	257	104	104	49	742	742	257	514	274	158	82	1762	1332	630		
Philadelphia	41	26	9	6	166	112	58	40	18	13	9	123	100	45	81	44	22	15	289	212	103		
Pittsburgh	47	41	2	4	247	113	86	46	25	13	8	173	134	58	93	66	15	12	420	247	144		
Quebec	24	14	5	5	105	77	33	24	8	14	2	82	93	18	48	22	19	7	187	170	51		
St. Louis	41	32	6	3	191	100	67	40	20	8	12	144	105	52	81	52	14	15	335	205	119		
Toronto	303	183	81	39	1072	740	405	304	105	155	44	780	913	254	607	288	236	83	1852	1653	659		
Vancouver	34	28	5	1	175	87	57	32	21	3	8	132	78	50	66	49	9	9	307	165	107		
Washington	27	23	1	3	150	52	49	28	14	8	6	107	67	34	55	37	9	9	257	119	83		
Winnipeg	11	9	2	0	61	29	18	12	6	3	3	53	38	15	23	15	5	3	114	67	33		
Defunct Clubs	231	148	58	25	779	469	321	230	98	97	35	586	606	231	461	246	155	60	1365	1075	552		
Totals	**2056**	**1307**	**458**	**291**	**7895**	**4864**	**2905**	**2056**	**865**	**830**	**361**	**5982**	**5857**	**2091**	**4112**	**2172**	**1288**	**652**	**13877**	**10721**	**4996**		

* Totals include those of Kansas City (1974-75, 1975-76) and Colorado (1976-77 through 1981-82)
** Totals include those of Atlanta (1972-73 through 1979-80)

Playoffs

	Series	W	L	GP	W	L	T	GF	GA	Last Mtg.	Round	Result
Boston	21	19	2	102	71	31	0	327	230	1986	DSF	W 3-0
Buffalo	3	1	2	15	6	9	0	52	45	1983	DSF	L 0-3
Calgary	1	1	0	5	4	1	0	15	13	1986	F	W 4-1
Chicago	17	12	5	81	50	29	2	261	185	1976	QF	W 4-0
Detroit	12	5	7	62	33	29	0	161	149	1978	QF	W 4-1
Edmonton	1	0	1	3	0	3	0	6	15	1981	P	L 0-3
Hartford	2	2	0	10	7	3	0	34	21	1986	DF	W 4-3
Minnesota	2	1	1	13	7	6	0	48	37	1980	QF	L 3-4
NY Islanders	3	2	1	17	10	7	0	48	44	1984	CF	L 2-4
NY Rangers	13	7	6	55	32	21	2	171	139	1986	CF	W 4-1
Philadelphia	2	2	0	9	8	1	0	33	22	1976	F	W 4-0
Quebec	3	1	2	18	9	9	0	60	48	1985	DF	L 3-4
St. Louis	3	3	0	12	12	0	0	42	14	1977	QF	W 4-0
Toronto	13	7	6	67	39	28	0	203	148	1979	QF	W 4-1
Vancouver	1	1	0	5	4	1	0	20	9	1975	QF	W 4-1
Defunct Clubs	3	1	2	6	1	2	3	5	9			
Totals	**100**	**65**	**35**	**480**	**293**	**180**	**7**	**1486**	**1128**			

Playoff Results 1986-82

Year	Round	Opponent	Result	GF	GA
1986	F	Calgary	W 4-1	15	13
	CF	NY Rangers	W 4-1	15	10
	DF	Hartford	W 4-3	17	13
	DSF	Boston	W 3-0	10	6
1985	DF	Quebec	L 3-4	24	24
	DSF	Boston	W 3-2	19	17
1984	CF	NY Islanders	L 2-4	12	17
	DF	Quebec	W 4-2	20	13
	DSF	Boston	W 3-0	10	2
1983	DSF	Buffalo	L 0-3	2	8
1982	DSF	Quebec	L 2-3	11	16

Abbreviations: Round: F – Final; CF – conference final; DF – division final; DSF – division semi-final; SF – semi-final; QF – quarter-final; P – preliminary round. GA – goals against; GF – goals for.

Entry Draft Selections 1986-72

1986
Pick
15	Mark Pederson
27	Benoit Brunet
57	Jyrkki Lumme
78	Brent Bobyck
94	Eric Aubertin
99	Mario Milani
120	Steve Bisson
141	Lyle Odelin
162	Rick Hayward
183	Antonin Routa
204	Eric Bohemier
225	Charlie Moore
246	Karel Svoboda

1985
Pick
12	Jose Charbonneau
16	Tom Chorske
33	Todd Richards
47	Rockey Dundas
75	Martin Desjardins
79	Brent Gilchrist
96	Tom Sagissor
117	Donald Dufresne
142	Ed Cristofoli
163	Mike Claringbull
184	Roger Beedon
198	Maurice Mansi
205	Chad Arthur
226	Mike Bishop
247	John Ferguson Jr.

1984
Pick
5	Petr Svoboda
9	Shayne Corson
29	Stephane Richer
51	Patrick Roy
54	Graeme Bonar
65	Lee Brodeur
95	Gerald Johannson
116	Jim Nesich
137	Scott MacTavish
158	Brad McCaughey
179	Eric Demers
199	Ron Annear
220	Dave Tanner
240	Troy Crosby

1983
Pick
17	Alfie Turcotte
26	Claude Lemieux
27	Sergio Momesso
35	Todd Francis
45	Daniel Letendre
78	John Kordic
98	Dan Wurst
118	Arto Javanainen
138	Vladislav Tretiak
158	Rob Bryden
178	Grant MacKay
198	Thomas Rundquist
218	Jeff Perpich
238	Jean Guy Bergeron

1982
Pick
19	Alain Heroux
31	Jocelyn Gauvreau
32	Kent Carlson
33	David Maley
40	Scott Sandelin
61	Scott Harlow
69	John Devoe
103	Kevin Houle
117	Ernie Vargas
124	Michael Dark
145	Hannu Jarvenpaa
150	Steve Smith
166	Tom Kolioupoulos
187	Brian Williams
208	Bob Emery
229	Darren Acheson
250	Bill Brauer

1981
Pick
7	Mark Hunter
18	Gilbert Delorme
19	Jan Ingman
32	Lars Eriksson

1981 (continued)
Pick
40	Chris Chelios
46	Dieter Hegen
82	Kjell Dahlin
88	Steve Rooney
124	Tom Anastos
145	Tom Kurvers
166	Paul Gess
187	Scott Ferguson
208	Danny Burrows

1980
Pick
1	Doug Wickenheiser
27	Ric Nattress
40	John Chabot
45	John Newberry
61	Craig Ludwig
82	Jeff Teal
103	Remi Gagne
124	Mike McPhee
145	Bill Norton
166	Steve Penney
187	John Schmidt
208	Scott Robinson

1979
Pick
27	Gaston Gingras
37	Mats Naslund
43	Craig Levie
44	Guy Carbonneau
58	Rick Wamsley
79	Dave Orleski
100	Yvon Joly
121	Greg Moffatt

1978
Pick
8	Dan Geoffrion
17	Dave Hunter
30	Dale Yakiwchuk
36	Ron Carter
42	Richard David
69	Kevin Reeves
86	Mike Boyd
103	Keith Acton
120	Jim Lawson
137	Larry Landon
154	Kevin Constantine
171	John Swain
186	Daniel Metivier
201	Vjacselev Fetisov
212	Jeff Mars
222	Greg Tignanelli
225	George Goulakos
227	Ken Moodie
229	Serge Leblanc
230	Bob Magnuson
231	Chris Nilan
232	Rick Wilson
233	Louis Sleigher
234	Doug Robb

1977
Pick
10	Mark Napier
18	Normand Dupont
36	Rod Langway
43	Alain Cote
46	Pierre Lagace
49	Moe Robinson
54	Gord Roberts
64	Bob Holland
90	Gaetan Rochette
108	Bill Himmelright
124	Richard Sevigny
137	Keith Hendrickson
140	Mike Reilly
152	Barry Barrett
154	Sid Tanchak
160	Mark Holden
162	Craig Laughlin
167	Daniel Poulin
169	Tom McDonnell
173	Cary Farelli
174	Carey Walker
176	Mark Wells
177	Stan Palmer
179	Jean Belisle
180	Bob Daly
182	Bob Boileau
183	John Costello

1976
Pick
12	Peter Lee
13	Rod Schutt
18	Bruce Baker
36	Barry Melrose
54	Bill Baker
72	Ed Clarey
90	Maurice Barrette
108	Pierre Brassard
118	Rich Gosselin
123	John Gregory
125	Bruce Horsch
127	John Tavella
129	Mark Davidson
131	Bill Wells
133	Ron Wilson

1975
Pick
9	Robin Sadler
15	Pierre Mondou
22	Brian Engblom
34	Kelly Greenbank
51	Paul Woods
52	Pat Hughes
70	Dave Gorman
88	Jim Turkiewicz
106	Michel Lachance
124	Tim Burke
142	Craig Norwich
158	Paul Clarke
173	Bob Ferriter
187	David Bell
198	Carl Jackson
204	Michel Brisebois
208	Roger Bourque
211	Jim Lundquist
214	Don Madson
215	Bob Bain

1974
Pick
5	Cam Connor
7	Doug Risebrough
10	Rick Chartraw
12	Mario Tremblay
15	Gord McTavish
30	Gary MacGregor
33	Gilles Lupien
51	Marty Howe
61	Barry Legge
69	Mike McKegney
105	John Stewart
123	Joe Micheletti
140	Jamie Hislop
157	Gord Stewart
172	Chuck Lucksa
187	Cliff Cox
199	Dave Lumley
209	Mike Hobin

1973
Pick
8	Bob Gainey
17	Glen Goldup
22	Peter Marrin
32	Ron Andruff
37	Ed Humphreys
56	Alan Hangsleban
64	Richard Latulippe
80	Gerry Gibbons
96	Dennis Patry
112	Michel Belisle
128	Mario Desjardins
143	Bob Wright
153	Alain Labrecque
166	Gord Halliday
167	Cap Raeder
168	Louis Chiasson

1972
Pick
4	Steve Shutt
6	Michel Larocque
8	Dave Gardner
14	John Van Boxmeer
46	Ed Gilbert
62	Dave Ellenbaas
66	Bill Nyrop
94	D'Arcy Ryan
110	Yves Archambault
126	Graham Parsons
142	Ed Bumbacco
151	Fred Riggall
152	Ron Leblanc

Club Directory

Montreal Forum
2313 St. Catherine Street West
Montreal, Quebec H3H 1N2
Phone 514/932-2528
TWX 610-421-3275
ENVOY ID   TM.MTL
Capacity: 16,074

Board of Directors

Morgan McCammon   Serge Savard
Ronald Corey   Jean Beliveau
Eric H. Molson

President	Ronald Corey
Managing Director	Serge Savard
Senior Vice-President, Corporate Affairs	Jean Beliveau
Special Ambassador	Maurice Richard
Senior Vice-President, Operations	Aldo Giampaolo
Vice-President, Finance and Administration	Fred Steer
Vice-President, Marketing	Francois-Xavier Seigneur
Head Coach	Jean Perron
Assistant Coach	Jacques Laperriere
Director of Hockey Personnel & Assistant to the Managing Director	Jacques Lemaire
Director of Recruitment & Assistant to the Managing Director	Andre Boudrias
Director of Player Development and Scout	Claude Ruel
Chief Scout	Doug Robinson
Director of Advertising Sales	Floyd Curry
Director of Public Relations	Claude Mouton
Director of Press Relations	Michéle Lapointe
Director of Special Events	Camil DesRoches
Director of Publications	Yvon Robert
Director of Purchasing	Robert Loiseau
Club Physician	Dr. D.G. Kinnear
Athletic Therapist	Gene Gaudet (PhD.)
Head Trainer	Eddy Palchak
Physiotherapist	Gene Gaudet
Assistant Athletic Therapist	Gaetan Lefebvre
Assistant Trainer	Sylvain Toupin
Box Office Supervisor	Rene St-Jacques
Location of Press Box	Suspended above ice — West Side
Location of Radio, TV Booth	Suspended above ice — East Side
Dimensions of Rink	200 x 85 feet
Ends of Rink	Herculite extends above boards all around rink
Club Colors	Red, White and Blue
Club trains at	Montreal Forum
Play-by-play, Radio/TV	Dick Irvin (English) Claude Quenneville, Lionel Duval, Richard Garneau, Gilles Tremblay (French)
TV Channels	CBMT (6), CBFT (2)
Radio Stations	CBF (690), CFCF (600)

Guy Carbonneau, Larry Robinson and Chris Chelios

New Jersey Devils

1985-86 Results: 28w-49L-3T 59 PTS. Sixth, Patrick Division

Year-by-Year Record

		Home			Road			Overall						
Season	GP	W	L	T	W	L	T	W	L	T	GF	GA	Pts.	Finished	Playoff Result
1985-86	80	17	21	2	11	28	1	28	49	3	300	374	59 6th,	Patrick Div.	Out of Playoffs
1984-85	80	13	21	6	7	31	2	22	48	10	264	346	54 5th,	Patrick Div.	Out of Playoffs
1983-84	80	10	28	2	7	28	5	17	56	7	231	350	41 5th,	Patrick Div.	Out of Playoffs
1982-83	80	11	20	9	6	29	5	17	49	14	230	338	48 5th,	Patrick Div.	Out of Playoffs
1981-82	80	14	21	5	4	28	8	18	49	13	241	362	49 5th,	Smythe Div.	Out of Playoffs
1980-81	80	15	16	9	7	29	4	22	45	13	258	344	57 5th,	Smythe Div.	Out of Playoffs
1979-80	80	12	20	8	7	28	5	19	48	13	234	308	51 6th,	Smythe Div.	Out of Playoffs
1978-79	80	8	24	8	7	29	4	15	53	12	210	331	42 4th,	Smythe Div.	Out of Playoffs
1977-78	80	17	14	9	2	26	12	19	40	21	257	305	59 2nd,	Smythe Div.	Lost Prelim. Round
1976-77	80	12	20	8	8	26	6	20	46	14	226	307	54 5th,	Smythe Div.	Out of Playoffs
1975-76	80	8	24	8	4	32	4	12	56	12	190	351	36 5th,	Smythe Div.	Out of Playoffs
1974-75	80	12	20	8	3	34	3	15	54	11	184	328	41 5th,	Smythe Div.	Out of Playoffs

Schedule

Home				Away			
Oct.	Sat.	11	Boston	**Oct.**	Thur.	9	NY Rangers
	Wed.	15	Vancouver		Sat.	18	Pittsburgh
	Fri.	17	Toronto		Tue.	21	NY Islanders
	Thur.	23	Los Angeles		Sat.	25	Washington
	Thur.	30	NY Islanders		Wed.	29	Pittsburgh
Nov.	Sat.	1	Buffalo	**Nov.**	Tue.	4	Philadelphia
	Thur.	6	Philadelphia		Sun.	9	Winnipeg
	Wed.	12	Detroit		Sat.	15	Boston
	Fri.	14	Pittsburgh		Wed.	19	Detroit
	Mon.	17	NY Rangers		Sat.	22	Minnesota
Dec.	Tue.	2	NY Rangers		Sun.	23	Chicago
	Thur.	4	Minnesota		Wed.	26	St. Louis
	Sat.	6	Buffalo		Sat.	29	Los Angeles
	Thur.	11	NY Islanders	**Dec.**	Tue.	9	Washington
	Sun.	14	Montreal		Sat.	13	NY Islanders
	Wed.	17	Toronto		Sat.	20	Montreal
	Fri.	19	Washington		Tue.	23	NY Rangers
	Fri.	26	NY Rangers		Sat.	27	Quebec
	Tue.	30	Calgary	**Jan.**	Sat.	3	Toronto
Jan.	Fri.	2	Boston		Tue.	6	Philadelphia
	Thur.	8	Quebec		Wed.	14	Chicago
	Sat.	10	Vancouver*		Tue.	20	Washington
	Mon.	12	Hartford		Mon.	26	NY Rangers
	Fri.	16	Winnipeg		Wed.	28	Los Angeles
	Sun.	18	Washington		Fri.	30	Vancouver
	Thur.	22	Calgary		Sat.	31	Calgary
	Sat.	24	Philadelphia	**Feb.**	Sat.	14	Detroit*
Feb.	Sat.	7	Philadelphia*		Sat.	21	Pittsburgh
	Sun.	8	Pittsburgh		Sat.	28	Montreal
	Wed.	18	Hartford	**Mar.**	Sun.	1	Hartford*
	Sun.	22	NY Islanders		Tue.	3	Washington
	Wed.	25	Edmonton	**Mar.**	Thur.	5	Buffalo
Mar.	Sat.	7	Chicago		Sun.	8	Philadelphia*
	Wed.	11	Philadelphia		Sat.	14	NY Islanders
	Fri.	13	NY Islanders		Tue.	17	Edmonton
	Mon.	23	Edmonton		Wed.	18	Winnipeg
	Fri.	27	Minnesota		Sat.	21	St. Louis
	Sun.	29	St. Louis*		Wed.	25	NY Rangers
	Tue.	31	Pittsburgh	**April**	Thur.	2	Pittsburgh
April	Sun.	5	Washington		Sat.	4	Quebec

* Denotes afternoon game.

Home Starting Times: . . . . 7:35 p.m.
Except Jan. 10, Feb. 7, Mar. 29 . . . . . 1:35 p.m.
Jan. 18, Feb. 22,
Mar. 7, Apr. 5 . . . . 5:05 p.m.

Franchise date: June 30, 1982. Transferred from Denver to New Jersey. Previously transferred from Kansas City to Denver, Colorado.

13th NHL Season

John Maclean

1986-87 Player Personnel

FORWARDS

	Ht.	Wt.	Place of Birth	Date	1985-86 Club
ADAMS, Greg	6-2	185	Nelson, B.C.	8/1/63	New Jersey
ANDERSEN, John	6-0	175	Toronto, Ont.	1/18/68	Oshawa
ANDERSON, Perry	6-0	195	Barrie, Ont.	10/14/61	New Jersey
BRADY, Neil	6-2	180	Montreal, Que.	4/12/68	Medicine Hat
BRICKLEY, Andy	6-0	195	Melrose, Mass.	8/9/61	Maine
BRIDGMAN, Mel	6-0	190	Trenton, Ont.	4/28/55	New Jersey
BROTEN, Aaron	5-10	175	Roseau, Minn.	11/14/60	New Jersey
CARLSSON, Anders	5-11	185	Galve, Sweden	11/25/60	Sodertalje (Sweden)
CHERNOMAZ, Rich	5-9	175	Selkirk, Man.	9/1/63	Maine
CONACHER, Pat	5-8	185	Edmonton, Alta.	5/1/59	New Jersey
CROWDER, Troy	6-4	200	Sudbury, Ont.	5/3/68	Hamilton
DORIAN, Dan	5-9	180	New York, N.Y.	3/2/63	New Jersey
EVTUSHEVSKI, Greg	5-8	180	St. Paul, Alta.	5/4/65	Maine-Kamloops
FLOYD, Larry	5-8	180	Peterborough, Ont.	5/1/61	Maine
GAGNE, Paul	5-10	180	Iroquois Falls, Ont.	2/6/62	New Jersey
HENDERSON, Archie	6-6	220	Calgary, Alta.	2/17/57	Maine
JOHNSON, Mark	5-9	160	Madison, Wis.	9/22/57	New Jersey
LOISELLE, Claude	5-11	190	Ottawa, Ont.	5/29/63	Detroit-Adirondack
LUDVIG, Jan	5-10	190	Liberec, Czech.	9/17/61	New Jersey
MacLEAN, John	6-0	195	Oshawa, Ont.	11/20/64	New Jersey
McKINLEY, Jamie	6-1	165	Moncton, N.B.	5/1/67	Guelph
McMILLAN, Bill	6-2	185	North Bay, Ont.	4/3/67	Peterborough
McNAB, Peter	6-3	205	Vancouver, B.C.	5/8/52	New Jersey
MULLER, Kirk	6-0	195	Kingston, Ont.	2/8/66	New Jersey
STEFANSKI, Bud	5-10	170	S. Porcupine, Ont.	4/28/55	Maine
STEWART, Al	5-11	175	Fort St. John, B.C.	1/31/64	New Jersey-Maine
SULLIMAN, Doug	5-9	195	Glace Bay, N.S.	8/29/59	New Jersey
TODD, Kevin	5-11	180	Winnipeg, Man.	5/4/68	Prince Albert
TROTTIER, Rocky	5-11	185	Climax, Sask.	4/11/64	Maine
TSUJIURA, Steve	5-5	155	Coaldale, Alta.	2/28/62	Maine
VERBEEK, Pat	5-9	190	Sarnia, Ont.	5/24/64	New Jersey

DEFENSEMEN

	Ht.	Wt.	Place of Birth	Date	1985-86 Club
BLOMQVIST, Timo	6-0	200	Helsinki, Finland	1/23/61	Binghamton
BOLDUC, Michel	6-2	210	Angegardian, Que.	3/13/61	Maine
CIRELLA, Joe	6-3	210	Hamilton, Ont.	5/9/63	New Jersey
DANEYKO, Ken	6-0	195	Windsor, Ont.	4/16/64	New Jersey-Maine
DAVEY, Neil	6-2	205	Edmonton, Alta.	12/29/65	Maine-Toledo
DRIVER, Bruce	6-0	185	Toronto, Ont.	4/29/62	New Jersey-Maine
FERGUSON, Ian	6-2	175	Winnipeg, Man.	6/24/66	Oshawa
HEPPLE, Alan	5-9	200	Blaydon-on-Tyne, Eng.	8/16/63	New Jersey-Maine
HIEMER, Uli	6-1	190	Fussen, W. Germany	9/21/62	New Jersey-Maine
HUSCROFT, Jamie	6-2	200	Creston, B.C.	1/9/67	Seattle
LANIEL, Marc	6-2	185	Oshawa, Ont.	1/6/68	Oshawa
MARK, Gordie	6-3	205	Edmonton, Alta.	9/10/64	Maine
PICHETTE, Dave	6-3	200	Grand Falls, Nfld.	2/4/60	New Jersey-Maine
RICHMOND, Steve	6-1	205	Chicago, Ill.	12/11/59	NY Rangers-New Haven-Detroit-Adirondack
VELISCHEK, Randy	6-1	205	Montreal, Que.	2/10/62	New Jersey-Maine
WOLANIN, Craig	6-3	205	Grosse Pointe, Mich.	7/27/67	New Jersey

GOALTENDERS

	Ht.	Wt.	Place of Birth	Date	1985-86 Club
BILLINGTON, Craig	5-10	150	London, Ont.	9/11/66	New Jersey-Belleville
BURKE, Sean	6-3	180	Windsor, Ont.	1/29/67	Toronto (OHL)
CHABOT, Frederic	5-10	160	Habartville, Que.	2/12/68	St. Foy (Quebec Midget)
CHEVRIER, Alain	5-8	170	Cornwall, Ont.	4/23/61	New Jersey
FRIESEN, Karl	6-0	165	Winnipeg, Man.	6/30/58	Maine
McLEAN, Kirk	6-0	175	Willowdale, Ont.	6/26/66	New Jersey-Oshawa
TERRERI, Chris	5-9	150	Warwick, R.I.	11/15/64	Providence College

Coach and General Manager

CARPENTER, DOUG
Coach, New Jersey Devils. Born in Cornwall, Ont., July 1, 1942.
Doug Carpenter will be entering his third season since being named coach of the Devils on May 31, 1984. A graduate of McGill University, Carpenter spent two seasons coaching the St. Catharines Black Hawks of the AHL. He started coaching in the International Hockey League with the Flint Generals. In 1980, he led the Cornwall Royals to the Memorial Cup Championships. Carpenter played nine seasons in the Eastern Hockey League before he started coaching.

NHL Coaching Record

Team	Season	Games	Regular Season				Playoffs			
			W	L	T	%	Games	W	L	%
New Jersey	1984-85	80	22	48	10	.338	....	....	....	....
New Jersey	1985-86	80	28	49	3	.369	....	....	....	....
NHL Totals		**160**	**50**	**97**	**13**	**.353**	....	....	....	....

McNAB, MAXWELL DOUGLAS (MAX)
General Manager, New Jersey Devils. Born in Watson, Sask., June 21, 1924.
Max McNab was named to the position of General Manager of the Devils on Nov. 22, 1983, replacing Billy MacMillan. McNab joined the Devils' organization in 1982 following a six-year tenure as general manager of the Washington Capitals. The Watson, Sask., native was appointed GM of the Capitals on Dec. 29, 1975 and played a major role in building the franchise into a Stanley Cup contender. Prior to his NHL front office career, McNab had a distinguished career in all phases of professional hockey. During his playing career, which included two seasons in the NHL with Detroit, he scored 292 goals. He began coaching in the Western Hockey League at New Westminster and continued in San Francisco and Vancouver. In 1966 he became coach and general manager at San Diego (WHL) and maintained the dual role until 1971 when he became vice-president and GM of the team. At the start of the 1974-75 season, McNab was named President of the Central Hockey League, a post he held until moving to Washington.

1985-86 Scoring

Regular Season

*—rookie

Pos	#	Player	Team	GP	G	A	Pts	+/-	PIM	PP	SH	GW	OT	S	%
F	24	Greg Adams	N.J	78	35	42	77	7−	30	10	0	2	0	202	17.3
F	9	Kirk Muller	N.J	77	25	41	66	20−	45	5	1	1	0	168	14.9
F	18	Mel Bridgman	N.J	78	23	40	63	1−	80	5	1	1	0	136	16.9
F	12	Mark Johnson	N.J	80	21	41	62	13−	16	6	1	3	0	167	12.6
F	15	John Maclean	N.J	74	21	36	57	3−	112	1	0	4	0	139	15.1
F	16	Pat Verbeek	N.J	76	25	28	53	24−	79	4	1	0	0	159	15.7
F	22	Doug Sulliman	N.J	73	21	22	43	10−	20	6	1	5	1	139	15.1
F	7	Peter McNab	N.J	71	19	24	43	11−	14	6	0	0	0	93	20.4
F	10	Aaron Broten	N.J	66	18	25	43	2	26	4	0	1	1	157	11.5
F	19	Rich Preston	N.J	76	19	22	41	3	65	3	0	2	0	117	16.2
F	17	Paul Gagne	N.J	47	19	19	38	15−	14	4	0	3	0	91	20.9
D	2	Joe Cirella	N.J	66	6	23	29	12−	147	2	0	0	0	89	6.7
D	20	Tim Higgins	N.J	59	9	17	26	7	47	2	0	1	0	90	10.0
D	28	Uli Hiemer	N.J	50	8	16	24	1−	61	6	0	1	0	100	8.0
D	8	Dave Pichette	N.J	33	7	12	19	11−	22	4	0	1	1	59	11.9
D	11	Perry Anderson	N.J	51	7	12	19	7−	91	1	0	1	0	61	11.5
D	23	Bruce Driver	N.J	40	3	15	18	9	32	1	0	0	0	64	4.7
D	6	*Craig Wolanin	N.J	44	2	16	18	7−	74	0	0	1	0	45	4.4
D	25	Dave Lewis	N.J	69	0	15	15	0	81	0	0	0	0	38	.0
F	29	Jan Ludvig	N.J	42	5	9	14	16−	63	0	0	0	0	72	6.9
D	3	*Ken Daneyko	N.J	44	0	10	10	0	100	0	0	0	0	48	.0
D	27	Randy Velischek	N.J	47	2	7	9	20−	39	0	0	0	0	24	8.3
D	4	Bob Lorimer	N.J	46	2	2	4	13−	52	0	0	0	0	28	7.1
G	30	*Alain Chevrier	N.J	37	0	3	3	0	6	0	0	0	0		
F	14	*Dan Dorion	N.J	3	1	1	2	1−	0	0	0	0	0	6	16.7
F	14	Pat Conacher	N.J	2	0	2	2	2	0	0	0	0	0	3	.0
D	5	*Don Dietrich	N.J	11	0	2	2	8−	10	0	0	0	0	14	.0
G	33	*Craig Billington	N.J	18	0	1	1	0	0	0	0	0	0		
D	8	Murray Brumwell	N.J	1	0	0	0	0	0	0	0	0	0		
D	5	*Alan Hepple	N.J	1	0	0	0	1−	0	0	0	0	0	3	.0
G	34	*Kirk McLean	N.J	2	0	0	0	0	0	0	0	0	0		
G	34	*Sam St. Laurent	N.J	4	0	0	0	0	0	0	0	0	0		
F	14	*Allan Stewart	N.J	4	0	0	0	1−	21	0	0	0	0		.0

Craig Wolanin

Club Records

Team

(Figures in brackets for season records are games played; records for fewest points, wins, ties, losses, goals, goals against are for 70 or more games)

Most Points	.59	1977-78 (80)
		1985-86 (80)
Most Wins	.28	1985-86 (80)
Most Ties	.21	1977-78 (80)
Most Losses	.56	1975-76 (80)
		1983-84 (80)
Most Goals	.300	1985-86 (80)
Most Goals Against	.374	1985-86 (80)
Fewest Points	.36	1975-76 (80)
Fewest Wins	.12	1975-76 (80)
Fewest Ties	.3	1985-86 (80)
Fewest Losses	.40	1977-78 (80)
Fewest Goals	.184	1974-75 (80)
Fewest Goals Against	.305	1977-78 (80)

Longest Winning Streak
Over-all . . . . 3 Several times
Home . . . . 4 Feb. 26-
Mar. 8/86
Mar. 27-
April 6/86

Away . . . . 3 Dec. 2-9/79

Longest Undefeated Streak
Over-all . . . . 9 Dec. 11-27/85
(5 wins, 4 ties)
Home . . . . 6 Feb. 24-
Mar. 19/78
(3 wins, 3 ties)
Dec. 7-27/85
(3 wins, 3 ties)

Away . . . . 4 Dec. 11-26/85
(2 wins, 2 ties)

Longest Losing Streak
Over-all . . . . 14 Dec. 30/75-
Jan. 29/76
Home . . . . 9 Dec. 22/85-
Feb. 6/86
Away . . . . 12 Oct. 19/83-
Dec. 1/83

Longest Winless Streak
Over-all . . . . 27 Feb. 12-
Apr. 4/76
Home . . . . 14 Feb. 12-
Mar. 30/76
(10 losses, 4 ties)
Feb. 4-
Mar. 31/79
(12 losses, 2 ties)

Away . . . . 32 Nov. 12/77-
Mar. 15/78
(22 losses, 10 ties)
Most Shutouts, Season 1983-84 (80)
Most Pen. Mins., 1980-81 (80)
Season 1,418
Most Goals, Game . . . . 9 Apr. 1/79
(St.L. 5 at Col. 9)
Feb. 12/82
(Que. 2 at Col. 9)

Individual

Most Seasons	.21	Mike Kitchen
Most Games	.474	Mike Kitchen
Most Goals, Career	.153	Wilf Paiement
Most Assists, Career	.183	Wilf Paiement
Most Points, Career	.336	Wilf Paiement
		(153 goals, 183 assists)
Most Pen. Mins., Career	.568	Wilf Paiement
Most Shutouts, Career	.1	Several players

Longest Consecutive
Games Streak . . . . .130 Aaron Broten
(Dec. 4/82-Apr. 1/84)
Most Goals, Season . . . . . . .41 Wilf Paiement
(1976-77)
Most Assists, Season . . . . . .56 Wilf Paiement
(1977-78)
Most Points, Season . . . . . . .87 Wilf Paiement
(1977-78)
(31 goals, 56 assists)
Most Pen. Mins., Season . . .209 Steve Durbano
(1975-76)
Most Points, Defenseman
Season . . . . .62 Rob Ramage
(1980-81)
(20 goals, 42 assists)
Most Points, Center
Season . . . . .71 Guy Charron
(1975-76)
(27 goals, 42 assists)
Most Points, Right Wing,
Season . . . . .87 Wilf Paiement
(1977-78)
(31 goals, 56 assists)
Most Points, Left Wing,
Season . . . . .60 Brent Ashton
(1981-82)
(24 goals, 36 assists)

Most Points, Rookie,
Season . . . . .60 Barry Beck
(1977-78)
(22 goals, 38 assists)
Most Shutouts, Season . . . . . .1 Several players
Most Goals, Game . . . . .4 Bob MacMillan
(Jan. 8/82)
Most Assists, Game . . . . . . .4 Several players
Most Points, Game . . . . . . .5 Several players
* NHL Record.

Coaching History

(Kansas City) Bep Guidolin, 1974-75; Bep Guidolin, Sid Abel, and Eddie Bush, 1975-76; (Colorado) John Wilson, 1976-77; Pat Kelly, 1977-78; Pat Kelly, Aldo Guidolin, 1978-79; Don Cherry, 1979-80; Bill MacMillan, 1980-81; Bert Marshall and Marshall Johnston, 1981-82; (New Jersey) Bill MacMillan, 1982-83; Bill MacMillan and Tom McVie, 1983-84; Doug Carpenter, 1984-85 to date.

Captains' History

Simon Nolet, 1974-75 to 1976-77; Wilf Paiement, 1977-78; Gary Croteau, 1978-79; Mike Christie, Rene Robert, Lanny McDonald, 1979-80; Lanny McDonald, 1980-81; Lanny McDonald, Rob Ramage, 1981-82; Don Lever, 1982-83; Don Lever, Mel Bridgman, 1983-84; Mel Bridgman, 1984-85, 1985-86.

All-time Record vs. Other Clubs

Regular Season

			At Home							On Road							Total					
	GP	W	L	T	GF	GA	PTS	GP	W	L	T	GF	GA	PTS	GP	W	L	T	GF	GA	PTS
Boston	21	1	13	7	53	81	9	22	6	16	0	63	99	12	43	7	29	7	116	180	21
Buffalo	21	1	16	4	57	92	6	22	2	18	2	58	110	6	43	3	34	6	115	202	12
**Calgary	26	6	17	3	69	101	15	26	2	20	4	61	125	8	52	8	37	7	130	226	23
Chicago	28	11	12	5	90	92	27	27	3	19	5	69	121	11	55	14	31	10	159	213	38
Detroit	22	11	6	5	82	62	27	21	6	14	1	63	98	13	43	17	20	6	145	160	40
Edmonton	14	6	7	1	50	52	13	14	2	10	2	49	79	6	28	8	17	3	99	121	19
Hartford	11	4	5	2	35	47	10	12	3	7	2	39	47	8	23	7	12	4	7	94	18
Los Angeles	24	8	12	4	78	96	20	24	1	19	4	70	136	6	48	9	31	8	148	232	26
Minnesota	26	12	11	3	86	84	27	27	4	18	5	62	115	13	53	16	29	8	148	199	40
Montreal	22	3	19	0	51	117	6	21	3	15	3	56	101	9	43	6	34	3	107	218	15
NY Islanders	32	7	20	5	94	138	19	32	1	28	3	75	172	5	64	8	48	8	169	310	24
NY Rangers	33	9	20	4	103	139	22	31	8	19	4	95	137	20	64	17	39	8	198	276	42
Philadelphia	31	9	20	2	106	144	20	32	0	29	1	54	145	5	63	11	49	3	160	289	25
Pittsburgh	29	12	11	6	107	111	30	30	9	19	2	96	123	20	59	21	30	8	203	234	50
Quebec	12	6	6	0	50	46	12	11	6	7	1	37	56	7	23	12	13	1	87	102	19
St. Louis	28	8	13	7	86	85	23	27	3	21	3	75	130	6	55	11	34	10	161	215	32
Toronto	21	5	7	9	72	73	19	22	4	16	2	71	102	10	43	9	23	11	143	175	29
Vancouver	30	11	14	5	91	107	27	30	5	15	10	94	117	20	60	16	29	15	185	224	47
Washington	30	10	14	6	92	93	26	29	4	22	3	74	136	11	59	14	36	9	166	229	37
Winnipeg	11	5	4	2	40	40	12	12	2	9	1	28	49	5	23	7	13	3	68	99	17
Defunct Clubs	8	4	2	2	25	19	10	8	2	3	3	19	27	7	16	6	5	5	44	46	17
Totals	4480	149	249	82	1517	1819	380	480	78	344	61	1308	2225	211	960	227	593	143	2825	4044	591

** Totals include those of Atlanta (1974-75 through 1979-80)

Playoffs

	Series	W	L	GP	W	L	T	GF	GA	Last Mtg.	Round	Result
Philadelphia	1	0	1	2	0	2	0	3	6	1978	P	L 0-2
Totals	1	0	1	2	0	2	0	3	6			

Abbreviations: Round: F – Final; **CF** – conference final; **DF** – division final; **DSF** – division semi-final; **SF** – semi-final; **QF** – quarter-final; **P** – preliminary round. **GA** – goals against; **GF** – goals for.

Entry Draft Selections 1986-74

1986
Pick
3	Neil Brady
24	Todd Copeland
45	Janne Ojanen
62	Marc Laniel
66	Anders Carlsson
108	Troy Crowder
129	Kevin Todd
150	Ryan Pardoski
171	Scott McCormack
192	Frederic Chabot
213	John Andersen
236	Doug Kirton

1985
Pick
3	Craig Wolanin
24	Sean Burke
32	Eric Weinrich
45	Myles O'Connor
66	Gregg Polak
108	Bill McMillan
129	Kevin Schrader
150	Ed Krayer
171	Jamie Huscroft
192	Terry Shold
213	Jamie McKinley
234	David Williams

1984
Pick
2	Kirk Muller
23	Craig Billington
44	Neil Davey
74	Paul Ysebaert
86	Jon Morris
107	Kirk McLean
128	Ian Ferguson
149	Vladimir Kames
170	Mike Roth
190	Mike Peluso
211	Jarkko Piiparinen
231	Chris Kiene

1983
Pick
6	John MacLean
24	Shawn Evans
87	Chris Terreri
108	Gordon Mark
129	Greg Evtushevski
150	Vjacselev Fetisov
171	Jay Octeau
192	Alexi Chernykh
213	Allan Stewart
234	Aleksei Kasatonov

1982
Pick
8	Rocky Trottier
18	Ken Daneyko
43	Pat Verbeek
54	Dave Kasper
85	Scott Brydges
106	Mike Moher
127	Paul Fulcher
148	John Hutchings
169	Alan Hepple
190	Brent Shaw
207	Tony Gilliard
211	Scott Fusco
232	Dan Dorian

1981
Pick
5	Joe Cirella
26	Rich Chernomaz
48	Ullie Hiemer
66	Gus Greco
87	Doug Speck
108	Bruce Driver
129	Jeff Larmer
150	Tony Arima
171	Tim Army
192	John Johannson

1980
Pick
19	Paul Gagne
22	Joe Ward
64	Rick LaFerriere
85	Ed Cooper
106	Aaron Broten
127	Dan Fascinato
148	Andre Hidi
169	Shawn MacKenzie
190	Bob Jansch

1979
Pick
1	Rob Ramage
64	Steve Peters
85	Gary Dillon
106	Bob Attwell

1978
Pick
4	Mike Gillis
27	Merlin Malinowski
41	Paul Messier
58	Dave Watson
73	Tim Thomlison
74	Rod Guimont
91	John Hynes
108	Andy Clark
125	John Oliver
142	Kevin Krook
159	Jeff Jensen
174	Bo Ericsson
190	Jari Viitala
204	Ulf Zetterstrom

1977
Pick
2	Barry Beck
38	Doug Berry
47	Randy Pierce
92	Daniel Lempe
110	Rick Doyle
126	Joe Contini
142	Jack Hughes

1976
Pick
11	Paul Gardner
38	Mike Kitchen
74	Rick McIntyre
92	Larry Skinner

1975
Pick
2	Barry Dean
20	Don Cairns
38	Neil Lyseng
56	Ron Delorme
74	Terry McDonald
92	Eric Sanderson
110	Bill Oleschuk
128	Joe Baker
145	Scott Williams

1974
Pick
2	Wilf Paiement
20	Glen Burdon
38	Bob Bourne
56	Roger Lemelin
74	Mark Lomenda
92	John Shewchuk
110	Mike Boland

Club Directory

Byrne Meadowlands Arena
P.O. Box 504
East Rutherford, N.J. 07073
Phone 201/935-6050
TWX 710-989-0295
ENVOY ID   TM.NJ
Capacity: 19,040

Chairman	John J. McMullen
President	Robert Butera
Vice President, Hockey Operations and General Manager	Max McNab
Vice President, Communications and Advertising	Larry Brooks
Vice President, Marketing and Sales	Jerry Dailey
Head Coach	Doug Carpenter
Assistant Coach	Ron Smith
Director of Player Personnel	Marshall Johnston
Assistant Director of Player Personnel	David Conte
Special Assignment Scout	Bob Hoffmeyer
Scouting Staff	David Conte, Frankie Jay, Russ LeClair, Ed Tomlinson, Claude Carrier
Athletic Trainer	Chris Ipson
Equipment Manager	Keith Parker
Physical Conditioning Consultant	Dimitri Lopuchin
Team Orthopedist	Dr. Barry Fisher
Team Internist	Dr. Richard Commentucci
Team Dentist	Dr. H. Hugh Gardy
Director, Public and Media Relations	David Freed
Director, Operations	Peter McMullen
Secretary	Susan Ross
Controller	Bob Wolff
Accountant	Ray Carlucci
Bookkeeper	Florence Dubers
Secretary	Patty Roy
Director of Ticket Operations	Terry Farmer
Administrative Assistant	Tom Shine
Regional Sales Managers	Mike Gerlowski, Sue Levy, Garry Albert, Ken Ferriter
Secretary to the President	Jill Polansky
Secretary to the General Manager	Marie Carnevale
Receptionist	Jelsa Belotta
Team Photographer	John Tremmel
Location of Press Box	Section 108, center ice
Location of Broadcast Booth	Front, Section 234
Dimensions of Rink	200 feet X 85 feet
Club Colors	Red, Green and White
Television Outlets	Sportschannel
Television Announcers	TBD
Radio Station	WMCA (570 AM)
Radio Announcers	TBD

Peter McNab (7) and Kirk Muller check Hartford's Kevin Dineen.

New York Islanders

1985-86 Results: 36w-38L-6T 78 PTS. Fourth, Patrick Division

Year-by-Year Record

Season	GP	Home W	L	T	Road W	L	T	Overall W	L	T	GF	GA	Pts.	Finished	Playoff Result
1985-86	80	22	11	7	17	18	5	39	29	12	327	284	90	3rd, Patrick Div.	Lost Div. Semi-Final
1984-85	80	26	11	3	14	23	3	40	34	6	345	312	86	3rd, Patrick Div.	Lost Div. Final
1983-84	80	28	11	1	22	15	3	50	26	4	357	269	104	1st, Patrick Div.	Lost Final
1982-83	**80**	**26**	**11**	**3**	**16**	**15**	**9**	**42**	**26**	**12**	**302**	**226**	**96**	**2nd, Patrick Div.**	**Won Stanley Cup**
1981-82	**80**	**33**	**3**	**4**	**21**	**13**	**6**	**54**	**16**	**10**	**385**	**250**	**118**	**1st, Patrick Div.**	**Won Stanley Cup**
1980-81	**80**	**23**	**6**	**11**	**25**	**12**	**3**	**48**	**18**	**14**	**355**	**260**	**110**	**1st, Patrick Div.**	**Won Stanley Cup**
1979-80	**80**	**26**	**9**	**5**	**13**	**19**	**8**	**39**	**28**	**13**	**281**	**247**	**91**	**2nd, Patrick Div.**	**Won Stanley Cup**
1978-79	80	31	3	6	20	12	8	51	15	14	358	214	116	1st, Patrick Div.	Lost Semi-Final
1977-78	80	29	3	8	19	14	7	48	17	15	334	210	111	1st, Patrick Div.	Lost Quarter-Final
1976-77	80	24	11	5	23	10	7	47	21	12	288	193	106	2nd, Patrick Div.	Lost Semi-Final
1975-76	80	24	8	8	18	13	9	42	21	17	297	190	101	2nd, Patrick Div.	Lost Semi-Final
1974-75	80	22	6	12	11	19	10	33	25	22	264	221	88	3rd, Patrick Div.	Lost Semi-Final
1973-74	78	13	17	9	6	24	9	19	41	18	182	247	56	8th, East Div.	Out of Playoffs
1972-73	78	10	25	4	2	35	2	12	60	6	170	347	30	8th, East Div.	Out of Playoffs

Schedule

		Home				Away
Oct.	Thur.	16 Washington		**Oct.**	Thur.	9 Chicago
	Sat.	18 NY Rangers			Sat.	11 Los Angeles
	Tue.	21 New Jersey			Sun.	19 NY Rangers
	Sat.	25 Los Angeles			Thur.	30 New Jersey
	Tue.	28 Philadelphia		**Nov.**	Wed.	5 Hartford
Nov.	Sat.	1 Winnipeg			Sun.	9 Buffalo
	Tue.	4 Washington			Sat.	15 Minnesota
	Sat.	8 Detroit			Sun.	16 Winnipeg
	Tue.	11 Edmonton			Tue.	18 Quebec
	Thur.	20 Toronto			Wed.	26 Pittsburgh
	Sat.	22 Hartford		**Dec.**	Tue.	2 Calgary
	Tue.	25 Pittsburgh			Wed.	3 Edmonton
	Sat.	29 Philadelphia			Fri.	5 Vancouver
Dec.	Tue.	9 Los Angeles			Sun.	7 Boston
	Sat.	13 New Jersey			Thur.	11 New Jersey
	Tue.	16 Minnesota			Thur.	18 Philadelphia
	Sat.	20 NY Rangers			Fri.	26 Washington
	Tue.	23 Pittsburgh			Sat.	27 Pittsburgh
	Tue.	30 Chicago			Wed.	31 NY Rangers
Jan.	Sat.	3 Boston		**Jan.**	Fri.	9 NY Rangers
	Tue.	6 Minnesota			Sun.	18 Philadelphia
	Sat.	10 Toronto			Wed.	21 Detroit
	Tue.	13 Pittsburgh			Sat.	24 Quebec
	Thur.	15 Washington			Fri.	30 Washington
	Sat.	17 Philadelphia		**Feb.**	Wed.	4 Vancouver
	Tue.	20 Calgary			Fri.	6 Edmonton
	Tue.	27 Winnipeg			Sat.	7 Calgary
	Sat.	31 Hartford			Wed.	18 Montreal
Feb.	Sat.	14 Buffalo			Sun.	22 New Jersey
	Tue.	17 Philadelphia			Tue.	24 St. Louis
	Sat.	21 Montreal		**Mar.**	Wed.	4 NY Rangers
	Thur.	26 Pittsburgh			Sat.	7 Toronto
	Sat.	28 St. Louis			Sun.	8 Chicago
Mar.	Tue.	3 Boston			Tue.	10 Pittsburgh
	Sat.	14 New Jersey			Fri.	13 New Jersey
	Sat.	21 NY Rangers			Mon.	16 Montreal
	Tue.	24 Washington			Thur.	19 Detroit
	Thur.	26 Vancouver			Fri.	27 Washington
April	Thur.	2 Quebec			Tue.	31 St. Louis
	Sat.	4 Buffalo		**April**	Sun.	5 Philadelphia

*Denotes afternoon game.

Home Starting Times:
Mondays through Fridays . . . . 8:05 p.m.
Saturdays & Sundays . . . . 7:05 p.m.
Except Jan. 17, Apr. 4 . . . . 5:05 p.m.

Franchise date: June 6, 1972

15th
NHL
Season

Duane Sutter

1986-87 Player Personnel

FORWARDS	Ht.	Wt.	Place of Birth	Date	1985-86 Club
BASSEN, Bob	5-10	180	Calgary, Alta.	5/6/65	NY Islanders-Springfield
BOSSY, Mike	6-0	185	Montreal, Que.	1/22/57	NY Islanders
BOURNE, Bob	6-3	197	Netherhill, Sask.	6/21/54	NY Islanders
COULTER, Neal	6-2	190	Toronto, Ont.	1/2/63	NY Islanders-Springfield
DALGARNO, Brad	6-3	205	Vancouver, B.C.	8/11/67	NY Islanders-Hamilton
DALLMAN, Rod	5-11	180	Quesnel, B.C.	1/26/67	Prince Albert
FLATLEY, Patrick	6-2	197	Toronto, Ont.	10/3/63	NY Islanders
GILBERT, Greg	6-1	192	Mississauga, Ont.	1/22/62	NY Islanders-Springfield
GILLIES, Clark	6-3	214	Moose Jaw, Sask.	4/7/54	NY Islanders
HAANPAA, Ari	6-1	185	Nokia, Finland	11/28/65	NY Islanders-Springfield
HAMWAY, Mark	6-0	190	Detroit, Mich.	8/9/61	NY Islanders-Springfield
HENRY, Dale	6-0	205	Prince Albert, Sask.	9/24/64	NY Islanders-Springfield
HEROM, Kevin	5-11	195	Regina, Sask.	7/6/67	Moose Jaw
KERR, Alan	5-11	195	Hazelton, B.C.	3/28/64	NY Islanders-Springfield
KING, Derek	6-1	205	Hamilton, Ont.	2/11/67	Oshawa
KORTKO, Roger	5-11	175	Hafford, Sask.	2/1/63	NY Islanders-Springfield
KROMM, Rich	5-11	180	Trail, B.C.	3/29/64	NY Islanders-Calgary
LaFONTAINE, Pat	5-10	177	St. Louis, Mo.	2/22/65	NY Islanders
LACEY, Garry	5-11	178	Sudbury, Ont.	5/24/64	Springfield
LACKTEN, Kurt	6-0	177	Kamsack, Sask.	5/20/67	Calgary (WHL)-Moose Jaw-Medicine Hat
LAUER, Brad	6-0	195	Humboldt, Sask.	10/27/66	Regina
MAKELA, Mikko	6-2	193	Tampere, Finland	2/28/65	NY Islanders-Springfield
McKECHNEY, Garnet	6-1	170	Swift Current, Sask.	4/28/65	London
SUTTER, Brent	5-11	176	Viking, Alta.	6/10/62	NY Islanders
SUTTER, Duane	6-1	195	Viking, Alta.	3/16/60	NY Islanders
TROTTIER, Bryan	5-11	195	Val Marie, Sask.	7/17/56	NY Islanders
WIECK, Doug	6-0	180	Rochester, Minn.	3/12/65	Colorado-Portland
WIEST, Rich	5-11	170	Lethbridge, Alta.	6/22/67	Calgary-Seattle-Lethbridge

DEFENSEMEN	Ht.	Wt.	Place of Birth	Date	1985-86 Club
BOUTILIER, Paul	6-0	200	Sydney, N.S.	5/3/63	NY Islanders
BOYD, Randy	5-11	192	Coniston, Ont.	1/23/62	NY Islanders
DIDUCK, Gerald	6-2	195	Edmonton, Alta.	4/6/65	NY Islanders-Springfield
DINEEN, Gord	6-0	195	Toronto, Ont.	9/21/62	NY Islanders-Springfield
FINLEY, Jeff	6-2	185	Edmonton, Alta.	4/14/67	Portland
JOHANNESEN, Glenn	6-2	220	Lac La Ronge, Sask.	2/15/62	NY Islanders-Springfield
JONSSON, Tomes	5-10	185	Falun, Sweden	4/12/60	NY Islanders
KONROYD, Steve	6-1	195	Scarborough, Ont.	2/10/61	NY Islanders-Calgary
LEITER, Ken	6-1	195	Detroit, Mich.	4/19/61	NY Islanders-Springfield
MacPHERSON, Duncan	6-1	195	Saskatoon, Sask.	2/3/66	Saskatoon
MORROW, Ken	6-4	205	Flint, Mich.	10/17/56	NY Islanders
NEILL, Mike	6-0	195	Kenora, Ont.	8/6/65	Springfield-Indianapolis
PADDOCK, Gord	6-0	180	Hamiota, Man.	2/15/64	Springfield-Indianapolis
POTVIN, Denis	6-0	205	Ottawa, Ont.	10/29/53	NY Islanders
SMITH, Vern	6-1	190	Winnipeg, Man.	5/30/64	Springfield
WARDEN, Tom	6-2	190	Darbshire, England	1/12/66	North Bay

GOALTENDERS	Ht.	Wt.	Place of Birth	Date	1985-86 Club
HRUDEY, Kelly	5-10	180	Edmonton, Alta.	1/13/61	NY Islanders
JOHNSON, Gary	5-10	165	Winnipeg, Man.	2/16/65	Brandon
SMITH, Bill	5-10	185	Perth, Ont.	12/12/50	NY Islanders
VOLPE, Mike	5-11	165	Vancouver, B.C.	1/2/67	Kitchener

1985-86 Scoring

Regular Season

*—rookie

Pos	#	Player	Team	GP	G	A	Pts	+/−	PIM	PP	SH	GW	OT	S	%
F	22	Mike Bossy	NYI	80	61	62	123	30	14	21	1	9	2	302	20.2
F	19	Bryan Trottier	NYI	78	37	59	96	29	72	5	1	3	0	185	20.0
D	5	Denis Potvin	NYI	74	21	38	59	34	78	8	1	4	0	168	12.5
F	21	Brent Sutter	NYI	61	24	31	55	11	74	10	0	2	2	135	17.8
F	16	Pat LaFontaine	NYI	65	30	23	53	16	43	2	0	4	0	172	17.4
F	12	Duane Sutter	NYI	80	20	33	53	15	157	4	0	1	0	151	13.2
F	26	Patrick Flatley	NYI	73	18	34	52	20	66	6	0	2	0	120	15.0
D	3	Tomas Jonsson	NYI	77	14	30	44	16	62	5	1	1	0	119	11.8
F	35	Rich Kromm	CGY	63	12	17	29	9	31	0	0	2	0	97	12.4
			NYI	14	7	7	14	8	4	0	0	0	0	23	30.4
			Total	77	19	24	43	17	35	0	0	2	0	120	15.8
F	24	*Mikko Makela	NYI	58	16	20	36	12	28	2	0	3	0	68	23.5
D	4	Paul Boutilier	NYI	77	4	30	34	5−	100	4	0	0	0	124	3.2
F	14	Bob Bourne	NYI	62	17	15	32	7−	36	2	0	5	0	100	17.0
D	33	Steve Konroyd	CGY	59	7	20	27	20	64	1	0	1	0	111	6.3
			NYI	14	0	5	5	4	16	0	0	0	0	13	.0
			Total	73	7	25	32	24	80	1	0	1	0	124	5.6
F	17	Greg Gilbert	NYI	60	9	19	28	5	82	1	0	2	0	58	15.5
D	7	Stefan Persson	NYI	56	1	19	20	3−	40	1	0	0	0	46	2.2
F	28	*Mark Hamway	NYI	49	5	12	17	5−	9	1	0	1	0	50	10.0
F	9	Clark Gillies	NYI	55	4	10	14	8−	55	1	0	0	0	74	5.4
D	8	Randy Boyd	NYI	55	2	12	14	9	79	0	0	0	0	52	3.8
F	11	Roger Kortko	NYI	52	5	8	13	11−	19	0	0	1	0	49	10.2
D	6	Ken Morrow	NYI	69	0	12	12	24	22	0	0	0	0	55	.0
D	2	Gord Dineen	NYI	57	1	8	9	15	81	0	0	0	0	52	1.9
F	32	*Neal Coulter	NYI	16	3	4	7	1−	4	0	0	0	0	17	17.6
F	25	*Ari Haanpaa	NYI	18	0	7	7	0	20	0	0	0	0	16	.0
F	20	Dale Henry	NYI	7	1	3	4	0	15	0	0	0	0	5	20.0
F	28	*Bob Bassen	NYI	11	2	1	3	0	6	0	0	0	0	5	40.0
D	29	Gerald Diduck	NYI	10	1	2	3	5	2	0	0	0	0	6	16.7
F	33	*Scott Howson	NYI	10	1	2	3	2	2	0	0	0	0	8	12.5
G	31	Billy Smith	NYI	41	0	3	3	0	49	0	0	0	0	0	.0
G	30	Kelly Hrudey	NYI	45	0	3	3	0	14	0	0	0	0	0	.0
D	35	*Ken Leiter	NYI	9	1	1	2	1	6	0	0	0	0	9	11.1
F	23	Bob Nystrom	NYI	14	1	1	2	4−	16	1	0	0	0	17	5.9
F	32	*Brad Dalgarno	NYI	2	1	0	1	1	0	0	0	0	0	3	33.3
F	10	*Alan Kerr	NYI	7	0	1	1	1	16	0	0	0	0	9	.0
F	36	*Glen Johannesen	NYI	2	0	0	0	1−	0	0	0	0	0	0	.0

Playoffs

* rookie

Pos	#	Player	Team	GP	G	A	Pts	+/−	PIM	PP	SH	GW	OT	S	%
F	22	Mike Bossy	NYI	3	1	2	3	2−	4	0	0	0	0	14	7.1
F	19	Bryan Trottier	NYI	3	1	1	2	1−	2	0	0	0	0	10	10.0
F	9	Clark Gillies	NYI	3	1	0	1	2−	6	0	0	0	0	7	14.3
F	16	Pat LaFontaine	NYI	3	1	0	1	2−	0	0	0	0	0	7	14.3
F	28	*Bob Bassen	NYI	3	0	1	1	1−	2	0	0	0	0	6	.0
D	3	Tomas Jonsson	NYI	3	0	1	1	2−	4	0	0	0	0	6	.0
F	35	Rich Kromm	NYI	3	0	1	1	0	0	0	0	0	0	4	.0
D	5	Denis Potvin	NYI	3	0	1	1	2−	0	0	0	0	0	4	.0
F	21	Brent Sutter	NYI	3	0	1	1	3−	2	0	0	0	0	6	.0
F	28	*Mark Hamway	NYI	1	0	0	0	0	0	0	0	0	0	0	.0
F	10	*Alan Kerr	NYI	1	0	0	0	0	0	0	0	0	0	0	.0
G	31	Billy Smith	NYI	1	0	0	0	0	0	0	0	0	0	0	.0
F	17	Greg Gilbert	NYI	2	0	0	0	1−	9	0	0	0	0	4	.0
G	30	Kelly Hrudey	NYI	2	0	0	0	0	4	0	0	0	0	0	.0
D	6	Ken Morrow	NYI	2	0	0	0	2−	4	0	0	0	0	5	.0
F	14	Bob Bourne	NYI	3	0	0	0	2−	0	0	0	0	0	5	.0
D	4	Paul Boutilier	NYI	3	0	0	0	2−	2	0	0	0	0	5	.0
D	8	Randy Boyd	NYI	3	0	0	0	1−	2	0	0	0	1	2	.0
D	2	Gord Dineen	NYI	3	0	0	0	1−	2	0	0	0	0	1	.0
F	26	Patrick Flatley	NYI	3	0	0	0	2−	21	0	0	0	0	4	.0
D	33	Steve Konroyd	NYI	3	0	0	0	1−	6	0	0	0	0	3	.0
F	12	Duane Sutter	NYI	3	0	0	0	1	16	0	0	0	0	4	.0

Coach and General Manager

TERRY SIMPSON
Coach, New York Islanders. Born in Brantford, Ont., August 30, 1943.

Named head coach of the New York Islanders on June 18, 1986, Terry Simpson brings to the NHL a most impressive 14-season amateur coaching background. During his first 10 seasons (1972-73 to 1981-82) as coach of the Prince Albert Raiders, then a Tier II squad, Simpson steered his team to eight league titles and four national Tier II championships, while winning Coach of the Year honors three times. In 1982-83, Prince Albert joined the Western Hockey League and within three seasons, he brought his club to national prominence with a WHL title and a Memorial Cup championship in 1984-85. Additionally, Simpson has also been a part of Canada's national junior team, serving as head coach for the last two years. He guided the junior team to gold and silver medals in 1984-85 and 1985-86, respectively.

TORREY, WILLIAM ARTHUR (BILL)
President and General Manager, New York Islanders. Born in Montreal, Que., June 23, 1934.

Although he never played professionally, Bill Torrey has been a valuable addition to professional hockey and was named winner of the 1983 Lester Patrick Trophy for his contribution to hockey in the United States. He attended St. Lawrence University in Canton, N.Y. where he played for the varsity team and graduated in 1957 with a Bachelor of Science degree. He joined the Pittsburgh Hornets of the American Hockey League in 1960 and served with that club until 1965, first as Director of Public Relations and later as Business Manager. In September 1968, Torrey moved to the California Seals of the NHL as Executive Vice-President and during his tenure, the Seals went from last place in the West Division to playoff berths the following two seasons. On February 15, 1972, he was appointed General Manager of the New York Islanders and has moulded the franchise into one of the greatest in the history of professional sports. His most satisfying season was 1979-80 when the Islanders won their first of four consecutive Stanley Cup titles.

Club Records

Team

(Figures in brackets for season records are games played; records for fewest points, wins, ties, losses, goals, goals against are for 70 or more games)

Most Points	118	1981-82 (80)
Most Wins	54	1981-82 (80)
Most Ties	22	1974-75 (80)
Most Losses	60	1972-73 (78)
Most Goals	385	1981-82 (80)
Most Goals Against	347	1972-73 (78)
Fewest Points	30	1972-73 (78)
Fewest Wins	12	1972-73 (78)
Fewest Ties	4	1983-84 (80)
Fewest Losses	15	1978-79 (80)
Fewest Goals	170	1972-73 (78)
Fewest Goals Against	190	1975-76 (80)

Longest Winning Streak
Over-all .... *15 Jan. 21/82-Feb. 20/82 Jan. 12-26/80

Home .... 14 Jan. 2/82-Feb. 25/82

Away .... 8 Feb. 27/81-Mar. 29/81

Longest Undefeated Streak
Over-all .... 15 Jan. 21-Feb. 20/82 (15 wins) Nov. 4-Dec. 2/80 (13 wins, 2 ties)

Home .... 23 Oct. 17/78-Jan. 20/79 (19 wins, 4 ties) Jan. 2/82-Apr. 3/82 (21 wins, 2 ties)

Away .... 8 Four times

Longest Losing Streak
Over-all .... 12 Dec. 27/72-Jan. 16/73

Home .... 5 Jan. 2-16/73 Feb. 28-Mar. 16/74

Away .... 15 Jan. 20-Mar. 31/73

Longest Winless Streak
Over-all .... 15 Nov. 22-Dec. 21/72 (12 losses, 3 ties)

Home .... 7 Oct. 14-Nov. 18/72 (6 losses, 1 tie) Nov. 28-Dec. 21/72 (5 losses, 2 ties)

Away .... 20 Nov. 3/72-Jan. 13/73 (19 losses, 1 tie)

Most Shutouts, Season 10 1975-76 (80) 1984-85 (80)
Most Pen. Mins., Season 1,512
Most Goals, Game .... 11 Dec. 20/83 (NYI 11 at Pit. 3) Mar. 3/84 (Tor. 6 at NYI 11)

Individual

Most Seasons	14	Bob Nystrom / Billy Smith
Most Games	929	Denis Potvin
Most Goals, Career	535	Mike Bossy
Most Assists, Career	698	Bryan Trottier
Most Points, Career	1,115	Bryan Trottier (417 goals, 698 assists)
Most Pen. Mins., Career	1,456	Garry Howatt

Most Shutouts, Career ..... 26 Glenn Resch
Longest Consecutive Games Streak .... 576 Bill Harris (Oct. 7/72-Nov. 30/79)
Most Goals, Season ...... 69 Mike Bossy (1978-79)
Most Assists, Season ..... 87 Bryan Trottier (1978-79)
Most Points, Season ..... 147 Mike Bossy (1981-82) (64 goals, 83 assists)
Most Pen. Mins., Season ... 219 Garry Howatt (1979-80)
Most Points, Defenseman, Season .... 101 Denis Potvin (1978-79) (31 goals, 70 assists)
Most Points, Center, Season .... 134 Bryan Trottier (1978-79) (47 goals, 87 assists)
Most Points, Right Wing, Season .... 147 Mike Bossy (1981-82) (64 goals, 83 assists)
Mot Points, Left Wing, Season .... 100 John Tonelli (1984-85) (42 goals, 58 assists)
Most Points, Rookie, Season .... 95 Bryan Trottier (1975-76) (32 goals, 63 assists)
Most Shutouts, Season ..... 7 Glenn Resch (1975-76)
Most Goals, Game .... 5 Bryan Trottier (Dec. 23/78) Bryan Trottier (Feb. 13/82)
Most Assists, Game .... 6 Mike Bossy (Jan. 6/81)
Most Points, Game .... 8 Bryan Trottier (Dec. 23/78)

* NHL Record.

Coaching History

Phil Goyette and Earl Ingarfield, 1972-73; Al Arbour, 1973-74 to 1985-86; Terry Simpson, 1986-87.

Captains' History

Ed Westfall, 1972-73 to 1975-76; Ed Westfall, Clark Gillies, 1976-77; Clark Gillies, 1977-78, 1978-79; Denis Potvin, 1979-80 to 1985-86.

All-time Record vs. Other Clubs

Regular Season

		At Home						On Road						Total					
	GP	W	L	T	GF	GA	PTS	GP	W	L	T	GF	GA	PTS	GP	W	L	T	GF	GA	PTS
Boston	27	12	14	1	86	92	25	28	5	15	8	79	110	18	55	17	29	9	165	202	43
Buffalo	28	11	13	4	81	81	26	28	8	16	4	74	97	20	56	19	29	8	155	178	46
**Calgary	33	18	6	9	133	83	45	32	10	13	9	104	113	29	65	28	19	18	237	196	74
Chicago	29	16	4	9	117	81	41	29	13	12	4	107	90	30	58	29	16	13	224	171	71
Detroit	27	17	10	0	114	74	34	26	13	11	2	89	85	28	53	30	21	2	203	159	62
Edmonton	12	5	1	6	61	53	16	11	5	6	3	44	41	11	23	10	6	7	105	94	27
Hartford	11	7	3	1	53	29	15	12	6	3	3	47	37	15	23	13	6	4	100	66	30
Los Angeles	26	15	7	4	102	68	34	27	10	10	7	86	92	27	53	25	17	11	188	160	61
Minnesota	28	14	7	7	113	79	35	29	15	9	5	108	81	35	57	29	16	12	221	160	70
Montreal	29	15	11	3	100	81	31	26	6	15	5	81	101	17	55	21	26	8	181	182	48
*New Jersey	32	28	1	3	172	75	59	32	20	7	5	138	94	45	64	48	8	8	310	169	104
NY Rangers	43	30	12	1	196	134	61	44	14	28	2	137	178	30	87	44	40	3	333	312	91
Philadelphia	43	24	11	8	179	118	56	43	13	25	5	118	155	31	86	37	36	13	297	273	87
Pittsburgh	37	24	8	5	164	101	53	37	14	15	8	120	127	36	74	38	23	13	284	228	89
Québec	12	8	3	1	53	41	17	11	3	7	1	40	54	7	23	11	10	2	93	95	24
St. Louis	30	19	4	7	125	64	45	28	14	8	6	106	90	34	58	33	12	13	231	154	79
Toronto	27	17	8	2	127	83	36	29	14	12	3	110	97	31	56	31	20	5	237	180	67
Vancouver	29	17	4	8	118	76	42	29	14	13	2	95	97	30	58	31	17	10	213	173	72
Washington	32	25	6	1	150	88	51	32	18	10	4	117	92	40	64	43	16	5	267	180	91
Winnipeg	11	5	2	4	41	28	14	12	8	3	1	50	36	17	23	13	5	5	91	64	31
Defunct Clubs	13	11	0	2	72	32	24	13	4	5	4	38	42	12	26	15	5	6	110	74	36
Totals	558	338	135	86	2357	1561	760	558	227	242	89	1888	1909	543	1116	565	377	175	4245	3470	1303

* Totals include those of Kansas City (1974-75, 1975-76) and Colorado (1976-77 through 1981-82)
** Totals include those of Atlanta (1972-73 through 1979-80)

Playoffs

	Series	W	L	GP	W	L	T	GF	GA	Last Mtg.	Round	Result
Boston	2	2	0	11	8	3	0	49	35	1983	CF	W 4-2
Buffalo	3	3	0	16	12	4	0	59	45	1980	SF	W 4-2
Chicago	2	2	0	6	6	0	0	21	6	1979	QF	W 4-0
Edmonton	3	2	1	15	9	6	0	58	47	1984	F	L 1-4
Los Angeles	1	1	0	4	3	1	0	21	10	1980	P	W 3-1
Minnesota	1	1	0	5	4	1	0	26	16	1981	F	W 4-1
Montreal	3	1	2	17	7	10	0	44	48	1984	CF	W 4-2
NY Rangers	6	5	1	30	19	11	0	113	88	1984	DSF	W 3-2
Philadelphia	3	1	2	18	8	10	0	53	60	1985	DF	L 1-4
Pittsburgh	2	2	0	12	7	5	0	43	31	1982	DSF	W 3-2
Quebec	1	1	0	4	4	0	0	18	9	1982	CF	W 4-0
Toronto	2	1	1	10	6	4	0	33	20	1981	P	W 3-0
Vancouver	2	2	0	6	6	0	0	26	14	1982	F	W 4-0
Washington	4	3	1	17	10	7	0	57	47	1986	DSF	L 0-3
Totals	35	27	8	171	109	62	0	621	476			

Playoff Results 1986-82

Year	Round	Opponent	Result	GF	GA
1986	DSF	Washington	L 0-3	4	11
1985	DF	Philadelphia	L 1-4	11	16
	DSF	Washington	W 3-2	14	12
1984	F	Edmonton	L 1-4	12	21
	CF	Montreal	W 4-2	17	12
	DF	Washington	W 4-1	20	13
	DSF	NY Rangers	W 3-2	3	14
1983	**F**	**Edmonton**	**W 4-0**	**17**	**6**
	CF	Boston	W 4-2	30	21
	DF	Ny Rangers	W 4-2	28	15
	DSF	Washington	W 3-1	19	11
1982	**F**	**Vancouver**	**W 4-0**	**18**	**10**
	CF	Quebec	W 4-0	18	9
	DF	NY Rangers	W 4-2	27	20
	DSF	Pittsburgh	W 3-2	22	13

Abbreviations: Round: F – Final; CF – conference final; DF – division final; DSF – division semi-final; SF – semi-final; QF – quarter-final; P – preliminary round. GA – goals against; GF – goals for.

Entry Draft Selections 1986-72

1986
Pick
17	Tom Fitzgerald
38	Dennis Vaske
59	Bill Berg
80	Shawn Byram
101	Dean Sexsmith
104	Todd McLellan
122	Tony Schmalzbauer
138	Will Anderson
143	Richard Pilon
164	Peter Harris
185	Jeff Jablonski
206	Kerry Clark
227	Dan Beaudette
248	Paul Thompson

1985
Pick
6	Brad Dalgarno
13	Derek King
34	Brad Lauer
55	Jeff Finley
76	Kevin Herom
89	Tommy Hedlund
97	Jeff Sveen
118	Rod Dallman
139	Kurt Lackten
160	Hank Lammens
181	Rich Wiest
202	Real Arsenault
223	Mike Volpe
244	Tony Grenier

1984
Pick
20	Duncan MacPherson
41	Bruce Melanson
62	Jeff Norton
70	Doug Wieck
83	Ari Eerik Haanpaa
104	Mike Murray
125	Jim Wilharm
146	Kelly Murphy
167	Franco Desantis
187	Tom Warden
208	David Volek
228	Russ Becker
249	Allister Brown

1983
Pick
3	Pat LaFontaine
16	Gerald Diduck
37	Garnet McKechney
57	Mike Neill
65	Mikko Makela
84	Bob Caulfield
97	Ron Viglasi
117	Darin Illikainen
137	Jim Sprenger
157	Dale Henry
177	Kevin Vescio
197	Dave Shellington
217	John Bjorkman
237	Peter McGeough

1982
Pick
21	Patrick Flatley
42	Vern Smith
63	Garry Lacey
84	Alan Kerr
105	Rene Breton
126	Roger Kortko
147	John Tiano
168	Todd Okerlund
189	Gord Paddock
210	Eric Faust
231	Pat Goff
252	Jim Koudys

1981
Pick
21	Paul Boutilier
42	Gord Dineen
57	Ron Handy
63	Neal Coulter
84	Todd Lumbard
94	Jacques Sylvestre
126	Chuck Brimmer
147	Teppo Virta
168	Bill Dowd
189	Scott MacLellan
210	Dave Randerson

1980
Pick
17	Brent Sutter
38	Kelly Hrudey
59	Dave Simpson
68	Monty Trottier
80	Greg Gilbert
101	Ken Leiter
122	Dan Revell
143	Mark Hamway
164	Morrison Gare
185	Peter Steblyk
206	Glen Johannesen

1979
Pick
17	Duane Sutter
25	Tomas Jonsson
38	Bill Carroll
59	Roland Melanson
80	Tom Lockridge
101	Glen Duncan
122	John Gibb

1978
Pick
15	Steve Tambellini
34	Randy Johnston
51	Dwayne Lowdermilk
84	Greg Hay
101	Kelly Davis
118	Richard Pepin
135	David Cameron
152	Paul Joswiak
169	Scott Cameron
184	Chris Lowdall
199	Gunnar Persson

1977
Pick
15	Mike Bossy
33	John Tonelli
50	Hector Marini
51	Bruce Andres
69	Steve Stoyanovich
87	Markus Mattsson
105	Steve Letzgus
121	Harold Luckner

1976
Pick
14	Alex McKendry
32	Mike Kaszycki
50	Garth McGuigan
68	Ken Morrow
86	Mike Hordy
104	Yvon Vautour

1975
Pick
11	Pat Price
29	David Salvian
47	Joe Fortunato
65	Andre Lepage
83	Denis McLean
101	Mike Sleep
119	Richie Hansen
137	Bob Sunderland
153	Dan Blair
168	Joey Girardin
183	Geoff Green
194	Kari Makkonen

1974
Pick
4	Clark Gillies
22	Bryan Trottier
40	Brad Anderson
76	Carlo Torresan
94	Sid Prysumka
112	Dave Langevin
129	David Inkpen
146	Jim Foubister
163	Bob Ferguson
178	Murray Fleck
192	David Rooke
204	Neil Smith
214	Stefan Persson
221	David Otness
226	Jim Murray
229	Mike Dibble
232	Brian Bye
235	Martti Jarko
238	Ron Phillips

1973
Pick
1	Denis Potvin
33	Dave Lewis
49	Andre St. Laurent
65	Ron Kennedy
81	Keith Smith
97	Don Cutts
110	Dennis Anderson
113	Mike Kennedy
126	Denis Desgagnes
129	Bob Lorimer

1972
Pick
1	Billy Harris
17	Lorne Henning
33	Bob Nystrom
49	Ron Smith
65	Richard Grenier
81	Derek Black
97	Richard Brodeur
101	Don McKaughlin
113	Derek Kuntz
117	Rene Lavasseur
129	Yvan Rolando
133	Bill Ennos
144	Garry Howatt
146	Rene Lambert

Denis Potvin and Mike Bossy

Club Directory

Nassau Veterans'
Memorial Coliseum
Uniondale, N.Y. 11553
Phone 516/794-4100
TWX 510-222-5575 (PR)
   510-221-1815 (EXEC)
ENVOY ID TM.NYI
Capacity: 16,265

Chairman of the Board, Governor.	John O. Pickett, Jr.
President and General Manager.	William A. Torrey
Vice-President — Finance.	Joseph H. Dreyer
Vice-President/Sales and Marketing	Arthur Adler
Vice-President/Player Development	Al Arbour
Coach.	Terry Simpson
Assistant Coaches.	TBD
Assistant General Manager/Director of Scouting	Gerry Ehman
Director of Hockey Administration.	Darcy Regier
Scouting Staff.	Harry Boyd, Fred Creighton, Richard Green, Earl Ingarfield, Hal Laycoe, Bert Marshall, Mario Saraceno, Jack Vivian
Publicity Director.	Les Wagner
Assistant Publicity Director	Greg Bouris
Publicity Assistant	Cathy Shutte
Director of Public Affairs.	Jill Knee
Communications Consultant	Barney Kremenko
Athletic Trainer	Craig Smith
Assistant Trainer.	Jim Pickard
Team Orthopedists	Jeffrey Minkoff, M.D., Barry Fisher, M.D.
Team Internist	George J. Gilbert, Jr., M.D.
Team Dentist	Bryce Michnick, D.D.S.
Team Photographer.	Bruce Bennett
Home Ice.	Nassau Coliseum
Location of Press Box	East Side of Building
Dimensions of Rink	200 feet by 85 feet
Ends of Rink	Herculite extends above boards around rink
Club Colors	Blue, Orange and White
Training Camp Site/Practice Facility	Cantiague Park, Hicksville, NY
Television Announcers.	Jiggs McDonald, Ed Westfall, Stan Fischler
Radio Announcers.	Barry Landers, Jean Potvin
Television Station	SportsChannel (Home and Away)
Radio Station.	WOR (710 AM)

New York Rangers

1985-86 Results: 36w-38L-6T 78 PTS. Fourth, Patrick Division

Schedule

	Home			Away	
Oct.	Thur.	9 New Jersey	**Oct.**	Sat.	11 Pittsburgh
	Mon.	13 Washington		Wed.	15 Chicago
	Sun.	19 NY Islanders		Sat.	18 NY Islanders
	Wed.	22 Los Angeles		Sat.	25 Montreal
	Sun.	26 Toronto		Wed.	29 St. Louis
Nov.	Sun.	2 Winnipeg	**Nov.**	Wed.	5 Detroit
	Wed.	12 Buffalo		Sat.	8 Philadelphia*
	Fri.	14 Philadelphia		Sun.	9 Quebec
	Sun.	16 Edmonton		Mon.	17 New Jersey
	Wed.	26 Quebec		Wed.	19 Edmonton
	Sun.	30 Pittsburgh		Fri.	21 Vancouver
Dec.	Wed.	10 Los Angeles		Sat.	22 Calgary
	Mon.	15 Minnesota		Sat.	29 Pittsburgh
	Wed.	17 Washington	**Dec.**	Tue.	2 New Jersey
	Sun.	21 Hartford		Fri.	5 Winnipeg
	Tue.	23 New Jersey		Thur.	11 Montreal
	Wed.	31 NY Islanders		Sun.	14 Washington*
Jan.	Mon.	5 Minnesota		Sat.	20 NY Islanders
	Wed.	7 Philadelphia		Fri.	26 New Jersey
	Fri.	9 NY Islanders		Sat.	27 St. Louis
	Sun.	11 Vancouver		Tue.	30 Pittsburgh
	Mon.	26 New Jersey	**Jan.**	Sat.	3 Quebec
	Wed.	28 Winnipeg		Mon.	12 Boston
Feb.	Sun.	1 Boston		Wed.	14 Calgary
	Wed.	4 Washington		Mon.	19 Los Angeles
	Sun.	8 Toronto		Wed.	21 Vancouver
	Sun.	15 Pittsburgh		Fri.	23 Edmonton
	Tue.	17 Detroit		Sat.	31 Philadelphia
	Fri.	20 Buffalo	**Feb.**	Sat.	7 Washington
	Sun.	22 Pittsburgh		Thur.	19 Chicago
Mar.	Wed.	4 NY Islanders		Tue.	24 Buffalo
	Sun.	8 Calgary		Wed.	25 Toronto
	Wed.	11 Boston		Sat.	28 Detroit*
	Sun.	15 Philadelphia	**Mar.**	Sun.	1 Washington*
	Wed.	18 Hartford		Thur.	12 Philadelphia
	Sun.	22 Chicago		Sat.	14 Pittsburgh
	Wed.	25 New Jersey		Tue.	17 Philadelphia
	Fri.	27 St. Louis		Sat.	21 NY Islanders
April	Wed.	1 Washington		Mon.	30 Minnesota
	Sun.	5 Montreal	**April**	Sat.	4 Hartford

*Denotes afternoon game.

Home Starting Times:
All Games . . . . 7:35 p.m.
Except Nov. 2, Nov. 30,
    Feb. 15 . . . . 8:35 p.m.
    Mar. 8 . . . . 9:05 p.m.

Franchise date: May 15, 1926

61st NHL Season

Vezina Trophy-winning goaltender John Vanbiesbrouck appeared in 61 games in the 1985-86 regular season.

Year-by-Year Record

Season	GP	Home			Road			Overall					Pts.	Finished		Playoff Result
		W	L	T	W	L	T	W	L	T	GF	GA				
1985-86	80	20	18	2	16	20	4	36	38	6	280	276	78	4th,	Patrick Div.	Lost Conf. Final
1984-85	80	16	18	6	10	26	4	26	44	10	295	345	62	4th,	Patrick Div.	Lost Div. Semi-Final
1983-84	80	27	12	1	15	17	8	42	29	9	314	304	93	4th,	Patrick Div.	Lost Div. Semi-Final
1982-83	80	24	13	3	11	22	7	35	35	10	306	287	80	4th,	Patrick Div.	Lost Div. Final
1981-82	80	19	15	6	20	12	8	39	27	14	316	306	92	2nd,	Patrick Div.	Lost Div. Final
1980-81	80	17	13	10	13	23	4	30	36	14	312	317	74	4th,	Patrick Div.	Lost Semi-Final
1979-80	80	22	10	8	16	22	2	38	32	10	308	284	86	3rd,	Patrick Div.	Lost Quarter-Final
1978-79	80	19	13	8	21	16	3	40	29	11	316	292	91	3rd,	Patrick Div.	Lost Final
1977-78	80	18	15	7	12	22	6	30	37	13	279	280	73	4th,	Patrick Div.	Lost Prelim. Round
1976-77	80	17	18	5	12	19	9	29	37	14	272	310	72	4th,	Patrick Div.	Out of Playoffs
1975-76	80	16	16	8	13	26	1	29	42	9	262	333	67	4th,	Patrick Div.	Out of Playoffs
1974-75	80	21	11	8	16	18	6	37	29	14	319	276	88	2nd,	Patrick Div.	Lost Prelim. Round
1973-74	78	26	7	6	14	17	8	40	24	14	300	251	94	3rd,	East Div.	Lost Semi-Final
1972-73	78	26	8	5	21	15	3	47	23	8	297	208	102	3rd,	East Div.	Lost Semi-Final
1971-72	78	26	6	7	22	11	6	48	17	13	317	192	109	2nd,	East Div.	Lost Final
1970-71	78	30	2	7	19	16	4	49	18	11	259	177	109	2nd,	East Div.	Lost Semi-Final
1969-70	76	22	8	8	16	14	8	38	22	16	246	189	92	4th,	East Div.	Lost Quarter-Final
1968-69	76	27	7	4	14	19	5	41	26	9	231	196	91	3rd,	East Div.	Lost Quarter-Final
1967-68	74	22	8	7	17	15	5	39	23	12	226	183	90	2nd,	East Div.	Lost Quarter-Final
1966-67	70	18	12	5	12	16	7	30	28	12	188	189	72	4th,		Lost Semi-Final
1965-66	70	12	16	7	6	25	4	18	41	11	195	261	47	6th,		Out of Playoffs
1964-65	70	8	19	8	12	19	4	20	38	12	179	246	52	5th,		Out of Playoffs
1963-64	70	14	13	8	8	25	2	22	38	10	186	242	54	5th,		Out of Playoffs
1962-63	70	12	17	6	10	19	6	22	36	12	211	233	56	5th,		Out of Playoffs
1961-62	70	16	11	8	10	21	4	26	32	12	195	207	64	4th,		Lost Semi-Final
1960-61	70	15	15	5	7	23	5	22	38	10	204	248	54	5th,		Out of Playoffs
1959-60	70	10	15	10	7	23	5	17	38	15	187	247	49	6th,		Out of Playoffs
1958-59	70	14	16	5	12	16	7	26	32	12	201	217	64	5th,		Out of Playoffs
1957-58	70	14	15	6	18	10	7	32	25	13	195	188	77	2nd,		Lost Semi-Final
1956-57	70	15	12	8	11	18	6	26	30	14	184	227	66	4th,		Lost Semi-Final
1955-56	70	20	7	8	12	21	2	32	28	10	204	203	74	3rd,		Lost Semi-Final
1954-55	70	10	12	13	7	23	5	17	35	18	150	210	52	5th,		Out of Playoffs
1953-54	70	18	12	5	11	19	5	29	31	10	161	182	68	5th,		Out of Playoffs
1952-53	70	11	14	10	6	23	6	17	37	16	152	211	50	6th,		Out of Playoffs
1951-52	70	16	13	6	7	21	7	23	34	13	192	219	59	5th,		Out of Playoffs
1950-51	70	14	11	10	6	18	11	20	29	21	169	201	61	5th,		Out of Playoffs
1949-50	70	19	12	4	9	19	7	28	31	11	170	189	67	4th,		Lost Final
1948-49	60	13	12	5	5	19	6	18	31	11	133	172	47	6th,		Out of Playoffs
1947-48	60	11	12	7	10	14	6	21	26	13	176	201	55	4th,		Lost Semi-Final
1946-47	60	11	14	5	11	18	1	22	32	6	167	186	50	5th,		Out of Playoffs
1945-46	50	8	12	5	5	16	4	13	28	9	144	191	35	6th,		Out of Playoffs
1944-45	50	7	11	7	4	18	3	11	29	10	154	247	32	6th,		Out of Playoffs
1943-44	50	4	17	4	2	22	1	6	39	5	162	310	17	6th,		Out of Playoffs
1942-43	50	7	13	5	4	18	3	11	31	8	161	253	30	6th,		Out of Playoffs
1941-42	48	15	8	1	14	9	1	29	17	2	177	143	60	1st,		Lost Semi-Final
1940-41	48	13	7	4	8	12	4	21	19	8	143	125	50	4th,		Lost Quarter-Final
1939-40	48	17	4	3	10	7	7	**27**	**11**	**10**	**136**	**92**	**64**	**2nd,**		**Won Stanley Cup**
1938-39	48	13	8	3	13	8	3	26	16	6	149	105	58	2nd,		Lost Semi-Final
1937-38	48	15	5	4	12	10	2	27	15	6	149	96	60	2nd,	Amn. Div.	Lost Quarter-Final
1936-37	48	9	7	8	10	13	1	19	20	9	117	106	47	3rd,	Amn. Div.	Lost Final
1935-36	48	11	6	7	8	11	5	19	17	12	91	96	50	4th,	Amn. Div.	Out of Playoffs
1934-35	48	11	8	5	11	12	1	22	20	6	137	139	50	3rd,	Amn. Div.	Lost Semi-Final
1933-34	48	11	7	6	10	12	2	21	19	8	120	113	50	3rd,	Amn. Div.	Lost Quarter-Final
1932-33	48	12	7	5	11	10	3	**23**	**17**	**8**	**135**	**107**	**54**	**3rd,**	**Amn. Div.**	**Won Stanley Cup**
1931-32	48	13	7	4	10	10	4	23	17	8	134	112	54	1st,	Amn. Div.	Lost Final
1930-31	44	10	9	3	9	7	6	19	16	9	106	87	47	3rd,	Amn. Div.	Lost Semi-Final
1929-30	44	11	5	6	6	12	4	17	17	10	136	143	44	3rd,	Amn. Div.	Lost Final
1928-29	44	12	6	4	9	7	6	21	13	10	72	65	52	2nd,	Amn. Div.	Lost Final
1927-28	44	10	8	4	9	8	5	**19**	**16**	**9**	**94**	**79**	**47**	**2nd,**	**Amn. Div.**	**Won Stanley Cup**
1926-27	44	13	5	4	12	8	2	25	13	6	95	72	56	1st,	Amn. Div.	Lost Quarter-Final

1986-87 Player Personnel

FORWARDS

	Ht.	Wt.	Place of Birth	Date	1985-86 Club
BERNARD, Larry	6-2	195	Prince George, B.C.	4/16/67	Seattle
BROOKE, Bob	6-2	205	Melrose, Mass.	12/18/60	NY Rangers
BROWN, Newell	5-9	178	Cornwall, Ont.	2/14/62	
CAUFIELD, Jay	6-4	240	Philadelphia, Pa.	7/17/60	New Haven-Toledo
CRAWFORD, Bob	5-11	175	Belleville, Ont.	4/6/59	Hartford-NY Rangers
ELIK, Todd	6-0	191	Brampton, Ont.	4/15/66	North Bay
ERIXON, Jan	6-0	190	Skellefttea, Sweden	7/8/62	NY Rangers
FILBEY, Ken	5-8	181	Prince Rupert, B.C.	1/5/63	Colorado College
GAGNER, Dave	5-10	180	Chatham, Ont.	12/11/64	NY Rangers
GROPP, Brent	5-11	195	Edmonton, Alta.	11/16/63	Colorado College
HELMINEN, Raimo	6-0	185	Tampere, Finland	3/11/64	NY Rangers
JENSEN, Chris	5-11	169	Salmon Arm, B.C.	10/28/63	U. of N. Dakota-NY Rangers
KISIO, Kelly	5-9	170	Wetaskwin, Alta.	9/18/59	Detroit
KOEBEL, Gerald	6-0	190	Edson, Alta.	12/7/64	U. of Alberta
KONTOS, Chris	6-1	195	Toronto, Ont.	12/10/63	Ilves (Finland)-New Haven
LAMBERT, Lane	5-11	178	Melfort, Sask.	11/18/64	Adirondack-Detroit
LAROUCHE, Pierre	5-11	175	Taschereau, Que.	11/16/55	Hershey-NY Rangers
MacLELLAN, Brian	6-3	212	Guelph, Ont.	10/17/58	Los Angeles-NY Rangers
MALONEY, Don	6-1	190	Lindsay, Ont.	9/5/58	NY Rangers
McPHEE, George	5-9	170	Guelph, Ont.	7/2/58	NY Rangers
MILLER, Kelly	5-11	185	Detroit, Mich.	3/3/63	NY Rangers
MOESER, Duanne	5-10	170	Waterloo, Ont.	4/3/63	Cornell
MONGEAU, Michel	5-10	175	Montreal, Que.	2/9/65	Laval
MORIA, Steve	6-0	175	Vancouver, B.C.	2/3/61	New Haven
NASHEIM, Rick	5-11	185	Regina, Sask.	1/15/63	U. of Regina
NATYSHAK, Peter	5-10	185	Oakville, Ont.	2/14/64	Cornell
NEMETH, Steve	5-8	162	Calgary, Alta.	2/11/67	Lethbridge
O'DWYER, Bill	6-0	190	S. Boston, Mass.	6/25/60	New Haven
OSBORNE, Mark	6-2	200	Toronto, Ont.	8/13/61	NY Rangers
PAIEMENT, Wilf	6-1	210	Earlton, Ont.	10/16/55	Quebec-NY Rangers
PODDUBNY, Walt	6-1	205	Thunder Bay, Ont.	2/14/60	Toronto-St. Catharines
POESCHEK, Rudy	6-1	208	Kamloops, B.C.	9/29/66	Kamloops
RAEDEKE, Mark	5-11	190	Regina, Sask.	1/7/63	U. of Regina
REIFENBERGER, Paul	5-11	191	St. Paul, Minn.	5/27/63	College of St. Thomas
RIDLEY, Mike	6-1	200	Winnipeg, Man.	7/8/63	NY Rangers
SANDSTROM, Tomas	6-2	200	Fagersta, Sweden	9/4/64	NY Rangers
SANKO, Ron	6-1	195	Windsor, Ont.	6/30/65	Kitchener
SHEA, Neil	5-11	194	Boston, Mass.	7/15/63	Boston College
STEPAN, Brad	5-11	185	Hastings, Minn.	8/27/67	
STRUEBY, Todd	6-1	190	Lannigan, Sask.	6/15/63	Muskegon
SUNDSTROM, Peter	6-0	180	Skellefttea, Sweden	12/14/61	NY Rangers
TAIT, Terry	6-2	190	Thunder Bay, Ont.	9/10/63	Springfield
TALAKOSKI, Ron	6-2	215	Thunder Bay, Ont.	6/1/62	
VINGE, Ken	5-10	175	Edmonton, Alta.	1/21/63	U. of Calgary
WALKER, Gordon	6-0	175	Castlegar, B.C.	8/12/65	New Haven

DEFENSEMEN

	Ht.	Wt.	Place of Birth	Date	1985-86 Club
ANDONOFF, Jim	6-2	200	Grosse Pointe, Mich.	8/7/65	Salt Lake-Flint-New Haven
BECK, Barry	6-3	215	Vancouver, B.C.	6/3/57	NY Rangers
BUMBACCO, Nick	6-2	200	Sault Ste. Marie, Ont.	4/19/64	Sault Ste. Marie Sr. A
CARKNER, Terry	6-3	200	Smith Falls, Ont.	3/7/66	Peterborough
DUGGAN, Ken	6-3	210	Toronto, Ont.	2/21/63	U. of Toronto
FELTRIN, Tony	6-1	185	Ladysmith, B.C.	12/6/61	New Haven-NY Rangers
GRESCHNER, Ron	6-2	205	Goodsoil, Sask.	12/22/54	NY Rangers
HUBER, Willie	6-5	225	Strasskirchen, W. Ger.	1/15/58	NY Rangers
LAIDLAW, Tom	6-2	215	Brampton, Ont.	4/15/58	NY Rangers
LEAVINS, Jim	5-11	185	Dinsmore, Sask.		Adirondack-Detroit
MECKLING, Brent	6-2	205	Kelowna, B.C.	9/14/64	U. of Calgary
MELNYK, Larry	6-0	180	Saskatoon, Sask.	2/21/60	Edmonton-NY Rangers
PATRICK, James	6-2	185	Winnipeg, Man.	6/14/63	NY Rangers
PILON, Neil	6-4	182	Merritt, B.C.	4/26/67	Moose Jaw
SAINT CYR, Chris	5-10	190	Winnipeg, Man.	9/14/63	U. of Manitoba
SALO, Vesa	6-2	194	Rauma, Finland	4/17/65	Lukko (Finland)
SAMUELSON, Kjell	6-6	227	Tyringe, Sweden	10/18/56	New Haven-NY Rangers
SMITH, Scott	6-1	185		10/16/62	U. of Maine-New Haven
WHISTLE, Rob	6-2	195	Thunder Bay, Ont.	4/30/61	New Haven-NY Rangers
WIEMER, Jim	6-4	200	Sudbury, Ont.	1/9/61	New Haven-NY Rangers

GOALTENDERS

	Ht.	Wt.	Place of Birth	Date	1985-86 Club
CROUSE, Peter	6-1	190	Trenton, Ont.	11/13/63	
KLEISINGER, Terry	6-0	190	Nanaimo, B.C.	10/22/60	Flint-New Haven-NY Rangers-Toledo
LABILLOIS, Judes	5-9	163	Nuvelle-Gaspesie, Que.	6/15/65	
SCOTT, Ron	5-8	155	Guelph, Ont.	7/21/60	New Haven-NY Rangers
SOETAERT, Doug	6-0	180	Edmonton, Alta.	4/21/55	Montreal
TRAKALO, Derril	5-9	165	Winnipeg, Man.	1/3/63	
VANBIESBROUCK, John	5-10	180	Detroit, Mich.	9/4/63	NY Rangers

1985-86 Scoring

Regular Season

*—rookie

Pos	#	Player	Team	GP	G	A	Pts	+/−	PIM	PP	SH	GW	OT	S	%
F	18	*Mike Ridley	NYR	80	22	43	65	0	69	7	0	6	1	150	14.7
D	29	Reijo Ruotsalainen	NYR	80	17	42	59	22	47	6	0	2	0	228	7.5
F	28	Tomas Sandstrom	NYR	73	25	29	54	4−	109	8	2	1	0	238	10.5
F	4	Ron Greschner	NYR	78	20	28	48	9	104	6	1	2	1	150	13.3
F	26	Brian MacLellan	L.A.	27	5	8	13	13−	19	4	0	0	0	53	9.4
			NYR	51	11	21	32	20−	47	8	0	1	0	112	9.8
			Total	78	16	29	45	33−	66	12	0	1	0	165	9.7
F	13	Bob Brooke	NYR	79	24	20	44	6	111	6	2	1	0	178	13.5
D	3	James Patrick	NYR	75	14	29	43	14	88	2	1	1	1	131	10.7
F	16	Mark Pavelich	NYR	59	20	20	40	3−	82	8	0	3	1	104	19.2
F	19	Mark Osborne	NYR	62	16	24	40	5	80	5	1	1	0	134	11.9
F	23	*Raimo Helminen	NYR	66	10	30	40	1−	10	4	0	2	0	125	8.0
F	32	Bob Crawford	HFD	57	14	20	34	16−	16	4	0	2	0	110	12.7
			NYR	11	1	2	3	2	10	0	0	0	0	15	6.7
			Total	68	15	22	37	14−	26	4	0	2	0	125	12.0
F	10	*Kelly Miller	NYR	74	13	20	33	3	52	0	1	3	0	112	11.6
F	12	Don Maloney	NYR	68	11	17	28	18	56	0	1	0	0	89	12.4
F	24	Pierre Larouche	NYR	28	20	7	27	6−	4	7	0	2	0	85	23.5
F	11	Wilf Paiement	QUE	44	7	12	19	0	145	2	0	0	1	75	9.3
			NYR	8	1	6	7	2	13	0	0	0	0	14	7.1
			Total	52	8	18	26	2	158	2	0	0	1	89	9.0
F	25	Peter Sundstrom	NYR	53	8	15	23	7	12	0	0	1	0	63	12.7
F	20	Jan Erixon	NYR	31	2	17	19	12	4	0	0	0	0	33	6.1
D	2	Tom Laidlaw	NYR	68	6	12	18	3−	103	0	1	0	0	50	12.0
D	27	Willie Huber	NYR	70	7	8	15	11−	85	1	0	2	0	124	5.6
F	14	Mike Allison	NYR	28	2	13	15	4	22	0	0	0	0	26	7.7
D	30	Larry Melnyk	EDM	6	2	3	5	8	11	0	0	0	0	4	50.0
			NYR	46	1	8	9	2	65	0	0	0	0	33	3.0
			Total	52	3	11	14	10	76	0	0	0	0	37	8.1
D	5	Barry Beck	NYR	25	4	8	12	7	24	3	0	1	0	53	7.5
F	9	Dave Gagner	NYR	32	4	6	10	1	19	0	0	0	0	41	9.8
F	21	George McPhee	NYR	30	4	4	8	5	63	0	0	1	0	31	12.9
F	17	*Rob Whistle	NYR	32	4	2	6	1	10	1	0	1	0	30	13.3
F	39	*Chris Jensen	NYR	9	1	3	4	1	0	0	0	1	0	18	5.6
D	6	Jim Wiemer	NYR	7	3	0	3	0	2	0	0	0	0	22	13.6
G	34	John Vanbiesbrouck	NYR	61	0	3	3	0	16	0	0	0	0	0	.0
F	40	*Randy Heath	NYR	1	0	1	1	1	0	0	0	0	0	1	.0
G	1	Glen Hanlon	NYR	23	0	1	1	0	4	0	0	0	0	0	.0
G	44	*Terry Kleisinger	NYR	4	0	0	0	0	2	0	0	0	0	0	.0
G	31	*Ron Scott	NYR	4	0	0	0	0	0	0	0	0	0	0	.0
D	8	*Kjell Samuelsson	NYR	9	0	0	0	1−	10	0	0	0	0	7	.0
D	32	Tony Feltrin	NYR	10	0	0	0	3−	21	0	0	0	0	8	.0

Playoffs

* rookie

Pos	#	Player	Team	GP	G	A	Pts	+/−	PIM	PP	SH	GW	OT	S	%
F	24	Pierre Larouche	NYR	16	8	9	17	5−	2	4	0	1	0	40	20.0
F	13	Bob Brooke	NYR	16	6	9	15	7	28	0	2	2	1	31	19.4
F	18	*Mike Ridley	NYR	16	6	8	14	5−	26	2	0	1	0	31	19.4
F	11	Wilf Paiement	NYR	16	5	5	10	2	45	4	0	0	0	31	16.1
F	28	Tomas Sandstrom	NYR	16	4	6	10	3−	20	0	0	1	0	52	7.7
D	29	Reijo Ruotsalainen	NYR	16	0	8	8	1−	6	0	0	0	0	29	.0
F	10	*Kelly Miller	NYR	16	3	4	7	1−	4	0	1	0	0	17	17.6
F	26	Brian MacLellan	NYR	16	2	4	6	1	15	0	0	1	1	31	6.5
D	3	James Patrick	NYR	16	1	5	6	1	34	0	0	0	0	16	6.3
D	27	Willie Huber	NYR	16	3	2	5	5−	16	2	0	0	0	25	12.0
F	19	Mark Osborne	NYR	15	3	2	5	2−	26	0	1	1	0	30	6.7
F	4	Ron Greschner	NYR	5	3	1	4	2	11	0	0	0	0	9	33.3
F	12	Don Maloney	NYR	16	2	1	3	6−	31	0	0	0	0	10	20.0
D	30	Larry Melnyk	NYR	16	1	2	3	9−	46	0	0	0	0	10	10.0
D	2	Tom Laidlaw	NYR	7	0	2	2	2	12	0	0	0	0	12	.0
F	14	Mike Allison	NYR	16	0	2	2	8−	38	0	0	0	0	13	.0
G	34	John Vanbiesbrouck	NYR	16	0	2	2	0	2	0	0	0	0	0	.0
D	6	Jim Wiemer	NYR	8	1	0	1	1−	6	1	0	1	0	16	6.3
F	32	Bob Crawford	NYR	7	0	1	1	0	8	0	0	0	0	9	.0
D	8	*Kjell Samuelsson	NYR	9	0	1	1	2−	8	0	0	0	0	4	.0
F	20	Jan Erixon	NYR	12	0	1	1	4	4	0	0	0	0	6	.0
F	25	Peter Sundstrom	NYR	1	0	0	0	1−	2	0	0	0	0	0	.0
F	23	*Raimo Helminen	NYR	2	0	0	0	2−	0	0	0	0	0	0	.0
G	1	Glen Hanlon	NYR	3	0	0	0	0	0	0	0	0	0	0	.0
F	17	*Rob Whistle	NYR	3	0	0	0	1	2	0	0	0	0	3	.0
F	21	George McPhee	NYR	11	0	0	0	2−	32	0	0	0	0	6	.0

Club Records
Team

(Figures in brackets for season records are games played; records for fewest points, wins, ties, losses, goals, goals against are for 70 or more games)

Most Points	109	1970-71 (78)
		1971-72 (78)
Most Wins	49	1970-71 (78)
Most Ties	21	1950-51 (70)
Most Losses	44	1984-85 (80)
Most Goals	319	1974-75 (80)
Most Goals Against	345	1984-85 (80)
Fewest Points	47	1965-66 (70)
Fewest Wins	17	1952-53; 54-55; 59-60 (70)
Fewest Ties	6	1985-86 (80)
Fewest Losses	17	1971-72 (78)
Fewest Goals	150	1954-55 (70)
Fewest Goals Against	177	1970-71 (78)

Longest Winning Streak

Over-all ... 10 Dec. 19/39-Jan. 13/40

Home ... 14 Dec. 19/39-Feb. 25/40

Away ... 7 Jan. 12-Feb. 12/35; Oct. 28-Nov. 29/78

Longest Undefeated Streak

Over-all ... 19 Nov. 23/39-Jan. 13/40 (14 wins, 5 ties)

Home ... 26 Mar. 29/70-Feb. 2/71 (19 wins, 7 ties)

Away ... 11 Nov. 5/39-Jan. 13/40 (6 wins, 5 ties)

Longest Losing Streak

Over-all ... 11 Oct. 30-Nov. 27/43

Home ... 7 Oct. 20-Nov. 14/76

Away ... 10 Oct. 30-Dec. 23/43

Longest Winless Streak

Over-all ... 21 Jan. 23-Mar. 19/44 (17 losses, 4 ties)

Home ... 10 Jan. 30-Mar. 19/44 (7 losses, 3 ties)

Away ... 16 Oct. 9-Dec. 20/52 (12 losses, 4 ties)

Most Shutouts, Season ... 13 1928-29 (44)

Most. Pen. Mins., Season ... 1,981 1980-81 (80)

Most Goals, Game ... 12 Nov. 21/71 (Cal. 1 at NYR 12)

Individual

Most Seasons	17	Harry Howell
Most Games	1,160	Harry Howell
Most Goals, Career	406	Rod Gilbert
Most Assists, Career	615	Rod Gilbert
Most Points, Career	1,021	Rod Gilbert (406 goals, 615 assists)
Most Pen. Mins., Career	1,147	Harry Howell
Most Shutouts, Career	49	Ed Giacomin

Longest Consecutive Games Streak ... 560 Andy Hebenton (Oct. 7/55-Mar. 24/63)

Most Goals, Season ... 50 Vic Hadfield (1971-72)

Most Assists, Season ... 65 Mike Rogers (1981-82)

Most Points, Season ... 109 Jean Ratelle (1971-72) (46 goals, 63 assists)

Most Pen. Mins., Season ... 231 Barry Beck (1980-81)

Most Points, Defenseman Season ... 82 Brad Park (1973-74) (25 goals, 57 assists)

Most Points, Center, Season ... 109 Jean Ratelle (1971-72) (46 goals, 63 assists)

Most Points, Right Wing, Season ... 97 Rod Gilbert (1971-72) (43 goals, 54 assists) Rod Gilbert (1974-75) (36 goals, 61 assists)

Most Points, Left Wing, Season ... 106 Vic Hadfield (1971-72) (50 goals, 56 assists)

Most Points, Rookie, Season ... 76 Mark Pavelich (1981-82) (33 goals, 43 assists)

Most Shutouts, Season ... 13 John Ross Roach (1928-29)

Most Goals, Game ... 5 Don Murdoch (Oct. 12/76) Mark Pavelich (Feb. 23/83)

Most Assists, Game ... 5 Walt Tkaczuk (Feb. 12/72) Rod Gilbert (Mar. 2/75; Mar. 30/75; Oct. 8/76)

Most Points, Game ... 7 Steve Vickers (Feb. 18/76)

Coaching History

Lester Patrick, 1926-27 to 1938-39; Frank Boucher, 1939-40 to 1947-48; Frank Boucher and Lynn Patrick, 1948-49; Lynn Patrick, 1949-50; Neil Colville, 1950-51; Neil Colville and Bill Cook, 1951-52; Bill Cook, 1952-53; Frank Boucher and Murray Patrick, 1953-54; Murray Patrick, 1954-55; Phil Watson, 1955-56 to 1958-59; Phil Watson and Alf Pike, 1959-60; Alf Pike, 1960-61; Doug Harvey, 1961-62; Murray Patrick and George Sullivan, 1962-63; George Sullivan, 1963-64 to 1964-65; George Sullivan and Emile Francis, 1965-66; Emile Francis, 1966-67 to 1967-68; Bernie Geoffrion and Emile Francis, 1968-69; Emile Francis, 1969-70 to 1972-73; Larry Popein and Emile Francis, 1973-74; Emile Francis, 1974-75; Ron Stewart and John Ferguson, 1975-76; John Ferguson, 1976-77; Jean-Guy Talbot, 1977-78; Fred Shero, 1978-79 to 1979-80; Fred Shero and Craig Patrick, 1980-81; Herb Brooks, 1981-82 to 1983-84; Herb Brooks and Craig Patrick, 1984-85; Ted Sator, 1985-86 to date.

All-time Record vs. Other Clubs
Regular Season

			At Home							On Road							Total				
	GP	W	L	T	GF	GA	PTS	GP	W	L	T	GF	GA	PTS	GP	W	L	T	GF	GA	PTS
Boston	268	115	101	52	809	748	282	267	83	147	37	745	982	203	535	198	248	89	1554	1730	485
Buffalo	33	14	10	9	122	96	37	35	9	21	5	112	159	23	68	23	31	14	234	255	60
**Calgary	33	14	15	4	117	118	32	32	9	17	6	93	138	24	65	23	32	10	210	256	56
Chicago	268	112	105	51	787	761	275	267	105	122	40	735	812	250	535	217	227	91	1522	1573	525
Detroit	266	127	83	56	812	672	310	266	73	150	43	648	926	189	532	200	233	99	1460	1598	499
Edmonton	12	4	7	1	51	45	9	11	5	5	1	38	41	11	23	9	12	2	89	86	20
Hartford	11	6	3	2	49	31	14	12	4	6	2	43	50	10	23	10	9	4	92	81	24
Los Angeles	40	23	12	5	157	111	51	41	17	16	8	145	131	42	81	40	28	13	302	242	93
Minnesota	42	26	8	8	153	115	60	43	24	13	6	172	129	54	85	50	21	14	325	244	114
Montreal	257	104	104	49	742	749	257	257	54	170	33	590	1013	141	514	158	274	82	1332	1762	398
*New Jersey	31	19	8	4	137	95	42	33	20	9	4	139	103	44	64	39	17	8	276	198	86
NY Islanders	44	28	14	2	178	137	58	43	12	30	1	134	197	25	87	40	44	3	312	334	83
Philadelphia	57	22	18	17	183	167	61	57	17	30	10	157	201	44	114	39	48	27	340	368	105
Pittsburgh	51	28	18	5	214	168	61	51	28	16	7	190	162	63	102	56	34	12	404	330	124
Québec	12	6	3	3	47	40	15	11	2	6	3	46	55	7	23	8	9	6	93	95	22
St. Louis	43	36	3	4	188	93	76	43	18	18	7	140	133	43	86	54	21	11	328	226	119
Toronto	257	106	98	53	771	744	265	257	73	147	37	656	889	183	514	179	245	90	1427	1633	448
Vancouver	36	27	6	3	161	87	57	34	23	9	2	135	105	48	70	50	15	5	296	192	105
Washington	32	18	10	4	156	119	40	32	9	16	7	109	138	25	64	27	26	11	265	257	65
Winnipeg	11	6	4	1	64	54	13	12	5	6	1	40	47	11	23	11	10	2	104	101	24
Defunct Clubs	139	87	30	22	460	290	196	139	82	34	23	441	291	187	278	169	64	45	901	581	383
Totals	1943	928	660	355	6358	5440	2211	1943	672	988	283	5508	6702	1627	3886	1600	1648	638	11866	12142	3838

* Totals include those of Kansas City (1974-75, 1975-76) and Colorado (1976-77 through 1981-82)

** Totals include those of Atlanta (1972-73 through 1979-80)

Playoffs

	Series	W	L	GP	W	L	T	GF	GA	Last Mtg.	Round	Result
Boston	9	3	6	42	18	22	2	104	114	1973	QF	W 4-1
Buffalo	1	0	1	3	1	2	0	6	11	1978	P	L 1-2
Calgary	1	1	0	4	3	1	0	14	8	1980	P	W 3-1
Chicago	5	1	4	24	10	14	0	54	66	1973	SF	L 1-4
Detroit	5	1	4	23	10	13	0	49	57	1950	F	L 3-4
Los Angeles	2	2	0	6	5	1	0	32	14	1981	P	W 3-1
Montreal	13	7	6	55	21	32	2	139	171	1986	CF	L 1-4
NY Islanders	6	1	5	30	11	19	0	87	114	1984	DSF	L 2-3
Philadelphia	7	4	3	32	17	15	0	117	97	1986	DSF	W 3-2
St. Louis	1	1	0	6	4	2	0	29	22	1981	QF	W 4-2
Toronto	8	5	3	35	19	16	0	86	86	1971	QF	W 4-2
Washington	1	1	0	6	4	2	0	20	25	1986	DF	W 4-2
Defunct Clubs	9	6	3	22	11	7	4	43	29			
Totals	63	32	31	264	124	132	8	726	748			

Playoff Results 1986-82

Year	Round	Opponent	Result	GF	GA
1985	DSF	Philadelphia	L 0-3	10	14
1984	DSF	NY Islanders	L 2-3	14	13
1983	DF	NY Islanders	L 2-4	15	28
	DSF	Philadelphia	W 3-0	18	9
1982	DF	NY Islanders	L 2-4	20	27
	DSF	Philadelphia	W 3-1	19	15

Abbreviations: Round: F – Final; CF – conference final; DF – division final; DSF – division semi-final; SF – semi-final; QF – quarter-final; P – preliminary round. GA – goals against. GF – goals for.

Captains' History

Bill Cook, 1926-27 to 1936-37; Art Coulter, 1937-38 to 1941-42; Ott Heller, 1942-43 to 1944-45; Neil Colville 1945-46 to 1948-49; Buddy O'Connor, 1949-50; Frank Eddolls, 1950-51; Frank Eddolls, Allan Stanley, 1951-52; Allan Stanley, 1952-53; Allan Stanley, Don Raleigh, 1953-54; Don Raleigh, 1954-55; Harry Howell, 1955-56, 1956-57; George Sullivan, 1957-58 to 1960-61; Andy Bathgate, 1961-61, 1962-63; Andy Bathgate, Camille Henry, 1963-64; Camille Henry, Bob Nevin, 1964-65; Bob Nevin 1965-66 to 1970-71; Vic Hadfield, 1971-72 to 1973-74; Brad Park, 1974-75; Brad Park, Phil Esposito, 1975-76; Phil Esposito, 1976-77, 1977-78; Dave Maloney, 1978-79, 1979-80; Dave Maloney, Walt Tkaczuk, Barry Beck, 1980-81; Barry Beck, 1981-82 to 1985-86.

Retired Numbers

7	Rod Gilbert	1960-1978

Entry Draft Selections 1986-72

1986
Pick
9	Brian Leetch
51	Bret Walter
53	Shawn Clouston
72	Mark Janssens
93	Jeff Bloemberg
114	Darren Turcotte
135	Robb Graham
156	Barry Chyzowski
177	Pat Scanlon
198	Joe Ranger
219	Russell Parent
240	Soren True

1985
Pick
7	Ulf Dahlen
28	Mike Richter
49	Sam Lindstahl
70	Pat Janostin
91	Brad Stephan
112	Brian McReynolds
133	Neil Pilon
154	Lary Bernard
175	Stephane Brochu
196	Steve Nemeth
217	Robert Burakovski
238	Rudy Poeschek

1984
Pick
14	Terry Carkner
35	Raimo Helminen
77	Paul Broten
98	Clark Donatelli
119	Kjell Samuelsson
140	Thomas Hussey
161	Brian Nelson
182	Ville Kentala
188	Heinz Ehlers
202	Kevin Miller
223	Tom Lorentz
243	Scott Brower

1983
Pick
12	Dave Gagner
33	Randy Heath
49	Vesa Salo
53	Gordie Walker
73	Peter Andersson
93	Jim Andonoff
113	Bob Alexander
133	Steve Orth
153	Peter Marcov
173	Paul Jerrard
213	Bryan Walker
233	Ulf Nilsson

1982
Pick
15	Chris Kontos
36	Tomas Sandstrom
57	Corey Millen
78	Chris Jensen
120	Tony Granato
141	Sergei Kapustin
160	Brian Glynn
162	Jan Karlsson
183	Kelly Miller
193	Simo Saarinen
204	Bob Lowes
225	Andy Otto
246	Dwayne Robinson

1981
Pick
9	James Patrick
30	Jan Erixon
50	Peter Sundstrom
51	Mark Morrison
72	John Vanbiesbrouck
114	Eric Magnuson
135	Mike Guentzel
156	Ari Lahtenmaki
177	Paul Reifenberger
198	Mario Proulx

1980
Pick
14	Jim Malone
35	Mike Allison
77	Kurt Kleinendorst
98	Scot Kleinendorst
119	Reijo Ruotsalainen
140	Bob Scurfield
161	Bart Wilson
182	Chris Wray
203	Anders Backstrom

1979
Pick
13	Doug Sulliman
34	Ed Hospodar
76	Pat Conacher
97	Dan Makuch
118	Stan Adams

1978
Pick
26	Don Maloney
43	Ray Markham
44	Dean Turner
59	Dave Silk
60	Andre Dore
76	Mike McDougall
93	Tom Laidlaw
110	Dan Clark
127	Greg Kostenko
144	Brian McDavid
161	Mark Rodrigues
176	Steve Weeks
192	Pierre Daigneault
206	Chris McLaughlin
217	Todd Johnson
223	Dan McCarthy

1977
Pick
8	Lucien DeBlois
13	Ron Duguay
26	Mike Keating
44	Steve Baker
62	Mario Marois
80	Benoit Gosselin
98	John Bethel
116	Robert Sullivan
131	Lance Nethery
146	Alex Jeans
157	Peter Raps
164	Mike Brown
171	Mark Miller

1976
Pick
6	Don Murdoch
24	Dave Farrish
42	Mike McEwen
60	Claude Periard
78	Doug Gaines
96	Barry Scully
112	Remi Levesque

1975
Pick
12	Wayne Dillon
30	Doug Soetaert
49	Greg Hickey
66	Bill Cheropita
84	Larry Huras
102	Randy Koch
120	Claude Larose
138	Bill Hamilton
154	Bud Stefanski
169	Daniel Beaulieu
184	John McMorrow
195	Tom McNamara
200	Steve Roberts
201	Paul Dionne
205	Cecil Luckern
209	John Corriveau
212	Tom Funke

1974
Pick
14	Dave Maloney
32	Ron Greschner
50	Jerry Holland
68	Boyd Anderson
86	Dennis Olmstead
104	Ed Johnstone
122	John Memryk
139	Greg Holst
156	Claude Arvisais
171	Ken Dodd
186	Ralph Krentz
198	Larry Jacques
208	Tom Gastle
218	Eric Brubacher
224	Russ Hall
227	Bill Kriski
230	Kevin Treacy
233	Ken Gassoff
236	Cliff Bast
239	Jim Mayer
241	Warren Miller
243	Kevin Walker
245	Jim Warner

1973
Pick
14	Rick Middleton
30	Pat Hickey
46	John Campbell
62	Brian Molvik
78	Pierre Laganiere
94	Dwayne Pentland

1972
Pick
10	Albert Blanchard
15	Bob MacMillan
21	Larry Sacharuk
31	Rene Villemure
47	Gerry Teeple
63	Doug Horbul
79	Martin Gateman
95	Ken Ireland
111	Jeff Hunt
127	Yvon Blais
137	Pierre Archambault

Club Directory

Madison Square Garden
4 Pennsylvania Plaza
New York, New York 10001
Phone 212/563-8000
TWX 710-581-4528
ENVOY ID TM.NYR
Capacity: 17,500

President	John H. Krumpe
Vice President & General Manager	Phil Esposito
Vice President & General Counsel	Kenneth W. Munoz
Assistant Vice President, Legal Affairs	Kevin Billet
Vice President, Alternate Governor	Mel Lowell
Treasurer	Stephen Schwartz
Vice-President, Communications	John Halligan
Coach	Ted Sator
Assistant Coaches	Jack Birch, Reg Higgs
Goaltending Coach/Special Assignment Scout	Ed Giacomin
Assistant to the General Manager	Joe Bucchino
Executive Asst. to Vice President and General Manager	Rita White
Administrative Asst. to Vice President & General Manager	Karen Zaneski
Public Relations Assistants	Barry Watkins, Matt Loughran
Statistician	Arthur Friedman
Scouting Staff	Wayne Cashman, Chuck Grillo, Lou Jankowski, Richard Rose, Lars Erik Sjoberg
Team Physician/Ortho Surgeon	Barton Nisonson, M.D.
Medical Consultants	James A. Nicholas, Anthony Maddalo, Howard Chester, Peter Bruno, Ronald Weissman, Irwin Miller, Gaetano T.A. Viti
Training Staff	Joe Murphy, Jerry Maloney, Dave Smith
Executive Offices	Madison Square Garden
Home Ice	Madison Square Garden
Press Facilities	33rd Street
Television Facilities	31st Street
Radio Facilities	33rd Street
Rink Dimensions	200 feet by 85 feet
Ends and Sides of Rink	Herculite Tempered Plate Glass
Club Colors	Blue, Red, White
Training Camp	Rye, New York
TV Announcers	Sam Rosen, Bruce Beck, John Davidson
Radio Announcers	Marv Albert, Sal Messina
Television Outlets	WOR-TV (9) and Madison Square Garden Cable Network
Radio Outlet	WNBC (66 AM)

Coach and General Manager

SATOR, THEODORE RICHARD (TED)
Coach, New York Rangers. Born in Utica, N.Y., November 18, 1949.
When Ted Sator was named head coach of the Rangers on June 19, 1985 he brought with him a wealth of experience. He served as an assistant coach with the United States entry in the 1984 Canada Cup tournament and was the first American to be invited to the Czechoslovokian National Team Symposium in 1983. Sator served two years as the Philadelphia Flyers' assistant coach under Bob McCammon and Mike Keenan. Sator had a brief playing career with New York Raiders of the WHA.

NHL Coaching Record

| Team | Season | Games | Regular Season | | | | Playoffs | | | |
			W	L	T	%	Games	W	L	%
New York Rangers	1985-86	80	36	38	6	.488	16	8	8	.500
NHL Totals		80	36	38	6	.488	16	8	8	.500

ESPOSITO, PHIL
General Manager, New York Rangers. Born in Sault Ste. Marie, Ont., February 20, 1942.
After an 18-year Hall of Fame career, including two Hart Trophies (League MVP), five Art Ross Trophies (top scorer) and eight All-Star selections, Phil Esposito brings to the New York Rangers' front office the same winning attitude that made him so extraordinary as a player. Named Vice-President and General Manager of the Rangers on July 14, 1986, Esposito began his professional career in 1963-64 with the Chicago Blackhawks, where he played for four seasons. He was traded to Boston, where he played for eight years and helped lead the Bruins to two Stanley Cup championships in 1970 and 1972. Dealt to the Rangers in November, 1975, Esposito skated in New York for the final six years of his career and played a major role on the club's last Stanley Cup Final appearance in 1979. The NHL's third all-time leading point-scorer with 1,590, he ranks second only to Gordie Howe in all-time goals with 717 and fourth in all-time assists with 873 in 1,282 regular-season contests. Esposito also added 61 goals and 76 assists for 137 points in 130 playoff games. During the 1968-69 campaign, he became the first player in NHL history to shatter the 100-point barrier. Immediately following his playing career, Esposito became an assistant coach with the Rangers until joining the Madison Square Garden Network as a color commentator in the Fall of 1981.

Philadelphia Flyers

1985-86 Results: 53w-23L-4T 110 PTS. First, Patrick Division

Year-by-Year Record

Season	GP	Home W	L	T	Road W	L	T	Overall W	L	T	GF	GA	Pts.	Finished	Playoff Result
1985-86	80	33	6	1	20	17	3	53	23	4	335	241	110	1st, Patrick Div.	Lost Div. Semi-Final
1984-85	80	32	4	4	21	16	3	53	20	7	348	241	113	1st, Patrick Div.	Lost Final
1983-84	80	25	10	5	19	16	5	44	26	10	350	290	98	3rd, Patrick Div.	Lost Div. Semi-Final
1982-83	80	29	8	3	20	15	5	49	23	8	326	240	106	1st, Patrick Div.	Lost Div. Semi-Final
1981-82	80	25	10	5	13	21	6	38	31	11	325	313	87	3rd, Patrick Div.	Lost Div. Semi-Final
1980-81	80	23	9	8	18	15	7	41	24	15	313	249	97	2nd, Patrick Div.	Lost Quarter-Final
1979-80	80	27	5	8	21	7	12	48	12	20	327	254	116	1st, Patrick Div.	Lost Final
1978-79	80	26	10	4	14	15	11	40	25	15	281	248	95	2nd, Patrick Div.	Lost Quarter-Final
1977-78	80	29	6	5	16	14	10	45	20	15	296	200	105	2nd, Patrick Div.	Lost Semi-Final
1976-77	80	33	6	1	15	10	15	48	16	16	323	213	112	1st, Patrick Div.	Lost Semi-Final
1975-76	80	36	2	2	15	11	14	51	13	16	348	209	118	1st, Patrick Div.	Lost Final
1974-75	**80**	**32**	**6**	**2**	**19**	**12**	**9**	**51**	**18**	**11**	**293**	**181**	**113**	**1st, Patrick Div.**	**Won Stanley Cup**
1973-74	**78**	**28**	**6**	**5**	**22**	**10**	**7**	**50**	**16**	**12**	**273**	**164**	**112**	**1st, West Div.**	**Won Stanley Cup**
1972-73	78	27	8	4	10	22	7	37	30	11	296	256	85	2nd, West Div.	Lost Semi-Final
1971-72	78	19	13	7	7	25	7	26	38	14	200	236	66	5th, West Div.	Out of Playoffs
1970-71	78	20	10	9	8	23	8	28	33	17	207	225	73	3rd, West Div.	Lost Quarter-Final
1969-70	76	11	14	13	6	21	11	17	35	24	197	225	58	5th, West Div.	Out of Playoffs
1968-69	76	14	16	8	6	19	13	20	35	21	174	225	61	3rd, West Div.	Lost Quarter-Final
1967-68	74	17	13	7	14	19	4	31	32	11	173	179	73	1st, West Div.	Lost Quarter-Final

Schedule

Home

Oct.	Thur.	9	Edmonton
	Thur.	16	Vancouver
	Sun.	19	Winnipeg
	Thur.	23	Pittsburgh
	Sun.	26	Minnesota
	Thur.	30	Quebec
Nov.	Sat.	1	Boston
	Tue.	4	New Jersey
	Sat.	8	NY Rangers*
	Thur.	13	Detroit
	Sun.	16	Washington
	Thur.	20	Chicago
	Sat.	22	Toronto
	Wed.	26	Montreal
Dec.	Tue.	2	St. Louis
	Thur.	4	Hartford
	Sun.	7	Edmonton
	Tue.	9	Vancouver
	Thur.	11	Calgary
	Thur.	18	NY Islanders
	Sun.	21	St. Louis
Jan.	Tue.	6	New Jersey
	Sun.	11	Washington
	Thur.	15	Montreal
	Sun.	18	NY Islanders
	Fri.	23	Chicago
	Thur.	29	Pittsburgh
	Sat.	31	NY Rangers*
Feb.	Mon.	16	Calgary*
	Thur.	19	Pittsburgh
Mar.	Tue.	3	Buffalo
	Thur.	5	Washington
	Sun.	8	New Jersey*
	Thur.	12	NY Rangers
	Tue.	17	NY Rangers
	Thur.	19	Los Angeles
	Sun.	22	Pittsburgh
	Thur.	26	Quebec
	Sat.	28	Detroit*
April	Sun.	5	NY Islanders

Away

Oct.	Sat.	11	Washington
	Sat.	18	Hartford
	Sat.	25	Pittsburgh
	Tue.	28	NY Islanders
Nov.	Thur.	6	New Jersey
	Fri.	14	NY Rangers
	Wed.	19	Toronto
	Fri.	28	Washington
	Sat.	29	NY Islanders
Dec.	Sat.	6	Boston*
	Sat.	13	Minnesota
	Sun.	14	Winnipeg
	Sat.	20	Pittsburgh
	Tue.	23	Buffalo
	Sat.	27	Vancouver
	Sun.	28	Edmonton
	Tue.	30	Los Angeles
Jan.	Sat.	3	Washington
	Wed.	7	NY Rangers
	Sat.	10	Boston*
	Sat.	17	NY Islanders
	Wed.	21	Chicago
	Sat.	24	New Jersey
	Wed.	28	Buffalo
Feb.	Mon.	2	Toronto
	Wed.	4	Winnipeg
	Sat.	7	New Jersey*
	Sat.	14	St. Louis
	Tue.	17	NY Islanders
	Sat.	21	Los Angeles
	Thur.	26	Calgary
Mar.	Sun.	1	Minnesota
	Sat.	7	Hartford
	Wed.	11	New Jersey
	Sat.	14	Montreal
	Sun.	15	NY Rangers
	Sat.	21	Quebec
	Tue.	24	Pittsburgh
April	Wed.	1	Detroit
	Sat.	4	Washington

*Denotes afternoon game.

Home Starting Times:

Weeknights & Saturdays	7:35 p.m.
Saturday Matinees	1:05 p.m.
Sundays	7:05 p.m.
Except Feb. 16	1:35 p.m.
Mar. 8	2:05 p.m.

Franchise date: June 5, 1967

20th NHL Season

Ron Sutter

1986-87 Player Personnel

FORWARDS	Ht.	Wt.	Place of Birth	Date	1985-86 Club
ALLISON, Ray	5-10	195	Cranbrook, B.C.	3/4/59	Hershey
BERUBE, Craig	6-2	195	Calihoo, Alta.	12/17/65	Medicine Hat
BROWN, Dave	6-5	205	Saskatoon, Sask.	10/12/62	Philadelphia
CARSON, Lindsay	6-2	195	N. Battleford, Sask.	11/21/60	Philadelphia
CRAVEN, Murray	6-2	175	Medicine Hat, Alta.	7/20/64	Philadelphia
DOBBIN, Brian	5-11	195	Petrolia, Ont.	8/18/66	London-Hershey
DZIKOWSKI, John	6-3	190	Point La Prairie, Man.	1/28/66	Seattle
EKLUND, Pelle	5-10	170	Stockholm, Sweden	3/22/63	Philadelphia
FITZPATRICK, Ross	6-1	195	Penticton, B.C.	10/7/60	Hershey-Philadelphia
HAWLEY, Kent	6-3	215	Kingston, Ont.	2/20/68	Ottawa
HILL, Al	6-1	175	Nanaimo, B.C.	4/22/55	Hershey
HOLMES, Daril	6-6	200	Cornwall, Ont.	2/15/67	Kingston
HORACEK, Tony	6-3	200	Vancouver, B.C.	3/3/67	Spokane
KERR, Tim	6-3	225	Windsor, Ont.	1/5/60	Philadelphia
KYPREOS, Nick	6-0	190	Toronto, Ont.	6/4/66	North Bay
LAMOREUX, Mitch	5-6	175	Ottawa, Ont.	8/22/62	Baltimore
MARTINSON, Steve	6-1	205	Minnetonka, Minn.	6/21/57	Hershey
MAXWELL, Kevin	5-9	170	Edmonton, Alta.	3/30/60	Maine
McLAY, Dave	5-11	175	Chilliwack, B.C.	5/13/66	Portland
MELLANBY, Scott	6-1	195	Montreal, Que.	6/11/66	U. of Wisconsin
MURRAY, Mike	6-0	185	Kingston, Ont.	8/29/66	Guelph
NACHBAUR, Don	6-2	200	Kitimat, B.C.	1/30/59	Hershey-Philadelphia
POULIN, Dave	5-11	180	Timmins, Ont.	12/17/58	Philadelphia
PROPP, Brian	5-10	190	Lanigan, Sask.	2/15/59	Philadelphia
SEABROOKE, Glen	6-1	175	Peterborough, Ont.	9/11/67	Peterborough
SEGUIN, Steve	6-1	191	Cornwall, Ont.	4/10/64	Hershey
SINISALO, Ilkka	6-1	190	Valeakoski, Fin.	7/10/58	Philadelphia
SMITH, Derrick	6-1	185	Scarborough, Ont.	1/22/65	Philadelphia
SUTTER, Ron	5-11	175	Viking, Alta.	12/2/63	Philadelphia
TOCCHET, Rick	6-0	195	Scarborough, Ont.	4/9/64	Philadelphia
TOOKEY, Tim	5-11	185	Edmonton, Alta.	8/29/60	Hershey
ZEZEL, Peter	5-9	200	Toronto, Ont.	4/22/65	Philadelphia
DEFENSEMEN					
ARMSTRONG, Ian	6-4	200	Peterborough, Ont.	1/25/65	Hershey
CHYCHRUN, Jeff	6-4	185	La Salle, Que.	5/3/66	Kingston
CROSSMAN, Doug	6-2	190	Peterborough, Ont.	6/30/60	Philadelphia
DAIGNEAULT, J.J.	5-11	180	Montreal, Que.	10/12/65	Vancouver
HOSPODAR, Ed	6-2	210	Bowling Green, Ohio	2/9/59	Philadelphia-Minnesota
HOWE, Mark	5-11	190	Detroit, Mich.	5/28/55	Philadelphia
HUFFMAN, Kerry	6-2	180	Peterborough, Ont.	1/3/68	Peterborough
MARSH, Brad	6-3	220	London, Ont.	3/31/58	Philadelphia
MAURICE, Paul	6-2	180	Sault Ste. Marie, Ont.	1/30/67	Windsor
MURPHY, Gordon	6-1	180	Willowdale, Ont.	2/23/67	Oshawa
McCARTHY, Kevin	5-11	195	Winnipeg, Man.	7/14/57	Hershey-Philadelphia
McCRIMMON, Brad	5-11	200	Dodsland, Sask.	3/29/59	Philadelphia
SMITH, Steve	5-9	200	Trenton, Ont.	4/4/63	Hershey-Philadelphia
SMYTH, Greg	6-3	194	Oakville, Ont.	4/23/66	London-Hershey
STANLEY, Daryl	6-2	200	Winnipeg, Man.	12/2/62	Philadelphia-Hershey
STEVENS, John	6-1	185	Completon, N.B.	5/4/66	Oshawa
STOTHERS, Mike	6-4	210	Toronto, Ont.	2/22/62	Hershey-Philadelphia
VILLENEUVE, Andre	6-0	190	Alma, Que.	1/19/63	Hershey
GOALTENDERS					
FROESE, Bob	5-11	180	St. Catharines, Ont.	6/30/58	Philadelphia
GILMORE, Darryl	5-11	160	Winnipeg, Man.	2/13/67	Moose Jaw
HEXTALL, Ron	6-3	180	Brandon, Man.	5/3/64	Hershey
JENSEN, Darren	5-9	165	Creston, B.C.	5/27/60	Philadelphia-Hershey
KEMP, John	6-0	185	Burlington, Ont.	7/31/63	Hershey
RESCH, Glenn	5-9	165	Moose Jaw, Sask.	7/10/48	Philadelphia-New Jersey

Coach and General Manager

KEENAN, MICHAEL (MIKE)
Coach, Philadelphia Flyers. Born in Toronto, Ont., October 21, 1949.

Mike Keenan was named coach of the Flyers on May 24, 1984, and in his first season led Philadelphia to a first place overall finish, and a Stanley Cup finals berth. Prior to joining the Flyers, he guided the University of Toronto Blues to a Canadian Intercollegiate Athletic Union Championship. He led the Rochester Americans to a Calder Cup victroy. Keenan is a graduate of St. Lawrence University and has coached at the international level with the 1980 and 1981 Canadian National Junior teams.

NHL Coaching Record

		Regular Season					Playoffs			
Team		Games	W	L	T	%	Games	W	L	%
Philadelphia	1984-85	80	53	20	7	.706	19	12	7	.632
Philadelphia	1985-86	80	53	23	4	.688	5	2	3	.400
NHL Total		**160**	**106**	**43**	**11**	**.697**	**24**	**14**	**10**	**.583**

CLARKE, ROBERT EARLE (BOBBY)
General Manager, Philadelphia Flyers. Born in Flin Flon, Man., August 13, 1949.

After 15 seasons with the Flyers, Bobby Clarke retired as a player to become the General Manager of the Philadelphia club. In his first season, the Flyers finished with 113 points and reached the Stanley Cup finals. As a player, the former Philadelphia captain led his club to Stanley Cup championships in 1974 and 1975 and captured numerous individual awards, including the Hart Trophy as the League's Most Valuable Player in 1973, 1975 and 1976. The four-time All-Star also received the Masterton Memorial Trophy (perseverence and dedication) in 1972 and Frank J. Selke Trophy (top defensive forward) in 1983. Drafted 17th overall in the 1969 Amateur Draft from the Flin Flon Bombers, Clarke appeared in 1,144 regular-season games, scoring 358 goals, 852 assists for 1210 points. He also added 119 points in 136 playoff games.

1985-86 Scoring

Regular Season

*–rookie

Pos	#	Player	Team	GP	G	A	Pts	+/–	PIM	PP	SH	GW	OT	S	%
F	26	Brian Propp	PHI	72	40	57	97	24	47	11	2	5	0	317	12.6
F	12	Tim Kerr	PHI	76	58	26	84	5–	79	34	0	8	0	285	20.4
D	2	Mark Howe	PHI	77	24	58	82	85	36	4	7	3	0	193	12.4
F	23	Ilkka Sinisalo	PHI	74	39	37	76	17	31	19	1	7	1	187	20.9
F	20	Dave Poulin	PHI	79	27	42	69	20	49	2	6	2	1	181	14.9
F	9	*Per-Erik Eklund	PHI	70	15	51	66	4–	12	8	0	5	0	141	10.6
F	14	Ron Sutter	PHI	75	18	41	59	26	159	0	0	4	0	145	12.4
D	10	Brad McCrimmon	PHI	80	13	43	56	83	85	2	0	2	0	162	8.0
F	32	Murray Craven	PHI	78	21	33	54	24	34	2	0	6	0	182	11.5
F	25	Peter Zezel	PHI	79	17	37	54	27	76	4	0	4	0	144	11.8
D	3	Doug Crossman	PHI	80	6	37	43	5–	55	2	0	1	0	134	4.5
F	15	Rich Sutter	PHI	78	14	25	39	28	199	0	0	2	0	124	11.3
F	22	Rick Tocchet	PHI	69	14	21	35	12	284	3	0	1	0	107	13.1
F	18	Lindsay Carson	PHI	50	9	12	21	10	84	0	0	0	0	59	15.3
F	21	Dave Brown	PHI	76	10	7	17	7	277	0	0	1	0	73	13.7
D	8	Brad Marsh	PHI	79	0	13	13	0	123	0	0	0	0	104	.0
F	24	Derrick Smith	PHI	69	6	6	12	14	57	0	0	2	0	108	5.6
D	34	Dave Richter	MIN	14	0	3	3	6–	29	0	0	0	0	5	.0
			PHI	50	0	2	2	2–	138	0	0	0	0	17	.0
			Total	64	0	5	5	8–	167	0	0	0	0	22	.0
F	37	Bo Berglund	MIN	3	2	0	2	0	2	1	0	0	1	6	33.3
			PHI	7	0	2	2	0	4	0	0	0	0	5	.0
			Total	10	2	2	4	0	6	1	0	0	1	11	18.2
D	27	Thomas Eriksson	PHI	43	0	4	4	12–	16	0	0	0	0	32	.0
F	42	Don Nachbaur	PHI	5	1	1	2	3	7	0	0	0	0	4	25.0
D	29	*Darryl Stanley	PHI	33	0	2	2	5–	69	0	0	0	0	7	.0
D	44	*Mike Stothers	PHI	6	0	1	1	1	6	0	0	0	0	1	.0
G	30	*Darren Jensen	PHI	29	0	1	1	0	2	0	0	0	0	0	.0
G	35	Bob Froese	PHI	51	0	1	1	0	8	0	0	0	0	0	.0
F	36	Carl Mokosak	PHI	1	0	0	0	0	5	0	0	0	0	0	.0
F	39	*Ross Fitzpatrick	PHI	2	0	0	0	1–	0	0	0	0	0	0	.0
F	19	*Scott Mellanby	PHI	2	0	0	0	1–	0	0	0	0	0	0	.0
D	5	*Steve Smith	PHI	2	0	0	0	1–	2	0	0	0	0	1	.0
D	5	Kevin McCarthy	PHI	4	0	0	0	0	4	0	0	0	0	0	.0
G	31	Pelle Lindbergh	PHI	8	0	0	0	0	0	0	0	0	0	0	.0
G	33	Glenn Resch	N.J	31	0	0	0	0	14	0	0	0	0	0	.0
			PHI	5	0	0	0	0	0	0	0	0	0	0	.0
			Total	36	0	0	0	0	14	0	0	0	0	0	.0

Playoffs

* rookie

Pos	#	Player	Team	GP	G	A	Pts	+/–	PIM	PP	SH	GW	OT	S	%
F	12	Tim Kerr	PHI	5	3	3	6	2–	8	1	0	0	0	22	13.6
F	25	Peter Zezel	PHI	5	3	1	4	2–	4	1	0	1	0	11	27.3
F	23	Ilkka Sinisalo	PHI	5	2	2	4	1	2	0	0	0	0	11	18.2
D	2	Mark Howe	PHI	5	0	4	4	0	0	0	0	0	0	16	.0
F	22	Rick Tocchet	PHI	5	1	2	3	1	26	0	0	0	0	10	10.0
F	32	Murray Craven	PHI	5	0	3	3	0	4	0	0	0	0	10	.0
D	10	Brad McCrimmon	PHI	5	2	0	2	1	2	0	0	1	0	14	14.3
F	20	Dave Poulin	PHI	5	2	0	2	4–	2	1	0	0	0	10	20.0
F	15	Rich Sutter	PHI	5	2	0	2	2	19	0	0	0	0	9	22.2
F	9	*Per-Erik Eklund	PHI	5	0	2	2	2	0	0	0	0	0	7	.0
F	26	Brian Propp	PHI	5	0	2	2	2–	4	0	0	0	0	12	.0
F	14	Ron Sutter	PHI	5	0	2	2	2	10	0	0	0	0	11	.0
D	3	Doug Crossman	PHI	5	0	1	1	0	4	0	0	0	0	8	.0
G	35	Bob Froese	PHI	5	0	1	1	0	0	0	0	0	0	0	.0
F	18	Lindsay Carson	PHI	1	0	0	0	0	5	0	0	0	0	1	.0
G	33	Glenn Resch	PHI	1	0	0	0	0	0	0	0	0	0	0	.0
D	29	*Darryl Stanley	PHI	1	0	0	0	0	2	0	0	0	0	1	.0
D	44	*Mike Stothers	PHI	3	0	0	0	0	4	0	0	0	0	4	.0
F	24	Derrick Smith	PHI	4	0	0	0	3–	10	0	0	0	0	5	.0
F	21	Dave Brown	PHI	5	0	0	0	3–	16	0	0	0	0	4	.0
D	8	Brad Marsh	PHI	5	0	0	0	1	2	0	0	0	0	8	.0
D	34	Dave Richter	PHI	5	0	0	0	0	21	0	0	0	0	2	.0

Mark Howe was selected a First Team All-Star in 1986. His plus/minus total of +85 was best in the NHL and earned him the Emery Edge Award.

Club Records

Team

(Figures in brackets for season records are games played; records for fewest points, wins, ties, losses, goals, goals against are for 70 or more games)

Most Points	118	1975-76 (80)
Most Wins	53	1984-85 (80)
		1985-86 (80)
Most Ties	*24	1969-70 (76)
Most Losses	38	1971-72 (78)
Most Goals	350	1983-84 (80)
Most Goals Against	313	1981-82 (78)
Fewest Points	58	1969-70 (76)
Fewest Wins	17	1969-70 (76)
Fewest Ties	4	1985-86 (80)
Fewest Losses	12	1979-80 (80)
Fewest Goals	173	1967-68 (74)
Fewest Goals Against	164	1973-74 (78)

Longest Winning Streak

Over-all	13	Oct. 19-Nov. 17/85
Home	*20	Jan. 4-Apr. 3/76
Away	8	Dec. 22/82-Jan. 16/83

Longest Undefeated Streak

Over-all	*35	Oct. 14/79-Jan. 6/80 (25 wins, 10 ties)
Home	26	Oct. 11/79-Feb. 3/80 (19 wins, 7 ties)
Away	16	Oct. 20/79-Jan. 6/80 (11 wins, 5 ties)

Longest Losing Streak

Over-all	6	Mar. 25-Apr. 4/70
Home	5	Jan. 30-Feb. 15/69
Away	8	Oct. 25-Nov. 26/72

Longest Winless Streak

Over-all	11	Nov. 21-Dec. 14/69 (9 losses, 2 ties) Dec. 10/70-Jan. 3/71 (9 losses, 2 ties)
Home	8	Dec. 19/68-Jan. 18/69 (4 losses, 4 ties)
Away	19	Oct. 23/71-Jan. 27/72 (15 losses, 4 ties)

Most Shutouts, Season	13	1974-75 (80)
Most Pen. Mins., Season	*2,621	1980-81 (80)
Most Goals, Game	13	Mar. 22/84 (Phi. 13 at Pit. 4) Oct. 18/84 (Van. 2 at Phil. 13)

Individual

Most Seasons	15	Bobby Clarke
Most Games	1,144	Bobby Clarke
Most Goals, Career	420	Bill Barber
Most Assists, Career	852	Bobby Clarke
Most Points, Career	1,210	Bobby Clarke (358 goals, 852 assists)
Most Pen Mins., Career	1,600	Paul Holmgren
Most Shutouts, Career	50	Bernie Parent

Longest Consecutive

Game Streak	287	Rick MacLeish (Oct. 6/72-Feb. 5/76)
Most Goals, Season	61	Reggie Leach (1975-76)
Most Assists, Season	89	Bobby Clarke (1974-75; 1975-76)
Most Points, Season	119	Bobby Clarke (1975-76) (30 goals, 89 assists)
Most Pen. Mins., Season	*472	Dave Schultz (1974-75)
Most Points, Defenseman, Season	82	Mark Howe (1985-86) (24 goals, 58 assists)
Most Points, Center, Season	119	Bobby Clarke (1975-76) (30 goals, 89 assists)
Most Points, Right Wing, Season	98	Tim Kerr (1984-85) (54 goals, 44 assists)
Most Points, Left Wing, Season	112	Bill Barber (1975-76) (50 goals, 62 assists)
Most Points, Rookie, Season	76	Dave Poulin (1983-84) (31 goals, 45 assists)
Most Shutouts, Season	12	Bernie Parent (1973-74; 1974-75)
Most Goals, Game	4	Rick MacLeish (Feb. 13/73; Mar. 4/72) Tom Bladon (Dec. 11/77) Tim Kerr (Oct. 25/84, Jan. 17/85)
Most Assists, Game	5	Bobby Clarke 53. 1/76)
Most Points, Game	8	Tom Bladon (Dec. 11/77)

* NHL Record.

All-time Record vs. Other Clubs

Regular Season

	At Home						On Road						Total					
	GP	W	L	T	GF	GA	PTS	GP	W	L	T	GF	GA	PTS	GP	W	L	T	GF	GA	PTS
Boston	41	17	18	6	142	130	40	41	7	28	6	122	177	20	82	24	46	12	264	307	60
Buffalo	34	21	7	6	126	85	48	32	11	15	6	93	109	28	66	32	22	12	219	195	76
**Calgary	33	27	5	1	149	75	55	33	11	15	7	114	135	29	66	38	20	8	263	210	84
Chicago	42	22	12	8	136	115	52	43	8	20	15	106	143	31	85	30	32	23	242	258	83
Detroit	40	25	6	9	164	104	59	41	15	19	7	128	137	37	81	40	25	16	292	241	96
Edmonton	11	9	2	0	60	36	18	12	5	5	2	41	42	12	23	14	7	2	101	78	30
Hartford	12	10	1	1	61	30	21	11	6	2	3	53	45	15	23	16	3	4	114	74	36
Los Angeles	46	28	11	7	178	112	63	46	27	12	7	154	122	61	92	55	23	14	332	234	124
Minnesota	49	32	7	10	189	103	74	47	18	17	12	156	142	48	96	50	24	22	345	245	122
Montreal	40	13	18	9	100	123	35	41	9	26	6	112	166	24	81	22	44	15	212	289	59
*New Jersey	32	29	2	1	145	54	59	31	20	9	2	144	106	42	63	49	11	3	289	160	101
NY Islanders	43	25	13	5	155	118	55	43	11	24	8	118	179	30	86	36	37	13	273	297	85
NY Rangers	57	30	17	10	201	157	70	57	18	22	17	167	183	53	114	48	39	27	368	340	123
Pittsburgh	57	47	5	5	270	119	99	56	23	21	12	176	167	58	113	70	26	17	446	286	157
Québec	11	8	2	1	43	28	17	12	4	3	5	38	37	13	23	12	5	6	81	65	30
St. Louis	48	33	7	8	185	102	74	49	23	19	7	141	135	53	97	56	26	15	326	237	127
Toronto	41	26	8	7	168	96	59	41	15	14	12	126	139	42	82	41	22	19	294	235	101
Vancouver	34	27	7	0	169	97	54	35	19	8	8	134	99	46	69	46	15	8	303	196	100
Washington	32	23	8	1	146	89	47	32	16	9	7	132	118	39	64	39	17	8	278	207	86
Winnipeg	12	10	2	0	65	38	20	11	5	6	0	39	41	10	23	15	8	0	104	79	30
Defunct Clubs	34	24	4	6	137	67	54	35	13	14	8	102	89	34	69	37	18	14	239	156	88
Totals	**749**	**486**	**162**	**101**	**2989**	**1878**	**1073**	**749**	**284**	**308**	**157**	**2396**	**2511**	**725**	**1498**	**770**	**470**	**258**	**5385**	**4389**	**1798**

* Totals include those of Kansas City (1974-75, 1975-76) and Colorado (1976-77 through 1981-82)
** Totals include those of Atlanta (1972-73 through 1979-80)

Playoffs

	Series	W	L	GP	W	L	T	GF	GA	Last Mtg.	Round	Result
Boston	4	2	2	20	9	11	0	57	60	1978	QF	L 1-4
Buffalo	2	2	0	11	8	3	0	35	23	1978	QF	W 4-1
Calgary	2	1	1	11	7	4	0	43	28	1981	QF	L 3-4
Chicago	1	0	1	4	0	4	0	8	20	1971	QF	L 0-4
Edmonton	2	1	1	8	4	4	0	26	27	1985	F	L 1-4
Minnesota	2	2	0	11	8	3	0	41	26	1980	SF	W 4-1
Montreal	2	0	2	9	1	8	0	22	33	1976	F	L 0-4
*New Jersey	1	1	0	2	2	0	0	6	3	1978	P	W 2-0
NY Islanders	3	2	1	18	10	8	0	60	53	1985	DF	W 4-1
NY Rangers	7	3	4	32	15	17	0	97	214	1986	DSF	L 3-2
Quebec	2	2	0	11	7	4	0	39	29	1985	CF	W 4-2
St. Louis	2	0	2	11	3	8	0	20	34	1969	QF	L 0-4
Toronto	3	3	0	17	12	5	0	67	47	1977	QF	W 4-2
Vancouver	1	1	0	3	2	1	0	15	9	1979	P	W 2-1
Washington	1	0	1	3	0	3	0	5	15	1984	DSF	L 0-3
Totals	**35**	**20**	**15**	**171**	**88**	**83**	**0**	**541**	**524**			

Playoff Results 1986-82

Year	Round	Opponent	Result	GF	GA
1986	DSF	NY Rangers	L 2-3	15	18
1985	F	Edmonton	L 1-4	14	21
	CF	Quebec	W 4-2	17	12
	DF	NY Islanders	W 4-1	16	11
	DSF	NY Rangers	W 3-0	14	10
1984	DSF	Washington	L 0-3	5	15
1983	DSF	NY Rangers	L 0-3	9	18
1982	DSF	NY Rangers	L 1-3	15	19

Abbreviations: Round: F – Final; CF – conference final; DF – division final; DSF – division semi-final; SF – semi-final; QF – quarter-final; P – preliminary round. GA – goals against; GF – goals for.

Coaching History

Keith Allen, 1967-68 to 1968-69; Vic Stasiuk, 1969-70 to 1970-71; Fred Shero, 1971-72 to 1977-78; Bob McCammon and Pat Quinn, 1978-79; Pat Quinn, 1979-80 to 1980-81; Pat Quinn and Bob McCammon, 1981-82; Bob McCammon, 1982-83 to 1983-84; Mike Keenan, 1984-85 to date.

Captains' History

Lou Angotti, 1967-68; Ed Van Impe, 1968-69 to 1971-72; Ed Van Impe, Bob Clarke, 1972-73; Bob Clarke, 1973-74 to 1978-79; Mel Bridgman, 1979-80, 1980-81; Bill Barber, 1981-82; Bill Barber, Bob Clarke, 1982-83; Bob Clarke, 1983-84; Dave Poulin, 1984-85, 1985-86.

Retired Numbers

1	Bernie Parent	1967-1971 and 1973-1979
4	Barry Ashbee	1970-1974
16	Bobby Clarke	1969-1984

Entry Draft Selections 1986-72

1986
Pick
20	Kerry Huffman
23	Jukka Seppo
28	Kent Hawley
83	Mark Bar
125	Steve Scheifele
146	Sami Wahlsten
167	Murray Baron
188	Blaine Rude
209	Shawn Sabol
230	Brett Lawrence
251	Daniel Stephano

1985
Pick
21	Glen Seabrooke
42	Bruce Rendall
48	Darryl Gilmour
63	Shane Whelan
84	Paul Marshall
105	Daril Holmes
126	Ken Alexander
147	Tony Horacek
168	Mike Cusack
189	Gordon Murphy
231	Rod Williams
252	Paul Maurice

1984
Pick
22	Greg Smyth
27	Scott Mellanby
37	Jeff Chychrun
43	Dave McLay
47	John Stevens
79	Dave Hanson
100	Brian Dobbin
121	John Dzikowski
142	Tom Allen
163	Luke Vitale
184	Bill Powers
205	Daryn Fersovitch
247	Juraj Bakos

1983
Pick
41	Peter Zezel
44	Derrick Smith
81	Alan Bourbeau
101	Jerome Carrier
121	Rick Tocchet
141	Bobby Mormina
161	Per-Erik Eklund
181	Rob Nichols
201	William McCormick
221	Brian Jopling
241	Harold Duvall

1982
Pick
4	Ron Sutter
46	Miroslav Dvorak
47	Bill Campbell
77	Mikael Hjalm
98	Todd Bergen
119	Ron Hextall
140	Dave Brown
161	Alain Lavigne
182	Magnus Roupe
203	Tom Allen
224	Rick Gal
245	Mark Vichorek

1981
Pick
16	Steve Smith
37	Rich Costello
47	Barry Tobobondung
58	Ken Strong
65	David Michayluk
79	Ken Latta
100	Justin Hanley
121	Andre Villeneuve
137	Vladimir Svitek
142	Gil Hudon
163	Steve Taylor
184	Len Hachborn
205	Steve Tsujiura

1980
Pick
21	Mike Stothers
42	Jay Fraser
63	Paul Mercier
84	Taras Zytynsky
105	Dan Held
126	Brian Tutt
147	Ross Fitzpatrick
168	Mark Botell
189	Peter Dineen
195	Bob O'Brien
210	Andy Brickley

1979
Pick
14	Brian Propp
22	Blake Wesley
35	Pelle Lindbergh
56	Lindsay Carson
77	Don Gillen
98	Thomas Eriksson
119	Gord Williams

1978
Pick
6	Behn Wilson
7	Ken Linseman
14	Dan Lucas
33	Mike Simurda
37	Gord Salt
50	Glen Cochrane
67	Russ Wilderman
83	Brad Tamblyn
100	Mark Taylor
117	Mike Ewanouski
126	Jerry Price
134	Darren Switzer
151	Greg Francis
167	Rick Berard
168	Don Lucia
182	Mark Berge
183	Ken Moore
195	Jim Olson
198	Anton Stastny

1977
Pick
17	Kevin McCarthy
35	Tom Gorence
53	Dave Hoyda
67	Yves Guillemette
71	Rene Hamelin
89	Dan Clark
107	Alain Chaput
123	Richard Dalpe
135	Pete Peeters
136	Clint Eccles
139	Mike Greeder
150	Tom Bauer
151	Mike Bauman
153	Bruce Crowder
158	Bob Nicholson
159	Dave Isherwood
161	Steve Jones
165	Jim Trainor
166	Barry Duench
168	Rob McNais
172	Mike Laycock

1976
Pick
17	Mark Suzor
35	Drew Callander
53	Craig Hammer
71	Dave Hynek
89	Robin Lang
107	Paul Klasinski
117	Ray Kurpis

1975
Pick
1	Mel Bridgman
54	Bob Ritchie
72	Rick St. Croix
90	Gary Morrison
108	Paul Holmgren
126	Dana Decker
160	Viktor Khatulev
175	Duffy Smith

1974
Pick
35	Don McLean
53	Bob Sirois
71	Randy Andreachuk
89	Dennis Sobchuk
107	Willie Friesen
125	Rejean Lemelin
142	Steve Short
159	Peter McKenzie
174	Marcel Labrosse
189	Scott Jesse
201	Richard Guay
211	Brad Morrow
219	Craig Arvidson

1973
Pick
20	Larry Goodenough
26	Brent Leavins
40	Bob Stumpf
42	Mike Clarke
58	Dale Cook
74	Michel Latreille
90	Doug Ferguson
106	Tom Young
122	Norm Barnes
137	Dan O'Donohue
153	Brian Dick

1972
Pick
7	Bill Barber
23	Tom Bladon
39	Jimmy Watson
55	Al MacAdam
71	Darryl Fedorak
87	Dave Hastings
103	Serge Beaudoin
119	Pat Russell
135	Ray Boutin

Tim Kerr's total of 34 power play goals was highest in the NHL in 1985-86.

Club Directory

The Spectrum
Pattison Place
Philadelphia, PA 19148
Phone 215/465-4500
TWX 910-997-2239
ENVOY ID TM.PHI
Capacity: 17,211

Board of Directors
Ed Snider, Jay Snider, Joe Scott, Keith Allen, Fred Shabel, Bob Clarke, Sylvan Tobin

Chairman of the Executive Committee	Ed Snider
Chairman of the Board Emeritus	Joe Scott
President	Jay Snider
Executive Vice-President	Keith Allen
Vice-President and General Manager	Bob Clarke
Assistant General Manager	Gary Darling
Head Coach	Mike Keenan
Assistant Coaches	E.J. McGuire, Paul Holmgren, Bill Barber
Goaltending Instructor	Bernie Parent
Physical Conditioning and Rehabilitation	Pat Croce, LPT, ATC
Scouts	Jerry Melnyk, Walt Atanas, Dennis Patterson, Red Sullivan, Ron Woody, Jim McMann
Vice President, Finance and Administration	Donn Patton
Vice President, Sales	Jack Betson
Assistant to the President	John Brogan
Director of Public Relations	Rodger Gottlieb
Assistant Director of Public Relations	Mark Piazza
Public Relations Assistant	Anita Doyle
Marketing Manager	Linda Panasci
Controller	Bob Baer
Director of Broadcast Sales	Pete Huver
Ticket Manager	Cecilia Baker
Director of Advertising	Ivan Schlictman
Director of Team Services	Joe Kadlec
Executive Assistants	Ilene Forcine, Barbara Gottesman, Dianna Taylor
Marketing Assistant	Lynn Burdulis
Ticket Office Assistant	Jeff Landis
Accountants	Kevin McGoldrick, Susan Schaffer
Advertising Sales	Bernadette Corcoran, Joe Watson
Advertising Assistant	Laura Green
Archivist	Mott Linn
Office Assistant	Leon Friedrich
Receptionist	Dolores McDermott
P.A. Announcer	Lou Nolan
Team Physician	Edward Viner, M.D.
Orthopedic Surgeon	John Gregg, M.D.
Oral Surgeon	Everett Borghesani, D.D.S.
Ophthalmologist	Lewis Karp, M.D.
Trainer	Dave Settlemyre
Assistant Trainer	Kurt Mundt
Dimensions of rink	200 feet by 85 feet
Location of Press Box	Mid-ice, North side, concourse level
Club colors	Orange, Black and White
Training camp site and Practice Center	The Coliseum, Voorhees, NJ
Play-by-Play Broadcaster	Gene Hart
Color Analyst	Bob Taylor
TV Channels	WTAF-TV Channel 29 (UHF) WPVI-TV, Channel 6 (VHF)
Cable TV Channel	PRISM
Radio Station	WIP-610 (AM)

Pittsburgh Penguins

1985-86 Results: 34w-38L-8T 76 pts. Fifth, Patrick Division

Year-by-Year Record

Season	GP	Home W	Home L	Home T	Road W	Road L	Road T	Overall W	L	T	GF	GA	Pts.	Finished	Playoff Result
1985-86	80	20	15	5	14	23	3	34	38	8	313	305	76	5th, Patrick Div.	Out of Playoffs
1984-85	80	17	20	3	7	31	2	24	51	5	276	385	53	6th, Patrick Div.	Out of Playoffs
1983-84	80	7	29	4	9	29	2	16	58	6	254	390	38	6th, Patrick Div.	Out of Playoffs
1982-83	80	14	22	4	4	31	5	18	53	9	257	394	45	6th, Patrick Div.	Lost Div. Semi-Final
1981-82	80	21	11	8	10	25	5	31	36	13	310	337	75	4th, Patrick Div.	Lost Prelim. Round
1980-81	80	21	16	3	9	21	10	30	37	13	302	345	73	3rd, Norris Div.	Lost Prelim. Round
1979-80	80	20	13	7	10	24	6	30	37	13	251	303	73	3rd, Norris Div.	Lost Prelim. Round
1978-79	80	23	12	5	13	19	8	36	31	13	281	279	85	2nd, Norris Div.	Lost Quarter-Final
1977-78	80	16	15	9	9	22	9	25	37	18	254	321	68	4th, Norris Div.	Out of Playoffs
1976-77	80	22	12	6	12	21	7	34	33	13	240	252	81	3rd, Norris Div.	Lost Prelim. Round
1975-76	80	23	11	6	12	22	6	35	33	12	339	303	82	3rd, Norris Div.	Lost Prelim. Round
1974-75	80	25	5	10	12	23	5	37	28	15	326	289	89	3rd, Norris Div.	Lost Quarter-Final
1973-74	78	15	18	6	13	23	3	28	41	9	242	273	65	5th, West Div.	Out of Playoffs
1972-73	78	24	11	4	8	26	5	32	37	9	257	265	73	5th, West Div.	Out of Playoffs
1971-72	78	18	15	6	8	23	8	26	38	14	220	258	66	4th, West Div.	Lost Quarter-Final
1970-71	78	18	12	9	3	25	11	21	37	20	221	240	62	6th, West Div.	Out of Playoffs
1969-70	76	17	13	8	9	25	4	26	38	12	182	238	64	2nd, West Div.	Lost Semi-Final
1968-69	76	12	20	6	8	25	5	20	45	11	189	252	51	5th, West Div.	Out of Playoffs
1967-68	74	15	12	10	12	22	3	27	34	13	195	216	67	5th, West Div.	Out of Playoffs

Schedule

Home

Oct. Thur. 9 Washington
Sat. 11 NY Rangers
Tue. 14 Los Angeles
Sat. 18 New Jersey
Wed. 22 Buffalo
Sat. 25 Philadelphia
Wed. 29 New Jersey
Nov. Tue. 4 Vancouver
Wed. 12 Boston
Sat. 15 Quebec
Wed. 26 NY Islanders
Sat. 29 NY Rangers
Dec. Fri. 5 Edmonton
Sat. 6 Minnesota
Wed. 10 Calgary
Fri. 12 Toronto
Sat. 20 Philadelphia
Sat. 27 NY Islanders
Tue. 30 NY Rangers
Jan. Sat. 3 Montreal
Wed. 7 Washington
Wed. 14 Winnipeg
Sun. 18 Detroit
Tue. 27 Washington
Feb. Sun. 1 Hartford
Sat. 7 Chicago
Sat. 14 Vancouver
Tue. 17 Calgary
Sat. 21 New Jersey
Tue. 24 Edmonton
Sat. 28 Chicago
Mar. Sun. 1 St. Louis
Tue. 10 NY Islanders
Thur. 12 Quebec
Sat. 14 NY Rangers
Wed. 18 St. Louis
Tue. 24 Philadelphia
Sun. 29 Montreal
April Thur. 2 New Jersey
Sat. 4 Detroit

Away

Oct. Sun. 12 Chicago
Fri. 17 Buffalo
Thur. 23 Philadelphia
Tue. 28 Hartford
Nov. Sat. 1 St. Louis
Sat. 8 Minnesota
Sun. 9 Detroit
Fri. 14 New Jersey
Tue. 18 Winnipeg
Thur. 20 Calgary
Sat. 22 Washington
Tue. 25 NY Islanders
Sun. 30 NY Rangers
Dec. Sat. 13 Toronto
Wed. 17 Los Angeles
Mon. 22 Montreal
Tue. 23 NY Islanders
Fri. 26 Buffalo
Jan. Thur. 1 Washington*
Fri. 9 Washington
Tue. 13 NY Islanders
Sat. 17 Boston*
Wed. 21 Los Angeles
Fri. 23 Vancouver
Sat. 24 Edmonton
Thur. 29 Philadelphia
Feb. Thur. 5 Boston
Sun. 8 New Jersey
Sun. 15 NY Rangers
Thur. 19 Philadelphia
Sun. 22 NY Rangers
Thur. 26 NY Islanders
Mar. Tue. 3 Quebec
Thur. 5 Toronto
Sat. 7 Minnesota
Sun. 8 Winnipeg
Fri. 20 Washington
Sun. 22 Philadelphia
Sat. 28 Hartford
Tue. 31 New Jersey

*Denotes afternoon game.

Home Starting Times:
All Games .... 7:35 p.m.

Franchise date: June 5, 1967

 **20th NHL Season**

Mario Lemieux won the Lester B. Pearson Award as the NHL's outstanding player as selected by the members of the NHL Players' Association.

1986-87 Player Personnel

FORWARDS	Ht.	Wt.	Place of Birth	Date	1985-86 Club
AITKEN, Brad	6-3	202	Scarborough, Ont.	10/30/67	Sault Ste. Marie
BELANGER, Roger	6-0	192	St. Catharines, Ont.	12/1/65	Baltimore
BLAISDELL, Mike	6-1	195	Moose Jaw, Sask.	1/18/60	Pittsburgh
BOURQUE, Phil	6-1	190	Chelmsford, Mass.	6/8/62	Pittsburgh-Baltimore
BROWN, Rob	5-11	170	Kingston, Ont.	4/10/68	Kamloops (WHL)
BULLARD, Mike	5-10	185	Ottawa, Ont.	3/10/61	Pittsburgh
CAIN, Kelly	5-6	180	Toronto, Ont.	4/19/68	London (OHL)
CAPUANO, Dave	6-2	188	Cranston, R. I.	7/27/68	Mt. St. Charles H.S.
CHABOT, John	6-3	190	Summerside, P.E.I.	5/18/62	Pittsburgh
CHOULES, Greg	5-9	190	Montreal, Que.	5/1/66	Chicoutimi
CLEMENS, Kevin	5-11	187	McLennan, Alta.	2/2/67	Regina
CUNNEYWORTH, Randy	6-0	180	Etobicoke, Ont.	5/10/61	Pittsburgh
DANIELS, Jeff	6-1	187	Oshawa, Ont.	6/24/68	Oshawa
DEL COL, John	5-10	190	St. Catharines, Ont.	5/11/65	Baltimore-Toledo
DRULIA, Stan	5-10	188	Elmira, N.Y.	1/5/68	Belleville
DUGUAY, Ron	6-2	210	Sudbury, Ont.	7/6/57	Detroit-Pittsburgh
ERREY, Bob	5-10	185	Montreal, Que.	9/21/64	Pittsburgh-Baltimore
FRAWLEY, Dan	6-0	170	Sturgeon Falls, Ont.	6/2/62	Pittsburgh
GIFFIN, Lee	5-11	170	Chatham, Ont.	4/1/67	Oshawa
GOTAAS, Steve	5-10	170	Camrose, Alta.	5/10/67	Prince Albert
HANNAN, Dave	5-10	175	Sudbury, Ont.	11/26/61	Pittsburgh
JOHNSON, Scott	5-11	185	New Hope, Minn.	10/12/63	Lake Superior
LEMIEUX, Mario	6-4	200	Montreal, Que.	10/5/65	Pittsburgh
LINDSTROM, Willy	6-0	180	Grunns, Sweden	5/5/51	Pittsburgh
LONEY, Troy	6-3	215	Bow Island, Alta.	9/21/63	Pittsburgh-Baltimore
MATHIASEN, Dwight	6-1	190	Brandon, Man.	5/12/65	Denver U.-Pittsburgh
McGEOUGH, Jim	5-8	170	Regina, Sask.	4/13/63	Pittsburgh-Baltimore
McILWAIN, Dave	6-0	189	Seaforth, Ont.	1/9/67	North Bay
MOKOSAK, Carl	6-1	180	Ft. Saskatchewan, Alt.	9/22/62	Hershey
RUSKOWSKI, Terry	5-9	180	Prince Albert, Sask.	12/31/54	Pittsburgh
SHAW, Brian	6-0	190	Edmonton, Alta.	5/20/62	Adirondack-Peoria
SIMPSON, Craig	6-2	185	London, Ont.	2/15/67	Pittsburgh
STEVENS, Kevin	6-3	207	Brockton, Mass.	4/15/64	Boston College
WILSON, Mitch	5-8	190	Kelowna, B.C.	7/5/57	Maine

DEFENSEMEN	Ht.	Wt.	Place of Birth	Date	1985-86 Club
BODGER, Doug	6-2	200	Chemainus, B.C.	6/18/66	Pittsburgh
BUSKAS, Rod	6-1	197	Wetaskiwin, Alta	1/7/61	Pittsburgh
CHARLESWORTH, Todd	6-1	190	Calgary, Alta.	3/22/65	Pittsburgh-Baltimore-Muskegon
DAHLQUIST, Chris	6-1	190	Fridley, Minn.	12/14/62	Pittsburgh-Baltimore
GOERTZ, Dave	5-11	210	Edmonton, Alta.	3/28/65	Baltimore
HILLIER, Randy	6-0	180	Toronto, Ont.	3/30/60	Pittsburgh-Baltimore
HOBSON, Doug	5-11	186	Prince Albert, Sask.	4/9/68	Prince Albert
JOHNSON, Jim	6-0	190	New Hope, Minn.	8/9/62	Pittsburgh
MANTHA, Moe	6-2	195	Lakewood, Ohio	1/21/61	Pittsburgh
MARSTON, Stuart	6-2	183	Montreal, Que.	5/9/67	Laval
McDONNELL, Joe	6-2	200	Kitchener, Ont.	5/11/61	Pittsburgh-Baltimore
PAEK, Jim	6-0	188	Seoul, Korea	4/7/67	Oshawa
ROWE, Mike	6-1	212	Kingston, Ont.	3/8/65	Pittsburgh-Baltimore
SCHMIDT, Norm	5-11	190	Sault Ste. Marie, Ont.	1/24/63	Pittsburgh
SIREN, Ville	6-1	185	Tempre, Finland	2/11/64	Pittsburgh
WILSON, Rob	6-3	187	Toronto, Ont.	7/18/68	Sudbury
ZALAPSKI, Zarley	6-1	196	Edmonton, Alta.	4/22/68	Team Canada-Ft. Saskatchewan (Midget)

GOALTENDERS	Ht.	Wt.	Place of Birth	Date	1985-86 Club
COOPER, Jeff	5-10	170	Ottawa, Ont.	6/12/62	Baltimore
FORD, Brian	5-10	170	Edmonton, Alta.	9/22/61	Baltimore-Muskegon
GUENETTE, Steve	5-9	170	Montreal, Que.	11/13/65	Guelph
MELOCHE, Gilles	5-9	185	Montreal, Que.	7/12/50	Pittsburgh
ROMANO, Roberto	5-6	170	Montreal, Que.	10/10/62	Pittsburgh
TITUS, Steve	5-10	151	St. John, N.B.	2/2/67	Cornwall

1985-86 Scoring

Regular Season

*—rookie

Pos	#	Player	Team	GP	G	A	Pts	+/−	PIM	PP	SH	GW	OT	S	%
F	66	Mario Lemieux	PIT	79	48	93	141	6−	43	17	0	4	0	276	17.4
F	22	Mike Bullard	PIT	77	41	42	83	16−	69	16	2	5	1	213	19.2
D	20	Moe Mantha	PIT	78	15	52	67	4−	102	11	2	0	0	224	6.7
F	8	Terry Ruskowski	PIT	73	26	37	63	10	162	11	0	7	0	91	28.6
F	35	Ron Duguay	DET	67	19	29	48	30−	26	8	0	2	0	153	12.4
			PIT	13	6	7	13	14−	6	3	0	0	1	33	18.2
			Total	80	25	36	61	44−	32	11	0	2	1	186	13.4
F	15	*Randy Cunneyworth	PIT	75	15	30	45	12	74	2	2	2	0	134	11.2
F	9	John Chabot	PIT	77	14	31	45	1−	6	1	2	3	0	89	15.7
D	3	Doug Bodger	PIT	79	4	33	37	3	63	1	0	1	0	140	2.9
F	32	Dave Hannan	PIT	75	17	18	35	4−	91	0	3	1	0	100	17.0
F	19	Willy Lindstrom	PIT	71	14	17	31	0	30	0	0	1	0	87	16.1
F	26	Mike Blaisdell	PIT	66	15	14	29	15	36	0	0	0	0	125	12.0
D	25	Norm Schmidt	PIT	66	15	14	29	7	57	3	0	0	0	141	10.6
D	6	*Jim Johnson	PIT	80	3	26	29	12	115	0	0	0	0	118	2.5
F	18	*Craig Simpson	PIT	76	11	17	28	1	49	2	1	0	0	74	14.9
F	28	Dan Frawley	PIT	69	10	11	21	19−	174	4	0	1	0	79	12.7
F	10	Bob Errey	PIT	37	11	6	17	1−	8	1	0	2	0	57	19.3
D	5	*Ville Siren	PIT	60	4	8	12	8−	32	1	0	0	0	58	6.9
F	11	Troy Loney	PIT	47	3	9	12	8−	95	0	0	1	0	50	6.0
D	7	Rod Buskas	PIT	72	2	7	9	9−	159	1	0	0	0	50	4.0
F	16	Jim McGeough	PIT	17	3	2	5	4−	8	0	1	0	0	29	10.3
D	2	*Chris Dahlquist	PIT	5	1	2	3	1	2	0	0	0	0	5	20.0
F	12	Tom O'Regan	PIT	9	1	2	3	1	0	0	0	0	0	7	14.3
F	23	Randy Hillier	PIT	28	0	3	3	3−	53	0	0	0	0	22	.0
F	34	Ted Nolan	PIT	18	1	1	2	1−	34	0	0	0	0	17	5.9
F	24	*Dwight Mathiason	PIT	4	1	0	1	4−	2	0	0	0	0	4	25.0
D	2	Todd Charlesworth	PIT	2	0	1	1	1−	0	0	0	0	0	1	.0
G	27	Gilles Meloche	PIT	34	0	1	1	0	2	0	0	0	0	0	.0
G	30	Roberto Romano	PIT	46	0	1	1	0	4	0	0	0	0	0	.0
G	1	Denis Herron	PIT	3	0	0	0	0	0	0	0	0	0	0	.0
D	33	Joe McDonnell	PIT	3	0	0	0	3−	2	0	0	0	0	1	.0
D	33	*Mike Rowe	PIT	3	0	0	0	1−	4	0	0	0	0	5	.0
D	4	*Phil Bourque	PIT	4	0	0	0	2−	2	0	0	0	0	6	.0
F	12	Tom Roulston	PIT	5	0	0	0	2−	2	0	0	0	0	6	.0

Jim Johnson

Coach and General Manager

BERRY, ROBERT VICTOR (BOB)
Coach, Pittsburgh Penguins. Born in Montreal, Que., November 29, 1943.

Bob Berry enters his ninth season of coaching in the NHL and third with Pittsburgh after being named to the Penguins' post on June 4, 1984. Berry's NHL coaching career began in 1978 with the Los Angeles Kings where he spent three seasons while compiling a record of 107 wins, 94 losses and 39 ties for a winning percentage of .527. He returned to his native Montreal on June 3, 1981 to assume the head coaching duties with the Canadiens, where in nearly three full seasons with Montreal, Berry guided his teams to a 116-71-36 record for a .601 winning percentage. Berry played seven seasons in the NHL with Montreal and Los Angeles, totalling 350 points.

NHL Coaching Record

Team		Games	Regular Season				Playoffs			
			W	L	T	%	Games	W	L	%
Los Angeles	1978-79	80	34	34	12	.500	2	0	2	.000
Los Angeles	1979-80	80	30	36	14	.462	4	1	3	.250
Los Angeles	1980-81	80	43	24	13	.619	4	1	3	.250
Montreal	1981-82	80	46	17	17	.681	5	2	3	.400
Montreal	1982-83	80	42	24	14	.612	3	0	3	.000
Montreal	1983-84	63	28	30	5	.484	....			
Pittsburgh	1984-85	80	24	51	5	.331	....			
Pittsburgh	1985-86	80	34	38	8	.475	....			
NHL Total		**623**	**281**	**254**	**88**	**.522**	**18**	**4**	**14**	**.222**

JOHNSTON, EDWARD JOSEPH (EDDIE)
General Manager, Pittsburgh Penguins. Born in Montreal, Que., November 24, 1935.

Eddie Johnston was appointed General Manager of the Pittsburgh Penguins on May 27, 1983, after serving as head coach for three seasons. Johnston's coaching career began in 1978-79 when he guided the New Brunswick Hawks of the American Hockey League to a 41-29-10 record and joined the Chicago Black Hawks for one season before assuming the coaching duties of the Penguins on July 15, 1980. Prior to stepping behind the bench, Johnston had spent 16 seasons as a goaltender in the NHL with Boston, Toronto, St. Louis and Chicago. He played on two Stanley Cup winning teams while with the Bruins (1970, 1972) and had a lifetime goals-against-average of 3.25.

Club Records

Team

(Figures in brackets for season records are games played; records for fewest points, wins, ties, losses, goals, goals against are for 70 or more games)

Most Points	.89	1974-75 (80)
Most Wins	.37	1974-75 (80)
Most Ties	.20	1970-71 (78)
Most Losses	.58	1983-84 (80)
Most Goals	.339	1975-76 (80)
Most Goals Against	.394	1982-83 (80)
Fewest Points	.38	1983-84 (80)
Fewest Wins	.16	1983-84 (80)
Fewest Ties	.6	1983-84 (80)
Fewest Losses	.28	1974-75 (80)
Fewest Goals	.182	1969-70 (76)
Fewest Goals Against	.216	1967-68 (74)

Longest Winning Streak
Over-all	.6	Feb. 22-Mar. 4/81
Home	.9	Feb. 26-Apr. 5/75
Away	.4	Oct. 14-Nov. 2/84

Longest Undefeated Streak
Over-all	.11	Feb. 7-28/76 (7 wins, 4 ties)
Home	.20	Nov. 30/74-Feb. 22/75 (12 wins, 8 ties)
Away	.7	Mar. 13-27/79 (5 wins, 2 ties)

Longest Losing Streak
Over-all	.11	Jan. 22/83-Feb. 10/83
Home	.7	Oct. 8-29/83
Away	.18	Dec. 23/82-Mar. 4/83

Longest Winless Streak
Over-all	.18	Jan. 2/83-Feb. 10/83 (17 losses, 1 tie)
Home	.11	Oct. 8-Nov. 19/83 (9 losses, 2 ties)

Away	.18	Oct. 25/70-Jan. 14/71 (11 losses, 7 ties) Dec. 23/82-Mar. 4/83 (18 losses)
Most Shutouts, Season	.6	1967-68 (74) 1976-77 (80) 1981-82 (80)
Most. Pen. Mins., Season	.2,210	
Most Goals, Game	.12	Mar. 15/75 (Wash. 1 at Pit. 12)

Individual

Most Seasons	.11	Rick Kehoe
Most Games	.753	Jean Pronovost
Most Goals, Career	.316	Jean Pronovost
Most Assists, Career	.349	Syl Apps
Most Points, Career	.636	Rick Kehoe (312 goals, 324 assists)
Most Pen. Mins., Career	.871	Bryan Watson
Most Shutouts, Career	.11	Les Binkley
Longest Consecutive Games Streak	.320	Ron Schock (Oct. 24/73-Apr. 3/77)
Most Goals, Season	.55	Rick Kehoe (1980-81)
Most Assists, Season	.93	Mario Lemieux (1985-86)
Most Points, Season	.141	Mario Lemieux (1985-86)
Most Pen. Mins., Season	.407	Paul Baxter (1981-82)
Most Points, Defenseman Season	.83	Randy Carlyle (1980-81) (16 goals, 67 assists)
Most Points, Center, Season	.141	Mario Lemieux (1985-86) (48 goals, 93 assists)

Most Points, Right Wing, Season	.104	Jean Pronovost (1975-76) (52 goals, 52 assists)
Most Points, Left Wing, Season	.82	Lowell MacDonald (1973-74) (43 goals, 39 assists)
Most Points, Rookie, Season	.100	Mario Lemieux (1984-85) (43 goals, 57 assists)
Most Shutouts, Season	.6	Les Binkley (1967-68)
Most Goals, Game	.4	Paul Gardner (Dec. 13/80) Mike Bullard (Dec. 5/84)
Most Assists, Game	.6	Ron Stackhouse (Mar. 8/75) Greg Malone (Nov. 28/79)
Most Points, Game	.6	Syl Apps (Dec. 13/72) Ron Stackhouse (Mar. 8/75) Greg Malone (Nov. 28/79)

Coaching History

George Sullivan, 1967-68 to 1968-69; Red Kelly, 1969-70 to 1971-72; Red Kelly and Ken Schinkel, 1972-73; Ken Schinkel and Marc Boileau, 1973-74; Marc Boileau, 1974-75; Marc Boileau and Ken Schinkel, 1975-76; Ken Schinkel, 1976-77; John Wilson, 1977-78 to 1979-80; Eddie Johnston, 1980-81 to 1982-83; Lou Angotti, 1983-84; Bob Berry, 1984-85 to date.

Captains' History

Ab McDonald, 1967-68; no captain, 1968-69 to 1972-73; Ron Schock, 1973-74 to 1976-77; Jean Pronovost, 1977-78; Orest Kindrachuk, 1978-79 to 1980-81; Randy Carlyle, 1981-82 to 1983-84; Mike Bullard, 1984-85, 1985-86.

All-time Record vs. Other Clubs

Regular Season

			At Home							On Road							Total				
	GP	W	L	T	GF	GA	PTS	GP	W	L	T	GF	GA	PTS	GP	W	L	T	GF	GA	PTS
Boston	43	11	23	9	130	173	31	42	5	33	4	113	201	14	85	16	56	13	243	374	45
Buffalo	35	11	12	12	125	128	34	34	4	19	11	83	156	19	69	15	31	23	208	284	53
**Calgary	27	12	7	8	97	94	32	27	5	16	6	71	109	16	54	17	23	14	168	203	48
Chicago	40	18	18	4	136	130	40	42	4	29	9	106	177	17	82	22	47	13	242	307	57
Detroit	46	31	12	3	200	136	65	47	8	31	8	123	184	24	93	39	43	11	323	320	89
Edmonton	11	4	6	1	40	59	9	12	1	10	1	43	78	3	23	5	16	2	83	137	12
Hartford	12	7	3	2	52	37	16	11	5	6	0	48	55	10	23	12	9	2	100	92	26
Los Angeles	53	31	16	6	199	158	68	57	13	30	8	131	181	34	104	44	46	14	330	339	102
Minnesota	46	28	13	5	173	120	61	45	14	27	4	145	176	32	91	42	40	9	318	296	93
Montreal	46	13	25	8	134	173	34	47	2	41	4	113	247	8	93	15	66	12	247	420	42
*New Jersey	30	19	9	2	123	96	40	29	11	12	6	111	107	28	59	30	21	8	234	203	68
NY Islanders	37	15	14	8	127	120	38	37	8	24	5	101	164	21	74	23	38	13	228	284	59
NY Rangers	51	16	28	7	162	190	39	51	18	28	5	168	214	41	102	34	56	12	330	404	80
Philadelphia	56	21	23	12	167	176	54	57	5	47	5	119	270	15	113	26	70	17	286	446	69
Québec	11	4	5	2	41	53	10	12	4	8	0	38	59	8	23	8	13	2	79	112	18
St. Louis	45	20	16	9	159	130	49	47	13	30	4	124	178	30	92	33	46	13	283	308	79
Toronto	43	21	17	5	157	140	47	42	14	18	10	137	165	38	85	35	35	15	294	305	85
Vancouver	32	21	7	4	146	112	46	33	15	15	3	130	126	33	65	36	22	7	276	238	79
Washington	38	14	19	5	148	128	33	38	14	21	3	138	170	31	76	28	40	8	286	298	64
Winnipeg	12	9	3	0	52	36	18	11	6	5	0	43	45	12	23	15	8	0	95	81	30
Defunct Clubs	35	22	6	7	148	93	51	34	13	10	11	108	101	37	69	35	16	18	256	194	88
Totals	749	348	282	119	2716	2482	815	749	182	460	107	2193	3163	471	1498	530	742	226	4909	5645	1286

* Totals include those of Kansas City (1974-75, 1975-76) and Colorado (1976-77 through 1981-82)
** Totals include those of Atlanta (1972-73 through 1979-80)

Playoffs

	Series	W	L	GP	W	L	T	GF	GA	Last Mtg.	Round	Result
Boston	2	0	2	9	2	7	0	21	37	1980	P	L 2-3
Buffalo	1	1	0	3	2	1	0	9	9	1979	P	W 2-1
Chicago	1	0	1	4	0	4	0	8	14	1972	QF	L 0-4
NY Islanders	2	0	2	12	5	7	0	31	43	1982	DSF	L 2-3
St. Louis	3	1	2	13	6	7	0	40	45	1981	P	W 3-2
Toronto	2	0	2	6	2	4	0	13	21	1977	P	L 2-1
Defunct Clubs	1	1	0	4	4	0	0	13	6			
Totals	12	3	9	51	21	30	0	135	175			

Playoff Results 1986-82

Year	Round	Opponent	Result	GF	GA
1982	DSF	NY Islanders	L 2-3	13	22

Abbreviations: Round: F – Final; **CF** – conference final; **DF** – division final; **DSF** – division semi-final; **SF** – semi-final; **QF** – quarter-final; **P** – preliminary round. **GA** – goals against; **GF** – goals for.

Retired Numbers

21	Michel Briere	1969-1970

Entry Draft Selections 1986-72

1986
Pick	
4	Zarley Zalapski
25	Dave Capuano
46	Brad Aitken
67	Rob Brown
88	Sandy Smith
109	Jeff Daniels
130	Doug Hobson
151	Steve Rohlik
172	Dave McLlwain
193	Kelly Cain
214	Stan Drulia
235	Rob Wilson

1985
Pick	
2	Craig Simpson
23	Lee Giffin
58	Bruce Racine
86	Steve Gotaas
107	Kevin Clemens
114	Stuart Marston
128	Steve Titus
149	Paul Stanton
170	Jim Paek
191	Steve Shaunessy
212	Doug Greschuk
233	Gregory Choules

1984
Pick	
1	Mario Lemieux
9	Doug Bodger
16	Roger Belanger
64	Mark Teevens
85	Arto Javanainen
127	Tom Ryan
169	John Del Col
189	Steve Hurt
210	Jim Steen
250	Mark Ziliotto

1983
Pick	
15	Bob Errey
22	Todd Charlesworth
58	Mike Rowe
63	Frank Pietrangelo
103	Patrick Emond
123	Paul Ames
163	Marty Ketola
183	Alec Haidy
203	Garth Hildebrand
223	Dave Goertz

1982
Pick	
10	Rich Sutter
38	Tim Hrynewich
52	Troy Loney
94	Grant Sasser
136	Grant Couture
157	Peter Derkson
178	Greg Gravel
199	Stu Wenaas
220	Chris McCauley
241	Stan Bautch

1981
Pick	
28	Steve Gatzos
49	Tom Thornbury
70	Norm Schmidt
109	Paul Edwards
112	Rod Buskas
133	Geoff Wilson
154	Mitch Lamoureaux
175	Dean Defazio
196	David Hannan

1980
Pick	
9	Mike Bullard
51	Randy Boyd
72	Tony Feltrin
93	Doug Shedden
114	Pat Graham
156	Robert Geale
177	Brian Lundberg
198	Steve McKenzie

1979
Pick	
31	Paul Marshall
52	Bennett Wolf
73	Brian Cross
94	Nick Ricci
115	Marc Chorney

1978
Pick	
25	Mike Meeker
61	Shane Pearsall
75	Rob Garner

1977
Pick	
30	Jim Hamilton
48	Kim Davis
66	Mark Johnson
102	Greg Millen

1976
Pick	
2	Blair Chapman
19	Greg Malone
29	Peter Marsh
47	Morris Lukowich
65	Greg Redquist
83	Brendan Lowe
101	Vic Sirko

1975
Pick	
13	Gord Laxton
31	Russ Anderson
49	Paul Baxter
67	Stu Younger
85	Kim Clackson
103	Peter Morris
121	Mike Will
139	Tapio Levo
155	Byron Shutt
170	Frank Salive
185	John Glynne
196	Lex Hudson
202	Dan Tsubouchi
206	Bronislav Stankovsky
217	Kelly Secord

1974
Pick	
8	Pierre Larouche
27	Jacques Cossette
62	Mario Faubert
80	Bruce Aberhart
98	Bill Schnedier
116	Robbie Laird
133	Larry Finck
150	James Chicoine
166	Rick Ulrich
181	Serge Gamelin
195	Richard Perron
206	Richard Hindmarch
216	Bill Davis
223	James Mathers

1973
Pick	
7	Blaine Stoughton
23	Wayne Bianchin
27	Colin Campbell
35	Dennis Owchar
71	Guido Tenesi
87	Don Seiling
103	Terry Ewasiuk
119	Fred Comrie
134	Gord Lane
150	Randy Aimde
164	Don McLeod

1972
Pick	
24	Jack Lynch
30	Bernie Lukowich
40	Denis Herron
56	Ron Lalonde
72	Brian Walker
88	Jeff Ablett
104	D'Arcy Keating
120	Yves Bergeron
136	Jay Babcock
149	Don Atchison

Ron Duguay

Club Directory

Civic Arena
Pittsburgh, PA 15219
Phone 412/642-1800
TWX 710-664-3081
ENVOY ID TM.PIT
Capacity: 16,033

Chairman of the Board & President	Edward J. DeBartolo, Sr.
Vice-President	Marie Denise DeBartolo York
Vice-President & General Counsel	J. Paul Martha
Vice-President & Treasurer	Thomas F. Rossetti
General Manager	Eddie Johnston
Director of Player Personnel, Assistant General Manager	Ken Schinkel
Director of Professional Scouting	Rick Kehoe
Coach	Bob Berry
Assistant Coach	Jim Roberts
Eastern Scouts	Paul Goulet & Doug Wood
Quebec Scout	Albert Mandanici
Western Scout	Bruce Haralson
Mid-Western Scout	John Gill
Director of Team Services	Terry Schiffhauer
Director of Marketing	Paul Steigerwald
Director of Press Relations	Cindy Himes
Ticket Manager	Tom Wood
Trainer	Steve Thomas
Equipment Manager	John Doolan
Strength Coach	Doug McKenney
Team Physicians	Dr. Chuck Stone, Dr. Russ Leslie, Dr. Larry Ellis & Dr. Lee Dameshek
Team Dentists	Dr. Stephen Todorovich & Dr. David Wessel
Executive Offices	Gate no. 7, Civic Arena
Location of Press Box	East Side of Building
Dimensions of Rink	200 feet by 85 feet
Club Colors	Black, Gold & White
Club Trains at	Pittsburgh, PA
Radio Station	KDKA (1020 AM)
Play-by-Play Announcer	Mike Lange
Television Station	WPGH-TV (53)
Television Commentators	Mike Lange & Paul Steigerwald

Quebec Nordiques

1985-86 Results: 43w-31L-6T 92 PTS. First, Adams Division

Year-by-Year Record

		Home			Road			Overall						
Season	GP	W	L	T	W	L	T	W	L	T	GF	GA	Pts.	Finished	Playoff Result
1985-86	80	23	13	4	20	18	2	43	31	6	330	289	92 1st,	Adams Div.	Lost Div. Semi-Final
1984-85	80	24	12	4	17	18	5	41	30	9	323	275	91 2nd,	Adams Div.	Lost Conf. Final
1983-84	80	24	11	5	18	17	5	42	28	10	360	278	94 3th,	Adams Div.	Lost Div. Final
1982-83	80	23	10	7	11	24	5	34	34	12	343	336	80 4th,	Adams Div.	Lost Div. Semi-Final
1981-82	80	24	13	3	9	18	13	33	31	16	356	345	82 4th,	Adams Div.	Lost Conf. Championship
1980-81	80	18	11	11	12	21	7	30	32	18	314	318	78 4th,	Adams Div.	Lost Prelim. Round
1979-80	80	17	16	7	8	28	4	25	44	11	248	313	61 5th,	Adams Div.	Out of Playoffs

Schedule

		Home				Away
Oct.	Thur.	9 Detroit	**Oct.**	Mon.	13 Vancouver
	Sat.	11 Minnesota		Wed.	15 Edmonton
	Tue.	21 Washington		Thur.	16 Calgary
	Sat.	25 Toronto		Sat.	18 St. Louis
	Tue.	28 Los Angeles		Wed.	22 Toronto
Nov.	Sun.	2 Hartford		Thur.	30 Philadelphia
	Tue.	4 Winnipeg	**Nov.**	Sat.	1 Hartford
	Sat.	8 Boston		Wed.	12 Montreal
	Sun.	9 NY Rangers		Fri.	14 Washington
	Tue.	18 NY Islanders		Sat.	15 Pittsburgh
	Sat.	22 Buffalo		Fri.	21 Buffalo
	Tue.	25 Montreal		Wed.	26 NY Rangers
	Sat.	29 Washington	**Dec.**	Wed.	3 Hartford
Dec.	Mon.	1 Hartford		Thur.	4 Boston
	Sat.	6 Calgary		Wed.	17 Edmonton
	Tue.	9 St. Louis		Thur.	18 Calgary
	Sat.	13 Buffalo		Sat.	20 Minnesota
	Sun.	14 Boston		Sun.	21 Winnipeg
	Sat.	27 New Jersey		Wed.	31 Montreal
	Tue.	30 Montreal	**Jan.**	Sun.	4 Buffalo
Jan.	Sat.	3 NY Rangers		Thur.	8 New Jersey
	Tue.	6 Vancouver		Sat.	10 Montreal
	Thur.	15 Edmonton		Sat.	17 Detroit
	Tue.	20 Boston		Sun.	18 Chicago
	Sat.	24 NY Islanders		Fri.	23 Hartford
	Tue.	27 Hartford		Fri.	30 Buffalo
Feb.	Sun.	1 Los Angeles	**Feb.**	Wed.	4 Montreal
	Tue.	3 Montreal		Sun.	8 Boston*
	Sat.	7 Buffalo*		Sun.	15 Chicago*
	Tue.	17 Winnipeg		Fri.	20 Detroit
	Tue.	24 Minnesota		Sat.	21 St. Louis
Mar.	Tue.	3 Pittsburgh		Thur.	26 Boston
	Sat.	7 Buffalo		Sat.	28 Hartford
	Tue.	10 Hartford	**Mar.**	Sun.	8 Buffalo
	Fri.	20 Toronto		Thur.	12 Pittsburgh
	Sat.	21 Philadelphia		Sat.	14 Los Angeles
	Tue.	24 Montreal		Tue.	17 Vancouver
	Sat.	28 Chicago		Thur.	26 Philadelphia
	Tue.	31 Boston	**April**	Thur.	2 NY Islanders
April	Sat.	4 New Jersey		Sun.	5 Boston

*Denotes afternoon game.

Home Starting Times:
All Games .... 7:35 p.m.
Except Matinees .... 2:05 p.m.

Franchise date: June 22, 1979

 7th NHL Season

Alain Cote

1986-87 Player Personnel

FORWARDS

	Ht.	Wt.	Place of Birth	Date	1985-86 Club
ASHTON, Brent	6-1	210	Saskatoon, Sask.	5/18/60	Quebec
COTA, Darren	5-11	193	McLellan, Alta.	4/7/66	Medicine Hat
COTE, Alain	5-10	203	Matane, Que.	5/3/57	Quebec
EAGLES, Mike	5-10	180	Sussex, N.B.	3/7/63	Quebec
GAULIN, Jean-Marc	5-10	182	Balve, Germany	3/3/62	Quebec-Fredericton
GERLITZ, Paul	5-11	205	Calgary, Alta.	3/23/63	Boston U.
GILLIS, Paul	5-11	190	Toronto, Ont.	12/31/63	Quebec
GOULET, Michel	6-1	185	Peribonka, Que.	4/21/60	Quebec
GROULX, Wayne	5-9	176	Welland, Ont.	2/2/65	Fredericton-Muskegon
HEROUX, Yves	5-11	185	Terrebonne, Que.	4/27/65	Fredericton-Muskegon
HOUGH, Mike	6-1	190	Montreal, Que.	2/6/63	Fredericton
HUNTER, Dale	5-9	190	Petrolia, Ont.	7/31/60	Quebec
KUMPEL, Mark	6-0	190	Wakefield, Mass.	3/7/61	Quebec-Fredericton
LAFRENIERE, Jason	5-11	185	St. Catharines, Ont.	12/6/66	Belleville
LATTA, David	6-0	185	Thunder Bay, Ont.	1/3/67	Quebec-Kitchener
MALONE, Greg	6-0	190	Fredericton, N.B.	3/8/56	Hartford-Quebec
MIDDENDORF, Max	6-4	194	Syracuse, N.Y.	9/18/67	Sudbury
PATRICK, Steve	6-4	205	Winnipeg, Man.	2/4/61	NY Rangers-Quebec
PEER, Brit	6-0	189	Toronto, Ont.	7/14/66	Windsor
PERKINS, Terry	6-1	190	Campbell River, B.C.	7/21/66	Spokane
QUINNEY, Ken	5-10	198	New Westminster, B.C.	5/23/65	Fredericton
STASTNY, Anton	6-0	185	Bratislava, Czech.	8/5/59	Quebec
STASTNY, Peter	6-1	195	Bratislava, Czech.	9/18/56	Quebec
STEINBURG, Trevor	6-1	185	Kingston, Ont.	5/13/66	Quebec-London
ZEMLAK, Richard	6-2	190	Wynard, Sask.	3/3/63	Muskegon-Fredericton

DEFENSEMEN

	Ht.	Wt.	Place of Birth	Date	1985-86 Club
ANDERSSON, Peter	6-2	200	Ferdertalve, Sweden	3/2/62	Washington-Quebec
BROWN, Jeff	6-1	185	Ottawa, Ont.	4/30/66	Quebec-Sudbury
DELORME, Gilbert	6-1	205	Boucherville, Que.	11/25/62	Sudbury-Quebec
DONNELLY, Gord	6-2	195	Montreal, Que.	4/5/62	Quebec-Fredericton
FINN, Steven	6-0	192	Laval, Que.	9/20/66	Quebec-Laval
KARALIS, Tom	6-1	190	Montreal, Que.	5/24/64	Fredericton-Muskegon
MOLLER, Randy	6-2	205	Red Deer, Alta.	9/23/63	Quebec
PICARD, Robert	6-2	205	Montreal, Que.	5/25/57	Winnipeg-Quebec
POUDRIER, Daniel	6-2	181	Thetford Mines, Que.	2/15/64	Quebec-Fredericton
PRICE, Pat	6-2	195	Nelson, B.C.	3/24/55	Quebec
ROCHEFORT, Normand	6-1	200	Trois-Rivieres, Que.	1/28/61	Quebec
SHAW, Dave	6-2	187	St. Thomas, Ont.	5/25/64	Quebec
SILTANEN, Risto	5-9	180	Tampere, Finland	10/31/58	Hartford-Quebec

GOALTENDERS

	Ht.	Wt.	Place of Birth	Date	1985-86 Club
BRUNETTA, Mario	6-3	180	Quebec, Que.	1/25/67	Laval
GOSSELIN, Mario	5-8	160	Thetford Mines, Que.	6/15/63	Quebec-Fredericton
GUENETTE, Luc	5-9	162	St-Jerome, Que.	7/22/64	Fredericton
MALARCHUK, Clint	5-10	172	Grande Prairie, Alta.	5/1/61	Quebec
SEVIGNY, Richard	5-8	178	Montreal, Que.	11/4/57	Quebec-Fredericton

Coach and General Manager

BERGERON, JOSEPH ROBERT (MICHEL)
Coach, Quebec Nordiques. Born in Montreal, Que., June 12, 1946.

Michel Bergeron was appointed coach of the Quebec Nordiques on October 20, 1980 after only days of professional hockey experience as assistant to general manager/coach Maurice Filion. When Filion relinquished the coaching duties, he named the youthful Bergeron as his replacement. After guiding a midget team in the Montreal area, Bergeron was named head coach of the Trois Rivieres Draveurs of the Quebec Major Junior Hockey League and led that club from last place to a pair of Memorial Cup Finals in 1978 and 1979. After the 1979-80 campaign, Bergeron was named assistant coach of the Nordiques.

NHL Coaching Record

NHL Coaching Record

Team		Games	Regular Season				Playoffs			
			W	L	T	%	Games	W	L	%
Quebec	1980-81	74	29	29	16	.500	5	2	3	.400
Quebec	1981-82	80	33	31	16	.512	16	7	9	.437
Quebec	1982-83	80	34	34	12	.500	4	1	3	.250
Quebec	1983-84	80	42	28	10	.588	9	5	4	.556
Quebec	1984-85	80	41	30	9	.569	18	9	9	.500
Quebec	1985-86	80	43	31	6	.575	3	0	3	.000
NHL Totals		**474**	**222**	**183**	**69**	**.541**	**55**	**24**	**31**	**.436**

FILION, MAURICE
General Manager, Quebec Nordiques. Born in Montreal, Que., February 12, 1932.

Maurice Filion was named general manager of the Quebec Nordiques, May 4, 1974 and was appointed coach following the 1979-80 season. Prior to that, Filion had been a scout with the club since its inception in 1972 and was head coach after three games of the 1972-73 season. Filion's coaching career began with the Montreal Olympiques in 1961-62 when he guided the Senior A club to the Allan Cup Final. He later coached several teams in Junior A, including Guy Lafleur and the Quebec Remparts when they won the Memorial Cup in 1970-71. Filion returned behind the bench with the Nordiques as interim coach for part of the 1976-77 season and early in the 1980-81 campaign. Although he played junior hockey with Trois-Rivières, he never turned pro. Filion relinquished the coaching duties to Michel Bergeron after only six games of the 1980-81 season (1 win, 3 losses, 2 ties.)

1985-86 Scoring

Regular Season

*–rookie

Pos	#	Player	Team	GP	G	A	Pts	+/-	PIM	PP	SH	GW	OT	S	%
F	26	Peter Stastny	QUE	76	41	81	122	2	60	15	0	8	0	207	19.8
F	16	Michel Goulet	QUE	75	53	51	104	6	64	28	0	3	1	244	21.7
F	20	Anton Stastny	QUE	74	31	43	74	8	19	8	0	4	0	163	19.0
F	32	Dale Hunter	QUE	80	28	42	70	6	265	7	0	4	0	152	18.4
F	9	Brent Ashton	QUE	77	26	32	58	7	64	5	2	5	0	207	12.6
F	15	J.F. Sauve	QUE	75	16	40	56	13–	20	13	0	1	0	100	16.0
F	23	Paul Gillis	QUE	80	19	24	43	2–	203	0	2	2	0	136	14.0
D	24	Robert Picard	WPG	20	2	5	7	2–	17	0	0	1	0	40	5.0
			QUE	48	7	27	34	2–	36	1	1	0	0	131	5.3
			Total	68	9	32	41	4–	53	1	1	1	0	171	5.3
D	12	Risto Siltanen	HFD	52	8	22	30	2	30	6	0	1	0	126	6.3
			QUE	13	2	5	7	1–	6	2	0	0	0	53	3.8
			Total	65	10	27	37	1	36	8	0	1	0	179	5.6
F	19	Alain Cote	QUE	78	13	21	34	3	29	0	3	2	0	119	10.9
D	29	Peter Andersson	WSH	61	6	16	22	8–	36	3	0	3	0	83	7.2
			QUE	12	1	8	9	8	4	1	0	0	0	16	6.3
			Total	73	7	24	31	0	40	4	0	3	0	99	7.1
D	4	*David Shaw	QUE	73	7	19	26	14	78	2	0	2	0	126	5.6
F	25	Steve Patrick	NYR	28	4	3	7	7–	37	0	0	0	0	20	20.0
			QUE	27	4	13	17	1	17	1	0	0	0	29	13.8
			Total	55	8	16	24	6–	54	1	0	0	0	49	16.3
F	11	*Mike Eagles	QUE	73	11	12	23	3	49	1	0	1	1	68	16.2
D	21	Randy Moller	QUE	69	5	18	23	9	141	0	0	1	0	105	4.8
F	17	Mark Kumpel	QUE	47	10	12	22	10	17	0	0	3	0	76	13.2
F	18	Greg Malone	HFD	22	6	7	13	5–	24	1	0	0	0	35	17.1
			QUE	27	3	5	8	3–	18	0	0	0	0	26	11.5
			Total	49	9	12	21	8–	42	1	0	0	0	61	14.8
D	6	Gilbert Delorme	QUE	64	2	18	20	1	51	1	0	0	0	102	2.0
D	7	Pat Price	QUE	54	3	13	16	0	82	0	0	0	0	49	6.1
D	5	Normand Rochefort	QUE	26	5	4	9	9	30	2	0	0	0	51	9.8
D	2	*Daniel Poudrier	QUE	13	1	5	6	2	10	0	0	1	0	6	16.7
D	28	*Jeff Brown	QUE	8	3	2	5	5	6	0	0	0	0	16	18.8
D	34	*Gord Donnelly	QUE	36	2	2	4	0	85	0	0	0	0	30	6.7
G	33	Mario Gosselin	QUE	31	0	3	3	0	2	0	0	0	0	0	.0
F	10	Jimmy Mann	QUE	35	0	3	3	2–	148	0	0	0	0	4	.0
G	30	Clint Malarchuk	QUE	46	0	2	2	0	21	0	0	0	0	0	.0
F	31	Jean Marc Gaulin	QUE	1	1	0	1	0	0	0	0	0	0	2	50.0
F	14	*Trevor Stienburg	QUE	2	1	0	1	0	6	0	0	0	0	6	16.7
D	12	*Claude Julien	QUE	13	0	1	1	2	25	0	0	0	0	4	.0
D	25	*Steven Finn	QUE	17	0	1	1	0	28	0	0	0	0	8	.0
F	27	*Dave Latta	QUE	1	0	0	0	0	0	0	0	0	0	1	.0
F	28	Alain Lemieux	QUE	7	0	0	0	1–	0	0	0	0	0	1	.0
G	1	Richard Sevigny	QUE	11	0	0	0	0	8	0	0	0	0	0	.0

Playoffs

* rookie

Pos	#	Player	Team	GP	G	A	Pts	+/-	PIM	PP	SH	GW	OT	S	%
F	9	Brent Ashton	QUE	3	2	1	3	1–	9	0	1	0	0	11	18.2
F	28	Alain Lemieux	QUE	1	1	0	1	0	2	0	0	0	0	2	50.0
F	16	Michel Goulet	QUE	3	1	2	3	2–	10	1	0	0	0	12	8.3
F	20	Anton Stastny	QUE	3	1	1	2	5–	0	0	0	0	0	5	20.0
F	23	Paul Gillis	QUE	3	0	2	2	0	14	0	0	0	0	6	.0
D	24	Robert Picard	QUE	3	0	2	2	4–	2	0	0	0	0	7	.0
F	17	Mark Kumpel	QUE	2	1	0	1	1–	0	0	0	0	0	3	33.3
F	19	Alain Cote	QUE	3	1	0	1	2–	0	0	0	0	0	8	12.5
D	29	Peter Andersson	QUE	3	0	1	1	1	4	0	0	0	0	0	.0
D	7	Pat Price	QUE	3	0	1	1	0	4	0	0	0	0	0	.0
D	12	Risto Siltanen	QUE	3	0	1	1	3–	2	0	0	0	0	9	.0
F	26	Peter Stastny	QUE	3	0	1	1	5–	2	0	0	0	0	10	.0
D	28	*Jeff Brown	QUE	1	0	0	0	0	0	0	0	0	0	0	.0
D	34	*Gord Donnelly	QUE	1	0	0	0	1–	0	0	0	0	0	0	.0
G	33	Mario Gosselin	QUE	3	0	0	0	0	0	0	0	0	0	0	.0
F	18	Greg Malone	QUE	1	0	0	0	1–	0	0	0	0	0	1	.0
F	3	*Trevor Stienburg	QUE	1	0	0	0	0	5	0	0	0	0	0	.0
D	6	Gilbert Delorme	QUE	2	0	0	0	1–	0	0	0	0	0	3	.0
F	10	Jimmy Mann	QUE	2	0	0	0	0	19	0	0	0	0	0	.0
F	15	J.F. Sauve	QUE	2	0	0	0	1–	2	0	0	0	0	4	.0
F	11	*Mike Eagles	QUE	3	0	0	0	1–	2	0	0	0	0	4	.0
F	32	Dale Hunter	QUE	3	0	0	0	1–	15	0	0	0	0	9	.0
G	30	Clint Malarchuk	QUE	3	0	0	0	0	0	0	0	0	0	0	.0
D	21	Randy Moller	QUE	3	0	0	0	1–	26	0	0	0	0	4	.0
F	25	Steve Patrick	QUE	3	0	0	0	1–	6	0	0	0	0	1	.0

Club Records

Team

(Figures in brackets for season records are games played; records for fewest points, wins, ties, losses, goals, goals against are for 70 or more games)

Most Points	.94	1983-84 (80)
Most Wins	.43	1985-86 (80)
Most Ties	.18	1980-81 (80)
Most Losses	.44	1979-80 (80)
Most Goals	.360	1983-84 (80)
Most Goals Against	.345	1981-82 (80)
Fewest Points	.61	1979-80 (80)
Fewest Wins	.25	1979-80 (80)
Fewest Ties	.6	1985-86 (80)
Fewest Losses	.28	1983-84 (80)
Fewest Goals	.248	1979-80 (80)
Fewest Goals Against	.275	1984-85 (80)

Longest Winning Streak
Over-all . . . . .7 Nov. 24-
Dec. 10/83
Home . . . . .10 Nov. 26/83-
Jan. 10/84
Away. . . . . .4 Feb. 17-22/81

Longest Undefeated Streak
Over-all . . . . .11 Mar. 10-31/81
(7 wins, 4 ties)
Home . . . . .14 Nov. 19/83
Jan. 21/84
(11 wins, 3 ties)
Away. . . . . .8 Feb. 17/81-
Mar. 22/81
(6 wins, 2 ties)

Longest Losing Streak
Over-all . . . . .7 Feb. 9-23/80
Home . . . . .4 Mar. 12-30/80
Away. . . . . .9 Feb. 2-
Mar. 19/80

Longest Winless Streak
Over-all . . . . .13 Oct. 12-
Nov. 11/80
(9 losses, 4 ties)
Home . . . . .8 Dec. 23/80-
Jan. 28/81
(4 losses, 4 ties)
Away. . . . . .13 Jan. 11-
Mar. 19/80
(12 losses, 1 tie)

Most Shutouts, Season 6 1985-86 (80)

Most Pen. Mins.,
Season 1,847 1985-86 (80)
Most Goals, Game . . . . . . .12 Feb. 1/83
(Hfd. 3 at Que. 12)
Oct. 20/84
(Que. 12 at Tor. 3)

Individual

Most Seasons . . . . .7 Several players
Most Games . . . . .532 Michel Goulet
Most Goals, Career . . . . . .317 Michel Goulet
Most Assists, Career . . . . .462 Peter Stastny
Most Points, Career . . . . .713 Peter Stastny
(210 goals, 381 assists)
Most Pen. Mins., Career . . 1,410 Dale Hunter
Most Shutouts, Career . . . . . .4 Clint Malarchuk
Daniel Bouchard

Longest Consecutive
Games Streak . . . . .312 Dale Hunter
(Oct. 9/80-Mar. 13/84)
Most Goals, Season . . . . . .57 Michel Goulet
(1982-83)
Most Assists, Season . . . . .93 Peter Stastny
(1980-81, 1981-82)
Most Points, Season . . . . .139 Peter Stastny
(1981-82)
(46 goals, 93 assists)
Most Pen. Mins., Season . . .272 Dale Hunter
(1981-82)
Most Points, Defenseman
Season . . . . .46 Mario Marois
(1983-84)
(13 goals, 36 assists)
Most Points, Center,
Season . . . . .139 Peter Stastny
(1981-82)
(46 goals, 93 assists)
Most Points, Right Wing,
Season . . . . .97 Réal Cloutier
(1981-82)
(37 goals, 60 assists)
Most Points, Left Wing,
Season . . . . .121 Michel Goulet
(1983-84)
(56 goals, 65 assists)

Most Points, Rookie,
Season . . . . .109 Peter Stastny
(1980-81)
(39 goals, 70 assists)
Most Shutouts, Season . . . . .4 Clint Malarchuk
(1985-86)
Most Goals, Game . . . . .4 Michel Goulet
(Dec. 14/85;
Mar. 17/86)
Most Assists, Game . . . . . . .5 Anton Stastny
(Feb. 22/81)
Most Points, Game . . . . .8 Peter Stastny
(Feb. 22/81)
Anton Stastny
(Feb. 22/81)

Coaching History

Jacques Demers, 1979-80; Maurice Filion and Michel Bergeron, 1980-81; Michel Bergeron, 1981-82 to date.

Captains' History

Marc Tardif, 1979-80, 1980-81; Robbie Ftorek, Andre Dupont, 1981-82; Mario Marois, 1982-83 to 1984-85; Mario Marois, Peter Stastny, 1985-86.

All-time Record vs. Other Clubs

Regular Season

	At Home							On Road							Total						
	GP	W	L	T	GF	GA	PTS	GP	W	L	T	GF	GA	PTS	GP	W	L	T	GF	GA	PTS
Boston	24	10	12	2	103	111	22	24	12	9	3	101	97	27	48	22	21	5	204	208	49
Buffalo	24	15	7	2	94	70	32	24	6	14	4	80	100	16	48	21	21	6	174	170	48
*Calgary	12	6	5	1	49	41	13	11	4	35	42	8	23	8	10	5	84	83	21
Chicago	12	6	3	3	55	41	15	11	4	7	0	36	51	8	23	10	10	3	91	92	23
Detroit	12	7	2	3	53	34	16	11	5	5	1	47	44	11	23	12	8	3	100	78	27
Edmonton	12	5	6	1	53	61	11	11	4	7	0	40	69	8	23	9	13	1	93	130	19
Hartford	24	15	7	2	126	73	36	24	7	10	7	98	105	21	48	24	15	9	224	178	57
Los Angeles	11	4	5	2	53	49	10	12	6	5	1	47	43	13	23	10	10	3	100	92	23
Minnesota	11	9	1	1	59	24	19	12	3	7	2	35	54	8	23	12	8	3	94	78	27
Montreal	24	14	8	2	93	82	30	24	5	14	5	77	105	15	48	19	22	7	170	187	45
*New Jersey	11	7	3	1	56	37	15	12	6	6	0	46	50	12	23	13	9	1	102	87	27
NY Islanders	11	7	3	1	54	40	15	12	3	8	1	41	53	7	23	10	11	2	95	93	22
NY Rangers	11	6	2	3	55	46	15	12	3	6	3	40	47	9	23	9	8	6	95	93	22
Philadelphia	12	3	4	5	37	38	11	11	2	8	1	28	43	5	23	5	12	6	65	81	16
Pittsburgh	12	8	4	0	59	38	16	11	5	4	2	53	41	12	23	13	8	2	112	79	28
St. Louis	12	8	2	2	52	32	18	11	3	7	1	38	50	7	23	11	9	3	90	82	25
Toronto	11	6	1	4	47	34	16	12	5	5	2	53	36	12	23	11	6	6	100	70	28
Vancouver	12	4	4	4	39	38	12	11	4	7	0	49	57	8	23	8	11	4	88	95	20
Washington	11	5	4	2	43	44	12	12	6	4	2	51	48	14	23	11	8	4	94	92	26
Winnipeg	11	6	4	1	50	37	13	12	4	6	2	49	49	10	23	10	10	3	99	86	23
Totals	**280**	**153**	**86**	**41**	**1230**	**970**	**347**	**280**	**95**	**144**	**41**	**1044**	**1184**	**231**	**560**	**248**	**230**	**82**	**2274**	**2154**	**578**

* Totals include those of Colorado Rockies (1979-80, 1980-81 and 1981-82)
** Totals include those of Atlanta (1979-80)

Playoffs

	Series	W	L	GP	W	L	T	GF	GA	Last Mtg.	Round	Result
Boston	2	1	1	11	5	6	0	36	37	1983	DSF	L 1-3
Buffalo	2	2	0	8	6	2	0	35	27	1985	DSF	W 3-2
Hartford	1	0	1	3	0	3	0	7	16	1986	DSF	L 0-3
Montreal	3	2	1	18	11	7	0	53	55	1985	DF	W 4-3
NY Islanders	1	0	1	4	0	4	0	9	18	1982	CF	L 0-4
Philadelphia	2	0	2	11	4	7	0	29	39	1985	CF	L 2-4
Totals	**11**	**5**	**6**	**55**	**26**	**29**	**6**	**169**	**192**			

Playoff Results 1986-82

Year	Round	Opponent	Result	GF	GA
1986	DSF	Hartford	L 0-3	7	16
1985	CF	Philadelphia	L 2-4	12	17
	DF	Montreal	W 4-3	24	24
	DSF	Buffalo	W 3-2	22	22
1984	DF	Montreal	L 2-4	13	20
	DSF	Buffalo	W 3-0	13	5
1983	DSF	Boston	L 1-3	8	11
1982	CF	NY Islanders	L 0-4	9	18
	DF	Boston	W 4-3	28	26
	DSF	Montreal	W 3-2	16	11

Abbreviations: Round: F – Final; **CF** – conference final; **DF** – division final; **DSF** – division semi-final; **SF** – semi-final; **QF** – quarter-final; **P** – preliminary round. **GA** – goals against; **GF** – goals for.

Retired Numbers

3	J.C. Tremblay	1972-1979
8	Marc Tardif	1979-1983

Entry Draft Selections 1986-79

1986
Pick
18	Ken McRae
39	Jean-M Routhier
41	Stephane Guerard
81	Ron Tugnutt
102	Gerald Bzdel
117	Scott White
123	Morgan Samuelsson
134	Mark Vermette
144	Jean-Francois Nault
165	Keith Miller
186	Pierre Millier
207	Chris Lappin
228	Martin Latreille
249	Sean Boudreault

1985
Pick
15	David Latta
36	Jason Lafreniere
57	Max Middendorf
65	Peter Massey
78	David Espe
99	Bruce Major
120	Andy Akervik
141	Mike Oliverio
162	Mario Brunetta
183	Brit Peer
204	Tom Sasso
225	Gary Murphy
246	Jean Bois

1984
Pick
15	Trevor Stienburg
36	Jeff Brown
57	Steve Finn
78	Terry Perkins
120	Darren Cota
141	Henrik Cedegren
162	Jyrki Maki
183	Guy Ouellette
203	Ken Quinney
244	Peter Loob

1983
Pick
32	Yves Heroux
52	Bruce Bell
54	Iiro Jarvi
92	Luc Guenette
112	Brad Walcott
132	Craig Mack
152	Tommy Albelin
172	Wayne Groulx
192	Scott Shaunessy
232	Bo Berglund
239	Dinorich Kokrement

1982
Pick
13	David Shaw
34	Paul Gillis
55	Mario Gosselin
76	Jiri Lala
97	Phil Stanger
131	Daniel Poudrier
181	Mike Hough
202	Vincent Lukac
223	Andre Martin
244	Jozef Lukac
248	Jan Jasko

1981
Pick
11	Randy Moller
53	Jean-Marc Gaulin
74	Clint Malarchuk
95	Ed Lee
116	Mike Eagles
158	Andre Cote
179	Marc Brisebois
200	Kari Takko

1980
Pick
24	Normand Rochefort
66	Jay Miller
108	Mark Kumpel
129	Gaston Therrien
150	Michel Bolduc
171	Christian Tanguay
192	William Robinson

1979
Pick
20	Michel Goulet
41	Dale Hunter
62	Lee Norwood
83	Anton Stastny
104	Pierre Lacroix
125	Scott McGeown

Club Directory

Colisée de Québec
2205 Ave du Colisée
Québec City, Quebec
G1L 4W7
Phone 418/529-8441
TWX 610-571-5743
ENVOY ID   TM.QUE
Capacity: 15,434

President, Governor	Marcel Aubut
General Manager	Maurice Filion
Director of Personnel Development	Gilles Léger
Director of Recruiting & Chief Scout	Martin Madden
Coach	Michel Bergeron
Associate Coaches	Simon Nolet, Ron Harris
Special Counsellor to hockey department	Charles Thiffault
Scouts	George Armstrong, Serge Aubry, Red Fleming, Pierre Gauthier
General Counsel	Jean Pelletier
Director of Finance and Administration	Jean Laflamme
Supervisor of Accounting	Marc Bélanger
Director of Communications & Press Relations	Bernard Brisset
Supervisor of Public Relations	Marius Fortier
Director of Marketing	Jean Méthot
Supervisor of Ticket Sales & Promotions	André Lestourneau
Supervisor of Novelties & Souvenirs	André Pelletier
Physiotherapist	Jacques Lavergne
Trainers	René Lacasse, René Lavigueur, Brian Turpin
Team Physician	Dr. Pierre Beauchemin
Location of Press Box	East & West side of building, upper level
Dimensions of Rink	200 feet by 85 feet
Club Colors	Blue, White & Red
Training Camp Site	Québec City
Radio Station	CHRC 80
Radio Announcers	Alain Crête, André Belisle
TV Station	CFCM (4) Télé-Capitale
TV Announcers	André Côté, Claude Bédard

Paul Gillis

St. Louis Blues

1985-86 Results: 37w-34L-9T 85 PTS. Third, Norris Division

Year-by-Year Record

Season	GP	Home W	L	T	Road W	L	T	Overall W	L	T	GF	GA	Pts.	Finished	Playoff Result
1985-86	80	23	11	6	14	23	3	37	34	9	302	291	85	3rd, Norris Div.	Lost Conf. Final
1984-85	80	21	12	7	16	19	5	37	31	12	299	288	86	1st, Norris Div.	Lost Div. Semi-Final
1983-84	80	23	14	3	9	27	4	32	41	7	293	316	71	2nd, Norris Div.	Lost Div. Final
1982-83	80	16	16	8	9	24	7	25	40	15	285	316	65	4th, Norris Div.	Lost Div. Semi-Final
1981-82	80	22	14	4	10	26	4	32	40	8	315	349	72	3rd, Norris Div.	Lost Div. Final
1980-81	80	29	7	4	16	11	13	45	18	17	352	281	107	1st, Smythe Div.	Lost Quarter-Final
1979-80	80	20	13	7	14	21	5	34	34	12	266	278	80	2nd, Smythe Div.	Lost Prelim. Round
1978-79	80	14	20	6	4	30	6	18	50	12	249	348	48	3rd, Smythe Div.	Out of Playoffs
1977-78	80	12	20	8	8	27	5	20	47	13	195	304	53	4th, Smythe Div.	Out of Playoffs
1976-77	80	22	13	5	10	26	4	32	39	9	239	276	73	1st, Smythe Div.	Lost Quarter-Final
1975-76	80	20	12	8	9	25	6	29	37	14	249	290	72	3rd, Smythe Div.	Lost Prelim. Round
1974-75	80	23	13	4	12	18	10	35	31	14	269	267	84	2nd, Smythe Div.	Lost Prelim. Round
1973-74	78	16	16	7	10	24	5	26	40	12	206	248	64	6th, West Div.	Out of Playoffs
1972-73	78	21	11	7	11	23	5	32	34	12	233	251	76	4th, West Div.	Lost Quarter-Final
1971-72	78	17	17	5	11	22	6	28	39	11	208	247	67	3rd, West Div.	Lost Semi-Final
1970-71	78	23	7	9	11	18	10	34	25	19	223	208	87	2nd, West Div.	Lost Quarter-Final
1969-70	76	24	9	5	13	18	7	37	27	12	224	179	86	1st, West Div.	Lost Final
1968-69	76	21	8	9	16	17	5	37	25	14	204	157	88	1st, West Div.	Lost Final
1967-68	74	18	12	7	9	19	9	27	31	16	177	191	70	3rd, West Div.	Lost Final

Schedule

	Home			Away	
Oct.	Sat. 18 Quebec		**Oct.**	Thur. 9 Los Angeles	
	Wed. 22 Minnesota			Sat. 11 Vancouver	
	Sat. 25 Detroit			Tue. 14 Toronto	
	Wed. 29 NY Rangers			Fri. 24 Detroit	
Nov.	Sat. 1 Pittsburgh		**Nov.**	Wed. 5 Toronto	
	Sun. 2 Chicago			Fri. 7 Winnipeg	
	Wed. 12 Toronto			Sun. 9 Chicago	
	Sat. 15 Chicago			Tue. 18 Minnesota	
	Wed. 19 Minnesota			Fri. 21 Hartford	
	Wed. 26 New Jersey			Sat. 22 Boston	
	Sat. 29 Detroit			Fri. 28 Detroit	
Dec.	Sun. 7 Toronto		**Dec.**	Tue. 2 Philadelphia	
	Sat. 13 Chicago			Wed. 3 Montreal	
	Tue. 16 Montreal			Fri. 5 Buffalo	
	Thur. 18 Winnipeg			Tue. 9 Quebec	
	Sat. 27 NY Rangers			Wed. 10 Hartford	
	Tue. 30 Boston			Sat. 20 Washington	
Jan.	Sat. 3 Calgary			Sun. 21 Philadelphia	
	Mon. 5 Washington			Fri. 26 Chicago	
	Wed. 7 Hartford		**Jan.**	Fri. 9 Edmonton	
	Fri. 16 Los Angeles			Sat. 10 Calgary	
	Sat. 17 Los Angeles			Mon. 12 Minnesota	
	Sat. 24 Detroit			Wed. 21 Toronto	
	Tue. 27 Montreal			Fri. 23 Detroit	
	Thur. 29 Toronto		**Feb.**	Thur. 5 Calgary	
	Sat. 31 Chicago			Fri. 6 Vancouver	
Feb.	Tue. 3 Edmonton			Sun. 8 Edmonton	
	Sat. 14 Philadelphia			Sun. 15 Minnesota	
	Tue. 17 Vancouver			Thur. 26 Buffalo	
	Thur. 19 Minnesota			Sat. 28 NY Islanders	
	Sat. 21 Quebec		**Mar.**	Sun. 1 Pittsburgh	
	Tue. 24 NY Islanders			Tue. 3 Toronto	
Mar.	Thur. 5 Winnipeg			Wed. 11 Chicago	
	Sat. 7 Detroit			Thur. 12 Boston	
	Mon. 9 Toronto			Wed. 18 Pittsburgh	
	Sat. 14 Washington			Mon. 23 Minnesota	
	Sat. 21 New Jersey			Wed. 25 Chicago	
	Tue. 31 NY Islanders			Fri. 27 NY Rangers	
April	Thur. 2 Buffalo			Sun. 29 New Jersey*	
	Sat. 4 Minnesota		**April**	Sun. 5 Detroit	

*Denotes afternoon game.

Home Starting Times:
Mondays through Saturdays . . . . 7:35 p.m.
Sundays . . . . 6:05 p.m.

Franchise date: June 5, 1967.

 **20th NHL Season**

Doug Wickenheiser

1986-87 Player Personnel

FORWARDS

	Ht.	Wt.	Place of Birth	Date	1985-86 Club
BARR, Dave	6-1	195	Toronto, Ont.	11/30/60	St. Louis
BEERS, Eddy	6-2	195	Merritt, B.C.	10/12/59	Calgary-St. Louis
BOZON, Phillipe	5-11	180	Chamoix, France	11/30/66	St. Jean
CARLSON, Kent	6-3	200	Concord, N.H.	1/11/62	Montreal-St. Louis
CAVALLINI, Gino	6-1	215	Toronto, Ont.	11/24/62	Calgary-St. Louis
DUMONT, Marc	6-1	185	Quebec City, Que.	1/28/67	Laval
EVANS, Doug	5-9	178	Peterborough, Ont.	6/2/63	Peoria-St. Louis
FEDERKO, Bernie	6-0	195	Foam Lake, Sask.	5/12/56	St. Louis
FLOCKHART, Ron	5-11	185	Smithers, B.C.	10/10/60	St. Louis
GILMOUR, Doug	5-11	160	Kingston, Ont.	6/25/63	St. Louis
HUNTER, Mark	6-0	205	Petrolia, Ont.	11/12/62	St. Louis
LEMIEUX, Jocelyn	5-11	207	Mont Laurier, Que.	11/18/67	Laval
MEAGHER, Rick	5-8	175	Belleville, Ont.	11/4/53	St. Louis
PASLAWSKI, Greg	5-11	189	Kindersley, Sask.	8/25/61	St. Louis
RAGLAN, Herb	6-0	204	Peterborough, Ont.	8/5/67	Kingston-St. Louis
REEDS, Mark	5-10	190	Toronto, Ont.	1/24/60	St. Louis
RONNING, Cliff	5-8	157	Vancouver, B.C.	10/1/65	Cdn. Olympic
SUTTER, Brian	5-11	180	Viking, Alta.	10/7/58	St. Louis
TRELOAR, Darren	5-10	180	Etobicoke, Ont.	5/14/66	Peterborough
WICKENHEISER, Doug	6-1	196	Regina, Sask.	3/30/61	St. Louis

DEFENSEMEN

ALLEN, Tom	6-3	200	London, Ont.	5/3/66	London
BELL, Bruce	6-0	190	Toronto, Ont.	2/15/65	St. Louis
BENNING, Brian	6-0	175	Edmonton, Alta.	6/10/66	Cdn. Olympic
BOURGEOIS, Charlie	6-4	220	Moncton, N.B.	11/19/59	Calgary-St. Louis
DARK, Michael	6-3	225	Sarnia, Ont.	9/17/63	RPI
DIRK, Robert	6-4	207	Regina, Sask.	8/20/66	Regina
EVANS, Shawn	6-2	195	Kingston, Ontario	9/7/65	Peoria-St. Louis
NATTRESS, Ric	6-2	210	Hamilton, Ontario	5/25/62	St. Louis
NORWOOD, Lee	6-0	195	Oakland, Calif.	2/2/60	St. Louis
PAVESE, Jim	6-2	205	New York, N.Y.	5/8/62	St. Louis
POSAVAD, Mike	5-11	196	Brantford, Ont.	1/3/64	Peoria-St. Louis
RAMAGE, Rob	6-2	210	Byron, Ontario	1/11/59	St. Louis
RUFF, Marty	6-1	195	Warburg, Alta.	5/19/53	Peoria

GOALTENDERS

JABLONSKI, Pat	6-0	170	Toledo, Ohio	6/20/67	Windsor
MAY, Darrell	6-0	175	Edmonton, Alta.	3/6/62	Peoria-St. Louis
MILLEN, Greg	5-9	175	Toronto, Ont.	6/25/57	St. Louis
PERRY, Alan	5-8	155	Providence, R.I.	8/30/66	Windsor
WAMSLEY, Rick	5-11	185	Simcoe, Ont.	5/25/59	St. Louis

Coach and General Manager

MARTIN, JACQUES
Coach, St. Louis Blues. Born in Rockland, Ont., October 1, 1952

When Jacques Martin was named coach of the St. Louis Blues on June 26, 1986, he brought with him a brief but successful coaching background. The youngest coach ever to lead the Blues in their 19 years and their 14th coach in club history, the 33-year-old Martin was named OHL Coach of the Year after he led the Guelph Platers to a 41-33-2 record en route to capturing the OHL championship and the Memorial Cup in 1985-86. His one year in Guelph was the best in team history as was their playoff mark of 18-4-2. In 1984-85, Martin coached the Peterborough Petes and led them to a first-place finish with a 42-20-4 record. In his first season with the Petes, 1983-84, he guided the club to a 43-23-4 mark.

CARON, RON
Vice President and Director of Player Personnel, St. Louis Blues. Born in Hull, Que., December 19, 1929

Ron Caron joined the St. Louis Blues on August 13, 1983 after a 26-year association with the Montreal Canadiens' organization. He joined the Canadiens in 1957 on a part-time scouting basis after coaching in the amateur ranks. In 1966, Caron was promoted to a full-time position as chief scout of the Montreal Junior Canadiens and was instrumental in assembling two Memorial Cup championship teams. In 1968, he was named chief scout of the parent club and served as an assistant to former manager Sam Pollock. In 1969 he added the responsibilities of general manager of the Montreal Voyageurs of the AHL and maintained that role until 1978 when he was named Director of Scouting and Player Personnel for the Canadiens. Caron remained with the Montreal organization until the conclusion of the 1982-83 campaign.

Bernie Federko led the Blues with 102 points.

1985-86 Scoring
Regular Season

*—rookie

Pos	#	Player	Team	GP	G	A	Pts	+/-	PIM	PP	SH	GW	OT	S	%
F	24	Bernie Federko	STL	80	34	68	102	10	34	16	0	2	0	167	20.4
F	20	Mark Hunter	STL	78	44	30	74	15	171	11	2	3	1	204	21.6
F	12	Ron Flockhart	STL	79	22	45	67	8	26	5	2	3	1	199	11.1
D	5	Rob Ramage	STL	77	10	56	66	18	171	7	0	2	0	227	4.4
F	9	Doug Gilmour	STL	74	25	28	53	-3	41	2	1	5	0	183	13.7
F	6	Dave Barr	STL	72	13	38	51	11	70	0	2	1	0	106	12.3
F	11	Brian Sutter	STL	44	19	23	42	-12	87	8	0	1	1	92	20.7
F	19	Eddy Beers	CGY	33	11	10	21	-3	8	4	0	1	0	83	13.3
			STL	24	7	11	18	-3	24	4	0	0	0	53	13.2
			Total	57	18	21	39	-6	32	8	0	1	0	136	13.2
F	16	Kevin LaVallee	STL	64	18	20	38	8	8	7	0	2	1	129	14.0
F	15	Mark Reeds	STL	78	10	28	38	11	28	0	1	0	0	108	9.3
F	28	Greg Paslawski	STL	56	22	11	33	-12	18	1	1	2	0	150	14.7
F	22	Rick Meagher	STL	79	11	19	30	1	28	0	3	3	0	109	10.1
D	23	Lee Norwood	STL	71	5	24	29	7	134	2	0	1	0	111	4.5
F	17	Gino Cavallini	CGY	27	7	7	14	-7	26	4	0	0	0	51	13.7
			STL	30	6	5	11	-2	36	1	0	0	0	44	13.6
			Total	57	13	12	25	-9	62	5	0	0	0	95	13.7
D	27	Ric Nattress	STL	78	4	20	24	-8	52	1	0	2	0	124	3.2
D	10	Bruce Bell	STL	75	2	18	20	2	43	2	0	0	0	96	2.1
F	14	Doug Wickenheiser	STL	36	8	11	19	11	16	0	0	2	0	53	15.1
D	4	Charles Bourgeois	CGY	29	5	5	10	9	128	0	0	0	0	30	16.7
			STL	31	2	7	9	9	116	1	0	1	0	34	5.9
			Total	60	7	12	19	18	244	1	0	1	0	64	10.9
D	35	Jim Pavese	STL	69	4	7	11	-3	116	0	0	0	0	51	7.8
F	17	Denis Cyr	STL	31	3	4	7	-11	2	0	0	0	0	21	14.3
D	33	Kent Carlson	MTL	2	0	0	0	0	0	0	0	0	0	0	.0
			STL	26	2	3	5	2	42	0	0	0	0	14	14.3
			Total	28	2	3	5	2	42	0	0	0	0	14	14.3
F	21	Normand Baron	STL	23	2	0	2	-7	39	0	0	0	0	13	15.4
F	18	*Doug Evans	STL	13	1	0	1	0	2	0	0	0	0	12	8.3
G	1	*Darrell May	STL	3	0	1	1	0	2	0	0	0	0	0	.0
G	29	Greg Millen	STL	36	0	1	1	0	8	0	0	0	0	0	.0
D	25	*Mike Posavad	STL	8	0	0	0	-1	0	0	0	0	0	2	.0
D	2	*Shawn Evans	STL	7	0	0	0	-1	2	0	0	0	1	0	.0
F	25	*Herb Raglan	STL	7	0	0	0	-3	5	0	0	0	0	4	.0
G	30	Rick Wamsley	STL	42	0	0	0	0	2	0	0	0	0	0	.0

Playoffs

* rookie

Pos	#	Player	Team	GP	G	A	Pts	+/-	PIM	PP	SH	GW	OT	S	%
F	9	Doug Gilmour	STL	19	9	12	21	3	25	1	2	2	0	55	16.4
F	24	Bernie Federko	STL	19	7	14	21	7	17	1	0	1	0	34	20.6
F	28	Greg Paslawski	STL	17	10	7	17	4	13	2	0	1	0	40	25.0
F	20	Mark Hunter	STL	19	7	7	14	-7	48	2	0	1	0	41	17.1
D	5	Rob Ramage	STL	19	1	10	11	2	66	0	0	0	0	36	2.8
F	17	Gino Cavallini	STL	17	4	5	9	2	10	0	0	2	0	28	14.3
D	23	Lee Norwood	STL	19	2	7	9	12	64	0	0	0	0	32	6.3
F	22	Rick Meagher	STL	19	4	4	8	8	12	0	1	0	0	34	11.8
F	15	Mark Reeds	STL	19	4	4	8	8	2	0	0	1	1	27	14.8
F	19	Eddy Beers	STL	19	3	4	7	4	8	2	0	1	0	32	9.4
F	14	Doug Wickenheiser	STL	19	2	5	7	1	12	1	0	1	1	40	5.0
D	27	Ric Nattress	STL	18	1	4	5	4	24	0	0	0	0	30	3.3
F	16	Kevin Lavallee	STL	13	2	2	4	0	2	1	0	0	0	23	8.7
D	4	Charles Bourgeois	STL	19	2	2	4	3	116	0	0	0	0	23	8.7
F	12	Ron Flockhart	STL	8	1	3	4	-6	6	0	0	0	0	14	7.1
D	18	*Brian Benning	STL	9	1	3	4	1	13	1	0	0	0	10	10.0
F	11	Brian Sutter	STL	6	1	2	3	-4	22	0	0	0	0	9	11.1
F	7	*Cliff Ronning	STL	5	1	1	2	0	2	1	0	0	0	11	9.1
F	25	*Herb Raglan	STL	10	1	1	2	1	24	0	0	0	0	7	14.3
F	6	Dave Barr	STL	11	1	1	2	1	14	1	0	0	0	12	8.3
D	10	Bruce Bell	STL	14	0	2	2	-5	13	0	0	0	0	11	.0
D	35	Jim Pavese	STL	19	0	2	2	-5	51	0	0	0	0	17	.0
D	33	Kent Carlson	STL	5	0	0	0	0	11	0	0	0	0	0	.0
G	29	Greg Millen	STL	10	0	0	0	0	0	0	0	0	0	0	.0
G	30	Rick Wamsley	STL	10	0	0	0	0	0	0	0	0	0	0	.0

Club Records

Team

(Figures in brackets for season records are games played; records for fewest points, wins, ties, losses, goals, goals against are for 70 or more games)

Most Points	107	1980-81 (80)
Most Wins	45	1980-81 (80)
Most Ties	19	1970-71 (78)
Most Losses	50	1978-79 (80)
Most Goals	352	1980-81 (80)
Most Goals Against	349	1981-82 (80)
Fewest Points	48	1978-79 (80)
Fewest Wins	18	1978-79 (80)
Fewest Ties	7	1983-84 (80)
Fewest Losses	18	1980-81 (80)
Fewest Goals	177	1967-68 (74)
Fewest Goals Against	157	1968-69 (76)

Longest Winning Streak

Over-all	5	Feb. 12-19/69 Jan. 6-16/72
Home	7	Nov. 28- Dec. 29/81
Away	4	Dec. 16/73- Jan. 8/74

Longest Undefeated Streak

Over-all	12	Nov. 10- Dec. 8/68 (5 wins, 7 ties)
Home	11	Feb. 12- Mar. 19/69 (5 wins, 6 ties) Feb. 7- Mar. 29/75 (9 wins, 2 ties)
Away	6	Feb. 1-17/81 (3 wins, 3 ties)

Longest Losing Streak

Over-all	7	Nov. 12-26/67
Home	5	Nov. 19- Dec. 6/77
Away	10	Jan. 20/82- Mar. 8/82

Longest Winless Streak

Over-all	12	Jan. 17- Feb. 15/78 (10 losses, 2 ties)
Home	7	Dec. 28/82- Jan. 25/83 (6 losses, 1 tie)
Away	17	Jan. 23- Apr. 7/74 (14 losses, 3 ties)

Most Shutouts, Season	13	1968-69 (76)
Most Pen. Mins., Season	1,657	1980-81 (80)
Most Goals, Game	10	Feb. 2/82 (Wpg. 6 at St.L. 10) Dec. 1/84 (Det. 5 at St. L. 10)

Individual

Most Seasons	11	Bob Plager
Most Games	718	Bernie Federko
Most Goals, Career	292	Garry Unger
Most Assists, Career	555	Bernie Federko
Most Points, Career	845	Bernie Federko
Most Pen. Mins., Career	1,621	Brian Sutter
Most Shutouts, Career	16	Glenn Hall
Longest Consecutive Games Streak	662	Garry Unger (Feb. 7/71-Apr. 8/79)
Most Goals, Season	54	Wayne Babych (1980-81)
Most Assists, Season	73	Bernie Federko (1980-81)
Most Points, Season	107	Bernie Federko (1983-84, 1984-85) (41 goals, 66 assists)
Most Pen. Mins., Season	306	Bob Gassoff (1975-76)

Most Points, Defenseman Season	66	Rob Ramage (1985-86) (10 goals, 56 assists)
Most Points, Center, Season	107	Bernie Federko (1983-84) (41 goals, 66 assists)
Most Points, Right Wing, Season	96	Wayne Babych (1980-81) (54 goals, 42 assists)
Most Points, Left Wing, Season	85	Chuck Lefley (1975-76) (43 goals, 42 assists)
Most Points, Rookie, Season	73	Jorgen Pettersson (1980-81) (37 goals, 36 assists)
Most Shutouts, Season	8	Glenn Hall (1968-69)
Most Goals, Game	6	Red Berenson (Nov. 7/68)
Most Assists, Game	4	Several players
Most Points, Game	7	Red Berenson (Nov. 7/68) Garry Unger (Mar. 13/71)

Coaching History

Lynn Patrick and Scott Bowman, 1967-68; Scott Bowman, 1968-69 to 1969-70; Al Arbour and Scott Bowman, 1970-71; Sid Abel, Bill McCreary, Al Arbour, 1971-72; Al Arbour and Jean-Guy Talbot, 1972-73; Jean-Guy Talbot and Lou Angotti, 1973-74; Lou Angotti, Lynn Patrick and Garry Young, 1974-75; Garry Young, Lynn Patrick and Leo Boivin, 1975-76; Emile Francis, 1976-77; Leo Boivin and Barclay Plager, 1977-78; Barclay Plager, 1978-79; Barclay Plager and Red Berenson, 1979-80; Red Berenson, 1980-81; Red Berenson and Emile Francis, 1981-82; Barclay Plager and Emile Francis, 1982-83; Jacques Demers, 1983-84 to 1985-86; Jacques Martin, 1986-87.

Captains' History

Al Arbour, 1967-68 to 1969-70; Red Berenson, Barclay Plager, 1970-71; Barclay Plager, 1971-72 to 1975-76; no captain, 1976-77; Red Berenson, 1977-78; Barry Gibbs, 1978-79; Brian Sutter, 1979-80 to 1985-86.

All-time Record vs. Other Clubs

Regular Season

	GP	W	L	T	GF	GA	PTS	GP	W	L	T	GF	GA	PTS	GP	W	L	T	GF	GA	PTS
			At Home							On Road							Total				
Boston	41	15	17	9	128	149	39	40	7	27	6	95	181	20	81	22	44	15	223	330	59
Buffalo	33	19	9	5	126	85	43	32	6	22	4	93	137	16	65	25	31	9	219	222	59
**Calgary	30	12	14	4	104	91	28	29	13	13	3	88	95	29	59	25	27	7	192	186	57
Chicago	58	26	22	10	200	194	62	60	13	40	7	163	241	33	118	39	62	17	363	435	95
Detroit	52	34	11	7	200	129	75	53	26	20	7	168	180	59	105	60	31	14	368	309	134
Edmonton	12	5	5	2	52	58	12	11	3	6	2	49	56	8	23	8	11	4	101	114	20
Hartford	12	6	5	1	46	43	13	11	5	5	1	40	41	11	23	11	10	2	86	84	24
Los Angeles	45	30	11	4	166	109	64	64	19	28	7	131	154	41	91	47	33	11	297	263	105
Minnesota	63	32	20	11	214	176	75	61	19	28	14	181	217	52	124	51	48	25	395	393	127
Montreal	40	8	20	12	105	144	28	41	6	32	3	100	191	15	81	14	52	15	205	335	43
*New Jersey	27	21	3	3	130	75	45	28	13	8	7	85	86	33	55	34	11	10	215	161	78
NY Islanders	28	8	14	6	90	106	22	30	4	19	7	64	125	15	58	12	33	13	154	231	37
NY Rangers	43	18	18	7	133	140	43	43	3	36	4	93	188	10	86	21	54	11	226	328	53
Philadelphia	49	19	23	7	135	141	45	48	7	33	8	102	185	22	97	26	56	15	237	326	67
Pittsburgh	47	30	13	4	178	124	64	45	16	20	9	130	159	41	92	46	33	13	308	283	105
Quebec	11	7	3	1	50	38	15	12	2	8	2	32	52	6	23	9	11	3	82	90	21
Toronto	53	30	14	9	188	147	69	52	11	35	6	147	213	28	105	41	49	15	335	360	97
Vancouver	39	24	9	6	155	110	54	38	18	16	4	127	122	40	77	42	25	10	282	232	94
Washington	21	10	6	5	94	63	25	22	9	12	1	71	86	19	43	19	18	6	165	149	44
Winnipeg	13	6	4	3	47	48	15	14	3	6	5	47	51	11	27	9	10	8	109	99	26
Defunct Clubs	32	25	4	3	131	55	53	33	11	10	12	95	100	34	65	36	14	15	226	155	87
Totals	749	385	245	119	2687	2225	889	749	212	418	119	2101	2860	543	1498	597	663	238	4788	5085	1432

* Totals include those of Kansas City (1974-75, 1975-76) and Colorado (1976-77 through 1981-82)
** Totals include those of Atlanta (1972-73 through 1979-80)

Playoffs

	Series	W	L	GP	W	L	T	GF	GA	Last Mtg.	Round	Result
Boston	2	0	2	8	0	8	0	15	48	1972	SF	L 0-4
Buffalo	1	0	1	3	1	2	0	8	7	1976	P	L 1-2
Calgary	1	0	1	7	3	4	0	22	28	1986	CF	L 3-4
Chicago	4	0	4	18	4	14	0	42	73	1983	DSF	L 1-3
Detroit	1	1	0	4	4	0	0	13	12	1984	DSF	W 3-1
Los Angeles	1	1	0	4	4	0	0	16	5	1969	SF	W 4-0
Minnesota	7	4	3	41	20	21	0	112	121	1986	DSF	W 3-2
Montreal	3	0	3	12	0	12	0	14	42	1977	QF	L 0-4
NY Rangers	1	0	1	4	1	3	0	29	1981		QF	L 2-4
Philadelphia	2	2	0	11	8	3	0	34	45	1969	QF	W 4-0
Pittsburgh	3	2	1	13	7	6	0	45	40	1981	P	W 3-2
Toronto	1	1	0	7	4	3	0	24	22	1986	DF	W 4-3
Winnipeg	1	1	0	4	3	1	0	20	13	1982	DSF	W 3-1
Totals	28	12	16	138	59	79	0	387	460			

Abbreviations: Round: F – Final; **CF** – conference final; **DF** – division final; **DSF** – division semi-final; **SF** – semi-final; **QF** – quarter-final; **P** – preliminary round. **GA** – goals against; **GF** – goals for.

Playoff Results 1986-82

Year	Round	Opponent	Result	GF	GA
1986	CF	Calgary	L 3-4	22	28
	DF	Toronto	W 4-3	24	22
	DSF	Minnesota	W 3-2	18	20
1985	DSF	Minnesota	L 0-3	5	9
1984	DF	Minnesota	L 3-4	17	19
	DSF	Detroit	W 3-1	13	12
1983	DSF	Chicago	L 1-3	10	16
1982	DF	Chicago	L 2-4	19	23
	DSF	Winnipeg	W 3-1	20	13

Retired Numbers

3	Bob Gassoff	1973-1977
8	Barclay Plager	1967-1977

Entry Draft Selections 1986-72

1986
Pick
10	Jocelyn Lemieux
31	Mike Posma
52	Tony Hejna
73	Glen Featherstone
87	Michael Wolak
115	Mike O'Toole
136	Andy May
157	Randy Skarda
178	Martyn Ball
199	Rod Thacker
220	Terry MacLean
234	Bill Butler
241	David Obrien

1985
Pick
37	Herb Raglan
44	Nelson Emerson
54	Ned Osmond
100	Dan Brooks
121	Rick Burchill
138	Pat Jablonski
159	Scott Brickey
180	Jeff Urban
201	Vince Guidotti
222	Ron Saatzer
243	Dave Jecha

1984
Pick
26	Brian Benning
32	Tony Hrkac
50	Toby Ducolon
53	Robert Dirk
56	Alan Perry
71	Graham Herring
92	Scott Paluch
113	Steve Tuttle
134	Cliff Ronning
148	Don Porter
155	Jim Vesey
176	Daniel Jomphe
196	Tom Tilley
217	Mark Cupolo
237	Mark Lanigan

1983
DID NOT DRAFT

1982
Pick
50	Mike Posavad
92	Scott Machej
113	Perry Ganchar
134	Doug Gilmour
155	Chris Delaney
176	Matt Christensen
197	John Shumski
218	Brian Ahern
239	Peter Smith

1981
Pick
20	Marty Ruff
36	Hakin Nordin
62	Gordon Donnelly
104	Mike Hickey
125	Peter Aslin
146	Erik Holmberg
167	Alain Vigneault
188	Dan Wood
209	Richard Zemlak

1980
Pick
12	Rik Wilson
54	Jim Pavese
75	Bob Brooke
96	Alain Lemieux
117	Perry Anderson
138	Roger Hagglund
159	Par Rabbitt
180	Peter Lindberg
201	John Smyth

1979
Pick
2	Perry Turnbull
65	Bob Crawford
86	Mark Reeds
107	Gilles Leduc

1978
Pick
3	Wayne Babych
39	Steve Harrison
72	Kevin Willison
89	Jim Nill
106	Steve Stockman
109	Paul MacLean
123	Denis Houle
140	Tony Meagher
143	Rick Simpson
157	Jim Lockhurst
160	Bob Froese
170	Dan Lerg
173	Risto Siltanen
175	Dan Hermansson
181	Jean-Francois Boutin
185	John Sullivan
188	Serge Menard
191	Don Boyd
197	Paul Stasiuk
200	Gerhard Truntscho
203	Victor Shkurdjuk
205	Carl Bloomberg
207	Terry Kitching
209	Brian O'Connor
210	Brian Crombeen
211	Mike Pidgeon
214	John Cochrane
216	Joe Casey
218	Jim Farrell
221	Blair Wheeler

1977
Pick
9	Scott Campbell
27	Neil Labatte
45	Tom Roulston
63	Tony Currie
81	Bruce Hamilton
99	Gary McMonagle
117	Matti Forss
132	Raimo Hirvonen
147	Bjorn Olsson

1976
Pick
7	Bernie Federko
20	Brian Sutter
25	John Smrke
43	Jim Kirkpatrick
56	Mike Liut
61	Paul Skidmore
97	Nels Goddard
113	Mike Eaves
121	Jacques Soquel
124	Dave Dornself
126	Brad Wilson
128	Dan Hoene
130	Goran Lindblom
132	Jim Bales
134	Anders Hakansson
135	Johani Wallenius

1975
Pick
27	Ed Staniowski
36	Jamie Masters
63	Rick Bourbonnais
81	Jim Gustafson
99	Jack Brownschidle
117	Doug Lindskog
135	Vic Lamby
151	David McNab

1974
Pick
26	Bob Hess
43	Gordon Buynak
79	Mike Zuke
87	Don Wheldon
97	Mike Thompson
115	Terry Casey
132	Ron Tordoff
149	Paul Touzin
165	Jack Ahearn
180	Mitch Babin
194	Doug Allan

1973
Pick
5	John Davidson
24	George Pesut
48	Bob Gassoff
72	Bill Laing
88	Randy Smith
104	John Wensink
120	John Tetreault

1972
Pick
9	Wayne Merrick
41	Jean Hamel
47	Murray Meyers
73	Dave Johnson
89	Tom Simpson
105	Brian Coughlin
121	Gary Winchester

Club Directory

St. Louis Arena
5700 Oakland Avenue
St. Louis, MO 63110
Phone 314/781-5300
Night line 314/781-5352
TWX 910-761-2141
ENVOY ID TM.STL
Capacity: 17,666

Board of Directors
Harry Ornest, Ruth Ornest, Maury Ornest, Michael Ornest, Jack Quinn, Cindy Ornest, Laura Ornest

Chairman of the Board and President	Harry Ornest
Vice-Chairman and Treasurer	Ruth L. Ornest
Executive Vice-President	Jack Quinn
Vice-President and Secretary	Michael Ornest
Vice-President, Administration	Cindy Ornest
Vice-President	Maury Ornest
Vice-President & General Manager	Ronald Caron
Head Coach	Jacques Martin
Assistant Coach	Barclay Plager
Special Assignment Scout/ Assistant to Ron Caron	Bob Plager
Director of Scouting	Ted Hampson
Assistant Director of Scouting	Jack Evans
Director of Public Relations	Susie Mathieu
Assistant Director of Public Relations	Charlie Hodges, Mark Niebling
Sales Staff	John Bauer, Lisa Beene, Tracy Lovasz, Dave Stalcup
Canadian Counsel	Robert R. Hall, Q.C., Toronto
Accountants	Margaret Steinmeyer, Donna Steinmeyer
Executive Secretary	Maggie Mersinger
Receptionist	Patty Manhart
M.D. Emeritus	Dr. J. G. Probstein
Orthopedic Surgeon	Dr. Jerome Gilden
Internist	Dr. Aaron Birenbaum
Team Dentist	Dr. Leslie Rich
Opthamologist	Dr. Michael Isserman
Head Trainer	Norm Mackie
Assistant Trainer	Dave Smith
Equipment Assistant	Frank Burns
Largest Hockey Attendance	20,009 (March 31/73)
Location of Press Box	East side of building, upper level
Club Colors	Blue, gold, red and white
Training Camp	Peoria Civic Center, Peoria, Illinois
Radio Station	KXOK Radio
Broadcaster	Dan Kelly
Television Station	KPLR-TV (Channel 11)
Broadcasters	Dan Kelly, Ken Wilson

Gino Cavallini

Toronto Maple Leafs

1985-86 Results: 25w-48L-7T 57 PTS. Fourth, Norris Division

Goaltender Ken Wregget appeared in 31 games in the regular season and all ten of the Leafs games in the playoffs.

Schedule

Home			Away		
Oct.	Thur.	9 Montreal	Oct.	Fri.	17 New Jersey
	Sat.	11 Buffalo		Sat.	25 Quebec
	Tue.	14 St. Louis		Sun.	26 NY Rangers
	Sat.	18 Chicago	Nov.	Thur.	6 Minnesota
	Wed.	22 Quebec		Wed.	12 St. Louis
	Tue.	28 Chicago		Sun.	16 Chicago
	Thur.	30 Hartford		Thur.	20 NY Islanders
Nov.	Sat.	1 Detroit		Sat.	22 Philadelphia
	Wed.	5 St. Louis		Wed.	26 Detroit
	Sat.	8 Vancouver		Fri.	28 Minnesota
	Sat.	15 Detroit	Dec.	Thur.	4 Los Angeles
	Wed.	19 Philadelphia		Sun.	7 St. Louis
	Mon.	24 Boston		Fri.	12 Pittsburgh
	Sat.	29 Minnesota		Wed.	17 New Jersey
Dec.	Wed.	10 Washington		Tue.	23 Minnesota
	Sat.	13 Pittsburgh		Fri.	26 Detroit
	Thur.	18 Minnesota	Jan.	Sun.	4 Hartford
	Sat.	20 Buffalo		Tue.	6 Detroit
	Sat.	27 Detroit		Wed.	7 Chicago
	Wed.	31 Winnipeg		Sat.	10 NY Islanders
Jan.	Sat.	3 New Jersey		Mon.	12 Montreal
	Wed.	14 Minnesota		Thur.	15 Detroit
	Sat.	17 Edmonton		Fri.	23 Winnipeg
	Wed.	21 St. Louis		Wed.	28 Chicago
	Sat.	24 Hartford		Thur.	29 St. Louis
	Mon.	26 Calgary	Feb.	Sat.	7 Boston*
	Sat.	31 Detroit		Sun.	8 NY Rangers
Feb.	Mon.	2 Philadelphia		Mon.	16 Los Angeles*
	Wed.	4 Los Angeles		Wed.	18 Edmonton
	Sat.	14 Boston		Fri.	20 Calgary
	Wed.	25 NY Rangers		Sun.	22 Vancouver
	Sat.	28 Vancouver	Mar.	Mon.	9 St. Louis
Mar.	Tue.	3 St. Louis		Wed.	11 Minnesota
	Thur.	5 Pittsburgh		Fri.	13 Washington
	Sat.	7 NY Islanders		Fri.	20 Quebec
	Sat.	14 Calgary		Sat.	21 Montreal
	Wed.	18 Chicago		Tue.	24 Buffalo
	Wed.	25 Minnesota		Sun.	29 Winnipeg
	Sat.	28 Edmonton		Tue.	31 Washington
April	Sat.	4 Chicago	April	Sun.	5 Chicago

* Denotes afternoon game.

Home Starting Times:
Weeknights . . . . 7:35 p.m.
Saturdays . . . . 8:05 p.m.
Sundays . . . . 7:05 p.m.

Franchise date: November 22, 1917

 **70th NHL Season**

Year-by-Year Record

Season	GP	Home W	L	T	Road W	L	T	Overall W	L	T	GF	GA	Pts.	Finished	Playoff Result
1985-86	80	16	21	3	9	27	4	25	48	7	311	386	57	4th, Norris Div.	Lost Div. Final
1984-85	80	10	28	2	10	24	6	20	52	8	253	358	48	5th, Norris Div.	Out of Playoffs
1983-84	80	17	16	7	9	29	2	26	45	9	303	287	61	5th, Norris Div.	Out of Playoffs
1982-83	80	20	15	5	8	25	7	28	40	12	293	330	68	3rd, Norris Div.	Lost Div. Semi-Final
1981-82	80	12	20	8	8	24	8	20	44	16	298	380	56	5th, Norris Div.	Out of Playoffs
1980-81	80	14	21	5	14	16	10	28	37	15	322	367	71	5th, Adams Div.	Lost Prelim. Round
1979-80	80	17	19	4	18	21	1	35	40	5	304	327	75	4th, Adams Div.	Lost Prelim. Round
1978-79	80	20	12	8	14	21	5	34	33	13	267	252	81	3rd, Adams Div.	Lost Quarter-Final
1977-78	80	21	13	6	20	16	4	41	29	10	271	237	92	3rd, Adams Div.	Lost Semi-Final
1976-77	80	18	13	9	15	19	6	33	32	15	301	285	81	3rd, Adams Div.	Lost Quarter-Final
1975-76	80	23	12	5	11	19	10	34	31	15	294	276	83	3rd, Adams Div.	Lost Quarter-Final
1974-75	80	19	12	9	12	21	7	31	33	16	280	309	78	3rd, Adams Div.	Lost Quarter-Final
1973-74	78	21	11	7	14	16	9	35	27	16	274	230	86	4th, East Div.	Lost Quarter-Final
1972-73	78	20	12	7	7	29	3	27	41	10	247	279	64	6th, East Div.	Out of Playoffs
1971-72	78	21	11	7	12	20	7	33	31	14	209	208	80	4th, East Div.	Lost Quarter-Final
1970-71	78	24	9	6	13	24	2	37	33	8	248	211	82	4th, East Div.	Lost Quarter-Final
1969-70	76	18	13	7	11	21	6	29	34	13	222	242	71	6th, East Div.	Out of Playoffs
1968-69	76	20	8	10	15	18	5	35	26	15	234	217	85	4th, East Div.	Lost Quarter-Final
1967-68	74	24	9	4	9	22	6	33	31	10	209	176	76	5th, East Div.	Out of Playoffs
1966-67	**70**	21	8	6	11	19	5	**32**	**27**	**11**	**204**	**211**	**75**	**3rd,**	**Won Stanley Cup**
1965-66	70	22	9	4	12	16	7	34	25	11	208	187	79	3rd,	Lost Semi-Final
1964-65	70	17	15	3	13	11	11	30	26	14	204	173	74	4th,	Lost Semi-Final
1963-64	**70**	22	7	6	11	18	6	**33**	**25**	**12**	**192**	**172**	**78**	**3rd,**	**Won Stanley Cup**
1962-63	**70**	21	8	6	14	15	6	**35**	**23**	**12**	**221**	**180**	**82**	**1st,**	**Won Stanley Cup**
1961-62	**70**	25	5	5	12	17	6	**37**	**22**	**11**	**232**	**180**	**85**	**2nd,**	**Won Stanley Cup**
1960-61	70	21	6	8	18	13	4	39	19	12	234	176	90	2nd,	Lost Semi-Final
1959-60	70	20	9	6	15	17	3	35	26	9	199	195	79	2nd,	Lost Final
1958-59	70	17	13	5	10	19	6	27	32	11	189	201	65	4th,	Lost Final
1957-58	70	12	16	7	9	22	4	21	38	11	192	226	53	6th,	Out of Playoffs
1956-57	70	12	16	7	9	18	8	21	34	15	174	192	57	5th,	Out of Playoffs
1955-56	70	19	10	6	5	23	7	24	33	13	153	181	61	4th,	Lost Semi-Final
1954-55	70	14	10	11	10	14	11	24	24	22	147	135	70	3rd,	Lost Semi-Final
1953-54	70	22	6	7	10	18	7	32	24	14	152	131	78	3rd,	Lost Semi-Final
1952-53	70	17	12	6	10	18	7	27	30	13	156	167	67	5th,	Out of Playoffs
1951-52	70	17	10	8	12	15	8	29	25	16	168	157	74	3rd,	Lost Semi-Final
1950-51	**70**	22	8	5	19	8	8	**41**	**16**	**13**	**212**	**138**	**95**	**2nd,**	**Won Stanley Cup**
1949-50	70	19	8	8	13	18	4	31	27	12	176	173	74	3rd,	Lost Semi-Final
1948-49	**60**	12	13	5	10	17	3	**22**	**25**	**13**	**147**	**161**	**57**	**4th,**	**Won Stanley Cup**
1947-48	**60**	22	3	5	10	12	8	**32**	**15**	**13**	**182**	**143**	**77**	**1st,**	**Won Stanley Cup**
1946-47	**60**	20	8	2	11	11	8	**31**	**19**	**10**	**209**	**172**	**72**	**2nd,**	**Won Stanley Cup**
1945-46	50	10	13	2	9	11	5	19	24	7	174	185	45	5th,	Out of Playoffs
1944-45	**50**	13	9	3	11	13	1	**24**	**22**	**4**	**183**	**161**	**52**	**3rd,**	**Won Stanley Cup**
1943-44	50	13	11	1	10	12	3	23	23	4	214	174	50	3rd,	Lost Semi-Final
1942-43	50	17	6	2	5	13	7	22	19	9	198	159	53	3rd,	Lost Semi-Final
1941-42	**48**	16	8	0	9	12	3	**27**	**18**	**3**	**158**	**136**	**57**	**2nd,**	**Won Stanley Cup**
1940-41	48	16	5	3	12	9	3	28	14	6	145	99	62	2nd,	Lost Semi-Final
1939-40	48	16	5	3	9	14	4	25	17	6	134	110	56	3rd,	Lost Final
1938-39	48	13	6	5	6	12	6	19	20	9	114	107	47	3rd,	Lost Final
1937-38	48	13	6	5	11	9	4	24	15	9	151	127	57	1st, Cdn. Div.	Lost Final
1936-37	48	14	9	1	8	12	4	22	21	5	119	115	49	3rd, Cdn. Div.	Lost Quarter-Final
1935-36	48	15	4	5	8	15	1	23	19	6	126	106	52	2nd, Cdn. Div.	Lost Final
1934-35	48	16	6	2	14	8	2	30	14	4	157	111	64	1st, Cdn. Div.	Lost Final
1933-34	48	19	2	3	7	11	6	26	13	9	174	119	61	1st, Cdn. Div.	Lost Semi-Final
1932-33	48	16	4	4	8	14	2	24	18	6	119	111	54	1st, Cdn. Div.	Lost Final
1931-32	**48**	17	4	3	6	14	4	**23**	**18**	**7**	**155**	**127**	**53**	**2nd, Cdn. Div.**	**Won Stanley Cup**
1930-31	44	15	4	3	7	9	6	22	13	9	118	99	53	2nd, Cdn. Div.	Lost Quarter-Final
1929-30	44	15	5	2	2	13	6	17	21	6	116	124	40	4th, Cdn. Div.	Out of Playoffs
1928-29	44	15	5	2	6	13	3	21	18	5	85	69	47	3rd, Cdn. Div.	Lost Semi-Final
1927-28	44	13	8	1	5	14	3	18	18	8	89	88	44	4th, Cdn. Div.	Out of Playoffs
1926-27*	44	10	10	2	5	14	3	15	24	5	79	94	35	5th, Cdn. Div.	Out of Playoffs
1925-26	36	11	5	2	1	16	1	12	21	3	92	114	27	6th,	Out of Playoffs
1924-25	30	10	5	0	9	6	0	19	11	0	90	84	38	2nd,	Lost NHL S-Final
1923-24	24	7	5	0	3	9	0	10	14	0	59	85	20	3rd,	Out of Playoffs
1922-23	24	10	1	1	3	9	0	13	10	1	82	88	27	3rd,	Out of Playoffs
1921-22	**24**	8	4	0	5	9	0	**13**	**10**	**1**	**98**	**97**	**27**	**2nd,**	**Won Stanley Cup**
1920-21	24	8	4	0	7	9	0	15	9	0	105	100	30	1st,	Lost NHL Playoffs
1919-20**	24	8	4	0	4	8	0	12	12	0	119	106	24	3rd,	Out of Cup Playoffs
1918-19	18	5	4	0	0	9	0	5	13	0	64	92	10	3rd,	Out of Playoffs
1917-18*	**22**	10	1	0	3	8	0	**13**	**9**	**0**	**108**	**109**	**26**	**2nd and 1st**	**Won Stanley Cup**

* Name changed from St. Patricks to Maple Leafs.
** Name changed from Arenas to St. Patricks.
*** Season played in two halves with no combined standing at end.

1986-87 Player Personnel

FORWARDS	Ht.	Wt.	Place of Birth	Date	1985-86 Club
ALLISON, Mike	6-0	200	Ft. Francis, Ont.	3/28/61	NY Rangers
ARMSTRONG, Tim	5-11	168	Toronto, Ont.	5/12/67	Toronto (OHL)
BEAN, Tim	6-0	194	Sault Ste. Marie, Ont.	3/9/67	North Bay
BELLEFEUILLE, Brian	6-2	185	Natick, Mass.	3/21/67	Canterbury
BRENNAN, Stephen	6-1	190	Winchester, Mass.	3/22/67	New Prep
CLARK, Wendel	5-11	197	Kelvington, Sask.	10/25/66	Toronto
COSTELLO, Rich	6-0	175	Framingham, Mass.	2/27/63	St. Catharines-Toronto
COURTNALL, Russ	5-11	179	Duncan, B.C.	6/2/65	Toronto
DAMPHOUSSE, Vincent	6-1	195	Montreal, Que.	12/17/67	Laval
DAOUST, Dan	5-11	160	Montreal, Que.	2/29/60	Toronto
DAVIDSON, Sean	5-11	177	Toronto, Ont.	4/13/68	Toronto
DONAHUE, Andy	6-1	180	Boston, Mass.	2/17/67	Dartmouth U.
FERGUS, Tom	6-1	200	Chicago, Ill.	6/16/62	Toronto
FRYCER, Miroslav	6-0	185	Opava, Czech.	9/27/59	Toronto
GIGUERE, Stephane	6-0	182	Montreal, Que.	2/21/68	St. Jean
HIE, Danny	6-0	178	Mississauga, Ont.	6/21/68	Ottawa
HODGSON, Dan	5-10	175	Ft. Vermillion, Alta.	8/29/65	Toronto-St. Catharines
HOLICK, Mark	6-2	185	Saskatoon, Sask.	8/6/68	Saskatoon
HULST, Kent	6-0	180	St. Thomas, Ont.	4/8/68	Windsor
IHNACAK, Miroslav	5-11	175	Poprad, Czech.	2/19/62	Toronto-St. Catharines
IHNACAK, Peter	6-1	195	Poprad, Czech.	5/3/57	Toronto
JACKSON, Jeff	6-1	193	Chatham, Ont.	4/24/65	Toronto-St. Catharines
JAMES, Val	6-2	205	Ocala, Fla.	2/14/57	St. Catharines
JARVIS, Wes	5-11	156	Toronto, Ont.	5/30/58	St. Catharines-Toronto
KORN, Jim	6-4	220	Hopkins, Minn.	7/28/57	Toronto
LAXDAL, Derek	6-2	195	St. Boniface, Man.	2/21/66	Brandon-New Westminster-St. Catharines-Toronto
LEEMAN, Gary	5-11	175	Toronto, Ont.	2/19/64	Toronto-St. Catharines
MacINNIS, Joseph	6-0	165	Cambridge, Mass.	5/25/66	Northeastern U.
MAGUIRE, Kevin	6-2	100	Toronto, Ont.	1/5/63	St. Catharines
McRAE, Chris	6-0	178	Beaverton, Ont.	8/25/65	St. Catharines
REYNOLDS, Bobby	5-11	175	Flint, Mich.	7/14/67	Michigan State
RUZICKA, Vladimir	6-1	175	Czechoslovakia	6/6/63	Czechoslovakia
SMITH, Brad	5-11	180	Quebec, Que.	7/31/54	Toronto-St. Catharines
TERRION, Greg	5-11	175	Marmora, Ont.	5/2/60	Toronto
THOMAS, Steve	5-10	185	Stockport, England	7/15/63	Toronto-St. Catharines
THOMLINSON, Dave	6-1	184	Edmonton, Alta.	10/22/66	Brandon
VAIVE, Rick	6-1	190	Ottawa, Ont.	5/14/59	Toronto
VERSTRAETE, Leigh	5-11	183	Pincher Creek, Alta.	1/6/62	St. Catharines
VEY, Greg	6-0	190	Toronto, Ont.	6/20/67	Peterborough
WASLEN, Gerrard	6-0	187	Humboldt, Sask.	10/5/62	Colgate
WHITTEMORE, Todd	6-1	175	Taunton, Mass.	6/20/67	Kent School
WURST, Mike	6-4	210	Edina, Minn.	10/5/64	Ohio State
DEFENSEMEN					
ALBRECHT, Cliff	6-0	200	Bramalea, Ont.	5/24/63	Princeton-St. Catharines
BENNING, Jim	6-0	183	Edmonton, Alta.	4/29/63	Toronto
BOLAND, Sean	6-3	180	Toronto, Ont.	2/18/68	Toronto (OHL)
BUCKLEY, David	6-4	195	Newton, Mass.	1/27/66	Boston College
CAPUANO, Jack	6-2	210	Cranston, R. I.	7/7/66	Maine
CLEMENTS, Scott	6-1	205	Sudbury, Ont.		St. Catharines
GILL, Todd	6-0	185	Brockville, Ont.	11/9/65	Toronto-St. Catharines
IAFRATE, Al	6-2	215	Dearborn, Mich.	3/21/66	Toronto
KITCHEN, Bill	6-2	198	Schomberg, Ont.	10/2/60	St. Catharines
KOTSOPOULOS, Chris	6-3	210	Scarborough, Ont.	11/27/58	Toronto
LATAL, Jiri				2/2/67	Sparta, Czech.
LOVEN, Tim	6-0	189	Red River, N.D.	10/14/63	U. of North Dakota
MAXWELL, Brad	6-2	195	Brandon, Man.	7/8/57	Toronto
McGILL, Bob	6-1	190	Edmonton, Alta.	4/27/62	Toronto
NYLUND, Gary	6-3	210	North Delta, B.C.	10/28/63	Toronto
PLANTE, Cam	6-0	195	Brandon, Man.	3/12/64	St. Catharines
ROOT, Bill	6-1	204	Toronto, Ont.	9/6/59	Toronto-St. Catharines
SALMING, Borje	6-1	195	Kiruna, Sweden	4/17/51	Toronto
SEROWIK, Jeff	6-0	190	Manchester, N.H.	10/1/67	Lawrence Academy
SHANNON, Darryl	6-2	190	Barrie, Ont.	6/21/68	Windsor
SLANINA, Peter	6-2	185	Czechoslovakia		
SPANGLER, Ken	5-11	196	Edmonton, Alta.	5/2/67	Calgary (WHL)-St. Catharines
TAYLOR, Scott	6-0	182	Toronto, Ont.	3/23/68	Kitchener
WESLEY, Blake	6-1	200	Red Deer, Alta.	7/10/59	Toronto-St. Catharines
GOALTENDERS					
BERNHARDT, Tim	5-9	164	Sarnia, Ont.	1/17/58	Toronto-St. Catharines
BESTER, Allan	5-7	155	Hamilton, Ont.	3/26/64	Toronto-St. Catharines
EDWARDS, Don	5-8	163	Hamilton, Ont.	9/28/55	Toronto
REESE, Jeff	5-9	150	Brantford, Ont.	3/24/66	London
WREGGET, Ken	6-1	195	Brandon, Man.	3/25/64	Toronto-St. Catharines

1985-86 Scoring

Regular Season

*–rookie

Pos	#	Player	Team	GP	G	A	Pts	+/–	PIM	PP	SH	GW	OT	S	%
F	14	Miroslav Frycer	TOR	73	32	43	75	24–	74	7	0	3	1	201	15.9
F	19	Tom Fergus	TOR	78	31	42	73	24–	64	3	2	3	1	168	18.5
F	22	Rick Vaive	TOR	61	33	31	64	19–	85	12	0	1	1	225	14.7
F	9	Russ Courtnall	TOR	73	22	38	60	0	52	3	1	4	0	203	10.8
F	32	*Steve Thomas	TOR	65	20	37	57	15–	36	5	0	5	0	197	10.2
F	10	Marian Stastny	TOR	70	23	30	53	6–	21	7	0	0	0	132	17.4
F	17	*Wendel Clark	TOR	66	34	11	45	27–	227	4	0	3	0	164	20.7
F	18	Peter Ihnacak	TOR	63	18	27	45	9–	16	5	0	1	1	96	18.8
F	8	Walt Poddubny	TOR	33	12	22	34	6	25	5	0	1	0	76	15.8
D	33	Al Iafrate	TOR	65	8	25	33	10–	40	2	0	2	0	94	8.5
F	7	Greg Terrion	TOR	76	10	22	32	5–	31	0	2	1	0	105	9.5
F	11	Gary Leeman	TOR	53	9	23	32	1–	20	1	1	0	0	123	7.3
D	4	Brad Maxwell	TOR	52	8	18	26	27–	108	4	0	0	0	93	8.6
F	16	*Dan Hodgson	TOR	40	13	12	25	5–	12	2	0	0	0	54	24.1
D	3	Jim Benning	TOR	52	4	21	25	4–	71	2	0	0	0	76	5.3
D	21	Borje Salming	TOR	41	7	15	22	7–	48	3	1	1	0	71	9.9
F	29	Brad Smith	TOR	42	5	17	22	8–	84	0	0	0	0	46	10.9
F	24	Dan Daoust	TOR	80	7	13	20	21–	88	1	0	0	0	92	7.6
D	2	Gary Nylund	TOR	79	2	16	18	32–	180	0	0	0	0	84	2.4
D	26	Chris Kotsopoulos	TOR	61	6	11	17	5–	83	0	0	0	0	69	8.7
F	12	Gary McAdam	TOR	15	1	6	7	11–	0	0	0	0	0	9	11.1
F	27	*Miroslav Ihnacak	TOR	21	2	4	6	6–	27	1	0	0	0	25	8.0
D	15	Bob McGill	TOR	61	1	4	5	17–	141	0	0	0	0	28	3.6
F	25	*Jeff Jackson	TOR	5	1	2	3	3	2	0	0	0	0	2	50.0
D	23	*Todd Gill	TOR	15	1	2	3	0	28	0	0	0	0	9	11.1
F	34	Wes Jarvis	TOR	2	1	0	1	1–	2	0	0	0	0	2	50.0
F	8	*Rich Costello	TOR	2	0	1	1	0	0	0	0	0	0	2	.0
D	34	*Craig Muni	TOR	6	0	1	1	3–	4	0	0	0	0	2	.0
G	1	Tim Bernhardt	TOR	23	0	1	1	0	0	0	0	0	0	0	.0
D	25	Bill Root	TOR	27	0	1	1	8–	29	0	0	0	0	34	.0
D	28	Blake Wesley	TOR	27	0	1	1	4–	21	0	0	0	0	11	.0
G	31	Allan Bester	TOR	1	0	0	0	0	0	0	0	0	0	0	.0
F	35	Rod Schutt	TOR	6	0	0	0	2–	0	0	0	0	0	2	.0
G	31	Ken Wregget	TOR	30	0	0	0	0	16	0	0	0	0	0	.0
G	30	Don Edwards	TOR	38	0	0	0	0	4	0	0	0	0	0	.0

Playoffs

* rookie

Pos	#	Player	Team	GP	G	A	Pts	+/–	PIM	PP	SH	GW	OT	S	%
F	32	*Steve Thomas	TOR	10	6	8	14	2	9	3	0	0	0	36	16.7
F	19	Tom Fergus	TOR	10	5	7	12	3	6	3	0	1	0	25	20.0
F	11	Gary Leeman	TOR	10	2	10	12	2	2	0	0	0	0	25	8.0
F	9	Russ Courtnall	TOR	10	3	6	9	2	8	1	0	0	0	32	9.4
F	22	Rick Vaive	TOR	9	6	2	8	2–	9	3	0	0	0	31	19.4
D	21	Borje Salming	TOR	10	1	6	7	13	14	0	0	0	0	23	4.3
F	17	*Wendel Clark	TOR	10	5	1	6	1	47	1	0	1	0	25	20.0
F	8	Walt Poddubny	TOR	9	4	1	5	0	4	0	0	3	0	22	18.2
F	18	Peter Ihnacak	TOR	10	2	3	5	1–	12	0	0	1	0	20	10.0
F	24	Dan Daoust	TOR	10	2	2	4	2	19	0	0	0	0	12	16.7
F	14	Miroslav Frycer	TOR	10	1	3	4	3–	10	0	0	0	0	20	5.0
F	29	Brad Smith	TOR	6	2	1	3	2	20	1	0	0	0	11	18.2
D	33	Al Iafrate	TOR	10	0	3	3	12	4	0	0	0	0	11	.0
F	7	Greg Terrion	TOR	10	0	3	3	1	17	0	0	0	0	9	.0
D	25	Bill Root	TOR	7	0	2	2	1–	13	0	0	0	0	6	.0
D	2	Gary Nylund	TOR	10	0	2	2	5–	25	0	0	0	0	8	.0
D	26	Chris Kotsopoulos	TOR	10	1	0	1	4–	14	0	0	0	0	7	14.3
D	4	Brad Maxwell	TOR	3	0	1	1	3–	12	0	0	0	0	2	.0
D	23	*Todd Gill	TOR	1	0	0	0	0	0	0	0	0	0	1	.0
F	10	Marian Stastny	TOR	3	0	0	0	1–	0	0	0	0	0	1	.0
D	15	Bob McGill	TOR	9	0	0	0	3–	35	0	0	0	0	6	.0
G	31	Ken Wregget	TOR	10	0	0	0	0	4	0	0	0	0	0	.0

Coach and General Manager

BROPHY, JOHN

Coach, Toronto Maple Leafs. Born in Antigonish. N.S., January 20, 1933.

John Brophy was named coach of the Maple Leafs after just two years in the Toronto organization. Brophy spent 1984-85 as an assistant coach with the Leafs before moving on in 1985-86 as coach of the club's AHL affiliate St. Catharines Saints. After a 21-year minor league playing career, Brophy began coaching in the mid-70's as an assistant coach with Hampton in the Southern League and then with the Cincinnati Stingers and Birmingham Bulls in the World Hockey Association.

In 1978-79, he took control of Birmingham and won Coach of the Year honors. Although the city's WHA team folded, Brophy stayed in Birmingham with the Calgary Flames' CHL affiliate until moving to his native Nova Scotia, where he coached the Montreal Canadiens' AHL affiliate from 1981-82 to 1983-84.

McNAMARA, GERALD L. (GERRY)

General Manager, Toronto Maple Leafs. Born in Sturgeon Falls, Ont., September 22, 1934.

Gerry McNamara was named general manager of the Maple Leafs in June, 1982 after serving as interim general manager since November, 1981. He originally joined the Maple Leafs in 1972 as a scout and would later become head scout of the organization. McNamara also spent the 1977-78 season coaching the Leafs minor league affiliate in Dallas and guided the Black Hawks to a third place finish in the Central Hockey League and were runners-up to Fort Worth in the Adams Cup Final. McNamara played professionally for eight seasons which included a brief stint with the Maple Leafs during the 1960-61 season and again in 1969-70.

Club Records

Team

(Figures in brackets for season records are games played; records for fewest points, wins, ties, losses, goals, goals against are for 70 or more games)

Most Points	95	1950-51 (70)
Most Wins	41	1950-51 (70)
		1977-78 (80)
Most Ties	22	1954-55 (70)
Most Losses	52	1984-85 (80)
Most Goals	322	1980-81 (80)
Most Goals Against	387	1983-84 (80)
Fewest Points	48	1984-85 (80)
Fewest Wins	20	1981-82, 1984-85 (80)
Fewest Ties	5	1979-80 (80)
Fewest Losses	16	1950-51 (70)
Fewest Goals	146	1954-55 (70)
Fewest Goals Against	*131	1953-54 (70)

Longest Winning Streak

Over-all .... 9 — Jan. 30-Feb. 28/25

Home .... 9 — Nov. 11-Dec. 26/53

Away .... 7 — Nov. 14-Dec. 15/40
Dec. 4/60-Jan. 5/61

Longest Undefeated Streak

Over-all .... 11 — Oct. 15-Nov. 8/50 (8 wins, 3 ties)

Home .... 18 — Nov. 28/33-Mar. 10/34 (15 wins, 3 ties)
Oct. 31/53-Jan. 23/54 (16 wins, 2 ties)

Away .... 9 — Nov. 30/47-Jan. 11/48 (4 wins, 5 ties)

Longest Losing Streak

Over-all .... 10 — Jan. 15-Feb. 8/67

Home .... 7 — Nov. 10-Dec. 5/84
Jan. 26-Feb. 25/85

Away .... 10 — Dec. 23/83-Feb. 1/84

Longest Winless Streak

Over-all .... 11 — Jan. 15-Feb. 11/67 (10 losses, 1 tie)

Home .... 10 — Oct. 27-Dec. 5/84 (8 losses, 2 ties)
Feb. 23-Mar. 20/82 (10 losses, 1 tie)

Away .... 18 — Oct. 6/82-Jan. 5/83 (14 losses, 4 ties)

Most Shutouts, Season	13	1953-54 (70)
Most Pen. Mins., Season	1,888	1981-82 (80)
Most Goals, Game	14	Mar. 16/57 (NYR 1 at Tor. 14)

Individual

Most Seasons	20	George Armstrong
Most Games	1,187	George Armstrong
Most Goals, Career	389	Darryl Sittler
Most Assists, Career	527	Darryl Sittler
Most Points, Career	916	Darryl Sittler (389 goals, 527 assists)
Most Pen. Mins., Career	1,670	Dave Williams
Most Shutouts, Career	62	Turk Broda
Longest Consecutive Games Streak	486	Tim Horton (Feb. 11/61-Feb. 4/68)

Most Goals, Season	54	Rick Vaive (1981-82)
Most Assists, Season	72	Darryl Sittler (1977-78)
Most Points, Season	117	Darryl Sittler (1977-78) (45 goals, 72 assists)
Most Pen. Mins., Season	351	Dave Williams (1977-78)
Most Points, Defenseman Season	79	Ian Turnbull (1976-77) (22 goals, 57 assists)
Most Points, Center Season	117	Darryl Sittler (1977-78) (45 goals, 72 assists)
Most Points, Right Wing, Season	97	Wilf Paiement (1980-81) (40 goals, 57 assists)
Most Points, Left Wing, Season	84	Frank Mahovlich (1960-61) (48 goals, 36 assists)
Most Points, Rookie, Season	66	Peter Ihnacak (1982-83) (28 goals, 38 assists)
Most Shutouts, Season	13	Harry Lumley (1953-54)
Most Goals, Game	6	Corb Denneny (Jan. 26/21) Darryl Sittler (Feb. 7/76)
Most Assists, Game	6	Babe Pratt (Jan. 8/44)
Most Points, Game	*10	Darryl Sittler (Feb. 7/76)

* NHL Record.

All-time Record vs. Other Clubs

Regular Season

		At Home						On Road						Total					
	GP	W	L	T	GF	GA	PTS	GP	W	L	T	GF	GA	PTS	GP	W	L	T	GF	GA	PTS
Boston	269	143	80	46	916	682	332	269	79	143	47	717	880	205	538	222	223	93	1633	1564	537
Buffalo	38	16	16	6	123	130	38	40	13	25	2	110	170	28	78	29	41	8	233	300	66
**Calgary	27	12	10	5	110	94	29	29	10	16	3	103	122	23	56	22	26	8	213	216	52
Chicago	269	146	76	47	929	665	339	268	102	128	38	693	789	242	537	248	204	85	1622	1454	581
Detroit	271	144	87	40	877	681	328	271	90	139	42	653	784	222	542	234	226	82	1530	1465	550
Edmonton	11	4	6	1	52	60	9	12	1	8	3	41	68	5	23	5	14	4	93	128	14
Hartford	11	4	7	0	55	55	8	12	3	7	2	45	63	8	23	7	14	2	90	118	16
Los Angeles	43	24	11	8	179	135	56	42	14	24	4	117	148	32	85	38	35	12	296	283	88
Minnesota	55	28	16	11	211	177	67	54	20	27	7	186	215	47	107	48	43	18	397	392	114
Montreal	304	155	105	44	913	780	354	303	81	183	39	740	1072	201	607	236	288	83	1653	1852	555
*New Jersey	22	16	4	2	102	71	34	21	7	5	9	73	72	23	43	23	9	11	175	143	57
NY Islanders	29	12	14	3	97	110	27	27	8	17	2	83	127	18	56	20	31	5	180	237	45
NY Rangers	257	147	73	37	889	658	331	257	98	106	53	744	771	249	514	245	179	90	1633	1427	580
Philadelphia	41	14	15	12	139	126	40	41	8	26	7	96	168	23	82	22	41	19	235	294	63
Pittsburgh	42	18	14	10	165	137	46	43	17	21	5	140	157	39	85	35	35	15	305	294	85
Quebec	12	5	5	2	36	53	12	11	1	6	4	34	47	6	23	6	11	6	70	100	18
St. Louis	52	35	11	6	213	147	76	53	14	30	9	147	188	37	105	49	41	15	360	335	113
Vancouver	33	13	13	7	121	114	33	34	10	17	7	114	125	27	67	23	30	14	235	239	60
Washington	24	13	8	3	108	85	29	23	9	12	2	72	89	20	47	22	20	5	180	174	49
Winnipeg	14	3	10	1	56	67	7	13	6	6	1	60	62	13	27	9	16	2	116	129	20
Defunct Clubs	232	158	53	21	860	515	337	233	84	120	29	607	745	197	465	242	173	50	1467	1260	534
Totals	**2056**	**1110**	**634**	**312**	**7141**	**5542**	**2532**	**2056**	**675**	**1066**	**315**	**5575**	**6862**	**1665**	**4112**	**1785**	**1700**	**627**	**12716**	**12404**	**4197**

* Totals include those of Kansas City (1974-75, 1975-76) and Colorado (1976-77 through 1981-82)
** Totals include those of Atlanta (1972-73 through 1979-80)

Playoffs

	Series	W	L	GP	W	L	T	GF	GA	Last Mtg.	Round	Result
Boston	13	8	5	62	31	30	1	150	153	1974	QF	L 0-4
Calgary	1	1	0	2	2	0	0	9	5	1979	P	W 2-0
Chicago	7	5	2	25	15	9	1	76	57	1986	DSF	W 3-0
Detroit	20	11	9	97	49	48	0	239	239	1964	F	W 4-3
Los Angeles	2	2	0	5	4	1	0	18	9	1978	P	W 2-0
Minnesota	2	0	2	7	1	6	0	26	35	1983	DSF	L 1-3
Montreal	13	6	7	67	28	39	0	138	184	1979	QF	L 0-4
NY Islanders	2	1	1	10	4	6	0	20	23	1981	P	L 0-3
NY Rangers	8	3	5	35	16	19	0	86	91	1971	QF	L 2-4
Philadelphia	3	0	3	17	5	12	0	47	67	1977	QF	L 2-4
Pittsburgh	2	2	0	6	4	2	0	21	13	1977	P	W 2-1
St. Louis	1	0	1	7	3	4	0	22	24	1986	DF	L 3-4
Defunct Clubs	4	3	1	10	5	4	1	20	16			
Totals	**78**	**42**	**36**	**350**	**167**	**180**	**3**	**882**	**911**			

Abbreviations: Round: F – Final; CF – conference final; DF – division final; DSF – division semi-final; SF – semi-final; QF – quarter-final; P – preliminary round. **GA** – goals against; **GF** – goals for.

Playoff Results 1986-82

Year	Round	Opponent	Result	GF	GA
1986	DSF	St. Louis	L 3-4	22	24
	DSF	Chicago	W 3-0	18	9
1983	DSF	Minnesota	L 1-3	18	18

Coaching History

Conn Smythe, 1927-28 to 1929-30; Conn Smythe and Art Duncan, 1930-31; Art Duncan and Dick Irvin, 1931-32; Dick Irvin, 1932-33 to 1939-40; Hap Day, 1940-41 to 1949-50; Joe Primeau, 1950-51 to 1952-53; "King" Clancy, 1953-54 to 1955-56; Howie Meeker, 1956-57; Billy Reay, 1957-58; Billy Reay and "Punch" Imlach, 1958-59; "Punch" Imlach, 1959-60 to 1968-69; John McLellan, 1969-70 to 1970-71; John McLellan and "King" Clancy, 1971-72; John McLellan, 1972-73; Red Kelly, 1973-74 to 1976-77; Roger Neilson, 1977-78 to 1978-79; Floyd Smith, Dick Duff and "Punch" Imlach, 1979-80; "Punch" Imlach and Mike Nykoluk, 1980-81; Mike Nykoluk, 1981-82 to 1983-84; Dan Maloney, 1984-85 to 1985-86; John Brophy, 1986-87.

Captains' History

Hap Day, 1927-28 to 1936-37; Charlie Conacher, 1937-38; Red Horner, 1938-39, 1939-40; Syl Apps, 1940-41 to 1942-43; Bob Davidson, 1943-44, 1944-45; Syl Apps, 1945-46 to 1947-48; Ted Kennedy, 1948-49 to 1954-55; Sid Smith, 1955-56; Ted Kennedy, Jim Thomson, 1956-57; George Armstrong, 1958-59 to 1968-69; Dave Keon, 1969-70 to 1974-75; Darryl Sittler, 1975-76 to 1980-81; Rick Vaive, 1981-82 to 1985-86.

Retired Numbers

5	Bill Barilko	1946-1951

Entry Draft Selections 1986-72

1986
Pick
6	Vincent Damphousse
36	Darryl Shannon
48	Sean Boland
69	Kent Hulst
90	Scott Taylor
111	Stephane Giguere
132	Danny Hie
153	Stephen Brennan
174	Brian Bellefeuille
195	Sean Davidson
216	Mark Holick
237	Brian Hoard

1985
Pick
1	Wendel Clark
22	Ken Spangler
43	Dave Thomlinson
64	Greg Vey
85	Jeff Serowik
106	Jiri Latal
127	Tim Bean
148	Andy Donahue
169	Todd Whittemore
190	Bob Reynolds
211	Tim Armstrong
232	Mitch Murphy

1984
Pick
4	Al Iafrate
25	Todd Gill
67	Jeff Reese
88	Jack Capuano
109	Joe Fabian
130	Joe McInnis
151	Derek Laxdal
172	Dan Turner
192	David Buckley
213	Mikael Wurst
233	Peter Slanina

1983
Pick
7	Russ Courtnall
28	Jeff Jackson
48	Alan Bester
83	Dan Hodgson
128	Cam Plante
148	Paul Bifano
168	Cliff Albrecht
184	Greg Rolston
188	Brian Ross
208	Mike Tomlak
228	Ron Choules

1982
Pick
3	Gary Nylund
24	Gary Leeman
25	Peter Ihnacak
45	Ken Wregget
73	Vaclav Ruzicka
87	Eduard Uvara
99	Sylvain Charland
108	Ron Dreger
115	Craig Kales
129	Dom Campedelli
139	Jeff Triano
171	Miroslav Ihnacak
192	Leigh Verstraete
213	Tim Loven
234	Jim Appleby

1981
Pick
6	Jim Benning
24	Gary Yaremchuk
55	Ernie Godden
90	Normand LeFrancois
102	Barry Brigley
132	Andrew Wright
153	Richard Turmel
174	Greg Barber
195	Marc Magnan

1980
Pick
25	Craig Muni
26	Bob McGill
43	Fred Boimistruck
74	Stewart Gavin
95	Hugh Larkin
116	Ron Dennis
137	Russ Adam
158	Fred Perlini
179	Darwin McCutcheon
200	Paul Higgins

1979
Pick
9	Laurie Boschman
51	Normand Aubin
72	Vincent Tremblay
93	Frank Nigro
114	Bill McCreary

1978
Pick
21	Joel Quenneville
48	Mark Kirton
65	Bob Parent
81	Jordy Douglas
92	Mel Hewitt
98	Normand Lefebvre
115	John Scammell
132	Kevin Reinhart
149	Mike Waghorne
166	Laurie Cuvelier

1977
Pick
11	John Anderson
12	Trevor Johansen
24	Bob Gladney
29	Rockey Saganiuk
65	Dan Eastman
83	John Wilson
101	Roy Sommer
119	Lynn Jorgenson

1976
Pick
30	Randy Carlyle
48	Alain Belanger
52	Gary McFayden
66	Tim Williams
84	Greg Hotham
102	Dan Dkjakalovic

1975
Pick
6	Don Ashby
24	Doug Jarvis
42	Bruce Boudreau
78	Ted Long
96	Kevin Campbell
114	Mario Rouillard
132	Ron Wilson
149	Paul Evans
165	Jean Latendresse
166	Paul Crowley
179	Dan D'Alvise
180	Jack Laine
188	Ken Holland

1974
Pick
13	Jack Valiquette
31	Dave Williams
49	P. Alexandersson
67	Peter Driscoll
85	Mike Palmateer
103	Bill Hassard
121	Kevin Devine
139	Kevin Kemp

1973
Pick
4	Lanny McDonald
10	Bob Neely
15	Ian Turnbull
52	Francois Rochon
68	Gord Titcomb
84	Doug Marit
100	Dan Follett
116	Les Burgess
132	Dave Pay
144	Lee Palmer
147	Bob Peace

1972
Pick
11	George Ferguson
27	Randy Osburn
43	Denis Deslauriers
59	Brian Bowles
75	Michel Plante
91	Dave Shardlow
107	Monte Miron
123	Peter Williams
139	Pat Boutette
143	Gary Schofield

Club Directory

Maple Leaf Gardens
60 Carlton Street
Toronto, Ontario M5B 1L1
Phone 416/977-1641
TWX 610-491-2177
ENVOY ID TM.TOR
Capacity: 16,182 (standing 200)

Board of Directors

Harold E. Ballard	Donald Giffin	Paul McNamara, Q.C.
Norman Bosworth	Jake Dunlap, Q.C.	Douglas H. Roxborough
Arthur Campbell Burgess	Edward Lawrence	Steve Stavro

President and Governor . . . . Harold E. Ballard
Alternate Governor . . . . Arthur Gans
Chairman of the Board. . . . . Paul McNamara, Q.C.
Vice-President . . . . Francis "King" Clancy
General Manager . . . . Gerry McNamara
Coach. . . . . John Brophy
Assistant Coach . . . . Garry Lariviere
Assistant to the General Manager . . . . Gord Stellick
Chief Scout . . . . Floyd Smith
Scouts. . . . . Johnny Bower, Frank Currie, Jacques Toupin,
Dick Duff, Jack Gardiner, Jim Bzdell
Director of Public Relations . . . . Bob Stellick
Treasurer . . . . Donald Crump
Box Office Manager. . . . . Gordon Finn
Building Superintendent . . . . Donald MacKenzie
Trainers. . . . . Guy Kinnear, Dan Lemelin
Team Doctors. . . . . Dr. Dave Hastings, Dr. Simon McGrail,
Dr. Murray Urowitz, Dr. Leith Douglas,
Dr. Ernie Lewis
Dimensions of rink. . . . . 200 feet by 85 feet
Club Colours . . . . Blue and White
Press Box . . . . East Side
Play-by-Play TV broadcasters . . . . Jim Hughson and Harry Neale (CBC-TV 5
and CHCH-TV 11)
Radio Network . . . . TBS
Radio Play-by-Play broadcaster . . . . Joe Bowen
Radio Color broadcaster . . . . Bill Watters, Brad Selwood

Russ Courtnall, left, and Wendel Clark, below, are two of Toronto's impressive group of talented, young players.

Vancouver Canucks

1985-86 Results: 23w-44l-13t 59 pts. Fourth, Smythe Division

Year-by-Year Record

		Home			Road			Overall							
Season	GP	W	L	T	W	L	T	W	L	T	GF	GA	Pts.	Finished	Playoff Result
1985-86	80	17	18	5	6	26	8	23	44	13	282	333	59	4th, Smythe Div.	Lost Div. Semi-Final
1984-85	80	15	21	4	10	25	5	25	46	9	284	401	59	5th, Smythe Div.	Out of Playoffs
1983-84	80	20	16	4	12	23	5	32	39	9	306	328	73	3rd, Smythe Div.	Lost Div. Semi-Final
1982-83	80	20	12	8	10	23	7	30	35	15	303	309	75	3rd, Smythe Div.	Lost Div. Semi-Final
1981-82	80	20	8	12	10	25	5	30	33	17	290	286	77	2nd, Smythe Div.	Lost Stanley Cup Final
1980-81	80	17	12	11	11	20	9	28	32	20	289	301	76	3rd, Smythe Div.	Lost Prelim. Round
1979-80	80	14	17	9	13	20	7	27	37	16	256	281	70	3rd, Smythe Div.	Lost Prelim. Round
1978-79	80	15	18	7	10	24	6	25	42	13	217	291	63	2nd, Smythe Div.	Lost Prelim. Round
1977-78	80	13	15	12	7	28	5	20	43	17	239	320	57	3rd, Smythe Div.	Out of Playoffs
1976-77	80	13	21	6	12	21	7	25	42	13	235	294	63	4th, Smythe Div.	Out of Playoffs
1975-76	80	22	11	7	11	21	8	33	32	15	271	272	81	2nd, Smythe Div.	Lost Prelim. Round
1974-75	80	23	12	5	15	20	5	38	32	10	271	254	86	1st, Smythe Div.	Lost Quarter-Final
1973-74	78	14	18	7	10	25	4	24	43	11	224	296	59	7th, East Div.	Out of Playoffs
1972-73	78	17	18	4	5	29	5	22	47	9	233	339	53	7th, East Div.	Out of Playoffs
1971-72	78	14	20	5	6	30	3	20	50	8	203	297	48	7th, East Div.	Out of Playoffs
1970-71	78	17	18	4	7	28	4	24	46	8	229	296	56	6th, East Div.	Out of Playoffs

Schedule

Home

Oct.	Sat.	11	St. Louis
	Mon.	13	Quebec
	Wed.	22	Boston
	Fri.	24	Chicago
	Tue.	28	Washington
	Fri.	31	Edmonton
Nov.	Sun.	2	Montreal
	Wed.	12	Hartford
	Fri.	14	Winnipeg
	Tue.	18	Calgary
	Fri.	21	NY Rangers
	Tue.	25	Los Angeles
	Sat.	29	Winnipeg
Dec.	Tue.	2	Chicago
	Fri.	5	NY Islanders
	Wed.	17	Detroit
	Sat.	20	Calgary
	Tue.	23	Los Angeles
	Sat.	27	Philadelphia
	Tue.	30	Edmonton
Jan.	Fri.	2	Los Angeles
	Fri.	16	Calgary
	Wed.	21	NY Rangers
	Fri.	23	Pittsburgh
	Tue.	27	Edmonton
	Fri.	30	New Jersey
Feb.	Sun.	1	Minnesota
	Wed.	4	NY Islanders
	Fri.	6	St. Louis
	Sun.	8	Calgary
	Fri.	20	Washington
	Sun.	22	Toronto
Mar.	Wed.	4	Edmonton
	Fri.	6	Montreal
	Tue.	10	Detroit
	Fri.	13	Buffalo
	Tue.	17	Quebec
	Fri.	20	Winnipeg
April	Fri.	3	Winnipeg
	Sun.	5	Los Angeles

Away

Oct.	Wed.	15	New Jersey
	Thur.	16	Philadelphia
	Sat.	18	Minnesota
	Sun.	26	Edmonton
Nov.	Tue.	4	Pittsburgh
	Wed.	5	Washington
	Fri.	7	Buffalo
	Sat.	8	Toronto
	Tue.	11	Calgary
	Sat.	22	Edmonton
	Wed.	26	Los Angeles
Dec.	Sun.	7	Winnipeg
	Tue.	9	Philadelphia
	Thur.	11	Boston
	Sat.	13	Hartford
	Sun.	14	Chicago
	Fri.	19	Edmonton
Jan.	Sun.	4	Winnipeg
	Tue.	6	Quebec
	Wed.	7	Montreal
	Sat.	10	New Jersey*
	Sun.	11	NY Rangers
	Wed.	14	Los Angeles
	Sat.	17	Calgary
	Mon.	19	Winnipeg
	Wed.	28	Edmonton
Feb.	Tue.	3	Calgary
	Sat.	14	Pittsburgh
	Tue.	17	St. Louis
	Wed.	18	Minnesota
	Tue.	24	Calgary
	Thur.	26	Detroit
	Sat.	28	Toronto
Mar.	Sun.	1	Buffalo
	Sun.	8	Los Angeles*
	Sun.	22	Winnipeg*
	Thur.	26	NY Islanders
	Sat.	28	Boston*
	Sun.	29	Hartford*
April	Wed.	1	Los Angeles

*Denotes afternoon game.

Home Starting Times:

Weeknights	7:35 p.m.
Saturdays	5:05 p.m.
Sundays	7:05 p.m.
Except Oct. 13	7:05 p.m.

Franchise date: May 22, 1970.

17th NHL Season

Petri Skriko was Vancouver's top scorer in 1985-86.

1986-87 Player Personnel

FORWARDS

	Ht.	Wt.	Place of Birth	Date	1985-86 Club
BERTUZZI, Brian	6-0	185	Vancouver, B.C.	11/24/66	New Westminster-Kalamazoo
BRUCE, Dave	5-11	177	Thunder Bay, Ont.	10/7/64	Fredericton-Vancouver
COXE, Craig	6-4	195	Chula Vista, Ca.	1/21/64	Vancouver
CRAWFORD, Marc	5-11	185	Belleville, Ont.	2/13/61	Fredericton-Vancouver
HALL, Taylor	5-11	185	Regina, Sask.	2/20/64	Vancouver-Fredericton
HAWKINS, Todd	6-1	195	Kingston, Ont.	8/2/66	Belleville
KIRTON, Mark	5-10	170	Regina, Sask.	2/3/58	Fredericton
KULAK, Stu	5-10	180	Edmonton, Alta.	3/10/63	Kalamazoo-Fredericton
LANTHIER, Jean-Marc	6-2	195	Montreal, Que.	3/27/63	Fredericton-Vancouver
LEBLANC, John	6-1	190	Campellton, N.B.	2/21/64	U. of New Brunswick-Team Canada
LEMAY, Moe	5-11	185	Saskatoon, Sask.	2/18/62	Vancouver
LOWRY, Dave	6-1	185	Sudbury, Ont.	1/14/65	Vancouver
MACINTYRE, Dunc	5-8	167	Cornwall, Ont.	7/3/64	Fredericton
NOBLE, Jeff	5-10	167	Mount Forest, Ont.	5/20/68	Kitchener
PEDERSON, Barry	5-11	185	Big River, Sask.	3/13/61	Boston
PETERSON, Brent	6-0	190	Calgary, Alta.	2/15/58	Vancouver
ROHLICEK, Jeff	6-0	180	Park Ridge, Ill.	1/27/66	Spokane
SANDLAK, Jim	6-3	209	Kitchener, Ont.	12/12/66	Vancouver-London
SISKA, Randy	6-2	195	Calgary, Alta.	6/1/67	Medicine Hat
SKRIKO, Petri	5-10	172	Lapeenranta, Finland	3/12/62	Vancouver
SMYL, Stan	5-8	185	Glendon, Alta.	1/28/58	Vancouver
STERN, Ronnie	6-0	195	St.-Agathe, Que.	1/11/67	Longueuil
STEVENS, Mike	5-11	193	Kitchener, Ont.	12/30/65	Fredericton
SUNDSTROM, Patrik	6-2	203	Skelleftea, Sweden	12/14/61	Vancouver
SUTTER, Rich	5-11	183	Viking, Alta.	12/2/63	Philadelphia
TAMBELLINI, Steve	6-0	184	Trail, B.C.	5/14/58	Vancouver
TANTI, Tony	5-9	185	Toronto, Ont.	9/7/63	Vancouver
TAYLOR, Darren	6-2	173	Calgary, Alta.	5/28/67	Calgary (WHL)-Seattle
TOTTLE, Scott	5-11	180	Brantford, Ont.	11/30/65	Fredericton
WOODLEY, Dan	6-0	190	Oklahoma City, Okla.	12/29/67	Portland

DEFENCEMEN

	Ht.	Wt.	Place of Birth	Date	1985-86 Club
AGNEW, Jim	6-1	185	Hartney, Man.	3/21/66	Portland
BARTEL, Robin	6-0	200	Drake, Sask.	5/16/61	Moncton-Calgary
BUTCHER, Garth	6-0	200	Regina, Sask.	1/8/63	Vancouver
COCHRANE, Glen	6-3	207	Kamloops, B.C.	1/29/58	Vancouver
DOYLE, Shane	6-1	200	Lindsay, Ont.	4/26/67	Belleville-Cornwall
DUNBAR, Dale	6-1	201	Winthrop, Mass.	10/14/61	Fredericton-Vancouver
HALWARD, Doug	6-1	197	Toronto, Ont.	11/1/55	Vancouver
HERNIMAN, Steve	6-3	199	Windsor, Ont.	6/9/68	Cornwall
HUNT, Curtis	6-0	180	North Battleford, Sask.	1/28/67	Prince Albert
LANZ, Rick	6-2	193	Karlouyvary, Czech.	9/16/61	Vancouver
LIDSTER, Doug	6-1	195	Kamloops, B.C.	10/18/60	Vancouver
LYONS, Marc	6-1	201	Toronto, Ont.	1/8/67	Kingston
MACDONALD, Brett	6-1	200	Bothwell, Ont.	1/5/66	Kitchener
MEASURES, Allan	6-0	170	Barrhead, Alta.	5/8/65	Calgary
PETIT, Michel	6-1	205	St. Malo, Que.	2/12/64	Fredericton-Vancouver
RICHTER, Dave	6-5	220	St. Boniface, Man.	4/8/60	Minnesota-Philadelphia

GOALTENDERS

	Ht.	Wt.	Place of Birth	Date	1985-86 Club
BRODEUR, Richard	5-7	175	Longueuil, Que.	9/15/52	Vancouver
CAPRICE, Frank	5-9	160	Hamilton, Ont.	5/2/62	Vancouver-Fredericton
GAMBLE, Troy	5-11	178	New Glasgow, N.S.	4/7/67	Medicine Hat
KILROY, Shawn	5-11	175	Ottawa, Ont.	9/22/64	Mohawk Valley
YOUNG, Wendell	5-8	185	Halifax, N.S.	9/1/63	Fredericton-Vancouver

1985-86 Scoring

Regular Season

*–rookie

Pos	#	Player	Team	GP	G	A	Pts	+/-	PIM	PP	SH	GW	OT	S	%
F	26	Petri Skriko	VAN	80	38	40	78	17–	34	12	1	2	1	192	19.8
F	9	Tony Tanti	VAN	77	39	33	72	8–	85	17	0	5	0	213	18.3
F	17	Patrik Sundstrom	VAN	79	18	48	66	8–	28	6	1	0	0	155	11.6
F	12	Stan Smyl	VAN	73	27	35	62	20–	144	3	4	1	0	165	16.4
D	4	Rick Lanz	VAN	75	15	38	53	26–	73	11	0	0	0	191	7.9
F	23	Thomas Gradin	VAN	71	14	27	41	16–	34	2	1	3	0	121	11.6
F	21	Cam Neely	VAN	73	14	20	34	30–	126	6	0	3	0	113	12.4
D	2	Doug Halward	VAN	70	8	25	33	19–	111	3	0	0	0	122	6.6
F	14	Moe Lemay	VAN	48	16	15	31	14–	92	6	0	1	0	112	14.3
F	10	Brent Peterson	VAN	77	8	23	31	10–	94	0	3	2	1	86	9.3
F	20	Steve Tambellini	VAN	48	15	15	30	18–	12	6	0	2	2	89	16.9
D	29	Jiri Bubla	VAN	43	6	24	30	25–	30	4	0	1	0	62	9.7
D	3	Doug Lidster	VAN	78	12	16	28	12–	56	1	1	0	0	151	7.9
D	15	J.J. Daigneault	VAN	64	5	23	28	20–	45	4	0	0	0	114	4.4
F	18	Marc Crawford	VAN	54	11	14	25	7–	92	0	0	0	0	80	13.8
F	22	*Dave Lowry	VAN	73	10	8	18	21–	143	1	0	1	0	66	15.2
F	28	Jean-Marc Lanthier	VAN	62	7	10	17	17–	12	3	0	1	0	50	14.0
D	24	Garth Butcher	VAN	70	4	7	11	25–	188	0	0	0	0	57	7.0
F	8	*Taylor Hall	VAN	19	5	5	10	11–	6	1	0	0	0	30	16.7
F	32	*Craig Coxe	VAN	57	3	5	8	13–	176	1	0	0	0	48	6.3
D	24	Michel Petit	VAN	32	1	6	7	6–	27	1	0	0	0	43	2.3
F	7	Gary Lupul	VAN	19	4	1	5	0	12	0	0	0	0	17	23.5
F	33	*Jim Sandlak	VAN	23	1	3	4	10–	10	0	0	0	0	34	2.9
D	34	Neil Belland	VAN	7	1	2	3	2–	4	1	0	1	0	10	10.0
D	27	Glen Cochrane	VAN	49	0	3	3	5–	125	0	0	0	0	24	.0
G	35	Richard Brodeur	VAN	64	0	2	2	0	16	0	0	0	0	0	.0
G	30	Frank Caprice	VAN	7	0	1	1	0	0	0	0	0	0	0	.0
F	25	*David Bruce	VAN	12	0	1	1	2–	14	0	0	0	0	17	.0
D	19	*Dale Dunbar	VAN	1	0	0	0	1–	0	0	0	0	0	0	.0
G	1	*Wendell Young	VAN	22	0	0	0	0	0	0	0	0	0	0	.0

Playoffs

* rookie

Pos	#	Player	Team	GP	G	A	Pts	+/-	PIM	PP	SH	GW	OT	S	%
F	23	Thomas Gradin	VAN	3	2	1	3	3–	2	0	0	0	0	9	22.2
F	10	Brent Peterson	VAN	3	2	0	2	4–	9	1	0	0	0	5	40.0
D	15	J.J. Daigneault	VAN	3	0	2	2	1–	0	0	0	0	0	4	.0
F	17	Patrik Sundstrom	VAN	3	1	0	1	3–	0	0	0	0	0	5	20.0
G	1	*Wendell Young	VAN	1	0	1	1	0	0	0	0	0	0	0	.0
F	18	Marc Crawford	VAN	3	0	1	1	2–	0	0	0	0	0	4	.0
D	3	Doug Lidster	VAN	3	0	1	1	1–	0	0	0	0	0	1	.0
F	33	*Jim Sandlak	VAN	3	0	1	1	2–	0	0	0	0	0	6	.0
F	9	Tony Tanti	VAN	3	0	1	1	4–	11	0	0	0	0	13	.0
F	25	*David Bruce	VAN	1	0	0	0	0	0	0	0	0	0	0	.0
G	35	Richard Brodeur	VAN	3	0	0	0	0	2	0	0	0	0	0	.0
D	27	Glen Cochrane	VAN	2	0	0	0	1–	0	0	0	0	0	4	.0
D	29	Jiri Bubla	VAN	3	0	0	0	6–	0	0	0	0	0	1	.0
D	5	Garth Butcher	VAN	3	0	0	0	6–	0	0	0	0	0	4	.0
F	32	*Craig Coxe	VAN	3	0	0	0	2–	2	0	0	0	0	4	.0
D	2	Doug Halward	VAN	3	0	0	0	6–	0	0	0	0	0	4	.0
D	4	Rick Lanz	VAN	3	0	0	0	6–	0	0	0	0	0	4	.0
F	22	*Dave Lowry	VAN	3	0	0	0	2–	2	0	0	0	0	1	.0
F	7	Gary Lupul	VAN	3	0	0	0	5–	0	0	0	0	0	0	.0
F	21	Cam Neely	VAN	3	0	0	0	3–	6	0	0	0	0	4	.0
F	26	Petri Skriko	VAN	3	0	0	0	6–	0	0	0	0	0	10	.0

Tony Tanti

Coach and General Manager

WATT, THOMAS (TOM)
Coach, Vancouver Canucks. Born in Toronto, Ont., June 17, 1935.

Tom Watt first served in the Vancouver Canucks' organization as an assistant coach in 1980-81. He returned to Vancouver in 1985 after three seasons as head coach of the Winnipeg Jets and, in 1984-85, a season as head coach of the University of Toronto Blues where Watt had previously won 11 conference titles and nine Canadian inter-collegiate championships in 14 seasons. In those 14 seasons, Watt's clubs accumulated a record of 378 wins, 96 losses and 29 ties in 503 games (.780). He was co-coach of the 1980 Canadian Olympic Team.

NHL Coaching Record

Team	Season	Games	Regular Season				Games	Playoffs			
			W	L	T	%		W	L	%
Winnipeg	1981-82	80	33	33	14	.500	4	1	3	.250
Winnipeg	1982-83	80	33	39	8	.463	3	0	3	.000
Winnipeg	1983-84	21	6	13	2	.333	....	....	....	....
Vancouver	1985-86	80	23	44	13	.369	3	0	3	.000
NHL Totals		**261**	**95**	**129**	**37**	**.435**	**10**	**1**	**9**	**.100**

GORDON, JOHN (JACK)
General Manager, Vancouver Canucks. Born in Winnipeg, Man., March 3, 1928.

Jack Gordon was appointed Director of Hockey Operations of the Canucks on June 4, 1985. Gordon played two seasons with New Haven of the AHL in the late 1940's and had a 36-game stint with the New York Rangers prior to spending 10 full seasons with Cleveland of the American league. With Cleveland in 1953-54, Gordon scored 31 goals and 71 assists for 102 points in 72 games, an AHL record which stood for many years. Before Gordon joined the Minnesota North Stars in 1970, he gained experience working as assistant general manager of the Rangers for four years. He coached the North Stars between 1970 and 1975, guiding them to a 116-124-50 record over that span. He was promoted to general manager in 1975-76, a position he held until 1978. Gordon was named assistant general manager of the Canucks in 1980.

Club Records

Team

(Figures in brackets for season records are games played; records for fewest points, wins, ties, losses, goals, goals against are for 70 or more games)

Most Points	86	1974-75 (80)
Most Wins	38	1974-75 (80)
Most Ties	20	1980-81 (80)
Most Losses	50	1971-72 (78)
Most Goals	306	1983-84 (80)
Most Goals Against	401	1984-85 (80)
Fewest Points	48	1971-72 (78)
Fewest Wins	20	1971-72 (78)
Fewest Ties	8	1970-71 (78)
		1971-72 (78)
Fewest Losses	32	1974-75 (80)
		1975-76 (80)
		1980-81 (80)
Fewest Goals	203	1971-72 (78)
Fewest Goals Against	254	1974-75 (80)

Longest Winning Streak
Over-all ....5 Mar. 2-12/83
Home ....8 Feb. 27/83-
Mar. 21/83
Away...............3 Eight times

Longest Undefeated Streak
Over-all ....10 Mar. 5-25/77
(5 wins, 5 ties)
Home ....12 Oct. 29-
Dec. 17/74
(11 wins, 1 tie)
Away...............5 Three times

Longest Losing Streak
Over-all ....9 Three times
Home ....6 Dec. 18/70-
Jan. 20/71
Nov. 3-18/78
Away...............12 Nov. 28/81-
Feb. 6/82

Longest Winless Streak
Over-all ....13 Nov. 9-
Dec. 7/73
(10 losses, 3 ties)
Home ....11 Dec. 18/70-
Feb. 6/71
(10 losses, 1 tie)

Away...............20 Jan. 2/86-
Apr. 2/86
(14 losses, 6 ties)
Most Shutouts, Season 8 1974-75 (80)
Most Pen. Mins.,
Season 1,892 1980-81 (80)
Most Goals, Game ....11 Mar. 28/71
(Cal. 5 at Van. 11)

Individual

Most Seasons	10	Dennis Kearns
		Harold Snepsts
Most Games	683	Harold Snepsts
Most Goals, Career	220	Stan Smyl
Most Assists, Career	353	Thomas Gradin
Most Points, Career	550	Thomas Gradin
		(197 goals, 353 assists)
Most Pen. Mins., Career	1,352	Harold Snepsts
Most Shutouts, Career	11	Gary Smith

Longest Consecutive
Games Streak ....437 Don Lever
(Oct. 7/72-Jan. 14/78)
Most Goals, Season ......45 Tony Tanti
(1983-84)
Most Assists, Deason .....62 André Boudrias
(1974-75)
Most Points, Season ......91 Patrik Sundstrom
(1983-84)
(38 goals, 53 assists)
Most Pen. Mins., Season ...343 Dave Williams
(1980-81)
Most Points, Defenseman,
Season ....60 Dennis Kearns
(1976-77)
(5 goals, 55 assists)
Most Points, Center,
Season ....91 Patrik Sundstrom
(1983-84)
(38 goals, 53 assists)
Most Points, Right Wing,
Season ....88 Stan Smyl
(1982-83)
(38 goals, 50 assists)

Most Points, Left Wing,
Season ....81 Darcy Rota
(1982-83)
(42 goals, 398 assists)
Most Points, Rookie,
Season ....60 Ivan Hlinka
(1981-82)
(23 goals, 37 assists)
Most Shutouts, Season .....6 Gary Smith
(1974-75)
Most Goals, Game ....4 Several players
Most Assists, Game ......6 Patrik Sundstrom
(Feb. 29/84)
Most Points, Game ....7 Patrik Sundstrom
(Feb. 29/84)

Coaching History

Hal Laycoe, 1970-71 to 1971-72; Vic Stasiuk, 1972-73; Bill McCreary and Phil Maloney, 1973-74; Phil Maloney, 1974-75 to 1975-76; Phil Maloney and Orland Kurtenbach, 1976-77; Orland Kurtenbach, 1977-78; Harry Neale, 1978-79 to 1981-82; Harry Neale and Roger Neilson, 1981-82; Roger Neilson 1982-83, 1983-84; Harry Neale, 1983-84; Bill Laforge, 1984-85; Tom Watt, 1985-86 to date.

Captains' History

Orland Kurtenbach, 1970-71 to 1973-74; Andre Boudrias, 1974-75, 1975-76; Chris Oddleifson, 1976-77; Don Lever, 1977-78; Don Lever, Kevin McCarthy, 1978-79; Kevin McCarthy, 1979-80, 1980-81; Stan Smyl, 1981-82 to 1985-86.

All-time Record vs. Other Clubs

Regular Season

			At Home							On Road							Total				
	GP	W	L	T	GF	GA	PTS	GP	W	L	T	GF	GA	PTS	GP	W	L	T	GF	GA	PTS
Boston	33	7	19	7	104	147	21	32	2	27	3	68	153	7	65	9	46	10	172	300	28
Buffalo	34	17	10	7	128	107	41	33	6	19	8	83	121	20	67	23	29	15	211	228	61
**Calgary	41	16	17	8	144	135	40	41	7	28	6	115	194	20	82	23	45	14	259	329	60
Chicago	38	16	12	10	115	115	42	39	10	24	5	86	136	25	77	26	36	15	201	251	67
Detroit	33	19	10	4	139	102	42	33	10	19	4	104	145	24	66	29	29	8	243	247	66
Edmonton	24	8	13	3	88	107	19	24	4	16	4	75	141	12	48	12	29	7	163	248	31
Hartford	12	7	2	3	51	32	17	11	4	5	2	47	43	10	23	11	7	5	98	75	27
Los Angeles	45	19	17	9	168	160	47	45	11	26	8	124	186	30	90	30	43	17	292	346	77
Minnesota	38	20	11	7	156	119	47	37	7	23	7	99	158	21	75	27	34	14	255	277	68
Montreal	32	3	21	8	78	132	14	34	5	28	1	87	175	11	66	8	49	9	165	307	25
*New Jersey	30	15	5	10	117	94	40	30	14	11	5	107	91	33	60	29	16	15	224	185	73
NY Islanders	29	13	14	2	97	97	28	29	4	17	8	76	118	16	58	17	31	10	173	213	44
NY Rangers	34	9	23	2	105	135	20	36	6	27	3	87	161	15	70	15	50	5	192	296	35
Philadelphia	35	8	19	8	99	134	24	34	7	27	0	97	169	14	69	15	46	8	196	303	38
Pittsburgh	33	15	15	3	126	130	33	32	7	21	4	112	146	18	65	22	36	7	238	276	51
Québec	11	7	4	0	57	49	14	12	4	4	4	38	39	12	23	11	8	4	95	88	26
St. Louis	38	16	18	4	122	127	36	39	9	24	6	110	155	24	77	25	42	10	232	282	60
Toronto	34	17	10	7	125	114	41	33	13	13	7	114	121	33	67	30	23	14	239	235	74
Washington	21	11	7	3	78	67	25	22	9	11	2	74	71	20	43	20	18	5	152	138	45
Winnipeg	22	14	5	3	93	70	31	21	6	10	5	86	88	17	43	20	15	8	179	158	48
Defunct Clubs	19	14	3	2	82	48	30	19	10	8	1	71	68	21	38	24	11	3	153	116	51
Totals	636	271	255	110	2272	2221	652	636	155	388	93	1860	2679	403	1272	426	643	203	4132	4898	1055

* Totals include those of Kansas City (1974-75, 1975-76) and Colorado (1976-77 through 1981-82)
** Totals include those of Atlanta (1972-73 through 1979-80)

Playoffs

	Series	W	L	GP	W	L	T	GF	GA	Last Mtg.	Round	Result
Buffalo	2	0	2	7	1	6	0	14	28	1981	P	L 0-3
**Calgary	3	1	2	11	5	6	0	35	36	1984	DSF	L 1-3
Chicago	1	1	0	5	4	1	0	18	13	1982	CF	W 4-1
Edmonton	1	0	1	3	0	3	0	5	17	1986	DSF	L 0-3
Los Angeles	1	1	0	5	4	1	0	19	14	1982	DF	W 4-1
Montreal	1	0	1	5	1	4	0	9	20	1975	QF	L 1-4
NY Islanders	2	0	2	6	0	6	0	14	26	1982	F	L 0-4
Philadelphia	1	0	1	3	1	2	0	9	15	1979	P	L 1-2
Totals	12	3	9	45	16	29	0	123	169			

** Totals include those of Atlanta (1972-73 through 1979-80)

Abbreviations: Round: F – Final; CF – conference final; DF – division final; DSF – division semi-final; SF – semi-final; QF – quarter-final; P – preliminary round. GA – goals against; GF – goals for.

Playoff Results 1986-82

Year	Round	Opponent	Result	GF	GA
1986	DSF	Edmonton	L 0-3	5	17
1984	DSF	Calgary	L 1-3	13	14
1983	DSF	Calgary	L 1-3	14	17
1982	F	NY Islanders	L 0-4	10	18
	CF	Chicago	W 4-1	18	13
	DF	Los Angeles	W 4-1	19	14
	DSF	Calgary	W 3-0	8	5

Retired Numbers

11   Wayne Maki   1971-1973

Entry Draft
Selections 1986-72

1986
Pick
7	Dan Woodley
49	Don Gibson
70	Ronnie Stern
91	Eric Murano
112	Steve Herniman
133	Jon Helgeson
154	Jeff Noble
175	Matt Merton
196	Marc Lyons
217	Todd Hawkins
238	Vladimir Krutov

1985
Pick
4	Jim Sandlak
25	Troy Gamble
46	Shane Doyle
67	Randy Siska
88	Robert Kron
109	Martin Hrstka
130	Brian McFarlane
151	Hakan Ahlund
172	Curtis Hunt
193	Carl Valimont
214	Igor Larionov
235	Darren Taylor

1984
Pick
10	J.J. Daigneault
31	Jeff Rolicek
52	Dave Saunders
55	Landis Chaulk
58	Mike Stevens
73	Brian Bertuzzi
94	Brett MacDonald
115	Jeff Korchinski
136	Blaine Chrest
157	Jim Agnew
178	Rex Grant
198	Ed Lowney
219	Doug Clarke
239	Ed Kister

1983
Pick
9	Cam Neely
30	Dave Bruce
50	Scott Tottle
70	Tim Lorentz
90	Doug Quinn
110	Dave Lowry
130	Terry Maki
150	John Labatt
170	Allan Measures
190	Roger Grillo
210	Steve Kayser
230	Jay Mazur

1982
Pick
11	Michel Petit
53	Yves Lapointe
71	Shawn Kilroy
116	Taylor Hall
137	Parie Proft
158	Newell Brown
179	Don McLaren
200	Al Raymond
221	Steve Driscoll
242	Shawn Green

1981
Pick
10	Garth Butcher
52	Jean-Marc Lanthier
73	Wendell Young
105	Moe Lemay
115	Stu Kulak
136	Bruce Holloway
175	Petri Skriko
178	Frank Caprice
199	Rejean Vignola

1980
Pick
7	Rick Lanz
49	Andy Schliebener
70	Marc Crawford
91	Darrel May
112	Ken Berry
133	Doug Lidster
154	John O'Connor
175	Patrik Sundstrom
196	Grant Martin

1979
Pick
5	Rick Vaive
26	Brent Ashton
47	Ken Ellacott
68	Art Rutland
89	Dirk Graham
110	Shane Swan

1978
Pick
4	Bill Derlago
22	Curt Fraser
40	Stan Smyl
56	Harold Luckner
57	Brad Smith
90	Gerry Minor
107	Dave Ross
124	Steve O'Neill
141	Charlie Antetomaso
158	Richard Martens

1977
Pick
4	Jere Gillis
22	Jeff Bandura
40	Glen Hanlon
56	Dave Morrow
58	Murray Bannerman
76	Steve Hazlett
94	Brian Drumm
112	Ray Creasey

1976
Pick
26	Bob Manno
44	Rob Flockhart
62	Elmer Ray
80	Rick Durston
98	Rob Tudor
114	Brad Rhiness
122	Stu Ostlund

1975
Pick
10	Rick Blight
28	Brad Gassoff
46	Norm Lapointe
64	Glen Richardson
100	Bob Watson
118	Brian Shmyr
136	Allan Fleck
152	Bob McNiece
182	Sid Veysey

1974
Pick
23	Ron Sedlbauer
41	John Hughes
59	Harold Snepsts
77	Mike Rogers
95	Andy Spruce
113	Jim Clarke
130	Robbie Watt
147	Marc Gaudreault

1973
Pick
3	Dennis Ververgaert
9	Bob Dailey
19	Paulin Bordeleau
35	Paul Sheard
51	Keith Mackie
67	Paul O'Neil
83	Jim Cowell
99	Clay Hebenton
115	John Senkpiel
131	Peter Folco
147	Terry McDougall

1972
Pick
3	Don Lever
19	Brian McSheffrey
35	Paul Raymer
51	Ron Homenuke
67	Larry Bolonchuk
83	Dave McLelland
99	Dan Gloor
115	Dennis McCord
131	Steve Stone

Club Directory

Pacific Coliseum
100 North Renfrew Street
Vancouver, B.C. V5K 3N7
Phone 604/254-5141
TWX 610-929-2054
ENVOY ID   TM.VAN
Capacity: 16,553

Northwest Sports Enterprises Ltd.
Board of Directors

J. Lawrence Dampier	W.L. McEwen	Andrew E. Saxton
Arthur R. Griffiths	David S. Owen	Peter W. Webster
Frank A. Griffiths, C.A.	Senator Ray Perrault	Sydney W. Welsh
F.W. Griffiths	J. Raymond Peters	D.A. Williams, C.A.
Coleman E. Hall	Peter Paul Saunders	D. Alexander Farac (Sec.)
Senator E.M. Lawson		

Chairman	Frank A. Griffiths, C.A.
Assistant to the Chairman	Arthur R. Griffiths
Director of Hockey Operations and General Manager	Jack Gordon
Vice-President, Finance	John Chesman
Vice-President, Marketing	John Whitman
Vice-President, Communications	Glen Ringdal
Assistant to the General Manager and Head Coach	Tom Watt
Assistant Coach	Jack McIlhargey
Director of Player Development	Darcy Rota
Director of Scouting	Mike Penny
Scouting Staff	Jack McCartan, Ken Slater, Ron Delorme
Director of Team Services	Norm Jewison
Assistant Director of Hockey Information	Frank Bohmer
Public Relations Assistant	Babe Pratt
Director of Community Relations	Lynn Harrison
Trainers	Ken Fleger, Larry Ashley
Marketing Representatives	Gord Robertson, Duke Dickson
Manager of Food and Beverage Operations	Terreeia Rauffman
Concessionaire	Irene Oakley
Club Doctors	Dr. David Harris, Dr. Ross Davidson
Club Dentist	Dr. Ken Walters
Club Colours	Black, Red, Gold
Club Trains at	Duncan, B.C.
Play-by-Play Broadcaster	Jim Robson (radio and TV)
Radio Station	CKNW (980)
TV Channel	CBC (2)

Stan Smyl

Washington Capitals

1985-86 Results: 50w-23L-7T 107 PTS. Second, Patrick Division

Year-by-Year Record

Season	GP	Home			Road			Overall						Finished		Playoff Result
		W	L	T	W	L	T	W	L	T	GF	GA	Pts.			
1985-86	80	30	8	2	20	15	5	50	23	7	315	272	107	2nd,	Patrick Div.	Lost Div. Final
1984-85	80	27	11	2	19	14	7	46	25	9	322	240	101	2nd,	Patrick Div.	Lost Div. Semi-Final
1983-84	80	26	11	3	22	16	2	48	27	5	308	226	101	2nd,	Patrick Div.	Lost Div. Final
1982-83	80	22	12	6	17	13	10	39	25	16	306	283	94	3rd,	Patrick Div.	Lost Div. Semi-Final
1981-82	80	16	16	8	10	25	5	26	41	13	319	338	65	5th,	Patrick Div.	Out of Playoffs
1980-81	80	16	17	7	10	19	11	26	36	18	286	317	70	5th,	Patrick Div.	Out of Playoffs
1979-80	80	20	14	6	7	26	7	27	40	13	261	293	67	5th,	Patrick Div.	Out of Playoffs
1978-79	80	15	19	6	9	22	9	24	41	15	273	338	63	4th,	Norris Div.	Out of Playoffs
1977-78	80	10	23	7	7	26	7	17	49	14	195	321	48	5th,	Norris Div.	Out of Playoffs
1976-77	80	17	15	8	7	27	6	24	42	14	221	307	62	4th,	Norris Div.	Out of Playoffs
1975-76	80	6	26	8	5	33	2	11	59	10	224	394	32	5th,	Norris Div.	Out of Playoffs
1974-75	80	7	28	5	1	39	0	8	67	5	181	446	21	5th,	Norris Div.	Out of Playoffs

Schedule

Home			Away		
Oct.	Sat.	11 Philadelphia	**Oct.**	Thur.	9 Pittsburgh
	Sat.	18 Buffalo		Mon.	13 NY Rangers
	Fri.	24 Minnesota		Thur.	16 NY Islanders
	Sat.	25 New Jersey		Mon.	20 Montreal
Nov.	Wed.	5 Vancouver		Tue.	21 Quebec
	Sat.	8 Chicago		Tue.	28 Vancouver
	Fri.	14 Quebec		Wed.	29 Edmonton
	Tue.	18 Los Angeles	**Nov.**	Sat.	1 Calgary
	Sat.	22 Pittsburgh		Tue.	4 NY Islanders
	Wed.	26 Boston		Tue.	11 Minnesota
	Fri.	28 Philadelphia		Wed.	12 Chicago
Dec.	Sat.	6 Montreal		Sun.	16 Philadelphia
	Tue.	9 New Jersey		Fri.	21 Detroit
	Sun.	14 NY Rangers*		Sat.	29 Quebec
	Sat.	20 St. Louis	**Dec.**	Mon.	1 Montreal
	Fri.	26 NY Islanders		Wed.	3 Winnipeg
	Tue.	30 Hartford		Wed.	10 Toronto
Jan.	Thur.	1 Pittsburgh*		Wed.	17 NY Rangers
	Sat.	3 Philadelphia		Fri.	19 New Jersey
	Fri.	9 Pittsburgh		Sun.	28 Chicago
	Tue.	13 Winnipeg	**Jan.**	Mon.	5 St. Louis
	Tue.	20 New Jersey		Wed.	7 Pittsburgh
	Sat.	24 Buffalo		Sun.	11 Philadelphia
	Fri.	30 NY Islanders		Thur.	15 NY Islanders
Feb.	Sun.	1 Winnipeg*		Sat.	17 Hartford
	Fri.	6 Hartford		Sun.	18 New Jersey
	Sat.	7 NY Rangers		Fri.	23 Buffalo
	Tue.	24 Detroit		Tue.	27 Pittsburgh
	Fri.	27 Edmonton		Wed.	28 Detroit
Mar.	Sun.	1 NY Rangers*	**Feb.**	Wed.	4 NY Rangers
	Tue.	3 New Jersey		Sun.	15 Edmonton
	Tue.	10 Calgary		Wed.	18 Los Angeles
	Fri.	13 Toronto		Fri.	20 Vancouver
	Tue.	17 Los Angeles		Sun.	22 Calgary
	Fri.	20 Pittsburgh	**Mar.**	Thur.	5 Philadelphia
	Sun.	22 Boston*		Sat.	7 Boston*
	Fri.	27 NY Islanders		Sat.	14 St. Louis
	Sun.	29 Minnesota*		Tue.	24 NY Islanders
	Tue.	31 Toronto	**April**	Wed.	1 NY Rangers
April	Sat.	4 Philadelphia		Sun.	5 New Jersey

*Denotes afternoon game.

Home Starting Times:
Weeknights & Saturdays	7:35 p.m.
Fridays	8:05 p.m.
Matinees	1:35 p.m.
Except Mar. 29	1:05 p.m.

Franchise date: June 11, 1974

 **13th NHL Season**

Pete Peeters

1986-87 Player Personnel

FORWARDS	Ht.	Wt.	Place of Birth	Date	1985-86 Club
ADAMS, Greg	6-1	195	Victoria, B.C.	5/31/60	Washington
CRAMAROSA, Vito	6-2	205	Toronto, Ont.	3/9/66	Toronto (OHL)
CARPENTER, Bob	6-0	190	Beverly, Mass.	7/13/63	Washington
CHRISTIAN, Dave	5-11	175	Warroad, Minn.	5/12/59	Washington
CORRIVEAU, Yvon	6-2	205	Welland, Ont.	2/8/67	Toronto (OHL)
DRUCE, John	6-1	187	Peterborough, Ont.	2/23/66	Peterborough
DUCHESNE, Gaetan	5-11	195	Les Saules, Que.	7/11/62	Washington
DUMAS, Claude	6-1	175	Thetford-Mines, Que.	1/10/67	Granby
FRANCESCHETTI, Lou	6-0	190	Toronto, Ont.	3/28/58	Washington
GARTNER, Mike	6-0	185	Barrie, Ont.	10/29/59	Washington
GOULD, Bob	5-11	195	Petrolia, Ont.	9/2/57	Washington
GREENLAW, Jeff	6-2	215	Toronto, Ont.	2/28/68	Team Canada
HAWORTH, Alan	5-10	190	Drummondville, Que.	9/1/60	Washington
HOLLETT, Steve	6-1	180	St. Johns, Nfld.	6/12/67	Sault Ste. Marie
JENSEN, David	6-1	185	Needham, Mass.	8/9/65	Binghamton-Washington
KASTELIC, Ed	6-2	215	Toronto, Ont.	1/29/64	Binghamton-Washington
KING, Kris	5-10	189	Bracebridge, Ont.	2/18/66	Peterborough
LAUGHLIN, Craig	5-11	198	Toronto, Ont.	9/14/57	Washington
LEACH, Steve	5-11	190	Cambridge, Mass.	1/16/66	U. of New Hampshire
MARTIN, Grant	5-10	190	Smooth Rock Fls, Ont.	3/13/62	Binghamton
MURRAY, Rob	6-1	175	Toronto, Ont.	4/4/67	Peterborough
PETTERSSON, Jorgen	6-2	185	Gothenburg, Sweden	7/11/56	Hartford-Washington
PIVONKA, Michal	6-2	192	Kladno, Czech.	1/28/66	Dukla-Jihlava
SAMPSON, Gary	6-0	190	Atikoken, Ont.	8/24/59	Binghamton
SCHOFIELD, Dwight	6-1	210	Waltham, Mass.	3/25/56	Washington
TAYLOR, Mark	5-11	180	Vancouver, B.C.	6/1/58	Binghamton-Washington
THOMSON, Jim	6-1	195	Edmonton, Alta.	12/30/65	Binghamton
DEFENSEMEN					
BARRETT, John	6-0	208	Ottawa, Ont.	7/1/58	Detroit-Washington
BEAUDOIN, Yves	6-0	190	Pte.-aux-Trembles, Que.	1/7/65	Binghamton
CAVALLINI, Paul	6-2	202	Toronto, Ont.	10/13/65	Team Canada
HATCHER, Kevin	6-4	212	Detroit, Mich.	9/9/66	Washington
HOULDER, Bill	6-2	205	Thunder Bay, Ont.	3/11/67	North Bay
JENNINGS, Grant	6-3	202	Hudson Bay, Sask.	5/5/65	Binghamton
KELLIN, Tony	6-2	205	Grand Rapids, Minn.	3/19/63	U. of Minnesota
LANGWAY, Rod	6-3	210	Formosa, Taiwan	5/3/57	Washington
MURPHY, Larry	6-2	206	Scarborough, Ont.	3/8/61	Washington
SHAW, Larry	6-0	200	Guelph, Ont.	2/10/67	Peterborough
SHOEBOTTOM, Bruce	6-1	200	Mississauga, Ont.	8/20/63	Binghamton
SMITH, Greg	6-0	195	Ponoka, Alta.	7/18/55	Detroit-Washington
STEVENS, Scott	6-1	210	Kitchener, Ont.	4/1/64	Washington
GOALTENDERS					
JENSEN, Al	5-10	180	Hamilton, Ont.	11/27/58	Washington
MASON, Bob	6-1	180	Intl. Falls, Minn.	4/22/61	Washington-Binghamton
PEETERS, Pete	6-1	207	Edmonton, Alta.	8/17/57	Boston-Washington
RAYMOND, Alain	5-10	177	Rimouski, Que.	6/24/65	Team Canada

Coach and General Manager

MURRAY, BRYAN CLARENCE
Coach, Washington Capitals. Born in Shawville, Que., December 5, 1942.

Bryan Murray was named coach of the Capitals on November 11, 1981, and less than two seasons later guided the Capitals to their first playoff appearance and the club's best record ever (39-25-16 94 pts.). He bettered that mark in 1983-84 (48-27-5 101 pts.) and received the Jack Adams Award (Coach of the Year). Murray was appointed to the coaching position with Washington after a successful season guiding the Hershey Bears of the American Hockey League to its winningest season in 43 years. Murray was named *Hockey News* Minor League Coach of the Year in his first full season at coaching professional hockey. Before joining the Capitals organization, Murray coached the Regina Pats of the Western Hockey League for the 1979-80 season and led the Pats to the WHL championship. Murray, a graduate of McGill University in Montreal, Quebec, also had extensive coaching experience at the collegiate and minor professional levels.

NHL Coaching Record

Team		Games	Regular Season				Playoffs			
			W	L	T	%	Games	W	L	%
Washington	1981-82	66	25	28	13	.477	....			....
Washington	1982-82	80	39	25	16	.588	4	1	3	.250
Washington	1983-84	80	48	27	5	.631	8	4	4	.500
Washington	1984-85	80	46	25	9	.631	5	2	3	.400
Washington	1985-86	80	50	23	7	.669	9	5	4	.556
NHL Totals		**386**	**208**	**128**	**50**	**.604**	**26**	**12**	**14**	**.462**

POILE, DAVID
Vice-President and General Manager, Washington Capitals. Born in Toronto, Ont., February 14, 1949.

David Poile was named to the position of General Manager of the Capitals on Aug. 30, 1982 and quickly built the franchise into a solid Stanley Cup contender. During his inaugural campaign (1982-83), he led the Caps' to their first winning season (39-25-16) and a first-time berth in the Stanley Cup playoffs. He received the *Sporting News* "Executive of the Year" award in 1982-83 for his efforts and duplicated the feat in 1983-84 following the Capitals' 48-27-5 season. Poile, a graduate of Northeastern University with a degree in Business Administration, began his professional hockey management career in 1972 as an Administrative Assistant for the Atlanta Flames organization where he served until joining the Washington franchise. A former collegiate hockey star at Northeastern, he won MVP and scoring honors during his senior year.

1985-86 Scoring
Regular Season
*—rookie

Pos	#	Player	Team	GP	G	A	Pts	+/–	PIM	PP	SH	GW	OT	S	%
F	27	Dave Christian	WSH	80	41	42	83	3	15	18	2	4	0	218	18.8
F	11	Mike Gartner	WSH	74	35	40	75	5 –	63	11	2	4	0	279	12.5
F	18	Craig Laughlin	WSH	75	30	45	75	24	43	10	0	4	1	114	26.3
F	16	Bengt Gustafsson	WSH	70	23	52	75	9	26	8	4	6	1	113	20.4
F	15	Alan Haworth	WSH	71	34	39	73	36	72	7	0	5	1	194	17.5
D	8	Larry Murphy	WSH	78	21	44	65	2	50	8	1	2	1	180	11.7
F	10	Bob Carpenter	WSH	80	27	29	56	12 –	105	7	0	3	0	205	13.2
F	22	Greg Adams	WSH	78	18	38	56	24	152	3	0	2	0	149	12.1
D	3	Scott Stevens	WSH	73	15	38	53	0	165	3	0	2	0	121	12.4
F	14	Gaetan Duchesne	WSH	80	11	28	39	10	39	0	1	3	0	119	9.2
F	23	Bob Gould	WSH	79	19	19	38	7	26	0	3	5	0	125	15.2
F	12	Jorgen Pettersson	HFD	23	5	5	10	12 –	2	2	0	0	0	27	18.5
			WSH	47	8	16	24	4 –	10	2	0	3	0	74	10.8
			Total	70	13	21	34	16 –	12	4	0	3	0	101	12.9
D	19	Greg Smith	DET	62	5	19	24	14 –	84	0	0	0	0	53	9.4
			WSH	14	0	3	3	3	10	0	0	0	0	6	.0
			Total	76	5	22	27	11 –	94	0	0	0	0	59	8.5
F	32	Lou Franceschetti	WSH	76	7	14	21	4 –	131	0	0	2	0	57	12.3
F	4	*Kevin Hatcher	WSH	79	9	10	19	6	119	1	0	1	0	132	6.8
D	5	Rod Langway	WSH	71	1	17	18	27	61	1	0	0	0	54	1.9
D	6	John Barrett	DET	65	2	12	14	29 –	125	0	0	0	0	60	3.3
			WSH	14	0	3	3	3	12	0	0	0	0	7	.0
			Total	79	2	15	17	26 –	137	0	0	0	0	67	3.0
F	20	Gary Sampson	WSH	19	1	4	5	3 –	2	0	0	1	0	15	5.9
F	28	Mark Taylor	WSH	30	2	1	3	4 –	4	0	0	0	0	23	8.7
D	2	Dwight Schofield	WSH	50	1	2	3	5	127	0	0	0	0	13	7.7
F	21	*Stephen Leach	WSH	11	1	1	2	0	2	0	0	0	0	4	25.0
G	1	Pete Peeters	BOS	8	0	2	2	0	4	0	0	0	0	0	.0
			WSH	34	0	0	0	0	8	0	0	0	0	0	.0
			Total	42	0	2	2	0	12	0	0	0	0	0	.0
F	9	*Dave Jensen	WSH	5	1	0	1	1	0	0	0	0	0	5	20.0
F	24	Daryl Evans	WSH	6	0	1	1	1 –	0	0	0	0	0	14	.0
F	30	Grant Martin	WSH	11	0	1	1	5 –	4	0	0	0	0	5	.0
G	35	Al Jensen	WSH	44	0	1	1	0	4	0	0	0	0	0	.0
G	31	Bob Mason	WSH	1	0	0	0	0	0	0	0	0	0	0	.0
F	26	*Yvon Corriveau	WSH	2	0	0	0	1 –	0	0	0	0	0	3	.0
D	30	*Yves Beaudoin	WSH	4	0	0	0	4 –	0	0	0	0	0	7	.0
F	29	*Ed Kastelic	WSH	15	0	0	0	0	73	0	0	0	0	2	.0

Playoffs
* rookie

Pos	#	Player	Team	GP	G	A	Pts	+/–	PIM	PP	SH	GW	OT	S	%
F	11	Mike Gartner	WSH	9	2	10	12	6	4	0	0	0	0	26	7.7
D	3	Scott Stevens	WSH	9	3	8	11	9	12	2	0	2	0	17	17.6
F	15	Alan Haworth	WSH	9	4	6	10	4	11	1	0	0	0	26	15.4
F	10	Bob Carpenter	WSH	9	5	4	9	4	12	2	0	1	0	24	20.8
F	27	Dave Christian	WSH	9	4	4	8	1	0	1	0	0	0	26	15.4
F	14	Gaetan Duchesne	WSH	9	4	3	7	5	12	0	1	0	0	18	22.2
F	23	Bob Gould	WSH	9	4	3	7	5	11	0	0	0	0	24	16.7
D	8	Larry Murphy	WSH	9	1	5	6	1	6	1	0	0	0	21	4.8
F	22	Greg Adams	WSH	9	1	3	4	1 –	27	0	0	0	0	10	10.0
D	6	John Barrett	WSH	9	2	1	3	1	35	0	0	1	0	6	33.3
D	19	Greg Smith	WSH	9	2	1	3	4	11	0	0	0	0	8	25.0
F	12	Jorgen Pettersson	WSH	8	1	2	3	2	0	1	0	0	0	11	9.1
D	5	Rod Langway	WSH	9	1	2	3	2	17	1	0	0	0	17	5.9
F	18	Craig Laughlin	WSH	9	1	2	3	2	10	0	0	1	0	13	7.7
F		*Yvon Corriveau	WSH	4	0	3	3	2	0	0	0	0	0	4	.0
F	4	*Kevin Hatcher	WSH	9	1	2	3	1 –	19	0	0	0	0	11	9.1
F	21	*Stephen Leach	WSH	6	0	1	1	2	0	0	0	0	0	6	.0
D	2	Dwight Schofield	WSH	3	0	1	1	0	14	0	0	0	0	1	.0
F	28	Mark Taylor	WSH	3	0	0	0	0	0	0	0	0	0	6	.0
F	9	*Dave Jensen	WSH	4	0	0	0	1	0	0	0	0	0	0	.0
F	32	Lou Franceschetti	WSH	8	0	0	0	1 –	15	0	0	0	0	5	.0
G	1	Pete Peeters	WSH	9	0	0	0	0	0	0	0	0	0	0	.0

Washington defensive star Rod Languay checks Dave Tippett of the Whalers.

Club Records

Team

(Figures in brackets for season records are games played; records for fewest points, wins, ties, losses, goals, goals against are for 70 or more games)

Most Points	107	1985-86 (80)
Most Wins	50	1985-86 (80)
Most Ties	18	1980-81 (80)
Most Losses	*67	1974-75 (80)
Most Goals	322	1984-85 (80)
Most Goals Against	*446	1974-75 (80)
Fewest Points	*21	1974-75 (80)
Fewest Wins	*8	1974-75 (80)
Fewest Ties	5	1974-75 (80)
		1983-84 (80)
Fewest Losses	23	1985-86 (80)
Fewest Goals	181	1974-75 (80)
Fewest Goals Against	226	1983-84 (80)

Longest Winning Streak
Over-all 10   Jan. 27-
                                       Feb. 18/84
Home 7   Jan. 17-
                                       Feb. 11/84
Away 6   Feb. 26-
                                       Apr. 1/84

Longest Undefeated Streak
Over-all 14   Nov. 12-
                                        Dec. 23/82
                                        (9 wins, 5 ties)
                                        Jan. 17-Feb. 18/84
                                        (13 wins, 1 tie)
Home 12   Nov. 7/82-
                                        Dec. 14/82
                                        (9 wins, 3 ties)
Away 10   Nov. 24/82-
                                        Jan. 8/83

Longest Losing Streak
Over-all . . . . *17   Feb. 18-
                                         Mar. 26/75
Home . . . . *11   Feb. 18-
                                         Mar. 30/75
Away . . . . *37   Oct. 9/74-
                                         Mar. 26/75

Longest Winless Streak
Over-all 25   Nov. 29/75-
                                        Jan. 21/76
                                        (22 losses, 3 ties)
Home 14   Dec. 3/75-
                                        Jan. 21/76
                                        (11 losses, 3 ties)

Away . . . . *37   Oct. 9/74-
                                         Mar. 26/75
                                         (37 losses)
Most Shutouts, Season 8   1983-84 (80)
Most Pen. Mins.,
Season 1,922   1981-82 (80)
Most Goals, Game 11   Dec. 11/81
                                       (Tor. 2 at Wash. 11)

Individual

Most Seasons	7	Yvon Labre
Most Games, Career	544	Mike Gartner
Most Goals, Career	282	Mike Gartner
Most Assists, Career	298	Mike Gartner
Most Points, Career	580	Mike Gartner

(282 goals, 298 assists)

Most Pen. Mins., Career . . . 782   Scott Stevens
Most Shutouts, Career 7   Al Jensen
Longest Consecutive
  Games Streak 245   Guy Charron
                                       (Oct. 5/76-Oct. 19/79)
Most Goals, Season 60   Dennis Maruk
                                       (1981-82)
Most Assists, Season 76   Dennis Maruk
                                       (1981-82)
Most Points, Season 136   Dennis Maruk
                                       (1981-82)
                                       (60 goals, 76 assists)
Most Pen. Mins., Season . . . 275   Randy Holt
                                       (1982-83)
Most Points, Defenseman,
  Season 65   Robert Picard
                                       (1978-79)
                                       (21 goals, 44 assists)
                                       Scott Stevens
                                       (1984-85)
                                       (21 goals, 44 assists)
Most Points, Center,
  Season 136   Dennis Maruk
                                         (1981-82)
                                         (60 goals, 76 assists)
Most Points, Right Wing,
  Season 102   Mike Gartner
                                         (1984-85)
                                         (50 goals, 52 assists)

Most Points, Left Wing,
  Season 87   Ryan Walter
                                        (1981-82)
                                        (38 goals, 49 assists)
Most Points, Rookie,
  Season 67   Bobby Carpenter
                                        (1981-82)
                                        (32 goals, 35 assists)
                                        Chris Valentine
                                        (1981-82)
                                        (30 goals, 37 assists)
Most Shutouts, Season 4   Al Jensen, Pat Riggin
                                       (1983-84)
Most Goals, Game 5   Bengt Gustafsson
                                      (Jan. 8/84)
Most Assists, Game 4   Several players
Most Points, Game 6   Several players

* NHL Record.

Coaching History

Jim Anderson, George Sullivan, Milt Schmidt, 1974-75; Milt Schmidt and Tom McVie, 1975-76; Tom McVie, 1976-77 to 1977-78; Danny Belisle, 1978-79; Danny Belisle and Gary Green, 1979-80; Gary Green, 1980-81; Gary Green and Bryan Murray, 1981-82; Bryan Murray, 1982-83 to date.

Captains' History

Doug Mohns, 1974-75; Bill Clement, Yvon Labre, 1975-76; Yvon Labre, 1976-77, 1977-78; Guy Charron, 1978-79; Ryan Walter, 1979-80 to 1981-82; Rod Langway, 1982-83 to 1985-86.

All-time Record vs. Other Clubs

Regular Season

		At Home								On Road								Total					
	GP	W	L	T	GF	GA	PTS	GP	W	L	T	GF	GA	PTS	GP	W	L	T	GF	GA	PTS			
Boston	23	5	13	5	69	98	15	24	5	16	3	56	108	13	47	10	29	8	125	206	28			
Buffalo	23	2	17	4	58	107	8	24	2	19	3	56	110	7	47	4	36	7	114	217	15			
**Calgary	22	10	9	3	85	84	23	21	4	16	1	47	90	9	43	14	25	4	132	174	32			
Chicago	22	12	7	3	89	74	27	21	5	12	4	64	90	14	43	17	19	7	153	164	41			
Detroit	28	15	10	3	107	87	33	27	6	13	8	80	106	20	55	21	23	11	187	193	53			
Edmonton	12	5	6	1	55	54	11	11	2	6	4	36	53	8	23	7	11	5	91	107	19			
Hartford	11	8	2	1	48	31	17	12	6	4	2	48	42	14	23	14	6	3	96	73	31			
Los Angeles	27	12	11	4	106	92	28	28	8	17	3	73	118	19	55	20	28	7	179	210	47			
Minnesota	21	7	8	6	62	69	20	22	5	12	5	63	92	15	43	12	20	11	125	161	35			
Montreal	28	8	14	6	67	107	22	27	1	23	3	52	150	5	55	9	37	9	119	257	27			
*New Jersey	29	22	4	3	136	74	47	30	14	10	6	93	92	34	59	36	14	9	229	166	81			
NY Islanders	32	10	18	4	92	117	24	32	6	25	1	88	150	13	64	16	43	5	180	267	37			
NY Rangers	32	16	9	7	138	109	39	32	10	18	4	119	156	24	64	26	27	11	257	265	63			
Philadelphia	32	9	16	7	118	132	25	32	8	23	1	89	158	17	64	17	39	8	207	290	42			
Pittsburgh	38	21	14	3	170	138	45	38	19	14	5	128	148	43	76	40	28	8	298	286	88			
Quebec	12	4	6	2	48	51	10	11	4	5	2	44	43	10	23	8	11	4	92	94	20			
St. Louis	22	12	9	1	86	71	25	21	6	10	5	63	94	17	43	18	19	6	149	165	42			
Toronto	23	12	9	2	89	72	26	24	8	13	3	85	108	19	47	20	22	5	174	180	45			
Vancouver	22	11	9	2	71	74	24	21	7	11	3	67	78	17	43	18	20	5	138	152	41			
Winnipeg	11	9	1	1	59	33	19	12	4	4	4	49	46	12	23	13	5	5	108	79	31			
Defunct Clubs	10	2	8	0	28	42	4	10	4	5	1	30	39	9	20	6	13	1	58	81	13			
Totals	480	212	200	68	1781	1716	492	480	134	275	71	1430	2071	339	960	346	475	139	3211	3787	831			

* Totals include those of Kansas City (1974-75, 1975-76) and Colorado (1976-77 through 1981-82)
** Totals include those of Atlanta (1974-75 through 1979-80) and (1976-77 through 1981-82)

Playoffs

	Series	W	L	GP	W	L	T	GF	GA	Last Mtg.	Round	Result
NY Islanders	1	1	0	3	3	0	0	11	4	1986	DSF	W 3-0
NY Rangers	5	1	4	23	8	14	0	61	73	1986	DF	L 2-4
Philadelphia	1	1	0	3	3	0	0	15	5	1984	DSF	W 3-0
Totals	7	3	4	29	14	14	0	87	82			

Playoff Results 1986-82

Year	Round	Opponent	Result	GF	GA
1986	DF	NY Rangers	L 2-4	25	20
	DSF	NY Islanders	W 3-0	11	4
1985	DSF	NY Islanders	L 2-3	12	14
1984	DF	NY Islanders	L 1-4	13	20
	DSF	Philadelphia	W 3-0	15	5
1983	DSF	NY Islanders	L 1-3	11	19

Abbreviations: Round: F – Final; CF – conference final; DF – division final; DSF – division semi-final; SF – semi-final; QF – quarter-final; P – preliminary round. GA – goals against; GF – goals for.

Retired Numbers

7	Yvon Labre	1973-1981

Entry Draft Selections 1986-74

1986
Pick
19	Jeff Greenlaw
40	Steve Seftel
60	Shawn Simpson
61	Jimmy Hrivnak
82	Erin Ginnell
103	John Purves
124	Stefan Nilsson
145	Peter Choma
166	Lee Davidson
187	Tero Toivola
208	Bobby Bobcock
229	John Schratz
250	Scott McCrory

1985
Pick
19	Yvon Corriveau
40	John Druce
61	Robert Murray
82	Bill Houlder
83	Larry Shaw
103	Claude Dumas
124	Doug Stromback
145	Jamie Nadjiwan
166	Mark Haarmann
187	Steve Hollett
208	Dallas Eakins
229	Steve Hrynewich
250	Frank DiMuzio

1984
Pick
17	Kevin Hatcher
34	Steve Leach
59	Michal Pivonka
80	Kris King
122	Vito Cramarossa
143	Timo Iijima
164	Frank Joo
185	Jim Thomson
205	Paul Cavallini
225	Mikhail Tatarinov
246	Per Schedrin

1983
Pick
75	Tim Bergland
95	Martin Bouliane
135	Dwaine Hutton
155	Marty Abrams
175	David Cowan
195	Yves Beaudoin
215	Alain Raymond
216	Anders Huss

1982
Pick
5	Scott Stevens
58	Milan Novy
89	Dean Evason
110	Ed Kastelic
152	Wally Schreiber
173	Jamie Reeves
194	Juha Nurmi
215	Wayne Prestage
236	John Holden
247	Marco Kallas

1981
Pick
3	Bob Carpenter
45	Eric Calder
68	Tony Kellin
89	Mike Siltala
91	Peter Sidorkiewicz
110	Jim McGeough
131	Risto Jalo
152	Gaetan Duchesne
173	George White
194	Chris Valentine

1980
Pick
5	Darren Veitch
47	Dan Miele
55	Torrie Robertson
89	Timo Blomqvist
110	Todd Bidner
131	Frank Perkins
152	Bruce Raboin
173	Peter Andersson
194	Tony Camazzola

1979
Pick
4	Mike Gartner
24	Errol Rausse
67	Harvie Pocza
88	Tim Tookey
109	Greg Theberge

1978
Pick
2	Ryan Walter
18	Tim Coulis
20	Paul Mulvey
23	Paul MacKinnon
38	Glen Currie
45	Jay Johnston
55	Bengt Gustafsson
71	Lou Franceschetti
88	Vince Magnan
105	Mats Hallin
122	Rick Sirois
139	Denis Pomerleau
156	Barry Heard
172	Mark Toffolo
187	Paul Hogan
189	Steve Barger
202	Rod Pacholsuk
213	Wes Jarvis
215	Ray Irwin

1977
Pick
3	Robert Picard
21	Mark Lofthouse
39	Eddy Godin
57	Nelson Burton
75	Denis Turcotte
93	Perry Schnarr
111	Rollie Bouton
127	Brent Tremblay
143	Don Micheletti
165	Archie Henderson

1976
Pick
1	Rick Green
15	Greg Carroll
37	Tom Rowe
55	Al Glendinning
73	Doug Patey
91	Jim Bedard
109	Dale Rideout
119	Allan Dumba

1975
Pick
18	Alex Forsyth
19	Peter Scammurra
55	Blair MacKasey
73	Craig Crawford
91	Roger Swanson
109	Clark Jantzie
127	Mike Fryia
144	Jim Ofrim
161	Mal Zinger

1974
Pick
1	Greg Joly
19	Mike Marson
37	John Paddock
55	Paul Nicholson
73	Jack Patterson
91	Brian Kinsella
109	Garth Malarchuk
127	John Nazar
144	Kelvin Erickson
161	Tony White
176	Ron Pronchuk
190	Dave McKee
202	Scott Mabley
212	Bernard Plante
220	Jacques Chiasson
225	Bill Bell
228	Robert Blanchet
231	Johnny Bower Jr.
234	Yves Plouffe
237	Terry Bozack
240	Gord Cole
242	Mike Cosentino
244	John Duncan
246	Barry Kerfoot
247	Ron Poole

Club Directory

Capital Centre
Landover, Maryland 20785
Phone 301/350-3400
TWX 710-827-9679
ENVOY ID TM.WSH
Capacity: 18,130

Board of Directors

Abe Pollin — Chairman	Albert H. Coheng	Edward Markowitz
David P. Bindeman	J. Martin Irving	Arthur K. Mason
Stewart L. Bindeman	James T. Lewis	Jack Meshel
James E. Cafritz	R. Robert Linowes	David M. Osnos
A. James Clark		Richard M. Patrick

Governor	Abe Pollin
President & Alternate Governor	Richard M. Patrick
Legal Counsel and Alternate Governors	David M. Osnos, Peter F. O'Malley
Vice President and General Manager	David Poile
Vice-President and Comptroller	Edmund Stelzer
Head Coach	Bryan Murray
Assistant Coach	Ron Lapointe, Terry Murray
Goaltending Coach	Warren Strelow
Director of Player Personnel and Recruitment	Jack Button
Assistant Director of Player Recruitment	Sam McMaster
Scouts	Bob Carpenter, Sr., Glen Dirk, Clare Rothernel, Bob Schmidt, Dick Todd
Head Trainer	Dick Young
Assistant Trainer	Doug Shearer
Director of Marketing	Lew Strudler
Assistant Director of Marketing	Debi Angus
Director of Public Relations	Lou Corletto
Director of Community Relations	Yvon Labre
Director of Promotions	Charles Copeland
Director of Season Subscriptions	Louise Robinson
Sales Representatives	Richard Merkle, Susan Hagman, Kerry Gregg
Administrative Assistant to General Manager	TBD
Assistant Comptroller	Aggie Ballard
Administrative Assistant to Marketing Director	Karen Merewitz
Administrative Assistant to PR Director	Pat Young
Administrative Assistant to Comptroller	Cathy Schwab
Accounting Assistants	David Berman, Crystal Coffren
Secretary/Receptionist	Heidi Swafford
Secretary to the Hockey Department	Denise Cox
Director of Telscreen/Television	Sheldon Shemer
Director of Clubhouse Operations	John "Chief" Gentry
Director of Program Sales	John Ross
Team Physicians	Dr. Stephen S. Haas, Dr. Carl C. MacCartee, Jr. Dr. Frank S. Melograna
Team Dentist	Dr. Howard Salob
Physical Therapist	John A. Romero R.P.T.
Dimensions of Rink	200 feet X 85 feet
Club Colors	Red, White and Blue
Radio Station/TV Station	WMAL (630 AM)/WDCA-TV (Channel 20) Home Team Sports (Cable)
Training Camp	Alexandria, Virginia

Below, left: Mike Gartner, left, and Bob Carpenter work in front off the Flyer goal.
Right: Dwight Schofield.

Winnipeg Jets

1985-86 Results: 26w-47L-7T 59 PTS. Third, Smythe Division

Year-by-Year Record

		Home			Road			Overall						
Season	GP	W	L	T	W	L	T	W	L	T	GF	GA	Pts.	Finished	Playoff Result
1985-86	80	18	19	3	8	28	4	26	47	7	295	372	59	3rd, Smythe Div.	Lost Div. Semi-Final
1984-85	80	21	13	6	22	14	4	43	27	10	358	332	96	2nd, Smythe Div.	Lost Div. Final
1983-84	80	17	15	8	14	23	3	31	38	11	340	374	73	4th, Smythe Div.	Lost Div. Semi-Final
1982-83	80	22	16	2	11	23	6	33	39	8	311	333	74	4th, Smythe Div.	Lost Div. Semi-Final
1981-82	80	18	13	9	15	20	5	33	33	14	319	332	80	2nd, Norris Div.	Lost Div. Semi-Final
1980-81	80	7	25	8	2	32	6	9	57	14	246	400	32	6th, Smythe Div.	Out of Playoffs
1979-80	80	13	19	8	7	30	3	20	49	11	214	314	51	5th, Smythe Div.	Out of Playoffs

Schedule

	Home			**Away**
Oct.	Thur. 9 Buffalo	**Oct.**	Thur. 16 Hartford
	Sun. 12 Edmonton		Sat. 18 Montreal
	Tue. 14 Boston		Sun. 19 Philadelphia
	Fri. 24 Calgary	**Nov.**	Sat. 1 NY Islanders
	Sun. 26 Chicago		Sun. 2 NY Rangers
	Wed. 29 Calgary		Tue. 4 Quebec
Nov.	Fri. 7 St. Louis		Tue. 11 Los Angeles
	Sun. 9 New Jersey		Thur. 13 Los Angeles
	Sun. 16 NY Islanders		Fri. 14 Vancouver
	Tue. 18 Pittsburgh		Wed. 26 Edmonton
	Fri. 21 Los Angeles		Thur. 27 Calgary
	Sun. 23 Los Angeles		Sat. 29 Vancouver
Dec.	Wed. 3 Washington	**Dec.**	Fri. 12 Edmonton
	Fri. 5 NY Rangers		Wed. 17 Chicago
	Sun. 7 Vancouver		Thur. 18 St. Louis
	Wed. 10 Edmonton		Tue. 23 Edmonton
	Sun. 14 Philadelphia		Fri. 26 Minnesota
	Sun. 21 Quebec		Wed. 31 Toronto
	Sun. 28 Minnesota	**Jan.**	Fri. 2 Buffalo
Jan.	Sun. 4 Vancouver		Sat. 10 Detroit
	Wed. 7 Buffalo		Tue. 13 Washington
	Fri. 9 Hartford		Wed. 14 Pittsburgh
	Sun. 18 Minnesota		Fri. 16 New Jersey
	Mon. 19 Vancouver		Tue. 27 NY Islanders
	Wed. 21 Edmonton		Wed. 28 NY Rangers
	Fri. 23 Toronto		Sat. 31 Boston*
Feb.	Wed. 4 Philadelphia	**Feb.**	Sun. 1 Washington
	Fri. 6 Los Angeles		Sat. 14 Montreal
	Sun. 8 Los Angeles*		Tue. 17 Quebec
	Fri. 20 Boston		Wed. 18 Detroit
	Sun. 22 Edmonton*		Tue. 24 Los Angeles
Mar.	Sun. 1 Calgary		Thur. 26 Los Angeles
	Sun. 8 Pittsburgh		Sat. 28 Calgary
	Wed. 11 Montreal	**Mar.**	Wed. 4 Chicago
	Fri. 13 Hartford		Thur. 5 St. Louis
	Sun. 15 Detroit*		Fri. 20 Vancouver
	Wed. 18 New Jersey		Thur. 26 Calgary
	Sun. 22 Vancouver*		Tue. 31 Edmonton
	Wed. 25 Calgary	**April**	Fri. 3 Vancouver
	Sun. 29 Toronto		Sun. 5 Calgary*

*Denotes afternoon game.

Home Starting Times:

Mondays through Fridays . . . . 7:35 p.m.
Saturdays & Sundays . . . . 7:05 p.m.
Matinees . . . . 2:35 p.m.

Franchise date: June 22, 1979

CAMPBELL CONFERENCE

7th NHL Season

Thomas Steen

1986-87 Player Personnel

FORWARDS	Ht.	Wt.	Place of Birth	Date	1985-86 Club
ACTON, Al	5-10	190	Unity, Sask.	8/28/65	Regina
ALEXANDER, Mike					
ANTONGIOVANNI, Patrick	6-3	220	Vancouver, B.C.	5/28/64	Auronzo (Italy)
BAILLARGEON, Joel	6-2	215	Charlesbourg, Que.	10/6/64	Sherbrooke
BOSCHMAN, Laurie	6-0	185	Major, Sask.	6/4/60	Winnipeg
CORNIER, Eric	6-2	201	Bathurst, N.B.	4/10/64	Moncton
DERLAGO, Bill	5-10	195	Birtle, Man.	8/25/58	Toronto-Boston-Winnipeg
DOURIS, Peter	6-1	192	Toronto, Ont.	2/19/66	Winnipeg
ELYNUIK, Pat	6-0	185	Foam Lake, Sask.	10/30/67	Prince Albert
ENDEAN, Craig	5-11	175	Kamloops, B.C.	4/13/68	Seattle
FLEMING, Gerry	6-5	225	Montreal, Que.	10/16/66	Verdun
GILHEN, Randy	5-10	190	Zweibrucken, W. Germany	6/13/63	Fort Wayne
HAMEL, Gilles	6-0	185	Asbestos, Que.	3/18/60	Buffalo
HAWERCHUK, Dale	5-11	185	Toronto, Ont.	4/4/63	Winnipeg
JARVENPAA, Hannu	6-0	193	Ilves, Finland	5/19/63	Karpat (Finland)
MACLEAN, Paul	6-0	205	Grostenquin, France	3/9/58	Winnipeg
MARTIN, Tom	6-2	195	Victoria, B.C.	5/11/64	Sherbrooke
McBAIN, Andrew	6-1	195	Toronto, Ont.	2/18/65	Winnipeg
MOXAM, Daran	5-10	180	Sudbury, Ont.	5/25/66	Belleville
MULLEN, Brian	5-10	180	New York, N.Y.	3/16/62	Winnipeg
NEWFELD, Ray	6-3	210	St. Boniface, Man.	4/15/59	Hartford-Winnipeg
NIELSEN, Len	5-9	170	Moose Jaw, Sask.	3/28/67	Regina
NILL, Jim	6-0	185	Hanna, Alta.	4/11/58	Winnipeg
POOLEY, Paul	6-0	175	Exeter, Ont.	8/2/60	Sherbrooke
POOLEY, Perry	6-0	175	Exeter, Ont.	8/2/60	Sherbrooke
RAY, Derek	5-11	200	Auburn, Wash.	10/30/63	Clarkson
SIMARD, Martin	6-3	210	Verdun, Que.	6/25/66	Hull
SMAIL, Doug	5-9	175	Moose Jaw, Sask.	9/2/57	Winnipeg
SPENCER, Michael	6-2	200	Weyburn, Sask.	4/12/63	N.A.I.T.
STEEN, Thomas	5-10	195	Tockmark, Sweden	6/8/60	Winnipeg
STEWART, Ryan	6-2	185	Prince George, B.C.	6/1/67	Prince Albert
TURNBULL, Perry	6-2	200	Bentley, Alta.	3/9/59	Winnipeg
VILGRAIN, Claude	6-1	195	Port-au-Prince, Haiti	3/1/63	Moncton
WILSON, Ron	5-9	175	Toronto, Ont.	5/13/56	Winnipeg
DEFENSEMEN					
BERRY, Brad	6-2	190	Bashaw, Alta.	4/1/65	Winnipeg
CAMPBELL, Scott	6-2	210	Toronto, Ont.	6/22/54	DID NOT PLAY
CARLYLE, Randy	5-10	200	Sudbury, Ont.	4/19/56	Winnipeg
CHANNELL, Craig	5-11	190	Moncton, N.B.	4/24/62	Ft. Wayne
DOLLAS, Bobby	6-2	215	Montreal, Que.	1/31/65	Winnipeg
ELLETT, Dave	6-1	200	Cleveland, Ohio	3/30/64	Winnipeg
KRC, Pavol	6-2	175	Banska Bystrica, Czech.	12/5/65	Banska Bystrica (Czech.)
KYTE, Jim	6-5	210	Ottawa, Ont.	3/21/64	Winnipeg
MAROIS, Mario	5-11	190	Ancienne Lorette, Que.	12/15/57	Quebec-Winnipeg
McFALL, Dan	6-0	192	Kenmore, N.Y.	4/8/63	Sherbrooke
OLAUSSON, Frederik	6-2	200	Vaxsjo, Sweden	10/5/66	Farjestad
PESSETTI, Ron	5-11	190	Laval, Que.	5/3/63	Western Michigan
SAMBRAY, James	6-1	185	Thunder Bay, Ont.	3/30/64	Thunder Bay
TAGLIANETTI, Peter	6-2	200	Framingham, Mass.	8/15/63	Winnipeg
WATTERS, Tim	5-11	180	Kamloops, B.C.	7/25/59	Winnipeg
GOALTENDERS					
BEHREND, Marc	6-1	185	Madison, Wis.	1/11/61	Sherbrooke
BERTHIAUME, Daniel	5-9	150	Longueuil, Que.	1/26/66	Chicoutimi
BOUCHARD, Daniel	6-0	190	Val d'Or, Que.	12/12/50	Winnipeg
DYCK, Larry	5-10	170	Winkler, Man.	12/15/65	Seattle
PENNEY, Steve	6-1	190	Ste-Foy, Que.	2/2/61	Montreal
QUIGLEY, David	5-10	155	Cap-de-la-Madelaine, Que.	1/17/65	Moncton
REDDICK, Eldon	5-8	170	Halifax, N.S.	10/6/64	Ft. Wayne
REIMER, Mark	5-11	168	Calgary, Alta.	3/23/67	Saskatoon
ROBERTSON, Tim	6-2	195	Regina, Sask.	11/29/64	York U.
VERSTAPPEN, Yannick	5-9	165	Geel, Belgium	9/30/67	Hyc Herentals (Belgium)

1985-86 Scoring

Regular Season

*–rookie

Pos	#	Player	Team	GP	G	A	Pts	+/–	PIM	PP	SH	GW	OT	S	%
F	10	Dale Hawerchuk	WPG	80	46	59	105	27–	44	18	2	2	1	313	14.7
F	16	Laurie Boschman	WPG	77	27	42	69	29–	241	3	2	2	0	158	17.1
F	25	Thomas Steen	WPG	78	17	47	64	29–	76	2	3	1	0	195	8.7
F	28	Ray Neufeld	HFD	16	5	10	15	3–	40	3	0	0	0	35	14.3
			WPG	60	20	28	48	17–	62	7	0	4	0	132	15.2
			Total	76	25	38	63	20–	102	10	0	4	0	167	15.0
F	19	Brian Mullen	WPG	79	28	34	62	17–	38	13	0	3	0	211	13.3
F	15	Paul MacLean	WPG	69	27	29	56	14–	74	11	0	2	0	168	16.1
F	27	Perry Turnbull	WPG	80	20	31	51	18–	183	6	0	2	0	168	11.9
D	8	Randy Carlyle	WPG	68	16	33	49	12–	93	3	0	2	1	152	10.5
D	2	Dave Ellett	WPG	80	15	31	46	38–	96	2	0	1	0	168	8.9
D	22	Mario Marois	QUE	20	1	12	13	10–	42	1	0	1	0	52	1.9
			WPG	56	4	28	32	22–	110	0	0	0	0	121	3.3
			Total	76	5	40	45	32–	152	1	0	1	0	173	2.9
F	11	Scott Arniel	WPG	80	18	25	43	8–	40	3	0	0	1	125	14.4
F	9	Doug Smail	WPG	73	16	26	42	10–	32	1	3	4	0	150	10.7
F	18	Bill Derlago	TOR	1	0	0	0	0	0	0	0	0	0	2	.0
			BOS	39	5	16	21	4	15	1	1	1	0	40	12.5
			WPG	27	5	5	10	13–	6	1	0	0	0	35	14.3
			Total	67	10	21	31	9–	21	2	1	1	0	77	13.0
D	7	Tim Watters	WPG	56	6	8	14	10–	97	0	0	0	0	37	16.2
F	17	Jim Nill	WPG	61	6	8	14	6–	75	0	0	1	1	35	17.1
F	24	Ron Wilson	WPG	54	6	7	13	2–	16	0	2	0	0	64	9.4
F	4	Bengt Lundholm	WPG	16	3	5	8	4–	6	0	1	0	0	14	21.4
F	20	Andrew McBain	WPG	28	3	3	6	11–	17	0	0	0	0	24	12.5
F	34	Dave Silk	WPG	32	2	4	6	6–	63	0	0	1	0	30	6.7
D	5	*Bobby Dollas	WPG	46	0	5	5	3–	66	0	0	0	0	50	.0
D	6	Jim Kyte	WPG	71	1	3	4	21–	126	0	0	0	0	28	3.6
F	14	*Anssi Melametsa	WPG	27	0	3	3	5–	2	0	0	0	0	20	.0
G	1	Brian Hayward	WPG	52	0	2	2	0	25	0	0	0	0	0	.0
F	28	*Ryan Stewart	WPG	3	1	0	1	0	0	0	0	0	0	5	20.0
F	26	Murray Eaves	WPG	4	1	0	1	2–	0	0	0	0	0	6	16.7
D	29	*Brad Berry	WPG	13	1	0	1	1	10	0	0	0	0	16	6.3
F	23	*Paul Pooley	WPG	3	0	1	1	1	0	0	0	0	0	2	.0
D	3	*Dan McFall	WPG	7	0	1	1	3–	0	0	0	0	0	2	.0
G	35	Dan Bouchard	WPG	32	0	1	1	0	38	0	0	0	0	0	.0
F	21	*Tom Martin	WPG	5	0	0	0	0	0	0	0	0	0	1	.0
G	31	Marc Behrend	WPG	9	0	0	0	0	0	0	0	0	0	0	.0
F	12	*Peter Douris	WPG	11	0	0	0	1–	0	0	0	0	0	0	.0
D	32	*Peter Taglianetti	WPG	18	0	0	0	1–	48	0	0	0	0	8	.0

Playoffs

* rookie

Pos	#	Player	Team	GP	G	A	Pts	+/–	PIM	PP	SH	GW	OT	S	%
D	22	Mario Marois	WPG	3	1	4	5	2–	6	1	0	0	0	12	8.3
F	19	Brian Mullen	WPG	3	1	2	3	1–	6	1	0	0	0	11	9.1
F	10	Dale Hawerchuk	WPG	3	0	3	3	2–	0	0	0	0	0	10	.0
F	28	Ray Neufeld	WPG	3	2	0	2	5–	10	1	0	0	0	5	40.0
F	25	Thomas Steen	WPG	3	1	1	2	0	4	0	1	0	0	5	20.0
F	15	Paul MacLean	WPG	2	1	0	1	2–	7	0	0	0	0	6	16.7
F	18	Bill Derlago	WPG	3	1	0	1	1	0	0	0	0	0	8	12.5
F	9	Doug Smail	WPG	3	1	0	1	0	0	0	0	0	0	7	14.3
F	16	Laurie Boschman	WPG	3	0	1	1	7–	6	0	0	0	0	3	.0
D	2	Dave Ellett	WPG	3	0	1	1	4–	0	0	0	0	0	7	.0
F	27	Perry Turnbull	WPG	3	0	1	1	5–	11	0	0	0	0	4	.0
G	31	Marc Behrend	WPG	1	0	0	0	0	0	0	0	0	0	0	.0
G		*Daniel Berthiaume	WPG	1	0	0	0	0	0	0	0	0	0	0	.0
G	35	Dan Bouchard	WPG	1	0	0	0	0	2	0	0	0	0	0	.0
F	34	Dave Silk	WPG	1	0	0	0	1	2	0	0	0	0	0	.0
F	24	Ron Wilson	WPG	1	0	0	0	0	0	0	0	0	0	1	.0
G	1	Brian Hayward	WPG	2	0	0	0	0	0	0	0	0	0	0	.0
F	4	Bengt Lundholm	WPG	2	0	0	0	0	2	0	0	0	0	1	.0
F	11	Scott Arniel	WPG	3	0	0	0	2–	12	0	0	0	0	3	.0
D	29	*Brad Berry	WPG	3	0	0	0	5–	0	0	0	0	0	2	.0
D	5	*Bobby Dollas	WPG	3	0	0	0	2–	2	0	0	0	0	0	.0
D	6	Jim Kyte	WPG	3	0	0	0	2–	12	0	0	0	0	4	.0
F	17	Jim Nill	WPG	3	0	0	0	3–	4	0	0	0	0	3	.0
D	32	*Peter Taglianetti	WPG	3	0	0	0	1–	2	0	0	0	0	0	.0

Coach and General Manager

MALONEY, DAN

Coach, Winnipeg Jets. Born in Barrie, Ont., September 24, 1950.

Dan Maloney was named coach of the Winnipeg Jets after guiding the Toronto Maple Leafs to their most successful season in nearly a decade in 1985-86. Maloney led the Leafs to the Norris Division Finals before losing to St. Louis in a dramatic seven-game series. Prior to his four-year stint with the Leafs which included two years as an assistant coach, Maloney played for 11 seasons in the NHL from 1970-71 through 1981-82. The rugged left-winger played for Chicago, Los Angeles and Detroit before finishing his career with Toronto. In 737 regular-season games, Maloney scored 192 goals and 259 assists for 451 points.

NHL Coaching Record

		Regular Season					Playoffs			
Team		Games	W	L	T	%	Games	W	L	%
Toronto	1984-85	80	20	52	8	.300	...	...	...	....
Toronto	1985-86	80	25	48	7	.356	10	6	4	.600
NHL Totals		**160**	**45**	**100**	**15**	**.328**	**10**	**6**	**4**	**.600**

FERGUSON, JOHN BOWIE

Vice-President and General Manager, Winnipeg Jets. Born in Vancouver, B.C., September 5, 1938.

John Ferguson was appointed general manager of the Jets on November 22, 1978 and was named the *Hockey News* Executive of the Year for the 1981-82 season after Winnipeg placed second in the Norris Division. After an eight-year career as a rugged left winger for the Montreal Canadiens, Ferguson retired from active play at the completion of the 1971-72 season. He moved to an assistant coaching position with Team Canada in September of 1972 for the dramatic eight game series against the Soviet Union. Over the next four-year period, Ferguson remained out of professional hockey to pursue private business interests and also served as coach and general manager of the Montreal Quebecois of the National Lacrosse League. He returned to the NHL in 1976 when he assumed coach and general manager duties with the New York Rangers and served in the dual capacities until joining the Jets in the fall of 1978.

Club Records

Team

(Figures in brackets for season records are games played; records for fewest points, wins, ties, losses, goals, goals against are for 70 or more games)

Most Points. 96 1984-85 (80)
Most Wins. 43 1984-85 (80)
Most Ties 14 1980-81 (80)
.................................1981-82 (80)
Most Losses 57 1980-81 (80)
Most Goals 358 1984-85 (80)
Most Goals Against. 400 1980-81 (80)
Fewest Points 32 1980-81 (80)
Fewest Wins 9 1980-81 (80)
Fewest Ties. 8 1982-83 (80)
Fewest Losses. 27 1984-85 (80)
Fewest Goals 214 1979-80 (80)
Fewest Goals Against 314 1979-80 (80)
Longest Winning Streak
  Over-all . . . . .9 Mar. 8-27/85
  Home . . . . .6 Feb. 28-Mar. 24/82
.................................Dec. 2-22/84
  Away. . . . . .8 Feb. 25-Apr. 6/85
Longest Undefeated Streak
  Over-all . . . . .13 Mar. 8-Apr. 7/85
.................................(10 wins, 3 ties)
  Home . . . . .11 Dec. 23/83
.................................Feb. 5/84
.................................(6 wins, 5 ties)
  Away. . . . . .9 Feb. 25-Apr. 7/85 (8
.................................wins, 1 tie)
Longest Losing Streak
  Over-all . . . . .10 Nov. 30-
.................................Dec. 20/80
  Home . . . . .4 Three times
  Away. . . . . .9 Dec. 26/79-
.................................Jan. 20/80
Longest Winless Streak
  Over-all . . . .*30 Oct. 19-
.................................Dec. 20/80
.................................(23 losses, 7 ties)
  Home . . . . .14 Oct. 19-
.................................Dec. 14/80
.................................(9 losses, 5 ties)
  Away. . . . . .18 Oct. 10-
.................................Dec. 20/80
.................................(16 losses, 2 ties)

Most Shutouts, Season 3 1981-82 (80)
Most Pen. Mins.,..................1985-86 (80)
  Season. 1,784
Most Goals, Game . . . . . . .12 Feb. 25/85
.................................(Wpg. 12 at NYR. 5)

Individual

Most Seasons . . . . .7 Ron Wilson
Most Games . . . . .431 Morris Lukowich
Most Goals, Career . . . . . .221 Dale Hawerchuk
Most Assists, Career . . . . .310 Dale Hawerchuk
Most Points, Career . . . . .531 Dale Hawerchuk
.................................(221 goals, 310 assists)
Most Pen. Mins., Career . . .598 Jimmy Mann
Most Shutouts, Career. . . . . .3 Markus Mattsson
Longest Consecutive
  Games Streak . . . . .212 Dave Christian
.................................(Mar. 2/80-Jan. 1/83)
Most Goals, Season . . . . . .53 Dale Hawerchuk
.................................(1984-85)
Most Assists, Season . . . .77 Dale Hawerchuk
.................................(1984-85)
Most Points, Season . . . . .130 Dale Hawerchuk
.................................(1984-85)
.................................(53 goals, 77 assists)
Most Pen. Mins., Season . . .287 Jimmy Mann
.................................(1979-80)
Most Points, Defenseman
  Season . . . . .74 David Babych
.................................(1982-83)
.................................(13 goals, 61 assists)
Most Points, Center,
  Season . . . . .130 Dale Hawerchuk
.................................(1984-85)
.................................(53 goals, 77 assists)
Most Points, Right Wing,
  Season . . . . .101 Paul Maclean
.................................(1984-85)
.................................(41 goals, 60 assists)
Most Points, Left Wing,
  Season . . . . .92 Morris Lukowich
.................................(1981-82)
.................................(43 goals, 49 assists)

Most Points, Rookie,
  Season . . . . .103 Dale Hawerchuk
.................................(1981-82)
.................................(45 goals, 58 assists)
Most Shutouts, Season . . . . .2 Markus Mattsson
.................................(1979-80)
.................................Doug Soetaert
.................................(1981-82)
.................................Dan Bouchard
.................................(1985-86)
Most Goals, Game . . . . .5 Willy Lindstrom
.................................(Mar. 2/82)
Most Assists, Game . . . . . .5 Dale Hawerchuk
.................................(Mar. 6/84)
Most Points, Game . . . . . . .6 Willy Lindstrom
.................................(Mar. 2/82)
.................................Dale Hawerchuk
.................................(Dec. 14/83)
.................................Thomas Steen
.................................(Oct. 24/84)

* NHL Record.

Coaching History

Tom McVie, 1979-80; Tom McVie and Bill Sutherland, 1980-81; Tom Watt, 1981-82 to 1982-83; Tom Watt, John Ferguson and Barry Long, 1983-84; Barry Long, and John Ferguson, 1985-86. Dan Maloney, 1986-87.

Captains' History

Lars-Erik Sjoberg, 1979-80; Morris Lukowich, 1980-81; Dave Christian, 1981-82; Dave Christian, Lucien DeBlois, 1982-83; Dale Hawerchuk, 1984-85, 1985-86.

All-time Record vs. Other Clubs
Regular Season

		At Home						On Road						Total					
	GP	W	L	T	GF	GA	PTS	GP	W	L	T	GF	GA	PTS	GP	W	L	T	GF	GA	Pts
Boston	11	5	5	1	41	43	11	12	1	9	2	41	63	4	23	6	14	3	82	106	15
Buffalo	11	4	5	2	39	40	10	12	0	11	1	28	63	1	23	4	16	3	67	103	11
**Calgary	21	5	11	5	82	94	15	22	2	17	3	67	123	7	28	8	149	217	22
Chicago	14	7	5	2	61	55	16	13	4	8	1	46	68	9	27	11	13	3	107	123	25
Detroit	14	6	4	4	53	40	16	13	6	5	2	55	47	14	27	12	9	6	108	87	30
Edmonton	21	5	15	1	92	119	11	22	5	17	0	76	123	10	43	10	32	1	168	242	21
Hartford	11	6	5	0	43	43	12	12	3	6	3	39	56	9	23	9	11	3	82	99	21
Los Angeles	22	10	7	5	106	93	25	21	12	7	2	96	88	26	43	22	14	7	202	181	51
Minnesota	13	4	8	1	46	49	9	14	5	8	1	40	63	11	27	9	16	2	86	112	20
Montreal	12	3	6	3	38	53	9	11	2	9	0	29	61	4	23	5	15	3	67	114	13
*New Jersey	12	9	2	1	49	28	19	11	4	5	2	40	40	10	23	13	7	3	89	68	29
NY Islanders	12	3	8	1	36	50	7	11	2	5	4	28	41	8	23	5	13	5	64	91	15
NY Rangers	12	6	5	1	47	40	13	11	4	6	1	54	64	9	23	10	11	2	101	104	22
Philadelphia	11	6	5	0	41	39	12	12	2	10	0	38	65	4	23	8	15	0	79	104	16
Pittsburgh	11	5	6	0	45	43	10	12	3	9	0	36	52	6	23	8	15	0	81	95	16
Quebec	12	6	4	2	49	49	14	11	4	6	1	37	50	9	23	10	10	3	86	99	23
St. Louis	14	6	3	5	51	47	17	13	4	6	3	48	62	11	27	10	9	8	99	109	28
Toronto	13	6	6	1	62	60	13	14	3	10	1	67	56	21	27	16	9	2	129	116	34
Vancouver	21	10	6	5	88	86	25	22	5	14	3	70	93	13	43	15	20	8	158	179	38
Washington	12	4	4	4	46	49	12	11	1	9	1	33	59	3	23	5	13	5	79	108	15
Totals	280	116	120	44	1115	1120	276	280	79	170	31	968	1337	189	560	195	290	75	2083	2457	465

* Totals include of Colorado Rockies (1979-80, 1980-81 and 1981-82)
** Totals include those of Atlanta Flames (1979-80)

Playoffs

	Series	W	L	GP	W	L	T	GF	GA	Last Mtg.	Round	Result
Calgary	2	1	1	7	3	3	0	23	28	1986	DSF	L 0-3
Edmonton	3	0	3	10	0	10	0	27	54	1985	DF	L 0-4
St. Louis	1	0	1	4	1	3	0	13	20	1982	DSF	L 1-3
Totals	6	1	5	21	4	16	0	63	132			

Playoff Results 1986-82

Year	Round	Opponent	Result	GF	GA
1985	DSF	Calgary	L 0-3	8	15
1985	DF	Edmonton	L 0-4	11	22
	DSF	Calgary	W 3-1	15	13
1984	DSF	Edmonton	L 0-3	7	18
1983	DSF	Edmonton	L 0-3	9	14
1982	DSF	St. Louis	L 1-3	20	13

Abbreviations: Round: F – Final; **CF** – conference final; **DF** – division final; **DSF** – division semi-final; **SF** – semi-final; **QF** – quarter-final; **P** – preliminary round. **GA** – goals against; **GF** – goals for.

Entry Draft
Selections 1986-79

1986
Pick
8	Pat Elynuik
29	Teppo Numminen
50	Esa Palosaari
71	Hannu Jarvenpaa
92	Craig Endean
113	Robertson Bateman
155	Frank Furlan
176	Mark Green
197	John Blue
218	Matt Cote
239	Arto Blomsten

1985
Pick
18	Ryan Stewart
39	Roger Ohman
60	Dan Berthiaume
81	Fredrik Olausson
102	John Borrell
123	Danton Cole
144	Brent Mowery
165	Tom Draper
186	Nevin Kardum
207	Dave Quigley
228	Chris Norton
249	Anssi Melametsa

1984
Pick
30	Peter Douris
68	Chris Mills
72	Sean Clement
93	Scott Schneider
114	Gary Lorden
135	Luciano Borsato
156	Brad Jones
177	Gord Whitaker
197	Rick Forst
218	Mike Warus
238	Jim Edmonds

1983
Pick
8	Andrew McBain
14	Bobby Dollas
29	Brad Berry
43	Peter Taglianetti
69	Bob Essensa
89	Harry Armstrong
109	Joel Baillargeon
129	Iain Duncan
149	Ron Pessetti
169	Todd Flichel
189	Cory Wright
209	Eric Cormier
229	Jamie Husgen

1982
Pick
12	Jim Kyte
74	Tom Martin
75	Dave Ellett
96	Tim Mishler
138	Derek Ray
159	Guy Gosselin
180	Tom Ward
201	Mike Savage
222	Bob Shaw
243	Jan Urban Ericson

1981
Pick
1	Dale Hawerchuk
22	Scott Arniel
43	Jyrki Seppa
64	Kirk McCaskill
85	Marc Behrend
106	Bob O'Connor
127	Peter Nilsson
148	Dan McFaul
169	Greg Dick
190	Vladimir Kadlec
211	Dave Kirwin

1980
Pick
2	David Babych
23	Moe Mantha
44	Murray Eaves
65	Guy Fournier
86	Glen Ostir
107	Ron Loustel
128	Brian Mullen
135	Mike Lauen
149	Sandy Beadle
170	Ed Christian
191	Dave Chartier

1979
Pick
19	Jimmy Mann
40	Dave Christian
61	Bill Whelton
82	Pat Daley
103	Thomas Steen
124	Tim Watters

Below, left: Paul MacLean; right: Dale Hawerchuk

Club Directory

Winnipeg Arena
15-1430 Maroons Road
Winnipeg, Manitoba R3G 0L5
Phone 204/772-9491
TWX 610-671-2586
ENVOY ID TM.WPG
Capacity: 15,250

Board of Directors
Barry L. Shenkarow	Bill Davis	Marvin Shenkarow
Harvey Sector	John B. Ferguson	Michael Dennehy
Don Henderson	Jerry Kruk	D.A. (Abe) Yanofsky

President & Governor. . . . . Barry L. Shenkarow

Hockey Operations
Vice-President & General Manager. . . . . John B. Ferguson
Assistant General Manager & Director of
Scouting & Recruitment . . . . Mike Smith
Assistant to the General Manager . . . . Barry Long
Coach. . . . . Dan Maloney
Assistant Coaches. . . . . Bill Sutherland, Rick Bowness
Chief Scout . . . . Les Binkley
Eastern Scout. . . . . Tom Savage
Western Scout . . . . Charlie Hodge
Special Assignments . . . . Bill Lesuk
Scouts. . . . . Joe Yannetti, Bruce Southern, Ken Chisholm, John O'Flaherty

Executive Ass't. to Vice President &
General Manager . . . . Pat MacDonald

Finance and Administration
Vice-President, Finance & Administration. . . . . Romeo Verrier
Accountant and Office Manager. . . . . Don Binda
Ticket Manager and Travel Co-Ordinator . . . . . Murray Harding
Assistant Accountant . . . . Glenda Leiske
Properties Manager . . . . Lori Kupskay
Novelty Store Attendant . . . . Trish Benson
Receptionist . . . . Val Kuhn

Public Relations
Director of Hockey & Media Information. . . . . . Ralph Carter
Director of Community & Media Relations . . . . . Lyle Moffat
Executive Assistant of
Public Relations and Marketing . . . . Lori Zahara

Marketing
Director of Marketing . . . . Madeline Hanson
Administrative Assistant . . . . Dianne Gabbs
Marketing Representatives . . . . Dianne Gabbs, Todd McLuckie, Val Overwater

Dressing Room
Athletic Therapist . . . . Chuck Badcock
Equipment Manager. . . . . Jack Stouffer
Assistant Equipment Manager . . . . Pat O'Neill
Dressing Room Co-ordinator . . . . Dave Mann
Team Doctor . . . . Dr. Wayne Hildahl
Team Dentist . . . . Dr. Gene Solmundson
Team Colors . . . . Blue, Red and White
Dimensions of Rink . . . . 200 feet by 85 feet
Training Camp . . . . Winnipeg
Press Box Location . . . . East Side
TV Channel . . . . CKY-TV
Radio Station . . . . CKY AM 580
Play-by-Play. . . . . Curt Keilback (TV and Radio)
Color Commentary . . . . TBA (TV), Ken Nicolson (Radio)

1985-86 Final Statistics

Standings

Abbreviations: * – rookie eligible for Calder Trophy; **GA** – goals against; **GF** – goals for; **GP** – games played; **L** – losses; **PTS** – points; **T** – ties; **W** – wins; **%** – percentage of games won.

CLARENCE CAMPBELL CONFERENCE

Norris Division

	GP	W	L	T	GF	GA	PTS	%
Chicago	80	39	33	8	351	349	86	.538
Minnesota	80	38	33	9	327	305	85	.531
St. Louis	80	37	34	9	302	291	83	.519
Toronto	80	25	48	7	311	386	57	.356
Detroit	80	17	57	6	266	415	40	.250

Smythe Division

	GP	W	L	T	GF	GA	PTS	%
Edmonton	80	56	17	7	426	310	119	.744
Calgary	80	40	31	9	354	315	89	.556
Winnipeg	80	26	47	7	295	372	59	.369
Vancouver	80	23	44	13	282	333	59	.369
Los Angeles	80	23	49	8	284	389	54	.338

PRINCE OF WALES CONFERENCE

Adams Division

	GP	W	L	T	GF	GA	PTS	%
Quebec	80	43	31	6	330	289	92	.575
Montreal	80	40	33	7	330	280	87	.544
Boston	80	37	31	12	311	288	86	.538
Hartford	80	40	36	4	332	302	84	.525
Buffalo	80	37	37	6	296	291	80	.500

Patrick Division

	GP	W	L	T	GF	GA	PTS	%
Philadelphia	80	53	23	4	335	241	110	.688
Washington	80	50	23	7	315	272	107	.669
NY Islanders	80	39	29	12	327	284	90	.563
NY Rangers	80	36	38	6	280	276	78	.488
Pittsburgh	80	34	38	8	313	305	76	.475
New Jersey	80	28	49	3	300	374	59	.369

Individual Leaders

Abbreviations: * – rookie eligible for Calder Trophy; **A** – assists; **G** – goals; **GP** – games played; **GT** – game-tying goals; **GW** – game-winning goals; **PIM** – penalties in minutes; **PP** – power play goals; **PTS** – points; **S** – shots on goal; **SH** – short-handed goals; **%** – percentage of shots resulting in goals; **+/−** – difference between Goals For (**GF**) scored when a player is on the ice with his team at even strength or short-handed and Goals Against (**GA**) scored when the same player is on the ice with his team at even strength or on a power play.

Scoring Leaders

Player	Team	GP	G	A	PTS	+/−	PIM	PP	SH	GW	GT	S	%
Wayne Gretzky	Edmonton	80	52	163	215	71	46	11	3	6	1	350	14.9
Mario Lemieux	Pittsburgh	79	48	93	141	6−	43	17	0	4	0	276	17.4
Paul Coffey	Edmonton	79	48	90	138	61	120	9	9	3	1	307	15.6
Jari Kurri	Edmonton	78	68	63	131	45	22	16	6	9	1	236	28.8
Mike Bossy	NY Islanders	80	61	62	123	30	14	21	1	9	2	302	20.2
Peter Stastny	Quebec	76	41	81	122	2	60	15	0	8	0	207	19.8
Denis Savard	Chicago	80	47	69	116	7	111	14	1	8	2	279	16.8
Mats Naslund	Montreal	80	43	67	110	11	16	19	0	7	1	223	19.3
Dale Hawerchuk	Winnipeg	80	46	59	105	27−	44	18	2	2	1	313	14.7
Neal Broten	Minnesota	80	29	76	105	14	47	6	0	0	0	193	15.0
Michel Goulet	Quebec	75	53	51	104	6	64	28	0	3	1	244	21.7
Glenn Anderson	Edmonton	72	54	48	102	38	90	18	2	9	0	243	22.2
Bernie Federko	St. Louis	80	34	68	102	10	34	16	0	2	0	167	20.4
Troy Murray	Chicago	80	45	54	99	32	94	9	5	7	0	197	22.8
Brian Propp	Philadelphia	72	40	57	97	24	47	11	2	5	0	317	12.6
Bernie Nicholls	Los Angeles	80	36	61	97	5−	78	10	4	0	0	281	12.8
Bryan Trottier	NY Islanders	78	37	59	96	29	72	5	1	3	0	185	20.0
Marcel Dionne	Los Angeles	80	36	58	94	22−	42	11	0	4	1	284	12.7
Joe Mullen	St. L/Cgy.	77	44	46	90	4−	21	14	0	8	0	203	21.7
Dino Ciccarelli	Minnesota	75	44	45	89	12	51	19	0	5	1	262	16.8
Dave Andreychuk	Buffalo	80	36	51	87	3	61	12	0	3	0	225	16.0
Bobby Smith	Montreal	79	31	55	86	10	55	5	0	7	1	202	15.3
Tim Kerr	Philadelphia	76	58	26	84	5−	79	34	0	8	0	285	20.4
Keith Crowder	Boston	78	38	46	84	14	177	20	0	4	1	184	20.7
Mark Messier	Edmonton	63	35	49	84	36	68	10	5	7	0	201	17.4

INDIVIDUAL LEADERS

Goals

Player	Team	GP	G
Jari Kurri	Edmonton	78	68
Mike Bossy	NY Islanders	80	61
Tim Kerr	Philadelphia	76	58
Glenn Anderson	Edmonton	72	54

Assists

Player	Team	GP	A
Wayne Gretzky	Edmonton	80	163
Mario Lemieux	Pittsburgh	79	93
Paul Coffey	Edmonton	79	90
Peter Stastny	Quebec	76	81

Power Play Goals

Player	Team	GP	PP
Tim Kerr	Philadelphia	76	34
Michel Goulet	Quebec	75	28
Mike Bossy	NY Islanders	80	21
Doug Shedden	Pit-Det	78	21
Keith Crowder	Boston	78	20

Short-Handed Goals

Player	Team	GP	SH
Paul Coffey	Edmonton	79	9
Mark Howe	Philadelphia	77	7
Jari Kurri	Edmonton	78	6
Dave Poulin	Philadelphia	79	6

Game-Winning Goals

Player	Team	GP	GW
Glenn Anderson	Edmonton	72	9
Mike Bossy	NY Islanders	80	9
Jari Kurri	Edmonton	78	9
Kevin Dineen	Hartford	57	8
Tim Kerr	Philadelphia	76	8
Joe Mullen	St.L-Cgy.	77	8
Denis Savard	Chicago	80	8
Peter Stastny	Quebec	76	8

Game-Tying Goals

Player	Team	GP	GT
Brian Bellows	Minnesota	77	2
Mike Bossy	NY Islanders	80	2
Denis Savard	Chicago	80	2
Brent Sutter	NY Islanders	61	2
Steve Tambellini	Vancouver	48	2

Shots

Player	Team	GP	S
Wayne Gretzky	Edmonton	80	350
Brian Propp	Philadelphia	72	317
Dale Hawerchuk	Winnipeg	80	313
Paul Coffey	Edmonton	79	307
Mike Bossy	NY Islanders	80	302

First Goals

Player	Team	GP	FG
Ilkka Sinisalo	Philadelphia	74	10
Peter Stastny	Quebec	76	10
Tim Kerr	Philadelphia	76	9
Mario Lemieux	Pittsburgh	79	9

Shooting Percentage (minimum 80 shots)

Player	Team	GP	G	S	%
Jari Kurri	Edmonton	78	68	236	28.8
Terry Ruskowski	Pittsburgh	73	26	91	28.6
Craig Laughlin	Washington	75	30	114	26.3
Charlie Simmer	Boston	55	36	141	25.5
Pierre Larouche	NY Rangers	28	20	85	23.5

CONSECUTIVE SCORING STREAKS

Goals

Games	Player	Team	G
10	Jari Kurri	Edmonton	10
9	Alan Haworth	Washington	11
7	Jari Kurri	Edmonton	12
7	Pierre Larouche	NY Rangers	10
7	Dave Taylor	Los Angeles	8
7	Geoff Courtnall	Boston	7
6	Jari Kurri	Edmonton	10
6	Mario Lemieux	Pittsburgh	10
6	Glenn Anderson	Edmonton	9
6	Kevin Dineen	Hartford	8
6	Michel Goulet	Quebec	8
6	Ilkka Sinisalo	Philadelphia	8
6	Mark Messier	Edmonton	7
6	Michel Goulet	Quebec	6
6	Al Secord	Chicago	6

Assists

Games	Player	Team	A
17	Paul Coffey	Edmonton	27
14	Wayne Gretzky	Edmonton	39
14	Mario Lemieux	Pittsburgh	23
12	Wayne Gretzky	Edmonton	24
12	Ken Linseman	Boston	19
11	Wayne Gretzky	Edmonton	24
9	Peter Stastny	Quebec	17
9	*Per-Erik Eklund	Philadelphia	14
9	Bengt Gustafsson	Washington	12
8	Wayne Gretzky	Edmonton	18
8	Denis Savard	Chicago	15
8	Neal Broten	Minnesota	14
8	Dale Hawerchuk	Winnipeg	11
8	Ron Sutter	Philadelphia	11
8	Dave Babych	Winnipeg	10
8	Denis Savard	Chicago	8

Points

Games	Player	Team	G	A	PTS
39	Wayne Gretzky	Edmonton	33	75	108
28	Mario Lemieux	Pittsburgh	21	38	59
28	Paul Coffey	Edmonton	16	39	55
20	Brian Bellows	Minnesota	11	18	29
19	Denis Savard	Chicago	16	21	37
18	Wayne Gretzky	Edmonton	10	45	55
18	Mats Naslund	Montreal	13	23	36
18	Bobby Smith	Montreal	12	17	29
15	Jari Kurri	Edmonton	18	13	31
15	J.F. Sauve	Quebec	6	21	27
15	Tim Kerr	Philadelphia	19	5	24
15	Ken Linseman	Boston	4	20	24
15	Mike Bossy	NY Islanders	10	13	23
15	Neal Broten	Minnesota	3	19	22
14	Michel Goulet	Quebec	11	7	18
13	Peter Stastny	Quebec	8	21	29
13	Marcel Dionne	Los Angeles	5	13	18

Three-or-More-Goal Games

Player	Team	Date	Final Score	G
Paul Gagne	New Jersey	Oct. 10	N.J. 6 PHI 5	3
Charlie Simmer	Boston	Oct. 12	BOS 9 DET 2	3
Jim Fox	Los Angeles	Oct. 12	NYI 5 L.A. 4	3
Rick Vaive	Toronto	Oct. 16	WSH 6 TOR 5	3
Charlie Simmer (2)	Boston	Oct. 19	BOS 6 CGY 3	3
Ron Francis	Hartford	Oct. 19	MTL 6 HFD 11	3
Perry Turnbull	Winnipeg	Oct. 23	EDM 9 WPG 3	3
Carey Wilson	Calgary	Oct. 26	DET 4 CGY 7	3
Glenn Anderson	Edmonton	Oct. 28	EDM 6 CGY 4	3
Mike Gartner	Washington	Oct. 29	STL 3 WSH 4	3
Danny Gare	Detroit	Oct. 30	PIT 3 DET 6	3
Wayne Gretzky	Edmonton	Nov. 3	TOR 1 EDM 7	3
Tim Kerr	Philadelphia	Nov. 3	L.A. 4 PHI 7	3
Patrick Flatley	NY Islanders	Nov. 6	NYI 5 TOR 4	4
Dave Lumley	Edmonton	Nov. 8	VAN 0 EDM 13	3
Tim Kerr	Philadelphia	Nov. 9	BOS 5 PHI 5	3
Tony Tanti	Vancouver	Nov. 13	PIT 6 VAN 5	3
Rick Vaive (2)	Toronto	Nov. 14	BOS 6 TOR 6	3
Greg Terrion	Toronto	Nov. 16	CHI 4 TOR 5	3
Neal Broten	Minnesota	Nov. 17	MIN 5 CHI 5	3
Petri Skriko	Vancouver	Nov. 19	VAN 7 DET 5	3
Bob Brooke	NY Rangers	Nov. 20	TOR 3 NYR 7	3
Gilbert Perreault	Buffalo	Nov. 22	QUE 5 BUF 7	3
Ron Francis (2)	Hartford	Nov. 23	WPG 1 HFD 8	3
Russ Courtnall	Toronto	Nov. 23	DET 3 TOR 9	3
Dave Poulin	Philadelphia	Nov. 24	PIT 4 PHI 7	3
Mark Hunter	St Louis	Nov. 26	TOR 1 STL 5	3
Mike Bossy	NY Islanders	Nov. 27	NYI 4 MIN 4	3
Peter Stastny	Quebec	Nov. 28	BOS 0 QUE 3	3
Craig MacTavish	Edmonton	Dec. 1	CGY 3 EDM 5	3
Tony McKegney	Minnesota	Dec. 3	CHI 2 MIN 9	3
Warren Young	Detroit	Dec. 7	DET 4 STL 5	3
Jari Kurri	Edmonton	Dec. 7	MIN 4 EDM 8	3
Carey Wilson (2)	Calgary	Dec. 10	L.A. 5 CGY 9	3
Greg Paslawski	St Louis	Dec. 10	EDM 3 STL 7	3
Glenn Anderson (2)	Edmonton	Dec. 11	EDM 12 CHI 9	3
Jari Kurri (2)	Edmonton	Dec. 11	EDM 12 CHI 9	3
Scott Bjugstad	Minnesota	Dec. 11	MIN 10 DET 2	3
Brian Bellows	Minnesota	Dec. 11	MIN 10 DET 2	4
Paul Lawless	Hartford	Dec. 13	HFD 6 BUF 4	3
Brent Ashton	Quebec	Dec. 14	N.J. 3 QUE 9	3
Michel Goulet	Quebec	Dec. 14	N.J. 3 QUE 9	4
Lindy Ruff	Buffalo	Dec. 15	QUE 2 BUF 6	4
Denis Savard	Chicago	Dec. 15	DET 4 CHI 6	3
Sylvain Turgeon	Hartford	Dec. 18	CGY 3 HFD 4	3
Larry Robinson	Montreal	Dec. 19	MTL 4 QUE 5	3
Paul Coffey	Edmonton	Dec. 20	L.A. 4 EDM 9	3
Jari Kurri (3)	Edmonton	Dec. 20	L.A. 4 EDM 9	4
Scott Bjugstad (2)	Minnesota	Dec. 22	MIN 8 N.J. 3	3
Greg Paslawski (2)	St Louis	Dec. 26	CHI 6 STL 9	3
Tim Kerr (3)	Philadelphia	Dec. 27	PHI 6 VAN 1	3
Steve Ludzik	Chicago	Dec. 28	CHI 7 WSH 4	3
Mike McPhee	Montreal	Dec. 28	N.J. 3 MTL 8	3
Mike Foligno	Buffalo	Dec. 29	NYI 3 BUF 6	3
Steve Kasper	Boston	Dec. 31	BOS 6 BUF 3	3
Wayne Gretzky (2)	Edmonton	Dec. 31	PHI 3 EDM 4	3
Mike Bullard	Pittsburgh	Dec. 31	PIT 8 STL 4	3
Mario Lemieux	Pittsburgh	Dec. 31	PIT 8 STL 4	4
Troy Murray	Chicago	Jan. 1	PIT 4 CHI 7	3
Al Secord	Chicago	Jan. 1	PIT 4 CHI 7	3
Mike Gartner (2)	Washington	Jan. 4	N.J. 3 WSH 9	3
*Kjell Dahlin	Montreal	Jan. 6	STL 2 MTL 9	3
Kevin Dineen	Hartford	Jan. 7	HFD 9 CGY 1	3
*Dean Evason	Hartford	Jan. 7	HFD 9 CGY 1	3
Wayne Gretzky (3)	Edmonton	Jan. 8	EDM 9 TOR 11	3
Miroslav Frycer	Toronto	Jan. 8	EDM 9 TOR 11	4
Tony Tanti (2)	Vancouver	Jan. 21	N.J. 3 VAN 5	3
Mike Bullard (2)	Pittsburgh	Jan. 22	PIT 7 EDM 4	3
Bryan Trottier	NY Islanders	Jan. 24	NYI 7 WSH 5	3
Rick Middleton	Boston	Jan. 25	DET 3 BOS 6	3
Bernie Nicholls	Los Angeles	Feb. 1	L.A. 9 WPG 6	3
Dave Andreychuk	Buffalo	Feb. 6	BUF 8 BOS 6	5
Neal Broten (2)	Minnesota	Feb. 6	TOR 7 MIN 8	3
Curt Fraser	Chicago	Feb. 13	TOR 4 CHI 5	3
Miroslav Frycer (2)	Toronto	Feb. 13	TOR 4 CHI 5	3
Mike Bossy (2)	NY Islanders	Feb. 15	N.J. 5 NYI 6	3
Doug Shedden	Pittsburgh	Feb. 15	VAN 4 PIT 9	3
Troy Murray (2)	Chicago	Feb. 19	MIN 6 CHI 5	3
Brian Lawton	Minnesota	Feb. 19	MIN 6 CHI 5	3
Mike Bullard (3)	Pittsburgh	Feb. 21	PIT 7 DET 3	3
Keith Crowder	Boston	Feb. 22	BOS 6 EDM 5	3
Mark Hunter (2)	St. Louis	Feb. 23	STL 8 HFD 2	3
Doug Gilmour	St. Louis	Feb. 23	STL 8 HFD 2	3
*Wendel Clark	Toronto	Feb. 25	NYR 3 TOR 7	3
Mark Messier	Edmonton	Feb. 26	EDM 8 WPG 2	3
Troy Murray (3)	Chicago	Feb. 27	CHI 6 L.A. 3	3
Walt Poddubny	Toronto	Feb. 28	TOR 7 DET 3	3
Charlie Simmer (3)	Boston	Mar. 1	N.J. 3 BOS 8	3
Dave Williams	Los Angeles	Mar. 1	MTL 6 L.A. 4	3
Mark Johnson	New Jersey	Mar. 3	WPG 4 N.J. 6	3
Dino Ciccarelli	Minnesota	Mar. 3	MIN 8 DET 1	3
*Peter Klima	Detroit	Mar. 5	DET 8 CHI 3	3
Pat Verbeek	New Jersey	Mar. 8	PHI 3 N.J. 7	3
Michel Goulet (2)	Quebec	Mar. 8	QUE 6 HFD 3	3
Glenn Anderson (3)	Edmonton	Mar. 9	EDM 7 L.A. 3	3
Mike Bossy (3)	NY Islanders	Mar. 11	CGY 4 NYI 8	4
Steve Larmer	Chicago	Mar. 12	BUF 7 CHI 4	3
Glenn Anderson (4)	Edmonton	Mar. 14	DET 3 EDM 12	3
Mike Gartner (3)	Washington	Mar. 15	WSH 5 STL 4	3
Jim Fox (2)	Los Angeles	Mar. 17	L.A. 5 TOR 7	3
Dino Ciccarelli (2)	Minnesota	Mar. 17	STL 5 MIN 6	3
*Stephane Richer	Montreal	Mar. 17	QUE 8 MTL 6	3
Michel Goulet (3)	Quebec	Mar. 17	QUE 8 MTL 6	3
John Anderson	QUE-HFD	Mar. 18	HFD 6 DET 4	3
Scott Bjugstad (3)	Minnesota	Mar. 19	MIN 6 CGY 5	3
Brian Mullen	Winnipeg	Mar. 19	MIN 6 DET 1	3
Mike Bossy (4)	NY Islanders	Mar. 20	NYI 7 TOR 1	3
*Peter Klima (2)	Detroit	Mar. 22	CHI 4 DET 5	3
Dino Ciccarelli (3)	Minnesota	Mar. 29	MIN 5 DET 4	3
Peter Stastny (2)	Quebec	Mar. 29	QUE 5 L.A. 3	3
Miroslav Frycer (3)	Toronto	Mar. 30	TOR 5 CHI 4	3
Ray Neufeld	HFD-WPG	Mar. 31	WPG 5 L.A. 2	3
Mark Johnson (2)	New Jersey	Apr. 2	QUE 5 N.J. 6	3
Brian Propp	Philadelphia	Apr. 6	WSH 3 PHI 5	3

NOTE: 114 Three-or-more-goal games recorded in 1985-86.

Scott Bjugstad of Minnesota had three three-goal games in 1985-86.

Individual Rookie Scoring Leaders

Scoring Leaders

Player	Team	GP	G	A	PTS	+/-	PIM	PP	SH	GW	GT	S	%
Kjell Dahlin	Montreal	77	32	39	71	10	4	14	0	3	0	172	18.6
Gary Suter	Calgary	80	18	50	68	11	141	9	0	4	0	195	9.2
Per-Erik Eklund	Philadelphia	70	15	51	66	4-	12	8	0	5	0	141	10.6
Mike Ridley	NY Rangers	80	22	43	65	0	69	7	0	6	1	150	14.7
Joel Otto	Calgary	79	25	34	59	22	188	9	0	2	1	147	17.0
Steve Thomas	Toronto	65	20	37	57	15-	36	5	0	5	0	197	10.2
Peter Klima	Detroit	74	32	24	56	39-	16	8	0	4	0	174	18.4
Dean Evason	Hartford	55	20	28	48	3	65	5	2	4	0	101	19.8
Wendel Clark	Toronto	66	34	11	45	27-	227	4	0	3	0	164	20.7
Randy Cunneyworth	Pittsburgh	75	15	30	45	12	74	2	2	2	0	134	11.2

Goal Scoring

Rookie	Team	GP	G
Wendel Clark	Toronto	66	34
Kjell Dahlin	Montreal	77	32
Peter Klima	Detroit	74	32
Joel Otto	Calgary	79	25
Mike Ridley	NY Rangers	80	22

Assists

Rookie	Team	GP	A
Per-Erik Eklund	Philadelphia	70	51
Gary Suter	Calgary	80	50
Mike Ridley	NY Rangers	80	43
Kjell Dahlin	Montreal	77	39
Steve Thomas	Toronto	65	37

Shots

Rookie	Team	GP	S
Steve Thomas	Toronto	65	197
Gary Suter	Calgary	80	195
Peter Klima	Detroit	74	174
Kjell Dahlin	Montreal	77	172

First Goals

Rookie	Team	GP	FG
Kjell Dahlin	Montreal	77	4
Dan Hodgson	Toronto	40	4
Peter Klima	Detroit	74	4
Joel Otto	Calgary	79	4

Shooting Percentage (minimum 80 shots)

Rookie	Team	GP	G	S	%
Raimo Summanen	Edmonton	73	19	83	22.9
Wendel Clark	Toronto	66	34	164	20.7
Dean Evason	Hartford	55	20	101	19.8
Randy Burridge	Boston	52	17	90	18.9
Stephane Richer	Montreal	65	21	112	18.8

CONSECUTIVE ROOKIE SCORING STREAKS

Goals

Games	Rookie	Team	G
5	Randy Burridge	Boston	5

Assists

Games	Rookie	Team	A
9	Per-Erik Eklund	Philadelphia	14
7	Mike Ridley	NY Rangers	11
7	Kjell Dahlin	Montreal	9
7	Gary Suter	Calgary	9
5	Ari Haanpaa	NY Islanders	6

Points

Games	Rookie	Team	G	A	PTS
9	Per-Erik Eklund	Philadelphia	2	14	16
8	Kjell Dahlin	Montreal	5	9	14
8	Mike Ridley	NY Rangers	3	11	14
7	Gary Suter	Calgary	2	9	11
7	Randy Burridge	Boston	6	3	9
6	Peter Klima	Detroit	5	7	12
6	Dan Hodgson	Toronto	5	6	11
6	Dean Evanson	Hartford	6	4	10
6	Steve Thomas	Toronto	6	4	10
6	Gary Suter	Calgary	5	4	9
6	Per-Erik Eklund	Philadelphia	2	6	8
6	Bob Probert	Detroit	3	5	8
6	Wayne Presley	Chicago	2	5	7

Gary Suter of Madison, Wisconsin won the Calder Trophy as the NHL's top rookie of 1985-86. After a college hockey career with the University of Wisconsin Badgers of the WCHA, Suter played on defense in all 80 games for the Calgary Flames in his first NHL season.

Goaltending Statistics

All goals against a team in any game are charged to the goaltender of that game for purposes of awarding the Bill Jennings Trophy.

Won-Lost-Tied record is based upon which goaltender was playing when the winning or tying goal was scored.

Empty-net goals are not counted in personal averages but are included in the team total and the shot(s) is included in the goaltender's shots against (SA) total.

(GPI) Games played in **(mins)** minutes played **(AVG)** 60 minute average
(ENG) Empty-net goals against **(SO)** shutouts **(GA)** goals against
(SA) Shots against **(S%)** save percentage

Goaltender	GPI	MINS	AVG	W	L	T	EN	SO	GA	SA	S%
Philadelphia											
Bob Froese	51	2728	2.55	31	10	3	1	5	116	1270	.909
Pelle Lindbergh	8	480	2.88	6	2	0	0	1	23	199	.884
Glenn Resch	5	187	3.21	1	2	0	0	0	10	84	.881
*Darren Jensen	29	1436	3.68	15	9	1	3	2	88	756	.883
TOTALS	80	4831	2.99	53	23	4		8	241	2309	.896
Washington											
Bob Mason	1	16	.00	1	0	0	0	0	0	5	1.000
Al Jensen	44	2437	3.18	28	9	3	3	2	129	1168	.889
Pete Peeters	34	2021	3.35	19	11	3	3	1	113	910	.875
Pat Riggin	7	369	3.74	2	3	1	1	0	23	133	.826
TOTALS	80	4843	3.37	50	23	7		3	272	2216	.877
NY Rangers											
John Vanbiesbrouck	61	3326	3.32	31	21	5	2	3	184	1625	.887
Glen Hanlon	23	1170	3.33	5	12	1	0	0	65	608	.893
*Ron Scott	4	156	4.23	0	3	0	0	0	11	56	.804
*Terry Kleisinger	4	191	4.40	0	2	0	0	0	14	109	.872
TOTALS	80	4843	3.42	36	38	6		3	276	2398	.885
Montreal											
Doug Soetaert	23	1215	2.77	11	7	2	1	3	56	533	.895
*Patrick Roy	47	2651	3.35	23	18	3	3	1	148	1185	.875
Steve Penney	18	990	4.36	6	8	2	0	0	72	447	.839
TOTALS	80	4856	3.46	40	33	7		4	280	2165	.871
NY Islanders											
Kelly Hrudey	45	2563	3.21	19	15	8	2	1	137	1455	.906
Billy Smith	41	2308	3.72	20	14	4	2	1	143	1204	.881
TOTALS	80	4871	3.50	39	29	12		2	284	2659	.893
Boston											
*Bill Ranford	4	240	2.50	3	1	0	0	0	10	106	.906
Pat Riggin	39	2272	3.35	17	11	8	1	1	127	973	.869
Doug Keans	30	1757	3.65	14	13	3	1	0	107	782	.863
Pete Peeters	8	485	3.84	3	4	1	1	0	31	245	.873
*Cleon Daskalakis	2	120	5.00	0	2	0	0	0	10	63	.841
TOTALS	80	4874	3.55	37	31	12		1	288	2169	.867
Quebec											
Clint Malarchuk	46	2657	3.21	26	12	4	0	4	142	1358	.895
Mario Gosselin	31	1726	3.86	14	14	1	3	2	111	796	.860
Richard Sevigny	11	468	4.23	3	5	1	0	0	33	242	.864
TOTALS	80	4851	3.57	43	31	6		6	289	2396	.879

Goaltender	GPI	MINS	AVG	W	L	T	EN	SO	GA	SA	S%
St. Louis											
Rick Wamsley	42	2517	3.43	22	16	3	0	1	144	1354	.894
Greg Millen	36	2168	3.57	14	16	6	5	1	129	1140	.886
*Darrell May	3	184	4.24	1	2	0	0	0	13	86	.849
TOTALS	80	4869	3.59	37	34	9		2	291	2580	.887
Buffalo											
*Darren Puppa	7	401	3.14	3	4	0	0	1	21	184	.886
Jacques Cloutier	15	872	3.37	5	9	1	2	1	49	428	.885
Tom Barrasso	60	3561	3.61	29	24	5	5	2	214	1778	.879
TOTALS	80	4834	3.61	37	27	6		4	291	2390	.878
Hartford											
Mike Liut	57	3282	3.62	27	23	4	3	2	198	1574	.874
Steve Weeks	27	1544	3.85	13	13	0	2	1	99	723	.863
TOTALS	80	4826	3.75	40	36	4		3	302	2297	.869
Minnesota											
*Kari Takko	1	60	3.00	0	1	0	1	0	3	34	.909
Don Beaupre	52	3073	3.55	25	20	6	2	1	182	1690	.892
*Jon Casey	26	1402	3.89	11	11	1	2	0	91	789	.884
Roland Melanson	6	325	4.43	2	1	2	0	0	24	175	.863
TOTALS	80	4860	3.77	38	33	9		1	305	2688	.887
Pittsburgh											
Roberto Romano	46	2684	3.55	21	20	3	6	2	159	1394	.885
Gilles Meloche	34	1989	3.59	13	15	5	5	0	119	1003	.884
Denis Herron	3	180	4.67	0	3	0	2	0	14	92	.844
TOTALS	80	4853	3.77	34	38	8		2	305	2489	.877
Edmonton											
Andy Moog	47	2664	3.69	27	9	7	2	1	164	1480	.889
Grant Fuhr	40	2184	3.93	29	8	0	1	0	143	1296	.890
TOTALS	80	4848	3.84	56	17	7		1	310	2776	.888
Calgary											
*Mike Vernon	18	921	3.39	9	3	3	0	1	52	417	.875
*Marc D'Amour	15	560	3.43	2	4	2	0	0	32	310	.897
Rejean Lemelin	60	3369	4.08	29	24	4	2	1	229	1787	.872
TOTALS	80	4850	3.90	40	31	9		2	315	2514	.875

Philadelphia allowed the fewest goals-against in 1985-86, as Bob Froese played in 51 games with a goals-against-average of 2.55.

Goaltender	GPI	MINS	AVG	W	L	T	EN	SO	GA	SA	S%
Vancouver											
*Wendell Young	22	1023	3.58	4	9	3	1	0	61	536	.886
Richard Brodeur	64	3541	4.07	19	32	8	3	2	240	1724	.861
Frank Caprice	7	308	5.45	0	3	2	0	0	28	155	.819
TOTALS	80	4872	4.10	23	44	13		2	333	2415	.862
Chicago											
Bob Sauve	38	2099	3.94	19	13	2	2	0	138	1210	.886
Murray Bannerman	48	2689	4.48	20	19	6	2	1	201	1538	.869
Warren Skorodenski	1	60	6.00	0	1	0	0	0	6	45	.867
TOTALS	80	4848	4.32	39	33	8		1	349	2793	.875
Winnipeg											
Dan Bouchard	32	1696	3.79	11	14	2	1	2	107	790	.864
Brian Hayward	52	2721	4.79	13	28	5	5	0	217	1373	.841
Marc Behrend	9	422	5.83	2	5	0	1	0	41	220	.813
TOTALS	80	4839	4.61	26	47	7		2	372	2383	.844
New Jersey											
*Sam St. Laurent	4	188	4.15	2	1	0	0	1	13	111	.883
Glenn Resch	31	1769	4.27	10	20	0	4	0	126	885	.857
*Alain Chevrier	37	1863	4.61	11	19	2	0	0	143	951	.850
*Craig Billington	18	901	5.13	4	9	1	0	0	77	482	.840
*Kirk Mclean	2	111	5.95	1	0	0	0	0	11	59	.814
TOTAL	80	4832	4.64	28	49	3		1	374	2488	.850
Toronto											
Ken Wregget	30	1566	4.33	9	13	4	3	0	113	901	.874
Don Edwards	38	2009	4.78	12	23	0	1	0	160	1140	.860
Tim Bernhardt	23	1266	5.07	4	12	3	0	0	107	727	.853
Allan Bester	1	20	6.00	0	0	0	0	0	2	5	.600
TOTALS	80	4861	4.76	25	48	7		0	386	2773	.861
Los Angeles											
Roland Melanson	22	1246	4.19	4	16	1	8	0	87	654	.865
Bob Janecyk	38	2083	4.67	14	16	4	2	0	162	1130	.856
Darren Eliot	27	1481	4.90	5	17	3	3	0	121	801	.848
*Glenn Healy	1	51	7.06	0	0	0	0	0	6	35	.829
TOTALS	80	4861	4.80	23	49	8		0	389	2620	.852
Detroit											
Greg Stefan	37	2068	4.50	10	20	5	3	1	155	1080	.856
*Chris Pusey	1	40	4.50	0	0	0	0	0	3	12	.750
*Mark Laforest	28	1383	4.95	4	21	0	5	1	114	742	.845
Corrado Micalef	11	565	5.52	1	9	1	0	0	52	342	.848
Ed Mio	18	788	6.32	2	7	0	0	0	83	453	.817
TOTALS	80	4844	5.14	17	57	6		2	415	2629	.842

Goaltending Leaders

Goals Against Average Minimum 25 games

Goaltender	Team	GPI	MINS	GA	AVG
Bob Froese	Philadelphia	51	2728	116	2.55
Al Jensen	Washington	44	2437	129	3.18
Kelly Hrudey	NY Islanders	45	2563	137	3.21
Clint Malarchuk	Quebec	46	2657	142	3.21
John Vanbiesbrouck	NY Rangers	61	3326	184	3.32

Wins

Goaltender	Team	GPI	MINS	W	L	T
John Vanbiesbrouck	NY Rangers	61	3326	31	21	5
Bob Froese	Philadelphia	51	2728	31	10	3
Tom Barrasso	Buffalo	60	3561	29	24	5
Rejean Lemelin	Calgary	60	3369	29	24	4
Grant Fuhr	Edmonton	40	2184	29	8	0

Save Percentage

Goaltender	Team	GPI	MINS	GA	SA	S%	W	L	T
Bob Froese	Philadelphia	51	2728	116	1270	.909	31	10	3
Kelly Hrudey	NY Islanders	45	2563	137	1455	.906	19	15	8
Clint Malarchuk	Quebec	46	2657	142	1358	.895	26	12	4
Rick Wamsley	St Louis	42	2517	144	1354	.894	22	16	3
Don Beaupre	Minnesota	52	3073	182	1690	.892	25	20	6

Shutouts

Goaltender	Team	GPI	MINS	SO	W	L	T
Bob Froese	Philadelphia	51	2728	5	31	10	3
Clint Malarchuk	Quebec	46	2657	4	26	12	4
Doug Soetaert	Montreal	23	1215	3	11	7	2
John Vanbiesbrouck	NY Rangers	61	3326	3	31	21	5

Steve Weeks

Team Statistics

TEAMS' HOME-AND-ROAD RECORD

Norris Division

	Home								Road							
	GP	W	L	T	GF	GA	PTS	%	GP	W	L	T	GF	GA	PTS	%
CHI	40	23	12	5	184	161	51	.638	40	16	21	3	167	188	35	.438
MIN	40	21	15	4	161	137	46	.575	40	17	18	5	166	168	39	.488
STL	40	23	11	6	171	144	52	.650	40	14	23	3	131	147	31	.388
TOR	40	16	21	3	173	188	35	.438	40	9	27	4	138	198	22	.275
DET	40	10	26	4	149	197	24	.300	40	7	31	2	117	218	16	.200
TOT	200	93	85	22	838	827	208	.520	200	63	120	17	719	919	143	.358

Smythe Division

	GP	W	L	T	GF	GA	PTS	%	GP	W	L	T	GF	GA	PTS	%
EDM	40	32	6	2	228	141	66	.825	40	24	11	5	198	169	53	.663
CGY	40	23	11	6	195	154	52	.650	40	17	20	3	159	161	37	.463
WPG	40	18	19	3	165	166	39	.488	40	8	28	4	130	206	20	.250
VAN	40	17	18	5	154	155	39	.488	40	6	26	8	128	178	20	.250
L.A	40	9	27	4	130	200	22	.275	40	14	22	4	154	189	32	.400
TOT	200	99	81	20	872	816	218	.545	200	69	107	24	769	903	162	.405

Adams Division

	GP	W	L	T	GF	GA	PTS	%	GP	W	L	T	GF	GA	PTS	%
QUE	40	23	13	4	174	142	50	.625	40	20	18	2	156	147	42	.525
MTL	40	25	11	4	176	123	54	.675	40	15	22	3	154	157	33	.413
BOS	40	24	9	7	155	118	55	.688	40	13	22	5	156	170	31	.388
HFD	40	21	17	2	181	153	44	.550	40	19	19	2	151	149	40	.500
BUF	40	23	16	1	169	147	47	.588	40	14	21	5	127	144	33	.413
TOT	200	116	66	18	855	683	250	.625	200	81	102	17	744	767	179	.488

Patrick Division

	GP	W	L	T	GF	GA	PTS	%	GP	W	L	T	GF	GA	PTS	%
PHI	40	33	6	1	186	101	67	.838	40	20	17	3	149	140	43	.538
WSH	40	30	8	2	171	124	62	.775	40	20	15	5	144	148	45	.563
NYI	40	22	11	7	179	131	51	.638	40	17	18	5	148	153	39	.488
NYR	40	20	18	2	147	123	42	.525	40	16	20	4	133	153	36	.450
PIT	40	20	15	5	155	133	45	.563	40	14	23	3	158	172	31	.388
N.J	40	17	21	2	156	170	36	.450	40	11	28	1	144	204	23	.288
TOT	240	142	79	19	994	782	303	.631	240	98	121	21	876	970	217	.452
TOT	840	450	311	79	3559	3108	979	.538	840	311	450	79	3108	3559	701	.417

TEAMS' DIVISIONAL RECORD

Norris Division

	Against Own Division								Against Other Divisions							
	GP	W	L	T	GF	GA	PTS	%	GP	W	L	T	GF	GA	PTS	%
CHI	32	16	14	2	147	144	34	.531	48	23	19	6	204	205	52	.524
MIN	32	20	7	5	165	122	45	.703	48	18	26	4	162	183	40	.417
STL	32	14	14	4	128	117	32	.500	48	23	20	5	174	174	51	.531
TOR	32	13	15	4	129	138	30	.469	48	12	33	3	182	248	27	.281
DET	32	8	21	3	124	172	19	.297	48	9	36	3	142	243	21	.219
TOT	160	71	71	18	693	693	160	.500	240	85	134	21	864	1053	191	.398

Smythe Division

	GP	W	L	T	GF	GA	PTS	%	GP	W	L	T	GF	GA	PTS	%
EDM	32	25	3	4	191	121	54	.844	48	31	14	3	235	189	65	.677
CGY	32	18	10	4	157	122	40	.625	48	22	21	5	197	193	49	.510
WPG	32	8	20	4	125	154	20	.313	48	18	27	3	170	218	39	.406
VAN	32	10	15	7	120	146	27	.422	48	13	29	6	162	187	32	.333
L.A	32	7	20	5	121	171	19	.297	48	16	29	3	163	218	35	.365
TOT	160	68	68	24	714	714	160	.500	240	100	120	20	927	1005	220	.458

Adams Division

	GP	W	L	T	GF	GA	PTS	%	GP	W	L	T	GF	GA	PTS	%
QUE	32	19	11	2	128	118	40	.625	48	24	20	4	202	171	52	.542
MTL	32	15	15	2	123	121	32	.500	48	25	18	5	207	159	55	.573
BOS	32	11	15	6	111	123	28	.438	48	26	16	6	200	165	58	.604
HFD	32	16	14	2	130	117	34	.531	48	24	22	2	202	185	50	.521
BUF	32	12	18	2	116	129	26	.406	48	25	19	4	180	162	54	.563
TOT	160	73	73	14	608	608	160	.500	240	124	95	21	991	842	269	.560

Patrick Division

	GP	W	L	T	GF	GA	PTS	%	GP	W	L	T	GF	GA	PTS	%
PHI	35	24	10	1	147	111	49	.700	45	29	13	3	188	130	61	.678
WSH	35	21	13	1	130	114	43	.614	45	29	10	6	185	158	64	.711
NYI	35	20	13	2	153	133	42	.600	45	19	16	10	174	151	48	.533
NYR	35	14	18	3	117	122	31	.443	45	22	20	3	163	154	47	.522
PIT	35	10	21	4	115	140	24	.343	45	24	17	4	198	165	52	.578
N.J	35	10	24	1	118	160	21	.300	45	18	25	2	182	214	38	.422
TOT	210	99	99	12	780	780	210	.500	270	141	101	28	1090	972	310	.574

DIVISION/CONFERENCE RECORDS

Clarence Campbell Conference

Norris vs Smythe

GP	W	L	T	GF	GA	PTS	%
75	25	39	11	298	334	61	.407

Smythe vs Norris

GP	W	L	T	GF	GA	PTS	%
75	39	25	11	334	298	89	.593

Campbell vs Wales Conference

GP	W	L	T	GF	GA	PTS	%
330	139	154	37	1215	1310	315	.477

Prince of Wales Conference

Adams vs Patrick

GP	W	L	T	GF	GA	PTS	%
90	50	26	14	347	275	114	.633

Patrick vs Adams

GP	W	L	T	GF	GA	PTS	%
90	26	50	14	275	347	66	.367

Wales vs Campbell Conference

GP	W	L	T	GF	GA	PTS	%
330	154	139	37	1310	1215	345	.523

Defenseman Mark Hardy of Los Angeles checks Minnesota's Brian Bellows.

TEAMS' POWER-PLAY RECORDS

Abbreviations: ADV – total advantages; PPGF – power-play goals for; % – percentage of advantages resulting in goals for.

	Home Team	ADV	PPGF	%	Road Team	ADV	PPGF	%	Overall Team	ADV	PPGF	%
1	CHI	165	47	28.5	BOS	195	53	27.2	EDM	295	78	26.4
2	MTL	178	49	27.5	EDM	134	35	26.1	CHI	332	85	25.6
3	EDM	161	43	26.7	MIN	194	48	24.7	MTL	343	87	25.4
4	CGY	181	47	26.0	NYI	170	41	24.1	CGY	372	92	24.7
5	PHI	202	51	25.2	QUE	194	46	23.7	PHI	380	91	23.9
6	WSH	185	46	24.9	CGY	191	45	23.6	MIN	370	88	23.8
7	VAN	220	53	24.1	MTL	165	38	23.0	QUE	423	99	23.4
8	BUF	197	46	23.4	CHI	167	38	22.8	BOS	412	95	23.1
9	QUE	229	53	23.1	PHI	178	40	22.5	WSH	360	82	22.8
10	MIN	176	40	22.7	HFD	174	39	22.4	NYI	332	73	22.0
11	PIT	235	53	22.6	PIT	190	40	21.1	HFD	378	83	22.0
12	STL	185	41	22.2	STL	177	37	20.9	PIT	425	93	21.9
13	DET	210	46	21.9	WSH	175	36	20.6	STL	362	78	21.5
14	HFD	204	44	21.6	WPG	183	37	20.2	VAN	419	89	21.2
15	N.J	184	38	20.7	L.A	184	36	19.6	DET	382	79	20.7
16	NYR	193	40	20.7	NYR	169	33	19.5	BUF	351	72	20.5
17	WPG	173	35	20.2	DET	172	33	19.2	WPG	356	72	20.2
18	NYI	162	32	19.8	N.J	171	32	18.7	NYR	362	73	20.2
19	TOR	192	38	19.8	VAN	199	36	18.1	N.J	355	70	19.7
20	BOS	217	42	19.4	BUF	154	26	16.9	TOR	364	67	18.4
21	L.A	209	33	15.8	TOR	172	29	16.9	L.A	393	69	17.6
TOTAL		4058	917	22.6		3708	798	21.5		7766	1715	22.1

TEAMS' PENALTY KILLING RECORDS

Abbreviations: TSH – times short-handed; PPGA – power-play goals against; % – percentage of times short-handed without a goal against.

	Home Team	TSH	PPGA	%	Road Team	TSH	PPGA	%	Overall Team	TSH	PPGA	%
1	PHI	202	29	85.6	HFD	188	30	84.0	PHI	418	71	83.0
2	EDM	200	30	85.0	QUE	200	34	83.0	QUE	379	71	81.3
3	MTL	158	25	84.2	BUF	178	34	80.9	EDM	409	77	81.2
4	WSH	164	30	81.7	MIN	217	42	80.6	HFD	376	72	80.9
5	PIT	163	31	81.0	PHI	216	42	80.6	WSH	348	67	80.7
6	VAN	161	31	80.7	NYI	210	42	80.0	BUF	342	66	80.7
7	BOS	185	36	80.5	WSH	184	37	79.9	MIN	387	80	79.3
8	BUF	164	32	80.5	CHI	201	43	78.6	MTL	307	64	79.2
9	STL	151	30	80.1	EDM	209	47	77.5	NYI	369	77	79.1
10	QUE	179	37	79.3	NYR	162	37	77.2	VAN	328	71	78.4
11	NYR	203	44	78.3	TOR	183	42	77.0	CHI	388	85	78.1
12	NYI	159	35	78.0	N.J	218	51	76.6	NYR	365	81	77.8
13	HFD	188	42	77.7	VAN	167	40	76.0	TOR	364	83	77.2
14	MIN	170	38	77.6	CGY	238	58	75.6	STL	324	74	77.2
15	CHI	187	42	77.5	DET	205	52	74.6	PIT	340	78	77.1
16	TOR	171	41	77.3	STL	173	44	74.6	CGY	427	101	76.3
17	CGY	189	43	77.2	L.A	187	48	74.3	BOS	402	97	75.9
18	WPG	170	38	76.9	MTL	149	39	73.8	WPG	335	83	75.2
19	N.J	182	52	71.4	WPG	179	47	73.7	N.J	400	103	74.3
20	L.A	177	55	68.9	PIT	177	47	73.4	DET	394	111	71.8
21	DET	189	59	68.8	BOS	217	61	71.9	L.A.	364	103	71.7
TOTAL		3708	798	78.5		4058	917	77.4		7766	1715	22.1

SHORT HAND GOALS FOR

	Home Team	SHGF	Road Team	SHGF	Overall Team	SHGF
1	EDM	17	CGY	11	EDM	27
2	PHI	11	EDM	10	PHI	17
3	QUE	9	HFD	8	CGY	16
4	WSH	9	CHI	7	CHI	15
5	WPG	9	STL	7	WSH	13
6	BUF	8	PHI	6	WPG	13
7	CHI	8	MIN	5	BUF	12
8	PIT	8	VAN	5	HFD	12
9	NYR	7	BOS	4	PIT	12
10	MIN	6	BUF	4	MIN	11
11	VAN	6	L.A	4	QUE	11
12	CGY	5	PIT	4	VAN	11
13	DET	5	TOR	4	L.A	9
14	L.A	5	WSH	4	NYR	9
15	MTL	5	WPG	4	STL	9
16	HFD	4	DET	3	DET	8
17	BOS	3	MTL	3	MTL	8
18	TOR	3	N.J	3	BOS	7
19	N.J	2	NYI	2	TOR	7
20	NYI	2	NYR	2	N.J	5
21	STL	2	QUE	2	NYI	4
		134		102		236

SHORT HAND GOALS AGAINST

	Home Team	SHGA	Road Team	SHGA	Overall Team	SHGA
1	BOS	2	MTL	1	NYR	4
2	N.J	2	NYR	1	BOS	5
3	PHI	2	WSH	2	N.J	5
4	TOR	2	BOS	3	WSH	6
5	HFD	3	N.J	3	HFD	8
6	NYR	3	NYI	4	MTL	8
7	CHI	4	HFD	5	NYI	9
8	DET	4	CGY	6	PHI	9
9	WSH	4	CHI	6	CHI	10
10	CGY	5	MIN	6	CGY	11
11	NYI	5	BUF	7	DET	11
12	WPG	5	DET	7	TOR	11
13	MIN	6	EDM	7	MIN	12
14	PIT	6	PHI	7	BUF	14
15	QUE	6	STL	7	STL	14
16	VAN	6	L.A	8	WPG	14
17	BUF	7	TOR	9	EDM	15
18	MTL	7	WPG	9	L.A	16
19	STL	7	PIT	11	PIT	17
20	EDM	8	VAN	11	VAN	17
21	L.A	8	QUE	14	QUE	20
		102		134		236

Peter Zezel of the Flyers.

TEAM STREAKS

Consecutive Wins

Games	Team	From	To
13	Philadelphia	Oct. 19	Nov. 17
8	Washington	Feb. 25	Mar. 11
7	Edmonton	Feb. 24	Mar. 9
7	Quebec	Oct. 10	Oct. 21
7	Quebec	Dec. 31	Jan. 11
6	Edmonton	Mar. 12	Mar. 26
6	NY Rangers	Feb. 8	Feb. 24
6	Philadelphia	Mar. 9	Mar. 22
6	Quebec	Nov. 28	Dec. 10
5	Buffalo	Jan. 31	Feb. 9
5	Calgary	Feb. 25	Mar. 4
5	Chicago	Dec. 28	Jan. 5
5	Edmonton	Oct. 10	Oct. 20
5	Edmonton	Dec. 29	Jan. 5
5	Hartford	Jan. 17	Jan. 25
5	Minnesota	Dec. 22	Jan. 2
5	Montreal	Jan. 23	Feb. 1
5	Philadelphia	Dec. 19	Dec. 28
5	Philadelphia	Mar. 29	Apr. 6
5	Pittsburgh	Nov. 27	Dec. 6
5	Washington	Nov. 30	Dec. 14

Consecutive Home Wins

Games	Team	From	To
11	Philadelphia	Oct. 19	Nov. 27
8	Edmonton	Feb. 24	Apr. 2
8	Philadelphia	Dec. 7	Jan. 14
8	Washington	Feb. 1	Mar. 11
6	Boston	Oct. 10	Nov. 10
6	Buffalo	Oct. 25	Nov. 13
6	Chicago	Dec. 15	Jan. 5
6	Edmonton	Oct. 10	Oct. 30
6	Edmonton	Jan. 24	Feb. 19
6	Montreal	Jan. 15	Feb. 1
6	Quebec	Nov. 30	Dec. 19
5	Boston	Jan. 16	Feb. 2
5	Calgary	Nov. 30	Dec. 12
5	Montreal	Dec. 18	Jan. 8
5	NY Islanders	Jan. 28	Feb. 15
5	NY Rangers	Feb. 12	Feb. 27
5	Philadelphia	Mar. 6	Mar. 22
5	St. Louis	Dec. 7	Dec. 26
5	Washington	Nov. 12	Nov. 27

Consecutive Home Wins

Games	Team	From	To
11	Philadelphia	Oct. 19	Nov. 27
8	Edmonton	Feb. 24	Apr. 2
8	Philadelphia	Dec. 7	Jan. 14
8	Washington	Feb. 1	Mar. 11
6	Boston	Oct. 10	Nov. 10
6	Buffalo	Oct. 25	Nov. 13
6	Chicago	Dec. 15	Jan. 5
6	Edmonton	Oct. 10	Oct. 30
6	Edmonton	Jan. 24	Feb. 19
6	Montreal	Jan. 15	Feb. 1
6	Quebec	Nov. 30	Dec. 19
5	Boston	Jan. 16	Feb. 2
5	Calgary	Nov. 30	Dec. 12
5	Montreal	Dec. 18	Jan. 8
5	NY Islanders	Jan. 28	Feb. 15
5	NY Rangers	Feb. 12	Feb. 27
5	Philadelphia	Mar. 6	Mar. 22
5	St. Louis	Dec. 7	Dec. 26
5	Washington	Nov. 12	Nov. 27

Consecutive Undefeated

Games	Team	W	T	From	To
13	Philadelphia	13	0	Oct. 19	Nov. 17
12	Edmonton	9	3	Nov. 16	Dec. 8
8	Hartford	6	2	Mar. 15	Apr. 1
8	Quebec	7	1	Nov. 28	Dec. 14
8	Washington	8	0	Feb. 25	Mar. 11
7	Edmonton	5	2	Jan. 24	Feb. 6
7	Edmonton	7	0	Feb. 24	Mar. 9
7	NY Islanders	6	1	Jan. 21	Feb. 2
7	Quebec	7	0	Oct. 10	Oct. 21
7	Quebec	7	0	Dec. 31	Jan. 11
7	Quebec	6	1	Mar. 6	Mar. 19
7	Vancouver	4	3	Jan. 18	Feb. 9
7	Washington	6	1	Nov. 12	Nov. 27
7	Washington	6	1	Nov. 30	Dec. 18

Consecutive Home Undefeated

Games	Team	W	T	From	To
11	Philadelphia	11	0	Oct. 19	Nov. 27
10	Calgary	8	2	Oct. 30	Dec. 12
10	Edmonton	8	2	Nov. 3	Dec. 15
10	Montreal	9	1	Nov. 23	Jan. 8
10	Pittsburgh	8	2	Jan. 6	Feb. 19
9	Boston	7	2	Oct. 10	Nov. 23
9	NY Islanders	8	1	Jan. 9	Feb. 15
8	Boston	6	2	Dec. 1	Jan. 4
8	Calgary	5	3	Jan. 9	Feb. 14
8	Edmonton	8	0	Feb. 24	Apr. 2
8	Philadelphia	8	0	Dec. 7	Jan. 14
8	Washington	8	0	Feb. 1	Mar. 11
7	Boston	4	3	Mar. 13	Apr. 3
7	Hartford	5	2	Mar. 15	Apr. 1
7	Philadelphia	6	1	Jan. 23	Feb. 22
7	St. Louis	5	2	Jan. 29	Feb. 18

Consecutive Road Undefeated

Games	Team	W	T	From	To
7	Edmonton	5	2	Jan. 11	Feb. 6
7	Philadelphia	7	0	Oct. 12	Nov. 16
7	Washington	5	2	Nov. 6	Dec. 18
5	NY Rangers	4	1	Jan. 14	Jan. 27
5	Edmonton	4	1	Nov. 16	Dec. 3
5	Quebec	5	0	Feb. 28	Mar. 24

Overtime Results

Team	1985-86 GP	W	L	T	1984-85 GP	W	L	T	1983-84 GP	W	L	T
Boston	17	2	3	12	18	4	4	10	7	1	0	6
Buffalo	9	1	2	6	17	0	3	14	13	5	1	7
Calgary	12	1	2	9	14	1	1	12	18	4	0	14
Chicago	12	3	1	8	12	2	3	7	9	0	1	8
Detroit	13	2	5	6	14	0	2	12	11	3	1	7
Edmonton	14	5	2	7	12	0	1	11	9	4	0	5
Hartford	7	1	2	4	17	4	4	9	15	2	3	10
Los Angeles	14	3	3	8	19	3	2	14	17	1	3	13
Minnesota	15	4	2	9	15	1	2	12	18	5	3	10
Montreal	14	1	6	7	18	3	3	12	7	1	1	5
New Jersey	10	4	3	3	12	0	2	10	15	1	7	7
NY Islanders	17	4	1	12	15	1	8	6	10	3	3	4
NY Rangers	13	0	7	6	17	2	5	10	17	5	3	9
Philadelphia	9	4	1	4	9	1	1	7	14	3	1	10
Pittsburgh	14	3	3	8	8	3	0	5	12	1	5	6
Quebec	11	4	1	6	14	3	2	9	15	0	5	10
St. Louis	17	5	3	9	15	2	1	12	11	3	1	7
Toronto	17	4	6	7	15	5	2	8	13	1	3	9
Vancouver	16	1	2	13	17	7	1	9	16	3	4	9
Washington	11	4	0	7	12	3	0	9	9	1	3	5
Winnipeg	8	0	1	7	14	3	1	10	24	7	6	11
Totals	**135**	**56**		**79**	**152**	**48**		**104**	**140**	**54**		**86**

Team Penalties

Abbreviations: GP – games played; PEN – total penalty minutes, including bench penalties; BMI – total bench penalty minutes; AVG – average penalty minutes per game.

Team	PEN	BMI	AVG	Team	PEN	BMI	AVG
NYI	1343	6	16.8	HFD	1759	24	22.0
MTL	1372	16	17.2	WPG	1774	24	22.2
WSH	1418	12	17.7	VAN	1813	20	22.7
NJ	1424	16	17.8	QUE	1847	28	23.1
STL	1478	10	18.5	BOS	1919	24	24.0
NYR	1496	22	18.7	EDM	1928	28	24.1
CHI	1537	16	19.2	LA	2004	16	25.1
PIT	1538	18	19.2	PHI	2025	10	25.3
BUF	1608	16	20.1	CGY	2297	18	28.7
MIN	1672	16	20.9	DET	2393	20	29.9
TOR	1716	10	21.5	**TOTAL**	**36361**	**370**	**43.3**

1985-86 Penalty Shots

Bo Berglund (Minnesota) scored against Corrado Micalef (Detroit) in 6-6 tie at Detroit, October 10.

Doug Smail (Winnipeg) unsuccessful against **Richard Sevigny** (Quebec) in 5-2 loss at Winnipeg, October 13.

Gerard Gallant (Detroit) scored against Brian Hayward (Winnipeg) in 4-3 loss at Detroit, October 16.

Denis Savard (Chicago) scored against Greg Stefan (Detroit) in 6-4 win at Chicago, December 15.

Brian Propp (Philadelphia) unsuccessful against **Glenn Resch** (New Jersey) in 6-3 win at Philadelphia, December 19.

Dan Daoust (Toronto) unsuccessful against **Patrick Roy** (Montreal) in 3-2 win at Toronto, January 1.

Ron Francis (Hartford) scored against Clint Malarchuk (Quebec) in 11-6 win at Hartford, January 17.

Steve Kasper (Boston) unsuccessful against **Mike Liut** (Hartford) in 6-3 win at Boston, January 27.

Bobby Smith (Montreal) unsuccessful against **Mario Gosselin** (Quebec) in 5-3 win at Montreal, January 29.

Mats Naslund (Montreal) scored against Glenn Resch (New Jersey) in 4-3 loss at New Jersey, February 13.

Pierre Larouche (NY Rangers) unsuccessful against **Corrado Micalef** (Detroit) in 3-1 win at New York, February 16.

Mike Ridley (NY Rangers) unsuccessful against **Corrado Micalef** (Detroit) in 3-1 win at New York, February 16.

Steve Kasper (Boston) unsuccessful against **Alain Chevrier** (New Jersey) in 8-3 win at Boston, March 1.

Peter Sundstrom (NY Rangers) scored against Al Jensen (Washington) in 4-2 loss at New York, March 2.

Dave Poulin (Philadelphia) unsuccessful against **Don Edwards** (Toronto) in 7-4 win at Philadelphia, March 6.

Summary: 15 penalty shots resulted in 6 goals.

1985-86 Schedule Results

* Denotes Afternoon Game

Game #	Visitor		Home	
Thur. Oct. 10				
1	Toronto	1	Boston	3
2	Hartford	5	Buffalo	4
3	Montreal	5	Pittsburgh	3
4	Chicago	2	Quebec	6
5	Washington	2	NY Rangers	4
6	New Jersey	6	Philadelphia	5
7	Minnesota	6	Philadelphia	5
7	Minnesota	6	Detroit	5
8	Winnipeg	2	Edmonton	4
9	Vancouver	6	Los Angeles	5
Fri. Oct. 11				
10	Winnipeg	3	Calgary	8
Sat. Oct. 12				
11	Boston	9	Detroit	2
12	NY Rangers	4	Hartford	8
13	Buffalo	6	Minnesota	5
14	Chicago	3	Montreal	6
15	Quebec	4	Toronto	0
16	NY Islanders	5	Los Angeles	4
17	Washington	4	New Jersey	1
18	Philadelphia	4	Pittsburgh	2
19	St. Louis	4	Vancouver	3
Sun. Oct. 13				
20	Montreal	2	Boston	7
21	Quebec	5	Winnipeg	2
22	New Jersey	3	NY Rangers	2
23	Philadelphia	4	Washington	1
24	Toronto	4	Chicago	1
25	St. Louis	3	Edmonton	6
26	Calgary	9	Los Angeles	2
Mon. Oct. 14				
27	Detroit	1	Buffalo	6
28	NY Islanders	1	Vancouver	4
Tues. Oct. 15				
29	Hartford	1	Quebec	4
30	Minnesota	2	Pittsburgh	3
Wed. Oct. 16				
31	Boston	3	Vancouver	3
32	Buffalo	6	Montreal	0
33	NY Islanders	4	Edmonton	6
34	NY Rangers	3	Los Angeles	4
35	Pittsburgh	5	Chicago	5
36	Washington	6	Toronto	0
37	Winnipeg	4	Detroit	3
38	St. Louis	2	Calgary	1
Thur. Oct. 17				
39	Hartford	4	New Jersey	3
40	Quebec	2	Philadelphia	1
41	Detroit	1	Minnesota	10
Fri. Oct. 18				
42	Boston	2	Edmonton	3
43	Washington	4	Buffalo	1
44	Los Angeles	4	Vancouver	5
Sat. Oct. 19				
45	Boston	6	Calgary	3
46	Montreal	6	Hartford	11
47	Buffalo	2	Washington	2
48	Pittsburgh	3	Quebec	4
49	NY Rangers	4	NY Islanders	5
50	New Jersey	3	St. Louis	4
51	Minnesota	3	Philadelphia	7
52	Winnipeg	4	Toronto	3
53	Chicago	6	Detroit	2
Sun. Oct. 20				
54	Vancouver	3	NY Rangers	4
55	Philadelphia	5	Chicago	2
56	Calgary	5	Winnipeg	8
57	Edmonton	8	Los Angeles	5
Mon. Oct. 21				
58	Quebec	3	Montreal	2
Tues. Oct. 22				
59	Boston	5	Los Angeles	2
60	Vancouver	2	NY Islanders	5
61	St. Louis	4	Minnesota	5
Wed. Oct. 23				
62	Hartford	2	Chicago	9
63	Montreal	5	Buffalo	4
64	New Jersey	1	NY Rangers	5
65	Pittsburgh	5	Toronto	4
66	Washington	3	Calgary	2
67	Vancouver	5	Detroit	0
68	Minnesota	4	St. Louis	4
69	Edmonton	3	Winnipeg	9
Thur. Oct. 24				
70	Hartford	0	Philadelphia	3
71	Quebec	3	NY Islanders	6
72	Chicago	6	New Jersey	4
73	Toronto	4	Pittsburgh	6
Fri. Oct. 25				
74	Vancouver	4	Buffalo	5
75	Los Angeles	0	NY Rangers	5
76	Washington	7	Winnipeg	7
77	Calgary	3	Edmonton	5

Game #	Visitor		Home	
Sat. Oct. 26				
78	Hartford	3	Montreal	5
79	Quebec	4	Pittsburgh	4
80	NY Islanders	5	St. Louis	2
81	Los Angeles	2	New Jersey	5
82	Minnesota	7	Toronto	5
83	Detroit	4	Calgary	7
Sun. Oct. 27				
84	Boston	1	NY Rangers	2
85	Minnesota	2	Buffalo	3
86	Vancouver	4	Philadelphia	7
87	Washington	4	Chicago	2
88	Detroit	3	Winnipeg	5
Mon. Oct. 28				
89	Edmonton	6	Calgary	4

Game #	Visitor		Home	
Tues. Oct. 29				
90	Boston	6	New Jersey	4
91	Hartford	4	Pittsburgh	3
92	Montreal	4	Quebec	6
93	Los Angeles	3	NY Islanders	2
94	St. Louis	3	Washington	6
Wed. Oct. 30				
95	Quebec	4	Hartford	6
96	Buffalo	5	Calgary	3
97	Philadelphia	5	Montreal	4
98	Pittsburgh	3	Detroit	6
99	Toronto	3	Vancouver	5
100	Chicago	3	Minnesota	5
101	Winnipeg	3	Edmonton	7
Thur. Oct. 31				
102	Los Angeles	4	Boston	7
103	Detroit	2	New Jersey	4

Game #	Visitor		Home	
Fri. Nov. 1				
104	Buffalo	2	Edmonton	0
105	NY Islanders	3	Washington	5
Sat. Nov. 2				
106	Chicago	4	Boston	5
107	Los Angeles	8	Hartford	1
108	Buffalo	3	Vancouver	6
109	Pittsburgh	4	Montreal	4
110	Philadelphia	4	Quebec	3
111	Washington	3	NY Islanders	5
112	NY Rangers	5	New Jersey	3
113	Toronto	2	Calgary	4
114	Detroit	5	St. Louis	5
115	Winnipeg	3	Minnesota	1
Sun. Nov. 3				
116	Los Angeles	4	Philadelphia	7
117	Toronto	1	Edmonton	7
118	St. Louis	4	Winnipeg	3

Game #	Visitor		Home	
Tues. Nov. 5				
119	Boston	5	Quebec	7
120	Montreal	8	Hartford	3
121	Calgary	4	NY Islanders	3
122	Chicago	4	Washington	8
123	Edmonton	6	Vancouver	4
Wed. Nov. 6				
124	Winnipeg	3	Buffalo	7
125	Montreal	3	Minnesota	4
126	NY Islanders	5	Toronto	4
127	Philadelphia	5	NY Rangers	4
128	Calgary	5	New Jersey	2
129	Washington	2	Pittsburgh	1
130	St. Louis	2	Detroit	3
131	Edmonton	4	Los Angeles	4
Thur. Nov. 7				
132	Hartford	1	Boston	2
133	Chicago	2	Philadelphia	6

Murray Bannerman

1985-86 NHL Schedule Results continued

Game #	Visitor		Home	
Fri. Nov. 8				
134	St. Louis	4	Buffalo	5
135	NY Rangers	7	Winnipeg	3
136	Pittsburgh	3	New Jersey	5
137	Toronto	3	Detroit	3
138	Vancouver	0	Edmonton	13
Sat. Nov. 9				
139	Boston	3	Philadelphia	5
140	Hartford	4	Quebec	3
141	Montreal	6	Los Angeles	0
142	New Jersey	2	NY Islanders	3
143	NY Rangers	3	Minnesota	4
144	Chicago	1	Pittsburgh	3
145	Calgary	5	Washington	4
146	St. Louis	2	Toronto	2
147	Vancouver	7	Winnipeg	2
Sun. Nov. 10				
148	Minnesota	1	Boston	2
149	Calgary	1	Buffalo	5
Mon. Nov. 11				
150	Chicago	5	NY Rangers	4
151	Detroit	0	Vancouver	5
Tues. Nov. 12				
152	Montreal	3	NY Islanders	2
153	Edmonton	4	Washington	2
154	Toronto	3	St. Louis	4
Wed. Nov. 13				
155	Boston	4	Buffalo	6
156	Minnesota	2	Hartford	5
157	Montreal	2	NY Rangers	5
158	Quebec	4	Chicago	6
159	Pittsburgh	6	Vancouver	3
160	Detroit	7	Los Angeles	2
161	Winnipeg	3	Calgary	3
Thur. Nov. 14				
162	Boston	6	Toronto	6
163	Quebec	3	St. Louis	5
164	Edmonton	3	Philadelphia	5
Fri. Nov. 15				
165	New Jersey	3	Winnipeg	5
166	Vancouver	3	Washington	5
Sat. Nov. 16				
167	Washington	2	Boston	2
168	Philadelphia	5	Hartford	2
169	Buffalo	1	Quebec	2
170	NY Rangers	2	Montreal	2
171	Edmonton	4	NY Islanders	4
172	New Jersey	2	Calgary	7
173	Pittsburgh	3	Los Angeles	4
174	Chicago	4	Toronto	6
175	Detroit	4	Minnesota	2
176	Vancouver	5	St. Louis	6
Sun. Nov. 17				
177	Toronto	3	Buffalo	5
178	NY Islanders	4	Philadelphia	5
179	Edmonton	3	NY Rangers	5
180	Minnesota	5	Chicago	4
181	Calgary	5	Winnipeg	4
Mon. Nov. 18				
182	Boston	2	Montreal	6
Tues. Nov. 19				
183	Buffalo	4	Hartford	0
184	Edmonton	5	Quebec	4
185	Philadelphia	6	NY Islanders	8
186	New Jersey	4	Los Angeles	5
187	Pittsburgh	3	Washington	4
188	Vancouver	7	Detroit	5
189	Minnesota	3	Calgary	3
Wed. Nov. 20				
190	Edmonton	5	Montreal	4
191	Toronto	3	NY Rangers	7
192	Washington	3	Pittsburgh	1
193	Vancouver	0	Chicago	2
194	St. Louis	1	Winnipeg	3
Thur. Nov. 21				
195	NY Islanders	4	Boston	4
196	Hartford	0	Philadelphia	3
197	Los Angeles	4	Detroit	4
198	St. Louis	5	Minnesota	2
Fri. Nov. 22				
199	Quebec	5	Buffalo	7
200	New Jersey	6	Vancouver	5
201	Winnipeg	1	Pittsburgh	8
Sat. Nov. 23				
202	*Philadelphia	4	Boston	5
203	Winnipeg	3	Hartford	8
204	Calgary	3	Montreal	4
205	Quebec	0	Washington	3
206	NY Rangers	3	NY Islanders	0
207	New Jersey	2	Edmonton	3
208	Detroit	3	Toronto	9
209	Chicago	7	St. Louis	3
210	Los Angeles	2	Minnesota	4
Sun. Nov. 24				
211	NY Islanders	4	NY Rangers	3
212	Pittsburgh	4	Philadelphia	7
213	Los Angeles	4	Chicago	3
Mon. Nov. 25				
214	Minnesota	4	Buffalo	3
Tues. Nov. 26				
215	Calgary	3	Quebec	1
216	Winnipeg	5	New Jersey	4
217	Toronto	1	St. Louis	5
218	Chicago	5	Vancouver	3
Wed. Nov. 27				
219	Hartford	9	Los Angeles	0
220	Buffalo	1	Detroit	7
221	Montreal	3	Washington	5
222	NY Islanders	4	Minnesota	4
223	Calgary	5	NY Rangers	2
224	Winnipeg	1	Philadelphia	6
225	Toronto	1	Pittsburgh	7
226	Vancouver	5	Edmonton	5
Thur. Nov. 28				
227	Quebec	3	Boston	0
Fri. Nov. 29				
228	Hartford	5	Vancouver	4
229	Montreal	5	Buffalo	2
230	NY Islanders	4	Winnipeg	1
231	NY Rangers	5	Washington	2
232	Philadelphia	4	Minnesota	1
233	St. Louis	3	Detroit	5
Sat. Nov. 30				
234	Boston	0	Quebec	2
235	Hartford	5	Edmonton	8
236	Buffalo	2	Toronto	3
237	Detroit	1	Montreal	10
238	NY Islanders	3	Calgary	4
239	NY Rangers	4	Pittsburgh	5
240	Washington	6	New Jersey	2
241	Chicago	4	Los Angeles	4
242	Minnesota	3	St. Louis	4
Sun. Dec. 1				
243	New Jersey	2	Boston	4
244	Philadelphia	1	Winnipeg	2
245	Calgary	3	Edmonton	5
Mon. Dec. 2				
246	Vancouver	0	Montreal	7
247	Pittsburgh	6	NY Rangers	0
Tues. Dec. 3				
248	Winnipeg	4	NY Islanders	4
249	Philadelphia	1	Detroit	4
250	Chicago	3	Minnesota	9
251	Edmonton	8	Los Angeles	4
Wed. Dec. 4				
252	Hartford	5	Calgary	8
253	Buffalo	6	St. Louis	3
254	Vancouver	4	Quebec	5
255	Winnipeg	4	NY Rangers	7
256	New Jersey	7	Toronto	10
257	Detroit	5	Pittsburgh	5
Thur. Dec. 5				
258	Montreal	6	Boston	8
259	Toronto	6	Philadelphia	3
260	St. Louis	2	Washington	3
261	Los Angeles	6	Edmonton	6
Fri. Dec. 6				
262	Pittsburgh	3	Buffalo	1
263	NY Islanders	3	Quebec	7
264	Vancouver	1	New Jersey	4
265	Chicago	2	Calgary	5

This page: Pierre Larouche of the Rangers emerged as one of the scoring stars of the 1986 Stanley Cup Playoffs after a regular season that saw him play only 28 games in the NHL. Facing page: Two more players with a scoring touch — Mike Bossy of the Islanders and Mats Naslund of the Canadiens.

* Denotes Afternoon Game

Game #	Visitor		Home	
Sat. Dec. 7				
266	Boston	2	Hartford	7
267	Montreal	6	Toronto	3
268	Quebec	4	NY Islanders	1
269	*NY Rangers	0	Philadelphia	4
270	New Jersey	5	Pittsburgh	1
271	Vancouver	1	Washington	2
272	Detroit	4	St. Louis	5
273	Minnesota	4	Edmonton	8
274	Los Angeles	3	Winnipeg	2
Sun. Dec. 8				
275	Buffalo	3	Boston	3
276	Philadelphia	1	NY Rangers	3
277	Chicago	4	Edmonton	4
278	Los Angeles	4	Winnipeg	1
Mon. Dec. 9				
279	New Jersey	6	Minnesota	4
Tues. Dec. 10				
280	Boston	4	Philadelphia	7
281	Buffalo	3	Quebec	4
282	Pittsburgh	4	NY Islanders	7
283	Toronto	4	Washington	3
284	New Jersey	3	St. Louis	4
285	Los Angeles	3	Calgary	6
Wed. Dec. 11				
286	Montreal	3	Hartford	1
287	NY Islanders	4	Pittsburgh	4
288	NY Rangers	4	New Jersey	2
289	St. Louis	2	Toronto	6
290	Minnesota	10	Detroit	9
291	Edmonton	12	Chicago	9
292	Winnipeg	6	Vancouver	3

Game #	Visitor		Home	
Thur. Dec. 12				
293	Quebec	1	Boston	1
294	Montreal	3	Philadelphia	6
295	Los Angeles	0	Calgary	5
Fri. Dec. 13				
296	Hartford	6	Buffalo	4
297	Edmonton	6	Winnipeg	3
Sat. Dec. 14				
298	*NY Rangers	2	Boston	5
299	Pittsburgh	4	Hartford	5
300	Chicago	3	Montreal	6
301	New Jersey	2	Quebec	9
302	St. Louis	2	NY Islanders	2
303	Philadelphia	4	Detroit	4
304	Washington	5	Los Angeles	4
305	*Toronto	3	Minnesota	6
306	Calgary	3	Vancouver	4
Sun. Dec. 15				
307	Quebec	2	Buffalo	6
308	Pittsburgh	5	NY Rangers	2
309	St. Louis	3	New Jersey	2
310	Toronto	3	Winnipeg	3
311	Detroit	3	Chicago	6
312	Vancouver	5	Edmonton	5
Mon. Dec. 16				
313	Hartford	4	Montreal	4
Tues. Dec. 17				
314	Buffalo	3	NY Islanders	7
315	Philadelphia	4	New Jersey	7
316	Calgary	3	Pittsburgh	4
317	Washington	3	Vancouver	4
318	Detroit	3	Minnesota	6
319	Winnipeg	6	St. Louis	8

Game #	Visitor		Home	
Wed. Dec. 18				
320	Calgary	3	Hartford	4
321	Buffalo	5	NY Rangers	10
322	Quebec	2	Montreal	3
323	Washington	5	Edmonton	2
324	Toronto	4	Los Angeles	4
325	Winnipeg	4	Chicago	5
Thur. Dec. 19				
326	Hartford	1	Boston	2
327	Montreal	4	Quebec	5
328	New Jersey	3	Philadelphia	6
329	Pittsburgh	4	Minnesota	2
Fri. Dec. 20				
330	NY Islanders	2	NY Rangers	2
331	Washington	4	Winnipeg	6
332	Toronto	3	Vancouver	5
333	Calgary	2	St. Louis	5
334	Los Angeles	4	Edmonton	9
Sat. Dec. 21				
335	*Minnesota	2	Boston	5
336	New Jersey	6	Hartford	7
337	Buffalo	1	NY Islanders	4
338	NY Rangers	5	Pittsburgh	2
339	Philadelphia	4	Pittsburgh	2
340	Chicago	3	Los Angeles	5
341	Vancouver	6	Los Angeles	2
Sun. Dec. 22				
342	Boston	3	Buffalo	5
343	*Washington	7	Quebec	5
344	Minnesota	4	New Jersey	3
345	Pittsburgh	2	Philadelphia	3
346	Calgary	4	Chicago	5
347	Winnipeg	7	Edmonton	6

Game #	Visitor		Home	
Mon. Dec. 23				
348	NY Islanders	6	Hartford	4
349	Detroit	2	NY Rangers	10
350	Winnipeg	3	Vancouver	5
Thur. Dec. 26				
351	Boston	3	Pittsburgh	4
352	Hartford	4	NY Islanders	3
353	NY Rangers	1	Buffalo	6
354	Quebec	5	Washington	4
355	Toronto	5	Detroit	4
356	Chicago	3	St. Louis	9
357	Minnesota	6	Winnipeg	5
Fri. Dec. 27				
358	Montreal	7	New Jersey	3
359	Philadelphia	6	Vancouver	3
Sat. Dec. 28				
360	Boston	5	St. Louis	1
361	Hartford	6	Toronto	3
362	New Jersey	3	Montreal	8
363	Detroit	3	Quebec	4
364	NY Islanders	5	Pittsburgh	2
365	*NY Rangers	1	Minnesota	3
366	Philadelphia	6	Calgary	3
367	Chicago	7	Washington	4
368	Winnipeg	4	Los Angeles	5
Sun. Dec. 29				
369	Boston	3	Chicago	4
370	Detroit	2	Hartford	4
371	NY Islanders	3	Buffalo	4
372	Washington	5	NY Rangers	3
373	Edmonton	5	Vancouver	3
Mon. Dec. 30				
374	Winnipeg	2	Los Angeles	4
Tues. Dec. 31				
375	Boston	6	Buffalo	6
376	Hartford	1	Quebec	5
377	NY Islanders	5	Detroit	4
378	Philadelphia	3	Edmonton	4
379	Pittsburgh	8	St. Louis	4
380	Calgary	3	Minnesota	6
Wed. Jan. 1				
381	Montreal	2	Toronto	3
382	*NY Rangers	0	Washington	7
383	Pittsburgh	4	Chicago	7
Thur. Jan. 2				
384	Boston	5	NY Islanders	7
385	Quebec	3	Hartford	2
386	Buffalo	2	Detroit	4
387	Philadelphia	7	Los Angeles	4
388	Vancouver	4	Minnesota	3
389	Edmonton	4	Calgary	3
Fri. Jan. 3				
390	Montreal	7	Winnipeg	3
391	Washington	3	New Jersey	2
Sat. Jan. 4				
392	Buffalo	0	Boston	4
393	Hartford	3	Edmonton	4
394	Montreal	4	Calgary	3
395	Quebec	7	Detroit	2
396	Chicago	4	NY Islanders	1
397	NY Rangers	4	Pittsburgh	3
398	New Jersey	3	Washington	9
399	Philadelphia	1	St. Louis	3
400	Los Angeles	6	Toronto	4
Sun. Jan. 5				
401	Los Angeles	3	Buffalo	2
402	Quebec	5	NY Rangers	4
403	Detroit	6	Toronto	5
404	Minnesota	2	Chicago	6
405	Vancouver	0	Winnipeg	3
406	Calgary	3	Edmonton	6
Mon. Jan. 6				
407	St. Louis	2	Montreal	9
408	New Jersey	3	Pittsburgh	4
Tues. Jan. 7				
409	Hartford	9	Calgary	1
410	St. Louis	4	Quebec	7
411	Minnesota	3	NY Islanders	2
412	Detroit	3	Washington	2
413	Vancouver	2	Winnipeg	2
Wed. Jan. 8				
414	Boston	3	Montreal	5
415	New Jersey	8	Chicago	4
416	Los Angeles	3	Pittsburgh	7
417	Edmonton	9	Toronto	11
Thur. Jan. 9				
418	St. Louis	7	Boston	2
419	Pittsburgh	0	NY Islanders	9
420	Washington	0	Philadelphia	4
421	Vancouver	4	Calgary	5
Fri. Jan. 10				
422	Hartford	4	Vancouver	3
423	Toronto	7	Buffalo	4
424	Montreal	4	NY Rangers	6
425	Edmonton	3	Quebec	6
426	Chicago	9	Detroit	4
427	Los Angeles	4	Minnesota	3

Game #	Visitor		Home	
Sat. Jan. 11				
428	*Winnipeg	4	Boston	8
429	Edmonton	6	Montreal	3
430	Quebec	5	Toronto	1
431	Detroit	2	NY Islanders	8
432	*Philadelphia	8	New Jersey	4
433	Washington	3	Minnesota	4
434	Los Angeles	4	St. Louis	4
Sun. Jan. 12				
435	Hartford	2	Chicago	4
436	St. Louis	2	NY Rangers	2
437	Calgary	0	Philadelphia	3
Mon. Jan. 13				
438	Edmonton	5	Boston	3
Sat. Jan. 11				
439	Buffalo	3	Pittsburgh	3
Mon. Jan. 13				
440	Detroit	4	Toronto	7
Tues. Jan. 14				
441	Winnipeg	5	Quebec	4
442	NY Rangers	2	Vancouver	1
443	New Jersey	2	Philadelphia	3
444	Calgary	4	Washington	3
445	Chicago	3	Minnesota	3
Wed. Jan. 15				
446	Edmonton	4	Hartford	1
447	Buffalo	2	Chicago	4
448	Winnipeg	0	Montreal	4
449	NY Islanders	4	Pittsburgh	6
450	NY Rangers	4	Los Angeles	3
451	New Jersey	4	Detroit	2
452	Toronto	1	St. Louis	10
Thur. Jan. 16				
453	Calgary	2	Boston	3
454	St. Louis	3	Minnesota	4
Fri. Jan. 17				
455	Quebec	6	Hartford	11
456	Montreal	4	Buffalo	5
457	NY Islanders	4	Philadelphia	5
458	Washington	4	New Jersey	3
459	Chicago	1	Winnipeg	5
460	Los Angeles	9	Vancouver	7
Sat. Jan. 18				
461	Hartford	5	Quebec	2
462	NY Islanders	0	Montreal	3
463	NY Rangers	4	Edmonton	5
464	Philadelphia	2	Washington	5
465	Pittsburgh	5	St. Louis	4
466	Minnesota	5	Toronto	2
467	*Calgary	4	Detroit	4
468	Vancouver	4	Los Angeles	4
Sun. Jan. 19				
469	Boston	2	Winnipeg	1
470	Buffalo	6	New Jersey	3
471	Minnesota	5	Pittsburgh	3
472	Calgary	9	Toronto	5
473	Detroit	4	Chicago	6
Mon. Jan. 20				
474	Hartford	5	NY Rangers	0
475	Montreal	2	Quebec	5
Tues. Jan. 21				
476	Philadelphia	3	NY Islanders	7
477	New Jersey	5	Vancouver	5
478	Minnesota	5	Washington	3
479	St. Louis	3	Los Angeles	6
Wed. Jan. 22				
480	Boston	5	Detroit	6
481	Winnipeg	3	Buffalo	6
482	Montreal	3	Chicago	3
483	NY Rangers	4	Toronto	2
484	New Jersey	6	Calgary	4
485	Pittsburgh	7	Edmonton	4
Thur. Jan. 23				
486	Winnipeg	5	Boston	7
487	Toronto	1	Hartford	4
488	Montreal	3	Minnesota	2
489	Quebec	4	NY Rangers	0
490	Detroit	2	Philadelphia	5
491	St. Louis	4	Los Angeles	3
Fri. Jan. 24				
492	Chicago	5	Buffalo	3
493	NY Islanders	7	Washington	5
494	New Jersey	3	Edmonton	7
495	Pittsburgh	3	Vancouver	4
Sat. Jan. 25				
496	*Detroit	3	Boston	6
497	Winnipeg	2	Hartford	7
498	Buffalo	3	Quebec	2
499	Toronto	2	Montreal	3
500	Chicago	3	NY Islanders	3
501	Philadelphia	1	St. Louis	0
502	Pittsburgh	2	Calgary	5
503	Washington	2	Minnesota	5
504	Los Angeles	2	Edmonton	5
Mon. Jan. 27				
505	Hartford	3	Boston	6
506	Buffalo	1	Montreal	6
507	NY Rangers	2	Quebec	6
508	New Jersey	2	Minnesota	6
509	Edmonton	4	Chicago	3
510	Los Angeles	3	Calgary	6

1985-86 NHL Schedule Results continued

Denotes Afternoon Game

Game # | Visitor | Home

Tues. Jan. 28
511 Toronto 2 NY Islanders 9
512 Philadelphia 2 Pittsburgh 2
513 Washington 0 Detroit 7

Wed. Jan. 29
514 Boston 5 Hartford 4
515 Buffalo 3 Winnipeg 5
516 Quebec 3 Montreal 5
517 NY Rangers 4 Chicago 5
518 Pittsburgh 4 New Jersey 1
519 Washington 4 Toronto 5
520 Edmonton 5 St. Louis 5
521 Minnesota 3 Los Angeles 4
522 Calgary 4 Vancouver 5

Thur. Jan. 30
523 Philadelphia 4 NY Islanders 8

Fri. Jan. 31
524 NY Rangers 3 Buffalo 5
525 St. Louis 4 Detroit 6
526 Minnesota 5 Vancouver 10
527 Calgary 4 Edmonton 7

Sat. Feb. 1
528 Boston 1 Montreal 2
529 NY Rangers 3 Hartford 4
530 Philadelphia 2 Quebec 2
531 Pittsburgh 5 NY Islanders 4
532 New Jersey 4 Washington 5
533 Chicago 7 Toronto 4
534 Detroit 3 St. Louis 4
535 Los Angeles 9 Winnipeg 6
536 Edmonton 4 Calgary 4

Sun. Feb. 2
537 Pittsburgh 2 Boston 3
538 Washington 4 Hartford 3
539 Quebec 3 Buffalo 5
540 NY Islanders 3 New Jersey 4
541 *Toronto 2 Chicago 3
542 Los Angeles 3 Winnipeg 6

Wed. Feb. 5
543 Montreal 2 Quebec 3
544 NY Islanders 2 Chicago 3
545 NY Rangers 3 St. Louis 4

Thur. Feb. 6
546 Buffalo 8 Boston 6
547 Hartford 3 Detroit 4
548 Edmonton 6 New Jersey 4
549 St. Louis 1 Philadelphia 4
550 Toronto 7 Minnesota 4
551 Los Angeles 2 Calgary 7

Fri. Feb. 7
552 Montreal 2 Washington 3
553 Winnipeg 2 Vancouver 5

Sat. Feb. 8
554 *NY Rangers 3 Boston 2
555 Buffalo 4 Hartford 2
556 Montreal 5 Detroit 4
557 *Chicago 5 Quebec 8
558 NY Islanders 4 Los Angeles 5
559 New Jersey 0 Pittsburgh 4
560 *Minnesota 3 Philadelphia 3
561 Edmonton 4 Washington 3
562 St. Louis 2 Toronto 3

Sun. Feb. 9
563 *Quebec 4 Boston 3
564 New Jersey 6 Hartford 3
565 Edmonton 2 Buffalo 3
566 *Philadelphia 2 Chicago 2
567 Winnipeg 3 Vancouver 5
568 Calgary 7 Los Angeles 3

Mon. Feb. 10
569 Minnesota 4 Montreal 3

Tues. Feb. 11
570 Boston 4 Chicago 5
571 Hartford 4 St. Louis 4
572 Vancouver 0 NY Islanders 1
573 Minnesota 4 Toronto 3
574 Edmonton 3 Detroit 2

Wed. Feb. 12
575 Philadelphia 4 Buffalo 0
576 Quebec 5 Los Angeles 2
577 Vancouver 4 NY Rangers 5
578 Washington 1 Pittsburgh 8
579 Winnipeg 2 Calgary 4

Thur. Feb. 13
580 Montreal 3 New Jersey 4
581 NY Islanders 4 Philadelphia 6
582 Toronto 4 Chicago 4
583 Minnesota 3 St. Louis 5

Fri. Feb. 14
584 Hartford 4 Winnipeg 5
585 Buffalo 3 Calgary 5
586 Quebec 2 Edmonton 8
587 NY Rangers 7 Detroit 5

Sat. Feb. 15
588 Boston 1 St. Louis 5
589 Hartford 4 Minnesota 5
590 Philadelphia 3 Montreal 5
591 New Jersey 4 NY Islanders 5
592 Vancouver 4 Pittsburgh 9
593 Washington 4 Los Angeles 1
594 Chicago 3 Toronto 4

Sun. Feb. 16
595 Boston 5 Minnesota 3
596 Buffalo 5 Edmonton 7
597 Quebec 6 Calgary 5
598 Detroit 1 NY Rangers 3
599 Pittsburgh 5 New Jersey 4
600 Vancouver 4 Toronto 4
601 St. Louis 2 Chicago 4

Mon. Feb. 17
602 Los Angeles 3 Montreal 2
603 *Winnipeg 4 Philadelphia 8

Tues. Feb. 18
604 Boston 4 Calgary 7
605 Vancouver 4 Hartford 5
606 Los Angeles 5 Quebec 4
607 Washington 3 NY Islanders 4
608 Detroit 0 St. Louis 5

Wed. Feb. 19
609 Hartford 6 Buffalo 4
610 Washington 4 Montreal 4
611 Winnipeg 2 Pittsburgh 5
612 Toronto 5 Edmonton 9
613 Minnesota 6 Chicago 5

Thur. Feb. 20
614 Quebec 3 New Jersey 4
615 St. Louis 3 NY Rangers 3
616 Los Angeles 3 Philadelphia 5
617 Toronto 7 Calgary 6

Fri. Feb. 21
618 NY Islanders 1 Buffalo 5
619 Quebec 2 Minnesota 5
620 Pittsburgh 7 Detroit 3
621 Chicago 5 Winnipeg 2
622 Calgary 4 Vancouver 0

Sat. Feb. 22
623 Boston 6 Edmonton 3
624 Hartford 3 Montreal 6
625 Detroit 2 NY Islanders 5
626 *Los Angeles 5 New Jersey 4
627 *Washington 1 Philadelphia 3
628 St. Louis 5 Pittsburgh 3

Sun. Feb. 23
629 Boston 6 Vancouver 1
630 *St. Louis 8 Hartford 2
631 Washington 1 Buffalo 4
632 *Quebec 2 Winnipeg 4
633 *Toronto 3 Minnesota 4
634 *Calgary 2 Chicago 6

Mon. Feb. 24
635 Montreal 2 Edmonton 3
636 Minnesota 5 NY Rangers 7
637 Los Angeles 1 Pittsburgh 6

Tues. Feb. 25
638 Boston 7 Quebec 4
639 NY Rangers 3 Toronto 7
640 Detroit 3 Washington 4
641 Calgary 4 St. Louis 1

Wed. Feb. 26
642 Minnesota 5 Hartford 2
643 Buffalo 2 Pittsburgh 5
644 Montreal 4 Vancouver 2
645 NY Islanders 3 New Jersey 7
646 Edmonton 8 Winnipeg 2

Thur. Feb. 27
647 Washington 2 Boston 1
648 Pittsburgh 3 NY Rangers 8
649 Philadelphia 5 Calgary 3
650 Chicago 6 Los Angeles 3

Fri. Feb. 28
651 Quebec 6 Buffalo 2
652 NY Islanders 6 Winnipeg 3
653 Philadelphia 1 Vancouver 3
654 Toronto 7 Detroit 3

Sat. Mar. 1
655 *New Jersey 3 Boston 8
656 Hartford 1 Pittsburgh 5
657 Buffalo 8 Quebec 4
658 Montreal 6 Los Angeles 4
659 NY Islanders 3 Minnesota 5
660 NY Rangers 0 Washington 5
661 Detroit 3 Toronto 6
662 Chicago 3 St. Louis 6
663 Vancouver 2 Calgary 3

Sun. Mar. 2
664 *Boston 1 Hartford 4
665 Washington 4 NY Rangers 2
666 Winnipeg 4 New Jersey 6
667 Philadelphia 1 Edmonton 2
668 *St. Louis 1 Chicago 4
669 Calgary 5 Los Angeles 1

Mon. Mar. 3
670 Winnipeg 1 Toronto 6
671 Minnesota 8 Detroit 5

Tues. Mar. 4
672 Buffalo 6 Philadelphia 4
673 Montreal 3 NY Islanders 4
674 St. Louis 6 Quebec 4
675 New Jersey 2 Washington 4
676 Pittsburgh 3 Calgary 5
677 Edmonton 6 Vancouver 2

Wed. Mar. 5
678 Buffalo 1 Hartford 5
679 NY Rangers 1 Winnipeg 4
680 Toronto 5 Minnesota 4
681 Detroit 8 Chicago 6
682 Los Angeles 3 Edmonton 6

Thur. Mar. 6
683 Quebec 5 Boston 4
684 St. Louis 7 Montreal 4
685 NY Rangers 5 Calgary 2
686 Detroit 2 New Jersey 7
687 Toronto 4 Philadelphia 7
688 Los Angeles 5 Vancouver 5

Fri. Mar. 7
689 Hartford 6 Buffalo 4
690 Pittsburgh 3 Edmonton 7

Sat. Mar. 8
691 Boston 3 Montreal 8
692 Quebec 6 NY Rangers 3
693 Washington 6 NY Islanders 3
694 *Philadelphia 3 New Jersey 4
695 Chicago 2 Toronto 4
696 Vancouver 3 St. Louis 7
697 *Winnipeg 4 Minnesota 3

Sun. Mar. 9
698 New Jersey 3 Buffalo 4
699 *NY Islanders 1 Washington 3
700 *Philadelphia 4 NY Rangers 5
701 *Pittsburgh 3 Winnipeg 5
702 *Calgary 3 Detroit 2
703 St. Louis 2 Chicago 4
704 *Edmonton 7 Los Angeles 3

Mon. Mar. 10
705 Hartford 5 Montreal 2

Tues. Mar. 11
706 Buffalo 2 St. Louis 5
707 Vancouver 1 Quebec 1
708 Calgary 3 NY Islanders 8
709 NY Rangers 6 New Jersey 3
710 Pittsburgh 3 Washington 5
711 Edmonton 0 Minnesota 4

Wed. Mar. 12
712 Boston 5 Pittsburgh 2
713 Buffalo 7 Chicago 6
714 Vancouver 2 Montreal 3
715 Calgary 3 NY Rangers 2
716 Detroit 3 Los Angeles 0
717 Edmonton 8 Winnipeg 5

Thur. Mar. 13
718 Montreal 2 Boston 3
719 NY Islanders 3 Hartford 2
720 Toronto 7 New Jersey 4
721 Washington 0 Philadelphia 2
722 Minnesota 3 St. Louis 2

Fri. Mar. 14
723 Calgary 2 Quebec 6
724 Detroit 3 Edmonton 12

Sat. Mar. 15
725 *Vancouver 1 Boston 1
726 Chicago 4 Hartford 11
727 Buffalo 3 Los Angeles 2
728 Calgary 5 Montreal 3
729 Minnesota 2 Pittsburgh 3
730 New Jersey 1 NY Islanders 3
731 NY Rangers 2 Pittsburgh 5
732 Philadelphia 6 Toronto 5
733 Washington 5 St. Louis 4

Sun. Mar. 16
734 NY Islanders 1 NY Rangers 3
735 New Jersey 1 Philadelphia 4
736 *Detroit 0 Winnipeg 6
737 Vancouver 4 Chicago 5

Mon. Mar. 17
738 Quebec 8 Montreal 6
739 Washington 5 Pittsburgh 3
740 Los Angeles 5 Toronto 7
741 St. Louis 5 Minnesota 6

Tues. Mar. 18
742 Hartford 6 Detroit 4
743 NY Rangers 2 NY Islanders 6
744 Los Angeles 3 Washington 2
745 Winnipeg 2 Edmonton 6

Wed. Mar. 19
746 Hartford 5 St. Louis 2
747 Buffalo 4 Vancouver 3
748 Montreal 4 Winnipeg 6
749 Toronto 2 Quebec 5
750 Pittsburgh 5 New Jersey 5
751 Minnesota 6 Calgary 5

Thur. Mar. 20
752 Los Angeles 3 Boston 6
753 NY Islanders 7 Toronto 1
754 Pittsburgh 1 Philadelphia 2
755 St. Louis 3 Detroit 4

Fri. Mar. 21
756 New Jersey 6 Buffalo 3
757 Winnipeg 3 Washington 5
758 Minnesota 4 Edmonton 5
759 Vancouver 5 Calgary 5

Sat. Mar. 22
760 *NY Islanders 3 Boston 3
761 Los Angeles 3 Hartford 6
762 Montreal 3 St. Louis 2
763 Pittsburgh 7 Quebec 3
764 *NY Rangers 2 Philadelphia 6
765 New Jersey 6 Toronto 5
766 *Chicago 4 Detroit 8
767 Minnesota 7 Vancouver 6

Sun. Mar. 23
768 *Boston 5 Hartford 3
769 Los Angeles 1 Buffalo 5
770 Chicago 5 NY Rangers 3
771 *Philadelphia 5 Washington 3
772 *Calgary 7 Winnipeg 4

Mon. Mar. 24
773 Quebec 3 Minnesota 0
774 Vancouver 4 Winnipeg 8

Tues. Mar. 25
775 Boston 3 Washington 6
776 St. Louis 3 NY Islanders 4
777 NY Rangers 5 New Jersey 4
778 Edmonton 7 Detroit 2

Wed. Mar. 26
779 Montreal 0 Hartford 3
780 Quebec 6 Vancouver 7
781 Edmonton 3 Pittsburgh 2
782 Minnesota 6 Toronto 1
783 Detroit 3 Chicago 5
784 Calgary 3 Los Angeles 7

Thur. Mar. 27
785 Montreal 3 Boston 3
786 Buffalo 1 Philadelphia 0
787 St. Louis 0 New Jersey 1

Fri. Mar. 28
788 NY Islanders 4 Washington 3
789 Edmonton 3 NY Rangers 4
790 Winnipeg 3 Calgary 6
791 Los Angeles 1 Vancouver 2

Sat. Mar. 29
792 *Buffalo 1 Boston 2
793 Washington 3 Hartford 4
794 Pittsburgh 3 Montreal 4
795 Quebec 3 NY Islanders 4
796 Edmonton 4 NY Islanders 4
797 NY Rangers 2 Philadelphia 8
798 *Chicago 2 New Jersey 3
799 St. Louis 1 Toronto 4
800 *Minnesota 5 Detroit 4

Sun. Mar. 30
801 Boston 2 Buffalo 5
802 Toronto 5 Chicago 3
803 Calgary 2 Vancouver 3

Mon. Mar. 31
804 New Jersey 0 NY Rangers 9
805 Winnipeg 5 Los Angeles 2

Tues. Apr. 1
806 Buffalo 3 Hartford 5
807 Detroit 0 Quebec 4
808 NY Islanders 2 Philadelphia 5
809 Pittsburgh 2 Washington 5
810 Toronto 2 St. Louis 4
811 Chicago 2 Minnesota 1
812 Vancouver 5 Calgary 6

Wed. Apr. 2
813 Detroit 2 Montreal 6
814 NY Islanders 7 Pittsburgh 2
815 Philadelphia 3 NY Rangers 5
816 Quebec 3 New Jersey 5
817 Minnesota 7 Chicago 5
818 Winnipeg 4 Los Angeles 5
819 Vancouver 4 Edmonton 8

Thur. Apr. 3
820 Toronto 2 Boston 5
821 Hartford 2 Washington 4

Fri. Apr. 4
822 Montreal 2 Buffalo 4
823 Edmonton 3 Calgary 9

Sat. Apr. 5
824 Boston 2 Quebec 2
825 Toronto 1 Hartford 7
826 Pittsburgh 2 Montreal 4
827 New Jersey 1 NY Islanders 7
828 NY Rangers 2 Washington 4
829 Philadelphia 4 Pittsburgh 3
830 Detroit 2 Minnesota 3
831 Chicago 5 St. Louis 7
832 Vancouver 5 Los Angeles 3

Sun. Apr. 6
833 Hartford 4 Boston 3
834 *NY Islanders 3 New Jersey 9
835 Pittsburgh 5 NY Rangers 3
836 Washington 3 Philadelphia 5
837 Toronto 2 Detroit 4
838 *St. Louis 1 Chicago 3
839 *Calgary 6 Winnipeg 4
840 Edmonton 2 Vancouver 2

Terry Ruskowski

NHL Record Book

All-Time Standings of NHL Teams
(ranked by percentage)

Team	Games	Won	Lost	Tied	Goals For	Goals Against	Points	%
Edmonton	560	314	167	79	2743	2181	707	.631
Montreal	4,112	2,172	1,288	652	13,877	10,721	4,996	.607
Philadelphia	1,498	770	470	258	5,385	4,389	1,798	.600
NY Islanders	1,116	564	377	175	4,245	3,470	1,303	.584
Buffalo	1,272	618	433	221	4,652	4,021	1,457	.573
Boston	3,952	1,874	1,475	603	12,856	11,621	4,351	.550
**Calgary	1,116	483	445	188	4,069	3,904	1,154	.517
Quebec	560	248	230	82	2,274	2,154	578	.516
Toronto	4,112	1,785	1,700	627	12,716	12,404	4,197	.510
NY Rangers	3,886	1,600	1,648	638	11,866	12,151	3,838	.494
Detroit	3,886	1,588	1,668	630	11,476	11,799	3,806	.490
Chicago	3,886	1,568	1,701	617	11,473	11,778	3,753	.483
St. Louis	1,498	597	663	238	4,788	5,085	1,432	.478
Minnesota	1,498	551	686	261	4,836	5,304	1,363	.455
Los Angeles	1,498	561	701	236	4,982	5,508	1,358	.453
Washington	960	346	475	139	3,211	3,775	831	.433
Pittsburgh	1,498	530	742	226	4,909	5,645	1,286	.429
Winnipeg	560	195	290	75	2,083	2,457	465	.415
Vancouver	1,272	426	643	203	4,132	4,898	1,055	.415
Hartford	560	186	289	85	2,008	2,378	457	.408
*New Jersey	960	224	593	143	2,826	4,044	591	.308

* Totals included those of Kansas City (1974-75, 1975-76) and Colorado (1976-77 through 1981-82)
** Totals include those of Atlanta (1972-73 through 1979-80)

Year-By-Year Final Standings & Leading Scorers

Note: Assists not tabulated until 1926-27.

1917-18
Final Standings

Team	GP	W	L	T	GF	GA	PTS
Montreal	22	13	9	0	115	84	26
Toronto	22	13	9	0	108	109	26
Ottawa	22	9	13	0	102	114	18
*Mtl. Wanderers	6	1	5	0	17	35	2

* Montreal Arena burned down and Wanderers forced to withdraw from League. Canadiens and Toronto each counted a win for defaulted games for Wanderers.

Leading Scorers

Player	Team	GP	G
Malone, Joe	Montreal	20	44
Denneny, Cy	Ottawa	22	36
Noble, Reg	Toronto	20	28
Lalonde, Newsy	Montreal	14	23
Denneny, Corbett	Toronto	21	20
Pitre, Didier	Montreal	19	17
Cameron, Harry	Toronto	20	17

1918-19
Final Standings

Team	GP	W	L	T	GF	GA	PTS
Ottawa	18	12	6	0	71	54	24
Montreal	18	10	8	0	88	78	20
Toronto	18	5	13	0	65	92	10

Leading Scorers

Player	Team	GP	G
Cleghorn, Odie	Montreal	17	24
Lalonde, Newsy	Montreal	17	21
Denneny, Cy	Ottawa	18	18
Nighbor, Frank	Ottawa	18	17
Pitre, Didier	Montreal	17	15
Alf Skinner	Toronto	17	13
Darragh, Jack	Ottawa	14	12

1919-20
Final Standings

Team	GP	W	L	T	GF	GA	PTS
Ottawa	24	19	5	0	121	64	38
Montreal	24	13	11	0	129	113	26
Toronto	24	12	12	0	119	106	24
Quebec	24	4	20	0	91	177	8

Leading Scorers

Player	Team	GP	G
Malone, Joe	Montreal	24	39
Lalonde, Newsy	Montreal	23	37
Nighbor, Frank	Ottawa	23	25
Denneny, Corbett	Toronto	23	25
Noble, Reg	Toronto	24	24
Darragh, Jack	Ottawa	22	24
Arbour, Amos	Montreal	20	21

1920-21
Final Standings

Team	GP	W	L	T	GF	GA	PTS
Toronto	24	15	9	0	105	100	30
Ottawa	24	14	10	0	97	75	28
Montreal	24	13	11	0	112	99	26
Hamilton	24	6	18	0	92	132	12

Leading Scorers

Player	Team	GP	G
Dye, Cecil	Tor.-Ham.	24	35
Denneny, Cy	Ottawa	24	34
Lalonde, Newsy	Montreal	24	32
Malone, Joe	Hamilton	20	28
Denneny, Corbett	Toronto	20	19
Noble, Reg	Toronto	24	19
Nighbor, Frank	Ottawa	24	19

1921-22
Final Standings

Team	GP	W	L	T	GF	GA	PTS
Ottawa	24	14	8	2	106	84	30
Toronto	24	13	10	1	98	97	27
Montreal	24	12	11	1	88	94	25
Hamilton	24	7	17	0	88	105	14

Leading Scorers

Player	Team	GP	G
Broadbent, Harry	Ottawa	24	30
Dye, Cecil	Toronto	24	30
Denneny, Cy	Ottawa	22	28
Malone, Joe	Hamilton	24	23
Cleghorn, Odie	Montreal	23	21
Denneny, Corbett	Toronto	24	20
Cameron, Harry	Toronto	24	18

Dick Irvin, Sr.

1922-23
Final Standings

Team	GP	W	L	T	GF	GA	PTS
Ottawa	24	14	9	1	77	54	29
Montreal	24	13	9	2	73	61	28
Toronto	24	13	10	1	82	88	27
Hamilton	24	6	18	0	81	110	12

Leading Scorers

Player	Team	GP	G
Dye, Cecil	Toronto	22	26
Boucher, Billy	Montreal	24	25
Denneny, Cy	Ottawa	24	23
Cleghorn, Odie	Montreal	24	18
Adams, Jack	Toronto	23	18
Roach, Mickey	Hamilton	23	17
Wilson, Cully	Hamilton	23	15

1923-24
Final Standings

Team	GP	W	L	T	GF	GA	PTS
Ottawa	24	16	8	0	74	54	32
Montreal	24	13	11	0	59	48	26
Toronto	24	10	14	0	59	85	20
Hamilton	24	9	15	0	63	68	18

Leading Scorers

Player	Team	GP	G
Denneny, Cy	Ottawa	21	22
Burch, Billy	Hamilton	24	16
Boucher, Billy	Montreal	23	16
Dye, Cecil	Toronto	19	16
Joliat, Aurel	Montreal	24	15
Boucher, George	Ottawa	21	13
Adams, Jack	Toronto	22	13
Morenz, Howie	Montreal	24	13

1924-25
Final Standings

Team	GP	W	L	T	GF	GA	PTS
Hamilton	30	19	10	1	90	60	39
Toronto	30	19	11	0	90	84	38
Montreal	30	17	11	2	93	56	36
Ottawa	30	17	12	1	83	66	35
Mtl. Maroons	30	9	19	2	45	65	20
Boston	30	6	24	0	49	119	12

Leading Scorers

Player	Team	GP	G
Dye, Cecil	Toronto	29	38
Morenz, Howie	Montreal	30	30
Joliat, Aurel	Montreal	24	29
Denneny, Cy	Ottawa	28	28
Adams, Jack	Toronto	27	21
Burch, Billy	Hamilton	27	21
Green, Redvers	Hamilton	30	19

1925-26
Final Standings

Team	GP	W	L	T	GF	GA	PTS
Ottawa	36	24	8	4	77	42	52
Mtl. Maroons	36	20	11	5	91	73	45
Pittsburgh	36	19	16	1	82	70	39
Boston	36	17	15	4	92	85	38
NY Americans	36	12	20	4	68	89	28
Toronto	36	12	21	3	92	114	27
Montreal	36	11	24	1	79	108	23

Leading Scorers

Player	Team	GP	G
Stewart, Nels	Mt.Maroons	36	34
Cooper, Carson	Boston	36	28
Herberts, Jimmy	Boston	36	26
Denneny, Cy	Ottawa	36	24
Morenz, Howie	Montreal	31	23
Adams, Jack	Toronto	36	22

1926-27
Final Standings
Canadian Division

Team	GP	W	L	T	GF	GA	PTS
Ottawa	44	30	10	4	86	69	64
Montreal	44	28	14	2	99	67	58
Mtl. Maroons	44	20	20	4	71	68	44
NY Americans	44	17	25	2	82	91	36
Toronto	44	15	24	5	79	94	35

American Division

Team	GP	W	L	T	GF	GA	PTS
New York	44	25	13	6	95	72	56
Boston	44	21	20	3	97	89	45
Chicago	44	19	22	3	115	116	41
Pittsburgh	44	15	26	3	79	108	33
Detroit	44	12	28	4	76	105	28

Leading Scorers

Player	Team	GP	G	A	PTS	PIM
Cook, Bill	New York	44	33	4	37	58
Irvin, Dick	Chicago	43	18	18	36	34
Morenz, Howie	Montreal	44	25	7	32	49
Fredrickson, Frank	Bos., Det.	41	18	13	31	46
Dye, Cecil	Chicago	41	25	5	30	14
Bailey, Ace	Toronto	42	15	13	28	82
Boucher, Frank	New York	44	13	15	28	17
Burch, Billy	NY Americans	43	19	8	27	40
Oliver, Harry	Boston	42	18	6	24	17
Keats, Gordon	Bos., Det.	42	16	8	24	52

1927-28
Final Standings
Canadian Division

Team	GP	W	L	T	GF	GA	PTS
Montreal	44	26	11	7	116	48	59
Mtl. Maroons	44	24	14	6	96	77	54
Ottawa	44	20	14	10	78	57	50
Toronto	44	18	18	8	89	88	44
NY Americans	44	11	27	6	63	128	28

American Division

Team	GP	W	L	T	GF	GA	PTS
Boston	44	20	13	11	77	70	51
New York	44	19	16	9	94	79	47
Pittsburgh	44	19	17	8	67	76	46
Detroit	44	19	19	6	88	79	44
Chicago	44	7	34	3	68	134	17

Leading Scorers

Player	Team	GP	G	A	PTS	PIM
Morenz, Howie	Montreal	43	33	18	51	66
Joliat, Aurel	Montreal	44	28	11	39	105
Boucher, Frank	New York	44	23	12	35	15
Hay, George	Detroit	42	22	13	35	20
Stewart, Nels	Mtl. Maroons	41	27	7	34	104
Gagne, Art	Montreal	44	20	10	30	75
Cook, Fred	New York	44	14	14	28	45
Carson, Bill	Toronto	32	20	6	26	36
Finnigan, Frank	Ottawa	38	20	5	25	34
Cook, Bill	New York	43	18	6	24	42
Keats, Gordon	Chi., Det.	38	14	10	24	60

1928-29
Final Standings
Canadian Division

Team	GP	W	L	T	GF	GA	PTS
Montreal	44	22	7	15	71	43	59
NY Americans	44	19	13	12	53	53	50
Toronto	44	21	18	5	85	69	47
Ottawa	44	14	17	13	54	67	41
Mtl. Maroons	44	15	20	9	67	65	39

American Division

Team	GP	W	L	T	GF	GA	PTS
Boston	44	26	13	5	89	52	57
New York	44	21	13	10	72	65	52
Detroit	44	19	16	9	72	63	47
Pittsburgh	44	9	27	8	46	80	26
Chicago	44	7	29	8	33	85	22

Leading Scorers

Player	Club	GP	G	A	PTS	PIM
Bailey, Ace	Toronto	44	22	10	32	78
Stewart, Nels	Mtl. Maroons	44	21	8	29	74
Cooper, Carson	Detroit	43	18	9	27	14
Morenz, Howie	Montreal	42	17	10	27	47
Blair, Andy	Toronto	44	12	15	27	41
Boucher, Frank	New York	44	10	16	26	8
Oliver, Harry	Boston	43	17	6	23	24
Cook, Bill	New York	43	15	8	23	41
Ward, Jimmy	Mtl. Maroons	43	14	8	22	46

1929-30
Final Standings
Canadian Division

Team	GP	W	L	T	GF	GA	PTS
Mtl. Maroons	44	23	16	5	141	114	51
Montreal	44	21	14	9	142	114	51
Ottawa	44	21	15	8	138	118	50
Toronto	44	17	21	6	116	124	40
NY Americans	44	14	25	5	113	161	33

American Division

Team	GP	W	L	T	GF	GA	PTS
Boston	44	38	5	1	179	98	77
Chicago	44	21	18	5	117	111	47
New York	44	17	17	10	136	143	44
Detroit	44	14	24	6	117	133	34
Pittsburgh	44	5	36	3	102	185	13

Leading Scorers

Name	Club	GP	G	A	PTS	PIM
Weiland, Ralph	Boston	44	43	30	73	27
Boucher, Frank	New York	42	26	36	62	16
Clapper, Aubrey	Boston	44	41	20	61	48
Cook, Bill	New York	44	29	30	59	56
Kilrea, Hec	Ottawa	44	36	22	58	72
Stewart, Nels	Mtl. Maroons	44	39	16	55	81
Morenz, Howie	Montreal	44	40	10	50	72
Himes, Norm	NY Americans	44	28	22	50	15
Lamb, Joe	Ottawa	44	29	20	49	119
Gainor, Norm	Boston	42	18	31	49	39

1930-31
Final Standings
Canadian Division

Team	GP	W	L	T	GF	GA	PTS
Montreal	44	26	10	8	129	89	60
Toronto	44	22	13	9	118	99	53
Mtl. Maroons	44	20	18	6	105	106	46
NY Americans	44	18	16	10	76	74	46
Ottawa	44	10	30	4	91	142	24

American Division

Team	GP	W	L	T	GF	GA	PTS
Boston	44	28	10	6	143	90	62
Chicago	44	24	17	3	108	78	51
New York	44	19	16	9	106	87	47
Detroit	44	16	21	7	102	105	39
Philadelphia	44	4	36	4	76	184	12

Leading Scorers

Player	Club	GP	G	A	PTS	PIM
Morenz, Howie	Montreal	39	28	23	51	49
Goodfellow, Ebbie	Detroit	44	25	23	48	32
Conacher, Charlie	Toronto	37	31	12	43	78
Bailey, Ace	Toronto	40	23	19	42	46
Cook, Bill	New York	43	30	12	42	39
Primeau, Joe	Toronto	38	9	32	41	18
Stewart, Nels	Mtl. Maroons	42	25	14	39	75
Boucher, Frank	New York	44	12	27	39	20
Weiland, Ralph	Boston	44	25	13	38	14
Cook, Fred	New York	44	18	17	35	72
Joliat, Aurel	Montreal	43	13	22	35	73

1931-32
Final Standings
Canadian Division

Team	GP	W	L	T	GF	GA	PTS
Montreal	48	25	16	7	128	111	57
Toronto	48	23	18	7	155	127	53
Mtl. Maroons	48	19	22	7	142	139	45
NY Americans	48	16	24	8	95	142	40

American Division

Team	GP	W	L	T	GF	GA	PTS
New York	48	23	17	8	134	112	54
Chicago	48	18	19	11	86	101	47
Detroit	48	18	20	10	95	108	46
Boston	48	15	21	12	122	117	42

Leading Scorers

Player	Club	GP	G	A	PTS	PIM
Jackson, Harvey	Toronto	48	28	25	53	63
Primeau, Joe	Toronto	46	13	37	50	25
Morenz, Howie	Montreal	48	24	25	49	46
Conacher, Charlie	Toronto	44	34	14	48	66
Cook, Bill	New York	48	34	14	48	33
Trottier, Dave	Mtl. Maroons	48	26	18	44	94
Smith, Reg	Mtl. Maroons	43	11	33	44	49
Siebert, Albert	Mtl. Maroons	48	21	18	39	64
Joliat, Aurel	Montreal	48	15	24	39	46
Clapper, Aubrey	Boston	48	17	22	39	21

1932-33
Final Standings
Canadian Division

Team	GP	W	L	T	GF	GA	PTS
Toronto	48	24	18	6	119	111	54
Mtl. Maroons	48	22	20	6	135	119	50
Montreal	48	18	25	5	92	115	41
NY Americans	48	15	22	11	91	118	41
Ottawa	48	11	27	10	88	131	32

American Division

Team	GP	W	L	T	GF	GA	PTS
Boston	48	25	15	8	124	88	58
Detroit	48	25	15	8	111	93	58
New York	48	23	17	8	135	107	54
Chicago	48	16	20	12	88	101	44

Leading Scorers

Player	Club	GP	G	A	PTS	PIM
Cook, Bill	New York	48	28	22	50	51
Jackson, Harvey	Toronto	48	27	17	44	43
Northcott, Lawrence	Mtl. Maroons	48	22	21	43	30
Smith, Reg	Mtl. Maroons	48	20	21	41	66
Haynes, Paul	Mtl. Maroons	48	16	25	41	18
Joliat, Aurel	Montreal	48	18	21	39	53
Barry, Marty	Boston	48	24	13	37	40
Cook, Fred	New York	48	22	15	37	35
Stewart, Nels	Boston	47	18	18	36	62
Shore, Eddie	Boston	48	8	27	35	102
Boucher, Frank	New York	47	7	28	35	4
Morenz, Howie	Montreal	46	14	21	35	32
Gagnon, Johnny	Montreal	48	12	23	35	64

1933-34
Final Standings
Canadian Division

Team	GP	W	L	T	GF	GA	PTS
Toronto	48	26	13	9	174	119	61
Montreal	48	22	20	6	99	101	50
Mtl. Maroons	48	19	18	11	117	122	49
NY Americans	48	15	23	10	104	132	40
Ottawa	48	13	29	6	115	143	32

American Division

Team	GP	W	L	T	GF	GA	PTS
Detroit	48	24	14	10	113	98	58
Chicago	48	20	17	11	88	83	51
New York	48	21	19	8	120	113	50
Boston	48	18	25	5	111	130	41

Leading Scorers

Player	Club	GP	G	A	PTS	PIM
Conacher, Charlie	Toronto	42	32	20	52	38
Primeau, Joe	Toronto	45	14	32	46	8
Boucher, Frank	New York	48	14	30	44	4
Barry, Marty	Boston	48	27	12	39	12
Dillon, Cecil	New York	48	13	26	39	10
Stewart, Nels	Boston	48	21	17	38	68
Jackson, Harvey	Toronto	38	20	18	38	38
Joliat, Aurel	Montreal	48	22	15	37	27
Smith, Reg	Mtl. Maroons	47	18	19	37	58
Thompson, Paul	Chicago	48	20	16	36	17

1934-35
Final Standings
Canadian Division

Team	GP	W	L	T	GF	GA	PTS
Toronto	48	30	14	4	157	111	64
Mtl. Maroons	48	24	19	5	123	92	53
Montreal	48	19	23	6	110	145	44
NY Americans	48	12	27	9	100	142	33
St. Louis	48	11	31	6	86	144	28

American Division

Team	GP	W	L	T	GF	GA	PTS
Boston	48	26	16	6	129	112	58
Chicago	48	26	17	5	118	88	57
New York	48	22	20	6	137	139	50
Detroit	48	19	22	7	127	114	45

Leading Scorers

Player	Club	GP	G	A	PTS	PIM
Conacher, Charlie	Toronto	47	36	21	57	24
Howe, Syd	St.L., Det.	50	22	25	47	34
Aurie, Larry	Detroit	48	17	29	46	24
Boucher, Frank	New York	48	13	32	45	2
Jackson, Harvey	Toronto	42	22	22	44	27
Chapman, Art	NY Americans	47	9	34	43	4
Lewis, Herb	Detroit	47	16	27	43	26
Schriner, David	NY Americans	48	18	22	40	6
Barry, Marty	Boston	48	20	20	40	33
Stewart, Nels	Boston	47	21	18	39	45
Thompson, Paul	Chicago	48	16	23	39	20

1935-36
Final Standings
Canadian Division

Team	GP	W	L	T	GF	GA	PTS
Mtl. Maroons	48	22	16	10	114	106	54
Toronto	48	23	19	6	126	106	52
NY Americans	48	16	25	7	109	122	39
Montreal	48	11	26	11	82	123	33

American Division

Team	GP	W	L	T	GF	GA	PTS
Detroit	48	24	16	8	124	103	56
Boston	48	22	20	6	92	83	50
Chicago	48	21	19	8	93	92	50
New York	48	19	17	12	91	96	50

Leading Scorers

Player	Club	GP	G	A	PTS	PIM
Schriner, David	NY Americans	48	19	26	45	8
Barry, Marty	Detroit	48	21	19	40	16
Thompson, Paul	Chicago	45	17	23	40	19
Romnes, Doc	Chicago	48	13	25	38	6
Thoms, Bill	Toronto	48	23	15	38	29
Conacher, Charlie	Toronto	44	23	15	38	74
Smith, Reg	Mtl. Maroons	47	19	19	38	75
Chapman, Art	NY Americans	47	10	28	38	14
Lewis, Herb	Detroit	45	14	23	37	25
Northcott, Lawrence	Mtl. Maroons	48	15	21	36	41

1936-37
Final Standings
Canadian Division

Team	GP	W	L	T	GF	GA	PTS
Montreal	48	24	18	6	115	111	54
Mtl. Maroons	48	22	17	9	126	110	53
Toronto	48	22	21	5	119	115	49
NY Americans	48	15	29	4	122	161	34

American Division

Team	GP	W	L	T	GF	GA	PTS
Detroit	48	25	14	9	128	102	59
Boston	48	23	18	7	120	110	53
New York	48	19	20	9	117	106	47
Chicago	48	14	27	7	99	131	35

Leading Scorers

Player	Club	GP	G	A	PTS	PIM
Schriner, David	NY Americans	48	21	25	46	17
Apps, Syl	Toronto	48	16	29	45	10
Barry, Marty	Detroit	48	17	27	44	6
Aurie, Larry	Detroit	45	23	20	43	20
Jackson, Harvey	Toronto	46	21	19	40	12
Gagnon, Johnny	Montreal	48	20	16	36	38
Gracie, Bob	Mtl. Maroons	47	11	25	36	18
Stewart, Nels	Bos., NYA	43	23	12	35	37
Thompson, Paul	Chicago	47	17	18	35	28
Cowley, Bill	Boston	46	13	22	35	4

1937-38
Final Standings
Canadian Division

Team	GP	W	L	T	GF	GA	PTS
Toronto	48	24	15	9	151	127	57
NY Americans	48	19	18	11	110	111	49
Montreal	48	18	17	13	123	128	49
Mtl. Maroons	48	12	30	6	101	149	30

American Division

Team	GP	W	L	T	GF	GA	PTS
Boston	48	30	11	7	142	89	67
New York	48	27	15	6	149	96	60
Chicago	48	14	25	9	97	139	37
Detroit	48	12	25	11	99	133	35

Leading Scorers

Player	Club	GP	G	A	PTS	PIM
Drillon, Gord	Toronto	48	26	26	52	4
Apps, Syl	Toronto	47	21	29	50	9
Thompson, Paul	Chicago	48	22	22	44	14
Mantha, Georges	Montreal	47	23	19	42	12
Dillon, Cecil	New York	48	21	18	39	6
Cowley, Bill	Boston	48	17	22	39	8
Schriner, David	NY Americans	49	21	17	38	22
Thoms, Bill	Toronto	48	14	24	38	14
Smith, Clint	New York	48	14	23	37	0
Colville, Neil	New York	45	17	19	36	11
Stewart, Nels	NY Americans	48	19	17	36	29

1938-39
Final Standings

Team	GP	W	L	T	GF	GA	PTS
Boston	48	36	10	2	156	76	74
New York	48	26	16	6	149	105	58
Toronto	48	19	20	9	114	107	47
NY Americans	48	17	21	10	119	157	44
Detroit	48	18	24	6	107	128	42
Montreal	48	15	24	9	115	146	39
Chicago	48	12	28	8	91	132	32

Leading Scorers

Player	Club	GP	G	A	PTS	PIM
Blake, Hector	Montreal	48	24	23	47	10
Schriner, David	NY Americans	48	13	31	44	20
Cowley, Bill	Boston	34	8	34	42	2
Barry, Marty	Detroit	48	13	28	41	4
Smith, Clint	New York	48	21	20	41	2
Anderson, Tom	NY Americans	48	13	27	40	14
Apps, Syl	Toronto	44	15	25	40	4
Gottselig, Johnny	Chicago	48	16	23	39	15
Haynes, Paul	Montreal	47	5	33	38	27
Carr, Lorne	NY Americans	46	19	18	37	16
Colville, Neil	New York	48	18	19	37	12
Conacher, Roy	Boston	47	26	11	37	12
Watson, Phil	New York	48	15	22	37	42

1939-40
Final Standings

Team	GP	W	L	T	GF	GA	PTS
Boston	48	31	12	5	170	98	67
New York	48	27	11	10	136	77	64
Toronto	48	25	17	6	134	110	56
Chicago	48	23	19	6	112	120	52
Detroit	48	16	26	6	90	126	38
NY Americans	48	15	29	4	106	140	34
Montreal	48	10	33	5	90	167	25

Leading Scorers

Player	Club	GP	G	A	PTS	PIM
Schmidt, Milt	Boston	48	22	30	52	37
Dumart, Woody	Boston	48	22	21	43	16
Bauer, Bob	Boston	48	17	26	43	2
Drillon, Gord	Toronto	43	21	19	40	13
Cowley, Bill	Boston	48	13	27	40	24
Hextall, Bryan	New York	48	24	15	39	52
Colville, Neil	New York	48	19	19	38	22
Howe, Syd	Detroit	46	14	23	37	17
Armstrong, Murray	NY Americans	48	16	20	36	12
Blake, Hector	Montreal	48	17	19	36	48

1940-41
Final Standings

Team	GP	W	L	T	GF	GA	PTS
Boston	48	27	8	13	168	102	67
Toronto	48	28	14	6	145	99	62
Detroit	48	21	16	11	112	102	53
New York	48	21	19	8	143	125	50
Chicago	48	16	25	7	112	139	39
Montreal	48	16	26	6	121	147	38
NY Americans	48	8	29	11	99	186	27

Leading Scorers

Player	Club	GP	G	A	PTS	PIM
Cowley, Bill	Boston	46	17	45	62	16
Hextall, Bryan	New York	48	26	18	44	16
Drillon, Gord	Toronto	42	23	21	44	2
Apps, Syl	Toronto	41	20	24	44	6
Patrick, Lynn	New York	48	20	24	44	12
Howe, Syd	Detroit	48	20	24	44	8
Colville, Neil	New York	48	14	28	42	28
Wiseman, Eddie	Boston	48	16	24	40	10
Bauer, Bobby	Boston	48	17	22	39	2
Schriner, David	Toronto	48	24	14	38	6
Conacher, Roy	Boston	40	24	14	38	7
Schmidt, Milt	Boston	44	13	25	38	23

1941-42
Final Standings

Team	GP	W	L	T	GF	GA	PTS
New York	48	29	17	2	177	143	60
Toronto	48	27	18	3	158	136	57
Boston	48	25	17	6	160	118	56
Chicago	48	22	23	3	145	155	47
Detroit	48	19	25	4	140	147	42
Montreal	48	18	27	3	134	173	39
NY Americans	48	16	29	3	133	175	35

Leading Scorers

Player	Club	GP	G	A	PTS	PIM
Hextall, Bryan	New York	48	24	32	56	30
Patrick, Lynn	New York	47	32	22	54	18
Grosso, Don	Detroit	48	23	30	53	13
Watson, Phil	New York	48	15	37	52	48
Abel, Sid	Detroit	48	18	31	49	45
Blake, Hector	Montreal	47	17	28	45	19
Thoms, Bill	Chicago	47	15	30	45	8
Drillon, Gord	Toronto	48	23	18	41	6
Apps, Syl	Toronto	38	18	23	41	0
Anderson, Tom	NY Americans	48	12	29	41	54

1942-43
Final Standings

Team	GP	W	L	T	GF	GA	PTS
Detroit	50	25	14	11	169	124	61
Boston	50	24	17	9	195	176	57
Toronto	50	22	19	9	198	159	53
Montreal	50	19	19	12	181	191	50
Chicago	50	17	18	15	179	180	49
New York	50	11	31	8	161	253	30

Leading Scorers

Player	Club	GP	G	A	PTS	PIM
Bentley, Doug	Chicago	50	33	40	73	18
Cowley, Bill	Boston	48	27	45	72	10
Bentley, Max	Chicago	47	26	44	70	2
Patrick, Lynn	New York	50	22	39	61	28
Carr, Lorne	Toronto	50	27	33	60	15
Taylor, Billy	Toronto	50	18	42	60	2
Hextall, Bryan	New York	50	27	32	59	28
Blake, Hector	Montreal	48	23	36	59	28
Lach, Elmer	Montreal	45	18	40	58	14
O'Connor, Herb	Montreal	50	15	43	58	2

Woody Dumart was on two Cup-winners with Boston in 1938-39 and 1940-41.

1943-44
Final Standings

Team	GP	W	L	T	GF	GA	PTS
Montreal	50	38	5	7	234	109	83
Detroit	50	26	18	6	214	177	58
Toronto	50	23	23	4	214	174	50
Chicago	50	22	23	5	178	187	49
Boston	50	19	26	5	223	268	43
New York	50	6	39	5	162	310	17

Leading Scorers

Player	Club	GP	G	A	PTS	PIM
Cain, Herb	Boston	48	36	46	82	4
Bentley, Doug	Chicago	50	38	39	77	22
Carr, Lorne	Toronto	50	36	38	74	9
Liscombe, Carl	Detroit	50	36	37	73	17
Lach, Elmer	Montreal	48	24	48	72	23
Smith, Clint	Chicago	50	23	49	72	4
Cowley, Bill	Boston	36	30	41	71	12
Mosienko, Bill	Chicago	50	32	38	70	10
Jackson, Art	Boston	49	28	41	69	8
Bodnar, Gus	Toronto	50	22	40	62	18

1944-45
Final Standings

Team	GP	W	L	T	GF	GA	PTS
Montreal	50	38	8	4	228	121	80
Detroit	50	31	14	5	218	161	67
Toronto	50	24	22	4	183	161	52
Boston	50	16	30	4	179	219	36
Chicago	50	13	30	7	141	194	33
New York	50	11	29	10	154	247	32

Leading Scorers

Player	Club	GP	G	A	PTS	PIM
Lach, Elmer	Montreal	50	26	54	80	37
Richard, Maurice	Montreal	50	50	23	73	36
Blake, Hector	Montreal	49	29	38	67	15
Cowley, Bill	Boston	49	25	40	65	2
Kennedy, Ted	Toronto	49	29	25	54	14
Mosienko, Bill	Chicago	50	28	26	54	0
Carveth, Joe	Detroit	50	26	28	54	6
DeMarco, Albert	New York	50	24	30	54	10
Smith, Clint	Chicago	50	23	31	54	0
Howe, Syd	Detroit	46	17	36	53	6

1945-46
Final Standings

Team	GP	W	L	T	GF	GA	PTS
Montreal	50	28	17	5	172	134	61
Boston	50	24	18	8	167	156	56
Chicago	50	23	20	7	200	178	53
Detroit	50	20	20	10	146	159	50
Toronto	50	19	24	7	174	185	45
New York	50	13	28	9	144	191	35

Leading Scorers

Player	Club	GP	G	A	PTS	PIM
Bentley, Max	Chicago	47	31	30	61	6
Stewart, Gaye	Toronto	50	37	15	52	8
Blake, Hector	Montreal	50	29	21	50	2
Smith, Clint	Chicago	50	26	24	50	2
Richard, Maurice	Montreal	50	27	21	48	50
Mosienko, Bill	Chicago	40	18	30	48	12
DeMarco, Albert	New York	50	20	27	47	20
Lach, Elmer	Montreal	50	13	34	47	34
Kaleta, Alex	Chicago	49	19	27	46	17
Taylor, Billy	Toronto	48	23	18	41	14
Horeck, Pete	Chicago	50	20	21	41	34

1946-47
Final Standings

Team	GP	W	L	T	GF	GA	PTS
Montreal	60	34	16	10	189	138	78
Toronto	60	31	19	10	209	172	72
Boston	60	26	23	11	190	175	63
Detroit	60	22	27	11	190	193	55
New York	60	22	32	6	167	186	50
Chicago	60	19	37	4	193	274	42

Leading Scorers

Player	Club	GP	G	A	PTS	PIM
Bentley, Max	Chicago	60	29	43	72	12
Richard, Maurice	Montreal	60	45	26	71	69
Taylor, Billy	Detroit	60	17	46	63	35
Schmidt, Milt	Boston	59	27	35	62	40
Kennedy, Ted	Toronto	60	28	32	60	27
Bentley, Doug	Chicago	52	21	34	55	18
Bauer, Bob	Boston	58	30	24	54	4
Conacher, Roy	Detroit	60	30	24	54	6
Mosienko, Bill	Chicago	59	25	27	52	2
Dumart, Woody	Boston	60	24	28	52	12

1947-48
Final Standings

Team	GP	W	L	T	GF	GA	PTS
Toronto	60	32	15	13	182	143	77
Detroit	60	30	18	12	187	148	72
Boston	60	23	24	13	167	168	59
New York	60	21	26	13	176	201	55
Montreal	60	20	29	11	147	169	51
Chicago	60	20	34	6	195	225	46

Leading Scorers

Player	Club	GP	G	A	PTS	PIM
Lach, Elmer	Montreal	60	30	31	61	72
O'Connor, Buddy	New York	60	24	36	60	8
Bentley, Doug	Chicago	60	20	37	57	16
Stewart, Gaye	Tor., Chi.	61	27	29	56	83
Bentley, Max	Chi., Tor.	59	26	28	54	14
Poile, Bud	Tor., Chi.	58	25	29	54	17
Richard, Maurice	Montreal	53	28	25	53	89
Apps, Syl	Toronto	55	26	27	53	12
Lindsay, Ted	Detroit	60	33	19	52	95
Conacher, Roy	Chicago	52	22	27	49	4

1948-49
Final Standings

Team	GP	W	L	T	GF	GA	PTS
Detroit	60	34	19	7	195	145	75
Boston	60	29	23	8	178	163	66
Montreal	60	28	23	9	152	126	65
Toronto	60	22	25	13	147	161	57
Chicago	60	21	31	8	173	211	50
New York	60	18	31	11	133	172	47

Leading Scorers

Player	Club	GP	G	A	PTS	PIM
Conacher, Roy	Chicago	60	26	42	68	8
Bentley, Doug	Chicago	58	23	43	66	38
Abel, Sid	Detroit	60	28	26	54	49
Lindsay, Ted	Detroit	50	26	28	54	97
Conacher, Jim	Det., Chi.	59	26	23	49	43
Ronty, Paul	Boston	60	20	29	49	11
Watson, Harry	Toronto	60	26	19	45	0
Reay, Billy	Montreal	60	22	23	45	33
Bodnar, Gus	Chicago	59	19	26	45	14
Peirson, John	Boston	59	22	21	43	45

1949-50
Final Standings

Team	GP	W	L	T	GF	GA	PTS
Detroit	70	37	19	14	229	164	88
Montreal	70	29	22	19	172	150	77
Toronto	70	31	27	12	176	173	74
New York	70	28	31	11	170	189	67
Boston	70	22	32	16	198	228	60
Chicago	70	22	38	10	203	244	54

Leading Scorers

Player	Club	GP	G	A	PTS	PIM
Lindsay, Ted	Detroit	69	23	55	78	141
Abel, Sid	Detroit	69	34	35	69	46
Howe, Gordie	Detroit	70	35	33	68	69
Richard, Maurice	Montreal	70	43	22	65	114
Ronty, Paul	Boston	70	23	36	59	8
Conacher, Roy	Chicago	70	25	31	56	16
Bentley, Doug	Chicago	64	20	33	53	28
Peirson, John	Boston	57	27	25	52	49
Prystai, Metro	Chicago	65	29	22	51	31
Guidolin, Bep	Chicago	70	17	34	51	42

1950-51
Final Standings

Team	GP	W	L	T	GF	GA	PTS
Detroit	70	44	13	13	236	139	101
Toronto	70	41	16	13	212	138	95
Montreal	70	25	30	15	173	184	65
Boston	70	22	30	18	178	197	62
New York	70	20	29	21	169	201	62
Chicago	70	13	47	10	171	280	36

Leading Scorers

Player	Club	GP	G	A	PTS	PIM
Howe, Gordie	Detroit	70	43	43	86	74
Richard, Maurice	Montreal	65	42	24	66	97
Bentley, Max	Toronto	67	21	41	62	34
Abel, Sid	Detroit	69	23	38	61	30
Schmidt, Milt	Boston	62	22	39	61	33
Kennedy, Ted	Toronto	63	18	43	61	32
Lindsay, Ted	Detroit	67	24	35	59	110
Sloan, Tod	Toronto	70	31	25	56	105
Kelly, Red	Detroit	70	17	37	54	24
Smith, Sid	Toronto	70	30	21	51	10
Gardner, Cal	Toronto	66	23	28	51	42

Ab DeMarco had 20-goal seasons in 1944-45 and 1945-46.

1951-52
Final Standings

Team	GP	W	L	T	GF	GA	PTS
Detroit	70	44	14	12	215	133	100
Montreal	70	34	26	10	195	164	78
Toronto	70	29	25	16	168	157	74
Boston	70	25	29	16	162	176	66
New York	70	23	34	13	192	219	59
Chicago	70	17	44	9	158	241	43

Leading Scorers

Player	Club	GP	G	A	PTS	PIM
Howe, Gordie	Detroit	70	47	39	86	78
Lindsay, Ted	Detroit	70	30	39	69	123
Lach, Elmer	Montreal	70	15	50	65	36
Raleigh, Don	New York	70	19	42	61	14
Smith, Sid	Toronto	70	27	30	57	6
Geoffrion, Bernie	Montreal	67	30	24	54	66
Mosienko, Bill	Chicago	70	31	22	53	10
Abel, Sid	Detroit	62	17	36	53	32
Kennedy, Ted	Toronto	70	19	33	52	33
Schmidt, Milt	Boston	69	21	29	50	57
Peirson, John	Boston	68	20	30	50	30

1952-53
Final Standings

Team	GP	W	L	T	GF	GA	PTS
Detroit	70	36	16	18	222	133	90
Montreal	70	28	23	19	155	148	75
Boston	70	28	29	13	152	172	69
Chicago	70	27	28	15	169	175	69
Toronto	70	27	30	13	156	167	67
New York	70	17	37	16	152	211	50

Leading Scorers

Player	Club	GP	G	A	PTS	PIM
Howe, Gordie	Detroit	70	49	46	95	57
Lindsay, Ted	Detroit	70	32	39	71	111
Richard, Maurice	Montreal	70	28	33	61	112
Hergesheimer, Wally	New York	70	30	29	59	10
Delvecchio, Alex	Detroit	70	16	43	59	28
Ronty, Paul	New York	70	16	38	54	20
Prystai, Metro	Detroit	70	16	34	50	12
Kelly, Red	Detroit	70	19	27	46	8
Olmstead, Bert	Montreal	69	17	28	45	83
Mackell, Fleming	Boston	65	27	17	44	63
McFadden, Jim	Chicago	70	23	21	44	29

1953-54
Final Standings

Team	GP	W	L	T	GF	GA	PTS
Detroit	70	37	19	14	191	132	88
Montreal	70	35	24	11	195	141	81
Toronto	70	32	24	14	152	131	78
Boston	70	32	28	10	177	181	74
New York	70	29	31	10	161	182	68
Chicago	70	12	51	7	133	242	31

Leading Scorers

Player	Club	GP	G	A	PTS	PIM
Howe, Gordie	Detroit	70	33	48	81	109
Richard, Maurice	Montreal	70	37	30	67	112
Lindsay, Ted	Detroit	70	26	36	62	110
Geoffrion, Bernie	Montreal	54	29	25	54	87
Olmstead, Bert	Montreal	70	15	37	52	85
Kelly, Red	Detroit	62	16	33	49	18
Reibel, Earl	Detroit	69	15	33	48	18
Sandford, Ed	Boston	70	16	31	47	42
Mackell, Fleming	Boston	67	15	32	47	60
Mosdell, Ken	Montreal	67	22	24	46	64
Ronty, Paul	New York	70	13	33	46	18

1954-55
Final Standings

Team	GP	W	L	T	GF	GA	PTS
Detroit	70	42	17	11	204	134	95
Montreal	70	41	18	11	228	157	93
Toronto	70	24	24	22	147	135	70
Boston	70	23	26	21	169	188	67
New York	70	17	35	18	150	210	52
Chicago	70	13	40	17	161	235	43

Leading Scorers

Player	Club	GP	G	A	PTS	PIM
Geoffrion, Bernie	Montreal	70	38	37	75	57
Richard, Maurice	Montreal	67	38	36	74	125
Beliveau, Jean	Montreal	70	37	36	73	58
Reibel, Earl	Detroit	70	25	41	66	15
Howe, Gordie	Detroit	64	29	33	62	68
Sullivan, George	Chicago	69	19	42	61	51
Olmstead, Bert	Montreal	70	10	48	58	103
Smith, Sid	Toronto	70	33	21	54	14
Mosdell, Ken	Montreal	70	22	32	54	82
Lewicki, Danny	New York	70	29	24	53	8

1955-56
Final Standings

Team	GP	W	L	T	GF	GA	PTS
Montreal	70	45	15	10	222	131	100
Detroit	70	30	24	16	183	148	76
New York	70	32	28	10	204	203	74
Toronto	70	24	33	13	153	181	61
Boston	70	23	34	13	147	185	59
Chicago	70	19	39	12	155	216	50

Leading Scorers

Player	Club	GP	G	A	PTS	PIM
Beliveau, Jean	Montreal	70	47	41	88	143
Howe, Gordie	Detroit	70	38	41	79	100
Richard, Maurice	Montreal	70	38	33	71	89
Olmstead, Bert	Montreal	70	14	56	70	94
Sloan, Tod	Toronto	70	37	29	66	100
Bathgate, Andy	New York	70	19	47	66	59
Geoffrion, Bernie	Montreal	59	29	33	62	66
Reibel, Earl	Detroit	68	17	39	56	10
Delvecchio, Alex	Detroit	70	25	26	51	24
Creighton, Dave	New York	70	20	31	51	43
Gadsby, Bill	New York	70	9	42	51	84

1956-57
Final Standings

Team	GP	W	L	T	GF	GA	PTS
Detroit	70	38	20	12	198	157	88
Montreal	70	35	23	12	210	155	82
Boston	70	34	24	12	195	174	80
New York	70	26	30	14	184	227	66
Toronto	70	21	34	15	174	192	57
Chicago	70	16	39	15	169	225	47

Leading Scorers

Player	Club	GP	G	A	PTS	PIM
Howe, Gordie	Detroit	70	44	45	89	72
Lindsay, Ted	Detroit	70	30	55	85	103
Beliveau, Jean	Montreal	69	33	51	84	105
Bathgate, Andy	New York	70	27	50	77	60
Litzenberger, Ed	Chicago	70	32	32	64	48
Richard, Maurice	Montreal	63	33	29	62	74
McKenney, Don	Boston	69	21	39	60	31
Moore, Dickie	Montreal	70	29	29	58	56
Richard, Henri	Montreal	63	18	36	54	71
Ullman, Norm	Detroit	64	16	36	52	47

Dean Prentice scored 391 goals in 22 NHL seasons.

1957-58
Final Standings

Team	GP	W	L	T	GF	GA	PTS
Montreal	70	43	17	10	250	158	96
New York	70	32	25	13	195	188	77
Detroit	70	29	29	12	176	207	70
Boston	70	27	28	15	199	194	69
Chicago	70	24	39	7	163	202	55
Toronto	70	21	38	11	192	226	53

Leading Scorers

Player	Club	GP	G	A	PTS	PIM
Moore, Dickie	Montreal	70	36	48	84	65
Richard, Henri	Montreal	67	28	52	80	56
Bathgate, Andy	New York	65	30	48	78	42
Howe, Gordie	Detroit	64	33	44	77	40
Horvath, Bronco	Boston	67	30	36	66	71
Litzenberger, Ed	Chicago	70	32	30	62	63
Mackell, Fleming	Boston	70	20	40	60	72
Beliveau, Jean	Montreal	55	27	32	59	93
Delvecchio, Alex	Detroit	70	21	38	59	22
McKenney, Don	Boston	70	28	30	58	22

1958-59
Final Standings

Team	GP	W	L	T	GF	GA	PTS
Montreal	70	39	18	13	258	158	91
Boston	70	32	29	9	205	215	73
Chicago	70	28	29	13	197	208	69
Toronto	70	27	32	11	189	201	65
New York	70	26	32	12	201	217	64
Detroit	70	25	37	8	167	218	58

Leading Scorers

Player	Club	GP	G	A	PTS	PIM
Moore, Dickie	Montreal	70	41	55	96	61
Beliveau, Jean	Montreal	64	45	46	91	67
Bathgate, Andy	New York	70	40	48	88	48
Howe, Gordie	Detroit	70	32	46	78	57
Litzenberger, Ed	Chicago	70	33	44	77	37
Geoffrion, Bernie	Montreal	59	22	44	66	30
Sullivan, George	New York	70	21	42	63	56
Hebenton, Andy	New York	70	33	29	62	8
McKenney, Don	Boston	70	32	30	62	20
Sloan, Tod	Chicago	59	27	35	62	79

1959-60
Final Standings

Team	GP	W	L	T	GF	GA	PTS
Montreal	70	40	18	12	255	178	92
Toronto	70	35	26	9	199	195	79
Chicago	70	28	29	13	191	180	69
Detroit	70	26	29	15	186	197	67
Boston	70	28	34	8	220	241	64
New York	70	17	38	15	187	247	49

Leading Scorers

Player	Club	GP	G	A	PTS	PIM
Hull, Bobby	Chicago	70	39	42	81	68
Horvath, Bronco	Boston	68	39	41	80	60
Beliveau, Jean	Montreal	60	34	40	74	57
Bathgate, Andy	New York	70	26	48	74	28
Richard, Henri	Montreal	70	30	43	73	66
Howe, Gordie	Detroit	70	28	45	73	46
Geoffrion, Bernie	Montreal	59	30	41	71	36
McKenney, Don	Boston	70	20	49	69	28
Stasiuk, Vic	Boston	69	29	39	68	121
Prentice, Dean	New York	70	32	34	66	43

1960-61
Final Standings

Team	GP	W	L	T	GF	GA	PTS
Montreal	70	41	19	10	254	188	92
Toronto	70	39	19	12	234	176	90
Chicago	70	29	24	17	198	180	75
Detroit	70	25	29	16	195	215	66
New York	70	22	38	10	204	248	54
Boston	70	15	42	13	176	254	43

Leading Scorers

Player	Club	GP	G	A	PTS	PIM
Geoffrion, Bernie	Montreal	64	50	45	95	29
Béliveau, Jean	Montreal	69	32	58	90	57
Mahovlich, Frank	Toronto	70	48	36	84	131
Bathgate, Andy	New York	70	29	48	77	22
Howe, Gordie	Detroit	64	23	49	72	30
Ullman, Norm	Detroit	70	28	42	70	34
Kelly, Red	Toronto	64	20	50	70	12
Moore, Dickie	Montreal	57	35	34	69	62
Richard, Henri	Montreal	70	24	44	68	91
Delvecchio, Alex	Detroit	70	27	35	62	26

1961-62
Final Standings

Team	GP	W	L	T	GF	GA	PTS
Montreal	70	42	14	14	259	166	98
Toronto	70	37	22	11	232	180	85
Chicago	70	31	26	13	217	186	75
New York	70	26	32	12	195	207	64
Detroit	70	23	33	14	184	219	60
Boston	70	15	47	8	177	306	38

Leading Scorers

Player	Club	GP	G	A	PTS	PIM
Hull, Bobby	Chicago	70	50	34	84	35
Bathgate, Andy	New York	70	28	56	84	44
Howe, Gordie	Detroit	70	33	44	77	54
Mikita, Stan	Chicago	70	25	52	77	97
Mahovlich, Frank	Toronto	70	33	38	71	87
Delvecchio, Alex	Detroit	70	26	43	69	18
Backstrom, Ralph	Montreal	66	27	38	65	29
Ullman, Norm	Detroit	70	26	38	64	54
Hay, Bill	Chicago	60	11	52	63	34
Provost, Claude	Montreal	70	33	29	62	22

1962-63
Final Standings

Team	GP	W	L	T	GF	GA	PTS
Toronto	70	35	23	12	221	180	82
Chicago	70	32	21	17	194	178	81
Montreal	70	28	19	23	225	183	79
Detroit	70	32	25	13	200	194	77
New York	70	22	36	12	211	233	56
Boston	70	14	39	17	198	281	45

Leading Scorers

Player	Club	GP	G	A	PTS	PIM
Howe, Gordie	Detroit	70	38	48	86	100
Bathgate, Andy	New York	70	35	46	81	54
Mikita, Stan	Chicago	65	31	45	76	69
Mahovlich, Frank	Toronto	67	36	37	73	56
Richard, Henri	Montreal	67	23	50	73	57
Beliveau, Jean	Montreal	69	18	49	67	68
Bucyk, John	Boston	69	27	39	66	36
Delvecchio, Alex	Detroit	70	20	44	64	8
Hull, Bobby	Chicago	65	31	31	62	27
Oliver, Murray	Boston	65	22	40	62	38

1963-64
Final Standings

Team	GP	W	L	T	GF	GA	PTS
Montreal	70	36	21	13	209	167	85
Chicago	70	36	22	12	218	169	84
Toronto	70	33	25	12	192	172	78
Detroit	70	30	29	11	191	204	71
New York	70	22	38	10	186	242	54
Boston	70	18	40	12	170	212	48

Leading Scorers

Player	Club	GP	G	A	PTS	PIM
Mikita, Stan	Chicago	70	39	50	89	146
Hull, Bobby	Chicago	70	43	44	87	50
Beliveau, Jean	Montreal	68	28	50	78	42
Bathgate, Andy	NYR., Tor.	71	19	58	77	34
Howe, Gordie	Detroit	69	26	47	73	70
Wharram, Ken	Chicago	70	39	32	71	18
Oliver, Murray	Boston	70	24	44	68	41
Goyette, Phil	New York	67	24	41	65	15
Gilbert, Rod	New York	70	24	40	64	62
Keon, Dave	Toronto	70	23	37	60	6

1964-65
Final Standings

Team	GP	W	L	T	GF	GA	PTS
Detroit	70	40	23	7	224	175	87
Montreal	70	36	23	11	211	185	83
Chicago	70	34	28	8	224	176	76
Toronto	70	30	26	14	204	173	74
New York	70	20	38	12	179	246	52
Boston	70	21	43	6	166	253	48

Leading Scorers

Player	Club	GP	G	A	PTS	PIM
Mikita, Stan	Chicago	70	28	59	87	154
Ullman, Norm	Detroit	70	42	41	83	70
Howe, Gordie	Detroit	70	29	47	76	104
Hull, Bobby	Chicago	61	39	32	71	32
Delvecchio, Alex	Detroit	68	25	42	67	16
Provost, Claude	Montreal	70	27	37	64	28
Gilbert, Rod	New York	70	25	36	61	52
Pilote, Pierre	Chicago	68	14	45	59	162
Bucyk, John	Boston	68	26	29	55	24
Backstrom, Ralph	Montreal	70	25	30	55	41
Esposito, Phil	Chicago	70	23	32	55	44

1965-66
Final Standings

Team	GP	W	L	T	GF	GA	PTS
Montreal	70	41	21	8	239	173	90
Chicago	70	37	25	8	240	187	82
Toronto	70	34	25	11	208	187	79
Detroit	70	31	27	12	221	194	74
Boston	70	21	43	6	174	275	48
New York	70	18	41	11	195	261	47

Leading Scorers

Player	Club	GP	G	A	PTS	PIM
Hull, Bobby	Chicago	65	54	43	97	70
Mikita, Stan	Chicago	68	30	48	78	58
Rousseau, Bobby	Montreal	70	30	48	78	20
Beliveau, Jean	Montreal	67	29	48	77	50
Howe, Gordie	Detroit	70	29	46	75	83
Ullman, Norm	Detroit	70	31	41	72	35
Delvecchio, Alex	Detroit	70	31	38	69	16
Nevin, Bob	New York	69	29	33	62	10
Richard, Henri	Montreal	62	22	39	61	47
Oliver, Murray	Boston	70	18	42	60	30

1966-67
Final Standings

Team	GP	W	L	T	GF	GA	PTS
Chicago	70	41	17	12	264	170	94
Montreal	70	32	25	13	202	188	77
Toronto	70	32	27	11	204	211	75
New York	70	30	28	12	188	189	72
Detroit	70	27	39	4	212	241	58
Boston	70	17	43	10	182	253	44

Leading Scorers

Player	Club	GP	G	A	PTS	PIM
Mikita, Stan	Chicago	70	35	62	97	12
Hull, Bobby	Chicago	66	52	28	80	52
Ullman, Norm	Detroit	68	26	44	70	26
Wharram, Ken	Chicago	70	31	34	65	21
Howe, Gordie	Detroit	69	25	40	65	53
Rousseau, Bobby	Montreal	68	19	44	63	58
Esposito, Phil	Chicago	69	21	40	61	40
Goyette, Phil	New York	70	12	49	61	6
Mohns, Doug	Chicago	61	25	35	60	58
Richard, Henri	Montreal	65	21	34	55	28
Delvecchio, Alex	Detroit	70	17	38	55	10

1967-68
Final Standings
East Division

Team	GP	W	L	T	GF	GA	PTS
Montreal	74	42	22	10	236	167	94
New York	74	39	23	12	226	183	90
Boston	74	37	27	10	259	216	84
Chicago	74	32	26	16	212	222	80
Toronto	74	33	31	10	209	176	76
Detroit	74	27	35	12	245	257	66

West Division

Team	GP	W	L	T	GF	GA	PTS
Philadelphia	74	31	32	11	173	179	73
Los Angeles	74	31	33	10	200	224	72
St. Louis	74	27	31	16	177	191	70
Minnesota	74	27	32	15	191	226	69
Pittsburgh	74	27	34	13	195	216	67
Oakland	74	15	42	17	153	219	47

Leading Scorers

Player	Club	GP	G	A	PTS	PIM
Mikita, Stan	Chicago	72	40	47	87	14
Esposito, Phil	Boston	74	35	49	84	21
Howe, Gordie	Detroit	74	39	43	82	53
Ratelle, Jean	New York	74	32	46	78	18
Gilbert, Rod	New York	73	29	48	77	12
Hull, Bobby	Chicago	71	44	31	75	39
Ullman, Norm	Det., Tor.	71	35	37	72	28
Delvecchio, Alex	Detroit	74	22	48	70	14
Bucyk, John	Boston	72	30	39	69	8
Wharram, Ken	Chicago	74	27	42	69	18

1968-69
Final Standings
East Division

Team	GP	W	L	T	GF	GA	PTS
Montreal	76	46	19	11	271	202	103
Boston	76	42	18	16	303	221	100
New York	76	41	26	9	231	196	91
Toronto	76	35	26	15	234	217	85
Detroit	76	33	31	12	239	221	78
Chicago	76	34	33	9	280	246	77

West Division

Team	GP	W	L	T	GF	GA	PTS
St. Louis	76	37	25	14	204	157	88
Oakland	76	29	36	11	219	251	69
Philadelphia	76	20	35	21	174	225	61
Los Angeles	76	24	42	10	185	260	58
Pittsburgh	76	20	45	11	189	252	51
Minnesota	76	18	43	15	189	270	51

Leading Scorers

Player	Club	GP	G	A	PTS	PIM
Esposito, Phil	Boston	74	49	77	126	79
Hull, Bobby	Chicago	74	58	49	107	48
Howe, Gordie	Detroit	76	44	59	103	58
Mikita, Stan	Chicago	74	30	67	97	52
Hodge, Ken	Boston	75	45	45	90	75
Cournoyer, Yvan	Montreal	76	43	44	87	31
Delvecchio, Alex	Detroit	72	25	58	83	8
Berenson, Red	St. Louis	76	35	47	82	43
Beliveau, Jean	Montreal	69	33	49	82	55
Mahovlich, Frank	Detroit	76	49	29	78	38
Ratelle, Jean	New York	75	32	46	78	26

1969-70
Final Standings
East Division

Team	GP	W	L	T	GF	GA	PTS
Chicago	76	45	22	9	250	170	99
Boston	76	40	17	19	277	216	99
Detroit	76	40	21	15	246	199	95
New York	76	38	22	16	246	189	92
Montreal	76	38	22	16	244	201	92
Toronto	76	29	34	13	222	242	71

West Division

Team	GP	W	L	T	GF	GA	PTS
St. Louis	76	37	27	12	224	179	86
Pittsburgh	76	26	38	12	182	238	64
Minnesota	76	19	35	22	224	257	60
Oakland	76	22	40	14	169	243	58
Philadelphia	76	17	35	24	197	225	58
Los Angeles	76	14	52	10	168	290	38

Leading Scorers

Player	Club	GP	G	A	PTS	PIM
Orr, Bobby	Boston	76	33	87	120	125
Esposito, Phil	Boston	76	43	56	99	50
Mikita, Stan	Chicago	76	39	47	86	50
Goyette, Phil	St. Louis	72	29	49	78	16
Tkaczuk, Walt	New York	76	27	50	77	38
Ratelle, Jean	New York	75	32	42	74	28
Berenson, Red	St. Louis	67	33	39	72	38
Parise, Jean-Paul	Minnesota	74	24	48	72	72
Howe, Gordie	Detroit	76	31	40	71	58
Mahovlich, Frank	Detroit	74	38	32	70	59
Balon, Dave	New York	76	33	37	70	100
McKenzie, John	Boston	72	29	41	70	114

1970-71
Final Standings
East Division

Team	GP	W	L	T	GF	GA	PTS
Boston	78	57	14	7	399	207	121
New York	78	49	18	11	259	177	109
Montreal	78	42	23	13	291	216	97
Toronto	78	37	33	8	248	211	82
Buffalo	78	24	39	15	217	291	63
Vancouver	78	24	46	8	229	296	56
Detroit	78	22	45	11	209	308	55

West Division

Team	GP	W	L	T	GF	GA	PTS
Chicago	78	49	20	9	277	184	107
St. Louis	78	34	25	19	223	208	87
Philadelphia	78	28	33	17	207	225	73
Minnesota	78	28	34	16	191	223	72
Los Angeles	78	25	40	13	239	303	63
Pittsburgh	78	21	37	20	221	240	62
California	78	20	53	5	199	320	45

Leading Scorers

Player	Club	GP	G	A	PTS	PIM
Esposito, Phil	Boston	78	76	76	152	71
Orr, Bobby	Boston	78	37	102	139	91
Bucyk, John	Boston	78	51	65	116	8
Hodge, Ken	Boston	78	43	62	105	113
Hull, Bobby	Chicago	78	44	52	96	32
Ullman, Norm	Toronto	73	34	51	85	24
Cashman, Wayne	Boston	77	21	58	79	100
McKenzie, John	Boston	65	31	46	77	120
Keon, Dave	Toronto	76	38	38	76	4
Beliveau, Jean	Montreal	70	25	51	76	40
Stanfield, Fred	Boston	75	24	52	76	12

1971-72
Final Standings
East Division

Team	GP	W	L	T	GF	GA	PTS
Boston	78	54	13	11	330	204	119
New York	78	48	17	13	317	192	109
Montreal	78	46	16	16	307	205	108
Toronto	78	33	31	14	209	208	80
Detroit	78	33	35	10	261	262	76
Buffalo	78	16	43	19	203	289	51
Vancouver	78	20	50	8	203	297	48

West Division

Team	GP	W	L	T	GF	GA	PTS
Chicago	78	46	17	15	256	166	107
Minnesota	78	37	29	12	212	191	86
St. Louis	78	28	39	11	208	247	67
Pittsburgh	78	26	38	14	220	258	66
Philadelphia	78	26	38	14	200	236	66
California	78	21	39	18	216	288	60
Los Angeles	78	20	49	9	206	305	49

Leading Scorers

Player	Club	GP	G	A	PTS	PIM
Esposito, Phil	Boston	76	66	67	133	76
Orr, Bobby	Boston	76	37	80	117	106
Ratelle, Jean	New York	63	46	63	109	4
Hadfield, Vic	New York	78	50	56	106	142
Gilbert, Rod	New York	73	43	54	97	64
Mahovlich, Frank	Montreal	76	43	53	96	36
Hull, Bobby	Chicago	78	50	43	93	24
Cournoyer, Yvan	Montreal	73	47	36	83	15
Bucyk, John	Boston	78	32	51	83	4
Clarke, Bobby	Philadelphia	78	35	46	81	87
Lemaire, Jacques	Montreal	77	32	49	81	26

1972-73
Final Standings
East Division

Team	GP	W	L	T	GF	GA	PTS
Montreal	78	52	10	16	329	184	120
Boston	78	51	22	5	330	235	107
NY Rangers	78	47	23	8	297	208	102
Buffalo	78	37	27	14	257	219	88
Detroit	78	37	29	12	265	243	86
Toronto	78	27	41	10	247	279	64
Vancouver	78	22	47	9	233	339	53
NY Islanders	78	12	60	6	170	347	30

West Division

Team	GP	W	L	T	GF	GA	PTS
Chicago	78	42	27	9	284	225	93
Philadelphia	78	37	30	11	296	256	85
Minnesota	78	37	30	11	254	230	85
St. Louis	78	32	34	12	233	251	76
Pittsburgh	78	32	37	9	257	265	73
Los Angeles	78	31	36	11	232	245	73
Atlanta	78	25	38	15	191	239	65
California	78	16	46	16	213	323	48

Leading Scorers

Player	Club	GP	G	A	PTS	PIM
Esposito, Phil	Boston	78	55	75	130	87
Clarke, Bobby	Philadelphia	78	37	67	104	80
Orr, Bobby	Boston	63	29	72	101	99
MacLeish, Rick	Philadelphia	78	50	50	100	69
Lemaire, Jacques	Montreal	77	44	51	95	16
Ratelle, Jean	NY Rangers	78	41	53	94	12
Redmond, Mickey	Detroit	76	52	41	93	24
Bucyk, John	Boston	78	40	53	93	12
Mahovlich, Frank	Montreal	78	38	55	93	51
Pappin, Jim	Chicago	76	41	51	92	82

1973-74
Final Standings
East Division

Team	GP	W	L	T	GF	GA	PTS
Boston	78	52	17	9	349	221	113
Montreal	78	45	24	9	293	240	99
NY Rangers	78	40	24	14	300	251	94
Toronto	78	35	27	16	274	230	86
Buffalo	78	32	34	12	242	250	76
Detroit	78	29	39	10	255	319	68
Vancouver	78	24	43	11	224	296	59
NY Islanders	78	19	41	18	182	247	56

West Division

Team	GP	W	L	T	GF	GA	PTS
Philadelphia	78	50	16	12	273	164	112
Chicago	78	41	14	23	272	164	105
Los Angeles	78	33	33	12	233	231	78
Atlanta	78	30	34	14	214	238	74
Pittsburgh	78	28	41	9	242	273	65
St. Louis	78	26	40	12	206	248	64
Minnesota	78	23	38	17	235	275	63
California	78	13	55	10	195	342	36

Leading Scorers

Player	Club	GP	G	A	PTS	PIM
Esposito, Phil	Boston	78	68	77	145	58
Orr, Bobby	Boston	74	32	90	122	82
Hodge, Ken	Boston	76	50	55	105	43
Cashman, Wayne	Boston	78	30	59	89	111
Clarke, Bobby	Philadelphia	77	35	52	87	113
Martin, Rick	Buffalo	78	52	34	86	38
Apps, Syl	Pittsburgh	75	24	61	85	37
Sittler, Darryl	Toronto	78	38	46	84	55
MacDonald, Lowell	Pittsburgh	78	43	39	82	14

1974-75
Final Standings
PRINCE OF WALES CONFERENCE

Norris Division

Team	GP	W	L	T	GF	GA	PTS
Montreal	80	47	14	19	374	225	113
Los Angeles	80	42	17	21	269	185	105
Pittsburgh	80	37	28	15	326	289	89
Detroit	80	23	45	12	259	335	58
Washington	80	8	67	5	181	446	21

Adams Division

Team	GP	W	L	T	GF	GA	PTS
Buffalo	80	49	16	15	354	240	113
Boston	80	40	26	14	345	245	94
Toronto	80	31	33	16	280	309	78
California	80	19	48	13	212	316	51

CLARENCE CAMPBELL CONFERENCE

Patrick Division

Team	GP	W	L	T	GF	GA	PTS
Philadelphia	80	51	18	11	293	181	113
NY Rangers	80	37	29	14	319	276	88
NY Islanders	80	33	25	22	264	221	88
Atlanta	80	34	31	15	243	233	83

Smythe Division

Team	GP	W	L	T	GF	GA	PTS
Vancouver	80	38	32	10	271	254	86
St. Louis	80	35	31	14	269	267	84
Chicago	80	37	35	8	268	241	82
Minnesota	80	23	50	7	221	341	53
Kansas City	80	15	54	11	184	328	41

Leading Scorers

Player	Club	GP	G	A	PTS	PIM
Orr, Bobby	Boston	80	46	89	135	101
Esposito, Phil	Boston	79	61	66	127	62
Dionne, Marcel	Detroit	80	47	74	121	14
Lafleur, Guy	Montreal	70	53	66	119	37
Mahovlich, Pete	Montreal	80	35	82	117	64
Clarke, Bobby	Philadelphia	80	27	89	116	125
Robert, Rene	Buffalo	74	40	60	100	75
Gilbert, Rod	NY Rangers	76	36	61	97	22
Perreault, Gilbert	Buffalo	68	39	57	96	53
Martin, Rick	Buffalo	68	52	43	95	72

Fred Stanfield finished 14 years in the NHL with 616 points.

1975-76
Final Standings
PRINCE OF WALES CONFERENCE
Norris Division

Team	GP	W	L	T	GF	GA	PTS
Montreal	80	58	11	11	337	174	127
Los Angeles	80	38	33	9	263	265	85
Pittsburgh	80	35	33	12	339	303	82
Detroit	80	26	44	10	226	300	62
Washington	80	11	59	10	224	394	32

Adams Division

Boston	80	48	15	17	313	237	113
Buffalo	80	46	21	13	339	240	105
Toronto	80	34	31	15	294	276	83
California	80	27	42	11	250	278	65

CLARENCE CAMPBELL CONFERENCE
Patrick Division

Philadelphia	80	51	13	16	348	209	118
NY Islanders	80	42	21	17	297	190	101
Atlanta	80	35	33	12	262	237	82
NY Rangers	80	29	42	9	262	333	67

Smythe Division

Chicago	80	32	30	18	254	261	82
Vancouver	80	33	32	15	271	272	81
St. Louis	80	29	37	14	249	290	72
Minnesota	80	20	53	7	195	303	47
Kansas City	80	12	56	12	190	351	36

Leading Scorers

Player	Club	GP	G	A	PTS	PIM
Lafleur, Guy	Montreal	80	56	59	125	36
Clarke, Bobby	Philadelphia	76	30	89	119	136
Perreault, Gilbert	Buffalo	80	44	69	113	36
Barber, Bill	Philadelphia	80	50	62	112	104
Larouche, Pierre	Pittsburgh	76	53	58	111	33
Ratelle, Jean	Bos., NYR	80	36	69	105	18
Mahovlich, Pete	Montreal	80	34	71	105	76
Pronovost, Jean	Pittsburgh	80	52	52	104	24
Sittler, Darryl	Toronto	79	41	59	100	90
Apps, Syl	Pittsburgh	80	32	67	99	24

1976-77
Final Standings
PRINCE OF WALES CONFERENCE
Norris Division

Team	GP	W	L	T	GF	GA	PTS
Montreal	80	60	8	12	387	171	132
Los Angeles	80	34	31	15	271	241	83
Pittsburgh	80	34	33	13	240	252	81
Washington	80	24	42	14	221	307	62
Detroit	80	16	55	9	183	309	41

Adams Division

Boston	80	49	23	8	312	240	106
Buffalo	80	48	24	8	301	220	104
Toronto	80	33	32	15	301	285	81
Cleveland	80	25	42	13	240	292	63

CLARENCE CAMPBELL CONFERENCE
Patrick Division

Philadelphia	80	48	16	16	323	213	112
NY Islanders	80	47	21	12	288	193	106
Atlanta	80	34	34	12	264	265	80
NY Rangers	88	29	37	14	272	310	72

Smythe Division

St. Louis	80	32	39	9	239	276	73
Minnesota	80	23	39	18	240	310	64
Chicago	80	26	43	11	240	298	63
Vancouver	80	25	42	13	235	294	63
Colorado	80	20	46	14	226	307	54

Leading Scorers

Player	Club	GP	G	A	PTS	PIM
Lafleur, Guy	Montreal	80	56	80	136	20
Dionne, Marcel	Los Angeles	80	53	69	122	12
Shutt, Steve	Montreal	80	60	45	105	28
MacLeish, Rick	Philadelphia	79	49	48	97	42
Perreault, Gilbert	Buffalo	80	39	56	95	30
Young, Tim	Minnesota	80	29	66	95	58
Ratelle, Jean	Boston	78	33	61	94	22
McDonald, Lanny	Toronto	80	46	44	90	77
Sittler, Darryl	Toronto	73	38	52	90	89
Clarke, Bobby	Philadelphia	80	27	63	90	71

1977-78
Final Standings
PRINCE OF WALES CONFERENCE
Norris Division

Team	GP	W	L	T	GF	GA	PTS
Montreal	80	59	10	11	359	183	129
Detroit	80	32	34	14	252	266	78
Los Angeles	80	31	34	15	243	245	77
Pittsburgh	80	25	37	18	254	321	68
Washington	80	17	49	14	195	321	48

Adams Division

Boston	80	51	18	11	333	218	113
Buffalo	80	44	19	17	288	215	105
Toronto	80	41	29	10	271	237	92
Cleveland	80	22	45	13	230	325	57

CLARENCE CAMPBELL CONFERENCE
Patrick Division

NY Islanders	80	48	17	15	334	210	111
Philadelphia	80	45	20	15	296	200	105
Atlanta	80	34	27	19	274	252	87
NY Rangers	80	30	37	13	279	280	73

Smythe Division

Chicago	80	32	29	19	230	220	83
Colorado	80	19	40	21	257	305	59
Vancouver	80	20	43	17	239	320	57
St. Louis	80	20	47	13	195	304	53
Minnesota	80	18	53	9	218	325	45

Leading Scorers

Player	Club	GP	G	A	PTS	PIM
Lafleur, Guy	Montreal	79	60	72	132	26
Trottier, Bryan	NY Islanders	77	46	77	123	46
Sittler, Darryl	Toronto	80	45	72	117	100
Lemaire, Jacques	Montreal	76	36	61	97	14
Potvin, Denis	NY Islanders	80	30	64	94	81
Bossy, Mike	NY Islanders	73	53	38	91	6
O'Reilly, Terry	Boston	77	29	61	90	211
Perreault, Gilbert	Buffalo	79	41	48	89	20
Clarke, Bobby	Philadelphia	71	21	68	89	83
McDonald, Lanny	Toronto	74	47	40	87	54
Paiement, Wilf	Colorado	80	31	56	87	114

1978-79
Final Standings
PRINCE OF WALES CONFERENCE
Norris Division

Team	GP	W	L	T	GF	GA	PTS
Montreal	80	52	17	11	337	204	115
Pittsburgh	80	36	31	13	281	279	85
Los Angeles	80	34	34	12	292	286	80
Washington	80	24	41	15	273	338	63
Detroit	80	23	41	16	252	295	62

Adams Division

Boston	80	43	23	14	316	270	100
Buffalo	80	36	28	16	280	263	88
Toronto	80	34	33	13	267	252	81
Minnesota	80	28	40	12	257	289	68

CLARENCE CAMPBELL CONFERENCE
Patrick Division

NY Islanders	80	51	15	14	358	214	116
Philadelphia	80	40	25	15	281	248	95
NY Rangers	80	40	29	11	316	292	91
Atlanta	80	41	31	8	327	280	90

Smythe Division

Chicago	80	29	36	15	244	277	73
Vancouver	80	25	42	13	217	291	63
St. Louis	80	18	50	12	249	348	48
Colorado	80	15	53	12	210	331	42

Leading Scorers

Player	Club	GP	G	A	PTS	PIM
Trottier, Bryan	NY Islanders	76	47	87	134	50
Dionne, Marcel	Los Angeles	80	59	71	130	30
Lafleur, Guy	Montreal	80	52	77	129	28
Bossy, Mike	NY Islanders	80	69	57	126	25
MacMillan, Bob	Atlanta	79	37	71	108	14
Chouinard, Guy	Atlanta	80	50	57	107	14
Potvin, Denis	NY Islanders	73	31	70	101	58
Federko, Bernie	St. Louis	74	31	64	95	14
Taylor, Dave	Los Angeles	78	43	48	91	124
Gillies, Clark	NY Islanders	75	35	56	91	68

1979-80
Final Standings
PRINCE OF WALES CONFERENCE
Norris Division

Team	GP	W	L	T	GF	GA	PTS
Montreal	80	47	20	13	328	240	107
Los Angeles	80	30	36	14	290	313	74
Pittsburgh	80	30	37	13	251	303	73
Hartford	80	27	34	19	303	312	73
Detroit	80	26	43	11	268	306	63

Adams Division

Buffalo	80	47	17	16	318	201	110
Boston	80	46	21	13	310	234	105
Minnesota	80	36	28	16	311	253	88
Toronto	80	35	40	5	304	327	75
Quebec	80	25	44	11	248	313	61

CLARENCE CAMPBELL CONFERENCE
Patrick Division

Philadelphia	80	48	12	20	327	254	116
NY Islanders	80	39	28	13	281	247	91
NY Rangers	80	38	32	10	308	284	86
Atlanta	80	35	32	13	282	269	83
Washington	80	27	40	13	261	293	67

Smythe Division

Chicago	80	34	27	19	241	250	87
St. Louis	80	34	34	12	266	278	80
Vancouver	80	27	37	16	256	281	70
Edmonton	80	28	39	13	301	322	69
Winnipeg	80	20	49	11	214	314	51
Colorado	80	19	48	13	234	308	51

Leading Scorers

Player	Club	GP	G	A	PTS	PIM
Dionne, Marcel	Los Angeles	80	53	84	137	32
Gretzky, Wayne	Edmonton	79	51	86	137	21
Lafleur, Guy	Montreal	74	50	75	125	12
Perreault, Gilbert	Buffalo	80	40	66	106	57
Rogers, Mike	Hartford	80	44	61	105	10
Trottier, Bryan	NY Islanders	78	42	62	104	68
Simmer, Charlie	Los Angeles	64	56	45	101	65
Stoughton, Blaine	Hartford	80	56	44	100	16
Sittler, Darryl	Toronto	73	40	57	97	62
MacDonald, Blair	Edmonton	80	46	48	94	6
Federko, Bernie	St. Louis	79	38	56	94	24

1980-81
Final Standings
PRINCE OF WALES CONFERENCE
Norris Division

Team	GP	W	L	T	GF	GA	PTS
Montreal	80	45	22	13	332	232	103
Los Angeles	80	43	24	13	337	290	99
Pittsburgh	80	30	37	13	302	345	73
Hartford	80	21	41	18	292	372	60
Detroit	80	19	43	18	252	339	56

Adams Division

Buffalo	80	39	20	21	327	250	99
Boston	80	37	30	13	316	272	87
Minnesota	80	35	28	17	291	263	87
Quebec	80	30	32	18	314	318	78
Toronto	80	28	37	15	322	367	71

CLARENCE CAMPBELL CONFERENCE
Patrick Division

NY Islanders	80	48	18	14	355	260	110
Philadelphia	80	41	24	15	313	249	97
Calgary	80	39	27	14	329	298	92
NY Rangers	80	30	36	14	312	317	74
Washington	80	26	36	18	286	317	70

Smythe Division

St. Louis	80	45	18	17	352	281	107
Chicago	80	31	33	16	304	315	78
Vancouver	80	28	32	20	289	301	76
Edmonton	80	29	35	16	328	327	74
Colorado	80	22	45	13	258	344	57
Winnipeg	80	9	57	14	246	400	32

Leading Scorers

Player	Club	GP	G	A	PTS	PIM
Gretzky, Wayne	Edmonton	80	55	109	164	28
Dionne, Marcel	Los Angeles	80	58	77	135	70
Nilsson, Kent	Calgary	80	49	82	131	26
Bossy, Mike	NY Islanders	79	68	51	119	32
Taylor, Dave	Los Angeles	72	47	65	112	130
Stastny, Peter	Quebec	77	39	70	109	37
Simmer, Charlie	Los Angeles	65	56	49	105	62
Rodgers, Mike	Hartford	80	40	65	105	32
Federko, Bernie	St. Louis	78	31	73	104	47
Richard, Jacques	Quebec	78	52	51	103	39
Middleton, Rick	Boston	80	44	59	103	16
Trottier, Bryan	NY Islanders	73	31	72	103	74

1981-82
Final Standings
CLARENCE CAMPBELL CONFERENCE

Norris Division

Team	GP	W	L	T	GF	GA	PTS
Minnesota	80	37	23	20	346	288	94
Winnipeg	80	33	33	14	319	332	80
St. Louis	80	32	40	8	315	349	72
Chicago	80	30	38	12	332	363	72
Toronto	80	20	44	16	298	380	56
Detroit	80	21	47	12	270	351	54

Smythe Division

Edmonton	80	48	17	15	417	295	111
Vancouver	80	30	33	17	290	286	77
Calgary	80	29	34	17	334	345	75
Los Angeles	80	24	41	15	314	369	63
Colorado	80	18	49	13	241	362	49

PRINCE OF WALES CONFERENCE

Adams Division

Montreal	80	46	17	17	360	223	109
Boston	80	43	27	10	323	285	96
Buffalo	80	39	26	15	307	273	93
Quebec	80	33	31	16	356	345	82
Hartford	80	21	41	18	264	351	60

Patrick Division

NY Islanders	80	54	16	10	385	250	118
NY Rangers	80	39	27	14	316	306	92
Philadelphia	80	38	31	11	325	313	87
Pittsburgh	80	31	36	13	310	337	75
Washington	80	26	41	13	319	338	65

Leading Scorers

Player	Club	GP	G	A	PTS	PIM
Gretzky, Wayne	Edmonton	80	92	120	212	26
Bossy, Mike	NY Islanders	80	64	83	147	22
Stastny, Peter	Quebec	80	46	93	139	91
Maruk, Dennis	Washington	80	60	76	136	128
Trottier, Bryan	NY Islanders	80	50	79	129	88
Savard, Denis	Chicago	80	32	87	119	82
Dionne, Marcel	Los Angeles	78	50	67	117	50
Smith, Bobby	Minnesota	80	43	71	114	82
Ciccarelli, Dino	Minnesota	76	55	51	106	138
Taylor, Dave	Los Angeles	78	39	67	106	130

1982-83
Final Standings
CLARENCE CAMPBELL CONFERENCE

Norris Division

Team	GP	W	L	T	GF	GA	PTS
Chicago	80	47	23	10	338	268	104
Minnesota	80	40	24	16	321	290	96
Toronto	80	28	40	12	293	330	68
St. Louis	80	25	40	15	285	316	65
Detroit	80	21	44	15	263	344	57

Smythe Division

Edmonton	80	47	21	12	424	315	106
Calgary	80	32	34	14	321	317	78
Vancouver	80	30	35	15	303	309	75
Winnipeg	80	33	39	8	311	333	74
Los Angeles	80	27	41	12	308	365	66

PRINCE OF WALES CONFERENCE

Adams Division

Boston	80	50	20	10	327	228	110
Montreal	80	42	24	14	350	286	98
Buffalo	80	38	29	13	318	285	89
Quebec	80	34	34	12	343	336	80
Hartford	80	19	54	7	261	403	45

Patrick Division

Philadelphia	80	49	23	8	326	240	106
NY Islanders	80	42	26	12	302	226	96
Washington	80	39	25	16	306	283	94
NY Rangers	80	35	35	10	306	287	80
New Jersey	80	17	49	14	230	338	48
Pittsburgh	80	18	53	9	257	394	45

Leading Scorers

Player	Club	GP	G	A	PTS	PIM
Gretzky, Wayne	Edmonton	80	71	125	196	59
Stastny, Peter	Quebec	75	47	77	124	78
Savard, Denis	Chicago	78	35	86	121	99
Bossy, Mike	NY Islanders	79	60	58	118	20
Dionne, Marcel	Los Angeles	80	56	51	107	22
Pederson, Barry	Boston	77	46	61	107	47
Messier, Mark	Edmonton	77	48	58	106	72
Goulet, Michel	Quebec	80	57	48	105	51
Anderson, Glenn	Edmonton	72	48	56	104	70
Nilsson, Kent	Calgary	80	46	58	104	10
Kurri, Jari	Edmonton	80	45	59	104	22

1983-84
Final Standings
CLARENCE CAMPBELL CONFERENCE

Norris Division

Team	GP	W	L	T	GF	GA	PTS
Minnesota	80	39	31	10	345	344	88
St. Louis	80	32	41	7	293	316	71
Detroit	80	31	42	7	298	323	69
Chicago	80	30	42	8	277	311	68
Toronto	80	26	45	9	303	387	61

Smythe Division

Edmonton	80	57	18	5	446	314	119
Calgary	80	34	32	14	311	314	82
Vancouver	80	32	39	9	306	328	73
Winnipeg	80	31	38	11	340	374	73
Los Angeles	80	23	44	13	309	376	59

PRINCE OF WALES CONFERENCE

Adams Division

Boston	80	49	25	6	336	261	104
Buffalo	80	48	25	7	315	257	103
Quebec	80	42	28	10	360	278	94
Montreal	80	35	40	5	286	295	75
Hartford	80	28	42	10	288	320	66

Patrick Division

NY Islanders	80	50	26	4	357	269	104
Washington	80	48	27	5	308	226	101
Philadelphia	80	44	26	10	350	290	98
NY Rangers	80	42	29	9	314	304	93
New Jersey	80	17	56	7	231	350	41
Pittsburgh	80	16	58	6	254	390	38

Leading Scorers

Player	Club	GP	G	A	PTS	PIM
Gretzky, Wayne	Edmonton	74	87	118	205	39
Coffey, Paul	Edmonton	80	40	86	126	104
Goulet, Michel	Quebec	75	56	65	121	76
Stastny, Peter	Quebec	80	46	73	119	73
Bossy, Mike	NY Islanders	67	51	67	118	8
Pederson, Barry	Boston	80	39	77	116	64
Kurri, Jari	Edmonton	64	52	61	113	14
Trottier, Bryan	NY Islanders	68	40	71	111	59
Federko, Bernie	St. Louis	79	41	66	107	43
Middleton, Rick	Boston	80	47	58	105	14

Barry Pederson

1984-85
Final Standings
CLARENCE CAMPBELL CONFERENCE

Norris Division

Team	GP	W	L	T	GF	GA	PTS
Minnesota	80	37	31	12	299	288	86
St. Louis	80	38	35	7	309	299	83
Detroit	80	27	41	12	313	357	66
Chicago	80	25	43	12	268	321	62
Toronto	80	20	52	8	253	358	48

Smythe Division

Edmonton	80	49	20	11	401	298	109
Calgary	80	43	27	10	358	332	96
Vancouver	80	41	27	12	363	302	94
Winnipeg	80	34	32	14	339	326	82
Los Angeles	80	25	46	9	284	401	59

PRINCE OF WALES CONFERENCE

Adams Division

Boston	80	41	27	12	309	262	94
Buffalo	80	41	30	9	323	275	91
Quebec	80	38	28	14	290	237	90
Montreal	80	36	34	10	303	287	82
Hartford	80	30	41	9	268	318	69

Patrick Division

NY Islanders	80	53	20	7	348	241	113
Washington	80	46	25	9	322	240	101
Philadelphia	80	40	34	6	345	312	86
NY Rangers	80	26	44	10	295	345	62
New Jersey	80	22	48	10	264	346	54
Pittsburgh	80	24	51	5	276	385	53

Leading Scorers

Player	Club	GP	G	A	PTS	PIM
Gretzky, Wayne	Edmonton	80	73	135	208	52
Kurri, Jari	Edmonton	73	71	64	135	30
Hawerchuk, Dale	Winnipeg	80	53	77	130	74
Dionne, Marcel	Los Angeles	80	46	80	126	46
Coffey, Paul	Edmonton	80	37	84	121	97
Bossy, Mike	NY Islanders	76	58	59	117	38
Ogrodnick, John	Detroit	79	55	50	105	30
Savard, Denis	Chicago	79	38	67	105	56
Federko, Bernie	St. Louis	76	30	73	103	27
Gartner, Mike	Washington	80	50	52	102	71

1985-86
Final Standings
CLARENCE CAMPBELL CONFERENCE

Norris Division

Team	GP	W	L	T	GF	GA	PTS
Chicago	80	39	33	8	351	349	86
Minnesota	80	38	33	9	327	305	85
St. Louis	80	37	34	9	302	291	83
Toronto	80	25	48	7	311	386	57
Detroit	80	17	57	6	266	415	40

Smythe Division

Edmonton	80	56	17	7	426	310	119
Calgary	80	40	31	9	354	315	89
Winnipeg	80	26	47	7	295	372	59
Vancouver	80	23	44	13	282	333	59
Los Angeles	80	23	49	8	284	389	54

PRINCE OF WALES CONFERENCE

Adams Division

Quebec	80	43	31	6	330	289	92
Montreal	80	40	33	7	330	280	87
Boston	80	37	31	12	311	288	86
Hartford	80	40	36	4	332	302	84
Buffalo	80	37	37	6	296	291	80

Patrick Division

Philadelphia	80	53	23	4	335	241	110
Washington	80	50	23	7	315	272	107
NY Islanders	80	39	29	12	327	284	90
NY Rangers	80	36	38	6	280	276	78
Pittsburgh	80	34	38	8	313	305	76
New Jersey	80	28	49	3	300	374	59

Leading Scorers

Player	Club	GP	G	A	PTS	PIM
Gretzky, Wayne	Edmonton	80	52	163	215	46
Lemieux, Mario	Pittsburgh	79	48	93	141	43
Coffey, Paul	Edmonton	79	48	90	138	120
Kurri, Jari	Edmonton	78	68	63	131	22
Bossy, Mike	NY Islanders	80	61	62	123	14
Stastny, Peter	Quebec	76	41	81	122	60
Savard, Denis	Chicago	80	47	69	116	111
Naslund, Mats	Montreal	80	43	67	110	16
Hawerchuk, Dale	Winnipeg	80	46	59	105	44
Broten, Neal	Minnesota	80	29	76	105	47

Note: Complete standings and leading scorers for 1985-86 are listed in the Final Statistics, 1985-86 section of the **NHL Guide & Record Book.**

NHL History

1917 — National Hockey League organized November 22 in Montreal following suspension of operations by the National Hockey Association of Canada Limited (NHA). Montreal Canadiens, Montreal Wanderers, Ottawa Senators and Quebec Bulldogs attended founding meeting. Delegates decided to use NHA rules.

Toronto Arenas were later admitted as fifth team; Quebec decided not to operate during the first season. Quebec players allocated to remaining four teams.

Frank Calder elected president and secretary-treasurer.

First NHL games played December 19, with Toronto only arena with artificial ice. Clubs played 22-game split schedule.

1918 — Emergency meeting held January 3 due to destruction by fire of Montreal Arena which was home ice for both Canadiens and Wanderers.

Wanderers withdrew, reducing the NHL to three teams; Canadiens played remaining home games at 3,250-seat Jubilee rink.

Quebec franchise sold to P.J. Quinn of Toronto on October 18 on the condition that the team operate in Quebec City for 1918-19 season. Quinn did not attend the November League meeting and Quebec did not play in 1918-19.

1919-20 — NHL reactivated Quebec Bulldogs franchise. Former Quebec players returned to the club. New Mount Royal Arena became home of Canadiens. Toronto Arenas changed name to St. Patricks. Clubs played 24-game split schedule.

1920-21 — H.P. Thompson of Hamilton, Ontario made application for the purchase of an NHL franchise. Quebec franchise shifted to Hamilton with other NHL teams providing players to strengthen the club.

1921-22 — Split schedule abandoned. First and second place teams at the end of full schedule to play for championship.

1922-23 — Clubs agreed that players could not be sold or traded to clubs in any other league without first being offered to all other clubs in the NHL. In March, Foster Hewitt broadcast radio's first hockey game.

1923-24 — Ottawa's new 10,000-seat arena opened. First U.S. franchise granted to Boston for following season.

Dr. Cecil Hart Trophy donated to NHL to be awarded to the player judged most useful to his team.

1924-25 — Canadian Arena Company of Montreal granted a franchise to operate Montreal Maroons. NHL now six team league with two clubs in Montreal. Inaugural game in new Montreal Forum played November 29, 1924 as Canadiens defeated Toronto 7-1. Forum was home rink for the Maroons, but no ice was available in the Canadiens arena November 29, resulting in shift to Forum.

Hamilton finished first in the standings, receiving a bye into the finals. But Hamilton players, demanding $200 each for additional games in the playoffs, went on strike. The NHL suspended all players, fining them $200 each. Stanley Cup finalist to be the winner of NHL semi-final between Toronto and Canadiens.

Prince of Wales and Lady Byng trophies donated to NHL.

Clubs played 30-game schedule.

1925-26 — Hamilton club dropped from NHL. Players signed by new New York Americans franchise. Franchise granted to Pittsburgh.

Clubs played 36-game schedule.

1926-27 — New York Rangers granted franchise April 17, 1926. Chicago Black Hawks and Detroit Cougars granted franchises May 15, 1926. NHL now ten-team league with an American and a Canadian Division.

Stanley Cup came under the control of NHL. In previous seasons, winners of the now-defunct Western or Pacific Coast leagues would play NHL champion in Cup finals.

Toronto franchise sold to a new company controlled by Hugh Aird and Conn Smythe. Name changed from St. Patricks to Maple Leafs.

Clubs played 44-game schedule.

The Montreal Canadiens donated the Vezina Trophy to be awarded to the team allowing the fewest goals-against in regular season play. The winning team would, in turn, present the trophy to the goaltender playing in the greatest number of games during the season.

1929-30 — Detroit franchise changed name from Cougars to Falcons.

1930-31 — Pittsburgh transferred to Philadelphia for one season. Pirates changed name to Philadelphia Quakers. Trading deadline for teams set at February 15 of each year. NHL approved operation of farm teams by Rangers, Americans, Falcons and Bruins. Four-sided electric arena clock first demonstrated.

1931-32 — Philadelphia dropped out. Ottawa withdrew for one season. New Maple Leaf Gardens completed.

Clubs played 48-game schedule

1932-33 — Franchise application received from St. Louis but refused because of additional travel costs. Ottawa team resumed play.

1933-34 — Detroit franchise changed name from Falcons to Red Wings. First all-star game played as a benefit for injured player Ace Bailey. Stanley Cup champion Leafs defeated All-Stars 7-3 in Toronto.

1934-35 — Ottawa franchise transferred to St. Louis. Team called St. Louis Eagles and consisted largely of Ottawa's players.

1935-36 — Ottawa-St. Louis franchise terminated. Montreal Canadiens finished season with very poor record. To strengthen the club, NHL gave Canadiens first call on the services of all French-Canadian players for three seasons.

1937-38 — Second benefit all-star game staged November 2 in Montreal in aid of the family of the late Canadiens star Howie Morenz.

Montreal Maroons withdrew from the NHL on June 22, 1938, leaving seven clubs in the League.

1938-39 — Expenses for each club regulated at $5 per man per day for meals and $2.50 per man per day for accommodation.

1939-40 — Benefit All-Star game played October 29, 1939 in Montreal for the children of the late Albert (Babe) Siebert.

1940-41 — Ross-Tyer puck adopted as the official puck of the NHL. Early in the season it was apparent that this puck was too soft. The Spalding puck was adopted in its place.

After the playoffs, Arthur Ross, NHL governor from Boston, donated a perpetual trophy to be awarded annually to the player voted outstanding in the league.

1941-42 — New York Americans changed name to Brooklyn Americans.

1942-43 — Brooklyn Americans withdrew from NHL, leaving six teams: Boston, Chicago, Detroit, Montreal, New York and Toronto. Playoff format saw first-place team play third-place team and second play fourth.

Clubs played 50-game schedule.

Frank Calder, president of the NHL since its inception, died in Montreal. Mervyn "Red" Dutton, former manager of the New York Americans, became president. The NHL commissioned the Calder Memorial Trophy to be awarded to the League's outstanding rookie each year.

1945-46 — Philadelphia, Los Angeles and San Fransisco applied for NHL franchises.

The Philadelphia Arena Company of the American Hockey League applied for an injunction to prevent the possible operation of an NHL franchise in that city.

1946-47 — Mervyn Dutton retired as president of the NHL prior to the start of the season. He was succeeded by Clarence S. Campbell.

Individual trophy winners and all-star team members to receive $1,000 awards.

Playoff guarantees for players introduced.

Clubs played 60-game schedule.

1947-48 — The first annual All-Star Game for the benefit of the players' pension fund was played when the All-Stars defeated the Stanley Cup Champion Toronto Maple Leafs 4-3 in Toronto on October 13, 1947.

Ross Trophy, awarded to the NHL's outstanding player since 1941, to be awarded annually to the League's scoring leader.

Philadelphia and Los Angeles franchise applications refused.

National Hockey League Pension Society formed.

1949-50 — Clubs played 70-game schedule

First intra-league draft held April 30, 1950. Clubs allowed to protect 30 players. Remaining players available for $25,000 each.

1951-52 — Referees included in the League's pension plan.

1952-53 — In May of 1952, City of Cleveland applied for NHL franchise. Application denied. In March of 1953, the Cleveland Barons of the AHL challenged the NHL champions for the Stanley Cup. The NHL governors did not accept this challenge, stating that Cleveland operated in a league of acknowledged lower standing.

1953-54 — The James Norris Memorial Trophy presented to the NHL for annual presentation to the League's best defenseman.

Intra-league draft rules amended to allow teams to protect 18 skaters and two goaltenders, claiming price reduced to $15,000.

1954-55 — Each arena to operate an "out-of-town" scoreboard. Referees and linesmen to wear shirts of black and white vertical stripes. Teams agree to wear white uniforms at home and colored uniforms on the road.

1956-57 — Standardized signals for referees and linesmen introduced.

1960-61 — Canadian National Exhibition, City of Toronto and NHL reach agreement for the construction of a Hockey Hall of Fame on the CNE grounds. Hall opens on August 26, 1961.

Visible time clocks were required in NHL arenas beginning with the 1933-34 season. This was the original clock used in Maple Leaf Gardens.

1963-64 — Player development league established with clubs operated by NHL franchises located in Minneapolis, St. Paul, Indianapolis, Omaha and, beginning in 1964-65, Tulsa. First universal amateur draft took place. All players of qualifying age (17) unaffected by sponsorship of junior teams available to be drafted.

1964-65 — Conn Smythe Trophy presented to the NHL to be awarded annually to the outstanding player in the Stanley Cup playoffs.
Minimum age of players subject ot amateur draft changed to 18.

1965-66 — NHL announced expansion plans for a second six-team division to begin play in 1967-68.

1966-67 — Fourteen applications for NHL franchises received.
Lester Patrick Trophy presented to the NHL to be awarded annually for outstanding service to hockey in the United States.
NHL sponsorship of junior teams ceased, making all players of qualifying age not already on NHL-sponsored lists eligible for the amateur draft.

1967-68 — Six new teams added: California Seals, Los Angeles Kings, Minnesota North Stars, Philadelphia Flyers, Pittsburgh Penguins, St. Louis Blues. New teams to play in West Division. Remaining six teams to play in East Division.
Minimum age of players subject to amateur draft changed to 20.
Clubs played 74-game schedule.
Clarence S. Campbell Trophy awarded to team finishing the regular season in first place in West Division.
California Seals changed name to Oakland Seals on December 8, 1967.

1968-69 — Clubs played 76-game schedule.
Amateur draft expanded to cover any amateur player of qualifying age throughout the world.

1970-71 — Two new teams added: Buffalo Sabres and Vancouver Canucks. These teams joined East Division: Chicago switched to West Division.
Clubs played 78-game schedule.

1971-72 — Playoff format amended. In each division, first to play fourth; second to play third.

1972-73 — Soviet Nationals and Canadian NHL stars play eight-game pre-season series. Canadians win 4-3-1.
Two new teams added. Atlanta Flames join West Division; New York Islanders join East Division.

1974-75 — Two new teams added: Kansas City Scouts and Washington Capitals. Teams realigned into two nine-team conferences, the Prince of Wales made up of the Norris and Adams Divisions, and the Clarence Campbell made up of the Smythe and Patrick Divisions.
Clubs played 80-game schedule.

1976-77 — California franchise transferred to Cleveland. Team named Cleveland Barons. Kansas City franchise transferred to Denver. Team named Colorado Rockies.

1977-78 — Clarence S. Campbell retires as NHL president. Succeeded by John A. Ziegler, Jr.

1978-79 — Cleveland and Minnesota franchises merge, leaving NHL with 17 teams. Merged team placed in Adams Division, playing home games in Minnesota.
Minimum age of players subject to amateur draft changed to 19.

1979-80 — Four new teams added: Edmonton Oilers, Hartford Whalers, Quebec Nordiques and Winnipeg Jets.
Minimum age of players subject to amateur draft changed to 18.

1980-81 — Atlanta franchise shifted to Calgary, retaining "Flames" name.

1981-82 — Unbalanced schedule adopted.

1982-83 — Colorado Rockies franchise shifted to East Rutherford, New Jersey. Team named New Jersey Devils.

Franchise History

Location	Club Name	NHL Seasons	Franchise Activity	Divisional Alignment
Atlanta	Flames	1973-80	transferred to Calgary	West 1973-79 Patrick 1980
Boston	Bruins	1925 to date		American 1927-38 East 1968-74 Adams 1975 to date
Brooklyn	Americans	1942	formerly NY Americans	Canadian
Buffalo	Sabres	1971 to date		East 1971-74 Adams 1975 to date
California	Seals	1968	renamed Oakland mid-season	West
Calgary	Flames	1981 to date	transferred from Atlanta	Smythe
Chicago	Black Hawks	1927 to date		American 1927-38 East 1968-70 West 1971-74 Smythe 1975-81 Norris 1982 to date
Cleveland	Barons	1977, 1978	transferred from Oakland merged with Minnesota	Adams
Colorado	Rockies	1977-82	transferred from Kansas City transferred to New Jersey	Smythe
Detroit	Cougars Falcons Red Wings	1927-30 1931-33 1934 to date	renamed Falcons 1931 renamed Red Wings 1934	American 1927-38 East 1968-74 Norris 1975 to date
Edmonton	Oilers	1980 to date	former WHA franchise	Smythe
Hamilton	Tigers	1921-25	sold to NY Americans	
Hartford	Whalers	1980 to date	former WHA franchise	Norris 1980, 1981 Adams 1982 to date
Kansas City	Scouts	1975, 1976	transferred to Colorado	Smythe
Long Island	NY Islanders	1973 to date		East 1973, 1974 Patrick 1975 to date
Los Angeles	Kings	1968 to date		West 1968-74 Norris 1975-81 Smythe 1982 to date
Minnesota	North Stars	1968 to date	merged with Cleveland	West 1968-74 Smythe 1975-78 Adams 1979-82 Norris 1982 to date
Montreal	Canadiens	1918 to date		Canadian 1927-38 East 1968-74 Norris 1975-81 Adams 1982 to date
	Wanderers Maroons	1918 1925-38		Canadian 1927-28
New Jersey	Devils	1982 to date	transferred from Colorado	Patrick
New York	Americans Rangers	1926-41 1927 to date	shifted to Brooklyn 1942	Canadian 1927-41 American 1927-38 East 1968-74 Patrick 1975 to date
Oakland	Seals	1968-76	formerly California transferred to Cleveland	West 1968-74 Adams 1975-76
Ottawa	Senators	1918-31 1933, 1934	did not play in 1932 transferred to St. Louis	Canadian 1927-31 Canadian 1933, 1934
Philadelphia	Quakers Flyers	1931 1968 to date		American East 1968-74 Patrick 1975 to date
Pittsburgh	Pirates Penguins	1926-30 1968 to date	transferred to Philadelphia	American 1927-30 West 1968-74 Norris 1975-81 Patrick 1982 to date
Quebec	Bulldogs Nordiques	1920 1980 to date	transferred to Hamilton former WHA franchise	Adams
St. Louis	Eagles Blues	1935 1968 to date	transferred from Ottawa	Canadian 1935 West 1967-74 Smythe 1975-81
Toronto	Arenas St. Patricks Maple Leafs	1918, 1919 1920-26 1927 to date	renamed St. Patricks renamed Maple Leafs	Canadian 1927-38 Norris 1982 to date
Vancouver	Canucks	1971 to date		East 1971-74 Smythe 1975 to date
Washington	Capitals	1975 to date		Patrick
Winnipeg	Jets	1980 to date	former WHA franchise	Smythe 1980, 1981 Norris 1982 Smythe 1983 to date

Note: All references to years in this table refer to the NHL season ending in the stated calendar year. "1918" refers to the 1917-18 NHL season. "1918, 1919" refers to the 1917-18 and 1918-19 NHL seasons.

Major Rule Changes

1910-11 — Game changed from two 30-minute periods to three 20-minute periods.

1911-12 — National Hockey Association (forerunner of the NHL) originated six-man hockey, replacing seven-man game.

1917-18 — Goalies permitted to fall to the ice to make saves. Previously a goaltender was penalized for dropping to the ice.

1918-19 — Penalty rules amended. For minor fouls, substitutes not allowed until penalized player had served three minutes. For major fouls, no substitutes for five minutes. For match fouls, no substitutes allowed for the remainder of the game.

With the addition of two lines painted on the ice twenty feet from center, three playing zones were created, producing a forty-foot neutral center ice area in which forward passing was permitted. Kicking the puck was permitted in this neutral zone.

Tabulation of assists began.

1921-22 — Goaltenders allowed to pass the puck forward up to their own blue line.

Overtime limited to twenty minutes.

Minor penalties changed from three minutes to two minutes.

1923-24 — Match foul defined as actions deliberately injuring or disableing an opponent. For such actions, a player was fined not less than $50 and ruled off the ice for the balance of the game. A player assessed a match penalty may be replaced by a substitute at the end of 20 minutes. Match penalty recipients must meet with the League president who can assess additional punishment.

1925-26 — Delayed penalty rules introduced. Each team must have a minimum of four players on the ice at all times.

Two rules were amended to encourage offense: No more than two defensemen permitted to remain inside a team's own blue line when the puck has left the defensive zone. A faceoff to be called for ragging the puck unless short-handed.

Team captains only players allowed to talk to referees.

Goaltender's leg pads limited to 12-inch width.

Timekeeper's gong to mark end of periods rather than referee's whistle. Teams to dress a maximum of 12 players for each game from a roster of no more than 14 players.

1926-27 — Blue lines repositioned to sixty feet from each goal-line, thereby enlarging the neutral zone and standardizing distance from blueline to goal.

Uniform goal nets adopted throughout NHL with goal posts securely fastened to the ice.

1927-28 — To further encourage offense, forward passes allowed in defending and neutral zones and goaltender's pads reduced in width from 12 to 10 inches.

Game standardized at three twenty-minute periods of stop-time separated by ten-minute intermissions.

Teams to change ends after each period.

Ten minutes of sudden-death overtime to be played if the score is tied after regulation time.

Minor penalty to be assessed to any player other than a goaltender for deliberately picking up the puck while it is in play. Minor penalty to be assessed for deliberately shooting the puck out of play.

The Art Ross goal net adopted as the official net of the NHL.

Maximum length of hockey sticks limited to 53 inches measured from heel of blade to end of handle. No minimum length stipulated.

Home teams given choice of goals to defend at start of game.

1928-29 — Forward passing permitted in defensive and neutral zones and into attacking zone if pass receiver is in neutral zone when pass is made. No forward passing allowed inside attacking zone.

Minor penalty to be assessed to any player who delays the game by passing the puck back into his defensive zone.

Ten-minute overtime without sudden-death provision to be played in games tied after regulation time. Games tied after this overtime period declared a draw.

Exclusive of goaltenders, team to dress at least 8 and no more than 12 skaters.

1929-30 — Forward passing permitted inside all three zones but not permitted across either blue line.

Kicking the puck allowed, but a goal cannot be scored by kicking the puck in.

No more than three players including the goaltender may remain in their defensive zone when the puck has gone up ice. Minor penalties to be assessed for the first two violations of this rule in a game; major penalties thereafter.

Goaltenders forbidden to hold the puck. Pucks caught must be cleared immediately. For infringement of this rule, a faceoff to be taken ten feet in front of the goal with no player except the goaltender standing between the faceoff spot and the goal-line.

Highsticking penalties introduced.

Maximum number of players in uniform increased from 12 to 15.

December 21, 1929 — Forward passing rules instituted at the beginning of the 1929-30 season more than doubled number of goals scored. Partway through the season, these rules were further amended to read, "No attacking player allowed to precede the play when entering the opposing defensive zone." This is similar to modern offside rule.

1930-31 — A player without a complete stick ruled out of play and forbidden from taking part in further action until a new stick is obtained. A player who has broken his stick must obtain a replacement at his bench.

A further refinement of the offside rule stated that the puck must first be propelled into the attacking zone before any player of the attacking side can enter that zone; for infringement of this rule a faceoff to take place at the spot where the infraction took place.

1931-32 — Though there is no record of a team attempting to play with two goaltenders on the ice, a rule was instituted which stated that each team was allowed only one goaltender on the ice at one time.

Attacking players forbidden to impede the movement or obstruct the vision of opposing goaltenders.

Defending players with the exception of the goaltender forbidden from falling on the puck within 10 feet of the net.

1932-33 — Each team to have captain on the ice at all times.

If the goaltender is removed from the ice to serve a penalty, the manager of the club to appoint a substitute.

Match penalty with substitution after five minutes instituted for kicking another player.

1933-34 — Number of players permitted to stand in defensive zone restricted to three including goaltender.

Visible time clocks required in each rink.

Two referees replace one referee and one linesman.

1934-35 — Penalty shot awarded when a player is tripped and thus prevented from having a clear shot on goal, having no player to pass to other than the offending player. Shot taken from inside a 10-foot circle located 38 feet from the goal. The goaltender must not advance more than one foot from his goal-line when the shot is taken.

1937-38 — Rules introduced governing icing the puck.

Penalty shot awarded when a player other than a goaltender falls on the puck within 10 feet of the goal.

1938-39 — Penalty shot modified to allow puck carrier to skate in before shooting.

One referee and one linesman replace two referee system.

Blue line widened to 12 inches.

Maximum number of players in uniform increased from 14 to 15.

1939-40 — A substitute replacing a goaltender removed from ice to serve a penalty may use a goaltender's stick and gloves but no other goaltending equipment.

1940-41 — Flooding ice surface between periods made obligatory.

1941-42 — Penalty shots classified as minor and major. Minor shot to be taken from a line 28 feet from the goal. Major shot, awarded when a player is tripped with only the goaltender to beat, permits the player taking the penalty shot to skate right into the goalkeeper and shoot from point-blank range.

One referee and two linesmen employed to officiate games.

For playoffs, standby minor league goaltenders employed by NHL as emergency substitutes.

1942-43 — Because of wartime restrictions on train scheduling, regular-season overtime was discontinued on November 21, 1941.

Player limit reduced from 15 to 14. Minimum of 12 men in uniform abolished.

1943-44 — Red line at center ice introduced to speed up the game and reduce offside calls. This rule is considered to mark the beginning of the modern era in the NHL.

Delayed penalty rules introduced.

1945-46 — Goal indicator lights synchronized with official time clock required at all rinks.

1946-47 — System of signals by officials to indicate infractions introduced.

Linesmen from neutral cities employed for all games.

1947-48 — Goal awarded when a player with the puck has an open net to shoot at and a thrown stick prevents the shot on goal. Major penalty to any player who throws his stick in any zone other than defending zone. If a stick is thrown by a player in his defending zone but the thrown stick is not considered to have prevented a goal, a penalty shot is awarded.

All playoff games played until a winner determined, with 20-minute sudden-death overtime periods separated by 10-minute intermissions.

1949-50 — Ice surface painted white.

Clubs allowed to dress 17 players exclusive of goaltenders.

Major penalties incurred by goaltenders served by a member of the goaltender's team instead of resulting in a penalty shot.

1950-51 — Each team required to provide an emergency goaltender in attendance with full equipment at each game for use by either team in the event of illness or injury to a regular goaltender.

1951-52 — Visiting teams to wear basic white uniforms; home teams basic colored uniforms.

Goal crease enlarged from 3 × 7 feet to 4 × 8 feet.

Number of players in uniform reduced to 15 plus goaltenders.

Faceoff circles enlarged from 10-foot to 15-foot radius.

1952-53 — Teams permitted to dress 15 skaters on the road and 16 at home.

1953-54 — Number of players in uniform set at 16 plus goaltenders.

1954-55 — Number of players in uniform set at 18 plus goaltenders up to December 1 and 16 plus goaltenders thereafter.

1956-57 — Player serving a minor penalty allowed to return to ice when a goal is scored by opposing team.

1959-60 — Players prevented from leaving their benches to enter into an altercation. Substitutions permitted providing substitutes do not enter into altercation.

1960-61 — Number of players in uniform set at 16 plus goaltenders.

1961-62 — Penalty shots to be taken by the player against whom the foul was committed. In the event of a penalty shot called in a situation where a particular player hasn't been fouled, the penalty shot to be taken by any player on the ice when the foul was committed.

1964-65 — No bodily contact on faceoffs.

In playoff games, each team to have its substitute goaltender dressed in his regular uniform except for leg pads and body protector. All previous rules governing standby goaltenders terminated.

1966-67 — Substitution allowed on coincidental major penalties.

Between-periods intermissions fixed at 15 minutes.

1967-68 — If a penalty incurred by a goaltender is a co-incident major, the penalty to be served by a player of the goaltender's team on the ice at the time the penalty was called.

1970-71 — Home teams to wear basic white uniforms; visiting teams basic colored uniforms.

Limit of curvature of hockey stick blade set at 1/2 inch.

Minor penalty for deliberately shooting the puck out of the playing area.

1971-72 — Number of players in uniform set at 17 plus 2 goaltenders.

Third man to enter an altercation assessed an automatic game misconduct penalty.

1972-73 — Minimum width of stick blade reduced to 2 inches from 2-1/2 inches.

1974-75 — Bench minor penalty imposed if a penalized player does not proceed directly and immediately to the penalty box.

1976-77 — Rule dealing with fighting amended to provide a major and game misconduct penalty for any player who is clearly the instigator of a fight.

1977-78 — Teams requesting a stick measurement to be assessed a minor penalty in the event that the measured stick does not violate the rules.

1981-82 — If both of a team's listed goaltenders are incapacitated, the team can dress and play any eligible goaltender who is available.

1983-84 — Five-minute sudden-death overtime to be played in regular-season games that are tied at the end of regulation time.

1985-86 — Substitutions allowed in the event of co-incidental minor penalties.

Team Records

BEST WINNING PERCENTAGE, ONE SEASON:
- .875 — **Boston Bruins,** 1929-30. Won 38, lost 5, tied 1. (77 points in 44 games)
- .830 — Montreal Canadiens, 1943-44. Won 38, lost 5, tied 7, (83 points in 50 games)
- .825 — Montreal Canadiens, 1976-77. Won 60, lost 8 tied 12 (132 points in 80 games)
- .806 — Montreal Canadiens, 1977-78. Won 59, lost 10, tied 11 (129 points in 80 games)
- .800 — Montreal Canadiens, 1944-45. Won 38, lost 8, tied 4 (80 points in 50 games)

MOST POINTS, ONE SEASON:
- 132 — **Montreal Canadiens,** 1976-77. Won 60, lost 8, tied 12. (80 games)
- 129 — Montreal Canadiens, 1977-78. Won 59, lost 10, tied 11. (80 games)
- 127 — Montreal Canadiens, 1975-76. Won 58, lost 11, tied 11. (80 games)

FEWEST POINTS, ONE SEASON:
- 8 — **Quebec Bulldogs,** 1919-20. Won 4, lost 20, tied 0. (24 games)
- 10 — Toronto Arenas, 1918-19. Won 5, lost 13, tied 0. (18 games)
- 12 — Hamilton Tigers, 1920-21. Won 6, lost 18, tied 0. (24 games)
  - — Hamilton Tigers, 1922-23. Won 6, lost 18, tied 0. (24 games)
  - — Boston Bruins, 1924-25. Won 6, lost 24, tied 0. (30 games)
  - — Philadelphia Quakers, 1930-31. Won 4, lost 36, tied 4. (44 games)

FEWEST POINTS, ONE SEASON (MINIMUM 70-GAME SCHEDULE):
- 21 — **Washington Capitals,** 1974-75. Won 8, lost 67, tied 5. (80 games)
- 30 — New York Islanders, 1972-73. Won 12, lost 60, tied 6. (78 games)
- 31 — Chicago Black Hawks, 1953-54. Won 12, lost 51, tied 7. (70 games)

MOST WINS, ONE SEASON:
- 60 — **Montreal Canadiens,** 1976-77. (80 games)
- 59 — Montreal Canadiens, 1977-78. (80 games)
- 58 — Montreal Canadiens, 1975-76. (80 games)

FEWEST WINS, ONE SEASON:
- 4 — **Quebec Bulldogs,** 1919-20. (24 games)
  - — **Philadelphia Quakers,** 1930-31. (44 games)
- 5 — Toronto Arenas, 1918-19. (18 games)
  - — Pittsburgh Pirates, 1929-30. (44 games)

FEWEST WINS, ONE SEASON (MINIMUM 70-GAME SCHEDULE):
- 8 — **Washington Capitals,** 1974-75. (80 games)
- 9 — Winnipeg Jets, 1980-81 (80 games)
- 11 — Washington Capitals, 1975-76. (80 games)

MOST LOSSES, ONE SEASON:
- 67 — **Washington Capitals,** 1974-75. (80 games)
- 60 — New York Islanders, 1972-73. (78 games)
- 59 — Washington Capitals, 1975-76. (80 games)

FEWEST LOSSES, ONE SEASON:
- 5 — **Ottawa Senators,** 1919-20. (24 games)
  - — **Boston Bruins,** 1929-30. (44 games)
  - — **Montreal Canadiens,** 1943-44. (50 games)

FEWEST LOSSES, ONE SEASON (MINIMUM 70-GAME SCHEDULE):
- 8 — **Montreal Canadiens,** 1976-77. (80 games)
- 10 — Montreal Canadiens, 1972-73. (78 games)
  - — Montreal Canadiens, 1977-78. (80 games)
- 11 — Montreal Canadiens, 1975-76. (80 games)

MOST TIES, ONE SEASON:
- 24 — **Philadelphia Flyers,** 1969-70. (76 games)
- 23 — Montreal Canadiens, 1962-63. (70 games)
  - — Chicago Black Hawks, 1973-74. (78 games)
- 22 — Toronto Maple Leafs, 1954-55. (70 games)
  - — New York Islanders, 1974-75. (80 games)
  - — Minnesota North Stars, 1969-70. (76 games)

FEWEST TIES, ONE SEASON (Since 1926-27):
- 1 — **Boston Bruins,** 1929-30. (44 games)
- 2 — New York Americans, 1926-27. (44 games)
  - — Montreal Canadiens, 1926-27. (44 games)
  - — Boston Bruins, 1938-39. (48 games)
  - — New York Rangers, 1941-42. (48 games)

FEWEST TIES, ONE SEASON (MINIMUM 70-GAME SCHEDULE):
- 3 — **New Jersey Devils,** 1985-86. (80 games)
- 4 — **Detroit Red Wings,** 1966-67. (70 games)
  - — New York Islanders, 1983-84. (80 games)
  - — Hartford Whalers, 1985-86. (80 games)
  - — Philadelphia Flyers, 1985-86. (80 games)

MOST HOME WINS, ONE SEASON:
- 36 — **Philadelphia Flyers,** 1975-76. (40 games)
- 33 — Boston Bruins, 1970-71. (39 games)
  - — Boston Bruins, 1973-74. (39 games)
  - — Montreal Canadiens, 1976-77. (40 games)
  - — Philadelphia Flyers, 1976-77. (40 games)
  - — New York Islanders, 1981-82. (40 games)
  - — Philadelphia Flyers,1985-86. (40 games)
- 32 — Philadelphia Flyers, 1974-75. (40 games)
  - — Montreal Canadiens, 1975-76. (40 games)
  - — Montreal Canadiens, 1977-78. (40 games)
  - — Philadelphia Flyers, 1984-85. (40 games)
  - — Edmonton Oilers, 1985-86. (40 games)

MOST ROAD WINS, ONE SEASON:
- 27 — **Montreal Canadiens,** 1976-77. (40 games)
  - — **Montreal Canadiens,** 1977-78. (40 games)
- 26 — Boston Bruins, 1971-72. (39 games)
  - — Montreal Canadiens, 1975-76. (40 games)
  - — Edmonton Oilers, 1983-84. (40 games)
- 25 — New York Islanders, 1980-81. (40 games)

MOST HOME LOSSES, ONE SEASON:
- 29 — **Pittsburgh Penguins,** 1983-84. (40 games)
- 28 — Washington Capitals, 1974-75. (40 games)
  - — New Jersey Devils, 1983-84. (40 games)
- 27 — Los Angeles Kings, 1985-86. (40 games)
- 26 — Washington Capitals, 1975-76. (40 games)
  - — Detroit Red Wings, 1985-86. (40 games)

MOST ROAD LOSSES, ONE SEASON:
- 39 — **Washington Capitals,** 1974-75. (40 games)
- 37 — California Seals, 1973-74. (39 games)
- 35 — New York Islanders, 1972-73. (39 games)

MOST HOME TIES, ONE SEASON:
- 13 — **New York Rangers,** 1954-55. (35 games)
  - — **Philadelphia Flyers,** 1969-70. (38 games)
  - — **California Seals,** 1971-72. (39 games)
  - — **California Seals,** 1972-73. (39 games)
  - — **Chicago Black Hawks,** 1973-74. (39 games)
- 12 — New York Islanders, 1974-75. (40 games)
  - — Vancouver Canucks, 1977-78. (40 games)
  - — Buffalo Sabres, 1980-81. (40 games)
  - — Minnesota North Stars, 1981-82. (40 games)
  - — Vancouver Canucks, 1981-82. (40 games)

MOST ROAD TIES, ONE SEASON:
- 15 — **Philadelphia Flyers,** 1976-77. (40 games)
- 14 — Montreal Canadiens, 1952-53. (35 games)
  - — Montreal Canadiens, 1974-75. (40 games)
  - — Philadelphia Flyers, 1975-76. (40 games)
- 13 — Montreal Canadiens, 1962-63. (35 games)
  - — Philadelphia Flyers, 1968-69. (38 games)
  - — Hartford Whalers, 1979-80. (40 games)
  - — St. Louis Blues, 1980-81. (40 games)
  - — Quebec Nordiques, 1981-82. (40 games)

FEWEST HOME WINS, ONE SEASON:
- 2 — **Chicago Black Hawks,** 1927-28. (22 games)
- 3 — Boston Bruins, 1924-25. (15 games)
  - — Chicago Black Hawks, 1928-29. (22 games)
  - — Philadelphia Quakers, 1930-31. (22 games)

FEWEST HOME WINS, ONE SEASON (MINIMUM 70-GAME SCHEDULE):
- 6 — **Chicago Black Hawks,** 1954-55. (35 games)
  - — **Washington Capitals,** 1975-76. (40 games)
- 7 — Boston Bruins, 1962-63. (35 games)
  - — Washington Capitals, 1974-75. (40 games)
  - — Winnipeg Jets, 1980-81. (40 games)
  - — Pittsburgh Penguins, 1983-84. (40 games)
- 8 — Chicago Black Hawks, 1950-51 and 1953-54. (35 games)
  - — New York Rangers, 1964-65. (35 games)
  - — Kansas City Scouts, 1975-76. (40 games)
  - — Colorado Rockies, 1978-79. (40 games)

FEWEST ROAD WINS, ONE SEASON:
- 0 — **Toronto Arenas,** 1918-19. (9 games)
  - — **Quebec Bulldogs,** 1919-20. (12 games)
  - — **Pittsburgh Pirates,** 1929-30. (22 games)
- 1 — Hamilton Tigers, 1921-22. (12 games)
  - — Toronto St. Patricks, 1925-26. (18 games)
  - — Philadelphia Quakers, 1930-31. (22 games)
  - — New York Americans, 1940-41. (24 games)
  - — Washington Capitals, 1974-75. (40 games)

FEWEST ROAD WINS, ONE SEASON (MINIMUM 70-GAME SCHEDULE):
- 1 — **Washington Capitals,** 1974-75. (40 games)
- 2 — Boston Bruins, 1960-61. (35 games)
  - — Los Angeles Kings, 1969-70. (38 games)
  - — New York Islanders, 1972-73. (39 games)
  - — California Seals, 1973-74. (39 games)
  - — Winnipeg Jets, 1980-81. (40 games)

FEWEST HOME LOSSES, ONE SEASON:
  0 — Ottawa Senators, 1922-23. (12 games)
  — Montreal Canadiens, 1943-44. (25 games)
  1 — Toronto Arenas, 1917-18. (11 games)
  — Ottawa Senators, 1918-19. (9 games)
  — Ottawa Senators, 1919-20. (12 games)
  — Toronto St. Patricks, 1922-23. (12 games)
  — Boston Bruins, 1929-30 and 1930-31. (22 games)
  — Montreal Canadiens, 1976-77. (40 games)

FEWEST HOME LOSSES, ONE SEASON (MINIMUM 70-GAME SCHEDULE):
  1 — Montreal Canadiens, 1976-77. (40 games)
  2 — Montreal Canadiens, 1961-62. (35 games)
  — New York Rangers, 1970-71. (39 games)
  — Philadelphia Flyers, 1975-76. (40 games)
  3 — Detroit Red Wings, 1950-51. (35 games)
  — Boston Bruins, 1968-69 and 1969-70. (38 games)
  — Montreal Canadiens, 1971-72. (39 games)
  — Chicago Black Hawks, 1971-72. (39 games)
  — Montreal Canadiens, 1975-76. (40 games)
  — New York Islanders, 1977-78. (40 games)
  — New York Islanders, 1978-79. (40 games)
  — New York Islanders, 1981-82. (40 games)

FEWEST ROAD LOSSES, ONE SEASON:
  3 — Montreal Canadiens, 1928-29. (22 games)
  4 — Ottawa Senators, 1919-20. (12 games)
  — Montreal Canadiens, 1927-28. (22 games)
  — Boston Bruins, 1929-30. (20 games)
  — Boston Bruins, 1940-41. (24 games)
  5 — Ottawa Senators, 1926-27. (22 games)
  — Montreal Canadiens, 1943-44. (25 games)

FEWEST ROAD LOSSES, ONE SEASON (MINIMUM 70-GAME SCHEDULE):
  6 — Montreal Canadiens, 1972-73. (39 games)
  — Montreal Canadiens, 1974-75. (40 games)
  — Montreal Canadiens, 1977-78. (40 games)
  7 — Detroit Red Wings, 1951-52. (35 games)
  — Montreal Canadiens, 1976-77. (40 games)
  — Philadelphia Flyers, 1979-80. (40 games)
  8 — Toronto Maple Leafs, 1950-51. (35 games)
  — Montreal Canadiens, 1962-63. (35 games)
  — Chicago Black Hawks, 1973-74. (39 games)
  — Montreal Canadiens, 1975-76. (40 games)

FEWEST HOME TIES, ONE SEASON:
  0 — Boston Bruins, 1926-27. (22 games)
  — Boston Bruins, 1929-30. (22 games)
  — Boston Bruins, 1934-35. (24 games)
  — Montreal Canadiens, 1936-37. (24 games)
  — Toronto Maple Leafs, 1941-42. (24 games)

FEWEST HOME TIES, ONE SEASON (MINIMUM 70-GAME SCHEDULE):
  1 — Montreal Canadiens, 1955-56. (35 games)
  — Montreal Canadiens, 1965-66. (35 games)
  — California Seals, 1970-71. (39 games)
  — Philadelphia Flyers, 1976-77. (40 games)
  — New York Islanders, 1983-84. (40 games)
  — New York Rangers, 1983-84. (40 games)
  — Buffalo Sabres, 1985-86. (40 games)
  — Philadelphia Flyers, 1985-86. (40 games)

FEWEST ROAD TIES, ONE SEASON:
  0 — Montreal Canadiens, 1926-27. (22 games)
  — New York Americans, 1926-27. (22 games)
  — Boston Bruins, 1938-39. (24 games)
  — Toronto Maple Leafs, 1939-40. (24 games)
  — Montreal Canadiens, 1939-40. (24 games)
  — Boston Bruins, 1964-65. (35 games)
  — California Seals, 1973-74. (39 games)
  — Washington Capitals, 1974-75. (40 games)

FEWEST ROAD TIES, ONE SEASON (MINIMUM 70-GAME SCHEDULE):
  0 — Boston Bruins, 1964-65. (35 games)
  — California Seals, 1973-74. (39 games)
  — Washington Capitals, 1974-75. (40 games)
  1 — Chicago Black Hawks, 1953-54. (35 games)
  — Detroit Red Wings, 1966-67. (35 games)
  — New York Rangers, 1975-76. (40 games)
  — Toronto Maple Leafs, 1979-80. (40 games)
  — Buffalo Sabres, 1983-84. (40 games)
  — Edmonton Oilers, 1983-84. (40 games)
  — New Jersey Devils, 1985-86. (40 games)

LONGEST WINNING STREAK:
15 Games — New York Islanders, Jan. 21, 1982, through Feb. 20, 1982.
14 Games — Boston Bruins, Dec. 3, 1929, through Jan. 9, 1930.
13 Games — Boston Bruins, Feb. 23, 1971, through March 20, 1971.
  — Philadelphia Flyers, Oct. 19, 1985, through Nov. 17, 1985.
12 Games — Boston Bruins, Feb. 4, 1930, through March 11, 1930.
  — Montreal Canadiens, Jan. 6, 1968, through Feb. 3, 1968.

LONGEST WINNING STREAK FROM START OF SEASON:
8 Games — Toronto Maple Leafs, 1934-35.
  — Buffalo Sabres, 1975-76.
7 Games — Edmonton Oilers, 1983-84.
  — Quebec Nordiques, 1985-86.
6 Games — Boston Bruins, 1937-38.
  — Toronto Maple Leafs, 1944-45.
  — St. Louis Blues, 1969-70.
  — Detroit Red Wings, 1972-73.

LONGEST WINNING STREAK, INCLUDING PLAYOFFS:
15 Games — Detroit Red Wings, Feb. 27, 1955, through April 5, 1955. Nine regular-season games, six playoff games.

LONGEST HOME WINNING STREAK (ONE SEASON):
20 Games — Boston Bruins, Dec. 3, 1929, through Mar. 18, 1930.
  — Philadelphia Flyers, Jan. 4, 1976, through April 3, 1976.

LONGEST HOME WINNING STREAK, INCLUDING PLAYOFFS:
24 Games — Philadelphia Flyers, Jan. 4, 1976, through April 25, 1976. 20 regular-season games, 4 playoff games.

LONGEST ROAD WINNING STREAK (ONE SEASON):
10 Games — Buffalo Sabres, Dec. 10, 1983, through Jan. 23, 1984.
8 Games — Boston Bruins, Feb. 17, 1972, through Mar. 8, 1972.
  — Los Angeles Kings, Dec. 18, 1974, through Jan. 16, 1975.
  — Montreal Canadiens, Dec. 18, 1977, through Jan. 18. 1978.
  — New York Islanders, Feb. 27, 1981, through March 29, 1981.
  — Montreal Canadiens, Jan. 21, 1982, through Feb. 21, 1982.
  — Philadelphia Flyers, Dec. 22, 1982, through Jan. 16, 1983.
  — Winnipeg Jets, Feb. 25, 1985 through Apr. 6, 1985.

LONGEST UNDEFEATED STREAK (ONE SEASON):
35 Games — Philadelphia Flyers, Oct. 14, 1979, through Jan. 6, 1980 (25 wins, 10 ties).
28 Games — Montreal Canadiens, Dec. 18, 1977, through Feb. 23, 1978. 23 wins, 5 ties.
23 Games — Boston Bruins, Dec. 22, 1940, through Feb. 23, 1941. 15 wins, 8 ties.
  — Philadelphia Flyers, Jan. 29, 1976, through Mar. 18, 1976. 17 wins, 6 ties.

LONGEST UNDEFEATED STREAK FROM START OF SEASON:
15 Games — Edmonton Oilers, 1984-85. (12 wins, 3 ties)
14 Games — Montreal Canadiens, 1943-44. (11 wins, 3 ties)
13 Games — Montreal Canadiens, 1972-73. (9 wins, 4 ties)
12 Games — Atlanta Flames, 1979-80. (10 wins, 2 ties)
10 Games — Buffalo Sabres, 1972-73. (6 wins, 4 ties)
  — Montreal Canadiens, 1981-82. (6 wins, 4 ties)
  — Detroit Red Wings, 1962-63. (8 wins, 2 ties)

LONGEST HOME UNDEFEATED STREAK (ONE SEASON):
34 Games — Montreal Canadiens, Nov. 1, 1976, through Apr. 2, 1977. (28 wins, 6 ties).
27 Games — Boston Bruins, Nov. 22, 1970, through Mar. 20, 1971. (26 wins, 1 tie).

LONGEST HOME UNDEFEATED STREAK, INCLUDING PLAYOFFS:
38 Games — Montreal Canadiens, Nov. 1, 1976, through April 26, 1977. (28 wins, 6 ties in regular season and 4 playoff wins.)

LONGEST ROAD UNDEFEATED STREAK (ONE SEASON):
23 Games — Montreal Canadiens, Nov. 27, 1974, through Mar. 12, 1975. (14 wins, 9 ties).
17 Games — Montreal Canadiens, Dec. 18, 1977, through March 1, 1978. (14 wins, 3 ties).
16 Games — Philadelphia Flyers, Oct. 20, 1979, through Jan. 6, 1980. (11 wins, 5 ties).

LONGEST LOSING STREAK (ONE SEASON):
17 Games — Washington Capitals, Feb. 18, 1975, through Mar. 26, 1975.
15 Games — Philadelphia Quakers, Nov. 29, 1930, through Jan. 8, 1931.

LONGEST LOSING STREAK FROM START OF SEASON:
11 Games — New York Rangers, 1943-44.
7 Games — Montreal Canadiens, 1938-39.
  — Chicago Black Hawks, 1947-48.
  — Washington Capitals, 1983-84.

LONGEST HOME LOSING STREAK (ONE SEASON):
11 Games — Boston Bruins, Dec. 8, 1924, through Feb. 17, 1925.
  — Washington Capitals, Feb. 18, 1975, through Mar. 30, 1975.

LONGEST ROAD LOSING STREAK (ONE SEASON):
37 Games — Washington Capitals, Oct. 9, 1974, through Mar. 26, 1975.

LONGEST WINLESS STREAK (ONE SEASON):
30 Games — Winnipeg Jets, Oct. 19, 1980, through Dec. 28, 1980. (23 losses, 7 ties).
27 Games — Kansas City Scouts, Feb. 12, 1976, through April 4, 1976. (21 losses, 6 ties).
25 Games — Washington Capitals, Nov. 29, 1975, through Jan. 21, 1976. (22 losses, 3 ties).

MOST GOALS, BOTH TEAMS, ONE GAME:
- 21 — **Montreal Canadiens, Toronto St. Patricks,** at Montreal, Jan. 10, 1920. Montreal won 14-7.
- — **Edmonton Oilers, Chicago Blackhawks,** at Chicago, Dec. 11, 1985. Edmonton won 12-9.
- 20 — Edmonton Oilers, Minnesota North North Stars, at Edmonton, Jan. 4, 1984. Edmonton won 12-8.
- — Toronto Maple Leafs, Edmonton Oilers, at Toronto, Jan. 8, 1986. Toronto won 11-9.
- 19 — Montreal Wanderers, Toronto Arenas, at Montreal, Dec. 19, 1917. Montreal won 10-9.
- — Montreal Canadiens, Quebec Bulldogs, at Quebec City, March 3, 1920, Montreal won 16-3.
- — Montreal Canadiens, Hamilton Tigers, at Montreal, Feb. 26, 1921. Canadiens won 13-6.
- — Boston Bruins, New York Rangers, at Boston, March 4, 1944, Boston won 10-9.
- — Boston Bruins, Detroit Red Wings, at Detroit, March 16, 1944. Detroit won 10-9.
- — Vancouver Canucks, Minnesota North Stars, at Vancouver, Oct. 7, 1983. Vancouver won 10-9.

MOST GOALS, ONE TEAM, ONE GAME:
- 16 — **Montreal Canadiens,** March 3, 1920, at Quebec City. Defeated Quebec Bulldogs 16-3.

MOST CONSECUTIVE GOALS, ONE TEAM, ONE GAME:
- 15 — **Detroit Red Wings,** Jan. 23, 1944, at Detroit. Defeated New York Rangers 15-0.

MOST POINTS, BOTH TEAMS, ONE GAME:
- 62 — **Edmonton Oilers, Chicago Blackhawks,** at Chicago, Dec. 11, 1985. Edmonton won 12-9. Edmonton had 24 assists, Chicago, 17.
- 53 — Quebec Nordiques, Washington Capitals, at Washington, Feb. 22, 1981. Quebec won 11-7. Quebec had 22 assists, Washington, 13.
- — Edmonton Oilers, Minnesota North Stars, at Edmonton, Jan. 4, 1984. Edmonton won 12-8. Edmonton had 20 assists, Minnesota 13.
- — Minnesota North Stars, St. Louis Blues, at St. Louis, Jan. 27, 1984. Minnesota won 10-8. Minnesota had 19 assists, St. Louis 16.
- 52 — Montreal Maroons, New York Americans, at New York, Feb. 18, 1936. 8-8 tie. New York had 20 assists, Montreal 16. (3 assists allowed for each goal.)
- — Vancouver Canucks, Minnesota North Stars, at Vancouver, Oct. 7, 1983. Vancouver won 10-9. Vancouver had 16 assists, Minnesota 17.

MOST POINTS, ONE TEAM, ONE GAME:
- 40 — **Buffalo Sabres,** Dec. 21, 1975, at Buffalo. Buffalo defeated Washington Capitals 14-2, receiving 26 assists.
- 39 — Minnesota North Stars, Nov. 11, 1981, at Minnesota. Minnesota defeated Winnipeg 15-2, receiving 24 assists.
- 36 — Detroit Red Wings, Jan. 23, 1944, at Detroit. Detroit defeated New York Rangers 15-0, receiving 22 assists.
- — Toronto Maple Leafs, March 16, 1957, at Toronto. Toronto defeated New York Rangers 14-1, receiving 23 assists.
- — Buffalo Sabres, Feb. 25, 1978, at Cleveland. Buffalo defeated Cleveland Barons 13-3, receiving 24 assists.
- — Edmonton Oilers, Dec. 11, 1985, at Chicago. Edmonton defeated Chicago 12-9, receiving 24 assists.

MOST SHOTS, BOTH TEAMS, ONE GAME:
- 141 — **New York Americans, Pittsburgh Pirates,** Dec. 26, 1925. Americans, who won game 3-1, had 73 shots; Pirates, 68 shots.

MOST SHOTS, ONE TEAM, ONE GAME:
- 83 — **Boston Bruins,** March 4, 1941, at Boston. Boston defeated Chicago 3-2. Chicago goaltender was Sam LoPresti.
- 73 — New York Americans, Dec. 26, 1925, at New York. Americans defeated Pittsburgh Pirates 3-1.
- 72 — Boston Bruins, Dec. 10, 1970, at Boston. Bruins defeated Buffalo 8-2.
- 68 — Pittsburgh Pirates, Dec. 26, 1925, at New York. Americans defeated Pirates 3-1.
- — Minnesota North Stars, March 24, 1981, at Minnesota. Los Angeles Kings defeated Minnesota 4-3.

MOST PENALTIES, BOTH TEAMS, ONE GAME: (AND)
MOST PENALTY MINUTES, BOTH TEAMS, ONE GAME:
- 84 Penalties; 406 Minutes — **Minnesota North Stars, Boston Bruins** at Boston, Feb. 26, 1981. Minnesota received 18 minors, 13 majors, 4 10-minute misconducts and 7 game misconducts; a total 42 penalties and 211 minutes. Boston received 20 minors, 13 majors, 3 10-minute misconducts and 6 game misconducts; a total 42 penalties and 195 minutes.

MOST PENALTIES, ONE TEAM, ONE GAME:
- 42 — **Minnesota North Stars,** Feb. 26, 1981, at Boston. Minnesota received 18 minors, 13 majors, 4 10-minute misconducts and 7 game misconducts.
- — **Boston Bruins,** Feb. 26, 1981, at Boston against Minnesota. Boston received 20 minors, 13 majors, 3 10-minute misconducts and 7 game misconducts.

MOST PENALTY MINUTES, ONE TEAM, ONE GAME:
- 211 — **Minnesota North Stars,** Feb. 26, 1981, at Boston. Minnesota received 18 minors, 13 majors, 4 10-minute misconducts and 7 game misconducts.

MOST GOALS, BOTH TEAMS, ONE PERIOD:
- 12 — **Buffalo Sabres, Toronto Maple Leafs,** at Buffalo, March 19, 1981, second period. Buffalo scored 9 goals, Toronto 3, during 14-4 win by Buffalo.
- — **Edmonton Oilers, Chicago Blackhawks,** at Chicago, Dec. 11, 1985, second period. Edmonton scored 6 goals, Chicago 6, during 12-9 win by Edmonton.
- 10 — New York Rangers, New York Americans, at New York, March 16, 1939, third period. Rangers scored seven goals, Americans three. Rangers won game 11-5.
- — Toronto Maple Leafs, Detroit Red Wings, at Detroit, March 17, 1946, third period. Toronto scored six goals, Detroit four. Toronto won game 11-7.
- — Vancouver Canucks, Buffalo Sabres, at Buffalo, Jan. 8, 1976, third period. Sabres scored six goals, Canucks four. Buffalo won game 8-5.
- — Buffalo Sabres, Montreal Canadiens, at Montreal, Oct. 26, 1982, first period. Canadiens scored five goals, Sabres five. Tie game 7-7.
- — Boston Bruins, Quebec Nordiques, at Quebec, Dec. 7, 1982, second period. Nordiques scored six goals, Bruins four. Quebec won game 10-5.

MOST GOALS, ONE TEAM, ONE PERIOD:
- 9 — **Buffalo Sabres,** March 19, 1981, at Buffalo against Toronto Maple Leafs, second period. Buffalo won 14-4.
- 8 — Detroit Red Wings, Jan. 23, 1944, at Detroit, third period during 15-0 win over New York Rangers.
- — Boston Bruins, March 16, 1969, at Boston, second period during 11-3 win over Toronto Maple Leafs.
- — New York Rangers, Nov. 21, 1971, at New York, third period during 12-1 win over California Seals.
- — Philadelphia Flyers, March 31, 1973, at Philadelphia, second period during 10-2 win over New York Islanders.
- — Buffalo Sabres, Dec. 21, 1975, at Buffalo, third period during 14-2 win over Washington Capitals.
- — Minnesota North Stars, Nov. 11, 1981, at Minnesota, second period during 15-2 win over Winnipeg.

MOST POINTS, BOTH TEAMS, ONE PERIOD:
- 35 — **Edmonton, Oilers, Chicago Blackhawks,** at Chicago, Dec. 11, 1985, second period. Edmonton had 6 goals, 12 assists; Chicago, 6 goals, 11 assists. Edmonton won game 12-9.
- 31 — Buffalo Sabres, Toronto Maple Leafs, at Buffalo, March 19, 1981, second period. Buffalo had 9 goals, 14 assists; Toronto, 3 goals, 5 assists. Buffalo won game 14-4.
- 27 — Boston Bruins, Quebec Nordiques, at Quebec, Dec. 7, 1982, second period. Quebec had six goals and 10 assists; Boston four goals and seven assists. Quebec won game 10-5.
- — Philadelphia Flyers, Hartford Whalers, at Hartford, Feb. 25, 1984, first period. Philadelphia had 4 goals, 8 assists; Hartford 5 goals, 10 assists. Hartford won game 9-7.
- — Minnesota North Stars, St. Louis Blues, at St. Louis, Jan. 27, 1984, third period. Minnesota had 6 goals, 12 assists; St. Louis 3 goals, 6 assists. Minnesota won game 10-8.
- — New York Rangers, Edmonton Oilers, at New York, Feb. 15, 1985, first period. New York had 6 goals, 12 assists; Edmonton, 3 goals, 6 assists. New York won game 8-7.

MOST POINTS, ONE TEAM, ONE PERIOD:
- 23 — **New York Rangers,** Nov. 21, 1971, at New York, third period during 12-1 win over California Seals. New York scored 8 goals and 15 assists.
- — **Buffalo Sabres,** Dec. 21, 1975, at Buffalo, third period during 14-2 win over Washington Capitals. Buffalo scored 8 goals and 15 assists.
- — **Buffalo Sabres,** March 19, 1981, at Buffalo against Toronto in second period. 9 goals, 14 assists. Buffalo won 14-4.
- 22 — Detroit Red Wings, Jan. 23, 1944, at Detroit, third period during 15-0 win over New York Rangers. Detroit scored 8 goals and 14 assists.
- — Boston Bruins, March 16, 1969, at Boston, second period during 11-3 win over Toronto Maple Leafs. Boston scored 8 goals and 14 assists.
- — Minnesota North Stars, Nov. 11, 1981, at Minnesota, second period during 15-2 win over Winnipeg. Minnesota scored 8 goals and 14 assists.

MOST SHOTS, ONE TEAM, ONE PERIOD:
- 37 — **Boston Bruins,** March 4, 1941, at Boston, first period. Boston defeated Chicago 3-2.

MOST PENALTY MINUTES, ONE SEASON:
- 2621 — **Philadelphia Flyers,** 1980-81. (80 games)
- 2493 — Philadelphia Flyers, 1981-82. (80 games)
- 2210 — Pittsburgh Penguins, 1981-82. (80 games)

MOST PENALTIES, BOTH TEAMS, ONE PERIOD:
- 67 — **Minnesota North Stars, Boston Bruins,** at Boston, Feb. 26, 1981, first period. Minnesota received 15 minors, 8 majors, 4 10-minute misconducts and 7 game misconducts, a total 34 penalties. Boston had 16 minors, 8 majors, 3 10-minute misconducts and 6 game misconducts, a total 33 penalties.

MOST PENALTY MINUTES, BOTH TEAMS, ONE PERIOD:
372 — **Los Angeles Kings, Philadelphia Flyers** at Philadelphia, March 11, 1979, first period. Philadelphia received 4 minors, 8 majors, 6 10-minute misconducts and 8 game misconducts for 188 minutes. Los Angeles received 2 minors, 8 majors, 6 10-minute misconducts and 8 game misconducts for 184 minutes.

MOST PENALTIES, ONE TEAM, ONE PERIOD:
34 — **Minnesota North Stars,** Feb. 26, 1981, at Boston, first period. 15 minors, 8 majors, 4 10-minute misconducts, 7 game misconducts.

MOST PENALTY MINUTES, ONE TEAM, ONE PERIOD:
188 — **Philadelphia Flyers,** March 11, 1979, at Philadelphia against Los Angeles, first period. Flyers received 4 minors, 8 majors, 6 10-minute misconducts and 8 game misconducts.

FASTEST SIX GOALS, BOTH TEAMS
3 Minutes, 15 Seconds — **Montreal Canadiens, Toronto Maple Leafs,** at Montreal, Jan. 4, 1944, first period. Montreal scored 4 goals, Toronto 2. Montreal won game 6-3.

FASTEST FIVE GOALS, BOTH TEAMS:
1 Minute, 24 Seconds — **Chicago Black Hawks, Toronto Maple Leafs,** at Toronto, Oct. 15, 1983, second period. Scorers were: Gaston Gingras, Toronto, 16:49; Denis Savard, Chicago, 17:12; Steve Larmer, Chicago, 17:27; Savard, 17:42; and John Anderson, Toronto, 18:13. Toronto won game 10-8.
1 Minute, 39 Seconds — Detroit Red Wings, Toronto Maple Leafs, at Toronto, Nov. 15, 1944, third period. Scorers were: Ted Kennedy, Toronto, 10:36 and 10:55; Hal Jackson, Detroit, 11:48; Steve Wochy, Detroit, 12:02; Don Grosso, Detroit, 12:15. Detroit won game 8-4.

FASTEST FIVE GOALS, ONE TEAM:
2 Minutes, 7 Seconds — **Pittsburgh Penguins,** at Pittsburgh, Nov. 22, 1972, third period. Scorers: Bryan Hextall, 12:00; Jean Pronovost, 12:18; Al McDonough, 13:40; Ken Schinkel, 13:49; Ron Schock, 14:07. Pittsburgh defeated St. Louis Blues 10-4.
2 Minutes, 55 Seconds — Boston Bruins, at Boston, Dec. 19, 1974. Scorers: Bobby Schmautz, 19:13 (first period); Ken Hodge, 0:18; Phil Esposito, 0:43; Don Marcotte, 0:58; John Bucyk, 2:08 (second period). Boston defeated New York Rangers 11-3.

FASTEST FOUR GOALS, BOTH TEAMS:
53 Seconds — **Chicago Black Hawks, Toronto Maple Leafs,** at Toronto, Oct. 15, 1983, second period. Scorers were: Gaston Gingras, Toronto, 16:49; Denis Savard, Chicago, 17:12; Steve Larmer, Chicago, 17:27; and Savard at 17:42. Toronto won game 10-8.
1 Minute, 1 Second — Colorado Rockies, New York Rangers, at New York, Jan. 15, 1980, first period. Scorers were: Doug Sulliman, Rangers, 7:52; Ed Johnstone, Rangers, 7:57; Warren Miller, Rangers, 8:20; Rob Ramage, Colorado, 8:53. Colorado 6, Rangers 6.
1 Minute, 5 Seconds — Montreal Canadiens, Toronto Maple Leafs, at Toronto, March 16, 1966, second period. Scorers were: Jean Beliveau, Montreal, 5:00; Dave Keon, Toronto, 5:21; Jean Beliveau, Montreal, 5:43; Ralph Backstrom, Montreal, 6:05. Montreal won game 7-2.

FASTEST FOUR GOALS, ONE TEAM:
1 Minute, 20 Seconds — **Boston Bruins,** at Boston, Jan. 21, 1945, second period. Scorers were: Bill Thoms at 6:34; Frank Mario at 7:08 and 7:27; and Ken Smith at 7:54. Boston defeated New York Rangers 14-3.

FASTEST THREE GOALS, BOTH TEAMS:
15 Seconds — **Minnesota North Stars, New York Rangers,** at Minnesota, Feb. 10, 1983, second period. Scorers were: Mark Pavelich, New York, 19:18; Ron Greschner, New York, 19:27; Willi Plett, Minnesota, 19:33. Minnesota won game 7-5.
18 Seconds — Montreal Canadiens, New York Rangers, at Montreal, Dec. 12, 1963, first period. Scorers were: Dave Balon, Montreal, 0:58; Gilles Tremblay, Montreal, 1:04; Camille Henry, New York, 1:16. Montreal won game 6-4.
18 Seconds — California Golden Seals, Buffalo Sabres, at California, Feb. 1, 1976, third period. Scorers were: Jim Moxey, California, 19:38; Wayne Merrick, California, 19:45; Danny Gare, Buffalo, 19:56. Buffalo won game 9-5.

FASTEST THREE GOALS, ONE TEAM:
20 Seconds — **Boston Bruins,** Feb. 25, 1971, against Vancouver Canucks, third period. John Bucyk scored at 4:50, Ed Westfall at 5:02 and Ted Green at 5:10. Bruins won game 8-3.
21 Seconds — Chicago Black Hawks, at New York, Mar. 23, 1952, third period. Bill Mosienko scored all three goals, at 6:09, 6:20 and 6:30. Chicago defeated Rangers 7-6.

FASTEST TWO GOALS, BOTH TEAMS:
4 Seconds — **Pittsburgh Penguins, Atlanta Flames,** at Atlanta, March 15, 1977, third period. Scorers were: Wayne Bianchin, Pittsburgh, at 15:31; Guy Chouinard, Atlanta, at 15:35. Atlanta won game 7-3.
— **Boston Bruins, Chicago Black Hawks,** at Chicago, Dec. 30, 1979, third period. Scorers were: Peter McNab, Boston, at 19:55; Grant Mulvey, Chicago, 19:59. Chicago won game 5-3.
— **Chicago Black Hawks, Hartford Whalers,** at Hartford, Jan. 19, 1980, third period. Scorers were: Bob Murray, Chicago, at 19:50; Jordy Douglas, Hartford, at 19:54. Hartford won game 5-3.
— **Buffalo Sabres, Quebec Nordiques,** at Quebec, Jan. 2, 1982, second period. Scorers were: Marian Stastny, Quebec, at 15:46; Dale McCourt, Buffalo, at 15:50. Quebec won 6-3.
— **Chicago Black Hawks, New York Rangers,** at New York, Feb. 24, 1982, third period. Scorers were: Denis Savard, Chicago, at 19:23; Mark Pavelich, New York, at 19:27. Rangers won 6-4.
— **Vancouver Canucks, Chicago Black Hawks,** at Vancouver, March 17, 1985, third period. Scorers were: Stan Smyl, Vancouver at 19:06; Ed Olczyk, Chicago at 19:10. Chicago won game 6-4.
5 Seconds — Pittsburgh Penguins, Buffalo Sabres, at Buffalo, Jan. 3, 1974, first period. Scorers were: Rick Martin, Buffalo, at 7:15; Greg Polis, Pittsburgh, at 7:20. Buffalo won game 6-1.
— Buffalo Sabres, St. Louis Blues, at Buffalo, March 7, 1976, third period. Scorers were: Danny Gare, Buffalo, 16:04; Garry Unger. St. Louis, 16:09. Buffalo and St. Louis tied 4-4.
— Boston Bruins, Philadelphia Flyers, at Boston, March 23, 1980, third period. Scorers were: Al Secord, Boston, at 1:42; Bob Kelly, Philadelphia, at 1:47. Boston won game 7-2.
— Los Angeles Kings, Calgary Flames, at Calgary, Jan. 4, 1981, third period. Scorers were: Marcel Dionne, Los Angeles, 19:30; Eric Vail, Calgary, 19:35. Calgary won 7-6.
— Calgary Flames, Montreal Canadiens, at Montreal, March 26, 1981, first period. Scorers: Pierre Larouche, Montreal 7:15; Kevin LaVallee, Calgary, 7:20. Montreal won 8-2.

FASTEST TWO GOALS, ONE TEAM:
4 Seconds — **Montreal Maroons,** at Montreal, Jan. 3, 1931, third period. Nels Stewart scored both goals, at 8:24 and 8:28. Maroons defeated Boston 5-3.
— **Buffalo Sabres,** at Buffalo, Oct. 17, 1974, third period. Scorers were: Lee Fogolin at 14:55 and Don Luce at 14:59. Buffalo defeated California 6-1.
5 Seconds — New York Rangers, at New York, March 5, 1961, first period. Pat Hannigan at 2:18 and Andy Bathgate at 2:23. Rangers defeated Detroit 8-3.
— Montreal Canadiens, at Montreal, Feb. 20, 1971, third period. Pete Mahovlich scored both goals, at 12:16 and 12:21. Montreal defeated Chicago 7-1.
— New York Rangers, at New York, Jan. 14, 1980, first period. Scorers were: Doug Sulliman at 7:52 and Ed Johnstone at 7:57. New York and Colorado tied 6-6.
— Buffalo Sabres, Dec. 7, 1980, at Buffalo, second period. Gilles Hamel scored at 2:32 and Ric Seiling at 2:37. Buffalo defeated Pittsburgh Penguins 10-1.
— Chicago Black Hawks, Jan. 1, 1931, at Philadelphia, third period. Vic Desjardins scored at 1:15 Frank Ingram at 1:20. Chicago defeated Philadelphia 10-3.

John Bucyk was a major contributor to the Bruins' powerful offensive teams in the early 1970s.

LONGEST WINLESS STREAK FROM START OF SEASON:
15 Games — New York Rangers, 1943-44. (14 losses, 1 tie)
12 Games — Pittsburgh Pirates, 1927-28. (9 losses, 3 ties)
11 Games — Minnesota North Stars, 1973-74. (5 losses, 6 ties)
10 Games — Detroit Red Wings, 1975-76. (7 losses, 3 ties)

LONGEST HOME WINLESS STREAK (ONE SEASON):
15 Games — Chicago Black Hawks, Dec. 16, 1928, through Feb. 28, 1929. (11 losses, 4 ties).
— **Montreal Canadiens,** Dec. 16, 1939, through Mar. 7, 1940. (12 losses, 3 ties).

LONGEST ROAD WINLESS STREAK (ONE SEASON):
37 Games — Washington Capitals, Oct. 9, 1974, through Mar. 26, 1975. (37 losses, 0 ties).

LONGEST NON-SHUTOUT STREAK:
264 Games — Calgary Flames, Nov. 12, 1981 through Jan. 9, 1985.
230 Games — Quebec Nordiques, Feb. 10, 1980, through Jan. 13, 1983.
229 Games — Edmonton Oilers, March 15, 1981, through Feb. 11, 1984.
228 Games — Chicago Black Hawks, March 14, 1970, through Feb. 21, 1973.
209 Games — Boston Bruins, Oct. 26, 1977, through Feb. 20, 1980.
187 Games — New York Islanders, Oct. 18, 1977, through Dec. 23, 1979.

LONGEST NON-SHUTOUT STREAK INCLUDING PLAYOFFS:
262 Games — Chicago Black Hawks, March 14, 1970, through Feb. 21, 1973. (8 playoff games in 1970; 18 in 1971; 8 in 1972).
251 Games — Quebec Nordiques, Feb. 10, 1980, through Jan. 13, 1983. (5 playoff games in 1981; 16 in 1982).
235 Games — Boston Bruins, Oct. 26, 1977, through Feb. 20, 1980. (15 playoff games in 1978; 11 in 1979).
198 Games — Edmonton Oilers, March 15, 1981, through May 3, 1983. (9 playoff games in 1981; 5 in 1982; 12 in 1983).
194 Games — Montreal Canadiens, May 26, 1971, through Nov. 8, 1973. (2 playoff games in 1971; 6 in 1972; 17 in 1973).

MOST CONSECUTIVE GAMES SHUT OUT:
8 — Chicago Black Hawks, 1928-29.

MOST SHUTOUTS, ONE SEASON:
22 — Montreal Canadiens, 1928-29. All by George Hainsworth. (44 games)
16 — New York Americans, 1928-29. Roy Worters had 13; Flat Walsh 3. (44 games)
15 — Ottawa Senators, 1925-26. All by Alex Connell. (36 games)
— Ottawa Senators, 1927-28. All by Alex Connell. (44 games)
— Boston Bruins, 1927-28. All by Hal Winkler. (44 games)
— Chicago Black Hawks, 1969-70. All by Tony Esposito. (76 games)

FEWEST SHUTOUTS, ONE SEASON (MINIMUM 44-GAME SCHEDULE):
(Prior to 1926-27 when the 44-game schedule was introduced, several teams went through a season without recording a shutout).
0 — Pittsburgh Pirates, 1929-30. (44 games)
— New York Rangers, 1943-44. (50 games)
— Boston Bruins, 1944-45. (50 games)
— Toronto Maple Leafs, 1945-46. (50 games)
— Chicago Black Hawks, 1947-48. (60 games)
— Chicago Black Hawks, 1954-55. (70 games)
— Vancouver Canucks, 1970-71. (78 games)
— New York Islanders, 1972-73. (78 games)
— New York Islanders, 1973-74. (78 games)
— Kansas City Scouts, 1974-75. (80 games)
— Kansas City Scouts, 1975-76. (80 games)
— Washington Capitals, 1975-76. (80 games)
— Colorado Rockies, 1976-77. (80 games)
— Pittsburgh Penguins, 1977-78. (80 games)
— Washington Capitals, 1978-79. (80 games)
— Washington Capitals, 1979-80. (80 games)
— Chicago Black Hawks, 1980-81. (80 games)
— Colorado Rockies, 1980-81. (80 games)
— Detroit Red Wings, 1980-81. (80 games)
— Edmonton Oilers, 1980-81. (80 games)
— Pittsburgh Penguins, 1980-81. (80 games)
— Toronto Maple Leafs, 1980-81. (80 games)
— New York Islanders, 1981-82. (80 games)
— Buffalo Sabres, 1981-82. (80 games)
— Colorado Rockies, 1981-82. (80 games)
— Detroit Red Wings, 1981-82. (80 games)
— Edmonton Oilers, 1981-82. (80 games)
— Hartford Whalers, 1981-82. (80 games)
— Philadelphia Flyers, 1981-82. (80 games)
— Toronto Maple Leafs, 1982-83. (80 games)
— New Jersey Devils, 1982-83. (80 games)
— Calgary Flames, 1983-84. (80 games)
— Toronto Maple Leafs, 1983-84. (80 games)
— Winnipeg Jets, 1983-84. (80 games)
— Detroit Red Wings, 1984-85. (80 games)
— Vancouver Canucks, 1984-85. (80 games)
— Toronto Maple Leafs, 1985-86. (80 games)
— Los Angeles Kings, 1985-86. (80 games)

MOST GOALS, ONE SEASON:
446 — Edmonton Oilers, 1983-84. (80 games)
426 — Edmonton Oilers, 1985-86. (80 games)
424 — Edmonton Oilers, 1982-83. (80 games)
417 — Edmonton Oilers, 1981-82. (80 games)
401 — Edmonton Oilers, 1984-85. (80 games)

HIGHEST GOALS-PER-GAME AVERAGE, ONE SEASON:
5.58 — Edmonton Oilers, 1983-84. 446 goals in 80 games.
5.38 — Montreal Canadiens, 1919-20. 129 goals in 24 games.
5.33 — Edmonton Oilers, 1985-86. 426 goals in 80 games.
5.30 — Edmonton Oilers, 1982-83. 424 goals in 80 games.
5.23 — Montreal Canadiens, 1917-18. 115 goals in 22 games.

FEWEST GOALS, ONE SEASON:
33 — Chicago Black Hawks, 1928-29. (44 games)
45 — Montreal Maroons, 1924-25. (30 games)
46 — Pittsburgh Pirates, 1928-29. (44 games)

FEWEST GOALS, ONE SEASON (MINIMUM 70-GAME SCHEDULE):
133 — Chicago Black Hawks, 1953-54. (70 games)
147 — Toronto Maple Leafs, 1954-55. (70 games)
— Boston Bruins, 1955-56. (70 games)
150 — New York Rangers, 1954-55. (70 games)

LOWEST GOALS-PER-GAME AVERAGE, ONE SEASON:
.75 — Chicago Black Hawks, 1928-29, 33 goals in 44 games.
1.05 — Pittsburgh Pirates, 1928-29. 46 goals in 44 games.
1.20 — New York Americans, 1928-29. 53 goals in 44 games.

MOST GOALS AGAINST, ONE SEASON:
446 — Washington Capitals, 1974-75. (80 games)
415 — Detroit Red Wings, 1985-86. (80 games)
403 — Hartford Whalers, 1982-83. (80 games)
401 — Vancouver Canucks, 1984-85. (80 games)
400 — Winnipeg Jets, 1980-81. (80 games)

HIGHEST GOALS-AGAINST-PER-GAME AVERAGE, ONE SEASON:
7.38 — Quebec Bulldogs, 1919-20, 177 goals against in 24 games.
6.20 — New York Rangers, 1943-44, 310 goals against in 50 games.
5.58 — Washington Capitals, 1974-75, 446 goals against in 80 games.

FEWEST GOALS AGAINST, ONE SEASON:
42 — Ottawa Senators, 1925-26. (36 games)
43 — Montreal Canadiens, 1928-29. (44 games)
48 — Montreal Canadiens, 1923-24. (24 games)
— Montreal Canadiens, 1927-28. (44 games)

FEWEST GOALS AGAINST, ONE SEASON (MINIMUM 70-GAME SCHEDULE):
131 — Toronto Maple Leafs, 1953-54. (70 games)
— Montreal Canadiens, 1955-56. (70 games)
132 — Detroit Red Wings, 1953-54. (70 games)
133 — Detroit Red Wings, 1951-52 (70 games)

LOWEST GOALS-AGAINST-PER-GAME AVERAGE, ONE SEASON:
.98 — Montreal Canadiens, 1928-29. 43 goals against in 44 games.
1.05 — Montreal Canadiens, 1927-28. 48 goals against in 44 games.
1.17 — Ottawa Senators, 1925-26. 42 goals against in 36 games.

MOST POWER-PLAY GOALS, ONE SEASON:
99 — Pittsburgh Penguins, 1981-82. (80 games)
— **Quebec Nordiques,** 1985-86. (80 games)
95 — Boston Bruins, 1985-86. (80 games)
93 — New York Islanders, 1980-81. (80 games)
— Washington Capitals, 1981-82. (80 games)
— Pittsburgh Penguins, 1985-86. (80 games)
92 — Montreal Canadiens, 1974-75. (80 games)
— New York Islanders, 1975-76. (80 games)
— Pittsburgh Penguins, 1980-81. (80 games)
— Minnesota North Stars, 1982-83. (80 games)
91 — Minnesota North Stars, 1983-84. (80 games)

MOST POWER-PLAY GOALS AGAINST, ONE SEASON:
111 — Detroit Red Wings, 1985-86. (80 games)
110 — Pittsburgh Penguins, 1982-83. (80 games)
103 — New Jersey Devils, 1985-86. (80 games)
— Los Angeles Kings, 1985-86. (80 games)
102 — Philadelphia Flyers, 1981-82. (80 games)

MOST SHORTHAND GOALS, ONE SEASON:
36 — Edmonton Oilers, 1983-84. (80 games)
27 — Edmonton Oilers, 1985-86. (80 games)
25 — Boston Bruins, 1970-71. (78 games)
— Edmonton Oilers, 1984-85. (80 games)

MOST SHORTHAND GOALS AGAINST, ONE SEASON:
22 — Pittsburgh Penguins, 1984-85. (80 games)
21 — Calgary Flames, 1984-85. (80 games)
20 — Minnesota North Stars, 1982-83. (80 games)
— Quebec Nordiques, 1985-86. (80 games)

MOST ASSISTS, ONE SEASON:
737 — Edmonton Oilers, 1985-86. (80 games)
736 — Edmonton Oilers, 1983-84. (80 games)
723 — Edmonton Oilers, 1982-83. (80 games)
706 — Edmonton Oilers, 1981-82. (80 games)
697 — Boston Bruins, 1970-71. (78 games)
690 — Edmonton Oilers, 1984-85. (80 games)

FEWEST ASSISTS, ONE SEASON:
45 — New York Rangers, 1926-27. (44 games)

FEWEST ASSISTS, ONE SEASON (MINIMUM 70-GAME SCHEDULE):
206 — Chicago Black Hawks, 1953-54. (70 games)

MOST SCORING POINTS, ONE SEASON:
1,182 — Edmonton Oilers, 1983-84. (80 games)
1,163 — Edmonton Oilers, 1985-86. (80 games)
1,129 — Edmonton Oilers, 1982-83. (80 games)
1,123 — Edmonton Oilers, 1981-82. (80 games)
1,096 — Boston Bruins, 1970-71. (78 games)

MOST 50-OR-MORE-GOAL SCORERS, ONE SEASON:
3 — **Edmonton Oilers,** 1983-84. Wayne Gretzky, 87; Glenn Anderson, 54; Jari Kurri, 52 (80 games).
— **Edmonton Oilers,** 1985-86. Jari Kurri, 68; Glenn Anderson, 54; Wayne Gretzky, 52. (80 games).
2 — Boston Bruins, 1970-71. Phil Esposito, 76; John Bucyk, 51. (78 games)
— Boston Bruins, 1973-74. Phil Esposito, 68; Ken Hodge, 50. (78 games)
— Philadelphia Flyers, 1975-76. Reggie Leach, 61; Bill Barber, 50. (80 games)
— Pittsburgh Penguins, 1975-76. Pierre Larouche, 53; Jean Pronovost, 52. (80 games)
— Montreal Canadiens, 1976-77. Steve Shutt, 60; Guy Lafleur, 56. (80 games)
— Los Angeles Kings, 1979-80. Charlie Simmer, 56; Marcel Dionne, 53. (80 games)
— Montreal Canadiens, 1979-80. Pierre Larouche, 50; Guy Lafleur, 50. (80 games)
— Los Angeles Kings, 1980-81. Marcel Dionne, 58; Charlie Simmer, 56. (80 games)
— Edmonton Oilers, 1981-82. Wayne Gretzky, 92; Mark Messier, 50. (80 games)
— New York Islanders, 1981-82. Mike Bossy, 64; Bryan Trottier, 50. (80 games)
— Edmonton Oilers, 1984-85. Wayne Gretzky, 73; Jari Kurri, 71. (80 games)
— Washington Capitals, 1984-85. Bob Carpenter, 53; Mike Gartner, 50. (80 games)

The 1982-83 Oilers became the first NHL team with four 40-goal scorers. Top: left, Mark Messier; right, Jari Kurri. Bottom: left, Wayne Gretzky; right, Glenn Anderson.

MOST 40-OR-MORE-GOAL SCORERS, ONE SEASON:
4 — **Edmonton Oilers,** 1982-83. Wayne Gretzky, 71; Glenn Anderson, 48; Mark Messier, 48; Jari Kurri, 45. (80 games).
— **Edmonton Oilers,** 1983-84. Wayne Gretzky, 87; Glenn Anderson, 54; Jari Kurri, 52; Paul Coffey, 40. (80 games).
— **Edmonton Oilers,** 1984-85. Wayne Gretzky, 73; Jari Kurri, 71; Mike Krushelnyski, 43; Glenn Anderson, 42. (80 games).
— **Edmonton Oilers,** 1985-86. Jari Kurri, 68; Glenn Anderson, 54; Wayne Gretzky, 52; Paul Coffey, 48. (80 games).
3 — Boston Bruins, 1970-71. Phil Esposito, 76; John Bucyk, 51; Ken Hodge, 43. (78 games)
— New York Rangers, 1971-72. Vic Hadfield, 50; Jean Ratelle, 46; Rod Gilbert, 43. (78 games)
— Buffalo Sabres, 1975-76. Danny Gare, 50; Rick Martin, 49; Gilbert Perreault, 44. (80 games)
— Montreal Canadiens, 1979-80. Guy Lafleur, 50; Pierre Larouche, 50; Steve Shutt, 47. (80 games)
— Buffalo Sabres, 1979-80. Danny Gare, 56; Rick Martin, 45; Gilbert Perreault, 40. (80 games)
— Los Angeles Kings, 1980-81. Marcel Dionne, 58; Charlie Simmer, 56; Dave Taylor, 47. (80 games)
— Los Angeles Kings, 1984-85. Marcel Dionne, 46; Bernie Nicholls, 46; Dave Taylor, 41. (80 games)
— New York Islanders, 1984-85. Mike Bossy, 58; Brent Sutter, 42; John Tonelli, 42. (80 games)
— Chicago Blackhawks, 1985-86. Denis Savard, 47; Troy Murray, 45; Al Secord, 40. (80 games)

MOST 30-OR-MORE GOAL SCORERS, ONE SEASON:
6 — **Buffalo Sabres,** 1974-75. Rick Martin, 52; René Robert, 40; Gilbert Perreault, 39; Don Luce, 33; Rick Dudley, Danny Gare, 31 each. (80 games)
— **New York Islanders,** 1977-78, Mike Bossy, 53; Bryan Trottier, 46; Clark Gillies, 35; Denis Potvin, Bob Nystrom, Bob Bourne, 30 each. (80 games)
— **Winnipeg Jets,** 1984-85. Dale Hawerchuk, 53; Paul MacLean, 41; Thomas Steen, 30; Laurie Boschman, 32; Brian Mullen, 32; Doug Smail, 31. (80 games)
5 — Chicago Black Hawks, 1968-69. (76 games)
— Boston Bruins, 1970-71. (78 games)
— Montreal Canadiens, 1971-72. (78 games)
— Philadelphia Flyers, 1972-73. (78 games)
— Boston Bruins, 1973-74. (78 games)
— Montreal Canadiens, 1974-75. (80 games)
— Montreal Canadiens, 1975-76. (80 games)
— Pittsburgh Penguins, 1975-76. (80 games)
— New York Islanders, 1978-79. (80 games)
— Detroit Red Wings, 1979-80. (80 games)
— Philadelphia Flyers, 1979-80. (80 games)
— New York Islanders, 1980-81. (80 games)
— St. Louis Blues, 1980-81. (80 games)
— Chicago Black Hawks, 1981-82. (80 games)
— Montreal Canadiens, 1981-82. (80 games)
— Washington Capitals, 1981-82. (80 games)
— Edmonton Oilers, 1982-83. (80 games)
— Edmonton Oilers, 1983-84. (80 games)
— Edmonton Oilers, 1984-85. (80 games)
— Edmonton Oilers, 1985-86. (80 games)

MOST 20-OR-MORE GOAL SCORERS, ONE SEASON:
11 — **Boston Bruins,** 1977-78; Peter McNab, 41; Terry O'Reilly, 29; Bobby Schmautz, Stan Jonathan, 27 each; Jean Ratelle, Rick Middleton, 25 each; Wayne Cashman, 24; Gregg Sheppard, 23; Brad Park, 22; Don Marcotte, Bob Miller, 20 each. (80 games)
10 — Boston Bruins, 1970-71. (78 games)
— Montreal Canadiens, 1974-75. (80 games)
— St. Louis Blues, 1980-81. (80 games)
9 — Boston Bruins, 1972-73. (78 games)
— Buffalo Sabres, 1974-75. (80 games)
— Pittsburgh Penguins, 1974-75. (80 games)
— New York Islanders, 1975-76. (80 games)
— Montreal Canadiens, 1982-83. (80 games)
— Edmonton Oilers, 1982-83. (80 games)
— Winnipeg Jets, 1983-84. (80 games)

MOST 100 OR-MORE-POINT SCORERS, ONE SEASON:
4 — **Boston Bruins,** 1970-71, Phil Esposito, 76 goals, 76 assists, 152 points; Bobby Orr, 37 goals, 102 assists, 139 points; John Bucyk, 51 goals, 65 assists, 116 points; Ken Hodge, 43 goals, 62 assists, 105 points. (78 games)
— **Edmonton Oilers,** 1982-83, Wayne Gretzky, 71 goals, 125 assists, 196 points; Mark Messier, 48 goals, 58 assists, 106 points; Glenn Anderson, 48 goals, 58 assists, 104 points; Jari Kurri, 45 goals, 59 assists, 104 points. (80 games)
— **Edmonton Oilers,** 1983-84, Wayne Gretzky, 87 goals, 118 assists, 205 points; Paul Coffey, 40 goals, 86 assists, 126 points; Jari Kurri, 52 goals, 61 assists, 113 points; Mark Messier, 37 goals, 64 assists, 101 points. (80 games).
— **Edmonton Oilers,** 1985-86. Wayne Gretzky, 52 goals, 163 assists, 215 points; Paul Coffey, 48 goals, 90 assists, 138 points; Jari Kurri, 68 goals, 63 assists, 131 points; Glenn Anderson, 54 goals, 48 assists, 102 points. (80 games)
3 — Boston Bruins, 1973-74, Phil Esposito, 68 goals, 77 assists, 145 points; Bobby Orr, 32 goals, 90 assists, 122 points; Ken Hodge, 50 goals, 55 assists, 105 points. (78 games)
— New York Islanders, 1978-79, Bryan Trottier, 47 goals, 87 assists, 134 points; Mike Bossy, 69 goals, 57 assists, 126 points; Denis Potvin, 31 goals, 70 assists, 101 points. (80 games)
— Los Angeles Kings, 1980-81, Marcel Dionne, 58 goals, 77 assists, 135 points; Dave Taylor, 47 goals, 65 assists, 112 points; Charlie Simmer, 56 goals, 49 assists, 105 points. (80 games)
— Edmonton Oilers, 1984-85, Wayne Gretzky, 73 goals, 135 assists, 208 points; Jari Kurri, 71 goals, 64 assists, 135 points; Paul Coffey, 37 goals, 84 assists, 121 points. (80 games)
— New York Islanders, 1984-85. Mike Bossy, 58 goals, 59 assists, 117 points; Brent Sutter, 42 goals, 60 assists, 102 points; John Tonelli, 42 goals, 58 assists, 100 points

MOST PENALTY MINUTES, ONE SEASON:
2621 — Philadelphia Flyers,1980-81. (80 games)
2493 — Philadelphia Flyers, 1981-82. (80 games)
2393 — Detroit Red Wings, 1985-86. (80 games)
2297 — Calgary Flames, 1985-86. (80 games)

FASTEST THREE GOALS FROM START OF GAME AND PERIOD, BOTH TEAMS:
1 Minute, 16 Seconds — Montreal Canadiens, New York Rangers, at Montreal, Dec. 12, 1963, first period. Scorers were: Dave Balon, Montreal, 0:58; Gilles Tremblay, Montreal, 1:04; Camille Henry, New York, 1:16. Montreal won game 6-4.

FASTEST TWO GOALS FROM START OF PERIOD, BOTH TEAMS:
14 Seconds — New York Rangers, Quebec Nordiques, at Quebec, Nov. 5, 1983, third period. Scorers: Andre Savard, Quebec, 8 seconds; Pierre Larouche, NY Rangers, 14 seconds. Rangers and Quebec tied 4-4.
35 Seconds — Boston Bruins, Pittsburgh Penguins, at Boston, Feb. 10, 1973, second period. Scorers: Lowell MacDonald, Pittsburgh, 7 seconds; Phil Esposito, Boston, 35 seconds. Boston won 6-3.
39 Seconds — Vancouver Canucks, Minnesota North Stars, at Vancouver, Jan. 29, 1977, third period. Scorers: Dennis Ververgaert, Vancouver, 16 seconds; Ernie Hicke, Minnesota, 39 seconds. Vancouver won game 4-3.
— Los Angeles Kings, Vancouver Canucks, at Vancouver, April 7, 1978, second period. Scorers: Mike Walton, Vancouver, 19 seconds; Marcel Dionne, Los Angeles, 39 seconds, Los Angeles and Vancouver tied 5-5.
41 Seconds — Montreal Maroons, New York Rangers, at Montreal, Nov. 25, 1930, third period. Scorers: Hooley Smith, Montreal, 24 seconds; Bill Cook, New York, 41 seconds. Maroons won game 5-2.

FASTEST TWO GOALS FROM START OF GAME, ONE TEAM:
24 Seconds — Edmonton Oilers, March 28, 1982, at Los Angeles. Mark Messier, at 14 seconds and Dave Lumley, at 24 seconds, scored in first period. Edmonton won 6-2.
29 Seconds — Pittsburgh Penguins, Dec. 6, 1981, at Pittsburgh against Chicago. George Ferguson, at 17 seconds, and Greg Malone, at 29 seconds, scored in first period. Pittsburgh won 6-4.
33 Seconds — Chicago Black Hawks, Nov. 13, 1975, at Philadelphia. John Marks scored at 14 seconds and again at 33 seconds, in the first period, as Chicago and Philadelphia tied 5-5.
37 Seconds — Boston Bruins, Jan. 31, 1943, at New York. Buzz Boll, at 14 seconds and Bill Cowley, at 37 seconds, scored in the first period as Boston defeated Rangers 7-2.

FASTEST TWO GOALS FROM START OF PERIOD, ONE TEAM:
21 Seconds — Chicago Black Hawks, Nov. 5, 1983, at Minnesota, second period. Ken Yaremchuk scored at 12 seconds and Darryl Sutter at 21 seconds. Minnesota defeated Chicago 10-5.
30 Seconds — Washington Capitals, Jan. 27, 1980, at Washington, second period. Mike Gartner scored at 8 seconds and Bengt Gustafsson at 30 seconds. Washington defeated New York Islanders 7-1.
31 Seconds — Buffalo Sabres, Jan. 10, 1974, at Buffalo, Rene Robert, at 21 seconds and Rick Martin, at 31 seconds, in third period as Buffalo defeated NY Rangers 7-2.
— New York Islanders, Feb. 22, 1986, at New York, third period Roger Kortko at 10 seconds and Bob Bourne at 31 seconds. New York defeated Detroit 5-2.

Individual Records

Career

MOST SEASONS:
26 — Gordie Howe, Detroit Red Wings, 1946-47 through 1970-71; Hartford Whalers, 1979-80.
23 — Alex Delvecchio, Detroit Red Wings, 1951-52 through 1973-74.
— John Bucyk, Detroit, Boston, 1955-56 through 1977-78.
22 — Tim Horton, Toronto, New York Rangers, Pittsburgh, Buffalo, 1952-53 through 1973-74.
— Dean Prentice, New York Rangers, Boston, Detroit, Pittsburgh, Minnesota, 1952-53 through 1973-74.
— Doug Mohns, Boston, Chicago, Minnesota, Atlanta, Washington, 1953-54 through 1974-75.
— Stan Mikita, Chicago Black Hawks, 1958-59 through 1979-80.

MOST GAMES:
1,767 — Gordie Howe, Detroit Red Wings, 1946-47 through 1970-71; Hartford Whalers, 1979-80.
1,549 — Alex Delvecchio, Detroit Red Wings, 1950-51 through 1973-74.
1,540 — John Bucyk, Detroit, Boston, 1955-56 through 1977-78.

MOST GOALS:
801 — Gordie Howe, Detroit Red Wings, Hartford Whalers, in 26 seasons, 1,767 games.
717 — Phil Esposito, Chicago Black Hawks, Boston Bruins, New York Rangers, in 18 seasons, 1,282 games.
665 — Marcel Dionne, Detroit Red Wings, Los Angeles Kings, in 15 seasons, 1,163 games.
610 — Bobby Hull, Chicago Black Hawks, Winnipeg Jets, Hartford Whalers, in 16 seasons, 1,063 games.

HIGHEST GOALS-PER-GAME AVERAGE, CAREER (AMONG PLAYERS WITH 200 OR MORE GOALS):
.870 — Wayne Gretzky, Edmonton Oilers, 481 goals, 553 games from 1979-80 through 1985-86.
.776 — Mike Bossy, New York Islanders, 535 goals, 689 games from 1977-78 through 1985-86.
.767 — Cy Denneny, Ottawa Senators, Boston Bruins, 250 goals, 326 games from 1917-18 through 1928-29.
.738 — Babe Dye, Toronto, Chicago, NY Americans, 200 goals, 271 games from 1919-20 through 1930-31.

MOST ASSISTS:
1,049 — Gordie Howe, Detroit Red Wings, Hartford Whalers in 26 seasons, 1,767 games.
934 — Marcel Dionne, Detroit, Los Angeles, in 15 seasons, 1,163 games.
926 — Stan Mikita, Chicago Blackhawks, in 22 seasons, 1,394 games.
873 — Phil Esposito, Chicago Black Hawks, Boston Bruins, NY Rangers in 18 seasons, 1,282 games.

HIGHEST ASSIST-PER-GAME AVERAGE, CAREER (AMONG PLAYERS WITH 300 OR MORE ASSISTS):
1.548 — Wayne Gretzky, Edmonton Oilers, 856 assists, 553 games, from 1979-80 through 1985-86.
.998 — Peter Stastny, Quebec Nordiques, 462 assists, 463 games, from 1980-81 through 1985-86.
.982 — Bobby Orr, Boston Bruins, Chicago Black Hawks, 645 assists, 657 games from 1966-67 through through 1978-79.
.845 — Bryan Trottier, New York Islanders, 639 assists, 756 games from 1975-76 through 1984-85.

MOST POINTS:
1,850 — Gordie Howe, Detroit Red Wings, Hartford Whalers, in 26 seasons, 1,767 games (801 goals, 1049 assists).
1,599 — Marcel Dionne, Detroit, Los Angeles, in 15 seasons, 1,163 games (665 goals, 934 assists).
1,590 — Phil Esposito, Chicago, Boston, NY Rangers in 18 seasons, 1,282 games (717 goals, 873 assists).
1,467 — Stan Mikita, Chicago in 22 seasons, 1,394 games (541 goals, 926 assists).

MOST GOALS BY A CENTER, CAREER
717 — Phil Esposito, Chicago, Boston, NY Rangers, in 18 seasons.
665 — Marcel Dionne, Detroit, Los Angeles, in 15 seasons
541 — Stan Mikita, Chicago, in 22 seasons.
507 — Jean Beliveau, Montreal, in 20 seasons.
503 — Gilbert Perreault, Buffalo, in 16 seasons.

MOST ASSISTS BY A CENTER, CAREER;
934 — Marcel Dionne, Detroit, Los Angeles, in 15 seasons.
926 — Stan Mikita, Chicago, in 22 seasons.
873 — Phil Esposito, Chicago, Boston, NY Rangers, in 18 seasons.
856 — Wayne Gretzky, Edmonton, in 7 seasons
852 — Bobby Clarke, Philadelphia, in 15 seasons.

MOST POINTS BY A CENTER, CAREER:
1,599 — Marcel Dionne, Detroit, Los Angeles, in 15 seasons
1,590 — Phil Esposito, Chicago, Boston, NY Rangers, in 18 seasons.
1,467 — Stan Mikita, Chicago, in 22 seasons
1,337 — Wayne Gretzky, Edmonton, in 7 seasons.
1,281 — Gilbert Perreault, Buffalo, in 16 seasons.

MOST GOALS BY A LEFT WING, CAREER:
610 — Bobby Hull, Chicago, Winnipeg, Hartford, in 16 seasons.
533 — Frank Mahovlich, Toronto, Detroit, Montreal, in 18 seasons.
424 — Steve Shutt, Montreal, Los Angeles, in 13 seasons.
420 — Bill Barber, Philadelphia, in 12 seasons.

MOST ASSISTS BY A LEFT WING, CAREER:
570 — Frank Mahovlich, Toronto, Detroit, Montreal, in 18 seasons.
560 — Bobby Hull, Chicago, Winnipeg, Hartford, in 16 seasons.
516 — Wayne Cashman, Boston, in 17 seasons.
472 — Ted Lindsay, Detroit, Chicago, in 17 seasons.
469 — Dean Prentice, NY Rangers, Boston, Detroit, Pittsburgh, Minnesota, in 22 seasons.

MOST POINTS BY A LEFT WING, CAREER:
1,170 — Bobby Hull, Chicago, Winnipeg, Hartford, in 16 seasons.
1,103 — Frank Mahovlich, Toronto, Detroit, Montreal, in 18 seasons.
883 — Bill Barber, Philadelphia, in 12 seasons.
860 — Dean Prentice, NY Rangers, Boston, Detroit, Pittsburgh, Minnesota, in 22 seasons.
851 — Ted Lindsay, Detroit, Chicago, in 17 seasons.

MOST GOALS BY A RIGHT WING, CAREER:
801 — Gordie Howe, Detroit, Hartford, in 26 seasons.
556 — John Bucyk, Detroit, Boston, in 23 seasons.
544 — Maurice Richard, Montreal, in 18 seasons.
535 — Mike Bossy, NY Islanders, in 9 seasons.
518 — Guy Lafleur, Montreal, in 14 seasons.

MOST ASSISTS BY A RIGHT WING, CAREER:
1,049 — Gordie Howe, Detroit, Hartford, in 26 seasons.
813 — John Bucyk, Detroit, Boston, in 23 seasons.
728 — Guy Lafleur, Montreal, in 14 seasons.
624 — Andy Bathgate, NY Rangers, Toronto, Detroit, Pittsburgh in 17 seasons.
615 — Rod Gilbert, NY Rangers, in 18 seasons.

MOST POINTS BY A RIGHT WING, CAREER:
1,850 — Gordie Howe, Detroit, Hartford, in 26 seasons.
1,369 — John Bucyk, Detroit, Boston, in 23 seasons.
1,246 — Guy Lafleur, Montreal, in 14 seasons.
1,051 — Mike Bossy, NY Islanders, in 9 seasons.
1,021 — Rod Gilbert, NY Rangers, in 18 seasons.

MOST GOALS BY A DEFENSEMAN, CAREER:
279 — Denis Potvin, NY Islanders, in 13 seasons.
270 — Bobby Orr, Boston, Chicago, in 12 seasons.
248 — Doug Mohns, Boston, Chicago, Minnesota, Atlanta, Washington, in 22 seasons.
213 — Brad Park, NY Rangers, Boston, Detroit, in 17 seasons.
192 — Paul Coffey, Edmonton, in 6 seasons

MOST ASSISTS BY A DEFENSEMAN, CAREER:
683 — Brad Park, NY Rangers, Boston, Detroit, in 17 seasons.
680 — Denis Potvin, NY Islanders, in 13 seasons.
645 — Bobby Orr, Bosotn, Chicago, in 12 seasons.
589 — Larry Robinson, Montreal, 14 seasons.
563 — Borje Salming, Toronto, in 13 seasons.

MOST POINTS BY A DEFENSEMAN, CAREER:
959 — Denis Potvin, NY Islanders, in 13 seasons.
915 — Bobby Orr, Boston, Chicago, in 12 seasons.
896 — Brad Park, NY Rangers, Boston, Detroit, in 17 seasons.
763 — Larry Robinson, Montreal, 14 seasons.
702 — Borje Salming, Toronto, in 13 seasons.

HIGHEST POINTS-PER-GAME AVERAGE, CAREER
(AMONG PLAYERS WITH 500 OR MORE POINTS):
2.418 — Wayne Gretzky, Edmonton Oilers, 1337 points (481 goals, 856 assists), 553 games from 1979-80 through 1985-86.
1.540 — Peter Stastny, Quebec Nordiques, 713 points (251 goals, 462 assists), 463 games from 1980-81 through 1985-86.
1.525 — Mike Bossy, New York Islanders, 1,051 points (535 goals, 516 assists), 689 games from 1977-78 through 1985-86.
1.460 — Jari Kurri, Edmonton Oilers, 644 points (300 goals, 344 assists), 441 games from 1980-81 through 1985-86.
1.393 — Bobby Orr, Boston Bruins, Chicago Black Hawks, 915 points (270 goals, 645 assists), 657 games from 1966-67 through 1978-79.
1.390 — Marcel Dionne, Detroit Red Wings, Los Angeles Kings, 1,505 points (629 goals, 876 assists), 1083 games from 1971-72 through 1984-85.
1.348 — Bryan Trottier, New York Islanders, 1019 points (380 goals, 639 assists), 756 games from 1975-76 through 1984-85.

MOST PENALTY MINUTES:
3,515 — Dave Williams, Toronto, Vancouver, Detroit, Los Angeles in 11 seasons, 858 games.
2,294 — Dave Schultz, Philadelphia, Los Angeles, Pittsburgh, Buffalo in 9 seasons, 533 games.
2,212 — Bryan Watson, Montreal, Detroit, California, Pittsburgh, St. Louis, Washington in 16 seasons, 878 games.

MOST GAMES, INCLUDING PLAYOFFS:
1,924 — Gordie Howe, Detroit Red Wings, Hartford Whalers, 1,767 regular-season and 157 playoff games.
1,670 — Alex Delvecchio, Detroit Red Wings, 1,549 regular-season and 121 playoff games.
1,664 — John Bucyk, Detroit, Boston, 1,540 regular-season and 124 playoff games.

MOST GOALS, INCLUDING PLAYOFFS:
869 — Gordie Howe, Detroit Red Wings, Hartford Whalers, 801 regular-season goals and 68 playoff goals.
778 — Phil Esposito, Chicago, Boston, NY Rangers, 717 regular-season and 61 playoff goals.
685 — Marcel Dionne, Detroit Red Wings, Los Angeles Kings, 665 regular-season and 20 playoff goals.
672 — Bobby Hull, Chicago, Winnipeg, Hartford, 610 regular-season and 62 playoff goals.

MOST ASSISTS, INCLUDING PLAYOFFS:
1,141 — Gordie Howe, Detroit Red Wings, Hartford Whalers, 1,049 regular-season and 92 playoff assists.
1,017 — Stan Mikita, Chicago, 926 regular-season and 91 playoff assists.
967 — Wayne Gretzky, Edmonton Oilers, 856 regular-season and 111 playoff assists.
957 — Marcel Dionne, Detroit, Los Angeles, 934 regular-season and 23 playoff assists.
949 — Phil Esposito, Chicago, Boston, NY Rangers, 873 regular-season and 76 playoff assists.

MOST POINTS, INCLUDING PLAYOFFS:
2,010 — Gordie Howe, Detroit Red Wings, Hartford Whalers, 1,850 regular-season and 160 playoff points.
1,727 — Phil Esposito, Chicago, Boston, NY Rangers, 1,590 regular-season and 137 playoff points.
1,642 — Marcel Dionne, Detroit, Los Angeles, 1,599 regular-season and 43 playoff points.
1,617 — Stan Mikita, Chicago, 1,467 regular-season and 150 playoff points.

Rod Gilbert

MOST PENALTY MINUTES, INCLUDING PLAYOFFS:
3,940 — Dave Williams, Toronto, Vancouver, Los Angeles, 3,515 in regular season; 425 in playoffs.
2,706 — Dave Schultz, Philadelphia, Los Angeles, Pittsburgh, Buffalo, 2,294 regular-season; 412 in playoffs.
2,531 — Willi Plett, Atlanta, Calgary, Minnesota, 2,139 in regular-season; 392 in playoffs.
2,338 — Andre Dupont, NY Rangers, St. Louis, Philadelphia, Quebec, 1,986 regular-season; 352 in playoffs.
2,282 — Bryan Watson, Montreal, Detroit, California, Pittsburgh, St. Louis, Washington, 2,212 regular-season; 70 in playoffs.

MOST CONSECUTIVE GAMES:
914 — Garry Unger, Toronto, Detroit, St. Louis, Atlanta from Feb. 24, 1968, through Dec. 21, 1979.
882 — Doug Jarvis, Montreal, Washington, Hartford, from Oct. 8, 1975 through Apr. 6, 1986.
776 — Craig Ramsay, Buffalo Sabres, from March 27, 1973, through Feb. 10, 1983.
630 — Andy Hebenton, NY Rangers, Boston, nine complete 70-game seasons from 1955-56 through 1963-64.
580 — John Wilson, Detroit, Chicago, Toronto, from Feb. 10, 1952 through Mar. 20, 1960.

MOST GAMES APPEARED IN BY A GOALTENDER, CAREER:
971 — Terry Sawchuk, Detroit, Boston, Toronto, Los Angeles, NY Rangers from 1949-50 through 1969-70.
906 — Glenn Hall, Detroit, Chicago, St. Louis from 1952-53 through 1970-71.
886 — Tony Esposito, Montreal, Chicago from 1968-69 through 1983-84.
860 — Lorne "Gump" Worsley, NY Rangers, Montreal, Minnesota from 1952-53 through 1973-74.

MOST CONSECUTIVE COMPLETE GAMES BY A GOALTENDER:
502 — Glenn Hall, Detroit, Chicago. Played 502 games from beginning of 1955-56 season through first 12 games of 1962-63. In his 503rd straight game, Nov. 7, 1962, at Chicago, Hall was removed from the game against Boston with a back injury in the first period.

MOST SHUTOUTS BY A GOALTENDER, CAREER:
103 — Terry Sawchuk, Detroit, Boston, Toronto, Los Angeles, NY Rangers in 20 seasons.
94 — George Hainsworth, Montreal Canadiens, Toronto in 10 seasons.
84 — Glenn Hall, Detroit, Chicago, St. Louis in 16 seasons.

MOST GAMES SCORING THREE-OR-MORE GOALS:
37 — Wayne Gretzky, Edmonton, in 7 seasons, 26 three-goal games, 8 four-goal games, 3 five-goal games
— **Mike Bossy,** NY Islanders, in 9 seasons, 28 three-goal games, 9 four-goal games.
32 — Phil Esposito, Chicago, Boston, NY Rangers, in 18 seasons, 27 three-goal games, 5 four-goal games.
28 — Bobby Hull, Chicago, Winnipeg, Hartford, in 16 seasons, 24 three-goal games, 4 four-goal games.
— Marcel Dionne, Detroit, Los Angeles, in 14 seasons, 25 three-goal games, 3 four-goal games.
26 — Cy Denneny, Ottawa Senators in 12 seasons. 20 three-goal games, 5 four-goal games, 1 six-goal game.
— Maurice Richard, Montreal, in 18 seasons, 23 three-goal games, 2 four-goal games, 1 five-goal game.

MOST 20-OR-MORE GOAL SEASONS:
22 — Gordie Howe, Detroit Red Wings, Hartford Whalers in 26 seasons.
16 — Phil Esposito, Chicago, Boston, NY Rangers, in 18 seasons.
— Norm Ullman, Detroit, Toronto, in 19 seasons.
— John Bucyk, Detroit, Boston, in 22 seasons.
15 — Frank Mahovlich, Toronto, Detroit, Montreal in 17 seasons.
— Marcel Dionne, Detroit, Los Angeles, in 15 seasons.
— Gilbert Perreault, Buffalo, in 16 seasons.
13 — Guy Lafleur, Montreal, in 14 seasons.

MOST CONSECUTIVE 20-OR-MORE GOAL SEASONS:
22 — Gordie Howe, Detroit Red Wings, 1949-50 through 1970-71.
16 — Phil Esposito, Chicago, Boston, NY Rangers, 1964-65 through 1979-80.
15 — Marcel Dionne, Detroit, Los Angeles, 1971-72 through 1985-86.
14 — Maurice Richard, Montreal, 1943-44 through 1956-57.
— Stan Mikita, Chicago Black Hawks, 1961-62 through 1974-75.
13 — Guy Lafleur, Montreal, 1971-72 through 1983-84.

MOST 30-OR-MORE GOAL SEASONS:
- **14 — Gordie Howe,** Detroit Red Wings, in 25 seasons.
- 13 — Bobby Hull, Chicago Black Hawks, in 16 seasons.
- — Phil Esposito, Chicago, Boston, NY Rangers, in 18 seasons.
- — Marcel Dionne, Detroit, Los Angeles, in 15 seasons.

MOST CONSECUTIVE 30-OR-MORE GOAL SEASONS:
- **13 — Bobby Hull,** Chicago Black Hawks, 1959-60 through 1971-72.
- — **Phil Esposito,** Boston, NY Rangers, 1967-68 through 1979-80.
- 12 — Marcel Dionne, Detroit, Los Angeles,1974-75 through 1985-86.
- 10 — Darryl Sittler, Toronto, Philadelphia, 1973-74 through 1982-83.
- 9 — Lanny McDonald, Toronto, Colorado, Calgary, 1975-76 through 1983-84.
- — Bryan Trottier, NY Islanders, 1975-76 through 1983-84.
- — Steve Shutt, Montreal, 1974-75 through 1982-83.
- 8 — Garry Unger, St. Louis Blues, 1971-72 through 1978-79.

MOST 40-OR-MORE GOAL SEASONS:
- **10 — Marcel Dionne,** Detroit, Los Angeles, in 14 seasons.
- 9 — Mike Bossy, NY Islanders, in 9 seasons.
- 8 — Bobby Hull, Chicago, Winnipeg, Hartford, in 16 seasons.
- — Phil Esposito, Chicago, Boston, NY Rangers, in 18 seasons.
- 7 — Wayne Gretzky, Edmonton Oilers, in 7 seasons.
- 6 — Guy Lafleur, Montreal Canadiens, in 13 seasons.
- — Lanny McDonald, Toronto, Colorado, Calgary in 12 seasons.
- 5 — Gordie Howe, Detroit, Hartford, in 26 seasons.
- — Richard Martin, Buffalo, Los Angeles, in 10 seasons.
- — Bryan Trottier, New York Islanders, in 10 seasons.
- — Rick Middleton, Boston, in 11 seasons.
- — Michel Goulet, Quebec, in 7 seasons.

Bobby Hull, in white, and Gordie Howe.

MOST CONSECUTIVE 40-OR-MORE GOAL SEASONS:
- **9 — Mike Bossy,** New York Islanders, 1977-78 through 1985-86.
- 7 — Phil Esposito, Boston Bruins, 1968-69 through 1974-75.
- — Wayne Gretzky, Edmonton, 1979-80 through 1985-86.
- 6 — Guy Lafleur, Montreal Canadiens, 1974-75 through 1979-80.
- 5 — Rick Middleton, Boston Bruins, 1979-80 through 1984-85.
- — Marcel Dionne, Los Angeles, 1978-79 through 1982-83.
- — Michel Goulet, Quebec, 1981-82 through 1985-86.
- 4 — Bobby Hull, Chicago Black Hawks, 1965-66 through 1968-69.
- — Lanny McDonald, Toronto, Colorado, 1976-77 through 1979-80.
- — Blaine Stoughton, Hartford Whalers, 1979-80 through 1982-83.

MOST 50-OR-MORE GOAL SEASONS:
- **9 — Mike Bossy,** New York Islanders, in 9 seasons.
- 7 — Wayne Gretzky, Edmonton, in 7 seasons.
- 6 — Guy Lafleur, Montreal Canadiens, in 13 seasons.
- — Marcel Dionne, Detroit, Los Angeles, in 15 seasons.
- 5 — Bobby Hull, Chicago, Winnipeg, Hartford, in 16 seasons.
- — Phil Esposito, Chicago, Boston, NY Rangers, in 18 seasons.

MOST CONSECUTIVE 50-OR-MORE GOAL SEASONS:
- **9 — Mike Bossy,** New York Islanders, 1977-78 through 1985-86.
- 7 — Wayne Gretzky, Edmonton, 1979-80 through 1985-86.
- 6 — Guy Lafleur, Montreal Canadiens, 1974-75 through 1979-80.
- 5 — Phil Esposito, Boston, 1970-71 through 1974-75.
- — Marcel Dionne, Los Angeles, 1978-79 through 1982-83.

MOST 100-OR-MORE POINT SEASONS:
- **8 — Marcel Dionne,** Detroit, 1974-75; Los Angeles, 1976-77; 1978-79 through 1982-83; 1984-85.
- 7 — Mike Bossy, NY Islanders, 1978-79; 1980-81 through 1985-86.
- — Wayne Gretzky, Edmonton, 1979-80 through 1985-86.
- 6 — Phil Esposito, Boston Bruins, 1968-69; 1970-71 through 1974-75.
- — Bobby Orr, Boston Bruins, 1969-70 through 1974-75.
- — Guy Lafleur, Montreal Canadiens, 1974-75 through 1979-80.
- — Bryan Trottier, New York Islanders, 1977-78 through 1981-82; 1983-84.
- — Peter Stastny, Quebec, 1980-81 through 1985-86.

MOST CONSECUTIVE 100-OR-MORE POINT SEASONS:
- **7 — Wayne Gretzky,** Edmonton Oilers,1979-80 through 1985-86.
- 6 — Bobby Orr,Boston Bruins, 1969-70 through 1974-75.
- — Guy Lafleur, Montreal Canadiens, 1974-75 through 1979-80.
- — Mike Bossy, NY Islanders,1980-81 through 1985-86.
- — Peter Stastny, Quebec Nordiques, 1980-81 through 1985-86.
- 5 — Phil Esposito, Boston Bruins, 1970-71 through 1974-75.
- — Bryan Trottier, New York Islanders, 1977-78 through 1981-82.
- — Marcel Dionne, Los Angeles Kings, 1978-79 through 1982-83.

Single Season

MOST GOALS, ONE SEASON:
- **92 — Wayne Gretzky,** Edmonton Oilers, 1981-82. (80 games)
- 87 — Wayne Gretzky, Edmonton Oilers, 1983-84. (80 games)
- 76 — Phil Esposito, Boston Bruins, 1970-71. (78 games)
- 73 — Wayne Gretzky, Edmonton Oilers, 1984-85. (80 games)
- 71 — Jari Kurri, Edmonton Oilers, 1984-85 (80 games)
- — Wayne Gretzky, Edmonton Oilers, 1982-83. (80 games)
- 69 — Mike Bossy, New York Islanders, 1978-79. (80 games)
- 68 — Phil Esposito, Boston Bruins, 1973-74. (78 games)
- — Mike Bossy, New York Islanders, 1980-81. (80 games)
- — Jari Kurri, Edmonton Oilers, 1985-86. (80 games).

MOST ASSISTS, ONE SEASON:
- **163 — Wayne Gretzky,** Edmonton Oilers, 1985-86. (80 games)
- 135 — Wayne Gretzky, Edmonton Oilers, 1984-85. (80 games)
- 125 — Wayne Gretzky, Edmonton Oilers, 1982-83. (80 games)
- 120 — Wayne Gretzky, Edmonton Oilers, 1981-82. (80 games)
- 118 — Wayne Gretzky, Edmonton Oilers, 1983-84. (80 games)
- 109 — Wayne Gretzky, Edmonton Oilers, 1980-81. (80 games)
- 102 — Bobby Orr, Boston Bruins, 1970-71. (78 games)
- 93 — Peter Stastny, Quebec Nordiques, 1981-82. (80 games)
- — Mario Lemieux, Pittsburgh Penguins, 1985-86. (80 games).

MOST POINTS, ONE SEASON:
- **215 — Wayne Gretzky,** Edmonton Oilers, 1985-86. (80 games)
- 212 — Wayne Gretzky, Edmonton Oilers, 1981-82. (80 games)
- 208 — Wayne Gretzky, Edmonton Oilers, 1984-85. (80 games)
- 205 — Wayne Gretzky, Edmonton Oilers, 1983-84. (80 games)
- 196 — Wayne Gretzky, Edmonton Oilers, 1982-83. (80 games)
- 164 — Wayne Gretzky, Edmonton Oilers, 1980-81. (80 games)
- 152 — Phil Esposito, Boston Bruins, 1970-71. (78 games)
- 147 — Mike Bossy, New York Islanders, 1981-82. (80 games)

MOST GAMES SCORING AT LEAST THREE GOALS, ONE SEASON:
- **10 — Wayne Gretzky,** Edmonton Oilers, 1981-82. 6 three-goal games, 3 four-goal games, 1 five-goal game.
- — **Wayne Gretzky,** Edmonton Oilers, 1983-84. 6 three-goal games, 4 four-goal games.
- 9 — Mike Bossy, New York Islanders, 1980-81. 6 three-goal games, 3 four-goal games.
- 7 — Joe Malone, Montreal Canadiens, 1917-18. 2 three-goal games, 2 four-goal games, 3 five-goal games.
- — Phil Esposito, Boston Bruins, 1970-71. 7 three-goal games.
- — Rick Martin, Buffalo Sabres, 1975-76. 6 three-goal games, 1 4-goal game.

**HIGHEST GOALS-PER-GAME AVERAGE, ONE SEASON
(AMONG PLAYERS WITH 20-OR-MORE GOALS):**
- **2.20 — Joe Malone,** Montreal Canadiens, 1917-18, with 44 goals in 20 games.
- 1.64 — Cy Denneny, Ottawa Senators, 1917-18, with 36 goals in 22 games.
- — Newsy Lalonde, Montreal Canadiens, 1917-18, with 23 goals in 14 games.
- 1.63 — Joe Malone, Quebec Bulldogs, 1919-20, with 39 goals in 24 games.

**HIGHEST ASSISTS-PER-GAME AVERAGE, ONE SEASON
(AMONG PLAYERS WITH 35-OR-MORE ASSISTS):**
- **2.04 — Wayne Gretzky,** Edmonton Oilers, 1985-86, with 163 assists in 80 games.
- 1.69 — Wayne Gretzky, Edmonton Oilers, 1984-85, with 135 assists in 80 games.
- 1.59 — Wayne Gretzky, Edmonton Oilers, 1983-84, with 118 assists in 74 games.
- 1.56 — Wayne Gretzky, Edmonton Oilers, 1982-83, with 125 assists in 80 games.
- 1.50 — Wayne Gretzky, Edmonton Oilers, 1981-82, with 120 assists in 80 games.
- 1.36 — Wayne Gretzky, Edmonton Oilers, 1980-81, with 109 assists in 80 games.
- 1.31 — Bobby Orr, Boston Bruins, 1970-71, with 102 assists in 78 games.
- 1.22 — Bobby Orr, Boston Bruins, 1973-74, with 90 assists in 74 games.
- 1.17 — Bobby Clarke, Philadelphia Flyers, 1975-76, with 89 assists in 76 games.

**HIGHEST POINTS-PER-GAME AVERAGE, ONE SEASON
(AMONG PLAYERS WITH 50 OR MORE POINTS):**
- **2.77 — Wayne Gretzky,** Edmonton Oilers, 1983-84, with 205 points in 74 games.
- 2.69 — Wayne Gretzky, Edmonton Oilers, 1985-86, with 215 points in 80 games.
- 2.65 — Wayne Gretzky, Edmonton Oilers, 1981-82, with 212 points in 80 games.
- 2.60 — Wayne Gretzky, Edmonton Oilers, 1984-85, with 208 points in 80 games.
- 2.45 — Wayne Gretzky, Edmonton Oilers, 1982-83, with 196 points in 80 games.
- 2.05 — Wayne Gretzky, Edmonton Oilers, 1980-81, with 164 points in 80 games.
- 1.97 — Bill Cowley, Boston Bruins, 1943-44, with 71 points in 36 games.
- 1.95 — Phil Esposito, Boston Bruins, 1970-71, with 152 points in 78 games.

MOST GOALS, ONE SEASON, INCLUDING PLAYOFFS:
100 — Wayne Gretzky, Edmonton Oilers, 1983-84, 87 goals in 74 regular-season games and 13 goals in 19 playoff games.
97 — Wayne Gretzky, Edmonton Oilers, 1981-82, 92 goals in 80 regular-season games and 5 goals in 5 playoff games.
90 — Wayne Gretzky, Edmonton Oilers, 1984-85, 73 goals in 80 regular season games and 17 goals in 18 playoff games.
— Jari Kurri, Edmonton Oilers, 1984-85, 71 goals in 80 regular season games and 19 goals in 18 playoff games.
85 — Mike Bossy, New York Islanders, 1980-81, 68 goals in 79 regular-season games and 17 goals in 18 playoff games.
83 — Wayne Gretzky, Edmonton Oilers, 1982-83, 71 goals in 80 regular-season games and 12 goals in 16 playoff games.
81 — Mike Bossy, New York Islanders, 1981-82, 64 goals in 80 regular-season games and 17 goals in 19 playoff games.
80 — Reggie Leach, Philadelphia Flyers, 1975-76, 61 goals in 80 regular-season games and 19 goals in 16 playoff games.

MOST ASSISTS, ONE SEASON, INCLUDING PLAYOFFS:
174 — Wayne Gretzky, Edmonton Oilers, 1985-86, 163 assists in 80 regular season games and 11 assists in 10 playoff games.
165 — Wayne Gretzky, Edmonton Oilers, 1984-85, 135 assists in 80 regular-season games and 30 assists in 18 playoff games.
151 — Wayne Gretzky, Edmonton Oilers, 1982-83, 125 assists in 80 regular-season games and 26 assists in 16 playoff games.
140 — Wayne Gretzky, Edmonton Oilers, 1983-84, 118 assists in 74 regular-season games and 22 in 19 playoff games.
127 — Wayne Gretzky, Edmonton Oilers, 1981-82, 120 assists in 80 regular-season games and 7 assists in 5 playoff games.
123 — Wayne Gretzky, Edmonton Oilers, 1980-81, 109 assists in 80 regular-season games and 14 assists in 9 playoff games.
109 — Bobby Orr, Boston Bruins, 1970-71, 102 assists in 78 regular-season games and 7 assists in 7 playoff games.
— Paul Coffey, Edmonton Oilers, 1984-85, 84 assists in 80 regular-season games and 47 points in 18 playoff games.

MOST POINTS, ONE SEASON, INCLUDING PLAYOFFS:
255 — Wayne Gretzky, Edmonton Oilers, 1984-85, 208 points in 80 regular-season games and 47 points in 18 playoff games.
240 — Wayne Gretzky, Edmonton Oilers, 1983-84, 205 points in 74 regular-season games and 35 points in 19 playoff games.
234 — Wayne Gretzky, Edmonton Oilers, 1982-83, 196 points in 80 regular-season games and 38 points in 16 playoff games.
— Wayne Gretzky, Edmonton Oilers, 1985-86, 215 points in 80 regular-season games and 19 points in 10 playoff games.
224 — Wayne Gretzky, Edmonton Oilers, 1981-82, 212 points in 80 regular-season games and 12 points in 5 playoff games.
185 — Wayne Gretzky, Edmonton Oilers, 1980-81, 164 points in 80 regular-season games and 21 points in 9 playoff games.
174 — Mike Bossy, New York Islanders, 1981-82, 147 points in 80 regular-season games and 27 points in 19 playoff games.
166 — Jari Kurri, Edmonton Oilers, 1984-85, 135 points in 80 regular season games, and 31 in 18 playoff games.
162 — Phil Esposito, Boston Bruins, 1970-71, 152 points in 78 regular-season games and 10 points in 7 playoff games.
— Guy Lafleur, Montreal Canadiens, 1976-77, 136 points in 80 regular-season games and 26 points in 14 playoff games.

MOST GOALS, ONE SEASON, BY A DEFENSEMAN:
48 — Paul Coffey, Edmonton Oilers, 1985-86. (80 games)
46 — Bobby Orr, Boston Bruins, 1974-75. (80 games)
40 — Paul Coffey, Edmonton Oilers, 1983-84. (80 games)
39 — Doug Wilson, Chicago Black Hawks, 1981-82. (80 games)
37 — Bobby Orr, Boston Bruins, 1970-71. (78 games)
— Bobby Orr, Boston Bruins, 1971-72. (78 games)
— Paul Coffey, Edmonton Oilers, 1984-85 (80 games).
33 — Bobby Orr, Boston Bruins, 1969-70. (76 games)
32 — Bobby Orr, Boston Bruins, 1973-74. (78 games)
31 — Denis Potvin, New York Islanders, 1975-76. (80 games)
— Denis Potvin, New York Islanders, 1978-79. (80 games)
— Raymond Bourque, Boston Bruins, 1983-84. (80 games)
— Phil Housley, Buffalo Sabres, 1983-84. (80 games)
30 — Denis Potvin, New York Islanders, 1979-80. (80 games)

MOST GOALS, ONE SEASON, BY A CENTER:
92 — Wayne Gretzky, Edmonton Oilers, 1981-82. (80 games)
87 — Wayne Gretzky, Edmonton Oilers, 1983-84. (80 games)
76 — Phil Esposito, Boston Bruins, 1970-71. (78 games)
73 — Wayne Gretzky, Edmonton Oilers, 1984-85. (80 games)
71 — Wayne Gretzky, Edmonton Oilers, 1982-83. (80 games)
68 — Phil Esposito, Boston Bruins, 1973-74. (78 games)
66 — Phil Esposito, Boston Bruins, 1971-72. (78 games)

MOST GOALS, ONE SEASON, BY A RIGHT WINGER:
71 — Jari Kurri, Edmonton Oilers, 1984-85. (80 games)
69 — Mike Bossy, New York Islanders, 1978-79. (80 games)
68 — Jari Kurri, Edmonton Oilers, 1985-86. (80 games).
— Mike Bossy, New York Islanders, 1980-81. (80 games)
66 — Lanny McDonald, Calgary Flames, 1982-83. (80 games)
64 — Mike Bossy, New York Islanders, 1981-82. (80 games)
61 — Reggie Leach, Philadelphia Flyers, 1975-76. (80 games)
60 — Guy Lafleur, Montreal Canadiens, 1977-78. (80 games)
— Mike Bossy, New York Islanders, 1982-83. (80 games)
58 — Mike Bossy, New York Islanders, 1984-85. (80 games)
56 — Guy Lafleur, Montreal Canadiens, 1975-76, 1976-77. (80 games)
— Blaine Stoughton, Hartford Whalers, 1979-80. (80 games)
— Danny Gare, Buffalo Sabres, 1979-80. (80 games)

MOST GOALS, ONE SEASON, BY A LEFT WINGER:
60 — Steve Shutt, Montreal Canadiens, 1976-77. (80 games)
58 — Bobby Hull, Chicago Black Hawks, 1968-69. (76 games)
57 — Michel Goulet, Quebec Nordiques, 1982-83. (80 games)
56 — Charlie Simmer, Los Angeles Kings, 1979-80. (80 games)
— Charlie Simmer, Los Angeles Kings, 1980-81. (80 games)
— Michel Goulet, Quebec Nordiques, 1983-84. (80 games)
55 — Michel Goulet, Quebec Nordiques, 1984-85. (80 games)
— John Ogrodnick, Detroit Red Wings, 1984-85. (80 games)
54 — Bobby Hull, Chicago Black Hawks, 1965-66. (70 games)
— Al Secord, Chicago Black Hawks, 1982-83. (80 games)

MOST GOALS, ONE SEASON, BY A ROOKIE:
53 — Mike Bossy, NY Islanders, 1977-78. (80 games)
45 — Dale Hawerchuk, Winnipeg Jets, 1981-82. (80 games)
44 — Richard Martin, Buffalo Sabres, 1971-72. (78 games)
— Barry Pederson, Boston Bruins, 1981-82. (80 games)
43 — Steve Larmer, Chicago Black Hawks, 1982-83. (80 games)
— Mario Lemieux, Pittsburgh Penguins, 1984-85. (80 games)
40 — Darryl Sutter, Chicago Black Hawks, 1980-81. (80 games)
— Sylvain Turgeon, Hartford Whalers, 1983-84. (80 games)
— Warren Young, Pittsburgh Penguins, 1984-85. (80 games)

MOST GOALS, ONE SEASON, BY A ROOKIE DEFENSEMAN:
22 — Barry Beck, Colorado Rockies, 1977-78. (80 games)
19 — Reed Larson, Detroit Red Wings, 1977-78. (80 games)
— Phil Housley, Buffalo Sabres, 1982-83. (80 games)
18 — Brad Maxwell, Minnesota North Stars, 1977-78. (80 games)
— Reijo Ruotsalainen, New York Rangers, 1981-82. (80 games)
— Gary Suter, Calgary Flames, 1985-86. (80 games).

MOST ASSISTS, ONE SEASON, BY A DEFENSEMAN:
102 — Bobby Orr, Boston Bruins, 1970-71. (78 games)
90 — Bobby Orr, Boston Bruins, 1973-74. (78 games)
89 — Bobby Orr, Boston Bruins, 1974-75. (80 games)

MOST ASSISTS, ONE SEASON, BY A CENTER:
163 — Wayne Gretzky, Edmonton Oilers, 1985-86. (80 games)
135 — Wayne Gretzky, Edmonton Oilers, 1984-85. (80 games)
125 — Wayne Gretzky, Edmonton Oilers, 1982-83. (80 games)
120 — Wayne Gretzky, Edmonton Oilers, 1981-82. (80 games)
118 — Wayne Gretzky, Edmonton Oilers, 1983-84. (80 games)
109 — Wayne Gretzky, Edmonton Oilers, 1980-81. (80 games)
93 — Peter Stastny, Quebec Nordiques, 1981-82. (80 games)
— Mario Lemieux, Pittsburgh Penguins, 1985-86. (80 games).

MOST ASSISTS, ONE SEASON, BY A RIGHT WINGER:
83 — Mike Bossy, New York Islanders, 1981-82. (80 games)
80 — Guy Lafleur, Montreal Canadiens, 1976-77. (80 games)
77 — Guy Lafleur, Montreal Canadiens, 1978-79. (80 games)

MOST ASSISTS, ONE SEASON, BY A LEFT WINGER:
65 — John Bucyk, Boston Bruins, 1970-71. (78 games)
— **Michel Goulet,** Quebec Nordiques, 1983-84. (80 games)
64 — Mark Messier, Edmonton Oilers, 1983-84. (80 games)
62 — Bill Barber, Philadelphia Flyers, 1975-76. (80 games)
60 — Anton Stastny, Quebec Nordiques, 1982-83. (80 games)
59 — Wayne Cashman, Boston Bruins, 1973-74. (78 games)

MOST ASSISTS, ONE SEASON, BY A ROOKIE:
70 — Peter Stastny, Quebec Nordiques, 1980-81. (80 games)
63 — Bryan Trottier, New York Islanders, 1975-76. (80 games)
60 — Larry Murphy, Los Angeles Kings, 1980-81. (80 games)

MOST ASSISTS, ONE SEASON, BY A ROOKIE DEFENSEMAN:
60 — Larry Murphy, Los Angeles Kings, 1980-81. (80 games)
55 — Chris Chelios, Montreal Canadiens, 1984-85. (80 games)
50 — Stefan Persson, New York Islanders, 1977-78. (80 games)
— Gary Suter, Calgary Flames, 1985-86. (80 games)
48 — Raymond Bourque, Boston Bruins, 1979-80. (80 games)

MOST ASSISTS, ONE SEASON, BY A GOALTENDER:
14 — Grant Fuhr, Edmonton Oilers, 1983-84.
8 — Mike Palmateer, Washington Capitals, 1980-81.
6 — Gilles Meloche, California Seals, 1974-75.
— Grant Fuhr, Edmonton Oilers, 1981-82.

MOST POINTS, ONE SEASON, BY A DEFENSEMAN:
139 — Bobby Orr, Boston Bruins, 1970-71. (78 games)
138 — Paul Coffey, Edmonton Oilers, 1985-86. (80 games)
135 — Bobby Orr, Boston Bruins, 1974-75. (80 games)
126 — Paul Coffey, Edmonton Oilers, 1983-84. (80 games)
122 — Bobby Orr, Boston Bruins, 1973-74. (78 games)

MOST POINTS, ONE SEASON, BY A CENTER:
215 — Wayne Gretzky, Edmonton Oilers, 1985-86. (80 games)
212 — Wayne Gretzky, Edmonton Oilers, 1981-82. (80 games)
208 — Wayne Gretzky, Edmonton Oilers, 1984-85. (80 games)
205 — Wayne Gretzky, Edmonton Oilers, 1983-84. (80 games)
196 — Wayne Gretzky, Edmonton Oilers, 1982-83. (80 games)
164 — Wayne Gretzky, Edmonton Oilers, 1980-81. (80 games)
152 — Phil Esposito, Boston Bruins, 1970-71. (78 games)

MOST POINTS, ONE SEASON, BY A RIGHT WINGER:
147 — Mike Bossy, New York Islanders, 1981-82. (80 games)
136 — Guy Lafleur, Montreal Canadiens, 1976-77. (80 games)
135 — Jari Kurri, Edmonton Oilers, 1984-85. (80 games)
132 — Guy Lafleur, Montreal Canadiens, 1977-78. (80 games)

MOST POINTS, ONE SEASON, BY A LEFT WINGER:
121 — Michel Goulet, Quebec Nordiques, 1983-84. (80 games)
116 — John Bucyk, Boston Bruins, 1970-71. (78 games)
112 — Bill Barber, Philadelphia Flyers, 1975-76. (80 games)
110 — Mats Naslund, Montreal Canadiens, 1985-86. (80 games).
107 — Bobby Hull, Chicago Black Hawks, 1968-69. (76 games)

MOST POINTS, ONE SEASON, BY A ROOKIE:
109 — Peter Stastny, Quebec Nordiques, 1980-81. (80 games)
103 — Dale Hawerchuk, Winnipeg Jets, 1981-82. (80 games)
100 — Mario Lemieux, Pittsburgh Penguins, 1984-85. (80 games)
97 — Neal Broten, Minnesota North Stars, 1981-82. (80 games)

MOST POINTS, ONE SEASON, BY A ROOKIE DEFENSEMAN:
76 — Larry Murphy, Los Angeles Kings, 1980-81. (80 games)
68 — Gary Suter, Calgary Flames, 1985-86. (80 games).
66 — Phil Housley, Buffalo Sabres, 1982-83. (80 games)
65 — Raymond Bourque, Boston Bruins, 1979-80. (80 games)
64 — Chris Chelios, Montreal Canadiens, 1984-85. (80 games)
60 — Barry Beck, Colorado Rockies, 1977-78. (80 games)
— Reed Larson, Detroit Red Wings, 1977-78. (80 games)

MOST POWER-PLAY GOALS, ONE SEASON:
34 — Tim Kerr, Philadelphia Flyers,1985-86. (80 games)
28 — Phil Esposito, Boston Bruins, 1971-72. (78 games)
— Mike Bossy, New York Islanders, 1980-81. (80 games)
— Michel Goulet, Quebec Nordiques, 1985-86. (80 games)
27 — Phil Esposito, Boston Bruins, 1974-75. (80 games)
— Mike Bossy, New York Islanders, 1978-79. (80 games)
25 — Phil Esposito, Boston Bruins, 1970-71. (78 games)
— Mike Bossy, New York Islanders, 1977-78. (80 games)

MOST SHORTHAND GOALS, ONE SEASON:
12 — Wayne Gretzky, Edmonton Oilers, 1983-84. (80 games)
11 — Wayne Gretzky, Edmonton Oilers, 1984-85. (80 games)
10 — Marcel Dionne, Detroit Red Wings, 1974-75. (80 games)
9 — Paul Coffey, Edmonton Oilers, 1985-86. (80 games).

MOST SHOTS ON GOAL, ONE SEASON:
550 — Phil Esposito, Boston Bruins, 1970-71. (78 games)
426 — Phil Esposito, Boston Bruins, 1971-72. (78 games)
414 — Bobby Hull, Chicago Black Hawks, 1968-69. (76 games)

MOST PENALTY MINUTES, ONE SEASON:
472 — Dave Schultz, Philadelphia Flyers, 1974-75. (80 games)
407 — Paul Baxter, Pittsburgh Penguins, 1981-82. (80 games)
405 — Dave Schultz, Los Angeles, Pittsburgh, 1977-78. (80 games)

MOST SHUTOUTS, ONE SEASON:
22 — George Hainsworth, Montreal Canadiens, 1928-29. (44 games)
15 — Alex Connell, Ottawa Senators, 1925-26. (36 games)
— Alex Connell, Ottawa Senators, 1927-28. (44 games)
— Hal Winkler, Boston Bruins, 1927-28. (44 games)
— Tony Esposito, Chicago Black Hawks, 1969-70. (76 games)
14 — George Hainsworth, Montreal Canadiens, 1926-27. (44 games)

LONGEST UNDEFEATED STREAK BY A GOALTENDER:
32 Games — Gerry Cheevers, Boston Bruins, 1971-72. 24 wins, 8 ties.
31 Games — Pete Peeters, Boston Bruins, 1982-83. 26 wins, 5 ties.
27 Games — Pete Peeters, Philadelphia Flyers, 1979-80. 22 wins, 5 ties.
23 Games — Frank Brimsek, Boston Bruins, 1940-41. 15 wins, 8 ties.
— Glenn Resch, New York Islanders, 1978-79. 15 wins, 8 ties.
— Grant Fuhr, Edmonton Oilers, 1981-82. 15 wins, 8 ties.

MOST GAMES, ONE SEASON, BY A GOALTENDER:
73 — Bernie Parent, Philadelphia, 1973-74.
72 — Gary Smith, Vancouver, 1974-75.
— Don Edwards, Buffalo, 1977-78.
71 — Gary Smith, California, 1970-71.
— Tony Esposito, Chicago, 1974-75.

MOST WINS, ONE SEASON, BY A GOALTENDER:
47 — Bernie Parent, Philadelphia, 1973-74.
44 — Bernie Parent, Philadelphia, 1974-75.
— Terry Sawchuk, Detroit, 1950-51.
— Terry Sawchuk, Detroit, 1951-52.

LONGEST WINNING STREAK, ONE SEASON, BY A GOALTENDER:
17 — Gilles Gilbert, Boston Bruins, 1975-76.
14 — Don Beaupre, Minnesota, 1985-86.
— Ross Brooks, Boston Bruins, 1973-74.
— Tiny Thompson, Boston Bruins, 1929-30.

MOST GOALS, 50 GAMES FROM START OF SEASON:
61 — Wayne Gretzky, Edmonton Oilers, 1981-82. Oct. 7, 1981 through Jan. 22, 1982. (80-game schedule)
— Wayne Gretzky, Edmonton Oilers, 1983-84. Oct. 5, 1983 through Jan. 25, 1984. (80-game schedule)
53 — Wayne Gretzky, Edmonton Oilers, 1984-85. Oct. 11, 1984 through Jan. 28, 1985. (80-game schedule).
50 — Maurice Richard, Montreal Canadiens, 1944-45. Oct. 28, 1944 through March 18, 1945. (50-game schedule)
— Mike Bossy, New York Islanders, 1980-81. Oct. 11, 1980 through Jan. 24, 1981. (80-game schedule)
49 — Charlie Simmer, Los Angeles Kings, 1980-81. Oct. 11, 1980 through Jan. 24, 1980. (80-game schedule)

LONGEST CONSECUTIVE POINT-SCORING STREAK FROM START OF SEASON:
51 Games — Wayne Gretzky, Edmonton Oilers, 1983-84. 61 goals, 92 assists, 153 points during streak which was stopped by goaltender Markus Mattsson and the Los Angeles Kings on Jan. 28, 1984.

LONGEST CONSECUTIVE POINT SCORING STREAK:
51 Games — Wayne Gretzky, Edmonton Oilers, 1983-84. 61 goals, 92 assists, 153 points during streak.
39 Games — Wayne Gretzky, Edmonton Oilers, 1985-86. 33 goals, 75 assists, 108 points during streak.
30 Games — Wayne Gretzky, Edmonton Oilers, 1982-83. 24 goals, 52 assists, 76 points during streak.
28 Games — Guy Lafleur, Montreal Canadiens, 1976-77. 19 goals, 42 assists, 61 points during streak.
— Wayne Gretzky, Edmonton Oilers, 1984-85. 20 goals, 43 assists, 63 points during streak.
— Mario Lemieux, Pittsburgh Penguins, 1985-86. 21 goals, 38 assists, 59 points during streak.
— Paul Coffey, Edmonton Oilers, 1985-86. 16 goals, 39 assists, 55 points during a streak.
25 Games — Bryan Trottier, New York Islanders, 1981-82. 28 goals, 27 assists, 55 points during streak.
— Bernie Nicholls, Los Angeles Kings, 1984-85. 21 goals, 19 assists, 40 points during streak.
24 Games — Wayne Gretzky, Edmonton Oilers, 1981-82. 28 goals, 38 assists, 66 points during streak.
23 Games — Guy Lafleur, Montreal Canadiens, 1978-79. 19 goals, 21 assists, 40 points during streak.
22 Games — Bronco Horvath, Boston Bruins, 1959-60. 16 goals, 17 assists, 33 points during streak.
— Bobby Clarke, Philadelphia Flyers, 1977-78. 5 goals, 26 assists, 31 points during streak.

LONGEST CONSECUTIVE POINT-SCORING STREAK BY A DEFENSEMAN:
28 Games — Paul Coffey, Edmonton Oilers, 1985-86. 16 goals, 39 assists, 55 points during streak.
17 Games — Ray Bourque, Boston Bruins, 1984-85. 4 goals, 24 assists, 28 points during streak.
15 Games — Bobby Orr, Boston Bruins, 1973-74. 8 goals, 15 assists, 23 points during streak.
15 Games — Bobby Orr, Boston Bruins, 1970-71. 10 goals, 23 assists, 33 points during streak.

LONGEST CONSECUTIVE GOAL-SCORING STREAK:
16 Games — Harry (Punch) Broadbent, Ottawa Senators, 1921-22. 25 goals during streak.
14 Games — Joe Malone, Montreal Canadiens, 1917-18. 35 goals during streak.
13 Games — Newsy Lalonde, Montreal Canadiens, 1920-21. 24 goals during streak.
— Charlie Simmer, Los Angeles Kings, 1979-80. 17 goals during streak.
12 Games — Cy Denneny, Ottawa Senators, 1917-18. 23 goals during streak.
— Dave Lumley, Edmonton Oilers, 1981-82. 15 goals during streak.
11 Games — Babe Dye, Toronto St. Patricks, Hamilton Tigers, 1920-21. 22 goals during streak.
— Babe Dye, Toronto St. Patricks, 1921-22. 15 goals during streak.
— Marcel Dionne, Los Angeles, 1982-83. 14 goals during streak.
10 Games — Andy Bathgate, New York Rangers, 1962-63. 11 goals during streak.
— Bobby Hull, Chicago Black Hawks, 1968-69. 15 goals during streak.
— Mike Bossy, New York Islanders, 1978-79. 12 goals during streak.
— Mike Bossy, New York Islanders, 1984-85. 17 goals during streak.
— John Anderson, Toronto Maple Leafs, 1984-85. 14 goals during streak.
— Jari Kurri, Edmonton Oilers, 1985-86. 10 goals during streak.

LONGEST CONSECUTIVE ASSIST-SCORING STREAK:
17 Games — Wayne Gretzky, Edmonton Oilers, 1983-84. 38 assists during streak.
— Paul Coffey, Edmonton Oilers, 1985-86. 27 assists during streak.
15 Games — Jari Kurri, Edmonton Oilers, 1983-84. 21 assists during streak.
14 Games — Stan Mikita, Chicago Black Hawks, 1967-68. 18 assists during streak.
— Bobby Orr, Boston Bruins, 1970-71. 23 assists during streak.
— Jude Drouin, Minnesota North Stars, 1971-72. 21 assists during streak.
— Wayne Gretzky, Edmonton Oilers, 1981-82. 26 assists during streak.
— Wayne Gretzky, Edmonton Oilers, 1985-86. 39 assists during streak.
— Mario Lemieux, Pittsburgh Penguins, 1985-86. 23 assists during streak.
12 Games — Norm Ullman, Toronto Maple Leafs, 1970-71. 15 assists during streak.
— Pete Mahovlich, Montreal Canadiens, 1974-75. 18 assists during streak.
— Bobby Clarke, Philadelphia Flyers, 1975-76. 20 assists during streak.
— Bobby Clarke, Philadelphia Flyers, 1977-78. 16 assists during streak.
— Guy Lafleur, Montreal Canadiens, 1979-80. 15 assists during streak.
— Wayne Gretzky, Edmonton Oilers, 1982-83. 20 assists during streak.
— Barry Pederson, Boston Bruins, 1982-83. 15 assists during streak.
— Wayne Gretzky, Edmonton Oilers, 1985-86. 24 assists during streak.
— Ken Linseman, Boston Bruins, 1985-86. 19 assists during streak.

LONGEST SHUTOUT SEQUENCE BY A GOALTENDER:

461 Minutes, 29 Seconds — Alex Connell, Ottawa Senators, 1927-28, six consecutive shutouts. (Forward passing not permitted in attacking zones in that era)

343 Minutes, 5 Seconds — George Hainsworth, Montreal Canadiens, 1928-29, four consecutive shutouts.

324 Minutes, 40 Seconds — Roy Wonters, New York Americans, 1930-31, four consecutive shutouts.

309 Minutes, 21 Seconds — Bill Durnan, Montreal Canadiens, 1948-49, four consecutive shutouts.

Single Game

MOST GOALS, ONE GAME:

7 — Joe Malone, Quebec Bulldogs, Jan. 31, 1920, at Quebec City. Quebec 10, Toronto St. Pats 6.

6 — Newsy Lalonde, Montreal Canadiens, Jan. 10, 1920, at Montreal. Canadiens 14, Toronto St. Pats 7.
— Joe Malone, Quebec Bulldogs, March 10, 1920, at Quebec City. Quebec 10, Ottawa Senators 4.
— Corb Denneny, Toronto St. Patricks, Jan. 26, 1921, at Toronto. Toronto 10, Hamilton Tigers 3.
— Cy Denneny, Ottawa Senators, March 7, 1921, at Ottawa. Ottawa 12, Hamilton Tigers 5.
— Syd Howe, Detroit Red Wings, Feb. 3, 1944, at Detroit. Detroit 12, New York Rangers 4.
— Red Berenson, St. Louis Blues, Nov. 7, 1968, at Philadelphia. St. Louis 8, Philadelphia 0
— Darryl Sittler, Toronto Maple Leafs, Feb. 7, 1976, at Toronto. Toronto 11, Boston 4.

MOST GOALS, ONE PERIOD:

4 — Harvey (Busher) Jackson, Toronto Maple Leafs, Nov. 20, 1934, at St. Louis, third period. Toronto 5, St. Louis Eagles 2.
— **Max Bentley,** Chicago Black Hawks, Jan. 28, 1943, at Chicago, third period. Chicago 10, New York Rangers 1.
— **Clint Smith,** Chicago Black Hawks, March 4, 1945, at Chicago, third period. Chicago 6, Montreal Canadiens 4.
— **Red Berenson,** St. Louis Blues, Nov. 7, 1968, at Philadelphia, second period. St. Louis 8, Philadelphia Flyers 0.
— **Wayne Gretzky,** Edmonton Oilers, Feb. 18, 1981, at Edmonton, third period. Edmonton 9, St. Louis 2.
— **Grant Mulvey,** Chicago Black Hawks, Feb. 3, 1982, at Chicago, first period. Chicago 9, St. Louis 5.
— **Bryan Trottier,** New York Islanders, Feb 13, 1982, at New York, second period. Islanders 8 Philadelphia 2.

MOST ASSISTS, ONE PERIOD:

5 — Dale Hawerchuk, Winnipeg Jets, Mar. 6, 1984, at Los Angeles, second period. Winnipeg 7, Los Angeles 3.

4 — Buddy O'Connor, Montreal Canadiens, Nov. 8, 1942, at Montreal, third period. Montreal 10, New York Rangers 4.
— Doug Bentley, Chicago Black Hawks, Jan. 28, 1943, at Chicago, third period. Chicago 10, New York Rangers 1.
— Joe Carveth, Detroit Red Wings, Jan. 23, 1944, at Detroit, third period. Detroit 15, New York Rangers 0.
— Phil Watson, Montreal Canadiens, March 18, 1944, at Montreal, third period. Montreal 11, New York Rangers 2.
— Bill Mosienko, Chicago Black Hawks, March 4, 1945, at Chicago, third period. Chicago 6, Montreal Canadiens 4.
— Jean-Claude Tremblay, Montreal Canadiens, Dec. 29, 1962, at Montreal, second period. Montreal 5, Detroit Red Wings 1.
— Phil Goyette, New York Rangers, Oct. 20, 1963, at New York, first period. New York 5, Boston 1
— Jim Wiste, Chicago Black Hawks, Nov. 9, 1969, at Chicago, third period. Chicago 9, Toronto 0.
— Cliff Koroll, Chicago Black Hawks, Dec. 16, 1970, at Chicago, second period. Chicago 8, St. Louis Blues 3.
— Syl Apps, Jr., Pittsburgh Penguins, March 24, 1971, at Pittsburgh, third period. Pittsburgh 8, Detroit Red Wings 2.
— Bobby Orr, Boston Bruins, Feb. 15, 1972, at Boston, first period. Boston 6, California 0.
— Jim Pappin, Chicago Black Hawks, March 24, 1973, at Chicago, second period. Chicago 7, Atlanta 0.
— Ron Stackhouse, Pittsburgh Penguins, March 8, 1975, at Pittsburgh, second period. Pittsburgh 8, Philadelphia 2.
— Chuck Lefley, St. Louis Blues, March 6, 1976, third period. St. Lous 7, Chicago 4.
— Clark Gillies, New York Islanders, Dec. 23, 1978, at New York, second period. New York Rangers 4 at New York Islanders 9.
— Brad Park, Boston Bruins, Mar. 17, 1979, at Boston, first period. Boston 4, Chicago 2.
— Mark Howe, Hartford Whalers, Jan. 30. 1980, at Hartford, second period. Hartford 8, Boston 2.
— Paul Mulvey, Washington Capitals, March 5, 1980, at Washington, first period. Washington 7, St. Louis 4.
— Mike Bossy, New York Islanders, Feb. 13, 1982, at New York, second period. Islanders 8, Philadelphia 2.
— Wayne Gretzky, Edmonton Oilers, Feb. 4, 1983, at Edmonton, first period. Edmonton 7, Montreal 3.
— Mark Messier, Edmonton Oilers, Jan. 4, 1984, at Edmonton, second period. Edmonton 12, Minnesota 8.
— Wayne Gretzky, Edmonton Oilers, October 26, 1984, at Edmonton, second period. Edmonton 8, Los Angeles 3.
— Wayne Gretzky, Edmonton Oilers, March 31, 1985, at Chicago, 3rd period. Edmonton 7, Chicago 3.
— Wayne Gretzky, Edmonton Oilers, Oct. 30, 1985, at Edmonton, second period. Edmonton 7, Winnipeg 3.

— Paul Gagne, New Jersey Devils, Feb. 9, 1986, at Hartford, third period. New Jersey 6, Hartford 3.
— Wayne Gretzky, Edmonton Oilers, Feb. 14, 1986, at Edmonton, third period. Edmonton 8, Quebec 2.
— Gary Suter, Calgary Flames, Apr. 4, 1986, at Calgary, second period. Calgary 9, Edmonton 3.

MOST POINTS, ONE PERIOD:

6 — Bryan Trottier, New York Islanders, Dec. 23, 1978, at New York, second period. 3 goals, 3 assists. New York Rangers 4 at New York Islanders 9.

5 — Les Cunningham, Chicago Black Hawks, Jan. 28, 1940, at Chicago, third period. 2 goals, 3 assists. Chicago 8, Montreal Canadiens 1.
— Max Bentley, Chicago Black Hawks, Jan. 28, 1943, at Chicago, third period. 4 goals, 1 assist, Chicago 10, New York Rangers 1.
— Leo Labine, Boston Bruins, Nov. 28, 1954, at Boston, second period, 3 goals, 2 assists. Boston 6, Detroit 2.
— Darryl Sittler, Toronto Maple Leafs, Feb. 7, 1976, at Toronto, second period. 3 goals, 2 assists. Toronto 11, Boston 4.
— Dale Hawerchuk, Winnipeg Jets, Mar. 6, 1984, at Los Angeles, second period. 5 assists. Winnipeg 7 Los Angeles 3.
— Jari Kurri, Edmonton Oilers, October 26, 1984 at Edmonton, 2nd period. Edmonton 8, Los Angeles 2.

MOST PENALTIES, ONE PERIOD:

9 — Randy Holt, Los Angeles Kings, Mar. 11, 1979, at Philadelphia, first period. 1 minor, 3 majors, 2 10-minute misconducts, 3 game misconducts.

MOST PENALTY MINUTES, ONE PERIOD:

67 — Randy Holt, Los Angeles Kings, Mar. 11, 1979, at Philadelphia, first period. 1 minor, 3 majors, 2 10-minute misconducts, 3 game misconducts.

FASTEST GOAL FROM START OF GAME BY A ROOKIE:

15 Seconds — Gus Bodnar, Toronto Maple Leafs, Oct. 30, 1943, at Toronto in his first NHL game. Toronto 5, New York Rangers 2.

18 Seconds — Danny Gare, Buffalo Sabres, Oct. 10, 1974, at Buffalo in his first NHL game. Buffalo 9, Boston 5.

36 Seconds — Al Hill, Philadelphia Flyers, Feb. 14, 1977, at Philadelphia in his first NHL game, Philadelphia 6, St. Louis 4.

FASTEST GOAL FROM START OF GAME:

5 Seconds — Bryan Trottier, New York Islanders, Mar. 22, 1984, at Boston. NY Islanders 3, Boston 3.
— **Doug Smail,** Winnipeg Jets, Dec. 20, 1981, at Winnipeg. Winnipeg 5, St. Louis 4.

6 Seconds — Henry Boucha, Detroit Red Wings, Jan. 28, 1973, at Montreal. Detroit 4, Montreal 2
— Jean Pronovost, Pittsburgh Penguins, March 25, 1976, at St. Louis. St. Louis 5, Pittsburgh 2

7 Seconds — Charlie Conacher, Toronto Maple Leafs, Feb. 6, 1932, at Toronto. Toronto 6, Boston 0
— Danny Gare, Buffalo Sabres, Dec. 17, 1978, at Buffalo. Buffalo 6, Vancouver 3

8 Seconds — Ron Martin, New York Americans, Dec. 4, 1932, at New York. Americans 4, Montreal 2
— Ted Kennedy, Toronto Maple Leafs, Oct. 24, 1953, at Toronto. Boston 3, Toronto 3
— Chuck Arnason, Colorado Rockies, Jan. 28, 1977, at Atlanta. Colorado 3, Atlanta 3
— Wayne Gretzky, Edmonton Oilers, Dec. 14, 1983, at New York. Edmonton 9, Rangers 4

FASTEST GOAL FROM START OF A PERIOD:

4 Seconds — Claude Provost, Montreal Canadiens, Nov. 9, 1957, at Montreal, second period. Montreal 4, Boston 2.
—**Denis Savard,** Chicago Blackhawks, Jan. 12, 1986, at Chicago, third period. Chicago 4, Hartford 2.

FASTEST TWO GOALS:

4 Seconds — Nels Stewart, Montreal Maroons, Jan. 3, 1931, at Montreal at 8:24 and 8:28, third period. Montreal 5, Boston 3.

5 Seconds — Pete Mahovlich, Montreal Canadiens, Feb. 20, 1971, at Montreal at 12:16 and 12:21, third period. Montreal 7, Chicago 1.

6 Seconds — Jim Pappin, Chicago Black Hawks, Feb. 16, 1972, at Chicago at 2:57 and 3:03, third period. Chicago and Philadelphia Tied 3-3.
— Ralph Backstrom, Los Angeles Kings, Nov. 2, 1972, at Los Angeles at 8:30 and 8:36, third period. Los Angeles 5, Boston 2.
— Lanny McDonald, Calgary Flames, Mar. 22, 1984, at Calgary at 16:23 and 16:29, first period. Detroit 6, Calgary 4.

FASTEST THREE GOALS:

21 Seconds — Bill Mosienko, Chicago Black Hawks, March 23, 1952, at New York, against goaltender Lorne Anderson. Mosienko scored at 6:09, 6:20 and 6:30, third period, all with both teams as full strength. Chicago 7, New York 6.

44 Seconds — Jean Béliveau, Montreal Canadiens, Nov. 5, 1955 at Montreal against goaltender Terry Sawchuk of Boston Bruins. Béliveau scored at 00:42, 1:08 and 1:26 of second period, all with Montreal holding a 6-4 man advantage. Montreal 4, Boston 2.

FASTEST THREE ASSISTS:

21 Seconds — Gus Bodnar, Chicago Black Hawks, March 23, 1952, at New York, Bodnar assisted on Bill Mosienko's three goals at 6:09, 6:20, 6:30 of third Period. Chicago 7, New York 6.

44 Seconds — Bert Olmstead, Montreal Canadiens, Nov. 5, 1955, at Montreal against Boston Bruins. Olmstead assisted on Jean Béliveau's three goals at 00:42, 1:08 and 1:26 of second period. Montreal 4, Boston 2.

MOST GOALS, ONE ROAD GAME:

6 — Red Berenson, St. Louis Blues, Nov. 7, 1968, at Philadelphia. St. Louis 8, Philadelphia 0.

5 — Joe Malone, Montreal Canadiens, Dec. 19, 1917, at Ottawa. Montreal 9, Ottawa 4.
 — Redvers Green, Hamilton Tigers, Dec. 5, 1924, at Toronto. Hamilton 10, Toronto 3.
 — Babe Dye, Toronto St. Patricks, Dec. 22, 1924, at Boston. Toronto 10, Boston 2.
 — Harry Broadbent, Montreal Maroons, Jan. 7, 1925, at Hamilton. Montreal 6, Hamilton 2.
 — Don Murdoch, New York Rangers, Oct. 12, 1976, at Minnesota. New York 10, Minnesota 4.
 — Tim Young, Minnesota North Stars, Jan. 15, 1979, at New York Rangers. Minnesota 8, New York 1.
 — Willy Lindstrom, Winnipeg Jets, March 2, 1982, at Philadelphia. Winnipeg 7, Philadelphia 6.
 — Bengt Gustafsson, Washington Capitals, Jan. 8, 1984, at Philadelphia. Washington 7, Philadelphia 1.
 — Dave Andreychuk, Buffalo Sabres, Feb. 6, 1986, at Boston. Buffalo 8, Boston 6.

MOST ASSISTS, ONE GAME:

7 — Billy Taylor, Detroit Red Wings, March 16, 1947, at Chicago. Detroit 10, Chicago 6.
 — **Wayne Gretzky,** Edmonton Oilers, Feb. 15, 1980, at Edmonton. Edmonton 8, Washington 2.
 — **Wayne Gretzky,** Edmonton Oilers, Dec. 11, 1985, at Chicago. Edmonton 12, Chicago 9.
 — **Wayne Gretzky,** Edmonton Oilers, Feb. 14, 1986, at Edmonton. Edmonton 8, Quebec 2.
6 — Elmer Lach, Montreal Canadiens, Feb. 6, 1943, at Montreal. Montreal 8, Boston 3.
 — Walter (Babe) Pratt, Toronto Maple Leafs, Jan. 8, 1944, at Toronto. Toronto 12, Boston 3.
 — Don Grosso, Detroit Red Wings, Feb. 3, 1944, at Detroit. Detroit 12, New York Rangers 2.
 — Pat Stapleton, Chicago Black Hawks, March 30, 1969, at Chicago 9, Detroit Red Wings 5.
 — Ken Hodge, Boston Bruins, Feb. 9, 1971, at Boston. Boston 6, New York Rangers 3.
 — Bobby Orr, Boston Bruins, Jan. 1, 1973, at Vancouver, Boston 8, Vancouver 2.
 — Ron Stackhouse, Pittsburgh, March 8, 1974, at Pittsburgh. Pittsburgh 8, Philadelphia 2.
 — Greg Malone, Pittsburgh, Nov. 28, 1979, at Pittsburgh. Pittsburgh 7, Quebec 2.
 — Mike Bossy, New York Islanders, Jan. 6, 1981, at New York. Islanders 6, Toronto 3.
 — Guy Chouinard, Calgary Flames, Feb. 25, 1981, at Calgary. Calgary 11, NY Islanders 4.
 — Mark Messier, Edmonton Oilers, Jan. 4, 1984, at Edmonton. Edmonton 12, Minnesota 8.
 — Patrik Sundstrom, Vancouver Canucks, Feb 29, 1984, at Pittsburgh. Vancouver 9, Pittsburgh 5.
 — Wayne Gretzky, Edmonton Oilers, Dec. 20, 1985, at Edmonton. Edmonton 9, Los Angeles 4.
 — Paul Coffey, Edmonton Oilers, Mar. 14, 1986 at Edmonton. Edmonton 12, Detroit 3.
 — Gary Suter, Calgary Flames, Apr. 4, 1986 at Calgary. Calgary 9, Edmonton 3.

MOST ASSISTS, ONE ROAD GAME:

7 — Billy Taylor, Detroit Red Wings, March 16, 1947, at Chicago. Detroit 10, Chicago 6.
 — **Wayne Gretzky,** Edmonton Oilers, Dec. 11, 1985, at Chicago. Edmonton 12, Chicago 9.
6 — Bobby Orr, Boston Bruins, Jan. 1, 1973, at Vancouver. Boston 8, Vancouver 2.
 — Patrik Sundstrom, Vancouver Canucks, Feb. 29, 1984, at Pittsburgh. Vancouver 9, Pittsburgh 5.

Ralph Backstrom, left, scored two goals in six seconds against Boston in 1972.

MOST POINTS, ONE GAME:

10 — Darryl Sittler, Toronto Maple Leafs, Feb. 7, 1976, at Toronto, 6 goals, 4 assists. Toronto 11, Boston 4.

8 — Maurice Richard, Montreal Canadiens, Dec. 28, 1944, at Montreal, 5 goals, 3 assists. Montreal 9, Detroit 1.
 — Bert Olmstead, Montreal Canadiens, Jan. 9, 1954, at Montreal, 4 goals, 4 assists. Montreal 12, Chicago 1.
 — Tom Bladon, Philadelphia Flyers, Dec. 11, 1977, at Philadelphia, 4 goals, 4 assists. Philadelphia 11, Cleveland 1.
 — Bryan Trottier, New York Islanders, Dec. 23, 1978, at New York, 5 goals, 3 assists. NY Rangers 4 NY Islanders 9.
 — Peter Stastny, Quebec Nordiques, Feb. 22, 1981, at Washington, 4 goals, 4 assists. Quebec 11, Washington 7.
 — Anton Stastny, Quebec Nordiques, Feb. 22, 1981, at Washington, 3 goals, 5 assists. Quebec 11, Washington 7.
 — Wayne Gretzky, Edmonton Oilers, Nov. 19, 1983, at Edmonton, 3 goals, 5 assists. Edmonton 13, New Jersey 4.
 — Wayne Gretzky, Edmonton Oilers, Jan. 4, 1984, at Edmonton, 4 goals, 4 assists. Edmonton 12 Minnesota 8.
 — Paul Coffey, Edmonton Oilers, Mar. 14, 1986, at Edmonton, 2 goals, 6 assists. Edmonton 12, Detroit 3.
7 — Joe Malone, Quebec Bulldogs, Jan. 31, 1920, at Quebec City, 7 goals, 0 assists. Quebec 10, Toronto St. Patrick 6.
 — Frank Fredrickson, Pittsburgh Pirates, Nov. 19, 1929, at Pittsburgh, 2 goals, 5 assists. Pittsburgh 10, Toronto 5.
 — Carl Liscombe, Detroit Red Wings, Nov. 5, 1942, at Detroit, 3 goals, 4 assists. Detroit 12, New York Rangers 5.
 — Max Bentley, Chicago Black Hawks, Jan. 28, 1943, at Chicago, 4 goals, 3 assists. Chicago 10, New York Rangers 1.
 — Don Grosso, Detroit Red Wings, Feb. 3, 1944, at Detroit, 1 goal, 6 assists. Detroit 12, New York Rangers 2.
 — Billy Taylor, Detroit Red Wings, March 16, 1947, at Chicago. 7 assists. Detroit 10, Chicago 6.
 — Jean Béliveau, Montreal Canadiens, March 7, 1959, at Montreal, 4 goals, 3 assists. Montreal 10, Detroit 2.
 — Red Berenson, St. Louis Blues, Nov. 7, 1968, at Philadelphia, 6 goals, 1 assist. St. Louis 8, Philadelphia 0.
 — Garry Unger, St. Louis Blues, March 13, 1971, at St. Louis, 3 goals, 4 assists. St. Louis 9, Buffalo Sabres 0.
 — Rick MacLeish, Philadelphia Flyers, March 4, 1973, at Philadelphia, 4 goals, 3 assists. Philadelphia 10, Toronto 0.
 — Bobby Orr, Boston Bruins, Nov. 15, 1973, at Boston, 3 goals, 4 assists. Boston 10, NY Rangers 2.
 — Phil Esposito, Boston Bruins, Dec. 19, 1974, at Boston, 3 goals, 4 assists. Boston 11, NY Rangers 3.
 — Yvan Cournoyer, Montreal Canadiens, Feb. 15, 1975, at Montreal, 5 goals, 2 assists. Montreal 12, Chicago 3.
 — Gilbert Perreault, Buffalo Sabres, Feb. 1, 1976, at California, 2 goals, 5 assists. Buffalo 9, California 5.
 — Steve Vickers, New York Rangers, Feb. 18, 1976, at New York, 3 goals, 4 assists. New York Rangers 11, Washington 4.
 — Darryl Sittler, Toronto Maple Leafs, Oct. 14, 1978, at Toronto, 3 goals, 4 assists. Toronto 10, NY Islanders 7.
 — Wayne Gretzky, Edmonton Oilers, Feb. 15, 1980, at Edmonton, 7 assists. Edmonton 8, Washington 2.
 — Wayne Gretzky, Edmonton Oilers, Feb. 18, 1981, at Edmonton. 5 goals, 2 assists. Edmonton 9, St. Louis 2.
 — Bobby Smith, Minnesota North Stars, Nov. 11, 1981, at Minnesota, 4 goals, 3 assists. Winnipeg 2, Minnesota 15.
 — Wayne Gretzky, Edmonton Oilers, Dec. 19, 1981, at Edmonton, 3 goals, 4 assists. Minnesota 6, Edmonton 9.
 — Grant Mulvey, Chicago Black Hawks, Feb. 3, 1982, at Chicago, 5 goals, 2 assists. St. Louis 5, Chicago 9.
 — Barry Pederson, Boston Bruins, April 4, 1982, at Boston, 3 goals, 4 assists. Hartford 2, Boston 7.
 — Peter Stastny, Quebec Nordiques, April 4, 1982, at Buffalo, 3 goals, 4 assists. Quebec 7, Buffalo 4.
 — Wayne Gretzky, Edmonton Oilers, Nov. 6, 1983, at Winnipeg, 4 goals, 3 assists. Edmonton 8, Winnipeg 5.
 — Patrik Sundstrom, Vancouver Canucks, Feb. 29, 1984, at Pittsburgh, 1 goal, 6 assists. Vancouver 9, Pittsburgh 5.
 — Wayne Gretzky, Edmonton Oilers, Dec. 11, 1985, at Chicago, 7 assists. Edmonton 12, Chicago 9.
 — Wayne Gretzky, Edmonton Oilers, Feb. 14, 1986, at Edmonton, 7 assists. Edmonton 8, Quebec 2.

MOST POINTS, ONE ROAD GAME:

8 — Peter Stastny, Quebec Nordiques, Feb. 22, 1981, at Washington, 4 goals, 4 assists. Quebec 11, Washington 7.
 — **Anton Stastny,** Quebec Nordiques, Feb. 22, 1981, at Washington, 3 goals, 5 assists. Quebec 11, Washington 7.
7 — Billy Taylor, Detroit Red Wings, March 16, 1947, at Chicago, 7 assists. Detroit 10, Chicago. 6.
 — Red Berenson, St. Louis Blues, Nov. 7, 1968, at Philadelphia, 6 goals, 1 assist. St. Louis 8, Philadelphia 0.
 — Gilbert Perreault, Buffalo Sabres, Feb. 1, 1976, at California, 2 goals, 5 assists. Buffalo 9, California 5.
 — Peter Stastny, Quebec Nordiques, April 1, 1982, at Boston, 3 goals, 4 assists. Quebec 8, Boston 5.
 — Wayne Gretzky, Edmonton Oilers, Nov. 6, 1984, at Winnipeg, 4 goals, 3 assists. Edmonton 8, Winnipeg 3.
 — Patrik Sundstrom, Vancouver Canucks, Feb. 29, 1984, at Pittsburgh, 1 goal, 6 assists. Vancouver 9, Pittsburgh 5.
 — Wayne Gretzky, Edmonton Oilers, Dec. 11, 1985, at Chicago. 7 assists, Edmonton 12, Chicago 9.

MOST GOALS, ONE GAME, BY A DEFENSEMAN:
5 — **Ian Turnbull,** Toronto Maple Leafs, Feb. 2, 1977, at Toronto. Toronto 9, Detroit 1.
4 — Harry Cameron, Toronto Arenas, Dec. 26, 1917, at Toronto. Toronto 7, Montreal Canadiens 5.
— Harry Cameron, Montreal Canadiens, March 3, 1920, at Quebec City. Montreal 16, Quebec Bulldogs 3.
— Sprague Cleghorn, Montreal Canadiens, Jan. 14, 1922, at Montreal. Montreal 10, Hamilton Tigers 6.
— Johnny McKinnon, Pittsburgh Pirates, Nov. 19, 1929, at Pittsburgh. Pittsburgh 10, Toronto 5.
— Hap Day, Toronto Maple Leafs, Nov. 19, 1929, at Pittsburgh. Pittsburgh 10, Toronto 5.
— Tom Bladon, Philadelphia Flyers, Dec. 11, 1977, at Philadelphia. Philadelphia 11, Cleveland 1.
— Ian Turnbull, Los Angeles Kings, Dec. 12, 1981, at Los Angeles. Los Angeles 7, Vancouver 5.

MOST GOALS BY ONE PLAYER IN HIS FIRST NHL GAME:
3 — **Alex Smart,** Montreal Canadiens, Jan. 14, 1943, at Montreal. Canadiens 5, Chicago 1.
— **Real Cloutier,** Quebec Nordiques, Oct. 10, 1979, at Quebec. Atlanta 5, Quebec 3.

Don Murdoch

MOST GOALS, ONE GAME, BY A PLAYER IN HIS FIRST NHL SEASON:
5 — **Howie Meeker,** Toronto Maple Leafs, Jan. 8, 1944, at Toronto. Toronto 10, Chicago 4.
— **Don Murdoch,** New York Rangers, Oct. 12, 1976, at Minnesota. NY Rangers 10, Minnesota 4.

MOST ASSISTS, ONE GAME, BY A DEFENSEMAN:
6 — **Babe Pratt,** Toronto Maple Leafs, Jan. 8, 1944, at Toronto. Toronto 12, Boston 3.
— **Pat Stapleton,** Chicago Black Hawks, March 30, 1969, at Chicago. Chicago 9, Detroit 5.
— **Bobby Orr,** Boston Bruins, Jan. 1, 1973, at Vancouver, Boston 8, Vancouver 2.
— **Ron Stackhouse,** Pittsburgh Penguins, March 8, 1975, at Pittsburgh. Pittsburgh 8, Philadelphia 2.
— **Paul Coffey,** Edmonton Oilers, Mar. 14, 1986, at Edmonton. Edmonton 12, Detroit 3.
— **Gary Suter,** Calgary Flames, Apr. 4, 1986, at Calgary. Calgary 9, Edmonton 3.

MOST ASSISTS BY ONE PLAYER IN HIS FIRST NHL GAME:
4 — **Earl (Dutch) Reibel,** Detroit Red Wings, Oct. 8, 1953, at Detroit. Detroit 4, New York Rangers 1.
— **Roland Eriksson,** Minnesota North Stars, Oct. 6, 1976, at New York. Rangers 6, Minnesota 5.
3 — Al Hill, Philadelphia Flyers, Feb. 14, 1977, at Philadelphia. Philadelphia 6, St. Louis 4.

MOST ASSISTS, ONE GAME, BY A PLAYER IN HIS FIRST NHL SEASON:
7 — **Wayne Gretzky,** Edmonton Oilers, Feb. 15, 1980, at Edmonton. Edmonton 8, Washington 2.
6 — Gary Suter, Calgary Flames, Apr. 4, 1986, at Calgary. Calgary 9, Edmonton 3.
5 — Jim McFadden, Detroit Red Wings, Nov. 23, 1947, at Chicago. Detroit 9, Chicago 3.
— Mark Howe, Hartford Whalers, Jan. 30, 1980, at Hartford. Hartford 8, Boston 2.
— Anton Stastny, Quebec Nordiques, Feb. 22, 1981, at Washington. Quebec 11, Washington 7.
— Mark Osborne, Detroit Red Wings, Feb. 7, 1982, at Detroit. St. Louis 5, Detroit 8.

MOST POINTS, ONE GAME, BY A DEFENSEMAN:
8 — **Tom Bladon,** Philadelphia Flyers, Dec. 11, 1977, at Philadelphia. 4 goals, 4 assists. Philadelphia 11, Cleveland 1.
— **Paul Coffey,** Edmonton Oilers, Mar. 14, 1986, at Edmonton. 2 goals, 6 assists. Edmonton 12, Detroit 3.
7 — Bobby Orr, Boston Bruins, Nov. 15, 1973, at Boston, 3 goals, 4 assists. Boston 10, NY Rangers 2.

MOST POINTS BY ONE PLAYER IN HIS FIRST NHL GAME:
5 — **Al Hill,** Philadelphia Flyers, Feb. 14, 1977, at Philadelphia. 2 goals, 3 assists. Philadelphia 6, St. Louis 4.
4 — Alex Smart, Montreal Canadiens, Jan. 14, 1943, at Montreal, 3 goals, 1 assist. Canadiens 5, Chicago 1.
— Earl (Dutch) Reibel, Detroit Red Wings, Oct. 8, 1953, at Detroit. 4 assists. Detroit 4, New York Rangers 1.

MOST POINTS, ONE GAME, BY A PLAYER IN HIS FIRST NHL SEASON:
8 — **Peter Stastny,** Quebec Nordiques, Feb. 22, 1981, at Washington. 4 goals, 4 assists. Quebec 11, Washington 7.
— **Anton Stastny,** Quebec Nordiques, Feb. 22, 1981, at Washington. 3 goals, 5 assists. Quebec 11, Washington 7.
7 — Wayne Gretzky, Edmonton Oilers, Feb. 15, 1980, at Edmonton. 7 assists. Edmonton 8, Washington 2.
6 — Wayne Gretzky, Edmonton Oilers, March 29, 1980, at Toronto. 2 goals, 4 assists. Edmonton 8, Toronto 5.
— Gary Suter, Calgary Flames, Apr. 4, 1986, at Calgary. Calgary 9, Edmonton 3.

MOST PENALTIES, ONE GAME:
9 — **Jim Dorey,** Toronto Maple Leafs, Oct. 16, 1968, at Toronto against Pittsburgh. 4 minors, 2 majors, 2 10-minute misconducts, 1 game misconduct.
— **Dave Schultz,** Pittsburgh Penguins, Apr. 6, 1978, at Detroit, 5 minors, 2 majors, 2 10-minute misconducts.
— **Randy Holt,** Los Angeles Kings, Mar. 11, 1979, at Philadelphia. 1 minor, 3 majors, 2 10-minute misconducts, 3 game misconducts.
— **Russ Anderson,** Pittsburgh Penguins, Jan. 19, 1980, at Pittsburgh. 3 minors, 3 majors, 3 game misconducts.
— **Kim Clackson,** Quebec Nordiques, March 8, 1981, at Quebec. 4 minors, 3 majors, 2 game misconducts.
— **Terry O'Reilly, Boston Bruins,** Dec. 19, 1984 at Hartford. 5 minors, 3 majors, 1 game misconduct.

MOST PENALTY MINUTES, ONE GAME:
67 — **Randy Holt,** Los Angeles Kings, Mar. 11, 1979, at Philadelphia. 1 minor, 3 majors, 2 10-minute misconducts, 3 game misconducts.
55 — Frank Bathe, Philadelphia Flyers, March 11, 1979, at Philadelphia. 3 majors, 2 10-minute misconducts, 2 game misconducts.
51 — Russ Anderson, Pittsburgh Penguins, Jan. 19, 1980, at Pittsburgh. 3 minors, 3 majors, 3 game misconducts.

NHL Attendance

| Season | Regular Season | | Playoffs | | Total |
	Games	Attendance	Games	Attendance	Attendance
1960-61	210	2,317,142	17	242,000	2,559,142
1961-62	210	2,435,424	18	277,000	2,712,424
1962-63	210	2,590,574	16	220,906	2,811,480
1963-64	210	2,732,642	21	309,149	3,041,791
1964-65	210	2,822,635	20	303,859	3,126,494
1965-66	210	2,941,164	16	249,000	3,190,184
1966-67	210	3,084,759	16	248,336	3,333,095
1967-68[1]	444	4,938,043	40	495,089	5,433,132
1968-69	456	5,550,613	33	431,739	5,982,352
1969-70	456	5,992,065	34	461,694	6,453,759
1970-71[2]	546	7,257,677	43	707,633	7,965,310
1971-72	546	7,609,368	36	582,666	8,192,034
1972-73[3]	624	8,575,651	38	624,637	9,200,288
1973-74	624	8,640,978	38	600,442	9,241,420
1974-75[4]	720	9,521,536	51	784,181	10,305,717
1975-76	720	9,103,761	48	726,279	9,830,040
1976-77	720	8,563,890	44	646,279	9,210,169
1977-78	720	8,526,564	45	686,634	9,213,198
1978-79	680	7,758,053	45	694,521	8,452,574
1979-80[5]	840	10,533,623	63	976,699	11,510,322
1980-81	840	10,726,198	68	966,390	11,692,588
1981-82	840	10,710,894	71	1,058,948	11,769,842
1982-83	840	11,020,610	66	1,088,222	12,028,832
1983-84	840	11,359,386	70	1,107,400	12,466,786
1984-85	840	11,633,730	70	1,107,500	12,741,230
1985-86	840	11,621,000	72	1,152,503	12,773,503

[1] First expansion: Los Angeles, Pittsburgh, California, Philadelphia, St. Louis and Minnesota
[2] Second expansion: Buffalo and Vancouver
[3] Third expansion: Atlanta and New York Islanders
[4] Fourth expansion: Kansas City (Colorado) and Washington
[5] Fifth expansion: Edmonton, Hartford, Quebec and Winnipeg

Top 100 All-Time Goal-Scoring Leaders

* active player
(figures in parentheses indicate ranking of top 10 by goals per game)

Player		Seasons	Games	Goals	Goals per game
1. **Gordie Howe**	Detroit	25	1,687	786	.466
	Hartford	1	80	15	.188
	Total	26	1,767	**801**	.453
2. **Phil Esposito**	Chicago	4	235	74	.315
	Boston	8 1/4	625	459	.734
	NY Rangers	5 3/4	422	184	.436
	Total	18	1,282	**717**	.572 (9)
* 3. **Marcel Dionne**	Detroit	4	309	139	.450
	Los Angeles	11	854	526	.615 (9)
	Total	14	1,163	**665**	.614 (5)
4. **Bobby Hull**	Chicago	15	1,036	604	.583
	Winnipeg	2/3	18	4	.222
	Hartford	1/3	9	2	.222
	Total	16	1,063	**610**	.574 (8)
5. **John Bucyk**	Detroit	2	104	11	.106
	Boston	21	1,436	545	.380
	Total	23	1,540	**556**	.361
6. **Maurice Richard**	Montreal	18	978	**544**	.556
7. **Stan Mikita**	Chicago	22	1,394	**541**	.388
* 8. **Mike Bossy**	NY Islanders	9	689	**535**	.776 (2)
9. **Frank Mahovlich**	Toronto	11 2/3	720	296	.411
	Detroit	2 2/3	198	108	.545
	Montreal	3 2/3	263	129	.490
	Total	18	1,181	**533**	.451
10. **Guy Lafleur**	Montreal	14	961	**518**	.539
11. **Jean Beliveau**, Montreal		18	1,125	**507**	.451
12. **Gilbert Perreault**, Buffalo		16	1,171	**503**	.429
13. **Jean Ratelle**, NY Rangers, Boston		21	1,281	**491**	.383
14. **Norm Ullman**, Detroit, Toronto		20	1,410	**490**	.348
15. **Darryl Sittler**, Toronto, Philadelphia, Detroit		15	1096	**484**	.442
* 16. **Wayne Gretzky**, Edmonton		7	553	**481**	.870 (1)
* 17. **Lanny McDonald**, Toronto, Colorado, Calgary		13	942	**465**	.494
18. **Alex Delvecchio**, Detroit		23	1,549	**456**	.294
19. **Yvan Cournoyer**, Montreal		16	968	**428**	.442
20. **Steve Shutt**, Montreal, Los Angeles		13	930	**424**	.456
21. **Bill Barber**, Philadelphia		12	903	**420**	.465
* 22. **Bryan Trottier**, NY Islanders		11	834	**417**	.500
23. **Garry Unger**, Toronto, Detroit, St. Louis, Atlanta, Los Angeles, Edmonton		16	1105	**413**	.374
24. **Rod Gilbert**, NY Rangers		18	1,065	**406**	.381
* 25. **Rick Middleton**, NY Rangers, Boston		12	870	**404**	.464
26. **Dave Keon**, Toronto, Hartford		18	1,296	**396**	.305
27. **Bernie Geoffrion**, Montreal, NY Rangers		16	883	**393**	.445
28. **Jean Pronovost**, Pittsburgh, Atlanta, Washington		13	998	**391**	.392
29. **Dean Prentice**, NY Rangers, Boston, Detroit, Pittsburgh, Minnesota		22	1378	**391**	.284
30. **Richard Martin**, Buffalo, Los Angeles		11	685	**384**	.561 (10)
31. **Reggie Leach**, Boston, California, Philadelphia, Detroit		13	934	**381**	.408
32. **Ted Lindsay**, Detroit, Chicago		17	1,068	**379**	.355
33. **Butch Goring**, Los Angeles, NY Islanders, Boston		16	1,107	**375**	.339
34. **Rick Kehoe**, Toronto, Pittsburgh		14	906	**371**	.409
35. **Jacques Lemaire**, Montreal		12	853	**366**	.429
* 36. **Pierre Larouche**, Pittsburgh, Montreal, Hartford, NY Rangers		12	729	**364**	.499
37. **Rick MacLeish**, Philadelphia, Hartford, Pittsburgh, Detroit		14	863	**361**	.418
* 38. **Ivan Boldirev**, Boston, California, Atlanta, Vancouver, Detroit		15	1052	**361**	.343
39. **Bobby Clarke**, Philadelphia		15	1,144	**358**	.313
40. **Henri Richard**, Montreal		20	1,256	**358**	.285
* 41. **Peter McNab**, Buffalo, Boston, Vancouver		13	908	**355**	.392
* 42. **Danny Gare**, Buffalo, Detroit		12	809	**353**	.436
43. **Andy Bathgate**, NY Rangers, Toronto, Detroit, Pittsburgh		16	1,069	**349**	.326
* 44. **Wilf Paiement**, Kansas City, Colorado, Toronto, Quebec, NY Rangers		12	867	**335**	.385
* 45. **Dennis Maruk**, California, Cleveland, Washington, Minnesota		11	793	**333**	.420
46. **Ron Ellis**, Toronto		16	1034	**332**	.321
47. **Ken Hodge**, Chicago, Boston, NY Rangers		14	881	**328**	.372
48. **Nels Stewart**, Montreal, Maroons, Boston, NY Americans		15	654	**324**	.498
49. **Pit Martin**, Detroit, Boston, Chicago, Vancouver		17	1,101	**324**	.294
50. **Vic Hadfield**, NY Rangers, Pittsburgh		16	1,002	**323**	.322
* 51. **Michel Goulet**, Quebec		7	532	**317**	.596 (7)
* 52. **Don Lever**, Vancouver, Atlanta, Calgary, Colorado, New Jersey, Buffalo		14	1,010	**310**	.309
53. **Bob Nevin**, Toronto, NY Rangers, Minnesota, Los Angeles		16	1,128	**307**	.272

Garry Unger is one of only 25 players to score more than 400 regular-season goals in the NHL.

Player	Seasons	Games	Goals	Goals per game
* 54. **Clark Gillies**, NY Islanders	12	872	**304**	.348
55. **Dennis Hull**, Chicago, Detroit	14	959	**303**	.316
56. **Dave Taylor**, Los Angeles	9	617	**303**	.476
* 57. **Charlie Simmer**, California, Cleveland, Los Angeles, Boston	12	582	**302**	.519
* 58. **Jari Kurri**, Edmonton	6	441	**300**	.680 (4)
59. **George Armstrong**, Toronto	20	1,187	**296**	.249
* 60. **Tom Lysiak**, Atlanta, Chicago	13	919	**292**	.318
* 61. **Bernie Federko**, St. Louis	10	718	**290**	.404
62. **Peter Mahovlich**, Detroit, Montreal, Pittsburgh	16	884	**288**	.326
* 63. **Brian Sutter**, St. Louis	10	692	**285**	.412
64. **Rene Robert**, Pittsburgh, Buffalo, Colorado, Toronto	12	744	**284**	.382
65. **Bill Goldsworthy**, Boston, Minnesota, NY Rangers	14	771	**283**	.367
66. **Dick Duff**, Toronto, NY Rangers, Montreal, Los Angeles, Buffalo	16	1,030	**283**	.275
* 67. **Mike Gartner**, Washington,	7	544	**282**	.518
68. **Bob Pulford**, Toronto, Los Angeles	16	1,079	**281**	.260
69. **Red Kelly**, Detroit, Toronto	20	1,316	**281**	.214
* 70. **Rick Vaive**, Vancouver, Toronto	7	508	**280**	.551
71. **Camille Henry**, NY Rangers, Chicago, St. Louis	12	727	**279**	.384
* 72. **Denis Potvin**, NY Islanders	13	930	**279**	.300
73. **Jim Pappin**, Toronto, Chicago, California, Cleveland	14	767	**278**	.362
74. **Ralph Backstrom**, Montreal, Los Angeles, Chicago	17	1,032	**278**	.362
75. **Wayne Cashman**, Boston	17	1,027	**277**	.270
76. **Ron Stewart**, Toronto, Boston, St. Louis, NY Rangers, Vancouver, NY Islanders	21	1,353	**276**	.204
77. **Murray Oliver**, Detroit, Boston, Toronto, Minnesota	16	1,127	**274**	.243
78. **Howie Morenz**, Montreal, Chicago, NY Rangers	14	550	**273**	.496
79. **Bobby Schmautz**, Chicago, Boston, Vancouver, Edmonton, Colorado	13	764	**271**	.355
80. **Bobby Orr**, Boston, Chicago	12	657	**270**	.411
81. **Aurel Joliat**, Montreal	16	654	**270**	.411
* 82. **Glenn Anderson**, Edmonton	6	442	**266**	.602 (6)
* 83. **Brian Propp**, Philadelphia	7	546	**266**	.487
84. **Don Marshall**, Montreal, NY Rangers, Buffalo, Toronto	18	1,176	**265**	.225
85. **Danny Grant**, Montreal, Minnesota, Detroit, Los Angeles	13	736	**263**	.357
86. **Dickie Moore**, Montreal, Toronto, St. Louis	14	719	**261**	.363
87. **Red Berenson**, Montreal, NY Rangers, St. Louis, Detroit	17	987	**261**	.264
88. **Blaine Stoughton**, Pittsburgh, Toronto, Hartford, NY Rangers	8	526	**258**	.490
89. **Bill Mosienko**, Chicago	13	711	**258**	.363
* 90. **Mario Tremblay**, Montreal	12	852	**258**	.303
91. **Ross Lonsberry**, Boston, Los Angeles, Philadelphia, Pittsburgh	15	968	**256**	.264
92. **Claude Provost**, Montreal	15	1,005	**254**	.253
93. **Ken Wharram**, Chicago	12	776	**252**	.329
94. **Craig Ramsay**, Buffalo	14	1,070	**252**	.235
* 95. **Peter Stastny**, Quebec	6	463	**251**	.542
96. **Cy Denneny**, Ottawa, Boston	12	326	**250**	.767 (3)
97. **Eric Nesterenko**, Toronto, Chicago	20	1,219	**250**	.205
98. **Doug Mohns**, Boston, Chicago, Minnesota, Atlanta, Washington	22	1,390	**248**	.178
* 99. **John Ogrodnick**, Detroit	7	500	**247**	.500
* 100. **Ron Duguay**, NY Rangers, Detroit, Pittsburgh	9	657	**247**	.376

Top 100 All-Time Career Assist Leaders

* active player

(figures in parentheses indicates ranking of top 10 in order of assists per game)

Bobby Clarke ranks sixth in all-time assists with 852.

	Player		Seasons	Games	Assists	Assists per game
	1. **Gordie Howe**	Detroit	25	1,687	1,023	.606
		Hartford	1	80	26	.325
		Total	26	1,767	**1,049**	.594
*	2. **Marcel Dionne** ...	Detroit	4	309	227	.735
		Los Angeles	11	854	707	.828
		Total	15	1,163	**934**	.803 (6)
	3. **Stan Mikita**	Chicago	22	1,394	**926**	.664
	4. **Phil Esposito**	Chicago	4	235	100	.426
		Boston	8¼	625	553	.885
		NY Rangers	5¾	422	220	.521
		Total	18	1,282	**873**	.681
*	5. **Wayne Gretzky** ..	Edmonton	7	553	**856**	1.547 (1)
	6. **Bobby Clarke** ..	Philadelphia	15	1,144	**852**	.745(10)
	7. **Alex Delvecchio** .	Detroit	23	1,549	**825**	.533
	8. **John Bucyk**	Detroit	2	104	19	.183
		Boston	21	1,436	794	.553
		Total	23	1,540	**813**	.528
	9. **Gilbert Perreault**	Buffalo	16	1,171	**807**	.689
	10. **Jean Ratelle,**	NY Rangers	15¼	862	481	.558
		Boston	5¾	419	295	.704
		Total	21	1,281	**776**	.605
	11. **Norm Ullman,**	Detroit, Toronto ..	20	1,410	**739**	.524
	12. **Guy Lafleur,**	Montreal	14	961	**728**	.757
	13. **Jean Beliveau,**	Montreal	20	1,125	**712**	.633
*	14. **Bryan Trottier,**	NY Islanders	11	834	**698**	.837 (5)
	15. **Henri Richard,**	Montreal	20	1,256	**688**	.548
	16. **Brad Park,**	NY Rangers, Boston, Detroit	17	1,113	**683**	.614
*	17. **Denis Potvin,**	NY Islanders	13	930	**680**	.731
	18. **Bobby Orr,**	Boston, Chicago	12	657	**645**	.982 (3)
	19. **Darryl Sittler,**	Toronto, Philadelphia, Detroit	15	1,096	**637**	.581
	20. **Andy Bathgate,**	NY Rangers, Toronto, Detroit, Pittsburgh	17	1,069	**624**	.584
	21. **Rod Gilbert,**	NY Rangers	18	1,065	**615**	.577
	22. **Dave Keon,**	Toronto, Hartford	18	1,296	**590**	.455
*	23. **Larry Robinson,**	Montreal	14	1,005	**589**	.595
	24. **Frank Mahovlich,**	Toronto, Detroit, Montreal	18	1,181	**570**	.483
*	25. **Borje Salming,**	Toronto	13	914	**563**	.616
	26. **Bobby Hull,**	Chicago, Winnipeg, Hartford	16	1,063	**560**	.527
*	27. **Bernie Federko,**	St. Louis	10	718	**555**	.773 (8)
*	28. **Tom Lysiak,**	Atlanta, Chicago	13	919	**551**	.596
	29. **Red Kelly,**	Detroit, Toronto	20	1,316	**542**	.412
*	30. **Mike Bossy,**	NY Islanders	9	689	**516**	.749 (9)
	31. **Wayne Cashman,**	Boston	17	1,027	**516**	.502
	32. **Butch Goring,**	Los Angeles, NY Islanders, Boston	16	1,107	**513**	.463
*	33. **Ivan Boldirev,**	Boston, California, Chicago, Atlanta, Vancouver, Detroit	15	1,052	**505**	.480
*	34. **Denis Maruk,**	California, Cleveland, Washington, Minnesota	11	793	**487**	.614 (6)
	35. **Peter Mahovlich,**	Montreal, Pittsburgh	16	884	**486**	.549
	36. **Pit Martin,**	Detroit, Boston, Chicago, Vancouver	17	1,101	**485**	.441
*	37. **Rick Middleton,**	NY Rangers, Boston	12	870	**484**	.556
*	38. **Lanny McDonald,**	Toronto, Colorado, Calgary	13	942	**474**	.537
	39. **Ken Hodge,**	Chicago, Boston, NY Rangers	14	881	**472**	.536
	40. **Ted Lindsay,**	Detroit, Chicago	17	1,068	**472**	.442
	41. **Jacques Lemaire,**	Montreal	12	853	**469**	.550
	42. **Dean Prentice,**	NY Rangers, Boston, Detroit, Pittsburgh, Minnesota	22	1,378	**469**	.340
	43. **Phil Goyette,**	Montreal, NY Rangers, St. Louis, Buffalo	16	941	**467**	.496
	44. **Bill Barber,**	Philadelphia	12	903	**463**	.513
	45. **Doug Mohns,**	Boston, Chicago, Minnesota, Atlanta, Washington	22	1,390	**462**	.332
*	46. **Peter Stastny,**	Quebec	6	463	**462**	.998 (2)
	47. **Bobby Rousseau,**	Montreal, Minnesota, NY Rangers	15	942	**458**	.486
	48. **Murray Oliver,**	Detroit, Boston, Toronto, Minnesota	17	1,127	**454**	.403
	49. **Doug Harvey,**	Montreal, NY Rangers, Detroit, St. Louis	19	1,113	**452**	.406
	50. **Guy Lapointe,**	Montreal, St. Louis, Boston	16	884	**451**	.510
	51. **Walt Tkaczuk,**	NY Rangers	14	945	**451**	.477
*	52. **Peter McNab,**	Buffalo, Boston, Vancouver, New Jersey	13	908	**438**	.482
	53. **Bill Gadsby,**	Chicago, NY Rangers, Detroit	20	1,248	**437**	.350
	54. **Yvan Cournoyer,**	Montreal	16	968	**435**	.449
*	55. **Wilf Paiement,**	Kansas City, Colorado, Toronto, Quebec, NY Rangers	12	867	**435**	.502
	56. **Bernie Geoffrion,**	Montreal, NY Rangers	16	883	**429**	.486

	Player	Seasons	Games	Assists	Assists per game
*	57. **Dave Taylor,** Los Angeles	9	617	**429**	.486
*	58. **Bobby Smith,** Minnesota, Montreal ...	8	600	**426**	.710
	59. **Syl Apps,** NY Rangers, Pittsburgh, Los Angeles	11	727	**423**	.582
	60. **Bert Olmstead,** Chicago, Montreal, Toronto	14	848	**421**	.496
	61. **Maurice Richard,** Montreal	18	978	**421**	.430
	62. **Craig Ramsay,** Buffalo	14	1,070	**420**	.392
	63. **Bob Nevin,** Toronto, NY Rangers, Minnesota, Los Angeles ..	18	1,128	**419**	.371
	64. **Rene Robert,** Pittsburgh, Buffalo, Colorado, Toronto	12	744	**418**	.562
	65. **Pierre Pilote,** Chicago, Toronto	14	890	**418**	.470
	66. **Carol Vadnais,** Montreal, Oakland, California, Boston, NY Rangers, New Jersey	17	1,087	**418**	.385
	67. **George Armstrong,** Toronto	21	1,187	**417**	.351
*	68. **Denis Savard,** Chicago	6	468	**413**	.882
	69. **Rick MacLeish,** Philadelphia, Hartford, Pittsburgh, Detroit	14	846	**410**	.485
*	70. **Paul Coffey,** Edmonton	6	473	**410**	.867 (4)
	71. **Elmer Lach,** Montreal	13	664	**408**	.614
	72. **Fred Stanfield,** Chicago, Boston, Minnesota, Buffalo	14	914	**405**	.443
	73. **Tim Horton,** Toronto, NY Rangers, Pittsburgh, Buffalo	22	1,446	**403**	.279
*	74. **Pierre Larouche,** Pittsburgh, Montreal, Hartford, NY Rangers	12	729	**403**	.553
	75. **Terry O'Reilly,** Boston	14	891	**402**	.451
*	76. **Mel Bridgman,** Philadelphia, Calgary, New Jersey	11	841	**401**	.477
	77. **Red Berenson,** Montreal, NY Rangers, St. Louis, Detroit	17	987	**397**	**.402**
	78. **Rick Kehoe,** Toronto, Pittsburgh	14	906	**396**	.437
	79. **Eddie Westfall,** Boston, NY Islanders	18	1,227	**394**	.323
	80. **Steve Shutt,** Montreal, Los Angeles ..	13	290	**393**	.422
	81. **Walt McKechnie,** Minnesota, California, Boston, Detroit, Washington, Cleveland, Toronto, Colorado	16	955	**392**	.411
	82. **Garry Unger,** Toronto, Detroit, St. Louis, Atlanta, Los Angeles, Edmonton	16	1,105	**391**	.354
	83. **Vic Hadfield,** NY Rangers, Pittsburgh	16	1,002	**389**	.388
*	84. **Reed Larson,** Detroit, Boston	10	721	**386**	.535
	85. **Jean Pronovost,** Pittsburgh, Atlanta, Washington	14	998	**383**	.384
*	86. **Kent Nilsson,** Atlanta, Calgary, Minnesota	7	486	**377**	.776 (7)
*	87. **Ron Greschner,** NY Rangers	12	757	**373**	.493
	88. **Ron Stackhouse,** California, Detroit, Pittsburgh	12	889	**372**	.418
*	89. **Doug Wilson,** Chicago	9	655	**372**	.568
	90. **Guy Chouinard,** Atlanta, Calgary, St. Louis.	10	578	**370**	.640
*	91. **Ray Bourque,** Boston	7	502	**365**	.727
*	92. **Don Lever,** Vancouver, Atlanta, Calgary, Colorado, New Jersey ...	14	1,010	**365**	.371
	93. **Bob Pulford,** Toronto, Los Angeles...	16	1,079	**362**	.335
	94. **Ralph Backstrom,** Montreal, Los Angeles, Chicago	17	1,032	**361**	.350
*	95. **Clark Gillies,** NY Islanders	12	872	**359**	.411
	96. **Jean-Paul Parise,** Boston, Toronto, Minnesota, NY Islanders, Cleveland	14	890	**356**	.400
	97. **Bill Cowley,** Boston, St. Louis, Pittsburgh, Buffalo	13	551	**353**	.641
*	98. **Thomas Gradin,** Vancouver	8	613	**353**	.575
	99. **Al MacAdam,** Philadelphia, California, Cleveland, Minnesota, Vancouver	13	864	**351**	.406
	100. **Ron Schock,** Boston, St. Louis, Pittsburgh, Detroit.	15	909	**351**	.386
	100. **Dennis Hull,** Chicago, Detroit	14	959	**351**	.366

Top 100 All-Time Point Leaders

* active player

(figures in parentheses indicate ranking of top 10 by points per game)

Player		Seasons	Games	Goals	Assists	Points	Points per game	
1. Gordie Howe,	Detroit....	25	1,687	786	1,023	1,809	1.072	
	Hartford...	1	80	15	26	41	.513	
	Total	26	1,767	801	1,049	**1,850**	1.047	
* 2. Marcel Dionne,	Detroit....	4	309	139	227	366	1.184	
	LA......	11	854	526	707	1,233	1.447	
	Total	15	1,163	665	934	**1,599**	1.374	(6)
3. Phil Esposito,	Chicago...	4	235	74	100	174	.740	
	Boston....	8¼	625	459	553	1,012	1.619	
	NYR.....	5¾	422	184	220	404	.957	
	Total	18	1,282	717	873	**1,590**	1.240	
4. Stan Mikita,	Chicago	22	1,394	541	926	**1,467**	1.052	
5. John Bucyk,	Detroit....	2	104	11	19	30	.288	
	Boston....	21	1,436	545	794	1,339	.932	
	Total	23	1,540	556	813	**1,369**	.889	
* 6. Wayne Gretzky,	Edmonton	7	553	481	856	**1,337**	2.417	(1)
7. Gilbert Perreault,	Buffalo....	16	1,171	503	807	**1,310**	1.187	
8. Alex Delvecchio,	Detroit...	24	1,549	456	825	**1,281**	.827	
9. Jean Ratelle,	NYR.....	15¼	862	336	481	817	.948	
	Boston....	5¾	419	155	295	450	1.074	
	Total	21	1,281	491	776	**1,267**	.989	
10. Guy Lafleur,	Montreal	14	961	518	728	**1,246**	1.296	(9)
11. Norm Ullman, Detroit, Toronto		20	1,410	490	739	**1,229**	.872	
12. Jean Beliveau, Montreal		20	1,125	507	712	**1,219**	1.084	
13. Bobby Clarke, Philadelphia..		15	1,144	358	852	**1,210**	1.057	
14. Bobby Hull, Chicago, Winnipeg, Hartford		16	1,063	610	560	**1,170**	1.100	
15. Darryl Sittler, Toronto, Philadelphia.		15	1,096	484	637	**1,121**	1.023	
* 16. Bryan Trottier, NY Islanders		11	834	417	698	**1,115**	1.337	(8)
17. Frank Mahovlich, Toronto, Detroit, Montreal		18	1,181	533	570	**1,103**	.934	
* 18. Mike Bossy, NY Islanders		9	689	535	516	**1,051**	1.525	(3)
19. Henri Richard, Montreal....		20	1,256	358	688	**1,046**	.833	
20. Rod Gilbert, NY Rangers		18	1,065	406	615	**1,021**	.959	
21. Dave Keon, Toronto, Hartford		18	1,296	396	590	**986**	.761	
22. Andy Bathgate, NY Rangers, Toronto, Detroit, Pittsburgh		17	1,069	349	624	**973**	.910	
23. Maurice Richard, Montreal		18	978	544	421	**965**	.987	
* 24. Denis Potvin, NY Islanders..		13	930	279	680	**959**	1.031	
* 25. Lanny McDonald, Toronto, Colorado, Calgary		13	942	465	474	**939**	.997	
26. Bobby Orr, Boston, Chicago		12	657	270	645	**915**	1.393	(5)
27. Brad Park, NY Rangers, Boston, Detroit		17	1,113	213	683	**896**	.805	
28. Butch Goring, Los Angeles, NY Islanders, Boston		16	1,107	375	513	**888**	.802	
* 29. Rick Middleton, NY Rangers, Boston.		12	870	404	484	**888**	1.020	
30. Bill Barber, Philadelphia		12	903	420	463	**883**	.978	
31. Ivan Boldirev, Boston, California, Chicago, Atlanta, Vancouver, Detroit		15	1,052	361	505	**866**	.823	
32. Yvan Cournoyer, Montreal...		16	968	428	435	**863**	.892	
33. Dean Prentice, NY Rangers, Boston, Detroit, Pittsburgh, Minnesota		22	1,318	391	469	**860**	.624	
34. Ted Lindsay, Detroit, Chicago		17	1,068	379	472	**851**	.797	
* 35. Bernie Federko, St. Louis...		10	718	290	555	**845**	1.177	
* 36. Tom Lysiak, Atlanta, Chicago		13	919	292	551	**843**	.917	
37. Jacques Lemaire, Montreal		12	853	366	469	**835**	.979	
38. Red Kelly, Detroit, Toronto...		20	1,316	281	542	**823**	.625	
39. Bernie Geoffrion, Montreal, NY Rangers		16	883	393	429	**822**	.931	
* 40. Denis Maruk, California, Cleveland, Washington, Minnesota		11	793	333	487	**820**	1.034	
41. Steve Shutt, Montreal, Los Angeles		13	930	424	393	**817**	.878	
42. Garry Unger, Toronto, Detroit, St. Louis, Atlanta, Los Angeles, Edmonton		16	1,105	413	391	**804**	.728	
43. Ken Hodge, Chicago, Boston, NY Rangers		14	881	328	472	**800**	.908	
44. Wayne Cashman, Boston		17	1,027	277	516	**793**	.772	
45. Peter McNab, Buffalo, Boston, Vancouver, New Jersey		13	908	355	438	**793**	.873	
46. Jean Pronovost, Pittsburgh, Atlanta, Washington		14	998	391	383	**774**	766	
47. Peter Mahovlich, Detroit, Montreal, Pittsburgh		16	884	288	485	**773**	.874	
* 48. Wilf Paiement, Kansas City, Colorado, Toronto, Quebec, NY Rangers		12	867	335	435	**770**	.887	
49. Rick Kehoe, Pittsburgh		14	906	371	396	**767**	.846	
* 50. Pierre Larouche, Pittsburgh, Montreal, Hartford, NY Rangers		12	729	364	403	**767**	1.052	

Player	Seasons	Games	Goals	Assists	Points	Points per game	
* 51. Larry Robinson, Montreal	14	1,005	174	589	**763**	.759	
52. Rick MacLeish, Philadelphia, Hartford, Pittsburgh, Detroit	14	846	349	410	**759**	.897	
* 53. Dave Taylor, Los Angeles	9	617	303	429	**732**	1.186	
54. Murray Oliver, Detroit, Boston, Toronto, Minnesota	17	1,127	274	454	**728**	.646	
55. Bob Nevin, Toronto, NY Rangers, Minnesota, Los Angeles	18	1,128	307	419	**726**	.644	
55. George Armstrong, Toronto	21	1,187	296	417	**713**	.601	
* 57. Peter Stastny, Quebec	6	463	251	462	**713**	1.539	(2)
58. Vic Hadfield, NY Rangers, Pittsburgh	16	1,002	323	289	**712**	.711	
59. Doug Mohns, Boston, Chicago, Minnesota, Atlanta, Washington	22	1,390	248	462	**710**	.511	
60. Bobby Rousseau, Montreal, Minnesota, NY Rangers	15	942	245	458	**703**	.746	
61. Rene Robert, Toronto, Pittsburgh, Buffalo, Colorado	12	744	284	418	**702**	.944	
* 62. Borje Salming, Toronto	13	914	139	563	**702**	.768	
63. Richard Martin, Buffalo, Los Angeles	11	685	384	317	**701**	1.023	
* 64. Danny Gare, Buffalo, Detroit	12	809	353	328	**681**	.842	
65. Walt Tkaczuk, NY Rangers	14	945	227	451	**678**	.717	
66. Phil Goyette, Montreal, NY Rangers, St. Louis, Buffalo	16	941	207	467	**674**	.716	
* 67. Don Lever, Vancouver, Atlanta, Calgary, Colorado, New Jersey, Buffalo	14	1,010	310	365	**675**	.668	
68. Craig Ramsay, Buffalo	14	1,070	252	420	**672**	.628	
69. Reggie Leach, Boston, California, Philadelphia, Detroit	13	934	381	285	**666**	.713	
* 70. Clark Gillies, NY Islanders..	12	872	304	359	**663**	.667	
71. Red Berenson, Montreal, NY Rangers, St. Louis, Detroit	17	987	261	397	**658**	.756	
* 72. Bobby Smith, Minnesota, Montreal	8	600	229	426	**655**	1.091	
73. Dennis Hull, Chicago, Detroit	14	959	303	351	**654**	.682	
* 74. Jari Kurri, Edmonton	6	441	300	344	**644**	1.460	(4)
75. Bob Pulford, Toronto, Los Angeles	16	1,079	281	362	**643**	.596	
76. Ron Ellis, Toronto	16	1,034	332	308	**640**	.618	
77. Ralph Backstrom, Montreal, Los Angeles, Chicago	17	1,032	278	361	**639**	.619	
* 78. Michel Goulet, Quebec	7	532	317	316	**633**	1.189	
79. Mel Bridgman, Philadelphia, Calgary, New Jersey	11	841	232	401	**633**	.752	
* 80. Denis Savard, Chicago	6	468	217	413	**630**	1.346	(7)
81. Eddie Westfall, Boston, Chicago	18	1,227	231	394	**625**	.512	
82. Elmer Lach, Montreal	13	664	215	408	**623**	.938	
83. Guy Lapointe, Montreal, St. Louis, Boston	16	884	171	451	**622**	.704	
* 84. Kent Nilsson, Calgary, Minnesota	17	486	245	377	**622**	1.279	(10)
85. Fred Stanfield, Chicago, Boston, Minnesota, Buffalo	14	914	211	405	**616**	.674	
* 86. Charlie Simmer, Los Angeles, Boston	11	582	302	311	**613**	1.053	
87. Pit Martin, Detroit, Boston, Chicago, Vancouver	17	1,011	324	485	**609**	.553	
88. Dickie Moore, Montreal, Toronto, St. Louis	14	719	261	347	**608**	.846	
89. Syl Apps, NY Rangers, Pittsburgh, Los Angeles	11	727	183	423	**606**	.834	
90. Walt McKechnie, Minnesota, California, Boston, Detroit, Washington, Cleveland, Toronto, Colorado	16	955	214	392	**606**	.635	
91. Terry O'Reilly, Boston	14	891	204	402	**606**	.680	
92. Bert Olmstead, Chicago, Montreal, Toronto	14	848	181	421	**602**	.710	
* 93. Paul Coffey, Edmonton	6	473	192	410	**602**	1.272	
94. Brian Propp, Philadelphia	7	546	266	333	**599**	1.097	
95. Jean Paul Parise, Boston, Toronto, Minnesota, NY Islanders, Cleveland	14	890	238	356	**594**	.667	
* 96. Brian Sutter, St. Louis	10	689	285	308	**593**	.860	
97. Al Mac Adam, Philadelphia, Calgary, Cleveland, Minnesota, Vancouver	11	864	204	351	**591**	.684	
98. Claude Provost, Montreal...	15	1,005	234	335	**589**	.501	
99. Don Marshall, Montreal, NY Islanders, Toronto, Buffalo	19	1,176	265	324	**589**	.501	
100. Carol Vadnais, Montreal, Oakland, California, Boston, NY Rangers, New Jersey	17	1,087	169	418	**587**	.540	

All-Time Games Played Leaders

* Active

(Regular Season)

	Player	Team	Seasons	GP
1.	**Gordie Howe**	Detroit	25	1,687
		Hartford	1	80
		Total	**26**	**1,767**
2.	**Alex Delvecchio**	**Detroit**	**23**	**1,549**
3.	**John Bucyk**	Detroit	2	104
		Boston	1	1,436
		Total	**23**	**1,540**
4.	**Tim Horton**	Toronto	17	1,185
		New York	1 1/2	93
		Pittsburgh	1	44
		Buffalo	2	124
		Total	**21 1/2**	**1,446**
5.	**Harry Howell**	NY Rangers	17	1,160
		California	1 1/2	83
		Los Angeles	2 1/2	168
		Total	**21**	**1,411**
6.	**Norm Ullman**	Detroit	12 1/2	875
		Toronto	7 1/2	535
		Total	20	1,410
7.	**Stan Mikita**	Chicago	21	1,394
8.	**Doug Mohns**	Boston	11	710
		Chicago	6 1/2	415
		Minnesota	2 1/2	162
		Atlanta	1	28
		Washington	1 1/2	75
		Total	**22**	**1,390**
9.	**Dean Prentice**	NY Rangers	10 1/2	666
		Boston	3	170
		Detroit	3 1/2	230
		Pittsburgh	2	144
		Minnesota	3	168
		Total	**22**	**1,378**
10.	**Ron Stewart**	Toronto	13	838
		Boston	2	126
		St. Louis	1/2	19
		NY Rangers	4	306
		Vancouver	1	42
		NY Islanders	1/2	22
		Total	**21**	**1,353**
11.	**Red Kelly**	Detroit	12	846
		Toronto	7 1/2	470
		Total	**20**	**1,316**
12.	**Dave Keon**	Toronto	15	1,062
		Hartford	3	234
		Total	**18**	**1,296**
13.	**Phil Esposito**	Chicago	4	235
		Boston	8 1/2	625
		NY Rangers	5 1/3	422
		Total	**18**	**1,282**
14.	**Jean Ratelle**	NY Rangers	13 1/3	862
		Boston	5 2/3	419
		Total	19	1,281
15.	**Henri Richard**	**Montreal**	**20**	**1,256**
16.	**Bill Gadsby**	Chicago	8 1/2	468
		NY Rangers	6 1/2	457
		Detroit	5	323
		Total	**20**	**1,248**
17.	**Allan Stanley**	NY Rangers	7	307
		Chicago	2	111
		Boston	2	129
		Toronto	9	633
		Philadelphia	1	64
		Total	**21**	**1,244**
18.	**Eddie Westfall**	Boston	11	734
		NY Rangers	7	493
		Total	**18**	**1,227**
19.	**Eric Nesterenko**	Toronto	4	206
		Chicago	16	1,013
		Total	**20**	**1,219**
20.	**Marcel Pronovost**	Detroit	15	983
		Toronto	5	223
		Total	**20**	**1,206**
21.	**George Armstrong**	**Toronto**	**20**	**1,187**
22.	**Frank Mahovlich**	Toronto	11	720
		Detroit	2 1/2	198
		Montreal	3 1/2	263
		Total	17	1,181
23.	**Don Marshall**	Monteal	9	585
		NY Rangers	7	479
		Buffalo	1	62
		Toronto	1	50
		Total	**18**	**1,176**
24.	**Gilbert Perreault**	**Buffalo**	**16**	**1,171**
*25.	**Marcel Dionne**	Detroit	4	309
		Los Angeles	11	854
		Total	**15**	**1,163**
26.	**Leo Boivin**	Toronto	2 1/2	137
		Boston	11	717
		Detroit	1 1/2	85
		Pittsburgh	1 1/2	114
		Minnesota	1 1/2	97
		Total	**18**	**1,150**
27.	**Bobby Clarke**	**Philadelphia**	**15**	**1,144**
28.	**Bob Nevin**	Toronto	4	250
		NY Rangers	7	505
		Minnesota	2	138
		Los Angeles	3	235
		Total	**16**	**1,128**
29.	**Butch Goring**	Los Angeles	10 3/4	736
		NY Islanders	4 3/4	359
		Boston	1/2	39
		Total	**16**	**1,134**
30.	**Murray Oliver**	Detroit	1 1/2	101
		Boston	6 1/2	429
		Toronto	3	226
		Minnesota	5	371
		Total	**16**	**1,127**
31.	**Jean Beliveau**	**Montreal**	**18**	**1,125**
32.	**Doug Harvey**	Montreal	14	890
		NY Rangers	2	151
		Detroit	1	2
		St. Louis	1	70
		Total	**18**	**1,113**
33.	**Brad Park**	NY Rangers	7 1/2	465
		Boston	7 1/2	501
		Detroit	2	147
		Total	**17**	**1,113**
34.	**Garry Unger**	Toronto	1/2	15
		Detroit	3	196
		St. Louis	8	662
		Atlanta	1	79
		Los Angeles	1/2	58
		Edmonton	2 1/3	75
		Total	**16**	**1,105**
35.	**Pit Martin**	Detroit	2 1/3	119
		Boston	1 2/3	111
		Chicago	10 1/3	740
		Vancouver	1 2/3	131
		Total	**16**	**1,101**
36.	**Darryl Sittler**	Toronto	11 1/2	844
		Philadelphia	2 1/2	191
		Detroit	1	61
		Total	**15**	**1,096**
37.	**Carol Vadnais**	**Montreal**	**1**	**42**
		Oakland	2	152
		California	2	94
		Boston	3 1/2	263
		NY Rangers	6 2/3	485
		New Jersey	1	51
		Total	**16**	**1,087**
38.	**Bob Pulford**	Toronto	14	947
		Los Angeles	2	132
		Total	**16**	**1,079**
39.	**Craig Ramsay**	**Buffalo**	**14**	**1,070**
40.	**Andy Bathgate**	NY Rangers	11	719
		Toronto	1	70
		Detroit	2	130
		Pittsburgh	2	150
		Total	**16**	**1,069**
41.	**Ted Lindsay**	Detroit	14	862
		Chicago	3	206
		Total	17	1,068
42.	**Terry Harper**	Montreal	9	554
		Los Angeles	3	234
		Detroit	4	252
		St. Louis	1	11
		Colorado	1/3	15
		Total	**17**	**1,066**
43.	**Rod Gilbert**	**NY Rangers**	**16**	**1,065**
44.	**Bobby Hull**	Chicago	15	1,036
		Winnipeg	2/3	18
		Hartford	1/3	9
		Total	**16**	**1,063**
45.	**Jean Guy Talbot**	Montreal	12	791
		Minnesota	1/3	4
		Detroit	1/3	32
		St. Louis	2 1/3	172
		Buffalo	1	57
		Total	**16**	**1,056**
46.	**Ivan Boldirev**	Boston	1/3	13
		California	2 2/3	191
		Chicago	5 2/3	384
		Atlanta	1 1/3	65
		Vancouver	2 2/3	216
		Detroit	2 1/2	183
		Total	**15**	**1,052**
47.	**Eddie Shack**	NY Rangers	2	141
		Toronto	8 1/2	504
		Boston	2	120
		Los Angeles	1 1/2	84
		Buffalo	1 1/2	111
		Pittsburgh	1 1/2	87
		Total	**17**	**1,047**
48.	**Serge Savard**	Montreal	15	917
		Winnipeg	2	123
		Total	**17**	**1,040**
49.	**Ron Ellis**	**Toronto**	**16**	**1,034**
50.	**Ralph Backstrom**	Montreal	13	844
		Los Angeles	2 2/3	172
		Chicago	1/3	16
		Total	**16**	**1,032**
51.	**Dick Duff**	Toronto	8 1/2	582
		NY Rangers	1	43
		Montreal	5	305
		Los Angeles	1/2	39
		Buffalo	2	61
		Total	**17**	**1,030**
52.	**Wayne Cashman**	**Boston**	**17**	**1,027**
53.	**Jim Neilson**	NY Rangers	12	810
		California	4	213
		Cleveland	2	115
		Total	**18**	**1,023**
*54.	**Don Lever**	Vancouver	7 2/3	593
		Atlanta	1/3	28
		Calgary	1 1/3	85
		Colorado	2/3	59
		New Jersey	3	216
		Buffalo	1	29
		Total	**14**	**1,010**
55.	**Jim Roberts**	Montreal	9 2/3	611
		St. Louis	5 1/3	395
		Total	**15**	**1,006**
*56.	**Larry Robinson**	**Montreal**	**14**	**1,005**
57.	**Vic Hadfield**	NY Rangers	13	839
		Pittsburgh	3	163
		Total	**16**	**1,002**

All-Time Penalty-Minute Leaders

(Regular season. Minimum 1,500 minutes)

Player Team	Seasons	Games	Penalty Minutes	Mins. per game
* **Dave Williams,** Toronto, Vancouver, Detroit, Los Angeles	11	858	**3,515**	4.09
Dave Schultz, Philadelphia, Los Angeles, Pittsburgh, Buffalo	9	535	**2,294**	4.29
Bryan Watson, Montreal, Detroit, California, Pittsburgh, St. Louis, Washington	16	878	**2,212**	2.52
* **Willi Plett,** Atlanta, Calgary, Minnesota	10	702	2,139	3.04
Terry O'Reilly, Boston	14	891	**2,095**	2.35
Andre Dupont, NY Rangers, St. Louis, Philadelphia, Quebec	13	810	**1,986**	2.45
Phil Russell, Chicago, Atlanta, Calgary, New Jersey	13	968	**1,963**	2.03
Garry Howatt, NY Islanders, Hartford, New Jersey	12	720	**1,836**	2.55
Carol Vadnais, Montreal, Oakland, California, Boston, NY Rangers, New Jersey	17	1,087	**1,813**	1.67
Ted Lindsay, Detroit, Chicago	17	1,068	**1,808**	1.69
* **Brian Sutter,** St. Louis	10	692	1,534	2.22
* **Chris Nilan,** Montreal	7	412	1,699	4.124
Gordie Howe, Detroit, Hartford	26	1,767	**1,685**	.95
Paul Holmgren, Philadelphia, Minnesota	9	527	**1,684**	3.23
Jerry Korab, Chicago, Vancouver, Buffalo, Los Angeles	15	975	**1,629**	1.67
Tim Horton, Toronto, NY Rangers, Pittsburgh, Buffalo	24	1,446	**1,611**	1.11
Wilf Paiement, Kansas City, Colorado, Toronto, Quebec, NY Rangers	12	867	**1,610**	1.89
Harold Snepsts, Vancouver, Minnesota	11	754	**1,583**	2.10
Dave Hutchison, Los Angeles, Toronto, Chicago, New Jersey	10	584	**1,550**	2.65
Bill Gadsby, Chicago, NY Rangers, Detroit	20	1,248	**1,539**	1.23

Year-by-Year Records
Point Totals of Scoring Champions

Season	Player and Club	Games Played	Goals	Assists	Points
1985-86	Wayne Gretzky, Edmonton	80	52	163	215
1984-85	Wayne Gretzky, Edmonton	80	73	135	208
1983-84	Wayne Gretzky, Edmonton	74	87	118	205
1982-83	Wayne Gretzky, Edmonton	80	71	125	196
1981-82	Wayne Gretzky, Edmonton	80	92	120	212
1980-81	Wayne Gretzky, Edmonton	80	55	109	164
1979-80	Marcel Dionne, Los Angeles	80	53	84	137
1978-79	Bryan Trottier, NY Islanders	76	47	87	134
1977-78	Guy Lafleur, Montreal	78	60	72	132
1976-77	Guy Lafleur, Montreal	80	56	80	136
1975-76	Guy Lafleur, Montreal	80	56	69	125
1974-75	Bobby Orr, Boston	80	46	89	135
1973-74	Phil Esposito, Boston	78	68	77	145
1972-73	Phil Esposito, Boston	78	55	75	130
1971-72	Phil Esposito, Boston	76	66	67	133
1970-71	Phil Esposito, Boston	78	76	76	152
1969-70	Bobby Orr, Boston	76	33	87	120
1968-69	Phil Esposito, Boston	74	49	77	126
1967-68	Stan Mikita, Chicago	72	40	47	87
1966-67	Stan Mikita, Chicago	70	35	62	97
1965-66	Bobby Hull, Chicago	65	54	43	97
1964-65	Stan Mikita, Chicago	70	28	59	87
1963-64	Stan Mikita, Chicago	70	39	50	89
1962-63	Gordie Howe, Detroit	70	38	48	86
1961-62	Bobby Hull, Chicago	70	50	34	84
1960-61	Bernie Geoffrion, Montreal	64	50	45	95
1959-60	Bobby Hull, Chicago	70	39	42	81
1958-59	Dickie Moore, Montreal	70	41	55	96
1957-58	Dickie Moore, Montreal	70	36	48	84
1956-57	Gordie Howe, Detroit	70	44	45	89
1955-56	Jean Beliveau, Montreal	70	47	41	88
1954-55	Bernie Geoffrion, Montreal	70	38	37	75
1953-54	Gordie Howe, Detroit	70	33	48	81
1952-53	Gordie Howe, Detroit	70	49	46	95
1951-52	Gordie Howe, Detroit	70	47	39	86
1950-51	Gordie Howe, Detroit	70	43	43	86
1949-50	Ted Lindsay, Detroit	69	23	55	78
1948-49	Roy Conacher, Chicago	60	26	42	68
1947-48	Elmer Lach, Montreal	60	30	31	61
1946-47	Max Bentley, Chicago	60	29	43	72
1945-46	Max Bentley, Chicago	47	31	30	61
1944-45	Elmer Lach, Montreal	50	26	54	80
1943-44	Herbie Cain, Boston	48	36	46	82
1942-43	Doug Bentley, Chicago	50	33	40	73
1941-42	Bryan Hextall, NY Rangers	48	24	32	56
1940-41	Bill Cowley, Boston	46	17	45	62
1939-40	Milt Schmidt, Boston	48	22	30	52
1938-39	Toe Blake, Montreal	48	24	23	47
1937-38	Gordie Drillon, Toronto	48	26	26	52
1936-37	Dave Schriner, NY Americans	48	21	25	46
1935-36	Dave Schriner, NY Americans	48	19	26	45
1934-35	Charlie Conacher, Toronto	48	36	21	57
1933-34	Charlie Conacher, Toronto	42	32	20	52
1932-33	Bill Cook, New York Rangers	48	28	22	50
1931-32	Harvey Jackson, Toronto	48	28	25	53
1930-31	Howie Morenz, Montreal	39	28	23	51
1929-30	Cooney Weiland, Boston	44	43	30	73
1928-29	Ace Bailey, Toronto	44	22	10	32
1927-28	Howie Morenz, Montreal	43	33	18	51
1926-27	Bill Cook, NY Rangers	44	33	4	37
1925-26	Nels Stewart, Mtl. Maroons	36	34	8	42
1924-25	Babe Dye, Toronto	29	38	6	44
1923-24	Cy Denneny, Ottawa	21	22	1	23
1922-23	Babe Dye, Toronto	22	26	11	37
1921-22	Punch Broadbent, Ottawa	24	32	14	46
1920-21	Newsy Lalonde, Montreal	24	33	8	41
1919-20	Joe Malone, Quebec	24	39	6	45
1918-19	Newsy Lalonde, Montreal	17	23	9	32
1917-18	Joe Malone, Montreal	20	44	**	44

** Number of assists not recorded

Goal-Scoring Leaders

Season	Player and Club	Games Played	Goals Scored
1985-86	Jari Kurri, Edmonton	78	68
1984-85	Wayne Gretzky, Edmonton	80	73
1983-84	Wayne Gretzky, Edmonton	74	87
1982-83	Wayne Gretzky, Edmonton	80	71
1981-82	Wayne Gretzky, Edmonton	80	92
1980-81	Mike Bossy, NY Islanders	79	68
1979-80	Charlie Simmer, Los Angeles	64	56
	Danny Gare, Buffalo	76	56
	Blaine Stoughton, Hartford	80	56
1978-79	Mike Bossy, NY Islanders	80	69
1977-78	Guy Lafleur, Montreal	78	60
1976-77	Steve Shutt, Montreal	80	60
1975-76	Reggie Leach, Philadelphia	80	61
1974-75	Phil Esposito, Boston	79	61
1973-74	Phil Esposito, Boston	78	68
1972-73	Phil Esposito, Boston	78	55
1971-72	Phil Esposito, Boston	76	66
1970-71	Phil Esposito, Boston	78	76
1969-70	Phil Esposito, Boston	76	43
1968-69	Bobby Hull, Chicago	74	58
1967-68	Bobby Hull, Chicago	71	44
1966-67	Bobby Hull, Chicago	66	52
1965-66	Bobby Hull, Chicago	65	54
1964-65	Norm Ullman, Detroit	70	42
1963-64	Bobby Hull, Chicago	70	43
1962-63	Gordie Howe, Detroit	70	38
1961-62	Bobby Hull, Chicago	70	50
1960-61	Bernie Geoffrion, Montreal	64	50
1959-60	Bobby Hull, Chicago	70	39
	Bronco Horvath, Boston	68	39
1958-59	Jean Beliveau, Montreal	64	45
1957-58	Dickie Moore, Montreal	70	36
1956-57	Gordie Howe, Detroit	70	44
1955-56	Jean Beliveau, Montreal	70	47
1954-55	Bernie Geoffrion, Montreal	67	38
	Maurice Richard, Montreal	70	38
1953-54	Maurice Richard, Montreal	70	37
1952-53	Gordie Howe, Detroit	70	49
1951-52	Gordie Howe, Detroit	70	47
1950-51	Gordie Howe, Detroit	70	43
1949-50	Maurice Richard, Montreal	70	43
1948-49	Sid Abel, Detroit	69	28
1947-48	Ted Lindsay, Detroit	60	33
1946-47	Maurice Richard, Montreal	60	45
1945-46	Gaye Stewart, Toronto	50	37
1944-45	Maurice Richard, Montreal	50	50
1943-44	Doug Bentley, Chicago	50	38
1942-43	Doug Bentley, Chicago	50	33
1941-42	Lynn Patrick, New York Rangers	47	32
1940-41	Bryan Hextall, New York Rangers	48	26
1939-40	Bryan Hextall, New York Rangers	48	24
1938-39	Roy Conacher, Boston	47	26
1937-38	Gordie Drillon, Toronto	48	26
1936-37	Larry Aurie, Detroit	45	23
	Nels Stewart, Bos., NY Americans	43	23
1935-36	Bill Thoms, Toronto	48	23
	Charlie Conacher, Toronto	44	23
1934-35	Charlie Conacher, Toronto	48	36
1933-34	Charlie Conacher, Toronto	42	32
1932-33	Bill Cook, New York Rangers	48	28
1931-32	Charlie Conacher, Toronto	45	34
1930-31	Charlie Conacher, Toronto	40	31
1929-30	Cooney Weiland, Boston	44	43
1928-29	"Ace" Bailey, Toronto	44	22
1927-28	Howie Morenz, Montreal	43	33
1926-27	Bill Cook, New York Rangers	44	33
1925-26	Nels Stewart, Mtl. Maroons	36	34
1924-25	Cecil Dye, Toronto	29	38
1923-24	Cy Denneny, Ottawa	21	22
1922-23	Cecil Dye, Toronto	22	26
1921-22	Harry Broadbent, Ottawa	24	30
	Cecil Dye, Toronto	24	30
1920-21	Cecil Dye, Toronto	24	35
1919-20	Joe Malone, Quebec	24	39
1918-19	Odie Cleghorn, Montreal	17	24
1917-18	Joe Malone, Montreal	20	44

Players' 500th Goals

Player	Team	Date	Game No.	Score		Opposing Goaltender	Total Goals	Total Games
Maurice Richard	Montreal	Oct. 19/57	863	Chi. 1	at Mtl. 3	Glenn Hall	544	978
Gordie Howe	Detroit	Mar. 14/62	1,045	Det. 2	at NYR 3	Gump Worsley	801	1,767
Bobby Hull	Chicago	Feb. 21/70	861	NYR. 2	at Chi. 4	Ed Giacomin	610	1,063
Jean Béliveau	Montreal	Feb. 11/71	1,101	Minn. 2	at Mtl. 6	Gilles Gilbert	507	1,125
Frank Mahovlich	Montreal	Mar. 21/73	1,105	Van. 2	at Mtl. 3	Dunc Wilson	533	1,181
Phil Esposito	Boston	Dec. 22/74	803	Det. 4	at Bos. 5	Jim Rutherford	710	1,241
John Bucyk	Boston	Oct. 30/75	1,370	St. L. 2	at Bos. 3	Yves Bélanger	556	1,540
Stan Mikita	Chicago	Feb. 27/77	1,221	Van. 4	at Chi. 3	Cesare Maniago	541	1,394
*Marcel Dionne	Los Angeles	Dec. 14/82	887	L.A. 2	at Wash. 7	Al Jensen	665	1,163
Guy Lafleur	Montreal	Dec. 20/83	918	Mtl. 5	at N.J. 2	Ron Low	516	942
*Mike Bossy	NY Islanders	Jan. 2/86	647	Bos. 5	at NYI 7	Doug Keans	535	689
Gilbert Perreault	Buffalo	Mar. 9/86	1,159	NJ 3	at Buf. 4	Alain Chevrier	503	1,171

* Active

Penalty Leaders

Season	Player and Club	Games Played	Penalties in Minutes
1985-86	Joey Kocur, Detroit	59	377
1984-85	Chris Nilan, Montreal	77	358
1983-84	Chris Nilan, Montreal	76	338
1982-83	Randy Holt, Washington	70	275
1981-82	Paul Baxter, Pittsburgh	76	409
1980-81	Dave Williams, Vancouver	77	343
1979-80	Jimmy Mann, Winnipeg	72	287
1978-79	Dave Williams, Toronto	77	298
1977-78	Dave Schultz, L.A., Pit.	74	405
1976-77	Dave Williams, Toronto	77	338
1975-76	Steve Durbano, Pit., K.C.	69	370
1974-75	Dave Schultz, Philadelphia	76	472
1973-74	Dave Schultz, Philadelphia	73	348
1972-73	Dave Schultz, Philadelphia	76	259
1971-72	Bryan Watson, Pittsburgh	75	212
1970-71	Keith Magnuson, Chicago	76	291
1969-70	Keith Magnuson, Chicago	76	213
1968-69	Forbes Kennedy, Phi., Tor.	77	219
1967-68	Barclay Plager, St. Louis	49	153
1966-67	John Ferguson, Montreal	67	177
1965-66	Reg Fleming, New York Rangers	69	166
1964-65	Carl Brewer, Toronto	70	177
1963-64	Vic Hadfield, New York Rangers	69	151
1962-63	Howie Young, Detroit	64	273
1961-62	Lou Fontinato, Montreal	54	167
1960-61	Pierre Pilote, Chicago	70	165
1959-60	Carl Brewer, Toronto	67	150
1958-59	Ted Lindsay, Chicago	70	184
1957-58	Lou Fontinato, New York Rangers	70	152
1956-57	Gus Mortson, Chicago	70	147
1955-56	Lou Fontinato, New York Rangers	70	202
1954-55	Fern Flaman, Boston	70	150
1953-54	Gus Mortson, Chicago	68	132
1952-53	Maurice Richard, Montreal	70	112
1951-52	Gus Kyle, Boston	69	127
1950-51	Gus Mortson, Toronto	60	142
1949-50	Bill Ezinicki, Toronto	67	144
1948-49	Bill Ezinicki, Toronto	52	145
1947-48	Bill Barilko, Toronto	57	147
1946-47	Gus Mortson, Toronto	60	133
1945-46	Jack Stewart, Detroit	47	73
1944-45	Pat Egan, Boston	48	86
1943-44	Mike McMahon, Montreal	42	98
1942-43	Jimmy Orlando, Detroit	40	89*
1941-42	Jimmy Orlando, Detroit	48	81**
1940-41	Jimmy Orlando, Detroit	48	99
1939-40	Red Horner, Toronto	30	87
1938-39	Red Horner, Toronto	48	85
1937-38	Red Horner, Toronto	47	82*
1936-37	Red Horner, Toronto	48	124
1935-36	Red Horner, Toronto	43	167
1934-35	Red Horner, Toronto	46	125
1933-34	Red Horner, Toronto	42	126*
1932-33	Red Horner, Toronto	48	144
1931-32	Red Dutton, New York Americans	47	107
1930-31	Harvey Rockburn, Detroit	42	118
1929-30	Joe Lamb, Ottawa	44	119
1928-29	Red Dutton, Montreal Maroons	44	139
1927-28	Eddie Shore, Boston	44	165
1926-27	Nels Stewart, Montreal Maroons	44	133

* Match Misconduct penalty not included in total penalty minutes.
** Three Match Misconduct penalties not included in total penalty minutes. 1946-47 was the first season that a Match penalty was automatically written into the player's total penalty minutes as 20 minutes. Now all penalties, Match, Game Misconduct, and Misconduct, are written as 10 minutes.

Players' 1,000th Points

Player	Team	Date	Game No.	G or A	Total Points G A PTS
Gordie Howe	Detroit	Nov. 27/60	938	(A)	801-1,049–1,850
Jean Béliveau	Montreal	Mar. 3/68	911	(G)	507-712–1,219
Alex Delvecchio	Detroit	Feb. 16/69	1,143	(A)	456-825–1,281
Norm Ullman	Toronto	Oct. 16/71	1,113	(A)	490-739–1,229
Bobby Hull	Chicago	Dec. 12/71	909	(A)	610-560–1,170
John Bucyk	Boston	Nov. 9/72	1,144	(G)	556-813–1,369
Frank Mahovlich	Montreal	Feb. 13/73	1,090	(A)	533-570–1,103
Stan Mikita	Chicago	Nov. 3/73	986	(A)	541-926–1,467
Henri Richard	Montreal	Dec. 20/73	1,194	(A)	358-688–1,046
Phil Esposito	Boston	Feb. 15/74	745	(A)	710-860–1,570
Rod Gilbert	NY Rangers	Feb. 19/77	1,027	(G)	406-615–1,021
Jean Ratelle	Boston	Apr. 3/77	1,007	(A)	480-750–1,230
Bobby Clarke	Philadelphia	Mar. 19/81	922	(G)	358-852–1,210
*Marcel Dionne	Los Angeles	Jan. 7/81	740	(G)	583-796–1,379
Guy Lafleur	Montreal	March 4/81	720	(G)	516-725–1,241
Gilbert Perreault	Buffalo	Apr. 3/82	871	(A)	452-715–1,167
Darryl Sittler	Philadelphia	Jan. 20/83	927	(A)	473-621–1,094
*Wayne Gretzky	Edmonton	Dec. 19/84	424	(A)	429-693–1,122
*Bryan Trottier	NY Islanders	Jan. 29/85	726	(G)	380-639–1,019
*Mike Bossy	NY Islanders	Jan. 24/86	656	(A)	535-516–1,051

* Active

Rookie Scoring Records
Top Goal-Scoring Rookies
(30 Goals or More)

	Rookie	Team	Position	Season	GP	G	A	PTS
1.	*Mike Bossy	NY Islanders	Right wing	1977-78	73	53	38	91
2.	*Dale Hawerchuk	Winnipeg	Center	1981-82	80	45	58	103
3.	Barry Pederson	Boston	Center	1981-82	80	44	48	92
	Rick Martin	Buffalo	Left wing	1971-72	73	44	30	74
5.	*Steve Larmer	Chicago	Right wing	1982-83	80	43	47	90
	*Mario Lemieux	Pittsburgh	Center	1984-85	73	43	57	100
7.	Darryl Sutter	Chicago	Left wing	1980-81	76	40	22	62
	Sylvain Turgeon	Hartford	Left wing	1983-84	76	40	32	72
	Warren Young	Pittsburgh	Left wing	1984-85	80	40	32	72
10.	Anton Stastny	Quebec	Left wing	1980-81	80	39	46	85
	Steve Yzerman	Detroit	Center	1983-84	80	39	48	87
	*Peter Stastny	Quebec	Center	1980-81	77	39	70	109
	*Eric Vail	Atlanta	Left wing	1974-75	72	39	21	60
14.	Neal Broten	Minnesota	Center	1981-82	73	38	59	97
	*Gilbert Perreault	Buffalo	Center	1970-71	78	38	34	72
16.	Jorgen Pettersson	St. Louis	Left wing	1980-81	62	37	36	73
	Mike Bullard	Pittsburgh	Center	1981-82	75	37	27	64
18.	Mike Foligno	Detroit	Right wing	1979-80	80	36	35	71
	Paul MacLean	Winnipeg	Right wing	1981-82	74	36	25	61
20.	Marian Stastny	Quebec	Right wing	1981-82	74	35	54	89
	Brian Bellows	Minnesota	Right wing	1982-83	80	35	30	60
22.	Nels Stewart	Mtl. Maroons	Center	1925-26	36	34	8	42
	*Danny Grant	Minnesota	Left wing	1968-69	75	34	31	65
	Norm Ferguson	Oakland	Right wing	1968-69	76	34	20	54
	Brian Propp	Philadelphia	Left wing	1979-80	80	34	41	75
	Wendel Clark	Toronto	Left wing	1985-86	66	34	11	45
27.	Mark Pavelich	NY Rangers	Center	1981-82	79	33	43	76
	*Willi Plett	Atlanta	Right wing	1976-77	64	33	23	56
	Dale McCourt	Detroit	Center	1977-78	76	33	39	72
	Ron Flockhart	Philadelphia	Center	1981-82	72	33	39	72
	Steve Bozek	Los Angeles	Center	1981-82	71	33	23	56
32.	Jari Kurri	Edmonton	Left wing	1980-81	75	32	43	75
	Bill Mosienko	Chicago	Right wing	1943-44	50	32	38	70
	Don Murdoch	NY Rangers	Right wing	1976-77	59	32	24	56
	Michel Bergeron	Detroit	Right wing	1975-76	72	32	27	59
	*Bryan Trottier	NY Islanders	Center	1975-76	80	32	63	95
	Kjell Dahlin	Montreal	Right wing	1985-86	77	32	39	71
	Peter Klima	Detroit	Left wing	1985-86	74	32	24	56
39.	Danny Gare	Buffalo	Right wing	1974-75	78	31	31	62
	Pierre Larouche	Pittsburgh	Center	1974-75	79	31	37	68
	Dave Poulin	Philadelphia	Center	1983-84	73	31	45	76

* Calder Trophy Winner.

All-Time Top Point-Scoring Rookies

	Rookie	Team	Position	Season	GP	G	A	PTS
1.	*Peter Stastny	Quebec	Center	1980-81	77	39	70	109
2.	*Dale Hawerchuk	Winnipeg	Center	1981-82	80	45	58	103
3.	*Mario Lemieux	Pittsburgh	Center	1984-85	73	43	57	100
4.	Neal Broten	Minnesota	Center	1981-82	73	38	59	97
5.	*Bryan Trottier	NY Islanders	Center	1975-76	80	32	63	95
6.	Barry Pederson	Boston	Center	1981-82	80	44	48	92
7.	*Mike Bossy	NY Islanders	Right wing	1977-78	73	53	38	91
8.	*Steve Larmer	Chicago	Right wing	1982-83	80	43	47	90
9.	Marian Stastny	Quebec	Right wing	1981-82	74	35	54	89
10.	Steve Yzerman	Detroit	Center	1983-84	80	39	48	87
11.	Anton Stastny	Quebec	Left wing	1980-81	80	39	46	85
12.	Marcel Dionne	Detroit	Center	1971-72	78	28	49	77
13.	Mark Pavelich	NY Rangers	Center	1981-82	79	33	43	76
	Larry Murphy	Los Angeles	Defense	1980-81	80	16	60	76
	Dave Poulin	Philadelphia	Center	1983-84	73	31	45	76
16.	Jari Kurri	Edmonton	Left wing	1980-81	75	32	43	75
	Brian Propp	Philadelphia	Left wing	1979-80	80	34	41	75
	Denis Savard	Chicago	Center	1980-81	76	28	47	75
19.	Rick Martin	Buffalo	Left wing	1971-72	73	44	30	74
	*Bobby Smith	Minnesota	Center	1978-79	80	30	44	74
21.	Jorgen Pettersson	St. Louis	Left wing	1980-81	62	37	36	73
22.	*Gilbert Perreault	Buffalo	Center	1970-71	78	38	34	72
	Ron Flockhart	Philadelphia	Center	1981-82	72	33	39	72
	Dale McCourt	Detroit	Center	1977-78	76	33	39	72
	Sylvain Turgeon	Hartford	Left wing	1983-84	76	40	32	72
	Warren Young	Pittsburgh	Left wing	1984-85	80	40	32	72
	Carey Wilson	Calgary	Center	1984-85	74	24	48	72
28.	Dave Christian	Winnipeg	Center	1980-81	80	28	43	71
	Mike Foligno	Detroit	Right wing	1979-80	80	36	35	71
	Mats Naslund	Montreal	Left wing	1982-83	74	26	45	71
	Kjell Dahlin	Montreal	Right wing	1985-86	77	32	39	71
32.	Bill Mosienko	Chicago	Right wing	1943-44	50	32	38	70
33.	Roland Eriksson	Minnesota	Center	1976-77	80	25	44	69
34.	Pierre Larouche	Pittsburgh	Center	1974-75	79	31	37	68
	Ron Francis	Hartford	Center	1981-82	59	25	43	68
	Jude Drouin	Minnesota	Center	1970-71	75	16	52	68
	*Gary Suter	Calgary	Defense	1985-86	80	18	50	68
38.	Bobby Carpenter	Washington	Center	1981-82	80	32	35	67
	Chris Valentine	Washington	Center	1981-82	60	30	37	67
	Tom Webster	Detroit	Right wing	1970-71	78	30	37	67
	Mark Osborne	Detroit	Left wing	1981-82	80	26	41	67
42.	Peter Ihnacak	Toronto	Center	1982-83	80	28	38	66
	Phil Housley	Buffalo	Defense	1982-83	77	19	47	66
	Per-Erik Eklund	Philadelphia	Center	1985-86	70	15	51	66
45.	Brian Bellows	Minnesota	Right wing	1982-83	78	35	30	65
	*Danny Grant	Minnesota	Left wing	1968-69	75	34	31	65
	Mike Krushelnyski	Boston	Center	1982-83	79	23	42	65
	*Raymond Bourque	Boston	Defense	1979-80	80	17	48	65
	Mike Ridley	NY Rangers	Center	1985-86	80	22	43	65

* Calder Trophy Winner.

Active Players' Three-Or-More-Goal Games

Regular Season

Teams named are the ones the players were with at the time of their multiple-scoring games.
Players listed alphabetically.

Player	Team	3-Goals	4-Goals	5-Goals
Acton, Keith	Mtl., Min.	3	—	—
Allison, Mike	NY Rangers	1	—	—
Anderson, Glen	Edmonton	14	1	—
Anderson, John	Toronto	3	—	—
Andreychuk, Dave	Buffalo	—	—	1
Arniel, Scott	Winnipeg	1	—	—
Ashton, Brent	Quebec	3	—	—
Babych, Wayne	St. Louis	3	—	—
Barr, Dave	St. Louis	1	—	—
Beck, Barry	Colorado	1	—	—
Beers, Ed	Calgary	4	1	—
Bellows, Brian	Minnesota	—	1	—
Bjugstad, Scott	Minnesota	3	—	—
Boschman, Laurie	Winnipeg	1	—	—
Bossy, Mike	NY Islanders	28	9	—
Boudreau, Bruce	Toronto	1	—	—
Bourne, Bob	NY Islanders	1	—	—
Bourque, Raymond	Boston	1	—	—
Boutette, Pat	Pittsburgh	2	—	—
Bozek, Steve	Los Angeles	2	—	—
Brickley, Andy	Pittsburgh	1	—	—
Bridgman, Mel	Calgary	1	—	—
Brooke, Bob	NY Rangers	1	—	—
Broten, Aaron	New Jersey	1	—	—
Broten, Neal	Minnesota	4	—	—
Bullard, Mike	Pittsburgh	7	—	—
Carbonneau, Guy	Montreal	1	—	—
Carpenter, Bob	Washington	—	1	—
Carroll, Billy	NY Islanders	1	—	—
Carson, Lindsay	Philadelphia	1	—	—
Christian, Dave	Winnipeg	2	—	—
Ciccarelli, Dino	Minnesota	10	1	—
Clark, Wendel	Toronto	1	—	—
Coffey, Paul	Edmonton	3	1	—
Cote, Alain	Quebec	1	—	—
Courtnall, Russ	Toronto	1	—	—
Crowder, Keith	Boston	1	—	—
Currie, Tony	St. L., Hfd.	2	—	—
Cyr, Paul	Buffalo	1	—	—
Dahlin, Kjell	Montreal	1	—	—
Daoust, Dan	Toronto	1	—	—
DeBlois, Lucien	Winnipeg	1	—	—
Derlago, Bill	Toronto	4	—	—
Dineen, Kevin	Hartford	1	—	—
Dionne, Marcel	Los Angeles	25	3	—
Douglas, Jordy	Hartford	1	1	—
Dufour, Luc	Boston	1	—	—
Duguay, Ron	NYR, Det.	9	—	—
Evason, Dean	Hartford	1	—	—
Federko, Bernie	St. Louis	9	—	—
Fergus, Tom	Toronto	1	—	—
Ferraro, Ray	Hartford	2	—	—
Flatley, Patrick	NY Islanders	—	1	—
Foligno, Mike	Det., Buf.	7	—	—
Foster, Dwight	Boston	2	—	—
Fox, Jimmy	Los Angeles	2	—	—
Francis, Ron	Hartford	4	1	—
Fraser, Curt	Chicago	1	—	—
Frycer, Miroslav	Que., Tor.	8	1	—
Gagne, Paul	New Jersey	1	—	—
Gare, Danny	Buf., Det.	12	—	—
Gartner, Mike	Washington	9	1	—
Gilbert, Greg	NY Islanders	1	—	—
Gillies, Clark	NY Islanders	3	—	—
Gillis, Jere	Vancouver	1	—	—
Gillis, Paul	Quebec	1	—	—
Gilmour, Doug	St. Louis	1	—	—
Gould, Bobby	Calgary	1	—	—
Goulet, Michel	Quebec	8	2	—
Gradin, Thomas	Vancouver	4	—	—
Greschner, Ron	NY Rangers	1	—	—
Gretzky, Wayne	Edmonton	27	7	3
Gustafsson, Bengt	Washington	1	—	1
Hallin, Mats	NY Islanders	1	—	—
Hamel, Gilles	Buffalo	1	—	—
Hawerchuk, Dale	Winnipeg	8	—	—
Haworth, Alan	Washington	2	—	—
Hiemer, Uli	New Jersey	1	—	—
Housley, Phil	Buffalo	1	—	—
Howe, Mark	Hartford	1	—	—
Hunter, Dale	Quebec	3	—	—
Hunter, Mark	St. Louis	2	—	—
Jarvis, Doug	Montreal	1	—	—
Johnson, Mark	Hfd., NJ	5	—	—
Kasper, Steve	Boston	2	—	—
Kelly, John Paul	Los Angeles	1	—	—
Kerr, Tim	Philadelphia	7	3	—
Klima, Petr	Detroit	2	—	—
Korn, Jim	Toronto	1	—	—
Krushelnyski, Mike	Edmonton	1	—	—
Kurri, Jari	Edmonton	15	1	1
LaFontaine, Pat	NY Islanders	1	—	—
Lambert, Lane	Detroit	1	—	—
Larmer, Steve	Chicago	3	—	—
Larouche, Pierre	Pit., Mtl., Hfd., NYR	12	1	—
Larson, Reed	Detroit	4	—	—
LaVallee, Kevin	St. Louis	1	—	—
Lawless, Paul	Hartford	1	—	—
Lawton, Brian	Minnesota	1	—	—
Lemieux, Alain	St. Louis	1	—	—
Lemieux, Mario	Pittsburgh	—	1	—
Lever, Don	Van., Col.	3	—	—
Lindstrom, Willy	Winnipeg	1	—	1
Linseman, Ken	Phi., Edm.	2	—	—
Lofthouse, Mark	Washington	1	—	—
Loob, Hakan	Calgary	1	—	—
Ludzik, Steve	Chicago	1	—	—
Lukowich, Morris	Winnipeg	1	—	—
Lumley, Dave	Edmonton	2	—	—
Lysiak, Tom	Atl., Chi.	3	—	—
MacLean, Paul	Winnipeg	2	—	—
MacLellan, Brian	LA, NYR	1	1	—
MacTavish, Craig	Edmonton	1	—	—
Malone, Greg	Pit., Hfd.	2	—	—
Maloney, Don	NY Rangers	4	—	—
Martin, Terry	Toronto	3	—	—
Maruk, Dennis	Cal., Clev., Wash.	8	4	—
McAdam, Gary	Pit., Cgy.	3	—	—
McCarthy, Tom	Minnesota	3	—	—
McDonald, Lanny	Tor., Col., Cgy.	16	—	—
McKegney, Tony	Buf., Que., Min.	4	—	—
McKenna, Sean	Buffalo	1	—	—
McNab, Peter	Boston	7	—	—
McPhee, Mike	Montreal	2	—	—
Meagher, Rick	Hartford	1	—	—
Messier, Mark	Edmonton	7	1	—
Middleton, Rick	NYR, Bos.	7	1	—
Mullen, Brian	Winnipeg	1	—	—
Mullen, Joe	St. Louis	2	—	—
Murray, Troy	Chicago	3	—	—
Napier, Mark	Montreal	1	1	—
Naslund, Mats	Montreal	1	1	—
Neufeld, Ray	Winnipeg	1	—	—
Nicholls, Bernie	Los Angeles	6	2	—
Nilsson, Kent	Atl., Cgy.	12	2	—
Nystrom, Bob	NY Islanders	3	—	—
Ogrodnick, John	Detroit	6	—	—
Osborne, Mark	Detroit	1	—	—
Paiement, Wilf	KC, Col., Tor., Que.	8	—	—
Paslawski, Greg	St. Louis	2	—	—
Payne, Steve	Minnesota	6	—	—
Pederson, Barry	Boston	6	1	—
Peplinski, Jim	Calgary	—	1	—
Perreault, Gilbert	Buffalo	18	—	—
Pettersson, Jorgen	St. Louis	5	—	—
Plett, Willi	Atl., Cgy., Min.	3	1	—
Poddubny, Walt	Toronto	2	—	—
Poulin, Dave	Philadelphia	4	—	—
Potvin, Denis	NY Islanders	5	—	—
Preston, Rich	New Jersey	1	—	—
Propp, Brian	Philadelphia	5	—	—
Reeds, Mark	St. Louis	1	—	—
Richer, Stephane	Montreal	1	—	—
Risebrough, Doug	Calgary	3	—	—
Robertson, Torrie	Hartford	1	—	—
Robinson, Larry	Montreal	1	—	—
Rogers, Mike	Hfd., NYR	6	—	—
Ruff, Lindy	Buffalo	1	1	—
Ruotsalainen, Reijo	NY Rangers	1	—	—
Saganiuk, Rocky	Toronto	1	—	—
Salming, Borje	Toronto	1	—	—
Savard, Denis	Chicago	5	—	—
Secord, Al	Chicago	2	1	—
Seiling, Ric	Buffalo	1	—	—
Semenko, Dave	Edmonton	1	—	—
Shedden, Doug	Pittsburgh	2	—	—
Sherven, Gord	Edmonton	1	—	—
Siltanen, Risto	Edmonton	1	—	—
Sinisalo, Ilkka	Philadelphia	3	—	—
Simmer, Charlie	LA, Bos.	7	1	—
Skriko, Petri	Vancouver	1	—	—
Smith, Bobby	Minnesota	3	1	—
Smyl, Stan	Vancouver	5	—	—
Stastny, Anton	Quebec	3	—	—
Stastny, Marian	Quebec	3	1	—
Stastny, Peter	Quebec	9	1	—
Steen, Thomas	Winnipeg	1	—	—
Sulliman, Doug	Hartford	1	—	—
Sundstrom, Patrik	Vancouver	2	—	—
Sundstrom, Peter	NY Rangers	2	—	—
Sutter, Brent	NY Islanders	4	—	—
Sutter, Brian	St. Louis	7	—	—

Active Players' Three-or-More Goal Games continued

Player	Team	3-Goals	4-Goals	5-Goals
Sutter, Darryl	Chicago	2	1	—
Tambellini, Steve	NJ, Cgy.	2	—	—
Tanti, Tony	Vancouver	4	—	—
Taylor, Dave	Los Angeles	5	1	—
Taylor, Mark	Pittsburgh	1	—	—
Terrion, Greg	Toronto	1	—	—
Tonelli, John	NY Islanders	2	—	1
Tremblay, Mario	Montreal	3	—	—
Trottier, Bryan	NY Islanders	12	1	2
Tucker, John	Buffalo	1	—	—
Turgeon, Sylvain	Hartford	2	—	—
Turnbull, Perry	St. L., Wpg.	2	1	—
Vaive, Rick	Toronto	6	3	—
Verbeek, Pat	New Jersey	1	—	—
Virta, Hannu	Buffalo	1	—	—
Walter, Ryan	Montreal	1	—	—
Wickenheiser, Doug	Mtl., St. L.	2	—	—
Williams, Dave	Vancouver	2	—	—
Wilson, Carey	Calgary	2	—	—
Wilson, Ron	Winnipeg	—	1	—
Young, Warren	Detroit	1	—	—
Yzerman, Steve	Detroit	2	—	—

Five-or-more-Goal Games

Player	Team	Date	Score			Opposing Goaltender
SEVEN GOALS						
Joe Malone	Quebec Bulldogs	Jan. 31/20	Tor.	6	at Que. 10	Ivan Mitchell
SIX GOALS						
Newsy Lalonde	Montreal	Jan. 10/20	Tor.	7	at Mtl. 14	Ivan Mitchell
Joe Malone	Quebec Bulldogs	Mar. 10/20	Ott.	4	at Que. 10	Clint Benedict
Corb Denneny	Toronto St. Pats	Jan. 26/21	Ham.	3	at Tor. 10	Howard Lockhart
Cy Denneny	Ottawa Senators	Mar. 7/21	Ham.	5	at Ott. 12	Howard Lockhart
Syd Howe	Detroit	Feb. 3/44	NYR	2	at Det. 12	Ken McAuley
Red Berenson	St. Louis	Nov. 7/68	St. L.	8	at Phil 0	Doug Favell
Darryl Sittler	Toronto	Feb. 7/76	Bos.	4	at Tor. 11	Dave Reece
FIVE GOALS						
Joe Malone	Montreal	Dec. 19/17	Mtl.	9	at Ott. 4	Clint Benedict
Harry Hyland	Mtl. Wanderers	Dec. 19/17	Tor.	9	at Mtl. 10	Arthur Brooks
Joe Malone	Montreal	Jan. 12/18	Ott.	4	at Mtl. 9	Clint Benedict
Joe Malone	Montreal	Feb. 2/18	Tor.	2	at Mtl. 9	Harry Holmes
Mickey Roach	Toronto St. Pats	Mar. 6/20	Que.	2	at Tor. 11	Frank Brophy
Newsy Lalonde	Montreal	Feb. 16/21	Ham.	5	at Mtl. 10	Howard Lockhart
Babe Dye	Toronto St. Pats	Dec. 16/22	Mtl.	2	at Tor. 7	Georges Vezina
Redvers Green	Hamilton Tigers	Dec. 5/24	Ham.	10	at Tor. 3	John Roach
Babe Dye	Toronto St. Pats	Dec. 22/24	Tor.	10	at Bos. 2	Charlie Stewart
Harry Broadbent	Mtl. Maroons	Jan. 7/25	Ham.	6	at Ham. 2	Vernon Forbes
Pit Lepine	Montreal	Dec. 14/29	Ott.	4	at Mtl. 6	Alex Connell
Howie Morenz	Montreal	Mar. 18/30	NYA	3	at Mtl. 8	Roy Worters
Charlie Conacher	Toronto	Jan. 19/32	NYA	3	at Tor. 11	Roy Worters
Ray Getliffe	Montreal	Feb. 6/43	Bos.	3	at Mtl. 8	Frank Brimsek
Maurice Richard	Montreal	Dec. 28/44	Det.	1	at Mtl. 9	Harry Lumley
Howie Meeker	Toronto	Jan. 8/47	Chi.	4	at Tor. 10	Paul Bibeault
Bernie Geoffrion	Montreal	Feb. 19/55	NYR	2	at Mtl. 10	Gump Worsley
Bobby Rousseau	Montreal	Feb. 1/64	Det.	3	at Mtl. 9	Roger Crozier
Yvan Cournoyer	Montreal	Feb. 15/75	Chi.	3	at Mtl. 12	Mike Veisor
Don Murdoch	NY Rangers	Oct. 12/76	NYR	10	at Min. 4	Gary Smith
Ian Turnbull	Toronto	Feb. 2/77	Det.	1	at Tor. 9	Ed Giacomin (2)
						Jim Rutherford (3)
*Bryan Trottier	NY Islanders	Dec. 23/78	NYR	4	at NYI 9	Wayne Thomas (4)
						John Davidson (1)
Tim Young	Minnesota	Jan. 15/79	Min.	8	at NYR 1	Doug Soetaert (3)
						Wayne Thomas (2)
*John Tonelli	NY Islanders	Jan. 6/81	Tor.	3	at NYI 6	Jiri Crha (5)
*Wayne Gretzky	Edmonton	Feb. 18/81	St.L.	2	at Edm. 9	Mike Liut (3)
						Ed Staniowski (2)
*Wayne Gretzky	Edmonton	Dec. 30/81	Phi.	5	at Edm. 7	Pete Peeters (4)
						Empty Net (1)
Grant Mulvey	Chicago	Feb. 3/82	St.L.	5	at Chi. 9	Mike Liut (4)
						Gary Edwards (1)
*Bryan Trottier	NY Islanders	Feb. 13/82	Phi.	2	at NYI 8	Pete Peeters
*Willy Lindstrom	Winnipeg	Mar. 2/82	Wpg.	7	at Phi. 6	Pete Peeters
Mark Pavelich	NY Rangers	Feb. 23/83	Hfd.	3	at NYR 11	Greg Millen
*Jari Kurri	Edmonton	Nov. 19/83	NJ.	4	at Edm. 13	Glenn Resch (3)
						Ron Low (2)
*Bengt Gustafsson	Washington	Jan. 8/84	Wash.	7	at Phi. 1	Pelle Lindbergh
*Pat Hughes	Edmonton	Feb. 3/84	Cgy.	5	at Edm. 10	Don Edwards (3)
						Rejean Lemelin (2)
*Wayne Gretzky	Edmonton	Dec. 15/84	Edm.	8	at St. L. 2	Rick Wamsley (4)
						Mike Liut(1)
*Dave Andreychuk	Buffalo	Feb. 6/86	Buf.	8	at Bos. 6	Pat Riggin (1)
						Doug Keans (4)

* Active.

One Season Scoring Records
Goals-Per-Game Leaders, One Season
(Among players with 20 goals or more in one season)

Player	Team	Season	Games	Goals	Average
Joe Malone	Montreal	1917-18	20	44	2.20
Newsy Lalonde	Montreal	1917-18	14	23	1.64
Cy Denneny	Ottawa	1917-18	22	36	1.64
Joe Malone	Quebec	1919-20	24	39	1.63
Newsy Lalonde	Montreal	1919-20	23	37	1.61
Cecil Dye	Toronto, Hamilton	1920-21	24	35	1.46
Cy Denneny	Ottawa	1920-21	24	34	1.42
Odie Cleghorn	Montreal	1918-19	17	24	1.41
Reg Noble	Toronto	1917-18	20	28	1.40
Joe Malone	Hamilton	1920-21	20	28	1.40
Newsy Lalonde	Montreal	1920-21	24	32	1.33
Cecil Dye	Toronto	1924-25	29	38	1.31
Cy Denneny	Ottawa	1921-22	22	28	1.27
Harry Broadbent	Ottawa	1921-22	24	30	1.25
Cecil Dye	Toronto	1921-22	24	30	1.25
Newsy Lalonde	Montreal	1918-19	17	21	1.25
Aurel Joliat	Montreal	1924-25	24	29	1.21
Wayne Gretzky	Edmonton	1983-84	74	87	1.18
Cecil Dye	Toronto	1922-23	22	26	1.18
Wayne Gretzky	Edmonton	1981-82	80	92	1.15
Jack Darragh	Ottawa	1919-20	22	24	1.09
Frank Nighbor	Ottawa	1919-20	23	25	1.09
Corb Denneny	Toronto	1919-20	23	25	1.09
Amos Arbour	Montreal	1919-20	20	21	1.05
Cy Denneny	Ottawa	1923-24	21	22	1.05
Billy Boucher	Montreal	1922-23	24	25	1.04
Maurice Richard	Montreal	1944-45	50	50	1.00
Howie Morenz	Montreal	1924-25	30	30	1.00
Cy Denneny	Ottawa	1924-25	28	28	1.00
Reg Noble	Toronto	1919-20	24	24	1.00

Points-Per-Game Leaders, One Season
(Among players with 50 points or more in one season)

Player	Team	Season	Games	Points	Average
Wayne Gretzky	Edmonton	1983-84	74	205	2.77
Wayne Gretzky	Edmonton	1985-86	80	215	2.69
Wayne Gretzky	Edmonton	1981-82	80	212	2.65
Wayne Gretzky	Edmonton	1984-85	80	208	2.60
Wayne Gretzky	Edmonton	1982-83	80	196	2.45
Wayne Gretzky	Edmonton	1980-81	80	164	2.05
Bill Cowley	Boston	1943-44	36	71	1.97
Phil Esposito	Boston	1970-71	78	152	1.95
Phil Esposito	Boston	1973-74	78	145	1.86
Jari Kurri	Edmonton	1984-85	73	135	1.85
Mike Bossy	NY Islanders	1981-82	80	147	1.84
Bobby Orr	Boston	1970-71	78	139	1.78
Mario Lemieux	Pittsburgh	1985-86	79	141	1.78
Jari Kurri	Edmonton	1983-84	64	113	1.77
Bryan Trottier	NY Islanders	1978-79	76	134	1.76
Mike Bossy	NY Islanders	1983-84	67	118	1.76
Paul Coffey	Edmonton	1985-86	79	138	1.75
Phil Esposito	Boston	1971-72	76	133	1.75
Peter Stastny	Quebec	1981-82	80	139	1.74
Wayne Gretzky	Edmonton	1979-80	79	137	1.73
Jean Ratelle	NY Rangers	1971-72	63	109	1.73
Marcel Dionne	Los Angeles	1979-80	80	137	1.71
Herb Cain	Boston	1943-44	48	82	1.71
Dennis Maruk	Washington	1981-82	80	136	1.70
Guy Lafleur	Montreal	1976-77	80	136	1.70
Phil Esposito	Boston	1968-69	74	126	1.70
Guy Lafleur	Montreal	1974-75	70	119	1.70
Bobby Orr	Boston	1974-75	80	135	1.69
Marcel Dionne	Los Angeles	1980-81	80	135	1.69
Guy Lafleur	Montreal	1977-78	78	132	1.69
Guy Lafleur	Montreal	1979-80	74	125	1.69
Jari Kurri	Edmonton	1985-86	78	131	1.68
Phil Esposito	Boston	1972-73	78	130	1.67
Cooney Weiland	Boston	1929-30	44	73	1.66
Peter Stastny	Quebec	1982-83	75	124	1.65
Bobby Orr	Boston	1973-74	74	122	1.65
Kent Nilsson	Calgary	1980-81	80	131	1.64
Marcel Dionne	Los Angeles	1978-79	80	130	1.63
Bryan Trottier	NY Islanders	1983-84	68	111	1.63
Dale Hawerchuk	Winnipeg	1984-85	80	130	1.63
Charlie Simmer	Los Angeles	1980-81	65	105	1.62
Guy Lafleur	Montreal	1978-79	80	129	1.61
Bryan Trottier	NY Islanders	1981-82	80	129	1.61
Phil Esposito	Boston	1974-75	79	127	1.61
Peter Stastny	Quebec	1985-86	76	122	1.61
Michel Goulet	Quebec	1983-84	75	121	1.61
Bryan Trottier	NY Islanders	1977-78	77	123	1.60
Bobby Orr	Boston	1972-73	63	101	1.60
Elmer Lach	Montreal	1944-45	50	80	1.60
Guy Chouinard	Calgary	1980-81	52	83	1.60
Mike Bossy	NY Islanders	1978-79	80	126	1.58
Paul Coffey	Edmonton	1983-84	80	126	1.58
Bobby Orr	Boston	1969-70	76	120	1.58
Charlie Simmer	Los Angeles	1979-80	64	101	1.58
Marcel Dionne	Los Angeles	1984-85	80	126	1.58
Bobby Clarke	Philadelphia	1975-76	76	119	1.57
Guy Lafleur	Montreal	1975-76	80	125	1.56
Dave Taylor	Los Angeles	1980-81	72	112	1.56
Denis Savard	Chicago	1982-83	78	121	1.55

Assists-Per-Game Leaders, One Season
(Among players with 35 assists or more in one season)

Player	Team	Season	Games	Assists	Average
Wayne Gretzky	Edmonton	1985-86	80	163	2.04
Wayne Gretzky	Edmonton	1984-85	80	135	1.68
Wayne Gretzky	Edmonton	1983-84	74	118	1.59
Wayne Gretzky	Edmonton	1982-83	80	125	1.56
Wayne Gretzky	Edmonton	1981-82	80	120	1.50
Wayne Gretzky	Edmonton	1980-81	80	109	1.36
Bobby Orr	Boston	1970-71	78	102	1.31
Bobby Orr	Boston	1973-74	74	90	1.22
Mario Lemieux	Pittsburgh	1985-86	79	93	1.18
Bobby Clarke	Philadelphia	1975-76	76	89	1.17
Peter Stastny	Quebec	1981-82	80	93	1.16
Bobby Orr	Boston	1969-70	76	87	1.15
Paul Coffey	Edmonton	1985-86	79	90	1.14
Bryan Trottier	NY Islanders	1978-79	76	87	1.14
Bobby Orr	Boston	1972-73	63	72	1.14
Bill Cowley	Boston	1943-44	36	41	1.14
Bobby Clarke	Philadelphia	1974-75	80	89	1.11
Bobby Orr	Boston	1974-75	80	89	1.11
Denis Savard	Chicago	1982-83	78	86	1.10
Wayne Gretzky	Edmonton	1979-80	79	86	1.09
Denis Savard	Chicago	1981-82	80	87	1.09
Paul Coffey	Edmonton	1983-84	80	86	1.08
Elmer Lach	Montreal	1944-45	50	54	1.08
Peter Stastny	Quebec	1985-86	76	81	1.07
Bobby Orr	Boston	1971-72	76	80	1.05
Marcel Dionne	Los Angeles	1979-80	80	84	1.05
Phil Esposito	Boston	1968-69	74	77	1.04
Mike Bossy	NY Islanders	1981-82	80	83	1.04
Bryan Trottier	NY Islanders	1983-84	68	71	1.04
Kent Nilsson	Calgary	1980-81	80	82	1.03
Peter Stastny	Quebec	1982-83	75	77	1.03
Pete Mahovlich	Montreal	1974-75	80	82	1.02
Guy Lafleur	Montreal	1979-80	74	75	1.01
Guy Lafleur	Montreal	1976-77	80	80	1.00
Bryan Trottier	NY Islanders	1977-78	77	77	1.00
Mike Bossy	NY Islanders	1983-84	67	67	1.00
Jean Ratelle	NY Rangers	1971-72	63	63	1.00
Guy Chouinard	Calgary	1980-81	52	52	1.00
Elmer Lach	Montreal	1943-44	48	48	1.00

Bobby Orr averaged more than one assist-per-game for six consecutive seasons.

50-Goal Seasons

Player	Team	Date of 50th Goal		Score	Goaltender	Player's Game No.	Team Game No.	Total Goals	Total Games	Age When First 50th Scored (Yrs. & Mos.)
Maurice Richard	Mtl.	18-3-45	Mtl. 4	at Bos. 2	Harvey Bennett	50	50	50	50	23.7
Bernie Geoffrion	Mtl.	16-3-61	Tor. 2	at Mtl. 5	Cesare Maniago	62	68	50	64	30.1
Bobby Hull	Chi.	25-3-62	Chi. 1	at NYR 4	Gump Worsley	70	70	50	70	23.2
Bobby Hull	Chi.	2-3-66	Det. 4	at Chi. 5	Hank Bassen	52	57	54	65	
Bobby Hull	Chi.	18-3-67	Chi. 5	at Tor. 9	Bruce Gamble	63	66	52	66	
Bobby Hull	Chi.	5-3-69	NYR 4	at Chi. 4	Ed Giacomin	64	66	58	74	
Phil Esposito	Bos.	20-2-71	Bos. 4	at L.A. 5	Denis DeJordy	58	58	76	78	29.0
John Bucyk	Bos.	16-3-71	Bos. 11	at Det. 4	Roy Edwards	69	69	51	78	35.1
Phil Esposito	Bos.	20-2-72	Bos. 3	at Chi. 1	Tony Esposito	60	60	66	76	
Bobby Hull	Chi.	2-4-72	Det. 1	at Chi. 6	Andy Brown	78	78	50	78	
Vic Hadfield	NYR	2-4-72	Mtl. 6	at NYR 5	Denis DeJordy	78	78	50	78	31.6
Phil Esposito	Bos.	25-3-73	Buf. 1	at Bos. 6	Roger Crozier	75	75	55	78	
Mickey Redmond	Det.	27-3-73	Det. 8	at Tor. 1	Ron Low	73	75	52	76	25.3
Rick MacLeish	Phi.	1-4-73	Phi. 4	at Pit. 5	Cam Newton	78	78	50	78	23.2
Phil Esposito	Bos.	20-2-74	Bos. 5	at Min. 5	Cesare Maniago	56	56	68	78	
Mickey Redmond	Det.	23-3-74	NYR 3	at Det. 5	Ed Giacomin	69	71	51	76	29.10
Ken Hodge	Bos.	6-4-74	Bos. 2	at Mtl. 6	Michel Larocque	75	77	50	78	22.9
Rick Martin	Buf.	7-4-74	St.L. 2	at Buf. 5	Wayne Stephenson	78	78	52	78	
Phil Esposito	Bos.	8-2-75	Bos. 8	at Det. 5	Jim Rutherford	54	54	61	79	
Guy Lafleur	Mtl.	29-3-75	K.C. 1	at Mtl. 4	Denis Herron	66	76	53	70	23.6
Danny Grant	Det.	2-4-75	Wash. 3	at Det. 8	John Adams	78	78	50	80	29.2
Rick Martin	Buf.	3-4-75	Bos. 2	at Buf. 4	Ken Broderick	67	79	52	68	
Reggie Leach	Phi.	14-3-76	Atl. 1	at Phi. 6	Daniel Bouchard	69	69	61	80	25.11
Jean Pronovost	Pit.	24-3-76	Bos. 5	at Pit. 5	Gilles Gilbert	74	74	52	80	31.3
Guy Lafleur	Mtl.	27-3-76	K.C. 2	at Mtl. 8	Denis Herron	76	76	56	80	
Bill Barber	Phi.	3-4-76	Buf. 2	at Phi. 5	Al Smith	79	79	50	80	23.9
Pierre Larouche	Pit.	3-4-76	Wash. 5	at Pit. 4	Ron Low	75	79	53	76	20.5
Danny Gare	Buf.	4-4-76	Tor. 2	at Buf. 5	Gord McRae	79	80	50	79	21.11
Steve Shutt	Mtl.	1-3-77	Mtl. 5	at NYI 4	Glenn Resch	65	65	60	80	24.8
Guy Lafleur	Mtl.	6-3-77	Mtl. 1	at Buf. 4	Don Edwards	68	68	56	80	
Marcel Dionne	L.A.	2-4-77	Min. 2	at L.A. 7	Pete LoPresti	79	79	53	80	25.8
Guy Lafleur	Mtl.	8-3-78	Wash. 3	at Mtl. 4	Jim Bedard	63	65	60	78	
Mike Bossy	NYI	1-4-78	Wash. 2	at NYI 3	Bernie Wolfe	69	76	53	73	21.2
Mike Bossy	NYI	24-2-79	Det. 1	at NYI 3	Rogie Vachon	58	58	69	80	
Marcel Dionne	L.A.	11-3-79	L.A. 3	at Phi. 6	Wayne Stephenson	68	68	59	80	
Guy Lafleur	Mtl.	31-3-79	Pit. 3	at Mtl. 5	Denis Herron	76	76	52	80	
Guy Chouinard	Atl.	6-4-79	NYR 2	at Atl. 9	John Davidson	79	79	50	80	22.5

Bernie Geoffrion was the second NHL player to score fifty goals in a single season.

50-Goal Seasons continued

Player	Team	Date of 50th Goal	Score		Goaltender	Player's Game No.	Team Game No.	Total Goals	Total Games	Age When First 50th Scored (Yrs. & Mos.)
Marcel Dionne	L.A.	12-3-80	L.A. 2	at Pit. 4	Nick Ricci	70	70	53	80	
Mike Bossy	NYI	16-3-80	NYI 6	at Chi. 1	Tony Esposito	68	71	51	75	
Charlie Simmer	L.A.	19-3-80	Det. 3	at L.A. 4	Jim Rutherford	57	73	56	64	26.0
Pierre Larouche	Mtl.	25-3-80	Chi. 4	at Mtl. 8	Tony Esposito	72	75	50	73	
Danny Gare	Buf.	27-3-80	Det. 1	at Buf. 10	Jim Rutherford	71	75	56	76	
Blaine Stoughton	Hfd.	28-3-80	Hfd. 4	at Van. 4	Glen Hanlon	75	75	56	80	27.0
Guy Lafleur	Mtl.	2-4-80	Mtl. 7	at Det. 2	Rogie Vachon	72	78	50	74	
Wayne Gretzky	Edm.	2-4-80	Min. 1	at Edm. 1	Gary Edwards	78	79	51	79	19.2
Reggie Leach	Phi.	3-4-80	Wash. 2	at Phi. 4	(empty net)	75	79	50	76	
Mike Bossy	NYI	24-1-81	Que. 3	at NYI 7	Ron Grahame	50	50	68	79	
Charlie Simmer	L.A.	26-1-81	L.A. 7	at Que. 5	Michel Dion	51	51	56	65	
Marcel Dionne	L.A.	8-3-81	L.A. 4	at Wpg. 3	Markus Mattsson	68	68	58	80	
Wayne Babych	St.L.	12-3-81	St.L. 3	at Mtl. 4	Richard Sevigny	70	68	54	78	22.9
Wayne Gretzky	Edm.	15-3-81	Edm. 3	at Cgy. 3	Pat Riggin	69	69	55	80	
Rick Kehoe	Pit.	16-3-81	Pit. 7	at Edm. 6	Eddie Mio	70	70	55	80	29.7
Jacques Richard	Que.	29-3-81	Mtl. 0	at Que. 4	Richard Sevigny	76	75	52	78	28.6
Dennis Maruk	Wash.	5-4-81	Det. 2	at Wash. 7	Larry Lozinski	80	80	50	80	25.3
Wayne Gretzky	Edm.	30-12-81	Phi. 5	at Edm. 7	(empty net)	39	39	92	80	
Dennis Maruk	Wash.	21-2-82	Wpg. 3	at Wash. 6	Doug Soetaert	61	61	60	80	
Mike Bossy	NYI	4-3-82	Tor. 1	at NYI 10	Michel Larocque	66	66	64	80	
Dino Ciccarelli	Min.	8-3-82	St.L. 1	at Min. 8	Mike Liut	67	68	55	76	21.7
Rick Vaive	Tor.	24-3-82	St.L. 3	at Tor. 4	Mike Liut	72	75	54	77	22.10
Rick Middleton	Bos.	28-3-82	Bos. 5	at Buf. 9	Paul Harrison	72	77	51	75	
Blaine Stoughton	Hfd.	28-3-82	Min. 5	at Hfd. 2	Gilles Meloche	76	76	52	80	29.1
Marcel Dionne	L.A.	30-3-82	Cgy. 7	at L.A. 5	Pat Riggin	75	77	50	78	
Mark Messier	Edm.	31-3-82	L.A. 3	at Edm. 7	Mario Lessard	78	79	50	78	21.3
Bryan Trottier	NYI	3-4-82	Phi. 3	at NYI 6	Pete Peeters	79	79	50	80	25.9
Lanny McDonald	Cgy.	18-2-83	Cgy. 1	at Buf. 5	Bob Sauve	60	60	66	80	30.0
Wayne Gretzky	Edm.	19-2-83	Edm. 10	at Pit. 7	Nick Ricci	60	60	71	80	
Michel Goulet	Que.	5-3-83	Que. 7	at Hfd. 3	Mike Veisor	67	67	57	80	22.11
Mike Bossy	NYI	12-3-83	Wash. 2	at NYI 6	Al Jensen	70	71	60	79	
Marcel Dionne	L.A.	17-3-83	Que. 3	at L.A. 4	Daniel Bouchard	71	71	56	80	
Al Secord	Chi.	20-3-83	Tor. 3	at Chi. 7	Mike Palmateer	73	73	54	80	25.0
Rick Vaive	Tor.	30-3-83	Tor. 4	at Det. 2	Gilles Gilbert	76	78	51	78	
Wayne Gretzky	Edm.	7-1-84	Hfd. 3	at Edm. 5	Greg Millen	42	42	87	74	
Michel Goulet	Que.	8-3-84	Que. 8	at Pit. 6	Denis Herron	63	69	56	75	
Rick Vaive	Tor.	14-3-84	Min. 3	at Tor. 3	Gilles Meloche	69	72	52	76	
Mike Bullard	Pit.	14-3-84	Pit. 6	at L.A. 7	Markus Mattsson	71	72	51	76	23.0
Jari Kurri	Edm.	15-3-84	Edm. 2	at Mtl. 3	Rick Wamsley	57	73	52	64	23.10
Glenn Anderson	Edm.	21-3-84	Hfd. 3	at Edm. 5	Greg Millen	76	76	54	80	23.6
Tim Kerr	Phi.	22-3-84	Pit. 4	at Phi. 13	Denis Herron	74	75	54	79	24.3
Mike Bossy	NYI	31-3-84	NYI 3	at Wash. 1	Pat Riggin	67	79	51	67	
Wayne Gretzky	Edm.	26-1-85	Pit. 3	at Edm. 6	Denis Herron	49	49	73	80	
Jari Kurri	Edm.	3-2-85	Hfd. 3	at Edm. 6	Greg Millen	50	53	71	73	
Mike Bossy	NYI	5-3-85	Phi. 5	at NYI 4	Bob Froese	61	65	58	76	
Tim Kerr	Phi.	7-3-85	Wash. 6	at Phi. 9	Pat Riggin	63	65	54	74	
John Ogrodnik	Det.	13-3-85	Det. 6	at Edm. 7	Grant Fuhr	69	69	55	79	25.9
Bob Carpenter	Wash.	21-3-85	Wash. 2	at Mtl. 3	Steve Penney	72	72	53	80	21.9
Michel Goulet	Que.	26-3-85	Buf. 3	at Que. 4	Tom Barrasso	62	73	55	69	
Dale Hawerchuk	Wpg.	29-4-85	Chi. 5	at Wpg. 5	W. Skorodenski	77	77	53	80	
Mike Gartner	Wash.	7-4-85	Pit. 3	at Wash. 7	Brian Ford	80	80	50	80	25.5
Jari Kurri	Edm.	4-3-86	Edm. 6	at Van. 2	Richard Brodeur	63	65	68	78	
Mike Bossy	NYI	11-3-86	Cgy. 4	at NYI 8	Rejean Lemelin	67	67	61	80	
Glenn Anderson	Edm.	14-3-86	Det. 3	at Edm. 12	Greg Stefan	63	71	54	72	
Michel Goulet	Que.	17-3-86	Que. 8	at Mtl. 6	Patrick Roy	67	72	53	75	
Wayne Gretzky	Edm.	18-3-86	Wpg. 2	at Edm. 6	Brian Hayward	72	72	52	80	
Tim Kerr	Phi.	20-3-86	Pit. 1	at Phi. 5	Roberto Romano	68	72	58	76	

Fifty-goal men: top, Al Secord of Chicago; above, Lanny McDonald of Calgary here checking Tom Lysiak; left, Dale Hawerchuck of Winnipeg.

100-Point Seasons

Player	Team	Date of 100th Point	G or A	Score		Player's Game No.	Team Game No.	Points G - A — PTS	Total Games	Age when first 100th point scored (Yrs. & Mos.)
Phil Esposito	Bos.	2-3-69	(G)	Pit. 0	at Bos. 4	60	62	49-77 — 126	74	27.1
Bobby Hull	Chi.	20-3-69	(G)	Chi. 5	at Bos. 5	71	71	58-49 — 107	76	30.2
Gordie Howe	Det.	30-3-69	(G)	Det. 5	at Chi. 9	76	76	44-59 — 103	76	41.0
Bobby Orr	Bos.	15-3-70	(G)	Det. 5	at Bos. 5	67	67	33-87 — 120	76	22.11
Phil Esposito	Bos.	6-2-71	(A)	Buf. 3	at Bos. 4	51	51	76-76 — 152	78	
Bobby Orr	Bos.	22-2-71	(A)	Bos. 4	at L.A. 5	58	58	37-102 — 139	78	
John Bucyk	Bos.	13-3-71	(G)	Bos. 6	at Van. 3	68	68	51-65 — 116	78	35.10
Ken Hodge	Bos.	21-3-71	(A)	Buf. 7	at Bos. 5	72	72	43-62 — 105	78	26.9
Jean Ratelle	NYR	18-2-72	(A)	NYR 2	at Cal. 2	58	58	46-63 — 109	63	31.4
Phil Esposito	Bos.	19-2-72	(A)	Bos. 6	at Min. 4	59	59	66-67 — 133	76	
Bobby Orr	Bos.	2-3-72	(A)	Van. 3	at Bos. 7	64	64	37-80 — 117	76	
Vic Hadfield	NYR	25-3-72	(A)	NYR 3	at Mtl. 3	74	74	50-56 — 106	78	31.5
Phil Esposito	Bos.	3-3-73	(A)	Bos. 1	at Mtl. 5	64	64	55-75 — 130	78	
Bobby Clarke	Phi.	29-3-73	(G)	Atl. 2	at Phi. 4	76	76	37-67 — 104	78	23.7
Bobby Orr	Bos.	31-3-73	(G)	Bos. 3	at Tor. 7	62	77	29-72 — 101	63	
Rick MacLeish	Phi.	1-4-73	(G)	Phi. 4	at Pit. 5	78	78	50-50 — 100	78	23.3
Phil Esposito	Bos.	13-2-74	(A)	Bos. 9	at Cal. 6	53	53	68-77 — 145	78	
Bobby Orr	Bos.	12-3-74	(A)	Buf. 0	at Bos. 4	62	66	32-90 — 122	74	
Ken Hodge	Bos.	24-3-74	(A)	Mtl. 3	at Bos. 6	72	72	50-55 — 105	76	
Phil Esposito	Bos.	8-2-75	(A)	Bos. 8	at Det. 5	54	54	61-66 — 127	79	
Bobby Orr	Bos.	13-2-75	(A)	Bos. 1	at Buf. 3	57	57	46-89 — 135	80	
Guy Lafleur	Mtl.	7-3-75	(G)	Wash. 4	at Mtl. 8	56	66	53-66 — 119	70	24.6
Pete Mahovlich	Mtl.	9-3-75	(G)	Mtl. 5	at NYR 3	67	67	35-82 — 117	80	29.5
Marcel Dionne	Det.	9-3-75	(A)	Det. 5	at Phi. 8	67	67	47-74 — 121	80	23.7
Bobby Clarke	Phi.	22-3-75	(A)	Min. 0	at Phi. 8	72	72	27-89 — 116	80	
René Robert	Buf.	5-4-75	(A)	Buf. 4	at Tor. 2	74	80	40-60 — 100	74	26.4
Guy Lafleur	Mtl.	10-3-76	(G)	Mtl. 5	at Chi. 1	69	69	56-69 — 125	80	
Bobby Clarke	Phi.	11-3-76	(A)	Buf. 1	at Phi. 6	64	68	30-89 — 119	76	
Bill Barber	Phi.	18-3-76	(A)	Van. 2	at Phi. 3	71	71	50-62 — 112	80	23.8
Gilbert Perreault	Buf.	21-3-76	(G)	K.C. 1	at Buf. 3	73	73	44-69 — 113	76	25.4
Pierre Larouche	Pit.	24-3-76	(G)	Bos. 5	at Pit. 5	70	74	53-58 — 111	76	20.4
Pete Mahovlich	Mtl.	28-3-76	(A)	Mtl. 2	at Bos. 2	77	77	34-71 — 105	80	
Jean Ratelle	Bos.	30-3-76	(G)	Buf. 4	at Bos. 4	77	77	36-69 — 105	80	
Jean Pronovost	Pit.	3-4-76	(A)	Wash. 5	at Pit. 4	79	79	52-52 — 104	80	30.4
Darryl Sittler	Tor.	3-4-76	(A)	Bos. 4	at Tor. 2	78	79	41-59 — 100	79	26.7
Guy Lafleur	Mtl.	26-2-77	(A)	Clev. 3	at Mtl. 5	63	63	56-80 — 136	80	
Marcel Dionne	L.A.	5-3-77	(G)	Pit. 3	at L.A. 3	67	67	53-69 — 122	80	
Steve Shutt	Mtl.	27-3-77	(A)	Mtl. 6	at Det. 0	77	77	60-45 — 105	80	24.9
Bryan Trottier	NYI	25-2-78	(A)	Chi. 1	at NYI 7	59	60	46-77 — 123	77	21.7
Guy Lafleur	Mtl.	28-2-78	(A)	Det. 3	at Mtl. 9	59	61	60-72 — 132	78	
Darryl Sittler	Tor.	12-3-78	(A)	Tor. 7	at Pit. 1	67	67	45-72 — 117	80	
Guy Lafleur	Mtl.	27-2-79	(A)	Mtl. 3	at NYI 7	61	61	52-77 — 129	80	
Bryan Trottier	NYI	6-3-79	(A)	Buf. 3	at NYI 2	59	63	47-87 — 134	76	
Marcel Dionne	L.A.	8-3-79	(G)	L.A. 4	at Buf. 6	66	66	59-71 — 130	80	
Mike Bossy	NYI	11-3-79	(G)	NYI 4	at Bos. 4	66	66	69-57 — 126	80	22.2
Bob MacMillan	Atl.	15-3-79	(A)	Atl. 4	at Phi. 5	68	69	37-71 — 108	79	26.6
Guy Chouinard	Atl.	30-3-79	(G)	L.A. 3	at Atl. 5	75	75	50-57 — 107	80	22.5
Denis Potvin	NYI	8-4-79	(A)	NYI 5	at NYR 2	73	80	31-70 — 101	73	25.5
Marcel Dionne	L.A.	6-2-80	(A)	L.A. 3	at Hfd. 7	53	53	53-84 — 137	80	
Guy Lafleur	Mtl.	10-2-80	(A)	Mtl. 3	at Bos. 2	55	55	50-75 — 125	74	
Wayne Gretzky	Edm.	24-2-80	(A)	Bos. 4	at Edm. 2	61	62	51-86 — 137	79	19.2
Bryan Trottier	NYI	30-3-80	(A)	NYI 9	at Que. 6	75	77	42-62 — 104	78	
Gilbert Perreault	Buf.	1-4-80	(A)	Buf. 5	at Atl. 2	77	77	40-66 — 106	80	
Mike Rogers	Hfd.	4-4-80	(A)	Que. 2	at Hfd. 9	79	79	44-61 — 105	80	25.5
Charlie Simmer	L.A.	5-4-80	(G)	Van. 5	at L.A. 3	64	80	56-45 — 101	64	26.0
Blaine Stoughton	Hfd.	6-4-80	(A)	Det. 3	at Hfd. 5	80	80	56-44 — 100	80	27.0
Wayne Gretzky	Edm.	6-2-81	(G)	Wpg. 4	at Edm. 10	53	53	55-109 — 164	80	
Marcel Dionne	L.A.	12-2-81	(A)	L.A. 5	at Chi. 5	58	58	58-77 — 135	80	
Charlie Simmer	L.A.	14-2-81	(A)	Bos. 5	at L.A. 4	59	59	56-49 — 105	65	
Kent Nilsson	Cgy.	27-2-81	(G)	Hfd. 1	at Cgy. 5	64	64	49-82 — 131	80	24.6
Mike Bossy	NYI	3-3-81	(G)	Edm. 8	at NYI 8	65	66	68-51 — 119	79	
Dave Taylor	L.A.	14-3-81	(G)	Min. 4	at L.A. 10	63	70	47-65 — 112	72	25.3
Mike Rogers	Hfd.	22-3-81	(G)	Tor. 3	at Hfd. 3	74	74	40-65 — 105	80	
Bernie Federko	St.L.	28-3-81	(A)	Buf. 4	at St.L. 7	74	76	31-73 — 104	78	24.10
Rick Middleton	Bos.	28-3-81	(A)	Chi. 2	at Bos. 5	76	76	44-59 — 103	80	27.4
Jacques Richard	Que.	29-3-81	(G)	Mtl. 0	at Que. 4	75	76	52-51 — 103	78	28.6
Bryan Trottier	NYI	29-3-81	(G)	NYI 5	at Wash. 4	69	76	31-72 — 103	73	
Peter Stastny	Que.	29-3-81	(A)	Mtl. 0	at Que. 4	73	76	39-70 — 109	77	24.6
Wayne Gretzky	Edm.	27-12-81	(G)	L.A. 3	at Edm. 10	38	38	92-120 — 212	80	
Mike Bossy	NYI	13-2-82	(A)	Phi. 2	at NYI 8	55	55	64-83 — 147	80	
Peter Stastny	Que.	16-2-82	(A)	Wpg. 3	at Que. 7	60	60	46-93 — 139	80	25.5
Dennis Maruk	Wash.	20-2-82	(A)	Wash. 3	at Min. 7	60	60	60-76 — 136	80	26.3
Bryan Trottier	NYI	23-2-82	(G)	Chi. 1	at NYI 5	61	61	50-79 — 129	80	
Denis Savard	Chi.	27-2-82	(A)	Chi. 5	at L.A. 3	64	64	32-87 — 119	80	21.1
Bobby Smith	Min.	3-3-82	(A)	Det. 4	at Min. 6	66	66	43-71 — 114	80	24.1
Marcel Dionne	L.A.	6-3-82	(G)	L.A. 6	at Hfd. 7	64	66	50-67 — 117	78	
Dave Taylor	L.A.	20-3-82	(A)	Pit. 5	at L.A. 7	71	72	39-67 — 106	78	
Dale Hawerchuk	Wpg.	24-3-82	(G)	L.A. 3	at Wpg. 5	74	74	45-58 — 103	80	19.0
Dino Ciccarelli	Min.	27-3-82	(A)	Min. 6	at Bos. 5	72	76	55-52 — 107	76	21.8
Glenn Anderson	Edm.	28-3-82	(G)	Edm. 6	at L.A. 2	78	78	38-67 — 105	80	21.7
Mike Rogers	NYR	2-4-82	(G)	Pit. 7	at NYR 5	79	79	38-65 — 103	80	

Top: Gil Perreault surpassed 100 points in 1976 and 1980; Peter Stastny, above, has done so every season since 1980-81.

Mike Bossy's goals and assists totals have each been greater than fifty in seven of his nine NHL seasons.

100-Point Seasons continued

Player	Team	Date of 100th Point	G or A		Score		Player's Game No.	Team Game No.	Points G - A	PTS	Total Games	Age when first 100th point scored (Yrs. & Mos.)
Wayne Gretzky	Edm.	5-1-83	(A)	Edm. 8	at	Wpg. 3	42	42	71-125 -	196	80	
Mike Bossy	NYI	3-3-83	(A)	Tor. 1	at	NYI. 5	66	67	60-58 —	118	79	
Peter Stastny	Que.	5-3-83	(A)	Hfd. 3	at	Que. 10	62	67	47-77 —	124	75	
Denis Savard	Chi.	6-3-83	(G)	Mtl. 4	at	Chi. 5	65	67	35-86 —	121	78	
Mark Messier	Edm.	23-3-83	(A)	Edm. 4	at	Wpg. 7	73	76	48-58 —	106	77	22.2
Barry Pederson	Bos.	26-3-83	(A)	Hfd. 4	at	Bos. 7	73	76	46-61 —	107	77	22.0
Marcel Dionne	L.A.	26-3-83	(A)	Edm. 9	at	L.A. 3	75	75	56-51 —	107	80	
Michel Goulet	Que.	27-3-83	(A)	Que. 6	at	Buf. 6	77	77	57-48 —	105	80	22.11
Glenn Anderson	Edm.	29-3-83	(A)	Edm. 7	at	Van. 4	70	78	48-56 —	104	72	
Jari Kurri	Edm.	29-3-83	(A)	Edm. 7	at	Van. 4	78	78	45-59 —	104	80	22.10
Kent Nilsson	Cgy.	29-3-83	(G)	L.A. 3	at	Cgy. 5	78	78	46-58 —	104	80	
Wayne Gretzky	Edm.	18-12-83	(G)	Edm. 7	at	Wpg. 5	34	34	87-118 —	205	74	
Paul Coffey	Edm.	4-3-84	(A)	Mtl. 1	at	Edm. 6	68	68	40-86 —	126	80	22.9
Michel Goulet	Que.	4-3-84	(A)	Que. 1	at	Buf. 1	62	67	56-65 —	121	75	
Jari Kurri	Edm.	7-3-84	(G)	Chi. 4	at	Edm. 7	53	69	52-61 —	113	64	
Peter Stastny	Que.	8-3-84	(A)	Que. 8	at	Pit. 6	69	69	46-73 —	119	80	
Mike Bossy	NYI	8-3-84	(G)	Tor. 5	at	NYI 9	56	68	51-67 —	118	67	
Barry Pederson	Bos.	14-3-84	(A)	Bos. 4	at	Det. 2	71	71	39-77 —	116	80	
Bryan Trottier	NYI	18-3-84	(A)	NYI 4	at	Hfd. 5	62	73	40-71 —	111	68	
Bernie Federko	St.L.	20-3-84	(A)	Wpg. 3	at	St.L. 9	75	76	41-66 —	107	79	
Rick Middleton	Bos.	27-3-84	(G)	Bos. 6	at	Que. 4	77	77	47-58 —	105	80	
Dale Hawerchuk	Wpg.	27-3-84	(A)	Wpg. 3	at	L.A. 3	77	77	37-65 —	102	80	
Mark Messier	Edm.	27-3-84	(G)	Edm. 9	at	Cgy. 2	72	79	37-64 —	101	73	
Wayne Gretzky	Edm.	29-12-84	(A)	Det. 3	at	Edm. 6	35	35	73-135 —	208	80	
Jari Kurri	Edm.	29-1-85	(G)	Edm. 4	at	Cgy. 2	48	51	71-64 —	135	73	
Mike Bossy	NYI	23-2-85	(G)	Bos. 1	at	NYI 7	56	60	58-59 —	117	76	
Dale Hawerchuk	Wpg.	25-2-85	(A)	Wpg. 12	at	NYR 5	64	64	53-77 —	130	80	
Marcel Dionne	L.A.	5-3-85	(A)	Pit. 0	at	L.A. 6	66	66	46-80 —	126	80	
Brent Sutter	NYI	12-3-85	(A)	NYI 6	at	St. L. 5	68	68	42-60 —	102	72	22.10
John Ogrodnik	Det.	22-3-85	(A)	NYR 3	at	Det. 5	73	73	55-50 —	105	79	25.9
Paul Coffey	Edm.	26-3-85	(G)	Edm. 7	at	NYI 5	74	74	37-84 —	121	80	
Denis Savard	Chi.	29-3-85	(A)	Chi. 5	at	Wpg. 5	75	76	38-67 —	105	79	
Peter Stastny	Que.	2-4-85	(A)	Que. 6	at	Que. 6	74	77	32-68 —	100	75	
Bernie Federko	St.L.	4-4-85	(A)	NYR 5	at	St.L. 4	74	78	30-73 —	103	76	
John Tonelli	NYI	6-4-85	(G)	NJ 5	at	NYI 5	80	80	42-58 —	100	80	28.1
Paul MacLean	Wpg.	6-4-85	(A)	Wpg. 6	at	Edm. 5	78	79	41-60 —	101	79	27.1
Mike Gartner	Wash.	7-4-85	(G)	Pit. 3	at	Wash. 7	80	80	50-52 —	102	80	25.6
Bernie Nicholls	L.A.	6-4-85	(A)	Van. 4	at	L.A. 4	80	80	46-54 —	100	80	22.9
Mario Lemieux	Pit.	7-4-85	(G)	Pit. 3	at	Wash. 7	73	80	43-57 —	100	73	19.6
Wayne Gretzky	Edm.	4-1-86	(A)	Hfd. 3	at	Edm. 4	39	39	52-163 —	215	80	
Mario Lemieux	Pit.	15-2-86	(A)	Van. 4	at	Pit. 9	55	56	48-93 —	141	79	
Paul Coffey	Edm.	19-2-86	(A)	Tor. 5	at	Edm. 9	59	60	48-90 —	138	79	
Jari Kurri	Edm.	2-3-86	(G)	Phi. 1	at	Edm. 2	62	64	68-63 —	131	78	
Peter Stastny	Que.	1-3-86	(A)	Buf. 8	at	Que. 4	66	68	41-81 —	122	80	
Mike Bossy	NYI	8-3-86	(G)	Wash. 6	at	NYI 2	65	65	61-62 —	123	80	
Denis Savard	Chi.	12-3-86	(A)	Buf. 7	at	Chi. 6	69	69	47-69 —	116	80	
Mats Naslund	Mtl.	13-3-86	(A)	Mtl. 2	at	Bos. 3	70	70	43-67 —	110	80	26.4
Michel Goulet	Que.	24-3-86	(A)	Que. 1	at	Minn. 0	70	75	53-50 —	103	75	
Glenn Anderson	Edm.	25-3-86	(A)	Edm. 7	at	Det. 2	66	74	54-48 —	102	72	
Neal Broten	Min.	26-3-86	(A)	Min. 6	at	Tor. 1	76	76	29-76 —	105	80	26.4
Dale Hawerchuk	Wpg.	31-3-86	(A)	Wpg. 5	at	L.A. 2	78	78	46-59 —	105	80	
Bernie Federko	St.L.	5-4-8	(G)	Chi. 5	at	St.L. 7	79	79	34-68 —	102	80	

Coaching Records

Following is a list of NHL coaches with 600-or-more regular-season games and their coaching records:

Coach	Team	Seasons	Games	Wins	Losses	Ties	%
Dick Irvin	Chicago	1930-31; 1955-56	114	43	56	15	.443
	Toronto	1931-40	427	216	152	59	.575
	Montreal	1940-55	896	431	313	152	.566
	Total		**1,437**	**690**	**521**	**226**	**.559**
Scott Bowman	St. Louis	1967-71	238	110	83	45	.557
	Montreal	1971-79	634	419	110	105	.744
	Buffalo	1979-85	355	189	109	57	.613
	Total		**1,227**	**718**	**302**	**207**	**.670**
Billy Reay	Toronto	1957-59	90	26	50	14	.367
	Chicago	1963-77	1,012	516	335	161	.589
	Total		**1,102**	**542**	**385**	**175**	**.571**
Al Arbour	St. Louis	1970-73	107	42	40	25	.509
	NY Islanders	1973-86	1,039	552	317	169	.612
	Total		**1,146**	**594**	**357**	**194**	**.603**
Jack Adams	Detroit	1927-44	**964**	**413**	**390**	**161**	**.512**
Sid Abel	Chicago	1952-54	140	39	79	22	.357
	Detroit	1957-68; 1969-70	810	340	338	132	.501
	St. Louis	1971-72	10	3	6	1	.350
	Kansas City	1975-76	3	0	3	0	.000
	Total		**963**	**382**	**426**	**155**	**.477**
Punch Imlach	Toronto	1958-69; 1979-80; 1980-81	840	391	311	138	.548
	Buffalo	1970-72	119	32	62	25	.374
	Total		**959**	**423**	**373**	**163**	**.526**
Toe Blake	Montreal	1955-68	**914**	**500**	**255**	**159**	**.634**
Milt Schmidt	Boston	1954-61; 1962-66	726	245	360	121	.421
	Washington	1974-76	43	5	33	5	.174
	Total		**769**	**250**	**393**	**126**	**.407**
Emile Francis	NY Rangers	1965-75	654	347	209	98	.606
	St. Louis	1976-77, 81-83	124	46	64	14	.427
	Total		**778**	**393**	**273**	**112**	**.577**
Red Kelly	Los Angeles	1967-69	150	55	75	20	.433
	Pittsburgh	1969-73	274	90	132	52	.423
	Toronto	1973-77	318	133	123	62	.516
	Total		**742**	**278**	**330**	**134**	**465**
Fred Shero	Philadelphia	1971-78	554	308	151	95	.642
	NY Rangers	1978-81	180	82	74	24	.522
	Total		**734**	**390**	**225**	**119**	**.612**
Art Ross	Boston	1924-45	**728**	**361**	**277**	**90**	**.558**
Bob Pulford	Los Angeles	1972-77	396	178	150	68	.535
	Chicago	1977-79; 1981-82; 1984-86	295	129	118	48	.518
	Total		**691**	**307**	**268**	**116**	**.528**
Bob Berry	Los Angeles	1978-81	240	107	94	39	.527
	Montreal	1981-84	223	116	71	36	.601
	Pittsburgh	1984-86	160	58	89	13	.403
	Total		**623**	**281**	**254**	**88**	**.521**
Tommy Ivan	Detroit	1947-54	470	262	118	90	.653
	Chicago	1956-58	140	40	78	22	.364
	Total		**610**	**302**	**196**	**112**	**.587**
Lester Patrick	NY Rangers	1926-39	**604**	**281**	**216**	**107**	**.554**

Goaltending Records

All-Time Shutout Leaders

Goaltender	Team	Seasons	Games	Shutouts
Terry Sawchuk (1949-1970)	Detroit	14	734	85
	Boston	2	102	11
	Toronto	3	91	4
	Los Angeles	1	36	2
	NY Rangers	1	8	1
	Total	21	971	**103**
George Hainsworth (1926-1937)	Montreal	7½	317	75
	Toronto	3½	145	19
	Total	11	464	**94**
Glenn Hall (1952-1971)	Detroit	4	148	17
	Chicago	10	618	51
	St. Louis	4	140	16
	Total	18	906	**84**
Jacques Plante (1952-1973)	Montreal	11	556	58
	NY Rangers	2	98	5
	St. Louis	2	69	10
	Toronto	2½	106	7
	Boston	½	8	2
	Total	18	837	**82**
Tiny Thompson (1928-1940)	Boston	10⅓	467	74
	Detroit	1⅔	85	7
	Total	12	552	**81**
Alex Connell (1925-1937)	Ottawa	8	292	63
	Detroit	1	48	6
	NY Americans	1	1	0
	Mtl. Maroons	2	75	11
	Total	12	416	**80**
Tony Esposito (1968-1984)	Montreal	1	13	2
	Chicago	15	873	74
	Total	16	886	**76**
Lorne Chabot (1926-1937)	NY Rangers	2	80	21
	Toronto	5	215	33
	Montreal	1	47	8
	Chicago	1	48	8
	Mtl. Maroons	1	16	2
	NY Americans	1	6	1
	Total	11	412	**73**
Harry Lumley (1943-1960)	Detroit	7	324	26
	Chicago	2	134	5
	Toronto	4	267	34
	Boston	3	78	6
	Total	16	803	**71**
Roy Worters (1925-1937)	Pittsburgh Pirates	3	123	22
	NY Americans	9	364	44
	*Montreal		1	0
	Total	12	488	**66**
Turk Broda (1936-1952)	Toronto	12	628	**62**
Clint Benedict (1917-1926)	Ottawa	7	158	19
	Mtl. Maroons	6	202	39
	Total	13	360	**58**
John Roach (1921-1935)	Toronto	7	223	13
	NY Rangers	4	89	30
	Detroit	3	180	15
	Total	14	492	**58**
Bernie Parent (1965-1979)	Boston	2	57	1
	Philadelphia	9½	486	50
	Toronto	1½	65	4
	Total	13	608	**55**
Ed Giacomin (1965-1978)	NY Rangers	10	539	49
	Detroit	3	71	5
	Total	13	610	**54**
David Kerr (1930-1941)	Mtl. Maroons	3	102	11
	NY Americans	1	1	0
	NY Rangers	7	324	40
	Total	11	427	**51**
Rogie Vachon (1966-1982)	Montreal	5½	206	13
	Los Angeles	6⅔	389	32
	Detroit	2	109	4
	Boston	2	91	2
	Total	16	795	**51**
Ken Dryden (1970-1979)	Montreal	8	397	**46**
Gump Worsley (1952-1974)	NY Rangers	10	582	24
	Montreal	6½	171	16
	Minnesota	4½	107	3
	Total	21	860	**43**
Chuck Gardiner (1927-1934)	Chicago	7	316	**42**
Frank Brimsek (1938-1950)	Boston	9	445	35
	Chicago	1	70	5
	Total	10	515	**40**
Johnny Bower (1953-1970)	NY Rangers	3	77	5
	Toronto	12	475	32
	Total	15	552	**37**
Bill Durnan (1943-1950)	Montreal	7	383	**34**
Eddie Johnston (1962-1978)	Boston	11	444	27
	Toronto	1	26	1
	St. Louis	3⅔	118	4
	Chicago	⅓	4	0
	Total	16	502	**32**
Roger Crozier (1963-1977)	Detroit	7	313	20
	Buffalo	6	202	10
	Washington	1	3	0
	Total	14	518	**30**
Cesare Maniago (1960-1978)	Toronto	⅓	7	0
	Montreal	⅓	14	0
	NY Rangers	2	34	2
	Minnesota	9	420	26
	Vancouver	2	93	2
	Total	14	568	**30**

*Played 1 game for Canadiens in 1929-30.

Ten or More Shutouts, One Season

Number of Shutouts	Goaltender	Team	Season	Length of Schedule
22	George Hainsworth	Montreal	1928-29	44
15	Alex Connell	Ottawa	1925-26	36
	Alex Connell	Ottawa	1927-28	44
	Hal Winkler	Boston	1927-28	44
	Tony Esposito	Chicago	1969-70	76
14	George Hainsworth	Montreal	1926-27	44
13	Clint Benedict	Mtl. Maroons	1926-27	44
	George Hainsworth	Montreal	1927-28	44
	Roy Worters	NY Americans	1927-28	44
	John Roach	NY Rangers	1928-29	44
	Roy Worters	NY Americans	1928-29	44
12	Alex Connell	Ottawa	1926-27	44
	Tiny Thompson	Boston	1928-29	44
	Lorne Chabot	Toronto	1928-29	44
	Chuck Gardiner	Chicago	1930-31	44
	Terry Sawchuk	Detroit	1951-52	70
	Terry Sawchuk	Detroit	1953-54	70
	Terry Sawchuk	Detroit	1954-55	70
	Glenn Hall	Detroit	1955-56	70
	Bernie Parent	Philadelphia	1973-74	78
	Bernie Parent	Philadelphia	1974-75	80
11	Lorne Chabot	NY Rangers	1927-28	44
	Harry Holmes	Detroit	1927-28	44
	Clint Benedict	Mtl. Maroons	1928-29	44
	Joe Miller	Pittsburgh Pirates	1928-29	44
	Tiny Thompson	Boston	1932-33	48
	Terry Sawchuk	Detroit	1950-51	70
10	Lorne Chabot	NY Rangers	1926-27	44
	Roy Worters	Pittsburgh Pirates	1927-28	44
	Clarence Dolson	Detroit	1928-29	44
	John Roach	Detroit	1932-33	48
	Chuck Gardiner	Chicago	1933-34	48
	Tiny Thompson	Boston	1935-36	48
	Frank Brimsek	Boston	1938-39	48
	Bill Durnan	Montreal	1948-49	60
	Gerry McNeil	Montreal	1952-53	70
	Harry Lumley	Toronto	1952-53	70
	Tony Esposito	Chicago	1973-74	78
	Ken Dryden	Montreal	1976-77	80

Jacques Plante hadn't adopted his famous mask in this 1957 photo. His goals-against-average in 112 playoff games is 2.16.

Goals Against Average Leaders

Season	Goaltender and Club	GP	MINS.	GA	SO	AVG.	Team GP	Totals GA
1985-86	Bob Froese, Philadelphia	51	2728	116	5	2.55	80	241
	Darren Jensen, Philadelphia	29	1436	88	2	3.68		
1984-85	Tom Barrasso, Buffalo	54	3248	144	5	2.66	80	237
	Bob Sauve, Buffalo	27	1564	84	0	3.22		
1983-84	Pat Riggin, Washington	41	2299	102	4	2.66	80	226
	Al Jensen, Washington	43	2414	117	4	2.91		
1982-83	Roland Melanson, NY Islanders	44	2460	109	1	2.66	80	231
	Billy Smith, NY Islanders	41	2340	112	1	2.87		
1981-82	Denis Herron, Montreal	27	1547	68	3	2.64	80	223
	Rick Wamsley, Montreal	38	2206	101	2	2.75		
1980-81	Richard Sevigny, Montreal	33	1777	71	2	2.40	80	232
	Michel Larocque, Montreal	28	1623	82	1	3.03		
	Denis Herron, Montreal	25	1147	67	1	3.50		
1979-80	Bob Sauvé, Buffalo	32	1880	74	4	2.36		201
	Don Edwards, Buffalo	49	2920	125	2	2.57		
1978-79	Ken Dryden, Montreal	47	2814	108	5	2.30	80	204
	Michel Larocque, Montreal	34	1986	94	3	2.84		
1977-78	Ken Dryden, Montreal	52	3071	105	5	2.05	80	183
	Michel Larocque, Montreal	30	1729	77	1	2.67		
1976-77	Michel Larocque, Montreal	26	1525	53	4	2.09	80	171
	Ken Dryden, Montreal	56	3275	117	10	2.14		
1975-76	Ken Dryden, Montreal	62	3580	121	8	2.03	80	174
1974-75	Bernie Parent, Philadelphia	68	4041	137	12	2.03	80	181
1973-74	Bernie Parent, Philadelphia	73	4314	136	12	1.89	78	164
	Tony Esposito, Chicago	70	4143	141	10	2.04	78	164
1972-73	Ken Dryden, Montreal	54	3165	119	6	2.26	78	184
1971-72	Tony Esposito, Chicago	48	2780	82	9	1.76	78	166
	Gary Smith, Chicago	28	1540	62	5	2.41		
1970-71	Ed Giacomin, NY Rangers	45	2641	95	8	2.15	78	177
	Gilles Villemure, NY Rangers	34	2039	78	4	2.29		
1969-70	Tony Esposito, Chicago	63	3763	136	15	2.17	76	170
1968-69	Jacques Plante, St. Louis	37	2139	70	5	1.96	76	157
	Glenn Hall, St. Louis	41	2354	85	8	2.17		
1967-68	Lorne Worsley, Montreal	40	2213	73	6	1.98	74	167
	Rogatien Vachon, Montreal	39	2227	92	4	2.48		
1966-67	Glenn Hall, Chicago	32	1664	66	2	2.38	70	170
	Denis DeJordy, Chicago	44	2536	104	4	2.46		
1965-66	Lorne Worsley, Montreal	51	2899	114	2	2.36	70	173
	Charlie Hodge, Montreal	26	1301	56	1	2.58		
1964-65	Johnny Bower, Toronto	34	2040	81	3	2.38	70	173
	Terry Sawchuk, Toronto	36	2160	92	1	2.56		
1963-64	Charlie Hodge, Montreal	62	3720	140	8	2.26	70	167
1962-63	Glenn Hall, Chicago	66	3910	166	5	2.51	70	178
1961-62	Jacques Plante, Montreal	70	4200	166	4	2.37	70	166
1960-61	Johnny Bower, Toronto	58	3480	145	2	2.50	70	176
1959-60	Jacques Plante, Montreal	69	4140	175	3	2.54	70	178
1958-59	Jacques Plante, Montreal	67	4000	144	9	2.18	70	158
1957-58	Jacques Plante, Montreal	57	3446	119	9	2.11	70	158
1956-57	Jacques Plante, Montreal	61	3660	123	9	2.02	70	155
1955-56	Jacques Plante, Montreal	64	3840	119	7	1.86	70	131
1954-55	Terry Sawchuk, Detroit	68	4080	132	12	1.94	70	134
1953-54	Harry Lumley, Toronto	69	4140	128	13	1.85	70	131
1952-53	Terry Sawchuk, Detroit	63	3780	120	9	1.90	70	133
1951-52	Terry Sawchuk, Detroit	70	4200	133	12	1.90	70	133
1950-51	Al Rollins, Toronto	40	2367	70	5	1.75	70	138
1949-50	Bill Durnan, Montreal	64	3840	141	8	2.20	70	150
1948-49	Bill Durnan, Montreal	60	3600	126	10	2.10	60	126
1947-48	Turk Broda, Toronto	60	3600	143	5	2.38	60	143
1946-47	Bill Durnan, Montreal	60	3600	138	4	2.30	60	138
1945-46	Bill Durnan, Montreal	40	2400	104	4	2.60	50	134
1944-45	Bill Durnan, Montreal	50	3000	121	1	2.42	50	121
1943-44	Bill Durnan, Montreal	50	3000	109	2	2.18	50	109
1942-43	Johnny Mowers, Detroit	50	3000	124	6	2.48	50	124
1941-42	Frank Brimsek, Boston	47	2820	115	3	2.44	48	118
1940-41	Turk Broda, Toronto	48	2880	99	5	2.06	48	99
1939-40	Dave Kerr, NY Rangers	48	2880	77	8	1.60	48	77
1938-39	Frank Brimsek, Boston	44	2640	70	10	1.59	48	76
1937-38	Tiny Thompson, Boston	48	2880	89	7	1.85	48	89
1936-37	Normie Smith, Detroit	48	2880	102	6	2.13	48	102
1935-36	Tiny Thompson, Boston	48	2880	83	10	1.73	48	83
1934-35	Lorne Chabot, Chicago	48	2880	88	8	1.83	48	88
1933-34	Chuck Gardiner, Chicago	48	2880	83	10	1.73	48	83
1932-33	Tiny Thompson, Boston	48	2880	88	11	1.83	48	88
1931-32	Chuck Gardiner, Chicago	48	2880	101	4	2.10	48	101
1930-31	Roy Worters, NY Americans	44	2640	74	8	1.68	44	74
1929-30	Tiny Thompson, Boston	44	2640	98	3	2.23	44	98
1928-29	George Hainsworth, Montreal	44	2640	43	22	0.98	44	43
1927-28	George Hainsworth, Montreal	44	2640	48	13	1.09	44	48
1926-27	George Hainsworth, Montreal	44	2640	67	14	1.52	44	67

* Goaltender(s) with lowest goals-against average awarded Vezina Trophy up to and including 1980-81 season. Beginning with 1982-83 season, William Jennings Trophy awarded.

Individual Awards

Hart Memorial Trophy

Art Ross Trophy

Calder Memorial Trophy

James Norris Memorial Trophy

HART MEMORIAL TROPHY

An annual award "to the player adjudged to be the most valuable to his team". Winner selected in poll by Professional Hockey Writers' Association in the 21 NHL cities at the end of the regular schedule. The winner receives $1,500 and the runner-up $750.

History: The Hart Memorial Trophy was presented by the National Hockey League in 1960 after the original Hart Trophy was retired to the Hockey Hall of Fame. The original Hart Trophy was donated to the NHL in 1923 by Dr. David A. Hart, father of Cecil Hart, former manager-coach of the Montreal Canadiens.

1985-86 Winner: Wayne Gretzky, Edmonton Oilers
Runners-up: Mario Lemieux, Pittsburgh Penguins
Mark Howe, Philadelphia Flyers

Gretzky extended his domination of the Hart Trophy to a record seventh straight season. The Oilers' center has won the award in each of his seven NHL seasons and is one short of the record for winning the same award the most times. Bobby Orr holds the distinction with eight consecutive Norris trophies from 1967-68 through 1974-75.

Gretzky polled 281 of a possible 300 points in the voting, while the Penguins' Mario Lemieux placed second with 163 points and the Flyers' Mark Howe was third with 32 points. Gretzky received 54 of a possible 60 first-place votes, while Lemieux (4), Paul Coffey (1) and John Vanbiesbrouck (1) received the remaining first-place votes.

Gretzky scored 52 goals, a record 163 assists for a record-breaking 215 points in 1985-86.

ART ROSS TROPHY

An annual award "to the player who leads the league in scoring points at the end of the regular season." Overall winner receives $1,000 and the overall runner-up $500. The leader at the end of first half of season and leader in second half each receive $500. The runners-up in each half each receive $250.

History: Arthur Howie Ross, former manager-coach of Boston Bruins, presented the trophy to the National Hockey League in 1947. If two players finish the schedule with the same number of points, the trophy is awarded in the following manner: 1. Player with most goals. 2. Player with fewer games played. 3. Player scoring first goal of the season.

1985-86 Winner: Wayne Gretzky, Edmonton Oilers
Runners-up: Mario Lemieux, Pittsburgh Penguins
Paul Coffey, Edmonton Oilers

Gretzky captured his record sixth consecutive Art Ross Trophy as the NHL's regular-season scoring champion after setting records for assists (163) and points (215). He also became the first player in NHL history to register a point on better than 50% of his team's goals — totalling 215 points on 426 Edmonton goals (50.5%).

Only Marcel Dionne of the Los Angeles Kings has kept Gretzky from winning the scoring crown in each of his seven NHL seasons. Dionne and Gretzky tied for the League-lead in points in 1979-80 (137), but Dionne was awarded the title based on two more goals (53 to 51).

The Penguins' Mario Lemieux finished second to Gretzky in points with 141 (48-93-141), while Coffey was third with 138 points (48-90-138).

CALDER MEMORIAL TROPHY

An annual award "to the player selected as the most proficient in his first year of competition in the National Hockey League". Winner selected in poll by Professional Hockey Writers' Association at the end of the regular schedule. The winner receives $1,500 and the runner-up $750.

History: From 1936-37 until his death in 1943, Frank Calder, NHL President, bought a trophy each year to be given permanently to the outstanding rookie. After Calder's death, the NHL presented the Calder Memorial Trophy in his memory and the trophy is to be kept in perpetuity. To be eligible for the award, a player cannot have played more than 25 games in any single preceding season nor in six or more games in each of any two preceding seasons in any major professional leagues.

1985-86 Winner: Gary Suter, Calgary Flames
Runners-up: Wendel Clark, Toronto Maple Leafs
Kjell Dahlin, Montreal Canadiens

Suter, a native of Madison, Wisconsin, becomes the sixth American-born player to capture the Calder Trophy in the 54-year history of the award. Other U.S.-born winners include: Tom Barrasso (Boston, MA) in 1983-84 with Buffalo; Frank Brimsek (Eveleth, MN) in 1938-39 with Boston; Cully Dahlstrom (Minneapolis, MN) in 1937-38 with Chicago; Mike Karakas (Aurora, MN) in 1935-36 with Chicago; and Carl Voss (Chelsea, MA) in 1932-33 with Detroit.

Suter, the first defenseman to win the Clader since Boston's Raymond Bourque in 1979-80, polled 230 of a possible 300 points, including 35 of 60 first-place votes, to outdistance Clark (165 points) and Dahlin (83 points).

JAMES NORRIS MEMORIAL TROPHY

An annual award "to the defense player who demonstrates throughout the season the greatest all-round ability in the position." Winner selected in poll by Professional Hockey Writers' Association at the end of the regular schedule. The winner receives $1,500 and the runner-up $750.

History: The James Norris Memorial Trophy was presented in 1953 by the four children of the late James Norris in memory of the former owner-president of the Detroit Red Wings.

1985-86 Winner: Paul Coffey, Edmonton Oilers
Runners-up: Mark Howe, Philadelphia Flyers
Larry Robinson, Montreal Canadiens

Coffey totalled 280 of a possible 300 points in the voting to capture his second consecutive Norris Trophy. Only six defensemen received votes for the award, fewest in the 33-year history of the Norris.

Coffey's 280 points in the balloting — 20 short of unanimous — was the closest a player has come to being a unanimous winner of the award since Bobby Orr captured 266 of a possible 270 points in 1974-75.

The Oilers' defenseman enjoyed another outstanding offensive season with a record 48 goals, 90 assists for 138 points. His goal total broke Orr's record of 46, while his point total was just one shy of Orr's record of 139, set in 1970-71.

Howe placed second in the voting with 172 points, while two-time Norris winner Larry Robinson was third with 43 points.

LADY BYNG MEMORIAL TROPHY

An annual award "to the player adjudged to have exhibited the best type of sportsmanship and gentlemanly conduct combined with a high standard of playing ability." Winner selected in poll by Professional Hockey Writers' Association at the end of the regular schedule. The winner receives $1,500 and the runner-up $750.

History: Lady Byng, wife of Canada's Governor-General at the time, presented the Lady Byng Trophy in 1925. After Frank Boucher of New York Rangers won the award seven times in eight seasons, he was given the trophy to keep and Lady Byng donated another trophy in 1936. After Lady Byng's death in 1949, the National Hockey League presented a new trophy, changing the name to Lady Byng Memorial Trophy.

1985-86 Winner: Mike Bossy, New York Islanders
Runners-up: Jari Kurri, Edmonton Oilers
Mats Naslund, Montreal Canadiens

Right winger Mike Bossy has won the Lady Byng Trophy for the third time in the last four seasons. In 1984-85, he finished fourth in the Lady Byng voting which was won by the Oilers' Jari Kurri.

In the 1985-86 balloting, Bossy totalled 217 points, including 33 of 60 first-place votes, to outdistance Kurri (100 points) and Naslund (99 points).

Bossy ranked fifth in League scoring with 123 points (61 goals, 62 assists) and accumulated only 14 penalty minutes — fewest among the NHL's top 25 scorers in 1985-86. During his outstanding career, Bossy has scored a total of 535 goals — 8th on the all-time list — and served only 177 penalty minutes in 689 games. He has averaged 19.7 penalty minutes per season during his nine-year career.

FRANK J. SELKE TROPHY

An annual award "to the forward who best excels in the defensive aspects of the game." Winner selected in poll by Professional Hockey Writers' Association at the end of the regular schedule. The winner receives $1,500 and the runner-up $750.

History: Presented to the National Hockey League in 1977 by the Board of Governors of the NHL in honour of Frank J. Selke, one of the great architects of NHL championship teams.

1985-86 Winner: Troy Murray, Chicago Blackhawks
Runners-up: Ron Sutter, Philadelphia Flyers
Guy Carbonneau, Montreal Canadiens

For the first time in the nine-year history of the Selke Trophy, a player from the Chicago Blackhawks has won the award. Center Troy Murray, who finished 10th in the voting for the 1984-85 Selke, totalled 179 of a possible 300 points to edge Ron Sutter (127 points) and Guy Carbonneau (52 points) for the award. A total of 28 players received votes in the balloting for the League's top defensive forward.

With a 99-point season (45 goals, 54 assists), Murray becomes the highest scoring player to ever capture the award. Bobby Clarke held the previous high with an 85-point season when he won the award in 1982-83. Murray, a University of North Dakota graduate, enjoyed his finest season since entering the NHL in 1981-82. His previous career high for points was 66 in 1984-85.

Vezina Trophy   *Lady Byng Memorial Trophy*   *Frank J. Selke Trophy*   *Conn Smythe Trophy*

VEZINA TROPHY

An annual award "to the goalkeeper adjudged to be the best at his position" as voted by the general managers of each of the 21 clubs. Over-all winner receives $1,500, runner-up $750.

History: Leo Dandurand, Louis Letourneau and Joe Cattarinich, former owners of the Montreal Canadiens, presented the trophy to the National Hockey League in 1926-27 in memory of Georges Vezina, outstanding goalkeeper of the Canadiens who collapsed during an NHL game November 28, 1925, and died of tuberculosis a few months later. Until the 1981-82 season, the goalkeeper(s) of the team allowing the fewest number of goals during the regular-season were awarded the Vezina Trophy.

1985-86 Winner: John Vanbiesbrouck, New York Rangers
Runners-up: Bob Froese, Philadelphia Flyers
Grant Fuhr, Edmonton Oilers

In the closest voting for the Vezina Trophy since it was first presented to the NHL's outstanding goaltender in 1981-82, Vanbiesbrouck polled 60 of a possible 105 points to edge Froese (58 points) and Fuhr (32 points).

In addition, Vanbiesbrouck's 1985-86 victory in the balloting, marks only the third time in the 60-year history of the award that a Rangers' goaltender has had his name inscribed on the Vezina. In 1970-71 Ed Giacomin and Gilles Villemure shared the Vezina and in 1939-40, Dave Kerr captured the award.

CONN SMYTHE TROPHY

An annual award "to the most valuable player for his team in the playoffs." Winner selected by the Professional Hockey Writers' Association at the conclusion of the final game in the Stanley Cup Finals. The winner receives $1,500.

History: Presented by Maple Leaf Gardens Limited in 1964 to honour Conn Smythe, the former coach, manager, president and owner-governor of the Toronto Maple Leafs.

1985-86 Winner: Patrick Roy, Montreal Canadiens

In leading the Canadiens to their record 23rd Stanley Cup Championship, Patrick Roy became the youngest player to receive the Conn Smythe Trophy in the 22-year history of the award. He appeared in all 20 Montreal post-season games and tied a Stanley Cup record with 15 victories. His 1.92 goals-against-average and .923 save percentage ranked second among playoff goaltenders.

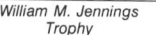

William M. Jennings
Trophy

Jack Adams
Award

Bill Masterton
Trophy

Lester Patrick
Trophy

Lester B. Pearson
Award

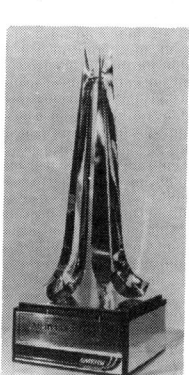

Emery Edge
Award

WILLIAM M. JENNINGS TROPHY

An annual award "to the goalkeeper(s) having played a minimum of 25 games for the team with the fewest goals scored against it." Winners selected on regular-season play. Overall winner receives $1,500, runner-up $750. Leader at end of first half of season and leader in second half each receive $250.

History: The Jennings Trophy was presented in 1981-82 by the National Hockey League's Board of Governors to honor the late William M. Jennings, longtime governor and president of the New York Rangers and one of the great builders of hockey in the United States.

1985-86 Winner: Bob Froese and Darren Jensen, Philadelphia Flyers
Runners-up: Al Jensen and Pete Peeters, Washington Capitals
John Vanbiesbrouck and Glen Hanlon, NY Rangers

Bob Froese and Darren Jensen combined to lead the Flyers to the best defensive record in the League as the club allowed an average of 2.99 goals-per-game. The Washington duo of Al Jensen and Pete Peeters finished second at 3.37, while John Vanbiesbrouck and Glen Hanlon helped lead the Rangers to the third best mark (3.42).

Froese led all goaltenders in average (2.55), save percentage (.909), shutouts (5) and tied with Vanbiesbrouck for the League lead in wins (31). Jensen compiled a 3.68 average and 15-9-1 record in 29 Flyers' appearances.

JACK ADAMS AWARD

An annual award presented by the National Hockey League Broadcasters' Association to "the NHL coach adjudged to have contributed the most to his team's success." Winner selected by poll among members of the NHL Broadcasters' Association at the end of the regular season. The winner receives $1,000 from the NHLBA.

History: The award was presented by the NHL Broadcasters' Association in 1974 to commemorate the late Jack Adams, longtime coach and general manager of Detroit Red Wings, whose lifetime dedication to hockey serves as an inspiration to all who would aspire to further the game.

1985-86 Winner: Glen Sather, Edmonton Oilers
Runners-up: Jacques Demers, St. Louis Blues
Lorne Henning, Minnesota North Stars

Edmonton Oilers' coach Glen Sather totalled 80 points in the balloting for the Jack Adams Award to edge runner-up Jacques Demers of St. Louis by 10 points. Minnesota North Stars' rookie coach Lorne Henning finished third with 42 points.

Sather guided the Oilers to a 56-17-7 record, best in the NHL in 1985-86, and their fifth consecutive Smythe Division title. In 560 career games as coach of the Oilers, Sather has compiled a 314-167-79 record.

BILL MASTERTON MEMORIAL TROPHY

An annual award under the trusteeship of the Professional Hockey Writers' Association to "the National Hockey League player who best exemplifies the qualities of perseverance, sportsmanship and dedication to hockey." Winner selected by poll among the 21 chapters of the PHWA at the end of the regular season. A $1,500 grant from the PHWA is awarded annually to the Bill Masterton Scholarship Fund, based in Bloomington, MN, in the name of the Masterton Trophy winner.

History: The trophy was presented by the NHL Writers' Association in 1968 to commemorate the late William Masterton, a player of the Minnesota North Stars, who exhibited to a high degree the qualities exemplified by the winner of the award, and who died January 15, 1968.

1985-86 Winner: Charlie Simmer, Boston Bruins

Despite missing 25 games in 1985-86 with a knee sprain and eye injury, Charlie Simmer averaged more than a point-per-game. The Bruins' left winger scored 36 goals and 23 assists for 59 points in 55 games.

The 12-year NHL veteran has played in all 80 regular-season games only once in his career (1982-83 with Los Angeles), but has been one of the League's most consistent pointgetters. In 582 career games with California, Los Angeles and the Bruins, Simmer has scored 302 goals, 311 assists for 613 points.

LESTER PATRICK TROPHY

An annual award "for outstanding service to hockey in the United States." Eligible recipients are players, officials, coaches, executives and referees. Winner selected by an award committee consisting of the President of the NHL, an NHL Governor, a hockey writer for a U.S. national news service, a nationally syndicated sports columnist, an ex-player in the Hockey Hall of Fame and a sports representative of a U.S. national radio-TV network. Each except the League president is rotated annually. The winner receives a miniature of the Trophy.

History: Presented by the New York Rangers in 1966 to honor the late Lester Patrick, longtime general manager and coach of the New York Rangers, whose teams finished out of the playoffs only once in his first 16 years with the club.

1985-86 Winners: John MacInnes and Jack Riley

The late John MacInnes coached for 26 seasons at Michigan Tech where his teams compiled a record of 555 wins, 295 losses and 39 ties. He was named WCHA Coach of the Year on six occasions and NCAA Coach of the Year twice. MacInnes guided Michigan Tech to three National Championships and a second place finish on three other occasions.

Jack Riley, a coach for 35 seasons at Army, has recorded more than 500 wins in his illustrious career. A graduate of Dartmouth ('47), Riley was a member of the 1948 U.S. Olympic Team and was later player/coach of the U.S. National Team. In 1960, he coached the U.S. Olympic Team to a gold medal at the Winter Olympics in Squaw Valley. Riley was inducted into the U.S. Hockey Hall of Fame in November, 1979.

LESTER B. PEARSON AWARD

An annual award presented to the NHL's outstanding player as selected by the members of the National Hockey League Players' Association.

History: The award was presented in 1970-71 by the NHLPA in honor of the late Lester B. Pearson, former Prime Minister of Canada.

1985-86 Winner: Mario Lemieux, Pittsburgh Penguins.

Mario Lemieux's second NHL season established him as one of the League's elite players. As a 20-year-old, the centerman scored 48 goals and 93 assists for 141 points in 79 games to finish as the second-leading scorer in the NHL. In addition, Lemieux placed second in voting for the Hart Memorial Trophy as the League's outstanding player.

EMERY EDGE AWARD

An annual award "to the player who appears in a minimum of 60 games and leads the National Hockey League in plus-minus statistics". Over-all winner receives $2,000. Each team leader receives $500, to be donated in his name to the charity of his choice.

History: The award was presented to the NHL in 1982-83 by Emery Worldwide, of Wilton, Connecticut, to recognize the League leader in plus-minus statistics. Plus-minus statistics are calculated by giving a player a "plus" when on-ice for an even-strength or shorthand goal scored by his team. He receives a "minus" when on-ice for an even-strength or shorthand goal scored by the opposing team.

1985-86 Winner: Mark Howe, Philadelphia Flyers
Runners-up: Brad McCrimmon, Philadelphia Flyers
Wayne Gretzky, Edmonton Oilers

Mark Howe compiled a plus-85 rating to edge teammate Brad McCrimmon by two points in the 1985-86 Emery Edge plus-minus race. Two-time Emery Edge winner Wayne Gretzky finished third with a plus-71. Individual team winners included: Barry Pederson, Boston; Mike Foligno, Buffalo; Al MacInnis, Calgary; Troy Murray, Chicago; Kelly Kisio, Detroit; Wayne Gretzky, Edmonton; Joel Quenneville, Hartford; Jay Wells, Los Angeles; Curt Giles, Minnesota; Larry Robinson, Montreal; Rich Preston, New Jersey; Denis Potvin, NY Islanders; Reijo Ruotsalainen, NY Rangers; Mark Howe, Philadelphia; Mike Blaisdell, Pittsburgh; David Shaw, Quebec; Rob Ramage, St. Louis; Russ Courtnall, Toronto; Tony Tanti and Patrick Sundstrom, Vancouver; Alan Haworth, Washington; Jim Nill, Winnipeg.

NATIONAL HOCKEY LEAGUE INDIVIDUAL AWARD WINNERS

HART TROPHY WINNERS

1986	Wayne Gretzky	Edmonton
1985	Wayne Gretzky	Edmonton
1984	Wayne Gretzky	Edmonton
1983	Wayne Gretzky	Edmonton
1982	Wayne Gretzky	Edmonton
1981	Wayne Gretzky	Edmonton
1980	Wayne Gretzky	Edmonton
1979	Bryan Trottier	NY Islanders
1978	Guy Lafleur	Montreal
1977	Guy Lafleur	Montreal
1976	Bobby Clarke	Philadelphia
1975	Bobby Clarke	Philadelphia
1974	Phil Esposito	Boston
1973	Bobby Clarke	Philadelphia
1972	Bobby Orr	Boston
1971	Bobby Orr	Boston
1970	Bobby Orr	Boston
1969	Phil Esposito	Boston
1968	Stan Mikita	Chicago
1967	Stan Mikita	Chicago
1966	Bobby Hull	Chicago
1965	Bobby Hull	Chicago
1964	Jean Béliveau	Montreal
1963	Gordie Howe	Detroit
1962	Jacques Plante	Montreal
1961	Bernie Geoffrion	Montreal
1960	Gordie Howe	Detroit
1959	Andy Bathgate	NY Rangers
1958	Gordie Howe	Detroit
1957	Gordie Howe	Detroit
1956	Jean Béliveau	Montreal
1955	Ted Kennedy	Toronto
1954	Al Rollins	Chicago
1953	Gordie Howe	Detroit
1952	Gordie Howe	Detroit
1951	Milt Schmidt	Boston
1950	Charlie Rayner	NY Rangers
1949	Sid Abel	Detroit
1948	Buddy O'Connor	NY Rangers
1947	Maurice Richard	Montreal
1946	Max Bentley	Chicago
1945	Elmer Lach	Montreal
1944	Babe Pratt	Toronto
1943	Bill Cowley	Boston
1942	Tom Anderson	NY Americans
1941	Bill Cowley	Boston
1940	Ebbie Goodfellow	Detroit
1939	Toe Blake	Montreal
1938	Eddie Shore	Boston
1937	Babe Siebert	Montreal
1936	Eddie Shore	Boston
1935	Eddie Shore	Boston
1934	Aurel Joliat	Montreal
1933	Eddie Shore	Boston
1932	Howie Morenz	Montreal
1931	Howie Morenz	Montreal
1930	Nels Stewart	Mtl. Maroons
1929	Roy Worters	NY Americans
1928	Howie Morenz	Montreal
1927	Herb Gardiner	Montreal
1926	Nels Stewart	Mtl. Maroons
1925	Billy Burch	Hamilton
1924	Frank Nighbor	Ottawa

ART ROSS TROPHY WINNERS

1986	Wayne Gretzky	Edmonton
1985	Wayne Gretzky	Edmonton
1984	Wayne Gretzky	Edmonton
1983	Wayne Gretzky	Edmonton
1982	Wayne Gretzky	Edmonton
1981	Wayne Gretzky	Edmonton
1980	Marcel Dionne	Los Angeles
1979	Bryan Trottier	NY Islanders
1978	Guy Lafleur	Montreal
1977	Guy Lafleur	Montreal
1976	Guy Lafleur	Montreal
1975	Bobby Orr	Boston
1974	Phil Esposito	Boston
1973	Phil Esposito	Boston
1972	Phil Esposito	Boston
1971	Phil Esposito	Boston
1970	Bobby Orr	Boston
1969	Phil Esposito	Boston
1968	Stan Mikita	Chicago
1967	Stan Mikita	Chicago
1966	Bobby Hull	Chicago
1965	Stan Mikita	Chicago
1964	Stan Mikita	Chicago
1963	Gordie Howe	Detroit
1962	Bobby Hull	Chicago
1961	Bernie Geoffrion	Montreal
1960	Bobby Hull	Chicago
1959	Dickie Moore	Montreal
1958	Dickie Moore	Montreal
1957	Gordie Howe	Detroit
1956	Jean Béliveau	Montreal
1955	Bernie Geoffrion	Montreal
1954	Gordie Howe	Detroit
1953	Gordie Howe	Detroit
1952	Gordie Howe	Detroit
1951	Gordie Howe	Detroit
1950	Ted Lindsay	Detroit
1949	Roy Conacher	Chicago
1948	Elmer Lach	Montreal
1947*	Max Bentley	Chicago
1946	Max Bentley	Chicago
1945	Elmer Lach	Montreal
1944	Herbie Cain	Boston
1943	Doug Bentley	Chicago
1942	Bryan Hextall	NY Rangers
1941	Bill Cowley	Boston
1940	Milt Schmidt	Boston
1939	Toe Blake	Montreal
1938	Gordie Drillon	Toronto
1937	Dave Schriner	NY Americans
1936	Dave Schriner	NY Americans
1935	Charlie Conacher	Toronto
1934	Charlie Conacher	Toronto
1933	Bill Cook	NY Rangers
1932	Harvey Jackson	Toronto
1931	Howie Morenz	Montreal
1930	Cooney Weiland	Boston
1929	Ace Bailey	Toronto
1928	Howie Morenz	Montreal
1927	Bill Cook	NY Rangers
1926	Nels Stewart	Mtl. Maroons
1925	Babe Dye	Toronto
1924	Cy Denneny	Ottawa
1923	Babe Dye	Toronto
1922	Punch Broadbent	Ottawa
1921	Newsy Lalonde	Montreal
1920	Joe Malone	Quebec
1919	Newsy Lalonde	Montreal
1918	Joe Malone	Montreal

* Scoring leaders prior to inception of Art Ross Trophy in 1947-48

CONN SMYTHE TROPHY WINNERS

1986	Patrick Roy	Montreal
1985	Wayne Gretzky	Edmonton
1984	Mark Messier	Edmonton
1983	Bill Smith	NY Islanders
1982	Mike Bossy	NY Islanders
1981	Butch Goring	NY Islanders
1980	Bryan Trottier	NY Islanders
1979	Bob Gainey	Montreal
1978	Larry Robinson	Montreal
1977	Guy Lafleur	Montreal
1976	Reggie Leach	Philadelphia
1975	Bernie Parent	Philadelphia
1974	Bernie Parent	Philadelphia
1973	Yvan Cournoyer	Montreal
1972	Bobby Orr	Boston
1971	Ken Dryden	Montreal
1970	Bobby Orr	Boston
1969	Serge Savard	Montreal
1968	Glenn Hall	St. Louis
1967	Dave Keon	Toronto
1966	Roger Crozier	Detroit
1965	Jean Béliveau	Montreal

CALDER MEMORIAL TROPHY WINNERS

1986	Gary Suter	Calgary
1985	Mario Lemieux	Pittsburgh
1984	Tom Barrasso	Buffalo
1983	Steve Larmer	Chicago
1982	Dale Hawerchuk	Winnipeg
1981	Peter Stastny	Quebec
1980	Raymond Bourque	Boston
1979	Bobby Smith	Minnesota
1978	Mike Bossy	NY Islanders
1977	Willi Plett	Atlanta
1976	Bryan Trottier	NY Islanders
1975	Eric Vail	Atlanta
1974	Denis Potvin	NY Islanders
1973	Steve Vickers	NY Rangers
1972	Ken Dryden	Montreal
1971	Gilbert Perreault	Buffalo
1970	Tony Esposito	Chicago
1969	Danny Grant	Minnesota
1968	Derek Sanderson	Boston
1967	Bobby Orr	Boston
1966	Brit Selby	Toronto
1965	Roger Crozier	Detroit
1964	Jacques Laperrière	Montreal
1963	Kent Douglas	Toronto
1962	Bobby Rousseau	Montreal
1961	Dave Keon	Toronto
1960	Bill Hay	Chicago
1959	Ralph Backstrom	Montreal
1958	Frank Mahovlich	Toronto
1957	Larry Regan	Boston
1956	Glenn Hall	Detroit
1955	Ed Litzenberger	Chicago
1954	Camille Henry	NY Rangers
1953	Lorne Worsley	NY Rangers
1952	Bernie Geoffrion	Montreal
1951	Terry Sawchuk	Detroit
1950	Jack Gelineau	Boston
1949	Pentti Lund	NY Rangers
1948	Jim McFadden	Detroit
1947	Howie Meeker	Toronto
1946	Edgar Laprade	NY Rangers
1945	Frank McCool	Toronto
1944	Gus Bodnar	Toronto
1943	Gaye Stewart	Toronto
1942	Grant Warwick	NY Rangers
1941	Johnny Quilty	Montreal
1940	Kilby MacDonald	NY Rangers
1939	Frank Brimsek	Boston
1938	Cully Dahlstrom	Chicago
1937	Syl Apps	Toronto
1936	Mike Karakas	Chicago
1935	Dave Schriner	NY Americans
1934	Russ Blinko	Mtl. Maroons
1933	Carl Voss	Detroit

JAMES NORRIS TROPHY WINNERS

1986	Paul Coffey	Edmonton
1985	Paul Coffey	Edmonton
1984	Rod Langway	Washington
1983	Rod Langway	Washington
1982	Doug Wilson	Chicago
1981	Randy Carlyle	Pittsburgh
1980	Larry Robinson	Montreal
1979	Denis Potvin	NY Islanders
1978	Denis Potvin	NY Islanders
1977	Larry Robinson	Montreal
1976	Denis Potvin	NY Islanders
1975	Bobby Orr	Boston
1974	Bobby Orr	Boston
1973	Bobby Orr	Boston
1972	Bobby Orr	Boston
1971	Bobby Orr	Boston
1970	Bobby Orr	Boston
1969	Bobby Orr	Boston
1968	Bobby Orr	Boston
1967	Harry Howell	NY Rangers
1966	Jacques Laperrière	Montreal
1965	Pierre Pilote	Chicago
1964	Pierre Pilote	Chicago
1963	Pierre Pilote	Chicago
1962	Doug Harvey	NY Rangers
1961	Doug Harvey	Montreal
1960	Doug Harvey	Montreal
1959	Tom Johnson	Montreal
1958	Doug Harvey	Montreal
1957	Doug Harvey	Montreal
1956	Doug Harvey	Montreal
1955	Doug Harvey	Montreal
1954	Red Kelly	Detroit

Doug Harvey is a seven-time winner of the Norris Trophy.

VEZINA TROPHY WINNERS

1986	John Vanbiesbrouck	NY Rangers
1985	Pelle Lindbergh	Philadelphia
1984	Tom Barrasso	Buffalo
1983	Pete Peeters	Boston
1982	Bill Smith	NY Islanders
1981	Richard Sevigny	Montreal
	Denis Herron	
	Michel Larocque	
1980	Bob Sauvé	Buffalo
	Don Edwards	
1979	Ken Dryden	Montreal
	Michel Larocque	
1978	Ken Dryden	Montreal
	Michel Larocque	
1977	Ken Dryden	Montreal
	Michel Larocque	
1976	Ken Dryden	Montreal
1975	Bernie Parent	Philadelphia
1974	Bernie Parent	Philadelphia
	Tony Esposito	Chicago
1973	Ken Dryden	Montreal
1972	Tony Esposito	Chicago
	Gary Smith	
1971	Ed Giacomin	NY Rangers
	Gilles Villemure	
1970	Tony Esposito	Chicago
1969	Jacques Plante	St. Louis
	Glenn Hall	
1968	Lorne Worsley	Montreal
	Rogie Vachon	
1967	Glenn Hall	Chicago
	Denis Dejordy	
1966	Lorne Worsley	Montreal
	Charlie Hodge	
1965	Terry Sawchuk	Toronto
	Johnny Bower	
1964	Charlie Hodge	Montreal
1963	Glenn Hall	Chicago
1962	Jacques Plante	Montreal
1961	Johnny Bower	Toronto
1960	Jacques Plante	Montreal
1959	Jacques Plante	Montreal
1958	Jacques Plante	Montreal
1957	Jacques Plante	Montreal
1956	Jacques Plante	Montreal
1955	Terry Sawchuk	Detroit
1954	Harry Lumley	Toronto
1953	Terry Sawchuk	Detroit
1952	Terry Sawchuk	Detroit
1951	Al Rollins	Toronto
1950	Bill Durnan	Montreal
1949	Bill Durnan	Montreal
1948	Turk Broda	Toronto
1947	Bill Durnan	Montreal
1946	Bill Durnan	Montreal
1945	Bill Durnan	Montreal
1944	Bill Durnan	Montreal
1943	Johnny Mowers	Detroit
1942	Frank Brimsek	Boston
1941	Turk Broda	Toronto
1940	Dave Kerr	NY Rangers
1939	Frank Brimsek	Boston
1938	Tiny Thompson	Boston
1937	Normie Smith	Detroit
1936	Tiny Thompson	Boston
1935	Lorne Chabot	Chicago
1934	Charlie Gardiner	Chicago
1933	Tiny Thompson	Boston
1932	Charlie Gardiner	Chicago
1931	Roy Worters	NY Americans
1930	Tiny Thompson	Boston
1929	George Hainsworth	Montreal
1928	George Hainsworth	Montreal
1927	George Hainsworth	Montreal

WILLIAM M. JENNINGS TROPHY WINNERS

1986	Bob Froese,	Philadelphia
	Darren Jensen	
1985	Tom Barrasso,	Buffalo
	Bob Sauve	
1984	Al Jensen,	Washington
	Pat Riggin	
1983	Roland Melanson,	NY Islanders
	Bill Smith	
1982	Rick Wamsley,	Montreal
	Denis Herron	

EMERY EDGE AWARD WINNERS

1986	Mark Howe	Philadelphia
1985	Wayne Gretzky	Edmonton
1984	Wayne Gretzky	Edmonton
1983	Charlie Huddy	Edmonton

LADY BYNG TROPHY WINNERS

1986	Mike Bossy	NY Islanders
1985	Jari Kurri	Edmonton
1984	Mike Bossy	NY Islanders
1983	Mike Bossy	NY Islanders
1982	Rick Middleton	Boston
1981	Rick Kehoe	Pittsburgh
1980	Wayne Gretzky	Edmonton
1979	Bob MacMillan	Atlanta
1978	Butch Goring	Los Angeles
1977	Marcel Dionne	Los Angeles
1976	Jean Ratelle	NY Rangers-Boston
1975	Marcel Dionne	Detroit
1974	John Bucyk	Boston
1973	Gilbert Perreault	Buffalo
1972	Jean Ratelle	NY Rangers
1971	John Bucyk	Boston
1970	Phil Goyette	St. Louis
1969	Alex Delvecchio	Detroit
1968	Stan Mikita	Chicago
1967	Stan Mikita	Chicago
1966	Alex Delvecchio	Detroit
1965	Bobby Hull	Chicago
1964	Ken Wharram	Chicago
1963	Dave Keon	Toronto
1962	Dave Keon	Toronto
1961	Red Kelly	Toronto
1960	Don McKenney	Boston
1959	Alex Delvecchio	Detroit
1958	Camille Henry	NY Rangers
1957	Andy Hebenton	NY Rangers
1956	Earl Reibel	Detroit
1955	Sid Smith	Toronto
1954	Red Kelly	Detroit
1953	Red Kelly	Detroit
1952	Sid Smith	Toronto
1951	Red Kelly	Detroit
1950	Edgar Laprade	NY Rangers
1949	Bill Quackenbush	Detroit
1948	Buddy O'Connor	NY Rangers
1947	Bobby Bauer	Boston
1946	Toe Blake	Montreal
1945	Bill Mosienko	Chicago
1944	Clint Smith	Chicago
1943	Max Bentley	Chicago
1942	Syl Apps	Toronto
1941	Bobby Bauer	Boston
1940	Bobby Bauer	Boston
1939	Clint Smith	NY Rangers
1938	Gordie Drillon	Toronto
1937	Marty Barry	Detroit
1936	Doc Romnes	Chicago
1935	Frank Boucher	NY Rangers
1934	Frank Boucher	NY Rangers
1933	Frank Boucher	NY Rangers
1932	Joe Primeau	Toronto
1931	Frank Boucher	NY Rangers
1930	Frank Boucher	NY Rangers
1929	Frank Boucher	NY Rangers
1928	Frank Boucher	NY Rangers
1927	Billy Burch	NY Americans
1926	Frank Nighbor	Ottawa
1925	Frank Nighbor	Ottawa

JACK ADAMS AWARD WINNERS

1986	Glen Sather	Edmonton
1985	Mike Keenan	Philadelphia
1984	Bryan Murray	Washington
1983	Orval Tessier	Chicago
1982	Tom Watt	Winnipeg
1981	Gordon (Red) Berenson	St. Louis
1980	Pat Quinn	Philadelphia
1979	Al Arbour	NY Islanders
1978	Bobby Kromm	Detroit
1977	Scott Bowman	Montreal
1976	Don Cherry	Boston
1975	Bob Pulford	Los Angeles
1974	Fred Shero	Philadelphia

FRANK J. SELKE TROPHY WINNERS

1986	Troy Murray	Chicago
1985	Craig Ramsay	Buffalo
1984	Doug Jarvis	Washington
1983	Bobby Clarke	Philadelphia
1982	Steve Kasper	Boston
1981	Bob Gainey	Montreal
1980	Bob Gainey	Montreal
1979	Bob Gainey	Montreal
1978	Bob Gainey	Montreal

LESTER PATRICK TROPHY WINNERS

1986	John MacInnes	
	Jack Riley	
1985	Jack Butterfield	
	Arthur M. Wirtz	
1984	John A. Ziegler Jr.	
	*Arthur Howie Ross	
1983	Bill Torrey	
1982	Emile P. Francis	
1981	Charles M. Schulz	
1980	Bobby Clarke	
	Edward M. Snider	
	Frederick A. Shero	
	1980 U.S. Olympic Hockey Team	
1979	Bobby Orr	
1978	Philip A. Esposito	
	Tom Fitzgerald	
	William T. Tutt	
	William W. Wirtz	
1977	John P. Bucyk	
	Murray A. Armstrong	
	John Mariucci	
1976	Stanley Mikita	
	George A. Leader	
	Bruce A. Norris	
1975	Donald M. Clark	
	William L. Chadwick	
	Thomas N. Ivan	
1974	Alex Delvecchio	
	Murray Murdoch	
	*Weston W. Adams, Sr.	
	*Charles L. Crovat	
1973	Walter L. Bush, Jr.	
1972	Clarence S. Campbell	
	John Kelly	
	Ralph "Cooney" Weiland	
	*James D. Norris	
1971	William M. Jennings	
	*John B. Sollenberger	
	*Terrance G. Sawchuk	
1970	Edward W. Shore	
	*James C. V. Hendy	
1969	Robert M. Hull	
	*Edward J. Jeremiah	
1968	Thomas F. Lockhart	
	*Walter A. Brown	
	*Gen. John R. Kilpatrick	
1967	Gordon Howe	
	*Charles F. Adams	
	*James Norris, Sr.	
1966	J.J. "Jack" Adams	

* Awarded Posthumously

BILL MASTERTON TROPHY WINNERS

1986	Charlie Simmer	Boston
1985	Anders Hedberg	NY Rangers
1984	Brad Park	Detroit
1983	Lanny McDonald	Calgary
1982	Glenn Resch	Colorado
1981	Blake Dunlop	St. Louis
1980	Al MacAdam	Minnesota
1979	Serge Savard	Montreal
1978	Butch Goring	Los Angeles
1977	Ed Westfall	NY Islanders
1976	Rod Gilbert	NY Rangers
1975	Don Luce	Buffalo
1974	Henri Richard	Montreal
1973	Lowell MacDonald	Pittsburgh
1972	Bobby Clarke	Philadelphia
1971	Jean Ratelle	NY Rangers
1970	Pit Martin	Chicago
1969	Ted Hampson	Oakland
1968	Claude Provost	Montreal

LESTER B. PEARSON AWARD WINNERS

1971	Phil Esposito	Boston
1972	Jean Ratelle	NY Rangers
1973	Phil Esposito	Boston
1974	Bobby Clark	Philadelphia
1975	Bobby Orr	Boston
1976	Guy Lafleur	Montreal
1977	Guy Lafleur	Montreal
1978	Guy Lafleur	Montreal
1979	Marcel Dionne	Los Angeles
1980	Marcel Dionne	Los Angeles
1981	Mike Liut	St. Louis
1982	Wayne Gretzky	Edmonton
1983	Wayne Gretzky	Edmonton
1984	Wayne Gretzky	Edmonton
1985	Wayne Gretzky	Edmonton
1986	Mario Lemieux	Pittsburgh

NHL Amateur and Entry Draft

History

Year	Site	Date	Total Players Drafted
1963	Queen Elizabeth Hotel	June 5	21
1964	Queen Elizabeth Hotel	June 11	24
1965	Queen Elizabeth Hotel	April 27	11
1966	Mount Royal Hotel	April 25	24
1967	Queen Elizabeth Hotel	June 7	18
1968	Queen Elizabeth Hotel	June 13	24
1969	Queen Elizabeth Hotel	June 12	84
1970	Queen Elizabeth Hotel	June 11	116
1971	Queen Elizabeth Hotel	June 10	117
1972	Queen Elizabeth Hotel	June 8	152
1973	Mount Royal Hotel	May 15	168
1974	NHL Montreal Office	May 28	247
1975	NHL Montreal Office	June 3	217
1976	NHL Montreal Office	June 1	135
1977	NHL Montreal Office	June 14	185
1978	Queen Elizabeth Hotel	June 15	234
1979	Queen Elizabeth Hotel	August 9	126
1980	Montreal Forum	June 11	210
1981	Montreal Forum	June 10	211
1982	Montreal Forum	June 9	252
1983	Montreal Forum	June 8	242
1984	Montreal Forum	June 9	250
1985	Toronto Convention Centre	June 15	252
1986	Montreal Forum	June 21	252

' The NHL Amateur Draft became the NHL Entry Draft in 1979

First Selections

Year	Player	Pos	Drafted By	Drafted From	Age
1969	Rejean Houle	LW	Montreal	Montreal Jr. Canadiens	19.7
1970	Gilbert Perreault	C	Buffalo	Montreal Jr. Canadiens	19.7
1971	Guy Lafleur	RW	Montreal	Quebec Remparts	19.8
1972	Billy Harris	RW	NY Islanders	Toronto Marlboros	20.4
1973	Denis Potvin	D	NY Islanders	Ottawa 67's	19.7
1974	Greg Joly	D	Washington	Regina Pats	20.0
1975	Mel Bridgman	C	Philadelphia	Victoria Cougars	20.1
1976	Rick Green	D	Washington	London Knights	20.3
1977	Dale McCourt	C	Detroit	St. Catharines Fincups	20.4
1978	Bobby Smith	C	Minnesota	Ottawa 67's	20.4
1979	Bob Ramage	D	Colorado	London Knights	20.5
1980	Doug Wickenheiser	C	Montreal	Regina Pats	19.2
1981	Dale Hawerchuk	C	Winnipeg	Cornwall Royals	18.2
1982	Gord Kluzak	D	Boston	Nanaimo Islanders	18.3
1983	Brian Lawton	C	Minnesota	Mount St. Charles HS	18.11
1984	Mario Lemieux	C	Pittsburgh	Laval Voisins	18.8
1985	Wendel Clark	LW/D	Toronto	Saskatoon Blades	18.7
1986	Joe Murphy	C	Detroit	Michigan State	18.8

Draft Summary

Following is a summary of the number of players drafted from the Ontario Hockey League (OHL), Western Hockey League (WHL), Quebec Major Junior Hockey League (QMJHL), United States Colleges, United States High Schools, European Leagues and other Leagues throughout North America since 1969:

	OHL	WHL	QMJHL	US Coll.	US HS	International	Other
1969	36	20	11	7	0	1	9
1970	51	22	13	16	0	0	13
1971	41	28	13	22	0	0	13
1972	46	44	30	21	0	0	11
1973	56	49	24	25	0	0	14
1974	69	66	40	41	0	6	24
1975	45	54	28	59	0	6	25
1976	47	33	18	26	0	8	3
1977	42	44	40	49	0	5	5
1978	59	48	22	71	0	15	19
1979	48	37	19	15	0	7	2
1980	73	41	24	42	7	13	10
1981	59	36	28	21	17	32	18
1982	60	55	17	20	47	35	18
1983	57	41	24	14	35	34	37
1984	55	38	16	22	44	40	35
1985	59	43	15	20	48	30	37
1986	66	32	22	22	40	28	42
Total	969	731	404	513	238	260	335

Ontario Hockey League

Club	'69	'70	'71	'72	'73	'74	'75	'76	'77	'78	'79	'80	'81	'82	'83	'84	'85	'86	Total
Peterborough	5	5	4	5	9	4	3	1	4	6	9	10	3	5	7	3	9	2	94
Toronto	3	7	6	5	6	8	4	4	7	5	4	10	2	6	4	3	4	6	92
Oshawa	5	4	3	5	5	7	6	6	1	3	3	2	9	5	5	6	6	6	87
Kitchener	1	6	2	8	4	13	3	1	3	4	4	4	5	5	8	2	6	3	84
Ottawa	2	4	3	4	6	5	6	5	5	5	3	8	4	9	2	2	3	3	79
London	4	9	1	5	6	6	3	5	4	3	6	2	5	5	3	7	1	3	78
Sault Ste. Marie	–	–	–	–	4	5	2	5	1	5	3	3	8	1	6	4	5	7	59
Sudbury	–	–	–	–	6	6	4	5	4	4	3	7	2	4	–	2	5	3	55
Kingston	–	–	–	–	4	4	6	4	9	2	8	5	2	1	3	3	4	–	55
Hamilton	2	3	5	4	6	4	7	3	–	8	1	–	–	–	–	3	6	–	52
St. Catharines	5	5	8	5	4	7	3	4	6	–	–	–	–	–	–	–	–	–	47
Niagara Falls	4	2	1	4	–	–	–	–	2	3	5	8	6	6	–	–	–	–	41
Windsor	–	–	–	–	–	–	–	2	1	4	2	3	5	3	2	2	3	7	34
Brantford	–	–	–	–	–	–	–	–	–	–	3	8	5	2	7	2	–	–	27
Montreal	5	6	8	1	–	–	–	–	–	–	–	–	–	–	–	–	–	–	20
Cornwall	–	–	–	–	–	–	–	–	–	–	–	–	7	4	3	2	2	2	20
Guelph	–	–	–	–	–	–	–	–	–	–	–	–	–	1	5	3	8	–	17
Belleville	–	–	–	–	–	–	–	–	–	–	–	–	–	–	3	4	4	5	16
North Bay	–	–	–	–	–	–	–	–	–	–	–	–	–	–	4	4	3	3	14

Year	Total Ontario Drafted	Total Players Drafted	Ontario %
1969	36	84	42.9
1970	51	116	44.0
1971	41	117	35.0
1972	46	152	30.3
1973	56	168	33.3
1974	69	247	27.9
1975	45	217	20.7
1976	47	135	34.8
1977	42	185	22.7
1978	59	234	25.2
1979	48	126	38.1
1980	73	210	34.8
1981	59	211	28.0
1982	60	252	23.8
1983	57	242	23.6
1984	55	250	22.0
1985	59	252	23.4
1986	66	252	26.2
Total	969	3450	28.1

Western Hockey League

Club	'69	'70	'71	'72	'73	'74	'75	'76	'77	'78	'79	'80	'81	'82	'83	'84	'85	'86	Total
Calgary	3	5	2	7	4	8	4	4	4	3	–	2	5	4	3	3	3	2	66
Regina	–	–	5	5	1	8	5	3	–	4	1	3	5	6	8	4	4	3	65
Portland	–	–	–	–	–	–	–	–	4	8	7	8	6	7	7	5	1	4	60
New Westminster	–	–	–	6	8	7	9	5	8	6	5	1	–	–	2	1	1	–	59
Saskatoon	1	–	1	3	8	4	5	3	4	1	2	3	5	5	3	1	5	–	56
Victoria	–	–	–	2	2	5	7	4	4	3	1	8	6	2	3	4	2	1	54
Brandon	–	3	1	5	2	7	4	–	3	1	10	5	2	1	3	2	1	–	52
Medicine Hat	–	–	–	4	6	4	5	3	5	4	–	4	2	1	2	1	6	2	49
Flin Flon	4	4	5	2	4	7	4	3	1	5	–	–	–	–	–	–	–	–	39
Lethbridge	–	–	–	–	–	–	–	2	3	5	4	1	4	7	2	1	5	1	35
Winnipeg	3	2	4	2	5	4	4	–	4	–	–	1	4	1	–	–	–	–	34
Edmonton	4	4	5	6	6	2	3	2	–	–	–	–	–	–	–	–	–	–	34
Kamloops	–	–	–	–	4	4	4	4	–	–	–	–	–	2	4	4	–	4	20
Seattle	–	–	–	–	–	–	–	–	4	2	3	–	6	–	2	2	1	–	20
Prince Albert	–	–	–	–	–	–	–	–	–	–	–	–	4	2	2	6	6	–	13
Billings	–	–	–	–	–	–	–	–	–	4	3	4	2	–	–	–	–	–	13
Estevan	4	4	4	–	–	–	–	–	–	–	–	–	–	–	–	–	–	–	12
Swift Current	1	–	1	–	3	6	–	–	–	–	–	–	–	–	–	–	–	–	11
Kelowna	–	–	–	–	–	–	–	–	–	–	–	–	–	–	2	4	4	–	10
Nanaimo	–	–	–	–	–	–	–	–	–	–	–	–	5	1	–	–	–	–	6
Vancouver	–	–	–	2	–	–	–	–	–	–	–	–	–	–	–	–	–	–	2
Moose Jaw	–	–	–	–	–	–	–	–	–	–	–	–	–	–	–	–	–	1	1

Year	Total Western Drafted	Total Players Drafted	Western %
1969	20	84	23.8
1970	22	116	19.0
1971	28	117	23.9
1972	44	152	28.9
1973	49	168	29.2
1974	66	247	26.7
1975	54	217	24.9
1976	33	135	24.4
1977	44	185	23.8
1978	48	234	20.5
1979	37	126	29.4
1980	41	210	19.5
1981	36	211	17.1
1982	55	252	21.8
1983	41	242	16.9
1984	38	250	15.2
1985	43	252	17.1
1986	32	252	12.7
Total	731	3450	21.2

United States Colleges

Club	'69	'70	'71	'72	'73	'74	'75	'76	'77	'78	'79	'80	'81	'82	'83	'84	'85	'86	Total
Minnesota	1	3	2	–	–	9	4	4	5	5	2	3	1	1	1	–	–	2	43
Michigan Tech	–	–	3	1	2	5	4	4	1	2	1	4	–	1	–	2	2	2	34
Wisconsin	–	1	2	4	5	4	4	2	3	–	1	–	3	2	–	1	1	–	33
Denver	1	3	2	4	2	3	1	2	2	2	2	1	–	1	–	–	1	2	29
North Dakota	2	3	3	1	4	2	1	–	1	2	3	3	1	–	–	1	–	–	27
Providence	–	–	–	–	–	–	3	2	3	4	–	5	4	1	2	–	1	1	26
New Hampshire	–	–	–	1	1	3	6	–	4	1	1	2	1	1	1	2	–	–	24
Boston U.	–	4	–	–	1	1	1	1	4	5	1	–	1	–	–	1	1	2	23
Michigan	1	–	–	–	2	2	3	3	1	4	–	4	–	–	–	1	1	–	22
Notre Dame	–	–	2	3	–	–	7	2	–	3	1	1	–	–	–	–	–	–	19
Clarkson	–	–	2	2	1	–	2	–	2	2	1	1	1	1	1	–	–	1	17
Colorado	2	1	–	–	1	3	1	2	2	–	1	–	–	–	3	–	1	–	17
Boston College	–	1	–	–	–	–	1	1	–	5	–	2	1	1	–	–	–	1	13
Vermont	–	–	–	–	1	–	4	–	1	1	–	1	1	–	1	1	2	–	13
Cornell	–	–	–	2	1	1	–	1	1	1	–	1	1	1	–	1	2	–	13
Harvard	–	–	2	–	–	–	2	–	2	2	–	–	–	1	1	–	2	–	12
Michigan State	–	–	1	–	1	1	1	1	–	–	–	2	–	2	–	2	–	1	12
Bowling Green	–	–	–	–	–	1	3	2	1	1	1	1	1	–	1	–	–	–	11
RPI	–	–	–	–	1	–	–	1	3	–	1	2	1	1	–	1	–	–	11
St. Lawrence	–	–	–	–	–	1	–	1	3	–	–	–	3	1	1	1	1	–	11
Brown	–	–	–	1	2	1	–	3	2	–	–	1	–	–	–	–	–	–	10
W. Michigan	–	–	–	–	–	–	–	2	–	2	–	2	–	2	2	2	–	–	10
Lake Superior	–	–	–	1	1	1	–	–	3	–	–	–	–	1	–	3	–	–	10
Northern Mich.	–	–	–	–	–	–	–	–	4	1	1	1	–	–	–	–	–	–	8
St. Louis	–	–	–	–	1	2	–	1	3	–	–	–	–	–	–	–	–	–	7
Minn.-Duluth	–	2	1	–	–	–	–	1	1	–	1	–	–	–	–	–	–	–	6
Yale	–	–	1	–	1	–	2	1	–	1	–	–	–	–	–	–	1	–	6
Northeastern	–	–	–	–	1	–	–	1	1	–	1	–	–	1	–	1	1	1	6
Princeton	–	–	–	–	–	1	1	1	1	1	–	–	–	–	–	–	–	–	5
Pennsylvania	–	–	–	1	2	1	–	–	1	–	–	1	–	–	–	–	–	–	5
Union College	–	–	–	–	–	–	4	–	–	–	–	–	–	–	–	–	–	–	4
Colgate	–	–	–	–	1	–	–	2	1	–	–	–	–	–	–	–	–	–	4
Ohio State	–	–	–	–	–	–	2	1	–	–	1	–	–	1	–	–	–	–	4
Lowell	–	–	–	–	–	1	1	–	1	–	1	–	–	–	1	–	–	–	4
Dartmouth	–	–	1	–	–	–	–	1	1	–	–	–	1	1	–	1	–	–	3
Maine	–	–	–	–	–	–	–	–	–	–	1	1	–	1	–	–	–	–	3
Merrimack	–	–	–	–	–	–	1	–	–	–	–	–	–	–	1	–	–	–	2
Salem State	–	–	–	–	–	–	1	–	–	–	–	–	–	–	–	–	–	–	1
Bemidji State	–	1	–	–	–	–	–	–	–	–	–	–	–	–	–	–	–	–	1
San Diego U.	–	–	–	–	–	–	–	–	–	–	–	–	–	–	–	1	–	–	1
Miami U.	–	–	–	–	–	–	–	–	–	–	–	–	–	–	–	1	–	–	1
U. of Ill.-Chicago	–	–	–	–	–	–	–	–	–	–	–	–	–	–	–	–	1	1	1
Babson College	–	–	–	–	–	–	–	–	–	–	–	–	–	–	–	–	1	–	1

Year	Total College Drafted	Total Players Drafted	College %
1969	7	84	8.3
1970	16	116	13.8
1971	22	117	18.8
1972	21	152	13.8
1973	25	168	14.9
1974	41	247	16.6
1975	59	217	26.7
1976	26	135	19.3
1977	49	185	26.5
1978	71	234	32.0
1979	15	126	11.9
1980	42	210	20.0
1981	21	211	10.0
1982	20	252	7.9
1983	14	242	5.8
1984	22	250	8.8
1985	20	252	7.9
1986	22	252	8.7
Total	**513**	**3450**	**14.9**

International

Country	'69	'70	'71	'72	'73	'74	'75	'76	'77	'78	'79	'80	'81	'82	'83	'84	'85	'86	Total
Sweden	–	–	–	–	5	2	5	2	8	6	9	13	14	10	14	20	9		117
Finland	1	–	–	–	1	3	2	3	2	–	4	13	5	9	10	5	10		68
Czechoslovakia	–	–	–	–	–	–	–	–	1	1	–	4	13	9	13	8	6		55
Soviet Union	–	–	–	–	–	1	–	–	2	–	–	3	5	1	1	1			14
West Germany	–	–	–	–	–	–	–	2	–	–	2	–	1	2	1	–			8
Switzerland	–	–	–	–	–	–	1	–	–	–	–	–	–	–	–	–			1
Denmark	–	–	–	–	–	–	–	–	–	–	–	–	–	–	–	1			1
Scotland	–	–	–	–	–	–	–	–	–	–	–	–	–	–	–	1			1

Year	Total International Drafted	Total Players Drafted	International %
1969	1	84	1.2
1970	0	116	0
1971	0	117	0
1972	0	152	0
1973	0	168	0
1974	7	247	2.8
1975	6	217	2.8
1976	8	135	5.9
1977	5	185	2.7
1978	15	234	6.4
1979	7	126	5.5
1980	13	210	6.2
1981	32	211	15.2
1982	35	252	13.9
1983	34	242	14.0
1984	40	250	17.6
1985	30	252	12.0
1986	28	252	11.1
Total	**260**	**3450**	**7.5**

Quebec Major Junior Hockey League

Club	'69	'70	'71	'72	'73	'74	'75	'76	'77	'78	'79	'80	'81	'82	'83	'84	'85	'86	Total
Quebec	1	1	2	4	6	6	1	3	7	1	3	2	2	1	2	2	2	–	47
Cornwall	2	1	2	6	4	8	1	3	1	6	1	5	5	–	–	–	–	–	45
Sherbrooke	–	–	2	2	4	3	7	5	6	3	4	1	5	2	–	–	–	–	44
Shawinigan	3	2	1	6	1	5	3	–	3	–	–	2	2	5	5	2	–	2	42
Trois Rivieres	–	1	2	2	2	3	2	6	3	2	2	2	1	3	–	3	–	3	36
Montreal	–	–	–	4	4	8	1	3	2	4	3	–	3	–	–	–	–	–	32
Sorel	2	3	1	3	1	8	1	1	3	–	–	–	5	–	–	–	–	–	28
Chicoutimi	–	–	–	–	1	–	–	5	1	1	3	6	1	3	–	3	1		25
Hull	–	–	–	–	–	–	3	2	2	3	–	3	1	–	3	1	–	4	22
Verdun	–	1	1	2	–	–	–	–	1	3	3	–	3	3	–	3	–	–	20
Drummondville	2	4	1	4	2	1	–	–	–	–	–	–	–	–	–	1	2	2	19
Granby	–	–	–	–	–	–	–	–	–	–	–	–	–	2	1	3	2	2	10
Longueuil	–	–	–	–	–	–	–	–	–	–	–	–	–	1	2	1	2		6
Laval	–	–	–	–	–	–	–	–	–	–	–	–	–	–	–	–	5		5
St. Jean	–	–	–	–	–	–	–	–	–	–	–	–	–	2	–	1	1		4
St. Jerome	1	–	1	–	–	–	–	–	–	–	–	–	–	–	–	–	–	–	2

Year	Total Quebec Drafted	Total Players Drafted	Quebec %
1969	11	84	13.1
1970	13	116	11.2
1971	13	117	11.1
1972	30	152	19.7
1973	24	168	14.3
1974	40	247	16.2
1975	28	217	12.9
1976	18	135	13.3
1977	40	185	21.6
1978	22	234	9.4
1979	19	126	15.1
1980	24	210	11.4
1981	28	211	13.3
1982	17	252	6.7
1983	24	242	9.9
1984	16	250	6.4
1985	15	252	5.9
1986	22	252	8.7
Total	**389**	**3450**	**11.3**

Center Joe Murphy of Michigan State was selected first overall by the Detroit Red Wings in the 1986 Entry Draft.

1986 Entry Draft

Transferred draft choice notation:
L.A.-Phi. represents a draft choice transferred **from** Los Angeles **to** Philadelphia.

ROUND # 1

Selection	Player	Claimed By	Amateur Club	Position
1	MURPHY, Joe	Detroit	Michigan State	C
2	CARSON, Jimmy	Los Angeles	Verdun	C
3	BRADY, Neil	New Jersey	Medicine Hat	C
4	ZALAPSKI, Zarley	Pittsburgh	Team Canada	LD
5	ANDERSON, Shawn	Buffalo	Team Canada	D
6	DAMPHOUSSE, Vincent	Toronto	Laval	LW
7	WOODLEY, Dan	Vancouver	Portland	C
8	ELYNUIK, Pat	Winnipeg	Prince Albert	RW
9	LEETCH, Brian	NY Rangers	Avon Old Farms	D
10	LEMIEUX, Jocelyn	St. Louis	Laval	RW
11	YOUNG, Scott	Hartford	Boston University	RW
12	BABE, Warren	Minnesota	Lethbridge	LW
13	JANNEY, Craig	Boston	Boston College	F
14	SANIPASS, Everett	Chicago	Verdun	LW
15	PEDERSON, Mark	Montreal	Medicine Hat	LW
16	PELAWA, George	Calgary	Bemidji HS	RW
17	FITZGERALD, Tom	NY Islanders	Austin Prep	C
18	McRAE, Ken	Quebec	Sudbury	C
19	GREENLAW, Jeff	Washington	Team Canada	LW
20	HUFFMAN, Kerry	Philadelphia	Guelph	LD
21	ISSEL, Kim	Edmonton	Prince Albert	RW

ROUND # 2

Selection	Player	Claimed By	Amateur Club	Position
22	GRAVES, Adam	Detroit	Windsor	C
23	SEPPO, Jukka	L.A.-Phi.	Vasa Sport, Finland	W
24	COPELAND, Todd	New Jersey	Belmont Hill	D
25	CAPUANO, Dave	Pittsburgh	Mt. St. Charles HS	C
26	BROWN, Greg	Buffalo	St. Mark's	D
27	BRUNET, Benoit	Tor.-Mtl.	Hull	LW
28	HAWLEY, Kent	Van.-Phi.	Ottawa	C
29	NUMMINEN, Teppo	Winnipeg	Tappara, Finland	D
30	WILKINSON, Neil	NYR.-Min.	Selkirk Settlers	D
31	POSMA, Mike	St. Louis	Buffalo Jr Sabres	RD
32	LaFORGE, Marc	Hartford	Kingston	D
33	KOLSTAD, Dean	Minnesota	Prince Albert	D
34	TIRKKONEN, Pekka	Boston	Sapko, Finland	C
35	KURZAWSKI, Mark	Chicago	Windsor	D
36	SHANNON, Darryl	Mtl.-Tor.	Windsor	LD
37	GLYNN, Brian	Calgary	Saskatoon	D
38	VASKE, Dennis	NY Islanders	Armstrong	LD
39	ROUTHIER, Jean-M	Quebec	Hull	RW
40	SEFTEL, Steve	Washington	Kingston	LW
41	GUERARD, Stephane	Phi.-Que.	Shawinigan	D
42	NICHOLS, Jamie	Edmonton	Portland	LW

ROUND # 3

Selection	Player	Claimed By	Amateur Club	Position
43	MAYER, Derek	Detroit	U. of Denver	RD
44	LAROCQUE, Denis	Los Angeles	Guelph	LD
45	OJANEN, Janne	New Jersey	Tappara, Finland	C
46	AITKEN, Brad	Pittsburgh	Sault Ste. Marie	LW
47	CORKUM, Bob	Buffalo	U. of Maine	F
48	BOLAND, Sean	Toronto	Toronto	RD
49	GIBSON, Don	Vancouver	Winkler	D
50	PALOSAARI, Esa	Winnipeg	Karpat, Finland	RW
51	WALTER, Bret	NY Rangers	U. of Alberta	C
52	HEJNA, Tony	St. Louis	Nichols	LW
53	CLOUSTON, Shawn	Hfd.-NYR.	U. of Alberta	RW
54	BENNETT, Eric	Minnesota	Wilbraham Monson	LW
55	ZETTLER, Rob	Bos.-Min.	Sault Ste. Marie	LD
56	KERR, Kevin	Chi.-Buf.	Windsor	RW
57	LUMME, Jyrki	Montreal	Ilves, Finland	D
58	TURNER, Brad	Cgy.-Min.	Calgary Canucks	RD
59	BERG, Bill	NY Islanders	Toronto	D
60	SIMPSON, Shawn	Que.-Wsh.	Sault Ste Marie	G
61	HRIVNAK, Jim	Washington	Merrimack College	G
62	LANIEL, Marc	Phi.-N.J.	Oshawa	LD
63	SHUDRA, Ron	Edmonton	Kamloops	D

ROUND # 4

Selection	Player	Claimed By	Amateur Club	Position
64	CHEVELDAE, Tim	Detroit	Saskatoon	G
65	COUTURIER, Sylvain	Los Angeles	Laval	LW
66	CARLSSON, Anders	New Jersey	Sodertalje	C
67	BROWN, Rob	Pittsburgh	Kamloops	C
68	BASEGGIO, David	Buffalo	Yale University	D
69	HULST, Kent	Toronto	Windsor	C
70	STERN, Ronnie	Vancouver	Longueuil	RW
71	JARVENPAA, Hannu	Winnipeg	Karpat	RW
72	JANSSENS, Mark	NY Rangers	Regina	C
73	FEATHERSTONE, Glen	St. Louis	Windsor	D
74	CHAPMAN, Brian	Hartford	Belleville	LD
75	TOMLINSON, Kirk	Minnesota	Hamilton	C
76	HALL, Dean	Boston	St. James Can.	C
77	FRANTISEK, Kucera	Chicago	Sparta Praha	D
78	BOBYCK, Brent	Montreal	Notre Dame	LW
79	QUINLAN, Tom	Calgary	Hill Murray HS	RW
80	BYRAM, Shawn	NY Islanders	Regina	LW
81	TUGNUTT, Ron	Quebec	Peterborough	G
82	GINNELL, Erin	Washington	Calgary	C
83	BAR, Mark	Philadelphia	Peterborough	LD
84	CURRIE, Dan	Edmonton	Sault Ste Marie	LW

ROUND # 5

Selection	Player	Claimed By	Amateur Club	Position
85	GARPENLOV, Johan	Detroit	Nacka, Sweden	F
86	GUDEN, Dave	Los Angeles	Roxbury Latin	LW
87	WOLAK, Michael	N.J.-St. L	Kitchener	C
88	SMITH, Sandy	Pittsburgh	Brainerd	F
89	ROONEY, Larry	Buffalo	Thayer	RD
90	TAYLOR, Scott	Toronto	Kitchener	C
91	MURANO, Eric	Vancouver	Calgary Canucks	LW
92	ENDEAN, Craig	Winnipeg	Seattle	RD
93	BLOEMBERG, Jeff	NY Rangers	North Bay	LW
94	AUBERTIN, Eric	St. L.-Mtl.	Granby	G
95	HORN, Bill	Hartford	Western Michigan U.	D
96	GRONSTAND, Jari	Minnesota	Tappara	LW
97	PESKLEWIS, Matt	Boston	St. Albert	LW
98	LOACH, Lonnie	Chicago	Guelph	RW
99	MILANI, Mario	Montreal	Verdun	LW
100	BLOOM, Scott	Calgary	Burnsville	C
101	SEXSMITH, Dean	NY Islanders	Brandon	D
102	BZDEL, Gerald	Quebec	Regina	D
103	PURVES, John	Washington	Hamilton	RW
104	McLELLAN, Todd	Phi.-NYI.	Saskatoon	C
105	HAAS, David	Edmonton	London	LW

ROUND # 6

Selection	Player	Claimed By	Amateur Club	Position
106	STARK, Jay	Detroit	Portland	D
107	STAUBER, Robb	Los Angeles	Duluth Denfield HS	G
108	CROWDER, Troy	New Jersey	Hamilton	RW
109	DANIELS, Jeff	Pittsburgh	Oshawa	LD
110	BALDRIS, Miguel	Buffalo	Shawinigan	D
111	GIGUERE, Stephane	Toronto	St. Jean	LW
112	HERNIMAN, Steve	Vancouver	Cornwall	D
113	BATEMAN, Robertson	Winnipeg	St. Laurent HS	RW
114	TURCOTTE, Darren	NY Rangers	North Bay	C
115	O'TOOLE, Mike	St. Louis	Markham	W
116	QUINN, Joe	Hartford	Calgary Canucks	RW
117	WHITE, Scott	Min.-Que.	Michigan Tech	D
118	PREMAK, Garth	Boston	New Westminster	D
119	DOYON, Mario	Chicago	Drummondville	D
120	BISSON, Steve	Montreal	Sault Ste Marie	LD
121	PARKER, John	Calgary	White Bear Lake	C
122	SCHMALZBAUER, Tony	NY Islanders	Hill Murray	LD
123	SAMUELSSON, Morgan	Quebec	Boden, Sweden	F
124	NILSSON, Stefan	Washington	Lulea, Sweden	C
125	SCHEIFELE, Steve	Philadelphia	Stratford Jr B	RW
126	ENNIS, Jim	Edmonton	Boston University	D

ROUND # 7

Selection	Player	Claimed By	Amateur Club	Position
127	DJOOS, Per	Detroit	Mora, Sweden	D
128	KRAKIWSKY, Sean	Los Angeles	Calgary	RW
129	TODD, Kevin	New Jersey	Prince Albert	C
130	HOBSON, Doug	Pittsburgh	Prince Albert	D
131	HARTMAN, Mike	Buffalo	North Bay	RW
132	HIE, Danny	Toronto	Ottawa	C
133	HELGESON, Jon	Vancouver	Rosseau H.S.	C
134	VERMETTE, Mark	Wpg.-Que.	Lake Superior State	RW
135	GRAHAM, Robb	NY Rangers	Guelph	RW
136	MAY, Andy	St. Louis	Bramalea Jr. B.	
137	TORREL, Steve	Hartford	Hibbing, H.S.	C
138	ANDERSON, Will	NY Islanders	Victoria	
139	BERALDO, Paul	Boston	Sault Ste. Marie	C
140	HUDSON, Mike	Chicago	Sudbury	LW
141	ODELIN, Lyle	Montreal	Moose Jaw	D
142	LESSARD, Rick	Calgary	Ottawa	D
143	PILON, Richard	NY Islanders	Prince Albert AAA	LD
144	NAULT, Jean-Francois	Quebec	Granby	C
145	CHOMA, Peter	Washington	Belleville	RW
146	WAHLSTEN, Sami	Philadelphia	TPS, Finland	W
147	MATULIK, Ivan	Edmonton	Slovan Bratislava	LW

ROUND # 8

Selection	Player	Claimed By	Amateur Club	Position
148	MORTON, Dean	Detroit	Oshawa	D
149	CHAPDELAINE, Rene	Los Angeles	Lake Superior State	D
150	PARDOSKI, Ryan	New Jersey	Calgary Canucks	LW
151	ROHLIK, Steve	Pittsburgh	Hill Murray	LW
152	GUAY, Francois	Buffalo	Laval	LW
153	BRENNAN, Stephen	Toronto	New Prep	W
154	NOBLE, Jeff	Vancouver	Kitchener	C
155	FURLAN, Frank	Winnipeg	Sherwood Park	G
156	CHYZOWSKI, Barry	NY Rangers	St. Albert	C
157	SKARDA, Randy	St. Louis	St. Thomas	D
158	HOOVER, Ron	Hartford	Western Michigan U.	C
159	MATHIAS, Scott	Minnesota	U. of Denver	C
160	FERREIRA, Brian	Boston	Falmouth HS	RW
161	NANNE, Marty	Chicago	U. of Minnesota	RW
162	HAYWARD, Rick	Montreal	Hull	D
163	OLSEN, Mark	Calgary	Colorado College	D
164	HARRIS, Peter	NY Islanders	Haverhill HS	G
165	MILLER, Keith	Quebec	Guelph	LW
166	DAVIDSON, Lee	Washington	Penticton	C
167	BARON, Murray	Philadelphia	Vernon	D
168	BEAULIEU, Nicolas	Edmonton	Drummondville	LW

1986 Entry Draft continued

ROUND # 9

169	POTVIN, Marc	Detroit	Stratford	RW
170	POCHIPINSKI, Trevor	Los Angeles	Penticton	D
171	McCORMACK, Scott	New Jersey	St. Pauls, H.S.	
172	McLLWAIN, Dave	Pittsburgh	North Bay	RW
173	WHITHAM, Shawn	Buffalo	Providence College	D
174	BELLEFEUILLE, Brian	Toronto	Canterbury	LW
175	MERTON, Matt	Vancouver	Stratford Jr B.	G
176	GREEN, Mark	Winnipeg	New Hampton	C
177	SCANLON, Pat	NY Rangers	Cretin, H.S.	
178	BALL, Martyn	St. Louis	St. Mikes Jr B.	LW
179	GLASGOW, Robert	Hartford	Sherwood Park	RW
180	PITLICK, Lance	Minnesota	Cooper H.S.	D
181	FLAHERTY, Jeff	Boston	Weymouth HS	RW
182	BENIC, Geoff	Chicago	Windsor	LW
183	ROUTA, Antonin	Montreal	C.S.S.R.	
184	SHARPLES, Warren	Calgary	Penticton	G
185	JABLONSKI, Jeff	NY Islanders	London Diamonds	LW
186	MILLIER, Pierre	Quebec	Chicoutimi	D
187	TOIVOLA, Tero	Washington	Tappara, Finland	W
188	RUDE, Blaine	Philadelphia	Fergus Falls	RW
189	GREENLAY, Mike	Edmonton	Calgary Mid AAA	G

ROUND # 10

190	KING, Scott	Detroit	Vernon	G
191	KELLY, Paul	Los Angeles	Guelph	D
192	CHABOT, Frederic	New Jersey	St. Foy Midget AAA	
193	CAIN, Kelly	Pittsburgh	London	C
194	REIN, Kenton	Buffalo	Prince Albert	G
195	DAVIDSON, Sean	Toronto	Toronto	RW
196	LYONS, Marc	Vancouver	Kingston	D
197	BLUE, John	Winnipeg	U. of Minnesota	G
198	RANGER, Joe	NY Rangers	London	D
199	THACKER, Rod	St. Louis	Hamilton	LD
200	EVOY, Sean	Hartford	Cornwall	G
201	KECZMER, Dan	Minnesota	Detroit Lit. Caesar	LD
202	HAWGOOD, Greg	Boston	Kamloops	D
203	LOWES, Glen	Chicago	Toronto Marlies	
204	BOHEMIER, Eric	Montreal	Hull	G
205	PICKELL, Doug	Calgary	Kamloops	LW
206	CLARK, Kerry	Ny Islanders	Saskatoon	RW
207	LAPPIN, Chris	Quebec	Canterbury HS	D
208	BABCOCK, Bobby	Washington	Sault Ste Marie	RD
209	SABOL, Shawn	Philadelphia	Fargo, N.D.	
210	LANZA, Matt	Edmonton	Winthrop	D

ROUND # 11

211	BISSETT, Tom	Detroit	Michigan Tech	C
212	MANN, Russ	Los Angeles	St. Lawrence Univ.	RD
213	ANDERSEN, John	New Jersey	Oshawa	LW
214	DRULIA, Stan	Pittsburgh	Belleville	RW
215	ARNDT, Troy	Buffalo	Portland	D
216	HOLICK, Mark	Toronto	Saskatoon	RW
217	HAWKINS, Todd	Vancouver	Belleville	RW
218	COTE, Matt	Winnipeg	Lake Superior	
219	PARENT, Russell	NY Rangers	South Winnipeg Blues	D
220	MacLEAN, Terry	St. Louis	Longueuil	C
221	BROWN, Cal	Hartford	Penticton	D
222	JOY, Garth	Minnesota	Hamilton	LD
223	MALMQUIST, Steffan	Boston	Leksand	
224	THAYER, Chris	Chicago	Kent School	C
225	MOORE, Charlie	Montreal	Belleville	LW
226	LINDSTROM, Anders	Calgary	Timra, Sweden	C
227	BEAUDETTE, Dan	NY Islanders	St. Thomas Academy	
228	LATREILLE, Martin	Quebec	Laval	LD
229	SCHRATZ, John	Washington	Amherst Jr B.	D
230	LAWRENCE, Brett	Philadelphia	Rochester Jr Amer	RW
231	BOZIK, Mojmir	Edmonton	Kosice, Czech	D

ROUND # 12

232	EKROTH, Peter	Detroit	Sodertalje, Sweden	D
233	HAYTON, Brian	Los Angeles	Guelph	LW
234	BUTLER, Bill	N.J.-St. L	Northwood Prep	LW
235	WILSON, Rob	Pittsburgh	Sudbury	LD
236	KIRTON, Doug	Buf.-N.J.	Orillia Tier II	W
237	HOARD, Brian	Toronto	Hamilton	D
238	KRUTOV, Vladimir	Vancouver	USSR Zska Moscow	W
239	BLOMSTEN, Arto	Winnipeg	Djurgarden, Sweden	D
240	TRUE, Soren	NY Rangers	Skobakken, Denmark	W
241	OBRIEN, David	St. Louis	Northeastern U.	RW
242	VERBEEK, Brian	Hartford	Kingston	C
243	STAHURA, Kurt	Minnesota	Williston Academy	LW
244	GARDNER, Joel	Boston	Sarnia	C
245	WILLIAMS, Sean	Chicago	Oshawa	C
246	SVOBODA, Karel	Montreal	CSSR	W
247	STAVJANA, Antonin	Calgary	Czech Nat. Team	D
248	THOMPSON, Paul	NY Islanders	Northern Manitoba AAA	D
249	BOUDREAULT, Sean	Quebec	Mt. St. Charles	F
250	McCRORY, Scott	Washington	Oshawa	C
251	STEPHANO, Daniel	Philadelphia	Northwood School	G
252	HAND, Tony	Edmonton	Murrayfield Racers	C

Draft Choices, 1985-69

1985

FIRST ROUND

Selection	Claimed By	Amateur Club
1. CLARK, Wendel	Toronto	Saskatoon Blades
2. SIMPSON, Craig	Pittsburgh	Michigan State
3. WOLANIN, Craig	New Jersey	Kitchener Rangers
4. SANDLAK, Jim	Vancouver	London Knights
5. MURZYN, Dana	Hartford	Calgary Wranglers
6. DALGARNO, Brad	NY Islanders	Hamilton Steelhawks
7. DAHLEN, Ulf	NY Rangers	Ostersund (Sweden)
8. FEDYK, Brent	Detroit	Regina Pats
9. DUNCANSON, Craig	Los Angeles	Sudbury Wolves
10. GRATTON, Dan	Los Angeles	Oshawa Generals
11. MANSON, David	Chicago	Prince Albert Raiders
12. CHARBONNEAU, Jose	Montreal	Drummondville Voltigeurs
13. KING, Derek	NY Islanders	Sault Ste. Marie Greyhounds
14. JOHANSSON, Carl	Buffalo	Vastra Frolunda (Sweden)
15. LATTA, Dave	Quebec	Kitchener Rangers
16. CHORSKE, Tom	Montreal	Minneapolis HS
17. BIOTTI, Chris	Calgary	Belmont Hill HS
18. STEWART, Ryan	Winnipeg	Kamloops Blazers
19. CORRIVEAU, Yvon	Washington	Toronto Marlboros
20. MELCALFE, Scott	Edmonton	Kingston Canadians
21. SEABROOKE, Glen	Philadelphia	Peterborough Petes

SECOND ROUND

22. SPANGLER, Ken	Toronto	Calgary Wranglers
23. GIFFIN, Lee	Pittsburgh	Oshawa Generals
24. BURKE, Sean	New Jersey	Toronto Marlboros
25. GAMBLE, Troy	Vancouver	Medicine Hat Tigers
26. WHITMORE, Kay	Hartford	Peterborough Petes
27. NIEUWENDYK, Joe	Calgary	Cornell Big Red
28. RICHTER, Mike	NY Rangers	Northwood Prep
29. SHARPLES, Jeff	Detroit	Kelowna Wings
30. EDLUND, Par	Los Angeles	Bjorkloven (Sweden)
31. COTE, Alain	Boston	Quebec Remparts
32. WEINRICH, Eric	New Jersey	North Yarmouth
33. RICHARD, Todd	Montreal	Armstrong HS
34. LAUER, Brad	NY Islanders	Regina Pats
35. HOGUE, Benoit	Buffalo	St Jean Castors
36. LAFRENIERE, Jason	Quebec	Hamilton Steelhawks
37. RAGLAN, Herb	St. Louis	Kingston Canadians
38. WENAAS, Jeff	Calgary	Medicine Hat Tigers
39. OHMAN, Roger	Winnipeg	Leksand Jr. (Sweden)
40. DRUCE, John	Washington	Peterborough Petes
41. CARNELLEY, Todd	Edmonton	Kamloops Blazers
42. RENDALL, Bruce	Philadelphia	Chatham Maroons

1984

FIRST ROUND

Selection	Claimed By	Amateur Club
1. LEMIEUX, Mario	Pittsburgh	Laval Voisins
2. MULLER, Kirk	New Jersey	Team Canada-Guelph
3. OLCZYK, Ed	Chicago	Team USA
4. IAFRATE, Al	Toronto	Team USA-Belleville Bulls
5. SVOBODA, Petr	Montreal	Czechoslovakia Jr.
6. REDMOND, Craig	Los Angeles	Team Canada
7. BURR, Shawn	Detroit	Kitchener Rangers
8. CORSON, Shayne	Montreal	Brantford Alexanders
9. BODGER, Doug	Pittsburgh	Kamloops Jr. Oilers
10. DAIGNEAULT, J.J.	Vancouver	Team Canada-Longueuil
11. COTE, Sylvain	Hartford	Quebec Remparts
12. ROBERTS, Gary	Calgary	Ottawa 67's
13. QUINN, David	Minnesota	Kent High School
14. CARKNER, Terry	NY Rangers	Peterborough Petes
15. STIENBURG, Trevor	Quebec	Guelph Platers
16. BELANGER, Roger	Pittsburgh	Kingston Canadians
17. HATCHER, Kevin	Washington	North Bay Centennials
18. ANDERSSON, Bo Mikael	Buffalo	Vastra Frolunda (Sweden)
19. PASIN, Dave	Boston	Prince Albert Raiders
20. MACPHERSON, Duncan	NY Islanders	Saskatoon Blades
21. ODELEIN, Selmar	Edmonton	Regina Pats

SECOND ROUND

22. SMYTH, Greg	Philadelphia	London Knights
23. BILLINGTON, Craig	New Jersey	Belleville Bulls
24. WILKS, Brian	Los Angeles	Kitchener Rangers
25. GILL, Todd	Toronto	Windsor Spitfires
26. BENNING, Brian	St. Louis	Portland Winter Hawks
27. MELLANBY, Scott	Philadelphia	Henry Carr Jr. B
28. HOUDA, Doug	Detroit	Calgary Wranglers
29. RICHER, Stephane	Montreal	Granby Bisons
30. DOURIS, Peter	Winnipeg	University of New Hampshire
31. ROHLICEK, Jeff	Vancouver	Portland Winter Hawks
32. HRKAC, Anthony	St. Louis	Orillia Jr. A
33. SABOURIN, Ken	Calgary	Sault Ste. Marie Greyhounds
34. LEACH, Stephen	Washington	Matignon High School
35. HELMINEN, Raimo Ilmari	NY Rangers	Ilves (Finland)
36. BROWN, Jeff	Quebec	Sudbury Wolves
37. CHYCHRUN, Jeff	Philadelphia	Kingston Canadians
38. RANHEIM, Paul	Calgary	Edina Hornets HS
39. TRAPP, Doug	Buffalo	Regina Pats
40. PODLOSKI, Ray	Boston	Portland Winter Hawks
41. MELANSON, Bruce	NY Islanders	Oshawa Generals
42. REAUGH, Daryl	Edmonton	Kamloops Jr. Oilers

1983
FIRST ROUND

Selection	Claimed By	Amateur Club
1. LAWTON, Brian	Minnesota	Mount St. Charles H.S.
2. TURGEON, Sylvain	Hartford	Hull Olympiques
3. LAFONTAINE, Pat	NY Islanders	Verdun Juniors
4. YZERMAN, Steve	Detroit	Peterborough Petes
5. BARRASSO, Tom	Buffalo	Acton-Boxboro High School
6. MacLEAN, John	New Jersey	Oshawa Generals
7. COURTNALL, Russ	Toronto	Victoria Cougars
8. McBAIN, Andrew	Winnipeg	North Bay Centennials
9. NEELY, Cam	Vancouver	Portland Winter Hawks
10. LACOMBE, Normand	Buffalo	University of New Hampshire
11. CREIGHTON, Adam	Buffalo	Ottawa 67's
12. GAGNER, Dave	NY Rangers	Brantford Alexanders
13. QUINN, Dan	Calgary	Belleville Bulls
14. DOLLAS, Bobby	Winnipeg	Laval Voisins
15. ERREY, Bob	Pittsburgh	Peterborough Petes
16. DIDUCK, Gerald	NY Islanders	Lethbridge Broncos
17. TURCOTTE, Alfie	Montreal	Portland Winter Hawks
18. CASSIDY, Bruce	Chicago	Ottawa 67's
19. BEUKEBOOM, Jeff	Edmonton	Sault Ste. Marie Greyhounds
20. JENSEN, David	Hartford	Lawrence Academy H.S.
21. MARKWART, Nevin	Boston	Regina Pats

SECOND ROUND

22. CHARLESWORTH, Todd	Pittsburgh	Oshawa Generals
23. SIREN, Ville	Hartford	Ilves (Finland)
24. EVANS, Shawn	New Jersey	Peterborough Petes
25. LAMBERT, Lane	Detroit	Saskatoon Blades
26. LEMIEUX, Claude	Montreal	Trois Rivieres Draveurs
27. MOMESSO, Sergio	Montreal	Shawinigan Cataractes
28. JACKSON, Jeff	Toronto	Brantford Alexanders
29. BERRY, Brad	Winnipeg	St. Albert Saints
30. BRUCE, Dave	Vancouver	Kitchener Rangers
31. TUCKER, John	Buffalo	Kitchener Rangers
32. HEROUX, Yves	Quebec	Chicoutimi Sagueneens
33. HEATH, Randy	NY Rangers	Portland Winter Hawks
34. HAJDU, Richard	Buffalo	Kamloops Jr. Oilers
35. FRANCIS, Todd	Montreal	Brantford Alexanders
36. PARKS, Malcolm	Minnesota	St. Albert Saints
37. McKECHNEY, Grant	NY Islanders	Kitchener Rangers
38. MUSIL, Frantisek	Minnesota	Czech. National Team
39. PRESLEY, Wayne	Chicago	Kitchener Rangers
40. GOLDEN, Mike	Edmonton	Reading High School
41. ZEZEL, Peter	Philadelphia	Toronto Malboros
42. JOHNSTON, Greg	Boston	Toronto Malboros

1982
FIRST ROUND

Selection	Claimed By	Amateur Club
1. KLUZAK, Gord	Boston	Nanaimo Islanders
2. BELLOWS, Brian	Minnesota	Kitchener Rangers
3. NYLUND, Gary	Toronto	Portland Winter Hawks
4. SUTTER, Ron	Philadelphia	Lethbridge Broncos
5. STEVENS, Scott	Washington	Kitchener Rangers
6. HOUSLEY, Phil	Buffalo	S. St. Paul High School
7. YAREMCHUK, Ken	Chicago	Portland Winter Hawks
8. TROTTIER, Rocky	New Jersey	Nanaimo Islanders
9. CYR, Paul	Buffalo	Victoria Cougars
10. SUTTER, Rich	Pittsburgh	Lethbridge Broncos
11. PETIT, Michel	Vancouver	Sherbrooke Castors
12. KYTE, Jim	Winnipeg	Cornwall Royals
13. SHAW, David	Quebec	Kitchener Rangers
14. LAWLESS, Paul	Hartford	Windsor Spitfires
15. KONTOS, Chris	NY Rangers	Toronto Marlboros
16. ANDREYCHUK, Dave	Buffalo	Oshawa Generals
17. CRAVEN, Murray	Detroit	Medicine Hat Tigers
18. DANEYKO, Ken	New Jersey	Seattle Breakers
19. HEROUX, Alain	Montreal	Chicoutimi Sagueneens
20. PLAYFAIR, Jim	Edmonton	Portland Winter Hawks
21. FLATLEY, Pat	NY Islanders	University of Wisconsin

SECOND ROUND

22. CURRAN, Brian	Boston	Portland Winter Hawks
23. COURTEAU, Yves	Detroit	Laval Voisins
24. LEEMAN, Gary	Toronto	Regina Pats
25. IHNACAK, Peter	Toronto	Czech National Team
26. ANDERSON, Mike	Buffalo	N. St. Paul High School
27. HEIDT, Mike	Los Angeles	Calgary Wranglers
28. BADEAU, Rene	Chicago	Quebec Remparts
29. REIERSON, Dave	Calgary	Prince Albert Raiders
30. JOHANSSON, Jens	Buffalo	Pitea (Sweden)
31. GAUVREAU, Jocelyn	Montreal	Granby Bisons
32. CARLSON, Kent	Montreal	St. Lawrence University
33. MALEY, David	Montreal	Edina High School
34. GILLIS, Paul	Quebec	Niagara Falls Flyers
35. PATERSON, Mark	Hartford	Ottawa 67's
36. SANDSTROM, Tomas	NY Rangers	Farjestads (Sweden)
37. KROMM, Richard	Calgary	Portland Winter Hawks
38. HRYNEWICH, Tim	Pittsburgh	Sudbury Wolves
39. BYERS, Lyndon	Boston	Regina Pats
40. SANDELIN, Scott	Montreal	Hibbing High School
41. GRAVES, Steve	Edmonton	Sault Ste. Marie Greyhounds
42. SMITH, Vern	NY Islanders	Lethbridge Broncos

1981
FIRST ROUND

Selection	Claimed By	Amateur Club
1. HAWERCHUK, Dale	Winnipeg	Cornwall Royals
2. SMITH, Doug	Los Angeles	Ottawa 67's
3. CARPENTER, Bobby	Washington	St. John's High School
4. FRANCIS, Ron	Hartford	Sault Ste. Marie Greyhounds
5. CIRELLA, Joe	Colorado	Oshawa Generals
6. BENNING, Jim	Toronto	Portland Winter Hawks
7. HUNTER, Mark	Montreal	Brantford Alexanders
8. FUHR, Grant	Edmonton	Victoria Cougars
9. PATRICK, James	NY Rangers	Prince Albert Raiders
10. BUTCHER, Garth	Vancouver	Regina Pats
11. MOLLER, Randy	Quebec	Lethbridge Broncos
12. TANTI, Tony	Chicago	Oshawa Generals
13. MEIGHAN, Ron	Minnesota	Niagara Falls Flyers
14. LEVEILLE, Normand	Boston	Chicoutimi Sagueneens
15. MacINNIS, Allan	Calgary	Kitchener Rangers
16. SMITH, Steve	Philadelphia	Sault Ste. Marie Greyhounds
17. DUDACEK, Jiri	Buffalo	Kladno (Czech.)
18. DELORME, Gilbert	Montreal	Chicoutimi Sagueneens
19. INGMAN, Jan	Montreal	Sweden
20. RUFF, Marty	St. Louis	Lethbridge Broncos
21. BOUTILIER, Paul	NY Islanders	Sherbrooke Castors

SECOND ROUND

22. ARNIEL, Scott	Winnipeg	Cornwall Royals
23. LOISELLE, Claude	Detroit	Windsor Spitfires
24. YAREMCHUK, Gary	Toronto	Portland Winter Hawks
25. GRIFFIN, Kevin	Chicago	Portland Winter Hawks
26. CHERNOMAZ, Rich	Colorado	Victoria Cougars
27. DONNELLY, Dave	Minnesota	St. Albert Saints
28. GATZOS, Steve	Pittsburgh	Sault Ste. Marie Greyhounds
29. STRUEBY, Todd	Edmonton	Regina Pats
30. ERIXON, Jan	NY Rangers	Skelleftea (Sweden)
31. SANDS, Mike	Minnesota	Sudbury Wolves
32. ERIKSSON, Lars	Montreal	Brynas (Sweden)
33. HIRSCH, Tom	Minnesota	Patrick Henry High School
34. PREUSS, Dave	Minnesota	St. Thomas Academy H.S.
35. DUFOUR, Luc	Boston	Chicoutimi Sagueneens
36. NORDIN, Hakan	St. Louis	Farjestads (Sweden)
37. COSTELLO, Rich	Philadelphia	Natick High School
38. VIRTA, Hannu	Buffalo	TPS Finland
39. KENNEDY, Dean	Los Angeles	Brandon Wheat Kings
40. CHELIOS, Chris	Montreal	Moose Jaw Canucks
41. WAHLSTEN, Jali	Minnesota	TPS Finland
42. DINEEN, Gord	NY Islanders	Sault Ste. Marie Greyhounds

1980
FIRST ROUND

Selection	Claimed By	Amateur Club
1. WICKENHEISER, Doug	Montreal	Regina Pats
2. BABYCH, Dave	Winnipeg	Portland Winter Hawks
3. SAVARD, Denis	Chicago	Montreal Juniors
4. MURPHY, Larry	Los Angeles	Peterborough Petes
5. VEITCH, Darren	Washington	Regina Pats
6. COFFEY, Paul	Edmonton	Kitchener Rangers
7. LANZ, Rick	Vancouver	Oshawa Generals
8. ARTHUR, Fred	Hartford	Cornwall Royals
9. BULLARD, Mike	Pittsburgh	Brantford Alexanders
10. FOX, Jimmy	Los Angeles	Ottawa 67's
11. BLAISDELL, Mike	Detroit	Regina Pats
12. WILSON, Rik	St. Louis	Kingston Canadians
13. CYR, Denis	Calgary	Montreal Juniors
14. MALONE, Jim	NY Rangers	Toronto Marlboros
15. DUPONT, Jerome	Chicago	Toronto Marlboros
16. PALMER, Brad	Minnesota	Victoria Cougars
17. SUTTER, Brent	NY Islanders	Red Deer Rustlers
18. PEDERSON, Barry	Boston	Victoria Cougars
19. GAGNE, Paul	Colorado	Windsor Spitfires
20. PATRICK, Steve	Buffalo	Brandon Wheat Kings
21. STOTHERS, Mike	Philadelphia	Kingston Canadians

SECOND ROUND

22. WARD, Joe	Colorado	Seattle Breakers
23. MANTHA, Moe	Winnipeg	Toronto Marlboros
24. ROCHEFORT, Normand	Quebec	Quebec Remparts
25. MUNI, Craig	Toronto	Kingston Canadians
26. McGILL, Bob	Toronto	Victoria Cougars
27. NATTRESS, Ric	Montreal	Brantford Alexanders
28. LUDZIK, Steve	Chicago	Niagara Falls Flyers
29. GALARNEAU, Michel	Hartford	Hull Olympiques
30. SOLHEIM, Ken	Chicago	Medicine Hat Tigers
31. CURTALE, Tony	Calgary	Brantford Alexanders
32. LaVALLEE, Kevin	Calgary	Brantford Alexanders
33. TERRION, Greg	Los Angeles	Brantford Alexanders
34. MORRISON, Dave	Los Angeles	Peterborough Petes
35. ALLISON, Mike	NY Rangers	Sudbury Wolves
36. DAWES, Len	Chicago	Victoria Cougars
37. BEAUPRE, Don	Minnesota	Sudbury Wolves
38. HRUDEY, Kelly	NY Islanders	Medicine Hat Tigers
39. KONROYD, Steve	Calgary	Oshawa Generals
40. CHABOT, John	Montreal	Hull Olympiques
41. MOLLER, Mike	Buffalo	Lethbridge Broncos
42. FRASER, Jay	Philadelphia	Ottawa 67's

1979
FIRST ROUND

Selection	Claimed By	Amateur Club
1. RAMAGE, Rob	Colorado	London Knights
2. TURNBULL, Perry	St. Louis	Portland Winter Hawks
3. FOLIGNO, Mike	Detroit	Sudbury Wolves
4. GARTNER, Mike	Washington	Niagara Falls Flyers
5. VAIVE, Rick	Vancouver	Sherbrooke Castors
6. HARTSBURG, Craig	Minnesota	Sault Ste. Marie Greyhounds
7. BROWN, Keith	Chicago	Portland Winter Hawks
8. BOURQUE, Raymond	Boston	Verdun Black Hawks
9. BOSCHMAN, Laurie	Toronto	Brandon Wheat Kings
10. McCARTHY, Tom	Minnesota	Oshawa Generals
11. RAMSEY, Mike	Buffalo	University of Minnesota
12. REINHART, Paul	Atlanta	Kitchener Rangers
13. SULLIMAN, Doug	NY Rangers	Kitchener Rangers
14. PROPP, Brian	Philadelphia	Brandon Wheat Kings
15. McCRIMMON, Brad	Boston	Brandon Wheat Kings
16. WELLS, Jay	Los Angeles	Kingston Canadians
17. SUTTER, Duane	NY Islanders	Lethbridge Broncos
18. ALLISON, Ray	Hartford	Brandon Wheat Kings
19. MANN, Jimmy	Winnipeg	Sherbrooke Beavers
20. GOULET, Michel	Quebec	Quebec Remparts
21. LOWE, Kevin	Edmonton	Quebec Remparts

SECOND ROUND

Selection	Claimed By	Amateur Club
22. WESLEY, Blake	Philadelphia	Portland Winter Hawks
23. PEROVICH, Mike	Atlanta	Brandon Wheat Kings
24. RAUSSE, Errol	Washington	Seattle Breakers
25. JONSSON, Tomas	NY Islanders	MoDo AIK (Sweden)
26. ASHTON, Brent	Vancouver	Saskatoon Blades
27. GINGRAS, Gaston	Montreal	Hamilton Fincups
28. TRIMPER, Tim	Chicago	Peterborough Petes
29. HOPKINS, Dean	Los Angeles	London Knights
30. HARDY, Mark	Los Angeles	Montreal Juniors
31. MARSHALL, Paul	Pittsburgh	Brantford Alexanders
32. RUFF, Lindy	Buffalo	Lethbridge Broncos
33. RIGGIN, Pat	Atlanta	London Knights
34. HOSPODAR, Ed	NY Rangers	Ottawa 67's
35. LINDBERGH, Pelle	Philadelphia	Solna (Sweden)
36. MORRISON, Doug	Boston	Lethbridge Broncos
37. NASLUND, Mats	Montreal	Brynas IFK (Sweden)
38. CARROLL, Billy	NY Islanders	London Knights
39. SMITH, Stuart	Hartford	Peterborough Petes
40. CHRISTIAN, Dave	Winnipeg	University of North Dakota
41. HUNTER, Dale	Quebec	Sudbury Wolves
42. BROTEN, Neal	Minnesota	University of Minnesota

1978
FIRST ROUND

Selection	Claimed By	Amateur Club
1. SMITH, Bobby	Minnesota	Ottawa 67's
2. WALTER, Ryan	Washington	Seattle Breakers
3. BABYCH, Wayne	St. Louis	Portland Winter Hawks
4. DERLAGO, Bill	Vancouver	Brandon Wheat Kings
5. GILLIS, Mike	Colorado	Kingston Canadians
6. WILSON, Behn	Philadelphia	Kingston Canadians
7. LINSEMAN, Ken	Philadelphia	Kingston Canadians
8. GEOFFRION, Danny	Montreal	Cornwall Royals
9. HUBER, Willie	Detroit	Hamilton Fincups
10. HIGGINS, Tim	Chicago	Ottawa 67's
11. MARSH, Brad	Atlanta	London Knights
12. PETERSON, Brent	Detroit	Portland Winter Hawks
13. PLAYFAIR, Larry	Buffalo	Portland Winter Hawks
14. LUCAS, Danny	Philadelphia	Sault Ste. Marie Greyhounds
15. TAMBELLINI, Steve	NY Islanders	Lethbridge Broncos
16. SECORD, Al	Boston	Hamilton Fincups
17. HUNTER, Dave	Montreal	Sudbury Wolves
18. COULIS, Tim	Washington	Hamilton Fincups

SECOND ROUND

Selection	Claimed By	Amateur Club
19. PAYNE, Steve	Minnesota	Ottawa 67's
20. MULVEY, Paul	Washington	Portland Winter Hawks
21. QUENNEVILLE, Joel	Toronto	Windsor Spitfires
22. FRASER, Curt	Vancouver	Victoria Cougars
23. MacKINNON, Paul	Washington	Peterborough Petes
24. CHRISTOFF, Steve	Minnesota	University of Minnesota
25. MEEKER, Mike	Pittsburgh	Peterborough Petes
26. MALONEY, Don	NY Rangers	Kitchener Rangers
27. MALINOWSKI, Merlin	Colorado	Medicine Hat Tigers
28. HICKS, Glenn	Detroit	Flin Flon Bombers
29. LECUYER, Doug	Chicago	Portland Winter Hawks
30. YAKIWCHUK, Dale	Montreal	Portland Winter Hawks
31. JENSEN, Al	Detroit	Hamilton Fincups
32. McKEGNEY, Tony	Buffalo	Kingston Canadians
33. SIMURDA, Mike	Philadelphia	Kingston Canadians
34. JOHNSTON, Randy	NY Islanders	Peterborough Petes
35. NICOLSON, Graeme	Boston	Cornwall Royals
36. CARTER, Ron	Montreal	Sherbrooke Castors

1977
FIRST ROUND

Selection	Claimed By	Amateur Club
1. McCOURT, Dale	Detroit	St. Catharines Fincups
2. BECK, Barry	Colorado	New Westminster Bruins
3. PICARD, Robert	Washington	Montreal Jrs.
4. GILLIS, Jere	Vancouver	Sherbrooke Castors
5. CROMBEEN, Mike	Cleveland	Kingston Canadians
6. WILSON, Doug	Chicago	Ottawa 67's
7. MAXWELL, Brad	Minnesota	New Westminster Bruins
8. DEBLOIS, Lucien	NY Rangers	Sorel Black Hawks
9. CAMPBELL, Scott	St. Louis	London Knights
10. NAPIER, Mark	Montreal	Toronto Marlboros
11. ANDERSON, John	Toronto	Toronto Marlboros
12. JOHANSON, Trevor	Toronto	Toronto Marlboros
13. DUGUAY, Ron	NY Rangers	Sudbury Wolves
14. SEILING, Ric	Buffalo	St. Catharines Fincups
15. BOSSY, Mike	NY Islanders	Laval Nationales
16. FOSTER, Dwight	Boston	Kitchener Rangers
17. McCARTHY, Kevin	Philadelphia	Winnipeg Monarchs
18. DUPONT, Norm	Montreal	Montreal Jrs.

SECOND ROUND

Selection	Claimed By	Amateur Club
19. SAVARD, Jean	Chicago	Quebec Remparts
20. ZAHARKO, Miles	Atlanta	New Westminster Bruins
21. LOFTHOUSE, Mark	Washington	New Westminster Bruins
22. BANDURA, Jeff	Vancouver	Portland Winter Hawks
23. CHICOINE, Daniel	Cleveland	Sherbrooke Castors
24. GLADNEY, Bob	Toronto	Oshawa Generals
25. SEMENKO, Dave	Minnesota	Brandon Wheat Kings
26. KEATING, Mike	NY Rangers	St. Catherines Fincups
27. LABATTE, Neil	St. Louis	Toronto Marlboros
28. LAURENCE, Don	Atlanta	Kitchener Rangers
29. SAGANIUK, Rocky	Toronto	Lethbridge Broncos
30. HAMILTON, Jim	Pittsburgh	London Knights
31. HILL, Brian	Atlanta	Medicine Hat Tigers
32. ARESHENKOFF, Ron	Buffalo	Medicine Hat Tigers
33. TONELLI, John	NY Islanders	Toronto Marlboros
34. PARRO, Dave	Boston	Saskatoon Blades
35. GORENCE, Tom	Philadelphia	University of Minnesota
36. LANGWAY, Rod	Montreal	University of New Hampshire

1976
FIRST ROUND

Selection	Claimed By	Amateur Club
1. GREEN, Rick	Washington	London Knights
2. CHAPMAN, Blair	Pittsburgh	Saskatoon Blades
3. SHARPLEY, Glen	Minnesota	Hull Festivals
4. WILLIAMS, Fred	Detroit	Saskatoon Blades
5. JOHANSSON, Bjorn	California	Sweden
6. MURDOCH, Don	NY Rangers	Medicine Hat Tigers
7. FEDERKO, Bernie	St. Louis	Saskatoon Blades
8. SHAND, Dave	Atlanta	Peterborough Petes
9. CLOUTIER, Real	Chicago	Quebec Remparts
10. PHILLIPOFF, Harold	Atlanta	New Westminster Bruins
11. GARDNER, Paul	Kansas City	Oshawa Generals
12. LEE, Peter	Montreal	Ottawa 67's
13. SCHUTT, Rod	Montreal	Sudbury Wolves
14. McKENDRY, Alex	NY Islanders	Sudbury Wolves
15. CARROLL, Greg	Washington	Medicine Hat Tigers
16. PACHAL, Clayton	Boston	New Westminster Bruins
17. SUZOR, Mark	Philadelphia	Kingston Canadians
18. BAKER, Bruce	Montreal	Ottawa 67's

SECOND ROUND

Selection	Claimed By	Amateur Club
19. MALONE, Greg	Pittsburgh	Oshawa Generals
20. SUTTER, Brian	St. Louis	Lethbridge Broncos
21. CLIPPINGDALE, Steve	Los Angeles	New Westminster Bruins
22. LARSON, Reed	Detroit	University of Minnesota
23. STENLUND, Vern	California	London Knights
24. FARRISH, Dave	NY Rangers	Sudbury Wolves
25. SMRKE, John	St. Louis	Toronto Marlboros
26. MANNO, Bob	Vancouver	St. Catharines Black Hawks
27. McDILL, Jeff	Chicago	Victoria Cougars
28. SIMPSON, Bobby	Atlanta	Sherbrooke Castors
29. MARSH, Peter	Pittsburgh	Sherbrooke Castors
30. CARLYLE, Randy	Toronto	Sudbury Wolves
31. ROBERTS, Jim	Minnesota	Ottawa 67's
32. KASZYCKI, Mike	NY Islanders	Sault Ste. Marie Greyhounds
33. KOWAL, Joe	Buffalo	Hamilton Fincups
34. GLOECKNER, Larry	Boston	Victoria Cougars
35. CALLANDER, Drew	Philadelphia	Regina Pats
36. MELROSE, Barry	Montreal	Kamloops Chiefs

1975

FIRST ROUND

Selection	Claimed By	Amateur Club
1. BRIDGMAN, Mel	Philadelphia	Victoria Cougars
2. DEAN, Barry	Kansas City	Medicine Hat Tigers
3. KLASSEN, Ralph	California	Saskatoon Blades
4. MAXWELL, Brian	Minnesota	Medicine Hat Tigers
5. LAPOINTE, Rick	Detroit	Victoria Cougars
6. ASHBY, Don	Toronto	Calgary Centennials
7. VAYDIK, Greg	Chicago	Medicine Hat Tigers
8. MULHERN, Richard	Atlanta	Sherbrooke Beavers
9. SADLER, Robin	Montreal	Edmonton Oil Kings
10. BLIGHT, Rick	Vancouver	Brandon Wheat Kings
11. PRICE, Pat	NY Islanders	Saskatoon Blades
12. DILLON, Wayne	NY Rangers	Toronto Marlboros
13. LAXTON, Gord	Pittsburgh	New Westminster Bruins
14. HALWARD, Doug	Boston	Peterborough Petes
15. MONDOU, Pierre	Montreal	Montreal Juniors
16. YOUNG, Tim	Los Angeles	Ottawa 67's
17. SAUVE, Bob	Buffalo	Laval Nationales
18. FORSYTH, Alex	Washington	Kingston Canadians

SECOND ROUND

Selection	Claimed By	Amateur Club
19. SCAMURRA, Peter	Washington	Peterborough Petes
20. CAIRNS, Don	Kansas City	Victoria Cougars
21. MARUK, Dennis	California	London Knights
22. ENGBLOM, Brian	Montreal	University of Wisconsin
23. ROLLINS, Jerry	Detroit	Winnipeg Jr. Jets
24. JARVIS, Doug	Toronto	Peterborough Petes
25. ARNDT, Daniel	Chicago	Saskatoon Blades
26. BOWNASS, Rick	Atlanta	Montreal Juniors
27. STANIOWSKI, Ed	St. Louis	Regina Pats
28. GASSOFF, Brad	Vancouver	Kamloops Chiefs
29. SALVIAN, David	NY Islanders	St. Catharines Black Hawks
30. SOETAERT, Doug	NY Rangers	Edmonton Oil Kings
31. ANDERSON, Russ	Pittsburgh	University of Minnesota
32. SMITH, Barry	Boston	New Westminster Bruins
33. BUCYK, Terry	Los Angeles	Lethbridge Broncos
34. GREENBANK, Kelvin	Montreal	Winnipeg Jr. Jets
35. BREITENBACH, Ken	Buffalo	St. Catharines Black Hawks
36. MASTERS, Jamie	St. Louis	Ottawa 67's

1974

FIRST ROUND

Selection	Claimed By	Amateur Club
1. JOLY, Greg	Washington	Regina Pats
2. PAIEMENT, Wilfred	Kansas City	St. Catharines Black Hawks
3. HAMPTON, Rick	California	St. Catharines Black Hawks
4. GILLIES, Clark	NY Islanders	Regina Pats
5. CONNOR, Cam	Montreal	Flin Flon Bombers
6. HICKS, Doug	Minnesota	Flin Flon Bombers
7. RISEBROUGH, Doug	Montreal	Kitchener Rangers
8. LAROUCHE, Pierre	Pittsburgh	Sorel Black Hawks
9. LOCHEAD, Bill	Detroit	Oshawa Generals
10. CHARTRAW, Rick	Montreal	Kitchener Rangers
11. FOGOLIN, Lee	Buffalo	Oshawa Generals
12. TREMBLAY, Mario	Montreal	Montreal Juniors
13. VALIQUETTE, Jack	Toronto	Sault Ste. Marie Greyhounds
14. MALONEY, Dave	NY Rangers	Kitchener Rangers
15. McTAVISH, Gord	Montreal	Sudbury Wolves
16. MULVEY, Grant	Chicago	Calgary Centennials
17. CHIPPERFIELD, Ron	California	Brandon Wheat Kings
18. LARWAY, Don	Boston	Swift Current Broncos

SECOND ROUND

Selection	Claimed By	Amateur Club
19. MARSON, Mike	Washington	Sudbury Wolves
20. BURDON, Glen	Kansas City	Regina Pats
21. AFFLECK, Bruce	California	University of Denver
22. TROTTIER, Bryan	NY Islanders	Swift Current Broncos
23. SEDLBAUER, Ron	Vancouver	Kitchener Rangers
24. NANTAIS, Rick	Minnesota	Quebec Remparts
25. HOWE, Mark	Boston	Toronto Marlboros
26. HESS, Bob	St. Louis	New Westminster Bruins
27. COSSETTE, Jacques	Pittsburgh	Sorel Black Hawks
28. CHOUINARD, Guy	Atlanta	Quebec Remparts
29. GARE, Danny	Buffalo	Calgary Centennials
30. MacGREGOR, Gary	Montreal	Cornwall Royals
31. WILLIAMS, Dave	Toronto	Swift Current Broncos
32. GRESCHNER, Ron	NY Rangers	New Westminster Bruins
33. LUPIEN, Gilles	Montreal	Montreal Juniors
34. DAIGLE, Alain	Chicago	Trois Rivières Draveurs
35. McLEAN, Don	Philadelphia	Sudbury Wolves
36. STURGEON, Peter	Boston	Kitchener Rangers

Ian Turnbull was drafted 15th in the 1973 Entry Draft.

1973

FIRST ROUND

Selection	Claimed By	Amateur Club
1. POTVIN, Denis	NY Islanders	Ottawa 67's
2. LYSIAK, Tom	Atlanta	Medicine Hat Tigers
3. VERVERGAERT, Dennis	Vancouver	London Knights
4. McDONALD, Lanny	Toronto	Medicine Hat Tigers
5. DAVIDSON, John	St. Louis	Calgary Centennials
6. SAVARD, Andre	Boston	Quebec Remparts
7. STOUGHTON, Blaine	Pittsburgh	Flin Flon Bombers
8. GAINEY, Bob	Montreal	Peterborough Petes
9. DAILEY, Bob	Vancouver	Toronto Marlboros
10. NEELEY, Bob	Toronto	Peterborough Petes
11. RICHARDSON, Terry	Detroit	New Westminster Bruins
12. TITANIC, Morris	Buffalo	Sudbury Wolves
13. ROTA, Darcy	Chicago	Edmonton Oil Kings
14. MIDDLETON, Rick	NY Rangers	Oshawa Generals
15. TURNBULL, Ian	Toronto	Ottawa 67's
16. MERCREDI, Vic	Atlanta	New Westminster Bruins

SECOND ROUND

Selection	Claimed By	Amateur Club
17. GOLDUP, Glen	Montreal	Toronto Marlboros
18. DUNLOP, Blake	Minnesota	Ottawa 67's
19. BORDELEAU, Paulin	Vancouver	Toronto Marlboros
20. GOODENOUGH, Larry	Philadelphia	London Knights
21. VAIL, Eric	Atlanta	Sudbury Wolves
22. MARRIN, Peter	Montreal	Toronto Marlboros
23. BIANCHIN, Wayne	Pittsburgh	Flin Flon Bombers
24. PESUT, George	St. Louis	Saskatoon Blades
25. ROGERS, John	Minnesota	Edmonton Oil Kings
26. LEVINS, Brent	Philadelphia	Swift Current Broncos
27. CAMPBELL, Colin	Pittsburgh	Peterborough Petes
28. LANDRY, Jean	Buffalo	Quebec Remparts
29. THOMAS, Reg	Chicago	London Knights
30. HICKEY, Pat	NY Rangers	Hamilton Red Wings
31. JONES, Jim	Boston	Peterborough Petes
32. ANDRUFF, Ron	Montreal	Flin Flon Bombers

1972
FIRST ROUND

Selection	Claimed By	Amateur Club
1. HARRIS, Billy	NY Islanders	Toronto Marlboros
2. RICHARD, Jacques	Atlanta	Quebec Remparts
3. LEVER, Don	Vancouver	Niagara Falls Flyers
4. SHUTT, Steve	Montreal	Toronto Marlboros
5. SCHOENFELD, Jim	Buffalo	Niagara Falls Flyers
6. LAROCQUE, Michel	Montreal	Ottawa 67's
7. BARBER, Bill	Philadelphia	Kitchener Rangers
8. GARDNER, Dave	Montreal	Toronto Marlboros
9. MERRICK, Wayne	St. Louis	Ottawa 67's
10. BLANCHARD, Albert	New York	Kitchener Rangers
11. FERGUSON, George	Toronto	Toronto Marlboros
12. BYERS, Jerry	Minnesota	Kitchener Rangers
13. RUSSELL, Phil	Chicago	Edmonton Oil Kings
14. VAN BOXMEER, John	Montreal	Guelph Juniors
15. MacMILLAN, Bobby	New York	St. Catharines Black Hawks
16. BLOOM, Mike	Boston	St. Catharines Black Hawks

SECOND ROUND

17. HENNING Lorne	NY Islanders	New Westminster Bruins
18. BIALOWAS, Dwight	Atlanta	Regina Pats
19. McSHEFFREY, Brian	Vancouver	Ottawa 67's
20. KOZAK, Don	Los Angeles	Edmonton Oil Kings
21. SACHARUK, Larry	New York	Saskatoon Blades
22. CASSIDY, Tom	California	Kitchener Rangers
23. BLADON, Tom	Philadelphia	Edmonton Oil Kings
24. LYNCH, Jack	Pittsburgh	Oshawa Generals
25. CARRIERE, Larry	Buffalo	Loyola College
26. GUITE, Pierre	Detroit	St. Catharines Black Hawks
27. OSBURN, Randy	Toronto	London Knights
28. WEIR, Stan	California	Medicine Hat Tigers
29. OGILVIE, Brian	Chicago	Edmonton Oil Kings
30. LUKOWICH, Bernie	Pittsburgh	New Westminster Royals
31. VILLEMURE, Rene	New York	Shawinigan Bruins
32. ELDER, Wayne	Boston	London Knights

1970
FIRST ROUND

Selection	Claimed By	Amateur Club
1. PERREAULT, Gilbert	Buffalo	Montreal Junior Canadiens
2. TALLON, Dale	Vancouver	Toronto Marlboros
3. LEACH, Reg	Boston	Flin Flon Bombers
4. MacLEISH, Rick	Boston	Peterborough Petes
5. MARTINIUK, Ray	Montreal	Flin Flon Bombers
6. LEFLEY, Chuck	Montreal	Canadian National Team
7. POLIS, Greg	Pittsburgh	Estevan Bruins
8. SITTLER, Darryl	Toronto	London Knights
9. PLUMB, Ron	Boston	Peterborough Petes
10. ODDLEIFSON, Chris	Oakland	Winnipeg Jets
11. GRATTON, Norm	New York	Montreal Junior Canadiens
12. LAJEUNESSE, Serge	Detroit	Montreal Junior Canadiens
13. STEWART, Bob	Boston	Oshawa Generals
14. MALONEY, Dan	Chicago	London Knights

SECOND ROUND

15. DEADMARSH, Butch	Buffalo	Brandon Wheat Kings
16. HARGREAVES, Jim	Vancouver	Winnipeg Jets
17. HARVEY, Fred	Minnesota	Hamilton Red Wings
18. CLEMENT, Bill	Philadelphia	Ottawa 67's
19. LAFRAMBOISE, Pete	Oakland	Ottawa 67's
20. BARRETT, Fred	Minnesota	Toronto Marlboros
21. STEWART, John	Pittsburgh	Flin Flon Bombers
22. THOMPSON, Errol	Toronto	Charlottetown Royals
23. KEOGAN, Murray	St. Louis	University of Minnesota
24. McDONOUGH, Al	Los Angeles	St. Catharines Black Hawks
25. MURPHY, Mike	New York	Toronto Marlboros
26. GUINDON, Bobby	Detroit	Montreal Junior Canadiens
27. BOUCHARD, Dan	Boston	London Knights
28. ARCHAMBAULT, Mike	Chicago	Drummondville Rangers

Murray Wilson, 11th choice in 1971.

Errol Thompson, 22nd choice in 1970.

1971
FIRST ROUND

Selection	Claimed By	Amateur Club
1. LAFLEUR, Guy	Montreal	Quebec Remparts
2. DIONNE, Marcel	Detroit	St. Catharines Black Hawks
3. GUEVREMONT, Jocelyn	Vancouver	Montreal Junior Canadiens
4. CARR, Gene	St. Louis	Flin Flon Bombers
5. MARTIN, Rick	Buffalo	Montreal Junior Canadiens
6. JONES, Ron	Boston	Edmonton Oil Kings
7. ARNASON, Chuck	Montreal	Flin Fon Bombers
8. WRIGHT, Larry	Philadelphia	Regina Pats
9. PLANTE, Pierre	Philadelphia	Drummondville Rangers
10. VICKERS, Steve	New York	Toronto Marlboros
11. WILSON, Murray	Montreal	Ottawa 67's
12. SPRING, Dan	Chicago	Edmonton Oil Kings
13. DURBANO, Steve	New York	Toronto Marlboros
14. O'REILLY, Terry	Boston	Oshawa Generals

SECOND ROUND

15. BAIRD, Ken	California	Flin Flon Bombers
16. BOUCHA, Henry	Detroit	U.S. Nationals
17. LALONDE, Bobby	Vancouver	Montreal Junior Canadiens
18. McKENZIE, Brian	Pittsburgh	St. Catharines Black Hawks
19. RAMSAY, Craig	Buffalo	Peterborough Petes
20. ROBINSON, Larry	Montreal	Kitchener Rangers
21. NORRISH, Rod	Minnesota	Regina Pats
22. KEHOE, Rick	Toronto	Hamilton Red Wings
23. FORTIER, Dave	Toronto	St. Catharines Black Hawks
24. DEGUISE, Michel	Montreal	Sorel Eperviers
25. FRENCH, Terry	Montreal	Ottawa 67's
26. KRYSKOW, Dave	Chicago	Edmonton Oil Kings
27. WILLIAMS, Tom	New York	Hamilton Red Wings
28. RIDLEY, Curt	Boston	Portage Terriers

1969
FIRST ROUND

Selection	Claimed By	Amateur Club
1. HOULE, Rejean	Montreal	Montreal Junior Canadiens
2. TARDIF, Marc	Montreal	Montreal Junior Canadiens
3. TANNAHILL, Don	Boston	Niagara Falls Flyers
4. SPRING, Frank	Boston	Edmonton Oil Kings
5. REDMOND, Dick	Minnesota	St. Catharines Black Hawks
6. CURRIER, Bob	Philadelphia	Cornwall Royals
7. FEATHERSTONE, Tony	Oakland	Peterborough Petes
8. DUPONT, André	New York	Montreal Junior Canadiens
9. MOSER, Ernie	Toronto	Estevan Bruins
10. RUTHERFORD, Jim	Detroit	Hamilton Red Wings
11. BOLDIREV, Ivan	Boston	Oshawa Generals
12. JARRY, Pierre	New York	Ottawa 67's
13. BORDELEAU, Jean-Pierre	Chicago	Montreal Junior Canadiens
14. O'BRIEN, Dennis	Minnesota	St. Catharines Black Hawks

SECOND ROUND

15. KESSELL, Rick	Pittsburgh	Oshawa Generals
16. HOGANSON, Dale	Los Angeles	Estevan Burins
17. CLARKE, Bobby	Philadelphia	Flin Flon Bombers
18. STACKHOUSE, Ron	Oakland	Peterborough Petes
19. LOWE, Mike	St. Louis	Loyola College
20. BRINDLEY, Doug	Toronto	Niagara Falls Flyers
21. GARWASIUK, Ron	Detroit	Regina Pats
22. QUOQUOCHI, Art	Boston	Montreal Junior Canadiens
23. WILSON, Bert	New York	London Knights
24. ROMANCHYCH, Larry	Chicago	Flin Flon Bombers
25. GILBERT, Gilles	Minnesota	London Knights
26. BRIERE, Michel	Pittsburgh	Shawinigan Falls Juniors
27. BODDY, Greg	Los Angeles	Edmonton Oil Kings
28. BROSSART, Bill	Philadelphia	Estevan Bruins

NHL All-Stars

Position Leaders in All-Star Selections

Position	Player	First Team	Second Team	Total
GOAL	Glenn Hall	7	4	11
	Frank Brimsek	2	6	8
	Jacques Plante	3	4	7
	Terry Sawchuk	3	4	7
	Bill Durnan	6	0	6
	Ken Dryden	5	1	6
DEFENSE	Doug Harvey	10	1	11
	Earl Seibert	4	6	10
	Bobby Orr	8	1	9
	Eddie Shore	7	1	8
	Red Kelly	6	2	8
	Pierre Pilote	5	3	8
LEFT WING	Bobby Hull	10	2	12
	Ted Lindsay	8	1	9
	Frank Mahovlich	3	6	9
	Harvey Jackson	4	1	5
	Toe Blake	3	2	5
RIGHT WING	Gordie Howe	12	9	21
	Maurice Richard	8	6	14
	*Mike Bossy	5	3	8
	Guy Lafleur	6	0	6
	Charlie Conacher	3	2	5
CENTER	Jean Beliveau	6	4	10
	Stan Mikita	6	2	8
	Phil Esposito	6	2	8
	Bill Cowley	6	2	8
	*Wayne Gretzky	6	1	7
	Elmer Lach	3	2	5
	Syl Apps	2	3	5

* — Active in Professional Hockey

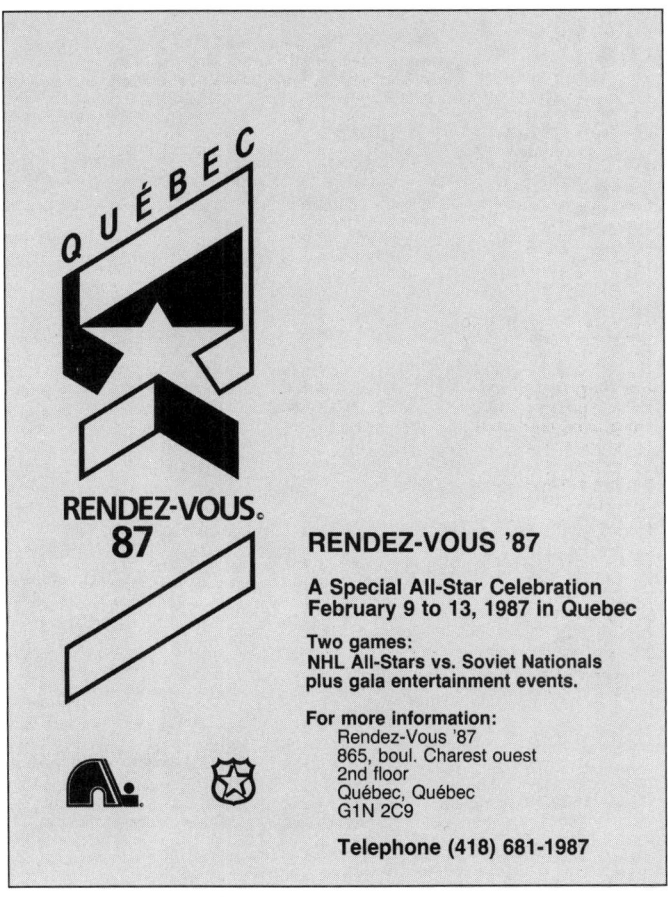

Active Players' All-Star Selection Records

GOALTENDERS

	First Team Selections	Second Team Selections	Total
Tom Barrasso	(1) 1983-84.	(1) 1984-85.	2
Glenn Resch	(0)	(2) 1975-76; 1978-79.	2
Don Edwards	(0)	(2) 1977-78; 1979-80.	2
Mike Liut	(1) 1980-81.	(0)	1
Bill Smith	(1) 1981-82.	(0)	1
Pete Peeters	(1) 1982-83.	(0)	1
J. Vanbiesbrouck	(1) 1985-86.	(0)	1
Grant Fuhr	(0)	(1) 1981-82.	1
R. Melanson	(0)	(1) 1982-83.	1
Pat Riggin	(0)	(1) 1983-84.	1
Bob Froese	(0)	(1) 1985-86.	1

DEFENSEMEN

	First Team Selections	Second Team Selections	Total
Denis Potvin	(5) 1974-75; 1975-76; 1977-78; 1978-79; 1980-81.	(2) 1976-77; 1983-84.	7
Borje Salming	(1) 1976-77.	(5) 1974-75; 1975-76; 1977-78; 1978-79; 1979-80.	6
Larry Robinson	(3) 1976-77; 1978-79; 1979-80.	(3) 1977-78; 1980-81; 1985-86.	6
Ray Bourque	(4) 1979-80; 1981-82; 1983-84; 1984-85.	(3) 1981-82; 1982-83; 1983-84	7
Paul Coffey	(2) 1984-85; 1985-86.	(3) 1981-82; 1982-83; 1983-84	5
Rod Langway	(2) 1982-83; 1983-84	(1) 1984-85.	3
Mark Howe	(2) 1982-83; 1985-86.	(0)	2
Randy Carlyle	(1) 1980-81.	(0)	1
Doug Wilson	(1) 1981-82.	(1) 1984-85.	2
Brian Engblom	(0)	(1) 1981-82.	1

CENTERS

	First Team Selections	Second Team Selections	Total
Wayne Gretzky	(6) 1980-81; 1981-82; 1982-83; 1983-84; 1984-85; 1985-86.	(1) 1979-80.	7
Marcel Dionne	(2) 1976-77; 1979-80.	(2) 1978-79; 1980-81.	4
Bryan Trottier	(2) 1977-78; 1978-79.	(2) 1981-82; 1983-84.	4
Denis Savard	(0)	(1) 1982-83.	1
Dale Hawerchuk	(0)	(1) 1984-85.	1
Mario Lemieux	(0)	(1) 1985-86.	1

RIGHT WINGERS

	First Team Selections	Second Team Selections	Total
Mike Bossy	(5) 1980-81; 1981-82; 1982-83; 1983-84; 1985-86.	(3) 1977-78; 1978-79; 1984-85.	8
L. McDonald	(0)	(2) 1976-77; 1982-83.	2
Danny Gare	(0)	(1) 1979-80.	1
Dave Taylor	(0)	(1) 1980-81.	1
Rick Middleton	(0)	(1) 1981-82.	1
Jari Kurri	(1) 1984-85.	(2) 1983-84; 1985-86.	3

LEFT WINGERS

	First Team Selections	Second Team Selections	Total
Mark Messier	(2) 1981-82; 1982-83.	(1) 1983-84.	3
Clark Gillies	(2) 1977-78; 1978-79.	(0)	2
Charlie Simmer	(2) 1979-80; 1980-81.	(0)	2
Michel Goulet	(2) 1983-84; 1985-86.	(1) 1982-83.	3
John Tonelli	(0)	(2) 1981-82; 1984-85.	2
John Ogrodnick	(1) 1984-85.	(0)	1
Mats Naslund	(0)	(1) 1985-86.	1

Leading All-Stars—1930-86

Player	Pos	Team	NHL Seasons	First Team Selections	Second Team Selections	Total Selections
Howe, Gordie	RW	Detroit	26	12	9	21
Richard, Maurice	RW	Montreal	18	8	6	14
Hull, Bobby	LW	Chicago	15	10	2	12
Harvey, Doug	Def	Mtl-NYR	19	10	1	11
Beliveau, Jean	Cen	Montreal	20	6	4	10
Seibert, Earl	Def	NYR-Chi	15	4	6	10
Orr, Bobby	Def	Boston	12	8	1	9
Lindsay, Ted	LW	Detroit	17	8	1	9
Hall, Glenn	Goal	Chi-St.L.	18	6	3	9
Mahovlich, Frank	LW	Tor-Det-Mtl	20	3	6	9
Shore, Eddie	Def	Boston	14	7	1	8
Mikita, Stan	Cen	Chicago	22	6	2	8
Kelly, Red	Def	Detroit	20	6	2	8
Esposito, Phil	Cen	Boston	18	6	2	8
Pilote, Pierre	Def	Chicago	14	5	3	8
Brimsek, Frank	Goal	Boston	10	2	6	8
*Bossy, Mike	RW	NY Islanders	9	5	3	8
*Gretzky, Wayne	Cen	Edmonton	7	6	1	7
*Potvin, Denis	Def	NY Islanders	12	5	2	7
Park, Brad	Def	NYR-Boston	16	5	2	7
*Bourque, Ray	Def	Boston	7	4	3	7
Plante, Jacques	Goal	Mtl-Tor	18	3	4	7
Gadsby, Bill	Def	Chi-NYR-Det	20	3	4	7
Sawchuk, Terry	Goal	Detroit	21	3	4	7
Durnan, Bill	Goal	Montreal	7	6	0	6
Lafleur, Guy	RW	Montreal	12	6	0	6
Dryden, Ken	Goal	Montreal	8	5	1	6
*Robinson, Larry	Def	Montreal	13	3	3	6
Clapper, Dit	Def	Boston	20	3	3	6
Horton, Tim	Def	Toronto	24	3	3	6
*Salming, Borje	Def	Toronto	11	1	5	6
Cowley, Bill	Cen	Boston	13	6	2	5
Jackson, Harvey	LW	Toronto	15	4	1	5
Conacher, Charlie	RW	Toronto	12	3	2	5
Stewart, Jack	Def	Detroit	12	3	2	5
Lach, Elmer	Cen	Montreal	14	3	2	5
Quackenbush, Bill	Def	Det-Bos	14	3	2	5
Blake, Toe	LW	Montreal	15	3	2	5
*Coffey, Paul	Def	Edmonton	6	2	3	5
Reardon, Ken	Def	Montreal	7	2	3	5
Apps, Syl	Cen	Toronto	10	2	3	5
Giacomin, Ed	Goal	NY Rangers	13	2	3	5

*Active in Professional Hockey

All-Star Teams
1930-86

Voting for the NHL All-Star Team is conducted among the representatives of the Professional Hockey Writers' Association at the end of the season.
Following is a list of the First and Second All-Star Teams since their inception in 1930-31.

First Team		Second Team

1985-86

First Team	Position	Second Team
Vanbiesbrouck, J., NY Rangers	Goal	Froese, Bob Philadelphia
Coffey, Paul, Edmonton	Defense	Robinson, Larry, Montreal
Howe, Mark, Philadelphia	Defense	Bourque, Raymond, Boston
Gretzky, Wayne, Edmonton	Center	Lemieux, Mario, Pittsburgh
Bossy, Mike, NY Islanders	Right Wing	Kurri, Jari, Edmonton
Goulet, Michel, Quebec	Left Wing	Naslund, Mats, Montreal

1984-85

First Team	Position	Second Team
Lindbergh, Pelle, Philadelphia	Goal	Barrasso, Tom Buffalo
Coffey, Paul, Edmonton	Defense	Langway, Rod, Washington
Bourque, Raymond, Boston	Defense	Wilson, Doug, Chicago
Gretzky, Wayne, Edmonton	Center	Hawerchuk, Dale, Winnipeg
Kurri, Jari, Edmonton	Right Wing	Bossy, Mike, NY Islanders
Ogrodnick, John, Detroit	Left Wing	Tonelli, John, NY Islanders

1983-84

First Team	Position	Second Team
Barrasso, Tom, Buffalo	Goal	Riggin, Pat Washington
Langway, Rod, Washington	Defense	Coffey, Paul, Edmonton
Bourque, Raymond, Boston	Defense	Potvin, Denis, NY Islanders
Gretzky, Wayne, Edmonton	Center	Trottier, Bryan, NY Islanders
Bossy, Mike, NY Islanders	Right Wing	Kurri, Jari, Edmonton
Goulet, Michel, Quebec	Left Wing	Messier, Mark, Edmonton

1982-83

First Team	Position	Second Team
Peeters, Pete, Boston	Goal	Melanson, Roland, NYI
Howe, Mark, Philadelphia	Defense	Bourque, Raymond, Boston
Langway, Rod, Washington	Defense	Coffey, Paul, Edmonton
Gretzky, Wayne, Edmonton	Center	Savard, Denis, Chicago
Bossy, Mike, NY Islanders	Right Wing	McDonald, Lanny, Calgary
Messier, Mark, Edmonton	Left Wing	Goulet, Michel, Quebec

1981-82

First Team	Position	Second Team
Smith, Bill, NY Islanders	Goal	Fuhr, Grant, Edmonton
Wilson, Doug, Chicago	Defense	Coffey, Paul, Edmonton
Bourque, Raymond, Boston	Defense	Engblom, Brian, Montreal
Gretzky, Wayne, Edmonton	Center	Trottier, Bryan, NY Islanders
Bossy, Mike, NY Islanders	Right Wing	Middleton, Rick, Boston
Messier, Mark, Edmonton	Left Wing	Tonelli, John, NY Islanders

1980-81

First Team	Position	Second Team
Liut, Mike, St. Louis	Goal	Lessard, Mario, Los Angeles
Potvin, Denis, NY Islanders	Defense	Robinson, Larry, Montreal
Carlyle, Randy, Pittsburgh	Defense	Bourque, Raymond, Boston
Gretzky, Wayne, Edmonton	Center	Dionne, Marcel, Los Angeles
Bossy, Mike, NY Islanders	Right Wing	Taylor, Dave, Los Angeles
Simmer, Charlie, Los Angeles	Left Wing	Barber, Bill, Philadelphia

1979-80

First Team	Position	Second Team
Esposito, Tony, Chicago	Goal	Edwards, Don, Buffalo
Robinson, Larry, Montreal	Defense	Salming, Borje, Toronto
Bourque, Raymond, Boston	Defense	Schoenfeld, Jim, Buffalo
Dionne, Marcel, Los Angeles	Center	Gretzky, Wayne, Edmonton
Lafleur, Guy, Montreal	Right Wing	Gare, Danny, Buffalo
Simmer, Charlie, Los Angeles	Left Wing	Shutt, Steve, Montreal

1978-79

First Team	Position	Second Team
Dryden, Ken, Montreal	Goal	Resch, Glenn, NY Islanders
Potvin, Denis, NY Islanders	Defense	Salming, Borje, Toronto
Robinson, Larry, Montreal	Defense	Savard, Serge, Montreal
Trottier, Bryan, NY Islanders	Center	Dionne, Marcel, Los Angeles
Lafleur, Guy, Montreal	Right Wing	Bossy, Mike, NY Islanders
Gillies, Clark, NY Islanders	Left Wing	Barber, Bill, Philadelphia

1977-78

First Team	Position	Second Team
Dryden, Ken, Montreal	Goal	Edwards, Don, Buffalo
Potvin, Denis, NY Islanders	Defense	Robinson, Larry, Montreal
Park, Brad, Boston	Defense	Salming, Borje, Toronto
Trottier, Bryan, NY Islanders	Center	Sittler, Darryl, Toronto
Lafleur, Guy, Montreal	Right Wing	Bossy, Mike, NY Islanders
Gillies, Clark, NY Islanders	Left Wing	Shutt, Steve, Montreal

1976-77

First Team	Position	Second Team
Dryden, Ken, Montreal	Goal	Vachon, Rogatien, Los Angeles
Robinson, Larry, Montreal	Defense	Potvin, Denis, NY Islanders
Salming, Borje, Toronto	Defense	Lapointe, Guy, Montreal
Dionne, Marcel, Los Angeles	Center	Perreault, Gilbert, Buffalo
Lafleur, Guy, Montreal	Right Wing	McDonald, Lanny, Toronto
Shutt, Steve, Montreal	Left Wing	Martin, Richard, Buffalo

1975-76

First Team	Position	Second Team
Dryden, Ken, Montreal	Goal	Resch, Glenn, NY Islanders
Potvin, Denis, NY Islanders	Defense	Salming, Borje, Toronto
Park, Brad, Boston	Defense	Lapointe, Guy, Montreal
Clarke, Bobby, Philadelphia	Center	Perreault, Gilbert, Buffalo
Lafleur, Guy, Montreal	Right Wing	Leach, Reggie, Philadelphia
Barber, Bill, Philadelphia	Left Wing	Martin, Richard, Buffalo

1974-75

First Team	Position	Second Team
Parent, Bernie, Philadelphia	Goal	Vachon, Rogie, Los Angeles
Orr, Bobby, Boston	Defense	Lapointe, Guy, Montreal
Potvin, Denis, NY Islanders	Defense	Salming, Borje, Toronto
Clarke, Bobby, Philadelphia	Center	Esposito, Phil, Boston
Lafleur, Guy, Montreal	Right Wing	Robert, René, Buffalo
Martin, Richard, Buffalo	Left Wing	Vickers, Steve, NY Rangers

1973-74

First Team	Position	Second Team
Parent, Bernie, Philadelphia	Goal	Esposito, Tony, Chicago
Orr, Bobby, Boston	Defense	White, Bill, Chicago
Park, Brad, NY Rangers	Defense	Ashbee, Barry, Philadelphia
Esposito, Phil, Boston	Center	Clarke, Bobby, Philadelphia
Hodge, Ken, Boston	Right Wing	Redmond, Mickey, Detroit
Martin, Richard, Buffalo	Left Wing	Cashman, Wayne, Boston

1972-73

First Team	Position	Second Team
Dryden, Ken, Montreal	Goal	Esposito, Tony, Chicago
Orr, Bobby, Boston	Defense	Park, Brad, NY Rangers
Lapointe, Guy, Montreal	Defense	White, Bill, Chicago
Esposito, Phil, Boston	Center	Clarke, Bobby, Philadelphia
Redmond, Mickey, Detroit	Right Wing	Cournoyer, Yvan, Montreal
Mahovlich, Frank, Montreal	Left Wing	Hull, Dennis, Chicago

1971-72

First Team	Position	Second Team
Esposito, Tony, Chicago	Goal	Dryden, Ken, Montreal
Orr, Bobby, Boston	Defense	White, Bill, Chicago
Park, Brad, New York	Defense	Stapleton, Pat, Chicago
Esposito, Phil, Boston	Center	Ratelle, Jean, New York
Gilbert, Rod, New York	Right Wing	Cournoyer, Yvan, Montreal
Hull, Bobby, Chicago	Left Wing	Hadfield, Vic, New York

1970-71

First Team	Position	Second Team
Giacomin, Ed, New York	Goal	Plante, Jacques, Toronto
Orr, Bobby, Boston	Defense	Park, Brad, New York
Tremblay, J.C., Montreal	Defense	Stapleton, Pat, Chicago
Esposito, Phil, Boston	Center	Keon, Dave, Toronto
Hodge, Ken, Boston	Right Wing	Cournoyer, Yvan, Montreal
Bucyk, John, Boston	Left Wing	Hull, Bobby, Chicago

1969-70

First Team	Position	Second Team
Esposito, Tony, Chicago	Goal	Giacomin, Ed, New York
Orr, Bobby, Boston	Defense	Brewer, Carl, Detroit
Park, Brad, New York	Defense	Laperrière, Jacques, Montreal
Esposito, Phil, Boston	Center	Mikita, Stan, Chicago
Howe, Gordie, Detroit	Right Wing	McKenzie, John, Boston
Hull, Bobby, Chicago	Left Wing	Mahovlich, Frank, Detroit

First Team		Second Team		First Team		Second Team

1968-69

Hall, Glenn, St. Louis	Goal	Giacomin, Ed, New York
Orr, Bobby, Boston	Defense	Green, Ted, Boston
Horton, Tim, Toronto	Defense	Harris, Ted, Montreal
Esposito, Phil, Boston	Center	Béliveau, Jean, Montreal
Howe, Gordie, Detroit	Right Wing	Cournoyer, Yvan, Montreal
Hull, Bobby, Chicago	Left Wing	Mahovlich, Frank, Detroit

1967-68

Worsley, Lorne, Montreal	Goal	Giacomin, Ed, New York
Orr, Bobby, Boston	Defense	Tremblay, J.C., Montreal
Horton, Tim, Toronto	Defense	Neilson, Jim, New York
Mikita, Stan, Chicago	Center	Esposito, Phil, Boston
Howe, Gordie, Detroit	Right Wing	Gilbert, Rod, New York
Hull, Bobby, Chicago	Left Wing	Bucyk, John, Boston

1966-67

Giacomin, Ed, New York	Goal	Hall, Glenn, Chicago
Pilote, Pierre, Chicago	Defense	Horton, Tim, Toronto
Howell, Harry, New York	Defense	Orr, Bobby, Boston
Mikita, Stan, Chicago	Center	Ullman, Norm, Detroit
Wharram, Ken, Chicago	Right Wing	Howe, Gordie, Detroit
Hull, Bobby, Chicago	Left Wing	Marshall, Don, New York

1965-66

Hall, Glenn, Chicago	Goal	Worsley, Lorne, Montreal
Laperrière, Jacques, Montreal	Defense	Stanley, Allan, Toronto
Pilote, Pierre, Chicago	Defense	Stapleton, Pat, Chicago
Mikita, Stan, Chicago	Center	Béliveau, Jean, Montreal
Howe, Gordie, Detroit	Right Wing	Rousseau, Bobby, Montreal
Hull, Bobby, Chicago	Left Wing	Mahovlich, Frank, Toronto

1964-65

Crozier, Roger, Detroit	Goal	Hodge, Charlie, Montreal
Pilote, Pierre, Chicago	Defense	Gadsby, Bill, Detroit
Laperrière, Jacques, Montreal	Defense	Brewer, Carl, Toronto
Ullman, Norm, Detroit	Center	Mikita, Stan, Chicago
Provost, Claude, Montreal	Right Wing	Howe, Gordie, Detroit
Hull, Bobby, Chicago	Left Wing	Mahovlich, Frank, Toronto

1963-64

Hall, Glenn, Chicago	Goal	Hodge, Charlie, Montreal
Pilote, Pierre, Chicago	Defense	Vasko, Elmer, Chicago
Horton, Tim, Toronto	Defense	Laperrière, Jacques, Montreal
Mikita, Stan, Chicago	Center	Béliveau, Jean, Montreal
Wharram, Ken, Chicago	Right Wing	Howe, Gordie, Detroit
Hull, Bobby, Chicago	Left Wing	Mahovlich, Frank, Toronto

1962-63

Hall, Glenn, Chicago	Goal	Sawchuk, Terry, Detroit
Pilote, Pierre, Chicago	Defense	Horton, Tim, Toronto
Brewer, Carl, Toronto	Defense	Vasko, Elmer, Chicago
Mikita, Stan, Chicago	Center	Richard, Henri, Montreal
Howe, Gordie, Detroit	Right Wing	Bathgate, Andy, New York
Mahovlich, Frank, Toronto	Left Wing	Hull, Bobby, Chicago

1961-62

Plante, Jacques, Montreal	Goal	Hall, Glenn, Chicago
Harvey, Doug, New York	Defense	Brewer, Carl, Toronto
Talbot, Jean-Guy, Montreal	Defense	Pilote, Pierre, Chicago
Mikita, Stan, Chicago	Center	Keon, Dave, Toronto
Bathgate, Andy, New York	Right Wing	Howe, Gordie, Detroit
Hull, Bobby, Chicago	Left Wing	Mahovlich, Frank, Toronto

1960-61

Bower, Johnny, Toronto	Goal	Hall, Glenn, Chicago
Harvey, Doug, Montreal	Defense	Stanley, Allan, Toronto
Pronovost, Marcel, Detroit	Defense	Pilote, Pierre, Chicago
Béliveau, Jean, Montreal	Center	Richard, Henri, Montreal
Geoffrion, Bernie, Montreal	Right Wing	Howe, Gordie, Detroit
Mahovlich, Frank, Toronto	Left Wing	Moore, Dickie, Montreal

1959-60

Hall, Glenn, Chicago	Goal	Plante, Jacques, Montreal
Harvey, Doug, Montreal	Defense	Stanley, Allan, Toronto
Pronovost, Marcel, Detroit	Defense	Pilote, Pierre, Chicago
Béliveau, Jean, Montreal	Center	Horvath, Bronco, Boston
Howe, Gordie, Detroit	Right Wing	Geoffrion, Bernie, Montreal
Hull, Bobby, Chicago	Left Wing	Prentice, Dean, New York

1958-59

Plante, Jacques, Montreal	Goal	Sawchuk, Terry, Detroit
Johnson, Tom, Montreal	Defense	Pronovost, Marcel, Detroit
Gadsby, Bill, New York	Defense	Harvey, Doug, Montreal
Béliveau, Jean, Montreal	Center	Richard, Henri, Montreal
Bathgate, Andy, New York	Right Wing	Howe, Gordie, Detroit
Moore, Dickie, Montreal	Left Wing	Delvecchio, Alex, Detroit

1957-58

Hall, Glenn, Chicago	Goal	Plante, Jacques, Montreal
Harvey, Doug, Montreal	Defense	Flaman, Fern, Boston
Gadsby, Bill, New York	Defense	Pronovost, Marcel, Detroit
Richard, Henri, Montreal	Center	Béliveau, Jean, Montreal
Howe, Gordie, Detroit	Right Wing	Bathgate, Andy, New York
Moore, Dickie, Montreal	Left Wing	Henry, Camille, New York

1956-57

Hall, Glenn, Detroit	Goal	Plante, Jacques, Montreal
Harvey, Doug, Montreal	Defense	Flaman, Fern, Boston
Kelly, Red, Detroit	Defense	Gadsby, Bill, New York
Béliveau, Jean, Montreal	Center	Litzenberger, Eddie, Chicago
Howe, Gordie, Detroit	Right Wing	Richard, Maurice, Montreal
Lindsay, Ted, Detroit	Left Wing	Chevrefils, Real, Boston

1955-56

Plante, Jacques, Montreal	Goal	Hall, Glenn, Detroit
Harvey, Doug, Montreal	Defense	Kelly, Red, Detroit
Gadsby, Bill, New York	Defense	Johnson, Tom, Montreal
Béliveau, Jean, Montreal	Center	Sloan, Tod, Toronto
Richard, Maurice, Montreal	Right Wing	Howe, Gordie, Detroit
Lindsay, Ted, Detroit	Left Wing	Olmstead, Bert, Montreal

Doug Harvey (left) and Alex Delvecchio

1954-55

Lumley, Harry, Toronto	Goal	Sawchuk, Terry, Detroit
Harvey, Doug, Montreal	Defense	Goldham, Bob, Detroit
Kelly, Red, Detroit	Defense	Flaman, Fern, Boston
Béliveau, Jean, Montreal	Center	Mosdell, Ken, Montreal
Richard, Maurice, Montreal	Right Wing	Geoffrion, Bernie, Montreal
Smith, Sid, Toronto	Left Wing	Lewicki, Danny, New York

First Team		Second Team

1953-54

Lumley, Harry, Toronto	Goal	Sawchuk, Terry, Detroit
Kelly, Red, Detroit	Defense	Gadsby, Bill, Chicago
Harvey, Doug, Montreal	Defense	Horton, Tim, Toronto
Mosdell, Ken, Montreal	Center	Kennedy, Ted, Toronto
Howe, Gordie, Detroit	Right Wing	Richard, Maurice, Montreal
Lindsay, Ted, Detroit	Left Wing	Sandford, Ed, Boston

1952-53

Sawchuk, Terry, Detroit	Goal	McNeil, Gerry, Montreal
Kelly, Red, Detroit	Defense	Quackenbush, Bill, Boston
Harvey, Doug, Montreal	Defense	Gadsby, Bill, Chicago
Mackell, Fleming, Boston	Center	Delvecchio, Alex, Detroit
Howe, Gordie, Detroit	Right Wing	Richard, Maurice, Montreal
Lindsay, Ted, Detroit	Left Wing	Olmstead, Bert, Montreal

1951-52

Sawchuk, Terry, Detroit	Goal	Henry, Jim, Boston
Kelly, Red, Detroit	Defense	Buller, Hy, New York
Harvey, Doug, Montreal	Defense	Thomson, Jim, Toronto
Lach, Elmer, Montreal	Center	Schmidt, Milt, Boston
Howe, Gordie, Detroit	Right Wing	Richard, Maurice, Montreal
Lindsay, Ted, Detroit	Left Wing	Smith, Sid, Toronto

1950-51

Sawchuk, Terry, Detroit	Goal	Rayner, Chuck, New York
Kelly, Red, Detroit	Defense	Thomson, Jim, Toronto
Quackenbush, Bill, Boston	Defense	Reise, Leo, Detroit
Schmidt, Milt, Boston	Center	Abel, Sid, Detroit
		Kennedy, Ted, Toronto
Howe, Gordie, Detroit	Right Wing	Richard, Maurice, Montreal
Lindsay, Ted, Detroit	Left Wing	Smith, Sid, Toronto

1949-50

Durnan, Bill, Montreal	Goal	Rayner, Chuck, New York
Mortson, Gus, Toronto	Defense	Reise, Leo, Detroit
Reardon, Kenny, Montreal	Defense	Kelly, Red, Detroit
Abel, Sid, Detroit	Center	Kennedy, Ted, Toronto
Richard, Maurice, Montreal	Right Wing	Howe, Gordie, Detroit
Lindsay, Ted, Detroit	Left Wing	Leswick, Tony, New York

1948-49

Durnan, Bill, Montreal	Goal	Rayner, Chuck, New York
Quackenbush, Bill, Detroit	Defense	Harmon, Glen, Montreal
Stewart, Jack, Detroit	Defense	Reardon, Kenny, Montreal
Abel, Sid, Detroit	Center	Bentley, Doug, Chicago
Richard, Maurice, Montreal	Right Wing	Howe, Gordie, Detroit
Conacher, Roy, Chicago	Left Wing	Lindsay, Ted, Detroit

1947-48

Broda, W. "Turk", Toronto	Goal	Brimsek, Frank, Boston
Quackenbush, Bill, Detroit	Defense	Reardon, Kenny, Montreal
Stewart, Jack, Detroit	Defense	Colville, Neil, New York
Lach, Elmer, Montreal	Center	O'Connor, "Buddy", New York
Richard, Maurice, Montreal	Right Wing	Poile, "Bud", Chicago
Lindsay, Ted, Detroit	Left Wing	Stewart, Gaye, Chicago

1946-47

Durnan, Bill, Montreal	Goal	Brimsek, Frank, Boston
Reardon, Kenny, Montreal	Defense	Stewart, Jack, Detroit
Bouchard, Emile, Montreal	Defense	Quackenbush, Bill, Detroit
Schmidt, Milt, Boston	Center	Bentley, Max, Chicago
Richard, Maurice, Montreal	Right Wing	Bauer, Bobby, Boston
Bentley, Doug, Chicago	Left Wing	Dumart, Woody, Boston

1945-46

Durnan, Bill, Montreal	Goal	Brimsek, Frank, Boston
Crawford, Jack, Boston	Defense	Reardon, Kenny, Montreal
Bouchard, Emile, Montreal	Defense	Stewart, Jack, Detroit
Bentley, Max, Chicago	Center	Lach, Elmer, Montreal
Richard, Maurice, Montreal	Right Wing	Mosienko, Bill, Chicago
Stewart, Gaye, Toronto	Left Wing	Blake, "Toe", Montreal
Irvin, Dick, Montreal	Coach	Gottselig, John, Chicago

1944-45

Durnan, Bill, Montreal	Goal	Karakas, Mike, Chicago
Bouchard, Emile, Montreal	Defense	Harmon, Glen, Montreal
Hollett, Bill, Detroit	Defense	Pratt, "Babe", Toronto
Lach, Elmer, Montreal	Center	Cowley, Bill, Boston
Richard, Maurice, Montreal	Right Wing	Mosienko, Bill, Chicago
Blake, "Toe", Montreal	Left Wing	Howe, Syd, Detroit
Irvin, Dick, Montreal	Coach	Adams, Jack, Detroit

1943-44

Durnan, Bill, Montreal	Goal	Bibeault, Paul, Toronto
Seibert, Earl, Chicago	Defense	Bouchard, Emile, Montreal
Pratt, "Babe", Toronto	Defense	Clapper, "Dit", Boston
Cowley, Bill, Boston	Center	Lach, Elmer, Montreal
Carr, Lorne, Toronto	Right Wing	Richard, Maurice, Montreal
Bentley, Doug, Chicago	Left Wing	Cain, Herb, Boston
Irvin, Dick, Montreal	Coach	Day, C.H., "Hap", Toronto

1942-43

Mowers, Johnny, Detroit	Goal	Brimsek, Frank, Boston
Seibert, Earl, Chicago	Defense	Crawford, Johnny, Boston
Stewart, Jack, Detroit	Defense	Hollett, Bill, Boston
Cowley, Bill, Boston	Center	Apps, Syl, Toronto
Carr, Lorne, Toronto	Right Wing	Hextall, Bryan, New York
Bentley, Doug, Chicago	Left Wing	Patrick, Lynn, New York
Adams, Jack, Detroit	Coach	Ross, Art, Boston

1941-42

Brimsek, Frank, Boston	Goal	Broda, W. "Turk", Toronto
Seibert, Earl, Chicago	Defense	Egan, Pat, NY Americans
Anderson, Tommy, NY Amer.	Defense	McDonald, Bucko, Toronto
Apps, Syl, Toronto	Center	Watson, Phil, NY Rangers
Hextall, Bryan, NY Rangers	Right Wing	Drillon, Gord, Toronto
Patrick, Lynn, NY Rangers	Left Wing	Abel, Sid, Detroit
Boucher, Frank, NY Rangers	Coach	Thompson, Paul, Chicago

Ott Heller

1940-41

Broda, W. "Turk", Toronto	Goal	Brimsek, Frank, Boston
Clapper, "Dit", Boston	Defense	Seibert, Earl, Chicago
Stanowski, Wally, Toronto	Defense	Heller, Ott, NY Rangers
Cowley, Bill, Boston	Center	Apps, Syl, Toronto
Hextall, Bryan, NY Rangers	Right Wing	Bauer, Bobby, Boston
Schriner, Dave, Toronto	Left Wing	Dumart, Woody, Boston
Weiland, "Cooney", Boston	Coach	Irvin, Dick, Montreal

First Team		Second Team	First Team		Second Team

1939-40

Kerr, Dave, NY Rangers	Goal	Brimsek, Frank, Boston
Clapper, "Dit", Boston	Defense	Coulter, Art, NY Rangers
Goodfellow, Ebbie, Detroit	Defense	Seibert, Earl, Chicago
Schmidt, Milt, Boston	Center	Colville, Neil, NY Rangers
Hextall, Bryan, NY Rangers	Right Wing	Bauer, Bobby, Boston
Blake, "Toe", Montreal	Left Wing	Dumart, Woody, Boston
Thompson, Paul, Chicago	Coach	Boucher, Frank, NY Rangers

1938-39

Brimsek, Frank, Boston	Goal	Robertson, Earl, NY Americans
Shore, Eddie, Boston	Defense	Seibert, Earl, Chicago
Clapper, "Dit", Boston	Defense	Coulter, Art, NY Rangers
Apps, Syl, Toronto	Center	Colville, Neil, NY Rangers
Drillon, Gord, Toronto	Right Wing	Bauer, Bobby, Boston
Blake, "Toe", Montreal	Left Wing	Gottselig, Johnny, Chicago
Ross, Art, Boston	Coach	Dutton, "Red", NY Americans

1937-38

Thompson, "Tiny", Boston	Goal	Kerr, Dave, N.Y. Rangers
Shore, Eddie, Boston	Defense	Coulter, Art, N.Y. Rangers
Seibert, "Babe", Montreal	Defense	Seibert, Eart, Chicago
Cowley, Bill, Boston	Center	Apps, Syl, Toronto
Dillon, Cecil, NY Rangers	Right Wing	Dillon, Cecil, N.Y. Rangers
Drillon, Gord, Toronto	(tied)	Drillon, Gord, Toronto
Thompson, Paul, Chicago	Left Wing	Blake, Toe, Mtl. Canadiens
Patrick, Lester, NY Rangers	Coach	Ross, Art, Boston

1936-37

Smith, Norm, Detroit	Goal	Cude, Wilf, Montreal
Siebert, "Babe", Montreal	Defense	Seibert, Earl, Chicago
Goodfellow, Ebbie, Detroit	Defense	Conacher, Lionel, Mtl. Maroons
Barry, Marty, Detroit	Center	Chapman, Art, NY Americans
Aurie, Larry, Detroit	Right Wing	Dillon, Cecil, NY Rangers
Jackson, Harvey, Toronto	Left Wing	Schriner, Dave, NY Americans
Adams, Jack, Detroit	Coach	Hart, Cecil, Montreal

1935-36

Thompson, "Tiny", Boston	Goal	Cude, Wilf, Montreal
Shore, Eddie, Boston	Defense	Seibert, Earl, Chicago
Seibert, "Babe", Boston	Defense	Goodfellow, Ebbie, Detroit
Smith, "Hooley", Mtl. Maroons	Center	Thoms, Bill, Toronto
Conacher, Charlie, Toronto	Right Wing	Dillon, Cecil, NY Rangers
Schriner, Dave, NY Americans	Left Wing	Thompson, Paul, Chicago
Patrick, Lester, NY Rangers	Coach	Gorman, T.P., Mtl. Maroons

Syl Apps

1934-35

Chabot, Lorne, Chicago	Goal	Thompson, "Tiny", Boston
Shore, Eddie, Boston	Defense	Wentworth, Cy, Mtl. Maroons
Seibert, Earl, NY Rangers	Defense	Coulter, Art, Chicago
Boucher, Frank, NY Rangers	Center	Weiland, "Cooney", Detroit
Conacher, Charlie, Toronto	Right Wing	Clapper, "Dit", Boston
Jackson, Harvey, Toronto	Left Wing	Joliat, Aurel, Montreal
Patrick, Lester, NY Rangers	Coach	Irvin, Dick, Toronto

1933-34

Gardiner, Charlie, Chicago	Goal	Worters, Roy, NY Americans
Clancy, "King", Toronto	Defense	Shore, Eddie, Boston
Conacher, Lionel, Chicago	Defense	Johnson, "Ching", NY Rangers
Boucher, Frank, NY Rangers	Center	Primeau, Joe, Toronto
Conacher, Charlie, Toronto	Right Wing	Cook, Bill, N.Y. Rangers
Jackson, Harvey, Toronto	Left Wing	Joliat, Aurel, Mtl. Canadiens
Patrick, Lester, NY Rangers	Coach	Irvin, Dick, Toronto

Lionel Conacher

1932-33

Roach, John Ross, Detroit	Goal	Gardiner, Charlie, Chicago
Shore, Eddie, Boston	Defense	Clancy, "King", Toronto
Johnson, "Ching", NY Rangers	Defense	Conacher, Lionel, Mtl. Maroons
Boucher, Frank, NY Rangers	Center	Morenz, Howie, Montreal
Cook, Bill, NY Rangers	Right Wing	Conacher, Charlie, Toronto
Northcott, "Baldy", Mtl. Maroons	Left Wing	Jackson, Harvey, Toronto
Patrick, Lester, NY Rangers	Coach	Irvin, Dick, Toronto

1931-32

Gardiner, Charlie, Chicago	Goal	Worters, Roy, NY Americans
Shore, Eddie, Boston	Defense	Mantha, Sylvio, Montreal
Johnson, "Ching", NY Rangers	Defense	Clancy, "King", Toronto
Morenz, Howie, Montreal	Center	Smith, "Hooley", Mtl. Maroons
Cook, Bill, NY Rangers	Right Wing	Conacher, Charlie, Toronto
Jackson, Harvey, Toronto	Left Wing	Joliat, Aurel, Montreal
Patrick, Lester, NY Rangers	Coach	Irvin, Dick, Toronto

1930-31

Gardiner, Charlie, Chicago	Goal	Thompson, "Tiny", Boston
Shore, Eddie, Boston	Defense	Mantha, Sylvio, Montreal
Clancy, "King", Toronto	Defense	Johnson, "Ching", NY Rangers
Morenz, Howie, Montreal	Center	Boucher, Frank, NY Rangers
Cook, Bill, NY Rangers	Right Wing	Clapper, "Dit", Boston
Joliet, Aurel, Montreal	Left Wing	Cook, "Bun", NY Rangers
Patrick, Lester, NY Rangers	Coach	Irvin, Dick, Chicago

All-Star Game Records 1947 through 1986

TEAM RECORDS

MOST GOALS, BOTH TEAMS, ONE GAME:
13 – Wales Conference 7, Campbell Conference 6, 1984 at New Jersey
12 – Campbell Conference 9, Wales Conference 3, 1983 at NY Islanders
– Wales Conference 7, Campbell Conference 5, 1976 at Philadelphia
10 – West Division 6, East Division 4, 1974 at Chicago
– Wales Conference 6, Campbell Conference 4, 1985 at Calgary
9 – Wales Conference 6, Campbell Conference 3, 1980 at Detroit
– East Division 5, West Division 4, 1973 at New York
– Montreal Canadiens 6, NHL All-Stars 3, 1958 at Montreal

FEWEST GOALS, BOTH TEAMS, ONE GAME:
2 – NHL All-Stars 1, Montreal Canadiens 1, 1956 at Montreal
– First Team All-Stars 1, Second Team All-Stars 1, 1952 at Detroit
3 – West Division 2, East Division 1, 1971 at Boston
– Montreal Canadiens 3, NHL All-Stars 0, 1967 at Montreal
– NHL All-Stars 2, Montreal Canadiens 1, 1960 at Montreal

MOST GOALS, ONE TEAM, ONE GAME:
9 – Campbell Conference 9, Wales Conference 3, 1983 at NY Islanders
7 – Wales Conference 7, Campbell Conference 5, 1976 at Philadelphia
– Wales Conference 7, Campbell Conference 1, 1975 at Montreal
– Detroit Red Wings 7, NHL All-Stars 1, 1950 at Detroit
– Wales Conference 7, Campbell Conference 6, 1984 at New Jersey

FEWEST GOALS, ONE TEAM, ONE GAME:
0 – NHL All-Stars 0, Montreal Canadiens 3, 1967 at Montreal
1 – 17 times (1981, 1975, 1971, 1970, 1962, 1961, 1960, 1959, both teams 1956, 1955, 1953, both teams 1952, 1950, 1949, 1948)

MOST SHOTS, BOTH TEAMS, ONE GAME (SINCE 1955):
81 – 1968 at Toronto – NHL All-Stars 3 (40 shots), Toronto Maple Leafs 4 (41 shots)
75 – 1955 at Detroit – NHL All-Stars 1 (31 shots), Detroit Red Wings 3 (44 shots)
74 – 1963 at Toronto – NHL All-Stars 3 (38 shots), Toronto Maple Leafs 3 (36 shots)
70 – 1957 at Montreal – NHL All-Stars 5 (38 shots), Montreal Canadiens 3 (32 shots)

FEWEST SHOTS, BOTH TEAMS, ONE GAME (SINCE 1955):
52 – 1978 at Buffalo – Campbell Conference 2 (12 shots), Wales Conference 3 (40 shots)
53 – 1960 at Montreal – NHL All-Stars 2 (27 shots), Montreal Canadiens 1 (26 shots)
55 – 1956 at Montreal – NHL All-Stars 1 (28 shots), Montreal Canadiens 1 (27 shots)
55 – 1971 at Boston – West Division 2 (28 shots), East Division 1 (27 shots)

MOST SHOTS, ONE TEAM, ONE GAME (SINCE 1955):
44 – 1955 at Detroit – Detroit Red Wings (3-1 vs. NHL All-Stars)
44 – 1970 at St. Louis – East Division (4-1 vs. West Division)
43 – 1981 at Los Angeles – Campbell Conference (4-1 vs. Wales)
42 – 1976 at Philadelphia – Wales Conference (7-5 vs. Campbell)

FEWEST SHOTS, ONE TEAM, ONE GAME (SINCE 1955):
12 – 1978 at Buffalo – Campbell Conference (2-3 vs. Wales)
17 – 1970 at St. Louis – West Division (1-4 vs. East)
23 – 1961 at Chicago – Chicago Black Hawks (1-3 vs. NHL All-Stars)
24 – 1976 at Philadelphia – Campbell Conference (5-7 vs. Wales)

MOST POWER-PLAY GOALS, BOTH TEAMS, ONE GAME (SINCE 1950):
3 – 1953 at Montreal – NHL All-Stars 3 (2 power-play goals), Montreal Canadiens 1 (1 power-play goal)
3 – 1954 at Detroit – NHL All-Stars 2 (1 power-play goal), Detroit Red Wings 2 (2 power-play goals)
3 – 1958 at Montreal – NHL All-Stars 3 (1 power-play goal), Montreal Canadiens 6 (2 power-play goals)

FEWEST POWER-PLAY GOALS, BOTH TEAMS, ONE GAME (SINCE 1950):
0 – 13 times (1952, 1959, 1960, 1967, 1968, 1969, 1972, 1973, 1976, 1980, 1981, 1984, 1985)

FASTEST TWO GOALS, BOTH TEAMS, FROM START OF GAME:
37 seconds – 1970 at St. Louis – Jacques Laperriere of East Division scored at 20 seconds and Dean Prentice of West Division scored at 37 seconds. Final score: East Division 4, West Division 1.
4:08 – 1963 at Toronto – Frank Mahovlich scored for Toronto Maple Leafs at 2:22 of first period and Henri Richard scored at 4:08 for NHL All-Stars. Final score: NHL All-Stars 3, Toronto Maple Leafs 3.
4:19 – 1980 at Detroit – Larry Robinson scored at 3:58 for Wales Conference and Steve Payne scored at 4:19 for Wales Conference. Final score: Wales Conference 6, Campbell Conference 3.

1985-86 All-Star Game Summary
February 4, 1986 at Hartford — Wales 4, Campbell 3
PLAYERS ON ICE: **Wales Conference** — *Gosselin, Froese, Mark Howe, *Langway, Ramsey, *Bourque, Robinson, *Lemieux, Muller, Gartner, *Kerr, Turgeon, *Goulet, Trottier, Poulin, Bossy, P. Stastny, Propp, Naslund, Ruotsalainen.
Campbell Conference — *Fuhr, Moog, Fogolin, Lowe, Ramage, *Coffey, Suter, *D. Wilson, *G. Anderson, Hawerchuk, Messier, N. Broten, Tanti, Clark, *Kurri, Taylor, Savard, M. Hunter, Ogrodnick, *Gretzky.
*Indicates voted to respective All-Star Team by fans.

GOALTENDERS   Wales: Gosselin   31 minutes   1 goal against
                         Froese   32 minutes   2 goals against
              Campbell: Fuhr   31 minutes   0 goals against
                         Moog   32 minutes   4 goals against

SUMMARY
First Period
   No scoring
       PENALTIES: Suter (C) 8:51; Gartner (W) 12:55
Second Period
   1. Campbell   Tanti   (unassisted)   7:56
   2. Wales   Propp   (Naslund, Bourque)   17:56
       PENALTIES: None
Third Period
   3. Wales   Stastny   (Robinson, Turgeon)   4:45
   4. Campbell   Gretzky   (Coffey, Savard)   17:09
   5. Wales   Propp   (Robinson)   17:38 PPG
   6. Campbell   Hawerchuk (Savard, Coffey)   19:17 PPG
       PENALTIES: Lowe (C) 6:14; Turgeon (W) 15:22,
                  Messier (C) 16:31; Gartner (W) 18:45
Overtime
   7. Wales   Trottier   (Bossy)   3:05
       PENALTIES: None
   SHOTS ON GOAL BY:
   Wales Conference   8   15   9   3   —   **35**
   Campbell Conference   6   11   10   2   —   **29**
   Attendance: 15,100

FASTEST TWO GOALS, BOTH TEAMS:
10 seconds – 1976 at Philadelphia – Dennis Ververgaert scored at 4:33 and at 4:43 of third period for Campbell Conference. Final score: Wales Conference 7, Campbell Conference 5.

17 seconds – 1970 at St. Louis – Jacques Laperriere of East Division scored at 20 seconds of first period and Dean Prentice of West Division scored at 37 seconds. Final score: East Division 4, West Division 1.

17 seconds – 1973 at New York – Paul Henderson of East Division scored at 19:12 of second period and Pit Martin of West Division scored at 19:29. Final score: East Division 5, West Division 4.

27 seconds – 1963 at Toronto – Ed Litzenberger scored at 2:56 of third period for Toronto and Marcel Pronovost scored at 3:23 for NHL All-Stars. Final score: NHL All-Stars 3, Toronto Maple Leafs 3.

FASTEST THREE GOALS, BOTH TEAMS:
1:32 – 1980 at Detroit – all by Wales Conference – Ron Stackhouse scored at 11:40 of third period, Craig Hartsburg scored at 12:40 and Reed Larson scored at 13:12. Final score: Wales Conference 6, Campbell Conference 3.
2:01 – 1976 at Philadelphia – Curt Bennett scored at 16:59 of first period for Campbell Conference; Pete Mahovlich scored at 18:31 for Wales Conference; Brad Park scored at 19:00 for Wales Conference. Final score: Wales Conference 7, Campbell Conference 5.
2:55 – 1964 at Toronto – Leo Boivin scored at 10:47 of second period for NHL All-Stars; Kent Douglas scored at 11:45 for Toronto; Jean Beliveau scored at 13:52 for All-Stars. Final score: NHL All-Stars 3, Toronto Maple Leafs 2.

FASTEST FOUR GOALS, BOTH TEAMS:
4:26 – 1980 at Detroit – all by Wales Conference – Ron Stackhouse scored at 11:40 of third period; Craig Hartsburg scored at 12:40; Reed Larson scored at 13:12; Real Cloutier scored at 16:06. Final score: Wales Conference 6, Campbell Conference 3.
5:14 – 1983 at NY Islanders – Don Maloney scored at 14:04 of third period for Wales Conference; Wayne Gretzky scored at 15:32 for Campbell Conference; Rick Vaive scored at 17:15 for Campbell Conference; Gretzky scored at 19:18 for Campbell Conference. Final score: Campbell Conference 9, Wales Conference 3.
6:44 – 1983 at NY Islanders – Wayne Gretzky scored at 10:31 of third period for Campbell Conference; Don Maloney scored at 14:04 for Wales Conference; Gretzky scored at 15:32 for Campbell Conference; Rick Vaive scored at 17:15 for Campbell Conference. Final score: Campbell Conference 9, Wales Conference 3.

FASTEST TWO GOALS, ONE TEAM, FROM START OF GAME:
4:19 – 1980 at Detroit – Prince of Wales Conference – Larry Robinson scored at 3:58 and Steve Payne scored at 4:19. Final score: Wales Conference 6, Campbell Conference 3.
4:38 – 1971 at Boston – West Division – Chico Maki scored at 36 seconds and Bobby Hull scored at 4:38. Final score: West Division 2, East Division 1.
5:25 – 1953 at Montreal – NHL All-Stars – Wally Hergesheimer scored at 4:06 and 5:25. Final score: NHL All-Stars 3, Montreal Canadiens 1.
5:31 – 1985 at Calgary – Wales Conference – Ron Francis scored at 1:40 and Tim Kerr scored at 5:31. Final score: Wales Conference 6, Campbell Conference 4.

AMERICAN EXPRESS/NHL ALL-ROOKIE TEAM

Voting for the NHL's All-Rookie Team is conducted among the representatives of the Professional Hockey Writers' Association at the end of the season. The rookie all-star team was first selected for the 1982-83 season.

1985-86		1984-85
Patrick Roy, Montreal	Goal	Steve Penney, Montreal
Gary Suter, Calgary	Defense	Chris Chelios, Montreal
Dana Murzyn, Hartford	Defense	Bruce Bell, Quebec
Mike Ridley, NY Rangers	Center	Mario Lemieux, Pittsburgh
Kjell Dahlin, Montreal	Right Wing	T. Sandstrom, NY Rangers
Wendel Clark, Toronto	Left Wing	Warren Young, Pittsburgh

1983-84		1982-83
Tom Barasso, Buffalo	Goal	Pelle Lindbergh, Philadelphia
Thomas Eriksson, Philadelphia	Defense	Scott Stevens, Washington
Jamie Macoun, Calgary	Defense	Phil Housley, Buffalo
Steve Yzerman, Detroit	Center	Dan Daoust, Montreal/Toronto
Hakan Loob, Calgary	Right Wing	Steve Larmer, Chicago
Sylvain Turgeon, Hartford	Left Wing	Mats Naslund, Montreal

FASTEST TWO GOALS, ONE TEAM:
10 seconds – 1976 at Philadelphia – Campbell Conference – Dennis Ververgaert scored at 4:33 and at 4:43 of third period. Final score: Wales Conference 7, Campbell Conference 5.

21 seconds – 1980 at Detroit – Wales Conference – Larry Robinson scored at 3:58 of first period and Steve Payne scored at 4:19. Final score: Wales Conference 6, Campbell Conference 3.

29 seconds – 1976 at Philadelphia – Campbell Conference – Denis Potvin scored at 14:17 of third period and Steve Vickers scored at 14:46. Final score: Wales Conference 7, Campbell Conference 5.

29 seconds – 1976 at Philadelphia – Wales Conference – Pete Mahovlich scored at 18:31 of first period and Brad Park scored at 19:00. Final score: Wales Conference 7, Campbell Conference 5.

FASTEST THREE GOALS, ONE TEAM:
1:32 – 1980 at Detroit – Wales Conference – Ron Stackhouse scored at 11:40 of third period; Craig Hartsburg scored at 12:40; Reed Larson scored at 13:12. Final score: Wales Conference 6, Campbell Conference 3.

3:05 – 1984 at New Jersey – Wales Conference – Rick Middleton scored at 14:49 of first period; Mats Naslund scored at 16:40; Pierre Larouche at 17:14. Final score: Wales Conference 7, Campbell Conference 6.

3:26 – 1980 at Detroit – Wales Conference – Craig Hartsburg scored at 12:40 of third period; Reed Larson scored at 13:12; Real Cloutier at 13:06. Final score: Wales Conference 6, Campbell Conference 3.

3:46 – 1983 at NY Islanders – Campbell Conference – Wayne Gretzky scored at 15:32 of third period; Rick Vaive at 17:15; Gretzky at 19:18. Final score: Campbell Conference 9, Wales Conference 3.

FASTEST FOUR GOALS, ONE TEAM:
4:26 – 1980 at Detroit – Wales Conference – Ron Stackhouse scored at 11:40 of third period; Craig Hartsburg scored at 12:40; Reed Larson scored at 13:12; Real Cloutier at 16:06. Final score: Wales Conference 6, Campbell Conference 3.

7:25 – 1976 at Philadelphia – Wales Conference – Al MacAdam scored at 9:34 of second period; Guy Lafleur at 11:54; Marcel Dionne at 13:51; Dan Maloney at 16:59. Final score: Wales Conference 7, Campbell Conference 5.

8:03 – 1975 at Montreal – Wales Conference – Phil Esposito scored at 19:16 of second period; Syl Apps at 3:25 of third period; Terry O'Reilly scored at 5:43; Bobby Orr scored at 7:19. Final score: Wales Conference 7, Campbell Conference 1.

MOST GOALS, BOTH TEAMS, ONE PERIOD:
7 – 1983 at NY Islanders – Third period – Campbell (6), Wales (1) Final score: Campbell Conference 9, Wales Conference 3.

5 – 1962 at Toronto – First period – Toronto (4), NHL All-Stars (1). Final score: Toronto Maple Leafs 4, NHL All-Stars 1.

5 – 1965 at Montreal – Second period – NHL All-Stars (3), Montreal (2). Final score: NHL All-Stars 5, Montreal Canadiens 2.

5 – 1973 at New York – Second period – East (3), West (2). Final score: East Division 5, West Division 4.

5 – 1974 at Chicago – Third period – West (3), East (2). Final score: West Division 6, East Division 4.

5 – 1980 at Detroit – Third period – Wales (4), Campbell (1). Final score: Wales Conference 6, Campbell Conference 3.

MOST GOALS, ONE TEAM, ONE PERIOD:
6 – 1983 at NY Islanders – Third period – Campbell Conference. Final score: Campbell Conference 9, Wales Conference 3.

5 – 1984 at New Jersey – First period – Wales Conference. Final score: Wales Conference 7, Campbell Conference 6.

4 – 1959 at Montreal – Third period – Montreal Canadiens. Final score: Montreal Canadiens 6, NHL All-Stars 1.

4 – 1962 at Toronto – First period – Toronto Maple Leafs. Final score: Toronto Maple Leafs 4, NHL All-Stars 1.

4 – 1976 at Philadelphia – Second period – Wales Conference. Final score: Wales Conference 7, Campbell Conference 5.

4 – 1976 at Philadelphia – Third period – Campbell Conference. Final score: Wales Conference 7, Campbell Conference 5.

4 – 1980 at Detroit – Third period – Wales Conference. Final score: Wales Conference 6, Campbell Conference 3.

MOST SHOTS, BOTH TEAMS, ONE PERIOD:
30 – 1959 at Montreal – Second period – NHL All-Stars (16), Montreal (14). Final score: Montreal Canadiens 6, NHL All-Stars 1.

29 – 1955 at Detroit – Third period – Detroit Red Wings (18), NHL All-Stars (11). Final score: Detroit Red Wings 3, NHL All-Stars 1.

29 – 1968 at Toronto – Second period – Toronto Maple Leafs (18), NHL All-Stars (11). Final score: Toronto Maple Leafs 4, NHL All-Stars 3.

29 – 1980 at Detroit – Third period – Wales Conference (17), Campbell Conference (12). Final score: Wales Conference 6, Campbell Conference 3

MOST SHOTS, ONE TEAM, ONE PERIOD:
20 – 1970 at St. Louis – Third period – East Division. Final score: East Division 4, West Division 1.

18 – 1955 at Detroit – Third period – Detroit Red Wings. Final score: Detroit Red Wings 3, NHL All-Stars 1.

18 – 1968 at Toronto – Second period – Toront Maple Leafs. Final score: Toronto Maple Leafs 4, NHL All-Stars 3.

18 – 1981 at Los Angeles – First period – Campbell Conference. Final score: Campbell Conference 4, Wales Conference 1.

FEWEST SHOTS, BOTH TEAMS, ONE PERIOD:
9 – 1971 at Boston – Third period – East (2), West (7). Final score: West Division 2, East Division 1.

9 – 1980 at Detroit – Second period – Campbell (4), Wales (5). Final score: Wales Conference 6, Campbell Conference 3.

13 – 1982 at Washington – Third period – Campbell (6), Wales (7). Final score: Wales Conference 4, Campbell Conference 2.

14 – 1978 at Buffalo – First period – Campbell (7), Wales (7). Final score: Wales Conference 3, Campbell Conference 2.

14 – 1986 at Hartford – First period – Campbell (6), Wales (8). Final score: Wales Conference 4, Campbell Conference 3.

FEWEST SHOTS, ONE TEAM, ONE PERIOD:
2 – 1971 at Boston – Third period – East Division Final score: West Division 2, East Division 1

2 – 1978 at Buffalo – Second period – Campbell Conference Final score: Wales Conference 3, Campbell Conference 2

3 – 1978 at Buffalo – Third period – Campbell Conference Final score: Wales Conference 3, Campbell Conference 2

4 – 1955 at Detroit – First period – NHL All-Stars Finalscore: Detroit Red Wings 3, NHL All-Stars 1

4 – 1980 at Detroit – Second period – Campbell Conference Final score: Wales Conference 6, Campbell Conference 3

All-Star Game Results

Year	Venue	Score	Coaches	Attendance
1986	Hartford	Wales 4, Campbell 3	Mike Keenan, Glen Sather	15,100
1985	Calgary	Wales 6, Campbell 4	Al Arbour, Glen Sather	16,825
1984	New Jersey	Wales 7, Campbell 6	Al Arbour, Glen Sather	18,939
1983	NY Islanders	Campbell 9, Wales 3	Roger Neilson, Al Arbour	15,230
1982	Washington	Wales 4, Campbell 2	Al Arbour, Glen Sonmor	18,130
1981	Los Angeles	Campbell 4, Wales 1	Pat Quinn, Scott Bowman	15,761
1980	Detroit	Wales 6, Campbell 3	Scott Bowman, Al Arbour	21,002
1978	Buffalo	Wales 3, Campbell 2	Scott Bowman, Fred Shero	16,433
1977	Vancouver	Wales 4, Campbell 3	Scott Bowman, Fred Shero	15,607
1976	Philadelphia	Wales 7, Campbell 5	Floyd Smith, Fred Shero	16,436
1975	Montreal	Wales 7, Campbell 1	Bep Guidolin, Fred Shero	16,080
1974	Chicago	West 6, East 4	Billy Reay, Scott Bowman	16,426
1973	New York	East 5, West 4	Tom Johnson, Billy Reay	16,986
1972	Minnesota	East 3, West 2	Al MacNeil, Billy Reay	15,423
1971	Boston	West 2, East 1	Scott Bowman, Harry Sinden	14,790
1970	St. Louis	East 4, West 1	Claude Ruel, Scott Bowman	16,587
1969	Montreal	East 3, West 3	Toe Blake, Scott Bowman	16,260
1968	Toronto	Toronto 4, All-Stars 3	Punch Imlach, Toe Blake	15,753
1967	Montreal	Montreal 3, All-Stars 0	Toe Blake, Sid Abel	14,284
1965	Montreal	All-Stars 5, Montreal 2	Billy Reay, Toe Blake	13,529
1964	Toronto	All-Stars 3, Toronto 2	Sid Abel, Punch Imlach	14,232
1963	Toronto	All-Stars 3, Toronto 3	Sid Abel, Punch Imlach	14,034
1962	Toronto	Toronto 4, All-Stars 1	Punch Imlach, Rudy Pilous	14,236
1961	Chicago	All-Stars 3, Chicago 1	Sid Abel, Rudy Pilous	14,534
1960	Montreal	All-Stars 2, Montreal 1	Punch Imlach, Toe Blake	13,949
1959	Montreal	Montreal 6, All-Stars 1	Toe Blake, Punch Imlach	13,818
1958	Montreal	Montreal 6, All-Stars 3	Toe Blake, Milt Schmidt	13,989
1957	Montreal	All-Stars 5, Montreal 3	Milt Schmidt, Toe Blake	13,003
1956	Montreal	All-Stars 1, Montreal 1	Jim Skinner, Toe Blake	13,095
1955	Detroit	Detroit 3, All-Stars 1	Jim Skinner, Dick Irvin	10,111
1954	Detroit	All-Stars 2, Detroit 2	King Clancy, Jim Skinner	10,689
1953	Montreal	All-Stars 3, Montreal 1	Lynn Patrick, Dick Irvin	14,153
1952	Detroit	1st team 1, 2nd team 1	Tommy Ivan, Dick Irvin	10,680
1951	Toronto	1st team 2, 2nd team 2	Joe Primeau, Hap Day	11,469
1950	Detroit	Detroit 7, All-Stars 1	Tommy Ivan, Lynn Patrick	9,166
1949	Toronto	All-Stars 3, Toronto 1	Tommy Ivan, Hap Day	13,541
1948	Chicago	All-Stars 3, Toronto 1	Tommy Ivan, Hap Day	12,794
1947	Toronto	All-Stars 4, Toronto 3	Dick Irvin, Hap Day	14,169

There was no All-Star contest during the calendar year of 1966 since the game was moved from the start of season to mid-season. In 1979, the Challenge Cup series between the Soviet Union and Team NHL replaced the All-Star Game.

INDIVIDUAL RECORDS
Career
MOST GAMES PLAYED:
23 – Gordie Howe from 1948 through 1980
15 – Frank Mahovlich from 1959 through 1974
13 – Jean Beliveau from 1953 through 1969
 – Alex Delvecchio from 1953 through 1967
 – Doug Harvey from 1951 through 1969
 – Maurice Richard from 1947 through 1959

MOST GOALS:
10 – Gordie Howe in 23 games
 8 – Frank Mahovlich in 15 games
 – Wayne Gretzky in 7 games
 7 – Maurice Richard in 13 games
 5 – Bobby Hull in 12 games
 – Ted Lindsay in 11 games
 – Denis Potvin in 8 games

MOST ASSISTS:
9 – Gordie Howe in 23 games
 7 – Doug Harvey in 13 games
 – Guy Lafleur in 5 games
 6 – Red Kelly in 11 games
 – Norm Ullman in 11 games

MOST POINTS:
19 – Gordie Howe (10 goals, 9 assists in 23 games)
13 – Frank Mahovlich (8 goals, 5 assists in 15 games)
10 – Bobby Hull (5 goals, 5 assists in 12 games)
 – Ted Lindsay (5 goals, 5 assists in 11 games)
 9 – Maurice Richard (7 goals, 2 assists in 13 games)
 – Henri Richard (4 goals, 5 assists in 10 games)
 – Denis Potvin (5 goals, 4 assists in 8 games)
 – Wayne Gretzky (8 goals, 1 assist in 7 games)
 8 – Norm Ullman (2 goals, 6 assists in 11 games)
 – Guy Lafleur (1 goal, 7 assists in 5 games)
 – Doug Harvey (1 goal, 7 assists in 13 games)

MOST PENALTY MINUTES:
27 – Gordie Howe in 23 games
21 – Gus Mortson in 9 games
16 – Harry Howell in 7 games

MOST POWER-PLAY GOALS:
6 – Gordie Howe in 23 games
3 – Bobby Hull in 12 games
2 – Maurice Richard in 13 games

Game
MOST GOALS, ONE GAME:
4 – Wayne Gretzky, Clarence Campbell Conference, 1983
3 – Ted Lindsay, Detroit Red Wings, 1950
2 – Wally Hergesheimer, NHL All-Stars, 1953
 – Earl Reibel, Detroit Red Wings, 1955
 – Andy Bathgate, NHL All-Stars, 1958
 – Maurice Richard, Montreal Canadiens, 1958
 – Frank Mahovlich, Toronto Maple Leafs, 1963
 – Gordie Howe, NHL All-Stars, 1965
 – John Ferguson, Montreal Canadiens, 1967
 – Frank Mahovlich, East Division All-Stars, 1969
 – Greg Polis, West Division All-Stars, 1973
 – Syl Apps, Prince of Wales Conference, 1975
 – Dennis Ververgaert, Clarence Campbell Conference, 1976
 – Richard Martin, Prince of Wales Conference, 1977
 – Lanny McDonald, Prince of Wales Conference, 1977
 – Mike Bossy, Prince of Wales Conference, 1982
 – Pierre Larouche, Prince of Wales Conference, 1984
 – Mario Lemieux, Prince of Wales Conference 1985
 – Brian Propp, Prince of Wales Conference, 1986

MOST ASSISTS, ONE GAME:
4 – Raymond Bourque, Prince of Wales Conference, 1985
3 – Dickie Moore, Montreal Canadiens, 1958
 – Doug Harvey, Montreal Canadiens, 1959
 – Guy Lafleur, Prince of Wales Conference, 1975
 – Pete Mahovlich, Prince of Wales Conference, 1976
 – Mark Messier, Clarence Campbell Conference, 1983
 – Rick Vaive, Clarence Campbell Conference, 1984
 – Mark Johnson, Prince of Wales Conference, 1984
 – Don Maloney, Prince of Wales Conference, 1984
 – Mike Krushelnyski, Campbell Conference, 1985

MOST POINTS, ONE GAME:
4 – Ted Lindsay, Detroit Red Wings, 1950 (3 goals, 1 assist)
 – Gordie Howe, NHL All-Stars, 1965 (2 goals, 2 assists)
 – Pete Mahovlich, Prince of Wales Conference, 1976 (1 goal, 3 assists)
 – Wayne Gretzky, Clarence Campbell Conference, 1983 (4 goals)
 – Don Maloney, Prince of Wales Conference, 1984 (1 goal, 3 assists)
 – Raymond Bourque, Prince of Wales Conference, 1985 (4 assists)

MOST GOALS, ONE PERIOD:
4 – Wayne Gretzky, Clarence Campbell Conference, Third period, 1983
2 – Ted Lindsay, Detroit Red Wings, First period, 1950
 – Wally Hergesheimer, NHL All-Stars, First period, 1953
 – Andy Bathgate, NHL All-Stars, Third period, 1958
 – Frank Mahovlich, Toronto Maple Leafs, First period, 1963
 – Dennis Ververgaert, Clarence Campbell Conference, Third period, 1976
 – Richard Martin, Prince of Wales Conference, Third period, 1977

MOST ASSISTS, ONE PERIOD:
3 – Mark Messier, Clarence Campbell Conference, Third period, 1983
2 – By several players

MOST POINTS, ONE PERIOD:
4 – Wayne Gretzky, Campbell Conference, Third period, 1983 (4 goals)
3 – Gordie Howe, Detroit, Second period, 1965 (1 goal, 2 assists)
 – Pete Mahovlich, Wales, First period, 1976 (1 goal, 2 assists)
 – Mark Messier, Campbell Conference, Third period, 1983 (4 assists)

FASTEST GOAL FROM START OF GAME:
19 seconds – Ted Lindsay, Detroit Red Wings, 1950
20 seconds – Jacques Laperriere, East Division All-Stars, 1970
36 seconds – Chico Maki, West Division All-Stars, 1971
37 seconds – Dean Prentice, West Division All-Star, 1970
45 seconds – Kent Nilsson, Campbell Conference, 1981

FASTEST GOAL FROM START OF A PERIOD:
19 seconds – Ted Lindsay, Detroit Red Wings, 1950 (first period)
20 seconds – Jacques Laperriere, East Division, 1970 (first period)
26 seconds – Wayne Gretzky, Campbell Conference, 1982 (second period)
28 seconds – Maurice Richard, NHL All-Stars, 1947 (third period)
33 seconds – Bert Olmstead, Montreal Canadiens, 1957 (second period)

FASTEST TWO GOALS FROM START OF GAME:
5:25 – Wally Hergesheimer, NHL All-Stars, 1953. Scored at 4:06 and 5:25 of first period.
12:11 – Frank Mahovlich, Toronto Maple Leafs, 1963. Scored at 2:22 and 12:11 of first period.

FASTEST TWO GOALS FROM START OF A PERIOD:
4:43 – Dennis Ververgaert, Campbell Conference, 1976. Scored at 4:33 and 4:43 of third period.
5:25 – Wally Hergesheimer, NHL All-Stars, 1953. Scored at 4:06 and 5:25 of first period.
12:11 – Frank Mahovlich, Toronto Maple Leafs, 1963. Scored at 2:22 and 12:11 of first period.
13:54 – Andy Bathgate, NHL All-Stars, 1958. Scored at 3:55 and 13:54 of third period.

FASTEST TWO GOALS:
10 seconds – Dennis Ververgaert, Campbell Conference, 1976. Scored at 4:33 and 4:43 of third period.
1:19 – Wally Hergesheimer, NHL All-Stars, 1953. Scored at 4:06 and 5:25 of first period.
4:09 – Mike Bossy, Wales Conference, 1982. Scored at 17:10 of second period and 1:19 of third period.

Goaltenders
MOST GAMES PLAYED:
13 – Glenn Hall from 1955 through 1969
11 – Terry Sawchuk from 1950 through 1968
 8 – Jacques Plante from 1956 through 1970
 6 – Tony Esposito from 1970 through 1980
 – Ed Giacomin from 1967 through 1973

MOST GOALS AGAINST:
22 – Glenn Hall in 13 games
19 – Terry Sawchuk in 11 games
18 – Jacques Plante in 8 games
14 – Turk Broda in 4 games

BEST GOALS-AGAINST-AVERAGE AMONG THOSE WITH AT LEAST TWO GAMES PLAYED:
0.68 – Gilles Villemure in 3 games
1.02 – Frank Brimsek in 2 games
1.59 – Johnny Bower in 4 games
1.64 – Lorne "Gump" Worsley in 4 games
1.98 – Gerry McNeil in 3 games
2.03 – Don Edwards in 2 games
2.44 – Terry Sawchuk in 11 games

MOST MINUTES PLAYED:
467 – Terry Sawchuk in 11 games
421 – Glenn Hall in 13 games
370 – Jacques Plante in 8 games
209 – Turk Broda in 4 games
182 – Ed Giacomin in 6 games
165 – Tony Esposito in 6 games

Don Maloney is one of only six players to score four points in a single All-Star Game.

Dave Keon, 14, above, won the Calder, Lady Byng and Conn Smythe Trophies during his 18 years in the NHL. Defensemen Leo Boivin, below, played 19 seasons with Toronto, Boston, Detroit, Pittsburgh and Minnesota. Along with Serge Savard, and OHA administrator Bill Hanley, Keon and Boivin were inducted into the Hockey Hall of Fame in September of 1986.

Hockey Hall of Fame

Location: Toronto's Exhibition Park, on the shore of Lake Ontario, adjacent to Ontario Place and Exhibition Stadium. The Hockey Hall of Fame building is in the middle of Exhibition Place, directly north of the stadium.

Telephone: (416) 595-1345.

Hours: Mid-May to mid-August - 10 am to 7 pm Tuesday through Sunday; Mondays 10 am to 5 pm. Mid-August to Labor Day - 10 am to 5:00 pm daily during annual Exhibition. September after Labor Day to mid-May - 10 am to 4:30 pm; closed Mondays. Also closed Christmas Day, New Year's Day and the day prior to the annual Exhibition.

Admission: Adults $2, Seniors & Students $1. Group rates, and reduced rate during Exhibition.

History: The Hockey Hall of Fame building was completed May 1, 1961, and officially opened August 26, 1961, by the Prime Minister of Canada, John G. Diefenbaker, and U.S. ambassador to Canada, Livingston T. Merchant. The six member clubs of the NHL operating at the time provided the funds required for construction. The City of Toronto, owner of the grounds, provided an ideal site, and the Canadian National Exhibition Association, as administrator of the park area, agreed to service and maintain the building in perpetuity for the purposes of the Hockey Hall of Fame. Hockey exhibits are provided and financed by the NHL with co-operative support of the Canadian Amateur Hockey Association. Staff and most administration costs are underwritten by the NHL.

Eligibility Requirements: Any person who is, or has been distinguished in hockey as a Player, Executive or Referee, shall be eligible for election. Player and Referee candidates will normally have completed their active participating careers three years prior to election, but in exceptional cases this period may be shortened by the Hockey Hall of Fame Governing Committee. Candidates for election as Executives and Referees shall be nominated only by the Governing Committee and upon election shall be known as Builders. Candidates for election shall be chosen on the basis of "playing ability, integrity, character and their contribution to their team and the game of hockey in general."

Honor Roll: There are 256 Honored Members of the Hockey Hall of Fame. Of the total, 179 are listed as players, 68 as Builders and nine as Referees. M. H. (Lefty) Reid is Director & Curator of the Hall.

(Year of election to the Hall is indicated in brackets after the Members' names).

PLAYERS

Abel, Sidney Gerald (1969)
*Adams, John James "Jack" (1959)
Apps, Charles Joseph Sylvanus "Syl" (1961)
Armstrong, George Edward (1975)
Bailey, Irvine Wallace "Ace" (1975)
*Bain, Donald H. "Dan" (1945)
*Baker, Hobart "Hobey" (1945)
*Barry, Martin J. "Marty" (1965)
Bathgate, Andrew James "Andy" (1978)
Beliveau, Jean Arthur (1972)
Benedict, Clinton S. (1965)
*Bentley, Douglas Wagner (1964)
*Bentley, Maxwell H. L. (1966)
Blake, Hector "Toe" (1966)
Boivin, Leo Joseph (1986)
*Boon, Richard R. "Dickie" (1952)
Bouchard, Emile Joseph "Butch" (1966)
*Boucher, Frank (1958)
*Boucher, George "Buck" (1960)
Bower, John William (1976)
*Bowie, Russell (1945)
Brimsek, Francis Charles (1966)
*Broadbent, Harry L. "Punch" (1962)
*Broda, Walter Edward "Turk" (1967)
Bucyk, John Paul (1981)
*Burch, Billy (1974)
*Cameron, Harold Hugh "Harry" (1962)
Cheevers, Gerald Michael "Gerry" (1985)
Clancy, Francis Michael "King" (1958)
*Clapper, Aubrey "Dit" (1945)
*Cleghorn, Sprague (1958)
Colville, Neil MacNeil (1967)
*Conacher, Charles W. (1961)
*Connell, Alex (1958)
*Cook, William Osser (1952)
Coulter, Arthur Edmund (1974)
Cournoyer, Yvan Serge (1982)
Cowley, William Mailes (1968)
*Crawford, Samuel Russell "Rusty" (1962)
*Darragh, John Proctor "Jack" (1962)
*Davidson, Allan M. "Scotty" (1950)
Day, Clarence Henry "Hap" (1961)
Delvecchio, Alex (1977)
*Denneny, Cyril "Cy" (1959)
Drillon, Gordon Arthur (1975)
*Drinkwater, Charles Graham (1950)
Dryden, Kenneth Wayne (1983)
*Dunderdale, Thomas (1974)
*Durnan, William Ronald (1964)
Dutton, Mervyn A. "Red" (1958)
*Dye, Cecil Henry "Babe" (1970)
Esposito, Philip Anthony (1984)
*Farrell, Arthur F. (1965)
*Foyston, Frank (1958)
*Frederickson, Frank (1958)
Gadsby, William Alexander (1970)

*Gardiner, Charles Robert "Chuck" (1945)
*Gardiner, Herbert Martin "Herb" (1958)
*Gardner, James Henry "Jimmy" (1962)
Geoffrion, Jos. A. Bernard "Boom Boom" (1972)
*Gerard, Eddie (1945)
Gilbert, Rodrigue Gabriel "Rod" (1982)
*Gilmour, Hamilton Livingstone "Billy" (1962)
*Goheen, Frank Xavier "Moose" (1952)
*Goodfellow, Ebenezer R. "Ebbie" (1963)
*Grant, Michael "Mike" (1950)
*Green, Wilfred "Shorty" (1962)
*Griffis, Silas Seth "Si" (1950)
*Hainsworth, George (1961)
Hall, Glenn Henry (1975)
*Hall, Joseph Henry (1961)
Harvey, Douglas Norman (1973)
*Hay, George (1958)
*Hern, William Milton "Riley" (1962)
*Hextall, Bryan Aldwyn (1969)
*Holmes, Harry "Hap" (1972)
*Hooper, Charles Thomas "Tom" (1962)
Horner, George Reginald "Red" (1965)
*Horton, Miles Gilbert "Tim" (1977)
Howe, Gordon (1972)
*Howe, Sydney Harris (1965)
Howell, Henry Vernon "Harry" (1979)
Hull, Robert Marvin (1983)
*Hutton, John Bower "Bouse" (1962)
*Hyland, Harry M. (1962)
*Irvin, James Dickenson "Dick" (1958)
*Jackson, Harvey "Busher" (1971)
*Johnson, Ernest "Moose" (1952)
*Johnson, Ivan "Ching" (1958)
Johnson, Thomas Christian (1970)
*Joliat, Aurel (1947)
*Keats, Gordon "Duke" (1958)
Kelly, Leonard Patrick "Red" (1969)
Kennedy, Theodore Samuel "Teeder" (1966)
Keon, David Michael (1986)
Lach, Elmer James (1966)
*Lalonde, Edouard Charles "Newsy" (1950)
*Laviolette, Jean Baptiste "Jack" (1962)
*Lehman, Hugh (1958)
Lemaire, Jacques Gerard (1984)
*LeSueur, Percy (1961)
Lindsay, Robert Blake Theodore "Ted" (1966)
Lumley, Harry (1980)
*MacKay, Duncan "Mickey" (1952)
Mahovlich, Frank William (1981)
*Malone, Joseph "Joe" (1950)
*Mantha, Sylvio (1960)
*Marshall, John "Jack" (1965)
*Maxwell, Fred G. "Steamer" (1962)
*McGee, Frank (1945)
*McGimsie, William George "Billy" (1962)
*McNamara, George (1958)

Mikita, Stanley (1983)
Moore, Richard Winston (1974)
*Moran, Patrick Joseph "Paddy" (1958)
*Morenz, Howie (1945)
*Mosienko, William "Billy" (1965)
*Nighbor, Frank (1945)
*Noble, Edward Reginald "Reg" (1962)

*Oliver, Harry (1967)
Olmstead, Murray Bert "Bert" (1985)
Orr, Robert Gordon (1979)
Parent, Bernard Marcel (1984)
*Patrick, Joseph Lynn (1980)
*Patrick, Lester (1945)
*Phillips, Tommy (1945)
Pilote, Joseph Albert Pierre Paul (1975)
*Pitre, Didier "Pit" (1962)
*Plante, Joseph Jacques Omer (1978)
Pratt, Walter "Babe" (1966)
Primeau, A. Joseph (1963)
Pronovost, Joseph René Marcel (1978)
*Pulford, Harvey (1945)
Quackenbush, Hubert George "Bill" (1976)
*Rankin, Frank (1961)
Ratelle, Joseph Gilbert Yvan Jean "Jean" (1985)
Rayner, Claude Earl "Chuck" (1973)
Reardon, Kenneth Joseph (1966)
Richard, Joseph Henri (1979)
Richard, Joseph Henri Maurice "Rocket" (1961)
*Richardson, George Taylor (1950)
Roberts, Gordon (1971)
*Ross, Arthur Howie (1945)
*Russel, Blair (1965)
*Russell, Ernest (1965)
*Ruttan, J.D. "Jack" (1962)
Savard, Serge A. (1986)
*Sawchuk, Terrance Gordon "Terry" (1971)
*Scanlan, Fred (1965)
Schmidt, Milton Conrad "Milt" (1961)
Schriner, David "Sweeney" (1962)
Seibert, Earl Walter (1963)
*Seibert, Oliver Levi (1961)
*Shore, Edward W. "Eddie" (1945)
*Siebert, Albert C. "Babe" (1964)
*Simpson, Harold Edward "Bullet Joe" (1962)
*Smith, Alfred E. (1962)
*Smith, Reginald "Hooley" (1972)
*Smith, Thomas James (1973)
Stanley, Allan Herbert (1981)
*Stanley, Russell "Barney" (1962)
*Stewart, John Sherratt "Black Jack" (1964)
*Stewart, Nelson "Nels" (1962)
*Stuart, Bruce (1961)
*Stuart, Hod (1945)
*Taylor, Frederic "Cyclone" (O.B.E.) (1945)
*Thompson, Cecil R. "Tiny" (1959)
*Trihey, Col. Harry J. (1950)
Ullman, Norman Victor Alexander "Norm" (1982)
*Vezina, Georges (1945)
*Walker, John Phillip "Jack" (1960)
*Walsh, Martin "Marty" (1962)
*Watson, Harry E. (1962)
*Weiland, Ralph "Cooney" (1971)
*Westwick, Harry (1962)
*Whitcroft, Fred (1962)
*Wilson, Gordon Allan "Phat" (1962)
Worsley, Lorne John "Gump" (1980)
*Worters, Roy (1969)

Fred "Cyclone" Taylor, at left, played in Renfrew and Ottawa before moving to Vancouver in 1913. Throughout his career he was one of hockey's fastest skaters, earning his nickname with swirling rushes from defense. He was part of a Cup-winner in 1909 and 1913. "Bullet" Joe Simpson, below, starred with the Edmonton Eskimos in the Western Canada Hockey League in the early 1920s. He joined the New York Americans in 1925, played until 1931 and then managed in New Haven and Minneapolis.

BUILDERS

*Adams, Charles Francis (1960)
*Adams, Weston W. (1972)
*Ahearn, Thomas Franklin "Frank" (1962)
*Ahearne, John Francis "Bunny" (1977)
*Allan, Sir Montague (C.V.O.) (1945)
Ballard, Harold Edwin (1977)
*Bickell, John Paris (1978)
*Brown, George V. (1961)
*Brown, Walter A. (1962)
Buckland, Frank (1975)
*Butterfield, Jack Arlington (1980)
*Calder, Frank (1945)
*Campbell, Angus D. (1964)
*Campbell, Clarence Sutherland (1966)
*Cattarinich, Joseph (1977)
*Dandurand, Joseph Viateur "Leo" (1963)
Dilio, Francis Paul (1964)
*Dudley, George S. (1958)
*Dunn, James A. (1968)
Francis, Emile (1982)
*Gibson, Dr. John L. "Jack" (1976)
*Gorman, Thomas Patrick "Tommy" (1963)
Hanley, William (1986)
*Hay, Charles (1974)
*Hendy, James C. (1968)
*Hewitt, Foster (1965)
*Hewitt, William Abraham (1945)

*Hume, Fred J. (1962)
Imlach, George "Punch" (1984)
Ivan, Thomas N. (1974)
*Jennings, William M. (1975)
Juckes, Gordon W. (1979)
*Kilpatrick, Gen. John Reed (1960)
*Leader, George Alfred (1969)
LeBel, Robert (1970)
*Lockhart, Thomas F. (1965)
*Loicq, Paul (1961)
*McLaughlin, Major Frederic (1963)
Mariucci, John (1985)
*Milford, John "Jake" (1984)
Molson, Hon. Hartland de Montarville (1973)
*Nelson, Francis (1945)
*Norris, Bruce A. (1969)
*Norris, Sr., James (1958)
*Norris, James Dougan (1962)
*Northey, William M. (1945)
*O'Brien, John Ambrose (1962)
*Patrick, Frank (1958)
*Pickard, Allan W. (1958)
Pilous, Rudy (1985)
Pollock, Samuel Patterson Smyth (1978)
*Raymond, Sen. Donat (1958)
*Robertson, John Ross (1945)
*Robinson, Claude C. (1945)

*Ross, Philip D. (1976)
*Selke, Frank J. (1960)
Sinden, Harry James (1983)
*Smith, Frank D. (1962)
*Smythe, Conn (1958)
*Stanley of Preston, Lord (G.C.B.) (1945)
*Sutherland, Cap. James T. (1945)
Tarasov, Anatoli V. (1974)
*Turner, Lloyd (1958)
Tutt, William Thayer (1978)
Voss, Carl Potter (1974)
*Waghorn, Fred C. (1961)
*Wirtz, Arthur Michael (1971)
Wirtz, William W. "Bill" (1976)

REFEREES
Ashley, John George (1981)
Chadwick, William L. (1964)
*Elliott, Chaucer (1961)
*Hewitson, Robert W. (1963)
*Ion, Fred J. "Mickey" (1961)
*Rodden, Michael J. "Mike" (1962)
*Smeaton, J. Cooper (1961)
Storey, Roy Alvin "Red" (1967)
Udvari, Frank Joseph (1973)

*Deceased

United States Hockey Hall of Fame

The United States Hockey Hall of Fame is located in Eveleth, Minnesota, 60 miles north of Duluth, on Highway 53. The facility is open Monday to Saturday 9 a.m. to 5 p.m. and Sundays noon to 5 p.m. from the day after Labor Day until June 14. During the remaining summer period the Monday to Saturday hours are 9 a.m. to 8 p.m. and Sundays 10 a.m. to 8 p.m.; Adult $2.00; Juniors $1.25; and Children 75 cents.

The Hall was dedicated and opened on June 21, 1973, largely as the result of the work of D. Kelly Campbell, Chairman of the Eveleth Civic Association's Project H Committee. The National Hockey League contributed $100,000 towards the construction of the building. There are now 66 enshrinees consisting of 42 players, 9 coaches, 14 administrators, and one referee. New members are inducted annually in October and must have made a significant contribution toward hockey in the United States through the vehicle of their careers. Roger Godin is the Director-Curator of the Hall.

Jack McCartan, right, gave the U.S. Olympic hockey team gold medal goaltending at the 1960 Winter Olympics in Squaw Valley, California. He played parts of two seasons with the New York Rangers in the NHL and played in the Eastern Professional Hockey League and the WHA.

Bill Moe, below, was the AHL's most valuable player with the Hershey Bears in 1943-44.

PLAYERS
*Abel, Clarence "Taffy"
*Baker, Hobart "Hobey"
Bartholome, Earl
Bessone, Peter
Blake, Robert
Brimsek, Frank
*Chaisson, Ray
Chase, John P.
Christian, William "Bill"
Cleary, Robert
Cleary, William
*Conroy, Anthony
Dahlstrom, Carl "Cully"
DesJardins, Victor
Dill, Robert
Everett, Doug
Garrison, John B.
Garrity, Jack
*Goheen, Frank "Moose"
Harding, Austin "Austie"
Iglehart, Stewart
Johnson, Virgil
Karakas, Mike
Lane, Myles J.
*Linder, Joseph
*LoPresti, Sam L.
Mariucci, John
Mayasich, John
McCartan, Jack
Moe, William
Moseley, Fred
*Nelson, Hubert "Hub"
Olson , Eddie
*Owen, Jr., George
*Palmer, Winthrop
Purpur, Clifford "Fido"
Riley, William
*Romnes, Elwin "Doc"
Rondeau, Richard
Williams, Thomas
*Winters, Frank "Coddy"
Yackel, Ken

COACHES
Almquist, Oscar
*Gordon, Malcolm K.
Heyliger, Victor
*Jeremiah, Edward J.
*Kelley, John "Snooks"
Riley, Jack
*Thompson, Clifford, R.
*Stewart, William
*Winsor, Alfred "Ralph"

ADMINISTRATORS
*Brown, George V.
*Brown, Walter A.
Bush, Walter
Clark, Donald
*Gibson, J.C. "Doc"
*Jennings, William M.
*Kahler, Nick
*Lockhart, Thomas F.
Marvin, Cal
Ridder, Robert
Trumble, Harold
Tutt, William Thayer
Wirtz, William W. "Bill"
*Wright, Lyle Z.

REFEREE
Chadwick, William

*Deceased

Notes

Patrick Roy, goaltender for the Montreal Canadiens, became the youngest player to win the Conn Smythe Trophy with his 1.92 goals-against-average in 20 games during the 1986 Stanley Cup Playoffs.

NHL AWARD MONEY BREAKDOWN

(All team awards are based on units of 21 per team)

Stanley Cup Playoffs

Division Semi-Final Losers	(8 teams)	$ 2,000	$ 336,000
Division Final Losers	(4 teams)	5,000	420,000
Conference Championship Losers	(2 teams)	10,000	420,000
Stanley Cup Championship Losers		15,000	315,000
Stanley Cup Winners		20,000	420,000
TOTAL PLAYOFF AWARD MONEY			$1,911,000

Final Standings, Regular Season

Division Winners	(4 teams)	$4,000	$336,000
Second Place	(4 teams)	$2,000	$168,000
Third Place	(4 teams)	$1,000	$ 84,000
Fourth Place	(4 teams)	$ 600	$ 50,400
TOTAL CHAMPIONSHIP POOL			$638,400

Individual Trophy Awards; Official All-Star Teams Award Money	$38,750
All-Star Game (21 units of $1,000 for winning team; 21 units of $750 for losing team)	36,750
TOTAL INDIVIDUAL AWARD MONEY	$73,250

1986 Stanley Cup Playoffs

Jim Peplinski of the Flames and Mats Naslund of the Canadiens in the Stanley Cup Finals. 1986 was the "Year of the Upset" in the NHL as many of the top teams in regular-season play were eliminated in the playoffs. Calgary's 22 games-played set a new record for one playoff year.

Team Playoff Records

	GP	W	L	GF	GA	%
Montreal	20	15	5	56	41	.750
Calgary	22	12	10	81	69	.545
St. Louis	19	10	9	64	70	.526
NY Rangers	16	8	8	47	55	.500
Edmonton	10	6	4	41	30	.600
Toronto	10	6	4	40	33	.600
Hartford	10	6	4	29	23	.600
Washington	9	5	4	36	24	.556
Minnesota	5	2	3	20	18	.400
Philadelphia	5	2	3	15	18	.400
Chicago	3	0	3	9	18	.000
Winnipeg	3	0	3	8	15	.000
Quebec	3	0	3	7	16	.000
Boston	3	0	3	6	10	.000
Vancouver	3	0	3	5	17	.000

Results

DIVISION SEMI-FINALS
(Best of five series)

Prince of Wales Conference

Series 'A'
Wed. Apr. 9	Hartford 3	at Quebec 2*
Thur. Apr. 10	Hartford 4	at Quebec 1
Sat. Apr. 12	Quebec 4	at Hartford 9

* Sylvain Turgeon scored at 2:36 of overtime
Hartford won series 3-0

Series 'B'
Wed. Apr. 9	Boston 1	at Montreal 3
Thur. Apr. 10	Boston 2	at Montreal 3
Sat. Apr. 12	Montreal 4	at Boston 3

Montreal won series 3-0

Series 'C'
Wed. Apr. 9	NY Rangers 6	at Philadelphia 2
Thur. Apr. 10	NY Rangers 1	at Philadelphia 2
Sat. Apr. 12	Philadelphia 2	at NY Rangers 5
Sun. Apr. 13	Philadelphia 7	at NY Rangers 1
Tues. Apr. 15	NY Rangers 5	at Philadelphia 2

NY Rangers won series 3-2

Series 'D'
Wed. Apr. 9	NY Islanders 1	at Washington 3
Thur. Apr. 10	NY Islanders 2	at Washington 5
Sat. Apr. 12	Washington 3	at NY Islanders 1

Washington won series 3-0

DIVISION FINALS
(Best-of-seven series)

Series 'I'
Thur. Apr. 17	Hartford 4	at Montreal 1
Sat. Apr. 19	Hartford 1	at Montreal 3
Mon. Apr. 21	Montreal 4	at Hartford 1
Wed. Apr. 23	Montreal 1	at Hartford 2*
Fri. Apr. 25	Hartford 3	at Montreal 5
Sun. Apr. 27	Montreal 0	at Hartford 1
Tues. Apr. 29	Hartford 1	at Montreal 2**

* Kevin Dineen scored at 1:07 of overtime
** Claude Lemieux scored at 5:55 of overtime
Montreal won series 4-3

Series 'J'
Thur. Apr. 17	NY Rangers 4	at Washington 3*
Sat. Apr. 19	NY Rangers 1	at Washington 8
Mon. Apr. 21	Washington 6	at NY Rangers 3
Wed. Apr. 23	Washington 5	at NY Rangers 6**
Fri. Apr. 25	NY Rangers 4	at Washington 2
Sun. Apr. 27	Washington 1	at NY Rangers 2

* Brian MacLellan scored at 1:16 of overtime
** Bob Brooke scored at 2:40 of overtime
NY Rangers won series 4-2

CONFERENCE CHAMPIONSHIPS
(Best-of-seven series)

Series 'M'
Thur. May 1	NY Rangers 1	at Montreal 2
Sat. May 3	NY Rangers 2	at Montreal 6
Mon. May 5	Montreal 4	at NY Rangers 3*
Wed. May 7	Montreal 0	at NY Rangers 2
Fri. May 9	NY Rangers 1	at Montreal 3

* Claude Lemieux scored at 9:41 of overtime
Montreal won series 4-1

Clarence Campbell Conference

Series 'E'
Wed. Apr. 9	Toronto 5	at Chicago 3
Thur. Apr. 10	Toronto 6	at Chicago 4
Sat. Apr. 12	Chicago 2	at Toronto 7

Toronto won series 3-0

Series 'F'
Wed. Apr. 9	St. Louis 2	at Minnesota 1
Thur. Apr. 10	St. Louis 1	at Minnesota 6
Sat. Apr. 12	Minnesota 3	at St. Louis 4
Sun. Apr. 13	Minnesota 7	at St. Louis 4
Tues. Apr. 15	St. Louis 6	at Minnesota 3

St. Louis won series 3-2

Series 'G'
Wed. Apr. 9	Vancouver 3	at Edmonton 7
Thur. Apr. 10	Vancouver 1	at Edmonton 5
Sat. Apr. 12	Edmonton 5	at Vancouver 1

Edmonton won series 3-0

Series 'H'
Wed. Apr. 9	Winnipeg 1	at Calgary 5
Thur. Apr. 10	Winnipeg 4	at Calgary 6
Sat. Apr. 12	Calgary 4	at Winnipeg 3*

* Lanny McDonald scored at 8:25 of overtime
Calgary won series 3-0

Series 'K'
Fri. Apr. 18	Toronto 1	at St. Louis 6
Sun. Apr. 20	Toronto 3	at St. Louis 0
Tues. Apr. 22	St. Louis 2	at Toronto 5
Thur. Apr. 24	St. Louis 7	at Toronto 4
Sat. Apr. 26	Toronto 3	at St. Louis 4*
Mon. Apr. 28	St. Louis 3	at Toronto 5
Wed. Apr. 30	Toronto 1	at St. Louis 2

* Mark Reeds scored at 7:11 of overtime
St. Louis won series 4-3

Series 'L'
Fri. Apr. 18	Calgary 4	at Edmonton 1
Sun. Apr. 20	Calgary 5	at Edmonton 6*
Tues. Apr. 22	Edmonton 2	at Calgary 3
Thur. Apr. 24	Edmonton 7	at Calgary 4
Sat. Apr. 26	Calgary 4	at Edmonton 1
Mon. Apr. 28	Edmonton 5	at Calgary 2
Wed. Apr. 30	Calgary 3	at Edmonton 2

* Glenn Anderson scored at 1:04 of overtime
Calgary won series 4-3

Series 'N'
Fri. May 2	St. Louis 3	at Calgary 2
Sun. May 4	St. Louis 2	at Calgary 8
Tues. May 6	Calgary 5	at St. Louis 3
Thur. May 8	Calgary 2	at St. Louis 5
Sat. May 10	St. Louis 2	at Calgary 4
Mon. May 12	Calgary 5	at St. Louis 6*
Wed. May 14	St. Louis 1	at Calgary 2

* Doug Wickenheiser scored at 7:30 of overtime
Calgary won series 4-3

STANLEY CUP CHAMPIONSHIP
(Best-of-seven series)

Series 'O'
Fri. May 16	Montreal 2	at Calgary 5
Sun. May 18	Montreal 3	at Calgary 2*
Tues. May 20	Calgary 3	at Montreal 5
Thur. May 22	Calgary 0	at Montreal 1
Sat. May 24	Montreal 4	at Calgary 3

* Brian Skrudland scored at 0:09 of overtime
Montreal won series 4-1

Individual Leaders

Abbreviations: * – rookie eligible for Calder Trophy; **A** – assists; **G** – goals; **GP** – games played; **GT** – game-tying goals; **GW** – game-winning goals; **PIM** – penalties in minutes; **PP** – power play goals; **PTS** – points; **S** – shots on goal; **SH** – short-handed goals; **%** – percentage of shots resulting in goals; **+/−** – difference between Goals For (**GF**) scored when a player is on the ice with his team at even strength or short-handed and Goals Against (**GA**) scored when the same player is on the ice with his team at even strength or on a power play.

Playoff Scoring Leaders

Player	Team	GP	G	A	Pts	+/−	PIM	PP	SH	GW	OT	S	%
Doug Gilmour	St. Louis	19	9	12	21	3	25	1	2	2	0	55	16.4
Bernie Federko	St. Louis	19	7	14	21	2	17	1	0	1	0	34	20.6
Joe Mullen	Calgary	21	12	7	19	3 −	4	4	0	2	0	53	22.6
Wayne Gretzky	Edmonton	10	8	11	19	0	2	4	1	2	0	42	19.0
Mats Naslund	Montreal	20	8	11	19	1 −	4	4	0	0	0	43	18.6
Al MacInnis	Calgary	21	4	15	19	11	30	2	0	0	0	79	5.1
Lanny McDonald	Calgary	22	11	7	18	5	30	4	0	2	1	70	15.7
Paul Reinhart	Calgary	21	5	13	18	2 −	4	4	0	0	0	34	14.7
Greg Paslawski	St. Louis	17	10	7	17	4	13	2	0	0	0	40	25.0
Pierre Larouche	NY Rangers	16	8	9	17	5 −	2	4	0	1	0	40	20.0
Doug Risebrough	Calgary	22	7	9	16	9	38	0	1	1	0	38	18.4
*Claude Lemieux	Montreal	20	10	5	15	1	68	4	0	4	2	51	19.6
John Tonelli	Calgary	22	7	9	16	3	49	1	0	1	0	44	15.9
Dan Quinn	Calgary	18	8	7	15	0	10	5	1	2	0	34	23.5
Bobby Smith	Montreal	20	7	8	15	2 −	22	3	0	3	0	44	15.9
Bob Brooke	NY Rangers	16	6	9	15	7 −	28	0	2	2	1	31	19.4
*Joel Otto	Calgary	22	5	10	15	5 −	80	3	0	1	0	41	12.2

Power-Play Goals

Player	Team	GP	PP
Dan Quinn	Calgary	18	5
Wayne Gretzky	Edmonton	10	4
Pierre Larouche	NY Rangers	16	4
*Claude Lemieux	Montreal	20	4
Lanny McDonald	Calgary	22	4
Joe Mullen	Calgary	21	4
Mats Naslund	Montreal	20	4
Wilf Paiement	NY Rangers	16	4
Paul Reinhart	Calgary	21	4

Short-Handed Goals

Player	Team	GP	SH
Bob Brooke	NY Rangers	16	2
Guy Carbonneau	Montreal	20	2
Doug Gilmour	St. Louis	19	2
Hakan Loob	Calgary	22	2
Mark Messier	Edmonton	10	2

Game-Winning Goals

Player	Team	GP	GW
*Claude Lemieux	Montreal	20	4
Bob Gainey	Montreal	20	3
Walt Poddubny	Toronto	9	3
Bobby Smith	Montreal	20	3

Overtime Goals

Player	Team	GP	OT
*Claude Lemieux	Montreal	20	2
Glenn Anderson	Edmonton	10	1
Bob Brooke	NY Rangers	16	1
Kevin Dineen	Hartford	10	1
Brian MacLellan	NY Rangers	16	1
Lanny McDonald	Calgary	22	1
Mark Reeds	St. Louis	19	1
*Brian Skrudland	Montreal	20	1
Sylvain Turgeon	Hartford	9	1
Doug Wickenheiser	St. Louis	19	1

Shots

Player	Team	GP	S
Al MacInnis	Calgary	21	79
Lanny McDonald	Calgary	22	70
Chris Chelios	Montreal	20	57
Hakan Loob	Calgary	22	56
Doug Gilmour	St. Louis	19	55

First Goals

Player	Team	GP	FG
Stewart Gavin	Hartford	10	3
Pierre Larouche	NY Rangers	16	3
Lanny McDonald	Calgary	22	3

Shooting Percentage

Player	Team	GP	G	S	%
Greg Paslawski	St. Louis	17	10	40	25.0
Dan Quinn	Calgary	18	8	34	23.5
Joe Mullen	Calgary	21	12	53	22.6
Kevin Dineen	Hartford	10	6	28	21.4
Glenn Anderson	Edmonton	10	8	38	21.1

(Minimum 20 shots)

Goal Scoring

Player	Team	GP	G
Joe Mullen	Calgary	21	12
Lanny McDonald	Calgary	22	11
*Claude Lemieux	Montreal	20	10
Greg Paslawski	St. Louis	17	10
Doug Gilmour	St. Louis	19	9

Assists

Player	Team	GP	A
Al MacInnis	Calgary	21	15
Bernie Federko	St. Louis	19	14
Paul Reinhart	Calgary	21	13
Larry Robinson	Montreal	20	13
Doug Gilmour	St. Louis	19	12

Lanny McDonald reached the Finals for the first time in his distinguished hockey career. His 11 goals in the playoffs included three first-goals, four scored on the power-play and one in overtime.

Individual Rookie Leaders

Playoff Rookie Scoring Leaders

Player	Team	GP	G	A	Pts	+/−	PIM	PP	SH	GW	OT	S	%
Claude Lemieux	Montreal	20	10	5	15	1	68	4	0	4	2	51	19.6
Joel Otto	Calgary	22	5	10	15	5−	80	3	0	1	0	41	12.2
Steve Thomas	Toronto	10	6	8	14	2−	9	3	0	0	0	36	16.7
Mike Ridley	NY Rangers	16	6	8	14	5−	26	2	0	1	0	31	19.4
Gary Suter	Calgary	10	2	8	10	1	8	0	0	1	0	17	11.8
Kelly Miller	NY Rangers	13	3	4	7	1−	4	0	1	0	0	17	17.6
Wendel Clark	Toronto	10	5	1	6	1	47	1	0	0	0	25	20.0
Brian Skrudland	Montreal	20	2	4	6	8	76	0	0	1	1	21	9.5
Stephane Richer	Montreal	16	4	1	5	3−	23	3	0	1	0	22	18.2
Esa Tikkanen	Edmonton	8	3	2	5	1	7	0	0	0	0	19	15.8
Kjell Dahlin	Montreal	16	2	3	5	1	4	0	0	0	0	20	10.0
Dean Evason	Hartford	10	1	4	5	4	10	0	0	0	0	11	9.1

Goal Scoring

Player	Team	GP	G
Claude Lemieux	Montreal	20	10
Mike Ridley	NY Rangers	16	6
Steve Thomas	Toronto	10	6
Wendel Clark	Toronto	10	5
Joel Otto	Calgary	22	5

Assists

Player	Team	GP	A
Joel Otto	Calgary	22	10
Mike Ridley	NY Rangers	16	8
Gary Suter	Calgary	10	8
Steve Thomas	Toronto	10	8
Claude Lemieux	Montreal	20	6

Shooting Percentage

Player	Team	GP	G	S	%
Wendel Clark	Toronto	10	5	25	20.0
Claude Lemieux	Montreal	20	10	51	19.6
Mike Ridley	NY Rangers	16	6	31	19.4
Stephane Richer	Montreal	16	4	22	18.2
Steve Thomas	Toronto	10	6	36	16.7

(Minimum 20 shots)

First Goals

Player	Team	GP	FG
Claude Lemieux	Montreal	20	2
Stephane Richer	Montreal	16	2
Kjell Dahlin	Montreal	16	1
Kelly Miller	NY Rangers	16	1
Herb Raglan	St. Louis	10	1
Mike Ridley	NY Rangers	16	1
Steve Thomas	Toronto	10	1

Shots

Player	Team	GP	S
Claude Lemieux	Montreal	20	51
Joel Otto	Calgary	22	41
Steve Thomas	Toronto	10	36
Mike Ridley	NY Rangers	16	31
Wendel Clark	Toronto	10	25
Stephane Richer	Montreal	16	22
Brian Skrudland	Montreal	20	21

Playoff Goaltending

Notes and Abbreviations: Empty-net goals are not counted in personal averages, but are included in the team's total. The shot(s) is (are) included in the goaltender's shots against (SA) total.
 GPI – games played in; **MINS** – minutes; **AVG** – goals allowed per 60 minutes played; **EN** – empty-net goals against; **SO** – shutouts; **GA** – goals against; **SA** – shots against; **S%** – percentage of shots saved; * – Rookie.

Goaltender	GPI	MINS	AVG	W	L	EN	SO	GA	SA	S%
Montreal										
*Patrick Roy	20	1218	1.92	15	5	2	1	39	506	.923
Totals	20	1218	2.02	15	5		1	41	506	.919
Hartford										
Mike Liut	8	441	1.90	5	2	0	1	14	226	.938
Steve Weeks	3	169	2.84	1	2	1	0	8	64	.873
Totals	10	610	2.26	6	4		1	23	290	.921
Washington										
Pete Peeters	9	544	2.65	5	4	0	0	24	253	.905
Edmonton										
Andy Moog	1	60	1.00	1	0	0	0	1	27	.963
Grant Fuhr	9	541	3.11	5	4	1	0	28	273	.897
Totals	10	601	3.00	6	4		0	30	300	.900
Calgary										
*Mike Vernon	21	1229	2.93	12	9	2	0	60	583	.897
Rejean Lemelin	3	109	3.85	0	1	0	0	7	48	.854
Totals	22	1338	3.09	12	10		0	69	631	.891
Toronto										
Ken Wregget	10	607	3.16	6	4	1	1	32	323	.901
Totals	10	607	3.26	6	4		1	33	323	.898
Boston										
Pat Riggin	1	60	3.00	0	1	0	0	3	23	.870
*Bill Ranford	2	120	3.50	0	2	0	0	7	44	.841
Totals	3	180	3.33	0	3		0	10	67	.851
NY Rangers										
John Vanbiesbrouck	16	899	3.27	8	8	0	1	49	477	.897
Glen Hanlon	3	75	4.80	0	0	0	0	6	32	.813
Totals	16	974	3.39	8	8		1	55	509	.892
Minnesota										
Don Beaupre	5	300	3.40	2	3	1	0	17	158	.892
Totals	5	300	3.60	2	3		0	18	158	.886
Philadelphia										
Bob Froese	5	293	3.07	2	3	2	0	15	125	.878
Glenn Resch	1	7	8.57	0	0	0	0	1	1	.000
Totals	5	300	3.60	2	3		0	18	126	.857
St. Louis										
Greg Millen	10	586	2.97	6	3	3	0	29	330	.911
Rick Wamsley	10	569	3.90	4	6	1	0	37	307	.879
Totals	19	1155	3.64	10	9		0	70	637	.890
NY Islanders										
Kelly Hrudey	2	120	3.00	0	2	0	0	6	59	.898
Billy Smith	1	60	4.00	0	1	1	0	4	34	.879
Totals	3	180	3.67	0	3		0	11	93	.882

Goaltender	GPI	MINS	AVG	W	L	EN	SO	GA	SA	S%
Winnipeg										
Marc Behrend	1	12	.00	0	0	0	0	0	7	1.000
*Daniel Berthiaume	1	68	3.53	0	1	0	0	4	43	.907
Brian Hayward	2	68	5.29	0	1	0	0	6	31	.806
Dan Bouchard	1	40	7.50	0	1	0	0	5	22	.773
Totals	3	188	4.79	0	3		0	15	103	.854
Quebec										
Clint Malarchuk	3	143	4.62	0	2	0	0	11	81	.864
Mario Gosselin	1	40	7.50	0	1	0	0	5	22	.773
Totals	3	183	5.25	0	3		0	16	103	.845
Vancouver										
*Wendell Young	1	60	5.00	0	1	0	0	5	32	.844
Richard Brodeur	2	120	6.00	0	2	0	0	12	79	.848
Totals	3	180	5.67	0	3		0	17	111	.847
Chicago										
Bob Sauve	2	99	4.85	0	2	1	0	8	61	.867
Murray Bannerman	2	81	6.67	0	1	0	0	9	40	.775
Totals	3	180	6.00	0	3		0	18	101	.822

Goals Against Average

Goaltender	Team	GPI	MINS	GA	AVG
Mike Liut	Hartford	8	441	14	1.90
*Patrick Roy	Montreal	20	1218	39	1.92
Pete Peeters	Washington	9	544	24	2.65
*Mike Vernon	Calgary	21	1229	60	2.93
Greg Millen	St. Louis	10	586	29	2.97

Wins

Goaltender	Team	GPI	MINS	W	L
*Patrick Roy	Montreal	20	1218	15	5
*Mike Vernon	Calgary	21	1229	12	9
John Vanbiesbrouck	NY Rangers	16	899	8	8
Greg Millen	St. Louis	10	586	6	3
Ken Wregget	Toronto	10	607	6	4

Save Percentage

Goaltender	Team	GPI	MINS	GA	SA	S%	W	L
Mike Liut	Hartford	8	441	14	226	.938	5	2
*Patrick Roy	Montreal	20	1218	39	506	.923	15	5
Greg Millen	St. Louis	10	586	29	330	.911	6	3
Pete Peeters	Washington	9	544	24	253	.905	5	4
Ken Wregget	Toronto	10	607	32	323	.901	6	4

Shutouts

Goaltender	Team	GPI	MINS	SO	W	L
Mike Liut	Hartford	8	441	1	5	2
*Patrick Roy	Montreal	20	1218	1	15	5
John Vanbiesbrouck	NY Rangers	16	899	1	8	8
Ken Wregget	Toronto	10	607	1	6	4

Team Statistics

TEAMS' HOME-AND-ROAD RECORD

			Home						Road				
	GP	W	L	GF	GA	%	GP	W	L	GF	GA	%
MTL	11	10	1	34	19	.909	9	5	4	22	22	.556
CGY	12	7	5	46	36	.583	10	5	5	35	33	.500
STL	9	6	3	34	30	.667	10	4	6	30	40	.400
NYR	7	4	3	22	25	.571	9	4	5	25	30	.444
EDM	6	3	3	22	20	.500	4	3	1	19	10	.750
TOR	4	3	1	21	14	.750	6	3	3	19	19	.500
HFD	4	3	1	13	9	.750	6	3	3	16	14	.500
WSH	5	3	2	21	12	.600	4	2	2	15	12	.500
MIN	3	1	2	10	10	.333	2	1	1	10	8	.500
PHI	3	1	2	6	12	.333	2	1	1	9	6	.500
CHI	2	0	2	7	11	.000	1	0	1	2	7	.000
WPG	1	0	1	3	4	.000	2	0	2	5	11	.000
QUE	2	0	2	3	7	.000	1	0	1	4	9	.000
BOS	1	0	1	3	4	.000	2	0	2	3	6	.000
VAN	1	0	1	1	5	.000	2	0	2	4	12	.000
NYI	1	0	1	1	3	.000	2	0	2	3	8	.000
TOTAL	72	41	31	247	221	.569	72	31	41	221	247	.431

TEAMS' POWER PLAY RECORD

Abbreviations: ADV-advantages; **PPGE**-power play goals for; **%**-success rate calculated by dividing PPGF by ADV.

			Home					Road						Overall		
	Team	GP	ADV	PPGF	%	Team	GP	ADV	PPGF	%	Team	GP	ADV	PPGF	%
1	WPG	1	5	2	40.0	MIN	2	11	4	36.4	MIN	5	24	6	25.0
2	CHI	2	10	3	30.0	EDM	2	12	4	33.3	TOR	10	48	12	25.0
3	TOR	4	25	6	24.0	WSH	4	17	5	29.4	CGY	22	109	25	22.9
4	HFD	4	18	4	22.2	CGY	10	42	12	28.6	WSH	9	40	9	22.5
5	MTL	11	51	11	21.6	TOR	6	23	6	26.1	EDM	10	39	8	20.5
6	NYR	7	33	7	21.2	QUE	1	8	2	25.0	WPG	3	15	3	20.0
7	CGY	12	67	13	19.4	PHI	2	9	2	22.2	CHI	3	16	3	18.8
8	STL	9	48	9	18.8	VAN	2	9	2	22.2	QUE	3	16	3	18.8
9	WSH	5	23	4	17.4	NYR	9	37	6	16.2	NYR	16	70	13	18.6
10	BOS	1	6	1	16.7	NYI	2	7	1	14.3	MTL	20	93	17	18.3
11	MIN	3	13	2	15.4	HFD	6	21	3	14.3	HFD	10	39	7	17.9
12	EDM	6	27	4	14.8	MTL	9	42	6	14.3	VAN	3	13	2	15.4
13	QUE	2	8	1	12.5	BOS	2	10	1	10.0	STL	19	91	13	14.3
14	PHI	3	20	1	5.0	WPG	2	10	1	10.0	BOS	3	16	2	12.5
15	NYI	1	4	0	.0	STL	10	43	4	9.3	PHI	5	29	3	10.3
16	VAN	1	4	0	.0	CHI	1	6	0	.0	NYI	3	11	1	9.1
	TOTAL	72	362	68	18.8		72	307	59	19.2		72	669	127	19.0

TEAMS' PENALTY KILLING RECORD

Abbreviations: ISH-times short-handed; **PPGA**-power play goals against; **%**-success rate calculated by dividing PPGA by ADV.

			Home					Road						Overall		
	Team	GP	ADV	PPGA	%	Team	GP	ADV	PPGA	%	Team	GP	ADV	PPGA	%
1	BOS	1	6	0	100.0	NYI	2	7	0	100.0	MIN	5	25	2	92.0
2	MIN	3	10	1	90.0	MTL	9	39	2	94.9	MTL	20	82	10	87.8
3	WSH	5	20	2	90.0	MIN	2	15	1	93.3	WPG	3	15	2	86.7
4	EDM	6	26	3	88.5	WPG	2	12	1	91.7	CGY	22	103	15	85.4
5	TOR	4	17	2	88.2	NYR	9	50	8	84.0	BOS	3	20	3	85.0
6	CGY	12	56	7	87.5	CGY	10	47	8	83.0	EDM	10	51	8	84.3
7	QUE	2	7	1	85.7	PHI	2	10	2	80.0	NYR	16	81	14	82.7
8	MTL	11	43	8	81.4	EDM	4	25	5	80.0	WSH	9	36	7	80.6
9	NYR	7	31	6	80.6	BOS	2	14	3	78.6	TOR	10	45	9	80.0
10	HFD	4	18	4	77.8	HFD	6	23	5	78.3	HFD	10	41	9	78.0
11	PHI	3	11	3	72.7	STL	10	55	12	78.2	NYI	3	13	3	76.9
12	VAN	1	3	1	66.7	TOR	6	28	7	75.0	PHI	5	21	5	76.2
13	WPG	1	3	1	66.7	WSH	4	16	5	68.8	STL	19	96	26	72.9
14	CHI	2	9	3	66.7	CHI	1	6	2	66.7	CHI	3	15	5	66.7
15	STL	9	41	14	65.9	VAN	2	8	3	62.5	QUE	3	14	5	64.3
16	NYI	1	6	3	50.0	QUE	1	7	4	42.9	VAN	3	11	4	63.6
	TOTAL	72	307	59	80.8		72	362	68	81.2		72	669	127	81.0

SHORT-HANDED GOALS

	For			Against	
Team	Games	Goals	Team	Games	Goals
CGY	22	5	CHI	3	0
EDM	10	4	NYI	3	0
NYR	16	4	WPG	3	0
MTL	20	4	BOS	3	1
STL	19	3	QUE	3	1
WSH	9	2	VAN	3	1
BOS	3	1	MIN	5	1
QUE	3	1	WSH	9	1
WPG	3	1	TOR	10	1
MIN	5	1	PHI	5	2
HFD	10	1	EDM	10	2
CHI	3	0	HFD	10	3
NYI	3	0	NYR	16	3
VAN	3	0	STL	19	3
PHI	5	0	MTL	20	3
TOR	10	0	CGY	22	5
TOTAL	72	27	**TOTAL**	72	27

Team Penalties

Abbreviations: GP – games played; **PEN** – total penalty minutes, including bench penalites; **BMI** – total bench penalty minutes; **AVG** – average penalty minutes per game.

Team	Games	PEN	BMI	AVG
VAN	3	55	2	18.3
WSH	9	209	0	23.2
HFD	10	260	4	26.0
NYR	16	426	4	26.6
NYI	3	84	0	28.0
TOR	10	284	0	28.4
MIN	5	142	2	28.4
PHI	5	145	0	29.0
CHI	3	87	0	29.0
WPG	3	88	0	29.3
STL	19	579	0	30.5
EDM	10	321	6	32.1
MTL	20	689	6	34.5
CGY	22	805	2	36.6
QUE	3	116	0	38.7
BOS	3	162	4	54.0
TOTAL	72	4452	30	61.8

The Prince of Wales Trophy, awarded to the winner of the Conference Championship series between the Adams and Patrick divisions, was won by the eventual 1986 Stanley Cup champion Montreal Canadiens. The Clarence S. Campbell Bowl was won by the Calgary Flames who, as winners of the Smythe Division, defeated the Norris Division champion St. Louis Blues to advance to the Finals.

Prince of Wales Trophy

Clarence S. Campbell Bowl

Stanley Cup

Stanley Cup Record Book

Championship Trophies

PRINCE OF WALES TROPHY

Beginning with the 1981-82 season, the club which advances to the Stanley Cup Finals as the winner of the Wales Conference is presented with the Prince of Wales Trophy.

History: His Royal Highnesss, the Prince of Wales, donated the trophy to the National Hockey League in 1924. From 1927-28 through 1937-38, the award was presented to the team finishing first in the American Division of the NHL. From 1938-39, when the NHL reverted to one section, to 1966-67, it was presented to the team winning the NHL championship. With expansion in 1967-68, it again became a divisional trophy through the 1973-74 season. Beginning in 1974-75, it was awarded to the regular-season winner of the conference bearing the name of the trophy. Starting with the 1981-82 season the trophy was presented to the playoff champion in the Wales Conference.

1985-86 Winner: Montreal Canadiens

The Montreal Canadiens captured the Prince of Wales Conference Championship by defeating the New York Rangers four games to one in the best-of-seven series. The Canadiens ended a streak which saw a Patrick Division club win the Prince of Wales Conference title in each of the last four years. Montreal took a 3-0 series lead with 2-1, 6-2 and 4-3 victories, before the Rangers won Game Four 2-0. The Canadiens clinched the series on home ice in Game Five with a 3-1 win.

PRINCE OF WALES TROPHY WINNERS

1985-86	Montreal Canadiens	1954-55	Detroit Red Wings
1984-85	Philadelphia Flyers	1953-54	Detroit Red Wings
1983-84	New York Islanders	1952-53	Detroit Red Wings
1982-83	New York Islanders	1951-52	Detroit Red Wings
1981-82	New York Islanders	1950-51	Detroit Red Wings
1980-81	Montreal Canadiens	1949-50	Detroit Red Wings
1979-80	Buffalo Sabres	1948-49	Detroit Red Wings
1978-79	Montreal Canadiens	1947-48	Toronto Maple Leafs
1977-78	Montreal Canadiens	1946-47	Montreal Canadiens
1976-77	Montreal Canadiens	1945-46	Montreal Canadiens
1975-76	Montreal Canadiens	1944-45	Montreal Canadiens
1974-75	Buffalo Sabres	1943-44	Montreal Canadiens
1973-74	Boston Bruins	1942-43	Detroit Red Wings
1972-73	Montreal Canadiens	1941-42	New York Rangers
1971-72	Boston Bruins	1940-41	Boston Bruins
1970-71	Boston Bruins	1939-40	Boston Bruins
1969-70	Chicago Black Hawks	1938-39	Boston Bruins
1968-69	Montreal Canadiens	1937-38	Boston Bruins
1967-68	Montreal Canadiens	1936-37	Detroit Red Wings
1966-67	Chicago Black Hawks	1935-36	Detroit Red Wings
1965-66	Montreal Canadiens	1934-35	Boston Bruins
1964-65	Detroit Red Wings	1933-34	Detroit Red Wings
1963-64	Montreal Canadiens	1932-33	Boston Bruins
1962-63	Toronto Maple Leafs	1931-32	New York Rangers
1961-62	Montreal Canadiens	1930-31	Boston Bruins
1960-61	Montreal Canadiens	1929-30	Boston Bruins
1959-60	Montreal Canadiens	1928-29	Boston Bruins
1958-59	Montreal Canadiens	1927-28	Boston Bruins
1957-58	Montreal Canadiens	1926-27	Ottawa Senators
1956-57	Detroit Red Wings	1925-26	Montreal Maroons
1955-56	Montreal Canadiens	1924-25	Montreal Canadiens

CLARENCE S. CAMPBELL BOWL

Beginning with the 1981-82 season, the club which advances to the Stanley Cup Finals as the winner of the Campbell Conference championship is presented with the Clarence S. Campbell Bowl.

History: Presented by the member clubs in 1968 for perpetual competition by the National Hockey League in recognition of the services of Clarence S. Campbell, President of the NHL from 1946 to 1977. From 1967-68 through 1973-74, the trophy was awarded to the champions of the West Division. The trophy itself is a hallmark piece made of sterling silver and was crafted by a British silversmith in 1878.

1985-86 Winner: Calgary Flames

The Calgary Flames won their first Clarence S. Campbell Conference Championship by defeating the St. Louis Blues four games to three. The Flames captured Game Two (8-2); Game Three (5-3); Game Five (4-2); and Game Seven (2-1). The Blues won the remaining three games by scores 3-2; 5-2; and 6-5.

The Flames advanced to the Conference Championship by defeating the Winnipeg Jets in three straight games and the Edmonton Oilers four games to three in the Smythe Division Final.

CLARENCE S. CAMPBELL BOWL WINNERS

1985-86	Calgary Flames	1975-76	Philadelphia Flyers
1984-85	Edmonton Oilers	1974-75	Philadelphia Flyers
1983-84	Edmonton Oilers	1973-74	Philadelphia Flyers
1982-83	Edmonton Oilers	1972-73	Chicago Black Hawks
1981-82	Vancouver Canucks	1971-72	Chicago Black Hawks
1980-81	New York Islanders	1970-71	Chicago Black Hawks
1979-80	Philadelphia Flyers	1969-70	St. Louis Blues
1978-79	New York Islanders	1968-69	St. Louis Blues
1977-78	New York Islanders	1967-68	Philadelphia Flyers
1976-77	Philadelphia Flyers		

THE STANLEY CUP

Awarded annually to the team winning the National Hockey League's best-of-seven final playoff round. It is symbolic of the World's Professional Hockey Championship.

The first four teams in each division at the end of the regular schedule advance to the playoffs. In each division, the first-place team opposes the fourth-place club while the second and third-place teams meet, all in best-of-five Division Semi-Finals. The winners oppose the other winners in each division in best-of-seven Division Final series. The division winners then play the opposite winners in each of the two conferences in best-of-seven Conference Championships. The Prince of Wales Conference champions then meet the Clarence Campbell Conference champions in the best-of-seven Stanley Cup Championship Series.

History: The Stanley Cup, the oldest trophy competed for by professional athletes in North America, was donated by Frederick Arthur, Lord Stanley of Preston and son of the Earl of Derby, in 1893. Lord Stanley purchased the trophy for 10 guineas ($50 at that time) for presentation to the amateur hockey champions of Canada. Since 1910, when the National Hockey Association took possession of the Stanley Cup, the trophy has been the symbol of professional hockey supremacy. It has been competed for only by NHL teams since 1926 and has been under the exclusive control of the NHL since 1946.

1985-86 Winner: Montreal Canadiens

The Montreal Canadiens won their record 23rd Stanley Cup Championship after defeating the Calgary Flames four games to one in the best-of-seven Final series. The Canadiens only loss in the series came in the opening game, 5-2. They rebounded to win the next four contests by scores of 3-2; 5-3; 1-0 and the series-clinching game on May 24, 4-3.

The Canadiens advanced to the Final by defeating Boston in three straight games, the Hartford Whalers in seven games (4-3) and the New York Rangers in the Wales Conference Championship four games to one.

Mats Naslund led the Canadiens in scoring with eight goals and 11 assists, while goaltender Patrick Roy posted a 1.92 goals-against-average and a 15-5 record.

STANLEY CUP WINNERS

Season	Champions	Season	Champions
1985-86	Montreal Canadiens	1950-51	Toronto Maple Leafs
1984-85	Edmonton Oilers	1949-50	Detroit Red Wings
1983-84	Edmonton Oilers	1948-49	Toronto Maple Leafs
1982-83	New York Islanders	1947-48	Toronto Maple Leafs
1981-82	New York Islanders	1946-47	Toronto Maple Leafs
1980-81	New York Islanders	1945-46	Montreal Canadiens
1979-80	New York Islanders	1944-45	Toronto Maple Leafs
1978-79	Montreal Canadiens	1943-44	Montreal Canadiens
1977-78	Montreal Canadiens	1942-43	Detroit Red Wings
1976-77	Montreal Canadiens	1941-42	Toronto Maple Leafs
1975-76	Montreal Canadiens	1940-41	Boston Bruins
1974-75	Philadelphia Flyers	1939-40	New York Rangers
1973-74	Philadelphia Flyers	1938-39	Boston Bruins
1972-73	Montreal Canadiens	1937-38	Chicago Black Hawks
1971-72	Boston Bruins	1936-37	Detroit Red Wings
1970-71	Montreal Canadiens	1935-36	Detroit Red Wings
1969-70	Boston Bruins	1934-35	Montreal Maroons
1968-69	Montreal Canadiens	1933-34	Chicago Black Hawks
1967-68	Montreal Canadiens	1932-33	New York Rangers
1966-67	Toronto Maple Leafs	1931-32	Toronto Maple Leafs
1965-66	Montreal Canadiens	1930-31	Montreal Canadiens
1964-65	Montreal Canadiens	1929-30	Montreal Canadiens
1963-64	Toronto Maple Leafs	1928-29	Boston Bruins
1962-63	Toronto Maple Leafs	1927-28	New York Rangers
1961-62	Toronto Maple Leafs	1926-27	Ottawa Senators
1960-61	Chicago Black Hawks	1925-26	Montreal Maroons
1959-60	Montreal Canadiens	1924-25	Victoria Cougars
1958-59	Montreal Canadiens	1923-24	Montreal Canadiens
1957-58	Montreal Canadiens	1922-23	Ottawa Senators
1956-57	Montreal Canadiens	1921-22	Toronto St. Pats
1955-56	Montreal Canadiens	1920-21	Ottawa Senators
1954-55	Detroit Red Wings	1919-20	Ottawa Senators
1953-54	Detroit Red Wings	1918-19	No decision*
1952-53	Montreal Canadiens	1917-18	Toronto Arenas
1951-52	Detroit Red Wings		

*In the spring of 1919 the Montreal Canadiens travelled to Seattle to meet Seattle, PCHL champions. After five games had been played — teams were tied at 2 wins and 1 tie — the series was called off by the local Department of Health because of the influenza epidemic and the death from influenza of Joe Hall.

STANLEY CUP WINNERS PRIOR TO FORMATION OF NHL IN 1917

Season	Champions	Season	Champions
1916-17	Seattle Metropolitans	1903-04	Ottawa Silver Seven
1915-16	Montreal Canadiens	1902-03	Ottawa Silver Seven
1914-15	Vancouver Millionaires	1901-02	Montreal A.A.A.
1913-14	Toronto Blueshirts	1900-01	Winnipeg Victorias
1912-13**	Quebec Bulldogs	1899-1900	Montreal Shamrocks
1911-12	Quebec Bulldogs	1898-99	Montreal Shamrocks
1910-11	Ottawa Senators	1897-98	Montreal Victorias
1909-10	Montreal Wanderers	1896-97	Montreal Victorias
1908-09	Ottawa Senators	1895-96	Montreal Victorias
1907-08	Montreal Wanderers		(December, 1896)
1906-07	Montreal Wanderers (March)	1895-96	Winnipeg Victorias
1906-07	Kenora Thistles (January)		(February)
1905-06	Montreal Wanderers	1894-95	Montreal Victorias
1904-05	Ottawa Silver Seven	1893-94	Montreal A.A.A.
		1892-93	Montreal A.A.A.

**Victoria defeated Quebec in challenge series.

Stanley Cup Winners:

Rosters and Final Series Scores

1985-86 — **Montreal Canadiens** — Bob Gainey, Doug Soetaert, Patrick Roy, Rick Green, David Maley, Ryan Walter, Serge Boisvert, Mario Tremblay, Bobby Smith, Craig Ludwig, Tom Kurvers, Kjell Dahlin, Larry Robinson, Guy Carbonneau, Chris Chelios, Petr Svoboda, Mats Naslund, Lucien DeBlois, Steve Rooney, Gaston Gingras, Mike Lalor, Chris Nilan, John Kordic, Claude Lemieux, Mike McPhee, Brian Skrudland, Stephane Richer, Ronald Corey (President), Serge Savard (General Manager), Jean Perron (Coach), Jacques Laperriere (Ass't. Coach), Jean Beliveau (Vice President), Francois-Xavier Seigneur (Vice President), Fred Steer (Vice President), Jacques Lemaire (Ass't. General Manager), Andre Boudrias (Ass't. General Manager), Claude Ruel, Yves Belanger (Athletic Therapist), Gaetan Lefebvre (Ass't. Athletic Therapist), Eddy Palchek (Trainer), Sylvain Toupin (Ass't. Trainer).

1986 —May 16 at Calgary — Calgary 5, Montreal 3; May 18 at Calgary — Montreal 3, Calgary 2; May 20 at Montreal — Montreal 5, Calgary 3; May 22 at Montreal — Montreal 1, Calgary 0; May 24 at Calgary — Montreal 4, Calgary 3.

1984-85 — **Edmonton Oilers** — Glenn Anderson, Bill Carrol, Paul Coffey, Lee Fogolin, Grant Fuhr, Randy Gregg, Wayne Gretzky, Charlie Huddy, Pat Hughes, Dave Hunter, Don Jackson, Mike Krushelnyski, Jari Kurri, Willy Lindstrom, Kevin Lowe, Dave Lumley, Kevin McClelland, Larry Melnyk, Mark Messier, Andy Moog, Mark Napier, Jaroslav Pouzar, Dave Semenko, Esa Tikkanen, Peter Pocklington (Owner), Glen Sather (General Manager/Coach), John Muckler (Ass't. Coach), Ted Green (Ass't. Coach), Bruce MacGregor (Ass't. General Manager), Barry Fraser (Director of Player Personnel/Chief Scout), Peter Millar (Athletic Therapist), Barrie Stafford, Lyle Kulchisky (Trainers)

1985 —May 21 at Philadelphia — Philadelphia 4, Edmonton 1; May 23 at Philadelphia — Edmonton 3, Philadelphia 1; May 25 at Edmonton — Edmonton 4, Philadelphia 3; May 28 at Edmonton — Edmonton 5, Philadelphia 3; May 30 at Edmonton — Edmonton 8, Philadelphia 3.

1983-84 — **Edmonton Oilers** — Glenn Anderson, Paul Coffey, Pat Conacher, Lee Fogolin, Grant Fuhr, Randy Gregg, Wayne Gretzky, Charlie Huddy, Pat Hughes, Dave Hunter, Don Jackson, Jari Kurri, Willy Lindstrom, Ken Linseman, Kevin Lowe, Dave Lumley, Kevin McClelland, Mark Messier, Andy Moog, Jaroslav Pouzar, Dave Semenko, Peter Pocklington (Owner), Glen Sather (General Manager/Coach), John Muckler (Ass't. Coach), Ted Green (Ass't. Coach), Bruce MacGregor (Ass't. General Manager), Barry Fraser (Director of Player Personnel/Chief Scout), Peter Millar (Athletic Therapist), Barrie Stafford (Trainer)

1984 —May 10 at New York — Edmonton 1, NY Islanders 0; May 12 at New York — NY Islanders 6, Edmonton 1; May 15 at Edmonton — Edmonton 7, NY Islanders 2; May 17 at Edmonton — Edmonton 7, NY Islanders 2; May 19 at Edmonton — Edmonton 5, NY Islanders 2.

1982-83 — **New York Islanders** — Mike Bossy, Bob Bourne, Paul Boutilier, Bill Carroll, Greg Gilbert, Clark Gillies, Butch Goring, Mats Hallin, Tomas Jonsson, Anders Kallur, Gord Lane, Dave Langevin, Mike McEwen, Roland Melanson, Wayne Merrick, Ken Morrow, Bob Nystrom, Stefan Persson, Denis Potvin, Bill Smith, Brent Sutter, Duane Sutter, John Tonelli, Bryan Trottier, Al Arbour (coach), Lorne Henning (ass't coach), Bill Torrey (general manager), Ron Waske, Jim Pickard (trainers)

1983 —May 10 at Edmonton — NY Islanders 2, Edmonton 0; May 12 at Edmonton — NY Islanders 6, Edmonton 3; May 14 at New York — NY Islanders 5, Edmonton 1; May 17 at New York — NY Islanders 4, Edmonton 2

1981-82 — **New York Islanders** — Mike Bossy, Bob Bourne, Bill Carroll, Butch Goring, Greg Gilbert, Clark Gillies, Tomas Jonsson, Anders Kallur, Gord Lane, Dave Langevin, Hector Marini, Mike McEwen, Roland Melanson, Wayne Merrick, Ken Morrow, Bob Nystrom, Stefan Persson, Denis Potvin, Bill Smith, Brent Sutter, Duane Sutter, John Tonelli, Bryan Trottier, Al Arbour (coach), Lorne Henning (ass't coach), Bill Torrey (general manager), Ron Waske, Jim Pickard (trainers)

1982 —May 8 at New York — NY Islanders 6, Vancouver 5; May 11 at New York — NY Islanders 6, Vancouver 4; May 13 at Vancouver — NY Islanders 3, Vancouver 0; May 16 at Vancouver — NY Islanders 3, Vancouver 1

1980-81 — **New York Islanders** — Denis Potvin, Mike McEwen, Ken Morrow, Gord Lane, Bob Lorimer, Stefan Persson, Dave Langevin, Mike Bossy, Bryan Trottier, Butch Goring, Wayne Merrick, Clark Gillies, John Tonelli, Bob Nystrom, Bill Carroll, Bob Bourne, Hector Marini, Anders Kallur, Duane Sutter, Garry Howatt, Lorne Henning, Bill Smith, Roland Melanson, Al Arbour (coach), Bill Torrey (general manager), Ron Waske, Jim Pickard (trainers).

1981 —May 12 at New York — NY Islanders 6, Minnesota 3; May 14 at New York — NY Islanders 6, Minnesota 3; May 17 at Minnesota — NY Islanders 7, Minnesota 5; May 19 at Minnesota — Minnesota 4, NY Islanders 2; May 21 at New York — NY Islanders 5, Minnesota 1.

1979-80 — **New York Islanders** — Gord Lane, Jean Potvin, Bob Lorimer, Denis Potvin, Stefan Persson, Ken Morrow, Dave Langevin, Duane Sutter, Garry Howatt, Clark Gillies, Lorne Henning, Wayne Merrick, Bob Bourne, Steve Tambellini, Bryan Trottier, Mike Bossy, Bob Nystrom, John Tonelli, Anders Kallur, Butch Goring, Alex McKendry, Glenn Resch, Billy Smith, Al Arbour (coach), Bill Torrey (general manager), Ron Waske, Jim Pickard (trainers).

1980 —May 13 at Philadelphia — NY Islanders 4, Philadelphia 3; May 15 at Philadelphia — Philadelphia 8, NY Islanders 3; May 17 at Long Island — NY Islanders 6, Philadelphia 2; May 19 at Long Island — NY Islanders 5, Philadelphia 2; May 22 at Philadelphia — Philadelphia 6, NY Islanders 3; May 24 at Long Island — NY Islanders 5, Philadelphia 4.

1978-79 — **Montreal Canadiens** — Ken Dryden, Larry Robinson, Serge Savard, Guy Lapointe, Brian Engblom, Gilles Lupien, Rick Chartraw, Guy Lafleur, Steve Shutt, Jacques Lemaire, Yvan Cournoyer, Rejean Houle, Pierre Mondou, Bob Gainey, Doug Jarvis, Yvon Lambert, Doug Risebrough, Pierre Larouche, Mario Tremblay, Cam Connor, Pat Hughes, Rod Langway, Mark Napier, Michel Larocque, Richard Sevigny, Scotty Bowman (coach), Irving Grundman (managing director), Eddy Palchak, Pierre Meilleur (trainers).

1979 —May 13 at Montreal — NY Rangers 4, Montreal 1; May 15 at Montreal — Montreal 6, NY Rangers 2; May 17 at New York — Montreal 4, NY Rangers 1; May 19 at New York — Montreal 4, NY Rangers 3; May 21 at Montreal — Montreal 4, NY Rangers 1.

1977-78 — **Montreal Canadiens** — Ken Dryden, Larry Robinson, Serge Savard, Guy Lapointe, Bill Nyrop, Pierre Bouchard, Brian Engblom, Gilles Lupien, Rick Chartraw, Guy Lafleur, Steve Shutt, Jacques Lemaire, Yvan Cournoyer, Rejean Houle, Pierre Mondou, Bob Gainey, Doug Jarvis, Yvon Lambert, Doug Risebrough, Pierre Larouche, Mario Tremblay, Michel Larocque, Scotty Bowman (coach), Sam Pollock (general manager), Eddy Palchak, Pierre Meilleur (trainers).

1978 —May 13 at Montreal — Montreal 4, Boston 1; May 16 at Montreal — Boston 4, Montreal 0; May 21 at Boston — Boston 4, Montreal 3; May 23 at Montreal — Montreal 4, Boston 1; May 25 at Boston — Montreal 4, Boston 1.

1976-77 — **Montreal Canadiens** — Ken Dryden, Guy Lapointe, Larry Robinson, Serge Savard, Jimmy Roberts, Rick Chartraw, Bill Nyrop, Pierre Bouchard, Brian Engblom, Yvan Cournoyer, Guy Lafleur, Jacques Lemaire, Steve Shutt, Pete Mahovlich, Murray Wilson, Doug Jarvis, Yvon Lambert, Bob Gainey, Doug Risebrough, Mario Tremblay, Rejean Houle, Pierre Mondou, Mike Polich, Michel Larocque, Scotty Bowman (coach), Sam Pollock (general manager), Eddy Palchak, Pierre Meilleur (trainers).

1977 —May 7 at Montreal — Montreal 7, Boston 3; May 10 at Montreal — Montreal 3, Boston 0; May 12 at Boston — Montreal 4, Boston 2; May 14 at Boston — Montreal 2, Boston 1.

1975-76 — **Montreal Canadiens** — Ken Dryden, Serge Savard, Guy Lapointe, Larry Robinson, Bill Nyrop, Pierre Bouchard, Jim Roberts, Guy Lafleur, Steve Shutt, Pete Mahovlich, Yvan Cournoyer, Jacques Lemaire, Yvon Lambert, Bob Gainey, Doug Jarvis, Doug Risebrough, Murray Wilson, Mario Tremblay, Rick Chartraw, Michel Larocque, Scotty Bowman (coach), Sam Pollock (general manager), Eddy Palchak, Pierre Meilleur (trainers).

1976 —May 9 at Montreal — Montreal 4, Philadelphia 3; May 11 at Montreal — Montreal 2, Philadelphia 1; May 13 at Philadelphia — Montreal 3, Philadelphia 2; May 16 at Philadelphia — Montreal 5, Philadelphia 3.

1974-75 — **Philadelphia Flyers** — Bernie Parent, Wayne Stephenson, Ed Van Impe, Tom Bladon, André Dupont, Joe Watson, Jim Watson, Ted Harris, Larry Goodenough, Rick MacLeish, Bobby Clarke, Bill Barber, Reggie Leach, Gary Dornhoefer, Ross Lonsberry, Bob Kelly, Terry Crisp, Don Saleski, Dave Schultz, Orest Kindrachuk, Bill Clement, Fred Shero (coach), Keith Allen (general manager), Frank Lewis, Jim McKenzie (trainers).

1975 —May 15 at Philadelphia — Philadelphia 4, Buffalo 1; May 18 at Philadelphia — Philadelphia 2, Buffalo 1; May 20 at Buffalo — Buffalo 5, Philadelphia 4; May 22 at Buffalo — Buffalo 4, Philadelphia 2; May 25 at Philadelphia — Philadelphia 5, Buffalo 1; May 27 at Buffalo — Philadelphia 2, Buffalo 0.

1973-74 — **Philadelphia Flyers** — Bernie Parent, Ed Van Impe, Tom Bladon, André Dupont, Joe Watson, Jim Watson, Barry Ashbee, Bill Barber, Dave Schultz, Don Saleski, Gary Dornhoefer, Terry Crisp, Bobby Clarke, Simon Nolet, Ross Lonsberry, Rick MacLeish, Bill Flett, Orest Kindrachuk, Bill Clement, Bob Kelly, Bruce Cowick, Al MacAdam, Bobby Taylor, Fred Shero (coach), Keith Allen (general manager), Frank Lewis, Jim McKenzie (trainers).

1974 —May 7 at Boston — Boston 3, Philadelphia 2; May 9 at Boston — Philadelphia 3, Boston 2; May 12 at Philadelphia — Philadelphia 4, Boston 1; May 14 at Philadelphia — Philadelphia 4, Boston 2; May 16 at Boston — Boston 5, Philadelphia 1; May 19 at Philadelphia — Philadelphia 1, Boston 0.

1972-73 — **Montreal Canadiens** — Ken Dryden, Guy Lapointe, Serge Savard, Larry Robinson, Jacques Laperriere, Bob Murdoch, Pierre Bouchard, Jim Roberts, Yvan Cournoyer, Frank Mahovlich, Jacques Lemaire, Pete Mahovlich, Marc Tardif, Henri Richard, Rejean Houle, Guy Lafleur, Chuck Lefley, Claude Larose, Murray Wilson, Steve Shutt, Michel Plasse, Scotty Bowman (coach), Sam Pollock (general manager), Ed Palchak, Bob Williams (trainers).

1973 —April 29 at Montreal — Montreal 8, Chicago 3; May 1 at Montreal — Montreal 4, Chicago 1; May 3 at Chicago — Chicago 7, Montreal 4; May 6 at Chicago — Montreal 4, Chicago 0; May 8 at Montreal — Chicago 8, Montreal 7; May 10 at Chicago — Montreal 6, Chicago 4.

1971-72 — **Boston Bruins** — Gerry Cheevers, Ed Johnston, Bobby Orr, Ted Green, Carol Vadnais, Dallas Smith, Don Awrey, Phil Esposito, Ken Hodge, John Bucyk, Mike Walton, Wayne Cashman, Garnet Bailey, Derek Sanderson, Fred Stanfield, Ed Westfall, John McKenzie, Don Marcotte, Garry Peters, Chris Hayes, Tom Johnson (coach), Milt Schmidt (general manager), Dan Canney, John Forristall (trainers).

1972 —April 30 at Boston — Boston 6, New York Rangers 5; May 2 at Boston — Boston 2, New York 1; May 4 at New York — New York 5, Boston 2; May 7 at New York — Boston 3, New York 2; May 9 at Boston — New York 3, Boston 2; May 11 at New York — Boston 3, New York 0.

1970-71 — Montreal Canadiens — Ken Dryden, Rogatien Vachon, Jacques Laperriere, Jean-Claude Tremblay, Guy Lapointe, Terry Harper, Pierre Bouchard, Jean Beliveau, Marc Tardif, Yvan Cournoyer, Rejean Houle, Claude Larose, Henri Richard, Phil Roberto, Pete Mahovlich, Leon Rochefort, John Ferguson, Bobby Sheehan, Jacques Lemaire, Frank Mahovlich, Bob Murdoch, Chuck Lefley, Al MacNeil (coach), Sam Pollock (general manager), Yvon Belanger, Ed Palchak (trainers).

1971 —May 4 at Chicago — Chicago 2, Montreal 1; May 6 at Chicago — Chicago 5, Montreal 3; May 9 at Montreal — Montreal 4, Chicago 2; May 11 at Montreal — Montreal 5, Chicago 2; May 13 at Chicago — Chicago 2, Montreal 0; May 16 at Montreal — Montreal 4, Chicago 3; May 18 at Chicago — Montreal 3, Chicago 2.

1969-70 — Boston Bruins — Gerry Cheevers, Ed Johnston, Bobby Orr, Rick Smith, Dallas Smith, Bill Speer, Gary Doak, Don Awrey, Phil Esposito, Ken Hodge, John Bucyk, Wayne Carleton, Wayne Cashman, Derek Sanderson, Fred Stanfield, Ed Westfall, John McKenzie, Jim Lorentz, Don Marcotte, Bill Lesuk, Dan Schock, Harry Sinden (coach), Milt Schmidt (general manager), Dan Canney, John Forristall (trainers).

1970 —May 3 at St. Louis — Boston 6, St. Louis 1; May 5 at St. Louis — Boston 6, St. Louis 2; May 7 at Boston — Boston 4, St. Louis 1; May 10 at Boston — Boston 4, St. Louis 3.

1968-69 — Montreal Canadiens — Lorne Worsley, Rogatien Vachon, Jacques Laperriere, Jean-Claude Tremblay, Ted Harris, Serge Savard, Terry Harper, Larry Hillman, Jean Beliveau, Ralph Backstrom, Dick Duff, Yvan Cournoyer, Claude Provost, Bobby Rousseau, Henri Richard, John Ferguson, Christian Bordeleau, Mickey Redmond, Jacques Lemaire, Lucien Grenier, Tony Esposito, Claude Ruel (coach), Sam Pollock (general manager), Larry Aubut, Eddy Palchak (trainers).

1969 —April 27 at Montreal — Montreal 3, St. Louis 1; April 29 at Montreal — Montreal 3, St. Louis 1; May 1 at St. Louis — Montreal 4, St. Louis 0; May 4 at St. Louis — Montreal 2, St. Louis 1.

1967-68 — Montreal Canadiens — Lorne Worsley, Rogatien Vachon, Jacques Laperriere, Jean-Claude Tremblay, Ted Harris, Serge Savard, Terry Harper, Carol Vadnais, Jean Beliveau, Gilles Tremblay, Ralph Backstrom, Dick Duff, Claude Larose, Yvan Cournoyer, Claude Provost, Bobby Rousseau, Henri Richard, John Ferguson, Danny Grant, Jacques Lemaire, Mickey Redmond, Toe Blake (coach), Sam Pollock (general manager), Larry Aubut, Eddy Palchak (trainers).

1968 —May 5 at St. Louis — Montreal 3, St. Louis 2; May 7 at St. Louis — Montreal 1, St. Louis 0; May 9 at Montreal — Montreal 4, St. Louis 3; May 11 at Montreal — Montreal 3, St. Louis 2.

1966-67 — Toronto Maple Leafs — Johnny Bower, Terry Sawchuk, Larry Hillman, Marcel Pronovost, Tim Horton, Bob Baun, Aut Erickson, Allan Stanley, Red Kelly, Ron Ellis, George Armstrong, Pete Stemkowski, Dave Keon, Mike Walton, Jim Pappin, Bob Pulford, Brian Conacher, Eddie Shack, Frank Mahovlich, Milan Marcetta, Larry Jeffrey, Bruce Gamble, Punch Imlach (manager-coach), Bob Haggart (trainer).

1967 —April 20 at Montreal — Toronto 2, Montreal 6; April 22 at Montreal — Toronto 3, Montreal 0; April 25 at Toronto — Toronto 3, Montreal 2; April 27 at Toronto — Toronto 6, Montreal 2; April 29 at Montreal — Toronto 4, Montreal 1; May 2 at Toronto — Toronto 3, Montreal 1.

1965-66 — Montreal Canadiens — Lorne Worsley, Charlie Hodge, Jean-Claude Tremblay, Ted Harris, Jean-Guy Talbot, Terry Harper, Jacques Laperriere, Noel Price, Jean Beliveau, Ralph Backstrom, Dick Duff, Gilles Tremblay, Claude Larose, Yvan Cournoyer, Claude Provost, Bobby Rousseau, Henri Richard, Dave Balon, John Ferguson, Leon Rochefort, Jim Roberts, Toe Blake (coach), Sam Pollock (general manager), Larry Aubut, Andy Galley (trainers).

1966 —April 24 at Montreal — Montreal 3, Detroit 2; April 26 at Montreal — Detroit 5, Montreal 2; April 28 at Detroit — Montreal 4, Detroit 2; May 1 at Detroit — Montreal 2, Detroit 1; May 3 at Montreal — Montreal 5, Detroit 1; May 5 at Detroit — Montreal 3, Detroit 2.

1964-65 — Montreal Canadiens — Lorne Worsley, Charlie Hodge, Jean-Claude Tremblay, Ted Harris, Jean-Guy Talbot, Terry Harper, Jacques Laperriere, Jean Gauthier, Noel Picard, Jean Beliveau, Ralph Backstrom, Dick Duff, Claude Larose, Yvan Cournoyer, Claude Provost, Bobby Rousseau, Henri Richard, Dave Balon, John Ferguson, Red Berenson, Jim Roberts, Toe Blake (coach), Sam Pollock (general manager), Larry Aubut, Andy Galley (trainers).

1965 —April 17 at Montreal — Montreal 3, Chicago 2; April 20 at Montreal — Montreal 2, Chicago 0; April 22 at Chicago — Montreal 1, Chicago 3; April 25 at Chicago — Montreal 1, Chicago 5; April 27 at Montreal — Montreal 6, Chicago 0; April 29 at Chicago — Montreal 1, Chicago 2; May 1 at Montreal — Montreal 4, Chicago 0.

1963-64 — Toronto Maple Leafs — Johnny Bower, Carl Brewer, Tim Horton, Bob Baun, Allan Stanley, Larry Hillman, Al Arbour, Red Kelly, Gerry Ehman, Andy Bathgate, George Armstrong, Ron Stewart, Dave Keon, Billy Harris, Don McKenney, Jim Pappin, Bob Pulford, Eddie Shack, Frank Mahovlich, Eddie Litzenberger, Punch Imlach (manager-coach), Bob Haggert (trainer).

1964 —April 11 at Toronto — Toronto 3, Detroit 2; April 14 at Toronto — Toronto 3, Detroit 4; April 16 at Detroit — Toronto 3, Detroit 4; April 18 at Detroit — Toronto 4, Detroit 2; April 21 at Toronto — Toronto 1, Detroit 2; April 23 at Detroit — Toronto 4, Detroit 3; April 25 at Toronto — Toronto 4, Detroit 0.

1962-63 — Toronto Maple Leafs — Johnny Bower, Don Simmons, Carl Brewer, Tim Horton, Kent Douglas, Allan Stanley, Bob Baun, Larry Hillman, Red Kelly, Dick Duff, George Armstrong, Bob Nevin, Ron Stewart, Dave Keon, Billy Harris, Bob Pulford, Eddie Shack, Ed Litzenberger, Frank Mahovlich, John MacMillan, Punch Imlach (manager-coach), Bob Haggert (trainer).

1963 —April 9 at Toronto — Toronto 4, Detroit 2; April 11 at Toronto — Toronto 4, Detroit 2; April 14 at Detroit — Toronto 2, Detroit 3; April 16 at Detroit — Toronto 4, Detroit 2; April 18 at Toronto — Toronto 3, Detroit 1.

1961-62 — Toronto Maple Leafs — Johnny Bower, Don Simmons, Carl Brewer, Tim Horton, Bob Baun, Allan Stanley, Al Arbour, Larry Hillman, Red Kelly, Dick Duff, George Armstrong, Frank Mahovlich, Bob Nevin, Ron Stewart, Bill Harris, Bert Olmstead, Bob Pulford, Eddie Shack, Dave Keon, Ed Litzenberger, John MacMillan, Punch Imlach (manager-coach), Bob Haggert (trainer).

1962 —April 10 at Toronto — Toronto 4, Chicago 1; April 12 at Toronto — Toronto 3, Chicago 2; April 15 at Chicago — Toronto 0, Chicago 3; April 17 at Chicago — Toronto 1, Chicago 4; April 19 at Toronto — Toronto 8, Chicago 4; April 22 at Chicago — Toronto 2, Chicago 1.

Ed Litzenberger

1960-61 — Chicago Black Hawks — Glenn Hall, Al Arbour, Pierre Pilote, Elmer Vasko, Jack Evans, Dollard St. Laurent, Reg Fleming, Tod Sloan, Ron Murphy, Eddie Litzenberger, Bill Hay, Bobby Hull, Ab McDonald, Eric Nesterenko, Ken Wharram, Earl Balfour, Stan Mikita, Murray Balfour, Chico Maki, Tommy Ivan (manager), Rudy Pilous (coach), Nick Garen (trainer).

1961 —April 6 at Chicago — Chicago 3, Detroit 2; April 8 at Detroit — Detroit 3, Chicago 1; April 10 at Chicago — Chicago 3, Detroit 1; April 12 at Detroit — Detroit 2, Chicago 1; April 14 at Chicago — Chicago 6, Detroit 3; April 16 at Detroit — Chicago 5, Detroit 1.

1959-60 — Montreal Canadiens — Jacques Plante, Charlie Hodge, Doug Harvey, Tom Johnson, Bob Turner, Jean-Guy Talbot, Albert Langlois, Ralph Backstrom, Jean Beliveau, Marcel Bonin, Bernie Geoffrion, Phil Goyette, Bill Hicke, Don Marshall, Ab McDonald, Dickie Moore, André Pronovost, Claude Provost, Henri Richard, Maurice Richard, Frank Selke (manager), Toe Blake (coach), Hector Dubois, Larry Aubut (trainers).

1960 —April 7 at Montreal — Canadiens 4, Toronto 2; April 9 at Montreal — Canadiens 2, Toronto 1; April 12 at Toronto — Canadiens 5, Toronto 2; April 14 at Toronto — Canadiens 4, Toronto 0.

1958-59 — Montreal Canadiens — Jacques Plante, Charlie Hodge, Doug Harvey, Tom Johnson, Bob Turner, Jean-Guy Talbot, Albert Langlois, Bernie Geoffrion, Ralph Backstrom, Bill Hicke, Maurice Richard, Dickie Moore, Claude Provost, Ab McDonald, Henri Richard, Marcel Bonin, Phil Goyette, Don Marshall, André Pronovost, Jean Béliveau, Frank Selke (manager), Toe Blake (coach), Hector Dubois, Larry Aubut (trainers).

1959 —April 9 at Montreal — Canadiens 5, Toronto 3; April 11 at Montreal — Canadiens 3, Toronto 1; April 14 at Toronto — Toronto 3, Canadiens 2; April 16 at Toronto — Canadiens 3, Toronto 2; April 18 at Montreal — Canadiens 5, Toronto 3.

1957-58 — Montreal Canadiens — Jacques Plante, Gerry McNeil, Doug Harvey, Tom Johnson, Bob Turner, Dollard St-Laurent, Jean-Guy Talbot, Albert Langlois, Jean Béliveau, Bernie Geoffrion, Maurice Richard, Dickie Moore, Claude Provost, Floyd Curry, Bert Olmstead, Henri Richard, Marcel Bonin, Phil Goyette, Don Marshall, André Pronovost, Connie Broden, Frank Selke (manager), Toe Blake (coach), Hector Dubois, Larry Aubut (trainers).

1958 —April 8 at Montreal — Canadiens 2, Boston 1; April 10 at Montreal — Boston 5, Canadiens 2; April 13 at Boston — Canadiens 3, Boston 0; April 15 at Boston — Boston 3, Canadiens 1; April 17 at Montreal — Canadiens 3, Boston 2; April 20 at Boston — Canadiens 5, Boston 3.

1956-57 — Montreal Canadiens — Jacques Plante, Gerry McNeil, Doug Harvey, Tom Johnson, Bob Turner, Dollard St. Laurent, Jean-Guy Talbot, Jean Béliveau, Bernie Geoffrion, Floyd Curry, Dickie Moore, Maurice Richard, Claude Provost, Bert Olmstead, Henri Richard, Phil Goyette, Don Marshall, André Pronovost, Connie Broden, Frank Selke (manager), Toe Blake (coach), Hector Dubois, Larry Aubut (trainers).

1957 —April 6, at Montreal — Canadiens 5, Boston 1; April 9, at Montreal — Canadiens 1, Boston 0; April 11, at Boston — Canadiens 4, Boston 2; April 14, at Boston — Boston 2, Canadiens 0; April 16, at Montreal — Canadiens 5, Boston 1.

1955-56 — Montreal Canadiens — Jacques Plante, Doug Harvey, Emile Bouchard, Bob Turner, Tom Johnson, Jean-Guy Talbot, Dollard St. Laurent, Jean Béliveau, Bernie Geoffrion, Bert Olmstead, Floyd Curry, Jackie Leclair, Maurice Richard, Dickie Moore, Henri Richard, Ken Mosdell, Don Marshall, Claude Provost, Frank Selke (manager), Toe Blake (coach), Hector Dubois (trainer).

1956 —March 31, at Montreal — Canadiens 6, Detroit 4; April 3, at Montreal — Canadiens 5, Detroit 1; April 5, at Detroit — Detroit 3, Canadiens 1; April 8, at Detroit — Canadiens 3, Detroit 0; April 10, at Montreal — Canadiens 3, Detroit 1.

1954-55 — Detroit Red Wings — Terry Sawchuk, Red Kelly, Bob Goldham, Marcel Pronovost, Ben Woit, Jim Hay, Larry Hillman, Ted Lindsay, Tony Leswick, Gordie Howe, Alex Delvecchio, Marty Pavelich, Glen Skov, Earl Reibel, John Wilson, Bill Dineen, Vic Stasiuk, Marcel Bonin, Jack Adams (manager), Jimmy Skinner (coach), Carl Mattson (trainer).

1955 —April 3, at Detroit — Detroit 4, Canadiens 2; April 5, at Detroit — Detroit 7, Canadiens 1, April 7 at Montreal — Canadiens 4, Detroit 2; April 9, at Montreal — Canadiens 5, Detroit 3; April 10, at Detroit — Detroit 5, Canadiens 1; April 12, at Montreal — Canadiens 6, Detroit 3; April 14, at Detroit — Detroit 3, Canadiens 1.

1953-54 — Detroit Red Wings — Terry Sawchuk, Red Kelly, Bob Goldham, Ben Woit, Marcel Pronovost, Al Arbour, Keith Allen, Tony Leswick, Gordie Howe, Marty Pavelich, Alex Delvecchio, Metro Prystai, Glen Skov, John Wilson, Bill Dineen, Jim Peters, Earl Reibel, Vic Stasiuk, Jack Adams (manager), Tommy Ivan (coach), Carl Mattson (trainer).

1954 —April 4, at Detroit — Detroit 3, Canadiens 1; April 6, at Detroit — Canadiens 3, Detroit 1; April 8, at Montreal — Detroit 5, Canadiens 2; April 10, at Montreal — Detroit 2, Canadiens 0; April 11, at Detroit — Canadiens 1, Detroit 0; April 13, at Montreal — Canadiens 4, Detroit 1; April 16, at Detroit — Detroit 2, Canadiens 1.

1952-53 — Montreal Canadiens — Gerry McNeil, Jacques Plante, Doug Harvey, Emile Bouchard, Tom Johnson, Dollard St. Laurent, Bud MacPherson, Maurice Richard, Elmer Lach, Bert Olmstead, Bernie Geoffrion, Floyd Curry, Paul Masnick, Billy Reay, Dickie Moore, Ken Mosdell, Dick Gamble, Johnny McCormack, Lorne Davis, Calum McKay, Eddie Mazur, Frank Selke (manager), Dick Irvin (coach), Hector Dubois (trainer).

1953 —April 9, at Montreal — Canadiens 4, Boston 2; April 11, at Montreal — Boston 4, Canadiens 1; April 12, at Boston — Canadiens 3, Boston 0; April 14, at Boston — Canadiens 7, Boston 3; April 16, at Montreal — Canadiens 1, Boston 0.

1951-52 — Detroit Red Wings — Terry Sawchuk, Bob Goldham, Ben Woit, Red Kelly, Leo Reise, Marcel Pronovost, Ted Lindsay, Tony Leswick, Gordie Howe, Metro Prystai, Marty Pavelich, Sid Abel, Glen Skov, Alex Delvecchio, John Wilson, Vic Stasiuk, Larry Zeidel, Jack Adams (manager) Tommy Ivan (coach), Carl Mattson (trainer).

1952 —April 10, at Montreal — Detroit 3, Canadiens 1; April 12 at Montreal — Detroit 2, Canadiens 1; April 13, at Detroit — Detroit 3, Canadiens 0; April 15, at Detroit — Detroit 3, Canadiens 0.

1950-51 — Toronto Maple Leafs — Turk Broda, Al Rollins, Jim Thomson, Gus Mortson, Bill Barilko, Bill Juzda, Fern Flaman, Hugh Bolton, Ted Kennedy, Sid Smith, Tod Sloan, Cal Gardner, Howie Meeker, Harry Watson, Max Bentley, Joe Klukay, Danny Lewicki, Ray Timgren, Fleming Mackell, Johnny McCormack, Bob Hassard, Conn Smythe (manager), Joe Primeau (coach), Tim Daly (trainer).

1951 —April 11, at Toronto — Toronto 3, Canadiens 2; April 14, at Toronto — Canadiens 3, Toronto 2; April 17, at Montreal — Toronto 2, Canadiens 1; April 19, at Montreal — Toronto 3, Canadiens 2; April 21 at Toronto — Toronto 3, Canadiens 2.

1949-50 — Detroit Red Wings — Harry Lumley, Jack Stewart, Leo Reise, Clare Martin, Al Dewsbury, Lee Fogolin, Marcel Pronovost, Red Kelly, Ted Lindsay, Sid Abel, Gordie Howe, George Gee, Jimmy Peters, Marty Pavelich, Jim McFadden, Pete Babando, Max McNab, Gerry Couture, Joe Carveth, Steve Black, John Wilson, Larry Wilson, Jack Adams (manager), Tommy Ivan (coach), Carl Mattson (trainer).

1950 —April 11, at Detroit — Detroit 4, Rangers 1; April 13, at Toronto* — Rangers 3, Detroit 1; April 15, at Toronto — Detroit 4, Rangers 0; April 18, at Detroit — Rangers 4, Detroit 3; April 20, at Detroit — Rangers 2, Detroit 1; April 22, at Detroit — Detroit 5, Rangers 4; April 23, at Detroit — Detroit 4, Rangers 3.

* Ice was unavailable in Madison Square Garden and Rangers elected to play second and third games on Toronto ice.

1948-49 — Toronto Maple Leafs — Turk Broda, Jim Thomson, Gus Mortson, Bill Barilko, Garth Boesch, Bill Juzda, Ted Kennedy, Howie Meeker, Vic Lynn, Harry Watson, Bill Ezinicki, Cal Gardner, Max Bentley, Joe Klukay, Sid Smith, Don Metz, Ray Timgren, Fleming Mackell, Harry Taylor, Bob Dawes, Tod Sloan, Conn Smythe (manager), Hap Day (coach), Tim Daly (trainer).

1949 —April 8, at Detroit — Toronto 3, Detroit 2; April 10, at Detroit — Toronto 3, Detroit 1; April 13, at Toronto — Toronto 3, Detroit 1; April 16, at Toronto — Toronto 3, Detroit 1.

1947-48 — Toronto Maple Leafs — Turk Broda, Jim Thomson, Wally Stanowski, Garth Boesch, Bill Barilko. Gus Mortson, Phil Samis, Syl Apps, Bill Ezinicki, Harry Watson, Ted Kennedy, Howie Meeker, Vic Lynn, Nick Metz, Max Bentley, Joe Klukay, Les Costello, Don Metz, Sid Smith, Conn Smythe (manager), Hap Day (coach), Tim Daly (trainer).

1948 —April 7, at Toronto — Toronto 5, Detroit 3; April 10, at Toronto — Toronto 4, Detroit 2; April 11, at Detroit — Toronto 2, Detroit 0; April 14, at Detroit — Toronto 7, Detroit 2.

1946-47 — Toronto Maple Leafs — Turk Broda, Garth Boesch, Gus Mortson, Jim Thomson, Wally Stanowski, Bill Barilko, Harry Watson, Bud Poile, Ted Kennedy, Syl Apps, Don Metz, Nick Metz, Bill Ezinicki, Vic Lynn, Howie Meeker, Gaye Stewart, Joe Klukay, Gus Bodnar, Bob Goldham, Conn Smythe (manager), Hap Day (coach), Tim Daly (trainer).

1947 —April 8, at Montreal — Canadiens 6, Toronto 0; April 10, at Montreal — Toronto 4, Canadiens 0; April 12, at Toronto — Toronto 4, Canadiens 2; April 15, at Toronto — Toronto 2, Canadiens 1; April 17, at Montreal — Canadiens 3, Toronto 1; April 19, at Toronto — Toronto 2, Canadiens 1.

Elmer Lach

1945-46 — Montreal Canadiens — Elmer Lach, Toe Blake, Maurice Richard, Bob Fillion, Dutch Hiller, Murph Chamberlain, Ken Mosdell, Buddy O'Connor, Glen Harmon, Jim Peters, Emile Bouchard, Bill Reay, Ken Reardon, Leo Lamoureux, Frank Eddolls, Gerry Plamondon, Bill Durnan, Tommy Gorman (manager), Dick Irvin (coach), Ernie Cook (trainer).

1946 —March 30, at Montreal — Canadiens 4, Boston 3; April 2, at Montreal — Canadiens 3, Boston 2; April 4, at Boston — Canadiens 4, Boston 2; April 7, at Boston — Boston 3, Canadiens 2; April 9, at Montreal — Canadiens 6, Boston 3.

1944-45 — Toronto Maple Leafs — Don Metz, Frank McCool, Wally Stanowski, Reg Hamilton, Elwyn Morris, Johnny McCreedy, Tommy O'Neill, Ted Kennedy, Babe Pratt, Gus Bodnar, Art Jackson, Jack McLean, Mel Hill, Nick Metz, Bob Davidson, Dave Schriner, Lorne Carr, Conn Smythe (manager), Frank Selke (business manager), Hap Day (coach), Tim Daly (trainer).

1945 —April 6, at Detroit — Toronto 1, Detroit 0; April 8, at Detroit — Toronto 2, Detroit 0; April 12, at Toronto — Toronto 1, Detroit 0; April 14, at Toronto — Detroit 5, Toronto 3; April 19, at Detroit — Detroit 2, Toronto 0; April 21 at Toronto — Detroit 1, Toronto 0; April 22, at Detroit — Toronto 2, Detroit 1.

1943-44 — Montreal Canadiens — Toe Blake, Maurice Richard, Elmer Lach, Ray Getliffe, Murph Chamberlain, Phil Watson, Emile Bouchard, Glen Harmon, Buddy O'Connor, Jerry Heffernan, Mike McMahon, Leo Lamoureux, Fernand Majeau, Bob Fillion, Bill Durnan, Tommy Gorman (manager), Dick Irvin (coach), Ernie Cook (trainer).

1944 —April 4, at Montreal — Canadiens 5, Chicago 1; April 6, at Chicago — Canadiens 3, Chicago 1; April 9 at Chicago — Canadiens 3, Chicago 2; April 13, at Montreal — Canadiens 5, Chicago 4.

1942-43 — Detroit Red Wings — Jack Stewart, Jimmy Orlando, Sid Abel, Alex Motter, Harry Watson, Joe Carveth, Mud Bruneteau, Eddie Wares, Johnny Mowers, Cully Simon, Don Grosso, Carl Liscombe, Connie Brown, Syd Howe, Les Douglas, Hal Jackson, Joe Fisher, Jack Adams (manager), Ebbie Goodfellow (playing-coach), Honey Walker (trainer).

1943 —April 1, at Detroit — Detroit 6, Boston 2; April 4, at Detroit — Detroit 4, Boston 3; April 7, at Boston — Detroit 4, Boston 0; April 8 at Boston — Detroit 2, Boston 0.

1941-42 — Toronto Maple Leafs — Wally Stanowski, Syl Apps, Bob Goldham, Gord Drillon, Hank Goldup, Ernie Dickens, Dave Schriner, Bucko McDonald, Bob Davidson, Nick Metz, Bingo Kampman, Don Metz, Gaye Stewart, Turk Broda, Johnny McCreedy, Lorne Carr, Pete Langelle, Billy Taylor, Conn Smythe (manager), Hap Day (coach), Frank Selke (business manager), Tim Daly (trainer).

1942 —April 4, at Toronto — Detroit 3, Toronto 2; April 7, at Toronto — Detroit 4, Toronto 2; April 9, at Detroit — Detroit 5, Toronto 2; April 12, at Detroit — Toronto 4, Detroit 3; April 14, at Toronto — Toronto 9, Detroit 3; April 16, at Detroit — Toronto 3, Detroit 0; April 18, at Toronto — Toronto 3, Detroit 1.

1940-41 — Boston Bruins — Bill Cowley, Des Smith, Dit Clapper, Frank Brimsek, Flash Hollett, John Crawford, Bobby Bauer, Pat McCreavy, Herb Cain, Mel Hill, Milt Schmidt, Woody Dumart, Roy Conacher, Terry Reardon, Art Jackson, Eddie Wiseman, Art Ross (manager), Cooney Weiland (coach), Win Green (trainer).

1941 —April 6, at Boston — Detroit 2, Boston 3; April 8, at Boston — Detroit 1, Boston 2; April 10, at Detroit — Boston 4, Detroit 2; April 12, at Detroit — Boston 3, Detroit 1.

1939-40 — New York Rangers — Dave Kerr, Art Coulter, Ott Heller, Alex Shibicky, Mac Colville, Neil Colville, Phil Watson, Lynn Patrick, Clint Smith, Muzz Patrick, Babe Pratt, Bryan Hextall, Kilby Macdonald, Dutch Hiller, Alf Pike, Sanford Smith, Lester Patrick (manager), Frank Boucher (coach), Harry Westerby (trainer).

1940 —April 2, at New York — Rangers 2, Toronto 1; April 3, at New York — Rangers 6, Toronto 2; April 6 — at Toronto — Rangers 1, Toronto 2; April 9, at Toronto — Rangers 0, Toronto 3; April 11, at Toronto — Rangers 2, Toronto 1; April 13, at Toronto — Rangers 3, Toronto 2.

1938-39 — Boston Bruins — Bobby Bauer, Mel Hill, Flash Hollett, Roy Conacher, Gord Pettinger, Milt Schmidt, Woody Dumart, Jack Crawford, Ray Getliffe, Frank Brimsek, Eddie Shore, Dit Clapper, Bill Cowley, Jack Portland, Red Hamill, Cooney Weiland, Art Ross (manager-coach), Win Green (trainer).

1939 —April 6, at Boston — Toronto 1, Boston 2; April 9, at Boston — Toronto 3, Boston 2; April 11, at Toronto — Toronto 1, Boston 3; April 13 at Toronto — Toronto 0, Boston 2; April 16, at Boston — Toronto 1, Boston 3.

1937-38 — Chicago Black Hawks — Art Wiebe, Carl Voss, Hal Jackson, Mike Karakas, Mush March, Jack Shill, Earl Seibert, Cully Dahlstrom, Alex Levinsky, Johnny Gottselig, Lou Trudel, Pete Palangio, Bill MacKenzie, Doc Romnes, Paul Thompson, Roger Jenkins, Alf Moore, Bert Connolly, Virgil Johnson, Paul Goodman, Bill Stewart (manager-coach), Eddie Froelich (trainer).

1938 —April 5, at Toronto — Chicago 3, Toronto 1; April 7, at Toronto — Chicago 1, Toronto 5; April 10 at Chicago — Chicago 2, Toronto 1; April 12, at Chicago — Chicago 4, Toronto 1.

1936-37 — Detroit Red Wings — Normie Smith, Pete Kelly, Larry Aurie, Herbie Lewis, Hec Kilrea, Mud Bruneteau, Syd Howe, Wally Kilrea, Jimmy Franks, Bucko McDonald, Gordon Pettinger, Ebbie Goodfellow, Johnny Gallagher, Scotty Bowman, Johnny Sorrell, Marty Barry, Earl Robertson, Johnny Sherf, Howard Mackie, Jack Adams (manager-coach), Honey Walker (trainer).

1937 —April 6, at New York — Detroit 1, Rangers 5; April 8, at Detroit — Detroit 4, Rangers 2; April 11, at Detroit — Detroit 0, Rangers 1; April 13, at Detroit — Detroit 1, Rangers 0; April 15, at Detroit — Detroit 3, Rangers 0.

1935-36 — Detroit Red Wings — Johnny Sorrell, Syd Howe, Marty Barry, Herbie Lewis, Mud Bruneteau, Wally Kilrea, Hec Kilrea, Gordon Pettinger, Bucko McDonald, Scotty Bowman, Pete Kelly, Doug Young, Ebbie Goodfellow, Normie Smith, Jack Adams (manager-coach), Honey Walker (trainer).

1936 —April 5, at Detroit — Detroit 3, Toronto 1; April 7, at Detroit — Detroit 9, Toronto 4; April 9, at Toronto — Detroit 3, Toronto 4; April 11, at Toronto — Detroit 3, Toronto 1.

1934-35 — Montreal Maroons — Marvin (Cy) Wentworth, Alex Connell, Toe Blake, Stew Evans, Earl Robinson, Bill Miller, Dave Trottier, Jimmy Ward, Larry Northcott, Hooley Smith, Russ Blinco, Allan Shields, Sammy McManus, Gus Marker, Bob Gracie, Herb Cain, Tommy Gorman (manager), Lionel Conacher (coach), Bill O'Brien (trainer).

1935 —April 4, at Toronto — Montreal 3, Toronto 2; April 6, at Toronto — Montreal 3, Toronto 1; April 9 at Montreal — Montreal 4, Toronto 1.

1933-34 — Chicago Black Hawks — Taffy Abel, Lolo Couture, Lou Trudel, Lionel Conacher, Paul Thompson, Leroy Goldsworthy, Art Coulter, Roger Jenkins, Don McFayden, Tommy Cook, Doc Romnes, Johnny Gottselig, Mush March, Johnny Sheppard, Chuck Gardiner (captain), Bill Kendall, Tommy Gorman (manager-coach), Eddie Froelich (trainer).

1934 —April 3, at Detroit — Detroit 1, Chicago 2; April 5, at Detroit — Detroit 1, Chicago 4; April 8 at Chicago — Detroit 5, Chicago 2; April 10, at Chicago — Detroit 0, Chicago 1.

1932-33 — New York Rangers — Ching Johnson, Butch Keeling, Frank Boucher, Art Somers, Babe Siebert, Bun Cook, Andy Aitkinhead, Ott Heller, Ozzie Asmundson, Gord Pettinger, Doug Brennan, Cecil Dillon, Bill Cook (captain), Murray Murdock, Earl Seibert, Lester Patrick (manager-coach), Harry Westerby (trainer).

1933 —April 4, at New York — Toronto 1, Rangers 5; April 8, at Toronto — Toronto 1, Rangers 3; April 11, at Toronto — Toronto 3, Rangers 2; April 13, at Toronto — Toronto 0, Rangers 1.

1931-32 — Toronto Maple Leafs — Charlie Conacher, Harvey Jackson, King Clancy, Andy Blair, Red Horner, Lorne Chabot, Alex Levinsky, Joe Primeau, Hal Darragh, Hal Cotton, Frank Finnigan, Hap Day, Ace Bailey, Bob Gracie, Fred Robertson, Earl Miller, Conn Smythe (manager), Dick Irvin (coach), Tim Daly (trainer).

1932 —April 5 at New York — Toronto 6, New York Rangers 4; April 7, at Boston* — Toronto 6, New York Rangers 2; April 9, at Toronto — Toronto 6, New York Rangers 4.

* Ice was unavailable in Madison Square Garden and Rangers elected to play the second game on neutral ice.

1930-31 — Montreal Canadiens — George Hainsworth, Wildor Larochelle, Marty Burke, Sylvio Mantha, Howie Morenz, Johnny Gagnon, Aurel Joliat, Armand Mondou, Pit Lepine, Albert Leduc, Georges Mantha, Art Lesieur, Nick Wasnie, Bert McCaffrey, Gus Rivers, Jean Pusie, Leo Dandurand (manager), Cecil Hart (coach), Ed Dufour (trainer).

1931 —April 3, at Chicago — Canadiens 2, Chicago 1; April 5, at Chicago — Canadiens 1, Chicago 2; April 9, at Chicago — Canadiens 3, Chicago 2; April 11, at Montreal — Canadiens 4, Chicago 2; April 14, at Montreal — Canadiens 2, Chicago 0.

1929-30 — Montreal Canadiens — George Hainsworth, Marty Burke, Sylvio Mantha, Howie Morenz, Bert McCaffrey, Aurel Joliat, Albert Leduc, Pit Lepine, Wildor Larochelle, Nick Wasnie, Gerald Carson, Armand Mondou, Georges Mantha, Gus Rivers, Leo Dandurand (manager), Cecil Hart (coach), Ed Dufour (trainer).

1930 —April 1 — Canadiens 3, Boston 0; April 3 — Canadiens 4, Boston 3.

1928-29 — Boston Bruins — Cecil (Tiny) Thompson, Eddie Shore, Lionel Hitchman, Perk Galbraith, Eric Pettinger, Frank Fredrickson, Mickey Mackay, Red Green, Dutch Gainor, Harry Oliver, Eddie Rodden, Dit Clapper, Cooney Weiland, Lloyd Klein, Cy Denneny, Bill Carson, George Owen, Myles Lane, Art Ross (manager-coach), Win Green (trainer).

1929 —March 28 — Rangers 0, Boston 2; March 29 — Rangers 1, Boston 2.

1927-28 — New York Rangers — Lorne Chabot, Taffy Abel, Leon Bourgault, Ching Johnson, Bill Cook, Bun Cook, Frank Boucher, Billy Boyd, Murray Murdoch, Paul Thompson, Alex Gray, Joe Miller, Patsy Callighen, Lester Patrick (manager-coach), Harry Westerby (trainer).

1928 —April 5 — Rangers 0, Montreal 2; April 7 — Rangers 2, Montreal 1; April 10 — Rangers 0, Montreal 2; April 12 — Rangers 1, Montreal 0; April 14 — Rangers 2, Montreal 1.

1926-27 — Ottawa Senators — Alex Connell, King Clancy, George (Buck) Boucher, Ed Gorman, Frank Finnigan, Alex Smith, Hec Kilrea, Hooley Smith, Cy Denneny, Frank Nighbor, Jack Adams, Milt Halliday, Dave Gil (manager-coach).

1927 —April 7 — Boston 0, Ottawa 0; April 9 — Boston 1, Ottawa 3; April 11 — Boston 1, Ottawa 1; April 13 — Boston 1, Ottawa 3.

1925-26 — Montreal Maroons — Clint Benedict, Reg Noble, Frank Carson, Dunc Munro, Nels Stewart, Harry Broadbent, Babe Siebert, Dinny Dinsmore, Bill Phillips, Hobart (Hobie) Kitchen, Sammy Rothschiel, Albert (Toots) Holway, Shorty Horne, Bern Brophy, Eddie Gerard (manager-coach), Bill O'Brien (trainer).

1926 —at Montreal, Maroons 3, Victoria 0; Maroons 3, Victoria 0; Victoria 3, Maroons 2; Maroons 2, Victoria 0. Total goals: Montreal 10, Victoria 3.

The series in the spring of 1926 ended the annual playoffs between the champions of the east and the champions of the west. The west coast league disbanded, selling its players to Chicago, Detroit and New York Rangers. Since 1926-27 the annual play-offs in the National Hockey League have decided the Stanley Cup champions.

1924-25 — Victoria Cougars — Harry (Happy) Holmes, Clem Loughlin, Gordie Fraser, Frank Fredrickson, Jack Walker, Harold (Gizzy) Hart, Harold (Slim) Halderson, Frank Foyston, Wally Elmer, Harry Meeking, Jocko Anderson, Lester Patrick (manager-coach).

1925 —at Victoria, Victoria 5, Montreal Canadiens 2; Victoria 3, Canadiens 1; Canadiens 4, Victoria 2; Victoria 6, Canadiens 1. Total goals: Victoria 16, Canadiens 8.

1923-24 — Montreal Canadiens — Georges Vezina, Sprague Cleghorn, Billy Couture, Howie Morenz, Aurel Joliat, Billy Boucher, Odie Cleghorn, Sylvio Mantha, Bobby Boucher, Billy Bell, Billy Cameron, Joe Malone, Fortier, Leo Dandurand (manager-coach).

1924 —at Montreal, Canadiens 3, Vancouver 2; Canadiens 2, Vancouver 1. Total goals, Canadiens 5, Vancouver 3. Canadiens 6, Calgary 1; (the second game was transferred to Ottawa to benefit from an artificial ice surface) Canadiens 3, Calgary 0. Total goals: Canadiens 9, Calgary 1. [Because of an agreement between the NHL and the two western Leagues (WCHL and PCHA) Canadiens had to play the champions of each league in the Stanley Cup series in 1924.]

1922-23 — Ottawa Senators — George (Buck) Boucher, Lionel Hitchman, Frank Nighbor, King Clancy, Harry Helman, Clint Benedict, Jack Darragh, Eddie Gerard, Cy Denneny, Harry Broadbent, Tommy Gorman (manager), Pete Green (coach), F. Dolan (trainer).

1923 —at Vancouver, Ottawa 1, Vancouver 0; Vancouver 4, Ottawa 1; Ottawa 3, Vancouver 2; Ottawa 5, Vancouver 1; Ottawa also met and defeated Edmonton Eskimos, Champions of the WCHL. The scores: Ottawa 2, Edmonton 1; Ottawa 1, Edmonton 0. Total goals: Ottawa 10, Vancouver 7; Ottawa 3, Edmonton 1.

1921-22 — Toronto St. Pats — Ted Stackhouse, Corb Denneny, Rod Smylie, Lloyd Andrews, John Ross Roach, Harry Cameron, Bill (Red) Stuart, Cecil (Babe) Dye, Ken Randall, Reg Noble, Eddie Gerard (borrowed for one game from Ottawa), Stan Jackson, Nolan Mitchell, Charlie Querrie (manager), Eddie Powers (coach).

1922 —at Toronto, Vancouver 4, Toronto 3; Toronto 2, Vancouver 1; Vancouver 3, Toronto 0; Toronto 6, Vancouver 0; Toronto 5, Vancouver 1. Total goals: Toronto 16, Vancouver 9.

1920-21 — Ottawa Senators — Jack McKell, Jack Darragh, Morley Bruce, George (Buck) Boucher, Eddie Gerard, Clint Benedict, Sprague Cleghorn, Frank Nighbor, Harry Broadbent, Cy Denneny, Leth Graham, Tommy Gorman (manager), Pete Green (coach), F. Dolan (trainer).

1921 —at Vancouver, Vancouver 2, Ottawa 1; Ottawa 4, Vancouver 3; Ottawa 3, Vancouver 2; Vancouver 3, Ottawa 2; Ottawa 2, Vancouver 1; Total goals: Ottawa 12, Vancouver 11.

1919-20 — Ottawa Senators — Jack McKell, Jack Darragh, Morley Bruce, Horrace Merrill, George (Buck) Boucher, Eddie Gerard, Clint Benedict, Sprague Cleghorn, Frank Nighbor, Harry Broadbent, Cy Denneny, Price, Tommy Gorman (manager), Pete Green (coach).

1920 —at Ottawa, Ottawa 3, Seattle 2; Ottawa 3, Seattle 0; Seattle 3, Ottawa 1. Mild weather ruined natural ice surface and necessitated the transfer of two games of the series to Toronto's artificial rink. At Toronto — Seattle 5, Ottawa 2; Ottawa 6, Seattle 1. Total goals: Ottawa 15, Seattle 11.

1918-19 — No decision, Series halted by Spanish influenza epidemic, illness of several players and death of Joe Hall of Montreal Canadiens from flu. Five games had been played when the series was halted, each team having won two and tied one. The results are shown:

1919 —at Seattle, Seattle 7, Canadiens 0; Canadiens 4, Seattle 2; Seattle 7, Canadiens 2; Seattle 0, Canadiens 0 (20 minutes overtime); Canadiens 4, Seattle 3 (15:57 overtime). Total goals: Seattle 19, Canadiens 10.

1917-18 — **Toronto Arenas** — Rusty Crawford, Harry Meeking, Ken Randall, Corb Denneny, Harry Cameron, Jack Adams, Alf Skinner, Harry Mummery, Harry (Happy) Holmes, Reg Noble, Sammy Hebert, Jack Marks, Jack Coughlin, Neville, Charlie Querrie (manager), Dick Carroll (coach), Frank Carroll (trainer).

1918 —at Toronto, Toronto 5, Vancouver 3; Vancouver 6, Toronto 4; Toronto 6, Vancouver 3; Vancouver 8, Toronto 1; Toronto 2, Vancouver 1. Total goals: Vancouver 21, Toronto 18.

1916-17 — **Seattle Metropolitans** — Harry (Happy) Holmes, Ed Carpenter, Cully Wilson, Jack Walker, Bernie Morris, Frank Foyston, Roy Rickey, Jim Riley, Bobby Rowe (captain), Peter Muldoon (manager).

1917 —at Seattle, Montreal Canadiens 8, Seattle 4; Seattle 6, Canadiens 1; Seattle 4, Canadiens 1; Seattle 9, Canadiens 1. Total goals: Seattle 23, Canadiens 11.

1915-16 — **Montreal Canadiens** — Georges Vezina, Bert Corbeau, Jack Laviolette, Newsy Lalonde, Louis Berlinguette, Goldie Prodgers, Howard McNamara, Didier Pitre, Skene Ronan, Amos Arbour, Skinner Poulin, Jack Fournier, George Kennedy (manager).

1916 —at Montreal, Portland 2, Canadiens 0; Canadiens 2, Portland 1; Canadiens 6, Portland 3; Portland 6, Canadiens 5; Canadiens 2, Portland 1. Total goals: Canadiens 15, Portland 13.

1914-15 — **Vancouver Millionaires** — Kenny Mallen, Frank Nighbor, Fred (Cyclone) Taylor, Hughie Lehman, Lloyd Cook, Mickey MacKay, Barney Stanley, Jim Seaborn, Si Griffis (captain), Jean Matz, Frank Patrick (playing manager).

1915 —at Vancouver, Vancouver 6, Ottawa 2; Vancouver 8, Ottawa 3; Vancouver 12, Ottawa 3. Total goals: Vancouver 26, Ottawa 8.

1913-14 — **Toronto Blueshirts** — Con Corbeau, F. Roy McGiffen, Jack Walker, George McNamara, Cully Wilson, Frank Foyston, Harry Cameron, Harry (Happy) Holmes, Alan M. Davidson (captain), Harriston, Jack Marshall (playing-manager), Frank and Dick Carroll (trainers).

1914 —at Toronto, Toronto 5, Victoria 2; Toronto 6, Victoria 5 (15 minutes overtime); Toronto 2, Victoria 1. Total goals: Toronto 13, Victoria 8.

1912-13 — **Quebec Bulldogs** — Joe Malone, Joe Hall, Paddy Moran, Harry Mummery, Tommy Smith, Jack Marks, Russell Crawford, Billy Creighton, Jeff Malone, Rocket Power, M.J. Quinn (manager), D. Beland (trainer).

1913 —at Quebec, March 8-10; Quebec 14, Sydney 3; Quebec 6, Sydney 2 (Quebec won best-of-three series 2-0). Victoria challenged Quebec but the Bulldogs refused to put the Stanley Cup in competition so the two teams played an exhibition series with Victoria winning two games to one by scores of 7-5, 3-6, 6-1. It was the first meeting between the Eastern champions and the Western champions. The following year, and until the Pacific Coast League disbanded after the 1926 playoffs, the Cup went to the winner of the series between East and West.

1911-12 — **Quebec Bulldogs** — Goldie Prodgers, Joe Hall, Walter Rooney, Paddy Moran, Jack Marks, Jack MacDonald, Eddie Oatman, Leonard, Joe Malone (captain), C. Nolan (coach), M.J. Quinn (manager), D. Beland (trainer).

1912 —at Quebec, Quebec 9, Moncton 3; Quebec 8, Moncton 0 (best-of-three series). Total goals: Quebec 17, Moncton 3. [Prior to 1912, teams could challenge the Stanley Cup champions for the title, thus there was more than one Championship Series played in most of the seasons between 1894 and 1911.]

1910-11 — **Ottawa Senators** — Hamby Shore, Percy LeSueur, Jack Darragh, Bruce Stuart, Marty Walsh, Bruce Ridpath, Fred Lake, Albert (Dubby) Kerr, Alex Currie, Horace Gaul.

1911 —at Ottawa, March 13, Ottawa 7, Galt 4. March 16, Ottawa 13, Port Arthur 4.

1909-10 — **Montreal Wanderers** — Cecil W. Blackford, Ernie (Moose) Johnson, Ernie Russell, Riley Hern, Harry Hyland, Jack Marshall, Frank (Pud) Glass (captain), Jimmy Gardner, R. R. Boon (manager).

1910 —at Montreal, March 12, Montreal 7, Berlin (Kitchener) 3.

1908-09 — **Ottawa Senators** — Fred Lake, Percy LeSueur, Fred (Cyclone) Taylor, H.L. (Billy) Gilmour, Albert Kerr, Edgar Dey, Marty Walsh, Bruce Stuart (captain).

1909 —Ottawa, as champions of the Eastern Canada Hockey Association took over the Stanley Cup in 1909 and, although a challenge was accepted by the Cup trustees from Winnipeg Shamrocks but could not be arranged because of the lateness of the season, no other challenges were made in 1909. The following season — 1909-10 — however, the Senators accepted two challenges as defending Cup Champions. The first was against Galt in a two-game, total-point series, and the second against Edmonton, also a two-game, total-point series. Details follow: at Ottawa, Jan. 5, Ottawa 12, Galt 3; Jan. 7, Ottawa 3, Galt 1. At Ottawa, Jan. 18, Ottawa 8, Edmonton 4; Jan. 20, Ottawa 13, Edmonton 7.

1907-08 — **Montreal Wanderers** — Riley Hern, Art Ross, Walter Small, Frank (Pud) Glass, Bruce Stuart, Ernie Russell, Ernie (Moose) Johnson, Cecil Blachford (captain), Tom Hooper, Larry Gilmour, Ernie Liffiton, R.R. Boon (manager).

1908 —Wanderers accepted four challenges for the Cup: at Montreal, Jan. 9, Wanderers 9, Ottawa Vics 3; Jan. 13, Wanderers 13, Ottawa 1. (Wanderers won two-game, total point series). At Montreal, March 10, Wanderers 11, Winnipeg Maple Leafs 5; March 12, Wanderers 9, Winnipeg 2 (Wanderers won two-game, total-point series). At Montreal, March 14 (sudden death), Wanderers 6, Toronto Maple Leafs (of Toronto Trolley League) 4. At start of following season, 1908-09, Wanderers were challenged by Edmonton. The results: At Montreal, Dec. 28, Wanderers 7, Edmonton 3; Dec. 30, Edmonton 7, Wanderers 6. (Wanderers won two-game, total-point series).

1906-07 — (March) — **Montreal Wanderers** — W. S. (Billy) Strachan, Riley Hern, Lester Patrick, Hod Stuart, Frank (Pud) Glass, Ernie Russell, Cecil Blachford (captain), Ernie (Moose) Johnson, Rod Kennedy, Jack Marshall, R. R. Boon (manager).

1907 —(March) — at Winnipeg, March 23, Wanderers 7, Kenora Thistles 2; March 25, Kenora 6, Wanderers 5 (Wanderers won two-game, total-point series).

1906-07 — (January) — **Kenora Thistles** — Eddie Geroux, Art Ross, Si Griffis, Tom Hooper, Billy McGimsie, Roxy Beaudro, Tom Phillips.

1907 —(January) — At Montreal, Jan. 17, Kenora 4, Wanderers 2; Jan. 21, Kenora 8, Wanderers 6. (Kenora won two-game, total-point series).

1905-06 — **Montreal Wanderers** — H. Menard, Billy Strachan, Rod Kennedy, Lester Patrick, Frank (Pud) Glass, Ernie Russell, Ernie (Moose) Johnson, Cecil Blachford (captain), Josh Arnold, R. R. Boon (manager).

1906 —at Montreal, March 14, Wanderers 9, Ottawa Silver Seven 1; March 17 at Ottawa, Ottawa 9, Wanderers 3 (Wanderers won two-game, total-point series). Wanderers accepted a challenge from New Glasgow, N.S., prior to the start of the 1906-07 season. The result: at Montreal, Dec. 27, Wanderers 10, New Glasgow 3; Dec. 29, Wanderers 7, New Glasgow 2.

1904-05 — **Ottawa Silver Seven** — Dave Finnie, Harvey Pulford (captain), Arthur Moore, Harry Westwick, Frank McGee, Alf Smith (playing coach), Billy Gilmour, Frank White, Horace Gaul, Hamby Shore, Allen.

1905 —at Ottawa, March 7, Rat Portage (Kenora) 9, Ottawa 3; March 9, Ottawa 4, Rat Portage 2; March 11, Ottawa 5, Rat Portage 4 (Ottawa won best-of-three series). As defending Cup champions, Ottawa was challenged twice during the following season, 1905-06, and accepted both. Here are the results: at Ottawa, Feb. 27, 28, Ottawa 16, Queen's University 7; Ottawa 12, Queen's 7 (Ottawa won two-game, total-point series). At Ottawa, March 6, 8, Ottawa 6, Smiths Falls 5; Ottawa 8, Smiths Falls 2 (Ottawa won two-game, total-point series).

1903-04 — **Ottawa Silver Seven** — S. C. (Suddy) Gilmour, Arthur Moore, Frank McGee, J.B. (Bouse) Hutton, H.L. (Billy) Gilmour, Jim McGee, Harry Westwick, E. H. (Harvey) Pulford (captain), Scott, A. T. (Alf) Smith (playing coach).

1904 —at Montreal, March 2, Wanderers 5, Ottawa 5. Following the tie game, a new two-game series was ordered to be played in Ottawa but Wanderers refused unless the tie-game was replayed in Montreal. When no settlement could be reached, the series was abandoned and Ottawa retained the Cup and accepted a two-game challenge from Brandon. The results: (both games at Ottawa), March 9, Ottawa 6, Brandon 3; March 11, Ottawa 9, Brandon 3. As defending Cup champions, Ottawa was challenged by Dawson City Klondikers and the two-game series was played at Ottawa the following season, 1904-05, Jan. 13 and 16. The results: Ottawa 9, Dawson City 2; Ottawa 23, Dawson City 2.

1902-03 — **Ottawa Silver Seven** — S. C. (Suddy) Gilmour, P.T. (Percy) Sims, J. B. (Bouse) Hutton, D. J. (Dave) Gilmour, H. L. (Billy) Gilmour, Harry Westwick, Frank McGee, F. H. Wood, A. A. Fraser, Charles D. Spittal, E. H. (Harvey) Pulford (captain), Arthur Moore, A. T. (Alf) Smith (coach.)

1903 —at Montreal, March 7, Montreal Victorias 1, Ottawa 1; at Ottawa, March 10, Ottawa 8, Montreal Vics 0 (Ottawa won two-game, total-point series). Ottawa was then challenged by Rat Portage in a two-game series. The results: at Ottawa, March 12, 14, Ottawa 6, Rat Portage 2; Ottawa 4, Rat Portage 2. The following season, 1903-04, Ottawa as defending Cup champions, accepted two more challenges. The results: at Ottawa, Dec. 30, 1903, Ottawa 9, Winnipeg Rowing Club 1; Jan. 1, 1904, Winnipeg 6, Ottawa 2; Jan. 4, Ottawa 2, Winnipeg 0 (Ottawa won best-of-three series). At Ottawa, Feb. 23, Ottawa 6, Toronto Marlboroughs 3; Feb. 25, Ottawa 11, Toronto 2 (Ottawa won two-game, total-point series).

1901-02 — **Montreal AAA** — Tom Hodge, R. R. (Dickie) Boon, W.C. (Billy) Nicholson, Art Hooper, W. J. (Billy) Bellingham, Charles A. Liffiton, Jack Marshall, Roland Elliott, Jim Gardner.

1902 —at Winnipeg, March 13, Winnipeg Victorias 1, Montreal 0; March 15, Montreal 5, Winnipeg 0; March 17, Montreal 2, Winnipeg 1 (Montreal won best-of-three series). Winnipeg challenged Montreal the following season, 1902-03, and, as defending Cup champions, Montreal accepted. The results: At Montreal, Jan. 29, Montreal 8, Winnipeg 1; Jan. 31, Winnipeg 2, Montreal 2 (27 minutes overtime); Feb. 2, Winnipeg 4, Montreal 2; Feb. 4, Montreal 4, Winnipeg 1.

1900-01 — **Winnipeg Victoria** — Burke Wood, Jack Marshall, A.B. (Tony) Gingras, Charles W. Johnstone, R. M. (Rod) Flett, Magnus L. Flett, Danny Bain (captain), A. Brown.

1901 —at Montreal, Jan. 29, Winnipeg 4, Montreal Shamrocks 3; Jan. 31, Winnipeg 2, Montreal 1 (4 minutes overtime) (Winnipeg won best-of-three series). The following season, 1901-02, Winnipeg, as defending Cup champions, defeated Toronto Wellingtons. The results: At Winnipeg, Jan. 21, Winnipeg 5, Toronto 3; Jan. 23, Winnipeg 5, Toronto 3 (Winnipeg won best-of-three series).

Stanley Cup Playoff Records

1918-1986
Team Records

MOST STANLEY CUP CHAMPIONSHIPS:
22 — Montreal Canadiens 1924-30-31-44-46-53-56-57-58-59-60-65-66-68-69-
71-73-76-77-78-79-86
11 — Toronto Maple Leafs
7 — Detroit Red Wings

MOST FINAL SERIES APPEARANCES:
30 — Montreal Canadiens in 69-year history.
19 — Toronto Maple Leafs in 68-year history.
18 — Detroit Red Wings in 59-year history.

MOST YEARS IN PLAYOFFS:
61 — Montreal Canadiens in 69-year history.
47 — Toronto Maple Leafs in 69-year history.
46 — Boston Bruins in 62-year history.

MOST CONSECUTIVE STANLEY CUP CHAMPIONSHIPS:
5 — Montreal Canadiens (1956-57-58-59-60)
4 — New York Islanders (1980-81-82-83) Montreal Canadiens (1976-77-78-79)

MOST CONSECUTIVE FINAL SERIES APPEARANCES:
10 — Montreal Canadiens (1951-60, inclusive)

MOST CONSECUTIVE PLAYOFF APPEARANCES:
21 — Montreal Canadiens (1949-69, inclusive)
20 — Detroit Red Wings (1939-58, inclusive)

MOST GOALS BOTH TEAMS, ONE PLAYOFF SERIES:
69 — Edmonton Oilers, Chicago Black Hawks in 1985 Campbell Conference Final. Edmonton won best-of-seven series 4-2, outscoring Chicago 44-25.
62 — Chicago Black Hawks, Minnesota North Stars in 1985 Norris Division Final. Chicago won best-of-seven series 4-2, outscoring Minnesota 33-29.
60 — Edmonton Oilers, Calgary Flames in 1984 Smythe Division Final. Edmonton won best-of-seven series 4-3, outscoring Calgary 33-27.

MOST GOALS ONE TEAM, ONE PLAYOFF SERIES:
44 — Edmonton Oilers in 1985 Campbell Conference Final. Edmonton won best-of-seven series 4-2, outscoring Chicago 44-25.
35 — Edmonton Oilers in 1983 Smythe Division Final. Edmonton won best-of-seven series 4-1, outscoring Calgary 35-13.

MOST GOALS, BOTH TEAMS, THREE-GAME SERIES:
33 — Minnesota North Stars, Boston Bruins in 1981 Preliminary Round. Minnesota won best-of-five series 3-0, outscoring Boston 20-13.
31 — Chicago Black Hawks, Detroit Red Wings in 1985 Norris Division Semi-Final. Chicago won best-of-five series 3-0, outscoring Detroit 23-8.
28 — Toronto Maple Leafs, New York Rangers in 1932 Final. Toronto won best-of-five series 3-0, outscoring New York 18-10.

MOST GOALS, ONE TEAM, THREE-GAME SERIES:
23 — Chicago Black Hawks in 1985 Norris Division Semi-Final. Chicago won best-of-five series 3-0, outscoring Detroit 23-8.
20 — Minnesota North Stars in 1981 Preliminary Round. Minnesota won best-of-five series 3-0, outscoring Boston 20-13.
— New York Islanders in 1981 Preliminary Round. New York won best-of-five series 3-0, outscoring Toronto 20-4.

MOST GOALS, BOTH TEAMS, FOUR-GAME SERIES:
36 — Boston Bruins, St. Louis Blues in 1972 Semi-Final. Boston won best-of-seven series 4-0, outscoring St. Louis 28-8.
35 — New York Rangers, Los Angeles Kings in 1981 Preliminary Round. New York won best-of-five series 3-1, outscoring Los Angeles 23-12.

MOST GOALS, ONE TEAM, FOUR-GAME SERIES:
28 — Boston Bruins in 1972 Semi-Final. Boston won best-of-seven series 4-0, outscoring St. Louis 28-8.

MOST GOALS, BOTH TEAMS, FIVE-GAME SERIES:
50 — Los Angeles Kings, Edmonton Oilers in 1982 Division Semi-Final. Los Angeles won best-of-five series 3-2, outscoring Edmonton 27-23.
48 — Edmonton Oilers, Calgary Flames in 1983 Smythe Division Final. Edmonton won best-of-seven series 4-1, outscoring Calgary 35-13.
44 — Quebec Nordiques, Buffalo Sabres in 1985 Adams Division Semi-Final. Quebec won best-of-five series 3-2, with each team scoring 22 goals.

MOST GOALS, ONE TEAM, FIVE-GAME SERIES:
35 — Edmonton Oilers in 1983 Smythe Division Final. Edmonton won best-of-seven series 4-1, outscoring Calgary 35-13.
28 — New York Rangers in 1979 Quarter-Final. New York won best-of-seven series 4-1, outscoring Philadelphia 28-8.
27 — Philadelphia Flyers in 1980 Semi-Final. Philadelphia won best-of-seven series 4-1, outscoring Minnesota 27-14.
— Los Angeles Kings in 1982 Division Semi-Final. Los Angeles won best-of-five series 3-2, outscoring Edmonton 27-23.

MOST GOALS, BOTH TEAMS, SIX-GAME SERIES:
69 — Edmonton Oilers, Chicago Black Hawks in 1985 Campbell Conference Final. Edmonton won best-of-seven series 4-2, outscoring Chicago 44-25.
62 — Chicago Black Hawks, Minnesota North Stars in 1985 Norris Division Final. Chicago won best-of-seven series 4-2, outscoring Minnesota 33-29.
56 — Montreal Canadiens, Chicago Black Hawks in 1973 Final. Montreal won best-of-seven series 4-2, outscoring Chicago 33-23.

Stanley Cup Standings

1918-1986

Team	Yrs.	Series	Won	Lost	Games	Won	Lost	Tied	GF	GA	Cup Wins	Winning %
Montreal	61	110*	71	38	511	311	192	8	1580	1229	22**	.616
Toronto	51	84	46	38	372	175	193	4	943	987	11	.476
Boston	47	76	34	42	358	172	180	6	1046	1032	5	.480
Chicago	41	68	30	38	295	134	156	5	824	939	3	.454
New York Rangers	38	68	32	36	288	134	146	8	788	813	3	.465
Detroit	36	60	31	29	281	135	145	1	722	742	7	.480
Philadelphia	17	35	20	15	171	88	83	0	541	524	2	.515
St. Louis	16	28	12	16	138	59	79	0	363	429	0	.428
Minnesota	13	24	11	13	124	59	65	0	419	438	0	.476
New York Islanders	12	35	27	8	171	109	62	0	621	473	4	.637
Los Angeles	12	16	4	12	69	24	45	0	189	265	0	.348
Buffalo	12	21	9	12	93	44	49	0	293	311	0	.473
Calgary***	12	19	7	12	82	37	45	0	257	311	0	.451
Pittsburgh	9	12	3	9	51	21	30	0	135	175	0	.412
Vancouver	9	12	3	9	45	16	29	0	125	175	0	.356
Edmonton	7	18	13	5	80	54	26	0	410	267	2	.675
Quebec	6	11	5	6	55	24	31	0	164	187	0	.436
Winnipeg	5	6	1	5	21	4	17	0	63	102	0	.190
Washington	4	6	2	4	26	12	14	0	85	82	0	.462
Hartford	2	3	1	2	13	6	7	0	37	41	0	.462
New Jersey****	1	1	0	1	2	0	2	0	3	6	0	.000

* 1919 final incomplete due to influenza epidemic.
** Canadiens also won the Stanley Cup in 1916.
*** Includes totals of Atlanta 1974-80.
**** Includes totals of Colorado 1976-82.

MOST GOALS, ONE TEAM, SIX-GAME SERIES:
44 — Edmonton Oilers in 1985 Campbell Conference Final vs. Chicago. Edmonton won best-of-seven series 4-2, outscoring Chicago 44-25.
33 — Chicago Black Hawks in 1985 Norris Division Final vs. Minnesota. Chicago won best-of-seven series 4-2, outscoring Minnesota 33-29.
— Montreal Canadiens in 1973 Final. Montreal won best-of-seven series 4-2, outscoring Chicago 33-23.

MOST GOALS, BOTH TEAMS, SEVEN-GAME SERIES:
60 — Edmonton Oilers, Calgary Flames in 1984 Smythe Division Final. Edmonton won best-of-seven series 4-3, outscoring Calgary 33-27.

MOST GOALS, ONE TEAM, SEVEN-GAME SERIES:
33 — Philadelphia Flyers in 1976 Quarter-Final against Toronto. Philadelphia won best-of-seven series 4-3, outscoring Toronto 33-23.
— Edmonton Oilers in 1984 Smythe Division Final against Calgary. Edmonton won best-of-seven series 4-3, outscoring Calgary 33-27.
— Boston Bruins in 1983 Adams Division Final vs. Buffalo. Boston won best-of-seven series 4-3, outscoring Buffalo 33-23.

FEWEST GOALS, BOTH TEAMS, TWO-GAME SERIES:
1 — New York Rangers, New York Americans, in 1929 Semi-Final. Rangers defeated Americans 1-0 in two-game, total-goal series.
— Montreal Maroons, Chicago Black Hawks in 1935 Semi-Final. Montreal defeated Chicago 1-0 in two-game, total-goal series.

FEWEST GOALS, ONE TEAM, TWO-GAME SERIES:
0 — Montreal Maroons in 1937 Semi-Final. Lost best-of-three series 2-0 to New York Rangers while being outscored 5-0.
— New York Americans in 1939 Quarter-Final. Lost best-of-three series 2-0 to Toronto while being outscored 6-0.
— New York Americans in 1929 Semi-Final. Lost two-game total series 1-0 against New York Rangers.
— Chicago Black Hawks in 1935 Semi-Final. Lost two-game total goal series 1-0 against Montreal Maroons.

FEWEST GOALS, BOTH TEAMS, THREE-GAME SERIES:
7 — Boston, Montreal Canadiens in 1929 Semi-Final. Boston won best-of-five series 3-0, outscoring Montreal 5-2.

FEWEST GOALS, ONE TEAM, THREE-GAME SERIES:
0 — Montreal Maroons in 1936 Semi-Final. Lost best-of-five series 3-0 to Detroit and were outscored 6-0.

FEWEST GOALS, BOTH TEAMS, FOUR-GAME SERIES:
9 — Toronto, Boston in 1935 Semi-Final. Toronto won best-of-five series 3-1, outscoring Boston 7-2.

FEWEST GOALS, ONE TEAM, FOUR-GAME SERIES:
2 — Boston Bruins in 1935 Semi-Final. Toronto won best-of-five series 3-1, outscoring Boston 7-2.
— Montreal Canadiens in 1952 Final. Detroit won best-of-seven series 4-0, outscoring Montreal 11-2.

FEWEST GOALS, BOTH TEAMS, FIVE-GAME SERIES:
11 — New York Rangers, Montreal Maroons in 1928 Final. New York won best-of-five series 3-2 , while outscored by Maroons 6-5.

FEWEST GOALS, ONE TEAM, FIVE-GAME SERIES:
5 — **New York Rangers** in 1928 Final. New York won best-of-five series 3-2, while outscored by Montreal Maroons 6-5.

FEWEST GOALS, BOTH TEAMS, SIX-GAME SERIES:
22 — **Toronto, Boston** in 1951 Semi-Final. Toronto won best-of-seven series 4-1 with one tie, outscoring Boston 17-5.

FEWEST GOALS, ONE TEAM, SIX-GAME SERIES:
5 — **Boston Bruins** in 1951 Semi-Final. Toronto won best-of-seven series 4-1 with one tie, outscoring Boston 17-5.

FEWEST GOALS, BOTH TEAMS, SEVEN-GAME SERIES:
18 — **Toronto, Detroit** in 1945 Final. Toronto won best-of-seven series 4-3; teams tied in scoring 9-9.

FEWEST GOALS, ONE TEAM, SEVEN-GAME SERIES:
9 — **Toronto Maple Leafs**, in 1945 Final. Toronto won best-of- seven series 4-3; teams tied in scoring 9-9.
— **Detroit Red Wings**, in 1945 Final. Toronto won best-of-seven series 4-3; teams tied in scoring 9-9.

MOST GOALS, BOTH TEAMS, ONE GAME:
18 — **Los Angeles, Edmonton** at Edmonton, April 7, 1982. Los Angeles 10, Edmonton 8. Los Angeles won best-of-five Division Semi-Final series 3-2.
15 — **Chicago, Montreal** at Montreal, May 8, 1973. Chicago 8, Montreal 7. Montreal won best-of-seven Final series 4-2.
— **Minnesota North Stars, Boston Bruins**, at Boston, April 9, 1981. Minnesota 9, Boston 6, Minnesota won best-of-five Preliminary Round series 3-0.
— **Edmonton, Chicago** at Edmonton, May 14, 1985. Edmonton 10, Chicago 5. Edmonton won best-of-seven Campbell Conference Final series 4-2.

MOST GOALS, ONE TEAM, ONE-GAME:
11 — **Montreal Canadiens** at Montreal, March 30, 1944. Canadiens 11, Toronto 0. Canadiens won best-of-seven Semi-Final 4-1.
— **Edmonton Oilers** at Edmonton May 4, 1985. Edmonton 11, Chicago 2. Edmonton won best-of-seven Campbell Conference Final 4-2.

MOST GOALS, BOTH TEAMS, ONE PERIOD:
9 — **New York Rangers, Philadelphia Flyers**, April 24, 1979, at Philadelphia, third period. Rangers won game 8-3 scoring six of nine third-period goals.
8 — Chicago, Montreal at Montreal, May 8, 1973, in the second period. Chicago won the game 8-7 scoring five of eight second-period goals.
— Chicago, Edmonton at Chicago, May 12, 1985 in the first period. Chicago won the game 8-6, scoring five of eight first-period goals.

MOST GOALS, ONE TEAM, ONE PERIOD:
7 — **Montreal Canadiens**, March 30, 1944, at Montreal in third period, during 11-0 win over Toronto.

LONGEST OVERTIME:
116 Minutes, 30 Seconds — **Detroit, Montreal Maroons** at Montreal, March 24-25, 1936. Detroit 1, Maroons 0. Mud Bruneteau scored, assisted by Hec Kilrea, at 16:30 of sixth overtime period, or after 176 minutes, 30 seconds from start of game, which ended at 2:25 a.m. Detroit won best-of-five semi-final 3-0.

SHORTEST OVERTIME:
9 Seconds — **Montreal Canadiens, Calgary Flames**, at Calgary, May 18, 1986. Montreal won game 3-2 on Brian Skrudland's goal and captured the best-of-seven Final series 4-1.
11 Seconds — **New York Islanders, New York Rangers**, at NY Rangers, April 11, 1975. NY Islanders won game 4-3 on Jean-Paul Parise's goal and captured the best-of-three series 2-1.

MOST OVERTIME GAMES, ONE PLAYOFF YEAR:
16 — **1982**. Of 71 games played, 16 went into overtime: one in Division Semi-Final won by Quebec 3-2 against Montreal; two in Division Semi-Final won by NY Islanders 3-2 against Pittsburgh; one in Division Semi-Final won by Chicago 3-1 against Minnesota; two in Division Semi-Final won by Los Angeles 3-2 against Edmonton; one in Division Semi-Final won by Vancouver 3-0 against Calgary; two in Division Final won by Quebec 4-3 against Boston; one in Division Final won by NY Islanders 4-2 against NY Rangers; one in Division Final won by Chicago 4-2 against St. Louis; two in Division Final won by Vancouver 4-1 against Los Angeles; one in Conference Championship won by NY Islanders 4-0 against Quebec; one in Conference Championship won by Vancouver 4-1 against Chicago; one in Stanley Cup Championship won by NY Islanders 4-0 against Vancouver.

FEWEST OVERTIME GAMES, ONE PLAYOFF YEAR:
0 — **1963**. None of the 16 games went into overtime, the only year since 1926 that no overtime was required in any playoff series.

MOST OVERTIME-GAME VICTORIES, ONE TEAM, ONE PLAYOFF YEAR:
6 — **New York Islanders**, 1980. One against Los Angeles in the Preliminary Round; two against Boston in the Quarter-Final; one against Buffalo in the Semi-Final; and two against Philadelphia in the Final. Islanders played 21 games.

MOST OVERTIME GAMES, FINAL SERIES:
5 — **Toronto, Montreal Canadiens** in 1951. Toronto defeated Canadiens 4-1 in best-of-seven series.

MOST OVERTIME GAMES, SEMI-FINAL SERIES:
4 — **Toronto, Boston** in 1933. Toronto won best-of-five series 3-2.
— **Boston, New York Rangers** in 1939. Boston won best-of-seven series 4-3.
— **St. Louis, Minnesota** in 1968. St. Louis won best-of-seven series 4-3.

MOST GAMES PLAYED BY ALL TEAMS, ONE PLAYOFF YEAR:
72 — **1986**. There were 28 Division Semi-Final games; 27 Division Final games; 12 Conference Championship games; and 5 Stanley Cup Final games.
71 — **1982**. There were 34 Division Semi-Final games; 24 Division Final games; 9 Conference Championship games; and 4 Stanley Cup Final games.

MOST GAMES PLAYED, ONE TEAM, ONE PLAYOFF YEAR:
22 — **Calgary Flames,** 1986. Won Div. SF series 3-0 against Winnipeg; Division Final 4-3 against Edmonton; Conf. Champ. 4-3 against St. Louis and lost Final 4-1 against Montreal.
21 — **New York Islanders**, 1980. Won a Preliminary Round series 3-1 against Los Angeles; a Quarter-Final 4-1 against Boston; a Semi-Final 4-2 against Buffalo; and the Final 4-2 against Philadelphia.
— **New York Islanders**, 1984. Won Div. SF series 3-2 against NY Rangers; Div. Final 4-1 against Washington; Conf. Champ. 4-2 against Montreal and lost Final 4-1 against Edmonton.

MOST ROAD VICTORIES, ONE TEAM, ONE PLAYOFF YEAR:
8 — **New York Islanders**, 1980. Won two at Los Angeles in a Preliminary Round series; three at Boston in a Quarter-Final series; two at Buffalo in a Semi-Final series; and one at Philadelphia in the Final series.

MOST HOME VICTORIES, ONE TEAM, ONE PLAYOFF YEAR:
10 — **Edmonton Oilers**, 1985 in 10 home-ice games.
— **Montreal Canadiens**, 1986
9 — Philadelphia Flyers, 1974.
— New York Islanders, 1981.
— New York Islanders, 1983.
— Edmonton Oilers, 1984.

MOST LOSSES BY HOME TEAMS, ONE PLAYOFF YEAR:
31 — **1986**. Of 72 games played, the home teams lost 31. 14 in Div. Semi-finals; 12 in Div. Finals; 3 in Conf.Championships and 2 in Final Series.
30 — **1980**. Of 67 games played, the home teams lost 30. 11 in eight Preliminary Round series; 12 in four Quarter-Final series; 6 in two Semi-Final series; and 1 in Final Series.
— **1984**. Of 70 games played, the home teams lost 30. 14 in Div. Semi-Finals; 12 in Div. Finals; 3 in Conf. Championships and 1 in Final series.

MOST CONSECUTIVE PLAYOFF GAME VICTORIES:
12 — **Edmonton Oilers.** Streak began May 15, 1984 at Edmonton with a 7-2 win over New York Islanders in third game of Final series, and ended May 9, 1985 when Chicago Black Hawks defeated Edmonton 5-2 at Chicago. Included in the streak were three wins over the Islanders, in 1984, three over the Los Angeles Kings, four over the Winnipeg Jets and two over the Black Hawks, all in 1985.

Marcel Bonin and coach Toe Blake celebrate the 1959 Stanley Cup victory.

11 — Montreal Canadiens. Streak began April 16, 1959, at Toronto with 3-2 win in fourth game of Final series, won by Canadiens 4-1, and ended March 23, 1961, when Chicago defeated Canadiens 4-3 in second game of Semi-Final series. Included in streak were eight straight victories in 1960.
— Montreal Canadiens. Streak began April 28, 1968, at Montreal with 4-3 win in fifth game of Semi-Final series, won by Canadiens 4-2, and ended April 17, 1969, at Boston when Bruins defeated them 5-0 in third game of Semi-Final series. Included in the streak were four straight wins over St. Louis in the 1968 Final and four straight wins over New York Rangers in a 1969 Quarter-Final series.
— Boston Bruins. Streak began April 14, 1970, at Boston with 3-2 victory over New York Rangers in fifth game of a Quarter-Final series, won by Bruins 4-2. It continued with a four-game victory over Chicago in the 1970 Semi-Final and a four-game win over St. Louis in the 1970 Final. Boston then won the first game of a 1971 Quarter-Final series against Montreal. Canadiens ended the streak April 8, 1971, at Boston with a 7-5 victory.
— Montreal Canadiens. Streak started May 6, 1976, at Montreal with 5-2 win in fifth game of a Semi-Final series against New York Islanders, won by Montreal 4-1. Continued with a four-game sweep over Philadelphia in the 1976 Final and a four-game win over St. Louis in the 1977 Quarter-Final. Canadiens won the first two games of a 1977 Semi-Final series against the Islanders before Islanders ended the streak, April 2, 1977 at Long Island with a 5-3 victory.

MOST CONSECUTIVE VICTORIES, ONE PLAYOFF YEAR:
10 — **Boston Bruins** in 1970. Bruins won last two games of best-of-seven Quarter-Final against New York Rangers to win series 4-2 and then defeated Chicago 4-0 in best-of-seven Semi-Final and St. Louis 4-0 in best-of-seven Final.

LONGEST PLAYOFF LOSING STREAK:
16 Games — Chicago Black Hawks. Streak started in 1975 Quarter-Final against Buffalo when Hawks lost last two games. Then Hawks lost four games to Montreal in 1976 Quarter-Final; two games to New York Islanders in 1977 Preliminary Round; four games to Boston in 1978 Quarter-Final and four games to New York Islanders in 1979 Quarter-Final. Streak ended on April 8, 1980 when Chicago defeated St. Louis 3-2 in the opening game of their 1980 Preliminary Round series.

12 Games — Toronto Maple Leafs. Streak started on April 16, 1979 as Toronto lost four straight games in a Quarter-Final series against Montreal. Continued with three-game Preliminary Round defeats versus Philadelphia and NY Islanders in 1980 and 1981 respectively. Toronto failed to qualify for the 1982 playoffs and lost the first two games of a 1983 Division Semi-Final against Minnesota. Toronto ended the streak with a 6-3 win against the North Stars on April 9, 1983.

10 Games — New York Rangers. Streak started in 1968 Quarter-Final against Chicago when Rangers lost last four games and continued through 1969 (four straight losses to Montreal in Quarter-Final) and 1970 (two straight losses to Boston in Quarter-Final) before ending with a 4-3 win against Boston, at New York, April 11, 1970.
— **Philadelphia Flyers.** Streak started on April 18, 1968, the last game in the 1968 Quarter-Final series against St. Louis, and continued through 1969 (four straight losses to Chicago in Quarter-Final) and 1973 (opening game loss to Minnesota in Quarter-Final) before ending with a 4-1 win against Minnesota, at Philadelphia, April 5, 1973.

MOST SHUTOUTS, ONE PLAYOFF YEAR, ALL TEAMS:
8 — 1937. Of 17 games played, New York Rangers had four. Detroit three, Boston one.
— **1975.** Of 51 games played, Philadelphia had five, Montreal two, New York Islanders one.
— **1980.** Of 67 games played, Buffalo had three, Philadelphia two, Montreal, NY Islanders and Minnesota one each.
— **1984.** Of 70 games played, Montreal had 3, Edmonton, Minnesota, NY Rangers, St. Louis and Vancouver one each.

FEWEST SHUTOUTS, ONE PLAYOFF YEAR, ALL TEAMS:
0 — 1959. Of 18 games played.

MOST SHUTOUTS, BOTH TEAMS, ONE SERIES:
5 — 1945 Final, Toronto, Detroit. Toronto had three shutouts, Detroit two. Toronto won best-of-seven series 4-3.
— **1950 Semi-Final, Toronto, Detroit.** Toronto had three shutouts, Detroit two. Detroit won best-of-seven series 4-3.

MOST PENALTIES, BOTH TEAMS, ONE SERIES:
167 — Calgary, St. Louis, in 1986 Conference Championship won by Calgary 4-3. Calgary received 69 minors, 8 majors, 7 10-minute misconducts. St. Louis received 68 minors, 9 majors, 6 10-minute misconducts.

MOST PENALTY MINUTES, BOTH TEAMS, ONE SERIES:
560 — Vancouver, Chicago in 1982 Conference Final won by Vancouver 4-1. Vancouver had 285 minutes, Chicago 275.

MOST PENALTIES, ONE TEAM, ONE SERIES:
92 — Philadelphia Flyers in 1976 Quarter-Final against Toronto. Philadelphia received 70 minors, 13 majors, three 10-minute misconducts and six game misconducts.

MOST PENALTY MINUTES, ONE TEAM, ONE SERIES:
295 — Philadelphia Flyers in 1976 Quarter-Final against Toronto. Philadelphia won series 4-3.

MOST PENALTIES, BOTH TEAMS, ONE GAME (AND) MOST PENALTY MINUTES, BOTH TEAMS, ONE GAME:
59 Penalties; 267 Minutes — New York Rangers, Los Angeles Kings, at Los Angeles, April 9, 1981. Rangers received 31 penalties for 142 minutes; Los Angeles 28 penalties for 125 minutes. Los Angeles won game 5-4.

MOST PENALTIES, ONE TEAM, ONE GAME:
31 — New York Rangers, at Los Angeles, April 9, 1981. Kings won game 5-4.
30 — Philadelphia Flyers, at Toronto, April 15, 1976. Toronto won game 5-4.

MOST PENALTY MINUTES, ONE TEAM, ONE GAME:
142 — New York Rangers, at Los Angeles, April 9, 1981. Los Angeles won game 5-4.

MOST PENALTIES, BOTH TEAMS, ONE PERIOD:
43 — New York Rangers, Los Angeles Kings, April 9, 1981, at Los Angeles, first period. Rangers had 24 penalties; Los Angeles 19. Los Angeles won game 5-4.

MOST PENALTY MINUTES, BOTH TEAMS, ONE PERIOD:
248 — New York Islanders, Boston Bruins, April 17, 1980, first period, at Boston. Each team received 124 minutes. Islanders won 5-4.

MOST PENALTIES, ONE TEAM, ONE PERIOD: (AND) MOST PENALTY MINUTES, ONE TEAM, ONE PERIOD:
24 Penalties; 125 Minutes — New York Rangers, April 9, 1981, at Los Angeles, first period. Los Angeles won game 5-4.

FEWEST PENALTIES, BOTH TEAMS, BEST-OF-SEVEN SERIES:
19 — Detroit, Toronto in 1945 Final, won by Toronto 4-3. Detroit received 10 minors. Toronto 9 minors.

FEWEST PENALTIES, ONE TEAM, BEST-OF-SEVEN SERIES:
9 — Toronto Maple Leafs in 1945 Final, won by Leafs 4-3 against Detroit.

MOST POWER-PLAY GOALS BY ALL TEAMS, ONE PLAYOFF YEAR:
150 — 1981 during 68 games.

MOST POWER-PLAY GOALS, ONE TEAM, ONE PLAYOFF YEAR:
31 — New York Islanders, 1981. 6 against Toronto in Preliminary Round, won by Islanders 3-0; 13 against Edmonton in Quarter-Final, won by Islanders 4-2; 7 against NY Rangers in Semi-Final, won by Islanders 4-0; and 5 in Final against Minnesota, won by Islanders 4-1.
25 — New York Islanders, 1980, during 21 games.
— **Calgary Flames,** 1986, during 22 games.
24 — Minnesota North Stars, 1981, during 19 games.

MOST POWER-PLAY GOALS, BOTH TEAMS, ONE SERIES:
21 — New York Islanders, Philadelphia Flyers in 1980 Final Series, won by Islanders 4-2. Islanders had 15 and Flyers 6.
— **New York Islanders, Edmonton Oilers** in 1981 Quarter-Final, won by Islanders 4-2. Islanders had 13 and Oilers 8.
20 — Toronto, Philadelphia in 1976 Quarter-Final series won by Philadelphia 4-3. Toronto had 12 power-play goals; Philadelphia 8.

MOST POWER-PLAY GOALS, ONE TEAM, ONE SERIES:
15 — New York Islanders in 1980 Final Series against Philadelphia. Islanders won series 4-2.
13 — New York Islanders in 1981 Quarter-Final against Edmonton. Islanders won series 4-2.
— **Calgary Flames** in 1986 Conference Championship against St. Louis. Calgary won series 4-3.
12 — Toronto Maple Leafs in 1976 Quarter-Final series won by Philadelphia 4-3.

Early Playoff Records

1893-1918
Team Records

MOST GOALS, BOTH TEAMS, ONE GAME:
25 — Ottawa Silver Seven, Dawson City at Ottawa, Jan. 16, 1905. Ottawa 23, Dawson City 2. Ottawa won best-of-three series 2-0.

MOST GOALS, ONE TEAM, ONE GAME:
23 — Ottawa Silver Seven at Ottawa, Jan. 16, 1905. Ottawa defeated Dawson City 23-2.

MOST GOALS, BOTH TEAMS, BEST-OF-THREE SERIES:
42 — Ottawa Silver Seven, Queen's at Ottawa, 1906. Ottawa defeated Queen's 16-7, Feb. 27, and 12-7, Feb. 28.

MOST GOALS, ONE TEAM, BEST-OF-THREE SERIES:
32 — Ottawa Silver Seven in 1905 at Ottawa. Defeated Dawson City 9-2, Jan. 13, and 23-2, Jan. 16.

MOST GOALS, BOTH TEAMS, BEST-OF-FIVE SERIES:
39 — Toronto Arenas, Vancouver at Toronto, 1918. Arenas won 5-3, Mar. 20; 6-3, Mar. 26; 2-1, Mar. 30. Vancouver won 6-4, Mar. 23, and 8-1, Mar. 28. Toronto scored 18 goals; Vancouver 21.

MOST GOALS, ONE TEAM, BEST-OF-FIVE SERIES:
26 — Vancouver in 1915 at Vancouver. Defeated Ottawa Senators 6-2, Mar. 22; 8-3, Mar. 24; and 12-3, Mar. 26.

Individual Records
MOST GOALS IN PLAYOFFS:
63 — Frank McGee, Ottawa Silver Seven, in 22 playoff games. Seven goals in four games, 1903; 21 goals in eight games, 1904; 18 goals in four games, 1905; 17 goals in six games, 1906.

MOST GOALS, ONE PLAYOFF SERIES:
15 — Frank McGee, Ottawa Silver Seven, in two games in 1905 at Ottawa. Scored one goal, Jan. 13, in 9-2 victory over Dawson City and 14 goals, Jan. 16, in 23-2 victory.

MOST GOALS, ONE PLAYOFF GAME:
14 — Frank McGee, Ottawa Silver Seven, Jan. 16, 1905 at Ottawa in 23-2 victory over Dawson City.

FASTEST THREE GOALS:
40 Seconds — Marty Walsh, Ottawa Senators, at Ottawa, March 16, 1911, at 3:00, 3:10, and 3:40 of third period. Ottawa defeated Port Arthur 13-4.

MOST POWER-PLAY GOALS, BOTH TEAMS, ONE GAME:
7 — Minnesota North Stars, Edmonton Oilers, April 28, 1984 at Minnesota. Minnesota had 4, Edmonton 3. Edmonton won game 8-5.
— **Philadelphia Flyers, New York Rangers,** April 13, 1985 at New York. Philadelphia had 4, New York 3. Philadelphia won game 6-5.
— **Edmonton Oilers, Chicago Black Hawks,** May 14, 1985 at Edmonton. Chicago had 5, Edmonton 2. Edmonton won game 10-5.
6 — Detroit Red Wings, Montreal Canadiens, March 23, 1939, at Detroit. Detroit had four power-play goals, Montreal two. Detroit won game 7-3.
— Boston Bruins, April 2, 1969, at Boston against Toronto Maple Leafs. Boston won game 10-0, scoring six power-play goals.
— Boston Bruins, Chicago Black Hawks, April 21, 1974, at Boston. Each had three power-play goals. Boston won game 8-6.
— Philadelphia, Toronto, April 15, 1976, at Toronto. Toronto had five power-play goals, Philadelphia had one. Toronto won game 5-4.
— New York Islanders, Edmonton Oilers, April 17, 1981, at New York. Islanders had four, Edmonton two power-play goals. Islanders won game 6-3.
— New York Rangers, Philadelphia Flyers, April 8, 1982, at New York. Rangers had four, Philadelphia two power-play goals. New York won game 7-3.

MOST POWER-PLAY GOALS, ONE TEAM, ONE GAME:
6 — Boston Bruins, April 2, 1969, at Boston against Toronto Maple Leafs. Boston won game 10-0.

MOST POWER-PLAY GOALS, BOTH TEAMS, ONE PERIOD:
5 — Minnesota North Stars, Edmonton Oilers, April 28, 1984, second period, at Minnesota. North Stars had four and Oilers one. Edmonton won game 8-5.
4 — Toronto Maple Leafs, Boston Bruins, March 26, 1936, second period, at Toronto. Maple Leafs scored four power-play goals and won game 8-3.
— Detroit Red Wings, Montreal Canadiens, March 23, 1939, second period at Detroit. Each had two power-play goals. Detroit won game 7-3.
— Detroit Red Wings, Chicago Black Hawks, April 4, 1965, third period at Detroit. Detroit had three power-play goals. Chicago one. Detroit won game 6-3.
— Minnesota North Stars, Toronto Maple Leafs, April 8, 1980, at Minnesota, first period. Each team had two. Minnesota won 6-3.
— New York Islanders, Edmonton Oilers, April 17, 1981, at Long Island, second period. Islanders had three power-play goals, Edmonton one. Islanders won game 6-3.
— Philadelphia Flyers, New York Rangers, April 13, 1985 at New York, second period. Philadelphia had three power-play goals, New York one. Philadelphia won game 6-5.

MOST POWER-PLAY GOALS, ONE TEAM, ONE PERIOD:
4 — Toronto Maple Leafs, March 26, 1936, second period against Boston at Toronto. Toronto won game 8-3.
— **Minnesota North Stars,** April 28, 1984, second period against Edmonton. Oilers won game 8-5.

MOST SHORTHAND GOALS BY ALL TEAMS, ONE PLAYOFF YEAR:
27 — 1986, during 72 games.
26 — 1981, during 68 games.

MOST SHORTHAND GOALS, ONE TEAM, ONE PLAYOFF YEAR:
10 — Edmonton Oilers 1983, in 16 games.
9 — New York Islanders, 1981, in 19 games.
7 — New York Islanders, 1980, in 21 games.
6 — New York Rangers, 1979, in 10 games.
— Minnesota North Stars, 1981, in 18 games.

MOST SHORT-HAND GOALS, BOTH TEAMS, ONE SERIES:
7 — Boston Bruins (4), New York Rangers (3), in 1958 semi-final, won by Boston 4-2.
— **Edmonton Oilers (5), Calgary Flames (2),** in 1983 Smythe Division Final won by Edmonton 4-1.

MOST SHORT-HAND GOALS, ONE TEAM, ONE SERIES:
5 — Edmonton Oilers in 1983 best-of-seven Smythe Division Final won by Edmonton 4-1.
— **New York Rangers** in 1979 against Philadelphia Flyers in best-of-seven Quarter-Final, won by Rangers 4-1.
4 — Boston Bruins in 1958 against New York Rangers in best-of-seven Semi-Final series, won by Boston 4-2.
— Minnesota North Stars in 1981 against Calgary Flames in best-of-seven Semi-Final, won by Minnesota 4-2.

MOST SHORTHAND GOALS, BOTH TEAMS, ONE GAME:
4 — New York Islanders, New York Rangers, April 17, 1983 at NY Rangers. The Islanders scored 3 shorthand goals, Rangers 1. The Rangers won 7-6.
— **Boston Bruins, Minnesota North Stars,** April 11, 1981, at Minnesota. Boston had 3 shorthand goals, Minnesota 1. Minnesota won 6-3.
3 — Toronto Maple Leafs, Detroit Red Wings, April 5, 1947, at Toronto. Toronto had 2 shorthand goals, Detroit, 1. Toronto won 6-1.
— New York Rangers, Boston Bruins, April 1, 1958, at Boston. New York had 2 shorthand goals, Boston, 1. New York won game 5-2.
— Minnesota North Stars, Philadelphia Flyers, May 4, 1980, at Minnesota. Minnesota had 2 shorthand goals, Philadelphia 1. Philadelphia won game 5-3.

MOST SHORTHAND GOALS, ONE TEAM, ONE GAME:
3 — Boston Bruins, April 11, 1981, at Minnesota. Minnesota won 6-3.

MOST SHORT-HAND GOALS, BOTH TEAMS, ONE PERIOD:
3 — Toronto Maple Leafs, Detroit Red Wings, April 5, 1947, at Toronto, first period. Toronto scored two short-hand goals; Detroit one. Toronto won game 6-1.

MOST SHORT-HAND GOALS ONE TEAM, ONE PERIOD:
2 — Toronto Maple Leafs, April 5, 1947, at Toronto against Detroit, first period. Toronto won game 6-1.
— **Toronto Maple Leafs,** April 13, 1965, at Toronto against Montreal, first period. Montreal won game 4-3.
— **Boston Bruins,** April 20, 1969, at Boston against Montreal, first period. Boston won game 3-2.
— **Boston Bruins,** April 8, 1970, at Boston against New York Rangers, second period. Boston won game 8-2.
— **Boston Bruins,** April 30, 1972, at Boston against New York Rangers, first period. Boston won game 6-5.
— **Chicago Black Hawks,** May 3, 1973, at Chicago against Montreal, first period. Chicago won game 7-4.
— **Montreal Canadiens,** April 23, 1978, at Detroit, first period. Montreal won game 8-0.
— **New York Islanders,** April 8, 1980, at New York against Los Angeles, second period. Islanders won 8-1.
— **Los Angeles Kings,** April 9, 1980, at New York Islanders, first period. Los Angeles won 6-3.
— **Boston Bruins,** April 13, 1980, at Pittsburgh, second period. Boston won 8-3.
— **Minnesota North Stars,** May 4, 1980, at Minnesota against Philadelphia, second period. Flyers won 5-3.
— **Boston Bruins,** April 11, 1981, at Minnesota, third period. Minnesota won 6-3.
— **New York Islanders,** May 12, 1981, at New York, first period. Islanders defeated Minnesota 6-3.
— **Montreal Canadiens,** April 7, 1982, at Montreal, third period. Montreal defeated Quebec 5-1.
— **Edmonton Oilers,** April 24, 1983, at Edmonton, third period. Edmonton defeated Chicago 8-4.
— **Winnipeg Jets,** April 14, 1985, at Calgary, second period. Winnipeg defeated Calgary 5-3.

FASTEST TWO GOALS, BOTH TEAMS:
5 Seconds — Pittsburgh, Buffalo at Buffalo, April 14, 1979. Gilbert Perreault scored for Buffalo at 12:59 and Jim Hamilton for Pittsburgh at 13:04 of first period. Pittsburgh won game 4-3 and best-of-three Preliminary Round 2-1.
9 seconds — New York Islanders, Washington Capitals at Washington, April 10, 1986. Bryan Trottier scored for New York at 18:26 of second period and Scott Stevens at 18:35 for Washington. Washington won game 5-2, and won best-of-five Division Semi-Final 3-0.
11 Seconds — Buffalo, Quebec at Buffalo, April 14, 1985. Phil Housley scored for Buffalo at 17:36 of second period and Mike Gillis at 17:47 for Quebec. Buffalo won game 7-4, and Quebec won best-of-five Division Semi-Final 3-2.
13 Seconds — Edmonton, Chicago at Edmonton, May 7, 1985. Glenn Anderson scored for Edmonton at 6:21 of first period and Bob Murray at 6:34 for Chicago. Edmonton won game 7-3 and best-of-seven Conference Final 4-2.

FASTEST TWO GOALS, ONE TEAM:
5 Seconds — Detroit Red Wings at Detroit, April 11, 1965, against Chicago. Norm Ullman scored at 17:35 and 17:40, 2nd period. Detroit won game 4-2. Chicago won best-of-seven Semi-Final 4-3.

FASTEST THREE GOALS, BOTH TEAMS:
21 Seconds — Edmonton, Chicago at Edmonton, May 7, 1985. Behn Wilson scored for Chicago at 19:22 of third period, Jari Kurri at 19:36 and Glenn Anderson at 19:43 for Edmonton. Edmonton Won game 7-3 and best-of-seven Conference Final 4-2.
36 Seconds — Los Angeles, Edmonton at Edmonton, April 7, 1982. Steve Bozek of Los Angeles scored at 6:00 of first period, Tom Roulston of Edmonton scored at 6:16, Risto Siltanen of Edmonton at 6:36. Los Angeles won game 10-8 and best-of-five Division Semi-Final 3-2.
38 Seconds — Toronto, Montreal at Toronto, April 13, 1965. Red Kelly of Toronto scored at 3:11 of first period, John Ferguson of Montreal at 3:32 and Ron Ellis of Toronto at 3:49. Montreal won game 4-3 in overtime and best-of-seven semi-final series 4-2.
— Boston, Philadelphia at Philadelphia, April 26, 1977. Mike Milbury of Boston scored at 15:01 of second period; Gary Dornhoefer of Philadelphia at 15:16; and Jean Ratelle of Boston at 15:39. Boston won game 5-4 and best-of-seven semi-final series 4-0.

FASTEST THREE GOALS, ONE TEAM:
23 Seconds — Toronto Maple Leafs at Toronto, April 12, 1979, against Atlanta Flames. Darryl Sittler scored at 4:04 and 4:16 and Ron Ellis at 4:27, first period. Leafs won game 7-4 and best-of-three Preliminary Round 2-0.
56 Seconds — Montreal Canadiens at Detroit, April 6, 1954. Dickie Moore scored at 15:03 of first period, Maurice Richard at 15:28 and again at 15:59. Canadiens won game 3-1 but Detroit won best-of-seven Final 4-3.

FASTEST FOUR GOALS, BOTH TEAMS:
1 minute, 34 seconds — Montreal, Calgary at Montreal, May 20, 1986. Joel Otto of Calgary scored at 17:59 of first period; Bobby Smith of Montreal at 18:25; Mats Naslund of Montreal at 19:17 and Bob Gainey of Montreal at 19:33. Montreal won game 5-3 and best-of-seven Final series 4-1.
1 Minute, 33 Seconds — Philadelphia, Toronto at Philadelphia, April 20, 1976. Don Saleski of Philadelphia scored at 10:04 of second period; Bob Neely of Toronto at 10:42; Gary Dornhoefer of Philadelphia at 11:24 and Don Saleski again at 11:37. Philadelphia won game 7-1 and best-of-seven Quarter-Final series 4-3.
1 Minute, 38 Seconds — Boston, Philadelphia at Philadelphia, April 26, 1977. Gregg Sheppard of Boston scored at 14:01 of second period; Mike Milbury of Boston at 15:01; Gary Dornhoefer of Philadelphia at 15:16 and Jean Ratelle of Boston at 15:39. Boston won game 5-4 and best-of-seven Semi-Final series 4-0.

FASTEST FOUR GOALS, ONE TEAM:
2 Minutes, 35 Seconds — Montreal Canadiens at Montreal, March 30, 1944, against Toronto. Toe Blake scored at 7:58 of third period and again at 8:37, Maurice Richard at 9:17, Ray Getliffe at 10:33. Canadiens won game 11-0 and best-of-seven Semi-Final 4-0.

FASTEST FIVE GOALS, BOTH TEAMS:
3 Minutes, 6 Seconds — Chicago, Minnesota, at Chicago April 21, 1985. Keith Brown scored for Chicago at 1:12, second period; Ken Yaremchuk, Chicago, at 1:27; Dino Ciccarelli, Minnesota, 2:48; Tony McKegney, Minnesota, 4:07; and Curt Fraser, Chicago, 4:18. Chicago won game 6-2.
3 Minutes, 20 Seconds — Minnesota, Philadelphia, at Philadelphia, April 29, 1980. Paul Shmyr scored for Minnesota at 13:20, first period; Steve Christoff, Minnesota, at 13:59; Ken Linseman, Philadelphia, at 14:54; Tom Gorence, Philadelphia, at 15:36; and Linseman, at 16:40. Minnesota won game 6-5.
4 Minutes, 19 Seconds — Toronto, New York Rangers at Toronto, April 9, 1932. Ace Bailey scored for Toronto at 15:07 of third period, Fred Cook at 16:32 for Rangers, Bob Gracie of Toronto at 17:36, Frank Boucher of Rangers at 18:26 and again at 19:26. Toronto won game 6-4 and best-of-five Final 3-0.

FASTEST FIVE GOALS, ONE TEAM:
3 Minutes, 36 Seconds — Montreal Canadiens at Montreal, March 30, 1944, against Toronto. Toe Blake scored at 7:58 of third period and 8:37, Maurice Richard at 9:17, Ray Getliffe at 10:33 and Buddy O'Connor at 11:34. Canadiens won game 11-0 and best-of-seven Semi-Final 4-0.

MOST THREE-OR-MORE-GOAL GAMES BY ALL TEAMS, ONE PLAYOFF YEAR:
12 — 1983 in 66 games.
11 — 1985 in 70 games.

MOST THREE-OR-MORE GOAL GAMES, ONE TEAM, ONE PLAYOFF YEAR:
6 — Edmonton Oilers in 16 games, 1983.
— Edmonton Oilers in 18 games, 1985.

Individual Records

Career

MOST YEARS IN PLAYOFFS:
20 — Gordie Howe, Detroit, Hartford (1947-58 incl.; 60-61; 63-66 incl.; 70 and 80)
19 — Red Kelly, Detroit, Toronto
18 — Stan Mikita, Chicago Black Hawks

MOST CONSECUTIVE YEARS IN PLAYOFFS:
17 — Brad Park, New York Rangers, Boston, Detroit (1969-1985 inclusive).
16 — Jean Beliveau, Montreal Canadiens (1954-69, inclusive).

MOST PLAYOFF GAMES:
180 — Henri Richard, Montreal Canadiens
167 — Denis Potvin, New York Islanders
164 — Red Kelly, Detroit, Toronto Maple Leafs
162 — Jean Béliveau, Montreal Canadiens

MOST POINTS IN PLAYOFFS (CAREER):
176 — Jean Beliveau, Montreal Canadiens, 79 goals, 97 assists.
175 — Wayne Gretzky, Edmonton Oilers, 64 goals, 111 assists.
160 — Gordie Howe, Detroit, Hartford, 68 goals, 92 assists.

MOST GOALS IN PLAYOFFS (CAREER):
83 — Mike Bossy, New York Islanders
82 — Maurice Richard, Montreal Canadiens
— Mike Bossy, New York Islanders
79 — Jean Beliveau, Montreal Canadiens

MOST GAME-WINNING GOALS IN PLAYOFFS (CAREER):
18 — Maurice Richard, Montreal Canadiens, in 15 playoff years.
17 — Mike Bossy, New York Islanders, in 7 playoff years.
15 — Jean Beliveau, Montreal Canadiens, in 17 playoff years.
— Yvan Cournoyer, Montreal Canadiens, in 12 playoff years.

MOST OVERTIME GOALS IN PLAYOFFS (CAREER):
6 — Maurice Richard, Montreal Canadiens. (1 in 1946; 3 in 1951; 1 in 1957; 1 in 1958.)
4 — Bob Nystrom, New York Islanders.
3 — Mel Hill, Boston Bruins.
— Rene Robert, Buffalo Sabres.
— Danny Gare, Buffalo Sabres.
— Jacques Lemaire, Montreal Canadiens.
— Bobby Clarke, Philadelphia Flyers.
— Terry O'Reilly, Boston Bruins.
— Mike Bossy, New York Islanders
— Dale Hunter, Quebec Nordiques
— Steve Payne, Minnesota North Stars
— Ken Morrow, New York Islanders
— Lanny McDonald, Toronto Maple Leafs, Calgary Flames.

Jean Beliveau leads the NHL with 176 points in 162 playoff games.

MOST POWER-PLAY GOALS IN PLAYOFFS (CAREER):
33 — Mike Bossy, New York Islanders, in 8 years.
26 — Jean Beliveau, Montreal Canadiens, in 17 years.
— Denis Potvin, New York Islanders, in 11 years.
22 — Bobby Hull, Chicago Black Hawks, in 13 years.
— Phil Esposito, Chicago, Boston, NY Rangers in 15 years.
21 — Bernie Geoffrion, Montreal Canadiens, NY Rangers, in 16 years.

MOST SHORTHAND GOALS IN PLAYOFFS (CAREER):
8 — Ed Westfall, Boston Bruins, New York Islanders, in 9 years.
— Wayne Gretzky, Edmonton Oilers, in 7 years.
7 — Mark Messier, Edmonton Oilers, in 7 years.
6 — Dave Keon, Toronto Maple Leafs, in 12 years.
— Derek Sanderson, Boston Bruins, in 8 years.
5 — Lorne Henning, New York Islanders, in 7 years.
— Bob Bourne, New York Islanders, in 9 years
— Anders Kallur, New York Islanders, in 6 years.

MOST THREE-OR-MORE-GOAL GAMES IN PLAYOFFS (CAREER):
7 — Maurice Richard, Montreal Canadiens. Four three-goal games; two four-goal games; one five-goal game.
6 — Wayne Gretzky, Edmonton Oilers. Two four-goal games; five three-goal games.
5 — Mike Bossy, New York Islanders. Four three-goal games; one four-goal game.
— Jari Kurri, Edmonton Oilers. One four-goal game; four three-goal games.

MOST ASSISTS IN PLAYOFFS (CAREER):
111 — Wayne Gretzky, Edmonton Oilers.
102 — Denis Potvin, New York Islanders
101 — Bryan Trottier, New York Islanders
97 — Jean Béliveau, Montreal Canadiens.
92 — Gordie Howe, Detroit, Hartford.
91 — Stan Mikita, Chicago Black Hawks.

MOST PENALTY MINUTES IN PLAYOFFS (CAREER):
425 — Dave Williams, Toronto Maple Leafs, Vancouver Canucks, Los Angeles Kings.
412 — Dave Schultz, Philadelphia Flyers, Los Angeles Kings, Buffalo Sabres.
392 — Willi Plett, Atlanta, Calgary Flames, Minnesota North Stars.
352 — Andre Dupont, Philadelphia Flyers, Quebec Nordiques.

MOST SHUTOUTS IN PLAYOFFS (CAREER):
14 — Jacques Plante, Montreal Canadiens, St. Louis Blues in 16 playoff years.
13 — Turk Broda, Toronto Maple Leafs, in 13 playoff years.
12 — Terry Sawchuk, Detroit, Toronto, Los Angeles in 15 playoff years.

MOST PLAYOFF GAMES APPEARED IN BY A GOALTENDER (CAREER):
129 — Bill Smith, NY Islanders, in 11 playoff years.
115 — Glenn Hall, Detroit, Chicago, St. Louis in 15 playoff years.
112 — Jacques Plante, Montreal, St. Louis, Toronto, Boston in 16 playoff years.
— Ken Dryden, Montreal, in eight playoff years.
106 — Terry Sawchuk, Detroit, Toronto, Los Angeles, New York Rangers in 15 playoff years.

MOST MINUTES PLAYED BY A GOALTENDER (CAREER):
7,518 — Bill Smith, NY Islanders in 11 playoff years.
6,899 — Glenn Hall, Detroit, Chicago, St. Louis in 15 playoff years.
6,841 — Ken Dryden, Montreal, in eight playoff years.
6,651 — Jacques Plante, Montreal, St. Louis, Toronto, Boston in 16 playoff years.

One-Playoff Year Records

MOST POINTS, ONE PLAYOFF YEAR:
47 — Wayne Gretzky, Edmonton Oilers, in 1985. 17 goals, 30 assists in 18 games.
38 — Wayne Gretzky, Edmonton Oilers, in 1983. 12 goals, 26 assists in 16 games.
37 — Paul Coffey, Edmonton Oilers, in 1985. 12 goals, 25 assists in 18 games.
35 — Mike Bossy, New York Islanders, in 1981. 17 goals, 18 assists in 18 games.
— Wayne Gretzky, Edmonton Oilers, in 1984. 13 goals, 22 assists in 19 games.
33 — Rick Middleton Boston Bruins, in 1983. 11 goals, 22 assists in 17 games.
32 — Barry Pederson, Boston Bruins, in 1983. 14 goals, 18 assists in 17 games.
31 — Jari Kurri, Edmonton Oilers, in 1985. 19 goals, 12 assists in 18 games.

MOST POINTS BY A DEFENSEMAN, ONE PLAYOFF YEAR:
37 — Paul Coffey, Edmonton Oilers, in 1985. 12 goals, 25 assists in 18 games against Los Angeles, Winnipeg, Chicago and Philadelphia.
25 — Denis Potvin, New York Islanders, in 1981. 8 goals, 17 assists in 18 games.
24 — Bobby Orr, Boston Bruins, in 1972. 5 goals, 19 assists in 15 games.

MOST POINTS BY A ROOKIE, ONE PLAYOFF YEAR:
21 — Dino Ciccarelli, Minnesota North Stars, in 1981. 14 goals, 7 assists in 19 games against Boston, Buffalo, Calgary and NY Islanders.
20 — Don Maloney, New York Rangers, in 1979. 7 goals, 13 assists in 18 games.

LONGEST CONSECUTIVE POINT-SCORING STREAK, ONE PLAYOFF YEAR:
18 games — Bryan Trottier, New York Islanders, 1981. 11 goals, 18 assists, 29 points.
14 games — Bobby Orr, Boston Bruins, 1970. 9 goals, 11 assists, 20 points.

LONGEST CONSECUTIVE POINT-SCORING STREAK, MORE THAN ONE PLAYOFF YEAR:
27 games — Bryan Trottier, New York Islanders, 1980, 1981 and 1982. 7 games in 1980 (3 goals, 5 assists, 8 points), 18 games in 1981 (11 goals, 18 assists, 29 points), and two games in 1982 (2 goals, 3 assists, 5 points) Total points in streak, 42.
18 games — Phil Esposito, Boston Bruins, 1970 and 1971. 13 goals, 20 assists, 33 points.

MOST GOALS, ONE PLAYOFF YEAR:
19 — Reggie Leach, Philadelphia Flyers, 1976. 16 games against Toronto, Boston and Montreal.
— **Jari Kurri, Edmonton Oilers,** 1985. 18 games against Los Angeles, Winnipeg, Chicago and Philadelphia.
17 — Mike Bossy, New York Islanders, 1981. 18 games.
— Steve Payne, Minnesota North Stars, 1981. 19 games.
— Mike Bossy, New York Islanders, 1982. 19 games.
— Mike Bossy, New York Islanders, 1983. 19 games
— Wayne Gretzky, Edmonton Oilers, 1985. 18 games.

MOST GOALS BY A DEFENSEMAN, ONE PLAYOFF YEAR:
12 — Paul Coffey, Edmonton Oilers, 1985. 18 games against Los Angeles, Winnipeg, Chicago and Philadelphia.
9 — Bobby Orr, Boston Bruins, 1970. 14 games against New York Rangers, Chicago and St. Louis.
— Brad Park, Boston Bruins, 1978. 15 games against Chicago, Philadelphia and Montreal.
8 — Denis Potvin, New York Islanders, 1981. 18 games.
— Raymond Bourque, Boston Bruins, 1983. 17 games.
— Denis Potvin, New York Islanders, 1983. 20 games.
— Paul Coffey, Edmonton Oilers, 1984. 19 games

MOST GOALS BY A ROOKIE, ONE PLAYOFF YEAR:
14 — Dino Ciccarelli, Minnesota North Stars, 1981. 19 games against Boston, Buffalo, Calgary and New York Islanders.
10 — Claude Lemieux, Montreal Canadiens, 1986. 20 games.
9 — Pat Flatley, NY Islanders, 1984. 21 games
8 — Steve Christoff, Minnesota North Stars, 1980. 14 games.
— Brad Palmer, Minnesota North Stars, 1981. 19 games.
— Mike Krushelnyski, Boston Bruins, 1983. 17 games.

MOST GAME-WINNING GOALS, ONE PLAYOFF YEAR:
5 — Mike Bossy, New York Islanders, 1983. 19 games against Washington, NY Rangers, Boston, and Edmonton.
4 — Maurice Richard, Montreal Canadiens, 1958. 10 games against Detroit and Boston.
— Jean Beliveau, Montreal Canadiens, 1965. 13 games against Toronto and Chicago.
— Rick MacLeish, Philadelphia, 1974. 17 games against Atlanta, NY Rangers and Boston.
— Guy Lafleur, Montreal Canadiens, 1975. 11 games against Vancouver and Buffalo.
— Clark Gillies, New York Islanders, 1977. 12 games against Chicago, Buffalo and Montreal.
— Bill Barber, Philadelphia Flyers, 1980. 19 games against Edmonton, NY Rangers, Minnesota and NY Islanders.
— Steve Payne, Minnesota North Stars, 1981. 19 games against Boston, Buffalo, Calgary and NY Islanders.
— Ken Linseman, Edmonton, 1984. 19 games against Winnipeg, Calgary, Minnesota and NY Islanders.
— Paul Coffey, Edmonton Oilers, 1985. 18 games against Los Angeles, Winnipeg, Chicago and Philadelphia.
— Darryl Sutter, Chicago Black Hawks, 1985. 15 games against Detroit, Minnesota and Edmonton.
— Claude Lemieux, Montreal Canadiens, 1986. 20 games, against Boston, Hartford, NY Rangers and Calgary.

MOST OVERTIME GOALS, ONE PLAYOFF YEAR:
3 — Mel Hill, Boston Bruins, 1939. All against New York Rangers in best-of-seven Semi-Final, won by Boston 4-3.
— **Maurice Richard, Montreal Canadiens,** 1951. 2 against Detroit Red Wings in best-of-seven Semi-Final, won by Montreal 4-2; 1 against Toronto Maple Leafs in best-of-seven Final, won by Toronto 4-1.

MOST POWER-PLAY GOALS, ONE PLAYOFF YEAR:
9 — Mike Bossy, New York Islanders, 1981. 18 games against Toronto, Edmonton, NY Rangers and Minnesota.
7 — Michel Goulet, Quebec Nordiques, 1985. 17 games.
6 — Andy Bathgate, Detroit Red Wings, 1966. 12 games.
— Bobby Hull, Chicago Black Hawks, 1971. 18 games.
— Jacques Lemaire, Montreal Canadiens, 1979. 16 games.
— Mike Bossy, New York Islanders, 1980. 21 games.
— Denis Potvin, New York Islanders, 1981. 18 games.
— Steve Payne, Minnesota North Stars, 1981. 19 games.
— Mike Bossy, New York Islanders, 1982. 19 games.
— Mike Bossy, New York Islanders, 1983. 19 games.

Derek Sanderson, left, had three shorthanded goals in the 1969 Playoffs.

MOST SHORTHAND GOALS, ONE PLAYOFF YEAR:
3 — Derek Sanderson, Boston Bruins, 1969. 1 against Toronto in Quarter-Final, won by Boston 4-0; 2 against Montreal in Semi-Final, won by Montreal, 4-2.
— **Bill Barber, Philadelphia Flyers,** 1980. All against Minnesota in Semi-Final, won by Philadelphia 4-1.
— **Lorne Henning, New York Islanders,** 1980. 1 against Boston in Quarter-Final won by NYI 4-1; 1 against Buffalo in Semi-Final, won by NYI 4-2, 1 against Philadelphia in Final, won by NYI 4-2.
— **Wayne Gretzky, Edmonton Oilers,** 1983. 2 against Winnipeg in Division Semi-Final won by Edmonton 3-0; 1 against Calgary in Division Final, won by Edmonton 4-1.

MOST THREE-OR-MORE GOAL GAMES, ONE PLAYOFF YEAR:
4 — Jari Kurri, Edmonton Oilers, 1985. 1 four-goal game, 3 three-goal games.
3 — Mark Messier, Edmonton Oilers, 1983. 3 three-goal games.
— Mike Bossy, New York Islanders, 1983. 3 three-goal games
2 — Maurice Richard, Montreal Canadiens, 1944. 1 five-goal game; 1 three-goal game.
— Doug Bentley, Chicago Black Hawks, 1944. 2 three-goal games.
— Norm Ullman, Detroit Red Wings, 1964. 2 three-goal games.
— Phil Esposito, Boston Bruins, 1970. 2 three-goal games.
— Pit Martin, Chicago Black Hawks, 1973. 2 three-goal games.
— Rick MacLeish, Philadelphia Flyers, 1975. 2 three-goal games.
— Lanny McDonald, Toronto Maple Leafs, 1977. 1 three-goal game; 1 four-goal game.
— Wayne Gretzky, Edmonton Oilers, 1981. 2 three-goal games.
— Wayne Gretzky, Edmonton Oilers, 1985. 2 three-goal games.
— Wayne Gretzky, Edmonton Oilers, 1983. 2 four-goal games.

LONGEST CONSECUTIVE GOAL-SCORING STREAK, ONE PLAYOFF YEAR:
9 Games — Reggie Leach, Philadelphia Flyers, 1976. Streak started April 17 at Toronto and ended May 9 at Montreal. He scored one goal in each of seven games; two in one game; and five in another; a total 14 goals.

MOST ASSISTS, ONE PLAYOFF YEAR:
30 — Wayne Gretzky, Edmonton Oilers, 1985. 18 games.
26 — Wayne Gretzky, Edmonton Oilers, 1983. 16 games.
25 — Paul Coffey, Edmonton Oilers, 1985. 18 games.
23 — Bryan Trottier, New York Islanders, 1982. 19 games.
22 — Rick Middleton, Boston Bruins, 1983. 17 games.
— Wayne Gretzky, Edmonton Oilers, 1984. 19 games.
20 — Bob Bourne, New York Islanders, 1983. 20 games.
19 — Bobby Orr, Boston Bruins, 1972. 15 games.

MOST ASSISTS BY A DEFENSEMAN, ONE PLAYOFF YEAR:
25 — Paul Coffey, Edmonton Oilers, 1985. 18 games.
19 — Bobby Orr, Boston Bruins, 1972. 15 games against Toronto, St. Louis and NY Rangers.
17 — Larry Robinson, Montreal Canadiens, 1978. 15 games.
— Denis Potvin, New York Islanders, 1981. 18 games.
— Charlie Huddy, Edmonton Oilers, 1985. 18 games.

MOST MINUTES PLAYED BY A GOALTENDER, ONE PLAYOFF YEAR:
1,229 — Mike Vernon, Calgary Flames, 1986. 21 games.
1,221 — Ken Dryden, Montreal Canadiens, 1971. 20 games.
1,218 — Patrick Roy, Montreal Canadiens, 1986. 20 games.
1,198 — Bill Smith, New York Islanders, 1980. 20 games.
1,190 — Bill Smith, New York Islanders, 1984. 21 games.

MOST WINS BY A GOALTENDER, ONE PLAYOFF YEAR:
15 — Bill Smith, New York Islanders, 1980. 20 games.
— Bill Smith, New York Islanders, 1982. 18 games.
— Grant Fuhr, Edmonton Oilers, 1985. 18 games.
— Patrick Roy, Montreal Canadiens, 1986. 20 games.
14 — Bill Smith, New York Islanders, 1981. 17 games.

MOST CONSECUTIVE WINS BY A GOALTENDER, ONE PLAYOFF YEAR:
10 — Gerry Cheevers, Boston Bruins, 1970. 2 wins against NY Rangers in Quarter-Final, won by Boston 4-2; 4 wins against Chicago in Semi-Final, won by Boston 4-0; and 4 wins against St. Louis in Final, won by Boston 4-0.

MOST SHUTOUTS, ONE PLAYOFF YEAR:
4 — Clint Benedict, Montreal Maroons, 1928. 9 games against Ottawa, Montreal Canadiens and NY Rangers.
— Dave Kerr, New York Rangers, 1937. 9 games against Montreal Maroons and Detroit.
— Frank McCool, Toronto Maple Leafs, 1945. 13 games against Montreal Canadiens and Detroit.
— Terry Sawchuk, Detroit Red Wings, 1952. 8 games against Toronto and Montreal Canadiens.
— Bernie Parent, Philadelphia Flyers, 1975. 17 games against Toronto, NY Islanders and Buffalo.
— Ken Dryden, Montreal Canadiens, 1977. 14 games against St. Louis, NY Islanders and Boston.

MOST CONSECUTIVE SHUTOUTS:
3 — Frank McCool, Toronto Maple Leafs, 1945. McCool shut out Detroit Red Wings 1-0, April 6; 2-0, April 8; 1-0, April 12. Toronto won the best-of-seven Final 4-3.

LONGEST SHUTOUT SEQUENCE:
248 Minutes, 32 Seconds — Norm Smith, Detroit Red Wings, 1936. In best-of-five Semi-Final, Smith shut out Montreal Maroons 1-0, March 24, in 116:30 overtime; shut out Maroons 3-0 in second game, March 26; and was scored against at 12:02 of first period, March 29, by Gus Marker. Detroit won series 3-0.

One-Series Records

MOST POINTS IN FINAL SERIES:
12 — Gordie Howe, Detroit Red Wings, in 1955, during 7 games against Montreal. 5 goals, 7 assists.
— Yvan Cournoyer, Montreal Canadiens, in 1973, during 6 games against Chicago. 6 goals, 6 assists.
— Jacques Lemaire, Montreal Canadiens, in 1973, during 6 games against Chicago. 3 goals, 9 assists.

MOST GOALS IN FINAL SERIES:
7 — Jean Beliveau, Montreal Canadiens, in 1956, during 5 games against Detroit.
— Mike Bossy, New York Islanders, in 1982, during 4 games against Vancouver.
— Wayne Gretzky, Edmonton Oilers, in 1985, during 5 games against Philadelphia.

MOST ASSISTS IN FINAL SERIES:
9 — Jacques Lemaire, Montreal Canadiens, in 1973, during 6 games against Chicago.

MOST POINTS IN ONE SERIES (OTHER THAN FINAL):
19 — Rick Middleton, Boston Bruins, in 1983, during 7 games against Buffalo. 5 goals, 14 assists.
18 — Wayne Gretzky, Edmonton Oilers, in 1985, during 6 games against Chicago. 4 goals, 14 assists.
16 — Barry Pederson, Boston Bruins, in 1983, during 7 games against Buffalo. 7 goals, 9 assists.
15 — Jari Kurri, Edmonton Oilers, in 1985, during 6 games against Chicago. 12 goals, 3 assists.

MOST GOALS IN ONE SERIES (OTHER THAN FINAL):
12 — Jari Kurri, Edmonton Oilers, in 1985, during 6 games against Chicago.
9 — Reggie Leach, Philadelphia, in 1976, during 5 games against Boston.
— Bill Barber, Philadelphia, in 1980, during 5 games against Minnesota.
— Mike Bossy, New York Islanders, in 1983, during 6 games against Boston.

MOST ASSISTS IN ONE SERIES (OTHER THAN FINAL):
14 — Rick Middleton, Boston Bruins, in 1983, during 7 games against Buffalo.
— Wayne Gretzky, Edmonton Oilers, in 1985, during 6 games against Chicago.
10 — Fleming Mackell, Boston Bruins, in 1958 during 6 games against NY Rangers.
— Stan Mikita, Chicago Black Hawks, in 1962, during 6 games against Montreal.
— Bob Bourne, New York Islanders, in 1983, during 6 games against New York Rangers.

MOST OVERTIME GOALS, ONE PLAYOFF SERIES:
3 — Mel Hill, Boston Bruins, 1939, in Semi-Final series against New York Rangers, won by Boston 4-3. Hill scored at 59:25 overtime March 21 for a 2-1 win; at 8:24, March 23 for a 3-2 win; and at 48:00 April 2 for a 2-1 win.

MOST POWER-PLAY GOALS, ONE PLAYOFF SERIES:
5 — Andy Bathgate, Detroit Red Wings, 1966, Semi-Final against Chicago, won by Detroit 4-2.
— Denis Potvin, New York Islanders, 1981, Quarter-Final against Edmonton, won by Islanders 4-2.
— Ken Houston, Calgary Flames, 1981, Quarter-Final against Philadelphia, won by Calgary 4-3.

MOST SHORTHAND GOALS, ONE PLAYOFF SERIES:
3 — Bill Barber, Philadelphia Flyers, 1980, Semi-Final against Minnesota, won by Philadelphia 4-1.
2 — Mac Colville, New York Rangers, 1940, Semi-Final against Boston, won by New York 4-2.
— Jerry Toppazzini, Boston Bruins, 1958, Semi-Final against New York Rangers, won by Boston 4-2.
— Dave Keon, Toronto Maple Leafs, 1963, Final Series against Detroit, won by Toronto 4-1.
— Bob Pulford, Toronto Maple Leafs, 1964, Final Series against Detroit, won by Toronto 4-3.
— Serge Savard, Montreal Canadiens, 1968, Final Series against St. Louis, won by Montreal 4-0.
— Derek Sanderson, Boston Bruins, 1969, Semi-Final against Montreal, won by Montreal 4-0.
— Bryan Trottier, New York Islanders, 1980, Preliminary Round against Los Angeles, won by Islanders 3-1.
— Bobby Lalonde, Boston Bruins, 1981, Preliminary Round against Minnesota, won by Minnesota 3-0.
— Butch Goring, New York Islanders, 1981, Semi-Final against New York Rangers, won by Islanders 4-0.
— Wayne Gretzky, Edmonton Oilers, 1983, Smythe Division Semi-Final against Winnipeg, won by Oilers 3-0.
— Mark Messier, Edmonton Oilers, 1983, Smythe Division Final against Calgary, won by Oilers 4-1.
— Jari Kurri, Edmonton Oilers, 1983, Campbell Conference Final against Chicago, won by Oilers 4-0.
— Wayne Gretzky, Edmonton Oilers, 1985, Smythe Division Final against Winnipeg, won by Oilers 4-0.

MOST THREE-OR-MORE-GOAL GAMES, ONE PLAYOFF SERIES:
3 — Jari Kurri, Edmonton Oilers, 1985, Campbell Conference Championship against Chicago. Kurri scored three goals May 7 in 7-3 win at Edmonton; three goals May 14 in 10-5 win at Edmonton; and four goals May 16 in 8-2 win at Chicago.
2 — Doug Bentley, Chicago Black Hawks, 1944, Semi-Final against Detroit, won by Chicago 4-1. Bentley scored three goals March 28 at Chicago in 7-1 win and three goals March 30 at Detroit in 5-2 win.
— Norm Ullman, Detroit Red Wings, 1964, Semi-Final against Chicago, won by Detroit 4-3. Ullman scored three goals March 29 at Chicago in 5-4 win and three goals April 7 at Detroit in 7-1 win.
— Mark Messier, Edmonton Oilers, 1983, Smythe Division Final against Calgary. Messier scored three goals April 14 in 6-3 win at Edmonton and three goals April 17 in 10-2 win at Calgary.
— Mike Bossy, NY Islanders, 1983, Wales Conference Final against Boston. Bossy scored three goals May 3 in 8-3 win at New York and four goals in 8-4 win May 7 at New York.

Single Playoff Game Records

MOST POINTS, ONE GAME:
7 — Wayne Gretzky, Edmonton Oilers, April 17, 1983 at Calgary during 10-2 win. Gretzky had 4 goals, 3 assists.
— Wayne Gretzky, Edmonton Oilers, April 25,1985 at Winnipeg during 8-3 win. Gretzky had 3 goals, 4 assists.
6 — Dickie Moore, Montreal Canadiens, March 25, 1954, at Montreal during 8-1 win over Boston. Moore had 2 goals, 4 assists.
— Phil Esposito, Boston Bruins, April 2, 1969, at Boston during 10-0 win over Toronto. Esposito had 4 goals, 2 assists.
— Darryl Sittler, Toronto Maple Leafs, April 22, 1976, at Toronto during 8-5 win over Philadelphia. Sittler had 5 goals, 1 assist.
— Guy Lafleur, Montreal Canadiens, April 11, 1977, at Montreal during 7-2 victory over St. Louis. Lafleur had 3 goals, 3 assists.
— Mikko Leinonen, New York Rangers, April 8, 1982, at New York during 7-3 win over Philadelphia. Leinonen had 6 assists.
— Paul Coffey, Edmonton Oilers, May 14, 1985 at Edmonton during 10-5 win over Chicago. Coffey had 1 goal, 5 assists.
— John Anderson, Hartford Whalers, April 12, 1986 at Hartford during 9-4 win over Quebec. Anderson had 2 goals, 4 assists.

MOST POINTS BY A DEFENSEMAN, ONE GAME:
6 — Paul Coffey, Edmonton Oilers, May 14, 1985 at Edmonton. 1 goal, 5 assists. Edmonton won 10-5.
5 — Eddie Bush, Detroit Red Wings, April 9, 1942, at Toronto. 1 goal, 4 assists. Detroit won 5-2.
— Bob Dailey, Philadelphia Flyers, May 1, 1980, at Philadelphia against Minnesota North Stars. 1 goal, 4 assists. Flyers won 7-0.
— Denis Potvin, New York Islanders, April 17, 1981, at New York against Edmonton Oilers. 3 goals, 2 assists. Islanders won 6-3.

MOST GOALS, ONE GAME:
5 — Maurice Richard, Montreal Canadiens, March 23, 1944, at Montreal. Final score: Canadiens 5, Toronto 1.
— Darryl Sittler, Toronto Maple Leafs, April 22, 1976, at Toronto. Final score: Toronto 8, Philadelphia 5.
— Reggie Leach, Philadelphia Flyers, May 6, 1976, at Philadelphia. Final score: Philadelphia 6, Boston 3.

MOST GOALS BY A DEFENSEMAN, ONE GAME:
3 — Bobby Orr, Boston Bruins, April 11, 1971 at Montreal. Final score: Boston 5, Montreal 2.
— Dick Redmond, Chicago Black Hawks, April 4, 1973 at Chicago. Final score: Chicago 7, St. Louis 1.
— Denis Potvin, NY Islanders, April 17, 1981 at Long Island. Final score: NY Islanders 6, Edmonton 3.
— Paul Reinhart, Calgary Flames, April 14, 1983 at Edmonton. Final score: Edmonton 6, Calgary 3.
— Paul Reinhart, Calgary, April 8, 1984 at Vancouver. Final score: Calgary 5, Vancouver 1.
— Doug Halward, Vancouver Canucks, April 7, 1984 at Vancouver. Final score: Vancouver 7, Calgary 0.

MOST POWER-PLAY GOALS, ONE GAME:

3 — **Syd Howe, Detroit Red Wings,** March 23, 1939, at Detroit against Montreal Canadiens. Detroit won 7-3.
— **Sid Smith, Toronto Maple Leafs,** April 10, 1949, at Toronto against Detroit Red Wings. Toronto won 3-1.
— **Phil Esposito, Boston Bruins,** April 2, 1969, at Boston against Toronto Maple Leafs. Boston won 10-0.
— **John Bucyk, Boston Bruins,** April 21, 1974, at Boston against Chicago Black Hawks. Boston won 8-6.
— **Denis Potvin, New York Islanders,** April 17, 1981, at New York against Edmonton Oilers. Islanders won 6-3.
— **Tim Kerr, Philadelphia Flyers,** April 13, 1985, at New York against Rangers. Philadelphia won 6-5.

MOST SHORTHAND GOALS, ONE GAME:

2 — **Dave Keon, Toronto Maple Leafs,** April 18, 1963, at Toronto, in 3-1 win against Detroit.
— **Bryan Trottier, New York Islanders,** April 8, 1980 at Long Island, in 8-1 win against Los Angeles.
— **Bobby Lalonde, Boston Bruins,** April 11, 1981 at Minnesota. Final score: Minnesota 6, Boston 3.
— **Wayne Gretzky, Edmonton Oilers,** April 6, 1983 at Edmonton, in 6-3 win against Winnipeg.
— **Jari Kurri, Edmonton, Oilers,** April 24, 1983, at Edmonton. Final score: Edmonton 8, Chicago 4.

St. Louis' Doug Gilmour had 21 points in the 1986 Playoffs including five assists in one game.

MOST ASSISTS, ONE GAME:

6 — **Mikko Leinonen, New York Rangers,** April 8, 1982, at New York. Final score: NY Rangers 7, Philadelphia 3.
5 — **Toe Blake, Montreal Canadiens,** March 23, 1944, at Montreal. Final score: Montreal 5, Toronto 1.
— **Maurice Richard, Montreal Canadiens,** March 27, 1956, at Montreal. Final score: Montreal, 7, NY Rangers 0.
— **Bert Olmstead, Montreal Canadiens,** March 30, 1957, at Montreal. Final score: Montreal 8, NY Rangers 3.
— **Don McKenney, Boston Bruins,** April 5, 1958, at Boston. Final score: Boston 8, NY Rangers 2.
— **Stan Mikita, Chicago Black Hawks,** April 4, 1973, at Chicago. Final score: Chicago 7, St. Louis 1.
— **Wayne Gretzky, Edmonton Oilers,** April 8, 1981, at Montreal. Final score: Edmonton 6, Montreal 3.
— **Paul Coffey, Edmonton Oilers,** May 14, 1985, at Edmonton. Fianl score: Edmonton 10, Chicago 5.
— **Doug Gilmour, St. Louis Blues,** April 15, 1986, at Minnesota. Final score: St. Louis 6, Minnesota 3.

MOST PENALTY MINUTES, ONE GAME:

42 — **Dave Schultz, Philadelphia Flyers,** April 22, 1976, at Toronto. One minor, two majors, one 10-minute misconduct and two game-misconducts. Final score: Toronto 8, Philadelphia 5.

MOST PENALTIES, ONE GAME:

8 — **Forbes Kennedy, Toronto Maple Leafs,** April 2, 1969, at Boston. Four minors, two majors, one 10-minute misconduct, one game misconduct. Final score: Boston 10, Toronto 0.
— **Kim Clackson, Pittsburgh Penguins,** April 14, 1980, at Boston. Five minors, two majors, one 10-minute misconduct.

MOST POINTS, ONE PERIOD:

4 — **Maurice Richard, Montreal Canadiens,** March 29, 1945, at Montreal against Toronto. Third period, three goals, one assist. Final score: Montreal 10, Toronto 3.
— **Dickie Moore, Montreal Canadiens,** March 25, 1954, at Montreal against Boston. First period, two goals, two assists. Final score: Montreal 8, Boston 1.
— **Barry Pederson, Boston Bruins,** April 8, 1982, at Boston against Buffalo. Second period, three goals, one assist. Final score: Boston 7, Buffalo 3.
— **Peter McNab, Boston Bruins,** April 11, 1982, at Buffalo. Second period, one goal, three assists. Final score: Boston 5, Buffalo 2.
— **Tim Kerr, Philadelphia Flyers,** April 13, 1985 at New York. Second period, four goals. Final score: Philadelphia 6, Rangers 5.
— **Ken Linseman, Boston Bruins,** April 14, 1985 at Boston against Montreal. Second period, two goals, two assists. Final score: Boston 7, Montreal 6.

MOST GOALS, ONE PERIOD:

4 — **Tim Kerr, Philadelphia Flyers,** April 13, 1985, at New York against Rangers, second period. Final score: Philadelphia 6, Rangers 5.
3 — **Harvey (Busher) Jackson, Toronto Maple Leafs,** April 5, 1932, at New York against Rangers, second period. Final score: Toronto 6, Rangers 4.
— **Maurice Richard, Montreal Canadiens,** March 23, 1944, at Montreal against Toronto, second period. Final score: Montreal 5, Toronto 1.
— **Maurice Richard, Montreal Canadiens,** March 29, 1945, at Montreal against Toronto, third period. Final score: Montreal 10, Toronto 3.
— **Maurice Richard, Montreal Canadiens,** April 6, 1957 at Montreal against Boston, second period. Final score: Montreal 5, Boston 1.
— **Ted Lindsay, Detroit Red Wings,** April 5, 1955, at Detroit against Canadiens, second period. Final score: Detroit 7, Montreal 1.
— **Red Berenson, St. Louis Blues,** April 15, 1969, at St. Louis against Los Angeles, second period. Final score: St. Louis 4, Los Angeles 0.
— **Jacques Lemaire, Montreal Canadiens,** April 20, 1971, at Montreal against Minnesota, second period. Final score: Montreal 7, Minnesota 2.
— **Rick MacLeish, Philadelphia Flyers,** April 11, 1974, at Philadelphia against Atlanta, second period. Final score: Philadelphia 5, Atlanta 1.
— **Tom Williams, Los Angeles Kings,** April 14, 1974, at Los Angeles against Chicago, third period. Final score: Los Angeles 5, Chicago 1.
— **Darryl Sittler, Toronto Maple Leafs,** April 22, 1976, at Toronto against Philadelphia, second period. Final score: Toronto 8, Philadelphia 5.
— **Reggie Leach, Philadelphia Flyers,** May 6, 1976, at Philadelphia against Boston, second period. Final score: Philadelphia 6, Boston 3.
— **Bobby Schmautz, Boston Bruins,** April 11, 1977, at Boston against Los Angeles, first period. Final score: Boston 8, Los Angeles 3.
— **George Ferguson, Toronto Maple Leafs,** April 11, 1978, at Toronto against Los Angeles, third period. Final score: Toronto 7, Los Angeles 3.
— **Barry Pederson, Boston Bruins,** April 8, 1982, at Boston against Buffalo, second period. Final score: Boston 7, Buffalo 3.
— **Peter Stastny, Quebec Nordiques,** April 5, 1983, at Boston, first period. Final score: Boston 4, Quebec 3.
— **Wayne Gretzky, Edmonton Oilers,** April 6, 1983 at Edmonton, second period. Final score: Edmonton 6, Winnipeg 3.
— **Mike Bossy, NY Islanders,** May 7, 1983 at Long Island, second period. Final score: NY Islanders 8, Boston 4.
— **Dave Andreychuk, Buffalo Sabres,** April 14, 1985, at Buffalo against Quebec, third period. Final score: Buffalo 7, Quebec 4.
— **Wayne Gretzky, Edmonton Oilers,** May 25, 1985, at Edmonton against Philadelphia, first period. Final score: Edmonton 4, Philadelphia 3.

MOST POWER PLAY GOALS, ONE PERIOD:

3 — **Tim Kerr, Philadelphia Flyers,** April 13, 1985 at New York, second period in 6-5 win against Rangers.
2 — Charlie Conacher, Toronto Maple Leafs, March 26, 1936, second period at Toronto in 8-3 win against Boston.
— Syd Howe, Detroit Red Wings, March 23, 1939, third period at Detroit in 7-3 win against Montreal Canadiens.
— Mac Colville, New York Rangers, March 22, 1942, third period at New York in 4-2 win by Toronto Maple Leafs.
— Sid Smith, Toronto Maple Leafs, April 10, 1949, first period at Toronto in 3-1 win against Detroit Red Wings.
— Maurice Richard, Montreal Canadiens, April 6, 1954, second period at Detroit in 3-1 win by Montreal.
— Bernie Geoffrion, Montreal Canadiens, April 7, 1955, first period at Montreal in 4-2 win against Detroit Red Wings.
— Don McKenney, Boston Bruins, March 29, 1958, first period at Boston in 5-0 win against New York Rangers.
— Floyd Smith, Detroit Red Wings, April 10, 1966, first period at Chicago in 7-0 win by Detroit.
— Gilles Tremblay, Montreal Canadiens, April 14, 1966, second period at Toronto in 4-1 win by Montreal.
— Rosaire Paiement, Philadelphia Flyers, April 13, 1968, third period at Philadelphia in 6-1 win against St. Louis Blues.
— Jean Béliveau, Montreal Canadiens, April 20, 1968, second period at Montreal in 4-1 win over Chicago Black Hawks.
— Phil Esposito, Boston Bruins, April 2, 1969, second period at Boston in 10-0 win against Toronto Maple Leafs.
— John Bucyk, Boston Bruins, April 23, 1970, second period at Boston in 5-2 win against Chicago Black Hawks.
— Bobby Hull, Chicago Black Hawks, April 10, 1971, third period at Philadelphia in 3-2 Chicago win.
— John McKenzie, Boston Bruins, April 23, 1972, second period at St. Louis during 7-2 Boston win.
— Brad Park, New York Rangers, May 4, 1972, first period at New York in 5-2 win against Boston Bruins.
— Pit Martin, Chicago Black Hawks, April 4, 1973, third period at Chicago in 7-1 win against St. Louis Blues.
— John Bucyk, Boston Bruins, April 21, 1974, first period at Boston in 8-6 win against Chicago Black Hawks.
— Rick MacLeish, Philadelphia Flyers, May 13, 1975, first period at Philadelphia in 4-1 win against New York Islanders.
— Denis Potvin, New York Islanders, April 17, 1981, at New York in 6-3 win against Edmonton Oilers.
— Mike Bossy, New York Islanders, May 5, 1981, first period at New York Rangers in 5-2 Islander win.
— Marcel Dionne, Los Angeles Kings, April 7, 1982, second period at Edmonton in 10-8 win.
— Denis Savard, Chicago Black Hawks, April 19, 1982, first period at Chicago in 7-4 win against St. Louis Blues.
— Larry Murphy, Washington Capitals, April 10, 1985, second period at Washington against New York Islanders in 4-3 Capitals win.
— Denis Savard, Chicago Blackhawks, April 10, 1986 at Chicago, first period in 6-4 Toronto win.
— Dan Quinn, Calgary Flames, May 12, 1986 at St. Louis, second period in 6-5 St. Louis win.

MOST SHORTHAND GOALS, ONE PERIOD:
2 — Bryan Trottier, New York Islanders, April 8, 1980, second period at New York in 8-1 win against Los Angeles Kings.
- **Bobby Lalonde, Boston Bruins,** April 11, 1981, third period at Minnesota in 6-3 win by North Stars.
- **Jari Kurri, Edmonton Oilers,** April 24, 1983, third period at Edmonton in 8-4 win against Chicago Black Hawks.

MOST ASSISTS, ONE PERIOD:
3 — Nick Metz, Toronto Maple Leafs, March 25, 1941, at Toronto against Boston, second period. Final score: Toronto 7, Boston 2.
- **Toe Blake, Montreal Canadiens,** March 23, 1944, at Montreal against Toronto, second period. Final score: Montreal 5, Toronto 1.
- **Toe Blake, Montreal Canadiens,** April 13, 1944, at Montreal against Chicago, third period. Final score: Montreal 5, Chicago 4.
- **Elmer Lach, Montreal Canadiens,** March 30, 1944, at Montreal against Toronto, third period. Final score: Montreal 11, Toronto 0.
- **Bobby Bauer, Boston Bruins,** March 24, 1946, at Boston against Detroit, third period. Final score: Boston 5, Detroit 2.
- **Jean Béliveau, Montreal Canadiens,** March 25, 1954, at Montreal against Boston, first period. Final score: Montreal 8, Boston 1.
- **Jean Béliveau, Montreal Canadiens,** April 27, 1971, at Montreal against Minnesota, third period. Final score: Montreal 6, Minnesota 1.
- **Maurice Richard, Montreal Canadiens,** March 27, 1956, at Montreal against Rangers, second period. Final score: Montreal 7, Rangers 0.
- **Doug Harvey, Montreal Canadiens,** April 6, 1957, at Montreal against Boston, second period. Final score: Canadiens 5, Boston 1.
- **Doug Harvey, Montreal Canadiens,** April 2, 1959, at Montreal against Chicago, third period. Final score: Montreal 4, Chicago 2.
- **Don McKenney, Boston Bruins,** April 5, 1958, at Boston against Rangers, third period. Final score: Boston 8, Rangers 2.
- **Dickie Moore, Montreal Canadiens,** April 2, 1959, at Montreal against Chicago, first period. Final score: Montreal 4, Chicago 2.
- **Henri Richard, Montreal Canadiens,** April 7, 1960, at Montreal against Toronto, first period. Final score: Montreal 4, Toronto 2.
- **Bobby Rousseau, Montreal Canadiens,** May 1, 1965, at Montreal against Chicago, first period. Final score: Montreal 4, Chicago 0.
- **Alex Delvecchio, Detroit Red Wings,** April 14, 1966, at Detroit against Chicago, third period. Final score: Detroit 5, Chicago 1.
- **Ab McDonald, St. Louis Blues,** April 21, 1970, at St. Louis, against Pittsburgh, first period. Final score: St. Louis 4, Pittsburgh 1.
- **Bobby Orr, Boston Bruins,** April 8, 1971, at Boston against Montreal, second period. Final score: Montreal 7, Boston 5.
- **Bobby Orr, Boston Bruins,** April 9, 1972, at Toronto, third period. Final score: Boston 5, Toronto 4.
- **Danny Grant, Minnesota North Stars,** April 22, 1971, at Montreal, first period. Final score: Minnesota 6, Montreal 3.
- **Jean Ratelle, New York Rangers,** April 22, 1971, at New York against Chicago, first period. Final score: New York 4, Chicago 1.
- **Barry Ashbee, Philadelphia Flyers,** April 5, 1973, at Philadelphia against Minnesota, second period. Final score: Philadelphia 4, Minnesota 1.
- **Pat Stapleton, Chicago Black Hawks,** April 29, 1973, at Montreal, first period. Final Score: Montreal 8, Chicago 3.
- **Jean-Paul Parise, New York Islanders,** April 17, 1975, at New York against Pittsburgh, third period. Final score: Pittsburgh 6, NY Islanders 4.
- **Wayne Gretzky, Edmonton Oilers,** April 8, 1981, at Montreal, first period. Final score: Edmonton 6, Montreal 3.
- **Wayne Gretzky, Edmonton Oilers,** April 24, 1983, at Edmonton, third period. Final score: Chicago 4, Edmonton 8.
- **Peter McNab, Boston Bruins,** April 11, 1982, at Buffalo, second period. Final score: Boston 5, Buffalo 2.
- **Mikko Leinonen, New York Rangers,** April 8, 1982, at New York, second period. Final score: Rangers 7, Philadelphia 3.
- **Joe Mullen, St. Louis Blues,** April 11, 1982, at St. Louis, first period. Final score: St. Louis 8, Winnipeg 2.
- **Bob Bourne, New York Islanders,** April 14, 1983 at Long Island, third period. Final score: NY Islanders 4, NY Rangers 1.
- **Rick Middleton, Boston Bruins,** April 18, 1983 at Buffalo, third period. Final score: Boston 6, Buffalo 2.
- **Raymond Bourque, Boston Bruins,** April 20, 1983 at Boston, first period. Final score: Boston 9, Buffalo 0.
- **Steve Payne, Minnesota North Stars,** April 26, 1984 at Edmonton, second period. Final score: Edmonton 4, Minnesota 3.
- **Peter Zezel, Philadelphia Flyers,** April 13, 1985 at New York, second period. Final score: Philadelphia 6, Rangers 5.
- **Raymond Bourque. Boston Bruins,** April 14, 1985 at Boston, second period. Final score: Boston 7, Montreal 6.
- **Tim Kerr, Philadelphia Flyers,** April 21, 1985 at Philadelphia, first period. Final score: Philadelphia 5, New York Islanders 2.
- **Wayne Gretzky, Edmonton Oilers,** April 25, 1985 at Winnipeg, second period. Final score: Edmonton 8, Winnipeg 3.
- **Randy Gregg, Edmonton Oilers,** May 4, 1985 at Edmonton, third period. Final score: Edmonton 11, Chicago 2.
- **Paul Coffey, Edmonton Oilers,** May 4, 1985 at Edmonton, second period. Final score: Edmonton 11 Chicago 2.

MOST PENALTIES, ONE PERIOD AND MOST PENALTY MINUTES, ONE PERIOD:
6 Penalties; 39 Minutes — Ed Hospodar, NY Rangers, April 9, 1981, at Los Angeles, first period. Two minors, one major, one 10-minute misconduct, two game misconducts. Final score: Los Angeles 5, NY Rangers 4.

FASTEST TWO GOALS:
5 Seconds — Norm Ullman, Detroit Red Wings, at Detroit, April 11, 1965, against Chicago and goaltender Glenn Hall. Ullman scored at 17:35 and 17:40 of second period. Detroit won game 4-2.

FASTEST GOAL FROM START OF GAME:
6 Seconds — Don Kozak, Los Angeles Kings, April 17, 1977, at Los Angeles against Boston and goaltender Gerry Cheevers during 7-4 Los Angeles victory.
7 Seconds — Bob Gainey, Montreal Canadiens, May 5, 1977, at New York against Islanders and goaltender Glenn Resch. Montreal won game 2-1.
- Terry Murray, Philadelphia Flyers, April 12, 1981, at Quebec against goaltender Dan Bouchard. Quebec won game 4-3 in overtime.
8 Seconds — Stan Smyl, Vancouver Canucks, April 7, 1982, at Vancouver against Calgary and goaltender Pat Riggin. Vancouver won game 5-3.

FASTEST GOAL FROM START OF PERIOD (OTHER THAN FIRST):
9 Seconds — Bill Collins, Minnesota North Stars, April 9, 1968, at Minnesota against Los Angeles and goaltender Wayne Rutledge, third period. Minnesota won game 7-5.
- **Dave Balon, Minnesota North Stars,** April 25, 1968, at St. Louis against goaltender Glenn Hall, third period. Minnesota won game 5-1.
- **Murray Oliver, Minnesota North Stars,** April 8, 1971, at St. Louis against goaltender Ernie Wakely, third period. St. Louis won game 4-2.
- **Clark Gillies, New York Islanders,** April 15, 1977, at Buffalo against goaltender Don Edwards, third period. Islanders won game 4-3.
- **Éric Vail, Atlanta Flames,** April 11, 1978, at Atlanta against Detroit and goaltender Ron Low, third period. Detroit won game 5-3.
- **Stan Smyl, Vancouver Canucks,** April 10, 1979, at Philadelphia against goaltender Wayne Stephenson, third period. Vancouver won game 3-2.
- **Wayne Gretzky, Edmonton Oilers,** April 6, 1983, at Edmonton against goaltender Brian Hayward, second period. Edmonton won game 6-3.
- **Mark Messier, Edmonton Oilers,** April 16, 1984, at Calgary against goaltender Don Edwards, third period. Edmonton won game 5-3.
- **Brian Skrudland, Montreal Canadiens,** May 18, 1986 at Calgary against Calgary and goaltender Mike Vernon, overtime. Montreal won game 3-2.

Dick Duff

FASTEST TWO GOALS FROM START OF GAME AND PERIOD:
1 Minute, 8 Seconds — Dick Duff, Toronto Maple Leafs, April 9, 1963, at Toronto against Detroit and goaltender Terry Sawchuk. Duff scored at 49 seconds and 1:08. Final score: Toronto 4, Detroit 2.

Officiating

MOST GAMES AS REFEREE AND LINESMAN:
233 — John D'Amico, 1965, 1966; 1970 through 1986. All as linesman.
220 — Matt Pavelich, 1957, 1958; 1961 through 1979. All as linesman.
205 — John D'Amico, 1965, 1966; 1970 through 1985. All as linesman.
198 — Neil Armstrong, 1959 through 1978. All as linesman.
149 — George Hayes, 1947 through 1964. 2 as referee; 147 as linesman.

MOST GAMES AS A REFEREE:
115 — Andy van Hellemond, 1975 through 1986.
111 — Bruce Hood, 1968 through 1973; 1975; 1977 through 1984.
105 — Bill Chadwick, 1941 through 1955.
89 — Andy van Hellemond, 1975 through 1984.
85 — Wally Harris, 1972 through 1983.

MOST GAMES AS A LINESMAN:
233 — John D'Amico, 1965, 1966; 1970 through 1986.
220 — Matt Pavelich, 1957, 1958; 1961 through 1979.
205 — John D'Amico, 1965, 1966; 1970 through 1985.
198 — Neil Armstrong, 1959 through 1978.

Penalty Shots in Stanley Cup Playoff Games

Date	Player	Goaltender
Mar. 25/37	Lionel Conacher, Mtl. Maroons	Tiny Thompson, Boston
Apr. 13/44	Virgil Johnson, Chicago	Bill Durnan, Montreal
Apr. 9/68	Wayne Connelly, Minnesota	Terry Sawchuk, Los Angeles
Apr. 27/68	Jim Roberts, St. Louis	Cesare Maniago, Minnesota
May 16/71	Frank Mahovlich, Montreal	Tony Esposito, Chicago
May 7/75	Bill Barber, Philadelphia	Glenn Resch, NY Islanders
Apr. 20/79	Mike Walton, Chicago	Glenn Resch, NY Islanders
Apr. 9/81	Peter McNab, Boston	Don Beaupre, Minnesota
Apr. 17/81	Anders Hedberg, NY Rangers	Mike Liut, St. Louis
Apr. 9/83	Denis Potvin, NY Islanders	Pat Riggin, Washington
Apr. 28/84	Wayne Gretzky, Edmonton	Don Beaupre, Minnesota
May 1/84	Mats Naslund, Montreal	Bill Smith, NY Islanders
Apr. 14/85	Bob Carpenter, Washington	Bill Smith, NY Islanders
May 28/85	Ron Sutter, Philadelphia	Grant Fuhr, Edmonton
May 30/85	Dave Poulin, Philadelphia	Grant Fuhr, Edmonton

Leading Playoff Scorers, 1926-27 – 1984-85

Season	Player and Club	Games Played	Goals	Assists	Points
1985-86	Doug Gilmour, St. Louis	19	9	12	21
	Bernie Federko, St. Louis	19	7	14	21
1984-85	Wayne Gretzky, Edmonton	18	17	30	47
1983-84	Wayne Gretzky, Edmonton	19	13	22	35
1982-83	Wayne Gretzky, Edmonton	16	12	26	38
1981-82	Bryan Trottier, NY Islanders	19	6	23	29
1980-81	Mike Bossy, NY Islanders	18	17	18	35
1979-80	Bryan Trottier, NY Islanders	21	12	17	29
1978-79	Jacques Lemaire, Montreal	16	11	12	23
	Guy Lafleur, Montreal	16	10	13	23
1977-78	Guy Lafleur, Montreal	15	10	11	21
	Larry Robinson, Montreal	15	4	17	21
1976-77	Guy Lafleur, Montreal	14	9	17	26
1975-76	Reggie Leach, Philadelphia	16	19	5	24
1974-75	Rick MacLeish, Philadelphia	17	11	9	20
1973-74	Rick MacLeish, Philadelphia	17	13	9	22
1972-73	Yvan Cournoyer, Montreal	17	15	10	25
1971-72	Phil Esposito, Boston	15	9	15	24
	Bobby Orr, Boston	15	5	19	24
1970-71	Frank Mahovlich, Montreal	20	14	13	27
1969-70	Phil Esposito, Boston	14	13	14	27
1968-69	Phil Esposito, Boston	10	8	10	18
1967-68	Bill Goldsworthy, Minnesota	14	8	7	15
1966-67	Jim Pappin, Toronto	12	7	8	15
1965-66	Norm Ullman, Detroit	12	6	9	15
1964-65	Bobby Hull, Chicago	14	10	7	17
1963-64	Gordie Howe, Detroit	14	9	10	19
1962-63	Gordie Howe, Detroit	11	7	9	16
	Norm Ullman, Detroit	11	4	12	16
1961-62	Stan Mikita, Chicago	12	6	15	21
1960-61	Gordie Howe, Detroit	11	4	11	15
	Pierre Pilote, Chicago	12	3	12	15
1959-60	Henri Richard, Montreal	8	3	9	12
	Bernie Geoffrion, Montreal	8	2	10	12
1958-59	Dickie Moore, Montreal	11	5	12	17
1957-58	Fleming Mackell, Boston	12	5	14	19
1956-57	Bernie Geoffrion, Montreal	11	11	7	18
1955-56	Jean Béliveau, Montreal	10	12	7	19
1954-55	Gordie Howe, Detroit	11	9	11	20
1953-54	Dickie Moore, Montreal	11	5	8	13
1952-53	Ed Sanford, Boston	11	8	3	11
1951-52	Ted Lindsay, Detroit	8	5	2	7
	Floyd Curry, Montreal	11	4	3	7
	Metro Prystai, Detroit	8	2	5	7
	Gordie Howe, Detroit	8	2	5	7
1950-51	Maurice Richard, Montreal	11	9	4	13
	Max Bentley, Toronto	11	2	11	13
1949-50	Pentti Lund, NY Rangers	12	6	5	11
1948-49	Gordie Howe, Detroit	11	8	3	11
1947-48	Ted Kennedy, Toronto	9	8	6	14
1946-47	Maurice Richard, Montreal	10	6	5	11
1945-46	Elmer Lach, Montreal	9	5	12	17
1944-45	Joe Carveth, Detroit	14	5	6	11
1943-44	Toe Blake, Montreal	9	7	11	18
1942-43	Carl Liscombe, Detroit	10	6	8	14
1941-42	Don Grosso, Detroit	12	8	6	14
1940-41	Milt Schmidt, Boston	11	5	6	11
1939-40	Phil Watson, NY Rangers	12	3	6	9
	Neil Colville, NY Rangers	12	2	7	9
1938-39	Bill Cowley, Boston	12	3	11	14
1937-38	Johnny Gottselig, Chicago	10	5	3	8
1936-37	Marty Barry, Detroit	10	4	7	11
1935-36	Buzz Boll, Toronto	9	7	3	10
1934-35	Baldy Northcott, Mtl. Maroons	7	4	1	5
	Harvey Jackson, Toronto	7	3	2	5
	Marvin Wentworth, Mtl. Maroons	7	3	2	5
1933-34	Larry Aurie, Detroit	9	3	7	10
1932-33	Cecil Dillon, NY Rangers	8	8	2	10
1931-32	Frank Boucher, NY Rangers	7	3	6	9
1930-31	Cooney Weiland, Boston	5	6	3	9
1929-30	Marty Barry, Boston	6	3	3	6
	Cooney Weiland, Boston	6	1	5	6
1928-29	Andy Blair, Toronto	4	3	0	3
	Butch Keeling, NY Rangers	6	3	0	3
	Ace Bailey, Toronto	4	1	2	3
1927-28	Frank Boucher, NY Rangers	9	7	3	10
1926-27	Harry Oliver, Boston	8	4	2	6
	Perk Galbraith, Boston	8	3	3	6
	Frank Fredrickson, Boston	8	2	4	6

Two playoff scoring leaders for the 1940s: Top, Don Grosso had 14 points in 12 games in 1940-41; at right, Pentti Lund had 11 in 12 games in 1949-50.

Clarence Campbell presents the Stanley Cup to Maurice Richard after the Canadiens' fifth consecutive win in 1960. Richard, who retired after the 1960 season, scored 82 goals in Stanley Cup play, twice leading the League in Playoff scoring.

All-Time Playoff Goal Leaders since 1918

(40 or more goals)

Player	Teams	Yrs.	GP	G
*Mike Bossy	NY Islanders	9	123	83
Maurice Richard	Montreal	15	133	82
Jean Beliveau	Montreal	17	162	79
Gordie Howe	Det., Hfd.	20	157	68
*Wayne Gretzky	Edmonton	7	80	64
Yvan Cournoyer	Montreal	12	147	64
Bobby Hull	Chi., Hfd.	14	119	62
Phil Esposito	Chi., Bos., NYR	15	130	61
Stan Mikita	Chicago	18	155	59
Bernie Geoffrion	Mtl., NYR	16	131	58
Guy Lafleur	Montreal	13	124	57
Bryan Trottier	NY Islanders	11	151	55
Rick MacLeish	Phi., Pit., Det.	11	114	54
Bill Barber	Philadelphia	11	129	53
*Denis Potvin	NY Islanders	12	170	53
Frank Mahovlich	Tor., Det., Mtl.	14	137	51
*Jari Kurri	Edmonton	6	77	50
Steve Shutt	Mtl., LA.	10	96	50
Henri Richard	Montreal	18	180	49
Reggie Leach	Philadelphia	8	96	47
Ted Lindsay	Det., Chi.	16	133	47
*Clark Gillies	NY Islanders	12	159	47
Dickie Moore	Mtl., Tor., St. L.	14	135	46
*Mark Messier	Edmonton	7	79	43
Bobby Clarke	Philadelphia	13	136	42
*Glenn Anderson	Edmonton	6	77	41
John Bucyk	Det., Bos.	14	124	41
*Lanny McDonald	Tor., Cgy.	10	89	40
*Peter McNab	Bos., Van.	10	107	40

All-Time Playoff Assist Leaders since 1918

(60 or more assists)

Player	Teams	Yrs.	GP	A
*Wayne Gretzky	Edmonton	7	80	111
*Denis Potvin	NY Islanders	12	170	102
*Bryan Trottier	NY Islanders	11	151	101
Jean Beliveau	Montreal	17	162	97
Gordie Howe	Det., Hfd.	20	157	92
Stan Mikita	Chicago	18	155	91
Brad Park	NYR, Bos., Det.	16	159	90
*Larry Robinson	Montreal	13	154	80
Henri Richard	Montreal	18	180	80
Jacques Lemaire	Montreal	11	145	78
Bobby Clarke	Philadelphia	13	136	77
Guy Lafleur	Montreal	13	124	76
Phil Esposito	Chi., Bos., NYR	15	130	76
*Mike Bossy	NY Islanders	9	123	72
Gilbert Perreault	Buffalo	11	85	70
Bobby Hull	Chi., Hfd.	14	119	67
Frank Mahovlich	Tor., Det., Mtl.	14	137	67
Bobby Orr	Boston	8	74	66
Jean Ratelle	NYR, Bos.	14	120	66
*John Tonelli	NYI, Cgy.	8	135	64
Dickie Moore	Mtl., Tor., St. L.	14	135	64
Doug Harvey	Mtl., NYR, St. L.	15	137	64
*Jari Kurri	Edmonton	6	77	63
Yvan Cournoyer	Montreal	12	147	63
John Bucyk	Det., Bos.	14	124	62
*Ken Linseman	Phi., Edm., Bos.	8	84	61

All-Time Playoff Point Leaders since 1918

(100 or more points)

Player	Teams	Yrs.	GP	G	A	Pts.
Jean Beliveau	Montreal	17	162	79	97	176
*Wayne Gretzky	Edmonton	7	80	64	111	175
Gordie Howe	Det., Hfd.	20	157	68	92	160
*Bryan Trottier	NY Islanders	11	151	55	101	156
*Mike Bossy	NY slanders	9	123	83	72	155
*Denis Potvin	NY slanders	12	170	53	102	155
Stan Mikita	Chicago	18	155	59	91	150
Jacques Lemaire	Montreal	11	145	61	78	139
Phil Esposito	Chi., Bos., NYR	15	130	61	76	137
Guy Lafleur	Montreal	13	124	57	76	133
Bobby Hull	Chi., Hfd.	14	119	62	67	129
Henri Richard	Montreal	18	180	49	80	129
Yvan Cournoyer	Montreal	12	147	64	63	127
Maurice Richard	Montreal	15	133	82	44	126
Brad Park	NYR, Bos., Det.	17	162	35	90	125
Bobby Clarke	Philadelphia	13	136	42	77	119
Frank Mahovlich	Tor., Det., Mtl.	14	137	51	67	118
Bernie Geoffrion	Mtl., NYR	16	131	58	59	117
*Jari Kurri	Edmonton	6	77	50	63	113
Dickie Moore	Mtl., Tor., St. L.	14	135	46	64	110
Bill Barber	Philadelphia	11	129	53	55	108
Rick MacLeish	Phi., Pit., Det.	11	114	54	53	107
Alex Delvecchio	Detroit	14	121	35	69	104
John Bucyk	Det., Bos.	14	124	41	62	103
Gilbert Perreault	Buffalo	14	90	33	70	103

* — Active

Stanley Cup-Winning Goals

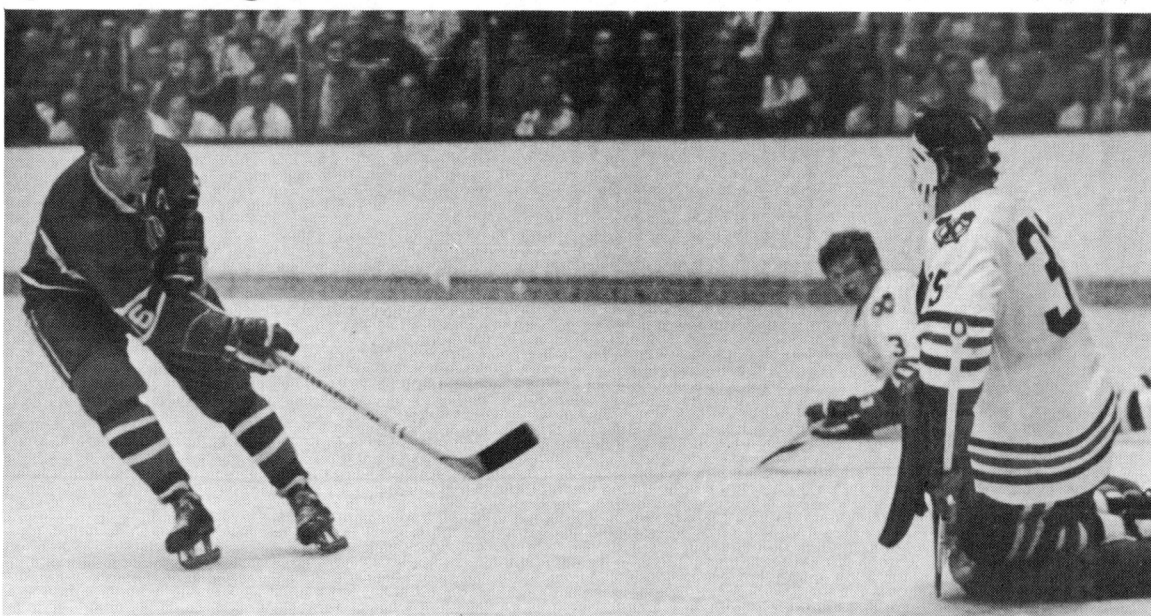

Henri Richard's second Cup-winning goal clinched the Canadiens' upset victory in the seventh game of the 1971 Finals against Chicago.

Only six players, four of them Montreal Canadiens, have twice scored the goals which proved to be the ones to give their team the Stanley Cup Championship.

The four Canadiens are: Hector (Toe) Blake, who scored Cup-winning goals in 1944 and 1946; Jean Béliveau, 1960 and 1965; Henri Richard, 1966 and 1971; and Jacques Lemaire, 1977 and 1979.

The only two non-Montreal players to score two Cup-winning goals are Bobby Orr of the Boston Bruins, who had the winning goals in 1970 and 1972; and Mike Bossy of the New York Islanders who scored winning goals in 1982 and 1983.

Bossy is the only player in playoff history to score Cup-winning goals in consecutive years.

The list of Cup-winning goal scorers contains the names of many stars through the years in which the National Hockey League has been the only League to compete for the Stanley Cup — since the 1926-27 season. Frank Boucher of New York Rangers, Howie Morenz of Montreal Canadiens, Ace Bailey of Toronto, Marty Barry of Detroit, Gordie Howe of Detroit, Maurice Richard of Canadiens, etc.

Of the last 60 Cup-winning goals, 12 were scored in overtime and of those, two were scored in the seventh and deciding game of the Final series. Pete Babando of Detroit dashed the Rangers' hopes of a Stanley Cup title in 1950 when he beat goaltender Chuck Rayner at the 8:31 mark of the second overtime period to give the Red Wings a 4-3 victory after the Rangers had taken a 2-0 lead in the first period. Babando was traded to Chicago the following summer.

In the seventh game of the 1954 Final, tough little Tony Leswick scored against Montreal goaltender Gerry McNeil at 4:29 of the first overtime period to give Detroit a 2-1 victory. Canadiens had led 1-0 early in the game.

The earliest winning goal was scored by Jean Beliveau in the seventh game of the 1965 Final. The Canadiens' captain beat Chicago goaltender Glenn Hall at the 14-second mark of the first period as Canadiens went on to defeat Chicago 4-0 in the game. Babando's goal in 1950 was the one scored in the longest deciding game.

Of the 60 goals, 13 were scored in the first period; 18 in the second; 17 in the third; and 12 in overtime.

The goaltender who suffered the most in respect to Cup-winning goals being scored against him was Glenn Hall, who had six such goals scored against him — with Detroit in 1956; with Chicago in 1962 and 1965; and with St. Louis in 1968, 1969 and 1970. Joining Hall as victim three straight years was Turk Broda of Toronto in 1938, 1939 and 1940.

Following a list of the Cup-winning goal-scorers since 1927:

Cup-Winning Goal Scorers

Year	Winning Team	Scorer	Losing Team	Period	Time	Game Score	Series Score
1927	Ottawa Senators	**Cy Denneny**	Boston	2nd	7:30	3-1	2-0. 2 ties
1928	New York Rangers	**Frank Boucher**	Montreal Maroons	3rd	3:35	2-1	3-2
1929	Boston	**Bill Carson**	New York Rangers	3rd	18:02	2-1	2-0
1930	Montreal Canadiens	**Howie Morenz**	Boston	2nd	1:00	4-3	2-0
1931	Montreal Canadiens	**Johnny Gagnon**	Chicago	2nd	9:59	2-0	3-2
1932	Toronto	**Ace Bailey**	New York Rangers	3rd	15:07	6-4	3-0
1933	New York Rangers	**Bill Cook**	Toronto	OT	7:34	1-0	3-1
1934	Chicago	**Mush March**	Detroit	OT	30:05	1-0	3-1
1935	Montreal Maroons	**Baldy Northcott**	Toronto	2nd	16:18	4-1	3-0
1936	Detroit	**Pete Kelly**	Toronto	3rd	9:45	3-2	3-1
1937	Detroit	**Marty Barry**	New York Rangers	1st	19:22	3-0	3-2
1938	Chicago	**Carl Voss**	Toronto	2nd	16:45	4-1	3-1
1939	Boston	**Roy Conacher**	Toronto	2nd	17:54	3-1	4-1
1940	New York Rangers	**Bryan Hextall**	Toronto	OT	2:07	3-2	4-2
1941	Boston	**Bobby Bauer**	Detroit	2nd	8:43	3-1	4-0
1942	Toronto	**Pete Langelle**	Detroit	3rd	9:48	3-1	4-3
1943	Detroit	**Joe Carveth**	Boston	1st	12:09	2-0	4-0
1944	Montreal	**Toe Blake**	Chicago	OT	9:12	5-4	4-0
1945	Toronto	**Babe Pratt**	Detroit	3rd	12:14	2-1	4-3
1946	Montreal	**Toe Blake**	Boston	3rd	11:06	6-3	4-1
1947	Toronto	**Ted Kennedy**	Montreal	3rd	14:39	2-1	4-2
1948	Toronto	**Harry Watson**	Detroit	1st	11:13	7-2	4-0
1949	Toronto	**Cal Gardner**	Detroit	2nd	19:45	3-1	4-0
1950	Detroit	**Pete Babando**	New York Rangers	OT	28:31	4-3	4-3
1951	Toronto	**Bill Barilko**	Montreal	OT	2:53	3-2	4-1
1952	Detroit	**Metro Prystai**	Montreal	1st	6:50	3-0	4-0
1953	Montreal	**Elmer Lach**	Boston	OT	1:22	1-0	4-1
1954	Detroit	**Tony Leswick**	Montreal	OT	4:29	2-1	4-3
1955	Detroit	**Gordie Howe**	Montreal	2nd	19:49	3-1	4-3
1956	Montreal	**Maurice Richard**	Detroit	2nd	15:08	3-1	4-1
1957	Montreal	**Dickie Moore**	Boston	2nd	00:14	5-1	4-1
1958	Montreal	**Bernie Geoffrion**	Boston	2nd	19:26	5-3	4-2
1959	Montreal	**Marcel Bonin**	Toronto	2nd	9:55	5-3	4-1
1960	Montreal	**Jean Béliveau**	Toronto	1st	8:16	4-0	4-0
1961	Chicago	**Ab McDonald**	Detroit	2nd	18:49	5-1	4-2
1962	Toronto	**Dick Duff**	Chicago	3rd	14:14	2-1	4-2
1963	Toronto	**Eddie Shack**	Detroit	3rd	13:28	3-1	4-1
1964	Toronto	**Andy Bathgate**	Detroit	1st	3:04	4-0	4-3
1965	Montreal	**Jean Béliveau**	Chicago	1st	00:14	4-0	4-3
1966	Montreal	**Henri Richard**	Detroit	OT	2:20	3-2	3-2
1967	Toronto	**Jim Pappin**	Montreal	2nd	19:24	3-1	4-2
1968	Montreal	**Jean-Claude Tremblay**	St. Louis	3rd	11:40	3-2	4-0
1969	Montreal	**John Ferguson**	St. Louis	3rd	3:02	2-1	4-0
1970	Boston	**Bobby Orr**	St. Louis	OT	00:40	4-3	4-0
1971	Montreal	**Henri Richard**	Chicago	3rd	2:34	3-2	4-3
1972	Boston	**Bobby Orr**	New York Rangers	1st	11:18	3-0	4-2
1973	Montreal	**Yvan Cournoyer**	Chicago	3rd	8:13	6-4	4-2
1974	Philadelphia	**Rick MacLeish**	Boston	1st	14:48	1-0	4-2
1975	Philadelphia	**Bob Kelly**	Buffalo	3rd	00:11	2-0	4-2
1976	Montreal	**Guy Lafleur**	Philadelphia	3rd	14:18	5-3	4-0
1977	Montreal	**Jacques Lemaire**	Boston	OT	4:32	2-1	4-0
1978	Montreal	**Mario Tremblay**	Boston	1st	9:20	4-1	4-2
1979	Montreal	**Jacques Lemaire**	New York Rangers	2nd	1:02	4-1	4-1
1980	New York Islanders	**Bob Nystrom**	Philadelphia	OT	7:11	5-4	4-2
1981	New York Islanders	**Wayne Merrick**	Minnesota	1st	5:37	5-1	4-1
1982	New York Islanders	**Mike Bossy**	Vancouver	2nd	5:00	3-1	4-0
1983	New York Islanders	**Mike Bossy**	Edmonton	1st	12:39	4-2	4-0
1984	Edmonton	**Ken Linseman**	New York Islanders	2nd	00:38	5-2	4-1
1985	Edmonton	**Paul Coffey**	Philadelphia	1st	17:57	8-3	4-1
1986	Montreal	**Bobby Smith**	Calgary	3rd	10:30	4-3	4-1

Three or more Goal Games, Playoffs 1926-27 – 1985-86

Player	Team	Date	City	Total Goals	Opposing Goaltender	Score	
Maurice Richard (7)	Mtl.	Mar. 23/44	Mtl.	5	Paul Bibeault	Mtl. 5	Tor. 1
		Apr. 7/44	Chi.	3	Mike Karakas	Mtl. 3	Chi. 1
		Mar. 29/45	Mtl.	4	Frank McCool	Mtl. 10	Tor. 3
		Apr. 14/53	Bos.	3	Gord Henry	Mtl. 7	Bos. 3
		Mar. 20/56	Mtl.	3	Lorne Worsley	Mtl. 7	NYR 1
		Apr. 6/57	Mtl.	4	Don Simmons	Mtl. 5	Bos. 1
		Apr. 1/58	Det.	3	Terry Sawchuk	Mtl. 4	Det. 3
Wayne Gretzky (7)	Edm.	Apr. 11/81	Edm.	3	Richard Sevigny	Edm. 6	Mtl. 2
		Apr. 19/81	Edm.	3	Billy Smith	Edm. 5	NYI 2
		Apr. 6/83	Edm.	4	Brian Hayward	Edm. 6	Wpg. 3
		Apr. 17/83	Cgy.	4	Rejean Lemelin	Edm. 10	Cgy. 2
		Apr. 25/85	Wpg.	3	Bryan Hayward (2) Marc Behrend (1)	Edm. 8	Wpg. 3
		May 25/85	Edm.	3	Pelle Lindbergh	Edm. 4	Phi. 3
		Apr. 24/86	Cgy.	3	Mike Vernon	Edm. 7	Cgy. 4
Mike Bossy (5)	NYI	Apr. 16/79	NYI	3	Tony Esposito	NYI 6	Chi. 2
		May 8/82	NYI	3	Richard Brodeur	NYI 6	Van. 5
		Apr. 10/83	Wash	3	Al Jensen	NYI 6	Wash. 3
		May 3/83	NYI	3	Pete Peeters	NYI 8	Bos. 3
		May 7/83	NYI	4	Pete Peeters	NYI 8	Bos. 4
Jari Kurri (5)	Edm.	Apr. 4/84	Edm.	3	Doug Soetaert (1) Mike Veisor (2)	Edm. 9	Wpg. 2
		Apr. 25/85	Wpg.	3	Bryan Hayward (2) Marc Behrend (1)	Edm. 8	Wpg. 3
		May 7/85	Edm.	3	Murray Bannerman	Edm. 7	Chi. 3
		May 14/85	Edm.	3	Murray Bannerman	Edm. 10	Chi. 5
		May 16/85	Chi.	3	Murray Bannerman	Edm. 8	Chi. 2
Phil Esposito (4)	Bos.	Apr. 2/69	Bos.	4	Bruce Gamble	Bos. 10	Tor. 0
		Apr. 8/70	Bos.	3	Ed Giacomin	Bos. 8	NYR 2
		Apr. 19/70	Chi.	3	Tony Esposito	Bos. 6	Chi. 3
		Apr. 8/75	Bos.	3	Tony Esposito (2) Michel Dumas (1)	Bos. 8	Chi. 2
Bernie Geoffrion (3)	Mtl.	Mar. 27/52	Mtl.	3	Jim Henry	Mtl. 4	Bos. 0
		Apr. 7/55	Mtl.	3	Terry Sawchuk	Mtl. 4	Det. 2
		Mar. 30/57	Mtl.	3	Lorne Worsley	Mtl. 8	NYR 3
Norm Ullman (3)	Det.	Mar. 29/64	Chi.	3	Glenn Hall	Det. 5	Chi. 4
		Apr. 7/64	Det.	3	Glenn Hall (2) Denis DeJordy (1)	Det. 7	Chi. 2
		Apr. 11/65	Det.	3	Glenn Hall	Det. 4	Chi. 2
John Bucyk (3)	Bos.	May 3/70	St. L.	3	Jacques Plante (1) Ernie Wakely (2)	Bos. 6	St.L. 1
		Apr. 20/72	Bos.	3	Jacques Caron (1) Ernie Wakely (2)	Bos. 10	St.L. 2
		Apr. 21/74	Bos.	3	Tony Esposito	Bos. 8	Chi. 6
Rick MacLeish (3)	Phil	Apr. 11/74	Phil	3	Phil Myre	Phi. 4	Atl. 1
		Apr. 13/75	Phil	3	Gord McRae	Phi. 6	Tor. 3
		May 13/75	Phil	3	Glenn Resch	Phi. 4	NYI 1
Mark Messier (3)	Edm.	Apr. 14/83	Edm.	4	Rejean Lemelin	Edm. 6	Cgy. 3
		Apr. 17/83	Cgy.	4	Rejean Lemelin (1) Don Edwards (2)	Edm. 10	Cgy. 3
		Apr. 26/83	Edm.	3	Murray Bannerman	Edm. 8	Chi. 2
Ted Kennedy (2)	Tor.	Apr. 14/45	Tor.	3	Harry Lumley	Det. 5	Tor. 3
		Mar. 27/48	Tor.	4	Frank Brimsek	Tor. 5	Bos. 3
Doug Bentley (2)	Chi.	Mar. 28/44	Chi.	3	Connie Dion	Chi. 7	Det. 1
		Mar. 30/44	Det.	3	Connie Dion	Chi. 5	Det. 2
Toe Blake (2)	Mtl.	Mar. 22/38	Mtl.	3	Mike Karakas	Mtl. 6	Chi. 4
		Mar. 26/46	Chi.	3	Mike Karakas	Mtl. 7	Chi. 2
Dino Ciccarelli (2)	Minn	May 5/81	Minn	3	Pat Riggin	Min. 7	Cgy. 4
		Apr. 10/82	Minn	3	Murray Bannerman	Min. 7	Chi. 1
Bobby Hull (2)	Chi.	Apr. 7/63	Det.	3	Terry Sawchuk	Det. 7	Chi. 4
		Apr. 9/72	Pitt	3	Jim Rutherford	Chi. 6	Pit. 5
F. St. Marseille (2)	St. L.	Apr. 28/70	St.L	3	Al Smith	St.L. 5	Pit. 0
		Apr. 6/72	Minn	3	Cesare Maniago	Min. 6	St.L. 5
Pit Martin (2)	Chi.	Apr. 4/73	Chi.	3	W. Stephenson	Chi. 7	St.L. 1
		May 10/73	Chi.	3	Ken Dryden	Mtl. 6	Chi. 4
Yvan Cournoyer (2)	Mtl.	May 5/73	Mtl.	3	Dave Dryden	Mtl. 7	Buf. 3
		Apr. 11/74	Mtl.	3	Ed Giacomin	Mtl. 4	NYR 1

Player	Team	Date	City	Total Goals	Opposing Goaltender	Score	
Lanny McDonald (2)	Tor.	Apr. 9/77	Pitt	3	Denis Herron	Tor. 5	Pit. 2
		Apr. 17/77	Tor.	4	W. Stephenson	Phi. 6	Tor. 5
Guy Lafleur (2)	Mtl.	May 1/75	Mtl.	3	Roger Crozier (1) Gerry Desjardins (2)	Mtl. 7	Buf. 0
		Apr. 11/77	Mtl.	3	Ed Staniowski	Mtl. 7	St.L. 2
Butch Goring (2)	L.A.	Apr. 9/77	L.A.	3	Phil Myre	L.A. 4	Atl. 2
	NYI	May 17/81	Minn	3	Gilles Meloche	NYI 7	Min. 5
Bryan Trottier (2)	NYI	Apr. 8/80	NYI	3	Doug Keans	NYI 8	L.A. 1
		Apr. 9/81	NYI	3	Michel Larocque	NYI 5	Tor. 1
Bill Barber (2)	Phil	May 4/80	Minn	3	Gilles Meloche	Phi. 5	Min. 3
		Apr. 9/81	Phil	3	Dan Bouchard	Phi. 8	Que. 5
Paul Reinhart (2)	Cgy	Apr. 14/83	Edm.	3	Andy Moog	Edm. 6	Cgy. 3
		Apr. 8/84	Van.	3	Richard Brodeur	Cgy. 5	Van. 1
Brain Propp (2)	Phi.	Apr. 22/81	Phi.	3	Pat Riggin	Phi. 9	Cgy. 4
		Apr. 21/85	Phi.	3	Billy Smith	Phi. 5	NYI 2
Denis Savard(2)	Chi.	Apr. 19/82	Chi.	3	Mike Liut	Chi. 7	StL. 4
		Apr. 10/86	Chi.	4	Ken Wregget	Tor. 6	Chi. 4
Perk Galbraith	Bos.	Mar. 31/27	Bos.	3	Hugh Lehman	Bos. 4	Chi. 4
Busher Jackson	Tor.	Apr. 5/32	NYR	3	John Ross Roach	Tor. 6	NYR 4
Frank Boucher	NYR	Apr. 9/32	Tor.	3	Lorne Chabot	Tor. 6	NYR 4
Charlie Conacher	Tor.	Mar. 26/36	Tor.	3	Tiny Thompson	Tor. 8	Bos. 3
Syd Howe	Det.	Mar. 23/39	Det.	3	Claude Bourque	Det. 7	Mtl. 3
Bryan Hextall	NYR	Apr. 3/40	NYR	3	Turk Broda	NYR 6	Tor. 2
Joe Benoit	Mtl.	Mar. 22/41	Mtl.	3	Sam LoPresti	Mtl. 4	Chi. 3
Syl Apps	Tor.	Mar. 25/41	Tor.	3	Frank Brimsek	Tor. 7	Bos. 2
Jack McGill	Bos.	Mar. 29/42	Bos.	3	Johnny Mowers	Det. 6	Bos. 4
Don Metz	Tor.	Apr. 14/42	Tor.	3	Johnny Mowers	Tor. 9	Det. 3
Mud Bruneteau	Det.	Apr. 1/43	Det.	3	Frank Brimsek	Det. 6	Bos. 2
Don Grosso	Det.	Apr. 7/43	Bos.	3	Frank Brimsek	Det. 4	Bos. 0
Carl Liscombe	Det.	Apr. 3/45	Bos.	4	Paul Bibeault	Det. 5	Bos. 3
Billy Reay	Mtl.	Apr. 1/47	Bos.	3	Frank Brimsek	Mtl. 5	Bos. 1
Gerry Plamondon	Mtl.	Mar. 24/49	Det.	3	Harry Lumley	Mtl. 4	Det. 3
Sid Smith	Tor.	Apr. 10/49	Det.	3	Harry Lumley	Tor. 3	Det. 1
Pentti Lund	NYR	Apr. 2/50	NYR	3	Bill Durnan	NYR 4	Mtl. 1
Ted Lindsay	Det.	Apr. 5/55	Det.	4	Charlie Hodge (1) Jacques Plante (3)	Det. 7	Mtl. 1
Gordie Howe	Det.	Apr. 10/55	Det.	3	Jacques Plante	Det. 5	Mtl. 1
Phil Goyette	Mtl.	Mar. 25/58	Mtl.	3	Terry Sawchuk	Mtl. 8	Det. 1
Jerry Toppazzini	Bos.	Apr. 5/58	Bos.	3	Lorne Worsley	Bos. 8	NYR 2
Bob Pulford	Tor.	Apr. 19/62	Tor.	3	Glenn Hall	Tor. 8	Chi. 4
Dave Keon	Tor.	Apr. 9/64	Mtl.	3	Charlie Hodge	Tor. 3	Mtl. 1
Henri Richard	Mtl.	Apr. 20/67	Mtl.	3	Terry Sawchuk (2) Johnny Bower (1)	Mtl. 6	Tor. 2
Rosaire Paiement	Phi.	Apr. 13/68	Phi.	3	Glenn Hall (1) Seth Martin (2)	Phi. 6	St. L. 1
Jean Béliveau	Mtl.	Apr. 20/68	Mtl.	3	Denis DeJordy	Mtl. 4	Chi. 1
Red Berenson	St. L.	Apr. 15/69	St. L.	3	Gerry Desjardins	St. L. 4	L.A. 0
Ken Schinkel	Pit.	Apr. 11/70	Oak.	3	Gary Smith	Pit. 5	Oak. 2
Jim Pappin	Chi.	Apr. 11/71	Chi.	3	Bruce Gamble	Chi. 6	Phi. 2
Bobby Orr	Bos.	Apr. 11/71	Bos.	3	Ken Dryden	Bos. 5	Mtl. 2
Jacques Lemaire	Mtl.	Apr. 20/71	Mtl.	3	Lorne Worsley	Mtl. 7	Min. 2
Vic Hadfield	NYR	Apr. 22/71	NYR	3	Tony Esposito	NYR 4	Chi. 1
Fred Stanfield	Bos.	Apr. 18/72	Bos.	3	Jacques Caron	Bos. 6	St. L. 1
Ken Hodge	Bos.	Apr. 30/72	Bos.	3	Ed Giacomin	Bos. 6	NYR 5
Steve Vickers	NYR	Apr. 10/73	Bos.	3	Ross Brooks (2) Ed Johnston (1)	NYR 6	Bos. 3
Dick Redmond	Chi.	Apr. 4/73	Chi.	3	Wayne Stephenson	Chi. 7	St.L. 1
Tom Williams	L.A.	Apr. 14/74	L.A.	3	Mike Veisor	L.A. 5	Chi. 1
Marcel Dionne	L.A.	Apr. 15/76	L.A.	3	Gilles Gilbert	L.A. 6	Bos. 4
Don Saleski	Phi.	Apr. 20/76	Phil	3	Wayne Thomas	Phi. 7	Tor. 1
Darryl Sittler	Tor.	Apr. 22/76	Tor.	5	Bernie Parent	Tor. 8	Phi. 5
Reggie Leach	Phi.	May 6/76	Phil	5	Gilles Gilbert	Phi. 6	Bos. 3
Jim Lorentz	Buf.	Apr. 7/77	Minn	3	Pete LoPresti (2) Gary Smith (1)	Buf. 7	Min. 1
Bobby Schmautz	Bos.	Apr. 11/77	Bos.	3	Rogatien Vachon	Bos. 8	L.A. 3
Billy Harris	NYI	Apr. 23/77	Mtl.	3	Ken Dryden	Mtl. 4	NYI 3
George Ferguson	Tor.	Apr. 11/78	Tor.	3	Rogatien Vachon	Tor. 7	L.A. 3
Jean Ratelle	Bos.	May 3/79	Bos.	3	Ken Dryden	Bos. 4	Mtl. 3
Stan Jonathan	Bos.	May 8/79	Bos.	3	Ken Dryden	Bos. 5	Mtl. 2
Ron Duguay	NYR	Apr. 20/80	NYR	3	Pete Peeters	NYR 4	Phi. 2
Steve Shutt	Mtl.	Apr. 22/80	Mtl.	3	Gilles Meloche	Mtl. 6	Min. 2
Gilbert Perreault	Buf.	May 6/80	NYI	3	Billy Smith (2) ENG (1)	Buf. 7	NYI 4
Paul Holmgren	Phi.	May 15/80	Phil	3	Billy Smith	Phi. 8	NYI 3
Steve Payne	Min.	Apr. 8/81	Bos.	3	Rogatien Vachon	Min. 5	Bos. 4
Denis Potvin	NYI	Apr. 17/81	NYI	3	Andy Moog	NYI 6	Edm. 3
Barry Pederson	Bos.	Apr. 8/82	Bos.	3	Don Edwards	Bos. 7	Buf. 3
Peter Stastny	Que.	Apr. 5/83	Bos.	3	Pete Peeters	Bos. 4	Que. 3
Duane Sutter	NYI	Apr. 15/83	NYI	3	Glen Hanlon	NYI 5	NYR 0
Glenn Anderson	Edm.	Apr. 26/83	Edm.	4	Murray Bannerman	Edm. 8	Chi. 2
Doug Halward	Van.	Apr. 7/84	Van.	3	Rejean Lemelin (2) Don Edwards (1)	Van. 7	Cgy. 0
Jorgen Pettersson	St. L.	Apr. 8/84	Det.	3	Ed Mio	St. L. 3	Det. 2
Clark Gillies	NYI	May 12/84	NYI	3	Grant Fuhr	NYI 6	Edm. 1
Tim Kerr	Phi.	Apr. 13/85	NYR	4	Glen Hanlon	Phi. 6	NYR 5
Ken Linseman	Bos.	Apr. 14/85	Bos.	3	Steve Penney	Bos. 7	Mtl. 6
Dave Andreychuk	Buf.	Apr. 14/85	Buf.	3	Dan Bouchard	Que. 4	Buf. 7
Michel Goulet	Que.	Apr. 23/85	Que.	3	Steve Penney	Que. 7	Mtl. 6
Peter Zezel	Phi.	Apr. 13/86	NYR	3	J. Vanbiesbrouck	Phi. 7	NYR 1
Greg Paslawski	StL.	Apr. 15/86	Min.	3	Don Beaupre	St. L. 6	Min. 3
Doug Risebrough	Cgy.	May 4/86	Cgy.	3	Rick Wamsley	Cgy. 8	StL. 2

Wayne Gretzky has seven three-goal games in Stanley Cup play.

Overtime Games since 1927

Abbreviations: CITIES — **Atl.** - Atlanta; **Bos.** - Boston; **Cgy.** - Calgary; **Chi.** - Chicago; **Det.** - Detroit; **Edm.** - Edmonton; **Hfd.** - Hartford; **Min.** - Minnesota; **Mtl.** - Montreal; **NY** - New York; **Oak.** - Oakland; **Ott.** - Ottawa; **Phi.** - Philadelphia; **Pit.** - Pittsburgh; **St.L.** - St. Louis; **Tor.** - Toronto.
TEAMS — **Atl.** - Atlanta; **Bos.** - Boston; **Buf.** - Buffalo; **Chi.** - Chicago; **Col.** - Colorado; **Det.** - Detroit; **Edm.** - Edmonton; **Hfd.** - Hartford; **L.A.** - Los Angeles; **Min.** - Minnesota; **Mtl.** - Montreal Canadiens; **Mtl. M.** - Montreal Maroons; **NYR** - New York Rangers; **NYA** - New York Americans; **NYI** - New York Islanders; **Oak** - Oakland; **Ott.** - Ottawa Senators; **Phi.** - Philadelphia Flyers; **Pit.** - Pittsburgh Penguins; **Que.** - Quebec Nordiques; **St.L.** - St. Louis Blues; **Tor.** - Toronto Maple Leafs.
SERIES — **Prelim.** - Preliminary round; — **QF** - Quarter-Final; **SF** - Semi-Final; **F** - Final; **DSF** - Division Semi-Final; **DF** - Division Final; **CF** - Conference Final.

Date	City	Series	Score		Scorer	Overtime	Series Winner
Mar. 31/27	Mtl.	QF	Mtl. 1	Mtl. M. 0	Howie Morenz	12:05	Mtl.
Apr. 7/27	Bos.	F	Ott. 0	Bos. 0	no scorer	20:00	Ott.
Apr. 11/27	Ott.	F	Bos. 1	Ott. 1			
Apr. 3/28	Mtl.	QF	Mtl. M. 1	Mtl. 0	Russ Oatman	8:20	Mtl. M.
Apr. 7/28	Mtl.	F	NYR 2	Mtl. M. 1	Frank Boucher	7:05	NYR
Mar. 21/29	NY	QF	NYR 1	NYA 0	Butch Keeling	29:50	NYR
Mar. 26/29	Tor.	SF	NYR 2	Tor. 1	Frank Boucher	2:03	NYR
Mar. 20/30	Mtl.	SF	Bos. 2	Mtl. M. 1	Harry Oliver	45:35	Bos.
Mar. 25/30	Bos.	SF	Mtl. M. 1	Bos. 0	Archie Wilcox	26:27	Bos.
Mar. 26/30	Mtl.	QF	Chi. 2	Mtl. 2	Howie Morenz (Mtl.)	51:43	Mtl.
Mar. 28/30	Mtl.	SF	Mtl. 2	NYR 1	Gus Rivers	68:52	Mtl.
Mar. 24/31	Bos.	SF	Bos. 5	Mtl. 4	Cooney Weiland	18:56	Mtl.
Mar. 26/31	Chi.	QF	Chi. 2	Tor. 1	Steward Adams	19:20	Chi.
Mar. 28/31	Mtl.	SF	Mtl. 4	Bos. 3	Georges Mantha	5:10	Mtl.
Apr. 1/31	Mtl.	SF	Mtl. 3	Bos. 2	Vildor Larochelle	19:00	Mtl.
Apr. 5/31	Chi.	F	Chi. 2	Mtl. 1	Johnny Gottselig	24:50	Mtl.
Apr. 9/31	Mtl.	F	Chi. 3	Mtl. 2	Cy Wentworth	53:50	Mtl.
Mar. 26/32	Mtl.	SF	NYR 4	Mtl. 3	Fred Cook	59:32	NYR
Apr. 2/32	Tor.	SF	Tor. 3	Mtl. M. 2	Bob Gracie	17:59	Tor.
Mar. 25/33	Bos.	SF	Bos. 2	Tor. 1	Marty Barry	14:14	Tor.
Mar. 28/33	Bos.	SF	Tor. 1	Bos. 0	Busher Jackson	15:03	Tor.
Mar. 30/33	Tor.	SF	Bos. 2	Tor. 1	Eddie Shore	4:23	Tor.
Apr. 3/33	Tor.	SF	Tor. 1	Bos. 0	Ken Doraty	104:46	Tor.
Apr. 13/33	Tor.	F	NYR 1	Tor. 0	Bill Cook	7:33	NYR
Mar. 22/34	Tor.	SF	Det. 2	Tor. 1	Herbie Lewis	1:33	Det.
Mar. 25/34	Chi.	QF	Chi. 1	Mtl. 1	Mush March (Chi)	11:05	Chi.
Apr. 3/34	Det.	F	Chi. 2	Det. 1	Paul Thompson	21:05	Chi.
Apr. 10/34	Chi.	F	Chi. 1	Det. 0	Mush March	30:05	Chi.
Mar. 23/35	Bos.	SF	Bos. 1	Tor. 0	Dit Clapper	33:26	Tor.
Mar. 26/35	Chi.	QF	Mtl. M. 1	Chi. 0	Baldy Northcott	4:02	Mtl. M
Mar. 30/35	Tor.	SF	Tor. 2	Bos. 1	Pep Kelly	1:36	Tor.
Apr. 4/35	Tor.	F	Mtl. M. 3	Tor. 2	Dave Trottier	5:2	Mtl. M.
Mar. 24/36	Mtl.	SF	Det. 1	Mtl. M. 0	Mud Bruneteau	116:30	Det.
Apr. 9/36	Tor.	F	Tor. 4	Det. 3	Buzz Boll	00:31	Det.
Mar. 25/37	NY	QF	NYR 2	Tor. 1	Babe Pratt	13:05	NYR
Apr. 1/37	Mtl.	SF	Det. 2	Mtl. 1	Hec Kilrea	51:49	Det.
Mar. 22/38	NY	QF	NYA 2	NYR 1	Johnny Sorrell	21:25	NYA
Mar. 25/38	Tor.	SF	Tor. 1	Bos. 0	George Parsons	21:31	Tor.
Mar. 26/38	Mtl.	QF	Chi. 3	Mtl. 2	Paul Thompson	11:49	Chi.
Mar. 27/38	NY	QF	NYA 3	NYR 2	Lorne Carr	60:40	NYA
Mar. 29/38	Bos.	SF	Tor. 3	Bos. 2	Gord Drillon	10:04	Tor.
Mar. 31/38	Chi.	SF	Chi. 1	NYA 0	Cully Dahlstrom	33:01	Chi.
Mar. 21/39	NY	SF	Bos. 2	NYR 1	Mel Hill	59:25	Bos.
Mar. 23/39	Bos.	SF	Bos. 3	NYR 2	Mel Hill	8:24	Bos.
Mar. 26/39	Det.	QF	Det. 1	Mtl. 0	Marty Barry	7:47	Det.
Mar. 30/39	Bos.	SF	NYR 2	Bos. 1	Snuffy Smith	17:19	Bos.
Apr. 1/39	Tor.	SF	Tor. 5	Det. 4	Gord Drillon	5:42	Tor.
Apr. 2/39	Bos.	SF	Bos. 2	NYR 1	Mel Hill	48:00	Bos.
Apr. 9/39	Bos.	F	Tor. 3	Bos. 2	Doc Romnes	10:38	Bos.
Mar. 19/40	Det.	QF	Det. 2	NYA 1	Syd Howe	00:25	Det.
Mar. 19/40	Tor.	QF	Tor. 3	Chi. 2	Syl Apps	6:35	Tor.
Apr. 2/40	NY	F	NYR 2	Tor. 1	Alf Pike	15:30	NYR
Apr. 11/40	Tor.	F	NYR 2	Tor. 1	Muzz Patrick	31:43	NYR
Apr. 13/40	Tor.	F	NYR 3	Tor. 2	Bryan Hextall	2:07	NYR
Mar. 20/41	Det.	QF	Det. 2	NYR 1	Gus Giesebrecht	12:01	Det.
Mar. 22/41	Mtl.	QF	Mtl. 4	Chi. 3	Charlie Sands	34:04	Chi.
Mar. 29/41	Bos.	SF	Tor. 2	Bos. 1	Pete Langelle	17:31	Bos.
Mar. 30/41	Chi.	SF	Det. 2	Chi. 1	Gus Giesebrecht	9:15	Det.
Mar. 22/42	Chi.	QF	Bos. 2	Chi. 1	Des Smith	9:51	Bos.
Mar. 21/43	Bos.	SF	Bos. 5	Mtl. 4	Don Gallinger	12:30	Bos.
Mar. 23/43	Det.	SF	Tor. 3	Det. 2	Jack McLean	70:18	Det.
Mar. 25/43	Mtl.	SF	Bos. 3	Mtl. 2	Harvey Jackson	3:20	Bos.
Mar. 30/43	Tor.	SF	Det. 3	Tor. 2	Adam Brown	9:21	Det.
Mar. 30/43	Bos.	SF	Bos. 5	Mtl. 4	Ab DeMarco	3:41	Bos.
Apr. 13/44	Mtl.	F	Mtl. 5	Chi. 4	Toe Blake	9:12	Mtl.
Mar. 27/45	Tor.	SF	Tor. 4	Mtl. 3	Gus Bodnar	12:36	Tor.
Mar. 29/45	Det.	SF	Det. 3	Bos. 2	Mud Bruneteau	17:12	Det.
Apr. 21/45	Tor.	F	Det. 1	Tor. 0	Ed Bruneteau	14:16	Tor.
Mar. 28/46	Bos.	SF	Bos. 4	Det. 3	Don Gallinger	9:51	Bos.
Mar. 30/46	Mtl.	F	Mtl. 4	Bos. 3	Maurice Richard	9:08	Mtl.
Apr. 2/46	Mtl.	F	Mtl. 3	Bos. 2	Jim Peters	16:55	Mtl.
Apr. 7/46	Bos.	F	Bos. 3	Mtl. 2	Terry Reardon	15:13	Mtl.
Mar. 26/47	Tor.	SF	Tor. 3	Det. 2	Howie Meeker	3:05	Tor.
Mar. 27/47	Mtl.	SF	Mtl. 2	Bos. 1	Ken Mosdell	5:38	Mtl.
Apr. 3/47	Mtl.	SF	Mtl. 4	Bos. 3	John Quilty	36:40	Mtl.
Apr. 15/47	Tor.	F	Tor. 2	Mtl. 1	Syl Apps	16:36	Tor.
Mar. 24/48	Tor.	SF	Tor. 5	Bos. 4	Nick Metz	17:03	Tor.
Mar. 22/49	Det.	SF	Det. 2	Mtl. 1	Max McNab	44:52	Det.
Mar. 24/49	Det.	SF	Mtl. 4	Det. 3	Gerry Plamondon	2:59	Det.
Mar. 26/49	Tor.	SF	Bos. 5	Tor. 4	Woody Dumart	16:14	Tor.
Apr. 8/49	Det.	F	Tor. 3	Det. 2	Joe Klukay	17:31	Tor.

Date	City	Series	Score		Scorer	Overtime	Series Winner
Apr. 4/50	Tor.	SF	Det. 2	Tor. 1	Leo Reise	20:38	Det.
Apr. 4/50	Mtl.	SF	Mtl. 3	NYR 2	Elmer Lach	15:19	Mtl.
Apr. 9/50	Det.	SF	Det. 1	Tor. 0	Leo Reise	8:39	Det.
Apr. 18/50	Det.	F	NYR 4	Det. 3	Don Raleigh	8:34	Det.
Apr. 20/50	Det.	F	NYR 2	Det. 1	Don Raleigh	1:38	Det.
Apr. 23/50	Det.	F	Det. 4	NYR 3	Pete Babando	28:31	Det.
Mar. 27/51	Det.	SF	Mtl. 3	Det. 2	Maurice Richard	61:09	Mtl.
Mar. 29/51	Det.	SF	Mtl. 1	Det. 0	Maurice Richard	42:20	Mtl.
Mar. 31/51	Tor.	SF	Bos. 1	Tor. 1	no scorer	20:00	Tor.
Apr. 11/51	Tor.	F	Tor. 3	Mtl. 2	Sid Smith	5:51	Tor.
Apr. 14/51	Tor.	F	Mtl. 3	Tor. 2	Maurice Richard	2:55	Tor.
Apr. 17/51	Mtl.	F	Tor. 2	Mtl. 1	Ted Kennedy	4:47	Tor.
Apr. 19/51	Mtl.	F	Tor. 3	Mtl. 2	Harry Watson	5:15	Tor.
Apr. 21/51	Tor.	F	Tor. 3	Mtl. 2	Bill Barilko	2:53	Tor.
Apr. 6/52	Bos.	SF	Mtl. 3	Bos. 2	Paul Masnick	27:49	Mtl.
Mar. 29/53	Bos.	SF	Bos. 2	Det. 1	Jack McIntyre	12:29	Bos.
Mar. 29/53	Chi.	SF	Chi. 2	Mtl. 1	Al Dewsbury	5:18	Mtl.
Apr. 16/53	Mtl.	F	Mtl. 1	Bos. 0	Elmer Lach	1:22	Mtl.
Apr. 1/54	Det.	SF	Det. 4	Tor. 3	Ted Lindsay	21:01	Det.
Apr. 11/54	Det.	F	Mtl. 1	Det. 0	Ken Mosdell	5:45	Det.
Apr. 16/54	Det.	F	Det. 2	Mtl. 1	Tony Leswick	4:29	Det.
Mar. 29/55	Bos.	SF	Mtl. 4	Bos. 3	Don Marshall	3:05	Mtl.
Mar. 24/56	Tor.	SF	Det. 5	Tor. 4	Ted Lindsay	4:22	Det.
Mar. 28/57	NY	SF	NYR 4	Mtl. 3	Andy Hebenton	13:38	Mtl.
Apr. 4/57	Mtl.	SF	Mtl. 4	NYR 3	Maurice Richard	1:11	Mtl.
Mar. 27/58	NY	SF	Bos. 4	NYR 3	Jerry Toppazzini	4:46	Bos.
Mar. 30/58	Det.	SF	Mtl. 2	Det. 1	André Pronovost	11:52	Mtl.
Apr. 17/58	Mtl.	F	Mtl. 3	Bos. 2	Maurice Richard	5:45	Mtl.
Mar. 28/59	Tor.	SF	Tor. 3	Bos. 2	Gerry Ehman	5:02	Tor.
Mar. 31/59	Tor.	SF	Tor. 3	Bos. 2	Frank Mahovlich	11:21	Tor.
Apr. 14/59	Tor.	F	Tor. 3	Mtl. 2	Dick Duff	10:06	Mtl.
Mar. 26/60	Mtl.	SF	Mtl. 4	Chi. 3	Doug Harvey	8:38	Mtl.
Mar. 27/60	Det.	SF	Tor. 5	Det. 4	Frank Mahovlich	43:00	Tor.
Mar. 29/60	Det.	SF	Det. 2	Tor. 1	Gerry Melnyk	1:54	Tor.
Mar. 22/61	Tor.	SF	Tor. 3	Det. 2	George Armstrong	24:51	Det.
Mar. 26/61	Chi.	SF	Chi. 2	Mtl. 1	Murray Balfour	52:12	Chi.
Apr. 5/62	Tor.	SF	Tor. 3	NYR 2	Red Kelly	24:23	Tor.
Apr. 2/64	Det.	SF	Chi. 3	Det. 2	Murray Balfour	8:21	Det.
Apr. 14/64	Tor.	F	Det. 3	Tor. 2	Larry Jeffrey	7:52	Tor.
Apr. 23/64	Det.	F	Tor. 4	Det. 3	Bobby Baun	1:43	Tor.
Apr. 6/65	Tor.	SF	Tor. 3	Mtl. 2	Dave Keon	4:17	Mtl.
Apr. 13/65	Tor.	SF	Mtl. 4	Tor. 3	Claude Provost	16:33	Mtl.
May 5/66	Det.	F	Mtl. 3	Det. 2	Henri Richard	2:20	Mtl.
Apr. 13/67	NY	SF	Mtl. 2	NYR 1	John Ferguson	6:28	Mtl.
Apr. 25/67	Tor.	F	Tor. 3	Mtl. 2	Bob Pulford	28:26	Tor.
Apr. 10/68	St. L.	QF	St. L. 3	Phi. 2	Larry Keenan	24:10	St. L.
Apr. 16/68	St. L.	QF	Phi. 2	St. L. 1	Don Blackburn	31:38	St. L.
Apr. 16/68	Min.	QF	Min. 4	L.A. 3	Milan Marcetta	9:11	Min.
Apr. 22/68	Min.	SF	Min. 3	St. L. 2	Parker MacDonald	3:41	St. L.
Apr. 27/68	St. L.	SF	St. L. 4	Min. 3	Gary Sabourin	1:32	St. L.
Apr. 28/68	Mtl.	SF	Mtl. 4	Chi. 3	Jacques Lemaire	2:14	Mtl.
Apr. 29/68	St. L.	SF	St. L. 3	Min. 2	Bill McCreary	17:27	St. L.
May 3/68	St. L.	SF	St. L. 2	Min. 1	Ron Schock	22:50	St. L.
May 5/68	St. L.	F	Mtl. 3	St. L. 2	Jacques Lemaire	1:41	Mtl.
May 9/68	Mtl.	F	Mtl. 4	St. L. 3	Bobby Rousseau	1:13	Mtl.
Apr. 2/69	Oak.	QF	L.A. 5	Oak. 4	Ted Irvine	00:19	L.A.
Apr. 10/69	Mtl.	SF	Mtl. 3	Bos. 2	Ralph Backstrom	00:42	Mtl.
Apr. 13/69	Mtl.	SF	Mtl. 4	Bos. 3	Mickey Redmond	4:55	Mtl.
Apr. 24/69	Bos.	SF	Mtl. 2	Bos. 1	Jean Béliveau	31:28	Mtl.
Apr. 12/70	Oak.	QF	Pit. 3	Oak. 2	Michel Briere	8:28	Pit.
May 10/70	Bos.	F	Bos. 4	St. L. 3	Bobby Orr	00:40	Bos.
Apr. 15/71	Tor.	QF	NYR 2	Tor. 1	Bob Nevin	9:07	NYR
Apr. 18/71	Chi.	SF	NYR 2	Chi. 1	Pete Stemkowski	1:37	Chi.
Apr. 27/71	Chi.	SF	Chi. 3	NYR 2	Bobby Hull	6:35	Chi.
Apr. 29/71	NY	SF	NYR 3	Chi. 2	Pete Stemkowski	41:29	Chi.
May 4/71	Chi.	F	Chi. 2	Mtl. 1	Jim Pappin	21:11	Mtl.
Apr. 6/72	Bos.	OF	Tor. 4	Bos. 3	Jim Harrison	2:58	Bos.
Apr. 6/72	Min.	QF	Min. 6	St. L. 5	Bill Goldsworthy	1:36	St. L.
Apr. 9/72	Pit.	QF	Chi. 6	Pit. 5	Pit Martin	00:12	Chi.
Apr. 16/72	Min.	QF	St. L. 2	Min. 1	Kevin O'Shea	10:07	St. L.
Apr. 01/73	Mtl.	QF	Buf. 3	Mtl. 2	René Robert	9:18	Mtl.
Apr. 10/73	Phi.	QF	Phi. 3	Min. 2	Gary Dornhoefer	8:35	Phi.
Apr. 14/73	Mtl.	SF	Phi. 5	Mtl. 4	Rick MacLeish	2:56	Mtl.
Apr. 17/73	Mtl.	SF	Mtl. 4	Phi. 3	Larry Robinson	6:45	Mtl.
Apr. 14/74	Tor.	QF	Bos. 4	Tor. 3	Ken Hodge	1:27	Bos.
Apr. 14/74	Atl.	QF	Phi. 4	Atl. 3	Dave Schultz	5:40	Phi.
Apr. 16/74	Mtl.	QF	NYR 3	Mtl. 2	Ron Harris	4:07	NYR
Apr. 23/74	Chi.	Sf	Chi. 4	Bos. 3	Jim Pappin	3:48	Bos.
Apr. 28/74	NY	SF	NYR 2	Phi. 1	Rod Gilbert	4:20	Phi.
May 9/74	Bos.	F	Phi. 3	Bos. 2	Bobby Clarke	12:01	Phi.
Apr. 8/75	L.A.	Prelim.	L.A. 3	Tor. 2	Mike Murphy	8:53	Tor.
Apr. 10/75	Tor.	Prelim.	Tor. 3	L.A. 2	Blaine Stoughton	10:19	Tor.
Apr. 10/75	Chi.	Prelim.	Chi. 4	Bos. 3	Ivan Boldirev	7:33	Chi.
Apr. 11/75	NY	Prelim.	NYI 4	NYR 3	Jean-Paul Parise	0:11	NYI
Apr. 19/75	Tor.	QF	Phi. 4	Tor. 3	André Dupont	1:45	Phi.
Apr. 17/75	Chi.	QF	Chi. 5	Buf. 4	Stan Mikita	2:31	Buf.
Apr. 22/75	Mtl.	QF	Mtl. 5	Van. 4	Guy Lafleur	17:06	Mtl.
May 1/75	Phi.	SF	Phi. 5	NYI 4	Bobby Clarke	2:56	Phi.
May 7/75	NYI	SF	NYI 4	Phi. 3	Jude Drouin	1:53	Phi.
Apr. 27/75	Buf.	SF	Buf. 6	Mtl. 5	Danny Gare	4:42	Buf.
May 6/75	Buf.	SF	Buf. 5	Mtl. 4	René Robert	5:56	Buf.
May 20/75	Buf.	F	Buf. 5	Phi. 4	René Robert	18:29	Phi.
Apr. 8/76	Buf.	Prelim.	Buf. 3	St. L. 2	Danny Gare	11:43	Buf.
Apr. 9/76	Buf.	Prelim.	Buf. 2	St. L. 1	Don Luce	14:27	Buf.
Apr. 13/76	Bos.	QF	L.A. 3	Bos. 2	Butch Goring	00:27	Bos.
Apr. 13/76	Buf.	QF	Buf. 3	NYI 2	Danny Gare	14:04	NYI
Apr. 22/76	L.A.	QF	L.A. 4	Bos. 3	Butch Goring	18:28	Bos.
Apr. 29/76	Phi.	SF	Phi. 2	Bos. 1	Reggie Leach	13:38	Phi.

Date	City	Series	Score	Scorer	Overtime	Series Winner
Apr. 15/77	Tor.	QF	Phi. 4 Tor. 3	Rick MacLeish	2:55	Phi.
Apr. 17/77	Tor.	QF	Phi. 6 Tor. 5	Reggie Leach	19:10	Phi.
Apr. 24/77	Phi.	SF	Bos. 4 Phi. 3	Rick Middleton	2:57	Bos.
Apr. 26/77	Phi.	SF	Bos. 5 Phi. 4	Terry O'Reilly	30:07	Bos.
May 3/77	Mtl.	SF	NYI 4 Mtl. 3	Billy Harris	3:58	Mtl.
May 14/77	Bos.	F	Mtl. 2 Bos. 1	Jacques Lemaire	4:32	Mtl.
Apr. 11/78	Phi.	Prelim.	Phi. 3 Col. 2	Mel Bridgman	0:23	Phi.
Apr. 13/78	NY	Prelim.	NYR 4 Buf. 3	Don Murdoch	1:37	Buf.
Apr. 19/78	Bos.	QF	Bos. 4 Chi. 3	Terry O'Reilly	1:50	Bos.
Apr. 19/78	NYI	QF	NYI 3 Tor. 2	Mike Bossy	2:50	Tor.
Apr. 21/78	Chi.	QF	Bos. 4 Chi. 3	Peter McNab	10:17	Bos.
Apr. 25/78	NYI	QF	NYI 2 Tor. 1	Bob Nystrom	8:02	Tor.
Apr. 29/78	NYI	QF	Tor. 2 NYI 1	Lanny McDonald	4:13	Tor.
May 2/78	Bos.	SF	Bos. 3 Phi. 2	Rick Middleton	1:43	Bos.
May 16/78	Mtl.	F	Mtl. 3 Bos. 2	Guy Lafleur	13:09	Mtl.
May 21/78	Bos.	F	Bos. 4 Mtl. 3	Bobby Schmautz	6:22	Mtl.
Apr. 12/79	L.A.	Prelim.	NYR 2 L.A. 1	Phil Esposito	6:11	NYR
Apr. 14/79	Buf.	Prelim.	Pit. 4 Buf. 3	George Ferguson	00:47	Pit.
Apr. 16/79	Phi.	QF	Phi. 3 NYR 2	Ken Linseman	00:44	NYR
Apr. 18/79	NYI	QF	NYI 1 Chi. 0	Mike Bossy	2:31	NYI
Apr. 21/79	Tor.	QF	Mtl. 5 Tor. 4	Cam Connor	25:25	Mtl.
Apr. 22/79	Tor.	QF	Mtl. 5 Tor. 4	Larry Robinson	4:14	Mtl.
Apr. 28/79	NYI	SF	NYI 4 NYR 3	Denis Potvin	8:02	NYR
May 3/79	NY	SF	NYI 3 NYR 2	Bob Nystrom	3:40	NYR
May 3/79	Bos.	SF	Bos. 4 Mtl. 3	Jean Ratelle	3:46	Mtl.
May 10/79	Mtl.	SF	Mtl. 5 Bos. 4	Yvon Lambert	9:33	Mtl.
May 19/79	NY	F	Mtl. 4 NYR 3	Serge Savard	7:25	Mtl.
Apr. 8/80	NY	Prelim.	NYR 2 Atl. 1	Steve Vickers	0:33	NYR
Apr. 8/80	Phi.	Prelim.	Phi. 4 Edm. 3	Bobby Clarke	8:06	Phi.
Apr. 8/80	Chi.	Prelim.	Chi. 3 St. L. 2	Doug Lecuyer	12:34	Chi.
Apr. 11/80	Hfd.	Prelim.	Mtl. 4 Hfd. 3	Yvon Lambert	0:29	Mtl.
Apr. 11/80	Tor.	Prelim.	Min. 4 Tor. 3	Al MacAdam	0:32	Min.
Apr. 11/80	L.A.	Prelim.	NYI 4 L.A. 3	Ken Morrow	6:55	NYI
Apr. 11/80	Edm.	Prelim.	Phi. 3 Edm. 2	Ken Linseman	23:56	Phi.
Apr. 16/80	Bos.	QF	NYI 2 Bos. 1	Clark Gillies	1:02	NYI
Apr. 17/80	Bos.	QF	NYI 5 Bos. 4	Bob Bourne	1:24	NYI
Apr. 21/80	NYI	QF	Bos. 4 NYI 3	Terry O'Reilly	17:13	NYI
May 1/80	Buf.	SF	NYI 2 Buf. 1	Bob Nystrom	21:20	NYI
May 13/80	Phi.	F	NYI 4 Phi. 3	Denis Potvin	4:07	NYI
May 24/80	NYI	F	NYI 5 Phi. 4	Bob Nystrom	7:11	NYI
Apr. 8/81	Buf.	Prelim.	Buf. 3 Van. 2	Alan Haworth	5:00	Buf.
Apr. 8/81	Bos.	Prelim.	Min. 5 Bos. 4	Steve Payne	3:34	Min.
Apr. 11/81	Chi.	Prelim.	Cgy. 5 Chi. 4	Willi Plett	35:17	Cgy.
Apr. 12/81	Que.	Prelim.	Que. 4 Phi. 3	Dale Hunter	:37	Phi.
Apr. 14/81	St. L.	Prelim.	St. L. 4 Pit. 3	Mike Crombeen	25:16	St. L.
Apr. 16/81	Buf.	QF	Min. 4 Buf. 3	Steve Payne	:22	Min.
Apr. 20/81	Min.	QF	Buf. 5 Min. 4	Craig Ramsay	16:32	Min.
Apr. 20/81	Edm.	QF	NYI 5 Edm. 4	Ken Morrow	5:41	NYI
Apr. 7/82	Min.	DSF	Chi. 3 Min. 2	Greg Fox	3:34	Chi.
Apr. 8/82	Edm.	DSF	Edm. 3 L.A. 2	Wayne Gretzky	6:20	L.A.
Apr. 8/82	Van.	DSF	Van. 2 Cgy. 1	Dave Williams	14:20	Van.
Apr. 10/82	Pit.	DSF	Pit. 2 NYI 1	Rick Kehoe	4:14	NYI
Apr. 10/82	L.A.	DSF	L.A. 6 Edm. 5	Daryl Evans	2:35	L.A.
Apr. 13/82	Mtl.	DSF	Que. 3 Mtl. 2	Dale Hunter	0:22	Que.
Apr. 16/82	Van.	DF	L.A. 3 Van. 2	Steve Bozek	4:33	Van.
Apr. 18/82	Que.	DF	Que. 3 Bos. 2	Wilf Paiement	11:44	Que.
Apr. 18/82	NY	DF	NYI 4 NYR 3	Bryan Trottier	3:00	NYI
Apr. 18/82	L.A.	DF	Van. 4 L.A. 3	Colin Campbell	1:23	Van.
Apr. 21/82	St. L.	DF	St. L. 3 Chi. 2	Bernie Federko	3:28	Chi.
Apr. 23/82	Que.	DF	Bos. 6 Que. 5	Peter McNab	10:54	Que.
Apr. 27/82	Chi.	CF	Van. 2 Chi. 1	Jim Nill	28:58	Van.
May 1/82	Que.	CF	NYI 5 Que. 4	Wayne Merrick	16:52	NYI
May 8/82	NYI	SCF	NYI 6 Van. 5	Mike Bossy	19:58	NYI
Apr. 5/83	Bos.	DSF	Bos. 4 Que. 3	Barry Pederson	1:46	Bos.
Apr. 6/83	Cgy.	DSF	Cgy. 4 Van. 3	Eddy Beers	12:27	Cgy.
Apr. 7/83	Min.	DSF	Min. 5 Tor. 4	Bobby Smith	5:03	Min.
Apr. 10/83	Tor.	DSF	Min. 5 Tor. 4	Dino Ciccarelli	8:05	Min.
Apr. 10/83	Van.	DSF	Cgy. 4 Van. 3	Greg Meredith	1:06	Cgy.
Apr. 18/83	Chi.	DF	Chi. 4 Min. 3	Rich Preston	10:34	Chi.
Apr. 24/83	Bos.	DF	Bos. 3 Buf. 3	Brad Park	1:52	Bos.
Apr. 5/84	Edm.	DSF	Edm. 5 Wpg. 4	Randy Gregg	0:21	Edm.
Apr. 7/84	Det.	DSF	St. L. 4 Det. 3	Mark Reeds	37:07	St. L.
Apr. 8/84	Det.	DSF	St. L. 3 Det. 2	Jorgen Pettersson	2:42	St. L.
Apr. 10/84	NYI	DSF	NYI 3 NYR 2	Ken Morrow	8:56	NYI
Apr. 13/84	Min.	DF	St. L. 4 Min. 3	Doug Gilmour	16:16	Min.
Apr. 13/84	Edm.	DF	Cgy. 6 Edm. 5	Carey Wilson	3:42	Edm.
Apr. 13/84	NYI	DF	NYI 5 Wash. 4	Anders Kallur	7:35	NYI
Apr. 16/84	Mtl.	DF	Que. 4 Mtl. 3	Bo Berglund	3:00	Mtl.
Apr. 20/84	Cgy.	DF	Cgy. 5 Edm. 4	Lanny McDonald	1:04	Edm.
Apr. 22/84	Min.	DF	Min. 4 St. L. 3	Steve Payne	6:00	Min.
Apr. 10/85	NYR	DSF	NYR 4 Phi. 5	Mark Howe	8:01	Phi.
Apr. 10/85	Wash.	DSF	NYI 3 Was. 4	Alan Haworth	2:28	NYI
Apr. 11/85	Wash.	DSF	NYI 1 Wash. 2	Mike Gartner	1:23	NYI
Apr. 10/85	Edm.	DSF	L.A. 2 Edm. 3	Lee Fogolin	3:01	Edm.
Apr. 13/85	L.A.	DSF	Edm. 4 L.A. 3	Glenn Anderson	0:46	Edm.
Apr. 18/85	Wpg.	DF	Cgy. 4 Wpg. 3	Brian Mullen	7:56	Wpg.
Apr. 18/85	Mtl.	DF	Que. 2 Mtl. 1	Mark Kumpel	12:23	Que.
Apr. 23/85	Que.	DF	Que. 7 Mtl. 6	Dale Hunter	18:36	Que.
May 2/85	Mtl.	DF	Que. 3 Mtl. 2	Peter Stastny	2:22	Que.
Apr. 25/85	Min.	DF	Chi. 7 Min. 6	Darryl Sutter	1:57	Chi.
Apr. 28/85	Chi.	DF	Chi. 4 Min. 5	Dennis Maruk	1:14	Chi.
Apr. 30/85	Min.	DF	Chi. 6 Min. 5	Darryl Sutter	15:41	Chi.
May 5/85	Que.	CF	Phi. 1 Que. 2	Peter Stastny	6:20	Phi.
Apr. 9/86	Que.	DSF	Hfd. 3 Que. 2	Sylvain Turgeon	2:36	Hfd.
Apr. 12/86	Wpg.	DSF	Cgy. 4 Wpg. 3	Lanny McDonald	8:25	Cgy.
Apr. 17/86	Wash.	DF	NYR 4 Wash. 3	Brian MacLellan	1:16	NYR
Apr. 20/86	Edm.	DF	Edm. 6 Cgy. 5	Glenn Anderson	1:04	Cgy.
Apr. 23/86	Hfd.	DF	Hfd. 2 Mtl. 1	Kevin Dineen	1:07	Mtl.
Apr. 23/86	NYR	DF	NYR 6 Wash. 5	Bob Brooke	2:40	NYR
Apr. 26/86	St. L.	DF	St. L. 4 Tor. 3	Mark Reeds	7:11	St. L.
Apr. 29/86	Mtl.	DF	Mtl. 2 Hfd. 1	Claude Lemieux	5:55	Mtl.
May 5/86	NYR	CF	Mtl. 4 NYR 3	Claude Lemieux	9:41	Mtl.
May 12/86	St. L.	CF	St. L. 6 Cgy. 5	Doug Wickenheiser	7:30	Cgy.
May 18/86	Cgy.	F	Mtl. 3 Cgy. 2	Brian Skrudland	0:09	Mtl.

Pete Stemkowski, left, scored at 1:29 of the third overtime period giving the New York Rangers a 3-2 win over Chicago in game six of the 1971 Semi-Finals.

Overtime Record of Current Teams

(Listed by number of OT games played)

Team	Overall				Home				Last OT Game	Road				Last OT Game
	GP	W	L	T	GP	W	L	T		GP	W	L	T	
Montreal	87	44	41	2	40	24	15	1	Apr. 19/86	47	20	26	1	May 18/86
Boston	73	30	40	3	34	17	16	1	Apr. 24/83	39	13	24	2	Apr. 23/82
Toronto	71	33	37	1	46	21	24	1	Apr. 10/83	25	12	13	0	Apr. 26/86
NY Rangers	46	23	23	0	19	9	10	0	May 5/86	27	14	13	0	Apr. 17/86
Detroit	42	19	23	0	26	10	16	0	Apr. 18/84	16	9	7	0	Apr. 14/64
Chicago	40	21	17	2	21	12	8	1	Apr. 28/85	19	9	9	1	Apr. 30/85
NY Islanders	28	21	7	0	12	10	2	0	Apr. 13/84	16	11	5	0	Apr. 11/85
Philadelphia	27	15	12	0	9	6	3	0	May 13/80	18	9	9	0	May 5/85
Minnesota	21	10	11	0	12	5	7	0	Apr. 30/85	9	5	4	0	Apr. 28/85
St. Louis	22	12	10	0	10	8	2	0	May 12/86	12	4	8	0	Apr. 22/84
Buffalo	15	9	6	0	10	7	3	0	Apr. 16/81	5	2	3	0	Apr. 24/83
Los Angeles	14	6	8	0	7	3	4	0	Apr. 13/85	7	3	4	0	Apr. 10/85
*Calgary	13	6	7	0	4	2	2	0	May 18/86	9	4	5	0	May 12/86
Quebec	12	8	4	0	7	4	3	0	Apr. 9/86	5	4	1	0	May 2/85
Edmonton	11	5	6	0	7	4	3	0	Apr. 20/86	4	1	3	0	Apr. 13/85
Vancouver	9	3	6	0	5	1	4	0	Apr. 10/83	4	2	2	0	Apr. 6/83
Pittsburgh	6	3	3	0	2	1	1	0	Apr. 10/82	4	2	2	0	Apr. 13/82
Washington	5	2	3	0	3	2	1	0	Apr. 17/86	2	0	2	0	Apr. 23/86
Hartford	4	2	2	0	2	1	1	0	Apr. 23/86	2	1	1	0	Apr. 29/86
Winnipeg	3	1	2	0	2	1	1	0	Apr. 12/86	1	0	1	0	Apr. 5/84
**New Jersey	1	0	1	0	0	0	0	0		1	0	1	0	Apr. 11/78

* Totals include those of Atlanta 1974-80.

** Totals include those of Colorado 1976-82.

Stanley Cup Coaching Records

Coaches listed in order of total games coached in playoffs. Minimum: 65 games.

Coach	Team	Years	Series	Series W	L	Games G	W	L	T	Cups	%
Irvin, Dick	Chicago	1	3	2	1	9	5	3	1	0	.611
	Toronto	9	20	12	8	66	33	32	1	1	.508
	Montreal	14	22	11	11	115	62	53	0	3	.539
	TOTALS	24	45	25	20	190	100	88	2	4	.532
Bowman, Scott	St. Louis	4	10	6	4	52	26	26	0	0	.500
	Montreal	8	19	16	3	98	70	28	0	5	.714
	Buffalo	5	8	3	5	36	18	18	0	0	.500
	TOTALS	17	37	25	12	186	114	72	0	5	.612
Arbour, Al	St. Louis	1	2	1	1	11	4	7	0	0	.364
	NY Islanders	12	35	27	8	171	109	62	0	4	.637
	TOTALS	13	37	28	9	182	113	69	0	4	.621
Blake, Toe	Montreal	13	23	18	5	119	82	37	0	8	.689
Reay, Billy	Chicago	12	22	10	12	117	57	60	0	0	.487
Shero, Fred	Philadelphia	6	16	12	4	83	48	35	0	2	.578
	NY Rangers	2	5	3	2	25	13	12	0	0	.520
	TOTALS	8	21	15	6	108	61	47	0	2	.565
Adams, Jack	Detroit	15	27	15	12	105	52	52	1	3	.500
Francis, Emile	NY Rangers	9	14	5	9	75	34	41	0	0	.453
	St. Louis	3	4	1	3	18	6	12	0	0	.333
	TOTALS	12	18	6	12	93	40	53	0	0	.430
Imlach, Punch	Toronto	11	17	10	7	92	44	48	0	4	.478
Sather, Glen	Edmonton	7	18	13	5	80	54	26	0	2	.675
Day, Hap	Toronto	9	14	10	4	80	49	31	0	5	.613
Abel, Sid	Chicago	1	1	0	1	7	3	4	0	0	.429
	Detroit	8	12	4	8	69	29	40	0	0	.420
	TOTALS	9	13	4	9	76	32	44	0	0	.421
Ross, Art	Boston	12	19	9	10	70	32	33	5	2	.493
Ivan, Tommy	Detroit	7	12	8	4	67	36	31	0	3	.537
Pulford, Bob	Los Angeles	4	6	2	4	26	11	15	0	0	.423
	Chicago	5	9	4	5	41	17	24	0	0	.415
	TOTALS	9	15	6	9	67	28	39	0	0	.418
Patrick, Lester	NY Rangers	12	24	14	10	65	31	26	8	2	.538

Late Additions to Player Register

ANDERSON, DAVID

Born, Vancouver, B.C., July 30, 1962.
Right wing. Shoots right. 6'0", 190 lbs.
Last amateur club: University of Denver Pioneers (WCHA).

				Regular Season						Playoffs			
Season	Club	Lea	GP	G	A	TP	PIM	GP	G	A	TP	PIM	
1981-82	Denver	WCHA	43	10	10	20	42	....	....	....	....	....	
1982-83	Denver	WCHA	30	5	10	15	27	....	....	....	....	....	
1983-84	Denver	WCHA	38	23	27	50	75	....	....	....	....	....	
1984-85	Denver	WCHA	34	16	23	39	48	....	....	....	....	....	
1985-86	Fort Wayne	IHL	79	33	41	74	156	15	4	7	11	55	

Signed as a free agent by **New Jersey**, August 6, 1986.

BROWN, DOUG

Born, Southboro, Mass., July 12, 1964.
Right wing. Shoots right. 5'11", 190 lbs.
Last amateur club: Boston College Eagles (H.E.).

				Regular Season						Playoffs			
Season	Club	Lea	GP	G	A	TP	PIM	GP	G	A	TP	PIM	
1982-83	Boston College	ECAC	22	9	8	17	0	....	....	....	....	....	
1983-84	Boston College	ECAC	38	11	10	21	6	....	....	....	....	....	
1984-85	Boston College	H.E.	45	37	31	68	10	....	....	....	....	....	
1985-86	Boston College	H.E.	38	16	40	56	16	16	....	....	....	....	

Signed as a free agent by **New Jersey**, August 6, 1986.

DONNELLY, MIKE

Born, Detroit, Mich., October 10, 1963.
Left wing. Shoots left. 5'11", 185 lbs.
Last amateur club: Michigan State University Spartans (CCHA).

				Regular Season						Playoffs			
Season	Club	Lea	GP	G	A	TP	PIM	GP	G	A	TP	PIM	
1982-83	Michigan St.	CCHA	24	7	13	20	8	....	....	....	....	....	
1983-84	Michigan St.	CCHA	44	18	14	32	40	....	....	....	....	....	
1984-85	Michigan St.	CCHA	44	26	21	47	48	....	....	....	....	....	
1985-86ab	Michigan St.	CCHA	44	59	38	97	65	....	....	....	....	....	

a CCHA First All-Star Team (1986)
b NCAA West First All-American Team (1986)

Signed as a free agent by **NY Rangers**, August 15, 1986.

LENARDON, TIM

Born, Trail, B.C., May 11, 1962.
Center. Shoots left. 6'2", 185 lbs.
Last amateur club: University of Brandon Bobcats (CWUAA).

				Regular Season						Playoffs			
Season	Club	Lea	GP	G	A	TP	PIM	GP	G	A	TP	PIM	
1983-84	U. Brandon	CWUAA	24	22	21	43	....	....	....	....	....	....	
1984-85	U. Brandon	CWUAA	24	21	39	60	....	....	....	....	....	....	
1985-86a	U. Brandon	CWUAA	26	26	40	66	33	....	....	....	....	....	

a Canadian University Player of the Year (1986).

Signed as a free agent by **New Jersey**, August 6, 1986.

OAKMAN, ERIC

Born, Virginia, Minn., November 15, 1963.
Left wing. Shoots left. 6'2", 185 lbs.
Last amateur club: College of St. Scholastia.

				Regular Season						Playoffs			
Season	Club	Lea	GP	G	A	TP	PIM	GP	G	A	TP	PIM	
1985-86	St. Scholastia		29	32	33	65	....	....	....	....	....	....	

Signed as a free agent by **NY Islanders**, March 22, 1986.

1986-87 Player Register

Leagues:

ACHL	Atlantic Coast Hockey League
AHL	American Hockey League
AJHL	Alberta Junior Hockey League
AUAA	Atlantic Universities Athletic Association
BCJHL	British Columbia Junior Hockey League
CCHA	Central Collegiate Hockey Association
CHL	Central Hockey League
COJHL	Central Ontario Junior Hockey League
CWUAA	Canada West Universities Athletic Association
ECAC	Eastern Collegiate Athletic Association
EHL	Eastern Hockey League
GPAC	Great Plains Athletic Conference
H.E.	Hockey East
IHL	International Hockey League
MJHA	(New York) Metropolitan Junior Hockey Association
MJHL	Manitoba Junior Hockey League
NAHL	North American Hockey League
NHL	National Hockey League
OHA	Ontario Hockey Association
OHL	Ontario Hockey League
OPJHL	Ontario Provincial Junior Hockey League
OUAA	Ontario Universities Athletic Association
QJHL, QMJHL	Quebec Major Junior Hockey League
SHL	Southern Hockey League
SJHL	Saskatchewan Junior Hockey League
SOHL	Southern Ontario Hockey League
WCHA	Western Collegiate Hockey Association
WHA	World Hockey Association
WHL	Western Hockey League

Abbreviations: A – assists; **G** – goals; **GP** – games played; **Lea** – league; **PIM** – penalties in minutes; **TP** – total points.

Goaltender Register begins on page 333.

Notes: The 1986-1987 Player Register lists forwards and defensemen only. Goaltenders are listed separately. The Player Register lists every skater who appeared in an NHL game in the 1985-86 season, every skater drafted in the first two rounds of the 1985 and 1986 Entry Drafts and other players on NHL Reserve Lists.

ACTON, KEITH EDWARD

Born, Stouffville, Ont., April 15, 1958.
Center. Shoots left. 5'8", 170 lbs.
Last amateur club: Peterborough Petes (OHA).
(Montreal's 8th choice, 103rd over-all, in 1978 Amateur Draft).

				Regular Season					Playoffs			
Season	Club	Lea	GP	G	A	TP	PIM	GP	G	A	TP	PIM
1976-77	Peterborough	OHA	65	52	69	121	93	4	1	4	5	6
1977-78	Peterborough	OHA	68	42	86	128	52	21	10	8	18	16
1978-79	Nova Scotia	AHL	79	15	26	41	22	10	4	2	6	4
1979-80	**Montreal**	**NHL**	2	0	1	1	0	....	....	....	....	....
	Nova Scotia	AHL	75	45	53	98	38	6	1	2	3	8
1980-81	**Montreal**	**NHL**	61	15	24	39	74	2	0	0	0	6
1981-82	**Montreal**	**NHL**	78	36	52	88	88	5	0	4	4	16
1982-83	**Montreal**	**NHL**	78	24	26	50	63	3	0	0	0	0
1983-84	**Montreal**	**NHL**	9	3	7	10	4	....	....	....	....	....
	Minnesota	**NHL**	62	17	38	55	60	15	4	7	11	12
1984-85	**Minnesota**	**NHL**	78	20	38	58	90	9	4	4	8	6
1985-86	**Minnesota**	**NHL**	79	26	32	58	100	5	0	3	3	6
	NHL Totals		447	141	218	359	479	39	8	18	26	46

Traded to **Minnesota** by **Montreal** with Mark Napier and Toronto's third round choice (Ken Hodge) in 1984 Entry Draft — Montreal's property via earlier transaction — for Bobby Smith, October 28, 1983.

ADAM, RUSSELL NORM (RUSS)

Born, Windsor, Ont., May 5, 1961.
Center. Shoots left. 5'10", 185 lbs.
Last amateur club: Kitchener Rangers (OHA).
(Toronto's 7th choice, 137th over-all, in 1980 Entry Draft).

				Regular Season					Playoffs			
Season	Club	Lea	GP	G	A	TP	PIM	GP	G	A	TP	PIM
1978-79	Kitchener	OHA	62	20	17	37	39	9	4	3	7	31
1979-80	Kitchener	OHA	54	37	34	71	143	....	....	....	....	....
1980-81	Kitchener	OHA	64	37	50	87	215	10	0	2	2	17
1981-82	New Brunswick	AHL	57	11	21	32	50	12	3	5	8	32
1982-83	**Toronto**	**NHL**	8	1	2	3	11	....	....	....	....	....
	St. Catharines	AHL	64	19	17	36	119	....	....	....	....	....
1983-84	St. Catharines	AHL	70	32	24	56	76	7	0	1	1	10
1984-85	Fort Wayne	IHL	60	28	46	74	56	....	....	....	....	....
1985-86	Fort Wayne	IHL	48	24	37	61	36	14	7	13	20	9
	NHL Totals		8	1	2	3	11	....	....	....	....	....

ADAMS, GREG

Born, Nelson, B.C., August 1, 1963.
Center. Shoots left. 6'2", 185 lbs.
Last amateur club: University of Northern Arizona Lumberjacks (NCAA).

				Regular Season					Playoffs			
Season	Club	Lea	GP	G	A	TP	PIM	GP	G	A	TP	PIM
1982-83	N. Arizona	NCAA	29	14	21	35	....	....	....	....	....	....
1983-84	N. Arizona	NCAA	26	44	29	73	....	....	....	....	....	....
1984-85	**New Jersey**	**NHL**	36	12	9	21	14	....	....	....	....	....
	Maine	AHL	41	15	20	35	12	....	....	....	....	....
1985-86	**New Jersey**	**NHL**	78	35	42	77	30	....	....	....	....	....
	NHL Totals		114	47	51	98	44	....	....	....	....	....

Signed as a Free agent by **New Jersey**, June 25, 1984.

ADAMS, GREGORY CHARLES (GREG)

Born, Duncan, B.C., May 31, 1960.
Left wing. Shoots left. 6'1", 195 lbs.
Last amateur club: Victoria Cougars (WHL).

				Regular Season					Playoffs			
Season	Club	Lea	GP	G	A	TP	PIM	GP	G	A	TP	PIM
1978-79	Victoria	WHL	71	23	31	54	151	14	5	0	5	59
1979-80	Victoria	WHL	71	62	48	110	212	16	9	11	20	71
1980-81	**Philadelphia**	**NHL**	6	3	0	3	8	....	....	....	....	....
	Maine	AHL	71	19	20	39	158	20	2	3	5	89
1981-82	**Philadelphia**	**NHL**	33	4	15	19	105	....	....	....	....	....
	Maine	AHL	45	16	21	37	241	4	0	3	3	28
1982-83	**Hartford**	**NHL**	79	10	13	23	216	....	....	....	....	....
1983-84	**Washington**	**NHL**	57	2	6	8	133	1	0	0	0	0
1984-85	**Washington**	**NHL**	51	6	12	18	72	5	0	0	0	9
	Binghamton	AHL	28	9	16	25	58	....	....	....	....	....
1985-86	**Washington**	**NHL**	78	18	38	56	152	9	1	3	4	27
	NHL Totals		304	43	84	127	686	15	1	3	4	36

Signed as a free agent by **Philadelphia**, September 28, 1979. Traded to **Hartford** by **Philadelphia** with Ken Linseman and Philadelphia's first (David Jensen) and third (Leif Karlsson) round choices in the 1983 Entry Draft for Mark Howe and Hartford's third round (Derrick Smith) choice in the 1983 Entry Draft, August 20, 1982. Traded to **Washington** by **Hartford** for Torrie Robertson, October 3, 1983.

AGNEW, JIM

Born, Deloraine, Man., March 21, 1966.
Defense. Shoots left. 6'1", 180 lbs.
Last amateur club: Portland Winterhawks (WHL).
(Vancouver's 10th choice, 157th over-all, in 1984 Entry Draft).

				Regular Season					Playoffs			
Season	Club	Lea	GP	G	A	TP	PIM	GP	G	A	TP	PIM
1982-83	Brandon	WHL	14	1	1	2	9	....	....	....	....	....
1983-84	Brandon	WHL	71	6	17	23	107	12	0	1	1	39
1984-85	Portland	WHL	63	8	39	47	305	6	0	2	2	44
1985-86a	Portland	WHL	70	6	30	36	386	9	0	1	1	48

a WHL First All-Star Team, West Division (1986)

AITKEN, BRAD

Born, Scarborough, Ont., October 30, 1967.
Left wing. Shoots left. 6'3", 200 lbs.
Last amateur club: Sault Ste. Marie Greyhounds (OHL).
(Pittsburgh's 3rd choice, 46th over-all, in 1986 Entry Draft).

				Regular Season					Playoffs			
Season	Club	Lea	GP	G	A	TP	PIM	GP	G	A	TP	PIM
1985-86	S.S. Marie	OHL	58	17	47	64	88	....	....	....	....	....

AKERVIK, ANDREW

Born, Duluth, Minn., August 11, 1967.
Center. Shoots right. 6'3", 190 lbs.
Last amateur club: University of Wisconsin Badgers (WCHA).
(Quebec's 7th choice, 120th over-all, in 1985 Entry Draft).

				Regular Season					Playoffs			
Season	Club	Lea	GP	G	A	TP	PIM	GP	G	A	TP	PIM
1985-86	Wisconsin	WCHA	22	2	0	2	2	....	....	....	....	....

ALBRECHT, CLIFF

Born, Toronto, Ont., May 24, 1963.
Defense. Shoots right. 6'0", 185 lbs.
Last amateur club: Princeton University Tigers (ECAC).
(Toronto's 7th choice, 168th over-all, in 1983 Entry Draft).

Season	Club	Lea	Regular Season GP	G	A	TP	PIM	Playoffs GP	G	A	TP	PIM
1982-83	Princeton	ECAC	24	4	10	14	52	....	....	....	....	....
1983-84	Princeton	ECAC	23	9	9	18	62	....	....	....	....	....
1984-85	Princeton	ECAC	26	6	22	28	31	....	....	....	....	....
1985-86ab	Princeton	ECAC	30	15	26	41	42	....	....	....	....	....
	St. Catharines	AHL	1	0	1	1	0	....	....	....	....	....

a NCAA East Second All-American Team (1986)
b ECAC First All-Star Team (1986)

ALDRED, JAMES (JIM)

Born, Toronto, Ont., April 28, 1963.
Left wing. Shoots left. 6'1", 185 lbs.
Last amateur club: Sault Ste. Marie Greyhounds (OHL).
(Buffalo's 3rd choice, 59th over-all, in 1981 Entry Draft).

Season	Club	Lea	Regular Season GP	G	A	TP	PIM	Playoffs GP	G	A	TP	PIM
1979-80	Kingston	OHA	16	0	1	1	9	....	....	....	....	....
1980-81	Kingston	OHA	67	20	28	48	140	12	4	2	6	10
1981-82	Kingston	OHL	10	2	4	6	18	....	....	....	....	....
	S. S. Marie	OHL	43	16	15	31	179	12	4	3	7	54
1982-83	S. S. Marie	OHL	63	22	22	44	176	16	2	8	10	46
1983-84	Rochester	AHL	64	10	9	19	57	11	2	0	2	33
1984-85	Rochester	AHL	2	0	0	0	0	....	....	....	....	....
	Toledo	IHL	24	7	3	10	16	....	....	....	....	....
	Flint	IHL	28	5	3	8	10	....	....	....	....	....
1985-86	Rochester	AHL	10	1	3	4	4	....	....	....	....	....
	Toledo	IHL	51	9	17	26	110	....	....	....	....	....

ALEXANDER, BOB

Born, St. Paul, Minn., October 31, 1964.
Defense. Shoots left. 5'10", 170 lbs.
Last amateur club: University of Minnesota-Duluth Bulldogs (WCHA).
(NY Rangers' 7th choice, 113th over-all, in 1983 Entry Draft).

Season	Club	Lea	Regular Season GP	G	A	TP	PIM	Playoffs GP	G	A	TP	PIM
1982-83	Rosemont	H.S.	22	14	40	54	....	....	....	....	....	....
1983-84	Minn-Duluth	WCHA	3	0	2	2	2	....	....	....	....	....
1984-85	DID NOT PLAY											
1985-86	Minn-Duluth	WCHA	6	1	1	2	4	....	....	....	....	....

ALLISON, DAVID BRYAN (DAVE)

Born, Fort Frances, Ont., April 14, 1959.
Defense. Shoots right. 6'1", 200 lbs.
Last amateur club: Cornwall Royals (QJHL).

Season	Club	Lea	Regular Season GP	G	A	TP	PIM	Playoffs GP	G	A	TP	PIM
1976-77	Cornwall	QJHL	63	2	11	13	180	12	0	4	4	60
1977-78	Cornwall	QJHL	60	9	29	38	302	5	2	3	5	32
1978-79	Cornwall	QJHL	66	7	31	38	407	7	1	6	7	34
1979-80	Nova Scotia	AHL	49	1	12	13	119	4	0	0	0	46
1980-81	Nova Scotia	AHL	70	5	12	17	298	6	0	0	0	15
1981-82	Nova Scotia	AHL	78	8	25	33	*332	9	0	3	3	*84
1982-83	Nova Scotia	AHL	70	3	22	25	180	7	0	2	2	2
1983-84	**Montreal**	**NHL**	**3**	**0**	**0**	**0**	**12**	....	....	....	....	....
	Nova Scotia	AHL	53	2	18	20	155	6	0	3	3	25
1984-85	Sherbrooke	AHL	4	0	1	1	19	....	....	....	....	....
	Nova Scotia	AHL	68	4	18	22	175	6	0	2	2	15
1985-86	Muskegon	IHL	66	7	30	37	247	14	2	9	11	46
	NHL Totals		**3**	**0**	**0**	**0**	**12**	....	....	....	....	....

Signed as a free agent by **Montreal**, October 4, 1979.

ALLISON, MICHAEL EARNEST (MIKE)

Born, Fort Frances, Ont., March 28, 1961.
Left wing. Shoots right. 6', 200 lbs.
Last amateur club: Sudbury Wolves (OHA).
(NY Rangers' 2nd choice, 35th over-all, in 1980 Entry Draft).

Season	Club	Lea	Regular Season GP	G	A	TP	PIM	Playoffs GP	G	A	TP	PIM
1978-79	Sudbury	OHA	59	24	32	56	41	10	4	2	6	18
1979-80	Sudbury	OHA	67	24	71	95	74	9	8	6	14	6
1980-81	**NY Rangers**	**NHL**	**75**	**26**	**38**	**64**	**83**	**14**	**3**	**1**	**4**	**20**
1981-82	Springfield	AHL	2	0	0	0	0	....	....	....	....	....
	NY Rangers	**NHL**	**48**	**7**	**15**	**22**	**74**	**10**	**1**	**3**	**4**	**18**
1982-83	Tulsa	CHL	6	2	2	4	2	....	....	....	....	....
	NY Rangers	**NHL**	**39**	**11**	**9**	**20**	**37**	**8**	**0**	**5**	**5**	**10**
1983-84	**NY Rangers**	**NHL**	**45**	**8**	**12**	**20**	**64**	**5**	**0**	**1**	**1**	**6**
1984-85	**NY Rangers**	**NHL**	**31**	**9**	**15**	**24**	**17**	....	....	....	....	....
1985-86	**NY Rangers**	**NHL**	**28**	**2**	**13**	**15**	**22**	**16**	**0**	**2**	**2**	**38**
	New Haven	AHL	9	6	6	12	4	....	....	....	....	....
	NHL Totals		**266**	**63**	**102**	**165**	**297**	**53**	**4**	**12**	**16**	**92**

Traded to **Toronto** by **NY Rangers** for Walt Poddubny, August 18, 1986.

ALLISON, RAYMOND PETER (RAY)

Born, Cranbrook, B.C., March 4, 1959.
Right wing. Shoots left. 5'10", 195 lbs.
Last amateur club: Brandon Wheat Kings (WHL).
(Hartford's 1st choice, 18th over-all, in 1979 Entry Draft).

Season	Club	Lea	Regular Season GP	G	A	TP	PIM	Playoffs GP	G	A	TP	PIM
1975-76	Brandon	WHL	36	9	17	26	50	5	2	1	3	0
1976-77	Brandon	WHL	71	45	92	137	198	14	9	11	20	37
1977-78	Brandon	WHL	71	74	86	160	254	8	7	8	15	35
1978-79	Brandon	WHL	62	60	93	153	191	22	18	19	37	28
1979-80	Springfield	AHL	13	6	9	15	18	....	....	....	....	....
	Hartford	**NHL**	**64**	**16**	**12**	**28**	**13**	**2**	**0**	**1**	**1**	**0**
1980-81	**Hartford**	**NHL**	**6**	**1**	**0**	**1**	**0**	....	....	....	....	....
	Binghamton	AHL	74	31	39	70	81	1	0	1	1	0
1981-82	Maine	AHL	26	15	13	28	75	....	....	....	....	....
	Philadelphia	**NHL**	**51**	**17**	**37**	**54**	**104**	**3**	**2**	**0**	**2**	**2**
1982-83	**Philadelphia**	**NHL**	**67**	**21**	**30**	**51**	**57**	**3**	**0**	**1**	**1**	**12**
1983-84	**Philadelphia**	**NHL**	**37**	**8**	**13**	**21**	**47**	**3**	**0**	**1**	**1**	**4**
1984-85	**Philadelphia**	**NHL**	**11**	**1**	**1**	**2**	**2**	**1**	**0**	**0**	**0**	**2**
	Hershey	AHL	49	17	22	39	61	....	....	....	....	....
1985-86	Hershey	AHL	77	32	46	78	131	18	4	6	10	28
	NHL Totals		**236**	**64**	**93**	**157**	**223**	**12**	**2**	**3**	**5**	**20**

Traded to **Philadelphia** by **Hartford** with Fred Arthur and Hartford's first (Ron Sutter), second (Peter Ihnacak, which was later transferred to **Toronto**) and third-round (Miroslav Dvorak) choices in the 1982 Entry Draft for Rick MacLeish, Blake Wesley, Don Gillen and Philadelphia's first (Paul Lawless), second (Mark Paterson) and third-round (Kevin Dineen) choices in the 1982 Entry Draft, July 3, 1981.

AMES, PAUL

Born, Woburn, Mass., March 12, 1965.
Defense. Shoots right. 6'0", 185 lbs.
Last amateur club: University of Lowell Chiefs (H.E.).
(Pittsburgh's 6th choice, 123rd over-all, in 1983 Entry Draft).

Season	Club	Lea	Regular Season GP	G	A	TP	PIM	Playoffs GP	G	A	TP	PIM
1983-84	Lowell	H.E.	31	1	13	14	16	....	....	....	....	....
1984-85	Lowell	H.E.	27	2	8	10	22	....	....	....	....	....
1985-86	Lowell	H.E.	41	7	20	27	39	....	....	....	....	....

ANASTOS, THOMAS (TOM)

Born, Dearborn, Mich., July 5, 1963.
Right wing. Shoots right. 6'3", 185 lbs.
Last amateur club: Michigan State University Spartans (CCHA).
(Montreal's 9th choice, 124th over-all, in 1981 Entry Draft).

Season	Club	Lea	Regular Season GP	G	A	TP	PIM	Playoffs GP	G	A	TP	PIM
1981-82	Michigan St.	CCHA	37	16	13	29	18	....	....	....	....	....
1982-83	Michigan St.	CCHA	27	3	5	8	13	....	....	....	....	....
1983-84	Michigan St.	CCHA	46	22	16	38	35	....	....	....	....	....
1984-85	Michigan St.	CCHA	41	29	39	68	36	....	....	....	....	....
1985-86	Sherbrooke	AHL	55	9	18	27	8	....	....	....	....	....

ANDERSON, GLENN CHRIS

Born, Vancouver, B.C., October 2, 1960.
Left/Right wing. Shoots left. 5'11", 180 lbs.
Last amateur club: 1980 Canadian Olympic Team.
(Edmonton's 3rd choice, 69th over-all, in 1979 Entry Draft).

Season	Club	Lea	Regular Season GP	G	A	TP	PIM	Playoffs GP	G	A	TP	PIM
1978-79	U. of Denver	WCHA	40	26	29	55	58	....	....	....	....	....
1979-80	Seattle	WHL	7	5	5	10	4	....	....	....	....	....
	Cdn. Olympic	...	49	21	21	42	46	....	....	....	....	....
1980-81	**Edmonton**	**NHL**	**58**	**30**	**23**	**53**	**24**	**9**	**5**	**7**	**12**	**12**
1981-82	**Edmonton**	**NHL**	**80**	**38**	**67**	**105**	**71**	**5**	**2**	**5**	**7**	**8**
1982-83	**Edmonton**	**NHL**	**72**	**48**	**56**	**104**	**70**	**16**	**10**	**10**	**20**	**32**
1983-84	**Edmonton**	**NHL**	**80**	**54**	**45**	**99**	**65**	**19**	**6**	**11**	**17**	**33**
1984-85	**Edmonton**	**NHL**	**80**	**42**	**39**	**81**	**69**	**18**	**10**	**16**	**26**	**38**
1985-86	**Edmonton**	**NHL**	**72**	**54**	**48**	**102**	**90**	**10**	**8**	**3**	**11**	**14**
	NHL Totals		**442**	**266**	**278**	**544**	**389**	**77**	**41**	**52**	**93**	**137**

ANDERSON, JOHN MURRAY

Born, Toronto, Ont., March 28, 1957.
Right wing. Shoots right. 5'11", 190 lbs.
Last amateur club: Toronto Marlboros (OHA).
(Toronto's 1st choice, 11th over-all, in 1977 Amateur Draft).

				Regula	r Seaso	n			Playoffs			
Season	Club	Lea	GP	G	A	TP	PIM	GP	G	A	TP	PIM
1973-74	Toronto	OHA	38	22	22	44	6	....	....	....	....	....
1974-75	Toronto	OHA	70	49	64	113	31	22	16	14	30	14
1975-76	Toronto	OHA	39	26	25	51	19	10	7	4	11	7
1976-77a	Toronto	OHA	64	57	62	119	42	6	3	5	8	0
1977-78	Toronto	NHL	17	1	2	3	2	2	0	0	0	0
	Dallas	CHL	55	22	23	45	6	13	*11	8	*19	2
1978-79	Toronto	NHL	71	15	11	26	10	6	0	2	2	0
1979-80	Toronto	NHL	74	25	28	53	22	3	1	1	2	0
1980-81	Toronto	NHL	75	17	26	43	31	2	0	0	0	0
1981-82	Toronto	NHL	69	31	26	57	30	....	....	....	....	....
1982-83	Toronto	NHL	80	31	49	80	24	4	2	4	6	0
1983-84	Toronto	NHL	73	37	31	68	22	....	....	....	....	....
1984-85	Toronto	NHL	75	32	31	63	27	....	....	....	....	....
1985-86	Quebec	NHL	65	21	28	49	26	....	....	....	....	....
	Hartford	NHL	1l2	10	5	8	13	0				
	NHL Totals		613	218	249	467	196	27	8	15	23	0

a OHA First All-Star Team (1977)
Traded to **Quebec** by **Toronto** for Brad Maxwell, August 21, 1985. Traded to **Hartford** by **Quebec** for Risto Siltanen, March 8, 1986.

ANDERSON, MIKE

Born, St. Paul, Minn., May 2, 1964.
Center. Shoots left. 6'1", 180 lbs.
Last amateur club: University of Minnesota Gophers (WCHA)
(Buffalo's 4th choice, 26th over-all, in 1982 Entry Draft).

				Regula	r Seaso	n				Playoffs		
Season	Club	Lea	GP	G	A	TP	PIM	GP	G	A	TP	PIM
1981-82	N. St. Paul HS	Minn.	24	19	31	50	18	....	....	....	....	....
1982-83	U. Minnesota	WCHA	38	8	11	19	18	....	....	....	....	....
1983-84	U. Minnesota	WCHA	24	1	7	8	4	....	....	....	....	....
1984-85	U. Minnesota	WCHA	23	4	6	10	6	....	....	....	....	....
1985-86	U. Minnesota	WCHA	12	3	3	6	4	....	....	....	....	....
	Rochester	AHL	25	3	1	4	2	....	....	....	....	....

ANDERSON, PERRY LYNN

Born, Barrie, Ont., October 14, 1961.
Left wing. Shoots left. 6', 210 lbs.
Last amateur club: Brantford Alexanders (OHA).
(St. Louis' 5th choice, 117th over-all, in 1980 Entry Draft).

				Regula	r Seaso	n				Playoffs		
Season	Club	Lea	GP	G	A	TP	PIM	GP	G	A	TP	PIM
1978-79	Kingston	OHA	61	6	13	19	85	5	2	1	3	6
1979-80	Kingston	OHA	63	17	16	33	52	3	0	0	0	6
1980-81	Kingston	OHA	38	9	13	22	118	....	....	....	....	....
	Brantford	OHA	31	8	27	35	43	6	4	2	6	15
1981-82	Salt Lake	CHL	71	32	32	64	117	2	1	0	1	2
	St. Louis	NHL	5	1	2	3	0	10	2	0	2	4
1982-83	St. Louis	NHL	18	5	2	7	14	....	....	....	....	....
	Salt Lake	CHL	57	23	19	42	140	....	....	....	....	....
1983-84	Montana	CHL	8	7	3	10	34	....	....	....	....	....
	St. Louis	NHL	50	7	5	12	195	9	0	0	0	27
1984-85	St. Louis	NHL	71	9	9	18	146	3	0	0	0	7
1985-86	New Jersey	NHL	51	7	12	19	91	....	....	....	....	....
	NHL Totals		195	29	30	59	446	22	2	0	2	38

Traded to **New Jersey** by **St. Louis** for Rick Meagher, August 29, 1985.

ANDERSON, SHAWN

Born, Montreal, Que., February 7, 1968.
Defense. Shoots left. 6'1", 180 lbs.
Last amateur club. Canadian Olympic Team
(Buffalo's 1st choice, 5th over-all, in 1986 Entry Draft).

				Regula	r Seaso	n				Playoffs		
Season	Club	Lea	GP	G	A	TP	PIM	GP	G	A	TP	PIM
1984-85	Lac St. Louis	Midget	42	23	42	65	100	....	....	....	....	....
1985-86	Maine	H.E.	16	5	8	13	22	....	....	....	....	....
	Cdn. Olympic	....	49	4	14	18	38	....	....	....	....	....

ANDERSSON, BO MIKAEL

Born, Malmo, Sweden, May 10, 1966.
Center. Shoots left. 5'9", 185 lbs.
Last amateur club: Vastra Frolunda (Sweden).
(Buffalo's 1st choice, 18th over-all, in 1984 Entry Draft).

				Regula	r Seaso	n				Playoffs		
Season	Club	Lea	GP	G	A	TP	PIM	GP	G	A	TP	PIM
1983-84	V. Frolunda	Swe.	12	0	2	2	6	....	....	....	....	....
1984-85	V. Frolunda	Swe.	32	16	11	27	18	....	....	....	....	....
1985-86	Buffalo	NHL	32	1	9	10	4	....	....	....	....	....
	Rochester	AHL	20	10	4	14	6	....	....	....	....	....
	NHL Totals		32	1	9	10	4	....	....	....	....	....

ANDERSSON, PETER

Born, Ferdertalve, Sweden, March 2, 1962.
Defense. Shoots right. 6'2", 200 lbs.
Last amateur club: Bjorkloven (Sweden)
(Washington's 8th choice, 173rd over-all, in 1980 Entry Draft).

				Regula	r Seaso	n				Playoffs		
Season	Club	Lea	GP	G	A	TP	PIM	GP	G	A	TP	PIM
1980-81	Bjorkloven	Swe.	31	1	2	3	16	....	....	....	....	....
1981-82	Bjorkloven	Swe.	33	7	7	14	36	7	1	1	2	8
	Swe. National		17	4	2	6	6	....	....	....	....	....
1982-83	Bjorkloven	Swe.	34	8	16	24	30	....	....	....	....	....
	Swe. National	...	25	3	1	4	18	....	....	....	....	....
1983-84	Washington	NHL	42	3	7	10	20	3	0	1	1	2
1984-85	Washington	NHL	57	0	10	10	21	2	0	0	0	0
	Binghamton	AHL	13	2	3	5	6	....	....	....	....	....
1985-86	Washington	NHL	61	6	16	22	36	....	....	....	....	....
	Quebec	NHL	12	1	8	9	4	2	0	1	1	0
	NHL Totals		172	10	41	51	80	7	0	2	2	2

Traded to **Quebec** by **Washington** for Quebec's third-round choice (Shawn Simpson) in 1986 Entry Draft, March 10, 1986.

ANDONOFF, JIM

Born, Warren, Mich., August 7, 1965.
Defense. Shoots right. 6'2", 190 lbs.
Last amateur club: Belleville Bulls (OHL).
(NY Rangers' 5th choice, 93rd over-all, in 1983 Entry Draft).

				Regula	r Seaso	n				Playoffs		
Season	Club	Lea	GP	G	A	TP	PIM	GP	G	A	TP	PIM
1981-82	Detroit	Midgets	78	75	115	190	77	....	....	....	....	....
1982-83	Belleville	OHL	69	17	24	41	36	4	0	0	0	0
1983-84	Belleville	OHL	68	7	24	31	55	3	1	0	1	0
1984-85	Belleville	OHL	64	10	52	62	82	14	4	5	9	10
1985-86	New Haven	AHL	38	5	7	12	25	5	0	0	0	19
	Flint	IHL	39	9	12	21	7	....	....	....	....	....
	Salt Lake	IHL	10	1	2	3	10	....	....	....	....	....

ANDREYCHUK, DAVID (DAVE)

Born, Hamilton, Ont., September 29, 1963.
Center. Shoots right. 6'3", 215 lbs.
Last amateur club: Oshawa Generals (OHL).
(Buffalo's 3rd choice, 16th over-all, in 1982 Entry Draft).

				Regula	r Seaso	n				Playoffs		
Season	Club	Lea	GP	G	A	TP	PIM	GP	G	A	TP	PIM
1980-81	Oshawa	OHA	67	22	22	44	80	10	3	2	5	20
1981-82	Oshawa	OHL	67	57	43	100	71	3	1	4	5	16
1982-83	Oshawa	OHL	14	8	24	32	6	....	....	....	....	....
	Buffalo	NHL	43	14	23	37	16	4	1	0	1	4
1983-84	Buffalo	NHL	78	38	42	80	42	2	0	1	1	2
1984-85	Buffalo	NHL	64	31	30	61	54	5	4	2	6	4
1985-86	Buffalo	NHL	80	36	51	87	61	....	....	....	....	....
	NHL Totals		265	119	146	265	173	11	5	3	8	10

ARCHIBALD, JAMES (JIM)

Born, Cralk, Sask., June 6, 1961.
Right wing. Shoots right. 5'11", 175 lbs.
Last amateur club: University of North Dakota Fighting Sioux (WCHA)
(Minnesota's 11th choice, 139th over-all, in 1981 Entry Draft).

				Regula	r Seaso	n				Playoffs		
Season	Club	Lea	GP	G	A	TP	PIM	GP	G	A	TP	PIM
1980-81	Moose Jaw	SJHL	52	46	42	88	308	....	....	....	....	....
1981-82	North Dakota	WCHA	41	10	16	26	96	....	....	....	....	....
1982-83	North Dakota	WCHA	23	4	11	15	77	....	....	....	....	....
1983-84	North Dakota	WCHA	44	21	15	36	156	....	....	....	....	....
1984-85	Minnesota	NHL	4	1	2	3	11	....	....	....	....	....
	Springfield	AHL	8	1	0	1	5	....	....	....	....	....
a	North Dakota	WCHA	41	37	24	61	197	....	....	....	....	....
1985-86	Minnesota	NHL	11	0	0	0	32	....	....	....	....	....
	Springfield	AHL	12	1	7	8	34	....	....	....	....	....
	NHL Totals		15	1	2	3	43	....	....	....	....	....

a WCHA Second All-Star Team (1985)

ARMSTRONG, HARRY

Born, Anchorage, AK, January 30, 1965.
Defense. Shoots right. 6'2", 195 lbs.
Last amateur club: University of Illinois at Chicago Flames (CCHA).
(Winnipeg's 6th choice, 89th over-all, in 1983 Entry Draft).

				Regula	r Seaso	n				Playoffs		
Season	Club	Lea	GP	G	A	TP	PIM	GP	G	A	TP	PIM
1983-84	Ill-Chicago	CCHA	25	4	11	15	21	....	....	....	....	....
1984-85	Ill-Chicago	CCHA	38	6	21	27	40	....	....	....	....	....
1985-86	Ill-Chicago	CCHA	34	6	13	19	21	....	....	....	....	....

ARMSTRONG, IAN

Born, Peterborough, Ont., January 25, 1965.
Defense. Shoots right. 6'4", 195 lbs.
Last amateur club: Peterborough Petes (OHL).
(Boston's 6th choice, 142nd over-all, in 1983 Entry Draft).

				Regula	r Seaso	n				Playoffs		
Season	Club	Lea	GP	G	A	TP	PIM	GP	G	A	TP	PIM
1982-83	Peterborough	OHL	63	1	6	7	29	4	0	0	0	0
1983-84	Peterborough	OHL	67	1	23	24	66	4	0	1	1	4
1984-85	Peterborough	OHL	66	13	21	34	63	17	3	9	12	17
1985-86	Hershey	AHL	66	0	8	8	42	1	0	0	0	0

Traded to **Philadelphia** by **Boston** for Philadelphia's tenth round choice in 1985 Entry Draft (Bob Beers), May 24, 1985.

ARMSTRONG, TIM

Born, Toronto, Ont., May 12, 1967.
Center. Shoots right. 5'11", 170 lbs.
Last amateur club: Toronto Marlboros (OHL).
(Toronto's 11th choice, 211th over-all, in 1985 Entry Draft).

			Regular Season					Playoffs			
Season	Club	Lea	GP	G	A	TP	PIM	GP	G	A	TP	PIM
1984-85	Toronto	OHL	63	17	45	62	28	5	5	2	7	0
1985-86	Toronto	OHL	64	35	69	104	36	4	1	3	4	9

ARMY, TIM

Born, Providence, Rhode Island, April 26, 1963.
Center. Shoots right. 6', 170 lbs.
Last amateur club: Providence College Friars (ECAC)
(Colorado's 9th choice, 171st over-all, in 1981 Entry Draft).

			Regular Season					Playoffs			
Season	Club	Lea	GP	G	A	TP	PIM	GP	G	A	TP	PIM
1981-82	Providence	ECAC	33	10	15	25	4	....	....	....	....	....
1982-83	Providence	ECAC	34	14	16	30	35	....	....	....	....	....
1983-84	Providence	ECAC	34	20	26	46	40	....	....	....	....	....
1984-85a	Providence	ECAC	37	25	41	66	16	....	....	....	....	....
1985-86	Maine	AHL	68	11	16	27	10	4	1	0	1	0

a NCAA All-American Team (1985)

ARNIEL, SCOTT   (ar-NEEL)

Born, Cornwall, Ont., September 17, 1962.
Center. Shoots left. 6'2", 190 lbs.
Last amateur club: Cornwall Royals (OHL).
(Winnipeg's 2nd choice, 22nd over-all, in 1981 Entry Draft).

			Regular Season					Playoffs			
Season	Club	Lea	GP	G	A	TP	PIM	GP	G	A	TP	PIM
1980-81	Cornwall	QJHL	68	52	71	123	102	19	14	19	33	24
1981-82	Cornwall	OHL	24	18	26	44	43	....	....	....	....	....
	Winnipeg	NHL	17	1	8	9	14	3	0	0	0	0
1982-83	Winnipeg	NHL	75	13	5	18	46	2	0	0	0	0
1983-84	Winnipeg	NHL	80	21	35	56	68	2	0	0	0	5
1984-85	Winnipeg	NHL	79	22	22	44	81	8	1	2	3	9
1985-86	Winnipeg	NHL	80	18	25	43	40	3	0	0	0	12
	NHL Totals		331	75	95	170	249	18	1	2	3	26

ARTHUR, CHAD

Born, Dekalb, Ill. February 18, 1967.
Right wing. Shoots right. 5'11", 195 lbs.
Last amateur club: Bowling Green State University Falcons (CCHA).
(Montreal's 13th choice, 205th over-all, in 1985 Entry Draft).

			Regular Season					Playoffs			
Season	Club	Lea	GP	G	A	TP	PIM	GP	G	A	TP	PIM
1985-86	Bowling Green	CCHA	35	3	4	7	50	....	....	....	....	....

ASHTON, BRENT KENNETH

Born, Saskatoon, Sask., May 18, 1960.
Left wing. Shoots left. 6'1", 210 lbs.
Last amateur club: Saskatoon Blades (WHL).
(Vancouver's 2nd choice, 26th over-all, in 1979 Entry Draft).

			Regular Season					Playoffs			
Season	Club	Lea	GP	G	A	TP	PIM	GP	G	A	TP	PIM
1977-78	Saskatoon	WHL	46	38	26	64	47	....	....	....	....	....
1978-79	Saskatoon	WHL	62	64	55	119	80	11	14	4	18	5
1979-80	Vancouver	NHL	47	5	14	19	11	4	1	0	1	6
1980-81	Vancouver	NHL	77	18	11	29	57	3	0	0	0	0
1981-82	Colorado	NHL	80	24	36	60	26	....	....	....	....	....
1982-83	New Jersey	NHL	76	14	19	33	47	....	....	....	....	....
1983-84	Minnesota	NHL	68	7	10	17	54	12	1	2	3	22
1984-85	Minnesota	NHL	29	4	7	11	15	....	....	....	....	....
	Quebec	NHL	49	27	24	51	38	18	6	4	10	13
1985-86	Quebec	NHL	77	26	32	58	64	3	2	1	3	9
	NHL Totals		503	125	153	278	312	40	10	7	17	50

Traded to **Winnipeg** by **Vancouver** with Vancouver's fourth-round choice (Tom Martin) in the 1982 Entry Draft as compensation for Vancouver's signing of Ivan Hlinka, July 15, 1981. Traded to **Colorado** by **Winnipeg** with Winnipeg's third round choice (Dave Kasper) in 1982 Entry Draft for Lucien DeBlois, July 15, 1981. Traded to **Minnesota** by **New Jersey** for Dave Lewis, October 3, 1983. Traded to **Quebec** by **Minnesota** with Brad Maxwell for Tony McKegney and Bo Berglund, December 14, 1984.

AUBRY, PIERRE   (oh-BREE)

Born, Cap-de-la-Madeleine, Que., April 15, 1960.
Left wing. Shoots left. 5'10", 175 lbs.
Last amateur club: Trois-Rivières Draveurs (QJHL).

			Regular Season					Playoffs			
Season	Club	Lea	GP	G	A	TP	PIM	GP	G	A	TP	PIM
1978-79	Trois Rivieres	QJHL	67	53	45	98	97	13	2	5	7	10
1979-80	Trois Rivieres	QJHL	72	85	62	147	118	7	5	3	8	14
1980-81	**Quebec**	**NHL**	1	0	0	0	0	....	....	....	....	....
	Rochester	AHL	7	0	1	1	4	....	....	....	....	....
	Erie	EHL	71	66	68	134	99	8	7	8	15	4
1981-82	Fredericton	AHL	11	6	5	11	10	....	....	....	....	....
	Quebec	**NHL**	62	10	13	23	27	15	1	1	2	30
1982-83	**Quebec**	**NHL**	77	7	9	16	48	2	0	0	0	0
1983-84	Fredericton	AHL	12	4	5	9	4	....	....	....	....	....
	Quebec	**NHL**	23	1	1	2	17	....	....	....	....	....
	Detroit	**NHL**	14	4	1	5	8	3	0	0	0	2
1984-85	**Detroit**	**NHL**	25	2	2	4	33	....	....	....	....	....
	Adirondack	AHL	29	13	10	23	74	....	....	....	....	....
1985-86	Adirondack	AHL	66	28	31	59	124	16	11	4	15	20
	NHL Totals		202	24	26	50	133	20	1	1	2	32

Signed as free agent by **Quebec**, October 10, 1980. Rights sold to **Detroit** by **Quebec**, February 29, 1984.

BABE, WARREN

Born, Medicine Hat, Alta., September 7, 1968
Left wing. Shoots left. 6'2", 190 lbs.
Last amateur club: Lethbridge Broncos (WHL).
(Minnesota's 1st choice, 12th overall, in 1986 Entry Draft).

			Regular Season					Playoffs			
Season	Club	Lea	GP	G	A	TP	PIM	GP	G	A	TP	PIM
1985-86	Lethbridge	WHL	63	33	24	57	125	....	....	....	....	....

BABYCH, DAVID MICHAEL (DAVE)   (BAB-itch)

Born, Edmonton, Alta., May 23, 1961.
Defense. Shoots left. 6'2", 215 lbs.
Last amateur club: Portland Winter Hawks (WHL).
(Winnipeg's 1st choice, 2nd over-all, in 1980 Entry Draft).

			Regular Season					Playoffs			
Season	Club	Lea	GP	G	A	TP	PIM	GP	G	A	TP	PIM
1978-79	Portland	WHL	67	20	59	79	63	25	7	22	29	22
1979-80ab	Portland	WHL	50	22	60	82	71	8	1	10	11	2
1980-81	**Winnipeg**	**NHL**	69	6	38	44	90	....	....	....	....	....
1981-82	**Winnipeg**	**NHL**	79	19	49	68	92	4	1	2	3	29
1982-83	**Winnipeg**	**NHL**	79	13	61	74	56	3	0	0	0	0
1983-84	**Winnipeg**	**NHL**	66	18	39	57	62	3	1	1	2	0
1984-85	**Winnipeg**	**NHL**	78	13	49	62	78	8	2	7	9	6
1985-86	**Winnipeg**	**NHL**	19	4	12	16	14	....	....	....	....	....
	Hartford	NHL	62	0	43	53	36	8	1	3	4	14
	NHL Totals		452	83	291	374	428	26	5	13	18	49

a WHL First All-Star Team (1980)
b Named WHL's Top Defenseman (1980)
Traded to **Hartford** by **Winnipeg** for Ray Neufeld, November 21, 1985.

BABYCH, WAYNE JOSEPH   (BAB-itch)

Born, Edmonton, Alta., June 6, 1958.
Right wing. Shoots right. 5'11", 190 lbs.
Last amateur club: Portland Winter Hawks (WHL).
(St. Louis' 1st choice, 3rd over-all, in 1978 Amateur Draft).

			Regular Season					Playoffs			
Season	Club	Lea	GP	G	A	TP	PIM	GP	G	A	TP	PIM
1976-77a	Portland	WHL	71	50	62	112	76	10	2	6	8	10
1977-78a	Portland	WHL	68	50	71	121	218	8	4	4	8	19
1978-79	**St. Louis**	**NHL**	67	27	36	63	75	....	....	....	....	....
1979-80	**St. Louis**	**NHL**	59	26	35	61	49	3	1	2	3	2
1980-81	**St. Louis**	**NHL**	78	54	42	96	93	11	2	0	2	8
1981-82	**St. Louis**	**NHL**	51	19	25	44	51	7	3	2	5	8
1982-83	**St. Louis**	**NHL**	71	16	23	39	62	....	....	....	....	....
1983-84	**St. Louis**	**NHL**	70	13	29	42	52	10	1	4	5	4
1984-85	Pittsburgh	NHL	65	20	34	54	35	....	....	....	....	....
1985-86	Pittsburgh	NHL	2	0	0	0	0	....	....	....	....	....
	Quebec	**NHL**	15	6	5	11	18	....	....	....	....	....
	Hartford	NHL	37	11	17	28	59	10	0	1	1	2
	NHL Totals		515	192	246	438	494	41	7	9	16	24

a WHL First All-Star Team (1977, 1978)
Claimed by **Pittsburgh** from **St. Louis** in NHL Waiver Draft, October 9, 1984. Traded to **Quebec** by **Pittsburgh** for future considerations, October 20, 1985. Traded to **Hartford** by **Quebec** for Greg Malone, January 17, 1986.

BAILLARGEON, JOEL

Born, Quebec City, Que., October 6, 1964.
Left Wing. Shoots left. 6'1", 205 lbs.
Last amateur club: Chicoutimi Sagueneens (QMJHL).
(Winnipeg's 5th choice, 109th over-all, in 1983 Entry Draft).

			Regular Season					Playoffs			
Season	Club	Lea	GP	G	A	TP	PIM	GP	G	A	TP	PIM
1981-82	Trois Rivieres	QMJHL	26	1	3	4	47	22	1	1	2	58
1982-83	Trois Rivieres	QMJHL	29	4	5	9	197	....	....	....	....	....
	Hull	QMJHL	25	15	7	22	76	7	0	1	1	16
1983-84	Chicoutimi	QMJHL	60	48	35	83	184	....	....	....	....	....
	Sherbrooke	AHL	8	0	0	0	26	....	....	....	....	....
1984-85	Granby	QMJHL	32	25	24	49	160	....	....	....	....	....
1985-86	Sherbrooke	AHL	56	6	12	18	115	....	....	....	....	....

BAKER, SEAN

Born, Los Angeles, Calif., May 21, 1966.
Defense. Shoots left. 6'0", 192 lbs.
Last amateur club: University of Michigan Wolverines (CCHA).
(Buffalo's 11th choice, 249th over-all, in 1984 Entry Draft).

Season	Club	Lea	Regular Season					Playoffs				
			GP	G	A	TP	PIM	GP	G	A	TP	PIM
1984-85	U. of Michigan	CCHA	20	1	3	4	18	....	....	....	....	....
1985-86	U. of Michigan	CCHA	32	1	7	8	24	....	....	....	....	....

BAKOVIC, PETER GEORGE

Born, Thunder Bay, Ont., January 31, 1965.
Right Wing. Shoots right. 6'2", 200 lbs.
Last amateur club: Windsor Compuware Spitfires (OHL).

Season	Club	Lea	Regular Season					Playoffs				
			GP	G	A	TP	PIM	GP	G	A	TP	PIM
1983-84	Windsor	OHL	63	12	31	43	161	3	0	2	2	14
1984-85	Windsor	OHL	58	26	48	74	259	3	0	0	0	12
1985-86	Moncton	AHL	80	18	36	54	349	10	2	2	4	30

Signed as a free agent by **Calgary**, October 10, 1985.

BARBE, MARIO

Born, Abitibi, Que., March 17, 1967.
Defense. Shoots left. 6'1", 195 lbs.
Last amateur club: Granby Bisons (QMJHL).
(Edmonton's 9th choice, 209th overall, in 1985 Entry Draft).

Season	Club	Lea	Regular Season					Playoffs				
			GP	G	A	TP	PIM	GP	G	A	TP	PIM
1984-85	Chicoutimi	QMJHL	64	2	13	15	211	14	0	2	2	36
1985-86	Granby	QMJHL	70	5	25	30	261	....	....	....	....	....

BARBER, DON

Born, Victoria, B.C., December 2, 1964.
Left wing. Shoots left. 6'1", 205 lbs.
Last amateur club: Bowling Green State University Falcons (CCHA).
(Edmonton's 5th choice, 120th over-all, in 1983 Entry Draft).

Season	Club	Lea	Regular Season					Playoffs				
			GP	G	A	TP	PIM	GP	G	A	TP	PIM
1984-85	Bowling Green	CCHA	39	15	22	37	44	....	....	....	....	....
1985-86	Bowling Green	CCHA	35	21	22	43	64	....	....	....	....	....

Traded to **Minnesota** by **Edmonton** with Marc Habscheid and Emanuel Viveiros for Gord Sherven and Don Biggs, December 20, 1985.

BARON, NORMAND   (BAIR-ohn, nor-MAHN)

Born, Verdun, Que., December 15, 1957.
Left wing. Shoots left. 6', 205 lbs.
Last amateur club: Nova Scotia Voyageurs (AHL).

Season	Club	Lea	Regular Season					Playoffs				
			GP	G	A	TP	PIM	GP	G	A	TP	PIM
1983-84	Nova Scotia	AHL	68	11	11	22	275	....	....	....	....	....
	Montreal	**NHL**	4	0	0	0	12	3	0	0	0	22
1984-85	Sherbrooke	AHL	39	5	5	10	98	2	0	0	0	25
1985-86	**St. Louis**	**NHL**	23	2	0	2	39	....	....	....	....	....
	Peoria	IHL	17	4	4	8	61	....	....	....	....	....
	Flint	IHL	11	1	7	8	43	....	....	....	....	....
	NHL Totals		27	2	0	2	51	3	0	0	0	22

Signed as free agent by **Montreal**, March 15, 1984. Rights sold to **St. Louis** by **Montreal**, September 30, 1985.

BARR, DAVID (DAVE)

Born, Edmonton, Alta., November 30, 1960.
Right wing. Shoots right. 6'1", 195 lbs.
Last amateur club: Lethbridge Broncos (WHL).

Season	Club	Lea	Regular Season					Playoffs				
			GP	G	A	TP	PIM	GP	G	A	TP	PIM
1979-80	Lethbridge	WHL	60	16	38	54	47	....	....	....	....	....
1980-81	Lethbridge	WHL	72	26	62	88	106	....	....	....	....	....
1981-82	Erie	AHL	76	18	48	66	29	....	....	....	....	....
	Boston	**NHL**	2	0	0	0	0	5	1	0	1	0
1982-83	Baltimore	AHL	72	27	51	78	67	....	....	....	....	....
	Boston	**NHL**	10	1	1	2	7	10	0	0	0	2
1983-84	**NY Rangers**	**NHL**	6	0	0	0	2	....	....	....	....	....
	St. Louis	**NHL**	1	0	0	0	0	....	....	....	....	....
	Tulsa	CHL	50	28	37	65	24	....	....	....	....	....
1984-85	**St. Louis**	**NHL**	75	16	18	34	32	2	0	0	0	2
1985-86	**St. Louis**	**NHL**	72	13	38	51	70	11	1	1	2	14
	NHL Totals		166	30	57	87	111	28	2	1	3	18

Signed as free agent by **Boston**, September 28, 1981. Traded to **NY Rangers** by **Boston** for Dave Silk, October 5, 1983. Traded to **St. Louis** by **NY Rangers** with NY Rangers' third-round choice (Alan Perry) in the 1984 Entry Draft for Larry Patey and Bob Brooke, March 5, 1984.

BARRETT, JOHN DAVID

Born, Ottawa, Ont., July 1, 1958
Defense. Shoots left. 6', 210 lbs.
Last amateur club: Windsor Spitfires (OHA).
(Detroit's 10th choice, 129th over-all, in 1978 Amateur Draft).

Season	Club	Lea	Regular Season					Playoffs				
			GP	G	A	TP	PIM	GP	G	A	TP	PIM
1976-77	Windsor	OHA	63	7	17	24	168	9	1	1	2	12
1977-78	Windsor	OHA	67	8	18	26	133	6	2	1	3	30
1978-79	Milwaukee	IHL	42	8	13	21	117	....	....	....	....	....
	Kalamazoo	IHL	31	1	12	13	54	15	2	11	13	48
1979-80	Kalamazoo	IHL	52	8	33	41	63	....	....	....	....	....
	Adirondack	AHL	28	0	4	4	59	5	1	2	3	6
1980-81	**Detroit**	**NHL**	56	3	10	13	60	....	....	....	....	....
	Adirondack	AHL	21	4	11	15	63	....	....	....	....	....
1981-82	**Detroit**	**NHL**	69	1	12	13	93	....	....	....	....	....
1982-83	**Detroit**	**NHL**	79	4	10	14	74	....	....	....	....	....
1983-84	**Detroit**	**NHL**	78	2	8	10	78	4	0	0	0	4
1984-85	**Detroit**	**NHL**	71	6	19	25	117	3	0	1	1	11
1985-86	**Detroit**	**NHL**	65	2	12	14	125	....	....	....	....	....
	Washington	**NHL**	14	0	3	3	12	9	2	1	3	35
	NHL Totals		432	18	74	92	599	16	2	2	4	50

Traded to **Washington** by **Detroit** with Greg Smith for Darren Veitch, March 10, 1986.

BARTEL, ROBIN DALE

Born, Drake, Sask., May 16, 1961
Defense. Shoots left. 6', 200 lbs.
Last amateur club: 1984 Canadian Olympic Team.

Season	Club	Lea	Regular Season					Playoffs				
			GP	G	A	TP	PIM	GP	G	A	TP	PIM
1980-81	Prince Albert	SJHL	86	22	63	85	N/A	....	....	....	....	....
1981-82	Prince Albert	SJHL	83	17	73	90	N/A	....	....	....	....	....
1982-83	U. of Sask.	CWUAA	24	4	14	18	N/A	....	....	....	....	....
1983-84	Cdn. National	...	51	4	6	10	50	....	....	....	....	....
	Cdn. Olympic	...	6	0	1	1	4	....	....	....	....	....
1984-85	Moncton	AHL	41	4	11	15	54	....	....	....	....	....
1985-86	**Calgary**	**NHL**	1	0	0	0	0	6	0	0	0	16
	Moncton	AHL	74	4	21	25	100	3	0	0	0	0
	NHL Totals		1	0	0	0	0	6	0	0	0	16

Signed as a free agent by **Calgary**, July 1, 1985. Signed as a free agent by **Vancouver**, June 27, 1986.

BASSEN, BOB

Born, Calgary, Alta., May 6, 1965.
Center. Shoots left. 5'10", 180 lbs.
Last amateur club: Medicine Hat Tigers (WHL).

Season	Club	Lea	Regular Season					Playoffs				
			GP	G	A	TP	PIM	GP	G	A	TP	PIM
1982-83	Medicine Hat	WHL	4	3	2	5	0	3	0	0	0	4
1983-84	Medicine Hat	WHL	72	29	29	58	93	14	5	11	16	12
1984-85a	Medicine Hat	WHL	65	32	50	82	143	10	2	8	10	39
1985-86	**NY Islanders**	**NHL**	11	2	1	3	6	3	0	1	1	0
	Springfield	AHL	54	13	21	34	111	....	....	....	....	....
	NHL Totals		11	2	1	3	6	3	0	1	1	0

a WHL First All-Star Team (1985)
Signed as a free agent by **NY Islanders**, October 19, 1984.

BAUMGARTNER, KEN

Born, Flin, Flon, Man., March 11, 1966.
Defense. Shoots left. 6'1", 200 lbs.
Last amateur club: Prince Albert Raiders (WHL).
(Buffalo's 12th choice, 245th over-all, in 1985 Entry Draft).

Season	Club	Lea	Regular Season					Playoffs				
			GP	G	A	TP	PIM	GP	G	A	TP	PIM
1984-85	Prince Albert	WHL	60	3	9	12	252	13	1	3	4	89
1985-86	Prince Albert	WHL	70	4	23	27	277	20	3	9	12	112

Traded to **Los Angeles** by **Buffalo** with Sean McKenna and Larry Playfair for Brian Engblom and Doug Smith, January 29, 1986.

BAXTER, PAUL GORDON

Born, Winnipeg, Man., October 28, 1955.
Defense. Shoots right. 5'11", 190 lbs.
Last amateur club: Winnipeg Clubs (WHL).
(Pittsburgh's 3rd choice, 49th over-all, in 1975 Amateur Draft).

			Regular Season					Playoffs				
Season	Club	Lea	GP	G	A	TP	PIM	GP	G	A	TP	PIM
1973-74	Winnipeg	WHL	63	10	30	40	384	....	....	....	....	....
1974-75	Cape Cod	NAHL	2	1	0	1	2	....	....	....	....	....
	Cleveland	WHA	5	0	0	0	37	....	....	....	....	....
1975-76	Syracuse	NAHL	3	1	2	3	9	....	....	....	....	....
	Cleveland	WHA	67	3	7	10	201	3	0	0	0	10
1976-77	Maine	NAHL	6	1	4	5	52	....	....	....	....	....
	Quebec	WHA	66	6	17	23	244	12	2	2	4	35
1977-78	Quebec	WHA	76	6	29	35	240	11	4	7	11	42
1978-79	Quebec	WHA	76	10	36	46	240	4	0	2	2	7
1979-80	**Quebec**	**NHL**	**61**	**7**	**13**	**20**	**145**	....	....	....	....	....
1980-81	**Pittsburgh**	**NHL**	**51**	**5**	**14**	**19**	**204**	**5**	**0**	**1**	**1**	**28**
1981-82	**Pittsburgh**	**NHL**	**76**	**9**	**34**	**43**	***409**	**5**	**0**	**0**	**0**	**14**
1982-83	**Pittsburgh**	**NHL**	**75**	**11**	**21**	**32**	**238**	....	....	....	....	....
1983-84	**Calgary**	**NHL**	**74**	**7**	**20**	**27**	**182**	**11**	**0**	**2**	**2**	**37**
1984-85	**Calgary**	**NHL**	**70**	**5**	**14**	**19**	**126**	**4**	**0**	**1**	**1**	**18**
1985-86	**Calgary**	**NHL**	**47**	**4**	**3**	**7**	**194**	**13**	**0**	**1**	**1**	**55**
	NHL Totals		**454**	**48**	**119**	**167**	**1498**	**38**	**0**	**5**	**5**	**152**
	WHA Totals		290	25	89	114	962	30	6	11	17	94

Reclaimed by **Pittsburgh** from **Quebec** prior to Expansion Draft, June 9, 1979. Claimed as priority selection by **Quebec**, June 9, 1979. Signed as free agent by **Pittsburgh** from **Quebec**, August 7, 1980. As compensation **Quebec** received Kim Clackson. Signed as free agent by **Calgary**, September 29, 1983.

BEAN, TIM

Born, Sault Ste. Marie, Ont., March 9, 1967.
Left wing. Shoots left. 6'1", 190 lbs.
Last amateur club: North Bay Centennials (OHL).
(Toronto's 7th choice, 127th over-all, in 1985 Entry Draft).

			Regular Season					Playoffs				
Season	Club	Lea	GP	G	A	TP	PIM	GP	G	A	TP	PIM
1983-84	Belleville	OHL	63	12	13	25	131	3	0	0	0	0
1984-85	Belleville	OHL	31	10	11	21	60	....	....	....	....	....
	North Bay	OHL	28	11	13	24	61	8	2	5	7	8
1985-86	North Bay	OHL	66	32	34	66	129	10	5	5	10	22

BECKER, RUSS

Born, Iowa City, Iowa, December 20, 1965
Defense. Shoots left. 6'3", 200 lbs.
Last amateur club: University of Michigan Tech Huskies (WCHA).
(NY Islanders' 12th choice, 228th over-all, in 1984 Entry Draft).

			Regular Season					Playoffs				
Season	Club	Lea	GP	G	A	TP	PIM	GP	G	A	TP	PIM
1984-85	Michigan Tech	WCHA	15	2	1	3	14	....	....	....	....	....
1985-86	Michigan Tech	WCHA	33	0	2	2	4	....	....	....	....	....

BEAUDOIN, YVES

Born, Pointe-aux-Trembles, Que., January 7, 1965.
Defense. Shoots right. 5'11", 180 lbs.
Last amateur club: Shawnigan Cataractes (QMJHL).
(Washington's 10th choice, 203rd over-all, in 1983 Entry Draft)

			Regular Season					Playoffs				
Season	Club	Lea	GP	G	A	TP	PIM	GP	G	A	TP	PIM
1983-84	Shawinigan	QMJHL	68	14	43	57	93	....	....	....	....	....
1984-85	Shawinigan	QMJHL	58	20	38	58	78	9	4	3	7	31
1985-86	**Washington**	**NHL**	**4**	**0**	**0**	**0**	**0**	....	....	....	....	....
	Binghamton	AHL	48	5	12	17	36	6	1	2	3	0
	NHL Totals		**4**	**0**	**0**	**0**	**0**	....	....	....	....	....

a Named QMJHL top defenseman (1985)
b QMJHL First All-Star Team (1985)

BECK, BARRY DAVID

Born, Vancouver, B.C., June 3, 1957.
Defense. Shoots left. 6'3", 215 lbs.
Last amateur club: New Westminster Bruins (WHL).
(Colorado's 1st choice, 2nd over-all, in 1977 Amateur Draft).

			Regular Season					Playoffs				
Season	Club	Lea	GP	G	A	TP	PIM	GP	G	A	TP	PIM
1974-75	N. Westminster	WHL	58	9	33	42	162	18	4	9	13	52
1975-76a	N. Westminster	WHL	68	19	80	99	325	17	3	9	12	58
1976-77abc	N. Westminster	WHL	61	16	46	62	167	12	4	6	10	39
1977-78	**Colorado**	**NHL**	**75**	**22**	**38**	**60**	**89**	**2**	**0**	**1**	**1**	**0**
1978-79	**Colorado**	**NHL**	**63**	**14**	**28**	**42**	**91**	....	....	....	....	....
1979-80	**Colorado**	**NHL**	**10**	**1**	**5**	**6**	**8**	....	....	....	....	....
	NY Rangers	**NHL**	**61**	**14**	**45**	**59**	**98**	**9**	**1**	**4**	**5**	**6**
1980-81	**NY Rangers**	**NHL**	**75**	**11**	**23**	**34**	**231**	**14**	**5**	**8**	**13**	**32**
1981-82	**NY Rangers**	**NHL**	**60**	**9**	**29**	**38**	**111**	**10**	**1**	**5**	**6**	**14**
1982-83	**NY Rangers**	**NHL**	**66**	**12**	**22**	**34**	**112**	**9**	**2**	**4**	**6**	**8**
1983-84	**NY Rangers**	**NHL**	**72**	**9**	**27**	**36**	**134**	**4**	**1**	**0**	**1**	**6**
1984-85	**NY Rangers**	**NHL**	**56**	**7**	**19**	**26**	**65**	**3**	**0**	**1**	**1**	**11**
1985-86	**NY Rangers**	**NHL**	**25**	**4**	**8**	**12**	**24**	....	....	....	....	....
	NHL Totals		**563**	**103**	**244**	**347**	**963**	**51**	**10**	**23**	**33**	**77**

a WHL First All-Star Team (1976, 1977)
b Named WHL's Top Defenseman (1977)
c Named WHL's Most Valuable Player (1977)

Traded to **NY Rangers** by **Colorado** for Pat Hickey, Lucien DeBlois, Mike McEwen, Dean Turner and future considerations (Bobby Crawford), November 2, 1979.

BECK, BRAD

Born, Vancouver, B.C., February 10, 1964.
Defense. Shoots right. 5'11", 180 lbs.
Last amateur club: Michigan State University Spartans (CCHA)
(Chicago's 5th choice, 91st over-all, in 1982 Entry Draft).

			Regular Season					Playoffs				
Season	Club	Lea	GP	G	A	TP	PIM	GP	G	A	TP	PIM
1981-82	Penticton	BCJHL	52	13	32	45	116	....	....	....	....	....
1982-83	Michigan State	CCHA	42	5	15	20	40	....	....	....	....	....
1983-84	Michigan State	CCHA	42	2	7	9	67	....	....	....	....	....
1984-85	Michigan State	CCHA	42	5	18	23	62	....	....	....	....	....
1985-86	Michigan State	CCHA	41	3	15	18	40	....	....	....	....	....

BEERS, EDWARD JOSEPH (EDDY)

Born, Merritt, B.C., October 12, 1959.
Left wing. Shoots left. 6'2", 195 lbs.
Last amateur club: University of Denver Pioneers (WCHA)

			Regular Season					Playoffs				
Season	Club	Lea	GP	G	A	TP	PIM	GP	G	A	TP	PIM
1980-81	U. of Denver	WCHA	39	24	15	39	63	....	....	....	....	....
1981-82	U. of Denver	WCHA	42	50	34	84	59	....	....	....	....	....
	Calgary	**NHL**	**5**	**1**	**1**	**2**	**21**	....	....	....	....	....
1982-83	Colorado	CHL	29	12	17	29	52	....	....	....	....	....
	Calgary	**NHL**	**41**	**11**	**15**	**26**	**21**	**8**	**1**	**1**	**2**	**27**
1983-84	**Calgary**	**NHL**	**73**	**36**	**39**	**75**	**88**	**11**	**2**	**5**	**7**	**12**
1984-85	**Calgary**	**NHL**	**74**	**28**	**40**	**68**	**94**	**3**	**1**	**0**	**1**	**0**
1985-86	**Calgary**	**NHL**	**33**	**11**	**10**	**21**	**8**	....	....	....	....	....
	St. Louis	**NHL**	**24**	**7**	**11**	**18**	**24**	**19**	**3**	**4**	**7**	**8**
	NHL Totals		**250**	**94**	**116**	**210**	**256**	**41**	**7**	**10**	**17**	**47**

Signed as free agent by **Calgary**, April 1, 1982. Traded to **St. Louis** by **Calgary** with Charles Bourgeois and Gino Cavallini for Joe Mullen, Terry Johnson and Rik Wilson, February 1, 1986.

BEKKERS, JOHN

Born, Halifax, N.S., May 18, 1965.
Center. Shoots left. 6'2", 195 lbs.
Last amateur club: St. Francis Xavier University X-men (AUAA).
(Calgary's 4th choice, 67th over-all, in 1983 Entry Draft).

			Regular Season					Playoffs				
Season	Club	Lea	GP	G	A	TP	PIM	GP	G	A	TP	PIM
1982-83	Regina	WHL	70	18	24	42	43	....	....	....	....	....
1983-84	Regina	WHL	32	8	1	9	25	....	....	....	....	....
	Portland	WHL	22	21	14	35	17	14	5	10	15	6
1984-85	St. Francis X.	AUAA	30	20	24	44	30	....	....	....	....	....
1985-86	St. Francis X.	AUAA	25	21	19	40	28	....	....	....	....	....

BELANGER, ROGER

Born, St. Catharines, Ont., December 1, 1965.
Center. Shoots right. 6', 190 lbs.
Last amateur club: Kingston Canadians (OHL).
(Pittsburgh's 3rd choice, 16th over-all, in 1984 Entry Draft).

			Regular Season					Playoffs				
Season	Club	Lea	GP	G	A	TP	PIM	GP	G	A	TP	PIM
1982-83	London	OHL	68	17	14	31	53	1	0	0	0	5
1983-84	Kingston	OHL	67	44	46	90	66	....	....	....	....	....
1984-85	**Pittsburgh**	**NHL**	**44**	**3**	**5**	**8**	**32**	....	....	....	....	....
	Hamilton	OHL	3	3	3	6	0	17	3	10	13	47
1985-86	Baltimore	AHL	69	17	21	38	61	....	....	....	....	....
	NHL Totals		**44**	**3**	**5**	**8**	**32**	....	....	....	....	....

BELL, BRUCE

Born, Toronto, Ont., February 15, 1965.
Defense. Shoots left. 6', 190 lbs.
Last amateur club: Brantford Alexanders (OHL).
(Quebec's 2nd choice, 52nd over-all, in 1983 Entry Draft).

			Regular Season					Playoffs				
Season	Club	Lea	GP	G	A	TP	PIM	GP	G	A	TP	PIM
1981-82	S. S. Marie	OHL	67	11	18	29	63	12	0	2	2	24
1982-83	S. S. Marie	OHL	5	0	2	2	2	....	....	....	....	....
	Windsor	OHL	61	10	35	45	39	3	0	4	4	0
1983-84a	Brantford	OHL	63	7	41	48	55	6	0	3	3	16
1984-85b	**Quebec**	**NHL**	**75**	**6**	**31**	**37**	**44**	**16**	**2**	**2**	**4**	**21**
1985-86	**St. Louis**	**NHL**	**75**	**2**	**18**	**20**	**43**	**14**	**0**	**2**	**2**	**13**
	NHL Totals		**150**	**8**	**49**	**57**	**87**	**30**	**2**	**4**	**6**	**34**

a OHL First All-Star Team (1984)
b NHL All-Rookie Team (1985)
Traded to **St. Louis** by **Quebec** for Gilbert Delorme, October 2, 1985.

BELLAND, BRAD

Born, Windsor, Ont., January 4, 1967.
Center. Shoots right. 6'0", 180 lbs.
Last amateur club: Hamilton Steelhawks (OHL).
(Chicago's 5th choice, 95th over-all, in 1985 Entry Draft).

			Regular Season					Playoffs				
Season	Club	Lea	GP	G	A	TP	PIM	GP	G	A	TP	PIM
1983-84	Windsor	OHL	43	26	25	51	63	....	....	....	....	....
1984-85	Sudbury	OHL	64	17	27	44	48	....	....	....	....	....
1985-86	Sudbury	OHL	7	0	6	6	0	....	....	....	....	....
	Hamilton	OHL	59	20	26	46	40	....	....	....	....	....

BELLAND, NEIL

Born, Parry Sound, Ont., April 3, 1961.
Defense. Shoots left. 5'11", 180 lbs.
Last amateur club: Kingston Canadians (OHA).

Season	Club	Lea	Regular Season GP	G	A	TP	PIM	Playoffs GP	G	A	TP	PIM
1979-80	Kingston	OHA	54	7	44	51	44	3	0	0	0	12
1980-81a	Kingston	OHA	53	28	54	82	54	14	5	6	11	23
1981-82	Dallas	CHL	27	2	20	22	18	....	....	....	....	....
	Vancouver	NHL	28	3	6	9	16	17	1	7	8	16
1982-83	Vancouver	NHL	14	2	4	6	4	....	....	....	....	....
	Fredericton	AHL	46	4	17	21	12	7	1	2	3	8
1983-84	Fredericton	AHL	17	3	15	18	2	....	....	....	....	....
	Vancouver	NHL	44	7	13	20	24	4	1	2	3	7
1984-85	Vancouver	NHL	13	0	6	6	6	....	....	....	....	....
b	Fredericton	AHL	57	7	34	41	31	6	0	2	2	4
1985-86	Vancouver	NHL	7	1	2	3	4	....	....	....	....	....
	Fredericton	AHL	36	6	18	24	10	6	1	6	7	2
	NHL Totals		106	13	31	44	54	21	2	9	11	23

Signed as free agent by **Vancouver**, October 1, 1980.
a OHA Third All-Star Team (1981)
b AHL Second All-Star Team (1985)

BELLOWS, BRIAN

Born, St. Catharines, Ont., September 1, 1964.
Right wing. Shoots right. 5'11", 195 lbs.
Last amateur club: Kitchener Rangers (OHL).
(Minnesota's 1st choice, 2nd over-all, in 1982 Entry Draft).

Season	Club	Lea	Regular Season GP	G	A	TP	PIM	Playoffs GP	G	A	TP	PIM
1980-81a	Kitchener	OHA	66	49	67	116	23	16	14	13	27	13
1981-82bc	Kitchener	OHL	47	45	52	97	23	15	16	13	29	11
1982-83	Minnesota	NHL	78	35	30	65	27	9	5	4	9	18
1983-84	Minnesota	NHL	78	41	42	83	66	16	2	12	14	9
1984-85	Minnesota	NHL	78	26	36	62	72	9	2	4	6	9
1985-86	Minnesota	NHL	77	31	48	79	46	5	5	0	5	16
	NHL Totals		311	133	156	289	217	39	14	20	34	49

a OHA Third All-Star Team (1981)
b OHL First All-Star Team (1982)
c Most Sportsmanlike Player, Memorial Cup Tournament (1982)

BENNET, ERIC

Born, Springfield, Mass. July 24, 1967.
Left wing. Shoots left. 6'3", 200 lbs.
Last amateur club: Wilbraham Monson Academy (HS).
(Minnesota's 4th choice, 54th over-all, in 1986 Entry Draft).

Season	Club	Lea	Regular Season GP	G	A	TP	PIM	Playoffs GP	G	A	TP	PIM
1985-86	Wilbraham	HS	57	9	40	49	95	9	1	5	6	14

BENNING, BRIAN

Born, Edmonton, Alta., June 10, 1966.
Defense. Shoots left. 6', 175 lbs.
Last amateur club: Canadian Olympic Team
(St. Louis' 1st choice, 26th over-all, in 1984 Entry Draft).

Season	Club	Lea	Regular Season GP	G	A	TP	PIM	Playoffs GP	G	A	TP	PIM
1982-83	St. Albert	SJHL	57	8	38	46	229	....	....	....	....	....
1983-84	Portland	WHL	38	6	41	47	108	....	....	....	....	....
1984-85	St. Louis	NHL	4	0	2	2	0	....	....	....	....	....
	Kamloops	WHL	17	3	18	21	26	6	1	2	3	13
1985-86	St. Louis	NHL	....	....	....	....	....	6	1	2	3	13
	Cdn. Olympic	....	60	6	13	19	43	....	....	....	....	....
	NHL Totals		4	0	2	2	0	6	1	2	3	13

BENNING, JAMES (JIM)

Born, Edmonton, Alta., April 29, 1963.
Defense. Shoots left. 6', 185 lbs.
Last amateur club: Portland Winter Hawks (WHL).
(Toronto's 1st choice, 6th over-all, in 1981 Entry Draft).

Season	Club	Lea	Regular Season GP	G	A	TP	PIM	Playoffs GP	G	A	TP	PIM
1979-80	Portland	WHL	71	11	60	71	42	8	3	9	12	6
1980-81ab	Portland	WHL	72	28	111	139	61	9	1	5	6	16
1981-82	Toronto	NHL	74	7	24	31	46	....	....	....	....	....
1982-83	Toronto	NHL	74	5	17	22	47	4	1	1	2	2
1983-84	Toronto	NHL	79	12	39	51	66	....	....	....	....	....
1984-85	Toronto	NHL	80	9	35	44	55	....	....	....	....	....
1985-86	Toronto	NHL	52	4	21	25	71	....	....	....	....	....
	NHL Totals		359	37	136	173	285	4	1	1	2	2

a WHL First All-Star Team (1981)
b Named WHL's Top Defenseman (1981)

BENOIT, GUY

Born, Ste. Hyacinthe, Que., June 18, 1965.
Center. Shoots left. 5'10", 185 lbs.
Last amateur club: Drummondville Voltigeurs (QMJHL).
(Los Angeles' 2nd choice, 67th over-all, in 1983 Entry Draft).

Season	Club	Lea	Regular Season GP	G	A	TP	PIM	Playoffs GP	G	A	TP	PIM
1982-83	Shawinigan	QMJHL	61	42	63	105	10	6	5	3	8	0
1983-84	Drummondville	QMJHL	61	26	56	82	25	10	4	4	8	2
1984-85	Drummondville	QMJHL	64	56	79	135	53	12	12	6	18	6
1985-86	New Haven	AHL	9	1	0	1	0	....	....	....	....	....
	Toledo	IHL	55	40	46	86	8	....	....	....	....	....
a	Muskegon	IHL	13	7	12	19	16	14	7	12	19	6

a IHL Rookie of the Year (1986)

BEREZAN, PERRY EDMUND   (BEAR-a-zan)

Born, Edmonton, Alta., December 25, 1964.
Center. Shoots right. 6'1", 190 lbs.
Last amateur club: University of North Dakota Fighting Sioux (WCHA)
(Calgary's 3rd choice, 56th over-all, in 1983 Entry Draft).

Season	Club	Lea	Regular Season GP	G	A	TP	PIM	Playoffs GP	G	A	TP	PIM
1983-84	North Dakota	WCHA	44	28	24	52	29	....	....	....	....	....
1984-85a	North Dakota	WCHA	42	23	35	58	32	....	....	....	....	....
	Calgary	NHL	9	3	2	5	4	2	1	0	1	4
1985-86	Calgary	NHL	55	12	21	33	39	8	1	1	2	6
	NHL Totals		64	15	23	38	43	10	2	1	3	10

a WCHA Second All-Star Team (1985)

BERG, BILL

Born, St. Catharines, Ont., October 21, 1967
Defense. Shoots left. 6'0", 185 lbs.
Last amateur club: Toronto Marlboros (OHL).
(NY Islanders' 3rd choice, 59th over-all, in 1986 Entry Draft).

Season	Club	Lea	Regular Season GP	G	A	TP	PIM	Playoffs GP	G	A	TP	PIM
1984-85	Grimsby	OPJHL	42	10	22	32	153	....	....	....	....	....
1985-86	Toronto	OHL	64	3	35	38	143	4	0	0	0	19

BERGEN, TODD

Born, Prince Albert, Sask., July 11, 1963.
Center. Shoots left. 6'3", 185 lbs.
Last amateur club: Prince Albert Raiders (WHL).
(Philadelphia's 5th choice, 98th over-all, in 1982 Entry Draft).

Season	Club	Lea	Regular Season GP	G	A	TP	PIM	Playoffs GP	G	A	TP	PIM
1981-82	Prince Albert	SJHL	59	30	62	92	35	....	....	....	....	....
1982-83	Prince Albert	WHL	70	34	47	81	17	....	....	....	....	....
1983-84	Prince Albert	WHL	43	57	39	96	15	5	2	5	7	4
	Springfield	AHL	1	0	0	0	0	....	....	....	....	....
1984-85	Philadelphia	NHL	14	11	5	16	4	17	4	9	13	8
	Hershey	AHL	38	20	19	39	2	....	....	....	....	....
1985-86	DID NOT PLAY											
	NHL Totals		14	11	5	16	4	17	4	9	13	8

Traded to **Minnesota** by **Philadelphia** with Ed Hospodar for Bo Berglund and Dave Richter, November 29, 1985.

BERGER, MIKE

Born, Edmonton, Alta., June 2, 1967.
Defense. Shoots right. 6'0", 195 lbs.
Last amateur club: Spokane Chiefs (WHL).
(Minnesota's 2nd choice, 69th over-all, in 1985 Entry Draft).

Season	Club	Lea	Regular Season GP	G	A	TP	PIM	Playoffs GP	G	A	TP	PIM
1982-83	Lethbridge	WHL	1	0	0	0	0	....	....	....	....	....
1983-84	Lethbridge	WHL	41	2	9	11	60	5	0	1	1	7
1984-85	Lethbridge	WHL	58	9	31	40	85	4	0	3	3	9
1985-86	Spokane	WHL	57	9	40	49	95	9	1	5	6	14

BERGERON, JEAN-GUY

Born, Montreal, Que., April 14, 1965
Defense. Shoots right. 5'11", 195 lbs.
Last amateur club: Drummondville Voltigeurs (QMJHL).
(Montreal's 14th choice, 238th over-all, in 1983 Entry Draft).

Season	Club	Lea	Regular Season GP	G	A	TP	PIM	Playoffs GP	G	A	TP	PIM
1982-83	Shawinigan	QMJHL	66	1	16	17	59	10	0	2	2	11
1983-84	St. Jean	QMJHL	71	9	34	43	126	4	1	4	5	0
1984-85	St. Jean	QMJHL	66	17	57	74	71	5	0	0	0	0
1985-86	Drummondville	QMJHL	61	12	52	64	40	23	3	7	10	10

BERGEVIN, MARC

Born, Montreal, Que., August 11, 1965.
Defense. Shoots right. 6'0", 185 lbs.
Last amateur club: Chicoutimi Sagueneens (QMJHL).
(Chicago's 3rd choice, 59th over-all, in 1983 Entry Draft).

| Season | Club | Lea | Regular Season | | | | | Playoffs | | | | |
			GP	G	A	TP	PIM	GP	G	A	TP	PIM
1982-83	Chicoutimi	QMJHL	64	3	27	30	113	....	....	....	....	....
1983-84	Chicoutimi	QMJHL	70	10	35	45	125	....	....	....	....	....
	Springfield	AHL	7	0	1	1	2	....	....	....	....	....
1984-85	Springfield	AHL	....	....	....	....	....	4	0	0	0	0
	Chicago	**NHL**	60	0	6	6	54	6	0	3	3	2
1985-86	**Chicago**	**NHL**	71	7	7	14	60	3	0	0	0	0
	NHL Totals		131	7	13	20	114	9	0	3	3	2

BERGLUND, BO

Born, Sjalevad, Sweden, April 6, 1955.
Right wing. Shoots left. 5'10", 175 lbs.
Last amateur club: Djurgardens (Sweden).
(Quebec's 11th choice, 232nd over-all, in 1983 Entry Draft).

| Season | Club | Lea | Regular Season | | | | | Playoffs | | | | |
			GP	G	A	TP	PIM	GP	G	A	TP	PIM
1981-82	Djurgardens	Swe.	....	33	16	36	42	....	....	....	....	....
1982-83	Djurgardens	Swe.	....	32	19	13	32	....	....	....	....	....
1983-84	**Quebec**	**NHL**	75	16	27	43	20	7	2	0	2	4
1984-85	**Quebec**	**NHL**	12	4	1	5	6	....	....	....	....	....
	Minnesota	**NHL**	33	6	9	15	8	2	0	0	0	2
	Springfield	AHL	3	1	2	3	0	....	....	....	....	....
1985-86	**Minnesota**	**NHL**	3	2	0	2	2	....	....	....	....	....
	Springfield	AHL	3	0	1	1	2	....	....	....	....	....
	Philadelphia	**NHL**	7	0	2	2	4	....	....	....	....	....
	Hershey	AHL	43	17	28	45	40	16	7	10	17	17
	NHL Totals		130	28	39	67	40	....	....	....	....	....

Traded to **Minnesota** by **Quebec** with Tony McKegney for Brad Maxwell and Brent Ashton, December 14, 1984. Traded to **Philadelphia** by **Minnesota** with Dave Richter for Todd Bergen and Ed Hospodar, November 29, 1985.

BERGLUND, TIM

Born, Crookston, Minn. January 11, 1965.
Center. Shoots right. 6'3", 180 lbs.
Last amateur club: University of Minnesota Golden Gophers (WCHA).
(Washington's 1st choice, 75th over-all, in 1983 Entry Draft).

| Season | Club | Lea | Regular Season | | | | | Playoffs | | | | |
			GP	G	A	TP	PIM	GP	G	A	TP	PIM
1983-84	U. Minnesota	WCHA	24	4	11	15	4	....	....	....	....	....
1984-85	U. Minnesota	WCHA	34	5	9	14	8	....	....	....	....	....
1985-86	U. Minnesota	WCHA	48	11	16	27	26	....	....	....	....	....

BERNARD, LARRY

Born, Prince George, B.C., April 16, 1967.
Left wing. Shoots left. 6'2", 195 lbs.
Last amateur club: Seattle Thunderbirds (WHL).
(NY Rangers' 8th choice, 154th over-all, in 1985 Entry Draft).

| Season | Club | Lea | Regular Season | | | | | Playoffs | | | | |
			GP	G	A	TP	PIM	GP	G	A	TP	PIM
1984-85	Seattle	WHL	63	18	26	44	66	....	....	....	....	....
1985-86	Seattle	WHL	54	17	25	42	64	5	1	3	4	10

BERRY, BRAD

Born, Bashaw, Alta., April 1, 1965.
Defense. Shoots left. 6'2", 190 lbs.
Last amateur club: University of North Dakota Fighting Sioux (WCHA).
(Winnipeg's 3rd choice, 29th over-all, in 1983 Entry Draft).

| Season | Club | Lea | Regular Season | | | | | Playoffs | | | | |
			GP	G	A	TP	PIM	GP	G	A	TP	PIM
1982-83	St. Albert	AJHL	55	9	33	42	97	....	....	....	....	....
1983-84	North Dakota	WCHA	32	2	7	9	8	....	....	....	....	....
1984-85	North Dakota	WCHA	40	4	26	30	26	....	....	....	....	....
1985-86	North Dakota	WCHA	40	6	29	35	26	....	....	....	....	....
	Winnipeg	**NHL**	13	1	0	1	10	3	0	0	0	0
	NHL Totals		13	1	0	1	10	3	0	0	0	0

BERTUZZI, BRIAN

Born, Vancouver, B.C., January 24, 1966.
Center. Shoots left. 5'11", 170 lbs.
Last amateur club: New Westminster Bruins (WHL)
(Vancouver's 6th choice, 73rd over-all, in 1984 Entry Draft).

| Season | Club | Lea | Regular Season | | | | | Playoffs | | | | |
			GP	G	A	TP	PIM	GP	G	A	TP	PIM
1983-84	Kamloops	WHL	69	29	21	50	99	16	1	5	6	17
1984-85	Kamloops	WHL	46	23	15	38	52	9	1	2	3	26
1985-86	Kalamazoo	IHL	4	2	0	2	2	....	....	....	....	....
	N. Westminster	WHL	47	24	24	48	58	....	....	....	....	....

BERUBE, CRAIG

Born, Calihoo, Alta., December 17, 1965.
Left wing. Shoots left. 6'1", 195 lbs.
Last amateur club: Medicine Hat Tigers (WHL).

| Season | Club | Lea | Regular Season | | | | | Playoffs | | | | |
			GP	G	A	TP	PIM	GP	G	A	TP	PIM
1982-83	Kamloops	WHL	4	0	0	0	0	....	....	....	....	....
1983-84	N. Westminster	WHL	70	11	20	31	104	8	1	2	3	5
1984-85	N. Westminster	WHL	70	25	44	69	191	10	3	2	5	4
1985-86	Medicine Hat	WHL	66	31	30	61	214	25	7	8	15	102

Signed as a free agent by **Philadelphia**, March 19, 1986.

BEUKEBOOM, JEFF

Born, Ajax, Ont., March 28, 1965.
Defense. Shoots right. 6'4", 210 lbs.
Last amateur club: Sault Ste. Marie Greyhounds (OHL).
(Edmonton's 1st choice, 19th over-all, in 1983 Entry Draft).

| Season | Club | Lea | Regular Season | | | | | Playoffs | | | | |
			GP	G	A	TP	PIM	GP	G	A	TP	PIM
1981-82	Newmarket	OPJHL	49	5	30	35	218	....	....	....	....	....
1982-83	S. S. Marie	OHL	70	0	25	25	143	16	1	4	5	46
1983-84	S. S. Marie	OHL	61	6	30	36	178	16	1	7	8	43
1984-85a	S. S. Marie	OHL	37	4	20	24	85	16	4	6	10	47
1985-86	**Edmonton**	**NHL**	....	....	....	....	....	1	0	0	0	4
	Nova Scotia	AHL	77	9	20	29	175	....	....	....	....	....
	NHL Totals		....	....	....	....	....	1	0	0	0	4

a OHL First All-Star Team (1985)

BEUKEBOOM, JOHN WILLIAM

Born, Ajax, Ont., January 1, 1961.
Defense. Shoots left. 6'2", 200 lbs.
Last amateur club: Peterborough Petes (OHA).
(Detroit's 6th choice, 151st over-all, in 1980 Entry Draft).

| Season | Club | Lea | Regular Season | | | | | Playoffs | | | | |
			GP	G	A	TP	PIM	GP	G	A	TP	PIM
1978-79	Peterborough	OHA	64	3	15	18	132	14	0	0	0	4
1979-80	Peterborough	OHA	61	12	23	35	115	14	2	3	5	48
1980-81	Peterborough	OHA	58	11	35	46	189	5	2	0	2	9
1981-82	Dallas	CHL	13	0	6	6	33	....	....	....	....	....
	Adirondack	AHL	59	2	10	12	123	5	0	1	1	2
1982-83	Adirondack	AHL	72	3	4	7	57	6	0	0	0	6
1983-84	Montana	CHL	59	6	26	32	166	....	....	....	....	....
	Adirondack	AHL	16	2	2	4	66	7	0	0	0	25
1984-85	Adirondack	AHL	63	4	17	21	167	....	....	....	....	....
1985-86	Kalamazoo	IHL	78	7	36	43	244	6	0	1	1	6

BIGGS, DON

Born, Mississauga, Ont., April 7, 1965.
Center. Shoots right. 5'8", 175 lbs.
Last amateur club: Oshawa Generals (OHL).
(Minnesota's 9th choice, 156th over-all, in 1983 Entry Draft).

| Season | Club | Lea | Regular Season | | | | | Playoffs | | | | |
			GP	G	A	TP	PIM	GP	G	A	TP	PIM
1981-82	Mississauga	Midget	54	49	67	116	125	....	....	....	....	....
1982-83	Oshawa	OHL	70	22	53	75	145	16	3	6	9	17
1983-84	Oshawa	OHL	58	31	60	91	149	7	4	4	8	18
1984-85	**Minnesota**	**NHL**	1	0	0	0	0	....	....	....	....	....
	Springfield	AHL	6	0	3	3	0	2	1	0	1	0
	Oshawa	OHL	60	48	69	117	105	5	3	4	7	6
1985-86	Springfield	AHL	28	15	16	31	46	....	....	....	....	....
	Nova Scotia	AHL	47	6	23	29	36	....	....	....	....	....
	NHL Totals		1	0	0	0	0	....	....	....	....	....

Traded to **Edmonton** by **Minnesota** with Gord Sherven for Marc Habscheid, Don Barber and Emanuel Viveiros, December 20, 1985.

BIOTTI, CHRIS

Born, Waltham, Mass., April 22, 1967.
Defense. Shoots left. 6'3", 195 lbs.
Last amateur club: Harvard University Crimson (ECAC).
(Calgary's 1st choice, 17th over-all, in 1985 Entry Draft).

| Season | Club | Lea | Regular Season | | | | | Playoffs | | | | |
			GP	G	A	TP	PIM	GP	G	A	TP	PIM
1983-84	Belmont HS	Mass.	23	10	20	30	N/A	....	....	....	....	....
1984-85	Belmont HS	Mass.	25	13	24	37	N/A	....	....	....	....	....
1985-86	Harvard	ECAC	15	3	5	8	18	....	....	....	....	....

BISHOP, MICHAEL

Born, Sarnia, Ont., June 15, 1966.
Defense. Shoots dleft. 6'2", 185 lbs.
Last amateur club: Colgate University Red Raiders (ECAC).
(Montreal's 14th choice, 226th over-all, in 1985 Entry Draft).

Season	Club	Lea	Regular Season					Playoffs				
			GP	G	A	TP	PIM	GP	G	A	TP	PIM
1985-86	Colgate	ECAC	17	5	6	11	47	....	....	....	....	....

BJORKMAN, JOHN

Born, Dover, NH, July 14, 1964.
Left wing. Shoots left. 6'1", 180 lbs.
Last amateur club: University of Michigan Wolverines (CCHA).
(NY Islanders' 13th choice, 217th over-all, in 1983 Entry Draft).

Season	Club	Lea	Regular Season					Playoffs				
			GP	G	A	TP	PIM	GP	G	A	TP	PIM
1983-84	Michigan	CCHA	36	9	12	21	33	....	....	....	....	....
1984-85	Michigan	CCHA	38	10	16	26	46	....	....	....	....	....
1985-86	Michigan	CCHA	7	0	0	0	6	....	....	....	....	....

BJUGSTAD, SCOTT   (BYOOK-stad)

Born, St. Paul, Minn., June 2, 1961.
Center. Shoots left. 6'1", 185 lbs.
Last amateur club: 1984 United States Olympic Team.
(Minnesota's 13th choice, 181st over-all, in 1981 Entry Draft).

Season	Club	Lea	Regular Season					Playoffs				
			GP	G	A	TP	PIM	GP	G	A	TP	PIM
1979-80	U. Minnesota	WCHA	18	2	2	4	2	....	....	....	....	....
1980-81	U. Minnesota	WCHA	35	12	23	25	34	....	....	....	....	....
1981-82	U. Minnesota	WCHA	36	29	14	43	24	....	....	....	....	....
1982-83a	U. Minnesota	WCHA	26	21	35	56	12	....	....	....	....	....
1983-84	U.S. National	...	54	31	20	51	28	....	....	....	....	....
	U.S. Olympic	...	6	3	2	5	6	....	....	....	....	....
	Minnesota	NHL	5	0	0	0	2	....	....	....	....	....
	Salt Lake	CHL	15	10	8	18	6	5	3	4	7	0
1984-85	Minnesota	NHL	72	11	4	15	32	....	....	....	....	....
	Springfield	AHL	5	2	3	5	2	....	....	....	....	....
1985-86	Minnesota	NHL	80	43	33	76	24	5	0	1	1	0
	NHL Totals		157	54	37	91	58	5	0	1	1	0

a WCHA First All-Star Team (1983)

BLAISDELL, MICHAEL WALTER (MIKE)   (BLAZE-dell)

Born, Moose Jaw, Sask., January 18, 1960.
Right wing. Shoots right. 6'1", 195 lbs.
Last amateur club: Regina Pats (WHL).
(Detroit's 1st choice, 11th over-all, in 1980 Entry Draft).

Season	Club	Lea	Regular Season					Playoffs				
			GP	G	A	TP	PIM	GP	G	A	TP	PIM
1977-78	Regina	WHL	6	5	5	10	2	13	4	7	11	0
1978-79	U. of Wisconsin	WCHA	20	7	1	8	4	....	....	....	....	....
1979-80	Regina	WHL	63	71	38	109	62	18	16	9	25	26
1980-81	Detroit	NHL	32	3	6	9	10	....	....	....	....	....
	Adirondack	AHL	41	10	4	14	8	12	2	2	4	5
1981-82	Detroit	NHL	80	23	32	55	48	....	....	....	....	....
1982-83	Detroit	NHL	80	18	23	41	22	....	....	....	....	....
1983-84	NY Rangers	NHL	36	5	6	11	31	....	....	....	....	....
	Tulsa	CHL	32	10	8	18	23	9	6	6	12	6
1984-85	NY Rangers	NHL	12	1	0	1	11	....	....	....	....	....
	New Haven	AHL	64	21	23	44	41	....	....	....	....	....
1985-86	Pittsburgh	NHL	66	15	14	29	36	....	....	....	....	....
	NHL Totals		306	65	81	146	158	....	....	....	....	....

Traded to **NY Rangers** by **Detroit** with Willie Huber and Mark Osborne for Ron Duguay, Eddie Mio and Eddie Johnstone, June 13, 1983. Claimed by **Pittsburgh** from **NY Rangers** in NHL Waiver Draft, October 7, 1985.

BLOMQVIST, TIMO   (BLOOM-quist)

Born, Helsinki, Finland, January 23, 1961.
Defense. Shoots right. 6', 200 lbs.
Last amateur club: Kiekkoreipas (Finland)
(Washington's 4th choice, 89th over-all, in 1980 Entry Draft).

Season	Club	Lea	Regular Season					Playoffs				
			GP	G	A	TP	PIM	GP	G	A	TP	PIM
1978-79	Jokerit	Fin.	36	4	2	6	35	....	....	....	....	....
1979-80	Jokerit	Fin.	32	3	1	4	52	....	....	....	....	....
1980-81	Kiekkoreipas	Fin.	30	6	7	13	14	....	....	....	....	....
1981-82	Hershey	AHL	13	0	8	8	14	....	....	....	....	....
	Washington	NHL	44	1	11	12	62	....	....	....	....	....
1982-83	Hershey	AHL	8	2	7	9	16	....	....	....	....	....
	Washington	NHL	61	1	17	18	67	3	0	0	0	16
1983-84	Washington	NHL	65	1	19	20	84	8	0	0	0	8
1984-85	Washington	NHL	53	1	4	5	51	2	0	0	0	0
1985-86	Binghamton	AHL	71	6	18	24	76	6	0	4	4	6
	NHL Totals		223	4	51	55	264	13	0	0	0	24

Signed as a free agent by **New Jersey** July 2, 1986.

BLUM, JOHN JOSEPH

Born, Detroit, Mich., October 8, 1959.
Defense. Shoots right. 6'3", 205 lbs.
Last amateur club: University of Michigan Wolverines (WCHA).

Season	Club	Lea	Regular Season					Playoffs				
			GP	G	A	TP	PIM	GP	G	A	TP	PIM
1980-81	U. of Michigan	WCHA	38	9	43	52	93	....	....	....	....	....
1981-82	Wichita	CHL	78	8	33	41	247	7	0	3	3	24
1982-83	Edmonton	NHL	5	0	3	3	24	....	....	....	....	....
	Moncton	AHL	76	10	30	40	219	....	....	....	....	....
1983-84	Moncton	AHL	57	3	22	25	202	....	....	....	....	....
	Edmonton	NHL	4	0	1	1	2	....	....	....	....	....
	Boston	NHL	12	1	1	2	30	3	0	0	0	4
1984-85	Boston	NHI	75	3	13	16	263	5	0	0	0	13
1985-86	Boston	NHL	61	1	7	8	80	3	0	0	0	6
	Moncton	AHL	12	1	5	6	37	....	....	....	....	....
	NHL Totals		157	5	25	30	399	11	0	0	0	23

Signed as free agent by **Edmonton**, May 5, 1981. Traded to **Boston** by **Edmonton** for Larry Melnyk, March 6, 1984.

BODGER, DOUG

Born, Chemainus, B.C., June 18, 1966
Defense. Shoots left. 6'2", 200 lbs.
Last amateur club: Kamloops Junior Oilers (WHL).
(Pittsburgh's 2nd choice, 9th over-all, in 1984 Entry Draft).

Season	Club	Lea	Regular Season					Playoffs				
			GP	G	A	TP	PIM	GP	G	A	TP	PIM
1982-83a	Kamloops	WHL	72	26	66	92	98	7	0	5	5	2
1983-84	Kamloops	WHL	70	21	77	98	90	17	2	15	17	12
1984-85	Pittsburgh	NHL	65	5	26	31	67	....	....	....	....	....
1985-86	Pittsburgh	NHL	79	4	33	37	63	....	....	....	....	....
	NHL Totals		144	9	59	68	130					

a WHL Second All-Star Team (1983)

BOETTGER, DWAYNE

Born, Brampton, Ont., February 6, 1963.
Defense. Shoots left. 6', 185 lbs.
Last amateur club: Toronto Marlboros (OHL).
(Edmonton's 5th choice, 104th over-all, in 1982 Entry Draft).

Season	Club	Lea	Regular Season					Playoffs				
			GP	G	A	TP	PIM	GP	G	A	TP	PIM
1981-82	Toronto	OHL	66	4	21	25	138	10	0	1	1	10
1982-83	Toronto	OHL	68	3	15	18	120	4	0	0	0	11
1983-84	Moncton	AHL	75	1	18	19	160	....	....	....	....	....
1984-85	Nova Scotia	AHL	70	3	11	14	71	5	0	0	0	5
1985-86	Nova Scotia	AHL	64	2	15	17	103	....	....	....	....	....

BOIS, JEAN

Born, Sherbrooke, Que., May 2, 1967.
Left wing. Shoots left. 5'11", 185 lbs.
Last amateur club: Shawinigan Cataractes (QMJHL).
(Quebec's 13th choice, 246th over-all, in 1985 Entry Draft).

Season	Club	Lea	Regular Season					Playoffs				
			GP	G	A	TP	PIM	GP	G	A	TP	PIM
1984-85	Trois Rivieres	QMJHL	67	33	51	84	103	7	2	6	8	2
1985-86	Shawinigan	QMJHL	69	31	65	96	111	5	0	0	0	9

BOISVERT, SERGE   (bwah-VAIR)

Born, Drummondville, Que., June 1, 1959.
Right wing. Shoots right. 5'9", 170 lbs.
Last amateur club: Sherbrooke Castors (QMJHL).

Season	Club	Lea	Regular Season					Playoffs				
			GP	G	A	TP	PIM	GP	G	A	TP	PIM
1977-78	Sherbrooke	QMJHL	55	17	33	50	19	10	2	2	4	2
1978-79	Sherbrooke	QMJHL	72	50	72	122	45	12	11	17	28	2
1979-80	Sherbrooke	QMJHL	70	52	72	124	45	15	14	18	32	4
1980-81	New Brunswick	AHL	60	19	27	46	31	5	0	0	0	2
1981-82	Yukijirushi	Japan	30	29	20	49		....	....	....	....	....
1982-83	Toronto	NHL	17	0	2	2	4	....	....	....	....	....
	St. Catharines	AHL	19	10	9	19	2	....	....	....	....	....
	Moncton	AHL	29	6	12	18	7	....	....	....	....	....
1983-84	Moncton	AHL	66	15	13	28	34	....	....	....	....	....
1984-85	Montreal	NHL	14	2	2	4	0	12	3	5	8	2
	Sherbrooke	AHL	63	38	41	79	8	10	1	9	10	12
1985-86	Montreal	NHL	9	2	2	4	2	8	0	1	1	0
a	Sherbrooke	NHL	69	40	48	88	18					
	NHL Totals		40	4	6	10	6	20	3	6	9	2

Signed as a free agent by **Toronto**, October 9, 1980. Traded to **Edmonton** by **Toronto** for Reid Bailey, January 15, 1983. Signed as a free agent by **Montreal**, February 8, 1985.

a AHL Second All-Star Team (1986)

BOLAND, SEAN

Born, Toronto, Ont., February 18, 1968.
Defense. Shoots right. 6'3", 180 lbs.
Last amateur club: Toronto Marlboros (OHL).
(Toronto's 3rd choice, 48th over-all, in 1986 Entry Draft).

Season	Club	Lea	Regular Season					Playoffs				
			GP	G	A	TP	PIM	GP	G	A	TP	PIM
1985-86	Toronto	OHL	52	2	10	12	85	4	0	0	0	13

BOLDUC, MICHEL

BOWL-duck

Born, Angegardien, Que., March 13, 1961.
Defense. Shoots left. 6'2", 190 lbs.
Last amateur club: Chicoutimi Saguneens (QJHL).
(Quebec's 6th choice, 150th over-all, in 1980 Entry Draft).

Season	Club	Lea	Regular Season					Playoffs				
			GP	G	A	TP	PIM	GP	G	A	TP	PIM
1979-80	Chicoutimi	QJHL	65	3	29	32	219	12	1	3	4	44
1980-81	Chicoutimi	QJHL	67	11	35	46	244	12	0	4	4	34
1981-82	**Quebec**	**NHL**	**3**	**0**	**0**	**0**	**0**	....	....	....	....	....
	Fredericton	AHL	69	4	9	13	130	....	....	....	....	....
1982-83	**Quebec**	**NHL**	**7**	**0**	**0**	**0**	**6**	....	....	....	....	....
	Fredericton	AHL	64	4	18	22	165	11	1	1	2	50
1983-84	Fredericton	AHL	70	2	15	17	96	7	0	1	1	19
1984-85	Fredericton	AHL	29	0	9	9	74	....	....	....	....	....
	Maine	AHL	31	1	7	8	86	11	1	1	2	23
1985-86	Maine	AHL	66	1	6	7	29	5	0	1	1	6
	NHL Totals		**10**	**0**	**0**	**0**	**6**	....	....	....	....	....

Claimed on waivers by **New Jersey** from **Quebec** January 25, 1985.

BONAR, GRAEME

Born, Toronto, Ont., January 21, 1966.
Right Wing. Shoots right. 6'3", 210 lbs.
Last amateur club: Peterborough Petes (OHL).
(Montreal's 5th choice, 54th over-all, in 1984 Entry Draft).

Season	Club	Lea	Regular Season					Playoffs				
			GP	G	A	TP	PIM	GP	G	A	TP	PIM
1983-84	S. S. Marie	OHL	65	15	39	54	80	16	6	4	10	15
1984-85a	S. S. Marie	OHL	66	66	71	137	93	16	13	20	33	10
1985-86b	Peterborough	OHL	56	53	40	93	41	16	11	10	21	15

a OHL First All-Star Team (1985)
b OHL Second All-Star Team (1986).

BORRELL, JOHN

Born, Shakopee, Minn., March 23, 1967.
Right wing. Shoots right. 6'2", 190 lbs.
Last amateur club: Lowell University Chiefs (H.E.).
(Winnipeg's 5th choice, 102nd over-all, in 1985 Entry Draft).

Season	Club	Lea	Regular Season					Playoffs				
			GP	G	A	TP	PIM	GP	G	A	TP	PIM
1985-86	Lowell	H.E.	41	3	15	18	12	....	....	....	....	....

BORSATO, LUCIANO

Born, Richmond Hill, Ont., January 7, 1966.
Center. Shoots right. 5'10", 165 lbs.
Last amateur club: Clarkson University Knights (ECAC).
(Winnipeg's 6th choice, 135th over-all, in 1984 Entry Draft).

Season	Club	Lea	Regular Season					Playoffs				
			GP	G	A	TP	PIM	GP	G	A	TP	PIM
1984-85	Clarkson	ECAC	33	15	17	32	37	....	....	....	....	....
1985-86	Clarkson	ECAC	28	14	17	31	44	....	....	....	....	....

BOSCHMAN, LAURIE JOSEPH

(BOSH-man)

Born, Major, Sask., June 4, 1960.
Center. Shoots left. 6', 185 lbs.
Last amateur club: Brandon Wheat Kings (WHL).
(Toronto's 1st choice, 9th over-all, in 1979 Entry Draft).

Season	Club	Lea	Regular Season					Playoffs				
			GP	G	A	TP	PIM	GP	G	A	TP	PIM
1976-77	Brandon	WHL	3	0	1	1	0	12	1	1	2	17
1977-78	Brandon	WHL	72	42	57	99	227	8	2	5	7	45
1978-79a	Brandon	WHL	65	66	83	149	215	22	11	23	34	56
1979-80	Toronto	NHL	80	16	32	48	78	3	1	1	2	18
1980-81	New Brunswick	AHL	4	4	1	5	47	....	....	....	....	....
	Toronto	NHL	53	14	19	33	178	3	0	0	0	7
1981-82	Toronto	NHL	54	9	19	28	150	....	....	....	....	....
	Edmonton	NHL	11	2	3	5	37	3	0	1	1	4
1982-83	Edmonton	NHL	62	8	12	20	183	....	....	....	....	....
	Winnipeg	NHL	12	3	5	8	36	3	0	1	1	12
1983-84	Winnipeg	NHL	61	28	46	74	234	3	0	1	1	5
1984-85	Winnipeg	NHL	80	32	44	76	180	8	2	1	3	21
1985-86	Winnipeg	NHL	77	27	42	69	241	3	0	1	1	6
	NHL Totals		**490**	**139**	**222**	**361**	**1317**	**26**	**3**	**6**	**9**	**73**

a WHL First All-Star Team (1979)

Traded to **Edmonton** by **Toronto** for Walt Poddubny and Phil Drouilliard, March 8, 1982. Traded to **Winnipeg** by **Edmonton** for Willy Lindstrom, March 7, 1983.

BOSSY, MICHAEL (MIKE)

Born, Montreal, Que., January 22, 1957.
Right wing. Shoots right. 6', 185 lbs.
Last amateur club: Laval Nationals (QJHL).
(NY Islanders' 1st choice, 15th over-all, in 1977 Amateur Draft).

Season	Club	Lea	Regular Season					Playoffs				
			GP	G	A	TP	PIM	GP	G	A	TP	PIM
1973-74	Laval	QJHL	68	70	48	118	45	11	6	16	22	2
1974-75	Laval	QJHL	67	84	65	149	42	16	18	20	38	2
1975-76	Laval	QJHL	64	79	57	136	25	....	....	....	....	....
1976-77	Laval	QJHL	61	75	51	126	12	7	5	5	10	12
1977-78abc	**NY Islanders**	**NHL**	**73**	**53**	**38**	**91**	**6**	**7**	**2**	**2**	**4**	**2**
1978-79c	**NY Islanders**	**NHL**	**80**	***69**	**57**	**126**	**25**	**10**	**6**	**2**	**8**	**2**
1979-80	**NY Islanders**	**NHL**	**75**	**51**	**41**	**92**	**12**	**16**	**10**	**13**	**23**	**8**
1980-81de	**NY Islanders**	**NHL**	**79**	***68**	**51**	**119**	**32**	**18**	***17**	***18**	***35**	**4**
1981-82df	**NY Islanders**	**NHL**	**80**	**64**	**83**	**147**	**22**	**19**	***17**	**10**	**27**	**0**
1982-83dg	**NY Islanders**	**NHL**	**79**	**60**	**58**	**118**	**20**	**19**	***17**	**9**	**26**	**10**
1983-84dg	**NY Islanders**	**NHL**	**67**	**51**	**67**	**118**	**8**	**21**	**8**	**10**	**18**	**4**
1984-85c	**NY Islanders**	**NHL**	**76**	**58**	**59**	**117**	**38**	**10**	**5**	**6**	**11**	**4**
1985-86dg	**NY Islanders**	**NHL**	**80**	**61**	**62**	**123**	**14**	**3**	**1**	**2**	**3**	**4**
	NHL Totals		**689**	**535**	**516**	**1051**	**177**	**123**	**83**	**72**	**155**	**38**

a NHL record for goals by a rookie (1978)
b Won Calder Memorial Trophy (1978)
c NHL Second All-Star Team (1978, 1979, 1985)
d NHL First All-Star Team (1981, 1982, 1983, 1984, 1986)
e Record for points in one playoff year (1981)
f Won Conn Smythe Trophy (1982)
g Won Lady Byng Memorial Trophy (1983, 1984, 1986).

BOTELL, MARK

Born, Scarborough, Ont., August 27, 1961.
Defense. Shoots left. 6'4", 220 lbs.
Last amateur club: Brantford Alexanders (OHA).
(Philadelphia's 8th choice, 168th over-all, in 1980 Entry Draft).

Season	Club	Lea	Regular Season					Playoffs				
			GP	G	A	TP	PIM	GP	G	A	TP	PIM
1978-79	Niagara Falls	OHA	55	2	8	10	122	14	2	1	3	6
1979-80	Niagara Falls	OHA	20	2	5	7	11	....	....	....	....	....
	Windsor	OHA	2	0	0	0	2	....	....	....	....	....
	Brantford	OHA	15	2	3	5	24	11	1	5	6	10
1980-81	Brantford	OHA	58	11	20	31	143	4	0	2	2	12
	Maine	AHL	2	0	1	1	0	20	4	4	8	36
1981-82	**Philadelphia**	**NHL**	**32**	**4**	**10**	**14**	**31**	....	....	....	....	....
	Maine	AHL	42	3	14	17	41	3	0	1	1	4
1982-83	Toledo	IHL	24	6	14	20	43	....	....	....	....	....
	Maine	AHL	30	1	4	5	26	....	....	....	....	....
1983-84	Montana	CHL	2	0	0	0	2	....	....	....	....	....
	Toledo	IHL	78	16	27	43	164	9	2	1	3	6
1984-85	Peoria	IHL	70	6	21	27	77	20	1	3	4	35
1985-86	St. Catharines	AHL	11	1	3	4	17	12	1	3	4	8
	NHL Totals		**32**	**4**	**10**	**14**	**31**	....	....	....	....	....

BOTHWELL, TIMOTHY (TIM)

Born, Vancouver, B.C., May 6, 1955.
Defense. Shoots left. 6'3", 190 lbs.
Last amateur club: Brown University Bruins (ECAC).

Season	Club	Lea	Regular Season					Playoffs				
			GP	G	A	TP	PIM	GP	G	A	TP	PIM
1976-77	Brown U.	ECAC	27	7	27	34	40	....	....	....	....	....
1977-78	Brown U.	ECAC	29	9	26	35	48	....	....	....	....	....
1978-79	**NY Rangers**	**NHL**	**1**	**0**	**0**	**0**	**2**	....	....	....	....	....
	New Haven	AHL	66	15	33	48	44	10	4	6	10	6
1979-80	New Haven	AHL	22	6	7	13	25	....	....	....	....	....
	NY Rangers	**NHL**	**45**	**4**	**6**	**10**	**20**	**9**	**0**	**0**	**0**	**8**
1980-81	**NY Rangers**	**NHL**	**3**	**0**	**1**	**1**	**0**	....	....	....	....	....
	New Haven	AHL	73	10	53	63	98	4	1	2	3	6
1981-82	**NY Rangers**	**NHL**	**13**	**0**	**3**	**3**	**10**	....	....	....	....	....
	Springfield	AHL	10	0	4	4	7	....	....	....	....	....
1982-83	**St. Louis**	**NHL**	**61**	**4**	**11**	**15**	**34**	....	....	....	....	....
1983-84	Montana	CHL	4	0	3	3	0	....	....	....	....	....
	St. Louis	**NHL**	**62**	**2**	**13**	**15**	**65**	**11**	**0**	**2**	**2**	**14**
1984-85	**St. Louis**	**NHL**	**79**	**4**	**22**	**26**	**62**	**3**	**0**	**0**	**0**	**2**
1985-86	**Hartford**	**NHL**	**62**	**2**	**8**	**10**	**53**	**6**	**0**	**0**	**0**	**0**
	NHL Totals		**326**	**16**	**64**	**80**	**246**	**33**	**0**	**2**	**2**	**32**

Signed as free agent by **NY Rangers**, June 8, 1978. Claimed by **St. Louis** from **NY Rangers** in NHL Waiver Draft, October 4, 1982. Rights sold to **Hartford** by **St. Louis**, October 4, 1985.

BOUDREAU, BRUCE ALLAN (BOO-droh)

Born, Toronto, Ont., January 9, 1955.
Center. Shoots left. 5'9", 175 lbs.
Last amateur club: Toronto Marlboros (OHA)
(Toronto's 3rd choice, 42nd over-all, in 1975 Amateur Draft).

			Regular Season					Playoffs				
Season	Club	Lea	GP	G	A	TP	PIM	GP	G	A	TP	PIM
1973-74	Toronto	OHA	53	46	67	113	51	....	....	....	....	....
1974-75	Toronto	OHA	69	*68	97	*165	52	22	12	*28	40	26
1975-76	Minnesota	WHA	30	3	6	9	4	....	....	....	....	....
	Johnstown	NAHL	34	25	35	60	14	....	....	....	....	....
1976-77	Dallas	CHL	58	*37	34	71	40	1	1	1	2	0
	Toronto	NHL	15	2	5	7	4	3	0	0	0	0
1977-78	Toronto	NHL	40	11	18	29	12	....	....	....	....	....
	Dallas	CHL	22	13	9	22	11	....	....	....	....	....
1978-79	Toronto	NHL	26	4	3	7	2	....	....	....	....	....
	New Brunswick	AHL	49	20	38	58	20	5	1	1	2	8
1979-80	Toronto	NHL	2	0	0	0	2	....	....	....	....	....
	New Brunswick	AHL	75	36	54	90	47	17	6	7	13	23
1980-81	Toronto	NHL	39	10	14	24	18	2	1	0	1	0
	New Brunswick	AHL	40	17	41	58	22	8	6	5	11	14
1981-82	Toronto	NHL	12	0	2	2	6	....	....	....	....	....
	Cincinnati	CHL	65	42	61	103	42	4	3	1	4	8
1982-83	St. Catharines	AHL	80	50	72	122	65	....	....	....	....	....
	Toronto	NHL	....	....	....	....	....	4	1	0	1	0
1983-84	St. Catharines	AHL	80	47	62	109	44	7	0	5	5	11
1984-85	Baltimore	AHL	17	4	7	11	4	15	3	9	12	4
1985-86	Chicago	NHL	7	1	0	1	2	....	....	....	....	....
	Nova Scotia	AHL	65	30	36	66	36	....	....	....	....	....
	NHL Totals		141	28	42	70	46	9	2	0	2	0
	WHA Totals		30	3	6	9	4	....	....	....	....	....

Claimed by **Toronto** as fill in Expansion Draft, June 13, 1979. Signed as a free agent by **Chicago**, October 10, 1985.

BOULIANE, MARTIN (boo-LEE-ann)

Born, Amqui, Que. April 9, 1965.
Center. Shoots right. 5'11", 170 lbs.
Last amateur club: Canadian Olympic Team.
(Washington's 5th choice, 98th over-all, in 1983 Entry Draft).

			Regular Season					Playoffs				
Season	Club	Lea	GP	G	A	TP	PIM	GP	G	A	TP	PIM
1983-84	Granby	QMJHL	62	41	41	82	6	....	....	....	....	....
1984-85	Granby	QMJHL	67	52	82	134	11	....	....	....	....	....
1985-86	Cdn. Olympic	....	67	16	23	39	28	....	....	....	....	....

BOURGEOIS, CHARLES MARC (CHARLIE) (boor-SHWAH)

Born, Moncton, N.B., November 19, 1959.
Defense. Shoots right. 6'4", 220 lbs.
Last amateur club: University of Moncton Blue Eagles (AUAA).

			Regular Season					Playoffs				
Season	Club	Lea	GP	G	A	TP	PIM	GP	G	A	TP	PIM
1980-81	U. of Moncton	AUAA	24	8	23	31	....	6	4	6	10	....
1981-82	Oklahoma City	CHL	13	2	2	4	17	....	....	....	....	....
	Calgary	NHL	54	2	13	15	112	3	0	0	0	7
1982-83	Calgary	NHL	15	2	3	5	21	....	....	....	....	....
	Colorado	CHL	51	10	18	28	128	6	2	3	5	30
1983-84	Colorado	CHL	54	12	32	44	133	....	....	....	....	....
	Calgary	NHL	17	1	3	4	35	8	0	1	1	27
1984-85	Calgary	NHL	47	2	10	12	134	4	0	0	0	17
1985-86	Calgary	NHL	29	5	5	10	128	....	....	....	....	....
	St. Louis	NHL	31	2	7	9	116	19	2	2	4	116
	NHL Totals		193	14	41	55	546	34	2	3	5	167

Signed as free agent by **Calgary**, April 19, 1981. Traded to **St. Louis** by **Calgary** with Eddy Beers and Gino Cavallini for Joe Mullen, Terry Johnson and Rik Wilson, February 1, 1986.

BOURNE, ROBERT GLEN (BOB) (BOORN)

Born, Kindersley, Sask., June 21, 1954.
Center. Shoots left. 6'3", 200 lbs.
Last amateur club: Saskatoon Blades (WHL).
(Kansas City's 3rd choice, 38th over-all, in 1974 Amateur Draft).

			Regular Season					Playoffs				
Season	Club	Lea	GP	G	A	TP	PIM	GP	G	A	TP	PIM
1972-73	Saskatoon	WHL	66	40	53	93	74	16	7	10	17	30
1973-74	Saskatoon	WHL	63	29	42	71	41	6	3	2	5	12
1974-75	NY Islanders	NHL	77	16	23	39	12	9	1	2	3	4
1975-76	NY Islanders	NHL	14	2	3	5	13	....	....	....	....	....
	Fort Worth	CHL	62	29	44	73	80	....	....	....	....	....
1976-77	NY Islanders	NHL	75	16	19	35	30	8	2	0	2	4
1977-78	NY Islanders	NHL	80	30	33	63	31	7	2	3	5	2
1978-79	NY Islanders	NHL	80	30	31	61	48	10	1	3	4	6
1979-80	NY Islanders	NHL	73	15	25	40	52	21	10	10	20	10
1980-81	NY Islanders	NHL	78	35	41	76	62	14	4	6	10	19
1981-82	NY Islanders	NHL	76	27	26	53	77	19	9	7	16	36
1982-83	NY Islanders	NHL	77	20	42	62	55	20	8	20	28	14
1983-84	NY Islanders	NHL	78	22	34	56	75	8	1	1	2	7
1984-85	NY Islanders	NHL	44	8	12	20	51	10	0	2	2	6
1985-86	NY Islanders	NHL	62	17	15	32	36	3	0	0	0	0
	NHL Totals		814	238	304	542	542	129	38	54	92	108

Traded to **NY Islanders** by **Kansas City** for Bart Crashley and the rights to Larry Hornung, September 13, 1974.

BOURQUE, PHILLIPPE RICHARD (PHIL) (BORK)

Born, Chelmsford, Mass., June 8, 1962.
Defense. Shoots left. 6', 185 lbs.
Last amateur club: Kingston Canadians (OHL).

			Regular Season					Playoffs				
Season	Club	Lea	GP	G	A	TP	PIM	GP	G	A	TP	PIM
1980-81	Kingston	OHL	47	4	4	8	46	6	0	0	0	10
1981-82	Kingston	OHL	67	11	40	51	111	4	0	0	0	0
1982-83	Baltimore	AHL	65	1	15	16	93	....	....	....	....	....
1983-84	Pittsburgh	NHL	5	0	1	1	12	....	....	....	....	....
	Baltimore	AHL	58	5	17	22	96	....	....	....	....	....
1984-85	Baltimore	AHL	79	6	15	21	164	13	2	5	7	23
1985-86	Pittsburgh	NHL	4	0	0	0	2	....	....	....	....	....
	Baltimore	AHL	74	8	18	26	226	....	....	....	....	....
	NHL Totals		9	0	1	1	14	....	....	....	....	....

Signed as free agent by **Pittsburgh**, October 4, 1982.

BOURQUE, RAYMOND JEAN (BORK)

Born, Montreal, Que., December 28, 1960.
Defense. Shoots left. 5'11", 205 lbs.
Last amateur club: Verdun Black Hawks (QJHL).
(Boston's 1st choice, 8th over-all, in 1979 Entry Draft).

			Regular Season					Playoffs				
Season	Club	Lea	GP	G	A	TP	PIM	GP	G	A	TP	PIM
1976-77	Sorel	QJHL	69	12	36	48	61	....	....	....	....	....
1977-78	Verdun	QJHL	72	22	57	79	90	4	2	1	3	0
1978-79	Verdun	QJHL	63	22	71	93	44	11	3	16	19	18
1979-80ab	Boston	NHL	80	17	48	65	73	10	2	9	11	27
1980-81c	Boston	NHL	67	27	29	56	96	3	0	1	1	2
1981-82b	Boston	NHL	65	17	49	66	51	9	1	5	6	16
1982-83c	Boston	NHL	65	22	51	73	20	17	8	15	23	10
1983-84b	Boston	NHL	78	31	65	96	57	3	0	2	2	0
1984-85b	Boston	NHL	73	20	66	86	53	5	0	3	3	4
1985-86c	Boston	NHL	74	19	57	76	68	3	0	0	0	0
	NHL Totals		502	153	365	518	418	50	11	35	46	59

a Won Calder Memorial Trophy (1980)
b NHL First All-Star Team (1980, 1982, 1984, 1985)
c NHL Second All-Star Team (1981, 1983, 1986).

BOUTILIER, PAUL ANDRE (boot-LEER)

Born, Sydney, N.S., May 3, 1963.
Defense. Shoots left. 6'0", 200 lbs.
Last amateur club: St. Jean Castors (QJHL).
(NY Islanders' 1st choice, 21st over-all, in 1981 Entry Draft).

			Regular Season					Playoffs				
Season	Club	Lea	GP	G	A	TP	PIM	GP	G	A	TP	PIM
1980-81	Sherbrooke	QJHL	72	10	29	39	95	14	3	7	10	10
1981-82ab	NY Islanders	NHL	1	0	0	0	0	....	....	....	....	....
	Sherbrooke	QJHL	57	20	60	80	62	21	7	31	38	12
1982-83	St. Jean	QJHL	22	5	14	19	30	....	....	....	....	....
	NY Islanders	NHL	29	4	5	9	24	2	0	0	0	2
1983-84	Indianapolis	CHL	50	6	17	23	56	....	....	....	....	....
	NY Islanders	NHL	28	0	11	11	36	21	1	7	8	10
1984-85	NY Islanders	NHL	78	12	23	35	90	10	0	2	2	16
1985-86	NY Islanders	NHL	77	4	30	34	100	3	0	0	0	2
	NHL Totals		213	20	69	89	250	36	1	9	10	30

a QMJHL First All-Star Team (1982)
b Named QMJHL's Top Defenseman (1982)

BOYD, RANDY KEITH

Born, Coniston, Ont., January 23, 1962.
Defense. Shoots left. 5'11", 190 lbs.
Last amateur club: Ottawa 67's (OHL).
(Pittsburgh's 2nd choice, 51st over-all, in 1980 Entry Draft).

			Regular Season					Playoffs				
Season	Club	Lea	GP	G	A	TP	PIM	GP	G	A	TP	PIM
1979-80	Ottawa	OHA	65	3	21	24	148	11	0	2	2	13
1980-81a	Ottawa	OHA	64	11	43	54	225	7	2	3	5	35
1981-82	Ottawa	OHL	26	9	29	38	51	....	....	....	....	....
	Pittsburgh	NHL	23	0	2	2	49	3	0	0	0	11
1982-83	Baltimore	AHL	21	5	10	15	43	....	....	....	....	....
	Pittsburgh	NHL	56	4	14	18	71	....	....	....	....	....
1983-84	Pittsburgh	NHL	5	0	1	1	6	....	....	....	....	....
	Baltimore	AHL	20	6	13	19	21	....	....	....	....	....
	Chicago	NHL	23	0	4	4	16	....	....	....	....	....
	Springfield	AHL	27	2	11	13	48	4	0	2	2	34
1984-85	Chicago	NHL	3	0	0	0	6	3	0	1	1	7
	Milwaukee	IHL	68	18	55	73	162	....	....	....	....	....
1985-86	NY Islanders	NHL	55	2	12	14	79	3	0	0	0	2
	NHL Totals		165	6	33	39	227	9	0	1	1	20

a OHA First All-Star Team (1981)

Traded to **Chicago** by **Pittsburgh** for Greg Fox, December 6, 1983. Claimed by **NY Islanders** from **Chicago** in NHL Waiver Draft, October 7, 1985.

BOZEK, STEVEN MICHAEL (STEVE)

Born, Kelowna, B.C., November 26, 1960.
Left wing. Shoots left. 5'11", 175 lbs.
Last amateur club: University of Northern Michigan Wildcats (CCHA)
(Los Angeles' 5th choice, 52nd over-all, in 1980 Entry Draft).

Season	Club	Lea	GP	G	A	TP	PIM	GP	G	A	TP	PIM
1979-80	U.N. Michigan	CCHA	41	42	47	89	32	....	....	....	....	....
1980-81	U.N. Michigan	CCHA	44	35	55	90	0	....	....	....	....	....
1981-82	Los Angeles	NHL	71	33	23	56	68	10	4	1	5	6
1982-83	Los Angeles	NHL	53	13	13	26	14	....	....	....	....	....
1983-84	Calgary	NHL	46	10	10	20	16	10	3	1	4	15
1984-85	Calgary	NHL	54	13	22	35	6	3	1	0	1	4
1985-86	Calgary	NHL	64	21	22	43	24	14	2	6	8	32
	NHL Totals		288	90	90	180	128	37	10	8	18	57

Traded to **Calgary** by **Los Angeles** for Carl Mokosak and Kevin LaVallee, June 20, 1983.

BOZON, PHILIPPE

Born, Charmonix, France, November 30, 1966.
Left wing. Shoots left. 5'10", 175 lbs.
Last amateur club: St. Jean Castors (QMJHL).

Season	Club	Lea	GP	G	A	TP	PIM	GP	G	A	TP	PIM
1984-85	St. Jean	QMJHL	67	32	50	82	82	5	0	5	5	4
1985-86a	St. Jean	QMJHL	65	59	52	111	72	10	10	6	16	16
	Peoria	IHL	....	....	....	....	....	5	1	0	1	0

a QMJHL Second All-Star team (1986).

Signed as a free agent by **St. Louis**, September 29, 1985.

BRADLEY, BRIAN WALTER RICHARD

Born, Kitchener, Ont., January 21, 1965.
Center. Shoots right. 5'10", 170 lbs.
Last amateur club: London Knights (OHL).
(Calgary's 2nd choice, 51st over-all, in 1983 Entry Draft).

Season	Club	Lea	GP	G	A	TP	PIM	GP	G	A	TP	PIM
1982-83	London	OHL	67	37	82	119	37	3	1	0	1	0
1983-84	London	OHL	49	40	60	100	24	4	2	4	6	0
1984-85	London	OHL	32	27	49	76	22	8	5	10	15	4
1985-86	Calgary	NHL	5	0	1	1	0	1	0	0	0	0
	Moncton	AHL	59	23	42	65	40	10	6	9	15	4
	NHL Totals		5	0	1	1	0	1	0	0	0	0

BRACCIA, RICK

Born, Revere, Mass., September 5, 1967.
Left wing. Shoots left. 6'0", 195 lbs.
Last amateur club: Boston College Eagles (H.E.).
(Chicago's 12th choice, 242nd over-all, in 1985 Entry Draft).

Season	Club	Lea	GP	G	A	TP	PIM	GP	G	A	TP	PIM
1985-86	Boston College	H.E.	9	0	3	3	20	....	....	....	....	....

BRADY, NEIL

Born, Montreal, Que., April 12, 1968.
Center. Shoots left. 6'2", 180 lbs.
Last amateur club: Medicine Hat Tigers (WHL).

Season	Club	Lea	GP	G	A	TP	PIM	GP	G	A	TP	PIM
1984-85	Calgary	Midget	37	25	50	75	75	....	....	....	....	....
1985-86a	Medicine Hat	WHL	72	21	60	81	104	21	9	11	20	23

a WHL Rookie of the Year (1986)

BRANT, CHRIS

Born, Belleville, Ont., August 26, 1965.
Left wing. Shoots left. 6'1", 190 lbs.
Last amateur club: Sault Ste. Marie Greyhounds (OHL).
(Hartford's 5th choice, 131st over-all, in 1985 Entry Draft).

Season	Club	Lea	GP	G	A	TP	PIM	GP	G	A	TP	PIM
1982-83	Kingston	OHL	67	1	17	18	53	....	....	....	....	....
1983-84	Kingston	OHL	7	4	4	8	14	....	....	....	....	....
	S.S. Marie	OHL	60	9	12	21	50	15	1	2	3	10
1984-85	S.S. Marie	OHL	52	16	33	49	110	16	8	9	17	15
1985-86	Binghamton	AHL	73	7	6	13	45	6	0	1	1	19

BRENNAN, DAN

Born, Dawson Creek, B.C., October 1, 1962.
Left wing. Shoots left. 6'3", 210 lbs.
Last amateur club: University of North Dakota Fighting Sioux (WCHA)
(Los Angeles' 7th choice, 165th over-all, in 1981 Entry Draft).

Season	Club	Lea	GP	G	A	TP	PIM	GP	G	A	TP	PIM
1980-81	North Dakota	WCHA	37	3	9	12	66	....	....	....	....	....
1981-82	North Dakota	WCHA	42	10	17	27	78	....	....	....	....	....
1982-83	North Dakota	WCHA	31	9	11	20	60	....	....	....	....	....
1983-84	North Dakota	WCHA	45	28	37	65	36	....	....	....	....	....
	Los Angeles	NHL	2	0	0	0	0	....	....	....	....	....
1984-85	New Haven	AHL	80	25	33	58	56	....	....	....	....	....
1985-86	Los Angeles	NHL	6	0	1	1	9	....	....	....	....	....
	New Haven	AHL	62	8	22	30	76	2	0	0	0	10
	NHL Totals		8	0	1	1	9	....	....	....	....	....

BRETON, RENE

Born, Princeville, Que., January 10, 1964.
Center. Shoots left. 5'11", 190 lbs.
Last amateur club: Granby Bisons (QMJHL).
(NY Islanders' 5th choice, 105th over-all, in 1982 Entry Draft).

Season	Club	Lea	GP	G	A	TP	PIM	GP	G	A	TP	PIM
1981-82	Granby	QMJHL	64	17	19	36	13	14	2	4	6	15
1982-83	Granby	QMJHL	59	38	48	86	21	....	....	....	....	....
1983-84	Granby	QMJHL	59	23	47	70	23	4	1	3	4	7
1984-85	Springfield	AHL	4	0	0	0	0	....	....	....	....	....
	Indianapolis	IHL	13	0	4	4	6	....	....	....	....	....
	Erie	ACHL	33	29	24	53	10	....	....	....	....	....
1985-86	Flint	IHL	73	8	24	32	19	....	....	....	....	....

BRICKLEY, ANDY

Born, Melrose, Mass., August 9, 1961.
Center. Shoots left. 6', 195 lbs.
Last amateur club: University of New Hampshire Wildcats (ECAC)
(Philadelphia's 10th choice, 210th over-all, in 1980 Entry Draft).

Season	Club	Lea	GP	G	A	TP	PIM	GP	G	A	TP	PIM
1979-80	N. Hampshire	ECAC	27	15	17	32	8	....	....	....	....	....
1980-81	N. Hampshire	ECAC	31	27	25	52	16	....	....	....	....	....
1981-82ab	N. Hampshire	ECAC	35	26	27	53	6	....	....	....	....	....
1982-83	Philadelphia	NHL	3	1	1	2	0	....	....	....	....	....
c	Maine	AHL	76	29	54	83	10	17	9	5	14	0
1983-84	Springfield	AHL	7	1	5	6	2	....	....	....	....	....
	Baltimore	AHL	4	0	5	5	2	....	....	....	....	....
	Pittsburgh	NHL	50	18	20	38	9	....	....	....	....	....
1984-85	Pittsburgh	NHL	45	7	15	22	10	....	....	....	....	....
	Baltimore	AHL	31	13	14	27	8	15	10	8	18	0
1985-86	Maine	AHL	60	26	34	60	20	5	0	4	4	0
	NHL Totals		98	26	36	62	19	....	....	....	....	....

a ECAC First All-Star Team (1982)
b Named to NCAA All-American Team (1982)
c AHL Second All-Star Team (1983)

Traded to **Pittsburgh** by **Philadelphia** with Mark Taylor, Ron Flockhart, Philadelphia's first round (Roger Belanger) and third round (Mike Stevens — later transferred to Vancouver) choices in 1984 Entry Draft for Rich Sutter, Philadelphia's second round (Greg Smyth) and third round (David McClay) choices in 1984 Entry Draft, October 23, 1983.

BRIDGMAN, MELVIN JOHN (MEL)   (BRIJ-man)

Born, Trenton, Ont., April 28, 1955.
Center. Shoots left. 6', 190 lbs.
Last amateur club: Victoria Cougars (WHL).
(Philadelphia's 1st choice and 1st over-all in 1975 Amateur Draft).

Season	Club	Lea	GP	G	A	TP	PIM	GP	G	A	TP	PIM
1972-73	Victoria	WHL	4	1	1	2	0	....	....	....	....	....
1973-74	Victoria	WHL	62	26	39	65	149	....	....	....	....	....
1974-75a	Victoria	WHL	66	66	91	*157	175	12	12	6	18	34
1975-76	Philadelphia	NHL	80	23	27	50	86	16	6	8	14	31
1976-77	Philadelphia	NHL	70	19	38	57	120	7	1	0	1	8
1977-78	Philadelphia	NHL	76	16	32	48	203	12	1	7	8	36
1978-79	Philadelphia	NHL	76	24	35	59	184	8	1	2	3	17
1979-80	Philadelphia	NHL	74	16	31	47	136	19	2	9	11	70
1980-81	Philadelphia	NHL	77	14	37	51	195	12	2	4	6	39
1981-82	Philadelphia	NHL	9	7	5	12	47	....	....	....	....	....
	Calgary	NHL	63	26	49	75	94	3	2	0	2	14
1982-83	Calgary	NHL	79	19	31	50	103	9	3	4	7	33
1983-84	New Jersey	NHL	79	23	38	61	121	....	....	....	....	....
1984-85	New Jersey	NHL	80	22	39	61	105	....	....	....	....	....
1985-86	New Jersey	NHL	78	23	40	63	80	....	....	....	....	....
	NHL Totals		841	232	402	634	1474	86	18	34	52	248

a Shared WHL First All-Star Team (1975) with Bryan Trottier (Lethbridge)

Traded to **Calgary** by **Philadelphia** for Brad Marsh, November 11, 1981. Traded to **New Jersey** by **Calgary** with Phil Russell for Steve Tambellini and Joel Quenneville, June 21, 1983.

BRITZ, GREG

Born, Buffalo, NY, January 3, 1961.
Right wing. Shoots left. 6', 190 lbs.
Last amateur club: Harvard University Crimson (ECAC).

Season	Club	Lea	GP	G	A	TP	PIM	GP	G	A	TP	PIM
1979-80	Harvard	ECAC	26	8	5	13	17	....	....	....	....	....
1980-81	Harvard	ECAC	17	3	4	7	10	....	....	....	....	....
1981-82	Harvard	ECAC	24	11	13	24	12	....	....	....	....	....
1982-83	Harvard	ECAC	33	16	23	39	18	....	....	....	....	....
1983-84	Toronto	NHL	6	0	0	0	2	....	....	....	....	....
	St. Catharines	AHL	44	23	16	39	25	7	1	0	1	0
1984-85	Toronto	NHL	1	0	0	0	2	....	....	....	....	....
	St. Catharines	AHL	74	15	17	32	31	....	....	....	....	....
1985-86	St. Catharines	AHL	72	17	19	36	52	13	3	3	6	17
	NHL Totals		7	0	0	0	4	....	....	....	....	....

Signed as free agent by **Toronto**, November 2, 1983.

BROCHU, STEPHANE

Born, Sherbrooke, Que., August 15, 1967.
Defense. Shoots left. 6'1", 185 lbs.
Last amateur club: St. Jean Castors (QMJHL).
(NY Rangers' 9th choice, 175th over-all, in 1985 Entry Draft).

Season	Club	Lea	GP	G	A	TP	PIM	GP	G	A	TP	PIM
1984-85	Quebec	QMJHL	59	2	16	18	56	4	0	2	2	2
1985-86	St. Jean	QMJHL	63	14	27	41	121	3	1	0	1	2

BRODEUR, LEE

Born, Grafton, N.D., February 14, 1966.
Right Wing. Shoots left. 6'1", 180 lbs.
Last amateur club: Western Michigan University Broncos (CCHA).
(Montreal's 6th choice, 65th over-all, in 1984 Entry Draft).

				Regular Season					Playoffs			
Season	Club	Lea	GP	G	A	TP	PIM	GP	G	A	TP	PIM
1984-85	North Dakota	WCHA	13	0	2	2	6	....	....	....	....	....
1985-86	North Dakota	WCHA	2	0	0	0	0	....	....	....	....	....
	W. Michigan	CCHA	20	1	4	5	22	....	....	....	....	....

BROOKE, ROBERT W. (BOB)

Born, Melrose, Mass., December 18, 1960.
Center. Shoots right. 6'2", 205 lbs.
Last amateur club: 1984 United States Olympic Team.
(St. Louis' 3rd choice, 75th over-all, in 1980 Entry Draft).

				Regular Season					Playoffs			
Season	Club	Lea	GP	G	A	TP	PIM	GP	G	A	TP	PIM
1979-80	Yale	ECAC	24	7	22	29	38	....	....	....	....	....
1980-81	Yale	ECAC	27	12	30	42	59	....	....	....	....	....
1981-82	Yale	ECAC	25	12	30	42	60	....	....	....	....	....
1982-83ab	Yale	ECAC	21	10	27	37	48	....	....	....	....	....
1983-84	U.S. National	....	54	7	18	25	75	....	....	....	....	....
	U.S. Olympic	....	6	1	2	3	10	....	....	....	....	....
	NY Rangers	NHL	9	1	2	3	4	5	0	0	0	7
1984-85	NY Rangers	NHL	72	7	9	16	79	3	0	0	0	8
1985-86	NY Rangers	NHL	79	24	20	44	111	16	6	9	15	28
	NHL Totals		160	32	31	63	194	24	6	9	15	43

a ECAC First All-Star Team (1983)
b NCAA All-American First Team (1983)
Rights traded to **NY Rangers** by **St. Louis** with Larry Patey for Dave Barr, NY Rangers' third round choice (Alan Perry) in 1984 Entry Draft and cash, March 5, 1984.

BROTEN, AARON   (BRAWT-en)

Born, Roseau, Minn., November 14, 1960.
Center. Shoots left. 5'10", 175 lbs.
Last amateur club: University of Minnesota Gophers (WCHA)
(Colorado's 5th choice, 106th over-all, in 1980 Entry Draft).

				Regular Season					Playoffs			
Season	Club	Lea	GP	G	A	TP	PIM	GP	G	A	TP	PIM
1979-80	U. Minnesota	WCHA	41	25	47	72	8	....	....	....	....	....
1980-81	U. Minnesota	WCHA	45	*47	*59	*106	24	....	....	....	....	....
	Colorado	NHL	2	0	0	0	0	....	....	....	....	....
1981-82	Fort Worth	CHL	19	15	21	36	11	....	....	....	....	....
	Colorado	NHL	58	15	24	39	6	....	....	....	....	....
1982-83	Wichita	CHL	4	0	4	4	0	....	....	....	....	....
	New Jersey	NHL	73	16	39	55	28	....	....	....	....	....
1983-84	New Jersey	NHL	80	13	23	36	36	....	....	....	....	....
1984-85	New Jersey	NHL	80	22	35	57	38	....	....	....	....	....
1985-86	New Jersey	NHL	66	18	25	43	26	....	....	....	....	....
	NHL Totals		359	84	146	230	134	....	....	....	....	....

BROTEN, NEAL LaMOY   (BRAWT-en)

Born, Roseau, Minn., November 29, 1959.
Center. Shoots left. 5'9", 170 lbs.
Last amateur club: University of Minnesota Gophers (WCHA)
(Minnesota's 3rd choice, 42nd over-all, in 1979 Entry Draft).

				Regular Season					Playoffs			
Season	Club	Lea	GP	G	A	TP	PIM	GP	G	A	TP	PIM
1978-79	U. Minnesota	WCHA	40	21	50	71	18	....	....	....	....	....
1979-80	U.S. National	...	55	25	30	55	20	....	....	....	....	....
	U.S. Olympic	...	7	2	1	3	2	....	....	....	....	....
1980-81ab	U. Minnesota	WCHA	36	17	54	71	56	....	....	....	....	....
	Minnesota	NHL	3	2	0	2	12	19	1	7	8	9
1981-82	Minnesota	NHL	73	38	60	98	42	4	0	2	2	0
1982-83	Minnesota	NHL	79	32	45	77	43	9	1	6	7	10
1983-84	Minnesota	NHL	76	28	61	89	43	16	5	5	10	4
1984-85	Minnesota	NHL	80	19	37	56	39	9	2	5	7	10
1985-86	Minnesota	NHL	80	29	76	105	47	5	3	2	5	2
	NHL Totals		391	148	279	427	226	62	12	27	39	35

a WCHA First All-Star Team (1981)
b Won Hobey Baker Memorial Trophy (Top U.S. College Player) (1981)

BROTEN, PAUL   (BRAWT-en)

Born, Roseau, Minn., October 27, 1965.
Center. Shoots right. 5'11", 155 lbs.
Last amateur club: University of Minnesota Gophers (WCHA)
(NY Rangers 3rd choice, 77th over-all, in 1984 Entry Draft)

				Regular Season					Playoffs			
Season	Club	Lea	GP	G	A	TP	PIM	GP	G	A	TP	PIM
1984-85	U. Minnesota	WCHA	34	6	6	12	24	....	....	....	....	....
1985-86	U. Minnesota	WCHA	38	6	16	22	24	....	....	....	....	....

BROWN, ALLISTER

Born, Cornwall, Ont., November 12, 1965.
Defense. Shoots right. 6'0", 185 lbs.
Last amateur club: University of New Hampshire Wildcats (H.E.).
(NY Islanders' 13th choice, 249th over-all, in 1984 Entry Draft).

				Regular Season					Playoffs			
Season	Club	Lea	GP	G	A	TP	PIM	GP	G	A	TP	PIM
1983-84	N. Hampshire	H.E.	36	1	7	8	12	....	....	....	....	....
1984-85	N. Hampshire	H.E.	42	4	7	11	18	....	....	....	....	....
1985-86	N. Hampshire	H.E.	36	2	5	7	28	....	....	....	....	....

BROWN, BILL

Born, Dayton, OH, October 9, 1966.
Center. Shoots right. 6'1", 170 lbs.
Last amateur club: Ohio State University Buckeyes (CCHA).
(Chicago's 11th choice, 216th over-all, in 1984 Entry Draft).

				Regular Season					Playoffs			
Season	Club	Lea	GP	G	A	TP	PIM	GP	G	A	TP	PIM
1984-85	Ohio State	CCHA	30	4	4	8	14	....	....	....	....	....
1985-86	Ohio State	CCHA	23	1	3	4	12	....	....	....	....	....

BROWN, DAVID

Born, Saskatoon, Sask., October 12, 1962.
Right wing. Shoots right. 6'5", 205 lbs.
Last amateur club: Saskatoon Blades (WHL).
(Philadelphia's 7th choice, 40th over-all, in 1982 Entry Draft).

				Regular Season					Playoffs			
Season	Club	Lea	GP	G	A	TP	PIM	GP	G	A	TP	PIM
1980-81	Spokane	WHL	9	2	2	4	21	....	....	....	....	....
1981-82	Saskatoon	WHL	62	11	33	44	344	5	1	0	1	4
1982-83	Philadelphia	NHL	2	0	0	0	5	....	....	....	....	....
	Maine	AHL	71	8	6	14	418	16	0	0	0	107
1983-84	Springfield	AHL	59	17	14	31	150	....	....	....	....	....
	Philadelphia	NHL	19	1	5	6	98	2	0	0	0	12
1984-85	Philadelphia	NHL	57	3	6	9	165	11	0	0	0	59
1985-86	Philadelphia	NHL	76	10	7	17	277	5	0	0	0	16
	NHL Totals		154	14	18	32	545	18	0	0	0	87

BROWN, GREG

Born, Hartford, Conn., March 7, 1968.
Defense. Shoots right. 5'11", 180 lbs.
Last amateur club: St. Mark's (HS).
(Buffalo's 2nd choice, 26th over-all, in 1986 Entry Draft).

				Regular Season					Playoffs			
Season	Club	Lea	GP	G	A	TP	PIM	GP	G	A	TP	PIM
1985-86	St. Mark's	HS	19	22	28	50	50	....	....	....	....	....

BROWN, JEFF

Born, Ottawa, Ont., April 30, 1966.
Defense. Shoots right. 6'1", 185 lbs.
Last amateur club: Sudbury Wolves (OHL).
(Quebec's 2nd choice, 36th over-all, in 1984 Entry Draft).

				Regular Season					Playoffs			
Season	Club	Lea	GP	G	A	TP	PIM	GP	G	A	TP	PIM
1982-83	Sudbury	OHL	65	9	37	46	39	....	....	....	....	....
1983-84	Sudbury	OHL	68	17	60	77	39	....	....	....	....	....
1984-85	Sudbury	OHL	56	16	48	64	26	....	....	....	....	....
1985-86	Quebec	NHL	8	3	2	5	6	1	0	0	0	0
a	Sudbury	OHL	45	22	28	50	24	4	0	2	2	11
	Fredericton	AHL	....	....	....	....	....	1	0	1	1	0
	NHL Totals		8	3	2	5	6	1	0	0	0	0

a OHL First All-Star Team (1986).

BROWN, KEITH JEFFREY

Born, Corner Brook, Nfld., May 6, 1960.
Defense. Shoots right. 6'1", 195 lbs.
Last amateur club: Portland Winter Hawks (WHL).
(Chicago's 1st choice, 7th over-all, in 1979 Entry Draft).

				Regular Season					Playoffs			
Season	Club	Lea	GP	G	A	TP	PIM	GP	G	A	TP	PIM
1977-78a	Portland	WHL	72	11	53	64	51	8	0	3	3	2
1978-79bc	Portland	WHL	70	11	85	96	75	25	3	*30	33	21
1979-80	Chicago	NHL	76	2	18	20	27	6	0	0	0	4
1980-81	Chicago	NHL	80	9	34	43	80	3	0	2	2	2
1981-82	Chicago	NHL	33	4	20	24	26	4	0	2	2	5
1982-83	Chicago	NHL	50	4	27	31	20	7	0	0	0	11
1983-84	Chicago	NHL	74	10	25	35	94	5	0	1	1	10
1984-85	Chicago	NHL	56	1	22	23	55	11	2	7	9	31
1985-86	Chicago	NHL	70	11	29	40	87	3	0	1	1	9
	NHL Totals		439	41	175	216	389	39	2	13	15	72

a Shared WHL's Rookie of the Year with John Ogrodnick (New Westminster) (1978)
b Named WHL's Top Defenseman (1979)
c WHL First All-Star Team (1979)

BROWN, NEWELL

Born, Cornwall, Ont., February 14, 1962.
Center. Shoots right. 5'9", 180 lbs.
Last amateur club: Michigan State University Spartans (CCHA).
(Vancouver's 6th choice, 158th over-all, in 1982 Entry Draft).

				Regular Season					Playoffs			
Season	Club	Lea	GP	G	A	TP	PIM	GP	G	A	TP	PIM
1980-81	Michigan State	CCHA	30	14	16	30	42	....	....	....	....	....
1981-82	Michigan State	CCHA	42	22	51	73	66	....	....	....	....	....
1982-83	Michigan State	CCHA	32	10	20	30	60	....	....	....	....	....
1983-84	Michigan State	CCHA	42	20	33	53	30	....	....	....	....	....
1984-85	Fredericton	AHL	46	5	8	13	17	....	....	....	....	....
	Muskegon	IHL	17	5	10	15	15	14	5	10	15	13
1985-86	Cdn. Olympic	....	72	15	21	36	60	....	....	....	....	....

BROWNSCHIDLE, JOHN J. (JR.) (JACK) (BROWNS-chy-del)

Born, Buffalo, NY, October 2, 1955.
Defense. Shoots left. 6'2", 195 lbs.
Last amateur club: University of Notre Dame Fighting Irish (WCHA)
(St. Louis' 5th choice, 99th over-all, in 1975 Amateur Draft).

			Regular Season					Playoffs				
Season	Club	Lea	GP	G	A	TP	PIM	GP	G	A	TP	PIM
1975-76	Notre Dame	WCHA	38	12	24	36	24	....	....	....	....	....
1976-77	Notre Dame	WCHA	38	13	35	48	30	....	....	....	....	....
1977-78	**St. Louis**	**NHL**	**40**	**2**	**15**	**17**	**23**	....	....	....	....	....
	Salt Lake	CHL	25	4	12	16	0	....	....	....	....	....
1978-79	Salt Lake	CHL	11	0	10	10	0	....	....	....	....	....
	St. Louis	**NHL**	**64**	**10**	**24**	**34**	**14**	....	....	....	....	....
1979-80	**St. Louis**	**NHL**	**77**	**12**	**32**	**44**	**8**	**3**	**0**	**0**	**0**	**0**
1980-81	**St. Louis**	**NHL**	**71**	**5**	**23**	**28**	**12**	**11**	**0**	**3**	**3**	**2**
1981-82	**St. Louis**	**NHL**	**80**	**5**	**33**	**38**	**26**	**8**	**0**	**2**	**2**	**14**
1982-83	**St. Louis**	**NHL**	**72**	**1**	**22**	**23**	**30**	**4**	**0**	**0**	**0**	**2**
1983-84	**St. Louis**	**NHL**	**51**	**1**	**7**	**8**	**19**	....	....	....	....	....
	Hartford	**NHL**	**13**	**2**	**2**	**4**	**10**	....	....	....	....	....
1984-85	**Hartford**	**NHL**	**17**	**1**	**4**	**5**	**5**	....	....	....	....	....
	Binghamton	AHL	56	4	17	21	8	....	....	....	....	....
1985-86	**Hartford**	**NHL**	**9**	**0**	**0**	**0**	**4**	....	....	....	....	....
a	Binghamton	AHL	58	5	26	31	18	6	0	3	3	0
	NHL Totals		**494**	**39**	**162**	**201**	**151**	....	....	....	....	....

Claimed on waivers by **Hartford** from **St. Louis**, March 2, 1984.

a AHL Second All-Star Team (1986)

BRUBAKER, JEFFREY J. (JEFF) (BREW-bake-er)

Born, Frederick, Maryland, February 24, 1958.
Left wing. Shoots left. 6'2", 210 lbs.
Last amateur club: Peterborough Petes (OHA).
(Boston's 6th choice, 102nd over-all, in 1978 Amateur Draft).

			Regular Season					Playoffs				
Season	Club	Lea	GP	G	A	TP	PIM	GP	G	A	TP	PIM
1976-77	Peterborough	OHA	26	0	5	5	143	4	0	2	2	7
1977-78	Peterborough	OHA	68	20	24	44	307	21	6	5	11	52
1978-79	Rochester	AHL	57	4	10	14	253	....	....	....	....	....
	New England	WHA	12	0	0	0	19	3	0	0	0	12
1979-80	**Hartford**	**NHL**	**3**	**0**	**1**	**1**	**2**	....	....	....	....	....
	Springfield	AHL	50	12	13	25	165	....	....	....	....	....
1980-81	**Hartford**	**NHL**	**43**	**5**	**3**	**8**	**93**	....	....	....	....	....
	Binghamton	AHL	33	18	11	29	138	....	....	....	....	....
1981-82	**Montreal**	**NHL**	**3**	**0**	**1**	**1**	**32**	**2**	**0**	**0**	**0**	**27**
	Nova Scotia	AHL	60	28	12	40	256	6	2	1	3	32
1982-83	Nova Scotia	AHL	78	31	27	58	183	7	1	1	2	25
1983-84	**Calgary**	**NHL**	**4**	**0**	**0**	**0**	**19**	....	....	....	....	....
	Colorado	CHL	57	16	19	35	218	6	3	1	4	15
1984-85	**Toronto**	**NHL**	**68**	**8**	**4**	**12**	**209**	....	....	....	....	....
1985-86	**Toronto**	**NHL**	**21**	**0**	**0**	**0**	**67**	....	....	....	....	....
	Edmonton	**NHL**	**4**	**1**	**0**	**1**	**12**	....	....	....	....	....
	Nova Scotia	AHL	19	4	3	7	41	....	....	....	..	....
	NHL Totals		**146**	**14**	**9**	**23**	**434**	....	....	....	....	....
	WHA Totals		12	0	0	0	19	3	0	0	0	12

Rights transferred to **Hartford** by **Boston**, June 22, 1979. Claimed by **Montreal** from **Hartford** in NHL Waiver Draft, October 5, 1981. Claimed by **Quebec** from **Montreal** in NHL Waiver Draft, October 3, 1983. Claimed by **Calgary** from **Quebec** in NHL Waiver Draft, October 3, 1983. Signed as a free agent by **Edmonton**, June 219, 1984. Claimed by **Toronto** from **Edmonton** in NHL Waiver Draft, October 9, 1984. Claimed on waivers by **Edmonton** from **Toronto**, December 5, 1985.

BRUCE, DAVID

Born, Thunder Bay, Ont., October 7, 1964.
Right wing/Center. Shoots right. 5'11", 180 lbs.
Last amateur club: Kitchener Rangers (OHL).
(Vancouver's 2nd choice, 30th over-all, in 1983 Entry Draft).

			Regular Season					Playoffs				
Season	Club	Lea	GP	G	A	TP	PIM	GP	G	A	TP	PIM
1982-83	Kitchener	OHL	67	36	35	71	199	12	7	9	16	27
1983-84	Kitchener	OHL	62	52	40	92	203	10	5	8	13	20
1984-85	Fredericton	AHL	56	14	11	25	104	5	0	0	0	37
1985-86	**Vancouver**	**NHL**	**12**	**0**	**1**	**1**	**14**	**1**	**0**	**0**	**0**	**0**
	Fredericton	AHL	66	25	16	41	51	2	0	1	1	12
	NHL Totals		**12**	**0**	**1**	**1**	**14**	**1**	**0**	**0**	**0**	**0**

BRUMWELL, JAMES (MURRAY)

Born, Calgary, Alta., March 31, 1960.
Defense. Shoots left. 6'1", 190 lbs.
Last amateur club: Billings Bighorns (WHL).

			Regular Season					Playoffs				
Season	Club	Lea	GP	G	A	TP	PIM	GP	G	A	TP	PIM
1978-79	Billings	WHL	61	11	32	43	62	....	....	....	....	....
1979-80	Billings	WHL	67	18	54	72	50	....	....	....	....	....
1980-81	**Minnesota**	**NHL**	**1**	**0**	**0**	**0**	**0**	....	....	....	....	....
	Oklahoma City	CHL	79	12	43	55	79	3	0	0	0	4
1981-82	**Minnesota**	**NHL**	**21**	**0**	**3**	**3**	**18**	**2**	**0**	**0**	**0**	**2**
	Nashville	CHL	55	4	21	25	66	....	....	....	....	....
1982-83	Wichita	CHL	11	4	1	5	4	....	....	....	....	....
	New Jersey	**NHL**	**59**	**5**	**14**	**19**	**34**	....	....	....	....	....
1983-84	**New Jersey**	**NHL**	**42**	**7**	**13**	**20**	**14**	....	....	....	....	....
	Maine	AHL	35	4	25	29	16	17	1	5	6	15
1984-85	Maine	AHL	64	8	31	39	12	10	4	5	9	19
1985-86	**New Jersey**	**NHL**	**1**	**0**	**0**	**0**	**0**	....	....	....	....	....
	Maine	AHL	66	9	28	37	35	5	0	3	3	2
	NHL Totals		**124**	**12**	**30**	**42**	**66**	**2**	**0**	**0**	**0**	**2**

Signed as free agent by **Minnesota**, August 7, 1980. Claimed by **New Jersey** from **Minnesota** in Waiver Draft, October 4, 1982.

BRUNET, BENOIT

Born, Montreal, Que., August 24, 1968.
Left wing. Shoots left. 5'10", 180 lbs.
Last amateur club: Hull Olympiques (QMJHL).
(Montreal's 2nd choice, 27th over-all, in 1986 Entry Draft).

			Regular Season					Playoffs				
Season	Club	Lea	GP	G	A	TP	PIM	GP	G	A	TP	PIM
1985-86	Hull	QMJHL	71	33	37	70	81	....	....	...	..	....

BRYDEN, ROB

Born, Toronto, Ont., April 5, 1963.
Left wing. Shoots left. 6'3", 205 lbs.
Last amateur club: Western Michigan University Broncos (CCHA).
(Montreal's 10th choice, 158th over-all, in 1983 Entry Draft).

			Regular Season					Playoffs				
Season	Club	Lea	GP	G	A	TP	PIM	GP	G	A	TP	PIM
1983-84	W. Michigan	CCHA	36	17	12	29	60	....	....	....	....	....
1984-85	W. Michigan	CCHA	39	18	19	37	59	....	....	....	....	....
1985-86	W. Michigan	CCHA	44	23	28	51	85	....	....	....	....	....

BRYDGES, PAUL

Born, Guelph, Ont., June 21, 1965.
Center. Shoots right. 5'11", 175 lbs.
Last amateur club: Guelph Platers (OHL).

			Regular Season					Playoffs				
Season	Club	Lea	GP	G	A	TP	PIM	GP	G	A	TP	PIM
1982-83	Guelph	OHL	56	13	13	26	27	....	....	....	....	....
1983-84	Guelph	OHL	68	27	23	50	37	....	....	....	....	....
1984-85	Guelph	OHL	57	22	24	46	39	....	....	....	....	....
1985-86	Guelph	OHL	62	17	40	57	88	19	10	15	25	22

Signed as a free agent by **Buffalo**, June 11, 1986.

BUBLA, JIRI (BOOB-la)

Born, Usti nad Labem, Czechoslovakia, January 27, 1950.
Defense. Shoots right. 5'11", 200 lbs.
Last amateur club: Sparta Praha (Czechoslovakia)

			Regular Season					Playoffs				
Season	Club	Lea	GP	G	A	TP	PIM	GP	G	A	TP	PIM
1980-81	Sparta Praha	Czech.	40	4	16	20	....	....	....	....	....	....
1981-82	**Vancouver**	**NHL**	**23**	**1**	**1**	**2**	**16**	....	....	....	....	....
1982-83	**Vancouver**	**NHL**	**72**	**2**	**28**	**30**	**59**	**1**	**0**	**0**	**0**	**5**
1983-84	**Vancouver**	**NHL**	**62**	**6**	**33**	**39**	**43**	**2**	**0**	**0**	**0**	**0**
1984-85	**Vancouver**	**NHL**	**56**	**2**	**15**	**17**	**54**	....	....	....	....	....
1985-86	**Vancouver**	**NHL**	**43**	**6**	**24**	**30**	**30**	**3**	**0**	**0**	**0**	**2**
	NHL Totals		**256**	**17**	**101**	**118**	**202**	**6**	**0**	**0**	**0**	**7**

Claimed in special Czechoslovakian Entry Draft by **Colorado**, May 28, 1981. Rights obtained by **Vancouver** from **Colorado**, when Vancouver sent Brent Ashton and their fourth round choice (Tom Martin) in 1982 Entry Draft to Winnipeg. Winnipeg then traded Ashton and their third round choice (Dave Kasper) in 1982 Entry Draft to Colorado for Lucien DeBlois, July 15, 1981.

BUCHBERGER, KELLY

Born, Langenburg, Sask., December 12, 1966.
Left wing. Shoots left. 6'2", 190 lbs.
Last amateur club: Moose Jaw Warriors (WHL).
(Edmonton's 8th choice, 188th over-all, in 1985 Entry Draft).

			Regular Season					Playoffs				
Season	Club	Lea	GP	G	A	TP	PIM	GP	G	A	TP	PIM
1984-85	Moose Jaw	WHL	51	12	17	29	114	....	....	....	....	....
1985-86	Moose Jaw	WHL	72	14	22	36	206	13	11	4	15	37

BUCKLEY, DAVID

Born, Newton, Mass., January 27, 1966.
Defense. Shoots left. 6'4", 195 lbs.
Last amateur club: Boston College Eagles (H.E.).
(Toronto's 9th choice, 192nd over-all, in 1984 Entry Draft).

			Regular Season					Playoffs				
Season	Club	Lea	GP	G	A	TP	PIM	GP	G	A	TP	PIM
1985-86	Boston College	H.E.	22	0	2	2	4	....	....	....	....	....

BUCYK, RANDY

Born, Edmonton, Alta., November 9, 1962.
Center. Shoots left. 5'11", 175 lbs.
Last amateur club: Northeastern University Huskies (ECAC).

			Regular Season					Playoffs				
Season	Club	Lea	GP	G	A	TP	PIM	GP	G	A	TP	PIM
1980-81	Northeastern	ECAC	31	18	17	35	0	....	....	....	....	....
1981-82	Northeastern	ECAC	33	19	17	36	10	....	....	....	....	....
1982-83	Northeastern	ECAC	28	16	20	36	16	....	....	....	....	....
1983-84	Northeastern	ECAC	29	16	13	29	11	....	....	....	....	....
1984-85	Sherbrooke	AHL	62	21	26	47	20	8	0	0	0	20
1985-86	Sherbrooke	AHL	43	18	33	51	22	....	....	....	....	....
	Montreal	**NHL**	**17**	**4**	**2**	**6**	**8**	**2**	**0**	**0**	**0**	**0**
	NHL Totals		**17**	**4**	**2**	**6**	**8**	**2**	**0**	**0**	**0**	**0**

Signed as a free agent by **Montreal**, January 15, 1986.

BUDA, DAVID

Born, Mississauga, Ont., March 14, 1966.
Center. Shoots left. 6'4", 190 lbs.
Last amateur club: Northeastern University Huskies (H.E.).
(Boston's 9th choice, 199th over-all, in 1985 Entry Draft).

			Regular Season					Playoffs				
Season	Club	Lea	GP	G	A	TP	PIM	GP	G	A	TP	PIM
1985-86	Northeastern	H.E.	39	4	4	8	39	....	....	....	....	....

BULLARD, MICHAEL BRIAN (MIKE)

(BULL-ard)

Born, Ottawa, Ont., March 10, 1961.
Center. Shoots left. 5'10", 185 lbs.
Last amateur club: Brantford Alexanders (OHA).
(Pittsburgh's 1st choice, 9th over-all, in 1980 Entry Draft).

				Regular Season					Playoffs			
Season	Club	Lea	GP	G	A	TP	PIM	GP	G	A	TP	PIM
1978-79	Brantford	OHA	66	43	56	99	66	....	....	....	....	....
1979-80a	Brantford	OHA	66	66	84	150	86	11	10	6	16	29
1980-81b	Brantford	OHA	42	47	60	107	55	6	4	5	9	10
	Pittsburgh	NHL	15	1	2	3	19	4	3	3	6	0
1981-82	Pittsburgh	NHL	75	36	27	63	91	5	1	1	2	4
1982-83	Pittsburgh	NHL	57	22	22	44	60	....	....	....	....	....
1983-84	Pittsburgh	NHL	76	51	41	92	57	....	....	....	....	....
1984-85	Pittsburgh	NHL	68	32	31	63	75	....	....	....	....	....
1985-86	Pittsburgh	NHL	77	41	42	83	69	....	....	....	....	....
	NHL Totals		368	183	165	348	371	....	....	....	....	...

a OHA Third All-Star Team (1979)
b OHA Second All-Star Team (1980)

BURNS, GARY

Born, Cambridge, Mass., January 16, 1955.
Left wing/Center. Shoots left. 6'1", 190 lbs.
Last amateur club: University of New Hampshire Wildcats (ECAC).
(Toronto's 15th choice, 191st over-all, in 1975 Amateur Draft).

				Regular Season					Playoffs			
Season	Club	Lea	GP	G	A	TP	PIM	GP	G	A	TP	PIM
1976-77	N. Hampshire	ECAC	38	9	6	15	24	....	....	....	....	....
1977-78	N. Hampshire	ECAC	29	9	19	28	55	....	....	....	....	....
1978-79	Rochester	AHL	79	16	30	46	99	....	....	....	....	....
1979-80	Binghamton	AHL	79	30	29	59	105	....	....	....	....	....
1980-81	New Haven	AHL	69	25	29	54	137	4	1	0	1	2
	NY Rangers	NHL	11	2	2	4	18	1	0	0	0	2
1981-82	Springfield	AHL	78	27	39	66	71	....	....	....	....	....
	NY Rangers	NHL	....	....	....	....	....	4	0	0	0	0
1982-83	Tulsa	CHL	80	21	33	54	61	....	....	....	....	....
1983-84	Tulsa	CHL	68	28	30	58	95	9	3	*9	12	2
1984-85	Rochester	AHL	76	22	27	49	64	2	0	1	1	6
1985-86	Salt Lake	IHL	78	23	35	58	85	4	1	0	1	6
	NHL Totals		11	2	2	4	18	5	0	0	0	2

Signed as free agent by **Boston**, October 10, 1978. Signed as free agent by **NY Rangers**, September 16, 1980.

BURR, SHAWN

Born, Sarnia, Ont., July 1, 1966.
Center. Shoots left. 6'1", 180 lbs.
Last amateur club: Kitchener Rangers (OHL).
(Detroit's 1st choice, 7th over-all, in 1984 Entry Draft).

				Regular Season					Playoffs			
Season	Club	Lea	GP	G	A	TP	PIM	GP	G	A	TP	PIM
1982-83	Sarnia Midgets	ONT	52	50	85	135	125	....	....	....	....	....
1983-84	Kitchener	OHL	68	41	44	85	50	16	5	12	17	22
1984-85	Detroit	NHL	9	0	0	0	2	....	....	....	....	....
	Adirondack	AHL	4	0	0	0	2	....	....	....	....	....
	Kitchener	OHL	48	24	42	66	50	4	3	3	6	2
1985-86	Detroit	NHL	5	1	0	1	4	....	....	....	....	....
	Adirondack	AHL	3	2	2	4	2	17	5	7	12	32
a	Kitchener	OHL	59	60	67	127	104	5	2	3	5	8
	NHL Totals		14	1	0	1	6	....	....	...	....	....

a OHL Second All-Star Team (1986)

BURRIDGE, RANDY

Born, Fort Erie, Ont., January 7, 1966.
Left Wing. Shoots left. 5'9", 170 lbs.
Last amateur club: Peterborough Petes (OHL).
(Boston's 7th choice, 157th over-all, in 1985 Entry Draft).

				Regular Season					Playoffs			
Season	Club	Lea	GP	G	A	TP	PIM	GP	G	A	TP	PIM
1983-84	Peterborough	OHL	55	6	7	13	44	8	3	2	5	7
1984-85	Peterborough	OHL	66	49	57	106	88	17	9	16	25	18.
1985-86	Peterborough	OHL	17	15	11	26	23	3	1	3	4	2
	Boston	NHL	52	17	25	42	17	3	0	4	4	12
	Moncton	AHL	....	....	....	....	....	3	0	2	2	2
	NHL Totals		52	17	25	42	17	3	0	4	4	12

BUSKAS, ROD

Born, Wetaskiwin, Alta., January 7, 1961.
Defense. Shoots right. 6'1", 200 lbs.
Last amateur club: Medicine Hat Tigers (WHL).
(Pittsburgh's 6th choice, 112th over-all, in 1981 Entry Draft).

				Regular Season					Playoffs			
Season	Club	Lea	GP	G	A	TP	PIM	GP	G	A	TP	PIM
1978-79	Billings	WHL	1	0	0	0	0	....	....	....	....	....
	Medicine Hat	WHL	34	1	12	13	60	....	....	....	....	....
1979-80	Medicine Hat	WHL	72	7	40	47	284	....	....	....	....	....
1980-81	Medicine Hat	WHL	72	14	46	60	164	5	1	1	2	8
1981-82	Erie	AHL	69	1	18	19	78	....	....	....	....	....
1982-83	Pittsburgh	NHL	41	2	2	4	102	....	....	....	....	....
	Baltimore	AHL	31	2	8	10	45	....	....	....	....	....
1983-84	Pittsburgh	NHL	47	2	4	6	60	....	....	....	....	....
	Baltimore	AHL	33	2	12	14	100	10	1	3	4	22
1984-85	Pittsburgh	NHL	69	2	7	9	191	....	....	....	....	....
1985-86	Pittsburgh	NHL	72	2	7	9	159	....	....	...	....	....
	NHL Totals		229	8	20	28	512	....	....	....	....	....

BUTCHER, GARTH

Born, Regina, Sask., January 8, 1963.
Defense. Shoots right. 6', 200 lbs.
Last amateur club: Regina Pats (WHL).
(Vancouver's 1st choice, 10th over-all, in 1981 Entry Draft).

				Regular Season					Playoffs			
Season	Club	Lea	GP	G	A	TP	PIM	GP	G	A	TP	PIM
1979-80	Regina	WHL	13	0	4	4	20	....	....	....	....	....
1980-81a	Regina	WHL	69	9	77	86	230	11	5	17	22	60
1981-82a	Regina	WHL	65	24	68	92	318	19	3	17	20	95
	Vancouver	NHL	5	0	0	0	9	1	0	0	0	0
1982-83	Vancouver	NHL	55	1	13	14	105	3	1	0	1	2
1983-84	Vancouver	NHL	28	2	0	2	34	....	....	....	....	....
	Fredericton	AHL	25	4	13	17	43	6	0	2	2	19
1984-85	Vancouver	NHL	75	3	9	12	152	....	....	....	....	....
	Fredericton	AHL	3	1	0	1	11	....	....	....	....	....
1985-86	Vancouver	NHL	70	4	7	11	188	3	0	0	0	0
	NHL Totals		233	10	29	39	488	7	1	0	1	0

a WHL First All-Star Team (1981, 1982)

BYERS, LYNDON

Born, Nipawin, Sask., February 29, 1964.
Right wing. Shoots right. 6'1", 190 lbs.
Last amateur club: Regina Pats (WHL).
(Boston's 3rd choice, 39th over-all, in 1982 Entry Draft).

				Regular Season					Playoffs			
Season	Club	Lea	GP	G	A	TP	PIM	GP	G	A	TP	PIM
1981-82	Regina	WHL	57	18	25	43	169	20	5	6	11	48
1982-83	Regina	WHL	70	32	38	70	153	5	1	1	2	16
1983-84	Boston	NHL	10	2	4	6	32	....	....	....	....	....
	Regina	WHL	58	32	57	89	154	23	17	18	35	78
1984-85	Boston	NHL	33	3	8	11	41	....	....	...	...	....
	Hershey	AHL	27	4	6	10	55	....	....	....	....	....
1985-86	Boston	NHL	5	0	2	2	9	....	....	....	....	....
	Moncton	AHL	14	2	4	6	26	....	....	....	....	....
	Milwaukee	IHL	8	0	2	2	22	....	....	....	....	....
	NHL Totals		48	5	14	19	82	....	....	....	....	....

BYRNES, BRIAN

Born, Manhassett, NY, March 30, 1962.
Defense. Shoots right. 5'11", 190 lbs.
Last amateur club: University of New Hampshire Wildcats (H.E.).

				Regular Season					Playoffs			
Season	Club	Lea	GP	G	A	TP	PIM	GP	G	A	TP	PIM
1981-82	N. Hampshire	ECAC	23	1	8	9	18	....	....	....	....	....
1982-83	N. Hampshire	ECAC	27	2	5	7	20	....	....	....	....	....
1983-84	N. Hampshire	ECAC	37	6	16	22	50	....	....	....	....	....
1984-85	N. Hampshire	H.E.	43	4	16	20	72	....	....	....	....	....
1985-86	Milwaukee	IHL						2	0	0	0	0

Signed as a free agent by **Boston**, October 10, 1985.

CALLAGHAN, GARY

Born, Oshawa, Ont., August 12, 1967.
Center. Shoots left. 5'11", 175 lbs.
Last amateur club: Belleville Bulls (OHL).
(Hartford's 3rd choice, 68th over-all, in 1985 Entry Draft).

				Regular Season					Playoffs			
Season	Club	Lea	GP	G	A	TP	PIM	GP	G	A	TP	PIM
1984-85	Belleville	OHL	57	24	25	49	42	14	2	4	6	5
1985-86	Belleville	OHL	53	29	16	45	42	24	4	6	10	28

CALLANDER, JOHN (JOCK)

Born, Regina, Sask., April 23, 1961.
Center. Shoots right. 6'1", 180 lbs.
Last amateur club: Regina Pats (WHL).

				Regular Season					Playoffs			
Season	Club	Lea	GP	G	A	TP	PIM	GP	G	A	TP	PIM
1979-80	Regina	WHL	39	9	11	20	25	18	8	5	13	0
1980-81	Regina	WHL	72	67	86	153	37	11	6	7	13	14
1981-82	Regina	WHL	71	79	111	*190	59	20	13	*26	39	37
1982-83	Salt Lake	CHL	68	20	27	47	26	6	0	1	1	9
1983-84	Montana	CHL	72	27	32	59	69	....	....	....	....	....
	Toledo	IHL	2	0	0	0	0	....	....	....	....	....
1984-85	Muskegon	IHL	82	39	68	107	86	17	8	13	21	33
1985-86a	Muskegon	IHL	82	39	72	111	121	14	12	11	23	12

a IHL playoff MVP (1986)

Signed as free agent by **St. Louis**, September 28, 1981.

CAMAZZOLA, ANTHONY BERT (TONY)

Born, Vancouver, B.C., September 11, 1962.
Defense. Shoots left. 6'2", 210 lbs.
Last amateur club: Brandon Wheat Kings (WHL).
(Washington's 9th choice, 194th over-all, in 1980 Entry Draft).

			Regular Season					Playoffs				
Season	Club	Lea	GP	G	A	TP	PIM	GP	G	A	TP	PIM
1979-80	Brandon	WHL	7	0	2	2	21	7	0	0	0	2
1980-81	Brandon	WHL	69	4	20	24	144	5	0	1	1	10
1981-82	**Washington**	**NHL**	**3**	**0**	**0**	**0**	**4**	....	....	....	....	....
	Brandon	WHL	64	6	23	29	210	4	1	1	2	26
1982-83	Hershey	AHL	52	3	8	11	106	....	....	....	....	....
1983-84	Hershey	AHL	63	6	10	16	138	....	....	....	....	....
1984-85	Fort Wayne	IHL	15	0	3	3	56	....	....	....	....	....
	Toledo	IHL	28	2	8	10	84	6	0	1	1	9
1985-86	Fort Wayne	IHL	54	5	7	12	144	14	6	0	6	7
	NHL Totals		**3**	**0**	**0**	**0**	**4**	....	....	....	....	....

CAMAZZOLA, JAMES

Born, Vancouver, B.C, January 5, 1964.
Left wing. Shoots left. 5'11", 190 lbs.
Last amateur club: Kamloops Junior Oilers (WHL).
(Chicago's 10th choice, 196th over-all, in 1982 Entry Draft).

			Regular Season					Playoffs				
Season	Club	Lea	GP	G	A	TP	PIM	GP	G	A	TP	PIM
1982-83	Kamloops	WHL	66	57	58	115	54	....	....	....	....	....
1983-84	**Chicago**	**NHL**	**1**	**0**	**0**	**0**	**0**	....	....	....	....	....
	Seattle	WHL	3	1	1	2	0	....	....	....	....	....
	Kamloops	WHL	29	26	24	50	25	17	12	19	31	44
1984-85	N. Westminster	WHL	25	19	29	48	25	11	10	12	22	4
1985-86	Nova Scotia	AHL	3	0	0	0	0	....	....	....	....	....
	Saginaw	IHL	42	16	22	38	10	8	0	3	3	15
	NHL Totals		**1**	**0**	**0**	**0**	**0**	....	....	....	....	....

CAMPEDELLI, DOM

Born, Cohasset, Mass., April 3, 1964.
Defense. Shoots right. 6'1", 185 lbs.
Last amateur club: Boston College Eagles (H.E.)
(Toronto's 10th choice, 129th over-all, in 1982 Entry Draft).

			Regular Season					Playoffs				
Season	Club	Lea	GP	G	A	TP	PIM	GP	G	A	TP	PIM
1982-83	Boston College	ECAC	26	1	10	11	26	....	....	....	....	....
1983-84	Boston College	ECAC	37	10	19	29	24	....	....	....	....	....
1984-85	Boston College	H.E.	44	5	44	49	74	....	....	....	....	....
1985-86	**Montreal**	**NHL**	**2**	**0**	**0**	**0**	**0**	....	....	....	....	....
	Sherbrooke	AHL	38	4	10	14	27	....	....	....	....	....
	NHL Totals		**2**	**0**	**0**	**0**	**0**	....	....	....	....	....

Traded to **Montreal** by **Toronto** for Montreal's second-round choice (Darryl Shannon) in 1986 Entry Draft and Toronto's fourth round choice (Kent Hulst) in 1986 Entry Draft-Montreal's property via earlier transaction, September 18, 1985.

CAMPBELL, WADE ALLAN

Born, Peace River, Alta., January 2, 1961.
Defense. Shoots right. 6'4", 220 lbs.
Last amateur club: University of Alberta Golden Bears (CWUAA)

			Regular Season					Playoffs				
Season	Club	Lea	GP	G	A	TP	PIM	GP	G	A	TP	PIM
1980-81	U. of Alberta	CWUAA	24	3	15	18	46	....	....	....	....	....
1981-82	U. of Alberta	CWUAA	24	6	12	18	10	....	....	....	....	....
1982-83	**Winnipeg**	**NHL**	**42**	**1**	**2**	**3**	**50**	....	....	....	....	....
	Sherbrooke	AHL	18	4	2	6	23	....	....	....	....	....
1983-84	**Winnipeg**	**NHL**	**79**	**7**	**14**	**21**	**147**	**3**	**0**	**0**	**0**	**7**
1984-85	**Winnipeg**	**NHL**	**40**	**1**	**6**	**7**	**21**	**3**	**0**	**0**	**0**	**2**
	Sherbrooke	AHL	28	2	6	8	70	....	....	....	....	....
1985-86	**Winnipeg**	**NHL**	**24**	**0**	**1**	**1**	**27**	....	....	....	....	....
	Sherbrooke	AHL	9	0	2	2	26	....	....	....	....	....
	Boston	**NHL**	**8**	**0**	**0**	**0**	**15**	....	....	....	....	....
	Moncton	AHL	17	2	2	4	21	10	0	0	0	16
	NHL Totals		**193**	**9**	**23**	**32**	**260**	**6**	**0**	**0**	**0**	**9**

Signed as a free agent by **Winnipeg**, October 5, 1982. Traded to **Boston** by **Winnipeg** for Bill Derlago, January 31, 1986.

CAMPBELL, WILLIAM (BILL)

Born, Montreal, Que., March 20, 1964.
Defense. Shoots right. 6', 175 lbs.
Last amateur club: Verdun Juniors (QMJHL).
(Philadelphia's 3rd choice, 47th over-all, in 1982 Entry Draft).

			Regular Season					Playoffs				
Season	Club	Lea	GP	G	A	TP	PIM	GP	G	A	TP	PIM
1980-81	Montreal	QMJHL	72	20	48	68	28	7	2	3	5	0
1981-82a	Montreal	QMJHL	64	21	41	62	30	14	1	6	7	6
1982-83	Verdun	QMJHL	67	35	64	99	34	10	5	8	13	10
1983-84	Verdun	QMJHL	65	24	66	90	59	10	2	5	7	4
1984-85	Hershey	AHL	80	6	43	49	34	....	....	....	....	....
1985-86	Hershey	AHL	37	0	8	8	18	....	....	....	....	....
	Sherbrooke	AHL	22	1	6	7	25	....	....	....	....	....

a QMJHL Second All-Star Team (1982)

Rights sold to **Montreal** by **Philadelphia**, February 14, 1986.

CAPUANO, DAVE

Born, Cranston, RI, July 27, 1968.
Center. Shoots left. 6'2", 190 lbs.
Last amateur club: Mt. St. Charles (HS)
(Pittsburgh's 2nd choice, 25th over-all, in 1986 Entry Draft).

			Regular Season					Playoffs				
Season	Club	Lea	GP	G	A	TP	PIM	GP	G	A	TP	PIM
1985-86	Mt. St. Charles	HS	25	43	42	85	10	....	....	....	....	....

CAPUANO, JACK

Born, Cranston, RI, July 7, 1966.
Defense. Shoots left. 6'2", 210 lbs.
Last amateur club: University of Maine Black Bears (H.E.).
(Toronto's 4th choice, 67th over-all, in 1984 Entry Draft).

			Regular Season					Playoffs				
Season	Club	Lea	GP	G	A	TP	PIM	GP	G	A	TP	PIM
1985-86	Maine	H.E.	39	9	18	27	51	....	....	....	....	....

CARBONNEAU, GUY (CAR-bon-oh, GEE)

Born, Sept Iles, Que., March 18, 1960.
Center. Shoots right. 5'11", 175 lbs.
Last amateur club: Chicoutimi Sagueneens (QJHL).
(Montreal's 4th choice, 44th over-all, in 1979 Entry Draft).

			Regular Season					Playoffs				
Season	Club	Lea	GP	G	A	TP	PIM	GP	G	A	TP	PIM
1976-77	Chicoutimi	QJHL	59	9	20	29	8	4	1	0	1	0
1977-78	Chicoutimi	QJHL	70	28	55	83	60	....	....	....	....	....
1978-79	Chicoutimi	QJHL	72	62	79	141	47	4	2	1	3	4
1979-80	Chicoutimi	QJHL	72	72	110	182	66	12	9	15	24	28
	Nova Scotia	AHL	....	....	....	....	....	2	1	1	2	2
1980-81	**Montreal**	**NHL**	**2**	**0**	**1**	**1**	**0**	....	....	....	....	....
	Nova Scotia	AHL	78	35	53	88	87	6	1	3	4	9
1981-82	Nova Scotia	AHL	77	27	67	94	124	9	2	7	9	8
1982-83	**Montreal**	**NHL**	**77**	**18**	**29**	**47**	**68**	**3**	**0**	**0**	**0**	**2**
1983-84	**Montreal**	**NHL**	**78**	**24**	**30**	**54**	**75**	**15**	**4**	**3**	**7**	**12**
1984-85	**Montreal**	**NHL**	**79**	**23**	**34**	**57**	**43**	**12**	**4**	**3**	**7**	**8**
1985-86	**Montreal**	**NHL**	**80**	**20**	**36**	**56**	**57**	**20**	**7**	**5**	**12**	**35**
	NHL Totals		**316**	**85**	**130**	**215**	**243**	**50**	**15**	**11**	**26**	**57**

CARKNER, TERRY

Born, Smiths Falls, Ont., March 7, 1966.
Defense. Shoots left. 6'3", 200 lbs.
Last amateur club: Peterborough Petes (OHL).
(NY Rangers' 1st choice, 14th over-all, in 1984 Entry Draft).

			Regular Season					Playoffs				
Season	Club	Lea	GP	G	A	TP	PIM	GP	G	A	TP	PIM
1982-83	Brockville	OPJHL	47	8	32	40	94	....	....	....	....	....
1983-84	Peterborough	OHL	58	4	19	23	77	8	0	6	6	13
1984-85a	Peterborough	OHL	64	14	47	61	125	17	2	10	12	11
1985-86b	Peterborough	OHL	54	12	32	44	106	16	1	7	8	17

a OHL Second All-Star Team (1985)
b OHL First All-Star Team (1986)

CARLILE, TODD

Born, St. Paul, Minn. January 22, 1964.
Defense. Shoots right. 5'11", 185 lbs.
Last amateur club: University of Michigan Wolverines (CCHA).
(Minnesota's 6th choice, 122nd over-all, in 1982 Entry Draft).

			Regular Season					Playoffs				
Season	Club	Lea	GP	G	A	TP	PIM	GP	G	A	TP	PIM
1982-83	U. of Michigan	CCHA	36	5	14	19	67	....	....	....	....	....
1983-84	U. of Michigan	CCHA	33	11	20	31	70	....	....	....	....	....
1984-85	U. of Michigan	CCHA	38	5	8	13	62	....	....	....	....	....
1985-86	U. of Michigan	CCHA	38	6	20	26	38	....	....	....	....	....

CARLSON, KENT

Born, Concord, New Hampshire, January 11, 1962.
Defense. Shoots left. 6'3", 200 lbs.
Last amateur club: St. Lawrence University Saints (ECAC)
(Montreal's 3rd choice, 32nd over-all, in 1982 Entry Draft).

			Regular Season					Playoffs				
Season	Club	Lea	GP	G	A	TP	PIM	GP	G	A	TP	PIM
1981-82	St. Lawrence	ECAC	28	8	14	22	0	....	....	....	....	....
1982-83	St. Lawrence	ECAC	36	10	23	33	56	....	....	....	....	....
1983-84	**Montreal**	**NHL**	**65**	**3**	**7**	**10**	**73**	....	....	....	....	....
1984-85	**Montreal**	**NHL**	**18**	**1**	**1**	**2**	**33**	....	....	....	....	....
	Sherbrooke	AHL	13	1	4	5	7	2	1	1	2	0
1985-86	**Montreal**	**NHL**	**2**	**0**	**0**	**0**	**0**	....	....	....	....	....
	Sherbrooke	AHL	35	11	15	26	79	....	....	....	....	....
	St. Louis	**NHL**	**26**	**2**	**3**	**5**	**42**	**5**	**0**	**0**	**0**	**11**
	NHL Totals		**111**	**6**	**11**	**17**	**148**	**5**	**0**	**0**	**0**	**11**

Traded to **St. Louis** by **Montreal** for Graham Herring and St. Louis' fifth-round choice (Eric Aubertin) in 1986 Entry Draft, January 31, 1986.

CARLSON, STEVE EDWARD

Born, Virginia, Minn., August 26, 1955.
Center. Shoots right. 6'3", 180 lbs.
Last amateur club: Johnstown Jets (NAHL).
(Detroit's 10th choice, 131st over-all, in 1975 Amateur Draft).

			Regular Season					Playoffs				
Season	Club	Lea	GP	G	A	TP	PIM	GP	G	A	TP	PIM
1974-75	Johnstown	NAHL	70	34	45	79	77	....	....	....	....	....
1975-76	Minnesota	WHA	10	0	1	1	23	....	....	....	....	....
	Johnstown	NAHL	40	22	24	46	55	....	....	....	....	....
1976-77	Minnesota	WHA	21	5	8	13	8	....	....	....	....	....
	New England	WHA	31	4	9	13	40	5	0	0	0	9
1977-78	Springfield	AHL	37	21	15	36	48	....	....	....	....	....
	New England	WHA	38	6	7	13	11	13	2	7	9	2
1978-79	Edmonton	WHA	73	18	22	40	50	11	1	1	2	12
1979-80	**Los Angeles**	**NHL**	**52**	**9**	**12**	**21**	**23**	**4**	**1**	**1**	**2**	**7**
1980-81	Houston	CHL	27	13	21	34	29	....	....	....	....	....
	Springfield	AHL	32	10	14	24	44	7	2	2	4	39
1981-82	Nashville	CHL	59	23	39	62	63	....	....	....	....	....
1982-83	Birmingham	CHL	69	25	42	67	73	9	1	4	5	4
1983-84	Baltimore	AHL	63	9	30	39	70	10	7	3	10	8
1984-85	Baltimore	AHL	76	18	29	47	69	15	2	6	8	4
1985-86	Baltimore	AHL	66	9	27	36	56	....	....	....	....	....
	NHL Totals		**52**	**9**	**12**	**21**	**23**	**4**	**1**	**1**	**2**	**7**
	WHA Totals		173	33	47	80	132	29	3	8	11	23

Rights transferred to **Los Angeles** by **Detroit** for Steve Short, December 6, 1978. Reclaimed by **Los Angeles** from **Edmonton** prior to Expansion Draft, June 9, 1979. Claimed by **Los Angeles** as fill in Expansion Draft, June 13, 1979. Signed as free agent by **Minnesota**, August 9, 1982. Signed as a free agent by **Pittsburgh**, August 15, 1983.

CARLSSON, ANDERS

Born, Gavle, Sweden, November 25, 1960.
Center. Shoots left. 5'11", 185 lbs.
Last amateur club: Sodertalje (Sweden).
(New Jersey's 5th choice, 66th over-all, in 1986 Entry Draft).

			Regular Season					Playoffs				
Season	Club	Lea	GP	G	A	TP	PIM	GP	G	A	TP	PIM
1985-86	Sodertalje	Swe.	36	12	26	38	20	....	....	....	....	....

CARLYLE, RANDY ROBERT

Born, Sudbury, Ont., April 19, 1956.
Defense. Shoots left. 5'10", 200 lbs.
Last amateur club: Sudbury Wolves (OHA).
(Toronto's 1st choice, 30th over-all, in 1976 Amateur Draft).

			Regular Season					Playoffs				
Season	Club	Lea	GP	G	A	TP	PIM	GP	G	A	TP	PIM
1974-75	Sudbury	OHA	67	17	47	64	118	15	3	6	9	21
1975-76a	Sudbury	OHA	60	15	64	79	126	17	6	13	19	50
1976-77	Dallas	CHL	26	2	7	9	63	....	....	....	....	....
	Toronto	**NHL**	**45**	**0**	**5**	**5**	**51**	**9**	**0**	**1**	**1**	**20**
1977-78	Dallas	CHL	21	3	14	17	31	....	....	....	....	....
	Toronto	**NHL**	**49**	**2**	**11**	**13**	**31**	**7**	**0**	**1**	**1**	**8**
1978-79	**Pittsburgh**	**NHL**	**70**	**13**	**34**	**47**	**78**	**7**	**0**	**0**	**0**	**12**
1979-80	**Pittsburgh**	**NHL**	**67**	**8**	**28**	**36**	**45**	**5**	**1**	**0**	**1**	**4**
1980-81bc	**Pittsburgh**	**NHL**	**76**	**16**	**67**	**83**	**136**	**5**	**4**	**5**	**9**	**9**
1981-82	**Pittsburgh**	**NHL**	**73**	**11**	**64**	**75**	**131**	**5**	**1**	**3**	**4**	**16**
1982-83	**Pittsburgh**	**NHL**	**61**	**15**	**41**	**56**	**110**	....	....	....	....	....
1983-84	**Pittsburgh**	**NHL**	**50**	**3**	**23**	**26**	**82**	....	....	....	....	....
	Winnipeg	**NHL**	**5**	**0**	**3**	**3**	**2**	**3**	**0**	**2**	**2**	**4**
1984-85	**Winnipeg**	**NHL**	**71**	**13**	**38**	**51**	**98**	**8**	**1**	**5**	**6**	**13**
1985-86	**Winnipeg**	**NHL**	**68**	**16**	**33**	**49**	**93**	....	....	....	....	....
	NHL Totals		**635**	**97**	**347**	**444**	**857**	**49**	**7**	**17**	**24**	**86**

a OHA Second All-Star Team (1976)
b Won James Norris Memorial Trophy (1981)
c NHL First All-Star Team (1981)

Traded to **Pittsburgh** by **Toronto** with George Ferguson for Dave Burrows, June 14, 1978. Traded to **Winnipeg** by **Pittsburgh** for Winnipeg's first round choice (Doug Bodger) in 1984 Entry Draft and future considerations (Moe Mantha), March 5, 1984.

CARNELLEY, TODD

Born, St. Albert, Alta., September 18, 1966.
Defense. Shoots right. 5'11", 195 lbs.
Last amateur club: Kamloops Blazers (WHL).
(Edmonton's 2nd choice, 41st over-all, in 1985 Entry Draft).

			Regular Season					Playoffs				
Season	Club	Lea	GP	G	A	TP	PIM	GP	G	A	TP	PIM
1983-84	Kamloops	WHL	70	7	23	30	66	17	0	6	6	4
1984-85a	Kamloops	WHL	56	18	29	47	69	15	8	19	27	19
1985-86	Kamloops	WHL	44	3	23	26	63	16	3	6	9	20

a WHL First All-Star Team, West Division (1985)

CARPENTER, ROBERT (BOB)

Born, Beverly, Mass., July 13, 1963.
Center. Shoots left. 6', 190 lbs.
Last amateur club: St. John's High School (Mass.).
(Washington's 1st choice, 3rd over-all, in 1981 Entry Draft).

			Regular Season					Playoffs				
Season	Club	Lea	GP	G	A	TP	PIM	GP	G	A	TP	PIM
1980-81	St. John's	HS	18	14	24	38	....	....	....	....	....	....
1981-82	**Washington**	**NHL**	**80**	**32**	**35**	**67**	**69**	....	....	....	....	....
1982-83	**Washington**	**NHL**	**80**	**32**	**37**	**69**	**64**	**4**	**1**	**0**	**1**	**2**
1983-84	**Washington**	**NHL**	**80**	**28**	**40**	**68**	**51**	**8**	**2**	**1**	**3**	**25**
1984-85	**Washington**	**NHL**	**80**	**53**	**42**	**95**	**87**	**5**	**1**	**4**	**5**	**8**
1985-86	**Washington**	**NHL**	**80**	**27**	**29**	**56**	**105**	**9**	**5**	**4**	**9**	**12**
	NHL Totals		**400**	**172**	**183**	**355**	**376**	**26**	**9**	**9**	**18**	**47**

CARROLL, WILLIAM ALLAN (BILLY)

Born, Toronto, Ont., January 19, 1959.
Center. Shoots left. 5'10", 190 lbs.
Last amateur club: London Knights (OHA).
(NY Islanders' 3rd choice, 38th over-all, in 1979 Entry Draft).

			Regular Season					Playoffs				
Season	Club	Lea	GP	G	A	TP	PIM	GP	G	A	TP	PIM
1977-78	London	OHA	68	37	46	73	42	11	3	6	9	6
1978-79a	London	OHA	63	35	50	85	38	7	1	5	6	14
1979-80	Indianapolis	CHL	49	9	17	26	19	7	0	1	1	0
1980-81	Indianapolis	CHL	59	27	37	64	67	....	....	....	....	....
	NY Islanders	**NHL**	**18**	**4**	**4**	**8**	**6**	**18**	**3**	**9**	**12**	**4**
1981-82	**NY Islanders**	**NHL**	**72**	**9**	**20**	**29**	**32**	**19**	**2**	**2**	**4**	**8**
1982-83	**NY Islanders**	**NHL**	**71**	**1**	**11**	**12**	**24**	**20**	**1**	**1**	**2**	**2**
1983-84	**NY Islanders**	**NHL**	**39**	**5**	**2**	**7**	**12**	**5**	**0**	**0**	**0**	**0**
1984-85	**Edmonton**	**NHL**	**65**	**8**	**9**	**17**	**22**	**9**	**0**	**0**	**0**	**4**
1985-86	**Edmonton**	**NHL**	**5**	**0**	**2**	**2**	**0**	....	....	....	....	....
	Nova Scotia	AHL	26	7	18	25	15	....	....	....	....	....
	Detroit	**NHL**	**21**	**2**	**4**	**6**	**11**	....	....	....	....	....
	NHL Totals		**291**	**29**	**52**	**81**	**107**	**71**	**6**	**12**	**18**	**18**

a OHA Second All-Star Team (1979)

Claimed by **Edmonton** from **NY Islanders** in NHL Waiver Draft, October 9, 1984. Traded to **Detroit** by **Edmonton** for Bruce Eakin, December 28, 1985.

CARSON, JIMMY

Born, Southfield, Mich., July 20, 1968.
Center. Shoots right. 6'0", 185 lbs.
Last amateur club: Verdun Junior Canadiens (QMJHL).
(Los Angeles' 1st choice, 2nd over-all, in 1986 Entry Draft).

			Regular Season					Playoffs				
Season	Club	Lea	GP	G	A	TP	PIM	GP	G	A	TP	PIM
1985-86a	Verdun	QMJHL	69	70	83	153	46	5	2	6	8	0

a QMJHL Second All-Star Team (1986)

CARSON, LINDSAY WARREN

Born, Oxbow, Sask., November 21, 1960.
Center. Shoots left. 6'2", 195 lbs.
Last amateur club: Billings Bighorns (WHL).
(Philadelphia's 4th choice, 56th over-all, in 1979 Entry Draft).

			Regular Season					Playoffs				
Season	Club	Lea	GP	G	A	TP	PIM	GP	G	A	TP	PIM
1978-79	Saskatoon	WHL	37	21	29	50	56	....	....	....	....	....
	Billings	WHL	30	13	22	35	50	....	....	....	....	....
1979-80	Billings	WHL	70	42	66	108	101	....	....	....	....	....
1980-81	Maine	AHL	79	11	25	36	84	20	4	12	16	45
1981-82	**Philadelphia**	**NHL**	**18**	**0**	**1**	**1**	**32**	....	....	....	....	....
	Maine	AHL	54	20	31	51	92	4	0	0	0	12
1982-83	**Philadelphia**	**NHL**	**78**	**18**	**19**	**37**	**67**	**1**	**0**	**0**	**0**	**0**
1983-84	Springfield	AHL	5	2	4	6	5	....	....	....	....	....
	Philadelphia	**NHL**	**16**	**1**	**3**	**4**	**10**	**1**	**0**	**0**	**0**	**5**
1984-85	**Philadelphia**	**NHL**	**77**	**20**	**19**	**39**	**123**	**17**	**0**	**3**	**3**	**24**
1985-86	**Philadelphia**	**NHL**	**50**	**9**	**12**	**21**	**84**	**1**	**0**	**0**	**0**	**5**
	NHL Totals		**239**	**48**	**54**	**102**	**316**	**20**	**0**	**3**	**3**	**34**

CARTER, JOHN

Born, Winchester, Mass., May 3, 1963.
Left wing. Shoots left. 5'10", 175 lbs.
Last amateur club: Rensselaer Polytechnic Institute Engineers (ECAC).

			Regular Season					Playoffs				
Season	Club	Lea	GP	G	A	TP	PIM	GP	G	A	TP	PIM
1982-83	RPI	ECAC	29	16	22	38	33	....	....	....	....	....
1983-84	RPI	ECAC	38	35	39	74	52	....	....	....	....	....
1984-85	RPI	ECAC	37	43	29	72	52	....	....	....	....	....
1985-86	RPI	ECAC	27	23	18	41	68	....	....	....	....	....
	Boston	**NHL**	**3**	**0**	**0**	**0**	**0**	....	....	....	....	....
	NHL Totals		**3**	**0**	**0**	**0**	**0**	....	....	....	....	....

Signed as a free agent by **Boston**, May 3, 1986.

CASSIDY, BRUCE

Born, Ottawa, Ont., May 20, 1965.
Defense. Shoots left. 5'11", 175 lbs.
Last amateur club: Ottawa 67's (OHL).
(Chicago's 1st choice, 18th over-all, in 1983 Entry Draft).

			Regular Season					Playoffs				
Season	Club	Lea	GP	G	A	TP	PIM	GP	G	A	TP	PIM
1981-82	Hawkesbury	COJHL	37	13	30	43	32	....	....	....	....	....
1982-83	Ottawa	OHL	70	25	86	111	33	9	3	9	12	10
1983-84	**Chicago**	**NHL**	**1**	**0**	**0**	**0**	**0**	....	....	....	....	....
a	Ottawa	OHL	67	27	68	95	58	13	6	16	22	6
1984-85	Ottawa	OHL	28	13	27	40	15	....	....	....	....	....
1985-86	**Chicago**	**NHL**	**1**	**0**	**0**	**0**	**0**	....	....	....	....	....
	Nova Scotia	AHL	4	0	0	0	0	....	....	....	....	....
	NHL Totals		**2**	**0**	**0**	**0**	**0**	....	....	....	....	....

a OHL Second All-Star Team (1984).

CAULFIELD, JAY

Born, Philadelphia, Penn., July 17, 1960.
Defense. Shoots right. 6'4", 240 lbs.
Last amateur club: University of North Dakota Fighting Sioux (WCHA).

				Regular Season					Playoffs			
Season	Club	Lea	GP	G	A	TP	PIM	GP	G	A	TP	PIM
1984-85	North Dakota	WCHA	1	0	0	0	0	....	....	....	....	....
1985-86	Toledo	IHL	30	5	4	9	54	....	....	....	....	....
	New Haven	AHL	40	2	3	5	40	1	0	0	0	0

Signed as a free agent by **NY Rangers**, October 8, 1985.

CAVALLINI, GINO JOHN

Born, Toronto, Ont., November 24, 1962.
Left wing. Shoots left. 6'1", 215 lbs.
Last amateur club: Bowling Green State University Falcons (CCHA).

				Regular Season					Playoffs			
Season	Club	Lea	GP	G	A	TP	PIM	GP	G	A	TP	PIM
1982-83	Bowling Green	CCHA	40	8	16	24	52	....	....	....	....	....
1983-84	Bowling Green	CCHA	43	25	23	48	16	....	....	....	....	....
1984-85	**Calgary**	**NHL**	**27**	**6**	**10**	**16**	**14**	**3**	**0**	**0**	**0**	**4**
	Moncton	AHL	51	29	19	48	28	....	....	....	....	....
1985-86	**Calgary**	**NHL**	**27**	**7**	**7**	**14**	**26**	....	....	....	....	....
	Moncton	AHL	4	3	2	5	7	....	....	....	....	....
	St. Louis	**NHL**	**30**	**6**	**5**	**11**	**36**	**17**	**4**	**5**	**9**	**10**
	NHL Totals		**84**	**19**	**22**	**41**	**76**	**20**	**4**	**5**	**9**	**14**

Signed as a free agent by **Calgary**, May 16, 1984. Traded to **St. Louis** by **Calgary** with Eddy Beers and Charles Bourgeois for Joe Mullen, Terry Johnson and Rik Wilson, February 1, 1986.

CAVALLINI, PAUL

Born, Toronto, Ont., October 13, 1965.
Defense. Shoots left. 6'2", 200 lbs.
Last amateur club: Providence College Friars (H.E.).
(Washington's 10th choice, 205th over-all, in 1984 Entry Draft).

				Regular Season					Playoffs			
Season	Club	Lea	GP	G	A	TP	PIM	GP	G	A	TP	PIM
1984-85	Providence	H.E.	37	4	10	14	52	....	....	....	....	....
1985-86	Binghamton	AHL	15	3	4	7	20	6	0	2	2	56
	Cdn. Olympic	....	52	1	11	12	95	....	....	....	....	....

CHABOT, JOHN DAVID   (sha-BAWT)

Born, Summerside, P.E.I., May 18, 1962.
Center. Shoots left. 6'2", 190 lbs.
Last amateur club: Sherbrooke Castors (QJHL).
(Montreal's 3rd choice, 40th over-all, in 1980 Entry Draft).

				Regular Season					Playoffs			
Season	Club	Lea	GP	G	A	TP	PIM	GP	G	A	TP	PIM
1979-80	Hull	QMJHL	68	26	57	83	28	4	1	2	3	0
1980-81	Hull	QMJHL	70	27	62	89	24	....	....	....	....	....
	Nova Scotia	AHL	1	0	0	0	0	2	0	0	0	0
1981-82ab	Sherbrooke	QMJHL	62	34	*109	143	42	19	6	26	32	6
1982-83	Nova Scotia	AHL	76	16	73	89	19	7	1	3	4	0
1983-84	**Montreal**	**NHL**	**56**	**18**	**25**	**43**	**13**	**11**	**1**	**4**	**5**	**0**
1984-85	**Montreal**	**NHL**	**10**	**1**	**6**	**7**	**2**	....	....	....	....	....
	Pittsburgh	**NHL**	**67**	**8**	**45**	**53**	**12**	....	....	....	....	....
1985-86	**Pittsburgh**	**NHL**	**77**	**14**	**31**	**45**	**6**	....	....	....	....	....
	NHL Totals		**210**	**41**	**107**	**148**	**33**	**11**	**1**	**4**	**5**	**0**

a QMJHL First All-Star Team (1982)
b QMJHL Most Valuable Player (1982)

Traded to **Pittsburgh** by **Montreal** for Ron Flockhart, November 9, 1984.

CHANNELL, CRAIG

Born, Moncton, N.B., April 24, 1962.
Defense. Shoots left. 5'11", 190 lbs.
Last amateur club: Seattle Breakers (WHL).

				Regular Season					Playoffs			
Season	Club	Lea	GP	G	A	TP	PIM	GP	G	A	TP	PIM
1979-80	Seattle	WHL	70	3	21	24	191	12	0	0	0	22
1980-81	Seattle	WHL	71	9	66	75	181	5	0	2	2	4
1981-82	Seattle	WHL	71	9	79	88	244	10	0	11	11	22
1982-83	Sherbrooke	AHL	65	0	15	15	109	....	....	....	....	....
1983-84	Sherbrooke	AHL	80	5	18	23	112	....	....	....	....	....
1984-85	Sherbrooke	AHL	1	0	0	0	0	....	....	....	....	....
	Fort Wayne	IHL	78	10	35	45	110	8	0	5	5	33
1985-86	Fort Wayne	IHL	69	7	28	35	116	15	3	12	15	41

Signed as a free agent by **Winnipeg**, November 9, 1981.

CHANNELL, TODD

Born, Naperville, Ont., October 8, 1963.
Right wing. Shoots right, 5'10", 180 lbs.
Last amateur club: University of Miami-Ohio Redskins (CCHA).

				Regular Season					Playoffs			
Season	Club	Lea	GP	G	A	TP	PIM	GP	G	A	TP	PIM
1982-83	Miami-Ohio	CCHA	34	8	18	26	6	....	....	....	....	....
1983-84	Miami-Ohio	CCHA	34	14	14	28	4	....	....	....	....	....
1984-85	Miami-Ohio	CCHA	40	15	32	47	22	....	....	....	....	....
1985-86	Miami-Ohio	CCHA	38	27	27	54	18	....	....	....	....	....

Signed as a free agent by **Hartford**, May, 1986.

CHAPMAN, WALLY

Born, Ft. Leonard Wood, Missouri, July 6, 1964.
Center. Shoots left. 6', 185 lbs.
Last amateur club: University of Minnesota Gophers (WCHA)
(Minnesota's 2nd choice, 59th over-all, in 1982 Entry Draft).

				Regular Season					Playoffs			
Season	Club	Lea	GP	G	A	TP	PIM	GP	G	A	TP	PIM
1981-82	Edina	HS	26	27	11	38	14	....	....	....	....	....
1982-83	U. Minnesota	WCHA	12	2	4	6	14	....	....	....	....	....
1983-84	U. Minnesota	WCHA	30	10	6	16	20	....	....	....	....	....
1984-85	U. Minnesota	WCHA	34	14	9	23	16	....	....	....	....	....
1985-86	U. Minnesota	WCHA	47	29	29	58	35	....	....	....	....	....

CHARBONNEAU, JOSE

Born, Ferme-Neuve, Que., November 21, 1966.
Right wing. Shoots right. 6', 195 lbs.
Last amateur club: Drummondville Voltigeurs (QMJHL).
(Montreal's 1st choice, 12th over-all, in 1985 Entry Draft).

				Regular Season					Playoffs			
Season	Club	Lea	GP	G	A	TP	PIM	GP	G	A	TP	PIM
1983-84	Drummondville	QMJHL	65	31	59	90	110	....	....	....	....	....
1984-85	Drummondville	QMJHL	46	34	40	74	91	12	5	10	15	20
1985-86	Drummondville	QMJHL	57	44	45	89	158	23	16	20	36	40

CHARLESWORTH, TODD

Born, Calgary, Alta., March 22, 1965.
Defense. Shoots left. 6'1", 185 lbs.
Last amateur club: Oshawa Generals (OHL).
(Pittsburgh's 2nd choice, 22nd over-all, in 1983 Entry Draft).

				Regular Season					Playoffs			
Season	Club	Lea	GP	G	A	TP	PIM	GP	G	A	TP	PIM
1981-82	Gloucester	COJHL	50	13	24	37	67	....	....	....	....	....
1982-83	Oshawa	OHL	70	6	23	29	55	17	0	4	4	20
1983-84	**Pittsburgh**	**NHL**	**10**	**0**	**0**	**0**	**8**	....	....	....	....	....
	Oshawa	OHL	57	11	35	46	54	7	0	4	4	4
1984-85	**Pittsburgh**	**NHL**	**67**	**1**	**8**	**9**	**31**	....	....	....	....	....
1985-86	**Pittsburgh**	**NHL**	**2**	**0**	**1**	**1**	**0**	....	....	....	....	....
	Baltimore	AHL	19	1	3	4	10	....	....	....	....	....
	Muskegon	IHL	51	9	27	36	78	14	3	8	11	14
	NHL Totals		**79**	**1**	**9**	**10**	**39**	....	....	....	....	....

CHAULK, LANDIS

Born, Swift Current, Sask., May 17, 1966.
Left wing. Shoots left. 6'1", 200 lbs.
Last amateur club: Lethbridge Broncos (WHL).
(Vancouver's 4th choice, 55th over-all, in 1984 Entry Draft).

				Regular Season					Playoffs			
Season	Club	Lea	GP	G	A	TP	PIM	GP	G	A	TP	PIM
1983-84	Calgary	WHL	72	21	28	49	123	4	3	1	4	12
1984-85	Calgary	WHL	65	25	40	65	174	8	1	4	5	16
1985-86	Lethbridge	WHL	44	8	10	18	79	....	....	....	....	....

CHELIOS, CHRIS   (CHELL-EE-ohs)

Born, Chicago, Illinois, January 25, 1962.
Defense. Shoots right. 6'1", 200 lbs.
Last amateur club: United States Olympic Team
(Montreal's 5th choice, 40th over-all, in 1981 Entry Draft).

				Regular Season					Playoffs			
Season	Club	Lea	GP	G	A	TP	PIM	GP	G	A	TP	PIM
1980-81	Moose Jaw	SJHL	54	23	64	87	175	....	....	....	....	....
1981-82	U. of Wisconsin	WCHA	43	6	43	49	50	....	....	....	....	....
1982-83ab	U. of Wisconsin	WCHA	26	9	17	26	50	....	....	....	....	....
1983-84	U.S. National	...	60	14	35	49	58	....	....	....	....	....
	U.S. Olympic	...	6	0	4	4	8	....	....	....	....	....
	Montreal	**NHL**	**12**	**0**	**2**	**2**	**12**	**15**	**1**	**9**	**10**	**17**
1984-85c	**Montreal**	**NHL**	**74**	**9**	**55**	**64**	**87**	**9**	**2**	**8**	**10**	**17**
1985-86	**Montreal**	**NHL**	**41**	**8**	**26**	**34**	**67**	**20**	**2**	**9**	**11**	**49**
	NHL Totals		**127**	**17**	**83**	**100**	**166**	**44**	**5**	**26**	**31**	**83**

a WCHA Second All-Star Team (1983)
b NCAA All-Tournament Team (1983)
c NHL All-Rookie Team (1985)

CHERNOMAZ, RICHARD (RICH)   (CHAIR-noh-maz)

Born, Selkirk, Man., September 1, 1963.
Right wing. Shoots right. 5'9", 175 lbs.
Last amateur club: Victoria Cougars (WHL).
(Colorado's 2nd choice, 26th over-all, in 1981 Entry Draft).

				Regular Season					Playoffs			
Season	Club	Lea	GP	G	A	TP	PIM	GP	G	A	TP	PIM
1980-81	Victoria	WHL	72	49	64	113	92	15	11	15	26	38
1981-82	**Colorado**	**NHL**	**2**	**0**	**0**	**0**	**0**	....	....	....	....	....
	Victoria	WHL	49	36	62	98	69	4	1	2	3	13
1982-83a	Victoria	WHL	64	71	53	124	113	12	10	5	15	18
1983-84	**New Jersey**	**NHL**	**7**	**2**	**1**	**3**	**2**	....	....	....	....	....
	Maine	AHL	69	17	29	46	39	2	0	1	1	0
1984-85	**New Jersey**	**NHL**	**3**	**0**	**2**	**2**	**2**	....	....	....	....	....
	Maine	AHL	64	17	34	51	64	10	2	2	4	4
1985-86	Maine	AHL	78	21	28	49	82	5	0	0	0	2
	NHL Totals		**12**	**2**	**3**	**5**	**4**	....	....	....	....	....

a WHL First All-Star Team (1983)

CHIASSON, STEVE

Born, Barrie, Ont., April 14, 1967.
Defense. Shoots left. 6′1″, 205 lbs.
Last amateur club: Guelph Platers (OHL).
(Detroit's 3rd choice, 50th over-all, in 1985 Entry Draft).

Season	Club	Lea	Regular Season					Playoffs				
			GP	G	A	TP	PIM	GP	G	A	TP	PIM
1984-85	Guelph	OHL	61	8	22	30	139	....	....	....	....	....
1985-86	Guelph	OHL	54	12	30	42	126	18	10	10	20	37

CHIATTO, CHARLES

Born, Pittsburgh, Penn., September 24, 1964.
Center. Shoots left. 5′8″, 160 lbs.
Last amateur club: Western Michigan University Broncos (CCHA).
(Detroit's 12th choice, 235th over-all, in 1983 Entry Draft).

Season	Club	Lea	Regular Season					Playoffs				
			GP	G	A	TP	PIM	GP	G	A	TP	PIM
1983-84	W. Michigan	CCHA	23	4	9	13	4	....	....	....	....	....
1984-85	W. Michigan	CCHA	32	6	7	13	24	....	....	....	....	....
1985-86	W. Michigan	CCHA	31	4	10	14	12	....	....	....	....	....

CHISHOLM, COLIN

Born, Edmonton, Alta., February 25, 1963.
Defense. Shoots right. 6′2″, 185 lbs.
Last amateur club: University of Alberta Golden Bears (CWUAA)
(Buffalo's 4th choice, 60th over-all, in 1981 Entry Draft).

Season	Club	Lea	Regular Season					Playoffs				
			GP	G	A	TP	PIM	GP	G	A	TP	PIM
1980-81	Calgary	WHL	70	0	18	18	156	22	2	3	5	34
1981-82	Calgary	WHL	70	1	15	16	150	9	0	3	3	24
1982-83	U. of Alberta	CWUAA	17	1	3	4	38	....	....	....	....	....
1983-84	U. of Alberta	CWUAA	24	8	14	22	12	....	....	....	....	....
1984-85	U. of Alberta	CWUAA	24	2	33	25	100	....	....	....	....	....
1985-86	DID NOT PLAY											

Signed as a free agent by **Minnesota**, June 11, 1986.

CHORSKE, TOM

Born, Minneapolis, Minn., September 18, 1966.
Left wing. Shoots right. 6′1″, 185 lbs.
Last amateur club: University of Minnesota Gophers (WCHA).
(Montreal's 2nd choice, 16th over-all, in 1985 Entry Draft).

Season	Club	Lea	Regular Season					Playoffs				
			GP	G	A	TP	PIM	GP	G	A	TP	PIM
1984-85	Mpls. S.W.	HS	23	44	26	70	24	....	....	....	....	....
1985-86	U. Minnesota	WCHA	39	6	4	10	16	....	....	....	....	....

CHREST, BLAINE

Born, Gainsborough, Sask., January 10, 1966.
Center. Shoots left. 5′11″, 175 lbs.
Last amateur club: Portland Winterhawks (WHL).
(Vancouver's 9th choice, 136th over-all, in 1984 Entry Draft).

Season	Club	Lea	Regular Season					Playoffs				
			GP	G	A	TP	PIM	GP	G	A	TP	PIM
1983-84	Portland	WHL	12	5	4	9	2	14	6	9	15	0
1984-85	Portland	WHL	68	27	39	66	13	6	2	5	7	2
1985-86	Portland	WHL	71	29	57	86	7	8	4	4	8	0

CHRISTENSEN, MATTHEW (MATT)

Born, Aurora, Minn., June 6, 1964.
Center. Shoots left. 6′, 180 lbs.
Last amateur club: University of Minnesota-Duluth Bulldogs (WCHA).
(St. Louis' 6th choice, 176th over-all, in 1982 Entry Draft).

Season	Club	Lea	Regular Season					Playoffs				
			GP	G	A	TP	PIM	GP	G	A	TP	PIM
1982-83	Minn.-Duluth	WCHA	45	6	16	22	10	....	....	....	....	....
1983-84	Minn.-Duluth	WCHA	42	24	39	63	16	....	....	....	....	....
1984-85a	Minn.-Duluth	WCHA	44	27	43	70	32	....	....	....	....	....
1985-86b	Minn.-Duluth	WCHA	33	16	41	57	36	....	....	....	....	....

a WCHA Second All-Star Team (1985)
b NCAA West Second All-American Team (1986)

CHRISTIAN, DAVID (DAVE)

Born, Warroad, Minn., May 12, 1959.
Center. Shoots right. 5′11″, 180 lbs.
Last amateur club: 1980 United States Olympic Team.
(Winnipeg's 2nd choice, 40th over-all, in 1979 Entry Draft).

Season	Club	Lea	Regular Season					Playoffs				
			GP	G	A	TP	PIM	GP	G	A	TP	PIM
1977-78	North Dakota	WCHA	38	8	16	24	14	....	....	....	....	....
1978-79	North Dakota	WCHA	40	22	24	46	22	....	....	....	....	....
1979-80	U.S. National	...	59	10	20	30	26	....	....	....	....	....
	U.S. Olympic	...	7	0	8	8	6	....	....	....	....	....
	Winnipeg	NHL	15	8	10	18	2	....	....	....	....	....
1980-81	**Winnipeg**	NHL	80	28	43	71	22	....	....	....	....	....
1981-82	**Winnipeg**	NHL	80	25	51	76	28	4	0	1	1	2
1982-83	**Winnipeg**	NHL	55	18	26	44	23	3	0	0	0	0
1983-84	**Washington**	NHL	80	29	52	81	28	8	5	4	9	5
1984-85	**Washington**	NHL	80	26	43	69	14	5	1	1	2	0
1985-86	**Washington**	NHL	80	41	42	83	15	9	4	4	8	0
	NHL Totals		470	175	267	442	132	29	10	10	20	7

Traded to **Washington** by **Winnipeg** for Washington's first round choice (Bob Dollas) in the 1983 Entry Draft, June 8, 1983.

CHURLA, SHANE

Born, Fernie, B.C., June 24, 1965.
Right wing. Shoots right. 6′1″, 200 lbs.
Last amateur club: Medicine Hat Tigers (WHL).
(Hartford's 4th choice, 110th over-all, in 1985 Entry Draft).

Season	Club	Lea	Regular Season					Playoffs				
			GP	G	A	TP	PIM	GP	G	A	TP	PIM
1983-84	Medicine Hat	WHL	48	3	7	10	115	14	1	5	6	41
1984-85	Medicine Hat	WHL	70	14	20	34	370	9	1	0	1	55
1985-86	Binghamton	AHL	52	4	10	14	306	3	0	0	0	22

CHYCHRUN, JEFF   (CHICK-run)

Born, LaSalle, Que., May 3, 1966.
Defense. Shoots right. 6′4″, 186 lbs.
Last amateur club: Kingston Canadians (OHL).
(Philadelphia's 3rd choice, 37th over-all, in 1984 Entry Draft).

Season	Club	Lea	Regular Season					Playoffs				
			GP	G	A	TP	PIM	GP	G	A	TP	PIM
1982-83	Nepean	COJHL	44	3	10	13	59	....	....	....	....	....
1983-84	Kingston	OHL	63	1	13	14	137	....	....	....	....	....
1984-85	Kingston	OHL	58	4	10	14	206	....	....	....	....	....
1985-86	Kingston	OHL	61	4	21	25	127	10	2	1	3	17
	Hershey	AHL	....	....	....	....	....	4	0	1	1	9
	Kalamazoo	IHL	....	....	....	....	....	3	1	0	1	0

CICCARELLI, DINO   (siss-ah-RELL-ee)

Born, Sarnia, Ont., February 8, 1960.
Right wing. Shoots right. 5′10″, 180 lbs.
Last amateur club: London Knights (OHA).

Season	Club	Lea	Regular Season					Playoffs				
			GP	G	A	TP	PIM	GP	G	A	TP	PIM
1977-78a	London	OHA	68	72	70	142	49	9	6	10	16	6
1978-79	London	OHA	30	8	11	19	35	7	3	5	8	0
1979-80	London	OHA	62	50	53	103	72	5	2	6	8	15
1980-81	Oklahoma City	CHL	48	32	25	57	45	....	....	....	....	....
	Minnesota	NHL	32	18	12	30	29	19	14	7	21	25
1981-82	**Minnesota**	NHL	76	55	51	106	138	4	3	1	4	2
1982-83	**Minnesota**	NHL	77	37	38	75	94	9	4	6	10	11
1983-84	**Minnesota**	NHL	79	38	33	71	58	16	4	5	9	27
1984-85	**Minnesota**	NHL	51	15	17	32	41	9	3	3	6	8
1985-86	**Minnesota**	NHL	75	44	45	89	51	5	0	1	1	6
	NHL Totals		390	207	196	403	411	62	28	23	51	79

a OHA Second All-Star Team (1978)
Signed as free agent by **Minnesota**, September 28, 1979.

CICHOCKI, CHRIS   (cha-HOCKEY)

Born, Detroit, Mich., September 17, 1963.
Right wing. Shoots right. 5′10″, 185 lbs.
Last amateur club: Michigan Tech University Huskies (CCHA).

Season	Club	Lea	Regular Season					Playoffs				
			GP	G	A	TP	PIM	GP	G	A	TP	PIM
1982-83	Michigan Tech	CCHA	36	12	10	22	10	....	....	....	....	....
1983-84	Michigan Tech	CCHA	40	25	20	45	36	....	....	....	....	....
1984-85	Michigan Tech	CCHA	40	30	24	54	14	....	....	....	....	....
1985-86	**Detroit**	NHL	59	10	11	21	21	....	....	....	....	....
	Adirondack	AHL	9	4	4	8	6	....	....	....	....	....
	NHL Totals		59	10	11	21	21					

Signed as a free agent by **Detroit**, June 28, 1985.

CIPRICK, TRENT

Born, Russell, Man., July 21, 1967.
Right wing. Shoots right. 6′1″, 175 lbs.
Last amateur club: Brandon Wheat Kings (WHL).
(Los Angeles' 9th choice, 219th over-all, in 1985 Entry Draft).

Season	Club	Lea	Regular Season					Playoffs				
			GP	G	A	TP	PIM	GP	G	A	TP	PIM
1984-85	Brandon	WHL	64	11	11	22	95	....	....	....	....	....
1985-86	Brandon	WHL	52	13	19	32	82	....	....	....	....	....

CIRELLA, JOE   (sir-ELL-ah)

Born, Hamilton, Ont., May 9, 1963.
Defense. Shoots right. 6′3″, 210 lbs.
Last amateur club: Oshawa Generals (OHL).
(Colorado's 1st choice, 5th over-all, in 1981 Entry Draft).

Season	Club	Lea	Regular Season					Playoffs				
			GP	G	A	TP	PIM	GP	G	A	TP	PIM
1980-81	Oshawa	OHA	56	5	31	36	220	11	0	2	2	41
1981-82	**Colorado**	NHL	65	7	12	19	52	....	....	....	....	....
	Oshawa	OHL	3	0	1	1	0	11	7	10	17	32
1982-83	**New Jersey**	NHL	2	0	1	1	4	....	....	....	....	....
a	Oshawa	OHL	56	13	55	68	110	17	4	16	20	37
1983-84	**New Jersey**	NHL	79	11	33	44	137	....	....	....	....	....
1984-85	**New Jersey**	NHL	66	6	18	24	143	....	....	....	....	....
1985-86	**New Jersey**	NHL	66	6	23	29	147	....	....	....	....	....
	NHL Totals		278	30	87	117	483	....	....	....	....	....

a OHL First All-Star Team (1983).

CLARINGBULL, MIKE

Born, St. Lawrence, Nfld., November 29, 1966.
Defense. Shoots right. 6'0", 185 lbs.
Last amateur club: Medicine Hat Tigers (WHL).
(Montreal's 10th choice, 163rd over-all, in 1985 Entry Draft).

Season	Club	Lea	Regular Season					Playoffs				
			GP	G	A	TP	PIM	GP	G	A	TP	PIM
1984-85	Medicine Hat	WHL	68	5	13	18	178	9	0	0	0	23
1985-86	Medicine Hat	WHL	69	2	15	17	123	24	1	8	9	65

CLARK, WENDEL

Born, Kelvington, Sask., October 25, 1966.
Left Wing. Shoots left. 5'11", 190 lbs.
Last amateur club: Saskatoon Blades (WHL).
(Toronto's 1st choice, 1st over-all, in 1985 Entry Draft).

Season	Club	Lea	Regular Season					Playoffs				
			GP	G	A	TP	PIM	GP	G	A	TP	PIM
1983-84	Saskatoon	WHL	72	23	45	68	225	....	....	....	....	....
1984-85a	Saskatoon	WHL	64	32	55	87	253	3	3	3	6	7
1985-86b	**Toronto**	**NHL**	66	34	11	45	227	10	5	1	6	47
	NHL Totals		66	34	11	45	227	10	5	1	6	47

a WHL First All-Star Team, East Division (1985).
b NHL All-Rookie Team (1986).

CLARKE, DOUG

Born, Toronto, Ont., February 29, 1964.
Defense. Shoots left. 6'0", 190 lbs.
Last amateur club: Canadian Olympic Team.
(Vancouver's 13th choice, 219th over-all, in 1984 Entry Draft).

Season	Club	Lea	Regular Season					Playoffs				
			GP	G	A	TP	PIM	GP	G	A	TP	PIM
1983-84	Colorado	WCHA	33	5	25	30	62	....	....	....	....	....
1984-85	Colorado	WCHA	37	12	36	48	77	....	....	....	....	....
1985-86	Cdn. Olympic	....	72	7	7	14	38	....	....	....	....	....

CLAVITER, WILLIAM (BILL)

Born, Virginia, Minn., March 24, 1965
Left-wing. Shoots left. 6'1", 175 lbs.
Last amateur club: University of North Dakota Fighting Sioux (WCHA)
(Calgary's 6th choice, 79th over-all, in 1983 Entry Draft).

Season	Club	Lea	Regular Season					Playoffs				
			GP	G	A	TP	PIM	GP	G	A	TP	PIM
1983-84	North Dakota	WCHA	18	2	5	7	4	....	....	....	....	....
1984-85	North Dakota	WCHA	34	6	8	14	10	....	....	....	....	....
1985-86	North Dakota	WCHA	35	4	10	14	34	....	....	....	....	....

CLEMENS, KEVIN

Born, McClennan, Alta., February 2, 1967.
Left wing. Shoots left. 5'11", 185 lbs.
Last amateur club: Regina Pats (WHL).
(Pittsburgh's 5th choice, 114th over-all, in 1985 Entry Draft).

Season	Club	Lea	Regular Season					Playoffs				
			GP	G	A	TP	PIM	GP	G	A	TP	PIM
1983-84	Regina	WHL	47	5	8	13	14	10	0	0	0	2
1984-85	Regina	WHL	70	31	16	47	40	8	3	2	5	2
1985-86	Regina	WHL	71	26	32	58	70	9	1	4	5	6

CLEMENT, SEAN

Born, Winnipeg, Man., February 26, 1966.
Defense. Shoots left. 6'2", 185 lbs.
Last amateur club: Michigan State University Spartans (CCHA).
(Winnipeg's 3rd choice, 72nd over-all, in 1984 Entry Draft).

Season	Club	Lea	Regular Season					Playoffs				
			GP	G	A	TP	PIM	GP	G	A	TP	PIM
1984-85	Michigan State	CCHA	44	5	13	18	24	....	....	....	....	....
1985-86	Michigan State	CCHA	40	4	7	11	40	....	....	....	....	....

CLEMENTS, SCOTT

Born, Sudbury, Ont., May 1, 1962.
Defense. Shoots left. 6'1", 205 lbs.
Last amateur club: University of New Brunswick Red Raiders (AUAA).

Season	Club	Lea	Regular Season					Playoffs				
			GP	G	A	TP	PIM	GP	G	A	TP	PIM
1984-85	St. Catharines	AHL	13	1	8	9	19	....	....	....	....	....
1985-86	St. Catharines	AHL	53	1	10	11	43	....	....	....	....	....
	Fredericton	AHL	20	0	2	2	4	6	1	2	3	2

Signed as a free agent by **Toronto**, May 24, 1985.

CLOUSTON, SEAN

Born, Viking, Alta., April 28, 1968.
Right wing. Shoots left. 6'0", 210 lbs.
Last amateur club: University of Alberta Golden Bears (CWUAA).
(NY Rangers' 3rd choice, 53rd over-all, in 1986 Entry Draft).

Season	Club	Lea	Regular Season					Playoffs				
			GP	G	A	TP	PIM	GP	G	A	TP	PIM
1985-86	Alberta	CWUAA	25	10	9	19	59	....	....	....	....	....

CLOUTIER, REJEAN

(KLOO-tee-ay, RAY-shahn)

Born, Windsor, Que., February 15, 1960.
Defense. Shoots left. 6'1", 185 lbs.
Last amateur club: Sherbrooke Beavers (QJHL).

Season	Club	Lea	Regular Season					Playoffs				
			GP	G	A	TP	PIM	GP	G	A	TP	PIM
1978-79	Sherbrooke	QJHL	70	6	31	37	93	12	2	11	13	13
1979-80	**Detroit**	**NHL**	3	0	1	1	0	....	....	....	....	....
	Sherbrooke	QJHL	65	11	57	68	163	15	3	11	14	44
1980-81	Adirondack	AHL	76	7	30	37	193	15	1	2	3	27
1981-82	**Detroit**	**NHL**	2	0	1	1	2	....	....	....	....	....
	Adirondack	AHL	64	11	27	38	140	5	0	2	2	6
1982-83	Adirondack	AHL	80	13	44	57	137	6	2	3	5	15
1983-84	Adirondack	AHL	77	9	30	39	208	7	2	4	6	9
1984-85	Adirondack	AHL	3	0	0	0	2	....	....	....	....	....
	Nova Scotia	AHL	72	8	19	27	152	6	1	1	2	14
1985-86	Sherbrooke	AHL	67	7	23	30	142	....	....	....	....	....
	Saginaw	IHL	2	0	0	0	4	....	....	....	....	....
	NHL Totals		5	0	2	2	2					

Signed as free agent by **Detroit**, October 30, 1979. Traded to **Edmonton** by **Detroit**, for Todd Bidner, October 17, 1984.

COCHRANE, GLEN MACLEOD

Born, Cranbrook, B.C., January 29, 1958.
Defense. Shoots left. 6'2", 205 lbs.
Last amateur club: Victoria Cougars (WHL).
(Philadelphia's 6th choice, 50th over-all, in 1978 Amateur Draft).

Season	Club	Lea	Regular Season					Playoffs				
			GP	G	A	TP	PIM	GP	G	A	TP	PIM
1976-77	Calgary	WHL	35	1	5	6	105	....	....	....	....	....
	Victoria	WHL	36	1	7	8	60	4	0	0	0	31
1977-78	Victoria	WHL	72	7	40	47	311	13	1	5	6	51
1978-79	**Philadelphia**	**NHL**	1	0	0	0	0	....	....	....	....	....
	Maine	AHL	76	1	22	23	320	10	3	4	7	24
1979-80	Maine	AHL	77	1	11	12	269	8	2	0	2	83
1980-81	Maine	AHL	38	4	13	17	201	....	....	....	....	....
	Philadelphia	**NHL**	31	1	8	9	219	6	1	1	2	18
1981-82	**Philadelphia**	**NHL**	63	6	12	18	329	2	0	0	0	2
1982-83	**Philadelphia**	**NHL**	77	2	22	24	237	3	0	0	0	4
1983-84	**Philadelphia**	**NHL**	67	7	16	23	225	....	....	....	....	....
1984-85	**Philadelphia**	**NHL**	18	0	3	3	100	....	....	....	....	....
	Hershey	AHL	9	0	8	8	35	....	....	....	....	....
1985-86	**Vancouver**	**NHL**	49	0	3	3	125	2	0	0	0	5
	NHL Totals		306	16	64	80	1235	13	1	1	2	29

Traded to **Vancouver** by **Philadelphia** for Vancouver's third round choice in 1986 Entry Draft, March 12, 1985.

COFFEY, PAUL DOUGLAS

Born, Weston, Ont., June 1, 1961.
Defense. Shoots left. 6'1", 205 lbs.
Last amateur club: Kitchener Rangers (OHA).
(Edmonton's 1st choice, 6th over-all, in the 1980 Entry Draft).

Season	Club	Lea	Regular Season					Playoffs				
			GP	G	A	TP	PIM	GP	G	A	TP	PIM
1978-79a	S. S. Marie	OHA	68	17	72	89	103	....	....	....	....	....
1979-80b	S. S. Marie	OHA	23	10	21	31	63	....	....	....	....	....
	Kitchener	OHA	52	19	52	71	130	....	....	....	....	....
1980-81	**Edmonton**	**NHL**	74	9	23	32	130	9	4	3	7	22
1981-82c	**Edmonton**	**NHL**	80	29	60	89	106	5	1	1	2	6
1982-83c	**Edmonton**	**NHL**	80	29	67	96	87	16	7	7	14	14
1983-84c	**Edmonton**	**NHL**	80	40	86	126	104	19	8	14	22	21
1984-85de	**Edmonton**	**NHL**	80	37	84	121	97	18	12	25	37	44
1985-86de	**Edmonton**	**NHL**	79	48	90	138	120	10	1	9	10	30
	NHL Totals		473	192	410	602	644	77	33	59	92	137

a OHA Third All-Star Team (1979)
b OHA Second All-Star Team (1980)
c NHL Second All-Star Team (1982, 1983, 1984).
d Won James Norris Memorial Trophy (1985, 1986)
e NHL First All-Star Team (1985, 1986)

COLE, DANTON

Born, Pontiac, Mich., January 10, 1967.
Right wing. Shoots right. 5'10", 180 lbs.
Last amateur club: Michigan State University Spartans (CCHA).
(Winnipeg's 6th choice, 123rd over-all, in 1985 Entry Draft).

Season	Club	Lea	Regular Season					Playoffs				
			GP	G	A	TP	PIM	GP	G	A	TP	PIM
1985-86	Michigan St.	CCHA	43	11	10	21	22	....	....	....	....	....

CONACHER, PATRICK JOHN (PAT)

Born, Edmonton, Alta., May 1, 1959.
Center. Shoots left. 5'8", 185 lbs.
Last amateur club: Saskatoon Blades (WHL).
(NY Rangers' 4th choice, 76th over-all, in 1979 Entry Draft).

Season	Club	Lea	Regular Season					Playoffs				
			GP	G	A	TP	PIM	GP	G	A	TP	PIM
1977-78	Billings	WHL	72	31	44	75	105	20	15	14	29	22
1978-79	Billings	WHL	39	25	37	62	50	....	....	....	....	....
	Saskatoon	WHL	33	15	32	47	37	....	....	....	....	....
1979-80	New Haven	AHL	53	11	14	25	43	7	1	1	2	4
	NY Rangers	**NHL**	17	0	5	5	4	3	0	1	1	2
1980-81	DID NOT PLAY											
1981-82	Springfield	AHL	77	23	22	45	38	....	....	....	....	....
1982-83	**NY Rangers**	**NHL**	5	0	1	1	4	....	....	....	....	....
	Tulsa	CHL	63	29	28	57	44	....	....	....	....	....
1983-84	Moncton	AHL	28	7	16	23	30	....	....	....	....	....
	Edmonton	**NHL**	45	2	8	10	31	3	1	0	1	2
1984-85	Nova Scotia	AHL	68	20	45	65	44	6	3	2	5	0
1985-86	**New Jersey**	**NHL**	2	0	2	2	2	....	....	....	....	....
	Maine	AHL	69	15	30	45	83	5	1	1	2	11
	NHL Totals		69	2	16	18	41	6	1	1	2	4

Signed as free agent by **Edmonton**, October 4, 1983. Signed as a free agent by **New Jersey**, August 14, 1985.

COPELAND, TODD

Born, Ridgewood, NJ, May 18, 1967.
Defense. Shoots left. 6'2", 210 lbs.
Last amateur club: Belmont-Hill (HS).
(New Jersey's 2nd choice, 24th over-all, in 1986 Entry Draft).

Season	Club	Lea	Regular Season					Playoffs				
			GP	G	A	TP	PIM	GP	G	A	TP	PIM
1984-85	Belmont-Hill	HS	23	8	25	33	18	....	....	....	....	....
1985-86	Belmont-Hill	HS	19	4	19	23	19	....	....	....	....	....

CORKUM, BOB

Born, Salisbury, Mass., December 18, 1967.
Right wing. Shoots right. 6'2", 195 lbs.
Last amateur club: University of Maine Black Bears (H.E.).
(Buffalo's 3rd choice, 57th over-all, in 1986 Entry Draft).

Season	Club	Lea	Regular Season					Playoffs				
			GP	G	A	TP	PIM	GP	G	A	TP	PIM
1984-85	Triton Regional	HS	18	35	36	71	....	....	....	....	....	....
1985-86	Maine	H.E.	39	7	26	33	53	....	....	....	....	....

CORNELIUS, JEFF

Born, Kingston, Ont. February 28, 1966.
Defense. Shoots left. 6'1", 185 lbs.
Last amateur club: Kingston Canadians (OHL).
(Boston's 3rd choice, 61st over-all, in 1984 Entry Draft).

Season	Club	Lea	Regular Season					Playoffs				
			GP	G	A	TP	PIM	GP	G	A	TP	PIM
1983-84	Toronto	OHL	64	2	14	16	117	9	0	2	2	28
1984-85	Toronto	OHL	24	1	5	6	74	....	....	....	....	....
	Kingston	OHL	29	1	4	5	49	....	....	....	....	....
1985-86	Kingston	OHL	59	2	17	19	143	10	1	5	6	22

CORRIVEAU, YVON

Born, Welland, Ont., February 8, 1967.
Left wing. Shoots left. 6'1", 195 lbs.
Last amateur club: Toronto Marlboros (OHL).
(Washington's 1st choice, 19th over-all, in 1985 Entry Draft).

Season	Club	Lea	Regular Season					Playoffs				
			GP	G	A	TP	PIM	GP	G	A	TP	PIM
1983-84	Welland	OPJHL	36	16	21	37	51	....	....	....	....	....
1984-85	Toronto	OHL	59	23	28	51	65	3	0	0	0	5
1985-86	**Washington**	**NHL**	2	0	0	0	0	4	0	3	3	2
	Toronto	OHL	59	54	36	90	75	4	1	1	2	0
	NHL Totals		2	0	0	0	0	4	0	3	3	2

CORSON, SHAYNE

Born, Barrie, Ont., August 13, 1966
Center. Shoots left. 6', 175 lbs.
Last amateur club: Hamilton Steelhawks (OHL).
(Montreal's 2nd choice, 8th over-all, in 1984 Entry Draft).

Season	Club	Lea	Regular Season					Playoffs				
			GP	G	A	TP	PIM	GP	G	A	TP	PIM
1982-83	Barrie	OPJHL	23	13	29	42	87	....	....	....	....	....
1983-84	Brantford	OHL	66	25	46	71	165	6	4	1	5	26
1984-85	Hamilton	OHL	54	27	63	90	154	11	3	7	10	19
1985-86	**Montreal**	**NHL**	3	0	0	0	2	....	....	....	....	....
	Hamilton	OHL	47	41	57	98	153	....	....	....	....	....
	NHL Totals		3	0	0	0	2	....	....	....	....	....

COSTELLO, RICHARD (RICH)

Born, Farmington, Mass., June 27, 1963.
Center. Shoots right. 6', 175 lbs.
Last amateur club: 1984 United States National Team.
(Philadelphia's 2nd choice, 37th over-all, in 1981 Entry Draft).

Season	Club	Lea	Regular Season					Playoffs				
			GP	G	A	TP	PIM	GP	G	A	TP	PIM
1981-82	Providence	ECAC	32	11	16	27	39	....	....	....	....	....
1982-83	Providence	ECAC	43	19	26	45	60	....	....	....	....	....
1983-84	U.S. National	...	38	17	19	26	31	....	....	....	....	....
	Toronto	**NHL**	10	2	1	3	2	....	....	....	....	....
	St. Catharines	AHL	20	0	0	0	12	4	1	0	1	0
1984-85	St. Catharines	AHL	80	8	6	14	45	....	....	....	....	....
1985-86	**Toronto**	**NHL**	2	0	1	1	0	....	....	....	....	....
	St. Catharines	AHL	76	18	22	40	87	13	3	6	9	30
	NHL Totals		12	2	2	4	2	....	....	....	....	....

Rights traded to **Toronto** by **Philadelphia** with Philadelphia's second round choice (Peter Ihnacak) in 1982 Entry Draft and future considerations (Ken Strong) for Darryl Sittler, January 20, 1982.

COTA, DARREN

Born, McLellan, Alta., April 7, 1966.
Right wing. Shoots right. 5'11", 195 lbs.
Last amateur club: Medicine Hat Tigers (WHL).
(Quebec's 5th choice, 120th over-all, in 1984 Entry Draft).

Season	Club	Lea	Regular Season					Playoffs				
			GP	G	A	TP	PIM	GP	G	A	TP	PIM
1982-83	Kelowna	WHL	49	5	13	18	141	....	....	....	....	....
1983-84	Kelowna	WHL	66	30	31	61	152	....	....	....	....	....
1984-85	Kelowna	WHL	34	26	20	46	75	....	....	....	....	....
	Medicine Hat	WHL	30	20	18	38	69	6	3	3	6	2
1985-86	Medicine Hat	WHL	59	34	37	71	258	20	8	8	16	52

COTE, ALAIN   (COH-tay)

Born, Matane, Que., May 3, 1957.
Left wing. Shoots left. 5'10", 205 lbs.
Last amateur club: Chicoutimi Sagueneens (QJHL).
(Montreal's 4th choice, 43rd over-all, in 1977 Amateur Draft).

Season	Club	Lea	Regular Season					Playoffs				
			GP	G	A	TP	PIM	GP	G	A	TP	PIM
1975-76	Chicoutimi	QJHL	72	35	49	84	93	5	3	3	6	2
1976-77	Chicoutimi	QJHL	56	42	45	87	86	8	1	5	6	14
1977-78	Hampton	AHL	36	15	17	32	38	....	....	....	....	....
	Quebec	WHA	27	3	5	8	8	11	1	2	3	0
1978-79	Quebec	WHA	79	14	13	27	23	4	0	0	0	2
1979-80	**Quebec**	**NHL**	41	5	11	16	13	....	....	....	....	....
	Syracuse	AHL	6	0	5	5	9	....	....	....	....	....
1980-81	Rochester	AHL	23	1	6	7	14	....	....	....	....	....
	Quebec	**NHL**	51	8	18	26	64	4	0	0	0	6
1981-82	**Quebec**	**NHL**	79	15	16	31	82	16	1	2	3	8
1982-83	**Quebec**	**NHL**	79	12	28	40	45	4	0	3	3	0
1983-84	**Quebec**	**NHL**	77	19	24	43	41	9	0	2	2	17
1984-85	**Quebec**	**NHL**	80	13	22	35	31	18	5	5	10	11
1985-86	**Quebec**	**NHL**	78	13	21	34	29	3	1	0	1	0
	NHL Totals		485	85	140	225	305	54	7	12	19	42
	WHA Totals		106	17	18	35	31	15	1	2	3	2

Reclaimed by **Montreal** from **Quebec** prior to Expansion Draft, June 9, 1979. Claimed by **Quebec** from **Montreal** in Expansion Draft, June 13, 1979.

COTE, ALAIN

Born, Montmagny, Que., April 14, 1967.
Defense. Shoots left. 5'11", 200 lbs.
Last amateur club: Granby Bisons (QMJHL).
(Boston's 1st choice, 31st over-all, in 1985 Entry Draft).

Season	Club	Lea	Regular Season					Playoffs				
			GP	G	A	TP	PIM	GP	G	A	TP	PIM
1983-84	Quebec	QMJHL	60	3	17	20	40	5	1	3	4	8
1984-85	Quebec	QMJHL	68	9	25	34	173	4	0	1	1	12
1985-86	Granby	QMJHL	22	4	12	16	48	....	....	....	....	....
	Boston	**NHL**	32	0	6	6	5	....	....	....	....	....
	NHL Totals		32	0	6	6	5	....	....	....	....	....

COTE, RAYMOND (RAY)   (COH-tay)

Born, Pincher Creek, Alta., May 31, 1961.
Center. Shoots right. 5'11", 170 lbs.
Last amateur club: Calgary Wranglers (WHL).

Season	Club	Lea	Regular Season					Playoffs				
			GP	G	A	TP	PIM	GP	G	A	TP	PIM
1979-80	Calgary	WHL	72	33	34	67	43	....	....	....	....	....
1980-81	Calgary	WHL	70	36	52	88	73	22	10	13	23	11
1981-82	Wichita	CHL	80	20	34	54	83	7	3	2	5	2
1982-83	Moncton	AHL	80	28	63	91	35	....	....	....	....	....
	Edmonton	**NHL**	....	....	....	....	....	14	3	2	5	0
1983-84	**Edmonton**	**NHL**	13	0	0	0	2	....	....	....	....	....
	Moncton	AHL	66	26	36	62	99	....	....	....	....	....
1984-85	**Edmonton**	**NHL**	2	0	0	0	2	....	....	....	....	....
	Nova Scotia	AHL	79	36	43	79	63	6	3	3	6	0
1985-86	Nova Scotia	AHL	20	7	3	10	17	....	....	....	....	....
	Cdn. Olympic	AHL	8	1	3	4	6	....	....	....	....	....
	NHL Totals		15	0	0	0	4	14	3	2	5	0

Signed as a free agent by **Edmonton**, October 6, 1981.

COTE, SYLVAIN

(COH-tay)

Born, Duberger, Que., January 19, 1966.
Defense. Shoots right. 6′, 175 lbs.
Last amateur club: Quebec Remparts (QMJHL).
(Hartford's 1st choice, 11th over-all, in 1984 Entry Draft).

Season	Club	Lea	GP	Regular Season G	A	TP	PIM	GP	Playoffs G	A	TP	PIM
1982-83	Quebec	QMJHL	66	10	24	34	50	....	....	....	....	....
1983-84	Quebec	QMJHL	66	15	50	65	89	5	1	1	2	0
1984-85	**Hartford**	**NHL**	67	3	9	12	17	....	....	....	....	....
1985-86	**Hartford**	**NHL**	2	0	0	0	0	....	....	....	....	....
a	Hull	QMJHL	26	10	33	43	14	13	6	28	34	22
	NHL Totals		69	3	9	12	17	....	....	....	....	....

a QMJHL First All-Star Team (1986).

COULIS, TIM

Born, Kenora, Ont., February 24, 1958.
Left wing. Shoots left. 6′, 200 lbs.
Last amateur club: Hamilton Fincups (OHA).
(Washington's 2nd choice, 18th over-all, in 1978 Amateur Draft).

Season	Club	Lea	GP	Regular Season G	A	TP	PIM	GP	Playoffs G	A	TP	PIM
1976-77	S. S. Marie	OHA	27	13	20	33	114	....	....	....	....	....
	St. Catharines	OHA	28	10	22	32	136	14	4	5	9	20
1977-78	Hamilton	OHA	46	27	25	52	203	11	6	3	9	64
1978-79	DID NOT PLAY											
1979-80	**Washington**	**NHL**	19	1	2	3	27	....	....	....	....	....
	Hershey	AHL	47	6	12	18	138	....	....	....	....	....
1980-81	Dallas	CHL	63	16	15	31	149	6	2	1	3	24
1981-82	Dallas	CHL	68	20	32	52	209	9	5	1	6	92
1982-83	DID NOT PLAY											
1983-84	**Minnesota**	**NHL**	2	0	0	0	4	....	....	....	....	....
	Salt Lake	CHL	63	25	35	60	225	4	1	2	3	35
1984-85	**Minnesota**	**NHL**	7	1	1	2	34	3	1	0	1	2
	Springfield	AHL	52	13	17	30	86	....	....	....	....	....
1985-86	**Minnesota**	**NHL**	19	2	2	4	73	....	....	....	....	....
	Springfield	AHL	13	5	7	12	42	....	....	....	....	....
	NHL Totals		47	4	5	9	138	3	1	0	1	2

Traded to **Toronto** by **Washington** with Robert Picard and Washington's second-round choice (Bob McGill) in the 1980 Entry Draft for Mike Palmateer and Toronto's third-round choice (Torrie Robertson) in 1980 Entry Draft, June 11, 1980. Signed as free agent by **Vancouver**, October 13, 1981. Signed as free agent by **Minnesota**, July 2, 1983.

COULTER, NEAL

Born, London, Ont., January 2, 1963.
Right wing. Shoots right. 6′2″, 180 lbs.
Last amateur club: Toronto Marlboros (OHL).
(NY Islanders' 4th choice, 63rd over-all, in 1981 Entry Draft).

Season	Club	Lea	GP	Regular Season G	A	TP	PIM	GP	Playoffs G	A	TP	PIM
1980-81	Toronto	OHA	19	4	3	7	22	5	0	3	3	0
1981-82	Toronto	OHL	62	14	16	30	79	....	....	....	....	....
1982-83	Toronto	OHL	59	13	37	50	60	4	2	1	3	2
1983-84	Toledo	IHL	5	1	3	4	0	....	....	....	....	....
	Indianapolis	CHL	58	7	10	17	25	4	2	0	2	0
1984-85	Springfield	AHL	2	1	0	1	0	....	....	....	....	....
	Indianapolis	IHL	82	31	26	57	95	7	3	1	4	9
1985-86	**NY Islanders**	**NHL**	16	3	4	7	4	....	....	....	....	....
	Springfield	AHL	60	17	9	26	92	....	....	....	....	....
	NHL Totals		16	3	4	7	4	....	....	....	....	....

COURTEAU, YVES

Born, Montreal, Que., April 25, l964.
Right wing. Shoots left. 6′, 195 lbs.
Last amateur club: Laval Voisins (QMJHL).
(Detroit's 2nd choice, 23rd over-all, in 1982 Entry Draft).

Season	Club	Lea	GP	Regular Season G	A	TP	PIM	GP	Playoffs G	A	TP	PIM
1980-81	Laval	QMJHL	70	24	39	63	80	....	....	....	....	....
1981-82	Laval	QMJHL	64	30	38	68	15	18	14	13	27	28
1982-83	Laval	QMJHL	68	44	78	122	52	12	4	11	15	0
1983-84	Laval	QMJHL	62	45	75	120	52	14	11	16	27	6
1984-85	**Calgary**	**NHL**	14	1	4	5	4	....	....	....	....	....
	Moncton	AHL	59	19	21	40	32	....	....	....	....	....
1985-86	**Calgary**	**NHL**	4	1	1	2	0	1	0	0	0	0
	Moncton	AHL	70	26	22	48	19	10	4	2	6	5
	NHL Totals		18	2	5	7	4	1	0	0	0	0

Rights traded to **Calgary** by **Detroit** for Bobby Francis, December 2, 1982.

COURTNALL, GEOFF

Born, Victoria, B.C., August 18, 1962.
Left wing. Shoots left. 6′, 165 lbs.
Last amateur club: Victoria Cougars (WHL).

Season	Club	Lea	GP	Regular Season G	A	TP	PIM	GP	Playoffs G	A	TP	PIM
1980-81	Victoria	WHL	11	3	4	7	6	15	2	1	3	7
1981-82	Victoria	WHL	72	35	57	90	100	4	1	0	1	2
1982-83	Victoria	WHL	71	41	73	114	186	12	6	7	13	42
1983-84	**Boston**	**NHL**	4	0	0	0	0	....	....	....	....	....
	Hershey	AHL	74	14	12	26	51	....	....	....	....	....
1984-85	**Boston**	**NHL**	64	12	16	28	82	5	0	2	2	7
	Hershey	AHL	9	8	4	12	4	....	....	....	....	....
1985-86	**Boston**	**NHL**	64	21	16	37	61	3	0	0	0	2
	Moncton	AHL	12	8	8	16	6	....	....	....	....	....
	NHL Totals		132	33	32	65	143	8	0	2	2	9

Signed as free agent by **Boston**, July 6, 1983.

COURTNALL, RUSSELL (RUSS)

Born, Duncan, B.C., June 2, 1964.
Center. Shoots right. 5′11″, 180 lbs.
Last amateur club: Victoria Cougars (WHL).
(Toronto's 1st choice, 7th over-all, in 1983 Entry Draft).

Season	Club	Lea	GP	Regular Season G	A	TP	PIM	GP	Playoffs G	A	TP	PIM
1981-82	Notre Dame	Midget	28	13	28	41		....	....	....	....	....
1982-83	Victoria	WHL	60	36	61	97	33	12	11	7	18	6
1983-84	Cdn. Olympic	...	16	4	7	11	10	....	....	....	....	....
	Victoria	WHL	32	29	37	16	63	....	....	....	....	....
	Toronto	**NHL**	14	3	9	12	6	....	....	....	....	....
1984-85	**Toronto**	**NHL**	69	12	10	22	44	....	....	....	....	....
1985-86	**Toronto**	**NHL**	73	22	38	60	52	10	3	6	9	8
	NHL Totals		156	37	57	94	102	10	3	6	9	8

COWAN, DAVID

Born, Minneapolis, Minn. July 23, 1965.
Left wing. Shoots left. 5′10″, 180 lbs.
Last amateur club: University of Minnesota-Duluth Bulldogs (WCHA).
(Washington's 5th choice, 175th over-all, in 1983 Entry Draft).

Season	Club	Lea	GP	Regular Season G	A	TP	PIM	GP	Playoffs G	A	TP	PIM
1983-84	Minn-Duluth	WCHA	12	1	2	3	8	....	....	....	....	....
1984-85	Minn-Duluth	WCHA	32	9	20	29	20	....	....	....	....	....
1985-86	Minn-Duluth	WCHA	41	9	16	25	8	....	....	....	....	....

COXE, CRAIG

Born, Chula Vista, Calif., January 21, 1964.
Center. Shoots left. 6′4″, 185 lbs.
Last amateur club: Belleville Bulls (OHL).
(Detroit's 4th choice, 66th over-all, in 1982 Entry Draft)

Season	Club	Lea	GP	Regular Season G	A	TP	PIM	GP	Playoffs G	A	TP	PIM
1982-83	Belleville	OHL	64	14	27	41	102	4	1	2	3	2
1983-84	Belleville	OHL	45	17	28	45	90	3	2	0	2	4
1984-85	**Vancouver**	**NHL**	9	0	0	0	49	....	....	....	....	....
	Fredericton	AHL	62	8	7	15	242	4	2	1	3	16
1985-86	**Vancouver**	**NHL**	57	3	5	8	176	3	0	0	0	2
	NHL Totals		66	3	5	8	225	3	0	0	0	2

Signed as a free agent by **Vancouver**, June 26, 1984.

CRAMAROSSA, VITO

Born, Toronto, Ont., March 9, 1966.
Right Wing. Shoots right. 6′, 195 lbs.
Last amateur club: Toronto Marlboros (OHL).
(Washington's 6th choice, 122nd over-all, in 1984 Entry Draft).

Season	Club	Lea	GP	Regular Season G	A	TP	PIM	GP	Playoffs G	A	TP	PIM
1983-84	Toronto	OHL	66	18	40	58	63	9	1	0	1	13
1984-85	Toronto	OHL	63	27	37	64	63	5	1	3	4	2
1985-86	Toronto	OHL	51	20	35	55	77	4	0	1	1	0
	Binghamton	AHL	....	....	....	....	....	4	0	0	0	0

CRAVEN, MURRAY

Born, Medicine Hat, Alta., July 20, 1964.
Left wing. Shoots left. 6′2″, 175 lbs.
Last amateur club: Medicine Hat Tigers (WHL).
(Detroit's 1st choice, 17th over-all, in 1982 Entry Draft).

Season	Club	Lea	GP	Regular Season G	A	TP	PIM	GP	Playoffs G	A	TP	PIM
1980-81	Medicine Hat	WHL	69	5	10	15	18	5	0	0	0	2
1981-82	Medicine Hat	WHL	72	35	46	81	49	....	....	....	....	....
1982-83	Medicine Hat	WHL	28	17	29	46	35	....	....	....	....	....
	Detroit	**NHL**	31	4	7	11	6	....	....	....	....	....
1983-84	**Detroit**	**NHL**	15	0	4	4	6	....	....	....	....	....
	Medicine Hat	WHL	48	38	56	94	53	4	5	3	8	4
1984-85	**Philadelphia**	**NHL**	80	26	35	61	30	19	4	6	10	11
1985-86	**Philadelphia**	**NHL**	78	21	33	54	34	5	0	3	3	4
	NHL Totals		204	51	79	130	76	24	4	9	13	15

Traded to **Philadelphia** by **Detroit** with Joe Paterson for Darryl Sittler, October 10, 1984.

CRAWFORD, LOUIS

Born, Belleville, Ont., November 5, 1962.
Left wing. Shoots left. 6', 185 lbs.
Last amateur club: Kitchener Rangers (OHL).

			Regular Season					Playoffs				
Season	Club	Lea	GP	G	A	TP	PIM	GP	G	A	TP	PIM
1980-81	Kitchener	OHA	53	2	7	9	134	....	....	....	....	....
1981-82	Kitchener	OHL	64	11	17	28	243	15	3	4	7	71
1982-83	Rochester	AHL	64	5	11	16	142	13	1	1	2	7
1983-84	Rochester	AHL	76	7	6	13	234	17	2	4	6	87
1984-85	Rochester	AHL	70	8	7	15	213	1	0	0	0	10
1985-86	Nova Scotia	AHL	78	8	11	19	214	....	....	....	....	....

Signed as free agent by **Buffalo**, August 23, 1984.

CRAWFORD, MARC JOSEPH JOHN

Born, Belleville, Ont., February 13, 1961.
Left wing. Shoots left. 5'11", 185 lbs.
Last amateur club: Cornwall Royals (QJHL).
(Vancouver's 3rd choice, 70th over-all, in 1980 Entry Draft).

			Regular Season					Playoffs				
Season	Club	Lea	GP	G	A	TP	PIM	GP	G	A	TP	PIM
1979-80	Cornwall	QJHL	54	27	36	63	127	18	8	20	28	48
1980-81	Cornwall	QJHL	63	42	57	99	242	19	20	15	35	27
1981-82	Dallas	CHL	34	13	21	34	71	....	....	....	....	....
	Vancouver	NHL	40	4	8	12	29	14	1	0	1	11
1982-83	Vancouver	NHL	41	4	5	9	28	3	0	1	1	25
	Fredericton	AHL	30	15	9	24	59	9	1	3	4	10
1983-84	Vancouver	NHL	19	0	1	1	9	....	....	....	....	....
	Fredericton	AHL	56	9	22	31	96	7	4	2	6	23
1984-85	Vancouver	NHL	1	0	0	0	4	....	....	....	....	....
1985-86	Vancouver	NHL	54	11	14	25	92	3	0	1	1	8
	Fredericton	AHL	26	10	14	24	55	....	....	....	....	....
	NHL Totals		155	19	28	47	162	20	1	2	3	44

CRAWFORD, ROBERT REMI (BOB)

Born, Belleville, Ont., April 6, 1959.
Right wing. Shoots right. 5'11", 180 lbs.
Last amateur club: Cornwall Royals (QJHL).
(St. Louis' 2nd choice, 65th over-all, in 1979 Entry Draft).

			Regular Season					Playoffs				
Season	Club	Lea	GP	G	A	TP	PIM	GP	G	A	TP	PIM
1977-78	Cornwall	QJHL	69	54	67	121	29	9	7	5	12	2
1978-79	Cornwall	QJHL	65	62	70	132	43	7	4	7	11	6
1979-80	St. Louis	NHL	8	1	0	1	2	....	....	....	....	....
	Salt Lake	CHL	67	30	21	51	32	13	3	5	8	9
1980-81	Salt Lake	CHL	79	35	26	61	27	17	7	8	15	2
1981-82	St. Louis	NHL	3	0	1	1	0	....	....	....	....	....
	Salt Lake	CHL	74	54	45	99	43	10	4	2	6	2
1982-83	Salt Lake	CHL	25	15	23	38	2	....	....	....	....	....
	St. Louis	NHL	27	5	9	14	2	4	0	0	0	0
1983-84	Hartford	NHL	80	36	25	61	32	....	....	....	....	....
1984-85	Hartford	NHL	45	14	14	28	8	....	....	....	....	....
1985-86	Hartford	NHL	57	14	20	34	16	....	....	....	....	....
	NY Rangers	NHL	11	1	2	3	10	7	0	1	1	8
	New Haven	AHL	27	7	8	15	6	5	0	0	0	2
	NHL Totals		231	71	71	142	70	11	0	1	1	8

Claimed by **Hartford** from **St. Louis** in NHL Waiver Draft, October 3, 1983. Traded to **NY Rangers** by **Hartford** for Mike McEwen, March 11, 1986.

CRAWFORD, WAYNE KENNETH

Born, Toronto, Ont., April 18, 1961.
Center. Shoots left. 5'11", 185 lbs.
Last amateur club: Toronto Marlboros (OHA).
(Detroit's 4th choice, 109th over-all, in 1980 Entry Draft).

			Regular Season					Playoffs				
Season	Club	Lea	GP	G	A	TP	PIM	GP	G	A	TP	PIM
1979-80	Niagara Falls	OHA	2	0	0	0	0	....	....	....	....	....
	Toronto	OHA	64	48	66	114	18	4	3	2	5	11
1980-81	Toronto	OHA	65	44	58	102	101	4	4	1	5	4
1981-82	Adirondack	AHL	65	14	26	40	42	3	0	1	1	2
1982-83	Adirondack	AHL	69	18	31	49	16	6	0	1	1	2
1983-84	Adirondack	AHL	67	28	25	53	97	7	3	4	7	4
1984-85	Kalamazoo	IHL	78	27	48	75	69	11	5	1	6	8
1985-86	Kalamazoo	IHL	77	51	51	102	83	6	2	4	6	2

CREIGHTON, ADAM   (CRAY-ton)

Born, Burlington, Ont., June 2, 1965.
Center. Shoots left. 6'5", 210 lbs.
Last amateur club: Ottawa 67's (OHL).
(Buffalo's 3rd choice, 11th over-all, in 1983 Entry Draft).

			Regular Season					Playoffs				
Season	Club	Lea	GP	G	A	TP	PIM	GP	G	A	TP	PIM
1981-82	Ottawa	OHL	60	15	27	42	73	17	7	1	8	40
1982-83	Ottawa	OHL	68	44	46	90	88	9	0	2	2	12
1983-84	**Buffalo**	NHL	7	2	2	4	4	....	....	....	....	....
	Ottawa	OHL	56	42	49	91	79	13	16	11	27	28
1984-85	**Buffalo**	NHL	30	2	8	10	33	....	....	....	....	....
	Rochester	AHL	6	5	3	8	2	5	2	1	3	20
	Ottawa	OHL	10	4	14	18	23	5	6	2	8	11
1985-86	**Buffalo**	NHL	19	1	1	2	2	....	....	....	....	....
	Rochester	AHL	32	17	21	38	27	....	....	....	....	....
	NHL Totals		56	5	11	16	39	....	....	....	....	....

CRISTOFOLI, ED

Born, Trail, B.C., May 14, 1967.
Center. Shoots left. 6'2", 205 lbs.
Last amateur club: University of Denver Pioneers (WCHA).
(Montreal's 9th choice, 142nd over-all, in 1985 Entry Draft).

			Regular Season					Playoffs				
Season	Club	Lea	GP	G	A	TP	PIM	GP	G	A	TP	PIM
1985-86	Denver	WCHA	46	10	9	19	32	....	....	....	....	....

CRONIN, SHAWN

Born, Flushing, Mich., August 20, 1963.
Defense. Shoots right. 6'2", 210 lbs.
Last amateur club: University of Illinois at Chicago Flames (CCHA).

			Regular Season					Playoffs				
Season	Club	Lea	GP	G	A	TP	PIM	GP	G	A	TP	PIM
1983-84	Ill-Chicago	CCHA	32	0	4	4	41	....	....	....	....	....
1984-85	Ill-Chicago	CCHA	31	2	6	8	52	....	....	....	....	....
1985-86	Ill-Chicago	CCHA	35	3	8	11	70	....	....	....	....	....

Signed as a free agent by **Hartford**, March, 1986.

CROSSMAN, DOUGLAS (DOUG)

Born, Peterborough, Ont., May 30, 1960.
Defense. Shoots left. 6'2", 190 lbs.
Last amateur club: Ottawa 67's (OHA).
(Chicago's 6th choice, 112th over-all, in 1979 Entry Draft).

			Regular Season					Playoffs				
Season	Club	Lea	GP	G	A	TP	PIM	GP	G	A	TP	PIM
1978-79	Ottawa	OHA	67	12	51	63	65	4	1	3	4	0
1979-80	Ottawa	OHA	66	20	96	116	48	11	7	6	13	19
1980-81	Chicago	NHL	9	0	2	2	2	....	....	....	....	....
	New Brunswick	AHL	70	13	43	56	90	13	5	6	11	36
1981-82	Chicago	NHL	70	12	28	40	24	11	0	3	3	4
1982-83	Chicago	NHL	80	13	40	53	46	13	3	7	10	6
1983-84	Philadelphia	NHL	78	7	28	35	63	3	0	0	0	0
1984-85	Philadelphia	NHL	80	4	33	37	65	19	4	6	10	38
1985-86	Philadelphia	NHL	80	6	37	43	55	5	0	1	1	4
	NHL Totals		397	42	168	210	255	51	7	17	24	42

Traded to **Philadelphia** by **Chicago** with Chicago's second round choice (Scott Mellanby) in the 1984 Entry Draft for Behn Wilson, June 8, 1983.

CROSSMAN, JEFF

Born, Toronto, Ont., December 3, 1967.
Left wing. shoots left. 6'0", 200 lbs.
Last amateur club: Western Michigan University Broncos (CCHA).
(Los Angeles' 10th choice, 191st over-all, in 1984 Entry Draft).

			Regular Season					Playoffs				
Season	Club	Lea	GP	G	A	TP	PIM	GP	G	A	TP	PIM
1982-83	W. Michigan	CCHA	30	3	2	5	43	....	....	....	....	....
1983-84	W. Michigan	CCHA	39	9	12	21	19	....	....	....	....	....
1984-85	W. Michigan	CCHA	35	5	12	17	87	....	....	....	....	....
1985-86	W. Michigan	CCHA	39	13	19	32	154	....	....	....	....	....

CROWDER, KEITH SCOTT

Born, Windsor, Ont., January 6, 1959.
Right wing. Shoots right. 6', 190 lbs.
Last amateur club: Peterborough Petes (OHA).
(Boston's 4th choice, 57th over-all, in 1979 Entry Draft).

			Regular Season					Playoffs				
Season	Club	Lea	GP	G	A	TP	PIM	GP	G	A	TP	PIM
1976-77	Peterborough	OHA	58	13	19	32	99	4	0	2	2	9
1977-78	Peterborough	OHA	58	30	30	60	139	14	3	5	8	21
1978-79	Peterborough	OHA	42	25	41	66	76	15	12	6	18	40
	Birmingham	WHA	5	1	0	1	17	....	....	....	....	....
1979-80	Binghamton	AHL	13	4	0	4	15	....	....	....	....	....
	Grand Rapids	IHL	20	10	13	23	22	....	....	....	....	....
1980-81	Springfield	AHL	26	12	18	30	34	....	....	....	....	....
	Boston	NHL	47	13	12	25	172	3	2	0	2	9
1981-82	**Boston**	NHL	71	23	21	44	101	11	2	2	4	14
1982-83	**Boston**	NHL	74	35	39	74	105	17	1	6	7	54
1983-84	**Boston**	NHL	63	24	28	52	128	3	0	0	0	7
1984-85	**Boston**	NHL	79	32	38	70	142	4	3	2	5	19
1985-86	**Boston**	NHL	78	38	46	84	177	3	2	0	2	21
	NHL Totals		412	165	184	349	823	41	10	10	20	124
	WHA Totals		5	1	0	1	17					

CRUICKSHANK, GORD

Born, Toronto, Ont., May 4, 1965.
Center. Shoots right. 5'11", 185 lbs.
Last amateur club: Providence College Friars (H.E.).
(Boston's 8th choice, 178th over-all, in 1985 Entry Draft).

			Regular Season					Playoffs				
Season	Club	Lea	GP	G	A	TP	PIM	GP	G	A	TP	PIM
1984-85	Providence	H.E.	40	8	9	17	32	....	....	....	....	....
1985-86a	Providence	H.E.	38	34	18	52	80	....	....	....	....	....

a Hockey East Second All-Star Team (1986).

CULHANE, JIM

Born, Haileyburg, Ont., August 8, 1960.
Defense. Shoots left. 6'0", 190 lbs.
Last amateur club: Western Michigan University Broncos (CCHA).
(Hartford's 6th choice, 214th over-all, in 1984 Entry Draft).

				Regular Season				Playoffs				
Season	Club	Lea	GP	G	A	TP	PIM	GP	G	A	TP	PIM
1983-84	W. Michigan	CCHA	42	1	14	15	88	....	....	....	....	....
1984-85	W. Michigan	CCHA	37	2	8	10	84	....	....	....	....	....
1985-86	W. Michigan	CCHA	40	1	21	22	61	....	....	....	....	....

CUNNEYWORTH, RANDY WILLIAM

Born, Etobicoke, Ont., May 10, 1961.
Center. Shoots left. 6', 180 lbs.
Last amateur club: Ottawa 67's (OHA).
(Buffalo's 9th choice, 167th over-all, in 1980 Entry Draft).

				Regular Season				Playoffs				
Season	Club	Lea	GP	G	A	TP	PIM	GP	G	A	TP	PIM
1979-80	Ottawa	OHA	63	16	25	41	145	11	0	1	1	13
1980-81	**Buffalo**	**NHL**	**1**	**0**	**0**	**0**	**2**	....	....	....	....	....
	Rochester	AHL	1	0	1	1	2	....	....	....	....	....
	Ottawa	OHA	67	54	74	128	240	15	5	8	13	35
1981-82	**Buffalo**	**NHL**	**20**	**2**	**4**	**6**	**47**	....	....	....	....	....
	Rochester	AHL	57	12	15	27	86	9	4	0	4	30
1982-83	Rochester	AHL	78	23	33	56	111	16	4	4	8	35
1983-84	Rochester	AHL	54	18	17	35	85	17	5	5	10	55
1984-85	Rochester	AHL	72	30	38	68	148	5	2	1	3	16
1985-86	**Pittsburgh**	**NHL**	**75**	**15**	**30**	**45**	**74**	....	....	....	....	....
	NHL Totals		**96**	**17**	**34**	**51**	**123**	....	....	....	....	....

Traded to **Pittsburgh** by **Buffalo** with Mike Moller for Pat Hughes, October 4, 1985.

CUPOLO, MARK

Born, Niagara Falls, Ont., November 17, 1965.
Left wing. Shoots left. 6'0", 180 lbs.
Last amateur club: Peterborough Petes (OHL).
(St. Louis' 13th choice, 217th over-all, in 1984 Entry Draft).

				Regular Season				Playoffs				
Season	Club	Lea	GP	G	A	TP	PIM	GP	G	A	TP	PIM
1982-83	Guelph	OHL	8	0	0	0	7	....	....	....	....	....
1983-84	Guelph	OHL	60	28	13	41	53	....	....	....	....	....
1984-85	Peterborough	OHL	47	18	14	32	51	17	7	9	16	12
1985-86	Peoria	IHL	60	9	14	23	87	3	0	0	0	2

CURRAN, BRIAN

Born, Toronto, Ont., November 5, 1963.
Defense. Shoots left. 6'3", 215 lbs.
Last amateur club: Portland Winter Hawks (WHL).
(Boston's 2nd choice, 22nd over-all, in 1982 Entry Draft).

				Regular Season				Playoffs				
Season	Club	Lea	GP	G	A	TP	PIM	GP	G	A	TP	PIM
1980-81	Portland	WHL	59	2	28	30	275	7	0	1	1	13
1981-82	Portland	WHL	51	2	16	18	132	14	1	7	8	63
1982-83	Portland	WHL	56	1	30	31	187	14	1	3	4	57
1983-84	Hershey	AHL	23	0	2	2	94	....	....	....	....	....
	Boston	**NHL**	**16**	**1**	**1**	**2**	**57**	**3**	**0**	**0**	**0**	**7**
1984-85	**Boston**	**NHL**	**56**	**0**	**1**	**1**	**158**	....	....	....	....	....
	Hershey	AHL	4	0	0	0	19	....	....	....	....	....
1985-86	**Boston**	**NHL**	**43**	**2**	**5**	**7**	**192**	**2**	**0**	**0**	**0**	**4**
	NHL Totals		**115**	**3**	**7**	**10**	**407**	**5**	**0**	**0**	**0**	**11**

CURRIE, GLEN ALLEN

Born, Montreal, Que., July 18, 1958.
Center. Shoots left. 6'2", 180 lbs.
Last amateur club: Laval Nationals (QJHL).
(Washington's 5th choice, 38th over-all, in 1978 Amateur Draft).

				Regular Season				Playoffs				
Season	Club	Lea	GP	G	A	TP	PIM	GP	G	A	TP	PIM
1976-77	Laval	QJHL	72	28	51	79	42	7	1	4	5	15
1977-78	Laval	QJHL	72	63	82	145	29	5	3	1	4	0
1978-79	Port Huron	IHL	69	27	36	63	43	7	5	4	9	2
1979-80	**Washington**	**NHL**	**32**	**2**	**0**	**2**	**2**	....	....	....	....	....
	Hershey	AHL	45	17	26	43	16	....	....	....	....	....
1980-81	**Washington**	**NHL**	**40**	**5**	**13**	**18**	**16**	....	....	....	....	....
	Hershey	AHL	35	18	21	39	10	....	....	....	....	....
1981-82	**Washington**	**NHL**	**43**	**7**	**7**	**14**	**14**	....	....	....	....	....
	Hershey	AHL	31	12	12	24	6	....	....	....	....	....
1982-83	Hershey	AHL	12	5	11	16	6	....	....	....	....	....
	Washington	**NHL**	**68**	**11**	**28**	**39**	**20**	**4**	**0**	**3**	**3**	**4**
1983-84	**Washington**	**NHL**	**80**	**12**	**24**	**36**	**20**	**8**	**1**	**0**	**1**	**0**
1984-85	**Washington**	**AHL**	**44**	**1**	**5**	**6**	**19**	....	....	....	....	....
	Binghampton	AHL	17	1	5	6	6	8	2	5	7	2
1985-86	**Los Angeles**	**NHL**	**12**	**1**	**2**	**3**	**9**	....	....	....	....	....
	New Haven	AHL	8	0	4	4	2	2	0	0	0	10
	NHL Totals		**319**	**39**	**79**	**118**	**100**	**12**	**1**	**3**	**4**	**4**

Traded to **Los Angeles** by **Washington** for Daryl Evans, September 9, 1985.

CURRIE, TONY

Born, Sydney Mines, N.S., November 12, 1957.
Right wing. Shoots right. 5'11", 165 lbs.
Last amateur club: Portland Winter Hawks (WHL).
(St. Louis' 4th choice, 63rd over-all, in 1977 Amateur Draft).

				Regular Season				Playoffs				
Season	Club	Lea	GP	G	A	TP	PIM	GP	G	A	TP	PIM
1975-76	Edmonton	WHL	71	41	40	81	56	5	0	1	1	5
1976-77	Portland	WHL	72	73	52	125	50	10	4	7	11	14
1977-78	**St. Louis**	**NHL**	**22**	**4**	**5**	**9**	**4**	....	....	....	....	....
	Salt Lake	CHL	53	33	17	50	17	....	....	....	....	....
1978-79	**St. Louis**	**NHL**	**36**	**4**	**15**	**19**	**0**	....	....	....	....	....
	Salt Lake	CHL	28	22	12	34	6	....	....	....	....	....
1979-80	Salt Lake	CHL	33	24	23	47	17	....	....	....	....	....
	St. Louis	**NHL**	**40**	**19**	**14**	**33**	**4**	**2**	**0**	**0**	**0**	**0**
1980-81	**St. Louis**	**NHL**	**61**	**23**	**32**	**55**	**38**	**11**	**4**	**12**	**16**	**4**
1981-82	**St. Louis**	**NHL**	**48**	**18**	**22**	**40**	**17**	....	....	....	....	....
	Vancouver	**NHL**	**12**	**5**	**3**	**8**	**2**	**3**	**0**	**0**	**0**	**10**
1982-83	**Vancouver**	**NHL**	**8**	**1**	**1**	**2**	**0**	....	....	....	....	....
	Fredericton	AHL	68	47	48	95	16	12	5	12	17	6
1983-84	Fredericton	AHL	12	6	11	17	16	....	....	....	....	....
	Vancouver	**NHL**	**18**	**3**	**3**	**6**	**2**	....	....	....	....	....
	Hartford	**NHL**	**32**	**12**	**16**	**28**	**4**	....	....	....	....	....
1984-85	**Hartford**	**NHL**	**13**	**3**	**8**	**11**	**12**	....	....	....	....	....
	Nova Scotia	AHL	53	16	31	47	8	6	1	3	4	0
1985-86	Fredericton	AHL	75	35	40	75	23	6	5	2	7	4
	NHL Totals		**300**	**92**	**119**	**211**	**83**	**16**	**4**	**12**	**16**	**14**

Traded to **Vancouver** by **St. Louis** with Jim Nill, Rick Heinz and St. Louis' fourth round choice (Shawn Kilroy) in 1982 Entry Draft for Glen Hanlon, March 9, 1982. Signed as free agent by **Hartford**, January 21, 1984. Claimed on waivers by **Edmonton** from **Hartford**, December 5 1984. Signed as a free agent by **Quebec**, August 25, 1985.

CURTALE, ANTHONY GLEN (TONY) (kerr-TAL-ee)

Born, Detroit, Mich., January 29, 1962.
Defense. Shoots left. 6', 185 lbs.
Last amateur club: Brantford Alexanders (OHL).
(Calgary's 2nd choice, 31st over-all, in 1980 Entry Draft).

				Regular Season				Playoffs				
Season	Club	Lea	GP	G	A	TP	PIM	GP	G	A	TP	PIM
1979-80	Brantford	OHA	59	10	35	45	227	5	0	4	4	4
1980-81	**Calgary**	**NHL**	**2**	**0**	**0**	**0**	**0**	....	....	....	....	....
	Brantford	OHA	59	14	71	85	141	6	1	4	5	26
1981-82	Brantford	OHL	36	17	32	49	118	8	1	2	3	35
	Oklahoma City	CHL	....	....	....	....	....	4	0	2	2	8
1982-83	Colorado	CHL	74	7	22	29	61	5	1	0	1	6
1983-84	Peoria	IHL	2	0	0	0	2	....	....	....	....	....
	Colorado	CHL	54	3	20	23	80	6	0	4	4	2
1984-85	Peoria	IHL	50	5	31	36	81	17	1	7	8	43
1985-86	Peoria	IHL	70	7	51	58	116	11	1	3	4	57
	NHL Totals		**2**	**0**	**0**	**0**	**0**	....	....	....	....	....

CUSACK, MIKE

Born, Los Angeles, Calif., September 25, 1966.
Right wing. Shoots right. 6'1", 175 lbs.
Last amateur club: University of Michigan Wolverines (CCHA).
(Philadelphia's 9th choice, 168th over-all, in 1985 Entry Draft).

				Regular Season				Playoffs				
Season	Club	Lea	GP	G	A	TP	PIM	GP	G	A	TP	PIM
1985-86	U. of Michigan	CCHA	37	8	2	10	51	....	....	....	....	....

CYR, DENIS (SEAR)

Born, Verdun, Que., February 4, 1961.
Right wing. Shoots left. 5'10", 180 lbs.
Last amateur club: Montreal Juniors (QJHL).
(Calgary's 1st choice, 13th over-all, in 1980 Entry Draft).

				Regular Season				Playoffs				
Season	Club	Lea	GP	G	A	TP	PIM	GP	G	A	TP	PIM
1978-79a	Montreal	QMJHL	70	46	112	158	88	11	7	5	12	26
1979-80b	Montreal	QMJHL	70	70	76	146	61	10	10	13	23	6
1980-81	**Calgary**	**NHL**	**10**	**1**	**4**	**5**	**0**	....	....	....	....	....
	Montreal	QMJHL	57	50	40	90	53	7	6	6	12	37
1981-82	Oklahoma City	CHL	14	10	4	14	16	....	....	....	....	....
	Calgary	**NHL**	**45**	**12**	**10**	**22**	**13**	....	....	....	....	....
1982-83	**Calgary**	**NHL**	**11**	**1**	**1**	**2**	**0**	....	....	....	....	....
	Chicago	**NHL**	**41**	**7**	**8**	**15**	**2**	**1**	**0**	**0**	**0**	**0**
1983-84	**Chicago**	**NHL**	**46**	**12**	**13**	**25**	**19**	....	....	....	....	....
	Springfield	AHL	17	4	13	17	11	3	0	0	0	0
1984-85	**St. Louis**	**NHL**	**9**	**5**	**3**	**8**	**0**	**3**	**0**	**0**	**0**	**0**
	Peoria	IHL	62	26	51	77	28	20	18	14	32	14
1985-86	**St. Louis**	**NHL**	**31**	**3**	**4**	**7**	**2**	....	....	....	....	....
	Peoria	IHL	34	15	26	41	15	11	5	4	9	2
	NHL Totals		**193**	**41**	**43**	**84**	**36**	**4**	**0**	**0**	**0**	**0**

a QMJHL Second All-Star Team (1979)
b QMJHL First All-Star Team (1980)

Traded to **Chicago** by **Calgary** for the rights to Carey Wilson, November 8, 1982. Signed as a free agent by **St. Louis**, September 14, 1984.

CYR, PAUL (SEAR)

Born, Port Alberni, B.C., October 31, 1963.
Left wing. Shoots left. 5'10", 185 lbs.
Last amateur club: Victoria Cougars (WHL).
(Buffalo's 2nd choice, 9th over-all, in 1982 Entry Draft).

			Regular Season					Playoffs				
Season	Club	Lea	GP	G	A	TP	PIM	GP	G	A	TP	PIM
1980-81	Victoria	WHL	64	36	23	59	85	14	6	5	11	46
1981-82	Victoria	WHL	58	52	56	108	167	4	3	2	5	12
1982-83	Victoria	WHL	20	21	22	43	61	....	....	....	....	....
	Buffalo	NHL	36	15	12	27	59	10	1	3	4	64
1983-84	Buffalo	NHL	71	16	27	43	52	3	0	1	1	0
1984-85	Buffalo	NHL	71	22	24	46	63	5	2	2	4	15
1985-86	Buffalo	NHL	71	20	31	51	120	....	....	....	....	....
	NHL Totals		249	73	94	167	294	18	3	6	9	79

DACHYSHYN, DEAN

Born, West Bank, B.C., May 4, 1959.
Left wing. Shoots left. 6'1", 195 lbs.
Last amateur club: University of North Dakota Fighting Sioux (WCHA).

			Regular Season					Playoffs				
Season	Club	Lea	GP	G	A	TP	PIM	GP	G	A	TP	PIM
1979-80	North Dakota	WCHA	40	12	8	20	88	....	....	....	....	....
1980-81	North Dakota	WCHA	35	8	13	21	91	....	....	....	....	....
1981-82	North Dakota	WCHA	30	6	13	19	82	....	....	....	....	....
1982-83	North Dakota	WCHA	20	5	1	6	28	....	....	....	....	....
1983-84	Moncton	AHL	74	9	7	16	90	....	....	....	....	....
1984-85	Nova Scotia	AHL	74	10	10	20	143	6	1	0	1	2
1985-86	Nova Scotia	AHL	55	2	9	11	148	....	....	....	....	....

Signed as free agent by **Edmonton**, July 19, 1983.

DAHLEN, ULF

Born, Ostersund, Sweden, January 12, 1967.
Center. Shoots left. 6'2", 195 lbs.
Last amateur club: Ostersund (Sweden).
(NY Rangers' 1st choice, 7th over-all, in 1985 Entry Draft).

			Regular Season					Playoffs				
Season	Club	Lea	GP	G	A	TP	PIM	GP	G	A	TP	PIM
1983-84	Ostersund	Swe.	36	15	11	26	10	....	....	....	....	....
1984-85	Ostersund	Swe.	36	33	26	59	20	....	....	....	....	....
1985-86	Ostersund	Swe.	21	4	3	7	8	....	....	....	....	....

DAHLIN, KJELL

Born, Timra, Sweden, February 2, 1963.
Right wing. Shoots left. 6'0", 175 lbs.
Last amateur club: Farjestad (Sweden).
(Montreal's 7th choice, 82nd overall, in 1981 Entry Draft).

			Regular Season					Playoffs				
Season	Club	Lea	GP	G	A	TP	PIM	GP	G	A	TP	PIM
1984-85	Farjestad	Swe.	35	21	26	47	....	....	....	....	....	....
1985-86a	Montreal	NHL	77	32	39	71	4	16	2	3	5	4
	NHL Totals		77	32	39	71	4	16	2	3	5	4

a NHL All-Rookie Team (1986).

DAHLQUIST, CHRIS

Born, Fridley, Minn., December 12, 1962.
Defense. Shoots left. 6'1", 190 lbs.
Last amateur club: Lake Superior State University Lakers (CCHA).

			Regular Season					Playoffs				
Season	Club	Lea	GP	G	A	TP	PIM	GP	G	A	TP	PIM
1981-82	Lake Superior	CCHA	39	4	10	14	62	....	....	....	....	....
1982-83	Lake Superior	CCHA	35	0	12	12	63	....	....	....	....	....
1983-84	Lake Superior	CCHA	40	4	19	23	76	....	....	....	....	....
1984-85	Lake Superior	CCHA	32	4	10	14	18	....	....	....	....	....
1985-86	Baltimore	AHL	65	4	21	25	64	....	....	....	....	....
	Pittsburgh	NHL	5	1	2	3	2	....	....	....	....	....
	NHL Totals		5	1	2	3	2	....	....	....	....	....

Signed as a free agent by **Pittsburgh**, May, 1985.

DAIGNEAULT, JEAN-JACQUES (DANE-yoh)

Born, Montreal, Que., October 12, 1965.
Defense. Shoots left. 5'11", 185 lbs.
Last amateur club: Longueuil Chevaliers (QMJHL).
(Vancouver's 1st choice, 10th over-all, in 1984 Entry Draft).

			Regular Season					Playoffs				
Season	Club	Lea	GP	G	A	TP	PIM	GP	G	A	TP	PIM
1981-82	Laval	QMJHL	64	4	25	29	41	18	1	3	4	2
1982-83ab	Longueuil	QMJHL	70	26	58	84	58	15	4	11	15	35
1983-84	Cdn. Olympic	...	62	6	15	21	40	....	....	....	....	....
	Longueuil	QMJHL	10	2	11	13	6	14	3	13	16	30
1984-85	Vancouver	NHL	67	4	23	27	69	....	....	....	....	....
1985-86	Vancouver	NHL	64	5	23	28	45	3	0	2	2	0
	NHL Totals		131	9	46	55	114	3	0	2	2	0

a QMJHL First All-Star Team (1983)
b Named QMJHL's Top Defenseman (1983)

Traded to **Philadelphia** by **Vancouver** with Vancouver's second-round choice (Kent Hawley) in 1986 Entry Draft for Dave Richter, Rich Sutter and Vancouver's third-round choice (Don Gibson) — acquired earlier — in 1986 Entry Draft, June 6, 1986.

DALGARNO, BRAD

Born, Vancouver, B.C., August 11, 1967.
Right wing. Shoots right. 6'3", 205 lbs.
Last amateur club: Hamilton Steelhawks (OHL).
(NY Islanders' 1st choice, 6th over-all, in 1985 Entry Draft).

			Regular Season					Playoffs				
Season	Club	Lea	GP	G	A	TP	PIM	GP	G	A	TP	PIM
1983-84	Markham	OPJHL	40	17	11	28	59	....	....	....	....	....
1984-85	Hamilton	OHL	66	23	30	53	86	17	5	5	10	12
1985-86	NY Rangers	NHL	2	1	0	1	0	....	....	....	....	....
	Hamilton	OHL	54	22	43	65	79	....	....	....	....	....
	NHL Totals		2	1	0	1	0	....	....	....	....	....

DALLMAN, MARTY

Born, Niagara Falls, Ont., February 15, 1963.
Center. Shoots right. 5'10", 180 lbs.
Last amateur club: Rensselaer Polytechnical Institute Engineers (ECAC)
(Los Angeles' 3rd choice, 81st over-all, in 1981 Entry Draft).

			Regular Season					Playoffs				
Season	Club	Lea	GP	G	A	TP	PIM	GP	G	A	TP	PIM
1980-81	RPI	ECAC	22	8	10	18	6	....	....	....	....	....
1981-82	RPI	ECAC	28	22	18	40	27	....	....	....	....	....
1982-83	RPI	ECAC	27	21	29	50	28	....	....	....	....	....
1983-84a	RPI	ECAC	38	30	24	54	32	....	....	....	....	....
1984-85	New Haven	AHL	78	18	39	57	26	....	....	....	....	....
1985-86	New Haven	AHL	69	23	33	56	92	5	0	4	4	4

a ECAC Second All-Star Team (1984)

DALLMAN, ROD

Born, Prince Albert, Sask., January 26, 1967.
Left wing. Shoots left. 5'10", 180 lbs.
Last amateur club: Prince Albert Raiders (WHL).
(NY Islanders' 8th choice, 118th over-all, in 1985 Entry Draft).

			Regular Season					Playoffs				
Season	Club	Lea	GP	G	A	TP	PIM	GP	G	A	TP	PIM
1984-85	Prince Albert	WHL	40	8	11	19	133	12	3	4	7	51
1985-86	Prince Albert	WHL	59	20	21	41	198	....	....	....	....	....

DANEYKO, KENNETH (KEN) (dan-EH-koh)

Born, Windsor, Ont., April 17, 1964.
Defense. Shoots left. 6', 195 lbs.
Last amateur club: Seattle Breakers (WHL).
(New Jersey's 2nd choice, 18th over-all, in 1982 Entry Draft).

			Regular Season					Playoffs				
Season	Club	Lea	GP	G	A	TP	PIM	GP	G	A	TP	PIM
1980-81	Spokane	WHL	62	6	13	19	40	4	0	0	0	6
1981-82	Spokane	WHL	26	1	11	12	147	....	....	....	....	....
	Seattle	WHL	38	1	22	23	151	14	1	9	10	49
1982-83	Seattle	WHL	69	17	43	60	150	4	1	3	4	14
1983-84	New Jersey	NHL	11	1	4	5	17	....	....	....	....	....
	Kamloops	WHL	19	6	28	34	52	17	4	9	13	28
1984-85	New Jersey	NHL	1	0	0	0	10	....	....	....	....	....
	Maine	AHL	80	4	9	13	206	11	1	3	4	36
1985-86	New Jersey	NHL	44	0	10	10	100	....	....	....	....	....
	Maine	AHL	21	3	2	5	75	....	....	....	....	....
	NHL Totals		56	1	14	15	127	....	....	....	....	....

DAMPHOUSSE, VINCENT

Born, Montreal, Que., December 17, 1967.
Left wing. Shoots left. 6'1", 190 lbs.
Last amateur club: Laval Titans (QMJHL).
(Toronto's 1st choice, 6th over-all, in 1986 Entry Draft).

			Regular Season					Playoffs				
Season	Club	Lea	GP	G	A	TP	PIM	GP	G	A	TP	PIM
1984-85	Laval	QMJHL	68	35	68	103	62	....	....	....	....	....
1985-86a	Laval	QMJHL	69	45	110	155	70	14	9	27	36	12

a QMJHL Second All-Star Team (1986)

DAOUST, DANIEL (DAN) (DOW-oo)

Born, Montreal, Que., February 29, 1960.
Center. Shoots left. 5'11", 165 lbs.
Last amateur club: Cornwall Royals (QJHL).

			Regular Season					Playoffs				
Season	Club	Lea	GP	G	A	TP	PIM	GP	G	A	TP	PIM
1978-79	Cornwall	QJHL	72	42	55	97	85	7	2	4	6	29
1979-80	Cornwall	QJHL	70	40	62	102	82	18	5	9	14	36
1980-81	Nova Scotia	AHL	80	38	60	98	106	6	1	3	4	10
1981-82	Nova Scotia	AHL	61	25	40	65	75	9	5	2	7	11
1982-83a	Montreal	NHL	4	0	1	1	4	....	....	....	....	....
	Toronto	NHL	48	18	33	51	31	....	....	....	....	....
1983-84	Toronto	NHL	78	18	56	74	88	....	....	....	....	....
1984-85	Toronto	NHL	79	17	37	54	98	....	....	....	....	....
1985-86	Toronto	NHL	80	7	13	20	88	10	2	2	4	19
	NHL Totals		289	60	140	200	309	10	2	2	4	19

a Named to NHL All-Rookie Team (1983)

Signed as free agent by **Montreal**, March 9, 1981. Traded to **Toronto** by **Montreal** for Toronto's third round choice (Ken Hodge — later transferred to Minnesota) in the 1984 Entry Draft, December 17, 1982.

DARK, MICHAEL

Born, Sarnia, Ont., September 17, 1963.
Defense. Shoots right. 6'3", 210 lbs.
Last amateur club: Rensselaer Polytechnical Institute Engineers (ECAC)
(Montreal's 10th choice, 124th over-all, in 1982 Entry Draft).

			Regular Season					Playoffs				
Season	Club	Lea	GP	G	A	TP	PIM	GP	G	A	TP	PIM
1981-82	Sarnia	SOJL	41	13	30	43	86	....	....	....	....	....
1982-83	RPI	ECAC	29	3	16	18	54	....	....	....	....	....
1983-84	RPI	ECAC	38	2	12	14	60	....	....	....	....	....
1984-85	RPI	ECAC	36	7	26	33	76	....	....	....	....	....
1985-86ab	RPI	ECAC	32	7	29	36	58	....	....	....	....	....

a NCAA East All-American Team (1986)
b ECAC First-All-Star Team (1986)

Traded to **St. Louis** by **Montreal** with Mark Hunter and Montreal's second (Herb Raglan); third (Nelson Emerson); fifth (Dan Brooks); and sixth (Rick Burchill) round choices in 1985 Entry draft for St. Louis' first (Jose Charbonneau); second (Todd Richard); fourth (Martin Desjardins); fifth (Tom Sagissor); and sixth (Don Dufresne) round choices in 1985 Entry draft, June 15, 1985.

DAVEY, NEIL

Born, Edmonton, Alta., December 29, 1965.
Defense. Shoots right. 6'2", 205 lbs.
Last amateur club: Prince Albert Raiders (WHL).
(New Jersey's 3rd choice, 44th over-all, in 1984 Entry Draft).

			Regular Season					Playoffs				
Season	Club	Lea	GP	G	A	TP	PIM	GP	G	A	TP	PIM
1983-84	Michigan State	CCHA	33	1	5	6	50	....	....	....	....	....
1984-85	Prince Albert	WHL	54	6	28	34	20	12	0	4	4	9
1985-86	Maine	AHL	7	0	0	0	8	....	....	....	....	....
	Toledo	IHL	49	5	8	13	35	....	....	....	....	....

DAVIS, MALCOLM STERLING (MAL)

Born, Lockeport, N.S., October 10, 1956.
Left wing. Shoots left. 5'11", 180 lbs.
Last amateur club: St. Mary's University Huskies (AUAA)

			Regular Season					Playoffs				
Season	Club	Lea	GP	G	A	TP	PIM	GP	G	A	TP	PIM
1978-79	Detroit	NHL	6	0	0	0	0	....	....	....	....	....
	Kansas City	CHL	71	42	24	66	29	4	2	0	2	4
1979-80	Adirondack	AHL	79	34	31	65	45	5	2	2	4	19
1980-81	**Detroit**	**NHL**	**5**	**2**	**0**	**2**	**0**	....	....	....	....	....
	Adirondack	AHL	58	23	12	35	48	17	6	4	10	9
1981-82	Rochester	AHL	75	32	33	65	14	9	2	3	5	2
1982-83	Rochester	AHL	57	43	32	75	15	....	....	....	....	....
	Buffalo	**NHL**	**24**	**8**	**12**	**20**	**0**	**6**	**1**	**0**	**1**	**0**
1983-84	**Buffalo**	**NHL**	**11**	**2**	**1**	**3**	**4**	**1**	**0**	**0**	**0**	**0**
	Rochester	AHL	71	55	48	103	53	15	6	9	15	33
1984-85	**Buffalo**	**NHL**	**47**	**17**	**9**	**26**	**26**	....	....	....	....	....
	Rochester	AHL	6	4	4	8	14	....	....	....	....	....
1985-86	**Buffalo**	**NHL**	**7**	**2**	**0**	**2**	**4**	....	....	....	....	....
	Rochester	AHL	38	21	15	36	23	....	....	....	....	....
	NHL Totals		**100**	**31**	**22**	**53**	**34**	**7**	**1**	**0**	**1**	**0**

Signed as free agent by **Detroit**, October 12, 1978. Signed as free agent by **Buffalo**, September 2, 1981.

DeBLOIS, LUCIEN (DEB-Lwah, loose-YEN)

Born, Joliette, Que., June 21, 1957.
Right wing. Shoots right. 5'11", 200 lbs.
Last amateur club: Sorel Black Hawks (QJHL).
(NY Rangers' 1st choice, 8th over-all, in 1977 Amateur Draft).

			Regular Season					Playoffs				
Season	Club	Lea	GP	G	A	TP	PIM	GP	G	A	TP	PIM
1975-76	Sorel	QJHL	70	56	55	111	112	5	1	1	2	32
1976-77	Sorel	QJHL	72	56	78	134	131	....	....	....	....	....
1977-78	**NY Rangers**	**NHL**	**71**	**22**	**8**	**30**	**27**	**3**	**0**	**0**	**0**	**2**
1978-79	New Haven	AHL	7	4	6	10	6	....	....	....	....	....
	NY Rangers	**NHL**	**62**	**11**	**17**	**28**	**26**	**9**	**2**	**0**	**2**	**4**
1979-80	**NY Rangers**	**NHL**	**6**	**3**	**1**	**4**	**7**	....	....	....	....	....
	Colorado	**NHL**	**70**	**24**	**19**	**43**	**36**	....	....	....	....	....
1980-81	**Colorado**	**NHL**	**74**	**26**	**16**	**42**	**78**	....	....	....	....	....
1981-82	**Winnipeg**	**NHL**	**65**	**25**	**27**	**52**	**87**	**4**	**2**	**1**	**3**	**4**
1982-83	**Winnipeg**	**NHL**	**79**	**27**	**27**	**54**	**69**	**3**	**0**	**0**	**0**	**5**
1983-84	**Winnipeg**	**NHL**	**80**	**34**	**45**	**79**	**50**	**3**	**0**	**1**	**1**	**4**
1984-85	**Montreal**	**NHL**	**51**	**12**	**11**	**23**	**20**	**8**	**2**	**4**	**6**	**4**
1985-86	**Montreal**	**NHL**	**61**	**14**	**17**	**31**	**48**	**11**	**0**	**0**	**0**	**7**
	NHL Totals		**619**	**198**	**188**	**386**	**448**	**41**	**6**	**6**	**12**	**30**

Traded to **Colorado** by **NY Rangers** with Pat Hickey, Mike McEwen, Dean Turner and future consideration (Bobby Crawford) for Barry Beck, November 2, 1979. Traded to **Winnipeg** by **Colorado** for Brent Ashton and Winnipeg's third-round choice (Dave Kasper) in the 1982 Entry Draft, July 15, 1981. Traded to **Montreal** by **Winnipeg** for Perry Turnbull, June 13, 1984.

DEEGAN, SHANNON

Born, Montreal, Que., March 19, 1966.
Center. Shoots left. 6'2", 190 lbs.
Last amateur club: University of Vermont Catamounts (ECAC).
(Los Angeles' 8th choice, 150th over-all, in 1984 Entry Draft).

			Regular Season					Playoffs				
Season	Club	Lea	GP	G	A	TP	PIM	GP	G	A	TP	PIM
1983-84	Vermont	ECAC	28	5	5	10	14	....	....	....	....	....
1984-85	Vermont	ECAC	9	0	3	3	6	....	....	....	....	....
1985-86	Vermont	ECAC	28	9	9	18	30	....	....	....	....	....

DEFAZIO, DEAN

Born, Ottawa, Ont., April 16, 1963.
Left wing. Shoots left. 5'11", 185 lbs.
Last amateur club: Oshawa Generals (OHL).
(Pittsburgh's 9th choice, 175th over-all, in 1981 Entry Draft).

			Regular Season					Playoffs				
Season	Club	Lea	GP	G	A	TP	PIM	GP	G	A	TP	PIM
1980-81	Brantford	OHA	60	6	13	19	104	6	1	0	1	19
1981-82	Brantford	OHL	10	2	6	8	30	....	....	....	....	....
	Sudbury	OHL	50	21	32	53	81	....	....	....	....	....
1982-83	Oshawa	OHL	52	22	23	45	108	17	8	9	17	16
1983-84	**Pittsburgh**	**NHL**	**22**	**0**	**2**	**2**	**28**	....	....	....	....	....
	Baltimore	AHL	46	18	13	31	114	10	2	2	4	19
1984-85	Baltimore	AHL	78	10	17	27	88	10	2	1	3	64
1985-86	Baltimore	AHL	75	14	24	38	171	....	....	....	....	....
	NHL Totals		**22**	**0**	**2**	**2**	**28**	....	....	....	....	....

DeGAETANO, PHIL

Born, Flushing, NY, August 9, 1963.
Defense. Shoots right. 6'1", 203 lbs.
Last amateur club: Northern Michigan University Wildcats (WCHA).

			Regular Season					Playoffs				
Season	Club	Lea	GP	G	A	TP	PIM	GP	G	A	TP	PIM
1981-82	N. Michigan	WCHA	36	4	10	14	34	....	....	....	....	....
1982-83	N. Michigan	WCHA	37	5	9	14	56	....	....	....	....	....
1983-84	N. Michigan	WCHA	35	2	9	11	45	....	....	....	....	....
1984-85	N. Michigan	WCHA	40	5	20	25	98	....	....	....	....	....
1985-86	Indianapolis	IHL	80	9	39	48	107	5	2	1	3	15

Signed as a free agent by **Detroit**, April 8, 1986.

DEGRAY, DALE EDWARD

Born, Oshawa, Ont., September 1, 1963.
Defense. Shoots right. 6', 200 lbs.
Last amateur club: Oshawa Generals (OHL).
(Calgary's 7th choice, 162nd over-all, in 1981 Entry Draft).

			Regular Season					Playoffs				
Season	Club	Lea	GP	G	A	TP	PIM	GP	G	A	TP	PIM
1980-81	Oshawa	OHA	61	11	10	21	93	8	1	1	2	19
1981-82	Oshawa	OHL	66	11	23	34	162	12	3	4	7	49
1982-83	Oshawa	OHL	69	20	30	50	149	17	7	7	14	36
1983-84	Colorado	CHL	67	16	14	30	67	6	1	1	2	2
1984-85a	Moncton	AHL	77	24	37	61	63	....	....	....	....	....
1985-86	**Calgary**	**NHL**	**1**	**0**	**0**	**0**	**0**	....	....	....	....	....
	Moncton	AHL	76	10	31	41	128	6	0	1	1	0
	NHL Totals		**1**	**0**	**0**	**0**	**0**	....	....	....	....	....

a AHL Second All-Star Team (1985)

DEGRIO, GARY

Born, Duluth, Minn., February 16, 1960.
Left/Right wing. Shoots left. 5'11", 180 lbs.
Last amateur club: University of Minnesota-Duluth Bulldogs (WCHA)

			Regular Season					Playoffs				
Season	Club	Lea	GP	G	A	TP	PIM	GP	G	A	TP	PIM
1978-79	Minn.-Duluth	WCHA	34	2	8	10	6	....	....	....	....	....
1979-80	Minn.-Duluth	WCHA	33	14	5	19	2	....	....	....	....	....
1980-81	Minn.-Duluth	WCHA	38	25	8	33	24	....	....	....	....	....
1981-82	Minn.-Duluth	WCHA	40	18	17	35	18	....	....	....	....	....
1982-83	Tulsa	CHL	77	18	21	39	25	....	....	....	....	....
1983-84	Tulsa	CHL	65	10	19	29	24	9	2	0	2	2
1984-85	Salt Lake	IHL	22	10	4	14	4	....	....	....	....	....
1985-86	Salt Lake	IHL	59	19	14	33	18	5	2	3	5	2

Signed as a free agent by **NY Rangers**, May 3, 1982.

DELCOL, JOHN

Born, St. Catharines, Ont., May 11, 1965.
Left wing. Shoots left. 5'10", 190 lbs.
Last amateur club: Toronto Marlboros (OHL).
(Pittsburgh's 8th choice, 169th over-all, in 1984 Entry Draft).

			Regular Season					Playoffs				
Season	Club	Lea	GP	G	A	TP	PIM	GP	G	A	TP	PIM
1983-84	Toronto	OHL	67	22	24	46	94	9	1	3	4	14
1984-85	Toronto	OHL	62	34	36	70	76	5	1	2	3	8
1985-86	Baltimore	AHL	26	1	2	3	16	....	....	....	....	....
	Muskegon	IHL	5	0	0	0	0	....	....	....	....	....
	Toledo	IHL	33	6	7	13	23	....	....	....	....	....

DELCOURT, GRANT

Born, Prince George, B.C., August 13, 1966.
Right wing. Shoots right. 5'11", 178 lbs.
Last amateur club: Spokane Chiefs (WHL).
(Buffalo's 10th choice, 228th over-all, in 1984 Entry Draft).

			Regular Season					Playoffs				
Season	Club	Lea	GP	G	A	TP	PIM	GP	G	A	TP	PIM
1983-84	Kelowna	WHL	72	22	53	75	55	....	....	....	....	....
1984-85	Kelowna	WHL	70	32	38	70	139	6	2	4	6	12
1985-86	Spokane	WHL	67	39	51	90	154	9	8	2	10	34

DELORME, GILBERT (de-LORM)

Born, Boucherville, Que., November 25, 1962.
Defense. Shoots right. 6'1", 205 lbs.
Last amateur club: Chicoutimi Sagueneens (QJHL).
(Montreal's 2nd choice, 18th over-all, in 1981 Entry Draft).

				Regular Season					Playoffs			
Season	Club	Lea	GP	G	A	TP	PIM	GP	G	A	TP	PIM
1979-80	Chicoutimi	QJHL	71	25	86	111	68	12	2	10	12	26
1980-81	Chicoutimi	QJHL	70	27	79	106	77	12	10	12	22	16
1981-82	**Montreal**	NHL	60	3	8	11	55	....	....	....	....	....
1982-83	**Montreal**	NHL	78	12	21	33	89	3	0	0	0	2
1983-84	**Montreal**	NHL	27	2	7	9	8	....	....	....	....	....
	St. Louis	NHL	44	0	5	5	41	11	1	3	4	11
1984-85	**St. Louis**	NHL	74	2	12	14	53	3	0	0	0	0
1985-86	**Quebec**	NHL	64	2	18	20	51	2	0	0	0	5
	NHL Totals		347	16	71	92	297	19	1	3	4	18

Traded to **St. Louis** by **Montreal** with Greg Paslawski and Doug Wickenheiser for Perry Turnbull, December 21, 1983. Traded to **Quebec** by **St. Louis** for Bruce Bell, October 2, 1985.

DEMERS, ERIC

Born, Montreal, Que., March 1, 1966.
Left wing. Shoots left. 6'3", 180 lbs.
Last amateur club: Drummondville Voltigeurs (QMJHL).
(Montreal's 11th choice, 179th over-all, in 1984 Entry Draft).

				Regular Season					Playoffs			
Season	Club	Lea	GP	G	A	TP	PIM	GP	G	A	TP	PIM
1983-84	Shawinigan	QMJHL	65	5	13	18	153	....	....	....	....	....
1984-85	Shawinigan	QMJHL	64	12	23	35	170	9	0	0	0	8
1985-86	Drummondville	QMJHL	55	13	10	23	243	15	4	6	10	43

DePALMA, LARRY

Born, Trenton, Mich., October 27, 1965.
Left wing. Shoots left. 6'0", 180 lbs.
Last amateur club: Saskatoon Blades (WHL).

				Regular Season					Playoffs			
Season	Club	Lea	GP	G	A	TP	PIM	GP	G	A	TP	PIM
1984-85	N. Westminster	WHL	65	14	16	30	87	10	1	1	2	25
1985-86	Saskatoon	WHL	65	61	51	112	232	13	7	9	16	58
	Minnesota	NHL	1	0	0	0	0	....	....	....	....	....
	NHL Totals		1	0	0	0	0	....	....	....	....	....

Signed as a free agent by **Minnesota**, May 12, 1986.

DERLAGO, WILLIAM ANTHONY (BILL) (der-LAG-oh)

Born, Birtle, Man., August 25, 1958.
Center. Shoots left. 5'10", 195 lbs.
Last amateur club: Brandon Wheat Kings (WHL).
(Vancouver's 1st choice, 4th over-all, in 1978 Amateur Draft).

				Regular Season					Playoffs			
Season	Club	Lea	GP	G	A	TP	PIM	GP	G	A	TP	PIM
1976-77a	Brandon	WHL	72	*96	82	*178	63	16	*14	*16	*30	31
1977-78b	Brandon	WHL	52	*89	63	152	105	8	9	13	22	10
1978-79	**Vancouver**	NHL	9	4	4	8	2	....	....	....	....	....
	Dallas	CHL	11	5	8	13	9	....	....	....	....	....
1979-80	**Vancouver**	NHL	54	11	15	26	27	....	....	....	....	....
	Toronto	NHL	23	5	12	17	13	3	0	0	0	4
1980-81	**Toronto**	NHL	80	35	39	74	26	3	1	0	1	2
1981-82	**Toronto**	NHL	75	34	50	84	42	....	....	....	....	....
1982-83	**Toronto**	NHL	58	13	24	37	27	4	3	0	3	2
1983-84	**Toronto**	NHL	79	40	20	60	50	....	....	....	....	....
1984-85	**Toronto**	NHL	62	31	31	62	21	....	....	....	....	....
1985-86	**Toronto**	NHL	1	0	0	0	0	....	....	....	....	....
	Boston	NHL	39	5	16	21	15	....	....	....	....	....
	Winnipeg	NHL	27	5	5	10	6	3	1	0	1	0
	NHL Totals		507	183	216	399	229	13	5	0	5	8

a WHL First All-Star Team (1977)
b WHL Second All-Star Team (1978)
Traded to **Toronto** by **Vancouver** with Rick Vaive for Dave Williams and Jerry Butler, February 18, 1980. Traded to **Boston** by **Toronto** for Tom Fergus, October 11, 1985. Traded to **Winnipeg** by **Boston** for Wade Campbell, January 31, 1986.

DESJARDINS, MARTIN

Born, Ste-Rose, Que., January 28, 1967.
Center. Shoots left. 5'11", 165 lbs.
Last amateur club: Trois Rivieres Draveurs (QMJHL).
(Montreal's 5th choice, 75th over-all, in 1985 Entry Draft).

				Regular Season					Playoffs			
Season	Club	Lea	GP	G	A	TP	PIM	GP	G	A	TP	PIM
1984-85	Trois Rivieres	QMJHL	66	29	34	63	76	7	4	6	10	6
1985-86	Trois Rivieres	QMJHL	71	49	69	118	103	4	2	4	6	4

DESMOND, NED

Born, New York, NY, February 18, 1966.
Defense. Shoots left. 6'3", 205 lbs.
Last amateur club: Dartmouth College Big Green (ECAC).
(St. Louis' 3rd choice, 54th over-all, in 1985 Entry Draft).

				Regular Season					Playoffs			
Season	Club	Lea	GP	G	A	TP	PIM	GP	G	A	TP	PIM
1985-86	Dartmouth	ECAC	23	4	12	16	4	....	....	....	....	....

DEVEREAUX, JOHN

Born, Scituate, Mass., June 8, 1965.
Center. Shoots right. 6'0", 175 lbs.
Last amateur club: Boston College Eagles (H.E.).
(Hartford's 4th choice, 173rd over-all, in 1984 Entry Draft).

				Regular Season					Playoffs			
Season	Club	Lea	GP	G	A	TP	PIM	GP	G	A	TP	PIM
1984-85	Boston College	H.E.	19	3	3	6	6	....	....	....	....	....
1985-86	Boston College	H.E.	41	8	6	14	24	....	....	....	....	....

DEVOE, JOHN

Born, Edina, Minn., November 1, 1963.
Left wing. Shoots right. 6'2", 190 lbs.
Last amateur club: Providence College Friars (H.E.).
(Montreal's 7th choice, 69th over-all, in 1984 Entry Draft).

				Regular Season					Playoffs			
Season	Club	Lea	GP	G	A	TP	PIM	GP	G	A	TP	PIM
1983-84	Providence	ECAC	28	14	6	20	18	....	....	....	....	....
1984-85	Providence	H.E.	36	4	4	8	28	....	....	....	....	....
1985-86	Providence	H.E.	39	1	10	11	34	....	....	....	....	....

DIDUCK, GERALD

Born, Edmonton, Alta., April 6, 1965.
Defense. Shoots right. 6'2", 195 lbs.
Last amateur club: Lethbridge Broncos (WHL).
(NY Islanders' 2nd choice, 16th over-all, in 1983 Entry Draft).

				Regular Season					Playoffs			
Season	Club	Lea	GP	G	A	TP	PIM	GP	G	A	TP	PIM
1981-82	Lethbridge	WHL	71	1	15	16	81	12	0	3	3	27
1982-83	Lethbridge	WHL	67	8	16	24	151	20	3	12	15	49
1983-84	Lethbridge	WHL	65	10	24	34	133	5	1	4	5	27
1984-85	**NY Islanders**	NHL	65	2	8	10	80	....	....	....	....	....
1985-86	**NY Islanders**	NHL	10	1	2	3	2	....	....	....	....	....
	Springfield	AHL	61	6	14	20	175	....	....	....	....	....
	NHL Totals		75	3	10	13	82	....	....	....	....	....

DIFIORE, RALPH

Born, Montreal, Que., April 20, 1966.
Defense. Shoots left. 6'1", 180 lbs.
Last amateur club: Trois Rivieres Draveurs (QMJHL).
(Chicago's 9th choice, 174th over-all, in 1984 Entry Draft).

				Regular Season					Playoffs			
Season	Club	Lea	GP	G	A	TP	PIM	GP	G	A	TP	PIM
1983-84	Shawinigan	QMJHL	65	6	22	28	38	....	....	....	....	....
1984-85	Shawinigan	QMJHL	55	4	30	34	38	9	2	5	7	10
1985-86	Trois Rivieres	QMJHL	41	0	21	21	110	5	1	0	1	4

DIETRICH, DON ARMOND

Born, Deloraine, Man., April 5, 1961.
Defense. Shoots left. 6'1", 195 lbs.
Last amateur club: Brandon Wheat Kings (WHL).
(Chicago's 14th choice, 183rd over-all, in 1980 Entry Draft).

				Regular Season					Playoffs			
Season	Club	Lea	GP	G	A	TP	PIM	GP	G	A	TP	PIM
1978-79	Brandon	WHL	69	6	37	43	29	....	....	....	....	....
1979-80	Brandon	WHL	63	15	45	60	56	....	....	....	....	....
1980-81	Brandon	WHL	72	16	64	80	84	....	....	....	....	....
1981-82	New Brunswick	AHL	62	1	5	6	14	2	0	0	0	0
1982-83	Springfield	AHL	76	6	26	32	26	....	....	....	....	....
1983-84	**Chicago**	NHL	17	0	5	5	0	....	....	....	....	....
	Springfield	AHL	50	14	21	35	14	....	....	....	....	....
1984-85	Maine	AHL	75	6	21	27	36	11	3	4	7	4
1985-86	**New Jersey**	NHL	11	0	2	2	10	....	....	....	....	....
	Maine	AHL	68	9	11	20	33	3	0	0	0	0
	NHL Totals		28	0	7	7	10	....	....	....	....	....

Traded to **New Jersey** by **Chicago** with Rich Preston for Bob MacMillan and New Jersey's fifth round choice in 1985 Entry Draft (Rick Herbert), June 12, 1984.

DIMUZIO, FRANK

Born, Toronto, Ont., August 12, 1967.
Left wing. Shoots right. 5'11", 185 lbs.
Last amateur club: Ottawa 67's (OHL).
(Washington's 13th choice, 250th over-all, in 1985 Entry Draft).

				Regular Season					Playoffs			
Season	Club	Lea	GP	G	A	TP	PIM	GP	G	A	TP	PIM
1984-85	Belleville	OHL	68	28	22	50	40	12	4	2	6	8
1985-86	Ottawa	OHL	63	29	26	55	105	....	....	....	....	....

DINEEN, GORDON (GORD)

Born, Toronto, Ont., September 21, 1962.
Defense. Shoots right. 5′11″, 195 lbs.
Last amateur club: Sault Ste. Marie Greyhounds (OHL).
(NY Islanders' 2nd choice, 42nd over-all, in 1981 Entry Draft).

Season	Club	Lea	Regular Season GP	G	A	TP	PIM	Playoffs GP	G	A	TP	PIM
1980-81	S. S. Marie	OHA	68	4	26	30	158	19	1	7	8	58
1981-82	S. S. Marie	OHL	68	9	45	54	185	13	1	2	3	52
1982-83	**NY Islanders**	**NHL**	**2**	**0**	**0**	**0**	**4**	....	....	....	....	....
abc	Indianapolis	CHL	73	10	47	57	78	13	2	10	12	29
1983-84	Indianapolis	CHL	26	4	13	17	63	....	....	....	....	....
	NY Islanders	**NHL**	**43**	**1**	**11**	**12**	**32**	**9**	**1**	**1**	**2**	**28**
1984-85	**NY Islanders**	**NHL**	**48**	**1**	**12**	**13**	**89**	**10**	**0**	**0**	**0**	**26**
	Springfield	AHL	25	1	8	9	46	....	....	....	....	....
1985-86	**NY Islanders**	**NHL**	**57**	**1**	**8**	**9**	**81**	**3**	**0**	**0**	**0**	**2**
	Springfield	AHL	11	2	3	5	20	....	....	....	....	....
	NHL Totals		**150**	**3**	**31**	**34**	**206**	**22**	**1**	**1**	**2**	**56**

a CHL First All-Star Team (1983)
b Won Bob Gassoff Trophy (CHL's Most Improved Defenseman) (1983)
c Won Bobby Orr Trophy (CHL's Top Defenseman) (1983)

DINEEN, KEVIN

Born, Toronto, Ont., October 28, 1963.
Right wing. Shoots right. 5′10″, 185 lbs.
Last amateur club: 1984 Canadian Olympic Team.
(Hartford's 3rd choice, 56th over-all, in 1982 Entry Draft).

Season	Club	Lea	Regular Season GP	G	A	TP	PIM	Playoffs GP	G	A	TP	PIM
1981-82	U. of Denver	WCHA	26	10	10	20	70	....	....	....	....	....
1982-83	U. of Denver	WCHA	36	16	13	29	108	....	....	....	....	....
1983-84	Cdn. Olympic	...	52	5	11	16	2	....	....	....	....	....
1984-85	**Hartford**	**NHL**	**57**	**25**	**16**	**41**	**120**	....	....	....	....	....
	Binghamton	AHL	25	15	8	23	41	....	....	....	....	....
1985-86	**Hartford**	**NHL**	**57**	**33**	**35**	**68**	**124**	**10**	**6**	**7**	**13**	**18**
	NHL Totals		**114**	**58**	**51**	**109**	**244**	**10**	**6**	**7**	**13**	**18**

DINEEN, PETER KEVIN

Born, Kingston, Ont., November 19, 1960.
Defense. Shoots right. 5′11″, 180 lbs.
Last amateur club: Kingston Canadians (OHA).
(Philadelphia's 9th choice, 189th over-all, in 1980 Entry Draft).

Season	Club	Lea	Regular Season GP	G	A	TP	PIM	Playoffs GP	G	A	TP	PIM
1978-79	Kingston	OHA	60	7	14	21	70	11	2	6	8	28
1979-80	Kingston	OHA	32	4	10	14	54	3	0	0	0	13
1980-81	Maine	AHL	41	6	7	13	100	16	1	2	3	82
1981-82	Maine	AHL	71	6	14	20	156	3	0	0	0	2
1982-83	Maine	AHL	2	0	0	0	0	....	....	....	....	....
	Moncton	AHL	57	0	10	10	76	....	....	....	....	....
1983-84	Moncton	AHL	63	0	10	10	120	....	....	....	....	....
	Hershey	AHL	12	0	1	1	32	....	....	....	....	....
1984-85	Hershey	AHL	79	4	19	23	144	....	....	....	....	....
1985-86	Binghamton	AHL	11	0	1	1	35	....	....	....	....	....
	Moncton	AHL	55	5	13	18	136	9	1	0	1	9

Traded to **Edmonton** by **Philadelphia** for Bob Hoffmeyer, October 22, 1982. Signed as a free agent by **Boston**, July 16, 1984. Signed as a free agent by Los Angeles, July 30, 1986.

DION, GRANT

Born, Tsawwassen, B.C., January 17, 1964.
Defense. Shoots right. 5′11″, 205 lbs.
Last amateur club: University of Denver Pioneers (WCHA).
(Edmonton's 10th choice, 209th over-all, in 1982 Entry Draft).

Season	Club	Lea	Regular Season GP	G	A	TP	PIM	Playoffs GP	G	A	TP	PIM
1982-83	Denver	WCHA	32	0	9	9	22	....	....	....	....	....
1983-84	Denver	WCHA	35	11	20	31	36	....	....	....	....	....
1984-85	Denver	WCHA	24	6	8	14	16	....	....	....	....	....
1985-86	Denver	WCHA	47	10	40	50	37	....	....	....	....	....

DIONNE, MARCEL ELPHEGE   (DEE-ahn)

Born, Drummondville, Que., August 3, 1951.
Center. Shoots right. 5′8″, 190 lbs.
Last amateur club: St. Catharines Black Hawks (OHA).
(Detroit's 1st choice, 2nd over-all, in 1971 Amateur Draft).

Season	Club	Lea	Regular Season GP	G	A	TP	PIM	Playoffs GP	G	A	TP	PIM
1969-70	St. Catharines	OHA	54	*55	*77	*132	46	....	....	....	....	....
1970-71	St. Catharines	OHA	46	62	81	*143	20	....	....	....	....	....
1971-72	**Detroit**	**NHL**	**78**	**28**	**49**	**77**	**14**	....	....	....	....	....
1972-73	**Detroit**	**NHL**	**77**	**40**	**50**	**90**	**21**	....	....	....	....	....
1973-74	**Detroit**	**NHL**	**74**	**24**	**54**	**78**	**10**	....	....	....	....	....
1974-75a	**Detroit**	**NHL**	**80**	**47**	**74**	**121**	**14**	....	....	....	....	....
1975-76	**Los Angeles**	**NHL**	**80**	**40**	**54**	**94**	**38**	**9**	**6**	**1**	**7**	**0**
1976-77ab	**Los Angeles**	**NHL**	**80**	**53**	**69**	**122**	**12**	**9**	**5**	**9**	**14**	**2**
1977-78	**Los Angeles**	**NHL**	**70**	**36**	**43**	**79**	**37**	**2**	**0**	**0**	**0**	**0**
1978-79cd	**Los Angeles**	**NHL**	**80**	**59**	**71**	**130**	**30**	**2**	**0**	**1**	**1**	**0**
1979-80bde	**Los Angeles**	**NHL**	**80**	**53**	**84**	***137**	**32**	**4**	**0**	**3**	**3**	**4**
1980-81c	**Los Angeles**	**NHL**	**80**	**58**	**77**	**135**	**70**	**4**	**1**	**3**	**4**	**7**
1981-82	**Los Angeles**	**NHL**	**78**	**50**	**67**	**117**	**50**	**10**	**7**	**4**	**11**	**0**
1982-83	**Los Angeles**	**NHL**	**80**	**56**	**51**	**107**	**22**	....	....	....	....	....
1983-84	**Los Angeles**	**NHL**	**66**	**39**	**53**	**92**	**28**	....	....	....	....	....
1984-85	**Los Angeles**	**NHL**	**80**	**46**	**80**	**126**	**46**	**3**	**1**	**2**	**3**	**2**
1985-86	**Los Angeles**	**NHL**	**80**	**36**	**58**	**94**	**42**	....	....	....	....	....
	NHL Totals		**1163**	**665**	**934**	**1599**	**466**	**43**	**20**	**23**	**43**	**15**

a Won Lady Byng Memorial Trophy (1975, 1977)
b NHL First All-Star Team (1977, 1980)
c NHL Second All-Star Team (1979, 1981)
d Won Lester B. Pearson Memorial Award (1979, 1980)
e Won Art Ross Trophy (1980)

Acquired as free agent by **Los Angeles** from **Detroit** with Bart Crashley for Terry Harper, Dan Maloney and Los Angeles' second choice — later transferred to Minnesota (Jimmy Roberts) — in 1976 Amateur Draft, June 23, 1975.

DIRK, ROBERT

Born, Regina, Sask., August 20, 1966.
Defense. Shoots left. 6′4″, 205 lbs.
Last amateur club: Regina Pats (WHL).
(St. Louis' 4th choice, 53rd over-all, in 1984 Entry Draft).

Season	Club	Lea	Regular Season GP	G	A	TP	PIM	Playoffs GP	G	A	TP	PIM
1982-83	Regina	WHL	1	0	0	0	0	....	....	....	....	....
1983-84	Regina	WHL	62	2	10	12	64	23	1	12	13	24
1984-85	Regina	WHL	69	10	34	44	97	8	0	0	0	4
1985-86	Regina	WHL	72	19	60	79	140	10	3	5	8	8

DOBBIN, BRIAN

Born, Petrolia, Ont., August 18, 1966.
Right wing. Shoots right. 5′11″, 195 lbs.
Last amateur club: London Knights (OHL).
(Philadelphia's 6th choice, 100th over-all, in 1984 Entry Draft).

Season	Club	Lea	Regular Season GP	G	A	TP	PIM	Playoffs GP	G	A	TP	PIM
1983-84	London	OHL	70	30	40	70	70	....	....	....	....	....
1984-85	London	OHL	53	42	57	99	63	8	7	4	11	2
1985-86	London	OHL	59	38	55	93	113	5	2	1	3.	9

DOBSON, JAMES (JIM)

Born, Winnipeg, Man., February 29, 1960.
Right wing. Shoots right. 6′1″, 195 lbs.
Last amateur club: Portland Winter Hawks (WHL).
(Minnesota's 5th choice, 90th over-all, in 1979 Entry Draft).

Season	Club	Lea	Regular Season GP	G	A	TP	PIM	Playoffs GP	G	A	TP	PIM
1978-79	Portland	WHL	71	38	39	77	143	....	....	....	....	....
1979-80a	Portland	WHL	72	66	68	134	181	....	....	....	....	....
	Minnesota	**NHL**	**1**	**0**	**0**	**0**	**0**	....	....	....	....	....
1980-81	**Minnesota**	**NHL**	**1**	**0**	**0**	**0**	**0**	....	....	....	....	....
	Oklahoma City	CHL	35	23	16	39	46	....	....	....	....	....
1981-82	Nashville	CHL	29	19	13	32	29	....	....	....	....	....
	Minnesota	**NHL**	**6**	**0**	**0**	**0**	**4**	....	....	....	....	....
	Colorado	**NHL**	**3**	**0**	**0**	**0**	**2**	....	....	....	....	....
	Fort Worth	CHL	34	15	12	27	65	....	....	....	....	....
1982-83	Birmingham	CHL	80	36	37	73	100	13	8	4	12	4
1983-84	**Quebec**	**NHL**	**1**	**0**	**0**	**0**	**0**	....	....	....	....	....
	Fredericton	AHL	75	33	44	77	74	7	3	2	5	2
1984-85	Fredericton	AHL	21	8	10	18	52	5	3	0	3	5
1985-86	New Haven	AHL	29	5	6	11	12	1	0	0	0	0
	NHL Totals		**12**	**0**	**0**	**0**	**6**	....	....	....	....	....

a WHL First All-Star Team (1980)

Rights traded to **Colorado** by **Minnesota**, December 31, 1981. Signed as free agent by **Minnesota**, September 20, 1982. Traded to **Quebec** by **Minnesota** for Jay Miller, June 29, 1983. Signed as a free agent by **NY Rangers**, December 13, 1985.

DOLLAS, BOBBY

Born, Montreal, Que., January 31, 1965.
Defense. Shoots left. 6'2", 210 lbs.
Last amateur club: Laval Nationales (QMJHL).
(Winnipeg's 2nd choice, 14th over-all, in 1983 Entry Draft).

Season	Club	Lea	Regular Season					Playoffs				
			GP	G	A	TP	PIM	GP	G	A	TP	PIM
1981-82	Lac St. Louis	Midget	44	9	31	40	138	....	....	....	....	....
1982-83a	Laval	QMJHL	63	16	45	61	144	11	5	5	10	23
1983-84	**Winnipeg**	**NHL**	1	0	0	0	0	....	....	....	....	....
	Laval	QMJHL	54	12	33	45	80	14	1	8	9	23
1984-85	**Winnipeg**	**NHL**	9	0	0	0	0	....	....	....	....	....
	Sherbrooke	AHL	8	1	3	4	4	17	3	6	9	17
1985-86	**Winnipeg**	**NHL**	46	0	5	5	66	3	0	0	0	2
	Sherbrooke	AHL	25	4	7	11	29	....	....	....	....	....
	NHL Totals		56	0	5	5	66	3	0	0	0	2

a QMJHL Second All-Star Team (1983).

DONAHUE, ANDY

Born, Boston, Mass., January 17, 1967.
Center. Shoots right. 6'1", 180 lbs.
Last amateur club: Dartmouth College Big Green (ECAC).
(Toronto's 8th choice, 148th over-all, in 1985 Entry Draft).

Season	Club	Lea	Regular Season					Playoffs				
			GP	G	A	TP	PIM	GP	G	A	TP	PIM
1985-86	Dartmouth	ECAC	25	12	7	19	14	....	....	....	....	....

DONATELLI, CLARK

Born, Providence, R.I., November 22, 1965.
Left wing. Shoots left. 5'10", 190 lbs.
Last amateur club: Boston University Terriers (H.E.).
(NY Ranger's 4th choice, 98th over-all, in 1984 Entry Draft).

Season	Club	Lea	Regular Season					Playoffs				
			GP	G	A	TP	PIM	GP	G	A	TP	PIM
1984-85	Boston U.	H.E.	40	17	18	35	46	....	....	....	....	....
1985-86ab	Boston U.	H.E.	43	28	34	62	30	....	....	....	....	....

a NCAA East Second All-American Team (1986)
b Hockey East Second All-Star Team (1986)

DONNELLY, DAVID (DAVE)

Born, Edmonton, Alta., February 2, 1962.
Center. Shoots left. 5'11", 185 lbs.
Last amateur club: 1984 Canadian Olympic Team.
(Minnesota's 2nd choice, 27th over-all, in 1981 Entry Draft).

Season	Club	Lea	Regular Season					Playoffs				
			GP	G	A	TP	PIM	GP	G	A	TP	PIM
1979-80	St. Albert	AJHL	59	27	33	60	146	....	....	....	....	....
1980-81	St. Albert	AJHL	53	39	55	94	243	....	....	....	....	....
1981-82	North Dakota	WCHA	38	10	15	25	38	....	....	....	....	....
1982-83	North Dakota	WCHA	34	18	16	34	106	....	....	....	....	....
1983-84	Cdn. Olympic	...	64	17	13	30	52	....	....	....	....	....
	Boston	**NHL**	16	3	4	7	2	3	0	0	0	0
1984-85	**Boston**	**NHL**	38	6	8	14	46	1	0	0	0	0
	Hershey	AHL	26	11	6	17	28	....	....	....	....	....
1985-86	**Boston**	**NHL**	8	0	0	0	17	....	....	....	....	....
	NHL Totals		62	9	12	21	65	4	0	0	0	0

Rights traded to **Boston** by **Minnesota** with Brad Palmer for past considerations, June 9, 1982.
Traded to **Detroit** by **Boston** for Dwight Foster, March 11, 1986.

DONNELLY, GORDON (GORD)

Born, Montreal, Que., April 5, 1962.
Defense. Shoots right. 6'1", 195 lbs.
Last amateur club: Sherbrooke Castors (QMJHL).
(St. Louis' 3rd choice, 62nd over-all, in 1981 Entry Draft).

Season	Club	Lea	Regular Season					Playoffs				
			GP	G	A	TP	PIM	GP	G	A	TP	PIM
1980-81	Sherbrooke	QMJHL	67	15	23	38	252	14	1	2	3	35
1981-82	Sherbrooke	QMJHL	60	8	41	49	250	22	2	7	9	106
1982-83	Salt Lake	CHL	67	3	12	15	222	6	1	1	2	8
1983-84	**Quebec**	**NHL**	38	0	5	5	60	....	....	....	....	....
	Fredericton	AHL	30	2	3	5	146	7	1	1	2	43
1984-85	**Quebec**	**NHL**	22	0	0	0	33	....	....	....	....	....
	Fredericton	AHL	42	1	5	6	134	6	0	1	1	25
1985-86	**Quebec**	**NHL**	36	2	2	4	85	1	0	0	0	0
	Fredericton	AHL	37	3	5	8	103	5	0	0	0	33
	NHL Totals		96	2	7	9	178	1	0	0	0	0

Rights transferred to **Quebec** by **St. Louis** with rights to Claude Julien when St. Louis signed Jacques Demers as coach, August 19, 1983.

DORE, ANDRE HECTOR   (door-AY)

Born, Montreal, Que., February 11, 1958.
Defense. Shoots right. 6'2", 200 lbs.
Last amateur club: Quebec Remparts (QJHL).
(NY Rangers' 5th choice, 60th over-all, in 1978 Amateur Draft).

Season	Club	Lea	Regular Season					Playoffs				
			GP	G	A	TP	PIM	GP	G	A	TP	PIM
1976-77	Hull	QJHL	72	9	42	51	178	3	0	3	3	29
1977-78	Hull	QJHL	15	3	9	12	22	....	....	....	....	....
	Trois Rivières	QJHL	27	2	14	16	61	....	....	....	....	....
	Quebec	QJHL	32	6	17	23	51	4	0	0	0	2
1978-79	**NY Rangers**	**NHL**	2	0	0	0	0	....	....	....	....	....
	New Haven	AHL	71	6	23	29	134	10	0	3	3	12
1979-80	**NY Rangers**	**NHL**	2	0	0	0	0	....	....	....	....	....
	New Haven	AHL	63	9	21	30	99	9	1	1	2	20
1980-81	**NY Rangers**	**NHL**	15	1	3	4	15	....	....	....	....	....
	New Haven	AHL	58	8	41	49	105	....	....	....	....	....
1981-82	Springfield	AHL	23	3	8	11	20	....	....	....	....	....
	NY Rangers	**NHL**	56	4	16	20	64	10	1	1	2	16
1982-83	**NY Rangers**	**NHL**	39	3	12	15	39	....	....	....	....	....
	St. Louis	**NHL**	38	2	15	17	25	4	0	1	1	8
1983-84	**St. Louis**	**NHL**	55	3	12	15	58	....	....	....	....	....
	Quebec	**NHL**	25	1	16	17	25	9	0	0	0	8
1984-85	**NY Rangers**	**NHL**	25	0	7	7	35	....	....	....	....	....
	New Haven	AHL	39	3	22	25	48	....	....	....	....	....
1985-86	Hershey	AHL	65	10	18	28	128	18	0	6	6	35
	NHL Totals		257	14	81	95	261	23	1	2	3	32

Traded to **St. Louis** by **NY Rangers** for Vaclav Nedomansky and Glen Hanlon, January 4, 1983. Traded to **Quebec** by **St. Louis** for Dave Pichette, February 10, 1984. Claimed by **NY Rangers** from **Quebec** in NHL Waiver Draft, October 9, 1984.

DORION, DAN

Born, Astoria, N.Y., March 2, 1963.
Center. Shoots right. 5'9", 175 lbs.
Last amateur club: Western Michigan University Broncos (CCHA).
(New Jersey's 10th choice, 232nd over-all, in 1982 Entry Draft).

Season	Club	Lea	Regular Season					Playoffs				
			GP	G	A	TP	PIM	GP	G	A	TP	PIM
1981-82	Austin	USHL	48	53	44	97	41	....	....	....	....	....
1982-83	W. Michigan	CCHA	34	11	20	31	23	....	....	....	....	....
1983-84	W. Michigan	CCHA	42	41	50	91	42	....	....	....	....	....
1984-85	W. Michigan	CCHA	39	21	46	67	28	....	....	....	....	....
1985-86abc	W. Michigan	CCHA	42	42	62	104	48	....	....	....	....	....
	New Jersey	**NHL**	3	1	1	2	0	....	....	....	....	....
	Maine	AHL	....	....	....	....	....	5	2	2	4	0
	NHL Totals		3	1	1	2	0	....	....	....	....	....

a NCAA West First All-American Team (1986)
b CCHA First All-Star Team (1986)
c CCHA Player of the Year (1986)

DORNBACH, GREG

Born, Huntington, W. Virginia, November 1, 1966.
Center. Shoots right. 5'11", 175 lbs.
Last amateur club: University of Miami (Ohio) Redskins (CCHA).
(Hartford's 7th choice, 173rd over-all, in 1985 Entry Draft).

Season	Club	Lea	Regular Season					Playoffs				
			GP	G	A	TP	PIM	GP	G	A	TP	PIM
1984-85	Miami-Ohio	CCHA	36	12	24	36	28	....	....	....	....	....
1985-86	Miami-Ohio	CCHA	35	13	18	31	42	....	....	....	....	....

DOUCET, BENOIT

Born, Montreal, Que., April 23, 1963.
Center. Shoots left. 5'10", 180 lbs.
Last amateur club: Hull Olympiques (QMJHL).

Season	Club	Lea	Regular Season					Playoffs				
			GP	G	A	TP	PIM	GP	G	A	TP	PIM
1985-86	Moncton	AHL	79	26	34	60	18	10	3	2	5	7

Signed as a free agent by **Calgary**, September 30, 1985.

DOURIS, PETER

Born, Toronto, Ont., February 19, 1966.
Center. Shoots right. 6'1", 192 lbs.
Last amateur club: Canadian Olympic Team
(Winnipeg's 1st choice, 30th over-all, in 1984 Entry Draft).

Season	Club	Lea	Regular Season					Playoffs				
			GP	G	A	TP	PIM	GP	G	A	TP	PIM
1983-84	N. Hampshire	ECAC	37	19	15	34	14	....	....	....	....	....
1984-85	N. Hampshire	H.E.	42	27	24	51	34	....	....	....	....	....
1985-86	**Winnipeg**	**NHL**	11	0	0	0	0	....	....	....	....	....
	Cdn. Olympic	....	33	16	7	23	18	....	....	....	....	....
	NHL Totals		11	0	0	0	0	....	....	....	....	....

DOYLE, SHANE

Born, Lindsay, Ont., April 26, 1967.
Defense. Shoots left. 6'1", 200 lbs.
Last amateur club: Cornwall Royals (OHL).
(Vancouver's 3rd choice, 46th over-all, in 1985 Entry Draft).

Season	Club	Lea	Regular Season					Playoffs				
			GP	G	A	TP	PIM	GP	G	A	TP	PIM
1984-85	Belleville	OHL	59	2	26	28	129	11	1	3	4	11
1985-86	Cornwall	OHL	55	4	28	32	206	6	1	0	1	17

DRISCOLL, STEVE

Born, Montreal, Que., June 7, 1964.
Left wing. Shoots left. 5'9", 170 lbs.
Last amateur club: Cornwall Royals (OHL).
(Vancouver's 9th choice, 221st over-all, in 1982 Entry Draft).

Season	Club	Lea	GP	Regular Season G	A	TP	PIM	GP	Playoffs G	A	TP	PIM
1981-82	Cornwall	OHL	65	24	50	74	28	....	....	....	....	....
1982-83a	Cornwall	OHL	64	49	77	126	34	8	4	9	13	2
1983-84	Cornwall	OHL	63	38	51	89	13	3	2	3	5	0
	Fredericton	AHL	2	0	0	0	0	1	0	0	0	0
1984-85	Fredericton	AHL	33	3	7	10	8	....	....	....	....	....
	St. Catharines	AHL	18	4	3	7	4	....	....	....	....	....
1985-86	Kalamazoo	IHL	11	3	4	7	4	....	....	....	....	....
	Toledo	IHL	68	26	28	54	8	....	....	....	....	....

a OHL Second All-Star Team (1983).

DRIVER, BRUCE

Born, Toronto, Ont., April 29, 1962.
Defense. Shoots right. 6', 185 lbs.
Last amateur club: 1984 Canadian Olympic Team.
(Colorado's 6th choice, 108th over-all, in 1981 Entry Draft).

Season	Club	Lea	GP	Regular Season G	A	TP	PIM	GP	Playoffs G	A	TP	PIM
1980-81	U. of Wisconsin	WCHA	42	5	15	20	42	....	....	....	....	....
1981-82ab	U. of Wisconsin	WCHA	46	7	37	44	84	....	....	....	....	....
1982-83	U. of Wisconsin	WCHA	39	16	34	50	50	10	3	8	11	....
1983-84	Cdn. Olympic	...	61	11	17	28	44	....	....	....	....	....
	New Jersey	**NHL**	4	0	2	2	0	....	....	....	....	....
	Maine	AHL	12	2	6	8	15	16	0	10	10	8
1984-85	**New Jersey**	**NHL**	67	9	23	32	36	....	....	....	....	....
1985-86	**New Jersey**	**NHL**	40	3	15	18	32	....	....	....	....	....
	Maine	AHL	15	4	7	11	16	....	....	....	....	....
	NHL Totals		111	12	40	52	68	....	....	....	....	....

a WCHA First All-Team (1982)
b NCAA All-Tournament Team (1982)

DRUCE, JOHN

Born, Peterborough, Ont., February 23, 1966.
Right wing. Shoots left. 6'1", 185 lbs.
Last amateur club: Peterborough Petes (OHL).
(Washington's 2nd choice, 40th over-all, in 1985 Entry Draft).

Season	Club	Lea	GP	Regular Season G	A	TP	PIM	GP	Playoffs G	A	TP	PIM
1984-85	Peterborough	OHL	54	12	14	26	90	17	6	2	8	21
1985-86	Peterborough	OHL	49	22	24	46	84	16	0	5	5	34

DUCHESNE, GAETAN   (dew-SHANE, gay-TAIN)

Born, Quebec City, Que., July 11, 1962.
Left wing. Shoots left. 5'11", 190 lbs.
Last amateur club: Quebec Remparts (QJHL).
(Washington's 8th choice, 152nd over-all, in 1981 Entry Draft).

Season	Club	Lea	GP	Regular Season G	A	TP	PIM	GP	Playoffs G	A	TP	PIM
1979-80	Quebec	QJHL	46	9	28	37	22	5	0	2	2	9
1980-81	Quebec	QJHL	72	27	45	72	63	7	1	4	5	6
1981-82	**Washington**	**NHL**	74	9	14	23	46	....	....	....	....	....
1982-83	Hershey	AHL	1	1	0	1	0	....	....	....	....	....
	Washington	**NHL**	77	18	19	37	52	4	1	1	2	4
1983-84	**Washington**	**NHL**	79	17	19	36	29	8	2	1	3	2
1984-85	**Washington**	**NHL**	67	15	23	38	32	5	0	1	1	7
1985-86	**Washington**	**NHL**	80	11	28	39	32	9	4	3	7	12
	NHL Totals		377	70	103	173	191	26	7	6	13	25

DUCHESNE, STEVE

Born, Sept-Iles, Que., June 30, 1965.
Defense. Shoots left. 5'11", 190 lbs.
Last amateur club: Drummondville Voltigeurs (QMJHL).

Season	Club	Lea	GP	Regular Season G	A	TP	PIM	GP	Playoffs G	A	TP	PIM
1983-84	Drummondville	QMJHL	67	1	34	35	79	....	....	....	....	....
1984-85a	Drummondville	QMJHL	65	22	54	76	94	5	4	7	11	8
1985-86	New Haven	AHL	75	14	35	49	76	5	0	2	2	9

a QMJHL First All-Star Team (1985)
Signed as a free agent by **Los Angeles,** October 1, 1984.

DUCOLON, TOBY

Born, St. Albans, Vt., June 18, 1966.
Right wing. Shoots right. 6', 195 lbs.
Last amateur club: University of Vermont Catamounts (ECAC).
(St. Louis' 3rd choice, 50th over-all, in 1984 Entry Draft).

Season	Club	Lea	GP	Regular Season G	A	TP	PIM	GP	Playoffs G	A	TP	PIM
1984-85	U. of Vermont	ECAC	24	7	4	11	14	....	....	....	....	....
1985-86	U. of Vermont	ECAC	30	10	6	16	48	....	....	....	....	....

DUFOUR, LUC   (DEW-for)

Born, Chicoutimi, Que., February 13, 1963.
Left wing. Shoots left. 5'11", 180 lbs.
Last amateur club: Chicoutimi Sagueneens (QMJHL).
(Boston's 2nd choice, 35th over-all, in 1981 Entry Draft).

Season	Club	Lea	GP	Regular Season G	A	TP	PIM	GP	Playoffs G	A	TP	PIM
1980-81	Chicoutimi	QMJHL	69	43	53	96	89	4	1	2	3	8
1981-82	Chicoutimi	QMJHL	62	55	60	115	94	20	12	19	31	26
1982-83	**Boston**	**NHL**	73	14	11	25	107	17	1	0	1	30
1983-84	**Boston**	**NHL**	41	6	4	10	47	....	....	....	....	....
	Hershey	AHL	37	9	19	28	51	....	....	....	....	....
1984-85	**Quebec**	**NHL**	30	2	3	5	27	....	....	....	....	....
	St. Louis	**NHL**	23	1	3	4	18	1	0	0	0	2
	Fredericton	AHL	12	2	0	2	13	....	....	....	....	....
	Hershey	AHL	6	1	1	2	10	....	....	....	....	....
1985-86	Maine	AHL	75	15	20	35	57	5	0	0	0	8
	NHL Totals		167	23	21	44	199	18	1	0	1	32

Traded to **Quebec** by **Boston** with Boston's fourth round choice in 1985 Entry Draft (Peter Massey) for Louis Sleigher, October 25, 1984. Traded to **St. Louis** by **Quebec** for Alain Lemieux, January 29, 1985.

DUFRESNE, DONALD

Born, Quebec City, Que., April 10, 1967.
Defense. Shoots left. 6'0", 190 lbs.
Last amateur club: Trois Rivieres Draveurs (QMJHL).
(Montreal's 8th choice, 117th over-all, in 1985 Entry Draft).

Season	Club	Lea	GP	Regular Season G	A	TP	PIM	GP	Playoffs G	A	TP	PIM
1983-84	Trois Rivieres	QMJHL	67	7	12	19	97	....	....	....	....	....
1984-85	Trois Rivieres	QMJHL	65	5	30	35	112	7	1	3	4	12
1985-86a	Trois Rivieres	QMJHL	63	8	32	40	160	1	0	0	0	0

a QMJHL Second All-Star Team (1986).

DUGUAY, RONALD (RON)   (doo-GAY)

Born, Sudbury, Ont., July 6, 1957.
Center. Shoots right. 6'2", 210 lbs.
Last amateur club: Sudbury Wolves (OHA).
(NY Rangers' 2nd choice, 13th over-all, in 1977 Amateur Draft).

Season	Club	Lea	GP	Regular Season G	A	TP	PIM	GP	Playoffs G	A	TP	PIM
1975-76a	Sudbury	OHA	61	42	92	134	101	17	11	9	20	37
1976-77	Sudbury	OHA	61	43	66	109	109	6	4	3	7	5
1977-78	**NY Rangers**	**NHL**	71	20	20	40	43	3	1	1	2	2
1978-79	**NY Rangers**	**NHL**	79	27	36	63	35	18	5	4	9	11
1979-80	**NY Rangers**	**NHL**	73	28	22	50	37	9	5	2	7	11
1980-81	**NY Rangers**	**NHL**	50	17	21	38	83	14	8	9	17	16
1981-82	**NY Rangers**	**NHL**	72	40	36	76	82	10	5	1	6	31
1982-83	**NY Rangers**	**NHL**	72	19	25	44	58	9	2	2	4	28
1983-84	**Detroit**	**NHL**	80	33	47	80	34	4	2	3	5	2
1984-85	**Detroit**	**NHL**	80	38	51	89	51	3	1	0	1	7
1985-86	**Detroit**	**NHL**	67	19	29	48	26	....	....	....	....	....
	Pittsburgh	**NHL**	13	6	7	13	6	....	....	....	....	....
	NHL Totals		657	247	294	541	455	70	29	22	51	108

a OHA Third All-Star Team (1976)
Traded to **Detroit** by **NY Rangers** with Eddie Mio and Eddie Johnstone for Willie Huber, Mark Osborne and Mike Blaisdell, June 13, 1983. Traded to **Pittsburgh** by **Detroit** for Doug Shedden, March 11, 1986.

DUMAS, CLAUDE

Born, Thetford Mines, Que., January 10, 1967.
Center. Shoots right. 6'1", 170 lbs.
Last amateur club: Granby Bisons (QMJHL).
(Washington's 6th choice, 103rd over-all, in 1985 Entry Draft).

Season	Club	Lea	GP	Regular Season G	A	TP	PIM	GP	Playoffs G	A	TP	PIM
1984-85	Granby	QMJHL	62	19	37	56	34	....	....	....	....	....
1985-86	Granby	QMJHL	64	31	58	89	78	....	....	....	....	....

DUMONT, MARC

Born, Beauport, Que., January 28, 1967.
Left wing. Shoots left. 6'0", 190 lbs.
Last amateur club: Laval Titans (QMJHL).

Season	Club	Lea	GP	Regular Season G	A	TP	PIM	GP	Playoffs G	A	TP	PIM
1984-85	Hull	QMJHL	59	8	13	21	43	5	1	1	2	0
1985-86	Laval	QMJHL	56	14	12	26	65	14	2	7	9	17

Signed as a free agent by **St. Louis,** September 29, 1985.

DUNBAR, DALE

Born, Winthrop, Mass., October 14, 1961.
Defense. Shoots left. 6', 200 lbs.
Last amateur club: Boston University Terriers (H.E.).

Season	Club	Lea	GP	Regular Season G	A	TP	PIM	GP	Playoffs G	A	TP	PIM
1982-83	Boston U.	ECAC	23	1	7	8	36	....	....	....	....	....
1983-84	Boston U.	ECAC	34	0	15	23	49	....	....	....	....	....
1984-85	Boston U.	H.E.	39	2	19	21	62	....	....	....	....	....
1985-86	**Vancouver**	**NHL**	1	0	0	0	2	....	....	....	....	....
	Fredericton	AHL	32	2	10	12	26	....	....	....	....	....
	NHL Totals		1	0	0	0	2	....	....	....	....	....

Signed as a free agent by **Vancouver,** May 10, 1985.

DUNCAN, IAIN

Born, Weston, Ont., August 4, 1963.
Left wing. Shoots left. 6'1", 180 lbs.
Last amateur club: Bowling Green State University Falcons (CCHA).
(Winnipeg's 8th choice, 129th over-all, in 1983 Entry Draft).

			Regular Season					Playoffs				
Season	Club	Lea	GP	G	A	TP	PIM	GP	G	A	TP	PIM
1983-84	Bowling Green	CCHA	44	11	20	31	65	....	....	....	....	....
1984-85	Bowling Green	CCHA	37	9	21	30	105	....	....	....	....	....
1985-86	Bowling Green	CCHA	41	26	26	52	124	....	....	....	....	....

DUNCANSON, CRAIG

Born, Sudbury, Ont., March 17, 1967.
Left wing. Shoots left. 6', 190 lbs.
Last amateur club: Sudbury Wolves (OHL).
(Los Angeles' 1st choice, 9th over-all, in 1985 Entry Draft).

			Regular Season					Playoffs				
Season	Club	Lea	GP	G	A	TP	PIM	GP	G	A	TP	PIM
1983-84	Sudbury	OHL	62	38	38	76	176	....	....	....	....	....
1984-85a	Sudbury	OHL	53	35	28	63	129	....	....	....	....	....
1985-86	**Los Angeles**	**NHL**	**2**	**0**	**1**	**1**	**0**	....	....	....	....	....
	Cornwall	OHL	61	43	67	110	190	6	4	7	11	2
	New Haven	AHL	....	....	....	....	....	2	0	0	0	5
	NHL Totals		**2**	**0**	**1**	**1**	**0**	....	....	....	....	....

a OHL Third All-Star Team (1985)

DUNDAS, ROCKY

Born, Regina, Sask., January 30, 1967.
Right wing. Shoots right. 6'0", 195 lbs.
Last amateur club: Spokane Chiefs (WHL).
(Montreal's 4th choice, 47th over-all, in 1985 Entry Draft).

			Regular Season					Playoffs				
Season	Club	Lea	GP	G	A	TP	PIM	GP	G	A	TP	PIM
1983-84	Kelowna	WHL	72	15	24	39	57	....	....	....	....	....
1984-85	Kelowna	WHL	71	32	44	76	117	6	1	1	2	14
1985-86	Spokane	WHL	71	31	70	101	160	9	2	5	7	28

DUNN, RICHARD L. (RICHIE)

Born, Boston, Mass., May 12, 1957.
Defense. Shoots left. 6', 195 lbs.
Last amateur club: Windsor Spitfires (OHA).

			Regular Season					Playoffs				
Season	Club	Lea	GP	G	A	TP	PIM	GP	G	A	TP	PIM
1975-76	Kingston	OHA	61	7	18	25	62	....	....	....	....	....
1976-77	Windsor	OHA	65	5	21	26	98	9	0	5	5	4
1977-78	Hershey	AHL	54	7	22	29	17	....	....	....	....	....
	Buffalo	**NHL**	**25**	**0**	**3**	**3**	**16**	**1**	**0**	**0**	**0**	**2**
1978-79	**Buffalo**	**NHL**	**24**	**0**	**3**	**3**	**14**	....	....	....	....	....
	Hershey	AHL	34	5	18	23	10	4	0	1	1	4
1979-80	**Buffalo**	**NHL**	**80**	**7**	**31**	**38**	**61**	**14**	**2**	**8**	**10**	**8**
1980-81	**Buffalo**	**NHL**	**79**	**7**	**42**	**49**	**34**	**8**	**0**	**5**	**5**	**6**
1981-82	**Buffalo**	**NHL**	**72**	**7**	**19**	**26**	**73**	**4**	**0**	**1**	**1**	**0**
1982-83	**Calgary**	**NHL**	**80**	**3**	**11**	**14**	**47**	**9**	**1**	**1**	**2**	**8**
1983-84	**Hartford**	**NHL**	**63**	**5**	**20**	**25**	**30**	....	....	....	....	....
1984-85	**Hartford**	**NHL**	**13**	**1**	**4**	**5**	**2**	....	....	....	....	....
ab	Binghamton	AHL	64	9	39	48	43	8	2	2	4	8
1985-86	**Buffalo**	**NHL**	**29**	**4**	**5**	**9**	**25**	....	....	....	....	....
	Rochester	AHL	34	6	17	23	12	....	....	....	....	....
	NHL Totals		**465**	**34**	**138**	**172**	**302**	**36**	**3**	**15**	**18**	**24**

a Won Eddie Shore Plaque (AHL Outstanding Defenseman 1985).
b AHL First All-Star Team (1985).
Signed as free agent by **Buffalo**, October 3, 1977. Traded to **Calgary** by **Buffalo** with Don Edwards and Buffalo's second round choice (Richard Kromm) in 1982 Entry Draft for Calgary's first round choice (Paul Cyr) and second round choice (Jens Johansson) in the 1982 Entry Draft and Calgary's second round choice (John Tucker) in 1983 Entry Draft, June 9, 1982. In addition, the two clubs exchanged first round draft choices in 1983 — Buffalo claimed Normand Lacombe and Calgary selected Dan Quinn. Traded to **Hartford** by **Calgary** with Joel Quenneville for Mickey Volcan, July 5, 1983. Signed as a free agent by **Buffalo**, July 10, 1986.

DUPONT, JEROME (JERRY) (DEW-paunt)

Born, Ottawa, Ont., February 21, 1962.
Defense. Shoots left. 6'3", 190 lbs.
Last amateur club: Toronto Marlboros (OHL).
(Chicago's 2nd choice, 15th over-all, in 1980 Entry Draft).

			Regular Season					Playoffs				
Season	Club	Lea	GP	G	A	TP	PIM	GP	G	A	TP	PIM
1980-81	Toronto	OHA	67	6	38	44	116	5	2	2	4	9
1981-82	**Chicago**	**NHL**	**34**	**0**	**4**	**4**	**51**	....	....	....	....	....
	Toronto	OHL	7	0	8	8	18	10	3	9	12	24
1982-83	**Chicago**	**NHL**	**1**	**0**	**0**	**0**	**0**	....	....	....	....	....
	Springfield	AHL	78	12	22	34	114	....	....	....	....	....
1983-84	Springfield	AHL	12	2	3	5	65	....	....	....	....	....
	Chicago	**NHL**	**36**	**2**	**2**	**4**	**116**	**4**	**0**	**0**	**0**	**15**
1984-85	**Chicago**	**NHL**	**55**	**3**	**10**	**13**	**105**	**15**	**0**	**2**	**2**	**41**
1985-86	**Chicago**	**NHL**	**75**	**2**	**13**	**15**	**173**	**1**	**0**	**0**	**0**	**0**
	NHL Totals		**201**	**7**	**29**	**36**	**445**	**20**	**0**	**2**	**2**	**56**

DURAND, BRIAN

Born, Duluth, Minn., August 5, 1965.
Center. Shoots left. 6'2", 175 lbs.
Last amateur club: University of Minnesota-Duluth Bulldogs (WCHA).
(Minnesota's 5th choice, 78th over-all, in 1983 Entry Draft).

			Regular Season					Playoffs				
Season	Club	Lea	GP	G	A	TP	PIM	GP	G	A	TP	PIM
1983-84	Minn-Duluth	WCHA	24	2	5	7	4	....	....	....	....	....
1984-85	Minn-Duluth	WCHA	16	1	0	1	2	....	....	....	....	....
1985-86	Minn-Duluth	WCHA	11	1	0	1	6	....	....	....	....	....

DUVALL, HAROLD

Born, Ogdenburg, NY, April 21, 1964.
Left wing. Shoots left. 5'11", 185 lbs.
Last amateur club: Colgate University Red Raiders (ECAC).
(Philadelphia's 11th choice, 241st over-all, in 1983 Entry Draft).

			Regular Season					Playoffs				
Season	Club	Lea	GP	G	A	TP	PIM	GP	G	A	TP	PIM
1983-84	Colgate	ECAC	26	1	9	10	37	....	....	....	....	....
1984-85	Colgate	ECAC	27	8	15	23	46	....	....	....	....	....
1985-86	Colgate	ECAC	18	5	6	11	47	....	....	....	....	....

DYKSTRA, STEVEN

Born, Edmonton, Alta., December 1, 1962.
Defense. Shoots left. 6'2", 210 lbs.
Last amateur club: Seattle Breakers (WHL).

			Regular Season					Playoffs				
Season	Club	Lea	GP	G	A	TP	PIM	GP	G	A	TP	PIM
1981-82	Seattle	WHL	57	8	26	34	139	10	3	1	4	42
1982-83	Rochester	AHL	70	2	16	18	100	15	0	5	5	27
1983-84	Rochester	AHL	63	3	19	22	141	6	0	0	0	46
1984-85	Flint	IHL	15	1	7	8	36	....	....	....	....	....
	Rochester	AHL	51	9	23	32	113	2	0	1	1	10
1985-86	**Buffalo**	**NHL**	**64**	**4**	**21**	**25**	**108**	....	....	....	....	....
	NHL Totals		**64**	**4**	**21**	**25**	**108**	....	....	....	....	....

Signed as a free agent by **Buffalo**, December 10, 1982.

DZIKOWSKI, JOHN

Born, Portage La Prairie, Man., January 28, 1966.
Left wing. Shoots left. 6'3", 190 lbs.
Last amateur club: Seattle Thunderbirds (WHL).
(Philadelphia's 7th choice, 125th over-all, in 1984 Entry Draft).

			Regular Season					Playoffs				
Season	Club	Lea	GP	G	A	TP	PIM	GP	G	A	TP	PIM
1983-84	Brandon	WHL	47	12	11	23	99	12	5	0	5	7
1984-85	Brandon	WHL	59	38	35	73	58	....	....	....	....	....
1985-86	Seattle	WHL	69	53	35	88	110	5	2	0	2	4

EAGLES, MICHAEL (MIKE)

Born, Sussex, N.B., March 7, 1963.
Center. Shoots left. 5'10", 180 lbs.
Last amateur club: Kitchener Rangers (OHL).
(Quebec's 5th choice, 116th over-all, in 1981 Entry Draft).

			Regular Season					Playoffs				
Season	Club	Lea	GP	G	A	TP	PIM	GP	G	A	TP	PIM
1980-81	Kitchener	OHA	56	11	27	38	64	18	4	2	6	36
1981-82	Kitchener	OHL	62	26	40	66	148	15	3	11	14	27
1982-83	**Quebec**	**NHL**	**2**	**0**	**0**	**0**	**2**	....	....	....	....	....
	Kitchener	OHL	58	26	36	62	133	12	5	7	12	27
1983-84	Fredericton	AHL	68	13	29	42	85	4	0	0	0	5
1984-85	Fredericton	AHL	36	4	20	24	80	3	0	0	0	2
1985-86	**Quebec**	**NHL**	**73**	**11**	**12**	**23**	**49**	**3**	**0**	**0**	**0**	**2**
	NHL Totals		**75**	**11**	**12**	**23**	**51**	**3**	**0**	**0**	**0**	**2**

EAKIN, BRUCE GLEN

Born, Winnipeg, Man., September 28, 1962.
Center. Shoots left. 5'11", 190 lbs.
Last amateur club: Saskatoon Blades (WHL).
(Calgary's 9th choice, 204th over-all, in 1981 Entry Draft).

			Regular Season					Playoffs				
Season	Club	Lea	GP	G	A	TP	PIM	GP	G	A	TP	PIM
1980-81	Saskatoon	WHL	52	18	46	64	54	....	....	....	....	....
1981-82	**Calgary**	**NHL**	**1**	**0**	**0**	**0**	**0**	....	....	....	....	....
a	Saskatoon	WHL	66	42	*125	167	120	5	4	6	10	0
	Oklahoma City	CHL	3	0	3	3	0	4	2	0	2	2
1982-83	Colorado	CHL	73	24	46	70	45	6	1	6	7	2
1983-84	**Calgary**	**NHL**	**7**	**2**	**1**	**3**	**4**	....	....	....	....	....
b	Colorado	CHL	67	33	69	102	18	6	4	2	6	0
1984-85	**Calgary**	**NHL**	**1**	**0**	**0**	**0**	**0**	....	....	....	....	....
	Moncton	AHL	78	35	48	83	60	....	....	....	....	....
1985-86	**Detroit**	**NHL**	**4**	**0**	**1**	**1**	**0**	....	....	....	....	....
	Adirondack	AHL	25	8	10	18	23	....	....	....	....	....
	Nova Scotia	AHL	14	6	12	18	12	....	....	....	....	....
	NHL Totals		**13**	**2**	**2**	**4**	**4**	....	....	....	....	....

a WHL First All-Star Team (1982)
b CHL Second All-Star Team (1984)
Traded to **Edmonton** by **Detroit** for Billy Carroll, December 28, 1985.

EAKINS, DALLAS

Born, Dade City, Florida, February 27, 1967.
Defense. Shoots left. 6'1", 185 lbs.
Last amateur club: Peterborough Petes (OHL).
(Washington's 11th choice, 208th over-all, in 1985 Entry Draft).

				Regular Season					Playoffs			
Season	Club	Lea	GP	G	A	TP	PIM	GP	G	A	TP	PIM
1984-85	Peterborough	OHL	48	0	8	8	96	7	0	0	0	18
1985-86	Peterborough	OHL	60	6	16	22	134	16	0	1	1	30

EAVES, MICHAEL GORDON (MIKE)

Born, Denver, Colorado, June 10, 1956.
Center. Shoots right. 5'10", 180 lbs.
Last amateur club: University of Wisconsin Badgers (WCHA)
(St. Louis' 8th choice, 113th over-all, in 1976 Amateur Draft).

				Regular Season					Playoffs			
Season	Club	Lea	GP	G	A	TP	PIM	GP	G	A	TP	PIM
1976-77	U. of Wisconsin	WCHA	45	28	53	81	18	....	....	....	....	....
1977-78	U. of Wisconsin	WCHA	43	31	58	89	16	....	....	....	....	....
1978-79	Minnesota	NHL	3	0	0	0	0	....	....	....	....	....
a	Oklahoma City	CHL	68	26	61	87	21	....	....	....	....	....
1979-80	Oklahoma City	CHL	12	9	8	17	2	....	....	....	....	....
	Minnesota	NHL	56	18	28	46	11	15	2	5	7	4
1980-81	Minnesota	NHL	48	10	24	34	18	....	....	....	....	....
1981-82	Minnesota	NHL	25	11	10	21	0	....	....	....	....	....
1982-83	Minnesota	NHL	75	16	16	32	21	9	0	0	0	0
1983-84	Calgary	NHL	61	14	36	50	20	11	4	4	8	2
1984-85	Calgary	NHL	56	14	29	43	10	....	....	....	....	....
1985-86	Calgary	NHL	....	....	....	....	....	8	1	1	2	8
	NHL Totals		324	83	143	226	80	43	7	10	17	14

a Won Ken McKenzie Trophy (CHL's Top Rookie) (1979).
Rights traded to **Cleveland** by **St. Louis** for Len Frig, August 17, 1977. Rights transferred to **Minnesota** Reserve List after Cleveland-Minnesota Dispersal Draft, June 15, 1978. Traded to **Calgary** by **Minnesota** with Keith Hanson for Steve Christoff and Calgary's second round choice (Frantisek Musil) in the 1983 Entry Draft, June 8, 1983.

EAVES, MURRAY

Born, Calgary, Alta., May 10, 1960.
Center. Shoots right. 5'10", 185 lbs.
Last amateur club: University of Michigan Wolverines (WCHA)
(Winnipeg's 3rd choice, 44th over-all, in 1980 Entry Draft).

				Regular Season					Playoffs			
Season	Club	Lea	GP	G	A	TP	PIM	GP	G	A	TP	PIM
1978-79	U. of Michigan	WCHA	23	12	22	34	14	....	....	....	....	....
1979-80	U. of Michigan	WCHA	33	36	49	85	34	....	....	....	....	....
1980-81	Winnipeg	NHL	12	1	2	3	5	....	....	....	....	....
	Tulsa	CHL	59	24	34	58	59	8	5	5	10	13
1981-82	Winnipeg	NHL	2	0	0	0	0	....	....	....	....	....
	Tulsa	CHL	68	30	49	79	33	3	0	2	2	0
1982-83	Winnipeg	NHL	26	2	7	9	2	....	....	....	....	....
	Sherbrooke	AHL	40	25	34	59	16	....	....	....	....	....
1983-84	Sherbrooke	AHL	78	47	68	115	40	....	....	....	....	....
	Winnipeg	NHL	2	0	0	0	0	2	0	0	0	2
1984-85	Winnipeg	NHL	3	0	3	3	0	2	0	1	1	0
	Sherbrooke	AHL	47	26	42	68	28	15	5	13	18	35
1985-86	Winnipeg	NHL	4	1	0	1	0	....	....	....	....	....
	Sherbrooke	AHL	68	22	51	73	26	....	....	....	....	....
	NHL Totals		49	4	12	16	7	4	0	1	1	2

EDLUND, PAR

Born, Sweden, April 9, 1967.
Right wing. Shoots right. 5'11", 180 lbs.
Last amateur club: Bjorkleven (Sweden).
(Los Angeles' 3rd choice, 30th over-all, in 1985 Entry Draft).

				Regular Season					Playoffs			
Season	Club	Lea	GP	G	A	TP	PIM	GP	G	A	TP	PIM
1983-84	Bjorkleven	Swe.	30	14	12	26	10	....	....	....	....	....
1984-85	Bjorkleven	Swe.	38	30	11	41	16	....	....	....	....	....
1985-86	Bjorkleven	Swe.	5	1	0	1	4	....	....	....	....	....

EIRICKSON, SHANE

Born, Lundbar, N.B., February 19, 1965.
Defense. Shoots left. 6'3", 190 lbs.
Last amateur club: Brandon Wheat Kings (WHL).

				Regular Season					Playoffs			
Season	Club	Lea	GP	G	A	TP	PIM	GP	G	A	TP	PIM
1985-86	Brandon	WHL	68	3	61	64	62	....	....	....	....	....

Signed as a free agent by **Minnesota**, September 25, 1985.

EKLUND, PER-ERIK

Born, Stockholm, Sweden, March 22, 1963.
Center. Shoots left. 5'10", 170 lbs.
Last amateur club: AIK (Sweden).
(Philadelphia's 8th choice, 167th over-all, in 1983 Entry Draft)

				Regular Season					Playoffs			
Season	Club	Lea	GP	G	A	TP	PIM	GP	G	A	TP	PIM
1983-84	AIK	Swe.	35	16	33	49	10	....	....	....	....	....
1984-85	AIK	Swe.	35	9	18	27	24	....	....	....	....	....
1985-86	Philadelphia	NHL	70	15	51	66	12	5	0	2	2	0
	NHL Totals		70	15	51	66	12	5	0	2	2	0

ELLETT, DAVID

Born, Cleveland, Ohio, March 30, 1964.
Defense. Shoots left. 6'1", 200 lbs.
Last amateur club: Bowling Green State University Falcons (CCHA)
(Winnipeg's 4th choice, 75th over-all, in 1982 Entry Draft).

				Regular Season					Playoffs			
Season	Club	Lea	GP	G	A	TP	PIM	GP	G	A	TP	PIM
1982-83	Bowling Green	CCHA	40	4	13	17	34	....	....	....	....	....
1983-84ab	Bowling Green	CCHA	43	15	39	54	96	....	....	....	....	....
1984-85	Winnipeg	NHL	80	11	27	38	85	8	1	5	6	4
1985-86	Winnipeg	NHL	80	15	31	46	96	3	0	1	1	0
	NHL Totals		160	26	58	84	181	11	1	6	7	4

a CCHA Second All-Star Team (1984).
b Named to NCAA All-Tournament Team (1984).

ELYNUIK, PAT

Born, Foam Lake, Sask., October 30, 1967.
Right wing. Shoots right. 6'0", 180 lbs.
Last amateur club: Prince Albert Raiders (WHL)
(Winnipeg's 1st choice, 7th over-all, in 1986 Entry Draft).

				Regular Season					Playoffs			
Season	Club	Lea	GP	G	A	TP	PIM	GP	G	A	TP	PIM
1984-85	Prince Albert	WHL	70	23	20	43	54	13	9	3	12	7
1985-86a	Prince Albert	WHL	68	53	53	106	62	20	7	9	16	17

a WHL East All-Star Team (1986).

EMERSON, NELSON

Born, Hamilton, Ont., August 17, 1967.
Center. Shoots right. 5'11", 165 lbs.
Last amateur club: Stratford Cullitans (OPJHL).
(St. Louis' 2nd choice, 44th over-all, in 1985 Entry Draft).

				Regular Season					Playoffs			
Season	Club	Lea	GP	G	A	TP	PIM	GP	G	A	TP	PIM
1985-86	Stratford	OPJHL	64	54	58	112	....	....	....	....	....	....

EMERY, ROBERT

Born, Somerville, Mass., March 4, 1964.
Defense. Shoots left. 6'1", 185 lbs.
Last amateur club: Boston College Eagles (H.E.)
(Montreal's 15th choice, 208th over-all, in 1982 Entry Draft).

				Regular Season					Playoffs			
Season	Club	Lea	GP	G	A	TP	PIM	GP	G	A	TP	PIM
1982-83	Boston College	ECAC	21	0	2	2	18	....	....	....	....	....
1983-84	Boston College	ECAC	35	2	7	9	32	....	....	....	....	....
1984-85	Boston College	H.E.	42	3	11	14	54	....	....	....	....	....
1985-86a	Boston College	H.E.	39	2	15	17	48	....	....	....	....	....

a Hockey East Second All-Star Team (1986)

ENGBLOM, BRIAN PAUL   (eng-BLOOM)

Born, Winnipeg, Man., January 27, 1955.
Defense. Shoots left. 6'2", 190 lbs.
Last amateur club: University of Wisconsin Badgers (WCHA)
(Montreal's 3rd choice, 22nd over-all, in 1975 Amateur Draft).

				Regular Season					Playoffs			
Season	Club	Lea	GP	G	A	TP	PIM	GP	G	A	TP	PIM
1973-74	U. of Wisconsin	WCHA	36	10	21	31	54	....	....	....	....	....
1974-75	U. of Wisconsin	WCHA	38	13	23	36	58	....	....	....	....	....
1975-76	Nova Scotia	AHL	73	4	34	38	79	9	1	7	8	26
1976-77	Nova Scotia	AHL	80	8	42	50	89	11	3	10	13	10
	Montreal	NHL	....	....	....	....	....	2	0	0	0	2
1977-78	Nova Scotia	AHL	7	1	5	6	4	....	....	....	....	....
	Montreal	NHL	28	1	2	3	23	5	0	0	0	2
1978-79	Montreal	NHL	62	3	11	14	60	16	0	1	1	11
1979-80	Montreal	NHL	70	3	20	23	43	10	2	4	6	4
1980-81	Montreal	NHL	80	3	25	28	96	3	1	0	1	4
1981-82a	Montreal	NHL	76	4	29	33	76	5	0	2	2	14
1982-83	Washington	NHL	73	5	22	27	59	4	0	2	2	2
1983-84	Washington	NHL	6	0	1	1	8	....	....	....	....	....
	Los Angeles	NHL	74	2	27	29	59	....	....	....	....	....
1984-85	Los Angeles	NHL	79	4	19	23	70	3	0	0	0	2
1985-86	Los Angeles	NHL	49	3	13	16	61	....	....	....	....	....
	Buffalo	NHL	30	1	4	5	16	....	....	....	....	....
	NHL Totals		627	29	173	202	571	48	3	9	12	43

a NHL Second All-Star Team (1982)

Traded to **Washington** by **Montreal** with Rod Langway, Doug Jarvis and Craig Laughlin for Ryan Walter and Rick Green, September 9, 1982. Traded to **Los Angeles** by **Washington** with Ken Houston for Larry Murphy, October 18, 1983. Traded to **Buffalo** by **Los Angeles** with Doug Smith For Larry Playfair, Sean McKenna and Ken Baumgartner, January 30, 1986.

ENGLISH, JOHN

Born, Toronto, Ont., May 13, 1966.
Defense. Shoots right. 6'2", 190 lbs.
Last amateur club: Ottawa 67's (OHL).
(Los Angeles' 3rd choice, 48th over-all, in 1984 Entry Draft).

				Regular Season					Playoffs			
Season	Club	Lea	GP	G	A	TP	PIM	GP	G	A	TP	PIM
1983-84	S. S. Marie	OHL	64	6	11	17	144	16	0	6	6	45
1984-85	S. S. Marie	OHL	15	0	3	3	61	....	....	....	....	....
	Hamilton	OHL	41	2	22	24	105	17	3	3	6	43
1985-86	Ottawa	OHL	54	10	37	47	175	....	....	....	....	....

ERICKSON, BRYAN

Born, Roseau, Minnesota, March 7, 1960.
Right wing. Shoots right. 5'9", 170 lbs.
Last amateur club: University of Minnesota Gophers (WCHA).

				Regular Season						Playoffs			
Season	Club	Lea	GP	G	A	TP	PIM	GP	G	A	TP	PIM
1979-80	U. Minnesota	WCHA	23	10	15	25	14	....	....	....	....	....
1980-81	U. Minnesota	WCHA	44	39	47	86	30	....	....	....	....	....
1981-82	U. Minnesota	WCHA	35	25	20	45	20	....	....	....	....	....
1982-83	U. Minnesota	WCHA	42	35	47	82	34	....	....	....	....	....
	Hershey	AHL	1	0	1	1	0	3	3	0	3	0
1983-84	Hershey	AHL	31	16	12	28	11	....	....	....	....	....
	Washington	**NHL**	45	12	17	29	16	8	2	3	5	7
1984-85	**Washington**	**NHL**	57	15	13	28	23	....	....	....	....	....
	Binghamton	AHL	13	6	11	17	8	8	1	4	5	6
1985-86	Binghamton	AHL	7	5	3	8	2	....	....	....	....	....
	New Haven	AHL	14	8	3	11	11	....	....	....	....	....
	Los Angeles	**NHL**	55	20	23	43	36	....	....	....	....	....
	NHL Totals		157	47	53	100	75	8	2	3	5	7

Signed as free agent by **Washington**, April 5, 1983. Traded to **Los Angeles** by **Washington** for Bruce Shoebottom, October 31, 1985.

ERIKSSON, THOMAS

Born, Stockholm, Sweden, October 16, 1959.
Defense. Shoots left. 6'2", 180 lbs.
Last amateur club: Djurgardens IF (Sweden)
(Philadelphia's 6th choice, 98th over-all, in 1979 Entry Draft).

				Regular Season						Playoffs			
Season	Club	Lea	GP	G	A	TP	PIM	GP	G	A	TP	PIM
1979-80	Djurgardens	Swe.	36	12	11	23	63	....	....	....	....	....
	Swe. National	...	22	5	0	5		....	....	....	....	....
1980-81	Maine	AHL	54	11	20	31	75	....	....	....	....	....
	Philadelphia	**NHL**	24	1	10	11	14	7	0	2	2	6
1981-82	**Philadelphia**	**NHL**	1	0	0	0	4	....	....	....	....	....
	Djurgardens	Swe.	27	7	5	12	48	....	....	....	....	....
1982-83	Djurgardens	Swe.	32	12	9	21	51	....	....	....	....	....
1983-84a	**Philadelphia**	**NHL**	68	11	33	44	37	3	0	1	1	0
1984-85	**Philadelphia**	**NHL**	72	10	29	39	36	9	0	0	0	6
1985-86	**Philadelphia**	**NHL**	43	0	4	4	16	....	....	....	....	....
	NHL Totals		208	22	76	98	107	19	0	3	3	6

a Named to NHL All-Rookie Team (1984)

ERIXON, JAN

Born, Skelleftea, Sweden, July 8, 1962.
Right wing. Shoots left. 6', 190 lbs.
Last amateur club: Skelleftea (Sweden).
(New York Rangers' 2nd choice, 30th over-all, in 1981 Entry Draft).

				Regular Season						Playoffs			
Season	Club	Lea	GP	G	A	TP	PIM	GP	G	A	TP	PIM
1979-80	Skelleftea	...	32	9	3	12	22	....	....	....	....	....
1980-81	Skelleftea	...	32	6	6	12	4	3	1	0	1	0
1981-82	Skelleftea	...	30	7	7	14	26	....	....	....	....	....
1982-83	Skelleftea	...	36	10	18	28	0	....	....	....	....	....
1983-84	**NY Rangers**	**NHL**	75	5	25	30	16	5	2	0	2	4
1984-85	**NY Rangers**	**NHL**	66	7	22	29	33	2	0	0	0	2
1985-86	**NY Rangers**	**NHL**	31	2	17	19	4	12	0	1	1	4
	NHL Totals		172	14	64	78	53	19	2	1	3	10

ERNST, GORDON

Born, Warwick,, R.I., January 25, 1967.
Center. Shoots left. 5'11", 170 lbs.
Last amateur club: Brown University Bruins (ECAC).
(Minnesota's 8th choice, 195th over-all, in 1985 Entry Draft).

				Regular Season						Playoffs			
Season	Club	Lea	GP	G	A	TP	PIM	GP	G	A	TP	PIM
1985-86	Brown	ECAC	22	4	10	14	6	....	....	....	....	....

ERREY, BOB

Born, Montreal, Que., September 21, 1964.
Left wing. Shoots left. 5'10", 180 lbs.
Last amateur club: Peterborough Petes (OHL)
(Pittsburgh's 1st choice, 15th over-all, in 1983 Entry Draft).

				Regular Season						Playoffs			
Season	Club	Lea	GP	G	A	TP	PIM	GP	G	A	TP	PIM
1981-82	Peterborough	OHL	68	29	31	60	39	9	3	1	4	9
1982-83a	Peterborough	OHL	67	53	47	100	74	4	1	3	4	7
1983-84	**Pittsburgh**	**NHL**	65	9	13	22	29	....	....	....	....	....
1984-85	**Pittsburgh**	**NHL**	16	0	2	2	7	....	....	....	....	....
	Baltimore	AHL	59	17	24	41	14	8	3	4	7	11
1985-86	**Pittsburgh**	**NHL**	37	11	6	17	8	....	....	....	....	....
	Baltimore	AHL	18	8	7	15	28	....	....	....	....	....
	NHL Totals		118	20	21	41	44	....	....	....	....	....

a OHL First All-Star Team (1983).

ESPE, DAVID

Born, St. Paul, Minn., November 3, 1966.
Defense. Shoots left. 6'0", 185 lbs.
Last amateur club: University of Minnesota Golden Gophers (WCHA).
(Quebec's 5th choice, 78th over-all, in 1985 Entry Draft).

				Regular Season						Playoffs			
Season	Club	Lea	GP	G	A	TP	PIM	GP	G	A	TP	PIM
1985-86	U. Minnesota	WCHA	27	0	6	6	18	....	....	....	....	....

EVANS, DARYL TOMAS

Born, Toronto, Ont., January 12, 1961.
Left wing. Shoots left. 5'9", 185 lbs.
Last amateur club: Brantford Alexanders (OHL).
(Los Angeles' 11th choice, 178th over-all, in 1980 Entry Draft).

				Regular Season						Playoffs			
Season	Club	Lea	GP	G	A	TP	PIM	GP	G	A	TP	PIM
1979-80	Niagara Falls	OHA	63	43	52	95	47	10	5	13	18	6
1980-81a	Niagara Falls	OHL	5	3	4	7	11	....	....	....	....	....
	Brantford	OHL	58	58	54	112	50	6	4	5	9	6
1981-82	New Haven	AHL	41	14	14	28	10	....	....	....	....	....
	Los Angeles	**NHL**	14	2	6	8	2	10	5	8	13	12
1982-83	**Los Angeles**	**NHL**	80	18	22	40	21	....	....	....	....	....
1983-84	**Los Angeles**	**NHL**	4	0	1	1	0	....	....	....	....	....
	New Haven	AHL	69	51	34	85	14	....	....	....	....	....
1984-85	**Los Angeles**	**NHL**	7	1	0	1	2	....	....	....	....	....
	New Haven	AHL	59	22	24	46	12	....	....	....	....	....
1985-86	**Washington**	**NHL**	6	0	1	1	0	....	....	....	....	....
	Binghamton	AHL	69	40	52	92	50	5	6	2	8	0
	NHL Totals		111	21	30	51	25	10	5	8	13	12

a OHL First All-Star Team (1981).

Traded to **Washington** by **Los Angeles** for Glen Currie, September 9, 1985.

EVANS, DOUG

Born, Peterborough, Ont., June 2, 1963.
Center. Shoots left. 5'9", 165 lbs.
Last amateur club: Peterborough Petes (OHL).

				Regular Season						Playoffs			
Season	Club	Lea	GP	G	A	TP	PIM	GP	G	A	TP	PIM
1981-82	Peterborough	OHL	56	17	49	66	176	9	0	2	2	41
1982-83	Peterborough	OHL	65	31	55	86	165	4	0	3	3	23
1983-84	Peterborough	OHL	61	45	79	124	98	8	4	12	16	26
1984-85	Peoria	IHL	81	36	61	97	189	20	18	14	32	14
1985-86a	Peoria	IHL	60	46	51	97	179	10	4	6	10	32
	St. Louis	**NHL**	13	1	0	1	2	....	....	....	....	....
	NHL Totals		13	1	0	1	2	....	....	....	....	....

a IHL First All-Star Team (1986).
Signed as a free agent by **St. Louis**, June 10, 1985.

EVANS, SHAWN

Born, Kingston, Ont., September 7, 1965.
Defense. Shoots left. 6'2", 195 lbs.
Last amateur club: Peterborough Petes (OHL).
(New Jersey's 2nd choice, 24th over-all, in 1983 Entry Draft).

				Regular Season						Playoffs			
Season	Club	Lea	GP	G	A	TP	PIM	GP	G	A	TP	PIM
1981-82	Kingston	OPJHL	21	9	13	22	55	....	....	....	....	....
1982-83	Peterborough	OHL	58	7	41	48	116	4	2	0	2	12
1983-84a	Peterborough	OHL	67	21	88	109	116	8	1	16	17	8
1984-85b	Peterborough	OHL	66	16	83	99	78	16	6	18	24	6
1985-86	**St. Louis**	**NHL**	7	0	0	0	2	....	....	....	....	....
	Peoria	IHL	55	8	26	34	36	....	....	....	....	....
	NHL Totals		7	0	0	0	2	....	....	....	....	....

a OHL Second All-Star Team (1984).
b OHL Third All-Star Team (1985).
Traded to **St. Louis** by **New Jersey** with New Jersey's fifth-round choice (Michael Wolak) in 1986 Entry Draft for Mark Johnson, September 19, 1985.

EVASON, DEAN

Born, Flin Flon, Man., August 22, 1964.
Center. Shoots left. 5'10", 180 lbs.
Last amateur club: Kamloops Junior Oilers (WHL).
(Washington's 3rd choice, 89th over-all, in 1982 Entry Draft).

				Regular Season						Playoffs			
Season	Club	Lea	GP	G	A	TP	PIM	GP	G	A	TP	PIM
1980-81	Spokane	WHL	3	1	1	2	0	....	....	....	....	....
1981-82	Spokane	WHL	26	8	14	22	65	....	....	....	....	....
	Kamloops	WHL	44	21	55	76	47	4	2	1	3	0
1982-83	Kamloops	WHL	70	71	93	164	102	7	5	7	12	18
1983-84	**Washington**	**NHL**	2	0	0	0	2	....	....	....	....	....
a	Kamloops	WHL	57	49	88	137	89	17	*21	20	41	33
1984-85	**Washington**	**NHL**	15	3	4	7	2	....	....	....	....	....
	Hartford	**NHL**	2	0	0	0	0	....	....	....	....	....
	Binghamton	AHL	65	27	49	76	38	8	3	5	8	9
1985-86	**Hartford**	**NHL**	55	20	28	48	65	10	1	4	5	10
	Binghamton	AHL	26	9	17	26	29	....	....	....	....	....
	NHL Totals		74	23	32	55	69	10	1	4	5	10

a WHL First All-Star Team, West Division (1984).
Traded to **Hartford** by **Washington** with Peter Sidorkiewicz for David Jensen, March 12, 1985.

EVTUSHEVSKI, GREG

Born, St. Paul, Alta., May 4, 1965.
Right wing. Shoots right. 5'10", 185 lbs.
Last amateur club: Kamloops Blazers (WHL).
(New Jersey's 5th choice, 125th over-all, in 1983 Entry Draft).

				Regular Season					Playoffs			
Season	Club	Lea	GP	G	A	TP	PIM	GP	G	A	TP	PIM
1982-83	Kamloops	WHL	70	32	49	81	245	7	2	3	5	37
1983-84	Kamloops	WHL	64	27	43	70	176	17	9	9	18	64
1984-85	Kamloops	WHL	71	47	93	140	167	15	11	14	25.	64
1985-86	Kamloops	WHL	34	29	47	76	100	16	11	18	29	53
	Maine	AHL	21	3	4	7	60	....	....	....	....	....

EWEN, TODD

Born, Saskatoon, Sask., March 26, 1966.
Right wing. Shoots right. 6'2", 180 lbs.
Last amateur club: New Westminster Bruins (WHL).
(Edmonton's 9th choice, 168th over-all, in 1984 Entry Draft).

				Regular Season					Playoffs			
Season	Club	Lea	GP	G	A	TP	PIM	GP	G	A	TP	PIM
1982-83	Kamloops	WHL	3	0	0	0	2	2	0	0	0	0
1983-84	N. Westminster	WHL	68	11	13	24	176	7	2	1	3	15
1984-85	N. Westminster	WHL	56	11	20	31	304	10	1	8	9	60
1985-86	N. Westminster	WHL	60	28	24	52	289	....	....	....	....	....
	Maine	AHL	....	....	....	....	....	3	0	0	0	7

FAIRFIELD, TONY

Born, Edmonton, Alta., July 2, 1967.
Right wing. Shoots right. 6'2", 195 lbs.
Last amateur club: U. of Northern Arizona Lumberjacks (NCAA).
(Edmonton's 7th choice, 167th over-all, in 1985 Entry Draft).

				Regular Season					Playoffs			
Season	Club	Lea	GP	G	A	TP	PIM	GP	G	A	TP	PIM
1985-86	N. Arizona	NCAA	26	4	2	6	71	....	....	....	....	....

FARRISH, DAVID ALLAN (DAVE)

Born, Wingham, Ont., August 1, 1956.
Defense. Shoots left. 6'1", 195 lbs.
Last amateur club: Sudbury Wolves (OHA).
(NY Rangers' 2nd choice, 24th over-all, in 1976 Amateur Draft).

				Regular Season					Playoffs			
Season	Club	Lea	GP	G	A	TP	PIM	GP	G	A	TP	PIM
1974-75	Sudbury	OHA	60	20	44	64	258	14	3	4	7	32
1975-76	Sudbury	OHA	66	27	48	75	155	17	3	12	15	22
1976-77	NY Rangers	NHL	80	2	17	19	102	....	....	....	....	....
1977-78	New Haven	AHL	10	0	3	3	4	....	....	....	....	....
	NY Rangers	NHL	66	3	5	8	62	3	0	0	0	0
1978-79	NY Rangers	NHL	71	1	19	20	61	7	0	2	2	14
1979-80	Quebec	NHL	4	0	0	0	0	....	....	....	....	....
	Syracuse	AHL	14	4	10	14	17	....	....	....	....	....
	New Brunswick	AHL	20	3	1	4	22	....	....	....	....	....
	Toronto	NHL	20	1	8	9	30	3	0	0	0	10
1980-81	Toronto	NHL	74	2	18	20	90	1	0	0	0	0
1981-82ab	New Brunswick	AHL	67	13	24	37	80	15	4	5	9	20
1982-83	Toronto	NHL	56	4	24	28	38	....	....	....	....	....
	St. Catharines	AHL	14	2	12	14	18	....	....	....	....	....
1983-84	Toronto	NHL	59	4	19	23	57	....	....	....	....	....
	St. Catharines	AHL	4	0	2	2	6	7	0	1	1	4
1984-85	St. Catharines	AHL	68	4	12	16	56	....	....	....	....	....
1985-86	Hershey	AHL	74	5	17	22	78	18	0	4	4	24
	NHL Totals		430	17	110	127	440	14	0	2	2	24

a AHL First All-Star Team (1982)
b Won Eddie Shore Plaque (AHL's Outstanding Defenseman) (1982)
Claimed by **Quebec** from **NY Rangers** in Expansion Draft, June 13, 1979. Traded to **Toronto** by **Quebec** with Terry Martin for Reggie Thomas, December 13, 1979. Signed as a free agent by **Philadelphia**, October 7, 1985.

FEDERKO, BERNARD ALLAN (BERNIE)

Born, Foam Lake, Sask., May 12, 1956.
Center. Shoots left. 6', 180 lbs.
Last amateur club: Saskatoon Blades (WHL).
(St. Louis' 1st choice, 7th over-all, in 1976 Amateur Draft).

				Regular Season					Playoffs			
Season	Club	Lea	GP	G	A	TP	PIM	GP	G	A	TP	PIM
1973-74	Saskatoon	WHL	68	22	28	50	19	6	0	0	0	2
1974-75	Saskatoon	WHL	66	39	68	107	30	17	*15	7	22	8
1975-76ab	Saskatoon	WHL	72	72	*115	*187	108	20	18	*27	*45	8
1976-77	Kansas City	CHL	42	30	39	69	41	....	....	....	....	....
	St. Louis	NHL	31	14	9	23	15	4	1	1	2	2
1977-78	St. Louis	NHL	72	17	24	41	27	....	....	....	....	....
1978-79	St. Louis	NHL	74	31	64	95	14	....	....	....	....	....
1979-80	St. Louis	NHL	79	38	56	94	24	3	1	0	1	2
1980-81	St. Louis	NHL	78	31	73	104	47	11	8	10	18	2
1981-82	St. Louis	NHL	74	30	62	92	70	10	3	15	18	10
1982-83	St. Louis	NHL	75	24	60	84	24	4	2	3	5	0
1983-84	St. Louis	NHL	79	41	66	107	43	11	4	4	4	10
1984-85	St. Louis	NHL	76	30	73	103	27	3	0	2	2	4
1985-86	St. Louis	NHL	80	34	68	102	34	19	7	14	21	17
	NHL Totals		718	290	555	845	325	65	26	49	75	47

a WHL First All-Star Team (1976)
b Named WHL's Most Valuable Player (1976)

FEDYK, BRENT   (FED-ick)

Born, Yorkton, Sask., March 8, 1967.
Right wing. Shoots right. 6' 180 lbs.
Last amateur club: Regina Pats (WHL).
(Detroit's 1st choice, 8th over-all, in 1985 Entry Draft).

				Regular Season					Playoffs			
Season	Club	Lea	GP	G	A	TP	PIM	GP	G	A	TP	PIM
1983-84	Regina	WHL	63	15	28	43	30	23	8	7	15	6
1984-85	Regina	WHL	66	35	35	70	48	8	5	4	9	0
1985-86	Regina	WHL	50	43	34	77	47	5	0	1	1	0

FELTRIN, ANTHONY LOUIS (TONY)

Born, Ladysmith, B.C., December 6, 1961.
Defense. Shoots left. 5'11", 185 lbs.
Last amateur club: Victoria Cougars (WHL).
(Pittsburgh's 3rd choice, 72nd over-all, in 1980 Entry Draft).

				Regular Season					Playoffs			
Season	Club	Lea	GP	G	A	TP	PIM	GP	G	A	TP	PIM
1978-79	Victoria	WHL	47	2	11	13	119	7	0	1	1	4
1979-80	Victoria	WHL	71	6	25	31	138	I7	0	8	8	21
1980-81	Victoria	WHL	43	4	25	29	81	....	....	....	....	....
	Pittsburgh	**NHL**	2	0	0	0	0	....	....	....	....	....
1981-82	**Pittsburgh**	**NHL**	4	0	0	0	4	....	....	....	....	....
	Erie	AHL	72	4	15	19	117	....	....	....	....	....
1982-83	**Pittsburgh**	**NHL**	32	3	3	6	40	....	....	....	....	....
	Baltimore	AHL	31	2	3	5	34	....	....	....	....	....
1983-84	Baltimore	AHL	4	0	0	0	2	....	....	....	....	....
	Salt Lake	CHL	65	8	22	30	94	5	2	0	2	5
1984-85	Salt Lake	IHL	81	8	19	27	125	7	2	1	3	14
1985-86	**NY Rangers**	**NHL**	10	0	0	0	21	....	....	....	....	....
	New Haven	AHL	22	0	2	2	38	....	....	....	....	....
	NHL Totals		48	3	3	6	65	....	....	....	....	....

Signed as a free agent by **NY Rangers**, October 8, 1985.

FENTON, PAUL JOHN

Born, Springfield, Mass., December 22, 1959.
Center. Shoots left. 5'11", 180 lbs.
Last amateur club: Boston University (ECAC).

				Regular Season					Playoffs			
Season	Club	Lea	GP	G	A	TP	PIM	GP	G	A	TP	PIM
1979-80	Boston U.	ECAC	24	8	17	25	14	....	....	....	....	....
1980-81	Boston U.	ECAC	5	3	2	5	0	....	....	....	....	....
1981-82	Boston U.	ECAC	28	20	13	33	20	....	....	....	....	....
1982-83	Peoria	IHL	82	60	51	111	53	....	....	....	....	....
	Colorado	CHL	1	0	1	1	0	3	2	0	2	2
1983-84	Binghamton	AHL	78	41	24	65	67	....	....	....	....	....
1984-85	**Hartford**	**NHL**	33	7	5	12	10	....	....	....	....	....
	Binghamton	AHL	45	26	21	47	18	....	....	....	....	....
1985-86	**Hartford**	**NHL**	1	0	0	0	0	....	....	....	....	....
a	Binghamton	AHL	75	53	35	88	87	6	2	0	2	2
	NHL Totals		34	7	5	12	10	....	....	....	....	....

a AHL First All-Star Team (1986)
Signed as free agent by **Hartford**, October 6, 1983.

FENYVES, DAVID   (FEN-vez)

Born, Dunnville, Ont., April 29, 1960.
Defense. Shoots left. 5'11", 190 lbs.
Last amateur club: Peterborough Petes (OHA).

				Regular Season					Playoffs			
Season	Club	Lea	GP	G	A	TP	PIM	GP	G	A	TP	PIM
1978-79	Peterborough	OHA	66	2	23	25	122	19	0	5	5	18
1979-80a	Peterborough	OHA	66	9	36	45	92	14	0	3	3	14
1980-81	Rochester	AHL	77	6	16	22	146	....	....	....	....	....
1981-82	Rochester	AHL	73	3	14	17	68	5	0	1	1	4
1982-83	Rochester	AHL	51	2	19	21	45	....	....	....	....	....
	Buffalo	**NHL**	24	0	8	8	14	4	0	0	0	0
1983-84	**Buffalo**	**NHL**	10	0	4	4	9	2	0	0	0	7
	Rochester	AHL	70	3	16	19	55	16	1	4	5	22
1984-85	**Buffalo**	**NHL**	60	1	8	9	27	5	0	0	0	2
	Rochester	AHL	9	0	3	3	8	....	....	....	....	....
1985-86	**Buffalo**	**NHL**	47	0	7	7	37	....	....	....	....	....
	NHL Totals		141	1	27	28	87	11	0	0	0	9

a OHA Second All-Star Team (1980)
Signed as free agent by **Buffalo**, October 31, 1979.

FERGUS, THOMAS JOSEPH (TOM)

Born, Chicago, Ill., June 16, 1962.
Center. Shoots left. 6',2", 205 lbs.
Last amateur club: Peterborough Petes (OHA).
(Boston's 2nd choice, 60th over-all, in 1980 Entry Draft).

				Regular Season					Playoffs			
Season	Club	Lea	GP	G	A	TP	PIM	GP	G	A	TP	PIM
1979-80	Peterborough	OHA	63	8	6	14	14	14	1	5	6	6
1980-81	Peterborough	OHA	63	43	45	88	33	5	1	4	5	2
1981-82	**Boston**	**NHL**	61	15	24	39	12	6	1	1	2	4
1982-83	**Boston**	**NHL**	80	28	35	63	39	15	2	2	4	15
1983-84	**Boston**	**NHL**	69	25	36	61	12	3	2	0	2	9
1984-85	**Boston**	**NHL**	79	30	43	73	75	5	0	0	0	0
1985-86	Toronto	NHL	78	31	42	73	64	10	5	7	12	6
	NHL Totals		367	129	180	309	201	39	12	9	21	34

Traded to **Toronto** by **Boston** for Bill Derlago, October 11, 1985.

FERGUSON, IAN

Born, Winnipeg, Man., June 24, 1966.
Defense. Shoots left. 6'2", 175 lbs.
Last amateur club: Oshawa Generals (OHL).
(New Jersey's 7th choice, 128th over-all, in 1984 Entry Draft).

			Regular Season					Playoffs				
Season	Club	Lea	GP	G	A	TP	PIM	GP	G	A	TP	PIM
1983-84	Oshawa	OHL	65	2	7	9	30	5	0	0	0	0
1984-85	Oshawa	OHL	65	6	19	25	78	5	1	1	2	4
1985-86	Oshawa	OHL	48	6	10	16	43	4	0	0	0	2

FERGUSON, JOHN JR.

Born, Winnipeg, Man., July 7, 1967.
Left wing. Shoots left. 6'0", 175 lbs.
Last amateur club: Providence College Friars (H.E.).
(Montreal's 15th choice, 247th overall, in 1985 Entry Draft).

			Regular Season					Playoffs				
Season	Club	Lea	GP	G	A	TP	PIM	GP	G	A	TP	PIM
1985-86	Providence	H.E.	18	1	2	3	2	....	....	....	....	....

FERNER, MARK

Born, Regina, Sask., September 5, 1965.
Defense. Shoots left. 6', 170 lbs.
Last amateur club: Kamloops Blazers (WHL)
(Buffalo's 12th choice, 194th over-all, in 1983 Entry Draft).

			Regular Season					Playoffs				
Season	Club	Lea	GP	G	A	TP	PIM	GP	G	A	TP	PIM
1982-83	Kamloops	WHL	69	6	15	21	81	7	0	0	0	7
1983-84	Kamloops	WHL	72	9	30	39	169	14	1	8	9	20
1984-85a	Kamloops	WHL	69	15	39	54	91	15	4	9	13	21
1985-86	Rochester	AHL	63	3	14	17	87	....	....	....	....	....

a WHL First All-Star Team, West Division (1985)

FERRARO, RAY

Born, Trail, B.C., August 23, 1964.
Center. Shoots left. 5'10", 160 lbs.
Last amateur club: Brandon Wheat Kings (WHL).
(Hartford's 5th choice, 88th over-all, in 1982 Entry Draft).

			Regular Season					Playoffs				
Season	Club	Lea	GP	G	A	TP	PIM	GP	G	A	TP	PIM
1981-82	Penticton	BCJHL	52	65	67	132	98	....	....	....	....	....
1982-83	Portland	WHL	50	41	49	90	39	14	14	10	24	13
1983-84a	Brandon	WHL	72	*108	84	*192	84	11	13	15	28	20
1984-85	**Hartford**	**NHL**	**44**	**11**	**17**	**28**	**40**	....	....	....	....	....
	Binghamton	AHL	37	20	13	33	29	....	....	....	....	....
1985-86	**Hartford**	**NHL**	**76**	**30**	**47**	**77**	**57**	**10**	**3**	**6**	**9**	**4**
	NHL Totals		**120**	**41**	**64**	**105**	**97**	**10**	**3**	**6**	**9**	**4**

a WHL First All-Star Team (1984)

FINLEY, JEFF

Born, Vernon, B.C., April 14, 1967.
Defense. Shoots left. 6'1", 185 lbs.
Last amateur club: Portland Winter Hawks (WHL).
(NY Islanders' 4th choice, 55th overall, in 1985 Entry Draft).

			Regular Season					Playoffs				
Season	Club	Lea	GP	G	A	TP	PIM	GP	G	A	TP	PIM
1983-84	Portland	WHL	5	0	0	0	5	5	0	1	1	4
1984-85	Portland	WHL	69	6	44	50	57	6	1	2	3	2
1985-86	Portland	WHL	70	11	59	70	83	15	1	7	8	16

FINN, STEVEN

Born, Laval, Que., August 20, 1966.
Defense. Shoots left. 6', 190 lbs.
Last amateur club: Laval Voisins (QMJHL)
(Quebec's 3rd choice, 57th over-all, in 1984 Entry Draft).

			Regular Season					Playoffs				
Season	Club	Lea	GP	G	A	TP	PIM	GP	G	A	TP	PIM
1982-83	Laval	QMJHL	69	7	30	37	108	6	0	2	2	6
1983-84	Laval	QMJHL	68	7	39	46	159	14	1	6	7	27
1984-85a	Laval	QMJHL	61	20	33	53	169	....	....	....	....	....
	Fredericton	AHL	4	0	0	0	14	6	1	1	2	4
1985-86	**Quebec**	**NHL**	**17**	**0**	**1**	**1**	**28**	....	....	....	....	....
	Laval	QMJHL	29	4	15	19	111	14	6	16	22	57
	NHL Totals		**17**	**0**	**1**	**1**	**28**	....	....	....	....	....

a QMJHL Second All-Star Team (1985).

FISHBACK, BRUCE

Born, St. Paul, Minn., January 19, 1965.
Right wing. Shoots right. 6'1", 185 lbs.
Last amateur club: University of Minnesota-Duluth Bulldogs (WCHA).
(Los Angeles' 9th choice, 173rd overall, in 1983 Entry Draft).

			Regular Season					Playoffs				
Season	Club	Lea	GP	G	A	TP	PIM	GP	G	A	TP	PIM
1983-84	Minn-Duluth	WCHA	13	2	2	4	4	....	....	....	....	....
1984-85	Minn-Duluth	WCHA	30	2	1	3	4	....	....	....	....	....
1985-86	Minn-Duluth	WCHA	37	2	3	5	4	....	....	....	....	....

FITZGERALD, TOM

Born, Melrose, Mass., August 28, 1968.
Center. Shoots right. 6'1", 195 lbs.
Last amateur club: Austin Prep (HS).
(NY Islanders' 1st choice, 17th overall, in 1986 Entry Draft).

			Regular Season					Playoffs				
Season	Club	Lea	GP	G	A	TP	PIM	GP	G	A	TP	PIM
1984-85	Austin Prep	HS	24	35	38	73	....	....	....	....	....	....
1985-86	Austin Prep	HS	18	20	21	41	....	....	....	....	....	....

FITZPATRICK, ROSS

Born, Penticton, B.C., October 7, 1960.
Center. Shoots left. 6', 195 lbs.
Last amateur club: Western Michigan University Broncos (CCHA).
(Philadelphia's 7th choice, 147th over-all, in 1980 Entry Draft).

			Regular Season					Playoffs				
Season	Club	Lea	GP	G	A	TP	PIM	GP	G	A	TP	PIM
1978-79	W. Michigan	CCHA	35	16	21	37	31	....	....	....	....	....
1979-80	W. Michigan	CCHA	34	26	33	59	22	....	....	....	....	....
1980-81a	W. Michigan	CCHA	36	28	43	71	22	....	....	....	....	....
1981-82	W. Michigan	CCHA	33	30	28	58	34	....	....	....	....	....
1982-83	**Philadelphia**	**NHL**	**1**	**0**	**0**	**0**	**0**	....	....	....	....	....
	Maine	AHL	66	29	28	57	32	12	5	1	6	12
1983-84	**Philadelphia**	**NHL**	**12**	**4**	**2**	**6**	**0**	....	....	....	....	....
	Springfield	AHL	45	33	30	63	28	4	3	2	5	2
1984-85	**Philadelphia**	**NHL**	**5**	**1**	**0**	**1**	**0**	....	....	....	....	....
	Hershey	AHL	35	26	15	41	8	....	....	....	....	....
1985-86	**Philadelphia**	**NHL**	**2**	**0**	**0**	**0**	**0**	....	....	....	....	....
b	Hershey	AHL	77	50	47	97	28	17	9	7	16	10
	NHL Totals		**20**	**5**	**2**	**7**	**0**	....	....	....	....	....

a CCHA First All-Star Team (1981)
b AHL Second All-Star Team (1986).

FITZSIMMONS, PAUL

Born, Wethersfield, Conn., August 25, 1963.
Defense. Shoots right. 6'2", 200 lbs.
Last amateur club: Northeastern University Huskies (H.E.).
(Boston's 10th choice, 202nd overall, in 1983 Entry Draft).

			Regular Season					Playoffs				
Season	Club	Lea	GP	G	A	TP	PIM	GP	G	A	TP	PIM
1982-83	Northeastern	ECAC	27	1	2	3	24	....	....	....	....	....
1983-84	Northeastern	ECAC	24	2	3	5	56	....	....	....	....	....
1984-85	Northeastern	ECAC	33	0	1	1	74	....	....	....	....	....
1985-86a	Northeastern	ECAC	38	3	18	21	44	....	....	....	....	....

a Hockey East First All-Star Team (1986)

FLANAGAN, MIKE

Born, Boston, Mass., April 27, 1965.
Defense. Shoots left. 6'4", 210 lbs.
Last amateur club: Providence College Friars (H.E.).
(Edmonton's 3rd choice, 60th overall, in 1983 Entry Draft).

			Regular Season					Playoffs				
Season	Club	Lea	GP	G	A	TP	PIM	GP	G	A	TP	PIM
1983-84	Providence	ECAC	19	1	0	1	2	....	....	....	....	....
1984-85	Providence	H.E.	25	0	1	1	12	....	....	....	....	....
1985-86	Providence	H.E.	33	0	4	4	45	....	....	....	....	....

FLANAGAN, TIM

Born, Red Deer, Alta., March 6, 1967.
Right wing. Shoots right. 6'0", 185 lbs.
Last amateur club: Michigan Tech University Huskies (WCHA).
(Los Angeles' 6th choice, 135th overall, in 1985 Entry Draft).

			Regular Season					Playoffs				
Season	Club	Lea	GP	G	A	TP	PIM	GP	G	A	TP	PIM
1984-85	Mich. Tech.	WCHA	27	5	5	10	34	....	....	....	....	....
1985-86	Mich. Tech.	WCHA	29	2	3	5	36	....	....	....	....	....

FLATLEY, PATRICK   (FLAT-lee)

Born, Toronto, Ont., October 3, 1963.
Right wing. Shoots right. 6'3", 205 lbs.
Last amateur club: 1984 Canadian Olympic Team.
(NY Islanders' 1st choice, 21st over-all, in 1982 Entry Draft).

			Regular Season					Playoffs				
Season	Club	Lea	GP	G	A	TP	PIM	GP	G	A	TP	PIM
1981-82	U. of Wisconsin	WCHA	17	10	9	19	40	....	....	....	....	....
1982-83ab	U. of Wisconsin	WCHA	26	17	24	41	48	....	....	....	....	....
1983-84	Cdn. Olympic	....	57	33	17	50	136	....	....	....	....	....
	NY Islanders	**NHL**	**16**	**2**	**7**	**9**	**6**	**21**	**9**	**6**	**15**	**14**
1984-85	**NY Islanders**	**NHL**	**78**	**20**	**31**	**51**	**106**	**4**	**1**	**0**	**1**	**6**
1985-86	**NY Islanders**	**NHL**	**73**	**18**	**34**	**52**	**66**	**3**	**0**	**0**	**0**	**21**
	NHL Totals		**167**	**40**	**72**	**112**	**178**	**28**	**10**	**6**	**16**	**41**

a WCHA First All-Star Team (1983)
b Named to NCAA All-Tournament Team (1983)

FLESCH, JOHN PATRICK

Born, Sudbury, Ont., July 15, 1953.
Left wing. Shoots left. 6'2", 200 lbs.
Last amateur club: Lake Superior State College Lakers (CCHA)
(Atlanta's 5th choice, 69th over-all, in 1973 Amateur Draft).

			Regular Season					Playoffs				
Season	Club	Lea	GP	G	A	TP	PIM	GP	G	A	TP	PIM
1972-73	Lake Superior	CCHA	29	28	32	60	108	....	....	....	....	....
1973-74	Omaha	CHL	69	27	27	54	98	5	1	2	3	4
1974-75	**Minnesota**	**NHL**	**57**	**8**	**15**	**23**	**47**	....	....	....	....	....
1975-76	**Minnesota**	**NHL**	**33**	**3**	**2**	**5**	**47**	....	....	....	....	....
	New Haven	AHL	31	11	10	21	95	3	1	0	1	2
1976-77	Columbus	IHL	74	34	39	73	210	7	1	5	6	15
1977-78	**Pittsburgh**	**NHL**	**29**	**7**	**5**	**12**	**19**	....	....	....	....	....
	Grand Rapids	IHL	43	11	19	30	106	....	....	....	....	....
1978-79	Grand Rapids	IHL	67	26	56	82	149	22	10	15	25	36
1979-80	**Colorado**	**NHL**	**5**	**0**	**1**	**1**	**4**	....	....	....	....	....
	Grand Rapids	IHL	6	39	54	93	66	....	....	....	....	....
1980-81	Milwaukee	IHL	70	27	44	71	70	7	1	3	4	6
1981-82	Milwaukee	IHL	82	39	54	93	45	5	2	2	4	4
1982-83	Milwaukee	IHL	51	24	31	55	56	11	5	7	12	10
1983-84	Milwaukee	IHL	81	43	44	87	27	4	0	2	2	0
1984-85	Kalamazoo	IHL	82	38	40	78	72	11	9	4	13	2
1985-86	Kalamazoo	IHL	48	15	15	30	33	6	0	3	3	2
	NHL Totals		**124**	**18**	**23**	**41**	**117**	....	....	....	....	....

Traded to **Minnesota** by **Atlanta** with Don Martineau for Buster Harvey and Jerry Byers, May 27, 1974. Signed as a free agent by **Pittsburgh**, February 4, 1978. Signed as free agent by **Colorado**, January 13, 1980.

FLICHEL, TODD

Born, Osgoode, Ont., September 14, 1964.
Defense. Shoots right. 6'3", 195 lbs.
Last amateur club: Bowling Green State University Falcons (CCHA).
(Winnipeg's 10th choice, 169th overall, in 1983 Entry Draft).

			Regular Season					Playoffs				
Season	Club	Lea	GP	G	A	TP	PIM	GP	G	A	TP	PIM
1983-84	Bowling Green	CCHA	44	1	3	4	12	....	....	....	....	....
1984-85	Bowling Green	CCHA	42	5	7	12	62	....	....	....	....	....
1985-86	Bowling Green	CCHA	42	3	10	13	84	....	....	....	....	....

FLOCKHART, RONALD (RON)

Born, Smithers, B.C., October 10, 1960.
Center. Shoots left. 5'11", 185 lbs.
Last amateur club: Regina Pats (WHL).

			Regular Season					Playoffs				
Season	Club	Lea	GP	G	A	TP	PIM	GP	G	A	TP	PIM
1979-80	Regina	WHL	65	54	76	130	63	17	11	23	34	18
1980-81	Maine	AHL	59	33	33	66	26	....	....	....	....	....
	Philadelphia	**NHL**	**14**	**3**	**7**	**10**	**11**	**3**	**1**	**0**	**1**	**2**
1981-82	**Philadelphia**	**NHL**	**72**	**33**	**39**	**72**	**44**	**4**	**0**	**1**	**1**	**2**
1982-83	**Philadelphia**	**NHL**	**73**	**29**	**31**	**60**	**49**	**2**	**1**	**1**	**2**	**2**
1983-84	**Philadelphia**	**NHL**	**8**	**0**	**3**	**3**	**4**	....	....	....	....	....
	Pittsburgh	**NHL**	**68**	**27**	**18**	**45**	**40**	....	....	....	....	....
1984-85	**Pittsburgh**	**NHL**	**12**	**0**	**5**	**5**	**4**	....	....	....	....	....
	Montreal	**NHL**	**42**	**10**	**12**	**22**	**14**	**2**	**1**	**1**	**2**	**2**
1985-86	**St. Louis**	**NHL**	**79**	**22**	**45**	**67**	**26**	**8**	**1**	**3**	**4**	**6**
	NHL Totals		**368**	**124**	**160**	**284**	**192**	**19**	**4**	**6**	**10**	**14**

Signed as free agent by **Philadelphia**, July 2, 1980. Traded to **Pittsburgh** by **Philadelphia** with Andy Brickley, Mark Taylor and Philadelphia's first round (Roger Belanger) and third round (Mike Stevens - later transferred to Vancouver) choices in 1984 Entry Draft for Rich Sutter and Pittsburgh's second round (Greg Smyth) and third round (David McClay) choices in 1984 Entry Draft, October 23, 1983. Traded to **Montreal** by **Pittsburgh** for John Chabot, November 9, 1984. Traded to **St. Louis** by **Montreal** for Perry Ganchar, August 26, 1985.

FLORIO, PERRY

Born, Glen Cove, NY, July 15, 1967.
Defense. Shoots left. 6'0", 190 lbs.
Last amateur club: Providence College Friars (H.E.).
(Los Angeles' 4th choice, 72nd overall, in 1985 Entry Draft).

			Regular Season					Playoffs				
Season	Club	Lea	GP	G	A	TP	PIM	GP	G	A	TP	PIM
1985-86	Providence	H.E.	39	4	5	9	90	....	....	....	....	....

FLOYD, LARRY DAVID

Born, Peterborough, Ont., May 1, 1961.
Center. Shoots left. 5'8", 180 lbs.
Last amateur club: Peterborough Petes (OHL).

			Regular Season					Playoffs				
Season	Club	Lea	GP	G	A	TP	PIM	GP	G	A	TP	PIM
1979-80	Peterborough	OHA	66	21	37	58	54	14	6	9	15	10
1980-81	Peterborough	OHA	44	26	37	63	43	5	2	2	4	0
1981-82	Peterborough	OHL	39	32	37	69	26	9	9	6	15	20
	Rochester	AHL	1	0	2	2	0	7	1	1	2	0
1982-83	**New Jersey**	**NHL**	**5**	**1**	**0**	**1**	**2**	....	....	....	....	....
a	Wichita	CHL	75	40	43	83	16	....	....	....	....	....
1983-84	**New Jersey**	**NHL**	**7**	**1**	**3**	**4**	**7**	....	....	....	....	....
	Maine	AHL	74	37	49	86	40	16	9	8	17	4
1984-85	Maine	AHL	72	30	51	81	24	3	0	1	1	2
1985-86	Maine	AHL	80	29	58	87	25	5	3	3	6	0
	NHL Totals		**12**	**2**	**3**	**5**	**9**	....	....	....	....	....

a Won Ken McKenzie Trophy (CHL's Rookie of the Year) (1983).

Signed as free agent by **New Jersey**, September 16, 1982.

FOGOLIN, LEE JOSEPH

Born, Chicago, Ill., February 7, 1955.
Defense. Shoots right. 6', 205 lbs.
Last amateur club: Oshawa Generals (OHA).
(Buffalo's 1st choice, 11th over-all, in 1974 Amateur Draft).

			Regular Season					Playoffs				
Season	Club	Lea	GP	G	A	TP	PIM	GP	G	A	TP	PIM
1972-73	Oshawa	OHA	55	5	21	26	132	....	....	....	....	....
1973-74	Oshawa	OHA	47	7	19	26	108	....	....	....	....	....
1974-75	**Buffalo**	**NHL**	**50**	**2**	**2**	**4**	**59**	**8**	**0**	**0**	**0**	**6**
1975-76	Hershey	AHL	20	1	8	9	61	....	....	....	....	....
	Buffalo	**NHL**	**58**	**0**	**9**	**9**	**64**	**9**	**0**	**4**	**4**	**23**
1976-77	**Buffalo**	**NHL**	**71**	**3**	**15**	**18**	**100**	**4**	**0**	**0**	**0**	**2**
1977-78	**Buffalo**	**NHL**	**76**	**0**	**23**	**23**	**98**	**6**	**0**	**2**	**2**	**23**
1978-79	**Buffalo**	**NHL**	**74**	**3**	**19**	**22**	**103**	**3**	**0**	**0**	**0**	**4**
1979-80	**Edmonton**	**NHL**	**80**	**5**	**10**	**15**	**104**	**3**	**0**	**0**	**0**	**4**
1980-81	**Edmonton**	**NHL**	**80**	**13**	**17**	**30**	**139**	**9**	**0**	**0**	**0**	**12**
1981-82	**Edmonton**	**NHL**	**80**	**4**	**25**	**29**	**154**	**5**	**1**	**1**	**2**	**14**
1982-83	**Edmonton**	**NHL**	**72**	**0**	**18**	**18**	**92**	**16**	**0**	**5**	**5**	**36**
1983-84	**Edmonton**	**NHL**	**80**	**5**	**16**	**21**	**125**	**19**	**1**	**4**	**5**	**23**
1984-85	**Edmonton**	**NHL**	**79**	**4**	**14**	**18**	**126**	**18**	**3**	**1**	**4**	**16**
1985-86	**Edmonton**	**NHL**	**80**	**4**	**22**	**26**	**129**	**8**	**0**	**2**	**2**	**10**
	NHL Totals		**880**	**43**	**190**	**233**	**1293**	**108**	**5**	**19**	**24**	**173**

Claimed by **Edmonton** from **Buffalo** in Expansion Draft, June 13, 1979.

FOLIGNO, MIKE ANTHONY (fo-LEEN-oh)

Born, Sudbury, Ont., January 29, 1959.
Right wing. Shoots right. 6'2", 195 lbs.
Last amateur club: Sudbury Wolves (OHA).
(Detroit's 1st choice, 3rd over-all, in 1979 Draft).

			Regular Season					Playoffs				
Season	Club	Lea	GP	G	A	TP	PIM	GP	G	A	TP	PIM
1977-78	Sudbury	OHA	67	47	39	86	112	....	....	....	....	....
1978-79a	Sudbury	OHA	68	65	85	*150	98	10	5	5	10	14
1979-80	**Detroit**	**NHL**	**80**	**36**	**35**	**71**	**109**	....	....	....	....	....
1980-81	**Detroit**	**NHL**	**80**	**28**	**35**	**63**	**210**	....	....	....	....	....
1981-82	**Detroit**	**NHL**	**26**	**13**	**13**	**26**	**28**	....	....	....	....	....
	Buffalo	**NHL**	**56**	**20**	**31**	**51**	**149**	**4**	**2**	**0**	**2**	**9**
1982-83	**Buffalo**	**NHL**	**66**	**22**	**25**	**47**	**135**	**10**	**2**	**3**	**5**	**39**
1983-84	**Buffalo**	**NHL**	**70**	**32**	**31**	**63**	**151**	**3**	**2**	**1**	**3**	**19**
1984-85	**Buffalo**	**NHL**	**77**	**27**	**29**	**56**	**154**	**5**	**1**	**3**	**4**	**12**
1985-86	**Buffalo**	**NHL**	**79**	**41**	**39**	**80**	**168**	....	....	....	....	....
	NHL Totals		**534**	**219**	**238**	**457**	**1104**	**22**	**7**	**7**	**14**	**79**

a OHL First All-Star Team (1979).
Traded to **Buffalo** by **Detroit** with Dale McCourt and Brent Peterson for Danny Gare, Jim Schoenfeld and Derek Smith, December 2, 1981.

FORST, RICK

Born, Esterhazy, Sask., June 6, 1965.
Left wing. Shoots left. 6'1", 175 lbs.
Last amateur club: University of North Dakota Fighting Sioux (WCHA).
(Winnipeg's 9th choice, 197th overall, in 1984 Entry Draft).

			Regular Season					Playoffs				
Season	Club	Lea	GP	G	A	TP	PIM	GP	G	A	TP	PIM
1984-85	North Dakota	WCHA	17	0	3	3	8	....	....	....	....	....
1985-86	North Dakota	WCHA	32	7	4	11	22	....	....	....	....	....

FOSTER, DWIGHT ALEXANDER

Born, Toronto, Ont., April 2, 1957.
Center/Right wing. Shoots right. 5'11", 195 lbs.
Last amateur club: Kitchener Rangers (OHA).
(Boston's 1st choice, 16th over-all, in 1977 Amateur Draft).

			Regular Season					Playoffs				
Season	Club	Lea	GP	G	A	TP	PIM	GP	G	A	TP	PIM
1975-76	Kitchener	OHA	61	36	58	94	110	8	4	6	10	28
1976-77a	Kitchener	OHA	64	60	83	143	88	3	2	4	6	2
1977-78	**Boston**	**NHL**	**14**	**2**	**1**	**3**	**6**	....	....	....	....	....
	Rochester	AHL	3	0	3	3	2	....	....	....	....	....
1978-79	Rochester	AHL	21	11	18	29	8	....	....	....	....	....
	Boston	**NHL**	**44**	**11**	**13**	**24**	**14**	**11**	**1**	**3**	**4**	**0**
1979-80	Binghamton	AHL	7	1	3	4	2	....	....	....	....	....
	Boston	**NHL**	**57**	**10**	**28**	**38**	**42**	**9**	**3**	**5**	**8**	**2**
1980-81	**Boston**	**NHL**	**77**	**24**	**28**	**52**	**62**	**3**	**1**	**1**	**2**	**0**
1981-82	**Colorado**	**NHL**	**70**	**12**	**19**	**31**	**41**	....	....	....	....	....
1982-83	**New Jersey**	**NHL**	**4**	**0**	**0**	**0**	**2**	....	....	....	....	....
	Wichita	CHL	2	0	1	1	2	....	....	....	....	....
	Detroit	**NHL**	**58**	**17**	**22**	**39**	**58**	....	....	....	....	....
1983-84	**Detroit**	**NHL**	**52**	**9**	**12**	**21**	**50**	**3**	**0**	**1**	**1**	**0**
1984-85	**Detroit**	**NHL**	**50**	**16**	**16**	**32**	**56**	**3**	**0**	**0**	**0**	**0**
1985-86	**Detroit**	**NHL**	**55**	**6**	**12**	**18**	**48**	....	....	....	....	....
	Boston	**NHL**	**13**	**0**	**0**	**0**	**4**	**3**	**0**	**2**	**2**	**2**
	NHL Totals		**494**	**107**	**151**	**258**	**383**	**32**	**5**	**12**	**17**	**4**

a OHA Third All-Star Team (1977)

Signed as free agent by **Colorado**, July 21, 1981. As compensation, **Boston** received Colorado's second-round choice (Brian Curran) in the 1982 Entry Draft and switched first round choices in the same draft. Boston claimed Gord Kluzak, while Colorado (New Jersey) selected Ken Daneyko. Rights sold to **Detroit** by **New Jersey**, October 29, 1982. Traded to **Boston** by **Detroit** for Dave Donnelly, March 11, 1986.

FOTIU, NICHOLAS EVLAMPIOS (NICK)   (foh-TEE-oo)

Born, Staten Island, N.Y., May 25, 1952.
Left wing. Shoots left. 6'2", 210 lbs.
Last amateur club: New Hyde Park Arrows (New York MJHA).

			Regular Season					Playoffs				
Season	Club	Lea	GP	G	A	TP	PIM	GP	G	A	TP	PIM
1971-72	New Hyde Park	MJHA	32	6	17	23	135	....	....	....	....	....
1972-73	DID NOT PLAY											
1973-74	Cape Cod	NAHL	72	12	24	36	371	....	....	....	....	....
1974-75	Cape Cod	NAHL	5	2	1	3	13	....	....	....	....	....
	New England	WHA	61	2	2	4	144	4	2	0	2	27
1975-76	Cape Cod	NAHL	6	2	1	3	15	....	....	....	....	....
	New England	WHA	49	3	2	5	94	16	3	2	5	57
1976-77	New York Rangers	NHL	70	4	8	12	174	....	....	....	....	....
1977-78	New Haven	AHL	5	1	1	2	9	....	....	....	....	....
	NY Rangers	NHL	59	2	7	9	105	3	0	0	0	5
1978-79	NY Rangers	NHL	71	3	5	8	190	4	0	0	0	6
1979-80	Hartford	NHL	74	10	8	18	107	3	0	0	0	6
1980-81	Hartford	NHL	42	4	3	7	79	....	....	....	....	....
	NY Rangers	NHL	27	5	6	11	91	2	0	0	0	4
1981-82	NY Rangers	NHL	70	8	10	18	151	10	0	2	2	6
1982-83	NY Rangers	NHL	72	8	13	21	90	5	0	1	1	6
1983-84	NY Rangers	NHL	40	7	6	13	115	....	....	....	....	....
1984-85	NY Rangers	NHL	46	4	7	11	54	....	....	....	....	....
1985-86	New Haven	AHL	9	4	2	6	21	....	....	....	....	....
	Calgary	NHL	9	0	1	1	21	11	0	1	1	34
	NHL Totals		**580**	**55**	**74**	**129**	**1177**	**38**	**0**	**4**	**4**	**67**

Signed as free agent by **NY Rangers**, July 23, 1976. Claimed by **Hartford** from **NY Rangers** in Expansion Draft, June 13, 1979. Traded to **NY Rangers** by **Hartford** for Rangers' fifth round choice (Bill Maguire) in 1981 Entry Draft, January 15, 1981. Traded to **Calgary** by **NY Rangers** for Calgary's sixth-round choice in 1987 Entry Draft, March 11, 1986.

FOX, JAMES CHARLES (JIMMY)

Born, Coniston, Ont., May 18, 1960.
Right wing. Shoots right. 5'8", 185 lbs.
Last amateur club: Ottawa 67's (OHA).
(Los Angeles' 2nd choice, 10th over-all, in 1980 Entry Draft).

			Regular Season					Playoffs				
Season	Club	Lea	GP	G	A	TP	PIM	GP	G	A	TP	PIM
1978-79	Ottawa	OHA	53	37	66	103	4	4	2	1	3	2
1979-80ab	Ottawa	OHA	52	65	*101	*166	30	11	6	14	20	2
1980-81	Los Angeles	NHL	71	18	25	43	8	4	0	1	1	0
1981-82	Los Angeles	NHL	77	30	38	68	23	9	1	4	5	0
1982-83	Los Angeles	NHL	77	28	40	68	8	....	....	....	....	....
1983-84	Los Angeles	NHL	80	30	42	72	26	....	....	....	....	....
1984-85	Los Angeles	NHL	79	30	53	83	10	3	0	1	1	0
1985-86	Los Angeles	NHL	39	14	17	31	2	....	....	....	....	....
	NHL Totals		**423**	**150**	**215**	**365**	**77**	**16**	**1**	**6**	**7**	**0**

a OHA First All-Star Team (1980)
b Named OHA Most Valuable Player (1980)

FRANCESCHETTI, LOU   (fran-se-SHETT-ee)

Born, Toronto, Ont., April 28, 1958.
Right wing. Shoots left. 6', 190 lbs.
Last amateur club: Niagara Falls Flyers (OHA).
(Washington's 8th choice, 71st over-all, in 1978 Amateur Draft).

			Regular Season					Playoffs				
Season	Club	Lea	GP	G	A	TP	PIM	GP	G	A	TP	PIM
1976-77	Niagara Falls	OHA	61	23	30	53	80	....	....	....	....	....
1977-78	Niagara Falls	OHA	62	40	50	90	46	....	....	....	....	....
1978-79	Saginaw	IHL	2	1	1	2	0	....	....	....	....	....
	Port Huron	IHL	76	45	58	103	131	....	....	....	....	....
1979-80	Port Huron	IHL	15	3	8	11	31	....	....	....	....	....
	Hershey	AHL	65	27	29	56	58	14	6	9	15	32
1980-81	Hershey	AHL	79	32	36	68	173	10	3	7	10	30
1981-82	Hershey	AHL	50	22	33	55	89	....	....	....	....	....
	Washington	NHL	30	2	10	12	23	....	....	....	....	....
1982-83	Hershey	AHL	80	31	44	75	176	5	1	2	3	16
1983-84	Hershey	AHL	73	26	34	60	130	....	....	....	....	....
	Washington	NHL	2	0	0	0	0	3	0	0	0	8
1984-85	Washington	NHL	22	4	7	11	45	5	1	1	2	15
	Binghamton	AHL	52	29	43	72	75	....	....	....	....	....
1985-86	Washington	NHL	76	7	14	21	131	8	0	0	0	15
	NHL Totals		**130**	**13**	**31**	**44**	**199**	**16**	**1**	**1**	**2**	**38**

FRANCIS, ROBERT EMILE (BOBBY)

Born, North Battleford, Sask., December 5, 1958.
Center. Shoots right. 5'9", 175 lbs.
Last amateur club: University of New Hampshire Wildcats (ECAC)

			Regular Season					Playoffs				
Season	Club	Lea	GP	G	A	TP	PIM	GP	G	A	TP	PIM
1978-79	N. Hampshire	ECAC	35	20	46	66	44	....	....	....	....	....
1979-80	N. Hampshire	ECAC	28	19	23	42	30	....	....	....	....	....
1980-81	Birmingham	CHL	18	6	21	27	20	....	....	....	....	....
	Muskegon	IHL	27	16	17	33	33	....	....	....	....	....
1981-82abc	Oklahoma City	CHL	80	48	66	*114	76	4	1	2	3	11
1982-83	Colorado	CHL	26	20	16	36	24	....	....	....	....	....
	Detroit	NHL	14	2	0	2	0	....	....	....	....	....
	Adirondack	AHL	17	3	8	11	0	....	....	....	....	....
1983-84	Colorado	CHL	68	32	50	82	53	1	0	1	1	0
1984-85	Salt Lake	IHL	53	24	16	40	36	6	1	1	2	0
1985-86	Salt Lake	IHL	82	32	44	76	163	5	0	4	4	10
	NHL Totals		**14**	**2**	**0**	**2**	**0**	....	....	....	....	....

a CHL First All-Star Team (1982)
b Won Tommy Ivan Trophy (CHL's Most Valuable Player) (1982)
c Won Ken McKenzie Trophy (CHL's Rookie of the Year) (1982)
Signed as free agent by **Calgary**, October 27, 1980. Traded to **Detroit** by **Calgary** for the rights to Yves Courteau, December 2, 1982.

FRANCIS, RONALD (RON)

Born, Sault Ste. Marie, Ont., March 1, 1963.
Center. Shoots left. 6'2", 200 lbs.
Last amateur club: Sault Ste. Marie Greyhounds (OHL).
(Hartford's 1st choice, 4th overall, in 1981 Entry Draft).

			Regular Season					Playoffs				
Season	Club	Lea	GP	G	A	TP	PIM	GP	G	A	TP	PIM
1980-81	S. S. Marie	OHA	64	26	43	69	33	19	7	8	15	34
1981-82	S. S. Marie	OHA	25	18	30	48	46	....	....	....	....	....
	Hartford	NHL	59	25	43	68	51	....	....	....	....	....
1982-83	**Hartford**	NHL	79	31	59	90	60	....	....	....	....	....
1983-84	**Hartford**	NHL	72	23	60	83	45	....	....	....	....	....
1984-85	**Hartford**	NHL	80	24	57	81	66	....	....	....	....	....
1985-86	**Hartford**	NHL	53	24	53	77	24	10	1	2	3	4
	NHL Totals		**343**	**127**	**272**	**399**	**246**	**10**	**1**	**2**	**3**	**4**

FRASER, CURT M.

Born, Cincinnati, Ohio, January 12, 1958.
Left wing. Shoots left. 6', 200 lbs.
Last amateur club: Victoria Cougars (WHL).
(Vancouver's 2nd choice, 22nd over-all, in 1978 Amateur Draft).

			Regular Season					Playoffs				
Season	Club	Lea	GP	G	A	TP	PIM	GP	G	A	TP	PIM
1976-77	Victoria	WHL	60	34	41	75	82	4	4	2	6	4
1977-78	Victoria	WHL	66	48	44	92	256	13	10	7	17	28
1978-79	Vancouver	NHL	78	16	19	35	116	3	0	2	2	6
1979-80	Vancouver	NHL	78	17	25	42	143	4	0	0	0	2
1980-81	Vancouver	NHL	77	25	24	49	118	3	1	0	1	2
1981-82	Vancouver	NHL	79	28	39	67	175	17	3	7	10	98
1982-83	Vancouver	NHL	36	6	7	13	99	....	....	....	....	....
	Chicago	NHL	38	6	13	19	77	13	4	4	8	18
1983-84	Chicago	NHL	29	5	12	17	28	5	0	0	0	14
1984-85	Chicago	NHL	73	25	25	50	109	15	6	3	9	36
1985-86	Chicago	NHL	61	29	39	68	84	3	0	1	1	12
	NHL Totals		**549**	**157**	**203**	**360**	**949**	**63**	**14**	**17**	**31**	**188**

Traded to **Chicago** by **Vancouver** for Tony Tanti, January 6, 1983.

FRAWLEY, WILLIAM DANIEL (DAN)

Born, Sturgeon Falls, Ont., June 2, l962.
Right wing. Shoots right. 6', 170 lbs.
Last amateur club: Cornwall Royals (OHL).
(Chicago's 15th choice, 204th over-all, in 1980 Entry Draft).

			Regular Season					Playoffs				
Season	Club	Lea	GP	G	A	TP	PIM	GP	G	A	TP	PIM
1979-80	Sudbury	OHA	63	21	26	47	67	8	0	1	1	2
1980-81	Cornwall	QMJHL	28	10	14	28	76	18	5	12	17	37
1981-82	Cornwall	OHL	64	27	50	77	239	5	3	8	11	19
1982-83	Springfield	AHL	80	30	27	57	107	....	....	....	....	....
1983-84	**Chicago**	NHL	3	0	0	0	0	....	....	....	....	....
	Springfield	AHL	69	22	34	56	137	4	0	1	1	12
1984-85	**Chicago**	NHL	30	4	3	7	64	1	0	0	0	0
	Milwaukee	IHL	26	11	12	23	125	....	....	....	....	....
1985-86	Pittsburgh	NHL	69	10	11	21	174	....	....	....	....	....
	NHL Totals		**102**	**14**	**14**	**28**	**238**	**1**	**0**	**0**	**0**	**0**

Claimed by **Pittsburgh** from **Chicago** in NHL Waiver Draft, October 7, 1985.

FRIDAY, TIM

Born, Burbank, Calif., March 5, 1961.
Defense. Shoots right. 6', 190 lbs.
Last amateur club: Rensselaer Polytechnic Institute Engineers (ECAC)

			Regular Season					Playoffs				
Season	Club	Lea	GP	G	A	TP	PIM	GP	G	A	TP	PIM
1981-82	RPI	ECAC	25	2	12	14	10	....	....	....	....	....
1982-83	RPI	ECAC	28	3	18	19	10	....	....	....	....	....
1983-84	RPI	ECAC	32	4	14	18	22	....	....	....	....	....
1984-85	RPI	ECAC	36	5	29	34	26	....	....	....	....	....
1985-86	**Detroit**	**NHL**	**23**	**0**	**3**	**3**	**6**	....	....	....	....	....
	Adirondack	AHL	43	2	31	33	23	16	0	6	6	6
	NHL Totals		**23**	**0**	**3**	**3**	**6**	....	....	....	....	....

Signed as a Free agent by **Detroit**, May 27, 1985

FRYCER, MIROSLAV (FREE-cher)

Born, Ostrava, Czechoslovakia, September 27, 1959.
Right wing. Shoots right. 6', 200 lbs.
Last amateur club: Vitkovice (Czechoslovakia)

			Regular Season					Playoffs				
Season	Club	Lea	GP	G	A	TP	PIM	GP	G	A	TP	PIM
1979-80	Vitkovice	Czech	44	31	15	46	....	....	....	....	....	....
1980-81	Vitkovice	Czech	34	33	24	57	....	....	....	....	....	....
1981-82	Fredericton	AHL	11	9	5	14	16	....	....	....	....	....
	Quebec	**NHL**	**49**	**20**	**17**	**37**	**47**	....	....	....	....	....
	Toronto	**NHL**	**10**	**4**	**6**	**10**	**31**	....	....	....	....	....
1982-83	**Toronto**	**NHL**	**67**	**25**	**30**	**55**	**90**	**4**	**2**	**5**	**7**	**0**
1983-84	**Toronto**	**NHL**	**46**	**9**	**16**	**25**	**55**	....	....	....	....	....
1984-85	**Toronto**	**NHL**	**65**	**25**	**30**	**55**	**55**	....	....	....	....	....
1985-86	**Toronto**	**NHL**	**73**	**32**	**43**	**75**	**74**	**10**	**1**	**3**	**4**	**10**
	NHL Totals		**310**	**115**	**142**	**257**	**352**	**14**	**3**	**8**	**11**	**10**

Signed as free agent by **Quebec**, April 21, 1980. Traded to **Toronto** by **Quebec** with Quebec's seventh round choice (Jeff Triano) in 1982 Entry Draft for Wilf Paiement, March 9, 1982.

FUSCO, SCOTT

Born, Burlington, Mass., January 21, 1963.
Center. Shoots left. 5'8", 160 lbs.
Last amateur club: 1984 United States Olympic Team.
(New Jersey's 11th choice, 211th over-all, in 1982 Entry Draft).

			Regular Season					Playoffs				
Season	Club	Lea	GP	G	A	TP	PIM	GP	G	A	TP	PIM
1981-82	Harvard	ECAC	28	16	20	36	20	....	....	....	....	....
1982-83ab	Harvard	ECAC	26	29	18	47	....	....	....	....	....	....
1983-84	U.S. National	...	59	21	28	49	55	....	....	....	....	....
	U.S. Olympic	...	6	1	3	4	4	....	....	....	....	....
1984-85ac	Harvard	ECAC	32	34	47	81	24	....	....	....	....	....
1985-86acd	Harvard	ECAC	31	24	44	68	37	....	....	....	....	....

a ECAC First All-Star Team (1983, 1986)
b Named to NCAA All-Tournament Team (1983)
c ECAC Player of the Year (1985, 1986)
d Won Hobey Baker Memorial Award (1986)
Rights traded to **Hartford** by **New Jersey** with Merlin Malinowski for Garry Howatt and Rick Meagher, October 15, 1982.

GAGE, JOSEPH WILLIAM (JODY)

Born, Toronto, Ont., November 29, 1959.
Right wing. Shoots right. 6', 185 lbs.
Last amateur club: Kitchener Rangers (OHA).
(Detroit's 2nd choice, 45th over-all, in 1979 Entry Draft).

			Regular Season					Playoffs				
Season	Club	Lea	GP	G	A	TP	PIM	GP	G	A	TP	PIM
1977-78	Hamilton	OHA	32	15	18	33	19	....	....	....	....	....
	Kitchener	OHA	36	17	27	44	21	9	4	3	7	4
1978-79	Kitchener	OHA	58	46	43	89	40	10	1	2	3	6
1979-80	Adirondack	AHL	63	25	21	46	15	5	2	1	3	0
1980-81	**Detroit**	**NHL**	**16**	**2**	**2**	**4**	**22**	....	....	....	....	....
	Adirondack	AHL	59	17	31	48	44	17	9	6	15	12
1981-82	Adirondack	AHL	47	21	20	41	21	....	....	....	....	....
	Detroit	**NHL**	**31**	**9**	**10**	**19**	**2**	....	....	....	....	....
1982-83	Adirondack	AHL	65	23	30	53	33	6	1	5	6	8
1983-84	**Detroit**	**NHL**	**3**	**0**	**0**	**0**	**0**	....	....	....	....	....
	Adirondack	AHL	73	40	32	72	32	6	3	4	7	2
1984-85	Adirondack	AHL	78	27	33	60	55	....	....	....	....	....
1985-86	**Buffalo**	**NHL**	**7**	**3**	**2**	**5**	**0**	....	....	....	....	....
a	Rochester	AHL	73	42	57	99	56	....	....	....	....	....
	NHL Totals		**57**	**14**	**14**	**28**	**24**	....	....	....	....	....

a AHL First All-Star Team (1986)

Signed as a free agent by **Buffalo**, July 31, 1985

GAGNE, PAUL (GONE-yay)

Born, Iroquois Falls, Ont., February 6, 1962.
Left wing. Shoots left. 5'10", 180 lbs.
Last amateur club: Windsor Spitfires (OHA).
(Colorado's 1st choice, 19th over-all, in 1980 Entry Draft).

			Regular Season					Playoffs				
Season	Club	Lea	GP	G	A	TP	PIM	GP	G	A	TP	PIM
1978-79	Windsor	OHA	67	24	18	42	64	7	1	1	2	2
1979-80a	Windsor	OHA	65	48	53	101	67	13	7	8	15	19
1980-81	**Colorado**	**NHL**	**61**	**25**	**16**	**41**	**12**	....	....	....	....	....
1981-82	**Colorado**	**NHL**	**59**	**10**	**12**	**22**	**17**	....	....	....	....	....
1982-83	**New Jersey**	**NHL**	**53**	**14**	**15**	**29**	**13**	....	....	....	....	....
	Wichita	CHL	16	1	9	10	9	....	....	....	....	....
1983-84	**New Jersey**	**NHL**	**66**	**14**	**18**	**32**	**33**	....	....	....	....	....
1984-85	**New Jersey**	**NHL**	**79**	**24**	**19**	**43**	**28**	....	....	....	....	....
1985-86	**New Jersey**	**NHL**	**47**	**19**	**19**	**38**	**14**	....	....	....	....	....
	NHL Totals		**365**	**106**	**99**	**205**	**117**	....	....	....	....	....

a OHA Second All-Star Team (1980)

GAGNER, DAVE

Born, Chatham, Ont., December 11, 1964.
Center. Shoots left. 5'10", 180 lbs.
Last amateur club: Brantford Alexanders (OHL).
(NY Rangers' 1st choice, 12th over-all, in 1983 Entry Draft).

			Regular Season					Playoffs				
Season	Club	Lea	GP	G	A	TP	PIM	GP	G	A	TP	PIM
1981-82	Brantford	OHL	68	30	46	76	31	11	3	6	9	6
1982-83a	Brantford	OHL	70	55	66	121	57	8	5	5	10	4
1983-84	Cdn. Olympic	...	50	19	18	37	26	....	....	....	....	....
	Brantford	OHL	12	7	13	20	4	6	0	4	4	6
1984-85	**NY Rangers**	**NHL**	**38**	**6**	**6**	**12**	**16**	....	....	....	....	....
	New Haven	AHL	38	13	20	33	23	....	....	....	....	....
1985-86	**NY Rangers**	**NHL**	**32**	**4**	**6**	**10**	**19**	....	....	....	....	....
	New Haven	AHL	16	10	11	21	11	4	1	2	3	2
	NHL Totals		**70**	**10**	**12**	**22**	**35**	....	....	....	....	....

a OHL Second All-Star Team (1983)

GAINEY, ROBERT MICHAEL (BOB)

Born, Peterborough, Ont., December 13, 1953.
Left wing. Shoots left. 6'1", 200 lbs.
Last amateur club: Peterborough Petes (OHA).
(Montreal's 1st choice, 8th over-all, in 1973 Amateur Draft).

			Regular Season					Playoffs				
Season	Club	Lea	GP	G	A	TP	PIM	GP	G	A	TP	PIM
1971-72	Peterborough	OHA	4	2	1	3	33	....	....	....	....	....
1972-73	Peterborough	OHA	52	22	21	43	99	....	....	....	....	....
1973-74	Nova Scotia	AHL	6	2	5	7	4	....	....	....	....	....
	Montreal	**NHL**	**66**	**3**	**7**	**10**	**34**	**6**	**0**	**0**	**0**	**6**
1974-75	**Montreal**	**NHL**	**80**	**17**	**20**	**37**	**49**	**11**	**2**	**4**	**6**	**4**
1975-76	**Montreal**	**NHL**	**78**	**15**	**13**	**28**	**57**	**13**	**1**	**3**	**4**	**20**
1976-77	**Montreal**	**NHL**	**80**	**14**	**19**	**33**	**41**	**14**	**4**	**1**	**5**	**25**
1977-78a	**Montreal**	**NHL**	**66**	**15**	**16**	**31**	**57**	**15**	**2**	**7**	**9**	**14**
1978-79ab	**Montreal**	**NHL**	**79**	**20**	**18**	**38**	**44**	**16**	**6**	**10**	**16**	**10**
1979-80a	**Montreal**	**NHL**	**64**	**14**	**19**	**33**	**32**	**10**	**1**	**1**	**2**	**4**
1980-81a	**Montreal**	**NHL**	**78**	**23**	**24**	**47**	**36**	**3**	**0**	**0**	**0**	**2**
1981-82	**Montreal**	**NHL**	**79**	**21**	**24**	**45**	**24**	**5**	**0**	**1**	**1**	**8**
1982-83	**Montreal**	**NHL**	**80**	**12**	**18**	**30**	**43**	**3**	**0**	**0**	**0**	**4**
1983-84	**Montreal**	**NHL**	**77**	**17**	**22**	**39**	**41**	**15**	**1**	**5**	**6**	**9**
1984-85	**Montreal**	**NHL**	**79**	**19**	**13**	**32**	**40**	**12**	**1**	**3**	**4**	**13**
1985-86	**Montreal**	**NHL**	**80**	**20**	**23**	**43**	**20**	**20**	**5**	**5**	**10**	**12**
	NHL Totals		**986**	**210**	**236**	**446**	**518**	**143**	**23**	**40**	**63**	**131**

a Won Frank J. Selke Trophy (1978, 1979, 1980, 1981)
b Won Conn Smythe Trophy (1979)

GALLANT, BERNARD (BERNIE) (ga-LAHNT)

Born, Montreal, Que., February 13, 1960.
Left wing. Shoots left. 5'11", 175 lbs.
Last amateur club: Sherbrooke Beavers (QJHL).

			Regular Season					Playoffs				
Season	Club	Lea	GP	G	A	TP	PIM	GP	G	A	TP	PIM
1978-79	Montreal	QJHL	11	1	2	3	2	....	....	....	....	....
	Trois Rivières	QJHL	44	23	62	85	38	13	10	18	28	9
1979-80	Laval	QJHL	17	4	8	12	25	....	....	....	....	....
	Sherbrooke	QJHL	50	28	52	80	82	15	13	16	29	22
1980-81	Rochester	AHL	69	8	18	26	64	....	....	....	....	....
1981-82	Flint	IHL	75	31	29	60	95	2	1	1	2	5
1982-83	Rochester	AHL	3	0	0	0	0	....	....	....	....	....
	Flint	IHL	79	27	54	81	19	5	0	3	3	29
1983-84	Flint	IHL	81	50	53	103	22	8	3	7	10	7
1984-85	Flint	IHL	81	26	37	63	80	7	3	4	7	11
1985-86	Saginaw	IHL	45	24	29	53	36	....	....	....	....	....

Signed as free agent by **Buffalo**, August 13, 1980.

GALLANT, GERARD

Born, Summerside, P.E.I., September 2, 1963.
Center. Shoots left. 5'10", 170 lbs.
Last amateur club: Verdun Juniors (QMJHL).
(Detroit's 4th choice, 107th over-all, in 1981 Entry Draft).

			Regular Season					Playoffs				
Season	Club	Lea	GP	G	A	TP	PIM	GP	G	A	TP	PIM
1980-81	Sherbrooke	QMJHL	68	41	59	100	265	14	6	13	19	46
1981-82	Sherbrooke	QMJHL	58	34	58	92	260	22	14	24	38	84
1982-83	St. Jean	QMJHL	33	28	25	53	139	....	....	....	....	....
	Verdun	QMJHL	29	26	49	75	105	15	14	19	33	84
1983-84	Adirondack	AHL	77	31	33	64	195	7	1	3	4	34
1984-85	**Detroit**	**NHL**	**32**	**6**	**12**	**18**	**66**	**3**	**0**	**0**	**0**	**11**
	Adirondack	AHL	46	18	29	47	131	....	....	....	....	....
1985-86	**Detroit**	**NHL**	**52**	**20**	**19**	**39**	**106**	....	....	....	....	....
	NHL Totals		**84**	**26**	**31**	**57**	**172**	**3**	**0**	**0**	**0**	**11**

GALLEY, GARRY

Born, Ottawa, Ont., April 16, 1963.
Defense. Shoots left. 5'11", 190 lbs.
Last amateur club: Bowling Green State University Falcons (CCHA).
(Los Angeles' 4th choice, 100th over-all, in 1983 Entry Draft).

			Regular Season					Playoffs				
Season	Club	Lea	GP	G	A	TP	PIM	GP	G	A	TP	PIM
1981-82	Bowling Green	CCHA	42	3	36	39	48	....	....	....	....	....
1982-83	Bowling Green	CCHA	40	17	29	46	40	....	....	....	....	....
1983-84ab	Bowling Green	CCHA	44	15	52	67	61	....	....	....	....	....
1984-85	**Los Angeles**	**NHL**	**78**	**8**	**30**	**38**	**82**	**3**	**1**	**0**	**1**	**2**
1985-86	**Los Angeles**	**NHL**	**49**	**9**	**13**	**22**	**46**	....	....	....	....	....
	New Haven	AHL	4	2	6	8	6	....	....	....	....	....
	NHL Totals		**127**	**17**	**43**	**60**	**128**	**3**	**1**	**0**	**1**	**2**

a CCHA First All-Star Team (1984)
b NCAA All-American (1984)

GANCHAR, PERRY

Born, Saskatoon, Sask., October 28, 1963.
Right wing. Shoots right. 5'9", 180 lbs.
Last amateur club: Saskatoon Blades (WHL).
(St. Louis' 3rd choice, 113th over-all, in 1982 Entry Draft).

				Regular Season					Playoffs			
Season	Club	Lea	GP	G	A	TP	PIM	GP	G	A	TP	PIM
1979-80	Saskatoon	WHL	27	9	14	23	60	.....	.....	.....	.....	.....
1980-81	Saskatoon	WHL	72	26	53	79	117	.....	.....	.....	.....	.....
1981-82	Saskatoon	WHL	53	38	52	90	82	5	3	3	6	17
1982-83	Saskatoon	WHL	68	68	48	116	105	6	1	4	5	24
	Salt Lake	CHL	.....	.....	.....	.....	.....	1	0	1	1	0
1983-84	Montana	CHL	59	23	22	45	77	.....	.....	.....	.....	.....
	St. Louis	NHL	1	0	0	0	0	7	3	1	4	0
1984-85	St. Louis	NHL	7	0	2	2	0	.....	.....	.....	.....	.....
a	Peoria	IHL	63	41	29	70	114	20	4	11	15	49
1985-86	Sherbrooke	AHL	75	25	29	54	42	.....	.....	.....	.....	.....
	NHL Totals		**8**	**0**	**2**	**2**	**0**	**7**	**3**	**1**	**4**	**0**

a IHL Second All-Star Team (1985)
Traded to **Montreal** by **St. Louis** for Ron Flockhart, August 26, 1985.

GANI, DARREN

Born, Perth, Australia, November 2, 1965.
Defense. Shoots left. 6'0", 180 lbs.
Last amateur club: Peterborough Petes (OHL).
(Edmonton's 11th choice, 250th overall, in 1984 Entry Draft).

				Regular Season					Playoffs			
Season	Club	Lea	GP	G	A	TP	PIM	GP	G	A	TP	PIM
1982-83	Belleville	OHL	63	1	21	22	22	4	0	0	0	0
1983-84	Belleville	OHL	67	16	40	56	22	3	0	0	0	0
1984-85	Belleville	OHL	45	17	32	49	27	14	2	3	5	14
1985-85	Peterborough	OHL	25	5	7	12	19	14	2	4	6	9

GANS, DAVID

Born, Brantford, Ont., June 6, 1964.
Center. Shoots right. 5'10", 180 lbs.
Last amateur club: Oshawa Generals (OHL).
(Los Angeles' 3rd choice, 64th over-all, in 1982 Entry Draft).

				Regular Season					Playoffs			
Season	Club	Lea	GP	G	A	TP	PIM	GP	G	A	TP	PIM
1981-82	Oshawa	OHL	66	23	51	74	112	12	3	6	9	45
1982-83	Los Angeles	NHL	3	0	0	0	0	.....	.....	.....	.....	.....
	Oshawa	OHL	64	41	64	105	90	17	14	24	38	27
1983-84	Oshawa	OHL	62	56	76	132	89	6	3	4	7	9
1984-85	Toledo	IHL	81	52	53	105	65	6	4	3	7	26
1985-86	Los Angeles	NHL	3	0	0	0	2	.....	.....	.....	.....	.....
	New Haven	AHL	17	11	12	23	14	.....	.....	.....	.....	.....
	Hershey	AHL	56	24	32	56	88	18	10	5	15	60
	NHL Totals		**6**	**0**	**0**	**0**	**2**	.....	.....	.....	.....	.....

GARDNER, PAUL MALONE

Born, Fort Erie, Ont., March 5, 1956.
Center. Shoots left. 6', 195 lbs.
Last amateur club: Oshawa Generals (OHA).
(Kansas City's 1st choice, 11th over-all, in 1976 Amateur Draft).

				Regular Season					Playoffs			
Season	Club	Lea	GP	G	A	TP	PIM	GP	G	A	TP	PIM
1974-75	Oshawa	OHA	64	27	36	63	54	5	0	0	0	9
1975-76	Oshawa	OHA	65	69	75	144	75	4	2	3	5	2
1976-77	Rhode Island	AHL	14	10	4	14	12	.....	.....	.....	.....	.....
	Colorado	NHL	60	30	29	59	25	.....	.....	.....	.....	.....
1977-78	Colorado	NHL	46	30	22	52	29	.....	.....	.....	.....	.....
1978-79	Colorado	NHL	64	23	26	49	32	.....	.....	.....	.....	.....
	Toronto	NHL	11	7	2	9	0	6	0	1	1	4
1979-80	Toronto	NHL	45	11	13	24	10	.....	.....	.....	.....	.....
	New Brunswick	AHL	20	11	16	27	14	15	10	5	15	2
1980-81	Springfield	AHL	14	9	12	21	6	.....	.....	.....	.....	.....
	Pittsburgh	NHL	62	34	40	74	59	5	1	0	1	8
1981-82	Pittsburgh	NHL	59	36	33	69	28	5	1	5	6	2
1982-83	Pittsburgh	NHL	70	28	27	55	12	.....	.....	.....	.....	.....
1983-84	Pittsburgh	NHL	16	0	5	5	6	.....	.....	.....	.....	.....
	Baltimore	AHL	54	32	48	80	14	10	12	10	22	0
1984-85	Washington	NHL	12	2	4	6	6	.....	.....	.....	.....	.....
abc	Binghamton	AHL	64	51	79	130	42	5	3	9	12	0
1985-86	**Buffalo**	NHL	2	0	0	0	0	.....	.....	.....	.....	.....
abd	Rochester	AHL	71	61	51	112	16	.....	.....	.....	.....	.....
	NHL Totals		**447**	**201**	**201**	**402**	**207**	**16**	**2**	**6**	**8**	**14**

Traded to **Toronto** by **Colorado** for Don Ashby and Trevor Johansen, March 13, 1979. Traded to **Pittsburgh** by **Toronto** with Dave Burrows for Kim Davis and Paul Marshall, November 8, 1980. Signed as free agent by **Washington**, July 17, 1984. Signed as a free agent by **Buffalo**, July 31, 1985.
a AHL First All-Star Team (1985, 1986)
b Won Les Cunningham Trophy (MVP – AHL 1985, 1986)
c Won Fred Hunt Trophy (sportsmanship – AHL 1985)
d Won John B. Sollenberger Trophy (Top Scorer — AHL 1986)

GARDNER, WILLIAM SCOTT (BILL)

Born, Toronto, Ont., March 18, 1960.
Center. Shoots left. 5'10", 180 lbs.
Last amateur club: Peterborough Petes (OHA).
(Chicago's 3rd choice, 49th over-all, in 1979 Entry Draft).

				Regular Season					Playoffs			
Season	Club	Lea	GP	G	A	TP	PIM	GP	G	A	TP	PIM
1978-79	Peterborough	OHA	68	33	71	104	19	18	4	20	24	6
1979-80a	Peterborough	OHA	59	43	63	106	17	14	13	14	27	8
1980-81	**Chicago**	NHL	1	0	0	0	0	.....	.....	.....	.....	.....
	New Brunswick	AHL	48	19	29	48	12	13	5	10	15	0
1981-82	Chicago	NHL	69	8	15	23	20	15	1	4	5	6
1982-83	Chicago	NHL	77	15	25	40	12	13	1	0	1	9
1983-84	Chicago	NHL	79	27	21	48	12	5	0	1	1	0
1984-85	Chicago	NHL	74	17	34	51	12	12	1	3	4	2
1985-86	Chicago	NHL	46	3	10	13	6	.....	.....	.....	.....	.....
	Hartford	NHL	18	1	8	9	4	.....	.....	.....	.....	.....
	NHL Totals		**364**	**71**	**113**	**184**	**66**	**45**	**3**	**8**	**11**	**17**

a OHA Third All-Star Team (1980)
Traded to **Hartford** by **Chicago** for Hartford's third-round choice in 1987 or 1988 Entry Draft, February 3, 1986.

GARE, DANIEL MIRL (DANNY)   (GEHR)

Born, Nelson, B.C., May 14, 1954.
Right wing. Shoots right. 5'9", 175 lbs.
Last amateur club: Calgary Centennials (WHL).
(Buffalo's 2nd choice, 29th over-all, in 1974 Amateur Draft).

				Regular Season					Playoffs			
Season	Club	Lea	GP	G	A	TP	PIM	GP	G	A	TP	PIM
1971-72	Calgary	WHL	56	10	17	27	15	13	1	1	2	2
1972-73	Calgary	WHL	65	45	43	88	107	6	5	5	10	18
1973-74a	Calgary	WHL	65	68	59	127	238	14	10	2	22	53
1974-75	**Buffalo**	NHL	78	31	31	62	75	17	7	6	13	19
1975-76	Buffalo	NHL	79	50	23	73	129	9	5	2	7	21
1976-77	Buffalo	NHL	35	11	15	26	73	4	0	0	0	18
1977-78	Buffalo	NHL	69	39	38	77	95	8	4	6	10	37
1978-79	Buffalo	NHL	71	27	40	67	90	3	0	0	0	9
1979-80b	Buffalo	NHL	76	*56	33	89	90	14	4	7	11	35
1980-81	Buffalo	NHL	73	46	39	85	109	3	3	0	3	8
1981-82	Buffalo	NHL	22	7	14	21	25	.....	.....	.....	.....	.....
	Detroit	NHL	36	13	9	22	74	.....	.....	.....	.....	.....
1982-83	Detroit	NHL	79	26	35	61	107	.....	.....	.....	.....	.....
1983-84	Detroit	NHL	63	13	13	26	147	4	2	0	2	38
1984-85	Detroit	NHL	71	27	29	56	163	2	0	0	0	10
1985-86	Detroit	NHL	57	7	9	16	102	.....	.....	.....	.....	.....
	NHL Totals		**809**	**353**	**328**	**681**	**1279**	**64**	**25**	**21**	**46**	**195**

a WHL First All-Star Team (1974)
b NHL Second All-Star Team (1980)
Traded to **Detroit** by **Buffalo** with Jim Schoenfeld and Derek Smith for Mike Foligno, Dale McCourt and Brent Peterson, December 2, 1981.

GARTNER, MICHAEL ALFRED (MIKE)

Born, Ottawa, Ont., October 29, 1959.
Right wing. Shoots right. 6', 185 lbs.
Last amateur club: Niagara Falls Flyers (OHA).
(Washington's 1st choice, 4th over-all, in 1979 Entry Draft).

				Regular Season					Playoffs			
Season	Club	Lea	GP	G	A	TP	PIM	GP	G	A	TP	PIM
1976-77	Niagara Falls	OHA	62	33	42	75	125	.....	.....	.....	.....	.....
1977-78a	Niagara Falls	OHA	64	41	49	90	56	.....	.....	.....	.....	.....
1978-79	Cincinnati	WHA	78	27	25	52	123	3	0	2	2	2
1979-80	Washington	NHL	77	36	32	68	66	.....	.....	.....	.....	.....
1980-81	Washington	NHL	80	48	46	94	100	.....	.....	.....	.....	.....
1981-82	Washington	NHL	80	35	45	80	121	.....	.....	.....	.....	.....
1982-83	Washington	NHL	73	38	38	76	54	4	0	0	0	4
1983-84	Washington	NHL	80	40	45	85	90	8	3	7	10	16
1984-85	Washington	NHL	80	50	52	102	71	5	4	3	7	9
1985-86	Washington	NHL	74	35	40	75	63	9	2	10	12	4
	NHL Totals		**544**	**282**	**298**	**580**	**565**	**26**	**9**	**20**	**29**	**33**
	WHA Totals		**78**	**27**	**25**	**52**	**123**	**3**	**0**	**2**	**2**	**2**

a OHA First All-Star Team (1978)

GASSEAU, JAMES

Born, Carleton, Que., May 4, 1966.
Defense. Shoots right. 6'2", 200 lbs.
Last amateur club: Drummondville Voltigeurs (QMJHL).
(Buffalo's 6nd choice, 123rd over-all, in 1984 Entry Draft).

				Regular Season					Playoffs			
Season	Club	Lea	GP	G	A	TP	PIM	GP	G	A	TP	PIM
1983-84	Drummondville	QMJHL	68	6	25	31	72	10	0	4	4	12
1984-85a	Drummondville	QMJHL	64	8	43	51	158	12	1	5	6	34
1985-86	Drummondville	QMJHL	46	20	31	51	155	23	1	13	14	18

a QMJHL Second All-Star Team (1985, 1986)

GATZOS, STEVE (GAT-zose)

Born, Toronto, Ont., June 22, 1961.
Right wing. Shoots right. 5'11", 185 lbs.
Last amateur club: Sault Ste. Marie Greyhounds (OHA).
(Pittsburgh's 1st choice, 28th over-all, in 1981 Entry Draft).

Season	Club	Lea	Regular Season GP	G	A	TP	PIM	Playoffs GP	G	A	TP	PIM
1979-80	S. S. Marie	OHA	64	36	38	74	64	....	....	....	....	....
1980-81	S. S. Marie	OHA	68	78	50	128	114	19	16	9	25	23
1981-82	Erie	AHL	54	18	19	37	67	....	....	....	....	....
	Pittsburgh	NHL	16	6	8	14	14	1	0	0	0	0
1982-83	Pittsburgh	NHL	44	6	7	13	52	....	....	....	....	....
	Baltimore	AHL	12	5	4	9	22	....	....	....	....	....
1983-84	Pittsburgh	NHL	23	3	3	6	15	....	....	....	....	....
	Baltimore	AHL	48	14	19	33	43	....	....	....	....	....
1984-85	Pittsburgh	NHL	6	0	2	2	2	....	....	....	....	....
	Muskegon	IHL	24	18	10	28	24	....	....	....	....	....
1985-86	Baltimore	AHL	53	25	8	33	34	....	....	....	....	....
	NHL Totals		**89**	**15**	**20**	**35**	**83**	**1**	**0**	**0**	**0**	**0**

GAULIN, JEAN-MARC

Born, Balve, Germany, March 3, 1962.
Right wing. Shoots right. 5'10", 180 lbs.
Last amateur club: Hull Olympiques (QMJHL).
(Quebec's 2nd choice, 53rd over-all, in 1981 Entry Draft).

Season	Club	Lea	Regular Season GP	G	A	TP	PIM	Playoffs GP	G	A	TP	PIM
1979-80	Sorel	QMJHL	59	21	40	61	119	....	....	....	....	....
1980-81	Sorel	QMJHL	70	50	40	90	157	7	0	3	3	6
1981-82	Hull	QMJHL	56	50	50	100	93	11	2	15	17	9
1982-83	Quebec	NHL	1	0	0	0	0	....	....	....	....	....
	Fredericton	AHL	67	11	17	28	58	9	0	0	0	21
1983-84	Quebec	NHL	2	0	0	0	0	....	....	....	....	....
	Fredericton	AHL	62	14	28	42	80	7	2	5	7	0
1984-85	Quebec	NHL	22	3	3	6	8	1	0	0	0	0
	Fredericton	AHL	27	10	9	19	32	5	1	3	4	2
1985-86	Quebec	NHL	1	1	0	1	0	....	....	....	....	....
	Fredericton	AHL	58	16	26	42	66	6	2	3	5	31
	NHL Totals		**26**	**4**	**3**	**7**	**8**	**1**	**0**	**0**	**0**	**0**

GAUME, DALLAS

Born, Innisfail, Alta., August 27, 1963.
Center. Shoots left. 5'10", 180 lbs.
Last amateur club: University of Denver Pioneers (WCHA).

Season	Club	Lea	Regular Season GP	G	A	TP	PIM	Playoffs GP	G	A	TP	PIM
1982-83	Denver	WCHA	37	19	47	66	12	....	....	....	....	....
1983-84	Denver	WCHA	32	12	25	37	22	....	....	....	....	....
1984-85	Denver	WCHA	39	15	48	63	28	....	....	....	....	....
1985-86	Denver	WCHA	47	32	67	99	18	....	....	....	....	....

Signed as a free agent by **Hartford**, July 10, 1986.

GAVIN, ROBERT (STEWART)

Born, Ottawa, Ont., March 15, 1960.
Left wing. Shoots left. 6', 185 lbs.
Last amateur club: Toronto Marlboros (OHA).
(Toronto's 4th choice, 74th over-all, in 1980 Entry Draft).

Season	Club	Lea	Regular Season GP	G	A	TP	PIM	Playoffs GP	G	A	TP	PIM
1978-79	Toronto	OHA	61	24	25	49	83	3	1	0	1	0
1979-80	Toronto	OHA	68	27	30	57	52	4	1	1	2	2
1980-81	Toronto	NHL	14	1	2	3	13	....	....	....	....	....
	New Brunswick	AHL	46	7	12	19	42	13	1	0	1	2
1981-82	Toronto	NHL	38	5	6	11	29	....	....	....	....	....
1982-83	St. Catharines	AHL	6	2	4	6	17	....	....	....	....	....
	Toronto	NHL	63	6	5	11	44	4	0	0	0	0
1983-84	Toronto	NHL	80	10	22	32	90	....	....	....	....	....
1984-85	Toronto	NHL	73	12	13	25	38	....	....	....	....	....
1985-86	Hartford	NHL	76	26	29	55	51	10	4	1	5	13
	NHL Totals		**344**	**60**	**77**	**137**	**265**	**14**	**4**	**1**	**5**	**13**

Traded to **Hartford** by **Toronto** for Chris Kotsopoulos, October 7, 1985.

GEALE, ROBERT CHARLES (BOB)

Born, Edmonton, Alta., April 17, 1962.
Center. Shoots right. 5'11", 175 lbs.
Last amateur club: Portland Winter Hawks (WHL).
(Pittsburgh's 8th choice, 156th over-all, in 1980 Entry Draft).

Season	Club	Lea	Regular Season GP	G	A	TP	PIM	Playoffs GP	G	A	TP	PIM
1980-81	Portland	WHL	54	30	32	62	54	....	....	....	....	....
1981-82	Portland	WHL	72	31	54	85	89	15	8	10	18	26
1982-83	Baltimore	AHL	56	4	10	14	6	....	....	....	....	....
1983-84	Baltimore	AHL	74	17	23	40	50	7	1	0	1	2
1984-85	Pittsburgh	NHL	1	0	0	0	2	....	....	....	....	....
	Baltimore	AHL	77	26	23	49	42	15	3	8	11	11
1985-86	Baltimore	AHL	21	5	7	12	9	....	....	....	....	....
	NHL Totals		**1**	**0**	**0**	**0**	**2**	....	....	....	....	....

GEIST, RICH

Born, St. Paul, Minn., November 17, 1964.
Center. Shoots left. 6'3", 190 lbs.
Last amateur club: Yale University Bulldogs (ECAC).
(Minnesota's 5th choice, 96th overall, in 1983 Entry Draft).

Season	Club	Lea	Regular Season GP	G	A	TP	PIM	Playoffs GP	G	A	TP	PIM
1983-84	U. Minnesota	WCHA	5	2	1	3	2	....	....	....	....	....
1984-85	U. Minnesota	WCHA	DID NOT PLAY					....	....	....	....	....
1985-86	Yale	ECAC	31	3	7	10	34	....	....	....	....	....

GERLITZ, PAUL

Born, Calgary, Alta., March 23, 1963.
Right wing. Shoots right. 5'11", 205 lbs.
Last amateur club: Boston University Terriers (H.E.).

Season	Club	Lea	Regular Season GP	G	A	TP	PIM	Playoffs GP	G	A	TP	PIM
1982-83	Boston U.	ECAC	19	6	6	12	14	....	....	....	....	....
1983-84	Boston U.	ECAC	40	14	13	27	46	....	....	....	....	....
1984-85	Boston U.	H.E.	39	5	14	19	26	....	....	....	....	....
1985-86	Boston U.	H.E.	34	6	7	13	17	....	....	....	....	....

Signed as a free agent by **Quebec**, May 29, 1986.

GIFFIN, LEE

Born, Chatham, Ont., April 1, 1967.
Right wing. Shoots right. 5'11", 175 lbs.
Last amateur club: Oshawa Generals (OHA).
(Pittsburgh's 2nd choice, 23rd over-all, in 1985 Entry Draft)

Season	Club	Lea	Regular Season GP	G	A	TP	PIM	Playoffs GP	G	A	TP	PIM
1983-84	Oshawa	OHL	70	23	27	50	88	7	1	4	5	12
1984-85	Oshawa	OHL	62	36	42	78	78	5	1	2	3	2
1985-86	Oshawa	OHL	54	29	37	66	28	6	0	5	5	8

GILBERT, GREGORY SCOTT (GREG)

Born, Mississauga, Ont., January 22, 1962.
Left wing. Shoots left. 6'1", 195 lbs.
Last amateur club: Toronto Marlboros (OHL).
(NY Islanders' 5th choice, 80th over-all, in 1980 Entry Draft).

Season	Club	Lea	Regular Season GP	G	A	TP	PIM	Playoffs GP	G	A	TP	PIM
1980-81	Toronto	OHA	64	30	37	67	73	5	2	6	8	16
1981-82 a	Toronto	OHL	65	41	67	108	119	10	4	12	16	23
	NY Islanders	NHL	1	1	0	1	0	4	1	1	2	2
1982-83	Indianapolis	CHL	24	11	16	27	23	....	....	....	....	....
	NY Islanders	NHL	45	8	11	19	30	10	1	0	1	14
1983-84	NY Islanders	NHL	79	31	35	66	59	21	5	7	12	39
1984-85	NY Islanders	NHL	58	13	25	38	36	....	....	....	....	....
1985-86	NY Islanders	NHL	60	9	19	28	82	2	0	0	0	9
	Springfield	AHL	2	0	0	0	2	....	....	....	....	....
	NHL Totals		**243**	**62**	**90**	**152**	**207**	**37**	**7**	**8**	**15**	**64**

a OHL Third All-Star Team (1982)

GILCHRIST, BRENT

Born, Moose Jaw, Sask., April 3, 1967.
Center. Shoots left. 5'10", 175 lbs.
Last amateur club: Spokane Chiefs (WHL).
(Montreal's 6th choice, 79th overall, in 1985 Entry Draft).

Season	Club	Lea	Regular Season GP	G	A	TP	PIM	Playoffs GP	G	A	TP	PIM
1983-84	Kelowna	WHL	69	16	11	27	16	....	....	....	....	....
1984-85	Kelowna	WHL	51	35	38	73	58	6	5	2	7	8
1985-86	Spokane	WHL	52	45	45	90	57	9	6	7	13	19

GILES, CURT (JYLES)

Born, The Pas, Man., November 30, 1958.
Defense. Shoots left. 5'8", 180 lbs.
Last amateur club: University of Minnesota-Duluth Bulldogs (WCHA)
(Minnesota's 4th choice, 54th over-all, in 1978 Amateur Draft).

Season	Club	Lea	Regular Season GP	G	A	TP	PIM	Playoffs GP	G	A	TP	PIM
1977-78	Minn-Duluth	WCHA	34	11	36	47	62	....	....	....	....	....
1978-79	Minn-Duluth	WCHA	30	3	38	41	38	....	....	....	....	....
1979-80	Oklahoma City	CHL	42	4	24	28	35	....	....	....	....	....
	Minnesota	NHL	37	2	7	9	31	12	2	4	6	10
1980-81	Minnesota	NHL	67	5	22	27	56	19	1	4	5	14
1981-82	Minnesota	NHL	74	3	12	15	87	4	0	0	0	2
1982-83	Minnesota	NHL	76	2	21	23	70	5	0	2	2	6
1983-84	Minnesota	NHL	70	6	22	28	59	16	1	3	4	25
1984-85	Minnesota	NHL	77	5	25	30	49	9	0	0	0	17
1985-86	Minnesota	NHL	69	6	21	27	30	5	0	1	1	10
	NHL Totals		**470**	**29**	**130**	**159**	**382**	**70**	**4**	**14**	**18**	**84**

GILHEN, RANDY

Born, Zweibrucken, West Germany, June 13, 1963.
Left wing. Shoots left. 5'10", 190 lbs.
Last amateur club: Winnipeg Warriors (WHL).
(Hartford's 6th choice, 109th over-all, in 1982 Entry Draft).

			Regular Season					Playoffs				
Season	Club	Lea	GP	G	A	TP	PIM	GP	G	A	TP	PIM
1980-81	Saskatoon	WHL	68	10	5	15	154	....	....	....	....	....
1981-82	Saskatoon	WHL	25	15	9	24	45	....	....	....	....	....
	Winnipeg	WHL	36	26	28	54	42	....	....	....	....	....
1982-83	**Hartford**	**NHL**	**2**	**0**	**1**	**1**	**0**	....	....	....	....	....
	Winnipeg	WHL	71	57	44	101	84	3	2	2	4	0
1983-84	Binghamton	AHL	73	8	12	20	72	....	....	....	....	....
1984-85	Salt Lake	IHL	57	20	20	40	28	....	....	....	....	....
	Binghamton	AHL	18	3	3	6	9	8	4	1	5	16
1985-86	Fort Wayne	IHL	82	44	40	84	48	15	10	8	18	6
	NHL Totals		**2**	**0**	**1**	**1**	**0**	....	....	....	....	....

GILL, TODD

Born, Brockville, Ont., November 9, 1965.
Defense. Shoots left. 6'1", 175 lbs.
Last amateur club: Windsor Spitfires (OHL).
(Toronto's 2nd choice, 25th over-all, in 1984 Entry Draft).

			Regular Season					Playoffs				
Season	Club	Lea	GP	G	A	TP	PIM	GP	G	A	TP	PIM
1982-83	Windsor	OHL	70	12	24	36	108	3	0	0	0	11
1983-84	Windsor	OHL	68	9	48	57	184	3	1	1	2	10
1984-85	**Toronto**	**NHL**	**10**	**1**	**0**	**1**	**13**	....	....	....	....	....
a	Windsor	OHL	53	17	40	57	148	4	0	1	1	14
1985-86	**Toronto**	**NHL**	**15**	**1**	**2**	**3**	**28**	**1**	**0**	**0**	**0**	**0**
	St. Catharines	AHL	58	8	25	33	90	10	1	6	7	17
	NHL Totals		**25**	**2**	**2**	**4**	**41**	**1**	**0**	**0**	**0**	**0**

a OHL Third All-Star Team (1985)

GILLIES, CLARK (GILL-eez)

Born, Moose Jaw, Sask., April 7, 1954.
Left wing. Shoots left. 6'3", 215 lbs.
Last amateur club: Regina Pats (WHL).
(NY Islanders' 1st choice, 4th over-all, in 1974 Amateur Draft).

			Regular Season					Playoffs				
Season	Club	Lea	GP	G	A	TP	PIM	GP	G	A	TP	PIM
1971-72	Regina	WHL	68	31	48	79	199	15	5	10	15	49
1972-73	Regina	WHL	68	40	52	92	192	4	0	3	3	34
1973-74a	Regina	WHL	65	46	66	112	179	16	9	8	17	32
1974-75	**NY Islanders**	**NHL**	**80**	**25**	**22**	**47**	**66**	**17**	**4**	**2**	**6**	**36**
1975-76	**NY Islanders**	**NHL**	**80**	**34**	**27**	**61**	**96**	**13**	**2**	**4**	**6**	**16**
1976-77	**NY Islanders**	**NHL**	**70**	**33**	**22**	**55**	**93**	**12**	**4**	**4**	**8**	**15**
1977-78b	**NY Islanders**	**NHL**	**80**	**35**	**50**	**85**	**76**	**7**	**2**	**0**	**2**	**15**
1978-79b	**NY Islanders**	**NHL**	**75**	**35**	**56**	**91**	**68**	**10**	**1**	**2**	**3**	**11**
1979-80	**NY Islanders**	**NHL**	**73**	**19**	**35**	**54**	**49**	**21**	**6**	**10**	**16**	**63**
1980-81	**NY Islanders**	**NHL**	**80**	**33**	**45**	**78**	**99**	**18**	**6**	**9**	**15**	**28**
1981-82	**NY Islanders**	**NHL**	**79**	**38**	**39**	**77**	**75**	**19**	**8**	**6**	**14**	**34**
1982-83	**NY Islanders**	**NHL**	**70**	**21**	**20**	**41**	**76**	**8**	**0**	**2**	**2**	**10**
1983-84	**NY Islanders**	**NHL**	**76**	**12**	**16**	**28**	**65**	**21**	**12**	**7**	**19**	**19**
1984-85	**NY Islanders**	**NHL**	**54**	**15**	**17**	**32**	**73**	**10**	**1**	**0**	**1**	**9**
1985-86	**NY Islanders**	**NHL**	**55**	**4**	**10**	**14**	**55**	**3**	**1**	**0**	**1**	**6**
	NHL Totals		**872**	**304**	**259**	**563**	**891**	**159**	**47**	**46**	**93**	**262**

a WHL First All-Star Team (1974)
b NHL First All-Star Team (1978, 1979)

GILLIS, JERE ALAN (GILL-is, JAIR-ee)

Born, Bend, Ore., January 18, 1957.
Left wing. Shoots left. 6', 190 lbs.
Last amateur club: Sherbrooke Castors (QJHL).
(Vancouver's 1st choice, 4th over-all, in 1977 Amateur Draft).

			Regular Season					Playoffs				
Season	Club	Lea	GP	G	A	TP	PIM	GP	G	A	TP	PIM
1975-76	Sherbrooke	QJHL	60	47	55	102	38	17	8	14	22	27
1976-77	Sherbrooke	QJHL	72	55	85	140	80	18	11	12	23	40
1977-78	**Vancouver**	**NHL**	**79**	**23**	**18**	**41**	**35**	....	....	....	....	....
1978-79	**Vancouver**	**NHL**	**78**	**13**	**12**	**25**	**33**	**1**	**0**	**1**	**1**	**0**
1979-80	**Vancouver**	**NHL**	**67**	**13**	**17**	**30**	**108**	....	....	....	....	....
1980-81	**Vancouver**	**NHL**	**11**	**0**	**4**	**4**	**4**	....	....	....	....	....
	NY Rangers	**NHL**	**35**	**10**	**10**	**20**	**4**	**14**	**2**	**5**	**7**	**9**
1981-82	**NY Rangers**	**NHL**	**26**	**3**	**9**	**12**	**16**	....	....	....	....	....
	Quebec	**NHL**	**12**	**2**	**1**	**3**	**0**	....	....	....	....	....
	Fredericton	AHL	28	2	17	19	10	....	....	....	....	....
1982-83	**Buffalo**	**NHL**	**3**	**0**	**0**	**0**	**0**	....	....	....	....	....
	Rochester	AHL	53	18	24	42	69	16	1	7	8	11
1983-84	Fredericton	AHL	36	22	28	50	35	....	....	....	....	....
	Vancouver	**NHL**	**37**	**9**	**13**	**22**	**7**	**4**	**2**	**1**	**3**	**0**
1984-85	**Vancouver**	**NHL**	**37**	**5**	**11**	**16**	**23**	....	....	....	....	....
	Fredericton	AHL	7	2	1	3	2	....	....	....	....	....
1985-86	Fredericton	AHL	29	4	14	18	21	....	....	....	....	....
	NHL Totals		**385**	**78**	**95**	**173**	**230**	**19**	**4**	**7**	**11**	**9**

Traded to **NY Rangers** by **Vancouver** with Jeff Bandura for Mario Marois and Jim Mayer, November 11, 1980. Traded to **Quebec** by **NY Rangers** with Dean Talafous (later Pat Hickey) for Robbie Ftorek and Quebec's eighth round choice (Brian Glynn) in 1982 Entry Draft, December 30, 1981. Signed as a free agent by **Buffalo**, September 11, 1982. Signed as free agent by **Vancouver**, September 26, 1983.

GILLIS, PAUL C.

Born, Toronto, Ont., December 31, 1963.
Center. Shoots left. 5'11", 190 lbs.
Last amateur club: North Bay Centennials (OHL).
(Quebec's 2nd choice, 34th over-all, in 1982 Entry Draft).

			Regular Season					Playoffs				
Season	Club	Lea	GP	G	A	TP	PIM	GP	G	A	TP	PIM
1980-81	Niagara Falls	OHA	59	14	19	33	165	....	....	....	....	....
1981-82	Niagara Falls	OHL	65	27	62	89	247	5	1	5	6	26
1982-83	**Quebec**	**NHL**	**7**	**0**	**2**	**2**	**2**	....	....	....	....	....
	North Bay	OHL	61	34	52	86	151	6	1	3	4	26
1983-84	Fredericton	AHL	18	7	8	15	47	....	....	....	....	....
	Quebec	**NHL**	**57**	**8**	**9**	**17**	**59**	**1**	**0**	**0**	**0**	**2**
1984-85	**Quebec**	**NHL**	**77**	**14**	**28**	**42**	**168**	**18**	**1**	**7**	**8**	**73**
1985-86	**Quebec**	**NHL**	**80**	**19**	**24**	**43**	**203**	**3**	**0**	**2**	**2**	**14**
	NHL Totals		**221**	**41**	**63**	**104**	**432**	**22**	**1**	**9**	**10**	**89**

GILMOUR, DOUGLAS (DOUG)

Born, Kingston, Ont., June 25, 1963.
Center. Shoots left. 5'11", 165 lbs.
Last amateur club: Cornwall Royals (OHL).
(St. Louis' 4th choice, 134th over-all, in 1982 Entry Draft).

			Regular Season					Playoffs				
Season	Club	Lea	GP	G	A	TP	PIM	GP	G	A	TP	PIM
1981-82	Cornwall	OHL	67	46	73	119	42	5	6	9	15	2
1982-83ab	Cornwall	OHL	68	70	*107	*177	62	8	8	10	18	16
1983-84	**St. Louis**	**NHL**	**80**	**25**	**28**	**53**	**57**	**11**	**2**	**9**	**11**	**10**
1984-85	**St. Louis**	**NHL**	**78**	**21**	**36**	**57**	**49**	**3**	**1**	**1**	**2**	**2**
1985-86	**St. Louis**	**NHL**	**74**	**25**	**28**	**53**	**41**	**19**	**9**	**12**	**21**	**25**
	NHL Totals		**232**	**71**	**92**	**163**	**147**	**33**	**12**	**22**	**34**	**37**

a OHL First All-Star Team (1983)
b Named OHL's Most Outstanding Player (1983)

GINGRAS, GASTON REGINALD (JING-rah)

Born, Temiscamingue, Que., February 13, 1959.
Defense. Shoots left. 6', 190 lbs.
Last amateur club: Hamilton Fincups (OHA).
(Montreal's 1st choice, 27th over-all, in 1979 Entry Draft).

			Regular Season					Playoffs				
Season	Club	Lea	GP	G	A	TP	PIM	GP	G	A	TP	PIM
1976-77	Kitchener	OHA	59	13	62	75	134	3	0	1	1	6
1977-78	Kitchener	OHA	32	13	24	37	31	....	....	....	....	....
	Hamilton	OHA	29	11	19	30	37	15	3	11	14	13
1978-79	Birmingham	WHA	60	13	21	34	35	....	....	....	....	....
1979-80	Nova Scotia	AHL	30	11	27	38	17	....	....	....	....	....
	Montreal	**NHL**	**34**	**3**	**7**	**10**	**18**	**10**	**1**	**6**	**7**	**8**
1980-81	**Montreal**	**NHL**	**55**	**5**	**16**	**21**	**22**	**1**	**1**	**0**	**1**	**0**
1981-82	**Montreal**	**NHL**	**34**	**6**	**18**	**24**	**28**	**5**	**0**	**1**	**1**	**0**
1982-83	**Montreal**	**NHL**	**22**	**1**	**8**	**9**	**8**	....	....	....	....	....
	Toronto	**NHL**	**45**	**10**	**18**	**28**	**10**	**3**	**1**	**2**	**3**	**2**
1983-84	**Toronto**	**NHL**	**59**	**7**	**20**	**27**	**16**	....	....	....	....	....
1984-85	**Toronto**	**NHL**	**5**	**0**	**2**	**2**	**0**	....	....	....	....	....
	St. Catharines	AHL	36	7	12	19	13	....	....	....	....	....
	Sherbrooke	AHL	21	3	14	17	6	17	5	4	9	4
1985-86	**Montreal**	**NHL**	**34**	**8**	**18**	**26**	**12**	**11**	**2**	**3**	**5**	**4**
	Sherbrooke	AHL	42	11	20	31	14	....	....	....	....	....
	NHL Totals		**288**	**40**	**107**	**147**	**114**	**30**	**5**	**12**	**17**	**14**
	WHA Totals		60	13	21	34	35	....	....	....	....	....

Traded to **Toronto** by **Montreal** for Toronto's second round choice in either 1985 or 1986 Entry Draft, December 17, 1982. Traded to **Montreal** by **Toronto** for Larry Landon, February 14, 1985

GLYNN, BRIAN

Born, Iserlohn, West Germany, November 23, 1967.
Defense. Shoots left. 6'4", 225 lbs.
Last amateur club: Saskatoon Blades (WHL).
(Calgary's 2nd choice, 37th overall, in 1986 Entry Draft).

			Regular Season					Playoffs				
Season	Club	Lea	GP	G	A	TP	PIM	GP	G	A	TP	PIM
1984-85	Saskatoon	WHL	12	1	0	1	2	3	0	0	0	0
1985-86	Saskatoon	WHL	66	7	25	32	131	13	0	3	3	30

GOERTZ, DAVE

Born, Edmonton, Alta., March 28, 1965.
Defense. Shoots right. 5'11", 210 lbs.
Last amateur club: Prince Albert Raiders (WHL).
(Pittsburgh's 10th choice, 212th over-all, in 1983 Entry Draft).

			Regular Season					Playoffs				
Season	Club	Lea	GP	G	A	TP	PIM	GP	G	A	TP	PIM
1981-82	Regina	WHL	67	5	19	24	181	19	1	2	3	61
1982-83	Regina	WHL	69	4	22	26	132	5	0	2	2	9
1983-84	Prince Albert	WHL	60	13	47	60	111	5	2	3	5	0
	Baltimore	AHL	1	0	0	0	2	6	0	0	0	0
1984-85	Prince Albert	WHL	48	3	48	51	62	13	4	14	18	29
1985-86	Baltimore	NHL	74	1	15	16	76	....	....	....	....	....

GOLDEN, MIKE

Born, Boston, Mass., June 14, 1965.
Center. Shoots right. 6'1", 190 lbs.
Last amateur club: University of Maine Black Bears (H.E.).
(Edmonton's 2nd choice, 40th overall, in 1983 Entry Draft).

Season	Club	Lea	Regular Season					Playoffs				
			GP	G	A	TP	PIM	GP	G	A	TP	PIM
1985-86	Maine	H.E.	24	3	16	29	10	....	....	....	....	....

GOFF, PATRICK (PAT)

Born, St. Paul, Minn., June 29, 1964.
Defense. Shoots left. 6'1", 1895 lbs.
Last amateur club: University of Michigan Wolverines (CCHA).
(NY Islanders' 11th choice, 231st overall, in 1982 Entry Draft).

Season	Club	Lea	Regular Season					Playoffs				
			GP	G	A	TP	PIM	GP	G	A	TP	PIM
1982-83	U. of Michigan	CCHA	36	2	18	20	20	....	....	....	....	....
1983-84	U. of Michigan	CCHA	37	4	17	21	38	....	....	....	....	....
1994-85	U. of Michigan	CCHA	34	3	4	7	26	....	....	....	....	....
1985-86	U. of Michigan	CCHA	38	2	12	14	30	....	....	....	....	....

GOSSELIN, GUY

Born, Rochester, Minn., January 6, 1964.
Defense. Shoots right. 5'11", 190 lbs.
Last amateur club: University of Minnesota-Duluth Bulldogs (WCHA).
(Winnipeg's 6th choice, 159th overall, in 1982 Entry Draft).

Season	Club	Lea	Regular Season					Playoffs				
			GP	G	A	TP	PIM	GP	G	A	TP	PIM
1982-83	Minn-Duluth	WCHA	4	0	0	0	0	....	....	....	....	....
1983-84	Minn-Duluth	WCHA	37	3	3	6	26	....	....	....	....	....
1984-85	Minn-Duluth	WCHA	47	3	7	10	25	....	....	....	....	....
1985-86	Minn-Duluth	WCHA	39	2	16	18	53	....	....	....	....	....

GOTAAS, STEVE

Born, Comrose, Sask., May 10, 1967.
Center. Shoots right. 5'9", 170 lbs.
Last amateur club: Prince Albert Raiders (WHL).
(Pittsburgh's 4th choice, 86th overall, in 1985 Entry Draft).

Season	Club	Lea	Regular Season					Playoffs				
			GP	G	A	TP	PIM	GP	G	A	TP	PIM
1983-84	Prince Albert	WHL	65	10	22	32	47	5	0	1	1	0
1984-85	Prince Albert	WHL	72	32	41	73	66	13	3	6	9	17
1985-86	Prince Albert	WHL	61	40	61	101	31	....	....	....	....	....

GOULD, ROBERT (BOBBY)

Born, Petrolia, Ont., September 2, 1957.
Right wing. Shoots right. 5'11", 190 lbs.
Last amateur club: University of New Hampshire Wildcats (ECAC)
(Atlanta's 7th choice, 118th over-all, in 1977 Amateur Draft).

Season	Club	Lea	Regular Season					Playoffs				
			GP	G	A	TP	PIM	GP	G	A	TP	PIM
1978-79a	N. Hampshire	ECAC	25	24	17	41	....	....	....	....	....	....
	Tulsa	CHL	5	2	0	2	4	....	....	....	....	....
1979-80	**Atlanta**	**NHL**	1	0	0	0	0	....	....	....	....	....
	Birmingham	CHL	79	27	33	60	73	4	2	4	6	0
1980-81	Birmingham	CHL	58	25	25	50	43	....	....	....	....	....
	Fort Worth	CHL	18	8	6	14	6	5	5	2	7	10
	Calgary	**NHL**	3	0	0	0	0	11	3	1	4	4
1981-82	Oklahoma City	CHL	1	0	1	1	0	....	....	....	....	....
	Calgary	**NHL**	16	3	0	3	4	....	....	....	....	....
	Washington	**NHL**	60	18	13	31	69	....	....	....	....	....
1982-83	**Washington**	**NHL**	80	22	18	40	43	4	5	0	5	4
1983-84	**Washington**	**NHL**	78	21	19	40	74	5	0	2	2	4
1984-85	**Washington**	**NHL**	78	14	19	33	69	5	0	1	1	2
1985-86	**Washington**	**NHL**	79	19	19	38	26	9	4	3	7	11
	NHL Totals		395	97	88	185	285	345	12	7	19	25

a ECAC Second All-Star Team (1979)
Traded to **Washington** by **Calgary** with Randy Holt for Pat Ribble and Washington's second round choice (Todd Francis — later transferred to Montreal in Doug Risebrough deal) in 1983 Entry Draft, November 25, 1981.

GOULET, MICHEL   (goo-LAY)

Born, Peribonqua, Que., April 21, 1960.
Left wing. Shoots left. 6'1", 185 lbs.
Last amateur club: Quebec Remparts (QJHL).
(Quebec's 1st choice, 20th over-all, in 1979 Entry Draft).

Season	Club	Lea	Regular Season					Playoffs				
			GP	G	A	TP	PIM	GP	G	A	TP	PIM
1976-77	Quebec	QJHL	37	17	18	35	9	14	3	8	11	19
1977-78	Quebec	QJHL	72	73	62	135	109	1	0	1	1	0
1978-79	Birmingham	WHA	78	28	30	58	65	....	....	....	....	....
1979-80	**Quebec**	**NHL**	77	22	32	54	48	....	....	....	....	....
1980-81	**Quebec**	**NHL**	76	32	39	71	45	4	3	4	7	7
1981-82	**Quebec**	**NHL**	80	42	42	84	48	16	8	5	13	6
1982-83a	**Quebec**	**NHL**	80	57	48	105	51	4	0	0	0	6
1983-84b	**Quebec**	**NHL**	75	56	65	121	76	9	2	4	6	17
1984-85	**Quebec**	**NHL**	69	55	40	95	55	17	11	10	21	17
1985-86b	**Quebec**	**NHL**	75	53	51	104	64	3	1	2	3	10
	NHL Totals		532	317	317	634	387	53	25	25	50	63
	WHA Totals		78	28	30	58	64	....	....	....	....	....

a NHL Second All-Star Team (1983)
b NHL First All-Star Team (1984, 1986)

GRADIN, THOMAS   (grah-DEEN)

Born, Solleftea, Sweden, February 18, 1956.
Center. Shoots right. 5'11", 170 lbs.
Last amateur club: Mo Do AIK (Sweden).
(Chicago's 3rd choice, 45th over-all, in 1976 Amateur Draft).

Season	Club	Lea	Regular Season					Playoffs				
			GP	G	A	TP	PIM	GP	G	A	TP	PIM
1976-77	AIK	Swe.	35	16	12	28	14	....	....	....	....	....
1977-78	AIK	Swe.	36	22	22	44	24	....	....	....	....	....
1978-79	Vancouver	NHL	76	20	31	51	22	3	4	1	5	4
1979-80	Vancouver	NHL	80	30	45	75	22	4	0	2	2	0
1980-81	Vancouver	NHL	79	21	48	69	34	3	1	3	4	0
1981-82	Vancouver	NHL	76	37	49	86	32	17	9	10	19	10
1982-83	Vancouver	NHL	80	32	54	86	61	4	1	3	4	2
1983-84	Vancouver	NHL	75	21	57	78	32	4	0	1	1	2
1984-85	Vancouver	NHL	76	22	42	64	43	....	....	....	....	....
1985-86	Vancouver	NHL	71	14	27	41	34	3	2	1	3	2
	NHL Totals		613	197	353	550	280	38	17	21	38	20

Rights traded to **Vancouver** by **Chicago** for Vancouver's second round choice (Steve Ludzik) in 1980 Entry Draft, June 14, 1978. Signed as a free agent by **Boston**, June 24, 1986.

GRAHAM, DIRK MILTON

Born, Regina, Sask., July 29, 1959.
Right wing. Shoots right. 5'11", 190 lbs.
Last amateur club: Regina Pats (WHL).
(Vancouver's 5th choice, 89th over-all, in 1979 Entry Draft).

Season	Club	Lea	Regular Season					Playoffs				
			GP	G	A	TP	PIM	GP	G	A	TP	PIM
1975-76	Regina	WHL	2	0	0	0	0	6	1	1	2	5
1976-77	Regina	WHL	65	37	28	65	66	....	....	....	....	....
1977-78	Regina	WHL	72	29	61	110	87	13	15	19	34	37
1978-79	Regina	WHL	71	48	60	108	252	....	....	....	....	....
1979-80	Dallas	CHL	62	17	15	32	96	....	....	....	....	....
1980-81	Fort Wayne	IHL	6	1	2	3	12	....	....	....	....	....
	Toledo	IHL	61	40	45	85	88	....	....	....	....	....
1981-82	Toledo	IHL	72	49	56	105	68	13	10	11	21	8
1982-83a	Toledo	IHL	78	70	55	125	88	11	13	7	20	30
1983-84	**Minnesota**	**NHL**	6	1	1	2	0	1	0	0	0	2
b	Salt Lake	CHL	57	37	57	94	72	5	3	8	11	2
1984-85	**Minnesota**	**NHL**	36	12	11	23	23	9	0	4	4	7
	Springfield	AHL	37	20	28	48	41	....	....	....	....	....
1985-86	**Minnesota**	**NHL**	80	22	33	55	87	5	3	1	4	2
	NHL Totals		122	35	45	80	110	15	3	5	8	11

a IHL First All-Star Team (1983)
b CHL First All-Star Team (1984)
Signed as free agent by **Minnesota**, August 17, 1983.

GRANATO, TONY

Born, Downers Grove, Ill., July 25, 1964.
Center. Shoots right. 5'10", 160 lbs.
Last amateur club: University of Wisconsin Badgers (WCHA).
(NY Rangers' 5th choice, 120th overall, in 1982 Entry Draft).

Season	Club	Lea	Regular Season					Playoffs				
			GP	G	A	TP	PIM	GP	G	A	TP	PIM
1983-84	Wisconsin	WCHA	35	14	17	31	48	....	....	....	....	....
1984-85	Wisconsin	WCHA	42	33	34	67	94	....	....	....	....	....
1985-86	Wisconsin	WCHA	33	25	24	49	36	....	....	....	....	....

GRANNIS, DAVID

Born, St. Paul, Minn., January 18, 1966.
Left wing. Shoots left. 6'0", 190 lbs.
Last amateur club: University of Minnesota Golden Gophers (WCHA).
(Los Angeles' 5th choice, 87th overall, in 1984 Entry Draft).

Season	Club	Lea	Regular Season					Playoffs				
			GP	G	A	TP	PIM	GP	G	A	TP	PIM
1984-85	Minnesota	WCHA	23	2	6	8	17	....	....	....	....	....
1985-86	Minnesota	WCHA	25	5	7	12	14	....	....	....	....	....

GRATTON, DAN

Born, Brantford, Ont., December 7, 1966.
Center. Shoots left. 6', 185 lbs.
Last amateur club: Oshawa Generals (OHL).
(Los Angeles' 2nd choice, 10th over-all, in 1985 Entry Draft).

Season	Club	Lea	Regular Season					Playoffs				
			GP	G	A	TP	PIM	GP	G	A	TP	PIM
1983-84	Oshawa	OHL	65	40	34	74	55	7	2	5	7	15
1984-85	Oshawa	OHL	56	24	48	72	67	5	3	3	6	0
1985-86	Belleville	OHL	54	33	37	70	45	24	20	9	29	16

GRAVES, ADAM

Born, Toronto, Ont., April 12, 1968.
Center. Shoots left. 5'11", 185 lbs.
Last amateur club: Windsor Spitfires (OHL).
(Detroit's 2nd choice, 22nd overall, in 1986 Entry Draft).

Season	Club	Lea	Regular Season					Playoffs				
			GP	G	A	TP	PIM	GP	G	A	TP	PIM
1985-86	Windsor	OHL	62	27	37	64	35	16	5	11	16	10

GRAVES, STEVE

Born, Trenton, Ont., April 7, 1964.
Center. Shoots left. 5'10", 175 lbs.
Last amateur club: Sault Ste. Marie Greyhounds (OHL).
(Edmonton's 2nd choice, 41st over-all, in 1982 Entry Draft).

			Regular Season					Playoffs				
Season	Club	Lea	GP	G	A	TP	PIM	GP	G	A	TP	PIM
1981-82	S. S. Marie	OHL	66	12	15	27	49	13	8	5	13	14
1982-83	S. S. Marie	OHL	60	21	20	41	48	5	0	0	0	4
1983-84	Edmonton	NHL	2	0	0	0	0	....	....	....	....	....
a	S. S. Marie	OHL	67	41	48	89	47	16	6	8	14	8
1984-85	Nova Scotia	AHL	80	17	15	32	20	6	0	1	1	4
1985-86	Nova Scotia	AHL	78	19	18	37	22	....	....	....	....	....
	NHL Totals		2	0	0	0	0	....	....	....	....	....

a OHL Third All-Star Team (1984)

GREEN, RICHARD DOUGLAS (RICK)

Born, Belleville, Ont., February 20, 1956.
Defense. Shoots left. 6'3", 220 lbs.
Last amateur club: London Knights (OHA).
(Washington's 1st choice and 1st over-all in 1976 Amateur Draft).

			Regular Season					Playoffs				
Season	Club	Lea	GP	G	A	TP	PIM	GP	G	A	TP	PIM
1974-75	London	OHA	65	8	45	53	68	....	....	....	....	....
1975-76ab	London	OHA	61	13	47	60	69	5	1	0	1	4
1976-77	Washington	NHL	45	3	12	15	16	....	....	....	....	....
1977-78	Washington	NHL	60	5	14	19	67	....	....	....	....	....
1978-79	Washington	NHL	71	8	33	41	62	....	....	....	....	....
1979-80	Washington	NHL	71	4	20	24	52	....	....	....	....	....
1980-81	Washington	NHL	65	8	23	31	91	....	....	....	....	....
1981-82	Washington	NHL	65	3	25	28	93	....	....	....	....	....
1982-83	Montreal	NHL	66	2	24	26	58	3	0	0	0	2
1983-84	Montreal	NHL	7	0	1	1	7	15	1	2	3	33
1984-85	Montreal	NHL	77	1	18	19	30	12	0	3	3	14
1985-86	Montreal	NHL	46	3	2	5	20	18	1	4	5	8
	NHL Totals		573	37	172	209	496	48	2	9	11	57

a OHA First All-Star Team (1976).
b Named OHA's Most Outstanding Defenseman (1976).
Traded to **Montreal** by **Washington** with Ryan Walter for Brian Engblom, Rod Langway, Doug Jarvis and Craig Laughlin, September 9, 1982.

GREENLAW, JEFF

Born, Toronto, Ont., February 28, 1968.
Left wing. Shoots left. 6'1", 1895 lbs.
Last amateur club: Canadian Olympic Team.
(Washington's 1st choice, 19th overall, in 1986 Entry Draft).

			Regular Season					Playoffs				
Season	Club	Lea	GP	G	A	TP	PIM	GP	G	A	TP	PIM
1985-86	Cdn. Olympic	...	57	3	16	19	43	....	....	....	....	....

GREENOUGH, GLENN

Born, Sudbury, Ont., July 20, 1966.
Right wing. Shoots right. 5'11", 200 lbs.
Last amateur club: Sudbury Wolves (OHL).
(Chicago's 8th choice, 153rd over-all, in 1984 Entry Draft).

			Regular Season					Playoffs				
Season	Club	Lea	GP	G	A	TP	PIM	GP	G	A	TP	PIM
1983-84	Sudbury	OHL	67	26	43	69	33	....	....	....	....	....
1984-85	Sudbury	OHL	15	12	11	23	13	....	....	....	....	....
1985-86	Sudbury	OHL	64	30	40	70	34	4	0	3	3	12

GREGG, RANDALL JOHN (RANDY)

Born, Edmonton, Alta., February 19, 1956.
Defense. Shoots left. 6'4", 215 lbs.
Last amateur club: Kikudo Bunnies (Japan).

			Regular Season					Playoffs				
Season	Club	Lea	GP	G	A	TP	PIM	GP	G	A	TP	PIM
1977-78	U. of Alberta	CWUAA	24	7	23	30	37	....	....	....	....	....
1978-79	U. of Alberta	CWUAA	24	5	16	21	47	....	....	....	....	....
1979-80	Cdn. National		56	7	17	24	36	....	....	....	....	....
	Cdn. Olympic	...	6	1	1	2	2	....	....	....	....	....
1980-81	Kikudo	Japan	35	12	18	30	30	....	....	....	....	....
1981-82	Kikudo	Japan	36	12	20	32	25	....	....	....	....	....
	Edmonton	NHL	....	....	....	....	....	4	0	0	0	0
1982-83	Edmonton	NHL	80	6	22	28	54	16	2	4	6	13
1983-84	Edmonton	NHL	80	13	27	40	56	19	3	7	10	21
1984-85	Edmonton	NHL	57	3	20	23	32	17	0	6	6	12
1985-86	Edmonton	NHL	64	2	26	28	47	10	1	0	1	12
	NHL Totals		281	24	95	119	189	66	6	17	23	58

Signed as a free agent by **Edmonton**, October 18, 1982.

GREGOIRE, BILL

Born, Penticton, B.C., April 9, 1967.
Defense. Shoots left. 6'0", 180 lbs.
Last amateur club: Victoria Cougars (WHL).
(Calgary's 13th choice, 248th overall, in 1985 Entry Draft).

			Regular xcSeason					Playoffs				
Season	Club	Lea	GP	G	A	TP	PIM	GP	G	A	TP	PIM
1984-85	Victoria	WHL	67	2	12	14	144	....	....	....	....	....
1985-86	Victoria	WHL	41	13	19	32	122	....	....	....	....	....

GRENIER, TONY

Born, St. Boniface, Man., January 23, 1965.
Center. Shoots left. 5'10", 175 lbs.
Last amateur club: Prince Albert Raiders (WHL).
(NY Islanders' 14th choice, 244th overall, in 1985 Entry Draft).

			Regular Season					Playoffs				
Season	Club	Lea	GP	G	A	TP	PIM	GP	G	A	TP	PIM
1982-83	Winnipeg	WHL	69	9	12	21	21	3	0	0	0	5
1983-84	Winnipeg	WHL	60	42	31	73	28	....	....	....	....	....
1984-85	Prince Albert	WHL	71	62	58	120	38	12	12	9	21	9
1985-86	Prince Albert	WHL	52	42	37	79	16	....	....	....	....	....

GRESCHNER, RONALD JOHN (RON)   (GRESH-nur)

Born, Goodsoil, Sask., December 22, 1954.
Defense. Shoots left. 6'2", 205 lbs.
Last amateur club: New Westminster Bruins (WHL).
(NY Rangers' 2nd choice, 32nd over-all, in 1974 Amateur Draft).

			Regular Season					Playoffs				
Season	Club	Lea	GP	G	A	TP	PIM	GP	G	A	TP	PIM
1972-73	N. Westminster	WHL	68	22	47	69	169	5	2	4	6	19
1973-74a	N. Westminster	WHL	67	33	70	103	170	11	5	6	11	18
1974-75	Providence	AHL	7	5	6	11	10	....	....	....	....	....
	NY Rangers	NHL	70	8	37	45	94	3	0	1	1	2
1975-76	NY Rangers	NHL	77	6	21	27	93	....	....	....	....	....
1976-77	NY Rangers	NHL	80	11	36	47	89	....	....	....	....	....
1977-78	NY Rangers	NHL	78	24	48	72	100	3	0	0	0	2
1978-79	NY Rangers	NHL	60	17	36	53	66	18	7	5	12	16
1979-80	NY Rangers	NHL	76	21	37	58	103	9	0	6	6	10
1980-81	NY Rangers	NHL	74	27	41	68	112	14	4	8	12	17
1981-82	NY Rangers	NHL	29	5	11	16	16	....	....	....	....	....
1982-83	NY Rangers	NHL	10	3	5	8	0	8	2	2	4	12
1983-84	NY Rangers	NHL	77	12	44	56	117	2	1	0	1	12
1984-85	NY Rangers	NHL	48	16	29	45	42	2	0	3	3	12
1985-86	NY Rangers	NHL	78	20	28	48	104	5	3	1	4	11
	NHL Totals		757	170	373	543	935	64	17	26	43	84

a WHL First All-Star Team (1974)

GRETZKY, KEITH

Born, Brantford, Ont., February 16, 1967.
Center. Shoots left. 5'8", 150 lbs.
Last amateur club: Windsor Compuware Spitfires (OHL).
(Buffalo's 3rd choice, 56th over-all, in 1985 Entry Draft).

			Regular Season					Playoffs				
Season	Club	Lea	GP	G	A	TP	PIM	GP	G	A	TP	PIM
1983-84	Windsor	OHL	70	15	38	53	8	3	0	1	1	2
1984-85	Windsor	OHL	66	31	62	93	12	4	2	2	4	4
1985-86	Belleville	OHL	61	27	47	74	12	24	8	13	21	2

GRETZKY, WAYNE   (GRETZ-kee)

Born, Brantford, Ont., January 26, 1961.
Center. Shoots left. 6', 170 lbs.
Last amateur club: Sault Ste. Marie Greyhounds (OHA).

			Regular Season					Playoffs				
Season	Club	Lea	GP	G	A	TP	PIM	GP	G	A	TP	PIM
1976-77	Peterborough	OHA	3	0	3	3	0	....	....	....	....	....
1977-78ab	S. S. Marie	OHA	64	70	112	182	14	13	6	20	26	0
1978-79	Indianapolis	WHA	8	3	3	6	0	....	....	....	....	....
cd	Edmonton	WHA	72	43	61	104	19	13	*10	10	*20	2
1979-80efg	Edmonton	NHL	79	51	*86	*137	21	3	2	1	3	0
1980-81 ehijk	Edmonton	NHL	80	55	*109	*164	28	9	7	14	21	4
1981-82 ehijklm	Edmonton	NHL	80	*92	*120	*212	26	5	5	7	12	8
1982-83 ehijmno	Edmonton	NHL	80	*71	*125	*196	59	16	12	*26	*38	4
1983-84ehim	Edmonton	NHL	74	*87	*118	*205	39	19	13	*22	*35	12
1984-85 ehijmnop	Edmonton	NHL	80	73	*135	*208	52	18	17	*30	*47	4
1985-86ehijk	Edmonton	NHL	80	52	*163	*215	46	10	8	11	19	2
	NHL Totals		553	481	856	1337	271	80	64	111	175	34
	WHA Totals		80	46	64	110	19	13	10	10	20	2

a OHA Second All-Star Team (1978)
b Named OHA's Rookie of the Year (1978)
c WHA Second All-Star Team (1979)
d Named WHA's Rookie of the Year (1979)
e Won Hart Trophy (1980, 1981, 1982, 1983, 1984, 1985, 1986)
f Won Lady Byng Trophy (1980)
g NHL Second All-Star Team (1980)
h NHL First All-Star Team (1981, 1982, 1983, 1984, 1985, 1986)
i Won Art Ross Trophy (1981, 1982, 1983, 1984, 1985, 1986)
j NHL record for assists in regular season (1981, 1982, 1983, 1985, 1986)
k NHL record for points in regular season (1981, 1982, 1986)
l NHL record for goals in regular season (1982)
m Won Lester B. Pearson Award (1982, 1983, 1984, 1985)
n NHL record for assists in one playoff year (1983, 1985)
o NHL record for points in one playoff year (1983, 1985)
p Won Conn Smythe Trophy (1985)

Reclaimed by **Edmonton** as an under-age junior prior to Expansion Draft, June 9, 1979.
Claimed as priority selection by **Edmonton**, June 9, 1979.

GRIMSON, STUART

Born, Vancouver, B.C., May 20, 1965.
Left wing. Shoots left. 6'5", 230 lbs.
Last amateur club: University of Manitoba Bisons (GPAC).
(Calgary's 8th choice, 143rd overall, in 1985 Entry Draft).

Season	Club	Lea	GP	G	A	TP	PIM	GP	G	A	TP	PIM
					Regular Season					Playoffs		
1982-83	Regina	WHL	48	0	1	1	105	5	0	0	0	14
1983-84	Regina	WHL	63	8	8	16	131	21	0	1	1	29
1984-85	Regina	WHL	71	24	32	56	248	8	1	2	3	14
1985-86	U. of Manitoba	GPAC	20	8	8	16	137	....	....	....	....	....

GROULX, WAYNE   (GREW)

Born, Welland, Ont., February 2, 1965.
Center. Shoots right. 6'1", 185 lbs.
Last amateur club: Sault Ste. Marie Greyhounds (OHL).
(Quebec's 8th choice, 179th over-all, in 1983 Entry Draft).

Season	Club	Lea	GP	G	A	TP	PIM	GP	G	A	TP	PIM
					Regular Season					Playoffs		
1981-82	S. S. Marie	OHL	66	25	41	66	66	13	6	8	14	8
1982-83	S. S. Marie	OHL	67	44	86	130	54	16	7	9	16	13
1983-84a	S. S. Marie	OHL	70	59	78	137	48	16	14	22	*36	13
1984-85	**Quebec**	**NHL**	1	0	0	0	0	....	....	....	....	....
bc	S. S. Marie	OHL	64	59	85	144	102	16	18	18	36	24
1985-86	Fredericton	AHL	15	2	6	8	12	....	....	....	....	....
	Muskegon	IHL	55	22	27	49	56	12	4	4	8	26
	NHL Totals		1	0	0	0	0	....	....	....	....	....

a OHL Second All-Star Team (1984)
b Won Red Tilson Trophy (Outstanding Player – OHL) (1985)
c OHL First All-Star Team (1985)

GRUHL, SCOTT KENNETH   (GROOL)

Born, Port Colborne, Ont., September 13, 1959.
Left wing. Shoots left. 5'11", 185 lbs.
Last amateur club: Sudbury Wolves (OHA).

Season	Club	Lea	GP	G	A	TP	PIM	GP	G	A	TP	PIM
					Regular Season					Playoffs		
1978-79	Sudbury	OHA	68	35	49	94	78	10	5	7	12	15
1979-80	Binghamton	AHL	4	1	0	1	0	....	....	....	....	....
	Saginaw	IHL	75	53	40	93	100	7	2	6	8	16
1980-81	Houston	CHL	4	0	0	0	0	....	....	....	....	....
	Saginaw	IHL	77	56	34	90	87	13	11	8	19	12
1981-82	**Los Angeles**	**NHL**	7	2	1	3	2	....	....	....	....	....
	New Haven	AHL	73	28	41	69	107	4	0	4	4	2
1982-83	**Los Angeles**	**NHL**	7	0	2	2	4	....	....	....	....	....
	New Haven	AHL	68	25	38	63	114	12	3	3	6	22
1983-84	Muskegon	IHL	56	40	56	96	46	....	....	....	....	....
1984-85a	Muskegon	IHL	82	62	64	126	102	17	7	16	23	25
1985-86b	Muskegon	IHL	82	59	50	109	178	14	7	13	20	22
	NHL Totals		14	2	3	5	6	....	....	....	....	....

Signed as free agent by **Los Angeles**, October 11, 1979.
a IHL First All-Star Team (1985)
b IHL Second All-Star Team (1986)

GUAY, PAUL   (GAY)

Born, Providence, Rhode Island, September 2, 1963.
Right wing. Shoots right. 5'11", 185 lbs.
Last amateur club: 1984 United States Olympic Team.
(Minnesota's 9th choice, 118th over-all, in 1981 Entry Draft).

Season	Club	Lea	GP	G	A	TP	PIM	GP	G	A	TP	PIM
					Regular Season					Playoffs		
1980-81	Mt. St. Charles	R.I.	23	28	38	66	....	....	....	....	....	....
1981-82	Providence	ECAC	33	23	17	40	38	....	....	....	....	....
1982-83a	Providence	ECAC	42	34	31	65	83	....	....	....	....	....
1983-84	U.S. National	...	62	20	18	38	44	....	....	....	....	....
	U.S. Olympic	...	6	1	0	1	8	....	....	....	....	....
	Philadelphia	NHL	14	2	6	8	14	3	0	0	0	4
1984-85	**Philadelphia**	**NHL**	2	0	1	1	0	....	....	....	....	....
	Hershey	AHL	74	23	30	53	123	....	....	....	....	....
1985-86	**Los Angeles**	**NHL**	23	3	3	6	18	....	....	....	....	....
	New Haven	AHL	57	16	35	51	101	5	3	0	3	11
	NHL Totals		39	5	10	15	32	3	0	0	0	4

a ECAC Second All-Star Team (1983)
Rights traded to **Philadelphia** by **Minnesota** with Minnesota's third round choice in 1985 Entry Draft for Paul Holmgren, February 23, 1984. Traded to **Los Angeles** by **Philadelphia** with Philadelphia's fourth-round choice (Sylvain Couturier) in 1986 Entry Draft for Steve Seguin and Los Angeles' second-round choice (Jukka Seppo) in 1986 Entry Draft, October 11, 1985.

GUERARD, STEPHANE

Born, St. Elizabeth, Que., April 12, 1968.
Defense. Shoots left. 6'2", 180 lbs.
Last amateur club: Shawinigan Cataractes (QMJHL).
(Quebec's 3rd choice, 41st overall, in 1986 Entry Draft).

Season	Club	Lea	GP	G	A	TP	PIM	GP	G	A	TP	PIM
					Regular Season					Playoffs		
1985-86	Shawinigan	QMJHL	59	4	16	20	167	3	1	1	2	0

GUIDOTTI, VINCENT

Born, Sacramento, Calif., April 29, 1967.
Left wing. Shoots left. 6'0", 180 lbs.
Last amateur club: University of Maine Black Bears (H.E.).
(St. Louis' 9th choice, 201st overall, in 1985 Entry Draft).

Season	Club	Lea	GP	G	A	TP	PIM	GP	G	A	TP	PIM
					Regular Season					Playoffs		
1985-86	Maine	H.E.	16	0	0	0	0	....	....	....	....	....

GUSTAFSSON, BENGT-AKE   (goose-TOFF-son)

Born, Karlskoga, Sweden, March 23, 1958.
Right wing. Shoots left. 6', 190 lbs.
Last amateur club: Farjestads BK (Sweden).
(Washington's 7th choice, 55th over-all, in 1978 Amateur Draft).

Season	Club	Lea	GP	G	A	TP	PIM	GP	G	A	TP	PIM
					Regular Season					Playoffs		
1977-78	Farjestads	Swe.	32	15	10	25	10	7	2	6	8	10
1978-79	Farjestads	Swe.	32	13	11	24	10	2	2	0	2	4
	Edmonton	WHA	....	....	....	....	....	2	1	2	3	0
1979-80	**Washington**	**NHL**	80	22	38	60	17	....	....	....	....	....
1980-81	**Washington**	**NHL**	72	21	34	55	26	....	....	....	....	....
1981-82	**Washington**	**NHL**	70	26	34	60	40	....	....	....	....	....
1982-83	**Washington**	**NHL**	67	22	42	64	16	4	0	1	1	4
1983-84	**Washington**	**NHL**	69	32	43	75	16	5	2	3	5	0
1984-85	**Washington**	**NHL**	51	14	29	43	8	5	1	3	4	0
1985-86	**Washington**	**NHL**	70	23	52	75	26	....	....	....	....	....
	NHL Totals		479	160	272	432	149	14	3	7	11	4
	WHA Totals							2	1	2	3	0

Reclaimed by **Washington** from **Edmonton** prior to Expansion Draft, June 9, 1979.

GUY, KEVAN

Born, Edmonton, Alta., July 16, 1965.
Defense. Shoots right. 6'2", 190 lbs.
Last amateur club: Medicine Hat Tigers (WHL).
(Calgary's 5th choice, 71st over-all, in 1983 Entry Draft).

Season	Club	Lea	GP	G	A	TP	PIM	GP	G	A	TP	PIM
					Regular Season					Playoffs		
1982-83	Medicine Hat	WHL	69	7	20	27	89	5	0	3	3	16
1983-84	Medicine Hat	WHL	72	15	42	57	117	14	3	4	7	14
1984-85	Medicine Hat	WHL	31	7	17	24	46	10	1	2	3	2
1985-86	Moncton	AHL	73	4	20	24	56	10	0	2	2	6

HAANPAA, ARI

Born, Nokia, Finland, November 28, 1965.
Right wing. Shoots right. 6'1", 185 lbs.
Last amateur club: Ilves-Tampere (Finland)
(NY Islanders' 5th choice, 83rd overall, in 1984 Entry Draft).

Season	Club	Lea	GP	G	A	TP	PIM	GP	G	A	TP	PIM
					Regular Season					Playoffs		
1984-85	Ilves	Fin.	13	5	0	5	2	....	....	....	....	....
1985-86	Springfield	AHL	20	3	1	4	13	....	....	....	....	....
	NY Islanders	**NHL**	18	0	7	7	20	....	....	....	....	....
	NHL Totals		18	0	7	7	20	....	....	....	....	....

HAARMANN, MARK

Born, Toronto, Ont., January 20, 1967.
Defense. Shoots left. 6'2", 200 lbs.
Last amateur club: Sault Ste. Marie Greyhounds (OHL).
(Washington's 9th choice, 166th overall, in 1985 Entry Draft).

Season	Club	Lea	GP	G	A	TP	PIM	GP	G	A	TP	PIM
					Regular Season					Playoffs		
1984-85	Oshawa	OHL	66	5	14	19	51	5	0	0	0	0
1985-86	S.S. Marie	OHL	56	7	20	27	59	....	....	....	....	....

HABSCHEID, MARC JOSEPH   (hab-SHIDE)

Born, Swift Current, Sask., March 1, 1963.
Center. Shoots right. 5'10", 170 lbs.
Last amateur club: Kamloops Junior Oilers (WHL).
(Edmonton's 6th choice, 113th over-all, in 1981 Entry Draft).

Season	Club	Lea	GP	G	A	TP	PIM	GP	G	A	TP	PIM
					Regular Season					Playoffs		
1980-81	Saskatoon	WHL	72	34	63	97	50	....	....	....	....	....
1981-82	**Edmonton**	**NHL**	7	1	3	4	2	....	....	....	....	....
a	Saskatoon	WHL	55	64	87	151	74	5	3	4	7	4
	Wichita	CHL	....	....	....	....	....	3	0	0	0	0
1982-83	Kamloops	WHL	6	7	16	23	8	....	....	....	....	....
	Edmonton	**NHL**	32	3	10	13	14	....	....	....	....	....
1983-84	**Edmonton**	**NHL**	9	1	0	1	6	....	....	....	....	....
	Moncton	AHL	71	19	37	56	32	....	....	....	....	....
1984-85	**Edmonton**	**NHL**	26	5	3	8	4	....	....	....	....	....
	Nova Scotia	AHL	48	29	29	58	65	6	4	3	7	9
1985-86	**Minnesota**	**NHL**	6	2	3	5	0	2	0	0	0	0
	Springfield	AHL	41	18	32	50	21	....	....	....	....	....
	NHL Totals		80	12	19	31	26	2	0	0	0	0

a WHL Second All-Star Team (1982)
Traded to **Minnesota** by **Edmonton** with Dan Barber and Emanuel Viveiros for Gord Sherven and Don Biggs, December 20, 1985.

HACHBORN, LEONARD (LEN)

Born, Brantford, Ont., September 4, 1961.
Center. Shoots left. 5'10", 175 lbs.
Last amateur club: Brantford Alexanders (OHL).
(Philadelphia's 9th choice, 184th over-all, in 1981 Entry Draft).

Season	Club	Lea	Regular Season GP	G	A	TP	PIM	Playoffs GP	G	A	TP	PIM
1980-81	Brantford	OHA	66	34	52	86	94	6	1	5	6	15
1981-82	Brantford	OHL	55	43	50	93	141	11	15	9	24	13
1982-83	Maine	AHL	75	28	55	83	32	17	2	7	9	2
1983-84	Springfield	AHL	28	18	42	60	15	....	....	....	....	....
	Philadelphia	NHL	38	11	21	32	4	3	0	0	0	7
1984-85	Philadelphia	NHL	40	5	17	22	23	4	0	3	3	0
	Hershey	AHL	14	6	7	13	14	....	....	....	....	....
1985-86	Hershey	AHL	23	12	22	34	34	....	....	....	....	....
	Los Angeles	NHL	24	4	1	5	2	....	....	....	....	....
	New Haven	AHL	12	5	8	13	21	3	0	1	1	26
	NHL Totals		102	20	39	59	29	7	0	3	3	7

Rights sold to **Los Angeles** by Philadelphia, December 6, 1985.

HAJDU, RICHARD

Born, Victoria, B.C., May 10, 1965.
Left wing. Shoots left. 6'1", 185 lbs.
Last amateur club: Victoria Cougars (WHL).
(Buffalo's 5th choice, 34th over-all, in 1983 Entry Draft).

Season	Club	Lea	Regular Season GP	G	A	TP	PIM	Playoffs GP	G	A	TP	PIM
1981-82	Kamloops	WHL	64	19	21	40	50	4	0	0	0	0
1982-83	Kamloops	WHL	70	22	36	58	101	5	0	0	0	4
1983-84	Victoria	WHL	42	17	10	27	106	....	....	....	....	....
1984-85	Victoria	WHL	24	12	16	28	33	....	....	....	....	....
	Rochester	AHL	2	0	2	2	0	....	....	....	....	....
1985-86	Buffalo	NHL	3	0	0	0	4	....	....	....	....	....
	Rochester	AHL	54	10	27	37	95	....	....	....	....	....
	NHL Totals		3	0	0	0	4					

HAJT, WILLIAM ALBERT (BILL)   (HYTE)

Born, Borden, Sask., November 18, 1951.
Defense. Shoots left. 6'3", 205 lbs.
Last amateur club: Saskatoon Blades (WHL).
(Buffalo's 3rd choice, 33rd over-all, in 1971 Amateur Draft).

Season	Club	Lea	Regular Season GP	G	A	TP	PIM	Playoffs GP	G	A	TP	PIM
1969-70	Saskatoon	WHL	60	10	21	31	40	7	2	3	5	8
1970-71	Saskatoon	WHL	66	19	53	72	50	5	1	4	5	2
1971-72	DID NOT PLAY											
1972-73	Cincinnati	AHL	69	4	31	35	40	15	2	9	11	14
1973-74	Buffalo	NHL	6	0	2	2	0	....	....	....	....	....
	Cincinnati	AHL	66	5	30	35	66	5	0	4	4	4
1974-75	Buffalo	NHL	76	3	26	29	68	17	1	4	5	18
1975-76	Buffalo	NHL	80	6	21	27	48	9	0	1	1	15
1976-77	Buffalo	NHL	79	6	20	26	56	6	0	1	1	4
1977-78	Buffalo	NHL	76	4	18	22	30	8	0	0	0	2
1978-79	Buffalo	NHL	40	3	8	11	20	....	....	....	....	....
1979-80	Buffalo	NHL	75	4	12	16	24	14	0	5	5	4
1980-81	Buffalo	NHL	68	2	19	21	42	8	0	2	2	17
1981-82	Buffalo	NHL	65	2	9	11	44	2	0	0	0	0
1982-83	Buffalo	NHL	72	3	12	15	26	10	0	0	0	4
1983-84	Buffalo	NHL	79	3	24	27	32	3	0	0	0	0
1984-85	Buffalo	NHL	57	5	13	18	14	3	1	3	4	6
1985-86	Buffalo	NHL	58	1	16	17	25	....	....	....	....	....
	NHL Totals		831	42	200	242	429	80	2	16	18	70

HAKANSSON, ANDERS

Born, Munkfors, Sweden, April 27, 1956.
Left wing. Shoots left. 6'2", 190 lbs.
Last amateur club: AIK Solna (Sweden).

Season	Club	Lea	Regular Season GP	G	A	TP	PIM	Playoffs GP	G	A	TP	PIM
1977-78	AIK Solna	Swe.	27	8	4	12	10	....	....	....	....	....
1978-79	AIK Solna	Swe.	36	12	8	20	37	....	....	....	....	....
1979-80	AIK Solna	Swe.	36	14	10	24	32	....	....	....	....	....
	Swe. National	...	5	0	2	2	7	....	....	....	....	....
1980-81	AIK Solna	Swe.	22	5	12	17	18	6	4	1	5	6
	Swe. National	...	10	6	1	7	12	....	....	....	....	....
1981-82	Minnesota	NHL	72	12	4	16	29	3	0	0	0	2
1982-83	Minnesota	NHL	5	0	0	0	9	....	....	....	....	....
	Pittsburgh	NHL	62	9	12	21	26	....	....	....	....	....
1983-84	Los Angeles	NHL	80	15	17	32	41	....	....	....	....	....
1984-85	Los Angeles	NHL	73	12	12	24	28	3	0	0	0	0
1985-86	Los Angeles	NHL	38	4	1	5	8	....	....	....	....	....
	NHL Totals		330	52	46	98	141	6	0	0	0	2

Signed as free agent by **Minnesota**, July 22, 1981. Traded to **Pittsburgh** by **Minnesota** with Ron Meighan and Minnesota's first round choice (Bob Errey) in 1983 Entry Draft for George Ferguson and Pittsburgh's first round choice (Brian Lawton) in 1983 Entry Draft, October 28, 1982. Traded to **Los Angeles** by **Pittsburgh** for the rights to Kevin Stevens, September 9, 1983.

HALKIDIS, BOB

Born, Toronto, Ont., March 5, 1966.
Defense. Shoots left. 5'11", 195 lbs.
Last amateur club: London Knights (OHL).
(Buffalo's 4th choice, 81st over-all, in 1984 Entry Draft).

Season	Club	Lea	Regular Season GP	G	A	TP	PIM	Playoffs GP	G	A	TP	PIM
1983-84	London	OHL	51	9	22	31	123	8	0	2	2	27
1984-85	Buffalo	NHL	....	....	....	....	....	4	0	0	0	19
ab	London	OHL	62	14	50	64	154	8	3	6	9	22
1985-86	Buffalo	NHL	37	1	9	10	115	....	....	....	....	....
	NHL Totals		37	1	9	10	115	4	0	0	0	19

a Named Outstanding Defenseman in OHL (1985)
b OHL First All-Star Team (1985)

HALL, TAYLOR

Born, Regina, Sask., February 20, 1964.
Left wing. Shoots left. 5'11", 180 lbs.
Last amateur club: Regina Pats (WHL).
(Vancouver's 4th choice, 116th over-all, in 1982 Entry Draft).

Season	Club	Lea	Regular Season GP	G	A	TP	PIM	Playoffs GP	G	A	TP	PIM
1981-82	Regina	WHL	48	14	15	29	43	11	2	3	5	14
1982-83	Regina	WHL	72	37	57	94	78	5	0	3	3	12
1983-84	Vancouver	NHL	4	1	0	1	0	....	....	....	....	....
a	Regina	WHL	69	63	79	142	42	23	*21	20	41	26
1984-85	Vancouver	NHL	7	1	4	5	19	....	....	....	....	....
1985-86	Vancouver	NHL	19	5	5	10	6	....	....	....	....	....
	Fredericton	AHL	45	21	14	35	28	1	0	0	0	0
	NHL Totals		30	7	9	16	25					

a WHL First All-Star Team, East Division (1984)

HALLIN, MATS   (HALL-een)

Born, Eskilstuna, Sweden, March 9, 1958.
Left wing. Shoots left. 6'2", 200 lbs.
Last amateur club: Sodertalje (Sweden).
(Washington's 9th choice, 105th over-all, in 1978 Amateur Draft).

Season	Club	Lea	Regular Season GP	G	A	TP	PIM	Playoffs GP	G	A	TP	PIM
1978-79	Sodertalje	Swe.	14	4	7	11	18	....	....	....	....	....
1979-80	Sodertalje	Swe.	31	22	19	41	84	9	8	5	13	36
1980-81	Sodertalje	Swe.	33	9	11	20	86	....	....	....	....	....
1981-82	Indianapolis	CHL	63	25	32	57	113	8	1	5	6	31
1982-83	Indianapolis	CHL	42	26	27	53	86	....	....	....	....	....
	NY Islanders	NHL	30	7	7	14	26	7	1	0	1	6
1983-84	NY Islanders	NHL	40	2	5	7	27	6	0	0	0	7
1984-85	NY Islanders	NHL	38	5	0	5	50	1	0	0	0	0
1985-86	Minnesota	NHL	38	3	2	5	86	1	0	0	0	0
	Springfield	AHL	2	1	1	2	0	....	....	....	....	....
	NHL Totals		146	17	14	31	189	15	1	0	1	13

Signed as free agent by **NY Islanders**, June 12, 1981.
Traded to **Minnesota** by **NY Islanders** for Minnesota's seventh-round choice (Will Anderson) in 1986 Entry Draft, September 9, 1985.

HALWARD, DOUGLAS ROBERT (DOUG)   (HALL-ward)

Born, Toronto, Ont., November 1, 1955.
Defense. Shoots left. 6'1", 200 lbs.
Last amateur club: Peterborough Petes (OHA).
(Boston's 1st choice, 14th over-all, in 1975 Amateur Draft).

Season	Club	Lea	Regular Season GP	G	A	TP	PIM	Playoffs GP	G	A	TP	PIM
1973-74	Peterborough	OHA	69	1	15	16	103	....	....	....	....	....
1974-75a	Peterborough	OHA	68	11	52	63	97	1	2	3	5	5
1975-76	Boston	NHL	22	1	5	6	6	1	0	0	0	0
	Rochester	AHL	54	6	11	17	51	4	1	0	1	4
1976-77	Rochester	AHL	54	4	28	32	26	....	....	....	....	....
	Boston	NHL	18	2	2	4	6	6	0	0	0	4
1977-78	Boston	NHL	25	0	2	2	2	....	....	....	....	....
	Rochester	AHL	42	8	14	22	17	6	0	3	3	2
1978-79	Springfield	AHL	14	5	1	6	10	....	....	....	....	....
	Los Angeles	NHL	27	1	5	6	13	1	0	0	0	12
1979-80	Los Angeles	NHL	63	11	45	56	52	1	0	0	0	2
1980-81	Los Angeles	NHL	51	4	15	19	96	....	....	....	....	....
	Vancouver	NHL	7	0	1	1	4	2	0	1	1	6
1981-82	Dallas	CHL	22	8	18	26	49	....	....	....	....	....
	Vancouver	NHL	37	4	13	17	40	15	2	4	6	44
1982-83	Vancouver	NHL	75	19	33	52	83	4	1	0	1	21
1983-84	Vancouver	NHL	54	7	16	23	35	3	1	3	4	2
1984-85	Vancouver	NHL	71	7	27	34	82	....	....	....	....	....
1985-86	Vancouver	NHL	70	8	25	33	111	3	0	0	0	4
	NHL Totals		520	64	189	253	530	37	6	6	12	95

a OHA Third All-Star Team (1975)

Traded to **Los Angeles** by **Boston** for future considerations, September 18, 1978. Claimed by **Los Angeles** as fill in Expansion Draft, June 13, 1979. Traded to **Vancouver** by **Los Angeles** for Vancouver's fifth-round choice (Ulf Isaksson) in 1982 Entry Draft, March 8, 1981.

HAMEL, GILLES

(A-mel, jyll)

Born, Asbestos, Que., March 18, 1960.
Left wing. Shoots left. 6', 185 lbs.
Last amateur club: Chicoutimi Sagueneens (QJHL).
(Buffalo's 5th choice, 74th over-all, in 1979 Entry Draft).

Season	Club	Lea	Regular Season GP	G	A	TP	PIM	Playoffs GP	G	A	TP	PIM
1978-79	Laval	QJHL	72	56	55	111	130	....	....	....	....	....
1979-80	Trois Rivieres	QJHL	12	13	8	21	8	....	....	....	....	....
	Chicoutimi	QJHL	57	73	62	135	87	12	10	6	16	20
	Rochester	AHL	....	....	....	....	....	1	0	0	0	0
1980-81	Rochester	AHL	14	8	7	15	7	....	....	....	....	....
	Buffalo	**NHL**	51	10	9	19	53	5	0	1	1	4
1981-82	**Buffalo**	**NHL**	16	2	7	9	2	....	....	....	....	....
	Rochester	AHL	57	31	44	75	55	....	....	....	....	....
1982-83	**Buffalo**	**NHL**	66	22	20	42	26	9	2	2	4	2
1983-84	**Buffalo**	**NHL**	75	21	23	44	37	3	0	2	2	2
1984-85	**Buffalo**	**NHL**	80	18	30	48	36	1	0	0	0	0
1985-86	**Buffalo**	**NHL**	77	19	25	44	61	....	....	....	....	....
	NHL Totals		365	92	114	206	215	18	2	5	7	8

Traded to **Winnipeg** by **Buffalo** for Scott Arniel, June 21, 1986.

HAMILTON, BRAD

Born, Calgary, Alta., March 30, 1967.
Defense. Shoots left. 6'0", 175 lbs.
Last amateur club: Michigan State University Spartans (CCHA).
(Chicago's 10th choice, 200th overall, in 1985 Entry Draft).

Season	Club	Lea	Regular Season GP	G	A	TP	PIM	Playoffs GP	G	A	TP	PIM
1984-85	Aurora	Tier II	43	9	29	38	149	....	....	....	....	....
1985-86	Michigan St.	CCHA	43	3	10	13	52	....	....	....	....	....

HAMILTON, JEFF

Born, Montreal, Que., February 23, 1964.
Left wing. Shoots left. 6', 180 lbs.
Last amateur club: Verdun Juniors (QMJHL).
(Buffalo's 7th choice, 79th over-all, in 1982 Entry Draft).

Season	Club	Lea	Regular Season GP	G	A	TP	PIM	Playoffs GP	G	A	TP	PIM
1981-82	Providence	ECAC	32	8	11	19	0	....	....	....	....	....
1982-83	Rochester	AHL	13	2	4	6	0	....	....	....	....	....
1983-84	Verdun	QMJHL	30	19	39	58	6	10	12	9	21	0
1984-85	Rochester	AHL	70	7	14	21	36	3	0	0	0	4
1985-86	Rochester	AHL	74	19	10	29	48	....	....	....	....	....

HAMMOND, KEN

Born, Port Credit, Ont., August 22, 1963.
Defense. Shoots left. 6'1", 190 lbs.
Last amateur club: Rensselaer Polytechnic Institute Engineers (ECAC)
(Los Angeles' 8th choice, 152nd over-all, in 1983 Entry Draft).

Season	Club	Lea	Regular Season GP	G	A	TP	PIM	Playoffs GP	G	A	TP	PIM
1982-83	RPI	ECAC	28	17	26	43	8	....	....	....	....	....
1983-84	RPI	ECAC	34	5	11	16	72	....	....	....	....	....
1984-85	**Los Angeles**	**NHL**	3	1	0	1	0	3	0	0	0	4
ab	RPI	ECAC	38	11	28	39	90	....	....	....	....	....
1985-86	**Los Angeles**	**NHL**	3	0	1	1	2	....	....	....	....	....
	New Haven	AHL	67	4	12	16	96	4	0	0	0	7
	NHL Totals		6	1	1	2	2	3	0	0	0	4

a ECAC First All-Star Team (1985)
b Named to NCAA All-American Team (1985)

HAMWAY, MARK

Born, Detroit, Mich., August 9, 1961.
Right wing. Shoots right. 6'0", 190 lbs.
Last amateur club: Michigan State University Spartans (CCHA).
(NY Islanders' 8th choice, 143rd over-all, in 1980 Entry Draft).

Season	Club	Lea	Regular Season GP	G	A	TP	PIM	Playoffs GP	G	A	TP	PIM
1979-80	Michigan State	WCHA	38	16	28	44	28	....	....	....	....	....
1980-81	Michigan State	WCHA	35	18	15	33	20	....	....	....	....	....
1981-82	Michigan State	CCHA	41	34	31	65	37	....	....	....	....	....
1982-83	Michigan State	CCHA	32	22	21	43	10	....	....	....	....	....
1983-84	Indianapolis	CHL	71	22	32	54	38	9	1	1	2	0
1984-85	**NY Islanders**	**NHL**	2	0	0	0	0	....	....	....	....	....
	Springfield	AHL	75	29	34	63	29	4	0	1	1	0
1985-86	**NY Islanders**	**NHL**	49	5	12	17	19	1	0	0	0	0
	Springfield	AHL	14	5	8	13	7	....	....	....	....	....
	NHL Totals		51	5	12	17	19	1	0	0	0	0

HANDY, RONALD (RON)

Born, Toronto, Ont., January 15, 1963.
Left wing. Shoots left. 5'10", 165 lbs.
Last amateur club: Kingston Canadians (OHL).
(NY Islanders' 3rd choice, 57th over-all, in 1981 Entry Draft).

Season	Club	Lea	Regular Season GP	G	A	TP	PIM	Playoffs GP	G	A	TP	PIM
1980-81	S. S. Marie	OHA	66	43	43	86	45	18	3	5	8	25
1981-82	S. S. Marie	OHL	20	15	10	25	20	....	....	....	....	....
	Kingston	OHL	44	35	38	73	23	4	1	1	2	16
1982-83	Kingston	OHL	67	52	96	148	64	....	....	....	....	....
	Indianapolis	CHL	9	2	7	9	0	10	3	8	11	18
1983-84a	Indianapolis	CHL	66	29	46	75	40	10	2	5	7	0
1984-85	**NY Islanders**	**NHL**	10	0	2	2	0	....	....	....	....	....
	Springfield	AHL	69	29	35	64	38	3	2	2	4	0
1985-86	Springfield	AHL	79	31	30	61	66	....	....	....	....	....
	NHL Totals		10	0	2	2	0	....	....	....	....	....

a CHL Second All-Star Team (1984).

HANLEY, TIMOTHY

Born, Greenfield, Mass., October 10, 1964.
Right wing. Shoots right. 6'0", 200 lbs.
Last amateur club: University of New Hampshire Wildcats (H.E.).
(Los Angeles' 7th choice, 129th overall, in 1984 Entry Draft).

Season	Club	Lea	Regular Season GP	G	A	TP	PIM	Playoffs GP	G	A	TP	PIM
1984-85	N. Hampshire	H.E.	42	22	18	40	21	....	....	....	....	....
1985-86	N. Hampshire	H.E.	29	9	13	22	22	....	....	....	....	....

HANNAN, DAVID (DAVE)

Born, Sudbury, Ont., November 26, 1961.
Center. Shoots left. 5'10", 175 lbs.
Last amateur club: Brantford Alexanders (OHA).
(Pittsburgh's 9th choice, 196th over-all, in 1981 Entry Draft).

Season	Club	Lea	Regular Season GP	G	A	TP	PIM	Playoffs GP	G	A	TP	PIM
1979-80	Brantford	OHA	53	16	20	36	57	....	....	....	....	....
1980-81	Brantford	OHA	56	46	35	81	155	6	2	4	6	20
1981-82	**Pittsburgh**	**NHL**	1	0	0	0	0	....	....	....	....	....
	Erie	AHL	76	33	37	70	129	....	....	....	....	....
1982-83	**Pittsburgh**	**NHL**	74	11	22	33	127	....	....	....	....	....
	Baltimore	AHL	5	2	2	4	13	....	....	....	....	....
1983-84	**Pittsburgh**	**NHL**	24	2	3	5	33	....	....	....	....	....
	Baltimore	AHL	47	18	24	42	98	10	2	6	8	27
1984-85	**Pittsburgh**	**NHL**	30	6	7	13	43	....	....	....	....	....
	Baltimore	AHL	49	20	25	45	91	....	....	....	....	....
1985-86	**Pittsburgh**	**NHL**	75	17	18	35	91	....	....	....	....	....
	NHL Totals		204	36	50	86	294	....	....	....	....	....

HANSON, DAVE

Born, Grand Forks, ND, July 18, 1966.
Center. Shoots left. 6'3", 220 lbs.
Last amateur club: University of Denver Pioneers (WCHA).
(Philadelphia's 6th choice, 79th overall, in 1984 Entry Draft).

Season	Club	Lea	Regular Season GP	G	A	TP	PIM	Playoffs GP	G	A	TP	PIM
1984-85	Denver	WCHA	36	3	7	10	28	....	....	....	....	....
1985-86	Denver	WCHA	45	12	14	26	45	....	....	....	....	....

HARDY, MARK LEA

Born, Semaden, Switzerland, February 1, 1959.
Defense. Shoots left. 5'11", 195 lbs.
Last amateur club: Montreal Juniors (QJHL).
(Los Angeles' 3rd choice, 30th over-all, in 1979 Entry Draft).

Season	Club	Lea	Regular Season GP	G	A	TP	PIM	Playoffs GP	G	A	TP	PIM
1977-78	Montreal	QJHL	72	25	57	82	150	13	3	10	13	22
1978-79	Montreal	QJHL	67	18	52	70	117	11	5	8	13	40
1979-80	Binghamton	AHL	56	3	13	16	32	....	....	....	....	....
	Los Angeles	**NHL**	15	0	1	1	10	4	1	1	2	9
1980-81	**Los Angeles**	**NHL**	77	5	20	25	77	4	1	2	3	4
1981-82	**Los Angeles**	**NHL**	77	6	39	45	130	10	1	2	3	9
1982-83	**Los Angeles**	**NHL**	74	5	34	39	101	....	....	....	....	....
1983-84	**Los Angeles**	**NHL**	79	8	41	49	122	....	....	....	....	....
1984-85	**Los Angeles**	**NHL**	78	14	39	53	97	3	0	1	1	2
1985-86	**Los Angeles**	**NHL**	55	6	21	27	71	....	....	....	....	....
	NHL Totals		455	44	195	239	608	21	3	6	9	24

HARLOW, SCOTT

Born, East Bridgewater, Mass., October 11, 1963.
Left wing. Shoots left. 6'1", 185 lbs.
Last amateur club: Boston College Eagles (ECAC)
(Montreal's 6th choice, 61st over-all, in 1982 Entry Draft).

Season	Club	Lea	Regular Season GP	G	A	TP	PIM	Playoffs GP	G	A	TP	PIM
1981-82	E. Bridgewater	Mass	22	58	57	115	0	....	....	....	....	....
1982-83	Boston College	ECAC	24	6	19	25	19	....	....	....	....	....
1983-84	Boston College	ECAC	39	27	20	47	17	....	....	....	....	....
1984-85a	Boston College	ECAC	44	34	38	72	45	....	....	....	....	....
1985-86bcd	Boston College	H.E.	42	38	41	79	48	....	....	....	....	....

a Hockey East Second All-Star Team
b NCAA East First All-American Team (1986)
c Hockey East First All-Star Team (1986)
d Hockey East Player of the Year (1986)

HARPER, WARREN

Born, Prince Albert, Sask., May 10, 1963.
Right wing. Shoots left. 6', 175 lbs.
Last amateur club: Prince Albert Raiders (WHL)
(Buffalo's 12th choice, 206th over-all, in 1981 Entry Draft.)

Season	Club	Lea	Regular Season					Playoffs				
			GP	G	A	TP	PIM	GP	G	A	TP	PIM
1980-81	Prince Albert	SJHL	60	35	35	70	158	....	....	....	....	....
1981-82	Prince Albert	SJHL	39	23	29	52	108	....	....	....	....	....
1982-83	Prince Albert	WHL	41	17	15	32	38	....	....	....	....	....
1983-84	Rochester	AHL	78	25	28	53	56	18	3	3	6	11
1984-85	Rochester	AHL	78	29	34	63	43	5	0	2	2	8
1985-86	Rochester	AHL	80	18	30	48	83	....	....	....	....	....

HARTSBURG, CRAIG

Born, Stratford, Ont., June 29, 1959.
Defense. Shoots left. 6'1", 200 lbs.
Last amateur club: Sault Ste. Marie Greyhounds (OHA).
(Minnesota's 1st choice, 6th over-all, in 1979 Entry Draft.)

Season	Club	Lea	Regular Season					Playoffs				
			GP	G	A	TP	PIM	GP	G	A	TP	PIM
1976-77a	S. S. Marie	OHA	61	29	64	93	142	9	0	11	11	27
1977-78b	S. S. Marie	OHA	36	15	42	57	101	13	4	8	12	24
1978-79	Birmingham	WHA	77	9	40	49	73	....	....	....	....	....
1979-80	Minnesota	NHL	79	14	30	44	81	15	3	1	4	17
1980-81	Minnesota	NHL	74	13	30	43	124	19	3	12	15	16
1981-82	Minnesota	NHL	76	17	60	77	117	4	1	2	3	14
1982-83	Minnesota	NHL	78	12	50	62	109	9	3	8	11	7
1983-84	Minnesota	NHL	26	7	7	14	37	....	....	....	....	....
1984-85	Minnesota	NHL	32	7	11	18	54	9	5	3	8	14
1985-86	Minnesota	NHL	75	10	47	57	127	5	0	1	1	2
	NHL Totals		440	80	235	315	649	61	15	27	42	70
	WHA Totals		77	9	40	49	73	....	....	....	....	....

a OHA Second All-Star Team (1977)
b OHA Third All-Star Team (1978)

HATCHER, KEVIN

Born, Detroit, Mich., September 9, 1966.
Defense. Shoots right. 6'3", 183 lbs.
Last amateur club: North Bay Centennials (OHL).
(Washington's 1st choice, 17th over-all, in 1984 Entry Draft.)

Season	Club	Lea	Regular Season					Playoffs				
			GP	G	A	TP	PIM	GP	G	A	TP	PIM
1982-83	Detroit	Midget	75	30	45	75	120	....	....	....	....	....
1983-84	North Bay	OHL	67	10	39	49	61	4	2	2	4	11
1984-85	Washington	NHL	2	1	0	1	0	1	0	0	0	0
a	North Bay	OHL	58	26	37	63	75	8	3	8	13	9
1985-86	Washington	NHL	79	9	10	19	119	9	1	1	2	19
	NHL Totals		81	10	10	20	119	10	1	1	2	19

a OHL Second All-Star Team (1985)

HAWERCHUK, DALE   (HOW-er-chuk)

Born, Toronto, Ont., April 4, 1963.
Center. Shoots left. 5'11", 180 lbs.
Last amateur club: Cornwall Royals (QJHL).
(Winnipeg's 1st choice and 1st over-all in 1981 Entry Draft.)

Season	Club	Lea	Regular Season					Playoffs				
			GP	G	A	TP	PIM	GP	G	A	TP	PIM
1979-80	Cornwall	QJHL	72	37	66	103	21	18	20	25	45	0
1980-81abc	Cornwall	QJHL	72	81	102	183	69	19	15	20	35	8
1981-82d	Winnipeg	NHL	80	45	58	103	47	4	1	7	8	5
1982-83	Winnipeg	NHL	79	40	51	91	31	3	1	4	5	8
1983-84	Winnipeg	NHL	80	37	65	102	73	3	1	1	2	0
1984-85e	Winnipeg	NHL	80	53	77	130	74	3	2	1	3	4
1985-86	Winnipeg	NHL	80	46	59	105	44	3	0	3	3	0
	NHL Totals		399	221	310	531	269	16	5	16	21	17

a QMJHL First All-Star Team (1981)
b QMJHL Player of the Year (1981)
c Canadian Major Junior Player of the Year (1981)
d Won Calder Memorial Trophy (1982)
e NHL Second All-Star Team (1985)

HAWLEY, KENT

Born, Kingston, Ont., February 20, 1968.
Center. Shoots left. 6'3", 215 lbs.
Last amateur club: Ottawa 67s (OHL).
(Philadelphia's 3rd choice, 28th overall, in 1986 Entry Draft.)

Season	Club	Lea	Regular Season					Playoffs				
			GP	G	A	TP	PIM	GP	G	A	TP	PIM
1985-86	Ottawa	OHL	64	21	30	51	96	....	....	....	....	....

HAWORTH, ALAN JOSEPH GORDON   (HAY-worth)

Born, Drummondville, Que., September 1, 1960.
Center. Shoots right. 5'10", 190 lbs.
Last amateur club: Sherbrooke Beavers (QJHL).
(Buffalo's 6th choice, 95th over-all, in 1979 Entry Draft.)

Season	Club	Lea	Regular Season					Playoffs				
			GP	G	A	TP	PIM	GP	G	A	TP	PIM
1976-77	Chicoutimi	QJHL	68	11	18	29	15	....	....	....	....	....
1977-78	Chicoutimi	QJHL	59	17	33	50	40	....	....	....	....	....
1978-79	Sherbrooke	QJHL	70	50	70	120	63	12	6	10	16	8
1979-80	Sherbrooke	QJHL	45	28	36	64	50	15	11	16	27	4
1980-81	Rochester	AHL	21	14	18	32	19	....	....	....	....	....
	Buffalo	**NHL**	49	16	20	36	34	7	4	4	8	2
1981-82	Rochester	AHL	14	5	12	17	10	....	....	....	....	....
	Buffalo	**NHL**	57	21	18	39	30	3	0	1	1	2
1982-83	Washington	NHL	74	23	27	50	34	4	0	0	0	2
1983-84	Washington	NHL	75	24	31	55	52	8	3	2	5	4
1984-85	Washington	NHL	76	23	26	49	48	5	1	0	1	0
1985-86	Washington	NHL	71	34	39	73	72	9	4	6	10	11
	NHL Totals		372	141	161	302	270	36	12	13	25	21

Traded to **Washington** by **Buffalo** with Buffalo's third round choice (Milan Novy) in 1982 Entry Draft for Washington's second round choice (Mike Anderson) and fourth round choice (Timo Jutila) in 1982 Entry Draft, June 9, 1982.

HAWRYLIW, NEIL

Born, Fielding, Sask., November 9, 1955.
Right wing. Shoots left. 5'11", 185 lbs.
Last amateur club: Muskegon Mohawks (IHL).

Season	Club	Lea	Regular Season					Playoffs				
			GP	G	A	TP	PIM	GP	G	A	TP	PIM
1977-78	Muskegon	IHL	75	37	32	69	84	....	....	....	....	....
1978-79	Muskegon	IHL	13	11	7	18	14	....	....	....	....	....
	Fort Worth	CHL	57	9	15	24	87	....	....	....	....	....
1979-80	Indianapolis	CHL	70	26	19	45	56	7	4	2	6	6
1980-81	Indianapolis	CHL	80	37	42	79	61	5	0	2	2	7
1981-82	**NY Islanders**	**NHL**	1	0	0	0	0	....	....	....	....	....
	Indianapolis	CHL	58	20	14	34	89	13	3	11	14	6
1982-83	Wichita	CHL	2	2	3	5	0	....	....	....	....	....
	Muskegon	IHL	68	33	24	57	42	4	0	1	1	4
1983-84	Muskegon	IHL	66	25	37	62	36	....	....	....	....	....
1984-85	Muskegon	IHL	80	17	22	39	93	14	4	3	5	29
1985-86	Muskegon	IHL	14	4	1	5	10	....	....	....	....	....
	Kalamazoo	IHL	68	32	23	55	67	6	1	3	4	17
	NHL Totals		1	0	0	0	0	....	....	....	....	....

Signed as free agent by **NY Islanders**, October 10, 1978.

HEADON, PETER

Born, Marystown, Nfld., January 18, 1967.
Center. Shoots left. 6'1", 180 lbs.
Last amateur club: Boston University Terriers (H.E.).
(Edmonton's 10th choice, 230th overall, in 1985 Entry Draft.)

Season	Club	Lea	Regular Season					Playoffs				
			GP	G	A	TP	PIM	GP	G	A	TP	PIM
1985-86	Boston U.	H.E.	2	0	0	0	0	....	....	....	....	....

HEATH, RANDY

Born, Vancouver, B.C., November 11, 1964.
Left wing. Shoots left. 5'8", 160 lbs.
Last amateur club: Portland Winter Hawks (WHL)
(NY Rangers' 2nd choice, 33rd over-all, in 1983 Entry Draft.)

Season	Club	Lea	Regular Season					Playoffs				
			GP	G	A	TP	PIM	GP	G	A	TP	PIM
1981-82	Portland	WHL	65	52	47	99	65	15	13	19	32	4
1982-83a	Portland	WHL	72	82	69	151	52	14	6	12	18	12
1983-84b	Portland	WHL	60	44	46	90	107	14	9	12	21	10
1984-85	**NY Rangers**	**NHL**	12	2	3	5	15	....	....	....	....	....
	New Haven	AHL	60	23	26	49	29	....	....	....	....	....
1985-86	**NY Rangers**	**NHL**	1	0	1	1	0	....	....	....	....	....
	New Haven	AHL	77	36	38	74	53	5	3	2	5	7
	NHL Totals		13	2	4	6	15	....	....	....	....	....

a WHL First All-Star Team (1983)
b WHL First All-Star Team, West Division (1984)

HEFFERNAN, KEVIN

Born, Weymouth, Mass., January 18, 1966.
Center. Shoots left. 6'1", 185 lbs.
Last amateur club: Northeastern University Huskies (H.E.).
(Boston's 9th choice, 186th overall, in 1984 Entry Draft.)

Season	Club	Lea	Regular Season					Playoffs				
			GP	G	A	TP	PIM	GP	G	A	TP	PIM
1984-85	Northeastern	ECAC	38	18	25	43	20	....	....	....	....	....
1985-86	Northeastern	ECAC	35	8	21	29	12	....	....	....	....	....

HELMER. TIM

Born, Woodstock, Ont., November 6, 1966.
Right wing. Shoots right. 6'1", 185 lbs.
Last amateur club: Ottawa 67's (OHL).
(Minnesota's 7th choice, 174th overall, in 1985 Entry Draft.)

Season	Club	Lea	Regular Season					Playoffs				
			GP	G	A	TP	PIM	GP	G	A	TP	PIM
1984-85	Ottawa	OHL	61	28	28	56	52	4	1	1	2	0
1985-86	Ottawa	OHL	28	13	12	25	30	....	....	....	....	....

HELMINEN, RAIMO ILMARI

Born, Tampere, Finland, March 11, 1964.
Center. Shoots left. 6', 183 lbs.
Last amateur club: Ilves-Tampere (Finland).
(New York Rangers' 2nd choice, 35th over-all, in 1984 Entry Draft).

			Regular Season					Playoffs				
Season	Club	Lea	GP	G	A	TP	PIM	GP	G	A	TP	PIM
1983-84	Ilves-Tampere	Fin.	37	17	13	30	14	....	....	....	....	....
1984-85	Ilves-Tampere	Fin.	36	21	36	57	20	....	....	....	....	....
1985-86	**NY Rangers**	**NHL**	**66**	**10**	**30**	**40**	**10**	**2**	**0**	**0**	**0**	**0**
	NHL Totals		**66**	**10**	**30**	**40**	**10**	**2**	**0**	**0**	**0**	**0**

HENDERSON, ARCHIE

Born, Calgary, Alta., February 17, 1957.
Right wing. Shoots right. 6'6", 220 lbs.
Last amateur club: Victoria Cougars (WHL).
(Washington's 10th choice, 156th over-all, in 1977 Amateur Draft).

			Regular Season					Playoffs				
Season	Club	Lea	GP	G	A	TP	PIM	GP	G	A	TP	PIM
1975-76	Victoria	WHL	31	8	7	15	205	....	....	....	....	....
1976-77	Victoria	WHL	47	14	10	24	208	....	....	....	....	....
1977-78	Port Huron	IHL	71	16	16	32	419	15	5	4	9	47
1978-79	Hershey	AHL	78	17	11	28	337	4	0	1	1	28
1979-80	Hershey	AHL	8	0	2	2	37	....	....	....	....	....
	Fort Worth	CHL	49	8	9	17	199	12	2	1	3	*58
1980-81	**Washington**	**NHL**	**7**	**1**	**0**	**1**	**28**	....	....	....	....	....
	Hershey	AHL	60	3	5	8	251	5	0	0	0	6
1981-82	**Minnesota**	**NHL**	**1**	**0**	**0**	**0**	**0**	....	....	....	....	....
	Nashville	CHL	77	12	23	35	*320	3	0	0	0	17
1982-83	**Hartford**	**NHL**	**15**	**2**	**1**	**3**	**64**	....	....	....	....	....
	Binghamton	AHL	50	8	9	17	172	....	....	....	....	....
1983-84	New Haven	AHL	48	1	8	9	164	....	....	....	....	....
1984-85	Nova Scotia	AHL	71	5	7	12	271	5	0	0	3	0
1985-86	Maine	AHL	57	4	6	10	172	5	0	0	0	24
	NHL Totals		**23**	**3**	**1**	**4**	**92**	....	....	....	....	....

Signed as free agent by **Minnesota**, July 15, 1981. Signed as free agent by **Hartford**, August 9, 1982. Signed as free agent by **Los Angeles**, August 29, 1983. Signed as a free agent by **New Jersey**, September 11, 1985.

HENRY, DALE

Born, Prince Albert, Sask., September 24, 1964.
Left wing. Shoots left. 6', 205 lbs.
Last amateur club: Saskatoon Blades (WHL).
(New York Islanders' 10th choice, 163rd over-all, in 1983 Entry Draft).

			Regular Season					Playoffs				
Season	Club	Lea	GP	G	A	TP	PIM	GP	G	A	TP	PIM
1981-82	Saskatoon	WHL	32	5	4	9	50	5	0	0	0	0
1982-83	Saskatoon	WHL	63	21	19	40	213	3	0	0	0	12
1983-84	Saskatoon	WHL	71	41	36	77	162	....	....	....	....	....
1984-85	**NY Islanders**	**NHL**	**16**	**2**	**1**	**3**	**19**	....	....	....	....	....
	Springfield	AHL	67	11	20	31	133	4	0	0	0	13
1985-86	**NY Islanders**	**NHL**	**7**	**1**	**3**	**4**	**15**	....	....	....	....	....
	Springfield	AHL	64	14	26	40	162	....	....	....	....	....
	NHL Totals		**23**	**3**	**4**	**7**	**34**	....	....	....	....	....

HEPPLE, ALAN

Born, Blaydon-on-Tyne, England, August 16, 1963.
Defense. Shoots left. 5'9", 200 lbs.
Last amateur club: Ottawa 67's (OHL).
(New Jersey's 9th choice, 169th over-all, in 1982 Entry Draft).

			Regular Season					Playoffs				
Season	Club	Lea	GP	G	A	TP	PIM	GP	G	A	TP	PIM
1980-81	Ottawa	OHL	64	3	13	16	110	6	0	1	1	2
1981-82	Ottawa	OHL	66	6	22	28	160	17	2	10	12	84
1982-83	Ottawa	OHL	64	10	26	36	168	9	2	1	3	24
1983-84	**New Jersey**	**NHL**	**1**	**0**	**0**	**0**	**7**	....	....	....	....	....
	Maine	AHL	64	4	23	27	117	....	....	....	....	....
1984-85	**New Jersey**	**NHL**	**1**	**0**	**0**	**0**	**0**	....	....	....	....	....
	Maine	AHL	80	7	17	24	125	11	0	3	3	30
1985-86	**New Jersey**	**NHL**	**1**	**0**	**0**	**0**	**0**	....	....	....	....	....
	Maine	AHL	69	4	21	25	104	5	0	0	0	11
	NHL Totals		**3**	**0**	**0**	**0**	**7**	....	....	....	....	....

HERBERT, RICK

Born, Toronto, Ont., July 10, 1967.
Defense. Shoots left. 6'1", 180 lbs.
Last amateur club: Spokane Chiefs (WHL).
(Chicago's 4th choice, 87th overall, in 1985 Entry Draft).

			Regular Season					Playoffs				
Season	Club	Lea	GP	G	A	TP	PIM	GP	G	A	TP	PIM
1982-83	Regina	WHL	63	0	7	7	55	2	0	0	0	0
1983-84	Regina	WHL	58	3	18	21	78	23	1	0	1	23
1984-85	Regina	WHL	70	7	39	46	192	6	0	0	0	10
1985-86	Spokane	WHL	71	4	37	41	132	....	....	....	....	....

HEROM, KEVIN

Born, Regina, Sask., July 6, 1967.
Left wing. Shoots left. 6'0", 195 lbs.
Last amateur club: Moose Jaw Warriors (WHL).
(NY Islanders' 5th choice, 76th overall, in 1985 Entry Draft).

			Regular Season					Playoffs				
Season	Club	Lea	GP	G	A	TP	PIM	GP	G	A	TP	PIM
1984-85	Moose Jaw	WHL	61	20	18	38	44	....	....	....	....	....
1985-86	Moose Jaw	WHL	66	22	18	40	103	13	3	3	6	19

HEROUX, YVES

Born, Terrebonne, Que., April 27, 1965.
Right wing. Shoots right. 5'11", 185 lbs.
Last amateur club: Chicoutimi Sagueneens (QMJHL).
(Quebec's 1st choice, 32nd over-all, in 1983 Entry Draft).

			Regular Season					Playoffs				
Season	Club	Lea	GP	G	A	TP	PIM	GP	G	A	TP	PIM
1981-82	Laurentides	Midget	48	53	53	106	84	....	....	....	....	....
1982-83	Chicoutimi	QMJHL	70	41	40	81	44	5	0	4	4	8
1983-84	Chicoutimi	QMJHL	56	28	25	53	67	....	....	....	....	....
	Fredericton	AHL	4	0	0	0	0	....	....	....	....	....
1984-85	Chicoutimi	QMJHL	66	42	54	96	123	14	5	8	13	16
1985-86	Fredericton	AHL	31	12	10	22	42	2	0	1	1	7
	Muskegon	IHL	42	14	8	22	41	....	....	....	....	....

HERRING, GRAHAM

Born, Montreal, Que., October 27, 1965.
Defense. Shoots left. 6'0", 170 lbs.
Last amateur club: Shawinigan Cataractes (QMJHL).
(St. Louis' 6th choice, 71st overall, in 1984 Entry Draft).

			Regular Season					Playoffs				
Season	Club	Lea	GP	G	A	TP	PIM	GP	G	A	TP	PIM
1983-84	Longueuil	QMJHL	68	9	44	53	101	....	....	....	....	....
1984-85	Shawinigan	QMJHL	20	5	10	15	28	9	0	1	1	13
1985-86	Shawinigan	QMJHL	24	0	9	9	19	....	....	....	....	....
	Peoria	IHL	39	1	7	10	22	....	....	....	....	....
	Sherbrooke	AHL	24	0	9	9	19	....	....	....	....	....

Traded to **Montreal** by **St. Louis** with St. Louis' fifth-round choice (Eric Aubertin) in 1986 Entry Draft for Kent Carlson, January 31, 1986.

HICKS, GLENN

Born, Red Deer, Alta., August 28, 1958.
Left wing. Shoots left. 5'10", 180 lbs.
Last amateur club: Flin Flon Bombers (WHL).
(Detroit's 3rd choice, 28th over-all, in 1978 Amateur Draft).

			Regular Season					Playoffs				
Season	Club	Lea	GP	G	A	TP	PIM	GP	G	A	TP	PIM
1976-77	Flin Flon	WHL	71	28	31	59	175	....	....	....	....	....
1977-78	Flin Flon	WHL	72	50	69	119	225	....	....	....	....	....
1978-79	Winnipeg	WHA	69	6	10	16	48	7	1	1	2	4
1979-80	**Detroit**	**NHL**	**50**	**1**	**2**	**3**	**43**	....	....	....	....	....
1980-81	**Detroit**	**NHL**	**58**	**5**	**10**	**15**	**84**	....	....	....	....	....
	Adirondack	AHL	19	10	6	16	56	....	....	....	....	....
1981-82	Tulsa	CHL	78	14	34	48	103	3	0	0	0	7
1982-83	Birmingham	CHL	80	13	26	39	40	13	0	7	7	23
1983-84	Salt Lake	CHL	62	4	26	30	87	5	0	1	1	16
1984-85	Springfield	AHL	11	3	4	7	4	....	....	....	....	....
1985-86	Salt Lake	IHL	82	14	40	54	75	5	0	4	4	6
	NHL Totals		**108**	**6**	**12**	**18**	**127**	....	....	....	....	....
	WHA Totals		69	6	10	16	48	7	1	1	2	4

Reclaimed by **Detroit** from **Winnipeg** prior to Expansion Draft, June 9, 1979. Signed as a free agent by **Minnesota**, September 2, 1983. Signed as a free agent by **NY Islanders**, March 6, 1985.

HIDI, ANDRE LAWRENCE (HAY-day)

Born, Toronto, Ont., June 5, 1960.
Left wing. Shoots left. 6'2", 205 lbs.
Last amateur club: University of Toronto Blues (OUAA)
(Colorado's 7th choice, 148th over-all, in 1980 Entry Draft).

			Regular Season					Playoffs				
Season	Club	Lea	GP	G	A	TP	PIM	GP	G	A	TP	PIM
1979-80	Peterborough	OHA	68	30	35	65	49	14	4	8	12	31
1980-81	U. of Toronto	OUAA	22	15	18	33	...	....	....	....	....	....
	Peterborough	OHA	3	1	1	2	2	5	2	3	5	11
1981-82	U. of Toronto	OUAA	22	27	26	53	52	....	....	....	....	....
1982-83	U. of Toronto	OUAA	24	23	29	52	50	....	....	....	....	....
1983-84	U. of Toronto	OUAA	24	30	30	60	66	....	....	....	....	....
	Washington	**NHL**	**1**	**0**	**0**	**0**	**0**	**2**	**0**	**0**	**0**	**0**
1984-85	**Washington**	**NHL**	**6**	**2**	**1**	**3**	**9**	....	....	....	....	....
	Binghamton	AHL	55	12	17	29	57	3	0	1	1	5
1985-86	Binghamton	AHL	66	19	24	43	104	6	1	4	5	13
	NHL Totals		**7**	**2**	**1**	**3**	**9**	**2**	**0**	**0**	**0**	**0**

Signed as free agent by **Washington**, March 29, 1984.

HEIMER, ULLRICH (ULLIE) (HEEM-er)

Born, Füssen, West Germany, September 21, 1962.
Defense. Shoots left. 6'1", 190 lbs.
Last amateur club: Koln (West Germany).
(Colorado's 3rd choice, 48th over-all, in 1981 Entry Draft).

			Regular Season					Playoffs				
Season	Club	Lea	GP	G	A	TP	PIM	GP	G	A	TP	PIM
1981-82	Köln	W. Ger.	36	19	27	46	N/A	....	....	....	....	....
1982-83	Köln	W. Ger.	45	10	23	33	N/A	....	....	....	....	....
1983-84	Köln	W. Ger.	50	23	23	46	N/A	....	....	....	....	....
1984-85	**New Jersey**	**NHL**	**53**	**5**	**24**	**29**	**70**	....	....	....	....	....
1985-86	**New Jersey**	**NHL**	**50**	**8**	**16**	**24**	**61**	....	....	....	....	....
	Maine	AHL	15	4	7	11	16	....	....	....	....	....
	NHL Totals		**103**	**13**	**40**	**53**	**131**	....	....	....	....	....

HIGGINS, TIM RAY

Born, Ottawa, Ont., February 7, 1958.
Right wing. Shoots right. 6'1", 185 lbs.
Last amateur club: Ottawa 67's (OHA).
(Chicago's 1st choice, 10th over-all, in 1978 Amateur Draft).

			Regular Season					Playoffs				
Season	Club	Lea	GP	G	A	TP	PIM	GP	G	A	TP	PIM
1976-77	Ottawa	OHA	66	35	52	87	80	19	10	14	24	39
1977-78	Ottawa	OHA	50	41	60	101	99	16	9	13	22	36
1978-79	New Brunswick	AHL	17	3	5	8	14	....	....	....	....	....
	Chicago	**NHL**	**36**	**7**	**16**	**23**	**30**	**4**	**0**	**0**	**0**	**0**
1979-80	**Chicago**	**NHL**	**74**	**13**	**12**	**25**	**50**	**7**	**0**	**3**	**3**	**10**
1980-81	**Chicago**	**NHL**	**78**	**24**	**35**	**59**	**86**	**3**	**0**	**0**	**0**	**0**
1981-82	**Chicago**	**NHL**	**74**	**20**	**30**	**50**	**85**	**12**	**3**	**1**	**4**	**15**
1982-83	**Chicago**	**NHL**	**64**	**14**	**9**	**23**	**63**	**13**	**1**	**3**	**4**	**10**
1983-84	**Chicago**	**NHL**	**32**	**1**	**4**	**5**	**21**	....	....	....	....	....
	New Jersey	**NHL**	**37**	**18**	**10**	**28**	**27**	....	....	....	....	....
1984-85	**New Jersey**	**NHL**	**71**	**19**	**29**	**48**	**30**	....	....	....	....	....
1985-86	**New Jersey**	**NHL**	**59**	**9**	**17**	**26**	**47**	....	....	....	....	....
	NHL Totals		**525**	**125**	**162**	**287**	**439**	**39**	**4**	**7**	**11**	**35**

Traded to **New Jersey** by **Chicago** for Jeff Larmer, January 11, 1984. Traded to **Detroit** by **New Jersey** for Claude Loiselle, June 25, 1986.

HILL, ALAN DOUGLAS (AL)

Born, Nanaimo, B.C., April 22, 1955.
Left wing/Center. Shoots left. 6'1", 175 lbs.
Last amateur club: Victoria Cougars (WHL).

			Regular Season					Playoffs				
Season	Club	Lea	GP	G	A	TP	PIM	GP	G	A	TP	PIM
1974-75	Victoria	WHL	70	21	36	57	75	12	5	2	7	21
1975-76	Victoria	WHL	68	26	40	66	172	15	5	10	15	94
1976-77	**Philadelphia**	**NHL**	**9**	**2**	**4**	**6**	**27**	....	....	....	....	....
	Springfield	AHL	63	13	28	41	125	....	....	....	....	....
1977-78	**Philadelphia**	**NHL**	**3**	**0**	**0**	**0**	**2**	....	....	....	....	....
	Maine	AHL	80	32	59	91	118	12	2	7	9	49
1978-79	Maine	AHL	35	11	14	25	59	....	....	....	....	....
	Philadelphia	**NHL**	**31**	**5**	**11**	**16**	**28**	**7**	**1**	**0**	**1**	**2**
1979-80	**Philadelphia**	**NHL**	**61**	**16**	**10**	**26**	**53**	**19**	**3**	**5**	**8**	**19**
1980-81	**Philadelphia**	**NHL**	**57**	**10**	**15**	**25**	**45**	**12**	**2**	**4**	**6**	**18**
1981-82	**Philadelphia**	**NHL**	**41**	**6**	**13**	**19**	**58**	**3**	**0**	**0**	**0**	**0**
1982-83	Moncton	AHL	78	22	22	44	78	....	....	....	....	....
1983-84	Maine	AHL	51	7	17	24	51	17	6	12	18	22
1984-85	Hershey	AHL	73	11	30	41	77	....	....	....	....	....
1985-86	Hershey	AHL	80	17	40	57	129	18	2	6	8	52
	NHL Totals		**202**	**39**	**53**	**92**	**213**	**41**	**6**	**9**	**15**	**39**

Signed as a free agent by **Philadelphia**, October 22, 1976. Signed as free agent by **Edmonton**, November 10, 1982. Signed as a free agent by **Philadelphia**, October 8, 1984.

HILL, BRUCE

Born, Olds, Alberta, May 11, 1965.
Left wing. Shoots left. 5'11", 165 lbs.
Last amateur club: University of Denver Pioneers (WCHA).
(Hartford's 10th choice, 236th overall, in 1985 Entry Draft).

			Regular Season					Playoffs				
Season	Club	Lea	GP	G	A	TP	PIM	GP	G	A	TP	PIM
1984-85	Denver	WCHA	34	11	16	27	36	....	....	....	....	....
1985-86	Denver	WCHA	24	7	13	20	20	....	....	....	....	....

HILLIER, RANDY GEORGE (HILL-yer)

Born, Toronto, Ont., March 30, 1960.
Defense. Shoots right. 6', 180 lbs.
Last amateur club: Sudbury Wolves (OHA).
(Boston's 4th choice, 102nd over-all, in 1980 Entry Draft).

			Regular Season					Playoffs				
Season	Club	Lea	GP	G	A	TP	PIM	GP	G	A	TP	PIM
1978-79	Sudbury	OHA	61	8	25	33	173	10	2	5	7	21
1979-80	Sudbury	OHA	60	16	49	65	143	9	3	6	9	14
1980-81	Springfield	AHL	64	3	17	20	105	6	0	2	2	36
1981-82	Erie	AHL	35	6	13	19	52	....	....	....	....	....
	Boston	**NHL**	**25**	**0**	**8**	**8**	**29**	**8**	**0**	**1**	**1**	**16**
1982-83	**Boston**	**NHL**	**70**	**0**	**10**	**10**	**99**	**3**	**0**	**0**	**0**	**4**
1983-84	**Boston**	**NHL**	**69**	**3**	**12**	**15**	**125**	....	....	....	....	....
1984-85	**Pittsburgh**	**NHL**	**45**	**2**	**19**	**21**	**56**	....	....	....	....	....
1985-86	**Pittsburgh**	**NHL**	**28**	**0**	**3**	**3**	**53**	....	....	....	....	....
	Baltimore	AHL	8	0	5	5	14	....	....	....	....	....
	NHL Totals		**237**	**5**	**52**	**57**	**362**	**11**	**0**	**1**	**1**	**20**

Traded to **Pittsburgh** by **Boston** for Pittsburgh's fourth round choice in 1985 Entry Draft (later traded to Quebec), October 15, 1984.

HIRSCH, TOM

Born, Minneapolis, Minn., January 27, 1963.
Defense. Shoots right. 6'3", 195 lbs.
Last amateur club: 1984 United States Olympic Team.
(Minnesota's 3rd choice, 33rd over-all, in 1981 Entry Draft).

			Regular Season					Playoffs				
Season	Club	Lea	GP	G	A	TP	PIM	GP	G	A	TP	PIM
1980-81	Patrick Henry	MINN	23	42	35	77	....	....	....	....	....	....
1981-82	U. Minnesota	WCHA	36	7	16	23	53	....	....	....	....	....
1982-83	U. Minnesota	WCHA	37	8	23	31	70	....	....	....	....	....
1983-84	U.S. National	...	56	8	25	33	72	....	....	....	....	....
	U.S. Olympic	...	6	1	2	3	10	....	....	....	....	....
	Minnesota	**NHL**	**15**	**1**	**3**	**4**	**20**	**12**	**0**	**0**	**0**	**6**
1984-85	**Minnesota**	**NHL**	**15**	**0**	**4**	**4**	**10**	....	....	....	....	....
	Springfield	AHL	19	4	5	9	2	....	....	....	....	....
1985-86	DID NOT PLAY											
	NHL Totals		**30**	**1**	**7**	**8**	**30**	**12**	**0**	**0**	**0**	**6**

HODGE, KENNETH JR. (KEN)

Born, Windsor, Ont., April 13, 1966.
Center. Shoots left. 6'2", 190 lbs.
Last amateur club: Boston College Eagles (H.E.).
(Minnesota's 2nd choice, 46th overall, in 1984 Entry Draft).

			Regular Season					Playoffs				
Season	Club	Lea	GP	G	A	TP	PIM	GP	G	A	TP	PIM
1984-85	Boston College	H.E.	41	20	44	64	28	....	....	....	....	....
1985-86	Boston College	H.E.	21	11	17	28	16	....	....	....	....	....

HODGSON, DANIEL (DAN)

Born, Fort Vermillion, Alta., August 29, 1965.
Center. Shoots right. 5'10", 175 lbs.
Last amateur club: Prince Albert Raiders (WHL).
(Toronto's 4th choice, 83rd over-all, in 1983 Entry Draft).

			Regular Season					Playoffs				
Season	Club	Lea	GP	G	A	TP	PIM	GP	G	A	TP	PIM
1982-83a	Prince Albert	WHL	72	56	74	130	66	....	....	....	....	....
1983-84b	Prince Albert	WHL	66	62	*119	181	65	5	5	3	8	7
1984-85c	Prince Albert	AHL	64	70	112	182	86	13	10	26	36	32
1985-86	**Toronto**	**NHL**	**40**	**13**	**12**	**25**	**12**	....	....	....	....	....
	St. Catharines	AHL	22	13	16	29	15	13	3	9	12	14
	NHL Totals		**40**	**13**	**12**	**25**	**12**	....	....	....	....	....

a WHL Rookie of the Year (1983)
b WHL Second Team All-Star (1984)
c WHL First Team All-Star (1985)

HOFFMAN, MICHAEL (MIKE)

Born, Barrie, Ont., February 26, 1963.
Left wing. Shoots left. 5'11", 190 lbs.
Last amateur club: Brantford Alexanders (OHL).
(Hartford's 3rd choice, 67th over-all, in 1981 Entry Draft).

			Regular Season					Playoffs				
Season	Club	Lea	GP	G	A	TP	PIM	GP	G	A	TP	PIM
1980-81	Brantford	OHA	68	15	19	34	71	6	1	0	1	5
1981-82	Brantford	OHL	66	34	47	81	169	11	5	8	13	9
1982-83	**Hartford**	**NHL**	**2**	**0**	**1**	**1**	**0**	....	....	....	....	....
	Brantford	OHL	63	26	49	75	128	8	5	4	9	18
	Binghamton	AHL	1	0	0	0	0	3	0	1	1	0
1983-84	Binghamton	AHL	64	11	13	24	92	....	....	....	....	....
1984-85	**Hartford**	**NHL**	**1**	**0**	**0**	**0**	**0**	....	....	....	....	....
	Binghamton	AHL	76	19	26	45	95	8	4	1	5	23
1985-86	**Hartford**	**NHL**	**6**	**1**	**2**	**3**	**2**	....	....	....	....	....
	Binghamton	AHL	40	14	14	28	79	2	1	0	1	2
	NHL Totals		**9**	**1**	**3**	**4**	**2**	....	....	....	....	....

HOFFMEYER, ROBERT FRANK (BOB)

Born, Dodsland, Sask., July 27, 1955.
Defense. Shoots left. 6', 180 lbs.
Last amateur club: Saskatoon Blades (WHL).
(Chicago's 5th choice, 79th over-all, in 1975 Amateur Draft).

			Regular Season					Playoffs				
Season	Club	Lea	GP	G	A	TP	PIM	GP	G	A	TP	PIM
1973-74	Saskatoon	WHL	62	2	10	12	198	6	0	1	1	20
1974-75	Saskatoon	WHL	64	4	38	42	242	17	2	10	12	69
1975-76	Dallas	CHL	5	0	0	0	11	....	....	....	....	....
	Flint	IHL	67	3	13	16	145	4	1	1	2	5
1976-77	Flint	IHL	78	12	51	63	213	5	0	7	7	22
1977-78	**Chicago**	**NHL**	**5**	**0**	**1**	**1**	**12**	....	....	....	....	....
	Dallas	CHL	67	5	11	16	172	13	1	3	4	40
1978-79	New Brunswick	AHL	41	3	6	9	104	....	....	....	....	....
	Chicago	**NHL**	**6**	**0**	**2**	**2**	**5**	....	....	....	....	....
1979-80	New Brunswick	AHL	77	3	20	23	161	17	0	3	3	38
1980-81	Schwenningen	W. Ger.	39	22	30	52	122	....	....	....	....	....
	Maine	AHL	2	1	1	2	0	20	2	11	13	68
1981-82	Maine	AHL	21	6	8	14	57	....	....	....	....	....
	Philadelphia	**NHL**	**57**	**7**	**20**	**27**	**142**	**2**	**0**	**1**	**1**	**25**
1982-83	Maine	AHL	23	5	10	15	79	....	....	....	....	....
	Philadelphia	**NHL**	**35**	**2**	**11**	**13**	**40**	**1**	**0**	**0**	**0**	**0**
1983-84	Maine	AHL	14	3	1	4	27	....	....	....	....	....
	New Jersey	**NHL**	**58**	**4**	**12**	**16**	**61**	....	....	....	....	....
1984-85	**New Jersey**	**NHL**	**37**	**1**	**6**	**7**	**65**	....	....	....	....	....
1985-86	Maine	AHL	8	0	0	0	6	5	0	0	0	6
	NHL Totals		**198**	**14**	**52**	**66**	**325**	**3**	**0**	**1**	**1**	**25**

Signed as free agent by **Philadelphia**, November 22, 1981. Claimed by **Edmonton** from **Philadelphia** in NHL Waiver Draft, October 4, 1982. Traded to **Philadelphia** by **Edmonton** for Peter Dineen, October 22, 1982. Signed as free agent by **New Jersey**, August 15, 1983.

HOFFORD, JAMES (JIM)

Born, Sudbury, Ont., October 4, 1964.
Defense. Shoots right. 6', 190 lbs.
Last amateur club: Windsor Spitfires (OHL).
(Buffalo's 8th choice, 114th over-all, in 1983 Entry Draft).

			Regular Season					Playoffs				
Season	Club	Lea	GP	G	A	TP	PIM	GP	G	A	TP	PIM
1982-83	Windsor	OHL	63	8	20	28	173	3	0	1	1	15
1983-84	Windsor	OHL	1	0	0	0	2	....	....	....	....	....
1984-85	Rochester	AHL	71	2	13	15	166	5	0	0	0	16
1985-86	**Buffalo**	**NHL**	**5**	**0**	**0**	**0**	**5**	....	....	....	....	....
	Rochester	AHL	40	2	7	9	148	....	....	....	....	....
	NHL Totals		**5**	**0**	**0**	**0**	**5**	....	....	....	....	....

HOGUE, BENOIT (HOAG)

Born, Repentigny, Que., October 28, 1966.
Center. Shoots left. 5'10", 165 lbs.
Last amateur club: St. Jean Castors (QMJHL).
(Buffalo's 2nd choice, 35th over-all, in 1985 Entry Draft).

			Regular Season					Playoffs				
Season	Club	Lea	GP	G	A	TP	PIM	GP	G	A	TP	PIM
1983-84	St. Jean	QMJHL	59	14	11	25	42	....	....	....	....	....
1984-85	St. Jean	QMJHL	63	46	44	90	92	....	....	....	....	....
1985-86	St. Jean	QMJHL	65	54	54	108	115	9	6	4	10	26

HOLLETT, STEVE

Born, St. John's, Nfld., June 12, 1967.
Center. Shoots left. 6'1", 175 lbs.
Last amateur club: Sault Ste. Marie Greyhounds (OHL).
(Washington's 10th choice, 187th overall, in 1985 Entry Draft).

			Regular Season					Playoffs				
Season	Club	Lea	GP	G	A	TP	PIM	GP	G	A	TP	PIM
1984-85	S. S. Marie	OHL	60	12	17	29	25	16	3	4	7	11
1985-86	S. S. Marie	OHL	63	31	34	65	81	....	....	....	....	....

HOLLOWAY, BRUCE

Born, Revelstoke, B.C., June 27, 1963.
Defense. Shoots left. 6', 200 lbs.
Last amateur club: Regina Pats (WHL).
(Vancouver's 6th choice, 136th over-all, in 1981 Entry Draft).

			Regular Season					Playoffs				
Season	Club	Lea	GP	G	A	TP	PIM	GP	G	A	TP	PIM
1978-79	Billings	WHL	9	0	1	1	0	4	0	0	0	0
1979-80	Billings	WHL	49	1	9	10	6	....	....	....	....	....
1980-81	Billings	WHL	2	0	2	2	0	....	....	....	....	....
	Regina	WHL	66	6	27	33	61	11	2	5	7	4
1981-82	Regina	WHL	69	4	28	32	111	2	0	2	2	17
1982-83	Brandon	WHL	7	0	5	5	8	....	....	....	....	....
	Kamloops	WHL	51	6	53	69	82	7	1	4	5	6
1983-84	Fredericton	AHL	66	3	30	33	29	5	0	0	0	0
1984-85	**Vancouver**	**NHL**	**2**	**0**	**0**	**0**	**0**	**....**	**....**	**....**	**....**	**....**
	Fredericton	AHL	31	2	4	6	16	....	....	....	....	....
	St. Catharines	AHL	13	1	0	1	0	....	....	....	....	....
1985-86	Kalamazoo	IHL	38	7	11	18	45	....	....	....	....	....
	Peoria	IHL	29	4	13	17	47	7	2	3	5	2
	NHL Totals		**2**	**0**	**0**	**0**	**0**	**....**	**....**	**....**	**....**	**....**

HOLMES, DARIL

Born, Cornwall, Ont., February 15, 1967.
Right wing. Shoots right. 6'6", 195 lbs.
Last amateur club: Kingston Canadians (OHL).
(Philadelphia's 6th choice, 105th overall, in 1985 Entry Draft).

			Regular Season					Playoffs				
Season	Club	Lea	GP	G	A	TP	PIM	GP	G	A	TP	PIM
1984-85	Kingston	OHL	57	11	22	33	50	....	....	....	....	....
1985-86	Kingston	OHL	66	25	37	62	97	10	2	2	4	4

HOLMES, WARREN

Born, Beeton, Ont., February 18, 1957.
Center. Shoots left. 6'1", 195 lbs.
Last amateur club: Ottawa 67's (OHA).
(Los Angeles' 2nd choice, 85th over-all, in 1977 Amateur Draft).

			Regular Season					Playoffs				
Season	Club	Lea	GP	G	A	TP	PIM	GP	G	A	TP	PIM
1975-76	Ottawa	OHA	28	3	11	14	6	....	....	....	....	....
1976-77	Ottawa	OHA	36	18	29	47	31	19	11	10	21	23
1977-78	Saginaw	IHL	78	48	33	81	51	5	3	3	6	14
1978-79	Springfield	AHL	4	0	0	0	0	....	....	....	....	....
	Milwaukee	IHL	31	11	17	28	33	....	....	....	....	....
	Saginaw	IHL	38	11	18	29	30	4	1	3	4	8
1979-80	Binghamton	AHL	2	0	0	0	0	....	....	....	....	....
	Saginaw	IHL	72	37	55	92	62	7	5	3	8	21
1980-81	Houston	CHL	25	7	7	14	18	....	....	....	....	....
	Saginaw	IHL	40	21	25	46	27	13	8	9	17	19
1981-82	**Los Angeles**	**NHL**	**3**	**0**	**2**	**2**	**0**	**....**	**....**	**....**	**....**	**....**
	New Haven	AHL	73	28	28	56	29	4	1	5	6	0
1982-83	**Los Angeles**	**NHL**	**39**	**8**	**16**	**24**	**7**	**....**	**....**	**....**	**....**	**....**
	New Haven	AHL	35	17	18	35	26	....	....	....	....	....
1983-84	**Los Angeles**	**NHL**	**3**	**0**	**0**	**0**	**0**	**....**	**....**	**....**	**....**	**....**
	New Haven	AHL	76	26	35	61	25	....	....	....	....	....
1984-85	Flint	IHL	80	23	44	67	70	7	3	3	6	11
1985-86	Saginaw	IHL	65	17	20	37	88	....	....	....	....	....
	NHL Totals		**45**	**8**	**18**	**26**	**7**	**....**	**....**	**....**	**....**	**....**

HOOEY, TODD BLAKLEY

Born, Oshawa, Ont., June 23, I963.
Right wing. Shoots right. 6'1", 190 lbs.
Last amateur club: Windsor Spitfires (OHL).
(Calgary's 5th choice, I20th over-all, in 1981 Entry Draft).

			Regular Season					Playoffs				
Season	Club	Lea	GP	G	A	TP	PIM	GP	G	A	TP	PIM
1980-81	Windsor	OHA	68	18	25	43	132	11	1	1	2	31
1981-82	Windsor	OHL	68	39	62	101	158	9	6	4	10	12
1982-83	Windsor	OHL	4	0	I	I	6	....	....	....	....	....
	Oshawa	OHL	62	31	34	65	64	17	6	7	13	34
1983-84	Colorado	CHL	67	19	21	40	40	6	1	0	1	2
1984-85	Moncton	AHL	61	4	14	18	52	....	....	....	....	....
1985-86	Salt Lake	IHL	80	15	23	38	95	5	1	1	2	9

HOOVER, TIM

Born, North Bay, Ont., January 9, 1965.
Defense. Shoots left. 5'10", 165 lbs.
Last amateur club: Sault Ste. Marie Greyhounds (OHL).
(Buffalo's 11th choice, 174th over-all, in 1983 Entry Draft).

			Regular Season					Playoffs				
Season	Club	Lea	GP	G	A	TP	PIM	GP	G	A	TP	PIM
1982-83	S. S. Marie	OHL	60	6	21	27	53	16	6	5	11	13
1983-84	S. S. Marie	OHL	70	8	34	42	50	16	2	6	8	10
1984-85	S. S. Marie	OHL	49	6	28	34	29	16	0	8	8	10
1985-86	Rochester	AHL	49	2	5	7	34	....	....	....	....	....

HOPKINS, DEAN ROBERT

Born, Cobourg, Ont., June 6, 1959.
Right wing. Shoots right. 6'1", 210 lbs.
Last amateur club: London Knights (OHA).
(Los Angeles' 2nd choice, 29th over-all, in 1979 Entry Draft).

			Regular Season					Playoffs				
Season	Club	Lea	GP	G	A	TP	PIM	GP	G	A	TP	PIM
1977-78	London	OHA	67	19	34	53	70	11	1	5	6	24
1978-79	London	OHA	65	37	55	92	149	7	6	0	6	27
1979-80	**Los Angeles**	**NHL**	**60**	**8**	**6**	**14**	**39**	**4**	**0**	**1**	**1**	**5**
1980-81	**Los Angeles**	**NHL**	**67**	**8**	**18**	**26**	**118**	**4**	**1**	**0**	**1**	**9**
1981-82	**Los Angeles**	**NHL**	**41**	**2**	**13**	**15**	**102**	**10**	**0**	**4**	**4**	**15**
1982-83	**Los Angeles**	**NHL**	**49**	**5**	**12**	**17**	**43**	**....**	**....**	**....**	**....**	**....**
	New Haven	AHL	20	9	8	17	58	....	....	....	....	....
1983-84	New Haven	AHL	79	35	47	82	162	....	....	....	....	....
1984-85	New Haven	AHL	20	7	10	17	38	....	....	....	....	....
	Nova Scotia	AHL	49	13	17	30	93	6	1	2	3	20
1985-86	**Edmonton**	**NHL**	**1**	**0**	**0**	**0**	**0**	**....**	**....**	**....**	**....**	**....**
	Nova Scotia	AHL	60	23	32	55	131	....	....	....	....	....
	NHL Totals		**218**	**23**	**49**	**72**	**302**	**18**	**1**	**5**	**6**	**29**

Traded to **Edmonton** by **Los Angeles** for cash, November 27, 1984. Traded to **Los Angeles** by **Edmonton** for future considerations, May 31, 1985. Signed as a free agent by **Edmonton**, September 27, 1985.

HORACHEK, PETER

Born, Stoney Creek, Ont., January 26, 1960.
Left wing. Shoots left. 6'1", 195 lbs.
Last amateur club: Oshawa Generals (OHA).

			Regular Season					Playoffs				
Season	Club	Lea	GP	G	A	TP	PIM	GP	G	A	TP	PIM
1978-79	Oshawa	OHA	67	15	35	50	50	5	3	1	4	2
1979-80	Oshawa	OHA	68	35	67	102	43	7	4	6	10	0
	Rochester	AHL	....	....	....	....	....	4	1	3	4	0
1980-81	Rochester	AHL	63	20	26	46	61	....	....	....	....	....
1981-82	Rochester	AHL	52	8	14	22	37	6	3	4	7	0
1982-83	Rochester	AHL	1	0	0	0	0	....	....	....	....	....
	Flint	IHL	51	27	28	55	23	5	4	1	5	2
1983-84	Flint	IHL	82	34	52	86	34	8	2	3	5	12
1984-85	Flint	IHL	77	38	30	68	30	7	2	3	5	4
1985-86	Saginaw	IHL	79	21	32	53	16	11	1	2	3	2

Signed as free agent by **Buffalo**, November 2, 1979.

HORACEK, TONY

Born, Vancouver, B.C., February 3, 1967.
Left wing. Shoots left. 6'3", 200 lbs.
Last amateur club: Spokane Chiefs (WHL).
(Philadelphia's 8th choice, 147th overall, in 1985 Entry Draft).

			Regular Season					Playoffs				
Season	Club	Lea	GP	G	A	TP	PIM	GP	G	A	TP	PIM
1984-85	Kelowna	WHL	67	9	18	27	114	6	0	1	1	11
1985-86	Spokane	IHL	64	19	28	47	129	9	4	5	9	29

HORNER, STEVE

Born, Cowansville, Que., June 4, 1966.
Right wing. Shoots right. 6'1", 195 lbs.
Last amateur club: University of New Hampshire Wildcats (H.E.).
(Los Angeles' 8th choice, 177th overall, in 1985 Entry Draft).

			Regular Season					Playoffs				
Season	Club	Lea	GP	G	A	TP	PIM	GP	G	A	TP	PIM
1985-86	N. Hampshire	H.E.	30	3	5	8	14	....	....	....	....	....

HOSPODAR, EDWARD DAVID (ED)

Born, Bowling Green, Ohio, February 9, 1959.
Defense. Shoots right. 6'2", 210 lbs.
Last amateur club: Ottawa 67's (OHA).
(NY Rangers' 2nd choice, 34th over-all, in 1979 Entry Draft).

			Regular Season					Playoffs				
Season	Club	Lea	GP	G	A	TP	PIM	GP	G	A	TP	PIM
1977-78	Ottawa	OHA	62	7	26	33	172	16	3	6	9	78
1978-79a	Ottawa	OHA	45	7	16	23	218	1	0	0	0	0
1979-80	New Haven	AHL	25	3	9	12	131	5	0	1	1	39
	NY Rangers	**NHL**	**20**	**0**	**1**	**1**	**76**	**7**	**1**	**0**	**1**	**42**
1980-81	**NY Rangers**	**NHL**	**61**	**5**	**14**	**19**	**214**	**12**	**2**	**0**	**2**	***93**
1981-82	**NY Rangers**	**NHL**	**41**	**3**	**8**	**11**	**152**	**....**	**....**	**....**	**....**	**....**
1982-83	**Hartford**	**NHL**	**72**	**1**	**9**	**10**	**199**	**....**	**....**	**....**	**....**	**....**
1983-84	**Hartford**	**NHL**	**59**	**0**	**9**	**9**	**163**	**....**	**....**	**....**	**....**	**....**
1984-85	**Philadelphia**	**NHL**	**50**	**3**	**4**	**7**	**130**	**18**	**1**	**1**	**2**	**69**
1985-86	**Philadelphia**	**NHL**	**17**	**3**	**1**	**4**	**55**	**....**	**....**	**....**	**....**	**....**
	Minnesota	**NHL**	**43**	**0**	**2**	**2**	**91**	**2**	**0**	**0**	**0**	**2**
	NHL Totals		**363**	**15**	**48**	**63**	**1080**	**39**	**4**	**1**	**5**	**204**

a OHA Second All-Star Team (1979)

Traded to **Hartford** by **NY Rangers** for Kent-Erik Andersson, October 1, 1982. Signed as free agent by **Philadelphia**, July 25, 1984. Traded to **Minnesota** by **Philadelphia** with Todd Bergen for Bo Berglund and Dave Richter, November 29, 1985.

HOTHAM, GREGORY (GREG) (HOTH-am)

Born, London, Ont., March 7, 1956.
Defense. Shoots right. 5'11", 185 lbs.
Last amateur club: Kingston Canadians (OHA)
(Toronto's 5th choice, 84th over-all, in 1976 Amateur Draft).

			Regular Season					Playoffs				
Season	Club	Lea	GP	G	A	TP	PIM	GP	G	A	TP	PIM
1974-75	Kingston	OHA	31	1	14	15	49	8	5	4	9	0
1975-76	Kingston	OHA	49	10	32	42	72	7	1	2	3	10
1976-77	Saginaw	IHL	60	4	33	37	100	....	....	....	....	....
1977-78	Saginaw	IHL	80	13	59	72	56	....	....	....	....	....
	Dallas	CHL	....	....	....	....	....	5	0	2	2	7
1978-79	New Brunswick	AHL	76	9	27	36	86	5	0	2	2	6
1979-80	**Toronto**	**NHL**	**46**	**3**	**10**	**13**	**10**	....	....	....	....	....
	New Brunswick	AHL	21	1	6	7	10	17	2	8	10	26
1980-81	**Toronto**	**NHL**	**11**	**1**	**1**	**2**	**11**	....	....	....	....	....
	New Brunswick	AHL	68	8	48	56	80	11	1	6	7	16
1981-82	**Toronto**	**NHL**	**3**	**0**	**0**	**0**	**0**	....	....	....	....	....
	Cincinnati	CHL	46	10	33	43	94	....	....	....	....	....
	Pittsburgh	**NHL**	**25**	**4**	**6**	**10**	**16**	**5**	**0**	**3**	**3**	**6**
1982-83	**Pittsburgh**	**NHL**	**58**	**2**	**30**	**32**	**39**	....	....	....	....	....
1983-84	**Pittsburgh**	**NHL**	**76**	**5**	**25**	**30**	**59**	....	....	....	....	....
1984-85	**Pittsburgh**	**NHL**	**11**	**0**	**2**	**2**	**4**	....	....	....	....	....
	Baltimore	AHL	44	4	27	31	43	15	4	4	8	34
1985-86	Baltimore	AHL	78	2	26	28	94	....	....	....	....	....
	NHL Totals		**230**	**15**	**74**	**89**	**139**	**5**	**0**	**3**	**3**	**6**

Traded to **Pittsburgh** by **Toronto** for Pittsburgh's sixth round choice (Craig Kales) in 1982 Entry Draft, February 3, 1982.

HOUCK, PAUL (HOWK)

Born, North Vancouver, B.C., August 12, 1963.
Right wing. Shoots right. 5'11", 185 lbs.
Last amateur club: University of Wisconsin Badgers (WCHA).
(Edmonton's 3rd choice, 71st over-all, in 1981 Entry Draft).

			Regular Season					Playoffs				
Season	Club	Lea	GP	G	A	TP	PIM	GP	G	A	TP	PIM
1981-82	U. of Wisconsin	WCHA	43	9	16	25	38	....	....	....	....	....
1982-83	U. of Wisconsin	WCHA	47	38	33	71	36	....	....	....	....	....
1983-84	U. of Wisconsin	WCHA	37	20	20	40	29	....	....	....	....	....
1984-85	U. of Wisconsin	WCHA	39	16	24	40	54	....	....	....	....	....
	Nova Scotia	AHL	10	1	0	1	0	....	....	....	....	....
1985-86	**Minnesota**	**NHL**	**3**	**1**	**0**	**1**	**0**	....	....	....	....	....
	Springfield	AHL	61	15	17	32	27	....	....	....	....	....
	NHL Totals		**3**	**1**	**0**	**1**	**0**	....	....	....	....	....

Traded to **Minnesota** by **Edmonton** for Gilles Meloche, May 31, 1985.

HOUDA, DOUG

Born, Blairmore, Alta., June 3, 1966.
Defense. Shoots right. 6'2", 200 lbs.
Last amateur club: Medicine Hat Tigers (WHL).
(Detroit's 2nd choice, 28th over-all, in 1984 Entry Draft).

			Regular Season					Playoffs				
Season	Club	Lea	GP	G	A	TP	PIM	GP	G	A	TP	PIM
1982-83	Calgary	WHL	71	5	23	28	99	16	1	3	4	44
1983-84	Calgary	WHL	69	6	30	36	195	4	0	0	0	7
1984-85a	Calgary	WHL	65	20	54	74	182	8	3	4	7	29
1985-86	**Detroit**	**NHL**	**6**	**0**	**0**	**0**	**4**	....	....	....	....	....
	Medicine Hat	WHL	51	13	33	46	140	25	4	19	23	64
	NHL Totals		**6**	**0**	**0**	**0**	**4**	....	....	....	....	....

a WHL Second All-Star Team, East Division (1985)

HOUGH, MIKE

Born, Montreal, Que., February 6, 1963.
Left wing. Shoots left. 6', 190 lbs.
Last amateur club: Kitchener Rangers (OHL).
(Quebec's 7th choice, 181st over-all, in 1982 Entry Draft).

			Regular Season					Playoffs				
Season	Club	Lea	GP	G	A	TP	PIM	GP	G	A	TP	PIM
1981-82	Kitchener	OHL	58	14	14	28	172	14	4	1	5	16
1982-83	Kitchener	OHL	61	17	27	44	156	12	5	4	9	30
1983-84	Fredericton	AHL	69	11	16	27	142	1	0	0	0	7
1984-85	Fredericton	AHL	76	21	27	48	49	6	1	1	2	2
1985-86	Fredericton	AHL	74	21	32	53	68	6	0	3	3	8

HOULDER, BILL

Born, Thunder Bay, Ont., March 11, 1967.
Defense. Shoots left. 6'2", 195 lbs.
Last amateur club: North Bay Centennials (OHL).
(Washington's 4th choice, 82nd overall, in 1985 Entry Draft).

			Regular Season					Playoffs				
Season	Club	Lea	GP	G	A	TP	PIM	GP	G	A	TP	PIM
1984-85	North Bay	OHL	66	4	20	24	37	8	0	0	0	2
1985-86	North Bay	OHL	59	5	30	35	97	10	1	6	7	12

HOULE, KEVIN

Born, Acton, Mass., April 21, 1964.
Left wing. Shoots right. 6'3", 205 lbs.
Last amateur club: Boston College Eagles (ECAC)
(Montreal's 8th choice, 103rd over-all, in 1982 Entry Draft).

			Regular Season					Playoffs				
Season	Club	Lea	GP	G	A	TP	PIM	GP	G	A	TP	PIM
1981-82	Acton High	Mass.	21	16	54	70	0	....	....	....	....	....
1982-83	Boston College	ECAC	18	3	4	7	6	....	....	....	....	....
1983-84	Boston College	ECAC	28	5	12	17	8	....	....	....	....	....
1984-85	Boston College	ECAC	21	1	6	7	20	....	....	....	....	....
1985-86	Boston College	H.E.	41	11	9	20	20	....	....	....	....	....

HOUSLEY, PHIL (HOWZ-lee)

Born, St. Paul, Minn., March 9, 1964.
Defense. Shoots left. 5'10", l80 lbs.
Last amateur club: South St. Paul High School (Minnesota).
(Buffalo's lst choice, 6th over-all, in 1982 Entry Draft).

			Regular Season					Playoffs				
Season	Club	Lea	GP	G	A	TP	PIM	GP	G	A	TP	PIM
1981-82	South St. Paul	MINN	22	31	34	65	18	....	....	....	....	....
1982-83a	**Buffalo**	**NHL**	**77**	**19**	**47**	**66**	**39**	**10**	**3**	**4**	**7**	**2**
1983-84	**Buffalo**	**NHL**	**75**	**31**	**46**	**77**	**33**	**3**	**0**	**0**	**0**	**6**
1984-85	**Buffalo**	**NHL**	**73**	**16**	**53**	**69**	**28**	**5**	**3**	**2**	**5**	**2**
1985-86	**Buffalo**	**NHL**	**79**	**15**	**47**	**62**	**54**	....	....	....	....	....
	NHL Totals		**304**	**81**	**193**	**274**	**154**	**18**	**6**	**6**	**12**	**10**

a Named to NHL All-Rookie Team (1983)

HOWARD, TAREK

Born, Tuscon, Arizona, February 6, 1965.
Defense. Shoots left. 6'1", 185 lbs.
Last amateur club: University of North Dakota Fighting Sioux (WCHA).
(Chicago's 4th choice, 79th overall, in 1983 Entry Draft).

			Regular Season					Playoffs				
Season	Club	Lea	GP	G	A	TP	PIM	GP	G	A	TP	PIM
1983-84	North Dakota	WCHA	24	0	1	1	14	....	....	....	....	....
1984-85	North Dakota	WCHA	24	1	3	4	17	....	....	....	....	....
1985-86	North Dakota	WCHA	32	2	11	13	28	....	....	....	....	....

HOWE, MARK STEVEN

Born, Detroit, Mich., May 28, 1955.
Defence. Shoots left. 5'11", 190 lbs.
Last amateur club: Toronto Marlboros (OHA).
(Boston's 2nd choice, 25th over-all, in 1974 Amateur Draft).

			Regular Season					Playoffs				
Season	Club	Lea	GP	G	A	TP	PIM	GP	G	A	TP	PIM
1972-73	Toronto	OHA	60	38	66	104	27	....	....	....	....	....
1973-74ab	Houston	WHA	76	38	41	79	20	14	9	10	19	4
1974-75	Houston	WHA	74	36	40	76	30	13	*10	12	*22	0
1975-76	Houston	WHA	72	39	37	76	38	17	6	10	16	18
1976-77a	Houston	WHA	57	23	52	75	46	10	4	10	14	2
1977-78	New England	WHA	70	30	61	91	32	14	8	7	15	18
1978-79c	New England	WHA	77	42	65	107	32	6	4	2	6	6
1979-80	**Hartford**	**NHL**	**74**	**24**	**56**	**80**	**20**	**3**	**1**	**2**	**3**	**2**
1980-81	**Hartford**	**NHL**	**63**	**19**	**46**	**65**	**54**	....	....	....	....	....
1981-82	**Hartford**	**NHL**	**76**	**8**	**45**	**53**	**18**	....	....	....	....	....
1982-83d	**Philadelphia**	**NHL**	**76**	**20**	**47**	**67**	**18**	**3**	**0**	**2**	**2**	**4**
1983-84	**Philadelphia**	**NHL**	**71**	**19**	**34**	**53**	**44**	**3**	**0**	**0**	**0**	**2**
1984-85	**Philadelphia**	**NHL**	**73**	**18**	**39**	**57**	**31**	**19**	**3**	**8**	**11**	**6**
1985-86de	**Philadelphia**	**NHL**	**77**	**24**	**58**	**82**	**36**	**5**	**0**	**4**	**4**	**0**
	NHL Totals		**510**	**132**	**325**	**457**	**221**	**33**	**4**	**16**	**20**	**14**
	WHA Totals		426	208	296	504	198	74	41	51	92	48

a WHA Second All-Star Team (1974, 1977)
b Named WHA's Rookie of the Year (1974)
c WHA First All-Star Team (1979)
d NHL First All-Star Team (1983, 1986)
e Won Emery Edge Award (1986)

Reclaimed by **Boston** from **Hartford** prior to Expansion Draft, June 9, 1979. Claimed as priority selection by **Hartford**, June 9, 1979. Traded to **Philadelphia** by **Hartford** with Hartford's third round choice (Derrick Smith) in 1983 Entry Draft for Ken Linseman, Greg Adams and Philadelphia's first (David Jensen) and third round choices (Leif Karlsson) in the 1983 Entry Draft, August 19, 1982.

HOWSON, DONALD (SCOTT)

Born, Toronto, Ont., April 9, 1960.
Center. Shoots right. 5'11", 160 lbs.
Last amateur club: Kingston Canadians (OHA).

			Regular Season					Playoffs				
Season	Club	Lea	GP	G	A	TP	PIM	GP	G	A	TP	PIM
1978-79	Kingston	OHA	58	27	47	74	45	11	0	10	10	12
1979-80	Kingston	OHA	68	38	50	88	52	3	0	4	4	0
1980-81	Kingston	OHA	66	57	83	140	53	14	9	10	19	2
1981-82	Indianapolis	CHL	8	2	1	3	5	....	....	....	....	....
	Toledo	IHL	71	55	65	120	14	12	10	9	19	6
1982-83	Indianapolis	CHL	67	34	40	74	22	13	12	9	21	21
1983-84	Indianapolis	CHL	71	34	34	68	40	7	1	3	4	2
1984-85	**NY Islanders**	**NHL**	**8**	**4**	**1**	**5**	**2**	....	....	....	....	....
	Springfield	AHL	57	20	40	60	31	4	1	3	4	2
1985-86	**NY Islanders**	**NHL**	**10**	**1**	**2**	**3**	**2**	....	....	....	....	....
	Springfield	AHL	53	15	19	34	10	....	....	....	....	....
	NHL Totals		**18**	**5**	**3**	**8**	**4**	....	....	....	....	....

Signed as free agent by **NY Islanders**, August 25, 1981.

HRKAC, ANTHONY (TONY)　　　　　　　　　　　　(HERK-is)

Born, Thunder Bay, Ont., July 7, 1966.
Center. Shoots left. 5'11", 165 lbs.
Last amateur club: Canadian Olympic Team
(St. Louis' 2nd choice, 32nd over-all, in 1984 Entry Draft).

				Regular Season					Playoffs			
Season	Club	Lea	GP	G	A	TP	PIM	GP	G	A	TP	PIM
1983-84	Orillia	OPJHL	42	52	55	107	16	.....	.....	.....	.....	.....
1984-85	North Dakota	WCHA	36	18	36	54	16	.....	.....	.....	.....	.....
1985-86	Cdn. Olympic	...	62	19	30	49	36	.....	.....	.....	.....	.....

HRYNEWICH, TIM　　　　　　　　　　　　　　(RINN-e-WICK)

Born, Leamington, Ont., October 2, 1963.
Left wing. Shoots left. 5'11", 190 lbs.
Last amateur club: Sudbury Wolves (OHL).
(Pittsburgh's 2nd choice, 38th over-all, in 1982 Entry Draft).

				Regular Season					Playoffs			
Season	Club	Lea	GP	G	A	TP	PIM	GP	G	A	TP	PIM
1980-81	Sudbury	OHA	65	25	17	42	104	.....	.....	.....	.....	.....
1981-82	Sudbury	OHL	64	29	41	70	144	.....	.....	.....	.....	.....
1982-83	Sudbury	OHL	23	21	16	37	65	.....	.....	.....	.....	.....
	Pittsburgh	NHL	30	2	3	5	48	.....	.....	.....	.....	.....
	Baltimore	AHL	9	2	1	3	6	.....	.....	.....	.....	.....
1983-84	Pittsburgh	NHL	25	4	5	9	34	.....	.....	.....	.....	.....
	Baltimore	AHL	52	13	17	30	65	.....	.....	.....	.....	.....
1984-85	Baltimore	AHL	21	4	3	7	31	.....	.....	.....	.....	.....
	Muskegon	IHL	30	10	13	23	42	.....	.....	.....	.....	.....
1985-86	Muskegon	IHL	67	25	26	51	110	.....	.....	.....	.....	.....
	Toledo	IHL	13	8	13	21	25	.....	.....	.....	.....	.....
	NHL Totals		55	6	8	14	82	.....	.....	.....	.....	.....

Traded to **Edmonton** by **Pittsburgh** with Marty McSorley for Gilles Meloche, September 12, 1985.

HRYNEWICH, STEVE

Born, Leamington, Ont., October 9, 1966.
Left wing. Shoots left. 6'1", 190 lbs.
Last amateur club: Ottawa 67's (OHL).
(Washington's 12th choice, 229th overall, in 1985 Entry Draft).

				Regular Season					Playoffs			
Season	Club	Lea	GP	G	A	TP	PIM	GP	G	A	TP	PIM
1984-85	Ottawa	OHL	47	18	14	32	43	5	0	0	0	7
1985-86	Ottawa	OHL	59	17	19	36	65	.....	.....	.....	.....	.....

HUBER, WILHELM HEINRICH (WILLIE)　　　　(HYOO-ber)

Born, Strasskirchen, West Germany, January 15, 1958.
Defense. Shoots right. 6'5", 230 lbs.
Last amateur club: Hamilton Fincups (OHA).
(Detroit's 1st choice, 9th over-all, in 1978 Amateur Draft).

				Regular Season					Playoffs			
Season	Club	Lea	GP	G	A	TP	PIM	GP	G	A	TP	PIM
1976-77	St. Catharines	OHA	36	10	24	34	111	10	2	4	6	29
1977-78a	Hamilton	OHA	61	12	45	57	168	20	6	12	18	45
1978-79	Kansas City	CHL	10	2	7	9	12	.....	.....	.....	.....	.....
	Detroit	NHL	68	7	24	31	114	.....	.....	.....	.....	.....
1979-80	Detroit	NHL	76	17	23	40	164	.....	.....	.....	.....	.....
	Adirondack	AHL	4	1	3	4	2	.....	.....	.....	.....	.....
1980-81	Detroit	NHL	80	15	34	49	130	.....	.....	.....	.....	.....
1981-82	Detroit	NHL	74	15	30	45	98	.....	.....	.....	.....	.....
1982-83	Detroit	NHL	74	14	29	43	106	.....	.....	.....	.....	.....
1983-84	NY Rangers	NHL	42	9	14	23	60	4	1	1	2	9
1984-85	NY Rangers	NHL	49	3	11	14	55	2	1	0	1	2
1985-86	NY Rangers	NHL	70	7	8	15	85	16	3	2	5	16
	NHL Totals		533	87	173	260	812	22	5	3	8	27

a OHA Second All-Star Team (1978)
Traded to **NY Rangers** by **Detroit** with Mike Blaisdell and Mark Osborne for Ron Duguay, Eddie Mio and Eddie Johnstone, June 13, 1983.

HUDDY, CHARLES WILLIAM (CHARLIE)

Born, Toronto, Ont., June 2, 1959.
Defense. Shoots left. 6', 200 lbs.
Last amateur club: Oshawa Generals (OHA).

				Regular Season					Playoffs			
Season	Club	Lea	GP	G	A	TP	PIM	GP	G	A	TP	PIM
1977-78	Oshawa	OHA	59	17	18	35	81	6	2	1	3	10
1978-79	Oshawa	OHA	64	20	38	58	108	5	3	4	7	12
1979-80	Houston	CHL	79	14	34	48	46	6	1	0	1	2
1980-81	Edmonton	NHL	12	2	5	7	6	.....	.....	.....	.....	.....
	Wichita	CHL	47	8	36	44	71	17	3	11	14	10
1981-82	Wichita	CHL	32	7	19	26	51	.....	.....	.....	.....	.....
	Edmonton	NHL	41	4	11	15	46	5	1	2	3	14
1982-83a	Edmonton	NHL	76	20	37	57	58	15	1	6	7	10
1983-84	Edmonton	NHL	75	8	34	42	43	12	1	9	10	8
1984-85	Edmonton	NHL	80	7	44	51	46	18	3	17	20	17
1985-86	Edmonton	NHL	76	6	35	41	55	7	0	2	2	0
	NHL Totals		360	47	166	213	254	57	6	36	42	49

a Won Emery Edge Trophy (1983)
Signed as a free agent by **Edmonton**, September 14, 1979.

HUFFMAN, KERRY

Born, Peterborough, Ont., January 3, 1968.
Defense. Shoots left. 6'2", 180 lbs.
Last amateur club: Guelph Platers (OHL).
(Philadelphia's 1st choice, 20th overall, in 1986 Entry Draft).

				Regular Season					Playoffs			
Season	Club	Lea	GP	G	A	TP	PIM	GP	G	A	TP	PIM
1984-85	Peterborough	OPJHL	24	2	5	7	53	.....	.....	.....	.....	.....
1985-86	Guelph	OHL	56	3	24	27	35	20	1	10	11	10

HUGHES, PATRICK (PAT)

Born, Calgary, Alta., March 25, 1955.
Right wing. Shoots right. 6'1", 180 lbs.
Last amateur club: University of Michigan Wolverines (WCHA)
(Montreal's 6th choice, 52nd over-all, in 1975 Amateur Draft).

				Regular Season					Playoffs			
Season	Club	Lea	GP	G	A	TP	PIM	GP	G	A	TP	PIM
1974-75	U. of Michigan	WCHA	38	24	19	43	64	.....	.....	.....	.....	.....
1975-76	U. of Michigan	WCHA	35	16	18	34	70	.....	.....	.....	.....	.....
1976-77	Nova Scotia	AHL	77	29	39	68	144	12	2	2	4	8
1977-78	Montreal	NHL	3	0	0	0	2	.....	.....	.....	.....	.....
a	Nova Scotia	AHL	74	40	28	68	128	11	5	*9	*14	24
1978-79	Montreal	NHL	41	9	8	17	22	8	1	2	3	4
1979-80	Pittsburgh	NHL	76	18	14	32	78	5	0	0	0	21
1980-81	Pittsburgh	NHL	58	10	9	19	161	.....	.....	.....	.....	.....
	Edmonton	NHL	2	0	0	0	0	5	0	5	5	16
1981-82	Edmonton	NHL	68	24	22	46	99	5	2	1	3	6
1982-83	Edmonton	NHL	80	25	20	45	85	16	2	5	7	14
1983-84	Edmonton	NHL	77	27	28	55	61	19	2	11	13	12
1984-85	Edmonton	NHL	73	12	13	25	85	10	1	1	2	4
1985-86	Buffalo	NHL	50	4	9	13	25	.....	.....	.....	.....	.....
	Rochester	AHL	10	3	3	6	7	.....	.....	.....	.....	.....
	NHL Totals		528	129	123	252	625	68	8	25	33	77

a AHL Second All-Star Team (1978)
Traded to **Pittsburgh** by **Montreal** with Robert Holland for Denis Herron and Pittsburgh's second round choice (Jocelyn Gauvreau) in the 1982 Entry Draft, August 30, 1979. Traded to **Edmonton** by **Pittsburgh** for Pat Price, March 10, 1981. Traded to **Pittsburgh** by **Edmonton** for Mike Moller, October 4, 1985. Traded to **Buffalo** by **Pittsburgh** for Mike Moller and Randy Cunneyworth, October 4, 1985.

HULL, BRETT

Born, Vancouver, B.C., August 9, 1964.
Right wing. Shoots right. 5'11", 200 lbs.
Last amateur club: University of Minnesota-Duluth Bulldogs (WCHA).
(Calgary's 6th choice, 117th overall, in 1984 Entry Draft).

				Regular Season					Playoffs			
Season	Club	Lea	GP	G	A	TP	PIM	GP	G	A	TP	PIM
1983-84	Penticton	BCJHL	56	105	83	188	20	.....	.....	.....	.....	.....
1984-85	Minn-Duluth	WCHA	48	32	28	60	24	.....	.....	.....	.....	.....
1985-86a	Minn-Duluth	WCHA	42	52	32	84	46	.....	.....	.....	.....	.....
	Calgary	NHL	.....	.....	.....	.....	.....	2	0	0	0	0
	NHL Totals		.....	.....	.....	.....	.....	2	0	0	0	0

a WCHA First All-Star Team (1986)

HUNT, CURTIS

Born, North Battleford, Sask., January 28, 1967.
Defense. Shoots left. 6'0", 180 lbs.
Last amateur club: Prince Albert Raiders (WHL).
(Vancouver's 9th choice, 172nd overall, in 1985 Entry Draft).

				Regular Season					Playoffs			
Season	Club	Lea	GP	G	A	TP	PIM	GP	G	A	TP	PIM
1984-85	Prince Albert	WHL	64	2	13	15	61	13	0	3	3	24
1985-86	Prince Albert	WHL	72	5	29	34	108	18	2	8	10	28

HUNTER, DALE ROBERT

Born, Petrolia, Ont., July 31, 1960.
Center. Shoots left. 5'9", 190 lbs.
Last amateur club: Sudbury Wolves (OHA).
(Quebec's 2nd choice, 41st over-all, in 1979 Entry Draft).

				Regular Season					Playoffs			
Season	Club	Lea	GP	G	A	TP	PIM	GP	G	A	TP	PIM
1978-79	Sudbury	OHA	59	42	68	110	188	10	4	12	16	47
1979-80	Sudbury	OHA	61	34	51	85	189	9	6	9	15	45
1980-81	Quebec	NHL	80	19	44	63	226	5	4	2	6	34
1981-82	Quebec	NHL	80	22	50	72	272	16	3	7	10	52
1982-83	Quebec	NHL	80	17	46	63	206	4	2	1	3	24
1983-84	Quebec	NHL	77	24	55	79	232	9	2	3	5	41
1984-85	Quebec	NHL	80	20	52	72	209	17	4	6	10	97
1985-86	Quebec	NHL	80	28	42	70	265	3	0	0	0	15
	NHL Totals		477	130	289	419	1410	54	15	19	34	263

HUNTER, DAVID (DAVE)

Born, Petrolia, Ont., January 1, 1958.
Left wing. Shoots left. 5'11", 195 lbs.
Last amateur club: Sudbury Wolves (OHA).
(Montreal's 2nd choice, 17th over-all, in 1978 Amateur Draft).

				Regular Season					Playoffs			
Season	Club	Lea	GP	G	A	TP	PIM	GP	G	A	TP	PIM
1976-77	Sudbury	OHA	62	30	56	86	140	6	1	3	4	9
1977-78	Sudbury	OHA	68	44	44	88	156	....	....	....	....	....
1978-79	Dallas	CHL	6	3	4	7	6	....	....	....	....	....
	Edmonton	WHA	72	7	25	32	134	13	2	3	5	42
1979-80	Edmonton	NHL	80	12	31	43	103	3	0	0	0	7
1980-81	Edmonton	NHL	78	12	16	28	98	9	0	0	0	28
1981-82	Edmonton	NHL	63	16	22	38	63	5	0	1	1	26
1982-83	Edmonton	NHL	80	13	18	31	120	16	4	7	11	60
1983-84	Edmonton	NHL	80	22	26	48	90	17	5	5	10	14
1984-85	Edmonton	NHL	80	17	19	36	122	18	2	5	7	33
1985-86	Edmonton	NHL	62	15	22	37	77	10	2	3	5	23
	NHL Totals		523	107	154	261	673	78	13	21	34	191
	WHA Totals		72	7	25	32	134	13	2	3	5	42

Claimed by **Edmonton** from **Montreal** in Expansion Draft, June 22, 1979.

HUNTER, MARK

Born, Petrolia, Ont., November 12, 1962.
Right wing. Shoots right. 6', 205 lbs.
Last amateur club: Brantford Alexanders (OHA).
(Montreal's 1st choice, 7th over-all, in 1981 Entry Draft).

				Regular Season					Playoffs			
Season	Club	Lea	GP	G	A	TP	PIM	GP	G	A	TP	PIM
1979-80	Brantford	OHA	66	34	56	90	171	11	2	8	10	27
1980-81	Brantford	OHA	53	39	40	79	157	6	3	3	6	27
1981-82	Montreal	NHL	71	18	11	29	143	5	0	0	0	20
1982-83	Montreal	NHL	31	8	8	16	73	....	....	....	....	....
1983-84	Montreal	NHL	22	6	4	10	42	14	2	1	3	69
1984-85	Montreal	NHL	72	21	12	33	123	11	0	3	3	13
1985-86	St. Louis	NHL	78	44	30	74	171	19	7	7	14	48
	NHL Totals		274	97	65	162	552	49	9	11	20	150

Traded to **St. Louis** by **Montreal** with Michael Dark and Montreal's second (Herb Raglan); third (Nelson Emerson); fifth (Dan Brooks); and sixth (Rick Burchill) round choices in 1985 Entry Draft, for St. Louis' first (Jose Charbonneau); second (Todd Richard); fourth (Martin Desjardins); fifth (Tom Sagissor); and sixth (Don Dufresne) round choices in 1985 Entry Draft, June 15, 1985.

HUNTER, TIMOTHY ROBERT (TIM)

Born, Calgary, Alta., September 10, 1960.
Right wing. Shoots right. 6'2", 202 lbs.
Last amateur club: Seattle Breakers (WHL).
(Atlanta's 4th choice, 54th over-all, in 1979 Entry Draft).

				Regular Season					Playoffs			
Season	Club	Lea	GP	G	A	TP	PIM	GP	G	A	TP	PIM
1979-80	Seattle	WHL	72	14	53	67	311	12	1	2	3	41
1980-81	Birmingham	CHL	58	3	5	8	*236	....	....	....	....	....
	Nova Scotia	AHL	17	0	0	0	62	6	0	1	1	45
1981-82	Calgary	NHL	2	0	0	0	9	....	....	....	....	....
	Oklahoma City	CHL	55	4	12	16	222	....	....	....	....	....
1982-83	Colorado	CHL	46	5	12	17	225	....	....	....	....	....
	Calgary	NHL	16	1	0	1	54	9	1	0	1	70
1983-84	Calgary	NHL	43	4	4	8	130	7	0	0	0	21
1984-85	Calgary	NHL	71	11	11	22	259	4	0	0	0	24
1985-86	Calgary	NHL	66	8	7	15	291	19	0	3	3	108
	NHL Totals		198	24	22	46	743	39	1	3	4	223

HURT, STEVE

Born, White Bear Lake, Minn., March 28, 1966.
Right wing. Shoots right. 6'3", 195 lbs.
Last amateur club: Lake Superior State University Lakers (CCHA).
(Pittsburgh's 8th choice, 189th overall, in 1984 Entry Draft).

				Regular Season					Playoffs			
Season	Club	Lea	GP	G	A	TP	PIM	GP	G	A	TP	PIM
1984-85	Lake Superior	CCHA	40	6	4	10	18	....	....	....	....	....
1985-86	Lake Superior	CCHA	12	1	1	2	4	....	....	....	....	....

HUSCROFT, JAMIE

Born, Lister, B.C., January 9, 1967.
Defense. Shoots right. 6'2", 195 lbs.
Last amateur club: Seattle Thunderbirds (WHL).
(New Jersey's 9th choice, 171st overall, in 1985 Entry Draft).

				Regular Season					Playoffs			
Season	Club	Lea	GP	G	A	TP	PIM	GP	G	A	TP	PIM
1983-84	Seattle	WHL	63	0	12	12	77	5	0	0	0	15
1984-85	Seattle	WHL	69	3	13	16	273	....	....	....	....	....
1985-86	Seattle	WHL	66	6	20	26	394	5	0	1	1	18

HUSGEN, JAMIE

Born, St. Louis, Missouri, October 13, 1964.
Defense. Shoots right. 6'3", 205 lbs.
Last amateur club: University of Illinois at Chicago Flames (CCHA).
(Winnipeg's 13th choice, 229th overall, in 1983 Entry Draft).

				Regular Season					Playoffs			
Season	Club	Lea	GP	G	A	TP	PIM	GP	G	A	TP	PIM
1983-84	Ill-Chicago	CCHA	35	6	17	23	76	....	....	....	....	....
1984-85	Ill-Chicago	CCHA	37	3	7	10	44	....	....	....	....	....
1985-86	Ill-Chicago	CCHA	29	2	5	7	51	....	....	....	....	....

HUSSEY, TOM

Born, Newmarket, Ont., July 12, 1966.
Left wing. Shoots left. 6'2", 190 lbs.
Last amateur club: Rensselaer Polytechnic Institute Engineers (ECAC).
(NY Rangers' 6th choice, 140th overall, in 1984 Entry Draft).

				Regular Season					Playoffs			
Season	Club	Lea	GP	G	A	TP	PIM	GP	G	A	TP	PIM
1984-85	RPI	ECAC	15	1	3	4	10	....	....	....	....	....
1985-86	RPI	ECAC	14	1	8	9	0	....	....	....	....	....

HUTTON, DWAINE

Born, Calgary, Alta., April 18, 1965.
Left wing. Shoots left. 5'11", 180 lbs.
Last amateur club: Spokane Chiefs (WHL).
(Washington's 7th choice, 140th overall, in 1983 Entry Draft).

				Regular Season					Playoffs			
Season	Club	Lea	GP	G	A	TP	PIM	GP	G	A	TP	PIM
1982-83	Kelowna	WHL	65	21	47	68	17	....	....	....	....	....
1983-84	Regina	WHL	14	2	2	4	2	....	....	....	....	....
	Saskatoon	WHL	49	15	32	47	18	....	....	....	....	....
1984-85	Kelowna	WHL	45	35	40	75	34	5	3	1	4	2
1985-86	Spokane	WHL	20	10	21	31	35	....	....	....	....	....
	Cdn. Olympic	...	19	3	4	7	24	....	....	....	....	....

HYNES, GORD

Born, Calgary, Alta., July 22, 1966.
Defense. Shoots left. 6'1", 170 lbs.
Last amateur club: Medicine Hat Tigers (WHL).
(Boston's 5th choice, 115th overall, in 1985 Entry Draft).

				Regular Season					Playoffs			
Season	Club	Lea	GP	G	A	TP	PIM	GP	G	A	TP	PIM
1983-84	Medicine Hat	WHL	72	5	14	19	39	14	0	0	0	0
1984-85	Medicine Hat	WHL	70	18	45	63	61	10	6	9	15	17
1985-86	Medicine Hat	WHL	58	22	39	61	45	25	8	15	23	32

IAFRATE, AL

(EYE-a-FRAT-ee)

Born, Dearborn, Mich., March 21, 1966.
Defense. Shoots left. 6'3", 215 lbs.
Last amateur club: Belleville Bulls (OHL).
(Toronto's 1st choice, 4th over-all, in 1984 Entry Draft).

				Regular Season					Playoffs			
Season	Club	Lea	GP	G	A	TP	PIM	GP	G	A	TP	PIM
1982-83	Detroit	Midget	66	30	45	75	90	....	....	....	....	....
1983-84	U.S. National	...	55	4	17	21	26	....	....	....	....	....
	U.S. Olympic	...	6	0	0	0	2	....	....	....	....	....
	Belleville	OHL	10	2	4	6	2	3	0	1	1	5
1984-85	Toronto	NHL	68	5	16	21	51	....	....	....	....	....
1985-86	Toronto	NHL	65	8	25	33	40	10	0	3	3	4
	NHL Totals		133	13	41	54	91	10	0	3	3	4

IHNACAK, PETER

(in-a-CHACK)

Born, Poprad, Czechoslovakia, May 3, 1957.
Center. Shoots right. 5'11", 180 lbs.
Last amateur club: Sparta Praha (Czechoslovakia)
(Toronto's 3rd choice, 25th over-all, in 1982 Entry Draft).

				Regular Season					Playoffs			
Season	Club	Lea	GP	G	A	TP	PIM	GP	G	A	TP	PIM
1979-80	Sparta Praha	Czech	44	22	12	34		....	....	....	....	....
1980-81	Sparta Praha	Czech	44	23	22	45	....	....	....	....	....	....
1981-82	Sparta Praha	Czech	39	16	22	38	30	....	....	....	....	....
1982-83	Toronto	NHL	80	28	38	66	44	....	....	....	....	....
1983-84	Toronto	NHL	47	10	13	23	24	....	....	....	....	....
1984-85	Toronto	NHL	70	22	22	44	24	....	....	....	....	....
1985-86	Toronto	NHL	63	18	27	45	16	10	2	3	5	12
	NHL Totals		260	78	100	178	108	10	2	3	5	12

IHNACAK, MIROSLAV

(Toronto's 12th choice, 171st over-all, in 1982 Entry Draft).

Born, Poprad, Czechoslovakia, November 19, 1962.
Left wing. Shoots left. 5'11", 175 lbs.
Last amateur club: Kocise (Czechoslovakia).

				Regular Season				Playoffs			PIM
Season	Club	Lea	GP	G	A	TP	PIM	GP	G	A	TP
1984-85	Kocise	Czech.	43	35	31	66	68	....	....	....	....
1985-86	Kocise	Czech.	21	16	16	32	....				
	Toronto	NHL	21	2	4	6	27	....	....	....	....
	St. Catharines	AHL	13	4	4	8	2	13	8	3	11	10
	NHL Totals		21	2	4	6	27	....	....	....	....

ILLIKAINEN, DARIN

Born, Hermantown, Minn., April 4, 1965.
Left wing. Shoots left. 6'3", 170 lbs.
Last amateur club: University of Minnesota-Duluth Bulldogs (WCHA).
(NY Islanders' 8th choice, 121st over-all, in 1983 Entry Draft).

				Regular Season					Playoffs			PIM
Season	Club	Lea	GP	G	A	TP	PIM	GP	G	A	TP	
1984-85	Minn-Duluth	WCHA	11	1	2	3	0	....	....	....	....	....
1985-86	Minn-Duluth	WCHA	31	6	6	12	6	....	....	....	....	....

ISSEL, KIM

Born, Regina, Sask., September 25, 1967.
Right wing. Shoots right. 6'3", 185 lbs.
Last amateur club: Prince Albert Raiders (WHL).
(Edmonton's 1st choice, 21st over-all, in 1986 Entry Draft).

Season	Club	Lea	Regular Season					Playoffs				
			GP	G	A	TP	PIM	GP	G	A	TP	PIM
1985-86	Prince Albert	WHL	68	29	39	68	41	19	6	7	13	6

JACKSON, DONALD CLINTON (DON)

Born, Minneapolis, Minn., September 2, 1956.
Defense. Shoots left. 6'3", 210 lbs.
Last amateur club: University of Notre Dame Fighting Irish (WCHA)
(Minnesota's 3rd choice, 39th over-all, in 1976 Amateur Draft).

Season	Club	Lea	Regular Season					Playoffs				
			GP	G	A	TP	PIM	GP	G	A	TP	PIM
1976-77	Notre Dame	WCHA	38	2	9	11	52	....	....	....	....	....
1977-78	Notre Dame	WCHA	37	10	23	33	69	....	....	....	....	....
	Minnesota	**NHL**	2	0	0	0	2	....	....	....	....	....
1978-79	Oklahoma City	CHL	73	8	23	31	108	....	....	....	....	....
	Minnesota	**NHL**	5	0	0	0	2	....	....	....	....	....
1979-80	Oklahoma City	CHL	33	5	9	14	54	....	....	....	....	....
	Minnesota	**NHL**	10	0	4	4	18	1	0	0	0	0
1980-81	**Minnesota**	**NHL**	10	0	3	3	19	....	....	....	....	....
	Oklahoma City	CHL	59	5	33	38	67	3	0	0	0	0
1981-82	**Edmonton**	**NHL**	8	0	0	0	18	....	....	....	....	....
	Wichita	CHL	71	7	37	44	116	7	0	1	1	21
1982-83	Birmingham	CHL	4	1	4	5	8	....	....	....	....	....
	Edmonton	**NHL**	71	2	8	10	136	16	3	3	6	30
1983-84	**Edmonton**	**NHL**	60	8	12	20	120	19	1	2	3	32
1984-85	**Edmonton**	**NHL**	78	3	17	20	141	9	0	0	0	64
1985-86	**Edmonton**	**NHL**	45	2	8	10	93	8	0	0	0	21
	NHL Totals		289	15	52	67	549	53	4	5	9	147

Traded to **Edmonton** by **Minnesota** with Edmonton's third round choice (Wally Chapman) in the 1982 Entry Draft (owned previously by Minnesota) for the rights to Don Murdoch, August 21, 1981.

JACKSON, JAMES KENNETH (JIM)

Born, Oshawa, Ont., February 1, 1960.
Left wing. Shoots right. 5'9", 190 lbs.
Last amateur club: Niagara Falls Flyers (OHL).

Season	Club	Lea	Regular Season					Playoffs				
			GP	G	A	TP	PIM	GP	G	A	TP	PIM
1976-77	Oshawa	OHA	65	13	40	53	26	....	....	....	....	....
1977-78	Oshawa	OHA	68	33	47	80	60	6	2	2	4	26
1978-79	Niagara Falls	OHA	62	26	39	65	73	20	6	9	15	16
1979-80	Niagara Falls	OHA	66	29	57	86	55	10	7	8	15	8
1980-81	Richmond	EHL	58	17	43	60	42	10	1	0	1	4
1981-82	Muskegon	IHL	82	44	51	75	72	....	....	....	....	....
1982-83	Colorado	CHL	30	10	16	26	4	....	....	....	....	....
	Calgary	**NHL**	48	8	12	20	7	8	2	1	3	2
1983-84	Colorado	CHL	25	5	27	32	4	....	....	....	....	....
	Calgary	**NHL**	49	6	14	20	13	6	1	1	2	4
1984-85	**Calgary**	**NHL**	10	1	4	5	0	....	....	....	....	....
	Moncton	CHL	24	2	5	7	6	....	....	....	....	....
1985-86	Rochester	AHL	65	16	32	48	10	....	....	....	....	....
	NHL Totals		107	15	30	45	20	14	3	2	5	6

Signed as free agent by **Calgary**, October 8, 1982. Signed as a free agent by **Buffalo**, September 26, 1985.

JACKSON, JEFF

Born, Chatham, Ont., April 24, 1965.
Left wing. Shoots left. 6', 195 lbs.
Last amateur club: Hamilton Steelhawks (OHL).
(Toronto's 2nd choice, 28th over-all, in 1983 Entry Draft).

Season	Club	Lea	Regular Season					Playoffs				
			GP	G	A	TP	PIM	GP	G	A	TP	PIM
1981-82	Newmarket	OPJHL	45	30	39	69	105	....	....	....	....	....
1982-83	Brantford	OHL	64	18	25	43	63	8	1	1	2	27
1983-84	Brantford	OHL	58	27	42	69	78	2	0	1	1	0
1984-85	**Toronto**	**NHL**	17	0	1	1	24	....	....	....	....	....
	Hamilton	OHL	20	13	14	27	51	17	8	12	20	26
1985-86	**Toronto**	**NHL**	5	1	2	3	2	....	....	....	....	....
	St. Catharines	AHL	74	17	28	45	122	13	5	2	7	30
	NHL Totals		22	1	3	4	26	....	....	....	....	....

JALO, RISTO

Born, Tampere, Finland, July 18, 1962.
Center. Shoots left. 5'11", 185 lbs.
Last amateur club: Ilves-Tampere (Finland)
(Washington's 7th choice, 131st over-all, in 1981 Entry Draft).

Season	Club	Lea	Regular Season					Playoffs				
			GP	G	A	TP	PIM	GP	G	A	TP	PIM
1984-85	Ilves	Fin.	36	17	21	38	18	....	....	....	....	....
1985-86	Ilves	Fin.	30	17	31	48	30	....	....	....	....	....
	Edmonton	**NHL**	3	0	3	3	0	....	....	....	....	....
	NHL Totals		3	0	3	3	0	....	....	....	....	....

Traded to **Edmonton** by **Washington** for **Edmonton's** fourth round choice (Larry Shaw) in 1985 Entry Draft, March 6, 1984.

JAMES, VALMORE (VAL)

Born, Ocala, Florida, February 14, 1957.
Left wing. Shoots left. 6'2", 205 lbs.
Last amateur club: Quebec Remparts (QJHL).
(Detroit's 15th choice, 184th over-all, in 1977 Amateur Draft).

Season	Club	Lea	Regular Season					Playoffs				
			GP	G	A	TP	PIM	GP	G	A	TP	PIM
1975-76	Quebec	QJHL	72	14	19	33	83	15	0	6	6	52
1976-77	Quebec	QJHL	68	16	16	32	99	10	1	1	2	48
1977-78	DID NOT PLAY											
1978-79	Erie	EHL	67	14	26	40	112	....	....	....	....	....
1979-80	Erie	EHL	69	12	13	25	117	....	....	....	....	....
1980-81	Rochester	AHL	3	0	0	0	12	....	....	....	....	....
	Erie	EHL	70	3	18	21	179	6	1	3	4	30
1981-82	**Buffalo**	**NHL**	7	0	0	0	16	....	....	....	....	....
	Rochester	AHL	65	5	4	9	204	6	0	2	2	16
1982-83	Rochester	AHL	68	3	4	7	88	16	1	0	1	27
1983-84	Rochester	AHL	62	1	2	3	122	....	....	....	....	....
1984-85	Rochester	AHL	55	1	4	5	70	3	0	0	0	15
1985-86	St. Catharines	AHL	80	0	3	3	162	13	1	1	2	53
	NHL Totals		7	0	0	0	16	....	....	....	....	....

Signed as free agent by **Buffalo**, July 22, 1981. Signed as a free agent by **Toronto**, October 3, 1985.

JANNEY, CRAIG

Born, Hartford, Conn., September 26, 1968.
Center. Shoots left. 6'0", 175 lbs.
Last amateur club: Boston College Eagles (H.E.).
(Boston's 1st choice, 13th over-all, in 1986 Entry Draft).

Season	Club	Lea	Regular Season					Playoffs				
			GP	G	A	TP	PIM	GP	G	A	TP	PIM
1984-85	Deerfield	HS	17	33	35	68	6	....	....	....	....	....
1985-86	Boston College	H.E.	34	13	14	27	8	....	....	....	....	....

JANOSTIK, PAT

Born, Battleford, Sask., November 17, 1966.
Defense. Shoots right. 6'0", 170 lbs.
Last amateur club: University of Minnesota-Duluth Bulldogs (WCHA).
(NY Rangers' 4th choice, 70th over-all, in 1985 Entry Draft).

Season	Club	Lea	Regular Season					Playoffs				
			GP	G	A	TP	PIM	GP	G	A	TP	PIM
1985-86	Minn-Duluth	WCHA	26	1	2	3	4	....	....	....	....	....

JARVIS, DOUGLAS (DOUG)

Born, Brantford, Ont., March 24, 1955.
Center. Shoots left. 5'9", 170 lbs.
Last amateur club: Peterborough Petes (OHA).
(Toronto's 2nd choice, 24th over-all, in 1975 Amateur Draft).

Season	Club	Lea	Regular Season					Playoffs				
			GP	G	A	TP	PIM	GP	G	A	TP	PIM
1973-74	Peterborough	OHA	70	31	53	84	27	....	....	....	....	....
1974-75a	Peterborough	OHA	64	45	88	133	38	11	4	11	15	8
1975-76	**Montreal**	**NHL**	80	5	30	35	16	13	2	1	3	2
1976-77	**Montreal**	**NHL**	80	16	22	38	14	14	0	7	7	2
1977-78	**Montreal**	**NHL**	80	11	28	39	23	15	3	5	8	12
1978-79	**Montreal**	**NHL**	80	10	13	23	16	12	1	3	4	4
1979-80	**Montreal**	**NHL**	80	13	11	24	28	10	4	4	8	2
1980-81	**Montreal**	**NHL**	80	16	22	38	34	3	0	0	0	0
1981-82	**Montreal**	**NHL**	80	20	28	48	20	5	1	0	1	4
1982-83	**Washington**	**NHL**	80	8	22	30	10	4	0	1	1	0
1983-84b	**Washington**	**NHL**	80	13	29	42	12	8	2	3	5	6
1984-85	**Washington**	**NHL**	80	9	28	37	32	5	1	0	1	2
1985-86	**Washington**	**NHL**	25	1	2	3	16	....	....	....	....	....
	Hartford	NHL	57	8	16	24	20	10	0	3	3	4
	NHL Totals		882	130	251	381	241	99	14	27	41	38

a OHA Second All-Star Team (1975)
b Won Frank J. Selke Trophy (1984)

Traded to **Montreal** by **Toronto** for Greg Hubick, June 26, 1975. Traded to **Washington** by **Montreal** with Rod Langway, Brian Engblom and Craig Laughlin for Ryan Walter and Rick Green, September 9, 1982. Traded to **Hartford** by **Washington** for Jorgen Pettersson, December 6, 1985.

JARVIS, WESLEY HERBERT (WES)

Born, Toronto, Ont., May 30, 1958.
Center. Shoots left. 5'11", 185 lbs.
Last amateur club: Windsor Spitfires (OHA).
(Washington's 18th choice, 213th over-all, in 1978 Amateur Draft).

			Regular Season					Playoffs				
Season	Club	Lea	GP	G	A	TP	PIM	GP	G	A	TP	PIM
1976-77	Sudbury	OHA	65	36	60	96	24	6	3	2	5	7
1977-78	Sudbury	OHA	21	7	16	23	16	....	....	....	....	....
	Windsor	OHA	44	27	51	78	37	6	0	2	2	0
1978-79	Port Huron	IHL	73	44	65	109	39	7	4	4	8	2
1979-80	**Washington**	**NHL**	**63**	**11**	**15**	**26**	**8**	....	....	....	....	....
	Hershey	AHL	16	6	14	20	4	....	....	....	....	....
1980-81	**Washington**	**NHL**	**55**	**9**	**14**	**23**	**30**	....	....	....	....	....
	Hershey	AHL	24	15	25	40	39	10	3	13	16	2
1981-82	**Washington**	**NHL**	**26**	**1**	**12**	**13**	**18**	....	....	....	....	....
	Hershey	AHL	56	31	61	92	44	5	3	4	7	4
1982-83	**Minnesota**	**NHL**	**3**	**0**	**0**	**0**	**2**	....	....	....	....	....
	Birmingham	CHL	75	40	*68	*108	36	13	8	8	16	4
1983-84	**Los Angeles**	**NHL**	**61**	**9**	**13**	**22**	**36**	....	....	....	....	....
1984-85	**Toronto**	**NHL**	**26**	**0**	**1**	**1**	**2**	....	....	....	....	....
	St. Catharines	AHL	52	29	44	73	22	....	....	....	....	....
1985-86	**Toronto**	**NHL**	**2**	**1**	**0**	**1**	**2**	....	....	....	....	....
	St. Catharines	AHL	74	36	60	96	38	13	5	8	13	12
	NHL Totals		**236**	**31**	**55**	**86**	**98**	....	....	....	....	....

Traded to **Minnesota** by **Washington** with Rollie Boutin for Robbie Moore and Minnesota's eleventh round choice (Anders Huss) in the 1983 Entry Draft, August 4, 1982. Signed as free agent by **Los Angeles**, August 10, 1983. Signed as a free agent by **Toronto**, October 2, 1984.

JENNINGS, GRANT

Born, Hudson Bay,Sask., May 5, 1965.
Defense. Shoots left. 6'3", 205 lbs.
Last amateur club: Saskatoon Blades (WHL)

			Regular Season					Playoffs				
Season	Club	Lea	GP	G	A	TP	PIM	GP	G	A	TP	PIM
1983-84	Saskatoon	WHL	64	5	13	18	102	....	....	....	....	....
1984-85	Saskatoon	WHL	47	10	24	34	134	2	1	0	1	2
1985-86	Binghamton	AHL	51	0	4	4	109	....	....	....	....	....

Signed as a free agent by **Washington**, June 25, 1985.

JENSEN, CHRIS

Born, Fort St. John, B.C., October 28, 1963.
Center. Shoots right. 5'10", 160 lbs.
Last amateur club: University of North Dakota Fighting Sioux (WCHA)
(NY Rangers' 4th choice, 78th over-all, in 1982 Entry Draft).

			Regular Season					Playoffs				
Season	Club	Lea	GP	G	A	TP	PIM	GP	G	A	TP	PIM
1981-82	Kelowna	BCJHL	48	46	46	92	212	....	....	....	....	....
1982-83	North Dakota	WCHA	13	3	3	6	28	....	....	....	....	....
1983-84	North Dakota	WCHA	44	24	25	49	100	....	....	....	....	....
1984-85	North Dakota	WCHA	40	25	27	52	80	....	....	....	....	....
1985-86	North Dakota	WCHA	34	25	40	65	53	....	....	....	....	....
	NY Rangers	**NHL**	**9**	**1**	**3**	**4**	**0**	....	....	....	....	....
	NHL Totals		**9**	**1**	**3**	**4**	**0**	....	....	....	....	....

JENSEN, DAVID A.

Born, Newton, Mass., August 19, 1965.
Center. Shoots left. 6', 175 lbs.
Last amateur club: 1984 United States Olympic Team.
(Hartford's 2nd choice, 20th over-all, in 1983 Entry Draft).

			Regular Season					Playoffs				
Season	Club	Lea	GP	G	A	TP	PIM	GP	G	A	TP	PIM
1982-83	Lawrence Prep.	Mass	23	41	48	89	....	....	....	....	....	....
1983-84	U.S. National	...	61	22	56	78	6	....	....	....	....	....
	U.S. Olympic	...	6	2	7	9	0	....	....	....	....	....
1984-85	**Hartford**	**NHL**	**13**	**0**	**4**	**4**	**6**	....	....	....	....	....
	Binghamton	AHL	40	8	9	17	2	....	....	....	....	....
1985-86	**Washington**	**NHL**	**5**	**1**	**0**	**1**	**0**	**4**	**0**	**0**	**0**	**0**
	Binghamton	AHL	41	17	14	31	4	4	2	4	6	0
	NHL Totals		**18**	**1**	**4**	**5**	**6**	**4**	**0**	**0**	**0**	**0**

Traded to **Washington** by **Hartford** for Dean Evason and Peter Sidorkiewicz, March 12, 1985.

JENSEN, DAVID HENRY (DAVE)

Born, Minneapolis, Minn., May 3, 1961.
Defense. Shoots left. 6'1", 185 lbs.
Last amateur club: 1984 United States Olympic Team.
(Minnesota's 5th choice, 100th over-all, in 1980 Entry Draft).

			Regular Season					Playoffs				
Season	Club	Lea	GP	G	A	TP	PIM	GP	G	A	TP	PIM
1979-80	U. Minnesota	WCHA	33	0	5	5	32	....	....	....	....	....
1980-81	U. Minnesota	WCHA	35	0	13	13	64	....	....	....	....	....
1981-82	U. Minnesota	WCHA	32	3	13	16	68	....	....	....	....	....
1982-83	U. Minnesota	WCHA	25	4	14	18	38	....	....	....	....	....
	Birmingham	CHL	....	....	....	....	....	2	0	0	0	0
1983-84	U.S. National	...	47	3	15	18	38	....	....	....	....	....
	U.S. Olympic	...	6	0	3	3	6	....	....	....	....	....
	Minnesota	**NHL**	**8**	**0**	**1**	**1**	**0**	....	....	....	....	....
	Salt Lake	CHL	13	0	7	7	6	5	0	1	1	5
1984-85	**Minnesota**	**NHL**	**5**	**0**	**1**	**1**	**4**	....	....	....	....	....
	Springfield	AHL	69	13	27	40	63	4	0	1	1	0
1985-86	**Minnesota**	**NHL**	**5**	**0**	**0**	**0**	**7**	....	....	....	....	....
	Springfield	AHL	40	4	18	22	31	....	....	....	....	....
	NHL Totals		**18**	**0**	**2**	**2**	**11**	....	....	....	....	....

JERRARD, PAUL

Born, Winnipeg, Man., April 30, 1965.
Defense. Shoots right. 6'1", 185 lbs.
Last amateur club: Lake Superior State University Lakers (CCHA).
(NY Rangers' 10th choice, 173rd over-all, in 1983 Entry Draft).

			Regular Season					Playoffs				
Season	Club	Lea	GP	G	A	TP	PIM	GP	G	A	TP	PIM
1983-84	Lake Superior	CCHA	40	8	18	26	48	....	....	....	....	....
1984-85	Lake Superior	CCHA	43	9	25	34	61	....	....	..	....	....
1985-86	Lake Superior	CCHA	38	13	11	24	34	....	....	....	....	....

JOHANNESEN, GLEN

Born, Lac Laronge, Sask., February 15, 1962.
Defense. Shoots right. 6'2", 220 lbs.
Last amateur club: Red Deer Rustlers (Tier II)
(NY Islanders' 11th choice, 206th over-all, in 1980 Entry Draft).

			Regular Season					Playoffs				
Season	Club	Lea	GP	G	A	TP	PIM	GP	G	A	TP	PIM
1984-85	Indianapolis	IHL	51	10	19	29	130	....	....	....	....	....
	Springfield	AHL	21	1	3	4	59	....	....	....	....	....
1985-86	Springfield	AHL	78	8	21	29	187	....	....	....	....	....
	NY Islanders	**NHL**	**2**	**0**	**0**	**0**	**0**	....	....	....	....	....
	NHL Totals		**2**	**0**	**0**	**0**	**0**	....	....	....	....	....

JOHANNSON, CARL

Born, Goteborg, Sweden., February 14, 1967.
Defense. Shoots left. 5'11", 200 lbs.
Last amateur club: Vastra Frolunda (Sweden).
(Buffalo's 1st choice, 14th over-all, in 1985 Entry Draft).

			Regular Season					Playoffs				
Season	Club	Lea	GP	G	A	TP	PIM	GP	G	A	TP	PIM
1983-84	V. Frolunda	Swe.	34	5	10	15	20	....	....	....	....	....
1984-85	V. Frolunda	Swe.	36	14	15	29	20	....	....	....	....	....
1985-86	DID NOT PLAY											

JOHNSON, JIM

Born, New Hope, Minn., August 9, 1962.
Defense. Shoots left. 6'0", 190 lbs.
Last amateur club: University of Minnesota-Duluth Bulldogs (WCHA).

			Regular Season					Playoffs				
Season	Club	Lea	GP	G	A	TP	PIM	GP	G	A	TP	PIM
1981-82	Minn-Duluth	WCHA	40	0	10	10	62	....	....	....	....	....
1982-83	Minn-Duluth	WCHA	44	3	18	21	118	....	....	....	....	....
1983-84	Minn-Duluth	WCHA	43	3	13	16	116	....	....	....	....	....
1984-85	Minn-Duluth	WCHA	47	7	29	36	49	....	....	....	....	....
1985-86	**Pittsburgh**	**NHL**	**80**	**3**	**26**	**29**	**115**	....	....	....	....	....
	NHL Totals		**80**	**3**	**26**	**29**	**115**	....	....	....	....	....

Signed as a free agent by **Pittsburgh**, June, 1985.

JOHNSON, MARK

Born, Madison, Wisconsin, September 22, 1957.
Left wing. Shoots left. 5'9", 160 lbs.
Last amateur club: 1984 United States Olympic Team.
(Pittsburgh's 3rd choice, 66th over-all, in 1977 Amateur Draft).

			Regular Season					Playoffs				
Season	Club	Lea	GP	G	A	TP	PIM	GP	G	A	TP	PIM
1977-78a	U. of Wisconsin	WCHA	42	*48	38	86	24	....	....	....	....	....
1978-79ab	U. of Wisconsin	WCHA	40	*41	49	*90	34	....	....	....	....	....
1979-80	U.S. National	...	53	33	48	81	25	....	....	....	....	....
	U.S. Olympic	...	7	5	6	11	6	....	....	....	....	....
	Pittsburgh	**NHL**	**17**	**3**	**5**	**8**	**4**	**5**	**2**	**2**	**4**	**0**
1980-81	**Pittsburgh**	**NHL**	**73**	**10**	**23**	**33**	**50**	**5**	**2**	**1**	**3**	**6**
1981-82	**Pittsburgh**	**NHL**	**46**	**10**	**11**	**21**	**30**	....	....	....	....	....
	Minnesota	**NHL**	**10**	**2**	**2**	**4**	**10**	**4**	**2**	**0**	**2**	**0**
1982-83	**Hartford**	**NHL**	**73**	**31**	**38**	**69**	**28**	....	....	....	....	....
1983-84	**Hartford**	**NHL**	**79**	**35**	**52**	**87**	**27**	....	....	....	....	....
1984-85	**Hartford**	**NHL**	**49**	**19**	**28**	**47**	**21**	....	....	....	....	....
	St. Louis	**NHL**	**17**	**4**	**6**	**10**	**2**	**3**	**0**	**1**	**1**	**0**
1985-86	**New Jersey**	**NHL**	**80**	**21**	**41**	**62**	**16**	....	....	....	....	....
	NHL Totals		**444**	**135**	**206**	**341**	**188**	**17**	**6**	**4**	**10**	**6**

a WCHA First All-Star Team (1978, 1979)
b WCHA Player of the Year (1979)

Traded to **Minnesota** by **Pittsburgh** for Minnesota's second round choice (Tim Hrynewich) in 1982 Entry Draft, March 2, 1982. Traded to **Hartford** by **Minnesota** with Kent-Erik Andersson for Jordy Douglas and Hartford's fifth round choice (Jiri Poner) in the 1984 Entry Draft, October 1, 1982. Traded to **St. Louis** by **Hartford** with Greg Millen for Mike Liut and Jorgen Pettersson, February 21, 1985. Traded to **New Jersey** by **St. Louis** for Shawn Evans and New Jersey's fifth-round choice (Michael Wolak) in 1986 Entry Draft, September 19, 1985.

JOHNSON, SCOTT

Born, New Hope, Minn., October 12, 1963.
Left wing. Shoots left. 5'11", 185 lbs.
Last amateur club: Lake Superior State Lakers (CCHA).

			Regular Season					Playoffs				
Season	Club	Lea	GP	G	A	TP	PIM	GP	G	A	TP	PIM
1982-83	Lake Superior	CCHA	32	2	7	9	9	....	....	....	....	....
1983-84	Lake Superior	CCHA	39	9	13	22	32	....	....	....	....	....
1984-85	Lake Superior	CCHA	44	21	23	44	70	....	....	....	....	....
1985-86	Lake Superior	CCHA	38	21	24	45	55	....	....	....	....	....

Signed as a free agent by **Pittsburgh**, July 3, 1986.

JOHNSON, TERRANCE (TERRY)

Born, Calgary, Alta., November 28, 1958.
Defense. Shoots left. 6'3", 210 lbs.
Last amateur club: University of Alberta Golden Bears (CWUAA)

			Regular Season					Playoffs				
Season	Club	Lea	GP	G	A	TP	PIM	GP	G	A	TP	PIM
1978-79	U. of Calgary	CWUAA	24	2	4	6	81	....	....	....	....	....
1979-80	**Quebec**	**NHL**	**3**	**0**	**0**	**0**	**2**	....	....	....	....	....
	Syracuse	AHL	74	0	13	13	163	4	0	0	0	7
1980-81	Hershey	AHL	63	1	7	8	207	9	0	1	1	14
	Quebec	**NHL**	**13**	**0**	**1**	**1**	**46**	**2**	**0**	**0**	**0**	**0**
1981-82	**Quebec**	**NHL**	**6**	**0**	**1**	**1**	**5**	....	....	....	....	....
	Fredericton	AHL	43	0	7	7	132	....	....	....	....	....
1982-83	**Quebec**	**NHL**	**3**	**0**	**0**	**0**	**2**	....	....	....	....	....
	Fredericton	AHL	78	2	15	17	181	12	1	1	2	12
1983-84	**St. Louis**	**NHL**	**65**	**2**	**6**	**8**	**143**	**11**	**0**	**1**	**1**	**25**
1984-85	**St. Louis**	**NHL**	**74**	**0**	**7**	**7**	**120**	**3**	**0**	**0**	**0**	**19**
1985-86	**St. Louis**	**NHL**	**49**	**0**	**4**	**4**	**87**	....	....	....	....	....
	Calgary	**NHL**	**24**	**1**	**4**	**5**	**71**	**17**	**0**	**3**	**3**	**64**
	NHL Totals		**237**	**3**	**23**	**26**	**476**	**33**	**0**	**4**	**4**	**108**

Signed as a free agent by **Quebec**, October 1, 1978. Claimed by **St. Louis** from **Quebec** in NHL Waiver Draft, October 3, 1983. Traded to **Calgary** by **St. Louis** with Joe Mullen and Rik Wilsonk for Ed Beers, Charles Bourgeois and Gino Cavallini, February 1, 1986.

JOHNSTON, GREG

Born, Barrie, Ont., January 14, 1965.
Right wing. Shoots right. 6'1", 190 lbs.
Last amateur club: Toronto Marlboros (OHL).
(Boston's 2nd choice, 42nd over-all, in 1983 Entry Draft).

			Regular Season					Playoffs				
Season	Club	Lea	GP	G	A	TP	PIM	GP	G	A	TP	PIM
1981-82	Barrie	Midget	42	31	46	77	74	....	....	....	....	....
1982-83	Toronto	OHL	58	18	19	37	58	4	1	0	1	4
1983-84	**Boston**	**NHL**	**15**	**2**	**1**	**3**	**2**	....	....	....	....	....
	Toronto	OHL	57	38	35	73	67	9	4	2	6	13
1984-85	**Boston**	**NHL**	**6**	**0**	**0**	**0**	**0**	....	....	....	....	....
	Hershey	AHL	3	1	0	1	0	....	....	....	....	....
	Toronto	OHL	42	22	28	50	55	5	1	3	4	4
1985-86	**Boston**	**NHL**	**20**	**0**	**2**	**2**	**0**	....	....	....	....	....
	Moncton	AHL	60	19	26	45	56	10	4	6	10	4
	NHL Totals		**41**	**2**	**3**	**5**	**2**	....	....	....	....	....

JOHNSTON, JOHN TIMOTHY (JAY)

Born, Hamilton, Ont., February 28, 1958.
Defense. Shoots left. 5'11", 195 lbs.
Last amateur club: Hamilton Fincups (OHA)
(Washington's 6th choice, 45th over-all, in 1978 Amateur Draft).

			Regular Season					Playoffs				
Season	Club	Lea	GP	G	A	TP	PIM	GP	G	A	TP	PIM
1976-77	St. Catharines	OHA	65	8	20	28	146	14	0	6	6	49
1977-78	Hamilton	OHA	48	2	12	14	163	18	0	3	3	59
1978-79	Port Huron	IHL	75	5	19	24	409	6	0	1	1	21
1979-80	Hershey	AHL	69	3	20	23	229	14	0	4	4	42
1980-81	**Washington**	**NHL**	**2**	**0**	**0**	**0**	**9**	....	....	....	....	....
	Hershey	AHL	61	1	11	12	187	4	0	0	0	4
1981-82	**Washington**	**NHL**	**6**	**0**	**0**	**0**	**4**	....	....	....	....	....
	Hershey	AHL	67	4	9	13	228	5	0	0	0	22
1982-83	Hershey	AHL	76	3	13	16	148	5	0	0	0	14
1983-84	Hershey	AHL	69	1	9	10	231	....	....	....	....	....
1984-85	Fort Wayne	IHL	69	1	12	13	211	13	1	4	5	36
1985-86	Fort Wayne	IHL	78	1	13	14	176	15	0	1	1	47
	NHL Totals		**8**	**0**	**0**	**0**	**13**	....	....	....	....	....

JOHNSTONE, EDWARD LAVERN (EDDIE)

Born, Brandon, Man., March 2, 1954.
Right wing. Shoots right. 5'9", 175 lbs.
Last amateur club: Medicine Hat Tigers (WHL).
(NY Rangers' 6th choice, 104th over-all, in 1974 Amateur Draft).

			Regular Season					Playoffs				
Season	Club	Lea	GP	G	A	TP	PIM	GP	G	A	TP	PIM
1972-73	Medicine Hat	WHL	68	58	44	102	70	17	13	10	23	21
1973-74	Medicine Hat	WHL	68	64	54	118	164	5	5	0	5	10
1974-75	Greensboro	SHL	25	21	25	46	21	....	....	....	....	....
	Michigan	WHA	23	4	4	8	43	....	....	....	....	....
	Providence	AHL	23	7	10	17	35	5	0	0	0	0
1975-76	**NY Rangers**	**NHL**	**10**	**2**	**1**	**3**	**4**	....	....	....	....	....
	Providence	AHL	58	23	33	56	102	3	0	0	0	14
1976-77	New Haven	AHL	80	40	58	98	79	6	3	6	9	7
1977-78	**NY Rangers**	**NHL**	**53**	**13**	**13**	**26**	**44**	....	....	....	....	....
	New Haven	AHL	17	10	12	22	20	....	....	....	....	....
1978-79	**NY Rangers**	**NHL**	**30**	**5**	**3**	**8**	**27**	**17**	**5**	**0**	**5**	**10**
1979-80	**NY Rangers**	**NHL**	**78**	**14**	**21**	**35**	**60**	**9**	**0**	**1**	**1**	**25**
1980-81	**NY Rangers**	**NHL**	**80**	**30**	**38**	**68**	**100**	**8**	**2**	**2**	**4**	**4**
1981-82	**NY Rangers**	**NHL**	**68**	**30**	**28**	**58**	**57**	**10**	**2**	**6**	**8**	**25**
1982-83	**NY Rangers**	**NHL**	**52**	**15**	**21**	**36**	**27**	**9**	**4**	**1**	**5**	**19**
1983-84	**Detroit**	**NHL**	**46**	**12**	**11**	**23**	**54**	**2**	**0**	**0**	**0**	**0**
1984-85	Adirondack	AHL	69	27	28	55	70	....	....	....	....	....
1985-86	**Detroit**	**NHL**	**3**	**1**	**0**	**1**	**2**	....	....	....	....	....
	Adirondack	AHL	62	29	31	60	74	17	5	7	12	4
	NHL Totals		**420**	**122**	**136**	**258**	**375**	**55**	**13**	**10**	**23**	**83**
	WHA Totals		23	4	4	8	43	....	....	....	....	....

Claimed by **NY Rangers** as fill in Expansion Draft, June 13, 1979. Traded to **Detroit** by **NY Rangers** with Ron Duguay and Eddie Mio for Willie Huber, Mark Osborne and Mike Blaisdell, June 13, 1983.

JOLY, GREGORY JAMES (GREG) (JAWL-ee)

Born, Calgary, Alta., May 30, 1954.
Defense. Shoots left. 6'1", 190 lbs.
Last amateur club: Regina Pats (WHL).
(Washington's 1st choice and 1st over-all in 1974 Amateur Draft).

			Regular Season					Playoffs				
Season	Club	Lea	GP	G	A	TP	PIM	GP	G	A	TP	PIM
1972-73a	Regina	WHL	67	14	54	68	94	....	....	....	....	....
1973-74a	Regina	WHL	67	21	71	92	103	....	....	....	....	....
1974-75	**Washington**	**NHL**	**44**	**1**	**7**	**8**	**44**	....	....	....	....	....
1975-76	Richmond	AHL	3	3	2	5	4	....	....	....	....	....
	Washington	**NHL**	**54**	**8**	**17**	**25**	**28**	....	....	....	....	....
1976-77	Springfield	AHL	22	0	8	8	16	....	....	....	....	....
	Detroit	**NHL**	**53**	**1**	**11**	**12**	**14**	....	....	....	....	....
1977-78	**Detroit**	**NHL**	**79**	**7**	**20**	**27**	**73**	**5**	**0**	**0**	**0**	**8**
1978-79	**Detroit**	**NHL**	**20**	**0**	**4**	**4**	**6**	....	....	....	....	....
1979-80	**Detroit**	**NHL**	**59**	**3**	**10**	**13**	**45**	....	....	....	....	....
	Adirondack	AHL	8	3	3	6	10	....	....	....	....	....
1980-81	**Detroit**	**NHL**	**17**	**0**	**2**	**2**	**10**	....	....	....	....	....
	Adirondack	AHL	62	3	34	37	158	17	4	12	16	38
1981-82	Adirondack	AHL	36	3	22	25	59	....	....	....	....	....
	Detroit	**NHL**	**37**	**1**	**5**	**6**	**30**	....	....	....	....	....
1982-83	**Detroit**	**NHL**	**2**	**0**	**0**	**0**	**0**	....	....	....	....	....
	Adirondack	AHL	71	8	40	48	118	6	1	0	1	0
1983-84	Adirondack	AHL	78	10	33	43	133	7	0	1	1	19
1984-85b	Adirondack	AHL	76	9	40	49	111	....	....	....	....	....
1985-86	Adirondack	AHL	65	0	22	22	68	16	0	4	4	38
	NHL Totals		**365**	**21**	**76**	**97**	**250**	**5**	**0**	**0**	**0**	**8**

a WHL First All-Star Team (1973, 1974)
b AHL First All-Star Team (1985)

Traded to **Detroit** by **Washington** for Bryan Watson, November 30, 1976.

JONES, BRAD

Born, Sterling Heights, Mich., June 26, 1965.
Center. Shoots left. 6'0", 195 lbs.
Last amateur club: University of Michigan Wolverines (CCHA).
(Winnipeg's 7th choice, 156th over-all, in 1984 Entry Draft).

			Regular Season					Playoffs				
Season	Club	Lea	GP	G	A	TP	PIM	GP	G	A	TP	PIM
1983-84	U. of Michigan	CCHA	37	8	26	34	32	....	....	....	....	....
1984-85	U. of Michigan	CCHA	34	21	27	48	66	....	....	....	....	....
1985-86a	U. of Michigan	CCHA	36	28	39	67	40	....	....	....	....	....

a CCHA Second All-Star Team (1986)

JONSSON, TOMAS (YAWN-son)

Born, Falun, Sweden, April 12, 1960.
Defense. Shoots left. 5'10", 176 lbs.
Last amateur club: MoDo AIK (Sweden).
(NY Islanders' 2nd choice, 25th over-all, in 1979 Entry Draft).

			Regular Season					Playoffs				
Season	Club	Lea	GP	G	A	TP	PIM	GP	G	A	TP	PIM
1977-78	MoDo AIK	Swe.	35	8	9	17	45	2	0	0	0	4
	Swe. National		4	0	0	0	0	....	....	....	....	....
1978-79	MoDo AIK	Swe.	34	11	10	21	77	5	1	2	3	13
	Swe. National		15	2	3	5	16	....	....	....	....	....
1979-80	MoDo AIK	Swe.	36	3	12	15	42	....	....	....	....	....
	Swe. National		18	2	4	6	24	....	....	....	....	....
1980-81	MoDo AIK	Swe.	35	8	12	20	58	....	....	....	....	....
	Swe. National		19	0	2	2	2	....	....	....	....	....
1981-82	**NY Islanders**	**NHL**	**70**	**9**	**25**	**34**	**51**	**10**	**0**	**2**	**2**	**21**
1982-83	**NY Islanders**	**NHL**	**72**	**13**	**35**	**48**	**50**	**20**	**2**	**10**	**12**	**18**
1983-84	**NY Islanders**	**NHL**	**72**	**11**	**36**	**47**	**54**	**21**	**3**	**5**	**8**	**22**
1984-85	**NY Islanders**	**NHL**	**69**	**16**	**34**	**50**	**58**	**7**	**1**	**2**	**3**	**10**
1985-86	**NY Islanders**	**NHL**	**77**	**14**	**30**	**44**	**62**	**3**	**0**	**1**	**1**	**4**
	NHL Totals		**360**	**63**	**160**	**223**	**275**	**61**	**6**	**20**	**26**	**75**

JOO, FRANK (yo)

Born, Regina, Sask., January 19, 1966.
Defense. Shoots left. 6', 185 lbs.
Last amateur club: Regina Pats (WHL)
(Washington's 8th choice, 164th over-all, in 1984 Entry Draft).

			Regular Season					Playoffs				
Season	Club	Lea	GP	G	A	TP	PIM	GP	G	A	TP	PIM
1983-84	Regina	WHL	50	2	7	9	90	17	0	1	1	15
1984-85	Regina	WHL	68	1	9	10	125	8	0	4	4	16
1985-86	Regina	WHL	22	1	8	9	39	10	0	1	1	19

JOSEPH, FABIAN

Born, Sydney, N.S., December 5, 1965.
Center. Shoots left. 5'8", 165 lbs.
Last amateur club: Canadian Olympic Team.
(Toronto's 5th choice, 109th over-all, in 1984 Entry Draft).

			Regular Season					Playoffs				
Season	Club	Lea	GP	G	A	TP	PIM	GP	G	A	TP	PIM
1982-83	Victoria	WHL	69	42	48	90	50	12	4	7	11	9
1983-84	Victoria	WHL	72	52	75	127	27	....	....	....	....	....
1984-85	Toronto	OHL	60	32	43	75	16	5	2	4	6	14
1985-86	Cdn. Olympic	...	71	26	18	44	51	....	....	....	....	....

JOYCE, ROBERT THOMAS (BOBBY)

Born, St. John, N.B., July 11, 1966.
Center. Shoots left. 6'1", 190 lbs.
Last amateur club: University of North Dakota Fighting Sioux (WCHA).
(Boston's 4th choice, 82nd over-all, in 1984 Entry Draft).

			Regular Season					Playoffs			
Season	Club	Lea	GP	G	A	TP	PIM	GP	G	A	TP	PIM
1984-85	North Dakota	WCHA	41	18	16	34	10	....	....	....	....	....
1985-86	North Dakota	WCHA	38	31	28	59	40	....	....	....	....	....

JULIEN, CLAUDE

Born, Blind River, Ont., April 23, 1960.
Defense. Shoots right. 5'11", 195 lbs.
Last amateur club: Windsor Spitfires (OHA).

			Regular Season					Playoffs			
Season	Club	Lea	GP	G	A	TP	PIM	GP	G	A	TP	PIM
1979-80	Windsor	OHA	68	14	37	51	148	16	5	11	16	23
1980-81	Windsor	OHA	3	1	1	2	21	....	....	....	....	....
	Port Huron	IHL	77	15	40	55	153	4	1	1	2	4
1981-82	Salt Lake	CHL	70	4	18	22	134	5	1	4	5	0
1982-83	Salt Lake	CHL	76	14	47	61	176	6	3	3	6	16
1983-84	Milwaukee	IHL	5	0	3	3	2	....	....	....	....	....
	Fredericton	AHL	57	7	22	29	58	7	0	4	4	6
1984-85	**Quebec**	**NHL**	1	0	0	0	0	....	....	....	....	....
	Fredericton	AHL	77	6	28	34	97	6	2	4	6	13
1985-86	**Quebec**	**NHL**	13	0	1	1	25	....	....	....	....	....
	Fredericton	AHL	49	3	18	21	74	6	1	4	5	19
	NHL Totals		14	0	1	1	25	....	....	....	....	....

Signed as free agent by **St. Louis**, September 28, 1981. Rights transferred to **Quebec** by St. Louis with rights to Gord Donnelly when St. Louis signed Jacques Demers as coach, August 19, 1983.

KAESE, TRENT

Born, Nanaimo, B.C., September 9, 1967.
Right wing. Shoots right. 5'11", 205 lbs.
Last amateur club: Lethbridge Broncos (WHL).
(Buffalo's 8th choice, 161st overall, in 1985 Entry Draft).

			Regular Season					Playoffs			
Season	Club	Lea	GP	G	A	TP	PIM	GP	G	A	TP	PIM
1983-84	Lethbridge	WHL	64	6	6	12	33	1	0	0	0	0
1984-85	Lethbridge	WHL	67	20	18	38	107	4	0	1	1	7
1985-86	Lethbridge	WHL	67	24	41	65	67	10	5	3	8	8

KARALIS, TOM

Born, Montreal, Que., May 24, 1964.
Defense. Shoots left. 6'1", 205 lbs.
Last amateur club: Drummondville Voltigeurs (QMJHL).

			Regular Season					Playoffs			
Season	Club	Lea	GP	G	A	TP	PIM	GP	G	A	TP	PIM
1981-82	Shawinigan	QMJHL	42	0	5	5	107	14	2	8	10	29
1982-83	Drummondville	QMJHL	64	6	11	17	218	....	....	....	....	....
1983-84	Drummondville	QMJHL	67	16	37	53	316	10	2	6	8	28
1984-85	Drummondville	QMJHL	64	21	59	80	184	9	0	7	7	12
1985-86	Fredericton	AHL	51	4	8	12	106	....	....	....	....	....
	Muskegon	IHL	21	5	8	13	81	11	1	3	4	32

Signed as a free agent by **Quebec**, June 6, 1985.

KARDUM, NEVIN

Born, Toronto, Ont., March 30, 1967.
Center. Shoots left. 6'1", 190 lbs.
Last amateur club: Providence College Friars (H.E.).
(Winnipeg's 9th choice, 186th overall, in 1985 Entry Draft).

			Regular Season					Playoffs			
Season	Club	Lea	GP	G	A	TP	PIM	GP	G	A	TP	PIM
1985-86	Providence	H.E.	12	1	0	1	0	....	....	....	....	....

KASPER, STEPHEN NEIL (STEVE)

Born, Montreal, Que., September 28, 1961.
Center. Shoots left. 5'8", 160 lbs.
Last amateur club: Sorel Black Hawks (QJHL).
(Boston's 3rd choice, 81st over-all, in 1980 Entry Draft).

			Regular Season					Playoffs			
Season	Club	Lea	GP	G	A	TP	PIM	GP	G	A	TP	PIM
1978-79	Verdun	QJHL	67	37	67	104	53	11	7	6	13	22
1979-80	Sorel	QJHL	70	57	65	122	117	....	....	....	....	....
1980-81	**Boston**	**NHL**	76	21	35	56	94	3	0	1	1	0
1981-82a	**Boston**	**NHL**	73	20	31	51	72	11	3	6	9	22
1982-83	**Boston**	**NHL**	24	2	6	8	24	12	2	1	3	10
1983-84	**Boston**	**NHL**	27	3	11	14	19	3	0	0	0	7
1984-85	**Boston**	**NHL**	77	16	24	40	33	5	1	0	1	9
1985-86	**Boston**	**NHL**	80	17	23	40	73	3	1	0	1	4
	NHL Totals		357	79	130	209	315	37	7	8	15	52

a Won Frank J. Selke Trophy (1982)

KASTELIC, EDWARD (ED)

Born, Toronto, Ont., January 29, 1964.
Right wing. Shoots right. 6'2", 200 lbs.
Last amateur club: London Knights (OHL).
(Washington's 4th choice, 110th over-all, in 1982 Entry Draft).

			Regular Season					Playoffs			
Season	Club	Lea	GP	G	A	TP	PIM	GP	G	A	TP	PIM
1981-82	London	OHL	68	5	18	23	63	4	0	1	1	4
1982-83	London	OHL	68	12	11	23	96	3	0	0	0	5
1983-84	London	OHL	68	17	16	33	218	8	0	2	2	41
1984-85	Moncton	AHL	62	5	11	16	187	....	....	....	....	....
	Binghamton	AHL	4	0	0	0	7	....	....	....	....	....
	Fort Wayne	IHL	5	1	0	1	37	....	....	....	....	....
1985-86	**Washington**	**NHL**	15	0	0	0	73	....	....	....	....	....
	Binghamton	AHL	23	7	9	16	76	....	....	....	....	....
	NHL Totals		15	0	0	0	73	....	....	....	....	....

KEANE, MIKE

Born, Winnipeg, Man., May 29, 1967.
Right wing. Shoots right. 6'0", 180 lbs.
Last amateur club: Moose Jaw Warriors (WHL).

			Regular Season					Playoffs			
Season	Club	Lea	GP	G	A	TP	PIM	GP	G	A	TP	PIM
1984-85	Moose Jaw	WHL	65	17	26	43	141	....	....	....	....	....
1985-86	Moose Jaw	WHL	67	34	49	83	162	13	6	8	14	9

Signed as a free agent by **Montreal**, September 25, 1985.

KELFER, MICHAEL (MIKE)

Born, Peabody, Mass., January 2, 1967.
Center. Shoots right. 5'10", 180 lbs.
Last amateur club: Boston University Terriers (H.E.).
(Minnesota's 5th choice, 132nd overall, in 1985 Entry Draft).

			Regular Season					Playoffs			
Season	Club	Lea	GP	G	A	TP	PIM	GP	G	A	TP	PIM
1985-86	Boston U.	H.E.	39	13	14	27	40	....	....	....	....	....

KELLER, DONALD (DON)

Born, Rocky Mountain House, Alta., December 4, 1961.
Left wing. Shoots left. 5'11", 195 lbs.
Last amateur club: Calgary Wranglers (WHL).

			Regular Season					Playoffs			
Season	Club	Lea	GP	G	A	TP	PIM	GP	G	A	TP	PIM
1980-81	Calgary	WHL	67	31	31	62	306	....	....	....	....	....
1981-82	Rochester	AHL	67	3	11	14	228	6	0	1	1	17
1982-83	Rochester	AHL	49	7	4	11	99	9	2	0	2	19
1983-84	Flint	IHL	29	6	8	14	93	....	....	....	....	....
	Peoria	IHL	13	4	7	11	56	....	....	....	....	....
	Rochester	AHL	3	0	0	0	0	....	....	....	....	....
1984-85	Peoria	IHL	75	21	27	48	140	9	2	1	3	30
1985-86	Peoria	IHL	31	8	4	12	80	....	....	....	....	....
	Muskegon	IHL	38	9	12	21	108	14	1	5	6	57

Signed as free agent by **Buffalo**, July 30, 1981.

KELLIN, TONY

Born, Grand Rapids, Minn., March 19, 1963.
Defense. Shoots right. 6'2", 195 lbs.
Last amateur club: University of Minnesota Gophers (WCHA).
(Washington's 3rd choice, 68th over-all, in 1981 Entry Draft).

			Regular Season					Playoffs			
Season	Club	Lea	GP	G	A	TP	PIM	GP	G	A	TP	PIM
1981-82	Grand Rapids	Minn	20	22	18	40	30	....	....	....	....	....
1982-83	U. Minnesota	WCHA	26	6	3	9	18	....	....	....	....	....
1983-84	U. Minnesota	WCHA	38	12	21	33	66	....	....	....	....	....
1984-85a	U. Minnesota	WCHA	32	3	15	18	70	....	....	....	....	....
1985-86	U. Minnesota	WCHA	44	10	24	34	61	....	....	....	....	....

a WCHA Second All-Star Team (1985)

KELLY, JOHN PAUL

Born, Edmonton, Alta., November 15, 1959.
Left wing. Shoots left. 6'1", 215 lbs.
Last amateur club: New Westminster Bruins (WHL).
(Los Angeles' 4th choice, 50th over-all, in 1979 Entry Draft).

			Regular Season					Playoffs			
Season	Club	Lea	GP	G	A	TP	PIM	GP	G	A	TP	PIM
1976-77	N. Westminster	WHL	68	35	24	59	62	5	2	2	4	0
1977-78	N. Westminster	WHL	70	26	30	56	124	20	10	15	25	51
1978-79	N. Westminster	WHL	70	25	22	47	207	5	0	1	1	15
1979-80	**Los Angeles**	**NHL**	40	2	5	7	28	3	0	0	0	2
1980-81	Houston	CHL	33	11	17	28	31	....	....	....	....	....
	Rochester	AHL	16	5	10	15	32	....	....	....	....	....
	Los Angeles	**NHL**	19	3	6	9	8	4	0	1	1	25
1981-82	**Los Angeles**	**NHL**	70	12	11	23	100	10	1	0	1	14
1982-83	**Los Angeles**	**NHL**	65	16	15	31	52	....	....	....	....	....
1983-84	**Los Angeles**	**NHL**	72	7	14	21	73	....	....	....	....	....
1984-85	**Los Angeles**	**NHL**	73	8	10	18	55	1	0	0	0	0
1985-86	**Los Angeles**	**NHL**	61	6	9	15	50	....	....	....	....	....
	NHL Totals		400	54	70	124	366	18	1	1	2	41

KEMPTHORNE, BRAD

Born, Boisevain, Man., May 2, 1960.
Center. Shoots right. 6'2", 190 lbs.
Last amateur club: Medicine Hat Tigers (WHL).
(Atlanta's 6th choice, 96th over-all, in 1979 Entry Draft).

				Regular Season					Playoffs			
Season	Club	Lea	GP	G	A	TP	PIM	GP	G	A	TP	PIM
1978-79	Brandon	WHL	56	22	31	53	89	....	....	....	....	....
1979-80	Medicine Hat	WHL	67	39	52	91	81	....	....	....	....	....
1980-81	Muskegon	IHL	13	3	7	10	42	....	....	....	....	....
	Birmingham	CHL	44	10	25	35	65	....	....	....	....	....
	Rochester	AHL	15	1	8	9	6	....	....	....	....	....
1981-82	Oklahoma City	CHL	72	17	29	46	78	4	0	0	0	5
1982-83	Peoria	IHL	69	39	65	104	101	....	....	....	....	....
	Colorado	CHL	3	0	0	0	0	....	....	....	....	....
1983-84	Peoria	IHL	80	15	47	62	47	....	....	....	....	....
1984-85	Peoria	IHL	70	13	45	58	60	20	4	8	12	21
1985-86	Peoria	IHL	45	9	26	35	27	10	1	3	4	8

KENNEDY, EDWARD (DEAN)

Born, Redver, Sask., January 18, 1963.
Defense. Shoots right. 6'2", 190 lbs.
Last amateur club: Brandon Wheat Kings (WHL).
(Los Angeles' 2nd choice, 39th over-all, in 1981 Entry Draft).

				Regular Season					Playoffs			
Season	Club	Lea	GP	G	A	TP	PIM	GP	G	A	TP	PIM
1980-81	Brandon	WHL	71	3	29	32	157	5	0	2	2	7
1981-82	Brandon	WHL	49	5	38	43	103	....	....	....	....	....
1982-83	Brandon	WHL	14	2	15	17	22	....	....	....	....	....
	Los Angeles	NHL	55	0	12	12	97	....	....	....	....	....
	Saskatoon	WHL	....	....	....	....	....	4	0	3	3	0
1983-84	Los Angeles	NHL	37	1	5	6	50	....	....	....	....	....
	New Haven	AHL	26	1	7	8	23	....	....	....	....	....
1984-85	New Haven	AHL	76	3	14	17	104	....	....	....	....	....
1985-86	Los Angeles	NHL	78	2	10	12	132	....	....	....	....	....
	NHL Totals		170	3	27	30	279	....	....	....	....	....

KERR, ALAN

Born, Hazelton, B.C., March 28, 1964.
Left wing. Shoots right. 5'11", 180 lbs.
Last amateur club: Seattle Breakers (WHL).
(NY Islanders' 4th choice, 84th over-all, in 1982 Entry Draft).

				Regular Season					Playoffs			
Season	Club	Lea	GP	G	A	TP	PIM	GP	G	A	TP	PIM
1981-82	Seattle	WHL	68	15	18	33	107	10	6	6	12	32
1982-83	Seattle	WHL	71	38	53	91	183	4	2	3	5	0
1983-84a	Seattle	WHL	66	46	66	112	141	5	1	4	5	12
1984-85	NY Islanders	NHL	19	3	1	4	24	4	1	0	1	4
	Springfield	AHL	62	32	27	59	140	4	1	2	3	2
1985-86	NY Islanders	NHL	7	0	1	1	16	1	0	0	0	0
	Springfield	AHL	71	35	36	71	127	....	....	....	....	....
	NHL Totals		26	3	2	5	40	5	1	0	1	4

a WHL First All-Star Team, West Division (1984)

KERR, TIM

Born, Windsor, Ont., January 5, 1960.
Center. Shoots right. 6'3", 225 lbs.
Last amateur club: Kingston Canadians (OHA).

				Regular Season					Playoffs			
Season	Club	Lea	GP	G	A	TP	PIM	GP	G	A	TP	PIM
1978-79	Kingston	OHA	57	17	25	42	27	6	1	1	2	2
1979-80	Kingston	OHA	63	40	33	73	39	3	0	1	1	16
	Maine	AHL	7	2	4	6	2	....	....	....	....	....
1980-81	Philadelphia	NHL	68	22	23	45	84	10	1	3	4	2
1981-82	Philadelphia	NHL	61	21	30	51	138	4	0	2	2	2
1982-83	Philadelphia	NHL	24	11	8	19	6	2	2	0	2	0
1983-84	Philadelphia	NHL	79	54	39	93	29	3	0	0	0	0
1984-85	Philadelphia	NHL	74	54	44	98	57	12	10	4	14	13
1985-86	Philadelphia	NHL	76	58	26	84	79	5	3	3	6	8
	NHL Totals		382	220	170	390	393	36	16	12	28	25

Signed as free agent by Philadelphia, October 25, 1979.

KETOLA, MARTY

Born, Cloquet, Minn., February 25, 1965.
Right wing. Shoots right. 5'11", 205 lbs.
Last amateur club: Colorado College Tigers (WCHA).
(Pittsburgh's 7th choice, 163rd overall, in 1983 Entry Draft).

				Regular Season					Playoffs			
Season	Club	Lea	GP	G	A	TP	PIM	GP	G	A	TP	PIM
1983-84	Colorado	WCHA	34	3	4	7	48	....	....	....	....	....
1984-85	Colorado	WCHA	38	1	11	12	63	....	....	....	....	....
1985-86	Colorado	WCHA	40	5	12	17	89	....	....	....	....	....

KIENE, CHRIS

Born, South Windsor, Conn., March 16, 1966.
Defense. Shoots left. 6'5", 215 lbs.
Last amateur club: Merrimack College Warriors (ECAC).
(New Jersey's 12th choice, 231st overall, in 1984 Entry Draft).

				Regular Season					Playoffs			
Season	Club	Lea	GP	G	A	TP	PIM	GP	G	A	TP	PIM
1985-86	Merrimack	ECAC	31	2	13	15	43	....	....	....	....	....

KING, DEREK

Born, Hamilton, Ont., February 11, 1967.
Left Wing. Shoots left. 6', 200 lbs.
Last amateur club: Sault Ste. Marie Greyhounds (OHL).
(NY Islanders' 2nd choice, 13th over-all, in 1985 Entry Draft).

				Regular Season					Playoffs			
Season	Club	Lea	GP	G	A	TP	PIM	GP	G	A	TP	PIM
1983-84	Hamilton	OPJHL	37	10	14	24	142	....	....	....	....	....
1984-85a	S.S. Marie	OHL	63	35	38	73	106	16	3	13	16	11
1985-86	Oshawa	OHL	44	20	30	50	48	6	3	2	5	13

a Named OHL Rookie of the year (1985)

KING, KRIS

Born, Bracebridge, Ont., February 18, 1966.
Center. Shoots left. 5'10", 190 lbs.
Last amateur club: Peterborough Petes (OHL).
(Washington's 4th choice, 80th over-all, in 1984 Entry Draft).

				Regular Season					Playoffs			
Season	Club	Lea	GP	G	A	TP	PIM	GP	G	A	TP	PIM
1983-84	Peterborough	OHL	62	13	18	31	168	8	3	3	6	14
1984-85	Peterborough	OHL	61	18	35	53	222	16	2	8	10	28
1985-86	Peterborough	OHL	58	19	40	59	254	8	4	0	4	21

KIRIAKOU, LOUIS (LOU)

Born, Toronto, Ont., April 2, I964.
Defense. Shoots left. 5'11", 175 lbs.
Last amateur club: Toronto Marlboros (OHL).
(Calgary's 6th choice, 93rd over-all, in 1982 Entry Draft.)

				Regular Season					Playoffs			
Season	Club	Lea	GP	G	A	TP	PIM	GP	G	A	TP	PIM
1981-82	Toronto	OHL	65	5	11	16	72	10	2	0	2	2
1982-83	Toronto	OHL	67	6	38	44	100	4	1	1	2	6
1983-84	Toronto	OHL	68	10	35	45	74	9	3	7	10	11
1984-85	Moncton	AHL	73	0	6	6	84	....	....	....	....	....
1985-86	Moncton	AHL	11	0	2	2	9	....	....	....	....	....

KIRTON, MARK ROBERT

Born, Regina, Sask., February 3, 1958
Center. Shoots right. 5'10", 170 lbs.
Last amateur club: Peterborough Petes (OHA).
(Toronto's 2nd choice, 48th over-all, in 1978 Amateur Draft).

				Regular Season					Playoffs			
Season	Club	Lea	GP	G	A	TP	PIM	GP	G	A	TP	PIM
1976-77	Peterborough	OHA	46	18	24	42	41	4	6	1	7	0
1977-78	Peterborough	OHA	68	27	44	71	29	21	12	14	26	14
1978-79	New Brunswick	AHL	80	20	30	50	14	5	0	0	0	2
1979-80	Toronto	NHL	2	1	0	1	2	....	....	....	....	....
	New Brunswick	AHL	61	19	42	61	33	17	7	11	18	16
1980-81	Toronto	NHL	11	0	0	0	0	....	....	....	....	....
	Detroit	NHL	50	18	13	31	24	....	....	....	....	....
1981-82	Detroit	NHL	74	14	28	42	62	....	....	....	....	....
1982-83	Detroit	NHL	10	1	1	2	6	....	....	....	....	....
	Adirondack	AHL	20	6	10	16	12	....	....	....	....	....
	Fredericton	AHL	3	2	0	2	2	....	....	....	....	....
	Vancouver	NHL	31	4	6	10	4	4	1	2	3	7
1983-84	Vancouver	NHL	26	2	3	5	2	....	....	....	....	....
	Fredericton	AHL	35	8	10	18	8	7	2	3	5	6
1984-85	Vancouver	NHL	62	17	5	22	21	....	....	....	....	....
	Fredericton	AHL	15	5	9	14	18	....	....	....	....	....
1985-86	Fredericton	AHL	77	23	36	59	33	6	2	2	4	4
	NHL Totals		266	57	56	113	121	4	1	2	3	7

Traded to **Detroit** by **Toronto** for Jim Rutherford, December 4, 1980. Traded to **Vancouver** by **Detroit** for Ivan Boldirev, January 17, 1983.

KISIO, KELLY W.

Born, Peace River, Alta., September 18, 1959.
Center. Shoots left. 5'9", 170 lbs.
Last amateur club: Calgary Wranglers (WHL).

				Regular Season					Playoffs			
Season	Club	Lea	GP	G	A	TP	PIM	GP	G	A	TP	PIM
1978-79	Calgary	WHL	70	60	61	121	73	....	....	....	....	....
1979-80	Calgary	WHL	71	65	73	138	64	....	....	....	....	....
1980-81	Adirondack	AHL	41	10	14	24	43	....	....	....	....	....
	Kalamazoo	IHL	31	27	16	43	48	8	7	7	14	13
1981-82	Dallas	CHL	78	*62	39	101	59	16	*12	*17	*29	38
1982-83	Davos	Swit.	35	40	33	73	....	....	....	....	....	....
	Detroit	NHL	15	4	3	7	0	....	....	....	....	....
1983-84	Detroit	NHL	70	23	37	60	34	4	1	0	1	4
1984-85	Detroit	NHL	75	20	41	61	56	3	0	2	2	2
1985-86	Detroit	NHL	76	21	48	69	85	....	....	....	....	....
	NHL Totals		236	68	129	197	175	7	1	2	3	6

Signed as a free agent by **Detroit**, May 2, 1983. Traded to **NY Rangers** by **Detroit** with Lane Lambert and Jim Leavins for Glen Hanlon and New York's third-round choices in 1987 and 1988 Entry Drafts, July 29, 1986.

KITCHEN, WILLIAM (BILL)

Born, Schomberg, Ont., October 2, 1960.
Defense. Shoots left. 6'1", 200 lbs.
Last amateur club: Ottawa 67's (OHA).

			Regular Season					Playoffs				
Season	Club	Lea	GP	G	A	TP	PIM	GP	G	A	TP	PIM
1978-79	Ottawa	OHA	55	3	16	19	188	4	0	1	1	14
1979-80	Ottawa	OHA	63	7	19	26	195	11	1	8	9	21
	Nova Scotia	AHL	....	....	....	....	....	2	0	1	1	0
1980-81	Nova Scotia	AHL	65	2	7	9	135	6	0	1	1	5
1981-82	**Montreal**	**NHL**	1	0	0	0	7	3	0	1	1	0
	Nova Scotia	AHL	71	3	17	20	135	6	2	0	2	11
1982-83	**Montreal**	**NHL**	8	0	0	0	4	....	....	....	....	....
	Nova Scotia	AHL	53	3	11	14	71	....	....	....	....	....
1983-84	**Montreal**	**NHL**	3	0	0	0	2	....	....	....	....	....
	Nova Scotia	AHL	68	4	20	24	193	10	1	1	2	8
1984-85	**Toronto**	**NHL**	29	1	4	5	27	....	....	....	....	....
	St. Catharines	AHL	31	3	7	10	52	....	....	....	....	....
1985-86	St. Catharines	AHL	72	7	32	39	109	12	0	2	2	19
	NHL Totals		41	1	4	5	40	3	0	1	1	0

Signed as free agent by **Montreal**, October 23, 1979. Signed as a free agent by **Toronto**, August 16, 1984.

KIVELL, ROB

Born, North Bay, Ont., January 14, 1965.
Defense. Shoots left. 6'1", 200 lbs.
Last amateur club: Victoria Cougars (WHL).
(Calgary's 11th choice, 178th over-all, in 1983 Entry Draft).

			Regular Season					Playoffs				
Season	Club	Lea	GP	G	A	TP	PIM	GP	G	A	TP	PIM
1982-83	Victoria	WHL	26	6	7	13	83	9	2	3	5	28
1983-84	Victoria	WHL	52	16	33	49	145	....	....	....	....	....
1984-85	Victoria	WHL	71	38	62	100	185	....	....	....	....	....
	Moncton	AHL	5	1	1	2	8	....	....	....	....	....
1985-86	Moncton	AHL	41	7	3	10	85	7	0	0	0	5

KLEINENDORST, KURT (KLINE-en-dost)

Born, Grand Rapids, Minn., December 31, 1961.
Center. Shoots left. 6'2", 190 lbs.
Last amateur club: Providence College Friars (ECAC).
(New York Rangers' 4th choice, 77th over-all, in 1980 Entry Draft).

			Regular Season					Playoffs				
Season	Club	Lea	GP	G	A	TP	PIM	GP	G	A	TP	PIM
1979-80	Providence	ECAC	32	10	17	27	4	....	....	....	....	....
1980-81	Providence	ECAC	32	16	20	36	18	....	....	....	....	....
1981-82a	Providence	ECAC	33	30	27	57	14	....	....	....	....	....
1982-83a	Providence	ECAC	41	33	39	72	30	....	....	....	....	....
1983-84	Tulsa	CHL	24	4	9	13	10	9	2	2	4	7
1984-85	New Haven	AHL	3	0	0	0	0	....	....	....	....	....
	Salt Lake	IHL	44	21	21	42	10	....	....	....	....	....
	Toledo	IHL	13	4	9	13	21	6	1	3	4	7
1985-86	Salt Lake	IHL	24	5	12	17	21	....	....	....	....	....
	Indianapolis	IHL	45	11	22	33	22	1	0	0	0	0

a ECAC First All-Star Team (1982, 1983).

KLEINENDORST, SCOT (KLINE-en-dorst)

Born, Grand Rapids, Minn., January 16, 1960.
Defense. Shoots left. 6'3", 205 lbs.
Last amateur club: Providence College Friars (ECAC).
(NY Rangers' 5th choice, 98th over-all, in 1980 Entry Draft).

			Regular Season					Playoffs				
Season	Club	Lea	GP	G	A	TP	PIM	GP	G	A	TP	PIM
1978-79	Providence	ECAC	25	4	4	8	27	....	....	....	....	....
1979-80a	Providence	ECAC	30	1	12	13	38	....	....	....	....	....
1980-81	Providence	ECAC	32	3	31	34	75	....	....	....	....	....
1981-82	Providence	ECAC	33	11	27	38	85	....	....	....	....	....
	Springfield	AHL	5	0	4	4	11	....	....	....	....	....
1982-83	Tulsa	CHL	10	0	7	7	2	....	....	....	....	....
	NY Rangers	**NHL**	30	2	9	11	8	6	0	2	2	2
1983-84	**NY Rangers**	**NHL**	23	0	2	2	35	....	....	....	....	....
	Tulsa	CHL	10	4	5	9	4	....	....	....	....	....
1984-85	**Hartford**	**NHL**	35	1	8	9	69	....	....	....	....	....
	Binghamton	AHL	30	3	7	10	42	....	....	....	....	....
1985-86	**Hartford**	**NHL**	41	2	7	9	62	10	0	1	1	18
	NHL Totals		129	5	26	31	174	16	0	3	3	20

a ECAC Second All-Star Team (1980)
Traded to **Hartford** by **NY Rangers** for Blaine Stoughton, February 27, 1984.

KLIMA, PETER (KLEE-ma)

Born, Chaomutov, Czechoslovakia, December 23, 1964.
Left Wing. Shoots left. 6', 190 lbs.
Last amateur club: Dukla Jihlava (Czechoslovakia)
(Detroit's 5th choice, 88th over-all, in 1983 Entry Draft).

			Regular Season					Playoffs				
Season	Club	Lea	GP	G	A	TP	PIM	GP	G	A	TP	PIM
1982-83	Czech. Jrs.	....	44	19	17	36	74	....	....	....	....	....
1983-84	Dukla Jihlava	Czech.	41	20	16	36	46	....	....	....	....	....
	Czech. Jrs.	....	7	6	5	11	NA	....	....	....	....	....
1984-85	Dukla Jihlava	Czech.	35	23	22	45	NA	....	....	....	....	....
	Czech. Nat'l	....	5	2	1	3	0	....	....	....	....	....
1985-86	**Detroit**	**NHL**	74	32	24	56	16	....	....	....	....	....
	NHL Totals		74	32	24	56	16	....	....	....	....	....

KLUZAK, GORDON (GORD) (KLOO-zak)

Born, Climax, Sask., March 4, 1964.
Defense. Shoots left. 6'4", 220 lbs.
Last amateur club: Billings Bighorns (WHL).
(Boston's 1st choice, 1st over-all, in 1982 Entry Draft).

			Regular Season					Playoffs				
Season	Club	Lea	GP	G	A	TP	PIM	GP	G	A	TP	PIM
1980-81	Billings	WHL	68	4	34	38	160	5	0	1	1	4
1981-82a	Billings	WHL	38	9	24	33	110	....	....	....	....	....
1982-83	**Boston**	**NHL**	70	1	6	7	105	17	1	4	5	54
1983-84	**Boston**	**NHL**	80	10	27	37	135	3	0	0	0	0
1984-85	DID NOT PLAY — INJURED											
1985-86	**Boston**	**NHL**	70	8	31	39	155	3	1	1	2	16
	NHL Totals		220	19	64	83	395	23	2	5	7	70

a WHL Second All-Star Team (1982)

KNUTSON, SCOTT

Born, Minneapolis, Minn., March 13, 1964.
Center. Shoots left. 5'11", 160 lbs.
Last amateur club: University of Illinois-Chicago Flames (CCHA)
(Minnesota's 11th choice, 227th over-all, in 1982 Entry Draft).

			Regular Season					Playoffs				
Season	Club	Lea	GP	G	A	TP	PIM	GP	G	A	TP	PIM
1982-83	U. Minnesota	WCHA	4	0	3	3	6	....	....	....	....	....
1983-84	U. Minnesota	WCHA	17	5	4	9	20	....	....	....	....	....
1984-85	U. of Ill.-Chi.	CCHA	40	20	22	42	22	....	....	....	....	....
1985-86	U. of Ill.-Chi.	NHL	39	19	21	40	34	....	....	....	....	....

KOCUR, JOEY (KOSH-er)

Born, Kelvington, Sask., December 21, 1964.
Right wing. Shoots right. 6', 205 lbs.
Last amateur club: Saskatoon Blades (WHL).
(Detroit's 6th choice, 91st over-all, in 1983 Entry Draft).

			Regular Season					Playoffs				
Season	Club	Lea	GP	G	A	TP	PIM	GP	G	A	TP	PIM
1982-83	Saskatoon	WHL	62	23	17	40	289	6	2	3	5	25
1983-84	Saskatoon	WHL	69	40	41	81	258	....	....	....	....	....
	Adirondack	AHL	....	....	....	....	....	5	0	0	0	20
1984-85	**Detroit**	**NHL**	17	1	0	1	64	3	1	0	1	5
	Adirondack	AHL	47	12	7	19	171	....	....	....	....	....
1985-86	**Detroit**	**NHL**	59	9	6	15	377	....	....	....	....	....
	Adirondack	AHL	9	6	2	8	34	....	....	....	....	....
	NHL Totals		76	10	6	16	441	3	1	0	1	5

KOLSTAD, DEAN

Born, Edmonton, Alta., June 16, 1968.
Defense. Shoots left. 6'6", 200 lbs.
Last amateur club: Prince Albert Raiders (WHL).
(Minnesota's 3rd choice, 33rd overall, in 1986 Entry Draft).

			Regular Season					Playoffs				
Season	Club	Lea	GP	G	A	TP	PIM	GP	G	A	TP	PIM
1985-86	Prince Albert	WHL	70	2	20	22	99	20	5	3	8	26

KONROYD, STEPHEN MARK (STEVE) (CON-royd)

Born, Scarborough, Ont., February 10, 1961.
Defense. Shoots left. 6'1", 195 lbs.
Last amateur club: Oshawa Generals (OHA).
(Atlanta's 4th choice, 39th over-all, in 1980 Entry Draft).

			Regular Season					Playoffs				
Season	Club	Lea	GP	G	A	TP	PIM	GP	G	A	TP	PIM
1979-80	Oshawa	OHA	62	11	23	34	133	7	0	2	2	14
1980-81	**Calgary**	**NHL**	4	0	0	0	4	....	....	....	....	....
	aOshawa	OHA	59	19	47	68	232	11	3	11	14	35
1981-82	Oklahoma City	CHL	14	2	3	5	15	....	....	....	....	....
	Calgary	**NHL**	63	3	14	17	78	3	0	0	0	12
1982-83	**Calgary**	**NHL**	79	4	13	17	73	9	2	1	3	18
1983-84	**Calgary**	**NHL**	80	1	13	14	94	8	1	2	3	8
1984-85	**Calgary**	**NHL**	64	3	23	26	73	4	1	4	5	2
1985-86	**Calgary**	**NHL**	59	7	20	27	64	....	....	....	....	....
	NY Islanders	**NHL**	14	0	5	5	16	3	0	0	0	6
	NHL Totals		363	18	88	106	402	27	4	7	11	46

a OHA Second All-Star Team (1981)
Traded to **NY Islanders** by **Calgary** with Richard Kromm for John Tonelli, March 11, 1986.

KONTOS, CHRISTOPHER (CHRIS) (CONN-toes)

Born, Toronto, Ont., December 10, 1963.
Center. Shoots left. 6'1", 195 lbs.
Last amateur club: Toronto Marlboros (OHL).
(NY Rangers' 1st choice, 15th over-all, in 1982 Entry Draft).

			Regular Season					Playoffs				
Season	Club	Lea	GP	G	A	TP	PIM	GP	G	A	TP	PIM
1980-81	Sudbury	OHA	57	17	27	44	36	....	....	....	....	....
1981-82	Sudbury	OHL	12	6	6	12	18	....	....	....	....	....
	Toronto	OHL	59	36	56	92	68	10	7	9	16	2
1982-83	Toronto	OHL	28	21	33	54	23	....	....	....	....	....
	NY Rangers	**NHL**	44	8	7	15	33	....	....	....	....	....
1983-84	**NY Rangers**	**NHL**	6	0	1	1	8	....	....	....	....	....
	Tulsa	CHL	21	5	13	18	8	....	....	....	....	....
1984-85	**NY Rangers**	**NHL**	28	4	8	12	24	....	....	....	....	....
	New Haven	AHL	48	19	24	43	30	....	....	....	....	....
1985-86	New Haven	AHL	21	8	15	23	12	5	4	2	6	4
	NHL Totals		78	12	16	28	65	....	....	....	....	....

KOPECKY, BILL

Born, Ipswich, Mass., January 11, 1966.
Center. Shoots left. 5'11", 170 lbs.
Last amateur club: Rensselaer Polytechnical Institute Engineers (ECAC).
(Boston's 11th choice, 227th overall, in 1984 Entry Draft).

			Regular Season					Playoffs				
Season	Club	Lea	GP	G	A	TP	PIM	GP	G	A	TP	PIM
1984-85	Boston Coll.	H.E.	29	6	10	16	18	....	....	....	....	....
1985-86	RPI	ECAC	29	9	15	24	26	....	....	....	....	....

KORCHINSKI, JEFF

Born, Ottawa, Ont., May 13, 1966.
Defense. Shoots left. 6'0", 190 lbs.
Last amateur club: Clarkson College Knights (ECAC).
(Vancouver's 8th choice, 115th overall, in 1984 Entry Draft).

			Regular Season					Playoffs				
Season	Club	Lea	GP	G	A	TP	PIM	GP	G	A	TP	PIM
1983-84	Clarkson	ECAC	34	1	5	6	12	....	....	....	....	....
1984-85	Clarkson	ECAC	33	0	11	11	20	....	....	....	....	....
1985-86	Clarkson	ECAC	25	2	4	6	18	....	....	....	....	....

KORDIC, JOHN

Born, Edmonton, Alta., March 22, 1965.
Defense. Shoots right. 6'1", 190 lbs.
Last amateur club: Seattle Breakers (WHL)
(Montreal's 6th choice, 80th over-all, in 1984 Entry Draft).

			Regular Season					Playoffs				
Season	Club	Lea	GP	G	A	TP	PIM	GP	G	A	TP	PIM
1982-83	Portland	WHL	72	3	22	25	235	14	1	6	7	30
1983-84	Portland	WHL	67	9	50	59	232	14	0	13	13	56
1984-85a	Seattle	WHL	46	17	36	53	154	....	....	....	....	....
	Portland	WHL	25	6	22	28	73	....	....	....	....	....
	Sherbrooke	AHL	4	0	0	0	4	4	0	0	0	11
1985-86	**Montreal**	**NHL**	**5**	**0**	**1**	**1**	**12**	**18**	**0**	**0**	**0**	**53**
	Sherbrooke	AHL	68	3	14	17	238	....	....	....	....	....
	NHL Totals		**5**	**0**	**1**	**1**	**12**	**18**	**0**	**0**	**0**	**53**

a WHL Second All-Star Team, West Division (1985).

KORN, JAMES A. (JIM)

Born, Hopkins, Minn., July 28, 1957.
Defense. Shoots left. 6'3", 210 lbs.
Last amateur club: Providence College Friars (ECAC)
(Detroit's 4th choice, 73rd over-all, in 1977 Amateur Draft).

			Regular Season					Playoffs				
Season	Club	Lea	GP	G	A	TP	PIM	GP	G	A	TP	PIM
1977-78	Providence	ECAC	33	7	14	21	47	....	....	....	....	....
1978-79	Providence	ECAC	27	5	19	24	72	....	....	....	....	....
1979-80	**Detroit**	**NHL**	**63**	**5**	**13**	**18**	**108**	....	....	....	....	....
	Adirondack	AHL	14	2	7	9	40	....	....	....	....	....
1980-81	Adirondack	AHL	9	3	7	10	53	....	....	....	....	....
	Detroit	**NHL**	**63**	**5**	**15**	**20**	**246**	....	....	....	....	....
1981-82	**Detroit**	**NHL**	**59**	**1**	**7**	**8**	**104**	....	....	....	....	....
	Toronto	**NHL**	**11**	**1**	**3**	**4**	**44**	....	....	....	....	....
1982-83	**Toronto**	**NHL**	**80**	**8**	**21**	**29**	**236**	**3**	**0**	**0**	**0**	**26**
1983-84	**Toronto**	**NHL**	**65**	**12**	**14**	**26**	**257**	....	....	....	....	....
1984-85	**Toronto**	**NHL**	**41**	**5**	**5**	**10**	**171**	....	....	....	....	....
1985-86	DID NOT PLAY											
	NHL Totals		**382**	**37**	**78**	**115**	**1115**	**3**	**0**	**0**	**0**	**26**

Traded to **Toronto** by **Detroit** for Toronto's fourth round choice (Craig Coxe) in 1982 Entry Draft and Toronto's fifth round choice (Joey Kocur) in 1983 Entry Draft, March 8, 1982.

KOROL, DAVID

Born, Winnipeg, Man., March 1, 1965.
Defense. Shoots right. 6'1", 185 lbs.
Last amateur club: Regina Pats (WHL).
(Detroit's 4th choice, 70th over-all, in 1983 Entry Draft).

			Regular Season					Playoffs				
Season	Club	Lea	GP	G	A	TP	PIM	GP	G	A	TP	PIM
1981-82	Winnipeg	WHL	64	4	22	26	55	....	....	....	....	....
1982-83	Winnipeg	WHL	72	14	32	57	90	3	0	1	1	0
1983-84	Winnipeg	WHL	57	15	48	63	49	....	....	....	....	....
	Adirondack	AHL	2	0	4	4	0	3	0	0	0	0
1984-85	Regina	WHL	48	4	30	34	61	3	0	0	0	0
1985-86	Adirondack	AHL	74	3	9	12	56	3	0	1	1	4

KORTKO, ROGER

Born, Hafford, Sask., February 1, 1963.
Center. Shoots left. 5'10", 180 lbs.
Last amateur club: Saskatoon Blades (WHL).
(NY Islanders' 6th choice, 126th over-all, in 1982 Entry Draft).

			Regular Season					Playoffs				
Season	Club	Lea	GP	G	A	TP	PIM	GP	G	A	TP	PIM
1980-81	Saskatoon	WHL	2	0	1	1	2	....	....	....	....	....
1981-82	Saskatoon	WHL	65	33	51	84	82	4	1	4	5	7
1982-83	Saskatoon	WHL	72	62	99	161	79	1	1	1	2	5
1983-84	Indianapolis	CHL	64	16	27	43	48	9	1	5	6	9
1984-85	**NY Islanders**	**NHL**	**27**	**2**	**9**	**11**	**9**	**10**	**0**	**3**	**3**	**17**
	Springfield	AHL	30	8	30	38	6	....	....	....	....	....
1985-86	**NY Islanders**	**NHL**	**52**	**5**	**8**	**13**	**19**	....	....	....	....	....
	Springfield	AHL	12	2	10	12	10	....	....	....	....	....
	NHL Totals		**79**	**7**	**17**	**24**	**28**	**10**	**0**	**3**	**3**	**17**

KOSTYNSKI, DOUGLAS (DOUG) (kah-STIN-skee)

Born, Castlegar, B.C., February 23, 1963.
Center. Shoots right. 6'1", 170 lbs.
Last amateur club: Kamloops Junior Oilers (WHL).
(Boston's 9th choice, 186th over-all, in 1982 Entry Draft).

			Regular Season					Playoffs				
Season	Club	Lea	GP	G	A	TP	PIM	GP	G	A	TP	PIM
1979-80	N. Westminster	WHL	11	1	4	5	12	....	....	....	....	....
1980-81	N. Westminster	WHL	64	18	40	58	51	....	....	....	....	....
1981-82	Kamloops	WHL	53	39	42	81	57	3	1	0	1	0
1982-83	Kamloops	WHL	75	57	59	116	55	7	2	7	9	6
1983-84	**Boston**	**NHL**	**9**	**3**	**1**	**4**	**2**	....	....	....	....	....
	Hershey	AHL	67	13	27	40	8	....	....	....	....	....
1984-85	**Boston**	**NHL**	**6**	**0**	**0**	**0**	**2**	....	....	....	....	....
	Hershey	AHL	55	17	27	44	26	....	....	....	....	....
1985-86	Moncton	AHL	72	18	36	54	24	8	3	1	4	9
	NHL Totals		**15**	**3**	**1**	**4**	**4**	....	....	....	....	....

KOTSOPOULOS, CHRISTOPHER (CHRIS) (kot-saw-POLE-us)

Born, Scarborough, Ont., November 27, 1958.
Defense. Shoots right. 6'3", 215 lbs.
Last amateur club: Acadia University Axemen (AUAA)

			Regular Season					Playoffs				
Season	Club	Lea	GP	G	A	TP	PIM	GP	G	A	TP	PIM
1978-79	Toledo	IHL	62	6	22	28	153	6	1	7	8	48
1979-80	New Haven	AHL	75	7	27	34	149	10	4	5	9	28
1980-81	**NY Rangers**	**NHL**	**54**	**4**	**12**	**16**	**153**	**14**	**0**	**3**	**3**	**63**
1981-82	**Hartford**	**NHL**	**68**	**13**	**20**	**33**	**147**	....	....	....	....	....
1982-83	**Hartford**	**NHL**	**68**	**6**	**24**	**30**	**125**	....	....	....	....	....
1983-84	**Hartford**	**NHL**	**72**	**5**	**13**	**18**	**118**	....	....	....	....	....
1984-85	**Hartford**	**NHL**	**33**	**5**	**3**	**8**	**553**	....	....	....	....	....
1985-86	**Toronto**	**NHL**	**61**	**6**	**11**	**17**	**83**	**10**	**1**	**0**	**1**	**14**
	NHL Totals		**356**	**39**	**83**	**122**	**679**	**24**	**1**	**3**	**4**	**77**

Signed as a free agent by **NY Rangers**, July 10, 1980. Traded to **Hartford** by **NY Rangers** with Gerry McDonald and Doug Sulliman for Mike Rogers and future considerations, October 2, 1981. Traded to **Toronto** by **Hartford** for Stewart Gavin, October 7, 1985.

KOUDYS, JAMES (JIM)

Born, Grimsby, Ont., January 9, 1964.
Defense. Shoots left. 5'10", 170 lbs.
Last amateur club: Sudbury Wolves (OHL).
(NY Islanders' 12th choice, 252nd over-all, in 1982 Entry Draft).

			Regular Season					Playoffs				
Season	Club	Lea	GP	G	A	TP	PIM	GP	G	A	TP	PIM
1981-82	Sudbury	OHL	68	10	29	39	25	....	....	....	....	....
1982-83	Sudbury	OHL	70	35	49	84	40	....	....	....	....	....
1983-84	Sudbury	OHL	70	46	45	91	34	....	....	....	....	....
1984-85	Springfield	AHL	26	0	0	0	2	....	....	....	....	....
	Indianapolis	IHL	24	5	14	19	7	3	2	1	3	0
1985-86	Springfield	AHL	40	3	10	13	32	....	....	....	....	....
	Indianapolis	IHL	32	4	13	17	23	5	0	1	1	0

KRAYER, ED

Born, Acton, Mass., June 6, 1967.
Left wing. Shoots left. 6'1", 175 lbs.
Last amateur club: Harvard University Crimson (ECAC)
(New Jersey's 8th choice, 150th overall, in 1985 Entry Draft).

			Regular Season					Playoffs				
Season	Club	Lea	GP	G	A	TP	PIM	GP	G	A	TP	PIM
1985-86	Harvard	ECAC	34	9	22	31	4	....	....	....	....	....

KRENTZ, DALE

Born, Steinbach, Man., December 19, 1961.
Left wing. Shoots left. 5'11", 190 lbs.
Last amateur club: Michigan State University Spartans (CCHA)

			Regular Season					Playoffs				
Season	Club	Lea	GP	G	A	TP	PIM	GP	G	A	TP	PIM
1982-83	Michigan State	CCHA	42	11	24	35	50	....	....	....	....	....
1983-84	Michigan State	CCHA	44	12	20	32	34	....	....	....	....	....
1984-85	Michigan State	CCHA	44	24	30	54	26	....	....	....	....	....
1985-86	Adirondack	AHL	79	19	27	46	27	13	2	6	8	9

Signed as a free agent by **Detroit**, June 5, 1985.

KROMM, RICHARD GORDON (RICH)

Born, Trail, B.C., March 29, 1964.
Left wing. Shoots left. 5'11", 190 lbs.
Last amateur club: Portland Winter Hawks (WHL).
(Calgary's 2nd choice, 37th over-all, in 1982 Entry Draft).

			Regular Season					Playoffs				
Season	Club	Lea	GP	G	A	TP	PIM	GP	G	A	TP	PIM
1981-82	Portland	WHL	60	16	38	54	30	14	0	3	3	17
1982-83	Portland	WHL	72	35	68	103	64	14	7	13	20	12
1983-84	Portland	WHL	10	10	4	14	13	....	....	....	....	....
	Calgary	**NHL**	**53**	**11**	**12**	**23**	**27**	**11**	**1**	**1**	**2**	**9**
1984-85	**Calgary**	**NHL**	**73**	**20**	**32**	**52**	**32**	**3**	**0**	**1**	**1**	**4**
1985-86	**Calgary**	**NHL**	**63**	**12**	**17**	**29**	**31**	....	....	....	....	....
	NY Islanders	**NHL**	**14**	**7**	**7**	**14**	**4**	**3**	**0**	**1**	**1**	**0**
	NHL Totals		**203**	**50**	**68**	**118**	**94**	**17**	**1**	**3**	**4**	**13**

Traded to **NY Islanders** by **Calgary** with Steve Konroyd for John Tonelli, March 11, 1986.

KRUSHELNYSKI, MICHAEL (MIKE) (KROOSH-el-NI-skee)

Born, Montreal, Que., April 27, 1960.
Center. Shoots left. 6'2", 200 lbs.
Last amateur club: Montreal Juniors (QMJHL).
(Boston's 7th choice, 120th over-all, in 1979 Entry Draft).

			Regular Season					Playoffs				
Season	Club	Lea	GP	G	A	TP	PIM	GP	G	A	TP	PIM
1978-79	Montreal	QJHL	46	15	29	44	42	11	3	4	7	8
1979-80	Montreal	QJHL	72	39	60	99	78	6	2	3	5	2
1980-81	Springfield	AHL	80	25	28	53	47	7	1	1	2	29
1981-82	Erie	AHL	62	31	52	83	44	....	....	....	....	....
	Boston	NHL	17	3	3	6	2	1	0	0	0	2
1982-83	Boston	NHL	79	23	42	65	43	17	8	6	14	12
1983-84	Boston	NHL	66	25	20	45	55	2	0	0	0	0
1984-85	Edmonton	NHL	80	43	45	88	60	18	5	8	13	22
1985-86	Edmonton	NHL	54	16	24	40	22	10	4	5	9	16
	NHL Totals		296	110	134	244	182	48	17	19	36	52

Traded to **Edmonton** by **Boston** for Ken Linseman, June 21, 1984.

KULAK, STUART (STU)

Born, Edmonton, Alta., March 10, 1963.
Right wing. Shoots right. 5'10", 180 lbs.
Last amateur club: Victoria Cougars (WHL).
(Vancouver's 5th choice, 115th over-all, in 1981 Entry Draft).

			Regular Season					Playoffs				
Season	Club	Lea	GP	G	A	TP	PIM	GP	G	A	TP	PIM
1979-80	Sherwood Park	AJHL	53	30	23	53	111	....	....	....	....	....
	Victoria	WHL	3	0	0	0	0	....	....	....	....	....
1980-81	Victoria	WHL	72	23	24	47	44	15	3	5	8	19
1981-82	Victoria	WHL	71	38	50	88	92	4	1	2	3	43
1982-83	Vancouver	NHL	4	1	1	2	0	....	....	....	....	....
	Victoria	WHL	50	29	33	62	130	10	10	9	19	29
1983-84	Fredericton	AHL	52	12	16	28	55	5	0	0	0	59
1984-85	DID NOT PLAY — INJURED											
1985-86	Fredericton	AHL	3	1	0	1	0	6	2	1	3	0
	Kalamazoo	IHL	30	14	8	22	38	2	2	0	2	0
	NHL Totals		4	1	1	2	0	....	....	....	....	....

KUMPEL, MARK

Born, Wakefield, Mass., March 7, 1961.
Right wing. Shoots right. 6', 190 lbs.
Last amateur club: 1984 United States Olympic Team.
(Quebec's 4th choice, 108th over-all, in 1980 Entry Draft).

			Regular Season					Playoffs				
Season	Club	Lea	GP	G	A	TP	PIM	GP	G	A	TP	PIM
1979-80	U. of Lowell	ECAC	30	18	18	36	12	....	....	....	....	....
1980-81	U. of Lowell	ECAC	1	2	0	2	0	....	....	....	....	....
1981-82	U. of Lowell	ECAC	35	17	13	30	23	....	....	....	....	....
1982-83	U. of Lowell	ECAC	7	8	5	13	0	....	....	....	....	....
	U.S. National	...	30	14	18	32	6	....	....	....	....	....
1983-84	U.S. National	...	61	14	19	33	19	....	....	....	....	....
	U.S. Olympic	...	6	1	0	1	2	....	....	....	....	....
	Fredericton	AHL	16	1	1	2	5	3	0	0	0	15
1984-85	Quebec	NHL	42	8	7	15	26	18	3	4	7	4
	Fredericton	AHL	18	9	6	15	17	....	....	....	....	....
1985-86	Quebec	NHL	47	10	12	22	17	2	1	0	1	0
	Fredericton	AHL	7	4	2	6	4	....	....	....	....	....
	NHL Totals		89	18	19	37	43	20	4	4	8	4

KURRI, JARI (COOR-ee, YAR-ee)

Born, Helsinki, Finland, May 18, 1960.
Right wing. Shoots right. 6'1", 185 lbs.
Last amateur club: Jokerit (Finland)
(Edmonton's 3rd choice, 69th over-all, in 1980 Entry Draft).

			Regular Season					Playoffs				
Season	Club	Lea	GP	G	A	TP	PIM	GP	G	A	TP	PIM
1978-79	Jokerit	Fin.	33	16	14	30	12	....	....	....	....	....
1979-80	Jokerit	Fin.	33	23	16	39	22	....	....	....	....	....
1980-81	Edmonton	NHL	75	32	43	75	40	9	5	7	12	4
1981-82	Edmonton	NHL	71	32	54	86	32	5	2	5	7	10
1982-83	Edmonton	NHL	80	45	59	104	22	16	8	15	23	8
1983-84a	Edmonton	NHL	64	52	61	113	14	19	*14	14	28	13
1984-85bc	Edmonton	NHL	73	71	64	135	30	18	*19	12	31	6
1985-86a	Edmonton	NHL	78	68	63	131	22	10	2	10	12	4
	NHL Totals		441	300	344	644	160	77	50	63	113	45

a NHL Second All-Star Team (1984, 1986)
b won Lady Byng Memorial Trophy (1985).
c NHL First All-Star Team (1985).

KURVERS, TOM

Born, Minneapolis, Minn., September 14, 1962.
Defense. Shoots left. 5'10", 180 lbs.
Last amateur club: University of Minnesota-Duluth Bulldogs (WCHA)
(Montreal's 10th choice, 145th over-all, in 1981 Entry Draft).

			Regular Season					Playoffs				
Season	Club	Lea	GP	G	A	TP	PIM	GP	G	A	TP	PIM
1980-81	Minn-Duluth	WCHA	39	6	24	30	48	....	....	....	....	....
1981-82	Minn-Duluth	WCHA	37	11	31	42	18	....	....	....	....	....
1982-83	Minn-Duluth	WCHA	26	4	23	27	24	....	....	....	....	....
1983-84a	Minn-Duluth	WCHA	43	18	58	76	46	....	....	....	....	....
1984-85	Montreal	NHL	75	10	35	45	30	12	0	6	6	6
1985-86	Montreal	NHL	62	7	23	30	36	....	....	....	....	....
	NHL Totals		137	17	58	75	66	12	0	6	6	6

a WCHA First All-Star Team (1984)

KURZAWSKI, MARK

Born, Chicago, Ill., February 25, 1968.
Defense. Shoots right. 6'3", 200 lbs.
Last amateur club: Windsor Compuware Spitfires (OHL).
(Chicago's 2nd choice, 35th overall, in 1986 Entry Draft).

			Regular Season					Playoffs				
Season	Club	Lea	GP	G	A	TP	PIM	GP	G	A	TP	PIM
1985-86	Windsor	OHL	66	11	25	36	66	16	3	5	8	23

KYPREOS, NICHOLAS (NICK)

Born, Toronto, Ontario, June 4, 1966.
Left Wing. Shoots left. 6', 190 lbs.
Last amateur club: North Bay Centennials (OHL).

			Regular Season					Playoffs				
Season	Club	Lea	GP	G	A	TP	PIM	GP	G	A	TP	PIM
1983-84	North Bay	OHL	51	12	11	23	36	4	3	2	5	9
1984-85	North Bay	OHL	64	41	36	77	71	8	2	2	4	15
1985-86a	North Bay	OHL	64	62	35	97	112	....	....	....	....	....

a OHL First All-Star Team (1986)

Signed as a free agent by **Philadelphia**, September 30, 1984.

KYTE, JAMES (JIM)

Born, Ottawa, Ont., March 21, 1964.
Defense. Shoots left. 6'5", 210 lbs.
Last amateur club: Cornwall Royals (OHL).
(Winnipeg's 1st choice, 12th over-all, in 1982 Entry Draft).

			Regular Season					Playoffs				
Season	Club	Lea	GP	G	A	TP	PIM	GP	G	A	TP	PIM
1981-82	Cornwall	OHL	52	4	13	17	148	5	0	0	0	10
1982-83	Winnipeg	NHL	2	0	0	0	0	....	....	....	....	....
	Cornwall	OHL	65	6	30	36	195	8	0	2	2	24
1983-84	Winnipeg	NHL	58	1	2	3	55	3	0	0	0	11
1984-85	Winnipeg	NHL	71	0	3	3	111	8	0	0	0	14
1985-86	Winnipeg	NHL	71	1	3	4	126	3	0	0	0	12
	NHL Totals		202	2	8	10	292	14	0	0	0	37

LACEY, GARRY

Born, Sudbury, Ont., May 24, 1964.
Left wing. Shoots left. 5'11", 180 lbs.
Last amateur club: Toronto Marlboros (OHL).
(NY Islanders' 3rd choice, 63rd over-all, in 1982 Entry Draft).

			Regular Season					Playoffs				
Season	Club	Lea	GP	G	A	TP	PIM	GP	G	A	TP	PIM
1981-82	Toronto	OHL	65	17	28	45	140	10	1	1	2	27
1982-83	Toronto	OHL	67	19	36	55	110	4	1	2	3	4
1983-84a	Toronto	OHL	59	41	60	101	77	6	4	3	7	22
1984-85	Indianapolis	IHL	76	17	21	38	88	7	2	0	2	28
1985-86	Springfield	AHL	52	12	11	23	41	....	....	....	....	....

a OHL First All-Star Team (1984)

LACKTEN, KURT

Born, Kamsack, Sask., May 20, 1967.
Right wing. Shoots right. 6'0", 180 lbs.
Last amateur club: Calgary Wranglers (WHL).
(NY Islanders' 9th choice, 139th overall, in 1985 Entry Draft).

			Regular Season					Playoffs				
Season	Club	Lea	GP	G	A	TP	PIM	GP	G	A	TP	PIM
1984-85	Moose Jaw	WHL	66	18	13	31	141	....	....	....	....	....
1985-86	Calgary	WHL	61	5	20	25	112	....	....	....	...	....

LACOMBE, NORMAND

Born, Pierrefonds, Que., October 18, 1964.
Right wing. Shoots right. 5'11", 205 lbs.
Last amateur club: University of N. Hampshire Wildcats (ECAC).
(Buffalo's 2nd choice, 10th over-all, in 1983 Entry Draft).

			Regular Season					Playoffs				
Season	Club	Lea	GP	G	A	TP	PIM	GP	G	A	TP	PIM
1981-82	N. Hampshire	ECAC	35	18	16	34	38	....	....	....	....	....
1982-83	N. Hampshire	ECAC	35	18	25	43	48	....	....	....	....	....
1983-84	Rochester	AHL	44	10	16	26	45	....	....	....	....	....
1984-85	Buffalo	NHL	30	2	4	6	25	....	....	....	....	....
	Rochester	AHL	33	13	16	29	33	5	3	1	4	4
1985-86	Buffalo	NHL	25	6	7	13	13	....	....	....	....	....
	Rochester	AHL	32	10	13	23	56	....	....	....	....	....
	NHL Totals		55	8	11	19	38	....	....	....	....	....

LADOUCEUR, RANDY (la-DEW-sir)

Born, Brockville, Ont., June 30, 1960.
Defense. Shoots left. 6'2", 220 lbs.
Last amateur club: Brantford Alexanders (OHA).

			Regular Season					Playoffs				
Season	Club	Lea	GP	G	A	TP	PIM	GP	G	A	TP	PIM
1978-79	Brantford	OHA	64	3	17	20	141	....	....	....	....	....
1979-80	Brantford	OHA	37	6	15	21	125	8	0	5	5	18
1980-81	Kalamazoo	IHL	80	7	30	37	52	8	1	3	4	10
1981-82	Adirondack	AHL	78	4	28	32	78	5	1	1	2	6
1982-83	Detroit	NHL	27	0	4	4	16	....	....	....	....	....
	Adirondack	AHL	48	11	21	32	54	....	....	....	....	....
1983-84	Adirondack	AHL	11	3	5	8	12	....	....	....	....	....
	Detroit	NHL	71	3	17	20	58	4	1	0	1	6
1984-85	Detroit	NHL	80	3	27	30	108	3	1	0	1	0
1985-86	Detroit	NHL	78	5	13	18	196	....	....	....	....	....
	NHL Totals		256	11	61	72	378	7	2	0	2	6

Signed as a free agent by **Detroit**, November 1, 1979.

LaFONTAINE, PAT

Born, St. Louis, Missouri, February 22, 1965.
Center. Shoots right. 5′9″, 170 lbs.
Last amateur club: 1984 United States Olympic Team.
(NY Islanders' 1st choice, 3rd over-all, in 1983 Entry Draft).

			Regular Season					Playoffs				
Season	Club	Lea	GP	G	A	TP	PIM	GP	G	A	TP	PIM
1981-82	Detroit Compu.	Midget	79	175	149	324	12	....	....	....	....	....
1982-83abcd	Verdun	QMJHL	70	*104	*130	*234	10	15	11	*24	*35	4
1983-84	U.S. National	...	58	56	55	111	22	....	....	....	....	....
	U.S. Olympic	...	6	5	5	10	0	....	....	....	....	....
	NY Islanders	**NHL**	15	13	6	19	6	16	3	6	9	8
1984-85	**NY Islanders**	**NHL**	67	19	35	54	32	9	1	2	3	4
1985-86	**NY Islanders**	**NHL**	65	30	23	53	43	3	1	0	1	0
	NHL Totals		147	62	64	126	81	28	5	8	13	12

a QMJHL First All-Star Team (1983).
b QMJHL Most Valuable Player (1983).
c QMJHL Most Valuable Player in Playoffs (1983).
d Canadian Major Junior Player of the Year (1983).

LAFORGE, MARC

Born, Sudbury, Ont., January 3, 1968.
Defense. Shoots left. 6′2″, 200 lbs.
Last amateur club: Kingston Canadians (OHL).
(Hartford's 2nd choice, 32nd overall, in 1986 Entry Draft).

			Regular Season					Playoffs				
Season	Club	Lea	GP	G	A	TP	PIM	GP	G	A	TP	PIM
1985-86	Kingston	OHL	60	1	13	14	248	10	0	1	1	30

LAFRENIERE, JASON

Born, St. Catharines, Ont., December 6, 1966.
Center. Shoots right. 5′11″, 185 lbs.
Last amateur club: Hamilton Steel Hawks (OHL).
(Quebec's 2nd choice, 36th over-all, in 1985 Entry Draft).

			Regular Season					Playoffs				
Season	Club	Lea	GP	G	A	TP	PIM	GP	G	A	TP	PIM
1983-84	Brantford	OHL	70	24	57	81	4	6	2	4	6	2
1984-85	Hamilton	OHL	59	26	69	95	10	17	12	16	28	0
1985-86a	Belleville	OHL	61	49	82	131	4	23	10	22	32	6

a OHL First All-Star Team (1986).

LAIDLAW, THOMAS (TOM)

Born, Brampton, Ont., April 15, 1958.
Defense. Shoots left. 6′2″, 215 lbs.
Last amateur club: University of Northern Michigan Wildcats (CCHA)
(NY Rangers' 7th choice, 93rd over-all, in 1978 Amateur Draft).

			Regular Season					Playoffs				
Season	Club	Lea	GP	G	A	TP	PIM	GP	G	A	TP	PIM
1978-79a	N. Michigan	CCHA	29	10	20	30	137	....	....	....	....	....
1979-80ab	N. Michigan	CCHA	39	8	30	38	83	....	....	....	....	....
	New Haven	AHL	1	0	0	0	0	10	1	6	7	27
1980-81	**NY Rangers**	**NHL**	80	6	23	29	100	14	1	4	5	18
1981-82	**NY Rangers**	**NHL**	79	3	18	21	104	10	0	3	3	14
1982-83	**NY Rangers**	**NHL**	80	0	10	10	75	9	1	1	2	10
1983-84	**NY Rangers**	**NHL**	79	3	15	18	62	5	0	0	0	8
1984-85	**NY Rangers**	**NHL**	61	1	11	12	52	3	0	2	2	4
1985-86	**NY Rangers**	**NHL**	68	6	12	18	103	7	0	2	2	12
	NHL Totals		447	19	89	108	496	38	2	9	11	52

a CCHA First All-Star Team (1979, 1980)
b NCAA All-Tournament Team (1980)

LAKSO, BOB

Born, Baltimore, Maryland. April 13, 1962.
Left wing. Shoots left. 5′11″, 180 lbs.
Last amateur club: University of Minnesota-Duluth Bulldogs (WCHA).
(Minnesota's 9th choice, 184th over-all, in 1980 Entry Draft).

			Regular Season					Playoffs				
Season	Club	Lea	GP	G	A	TP	PIM	GP	G	A	TP	PIM
1980-81	Minn.-Duluth	WCHA	25	5	3	8	2	....	....	....	....	....
1981-82	Minn.-Duluth	WCHA	22	8	10	18	6	....	....	....	....	....
1982-83	Minn.-Duluth	WCHA	26	11	17	28	4	....	....	....	....	....
1983-84	Minn.-Duluth	WCHA	26	20	18	38	8	....	....	....	....	....
1984-85	Springfield	AHL	8	2	1	3	0	....	....	....	....	....
	Indianapolis	IHL	76	26	32	58	4	6	3	2	5	2
1985-86	Springfield	AHL	17	3	6	9	2	....	....	....	....	....
	Indianapolis	IHL	58	41	35	76	4	5	4	2	6	0

LALOR, MIKE

Born, Fort Erie, Ont., March 8, 1963.
Defense. Shoots left. 6′0″, 190 lbs.
Last amateur club: Brantford Alexanders (OHL).

			Regular Season					Playoffs				
Season	Club	Lea	GP	G	A	TP	PIM	GP	G	A	TP	PIM
1981-82	Brantford	OHL	64	3	13	16	114	11	0	6	6	11
1982-83	Brantford	OHL	65	10	30	40	113	8	1	3	4	20
1983-84	Nova Scotia	AHL	67	5	11	16	80	12	0	2	2	13
1984-85	Sherbrooke	AHL	79	9	23	32	114	17	3	5	8	36
1985-86	**Montreal**	**NHL**	62	3	5	8	56	17	1	1	2	29
	NHL Totals		62	3	5	8	56	17	1	1	2	29

Signed as a free agent by **Montreal**, September, 1983.

LAMB, MARK

Born, Ponteix, Sask., August 3, l964.
Center. Shoots left. 5′9″, 180 lbs.
Last amateur club: Medicine Hat Tigers (WHL).
(Calgary's 5th choice, 72nd over-all, in 1982 Entry Draft).

			Regular Season					Playoffs				
Season	Club	Lea	GP	G	A	TP	PIM	GP	G	A	TP	PIM
1981-82	Billings	WHL	72	45	56	101	46	5	4	6	10	4
1982-83	Nanaimo	WHL	30	14	37	51	16	....	....	....	....	....
	Medicine Hat	WHL	46	22	43	65	33	5	3	2	5	4
	Colorado	CHL	....	....	....	....	....	6	0	2	2	0
1983-84a	Medicine Hat	WHL	72	59	77	136	30	14	12	11	23	6
1984-85	Moncton	AHL	80	23	49	72	53	....	....	....	....	....
1985-86	**Calgary**	**NHL**	1	0	0	0	0	....	....	....	....	....
	Moncton	AHL	79	26	50	76	51	10	2	6	8	17
	NHL Totals		1	0	0	0	0	....	....	....	....	....

a WHL First All-Star Team, East Division (1984)

LAMBERT, LANE

Born, Melfort, Sask., November 18, 1964.
Right wing. Shoots right. 5′11″, 180 lbs.
Last amateur club: Saskatoon Blades (WHL).
(Detroit's 2nd choice, 25th over-all, in 1983 Entry Draft).

			Regular Season					Playoffs				
Season	Club	Lea	GP	G	A	TP	PIM	GP	G	A	TP	PIM
1981-82	Saskatoon	WHL	72	45	69	114	111	5	1	1	2	25
1982-83a	Saskatoon	WHL	64	59	60	119	126	6	4	3	7	7
1983-84	**Detroit**	**NHL**	73	20	15	35	115	4	0	0	0	10
1984-85	**Detroit**	**NHL**	69	14	11	25	104	....	....	....	....	....
1985-86	**Detroit**	**NHL**	34	2	3	5	130	....	....	....	....	....
	Adirondack	AHL	45	16	25	41	69	16	5	5	10	9
	NHL Totals		176	36	29	65	349	4	0	0	0	10

a WHL Second All-Star Team (1983).
Traded to **NY Rangers** by **Detroit** with Kelly Kisio and Jim Leavins for Glen Hanlon and New York's third round choices in 1987 and 1988 Entry Drafts, July 29, 1986.

LAMBERT, RICHARD

Born, Toronto, Ont., September 9, 1966.
Left wing. Shoots left. 6′0″, 195 lbs.
Last amateur club: University of New Hampshire Wildcats (H.E.).
(Edmonton's 5th choice, 105th overall, in 1984 Entry Draft).

			Regular Season					Playoffs				
Season	Club	Lea	GP	G	A	TP	PIM	GP	G	A	TP	PIM
1985-86	N. Hampshire	H.E.	37	9	7	16	39	....	....	....	....	....

LAMMENS, HANK

Born, Brockville, Ont., February 21, 1966.
Defense. Shoots left. 6′2″, 195 lbs.
Last amateur club: St. Lawrence University Saints (ECAC).
(NY Islanders' 10th choice, 169th overall, in 1985 Entry Draft).

			Regular Season					Playoffs				
Season	Club	Lea	GP	G	A	TP	PIM	GP	G	A	TP	PIM
1984-85	St. Lawrence	ECAC	21	1	7	8	16	....	....	....	....	....
1985-86	St. Lawrence	ECAC	30	3	14	17	60	....	....	....	....	....

LAMOUREUX, MITCH

Born, Ottawa, Ont., August 22, 1962.
Center. Shoots left. 5′6″, 175 lbs.
Last amateur club: Oshawa Generals (OHL).
(Pittsburgh's 8th choice, 154th over-all, in 1981 Entry Draft).

			Regular Season					Playoffs				
Season	Club	Lea	GP	G	A	TP	PIM	GP	G	A	TP	PIM
1979-80	Oshawa	OHA	67	28	48	76	63	7	2	1	3	16
1980-81	Oshawa	OHA	63	50	69	119	256	11	11	13	24	57
1981-82a	Oshawa	OHL	66	43	78	121	275	12	4	17	21	68
1982-83bc	Baltimore	AHL	80	57	50	107	107	....	....	....	....	....
1983-84	**Pittsburgh**	**NHL**	8	1	1	2	6	....	....	....	....	....
	Baltimore	AHL	68	30	38	68	136	9	1	3	4	2
1984-85	**Pittsburgh**	**NHL**	62	10	8	18	53	....	....	....	....	....
	Baltimore	AHL	18	10	14	24	34	....	....	....	....	....
1985-86	Baltimore	AHL	75	22	31	53	129	....	....	....	....	....
	NHL Totals		70	11	9	20	59	....	....	....	....	....

a OHL Third All-Star Team (1982)
b Won Dudley "Red Garrett Memorial Trophy (AHL's Rookie of the Year) (1983)
c AHL Second All-Star Team (1983)

LANGEVIN, CHRIS

Born, Montreal, Que., November 27, 1959.
Left wing. Shoots left. 6′, 190 lbs.
Last amateur club: Chicoutimi Sagueneens (QMJHL).

			Regular Season					Playoffs				
Season	Club	Lea	GP	G	A	TP	PIM	GP	G	A	TP	PIM
1977-78	Chicoutimi	QJHL	67	8	20	28	183	....	....	....	....	....
1978-79	Chicoutimi	QJHL	65	24	23	47	182	4	0	2	2	19
1979-80	Chicoutimi	QJHL	46	22	30	52	97	2	0	3	3	14
1980-81	Saginaw	IHL	75	35	48	83	179	13	2	5	7	24
1981-82	Rochester	AHL	33	3	5	8	150	9	4	5	9	33
1982-83	Rochester	AHL	71	18	25	43	255	11	0	3	3	24
1983-84	**Buffalo**	**NHL**	6	1	0	1	2	....	....	....	....	....
	Rochester	AHL	41	11	14	25	133	15	3	2	5	39
1984-85	Rochester	AHL	63	19	21	40	212	5	2	1	3	16
1985-86	**Buffalo**	**NHL**	16	2	1	3	20	....	....	....	....	....
	NHL Totals		22	3	1	4	22	....	....	....	....	....

Signed as free agent by **Buffalo**, October 14, 1983.

LANGEVIN, DAVID (DAVE) (LAWN-je-vin)

Born, St. Paul, Minn., May 15, 1954.
Defense. Shoots left. 6'2", 200 lbs.
Last amateur club: University of Minnesota-Duluth Bulldogs (WCHA)
(NY Islanders' 6th choice, 112th over-all, in 1974 Amateur Draft).

			Regular Season					Playoffs				
Season	Club	Lea	GP	G	A	TP	PIM	GP	G	A	TP	PIM
1974-75	Minn Duluth	WCHA	35	8	24	32	91	....	....	....	....	....
1975-76	Minn-Duluth	WCHA	34	19	26	45	82	....	....	....	....	....
1976-77	Edmonton	WHA	77	7	16	23	94	5	2	1	3	9
1977-78	Edmonton	WHA	62	6	22	28	90	5	0	2	2	10
1978-79	Edmonton	WHA	77	6	21	27	76	13	0	1	1	25
1979-80	**NY Islanders**	**NHL**	**76**	**3**	**13**	**16**	**109**	**21**	**0**	**3**	**3**	**32**
1980-81	**NY Islanders**	**NHL**	**75**	**1**	**16**	**17**	**122**	**18**	**0**	**3**	**3**	**25**
1981-82	**NY Islanders**	**NHL**	**73**	**1**	**20**	**21**	**82**	**19**	**2**	**4**	**6**	**16**
1982-83	**NY Islanders**	**NHL**	**73**	**4**	**17**	**21**	**64**	**8**	**0**	**2**	**2**	**2**
1983-84	**NY Islanders**	**NHL**	**69**	**3**	**16**	**19**	**53**	**12**	**0**	**4**	**4**	**18**
1984-85	**NY Islanders**	**NHL**	**56**	**0**	**13**	**13**	**35**	**4**	**0**	**0**	**0**	**4**
1985-86	**Minnesota**	**NHL**	**80**	**0**	**8**	**8**	**58**	**5**	**0**	**1**	**1**	**9**
	NHL Totals		**502**	**12**	**103**	**115**	**523**	**87**	**2**	**15**	**17**	**106**
	WHA Totals		216	19	59	78	260	23	2	4	6	44

Reclaimed by **NY Islanders** from **Edmonton** prior to Expansion Draft, June 9, 1979. Claimed by **Minnesota** from **NY Islanders** in NHL Waiver Draft, October 7, 1985.

LANGWAY, ROD CORRY

Born, Formosa, Taiwan, May 3, 1957.
Defense. Shoots left. 6'3", 215 lbs.
Last amateur club: University of N. Hampshire Wildcats (ECAC)
(Montreal's 3rd choice, 36th over-all, in 1977 Amateur Draft).

			Regular Season					Playoffs				
Season	Club	Lea	GP	G	A	TP	PIM	GP	G	A	TP	PIM
1976-77	N. Hampshire	ECAC	34	10	43	53	52	....	....	....	....	....
1977-78	Hampton	AHL	30	6	16	22	50	....	....	....	....	....
	Birmingham	WHA	52	3	18	21	52	4	0	0	0	9
1978-79	Nova Scotia	AHL	18	6	13	19	29	....	....	....	....	....
	Montreal	**NHL**	**45**	**3**	**4**	**7**	**30**	**8**	**0**	**0**	**0**	**16**
1979-80	**Montreal**	**NHL**	**77**	**7**	**29**	**36**	**81**	**10**	**3**	**3**	**6**	**2**
1980-81	**Montreal**	**NHL**	**80**	**11**	**34**	**45**	**120**	**3**	**0**	**0**	**0**	**6**
1981-82	**Montreal**	**NHL**	**66**	**5**	**34**	**39**	**116**	**5**	**0**	**3**	**3**	**18**
1982-83ab	**Washington**	**NHL**	**80**	**3**	**29**	**32**	**75**	**4**	**0**	**0**	**0**	**0**
1983-84ab	**Washington**	**NHL**	**80**	**9**	**24**	**33**	**61**	**8**	**0**	**5**	**5**	**7**
1984-85c	**Washington**	**NHL**	**79**	**4**	**22**	**26**	**54**	**5**	**0**	**1**	**1**	**6**
1985-86	**Washington**	**NHL**	**71**	**1**	**17**	**18**	**61**	**9**	**1**	**2**	**3**	**6**
	NHL Totals		**578**	**43**	**193**	**236**	**598**	**52**	**4**	**14**	**18**	**60**
	WHA Totals		52	3	18	21	52	4	0	0	0	9

a Won James Norris Memorial Trophy (1983, 1984)
b NHL First All-Star Team (1983, 1984)
c NHL Second All-Star Team (1985)

Claimed by **Montreal** as fill in Expansion Draft, June 13, 1979. Traded to **Washington** by **Montreal** with Doug Jarvis, Craig Laughlin and Brian Engblom for Ryan Walter and Rick Green, September 9, 1982.

LANIEL, MARC

Born, Oshawa, Ont., January 16, 1968.
Defense. Shoots left. 6'2", 190 lbs.
Last amateur club: Oshawa Generals (OHL).
(New Jersey's 4th choice, 62nd overall, in 1986 Entry Draft).

			Regular Season					Playoffs				
Season	Club	Lea	GP	G	A	TP	PIM	GP	G	A	TP	PIM
1985-86	Oshawa	OHL	66	9	25	34	27	6	2	3	5	6

LANIGAN, MARK

Born, Waterloo, Iowa, December 29, 1964.
Defense. Shoots left. 6'2", 180 lbs.
Last amateur club: Northern Michigan University Wildcats (WCHA).
(St. Louis' 15th choice, 237th overall, in 1984 Entry Draft).

			Regular Season					Playoffs				
Season	Club	Lea	GP	G	A	TP	PIM	GP	G	A	TP	PIM
1984-85	N. Michigan	WCHA	28	1	5	6	14	....	....	....	....	....
1985-86	N. Michigan	WCHA	38	1	7	8	18	....	....	....	....	....

LANTHIER, JEAN-MARC

Born, Montreal, Que., March 27, 1963.
Right wing. Shoots right. 6'2", 195 lbs.
Last amateur club: Laval Voisins (QMJHL).
(Vancouver's 2nd choice, 52nd over-all, in 1981 Entry Draft).

			Regular Season					Playoffs				
Season	Club	Lea	GP	G	A	TP	PIM	GP	G	A	TP	PIM
1980-81	Quebec	QMJHL	37	13	32	45	18	....	....	....	....	....
	Sorel	QMJHL	35	6	33	39	29	7	1	4	5	4
1981-82	Laval	QMJHL	60	44	34	78	48	18	8	11	19	8
1982-83	Laval	QMJHL	69	39	71	110	54	12	6	17	23	8
1983-84	**Vancouver**	**NHL**	**11**	**2**	**1**	**3**	**2**	....	....	....	....	....
	Fredericton	AHL	60	25	17	42	29	7	4	6	10	0
1984-85	**Vancouver**	**NHL**	**27**	**6**	**4**	**10**	**13**	....	....	....	....	....
	Fredericton	AHL	38	8	5	13	15	....	....	....	....	....
1985-86	**Vancouver**	**NHL**	**62**	**7**	**10**	**17**	**12**	....	....	....	....	....
	Fredericton	AHL	7	5	5	10	2	....	....	....	....	....
	NHL Totals		**100**	**15**	**15**	**30**	**27**	....	....	....	....	....

LANZ, RICK ROMAN

Born, Karlouyvary, Czechoslovakia, September 16, 1961.
Defense. Shoots right. 6'2", 200 lbs.
Last amateur club: Oshawa Generals (OHA).
(Vancouver's 1st choice, 7th over-all, in 1980 Entry Draft).

			Regular Season					Playoffs				
Season	Club	Lea	GP	G	A	TP	PIM	GP	G	A	TP	PIM
1978-79	Oshawa	OHA	65	12	47	59	88	5	1	3	4	14
1979-80a	Oshawa	OHA	52	18	38	56	51	7	2	3	5	6
1980-81	**Vancouver**	**NHL**	**76**	**7**	**22**	**29**	**40**	**3**	**0**	**0**	**0**	**4**
1981-82	**Vancouver**	**NHL**	**39**	**3**	**11**	**14**	**48**	....	....	....	....	....
1982-83	**Vancouver**	**NHL**	**74**	**10**	**38**	**48**	**46**	**4**	**2**	**1**	**3**	**0**
1983-84	**Vancouver**	**NHL**	**79**	**18**	**39**	**57**	**45**	**4**	**0**	**4**	**4**	**2**
1984-85	**Vancouver**	**NHL**	**57**	**2**	**17**	**19**	**69**	....	....	....	....	....
1985-86	**Vancouver**	**NHL**	**75**	**15**	**38**	**53**	**73**	**3**	**0**	**0**	**0**	**0**
	NHL Totals		**400**	**55**	**165**	**220**	**321**	**14**	**2**	**5**	**7**	**6**

a OHA Third All-Star Team (1980).

LAPLANTE, RICHARD

Born, Boucherville, Que., March 15, 1967.
Center. Shoots right. 5'11", 175 lbs.
Last amateur club: University of Vermont Catamounts (ECAC).
(Chicago's 9th choice, 179th overall, in 1985 Entry Draft).

			Regular Season					Playoffs				
Season	Club	Lea	GP	G	A	TP	PIM	GP	G	A	TP	PIM
1984-85	Vermont	ECAC	29	8	16	24	6	....	....	....	....	....
1985-86	Vermont	ECAC	28	1	17	18	14	....	....	....	....	....

LaPOINTE, RICHARD PAUL (RICK) (la-POINT)

Born, Victoria, B.C., August 2, 1955.
Defense. Shoots left. 6'2", 200 lbs.
Last amateur club: Victoria Cougars (WHL).
(Detroit's 1st choice, 5th over-all, in 1975 Amateur Draft).

			Regular Season					Playoffs				
Season	Club	Lea	GP	G	A	TP	PIM	GP	G	A	TP	PIM
1973-74	Victoria	WHL	66	8	18	26	207	....	....	....	....	....
1974-75a	Victoria	WHL	67	19	51	70	177	12	1	12	13	26
1975-76	**Detroit**	**NHL**	**80**	**10**	**23**	**33**	**95**	....	....	....	....	....
1976-77	**Detroit**	**NHL**	**49**	**2**	**11**	**13**	**80**	....	....	....	....	....
	Kansas City	CHL	6	0	0	0	6	....	....	....	....	....
	Philadelphia	**NHL**	**22**	**1**	**8**	**9**	**39**	**10**	**0**	**0**	**0**	**7**
1977-78	**Philadelphia**	**NHL**	**47**	**4**	**16**	**20**	**91**	**12**	**0**	**3**	**3**	**19**
1978-79	**Philadelphia**	**NHL**	**77**	**3**	**18**	**21**	**53**	**7**	**0**	**1**	**1**	**14**
1979-80	**St. Louis**	**NHL**	**80**	**6**	**19**	**25**	**87**	**3**	**0**	**1**	**1**	**6**
1980-81	**St. Louis**	**NHL**	**80**	**8**	**25**	**33**	**124**	**8**	**2**	**2**	**4**	**12**
1981-82	**St. Louis**	**NHL**	**71**	**2**	**20**	**22**	**127**	**3**	**0**	**0**	**0**	**6**
1982-83	**Quebec**	**NHL**	**43**	**2**	**9**	**11**	**59**	....	....	....	....	....
	Fredericton	AHL	31	4	14	18	50	12	0	6	6	8
1983-84	Fredericton	AHL	54	8	22	30	79	....	....	....	....	....
	Quebec	**NHL**	**22**	**2**	**10**	**12**	**12**	**3**	**0**	**0**	**0**	**0**
1984-85	**Los Angeles**	**NHL**	**73**	**4**	**13**	**17**	**46**	....	....	....	....	....
1985-86	**Los Angeles**	**NHL**	**20**	**0**	**4**	**4**	**18**	....	....	....	....	....
	NHL Totals		**664**	**44**	**176**	**220**	**831**	**46**	**2**	**7**	**9**	**64**

a WHL First All-Star Team (1975).

Traded to **Philadelphia** by **Detroit** with Mike Korney for Terry Murray, Bob Ritchie, Steve Coates and Dave Kelly, February 17, 1977. Traded to **St. Louis** by **Philadelphia** with Blake Dunlop for goaltender Phil Myre, June 7, 1979. Traded to **Quebec** by **St. Louis** for Pat Hickey, August 4, 1982. Signed as a free agent by **Los Angeles**, October 10, 1984.

LARIVIERE, GARRY JOSEPH

Born, St. Catharines, Ont., December 6, 1954.
Defense. Shoots right. 6', 190 lbs.
Last amateur club: St. Catharines Black Hawks (OHA).
(Buffalo's 5th choice, 83rd over-all, in 1974 Amateur Draft).

			Regular Season					Playoffs				
Season	Club	Lea	GP	G	A	TP	PIM	GP	G	A	TP	PIM
1972-73	St. Catharines	OHA	55	5	32	37	140	....	....	....	....	....
1973-74	St. Catharines	OHA	60	3	35	38	153	....	....	....	....	....
1974-75	Tulsa	CHL	76	15	38	53	168	....	....	....	....	....
	Phoenix	WHA	4	0	1	1	28	1	0	0	0	0
1975-76	Phoenix	WHA	79	7	17	24	100	5	0	2	2	2
1976-77	Phoenix	WHA	61	7	23	30	48	....	....	....	....	....
	Quebec	WHA	15	0	3	3	8	17	0	10	10	10
1977-78	Quebec	WHA	80	7	49	56	78	11	3	2	5	4
1978-79	Quebec	WHA	50	5	33	38	54	4	0	1	1	2
1979-80	**Quebec**	**NHL**	**75**	**2**	**19**	**21**	**56**	....	....	....	....	....
1980-81	**Quebec**	**NHL**	**52**	**3**	**13**	**16**	**50**	....	....	....	....	....
	Edmonton	**NHL**	**13**	**0**	**2**	**2**	**6**	**9**	**0**	**3**	**3**	**8**
1981-82	**Edmonton**	**NHL**	**62**	**1**	**21**	**22**	**41**	**4**	**0**	**1**	**1**	**0**
1982-83	**Edmonton**	**NHL**	**17**	**0**	**2**	**2**	**14**	**1**	**0**	**1**	**1**	**0**
1983-84	St. Catharines	AHL	65	7	35	42	41	7	0	3	3	2
1984-85	St. Catharines	AHL	72	4	32	36	47	....	....	....	....	....
1985-86	St. Catharines	AHL	52	0	9	9	10	6	0	1	1	6
	NHL Totals		**219**	**6**	**57**	**63**	**167**	**14**	**0**	**5**	**5**	**8**
	WHA Totals		289	26	126	152	316	38	3	15	18	18

Rights traded to **NY Islanders** by **Buffalo** for cash and future considerations, February 19, 1975. Reclaimed by **NY Islanders** from **Quebec** prior to Expansion Draft, June 9, 1979. Claimed as priority selection by **Quebec**, June 9, 1979. Traded to **Vancouver** by **Quebec** for Mario Marois, March 10, 1981. Traded to **Edmonton** by **Vancouver** with the rights to Lars Gunnar Pettersson for Blair MacDonald and the rights to Ken Berry, March 10, 1981.

LARMER, JEFF

Born, Peterborough, Ont., November 10, 1962.
Left wing. Shoots left. 5'10", 175 lbs.
Last amateur club: Kitchener Rangers (OHL).
(Colorado's 7th choice, 129th over-all, in 1981 Entry Draft).

				Regular Season					Playoffs			
Season	Club	Lea	GP	G	A	TP	PIM	GP	G	A	TP	PIM
1980-81a	Kitchener	OHA	68	54	54	108	103	16	12	16	28	27
1981-82 b	Kitchener	OHL	49	51	44	95	95	15	*21	14	*35	16
	Colorado	NHL	8	1	1	2	8	....	....	....	....	....
1982-83	New Jersey	NHL	65	21	24	45	21	....	....	....	....	....
	Wichita	CHL	10	6	5	11	2	....	....	....	....	....
1983-84	New Jersey	NHL	40	6	13	19	8	....	....	....	....	....
	Chicago	NHL	36	9	13	22	80	5	1	0	1	2
1984-85	Chicago	NHL	7	0	0	0	0	....	....	....	....	....
	Milwaukee	IHL	61	24	37	61	30	....	....	....	....	....
1985-86	Chicago	NHL	2	0	0	0	0	....	....	....	....	....
	Nova Scotia	AHL	77	20	44	64	46	....	....	....	....	....
	NHL Totals		158	37	51	88	57	5	1	0	1	2

a OHA Third All-Star Team (1981).
b OHL Second All-Star Team (1982).

Traded to **Chicago** by **New Jersey** for Tim Higgins, January 11, 1984.

LARMER, STEVE DONALD

Born, Peterborough, Ont., June 16, 1961.
Right wing. Shoots left. 5'10", 185 lbs.
Last amateur club: Niagara Falls Flyers (OHA).
(Chicago's 11th choice, 120th over-all, in 1980 Entry Draft).

				Regular Season					Playoffs			
Season	Club	Lea	GP	G	A	TP	PIM	GP	G	A	TP	PIM
1979-80	Niagara Falls	OHA	67	45	69	114	71	10	5	9	14	15
1980-81	Chicago	NHL	4	0	1	1	0	....	....	....	....	....
a	Niagara Falls	OHA	61	55	78	133	73	12	13	8	21	24
1981-82	Chicago	NHL	3	0	0	0	0	....	....	....	....	....
b	New Brunswick	AHL	74	38	44	82	46	15	6	6	12	0
1982-83cd	Chicago	NHL	80	43	47	90	28	11	5	7	12	8
1983-84	Chicago	NHL	80	35	40	75	34	5	2	2	4	7
1984-85	Chicago	NHL	80	46	40	86	16	15	9	13	22	14
1985-86	Chicago	NHL	80	31	45	76	47	3	0	3	3	4
	NHL Totals		327	155	173	328	125	34	16	25	41	33

a OHA Second All-Star Team (1981)
b AHL Second All-Star Team (1982)
c Won Calder Trophy (1983)
d Named to NHL All-Rookie Team (1983)

LAROCQUE, DENIS

Born, Hawkesbury, Ont., October 5, 1967.
Defense. Shoots left. 6'1", 195 lbs.
Last amateur club: Guelph Platers (OHL).
(Los Angeles' 2nd choice, 44th overall, in 1986 Entry Draft).

				Regular Season					Playoffs			
Season	Club	Lea	GP	G	A	TP	PIM	GP	G	A	TP	PIM
1984-85	Guelph	OHL	62	1	15	16	67	....	....	....	....	....
1985-86	Guelph	OHL	66	2	17	19	144	....	....	....	....	....

LAROSE, CLAUDE ANDRE

Born, St. Jean, Que., May 17, 1955.
Left wing. Shoots left. 5'10", 175 lbs.
Last amateur club: Sherbrooke Beavers (QJHL).
(NY Rangers' 7th choice, 120th over-all, in 1975 Amateur Draft).

				Regular Season					Playoffs			
Season	Club	Lea	GP	G	A	TP	PIM	GP	G	A	TP	PIM
1972-73	Drummondville	QJHL	61	63	50	113	12	....	....	....	....	....
1973-74	Drummondville	QJHL	68	56	77	133	16	....	....	....	....	....
1974-75	Shawinigan	QJHL	35	29	31	60	6	....	....	....	....	....
	Sherbrooke	QJHL	29	40	45	85	6	....	....	....	....	....
1975-76	Cincinnati	WHA	79	28	24	52	19	....	....	....	....	....
1976-77	Cincinnati	WHA	81	30	46	76	8	4	2	1	3	0
1977-78	Cincinnati	WHA	51	11	20	31	6	....	....	....	....	....
	Indianapolis	WHA	13	5	8	13	0	....	....	....	....	....
1978-79	Indianapolis	WHA	13	5	8	13	0	....	....	....	....	....
	New Haven	AHL	42	25	25	50	7	10	7	5	12	2
1979-80	NY Rangers	NHL	25	4	7	11	2	....	....	....	....	....
	New Haven	AHL	31	16	27	43	4	....	....	....	....	....
1980-81	New Haven	AHL	80	30	27	57	12	4	1	2	3	0
1981-82	Springfield	AHL	76	30	36	66	12	....	....	....	....	....
	NY Rangers	NHL	....	....	....	....	....	2	0	0	0	0
1982-83		DID NOT PLAY										
1983-84	Sherbrooke	AHL	80	53	67	120	6	....	....	....	....	....
1984-85	Sherbrooke	AHL	77	36	43	79	4	17	10	6	16	8
1985-86	Sherbrooke	AHL	65	38	39	77	2	....	....	....	....	....
	NHL Totals		25	4	7	11	2	2	0	0	0	0

LAROSE, GUY

Born, Hull, Que., August 31, 1967.
Center. Shoots left. 5'9", 175 lbs.
Last amateur club: Ottawa 67s (OHL).
(Buffalo's 11th choice, 224th overall, in 1985 Entry Draft).

				Regular Season					Playoffs			
Season	Club	Lea	GP	G	A	TP	PIM	GP	G	A	TP	PIM
1984-85	Guelph	OHL	58	30	30	60	63	....	....	....	....	....
1985-86	Ottawa	OHL	65	31	61	92	118	....	....	....	....	....

LAROUCHE, PIERRE

(la-ROOSH)

Born, Taschereau, Que., November 16, 1955.
Center. Shoots right. 5'11", 175 lbs.
Last amateur club: Sorel Black Hawks (QJHL).
(Pittsburgh's 1st choice, 8th over-all, in 1974 Amateur Draft).

				Regular Season					Playoffs			
Season	Club	Lea	GP	G	A	TP	PIM	GP	G	A	TP	PIM
1972-73	Quebec	QJHL	20	6	7	13	0	....	....	....	....	....
	Sorel	QJHL	43	47	54	101	44	10	7	6	13	2
1973-74	Sorel	QJHL	67	94	*157	*251	53	13	15	18	33	20
1974-75	Pittsburgh	NHL	79	31	37	68	52	9	2	5	7	2
1975-76	Pittsburgh	NHL	76	53	58	111	33	3	0	1	1	0
1976-77	Pittsburgh	NHL	65	29	34	63	14	3	0	3	3	0
1977-78	Pittsburgh	NHL	20	6	5	11	0	....	....	....	....	....
	Montreal	NHL	44	17	32	49	11	5	2	1	3	4
1978-79	Montreal	NHL	36	9	13	22	4	6	1	3	4	0
1979-80	Montreal	NHL	73	50	41	91	16	9	1	7	8	2
1980-81	Montreal	NHL	61	25	28	53	28	2	0	2	2	0
1981-82	Montreal	NHL	22	9	12	21	0	....	....	....	....	....
	Hartford	NHL	45	25	25	50	12	....	....	....	....	....
1982-83	Hartford	NHL	38	18	22	40	8	....	....	....	....	....
1983-84	NY Rangers	NHL	77	48	33	81	22	5	3	1	4	2
1984-85	NY Rangers	NHL	65	24	36	60	8	....	....	....	....	....
1985-86	NY Rangers	NHL	28	20	7	27	4	16	8	9	17	2
	Hershey	AHL	32	22	17	39	16	....	....	....	....	....
	NHL Totals		729	364	383	747	212	58	17	32	49	12

Traded to **Montreal** by **Pittsburgh** with a player to be named later (Peter Marsh, December 15, 1977) for Pete Mahovlich and Peter Lee, November 29, 1977. Traded to **Hartford** by **Montreal** for a switch in first round selections in 1984 Entry Draft (Montreal selected Petr Svoboda and Hartford chose Sylvain Cote); Hartford's second round choice — (Brian Benning) which was later transferred to St. Louis — in 1984 Entry Draft; and a switch in third round choices in 1985 Entry Draft, December 21, 1981. Signed as free agent by **NY Rangers**, September 12, 1983.

LARSON, REED DAVID

Born, Minneapolis, Minn., July 30, 1956.
Defense. Shoots right. 6', 195 lbs.
Last amateur club: University of Minnesota Gophers (WCHA)
(Detroit's 2nd choice, 22nd over-all, in 1976 Amateur Draft).

				Regular Season					Playoffs			
Season	Club	Lea	GP	G	A	TP	PIM	GP	G	A	TP	PIM
1975-76	U. Minnesota	WCHA	42	13	29	42	94	....	....	....	....	....
1976-77	U. Minnesota	WCHA	21	10	15	25	30	....	....	....	....	....
	Detroit	NHL	14	0	1	1	23	....	....	....	....	....
1977-78	Detroit	NHL	75	19	41	60	95	7	0	2	2	4
1978-79	Detroit	NHL	79	18	49	67	169	....	....	....	....	....
1979-80	Detroit	NHL	80	22	44	66	101	....	....	....	....	....
1980-81	Detroit	NHL	78	27	31	58	153	....	....	....	....	....
1981-82	Detroit	NHL	80	21	39	60	112	....	....	....	....	....
1982-83	Detroit	NHL	80	22	52	74	104	....	....	....	....	....
1983-84	Detroit	NHL	78	23	39	62	122	4	2	0	2	21
1984-85	Detroit	NHL	77	17	45	62	139	3	1	2	3	20
1985-86	Detroit	NHL	67	19	41	60	109	....	....	....	....	....
	Boston	NHL	13	3	4	7	8	3	1	0	1	6
	NHL Totals		721	191	386	577	1135	17	4	4	8	51

Traded to **Boston** by **Detroit** for Mike O'Connell, March 10, 1986.

LATTA, DAVID

Born, Thunder Bay, Ont., January 3, 1967.
Left wing. Shoots left. 5'11", 185 lbs.
Last amateur club: Kitchener Rangers (OHL).
(Quebec's 1st choice, 15th over-all, in 1985 Entry Draft).

				Regular Season					Playoffs			
Season	Club	Lea	GP	G	A	TP	PIM	GP	G	A	TP	PIM
1983-84	Kitchener	OHL	66	17	26	43	54	16	3	6	9	9
1984-85	Kitchener	OHL	52	38	27	65	26	4	2	4	6	4
1985-86	Quebec	NHL	1	0	0	0	0	....	....	....	....	....
	Fredericton	AHL	3	1	0	1	0	5	0	3	3	0
	Kitchener	OHL	55	36	34	70	60	5	7	1	8	15
	NHL Totals		1	0	0	0	0	....	....	....	....	....

LAUEN, MICHAEL ARTHUR (MIKE)

Born, Edina, Minn., February 9, 1961.
Right wing. Shoots right. 6'1", 185 lbs.
Last amateur club: Michigan Tech Huskies (CCHA).
(Winnipeg's 8th choice, 135th over-all, in 1980 Entry Draft).

				Regular Season					Playoffs			
Season	Club	Lea	GP	G	A	TP	PIM	GP	G	A	TP	PIM
1979-80	Michigan Tech	CCHA	35	24	21	45	16	....	....	....	....	....
1980-81	Michigan Tech	CCHA	44	24	20	44	14	....	....	....	....	....
1981-82	Michigan Tech	CCHA	30	13	15	28	28	....	....	....	....	....
1982-83	Michigan Tech	CCHA	30	17	14	31	18	....	....	....	....	....
	Sherbrooke	AHL	5	0	3	3	0	....	....	....	....	....
1983-84	Winnipeg	NHL	4	0	1	1	0	....	....	....	....	....
	Sherbrooke	AHL	62	23	29	52	13	....	....	....	....	....
1984-85	Sherbrooke	AHL	25	6	10	16	2	....	....	....	....	....
1985-86	Toledo	IHL	27	4	10	14	16	....	....	....	....	....
	NHL Totals		4	0	1	1	0	....	....	....	....	....

LAUER, BRAD (LAU-er)

Born, Humboldt, Sask., October 27, 1966.
Right wing. Shoots left. 6', 195 lbs.
Last amateur club: Regina Pats (WHL).
(NY Islander's 2nd choice, 34th over-all, in 1985 Entry Draft).

			Regular Season					Playoffs				
Season	Club	Lea	GP	G	A	TP	PIM	GP	G	A	TP	PIM
1983-84	Regina	WHL	60	5	7	12	51	16	0	1	1	24
1984-85	Regina	WHL	72	33	46	79	57	8	6	6	12	9
1985-86	Regina	WHL	57	36	38	74	69	10	4	5	9	2

LAUGHLIN, CRAIG (LOCK-lin)

Born, Toronto, Ont., September 19, 1957.
Right wing. Shoots right. 6', 190 lbs.
Last amateur club: Clarkson College Golden Knights (ECAC)
(Montreal's 17th choice, 162nd over-all, in 1977 Amateur Draft).

			Regular Season					Playoffs				
Season	Club	Lea	GP	G	A	TP	PIM	GP	G	A	TP	PIM
1976-77	Clarkson	ECAC	33	12	13	25	44	....	....	....	....	....
1977-78	Clarkson	ECAC	30	17	31	48	56	....	....	....	....	....
1978-79	Clarkson	ECAC	30	18	29	47	22	....	....	....	....	....
1979-80	Clarkson	ECAC	34	18	30	48	38	....	....	....	....	....
	Nova Scotia	AHL	2	0	0	0	2	....	....	....	....	....
1980-81	Nova Scotia	AHL	46	32	29	61	15	6	0	1	1	6
1981-82	Nova Scotia	AHL	26	14	15	29	16	....	....	....	....	....
	Montreal	NHL	36	12	11	23	33	3	0	1	1	0
1982-83	Washington	NHL	75	17	27	44	41	4	1	0	1	0
1983-84	Washington	NHL	80	20	32	52	69	8	4	2	6	6
1984-85	Washington	NHL	78	16	34	50	38	5	0	0	0	2
1985-86	Washington	NHL	75	30	45	75	43	9	1	2	3	10
	NHL Totals		344	95	149	244	224	29	6	5	11	18

Traded to **Washington** by **Montreal** with Brian Engblom, Doug Jarvis and Rod Langway for Rick Green and Ryan Walter, September 9, 1982.

LaVALLEE, KEVIN A. (la-VALL-ee)

Born, Sudbury, Ont., September 16, 1961.
Left wing. Shoots left. 5'8", 180 lbs.
Last amateur club: Brantford Alexanders (OHA).
(Calgary's 3rd choice, 32nd over-all, in 1980 Entry Draft).

			Regular Season					Playoffs				
Season	Club	Lea	GP	G	A	TP	PIM	GP	G	A	TP	PIM
1978-79	Brantford	OHA	66	27	23	50	30	....	....	....	....	....
1979-80a	Brantford	OHA	65	65	70	135	50	10	10	4	14	7
1980-81	Calgary	NHL	77	15	20	35	16	8	2	3	5	4
1981-82	Calgary	NHL	75	32	29	61	30	3	0	0	0	7
1982-83	Colorado	CHL	5	5	4	9	0	....	....	....	....	....
	Calgary	NHL	60	19	16	35	17	8	1	3	4	4
1983-84	Los Angeles	NHL	19	3	3	6	2	....	....	....	....	....
	New Haven	AHL	47	29	23	52	25	....	....	....	....	....
1984-85	St. Louis	NHL	38	15	17	32	8	....	....	....	....	....
1985-86	St. Louis	NHL	64	18	20	38	8	13	2	2	4	6
	NHL Totals		273	83	79	172	64	24	4	5	9	17

a OHA Third All-Star Team (1980)
Traded to **Los Angeles** by **Calgary** with Carl Mokosak for Steve Bozek, June 20, 1983. Signed as a free agent by **St. Louis**, September 13, 1984.

LAVARRE, MARK

Born, Evanston, Ill., February 21, 1965.
Right wing. Shoots right. 5'11", 170 lbs.
Last amateur club: Windsor Compuware Spitfires(OHL).
(Chicago's 7th choice, 123rd over-all, in 1983 Entry Draft).

			Regular Season					Playoffs				
Season	Club	Lea	GP	G	A	TP	PIM	GP	G	A	TP	PIM
1983-84	North Bay	OHL	41	19	22	41	15	....	....	....	....	....
1984-85	Windsor	OHL	46	15	30	45	30	4	0	0	0	0
1985-86	Chicago	NHL	2	0	0	0	0	....	....	....	....	....
	Nova Scotia	AHL	62	15	19	34	32	....	....	....	....	....
	NHL Totals		2	0	0	0	0	....	....	....	....	....

LAWLESS, PAUL

Born, Scarborough, Ont., July 2, 1964.
Left wing. Shoots left. 6', 185 lbs.
Last amateur club: Windsor Spitfires (OHL).
(Hartford's 1st choice, 14th over-all, in 1982 Entry Draft).

			Regular Season					Playoffs				
Season	Club	Lea	GP	G	A	TP	PIM	GP	G	A	TP	PIM
1981-82	Windsor	OHL	68	24	25	49	47	9	1	1	2	4
1982-83	Windsor	OHL	33	15	20	35	25	....	....	....	....	....
	Hartford	NHL	47	6	9	15	4	....	....	....	....	....
1983-84	Hartford	NHL	6	0	3	3	0	....	....	....	....	....
a	Windsor	OHL	55	31	49	80	26	2	0	1	1	0
1984-85	Binghamton	AHL	8	1	1	2	0	....	....	....	....	....
	Salt Lake	IHL	72	49	48	97	14	7	5	3	8	20
1985-86	Hartford	NHL	64	17	21	38	20	1	0	0	0	0
	NHL Totals		117	23	33	56	24	1	0	0	0	0

a OHL Second All-Star Team (1984)

LAWTON, BRIAN

Born, New Brunswick, New Jersey, June 29, 1964.
Center. Shoots left. 6', 180 lbs.
Last amateur club: Mount St. Charles High School (Rhode Island)
(Minnesota's 1st choice and 1st over-all in 1983 Entry Draft).

			Regular Season					Playoffs				
Season	Club	Lea	GP	G	A	TP	PIM	GP	G	A	TP	PIM
1981-82	Mt. St. Charles	R.I.	26	45	43	88	....	....	....	....	....	....
1982-83	Mt. St. Charles	R.I.	23	40	43	83	....	....	....	....	....	....
1983-84	Minnesota	NHL	58	10	21	31	33	5	0	0	0	10
1984-85	Minnesota	NHL	40	5	6	11	24	....	....	....	....	....
	Springfield	AHL	42	14	28	42	37	4	1	1	2	2
1985-86	Minnesota	NHL	65	18	17	35	36	3	0	1	1	2
	NHL Totals		163	33	44	77	93	8	0	1	1	12

LAXDAL, DEREK

Born, St. Boniface, Man., February 21, 1966.
Right wing. Shoots right. 6'1', 175 lbs.
Last amateur club: New Westminster Bruins (WHL).

			Regular Season					Playoffs				
Season	Club	Lea	GP	G	A	TP	PIM	GP	G	A	TP	PIM
1982-83	Portland	WHL	39	4	9	13	27	14	0	2	2	2
1983-84	Brandon	WHL	70	23	20	43	86	12	0	4	4	10
1984-85	Toronto	NHL	3	0	0	0	6	....	....	....	....	....
	Brandon	WHL	69	61	41	102	74	....	....	....	....	....
	St. Catherines	AHL	5	3	2	5	2	....	....	....	....	....
1985-86	N. Westminster	WHL	60	43	41	84	76	....	....	....	....	....
	St. Catharines	AHL	7	0	1	1	15	12	1	1	2	24
	NHL Totals		3	0	0	0	6	....	....	....	....	....

LEACH, STEPHEN

Born, Cambridge, Mass., January 16, 1966.
Right Wing. Shoots right. 5'11", 180 lbs.
Last amateur club: University of N. Hampshire Wildcats (H.E.).
(Washington's 2nd choice, 34th over-all, in 1984 Entry Draft).

			Regular Season					Playoffs				
Season	Club	Lea	GP	G	A	TP	PIM	GP	G	A	TP	PIM
1982-83	Matignon HS	Mass.	23	17	21	39	...	....	....	....	....	....
1983-84	Matignon HS	Mass.	21	27	22	49	...	....	....	....	....	....
1984-85	N. Hampshire	H.E.	41	12	25	37	53	....	....	....	....	....
1985-86	Washington	NHL	11	1	1	2	2	6	0	1	1	0
	N. Hampshire	H.E.	25	22	6	28	30	....	....	....	....	....
	NHL Totals		11	1	1	2	2	6	0	1	1	0

LEAVINS, JIM

Born, Dinsmore, Sask., July 28, 1960.
Defense. Shoots left. 5'11", 185 lbs.
Last amateur club: University of Denver Pioneers (WCHA).

			Regular Season					Playoffs				
Season	Club	Lea	GP	G	A	TP	PIM	GP	G	A	TP	PIM
1981-82	Denver	WCHA	41	8	34	42	56	....	....	....	....	....
1982-83	Denver	WCHA	33	16	24	40	20	....	....	....	....	....
1983-84	Denver	WCHA	39	13	26	39	38	....	....	....	....	....
1984-85	Fort Wayne	IHL	76	5	20	25	57	13	3	8	11	10
1985-86	Adirondack	AHL	36	4	21	25	19	....	....	....	....	....
	Detroit	NHL	37	2	11	13	26	....	....	....	....	....
	NHL Totals		37	2	11	13	26	....	....	....	....	....

Signed as a free agent by **Detroit**, November 9, 1985. Traded to **NY Rangers** by **Detroit** with Kelly Kisio and Lane Lambert for Glen Hanlon and **New York's** third-round choices in 1986 and 1987 Entry Drafts, July 29, 1986.

LeBLANC, JEAN GLENN

Born, Campbellton, N.B., January 21, 1964.
Left Wing. Shoots left. 6'1", 195 lbs.
Last amateur club: University of New Brunswick Red Devils (AUAA).

			Regular Season					Playoffs				
Season	Club	Lea	GP	G	A	TP	PIM	GP	G	A	TP	PIM
1983-84	Hull	QMJHL	69	39	35	74	32	....	....	....	....	....
1984-85	New Brunswick	AUAA	24	25	34	59	32	....	....	....	....	....
1985-86	New Brunswick	AUAA	24	38	28	66	35	....	....	....	....	....

Signed as a free agent by **Vancouver**, April 12, 1986.

LEDYARD, GRANT

Born, Winnipeg, Man., November 19, 1961.
Defense. Shoots left. 6'2", 190 lbs.
Last amateur club: Fort Garry (Manitoba Tier II Jrs.)

			Regular Season					Playoffs				
Season	Club	Lea	GP	G	A	TP	PIM	GP	G	A	TP	PIM
1980-81	Saskatoon	WHL	71	9	28	37	148	....	....	....	....	....
1981-82	Fort Garry	MJHL	63	25	45	70	150	....	....	....	....	....
1982-83	Tulsa	CHL	80	13	29	42	115	....	....	....	....	....
1983-84a	Tulsa	CHL	58	9	17	26	71	9	5	4	9	10
1984-85	NY Rangers	NHL	42	8	12	20	53	3	0	2	2	4
	New Haven	AHL	36	6	20	26	18	....	....	....	....	....
1985-86	NY Rangers	NHL	27	2	9	11	20	....	....	....	....	....
	Los Angeles	NHL	52	7	18	25	78	....	....	....	....	....
	NHL Totals		121	17	39	56	151	3	0	2	2	4

a Won Bob Gassoff Trophy (CHL's Most Improved Defenseman) (1984)

Signed as a free agent by **NY Rangers**, July 7, 1982. Traded to **Los Angeles** by **NY Rangers** with Roland Melanson for Los Angeles' fourth-round choice in 1987 Entry Draft and Brian MacLellan, December 7, 1985.

LEE, EDWARD (ED)

Born, Rochester, N.Y., December 17, 1961.
Right wing. Shoots right. 6'2", 180 lbs.
Last amateur club: Princeton Universtiy Tigers (ECAC).
(Quebec's 4th choice, 95th over-all, in 1981 Entry Draft).

Season	Club	Lea	Regular Season					Playoffs				
			GP	G	A	TP	PIM	GP	G	A	TP	PIM
1980-81	Princeton U.	ECAC	21	6	8	14	34	....	....	....	....	....
1981-82	Princeton U.	ECAC	26	12	21	33	46	....	....	....	....	....
1982-83	Princeton U.	ECAC	25	19	25	44	51	....	....	....	....	....
1983-84	Princeton U.	ECAC	11	10	18	28	22	....	....	....	....	....
	Fredericton	AHL	6	0	4	4	4	....	....	....	....	....
1984-85	**Quebec**	**NHL**	**2**	**0**	**0**	**0**	**5**	....	....	....	....	....
	Fredericton	AHL	21	11	7	18	45	....	....	....	....	....
1985-86	Fredericton	AHL	6	3	1	4	2	....	....	....	....	....
	Springfield	AHL	24	3	4	7	26	....	....	....	....	....
	Indianapolis	IHL	2	0	0	0	0	....	....	....	....	....
	NHL Totals		**2**	**0**	**0**	**0**	**5**					

Traded to **Minnesota** by **Quebec** for Minnesota's sixth-round choice (Scott White) in 1986 Entry Draft, November 15, 1985.

LEEMAN, GARY

Born, Toronto, Ont., February 19, 1964.
Right wing/Defense. Shoots right. 5'11", 170 lbs.
Last amateur club: Regina Pats (WHL).
(Toronto's 2nd choice, 24th over-all, in 1982 Entry Draft).

Season	Club	Lea	Regular Season					Playoffs				
			GP	G	A	TP	PIM	GP	G	A	TP	PIM
1981-82	Regina	WHL	72	19	41	60	112	3	2	2	4	0
1982-83ab	Regina	WHL	63	24	62	86	88	5	1	5	6	4
	Toronto	**NHL**	....	....	....	....	....	2	0	0	0	0
1983-84	**Toronto**	**NHL**	52	4	8	12	31	....	....	....	....	....
1984-85	**Toronto**	**NHL**	53	5	26	31	72	....	....	....	....	....
	St. Catharines	AHL	7	2	2	4	11	....	....	....	....	....
1985-86	**Toronto**	**NHL**	53	9	23	32	20	10	2	10	12	2
	St. Catharines	AHL	25	15	13	28	6	....	....	....	....	....
	NHL Totals		**158**	**18**	**57**	**75**	**123**	**12**	**2**	**10**	**12**	**2**

a WHL First All-Star Team (1983)
b Named WHL's Top Defenseman (1983)

LEETCH, BRIAN

Born, Corpus Christi, Texas, March 3, 1968.
Defense. Shoots left. 5'11", 170 lbs.
Last amateur club: Avon Old Farms (HS).
(NY Rangers' 1st choice, 9th overall, in 1986 Entry Draft).

Season	Club	Lea	Regular Season					Playoffs				
			GP	G	A	TP	PIM	GP	G	A	TP	PIM
1984-85	Avon O. Farms	HS	26	30	46	76	15	....	....	....	....	....
1985-86	Avon O. Farms	HS	28	40	44	84	18	....	....	....	....	....

LEIME, HEIKKI

(LEE-me, Hike-ee)

Born, Turku, Finland, May 7, 1962.
Defense. Shoots left. 6'1", 195 lbs.
Last amateur club: TPS (Finland).
(Buffalo's 9th choice, 143rd over-all, in 1981 Entry Draft).

Season	Club	Lea	Regular Season					Playoffs				
			GP	G	A	TP	PIM	GP	G	A	TP	PIM
1984-85	Rochester	AHL	76	4	18	22	30	4	0	0	0	4
1985-86	Rochester	AHL	53	0	17	17	51	....	....	....	....	....

LEITER, KEN

Born, Detroit, Mich., April 19, 1961.
Defense. Shoots right. 6'1", 195 lbs.
Last amateur club: Michigan State University Spartans (CCHA).
(New York Islanders' 6th choice, 101st over-all, in 1980 Entry Draft).

Season	Club	Lea	Regular Season					Playoffs				
			GP	G	A	TP	PIM	GP	G	A	TP	PIM
1979-80	Michigan State	WCHA	38	0	10	10	96	....	....	....	....	....
1980-81	Michigan State	WCHA	31	2	12	14	48	....	....	....	....	....
1981-82	Michigan State	CCHA	31	7	13	20	50	....	....	....	....	....
1982-83a	Michigan State	CCHA	40	3	28	31	47	....	....	....	....	....
1983-84	Indianapolis	CHL	68	10	26	36	46	10	3	4	7	0
1984-85	**NY Islanders**	**NHL**	5	0	2	2	2	....	....	....	....	....
	Springfield	AHL	39	3	12	15	12	4	0	3	3	2
1985-86	**NY Islanders**	**NHL**	9	1	1	2	6	....	....	....	....	....
	Springfield	AHL	68	7	27	34	51	....	....	....	....	....
	NHL Totals		**14**	**1**	**3**	**4**	**8**	....	....	....	....	....

a CCHA First All-Star Team (1983)

LEMAY, MAURICE (MOE)

(le-MAY)

Born, Saskatoon, Sask., February 18, 1962.
Left wing. Shoots left. 5'11", 185 lbs.
Last amateur club: Ottawa 67's (OHL).
(Vancouver's 4th choice, 105th over-all, in 1981 Entry Draft).

Season	Club	Lea	Regular Season					Playoffs				
			GP	G	A	TP	PIM	GP	G	A	TP	PIM
1979-80	Ottawa	OHA	62	16	23	39	20	10	2	3	5	19
1980-81	Ottawa	OHA	63	32	45	77	102	7	3	5	8	17
1981-82a	Ottawa	OHL	62	*68	70	138	48	17	9	19	28	18
	Vancouver	**NHL**	5	1	2	3	0	....	....	....	....	....
1982-83	**Vancouver**	**NHL**	44	11	9	20	41	....	....	....	....	....
	Fredericton	AHL	26	7	8	15	6	9	0	2	2	10
1983-84	Fredericton	AHL	23	9	7	16	32	....	....	....	....	....
	Vancouver	**NHL**	56	12	18	30	38	4	0	0	0	12
1984-85	**Vancouver**	**NHL**	74	21	31	52	68	....	....	....	....	....
1985-86	**Vancouver**	**NHL**	48	16	15	31	92	....	....	....	....	....
	NHL Totals		**227**	**61**	**75**	**136**	**239**	**4**	**0**	**0**	**0**	**12**

a OHL First All-Star Team (1982)

LEMIEUX, ALAIN

(le-MYEW)

Born, Montreal, Que., May 24, 1961.
Center. Shoots left. 6', 185 lbs.
Last amateur club: Trois Rivieres Draveurs (QJHL).
(St. Louis' 4th choice, 96th over-all, in 1980 Entry Draft).

Season	Club	Lea	Regular Season					Playoffs				
			GP	G	A	TP	PIM	GP	G	A	TP	PIM
1979-80	Chicoutimi	QJHL	72	47	95	142	36	12	8	12	20	8
1980-81	Chicoutimi	QJHL	11	0	0	0	2	....	....	....	....	....
	Trois Rivières	QJHL	69	68	98	166	62	19	18	31	49	38
1981-82	**St. Louis**	**NHL**	3	0	1	1	0	....	....	....	....	....
	Salt Lake	CHL	74	41	42	83	61	10	6	4	10	14
1982-83	Salt Lake	CHL	29	20	24	44	35	....	....	....	....	....
	St. Louis	**NHL**	42	9	25	34	18	4	0	1	1	0
1983-84	**St. Louis**	**NHL**	17	4	5	9	6	....	....	....	....	....
	Montana	CHL	38	28	41	69	36	....	....	....	....	....
	Springfield	AHL	14	11	14	25	18	4	0	3	3	2
1984-85	**St. Louis**	**NHL**	19	4	2	6	0	....	....	....	....	....
	Peoria	IHL	2	1	0	1	0	....	....	....	....	....
	Quebec	**NHL**	30	11	11	22	12	14	3	3	6	0
1985-86	**Quebec**	**NHL**	7	0	0	0	2	1	1	2	3	0
	Fredericton	AHL	64	29	45	74	54	5	5	2	7	5
	NHL Totals		**118**	**28**	**44**	**72**	**38**	**19**	**4**	**6**	**10**	**0**

Traded to **Quebec** by **St. Louis** for Luc Dufour, January 29, 1985.

LEMIEUX, CLAUDE

Born, Buckingham, Que., July 16, 1965.
Right wing. Shoots right. 6', 220 lbs.
Last amateur club: Trois Rivières Draveurs (QMJHL).
(Montreal's 2nd choice, 26th over-all, in 1983 Entry Draft).

Season	Club	Lea	Regular Season					Playoffs				
			GP	G	A	TP	PIM	GP	G	A	TP	PIM
1981-82	Richelieu	Midget	48	24	48	72	96	....	....	....	....	....
1982-83	Trois Rivières	QMJHL	62	28	38	66	187	4	1	0	1	30
1983-84	**Montreal**	**NHL**	8	1	1	2	12	....	....	....	....	....
	Verdun	QMJHL	51	41	45	86	225	9	8	12	20	63
	Nova Scotia	AHL	....	....	....	....	....	2	1	0	1	0
1984-85	**Montreal**	**NHL**	1	0	1	1	7	....	....	....	....	....
ab	Verdun	QMJHL	52	58	66	124	152	14	23	17	40	38
1985-86	**Montreal**	**NHL**	10	1	2	3	22	20	10	6	16	68
	Sherbrooke	AHL	58	21	32	53	145	....	....	....	....	....
	NHL Totals		**19**	**2**	**4**	**6**	**41**	**20**	**10**	**6**	**16**	**68**

a Named Most Valuable Player in QMJHL Playoffs (1985).
b QMJHL First All-Star Team (1985).

LEMIEUX, JOCELYN

Born, Mont Laurier, Que., November 18, 1967.
Right wing. Shoots left. 5'10", 200 lbs.
Last amateur club: Laval Titans (QMJHL).
(St. Louis' 1st choice, 10th overall, in 1986 Entry Draft).

Season	Club	Lea	Regular Season					Playoffs				
			GP	G	A	TP	PIM	GP	G	A	TP	PIM
1984-85	Laval	QMJHL	68	13	19	32	92	....	....	....	....	....
1985-86a	Laval	QMJHL	71	57	68	125	131	14	9	15	24	37

a QMJHL First All-Star Team (1986).

LEMIEUX, MARIO

(le-MYEW)

Born, Montreal, Que., October 5, 1965.
Center. Shoots right. 6'4", 200 lbs.
Last amateur club: Laval Voisins (QMJHL).
(Pittsburgh's 1st choice and 1st over-all in 1984 Entry Draft).

Season	Club	Lea	Regular Season					Playoffs				
			GP	G	A	TP	PIM	GP	G	A	TP	PIM
1981-82	Laval	QMJHL	64	30	66	96	22	18	5	9	14	31
1982-83a	Laval	QMJHL	66	84	100	184	76	12	14	18	32	18
1983-84bcd	Laval	QMJHL	70	*133	*149	*282	92	14	*29	*23	*52	29
1984-85ef	**Pittsburgh**	**NHL**	73	43	57	100	54	....	....	....	....	....
1985-86gh	**Pittsburgh**	**NHL**	79	48	93	141	43	....	....	....	....	....
	NHL Totals		**152**	**91**	**150**	**241**	**97**	....	....	....	....	....

a QMJHL Second All-Star Team (1983)
b QMJHL First All-Star Team (1984)
c QMJHL Most Valuable Player (1984)
d Canadian Major Junior Player of the Year (1984)
e won Calder Memorial Trophy (1985).
f Named to NHL All-Rookie Team (1985).
g NHL Second All-Star Team (1986).
h Won Lester B. Pearson Award (1986).

LETENDRE, DANIEL   (le-TAHND-dre)

Born, Sorel, Que., January 21, 1965.
Right wing. Shoots right. 6', 200 lbs.
Last amateur club: Quebec Remparts (QMJHL).
(Montreal's 5th choice, 45th over-all, in 1983 Entry Draft).

				Regular Season					Playoffs			
Season	Club	Lea	GP	G	A	TP	PIM	GP	G	A	TP	PIM
1982-83	Quebec	QMJHL	61	28	25	53	22	....	....	....	....	....
1983-84	Quebec	QMJHL	67	25	41	66	35	5	2	3	5	4
1984-85	Flint	IHL	2	0	0	0	0	7	1	0	1	2
	Trois Rivieres	QMJHL	61	36	35	71	39	7	6	2	8	2
1985-86	Saginaw	IHL	40	8	7	15	2	....	....	....	....	....

LEVER, DONALD RICHARD (DON)   (LEE-ver)

Born, South Porcupine, Ont., November 14, 1952.
Left wing. Shoots left. 5'11", 185 lbs.
Last amateur club: Niagara Falls Flyers (OHA).
(Vancouver's 1st choice, 3rd over-all, in 1972 Amateur Draft).

				Regular Season					Playoffs			
Season	Club	Lea	GP	G	A	TP	PIM	GP	G	A	TP	PIM
1970-71	Niagara Falls	OHA	59	35	36	71	112	....	....	....	....	....
1971-72	Niagara Falls	OHA	63	61	65	126	69	....	....	....	....	....
1972-73	Vancouver	NHL	78	12	26	38	49	....	....	....	....	....
1973-74	Vancouver	NHL	78	23	25	48	28	....	....	....	....	....
1974-75	Vancouver	NHL	80	38	30	68	49	5	0	1	1	4
1975-76	Vancouver	NHL	80	25	40	65	93	2	0	0	0	0
1976-77	Vancouver	NHL	80	27	30	57	28	....	....	....	....	....
1977-78	Vancouver	NHL	75	17	32	49	58	....	....	....	....	....
1978-79	Vancouver	NHL	71	23	21	44	17	3	2	1	3	2
1979-80	Vancouver	NHL	51	21	17	38	32	....	....	....	....	....
	Atlanta	NHL	28	14	16	30	4	4	1	1	2	0
1980-81	Calgary	NHL	62	26	31	57	56	16	4	7	11	20
1981-82	Calgary	NHL	23	8	11	19	6	....	....	....	....	....
	Colorado	NHL	59	22	28	50	20	....	....	....	....	....
1982-83	New Jersey	NHL	79	23	30	53	68	....	....	....	....	....
1983-84	New Jersey	NHL	70	14	19	33	44	....	....	....	....	....
1984-85	New Jersey	NHL	67	10	8	18	31	....	....	....	....	....
1985-86	Buffalo	NHL	29	7	1	8	6	....	....	....	....	....
	Rochester	AHL	29	6	11	17	16	....	....	....	....	....
	NHL Totals		**1010**	**310**	**365**	**675**	**589**	**30**	**7**	**10**	**17**	**26**

Traded to **Atlanta** by **Vancouver** with Brad Smith for Ivan Boldirev and Darcy Rota, February 8, 1980. Traded to **Colorado** by **Calgary** with Bob MacMillan for Lanny McDonald and Colorado's fourth round choice — (Mikko Makela) later transferred to NY Islanders — in 1983 Entry Draft, November 25, 1981. Rights sold to **Buffalo** by **New Jersey**, September 9, 1985.

LEVIE, CRAIG DEAN   (LEE-vee)

Born, Calgary, Alta., August 17, 1959.
Defense. Shoots right. 5'11", 190 lbs.
Last amateur club: Edmonton Oilers (WHL).
(Montreal's 3rd choice, 43rd over-all, in 1979 Entry Draft).

				Regular Season					Playoffs			
Season	Club	Lea	GP	G	A	TP	PIM	GP	G	A	TP	PIM
1977-78	Flin Flon	WHL	72	25	64	89	167	16	3	7	10	58
1978-79	Edmonton	WHL	69	29	63	92	200	7	4	6	10	11
1979-80	Nova Scotia	AHL	72	6	21	27	74	6	0	2	2	17
1980-81ab	Nova Scotia	AHL	80	20	*62	82	162	6	5	2	7	16
1981-82	Tulsa	CHL	14	7	11	17	17	....	....	....	....	....
	Winnipeg	NHL	40	4	9	13	48	....	....	....	....	....
1982-83	**Winnipeg**	NHL	22	4	5	9	31	....	....	....	....	....
	Sherbrooke	AHL	44	3	27	30	52	....	....	....	....	....
1983-84	Salt Lake	CHL	37	8	20	28	101	....	....	....	....	....
	Minnesota	NHL	37	6	13	19	44	15	2	3	5	32
1984-85	**St. Louis**	NHL	61	6	23	29	33	1	0	0	0	0
1985-86	**Minnesota**	NHL	14	2	2	4	8	....	....	....	....	....
	Springfield	AHL	36	5	23	28	82	....	....	....	....	....
	NHL Totals		**174**	**22**	**52**	**74**	**164**	**16**	**2**	**3**	**5**	**32**

a AHL First All-Star Team (1981).
b Won Eddie Shore Plaque (AHL's Most Outstanding Defenseman) (1981).
Claimed by **Winnipeg** from **Montreal** in NHL Waiver Draft, October 5, 1981. Traded to **Minnesota** by **Winnipeg** with the rights to Tom Ward for Tim Young, August 3, 1983. Claimed by **St. Louis** from **Minnesota** in NHL Waiver Draft, October 9, 1984. Claimed by **Calgary** from **St. Louis** in NHL Waiver Draft, October 7, 1985.

LEWIS, DAVID RODNEY (DAVE)

Born, Kindersley, Sask., July 3, 1953.
Defense. Shoots left. 6'2", 205 lbs.
Last amateur club: Saskatoon Blades (WHL).
(New York Islanders' 2nd choice, 33rd over-all, in 1973 Amateur Draft).

				Regular Season					Playoffs			
Season	Club	Lea	GP	G	A	TP	PIM	GP	G	A	TP	PIM
1971-72	Saskatoon	WHL	52	2	9	11	68	8	2	3	5	4
1972-73	Saskatoon	WHL	67	10	35	45	89	16	3	12	15	44
1973-74	NY Islanders	NHL	66	2	15	17	58	....	....	....	....	....
1974-75	NY Islanders	NHL	78	5	14	19	98	17	0	1	1	28
1975-76	NY Islanders	NHL	73	0	19	19	54	13	0	1	1	44
1976-77	NY Islanders	NHL	79	4	24	28	44	12	1	6	7	4
1977-78	NY Islanders	NHL	77	3	11	14	58	7	0	1	1	11
1978-79	NY Islanders	NHL	79	5	18	23	43	10	0	0	0	4
1979-80	NY Islanders	NHL	62	5	16	21	54	....	....	....	....	....
	Los Angeles	NHL	11	1	1	2	12	4	0	1	1	2
1980-81	Los Angeles	NHL	67	1	12	13	98	4	0	2	2	4
1981-82	Los Angeles	NHL	64	1	13	14	75	10	0	4	4	36
1982-83	Los Angeles	NHL	79	2	10	12	53	....	....	....	....	....
1983-84	New Jersey	NHL	66	2	5	7	63	....	....	....	....	....
1984-85	New Jersey	NHL	74	3	9	12	78	....	....	....	....	....
1985-86	New Jersey	NHL	69	0	15	15	81	....	....	....	....	....
	NHL Totals		**944**	**34**	**182**	**216**	**869**	**77**	**1**	**16**	**17**	**133**

Traded to **Los Angeles** by **NY Islanders** with Billy Harris for Butch Goring, March 10, 1980.
Traded to **Minnesota** by **Los Angeles** with Los Angeles' second round choice in 1985 Entry Draft for Steve Christoff and Minnesota's fifth round choice in 1985 Entry Draft, October 3, 1983. Traded to **New Jersey** by **Minnesota** for Brent Ashton, October 3, 1983. Signed as a free agent by **Detroit**, July 27, 1986.

LIDSTER, DOUG

Born, Kamloops, B.C., October 18, 1960.
Defense. Shoots right. 6'1", 195 lbs.
Last amateur club: 1984 Canadian Olympic Team.
(Vancouver's 6th choice, 133rd over-all, in 1980 Entry Draft).

				Regular Season					Playoffs			
Season	Club	Lea	GP	G	A	TP	PIM	GP	G	A	TP	PIM
1979-80	Colorado	WCHA	39	18	25	43	52	....	....	....	....	....
1980-81	Colorado	WCHA	36	10	30	40	54	....	....	....	....	....
1981-82	Colorado	WCHA	36	13	22	35	32	....	....	....	....	....
1982-83	Colorado	WCHA	34	15	41	56	30	....	....	....	....	....
1983-84	Cdn. Olympic	...	59	6	20	26	28	....	....	....	....	....
	Vancouver	NHL	8	0	0	0	4	2	0	1	1	0
1984-85	Vancouver	NHL	78	6	24	30	55	....	....	....	....	....
1985-86	Vancouver	NHL	78	12	16	28	56	3	0	1	1	2
	NHL Totals		**164**	**18**	**40**	**58**	**115**	**5**	**0**	**2**	**2**	**2**

LINDSTROM, BO MORGAN WILLY   (LIND-strum, WILLY)

Born, Grunns, Sweden, May 5, 1951.
Right wing. Shoots left. 6', 180 lbs.
Last amateur club: Swedish National Team.

				Regular Season					Playoffs			
Season	Club	Lea	GP	G	A	TP	PIM	GP	G	A	TP	PIM
1973-74	V. Frolunda	Swe.	27	19	11	30	22	....	....	....	....	....
	Swe. National	...	15	8	6	14	8	....	....	....	....	....
1974-75	V. Frolunda	Swe.	29	18	15	33	24	....	....	....	....	....
	Swe. National	...	27	7	5	12	10	....	....	....	....	....
1975-76	Winnipeg	WHA	81	23	36	59	32	13	4	7	11	2
1976-77	Winnipeg	WHA	79	44	36	80	37	20	9	6	15	22
	Swe. National	...	5	0	0	0	9	....	....	....	....	....
1977-78	Winnipeg	WHA	77	30	30	60	42	8	3	4	7	17
1978-79	Winnipeg	WHA	79	26	36	62	22	10	*10	5	15	9
1979-80	Winnipeg	NHL	79	23	26	49	20	....	....	....	....	....
1980-81	Winnipeg	NHL	72	22	13	35	45	....	....	....	....	....
1981-82	Winnipeg	NHL	74	32	27	59	33	4	1	3	2	2
1982-83	Winnipeg	NHL	63	20	25	45	8	....	....	....	....	....
	Edmonton	NHL	10	6	5	11	2	16	2	11	13	4
1983-84	Edmonton	NHL	73	22	16	38	38	19	5	5	10	10
1984-85	Edmonton	NHL	80	12	20	32	18	18	1	5	6	0
1985-86	Pittsburgh	NHL	71	14	17	31	30	....	....	....	....	....
	NHL Totals		**522**	**151**	**149**	**300**	**194**	**57**	**14**	**18**	**32**	**24**
	WHA Totals		**316**	**123**	**138**	**261**	**133**	**51**	**26**	**22**	**48**	**50**

Signed as free agent by **Winnipeg**, July 25, 1979. Traded to **Edmonton** by **Winnipeg** for Laurie Boschman, March 8, 1983. Claimed by **Pittsburgh** from **Edmonton** in NHL Waiver Draft, October 7, 1985.

LINSEMAN, KEN   (LINZ-man)

Born, Kingston, Ont., August 11, 1958.
Center. Shoots left. 5'11", 175 lbs.
Last amateur club: Kingston Canadians (OHA).
(Philadelphia's 2nd choice, 7th over-all, in 1978 Amateur Draft).

				Regular Season					Playoffs			
Season	Club	Lea	GP	G	A	TP	PIM	GP	G	A	TP	PIM
1975-76	Kingston	OHA	65	61	51	112	92	7	5	0	5	18
1976-77a	Kingston	OHA	63	53	74	127	210	10	9	12	21	54
1977-78	Birmingham	WHA	71	38	38	76	126	5	2	2	4	15
1978-79	Maine	AHL	38	17	22	39	106	....	....	....	....	....
	Philadelphia	NHL	30	5	20	25	23	8	2	6	8	22
1979-80	Philadelphia	NHL	80	22	57	79	107	17	4	*18	22	40
1980-81	Philadelphia	NHL	51	17	30	47	150	12	4	16	20	67
1981-82	Philadelphia	NHL	79	24	68	92	275	4	1	2	3	6
1982-83	Edmonton	NHL	72	33	42	75	181	16	6	8	14	22
1983-84	Edmonton	NHL	72	18	49	67	119	19	10	4	14	65
1984-85	Boston	NHL	75	24	49	74	126	5	4	6	10	8
1985-86	Boston	NHL	64	23	58	81	97	3	0	1	1	17
	NHL Totals		522	167	373	540	1078	84	31	61	92	247
	WHA Totals		71	38	38	76	126	5	2	2	4	15

a OHA Second All-Star Team (1977).
Traded to **Hartford** by **Philadelphia** with Greg Adams and Philadelphia's first (David Jensen) and third round choices (Leif Karlsson) in 1983 Entry Draft for Mark Howe and Hartford's third round choice (Derrick Smith) in the 1983 Entry Draft, August 19, 1982. Traded to **Edmonton** by **Hartford** with Don Nachbaur for Risto Siltanen and Brent Loney, August 19, 1982. Traded to **Boston** by **Edmonton** for Mike Krushelnyski, June 21, 1984.

LOFTHOUSE, MARK   (LOFT-house)

Born, New Westminster, B.C., April 21, 1957.
Right wing/Center. Shoots right. 6'2", 195 lbs.
Last amateur club: New Westminster Bruins (WHL).
(Washington's 2nd choice, 21st over-all, in 1977 Amateur Draft).

				Regular Season					Playoffs			
Season	Club	Lea	GP	G	A	TP	PIM	GP	G	A	TP	PIM
1974-75	N. Westminster	WHL	61	36	28	64	53	....	....	....	....	....
1975-76	N. Westminster	WHL	72	68	48	116	55	17	9	12	21	22
1976-77	N. Westminster	WHL	70	54	58	112	59	14	10	8	18	19
1977-78	Washington	NHL	18	2	1	3	8	....	....	....	....	....
	Hershey	AHL	35	8	6	14	39	....	....	....	....	....
	Salt Lake	CHL	13	0	1	1	4	5	0	1	1	6
1978-79	Washington	NHL	52	13	10	23	10	....	....	....	....	....
	Hershey	AHL	16	7	7	14	6	4	0	1	1	2
1979-80	Washington	NHL	68	15	18	33	20	....	....	....	....	....
	Hershey	AHL	9	7	3	10	6	....	....	....	....	....
1980-81	Washington	NHL	3	1	1	2	4	....	....	....	....	....
ab	Hershey	AHL	72	*48	55	*103	131	10	6	9	15	24
1981-82	Detroit	NHL	12	3	4	7	13	....	....	....	....	....
	Adirondack	AHL	69	33	38	71	75	5	2	3	5	2
1982-83	Detroit	NHL	28	8	4	12	18	....	....	....	....	....
	Adirondack	AHL	39	27	18	45	20	....	....	....	....	....
1983-84	New Haven	AHL	79	37	64	101	45	....	....	....	....	....
1984-85	New Haven	AHL	12	11	4	15	4	....	....	....	....	....
1985-86	New Haven	AHL	70	32	35	67	56	5	2	1	3	0
	NHL Totals		181	42	38	80	73	....	....	....	....	....

a AHL First All-Star Team (1981).
b Won John B. Sollenberger Trophy (AHL's leading scorer) (1981)
Traded to **Detroit** by **Washington** for Al Jensen, July 23, 1981. Signed as free agent by **Los Angeles**, August 10, 1983.

LOGAN, ROBERT

Born, Montreal, Que., February 22, 1964.
Right wing. Shoots right. 6', 180 lbs.
Last amateur club: Yale University Bulldogs (ECAC)
(Buffalo's 8th choice, 100th over-all, in 1982 Entry Draft.)

				Regular Season					Playoffs			
Season	Club	Lea	GP	G	A	TP	PIM	GP	G	A	TP	PIM
1982-83	Yale	ECAC	28	13	12	25	8	....	....	....	....	....
1983-84	Yale	ECAC	22	9	13	22	25	....	....	....	....	....
1984-85	Yale	ECAC	32	19	12	31	18	....	....	....	....	....
1985-86a	Yale	ECAC	27	19	21	40	22	....	....	....	....	....

a ECAC Second All-Star Team (1986).

LOISELLE, CLAUDE   (LOY-zell)

Born, Ottawa, Ont., May 29, 1963.
Center. Shoots left. 5'11", 190 lbs.
Last amateur club: Windsor Spitfires (OHL).
(Detroit's 1st choice, 23rd over-all, in 1981 Entry Draft.)

				Regular Season					Playoffs			
Season	Club	Lea	GP	G	A	TP	PIM	GP	G	A	TP	PIM
1980-81	Windsor	OHA	68	38	56	94	103	11	3	3	6	40
1981-82	Detroit	NHL	4	1	0	1	2	....	....	....	....	....
	Windsor	OHL	68	36	73	109	192	9	2	10	12	42
1982-83	Detroit	NHL	18	2	0	2	15	....	....	....	....	....
	Adirondack	AHL	6	1	7	8	0	6	2	4	6	0
1983-84	Detroit	NHL	28	4	6	10	32	....	....	....	....	....
	Adirondack	AHL	29	13	16	29	59	....	....	....	....	....
1984-85	Detroit	NHL	30	8	1	9	45	3	0	2	2	0
	Adirondack	AHL	47	22	29	51	24	....	....	....	....	....
1985-86	Detroit	NHL	48	7	15	22	142	....	....	....	....	....
	Adirondack	AHL	21	15	11	26	32	16	5	10	15	38
	NHL Totals		128	22	22	44	236	3	0	2	2	0

Traded to **New Jersey** by **Detroit** for Tim Higgins, June 25, 1986.

LOMOW, BYRON

Born, Sherwood Park, Alta., April 27, 1965.
Center. Shoots right. 5'11", 180 lbs.
Last amateur club: Brandon Wheat Kings (WHL).

				Regular Season					Playoffs			
Season	Club	Lea	GP	G	A	TP	PIM	GP	G	A	TP	PIM
1982-83	Brandon	OHA	62	19	26	45	21	....	....	....	....	....
1983-84	Brandon	WHL	71	44	57	101	44	12	1	5	6	16
1984-85	Brandon	WHL	71	42	70	112	90	....	....	....	....	....
1985-86	Brandon	WHL	72	52	67	119	77	....	....	....	....	....
	Indianapolis	IHL	9	8	3	11	10	5	2	11	3	2

Signed a free agent by **Minnesota**, April 21, 1986.

LONEY, BRENT

Born, Cornwall, Ont., May 25, 1964.
Left wing. Shoots left. 6', 155 lbs.
Last amateur club: Cornwall Royals (OHL).
(Edmonton's 3rd choice, 62nd over-all, in 1982 Entry Draft).

				Regular Season					Playoffs			
Season	Club	Lea	GP	G	A	TP	PIM	GP	G	A	TP	PIM
1981-82	Cornwall	OHL	65	13	12	25	57	5	2	0	2	0
1982-83	Cornwall	OHL	47	11	24	35	69	8	1	0	1	2
1983-84	Cornwall	OHL	62	24	38	62	56	3	0	0	0	0
1984-85	Salt Lake	IHL	11	2	0	2	2	....	....	....	....	....
	Hamilton	IHL	13	11	8	19	19	....	....	....	....	....
	Oshawa	OHL	32	13	16	29	21	5	2	2	4	4
	Binghamton	AHL	4	0	0	0	0	3	0	0	0	0
1985-86	Hershey	AHL	59	0	8	8	113	1	0	0	0	0

Rights traded to **Hartford** by **Edmonton** with Risto Siltanen for Ken Linseman and Don Nachbaur, August 19, 1982.

LONEY, TROY

Born, Bow Island, Alta., September 21, 1963.
Left wing. Shoots left. 6'3", 215 lbs.
Last amateur club: Lethbridge Broncos (WHL).
(Pittsburgh's 3rd choice, 52nd over-all, in 1982 Entry Draft).

				Regular Season					Playoffs			
Season	Club	Lea	GP	G	A	TP	PIM	GP	G	A	TP	PIM
1980-81	Lethbridge	WHL	71	18	13	31	100	9	2	2	5	14
1981-82	Lethbridge	WHL	71	26	33	59	152	12	3	3	6	14
1982-83	Lethbridge	WHL	72	33	34	67	156	20	10	7	17	43
1983-84	Pittsburgh	NHL	13	0	0	0	9	....	....	....	....	....
	Baltimore	AHL	63	18	13	31	147	10	0	2	2	19
1984-85	Pittsburgh	NHL	46	10	8	18	59	....	....	....	....	....
	Baltimore	AHL	15	4	2	6	25	....	....	....	....	....
1985-86	Pittsburgh	NHL	47	3	9	12	95	....	....	....	....	....
	Baltimore	AHL	33	12	11	23	84	....	....	....	....	....
	NHL Totals		106	13	17	30	163	....	....	....	....	....

LOOB, HAKAN   (LEWB, HOH-kan)

Born, Karlstad, Sweden, July 3, 1960.
Right wing. Shoots right. 5'9", 175 lbs.
Last amateur club: Farjestads BK (Sweden).
(Calgary's 10th choice, 181st over-all, in 1980 Entry Draft).

				Regular Season					Playoffs			
Season	Club	Lea	GP	G	A	TP	PIM	GP	G	A	TP	PIM
1979-80	Farjestads	Swe.	36	15	4	19	20	....	....	....	....	....
1980-81	Farjestads	Swe.	36	23	6	29	14	7	5	3	8	6
	Swe. National	...	6	0	1	1	0	....	....	....	....	....
1981-82	Farjestads	Swe.	36	26	15	41	28	2	1	0	1	0
	Swe. National	...	21	8	3	11	8	....	....	....	....	....
1982-83	Farjestads	Swe.	36	42	34	76	29	8	10	4	14	6
	Swe. National	...	11	2	2	4	8	....	....	....	....	....
1983-84a	Calgary	NHL	77	30	25	55	22	11	2	3	5	2
1984-85	Calgary	NHL	78	37	35	72	14	4	3	3	6	0
1985-86	Calgary	NHL	68	31	36	67	36	22	4	10	14	6
	NHL Totals		223	98	96	194	72	37	9	16	25	8

a Named to NHL All-Rookie Team (1984)

LORDEN, GARY

Born, Providence, RI, January 17, 1966.
Center. Shoots left. 6'2", 190 lbs.
Last amateur club: University of Michigan Wolverines (CCHA).
(Winnipeg's 5th choice, 114th overall, in 1984 Entry Draft).

				Regular Season					Playoffs			
Season	Club	Lea	GP	G	A	TP	PIM	GP	G	A	TP	PIM
1985-86	U. of Michigan	CCHA	38	1	2	3	22	....	....	....	....	....

LORENTZ, TOM

Born, St. Paul, Minn., November 18, 1966.
Center. Shoots left. 5'11", 160 lbs.
Last amateur club: University of Minnesota-Duluth Bulldogs (WCHA).
(NY Rangers' 11th choice, 223rd overall, in 1984 Entry Draft).

				Regular Season					Playoffs			
Season	Club	Lea	GP	G	A	TP	PIM	GP	G	A	TP	PIM
1984-85	Minn-Duluth	WCHA	DID NOT PLAY — INJURED									
1985-86	Minn-Duluth	WCHA	17	4	1	5	6	....	....	....	....	....

LORIMER, ROBERT ROY (BOB)

Born, Toronto, Ont., August 25, 1953.
Defense. Shoots right. 6'1", 200 lbs.
Last amateur club: Michigan Tech University Huskies (WCHA).
(NY Islanders' 10th choice, 129th over-all, in 1973 Amateur Draft).

			Regular Season					Playoffs				
Season	Club	Lea	GP	G	A	TP	PIM	GP	G	A	TP	PIM
1973-74	Michigan Tech	WCHA	39	3	18	21	46	....	....	....	....	....
1974-75	Michigan Tech	WCHA	38	10	21	31	68	....	....	....	....	....
1975-76	Muskegon	IHL	78	6	21	27	94	....	....	....	....	....
	Fort Worth	CHL	2	0	0	0	2	....	....	....	....	....
1976-77	NY Islanders	NHL	1	0	1	1	0	....	....	....	....	....
	Fort Worth	CHL	28	4	6	10	38	6	0	0	0	17
1977-78	NY Islanders	NHL	5	1	0	1	0	....	....	....	....	....
	Fort Worth	CHL	71	6	13	19	81	14	1	7	8	25
1978-79	NY Islanders	NHL	67	3	18	21	42	10	1	3	4	15
1979-80	NY Islanders	NHL	74	3	16	19	53	21	1	3	4	41
1980-81	NY Islanders	NHL	73	1	12	13	77	18	1	4	5	27
1981-82	Colorado	NHL	79	5	15	20	68	....	....	....	....	....
1982-83	New Jersey	NHL	66	3	10	13	42	....	....	....	....	....
1983-84	New Jersey	NHL	72	2	10	12	62	....	....	....	....	....
1984-85	New Jersey	NHL	46	2	6	8	35	....	....	....	....	....
1985-86	New Jersey	NHL	46	2	2	4	52	....	....	....	....	....
	NHL Totals		**529**	**22**	**90**	**112**	**431**	**49**	**3**	**10**	**13**	**83**

Traded to **Colorado** by **NY Islanders** with Dave Cameron for Colorado's first round choice (Pat LaFontaine) in 1983 Entry Draft, October 1, 1981.

LOVEN, TIM

Born, Grand Forks, ND, October 14, 1963.
Defense. Shoots left. 6'0", 205 lbs.
Last amateur club: University of North Dakota Fighting Sioux (WCHA).
(Toronto's 14th choice, 213th overall, in 1982 Entry Draft).

			Regular Season					Playoffs				
Season	Club	Lea	GP	G	A	TP	PIM	GP	G	A	TP	PIM
1982-83	North Dakota	WCHA	9	1	2	3	2	....	....	....	....	....
1983-84	North Dakota	WCHA	35	0	7	7	14	....	....	....	....	....
1984-85	North Dakota	WCHA	36	0	9	9	10	....	....	....	....	....
1985-86	North Dakota	WCHA	16	0	1	1	4	....	....	....	....	....

LOWE, KEVIN HUGH (LOH)

Born, Lachute, Que., April 15, 1959.
Defense. Shoots left. 6'2", 200 lbs.
Last amateur club: Quebec Remparts (QJHL).
(Edmonton's 1st choice, 21st over-all, in 1979 Entry Draft).

			Regular Season					Playoffs				
Season	Club	Lea	GP	G	A	TP	PIM	GP	G	A	TP	PIM
1977-78	Quebec	QJHL	64	13	52	65	86	4	1	2	3	6
1978-79a	Quebec	QJHL	68	26	60	86	120	6	1	7	8	36
1979-80	Edmonton	NHL	64	2	19	21	70	3	0	1	1	0
1980-81	Edmonton	NHL	79	10	24	34	94	9	0	2	2	11
1981-82	Edmonton	NHL	80	9	31	40	63	5	0	3	3	0
1982-83	Edmonton	NHL	80	6	34	40	43	16	1	8	9	10
1983-84	Edmonton	NHL	80	4	42	46	59	19	3	7	10	16
1984-85	Edmonton	NHL	80	4	21	25	104	16	0	5	5	8
1985-86	Edmonton	NHL	74	2	16	18	90	10	1	3	4	15
	NHL Totals		**537**	**37**	**187**	**224**	**523**	**78**	**5**	**29**	**34**	**50**

a QMJHL Second All-Star Team (1979)

LOWNEY, ED

Born, Revere, Mass., June 10, 1965.
Right wing. Shoots right. 5'11", 180 lbs.
Last amateur club: Boston University Terriers (H.E.).
(Vancouver's 12th choice, 198th overall, in 1984 Entry Draft).

			Regular Season					Playoffs				
Season	Club	Lea	GP	G	A	TP	PIM	GP	G	A	TP	PIM
1983-84	Boston U.	H.E.	30	16	8	24	26	....	....	....	....	....
1984-85	Boston U.	H.E.	42	18	21	39	10	....	....	....	....	....
1985-86	Boston U.	H.E.	43	18	20	38	14	....	....	....	....	....

LOWRY, DAVE

Born, Sudbury, Ont., January 14, 1965.
Left wing. Shoots left. 6'1", 185 lbs.
Last amateur club: London Knights (OHL).
(Vancouver's 6th choice, 110th over-all, in 1983 Entry Draft).

			Regular Season					Playoffs				
Season	Club	Lea	GP	G	A	TP	PIM	GP	G	A	TP	PIM
1982-83	London	OHL	42	11	16	27	48	3	0	0	0	14
1983-84	London	OHL	66	29	47	76	125	8	6	6	12	41
1984-85a	London	OHL	61	60	60	120	94	8	6	5	11	10
1985-86	Vancouver	NHL	73	10	8	18	143	3	0	0	0	0
	NHL Totals		**73**	**10**	**8**	**18**	**143**	**3**	**0**	**0**	**0**	**0**

a OHL First All-Star Team (1985).

LUDVIG, JAN (LOOD-vig)

Born, Liberec, Czechoslovakia, September 17, 1961.
Right wing. Shoots right. 5'10", 190 lbs.
Last amateur club: Kamloops Junior Oilers (WHL).

			Regular Season					Playoffs				
Season	Club	Lea	GP	G	A	TP	PIM	GP	G	A	TP	PIM
1980-81	CHZ Litvinov	Czech	3	0	0	0	0	....	....	....	....	....
1981-82	St. Albert	AJHL	4	2	4	6	20	....	....	....	....	....
	Kamloops	WHL	37	31	34	65	36	4	2	0	2	7
	Wichita	CHL	....	....	....	....	....	3	2	0	2	0
1982-83	New Jersey	NHL	51	7	10	17	30	....	....	....	....	....
	Wichita	CHL	9	3	0	3	19	....	....	....	....	....
1983-84	New Jersey	NHL	74	22	32	54	70	....	....	....	....	....
1984-85	New Jersey	NHL	74	12	19	31	53	....	....	....	....	....
1985-86	New Jersey	NHL	42	5	9	14	63	....	....	....	....	....
	NHL Totals		**241**	**46**	**70**	**116**	**216**					

Signed as a free agent by **New Jersey**, October 28, 1982.

LUDWIG, CRAIG LEE

Born, Rinelander, Wisconsin, March 15, 1961.
Defense. Shoots left. 6'3", 215 lbs.
Last amateur club: University of North Dakota Fighting Sioux (WCHA)
(Montreal's 5th choice, 61st over-all, in 1980 Entry Draft).

			Regular Season					Playoffs				
Season	Club	Lea	GP	G	A	TP	PIM	GP	G	A	TP	PIM
1979-80	North Dakota	WCHA	33	1	8	9	32	....	....	....	....	....
1980-81	North Dakota	WCHA	34	4	8	12	48	....	....	....	....	....
1981-82	North Dakota	WCHA	37	4	17	21	42	....	....	....	....	....
1982-83	Montreal	NHL	80	0	25	25	59	3	0	0	0	2
1983-84	Montreal	NHL	80	7	18	25	52	15	0	3	3	23
1984-85	Montreal	NHL	72	5	14	19	90	12	0	1	1	6
1985-86	Montreal	NHL	69	2	4	6	63	20	0	1	1	48
	NHL Totals		**301**	**14**	**61**	**75**	**264**	**50**	**0**	**5**	**5**	**79**

LUDZIK, STEVE

Born, Toronto, Ont., April 3, 1962.
Center. Shoots left. 5'11", 185 lbs.
Last amateur club: Niagara Falls Flyers (OHA).
(Chicago's 3rd choice, 28th over-all, in 1980 Entry Draft).

			Regular Season					Playoffs				
Season	Club	Lea	GP	G	A	TP	PIM	GP	G	A	TP	PIM
1979-80	Niagara Falls	OHA	67	43	76	119	102	10	6	6	12	16
1980-81	Niagara Falls	OHA	58	50	92	142	108	12	5	9	14	40
1981-82	Chicago	NHL	8	2	1	3	2	....	....	....	....	....
	New Brunswick	AHL	73	21	41	62	142	15	3	7	10	6
1982-83	Chicago	NHL	66	6	19	25	63	13	3	5	8	20
1983-84	Chicago	NHL	80	9	20	29	73	4	0	1	1	9
1984-85	Chicago	NHL	79	11	20	31	86	15	1	1	2	16
1985-86	Chicago	NHL	49	6	5	11	21	3	0	0	0	12
	NHL Totals		**282**	**34**	**65**	**99**	**245**	**35**	**4**	**7**	**11**	**57**

LUKOWICH, EUGENE (MORRIS) (LUKE-oh-witch)

Born, Speers, Sask., June 1, 1956.
Left wing. Shoots left. 5'9", 170 lbs.
Last amateur club: Medicine Hat Tigers (WHL).
(Pittsburgh's 4th choice, 47th over-all, in 1976 Amateur Draft).

			Regular Season					Playoffs				
Season	Club	Lea	GP	G	A	TP	PIM	GP	G	A	TP	PIM
1974-75	Medicine Hat	WHL	70	40	54	94	111	5	4	1	5	2
1975-76a	Medicine Hat	WHL	72	65	77	142	195	9	5	8	13	20
1976-77	Houston	WHA	62	27	18	45	67	11	6	4	10	19
1977-78	Houston	WHA	80	40	35	75	131	6	1	2	3	17
1978-79b	Winnipeg	WHA	80	65	34	99	119	10	8	7	15	21
1979-80	Winnipeg	NHL	78	35	39	74	77	....	....	....	....	....
1980-81	Winnipeg	NHL	80	33	34	67	90	....	....	....	....	....
1981-82	Winnipeg	NHL	77	43	49	92	102	4	0	2	2	16
1982-83	Winnipeg	NHL	69	22	21	43	67	....	....	....	....	....
1983-84	Winnipeg	NHL	80	30	25	55	71	3	0	0	0	0
1984-85	Winnipeg	NHL	47	5	9	14	31	....	....	....	....	....
	Boston	NHL	22	5	8	13	21	1	0	0	0	0
1985-86	Boston	NHL	14	1	4	5	10	....	....	....	....	....
	Los Angeles	NHL	55	9	11	20	51	....	....	....	....	....
	NHL Totals		**522**	**185**	**198**	**383**	**520**	**8**	**0**	**2**	**2**	**16**
	WHA Totals		**222**	**132**	**87**	**219**	**317**	**27**	**15**	**13**	**28**	**57**

a WHL First All-Star Team (1976)
b WHA Second All-Star Team (1979)

Reclaimed by **Pittsburgh** from **Winnipeg** prior to Expansion Draft, June 9, 1979. Claimed as priority selection by **Winnipeg**, June 9, 1979. Traded to **Boston** by **Winnipeg** for Jim Nill, February 4, 1985. Claimed on waivers by **Los Angeles** from **Boston**, November 15, 1985.

LUMLEY, DAVID (DAVE)   (LUM-lee)

Born, Toronto, Ont., September 1, 1954.
Right wing. Shoots right. 6', 185 lbs.
Last amateur club: University of New Hampshire Wildcats (ECAC)
(Montreal's 17th choice, 199th over-all, in 1974 Amateur Draft).

Season	Club	Lea	GP	G	A	TP	PIM	GP	G	A	TP	PIM
1975-76	N. Hampshire	ECAC	30	9	32	41	55	....	....	....	....	....
1976-77	N. Hampshire	ECAC	39	22	38	60	42	....	....	....	....	....
1977-78	Nova Scotia	AHL	58	22	21	43	58	2	0	1	1	5
1978-79	**Montreal**	**NHL**	3	0	0	0	0	....	....	....	....	....
	Nova Scotia	AHL	61	22	58	80	160	10	6	8	14	35
1979-80	Edmonton	NHL	80	20	38	58	138	3	1	0	1	12
1980-81	Edmonton	NHL	53	7	9	16	74	7	1	0	1	4
1981-82	Edmonton	NHL	66	32	42	74	96	5	2	1	3	21
1982-83	Edmonton	NHL	72	13	24	37	158	16	0	1	1	19
1983-84	Edmonton	NHL	56	6	15	21	68	19	2	5	7	44
1984-85	Hartford	NHL	48	8	20	28	98	....	....	....	....	....
	Edmonton	NHL	12	1	3	4	13	8	0	0	0	29
1985-86	Edmonton	NHL	46	11	9	20	35	3	0	2	2	2
	NHL Totals		436	98	160	258	680	61	6	8	14	131

Traded to **Edmonton** by **Montreal** with Dan Newman for Edmonton's second-round choice (Ric Nattress) in 1980 Entry Draft, June 13, 1979. Claimed by **Hartford** from **Edmonton** in NHL Waiver Draft, October 9, 1984. Acquired by **Edmonton** from **Hartford** on waivers, February 6, 1985.

LUMME, JYRKKI

Born, Tampere, Finland, July 16, 1966.
Defense. Shoots left. 6'1", 190 lbs.
Last amateur club: Ilves-Tampere (FINLAND)
(Montreal's 3rd choice, 57th overall, in 1986 Entry Draft).

Season	Club	Lea	GP	G	A	TP	PIM	GP	G	A	TP	PIM
1984-85	KooVee	Fin.	30	6	4	10	44	....	....	....	....	....
1985-86	Ilves	Fin.	31	1	5	6	4	....	....	....	....	....

LUNDHOLM, BENGT   (LOOND-holm)

Born, Falun, Sweden, August 4, 1955.
Left wing. Shoots left. 6', 180 lbs.
Last amateur club: AIK Solna (Sweden)

Season	Club	Lea	GP	G	A	TP	PIM	GP	G	A	TP	PIM
1978-79	AIK Solna	Swe.	34	10	10	20	24	....	....	....	....	....
	Swe. National	...	17	2	6	8	8	....	....	....	....	....
1979-80	AIK Solna	Swe.	35	16	16	32	32	....	....	....	....	....
	Swe. National	...	6	1	0	1	0	....	....	....	....	....
1980-81	AIK Solna	Swe.	24	7	8	15	40	5	1	0	1	2
	Swe. National	...	4	1	1	2	0	....	....	....	....	....
1981-82	**Winnipeg**	**NHL**	66	14	30	44	10	4	1	1	2	2
1982-83	Winnipeg	NHL	58	14	28	42	16	3	0	1	1	2
1983-84	Winnipeg	NHL	57	5	14	19	20	....	....	....	....	....
1984-85	Winnipeg	NHL	78	12	18	30	20	5	2	2	4	8
1985-86	Winnipeg	NHL	16	3	5	8	6	2	0	0	0	2
	NHL Totals		275	48	95	143	72	14	3	4	7	14

Signed as free agent by **Winnipeg**, June 19, 1981.

LUNDMARK, DAVE

Born, Minneapolis, Minn., February 14, 1965.
Defense. Shoots left. 6', 190 lbs.
Last amateur club: Kingston Canadians (OHL).
(Los Angeles' 5th choice, 107th over-all, in 1983 Entry Draft).

Season	Club	Lea	GP	G	A	TP	PIM	GP	G	A	TP	PIM
1983-84	Kingston	OHL	65	2	9	11	1	....	....	....	....	....
1984-85	New Haven	AHL	2	0	0	0	0	....	....	....	....	....
	Kingston	OHL	12	1	2	3	44	....	....	....	....	....
	Sudbury	OHL	45	0	8	8	39	....	....	....	....	....
1985-86	Toledo	IHL	12	0	1	1	7	....	....	....	....	....

LUONGO, CHRISTOPHER (CHRIS)

Born, Detroit, Mich., March 17, 1967.
Defense. Shoots right. 6'0", 180 lbs.
Last amateur club: Michigan State University Spartans (CCHA).
(Detroit's 5th choice, 92nd overall, in 1985 Entry Draft).

Season	Club	Lea	GP	G	A	TP	PIM	GP	G	A	TP	PIM
1985-86	Michigan St.	CCHA	38	1	5	6	29	....	....	....	....	....

LUPUL, GARY JOHN   (LOO-pull)

Born, Powell River, B.C., April 4, 1959.
Center/Left wing. Shoots left. 5'8", 175 lbs.
Last amateur club: Victoria Cougars (WHL).

Season	Club	Lea	GP	G	A	TP	PIM	GP	G	A	TP	PIM
1977-78	Victoria	WHL	59	37	49	86	79	13	6	15	21	2
1978-79	Victoria	WHL	71	53	54	107	85	15	10	14	24	19
1979-80	Dallas	CHL	26	9	15	24	4	....	....	....	....	....
	Vancouver	NHL	51	9	11	20	24	4	1	0	1	0
1980-81	Vancouver	NHL	7	0	2	2	2	....	....	....	....	....
	Dallas	CHL	53	25	32	57	27	6	4	1	5	5
1981-82	Dallas	CHL	31	22	17	39	76	....	....	....	....	....
	Vancouver	NHL	41	10	7	17	26	10	2	3	5	4
1982-83	Fredericton	AHL	35	16	26	42	48	....	....	....	....	....
	Vancouver	NHL	40	18	10	28	46	4	1	3	4	0
1983-84	Vancouver	NHL	69	17	27	44	51	4	0	1	1	7
1984-85	Vancouver	NHL	66	12	17	29	82	....	....	....	....	....
1985-86	Vancouver	NHL	19	4	1	5	12	3	0	0	0	0
	Fredericton	AHL	43	13	22	35	76	3	2	0	2	4
	NHL Totals		293	70	75	145	243	25	4	7	11	11

Signed as free agent by **Vancouver**, September 14, 1979.

LYSIAK, THOMAS JAMES (TOM)   (LIE-see-ak)

Born, High Prairie, Alta., April 22, 1953.
Center. Shoots left. 6'1", 205 lbs.
Last amateur club: Medicine Hat Tigers (WHL).
(Atlanta's 1st choice, 2nd over-all, in 1973 Amateur Draft).

Season	Club	Lea	GP	G	A	TP	PIM	GP	G	A	TP	PIM
1971-72a	Medicine Hat	WHL	68	46	*97	*143	96	7	7	5	12	18
1972-73a	Medicine Hat	WHL	67	58	*96	*154	104	17	12	*27	*39	48
1973-74	Atlanta	NHL	77	19	45	64	54	4	0	2	2	0
1974-75	Atlanta	NHL	77	25	52	77	73	....	....	....	....	....
1975-76	Atlanta	NHL	80	31	51	82	60	2	0	0	0	2
1976-77	Atlanta	NHL	79	30	51	81	52	3	1	3	4	8
1977-78	Atlanta	NHL	80	27	42	69	54	2	1	0	1	2
1978-79	Atlanta	NHL	52	23	35	58	36	....	....	....	....	....
	Chicago	NHL	14	0	10	10	14	4	0	0	0	2
1979-80	Chicago	NHL	77	26	43	69	31	7	4	4	8	0
1980-81	Chicago	NHL	72	21	55	76	20	3	0	3	3	0
1981-82	Chicago	NHL	71	32	50	82	84	15	6	9	15	13
1982-83	Chicago	NHL	61	23	38	61	27	13	6	7	13	8
1983-84	Chicago	NHL	54	17	30	47	35	5	1	1	2	2
1984-85	Chicago	NHL	74	16	30	46	13	15	4	8	12	10
1985-86	Chicago	NHL	51	2	19	21	14	3	2	1	3	2
	NHL Totals		919	292	551	843	567	78	25	38	63	49

a WHL First All-Star Team (1972, 1973)
Traded to **Chicago** by **Atlanta** with Harold Phillipoff, Pat Ribble, Greg Fox and Miles Zaharko for Ivan Boldirev, Phil Russell and Darcy Rota, March 13, 1979.

MacDERMID, PAUL

Born, Chesley, Ont., April 14, 1963.
Center. Shoots right. 6'1", 200 lbs.
Last amateur club: Windsor Spitfires (OHL).
(Hartford's 2nd choice, 61st over-all, in 1981 Entry Draft).

Season	Club	Lea	GP	G	A	TP	PIM	GP	G	A	TP	PIM
1980-81	Windsor	OHA	68	15	17	32	106	....	....	....	....	....
1981-82	**Hartford**	**NHL**	3	1	0	1	2	....	....	....	....	....
	Windsor	OHL	65	26	45	71	179	9	6	4	10	17
1982-83	Hartford	NHL	7	0	0	0	2	....	....	....	....	....
	Windsor	OHL	42	35	45	80	9	....	....	....	....	....
1983-84	Hartford	NHL	3	0	1	1	0	....	....	....	....	....
	Binghamton	AHL	70	31	30	61	130	....	....	....	....	....
1984-85	Hartford	NHL	31	4	7	11	29	....	....	....	....	....
	Binghamton	AHL	48	9	31	40	87	....	....	....	....	....
1985-86	Hartford	NHL	74	13	10	23	160	10	2	1	3	20
	NHL Totals		118	18	18	36	193	10	2	1	3	20

MACDONALD, BRETT

Born, Bothwell, Ont., January 5, 1966.
Defense. Shoots left. 6', 195 lbs.
Last amateur club: Kitchener Rangers (OHL).
(Vancouver's 7th choice, 94th over-all, in 1984 Entry Draft).

Season	Club	Lea	GP	G	A	TP	PIM	GP	G	A	TP	PIM
1983-84	North Bay	OHL	70	8	18	26	83	4	0	1	1	0
1984-85	North Bay	OHL	58	6	27	33	72	8	1	1	2	11
1985-86	Kitchener	OHL	68	10	33	43	94	5	3	7	10	6

MacDONALD, CHRIS

Kingston, Ont., July 9, 1963.
Defense. Shoots right. 6'9", 185 lbs.
Last amateur club: Western Michigan University Broncos (CCHA).
(Calgary's 10th choice, 151st overall, in 1983 Entry Draft).

Season	Club	Lea	GP	G	A	TP	PIM	GP	G	A	TP	PIM
1982-83	W. Michigan	CCHA	30	1	13	14	26	....	....	....	....	....
1983-84	W. Michigan	CCHA	23	0	10	10	32	....	....	....	....	....
1984-85	W. Michigan	CCHA	34	7	24	31	44	....	....	....	....	....
1985-86a	W. Michigan	CCHA	42	12	38	50	54	....	....	....	....	....

a CCHA Second All-Star Team (1986)

MacINNIS, ALLAN

Born, Inverness, N.S., July 11, 1963.
Defense. Shoots right. 6'1", 195 lbs.
Last amateur club: Kitchener Rangers (OHL).
(Calgary's 1st choice, 15th over-all, in 1981 Entry Draft).

			Regular Season					Playoffs				
Season	Club	Lea	GP	G	A	TP	PIM	GP	G	A	TP	PIM
1980-81	Kitchener	OHA	47	11	28	39	59	18	4	12	16	20
1981-82	Calgary	NHL	2	0	0	0	0	....	....	....	....	....
a	Kitchener	OHL	59	25	50	75	145	15	5	10	15	44
1982-83	Calgary	NHL	14	1	3	4	9	....	....	....	....	....
a	Kitchener	OHL	51	38	46	84	67	8	3	8	11	9
1983-84	Colorado	CHL	19	5	14	19	22	....	....	....	....	....
	Calgary	NHL	51	11	34	45	42	11	2	12	14	13
1984-85	Calgary	NHL	67	14	52	66	75	4	1	2	3	8
1985-86	Calgary	NHL	77	11	57	68	76	21	4	15	19	30
	NHL Totals		211	37	146	183	202	36	7	29	36	51

a OHL First All-Star Team (1982, 1983)

MacINNIS, JOSEPH

Born, Cambridge, Mass., May 25, 1966.
Left wing. Shoots left. 6'0", 165 lbs.
Last amateur club: Northeastern University Huskies (H.E.).
(Toronto's 6th choice, 130th overall, in 1984 Entry Draft).

			Regular Season					Playoffs				
Season	Club	Lea	GP	G	A	TP	PIM	GP	G	A	TP	PIM
1984-85	Northeastern	H.E.	31	3	2	5	20	....	....	....	....	....
1985-86	Northeastern	H.E.	20	4	3	7	10	....	....	....	....	....

MacINTYRE, DUNCAN

Born, Brockville, Ont., July 3, 1964.
Center. Shoots right. 5'8", 170 lbs.
Last amateur club: Belleville Bulls (OHL).

			Regular Season					Playoffs				
Season	Club	Lea	GP	G	A	TP	PIM	GP	G	A	TP	PIM
1981-82	Belleville	OHL	66	28	53	81	123	....	....	....	....	....
1982-83	Belleville	OHL	65	36	38	74	73	4	2	2	4	6
1983-84	Belleville	OHL	70	34	53	87	52	3	2	1	3	2
1984-85	Belleville	OHL	66	44	62	106	27	14	2	9	11	6
1985-86	Fredericton	AHL	80	23	22	45	31	6	3	3	6	4

Signed as a free agent by Vancouver, October 1, 1985.

MACK, CRAIG

Born, Grand Forks, North Dakota, March 27, 1965.
Defense. Shoots right. 6'1", 195 lbs.
Last amateur club: University of Minnesota Golden Gophers (WCHA).
(Quebec's 6th choice, 132nd overall, in 1983 Entry Draft).

			Regular Season					Playoffs				
Season	Club	Lea	GP	G	A	TP	PIM	GP	G	A	TP	PIM
1983-84	U. Minnesota	WCHA	21	0	3	3	14	....	....	....	....	....
1984-85	U. Minnesota	WCHA	24	0	2	2	12	....	....	....	....	....
1985-86	U. Minnesota	WCHA	45	2	15	17	32	....	....	....	....	....

MACKEY, DAVID

Born, Richmond, B.C., July 24, 1966.
Left wing. Shoots left. 6'4", 200 lbs.
Last amateur club: Medicine Hat Tigers (WHL).
(Chicago's 12th choice, 224th overall, in 1984 Entry Draft).

			Regular Season					Playoffs				
Season	Club	Lea	GP	G	A	TP	PIM	GP	G	A	TP	PIM
1982-83	Victoria	WHL	69	16	16	32	53	12	11	1	2	4
1983-84	Victoria	WHL	69	15	15	30	97	....	....	....	....	....
1984-85	Victoria	WHL	16	5	6	11	45	....	....	....	....	....
	Portland	WHL	56	28	32	60	122	6	2	1	3	13
1985-86	Medicine Hat	WHL	69	28	36	64	180	25	6	3	9	72

MacLEAN, DAVE

Born, Brantford, Ont., January 12, 1965.
Right wing. Shoots right. 6', 190 lbs.
Last amateur club: Belleville Bulls (OHL).
(Hartford's 5th choice, 64th over-all, in 1983 Entry Draft).

			Regular Season					Playoffs				
Season	Club	Lea	GP	G	A	TP	PIM	GP	G	A	TP	PIM
1981-82	Oshawa	OHL	54	6	8	14	38	8	2	2	4	0
1982-83	Oshawa	OHL	11	8	6	14	6	....	....	....	....	....
	Belleville	OHL	51	34	46	80	28	4	2	2	4	0
1983-84	Belleville	OHL	70	58	51	109	47	3	0	0	0	0
1984-85ab	Belleville	OHL	63	64	90	*154	41	14	11	8	19	17
1985-86	Binghamton	AHL	23	0	0	0	7	....	....	....	....	....
	Salt Lake	IHL	41	9	14	23	14	5	1	1	2	8

a OHL Second All-Star Team (1985)
b Named OHL Player of the Year (1985)

MacLEAN, JOHN

Born, Oshawa, Ont., November 20, 1964.
Right wing. Shoots right. 6', 195 lbs.
Last amateur club: Oshawa Generals (OHL).
(New Jersey's 1st choice, 6th over-all, in 1983 Entry Draft).

			Regular Season					Playoffs				
Season	Club	Lea	GP	G	A	TP	PIM	GP	G	A	TP	PIM
1981-82	Oshawa	OHL	67	17	22	39	197	12	3	6	9	63
1982-83	Oshawa	OHL	66	47	51	98	138	17	*18	20	*38	35
1983-84	New Jersey	NHL	23	1	0	1	10	....	....	....	....	....
	Oshawa	OHL	30	23	36	59	58	7	2	5	7	18
1984-85	New Jersey	NHL	61	13	20	33	44	....	....	....	....	....
1985-86	New Jersey	NHL	74	21	36	57	112	....	....	....	....	....
	NHL Totals		158	35	56	91	66	....	....	....	....	....

MacLEAN, PAUL   (mac-LANE)

Born, Grostenquin, France, March 9, 1958.
Right wing. Shoots right. 6', 190 lbs.
Last amateur club: 1980 Canadian Olympic Team.
(St. Louis' 6th choice, 109th over-all, in 1978 Amateur Draft).

			Regular Season					Playoffs				
Season	Club	Lea	GP	G	A	TP	PIM	GP	G	A	TP	PIM
1977-78	Hull	QJHL	66	38	33	71	125	....	....	....	....	....
1979-80	Cdn. National	...	50	21	11	32	90	....	....	....	....	....
	Cdn. Olympic	...	6	2	3	5	6	....	....	....	....	....
1980-81	St. Louis	NHL	1	0	0	0	0	....	....	....	....	....
	Salt Lake	CHL	80	36	42	78	160	17	11	5	16	47
1981-82	Winnipeg	NHL	74	36	25	61	106	4	3	2	5	20
1982-83	Winnipeg	NHL	80	32	44	76	121	3	1	2	3	6
1983-84	Winnipeg	NHL	76	40	31	71	155	3	1	0	1	0
1984-85	Winnipeg	NHL	79	41	60	101	119	8	3	4	7	4
1985-86	Winnipeg	NHL	69	27	29	56	74	2	1	0	1	7
	NHL Totals		379	176	189	365	575	20	9	8	17	37

Traded to Winnipeg by St. Louis with Bryan Maxwell and Ed Staniowski for Scott Campbell and John Markell, July 3, 1981.

MacLELLAN, BRIAN

Born, Guelph, Ont., October 27, 1958.
Left wing. Shoots left. 6'3", 210 lbs.
Last amateur club: Bowling Green State University Falcons (CCHA)

			Regular Season					Playoffs				
Season	Club	Lea	GP	G	A	TP	PIM	GP	G	A	TP	PIM
1980-81	Bowling Green	CCHA	37	11	14	25	96	....	....	....	....	....
1981-82	Bowling Green	CCHA	41	11	21	33	109	....	....	....	....	....
1982-83	Los Angeles	NHL	8	0	3	3	7	....	....	....	....	....
	New Haven	AHL	71	11	15	26	40	12	5	3	8	4
1983-84	New Haven	AHL	2	0	2	2	0	....	....	....	....	....
	Los Angeles	NHL	72	25	29	54	45	....	....	....	....	....
1984-85	Los Angeles	NHL	80	31	54	85	53	3	0	1	1	0
1985-86	Los Angeles	NHL	27	5	8	13	19	....	....	....	....	....
	NY Rangers	NHL	51	11	21	32	47	16	2	4	6	15
	NHL Totals		238	72	115	187	171	19	2	5	7	15

Signed as a free agent by Los Angeles, May 12, 1982. Traded to NY Rangers by Los Angeles with Los Angeles' fourth-round draft choice in 1987 for Roland Melanson and Grant Ledyard, December 9, 1985.

MACOUN, JAMIE   (ma-COWN)

Born, Newmarket, Ont., August 7, 1961.
Defense. Shoots left. 6'2", 197 lbs.
Last amateur club: Ohio State University Buckeyes (CCHA)

			Regular Season					Playoffs				
Season	Club	Lea	GP	G	A	TP	PIM	GP	G	A	TP	PIM
1980-81	Ohio State	CCHA	38	9	20	29	83	....	....	....	....	....
1981-82	Ohio State	CCHA	25	2	18	20	89	....	....	....	....	....
1982-83	Ohio State	CCHA	19	6	21	27	54	....	....	....	....	....
	Calgary	NHL	22	1	4	5	25	9	0	2	2	8
1983-84a	Calgary	NHL	72	9	23	32	97	11	1	0	1	0
1984-85	Calgary	NHL	70	9	30	39	67	4	0	1	1	4
1985-86	Calgary	NHL	77	11	21	32	81	22	1	6	7	23
	NHL Totals		241	30	78	108	270	46	3	8	11	35

a Named to the NHL All-Rookie Team (1984).
Signed as free agent by Calgary, January 31, 1983.

MacPHERSON, DUNCAN A.

Born, Saskatoon, Sask., February 3, 1966.
Defense. Shoots left. 6'1", 188 lbs.
Last amateur club: Saskatoon Blades (WHL).
(New York Islanders' 1st choice, 20th over-all, in 1984 Entry Draft).

			Regular Season					Playoffs				
Season	Club	Lea	GP	G	A	TP	PIM	GP	G	A	TP	PIM
1982-83	N. Battleford	SJHL	59	6	11	17	215	....	....	....	....	....
1983-84	Saskatoon	WHL	45	0	14	14	74	....	....	....	....	....
1984-85	Saskatoon	WHL	69	9	26	35	116	3	0	0	0	4
1985-86	Saskatoon	WHL	70	10	54	64	147	13	3	8	11	38

MacTAVISH, CRAIG

Born, London, Ont., August 15, 1958.
Center. Shoots left. 6', 185 lbs.
Last amateur club: University of Lowell Chiefs (ECAC).
(Boston's 9th choice, 153rd over-all, in 1984 Entry Draft).

Season	Club	Lea	Regular Season					Playoffs				
			GP	G	A	TP	PIM	GP	G	A	TP	PIM
1979-80	Binghamton	AHL	34	17	15	32	29					
	Boston	**NHL**	46	11	17	28	8	10	2	3	5	7
1980-81	**Boston**	**NHL**	24	3	5	8	13	....	....	....	....	....
	Springfield	AHL	53	19	24	43	81	7	5	4	9	8
1981-82	**Boston**	**NHL**	2	0	1	1	0	....	....	....	....	....
	Erie	AHL	72	23	32	55	37	....	....	....	....	....
1982-83	**Boston**	**NHL**	75	10	20	30	18	17	3	1	4	18
1983-84	**Boston**	**NHL**	70	20	23	43	35	1	0	0	0	0
1984-85	DID NOT PLAY											
1985-86	**Edmonton**	**NHL**	74	23	24	47	70	10	4	4	8	11
	NHL Totals		291	67	90	157	144	38	9	8	17	36

Signed as a free agent by **Edmonton**, February 1, 1985.

MacTAVISH, SCOTT

Born, Fredericton, N.B., January 25, 1966.
Defense. Shoots right. 6'3", 205 lbs.
Last amateur club: Verdun Juniors (QMJHL).
(Montreal's 9th choice, 137th over-all, in 1984 Entry Draft).

Season	Club	Lea	Regular Season					Playoffs				
			GP	G	A	TP	PIM	GP	G	A	TP	PIM
1984-85	Verdun	QMJHL	52	5	15	20	200	10	1	1	2	53
1985-86	Verdun	QMJHL	50	7	14	21	145	5	1	3	4	22

MAGNAN, MARC

Born, Beaumont, Alta., February 17, 1962.
Left wing. Shoots left. 5'11", 195 lbs.
Last amateur club: Lethbridge Broncos (WHL).
(Toronto's 9th choice, 195th over-all, in 1981 Entry Draft).

Season	Club	Lea	Regular Season					Playoffs				
			GP	G	A	TP	PIM	GP	G	A	TP	PIM
1979-80	St. Albert	AJHL	42	14	23	37	178	....	....	....	....	....
	Lethbridge	WHL	1	0	1	1	0	....	....	....	....	....
1980-81	Lethbridge	WHL	66	16	30	46	284	9	4	1	5	78
1981-82	Lethbridge	WHL	64	33	38	71	406	12	10	5	15	60
1982-83	**Toronto**	**NHL**	4	0	1	1	5	....	....	....	....	....
	St. Catharines	AHL	67	6	10	16	229	....	....	....	....	....
1983-84	St. Catharines	AHL	54	3	6	9	170	....	....	....	....	....
	Muskegon	IHL	19	3	10	13	30	....	....	....	....	....
1984-85	Indianapolis	IHL	72	9	24	33	244	7	1	3	4	13
1985-86	Indianapolis	IHL	69	15	22	37	279	5	0	1	1	48
	NHL Totals		4	0	1	1	5	....	....	....	....	....

MAGUIRE, KEVIN

Born, Trenton, Ont., January 5, 1963.
Right Wing. Shoots right. 6'2", 200 lbs.
Last amateur club: Orilla Travelways (Tier II Jr.).

Season	Club	Lea	Regular Season					Playoffs				
			GP	G	A	TP	PIM	GP	G	A	TP	PIM
1983-84	Orilla	OPJHL	35	42	77	119	NA	....	....	....	....	....
1984-85	St. Catharines	AHL	76	10	15	25	112	....	....	....	....	....
1985-86	St. Catharines	AHL	61	6	9	15	161	1	0	0	0	0

Signed as a free agent by **Toronto**, October 10, 1984.

MAJOR, BRUCE

Born, Vernon, B.C., January 3, 1967.
Center. Shoots left. 6'3", 180 lbs.
Last amateur club: University of Maine Black Bears (H.E.).
(Quebec's 6th choice, 99th overall, in 1985 Entry Draft).

Season	Club	Lea	Regular Season					Playoffs				
			GP	G	A	TP	PIM	GP	G	A	TP	PIM
1985-86	Maine	H.E.	38	14	14	28	39	....	....	....	....	....

MAKELA, MIKKO

Born, Tampere, Finland, February 28, 1965.
Center. Shoots left. 6'2", 193 lbs.
Last amateur club: Ilves (Finland).
(NY Islanders' 5th choice, 66th over-all, in 1983 Entry Draft).

Season	Club	Lea	Regular Season					Playoffs				
			GP	G	A	TP	PIM	GP	G	A	TP	PIM
1983-84	Ilves	Fin.	35	17	11	28	16	....	....	....	....	....
1984-85	Ilves	Fin.	36	25	34	59	24	9	4	7	11	NA
1985-86	**NY Islanders**	**NHL**	58	16	20	36	28	....	....	....	....	....
	Springfield	AHL	2	1	1	2	0	....	....	..	....	....
	NHL Totals		58	16	20	36	28	....	....	....	....	....

MAKI, JYRKI

Born, Helsinki, Finland, February 8, 1966.
Defense. Shoots left. 6'0", 170 lbs.
Last amateur club: Lowell University Chiefs (H.E.).
(Quebec's 7th choice, 162nd overall, in 1984 Entry Draft).

Season	Club	Lea	Regular Season					Playoffs				
			GP	G	A	TP	PIM	GP	G	A	TP	PIM
1984-85	Lowell	H.E.	33	0	5	5	12	....	....	....	....	....
1985-86	Lowell	H.E.	26	1	2	3	9	....	....	....	....	....

MALEY, DAVID

Born, Beaver Dam, Wisconsin, April 24, 1963.
Center. Shoots left. 6'2", 195 lbs.
Last amateur club: University of Wisconsin Badgers (WCHA)
(Montreal's 4th choice, 33rd over-all, in 1982 Entry Draft).

Season	Club	Lea	Regular Season					Playoffs				
			GP	G	A	TP	PIM	GP	G	A	TP	PIM
1981-82	Edina HS	Minn.	26	22	28	50	26	....	....	....	....	....
1982-83	U. of Wisconsin	WCHA	25	4	12	16	4	....	....	....	....	....
1983-84	U. of Wisconsin	WCHA	38	10	28	38	56	....	....	....	....	....
1984-85	U. of Wisconsin	WCHA	38	19	9	28	86	....	....	....	....	....
1985-86	U. of Wisconsin	WCHA	42	20	40	60	135	....	....	....	....	....
	Montreal	**NHL**	3	0	0	0	0	7	1	3	4	2
	NHL Totals		3	0	0	0	0	7	1	3	4	2

MALONE, WILLIAM GREGORY (GREG)   (MA-loan)

Born, Fredericton, N.B., March 8, 1956.
Center. Shoots left. 6', 190 lbs.
Last amateur club: Oshawa Generals (OHA).
(Pittsburgh's 2nd choice, 19th over-all, in 1976 Amateur Draft).

Season	Club	Lea	Regular Season					Playoffs				
			GP	G	A	TP	PIM	GP	G	A	TP	PIM
1974-75	Oshawa	OHA	68	37	41	78	86	5	1	3	4	9
1975-76	Oshawa	OHA	61	36	36	72	75	5	3	2	5	2
1976-77	**Pittsburgh**	**NHL**	66	18	19	37	43	3	1	1	2	2
1977-78	**Pittsburgh**	**NHL**	78	18	43	61	80	....	....	....	....	....
1978-79	**Pittsburgh**	**NHL**	80	35	30	65	52	7	0	1	1	10
1979-80	**Pittsburgh**	**NHL**	51	19	32	51	46	....	....	....	....	....
1980-81	**Pittsburgh**	**NHL**	62	21	29	50	68	5	2	3	5	16
1981-82	**Pittsburgh**	**NHL**	78	15	24	39	125	3	0	0	0	4
1982-83	**Pittsburgh**	**NHL**	80	17	44	61	82	....	....	....	....	....
1983-84	**Hartford**	**NHL**	78	17	37	54	56	....	....	....	....	....
1984-85	**Hartford**	**NHL**	76	22	39	61	67	....	....	....	....	....
1985-86	**Hartford**	**NHL**	22	6	7	13	24	....	....	....	....	....
	Quebec	**NHL**	27	3	5	8	18	1	0	0	0	0
	NHL Totals		698	191	309	500	661	19	3	5	8	32

Traded to **Hartford** by **Pittsburgh** for a third round choice in 1985 Entry Draft, September 30, 1983. Traded to **Quebec** by **Hartford** for Wayne Babych, January 17, 1986.

MALONEY, DONALD MICHAEL (DON)   (ma-LOAN-ee)

Born, Lindsay, Ont., September 5, 1958.
Left wing. Shoots left. 6'1", 190 lbs.
Last amateur club: Kitchener Rangers (OHA).
(NY Rangers' 1st choice, 26th over-all, in 1978 Amateur Draft).

Season	Club	Lea	Regular Season					Playoffs				
			GP	G	A	TP	PIM	GP	G	A	TP	PIM
1976-77	Kitchener	OHA	38	22	34	56	126	....	....	....	....	....
1977-78	Kitchener	OHA	62	30	74	104	143	9	4	9	13	40
1978-79	New Haven	AHL	38	18	26	44	62	....	....	....	....	....
	NY Rangers	**NHL**	28	9	17	26	39	18	7	*13	20	19
1979-80	**NY Rangers**	**NHL**	79	25	48	73	97	9	0	4	4	10
1980-81	**NY Rangers**	**NHL**	61	29	23	52	99	13	1	6	7	13
1981-82	**NY Rangers**	**NHL**	54	22	36	58	73	10	5	5	10	10
1982-83	**NY Rangers**	**NHL**	78	29	40	69	88	5	0	1	1	0
1983-84	**NY Rangers**	**NHL**	79	24	42	66	62	5	1	4	5	0
1984-85	**NY Rangers**	**NHL**	37	11	16	27	32	3	4	0	4	2
1985-86	**NY Rangers**	**NHL**	68	11	17	28	56	16	2	1	3	31
	NHL Totals		484	160	239	399	546	79	20	34	54	85

MANDICH, DANIEL (DAN)

Born, Brantford, Ont., June 12, 1960.
Defense. Shoots right. 6'3", 205 lbs.
Last amateur club: Ohio State University Buckeyes (CCHA)

Season	Club	Lea	Regular Season					Playoffs				
			GP	G	A	TP	PIM	GP	G	A	TP	PIM
1980-81	Ohio State	CCHA	39	20	26	46	188	....	....	....	....	....
1981-82	Ohio State	CCHA	33	14	26	40	157	....	....	....	....	....
	Nashville	CHL	16	2	5	7	24	3	0	0	0	26
1982-83	Birmingham	CHL	6	0	4	4	18	....	....	....	....	....
	Minnesota	**NHL**	67	3	4	7	169	7	0	0	0	2
1983-84	**Minnesota**	**NHL**	31	2	7	9	77	....	....	....	....	....
	Salt Lake	CHL	3	2	2	4	13	....	....	....	....	....
1984-85	**Minnesota**	**NHL**	10	0	0	0	32	....	....	....	....	....
1985-86	**Minnesota**	**NHL**	3	0	0	0	25	....	....	....	....	....
	Springfield	AHL	3	0	0	0	4	....	....	....	....	....
	NHL Totals		111	5	11	16	303	7	0	0	0	2

Signed as a free agent by **Minnesota**, July 19, 1982.

MANN, JAMES EDWARD (JIMMY)

Born, Montreal, Que., April 17, 1959.
Right wing. Shoots right. 6', 205 lbs.
Last amateur club: Sherbrooke Beavers (QJHL).
(Winnipeg's 1st choice, 19th over-all, in 1979 Entry Draft).

Season	Club	Lea	Regular Season					Playoffs				
			GP	G	A	TP	PIM	GP	G	A	TP	PIM
1977-78	Sherbrooke	QJHL	67	27	54	81	277	7	3	9	12	14
1978-79	Sherbrooke	QJHL	65	35	47	82	260	12	14	12	26	83
1979-80	Winnipeg	NHL	72	3	5	8	*287	....	....	....	....	....
1980-81	Winnipeg	NHL	37	3	3	6	105	....	....	....	....	....
	Tulsa	CHL	26	4	7	11	175	5	0	0	0	21
1981-82	Winnipeg	NHL	37	3	2	5	79	3	0	0	0	7
1982-83	Winnipeg	NHL	40	0	1	1	73	1	0	0	0	0
1983-84	Winnipeg	NHL	16	0	1	1	54	....	....	....	....	....
	Sherbrooke	AHL	20	6	3	9	94	....	....	....	....	....
	Quebec	NHL	22	1	1	2	42	3	0	0	0	22
1984-85	Quebec	NHL	25	0	4	4	54	13	0	0	0	41
	Fredericton	AHL	13	4	4	8	97	....	....	....	....	....
1985-86	Quebec	NHL	35	0	3	3	148	2	0	0	0	19
	NHL Totals		284	10	20	30	842	22	0	0	0	89

Traded to **Quebec** by **Winnipeg** for Quebec's fifth round choice (Brent Severyn) in 1984 Entry Draft, February 6, 1984.

MANSI, MAURICE

Born, Montreal, Que., September 3, 1965.
Center. Shoots left. 5'11", 170 lbs.
Last amateur club: Rensselaer Polytechnic Institute Engineers (ECAC).
(Montreal's 12th choice, 198th overall, in 1985 Entry Draft).

Season	Club	Lea	Regular Season					Playoffs				
			GP	G	A	TP	PIM	GP	G	A	TP	PIM
1984-85	RPI	ECAC	21	4	6	10	12	....	....	....	....	....
1985-86	RPI	ECAC	31	16	21	37	35	....	....	....	....	....

MANSON, DAVE

Born, Prince Albert, Sask., January 27, 1967.
Defense. Shoots left. 6'2", 190 lbs.
Last amateur club: Prince Albert Raiders (WHL).
(Chicago's 1st choice, 11th over-all, in 1985 Entry Draft).

Season	Club	Lea	Regular Season					Playoffs				
			GP	G	A	TP	PIM	GP	G	A	TP	PIM
1983-84	Prince Albert	WHL	70	2	7	9	233	5	0	0	0	4
1984-85	Prince Albert	WHL	72	8	30	38	247	13	1	0	1	34
1985-86	Prince Albert	WHL	70	14	34	48	177	20	1	8	9	63

MANTHA, MAURICE WILLIAM (MOE) (MAN-tha)

Born, Lakewood, Ohio, January 21, 1961.
Defense. Shoots right. 6'2", 195 lbs.
Last amateur club: Toronto Marlboros (OHA).
(Winnipeg's 2nd choice, 23rd over-all, in 1980 Entry Draft).

Season	Club	Lea	Regular Season					Playoffs				
			GP	G	A	TP	PIM	GP	G	A	TP	PIM
1978-79	Toronto	OHA	68	10	38	48	57	4	0	2	2	11
1979-80	Toronto	OHA	58	8	38	46	86	....	....	....	....	....
1980-81	Winnipeg	NHL	58	2	23	25	35	....	....	....	....	....
1981-82	Tulsa	CHL	33	8	15	23	56	....	....	....	....	....
	Winnipeg	NHL	25	0	12	12	28	4	1	3	4	16
1982-83	Sherbrooke	AHL	13	1	4	5	13	....	....	....	....	....
	Winnipeg	NHL	21	2	7	9	6	2	2	2	4	0
1983-84	Sherbrooke	AHL	7	1	1	2	10	....	....	....	....	....
	Winnipeg	NHL	72	16	38	54	67	3	1	0	1	0
1984-85	Pittsburgh	NHL	71	11	40	51	54	....	....	....	....	....
1985-86	Pittsburgh	NHL	78	15	52	67	102	....	....	....	....	....
	NHL Totals		325	46	172	218	292	9	4	5	9	16

Traded to **Pittsburgh** by **Winnipeg**, May 1, 1984 to complete deal of March 6, 1984 when Pittsburgh traded Randy Carlyle to Winnipeg.

MARCOV, PETER

Born, Welland, Ont., March 4, 1965.
Left wing. Shoots left. 5'9", 180 lbs.
Last amateur club: Cornell University Big Red (ECAC).
(NY Rangers' 9th choice, 153rd overall, in 1983 Entry Draft).

Season	Club	Lea	Regular Season					Playoffs				
			GP	G	A	TP	PIM	GP	G	A	TP	PIM
1983-84	Cornell	ECAC	26	11	11	22	6	....	....	....	....	....
1984-85	Cornell	ECAC	29	6	17	23	16	....	....	....	....	....
1985-86	Cornell	ECAC	21	3	14	17	55	....	....	....	....	....

MARINI, HECTOR (ma-REEN-ee)

Born, Timmins, Ont., January 27, 1957.
Right wing. Shoots right. 6'1", 200 lbs.
Last amateur club: Sudbury Wolves (OHA).
(NY Islanders' 3rd choice, 50th over-all, in 1977 Amateur Draft).

Season	Club	Lea	Regular Season					Playoffs				
			GP	G	A	TP	PIM	GP	G	A	TP	PIM
1975-76	Sudbury	OHA	66	32	45	77	102	17	7	5	12	32
1976-77	Sudbury	OHA	64	32	58	90	89	6	1	3	4	9
1977-78	Fort Worth	CHL	2	0	0	0	4	....	....	....	....	....
	Muskegon	IHL	80	33	60	93	127	6	7	4	11	5
1978-79	Fort Worth	CHL	74	21	27	48	172	5	1	4	5	7
	NY Islanders	NHL	1	0	0	0	2	1	0	0	0	0
1979-80	Indianapolis	CHL	76	29	34	63	144	7	1	4	5	20
1980-81	Indianapolis	CHL	54	15	37	52	85	....	....	....	....	....
	NY Islanders	NHL	14	4	7	11	39	9	3	6	9	14
1981-82	NY Islanders	NHL	30	4	9	13	53	....	....	....	....	....
1982-83	New Jersey	NHL	77	17	28	45	105	....	....	....	....	....
1983-84	New Jersey	NHL	32	2	2	4	47	....	....	....	....	....
	Maine	AHL	17	7	4	11	23	....	....	....	....	....
1984-85	Maine	AHL	30	1	5	6	67	....	....	....	....	....
1985-86	Maine	AHL	6	0	5	5	17	....	....	....	....	....
	Fort Wayne	IHL	7	1	1	2	5	....	....	....	....	....
	NHL Totals		154	27	46	73	246	10	3	6	9	14

Traded to **New Jersey** by **NY Islanders** with New York's fourth round choice (Bill Clavier) in 1983 Entry Draft (later transferred to Calgary) for New Jersey's fourth round choice (Mikko Makela) in 1983 Entry Draft, October 1, 1982.

MARK, GORDON

Born, Edmonton, Alta., September 10, 1964.
Defense. Shoots right. 6'3", 205 lbs.
Last amateur club: Kamloops Junior Oilers (WHL).
(New Jersey's 4th choice, 108th over-all, in 1983 Entry Draft).

Season	Club	Lea	Regular Season					Playoffs				
			GP	G	A	TP	PIM	GP	G	A	TP	PIM
1982-83	Kamloops	WHL	71	12	20	32	135	7	1	1	2	8
1983-84	Kamloops	WHL	67	12	30	42	202	17	2	6	8	27
1984-85	Kamloops	WHL	32	11	23	34	68	7	1	2	3	10
1985-86	Maine	AHL	77	9	13	22	134	5	0	1	1	9

MARKWART, NEVIN

Born, Toronto, Ont., December 9, 1964.
Left wing. Shoots left. 5'10", 170 lbs.
Last amateur club: Regina Pats (WHL).
(Boston's 1st choice, 21st over-all, in 1983 Entry Draft).

Season	Club	Lea	Regular Season					Playoffs				
			GP	G	A	TP	PIM	GP	G	A	TP	PIM
1981-82	Regina	WHL	25	2	12	14	56	20	2	2	4	82
1982-83	Regina	WHL	43	27	39	66	91	1	0	0	0	0
1983-84	Boston	NHL	70	14	16	30	121	....	....	....	....	....
1984-85	Boston	NHL	26	0	4	4	36	1	0	0	0	0
	Hershey	AHL	38	13	18	31	79	....	....	....	....	....
1985-86	Boston	NHL	65	7	15	22	207	1	0	0	0	0
	NHL Totals		161	21	35	56	364	1	0	0	0	0

MAROIS, MARIO (MAIR-wah)

Born, Ancienne Lorette, Que., December 15, 1957.
Defense. Shoots right. 5'11", 190 lbs.
Last amateur club: Quebec Remparts (QJHL).
(NY Rangers' 5th choice, 62nd over-all, in 1977 Amateur Draft).

Season	Club	Lea	Regular Season					Playoffs				
			GP	G	A	TP	PIM	GP	G	A	TP	PIM
1975-76	Quebec	QJHL	67	11	42	53	270	15	2	3	5	86
1976-77	Quebec	QJHL	72	17	67	84	239	14	1	17	18	75
1977-78	NY Rangers	NHL	8	1	1	2	15	1	0	0	0	5
	New Haven	AHL	52	8	23	31	147	12	5	3	8	31
1978-79	NY Rangers	NHL	71	5	26	31	153	18	0	6	6	29
1979-80	NY Rangers	NHL	79	8	23	31	142	9	0	2	2	8
1980-81	NY Rangers	NHL	8	1	2	3	46	....	....	....	....	....
	Vancouver	NHL	50	4	12	16	115	....	....	....	....	....
	Quebec	NHL	11	0	7	7	20	5	0	1	1	6
1981-82	Quebec	NHL	71	11	32	43	161	13	1	2	3	44
1982-83	Quebec	NHL	36	2	12	14	108	....	....	....	....	....
1983-84	Quebec	NHL	80	13	36	49	151	9	1	4	5	6
1984-85	Quebec	NHL	76	6	37	43	91	18	0	8	8	12
1985-86	Quebec	NHL	20	1	12	13	42	....	....	....	....	....
	Winnipeg	NHL	56	4	28	32	110	3	1	4	5	6
	NHL Totals		566	56	228	284	1154	76	3	27	30	116

Traded to **Vancouver** by **NY Rangers** with Jim Mayer for Jere Gillis and Jeff Bandura, November 11, 1980. Traded to **Quebec** by **Vancouver** for Garry Lariviere, March 10, 1981. Traded to **Winnipeg** by **Quebec** for Robert Picard, November 27, 1985.

MARSH, CHARLES BRADLEY (BRAD)

Born, London, Ont., March 31, 1958.
Defense. Shoots left. 6'3", 220 lbs.
Last amateur club: London Knights (OHA).
(Atlanta's 1st choice, 11th over-all, in 1978 Amateur Draft).

Season	Club	Lea	GP	G	A	TP	PIM	GP	G	A	TP	PIM
1976-77a	London	OHA	63	7	33	40	121	20	3	5	8	47
1977-78b	London	OHA	62	8	55	63	192	11	2	10	12	21
1978-79	Atlanta	NHL	80	0	19	19	101	2	0	0	0	17
1979-80	Atlanta	NHL	80	2	9	11	119	4	0	1	1	2
1980-81	Calgary	NHL	80	1	12	13	87	16	0	5	5	8
1981-82	Calgary	NHL	17	0	1	1	10	....	....	....	....	....
	Philadelphia	NHL	66	2	22	24	106	4	0	0	0	2
1982-83	Philadelphia	NHL	68	2	11	13	52	2	0	1	1	0
1983-84	Philadelphia	NHL	77	3	14	17	83	3	1	1	2	2
1984-85	Philadelphia	NHL	77	2	18	20	91	19	0	6	6	65
1985-86	Philadelphia	NHL	79	0	13	13	123	5	0	0	0	2
	NHL Totals		624	12	119	131	772	55	1	14	15	98

a OHA Third All-Star Team (1977).
b OHA First All-Star Team (1978)
Claimed by **Atlanta** as fill in Expansion Draft, June 13, 1979. Traded to **Philadelphia** by **Calgary** for Mel Bridgman, November 11, 1981.

MARSHALL, PAUL

Born, Quincy, Mass., October 22, 1966.
Defense. Shoots right. 6'2", 180 lbs.
Last amateur club: Boston College Eagles (H.E.).
(Philadelphia's 5th choice, 84th overall, in 1985 Entry Draft).

Season	Club	Lea	GP	G	A	TP	PIM	GP	G	A	TP	PIM
1985-86	Boston College	H.E.	40	0	12	12	28	....	....	....	....	....

MARSTON, STUART

Born, Montreal, Que., May 9, 1967.
Defense. Shoots left. 6'2", 185 lbs.
Last amateur club: Laval Titans (QMJHL).
(Pittsburgh's 6th choice, 114th overall, in 1985 Entry Draft).

Season	Club	Lea	GP	G	A	TP	PIM	GP	G	A	TP	PIM
1984-85	Longueuil	QMJHL	62	4	16	20	84	....	....	....	....	....
1985-86	Laval	QMJHL	32	7	18	25	48	12	4	4	8	16

MARTIN, BRIAN

Born, St. Catharines, Ont., March 27, 1966.
Left wing. Shoots left. 6'0", 180 lbs.
Last amateur club: Windsor Compuware Spitfires (OHL).
(Los Angeles' 12th choice, 236th overall, in 1983 Entry Draft).

Season	Club	Lea	GP	G	A	TP	PIM	GP	G	A	TP	PIM
1983-84	Belleville	OHL	69	21	41	62	32	3	0	2	2	0
1984-85	Windsor	OHL	59	28	25	53	64	4	2	1	3	7
1985-86	Windsor	OHL	60	42	41	83	115	12	7	4	11	23

MARTIN, GRANT MICHAEL

Born, Smooth Rock Falls, Ont., March 13, 1962.
Left wing. Shoots left. 5'10", 190 lbs.
Last amateur club: Kitchener Rangers (OHL).
(Vancouver's 9th choice, 196th over-all, in 1980 Entry Draft).

Season	Club	Lea	GP	G	A	TP	PIM	GP	G	A	TP	PIM
1979-80	Kitchener	OHA	65	31	21	52	62	....	....	....	....	....
1980-81	Kitchener	OHA	66	41	57	98	77	18	9	20	29	42
1981-82	Kitchener	OHL	54	33	63	96	97	12	3	15	18	33
1982-83	Fredericton	AHL	80	19	27	46	73	12	4	1	5	14
1983-84	Vancouver	NHL	12	0	2	2	6	....	....	....	....	....
	Fredericton	AHL	57	36	24	60	46	7	4	5	9	16
1984-85	Vancouver	NHL	12	0	1	1	39	....	....	....	....	....
	Fredericton	AHL	65	31	47	78	78	6	1	4	5	8
	Salt Lake	IHL	2	0	0	0	0	....	....	....	....	....
1985-86	Washington	NHL	11	0	1	1	6	....	....	....	....	....
	Baltimore	AHL	54	27	49	76	97	6	1	3	4	14
	NHL Totals		35	0	4	4	51	....	....	....	....	....

Signed as a free agent by **Washington**, August 6, 1985.

MARTIN, TERRY GEORGE

Born, Barrie, Ont., October 25, 1955.
Left wing. Shoots left. 5'11", 195 lbs.
Last amateur club: London Knights (OHA).
(Buffalo's 3rd choice, 44th over-all, in 1975 Amateur Draft).

Season	Club	Lea	GP	G	A	TP	PIM	GP	G	A	TP	PIM
1973-74	London	OHA	63	33	24	57	38	....	....	....	....	....
1974-75	London	OHA	70	43	57	100	118	....	....	....	....	....
1975-76	Buffalo	NHL	1	0	0	0	0	....	....	....	....	....
	Charlotte	SHL	25	12	10	22	30	....	....	....	....	....
	Hershey	AHL	19	3	6	9	18	....	....	....	....	....
1976-77	Hershey	AHL	12	1	4	5	12	....	....	....	....	....
	Buffalo	NHL	62	11	12	23	8	3	0	2	2	5
1977-78	Hershey	AHL	4	2	1	3	2	....	....	....	....	....
	Buffalo	NHL	21	3	2	5	9	8	2	0	2	5
1978-79	Buffalo	NHL	64	6	8	14	33	....	....	....	....	....
1979-80	Syracuse	AHL	18	9	9	18	6	....	....	....	....	....
	Quebec	NHL	3	0	0	0	0	....	....	....	....	....
	New Brunswick	AHL	3	0	1	1	0	....	....	....	....	....
	Toronto	NHL	37	6	15	21	2	3	2	0	2	7
1980-81	Toronto	NHL	69	23	14	37	32	3	0	0	0	0
1981-82	Toronto	NHL	72	25	24	49	39	....	....	....	....	....
1982-83	Toronto	NHL	76	14	13	27	28	4	0	0	0	9
1983-84	Toronto	NHL	63	15	10	25	51	....	....	....	....	....
1984-85	Edmonton	NHL	4	0	2	2	0	....	....	....	....	....
	Nova Scotia	AHL	28	17	11	28	4	....	....	....	....	....
	Minnesota	NHL	7	1	1	2	0	....	....	....	....	....
1985-86	Springfield	AHL	72	19	22	41	17	....	....	....	....	....
	NHL Totals		479	104	101	205	202	21	4	2	6	26

Claimed by **Quebec** from **Buffalo** in Expansion Draft, June 13, 1979. Traded to **Toronto** by **Quebec** with Dave Farrish for Reggie Thomas, December 13, 1979. Claimed by **Edmonton** from **Toronto** in NHL Waiver Draft, October 9, 1984. Traded to **Minnesota** by **Edmonton** with Gord Sherven for Mark Napier, January 24, 1985.

MARTIN, TOM

Born, Victoria, B.C., May 11, 1964.
Left wing. Shoots left. 6'2", 195 lbs.
Last amateur club: Victoria Cougars (WHL).
(Winnipeg's 2nd choice, 74th over-all, in 1982 Entry Draft).

Season	Club	Lea	GP	G	A	TP	PIM	GP	G	A	TP	PIM
1981-82	Kelowna	BCJHL	51	35	45	80	293	....	....	....	....	....
1982-83	U. of Denver	WCHA	37	8	18	26	128	....	....	....	....	....
1983-84	Victoria	WHL	60	30	45	75	261	....	....	....	....	....
	Sherbrooke	AHL	5	0	0	0	16	....	....	....	....	....
1984-85	Winnipeg	NHL	8	1	0	1	42	3	0	0	0	2
	Sherbrooke	AHL	58	4	15	19	212	12	1	1	2	72
1985-86	Winnipeg	NHL	5	0	0	0	0	....	....	....	....	....
	Sherbrooke	AHL	69	11	18	29	227	....	....	....	....	....
	NHL Totals		13	1	0	1	42	3	0	0	0	2

MARTINSON, STEVEN

Born, Minnetonka, Minn., June 21, 1957.
Left wing. Shoots left. 6'1", 205 lbs.
Last amateur club: Toledo Golddiggers (IHL).

Season	Club	Lea	GP	G	A	TP	PIM	GP	G	A	TP	PIM
1982-83	Toledo	IHL	32	9	10	19	111	....	....	....	....	....
	Birmingham	CHL	43	4	5	9	184	13	1	2	3	80
1983-84	Tulsa	CHL	42	3	6	9	240	6	0	0	0	43
1984-85	Toledo	IHL	54	4	10	14	300	2	0	0	0	21
1985-86	Hershey	AHL	69	3	6	9	432	3	0	0	0	56

Signed as a free agent by **Philadelphia**, September 30, 1985.

MARUK, DENNIS JOHN

(ma-ROOK)

Born, Toronto, Ont., November 17, 1955.
Center. Shoots left. 5'8", 175 lbs.
Last amateur club: London Knights (OHA).
(California's 2nd choice, 21st over-all, in 1975 Amateur Draft).

Season	Club	Lea	GP	G	A	TP	PIM	GP	G	A	TP	PIM
1973-74	London	OHA	67	47	65	112	61	....	....	....	....	....
1974-75	London	OHA	65	66	79	145	53	....	....	....	....	....
1975-76	California	NHL	80	30	32	62	44	....	....	....	....	....
1976-77	Cleveland	NHL	80	28	50	78	68	....	....	....	....	....
1977-78	Cleveland	NHL	76	36	35	71	50	....	....	....	....	....
1978-79	Minnesota	NHL	2	0	0	0	0	....	....	....	....	....
	Washington	NHL	76	31	59	90	71	....	....	....	....	....
1979-80	Washington	NHL	27	10	17	27	8	....	....	....	....	....
1980-81	Washington	NHL	80	50	47	97	87	....	....	....	....	....
1981-82	Washington	NHL	80	60	76	136	128	....	....	....	....	....
1982-83	Washington	NHL	80	31	50	81	71	4	1	1	2	2
1983-84	Minnesota	NHL	71	17	43	60	42	16	5	5	10	8
1984-85	Minnesota	NHL	71	19	41	60	56	9	4	7	11	12
1985-86	Minnesota	NHL	70	21	37	58	67	5	4	9	13	4
	NHL Totals		793	333	487	820	692	34	14	22	36	26

Protected by **Minnesota** prior to Cleveland-Minnesota Dispersal Draft, June 15, 1978. Traded to **Washington** by **Minnesota** for Pittsburgh's first round choice (Tom McCarthy) in 1979 Entry Draft — Washington's property via earlier deal — October 18, 1978. Traded to **Minnesota** by **Washington** for Minnesota's second round choice (Stephen Leach) in 1984 Entry Draft, July 5, 1983.

MASSEY, PETER

Born, Lynn, Mass., June 16, 1966.
Left wing. Shoots left. 6′3″, 200 lbs.
Last amateur club: Northeastern University Huskies (H.E.).
(Quebec's 4th choice, 65th overall, in 1985 Entry Draft).

Season	Club	Lea	Regular Season					Playoffs				
			GP	G	A	TP	PIM	GP	G	A	TP	PIM
1985-86	Northeastern	H.E.	36	4	0	4	22	....	....	....	....	....

MATHIASON, DWIGHT

Born, Brandon, Man., May 12, 1963.
Right wing. Shoots right. 6′1″, 190 lbs.
Last amateur club: University of Denver Pioneers (WCHA).

Season	Club	Lea	Regular Season					Playoffs				
			GP	G	A	TP	PIM	GP	G	A	TP	PIM
1983-84	Denver	CCHA	36	24	27	51	48	....	....	....	....	....
1984-85	Denver	CCHA	39	26	32	58	64	....	....	....	....	....
1985-86ab	Denver	CCHA	48	40	49	89	48	....	....	....	....	....
	Pittsburgh	NHL	4	1	0	1	2	....	....	....	....	....
	NHL Totals		**4**	**1**	**0**	**1**	**2**	....	....	....	....	....

a NCAA West Second All-Star Team (1986).
b WCHA Second All-Star Team (1986).
Signed as a free agent by **Pittsburgh**, March 31, 1986.

MATIKAINEN, PETRI

Born, Savonlinna, Finland, January 7, 1967.
Defense. Shoots left. 6′0″, 185 lbs.
Last amateur club: Oshawa Generals (OHL).
(Buffalo's 7th choice, 140th overall, in 1985 Entry Draft).

Season	Club	Lea	Regular Season					Playoffs				
			GP	G	A	TP	PIM	GP	G	A	TP	PIM
1984-85	Sapko	Fin.	24	0	4	4	34	....	....	....	....	....
1985-86	Oshawa	OHL	53	14	42	56	27	....	....	....	....	....

MAURICE, PAUL

Born, Sault Ste. Marie, Ont., January 30, 1967.
Defense. Shoots right. 6′2″, 180 lbs.
Last amateur club: Windsor Compuware Spitfires (OHL).
(Philadelphia's 12th choice, 252nd overall, in 1985 Entry Draft).

Season	Club	Lea	Regular Season					Playoffs				
			GP	G	A	TP	PIM	GP	G	A	TP	PIM
1984-85	Windsor	OHL	38	0	3	3	47	4	0	0	0	19
1985-86	Windsor	OHL	56	3	10	13	89	16	0	2	2	8

MAXWELL, BRAD ROBERT

Born, Brandon, Man., July 8, 1957.
Defense. Shoots right. 6′2″, 195 lbs.
Last amateur club: New Westminster Bruins (WHL).
(Minnesota's 1st choice, 7th over-all, in 1977 Amateur Draft).

Season	Club	Lea	Regular Season					Playoffs				
			GP	G	A	TP	PIM	GP	G	A	TP	PIM
1975-76	N. Westminster	WHL	72	19	80	99	239	17	3	12	15	86
1976-77	N. Westminster	WHL	70	21	58	79	205	14	7	15	22	39
1977-78	Minnesota	NHL	75	18	29	47	100	....	....	....	....	....
1978-79	Oklahoma City	CHL	2	0	1	1	21	....	....	....	....	....
	Minnesota	NHL	70	9	28	37	145	....	....	....	....	....
1979-80	Minnesota	NHL	58	7	30	37	126	11	0	8	8	20
1980-81	Minnesota	NHL	27	3	13	16	98	18	3	11	14	35
1981-82	Minnesota	NHL	51	10	21	31	96	4	0	3	3	13
1982-83	Minnesota	NHL	77	11	28	39	157	9	5	6	11	23
1983-84	Minnesota	NHL	78	19	54	73	225	16	2	11	13	40
1984-85	Minnesota	NHL	18	3	7	10	53	....	....	....	....	....
	Quebec	NHL	50	7	24	31	119	18	2	9	11	35
1985-86	Toronto	NHL	52	8	18	26	108	3	0	1	1	12
	NHL Totals		**556**	**95**	**252**	**347**	**1227**	**79**	**12**	**49**	**61**	**178**

Traded to **Quebec** by **Minnesota** with Brent Ashton for Tony McKegney and Bo Berglund, December 14, 1984. Traded to **Toronto** by **Quebec** for John Anderson, August 22, 1985.

MAXWELL, KEVIN

Born, Edmonton, Alta., March 30, 1960.
Center. Shoots right. 5′9″, 165 lbs.
Last amateur club: 1980 Canadian Olympic Team.
(Minnesota's 4th choice, 63rd over-all, in 1979 Entry Draft).

Season	Club	Lea	Regular Season					Playoffs				
			GP	G	A	TP	PIM	GP	G	A	TP	PIM
1978-79ab	North Dakota	WCHA	42	31	51	82	79	....	....	....	....	....
1979-80	Cdn. National	...	47	25	46	71	28	....	....	....	....	....
	Cdn. Olympic	...	6	0	5	5	4	....	....	....	....	....
1980-81	Oklahoma City	CHL	31	8	13	21	38	....	....	....	....	....
	Minnesota	NHL	6	0	3	3	7	16	3	4	7	24
1981-82	Nashville	CHL	5	4	2	6	6	....	....	....	....	....
	Minnesota	NHL	12	1	4	5	8	....	....	....	....	....
	Colorado	NHL	34	5	5	10	44	....	....	....	....	....
1982-83	Wichita	CHL	68	24	41	65	47	....	....	....	....	....
1983-84	New Jersey	NHL	14	0	3	3	2	....	....	....	....	....
	Maine	AHL	56	21	27	48	59	17	5	11	16	36
1984-85	Maine	AHL	52	25	21	46	70	11	7	7	14	4
1985-86	Maine	AHL	49	14	17	31	77	5	2	1	3	9
	NHL Totals		**66**	**6**	**15**	**21**	**61**	**16**	**3**	**4**	**7**	**24**

a WCHA Rookie of the Year (1979)
b WCHA First All-Star Team (1979)
Sold to **Colorado** by **Minnesota**, December 31, 1981.

MAYER, DEREK

Born, Rossland, B.C., May 21, 1967.
Defense. Shoots right. 6′0″, 185 lbs.
Last amateur club: University of Denver Pioneers (WCHA).
(Detroit's 3rd choice, 43rd overall, in 1986 Entry Draft).

Season	Club	Lea	Regular Season					Playoffs				
			GP	G	A	TP	PIM	GP	G	A	TP	PIM
1985-86	Denver	WCHA	44	2	7	9	42	....	....	....	....	....

McADAM, GARY

Born, Smiths Falls, Ont., December 31, 1955.
Left wing. Shoots left. 5′11″, 175 lbs.
Last amateur club: St. Catharines Black Hawks (OHA).
(Buffalo's 4th choice, 53rd over-all, in 1975 Amateur Draft).

Season	Club	Lea	Regular Season					Playoffs				
			GP	G	A	TP	PIM	GP	G	A	TP	PIM
1974-75	St. Catharines	OHA	65	24	53	77	111	4	4	0	4	4
1975-76	Buffalo	NHL	31	1	2	3	2	1	0	0	0	0
	Hershey	AHL	24	14	13	27	45	10	3	2	5	9
1976-77	Buffalo	NHL	73	13	16	29	17	6	1	0	1	0
1977-78	Buffalo	NHL	79	19	22	41	44	8	2	2	4	7
1978-79	Buffalo	NHL	40	6	5	11	13	....	....	....	....	....
	Pittsburgh	NHL	28	5	9	14	2	7	2	1	3	0
1979-80	Pittsburgh	NHL	78	19	22	41	63	5	1	2	3	9
1980-81	Pittsburgh	NHL	34	3	9	12	30	....	....	....	....	....
	Detroit	NHL	40	5	14	19	27	....	....	....	....	....
1981-82	Dallas	CHL	12	10	10	20	14	....	....	....	....	....
	Calgary	NHL	46	12	15	27	18	3	0	0	0	0
1982-83	Buffalo	NHL	4	1	0	1	0	....	....	....	....	....
	Rochester	AHL	73	40	29	69	58	16	3	4	7	4
1983-84	Maine	AHL	10	3	4	7	18	....	....	....	....	....
	Washington	NHL	24	1	5	6	12	....	....	....	....	....
	New Jersey	NHL	38	9	6	15	15	....	....	....	....	....
1984-85	New Jersey	NHL	4	1	1	2	0	....	....	....	....	....
	Maine	AHL	70	32	20	52	39	10	4	6	10	0
1985-86	Toronto	NHL	15	1	6	7	0	....	....	....	....	....
	St. Catharines	AHL	27	15	18	33	16	....	....	....	....	....
	NHL Totals		**534**	**96**	**132**	**228**	**243**	**30**	**6**	**5**	**11**	**16**

Traded to **Pittsburgh** by **Buffalo** for Dave Schultz, February 6, 1979. Traded to **Detroit** by **Pittsburgh** for Errol Thompson, January 8, 1981. Traded to **Calgary** by **Detroit** with Detroit's fourth round choice (John Bekkers) in 1983 Entry Draft for Eric Vail, November 10, 1981. Signed as a free agent by **Buffalo**, September 1, 1982. Signed as free agent by **New Jersey**, August 4, 1983. Claimed on waivers by **Washington** from **New Jersey**, November 17, 1983. Rights sold to **New Jersey** by **Washington**, January 18, 1984. Signed as a free agent by **Toronto**, July 31, 1985.

McBAIN, ANDREW

Born, Scarborough, Ont., January 18, 1965.
Right wing. Shoots right. 6′1″, 190 lbs.
Last amateur club: North Bay Centennials (OHL).
(Winnipeg's 1st choice, 8th over-all, in 1983 Entry Draft).

Season	Club	Lea	Regular Season					Playoffs				
			GP	G	A	TP	PIM	GP	G	A	TP	PIM
1981-82	Niagara Falls	OHL	68	19	25	44	35	5	0	3	3	4
1982-83a	North Bay	OHL	67	33	87	120	61	8	2	6	8	17
1983-84	Winnipeg	NHL	78	11	19	30	37	3	2	0	2	0
1984-85	Winnipeg	NHL	77	7	15	22	45	7	1	0	1	0
1985-86	Winnipeg	NHL	28	3	3	6	17	....	....	....	....	....
	NHL Totals		**183**	**21**	**37**	**58**	**99**	**10**	**3**	**0**	**3**	**0**

a OHL Second All-Star Team (1983).

McCARTHY, DANIEL (DAN)

Born, St. Mary's, Ont., April 7, 1958.
Center. Shoots left. 5′9″, 185 lbs.
Last amateur club: Sudbury Wolves (OHA).
(NY Rangers' 16th choice, 223rd over-all, in 1978 Amateur Draft).

Season	Club	Lea	Regular Season					Playoffs				
			GP	G	A	TP	PIM	GP	G	A	TP	PIM
1976-77	Sudbury	OHA	54	23	32	55	76	6	0	3	3	12
1977-78	Sudbury	OHA	68	30	51	81	96	....	....	....	....	....
1978-79	Flint	IHL	75	38	42	80	80	....	....	....	....	....
1979-80	New Haven	AHL	26	6	3	9	8	....	....	....	....	....
	Richmond	EHL	8	6	4	10	7	2	1	0	1	22
1980-81	NY Rangers	NHL	5	4	0	4	4	....	....	....	....	....
	New Haven	AHL	71	28	17	45	54	4	0	0	0	4
1981-82	Springfield	AHL	78	26	32	58	57	....	....	....	....	....
1982-83	Birmingham	CHL	76	30	35	65	67	13	4	5	9	15
1983-84	Baltimore	AHL	27	8	11	19	8	....	....	....	....	....
1984-85	Baltimore	AHL	32	3	11	19	15	3	4	7	18	
1985-86	Springfield	AHL	33	7	9	16	46	....	....	....	....	....
	NHL Totals		**5**	**4**	**0**	**4**	**4**	....	....	....	....	....

Traded to **Minnesota** by **NY Rangers** for Shawn Dineen, August 23, 1982.

McCARTHY, KEVIN

Born, Winnipeg, Man., July 14, 1957.
Defense. Shoots right. 5'11", 195 lbs.
Last amateur club: Winnipeg Monarchs (WHL).
(Philadelphia's 1st choice, 17th over-all, in 1977 Amateur Draft).

Season	Club	Lea	GP	G	A	TP	PIM	GP	G	A	TP	PIM
1975-76ab	Winnipeg	WHL	72	33	88	121	160	6	2	9	11	8
1976-77ac	Winnipeg	WHL	72	22	*105	127	110	7	0	4	4	27
1977-78	**Philadelphia**	NHL	62	2	15	17	32	10	0	1	1	8
1978-79	**Philadelphia**	NHL	22	1	2	3	21	....	....	....	....	....
	Vancouver	NHL	1	0	0	0	0	....	....	....	....	....
1979-80	**Vancouver**	NHL	79	15	30	45	70	4	1	0	1	0
1980-81	**Vancouver**	NHL	80	16	37	53	85	3	0	1	1	0
1981-82	**Vancouver**	NHL	71	6	39	45	84	....	....	....	....	....
1982-83	**Vancouver**	NHL	74	12	28	40	88	4	1	1	2	12
1983-84	**Vancouver**	NHL	47	2	14	16	61	....	....	....	....	....
	Pittsburgh	NHL	31	4	16	20	52	....	....	....	....	....
1984-85	**Pittsburgh**	NHL	64	9	10	19	30	....	....	....	....	....
1985-86	**Philadelphia**	NHL	4	0	0	0	4	....	....	....	....	....
d	Hershey	AHL	64	15	40	55	157	17	1	10	11	12
	NHL Totals		535	67	191	258	527	21	2	3	5	20

a WHL First All-Star Team (1976, 1977)
b Named WHL's Top Defenseman (1976)
c Named WHL Player of the Year (1977)
d AHL First All-Star Team (1986).

Traded to **Vancouver** by **Philadelphia** with Drew Callander for Dennis Ververgaert, December 29, 1978. Traded to **Pittsburgh** by **Vancouver** for Philadelphia's third round choice (David McClay) — Pittsburgh property via earlier deal — January 26, 1984. Signed as a free agent by **Philadelphia**, July 19, 1985.

McCARTHY, TOM JOSEPH

Born, Toronto, Ont., July 31, 1960.
Left wing. Shoots left. 6'2", 210 lbs.
Last amateur club: Oshawa Generals (OHA).
(Minnesota's 2nd choice, 10th over-all, in 1979 Entry Draft).

Season	Club	Lea	GP	G	A	TP	PIM	GP	G	A	TP	PIM
1977-78	Oshawa	OHA	62	47	46	93	72	6	3	5	8	4
1978-79a	Oshawa	OHA	63	69	75	141	98	3	1	0	1	9
1979-80	**Minnesota**	NHL	68	16	20	36	39	15	5	6	11	20
1980-81	**Minnesota**	NHL	62	23	25	48	62	8	0	3	3	6
1981-82	**Minnesota**	NHL	40	12	30	42	36	4	0	2	2	4
1982-83	**Minnesota**	NHL	80	28	48	76	59	9	2	4	6	9
1983-84	**Minnesota**	NHL	66	39	31	70	49	8	1	4	5	6
1984-85	**Minnesota**	NHL	44	16	21	37	36	7	0	2	2	0
1985-86	**Minnesota**	NHL	25	12	12	24	12	....	....	....	....	....
	NHL Totals		385	146	187	333	293	51	8	21	29	45

a OHA First All-Star Team (1979)

Traded to **Boston** by **Minnesota** for Boston's third-round choice (Rob Zettler) in 1986 Entry Draft, May 16, 1986.

McCAUGHEY, BRAD

Born, Ann Arbor, Mich., June 10, 1966.
Right wing. Shoots right. 6'0", 180 lbs.
Last amateur club: University of Michigan Wolverines (CCHA).
(Montreal's 10th choice, 158th overall, in 1984 Entry Draft).

Season	Club	Lea	GP	G	A	TP	PIM	GP	G	A	TP	PIM
1984-85	U. of Michigan	CCHA	35	16	11	27	49	....	....	....	....	....
1985-86	U. of Michigan	CCHA	32	24	26	50	51	....	....	....	....	....

McCLELLAND, KEVIN WILLIAM

Born, Oshawa, Ont., July 4, 1962.
Center. Shoots right. 6', 180 lbs.
Last amateur club: Niagara Falls Flyers (OHL).
(Hartford's 4th choice, 71st over-all, in 1980 Entry Draft).

Season	Club	Lea	GP	G	A	TP	PIM	GP	G	A	TP	PIM
1980-81	Niagara Falls	OHA	68	36	72	108	186	12	8	13	21	42
1981-82	Niagara Falls	OHL	46	36	47	83	184	....	....	....	....	....
	Pittsburgh	NHL	10	1	4	5	4	5	1	1	2	5
1982-83	**Pittsburgh**	NHL	38	5	4	9	73	....	....	....	....	....
1983-84	Baltimore	AHL	3	1	1	2	0	....	....	....	....	....
	Pittsburgh	NHL	24	2	4	6	62	....	....	....	....	....
	Edmonton	NHL	52	8	20	28	127	18	4	6	10	42
1984-85	**Edmonton**	NHL	62	8	15	23	205	18	1	3	4	75
1985-86	**Edmonton**	NHL	79	11	25	36	266	10	1	1	2	32
	NHL Totals		265	35	72	107	737	51	7	10	17	154

Traded to **Pittsburgh** by **Hartford** with Pat Boutette as compensation for Hartford's signing of free agent goaltender Greg Millen, June 29, 1981. Traded to **Edmonton** by **Pittsburgh** with Pittsburgh's sixth round choice (Emanuel Viveiros) in 1984 Entry Draft for Tom Roulston, December 5, 1983.

McCOLGAN, GARY

Born, Scarborough, Ont., March 27, 1966.
Left wing. Shoots left. 6'0", 195 lbs.
Last amateur club: Oshawa Generals (OHL).
(Minnesota's 6th choice, 118th overall, in 1984 Entry Draft).

Season	Club	Lea	GP	G	A	TP	PIM	GP	G	A	TP	PIM
1983-84	Oshawa	OHL	66	11	28	39	14	....	....	....	....	....
1984-85	Oshawa	OHL	63	29	26	55	17	5	1	3	4	0
1985-86	Oshawa	OHL	57	49	54	103	22	6	7	4	11	2

McCOMB, TOM

Born, Norwood, Mass., January 20, 1965.
Defense. Shoots right. 6'1", 190 lbs.
Last amateur club: University of Maine Black Bears (H.E.).
(Minnesota's 7th choice, 116th overall, in 1983 Entry Draft).

Season	Club	Lea	GP	G	A	TP	PIM	GP	G	A	TP	PIM
1985-86	Maine	H.E.	21	0	4	4	6	....	....	....	....	....

McCORMACK, BILL

Born, Winchester, Mass., January 16, 1964.
Center. Shoots left. 6'1", 185 lbs.
Last amateur club: University of Vermont Catamounts (ECAC).
(Philadelphia's 9th choice, 201st overall, in 1983 Entry Draft).

Season	Club	Lea	GP	G	A	TP	PIM	GP	G	A	TP	PIM
1983-84	Vermont	ECAC	22	0	1	1	10	....	....	....	....	....
1984-85	Vermont	ECAC	23	3	5	8	22	....	....	....	....	....
1985-86	Vermont	ECAC	30	8	7	15	36	....	....	....	....	....

McCREARY, WILLIAM (BILL)

Born, Springfield, Mass., April 15, 1960.
Right wing. Shoots right. 6', 190 lbs.
Last amateur club: Colgate University Red Raiders (ECAC).
(Toronto's 5th choice, 114th over-all, in 1979 Entry Draft).

Season	Club	Lea	GP	G	A	TP	PIM	GP	G	A	TP	PIM
1978-79	Colgate	ECAC	24	19	25	44	70	....	....	....	....	....
1979-80	Colgate	ECAC	12	7	13	20	44	....	....	....	....	....
1980-81	**Toronto**	NHL	12	1	0	1	4	....	....	....	....	....
	New Brunswick	AHL	61	19	24	43	120	12	2	0	2	13
1981-82	Cincinnati	CHL	69	8	27	35	61	4	0	4	4	2
1982-83	Peoria	IHL	76	23	34	57	28	....	....	....	....	....
	St. Catharines	AHL	4	0	1	1	2	....	....	....	....	....
1983-84	Milwaukee	IHL	81	28	35	63	44	4	0	2	2	2
1984-85	Milwaukee	IHL	10	1	0	1	4	....	....	....	....	....
1985-86	Milwaukee	IHL	80	30	31	61	83	5	3	0	3	6
	NHL Totals		12	1	0	1	4	....	....	....	....	....

McCRIMMON, BYRON (BRAD)

Born, Dodsland, Sask., March 29, 1959.
Defense. Shoots left. 5'11", 195 lbs.
Last amateur club: Brandon Wheat Kings (WHL).
(Boston's 2nd choice, 15th over-all, in 1979 Entry Draft).

Season	Club	Lea	GP	G	A	TP	PIM	GP	G	A	TP	PIM
1977-78ab	Brandon	WHL	65	19	78	97	245	8	2	11	13	20
1978-79a	Brandon	WHL	66	24	74	98	139	22	9	19	28	34
1979-80	**Boston**	NHL	72	5	11	16	94	10	1	1	2	28
1980-81	**Boston**	NHL	78	11	18	29	148	3	0	1	1	2
1981-82	**Boston**	NHL	78	1	8	9	83	2	0	0	0	2
1982-83	**Philadelphia**	NHL	79	4	21	25	61	3	0	0	0	4
1983-84	**Philadelphia**	NHL	71	0	24	24	76	1	0	0	0	4
1984-85	**Philadelphia**	NHL	66	8	35	43	81	11	2	1	3	15
1985-86	**Philadelphia**	NHL	80	13	43	56	85	5	2	0	2	2
	NHL Totals		524	42	160	202	628	35	5	3	8	57

a WHL First All-Star Team (1978, 1979)
b Named WHL's Top Defenseman (1978)

Traded to **Philadelphia** by **Boston** for Pete Peeters, June 9, 1982.

McCUTCHEON, DARWIN

Born, Listowel, Ont., April 19, 1962.
Defense. Shoots left. 6'4", 190 lbs.
Last amateur club: University of Prince Edward Island Panthers (AUAA).
(Toronto's 8th choice, 179th overall, in 1980 Entry Draft).

Season	Club	Lea	GP	G	A	TP	PIM	GP	G	A	TP	PIM
1984-85	U. PEI	AUAA	24	5	30	35	73	....	....	....	....	....
1985-86	Moncton	AHL	12	0	2	2	31	9	0	0	0	9

Signed by as a free agent by **Calgary**, March 19, 1986.

McDONALD, LANE

Born, Mequon, Wisconsin, March 3, 1966.
Left wing. Shoots left. 5'11", 170 lbs.
Last amateur club: Harvard University Crimson (ECAC).
(Calgary's 4th choice, 58th overall in 1985 Entry Draft).

Season	Club	Lea	GP	G	A	TP	PIM	GP	G	A	TP	PIM
1984-85	Harvard	ECAC	24	17	25	42	0	....	....	....	....	....
1985-86	Harvard	ECAC	30	22	24	46	45	....	....	....	....	....

McDONALD, LANNY KING

Born, Hanna, Alta., February 16, 1953.
Right wing. Shoots right. 6', 190 lbs.
Last amateur club: Medicine Hat Tigers (WHL).
(Toronto's 1st choice, 4th over-all, in 1973 Amateur Draft).

			Regular Season					Playoffs				
Season	Club	Lea	GP	G	A	TP	PIM	GP	G	A	TP	PIM
1971-72	Medicine Hat	WHL	68	50	64	114	54	7	2	2	4	6
1972-73a	Medicine Hat	WHL	68	62	77	139	84	17	*18	19	37	6
1973-74	Toronto	NHL	70	14	16	30	43					
1974-75	Toronto	NHL	64	17	27	44	86	7	0	0	0	2
1975-76	Toronto	NHL	75	37	56	93	70	10	4	4	8	4
1976-77b	Toronto	NHL	80	46	44	90	77	9	10	7	17	6
1977-78	Toronto	NHL	74	47	40	87	54	13	3	4	7	10
1978-79	Toronto	NHL	79	43	42	85	32	6	3	2	5	0
1979-80	Toronto	NHL	35	15	15	30	10					
	Colorado	NHL	46	25	20	45	43					
1980-81	Colorado	NHL	80	35	46	81	56					
1981-82	Colorado	NHL	16	6	9	15	20					
	Calgary	NHL	55	34	33	67	37	3	0	1	1	6
1982-83bc	Calgary	NHL	80	66	32	98	90	7	3	4	7	19
1983-84	Calgary	NHL	65	33	33	66	64	11	6	7	13	6
1984-85	Calgary	NHL	43	19	18	37	36	1	0	0	0	0
1985-86	Calgary	NHL	80	28	43	71	44	22	11	7	18	30
	NHL Totals		942	465	474	939	762	89	40	36	76	83

a WHL First All-Star Team (1973)
b NHL Second All-Star Team (1977, 1983)
c Won Bill Masterton Memorial Trophy (1983)

Traded to **Colorado** by **Toronto** with Joel Quenneville for Pat Hickey and Wilf Paiement, December 29, 1979. Traded to **Calgary** by **Colorado** with Colorado's fourth round choice (Mikko Makela — later transferred to NY Islanders) in 1983 Entry Draft for Bob MacMillan and Don Lever, November 25, 1981.

McDONNELL, JOSEPH PATRICK (JOE)

Born, Kitchener, Ont., May 11, 1961.
Defense. Shoots right. 6'2", 200 lbs.
Last amateur club: Kitchener Rangers (OHA).

			Regular Season					Playoffs				
Season	Club	Lea	GP	G	A	TP	PIM	GP	G	A	TP	PIM
1979-80	Kitchener	OHA	62	6	21	27	81					
1980-81	Kitchener	OHA	66	15	50	65	103	16	4	9	13	8
1981-82	Vancouver	NHL	7	0	1	1	12					
	Dallas	CHL	60	13	24	37	46	9	2	1	3	12
1982-83	Moncton	AHL	79	14	21	35	44					
1983-84	Moncton	AHL	78	12	33	45	44					
1984-85	Pittsburgh	NHL	40	2	9	11	20					
	Baltimore	AHL	41	7	27	34	22					
1985-86	Pittsburgh	NHL	3	0	0	0	2					
	Baltimore	AHL	31	1	13	14	20					
	NHL Totals		50	2	10	12	34					

Signed as free agent by **Vancouver**, September 22, 1980. Signed as free agent by **Edmonton**, August 16, 1982. Signed as a free agent by **Pittsburgh**, December 30, 1984.

McEWEN, MICHAEL TODD (MIKE) (mc-YOU-en)

Born, Hornepayne, Ont., August 10, 1956.
Defense. Shoots left. 6'1", 185 lbs.
Last amateur club: Toronto Marlboros (OHA).
(NY Rangers' 3rd choice, 42nd over-all, in 1976 Amateur Draft).

			Regular Season					Playoffs				
Season	Club	Lea	GP	G	A	TP	PIM	GP	G	A	TP	PIM
1974-75	Toronto	OHA	68	18	63	81	52	23	5	14	19	33
1975-76	Toronto	OHA	65	23	40	63	63	10	3	9	12	20
1976-77	NY Rangers	NHL	80	14	29	43	38					
1977-78	NY Rangers	NHL	57	5	13	18	52					
1978-79	NY Rangers	NHL	80	20	38	58	35	18	2	11	13	8
1979-80	NY Rangers	NHL	9	1	7	8	8					
	Colorado	NHL	67	11	40	51	33					
1980-81	Colorado	NHL	65	11	35	46	84					
	NY Islanders	NHL	13	0	3	3	10	17	6	8	14	6
1981-82	NY Islanders	NHL	73	10	39	49	50	15	3	7	10	18
1982-83	NY Islanders	NHL	42	2	11	13	16	12	0	2	2	4
1983-84	NY Islanders	NHL	15	0	2	2	6					
	Los Angeles	NHL	47	10	24	34	14					
	New Haven	AHL	9	3	7	10	26					
1984-85	Washington	NHL	56	11	27	38	42	5	0	1	1	4
	Binghamton	AHL	14	2	10	12	14					
1985-86	Detroit	NHL	29	0	10	10	16					
	NY Rangers	NHL	16	2	5	7	8					
	New Haven	AHL	2	0	3	3	2					
	Hartford	NHL	10	3	2	5	6	8	0	4	4	6
	NHL Totals		659	100	285	385	418	75	11	33	44	46

Traded to **Colorado** by **NY Rangers** with Pat Hickey, Lucien DeBlois, Dean Turner and future considerations (Bobby Crawford) for Barry Beck, November 2, 1979. Traded to **NY Islanders** by **Colorado** with Jari Kaarela for Glenn Resch and Steve Tambellini, March 10, 1981. Traded to **Los Angeles** by **NY Islanders** for Detroit's fourth round choice (Doug Wieck) — Los Angeles property via earlier deal — November 17, 1983. Signed as a free agent by **Detroit,** August 12, 1985. Traded to **NY Rangers**, by **Detroit** for Steve Richmond, December 26,1985. Traded to **Hartford** by **NY Rangers** for Bob Crawford, March 11, 1986.

McFALL, DAN

Born, Kenmore, N.Y., April 8, 1963.
Defense. Shoots right. 6', 180 lbs.
Last amateur club: Michigan State University Spartans (CCHA).
(Winnipeg's 8th choice, 148th over-all, in 1981 Entry Draft).

			Regular Season					Playoffs				
Season	Club	Lea	GP	G	A	TP	PIM	GP	G	A	TP	PIM
1981-82	Mich. State U.	CCHA	40	3	17	20	28					
1982-83	Mich. State U.	CCHA	36	12	14	26	22					
1983-84	Mich. State U.	CCHA	46	14	20	34	56					
1984-85	Winnipeg	NHL	2	0	0	0	0					
ab	Mich. State U.	CCHA	44	7	25	32	32					
1985-86	Winnipeg	NHL	7	0	1	1	0					
	Sherbrooke	AHL	50	2	10	12	16					
	NHL Totals		9	0	1	1	0					

a CCHA Second All-Star Team (1985)
b Named to NCAA All-American Team (1985)

McGEOUGH, JAMES (JIM) (meh-GOO)

Born, Regina, Sask., April 13, 1963.
Center. Shoots left. 5'8", 170 lbs.
Last amateur club: Nanaimo Islanders (WHL).
(Washington's 6th choice, 110th over-all, in 1981 Entry Draft).

			Regular Season					Playoffs				
Season	Club	Lea	GP	G	A	TP	PIM	GP	G	A	TP	PIM
1980-81	Regina	WHL	4	1	2	3	2					
	Billings	WHL	67	49	42	91	139	5	2	5	7	15
1981-82	Washington	NHL	4	0	0	0	0					
	Billings	WHL	71	*93	66	159	142	5	2	1	3	4
1982-83	Nanaimo	WHL	72	76	56	132	126					
	Hershey	AHL	5	1	1	2	10	5	0	2	2	25
1983-84	Hershey	AHL	79	40	36	76	108					
1984-85	Washington	NHL	11	3	0	3	12					
	Pittsburgh	NHL	14	0	4	4	4					
	Binghamton	AHL	57	32	21	53	26					
1985-86	Pittsburgh	NHL	17	3	2	5	8					
	Baltimore	AHL	38	14	13	27	20					
	NHL Totals		46	6	6	12	24					

Traded to **Pittsburgh** by **Washington** for Mark Taylor, March 12, 1985.

MacGEOUGH, PETER

Born, Watertown, NY, April 15, 1965.
Defense. Shoots left. 6'1", 190 lbs.
Last amateur club: St. Lawrence University Saints (ECAC).
(NY Islanders' 14th choice, 247th overall, in 1983 Entry Draft).

			Regular Season					Playoffs				
Season	Club	Lea	GP	G	A	TP	PIM	GP	G	A	TP	PIM
1984-85	St. Lawrence	ECAC	32	1	8	9	70					
1985-86	St. Lawrence	ECAC	27	9	8	17	83					

McGILL, ROBERT PAUL (BOB)

Born, Edmonton, Alta., April 27, 1962.
Defense. Shoot right. 6', 190 lbs.
Last amateur club: Victoria Cougars (WHL).
(Toronto's 2nd choice, 26th over-all, in 1980 Entry Draft).

			Regular Season					Playoffs				
Season	Club	Lea	GP	G	A	TP	PIM	GP	G	A	TP	PIM
1979-80	Victoria	WHL	70	3	18	21	230	15	0	5	5	64
1980-81	Victoria	WHL	66	5	36	41	295	11	1	5	6	67
1981-82	Toronto	NHL	68	1	10	11	263					
1982-83	Toronto	NHL	30	0	0	0	146					
	St. Catharines	AHL	32	2	5	7	95					
1983-84	Toronto	NHL	11	0	2	2	51					
	St. Catharines	AHL	55	1	15	16	217	6	0	0	0	26
1984-85	Toronto	NHL	72	0	5	5	250					
1985-86	Toronto	NHL	61	1	4	5	141	9	0	0	0	35
	NHL Totals		242	2	21	23	851	9	0	0	0	35

McKAY, DARREN DOYLE

Born, Lloydminster, Sask., February 10, 1962.
Defense. Shoots left. 5'9", 190 lbs.
Last amateur club: Billings Bighorns (WHL).

			Regular Season					Playoffs				
Season	Club	Lea	GP	G	A	TP	PIM	GP	G	A	TP	PIM
1979-80	Billings	WHL	14	6	2	8	23					
1980-81	Billings	WHL	68	10	29	39	183	5	1	0	1	8
1981-82	Billings	WHL	70	12	64	76	176	5	0	1	1	35
1982-83	Binghamton	AHL	65	4	32	36	113					
1983-84	Binghamton	AHL	71	11	40	51	206					
1984-85	Muskegon	IHL	64	8	28	36	90	17	5	8	13	39
1985-86	Muskegon	IHL	36	4	22	26	62					
	Indianapolis	IHL	30	4	14	18	42	4	0	1	1	17

Signed as a free agent by **Hartford**, December 28, 1982.

McKAY, RANDY

Born, Montreal, Que., January 25, 1967.
Right wing. Shoots right. 6'1", 170 lbs.
Last amateur club: Michigan Tech University Huskies (WCHA).
(Detroit's 6th choice, 113th overall, in 1985 Entry Draft).

			Regular Season					Playoffs				
Season	Club	Lea	GP	G	A	TP	PIM	GP	G	A	TP	PIM
1984-85	Michigan	WCHA	25	4	5	9	32					
1985-86	Michigan	WCHA	40	12	22	34	46					

McKECHNEY, GARNET

Born, Swift Current, Sask., April 28, 1965.
Right wing. Shoots right. 6'1", 175 lbs.
Last amateur club: Kitchener Rangers (OHL).
(NY Islanders' 3rd choice, 37th over-all, in 1983 Entry Draft).

Season	Club	Lea	Regular Season GP	G	A	TP	PIM	Playoffs GP	G	A	TP	PIM
1981-82	Thunder Bay	Midget	62	40	30	70	54	....	....	....	....	....
1982-83	Kitchener	OHL	66	20	20	40	95	12	4	1	5	11
1983-84	Kitchener	OHL	68	31	45	76	107	16	6	4	10	8
1984-85	Kitchener	OHL	40	12	25	37	52	....	....	....	....	....
	London	OHL	23	10	9	19	23	8	4	2	6	11
1985-86	London	OHL	27	16	14	30	50	5	0	0	0	20
	Indianapolis	IHL	3	0	1	1	2	....	....	....	....	....
	Milwaukee	IHL	15	0	2	2	11	....	....	....	....	....
	Saginaw	IHL	8	2	2	4	2	....	....	....	....	....

McKEGNEY, ANTHONY SYIIYD (TONY)   (ma-KEG-nee)

Born, Montreal, Que., February 15, 1958.
Left wing. Shoots left. 6'1", 200 lbs.
Last amateur club: Kingston Canadians (OHA).
(Buffalo's 2nd choice, 32nd over-all, in 1978 Amateur Draft).

Season	Club	Lea	Regular Season GP	G	A	TP	PIM	Playoffs GP	G	A	TP	PIM
1976-77a	Kingston	OHA	66	58	77	135	30	14	13	10	23	14
1977-78b	Kingston	OHA	55	43	49	92	19	5	3	3	6	0
1978-79	Hershey	AHL	24	21	18	39	4	1	0	0	0	0
	Buffalo	NHL	52	8	14	22	10	2	0	1	1	0
1979-80	Buffalo	NHL	80	23	29	52	24	14	3	4	7	2
1980-81	Buffalo	NHL	80	37	32	69	24	8	5	3	8	2
1981-82	Buffalo	NHL	73	23	29	52	41	4	0	0	0	2
1982-83	Buffalo	NHL	78	36	37	73	18	10	3	1	4	4
1983-84	Quebec	NHL	75	24	27	51	23	7	0	0	0	0
1984-85	Quebec	NHL	30	12	9	21	12	....	....	....	....	....
	Minnesota	NHL	27	11	13	24	4	9	8	6	14	0
1985-86	Minnesota	NHL	70	15	25	40	48	5	2	1	3	22
	NHL Totals		**565**	**189**	**215**	**404**	**204**	**59**	**21**	**16**	**37**	**32**

a OHA First All-Star Team (1977).
b OHA Second All-Star Team (1978).
Traded to **Quebec** by **Buffalo** with Andre Savard, J.F. Sauve and Buffalo's third round choice (Iiirvo Jarvi) in 1983 Entry Draft for Real Cloutier and Quebec's first round choice (Adam Creighton) in 1983 Entry Draft, June 8, 1983. Traded to **Minnesota** by **Quebec** with Bo Berglund for Brent Ashton and Brad Maxwell, December 14, 1984.

McKENNA, SEAN MICHAEL

Born, Asbestos, Que., March 7, 1962.
Right wing. Shoots right. 6', 190 lbs.
Last amateur club: Sherbrooke Beavers (QMJHL).
(Buffalo's 3rd choice, 56th over-all, in 1980 Entry Draft).

Season	Club	Lea	Regular Season GP	G	A	TP	PIM	Playoffs GP	G	A	TP	PIM
1980-81a	Sherbrooke	QJHL	71	57	47	104	122	14	9	9	18	12
1981-82	Buffalo	NHL	3	0	1	1	2	....	....	....	....	....
bc	Sherbrooke	QJHL	59	57	33	90	29	22	26	18	44	28
1982-83	Buffalo	NHL	46	10	14	24	4	....	....	....	....	....
	Rochester	AHL	26	16	10	26	14	16	14	8	22	18
1983-84	Buffalo	NHL	78	20	10	30	45	3	1	0	1	2
1984-85	Buffalo	NHL	65	20	16	36	41	5	0	1	1	0
1985-86	Buffalo	NHL	45	6	12	18	28	....	....	....	....	....
	Los Angeles	NHL	30	4	0	4	7	....	....	....	....	....
	NHL Totals		**267**	**60**	**53**	**113**	**127**	**8**	**1**	**1**	**2**	**2**

a QMJHL First All-Star Team (1981).
b QMJHL Second All-Star Team (1982).
c Named Most Valuable Player, 1982 Memorial Cup.
Traded to **Los Angeles** by **Buffalo** with Larry Playfair and Ken Baumgartner for Brian Engblom and Doug Smith, January 30, 1986.

McKINLEY, JAMIE

Born, Moncton, N.B., May 1, 1967.
Right wing. Shoots right. 6'1", 165 lbs.
Last amateur club: Guelph Platers (OHL).
(New Jersey's 10th choice, 192nd overall, in 1985 Entry Draft).

Season	Club	Lea	Regular Season GP	G	A	TP	PIM	Playoffs GP	G	A	TP	PIM
1984-85	Guelph	OHL	62	25	23	48	9	....	....	....	....	....
1985-86	Guelph	OHL	66	23	29	52	48	20	9	15	24	12

McKINNON, BRIAN

Born, Toronto, Ont., October 4, 1964.
Center. Shoots left. 5'11", 185 lbs.
Last amateur club: Ottawa 67's (OHL).
(Buffalo's 9th choice, 207th over-all, in 1984 Entry Draft).

Season	Club	Lea	Regular Season GP	G	A	TP	PIM	Playoffs GP	G	A	TP	PIM
1983-84	Ottawa	OHL	58	31	27	58	27	13	0	7	7	12
1984-85	Rochester	AHL	62	6	8	14	16	....	....	....	....	....
1985-86	Rochester	AHL	51	4	7	11	14	....	....	....	....	....

McLAY, DAVID

Born, Chilliwack, B.C., May 13, 1966.
Left wing. Shoots left. 5'11", 175 lbs.
Last amateur club: Portland Winterhawks (WHL).
(Philadelphia's 4th choice, 43rd over-all, in 1984 Entry Draft).

Season	Club	Lea	Regular Season GP	G	A	TP	PIM	Playoffs GP	G	A	TP	PIM
1983-84	Kelowna	WHL	71	34	34	68	112	....	....	....	....	....
1984-85	Portland	WHL	70	32	36	68	220	6	3	2	5	12
1985-86	Portland	WHL	70	37	49	86	219	15	6	3	9	30

McMILLAN, BILL

Born, North Bay, Ont., April 3, 1967.
Right wing. Shoots right. 6'2", 185 lbs.
Last amateur club: Peterborough Petes (OHL).
(New Jersey's 6th choice, 108th overall, in 1985 Entry Draft).

Season	Club	Lea	Regular Season GP	G	A	TP	PIM	Playoffs GP	G	A	TP	PIM
1984-85	Peterborough	OHL	61	12	22	34	10	9	1	1	2	0
1985-86	Peterborough	OHL	56	16	33	49	67	6	1	1	2	4

McMURCHY, THOMAS (TOM)

Born, New Westminster, B.C., December 2, 1963.
Right wing. Shoots left. 5'9", 165 lbs.
Last amateur club: Brandon Wheat Kings (WHL).
(Chicago's 3rd choice, 49th over-all, in 1982 Entry Draft).

Season	Club	Lea	Regular Season GP	G	A	TP	PIM	Playoffs GP	G	A	TP	PIM
1980-81	Medicine Hat	WHL	14	5	0	5	46	....	....	....	....	....
	Brandon	WHL	46	20	33	53	101	5	2	2	4	4
1981-82	Brandon	WHL	68	59	63	122	179	4	7	3	10	4
1982-83	Brandon	WHL	42	43	38	81	48	....	....	....	....	....
	Springfield	AHL	8	2	2	4	0	....	....	....	....	....
1983-84	Chicago	NHL	27	3	1	4	42	....	....	....	....	....
	Springfield	AHL	43	16	14	30	54	4	4	0	4	0
1984-85	Chicago	NHL	15	1	2	3	13	....	....	....	....	....
	Milwaukee	IHL	69	30	26	56	61	....	....	....	....	....
1985-86	Chicago	NHL	4	0	0	0	2	....	....	....	....	....
	Nova Scotia	AHL	49	26	21	47	73	....	....	....	....	....
	Moncton	AHL	16	7	3	10	27	2	0	1	1	6
	NHL Totals		**46**	**4**	**3**	**7**	**57**	....	....	....	....	....

Traded to **Calgary** by **Chicago** for Rik Wilson, March 11, 1986.
Signed as a free agent by **Edmonton**, August 18, 1986.

McNAB, PETER MAXWELL

Born, Vancouver, B.C., May 8, 1952.
Center. Shoots left. 6'3", 205 lbs.
Last amateur club: University of Denver Pioneers (WCHA).
(Buffalo's 6th choice, 85th over-all, in 1972 Amateur Draft).

Season	Club	Lea	Regular Season GP	G	A	TP	PIM	Playoffs GP	G	A	TP	PIM
1971-72	U. of Denver	WCHA	38	27	38	65	16	....	....	....	....	....
1972-73	U. of Denver	WCHA	28	23	29	52	12	....	....	....	....	....
1973-74	Buffalo	NHL	22	3	6	9	2	....	....	....	....	....
	Cincinnati	AHL	49	34	39	73	16	5	2	6	8	0
1974-75	Buffalo	NHL	53	22	21	43	8	17	2	6	8	4
1975-76	Buffalo	NHL	79	24	32	56	16	8	0	0	0	0
1976-77	Boston	NHL	80	38	48	86	11	14	5	3	8	2
1977-78	Boston	NHL	79	41	39	80	4	15	8	11	19	2
1978-79	Boston	NHL	76	35	45	80	10	11	5	3	8	0
1979-80	Boston	NHL	74	40	38	78	10	10	8	6	14	2
1980-81	Boston	NHL	80	37	46	83	24	3	3	0	3	0
1981-82	Boston	NHL	80	36	40	76	19	11	8	6	14	6
1982-83	Boston	NHL	74	22	52	74	23	15	3	5	8	4
1983-84	Boston	NHL	52	14	16	30	10	....	....	....	....	....
	Vancouver	NHL	13	1	6	7	10	3	0	0	0	0
1984-85	Vancouver	NHL	75	23	25	48	10	....	....	....	....	....
1985-86	New Jersey	NHL	71	19	24	43	10	....	....	....	....	....
	NHL Totals		**908**	**355**	**438**	**793**	**171**	**107**	**40**	**42**	**82**	**20**

Signed as free agent by **Boston** from **Buffalo**, June 11, 1976. Traded to **Vancouver** by **Boston** for Jim Nill, February 3, 1984. Signed as a free agent by **New Jersey**, August 20, 1985.

McPHEE, GEORGE

Born, Guelph, Ont., July 2, 1958.
Left wing. Shoots left. 5'9", 170 lbs.
Last amateur club: Bowling Green State University Falcons (CCHA).

Season	Club	Lea	Regular Season GP	G	A	TP	PIM	Playoffs GP	G	A	TP	PIM
1978-79ab	Bowling Green	CCHA	43	*40	48	*88	58	....	....	....	....	....
1979-80	Bowling Green	CCHA	34	21	24	45	51	....	....	....	....	....
1980-81b	Bowling Green	CCHA	36	25	29	54	68	....	....	....	....	....
1981-82cde	Bowling Green	CCHA	40	28	52	80	57	....	....	....	....	....
1982-83	Tulsa	CHL	61	17	43	60	145	7	1	1	2	14
	NY Rangers	NHL	....	....	....	....	....	9	3	3	6	2
1983-84	NY Rangers	NHL	9	1	1	2	11	....	....	....	....	....
	Tulsa	CHL	49	20	28	48	133	....	....	....	....	....
1984-85	NY Rangers	NHL	49	12	15	27	139	3	1	0	1	7
	New Haven	AHL	8	2	4	6	13	....	....	....	....	....
1985-86	NY Rangers	NHL	30	4	4	8	63	11	0	0	0	32
	NHL Totals		**88**	**17**	**20**	**37**	**213**	**23**	**4**	**3**	**7**	**41**

a CCHA Rookie of the Year (1979)
b CCHA Second All-Star Team (1979, 1980)
c CCHA First All-Star Team (1982)
d CCHA Player of the Year (1982)
e Winner of the 1982 Hobey Baker Memorial Trophy (Top U.S. College Player).
Signed as a free agent by **NY Rangers**, July 1, 1982.

McPHEE, MICHAEL JOSEPH (MIKE)

Born, Rivière Bourgeois, N.S., July 14, 1960.
Left wing. Shoots left. 6'2", 205 lbs.
Last amateur club: Rensselaer Polytechnical Institute Engineers (ECAC)
(Montreal's 8th choice, 124th over-all, in 1980 Entry Draft).

Season	Club	Lea	Regular Season					Playoffs				
			GP	G	A	TP	PIM	GP	G	A	TP	PIM
1980-81	RPI	ECAC	29	28	18	46	22	....	....	....	....	....
1981-82	RPI	ECAC	6	0	3	3	4	....	....	....	....	....
1982-83	Nova Scotia	AHL	42	10	15	25	29	7	1	1	2	14
1983-84	Nova Scotia	AHL	67	22	33	55	101	....	....	....	....	....
	Montreal	**NHL**	14	5	2	7	41	15	1	0	1	31
1984-85	Montreal	NHL	70	17	22	39	120	12	4	1	5	32
1985-86	Montreal	NHL	70	19	21	40	69	20	3	4	7	45
	NHL Totals		154	41	45	86	230	47	8	5	13	110

McRAE, BASIL PAUL

Born, Beaverton, Ont., January 5, 1961.
Left wing. Shoots left. 6'2", 205 lbs.
Last amateur club: London Knights (OHA).
(Quebec's 3rd choice, 87th over-all, in 1980 Entry Draft).

Season	Club	Lea	Regular Season					Playoffs				
			GP	G	A	TP	PIM	GP	G	A	TP	PIM
1979-80	London	OHA	67	24	36	60	116	5	0	0	0	18
1980-81	London	OHA	65	29	23	52	266	....	....	....	....	....
1981-82	Fredericton	AHL	47	11	15	26	175	....	....	....	....	....
	Quebec	**NHL**	20	4	3	7	69	9	1	0	1	34
1982-83	Quebec	NHL	22	1	1	2	59	....	....	....	....	....
	Fredericton	AHL	53	22	19	41	146	12	1	5	6	75
1983-84	**Toronto**	**NHL**	3	0	0	0	19	....	....	....	....	....
	St. Catharines	AHL	78	14	25	39	187	6	0	0	0	40
1984-85	Toronto	NHL	1	0	0	0	0	....	....	....	....	....
	St. Catharines	AHL	72	30	25	55	186	....	....	....	....	....
1985-86	**Detroit**	**NHL**	4	0	0	0	5	....	....	....	....	....
	Adirondack	AHL	69	22	30	52	259	17	5	4	9	101
	NHL Totals		50	5	4	9	154	9	1	0	1	34

Traded to **Toronto** by **Quebec** for Richard Turmel, August 12, 1983.
Signed as a free agent by **Detroit**, July 17, 1985.

McRAE, CHRIS

Born, Newmarket, Ont., August 26, 1965.
Left wing. Shoots left. 6'0", 180 lbs.
Last amateur club: Oshawa Generals (OHL).

Season	Club	Lea	Regular Season					Playoffs				
			GP	G	A	TP	PIM	GP	G	A	TP	PIM
1983-84	Sudbury	OHL	62	14	31	45	139	....	....	....	....	....
1984-85	Oshawa	OHL	49	8	9	17	128	5	0	1	1	2
	St. Catharines	AHL	6	4	3	7	24	....	....	....	....	....
1985-86	St. Catharines	AHL	59	1	1	2	233	11	0	1	1	65

Signed as a free agent by **Toronto**, October 16, 1985.

McRAE, KEN

Born, Winchester, Ont., April 23, 1968.
Center. Shoots right. 6'1", 195 lbs.
Last amateur club: Sudbury Wolves (OHL).
(Quebec's 1st choice, 18th overall, in 1986 Entry Draft).

Season	Club	Lea	Regular Season					Playoffs				
			GP	G	A	TP	PIM	GP	G	A	TP	PIM
1985-86	Sudbury	OHL	66	25	49	74	127	4	2	1	3	12

McREYNOLDS, BRIAN

Born, Penetanguishene, Ont., January 5, 1965.
Center. Shoots left. 6'1", 180 lbs.
Last amateur club: Michigan State University Spartans (CCHA).
(NY Rangers' 6th choice, 112th overall, in 1985 Entry Draft).

Season	Club	Lea	Regular Season					Playoffs				
			GP	G	A	TP	PIM	GP	G	A	TP	PIM
1985-86	Michigan St.	CCHA	45	14	24	38	78	....	....	....	....	....

McSORLEY, CHRISTOPHER

Born, Hamilton, Ont., March 22, 1962.
Center. Shoots right. 5'11", 185 lbs.
Last amateur club: Mohawk College.

Season	Club	Lea	Regular Season					Playoffs				
			GP	G	A	TP	PIM	GP	G	A	TP	PIM
1984-85	Toledo	IHL	51	15	14	29	285	....	....	....	....	....
1985-86	Toledo	IHL	75	27	28	55	546	....	....	....	....	....

Signed as free agent by **Los Angeles**, May 9, 1986.

McSORLEY, MARTIN J. (MARTY)

Born, Hamilton, Ont., May 18, 1963.
Defense. Shoots right. 6'1", 190 lbs.
Last amateur club: Belleville Bulls (OHL).

Season	Club	Lea	Regular Season					Playoffs				
			GP	G	A	TP	PIM	GP	G	A	TP	PIM
1981-82	Belleville	OHL	58	6	13	19	234	....	....	....	....	....
1982-83	Belleville	OHL	70	10	41	51	183	4	0	0	0	7
	Baltimore	AHL	2	0	0	0	22	....	....	....	....	....
1983-84	**Pittsburgh**	**NHL**	72	2	7	9	224	....	....	....	....	....
1984-85	**Pittsburgh**	**NHL**	15	0	0	0	15	....	....	....	....	....
	Baltimore	AHL	58	6	24	30	154	14	0	7	7	47
1985-86	**Edmonton**	**NHL**	59	11	12	23	265	8	0	2	2	50
	Nova Scotia	AHL	9	2	4	6	34	....	....	....	....	....
	NHL Totals		146	13	19	32	504	8	0	2	2	50

Signed as free agent by **Pittsburgh**, July 30, 1982. Traded to **Edmonton** by **Pittsburgh** with Tim Hrynewich for Gilles Meloche, September, 12, 1985.

McSWEEN, DON

Born, Detroit, Michigan, June 9, 1964.
Defense; Shoots left. 5'10", 190 lbs.
Last amateur club: Michigan State University Spartans (CCHA).
(Buffalo's 10th choice, 154th overall, in 1983 Entry Draft).

Season	Club	Lea	Regular Season					Playoffs				
			GP	G	A	TP	PIM	GP	G	A	TP	PIM
1983-84	Michigan St.	CCHA	46	10	26	36	30	....	....	....	....	....
1984-85	Michigan St.	CCHA	44	2	23	25	52	....	....	....	....	....
1985-86a	Michigan St.	CCHA	45	9	29	38	18	....	....	....	....	....

a CCHA First All-Star Team (1986).

MEAGHER, RICHARD (RICK)   (ma-HAR)

Born, Belleville, Ont., November 4, 1953.
Center. Shoots left. 5'8", 175 lbs.
Last amateur club: Boston University Terriers (ECAC).

Season	Club	Lea	Regular Season					Playoffs				
			GP	G	A	TP	PIM	GP	G	A	TP	PIM
1975-76	Boston U.	ECAC	28	12	25	37	22	....	....	....	....	....
1976-77	Boston U.	ECAC	34	34	46	80	42	....	....	....	....	....
1977-78	Nova Scotia	AHL	57	20	27	47	33	11	5	3	8	11
1978-79	Nova Scotia	AHL	79	35	46	81	57	10	1	6	7	11
1979-80	**Montreal**	**NHL**	2	0	0	0	0	....	....	....	....	....
	Nova Scotia	AHL	64	32	44	76	53	6	3	4	7	2
1980-81	**Hartford**	**NHL**	27	7	10	17	19	....	....	....	....	....
	Binghamton	AHL	50	23	35	58	54	....	....	....	....	....
1981-82	Hartford	NHL	65	24	19	43	51	....	....	....	....	....
1982-83	**Hartford**	**NHL**	4	0	0	0	0	....	....	....	....	....
	New Jersey	**NHL**	57	15	14	29	11	....	....	....	....	....
1983-84	Maine	AHL	10	6	4	10	2	....	....	....	....	....
	New Jersey	NHL	52	14	14	28	16	....	....	....	....	....
1984-85	New Jersey	NHL	71	11	20	31	22	....	....	....	....	....
1985-86	**St. Louis**	**NHL**	79	11	19	30	28	19	4	4	8	12
	NHL Totals		357	82	96	178	147	19	4	4	8	12

Signed as a free agent by **Montreal**, June 27, 1977. Traded to **Hartford** by **Montreal** with Montreal's third round (Paul MacDermid) and fifth round (Dan Bourbonnais) choices in 1981 Entry Draft for Hartford's third round (Dieter Hegen) and fifth round (Steve Rooney) choices in 1981 Entry Draft, June 5, 1980. Traded to **New Jersey** by **Hartford** with the rights to Garry Howatt for Merlin Malinowski and the rights to Scott Fusco, October 15, 1982. Traded to **St. Louis** by **New Jersey** for Perry Anderson, August 29, 1985.

MEASURES, ALLAN

Born, Barrhead, Alta., May 8, 1965.
Defense. Shoots left. 5'11", 165 lbs.
Last amateur club: Calgary Wranglers (WHL).
(Vancouver's 9th choice, 170th over-all, in 1983 Entry Draft).

Season	Club	Lea	Regular Season					Playoffs				
			GP	G	A	TP	PIM	GP	G	A	TP	PIM
1982-83	Calgary	WHL	63	5	23	28	43	16	0	5	5	12
1983-84	Calgary	WHL	69	17	36	53	96	4	3	4	7	0
1984-85	Calgary	WHL	65	25	58	83	84	8	2	4	6	11
1985-86	Calgary	WHL	46	23	34	57	50	....	....	....	....	....

MELAMETSA, ANSSI

Born, Jyvaskyla, Finland, June 21, 1961.
Left wing. Shoots left. 6'0", 190 lbs.
Last amateur club: IFK Helsinki (Finland).
(Winnipeg's 12th choice, 249th overall, in 1985 Entry Draft).

Season	Club	Lea	Regular Season					Playoffs				
			GP	G	A	TP	PIM	GP	G	A	TP	PIM
1983-84	IFK	Fin.	36	13	20	33	59	....	....	....	....	....
1984-85	IFK	Fin.	36	16	15	31	18	....	....	....	....	....
1985-86	Sherbrooke	AHL	14	7	5	12	16	....	....	....	....	....
	Winnipeg	**NHL**	27	0	3	3	2	....	....	....	....	....
	NHL Totals		27	0	3	3	2	....	....	....	....	....

MELLANBY, SCOTT

Born, Montreal, Que., June 11, 1966.
Right wing. Shoots right. 6'1", 195 lbs.
Last amateur club: University of Wisconsin Badgers (WCHA).
(Philadelphia's 2nd choice, 27th over-all, in 1984 Entry Draft).

			Regular Season					Playoffs				
Season	Club	Lea	GP	G	A	TP	PIM	GP	G	A	TP	PIM
1983-84	Henry Carr	Ont.	39	37	37	74	97	....	....	....	....	....
1984-85	U. of Wisconsin	WCHA	40	14	24	38	60	....	....	....	....	....
1985-86	U. of Wisconsin	WCHA	32	21	23	44	89	....	....	....	....	....
	Philadelphia	NHL	2	0	0	0	0	....	....	....	....	....
	NHL Totals		2	0	0	0	0	....	....	....	....	....

MELNYK, LARRY JOSEPH (MEL-nick)

Born, New Westminster, B.C., February 21, 1960.
Defense. Shoots left. 6', 180 lbs.
Last amateur club: New Westminster Bruins (WHL).
(Boston's 5th choice, 78th over-all, in 1979 Entry Draft).

			Regular Season					Playoffs				
Season	Club	Lea	GP	G	A	TP	PIM	GP	G	A	TP	PIM
1978-79	N. Westminster	WHL	71	7	33	40	142	8	1	4	5	14
1979-80	N. Westminster	WHL	67	13	38	51	236	....	....	....	....	....
1980-81	Boston	NHL	26	0	4	4	39	....	....	....	....	....
	Springfield	AHL	47	1	10	11	109	1	0	0	0	0
1981-82	Erie	AHL	10	0	3	3	36	....	....	....	....	....
	Boston	NHL	48	0	8	8	84	11	0	3	3	40
1982-83	Baltimore	AHL	72	2	24	26	215	....	....	....	....	....
	Boston	NHL	1	0	0	0	0	11	0	0	0	9
1983-84	Hershey	AHL	50	0	18	18	156	....	....	....	....	....
	Moncton	AHL	14	0	3	3	17	....	....	....	....	....
	Edmonton	NHL	....	....	....	....	....	6	0	1	1	0
1984-85	Edmonton	NHL	28	0	0	11	25	12	1	3	4	26
	Nova Scotia	AHL	37	2	10	12	97	....	....	....	....	....
1985-86	Edmonton	NHL	6	2	3	5	11	....	....	....	....	....
	Nova Scotia	AHL	19	2	8	10	72	....	....	....	....	....
	NY Rangers	NHL	46	1	8	9	65	16	1	2	3	46
	NHL Totals		155	3	34	37	224	56	2	9	11	121

Traded to **Edmonton** by **Boston** for John Blum, March 6, 1984. Traded to **NY Rangers** by **Edmonton** with Todd Strueby for Mike Rogers, December 20, 1985.

MELROSE, BARRY

Born, Kelvington, Sask., July 15, 1956.
Defense. Shoots right. 6', 205 lbs.
Last amateur club: Kamloops Chiefs (WHL).
(Montreal's 4th choice, 36th over-all, in 1976 Amateur Draft).

			Regular Season					Playoffs				
Season	Club	Lea	GP	G	A	TP	PIM	GP	G	A	TP	PIM
1974-75	Kamloops	WHL	70	6	18	24	95	6	1	1	2	21
1975-76	Kamloops	WHL	72	12	49	61	112	12	4	6	10	14
1976-77	Springfield	AHL	23	0	3	3	17	....	....	....	....	....
	Cincinnati	WHA	29	1	4	5	8	2	0	0	0	0
1977-78	Cincinnati	WHA	69	2	9	11	113	....	....	....	....	....
1978-79	Cincinnati	WHA	80	2	14	16	222	3	0	1	1	8
1979-80	Winnipeg	NHL	74	4	6	10	124	....	....	....	....	....
1980-81	Winnipeg	NHL	18	1	1	2	40	....	....	....	....	....
	Toronto	NHL	57	2	5	7	166	3	0	1	1	15
1981-82	Toronto	NHL	64	1	5	6	186	....	....	....	....	....
1982-83	St. Catharines	AHL	25	1	10	11	106	....	....	....	....	....
	Toronto	NHL	52	2	5	7	68	4	0	1	1	23
1983-84	Adirondack	AHL	16	2	1	3	37	....	....	....	....	....
	Detroit	NHL	21	0	1	1	74	....	....	....	....	....
1984-85	Adirondack	AHL	72	3	13	16	226	....	....	....	....	....
1985-86	Detroit	NHL	14	0	0	0	70	....	....	....	....	....
	Adirondack	AHL	57	4	4	8	204	....	....	....	....	....
	NHL Totals		300	10	23	33	728	7	0	2	2	38
	WHA Totals		178	5	27	32	343	5	0	1	1	8

Transferred from **Montreal** Reserve List to **Winnipeg** Reserve List, June 22, 1979. Claimed on waivers by **Toronto** from **Winnipeg**, November 30, 1980. Signed as a free agent by **Detroit**, July 5, 1983.

MELROSE, KEVAN

Born, Calgary, Alta., March 28, 1966.
Defense. Shoots left. 5'10", 180 lbs.
Last amateur club: Penticton Knights (BCJHL).
(Calgary's 7th choice, 138th overall in 1984 Entry Draft).

			Regular Season					Playoffs				
Season	Club	Lea	GP	G	A	TP	PIM	GP	G	A	TP	PIM
1983-84	Red Deer	AJHL	42	9	26	35	89	....	....	....	....	....
1984-85	Penticton	BCJHL	24	15	10	25	42	....	....	....	....	....
1985-86	Penticton	BCJHL	22	18	15	33	56	29	22	25	47	72

MERCIER, DON

Born, Grimshaw, Alta., January 21, 1963.
Defense. Shoots left. 6'4", 210 lbs.
Last amateur club: University of Denver Pioneers (WCHA).

			Regular Season					Playoffs				
Season	Club	Lea	GP	G	A	TP	PIM	GP	G	A	TP	PIM
1982-83	St. Albert	AJHL	28	5	14	19	44	....	....	....	....	....
1983-84	Denver	WCHA	35	2	10	12	44	....	....	....	....	....
1984-85	Denver	WCHA	33	4	12	16	62	....	....	....	....	....
1985-86	Denver	WCHA	48	3	10	13	60	....	....	....	....	....

Signed as a free agent by **Calgary**, July 17, 1986.

MERKOSKY, GLENN (mer-KAUS-kee)

Born, Edmonton, Alta., April 8, 1960.
Center. Shoots left. 5'10", 175 lbs.
Last amateur club: Calgary Wranglers (WHL).

			Regular Season					Playoffs				
Season	Club	Lea	GP	G	A	TP	PIM	GP	G	A	TP	PIM
1979-80	Calgary	WHL	72	49	40	89	95	7	4	6	10	14
1980-81	Binghamton	AHL	80	26	35	61	61	5	0	2	2	2
1981-82	Hartford	NHL	7	0	0	0	2	....	....	....	....	....
	Binghamton	AHL	72	29	40	69	83	10	0	2	2	2
1982-83	New Jersey	NHL	34	4	10	14	20	....	....	....	....	....
	Wichita	CHL	45	26	23	49	15	....	....	....	....	....
1983-84	New Jersey	NHL	5	1	0	1	0	....	....	....	....	....
	Maine	AHL	75	28	28	56	56	17	11	10	21	20
1984-85a	Maine	AHL	80	38	38	76	19	11	2	3	5	13
1985-86	Detroit	NHL	17	0	2	2	0	....	....	....	....	....
	Adirondack	AHL	59	24	33	57	22	17	5	7	12	15
	NHL Totals		63	5	12	17	22	....	....	....	....	....

a AHL Second All-Star Team (1985)
Signed as free agent by **Hartford**, August 10, 1980. Signed as a free agent by **New Jersey**, September 14, 1982. Signed as a free agent by **Detroit**, July 15, 1985.

MESSIER, MARK DOUGLAS (MESS-yay)

Born, Edmonton, Alta., January 18, 1961.
Left wing. Shoots left. 6', 205 lbs.
Last amateur club: St. Albert Saints (Tier II Jrs.).
(Edmonton's 2nd choice, 48th over-all, in 1979 Entry Draft).

			Regular Season					Playoffs				
Season	Club	Lea	GP	G	A	TP	PIM	GP	G	A	TP	PIM
1978-79	Indianapolis	WHA	5	0	0	0	0	....	....	....	....	....
	Cincinnati	WHA	47	1	10	11	58	....	....	....	....	....
1979-80	Houston	CHL	4	0	3	3	4	....	....	....	....	....
	Edmonton	NHL	75	12	21	33	120	3	1	2	3	2
1980-81	Edmonton	NHL	72	23	40	63	102	9	2	5	7	13
1981-82a	Edmonton	NHL	78	50	38	88	119	5	1	2	3	8
1982-83a	Edmonton	NHL	77	48	58	106	72	15	15	6	21	14
1983-84bc	Edmonton	NHL	73	37	64	101	165	19	8	18	26	19
1984-85	Edmonton	NHL	55	23	31	54	57	18	12	13	25	12
1985-86	Edmonton	NHL	63	35	49	84	68	10	4	6	10	18
	NHL Totals		493	228	301	529	703	79	43	52	95	86
	WHA Totals		52	1	10	11	58	....	....	....	....	....

a NHL First All-Star Team (1982, 1983)
b NHL Second All-Star Team (1984)
c Won Conn Smythe Trophy (1984)

MESSIER, MITCH

Born, Regina, Sask., August 21, 1965.
Right wing. Shoots right. 6'2", 185 lbs.
Last amateur club: Michigan State University Spartans (CCHA).
(Minnesota's 4th choice, 56th overall, in 1983 Entry Draft).

			Regular Season					Playoffs				
Season	Club	Lea	GP	G	A	TP	PIM	GP	G	A	TP	PIM
1983-84	Michigan St.	CCHA	37	6	15	21	22	....	....	....	....	....
1984-85	Michigan St.	CCHA	42	12	21	33	46	....	....	....	....	....
1985-86	Michigan St.	CCHA	38	24	40	64	36	....	....	....	....	....

METCALFE, SCOTT

Born, Toronto, Ont., January 6, 1967.
Left wing. Shoots left. 6', 195 lbs.
Last amateur club: Kingston Canadians (OHL).
(Edmonton's 1st choice, 20th over-all, in 1985 Entry Draft).

			Regular Season					Playoffs				
Season	Club	Lea	GP	G	A	TP	PIM	GP	G	A	TP	PIM
1983-84	Kingston	OHL	68	25	49	74	154	....	....	....	....	....
1984-85	Kingston	OHL	58	27	33	60	100	....	....	....	....	....
1985-86	Kingston	OHL	66	36	43	79	213	10	3	6	9	21

MEULENBROEKS, JOHN

Born, Kingston, Ont., April 3, 1964.
Defense. Shoots left. 6', 180 lbs.
Last amateur club: Brantford Alexanders (OHL).
(Boston's 7th choice, 144th over-all, in 1982 Entry Draft).

			Regular Season					Playoffs				
Season	Club	Lea	GP	G	A	TP	PIM	GP	G	A	TP	PIM
1981-82	Brantford	OHL	58	4	4	8	45	11	1	3	4	6
1982-83	Brantford	OHL	69	1	18	19	55	8	0	0	0	4
1983-84	Brantford	OHL	68	7	25	32	39	6	0	1	1	12
1984-85	Hershey	AHL	74	1	17	18	19	....	....	....	....	....
1985-86	Moncton	AHL	51	1	4	5	51	8	0	0	0	11

MEYER, JAYSON

Born, Regina, Sask., February 21, 1965.
Defense. Shoots left. 5'10", 185 lbs.
Last amateur club: New Westminster Bruins (WHL).
(Buffalo's 7th choice, 94th over-all, in 1983 Entry Draft).

			Regular Season					Playoffs				
Season	Club	Lea	GP	G	A	TP	PIM	GP	G	A	TP	PIM
1981-82	Regina	WHL	59	3	20	23	106	20	2	9	11	20
1982-83	Regina	WHL	72	10	45	55	89	5	0	6	6	4
1983-84	Regina	WHL	70	16	67	83	39	6	1	3	4	10
1984-85	N. Westminster	WHL	63	20	51	71	67	11	3	9	12	11
1985-86	Rochester	AHL	76	7	28	35	74	....	....	....	....	....

MICHAYLUK, DAVID (DAVE)   (mi-KIE-luck)

Born, Wakaw, Sask., May 18, 1962.
Right wing. Shoots left. 5'10", 180 lbs.
Last amateur club: Regina Pats (WHL).
(Philadelphia's 5th choice, 65th over-all, in 1981 Entry Draft).

				Regular Season					Playoffs			
Season	Club	Lea	GP	G	A	TP	PIM	GP	G	A	TP	PIM
1980-81	Regina	WHL	72	62	71	133	39	11	5	12	17	8
1981-82	**Philadelphia**	**NHL**	1	0	0	0	0	....	....	....	....	....
a	Regina	WHL	72	62	111	172	128	12	16	24	*40	23
1982-83	**Philadelphia**	**NHL**	13	2	6	8	8					
	Maine	AHL	69	32	40	72	16	8	0	2	2	0
1983-84	Springfield	AHL	79	18	44	62	37	4	0	0	0	2
1984-85	Hershey	AHL	3	0	2	2	2	....	....	....	....	....
b	Kalamazoo	IHL	82	66	33	99	49	11	7	7	14	0
1985-86	Nova Scotia	AHL	3	0	1	1	0	....	....	....	....	....
	Muskegon	IHL	77	52	52	104	73	14	6	9	15	12
	NHL Totals		**14**	**2**	**6**	**8**	**8**	....	....	....	....	....

a WHL Second All-Star Team (1982)
b IHL Second All-Star Team (1985)

MICHELETTI, PATRICK

Born, Hibbing, Minn., December 11, 1963.
Center. Shoots left. 5'10", 175 lbs.
Last amateur club: University of Minnesota Gophers (WCHA)
(Minnesota's 9th choice, 185th over-all, in 1982 Entry Draft).

				Regular Season					Playoffs			
Season	Club	Lea	GP	G	A	TP	PIM	GP	G	A	TP	PIM
1981-82	Hibbing	HS	22	26	39	6	50	....	....	....	....	....
1982-83	U. Minnesota	WCHA	20	11	11	22	52	....	....	....	....	....
1983-84	U. Minnesota	WCHA	39	26	34	60	62	....	....	....	....	....
1984-85ab	U. Minnesota	WCHA	32	40	34	74	120	....	....	....	....	....
1985-86c	U. Minnesota	WCHA	48	32	48	80	113	....	....	....	....	....
	Springfield	AHL	2	1	0	1	0	....	....	....	....	....

a WCHA First Team All-Star (1985)
b named to NCAA All-American Team (1985)
c WCHA Second All-Star Team (1986).

MIDDENDORF, MAX

Born, Syracuse, NY, August 18, 1967.
Right wing. Shoots right. 6'4", 195 lbs.
Last amateur club: Sudbury Wolves (OHL).
(Quebec's 3rd choice, 57th overall, in 1985 Entry Draft).

				Regular Season					Playoffs			
Season	Club	Lea	GP	G	A	TP	PIM	GP	G	A	TP	PIM
1984-85	Sudbury	OHL	63	16	28	44	106	....	....	....	....	....
1985-86	Sudbury	OHL	61	40	42	82	71	4	4	2	6	11

MIDDLETON, RICHARD DAVID (RICK)

Born, Toronto, Ont., December 4, 1953.
Right wing. Shoots right. 5'11", 170 lbs.
Last amateur club: Oshawa Generals (OHA).
(NY Rangers' 1st choice, 14th over-all, in 1973 Amateur Draft).

				Regular Season					Playoffs			
Season	Club	Lea	GP	G	A	TP	PIM	GP	G	A	TP	PIM
1971-72	Oshawa	OHA	53	36	34	70	24	....	....	....	....	....
1972-73	Oshawa	OHA	62	67	70	137	14	....	....	....	....	....
1973-74a	Providence	AHL	63	36	48	84	14	15	9	6	15	2
1974-75	**NY Rangers**	**NHL**	47	22	18	40	19	3	0	0	0	2
1975-76	**NY Rangers**	**NHL**	77	24	26	50	14	....	....	....	....	....
1976-77	**Boston**	**NHL**	72	20	22	42	2	13	5	4	9	0
1977-78	**Boston**	**NHL**	79	25	35	60	8	15	5	2	7	0
1978-79	**Boston**	**NHL**	71	38	48	86	7	11	4	8	12	0
1979-80	**Boston**	**NHL**	80	40	52	92	24	10	4	2	6	5
1980-81	**Boston**	**NHL**	80	44	59	103	16	3	0	1	1	2
1981-82bc	**Boston**	**NHL**	75	51	43	94	12	11	6	9	15	0
1982-83	**Boston**	**NHL**	80	49	47	96	8	17	11	22	33	6
1983-84	**Boston**	**NHL**	80	47	58	105	14	3	0	0	0	0
1984-85	**Boston**	**NHL**	80	30	46	76	6	5	3	0	3	0
1985-86	**Boston**	**NHL**	49	14	30	44	10	....	....	....	....	....
	NHL Totals		**870**	**404**	**484**	**888**	**140**	**91**	**38**	**48**	**86**	**15**

a Won Dudley "Red" Garrett Memorial Trophy (AHL Rookie of the Year) (1974)
b Won Lady Byng Memorial Trophy (1982)
c NHL Second All-Star Team (1982)
Traded to **Boston** by **NY Rangers** for Ken Hodge, May 26, 1976.

MIELE, DAN

Born, LaSalle, Que., April 12, 1962.
Right wing. Shoots right. 6'2", 190 lbs.
Last amateur club: Providence College Friars (ECAC).
(Washington's 2nd choice, 47th over-all, in 1980 Entry Draft).

				Regular Season					Playoffs			
Season	Club	Lea	GP	G	A	TP	PIM	GP	G	A	TP	PIM
1979-80	Providence	ECAC	30	11	13	24	30	....	....	....	....	....
1980-81	Providence	ECAC	28	16	13	29	20	....	....	....	....	....
1981-82	Hershey	AHL	67	7	11	18	25	....	....	....	....	....
1982-83	Hershey	AHL	74	11	11	22	62	5	0	1	1	0
1983-84	Hershey	AHL	65	23	17	40	18	....	....	....	....	....
1984-85	Fort Wayne	IHL	34	7	14	21	21	13	3	8	11	12
1985-86	Indianapolis	IHL	55	5	11	16	68	....	....	....	....	....

MILBURY, MICHAEL JAMES (MIKE)

Born, Brighton, Mass., June 17, 1952.
Defense. Shoots left. 6'1", 200 lbs.
Last amateur club: Colgate University Red Raiders (ECAC).

				Regular Season					Playoffs			
Season	Club	Lea	GP	G	A	TP	PIM	GP	G	A	TP	PIM
1972-73	Colgate	ECAC	27	4	25	29	81	....	....	....	....	....
1973-74	Colgate	ECAC	23	2	19	21	68	....	....	....	....	....
	Boston	AHL	5	0	0	0	7	....	....	....	....	....
1974-75	Rochester	AHL	71	2	15	17	246	8	0	3	3	24
1975-76	Rochester	AHL	73	3	15	18	199	3	0	1	1	13
	Boston	**NHL**	3	0	0	0	9	11	0	0	0	29
1976-77	**Boston**	**NHL**	77	6	18	24	166	13	2	2	4	*47
1977-78	**Boston**	**NHL**	80	8	30	38	151	15	1	8	9	27
1978-79	**Boston**	**NHL**	74	1	34	35	149	11	1	7	8	7
1979-80	**Boston**	**NHL**	72	10	13	23	59	10	0	2	2	50
1980-81	**Boston**	**NHL**	77	0	18	18	222	2	0	1	1	10
1981-82	**Boston**	**NHL**	51	2	10	12	71	11	0	4	4	6
1982-83	**Boston**	**NHL**	78	9	15	24	216	....	....	....	....	....
1983-84	**Boston**	**NHL**	74	2	17	19	159	3	0	0	0	12
1984-85	**Boston**	**NHL**	78	3	13	16	152	5	0	0	0	10
1985-86	**Boston**	**NHL**	22	2	5	7	102	1	0	0	0	17
	NHL Totals		**686**	**43**	**173**	**216**	**1456**	**82**	**4**	**24**	**28**	**215**

Signed as a free agent by **Boston**, November 5, 1974.

MILLAR, MIKE

Born, St. Catharines, Ont., April 28, 1965.
Right wing. Shoots left. 5'10", 170 lbs.
Last amateur club: Canadian Olympic Team
(Hartford's 2nd choice, 110th over-all, in 1984 Entry Draft).

				Regular Season					Playoffs			
Season	Club	Lea	GP	G	A	TP	PIM	GP	G	A	TP	PIM
1982-83	Brantford	OHL	53	20	29	49	10	8	0	5	5	2
1983-84	Brantford	OHL	69	50	45	95	48	6	4	0	4	2
1984-85	Hamilton	OHL	63	66	60	126	54	17	9	10	19	14
1985-86	Cdn. Olympic	...	69	50	38	88	74	....	....	....	....	....

MILLEN, CORY

Born, Cloquet, Minn., April 29, 1964.
Center. Shoots right. 5'7", 165 lbs.
Last amateur club: University of Minnesota Golden Gophers (WCHA).
(NY Rangers' 3rd choice, 57th overall, in 1982 Entry Draft).

				Regular Season					Playoffs			
Season	Club	Lea	GP	G	A	TP	PIM	GP	G	A	TP	PIM
1982-83	U. Minnesota	WCHA	21	14	15	29	18	....	....	....	....	....
1983-84	U.S. Olympic	...	45	15	11	26	10	....	....	....	....	....
1984-85	U. Minnesota	WCHA	38	28	36	64	60	....	....	....	....	....
1985-86ab	U. Minnesota	WCHA	48	41	42	83	64	....	....	....	....	....

a NCAA West Second All-American Team (1986).
b WCHA Second All-Star Team (1986).

MILLER, JAY

Born, Wellesley, Mass., July 16, 1960.
Left wing. Shoots right. 6'2", 205 lbs.
Last amateur club: University of New Hampshire Wildcats (ECAC).
(Quebec's 2nd choice, 66th overall, in 1980 Entry Draft).

				Regular Season					Playoffs			
Season	Club	Lea	GP	G	A	TP	PIM	GP	G	A	TP	PIM
1981-82	N. Hampshire	ECAC	24	6	4	10	34	....	....	....	....	....
1982-83	N. Hampshire	ECAC	28	6	4	10	28	....	....	....	....	....
1983-84	Toledo	IHL	2	0	0	0	2	....	....	....	....	....
	Maine	AHL	15	1	1	2	27	....	....	....	....	....
1984-85	Muskegon	IHL	56	5	29	34	177	17	1	1	2	56
1985-86	Moncton	AHL	18	4	6	10	113	....	....	....	....	....
	Boston	**NHL**	46	3	0	3	178	2	0	0	0	17
	NHL Totals		**46**	**3**	**0**	**3**	**178**	**2**	**0**	**0**	**0**	**17**

Signed as a free agent by **Boston**, October 1, 1985.

MILLER, KELLY

Born, Detroit, Michigan, March 3, 1963.
Center. Shoots left. 5'10", 185 lbs.
Last amateur club: Michigan State University Spartans (CCHA).
(NY Rangers' 9th choice, 183rd overall, in 1982 Entry Draft).

				Regular Season					Playoffs			
Season	Club	Lea	GP	G	A	TP	PIM	GP	G	A	TP	PIM
1981-82	Mich. State U.	CCHA	38	11	18	29	17	....	....	....	....	....
1982-83	Mich. State U.	CCHA	36	16	19	35	12	....	....	....	....	....
1983-84	Mich. State U.	CCHA	46	28	21	49	12	....	....	....	....	....
1984-85	**NY Rangers**	**NHL**	5	0	2	2	2	3	0	0	0	2
ab	Mich. State U.	CCHA	43	27	23	50	21	....	....	....	....	....
1985-86	**NY Rangers**	**NHL**	74	13	20	33	52	16	3	4	7	4
	NHL Totals		**79**	**13**	**22**	**35**	**54**	**19**	**3**	**4**	**7**	**6**

a CCHA First All-Star Team (1985)
b Named to NCAA All-American Team (1985)

MILLER, KEVIN

Born, Lansing, Mich., August 9, 1965.
Center. Shoots right. 5'9", 170 lbs.
Last amateur club: Michigan State University Spartans (CCHA).
(NY Rangers' 10th choice, 202nd overall, in 1984 Entry Draft).

				Regular Season					Playoffs			
Season	Club	Lea	GP	G	A	TP	PIM	GP	G	A	TP	PIM
1984-85	Michigan St.	CCHA	44	11	29	40	84	....	....	....	....	....
1985-86	Michigan St.	CCHA	45	19	52	71	112	....	....	....	....	....

MILLS, CHRIS

Born, Scarborough, Ont., May 30, 1966.
Defense. Shoots left. 6'1", 185 lbs.
Last amateur club: Clarkson University Knights (ECAC).
(Winnipeg's 2nd choice, 68th overall, in 1984 Entry Draft).

			Regular Season					Playoffs				
Season	Club	Lea	GP	G	A	TP	PIM	GP	G	A	TP	PIM
1984-85	Clarkson	ECAC	29	0	1	1	22	....	....	....	....	....
1985-86	Clarkson	ECAC	28	2	3	5	6	....	....	....	....	....

MINER, JOHN

Born, Moose Jaw, Sask., August 28, 1965.
Defense. Shoots right. 5'10", 180 lbs.
Last amateur club: Regina Pats (WHL).
(Edmonton's 10th choice, 229th over-all, in 1983 Entry Draft).

			Regular Season					Playoffs				
Season	Club	Lea	GP	G	A	TP	PIM	GP	G	A	TP	PIM
1982-83	Regina	WHL	71	11	23	34	126	5	1	1	2	20
1983-84	Regina	WHL	70	27	42	69	132	23	9	25	34	54
1984-85	Regina	WHL	66	30	54	84	128	8	4	10	14	12
1985-86	Nova Scotia	AHL	79	10	33	43	90	....	....	....	....	....

MINOR, GERALD (GERRY) (MY-nor)

Born, Regina, Sask., October 27, 1958.
Center. Shoots left. 5'8", 175 lbs.
Last amateur club: Regina Pats (WHL).
(Vancouver's 6th choice, 90th over-all, in 1978 Amateur Draft).

			Regular Season					Playoffs				
Season	Club	Lea	GP	G	A	TP	PIM	GP	G	A	TP	PIM
1976-77	Regina	WHL	48	22	32	59	120	....	....	....	....	....
1977-78	Regina	WHL	66	54	75	129	238	13	5	22	*37	31
1978-79	Fort Wayne	IHL	42	18	28	46	67	....	....	....	....	....
	Dallas	CHL	37	14	25	39	76	9	3	4	7	31
1979-80	**Vancouver**	**NHL**	**5**	**0**	**1**	**1**	**2**	....	....	....	....	....
	Dallas	CHL	73	31	52	83	162	....	....	....	....	....
1980-81	**Vancouver**	**NHL**	**74**	**10**	**14**	**24**	**108**	**3**	**0**	**0**	**0**	**8**
1981-82	Dallas	CHL	12	5	8	13	92	....	....	....	....	....
	Vancouver	**NHL**	**13**	**0**	**1**	**1**	**6**	**9**	**1**	**3**	**4**	**17**
1982-83	**Vancouver**	**NHL**	**39**	**1**	**5**	**6**	**57**	....	....	....	....	....
	Fredericton	AHL	17	4	17	21	14	....	....	....	....	....
1983-84	**Vancouver**	**NHL**	**9**	**0**	**0**	**0**	**0**	....	....	....	....	....
	Fredericton	AHL	66	16	42	58	85	7	1	4	5	20
1984-85	Nova Scotia	AHL	21	4	10	14	8	....	....	....	....	....
	New Haven	AHL	52	11	29	40	65	....	....	....	....	....
1985-86	Indianapolis	IHL	72	28	46	74	108	5	3	4	7	8
	NHL Totals		**140**	**11**	**21**	**32**	**173**	**12**	**1**	**3**	**4**	**25**

MOKOSAK, CARL (moh-KA-sack)

Born, Fort Saskatchewan, Alta., September 22, 1962.
Left wing. Shoots left. 6'1", 180 lbs.
Last amateur club: Brandon Wheat Kings (WHL).

			Regular Season					Playoffs				
Season	Club	Lea	GP	G	A	TP	PIM	GP	G	A	TP	PIM
1979-80	Brandon	WHL	61	12	21	33	226	11	0	4	4	66
1980-81	Brandon	WHL	70	28	44	72	363	5	1	3	4	12
1981-82	**Calgary**	**NHL**	**1**	**0**	**1**	**1**	**0**	....	....	....	....	....
	Brandon	WHL	69	46	61	107	363	4	0	1	1	11
	Oklahoma City	CHL	2	1	1	2	2	4	1	1	2	0
1982-83	**Calgary**	**NHL**	**41**	**7**	**6**	**13**	**87**	....	....	....	....	....
	Colorado	CHL	28	10	12	22	106	5	1	0	1	12
1983-84	New Haven	AHL	80	18	21	39	206	....	....	....	....	....
1984-85	**Los Angeles**	**NHL**	**30**	**4**	**8**	**12**	**43**	....	....	....	....	....
	New Haven	AHL	11	6	6	12	26	....	....	....	....	....
1985-86	**Philadelphia**	**NHL**	**1**	**0**	**0**	**0**	**5**	....	....	....	....	....
	Hershey	AHL	79	30	42	72	312	16	0	4	4	111
	NHL Totals		**73**	**11**	**15**	**26**	**135**	....	....	....	....	....

Signed as free agent by **Calgary**, July 21, 1981. Traded to **Los Angeles** by **Calgary** with Kevin LaVallee for Steve Bozek, June 20, 1983. Signed as a free agent by **Philadelphia**, July 23, 1985. Signed as a free agent by **Pittsburgh**, July 23, 1986.

MOKOSAK, JOHN (moh-KA-sack)

Born, Edmonton, Alta., September 7, 1963.
Defense. Shoots left. 5'11", 200 lbs.
Last amateur club: Victoria Cougars (WHL).
(Hartford's 6th choice, 130th over-all, in 1981 Entry Draft).

			Regular Season					Playoffs				
Season	Club	Lea	GP	G	A	TP	PIM	GP	G	A	TP	PIM
1980-81	Victoria	WHL	71	2	18	20	59	15	0	3	3	53
1981-82	Victoria	WHL	69	6	45	51	102	4	1	1	2	0
1982-83	Victoria	WHL	70	10	33	43	102	12	0	0	0	8
1983-84	Binghamton	AHL	79	3	21	24	80	....	....	....	....	....
1984-85	Binghamton	AHL	54	1	13	14	109	7	0	0	0	12
	Salt Lake	IHL	22	1	10	11	41	....	....	....	....	....
1985-86	Binghamton	AHL	64	0	9	9	196	6	0	0	0	6

Signed as a free agent by **Pittsburgh**, July 23, 1986.

MOLLER, MICHAEL JOHN (MIKE) (MOH-ler)

Born, Calgary, Alta., June 16, 1962.
Right wing. Shoots right. 6', 190 lbs.
Last amateur club: Lethbridge Broncos (WHL).
(Buffalo's 2nd choice, 41st over-all, in 1980 Entry Draft).

			Regular Season					Playoffs				
Season	Club	Lea	GP	G	A	TP	PIM	GP	G	A	TP	PIM
1979-80	Lethbridge	WHL	72	30	41	71	55	4	0	6	6	0
1980-81a	Lethbridge	WHL	70	39	69	108	71	9	6	10	16	12
	Buffalo	**NHL**	**5**	**2**	**2**	**4**	**0**	**3**	**0**	**1**	**1**	**0**
1981-82	**Buffalo**	**NHL**	**9**	**0**	**0**	**0**	**0**	....	....	....	....	....
a	Lethbridge	WHL	49	41	81	122	38	12	5	12	17	9
1982-83	**Buffalo**	**NHL**	**49**	**6**	**12**	**18**	**14**	....	....	....	....	....
	Rochester	AHL	10	1	6	7	2	11	2	4	6	4
1983-84	**Buffalo**	**NHL**	**59**	**5**	**11**	**16**	**27**	....	....	....	....	....
1984-85	**Buffalo**	**NHL**	**5**	**0**	**2**	**2**	**0**	....	....	....	....	....
	Rochester	AHL	73	19	46	65	27	5	1	1	2	0
1985-86	**Edmonton**	**NHL**	**1**	**0**	**0**	**0**	**0**	....	....	....	....	....
	Nova Scotia	AHL	62	16	15	31	24	....	....	....	....	....
	NHL Totals		**128**	**13**	**27**	**40**	**41**	**3**	**0**	**1**	**1**	**0**

a WHL First All-Star Team (1981, 1982)

Traded to **Pittsburgh** by **Buffalo** with Randy Cunneyworth for Pat Hughes, October 4, 1985.
Traded to **Edmonton** by **Pittsburgh** for Pat Hughes, October 4, 1985.

MOLLER, RANDY

Born, Red Deer, Alta., August 23, 1963.
Defense. Shoots right. 6'2", 205 lbs.
Last amateur club: Lethbridge Broncos (WHL).
(Quebec's 1st choice, 11th over-all, in 1981 Entry Draft).

			Regular Season					Playoffs				
Season	Club	Lea	GP	G	A	TP	PIM	GP	G	A	TP	PIM
1979-80	Lethbridge	WHL	46	4	21	25	176	9	0	4	4	24
1980-81	Lethbridge	WHL	60	20	55	75	249	12	4	6	10	65
1981-82	**Quebec**	**NHL**	....	....	....	....	....	**1**	**0**	**0**	**0**	**0**
a	Lethbridge	WHL	60	20	55	75	249	12	4	6	10	65
1982-83	**Quebec**	**NHL**	**75**	**2**	**12**	**14**	**145**	**4**	**1**	**0**	**1**	**4**
1983-84	**Quebec**	**NHL**	**74**	**4**	**14**	**18**	**147**	**9**	**1**	**0**	**1**	**45**
1984-85	**Quebec**	**NHL**	**79**	**7**	**22**	**29**	**120**	**18**	**2**	**2**	**4**	**40**
1985-86	**Quebec**	**NHL**	**69**	**5**	**18**	**23**	**141**	**3**	**0**	**0**	**0**	**26**
	NHL Totals		**297**	**18**	**66**	**84**	**553**	**35**	**4**	**2**	**6**	**115**

a WHL Second All-Star Team (1982)

MOMESSO, SERGIO

Born, Montreal, Que., September 4, 1965.
Center. Shoots left. 6'3", 200 lbs.
Last amateur club: Shawinigan Cataractes (QMJHL).
(Montreal's 3rd choice, 27th over-all, in 1983 Entry Draft).

			Regular Season					Playoffs				
Season	Club	Lea	GP	G	A	TP	PIM	GP	G	A	TP	PIM
1981-82	Montreal	Midget	45	30	38	68	63	....	....	....	....	....
1982-83	Shawinigan	QMJHL	70	27	42	69	93	10	5	4	9	55
1983-84	**Montreal**	**NHL**	**1**	**0**	**0**	**0**	**0**	....	....	....	....	....
	Shawinigan	QMJHL	68	42	88	130	235	6	4	4	8	13
	Nova Scotia	AHL	....	....	....	....	....	8	0	2	2	0
1984-85a	Shawinigan	QMJHL	64	56	90	146	216	8	7	8	15	17
1985-86	**Montreal**	**NHL**	**24**	**8**	**7**	**15**	**46**	....	....	....	....	....
	NHL Totals		**25**	**8**	**7**	**15**	**46**	....	....	....	....	....

a QMJHL First All-Star Team (1985)

MONGRAIN, ROBERT (MAWN-grain)

Born, La Sarre, Que., August 31, 1959.
Center. Shoots left. 5'10", 165 lbs.
Last amateur club: Trois-Rivières Draveurs (QMJL).

			Regular Season					Playoffs				
Season	Club	Lea	GP	G	A	TP	PIM	GP	G	A	TP	PIM
1977-78	Trois Rivières	QJHL	72	35	43	78	77	13	2	4	6	7
1978-79	Trois Rivières	QJHL	72	66	76	142	55	13	4	14	18	13
1979-80	Rochester	AHL	39	25	24	49	58	....	....	....	....	....
	Buffalo	**NHL**	**34**	**4**	**6**	**10**	**4**	**9**	**1**	**2**	**3**	**2**
1980-81	**Buffalo**	**NHL**	**4**	**0**	**0**	**0**	**2**	....	....	....	....	....
	Rochester	AHL	69	21	29	50	101	....	....	....	....	....
1981-82	Rochester	AHL	56	37	37	74	45	....	....	....	....	....
	Buffalo	**NHL**	**24**	**6**	**4**	**10**	**6**	**1**	**0**	**0**	**0**	**0**
1982-83	Rochester	AHL	80	29	52	81	72	16	3	5	8	24
1983-84	**Buffalo**	**NHL**	....	....	....	....	....	**1**	**0**	**0**	**0**	**0**
	Rochester	AHL	78	41	44	85	154	18	11	9	20	46
1984-85	**Buffalo**	**NHL**	**8**	**1**	**1**	**2**	**0**	....	....	....	....	....
1985-86	**Los Angeles**	**NHL**	**11**	**2**	**3**	**5**	**2**	....	....	....	....	....
	NHL Totals		**83**	**13**	**14**	**27**	**14**	**11**	**1**	**2**	**3**	**2**

Signed as a free agent by **Buffalo**, September 16, 1979. Signed as a free agent by **Los Angeles**, March 4, 1986.

MOORE, STEVE

Born, Toronto, Ont., January 21, 1967.
Defense. Shoots right. 6'2", 185 lbs.
Last amateur club: Rensselaer Polytechnical Institute Engineers (ECAC).
(Boston's 4th choice, 94th overall, in 1985 Entry Draft).

			Regular Season					Playoffs				
Season	Club	Lea	GP	G	A	TP	PIM	GP	G	A	TP	PIM
1984-85	London	OHL	46	12	26	38	112	....	....	....	....	....
1985-86	RPI	ECAC	24	4	3	7	32	....	....	....	....	....

MORIA, STEVE

Born, Vancouver, B.C., February 3, 1961.
Center. Shoots left. 6', 175 lbs.
Last amateur club: University of Alaska-Fairbanks Nanooks (NCAA).

			Regular Season					Playoffs				
Season	Club	Lea	GP	G	A	TP	PIM	GP	G	A	TP	PIM
1982-83	Alaska-Fair.	NCAA	26	29	46	75	....	....	....	....	....	....
1983-84	Alaska-Fair.	NCAA	26	36	51	87	....	....	....	....	....	....
1984-85	Alaska-Fair.	NCAA	34	43	66	109	6	....	....	....	....	....
1985-86	New Haven	AHL	74	19	37	56	29	5	0	1	1	4

Signed as a free agent by **NY Rangers**, August 7, 1985.

MORRIS, JON

Born, Lowell, Mass., May 6, 1966.
Center. Shoots right. 6'0", 165 lbs.
Last amateur club: University of Lowell Chiefs (H.E.).
(New Jersey's 5th choice, 86th overall, in 1984 Entry Draft).

			Regular Season					Playoffs				
Season	Club	Lea	GP	G	A	TP	PIM	GP	G	A	TP	PIM
1984-85	Lowell	H.E.	42	29	31	60	16	....	....	....	....	....
1985-86	Lowell	H.E.	39	25	31	56	52	....	....	....	....	....

MORRISON, DOUGLAS (DOUG)

Born, Vancouver, B.C., February 1, 1960.
Right wing. Shoots right. 5'11", 185 lbs.
Last amateur club: Lethbridge Broncos (WHL).
(Boston's 3rd choice, 36th over-all, in 1979 Entry Draft).

			Regular Season					Playoffs				
Season	Club	Lea	GP	G	A	TP	PIM	GP	G	A	TP	PIM
1978-79	Lethbridge	WHL	64	56	67	123	159	19	20	15	35	7
1979-80	**Boston**	**NHL**	1	0	0	0	0	....	....	....	....	....
	Lethbridge	WHL	68	58	59	117	188	4	5	3	8	15
1980-81	**Boston**	**NHL**	18	7	3	10	13	....	....	....	....	....
	Springfield	AHL	42	19	30	49	28	7	4	5	9	2
1981-82	**Boston**	**NHL**	3	0	0	0	0	....	....	....	....	....
	Erie	AHL	75	23	35	58	31	....	....	....	....	....
1982-83	Maine	AHL	61	38	29	67	44	14	5	1	6	4
1983-84	Hershey	AHL	72	38	40	78	42	....	....	....	....	....
1984-85	**Boston**	**NHL**	1	0	0	0	2	....	....	....	....	....
	Hershey	AHL	65	28	25	53	25	....	....	....	....	....
1985-86	Salt Lake	IHL	80	27	34	61	30	5	7	3	10	14
	NHL Totals		23	7	3	10	15	....	....	....	....	....

MORROW, KEN

Born, Flint, Mich., October 17, 1956.
Defense. Shoots right. 6'4", 210 lbs.
Last amateur club: 1980 United States Olympic Team.
(NY Islanders' 4th choice, 68th over-all, in 1976 Amateur Draft).

			Regular Season					Playoffs				
Season	Club	Lea	GP	G	A	TP	PIM	GP	G	A	TP	PIM
1978-79ab	Bowling Green	CCHA	45	15	37	52	22	....	....	....	....	....
1979-80	U.S. National	...	56	4	18	22	6	....	....	....	....	....
	U.S. Olympic	...	7	1	2	3	6	....	....	....	....	....
	NY Islanders	**NHL**	18	0	3	3	4	20	1	2	3	12
1980-81	**NY Islanders**	**NHL**	80	2	11	13	20	18	3	4	7	8
1981-82	**NY Islanders**	**NHL**	75	1	18	19	56	19	0	4	4	8
1982-83	**NY Islanders**	**NHL**	79	5	11	16	44	19	5	7	12	18
1983-84	**NY Islanders**	**NHL**	63	3	11	14	45	20	1	2	3	20
1984-85	**NY Islanders**	**NHL**	15	1	7	8	14	10	0	0	0	17
1985-86	**NY Islanders**	**NHL**	69	0	12	12	22	2	0	0	0	4
	NHL Totals		339	12	73	85	205	108	10	19	29	87

a CCHA First All-Star Team (1979)
b CCHA Player of the Year (1979)

MOYLAN, DAVE

Born, Tillsonburg, Ont., August 13, 1967.
Defense. Shoots left. 6'1", 195 lbs.
Last amateur club: Sudbury Wolves (OHL).
(Buffalo's 4th choice, 77th overall, in 1985 Entry Draft).

			Regular Season					Playoffs				
Season	Club	Lea	GP	G	A	TP	PIM	GP	G	A	TP	PIM
1984-85	Sudbury	OHL	66	1	15	16	108	....	....	....	....	....
1985-86	Sudbury	OHL	52	10	25	35	87	4	0	0	0	15

MULLEN, BRIAN

Born, New York, NY, March 16, 1962.
Left wing. Shoots left. 5'10", 180 lbs.
Last amateur club: University of Wisconsin Badgers (WCHA).
(Winnipeg's 7th choice, 128th over-all, in 1980 Entry Draft).

			Regular Season					Playoffs				
Season	Club	Lea	GP	G	A	TP	PIM	GP	G	A	TP	PIM
1980-81	U. of Wisconsin	WCHA	38	11	13	24	28	....	....	....	....	....
1981-82	U. of Wisconsin	WCHA	33	20	17	37	10	....	....	....	....	....
1982-83	**Winnipeg**	**NHL**	80	24	26	50	14	3	1	0	1	0
1983-84	**Winnipeg**	**NHL**	75	21	41	62	28	3	0	3	3	6
1984-85	**Winnipeg**	**NHL**	69	32	39	71	32	8	1	2	3	4
1985-86	**Winnipeg**	**NHL**	79	28	34	62	38	3	1	2	3	6
	NHL Totals		303	105	140	245	112	17	3	7	10	16

MULLEN, JOE

Born, New York, NY, February 26, 1957.
Right wing. Shoots right. 5'9", 180 lbs.
Last amateur club: Boston College Eagles (ECAC)

			Regular Season					Playoffs				
Season	Club	Lea	GP	G	A	TP	PIM	GP	G	A	TP	PIM
1977-78a	Boston College	ECAC	34	34	34	68	12	....	....	....	....	....
1978-79a	Boston College	ECAC	25	32	24	56	8	....	....	....	....	....
1979-80bc	Salt Lake	CHL	75	40	32	72	21	13	*9	11	20	0
	St. Louis	**NHL**	....	....	....	....	....	1	0	0	0	0
1980-81de	Salt Lake	CHL	80	59	58	*117	8	17	11	9	20	0
1981-82	Salt Lake	CHL	27	21	27	48	12	....	....	....	....	....
	St. Louis	**NHL**	45	25	34	59	4	10	7	11	18	4
1982-83	**St. Louis**	**NHL**	49	17	30	47	6	....	....	....	....	....
1983-84	**St. Louis**	**NHL**	80	41	44	85	19	6	2	0	2	0
1984-85	**St. Louis**	**NHL**	79	40	52	92	6	3	0	0	0	0
1985-86	**St. Louis**	**NHL**	48	28	24	52	10	....	....	....	....	....
	Calgary	NHL	29	16	22	38	11	21	12	7	19	4
	NHL Totals		330	167	206	373	56	41	21	18	39	8

a ECAC First All-Star Team (1978, 1979)
b CHL Second All-Star Team (1980)
c Won Ken McKenzie Trophy (CHL's Top Rookie) (1980)
d CHL First All-Star Team (1981)
e Won Tommy Ivan Trophy (CHL's Most Valuable Player) (1981)
Signed as a free agent by **St. Louis**, August 16, 1979. Traded to **Calgary** by **St. Louis** with Terry Johnson and Rik Wilson for Ed Beers, Charles Bourgeois and Gino Cavallini, February 1, 1986.

MULLER, KIRK

Born, Kingston, Ont., February 8, 1966.
Center. Shoots left. 6'0", 195 lbs.
Last amateur club: Guelph Platers (OHL).
(New Jersey's 1st choice, 2nd over-all, in 1984 Entry Draft).

			Regular Season					Playoffs				
Season	Club	Lea	GP	G	A	TP	PIM	GP	G	A	TP	PIM
1981-82	Kingston	OHL	67	12	39	51	27	4	5	1	6	4
1982-83ab	Guelph	OHL	66	52	60	112	41	....	....	....	....	....
1983-84b	Cdn. Olympic	...	21	4	3	7	6	....	....	....	....	....
	Guelph	OHL	49	31	63	94	27	....	....	....	....	....
1984-85	**New Jersey**	**NHL**	80	17	37	54	69	....	....	....	....	....
1985-86	**New Jersey**	**NHL**	77	25	41	66	45	....	....	....	....	....
	NHL Totals		157	42	78	120	114	....	....	....	....	....

a OHL's Most Gentlemanly Player (1983)
b OHL Third All-Star Team (1983, 1984).

MULLINS, DWIGHT

Born, Calgary, Alta., February 28, 1967.
Right wing. Shoots right. 5'11", 190 lbs.
Last amateur club: Lethbridge Broncos (WHL).
(Minnesota's 3rd choice, 90th overall, in 1985 Entry Draft).

			Regular Season					Playoffs				
Season	Club	Lea	GP	G	A	TP	PIM	GP	G	A	TP	PIM
1982-83	Lethbridge	WHL	66	5	2	7	71	20	4	6	10	17
1983-84	Lethbridge	WHL	70	20	23	43	101	5	0	0	0	9
1984-85	Lethbridge	WHL	62	21	18	39	94	4	1	2	3	7
1985-86	Lethbridge	WHL	72	52	37	89	99	10	3	4	7	12

MULLOWNEY, MICHAEL

Born, Brighton, Mass., January 17, 1966.
Defense. Shoots left. 6'1", 190 lbs.
Last amateur club: Boston College Eagles (H.E.).
(Minnesota's 4th choice, 111th overall, in 1985 Entry Draft).

			Regular Season					Playoffs				
Season	Club	Lea	GP	G	A	TP	PIM	GP	G	A	TP	PIM
1985-86	Boston College	H.E.	26	0	2	2	20	....	....	....	....	....

MUNI, CRAIG DOUGLAS (MYEWN-ee)

Born, Toronto, Ont., July 19, 1962.
Defense. Shoots left. 6'2", 200 lbs.
Last amateur club: Windsor Spitfires (OHL).
(Toronto's 1st choice, 25th over-all, in 1980 Entry Draft).

			Regular Season					Playoffs				
Season	Club	Lea	GP	G	A	TP	PIM	GP	G	A	TP	PIM
1980-81	Kingston	OHA	38	2	14	16	65	....	....	....	....	....
	Windsor	OHA	25	5	11	16	41	11	1	4	5	14
	New Brunswick	AHL	....	....	....	....	....	2	0	1	1	10
1981-82	**Toronto**	**NHL**	3	0	0	0	2	....	....	....	....	....
	Windsor	OHL	49	5	32	37	92	9	2	3	5	16
	Cincinnati	CHL	....	....	....	....	....	3	0	2	2	2
1982-83	**Toronto**	**NHL**	2	0	1	1	0	....	....	....	....	....
	St. Catharines	AHL	64	6	32	38	52	....	....	....	....	....
1983-84	St. Catharines	AHL	64	4	16	20	79	7	0	1	1	0
1984-85	**Toronto**	**NHL**	8	0	0	0	0	....	....	....	....	....
	St. Catharines	AHL	68	7	17	24	54	....	....	....	....	....
1985-86	**Toronto**	**NHL**	6	0	1	1	4	....	....	....	....	....
	St. Catharines	AHL	73	3	34	37	91	13	0	5	5	16
	NHL Totals		19	0	2	2	6	....	....	....	....	....

Signed as a free agent by **Edmonton**, August 18, 1986.

MURDOCH, DONALD WALTER (DON)　　　　　　　　　(MURR-dock)

Born, Cranbrook, B.C., October 25, 1956.
Right wing. Shoots right. 5'11", 180 lbs.
Last amateur club: Medicine Hat Tigers (WHL).
(NY Rangers' 1st choice, 6th over-all, in 1976 Amateur Draft).

Season	Club	Lea	GP	Regular Season G	A	TP	PIM	GP	Playoffs G	A	TP	PIM
1974-75a	Medicine Hat	WHL	70	*82	59	141	83	5	1	5	6	15
1975-76a	Medicine Hat	WHL	70	*88	77	165	202	7	4	3	7	23
1976-77	**NY Rangers**	**NHL**	59	32	24	56	47	....	....	....	....	....
1977-78	**NY Rangers**	**NHL**	66	27	28	55	41	3	1	3	4	4
1978-79	**NY Rangers**	**NHL**	40	15	22	37	6	18	7	5	12	12
1979-80	**NY Rangers**	**NHL**	56	23	19	42	16	....	....	....	....	....
	Edmonton	NHL	10	5	2	7	4	3	2	0	2	0
1980-81	**Edmonton**	**NHL**	40	10	9	19	18	....	....	....	....	....
	Wichita	CHL	22	15	10	25	48	18	*17	7	24	24
1981-82	**Detroit**	**NHL**	49	9	13	22	23	....	....	....	....	....
	Adirondack	AHL	24	11	13	24	24	4	5	0	5	14
1982-83	Adirondack	AHL	35	10	12	22	19	....	....	....	....	....
1983-84	Adirondack	AHL	59	26	20	46	19	....	....	....	....	....
	Montana	CHL	17	10	10	20	2	....	....	....	....	....
1984-85	Muskegon	IHL	32	18	13	31	4	16	6	3	9	26
1985-86	Indianapolis	IHL	11	4	3	7	4	....	....	....	....	....
	Toledo	IHL	37	15	23	38	8	....	....	....	....	....
	Muskegon	IHL	12	4	4	8	0	....	....	....	....	....
	NHL Totals		320	121	117	238	155	24	10	8	18	16

a WHL First All-Star Team (1975, 1976)
Traded to **Edmonton** by **NY Rangers** for Cam Connor and Edmonton's third round choice (Peter Sundstrum) in 1981 Entry Draft, March 11, 1980. Rights traded to **Minnesota** by **Edmonton** for Don Jackson, August 21, 1981. Rights traded to **Detroit** by **Minnesota** with Greg Smith and Minnesota's first round choice (Murray Craven) in 1982 Entry Draft for Detroit's first round choice (Brian Bellows) in 1982 Entry Draft, August 21, 1981.

MURPHY, GARY

Born, Winchester, Mass., March 23, 1967.
Defense. Shoots left. 6'1", 175 lbs.
Last amateur club: Lowell University Chiefs; (H.E.).
(Quebec's 12th choice, 225th overall, in 1985 Entry Draft).

Season	Club	Lea	GP	Regular Season G	A	TP	PIM	GP	Playoffs G	A	TP	PIM
1985-86	Lowell	H.E.	27	0	9	9	32	....	....	....	....	....

MURPHY, GORDON

Born, Willowdale, Ont., February 23, 1967.
Defense. Shoots right. 6'1", 180 lbs.
Last amateur club: Oshawa Generals (OHL).
(Philadelphia's 10th choice, 189th overall, in 1985 Entry Draft).

Season	Club	Lea	GP	Regular Season G	A	TP	PIM	GP	Playoffs G	A	TP	PIM
1984-85	Oshawa	OHL	59	3	12	15	25	....	....	....	....	....
1985-86	Oshawa	OHL	64	7	15	22	56	6	1	1	2	6

MURPHY, JOE

Born, London, Ont., October 16, 1967.
Center. Shoots left. 6'1", 190 lbs.
Last amateur club: Michigan State University Spartans (CCHA).
(Detroit's 1st choice, 1st overall, in 1986 Entry Draft).

Season	Club	Lea	GP	Regular Season G	A	TP	PIM	GP	Playoffs G	A	TP	PIM
1985-86	Cdn. Olympic	...	8	3	3	6	2	....	....	....	....	....
	Michigan St.	CCHA	35	24	37	61	50	....	....	....	....	....

a CCHA Rookie of the year (1986).

MURPHY, KELLY

Born, Regina, Sask., April 24, 1966.
Defense. Shoots right. 6'1", 175 lbs.
Last amateur club: Michigan Tech University Huskies (WCHA).
(NY Islanders' 8th choice, 146th overall, in 1984 Entry Draft).

Season	Club	Lea	GP	Regular Season G	A	TP	PIM	GP	Playoffs G	A	TP	PIM
1984-85	Michigan Tech	WCHA	40	2	8	10	16	....	....	....	....	....
1985-86	Michigan Tech	WCHA	40	0	11	11	20	....	....	....	....	....

MURPHY, LAWRENCE THOMAS (LARRY)

Born, Scarborough, Ont., March 8, 1961.
Defense. Shoots right. 6'1", 210 lbs.
Last amateur club: Peterborough Petes (OHA).
(Los Angeles' 1st choice, 4th over-all, in 1980 Entry Draft).

Season	Club	Lea	GP	Regular Season G	A	TP	PIM	GP	Playoffs G	A	TP	PIM
1978-79	Peterborough	OHA	66	6	21	27	82	19	1	9	10	42
1979-80a	Peterborough	OHA	68	21	68	89	88	14	4	13	17	20
1980-81	**Los Angeles**	**NHL**	80	16	60	76	79	4	3	0	3	2
1981-82	**Los Angeles**	**NHL**	79	22	44	66	95	10	2	8	10	12
1982-83	**Los Angeles**	**NHL**	77	14	48	62	81	....	....	....	....	....
1983-84	**Los Angeles**	**NHL**	6	0	3	3	0	....	....	....	....	....
	Washington	NHL	72	13	33	46	50	8	0	3	3	6
1984-85	**Washington**	**NHL**	79	13	42	55	51	5	2	3	5	0
1985-86	**Washington**	**NHL**	78	21	44	65	50	9	1	5	6	6
	NHL Totals		471	99	274	373	406	36	8	19	27	26

a OHA First All-Star Team (1980)
Traded to **Washington** by **Los Angeles** for Ken Houston and Brian Engblom, October 18, 1983.

MURRAY, MIKE

Born, Kingston, Ont., August 29, 1966.
Center. Shoots left. 6', 185 lbs.
Last amateur club: London Knights (OHL).
(NY Islanders' 6th choice, 104th over-all, in 1984 Entry Draft).

Season	Club	Lea	GP	Regular Season G	A	TP	PIM	GP	Playoffs G	A	TP	PIM
1983-84	London	OHL	70	8	24	32	14	8	1	4	5	2
1984-85	London	OHL	43	21	35	56	19	....	....	....	....	....
	Guelph	OHL	23	10	9	19	8	....	....	....	....	....
1985-86	Guelph	OHL	56	27	38	65	19	20	7	13	20	0

MURRAY, ROB

Born, Toronto, Ont., April 4, 1967.
Center. Shoots right. 6'1", 175 lbs.
Last amateur club: Peterborough Petes (OHL).
(Washington's 3rd choice, 61st overall, in 1985 Entry Draft).

Season	Club	Lea	GP	Regular Season G	A	TP	PIM	GP	Playoffs G	A	TP	PIM
1984-85	Peterborough	OHL	63	12	9	21	155	17	2	7	9	45
1985-86	Peterborough	OHL	52	14	18	32	125	16	1	2	3	50

MURRAY, ROBERT FREDERICK (BOB)

Born, Kingston, Ont., November 26, 1954.
Defense. Shoots right. 5'10", 185 lbs.
Last amateur club: Cornwall Royals (QJHL).
(Chicago's 3rd choice, 52nd over-all, in 1974 Amateur Draft).

Season	Club	Lea	GP	Regular Season G	A	TP	PIM	GP	Playoffs G	A	TP	PIM
1972-73	Cornwall	QJHL	32	9	26	35	34	12	1	21	22	43
1973-74	Cornwall	QJHL	63	23	76	99	88	5	0	6	6	6
1974-75	Dallas	CHL	75	14	43	57	130	10	2	6	8	13
1975-76	**Chicago**	**NHL**	64	1	2	3	44	....	....	....	....	....
1976-77	**Chicago**	**NHL**	77	10	11	21	71	2	0	1	1	2
1977-78	**Chicago**	**NHL**	70	14	17	31	41	4	1	4	5	2
1978-79	**Chicago**	**NHL**	79	19	32	51	38	4	1	0	1	6
1979-80	**Chicago**	**NHL**	74	16	34	50	60	7	2	4	6	6
1980-81	**Chicago**	**NHL**	77	13	47	60	93	3	0	0	0	2
1981-82	**Chicago**	**NHL**	45	8	22	30	48	15	1	6	7	16
1982-83	**Chicago**	**NHL**	79	7	32	39	73	13	2	3	5	10
1983-84	**Chicago**	**NHL**	78	11	37	48	78	5	3	1	4	6
1984-85	**Chicago**	**NHL**	80	5	38	43	56	15	3	6	9	20
1985-86	**Chicago**	**NHL**	80	9	29	38	75	3	0	2	2	0
	NHL Totals		803	113	301	414	677	71	13	27	40	70

MURRAY, TROY NORMAN

Born, Calgary, Alta., July 31, 1962.
Center. Shoots right. 6'1", 195 lbs.
Last amateur club: University of North Dakota Fighting Sioux (WCHA).
(Chicago's 6th choice, 51st over-all, in 1980 Entry Draft).

Season	Club	Lea	GP	Regular Season G	A	TP	PIM	GP	Playoffs G	A	TP	PIM
1980-81ab	North Dakota	WCHA	38	33	45	78	28	....	....	....	....	....
1981-82b	North Dakota	WCHA	26	13	17	30	62	....	....	....	....	....
	Chicago	NHL	1	0	0	0	0	7	1	0	1	5
1982-83	**Chicago**	**NHL**	54	8	8	16	27	2	0	0	0	0
1983-84	**Chicago**	**NHL**	61	15	15	30	45	5	1	0	1	7
1984-85	**Chicago**	**NHL**	80	26	40	66	82	15	5	14	19	24
1985-86c	**Chicago**	**NHL**	80	45	54	99	94	2	0	0	0	2
	NHL Totals		276	94	117	211	248	31	7	14	21	38

a WCHA Rookie of the Year (1981)
b WCHA Second All-Star Team (1981, 1982)
c Won Frank J. Selke Memorial Trophy (1986).

MURZYN, DANA　　　　　　　　　(MIRR-zin)

Born, Calgary, Alta., December 9, 1966.
Defense. Shoots left. 6'2", 200 lbs.
Last amateur club: Calgary Wranglers (WHL).
(Hartford's 1st choice, 5th over-all, in 1985 Entry Draft).

Season	Club	Lea	GP	Regular Season G	A	TP	PIM	GP	Playoffs G	A	TP	PIM
1983-84	Calgary	WHL	65	11	20	31	135	2	0	0	0	10
1984-85a	Calgary	WHL	72	32	60	92	233	8	1	11	12	16
1985-86b	**Hartford**	**NHL**	78	3	23	26	125	4	0	0	0	10
	NHL Totals		78	3	23	26	125	4	0	0	0	10

a WHL First All-Star Team, East Division (1985).
b NHL All-Rookie Team (1986).

NACHBAUR, DONALD KENNETH (DON) (KNOCK-bow-er)

Born, Kitimat, B.C., January 30, 1959.
Center. Shoots left. 6'2", 200 lbs.
Last amateur club: Billings Bighorns (WHL).
(Hartford's 3rd choice, 60th over-all, in 1979 Entry Draft).

				Regu	lar Se	ason			Play	offs		
Season	Club	Lea	GP	G	A	TP	PIM	GP	G	A	TP	PIM
1977-78	Billings	WHL	68	23	27	50	128	20	*18	7	25	37
1978-79	Billings	WHL	69	44	52	96	175	8	2	3	5	10
1979-80	Springfield	AHL	70	12	17	29	119	....	....	....	....	....
1980-81	**Hartford**	**NHL**	77	16	17	33	139	....	....	....	....	....
1981-82	**Hartford**	**NHL**	77	5	21	26	117	....	....	....	....	....
1982-83	Moncton	AHL	70	33	32	65	125	....	....	....	....	....
	Edmonton	**NHL**	4	0	0	0	17	2	0	0	0	7
1983-84	New Haven	AHL	70	33	32	65	194	....	....	....	....	....
1984-85	Hershey	AHL	7	2	3	5	21	....	....	....	....	....
1985-86	**Philadelphia**	**NHL**	5	1	1	2	7	....	....	....	....	....
	Hershey	AHL	74	23	24	47	301	18	5	4	9	70
	NHL Totals		163	22	39	61	280	2	0	0	0	7

Traded to **Edmonton** by **Hartford** with Ken Linseman for Risto Siltanen and the rights to Brent Loney, August 19, 1982. Claimed by **Los Angeles** from **Edmonton** in NHL Waiver Draft, October 3, 1983. Signed as a free agent by **Philadelphia**, October 4, 1984.

NADJIWAN, JAMIE

Born, Sudbury, Ont., January 2, 1966.
Left wing. Shoots left. 6'1", 195 lbs.
Last amateur club: Hamilton Steelhawks (OHL).
(Washington's 8th choice, 145th overall, in 1985 Entry Draft).

				Regu	lar Se	ason			Play	offs		
Season	Club	Lea	GP	G	A	TP	PIM	GP	G	A	TP	PIM
1984-85	Sudbury	OHL	62	29	21	50	42	....	....	....	....	....
1985-86	Hamilton	OHL	49	23	28	51	22	....	....	....	....	....

NAPIER, ROBERT MARK (NAY-pyeer) (MARK)

Born, Toronto, Ont., January 28, 1957.
Right wing. Shoots left. 5'10", 185 lbs.
Last amateur club: Toronto Marlboros (OHA).
(Montreal's 1st choice, 10th over-all, in 1977 Amateur Draft).

				Regu	lar Se	ason			Play	offs		
Season	Club	Lea	GP	G	A	TP	PIM	GP	G	A	TP	PIM
1973-74	Toronto	OHA	70	47	46	93	63	....	....	....	....	....
1974-75a	Toronto	OHA	61	66	64	130	106	23	*24	24	*48	13
1975-76b	Toronto	WHA	78	43	50	93	20	....	....	....	....	....
1976-77	Birmingham	WHA	80	60	36	96	24	....	....	....	....	....
1977-78	Birmingham	WHA	79	33	32	65	9	5	0	2	2	14
1978-79	**Montreal**	**NHL**	54	11	20	31	11	12	3	2	5	2
1979-80	**Montreal**	**NHL**	76	16	33	49	7	10	2	6	8	0
1980-81	**Montreal**	**NHL**	79	35	36	71	24	3	0	0	0	2
1981-82	**Montreal**	**NHL**	80	40	41	81	14	5	3	2	5	0
1982-83	**Montreal**	**NHL**	73	40	27	67	6	3	0	0	0	0
1983-84	**Montreal**	**NHL**	5	3	2	5	0	....	....	....	....	....
	Minnesota	**NHL**	58	13	28	41	17	12	3	2	5	0
1984-85	**Minnesota**	**NHL**	39	10	18	28	2	....	....	....	....	....
	Edmonton	**NHL**	33	9	26	35	19	18	5	5	10	7
1985-86	**Edmonton**	**NHL**	80	24	32	56	14	10	1	4	5	0
	NHL Totals		577	201	263	464	114	73	17	21	38	11
	WHA Totals		237	136	118	254	134	9	0	2	2	14

a OHA First All-Star Team (1975)
b Named WHA Rookie of the Year (1976)

Traded to **Minnesota** by **Montreal** with Keith Acton and Toronto's third round choice (Ken Hodge) — Montreal's property via earlier deal — for Bobby Smith, October 28, 1983. Traded to **Edmonton** by **Minnesota** for Gord Sherven and Terry Martin, January 24, 1985.

NASLUND, MATS (NAZ-lund)

Born, Timra, Sweden, October 31, 1959.
Left wing. Shoots left. 5'7", 160 lbs.
Last amateur club: Brynas IF (Sweden)
(Montreal's 2nd choice, 37th over-all, in 1979 Entry Draft).

				Regu	lar Se	ason			Play	offs		
Season	Club	Lea	GP	G	A	TP	PIM	GP	G	A	TP	PIM
1978-79	Brynas IF	Swe.	36	12	12	24	19	....	....	....	....	....
	Swe. National	...	13	8	3	11	12	....	....	....	....	....
1979-80	Brynas IF	Swe.	36	18	19	37	34	7	2	2	4	4
	Swe. Olympic	...	7	3	7	10	6	....	....	....	....	....
	Swe. National	...	21	3	11	14	10	....	....	....	....	....
1980-81	Brynas IF	Swe.	36	17	*25	*42	34	....	....	....	....	....
	Swe. National	...	25	6	10	20	....	....	....	....	....	....
1981-82	Brynas IF (Sweden)	Swe.	36	24	18	42	16	....	....	....	....	....
	Swe. National	...	24	6	9	15	40	....	....	....	....	....
1982-83a	**Montreal**	**NHL**	74	26	45	71	10	3	1	0	1	0
1983-84	**Montreal**	**NHL**	77	29	35	64	4	15	6	8	14	4
1984-85	**Montreal**	**NHL**	80	42	37	79	14	12	7	4	11	6
1985-86b	**Montreal**	**NHL**	80	43	67	110	16	20	8	11	19	4
	NHL Totals		311	140	184	324	44	50	22	23	45	14

a Named to NHL All-Rookie Team (1983)
b NHL Sejcond All-Star Team (1986).

NATTRESS, ERIC RIC (RIC)

Born, Hamilton, Ont., May 25, 1962.
Defense. Shoots right. 6'2", 210 lbs.
Last amateur club: Brantford Alexanders (OHL).
(Montreal's 2nd choice, 27th over-all, in 1980 Entry Draft).

				Regu	lar Se	ason			Play	offs		
Season	Club	Lea	GP	G	A	TP	PIM	GP	G	A	TP	PIM
1979-80	Brantford	OHA	65	3	21	24	94	11	1	6	7	38
1980-81	Brantford	OHA	51	8	34	42	106	6	1	4	5	19
1981-82	Brantford	OHL	59	11	50	61	126	11	3	7	1	17
	Nova Scotia	AHL	....	....	....	....	....	5	0	1	1	7
1982-83	Nova Scotia	AHL	9	0	4	4	16	....	....	....	....	....
	Montreal	**NHL**	40	1	3	4	19	3	0	0	0	10
1983-84	**Montreal**	**NHL**	34	0	12	12	15	....	....	....	....	....
1984-85	**Montreal**	**NHL**	5	0	1	1	2	2	0	0	0	2
	Sherbrooke	AHL	72	8	40	48	37	16	4	13	17	20
1985-86	**St. Louis**	**NHL**	78	4	20	24	52	18	1	4	5	24
	NHL Totals		157	5	36	41	88	23	1	4	5	36

Rights sold to **St. Louis** by **Montreal**, October 7, 1985.

NAUD, DANIEL (DAN)

Born, Trois Rivières, Que., February 20, 1962.
Defense. Shoots right. 5'10", 185 lbs.
Last amateur club: Hull Olympiques (QMJHL).
(Buffalo's 7th choice, 125th over-all, in 1980 Entry Draft).

				Regu	lar Se	ason			Play	offs		
Season	Club	Lea	GP	G	A	TP	PIM	GP	G	A	TP	PIM
1979-80	Sorel	QMJHL	72	17	53	70	30	....	....	....	....	....
1980-81	Sorel	QMJHL	62	17	32	49	28	7	1	2	3	2
1981-82	Hull	QMJHL	64	20	51	71	68	14	6	4	10	10
1982-83	Rochester	AHL	71	6	52	58	34	15	3	5	8	4
1983-84	Rochester	AHL	79	15	44	59	29	18	4	12	16	4
1984-85	Flint	IHL	82	20	44	64	38	7	1	2	3	2
1985-86a	Muskegon	IHL	80	13	52	65	34	14	2	10	12	10

a IHL Second All-Star Team (1986).

NEELY, CAM

Born, Comox, B.C., June 6, 1965.
Right wing. Shoots right. 6'1", 205 lbs.
Last amateur club: Portland Winter Hawks (WHL).
(Vancouver's 1st choice, 9th over-all, in 1983 Entry Draft).

				Regu	lar Se	ason			Play	offs		
Season	Club	Lea	GP	G	A	TP	PIM	GP	G	A	TP	PIM
1981-82	Maple Ridge	Midget	64	73	68	141	134	....	....	....	....	....
1982-82	Portland	WHL	72	56	64	120	130	14	9	11	20	17
1983-84	Portland	WHL	19	8	18	26	29	....	....	....	....	....
	Vancouver	**NHL**	56	16	15	31	57	4	2	0	2	2
1984-85	**Vancouver**	**NHL**	72	21	18	39	137	....	....	....	....	....
1985-86	**Vancouver**	**NHL**	73	14	20	34	126	3	0	0	0	6
	NHL Totals		201	51	53	104	320	7	2	0	2	8

Traded to **Boston** by **Vancouver** with Vancouver's first-round choice in 1987 for Barry Pederson, June 6, 1986.

NEILL, MIKE

Born, Kenora, Ont., August 6, 1965.
Defense. Shoots left. 6'1", 190 lbs.
Last amateur club: Windsor Spitfires (OHL).
(New York Islanders' 4th choice, 57th over-all, in 1983 Entry Draft).

				Regu	lar Se	ason			Play	offs		
Season	Club	Lea	GP	G	A	TP	PIM	GP	G	A	TP	PIM
1982-83	S. S. Marie	OHL	65	4	13	17	115	15	0	0	0	22
1983-84	S. S. Marie	OHL	20	2	6	8	42	....	....	....	....	....
	Windsor	OHL	49	9	17	26	101	3	1	0	1	2
1984-85	Springfield	AHL	7	0	0	0	16	1	0	0	0	0
	Windsor	OHL	63	3	17	20	143	4	0	1	1	11
1985-86	Springfield	AHL	8	0	2	2	11	....	....	....	....	....
	Indianapolis	IHL	71	2	11	13	117	3	0	0	0	4

NELSON, BRIAN

Born, Willmar, Minn., October 5, 1965.
Center. Shoots left. 5'11", 170 lbs.
Last amateur club: University of Minnesota-Duluth Bulldogs (WCHA).
(NY Rangers' 7th choice, 161st overall, in 1984 Entry Draft).

				Regu	lar Se	ason			Play	offs		
Season	Club	Lea	GP	G	A	TP	PIM	GP	G	A	TP	PIM
1984-85	Minn-Duluth	WCHA	3	0	0	0	2	....	....	....	....	....
1985-86	Minn-Duluth	WCHA	14	1	2	3	2	....	....	....	....	....

NEMETH, STEVE

Born, Calgary, Alta., February 11, 1967.
Center. Shoots left. 5'8", 170 lbs.
Last amateur club: Lethbridge Broncos (WHL).
(NY Rangers' 10th choice, 196th overall, in 1985 Entry Draft).

				Regu	lar Se	ason			Play	offs		
Season	Club	Lea	GP	G	A	TP	PIM	GP	G	A	TP	PIM
1982-83	Lethbridge	WHL	2	0	1	1	0	....	....	....	....	....
1983-84	Lethbridge	WHL	68	22	20	42	33	5	1	1	2	2
1984-85	Lethbridge	WHL	67	39	55	94	39	4	2	3	5	13
1985-86	Lethbridge	WHL	70	42	69	111	47	10	5	5	10	6

NESICH, JIM

Born, Dearborn, Mich., February 22, 1966.
Right wing. Shoots right. 5'11", 160 lbs.
Last amateur club: Verdun Junior Canadiens (QMJHL).
(Montreal's 8th choice, 116th overall, in 1984 Entry Draft).

			Regular Season					Playoffs				
Season	Club	Lea	GP	G	A	TP	PIM	GP	G	A	TP	PIM
1983-84	Verdun	QMJHL	70	22	24	46	35	10	11	5	16	2
1984-85	Verdun	QMJHL	65	19	33	52	72	14	1	6	7	25
1985-86	Verdun	QMJHL	71	26	55	81	114	5	0	0	0	8

NEUFELD, RAY MATTHEW   (NEW-feld)

Born, St. Boniface, Man. April 15, 1959.
Right wing. Shoots right. 6'3", 210 lbs.
Last amateur club: Edmonton Oil Kings (WHL).
(Hartford's 4th choice, 81st over-all, in 1979 Entry Draft).

			Regular Season					Playoffs				
Season	Club	Lea	GP	G	A	TP	PIM	GP	G	A	TP	PIM
1977-78	Flin Flon	WHL	72	23	46	69	224	15	4	4	8	39
1978-79	Edmonton	WHL	57	54	48	102	138	8	5	1	6	2
1979-80	Springfield	AHL	73	23	29	52	51	....	....	....	....	....
	Hartford	NHL	8	1	0	1	0	2	1	0	1	0
1980-81	Hartford	NHL	52	5	10	15	44	....	....	....	....	....
	Binghamton	AHL	25	7	7	14	43	6	2	0	2	0
1981-82	Hartford	NHL	19	4	3	7	4	....	....	....	....	....
	Binghamton	AHL	61	28	31	59	81	15	*9	8	17	10
1982-83	Hartford	NHL	80	26	31	57	86	....	....	....	....	....
1983-84	Hartford	NHL	80	27	42	69	97	....	....	....	....	....
1984-85	Hartford	NHL	76	27	35	62	129	....	....	....	....	....
1985-86	Hartford	NHL	16	5	10	15	40	....	....	....	....	....
	Winnipeg	NHL	60	20	28	48	62	3	2	0	2	10
	NHL Totals		391	115	159	274	462	5	3	0	3	10

Traded to **Winnipeg** by **Hartford** for Dave Babych, November 21, 1985.

NEWBERRY, JOHN

Born, Port Alberni, B.C., April 8, 1962.
Center. Shoots left. 6', 190 lbs.
Last amateur club: University of Wisconsin Badgers (WCHA)
(Montreal's 4th choice, 45th over-all, in 1980 Entry Draft).

			Regular Season					Playoffs				
Season	Club	Lea	GP	G	A	TP	PIM	GP	G	A	TP	PIM
1980-81	U. of Wisconsin	WCHA	39	30	32	62	77	....	....	....	....	....
1981-82a	U. of Wisconsin	WCHA	39	38	27	65	....	....	....	....	....	....
1982-83	Nova Scotia	AHL	71	29	29	58	43	6	3	1	4	2
	Montreal	NHL	....	....	....	....	....	2	0	0	0	0
1983-84	Montreal	NHL	3	0	0	0	0	....	....	....	....	....
	Nova Scotia	AHL	78	25	37	62	116	12	7	12	19	22
1984-85	Montreal	NHL	16	0	4	4	6	....	....	....	....	....
	Sherbrooke	AHL	58	23	40	63	30	17	6	14	20	18
1985-86	Hartford	NHL	3	0	0	0	0	....	....	....	....	....
	Binghamton	AHL	21	6	11	17	38	....	....	....	....	....
	Moncton	AHL	44	10	24	34	31	9	1	4	5	2
	NHL Totals		22	0	4	4	6	2	0	0	0	0

a WCHA First All-Star Team (1982)
Signed as a free agent by **Hartford**, September 19, 1985.

NEWHOUSE, JIM

Born, Winchester, Mass., April 1, 1966.
Left wing. Shoots left. 5'10", 180 lbs.
Last amateur club: University of Lowell Chiefs (H.E.).
(Boston's 112th choice, 248th overall, in 1984 Entry Draft).

			Regular Season					Playoffs				
Season	Club	Lea	GP	G	A	TP	PIM	GP	G	A	TP	PIM
1984-85	Lowell	H.E.	37	6	7	13	16	....	....	....	....	....
1985-86	Lowell	H.E.	39	20	13	33	32	....	....	....	....	....

NICHOLLS, BERNIE IRVINE   (NICK-els)

Born, Haliburton, Ont., June 24, 1961.
Center. Shoots right. 6', 185 lbs.
Last amateur club: Kingston Canadians (OHA).
(Los Angeles' 6th choice, 73rd over-all, in 1980 Entry Draft).

			Regular Season					Playoffs				
Season	Club	Lea	GP	G	A	TP	PIM	GP	G	A	TP	PIM
1979-80	Kingston	OHA	68	36	43	79	85	3	1	0	1	10
1980-81	Kingston	OHA	65	63	89	152	109	14	8	10	18	17
1981-82	New Haven	AHL	55	41	30	71	31	....	....	....	....	....
	Los Angeles	NHL	22	14	18	32	27	10	4	0	4	23
1982-83	Los Angeles	NHL	71	28	22	50	124	....	....	....	....	....
1983-84	Los Angeles	NHL	78	41	54	95	83	....	....	....	....	....
1984-85	Los Angeles	NHL	80	46	54	100	76	3	1	1	2	9
1985-86	Los Angeles	NHL	80	36	61	97	78	....	....	....	....	....
	NHL Totals		331	165	209	374	388	13	5	1	6	32

NICHOLS, JAMIE

Born, Vancouver, B.C., March 27, 1968.
Left wing. Shoots left. 6'0", 185 lbs.
Last amateur club: Portland Winter Hawks (WHL).
(Edmonton's 2nd choice, 42nd overall, in 1986 Entry Draft).

			Regular Season					Playoffs				
Season	Club	Lea	GP	G	A	TP	PIM	GP	G	A	TP	PIM
1985-86	Portland	WHL	65	15	37	52	60	15	2	10	12	7

NICKOLAU, TOM

Born, Scarborough, Ont., April 11, 1966.
Center. Shoots left. 6'2", 190 lbs.
Last amateur club: Guelph Platers (OHL).
(Detroit's 12th choice, 236th over-all, in 1984 Entry Draft).

			Regular Season					Playoffs				
Season	Club	Lea	GP	G	A	TP	PIM	GP	G	A	TP	PIM
1983-84	Guelph	OHL	61	5	13	18	98	....	....	....	....	....
1984-85	Guelph	OHL	48	17	24	41	71	....	....	....	....	....
1985-86	Guelph	OHL	39	6	26	32	81	....	....	....	....	....

NIELSON, LEN

Born, Moose Jaw, Sask., March 28, 1967.
Center. Shoots left. 5'9", 170 lbs.
Last amateur club: Regina Pats (WHL).

			Regular Season					Playoffs				
Season	Club	Lea	GP	G	A	TP	PIM	GP	G	A	TP	PIM
1983-84	Regina	WHL	57	9	15	24	20	23	0	2	2	4
1984-85	Regina	WHL	72	35	74	109	48	8	5	7	12	4
1985-86	Regina	WHL	66	30	77	107	49	10	4	4	8	6

Signed as a free agent by **Winnipeg**, September 30, 1985.

NIENHUIS, KRAIG

Born, Sarnia, Ont., May 9, 1961.
Left wing. Shoots left. 6'2", 205 lbs.
Last amateur club: Rensselaer Polytechnic Institute Engineers (ECAC).

			Regular Season					Playoffs				
Season	Club	Lea	GP	G	A	TP	PIM	GP	G	A	TP	PIM
1982-83	RPI	ECAC	24	9	11	20	34	....	....	....	....	....
1983-84	RPI	ECAC	35	10	12	22	26	....	....	....	....	....
1984-85	RPI	ECAC	36	11	10	21	55	....	....	....	....	....
1985-86	Boston	NHL	70	16	14	30	37	2	0	0	0	14
	NHL Totals		70	16	14	30	37	2	0	0	0	14

Signed as a free agent by **Boston**, May 28, 1985.

NIEUWENDYK, JOE

Born, Oshawa, Ont., September 10, 1966.
Center. Shoots left. 6'1", 175 lbs.
Last amateur club: Cornell University Big Red (ECAC).
(Calgary's 2nd choice, 27th over-all, in 1985 Entry Draft).

			Regular Season					Playoffs				
Season	Club	Lea	GP	G	A	TP	PIM	GP	G	A	TP	PIM
1983-84	Pickering	OPJHL	38	30	28	58	35	....	....	....	....	....
1984-85a	Cornell	ECAC	23	18	21	39	20	....	....	....	....	....
1985-86bc	Cornell	ECAC	21	21	21	42	45	....	....	....	....	....

a ECAC Rookie of the Year (1985).
b NCAA East First All-Star Team (1986).
c ECAC First All-Star Team (1986).

NIGHTENGALE, MIKE

Born, South St. Paul, Minn., June 12, 1966.
Defense. Shoots left. 6'1", 180 lbs.
Last amateur club: Ohio State University Buckeyes (CCHA).
(Minnesota's 12th choice, 242nd overall, in 1984 Entry Draft).

			Regular Season					Playoffs				
Season	Club	Lea	GP	G	A	TP	PIM	GP	G	A	TP	PIM
1984-85	Ohio State	CCHA	18	0	2	2	2	....	....	....	....	....
1985-86	Ohio State	CCHA	DID NOT PLAY — INJURED									

NILAN, CHRISTOPHER JOHN (CHRIS)   (NIGH-lan)

Born, Boston, Mass., February 9, 1958.
Right wing. Shoots right. 6', 205 lbs.
Last amateur club: Northeastern University Huskies (ECAC)
(Montreal's 21st choice, 231st over-all, in 1978 Amateur Draft).

			Regular Season					Playoffs				
Season	Club	Lea	GP	G	A	TP	PIM	GP	G	A	TP	PIM
1978-79	Northeastern	ECAC	32	9	17	26	....	....	....	....	....	....
1979-80	Nova Scotia	AHL	49	15	10	25	*304	....	....	....	....	....
	Montreal	NHL	15	0	2	2	50	5	0	0	0	2
1980-81	Montreal	NHL	57	7	8	15	262	2	0	0	0	0
1981-82	Montreal	NHL	49	7	4	11	204	5	1	1	2	22
1982-83	Montreal	NHL	66	6	8	14	213	3	0	0	0	5
1983-84	Montreal	NHL	76	16	10	26	338	15	1	0	1	81
1984-85	Montreal	NHL	77	21	16	37	358	12	2	1	3	81
1985-86	Montreal	NHL	72	19	15	34	274	18	1	2	3	14
	NHL Totals		412	76	63	139	1699	60	5	4	9	332

NILL, JAMES EDWARD (JIM)

Born, Hanna, Alta., April 11, 1958.
Right wing. Shoots right. 6', 185 lbs.
Last amateur club: 1980 Canadian Olympic Team.
(St. Louis' 4th choice, 89th over-all, in 1978 Amateur Draft).

			Regular Season					Playoffs				
Season	Club	Lea	GP	G	A	TP	PIM	GP	G	A	TP	PIM
1975-76	Medicine Hat	WHL	62	5	11	16	69	9	1	1	2	20
1976-77	Medicine Hat	WHL	71	23	24	47	140	4	2	2	4	4
1977-78	Medicine Hat	WHL	72	47	46	93	252	12	8	7	15	37
1978-79	DID NOT PLAY											
1979-80	Cdn. National	...	45	13	19	32	54	....	....	....	....	....
	Cdn. Olympic	...	6	1	2	3	4	....	....	....	....	....
1980-81	Salt Lake	CHL	79	28	34	62	222	16	9	8	17	38
1981-82	St. Louis	NHL	61	9	12	21	127	....	....	....	....	....
	Vancouver	NHL	8	1	2	3	5	16	4	3	7	67
1982-83	Vancouver	NHL	65	7	15	22	136	4	0	0	0	6
1983-84	Vancouver	NHL	51	9	6	15	78	....	....	....	....	....
	Boston	NHL	27	3	2	5	81	3	0	0	0	4
1984-85	Boston	NHL	49	1	9	10	62	....	....	....	....	....
	Winnipeg	NHL	20	8	8	16	38	8	0	1	1	28
1985-86	Winnipeg	NHL	61	6	8	14	75	3	0	0	0	4
	NHL Totals		342	44	62	106	602	34	4	4	8	109

Traded to **Vancouver** by **St. Louis** with Tony Currie, Rick Heinz and St. Louis' fourth round choice (Shawn Kilroy) in 1982 Entry Draft for Glen Hanlon, March 9, 1982. Traded to **Boston** by **Vancouver** for Peter McNab, February 3, 1984. Traded to **Winnipeg** by **Boston** for Morris Lukowich, February 14, 1985.

NILSSON, KENT

Born, Nynashamn, Sweden, August 31, 1956.
Center. Shoots left. 6'1", 195 lbs.
Last amateur club: AIK (Sweden).
(Atlanta's 5th choice, 64th over-all, in 1976 Amateur Draft).

			Regular Season					Playoffs				
Season	Club	Lea	GP	G	A	TP	PIM	GP	G	A	TP	PIM
1975-76	Djurgardens	Swe.	36	28	27	55	10	....	....	....	....	....
	Swe. National	...	6	0	0	0	0	....	....	....	....	....
1976-77	AIK	Swe.	36	30	18	48	18	....	....	....	....	....
1977-78	Winnipeg	WHA	80	42	65	107	8	9	2	8	10	10
1978-79	Winnipeg	WHA	78	39	68	107	8	10	3	11	14	4
1979-80	Atlanta	NHL	80	40	53	93	10	4	0	0	0	2
1980-81	Calgary	NHL	80	49	82	131	26	14	3	9	12	2
1981-82	Calgary	NHL	41	26	29	55	8	3	0	3	3	2
1982-83	Calgary	NHL	80	46	58	104	10	9	1	11	12	2
1983-84	Calgary	NHL	67	31	49	80	22	....	....	....	....	....
1984-85	Calgary	NHL	77	37	62	99	14	3	0	1	1	0
1985-86	Minnesota	NHL	61	16	44	60	10	5	1	4	5	0
	NHL Totals		486	245	377	622	100	38	5	28	33	8
	WHA Totals		158	81	133	214	16	19	5	19	24	14

Reclaimed by **Atlanta** from **Winnipeg** prior to Expansion Draft, June 9, 1979. Traded to **Minnesota** by **Calgary** with Calgary's second round choice in 1987, for Minnesota's second round choice in 1985 (Joe Nieuwendyk) and second round choice in 1987 Entry Draft, June 15, 1985.

NOLAN, THEODORE JOHN (TED)   (KNOW-lan)

Born, Sault Ste. Marie, Ont., April 7, 1958.
Center. Shoots left. 6', 185 lbs.
Last amateur club: Sault Ste. Marie Greyhounds (OHA).
(Detroit's 7th choice, 78th over-all, in 1978 Amateur Draft).

			Regular Season					Playoffs				
Season	Club	Lea	GP	G	A	TP	PIM	GP	G	A	TP	PIM
1976-77	S.S. Marie	OHA	60	8	16	24	109	9	1	2	3	19
1977-78	S.S. Marie.	OHA	66	14	30	44	106	13	1	3	4	20
1978-79	Kansas City	CHL	73	12	38	50	66	4	1	2	3	0
1979-80	Adirondack	AHL	75	16	24	40	106	5	0	1	1	0
1980-81	Adirondack	AHL	76	22	28	50	86	18	6	10	16	11
1981-82	Adirondack	AHL	39	12	18	30	81	....	....	....	....	....
	Detroit	NHL	41	4	13	17	45	....	....	....	....	....
1982-83	Adirondack	AHL	78	24	40	64	103	6	2	5	7	14
1983-84	Detroit	NHL	19	1	2	3	26	....	....	....	....	....
	Adirondack	AHL	31	10	16	26	76	7	2	3	5	18
1984-85	Rochester	AHL	65	28	34	62	152	5	4	0	4	18
1985-86	Pittsburgh	NHL	18	1	1	2	34	....	....	....	....	....
	Baltimore	AHL	10	4	4	8	19	....	....	....	....	....
	NHL Totals		78	6	16	22	105	....	....	....	....	....

Signed as a free agent by **Buffalo**, March 7, 1985. Rights sold to **Pittsburgh** by **Buffalo**, September 16, 1985.

NOONAN, BRIAN

Born, Boston, Mass., May 29, 1965.
Center. Shoots right. 6'1", 180 lbs.
Last amateur club: New Westminster Bruins (WHL).
(Chicago's 10th choice, 186th over-all, in 1983 Entry Draft).

			Regular Season					Playoffs				
Season	Club	Lea	GP	G	A	TP	PIM	GP	G	A	TP	PIM
1984-85	N. Westminster	WHL	72	50	66	116	76	11	8	7	15	4
1985-86	Nova Scotia	AHL	2	0	0	0	0	....	....	....	....	....
	Saginaw	IHL	76	39	39	78	69	11	6	3	9	6

NORMAN, TODD

Born, St. Paul, Minn., February 26, 1966.
Center. Shoots left. 6'0", 170 lbs.
Last amateur club: University of North Dakota Fighting Sioux (WCHA).
(Edmonton's 3rd choice, 63rd overall, in 1984 Entry Draft).

			Regular Season					Playoffs				
Season	Club	Lea	GP	G	A	TP	PIM	GP	G	A	TP	PIM
1984-85	North Dakota	WCHA	42	10	6	16	46	....	....	....	....	....
1985-86	North Dakota	WCHA	19	4	1	5	32	....	....	....	....	....

NORTON, CHRIS

Born, Oakville, Ont., March 11, 1965.
Defense. Shoots right. 6'2", 200 lbs.
Last amateur club: Cornell University Big Red (ECAC).
(Winnipeg's 11th choice, 228th overall, in 1985 Entry Draft).

			Regular Season					Playoffs				
Season	Club	Lea	GP	G	A	TP	PIM	GP	G	A	TP	PIM
1984-85	Cornell	ECAC	29	4	19	23	34	....	....	....	....	....
1985-86a	Cornell	ECAC	21	8	15	23	56	....	....	....	....	....

a ECAC Second All-Star Team (1986).

NORTON, JEFF

Born, Cambridge, Mass., November 25, 1965.
Defense. Shoots left. 6'2", 190 lbs.
Last amateur club: University of Michigan Wolverines (CCHA).
(NY Islanders' 3rd choice, 62nd overall, in 1984 Entry Draft).

			Regular Season					Playoffs				
Season	Club	Lea	GP	G	A	TP	PIM	GP	G	A	TP	PIM
1984-85	U. of Michigan	CCHA	37	8	16	24	103	....	....	....	....	....
1985-86	U. of Michigan	CCHA	37	15	30	45	99	....	....	....	....	....

NORWOOD, LEE CHARLES

Born, Oakland, Calif., February 2, 1960.
Defense. Shoots left. 6', 195 lbs.
Last amateur club: Oshawa Generals (OHA).
(Quebec's 3rd choice, 62nd over-all, in 1979 Entry Draft).

			Regular Season					Playoffs				
Season	Club	Lea	GP	G	A	TP	PIM	GP	G	A	TP	PIM
1978-79	Oshawa	OHA	61	23	38	61	171	5	2	2	4	17
1979-80	Oshawa	OHA	60	13	39	52	143	6	2	7	9	15
1980-81	Hershey	AHL	52	11	32	43	78	8	0	4	4	14
	Quebec	NHL	11	1	1	2	9	3	0	0	0	2
1981-82	Fredericton	AHL	29	6	13	19	74	....	....	....	....	....
	Quebec	NHL	2	0	0	0	2	....	....	....	....	....
	Washington	NHL	26	7	10	17	125	....	....	....	....	....
1982-83	Washington	NHL	8	0	1	1	14	....	....	....	....	....
	Hershey	AHL	67	12	36	48	90	5	0	1	1	2
1983-84	St. Catharines	AHL	75	13	46	59	91	7	0	5	5	31
1984-85ab	Peoria	IHL	80	17	60	77	229	18	1	11	12	62
1985-86	St. Louis	NHL	71	5	24	29	134	19	2	7	9	64
	NHL Totals		118	13	36	49	284	22	2	7	9	66

a Won Governors' Trophy (outstanding defenseman) 1985.
b IHL First All-Star Team (1985).

Traded to **Washington** by **Quebec** for Tim Tookey and Washington's seventh round choice (Daniel Poudrier) in 1982 Entry Draft, February 1, 1982. Traded to **Toronto** by **Washington** for Dave Shand, October 6, 1983. Signed as a free agent by **St. Louis**, August 13, 1985. Traded to **Detroit** by **St. Louis** for Larry Trader, August 7, 1986.

NOVAK, RICHARD

Born, Squamish, B.C., February 19, 1966.
Right wing. Shoots right. 6'1", 170 lbs.
Last amateur club: Michigan Tech University Huskies (WCHA).
(Edmonton's 4th choice, 84th overall, in 1984 Entry Draft).

			Regular Season					Playoffs				
Season	Club	Lea	GP	G	A	TP	PIM	GP	G	A	TP	PIM
1984-85	Michigan Tech.	WCHA	40	9	10	19	16	....	....	....	....	....
1985-86	Michigan Tech.	WCHA	38	9	20	29	20	....	....	....	....	....

NUMMINEN, TEPPO

Born, Tampere, Finland, July 3, 1968.
Defense. Shoots right. 6'1", 175 lbs.
Last amateur club: Tappara (Finland)
(Winnipeg's 2nd choice, 29th overall, in 1986 Entry Draft).

			Regular Season					Playoffs				
Season	Club	Lea	GP	G	A	TP	PIM	GP	G	A	TP	PIM
1985-86	Tappara	Fin.	39	2	4	6	6	....	....	....	....	....

NYLUND, GARY   (NIGH-lund)

Born, Surrey, B.C., October 28, 1963.
Defense. Shoots left. 6'4", 210 lbs.
Last amateur club: Portland Winter Hawks (WHL).
(Toronto's 1st choice, 3rd over-all, in 1982 Entry Draft).

			Regular Season					Playoffs				
Season	Club	Lea	GP	G	A	TP	PIM	GP	G	A	TP	PIM
1979-80	Portland	WHL	72	5	21	26	59	8	0	1	1	2
1980-81a	Portland	WHL	70	6	40	46	186	9	1	7	8	17
1981-82bc	Portland	WHL	65	7	59	66	267	15	3	16	19	74
1982-83	Toronto	NHL	16	0	3	3	16	....	....	....	....	....
1983-84	Toronto	NHL	47	2	14	16	103	....	....	....	....	....
1984-85	Toronto	NHL	76	3	17	20	99	....	....	....	....	....
1985-86	Toronto	NHL	79	2	16	18	180	10	0	2	2	25
	NHL Totals		218	7	50	57	398	10	0	2	2	25

a WHL Second All-Star Team (1981)
b WHL First All-Star Team (1982)
c Named WHL's Top Defenseman (1982)

NYSTROM, THORE ROBERT (BOB) (NIGH-struhm)

Born, Stockholm, Sweden, October 10, 1952.
Right wing. Shoots right. 6'1", 200 lbs.
Last amateur club: Calgary Centennials (WHL).
(NY Islanders' 3rd choice, 33rd over-all, in 1972 Amateur Draft).

				Regular Season					Playoffs			
Season	Club	Lea	GP	G	A	TP	PIM	GP	G	A	TP	PIM
1970-71	Calgary	WHL	66	15	16	31	153	10	2	3	5	32
1971-72	Calgary	WHL	64	27	25	52	178	11	3	6	9	27
1972-73	NY Islanders	NHL	11	1	1	2	10	....	....	....	....	....
	New Haven	AHL	60	12	10	22	114	....	....	....	....	....
1973-74	NY Islanders	NHL	77	21	20	41	118	....	....	....	....	....
1974-75	NY Islanders	NHL	76	27	28	55	122	17	1	3	4	27
1975-76	NY Islanders	NHL	80	23	25	48	106	13	3	6	9	30
1976-77	NY Islanders	NHL	80	29	27	56	91	12	0	2	2	7
1977-78	NY Islanders	NHL	80	30	29	59	94	7	3	1	4	14
1978-79	NY Islanders	NHL	78	19	20	39	113	10	3	2	5	4
1979-80	NY Islanders	NHL	67	21	18	39	94	20	9	9	18	50
1980-81	NY Islanders	NHL	79	14	30	44	145	18	6	6	12	20
1981-82	NY Islanders	NHL	74	22	25	47	103	15	5	5	10	32
1982-83	NY Islanders	NHL	74	10	20	30	98	20	7	6	13	15
1983-84	NY Islanders	NHL	74	15	29	44	80	15	0	2	2	8
1984-85	NY Islanders	NHL	36	2	5	7	58	10	2	2	4	29
1985-86	NY Islanders	NHL	14	1	1	2	16	....	....	....	....	....
	NHL Totals		900	235	278	513	1248	157	39	44	83	236

OATES, ADAM

Born, Weston, Ont., August 27, 1962.
Center. Shoots right. 5'11", 190 lbs.
Last amateur club: Rensselaer Polytechnic Institute Engineers (ECAC).

				Regular Season					Playoffs			
Season	Club	Lea	GP	G	A	TP	PIM	GP	G	A	TP	PIM
1982-83	RPI	ECAC	22	9	33	42	8	....	....	....	....	....
1983-84	RPI	ECAC	38	26	57	83	15	....	....	....	....	....
1984-85ab	RPI	ECAC	38	31	60	91	29	....	....	....	....	....
1985-86	Detroit	NHL	38	9	11	20	10	....	....	....	....	....
	Adirondack	AHL	34	18	28	46	4	17	7	14	21	4
	NHL Totals		38	9	11	20	10	....	....	....	....	....

a ECAC First All-Star Team (1985)
b Named to NCAA All-American Team (1985)
Signed as a free agent by **Detroit**, June 28, 1985.

O'CALLAHAN, JACK

Born, Charleston, Mass., July 24, 1957.
Defense. Shoots right. 6'1", 190 lbs.
Last amateur club: 1980 United States Olympic Team.
(Chicago's 5th choice, 96th over-all, in 1977 Amateur Draft).

				Regular Season					Playoffs			
Season	Club	Lea	GP	G	A	TP	PIM	GP	G	A	TP	PIM
1978-79	Boston U.	ECAC	....	....	....	....	....	....	....	....	....	....
1979-80	U.S. National	...	51	7	29	36	83	....	....	....	....	....
	U.S. Olympic	...	4	0	1	1	2	....	....	....	....	....
1980-81	New Brunswick	AHL	78	9	25	34	167	13	1	6	7	36
1981-82	New Brunswick	AHL	79	15	33	48	130	15	2	6	8	24
1982-83	Springfield	AHL	35	2	24	26	25	....	....	....	....	....
	Chicago	NHL	39	0	11	11	46	5	0	2	2	2
1983-84	Chicago	NHL	70	4	13	17	67	2	0	0	0	2
1984-85	Chicago	NHL	66	6	8	14	105	15	3	5	8	25
1985-86	Chicago	NHL	80	4	19	23	116	3	0	1	1	4
	NHL Totals		255	14	51	65	334	25	3	8	11	33

O'CONNELL, MICHAEL THOMAS (MIKE)

Born, Chicago, Ill., November 25, 1955.
Defense. Shoots right. 5'9", 180 lbs.
Last amateur club: Kingston Canadians (OHA).
(Chicago's 3rd choice, 43rd over-all, in 1975 Amateur Draft).

				Regular Season					Playoffs			
Season	Club	Lea	GP	G	A	TP	PIM	GP	G	A	TP	PIM
1973-74	Kingston	OHA	70	16	43	59	81	....	....	....	....	....
1974-75a	Kingston	OHA	50	18	55	73	47	8	1	9	3	4
1975-76	Dallas	CHL	70	6	37	43	50	10	2	*8	10	8
1976-77	Dallas	CHL	63	15	53	68	30	5	1	4	5	0
1977-78	Chicago	NHL	6	1	1	2	2	....	....	....	....	....
	Dallas	CHL	62	6	45	51	75	13	1	*11	12	8
1978-79	New Brunswick	AHL	35	5	19	24	19	....	....	....	....	....
	Chicago	NHL	48	4	22	26	20	4	0	0	0	4
1979-80	Chicago	NHL	78	8	22	30	52	7	0	1	1	0
1980-81	Chicago	NHL	34	5	16	21	32	....	....	....	....	....
	Boston	NHL	48	10	22	32	42	3	1	3	4	2
1981-82	Boston	NHL	80	5	34	39	75	11	2	2	4	20
1982-83	Boston	NHL	80	14	39	53	42	17	3	5	8	12
1983-84	Boston	NHL	75	18	42	60	42	3	0	0	0	0
1984-85	Boston	NHL	78	15	40	55	64	5	1	5	6	0
1985-86	Boston	NHL	63	8	21	29	47	....	....	....	....	....
	Detroit	NHL	13	1	7	8	16	....	....	....	....	....
	NHL Totals		603	89	266	355	434	50	7	16	23	38

a OHA First All-Star Team (1975).
Traded to **Boston** by **Chicago** for Al Secord, December 18, 1980. Traded to **Detroit** by **Boston** for Reed Larson, March 10, 1986.

O'CONNOR, MYLES

Born, Calgary, Alta., April 2, 1967.
Defense. Shoots left. 5'11", 165 lbs.
Last amateur club: University of Michigan Wolverines (CCHA).
(New Jersey's 4th choice, 45th overall, in 1985 Entry Draft).

				Regular Season					Playoffs			
Season	Club	Lea	GP	G	A	TP	PIM	GP	G	A	TP	PIM
1985-86	U. of Michigan	CCHA	37	6	19	25	73	....	....	....	....	....

OCTEAU, JAY

Born, Providence, RI, March 24, 1965.
Defense. Shoots right. 5'10", 180 lbs.
Last amateur club: Boston University Terriers (H.E.).
(New Jersey's 7th choice, 171st overall, in 1983 Entry Draft).

				Regular Season					Playoffs			
Season	Club	Lea	GP	G	A	TP	PIM	GP	G	A	TP	PIM
1983-84	Boston U.	H.E.	27	1	6	7	20	....	....	....	....	....
1984-85	Boston U.	H.E.	38	2	14	16	42	....	....	....	....	....
1985-86a	Boston U.	H.E.	41	8	27	35	47	....	....	....	....	....

a NCAA East Sejcond All-Star Team (1986).

ODELEIN, SELMAR (OH-de-leen)

Born, Quill Lake, Sask., April 11, 1966.
Defense. Shoots right. 6', 195 lbs.
Last amateur club: Regina Pats (WHL).
(Edmonton's 1st choice, 21st over-all, in 1984 Entry Draft).

				Regular Season					Playoffs			
Season	Club	Lea	GP	G	A	TP	PIM	GP	G	A	TP	PIM
1982-83	Regina	Midget	70	30	84	114	38	....	....	....	....	....
1983-84	Regina	WHL	71	9	42	51	45	23	4	11	15	45
1984-85	Regina	WHL	64	24	35	59	121	8	3	4	7	13
1985-86	Edmonton	NHL	4	0	0	0	0	....	....	....	....	....
	Regina	WHL	36	13	28	41	57	8	5	2	7	24
	NHL Totals		4	0	0	0	0	....	....	....	....	....

OJANEN, JANNE

Born, Tampere, Finland, April 9, 1968.
Center. Shoots left. 6'2", 185 lbs.
Last amateur club: Tappara (Finland).
(New Jersey's 3rd choice, 45th over-all, in 1986 Entry Draft).

				Regular Season					Playoffs			
Season	Club	Lea	GP	G	A	TP	PIM	GP	G	A	TP	PIM
1985-86	Tappara	Fin.	14	5	17	22	....	....	....	....	....	....

O'DWYER, BILL

Born, South Boston, Mass., June 25, 1960.
Center. Shoots left. 6', 190 lbs.
Last amateur club: Boston College Eagles (ECAC).
(Los Angeles' 10th choice, 157th over-all, in 1980 Entry Draft).

				Regular Season					Playoffs			
Season	Club	Lea	GP	G	A	TP	PIM	GP	G	A	TP	PIM
1978-79	Boston College	ECAC	30	9	30	39	14	....	....	....	....	....
1979-80	Boston College	ECAC	33	20	22	42	22	....	....	....	....	....
1980-81	Boston College	ECAC	31	20	20	40	6	....	....	....	....	....
1981-82	Boston College	ECAC	30	15	26	41	10	....	....	....	....	....
1982-83	New Haven	AHL	77	24	23	47	29	11	3	4	7	9
1983-84	Los Angeles	NHL	5	0	0	0	0	....	....	....	....	....
	New Haven	AHL	58	15	42	57	39	....	....	....	....	....
1984-85	Los Angeles	NHL	13	1	0	1	15	....	....	....	....	....
	New Haven	AHL	46	19	24	43	27	....	....	....	....	....
1985-86	New Haven	AHL	41	10	15	25	41	5	0	1	1	2
	NHL Totals		18	1	0	1	15	....	....	....	....	....

Signed as a free agent by **NY Rangers**, July 13, 1985.

OGRODNICK, JOHN ALEXANDER (oh-GRAHD-nik)

Born, Ottawa, Ont., June 20, 1959.
Left wing. Shoots left. 6', 190 lbs.
Last amateur club: New Westminster Bruins (WHL).
(Detroit's 4th choice, 66th over-all, in 1979 Entry Draft).

				Regular Season					Playoffs			
Season	Club	Lea	GP	G	A	TP	PIM	GP	G	A	TP	PIM
1977-78a	N. Westminster	WHL	72	59	29	88	47	21	14	7	21	14
1978-79	N. Westminster	WHL	72	48	36	84	38	6	2	0	2	4
1979-80	Detroit	NHL	41	8	24	32	8	....	....	....	....	....
	Adirondack	AHL	39	13	20	33	21	....	....	....	....	....
1980-81	Detroit	NHL	80	35	35	70	14	....	....	....	....	....
1981-82	Detroit	NHL	80	28	26	54	28	....	....	....	....	....
1982-83	Detroit	NHL	80	41	44	85	30	....	....	....	....	....
1983-84	Detroit	NHL	64	42	36	78	14	4	0	0	0	0
1984-85b	Detroit	NHL	79	55	50	105	30	3	1	1	2	0
1985-86	Detroit	NHL	76	38	32	70	18	....	....	....	....	....
	NHL Totals		500	247	247	494	142	7	1	1	2	0

a Shared WHL Rookie of the Year Award with Keith Brown (Portland) (1978)
b NHL First All-Star Team (1985)

OKERLUND, TODD

Born, Burnsville, Minn., September 6, 1964.
Right wing. Shoots right. 5'10", 190 lbs.
Last amateur club: University of Minnesota Golden Gophers (WCHA).
(NY Islanders' 8th choice, 168th overall, in 1982 Entry Draft).

				Regular Season					Playoffs			
Season	Club	Lea	GP	G	A	TP	PIM	GP	G	A	TP	PIM
1983-84	U. Minnesota	WCHA	34	11	20	31	18	.....	.....	.....	.....	.....
1984-85	U. Minnesota	WCHA	47	16	27	43	80	.....	.....	.....	.....	.....
1985-86	U. Minnesota	WCHA	48	17	32	49	58	.....	.....	.....	.....	.....

OHMAN, ROGER

Born, Stockholm, Sweden, June 5, 1967.
Defense. Shoots left. 6'2", 200 lbs.
Last amateur club: Leksand (Sweden).
(Winnipeg's 2nd choice, 39th over-all, in 1985 Entry Draft).

				Regular Season					Playoffs			
Season	Club	Lea	GP	G	A	TP	PIM	GP	G	A	TP	PIM
1983-84	Leksand	Swe.	36	31	21	52	80	.....	.....	.....	.....	.....
1984-85	Leksand	Swe.	40	32	44	76	60	.....	.....	.....	.....	.....
1985-86	DID NOT PLAY											

OLCZYK, ED   (ohl-CHUCK)

Born, Chicago, Illinois, August 16, 1966.
Right wing. Shoots left. 6'2", 195 lbs.
Last amateur club: 1984 United States Olympic Team.
(Chicago's 1st choice, 3rd over-all, in 1984 Entry Draft).

				Regular Season					Playoffs			
Season	Club	Lea	GP	G	A	TP	PIM	GP	G	A	TP	PIM
1982-83	Stratford	OPJHL	42	50	92	*141	54	.....	.....	.....	.....	.....
1983-84	U.S. Olympic	...	62	21	47	68	36	.....	.....	.....	.....	.....
1984-85	**Chicago**	**NHL**	70	20	30	50	67	15	6	5	11	11
1985-86	**Chicago**	**NHL**	79	29	50	79	47	3	0	0	0	0
	NHL Totals		149	49	80	129	114	18	6	5	11	11

OLIVERIO, MICHAEL

Born, Sault Ste. Marie, Ont., June 10, 1967.
Center. Shoots left. 5'10", 180 lbs.
Last amateur club: Sault Ste. Marie Greyhounds (OHL).
(Quebec's 8th choice, 141st overall, in 1985 Entry Draft).

				Regular Season					Playoffs			
Season	Club	Lea	GP	G	A	TP	PIM	GP	G	A	TP	PIM
1984-85	S.S. Marie	OHL	66	38	48	86	24	16	3	14	17	6
1985-86	S.S. Marie	OHL	64	26	56	82	45	.....	.....	.....	.....	.....

OLLSON, JOHN

Born, Nepean, Ont., July 31, 1963.
Center. Shoots left. 5'9", 175 lbs.
Last amateur club: Ottawa 67's (OHL).

				Regular Season					Playoffs			
Season	Club	Lea	GP	G	A	TP	PIM	GP	G	A	TP	PIM
1980-81	Ottawa	OHA	31	6	6	12	12	.....	.....	.....	.....	.....
1981-82	Ottawa	OHL	67	36	42	78	49	17	6	8	14	15
1982-83	Ottawa	OHL	68	46	76	122	41	9	2	10	12	14
1983-84	Springfield	AHL	75	29	43	72	51	4	1	2	3	12
1984-85	Indianapolis	IHL	17	9	11	20	6	7	1	1	2	4
	Milwaukee	IHL	55	17	24	41	23	.....	.....	.....	.....	.....
1985-86	Nova Scotia	AHL	60	19	21	40	10	.....	.....	.....	.....	.....
	Saginaw	IHL	13	6	6	12	9	11	6	5	11	4

Signed as free agent by **Chicago**, August 12, 1983.

OLSEN, DARRYL

Born, Calgary, Alta., October 7, 1966.
Defense. Shoots left. 6'0", 180 lbs.
Last amateur club: Northern Michigan University Wildcats (WCHA).
(Calgary's 10th choice, 185th overall in 1985 Entry Draft).

				Regular Season					Playoffs			
Season	Club	Lea	GP	G	A	TP	PIM	GP	G	A	TP	PIM
1984-85	St. Albert	AJHL	57	19	48	67	77	.....	.....	.....	.....	.....
1985-86	N. Michigan	WCHA	37	5	20	25	46	.....	.....	.....	.....	.....

O'REGAN, THOMAS PATRICK (TOM)

Born, Cambridge, Mass., December 29, 1961.
Center. Shoots left. 5'10", 180 lbs.
Last amateur club: Boston University Terriers (ECAC).

				Regular Season					Playoffs			
Season	Club	Lea	GP	G	A	TP	PIM	GP	G	A	TP	PIM
1981-82	Boston U.	ECAC	28	18	34	52	67	.....	.....	.....	.....	.....
1982-83	Boston U.	ECAC	27	15	17	32	43	.....	.....	.....	.....	.....
1983-84	**Pittsburgh**	**NHL**	51	4	10	14	8	.....	.....	.....	.....	.....
	Baltimore	AHL	25	13	14	27	15	.....	.....	.....	.....	.....
1984-85	**Pittsburgh**	**NHL**	1	0	0	0	0	.....	.....	.....	.....	.....
	Baltimore	AHL	62	28	28	56	62	15	4	5	9	0
1985-86	**Pittsburgh**	**NHL**	9	1	2	3	2	.....	.....	.....	.....	.....
	Baltimore	AHL	61	23	31	54	65	.....	.....	.....	.....	.....
	NHL Totals		60	5	12	17	10	.....	.....	.....	.....	.....

Signed as free agent by **Pittsburgh**, September 4, 1983.

ORLANDO, GAETANO (GATES)

Born, Montreal, Que., November 13, 1962.
Center. Shoots left. 5'8", 180 lbs.
Last amateur club: Providence College Friars (ECAC)
(Buffalo's 10th choice, 164th over-all, in 1981 Entry Draft).

				Regular Season					Playoffs			
Season	Club	Lea	GP	G	A	TP	PIM	GP	G	A	TP	PIM
1980-81	Providence	ECAC	31	24	32	56	45	.....	.....	.....	.....	.....
1981-82	Providence	ECAC	28	18	18	36	31	.....	.....	.....	.....	.....
1982-83	Providence	ECAC	40	30	39	69	32	.....	.....	.....	.....	.....
1983-84	Providence	ECAC	30	21	28	49	N/A	.....	.....	.....	.....	.....
	Rochester	AHL	11	8	7	15	2	18	4	10	14	6
1984-85	**Buffalo**	**NHL**	11	3	6	9	6	5	0	4	4	14
	Rochester	AHL	49	26	30	56	62	2	0	1	1	6
1985-86	**Buffalo**	**NHL**	60	13	12	25	29	.....	.....	.....	.....	.....
	Rochester	AHL	3	4	0	4	10	.....	.....	.....	.....	.....
	NHL Totals		71	16	18	34	35	5	0	4	4	14

ORN, MIKE

Born, Moorehead, Minn., April 26, 1966.
Center. Shoots left. 5'11", 170 lbs.
Last amateur club: University of Miami - Ohio Redkins (CCHA).
(Minnesota's 10th choice, 201st overall, in 1984 Entry Draft).

				Regular Season					Playoffs			
Season	Club	Lea	GP	G	A	TP	PIM	GP	G	A	TP	PIM
1984-85	Miami-Ohio	CCHA	40	13	15	28	52	.....	.....	.....	.....	.....
1985-86	Miami-Ohio	CCHA	31	13	19	32	58	.....	.....	.....	.....	.....

ORTH, STEVE

Born, St. Cloud, Minn., January 17, 1965.
Center. Shoots left. 5'8", 150 lbs.
Last amateur club: University of Minnesota Golden Gophers (WCHA).
(NY Rangers' 8th choice, 133rd overall, in 1983 Entry Draft).

				Regular Season					Playoffs			
Season	Club	Lea	GP	G	A	TP	PIM	GP	G	A	TP	PIM
1983-84	U. Minnesota	WCHA	8	4	4	8	2	.....	.....	.....	.....	.....
1984-85	U. Minnesota	WCHA	38	7	14	21	8	.....	.....	.....	.....	.....
1985-86	U. Minnesota	WCHA	38	6	7	13	4	.....	.....	.....	.....	.....

OSBORNE, MARK ANATOLE   (AHS-born)

Born, Toronto, Ont., August 13, 1961.
Left wing. Shoots left. 6'1", 185 lbs.
Last amateur club: Niagara Falls Flyers (OHA).
(Detroit's 2nd choice, 46th over-all, in 1980 Entry Draft).

				Regular Season					Playoffs			
Season	Club	Lea	GP	G	A	TP	PIM	GP	G	A	TP	PIM
1979-80	Niagara Falls	OHA	52	10	33	43	104	10	2	1	3	23
1980-81	Niagara Falls	OHA	54	39	41	80	140	12	11	10	21	20
	Adirondack	AHL	.....	.....	.....	.....	.....	13	2	3	5	2
1981-82	**Detroit**	**NHL**	80	26	41	67	61	.....	.....	.....	.....	.....
1982-83	**Detroit**	**NHL**	80	19	24	43	83	.....	.....	.....	.....	.....
1983-84	**NY Rangers**	**NHL**	73	23	28	51	88	5	0	1	1	7
1984-85	**NY Rangers**	**NHL**	23	4	4	8	33	3	0	0	0	4
1985-86	**NY Rangers**	**NHL**	62	16	24	40	80	15	2	3	5	26
	NHL Totals		318	88	121	209	345	23	2	4	6	37

Traded to **NY Rangers** by **Detroit** with Willie Huber and Mike Blaisdell for Ron Duguay, Eddie Mio and Eddie Johnstone, June 13, 1983.

OSWALD, RANDY

Born, Bowmanville, Ont., January 5, 1966.
Defense. Shoots left. 6'3", 185 lbs.
Last amateur club: Michigan Tech University Huskies (WCHA).
(Boston's 6th choice, 124th overall, in 1984 Entry Draft).

				Regular Season					Playoffs			
Season	Club	Lea	GP	G	A	TP	PIM	GP	G	A	TP	PIM
1983-84	Michigan Tech	WCHA	41	0	2	2	44	.....	.....	.....	.....	.....
1984-85	Michigan Tech	WCHA	37	0	4	4	60	.....	.....	.....	.....	.....
1985-86	Michigan Tech	WCHA	30	4	9	13	58	.....	.....	.....	.....	.....

OTTO, ANDY

Born, Park Ridge, Ill., May 8, 1963.
Defense. Shoots left. 5'10", 180 lbs.
Last amateur club: Clarkson University Knights (ECAC).
(NY Rangers' 12th choice, 225th overall, in 1982 Entry Draft).

				Regular Season					Playoffs			
Season	Club	Lea	GP	G	A	TP	PIM	GP	G	A	TP	PIM
1982-83	Clarkson	ECAC	29	5	10	15	24	.....	.....	.....	.....	.....
1983-84	Clarkson	ECAC	34	8	19	27	16	.....	.....	.....	.....	.....
1984-85	Clarkson	ECAC	33	5	10	15	44	.....	.....	.....	.....	.....
1985-86a	Clarkson	ECAC	28	4	24	28	20	.....	.....	.....	.....	.....

a NCAA Second All-American Team (1986).

OTTO, JOEL STUART

Born, St. Cloud, Minn., October 29, 1961.
Left Wing. Shoots right. 6′4″, 220 lbs.
Last amateur club: Bemidji State Beavers (NCAA II).

			Regular Season					Playoffs				
Season	Club	Lea	GP	G	A	TP	PIM	GP	G	A	TP	PIM
1980-81	Bemidji S.	NCAA	23	5	11	16	10	....	....	....	....	....
1981-82	Bemidji S.	NCAA	31	19	33	52	24	....	....	....	....	....
1982-83	Bemidji S.	NCAA	37	33	28	61	68	....	....	....	....	....
1983-84	Bemidji S.	NCAA	31	32	43	75	32	....	....	....	....	....
1984-85	Calgary	NHL	17	4	8	12	30	3	2	1	3	10
	Moncton	AHL	56	27	36	63	89	....	....	....	....	....
1985-86	Calgary	NHL	79	25	34	59	188	22	5	10	15	80
	NHL Totals		96	29	42	71	218	25	7	11	18	90

Signed as a free agent by **Calgary**, September 11, 1984.

PADDOCK, GORDON

Born, Hamiota, Man., February 15, 1964.
Defense. Shoots right. 5′11″, 180 lbs.
Last amateur club: Brandon Wheat Kings (WHL).
(NY Islanders' 9th choice, 189th over-all, in 1982 Entry Draft).

			Regular Season					Playoffs				
Season	Club	Lea	GP	G	A	TP	PIM	GP	G	A	TP	PIM
1981-82	Saskatoon	WHL	59	8	21	29	232	3	0	0	0	17
1982-83	Saskatoon	WHL	67	4	25	29	158	6	0	2	2	16
1983-84	Brandon	WHL	72	14	37	51	151	12	1	5	6	23
1984-85	Springfield	AHL	12	0	2	2	24	3	0	0	0	6
	Indianapolis	IHL	65	10	21	31	92	7	2	1	3	23
1985-86	Springfield	AHL	20	1	1	2	52	....	....	....	....	....
	Indianapolis	IHL	11	1	1	2	11	....	....	....	....	....
	Muskegon	IHL	47	1	20	21	87	....	....	....	....	....

PAEK, JIM

Born, Soeul, Korea, April 7, 1967.
Defense. Shoots left. 6′0″, 190 lbs.
Last amateur club: Oshawa Generals (OHL).
(Pittsburgh's 9th choice, 170th overall,l in 1985 Entry Draft).

			Regular Season					Playoffs				
Season	Club	Lea	GP	G	A	TP	PIM	GP	G	A	TP	PIM
1984-85	Oshawa	OHL	54	2	13	15	57	5	1	0	1	9
1985-86	Oshawa	OHL	64	5	21	26	122	6	0	1	1	9

PAIEMENT, WILFRID, JR. (WILF)   (PAY-mahn)

Born, Earlton, Ont., October 16, 1955.
Right wing. Shoots right. 6′1″, 210 lbs.
Last amateur club: St. Catharines Black Hawks (OHA).
(Kansas City's 1st choice, 2nd over-all, in 1974 Amateur Draft).

			Regular Season					Playoffs				
Season	Club	Lea	GP	G	A	TP	PIM	GP	G	A	TP	PIM
1972-73	St. Catharines	OHA	61	18	27	45	173	....	....	....	....	....
1973-74a	St. Catharines	OHA	70	50	73	123	134	....	....	....	....	....
1974-75	Kansas City	NHL	78	26	13	39	101	....	....	....	....	....
1975-76	Kansas City	NHL	57	21	22	43	121	....	....	....	....	....
1976-77	Colorado	NHL	78	41	40	81	101	....	....	....	....	....
1977-78	Colorado	NHL	80	31	56	87	114	2	0	0	0	7
1978-79	Colorado	NHL	65	24	36	60	80	....	....	....	....	....
1979-80	Colorado	NHL	34	10	16	26	41	....	....	....	....	....
	Toronto	NHL	41	20	28	48	72	3	0	2	2	17
1980-81	Toronto	NHL	77	40	57	97	145	3	0	0	0	2
1981-82	Toronto	NHL	69	18	40	58	203	....	....	....	....	....
	Quebec	NHL	8	7	6	13	18	14	6	6	12	28
1982-93	Quebec	NHL	80	26	38	64	170	4	0	1	1	4
1983-84	Quebec	NHL	80	39	37	76	121	9	3	1	4	24
1984-85	Quebec	NHL	68	23	28	51	165	18	4	2	6	58
1985-86	Quebec	NHL	44	7	12	19	145	....	....	....	....	....
	NY Rangers	NHL	8	1	6	7	13	16	5	5	10	45
	NHL Totals		867	334	435	769	1610	69	18	17	35	185

a OHA First All-Star Team (1974)

Traded to **Toronto** by **Colorado** with Pat Hickey for Lanny McDonald and Joel Quenneville, December 29, 1979. Traded to **Quebec** by **Toronto** for Miroslav Frycer and Quebec's seventh round choice (Jeff Triano) in 1982 Entry Draft, March 9, 1982. Traded to **NY Rangers** by **Quebec** for Steve Patrick, February 6, 1986.

PALMER, ROBERT ROSS (ROB)

Born, Sarnia, Ont., September 10, 1956.
Defense. Shoots right. 5′11″, 190 lbs.
Last amateur club: University of Michigan Wolverines (WCHA)
(Los Angeles' 4th choice, 85th over-all, in 1976 Amateur Draft).

			Regular Season					Playoffs				
Season	Club	Lea	GP	G	A	TP	PIM	GP	G	A	TP	PIM
1975-76	U. of Michigan	WCHA	42	5	16	21	58	....	....	....	....	....
1976-77	U. of Michigan	WCHA	45	5	37	42	32	....	....	....	....	....
	Fort Worth	CHL	3	0	2	2	0	5	0	0	0	0
1977-78	Springfield	AHL	19	1	7	8	18	....	....	....	....	....
	Los Angeles	NHL	48	0	3	3	27	2	0	0	0	0
1978-79	**Los Angeles**	NHL	78	4	41	45	26	2	0	0	0	2
1979-80	**Los Angeles**	NHL	78	4	36	40	18	4	1	2	3	4
1980-81	**Los Angeles**	NHL	13	0	4	4	13	....	....	....	....	....
	Houston	CHL	28	3	10	13	23	....	....	....	....	....
	Indianapolis	CHL	27	1	9	10	16	5	1	1	2	0
1981-82	**Los Angeles**	NHL	5	0	2	2	0	....	....	....	....	....
	New Haven	AHL	41	2	23	25	22	4	1	4	5	2
1982-83	**New Jersey**	NHL	60	1	10	11	21	....	....	....	....	....
1983-84	**New Jersey**	NHL	38	0	5	5	10	....	....	....	....	....
	Maine	AHL	33	5	10	15	10	17	3	10	13	8
1984-85	Maine	AHL	79	1	23	24	22	11	0	3	3	2
1985-86	Maine	AHL	73	2	10	12	18	5	0	0	0	0
	NHL Totals		320	9	101	110	115	8	1	2	3	6

Signed as a free agent by **New Jersey**, September 9, 1982.

PALOSAARI, ESA

Born, Oulu, Finland, June 10, 1965.
Right wing. Shoots right. 6′4″, 210 lbs.
Last amateur club: Karpat (Finland).
(Winnipeg's 3rd choice, 50th overall, in 1986 Entry Draft).

			Regular Season					Playoffs				
Season	Club	Lea	GP	G	A	TP	PIM	GP	G	A	TP	PIM
1985-86	Karpat	Fin.	26	9	8	17	40	....	....	....	....	....

PALUCH, SCOTT

Born, Chicago, Ill., March 9, 1966.
Defense. Shoots left. 6′3″, 185 lbs.
Last amateur club: Bowling Green State University Falcons (CCHA).
(St. Louis' 7th choice, 92nd overall, in 1984 Entry Draft).

			Regular Season					Playoffs				
Season	Club	Lea	GP	G	A	TP	PIM	GP	G	A	TP	PIM
1984-85	Bowling Green	CCHA	42	11	25	36	64	....	....	....	....	....
1985-86	Bowling Green	CCHA	34	10	11	21	44	....	....	....	....	....

PARKER, JEFF

Born, St. Paul, Minn., September 7, 1964.
Center. Shoots left. 6′3″, 175 lbs.
Last amateur club: Michigan State University Spartans (CCHA).
(Buffalo's 9th choice, 111th overalll, in 1982 Entry Draft).

			Regular Season					Playoffs				
Season	Club	Lea	GP	G	A	TP	PIM	GP	G	A	TP	PIM
1983-84	Michigan St.	CCHA	44	8	13	21	82	....	....	....	....	....
1984-85	Michigan St.	CCHA	42	10	12	22	89	....	....	....	....	....
1985-86	Michigan St.	CCHA	41	15	20	35	88	....	....	....	....	....

PARKS, MALCOLM

Born, Edmonton, Alta., January 20, 1965.
Center/Right wing. Shoots right. 6′, 185 lbs.
Last amateur club: University of North Dakota Fighting Sioux (WCHA).
(Minnesota's 2nd choice, 36th over-all, in 1983 Entry Draft).

			Regular Season					Playoffs				
Season	Club	Lea	GP	G	A	TP	PIM	GP	G	A	TP	PIM
1982-83	St. Albert	AJHL	54	59	57	116	185	....	....	....	....	....
1983-84	North Dakota	WCHA	23	5	6	11	32	....	....	....	....	....
1984-85	North Dakota	WCHA	39	4	7	11	41	....	....	....	....	....
1985-86	North Dakota	WCHA	39	6	14	20	38	....	....	....	....	....

PASIN, DAVE

Born, Edmonton, Alta., July 8, 1966.
Right wing. Shoots right. 6′2″, 195 lbs.
Last amateur club: Prince Albert Raiders (WHL).
(Boston's 1st choice, 19th over-all, in 1984 Entry Draft).

			Regular Season					Playoffs				
Season	Club	Lea	GP	G	A	TP	PIM	GP	G	A	TP	PIM
1982-83	Prince Albert	WHL	62	40	42	82	48	....	....	....	....	....
1983-84	Prince Albert	WHL	71	68	54	122	68	5	1	4	5	0
1984-85a	Prince Albert	WHL	65	64	52	116	88	10	10	11	21	10
1985-86	**Boston**	NHL	71	18	19	37	50	3	0	1	1	0
	NHL Totals		71	18	19	37	50	3	0	1	1	0

a WHL Second All-Star Team, East Division (1985).

PASLAWSKI, GREGORY STEPHEN (GREG)   (paz-LAWS-kee)

Born, Kindersley, Sask., August 25, 1961.
Right wing. Shoots right. 5'11", 190 lbs.
Last amateur club: Prince Albert Raiders (Tier II).

Season	Club	Lea	GP	G	A	TP	PIM	GP	G	A	TP	PIM
					Regular Season					Playoffs		
1981-82	Nova Scotia	AHL	43	15	11	26	31	....	....	....	....	....
1982-83	Nova Scotia	AHL	75	46	42	88	32	6	1	3	4	8
1983-84	**Montreal**	**NHL**	26	1	4	5	4	....	....	....	....	....
	St. Louis	NHL	34	8	6	14	17	9	1	0	1	2
1984-85	St. Louis	NHL	72	22	20	42	21	3	0	0	0	2
1985-86	St. Louis	NHL	56	22	11	33	18	17	10	7	17	13
	NHL Totals		188	53	41	94	60	29	11	7	18	17

Signed as free agent by **Montreal**, October 5, 1981. Traded to **St. Louis** by **Montreal** with Gilbert Delorme and Doug Wickenheiser for Perry Turnbull, December 21, 1983.

PATERSON, JOSEPH (JOE)

Born, Toronto, Ont., June 25, 1960.
Left wing. Shoots left. 6'2", 205 lbs.
Last amateur club: London Knights (OHA).
(Detroit's 5th choice, 87th over-all, in 1979 Entry Draft).

Season	Club	Lea	GP	G	A	TP	PIM	GP	G	A	TP	PIM
					Regular Season					Playoffs		
1978-79	London	OHA	59	22	19	41	158	7	2	3	5	13
1979-80	London	OHA	62	21	50	71	156	....	....	....	....	....
	Kalamazoo	IHL	4	1	2	3	2	3	2	1	3	11
1980-81	**Detroit**	**NHL**	38	2	5	7	53	....	....	....	....	....
	Adirondack	AHL	39	9	16	25	68	....	....	....	....	....
1981-82	**Detroit**	**NHL**	3	0	0	0	0	....	....	....	....	....
	Adirondack	AHL	74	22	28	50	132	5	1	4	5	6
1982-83	**Detroit**	**NHL**	33	2	1	3	14	....	....	....	....	....
	Adirondack	AHL	36	11	10	21	85	6	1	2	3	21
1983-84	Adirondack	AHL	20	10	15	25	43	....	....	....	....	....
	Detroit	**NHL**	41	2	5	7	148	3	0	0	0	7
1984-85	**Philadelphia**	**NHL**	6	0	0	0	31	17	3	4	7	70
	Hershey	AHL	67	26	27	53	173	....	....	....	....	....
1985-86	**Philadelphia**	**NHL**	5	0	0	0	12	....	....	....	....	....
	Hershey	AHL	20	5	10	15	68	....	....	....	....	....
	Los Angeles	NHL	47	9	18	27	153	....	....	....	....	....
	NHL Totals		173	15	29	44	411	20	3	4	7	77

Traded to **Philadelphia** by **Detroit** with Murray Craven for Darryl Sittler, October 19, 1984. Traded to **Los Angeles** by **Philadelphia** for Philadelphia's fourth-round choice (Mark Bar) — acquired earlier — in 1986 Entry Draft, December 18, 1985.

PATERSON, MARK

Born, Ottawa, Ont., February 22, 1964.
Defense. Shoots left. 5'11", 180 lbs.
Last amateur club: Ottawa 67's (OHL).
(Hartford's 2nd choice, 35th over-all, in 1982 Entry Draft).

Season	Club	Lea	GP	G	A	TP	PIM	GP	G	A	TP	PIM
					Regular Season					Playoffs		
1981-82	Ottawa	OHL	64	4	13	17	59	17	1	5	6	40
1982-83	**Hartford**	**NHL**	2	0	0	0	0	....	....	....	....	....
a	Ottawa	OHL	57	7	14	21	140	9	1	4	5	31
1983-84	**Hartford**	**NHL**	9	2	0	2	4	....	....	....	....	....
a	Ottawa	OHL	45	8	16	24	114	13	2	7	9	16
1984-85	**Hartford**	**NHL**	13	1	3	4	24	....	....	....	....	....
	Binghamton	AHL	44	2	18	20	74	....	....	....	....	....
1985-86	**Hartford**	**NHL**	5	0	0	0	5	....	....	....	....	....
	Binghamton	AHL	67	6	12	18	121	6	0	0	0	6
	NHL Totals		29	3	3	6	33	....	....	....	....	....

a OHL Third Team All-Star (1983, 1984).

PATERSON, RICHARD DAVID (RICK)

Born, Kingston, Ont., February 10, 1958.
Center. Shoots right. 5'9", 190 lbs.
Last amateur club: Cornwall Royals (QJHL).
(Chicago's 3rd choice, 46th over-all, in 1978 Amateur Draft).

Season	Club	Lea	GP	G	A	TP	PIM	GP	G	A	TP	PIM
					Regular Season					Playoffs		
1976-77	Cornwall	QJHL	72	31	63	94	90	12	6	9	15	22
1977-78	Cornwall	QJHL	71	58	80	138	105	9	3	7	10	27
1978-79	New Brunswick	AHL	73	21	19	40	30	5	0	1	1	9
	Chicago	**NHL**	....	....	....	....	....	1	0	1	1	0
1979-80	New Brunswick	AHL	55	22	30	52	18	12	5	6	11	9
	Chicago	**NHL**	11	0	2	2	0	7	0	0	0	5
1980-81	New Brunswick	AHL	21	7	8	15	6	....	....	....	....	....
	Chicago	**NHL**	49	8	2	10	18	2	1	0	1	0
1981-82	**Chicago**	**NHL**	48	4	7	11	8	15	3	2	5	21
1982-83	**Chicago**	**NHL**	79	14	9	23	14	13	1	1	2	4
1983-84	**Chicago**	**NHL**	72	7	6	13	41	5	1	1	2	6
1984-85	**Chicago**	**NHL**	79	7	12	19	25	15	1	5	6	15
1985-86	**Chicago**	**NHL**	70	9	3	12	24	3	0	0	0	0
	NHL Totals		408	49	41	90	130	61	7	10	17	51

PATRICK, JAMES

Born, Winnipeg, Man., June 14, 1963.
Defense. Shoots right. 6'2", 185 lbs.
Last amateur club: 1984 Canadian Olympic Team.
(NY Rangers' 1st choice, 9th over-all, in 1981 Entry Draft).

Season	Club	Lea	GP	G	A	TP	PIM	GP	G	A	TP	PIM
					Regular Season					Playoffs		
1980-81ab	Prince Albert	SJHL	59	21	61	82	162	4	1	6	7	....
1981-82cde	North Dakota	WCHA	42	5	24	29	26	....	....	....	....	....
1982-83fg	North Dakota	WCHA	36	12	36	48	29	....	....	....	....	....
1983-84	Cdn. Olympic	....	63	7	24	31	52	....	....	....	....	....
	NY Rangers	**NHL**	12	1	7	8	2	5	0	3	3	2
1984-85	**NY Rangers**	**NHL**	75	8	28	36	71	3	0	0	0	4
1985-86	**NY Rangers**	**NHL**	75	14	29	43	88	16	1	5	6	34
	NHL Totals		162	23	64	87	161	24	1	8	9	40

a Most Valuable Player, 1981 Centennial Cup Tournament.
b First All-Star Team, 1981 Centennial Cup Tournament.
c WCHA Rookie of the Year (1982)
d WCHA Second All-Star Team (1982)
e Named to NCAA All-Tournament Team (1982)
f WCHA First All-Star Team (1983)
g NCAA All American (West) (1983)

PATRICK, STEPHEN GARY (STEVE)

Born, Winnipeg, Man., February 4, 1961.
Right wing. Shoots right. 6'4", 205 lbs.
Last amateur club: Brandon Wheat Kings (WHL).
(Buffalo's 1st choice, 20th over-all, in 1980 Entry Draft).

Season	Club	Lea	GP	G	A	TP	PIM	GP	G	A	TP	PIM
					Regular Season					Playoffs		
1979-80	Brandon	WHL	71	28	38	66	185	11	6	6	12	19
1980-81	Brandon	WHL	34	29	30	59	56	....	....	....	....	....
	Buffalo	**NHL**	30	1	7	8	25	5	0	1	1	6
1981-82	**Buffalo**	**NHL**	41	8	8	16	64	....	....	....	....	....
	Rochester	AHL	38	11	9	20	15	5	3	2	5	12
1982-83	**Buffalo**	**NHL**	56	9	13	22	26	2	0	0	0	0
1983-84	**Buffalo**	**NHL**	11	1	4	5	6	1	0	0	0	0
	Rochester	AHL	30	8	14	22	33	13	2	1	3	18
1984-85	**Buffalo**	**NHL**	14	2	2	4	4	....	....	....	....	....
	NY Rangers	**NHL**	43	11	18	29	63	1	0	0	0	0
1985-86	**NY Rangers**	**NHL**	28	4	3	7	37	....	....	....	....	....
	Quebec	NHL	27	4	13	17	17	3	0	0	0	6
	NHL Totals		250	40	68	108	242	12	0	1	1	12

Traded to **NY Rangers** by **Buffalo** with Jim Wiemer, for Dave Maloney and Chris Renaud, December 6, 1984. Traded to **Quebec** by **NY Rangers** for Wilf Paiement, February 6, 1986.

PATTERSON, COLIN

Born, Rexdale, Ont., May 11, 1960.
Right wing. Shoots right. 6'2", 195 lbs.
Last amateur club: Clarkson College Golden Knights (ECAC)
(Calgary's 14th choice, 240th over-all, in 1982 Entry Draft).

Season	Club	Lea	GP	G	A	TP	PIM	GP	G	A	TP	PIM
					Regular Season					Playoffs		
1980-81	Clarkson	ECAC	34	20	31	51	8	....	....	....	....	....
1981-82	Clarkson	ECAC	35	21	31	52	32	....	....	....	....	....
1982-83	Clarkson	ECAC	31	23	29	52	30	....	....	....	....	....
	Colorado	CHL	2	1	1	2	0	....	....	....	....	....
1983-84	Colorado	CHL	6	2	3	5	9	....	....	....	....	....
	Calgary	**NHL**	56	13	14	27	15	11	1	1	2	6
1984-85	**Calgary**	**NHL**	57	22	21	43	5	4	0	0	0	5
1985-86	**Calgary**	**NHL**	61	14	13	27	22	19	6	3	9	10
	NHL Totals		174	49	48	97	42	34	7	4	11	21

PAVELICH, MARK   (PAV-lich)

Born, Eveleth, Minn., February 28, 1958.
Center. Shoots right. 5'8", 170 lbs.
Last amateur club: 1980 United States Olympic Team.
(St. Louis' 5th choice, 117th over-all, in 1980 Entry Draft).

Season	Club	Lea	GP	G	A	TP	PIM	GP	G	A	TP	PIM
					Regular Season					Playoffs		
1978-79a	Minn.-Duluth	WCHA	37	31	48	79	52	....	....	....	....	....
1979-80	U.S. National	...	53	15	30	45	12	....	....	....	....	....
	U.S. Olympic	...	7	1	6	7	2	....	....	....	....	....
1980-81	Lugano	Swit.	60	24	49	73	....	....	....	....	....	....
1981-82	**NY Rangers**	**NHL**	79	33	43	76	67	6	1	5	6	0
1982-83	**NY Rangers**	**NHL**	78	37	38	75	52	9	4	5	9	12
1983-84	**NY Rangers**	**NHL**	77	29	53	82	96	5	2	4	6	0
1984-85	**NY Rangers**	**NHL**	48	14	31	45	29	3	0	3	3	2
1985-86	**NY Rangers**	**NHL**	59	20	20	40	82	....	....	....	....	....
	NHL Totals		341	133	185	318	326	23	7	17	24	14

a WCHA First All-Star Team (1979)

Signed as free agent by **NY Rangers**, June 5, 1981.

PAVESE, JAMES PETER (JIM) (pa-VEEZ-ee)

Born, New York, N.Y., May 8, 1962.
Defense. Shoots left. 6′2″, 205 lbs.
Last amateur club: Sault Ste. Marie Greyhounds (OHL).
(St. Louis' 2nd choice, 54th over-all, in 1980 Entry Draft).

Season	Club	Lea	Regular Season GP	G	A	TP	PIM	Playoffs GP	G	A	TP	PIM
1980-81	Kitchener	OHA	19	3	12	15	93	....	....	....	....	....
	S.S. Marie	OHA	43	3	25	28	127	19	1	3	4	69
1981-82	S.S. Marie	OHL	26	4	21	25	110	13	2	12	14	38
	St. Louis	**NHL**	42	2	9	11	101	3	0	3	3	2
	Salt Lake	CHL	....	....	....	....	....	1	0	0	0	17
1982-83	**St. Louis**	**NHL**	24	0	2	2	45	4	0	0	0	6
	Salt Lake	CHL	36	5	6	11	165	4	1	3	4	2
1983-84	**St. Louis**	**NHL**	4	0	1	1	19	....	....	....	....	....
	Montana	CHL	47	1	19	20	147					
1984-85	**St. Louis**	**NHL**	51	2	5	7	69	1	0	0	0	5
1985-86	**St. Louis**	**NHL**	69	4	7	11	116	19	0	2	2	51
	NHL Totals		190	8	24	32	350	27	0	5	5	64

PAYNE, STEVEN JOHN (STEVE)

Born, Toronto, Ont., August 16, 1958.
Left wing. Shoots left. 6′2″, 210 lbs.
Last amateur club: Ottawa 67's (OHA).
(Minnesota's 2nd choice, 19th over-all, in 1978 Amateur Draft).

Season	Club	Lea	Regular Season GP	G	A	TP	PIM	Playoffs GP	G	A	TP	PIM
1976-77	Ottawa	OHA	61	25	26	47	22	19	4	14	18	5
1977-78a	Ottawa	OHA	52	57	37	94	22	16	12	8	20	4
1978-79	Oklahoma City	CHL	5	3	4	7	2	....	....	....	....	....
	Minnesota	**NHL**	70	23	17	40	29	....	....	....	....	....
1979-80	**Minnesota**	**NHL**	80	42	43	85	40	15	7	7	14	9
1980-81	**Minnesota**	**NHL**	76	30	28	58	88	19	17	12	29	6
1981-82	**Minnesota**	**NHL**	74	33	45	78	76	4	4	2	6	2
1982-83	**Minnesota**	**NHL**	80	30	39	69	53	9	3	6	9	19
1983-84	**Minnesota**	**NHL**	78	28	31	59	49	15	3	6	9	18
1984-85	**Minnesota**	**NHL**	76	29	22	51	61	9	1	2	3	6
1985-86	**Minnesota**	**NHL**	22	8	4	12	8	....	....	....	....	....
	NHL Totals		556	223	229	452	404	71	35	35	70	60

a OHA Third All-Star Team (1978)

PAWLOWSKI, JERRY

Born, Northville, Mich., September 18, 1965.
Left wing. Shoots left. 5′11″, 180 lbs.
Last amateur club: Harvard University Crimson (ECAC).
(Hartford's 9th choice, 215th overall, in 1985 Entry Draft).

Season	Club	Lea	Regular Season GP	G	A	TP	PIM	Playoffs GP	G	A	TP	PIM
1984-85	Harvard	ECAC	24	0	9	9	26	....	....	....	....	....
1985-86	Harvard	ECAC	34	3	19	22	22	....	....	....	....	....

PAYNTER, KENT

Born, Summerside, PEI, April 17, 1965.
Defense. Shoots left. 6′0″, 185 lbs.
Last amateur club: Kitchener Rangers (OHL).
(Chicago's 9th choice, 159th overall, in 1983 Entry Draft).

Season	Club	Lea	Regular Season GP	G	A	TP	PIM	Playoffs GP	G	A	TP	PIM
1982-83	Kitchener	OHL	65	4	11	15	97	12	1	0	1	20
1983-84	Kitchener	OHL	65	9	27	36	94	16	4	9	13	18
1984-85	Kitchener	OHL	58	7	28	35	93	4	2	1	3	4
1985-86	Nova Scotia	AHL	23	1	2	3	36	....	....	....	....	....

PEARSON, PAUL THEODORE (TED)

Born, Edina, Minn., January 9, 1962.
Left Wing. Shoots left. 5′10″, 175 lbs.
Last amateur club: University of Wisconsin Badgers (WCHA).
(Calgary's 12th choice, 177th over-all, in 1982 Entry Draft).

Season	Club	Lea	Regular Season GP	G	A	TP	PIM	Playoffs GP	G	A	TP	PIM
1981-82	U. of Wisconsin	WCHA	41	15	23	38	85	....	....	....	....	....
1982-83	U. of Wisconsin	WCHA	42	6	9	15	90	....	....	....	....	....
1983-84	U. of Wisconsin	WCHA	35	13	20	33	60	....	....	....	....	....
1984-85	Moncton	AHL	65	9	17	26	70	....	....	....	....	....
1985-86	Salt Lake	NHL	77	28	27	55	68	5	2	4	6	0

PEDERSON, ALLAN

Born, Edmonton, Alta., January 13, 1965.
Defense. Shoots left. 6′3″, 180 lbs.
Last amateur club: Medicine Hat Tigers (WHL).
(Boston's 5th choice, 105th over-all, in 1983 Entry Draft).

Season	Club	Lea	Regular Season GP	G	A	TP	PIM	Playoffs GP	G	A	TP	PIM
1982-83	Medicine Hat	WHL	63	3	10	13	49	5	0	0	0	7
1983-84	Medicine Hat	WHL	44	0	11	11	47	14	0	2	2	24
1984-85	Medicine Hat	WHL	72	6	16	22	66	10	0	0	0	9
1985-86	Moncton	AHL	59	1	8	9	39	3	0	0	0	0

PEDERSON, BARRY ALAN (PEE-der-son)

Born, Big River, Sask., March 13, 1961.
Center. Shoots right. 5′11″, 170 lbs.
Last amateur club: Victoria Cougars (WHL).
(Boston's 1st choice, 18th over-all, in 1980 Entry Draft).

Season	Club	Lea	Regular Season GP	G	A	TP	PIM	Playoffs GP	G	A	TP	PIM
1978-79	Victoria	WHL	72	31	53	84	41	....	....	....	....	....
1979-80	Victoria	WHL	72	52	88	140	50	16	13	14	27	31
1980-81a	Victoria	WHL	55	65	82	147	65	15	15	21	36	10
	Boston	**NHL**	9	1	4	5	6	....	....	....	....	....
1981-82	**Boston**	**NHL**	80	44	48	92	53	11	7	11	18	2
1982-83	**Boston**	**NHL**	77	46	61	107	47	17	14	18	32	21
1983-84	**Boston**	**NHL**	80	39	77	116	64	3	0	1	1	2
1984-85	**Boston**	**NHL**	22	4	8	12	10	....	....	....	....	....
1985-86	**Boston**	**NHL**	79	29	47	76	60	3	1	0	1	0
	NHL Totals		347	163	245	408	240	34	22	30	52	25

a WHL First All-Star Team (1981)
Traded to **Vancouver** by **Boston** for Cam Neely and Vancouver's first-round choice in 1987 Entry Draft, June 6, 1986.

PEDERSON, MARK

Born, Prelate, Sask., January 14, 1968.
Left wing. Shoots left. 6′1″, 200 lbs.
Last amateur club: Medicine Hat Tigers (WHL).
(Montreal's 1st choice, 15th overall, in 1986 Entry Draft).

Season	Club	Lea	Regular Season GP	G	A	TP	PIM	Playoffs GP	G	A	TP	PIM
1984-85	Medicine Hat	WHL	71	42	40	82	63	10	3	2	5	0
1985-86	Medicine Hat	WHL	72	46	60	106	46	25	12	6	18	25

PEER, BRIT

Born, Mississauga, Ont., June 14, 1966.
Right wing. Shoots right. 5′10″, 180 lbs.
Last amateur club: Windsor Compuware Spitfires (OHL).
(Quebec's 10th choice, 183rd overall, in 1985 Entry Draft).

Season	Club	Lea	Regular Season GP	G	A	TP	PIM	Playoffs GP	G	A	TP	PIM
1983-84	S.S. Marie	OHL	34	1	9	10	45	7	0	0	0	0
1984-85	S.S. Marie	OHL	55	19	40	59	92	16	9	6	15	19
1985-86	Windsor	OHL	45	22	33	55	92	16	6	13	19	6

PEERLESS, BLAINE STEPHEN

Born, Edmonton, Alta., October 13, 1961.
Defense. Shoots left. 6′, 195 lbs.
Last amateur club: Spokane Flyers (WHL).

Season	Club	Lea	Regular Season GP	G	A	TP	PIM	Playoffs GP	G	A	TP	PIM
1980-81	Spokane	WHL	70	14	32	48	228	....	....	....	....	....
1981-82	Milwaukee	IHL	80	12	38	50	127	5	0	3	3	25
1982-83	Salt Lake	CHL	45	1	8	9	38	3	0	1	1	0
1983-84	Montana	CHL	73	6	18	24	80	....	....	....	....	....
1984-85	Toledo	IHL	70	5	17	22	137	6	0	0	0	22
1985-86	Milwaukee	IHL	80	10	39	49	110	5	0	3	3	2

Signed as free agent by **St. Louis**, December 28, 1982.

PELUSO, MIKE

Born, Hibbing, Minn., November 8, 1965.
Defense. Shoots left. 6′4″, 200 lbs.
Last amateur club: University of Alaska (Anchorage) Seawolves (G.N.).
(New Jersey's 10th choice, 190th overall, in 1984 Entry Draft).

Season	Club	Lea	Regular Season GP	G	A	TP	PIM	Playoffs GP	G	A	TP	PIM
1984-85	Stratford	OPJHL	52	11	45	56	114	....	....	....	....	....
1985-86	Alaska-Anch.	G.N.	32	2	11	13	59	....	....	....	....	....

PEPLINSKI, JAMES DESMOND (JIM) (peh-PLINS-kee)

Born, Renfrew, Ont., October 24, 1960.
Right wing. Shoots right. 6′3″, 209 lbs.
Last amateur club: Toronto Marlboros (OHA).
(Atlanta's 5th choice, 75th over-all, in 1979 Entry Draft).

Season	Club	Lea	Regular Season GP	G	A	TP	PIM	Playoffs GP	G	A	TP	PIM
1978-79	Toronto	OHA	66	23	32	55	88	3	0	1	1	0
1979-80	Toronto	OHA	67	35	66	101	89	4	1	2	3	14
1980-81	**Calgary**	**NHL**	80	13	25	38	108	16	2	3	5	41
1981-82	**Calgary**	**NHL**	74	30	37	67	115	3	0	1	1	13
1982-83	**Calgary**	**NHL**	80	15	26	41	134	8	1	1	2	45
1983-84	**Calgary**	**NHL**	74	11	22	33	114	11	3	4	7	21
1984-85	**Calgary**	**NHL**	80	16	29	45	111	4	1	3	4	11
1985-86	**Calgary**	**NHL**	77	24	35	59	214	22	5	9	14	107
	NHL Totals		465	109	174	283	796	64	13	20	33	238

PERKINS, TERRY

Born, Campbell River, B.C., June 21, 1966.
Right wing. Shoots right. 6'1", 190 lbs.
Last amateur club: Portland Winterhawks (WHL).
(Quebec's 4th choice, 78th over-all, in 1984 Entry Draft).

				Regular Season					Playoffs			
Season	Club	Lea	GP	G	A	TP	PIM	GP	G	A	TP	PIM
1983-84	Portland	WHL	30	10	10	20	0	14	8.	4	12	2
1984-85	Portland	WHL	63	33	38	71	81	6	0	4	4	5
1985-86	Spokane	WHL	69	71	46	117	74	9	2	5	7	24

PERLINI, FRED   (purr-LEE-nee)

Born, Sault Ste. Marie, Ont., April 12, 1962.
Center. Shoots left. 6'2", 175 lbs.
Last amateur club: Toronto Marlboros (OHL).
(Toronto's 8th choice, 158th over-all, in 1980 Entry Draft).

				Regular Season					Playoffs			
Season	Club	Lea	GP	G	A	TP	PIM	GP	G	A	TP	PIM
1979-80	Toronto	OHA	67	13	18	31	12	4	0	1	1	5
1980-81	Toronto	OHA	35	37	29	66	48	5	0	0	0	4
1981-82	**Toronto**	**NHL**	7	2	3	5	0	....	....	....	....	....
	Toronto	OHL	68	47	64	111	75	10	4	9	13	9
1982-83	St. Catharines	AHL	76	8	22	30	24	....	....	....	....	....
1983-84	**Toronto**	**NHL**	1	0	0	0	0	....	....	....	....	....
	St. Catharines	AHL	79	21	31	52	67	7	1	1	2	17
1984-85	St. Catharines	AHL	77	21	28	49	26	....	....	....	....	....
1985-86	Baltimore	AHL	25	6	4	10	6	....	....	....	....	....
	NHL Totals		**8**	**2**	**3**	**5**	**0**	....	....	....	....	....

PERREAULT, GILBERT (GIL)   (PAIR-oh, ZHIL-behr)

Born, Victoriaville, Que., November 13, 1950.
Center. Shoots left. 6', 200 lbs.
Last amateur club: Montreal Junior Canadiens (OHA).
(Buffalo's 1st choice and 1st over-all in 1970 Amateur Draft).

				Regular Season					Playoffs			
Season	Club	Lea	GP	G	A	TP	PIM	GP	G	A	TP	PIM
1968-69a	Montreal	OHA	54	37	60	97	29	....	....	....	....	....
1969-70ab	Montreal	OHA	54	51	70	121	26	....	....	....	....	....
1970-71c	**Buffalo**	**NHL**	78	38	34	72	19	....	....	....	....	....
1971-72	**Buffalo**	**NHL**	76	26	48	74	24	....	....	....	....	....
1972-73d	**Buffalo**	**NHL**	78	28	60	88	10	6	3	7	10	2
1973-74	**Buffalo**	**NHL**	55	18	33	51	10	....	....	....	....	....
1974-75	**Buffalo**	**NHL**	68	39	57	96	36	17	6	9	15	10
1975-76e	**Buffalo**	**NHL**	80	44	69	113	36	9	4	4	8	4
1976-77e	**Buffalo**	**NHL**	80	39	56	95	30	6	1	8	9	4
1977-78	**Buffalo**	**NHL**	79	41	48	89	20	8	3	2	5	0
1978-79	**Buffalo**	**NHL**	79	27	58	85	20	3	1	0	1	2
1979-80	**Buffalo**	**NHL**	80	40	66	106	57	14	10	11	21	8
1980-81	**Buffalo**	**NHL**	56	20	39	59	56	8	2	10	12	2
1981-82	**Buffalo**	**NHL**	62	31	42	73	40	4	0	7	7	0
1982-83	**Buffalo**	**NHL**	77	30	46	76	34	10	0	7	7	8
1983-84	**Buffalo**	**NHL**	73	31	59	90	32	....	....	....	....	....
1984-85	**Buffalo**	**NHL**	78	30	53	83	42	5	3	5	8	4
1985-86	**Buffalo**	**NHL**	72	21	39	60	28	....	....	....	....	....
	NHL Totals		**1171**	**503**	**807**	**1310**	**494**	**90**	**33**	**70**	**103**	**44**

a OHA First All-Star Team (1969, 1970)
b Named OHA's Most Valuable Player (1970)
c Won Calder Memorial Trophy (1971)
d Won Lady Byng Memorial Trophy (1973)
e NHL Second All-Star Team (1976, 1977)

PERSSON, STEFAN   (PAIR-son)

Born, Umea, Sweden, December 22, 1954.
Defense. Shoots left. 6'1", 190 lbs.
Last amateur club: Swedish National Team.
(NY Islanders' 13th choice, 214th over-all, in 1974 Amateur Draft).

				Regular Season					Playoffs			
Season	Club	Lea	GP	G	A	TP	PIM	GP	G	A	TP	PIM
1974-75	Brynas	Swe.	30	5	7	12	34	6	1	0	1	2
	Swe. National	...	11	0	1	1	0	....	....	....	....	....
1975-76	Brynas	Swe.	34	8	9	17	51	4	0	2	2	10
1976-77	Brynas	Swe.	31	5	11	16	70	4	1	0	1	2
	Swe. National	...	18	4	1	5	34	....	....	....	....	....
1977-78	**NY Islanders**	**NHL**	66	6	50	56	54	7	0	2	2	6
1978-79	**NY Islanders**	**NHL**	78	10	56	66	57	10	0	4	4	8
1979-80	**NY Islanders**	**NHL**	73	4	35	39	76	21	5	10	15	16
1980-81	**NY Islanders**	**NHL**	80	9	52	61	82	7	0	5	5	6
1981-82	**NY Islanders**	**NHL**	70	6	37	43	99	13	1	14	15	9
1982-83	**NY Islanders**	**NHL**	70	4	25	29	71	18	1	5	6	18
1983-84	**NY Islanders**	**NHL**	75	9	24	33	65	10	0	6	6	2
1984-85	**NY Islanders**	**NHL**	54	3	19	22	30	10	0	4	4	4
1985-86	**NY Islanders**	**NHL**	56	1	19	20	40	....	....	....	....	....
	NHL Totals		**622**	**52**	**317**	**369**	**574**	**102**	**7**	**50**	**57**	**69**

PETERSON, BRENT RONALD   (PEE-ter-son)

Born, Calgary, Alta., February 15, 1958.
Center. Shoots right. 6', 190 lbs.
Last amateur club: Portland Winter Hawks (WHL).
(Detroit's 2nd choice, 12th over-all, in 1978 Amateur Draft).

				Regular Season					Playoffs			
Season	Club	Lea	GP	G	A	TP	PIM	GP	G	A	TP	PIM
1976-77	Portland	WHL	69	34	78	112	98	10	3	8	11	8
1977-78	Portland	WHL	51	33	50	83	95	3	1	1	2	2
1978-79	**Detroit**	**NHL**	5	0	0	0	0	....	....	....	....	....
1979-80	**Detroit**	**NHL**	18	1	2	3	2	....	....	....	....	....
	Adirondack	AHL	52	9	22	31	61	5	0	0	0	6
1980-81	**Detroit**	**NHL**	53	6	18	24	24	....	....	....	....	....
	Adirondack	AHL	3	1	0	1	10	....	....	....	....	....
1981-82	**Detroit**	**NHL**	15	1	0	1	6	....	....	....	....	....
	Buffalo	**NHL**	46	9	5	14	43	4	1	0	1	12
1982-83	**Buffalo**	**NHL**	75	13	24	37	38	10	1	2	3	28
1983-84	**Buffalo**	**NHL**	70	9	12	21	52	3	0	1	1	4
1984-85	**Buffalo**	**NHL**	74	12	22	34	47	5	0	0	0	6
1985-86	**Vancouver**	**NHL**	77	8	23	31	94	3	2	0	2	9
	NHL Totals		**433**	**59**	**106**	**165**	**306**	**25**	**4**	**3**	**7**	**59**

Traded to **Buffalo** by **Detroit** with Mike Foligno and Dale McCourt for Danny Gare, Jim Schoenfeld and Derek Smith, December 2, 1981. Claimed by **Vancouver** from **Buffalo** in NHL Waiver Draft, October 7, 1985.

PETIT, MICHEL   (pe-TEE)

Born, St. Malo, Que., February 12, 1964.
Defense. Shoots right. 6'1", 190 lbs.
Last amateur club: St. Jean Castors (QMJHL).
(Vancouver's 1st choice, 11th over-all, in 1982 Entry Draft).

				Regular Season					Playoffs			
Season	Club	Lea	GP	G	A	TP	PIM	GP	G	A	TP	PIM
1981-82a	Sherbrooke	QMJHL	63	10	39	49	106	22	5	20	25	24
1982-83	**Vancouver**	**NHL**	2	0	0	0	0	....	....	....	....	....
a	St. Jean	QMJHL	62	19	67	86	196	3	0	0	0	35
1983-84	Cdn. Olympic	....	19	3	10	13	58	....	....	....	....	....
	Vancouver	**NHL**	44	6	9	15	53	1	0	0	0	0
1984-85	**Vancouver**	**NHL**	69	5	26	31	127	....	....	....	....	....
1985-86	**Vancouver**	**NHL**	32	1	6	7	27	....	....	....	....	....
	Fredericton	AHL	25	0	13	13	79	....	....	....	....	....
	NHL Totals		**147**	**12**	**41**	**53**	**207**	**1**	**0**	**0**	**0**	**0**

a QMJHL First All-Star Team (1982, 1983)

PETTERSSON, JORGEN   (PEH-turr-son, YOR-gen)

Born, Gothenburg, Sweden, July 11, 1956.
Left wing. Shoots left. 6'2", 185 lbs.
Last amateur club: Vastra Frolunda (Sweden).

				Regular Season					Playoffs			
Season	Club	Lea	GP	G	A	TP	PIM	GP	G	A	TP	PIM
1978-79	V. Frolunda	Swe.	35	23	11	34	12	....	....	....	....	....
1979-80	V. Frolunda	Swe.	33	17	15	32	18	8	4	4	8	8
1980-81	**St. Louis**	**NHL**	62	37	36	73	24	11	4	3	7	0
1981-82	**St. Louis**	**NHL**	77	38	31	69	28	7	1	2	3	0
1982-83	**St. Louis**	**NHL**	74	35	38	73	4	4	1	1	2	0
1983-84	**St. Louis**	**NHL**	77	28	34	62	29	11	7	3	10	2
1984-85	**St. Louis**	**NHL**	75	23	32	55	20	3	1	1	2	0
1985-86	**Hartford**	**NHL**	23	5	5	10	2	....	....	....	....	....
	Washington	**NHL**	47	8	16	24	10	8	1	2	3	2
	NHL Totals		**435**	**174**	**192**	**366**	**117**	**44**	**15**	**12**	**27**	**4**

Signed as free agent by **St. Louis**, May 8, 1980. Traded to **Hartford** by **St. Louis** with Mike Liut for Mark Johnson and Greg Millen, February 21, 1985. Traded to **Washington** by **Hartford** for Doug Jarvis, December 6, 1985.

PHAIR, LYLE

Born, Pilot Mound, Man., August 31, 1961.
Left wing. Shoots left. 6'1", 190 lbs.
Last amateur club: Michigan State University Spartans (CCHA).

				Regular Season					Playoffs			
Season	Club	Lea	GP	G	A	TP	PIM	GP	G	A	TP	PIM
1981-82	Michigan St.	CCHA	42	19	24	43	49	....	....	....	....	....
1982-83	Michigan St.	CCHA	42	20	15	35	64	....	....	....	....	....
1983-84	Michigan St.	CCHA	45	15	16	31	58	....	....	....	....	....
1984-85	Michigan St.	CCHA	43	23	27	50	86	....	....	....	....	....
1985-86	New Haven	AHL	35	9	9	18	15	2	0	0	0	0
	Los Angeles	**NHL**	15	0	1	1	2	....	....	....	....	....
	NHL Totals		**15**	**0**	**1**	**1**	**2**	....	....	....	....	....

Signed as a free agent by **Los Angeles**, June 7, 1985.

PICARD, ROBERT RENE JOSEPH   (PEE-car, roh-BEAR)

Born, Montreal, Que., May 25, 1957.
Defense. Shoots left. 6'2", 205 lbs.
Last amateur club: Montreal Juniors (QJHL).
(Washington's 1st choice, 3rd over-all, in 1977 Amateur Draft).

			Regular Season					Playoffs				
Season	Club	Lea	GP	G	A	TP	PIM	GP	G	A	TP	PIM
1975-76a	Montreal	QJHL	72	14	67	81	282	6	2	9	11	25
1976-77bc	Montreal	QJHL	70	32	60	92	267	13	2	10	12	20
1977-78	Washington	NHL	75	10	27	37	101	....	....	....	....	....
1978-79	Washington	NHL	77	21	44	65	85	....	....	....	....	....
1979-80	Washington	NHL	78	11	43	54	122	....	....	....	....	....
1980-81	Toronto	NHL	59	6	19	25	68	....	....	....	....	....
	Montreal	NHL	8	2	2	4	6	1	0	0	0	0
1981-82	Montreal	NHL	62	2	26	28	106	5	1	1	2	7
1982-83	Montreal	NHL	64	7	31	38	60	3	0	0	0	0
1983-84	Montreal	NHL	7	0	2	2	0	....	....	....	....	....
	Winnipeg	NHL	62	6	16	22	34	3	0	0	0	12
1984-85	Winnipeg	NHL	78	12	22	34	107	8	2	2	4	8
1985-86	Winnipeg	NHL	20	2	5	7	17	....	....	....	....	....
	Quebec	NHL	48	7	27	34	36	3	0	2	2	2
	NHL Totals		638	86	264	350	742	23	3	5	8	29

a QJHL Second All-Star Team (1976)
b QJHL First All-Star Team (1977)
c Named QJHL's Top Defenseman (1977)
Traded to **Toronto** by **Washington** with Tim Coulis and Washington's second round choice (Bob McGill) in 1980 Entry Draft for Mike Palmateer and Toronto's third round choice (Torrie Robertson) in 1980 Entry Draft, June 11, 1980. Traded to **Montreal** by **Toronto** for Michel Larocque, March 10, 1981. Traded to **Winnipeg** by **Montreal** for Winnipeg's third round choice (Patrick Roy) in 1984 Entry Draft, November 4, 1983. Traded to **Quebec** by **Winnipeg** for Mario Marois, November 27, 1985.

PICHETTE, DAVE   (pee-SHETT)

Born, Grand Falls, Nfld., February 4, 1960.
Defense. Shoots left. 6'3", 190 lbs.
Last amateur club: Quebec Remparts (QJHL).

			Regular Season					Playoffs				
Season	Club	Lea	GP	G	A	TP	PIM	GP	G	A	TP	PIM
1978-79	Quebec	QJHL	57	10	16	26	134	6	1	1	2	35
1979-80	Quebec	QJHL	56	8	19	27	129	5	1	3	4	8
1980-81	Hershey	AHL	20	2	3	5	37	....	....	....	....	....
	Quebec	NHL	46	4	16	20	62	1	0	0	0	14
1981-82	Quebec	NHL	67	7	30	37	152	16	2	4	6	22
1982-83	Fredericton	AHL	16	3	11	14	14	....	....	....	....	....
	Quebec	NHL	53	3	21	24	49	2	0	1	1	0
1983-84	Quebec	NHL	23	2	7	9	12	....	....	....	....	....
	Fredericton	AHL	10	2	1	3	13	....	....	....	....	....
	St. Louis	NHL	23	0	11	11	6	9	1	2	3	18
1984-85	New Jersey	NHL	71	17	40	57	41	....	....	....	....	....
1985-86	New Jersey	NHL	33	7	12	19	22	....	....	....	....	....
	Maine	AHL	25	4	15	19	28	....	....	....	....	....
	NHL Totals		316	40	137	177	344	28	3	7	10	54

Signed as free agent by **Quebec**, October 31, 1979. Traded to **St. Louis** by **Quebec** for Andre Dore, February 10, 1984. Claimed by **New Jersey** from **St. Louis** in NHL Waiver Draft, October 9, 1984.

PIERCE, RANDY STEPHEN

Born, Arnprior, Ont., November 23, 1957.
Right wing. Shoots right. 5'11", 185 lbs.
Last amateur club: Sudbury Wolves (OHA).
(Colorado's 3rd choice, 47th over-all, in 1977 Amateur Draft).

			Regular Season					Playoffs				
Season	Club	Lea	GP	G	A	TP	PIM	GP	G	A	TP	PIM
1975-76	Sudbury	OHA	56	21	44	65	72	15	9	16	25	13
1976-77	Sudbury	OHA	60	38	60	98	67	6	2	3	5	7
1977-78	Phoenix	CHL	12	3	1	4	11	....	....	....	....	....
	Hampton	AHL	3	0	1	1	2	....	....	....	....	....
	Colorado	NHL	35	9	10	19	15	2	0	0	0	0
1978-79	Colorado	NHL	70	19	17	36	35	....	....	....	....	....
	Philadelphia	AHL	1	0	0	0	0	....	....	....	....	....
1979-80	Colorado	NHL	75	16	23	39	100	....	....	....	....	....
1980-81	Colorado	NHL	55	9	21	30	52	....	....	....	....	....
1981-82	Colorado	NHL	5	0	0	0	4	....	....	....	....	....
	Fort Worth	CHL	15	6	6	12	19	....	....	....	....	....
1982-83	New Jersey	NHL	3	0	0	0	0	....	....	....	....	....
	Wichita	CHL	14	4	8	12	4	....	....	....	....	....
	Binghamton	AHL	46	14	41	55	33	2	0	1	1	0
1983-84	Hartford	NHL	17	6	3	9	9	....	....	....	....	....
	Binghamton	AHL	46	22	24	46	41	....	....	....	....	....
1984-85	Hartford	NHL	17	3	2	5	8	....	....	....	....	....
	Binghamton	AHL	31	6	10	16	45	6	2	1	3	6
1985-86	Salt Lake	IHL	20	5	5	10	25	....	....	....	....	....
	NHL Totals		277	62	76	138	223	2	0	0	0	0

Signed as free agent by **Hartford**, October 6, 1983.

PILON, NEIL

Born, Merritt, B.C., April 26, 1967.
Defense. Shoots right. 6'4", 185 lbs.
Last amateur club: Moose Jaw Warriors (WHL).
(NY Rangers' 7th choice, 133rd overall, in 1985 Entry Draft).

			Regular Season					Playoffs				
Season	Club	Lea	GP	G	A	TP	PIM	GP	G	A	TP	PIM
1983-84	Moose Jaw	WHL	9	0	2	2	0	2	0	0	0	2
1984-85	Moose Jaw	WHL	52	1	6	7	40	14	0	3	3	6
1985-86	Moose Jaw	WHL	59	2	18	20	112	13	1	1	2	19

PIVONKA, MICHAL

Born, Kladno, Czechoslovakia, January 28, 1967.
Center. Shoots left. 6'2", 190 lbs.
Last amateur club: Dukla-Jihlava (Czechoslovakia).
(Washington's 3rd choice, 59th over-all, in 1984 Entry Draft).

			Regular Season					Playoffs				
Season	Club	Lea	GP	G	A	TP	PIM	GP	G	A	TP	PIM
1985-86	Dukla-Jihlava	Czech			UNAVAILABLE							

PLANTE, CAM

Born, Brandon, Man., March 12, 1964.
Defense. Shoots left. 6'1", 195 lbs.
Last amateur club: Brandon Wheat Kings (WHL).
(Toronto's 5th choice, 128th over-all, in 1983 Entry Draft).

			Regular Season					Playoffs				
Season	Club	Lea	GP	G	A	TP	PIM	GP	G	A	TP	PIM
1980-81	Brandon	WHL	70	3	14	17	17	5	0	2	2	0
1981-82	Brandon	WHL	36	4	12	16	22	4	0	6	6	4
1982-83	Brandon	WHL	56	19	56	75	71	....	....	....	....	....
1983-84a	Brandon	WHL	72	22	118	140	96	11	4	16	20	14
1984-85	Toronto	NHL	2	0	0	0	0	....	....	....	....	....
	St. Catharines	AHL	54	5	31	36	42	....	....	....	....	....
1985-86	St. Catharines	AHL	49	6	15	21	28	5	0	3	3	2
	NHL Totals		2	0	0	0	0	....	....	....	....	....

a WHL First All-Star Team, East Division (1984)

PLAYFAIR, JAMES (JIM)

Born, Fort St. James, B.C., May 22, 1964.
Defense. Shoots left. 6'4", 200 lbs.
Last amateur club: Portland Winter Hawks (WHL).
(Edmonton's 1st choice, 20th over-all, in 1982 Entry Draft).

			Regular Season					Playoffs				
Season	Club	Lea	GP	G	A	TP	PIM	GP	G	A	TP	PIM
1981-82	Portland	WHL	70	4	13	17	121	15	1	2	3	21
1982-83	Portland	WHL	63	8	27	35	218	14	0	5	5	16
1983-84	Edmonton	NHL	2	1	1	2	2	....	....	....	....	....
	Portland	WHL	16	5	6	11	38	....	....	....	....	....
	Calgary	WHL	60	11	15	26	134	4	0	1	1	2
1984-85	Nova Scotia	AHL	41	0	4	4	107	....	....	....	....	....
1985-86	Nova Scotia	AHL	73	2	12	14	160	....	....	....	....	....
	NHL Totals		2	1	1	2	2	....	....	....	....	....

PLAYFAIR, LARRY WILLIAM

Born, Fort St. James, B.C., June 23, 1958.
Defense. Shoots left. 6'4", 200 lbs.
Last amateur club: Portland Winter Hawks (WHL).
(Buffalo's 1st choice, 13th over-all, in 1978 Amateur Draft).

			Regular Season					Playoffs				
Season	Club	Lea	GP	G	A	TP	PIM	GP	G	A	TP	PIM
1976-77	Portland	WHL	65	2	17	19	199	8	0	0	0	4
1977-78a	Portland	WHL	71	13	19	32	402	8	0	2	2	58
1978-79	Buffalo	NHL	26	0	3	3	60	....	....	....	....	....
	Hershey	AHL	45	0	12	12	148	....	....	....	....	....
1979-80	Buffalo	NHL	79	2	10	12	145	14	0	2	2	29
1980-81	Buffalo	NHL	75	3	9	12	169	8	0	0	0	26
1981-82	Buffalo	NHL	77	6	10	16	258	4	0	0	0	22
1982-83	Buffalo	NHL	79	4	13	17	180	5	0	1	1	11
1983-84	Buffalo	NHL	76	5	11	16	211	3	0	0	0	0
1984-85	Buffalo	NHL	72	3	14	17	157	5	0	3	3	9
1985-86	Buffalo	NHL	47	1	2	3	100	....	....	....	....	....
	Los Angeles	NHL	14	0	1	1	26	....	....	....	....	....
	NHL Totals		545	24	73	97	1306	39	0	6	6	97

a WHL First All-Star Team (1978)

Traded to **Los Angeles** by **Buffalo** with Sean McKenna and Ken Baumgartner for Brian Engblom and Doug Smith, January 30, 1986.

PLETT, WILLI

Born, Paraguay, South America, June 7, 1955.
Right wing. Shoots right. 6'3", 205 lbs.
Last amateur club: St. Catharines Black Hawks (OHA).
(Atlanta's 4th choice, 80th over-all, in 1975 Amateur Draft).

			Regular Season					Playoffs				
Season	Club	Lea	GP	G	A	TP	PIM	GP	G	A	TP	PIM
1974-75	St. Catharines	OHA	22	6	8	14	63	4	1	1	2	42
1975-76	Atlanta	NHL	4	0	0	0	0	....	....	....	....	....
	Tulsa	CHL	73	30	20	50	163	9	*5	4	9	21
1976-77	Tulsa	CHL	14	8	4	12	68	....	....	....	....	....
a	Atlanta	NHL	64	33	23	56	123	3	1	0	1	19
1977-78	Atlanta	NHL	78	22	21	43	171	....	....	....	....	....
1978-79	Atlanta	NHL	74	23	20	43	213	2	1	0	1	29
1979-80	Atlanta	NHL	76	13	19	32	231	4	1	0	1	15
1980-81	Calgary	NHL	78	38	30	68	239	15	8	4	12	89
1981-82	Calgary	NHL	78	21	36	57	288	3	1	2	3	39
1982-83	Minnesota	NHL	71	25	14	39	170	9	1	3	4	38
1983-84	Minnesota	NHL	73	15	23	38	316	16	6	2	8	51
1984-85	Minnesota	NHL	47	14	14	28	157	9	3	6	9	67
1985-86	Minnesota	NHL	59	10	7	17	231	5	0	1	1	45
	NHL Totals		702	214	207	421	2139	66	22	18	40	392

a Won Calder Memorial Trophy (1977)

Traded to **Minnesota** by **Calgary** with Calgary's fourth choice (Dusan Pasek) in 1982 Entry Draft for Steve Christoff, Bill Nyrop and Minnesota's second choice (Dave Reierson) in 1982 Entry Draft, June 7, 1982.

PODDUBNY, WALTER MICHAEL (WALT)   (puh-DUBB-nee)

Born, Thunder Bay, Ont., February 14, 1960.
Center. Shoots left. 6'1", 205 lbs.
Last amateur club: Kingston Canadians (OHA.).
(Edmonton's 4th choice, 90th over-all, in 1980 Entry Draft).

			Regular Season					Playoffs				
Season	Club	Lea	GP	G	A	TP	PIM	GP	G	A	TP	PIM
1979-80	Kitchener	OHA	19	3	9	12	35	....	....	....	....	....
	Kingston	OHA	43	30	17	47	36	3	0	2	2	0
1980-81	Milwaukee	IHL	5	4	2	6	4	....	....	....	....	....
	Wichita	CHL	70	21	29	50	207	11	1	6	7	26
1981-82	Wichita	CHL	60	35	46	81	79	....	....	....	....	....
	Edmonton	**NHL**	4	0	0	0	0	....	....	....	....	....
	Toronto	**NHL**	11	3	4	7	8	....	....	....	....	....
1982-83	Toronto	NHL	72	28	31	59	71	4	3	1	4	0
1983-84	Toronto	NHL	38	11	14	25	48	....	....	....	....	....
1984-85	Toronto	NHL	32	5	15	20	26	....	....	....	....	....
	St. Catharines	AHL	8	5	7	12	10	....	....	....	....	....
1985-86	Toronto	NHL	33	12	22	34	25	9	4	1	5	4
	St. Catharines	AHL	37	28	27	55	52	....	....	....	....	....
	NHL Totals		190	59	86	145	178	13	7	2	9	4

Traded to **Toronto** by **Edmonton** with Phil Drouilliard for Laurie Boschman, March 28, 1982.
Traded to **NY Rangers** by **Toronto** for Mike Allison, August 18, 1986.

PODLOSKI, RAY

Born, Edmonton, Alta., January 5, 1966.
Center. Shoots left. 6'1", 200 lbs.
Last amateur club: Portland Winter Hawks (WHL).
(Boston's 2nd choice, 40th over-all, in 1984 Entry Draft).

			Regular Season					Playoffs				
Season	Club	Lea	GP	G	A	TP	PIM	GP	G	A	TP	PIM
1982-83	Red Deer	AJHL	59	49	49	97	47	....	....	....	....	....
1983-84	Portland	WHL	66	46	50	96	44	14	8	14	22	14
1984-85	Portland	WHL	67	63	75	138	41	6	3	1	4	7
1985-86	Portland	WHL	66	59	75	134	68	7	1	9	10	8

POESCHEK, RUDY

Born, Terrace, B.C., September 29, 1966.
Defense. Shoots right. 6'2", 210 lbs.
Last amateur club: Kamloops Blazers (WHL).
(NY Rangers' 12th choice, 238th overall, in 1985 Entry Draft).

			Regular Season					Playoffs				
Season	Club	Lea	GP	G	A	TP	PIM	GP	G	A	TP	PIM
1983-84	Kamloops	WHL	47	3	9	12	93	8	0	2	2	7
1984-85	Kamloops	WHL	34	6	7	13	100	15	0	3	3	56
1985-86	Kamloops	WHL	32	3	13	16	92	16	3	7	10	40

POLAK, GREGG

Born, Providence, RI, July 16, 1967.
Right wing. Shoots left. 6'2", 186 lbs.
Last amateur club. Northeastern University Huskies (H.E.).
(New Jersey's 5th choice, 66th overall, in 1985 Entry Draft).

			Regular Season					Playoffs				
Season	Club	Lea	GP	G	A	TP	PIM	GP	G	A	TP	PIM
1985-86	Northeastern	H.E.	4	1	1	2	6	....	....	....	....	....

POLONICH, DENNIS DANIEL   (poh-LAHN-itch)

Born, Foam Lake, Sask., December 4, 1953.
Center/Right wing. Shoots right. 5'6", 165 lbs.
Last amateur club: Flin Flon Bombers (WHL).
(Detroit's 8th choice, 118th over-all, in 1973 Amateur Draft).

			Regular Season					Playoffs				
Season	Club	Lea	GP	G	A	TP	PIM	GP	G	A	TP	PIM
1971-72	Flin Flon	WHL	65	9	21	30	200	7	0	1	1	41
1972-73	Flin Flon	WHL	68	26	48	74	222	....	....	....	....	....
1973-74	London	Eng.	67	17	43	60	57	....	....	....	....	....
1974-75	**Detroit**	**NHL**	4	0	0	0	0	....	....	....	....	....
	Virginia	AHL	60	14	20	34	194	5	0	2	2	30
1975-76	Kalamazoo	IHL	5	1	8	9	32	....	....	....	....	....
	Detroit	**NHL**	57	11	12	23	302	....	....	....	....	....
1976-77	**Detroit**	**NHL**	79	18	28	46	274	....	....	....	....	....
1977-78	**Detroit**	**NHL**	79	16	19	35	254	7	1	0	1	19
1978-79	**Detroit**	**NHL**	62	10	12	22	208	....	....	....	....	....
1979-80	**Detroit**	**NHL**	66	2	8	10	127	....	....	....	....	....
1980-81	**Detroit**	**NHL**	32	2	2	4	77	....	....	....	....	....
	Adirondack	AHL	40	16	13	29	99	14	9	5	14	95
1981-82	Adirondack	AHL	80	30	26	56	202	5	2	2	4	0
1982-83	**Detroit**	**NHL**	11	0	1	1	0	....	....	....	....	....
	Adirondack	AHL	61	18	22	40	128	6	2	2	4	10
1983-84	Adirondack	AHL	66	14	26	40	122	....	....	....	....	....
1984-85	Adirondack	AHL	53	18	17	35	133	....	....	....	....	....
1985-86	Muskegon	IHL	78	32	36	68	222	14	8	10	18	36
	NHL Totals		390	59	82	141	1242	7	1	0	1	19

PONER, JIRI

Born, Pardubice, Czechoslovakia., February 9, 1964.
Left Wing. Shoots left. 6'0", 175 lbs.
Last amateur club: Landshut (West Germany).
(Minnesota's 8th choice, 89th over-all, in 1984 Entry Draft).

			Regular Season					Playoffs				
Season	Club	Lea	GP	G	A	TP	PIM	GP	G	A	TP	PIM
1983-84	Landshut	W. Ger.	44	72	75	147	N/A	....	....	....	....	....
1984-85	Springfield	AHL	27	2	4	6	17	....	....	....	....	....
	Indianapolis	IHL	26	3	10	13	26	....	....	....	....	....
1985-86	Indianapolis	IHL	3	0	0	0	2	....	....	....	....	....
	Muskegon	IHL	70	17	43	60	118	9	5	3	8	6

POOLEY, PAUL

Born, Exeter, Ont., August 2, 1960.
Center. Shoots right. 6', 177 lbs.
Last amateur club: Ohio State University Buckeyes (CCHA).

			Regular Season					Playoffs				
Season	Club	Lea	GP	G	A	TP	PIM	GP	G	A	TP	PIM
1980-81a	Ohio State	CCHA	38	28	30	60	41	....	....	....	....	....
1981-82	Ohio State	CCHA	34	21	24	45	34	....	....	....	....	....
1982-83	Ohio State	CCHA	36	33	36	69	50	....	....	....	....	....
1983-84bc	Ohio State	CCHA	41	32	64	96	40	....	....	....	....	....
1984-85	**Winnipeg**	**NHL**	12	0	2	2	0	....	....	....	....	....
	Sherbrooke	AHL	57	18	17	35	16	17	2	2	4	7
1985-86	**Winnipeg**	**NHL**	3	0	1	1	0	....	....	....	....	....
	Sherbrooke	AHL	70	20	21	41	31	....	....	....	....	....
	NHL Totals		15	0	3	3	0	....	....	....	....	....

a CCHA Rookie of the Year (1981)
b CCHA First All-Star Team (1984)
c CCHA Player of the Year (1984)
Signed as free agent by **Winnipeg**, May 24, 1984.

POOLEY, PERRY

Born, Exeter, Ont., August 2, 1960.
Right wing. Shoots right. 6', 177 lbs.
Last amateur club: Ohio State University Buckeyes (CCHA).

			Regular Season					Playoffs				
Season	Club	Lea	GP	G	A	TP	PIM	GP	G	A	TP	PIM
1980-81	Ohio State	CCHA	37	9	15	24	62	....	....	....	....	....
1981-82	Ohio State	CCHA	34	8	8	16	24	....	....	....	....	....
1982-83	Ohio State	CCHA	40	29	26	55	36	....	....	....	....	....
1983-84	Ohio State	CCHA	41	39	40	79	28	....	....	....	....	....
1984-85	Sherbrooke	AHL	69	10	18	28	16	13	1	1	2	0
1985-86	Sherbrooke	AHL	67	12	19	31	15	....	....	....	....	....

Signed as free agent by **Winnipeg**, May 24, 1984.

PORTER, DON

Born, Geraldton, Ont., May 25, 1966.
Left wing. Shoots left. 6'3", 190 lbs.
Last amateur club: Michigan Tech University Huskies (WCHA).
(St. Louis' 10th choice, 148th overall, in 1984 Entry Draft).

			Regular Season					Playoffs				
Season	Club	Lea	GP	G	A	TP	PIM	GP	G	A	TP	PIM
1983-84	Michigan Tech	WCHA	31	4	4	8	8	....	....	....	....	....
1984-85	Michigan Tech	WCHA	34	12	11	23	10	....	....	....	....	....
1985-86	Michigan Tech	WCHA	40	17	10	27	28	....	....	....	....	....

POSA, VICTOR

Born, Bari, Italy, November 5, 1966.
Left wing/defense. Shoots left. 6'0", 195 lbs.
Last amateur club: Toronto Marlboros (OHL).
(Chicago's 7th choice, 137th overall, in 1985 Entry Draft).

			Regular Season					Playoffs				
Season	Club	Lea	GP	G	A	TP	PIM	GP	G	A	TP	PIM
1984-85	Wisconsin	WCHA	33	1	5	6	47	....	....	....	....	....
1985-86	Toronto	OHL	48	28	39	62	116	....	....	....	....	....

POSAVAD, MIKE

Born, Brantford, Ont., January 3, 1964.
Defense. Shoots right. 5'11", 195 lbs.
Last amateur club: Peterborough Petes (OHL).
(St. Louis' 1st choice, 50th over-all, in 1982 Entry Draft).

			Regular Season					Playoffs				
Season	Club	Lea	GP	G	A	TP	PIM	GP	G	A	TP	PIM
1981-82a	Peterborough	OHL	64	7	23	30	110	9	3	4	7	15
1982-83b	Peterborough	OHL	70	1	36	37	68	4	0	2	2	2
1983-84	Peterborough	OHL	63	3	25	28	78	8	3	2	5	8
1984-85	Peoria	IHL	67	2	19	21	58	19	1	5	6	42
1985-86	**St. Louis**	**NHL**	6	0	0	0	0	....	....	....	....	....
	Peoria	IHL	72	1	17	18	75	11	0	1	1	13
	NHL Totals		6	0	0	0	0	....	....	....	....	....

a OHL Second All-Star Team (1982)
b OHL Third All-Star Team (1983)

POSMA, MIKE

Born, Utica, NY, December 16, 1967.
Defense. Shoots right. 6'1", 190 lbs.
Last amateur club: Buffalo Jr. Sabres (Jr. B).
(St. Louis' 2nd choice, 31st overall, in 1986 Entry Draft).

			Regular Season					Playoffs				
Season	Club	Lea	GP	G	A	TP	PIM	GP	G	A	TP	PIM
1985-86	Buffalo Jr.	Jr. B	40	16	47	63	62	....	....	....	....	....

POTVIN, DENIS CHARLES (POT-vahn)

Born, Ottawa, Ont., October 29, 1953.
Defense. Shoots left. 6', 205 lbs.
Last amateur club: Ottawa 67's (OHA).
(NY Islanders' 1st choice and 1st over-all in 1973 Amateur Draft).

Season	Club	Lea	GP	G	A	TP	PIM	GP	G	A	TP	PIM
1968-69	Ottawa	OHA	46	12	25	37	83	....	....	....	....	....
1969-70	Ottawa	OHA	42	13	18	31	97	....	....	....	....	....
1970-71	Ottawa	OHA	57	20	58	78	200	....	....	....	....	....
1971-72a	Ottawa	OHA	48	15	45	60	188	....	....	....	....	....
1972-73a	Ottawa	OHA	61	35	88	123	232	....	....	....	....	....
1973-74b	NY Islanders	NHL	77	17	37	54	175	....	....	....	....	....
1974-75c	NY Islanders	NHL	79	21	55	76	105	17	5	9	14	30
1975-76cd	NY Islanders	NHL	78	31	67	98	100	13	5	*14	19	32
1976-77e	NY Islanders	NHL	80	25	55	80	103	12	6	4	10	20
1977-78cd	NY Islanders	NHL	80	30	64	94	81	7	2	2	4	6
1978-79cd	NY Islanders	NHL	73	31	70	101	58	10	4	7	11	8
1979-80	NY Islanders	NHL	31	8	33	41	44	21	6	13	19	24
1980-81c	NY Islanders	NHL	74	20	56	76	104	18	8	17	25	16
1981-82	NY Islanders	NHL	60	24	37	61	83	19	5	16	21	30
1982-83e	NY Islanders	NHL	69	12	54	66	60	20	8	12	20	22
1983-84	NY Islanders	NHL	78	22	63	85	87	20	1	5	6	28
1984-85	NY Islanders	NHL	77	17	51	68	96	10	3	2	5	10
1985-86	NY Islanders	NHL	74	21	38	59	78	3	0	1	1	0
	NHL Totals		930	279	680	959	1174	170	53	102	155	226

a OHA First All-Star Team (1972, 1973)
b Won Calder Memorial Trophy (1974)
c NHL First All-Star Team (1975, 1976, 1978, 1979, 1981)
d Won James Norris Memorial Trophy (1976, 1978, 1979)
e NHL Second All-Star Team (1977, 1983).

POUDRIER, DANIEL (POOH-dree-ay)

Born, Thetford Mines, Que., February 15, 1964.
Defense. Shoots left. 6'2", 175 lbs.
Last amateur club: Drummondville Volitgeurs (QMJHL).
(Quebec's 6th choice, 131st over-all, in 1982 Entry Draft).

Season	Club	Lea	GP	G	A	TP	PIM	GP	G	A	TP	PIM
1981-82	Shawinigan	QMJHL	64	6	18	24	20	14	1	1	2	2
1982-83	Shawinigan	QMJHL	67	6	28	34	31	10	1	2	3	2
1983-84	Drummondville	QMJHL	64	7	28	35	15	10	2	3	5	4
1984-85	Fredericton	AHL	1	0	0	0	0	....	....	....	....	....
	Muskegon	IHL	82	9	30	39	12	17	2	6	8	2
1985-86	Quebec	NHL	13	1	5	6	10	....	....	....	....	....
	Fredericton	AHL	65	5	26	31	9	6	0	3	3	0
	NHL Totals		13	1	5	6	10	....	....	....	....	....

POULIN, DAVID JAMES (DAVE) (POOL-in)

Born, Timmins, Ont., December 17, 1958.
Center. Shoots left. 5'11", 180 lbs.
Last amateur club: University of Notre Dame Fighting Irish (CCHA).

Season	Club	Lea	GP	G	A	TP	PIM	GP	G	A	TP	PIM
1978-79	Notre Dame	WCHA	37	28	31	59	32	....	....	....	....	....
1979-80	Notre Dame	WCHA	24	19	24	43	46	....	....	....	....	....
1980-81	Notre Dame	WCHA	35	13	22	35	53	....	....	....	....	....
1981-82a	Notre Dame	CCHA	39	29	30	59	44	....	....	....	....	....
1982-83	Rogle	Swe.	32	35	27	62	64	....	....	....	....	....
	Maine	AHL	16	7	9	16	2	....	....	....	....	....
	Philadelphia	NHL	2	2	0	2	2	3	1	3	4	9
1983-84	Philadelphia	NHL	73	31	45	76	47	3	0	0	0	2
1984-85	Philadelphia	NHL	73	30	44	74	59	11	3	5	8	6
1985-86	Philadelphia	NHL	79	27	42	69	49	5	2	0	2	2
	NHL Totals		227	90	131	221	157	22	6	8	14	19

a CCHA Second All-Star Team (1982).
Signed as free agent by **Philadelphia**, March 8, 1983.

POUND, IAN

Born, Brockville, Ont., January 22, 1967.
Defense. Shoots left. 6'1", 185 lbs.
Last amateur club: Kitchener Rangers (OHL).
(Chicago's 11th choice, 221st overall, in 1985 Entry Draft).

Season	Club	Lea	GP	G	A	TP	PIM	GP	G	A	TP	PIM
1984-85	Kitchener	OHL	57	1	9	10	60	4	0	0	0	0
1985-86	Kitchener	OHL	63	2	12	14	87	3	1	0	1	6

POWERS, WILLIAM (BILL)

Born, Cambridge, Mass., April 10, 1966.
Center. Shoots right. 6'0", 175 lbs.
Last amateur club: University of Michigan Wolverines (CCHA).
(Philadelphia's 11th choice, 184th overall, in 1984 Entry Draft).

Season	Club	Lea	GP	G	A	TP	PIM	GP	G	A	TP	PIM
1985-86	U. of Michigan	CCHA	38	15	28	43	10	....	....	....	....	....

PRATT, TOM

Born, Lake Placid, N.Y., August 28, 1965.
Defense. Shoots left. 6', 190 lbs.
Last amateur club: Bowling Green State University Falcons (CCHA).
(Calgary's 12th choice, 191st overall in 1983 Entry Draft).

Season	Club	Lea	GP	G	A	TP	PIM	GP	G	A	TP	PIM
1983-84	St. Lawrence	ECAC	32	4	8	12	70	....	....	....	....	....
1984-85	St. Lawrence	ECAC	31	2	4	6	32	....	....	....	....	....
1985-86	Bowling Green	CCHA	38	1	4	5	74	....	....	....	....	....

PRESLEY, WAYNE

Born, Dearborn, Michigan, March 23, 1965.
Right wing. Shoots right. 5'11", 170 lbs.
Last amateur club: Kitchener Rangers (OHL).
(Chicago's 2nd choice, 39th over-all, in 1983 Entry Draft).

Season	Club	Lea	GP	G	A	TP	PIM	GP	G	A	TP	PIM
1981-82	Detroit Little Caesars	Midget	61	38	56	94	146	....	....	....	....	....
1982-83	Kitchener	OHL	70	39	48	87	99	12	1	4	5	9
1983-84a	Kitchener	OHL	70	63	76	139	156	16	12	16	28	38
1984-85	Chicago	NHL	3	0	1	1	0	....	....	....	....	....
	Kitchener	OHL	31	25	21	46	77	....	....	....	....	....
	S.S. Marie	OHL	11	5	9	14	14	16	13	9	22	13
1985-86	Chicago	NHL	38	7	8	15	38	3	0	0	0	0
	Nova Scotia	AHL	29	6	9	15	22	....	....	....	....	....
	NHL Totals		41	7	9	16	38	3	0	0	0	0

a OHL First All-Star Team (1984)

PRESTIDGE, MICHAEL DAVID (MIKE)

Born, Weston, Ont., August 14, 1959.
Center. Shoots left. 6'3", 205 lbs.
Last amateur club: Clarkson College Golden Knights (ECAC)

Season	Club	Lea	GP	G	A	TP	PIM	GP	G	A	TP	PIM
1978-79	Clarkson	ECAC	31	16	24	40	2	....	....	....	....	....
1979-80	Clarkson	ECAC	34	28	30	58	24	....	....	....	....	....
1980-81	Clarkson	ECAC	31	13	17	30	22	....	....	....	....	....
1981-82	Oklahoma City	CHL	53	20	19	39	6	4	3	1	4	0
1982-83	Colorado	CHL	62	13	26	39	17	2	0	1	1	0
1983-84	Peoria	IHL	68	40	40	80	4	....	....	....	....	....
1984-85	Peoria	IHL	82	42	48	90	27	17	6	9	15	11
1985-86	Peoria	IHL	81	31	56	87	16	10	1	7	8	7

Signed as free agent by **Calgary**, October 5, 1981.

PRESTON, RICHARD JOHN (RICH)

Born, Regina, Sask., May 22, 1952.
Right wing. Shoots right. 5'11", 185 lbs.
Last amateur club: University of Denver Pioneers (WCHA).

Season	Club	Lea	GP	G	A	TP	PIM	GP	G	A	TP	PIM
1972-73	U. of Denver	WCHA	39	23	25	48	24	....	....	....	....	....
1973-74	U. of Denver	WCHA	38	20	25	45	36	....	....	....	....	....
1974-75	Houston	WHA	78	20	21	41	10	13	1	6	7	6
1975-76	Houston	WHA	77	22	33	55	33	17	4	6	10	8
1976-77	Houston	WHA	80	38	41	79	54	11	3	5	8	10
1977-78	Houston	WHA	73	25	25	50	52	....	....	....	....	....
1978-79	Winnipeg	WHA	80	28	32	60	88	10	8	5	13	15
1979-80	Chicago	NHL	80	31	30	61	70	7	0	3	3	2
1980-81	Chicago	NHL	47	7	14	21	24	3	0	1	1	0
1981-82	Chicago	NHL	75	15	28	43	30	15	2	4	6	21
1982-83	Chicago	NHL	79	25	28	53	64	13	2	7	9	25
1983-84	Chicago	NHL	75	10	18	28	50	5	0	1	1	4
1984-85	New Jersey	NHL	75	12	15	27	26	....	....	....	....	....
1985-86	New Jersey	NHL	76	19	22	41	65	....	....	....	....	....
	NHL Totals		507	119	155	274	329	43	4	16	20	52
	WHA Totals		388	133	152	285	237	51	16	22	38	39

Claimed by **Chicago** from **Winnipeg** in Expansion Draft, June 13, 1979. Traded to **New Jersey** by **Chicago** with Don Dietrich for Bob MacMillan, and New Jersey's fifth round draft choice in 1985 (Rick Herbert), June 19, 1984.

PRICE, SHAUN PATRICK (PAT)

Born, Nelson, B.C., March 24, 1955.
Defense. Shoots left. 6'2", 195 lbs.
Last amateur club: Saskatoon Blades (WHL).
(NY Islanders' 1st choice, 11th over-all, in 1975 Amateur Draft).

			Regular Season					Playoffs				
Season	Club	Lea	GP	G	A	TP	PIM	GP	G	A	TP	PIM
1972-73	Saskatoon	WHL	67	12	56	68	134	16	4	17	21	24
1973-74a	Saskatoon	WHL	67	27	68	95	147	6	3	4	7	13
1974-75	Vancouver	WHA	68	5	29	34	15	....	....	....	....	....
1975-76	NY Islanders	NHL	4	0	2	2	2	....	....	....	....	....
	Fort Worth	CHL	72	6	44	50	119	....	....	....	....	....
1976-77	NY Islanders	NHL	71	3	22	25	25	10	0	1	1	2
1977-78	Rochester	AHL	5	2	1	3	9	....	....	....	....	....
	NY Islanders	NHL	52	2	10	12	27	5	0	1	1	2
1978-79	NY Islanders	NHL	55	3	11	14	50	7	0	1	1	25
1979-80	Edmonton	NHL	75	11	21	32	134	3	0	0	0	11
1980-81	Edmonton	NHL	59	8	24	32	193	....	....	....	....	....
	Pittsburgh	NHL	13	0	10	10	33	5	1	1	2	21
1981-82	Pittsburgh	NHL	77	7	31	38	322	5	0	0	0	28
1982-83	Pittsburgh	NHL	38	1	11	12	104	....	....	....	....	....
	Quebec	NHL	14	1	2	3	28	4	0	0	0	14
1983-84	Quebec	NHL	72	3	25	28	188	9	1	0	1	10
1984-85	Quebec	NHL	68	1	26	27	118	17	0	4	4	51
1985-86	Quebec	NHL	54	3	13	16	82	3	0	1	1	4
	NHL Totals		652	43	208	251	1306	68	2	9	11	168
	WHA Totals		68	5	29	34	15	....	....	....	....	....

a WHL First All-Star Team (1974)

Claimed by **Edmonton** from **NY Islanders** in Expansion Draft, June 13, 1979. Traded to **Pittsburgh** by **Edmonton** for Pat Hughes, March 10, 1981. Claimed on waivers by **Quebec** from **Pittsburgh**, December 31, 1982.

PRIESTLAY, KEN

Born, Richmond, B.C., August 24, 1967.
Center. Shoots left. 5'11", 180 lbs.
Last amateur club: Victoria Cougars (WHL).
(Buffalo's 5th choice, 98th overall, in 1985 Entry Draft).

			Regular Season					Playoffs				
Season	Club	Lea	GP	G	A	TP	PIM	GP	G	A	TP	PIM
1983-84	Victoria	WHL	55	10	18	28	31	....	....	....	....	....
1984-85	Victoria	WHL	50	25	37	62	48	....	....	....	....	....
1985-86	Victoria	WHL	72	73	72	145	45	....	....	....	....	....
	Rochester	AHL	4	0	2	2	0	....	....	....	....	....

PROBERT, BOB

Born, Windsor, Ont., June 5, 1965.
Left wing. Shoots left. 6'3", 210 lbs.
Last amateur club: Brantford Alexanders (OHL).
(Detroit's 3rd choice, 46th over-all, in 1983 Entry Draft).

			Regular Season					Playoffs				
Season	Club	Lea	GP	G	A	TP	PIM	GP	G	A	TP	PIM
1982-83	Brantford	OHL	51	12	16	28	133	8	2	2	4	23
1983-84	Brantford	OHL	65	35	38	73	189	6	0	3	3	16
1984-85	S.S. Marie	OHL	44	20	52	72	172	....	....	....	....	....
	Hamilton	OHL	4	0	1	1	21	....	....	....	....	....
1985-86	Detroit	NHL	44	8	13	21	186	....	....	....	....	....
	Adirondack	AHL	32	12	15	27	152	10	2	3	5	68
	NHL Totals		44	8	13	21	186	....	....	....	....	....

PROFT, PARIE

Born, Barrhead, Alta., January 22, 1964.
Defense. Shoots right. 5'9", 185 lbs.
Last amateur club: Canadian Olympic Team.
(Vancouver's 5th choice, 137th overall, in 1982 Entry Draft).

			Regular Season					Playoffs				
Season	Club	Lea	GP	G	A	TP	PIM	GP	G	A	TP	PIM
1982-83	Calgary	WHL	71	16	50	66	75	16	3	13	16	20
1983-84	Alberta	CWUAA	40	12	20	32	47	....	....	....	....	....
1984-85	Alberta	CWUAA	42	13	35	48	63	....	....	....	....	....
1985-86	Cdn. Olympic	...	61	9	12	21	17	....	....	....	....	....

PROPP, BRIAN PHILIP

Born, Lanigan, Sask., February 15, 1959.
Left wing. Shoots left. 5'9", 190 lbs.
Last amateur club: Brandon Wheat Kings (WHL).
(Philadelphia's 1st choice, 14th over-all, in 1979 Entry Draft).

			Regular Season					Playoffs				
Season	Club	Lea	GP	G	A	TP	PIM	GP	G	A	TP	PIM
1976-77	Brandon	WHL	72	55	80	135	47	16	*14	12	26	5
1977-78a	Brandon	WHL	70	70	*112	*182	200	8	7	6	13	12
1978-79ab	Brandon	WHL	71	*94	*100	*194	127	22	15	23	*38	40
1979-80	Philadelphia	NHL	80	34	41	75	54	19	5	10	15	29
1980-81	Philadelphia	NHL	79	26	40	66	110	12	6	6	12	32
1981-82	Philadelphia	NHL	80	44	47	91	117	4	2	2	4	4
1982-83	Philadelphia	NHL	80	40	42	82	72	3	1	2	3	8
1983-84	Philadelphia	NHL	79	39	53	92	37	3	0	1	1	6
1984-85	Philadelphia	NHL	76	43	53	96	43	19	8	10	18	6
1985-86	Philadelphia	NHL	72	40	57	97	47	5	0	2	2	4
	NHL Totals		546	266	333	599	480	65	22	33	55	89

a WHL First All-Star Team (1978, 1979)
b WHL Player of the Year (1979)

PRYOR, CHRIS

Born, St. Paul, Minn., January 23, 1961.
Defense. Shoots right. 6'0", 200 lbs.
Last amateur club: University of New Hampshire Wildcats (ECAC).

			Regular Season					Playoffs				
Season	Club	Lea	GP	G	A	TP	PIM	GP	G	A	TP	PIM
1979-80	N. Hampshire	ECAC	27	9	13	22	27	....	....	....	....	....
1980-81	N. Hampshire	ECAC	33	10	27	37	36	....	....	....	....	....
1981-82	N. Hampshire	ECAC	35	3	16	19	36	....	....	....	....	....
1982-83	N. Hampshire	ECAC	34	4	9	13	23	....	....	....	....	....
1983-84	Salt Lake	CHL	72	7	21	28	215	5	1	2	3	11
1984-85	Minnesota	NHL	4	0	0	0	16	....	....	....	....	....
	Springfield	AHL	77	3	21	24	158	....	....	....	....	....
1985-86	Minnesota	NHL	7	0	1	1	0	....	....	....	....	....
	Springfield	AHL	55	4	16	20	104	....	....	....	....	....
	NHL Totals		11	0	1	1	16	....	....	....	....	....

Signed as a free agent by **Minnesota**, January 10, 1985.

PULIS, PAUL

Born, Duluth, Minn., January 14, 1965.
Left wing. Shoots left. 6'5", 200 lbs.
Last amateur club: University of Illinois at Chicago Flames (CCHA).
(Minnesota's 10th choice, 176th overall, in 1983 Entry Draft).

			Regular Season					Playoffs				
Season	Club	Lea	GP	G	A	TP	PIM	GP	G	A	TP	PIM
1983-84	Ill-Chicago	CCHA	25	1	2	3	12	....	....	....	....	....
1984-85	Ill-Chicago	CCHA	31	0	2	2	11	....	....	....	....	....
1985-86	Ill-Chicago	CCHA	28	7	2	9	14	....	....	....	....	....

QUENNEVILLE, JOEL NORMAN (KWEN-vil)

Born, Windsor, Ont., September 15, 1958.
Defense. Shoots left. 6', 190 lbs.
Last amateur club: Windsor Spitfires (OHA).
(Toronto's 1st choice, 21st over-all, in 1978 Amateur Draft).

			Regular Season					Playoffs				
Season	Club	Lea	GP	G	A	TP	PIM	GP	G	A	TP	PIM
1975-76	Windsor	OHA	66	15	33	48	61	....	....	....	....	....
1976-77	Windsor	OHA	65	19	59	78	169	9	6	5	11	112
1977-78a	Windsor	OHA	66	27	76	103	114	6	2	3	5	17
1978-79	New Brunswick	AHL	16	1	10	11	10	....	....	....	....	....
	Toronto	NHL	61	2	9	11	60	6	0	1	1	4
1979-80	Toronto	NHL	32	1	4	5	24	....	....	....	....	....
	Colorado	NHL	35	5	7	12	26	....	....	....	....	....
1980-81	Colorado	NHL	71	10	24	34	86	....	....	....	....	....
1981-82	Colorado	NHL	64	5	10	15	55	....	....	....	....	....
1982-83	New Jersey	NHL	74	5	12	17	46	....	....	....	....	....
1983-84	Hartford	NHL	80	5	8	13	95	....	....	....	....	....
1984-85	Hartford	NHL	79	6	16	22	96	....	....	....	....	....
1985-86	Hartford	NHL	71	5	20	25	83	10	0	2	2	12
	NHL Totals		567	44	110	154	571	16	0	3	3	6

a OHA Second All-Star Team (1978)

Traded to **Colorado** by **Toronto** with Lanny McDonald for Pat Hickey and Wilf Paiement, December 29, 1979. Traded to **Calgary** by **New Jersey** with Steve Tambellini for Phil Russell and Mel Bridgman, June 20, 1983. Traded to **Hartford** by **Calgary** with Richie Dunn for Mickey Volcan, July 5, 1983.

QUINN, DAN

Born, Ottawa, Ont., June 1, 1965.
Center. Shoots left. 5'10", 176 lbs.
Last amateur club: Belleville Bulls (OHL).
(Calgary's 1st choice, 13th over-all, in 1983 Entry Draft).

			Regular Season					Playoffs				
Season	Club	Lea	GP	G	A	TP	PIM	GP	G	A	TP	PIM
1981-82	Belleville	OHL	67	19	32	51	41	....	....	....	....	....
1982-83	Belleville	OHL	70	59	88	147	27	4	2	6	8	2
1983-84	Belleville	OHL	24	23	36	59	12	....	....	....	....	....
	Calgary	NHL	54	19	33	52	20	8	3	5	8	4
1984-85	Calgary	NHL	74	20	38	58	22	3	0	0	0	0
1985-86	Calgary	NHL	78	30	42	72	44	18	8	7	15	10
	NHL Totals		206	69	113	182	86	29	11	12	23	14

QUINN, DAVID

Born, Cranston, Rhode Island, July 30, 1966.
Defense. Shoots left. 6', 205 lbs.
Last amateur club: Boston University Terriers (H.E.)
(Minnesota's 1st choice, 13th over-all, in 1984 Entry Draft).

			Regular Season					Playoffs				
Season	Club	Lea	GP	G	A	TP	PIM	GP	G	A	TP	PIM
1984-85	Boston U.	H.E.	30	3	11	14	26	....	....	....	....	....
1985-86a	Boston U.	H.E.	37	2	20	22	58	....	....	....	....	....

a Hockey East First All-Star Team (1986)

QUINNEY, KEN

Born, New Westminster, B.C., May 23, 1965.
Right wing. Shoots right. 5'10", 195 lbs.
Last amateur club: Calgary Wranglers (WHL).
(Quebec's 8th choice, 204th over-all, in 1984 Entry Draft).

			Regular Season					Playoffs				
Season	Club	Lea	GP	G	A	TP	PIM	GP	G	A	TP	PIM
1981-82	Calgary	WHL	63	11	17	28	55	2	0	0	0	15
1982-83	Calgary	WHL	71	26	25	51	71	16	6	1	7	46
1983-84	Calgary	WHL	71	64	54	118	38	4	5	2	7	0
1984-85a	Calgary	WHL	56	47	67	114	65	7	6	4	10	15
1985-86	Fredericton	AHL	61	11	26	37	34	6	2	2	4	9

a WHL First All-Star Team, Division (1985)

RAGLAN, HERB

Born, Peterborough, Ont., August 5, 1967.
Right wing. Shoots right. 6', 205 lbs.
Last amateur club: Kingston Canadians (OHL).
(St. Louis' 1st choice, 37th over-all, in 1985 Entry Draft).

			Regular Season					Playoffs				
Season	Club	Lea	GP	G	A	TP	PIM	GP	G	A	TP	PIM
1984-85	Peterborough	OHL	58	20	22	42	166	....	....	....	....	....
1985-86	**St. Louis**	**NHL**	7	0	0	0	5	10	1	1	2	24
	Kingston	OHL	28	10	9	19	88	10	5	2	7	30
	NHL Totals		7	0	0	0	5	10	1	1	2	24

RAMAGE, GEORGE (ROB)   (RAM-aj)

Born, Byron, Ont., January 11, 1959.
Defense. Shoots right. 6'2", 195 lbs.
Last amateur club: London Knights (OHA).
(Colorado's 1st choice and 1st over-all 1979 Entry Draft).

			Regular Season					Playoffs				
Season	Club	Lea	GP	G	A	TP	PIM	GP	G	A	TP	PIM
1975-76	London	OHA	65	12	31	43	113	5	0	1	1	11
1976-77a	London	OHA	65	15	58	73	177	20	3	11	14	55
1977-78b	London	OHA	59	17	48	64	162	11	4	5	9	29
1978-79	Birmingham	WHA	80	12	36	48	165	....	....	....	....	....
1979-80	**Colorado**	**NHL**	75	8	20	28	135	....	....	....	....	....
1980-81	**Colorado**	**NHL**	79	20	42	62	193	....	....	....	....	....
1981-82	**Colorado**	**NHL**	80	13	29	42	201	....	....	....	....	....
1982-83	**St. Louis**	**NHL**	78	16	35	51	193	4	0	3	3	22
1983-84	**St. Louis**	**NHL**	80	15	45	60	121	11	1	8	9	32
1984-85	**St. Louis**	**NHL**	80	7	31	38	178	3	1	3	4	6
1985-86	**St. Louis**	**NHL**	77	10	56	66	171	19	1	10	11	66
	NHL Totals		549	89	258	347	1192	37	3	24	27	126
	WHA Totals		80	12	36	48	165					

a OHA Third All-Star Team (1977)
b OHA First All-Star Team (1978)
Traded to **St. Louis** by **New Jersey** for St. Louis' first round choice (Rocky Trottier) in 1982 Entry Draft and first round choice (John MacLean) in 1983 Entry Draft, June 9, 1982.

RAMSEY, MICHAEL ALLEN (MIKE)

Born, Minneapolis, Minn., December 3, 1960.
Defense. Shoots left. 6'3", 190 lbs.
Last amateur club: 1980 United States Olympic Team.
(Buffalo's 1st choice, 11th over-all, in 1979 Entry Draft).

			Regular Season					Playoffs				
Season	Club	Lea	GP	G	A	TP	PIM	GP	G	A	TP	PIM
1978-79	U. Minnesota	WCHA	26	6	11	17	30	....	....	....	....	....
1979-80	U.S. National	...	56	11	22	33	55	....	....	....	....	....
	U.S. Olympic	...	7	0	2	2	8	....	....	....	....	....
	Buffalo	**NHL**	13	1	6	7	6	13	1	2	3	12
1980-81	**Buffalo**	**NHL**	72	3	14	17	56	8	0	3	3	20
1981-82	**Buffalo**	**NHL**	80	7	23	30	56	4	1	1	2	14
1982-83	**Buffalo**	**NHL**	77	8	30	38	55	10	4	4	8	15
1983-84	**Buffalo**	**NHL**	72	9	22	31	82	3	0	1	1	6
1984-85	**Buffalo**	**NHL**	79	8	22	30	102	5	0	1	1	23
1985-86	**Buffalo**	**NHL**	76	7	21	28	117	....	....	....	....	....
	NHL Totals		469	43	138	181	474	43	6	12	18	90

RANGER, JOE

Born, Sudbury, Ont., January 11, 1968.
Defense. Shoots left. 6'4", 225 lbs.
Last amateur club: London Knights (OHL).
(NY Rangers' 10th choice, 198th overall, in 1986 Entry Draft).

			Regular Season					Playoffs				
Season	Club	Lea	GP	G	A	TP	PIM	GP	G	A	TP	PIM
1985-86	London	OHL	22	0	5	5	31	....	....	....	....	....

RANHEIM, PAUL

Born, St. Louis, Missouri, January 25, 1966.
Center. Shoots right. 6', 195 lbs.
Last amateur club: University of Wisconsin Badgers (WCHA).
(Calgary's 3rd choice, 38th over-all, in 1984 Entry Draft).

			Regular Season					Playoffs				
Season	Club	Lea	GP	G	A	TP	PIM	GP	G	A	TP	PIM
1982-83	Edina HS	...	26	12	25	37	4	....	....	....	....	....
1983-84	Edina HS	...	26	16	24	40	6	....	....	....	....	....
1984-85	U. of Wisconsin	WCHA	42	11	11	22	40	....	....	....	....	....
1985-86	U. of Wisconsin	WCHA	33	17	17	34	34	....	....	....	....	....

RAY, DEREK

Born, Auburn, Mass., October 30, 1963.
Right wing. Shoots right. 5'11", 200 lbs.
Last amateur club: Clarkson University Knights (ECAC).
(Winnipeg's 5th choice, 138th overall, in 1982 Entry Draft).

			Regular Season					Playoffs				
Season	Club	Lea	GP	G	A	TP	PIM	GP	G	A	TP	PIM
1982-83	Clarkson	ECAC	30	1	5	6	50	....	....	....	....	....
1983-84	Clarkson	ECAC	33	12	16	28	102	....	....	....	....	....
1984-85	Clarkson	ECAC	31	6	6	12	94	....	....	....	....	....
1985-86	Clarkson	ECAC	28	8	4	12	142	....	....	....	....	....

REDMOND, CRAIG

Born, Dawson Creek, B.C., September 22, 1965.
Defense. Shoots left. 5'11", 190 lbs.
Last amateur club: 1984 Canadian Olympic Team.
(Los Angeles' 1st choice, 6th over-all, in 1984 Entry Draft).

			Regular Season					Playoffs				
Season	Club	Lea	GP	G	A	TP	PIM	GP	G	A	TP	PIM
1982-83ab	U. of Denver	WCHA	34	16	38	54	44	....	....	....	....	....
1983-84	Cdn. Olympic	...	55	10	11	21	38	....	....	....	....	....
1984-85	**Los Angeles**	**NHL**	79	6	33	39	57	3	1	0	1	2
1985-86	**Los Angeles**	**NHL**	73	6	18	24	57	....	....	....	....	....
	NHL Totals		152	12	51	63	114	3	1	0	1	2

a WCHA Rookie of the Year (1983).
b WCHA Second All-Star Team (1983).

REEDS, MARK

Born, Burlington, Ont., January 24, 1960.
Right wing. Shoots right. 5'10", 190 lbs.
Last amateur club: Peterborough Petes (OHA).
(St. Louis' 3rd choice, 86th over-all, in 1979 Entry Draft).

			Regular Season					Playoffs				
Season	Club	Lea	GP	G	A	TP	PIM	GP	G	A	TP	PIM
1978-79	Peterborough	OHA	66	25	25	50	96	11	0	5	5	19
1979-80	Peterborough	OHA	54	34	45	79	51	14	9	10	19	19
1980-81	Salt Lake	CHL	74	15	45	60	81	17	5	8	13	28
1981-82	Salt Lake	CHL	59	22	24	46	55	....	....	....	....	....
	St. Louis	**NHL**	9	1	3	4	0	10	0	1	1	2
1982-83	Salt Lake	CHL	55	16	26	42	32	....	....	....	....	....
	St. Louis	**NHL**	20	5	14	19	6	4	1	0	1	2
1983-84	**St. Louis**	**NHL**	65	11	14	25	23	11	3	3	6	15
1984-85	**St. Louis**	**NHL**	80	9	30	39	25	3	0	0	0	0
1985-86	**St. Louis**	**NHL**	78	10	28	38	28	19	4	4	8	2
	NHL Totals		252	36	89	125	82	47	8	8	16	21

REEKIE, JOE

Born, Petawawa, Ont., February 22, 1965.
Defense. Shoots left. 6'3", 195 lbs.
Last amateur club: Cornwall Royals (OHL).
(Buffalo's 6th choice, 119th overall, in 1985 Entry Draft)

			Regular Season					Playoffs				
Season	Club	Lea	GP	G	A	TP	PIM	GP	G	A	TP	PIM
1982-83	North Bay	OHL	59	2	9	11	49	8	0	1	1	11
1983-84	Cornwall	OHL	62	7	27	34	184	3	0	0	0	4
1984-85	Cornwall	OHL	65	19	63	82	134	9	4	13	17	18
1985-86	Rochester	AHL	77	3	25	28	178	....	....	....	....	....
	Buffalo	**NHL**	3	0	0	0	14	....	....	....	....	....
	NHL Totals		3	0	0	0	14					

REGAN, BRENT

Born, Edmonton, Alta., March 4, 1966.
Left wing. Shoots left. 6'0", 175 lbs.
Last amateur club: Bowling Green State University Falcons (CCHA).
(Hartford's 5th choice, 194th overall, in 1984 Entry Draft).

			Regular Season					Playoffs				
Season	Club	Lea	GP	G	A	TP	PIM	GP	G	A	TP	PIM
1984-85	Bowling Green	CCHA	42	6	18	24	12	....	....	....	....	....
1985-86	Bowling Green	CCHA	32	4	2	6	28	....	....	....	....	....

REID, DAVID

Born, Toronto, Ont., May 15, 1964.
Left wing. Shoots left. 6', 205 lbs.
Last amateur club: Peterborough Petes (OHL).
(Boston's 4th choice, 60th over-all, in 1982 Entry Draft).

			Regular Season					Playoffs				
Season	Club	Lea	GP	G	A	TP	PIM	GP	G	A	TP	PIM
1981-82	Peterborough	OHL	68	10	32	42	41	9	2	3	5	11
1982-83	Peterborough	OHL	70	23	34	57	33	4	3	1	4	0
1983-84	**Boston**	**NHL**	8	1	0	1	2	....	....	....	....	....
	Peterborough	OHL	60	33	64	97	12	....	....	....	....	....
1984-85	**Boston**	**NHL**	35	14	13	27	27	5	1	0	1	0
	Hershey	AHL	43	10	14	24	6	....	....	....	....	....
1985-86	**Boston**	**NHL**	37	10	10	20	10	....	....	....	....	....
	Moncton	AHL	26	14	18	32	4	....	....	....	....	....
	NHL Totals		80	25	23	48	39	5	1	0	1	0

REIERSON, DAVID (DAVE)

Born, Bashaw, Alta., August 30, 1964.
Defense. Shoots right. 5'11", 165 lbs.
Last amateur club: Michigan Tech University Huskies (CCHA)
(Calgary's 1st choice, 29th over-all, in 1982 Entry Draft).

			Regular Season					Playoffs				
Season	Club	Lea	GP	G	A	TP	PIM	GP	G	A	TP	PIM
1981-82	Prince Albert	SJHL	60	20	51	71	163	....	....	....	....	....
1982-83	Michigan Tech	CCHA	38	2	14	16	52	....	....	....	....	....
1983-84	Michigan Tech	CCHA	38	4	15	19	63	....	....	....	....	....
1984-85	Michigan Tech	CCHA	36	5	27	32	76	....	....	....	....	....
1985-86	Michigan Tech.	WCHA	39	7	16	23	51	....	....	....	....	....

REINHART, PAUL (RINE-hart)

Born, Kitchener, Ont., January 8, 1960.
Defense. Shoots left. 5'11", 205 lbs.
Last amateur club: Kitchener Rangers (OHA).
(Atlanta's 1st choice, 12th over-all, in 1979 Entry Draft).

			Regular Season					Playoffs				
Season	Club	Lea	GP	G	A	TP	PIM	GP	G	A	TP	PIM
1975-76	Kitchener	OHA	53	6	33	39	42	8	1	2	3	4
1976-77	Kitchener	OHA	51	4	14	18	16	3	0	2	2	4
1977-78	Kitchener	OHA	47	17	28	45	15	9	4	6	10	29
1978-79	Kitchener	OHA	66	51	78	129	57	10	3	10	13	16
1979-80	Atlanta	NHL	79	9	38	47	31	....	....	....	....	....
1980-81	Calgary	NHL	74	18	49	67	52	16	1	14	15	16
1981-82	Calgary	NHL	62	13	48	61	17	3	0	1	1	2
1982-83	Calgary	NHL	78	17	58	75	28	9	6	3	9	2
1983-84	Calgary	NHL	27	6	15	21	10	11	6	11	17	2
1984-85	Calgary	NHL	75	23	46	69	18	4	1	1	2	0
1985-86	Calgary	NHL	32	8	25	33	15	21	5	13	18	4
	NHL Totals		427	94	279	373	171	64	19	43	62	26

RENDALL, BRUCE

Born, Thunder Bay, Ont., April 18, 1967.
Left wing. Shoots left. 6'1", 180 lbs.
Last amateur club: Chatham Maroons (Tier II Jr.)
(Philadelphia's 2nd choice, 42nd over-all, in 1985 Entry Draft).

			Regular Season					Playoffs				
Season	Club	Lea	GP	G	A	TP	PIM	GP	G	A	TP	PIM
1984-85	Chatham	OPJHL	46	32	33	65	62	....	....	....	....	....
1985-86	Michigan State	CCHA	45	14	18	32	68	....	....	....	....	....

REYNOLDS, BOBBY

Born, Flint, Mich., July 14, 1967.
Left wing. Shoots left. 5'11", 175 lbs.
Last amateur club: Michigan State University Spartans (CCHA).
(Toronto's 10th choice, 190th overall, in 1985 Entry Draft).

			Regular Season					Playoffs				
Season	Club	Lea	GP	G	A	TP	PIM	GP	G	A	TP	PIM
1985-86	Michigan St.	CCHA	45	9	10	19	26	....	....	....	....	....

REZANSOFF, GRANT

Born, Surrey, B.C., March 3, 1961.
Center. Shoots right. 5'11", 180 lbs.
Last amateur club: Victoria Cougars (WHL).

			Regular Season					Playoffs				
Season	Club	Lea	GP	G	A	TP	PIM	GP	G	A	TP	PIM
1979-80	Victoria	WHL	67	17	19	36	7	....	....	....	....	....
1980-81	Victoria	WHL	72	40	57	97	27	15	14	13	27	14
1981-82	Oklahoma City	CHL	45	15	20	35	10	....	....	....	....	....
	Muskegon	IHL	37	15	11	26	4	....	....	....	....	....
1982-83	Colorado	CHL	22	4	3	7	16	1	0	0	0	2
1983-84	Peoria	IHL	82	36	46	82	11	....	....	....	....	....
1984-85	Salt Lake	IHL	37	12	17	29	2	7	2	0	2	0
	Toledo	IHL	25	9	10	19	0	....	....	....	....	....
1985-86	Peoria	IHL	80	30	47	77	23	11	3	5	8	2

Signed as free agent by **Calgary**, October 5, 1981.

RIBBLE, PATRICK WAYNE (PAT)

Born, Leamington, Ont., April 26, 1954.
Defense. Shoots left. 6'4", 210 lbs.
Last amateur club: Oshawa Generals (OHA).
(Atlanta's 3rd choice, 58th over-all, in 1974 Amateur Draft).

			Regular Season					Playoffs				
Season	Club	Lea	GP	G	A	TP	PIM	GP	G	A	TP	PIM
1972-73	Oshawa	OHA	61	11	27	38	110	....	....	....	....	....
1973-74	Oshawa	OHA	70	8	16	24	134	....	....	....	....	....
1974-75	Omaha	CHL	77	5	17	22	164	6	0	1	1	23
1975-76	Atlanta	NHL	3	0	0	0	0	....	....	....	....	....
	Tulsa	CHL	73	3	22	25	98	9	0	3	3	10
1976-77	Tulsa	CHL	51	9	20	29	140	....	....	....	....	....
	Atlanta	NHL	23	2	2	4	31	2	0	0	0	6
1977-78	Atlanta	NHL	80	5	12	17	68	2	0	1	1	2
1978-79	Atlanta	NHL	66	5	16	21	69	....	....	....	....	....
	Chicago	NHL	12	1	3	4	8	4	0	0	0	4
1979-80	Chicago	NHL	23	1	2	3	14	....	....	....	....	....
	Toronto	NHL	13	0	2	2	8	....	....	....	....	....
	Washington	NHL	19	1	5	6	30	....	....	....	....	....
1980-81	Washington	NHL	67	3	15	18	103	....	....	....	....	....
1981-82	Washington	NHL	12	1	2	3	14	....	....	....	....	....
	Calgary	NHL	3	0	0	0	2	....	....	....	....	....
	Oklahoma City	CHL	43	1	9	10	44	2	0	0	0	6
1982-83	Calgary	NHL	28	0	1	1	18	....	....	....	....	....
	Colorado	CHL	10	1	4	5	8	....	....	....	....	....
1983-84	Colorado	CHL	53	4	27	31	60	6	0	2	2	4
1984-85	Indianapolis	IHL	24	10	14	24	18	7	0	2	2	4
	Salt Lake	IHL	54	4	23	27	50	....	....	....	....	....
1985-86	Indianapolis	IHL	52	6	21	27	45	2	0	1	1	2
	NHL Totals		349	19	60	79	365	8	0	1	1	12

Traded to **Chicago** by **Atlanta** with Tom Lysiak, Harold Phillipoff, Greg Fox and Miles Zaharko for Ivan Boldirev, Phil Russell and Darcy Rota, March 13, 1979. Traded to **Toronto** by **Chicago** for Dave Hutchison, January 10, 1980. Traded to **Washington** by **Toronto** for Mike Kaszycki, February 16, 1980. Traded to **Calgary** by **Washington** with Washington's second round choice (Todd Francis — later transferred to Montreal) in 1983 Entry Draft for Randy Holt and Bobby Gould, November 25, 1981.

RICHARD, TODD

Born, Robindale, Minn., October, 20, 1966.
Defense. Shoots right. 6', 180 lbs.
Last amateur club: Armstrong H.S. (Minnesota)
(Montreal's 3rd choice, 33rd over-all, in 1985 Entry Draft).

			Regular Season					Playoffs				
Season	Club	Lea	GP	G	A	TP	PIM	GP	G	A	TP	PIM
1984-85	Armstrong	HS	24	10	23	33	24	....	....	....	....	....
1985-86	U. Minnesota	WCHA	38	6	23	29	38	....	....	....	....	....

RICHER, STEPHANE

Born, Buckingham, Que., June 7, 1966.
Center. Shoots right. 6'2", 200 lbs.
Last amateur club: Granby Bisons (QMJHL).
(Montreal's 3rd choice, 29th over-all, in 1984 Entry Draft).

			Regular Season					Playoffs				
Season	Club	Lea	GP	G	A	TP	PIM	GP	G	A	TP	PIM
1982-83	Laval	Midget	48	47	54	101	86	....	....	....	....	....
1983-84	Granby	QMJHL	67	39	37	76	58	3	1	1	2	4
1984-85	Montreal	NHL	1	0	0	0	0	....	....	....	....	....
a	Chicoutimi	QMJHL	57	61	59	120	71	12	13	13	26	25
1985-86	Montreal	NHL	65	21	16	37	50	16	4	1	5	23
	NHL Totals		66	21	16	37	50	16	4	1	5	23

a QMJHL Second All-Star Team (1985)

RICHMOND, STEVE

Born, Chicago, Illinois, December 11, 1959.
Defense. Shoots left. 6'1", 205 lbs.
Last amateur club: University of Michigan Wolverines (CCHA).

			Regular Season					Playoffs				
Season	Club	Lea	GP	G	A	TP	PIM	GP	G	A	TP	PIM
1978-79	U. of Michigan	CCHA	34	2	5	7	38	....	....	....	....	....
1979-80	U. of Michigan	CCHA	38	10	19	29	26	....	....	....	....	....
1980-81	U. of Michigan	CCHA	39	22	32	54	56	....	....	....	....	....
1981-82a	U. of Michigan	CCHA	38	6	30	36	68	....	....	....	....	....
1982-83	Tulsa	CHL	68	5	13	18	187	....	....	....	....	....
1983-84	Tulsa	CHL	38	1	17	18	114	....	....	....	....	....
	NY Rangers	NHL	26	2	5	7	110	4	0	0	0	12
1984-85	NY Rangers	NHL	34	0	5	5	90	....	....	....	....	....
	New Haven	AHL	37	3	10	13	122	....	....	....	....	....
1985-86	NY Rangers	NHL	17	0	2	2	63	....	....	....	....	....
	New Haven	AHL	11	2	6	8	32	....	....	....	....	....
	Detroit	NHL	29	1	2	3	82	....	....	....	....	....
	Adirondack	AHL	20	1	7	8	23	17	2	9	11	34
	NHL Totals		106	3	14	17	345	4	0	0	0	12

a CCHA Second All-Star Team (1982)

Signed as a free agent by **NY Rangers**, June 22, 1982. Traded to **Detroit** by **NY Rangers** for Mike McEwen, December 26, 1985.
Traded to **New Jersey** by **Detroit** for Sam St. Laurent, August 18, 1986.

RICHTER, DAVE (RICK-ter)

Born, St. Boniface, Man., April 8, 1960.
Defense. Shoots right. 6'5", 220 lbs.
Last amateur club: University of Michigan Wolverines (WCHA)
(Minnesota's 10th choice, 205th over-all, in 1980 Entry Draft).

			Regular Season					Playoffs				
Season	Club	Lea	GP	G	A	TP	PIM	GP	G	A	TP	PIM
1980-81	U. of Michigan	WCHA	36	2	13	15	56	....	....	....	....	....
1981-82	U. of Michigan	WCHA	36	9	12	21	78	....	....	....	....	....
	Nashville	CHL	2	0	1	1	0	....	....	....	....	....
	Minnesota	NHL	3	0	0	0	11	....	....	....	....	....
1982-83	Minnesota	NHL	6	0	0	0	4	....	....	....	....	....
	Birmingham	CHL	69	6	17	23	211	13	3	1	4	36
1983-84	Salt Lake	CHL	10	1	4	5	39	....	....	....	....	....
	Minnesota	NHL	42	2	3	5	132	8	0	0	0	20
1984-85	Minnesota	NHL	55	2	8	10	221	9	1	0	1	39
	Springfield	AHL	3	0	0	0	2	....	....	....	....	....
1985-86	Minnesota	NHL	14	0	3	3	29	....	....	....	....	....
	Philadelphia	NHL	50	0	2	2	138	5	0	0	0	21
	NHL Totals		170	4	16	20	535	22	1	0	1	80

Traded to **Philadelphia** by **Minnesota** with Bo Berglund for Ed Hospodar and Todd Bergen, November 29, 1985. Traded to **Vancouver** by **Philadelphia** with Rich Sutter and Vancouver's third-round choice (Don Gibson) — acquired earlier — in 1986 Entry Draft for J.J. Daigneault and Vancouver's second-round choice (Kent Hawley) in 1986 Entry Draft, June 6, 1986.

RIDLEY, MIKE

Born, Winnipeg, Man., July 8, 1963.
Center. Shoots left. 6'1", 200 lbs.
Last amateur club: University of Manitoba Bisons (GPAC).

			Regular Season					Playoffs				
Season	Club	Lea	GP	G	A	TP	PIM	GP	G	A	TP	PIM
1983-84a	Manitoba	GPAC	46	39	41	80	...	....	....	....	....	....
1984-85	Manitoba	GPAC	30	29	38	67	48	....	....	....	....	....
1985-86b	NY Rangers	NHL	80	22	43	65	69	16	6	8	14	26
	NHL Totals		80	22	43	65	69	16	6	8	14	26

a Canadian University Player of the Year (1984).
b NHL All-Rookie Team (1986).

Signed as a free agent by **NY Rangers**, September 26, 1985.

RIOUX, PIERRE (ree-OO)

Born, Quebec City, Que., February I, I962.
Right wing. Shoots right. 5'9", 165 lbs.
Last amateur club: Shawinigan Cataractes (QMJHL).

			Regular Season					Playoffs				
Season	Club	Lea	GP	G	A	TP	PIM	GP	G	A	TP	PIM
1980-81	Shawinigan	QMJHL	69	53	77	130	16	5	2	3	5	6
1981-82	Shawinigan	QMJHL	57	66	86	152	50	14	15	26	41	8
1982-83	**Calgary**	**NHL**	**14**	**1**	**2**	**3**	**4**	....	....	....	....	....
	Colorado	CHL	59	26	36	62	18	....	....	....	....	....
1983-84	Colorado	CHL	65	37	46	83	22	6	2	7	9	4
1984-85a	Moncton	AHL	69	25	66	91	14	....	....	....	....	....
1985-86	Moncton	AHL	5	0	0	0	0	....	....	....	....	....
	Binghamton	AHL	6	0	2	2	0	....	....	....	....	....
	NHL Totals		**14**	**1**	**2**	**3**	**4**	....	....	....	....	....

Signed as free agent by **Calgary**, August 24, 1982.

a AHL First All-Star Team (1985)

RISEBROUGH, DOUGLAS (DOUG) (RYZ-brow)

Born, Kitchener, Ont., January 29, 1954.
Center. Shoots left. 5'11", 180 lbs.
Last amateur club: Kitchener Rangers (OHA).
(Montreal's 2nd choice, 7th over-all, in 1974 Amateur Draft).

			Regular Season					Playoffs				
Season	Club	Lea	GP	G	A	TP	PIM	GP	G	A	TP	PIM
1972-73	Guelph (Tier II)	OHA	60	47	60	107	229	....	....	....	....	....
1973-74	Kitchener	OHA	46	25	27	52	114	....	....	....	....	....
1974-75	Nova Scotia	AHL	7	5	4	9	55	....	....	....	....	....
	Montreal	**NHL**	**64**	**15**	**32**	**47**	**198**	**11**	**3**	**5**	**8**	**37**
1975-76	**Montreal**	**NHL**	**80**	**16**	**28**	**44**	**180**	**13**	**0**	**3**	**3**	**30**
1976-77	**Montreal**	**NHL**	**78**	**22**	**38**	**60**	**132**	**12**	**2**	**3**	**5**	**16**
1977-78	**Montreal**	**NHL**	**72**	**18**	**23**	**41**	**97**	**15**	**2**	**2**	**4**	**17**
1978-79	**Montreal**	**NHL**	**48**	**10**	**15**	**25**	**62**	**15**	**1**	**6**	**7**	**32**
1979-80	**Montreal**	**NHL**	**44**	**8**	**10**	**18**	**81**	....	....	....	....	....
1980-81	**Montreal**	**NHL**	**48**	**13**	**21**	**34**	**93**	**3**	**1**	**0**	**1**	**0**
1981-82	**Montreal**	**NHL**	**59**	**15**	**18**	**33**	**116**	**5**	**2**	**1**	**3**	**11**
1982-83	**Calgary**	**NHL**	**71**	**21**	**37**	**58**	**138**	**9**	**1**	**3**	**4**	**18**
1983-84	**Calgary**	**NHL**	**77**	**23**	**28**	**51**	**161**	**11**	**2**	**1**	**3**	**25**
1984-85	**Calgary**	**NHL**	**15**	**7**	**5**	**12**	**49**	**4**	**0**	**3**	**3**	**12**
1985-86	**Calgary**	**NHL**	**62**	**15**	**28**	**43**	**169**	**22**	**7**	**9**	**16**	**38**
	NHL Totals		**718**	**183**	**283**	**466**	**1476**	**120**	**21**	**36**	**57**	**236**

Traded to **Calgary** by **Montreal** with Montreal's second round choice (Frantisek Musil — later transferred to Minnesota) in the 1983 Entry Draft for Washington's second round choice (Todd Francis) — which Calgary acquired in a previous deal — in 1983 Entry Draft and Calgary's third round choice (Graeme Bonar) in 1984 Entry Draft, September 11, 1982.

RISSLING, GARY DANIEL

Born, Saskatoon, Sask., August 8, 1956.
Left wing. Shoots left. 5'9", 175 lbs.
Last amateur club: Calgary Wranglers (WHL).

			Regular Season					Playoffs				
Season	Club	Lea	GP	G	A	TP	PIM	GP	G	A	TP	PIM
1975-76	Edmonton	WHL	18	5	9	14	25	....	....	....	....	....
	Calgary	WHL	47	29	38	67	196	....	....	....	....	....
1976-77	Calgary	WHL	68	40	40	80	317	9	9	7	16	12
1977-78	Port Huron	IHL	79	29	36	63	341	....	....	....	....	....
1978-79	**Washington**	**NHL**	**26**	**3**	**3**	**6**	**127**	....	....	....	....	....
	Hershey	AHL	52	14	20	34	337	4	0	0	0	18
1979-80	**Washington**	**NHL**	**11**	**0**	**1**	**1**	**49**	....	....	....	....	....
	Hershey	AHL	46	16	24	40	279	14	3	5	8	*87
1980-81	Birmingham	CHL	19	5	7	12	161	....	....	....	....	....
	Hershey	AHL	4	1	1	2	74	....	....	....	....	....
	Pittsburgh	**NHL**	**25**	**1**	**0**	**1**	**143**	**5**	**0**	**1**	**1**	**4**
1981-82	**Pittsburgh**	**NHL**	**16**	**0**	**0**	**0**	**55**	....	....	....	....	....
	Erie	AHL	29	7	15	22	185	....	....	....	....	....
1982-83	**Pittsburgh**	**NHL**	**40**	**5**	**4**	**9**	**128**	....	....	....	....	....
	Baltimore	AHL	38	14	17	31	136	....	....	....	....	....
1983-84	**Pittsburgh**	**NHL**	**47**	**4**	**13**	**17**	**297**	....	....	....	....	....
	Baltimore	AHL	30	12	13	25	47	....	....	....	....	....
1984-85	**Pittsburgh**	**NHL**	**56**	**10**	**9**	**19**	**209**	....	....	....	....	....
	Baltimore	AHL	22	9	17	26	60	....	....	....	....	....
1985-86	Baltimore	AHL	76	19	34	53	340	....	....	....	....	....
	NHL Totals		**221**	**23**	**30**	**53**	**1008**	**5**	**0**	**1**	**1**	**4**

Signed as free agent by **Washington**, December 4, 1978. Traded to **Pittsburgh** by **Washington** for Pittsburgh's fifth-round choice (Peter Sidorkiewicz) in the 1981 Entry Draft, January 2, 1981.

RISTAU, ANDREW

Born, Winnipeg, Man., January 28, 1961.
Right wing. Shoots right. 6'5", 230 lbs.
Last amateur club: Rochester Americans (AHL).

			Regular Season					Playoffs				
Season	Club	Lea	GP	G	A	TP	PIM	GP	G	A	TP	PIM
1985-86	Rochester	AHL	46	1	2	3	170	....	....	....	....	....

Signed as a free agent by **Buffalo**, March 7, 1986.

RIVINGTON, DALE

Born, Ottawa, Ont., March 7, 1964.
Defense. Shoots right. 6'1", 195 lbs.
Last amateur club: Rochester Institute of Technology (ECAC).

			Regular Season					Playoffs				
Season	Club	Lea	GP	G	A	TP	PIM	GP	G	A	TP	PIM
1985-86	RIT	ECAC	37	16	23	39	52	....	....	....	....	....

Signed as a free agent by **Calgary**, July 17, 1986.

ROBERTS, GARY

Born, North York, Ont., May 23, 1966.
Left wing. Shoots left. 6'1", 185 lbs.
Last amateur club: Ottawa 67's (OHL).
(Calgary's 1st choice, 12th over-all, in 1984 Entry Draft).

			Regular Season					Playoffs				
Season	Club	Lea	GP	G	A	TP	PIM	GP	G	A	TP	PIM
1982-83	Ottawa	OHL	53	12	8	20	83	5	1	0	1	19
1983-84	Ottawa	OHL	48	27	30	57	144	13	10	7	17	62
1984-85	Moncton	AHL	7	4	2	6	7	....	....	....	....	....
a	Ottawa	OHL	59	44	62	106	186	5	2	8	10	10
1985-86a	Guelph	OHL	47	44	40	84	148	20	18	13	31	43

a OHL Second All-Star Team (1985, 1986)

ROBERTS, GORDON (GORDIE)

Born, Detroit, Mich., October 2, 1957.
Defense. Shoots left. 6'1", 195 lbs.
Last amateur club: Victoria Cougars (WHL).
(Montreal's 7th choice, 54th over-all, in 1977 Amateur Draft).

			Regular Season					Playoffs				
Season	Club	Lea	GP	G	A	TP	PIM	GP	G	A	TP	PIM
1974-75	Victoria	WHL	53	19	45	64	145	12	1	9	10	42
1975-76	New England	WHA	77	3	19	22	102	17	2	9	11	36
1976-77	New England	WHA	77	13	33	46	169	5	2	2	4	6
1977-78	New England	WHA	78	15	46	61	118	14	0	5	5	29
1978-79	New England	WHA	79	11	46	57	113	10	0	4	4	10
1979-80	**Hartford**	**NHL**	**80**	**8**	**28**	**36**	**89**	**3**	**1**	**1**	**2**	**2**
1980-81	**Hartford**	**NHL**	**27**	**2**	**11**	**13**	**81**	....	....	....	....	....
	Minnesota	**NHL**	**50**	**6**	**31**	**37**	**94**	**19**	**1**	**5**	**6**	**17**
1981-82	**Minnesota**	**NHL**	**79**	**4**	**30**	**34**	**119**	**4**	**0**	**3**	**3**	**27**
1982-83	**Minnesota**	**NHL**	**80**	**3**	**41**	**44**	**103**	**9**	**1**	**5**	**6**	**14**
1983-84	**Minnesota**	**NHL**	**77**	**8**	**45**	**53**	**132**	**15**	**3**	**7**	**10**	**23**
1984-85	**Minnesota**	**NHL**	**78**	**6**	**36**	**42**	**112**	**9**	**1**	**6**	**7**	**6**
1985-86	**Minnesota**	**NHL**	**76**	**2**	**21**	**23**	**101**	**5**	**0**	**4**	**4**	**8**
	NHL Totals		**547**	**39**	**243**	**282**	**831**	**64**	**7**	**31**	**38**	**97**
	WHA Totals		311	42	144	186	502	46	4	20	24	81

Claimed by **Hartford** from **Montreal** in 1979 Expansion Draft, June 22, 1979. Traded to **Minnesota** by **Hartford** for Mike Fidler, December 16, 1980.

ROBERTSON, GEORDIE

Born, Victoria, B.C., August 1, 1959.
Right wing. Shoots right. 6', 165 lbs.
Last amateur club: Victoria Cougars (WHL).

			Regular Season					Playoffs				
Season	Club	Lea	GP	G	A	TP	PIM	GP	G	A	TP	PIM
1977-78	Victoria	WHL	61	64	72	136	85	13	15	11	26	42
1978-79	Victoria	WHL	54	31	42	73	94	14	15	10	25	22
1979-80	Rochester	AHL	55	26	26	52	66	4	1	4	5	2
1980-81	Rochester	AHL	20	3	3	6	19	....	....	....	....	....
1981-82	Flint	IHL	11	6	14	20	19	....	....	....	....	....
	Rochester	AHL	46	14	15	29	45	9	1	3	4	13
1982-83	**Buffalo**	**NHL**	**5**	**1**	**2**	**3**	**7**	....	....	....	....	....
	Rochester	AHL	72	46	73	119	83	16	8	6	14	23
1983-84	Rochester	AHL	64	37	54	91	103	18	9	9	18	42
1984-85	Rochester	AHL	70	27	48	75	91	5	0	1	1	4
1985-86	Adirondack	AHL	79	36	56	92	99	15	4	6	10	25
	NHL Totals		**5**	**1**	**2**	**3**	**7**	....	....	....	....	....

Signed as free agent by **Buffalo**, September 5, 1979. Signed as a free agent by **Detroit**, July 9, 1985.

ROBERTSON, TORRIE ANDREW

Born, Victoria, B.C., August 2, 1961.
Left wing. Shoots left. 5'11", 190 lbs.
Last amateur club: Victoria Cougars (WHL).
(Washington's 3rd choice, 55th over-all, in 1980 Entry Draft).

			Regular Season					Playoffs				
Season	Club	Lea	GP	G	A	TP	PIM	GP	G	A	TP	PIM
1978-79	Victoria	WHL	69	18	23	41	141	15	1	2	3	29
1979-80	Victoria	WHL	72	23	24	47	298	17	5	7	12	117
1980-81	**Washington**	**NHL**	**3**	**0**	**0**	**0**	**0**	....	....	....	....	....
	Victoria	WHL	59	45	66	111	274	15	10	13	23	55
1981-82	Hershey	AHL	21	5	3	8	60	....	....	....	....	....
	Washington	**NHL**	**54**	**8**	**13**	**21**	**204**	....	....	....	....	....
1982-83	**Washington**	**NHL**	**5**	**2**	**0**	**2**	**4**	....	....	....	....	....
	Hershey	AHL	69	21	33	54	187	5	1	2	3	8
1983-84	**Hartford**	**NHL**	**66**	**7**	**13**	**20**	**198**	....	....	....	....	....
1984-85	**Hartford**	**NHL**	**74**	**11**	**30**	**41**	**337**	....	....	....	....	....
1985-86	**Hartford**	**NHL**	**76**	**13**	**24**	**37**	**358**	**10**	**1**	**0**	**1**	**67**
	NHL Totals		**278**	**41**	**80**	**121**	**1101**	**10**	**1**	**0**	**1**	**67**

Traded to **Hartford** by **Washington** for Greg Adams, October 3, 1983.

ROBIDOUX, FLORENT (ROB-ee-doo)

Born, Treheme, Man., May 5, 1960.
Left wing. Shoots left. 6'2", 190 lbs.
Last amateur club: Portland Winter Hawks (WHL).

			Regular Season					Playoffs				
Season	Club	Lea	GP	G	A	TP	PIM	GP	G	A	TP	PIM
1978-79	Portland	WHL	70	36	41	77	73	25	11	16	27	20
1979-80a	Portland	WHL	70	43	57	100	157	8	5	2	7	10
1980-81	Chicago	NHL	39	6	2	8	75	....	....	....	....	....
	New Brunswick	AHL	35	12	11	23	110	13	2	7	9	38
1981-82	Chicago	NHL	4	1	2	3	0	....	....	....	....	....
	New Brunswick	AHL	69	31	35	66	200	15	*9	10	19	21
1982-83	DID NOT PLAY — INJURED											
1983-84	Chicago	NHL	9	0	0	0	0	....	....	....	....	....
	Springfield	AHL	68	26	22	48	123	4	0	1	1	6
1984-85	Milwaukee	IHL	76	29	35	64	184	....	....	....	....	....
1985-86	Hershey	AHL	47	6	3	9	81	3	0	0	0	15
	NHL Totals		52	7	4	11	75	....	....	....	....	....

a WHL First All-Star Team (1980)

Signed as free agent by **Chicago**, October 20, 1979. Signed as a free agent by **Philadelphia**, October 8, 1985.

ROBINSON, DWAYNE

Born, Montreal, Que., March 16, 1964.
Defense. Shoots right. 5'10", 180 lbs.
Last amateur club: University of N. Hampshire Wildcats (H.E.).
(NY Rangers' 13th choice, 246th over-all, in 1982 Entry Draft).

			Regular Season					Playoffs				
Season	Club	Lea	GP	G	A	TP	PIM	GP	G	A	TP	PIM
1981-82	N. Hampshire	ECAC	29	1	7	8	0	....	....	....	....	....
1982-83	N. Hampshirer	ECAC	33	3	1	4	14	....	....	....	....	....
1983-84	N. Hampshire	ECAC	37	4	9	13	26	....	....	....	....	....
1984-85	N. Hampshire	H.E.	43	4	10	14	30	....	....	....	....	....
1985-86	Muskegon	IHL	12	1	2	3	0	....	....	....	....	....
	Saginaw	IHL	46	6	9	15	11	7	1	3	4	4

ROBINSON, KEVIN

Born, Toronto, Ont., January 24, 1964.
Left Wing. Shoots left. 5'11", 170 lbs.
Last amateur club: Toronto Marlboros (OHL).
(Chicago's 5th choice, 99th over-all, in 1983 Entry Draft).

			Regular Season					Playoffs				
Season	Club	Lea	GP	G	A	TP	PIM	GP	G	A	TP	PIM
1982-83	Toronto	OHL	70	35	40	75	85	4	0	2	2	2
1983-84	Toronto	OHL	65	40	45	85	55	9	1	2	3	7
1984-85	Milwaukee	IHL	82	39	22	61	21	....	....	....	....	....
1985-86	Saginaw	IHL	81	34	36	70	43	11	5	4	9	32

ROBINSON, LARRY CLARK

Born, Winchester, Ont., June 2, 1951.
Defense. Shoots left. 6'3", 220 lbs.
Last amateur club: Kitchener Rangers (OHA).
(Montreal's 4th choice, 20th over-all, in 1971 Amateur Draft).

			Regular Season					Playoffs				
Season	Club	Lea	GP	G	A	TP	PIM	GP	G	A	TP	PIM
1969-70	Brockville	OHA	40	22	29	51	74	....	....	....	....	....
1970-71	Kitchener	OHA	61	12	39	51	65	....	....	....	....	....
1971-72	Nova Scotia	AHL	74	10	14	24	54	15	2	10	12	31
1972-73	Nova Scotia	AHL	38	6	33	39	33	....	....	....	....	....
	Montreal	NHL	36	2	4	6	20	11	1	4	5	9
1973-74	Montreal	NHL	78	6	20	26	66	6	0	1	1	26
1974-75	Montreal	NHL	80	14	47	61	76	11	0	4	4	27
1975-76	Montreal	NHL	80	10	30	40	59	13	3	3	6	10
1976-77ab	Montreal	NHL	77	19	66	85	45	14	2	10	12	12
1977-78cd	Montreal	NHL	80	13	52	65	39	15	4	*17	*21	6
1978-79b	Montreal	NHL	67	16	45	61	33	16	6	9	15	8
1979-80ab	Montreal	NHL	72	14	61	75	39	10	0	4	4	2
1980-81d	Montreal	NHL	65	12	38	50	37	3	0	1	1	2
1981-82	Montreal	NHL	71	12	47	59	41	5	0	1	1	8
1982-83	Montreal	NHL	71	14	49	63	33	3	0	0	0	2
1983-84	Montreal	NHL	74	9	34	43	39	15	0	5	5	22
1984-85	Montreal	NHL	76	14	33	47	44	12	3	8	11	8
1985-86d	Montreal	NHL	78	19	63	82	39	20	0	13	13	22
	NHL Totals		1005	174	589	763	610	154	19	80	99	164

a Won James Norris Memorial Trophy (1977, 1980)
b NHL First All-Star Team (1977, 1979, 1980)
c Won Conn Smythe Trophy (1978)
d NHL Second All-Star Team (1978, 1981, 1986)

ROBITAILLE, LUC

Born, Montreal, Que., February 17, 1966.
Left wing. Shoots left. 6', 180 lbs.
Last amateur club: Hull Olympiques (QMJNL).
(Los Angeles' 9th choice, 171st over-all, in 1984 Entry Draft).

			Regular Season					Playoffs				
Season	Club	Lea	GP	G	A	TP	PIM	GP	G	A	TP	PIM
1983-84	Hull	QMJHL	70	32	53	85	48	....	....	....	....	....
1984-85a	Hull	QMJHL	64	55	94	149	115	5	4	2	6	27
1985-86bcd	Hull	QMJHL	63	68	123	91	191	15	17	27	44	28

a QMJHL Second All-Star Team (1985)
b QMJHL First All-Star Team (1986)
c QMJHL Player of the Year (1986)
d Canadian Major Junior Player of the Year (1986)

ROCHEFORT, NORMAND (ROASH-four)

Born, Trois Rivieres, Que., January 28, 1961.
Defense. Shoots left. 6'1", 200 lbs.
Last amateur club: Quebec Remparts (QMJHL).
(Quebec's 1st choice, 24th over-all, in 1980 Entry Draft).

			Regular Season					Playoffs				
Season	Club	Lea	GP	G	A	TP	PIM	GP	G	A	TP	PIM
1978-79	Trois Rivières	QJHL	72	17	57	74	30	13	3	11	14	17
1979-80	Trois Rivières	QJHL	20	5	25	30	22	....	....	....	....	....
a	Quebec	QJHL	52	8	39	47	68	5	1	3	4	8
1980-81	Quebec	QJHL	9	2	6	8	14	....	....	....	....	....
	Quebec	NHL	56	3	7	10	51	5	0	0	0	4
1981-82	Quebec	NHL	72	4	14	18	115	16	0	2	2	10
1982-83	Quebec	NHL	62	6	17	23	40	1	0	0	0	2
1983-84	Quebec	NHL	75	2	22	24	47	6	1	0	1	6
1984-85	Quebec	NHL	73	3	21	24	74	18	2	1	3	8
1985-86	Quebec	NHL	26	5	4	9	30	....	....	....	....	....
	NHL Totals		364	23	85	108	357	46	3	3	6	30

a QMJHL Second All-Star Team (1980)

ROGERS, MICHAEL (MIKE)

Born, Calgary, Alta., October 24, 1954.
Center. Shoots left. 5'9", 170 lbs.
Last amateur club: Calgary Centennials (WHL).
(Vancouver's 4th choice, 77th over-all, in 1974 Amateur Draft).

			Regular Season					Playoffs				
Season	Club	Lea	GP	G	A	TP	PIM	GP	G	A	TP	PIM
1972-73	Calgary	WHL	67	54	58	122	44	6	8	5	13	2
1973-74a	Calgary	WHL	66	67	73	140	32	14	13	16	29	6
1974-75	Edmonton	WHA	78	35	48	83	2	....	....	....	....	....
1975-76	Edmonton	WHA	44	12	15	27	10	....	....	....	....	....
	New England	WHA	36	18	14	32	10	17	5	8	13	2
1976-77	New England	WHA	78	25	57	82	10	5	1	1	2	2
1977-78	New England	WHA	80	28	43	71	46	14	5	6	11	8
1978-79	New England	WHA	80	27	45	72	31	10	2	6	8	2
1979-80	Hartford	NHL	80	44	61	105	10	3	0	3	3	0
1980-81	Hartford	NHL	80	40	65	105	32	....	....	....	....	....
1981-82	NY Rangers	NHL	80	38	65	103	43	9	1	6	7	2
1982-83	NY Rangers	NHL	71	29	47	76	28	1	0	0	0	0
1983-84	NY Rangers	NHL	78	23	38	61	45	1	0	0	0	0
1984-85	NY Rangers	NHL	78	26	38	64	24	3	0	4	4	4
1985-86	NY Rangers	NHL	9	1	3	4	2	....	....	....	....	....
	New Haven	AHL	20	9	15	24	28	....	....	....	..	..
	Edmonton	NHL	8	1	0	1	0	....	....	....	....	....
	Nova Scotia	AHL	33	15	28	43	14	....	....	....	....	....
	NHL Totals		484	202	317	519	184	17	1	13	14	6
	WHA Totals		396	145	222	367	109	46	13	21	34	14

a WHL's Most Gentlemanly Player (1974)

Rights transferred to **Hartford** by **Vancouver**, June 22, 1979. Traded to **NY Rangers** by **Hartford** with Hartford's tenth round choice (Simo Saarinen) in 1982 Entry Draft for Chris Kotsopoulos, Gerry McDonald and Doug Sulliman, October 2, 1981. Traded to **Edmonton** by **NY Rangers** for Larry Melnyk and Todd Strueby, December 20, 1985.

ROHLICEK, JEFF (ROW-li-check)

Born, Park Ridge, Illinois, January 27, 1966.
Left wing. Shoots left. 5'11", 164 lbs.
Last amateur club: Spokane Chiefs (WHL).
(Vancouver's 2nd choice, 31st over-all, in 1984 Entry Draft).

			Regular Season					Playoffs				
Season	Club	Lea	GP	G	A	TP	PIM	GP	G	A	TP	PIM
1982-83	Chicago Jets	Midget	35	57	73	130	...	....	....	....	....	....
	Main West HS	...	25	60	60	120	...	....	....	....	....	....
1983-84	Portland	WHL	71	44	53	97	22	14	13	8	21	10
1984-85a	Kelowna	WHL	65	39	52	91	26	6	3	6	9	2
	Portland	WHL	16	5	13	18	2	....	....	....	....	....
1985-86	Spokane	WHL	57	50	52	102	39	9	6	2	8	16

a WHL Second All-Star Team, West Division (1985)

RONNING, CLIFF

Born, Vancouver, B.C., October 1, 1965.
Center. Shoots left. 5'8", 175 lbs.
Last amateur club: Canadian Olympic Team
(St. Louis' 9th choice, 134th over-all, in 1984 Entry Draft)

			Regular Season					Playoffs				
Season	Club	Lea	GP	G	A	TP	PIM	GP	G	A	TP	PIM
1983-84	N. Westminster	WHL	71	69	67	136	10	9	8	13	21	10
1984-85ab	N. Westminster	WHL	70	89	108	197	20	11	10	14	24	4
1985-86	St. Louis	NHL	....	....	....	....	....	5	1	1	2	2
	Cdn. Olympic	...	71	55	63	118	53	....	....	....	....	....
	NHL Totals		....	....	....	....	....	5	1	1	2	2

a WHL First All-Star Team (1985)
b WHL Most Valuable Player (1985)

ROONEY, STEVE

Born, Canton, Mass., June 28, 1962.
Left Wing. Shoots left. 6'2", 195 lbs.
Last amateur club: Providence College Friars (H.E.)
Montreal's 8th choice, 88th over-all, in 1981 Entry Draft)

Season	Club	Lea	GP	G	A	TP	PIM	GP	G	A	TP	PIM
						Regular Season				Playoffs		
1981-82	Providence	ECAC	31	7	10	17	41	....	....	....	....	....
1982-83	Providence	ECAC	42	10	20	30	31	....	....	....	....	....
1983-84	Providence	ECAC	33	11	16	27	46	....	....	....	....	....
1984-85	**Montreal**	**NHL**	**3**	**1**	**0**	**1**	**7**	**11**	**2**	**2**	**4**	**19**
	Providence	H.E.	31	7	10	17	41	....	....	....	....	....
1985-86	**Montreal**	**NHL**	**38**	**2**	**3**	**5**	**114**	**1**	**0**	**0**	**0**	**0**
	NHL Totals		**41**	**3**	**3**	**6**	**121**	**12**	**2**	**2**	**4**	**19**

ROOT, WILLIAM JOHN (BILL)

Born, Toronto, Ont., September 6, 1959.
Defense. Shoots right. 6', 210 lbs.
Last amateur club: Niagara Falls Flyers (OHA).

Season	Club	Lea	GP	G	A	TP	PIM	GP	G	A	TP	PIM
						Regular Season				Playoffs		
1977-78	Niagara Falls	OHA	67	6	11	17	61	....	....	....	....	....
1978-79	Niagara Falls	OHA	67	4	31	35	119	20	4	7	11	42
1979-80	Nova Scotia	AHL	55	4	15	19	57	6	1	1	2	2
1980-81	Nova Scotia	AHL	63	3	12	15	76	6	0	1	1	2
1981-82	Nova Scotia	AHL	77	6	25	31	105	9	1	0	1	4
1982-83	**Montreal**	**NHL**	**46**	**2**	**3**	**5**	**24**	....	....	....	....	....
	Nova Scotia	AHL	24	0	7	7	29	....	....	....	....	....
1983-84	**Montreal**	**NHL**	**72**	**4**	**13**	**17**	**45**	....	....	....	....	....
1984-85	**Toronto**	**NHL**	**35**	**1**	**1**	**2**	**23**	....	....	....	....	....
	St. Catharines	AHL	28	5	9	14	10	....	....	....	....	....
1985-86	**Toronto**	**NHL**	**27**	**0**	**1**	**1**	**29**	**7**	**0**	**2**	**2**	**13**
	St. Catharines	AHL	14	7	4	11	11	....	....	....	....	....
	NHL Totals		**180**	**7**	**18**	**25**	**121**	**7**	**0**	**2**	**2**	**13**

Signed as free agent by **Montreal**, October 4, 1979.
Traded to **Toronto** by **Montreal** with Montreal's second-round choice (Darryl Shannnon) in 1986 Entry Draft for Dom Campedelli, August 21, 1984.

ROSE, JAY

Born, Newton, Mass., July 6, 1966.
Defense. Shoots right. 6'0", 180 lbs.
Last amateur club: Clarkson University Golden Knights (ECAC).
(Detroit's 10th choice, 195th overall, in 1984 Entry Draft).

Season	Club	Lea	GP	G	A	TP	PIM	GP	G	A	TP	PIM
						Regular Season				Playoffs		
1984-85	Clarkson	ECAC	15	1	4	5	18	....	....	....	....	....
1985-86	Clarkson	ECAC	28	0	7	7	34	....	....	....	....	....

ROTH, MIKE

Born, St. Paul, Minn., September 7, 1966.
Defense. Shoots left. 6'1", 215 lbs.
Last amateur club: University of New Hampshire Wildcats (H.E.).
(New Jersey's 9th choice, 170th overall, in 1984 Entry Draft).

Season	Club	Lea	GP	G	A	TP	PIM	GP	G	A	TP	PIM
						Regular Season				Playoffs		
1985-86	N. Hampshire	H.E.	27	0	3	3	20	....	....	....	....	....

ROULEAU, GUY

Born, Beloeil, Que., February 16, 1965.
Center. Shoots left. 5'9", 175 lbs.
Last amateur club: Hull Olympiques (QMJHL).

Season	Club	Lea	GP	G	A	TP	PIM	GP	G	A	TP	PIM
						Regular Season				Playoffs		
1982-83	Longueuil	QMJHL	68	25	31	56	23	15	3	4	7	13
1983-84	Longueuil	QMJHL	70	60	73	133	28	17	9	20	29	42
1984-85	Longueuil	QMJHL	60	76	87	163	68	....	....	....	....	....
1985-86	Hull	QMJHL	62	92	99	191	72	15	23	20	43	21

Signed as a free agent by **Montreal**, April 30, 1986.

ROULSTON, THOMAS (TOM)   (ROLL-ston)

Born, Winnipeg, Man., November 20, 1957.
Center/Right wing. Shoots right. 6'1", 185 lbs.
Last amateur club: Winnipeg Monarchs (WHL).
(St. Louis' 3rd choice, 45th over-all, in 1977 Amateur Draft).

Season	Club	Lea	GP	G	A	TP	PIM	GP	G	A	TP	PIM
						Regular Season				Playoffs		
1975-76	Winnipeg	WHL	60	18	17	35	56	....	....	....	....	....
1976-77	Winnipeg	WHL	72	56	53	109	35	....	....	....	....	....
1977-78	Salt Lake	CHL	21	2	1	3	2	....	....	....	....	....
	Port Huron	IHL	49	27	36	63	24	16	*17	7	24	10
1978-79	Dallas	CHL	73	26	29	55	57	9	*6	6	12	11
1979-80	Houston	CHL	72	29	41	70	46	6	2	4	6	4
1980-81	**Edmonton**	**NHL**	**11**	**1**	**1**	**2**	**2**	....	....	....	....	....
a	Wichita	CHL	69	*63	44	107	93	18	15	11	*26	44
1981-82	Wichita	CHL	30	22	28	50	46	....	....	....	....	....
	Edmonton	**NHL**	**35**	**11**	**3**	**14**	**22**	**5**	**1**	**0**	**1**	**2**
1982-83	**Edmonton**	**NHL**	**67**	**19**	**21**	**40**	**24**	**16**	**1**	**2**	**3**	**0**
1983-84	**Edmonton**	**NHL**	**24**	**5**	**7**	**12**	**16**	....	....	....	....	....
	Pittsburgh	**NHL**	**53**	**11**	**17**	**28**	**8**	....	....	....	....	....
1984-85	Baltimore	AHL	78	31	39	70	48	15	4	8	12	6
1985-86	**Pittsburgh**	**NHL**	**5**	**0**	**0**	**0**	**2**	....	....	....	....	....
	Baltimore	AHL	73	38	49	87	38	....	....	....	....	....
	NHL Totals		**195**	**47**	**49**	**96**	**74**	**21**	**2**	**2**	**4**	**2**

a CHL First All-Star Team (1981).
Traded to **Edmonton** by **St. Louis** with Risto Siltanen for Joe Micheletti, August 7, 1979. Traded to **Pittsburgh** by **Edmonton** for Kevin McClelland and Pittsburgh's sixth round choice (Emanuel Viveiros) in 1984 Entry Draft, December 5, 1983.

ROUSE, ROBERT (BOB)

Born, Surrey, B.C., June 18, 1964.
Defense. Shoots right. 6'2", 210 lbs.
Last amateur club: Lethbridge Broncos (WHL).
(Minnesota's 3rd choice, 80th over-all, in 1982 Entry Draft).

Season	Club	Lea	GP	G	A	TP	PIM	GP	G	A	TP	PIM
						Regular Season				Playoffs		
1980-81	Billings	WHL	70	0	13	13	116	5	0	0	0	2
1981-82	Billings	WHL	71	7	22	29	209	5	0	2	2	10
1982-83	Nanaimo	WHL	29	7	20	27	86	....	....	....	....	....
	Lethbridge	WHL	42	8	30	38	82	20	2	13	15	55
1983-84	**Minnesota**	**NHL**	**1**	**0**	**0**	**0**	**0**	....	....	....	....	....
a	Lethbridge	WHL	71	18	42	60	101	5	0	1	1	28
1984-85	**Minnesota**	**NHL**	**63**	**2**	**9**	**11**	**113**	....	....	....	....	....
	Springfield	AHL	8	0	3	3	6	....	....	....	....	....
1985-86	**Minnesota**	**NHL**	**75**	**1**	**14**	**15**	**151**	**3**	**0**	**0**	**0**	**0**
	NHL Totals		**139**	**3**	**23**	**26**	**264**	**3**	**0**	**0**	**0**	**2**

a WHL First All-Star Team, East Division (1984)

ROUTHIER, JEAN-MARC

Born, Quebec, Que., February 2, 1968.
Right wing. Shoots right. 6'1", 175 lbs.
Last amateur club: Hull Olympiques (QMJHL).
(Quebec's 2nd choice, 39th overall, in 1986 Entry Draft).

Season	Club	Lea	GP	G	A	TP	PIM	GP	G	A	TP	PIM
						Regular Season				Playoffs		
1985-86	Hull	QMJHL	71	18	16	34	111	15	3	6	9	27

ROWE, MIKE

Born, Kingston, Ont., March 8, 1965.
Defense. Shoots left. 6'1", 208 lbs.
Last amateur club: Toronto Marlboros (OHL).
(Pittsburgh's 3rd choice, 58th over-all, in 1983 Entry Draft).

Season	Club	Lea	GP	G	A	TP	PIM	GP	G	A	TP	PIM
						Regular Season				Playoffs		
1981-82	Toronto	OHL	58	4	4	8	214	10	0	0	0	63
1982-83	Toronto	OHL	64	4	29	33	262	4	0	1	1	19
1983-84	Toronto	OHL	59	9	36	45	208	9	0	5	5	45
1984-85	**Pittsburgh**	**NHL**	**6**	**0**	**0**	**0**	**7**	....	....	....	....	....
	Toronto	OHL	66	17	34	51	202	....	....	....	....	....
1985-86	**Pittsburgh**	**NHL**	**3**	**0**	**0**	**0**	**4**	....	....	....	....	....
	Baltimore	AHL	67	0	5	5	107	....	....	....	....	....
	NHL Totals		**9**	**0**	**0**	**0**	**11**	....	....	....	....	....

ROY, DARCY

Born, Haileybury, Ont., May 10, 1964.
Left wing. Shoots left. 5'11", 190 lbs.
Last amateur club: Ottawa 67's (OHL).
(Los Angeles' 5th choice, 90th over-all, in 1982 Entry Draft).

Season	Club	Lea	GP	G	A	TP	PIM	GP	G	A	TP	PIM
						Regular Season				Playoffs		
1981-82	Ottawa	OHL	65	22	20	42	79	16	0	4	4	37
1982-83	Ottawa	OHL	70	28	40	68	151	9	2	0	2	19
1983-84	Ottawa	OHL	70	21	41	62	98	13	9	10	19	16
1984-85	Toledo	IHL	80	17	28	45	115	6	2	0	2	27
	New Haven	AHL	2	0	0	0	2	....	....	....	....	....
1985-86	New Haven	AHL	38	1	10	11	43	....	....	....	....	....
	Toledo	IHL	3	0	0	0	4	....	....	....	....	....

ROY, STEPHANE

Born, Ste. Foy, Que., June 29, 1967.
Center. Shoots left. 5'11", 185 lbs.
Last amateur club: Granby Bisons (QMJHL).
(Minnesota's 1st choice, 51st overall, in 1985 Entry Draft).

			Regular Season					Playoffs				
Season	Club	Lea	GP	G	A	TP	PIM	GP	G	A	TP	PIM
1984-85	Granby	QMJHL	68	28	53	81	34	....	....	....	....	....
1985-86	Granby	QMJHL	61	33	52	85	68	....	....	....	....	....
	Cdn. Olympic	...	10	0	1	1	4	....	....	....	....	....

RUFF, LINDY CAMERON

Born, Warburg, Alta., February 17, 1960.
Defense. Shoots left. 6'2", 200 lbs.
Last amateur club: Lethbridge Broncos (WHL).
(Buffalo's 2nd choice, 32nd over-all, in 1979 Entry Draft).

			Regular Season					Playoffs				
Season	Club	Lea	GP	G	A	TP	PIM	GP	G	A	TP	PIM
1977-78	Lethbridge	WHL	66	9	24	33	219	8	2	8	10	4
1978-79	Lethbridge	WHL	24	9	18	27	108	6	0	1	1	0
1979-80	Buffalo	NHL	63	5	14	19	38	8	1	1	2	19
1980-81	Buffalo	NHL	65	8	18	26	121	6	3	1	4	23
1981-82	Buffalo	NHL	79	16	32	48	194	4	0	0	0	28
1982-83	Buffalo	NHL	60	12	17	29	130	10	4	2	6	47
1983-84	Buffalo	NHL	58	14	31	45	101	3	1	0	1	9
1984-85	Buffalo	NHL	39	13	11	24	45	5	2	4	6	15
1985-86	Buffalo	NHL	54	20	12	32	158	....	....	....	....	....
	NHL Totals		418	88	135	223	787	36	11	8	19	141

RUFF, MARTY

Born, Warburg, Alta., May 19, 1963.
Defense. Shoots right. 6'1", 195 lbs.
Last amateur club: Lethbridge Broncos (WHL).
(St. Louis' 1st choice, 20th over-all, in 1981 Entry Draft).

			Regular Season					Playoffs				
Season	Club	Lea	GP	G	A	TP	PIM	GP	G	A	TP	PIM
1980-81	Lethbridge	WHL	71	9	37	46	222	7	0	2	2	17
1981-82	Lethbridge	WHL	46	7	28	35	188	12	0	5	5	35
1982-83	Lethbridge	WHL	53	7	23	30	128	20	2	5	7	43
1983-84	Montana	CHL	1	0	0	0	2	....	....	....	....	....
	Muskegon	IHL	44	3	15	18	44	....	....	....	....	....
	Toledo	IHL	2	0	1	1	0	....	....	....	....	....
1984-85	Peoria	IHL	5	0	1	1	0	....	....	....	....	....
1985-86	Peoria	IHL	44	3	6	9	34	5	1	0	1	2

RUOTSALAINEN, REIJO   (roo-OTT-sa-LAY-nen)

Born, Oulu, Finland, April 1, 1960.
Defense. Shoots right. 5'8", 170 lbs.
Last amateur club: Karpat (Finland).
(NY Rangers' 5th choice, 119th over-all, in 1980 Entry Draft).

			Regular Season					Playoffs				
Season	Club	Lea	GP	G	A	TP	PIM	GP	G	A	TP	PIM
1979-80a	Karpat	Fin.	30	15	13	28	31	6	5	2	7	0
1980-81a	Karpat	Fin.	36	28	23	51	28	12	7	4	11	6
1981-82	NY Rangers	NHL	78	18	38	56	27	10	4	5	9	2
1982-83	NY Rangers	NHL	77	16	53	69	22	9	4	2	6	6
1983-84	NY Rangers	NHL	74	20	39	59	26	5	1	1	2	2
1984-85	NY Rangers	NHL	80	28	45	73	32	3	2	0	2	6
1985-86	NY Rangers	NHL	80	17	42	59	147	16	0	8	8	6
	NHL Totals		389	99	217	316	154	43	11	16	27	22

a Named to Finnish League All-Star Team (1980, 1981)

RUSKOWSKI, TERRY WALLACE

Born, Prince Albert, Sask., December 31, 1954.
Center. Shoots left. 5'9", 180 lbs.
Last amateur club: Swift Current Broncos (WHL).
(Chicago's 4th choice, 70th over-all, in 1974 Amateur Draft).

			Regular Season					Playoffs				
Season	Club	Lea	GP	G	A	TP	PIM	GP	G	A	TP	PIM
1972-73	Swift Current	WHL	53	25	64	89	136	....	....	....	....	....
1973-74	Swift Current	WHL	68	40	93	133	243	13	5	*23	28	23
1974-75	Houston	WHA	71	10	36	46	134	13	4	2	6	15
1975-76	Houston	WHA	65	14	35	49	100	16	6	10	16	*64
1976-77	Houston	WHA	80	24	60	84	146	11	6	11	17	*67
1977-78	Houston	WHA	78	15	57	72	170	4	1	1	2	5
1978-79	Winnipeg	WHA	75	20	66	86	211	8	1	*12	13	23
1979-80	Chicago	NHL	74	15	55	70	252	4	0	0	0	22
1980-81	Chicago	NHL	72	8	51	59	225	3	0	2	2	11
1981-82	Chicago	NHL	60	7	30	37	120	11	1	2	3	53
1982-83	Chicago	NHL	5	0	2	2	12	....	....	....	....	....
	Los Angeles	NHL	71	14	30	44	127	....	....	....	....	....
1983-84	Los Angeles	NHL	77	7	25	32	89	....	....	....	....	....
1984-85	Los Angeles	NHL	78	16	33	49	144	3	0	2	2	0
1985-86	Pittsburgh	NHL	73	26	37	63	162	....	....	....	....	....
	NHL Totals		510	93	263	356	1131	21	1	6	7	86
	WHA Totals		369	83	254	337	761	52	18	36	54	174

Reclaimed by **Chicago** from **Winnipeg** prior to Expansion Draft, June 9, 1979. Traded to **Los Angeles** by **Chicago** for Larry Goodenough and Los Angeles' third round choice (Trent Yawney) in the 1984 Entry Draft, October 24, 1982. Signed as a free agent by **Pittsburgh**, October 3, 1985.

RUSSELL, PHILLIP DOUGLAS (PHIL)

Born, Edmonton, Alta., July 21, 1952.
Defense. Shoots left. 6'2", 205 lbs.
Last amateur club: Edmonton Oil Kings (WHL).
(Chicago's 1st choice, 13th over-all, in 1972 Amateur Draft).

			Regular Season					Playoffs				
Season	Club	Lea	GP	G	A	TP	PIM	GP	G	A	TP	PIM
1970-71	Edmonton	WHL	34	4	16	20	113	17	1	7	8	47
1971-72a	Edmonton	WHL	64	14	45	59	*331	16	1	9	10	15
1972-73	Chicago	NHL	76	6	19	25	156	15	0	3	3	49
1973-74	Chicago	NHL	75	10	25	35	184	9	0	1	1	41
1974-75	Chicago	NHL	80	5	24	29	260	8	1	3	4	23
1975-76	Chicago	NHL	74	9	29	38	194	4	0	1	1	17
1976-77	Chicago	NHL	76	9	36	45	233	2	0	1	1	2
1977-78	Chicago	NHL	57	6	20	26	139	....	....	....	....	....
1978-79	Chicago	NHL	66	8	23	31	122	....	....	....	....	....
	Atlanta	NHL	13	1	6	7	28	2	0	0	0	9
1979-80	Atlanta	NHL	80	5	31	36	115	4	0	1	1	6
1980-81	Calgary	NHL	80	6	23	29	104	16	2	7	9	29
1981-82	Calgary	NHL	71	4	25	29	110	3	0	1	1	2
1982-83	Calgary	NHL	78	13	18	31	112	9	1	4	5	24
1983-84	New Jersey	NHL	76	9	22	31	96	....	....	....	....	....
1984-85	New Jersey	NHL	66	4	16	20	110	....	....	....	....	....
1985-86	New Jersey	NHL	30	2	3	5	51	....	....	....	....	....
	Buffalo	NHL	12	2	3	5	12	....	....	....	....	....
	NHL Totals		1010	99	323	422	2026	73	4	22	26	202

a WHL First All-Star Team (1972)

Traded to **Atlanta** by **Chicago** with Ivan Boldirev and Darcy Rota for Harold Phillipoff, Tom Lysiak, Pat Ribble, Greg Fox and Miles Zaharko, March 13, 1979. Traded to **New Jersey** by **Calgary** with Mel Bridgman for Steve Tambellini and Joel Quenneville, June 20, 1983. Traded to **Buffalo** by **New Jersey** for Buffalo's twelfth-round choice (Doug Kirton) in 1986 Entry Draft, March 11, 1986.

RYAN, TOM

Born, Boston, Mass., January 12, 1966.
Defense. Shoots right. 5'11", 180 lbs.
Last amateur club: Boston University Terriers (H.E.).
(Pittsburgh's 6th choice, 127th overall, in 1984 Entry Draft).

			Regular Season					Playoffs				
Season	Club	Lea	GP	G	A	TP	PIM	GP	G	A	TP	PIM
1984-85	Boston U.	H.E.	34	6	8	14	14	....	....	....	....	....
1985-86	Boston U.	H.E.	42	2	8	10	22	....	....	....	....	....

SAARINEN, SIMO

Born, Helsinki, Finland, February 14, 1963.
Defense. Shoots left. 5'8", 185 lbs.
Last amateur club: IFK Helsinki (Finland).
(NY Rangers' 10th choice, 193rd over-all, in 1982 Entry Draft).

			Regular Season					Playoffs				
Season	Club	Lea	GP	G	A	TP	PIM	GP	G	A	TP	PIM
1980-81	IFK	Fin.	20	1	0	1	4	....	....	....	....	....
1981-82	IFK	Fin.	36	5	10	15	20	....	....	....	....	....
1983-84	IFK	Fin.	36	9	6	15	24	19	1	4	5	20
1983-84	IFK	Fin.	36	7	7	14	32	....	....	....	....	....
1984-85	NY Rangers	NHL	8	0	0	0	0	....	....	....	....	....
1985-86	New Haven	AHL	13	3	4	7	11	....	....	....	....	....
	NHL Totals		8	0	0	0	0	....	....	....	....	....

SAATZER, RON

Born, Minnetonka, MN, September 5, 1966.
Center. Shoots left. 6'1", 175 lbs.
Last amateur club: University of Miami-Ohio Redskins (CCHA).
(St. Louis' 10th choice, 222nd overall, in 1985 Entry Draft).

			Regular Season					Playoffs				
Season	Club	Lea	GP	G	A	TP	PIM	GP	G	A	TP	PIM
1985-86	Miami-Ohio	CCHA	23	7	9	16	16	....	....	....	....	....

SABOURIN, KEN

Born, Scarborough, Ont. April 28, 1966.
Defense. Shoots left. 6'4", 200 lbs.
Last amateur club: Sault Ste. Marie Greyhounds (OHL).
(Calgary's 2nd choice, 33rd over-all, in 1984 Entry Draft).

			Regular Season					Playoffs				
Season	Club	Lea	GP	G	A	TP	PIM	GP	G	A	TP	PIM
1982-83	S.S. Marie	OHL	58	0	8	8	90	10	0	0	0	14
1983-84	S.S. Marie	OHL	63	7	13	20	157	9	0	1	1	25
1984-85	S.S. Marie	OHL	63	5	19	24	139	16	1	4	5	10
1985-86	Moncton	AHL	3	0	0	0	0	6	0	1	1	2
	Cornwall	OHL	62	4	17	21	171	6	1	2	3	6

SAGISSOR, THOMAS (TOM)

Born, Hastings, Minn., September 12, 1967.
Center. Shoots left. 5'11", 180 lbs.
Last amateur club: Hastings (HS).
(Montreal's 7th choice, 96th overall, in 1985 Entry Draft).

			Regular Season					Playoffs				
Season	Club	Lea	GP	G	A	TP	PIM	GP	G	A	TP	PIM
1985-86	Hastings	HS	25	26	38	64	28	....	....	....	....	....

SALMING, ANDERS BORJE (SAHL-ming, BOR-yah)

Born, Kiruna, Sweden, April 17, 1951.
Defense. Shoots left. 6′1″, 185 lbs.
Last amateur club: Swedish National Team.

				Regular Season					Playoffs			
Season	Club	Lea	GP	G	A	TP	PIM	GP	G	A	TP	PIM
1973-74	Toronto	NHL	76	5	34	39	48	4	0	1	1	4
1974-75a	Toronto	NHL	60	12	25	37	34	7	0	4	4	6
1975-76a	Toronto	NHL	78	16	41	57	70	10	3	4	7	9
1976-77b	Toronto	NHL	76	12	66	78	46	9	3	6	9	6
1977-78a	Toronto	NHL	80	16	60	76	70	6	2	2	4	6
1978-79a	Toronto	NHL	78	17	56	73	76	6	0	1	1	8
1979-80a	Toronto	NHL	74	19	52	71	94	3	1	1	2	2
1980-81	Toronto	NHL	72	5	61	66	154	3	0	2	2	4
1981-82	Toronto	NHL	69	12	44	56	170	....	....	....	....	....
1982-83	Toronto	NHL	69	7	38	45	104	4	1	4	5	10
1983-84	Toronto	NHL	68	5	38	43	92	....	....	....	....	....
1984-85	Toronto	NHL	73	6	33	39	76	....	....	....	....	....
1985-86	Toronto	NHL	41	7	15	22	48	10	1	6	7	14
	NHL Totals		914	139	563	702	1082	62	11	31	42	69

a NHL Second All-Star Team (1975, 1976, 1978, 1979, 1980)
b NHL First All-Star Team (1977)
Signed as free agent by **Toronto**, May 12, 1973.

SAMPSON, GARY EDWARD

Born, Atikokan, Ont., August 24, 1959.
Left wing. Shoots left. 6′, 190 lbs.
Last amateur club: 1984 United States Olympic Team.

				Regular Season					Playoffs			
Season	Club	Lea	GP	G	A	TP	PIM	GP	G	A	TP	PIM
1978-79	Boston College	ECAC	30	10	18	28	4	....	....	....	....	....
1979-80	Boston College	ECAC	24	6	18	24	8	....	....	....	....	....
1980-81	Boston College	ECAC	31	8	16	24	8	....	....	....	....	....
1981-82	Boston College	ECAC	21	7	11	18	22	....	....	....	....	....
1982-83	U.S. National	...	40	11	20	31	8	....	....	....	....	....
1983-84	U.S. National	...	57	21	18	39	10	....	....	....	....	....
	U.S. Olympic	...	7	1	3	4	0	....	....	....	....	....
	Washington	NHL	15	1	1	2	6	8	1	0	1	0
1984-85	Washington	NHL	46	10	15	25	13	4	0	0	0	0
	Binghamton	AHL	5	2	2	4	2	....	....	....	....	....
1985-86	Washington	NHL	19	1	4	5	2	....	....	....	....	....
	Binghamton	AHL	49	9	21	30	16	6	2	2	4	4
	NHL Totals		80	12	20	32	21	12	1	0	1	0

Signed as free agent by **Washington**, February 21, 1984.

SAMEULSSON, KJELL

Born, Tingsryd, Sweden, October 18, 1966.
Defense. Shoots left. 6′6″, 225 lbs.
Last amateur club: Leksand (Sweden).
(NY Rangers' 5th choice, 119th overall, in 1984 Entry Draft).

				Regular Season					Playoffs			
Season	Club	Lea	GP	G	A	TP	PIM	GP	G	A	TP	PIM
1983-84	Leksand	Swe.	36	6	7	13	59	....	....	....	....	....
1984-85	Leksand	Swe.	35	9	5	14	34	....	....	....	....	....
1985-86	New Haven	AHL	56	6	21	27	87	3	0	0	0	10
	NY Rangers	NHL	9	0	0	0	10	9	0	1	1	8
	NHL Totals		9	0	0	0	10	9	0	1	1	8

SAMUELSSON, ULF

Born, Leksands, Sweden, March 26, 1964.
Defense. Shoots left. 6′1″, 187 lbs.
Last amateur club: Leksands IF (Sweden).
(Hartford's 4th choice, 67th over-all, in 1982 Entry Draft).

				Regular Season					Playoffs			
Season	Club	Lea	GP	G	A	TP	PIM	GP	G	A	TP	PIM
1981-82	Leksands	Swe.	31	3	1	4	40	....	....	....	....	....
1982-83	Leksands	Swe.	33	9	6	15	72	....	....	....	....	....
1983-84	Leksands	Swe.	36	5	10	15	53	....	....	....	....	....
1984-85	Hartford	NHL	41	2	6	8	83	....	....	....	....	....
	Binghamton	AHL	36	5	11	16	92	....	....	....	....	....
1985-86	Hartford	NHL	80	5	19	24	174	10	1	2	3	38
	NHL Totals		121	7	25	32	257	10	1	2	3	38

SANDELIN, SCOTT

Born, Hibbing, Minn., August 8, 1964.
Defense. Shoots right. 6′, 180 lbs.
Last amateur club: University of North Dakota Fighting Sioux (WCHA).
(Montreal's 5th choice, 48th over-all, in 1982 Entry Draft).

				Regular Season					Playoffs			
Season	Club	Lea	GP	G	A	TP	PIM	GP	G	A	TP	PIM
1981-82	Hibbing HS	Minn.	20	5	15	20	30	....	....	....	....	....
1982-83	North Dakota	WCHA	21	0	4	4	10	....	....	....	....	....
1983-84	North Dakota	WCHA	41	4	23	27	24	....	....	....	....	....
1984-85	North Dakota	WCHA	38	4	17	21	30	....	....	....	....	....
1985-86ab	North Dakota	WCHA	40	7	31	38	38	....	....	....	....	....
	Sherbrooke	AHL	6	0	2	2	2	....	....	....	....	....

a NCAA West Second All-Star Team (1986)
b WCHA First All-Star Team (1986).

SANDLAK, JIM

Born, Kitchener, Ont., December 12, 1966.
Right wing. Shoots right. 6′3″, 205 lbs.
Last amateur club: London Knights (OHL)
(Vancouver's 1st choice, 4th over-all, in 1985 Entry Draft)

				Regular Season					Playoffs			
Season	Club	Lea	GP	G	A	TP	PIM	GP	G	A	TP	PIM
1983-84	London	OHL	68	23	18	41	143	8	1	11	12	13
1984-85a	London	OHL	58	40	24	64	128	8	3	2	5	14
1985-86	Vancouver	NHL	23	1	3	4	10	3	0	1	1	0
	London	OHL	16	8	14	22	38	5	2	3	5	24
	NHL Totals		23	1	3	4	10	3	0	1	1	0

a OHL Third All-Star Team (1985)

SANDSTROM, TOMAS

Born, Fagersta, Sweden, September 4, 1964.
Right wing. Shoots left. 6′2″, 200 lbs.
Last amateur club: Brynas (Sweden).
(NY Rangers' 2nd choice, 36th over-all, in 1982 Entry Draft).

				Regular Season					Playoffs			
Season	Club	Lea	GP	G	A	TP	PIM	GP	G	A	TP	PIM
1982-83	Brynas	Swe.	36	22	14	36	36	....	....	....	....	....
1983-84	Brynas	Swe.	43	20	10	30	81	....	....	....	....	....
1984-85a	NY Rangers	NHL	74	29	29	58	51	3	0	2	2	0
1985-86	NY Rangers	NHL	73	25	29	54	109	16	4	6	10	20
	NHL Totals		147	54	58	112	160	19	4	8	12	20

a Named to NHL All-Rookie Team (1985)

SANIPASS, EVERETT

Born, Big Cove, N.B., February 13, 1968.
Left wing. Shoots left. 6′1″, 190 lbs.
Last amateur club: Verdun Junior Canadiens (QMJHL).
(Chicago's 1st choice, 14th overall, in 1986 Entry Draft).

				Regular Season					Playoffs			
Season	Club	Lea	GP	G	A	TP	PIM	GP	G	A	TP	PIM
1985-86	Verdun	QMJHL	67	23	66	89	320	5	0	2	2	16

SASSO, TOM

Born, Malden, Mass., November 20, 1966.
Center. Shoots right. 6′1″, 185 lbs.
Last amateur club: Babson College Beavers (ECAC).
(Quebec's 11th choice, 204th overall, in 1985 Entry Draft).

				Regular Season					Playoffs			
Season	Club	Lea	GP	G	A	TP	PIM	GP	G	A	TP	PIM
1984-85	Babson	ECAC	31	18	36	54	4	....	....	....	....	....
1985-86	Babson	ECAC	28	25	33	58	6	....	....	....	....	....

SAUNDERS, DAVID

Born, Ottawa, Ont., May 20, 1966.
Left wing. Shoots left. 6′1″, 195 lbs.
Last amateur club: St. Lawrence University Saints (ECAC).
(Vancouver's 3rd choice, 52nd overall, in 1984 Entry Draft).

				Regular Season					Playoffs			
Season	Club	Lea	GP	G	A	TP	PIM	GP	G	A	TP	PIM
1983-84	St. Lawrence	ECAC	32	10	21	31	24	....	....	....	....	....
1984-85	St. Lawrence	ECAC	27	7	9	16	16	....	....	....	....	....
1985-86	St. Lawrence	ECAC	29	15	19	34	26	....	....	....	....	....

SAUVE, JEAN-FRANÇOIS (SEW-vay)

Born, Ste-Geneviève, Que., January 23, 1960.
Center. Shoots left. 5′6″, 175 lbs.
Last amateur club: Trois-Rivières Draveurs (QMJHL).

				Regular Season					Playoffs			
Season	Club	Lea	GP	G	A	TP	PIM	GP	G	A	TP	PIM
1978-79a	Trois Rivières	QJHL	72	65	111	*176	31	13	*19	*19	*38	4
1979-80b	Trois Rivières	QJHL	72	63	*124	*187	31	7	5	9	14	0
1980-81c	Rochester	AHL	56	29	54	83	21	....	....	....	....	....
	Buffalo	NHL	20	5	9	14	12	5	2	0	2	0
1981-82	Rochester	AHL	7	5	8	13	6	....	....	....	....	....
	Buffalo	NHL	69	19	36	55	49	2	0	2	2	0
1982-83	Buffalo	NHL	9	0	4	4	9	....	....	....	....	....
	Rochester	AHL	73	30	69	99	10	16	7	21	28	2
1983-84	Fredericton	AHL	26	19	31	50	23	....	....	....	....	....
	Quebec	NHL	39	10	17	27	2	9	2	5	7	2
1984-85	Quebec	NHL	64	13	29	42	21	18	5	5	10	8
1985-86	Quebec	NHL	75	16	40	56	20	2	0	0	0	0
	NHL Totals		276	63	135	198	113	36	9	12	21	10

a QMJHL Second All-Star Team (1979)
b QMJHL First All-Star Team (1980)
c AHL Second All-Star Team (1981)

Signed as free agent by **Buffalo**, November 1, 1979. Traded to **Quebec** by **Buffalo** with Tony McKegney, Andre Savard and Buffalo's third round choice (Iiro Jarvi) in 1983 Entry Draft for Real Cloutier and Quebec's first round choice (Adam Creighton) in 1983 Entry Draft, June 8, 1983.

SAVARD, DENIS JOSEPH

(sa-VARH, den-NY)

Born, Pointe Gatineau, Que., February 4, 1961.
Center. Shoots right. 5'10", 175 lbs.
Last amateur club: Montreal Juniors (QMJHL).
(Chicago's 1st choice, 3rd over-all, in 1980 Entry Draft).

Season	Club	Lea	Regular Season					Playoffs				
			GP	G	A	TP	PIM	GP	G	A	TP	PIM
1978-79	Montreal	QJHL	70	46	*112	158	88	11	5	6	11	46
1979-80ab	Montreal	QJHL	72	63	118	181	93	10	7	16	23	8
1980-81	**Chicago**	**NHL**	76	28	47	75	47	3	0	0	0	0
1981-82	**Chicago**	**NHL**	80	32	87	119	82	15	11	7	18	52
1982-83c	**Chicago**	**NHL**	78	35	86	121	99	13	8	9	17	22
1983-84	**Chicago**	**NHL**	75	37	57	94	71	5	1	3	4	9
1984-85	**Chicago**	**NHL**	79	38	67	105	56	15	9	20	29	20
1985-86	**Chicago**	**NHL**	80	47	69	116	111	3	4	1	5	6
	NHL Totals		468	217	413	630	466	54	33	40	73	109

a QMJHL First All-Star Team (1980).
b Named QMJHL's Most Valuable Player (1980).
c NHL Second All-Star Team (1983).

SAWKINS, PETER

Born, Skagen, Denmark, August 9, 1963.
Defense. Shoots right. 6'3", 190 lbs.
Last amateur club: Yale University Bulldogs (ECAC).
(Los Angeles' 6th choice, 144th over-all, in 1981 Entry Draft).

Season	Club	Lea	Regular Season					Playoffs				
			GP	G	A	TP	PIM	GP	G	A	TP	PIM
1981-82	Yale	ECAC	24	0	5	5	20	....	....	....	....	....
1982-83	Yale	ECAC	26	2	8	10	10	....	....	....	....	....
1983-84	Yale	ECAC	25	2	14	16	24	....	....	....	....	....
1984-85	Yale	ECAC	28	1	11	12	20	....	....	....	....	....
1985-86	New Haven	AHL	7	1	2	3	14	....	....	....	....	....
	Toledo	IHL	25	4	8	12	25	....	....	....	....	....

SCEVIOUR, DARIN

Born, Lacombe, Alta., November 30, 1965.
Right wing. Shoots right. 5'10", 185 lbs.
Last amateur club: Lethbridge Broncos (WHL).
(Chicago's 5th choice, 101st over-all, in 1984 Entry Draft).

Season	Club	Lea	Regular Season					Playoffs				
			GP	G	A	TP	PIM	GP	G	A	TP	PIM
1982-83	Lethbridge	WHL	64	9	17	26	45	17	8	0	8	9
1983-84	Lethbridge	WHL	71	37	28	65	28	5	2	2	4	0
1984-85	Lethbridge	WHL	67	39	36	75	37	4	2	2	4	0
1985-86	Nova Scotia	AHL	31	4	3	7	6	....	....	....	....	....
	Saginaw	IHL	24	9	11	20	7	11	8	5	13	5

SCHAFHAUSER, WILLIAM (BILL)

Born, St. Paul, Minn., March 12, 1962.
Defense. Shoots right. 6', 190 lbs.
Last amateur club: Northern Michigan University Wildcats (CCHA).
(Chicago's 6th choice, 117th over-all, in 1981 Entry Draft).

Season	Club	Lea	Regular Season					Playoffs				
			GP	G	A	TP	PIM	GP	G	A	TP	PIM
1980-81	N. Michigan	CCHA	44	3	12	15	38	....	....	....	....	....
1981-82	N. Michigan	CCHA	35	12	15	27	33	....	....	....	....	....
1982-83	N. Michigan	CCHA	40	6	18	24	30	....	....	....	....	....
1983-84	N. Michigan	CCHA	39	6	21	27	34	....	....	....	....	....
1984-85	Kalamazoo	IHL	82	11	30	41	87	11	0	6	6	4
1985-86	Hershey	AHL	8	0	1	1	2	....	....	....	....	....
	Kalamazoo	IHL	75	9	45	54	46	6	1	2	3	2

SCHAMEHORN, KEVIN DEAN

(SHAME-horn)

Born, Calgary, Alta., July 28, 1956.
Right wing. Shoots right. 5'9", 185 lbs.
Last amateur club: New Westminster Bruins (WHL).
(Detroit's 4th choice, 58th over-all, in 1976 Amateur Draft).

Season	Club	Lea	Regular Season					Playoffs				
			GP	G	A	TP	PIM	GP	G	A	TP	PIM
1974-75	N. Westminster	WHL	37	14	6	20	175	....	....	....	....	....
1975-76	N. Westminster	WHL	62	32	42	74	276	....	....	....	....	....
1976-77	**Detroit**	**NHL**	3	0	0	0	9	....	....	....	....	....
	Kalamazoo	IHL	77	27	32	59	314	10	3	9	12	76
1977-78	Kansas City	CHL	36	5	3	8	113	....	....	....	....	....
	Kalamazoo	IHL	39	18	14	32	144	7	1	3	4	65
1978-79	Kalamazoo	IHL	80	45	57	102	245	15	*15	9	24	60
1979-80	**Detroit**	**NHL**	2	0	0	0	4	....	....	....	....	....
	Adirondack	AHL	60	10	13	23	145	5	0	0	0	13
1980-81	**Los Angeles**	**NHL**	5	0	0	0	4	....	....	....	....	....
	Rochester	AHL	27	6	10	16	44	....	....	....	....	....
	Houston	CHL	26	7	9	16	43	....	....	....	....	....
1981-82	Kalamazoo	IHL	75	38	27	65	113	5	1	2	3	25
1982-83	Kalamazoo	IHL	58	38	29	67	78	9	6	3	9	24
1983-84	Kalamazoo	IHL	76	37	31	68	154	3	0	2	2	9
1984-85	Kalamazoo	IHL	80	35	43	78	154	11	4	3	7	31
1985-86	Milwaukee	IHL	82	47	34	81	101	5	1	3	4	4
	NHL Totals		10	0	0	0	17	....	....	....	....	....

Signed as free agent by **Los Angeles**, October 18, 1980.

SCHENNA, ROB

Born, Saugus, Mass., February 5, 1967.
Defense. Shoots left. 6'1", 190 lbs.
Last amateur club: Rensselaer Polytechnic Institute Engineers (ECAC).
(Detroit's 9th choice, 197th overall, in 1985 Entry Draft).

Season	Club	Lea	Regular Season					Playoffs				
			GP	G	A	TP	PIM	GP	G	A	TP	PIM
1985-86	RPI	ECAC	32	0	6	6	63	....	....	....	....	....

SCHLIEBENER, ANDREAS (ANDY)

(SHLEEB-ner)

Born, Ottawa, Ont., August 16, 1962.
Defense. Shoots left. 6', 200 lbs.
Last amateur club: Niagara Falls Flyers (OHL).
(Vancouver's 2nd choice, 49th over-all, in 1980 Entry Draft).

Season	Club	Lea	Regular Season					Playoffs				
			GP	G	A	TP	PIM	GP	G	A	TP	PIM
1980-81	Peterborough	OHA	68	9	48	57	144	5	1	3	4	4
1981-82	Peterborough	OHL	14	1	9	10	25	....	....	....	....	....
	Niagara Falls	OHL	27	6	26	32	33	5	3	5	8	14
	Vancouver	**NHL**	22	0	1	1	10	3	0	0	0	0
	Dallas	CHL	8	2	2	4	4	9	0	4	4	10
1982-83	Fredericton	AHL	76	4	15	19	20	10	0	3	3	7
1983-84	Fredericton	AHL	27	1	6	7	27	....	....	....	....	....
	Vancouver	**NHL**	51	2	10	12	48	3	0	0	0	0
1984-85	**Vancouver**	**NHL**	11	0	0	0	16	....	....	....	....	....
	Fredericton	AHL	47	1	11	12	58	....	....	....	....	....
1985-86	Fredericton	AHL	73	3	9	12	60	6	0	1	1	10
	NHL Totals		84	2	11	13	74	6	0	0	0	0

SCHMIDT, NORM

Born, Sault Ste. Marie, Ont., January 24, 1963.
Defense. Shoots right. 5'11", 190 lbs.
Last amateur club: Oshawa Generals (OHL).
(Pittsburgh's 4th choice, 70th over-all, in 1981 Entry Draft).

Season	Club	Lea	Regular Season					Playoffs				
			GP	G	A	TP	PIM	GP	G	A	TP	PIM
1980-81	Oshawa	OHA	65	12	25	37	73	11	2	5	7	25
1981-82a	Oshawa	OHL	67	13	48	61	172	....	....	....	....	....
1982-83b	Oshawa	OHL	61	21	49	70	114	17	1	16	20	47
1983-84	**Pittsburgh**	**NHL**	34	6	12	18	12	....	....	....	....	....
	Baltimore	AHL	43	4	12	16	31	....	....	....	....	....
1984-85	Baltimore	AHL	33	0	22	22	31	....	....	....	....	....
1985-86	**Pittsburgh**	**NHL**	66	15	14	29	57	....	....	....	....	....
	NHL Totals		100	21	26	47	69	....	....	....	....	....

a OHL Third All-Star Team (1982)
b OHL Second All-Star Team (1983)

SCHNEIDER, SCOTT

Born, Rochester, Minn., May 18, 1965.
Center. Shoots right. 6'1", 175 lbs.
Last amateur club: Colorado College Tigers (WCHA).
(Winnipeg's 4th choice, 93rd overall, in 1984 Entry Draft).

Season	Club	Lea	Regular Season					Playoffs				
			GP	G	A	TP	PIM	GP	G	A	TP	PIM
1983-84	Colorado	WCHA	35	19	14	33	24	....	....	....	....	....
1984-85	Colorado	WCHA	33	16	13	29	60	....	....	....	....	....
1985-86	Colorado	WCHA	40	16	22	38	32	....	....	....	....	....

SCHOFIELD, DWIGHT HAMILTON

Born, Waltham, Mass., March 25, 1956.
Defense. Shoots left. 6'3", 195 lbs.
Last amateur club: London Knights (OHA).
(Detroit's 5th choice, 76th over-all, in 1976 Amateur Draft).

Season	Club	Lea	Regular Season					Playoffs				
			GP	G	A	TP	PIM	GP	G	A	TP	PIM
1974-75	London	OHA	70	6	16	22	124	....	....	....	....	....
1975-76	London	OHA	59	14	29	43	121	....	....	....	....	....
1976-77	**Detroit**	**NHL**	3	1	0	1	2	10	4	7	11	61
	Kalamazoo	IHL	73	20	41	61	180					
1977-78	Kalamazoo	IHL	3	3	6	9	21	....	....	....	....	....
	Kansas City	CHL	22	3	7	10	58	....	....	....	....	....
1978-79	Kansas City	CHL	13	1	4	5	20	....	....	....	....	....
	Kalamazoo	IHL	47	8	29	37	199	....	....	....	....	....
	Fort Wayne	IHL	14	2	3	5	54	13	0	9	9	28
1979-80	Dayton	IHL	71	15	47	62	257	....	....	....	....	....
	Tulsa	CHL	1	0	0	0	0	....	....	....	....	....
1980-81	Milwaukee	IHL	82	18	41	59	327	7	2	5	7	25
1981-82	Nova Scotia	AHL	75	7	24	31	335	9	1	3	4	41
1982-83	**Montreal**	**NHL**	2	0	0	0	7	....	....	....	....	....
	Nova Scotia	AHL	73	10	21	31	248	7	0	3	3	21
1983-84	**St. Louis**	**NHL**	70	4	10	14	219	4	0	0	0	26
1984-85	**St. Louis**	**NHL**	43	1	4	5	184	2	0	0	0	15
1985-86	**Washington**	**NHL**	50	1	2	3	127	3	0	0	0	14
	NHL Totals		168	7	16	23	539	9	0	0	0	55

Signed as a free agent by **Montreal**, September 20, 1982. Claimed by **St. Louis** from **Montreal** in NHL Waiver Draft, October 3, 1983. Claimed by **Washington** from **St. Louis** in NHL Waiver Draft, October 7, 1985.

SCHRADER, KEVIN

Born, Wells, Minn., February 1, 1967.
Defense. Shoots right. 6'2", 200 lbs.
Last amateur club: University of New Hampshire Wildcats (H.E.).
(New Jersey's 7th choice, 129th overall, in 1985 Entry Draft).

			Regular Season					Playoffs			
Season	Club	Lea	GP	G	A	TP	PIM	GP	G	A	TP	PIM
1985-86	N. Hampshire	H.E.	32	1	0	1	22	....	....	....	....	....

SCHUTT, RODNEY (ROD)   (SHUT)

Born, Bancroft, Ont., October 13, 1956.
Left wing. Shoots left. 5'10", 185 lbs.
Last amateur club: Sudbury Wolves (OHA).
(Montreal's 2nd choice, 13th over-all, in 1976 Amateur Draft).

			Regular Season					Playoffs				
Season	Club	Lea	GP	G	A	TP	PIM	GP	G	A	TP	PIM
1974-75a	Sudbury	OHA	69	43	61	104	66	15	13	9	22	2
1975-76a	Sudbury	OHA	63	72	63	135	42	17	18	16	34	13
1976-77b	Nova Scotia	AHL	80	33	51	84	56	12	8	*8	8	16	4
1977-78	**Montreal**	**NHL**	2	0	0	0	0	....	....	....	....	....
	Nova Scotia	AHL	77	36	44	80	57	11	4	7	11	2
1978-79	**Pittsburgh**	**NHL**	74	24	21	45	33	7	2	0	2	4
1979-80	**Pittsburgh**	**NHL**	73	18	21	39	43	5	2	1	3	6
1980-81	**Pittsburgh**	**NHL**	80	25	35	60	55	5	3	3	6	16
1981-82	Erie	AHL	35	12	15	27	40	....	....	....	....	....
	Pittsburgh	**NHL**	35	9	12	21	42	5	1	2	3	0
1982-83	**Pittsburgh**	**NHL**	5	0	0	0	0	....	....	....	....	....
	Baltimore	AHL	64	34	53	87	24	....	....	....	....	....
1983-84	**Pittsburgh**	**NHL**	11	1	3	4	4	....	....	....	....	....
	Baltimore	AHL	36	15	19	34	48	10	3	1	4	22
1984-85	Muskegon	IHL	79	44	46	90	58	17	10	13	23	10
1985-86	**Toronto**	**NHL**	6	0	0	0	0	....	....	....	....	....
	St. Catharines	AHL	70	21	28	49	44	13	7	4	11	18
	NHL Totals		**286**	**77**	**92**	**169**	**177**	**22**	**8**	**6**	**14**	**26**

a OHA First All-Star Team (1975, 1976).
b Won Dudley (Red) Garrett Memorial Trophy (AHL's Rookie of the Year) (1977).
Traded to **Pittsburgh** by **Montreal** for Pittsburgh's first-round choice (Mark Hunter) in the 1981 Entry Draft, October 18, 1978. Signed as a free agent by **Toronto**, October 3, 1985.

SEABROOKE, GLEN

Born, Peterborough, Ont., September 11, 1967.
Center. Shoots left. 6'1", 175 lbs.
Last amateur club: Peterbourough Petes (OHL).
(Philadelphia's 1st choice, 21st over-all, in 1985 Entry Draft).

			Regular Season					Playoffs				
Season	Club	Lea	GP	G	A	TP	PIM	GP	G	A	TP	PIM
1983-84	Peterborough	Midget	29	36	31	67	31	....	....	....	....	....
1984-85	Peterborough	OHL	45	21	13	34	49	16	3	5	8	4
1985-86	Peterborough	OHL	19	8	12	20	33	14	9	7	16	14

SECORD, ALAN WILLIAM (AL)   (SEE-cord)

Born, Sudbury, Ont., March 3, 1958.
Left wing. Shoots left. 6'1", 205 lbs.
Last amateur club: Hamilton Fincups (OHA).
(Boston's 1st choice, 16th over-all, in 1978 Amateur Draft).

			Regular Season					Playoffs				
Season	Club	Lea	GP	G	A	TP	PIM	GP	G	A	TP	PIM
1976-77	St. Catharines	OHA	57	32	34	66	343	14	4	3	7	46
1977-78	Hamilton	OHA	59	28	22	50	185	20	8	11	19	71
1978-79	Rochester	AHL	4	4	2	6	40	....	....	....	....	....
	Boston	**NHL**	71	16	7	23	125	4	0	0	0	4
1979-80	**Boston**	**NHL**	77	23	16	39	170	10	0	3	3	65
1980-81	Springfield	AHL	8	3	5	8	21	....	....	....	....	....
	Boston	**NHL**	18	0	3	3	42	....	....	....	....	....
	Chicago	**NHL**	41	13	9	22	145	3	4	0	4	14
1981-82	**Chicago**	**NHL**	80	44	31	75	303	15	2	5	7	61
1982-83	**Chicago**	**NHL**	80	54	32	86	180	12	4	7	11	66
1983-84	**Chicago**	**NHL**	14	4	4	8	77	5	3	4	7	28
1984-85	**Chicago**	**NHL**	51	15	11	26	193	15	7	9	16	42
1985-86	**Chicago**	**NHL**	80	40	36	76	201	2	0	2	2	26
	NHL Totals		**512**	**209**	**149**	**358**	**1436**	**66**	**22**	**30**	**52**	**306**

Traded to **Chicago** by **Boston** for Mike O'Connell, December 18, 1980.

SEFTEL, STEVE

Born, Kitchener, Ont., May 14, 1968.
Left wing. Shoots left. 6'1", 185 lbs.
Last amateur club: Kingston Canadians (OHL).
(Washington's 2nd choice, 40th overall, in 1986 Entry Draft).

			Regular Season					Playoffs				
Season	Club	Lea	GP	G	A	TP	PIM	GP	G	A	TP	PIM
1985-86	Kingston	OHL	42	11	16	27	53	....	....	....	....	....

SEGUIN, STEVE

Born, Cornwall, Ont., April 10, 1964.
Right wing. Shoots right. 6'2", 200 lbs.
Last amateur club: Peterborough Petes (OHL).
(Los Angeles' 2nd choice, 48th over-all, in 1982 Entry Draft).

			Regular Season					Playoffs				
Season	Club	Lea	GP	G	A	TP	PIM	GP	G	A	TP	PIM
1981-82	Kingston	OHL	62	23	31	54	75	4	0	2	2	4
1982-83	Kingston	OHL	19	8	17	25	42	....	....	....	....	....
	Peterborough	OHL	44	16	30	46	22	4	0	1	1	2
1983-84	Peterborough	OHL	67	55	51	106	84	8	8	8	16	11
1984-85	**Los Angeles**	**NHL**	5	0	0	0	9	....	....	....	....	....
	New Haven	AHL	58	18	7	25	39	....	....	....	....	....
1985-86	New Haven	AHL	2	0	0	0	0	....	....	....	....	....
	Hershey	AHL	75	25	29	54	91	15	2	0	2	22
	NHL Totals		**5**	**0**	**0**	**0**	**9**	....	....	....	....	....

Traded to **Philadelphia** by **Los Angeles** with Los Angeles' second-round choice (Jukka Seppo) in 1986 Entry Draft for Paul Guay and Joe Paterson, October 11, 1985.

SEILING, RICHARD JAMES (RIC)   (SEE-ling)

Born, Elmira, Ont., December 15, 1957.
Right wing/Center. Shoots right. 6'1", 180 lbs.
Last amateur club: St. Catharines Fincups (OHA).
(Buffalo's 1st choice, 14th over-all, in 1977 Amateur Draft).

			Regular Season					Playoffs				
Season	Club	Lea	GP	G	A	TP	PIM	GP	G	A	TP	PIM
1975-76	Hamilton	OHA	59	35	51	86	49	14	14	13	27	19
1976-77a	St. Catharines	OHA	62	49	61	110	103	14	6	6	12	36
1977-78	**Buffalo**	**NHL**	80	19	19	38	33	8	0	2	2	7
1978-79	**Buffalo**	**NHL**	78	20	22	42	56	3	0	1	1	2
1979-80	**Buffalo**	**NHL**	80	25	35	60	54	14	5	4	9	6
1980-81	**Buffalo**	**NHL**	74	30	27	57	80	8	2	2	4	2
1981-82	**Buffalo**	**NHL**	57	22	25	47	58	4	1	1	2	2
1982-83	**Buffalo**	**NHL**	75	19	22	41	41	10	2	3	5	6
1983-84	**Buffalo**	**NHL**	78	13	22	35	42	3	0	0	0	6
1984-85	**Buffalo**	**NHL**	73	16	15	31	86	5	4	1	5	4
1985-86	**Buffalo**	**NHL**	69	12	13	25	74	....	....	....	....	....
	NHL Totals		**664**	**176**	**200**	**376**	**524**	**55**	**14**	**14**	**28**	**31**

a OHA Third All-Star Team (1977)

SEMENKO, DAVID (DAVE)   (se-MENK-oh)

Born, Winnipeg, Man., July 12, 1957.
Left wing. Shoots left. 6'3", 200 lbs.
Last amateur club: Brandon Wheat Kings (WHL).
(Minnesota's 2nd choice, 25th over-all, in 1977 Amateur Draft).

			Regular Season					Playoffs				
Season	Club	Lea	GP	G	A	TP	PIM	GP	G	A	TP	PIM
1976-77	Brandon	WHL	61	27	33	60	265	16	3	4	7	61
1977-78	Brandon	WHL	7	10	5	15	40	....	....	....	....	....
	Edmonton	WHA	65	6	6	12	140	5	0	0	0	8
1978-79	Edmonton	WHA	77	10	14	24	158	11	4	2	6	29
1979-80	**Edmonton**	**NHL**	67	6	7	13	135	3	0	0	0	2
1980-81	Wichita	CHL	14	1	2	3	40	....	....	....	....	....
	Edmonton	**NHL**	58	11	8	19	80	8	0	0	0	5
1981-82	**Edmonton**	**NHL**	59	12	12	24	194	4	0	0	0	2
1982-83	**Edmonton**	**NHL**	75	12	15	27	141	15	1	1	2	69
1983-84	**Edmonton**	**NHL**	52	6	11	17	118	19	5	5	10	44
1984-85	**Edmonton**	**NHL**	69	6	12	18	172	14	0	0	0	39
1985-86	**Edmonton**	**NHL**	69	6	12	18	141	6	0	0	0	32
	NHL Totals		**449**	**59**	**77**	**136**	**981**	**69**	**6**	**6**	**12**	**193**
	WHA Totals		**142**	**16**	**20**	**36**	**298**	**16**	**4**	**2**	**6**	**37**

Reclaimed by **Minnesota** from **Edmonton** prior to Expansion Draft, June 9, 1979. Traded to **Edmonton** by **Minnesota** for Edmonton's second round (Neal Broten) and third round (Kevin Maxwell) choices in 1979 Entry Draft, August 9, 1979.

SEPPO, JUKKA

Born, Vassa Finland, January 2, 1968.
Forward. Shoots left. 6'1", 180 lbs.
Last amateur club: Vaasa Sport (Finland).
(Philadelphia's 2nd choice, 23rd over-all, in 1986 Entry Draft).

			Regular Season					Playoffs				
Season	Club	Lea	GP	G	A	TP	PIM	GP	G	A	TP	PIM
1985-86	Vassa Sport	Fin.	36	33	34	67	83	....	....	....	....	....

SERVINIS, GEORGE

Born, Toronto, Ont., April 29, 1962.
Left wing. Shoots left. 5'11", 180 lbs.
Last amateur club: Rensselaer Polytechnic Institute Engineers (ECAC).

			Regular Season					Playoffs				
Season	Club	Lea	GP	G	A	TP	PIM	GP	G	A	TP	PIM
1982-83	RPI	ECAC	28	35	29	64	22	....	....	....	....	....
1983-84	Cdn. Olympic		43	13	11	24	33	....	....	....	....	....
	RPI	ECAC	12	5	13	18	14	....	....	....	....	....
1984-85	RPI	ECAC	35	34	25	59	44	....	....	....	....	....
1985-86	Springfield	AHL	30	2	14	16	19	....	....	....	....	....

Signed as a free agent by **Minnesota**, August 13, 1985.

SHANNON, DARRYL

Born, Barrie, Ont., June 21, 1968.
Defense. Shoots left. 6'2", 190 lbs.
Last amateur club: Windsor Compuware Spitfires (OHL).
(Toronto's 2nd choice, 36th over-all, in 1986 Entry Draft).

			Regular Season					Playoffs				
Season	Club	Lea	GP	G	A	TP	PIM	GP	G	A	TP	PIM
1985-86	Windsor	OHL	57	6	21	27	52	16	5	6	11	22

SHARPLES, JEFF

Born, Terrace, B.C., July 28, 1967.
Defense. Shoots left. 6'0", 185 lbs.
Last Winter club: Portland Winter Hawks (WHL)
(Detroit's 2nd choice, 29th over-all, in 1985 Entry Draft)

			Regular Season					Playoffs				
Season	Club	Lea	GP	G	A	TP	PIM	GP	G	A	TP	PIM
1983-84	Kelowna	WHL	72	9	24	33	51	....	....	....	....	....
1984-85a	Kelowna	WHL	72	12	41	53	90	6	0	1	1	6
1985-86	Portland	WHL	22	2	6	8	48	15	2	6	8	6

a WHL Second All-Star Team, West Division (1985)

SHAUNESSY, SCOTT

Born, Newport, RI, January 22, 1964.
Defense. Shoots left. 6'4", 220 lbs.
Last amateur club: Boston University Terriers (H.E.).
(Quebec's 9th choice, 192nd over-all, in 1983 Entry Draft).

			Regular Season					Playoffs				
Season	Club	Lea	GP	G	A	TP	PIM	GP	G	A	TP	PIM
1983-84	Boston U.	H.E.	40	6	22	28	48	....	....	....	....	....
1984-85	Boston U.	H.E.	42	7	15	22	87	....	....	....	....	....
1985-86a	Boston U.	H.E.	38	16	13	19	31	....	....	....	....	....

a Hockey East First All-Star Team (1986)

SHAW, BRAD

Born, Cambridge, Ont., April 28, 1964.
Defense. Shoots right. 5'11", 160 lbs.
Last amateur club: Ottawa 67's (OHL).
(Detroit's 5th choice, 86th over-all, in 1982 Entry Draft).

			Regular Season					Playoffs				
Season	Club	Lea	GP	G	A	TP	PIM	GP	G	A	TP	PIM
1981-82	Ottawa	OHL	68	13	59	72	24	15	1	13	14	4
1982-83	Ottawa	OHL	63	12	66	78	24	9	2	9	11	4
1983-84a	Ottawa	OHL	68	11	71	82	75	13	2	*27	29	9
1984-85	Binghamton	AHL	24	1	10	11	4	8	1	8	9	6
	Salt Lake	IHL	44	3	29	32	25	....	....	....	....	....
1985-86	Hartford	NHL	8	0	2	2	4	....	....	....	....	....
	Binghamton	AHL	64	10	44	54	33	5	0	2	2	6
	NHL Totals		8	0	2	2	4	....	....	....	....	....

a OHL First All-Star Team (1984)
Rights traded to Hartford by Detroit for Hartford's eighth round choice (Urban Nordin) in 1984 Entry Draft, May 29, 1984.

SHAW, LARRY

Born, Guelph, Ont., February 10, 1967.
Defense. Shoots right. 6'1", 200 lbs.
Last amateur club: Peterborough Petes (OHL).
(Washington's 5th choice, 83rd over-all, in 1985 Entry Draft).

			Regular Season					Playoffs				
Season	Club	Lea	GP	G	A	TP	PIM	GP	G	A	TP	PIM
1984-85	Peterborough	OHL	54	1	11	12	93	16	0	1	1	9
1985-86	Peterborough	OHL	66	2	17	19	106	16	1	1	2	24

SHAW, BRIAN JAMES

Born, Edmonton, Alta., May 20, 1962.
Right wing. Shoots right. 6', 190 lbs.
Last amateur club: Portland Winter Hawks (WHL).
(Chicago's 9th choice, 78th over-all, in 1980 Entry Draft).

			Regular Season					Playoffs				
Season	Club	Lea	GP	G	A	TP	PIM	GP	G	A	TP	PIM
1979-80	Portland	WHL	68	20	25	45	161	3	1	1	2	0
1980-81	Portland	WHL	72	53	65	118	176	9	3	7	10	29
1981-82	Portland	WHL	69	56	76	132	193	15	*18	9	27	30
1982-83	Springfield	AHL	79	15	17	32	62	....	....	....	....	....
1983-84	Springfield	AHL	4	2	2	4	2	....	....	....	....	....
	Peoria	IHL	54	27	27	54	49	....	....	....	....	....
1984-85	Peoria	IHL	63	31	14	45	163	20	9	9	18	77
1985-86	Adirondack	AHL	23	3	1	4	14	....	....	....	....	....
	Peoria	IHL	54	41	23	64	139	10	3	4	7	32

Signed as a free agent by Detroit, August 14, 1985.

SHAW, DAVID

Born, St. Thomas, Ont., May 25, 1964.
Defense. Shoots right. 6'1", 190 lbs.
Last amateur club: Kitchener Rangers (OHL).
(Quebec's 1st choice, 13th over-all, in 1982 Entry Draft).

			Regular Season					Playoffs				
Season	Club	Lea	GP	G	A	TP	PIM	GP	G	A	TP	PIM
1981-82	Kitchener	OHL	68	6	25	31	94	15	2	2	4	51
1982-83	Quebec	NHL	2	0	0	0	0	....	....	....	....	....
	Kitchener	OHL	57	18	56	74	78	12	2	10	12	18
1983-84	Quebec	NHL	3	0	0	0	0	....	....	....	....	....
a	Kitchener	OHL	58	14	34	48	73	16	4	9	13	12
1984-85	Quebec	NHL	14	0	0	0	11	....	....	....	....	....
	Fredericton	AHL	48	7	6	13	73	2	0	0	0	7
1985-86	Quebec	NHL	73	7	19	26	78	....	....	....	....	....
	NHL Totals		90	7	19	26	89	....	....	....	....	....

a OHL First All-Star Team (1984)

SHEDDEN, DOUGLAS ARTHUR (DOUG)

Born, Wallaceburg, Ont., April 29, 1961.
Center. Shoots right. 6', 185 lbs.
Last amateur club: Sault Ste. Marie Greyhounds (OHA).
(Pittsburgh's 5th choice, 93rd over-all, in 1980 Entry Draft).

			Regular Season					Playoffs				
Season	Club	Lea	GP	G	A	TP	PIM	GP	G	A	TP	PIM
1979-80	Kitchener	OHA	16	10	16	26	26	....	....	....	....	....
	S. S. Marie	OHA	45	30	44	74	59	....	....	....	....	....
1980-81	S. S. Marie	OHA	66	51	72	123	114	19	16	22	38	10
1981-82	Erie	AHL	17	4	6	10	14	....	....	....	....	....
	Pittsburgh	NHL	38	10	15	25	12	....	....	....	....	....
1982-83	Pittsburgh	NHL	80	24	43	67	54	....	....	....	....	....
1983-84	Pittsburgh	NHL	67	22	35	57	20	....	....	....	....	....
1984-85	Pittsburgh	NHL	80	35	32	67	30	....	....	....	....	....
1985-86	Pittsburgh	NHL	67	32	34	66	32	....	....	....	....	....
	Detroit	NHL	11	2	3	5	2	....	....	....	....	....
	NHL Totals		343	125	162	287	150	....	....	....	....	....

Traded to Detroit by Pittsburgh for Ron Duguay, March 11, 1986.

SHEEHY, NEIL

Born, Fort Frances, Ont., February 9, 1960.
Defense. Shoots right. 6'2", 210 lbs.
Last amateur club: Harvard University Crimson (ECAC).

			Regular Season					Playoffs				
Season	Club	Lea	GP	G	A	TP	PIM	GP	G	A	TP	PIM
1979-80	Harvard	ECAC	13	0	0	0	10	....	....	....	....	....
1980-81	Harvard	ECAC	26	4	8	12	22	....	....	....	....	....
1981-82	Harvard	ECAC	30	7	11	18	46	....	....	....	....	....
1982-83	Harvard	ECAC	34	5	13	18	48	....	....	....	....	....
1983-84	Calgary	NHL	1	1	0	1	2	....	....	....	....	....
	Colorado	CHL	74	5	18	23	151	....	....	....	....	....
1984-85	Calgary	NHL	31	3	4	7	109	....	....	....	....	....
	Moncton	AHL	34	6	9	15	101	....	....	....	....	....
1985-86	Calgary	NHL	65	2	16	18	271	22	0	2	2	79
	Moncton	AHL	4	1	1	2	21	....	....	....	....	....
	NHL Totals		97	6	20	26	382	22	0	2	2	79

Signed as free agent by Calgary, August 16, 1983.

SHEPPARD, RAY

Born, Pembroke, Ont., May 27, 1966.
Right wing. Shoots right. 5'11", 180 lbs.
Last amateur club: Cornwall Royals (OHL).
(Buffalo's 3rd choice, 60th over-all, in 1984 Entry Draft).

			Regular Season					Playoffs				
Season	Club	Lea	GP	G	A	TP	PIM	GP	G	A	TP	PIM
1983-84	Cornwall	OHL	68	44	36	80	69	....	....	....	....	....
1984-85	Cornwall	OHL	49	25	33	58	51	9	2	12	14	4
1985-86ab	Cornwall	OHL	63	81	61	142	25	6	7	4	11	0

a OHL Player of the Year (1986)
b OHL First All-Star Team (1986)

SHERVEN, GORD

Born, Gravelbourg, Sask., August 21, 1963.
Center. Shoots right. 6', 185 lbs.
Last amateur club: University of North Dakota Fighting Sioux (WCHA)
(Edmonton's 9th choice, 197th over-all, in 1981 Entry Draft).

			Regular Season					Playoffs				
Season	Club	Lea	GP	G	A	TP	PIM	GP	G	A	TP	PIM
1981-82	North Dakota	WCHA	46	18	25	43	16	....	....	....	....	....
1982-83	North Dakota	WCHA	36	12	21	33	16	....	....	....	....	....
1983-84	Cdn. Olympic	...	46	9	13	22	13	....	....	....	....	....
	Edmonton	NHL	2	1	0	1	0	....	....	....	....	....
1984-85	Edmonton	NHL	37	9	7	16	10	....	....	....	....	....
	Minnesota	NHL	32	2	12	14	8	3	0	0	0	0
	Nova Scotia	AHL	5	4	5	9	5	....	....	....	....	....
1985-86	Minnesota	NHL	13	0	2	2	11	....	....	....	....	....
	Springfield	AHL	11	3	7	10	8	....	....	....	....	....
	Edmonton	NHL	5	1	1	2	4	....	....	....	....	....
	Nova Scotia	AHL	38	14	17	31	4	....	....	....	....	....
	NHL Totals		89	13	22	35	33	....	....	....	....	....

Traded to Minnesota by Edmonton with Terry Martin for Mark Napier, January 24, 1985.
Traded to Edmonton by Minnesota with Don Biggs for Marc Habscheid, Dan Barber and Emanuel Viveiros, December 20, 1985.

SHIBICKY, BILL

Born, Burnaby, B.C., January 25, 1964.
Center. Shoots right. 5'9", 165 lbs.
Last amateur club: Michigan State University Spartans (CCHA).
(Detroit's 9th choice, 175th over-all, in 1984 Entry Draft).

			Regular Season					Playoffs				
Season	Club	Lea	GP	G	A	TP	PIM	GP	G	A	TP	PIM
1983-84	Michigan St.	CCHA	43	18	37	55	59	....	....	....	....	....
1984-85	Michigan St.	CCHA	32	8	24	32	60	....	....	....	....	....
1985-86	Michigan St.	CCHA	44	17	39	56	104	....	....	....	....	....

SHOEBOTTOM, BRUCE

Born, Windsor, Ont., August 20, 1965.
Defense, Shoots left. 6'2", 200 lbs.
Amateur club: Peterborough Petes (OHL)
(Los Angeles' 1st choice, 47th over-all, in 1983 Entry Draft).

Season	Club	Lea	GP	G	A	TP	PIM	GP	G	A	TP	PIM
				Regular Season					Playoffs			
1982-83	Peterborough	OHL	34	2	10	12	106	....	....	....	....	....
1983-84	Peterborough	OHL	16	0	5	5	73	....	....	....	....	....
1984-85	Perterborough	OHL	60	2	15	17	143	17	0	4	4	26
1985-86	New Haven	AHL	6	2	0	2	12	....	....	....	....	....
	Binghamton	AHL	62	7	5	12	249	....	....	....	....	....

Traded to **Washington** by **Los Angeles** for Bryan Erickson, October 31, 1985.

SHOLD, TERRY

Born, Grand Marais, Minn., July 29, 1966.
Left wing. Shoots left. 6'1", 185 lbs.
Last amateur club: University of Minnesota-Duluth Bulldogs (WCHA).
(New Jersey's 10th choice, 192nd over-all, in 1985 Entry Draft).

Season	Club	Lea	GP	G	A	TP	PIM	GP	G	A	TP	PIM
				Regular Season					Playoffs			
1985-86	Minn-Duluth	WCHA	18	1	1	2	2	....	....	....	....	....

SHUDRA, RON

Born, Winnipeg, Man., November 28, 1967.
Defense. Shoots left. 6'1", 180 lbs.
Last amateur club: Kamloops Blazers (WHL).
(Edmonton's 3rd choice, 63rd over-all, in 1986 Entry Draft).

Season	Club	Lea	GP	G	A	TP	PIM	GP	G	A	TP	PIM
				Regular Season					Playoffs			
1985-86a	Kamloops	WHL	72	10	40	50	81	16	1	11	12	11

a WHL Rookie of the Year (1986)

SHUMSKI, JOHN

Born, Stoneham, Mass., October 10, 1963.
Center. Shoots right. 6'3", 205 lbs.
Last amateur club: University of Lowell Chiefs (H.E.)
(St. Louis' 7th choice, 197th over-all, in 1982 Entry Draft).

Season	Club	Lea	GP	G	A	TP	PIM	GP	G	A	TP	PIM
				Regular Season					Playoffs			
1981-82	RPI	ECAC	28	8	15	23	12	....	....	....	....	....
1982-83	RPI	ECAC	14	5	4	9	12	....	....	....	....	....
1983-84	DID NOT PLAY											
1984-85	U. of Lowell	ECAC	41	22	31	53	66	....	....	....	....	....
1985-86	U. of Lowell	H.E.	16	1	6	7	10	....	....	....	....	....

SILK, DAVID (DAVE)

Born, Scituate, Mass., January 1, 1958.
Right wing. Shoots right. 5'11", 190 lbs.
Last amateur club: 1980 United States Olympic Team.
(NY Rangers' 4th choice, 59th over-all, in 1978 Amateur Draft).

Season	Club	Lea	GP	G	A	TP	PIM	GP	G	A	TP	PIM
				Regular Season					Playoffs			
1977-78a	Boston U.	ECAC	28	27	31	58	57	....	....	....	....	....
1978-79	Boston U.	ECAC	23	8	12	20	20	....	....	....	....	....
1979-80	U.S. National	...	56	12	36	48	32	....	....	....	....	....
	U.S. Olympic	...	7	2	3	5	0	....	....	....	....	....
	NY Rangers	NHL	2	0	0	0	0	....	....	....	....	....
	New Haven	AHL	11	1	9	10	0	9	1	2	3	12
1980-81	**NY Rangers**	NHL	59	14	12	26	58	....	....	....	....	....
	New Haven	AHL	12	0	4	4	34	3	0	0	0	0
1981-82	**NY Rangers**	NHL	64	15	20	35	39	9	2	4	6	4
1982-83	**NY Rangers**	NHL	16	1	1	2	15	....	....	....	....	....
	Tulsa	CHL	40	28	29	57	67	....	....	....	....	....
	Binghamton	AHL	9	1	2	3	29	....	....	....	....	....
1983-84	Hershey	AHL	15	11	10	21	22	....	....	....	....	....
	Boston	NHL	35	13	17	30	64	3	0	0	0	7
1984-85	**Boston**	NHL	29	7	5	12	22	....	....	....	....	....
	Detroit	NHL	12	2	0	2	10	....	....	....	....	....
1985-86	**Winnipeg**	NHL	32	2	4	6	63	1	0	0	0	2
	Sherbrooke	AHL	18	5	14	19	18	....	....	....	....	....
	NHL Totals		249	54	59	113	271	13	2	4	6	13

a ECAC Second All-Star Team (1978)

Traded to **Boston** by **NY Rangers** for Dave Barr, October 5, 1983. Claimed by **Detroit** from **Boston** on waivers, December 21, 1984. Signed as a free agent by **Winnipeg**, September 30, 1985.

SILTALA, MICHAEL

Born, Toronto, Ont., August 5, 1963.
Right wing. Shoots right. 5'9", 170 lbs.
Last amateur club: Kingston Canadians (OHL)
(Washington's 4th choice, 89th over-all, in 1981 Entry Draft).

Season	Club	Lea	GP	G	A	TP	PIM	GP	G	A	TP	PIM
				Regular Season					Playoffs			
1980-81	Kingston	OHA	63	18	22	40	23	14	5	6	11	20
1981-82	**Washington**	NHL	3	1	0	1	2	....	....	....	....	....
	Kingston	OHL	59	38	49	87	70	4	2	3	5	9
1982-83a	Kingston	OHL	50	53	61	114	45	....	....	....	....	....
	Hershey	AHL	9	0	3	3	2	....	....	....	....	....
1983-84	Hershey	AHL	50	15	17	32	29	....	....	....	....	....
1984-85	Binghamton	AHL	75	42	36	78	53	5	5	5	10	0
1985-86	Binghamton	AHL	50	25	22	47	36	2	3	0	3	0
	NHL Totals		3	1	0	1	2	....	....	....	....	....

a OHL First All-Star Team (1983).
b AHL Second All-Star Team (1985)
Signed as a free agent by **NY Rangers**, August 15, 1986.

SILTANEN, RISTO

(SIL-ta-nen)

Born, Tampere, Finland, October 31, 1958.
Defense. Shoots right. 5'9", 180 lbs.
Last amateur club: Finnish National Team
(St. Louis' 13th choice, 173rd over-all, in 1978 Amateur Draft).

Season	Club	Lea	GP	G	A	TP	PIM	GP	G	A	TP	PIM
				Regular Season					Playoffs			
1976-77	Ilves	Fin.	36	10	7	17	28	....	....	....	....	....
1977-78	Ilves	Fin.	36	7	8	15	42	....	....	....	....	....
1978-79	Fin. National	...	11	2	0	2	6	....	....	....	....	....
	Edmonton	WHA	20	3	4	7	4	11	0	9	9	4
1979-80	**Edmonton**	NHL	64	6	29	35	26	2	0	0	0	0
1980-81	**Edmonton**	NHL	79	17	36	53	54	9	2	0	2	8
1981-82	**Edmonton**	NHL	63	15	48	63	26	5	3	2	5	10
1982-83	**Hartford**	NHL	74	5	25	30	28	....	....	....	....	....
1983-84	**Hartford**	NHL	75	15	38	53	34	....	....	....	....	....
1984-85	**Hartford**	NHL	76	12	33	45	30	....	....	....	....	....
1985-86	**Hartford**	NHL	52	8	22	30	30	....	....	....	....	....
	Quebec	NHL	13	2	5	7	6	3	0	1	1	2
	NHL Totals		496	80	236	316	234	19	5	3	8	22
	WHA Totals		20	3	4	7	4	11	0	9	9	4

Reclaimed by **St. Louis** from **Edmonton** prior to Expansion Draft, June 9, 1979. Traded to **Edmonton** by **St. Louis** with Tom Roulston for Joe Micheletti, August 19, 1979. Traded to **Hartford** by **Edmonton** with the rights to Brent Loney for Ken Linseman and Don Nachbaur, August 19, 1982. Traded to **Quebec** by **Hartford** for John Anderson, March 8, 1986.

SIMMER, CHARLES ROBERT (CHARLIE)

Born, Terrace Bay, Ont., March 20, 1954.
Left wing. Shoots left. 6'3", 210 lbs.
Last amateur club: Sault Ste. Marie Greyhounds (OHA).
(California's 4th choice, 39th over-all, in 1974 Amateur Draft).

Season	Club	Lea	GP	G	A	TP	PIM	GP	G	A	TP	PIM
				Regular Season					Playoffs			
1973-74	S. S. Marie	OHA	70	45	54	99	137	....	....	....	....	....
1974-75	Salt Lake	CHL	47	12	29	41	86	....	....	....	....	....
	California	NHL	35	8	13	21	26	....	....	....	....	....
1975-76	Salt Lake	CHL	42	23	16	39	96	....	....	....	....	....
	California	NHL	21	1	1	2	22	....	....	....	....	....
1976-77	**Cleveland**	NHL	24	2	0	2	16	....	....	....	....	....
a	Salt Lake	CHL	51	32	30	62	37	....	....	....	....	....
1977-78	**Los Angeles**	NHL	3	0	0	0	2	....	....	....	....	....
b	Springfield	AHL	75	42	41	83	100	4	0	1	1	5
1978-79	Springfield	AHL	39	13	23	36	33	....	....	....	....	....
	Los Angeles	NHL	38	21	27	48	16	2	1	0	1	2
1979-80c	**Los Angeles**	NHL	64	*56	45	101	65	3	2	0	2	0
1980-81c	**Los Angeles**	NHL	65	56	49	105	62	....	....	....	....	....
1981-82	**Los Angeles**	NHL	50	15	24	39	42	10	4	7	11	22
1982-83	**Los Angeles**	NHL	80	29	51	80	51	....	....	....	....	....
1983-84	**Los Angeles**	NHL	79	44	48	92	78	....	....	....	....	....
1984-85	**Los Angeles**	NHL	5	1	1	4		....	....	....	....	....
	Boston	NHL	63	33	30	63	35	5	2	2	4	2
1985-86d	**Boston**	NHL	55	36	24	60	42	3	0	0	0	4
	NHL Totals		582	302	312	614	461	23	9	9	18	30

a CHL Second All-Star Team (1977)
b AHL Second All-Star Team (1978)
c NHL Second All-Star Team (1980, 1981)
d Won Bill Masterton Award (1986)
Traded to **Boston** by **Los Angeles** for Boston's first-round choice (Dan Gratton) in 1985 Entry Draft, October 24, 1985.

SIMONETTI, FRANK

Born, Melrose, Mass., September 11, 1962.
Defense. Shoots right. 6'1", 190 lbs.
Last amateur club: Norwich university Cadets (ECAC)

Season	Club	Lea	GP	G	A	TP	PIM	GP	G	A	TP	PIM
				Regular Season					Playoffs			
1983-84	Norwich U.	ECAC	18	9	19	28	32	....	....	....	....	....
1984-85	**Boston**	NHL	43	1	5	6	26	5	0	1	1	2
	Hershey	AHL	31	0	6	6	14	....	....	....	....	....
1985-86	**Boston**	NHL	17	1	0	1	14	3	0	0	0	0
	Moncton	AHL	5	0	0	0	2	....	....	....	....	....
	NHL Totals		60	2	5	7	40	8	0	1	1	2

Signed as a free agent by **Boston**, October 4, 1984.

SIMPSON, CRAIG

Born, London, Ont., February 15, 1967.
Center. Shoots right. 6'2", 185 lbs.
Last amateur club: Michigan State University Spartans (CCHA)
(Pittsburgh's 1st choice, 2nd over-all, in 1985 Entry Draft)

				Regular Season					Playoffs			
Season	Club	Lea	GP	G	A	TP	PIM	GP	G	A	TP	PIM
1983-84	Michigan State	CCHA	46	14	43	57	38	....	....	....	....	....
1984-85ab	Michigan State	CCHA	42	31	53	84	33	....	....	....	....	....
1985-86	Pittsburgh	NHL	76	11	17	28	49	....	....	....	....	....
	NHL Totals		76	11	17	28	49	....	....	....	....	....

a CCHA First All-Star Team (1985)
b NCAA All-American (1985)

SIMPSON, DAVID STEWART (DAVE)

Born, London, Ont., March 3, 1962.
Center. Shoots left. 6', 190 lbs.
Last amateur club: London Knights (OHL).
(NY Islanders' 3rd choice, 59th over-all, in 1980 Amateur Draft).

				Regular Season					Playoffs			
Season	Club	Lea	GP	G	A	TP	PIM	GP	G	A	TP	PIM
1978-79	London	OHA	9	1	1	2	2	3	0	1	1	4
1979-80	London	OHA	68	29	44	73	38	5	3	4	7	0
1980-81	London	OHA	67	34	56	90	80	....	....	....	....	....
1981-82a	London	OHL	68	67	88	*155	18	4	3	3	6	2
	Indianapolis	CHL	3	0	1	1	0	....	....	....	....	....
1982-83	Indianapolis	CHL	70	29	39	68	69	13	7	13	20	12
1983-84	Indianapolis	CHL	72	24	43	67	26	10	1	5	6	2
1984-85	Cdn. Olympic	...	10	1	5	6	2	....	....	....	....	....
1985-86	Baltimore	AHL	79	13	19	32	56	....	....	....	....	....

a OHL First All-Star Team (1982)
Traded to **Pittsburgh** by **NY Islanders** for future considerations, September 11, 1985.

SIMPSON, ROBERT (BOBBY)

Born, Caughnawaga, Que., November 17, 1956.
Left wing. Shoots left. 6', 190 lbs.
Last amateur club: Sherbrooke Beavers (QJHL).
(Atlanta's 3rd choice, 28th over-all, in 1976 Amateur Draft).

				Regular Season					Playoffs			
Season	Club	Lea	GP	G	A	TP	PIM	GP	G	A	TP	PIM
1974-75	Sherbrooke	QJHL	69	38	47	85	146	13	10	12	22	26
1975-76	Sherbrooke	QJHL	68	56	77	133	126	17	11	14	25	19
1976-77	Atlanta	NHL	72	13	10	23	45	2	0	1	1	0
1977-78	Tulsa	CHL	14	8	8	16	34	....	....	....	....	....
	Atlanta	NHL	55	10	8	18	49	2	0	0	0	2
1978-79	Tulsa	CHL	49	14	19	33	38	....	....	....	....	....
1979-80	St. Louis	NHL	18	2	2	4	0	....	....	....	....	....
	Salt Lake	CHL	41	19	12	31	58	12	4	5	9	9
1980-81	Salt Lake	CHL	8	2	1	3	4	....	....	....	....	....
	Muskegon	IHL	42	17	26	43	42	3	0	3	3	0
1981-82	Erie	AHL	48	25	23	48	45	....	....	....	....	....
	Pittsburgh	NHL	26	9	9	18	4	2	0	0	0	0
1982-83	Pittsburgh	NHL	4	1	0	1	0	....	....	....	....	....
	Baltimore	AHL	61	24	27	51	24	....	....	....	....	....
1983-84	Baltimore	AHL	71	16	16	32	36	10	7	5	12	8
1984-85	Indianapolis	IHL	55	16	24	40	65	....	....	....	....	....
	Salt Lake	IHL	28	7	11	18	25	7	1	0	1	19
1985-86	Salt Lake	IHL	74	6	38	44	37	5	2	3	5	8
	NHL Totals		175	35	29	64	98	6	0	1	1	2

Traded to **St. Louis** by **Atlanta** for Curt Bennett, May 24, 1979. Claimed by **St. Louis** as fill in Expansion Draft, June 13, 1979. Signed as a free agent by **Pittsburgh**, October 1, 1981.

SINISALO, ILKKA

(sin-i-SAL-oh)

Born, Helsinki, Finland, July 10, 1958.
Left wing. Shoots left. 6'1", 190 lbs.
Last amateur club: Helsinki IFK (Finland).

				Regular Season					Playoffs			
Season	Club	Lea	GP	G	A	TP	PIM	GP	G	A	TP	PIM
1979-80	Helsinki IFK	Fin.	35	16	9	25	16	7	1	3	4	4
1980-81	Helsinki IFK	Fin.	36	27	17	44	14	6	5	3	8	4
1981-82	Philadelphia	NHL	66	15	22	37	22	4	0	2	2	0
1982-83	Philadelphia	NHL	61	21	29	50	16	3	1	1	2	0
1983-84	Philadelphia	NHL	73	29	17	46	29	2	2	0	2	0
1984-85	Philadelphia	NHL	70	36	37	73	16	19	6	1	7	0
1985-86	Philadelphia	NHL	74	39	37	76	31	5	2	2	4	2
	NHL Totals		344	140	142	282	114	33	11	6	17	2

Signed as free agent by **Philadelphia**, February 14, 1981.

SIREN, VILLE

Born, Tampere, Finland, February 10, 1964.
Defense. Shoots left. 6'1", 185 lbs.
Last amateur club: Ilves-Tampere (Finland).
(Hartford's 3rd choice, 23rd overall, in 1983 Entry Draft).

				Regular Season					Playoffs			
Season	Club	Lea	GP	G	A	TP	PIM	GP	G	A	TP	PIM
1984-85	Ilves	Fin	36	11	13	24	...	....	....	....	....	....
1985-86	Pittsburgh	NHL	60	4	8	12	32	....	....	....	....	....
	NHL Totals		60	4	8	12	32	....	....	....	....	....

Traded to **Pittsburgh** by **Hartford** for Pat Boutette, November 16, 1984.

SISKA, RANDY

Born, Calgary, Alta., June 1, 1967.
Center. Shoots left. 6'2", 195 lbs.
Last amateur club: Medicine Hat Tigers (WHL).
(Vancouver's 4th choice, 67th overall, in 1985 Entry Draft).

				Regular Season					Playoffs			
Season	Club	Lea	GP	G	A	TP	PIM	GP	G	A	TP	PIM
1983-84	Victoria	WHL	57	3	4	7	4	....	....	....	....	....
1984-85	Medicine Hat	WHL	67	20	12	32	39	10	2	0	2	6
1985-86	Medicine Hat	WHL	41	11	13	24	19	22	3	3	6	12

SKRIKO, PETRI

Born, Laapeenrenta, Finland, March 12, 1962.
Right wing. Shoots left. 5'10", 170 lbs.
Last amateur club: Saipa (Finland)
(Vancouver's 7th choice, 157th over-all, in 1981 Entry Draft)

				Regular Season					Playoffs			
Season	Club	Lea	GP	G	A	TP	PIM	GP	G	A	TP	PIM
1980-81	Saipa	Fin.	36	20	13	33	14	....	....	....	....	....
1981-82	Saipa	Fin.	33	19	27	46	24	....	....	....	....	....
1982-83	Saipa	Fin.	36	23	12	35	12	....	....	....	....	....
1983-84	Saipa	Fin.	32	25	26	51	13	....	....	....	....	....
1984-85	Vancouver	NHL	72	21	14	35	10	....	....	....	....	....
1985-86	Vancouver	NHL	80	38	40	78	34	3	0	0	0	0
	NHL Totals		152	59	54	113	44	3	0	0	0	0

SKRUDLAND, BRIAN

Born, Peace River, Alta., July 31, 1963.
Center. Shoots left. 6'1", 180 lbs.
Last amateur club: Saskatoon Blades (WHL).

				Regular Season					Playoffs			
Season	Club	Lea	GP	G	A	TP	PIM	GP	G	A	TP	PIM
1980-81	Saskatoon	WHL	66	15	27	42	97	....	....	....	....	....
1981-82	Saskatoon	WHL	71	27	29	56	135	5	0	1	1	2
1982-83	Saskatoon	WHL	71	35	59	94	42	6	1	3	4	19
1983-84	Nova Scotia	AHL	56	13	12	25	55	12	2	8	10	14
1984-85	Sherbrooke	AHL	70	22	28	50	109	17	9	8	17	23
1985-86	Montreal	NHL	65	9	13	22	57	20	2	4	6	76
	NHL Totals		65	9	13	22	57	20	2	4	6	76

Signed as a free agent by **Montreal**, September 13, 1983.

SLEIGHER, LOUIS

(SLAIG-er)

Born, Nouvelle, Que., October 23, 1958.
Right wing. Shoots right. 5'11", 200 lbs.
Last amateur club: Chicoutimi Sagueneens (QMJHL).
(Montreal's 23rd choice, 233rd over-all, in 1978 Amateur Draft)

				Regular Season					Playoffs			
Season	Club	Lea	GP	G	A	TP	PIM	GP	G	A	TP	PIM
1976-77	Chicoutimi	QJHL	70	53	48	101	49	8	5	3	8	9
1977-78	Chicoutimi	QJHL	71	65	54	119	125	....	....	....	....	....
1978-79	Birmingham	WHA	62	26	12	38	46	....	....	....	....	....
1979-80	Syracuse	AHL	58	28	15	43	37	1	0	1	1	15
	Quebec	NHL	2	0	1	1	0	....	....	....	....	....
1980-81	Erie	EHL	50	39	29	68	129	8	6	4	10	12
1981-82	Quebec	NHL	8	0	0	0	0	....	....	....	....	....
	Fredericton	AHL	59	32	34	66	37	4	0	0	0	4
1982-83	Fredericton	AHL	12	8	2	10	9	....	....	....	....	....
	Quebec	NHL	51	14	10	24	49	4	0	0	0	4
1983-84	Quebec	NHL	44	15	19	34	32	7	1	1	2	42
1984-85	Quebec	NHL	6	1	2	3	0	....	....	....	....	....
	Boston	NHL	70	12	19	31	45	5	0	0	0	4
1985-86	Boston	NHL	13	4	2	6	20	1	0	0	0	14
	NHL Totals		194	46	53	99	146	17	1	1	2	64
	WHA Totals		62	26	12	38	46	....	....	....	....	....

Signed as free agent by **Quebec**, September 11, 1980. Traded to **Boston** by **Quebec** for Luc Dufour and Boston's fourth round choice in 1985 Entry draft (Peter Massey), October 25, 1984.

SMAIL, DOUGLAS (DOUG)

Born, Moose Jaw, Sask., September 2, 1957.
Left wing. Shoots left. 5'9", 175 lbs.
Last amateur club: University of North Dakota Fighting Sioux (WCHA)

				Regular Season					Playoffs			
Season	Club	Lea	GP	G	A	TP	PIM	GP	G	A	TP	PIM
1978-79	North Dakota	WCHA	35	24	34	58	46	....	....	....	....	....
1979-80ab	North Dakota	WCHA	40	43	44	87	70	....	....	....	....	....
1980-81	Winnipeg	NHL	30	10	8	18	45	....	....	....	....	....
1981-82	Winnipeg	NHL	72	17	18	35	55	4	0	0	0	0
1982-83	Winnipeg	NHL	80	15	29	44	32	3	0	0	0	6
1983-84	Winnipeg	NHL	66	20	17	37	62	3	0	1	1	7
1984-85	Winnipeg	NHL	80	31	35	66	45	8	2	1	3	4
1985-86	Winnipeg	NHL	73	16	26	42	32	3	1	0	1	0
	NHL Totals		401	109	133	242	271	21	3	2	5	17

a WCHA Second All-Star Team (1980).
b Most Valuable Player, NCAA Tournament (1980).
Signed as free agent by **Winnipeg**, May 22, 1980.

SMITH, BRAD ALLAN

Born, Windsor, Ont., April 13, 1958.
Right wing. Shoots right. 6'1", 195 lbs.
Last amateur club: Sudbury Wolves (OHA).
(Vancouver's 5th choice, 57th over-all, in 1978 Amateur Draft).

			Regular Season					Playoffs				
Season	Club	Lea	GP	G	A	TP	PIM	GP	G	A	TP	PIM
1976-77	Windsor	OHA	66	37	53	90	154	9	4	10	14	20
1977-78	Windsor	OHA	20	8	26	34	39	....	....	....	....	....
	Sudbury	OHA	46	21	21	42	183	....	....	....	....	....
1978-79	**Vancouver**	**NHL**	**2**	**0**	**0**	**0**	**2**	....	....	....	....	....
	Dallas	CHL	60	17	18	35	143	9	1	3	4	22
1979-80	**Vancouver**	**NHL**	**19**	**1**	**3**	**4**	**50**	....	....	....	....	....
	Atlanta	**NHL**	**4**	**0**	**0**	**0**	**4**	....	....	....	....	....
	Dallas	CHL	51	26	16	42	138	....	....	....	....	....
1980-81	Birmingham	CHL	10	5	6	11	13	....	....	....	....	....
	Calgary	**NHL**	**45**	**7**	**4**	**11**	**65**	....	....	....	....	....
	Detroit	**NHL**	**20**	**5**	**2**	**7**	**93**	....	....	....	....	....
1981-82	**Detroit**	**NHL**	**33**	**2**	**0**	**2**	**80**	....	....	....	....	....
	Adirondack	AHL	34	10	5	15	126	5	0	0	0	8
1982-83	**Detroit**	**NHL**	**1**	**0**	**0**	**0**	**0**	....	....	....	....	....
	Adirondack	AHL	74	20	30	50	132	6	1	1	2	10
1983-84	**Detroit**	**NHL**	**8**	**2**	**1**	**3**	**36**	....	....	....	....	....
	Adirondack	AHL	46	15	29	44	128	7	1	1	2	26
1984-85	**Detroit**	**NHL**	**1**	**1**	**0**	**1**	**5**	**3**	**0**	**1**	**1**	**5**
	Adirondack	AHL	75	33	39	72	89	....	....	....	....	....
1985-86	**Toronto**	**NHL**	**42**	**5**	**17**	**22**	**84**	**6**	**2**	**1**	**3**	**20**
	St. Catharines	AHL	31	13	29	42	79	....	....	....	....	....
	NHL Totals		**175**	**23**	**27**	**50**	**419**	**9**	**2**	**2**	**4**	**25**

Traded to **Atlanta** by **Vancouver** with Don Lever for Ivan Boldirev and Darcy Rota, February 8, 1980. Traded to **Detroit** by **Calgary** for future considerations (Rick Vasko, May 28, 1981), February 24, 1981. Signed as a free agent by **Toronto**, July 2, 1985.

SMITH, DERRICK

Born, Scarborough, Ont., January 22, 1965.
Left wing. Shoots left. 6'1", 185 lbs.
Last amateur club: Peterborough Petes (OHL).
(Philadelphia's 2nd choice, 44th over-all, in 1983 Entry Draft).

			Regular Season					Playoffs				
Season	Club	Lea	GP	G	A	TP	PIM	GP	G	A	TP	PIM
1982-83	Peterborough	OHL	70	16	19	35	47	....	....	....	....	....
1983-84	Peterborough	OHL	70	30	36	66	31	8	4	4	8	7
1984-85	**Philadelphia**	**NHL**	**77**	**17**	**22**	**39**	**31**	**19**	**2**	**5**	**7**	**16**
1985-86	**Philadelphia**	**NHL**	**69**	**6**	**6**	**12**	**57**	**4**	**0**	**0**	**0**	**10**
	NHL Totals		**146**	**23**	**28**	**51**	**88**	**23**	**2**	**5**	**7**	**26**

SMITH, DOUGLAS ERIC (DOUG)

Born, Ottawa, Ont., May 17, 1963.
Center. Shoots right. 5'11", 180 lbs.
Last amateur club: Ottawa 67's (OHA).
(Los Angeles' 1st choice, 2nd over-all, in 1981 Entry Draft).

			Regular Season					Playoffs				
Season	Club	Lea	GP	G	A	TP	PIM	GP	G	A	TP	PIM
1979-80	Ottawa	OHA	64	23	34	57	45	11	2	0	2	33
1980-81	Ottawa	OHA	54	45	56	101	61	7	5	6	11	13
1981-82	**Los Angeles**	**NHL**	**80**	**16**	**14**	**30**	**64**	**10**	**3**	**2**	**5**	**11**
1982-83	**Los Angeles**	**NHL**	**42**	**11**	**11**	**22**	**12**	....	....	....	....	....
1983-84	**Los Angeles**	**NHL**	**72**	**16**	**20**	**36**	**28**	....	....	....	....	....
1984-85	**Los Angeles**	**NHL**	**62**	**21**	**20**	**41**	**58**	**3**	**1**	**0**	**1**	**4**
1985-86	**Los Angeles**	**NHL**	**48**	**8**	**9**	**17**	**56**	....	....	....	....	....
	Buffalo	**NHL**	**30**	**10**	**11**	**21**	**73**	....	....	....	....	....
	NHL Totals		**334**	**82**	**85**	**167**	**291**	**13**	**4**	**2**	**6**	**15**

Traded to **Buffalo** by **Los Angeles** with Brian Engblom for Sean McKenna, Larry Playfair and Ken Baumgartner, January 30, 1986.

SMITH, GREGORY JAMES (GREG)

Born, Ponoka, Alta., July 8, 1955.
Defense. Shoots left. 6', 195 lbs.
Last amateur club: Colorado College Tigers (WCHA)
(California's 4th choice, 57th over-all, 1975 Amateur Draft).

			Regular Season					Playoffs				
Season	Club	Lea	GP	G	A	TP	PIM	GP	G	A	TP	PIM
1973-74	Colorado	WCHA	31	7	13	20	80	....	....	....	....	....
1974-75	Colorado	WCHA	36	10	24	34	75	....	....	....	....	....
1975-76	Colorado	WCHA	34	18	19	37	123	....	....	....	....	....
	California	**NHL**	**1**	**0**	**1**	**1**	**2**	....	....	....	....	....
	Salt Lake	CHL	5	0	2	2	2	5	1	2	3	4
1976-77	**Cleveland**	**NHL**	**74**	**9**	**17**	**26**	**65**	....	....	....	....	....
1977-78	**Cleveland**	**NHL**	**80**	**7**	**30**	**37**	**92**	....	....	....	....	....
1978-79	**Minnesota**	**NHL**	**80**	**5**	**27**	**32**	**147**	....	....	....	....	....
1979-80	**Minnesota**	**NHL**	**55**	**5**	**13**	**18**	**103**	**12**	**0**	**1**	**1**	**9**
1980-81	**Minnesota**	**NHL**	**74**	**5**	**21**	**26**	**126**	**19**	**1**	**5**	**6**	**39**
1981-82	**Detroit**	**NHL**	**69**	**10**	**22**	**32**	**79**	....	....	....	....	....
1982-83	**Detroit**	**NHL**	**73**	**4**	**26**	**30**	**79**	....	....	....	....	....
1983-84	**Detroit**	**NHL**	**75**	**3**	**20**	**23**	**108**	**4**	**1**	**0**	**1**	**8**
1984-85	**Detroit**	**NHL**	**73**	**2**	**18**	**20**	**117**	**3**	**0**	**0**	**0**	**7**
1985-86	**Detroit**	**NHL**	**62**	**5**	**19**	**24**	**84**	....	....	....	....	....
	Washington	**NHL**	**14**	**0**	**3**	**3**	**10**	**9**	**2**	**1**	**3**	**9**
	NHL Totals		**730**	**55**	**217**	**272**	**1012**	**47**	**4**	**7**	**11**	**72**

Protected by **Minnesota** prior to Cleveland-Minnesota Dispersal Draft, June 15, 1978. Traded to **Detroit** by **Minnesota** with the rights to Don Murdoch and Minnesota's first round choice (Murray Craven) in 1982 Entry Draft for Detroit's first round choice (Brian Bellows) in 1982 Entry Draft, August 21, 1981. Traded to **Washington** by **Detroit** with John Barrett for Darren Veitch, March 10, 1986.

SMITH, JAMES STEPHEN (STEVE)

Born, Glasgow, Scotland, April 30, 1963.
Defense. Shoots left. 6'2", 180 lbs.
Last amateur club: London Knights (OHL).
(Edmonton's 5th choice, 111th over-all, in 1981 Entry Draft).

			Regular Season					Playoffs				
Season	Club	Lea	GP	G	A	TP	PIM	GP	G	A	TP	PIM
1980-81	London	OHA	62	4	12	16	141	....	....	....	....	....
1981-82	London	OHL	58	10	36	46	207	4	1	2	3	13
1982-83	Moncton	AHL	2	0	0	0	0	....	....	....	....	....
	London	OHL	50	6	35	41	133	3	1	0	1	10
1983-84	Moncton	AHL	64	1	8	9	176	....	....	....	....	....
1984-85	**Edmonton**	**NHL**	**2**	**0**	**0**	**0**	**2**	....	....	....	....	....
	Nova Scotia		68	2	28	30	161	5	0	3	3	40
1985-86	**Edmonton**	**NHL**	**55**	**4**	**20**	**24**	**166**	**6**	**0**	**1**	**1**	**14**
	Nova Scotia	AHL	4	0	2	2	11	....	....	....	....	....
	NHL Totals		**57**	**4**	**20**	**24**	**168**	**6**	**0**	**1**	**1**	**14**

SMITH, JIM

Born, Castlegar, B.C., November 27, 1964.
Defense. Shoots left. 6'1", 200 lbs.
Last amateur club: University of Denver Pioneers (WCHA).

			Regular Season					Playoffs				
Season	Club	Lea	GP	G	A	TP	PIM	GP	G	A	TP	PIM
1982-83	Denver	WCHA	36	10	18	28	10	....	....	....	....	....
1983-84	Denver	WCHA	36	5	15	20	24	....	....	....	....	....
1984-85	Denver	WCHA	37	7	18	25	40	....	....	....	....	....
1985-86	Denver	WCHA	47	10	40	50	37	....	....	....	....	....

Signed as a free agent by **Detroit**, July 3, 1986.

SMITH, NATHAN (NATE)

Born, Brunswick, Maine, July 13, 1967.
Defense. Shoots left. 6'1", 190 lbs.
Last amateur club: Lawrence Academy (HS).
(Calgary's 9th choice, 164th overall in 1985 Entry Draft).

			Regular Season					Playoffs				
Season	Club	Lea	GP	G	A	TP	PIM	GP	G	A	TP	PIM
1984-85	Lawrence	HS	24	5	19	24	4	....	....	....	....	....
1985-86	Lawrence	HS	22	10	21	31	22	....	....	....	....	....

SMITH, RANDY

Born, Saskatoon, Sask., July 7, 1965.
Center. Shoots left. 6'3", 175 lbs.
Last amateur club: Saskatoon Blades (WHL).

			Regular Season					Playoffs				
Season	Club	Lea	GP	G	A	TP	PIM	GP	G	A	TP	PIM
1983-84	Saskatoon	WHL	69	19	21	40	53	....	....	....	....	....
1984-85	Saskatoon	WHL	71	34	51	85	26	8	4	3	7	0
1985-86	Saskatoon	WHL	70	60	86	146	44	9	4	9	13	4
	Minnesota	**NHL**	**1**	**0**	**0**	**0**	**0**	....	....	....	..	....
	NHL Totals		**1**	**0**	**0**	**0**	**0**	....	....	....	....	....

Signed as a free agent by **Minnesota**, May 12, 1986.

SMITH, ROBERT DAVID (BOBBY)

Born, North Sydney, N.S., February 12, 1958.
Center. Shoots left. 6'4", 210 lbs.
Last amateur club: Ottawa 67's (OHA).
(Minnesota's 1st choice and 1st over-all in 1978 Amateur Draft).

			Regular Season					Playoffs				
Season	Club	Lea	GP	G	A	TP	PIM	GP	G	A	TP	PIM
1976-77a	Ottawa	OHA	64	*65	70	135	52	19	16	16	32	29
1977-78bc	Ottawa	OHA	61	69	*123	*192	44	16	15	15	30	10
1978-79d	**Minnesota**	**NHL**	**80**	**30**	**44**	**74**	**39**	....	....	....	....	....
1979-80	**Minnesota**	**NHL**	**61**	**27**	**56**	**83**	**24**	**15**	**1**	**13**	**14**	**9**
1980-81	**Minnesota**	**NHL**	**78**	**29**	**64**	**93**	**73**	**19**	**8**	**17**	**25**	**13**
1981-82	**Minnesota**	**NHL**	**80**	**43**	**71**	**114**	**82**	**4**	**2**	**4**	**6**	**5**
1982-83	**Minnesota**	**NHL**	**77**	**24**	**53**	**77**	**81**	**9**	**6**	**4**	**10**	**17**
1983-84	**Minnesota**	**NHL**	**10**	**3**	**6**	**9**	**9**	....	....	....	....	....
	Montreal	**NHL**	**70**	**26**	**37**	**63**	**62**	**15**	**2**	**7**	**9**	**8**
1984-85	**Montreal**	**NHL**	**65**	**16**	**40**	**56**	**59**	**12**	**5**	**6**	**11**	**30**
1985-86	**Montreal**	**NHL**	**79**	**31**	**55**	**86**	**55**	**20**	**7**	**8**	**15**	**22**
	NHL Totals		**600**	**229**	**426**	**655**	**484**	**94**	**31**	**59**	**90**	**104**

a OHA Second All-Star Team (1977)
b OHA First All-Star Team (1978)
c Named Canadian Major Junior Player of the Year (1978).
d Won Calder Memorial Trophy (1979)

Traded to **Montreal** by **Minnesota** for Keith Acton, Mark Napier and Toronto's third round choice (Ken Hodge) in 1984 Entry Draft — Montreal's property via earlier deal — October 28, 1983.

SMITH, SCOTT

Born, St. Paul, Minn., October 16, 1962.
Defense. Shoots right. 6'1", 185 lbs.
Last amateur club: University of Maine Black Bears (H.E.).

			Regular Season					Playoffs				
Season	Club	Lea	GP	G	A	TP	PIM	GP	G	A	TP	PIM
1992-83	Maine	H.E.	19	1	3	4	40	....	....	....	....	....
1983-84	Maine	H.E.	32	1	9	10	62	....	....	....	....	....
1984-85	Maine	H.E.	41	4	14	18	83	....	....	....	....	....
1985-86	Maine	H.E.	39	6	15	21	102	....	....	....	....	....
	New Haven	AHL	5	0	0	0	7	3	0	0	0	0

Signed as a free agent by **NY Rangers**, March 26, 1986.

SMITH, STEVE

Born, Trenton, Ont., April 4, 1963.
Defense. Shoots left. 5'9", 195 lbs.
Last amateur club: Sault Ste. Marie Greyhounds (OHL).
(Philadelphia's 1st choice, 16th over-all, in 1981 Entry Draft).

			Regular Season					Playoffs				
Season	Club	Lea	GP	G	A	TP	PIM	GP	G	A	TP	PIM
1980-81a	S. S. Marie	OHA	61	3	37	40	143	19	0	6	6	60
1981-82b	**Philadelphia**	**NHL**	**8**	**0**	**1**	**1**	**0**	....	....	....	....	....
	S. S. Marie	OHL	50	7	20	27	179	12	0	2	2	23
1982-83b	S. S. Marie	OHL	55	11	33	44	139	16	0	8	8	28
1983-84	Springfield	AHL	70	4	25	29	77	4	0	0	0	0
1984-85	**Philadelphia**	**NHL**	**2**	**0**	**0**	**0**	**7**	....	....	....	....	....
	Hershey	AHL	65	10	20	30	83	....	....	....	....	....
1985-86	**Philadelphia**	**NHL**	**2**	**0**	**0**	**0**	**2**	....	....	....	....	....
	Hershey	AHL	49	1	11	12	96	16	2	4	6	43
	NHL Totals		**12**	**0**	**1**	**1**	**9**	....	....	....	....	....

a OHA Second All-Star Team (1981).
b OHL Second All-Star Team (1982, 1983).

SMITH, STEVEN M.

Born, Ann Arbor, Michigan, May 11, 1962.
Defense. Shoots right. 6'2", 190 lbs.
Last amatejur club: St. Lawrence University Saints (ECAC).
(Montreal's 12th choice, 150th over-all, in 1982 Entry Draft).

			Regular Season					Playoffs				
Season	Club	Lea	GP	G	A	TP	PIM	GP	G	A	TP	PIM
1980-81	St. Lawrence	ECAC	31	1	6	7	18	....	....	....	....	....
1981-82	St. Lawrence	ECAC	31	5	8	13	44	....	....	....	....	....
1982-83	St. Lawrence	ECAC	29	7	11	18	37	....	....	....	....	....
1983-84	St. Lawrence	ECAC	32	7	18	25	46	....	....	....	....	....
1984-85	Sherbrooke	AHL	51	0	13	13	25	....	....	....	....	....
1985-86	Sherbrooke	AHL	63	5	31	36	37	....	....	....	....	....

SMITH, VERN

Born, Winnipeg, Man., May 30, 1964.
Defense. Shoots left. 6'1", 190 lbs.
Last amateur club: New Westminster Bruins (WHL).
(NY Islanders' 2nd choice, 42nd over-all, in 1982 Entry Draft).

			Regular Season					Playoffs				
Season	Club	Lea	GP	G	A	TP	PIM	GP	G	A	TP	PIM
1981-82	Lethbridge	WHL	72	5	38	43	73	12	0	2	2	8
1982-83	Lethbridge	WHL	30	2	10	12	54	....	....	....	....	....
	Nanaimo	WHL	42	6	21	27	62	....	....	....	....	....
1983-84	N. Westminster	WHL	69	13	44	57	94	9	6	6	12	12
1984-85	**NY Islanders**	**NHL**	**1**	**0**	**0**	**0**	**0**	....	....	....	....	....
	Springfield	AHL	76	6	20	26	115	4	0	2	2	9
1985-86	Springfield	AHL	55	3	11	14	83	....	....	....	....	....
	NHL Totals		**1**	**0**	**0**	**0**	**0**	....	....	....	....	....

SMYL, STANLEY PHILLIP (STAN) (SMEEL)

Born, Glendon, Alta., January 28, 1958.
Right wing. Shoots right. 5'8", 190 lbs.
Last amateur club: New Westminster Bruins (WHL).
(Vancouver's 3rd choice, 40th over-all, in 1978 Amateur Draft).

			Regular Season					Playoffs				
Season	Club	Lea	GP	G	A	TP	PIM	GP	G	A	TP	PIM
1975-76	N. Westminster	WHL	72	32	42	74	169	19	8	6	14	58
1976-77	N. Westminster	WHL	72	36	31	66	200	13	6	7	13	51
1977-78	N. Westminster	WHL	53	29	47	76	211	20	14	21	35	43
1978-79	Dallas	CHL	3	1	1	2	9	....	....	....	....	....
	Vancouver	**NHL**	**62**	**14**	**24**	**38**	**89**	**2**	**1**	**1**	**2**	**0**
1979-80	**Vancouver**	**NHL**	**77**	**31**	**47**	**78**	**204**	**4**	**0**	**2**	**2**	**14**
1980-81	**Vancouver**	**NHL**	**80**	**25**	**38**	**63**	**171**	**3**	**1**	**2**	**3**	**0**
1981-82	**Vancouver**	**NHL**	**80**	**34**	**44**	**78**	**144**	**17**	**9**	**9**	**18**	**25**
1982-83	**Vancouver**	**NHL**	**74**	**38**	**50**	**88**	**114**	**4**	**3**	**2**	**5**	**12**
1983-84	**Vancouver**	**NHL**	**80**	**24**	**43**	**67**	**136**	**4**	**2**	**1**	**3**	**4**
1984-85	**Vancouver**	**NHL**	**80**	**27**	**37**	**64**	**100**	....	....	....	....	....
1985-86	**Vancouver**	**NHL**	**73**	**27**	**35**	**62**	**144**	....	....	....	....	....
	NHL Totals		**606**	**220**	**318**	**538**	**1102**	**34**	**16**	**17**	**33**	**55**

SMYTH, GREG (smith)

Born, Oakville, Ont., April 23, 1966.
Defense. Shoots right. 6'3", 194 lbs.
Last amateur club: London Knights (OHL).
(Philadelphia's 1st choice, 22nd over-all, in 1984 Entry Draft).

			Regular Season					Playoffs				
Season	Club	Lea	GP	G	A	TP	PIM	GP	G	A	TP	PIM
1983-84	London	OHL	64	4	21	25	252	6	1	0	1	24
1984-85	London	OHL	47	7	16	23	188	8	2	2	4	27
1985-86	Hershey	AHL	2	0	1	1	5	8	0	0	0	60
a	London	OHL	46	12	42	54	199	4	1	2	3	28

a OHL Second All-Star Team (1986).

SNEPSTS, HAROLD JOHN (SNEPS)

Born, Edmonton, Alta., October 24, 1954.
Defense. Shoots left. 6'3", 215 lbs.
Last amateur club: Edmonton Oil Kings (WHL).
(Vancouver's 3rd choice, 59th over-all, in 1974 Amateur Draft).

			Regular Season					Playoffs				
Season	Club	Lea	GP	G	A	TP	PIM	GP	G	A	TP	PIM
1972-73	Edmonton	WHL	68	2	24	26	155	11	0	1	1	54
1973-74	Edmonton	WHL	68	8	41	49	239	....	....	....	....	....
1974-75	Seattle	CHL	19	1	6	7	58	....	....	....	....	....
	Vancouver	**NHL**	**27**	**1**	**2**	**3**	**30**	....	....	....	....	....
1975-76	**Vancouver**	**NHL**	**78**	**3**	**15**	**18**	**125**	**2**	**0**	**0**	**0**	**4**
1976-77	**Vancouver**	**NHL**	**79**	**4**	**18**	**22**	**149**	....	....	....	....	....
1977-78	**Vancouver**	**NHL**	**75**	**4**	**16**	**20**	**118**	....	....	....	....	....
1978-79	**Vancouver**	**NHL**	**76**	**7**	**24**	**31**	**130**	**3**	**0**	**0**	**0**	**0**
1979-80	**Vancouver**	**NHL**	**79**	**3**	**20**	**23**	**202**	**4**	**0**	**2**	**2**	**8**
1980-81	**Vancouver**	**NHL**	**76**	**3**	**16**	**19**	**212**	**3**	**0**	**0**	**0**	**8**
1981-82	**Vancouver**	**NHL**	**68**	**3**	**14**	**17**	**153**	**17**	**0**	**4**	**4**	**50**
1982-83	**Vancouver**	**NHL**	**46**	**2**	**8**	**10**	**80**	**4**	**1**	**1**	**2**	**8**
1983-84	**Vancouver**	**NHL**	**79**	**4**	**16**	**20**	**152**	**4**	**0**	**1**	**1**	**15**
1984-85	**Minnesota**	**NHL**	**71**	**0**	**7**	**7**	**232**	**9**	**0**	**0**	**0**	**24**
1985-86	**Detroit**	**NHL**	**35**	**0**	**6**	**6**	**75**	....	....	....	....	....
	NHL Totals		**789**	**34**	**162**	**196**	**1658**	**46**	**1**	**8**	**9**	**117**

Traded to **Minnesota** by **Vancouver** for Al MacAdam, June 21, 1984. Signed as a free agent by **Detroit**, July 31, 1985.

SOLHEIM, KENNETH LAWRENCE (KEN) (SOUL-hime)

Born, Hythe, Alta., March 27, 1961.
Left wing. Shoots left. 6'3", 210 lbs.
Last amateur club: Medicine Hat Tigers (WHL).
(Chicago's 4th choice, 24th over-all, in 1980 Entry Draft).

			Regular Season					Playoffs				
Season	Club	Lea	GP	G	A	TP	PIM	GP	G	A	TP	PIM
1979-80	Medicine Hat	WHL	72	54	33	87	50	13	1	6	7	6
1980-81a	Medicine Hat	WHL	64	*68	43	111	87	5	5	4	9	2
	Chicago	**NHL**	**5**	**2**	**0**	**2**	**0**	....	....	....	....	....
	Minnesota	**NHL**	**5**	**2**	**1**	**3**	**0**	**2**	**1**	**0**	**1**	**0**
1981-82	Nashville	CHL	44	23	18	41	40	....	....	....	....	....
	Minnesota	**NHL**	**29**	**4**	**5**	**9**	**4**	**1**	**0**	**1**	**1**	**2**
1982-83	Birmingham	CHL	22	14	3	17	4	....	....	....	....	....
	Minnesota	**NHL**	**25**	**2**	**4**	**6**	**4**	....	....	....	....	....
	Detroit	**NHL**	**10**	**0**	**0**	**0**	**2**	....	....	....	....	....
1983-84	Adirondack	AHL	61	24	20	44	13	7	1	1	2	0
1984-85	**Minnesota**	**NHL**	**55**	**8**	**10**	**18**	**19**	....	....	....	....	....
	Springfield	AHL	17	6	8	14	0	4	2	0	2	2
1985-86	**Edmonton**	**NHL**	**6**	**1**	**0**	**1**	**5**	....	....	....	....	....
	Nova Scotia	AHL	71	19	27	46	45	....	....	....	....	....
	NHL Totals		**135**	**19**	**20**	**39**	**34**	**3**	**1**	**1**	**2**	**2**

a WHL First All-Star Team (1981)

Traded to **Minnesota** by **Chicago** with Chicago's second-round choice (Tom Hirsch) in 1981 Entry Draft for Glen Sharpley, December 29, 1980. Traded to **Detroit** by **Minnesota** for future considerations, March 8, 1983. Signed as a free agent by **Edmonton**, August 15, 1985.

SOMMER, ROY

Born, Oakland, California, April 5, 1957.
Center. Shoots left. 6', 180 lbs.
Last amateur club: Calgary Centennials (WHL).
(Toronto's 7th choice, 101st over-all, in 1977 Amateur Draft).

			Regular Season					Playoffs				
Season	Club	Lea	GP	G	A	TP	PIM	GP	G	A	TP	PIM
1975-76	Calgary	WHL	70	13	24	37	155	....	....	....	....	....
1976-77	Calgary	WHL	50	16	22	38	111	9	5	9	14	8
1977-78	Saginaw	IHL	12	2	3	5	2	....	....	....	....	....
	Grand Rapids	IHL	45	20	18	38	67	....	....	....	....	....
1978-79	DID NOT PLAY											
1979-80	Grand Rapids	IHL	9	1	4	5	32	....	....	....	....	....
	Houston	CHL	69	24	31	55	246	6	2	2	4	8
1980-81	**Edmonton**	**NHL**	**3**	**1**	**0**	**1**	**7**	....	....	....	....	....
	Wichita	CHL	57	13	22	35	212	14	3	2	5	61
1981-82	Wichita	CHL	76	17	28	45	193	....	....	....	....	....
1982-83	Wichita	CHL	73	22	39	61	130	....	....	....	....	....
1983-84	Maine	AHL	67	7	10	17	202	14	6	1	7	24
1984-85	Maine	AHL	80	12	13	25	175	11	4	2	6	27
1985-86	Indianapolis	IHL	37	9	10	19	118	....	....	....	....	....
	Muskegon	IHL	27	5	8	13	109	12	2	4	6	92
	NHL Totals		**3**	**1**	**0**	**1**	**7**	....	....	....	....	....

Signed as a free agent by **Edmonton**, January 1, 1980. Signed as free agent by **New Jersey**, September 25, 1982.

SPANGLER, KEN

Born, Edmonton, Alta., May 2, 1967.
Defense. Shoots right. 5'11", 190 lbs.
Last amateur club: Calgary Wranglers (WHL).
(Toronto's 2nd choice, 22nd over-all, in 1985 Entry Draft).

			Regular Season					Playoffs				
Season	Club	Lea	GP	G	A	TP	PIM	GP	G	A	TP	PIM
1983-84	Calgary	WHL	71	1	12	13	119	4	0	0	0	6
1984-85	Calgary	WHL	71	5	30	35	251	8	6	2	8	18
1985-86a	Calgary	WHL	66	19	36	55	237	....	....	....	....	....
	St. Catharines	AHL	7	0	0	0	16	2	0	0	0	15

a WHL East All-Star Team (1986).

SPEERS, TED

Born, Ann Arbor, Mich., January 28, 1961.
Right wing. Shoots right. 5'11", 200 lbs.
Last amateur club: University of Michigan Wolverines (CCHA).

Season	Club	Lea	GP	G	A	TP	PIM	GP	G	A	TP	PIM
						Regular Season				Playoffs		
1979-80	U. of Michigan	WCHA	30	13	16	29	16	....	....	....	....	....
1980-81	U. of Michigan	WCHA	39	22	23	45	20	....	....	....	....	....
1981-82	U. of Michigan	CCHA	38	23	16	39	46	....	....	....	....	....
1982-83a	U. of Michigan	CCHA	36	18	41	59	40	....	....	....	....	....
1983-84	Adirondack	AHL	79	15	25	40	27	7	2	1	3	9
1984-85	Adirondack	AHL	80	22	31	53	40	....	....	....	....	....
1985-86	Detroit	NHL	4	1	1	2	0	....	....	....	....	....
	Adirondack	AHL	74	32	35	67	20	15	7	5	12	9
	NHL Totals		4	1	1	2	0	....	....	....	....	....

a CCHA First All-Star Team (1983).
Signed as free agent by **Detroit**, September 14, 1983.

SPRENGER, JIM

Born, Cloquet, Minn., May 28, 1965.
Defense. Shoots right. 5'11", 175 lbs.
Last amateur club: University of Minnesota-Duluth Bulldogs (WCHA).
(NY Islanders' 9th choice, 137th overall, in 1983 Entry Draft).

Season	Club	Lea	GP	G	A	TP	PIM	GP	G	A	TP	PIM
						Regular Season				Playoffs		
1983-84	Minn-Duluth	WCHA	42	2	7	9	22	....	....	....	....	....
1984-85	Minn-Duluth	WCHA	48	6	12	18	32	....	....	....	....	....
1985-86	Minn-Duluth	WCHA	42	6	11	17	24	....	....	....	....	....

STAFFORD, GORDON DALE (GORD)

Born, Banff, Alta., October 10, 1960.
Center. Shoots right. 5'10", 180 lbs.
Last amateur club: Billings Bighorns (WHL).

Season	Club	Lea	GP	G	A	TP	PIM	GP	G	A	TP	PIM
						Regular Season				Playoffs		
1977-78	Billings	WHL	59	11	22	33	54	20	4	10	14	17
1978-79	Billings	WHL	72	37	66	103	70	8	7	6	13	2
1979-80	Billings	WHL	68	52	58	110	91	....	....	....	....	....
1980-81	Milwaukee	IHL	40	24	32	56	30	....	....	....	....	....
	Wichita	CHL	27	5	3	8	34	10	3	4	7	10
1981-82	Wichita	CHL	49	9	16	25	42	....	....	....	....	....
1982-83	Milwaukee	IHL	77	23	49	72	81	11	3	5	8	30
1983-84	Milwaukee	IHL	79	36	45	81	35	4	1	1	2	2
1984-85	Milwaukee	IHL	6	0	2	2	0	....	....	....	....	....
1985-86	Milwaukee	IHL	82	20	57	77	40	5	1	2	3	2

Signed as free agent by **Edmonton**, October 31, 1979.

STANLEY, DARRYL

Born, Winnipeg, Man., December 2, 1962.
Defense. Shoots left. 6'2", 200 lbs.
Last amateur club: Saskatoon Blades (WHL).

Season	Club	Lea	GP	G	A	TP	PIM	GP	G	A	TP	PIM
						Regular Season				Playoffs		
1980-81	N. Westminster	WHL	66	7	27	34	127	....	....	....	....	....
1981-82	Saskatoon	WHL	65	7	25	32	175	5	1	1	2	14
	Maine	AHL	....	....	....	....	....	2	0	2	2	2
1982-83	Maine	AHL	44	2	5	7	95	2	0	0	0	0
1983-84	Springfield	AHL	51	4	10	14	122	....	....	....	....	....
	Philadelphia	NHL	23	1	4	5	71	3	0	0	0	19
1984-85	Hershey	AHL	24	0	7	7	33	....	....	....	....	....
1985-86	Philadelphia	NHL	33	0	2	2	69	1	0	0	0	2
	Hershey	AHL	27	0	4	4	88	....	....	....	....	....
	NHL Totals		56	1	6	7	140	4	0	0	0	21

Signed as a free agent by **Philadelphia**, October 9, 1981.

STANTON, PAUL

Born, Boston, Mass., June 22, 1967.
Defense. Shoots right. 6'0", 175 lbs.
Last amateur club: University of Wisconsin Badgers (WCHA).
(Pittsburgh's 8th choice, 149th overall, in 1985 Entry Draft).

Season	Club	Lea	GP	G	A	TP	PIM	GP	G	A	TP	PIM
						Regular Season				Playoffs		
1985-86	Wisconsin	WCHA	36	4	6	10	16	....	....	....	....	....

STAPLETON, MIKE

Born, Sarnia, Ont., May 5, 1966.
Center. Shoots right. 5'10", 165 lbs.
Last amateur club: Cornwall Royals (OHL).
(Chicago's 7th choice, 132nd over-all, in 1984 Entry Draft).

Season	Club	Lea	GP	G	A	TP	PIM	GP	G	A	TP	PIM
						Regular Season				Playoffs		
1983-84	Cornwall	OHL	70	24	45	69	94	3	1	2	3	4
1984-85	Cornwall	OHL	56	41	44	85	68	9	2	4	6	23
1985-86	Cornwall	OHL	56	39	64	103	74	6	2	3	5	2

STASTNY, ANTON   (STASH-nee)

Born, Bratislava, Czechoslovakia, August 5, 1959.
Left wing. Shoots left. 6', 185 lbs.
Last amateur club: Slovan Bratislava (Czechoslovakia)
(Quebec's 4th choice, 83rd over-all, in 1979 Entry Draft).

Season	Club	Lea	GP	G	A	TP	PIM	GP	G	A	TP	PIM
						Regular Season				Playoffs		
1978-79	Slovan	Czech.	44	32	19	51		....	....	....	....	....
1979-80	Slovan	Czech.	40	30	30	60		....	....	....	....	....
	Czech. Olympic	....	6	4	4	8	2					
1980-81	**Quebec**	**NHL**	80	39	46	85	12	5	4	3	7	2
1981-82	**Quebec**	**NHL**	68	26	46	72	16	16	5	10	15	10
1982-83	**Quebec**	**NHL**	79	32	60	92	25	4	2	2	4	0
1983-84	**Quebec**	**NHL**	69	25	37	62	14	9	2	5	7	7
1984-85	**Quebec**	**NHL**	79	38	42	80	30	16	3	3	6	6
1985-86	**Quebec**	**NHL**	74	31	43	74	19	3	1	1	2	0
	NHL Totals		449	191	274	465	116	53	17	24	41	25

STASTNY, MARIAN   (STASH-nee)

Born, Bratislava, Czechoslovakia, January 8, 1953.
Right wing. Shoots left. 5'10", 195 lbs.
Last amateur club: Slovan Bratislava (Czechoslovakia)

Season	Club	Lea	GP	G	A	TP	PIM	GP	G	A	TP	PIM
						Regular Season				Playoffs		
1979-80	Slovan	Czech.	13	7	8	15		....	....	....	....	....
	Czech. Olympic	....	6	5	6	11	4	....	....	....	....	....
1980-81	DID NOT PLAY											
1981-82	**Quebec**	**NHL**	74	35	54	89	27	16	3	14	17	5
1982-83	**Quebec**	**NHL**	60	36	43	79	32	2	0	0	0	0
1983-84	**Quebec**	**NHL**	68	20	32	52	26	9	2	3	5	2
1984-85	**Quebec**	**NHL**	50	7	14	21	4	2	0	0	0	0
1985-86	**Toronto**	**NHL**	70	23	30	53	21	3	0	0	0	0
	NHL Totals		322	121	173	294	110	32	5	17	22	7

Signed as free agent by **Quebec**, August 26, 1980. Signed as a free agent by **Toronto**, August 12, 1985.

STASTNY, PETER   (STASH-nee)

Born, Bratislava, Czechoslovakia, September 18, 1956.
Center. Shoots left. 6'1", 195 lbs.
Last amateur club: Slovan Bratislava (Czechoslovakia)

Season	Club	Lea	GP	G	A	TP	PIM	GP	G	A	TP	PIM
						Regular Season				Playoffs		
1978-79	Slovan	Czech.	44	32	19	51		....	....	....	....	....
1979-80a	Slovan	Czech.	40	30	30	60		....	....	....	....	....
	Czech. Olympic	...	6	7	7	14	6	....	....	....	....	....
1980-81bcd	**Quebec**	**NHL**	77	39	70	109	37	5	2	8	10	7
1981-82	**Quebec**	**NHL**	80	46	93	139	91	12	7	11	18	10
1982-83	**Quebec**	**NHL**	75	47	77	124	78	4	3	2	5	10
1983-84	**Quebec**	**NHL**	80	46	73	119	73	9	2	7	9	31
1984-85	**Quebec**	**NHL**	75	32	68	100	95	18	4	19	23	24
1985-86	**Quebec**	**NHL**	76	41	81	122	60	3	0	1	1	2
	NHL Totals		463	251	462	713	434	51	18	48	66	84

a Czechoslovakian League Player of the Year (1980)
b Won Calder Memorial Trophy (1981)
c NHL record for assists by a rookie (1981)
d NHL record for points by a rookie (1981)
Signed as free agent by **Quebec**, August 26, 1980.

STASZAK, RAY   (STAY-zak)

Born, Philadelphia, Pa., December 1, 1962.
Right wing. Shoots right. 6'0", 200 lbs.
Last amateur club: University of Illinois-Chicago Flames (CCHA).

Season	Club	Lea	GP	G	A	TP	PIM	GP	G	A	TP	PIM
						Regular Season				Playoffs		
1982-83	Austin	USHL	30	18	13	31	NA	....	....	....	....	....
1983-84	U. of Ill.-Chi.	CCHA	31	15	17	32	42	....	....	....	....	....
1984-85	U. of Ill.-Chi.	CCHA	38	37	35	72	98	....	....	....	....	....
1985-86	**Detroit**	**NHL**	4	0	1	1	7	....	....	....	....	....
	Adirondack	AHL	26	13	8	21	41	16	2	3	5	70
	NHL Totals		4	0	1	1	7	....	....	....	....	....

a CCHA Player of the Year (1985)
b CCHA First All-Star Team (1985)
Signed as a free agent by **Detroit**, July 31, 1985.

STEEN, JIM

Born, Moorehead, Minn., January 26, 1966.
Center. Shoots left. 6'3", 195 lbs.
Last amateur club: University of North Dakota Fighting Sioux (WCHA).
(Pittsburgh's 9th choice, 210th overall, in 1984 Entry Draft).

Season	Club	Lea	GP	G	A	TP	PIM	GP	G	A	TP	PIM
						Regular Season				Playoffs		
1985-86	North Dakota	WCHA	8	0	0	0	2	....	....	....	....	....

STEEN, THOMAS

Born, Tocksmark, Sweden, June 8, 1960.
Center. Shoots left. 5'10", 195 lbs.
Last amateur club: Farjestads (Sweden).
(Winnipeg's 5th choice, 103rd over-all, in 1979 Entry Draft).

				Regular Season					Playoffs			
Season	Club	Lea	GP	G	A	TP	PIM	GP	G	A	TP	PIM
1976-77	Leksands	Swe.	3	1	1	2	2	....	....	....	....	....
1977-78	Leksands	Swe.	35	5	6	11	30	....	....	....	....	....
1978-79	Leksands	Swe.	23	13	4	17	35	5	1	2	3	13
	Swe. National	...	2	0	0	0	0	....	....	....	....	....
1979-80	Leksands	Swe.	18	7	7	14	14	2	0	0	0	6
1980-81	Farjestads	Swe.	32	16	23	39	30	7	4	2	6	8
	Swe. National	...	19	2	5	7	12	....	....	....	....	....
1981-82	Winnipeg	NHL	73	15	29	44	42	4	0	4	4	2
1982-83	Winnipeg	NHL	75	26	33	59	60	3	0	2	2	0
1983-84	Winnipeg	NHL	78	20	45	65	69	3	0	1	1	9
1984-85	Winnipeg	NHL	79	30	54	84	80	8	2	3	5	17
1985-86	Winnipeg	NHL	78	17	47	64	76	3	1	1	2	4
	NHL Totals		383	108	208	316	327	21	3	11	14	32

STEFANSKI, ED STANLEY MICHAEL (BUD)　　　　(ste-FAN-skee)

Born, South Porcupine, Ont., April 28, 1955.
Center. Shoots left. 5'10", 170 lbs.
Last amateur club: Oshawa Generals (OHA).
(NY Rangers' 9th choice, 154th over-all, in 1975 Amateur Draft).

				Regular Season					Playoffs			
Season	Club	Lea	GP	G	A	TP	PIM	GP	G	A	TP	PIM
1973-74	Oshawa	OHA	67	25	32	57	22	....	....	....	....	....
1974-75	Oshawa	OHA	61	18	48	66	35	5	2	2	4	14
1975-76	Port Huron	IHL	71	26	30	56	59	15	4	4	8	16
1976-77	Port Huron	IHL	77	49	54	103	61	....	....	....	....	....
	New Haven	AHL						2	1	0	1	0
1977-78	NY Rangers	NHL	1	0	0	0	0	....	....	....	....	....
	New Haven	AHL	79	27	37	64	61	15	5	4	9	6
1978-79	New Haven	AHL	51	18	40	58	71	10	3	7	10	21
1979-80	Tulsa	CHL	71	19	44	63	61	3	0	0	0	9
1980-81	New Haven	AHL	20	9	18	27	46	4	0	1	1	8
1981-82	New Haven	AHL	16	6	5	11	24	4	2	1	3	11
1982-83	Springfield	AHL	80	30	40	70	65	....	....	....	....	....
1983-84	Maine	AHL	57	26	24	50	47	17	12	9	21	16
1984-85	Maine	AHL	75	19	34	53	67	11	1	7	8	12
1985-86	Maine	AHL	68	32	39	71	70	2	0	0	0	6
	NHL Totals		1	0	0	0	0	....	....	....	....	....

Traded to **Winnipeg** by **NY Rangers** for future considerations, October 12, 1979. Signed as free agent by **Chicago**, September 27, 1982. Signed as free agent by **New Jersey**, July 22, 1984.

STEVENS, JOHN

Born, Completon, N.B., May 4, 1966.
Defense. Shoots left. 6'1", 185 lbs.
Last amateur club: Oshawa Generals (OHL).
(Philadelphia's 5th choice, 47th over-all, in 1984 Entry Draft).

				Regular Season					Playoffs			
Season	Club	Lea	GP	G	A	TP	PIM	GP	G	A	TP	PIM
1983-84	Oshawa	OHL	70	1	10	11	71	7	0	1	1	6
1984-85	Oshawa	OHL	44	2	10	12	61	5	0	2	2	4
	Hershey	AHL	3	0	0	0	0	....	....	....	....	....
1985-86	Kalamazoo	IHL	6	0	1	1	8	6	0	3	3	9
	Oshawa	OHL	65	1	7	8	146	6	0	2	2	14

STEVENS, KEVIN

Born, Brockton, Mass., April 15, 1965.
Center. Shoots left. 6'3", 210 lbs.
Last amateur club: Boston College Eagles (H.E.).
(Los Angeles' 6th choice, 108th overall, in 1983 Entry Draft).

				Regular Season					Playoffs			
Season	Club	Lea	GP	G	A	TP	PIM	GP	G	A	TP	PIM
1983-84	Boston College	ECAC	37	6	14	20	36	....	....	....	....	....
1984-85	Boston College	H.E.	40	13	23	36	36	....	....	....	....	....
1985-86	Boston College	H.E.	42	17	27	44	56	....	....	....	....	....

Rights traded to **Pittsburgh** by **Los Angeles** for Anders Hakansson, September 9, 1983.

STEVENS, MIKE

Born, Kitchener, Ont., December 30, 1965.
Left wing. Shoots left. 5'11", 195 lbs.
Last amateur club: Kitchener Rangers (OHL).
(Vancouver's 5th choice, 58th over-all, in 1984 Entry Draft).

				Regular Season					Playoffs			
Season	Club	Lea	GP	G	A	TP	PIM	GP	G	A	TP	PIM
1982-83	Kitchener	OHL	13	0	4	4	16	12	0	1	1	9
1983-84	Kitchener	OHL	66	19	21	40	109	16	10	7	17	40
1984-85	Vancouver	NHL	6	0	3	3	6	....	....	....	....	....
	Kitchener	OHL	37	17	18	35	121	4	1	1	2	8
1985-86	Fredericton	AHL	79	12	19	31	208	6	1	1	2	35
	NHL Totals		6	0	3	3	6	....	....	....	....	....

STEVENS, SCOTT

Born, Kitchener, Ont., April 1, 1964.
Defense. Shoots left. 5'11", 200 lbs.
Last amateur club: Kitchener Rangers (OHL).
(Washington's 1st choice, 5th over-all, in 1982 Entry Draft).

				Regular Season					Playoffs			
Season	Club	Lea	GP	G	A	TP	PIM	GP	G	A	TP	PIM
1980-81	Kitchener	OPJHL	39	7	33	40	82	....	....	....	....	....
	Kitchener	OHA	1	0	0	0	0	....	....	....	....	....
1981-82	Kitchener	OHL	68	6	36	42	158	15	1	10	11	71
1982-83a	Washington	NHL	77	9	16	25	195	4	1	0	1	26
1983-84	Washington	NHL	78	13	32	45	201	8	1	8	9	21
1984-85	Washington	NHL	80	21	44	65	221	5	0	1	1	20
1985-86	Washington	NHL	73	15	38	53	165	9	3	8	11	12
	NHL Totals		308	58	130	188	782	26	5	17	22	79

a Named to NHL All-Rookie Team (1983)

STEWART, ALLAN

Born, Grande Centre, Alta., January 31, 1964.
Left wing. Shoots left. 6', 175 lbs.
Last amateur club: Prince Albert Raiders (WHL).
(New Jersey's 9th choice, 205th over-all, in 1983 Entry Draft).

				Regular Season					Playoffs			
Season	Club	Lea	GP	G	A	TP	PIM	GP	G	A	TP	PIM
1982-83	Prince Albert	WHL	70	25	34	59	272	....	....	....	....	....
1983-84	Prince Albert	WHL	67	44	39	83	216	5	1	2	3	29
	Maine	AHL	....	....	....	....	....	3	0	0	0	0
1984-85	Maine	AHL	75	8	11	19	241	11	1	2	3	58
1985-86	New Jersey	NHL	4	0	0	0	21	....	....	....	....	....
	Maine	AHL	58	7	12	19	181	....	....	....	....	....
	NHL Totals		4	0	0	0	21	....	....	....	....	....

STEWART, RYAN

Born, Houston, B.C., June 1, 1967.
Center. Shoots right. 6'1", 175 lbs.
Last amateur club: Kamloops Blazers (WHL).
(Winnipeg's 1st choice, 18th over-all, in 1985 Entry Draft).

				Regular Season					Playoffs			
Season	Club	Lea	GP	G	A	TP	PIM	GP	G	A	TP	PIM
1983-84	Kamloops	WHL	69	31	38	69	88	16	7	7	14	19
1984-85	Kamloops	WHL	54	33	37	70	92	11	6	6	12	34
1985-86	Winnipeg	NHL	3	1	0	1	0	....	....	....	....	....
	Prince Albert	WHL	62	52	44	96	82	15	7	8	15	21
	NHL Totals		3	1	0	1	0	....	....	....	....	....

STEWART, WILLIAM DONALD (BILL)

Born, Toronto, Ont., October 6, 1957.
Defense. Shoots right. 6'2", 180 lbs.
Last amateur club: Niagara Falls Flyers (OHA).
(Buffalo's 3rd choice, 68th over-all, in 1977 Amateur Draft).

				Regular Season					Playoffs			
Season	Club	Lea	GP	G	A	TP	PIM	GP	G	A	TP	PIM
1975-76	Kitchener	OHA	1	3	4	4	4	....	....	....	....	....
	St. Catharines	OHA	48	9	31	40	57	4	0	3	3	8
1976-77	Niagara Falls	OHA	59	18	37	55	202	....	....	....	....	....
1977-78	Hershey	AHL	54	6	18	24	92	....	....	....	....	....
	Buffalo	NHL	13	2	0	2	15	8	0	2	2	0
1978-79	Buffalo	NHL	68	1	17	18	101	1	0	1	1	0
1979-80	Rochester	AHL	63	12	28	40	189	4	1	2	3	42
1980-81	Rochester	AHL	6	1	6	7	12	....	....	....	....	....
	St. Louis	NHL	60	2	21	23	114	4	1	0	1	11
1981-82	St. Louis	NHL	22	0	5	5	25	....	....	....	....	....
	Salt Lake	CHL	40	2	12	14	93	10	0	6	6	12
1982-83	St. Louis	NHL	7	0	0	0	8	....	....	....	....	....
	Salt Lake	CHL	62	10	42	52	143	5	1	4	5	8
1983-84	Toronto	NHL	56	2	17	19	116	....	....	....	....	....
1984-85	Toronto	NHL	27	0	2	2	32	....	....	....	....	....
	St. Catharines	AHL	12	2	5	7	11	....	....	....	....	....
1985-86	Minnesota	NHL	8	0	2	2	13	....	....	....	....	....
	Springfield	AHL	59	7	19	26	135	....	....	....	....	....
	NHL Totals		261	7	64	71	424	13	1	3	4	11

Claimed by **Buffalo** as fill in Expansion Draft, June 13, 1979. Traded to **St. Louis** by **Buffalo** for Bob Hess, October 30, 1980. Signed as free agent by **Toronto**, September 10, 1983. Signed as a free agent by **Minnesota**, September 15, 1985.

STIENBURG, TREVOR

Born, Kingston, Ont., May 13, 1966.
Right wing. Shoots right. 6'1", 180 lbs.
Last amateur club: Guelph Platers (OHL).
(Quebec's 1st choice, 15th over-all, in 1984 Entry Draft).

				Regular Season					Playoffs			
Season	Club	Lea	GP	G	A	TP	PIM	GP	G	A	TP	PIM
1982-83	Brockville	OPJHL	47	39	30	69	182	....	....	....	....	....
1983-84	Guelph	OHL	65	33	18	51	104	....	....	....	....	....
1984-85	Guelph	OHL	18	7	12	19	38	....	....	....	....	....
	London	OHL	22	9	11	20	45	8	1	3	4	22
1985-86	Quebec	NHL	2	1	0	1	0	....	....	....	....	....
	London	OHL	31	12	18	30	88	5	0	0	0	20
	NHL Totals		2	1	0	1	0	1	0	0	0	0

STILES, TONY

Born, Carstairs, Alta., August I2, I959.
Defense. Shoots left. 5'11", 200 lbs.
Last amateur club: Michigan Tech University Huskies (CCHA)

			Regular Season					Playoffs				
Season	Club	Lea	GP	G	A	TP	PIM	GP	G	A	TP	PIM
1980-81	Michigan Tech	CCHA	44	10	20	30	58	....	....	....	....	....
1981-82	Michigan Tech	CCHA	38	7	14	21	26	....	....	....	....	....
1982-83	Colorado	CHL	58	2	7	9	53	1	0	0	0	0
1983-84	**Calgary**	**NHL**	**30**	**2**	**7**	**9**	**20**	....	....	....	....	....
	Colorado	CHL	39	3	18	21	24	1	0	0	0	0
1984-85	Moncton	AHL	79	5	9	14	46	....	....	....	....	....
1985-86	Moncton	AHL	20	0	2	2	18	....	....	....	....	....
	Fredericton	AHL	9	0	1	1	9	....	....	....	....	....
	NHL Totals		**30**	**2**	**7**	**9**	**20**	....	....	....	....	....

Signed as free agent by **Calgary**, September 17, 1982. Traded to **Quebec** to **Calgary** for Tom Thornbury, January 16, 1986.

STOTHERS, MICHAEL PATRICK (MIKE)

Born, Toronto, Ont., February 22, 1962.
Defense. Shoots left. 6'4", 210 lbs.
Last amateur club: Kingston Canadians (OHL).
(Philadelphia's 1st choice, 21st over-all, in 1980 Entry Draft).

			Regular Season					Playoffs				
Season	Club	Lea	GP	G	A	TP	PIM	GP	G	A	TP	PIM
1979-80	Kingston	OHA	66	4	23	27	137	....	....	....	....	....
1980-81	Kingston	OHA	65	4	22	26	237	14	0	3	3	27
1981-82	Kingston	OHL	61	1	20	21	203	4	0	1	1	8
	Maine	AHL	5	0	0	0	4	1	0	0	0	0
1982-83	Maine	AHL	80	2	16	18	139	12	0	0	0	21
1983-84	Maine	AHL	61	2	10	12	109	17	0	1	1	34
1984-85	**Philadelphia**	**NHL**	**1**	**0**	**0**	**0**	**0**	....	....	....	....	....
	Hershey	AHL	59	8	18	26	142	....	....	....	....	....
1985-86	**Philiadelphia**	**NHL**	**6**	**0**	**1**	**1**	**6**	**3**	**0**	**0**	**0**	**4**
	Hershey	AHL	66	4	9	13	221	13	0	3	3	88
	NHL Totals		**7**	**0**	**1**	**1**	**6**	**3**	**0**	**0**	**0**	**4**

STROMBACK, DOUG

Born, Farmington, Mich., March 3, 1967.
Right wing. Shoots right. 6'0", 175 lbs.
Last amateur club: North Bay Centennials (OHL).
(Washington's 7th choice, 124th overall, in 1985 Entry Draft).

			Regular Season					Playoffs				
Season	Club	Lea	GP	G	A	TP	PIM	GP	G	A	TP	PIM
1984-85	Kitchener	OHL	66	20	24	44	48	4	2	1	3	0
1985-86	North Bay	OHL	63	26	32	58	63	10	0	0	0	14

STRONG, KEN

Born, Toronto, Ont., May 9, 1963.
Left wing. Shoots left. 5'11", 185 lbs.
Last amateur club: Peterborough Petes (OHL).
(Philadelphia's 4th choice, 58th over-all, in 1981 Entry Draft).

			Regular Season					Playoffs				
Season	Club	Lea	GP	G	A	TP	PIM	GP	G	A	TP	PIM
1980-81	Peterborough	OHA	64	17	36	53	52	5	2	1	3	18
1981-82	Peterborough	OHL	42	21	22	43	69	9	8	11	19	23
1982-83	**Toronto**	**NHL**	**2**	**0**	**0**	**0**	**0**	....	....	....	....	....
	Peterborough	OHL	57	41	48	89	80	4	2	2	4	4
1983-84	**Toronto**	**NHL**	**2**	**0**	**2**	**2**	**2**	....	....	....	....	....
	St. Catharines	AHL	78	27	45	72	78	7	3	3	6	4
1984-85	**Toronto**	**NHL**	**11**	**2**	**0**	**2**	**4**	....	....	....	....	....
	St. Catharines	AHL	45	15	19	34	41	....	....	....	....	....
1985-86	St. Catharines	AHL	33	16	25	41	14	3	0	1	1	0
	NHL Totals		**15**	**2**	**2**	**4**	**6**	....	....	....	....	....

Acquired by **Toronto** from **Philadelphia** as part of earlier deal (Darryl Sittler), January 20, 1982.

STRUEBY, TODD KENNETH (STROO-bee)

Born, Lannigan, Sask., June 15, 1963.
Left wing. Shoots left. 6'1", 185 lbs.
Last amateur club: Saskatoon Blades (WHL).
(Edmonton's 2nd choice, 29th over-all, in 1981 Entry Draft).

			Regular Season					Playoffs				
Season	Club	Lea	GP	G	A	TP	PIM	GP	G	A	TP	PIM
1980-81	Regina	WHL	71	18	27	45	99	11	3	6	9	19
1981-82a	Saskatoon	WHL	61	60	58	118	160	5	2	2	4	6
	Edmonton	**NHL**	**3**	**0**	**0**	**0**	**0**	....	....	....	....	....
1982-83	**Edmonton**	**NHL**	**1**	**0**	**0**	**0**	**0**	....	....	....	....	....
b	Saskatoon	WHL	65	40	70	110	119	6	3	3	6	19
1983-84	**Edmonton**	**NHL**	**1**	**0**	**1**	**1**	**2**	....	....	....	....	....
	Moncton	AHL	72	17	25	42	38	....	....	....	....	....
1984-85	Nova Scotia	AHL	38	2	3	5	29	....	....	....	....	....
	Muskegon	IHL	27	19	12	31	55	17	4	10	14	27
1985-86	Muskegon	IHL	58	25	40	65	191	14	7	5	12	51
	NHL Totals		**5**	**0**	**1**	**1**	**2**	....	....	....	....	....

a WHL First All-Star Team (1982)
b WHL Second All-Star Team (1983)
Traded to **NY Rangers** by **Edmonton** with Larry Melnyk for Mike Rogers, December 20, 1985.

SULLIMAN, SIMON DOUGLAS (DOUG)

Born, Glace Bay, N.S., August 29, 1959.
Right wing. Shoots left. 5'9", 195 lbs.
Last amateur club: Kitchener Rangers (OHA).
(NY Rangers' 1st choice, 13th over-all, in 1979 Entry Draft).

			Regular Season					Playoffs				
Season	Club	Lea	GP	G	A	TP	PIM	GP	G	A	TP	PIM
1977-78	Kitchener	OHA	68	50	39	89	87	9	5	7	12	24
1978-79	Kitchener	OHA	68	38	77	115	88	10	5	7	12	7
1979-80	**NY Rangers**	**NHL**	**31**	**4**	**7**	**11**	**2**	....	....	....	....	....
	New Haven	AHL	31	9	7	16	9	....	....	....	....	....
1980-81	New Haven	AHL	45	10	16	26	18	1	0	0	0	0
	NY Rangers	**NHL**	**32**	**4**	**1**	**5**	**32**	**3**	**1**	**0**	**1**	**0**
1981-82	**Hartford**	**NHL**	**77**	**29**	**40**	**69**	**39**	....	....	....	....	....
1982-83	**Hartford**	**NHL**	**77**	**22**	**19**	**41**	**14**	....	....	....	....	....
1983-84	**Hartford**	**NHL**	**67**	**6**	**13**	**19**	**20**	....	....	....	....	....
1984-85	**New Jersey**	**NHL**	**57**	**22**	**16**	**38**	**4**	....	....	....	....	....
1985-86	**New Jersey**	**NHL**	**73**	**21**	**22**	**43**	**20**	....	....	....	....	....
	NHL Totals		**414**	**108**	**118**	**226**	**131**	**3**	**1**	**0**	**1**	**0**

Traded to **Hartford** by **NY Rangers** with Chris Kotsopoulos and Gerry McDonald for Mike Rogers and NY Rangers' tenth round choice (Simo Saarinen) in 1982 Entry Draft, October 2, 1981. Signed as free agent by **New Jersey**, July 11, 1984.

SUMMANEN, RAIMO (SOO-ma-nen, RYE-moh)

Born, Jyvaskyla, Finland, March 2, 1962.
Left wing. Shoots left. 5'11", 185 lbs.
Last amateur club: Tampere Ilves (Finland).
(Edmonton's 6th choice, 125th over-all, in 1982 Entry Draft).

			Regular Season					Playoffs				
Season	Club	Lea	GP	G	A	TP	PIM	GP	G	A	TP	PIM
1982-83	Tampere	Fin.	36	45	15	60	36	....	....	....	....	....
1983-84	Tampere	Fin.	37	28	19	47	26	....	....	....	....	....
	Edmonton	**NHL**	**2**	**1**	**4**	**5**	**2**	**5**	**1**	**4**	**5**	**0**
1984-85	**Edmonton**	**NHL**	**9**	**0**	**4**	**4**	**0**	....	....	....	....	....
	Nova Scotia	AHL	66	20	33	53	2	5	1	2	3	0
1985-86	**Edmonton**	**NHL**	**73**	**19**	**18**	**37**	**16**	**5**	**1**	**1**	**2**	**0**
	NHL Totals		**84**	**20**	**26**	**46**	**18**	**10**	**2**	**5**	**7**	**0**

SUNDSTROM, PATRIK

Born, Skelleftea, Sweden, December 14, 1961.
Center/Right wing. Shoots left. 6', 200 lbs.
Last amateur club: Bjorkloven (Sweden).
(Vancouver's 8th choice, 175th over-all, in 1980 Entry Draft).

			Regular Season					Playoffs				
Season	Club	Lea	GP	G	A	TP	PIM	GP	G	A	TP	PIM
1978-79	Bjorkloven	Swe.	1	0	0	0	0	....	....	....	....	....
1979-80	Bjorkloven	Swe.	26	5	7	12	20	....	....	....	....	....
1980-81	Bjorkloven	Swe.	36	10	18	28	30	3	1	0	1	4
	Swe. National	...	15	4	2	6	6	....	....	....	....	....
1981-82	Bjorkloven	Swe.	36	22	13	35	38	7	3	4	7	6
	Swe. National	...	36	17	7	24	24	....	....	....	....	....
1982-83	**Vancouver**	**NHL**	**74**	**23**	**23**	**46**	**30**	**4**	**0**	**0**	**0**	**2**
1983-84	**Vancouver**	**NHL**	**78**	**38**	**53**	**91**	**37**	**4**	**0**	**1**	**1**	**7**
1984-85	**Vancouver**	**NHL**	**71**	**25**	**43**	**68**	**46**	....	....	....	....	....
1985-86	**Vancouver**	**NHL**	**79**	**18**	**48**	**66**	**28**	**3**	**1**	**0**	**1**	**0**
	NHL Totals		**302**	**104**	**167**	**271**	**141**	**11**	**1**	**1**	**2**	**9**

SUNDSTROM, PETER

Born, Skelleftea, Sweden, December 14, 1961.
Left wing. Shoots left. 6', 180 lbs.
Last amateur club: Bjorkloven (Sweden).
(New York Rangers' 3rd choice, 50th over-all, in 1981 Entry Draft).

			Regular Season					Playoffs				
Season	Club	Lea	GP	G	A	TP	PIM	GP	G	A	TP	PIM
1979-80	Bjorkloven	Swe.	8	0	0	0	2	....	....	....	....	....
1980-81	Bjorkloven	Swe.	29	7	2	9	8	....	....	....	....	....
1981-82	Bjorkloven	Swe.	35	10	14	24	18	7	2	1	3	0
1982-83	Bjorkloven	Swe.	36	17	10	27	...	....	....	....	....	....
1983-84	**NY Rangers**	**NHL**	**77**	**22**	**22**	**44**	**24**	**5**	**1**	**3**	**4**	**0**
1984-85	**NY Rangers**	**NHL**	**76**	**18**	**25**	**43**	**34**	**3**	**0**	**0**	**0**	**0**
1985-86	**NY Rangers**	**NHL**	**53**	**8**	**15**	**23**	**12**	**1**	**0**	**0**	**0**	**2**
	New Haven	AHL	8	3	6	9	4	....	....	....	....	....
	NHL Totals		**206**	**48**	**62**	**110**	**70**	**9**	**1**	**3**	**4**	**2**

SUTER, GARY

Born, Madison, Wisc., June 24, 1964.
Defense. Shoots left. 6'0", 190 lbs.
Last amateur club: University of Wisconsin Badgers (WCHA).
(Calgary's 10th choice, 180th over-all, in 1984 Entry Draft).

			Regular Season					Playoffs				
Season	Club	Lea	GP	G	A	TP	PIM	GP	G	A	TP	PIM
1983-84	U. of Wisconsin	WCHA	35	4	18	22	68	....	....	....	....	....
1984-85	U. of Wisconsin	WCHA	39	12	39	51	110	....	....	....	....	....
1985-86a	**Calgary**	**NHL**	**80**	**18**	**50**	**68**	**141**	**10**	**2**	**8**	**10**	**8**
	NHL Totals		**80**	**18**	**50**	**68**	**141**	**10**	**2**	**8**	**10**	**2**

a Won Calder Memorial Trophy (1986)

SUTTER, BRENT COLIN (SUTT-er)

Born, Viking, Alta., June 10, 1962.
Center. Shoots right. 5'11", 175 lbs.
Last amateur club: Lethbridge Broncos (WHL).
(NY Islanders' 1st choice, 17th over-all, in 1980 Entry Draft).

Season	Club	Lea	Regular Season					Playoffs				
			GP	G	A	TP	PIM	GP	G	A	TP	PIM
1979-80	Red Deer	AJHL	59	70	101	171	....	....	....	....	....	....
	Lethbridge	WHL	5	1	0	1	2	....	....	....	....	....
1980-81	NY Islanders	NHL	3	2	2	4	0	....	....	....	....	....
	Lethbridge	WHL	68	54	54	108	116	9	6	4	10	51
1981-82	Lethbridge	WHL	34	46	34	80	162	....	....	....	....	....
	NY Islanders	NHL	43	21	22	43	114	19	2	6	8	36
1982-83	NY Islanders	NHL	80	21	19	40	128	20	10	11	21	26
1983-84	NY Islanders	NHL	69	34	15	49	69	20	4	10	14	18
1984-85	NY Islanders	NHL	72	42	60	102	51	10	3	3	6	14
1985-86	NY Islanders	NHL	61	24	31	55	74	3	0	1	1	2
	NHL Totals		328	144	149	293	436	72	19	31	50	96

SUTTER, BRIAN LOUIS ALLEN (SUTT-er)

Born, Viking, Alta., October 7, 1956.
Left wing. Shoots left. 5'11", 175 lbs.
Last amateur club: Lethbridge Broncos (WHL).
(St. Louis' 2nd choice, 20th over-all, in 1976 Amateur Draft).

Season	Club	Lea	Regular Season					Playoffs				
			GP	G	A	TP	PIM	GP	G	A	TP	PIM
1974-75	Lethbridge	WHL	53	34	47	81	134	6	0	1	1	39
1975-76	Lethbridge	WHL	72	36	56	92	233	7	3	4	7	45
1976-77	Kansas City	CHL	38	15	23	38	47	....	....	....	....	....
	St. Louis	NHL	35	4	10	14	82	4	1	0	1	14
1977-78	St. Louis	NHL	78	9	13	22	123	....	....	....	....	....
1978-79	St. Louis	NHL	77	41	39	80	165	....	....	....	....	....
1979-80	St. Louis	NHL	71	23	35	58	156	3	0	0	0	4
1980-81	St. Louis	NHL	78	35	34	69	232	11	6	3	9	77
1981-82	St. Louis	NHL	74	39	36	75	239	10	8	6	14	49
1982-83	St. Louis	NHL	79	46	30	76	254	4	2	1	3	10
1983-84	St. Louis	NHL	76	32	51	83	162	11	1	5	6	22
1984-85	St. Louis	NHL	77	37	37	74	121	3	2	1	3	2
1985-86	St. Louis	NHL	44	19	23	42	87	9	1	2	3	22
	NHL Totals		689	285	308	593	1621	55	21	18	39	200

SUTTER, DARRYL JOHN (SUTT-er)

Born, Viking, Alta., August 19, 1958.
Left wing. Shoots left. 5'11", 180 lbs.
Last amateur club: Lethbridge Broncos (WHL).
(Chicago's 11th choice, 179th over-all, in 1978 Amateur Draft).

Season	Club	Lea	Regular Season					Playoffs				
			GP	G	A	TP	PIM	GP	G	A	TP	PIM
1976-77	Lethbridge	WHL	1	1	0	1	0	15	3	7	10	13
1977-78	Lethbridge	WHL	68	33	48	81	119	8	4	9	13	2
1978-79	New Brunswick	AHL	19	7	6	13	6	5	1	2	3	0
1979-80ab	New Brunswick	AHL	69	35	31	66	69	12	6	6	12	8
	Chicago	NHL	8	2	0	2	2	7	3	1	4	2
1980-81	Chicago	NHL	76	40	22	62	86	3	3	1	4	2
1981-82	Chicago	NHL	40	23	12	35	31	3	0	1	1	2
1982-83	Chicago	NHL	80	31	30	61	53	13	4	6	10	8
1983-84	Chicago	NHL	59	20	20	40	44	5	1	1	2	0
1984-85	Chicago	NHL	49	20	18	38	12	15	12	7	19	12
1985-86	Chicago	NHL	50	17	10	27	44	3	1	2	3	0
	NHL Totals		362	153	112	265	272	49	24	19	43	26

a AHL Second All-Star Team (1980)
b Won Dudley "Red" Garrett Memorial Trophy (AHL's Rookie of the Year) (1980)

SUTTER, DUANE CALVIN (SUTT-er)

Born, Viking, Alta., March 16, 1960.
Right wing. Shoots right. 6'1", 185 lbs.
Last amateur club: Lethbridge Broncos (WHL).
(NY Islanders' 1st choice, 17th over-all, in 1979 Entry Draft).

Season	Club	Lea	Regular Season					Playoffs				
			GP	G	A	TP	PIM	GP	G	A	TP	PIM
1976-77	Lethbridge	WHL	1	0	1	1	2	8	0	1	1	15
1977-78	Lethbridge	WHL	5	1	5	6	19	8	1	4	5	10
1978-79	Lethbridge	WHL	71	50	75	125	212	19	11	12	23	43
1979-80	Lethbridge	WHL	21	18	16	34	74	....	....	....	....	....
	NY Islanders	NHL	56	15	9	24	55	21	3	7	10	74
1980-81	NY Islanders	NHL	23	7	11	18	26	12	3	1	4	10
1981-82	NY Islanders	NHL	77	18	35	53	100	19	5	5	10	57
1982-83	NY Islanders	NHL	75	13	19	32	118	20	9	12	21	43
1983-84	NY Islanders	NHL	78	17	23	40	94	21	1	3	4	48
1984-85	NY Islanders	NHL	78	17	24	41	174	10	2	0	2	47
1985-86	NY Islanders	NHL	80	20	33	53	157	3	0	0	0	16
	NHL Totals		467	107	154	261	725	106	21	30	51	295

SUTTER, RICHARD (RICH) (SUTT-er)

Born, Viking, Alta., December 2, 1963.
Right wing. Shoots right. 5'11", 165 lbs.
Last amateur club: Lethbridge Broncos (WHL).
(Pittsburgh's 1st choice, 10th over-all, in 1982 Entry Draft).

Season	Club	Lea	Regular Season					Playoffs				
			GP	G	A	TP	PIM	GP	G	A	TP	PIM
1980-81	Lethbridge	WHL	72	23	18	41	255	9	3	1	4	35
1981-82	Lethbridge	WHL	57	38	31	69	263	12	3	3	6	55
1982-83	Pittsburgh	NHL	4	0	0	0	0	....	....	....	....	....
	Lethbridge	WHL	64	37	30	67	200	17	14	9	23	43
1983-84	Baltimore	AHL	2	0	1	1	0	....	....	....	....	....
	Pittsburgh	NHL	5	0	0	0	0	....	....	....	....	....
	Philadelphia	NHL	70	16	12	28	93	3	0	0	0	15
1984-85	Philadelphia	NHL	56	6	10	16	89	11	3	0	3	10
	Hershey	AHL	13	3	7	10	14	....	....	....	....	....
1985-86	Philadelphia	NHL	78	14	25	39	199	5	2	0	2	19
	NHL Totals		213	36	47	83	381	19	5	0	5	44

Traded to **Philadelphia** by **Pittsburgh** with Pittsburgh's second round (Greg Smyth) and third round (David McClay) choices in 1984 Entry Draft for Andy Brickley, Mark Taylor, Ron Flockhart, Philadelphia's first round (Roger Belanger) and third round (Mike Stevens — later transferred to Vancouver) choices in 1984 Entry Draft, October 23, 1983. Traded to **Vancouver** by **Philadelphia**, with Dave Richter and Vancouver's third-round choice (Don Gibson) in 1986 Entry Draft — acquired earlier — for J.J. Daigneault and Vancouver's second-round choice (Kent Hawley) in 1986 Entry Draft, June 6, 1986.

SUTTER, RONALD (RON) (SUTT-er)

Born, Viking, Alta., December 2, 1963.
Center. Shoots right. 5'11", 175 lbs.
Last amateur club: Lethbridge Broncos (WHL).
(Philadelphia's 1st choice, 4th over-all, in 1982 Entry Draft).

Season	Club	Lea	Regular Season					Playoffs				
			GP	G	A	TP	PIM	GP	G	A	TP	PIM
1980-81	Lethbridge	WHL	72	13	32	45	152	9	2	5	7	29
1981-82	Lethbridge	WHL	59	38	54	92	207	12	6	5	11	28
1982-83	Philadelphia	NHL	10	1	1	2	9	....	....	....	....	....
	Lethbridge	WHL	58	35	48	83	98	20	22	19	41	45
1983-84	Philadelphia	NHL	79	19	32	51	101	3	0	0	0	22
1984-85	Philadelphia	NHL	73	16	29	45	94	19	4	8	12	28
1985-86	Philadelphia	NHL	75	18	42	60	159	5	0	2	2	10
	NHL Totals		237	54	104	158	363	27	4	10	14	60

SUTTON, BOYD

Born, Anchorage, Alaska, December 6, 1966.
Center/Left wing. Shoots left. 5'10", 175 lbs.
Last amateur club: University of Miami-Ohio Redskins (CCHA).
(Buffalo's 10th choice, 203rd overall, in 1985 Entry Draft).

Season	Club	Lea	Regular Season					Playoffs				
			GP	G	A	TP	PIM	GP	G	A	TP	PIM
1985-86	Miami-Ohio	CCHA	33	8	13	21	24	....	....	....	....	....

SVEEN, JEFF

Born, Barrhead, Alta., February 5, 1967.
Center. Shoots right. 5'11", 175 lbs.
Last amateur club: Boston University Terriers (H.E.).
(NY Islanders' 7th choice, 97th overall, in 1985 Entry Draft).

Season	Club	Lea	Regular Season					Playoffs				
			GP	G	A	TP	PIM	GP	G	A	TP	PIM
1984-85	Boston U.	H.E.	42	14	10	24	10	....	....	....	....	....
1985-86	Boston U.	H.E.	35	15	8	23	18	....	....	....	....	....

SVOBODA, PETR (sza-BOH-da)

Born, Most, Czechoslovakia, February 14, 1966.
Defense. Shoots left. 6'1", 165 lbs.
Last amateur club: Czechoslovakian National Junior Team.
(Montreal's 1st choice, 5th over-all, in 1984 Entry Draft).

Season	Club	Lea	Regular Season					Playoffs				
			GP	G	A	TP	PIM	GP	G	A	TP	PIM
1983-84	Czech. Jrs.	...	40	15	21	36	14	....	....	....	....	....
1984-85	Montreal	NHL	73	4	27	31	65	7	1	1	2	12
1985-86	Montreal	NHL	73	1	18	19	93	8	0	0	0	21
	NHL Totals		146	5	45	50	158	15	1	1	2	33

SWEENEY, DON

Born, St. Stephen, N.B., August 17, 1966.
Defense. Shoots left. 5'11", 170 lbs.
Last amateur club: University of Harvard Crimson (ECAC).
(Boston's 8th choice, 166th overall, in 1984 Entry Draft).

Season	Club	Lea	Regular Season					Playoffs				
			GP	G	A	TP	PIM	GP	G	A	TP	PIM
1984-85	Harvard	ECAC	29	3	7	10	30	....	....	....	....	....
1985-86	Harvard	ECAC	31	4	5	9	12	....	....	....	....	....

SWEENEY, ROBERT (BOB)

Born, Boxboro, Mass., January 25, 1964.
Center. Shoots right. 6'3", 190 lbs.
Last amateur club: Boston College Eagles (ECAC)
(Boston's 6th choice, 123rd over-all, in 1982 Entry Draft).

				Regular Season					Playoffs			
Season	Club	Lea	GP	G	A	TP	PIM	GP	G	A	TP	PIM
1982-83	Boston College	ECAC	30	17	11	28	10	....	....	....	....	....
1983-84	Boston College	ECAC	23	14	7	21	10	....	....	....	....	....
1984-85a	Boston College	ECAC	44	32	32	64	43	....	....	....	....	....
1985-86	Boston College	H.E.	41	15	24	39	52	....	....	....	....	....

a ECAC Second Team All-Star.

SWEENEY, TIM

Born, Boston. Mass., April 12, 1967.
Center. Shoots left. 5'11", 180 lbs.
Last amateur club: Boston College Eagles (H.E.).
(Calgary's 7th choice, 122nd over-all, in 1985 Entry Draft).

				Regular Season					Playoffs			
Season	Club	Lea	GP	G	A	TP	PIM	GP	G	A	TP	PIM
1985-86	Boston College	H.E.	32	8	4	12	8	....	....	....	....	....

SYKES, PHIL

Born, Dawson Creek, B.C., May 18, 1959.
Left wing. Shoots left. 6', 185 lbs.
Last amateur club: University of North Dakota Fighting Sioux (WCHA)

				Regular Season					Playoffs			
Season	Club	Lea	GP	G	A	TP	PIM	GP	G	A	TP	PIM
1979-80	North Dakota	WCHA	37	22	27	49	34	....	....	....	....	....
1980-81	North Dakota	WCHA	38	28	34	62	22	....	....	....	....	....
1981-82abc	North Dakota	WCHA	37	22	27	49	34	....	....	....	....	....
1982-83	Los Angeles	NHL	7	2	0	2	2	....	....	....	....	....
	New Haven	AHL	71	19	26	45	111	12	2	2	4	21
1983-84	Los Angeles	NHL	3	0	0	0	2	....	....	....	....	....
	New Haven	AHL	77	29	37	66	101	....	....	....	....	....
1984-85	Los Angeles	NHL	79	17	15	32	38	3	0	1	1	4
1985-86	Los Angeles	NHL	76	20	24	44	97	....	....	....	....	....
	NHL Totals		165	39	39	78	139	3	0	1	1	4

a WCHA First All-Star Team (1982)
b Named WCHA Player of the Year (1982)
c Named Most Valuable Player, NCAA Tournament (1982)
Signed as a free agent by **Los Angeles**, April 5, 1982.

TAGLIANETTI, PETER

Born, Framingham, Mass., August 15, 1963.
Defense. Shoots left. 6'2", 195 lbs.
Last amateur club: Providence College Friars (H.E.).
(Winnipeg's 4th choice, 43rd over-all, in 1983 Entry Draft).

				Regular Season					Playoffs			
Season	Club	Lea	GP	G	A	TP	PIM	GP	G	A	TP	PIM
1981-82	Providence	ECAC	2	0	0	0	2	....	....	....	....	....
1982-83	Providence	ECAC	43	4	17	21	68	....	....	....	....	....
1983-84	Providence	ECAC	30	4	25	29	68	....	....	....	....	....
1984-85	Winnipeg	NHL	1	0	0	0	0	1	0	0	0	0
a	Providence	H.E.	35	6	18	24	32	....	....	....	....	....
1985-86	Winnipeg	NHL	18	0	0	0	48	3	0	0	0	2
	Sherbrooke	AHL	24	1	18	9	75	....	....	....	....	....
	NHL Totals		19	0	0	0	48	4	0	0	0	2

a Hockey East First All-Star Team (1985).

TAIT, TERRY

Born, Thunder Bay, Ont., September 10, 1963.
Center. Shoots left. 6'1", 195 lbs.
Last amateur club: Sault Ste. Marie Greyhounds (OHL).
(Minnesota's 6th choice, 69th over-all, in 1981 Entry Draft).

				Regular Season					Playoffs			
Season	Club	Lea	GP	G	A	TP	PIM	GP	G	A	TP	PIM
1980-81	S. S. Marie	OHA	54	5	10	15	90	12	2	2	4	4
1981-82	S. S. Marie	OHL	60	18	17	35	96	13	3	4	7	6
1982-83	S. S. Marie	OHL	65	29	47	76	59	16	5	1	16	22
1983-84	Salt Lake	CHL	36	1	7	8	7	....	....	....	....	....
	Toledo	IHL	5	0	0	0	2	....	....	....	....	....
1984-85	Springfield	AHL	75	19	25	44	18	4	0	0	0	7
1985-86	Springfield	AHL	62	11	19	30	34	....	....	....	....	....

TAMBELLINI, STEVEN ANTHONY (STEVE)

(TAM-be-lee-nee)

Born, Trail, B.C., May 14, 1958.
Center. Shoots left. 6', 184 lbs.
Last amateur club: Lethbridge Broncos (WHL).
(NY Islanders' 1st choice, 15th over-all, in 1978 Amateur Draft).

				Regular Season					Playoffs			
Season	Club	Lea	GP	G	A	TP	PIM	GP	G	A	TP	PIM
1975-76a	Lethbridge	WHL	72	38	59	97	42	7	3	6	9	2
1976-77b	Lethbridge	WHL	55	42	42	84	23	15	10	11	21	0
1977-78b	Lethbridge	WHL	66	75	80	155	32	8	10	5	15	5
1978-79	NY Islanders	NHL	1	0	0	0	0	....	....	....	....	....
	Fort Worth	CHL	73	25	27	52	32	5	0	1	1	0
1979-80	NY Islanders	NHL	45	5	8	13	4	....	....	....	....	....
1980-81	NY Islanders	NHL	61	19	17	36	17	....	....	....	....	....
	Colorado	NHL	13	6	12	18	2	....	....	....	....	....
1981-82	Colorado	NHL	79	29	30	59	14	....	....	....	....	....
1982-83	New Jersey	NHL	73	25	18	43	14	....	....	....	....	....
1983-84	Calgary	NHL	73	15	10	25	16	2	0	1	1	0
1984-85	Calgary	NHL	47	19	10	29	4	....	....	....	....	....
	Moncton	AHL	7	2	5	7	0	....	....	....	....	....
1985-86	Vancouver	NHL	48	15	15	30	12	....	....	....	....	....
	NHL Totals		440	133	120	253	83	2	0	1	1	0

a WHL Rookie of the Year (1976)
b WHL Most Gentlemanly Player (1977, 1978)
Traded to **Colorado** by **NY Islanders** with Glenn Resch for Mike McEwen and Jari Kaarela, March 10, 1981. Traded to **Calgary** by **New Jersey** with Joel Quenneville for Mel Bridgman and Phil Russell, June 20, 1983. Signed as a free agent by **Vancouver**, August 28, 1985.

TANNER, DAVID

Born, Winnipeg, Man., March 5, 1966.
Defense. Shoots left. 6'0", 185 lbs.
Last amateur club: Yale University Bulldogs (ECAC).
(Montreal's 13th choice, 220th over-all, in 1984 Entry Draft).

				Regular Season					Playoffs			
Season	Club	Lea	GP	G	A	TP	PIM	GP	G	A	TP	PIM
1984-85	Yale	ECAC	31	2	10	12	4	....	....	....	....	....
1985-86	Yale	ECAC	22	6	20	26	11	....	....	....	....	....

TANTI, TONY

(TAN-tee)

Born, Toronto, Ont., September 7, 1963.
Right wing. Shoots left. 5'9", 190 lbs.
Last amateur club: Oshawa Generals (OHL).
(Chicago's 1st choice, 12th over-all, in 1981 Entry Draft).

				Regular Season					Playoffs			
Season	Club	Lea	GP	G	A	TP	PIM	GP	G	A	TP	PIM
1980-81a	Oshawa	OHA	67	81	69	150	197	11	7	8	15	41
1981-82	Chicago	NHL	2	0	0	0	0	....	....	....	....	....
b	Oshawa	OHL	57	62	64	126	138	12	14	12	26	15
1982-83	Oshawa	OHL	30	34	28	62	35	....	....	....	....	....
	Chicago	NHL	1	1	0	1	0	....	....	....	....	....
	Vancouver	NHL	39	8	8	16	16	4	0	1	1	0
1983-84	Vancouver	NHL	79	45	41	86	50	4	1	2	3	0
1984-85	Vancouver	NHL	68	39	20	59	45	....	....	....	....	....
1985-86	Vancouver	NHL	77	39	33	72	85	3	0	1	1	11
	NHL Totals		266	132	102	234	196	11	1	4	5	11

a OHA First All-Star Team (1981)
b OHL Second All-Star Team (1982)
Traded to **Vancouver** by **Chicago** for Curt Fraser, January 6, 1983.

TAYLOR, DARREN

Born, Calgary, Alta., May 28, 1967.
Center. Shoots left. 6'1", 170 lbs.
Last amateur club: Seattle Thunderbirds (WHL).
(Vancouver's 12th choice, 235th over-all, in 1985 Entry Draft).

				Regular Season					Playoffs			
Season	Club	Lea	GP	G	A	TP	PIM	GP	G	A	TP	PIM
1984-85	Calgary	WHL	72	11	5	16	54	7	1	0	1	10
1985-86	Seattle	WHL	68	11	19	30	137	5	0	0	0	8

TAYLOR, DAVID ANDREW (DAVE)

Born, Levack, Ont., December 4, 1955.
Right wing. Shoots right. 6', 195 lbs.
Last amateur club: Clarkson College Golden Knights (ECAC).
(Los Angeles' 14th choice, 210th over-all, in 1975 Amateur Draft).

				Regular Season					Playoffs			
Season	Club	Lea	GP	G	A	TP	PIM	GP	G	A	TP	PIM
1976-77	Clarkson	ECAC	34	41	67	108	....	....	....	....	....	....
	Fort Worth	CHL	7	2	4	6	6	....	....	....	....	....
1977-78	Los Angeles	NHL	64	22	21	43	47	2	0	0	0	5
1978-79	Los Angeles	NHL	78	43	48	91	124	2	0	0	0	2
1979-80	Los Angeles	NHL	61	37	53	90	72	4	2	1	3	4
1980-81a	Los Angeles	NHL	72	47	65	112	130	4	2	2	4	10
1981-82	Los Angeles	NHL	78	39	67	106	130	10	4	6	10	20
1982-83	Los Angeles	NHL	46	21	37	58	76	....	....	....	....	....
1983-84	Los Angeles	NHL	63	20	49	69	91	....	....	....	....	....
1984-85	Los Angeles	NHL	79	41	51	92	132	3	2	2	4	8
1985-86	Los Angeles	NHL	76	33	38	71	110	....	....	....	....	....
	NHL Totals		617	303	429	732	912	25	10	11	21	49

a NHL Second All-Star Team (1981)

TAYLOR, MARK

Born, Vancouver, B.C., January 26, 1958.
Center. Shoots left. 5'11", 185 lbs.
Last amateur club: University of North Dakota Fighting Sioux (WCHA).
(Philadelphia's 9th choice, 100th over-all, in 1978 Amateur Draft).

				Regular Season					Playoffs			
Season	Club	Lea	GP	G	A	TP	PIM	GP	G	A	TP	PIM
1978-79a	North Dakota	WCHA	42	24	59	83	28	....	....	....	....	....
1979-80	North Dakota	WCHA	40	33	59	92	30	....	....	....	....	....
1980-81	Maine	AHL	79	19	50	69	56	20	5	16	*21	20
1981-82	**Philadelphia**	**NHL**	2	0	0	0	0	....	....	....	....	....
	Maine	AHL	75	32	48	80	42	4	2	3	5	4
1982-83	**Philadelphia**	**NHL**	61	8	25	33	24	3	0	0	0	0
1983-84	**Philadelphia**	**NHL**	1	0	0	0	0	....	....	....	....	....
	Pittsburgh	**NHL**	59	24	31	55	24	....	....	....	....	....
1984-85	**Pittsburgh**	**NHL**	47	7	10	17	19	....	....	....	....	....
	Washington	**NHL**	9	1	1	2	2	....	....	....	....	....
1985-86	**Washington**	**NHL**	30	2	1	3	4	3	0	0	0	0
	Binghamton	AHL	43	19	38	57	27	....	....	....	....	....
	NHL Totals		**209**	**42**	**68**	**110**	**73**	**6**	**0**	**0**	**0**	**0**

a Named to NCAA All-Tournament Team (1979)
Traded to **Pittsburgh** by **Philadelphia** with Ron Flockhart, Andy Brickley and Philadelphia's first round choice (Roger Belanger) and third round (Mike Stevens — later transferred to Vancouver) choices in 1984 Entry Draft for Ron Sutter and Pittsburgh's second round (Greg Smyth) and third round (David McClay) choices in 1984 Entry Draft, October 23, 1983. Traded to **Washington** by **Pittsburgh** for Jim McGeough, March 12, 1985.

TEBBUTT, GREGORY (GREG)

Born, North Vancouver, B.C., May 11, 1957.
Defense. Shoots left. 6'2", 215 lbs.
Last amateur club: Flin Flon Bombers (WHL).
(Minnesota's 7th choice, 130th over-all, in 1977 Amateur Draft).

				Regular Season					Playoffs			
Season	Club	Lea	GP	G	A	TP	PIM	GP	G	A	TP	PIM
1975-76	Victoria	WHL	51	3	4	7	217	15	2	0	2	43
1976-77	Victoria	WHL	29	7	12	19	98	....	....	....	....	....
	Regina	WHL	40	8	17	25	138	....	....	....	....	....
1977-78	Flin Flon	WHL	55	28	46	74	270	15	11	17	28	45
1978-79	Birmingham	WHA	38	2	5	7	83	....	....	....	....	....
	Binghamton	AHL	33	8	9	17	50	....	....	....	....	....
1979-80	**Quebec**	**NHL**	2	0	1	1	4	....	....	....	....	....
	Syracuse	AHL	14	2	3	5	35	....	....	....	....	....
	Erie	EHL	48	20	53	73	138	....	....	....	....	....
1980-81	Erie	EHL	35	16	37	53	93	....	....	....	....	....
1981-82	Fort Wayne	IHL	49	13	34	47	148	....	....	....	....	....
1982-83ab	Baltimore	AHL	80	28	56	84	140	....	....	....	....	....
1983-84	**Pittsburgh**	**NHL**	24	0	2	2	31	....	....	....	....	....
	Baltimore	AHL	44	12	42	54	125	10	0	6	6	20
1984-85	Baltimore	AHL	2	0	0	0	4	....	....	....	....	....
c	Muskegon	IHL	73	23	55	78	220	17	3	9	12	87
1985-86	Milwaukee	IHL	77	20	49	69	226	5	0	3	3	8
	NHL Totals		**26**	**0**	**3**	**3**	**35**	....	....	....	....	....
	WHA Totals		**38**	**2**	**5**	**7**	**83**	....	....	....	....	....

a AHL First All-Star Team (1983).
b Won Eddie Shore Plaque (AHL's Most Outstanding Defenseman) (1983).
c IHL Second All-Star Team (1985).
Claimed on waivers by **Quebec** from **Minnesota**, August 13, 1979. Signed as free agent by **Pittsburgh**, July 22, 1983.

TEEVENS, MARK

Born, Ottawa, Ont., June 17, 1966.
Right wing. Shoots left. 6', 180 lbs.
Last amateur club: Peterborough Petes (OHL).
(Pittsburgh's 4th choice, 64th over-all, in 1984 Entry Draft).

				Regular Season					Playoffs			
Season	Club	Lea	GP	G	A	TP	PIM	GP	G	A	TP	PIM
1983-84	Peterborough	OHL	70	27	37	64	70	8	3	4	7	4
1984-85	Peterborough	OHL	65	43	90	133	70	17	10	12	22	24
1985-86	Peterborough	OHL	50	31	50	81	106	16	4	21	25	19

TERRION, GREG PATRICK   (TERRY-on)

Born, Marmora, Ont., May 2, 1960.
Left wing. Shoots left. 5'11", 190 lbs.
Last amateur club: Brantford Alexanders (OHA).
(Los Angeles' 3rd choice, 33rd over-all, in 1980 Entry Draft).

				Regular Season					Playoffs			
Season	Club	Lea	GP	G	A	TP	PIM	GP	G	A	TP	PIM
1978-79	Brantford	OHA	59	27	28	55	48	....	....	....	....	....
1979-80	Brantford	OHA	67	44	78	122	13	11	4	7	11	14
1980-81	**Los Angeles**	**NHL**	73	12	25	37	99	3	1	0	1	4
1981-82	**Los Angeles**	**NHL**	61	15	22	37	23	....	....	....	....	....
1982-83	New Haven	AHL	4	0	1	1	7	....	....	....	....	....
	Toronto	**NHL**	74	16	16	32	59	4	1	2	3	2
1983-84	**Toronto**	**NHL**	79	15	24	39	36	....	....	....	....	....
1984-85	**Toronto**	**NHL**	72	14	17	31	20	....	....	....	....	....
1985-86	**Toronto**	**NHL**	76	10	22	32	31	10	0	3	3	17
	NHL Totals		**430**	**82**	**126**	**208**	**268**	**17**	**2**	**5**	**7**	**23**

Traded to **Toronto** by **Los Angeles** for Toronto's fourth round choice (David Korol) in 1983 Entry Draft (later transferred to Detroit), October 19, 1982.

TERWILLIGER, TOM

Born, Denver, Colo., September 1, 1965.
Defense. Shoots right. 6'2", 185 lbs.
Last amateur club: University of Miami-Ohio Redskins (CCHA).
(Minnesota's 11th choice, 222nd overall, in 1984 Entry Draft).

				Regular Season					Playoffs			
Season	Club	Lea	GP	G	A	TP	PIM	GP	G	A	TP	PIM
1984-85	Miami-Ohio	CCHA	29	2	3	5	18	....	....	....	....	....
1985-86	Miami-Ohio	CCHA	32	1	3	4	35	....	....	....	....	....

THELIN, MATS   (tay-LEEN)

Born, Stockholm, Sweden, March 30, 1961.
Defense. Shoots left. 5'10", 185 lbs.
Last amateur club: AIK (Sweden).
(Boston's 6th choice, 140th over-all, in 1981 Entry Draft).

				Regular Season					Playoffs			
Season	Club	Lea	GP	G	A	TP	PIM	GP	G	A	TP	PIM
1980-81	AIK	Swe.	9	0	0	0	4	....	....	....	....	....
1981-82	AIK	Swe.	36	2	2	4	28	....	....	....	....	....
1982-83	AIK	Swe.	28	6	4	10	50	....	....	....	....	....
1983-84	AIK	Swe.	16	4	1	5	20	....	....	....	....	....
1984-85	**Boston**	**NHL**	73	6	13	19	9	5	0	0	0	6
1985-86	**Boston**	**NHL**	31	2	3	5	29	....	....	....	....	....
	Moncton	AHL	2	0	1	1	0	....	....	....	....	....
	NHL Totals		**104**	**7**	**16**	**23**	**38**	**5**	**0**	**0**	**0**	**6**

THELVEN, MICHAEL   (tell-VAIN)

Born, Stockholm, Sweden, January 7, 1961.
Defense. Shoots right. 5'11", 180 lbs.
Last amateur club: Djurgardens (Sweden).
(Boston's 8th choice, 186th over-all, in 1980 Entry Draft).

				Regular Season					Playoffs			
Season	Club	Lea	GP	G	A	TP	PIM	GP	G	A	TP	PIM
1981-82	Djurgardens	Swe.	34	5	3	8	53	....	....	....	....	....
1982-83	Djurgardens	Swe.	30	3	14	17	50	....	....	....	....	....
1983-84	Djurgardens	Swe.	27	6	8	14	51	....	....	....	....	....
1984-85	Djurgardens	Swe.	33	8	13	21	54	....	....	....	....	....
1985-86	**Boston**	**NHL**	60	6	20	26	48	3	0	0	0	0
	NHL Totals		**60**	**6**	**20**	**26**	**48**	**3**	**0**	**0**	**0**	**0**

THOMAS, STEVE

Born, Stockport, England, July 15, 1963.
Left Wing. Shoots left. 5'10", 180 lbs.
Last amateur club: Toronto Marlboros (OHL).

				Regular Season					Playoffs			
Season	Club	Lea	GP	G	A	TP	PIM	GP	G	A	TP	PIM
1983-84	Toronto	OHL	70	51	54	105	77	....	....	....	....	....
1984-85	**Toronto**	**NHL**	18	1	1	2	2	....	....	....	....	....
ab	St. Catharines	AHL	64	42	48	90	56	....	....	....	....	....
1985-86	**Toronto**	**NHL**	65	20	37	57	36	10	6	8	14	9
	St. Catharines	AHL	19	18	14	32	35	....	....	....	....	....
	NHL Totals		**83**	**21**	**38**	**59**	**38**	**10**	**6**	**8**	**14**	**9**

a Won AHL Rookie of the Year (1985)
b AHL First All-Star Team (1985)
Signed as a free agent by **Toronto**, May 12, 1984.

TOMLINSON, DAVE

Born, Edmonton, Alta., October 22, 1966.
Left wing. Shoots left. 6'1", 185 lbs.
Last amateur club: Brandon Wheat Kings (WHL).
(Toronto's 3rd choice, 43rd overall, in 1985 Entry Draft).

				Regular Season					Playoffs			
Season	Club	Lea	GP	G	A	TP	PIM	GP	G	A	TP	PIM
1984-85	Brandon	WHL	26	13	14	27	70	....	....	....	....	....
1985-86	Brandon	WHL	53	25	20	45	116	....	....	....	....	....

THOMSON, JIM

Born, Edmonton, Alta., December 30, 1965.
Right Wing. Shoots right. 6', 180 lbs.
Last amateur club: Toronto Marlboros (OHL).
(Washington's 9th choice, 185th over-all, in 1984 Entry Draft).

				Regular Season					Playoffs			
Season	Club	Lea	GP	G	A	TP	PIM	GP	G	A	TP	PIM
1983-84	Toronto	OHL	60	10	18	28	68	9	1	0	1	26
1984-85	Toronto	OHL	63	23	28	51	122	5	3	1	4	25
	Binghamton	AHL	4	0	0	0	2	....	....	....	....	....
1985-86	Binghamton	AHL	59	15	9	24	195	....	....	....	....	....

THORNBURY, TOM

Born, Lindsay, Ont., March 17, 1963.
Defense. Shoots right. 5'11", 175 lbs.
Last amateur club: Cornwall Royals (OHL).
(Pittsburgh's 3rd choice, 49th over-all, in 1981 Entry Draft).

Season	Club	Lea	Regular Season GP	G	A	TP	PIM	Playoffs GP	G	A	TP	PIM
1980-81	Niagara Falls	OHA	60	15	2	37	136	12	1	5	6	31
1981-82	Niagara Falls	OHL	43	11	22	33	65	1	0	0	0	2
1982-83	North Bay	OHL	17	6	9	15	30	....	....	....	....	....
	Cornwall	OHL	50	21	35	56	66	8	2	4	6	8
1983-84	**Pittsburgh**	**NHL**	14	1	8	9	16	....	....	....	....	....
	Baltimore	AHL	65	17	46	63	64	10	2	15	17	8
1984-85	Baltimore	AHL	22	4	12	16	21	....	....	....	....	....
	Fredericton	AHL	53	11	16	27	26	6	0	2	2	5
1985-86	Fredericton	AHL	24	0	15	15	30	....	....	....	....	....
	Muskegon	IHL	9	0	8	8	8	....	....	....	....	....
	Moncton	AHL	40	6	12	18	38	7	0	2	2	10
	NHL Totals		14	1	8	9	16	....	....	....	....	....

Traded to **Quebec** by **Pittsburgh** for Brian Ford, December 6, 1984. Traded to **Calgary** by **Quebec** for Tony Stiles, January 16, 1986.

TIANO, JOHN

Born, Winthrop, Mass., April 25, 1964.
Center. Shoots left. 5'11", 180 lbs.
Last amateur club: Rensselaer Polytechnic Institute Engineers (ECAC).
(NY Islanders' 7th choice, 147th overall, in 1982 Entry Draft).

Season	Club	Lea	Regular Season GP	G	A	TP	PIM	Playoffs GP	G	A	TP	PIM
1984-85	RPI	ECAC	36	13	16	29	28	....	....	....	....	....
1985-86	RPI	ECAC	32	6	19	25	22	....	....	....	....	....

TIKKANEN, ESA

(TIK-a-nen)

Born, Helsinki, Finland, January 25, 1965.
Left Wing. Shoots left. 5'11", 185 lbs.
Last amateur club: IFK Helsinki (Findland).
(Edmonton's 4th choice, 82nd over-all, in 1983 Entry Draft).

Season	Club	Lea	Regular Season GP	G	A	TP	PIM	Playoffs GP	G	A	TP	PIM
1983-84	IFK Jrs.	Fin.	36	21	33	54	42	....	....	....	....	....
1984-85	IFK Helsinki	Fin.	36	21	34	55	42	....	....	....	....	....
	Edmonton	NHL	....	....	....	....	....	3	0	0	0	2
1985-86	**Edmonton**	**NHL**	35	7	6	13	28	8	3	2	5	7
	Nova Scotia	AHL	15	4	8	12	17	....	....	....	....	....
	NHL Totals		35	7	6	13	28	11	3	2	5	9

TILLEY, TOM

Born, Trenton, Ont., March 28, 1965.
Defense. Shoots right. 6'0", 180 lbs.
Last amateur club: Michigan State University Spartans (CCHA).
(St. Louis' 13th choice, 196th overall, in 1984 Entry Draft).

Season	Club	Lea	Regular Season GP	G	A	TP	PIM	Playoffs GP	G	A	TP	PIM
1984-85	Michigan State	CCHA	37	1	5	6	58	....	....	....	....	....
1985-86	Michigan State	CCHA	42	9	25	34	48	....	....	....	....	....

TIPPETT, DAVE

Born, Moosomin, Sask., August 25, 1961.
Center. Shoots left. 5'10", 175 lbs.
Last amateur club: 1984 Canadian Olymic Team.

Season	Club	Lea	Regular Season GP	G	A	TP	PIM	Playoffs GP	G	A	TP	PIM
1981-82	North Dakota	WCHA	43	13	28	41	20	....	....	....	....	....
1982-83	North Dakota	WCHA	36	15	31	46	24	....	....	....	....	....
1983-84	Cdn. Olympic	...	66	14	19	33	24	....	....	....	....	....
	Hartford	**NHL**	17	4	2	6	2	....	....	....	....	....
1984-85	**Hartford**	**NHL**	80	7	12	19	12	....	....	....	....	....
1985-86	**Hartford**	**NHL**	80	14	20	34	18	10	2	2	4	4
	NHL Totals		177	25	34	59	32	10	2	2	4	4

Signed as free agent by **Hartford**, February 29, 1984.

TIRKKONEN, PEKKA

Born, Savonlinna, Finland, July 17, 1968.
Center. Shoots left. 6'1", 195 lbs.
Last amateur club: Sapko (Finland)
(Boston's 2nd choice, 34th overall, in 1986 Entry Draft).

Season	Club	Lea	Regular Season GP	G	A	TP	PIM	Playoffs GP	G	A	TP	PIM
1984-85	Sapko	Fin.	30	9	5	14	...	....	....	....	....	....
1985-86	Sapko	Fin.	40	14	13	27	...	....	....	....	....	....

TOCCHET, RICK

(TOCK-ett)

Born, Scarborough, Ont., April 9, 1964.
Right wing. Shoots right. 6', 195 lbs.
Last amateur club: Sault Ste. Marie Greyhounds (OHL).
(Phiadelphia's 5th choice, 121st over-all, in 1983 Entry Draft).

Season	Club	Lea	Regular Season GP	G	A	TP	PIM	Playoffs GP	G	A	TP	PIM
1981-82	S. S. Marie	OHL	59	7	15	22	184	11	1	1	2	28
1982-83	S. S. Marie	OHL	66	32	34	66	146	16	4	13	17	67
1983-84	S. S. Marie	OHL	64	44	64	108	209	16	*22	14	*36	41
1984-85	**Philadelphia**	**NHL**	75	14	25	39	181	19	3	4	7	72
1985-86	**Philadelphia**	**NHL**	69	14	21	35	284	5	1	2	3	26
	NHL Totals		144	28	46	74	465	24	4	6	10	98

TONELLI, JOHN

(TAH-nel-ee)

Born, Milton, Ont., March 23, 1957.
Left wing. Shoots left. 6'1", 200 lbs.
Last amateur club: Toronto Marlboros (OHA).
(NY Islanders' 2nd choice, 33rd over-all, in 1977 Amateur Draft).

Season	Club	Lea	Regular Season GP	G	A	TP	PIM	Playoffs GP	G	A	TP	PIM
1973-74	Toronto	OHA	69	18	37	55	62	....	....	....	....	....
1974-75a	Toronto	OHA	70	49	86	135	85	....	....	....	....	....
1975-76	Houston	WHA	79	17	14	31	66	17	7	7	14	18
1976-77	Houston	WHA	80	24	31	55	109	11	3	4	7	12
1977-78	Houston	WHA	65	23	41	64	103	6	1	3	4	8
1978-79	**NY Islanders**	**NHL**	73	17	39	56	44	10	1	6	7	0
1979-80	**NY Islanders**	**NHL**	77	14	30	44	49	21	7	9	16	18
1980-81	**NY Islanders**	**NHL**	70	20	32	52	57	16	5	8	13	16
1981-82b	**NY Islanders**	**NHL**	80	35	58	93	57	19	6	10	16	18
1982-83	**NY Islanders**	**NHL**	76	31	40	71	55	20	7	11	18	20
1983-84	**NY Islanders**	**NHL**	73	27	40	67	66	17	1	3	4	31
1984-85b	**NY Islanders**	**NHL**	80	42	58	100	95	10	1	8	9	10
1985-86	**NY Islanders**	**NHL**	65	20	41	61	50	....	....	....	....	....
	Calgary	NHL	9	3	4	7	10	22	7	9	16	49
	NHL Totals		603	209	342	551	483	135	35	64	99	162
	WHA Totals		224	64	86	150	278	34	11	14	25	38

a OHA First All-Star Team (1975)
b NHL Second Team All-Star (1982, 1985)
Traded to **Calgary** by **NY Islanders** for Richard Kromm and Steve Konroyd, March 11, 1986.

TOOKEY, TIMOTHY RAYMOND (TIM)

Born, Edmonton, Alta., August 29, 1960.
Center. Shoots left. 5'11", 180 lbs.
Last amateur club: Portland Winter Hawks (WHL).
(Washington's 4th choice, 88th over-all, in 1979 Entry Draft).

Season	Club	Lea	Regular Season GP	G	A	TP	PIM	Playoffs GP	G	A	TP	PIM
1977-78	Portland	WHL	72	16	15	31	55	8	2	2	4	5
1978-79	Portland	WHL	56	33	47	80	55	25	6	14	20	6
1979-80	Portland	WHL	70	58	83	141	55	8	2	5	7	4
1980-81	**Washington**	**NHL**	29	10	13	23	18	....	....	....	....	....
	Hershey	AHL	47	20	38	58	129	....	....	....	....	....
1981-82	**Washington**	**NHL**	28	8	8	16	35	....	....	....	....	....
	Hershey	AHL	14	4	9	13	10	....	....	....	....	....
	Fredericton	AHL	16	6	10	16	16	....	....	....	....	....
1982-83	**Quebec**	**NHL**	12	1	6	7	4	....	....	....	....	....
	Fredericton	AHL	53	24	43	67	24	9	5	4	9	0
1983-84	**Pittsburgh**	**NHL**	8	0	2	2	2	....	....	....	....	....
	Baltimore	AHL	58	16	28	44	25	8	1	1	2	2
1984-85	Baltimore	AHL	74	25	43	68	74	15	8	10	18	13
1985-86ab	Hershey	AHL	69	35	62	97	66	18	11	8	19	10
	NHL Totals		77	19	29	48	59	....	....	....	....	....

a AHL Second All-Star Team (1986)
b AHL Playoff MVP (1986)
Traded to **Quebec** by **Washington** with Washington's seventh round choice (Daniel Poudrier) in 1982 Entry Draft for Lee Norwood and Quebec's sixth round choice (Mats Kihlstron) —later transferred to Calgary— in 1982 Entry Draft, February 1, 1982. Signed as free agent by **Pittsburgh**, September 12, 1983. Signed as a free agent by **Philadelphia**, July 23, 1985.

TOOMEY, SEAN

Born, St. Paul, Minn., June 27, 1965.
Left wing. Shoots left. 6'2", 190 lbs.
Last amateur club: University of Minnesota-Duluth Bulldogs (WCHA).
(Minnesota's 8th choice, 136th overall, in 1983 Entry Draft).

Season	Club	Lea	Regular Season GP	G	A	TP	PIM	Playoffs GP	G	A	TP	PIM
1983-84	Minn-Duluth	WCHA	29	3	5	8	8	....	....	....	....	....
1984-85	Minn-Duluth	WCHA	43	6	7	13	14	....	....	....	....	....
1985-86	Minn-Duluth	WCHA	33	23	11	34	10	....	....	....	....	....

TORY, PAUL

Born, Coquitlam, B.C., January 13, 1966.
Right wing. Shoots right. 6'0", 175 lbs.
Last amateur club: University of Illinois at Chicago Flames (CCHA).
(Hartford's 8th choice, 194th overall, in 1985 Entry Draft).

Season	Club	Lea	Regular Season GP	G	A	TP	PIM	Playoffs GP	G	A	TP	PIM
1984-85	Ill-Chicago	CCHA	40	13	14	27	60	....	....	....	....	....
1985-86	Ill-Chicago	CCHA	40	21	14	35	45	....	....	....	....	....

TOTTLE, SCOTT

Born, Brantford, Ont., January 30, 1964.
Right wing. Shoots right. 5'11", 170 lbs.
Last amateur club: Peterborough Petes (OHL).
(Vancouver's 3rd choice, 50th over-all, in 1983 Entry Draft).

Season	Club	Lea	Regular Season GP	G	A	TP	PIM	Playoffs GP	G	A	TP	PIM
1982-83	Peterborough	OHL	68	25	49	74	36	4	2	1	3	4
1983-84	Peterborough	OHL	70	63	47	110	24	8	10	5	15	5
1984-85a	Peterborough	OHL	64	55	71	126	19	13	9	14	23	0
1985-86	Fredericton	AHL	69	15	22	37	12	3	1	1	2	0

a won William Hanley Trophy (most gentlemanly player - OHL 1985)

TRADER, LARRY

Born, Barry's Bay, Ont., July 7, 1963.
Defense. Shoots left. 6'1", 180 lbs.
Last amateur club: London Knights (OHL).
(Detroit's 3rd choice, 86th over-all, in 1981 Entry Draft)

			Regular Season					Playoffs				
Season	**Club**	**Lea**	**GP**	**G**	**A**	**TP**	**PIM**	**GP**	**G**	**A**	**TP**	**PIM**
1980-81	London	OHA	68	5	23	28	132	....	....	....	....	....
1981-82	London	OHL	68	19	37	56	161	4	0	1	1	6
1982-83	**Detroit**	**NHL**	**15**	**0**	**2**	**2**	**6**	....	....	....	....	....
	London	OHL	39	16	28	44	67	3	0	1	1	6
	Adirondack	AHL	6	2	2	4	4	6	2	1	3	10
1983-84	Adirondack	AHL	80	13	28	41	89	6	1	1	2	4
1984-85	**Detroit**	**NHL**	**40**	**3**	**7**	**10**	**39**	**3**	**0**	**0**	**0**	**0**
	Adirondack	AHL	6	0	4	4	0	....	....	....	....	....
1985-86a	Adirondack	AHL	64	10	46	56	77	17	6	16	22	14
	NHL Totals		**55**	**3**	**9**	**12**	**45**	**3**	**0**	**0**	**0**	**0**

a AHL Second All-Star Team (1986)
Traded to **St. Louis** by **Detroit** for Lee Norwood, August 7, 1986.

TRAPP, DOUG

Born, Balcarres, Sask., November 28, 1965.
Left wing. Shoots left. 6', 180 lbs.
Last amateur club: Regina Pats (WHL).
(Buffalo's 2nd choice, 39th over-all, in 1984 Entry Draft).

			Regular Season					Playoffs				
Season	**Club**	**Lea**	**GP**	**G**	**A**	**TP**	**PIM**	**GP**	**G**	**A**	**TP**	**PIM**
1982-83	Regina	WHL	71	23	28	51	123	5	0	2	2	18
1983-84	Regina	WHL	59	43	50	93	44	23	12	12	24	38
1984-85	Regina	WHL	72	48	60	108	81	8	7	7	14	2
1985-86	Rochester	AHL	75	21	42	63	86	....	....	....	....	....

TREMBLAY, MARIO (TRAHM-blay)

Born, Alma, Que., September 2, 1956.
Right wing. Shoots right. 6', 190 lbs.
Last amateur club: Montreal Juniors (QJHL).
(Montreal's 4th choice, 12th over-all, in 1974 Amateur Draft).

			Regular Season					Playoffs				
Season	**Club**	**Lea**	**GP**	**G**	**A**	**TP**	**PIM**	**GP**	**G**	**A**	**TP**	**PIM**
1972-73	Montreal	QJHL	56	43	37	80	155	4	0	1	1	4
1973-74	Montreal	QJHL	47	49	51	100	154	7	1	3	4	17
1974-75	Nova Scotia	AHL	15	10	8	18	47	....	....	....	....	....
	Montreal	**NHL**	**63**	**21**	**18**	**39**	**108**	**11**	**0**	**1**	**1**	**7**
1975-76	**Montreal**	**NHL**	**71**	**11**	**16**	**27**	**88**	**10**	**0**	**1**	**1**	**27**
1976-77	**Montreal**	**NHL**	**74**	**18**	**28**	**46**	**61**	**14**	**3**	**0**	**3**	**9**
1977-78	**Montreal**	**NHL**	**56**	**10**	**14**	**24**	**44**	**5**	**2**	**1**	**3**	**16**
1978-79	**Montreal**	**NHL**	**76**	**30**	**29**	**59**	**74**	**13**	**3**	**4**	**7**	**13**
1979-80	**Montreal**	**NHL**	**77**	**16**	**26**	**42**	**105**	**10**	**0**	**11**	**11**	**14**
1980-81	**Montreal**	**NHL**	**77**	**25**	**38**	**63**	**123**	**3**	**0**	**0**	**0**	**9**
1981-82	**Montreal**	**NHL**	**80**	**33**	**40**	**73**	**66**	**5**	**4**	**1**	**5**	**24**
1982-83	**Montreal**	**NHL**	**80**	**30**	**37**	**67**	**87**	**3**	**0**	**1**	**1**	**7**
1983-84	**Montreal**	**NHL**	**67**	**14**	**25**	**39**	**112**	**15**	**6**	**3**	**9**	**31**
1984-85	**Montreal**	**NHL**	**75**	**31**	**35**	**66**	**120**	**12**	**2**	**6**	**8**	**30**
1985-86	**Montreal**	**NHL**	**56**	**19**	**20**	**39**	**55**	....	....	....	....	....
	NHL Totals		**852**	**258**	**326**	**584**	**1043**	**100**	**20**	**29**	**49**	**187**

TROTTIER, BRYAN JOHN (TROTZ-yay)

Born, Val Marie, Sask., July 17, 1956.
Center. Shoots left. 5'10", 195 lbs.
Last amateur club: Lethbridge Broncos (WHL).
(NY Islanders' 2nd choice, 22nd over-all, in 1974 Amateur Draft).

			Regular Season					Playoffs				
Season	**Club**	**Lea**	**GP**	**G**	**A**	**TP**	**PIM**	**GP**	**G**	**A**	**TP**	**PIM**
1972-73	Swift Current	WHL	67	16	29	45	10	....	....	....	....	....
1973-74	Swift Current	WHL	68	41	71	112	76	13	7	8	15	8
1974-75ab	Lethbridge	WHL	67	46	*98	144	103	6	2	5	7	14
1975-76c	**NY Islanders**	**NHL**	**80**	**32**	**63**	**95**	**21**	**13**	**1**	**7**	**8**	**8**
1976-77	**NY Islanders**	**NHL**	**76**	**30**	**42**	**72**	**34**	**12**	**2**	**8**	**10**	**2**
1977-78d	**NY Islanders**	**NHL**	**77**	**46**	***77**	**123**	**46**	**7**	**0**	**3**	**3**	**4**
1978-79def	**NY Islanders**	**NHL**	**76**	**47**	***87**	***134**	**50**	**10**	**2**	**4**	**6**	**13**
1979-80g	**NY Islanders**	**NHL**	**78**	**42**	**62**	**104**	**68**	**21**	***12**	**17**	***29**	**16**
1980-81	**NY Islanders**	**NHL**	**73**	**31**	**72**	**103**	**74**	**18**	**11**	**18**	**29**	**34**
1981-82h	**NY Islanders**	**NHL**	**80**	**50**	**79**	**129**	**88**	**19**	**6**	***23**	***29**	**40**
1982-83	**NY Islanders**	**NHL**	**80**	**34**	**55**	**89**	**68**	**17**	**8**	**12**	**20**	**18**
1983-84h	**NY Islanders**	**NHL**	**68**	**40**	**71**	**111**	**59**	**21**	**8**	**6**	**14**	**49**
1984-85	**NY Islanders**	**NHL**	**68**	**28**	**31**	**59**	**47**	**10**	**4**	**2**	**6**	**8**
1985-86	**NY Islanders**	**NHL**	**78**	**37**	**59**	**96**	**72**	**3**	**1**	**1**	**2**	**2**
	NHL Totals		**834**	**417**	**698**	**1115**	**627**	**151**	**55**	**101**	**156**	**194**

a WHL Most Valuable Player (1975)
b WHL First All-Star Team (1975)
c Won Calder Memorial Trophy (1976)
d NHL First All-Star Team (1978, 1979)
e Won Art Ross Trophy (1979)
f Won Hart Trophy (1979)
g Won Conn Smythe Trophy (1980)
h NHL Second All-Star Team (1982, 1984)

TROTTIER, MONTY LEE (TROTZ-yay)

Born, Val Marie, Sask., July 25, 1961.
Right wing. Shoots right. 5'8", 160 lbs.
Last amateur club: Billings Bighorns (WHL).
(NY Islanders' 4th choice, 68th over-all, in 1980 Entry Draft).

			Regular Season					Playoffs				
Season	**Club**	**Lea**	**GP**	**G**	**A**	**TP**	**PIM**	**GP**	**G**	**A**	**TP**	**PIM**
1979-80	Billings	WHL	60	18	32	50	168	7	2	0	2	31
1980-81	Billings	WHL	58	15	37	52	289	....	....	....	....	....
1981-82	Indianapolis	CHL	72	10	15	25	142	9	2	2	4	14
1982-83	Indianapolis	CHL	63	17	23	40	69	13	1	4	5	11
1983-84	Indianapolis	CHL	69	18	23	41	135	10	1	7	8	2
1984-85	Springfield	AHL	60	6	12	18	40	3	0	1	1	8
1985-86	Indianapolis	IHL	81	27	38	65	106	5	1	2	3	17

TROTTIER, ROCKY (TROTZ-yay)

Born, Climax, Sask., April 11, 1964.
Right wing. Shoots left. 5'11", 185 lbs.
Last amateur club: Medicine Hat Tigers (WHL).
(New Jersey's 1st choice, 8th over-all, in 1982 Entry Draft).

			Regular Season					Playoffs				
Season	**Club**	**Lea**	**GP**	**G**	**A**	**TP**	**PIM**	**GP**	**G**	**A**	**TP**	**PIM**
1980-81	Saskatoon	WHL	34	9	15	24	26	....	....	....	....	....
	Billings	WHL	28	2	11	13	41	5	0	0	0	0
1981-82	Billings	WHL	28	13	21	34	36	....	....	....	....	....
1982-83	Nanaimo	WHL	34	13	22	35	12	....	....	....	....	....
	Medicine Hat	WHL	20	5	9	14	11	5	0	2	2	2
	Wichita	CHL	2	0	1	1	0	....	....	....	....	....
1983-84	**New Jersey**	**NHL**	**5**	**1**	**1**	**2**	**0**	....	....	....	....	....
	Medicine Hat	WHL	65	34	50	84	41	14	5	10	15	13
1984-85	**New Jersey**	**NHL**	**33**	**5**	**3**	**8**	**2**	....	....	....	....	....
	Maine	AHL	34	17	16	33	4	10	2	0	2	15
1985-86	Maine	AHL	66	12	19	31	42	....	....	....	....	....
	NHL Totals		**38**	**6**	**4**	**10**	**2**	....	....	....	....	....

TSUJIURA, STEVE

Born, Goaldale, Alta., February 28, 1962.
Center. Shoots left. 5'5", 155 lbs.
Last amateur club: University of Calgary Dinosaurs (CWUAA)
(Philadelphia's 10th choice, 205th over-all, in 1981 Entry Draft).

			Regular Season					Playoffs				
Season	**Club**	**Lea**	**GP**	**G**	**A**	**TP**	**PIM**	**GP**	**G**	**A**	**TP**	**PIM**
1978-79	Medicine Hat	WHL	62	24	45	69	14	....	....	....	....	....
1979-80	Medicine Hat	WHL	72	25	77	102	36	16	9	4	13	14
1980-81	Medicine Hat	WHL	72	55	84	139	60	5	4	4	8	0
1981-82	U. of Calgary	CWUAA	37	26	53	79	33	....	....	....	....	....
1982-83	Maine	AHL	78	15	51	66	46	14	3	4	7	8
1983-84	Springfield	AHL	78	24	56	80	27	4	4	3	7	2
1984-85	Maine	AHL	69	28	38	66	40	11	3	8	11	14
1985-86a	Maine	AHL	80	31	55	86	34	5	2	3	5	2

a AHL Most Sportsmanlike Player of the Year (1986)
Signed as free agent by **New Jersey**, July 15, 1984.

TUCKER, JOHN

Born, Windsor, Ont., September 29, 1964.
Center. Shoots right. 6', 190 lbs.
Last amateur club: Kitchener Rangers (OHL)
(Buffalo's 4th choice, 31st over-all, in 1983 Entry Draft).

			Regular Season					Playoffs				
Season	**Club**	**Lea**	**GP**	**G**	**A**	**TP**	**PIM**	**GP**	**G**	**A**	**TP**	**PIM**
1981-82	Kitchener	OHL	67	16	32	48	32	15	2	3	5	2
1982-83	Kitchener	OHL	70	60	80	140	33	11	5	9	14	10
1983-84ab	**Buffalo**	**NHL**	**21**	**12**	**4**	**16**	**4**	**3**	**1**	**0**	**1**	**0**
	Kitchener	OHL	39	40	60	100	25	12	12	18	30	8
1984-85	**Buffalo**	**NHL**	**64**	**22**	**27**	**49**	**21**	**5**	**1**	**5**	**6**	**0**
1985-86	**Buffalo**	**NHL**	**75**	**31**	**34**	**65**	**39**	....	....	....	....	....
	NHL Totals		**160**	**65**	**65**	**130**	**64**	**8**	**2**	**5**	**7**	**0**

a OHL First All-Star Team (1984)
b OHL Player of the Year (1984)

TUDOR, ROBERT ALAN (ROB)

Born, Cupar, Sask., June 30, 1956.
Right wing/Center. Shoots right. 5'11", 190 lbs.
Last amateur club: Regina Pats (WHL).
(Vancouver's 5th choice, 98th over-all, in 1976 Amateur Draft).

			Regular Season					Playoffs				
Season	**Club**	**Lea**	**GP**	**G**	**A**	**TP**	**PIM**	**GP**	**G**	**A**	**TP**	**PIM**
1974-75	Regina	WHL	68	48	48	96	125	11	5	6	11	20
1975-76	Regina	WHL	72	46	60	106	228	6	6	3	9	15
1976-77	Fort Wayne	IHL	78	34	60	94	108	9	11	8	19	26
1977-78	Tulsa	CHL	65	23	33	56	58	7	1	2	3	37
1978-79	Dallas	CHL	51	27	37	64	80	....	....	....	....	....
	Vancouver	**NHL**	**24**	**4**	**4**	**8**	**19**	**2**	**0**	**0**	**0**	**0**
1979-80	Dallas	CHL	74	39	41	80	177	....	....	....	....	....
	Vancouver	**NHL**	**2**	**0**	**0**	**0**	**0**	**1**	**0**	**0**	**0**	**0**
1980-81	Dallas	CHL	79	31	32	63	155	6	0	1	1	25
1981-82	Dallas	CHL	80	32	47	79	132	15	7	13	20	56
1982-83	**St. Louis**	**NHL**	**2**	**0**	**0**	**0**	**0**	....	....	....	....	....
	Salt Lake	CHL	76	37	30	67	168	6	1	4	5	2
1983-84	Salt Lake	CHL	32	10	12	22	35	5	1	2	3	21
1984-85	Nova Scotia	AHL	22	6	6	12	40	....	....	....	....	....
	New Haven	AHL	52	9	11	20	45	....	....	....	....	....
1985-86	Fort Wayne	IHL	13	6	8	14	7	15	4	2	6	35
	NHL Totals		**28**	**4**	**4**	**8**	**19**	**3**	**0**	**0**	**0**	**0**

Signed as a free agent by **St. Louis**, July 22, 1982.

TUER, ALLAN (AL)

Born, North Battleford, Sask., July 19, 1963.
Defense. Shoots left. 6', 175 lbs.
Last amateur club: Regina Pats (WHL).
(Los Angeles' 8th choice, 186th over-all, in 1981 Entry Draft).

			Regular Season					Playoffs				
Season	Club	Lea	GP	G	A	TP	PIM	GP	G	A	TP	PIM
1980-81	Regina	WHL	31	0	7	7	58	8	0	1	1	37
1981-82	Regina	WHL	63	2	18	20	*486	13	0	3	3	117
1982-83	Regina	WHL	71	3	27	30	229	5	0	0	0	37
1983-84	New Haven	AHL	78	0	20	20	195	....	....	....	....	....
1984-85	New Haven	AHL	56	0	7	7	241	....	....	....	....	....
1985-86	**Los Angeles**	**NHL**	**45**	**0**	**1**	**1**	**150**	....	....	....	....	....
	New Haven	AHL	8	1	0	1	53	....	....	....	....	....
	NHL Totals		**45**	**0**	**1**	**1**	**150**	....	....	....	....	....

Signed as a free agent by **Edmonton**, August 18, 1986.

TUUITE, STEVE

Born, Brockton, Mass., January 14, 1962.
Defefnse. Shoots right. 6'1", 205 lbs.
Last amateur club: St. Lawrence University Saints (ECAC).

			Regular Season					Playoffs				
Season	Club	Lea	GP	G	A	TP	PIM	GP	G	A	TP	PIM
1981-82	St. Lawrence	ECAC	21	2	4	6	8	....	....	....	....	....
1982-83	St. Lawrence	ECAC	36	2	11	13	12	....	....	....	....	....
1983-84	St. Lawrence	ECAC	32	10	18	28	24	....	....	....	....	....
1984-85	St. Lawrence	ECAC	32	3	14	17	26	....	....	....	....	....
1985-86	New Haven	AHL	14	0	2	2	6	....	....	....	....	....
	Toledo	IHL	47	5	31	36	36	....	....	....	....	....

Signed as a free agent by **Los Angeles**, June 7, 1985.

TURCOTTE, ALFIE

Born, Gary, Indiana, June 5, 1965.
Center. Shoots left. 5'9", 170 lbs.
Last amateur club: Portland Winter Hawks (WHL).
(Montreal's 1st choice, 17th over-all, in 1983 Entry Draft).

			Regular Season					Playoffs				
Season	Club	Lea	GP	G	A	TP	PIM	GP	G	A	TP	PIM
1981-82	Detroit Compu.	Midget	93	131	152	283	40	....	....	....	....	....
1982-83	Nanaimo	WHL	36	23	27	50	22	....	....	....	....	....
	Portland	WHL	39	26	51	77	26	14	14	18	32	9
1983-84	Portland	WHL	32	22	41	63	39	....	....	....	....	....
	Montreal	**NHL**	**30**	**7**	**7**	**14**	**10**	....	....	....	....	....
1984-85	**Montreal**	**NHL**	**53**	**8**	**16**	**24**	**35**	**5**	**0**	**0**	**0**	**0**
1985-86	**Montreal**	**NHL**	**2**	**0**	**0**	**0**	**2**	....	....	....	....	....
	Sherbrooke	AHL	75	29	36	65	60	....	....	....	....	....
	NHL Totals		**85**	**15**	**23**	**38**	**47**	**5**	**0**	**0**	**0**	**0**

Traded to **Edmonton** by **Montreal** for future considerations, June 25, 1986.

TURGEON, SYLVAIN

Born, Noranda, Que., January 17, 1965.
Left wing. Shoots left. 6', 190 lbs.
Last amateur club: Hull Olympiques (QMJHL).
(Hartford's 1st choice, 2nd over-all, in 1983 Entry Draft).

			Regular Season					Playoffs				
Season	Club	Lea	GP	G	A	TP	PIM	GP	G	A	TP	PIM
1981-82	Hull	QMJHL	57	33	40	73	78	14	11	11	22	16
1982-83a	Hull	QMJHL	67	54	109	163	103	7	8	7	15	10
1983-84b	**Hartford**	**NHL**	**76**	**40**	**32**	**72**	**55**	....	....	....	....	....
1984-85	**Hartford**	**NHL**	**64**	**31**	**31**	**62**	**67**	....	....	....	....	....
1985-86	**Hartford**	**NHL**	**76**	**45**	**34**	**79**	**88**	**9**	**2**	**3**	**5**	**4**
	NHL Totals		**216**	**116**	**97**	**213**	**210**	**9**	**2**	**3**	**5**	**4**

a QMJHL First All-Star Team (1983).
b Named to NHL All-Rookie Team (1984).

TURNBULL, PERRY JOHN

Born, Bentley, Alta., March 9, 1959.
Center. Shoots left. 6'2", 200 lbs.
Last amateur club: Portland Winter Hawks (WHL).
(St. Louis' 1st choice, 2nd over-all, in 1979 Entry Draft).

			Regular Season					Playoffs				
Season	Club	Lea	GP	G	A	TP	PIM	GP	G	A	TP	PIM
1975-76	Calgary	WHL	19	6	7	13	14	....	....	....	....	....
1976-77	Calgary	WHL	10	8	5	13	33	....	....	....	....	....
	Portland	WHL	58	23	30	53	249	10	2	1	3	36
1977-78	Portland	WHL	57	36	27	63	318	8	2	3	5	44
1978-79ab	Portland	WHL	70	75	43	118	191	20	10	8	18	33
1979-80	**St. Louis**	**NHL**	**80**	**16**	**19**	**35**	**124**	**3**	**1**	**1**	**2**	**2**
1980-81	**St. Louis**	**NHL**	**75**	**34**	**22**	**56**	**209**	....	....	....	....	....
1981-82	**St. Louis**	**NHL**	**79**	**33**	**26**	**59**	**161**	**5**	**3**	**2**	**5**	**11**
1982-83	**St. Louis**	**NHL**	**79**	**32**	**15**	**47**	**172**	**4**	**1**	**0**	**1**	**14**
1983-84	**St. Louis**	**NHL**	**32**	**14**	**8**	**22**	**81**	....	....	....	....	....
	Montreal	**NHL**	**40**	**6**	**7**	**13**	**59**	**9**	**1**	**2**	**3**	**10**
1984-85	**Winnipeg**	**NHL**	**66**	**22**	**21**	**43**	**130**	**8**	**0**	**1**	**1**	**26**
1985-86	**Winnipeg**	**NHL**	**80**	**20**	**31**	**51**	**183**	**3**	**0**	**1**	**1**	**11**
	NHL Totals		**531**	**177**	**149**	**326**	**1119**	**32**	**6**	**7**	**13**	**74**

a WHL Second All-Star Team (1979)
b WHL Most Valuable Player (1979)

Traded to **Montreal** by **St. Louis** for Doug Wickenheiser, Gilbert Delorme and Greg Paslawski, December 21, 1983. Traded to **Winnipeg** by **Montreal** for Lucien DeBlois, June 14, 1984.

TURNBULL, RANDY LAYNE

Born, Bentley, Alta., February 7, 1962.
Defense. Shoots left. 6', 185 lbs.
Last amateur club: Portland Winter Hawks (WHL).
(Calgary's 6th choice, 97th over-all, in 1980 Entry Draft).

			Regular Season					Playoffs				
Season	Club	Lea	GP	G	A	TP	PIM	GP	G	A	TP	PIM
1978-79	Portland	WHL	1	0	0	0	7	4	0	0	0	2
1979-80	Portland	WHL	72	4	25	29	355	8	0	1	1	50
1980-81	Portland	WHL	56	1	31	32	295	8	0	1	1	86
1981-82	**Calgary**	**NHL**	**1**	**0**	**0**	**0**	**2**	....	....	....	....	....
	Portland	WHL	69	5	19	24	430	15	1	9	10	100
1982-83	Colorado	CHL	65	2	1	3	292	6	0	1	1	7
1983-84	New Haven	AHL	8	0	0	0	46	....	....	....	....	....
	Peoria	IHL	73	3	18	21	213	....	....	....	....	....
1984-85	Salt Lake	IHL	81	10	14	24	282	7	0	0	0	41
1985-86	Salt Lake	IHL	77	6	14	20	236	5	0	1	1	15
	NHL Totals		**1**	**0**	**0**	**0**	**2**	....	....	....	....	....

TURNER, BRAD

Born, Winnipeg, Man., May 25, 1968.
Defense. Shoots right. 6'2", 190 lbs.
Last amateur club: Calgary Canucks (AJHL).
(Minnesota's 6th choice, 58th overall, in 1986 Entry Draft).

			Regular Season					Playoffs				
Season	Club	Lea	GP	G	A	TP	PIM	GP	G	A	TP	PIM
1985-86	Calgary	AJHL	54	14	21	35	109	....	....	....	....	....

TUTT, BRIAN

Born, Small Well, Alta., June 9, 1962.
Defense. Shoots left. 6'1", 195 lbs.
Last amateur club: Calgary Wranglers (WHL).
(Philadelphia's 6th choice, 126th over-all, in 1980 Entry Draft).

			Regular Season					Playoffs				
Season	Club	Lea	GP	G	A	TP	PIM	GP	G	A	TP	PIM
1979-80	Calgary	WHL	2	0	0	0	0	4	0	1	1	6
1980-81	Calgary	WHL	72	10	41	51	111	22	3	11	14	30
1981-82	Calgary	WHL	40	2	16	18	85	9	2	2	4	22
1982-83	Maine	AHL	31	0	0	0	28	....	....	....	....	....
	Toledo	IHL	23	5	10	15	26	11	1	7	8	16
1983-84	Springfield	AHL	1	0	0	0	2	....	....	....	....	....
a	Toledo	IHL	82	7	44	51	79	13	0	6	6	16
1984-85	Hershey	AHL	3	0	0	0	8	....	....	....	....	....
a	Kalamazoo	IHL	80	8	45	53	62	11	2	4	6	19
1985-86	Kalamazoo	IHL	82	11	39	50	129	6	1	6	7	11

a IHL Second All-Star Team (1984, 1985)

TUTTLE, STEVE

Born, Vancouver, B.C., January 5, 1966.
Right wing. Shoots right. 6'1", 180 lbs.
Last amateur club: University of Wisconsin Badgers (WCHA).
(St. Louis' 8th choice, 113th overall, in 1984 Entry Draft).

			Regular Season					Playoffs				
Season	Club	Lea	GP	G	A	TP	PIM	GP	G	A	TP	PIM
1984-85	Wisconsin	WCHA	28	3	4	7	0	....	....	....	....	....
1985-86	Wisconsin	WCHA	32	2	10	12	2	....	....	....	....	....

TYERS, SHAWN

Born, Toronto, Ont., January 14, 1967.
Right wing. Shoots right. 6'1", 195 lbs.
Last amateur club: Kitchener Rangers (OHL).
(Edmonton's 6th choice, 146th overall, in 1985 Entry Draft).

			Regular Season					Playoffs				
Season	Club	Lea	GP	G	A	TP	PIM	GP	G	A	TP	PIM
1984-85	Kitchener	OHL	57	13	26	39	26	4	0	4	4	0
1985-86	Kitchener	OHL	26	2	3	5	14	....	....	....	....	....

URBAN, JEFF

Born, Edina, Minn., March 23, 1967.
Left wing. Shoots left. 6'2", 185 lbs.
Last amateur club: University of Michigan Wolverines (CCHA).
(St. Louis' 8th choice, 180th overall, in 1985 Entry Draft).

			Regular Season					Playoffs				
Season	Club	Lea	GP	G	A	TP	PIM	GP	G	A	TP	PIM
1985-86	U. of Michigan	CCHA	36	9	6	15	23	....	....	....	....	....

VAIVE, RICHARD CLAUDE (RICK) (VIHV)

Born, Ottawa, Ont., May 14, 1959.
Right wing. Shoots right. 6', 180 lbs.
Last amateur club: Sherbrooke Castors (QJHL).
(Vancouver's 1st choice, 5th over-all, in 1979 Entry Draft).

			Regular Season					Playoffs				
Season	Club	Lea	GP	G	A	TP	PIM	GP	G	A	TP	PIM
1976-77	Sherbrooke	QJHL	67	51	59	110	91	18	10	13	23	78
1977-78	Sherbrooke	QJHL	68	76	79	155	199	9	8	4	12	38
1978-79	Birmingham	WHA	75	26	33	59	*248	....	....	....	....	....
1979-80	Vancouver	NHL	47	13	8	21	111	....	....	....	....	....
	Toronto	NHL	22	9	7	16	77	3	1	0	1	11
1980-81	Toronto	NHL	75	33	29	62	229	3	1	0	1	4
1981-82	Toronto	NHL	77	54	35	89	157	....	....	....	....	....
1982-83	Toronto	NHL	78	51	28	79	105	4	2	5	7	6
1983-84	Toronto	NHL	76	52	41	93	114	....	....	....	....	....
1984-85	Toronto	NHL	72	35	33	68	112	....	....	....	....	....
1985-86	Toronto	NHL	61	33	31	64	85	9	6	2	8	9
	NHL Totals		508	280	212	492	990	19	10	7	17	30
	WHA Totals		75	26	33	59	248	....	....	....	....	....

Traded to **Toronto** by **Vancouver** with Bill Derlago for Dave Williams and Jerry Butler, February 18, 1980.

VALIMONT, CARL

Born, Southington, Conn., March 1, 1966.
Defense. Shoots left. 6'1", 180 lbs.
Last amateur club: Lowell University Chiefs (H.E.).
(Vancouver's 10th choice, 193rd overall, in 1985 Entry Draft).

			Regular Season					Playoffs				
Season	Club	Lea	GP	G	A	TP	PIM	GP	G	A	TP	PIM
1984-85	Lowell	H.E.	40	4	11	15	24	....	....	....	....	....
1985-86	Lowell	H.E.	26	1	9	10	12	....	....	....	....	....

VANI, CARMINE

Born, Toronto, Ont., August 7, 1964.
Center. Shoots left. 5'11", 175 lbs.
Last amateur club: Kitchener Rangers (OHL).
(Detroit's 3rd choice, 44th overall, in 1982 Entry Draft).

			Regular Season					Playoffs				
Season	Club	Lea	GP	G	A	TP	PIM	GP	G	A	TP	PIM
1981-82	Kingston	OHL	49	11	16	27	138	4	1	0	1	9
1982-83	Kingston	OHL	21	7	11	18	56	....	....	....	....	....
	North Bay	OHL	25	22	22	44	84	8	1	6	7	23
1983-84	North Bay	OHL	17	14	3	17	58	....	....	....	....	....
	Kitchener	OHL	24	15	8	23	75	10	6	6	12	17
1984-85	Adirondack	AHL	45	10	5	15	53	....	....	....	....	....
1985-86	Flint	IHL	58	27	26	53	100	....	....	....	....	....
	Milwaukee	IHL	3	1	0	1	4	....	....	....	....	....

VARGAS, ERNIE

Born, St. Paul, Minn., March 1, 1964.
Center. Shoots left. 6'1", 180 lbs.
Last amateur club: University of Wisconsin Badgers (WCHA).
(Montreal's 9th choice, 117th over-all, in 1982 Entry Draft).

			Regular Season					Playoffs				
Season	Club	Lea	GP	G	A	TP	PIM	GP	G	A	TP	PIM
1982-83	U. of Wisconsin	WCHA	25	1	4	5	30	....	....	....	....	....
1983-84	U. of Wisconsin	WCHA	36	5	15	20	32	....	....	....	....	....
1984-85	U. of Wisconsin	WCHA	42	8	16	24	68	....	....	....	....	....
1985-86	U. of Wisconsin	WCHA	41	20	23	43	67	....	....	....	....	....

VASKE, DENNIS

Born, Rockford, Ill., October 11, 1967.
Defense. Shoots left. 6'2", 210 lbs.
Last amateur club: Armstrong (HS).
(NY Islanders' 2nd choice, 38th overall, in 1986 Entry Draft).

			Regular Season					Playoffs				
Season	Club	Lea	GP	G	A	TP	PIM	GP	G	A	TP	PIM
1984-85	Armstrong	HS	22	5	18	23	...	....	....	....	....	....
1985-86	Armstrong	HS	20	9	13	22	...	....	....	....	....	....

VEITCH, DARREN WILLIAM (VEETCH)

Born, Saskatoon, Sask., April 24, 1960.
Defense. Shoots right. 6', 190 lbs.
Last amateur club: Regina Pats (WHL).
(Washington's 1st choice, 5th over-all, in 1980 Entry Draft).

			Regular Season					Playoffs				
Season	Club	Lea	GP	G	A	TP	PIM	GP	G	A	TP	PIM
1976-77	Regina	WHL	1	0	0	0	0	....	....	....	....	....
1977-78	Regina	WHL	71	13	32	45	135	9	0	2	2	4
1978-79	Regina	WHL	51	11	36	47	80	....	....	....	....	....
1979-80a	Regina	WHL	71	29	*93	122	118	18	13	18	31	13
1980-81	Washington	NHL	59	4	21	25	46	....	....	....	....	....
	Hershey	AHL	26	6	22	28	12	10	6	3	9	15
1981-82	Hershey	AHL	10	5	10	15	16	....	....	....	....	....
	Washington	NHL	67	9	44	53	54	....	....	....	....	....
1982-83	Washington	NHL	10	0	8	8	0	....	....	....	....	....
	Hershey	AHL	5	0	1	1	2	....	....	....	....	....
1983-84	Hershey	AHL	11	1	6	7	4	....	....	....	....	....
	Washington	NHL	46	6	18	24	17	5	0	1	1	15
1984-85	Washington	NHL	75	3	18	21	37	5	0	1	1	4
1985-86	Washington	NHL	62	3	9	12	27	....	....	....	....	....
	Detroit	NHL	13	0	5	5	2	....	....	....	....	....
	NHL Totals		332	25	123	148	183	10	0	2	2	19

a WHL First All-Star Team (1980)
Traded to **Detroit** by **Washington** for John Barrett and Greg Smith, March 10, 1986.

VELISCHEK, RANDY

Born, Montreal, Que., February 10, 1962.
Defense. Shoots left. 6', 200 lbs.
Last amateur club: Providence College Friars (ECAC).
(Minnesota's 3rd choice, 53rd over-all, in 1980 Entry Draft).

			Regular Season					Playoffs				
Season	Club	Lea	GP	G	A	TP	PIM	GP	G	A	TP	PIM
1979-80	Providence	ECAC	31	5	5	10	20	....	....	....	....	....
1980-81	Providence	ECAC	33	3	12	15	26	....	....	....	....	....
1981-82a	Providence	ECAC	33	1	14	15	38	....	....	....	....	....
1982-83bc	Providence	ECAC	41	18	34	52	50	....	....	....	....	....
	Minnesota	NHL	3	0	0	0	2	9	0	0	0	0
1983-84	Salt Lake	CHL	43	7	21	28	54	5	0	3	3	2
	Minnesota	NHL	33	2	2	4	10	1	0	0	0	0
1984-85	Minnesota	NHL	52	4	9	13	26	9	2	3	5	8
	Springfield	AHL	26	2	7	9	22	....	....	....	....	....
1985-86	New Jersey	NHL	47	2	7	9	39	....	....	....	....	....
	Maine	AHL	21	0	4	4	4	....	....	....	....	....
	NHL Totals		135	8	18	26	77	19	2	3	5	8

a ECAC Second All-Star Team (1982)
b ECAC First All-Star Team (1983)
c Named ECAC Player of the Year (1983)
Claimed by **New Jersey** from **Minnesota** in NHL Waiver Draft, October 7, 1985

VELLUCCI, MIKE

Born, Farmington, Mich., August 11, 1966.
Defense. Shoots left. 6'1", 180 lbs.
Last amateur club: Belleville Bulls (OHL).
(Hartford's 3rd choice, 131st overall, in 1984 Entry Draft).

			Regular Season					Playoffs				
Season	Club	Lea	GP	G	A	TP	PIM	GP	G	A	TP	PIM
1983-84	Belleville	OHL	67	2	20	22	83	3	1	0	1	6
1984-85	DID NOT PLAY — INJURED											
1985-86	Belleville	OHL	64	11	32	43	154	24	2	5	7	45

VERBEEK, PATRICK (PAT) (ver-BEEK)

Born, Sarnia, Ont., May 24, 1964.
Center. Shoots right. 5'9", 190 lbs.
Last amateur club: Sudbury Wolves (OHL).
(New Jersey's 3rd choice, 43rd over-all, in 1982 Entry Draft).

			Regular Season					Playoffs				
Season	Club	Lea	GP	G	A	TP	PIM	GP	G	A	TP	PIM
1980-81	Petrolia	OPJHL	42	44	44	88	155	....	....	....	....	....
1981-82	Sudbury	OHL	66	37	51	88	180	....	....	....	....	....
1982-83	Sudbury	OHL	61	40	67	107	184	....	....	....	....	....
	New Jersey	NHL	6	3	2	5	8	....	....	....	....	....
1983-84	New Jersey	NHL	79	20	27	47	158	....	....	....	....	....
1984-85	New Jersey	NHL	78	15	18	33	162	....	....	....	....	....
1985-86	New Jersey	NHL	76	25	28	53	79	....	....	....	....	....
	NHL Totals		239	63	75	138	407	....	....	....	....	....

VERRET, CLAUDE (ver-ETT)

Born, Lachine, Que., April 20, 1963.
Center. Shoots left. 5'9", 165 lbs.
Last amateur club: Trois Rivières Draveurs (QMJHL).
(Buffalo's 12th choice, 163rd over-all, in 1982 Entry Draft).

			Regular Season					Playoffs				
Season	Club	Lea	GP	G	A	TP	PIM	GP	G	A	TP	PIM
1980-81ab	Trois Rivieres	QMJHL	68	39	73	112	4	19	13	24	37	7
1981-82bc	Trois Rivières	QMJHL	64	54	108	*162	14	23	13	*35	*48	4
1982-83	Trois Rivières	QMJHL	68	73	115	188	21	4	3	6	9	4
1983-84	Buffalo	NHL	11	2	5	7	2	....	....	....	....	....
	Rochester	AHL	65	39	51	90	4	18	5	9	14	4
1984-85	Buffalo	NHL	3	0	0	0	0	....	....	....	....	....
d	Rochester	AHL	76	40	53	93	12	5	2	5	7	0
1985-86	Rochester	AHL	52	19	32	51	14	....	....	....	....	....
	NHL Totals		14	2	5	7	2	....	....	....	....	....

a Named QMJHL Rookie of the Year (1981).
b Named QMJHL's Most Gentlemanly Player (1981, 1982).
c QMJHL First All-Star Team (1982).
d AHL Second All-Star Team (1985)

VERSTRAETE, LEIGH (VAIR-straight)

Born, Pincher Creek, Alta., January 6, 1962.
Right wing. Shoots right. 5'11", 185 lbs.
Last amateur club: Calgary Wranglers (WHL).
(Toronto's 13th choice, 192nd over-all, in 1982 Entry Draft).

				Regular Season					Playoffs			
Season	Club	Lea	GP	G	A	TP	PIM	GP	G	A	TP	PIM
1978-79	Billings	WHL	32	4	4	8	58	2	0	0	0	5
1979-80	Billings	WHL	10	1	0	1	47	....	....	....	....	....
	Calgary	WHL	56	12	14	26	168	7	2	2	4	23
1980-81	Calgary	WHL	71	22	18	40	372	21	6	5	11	155
1981-82	Calgary	WHL	49	19	20	39	385	8	4	4	8	43
1982-83	**Toronto**	**NHL**	**3**	**0**	**0**	**0**	**5**	....	....	....	....	....
	St. Catharines	AHL	61	5	3	8	221	....	....	....	....	....
1983-84	St. Catharines	AHL	51	0	7	7	183	....	....	....	....	....
1984-85	**Toronto**	**NHL**	**2**	**0**	**0**	**0**	**0**	....	....	....	....	....
	St. Catharines	AHL	43	5	8	13	164	....	....	....	....	....
1985-86	St. Catharines	AHL	75	8	12	20	300	11	2	3	5	114
	NHL Totals		**5**	**0**	**0**	**0**	**5**	....	....	....	....	....

VESEY, JIM

Born, Columbus, Mass., September 29, 1965.
Center. Shoots right. 6'1", 200 lbs..
Last amateur club: Merrimack College Warriors (ECAC).
(St. Louis' 11th choice, 155th over-all, in 1984 Entry Draft).

				Regular Season					Playoffs			
Season	Club	Lea	GP	G	A	TP	PIM	GP	G	A	TP	PIM
1984-85	Merrimack	ECAC	33	19	11	30	28	....	....	....	....	....
1985-86	Merrimack	ECAC	32	29	32	61	67	....	....	....	....	....

VEY, GREG

Born, Toronto, Ont., June 20, 1967.
Center. Shoots left. 6'1", 190 lbs.
Last amateur club: Peterborough Petes (OHL).
(Toronto's 4th choice, 64th over-all, in 1985 Entry Draft).

				Regular Season					Playoffs			
Season	Club	Lea	GP	G	A	TP	PIM	GP	G	A	TP	PIM
1984-85	Peterborough	OHL	61	11	15	26	25	16	3	1	4	0
1985-86	Peterborough	OHL	61	14	20	34	49	10	5	1	6	12

VINCELETTE, DANIEL

Born, Verdun, Que., August 1, 1967.
Left wing. Shoots left. 6'1", 200 lbs.
Last amateur club: Drummondville Voltigeurs (QMJHL).
(Chicago's 3rd choice, 74th over-all, in 1985 Entry Draft).

				Regular Season					Playoffs			
Season	Club	Lea	GP	G	A	TP	PIM	GP	G	A	TP	PIM
1984-85	Drummondville	QMJHL	64	11	24	35	124	12	0	1	1	11
1985-86	Drummondville	QMJHL	70	37	47	84	234	22	11	14	25	40

VIRTA, HANNU (VIR-ta HAN-oo)

Born, Turku, Finland, March 22, 1963.
Defense. Shoots left. 6', 180 lbs.
Last amateur club: T.P.S. (Finland).
(Buffalo's 2nd choice, 38th over-all, in 1981 Entry Draft).

				Regular Season					Playoffs			
Season	Club	Lea	GP	G	A	TP	PIM	GP	G	A	TP	PIM
1980-81a	T.P.S.	Fin.	1	0	1	1	0	4	0	1	1	4
1981-82b	T.P.S.	Fin.	36	5	12	17	6	....	....	....	....	....
	Buffalo	**NHL**	**3**	**0**	**1**	**1**	**4**	**4**	**0**	**1**	**1**	**0**
1982-83c	**Buffalo**	**NHL**	**74**	**13**	**24**	**37**	**18**	**10**	**1**	**2**	**3**	**4**
1983-84	**Buffalo**	**NHL**	**70**	**6**	**30**	**36**	**12**	**3**	**0**	**0**	**0**	**2**
1984-85	**Buffalo**	**NHL**	**51**	**1**	**23**	**24**	**16**	....	....	....	....	....
1985-86	**Buffalo**	**NHL**	**47**	**5**	**23**	**28**	**16**	....	....	....	....	....
	NHL Totals		**245**	**25**	**101**	**126**	**66**	**17**	**1**	**3**	**4**	**6**

a Named to All-Star Team, 1981 European Junior Championships
b Named Rookie of the Year in Finnish National League (1982)
c Named to NHL All-Rookie Team (1983)

VITALE, LUKE

Born, Toronto, Ont., April 17, 1966.
Center. Shoots left. 5'11", 180 lbs.
Last amateur club: Providence College Friars (H.E.).
(Philadelphia's 10th choice, 163rd over-all, in 1984 Entry Draft).

				Regular Season					Playoffs			
Season	Club	Lea	GP	G	A	TP	PIM	GP	G	A	TP	PIM
1985-86	Providence	H.E.	39	9	7	16	16	....	....	....	....	....

VIVEIROS, EMMANUEL

Born, St. Albert, Alta., January 8, 1966.
Defense. Shoots left. 5'11", 175 lbs.
Last amateur club: Prince Albert Raiders (WHL).
(Edmonton's 6th choice, 106th over-all, in 1984 Entry Draft).

				Regular Season					Playoffs			
Season	Club	Lea	GP	G	A	TP	PIM	GP	G	A	TP	PIM
1982-83	Prince Albert	WHL	59	6	26	32	55	....	....	....	....	....
1983-84	Prince Albert	WHL	67	15	94	109	48	2	0	3	3	6
1984-85a	Prince Albert	WHL	68	17	71	88	94	13	2	9	11	14
1985-86	**Minnesota**	**NHL**	**4**	**0**	**1**	**1**	**0**	....	....	....	....	....
bc	Prince Albert	WHL	57	22	70	92	30	20	4	24	28	4
	NHL Totals		**4**	**0**	**1**	**1**	**0**	....	....	....	....	....

a WHL Second All-Star Team, East Division (1985)
b WHL East All-Star Team (1986)
c WHL Player of the Year (1986)
Traded to **Minnesota** by **Edmonton** with Marc Habscheid, Dan Barber for Gord Sherven and Don Biggs, December 20, 1985.

VOLCAN, MICHAEL STEPHEN (MICKEY)

Born, Edmonton, Alta., March 3, 1962.
Defense. Shoots right. 6', 190 lbs.
Last amateur club: University of North Dakota Fighting Sioux (WCHA).
(Hartford's 3rd choice, 50th over-all, in 1980 Entry Draft).

				Regular Season					Playoffs			
Season	Club	Lea	GP	G	A	TP	PIM	GP	G	A	TP	PIM
1978-79	St. Albert	AJHL	50	20	47	67	109	....	....	....	....	....
1979-80	North Dakota	WCHA	33	2	14	16	38	....	....	....	....	....
1980-81	**Hartford**	**NHL**	**49**	**2**	**11**	**13**	**26**	....	....	....	....	....
	Binghamton	AHL	24	1	9	10	26	6	0	0	0	14
1981-82	**Hartford**	**NHL**	**26**	**1**	**5**	**6**	**29**	....	....	....	....	....
	Binghamton	AHL	33	4	13	17	47	14	4	8	12	40
1982-83	**Hartford**	**NHL**	**68**	**4**	**13**	**17**	**73**	....	....	....	....	....
1983-84	**Calgary**	**NHL**	**19**	**1**	**4**	**5**	**18**	....	....	....	....	....
	Colorado	CHL	30	8	9	17	20	5	0	0	0	11
1984-85	Moncton	AHL	63	8	14	22	44	....	....	....	....	....
1985-86	Nova Scotia	AHL	66	12	36	48	114	....	....	....	....	....
	NHL Totals		**162**	**8**	**33**	**41**	**146**	....	....	....	....	....

Traded to **Calgary** by **Hartford** for Joel Quenneville and Richie Dunn, July 5, 1983.

VOS, RALPH

Born, Guelph, Ont., January 5, 1964.
Left wing. Shoots right. 6'2", 185 lbs.
Last amateur club: University of Northern Michigan Wildcats (WCHA).
(Edmonton's 7th choice, 166th over-all, in 1983 Entry Draft).

				Regular Season					Playoffs			
Season	Club	Lea	GP	G	A	TP	PIM	GP	G	A	TP	PIM
1983-84	N. Michigan	WCHA	39	7	28	35	26	....	....	....	....	....
1984-85	N. Michigan	WCHA	39	12	37	49	52	....	....	....	....	....
1985-86	N. Michigan	WCHA	39	12	36	48	42	....	....	....	....	....

WAHLIN, DUANE

Born, St. Paul, Minn., June 3, 1965.
Defense. Shoots right. 5'11", 165 lbs.
Last amateur club: University of Maine Black Bears (H.E.).
(Minnesota's 9th choice, 181st over-all, in 1984 Entry Draft).

				Regular Season					Playoffs			
Season	Club	Lea	GP	G	A	TP	PIM	GP	G	A	TP	PIM
1984-85	Maine	H.E.	38	12	6	18	36	....	....	....	....	....
1985-86	Maine	H.E.	12	0	3	3	14	....	....	....	....	....

WALKER, BRIAN

Born, Red Deer Alta., January 21, 1965.
Defense. Shoots right. 6'2", 205 lbs.
Last amateur club: Moose Jaw Warriors (WHL).
(NY Rangers' 11th choice, 222nd over-all, in 1983 Entry Draft).

				Regular Season					Playoffs			
Season	Club	Lea	GP	G	A	TP	PIM	GP	G	A	TP	PIM
1981-82	Lethbridge	WHL	6	1	3	4	2	3	0	0	0	0
1982-83	Lethbridge	WHL	13	0	1	1	14	....	....	....	....	....
	Portland	WHL	47	4	13	17	45	13	0	2	2	15
1983-84	Portland	WHL	67	6	25	31	182	14	0	8	8	41
1984-85	Moose Jaw	WHL	65	12	59	71	109	....	....	....	....	....
1985-86	Toledo	IHL	12	0	2	2	11	....	....	....	....	....

WALKER, GORD

Born, Castlegar, B.C., August 12, 1965.
Left wing. Shoots left. 6', 175 lbs.
Last amateur club: Portland Winter Hawks (WHL).
(New York Rangers' 3rd choice, 54th over-all, in 1983 Entry Draft).

				Regular Season					Playoffs			
Season	Club	Lea	GP	G	A	TP	PIM	GP	G	A	TP	PIM
1982-83	Portland	WHL	66	24	30	54	95	14	5	8	13	12
1983-84	Portland	WHL	58	28	41	69	65	14	8	11	19	18
1984-85a	Kamloops	WHL	66	67	67	134	76	15	13	14	27	34
1985-86	New Haven	AHL	46	11	28	39	66	....	....	....	....	....

a WHL First All-Star Team (1985)

WALTER, BRET
Born, Calgary, Alta., April 28, 1968.
Center. Shoots right. 6'1", 195 lbs.
Last amateur club: University of Alberta Golden Bears (GPAC).
(NY Rangers' 2nd choice, 51st over-all, in 1986 Entry Draft).

				Regular Season					Playoffs			
Season	Club	Lea	GP	G	A	TP	PIM	GP	G	A	TP	PIM
1984-85	Ft. Sask.	Midget	32	38	39	77	44	....	....	....	....	....
1985-86	Alberta	GPAC	18	3	11	14	6	....	....	....	....	....

WALTER, RYAN WILLIAM
Born, New Westminster, B.C., April 23, 1958.
Center/Left wing. Shoots left. 6', 195 lbs.
Last amateur club: Seattle Breakers (WHL).
(Washington's 1st choice, 2nd over-all, in 1978 Amateur Draft).

				Regular Season					Playoffs			
Season	Club	Lea	GP	G	A	TP	PIM	GP	G	A	TP	PIM
1974-75	Kamloops	WHL	9	8	4	12	2	2	1	1	2	2
1975-76	Kamloops	WHL	72	35	49	84	96	12	3	9	12	10
1976-77	Kamloops	WHL	71	41	58	99	100	5	1	3	4	11
1977-78abc	Seattle	WHL	62	54	71	125	148	....	....	....	....	....
1978-79	Washington	NHL	69	28	28	56	70	....	....	....	....	....
1979-80	Washington	NHL	80	24	42	66	106	....	....	....	....	....
1980-81	Washington	NHL	80	24	44	68	150	....	....	....	....	....
1981-82	Washington	NHL	78	38	49	87	142	....	....	....	....	....
1982-83	Montreal	NHL	80	29	46	75	40	3	0	0	0	11
1983-84	Montreal	NHL	73	20	29	49	83	15	2	1	3	4
1984-85	Montreal	NHL	72	19	19	38	59	12	2	7	9	13
1985-86	Montreal	NHL	69	15	34	49	45	5	0	1	1	2
	NHL Totals		601	197	291	486	695	35	4	9	13	30

a WHL Most Valuable Player (1978)
b WHL Player of the Year (1978)
c WHL First All-Star Team (1978)
Traded to **Montreal** by **Washington** with Rick Green for Rod Langway, Brian Engblom, Doug Jarvis and Craig Laughlin, September 9, 1982.

WARE, MICHAEL
Born, York, Ont., March 22, 1967.
Right wing. Shoots right. 6'5", 200 lbs.
Last amateur club: Hamilton Steelhawks (OHL).
(Edmonton's 3rd choice, 62nd over-all, in 1985 Entry Draft).

				Regular Season					Playoffs			
Season	Club	Lea	GP	G	A	TP	PIM	GP	G	A	TP	PIM
1984-85	Hamilton	OHL	57	4	14	18	225	12	0	1	1	29
1985-86	Hamilton	OHL	44	8	11	19	155	....	....	....	....	....

WARUS, MIKE
Born, Sudbury, Ont., January 16, 1964.
Right wing. Shoots right. 6'1", 190 lbs.
Last amateur club: Lake Superior State Lakers (CCHA).
(Winnipeg's 10th choice, 218th over-all, in 1984 Entry Draft).

				Regular Season					Playoffs			
Season	Club	Lea	GP	G	A	TP	PIM	GP	G	A	TP	PIM
1983-84	Lake Superior	CCHA	35	6	4	10	33	....	....	....	....	....
1984-85	Lake Superior	CCHA	43	4	11	15	36	....	....	....	....	....
1985-86	Lake Superior	CCHA	38	5	6	11	85	....	....	....	....	....

WASLEN, GERARD
Born, Humboldt, Sask., October 5, 1962.
Right wing. Shoots right. 6'0", 190 lbs.
Last amateur club: Colgate University Red Raiders (ECAC).

				Regular Season					Playoffs			
Season	Club	Lea	GP	G	A	TP	PIM	GP	G	A	TP	PIM
1982-83	Colgate	ECAC	28	17	38	55	10	....	....	....	....	....
1983-84	Colgate	ECAC	35	28	33	61	64	....	....	....	....	....
1984-85	Colgate	ECAC	28	10	20	30	55	....	....	....	....	....
1985-86a	Colgate	ECAC	21	14	21	35	36	....	....	....	....	....

a ECAC Second All-Star Team (1986)
Signed as a free agent by **Toronto**, June 27, 1986.

WATSON, WILLIAM (BILL)
Born, Pine Falls, Man., March 30, 1964.
Right wing. Shoots right. 6', 185 lbs.
Last amateur club: University of Minnesota-Duluth Bulldogs (WCHA).
(Chicago's 4th choice, 70th over-all, in 1982 Entry Draft).

				Regular Season					Playoffs			
Season	Club	Lea	GP	G	A	TP	PIM	GP	G	A	TP	PIM
1980-81	Prince Albert	SJHL	54	30	39	69	27	....	....	....	....	....
1981-82	Prince Albert	SJHL	47	43	41	84	37	....	....	....	....	....
1982-83	Minn.-Duluth	WCHA	22	5	10	15	10	....	....	....	....	....
1983-84a	Minn.-Duluth	WCHA	40	35	51	86	12	....	....	....	....	....
1984-85b	Minn.-Duluth	WCHA	42	46	54	100	46	....	....	....	....	....
1985-85	Chicago	NHL	52	8	16	24	2	2	0	1	1	0
	NHL Totals		52	8	16	24	2	2	0	1	1	0

a WCHA First All-Star Team (1984)
b Named winner of 1985 Hobey Baker Trophy (Top U.S. Collegiate Player)

WATTERS, TIMOTHY J. (TIM)
Born, Kamloops, B.C., July 25, 1959.
Defense. Shoots left. 5'11", 180 lbs.
Last amateur club: Michigan Tech University Huskies (WCHA).
(Winnipeg's 6th choice, 124th over-all, in 1979 Entry Draft).

				Regular Season					Playoffs			
Season	Club	Lea	GP	G	A	TP	PIM	GP	G	A	TP	PIM
1978-79	Michigan Tech.	WCHA	38	6	21	27	48	....	....	....	....	....
1979-80	Cdn. National	...	56	8	21	29	43	....	....	....	....	....
	Cdn. Olympic	...	6	1	1	2	0	....	....	....	....	....
1980-81ab	Michigan Tech	WCHA	43	12	38	50	36	....	....	....	....	....
1981-82	Tulsa	CHL	5	1	2	3	0	....	....	....	....	....
	Winnipeg	NHL	69	2	22	24	97	4	0	1	1	8
1982-83	Winnipeg	NHL	77	5	18	23	98	3	0	0	0	2
1983-84	Winnipeg	NHL	74	3	20	23	169	3	1	0	1	2
1984-85	Winnipeg	NHL	63	2	20	22	74	8	0	1	1	16
1985-86	Winnipeg	NHL	56	6	8	14	97	....	....	....	....	....
	NHL Totals		339	18	88	106	535	18	1	2	3	28

a WCHA First All-Star Team (1981)
b Named to NCAA All-Tournament Team (1981)

WEINRICH, ERIC
Born, Roanoke, Virginia, December 19, 1966.
Defense. Shoots left. 6'1", 195 lbs.
Last amateur club: University of Maine Black Bears (H.E.).
(New Jersey's 2nd choice, 32nd over-all, in 1985 Entry Draft).

				Regular Season					Playoffs			
Season	Club	Lea	GP	G	A	TP	PIM	GP	G	A	TP	PIM
1983-84	N. Yarmouth	Mass.	17	23	33	56	32	....	....	....	....	....
1984-85	N. Yarmouth	Mass.	20	6	21	27	28	....	....	....	....	....
1985-86	U. of Maine	H.E.	34	0	15	15	26	....	....	....	....	....

WEIR, WALLY
Born, Verdun, Que. June 3, 1954.
Defense. Shoots left. 6'2", 205 lbs.
Last amateur club: Beauce Jaros (NAHL).

				Regular Season					Playoffs			
Season	Club	Lea	GP	G	A	TP	PIM	GP	G	A	TP	PIM
1975-76	Beauce	NAHL	56	6	20	26	180	....	....	....	....	....
1976-77	Quebec	WHA	69	3	17	20	197	17	1	5	6	13
1977-78	Quebec	WHA	13	0	0	0	47	11	1	2	3	50
1978-79	Quebec	WHA	68	2	7	9	166	4	0	1	1	4
1979-80	Quebec	NHL	73	3	12	15	133	....	....	....	....	....
1980-81	Rochester	AHL	7	1	1	2	79	....	....	....	....	....
	Quebec	NHL	54	6	8	14	77	3	0	0	0	15
1981-82	Quebec	NHL	62	3	5	8	173	15	0	0	0	45
1982-83	Quebec	NHL	58	5	11	16	135	4	0	1	1	19
1983-84	Quebec	NHL	25	2	3	5	17	1	0	0	0	17
	Fredericton	AHL	44	6	17	23	45	7	2	2	4	14
1984-85	Hartford	NHL	34	2	3	5	56	....	....	....	....	....
	Pittsburgh	NHL	14	0	3	3	34	....	....	....	....	....
1985-86	Baltimore	AHL	67	5	12	17	300	....	....	....	....	....
	NHL Totals		320	21	45	66	625	23	0	1	1	96
	WHA Totals		150	5	24	29	410	32	2	8	10	67

Claimed by **Hartford** from **Quebec** in NHL waiver draft, October 9, 1984. Claimed by **Pittsburgh** from **Hartford** on waivers, March 1, 1985.

WELLS, GORDON (JAY)
Born, Paris, Ont., May 18, 1959.
Defense. Shoots left. 6'1", 205 lbs.
Last amateur club: Kingston Canadians (OHA).
(Los Angeles' 1st choice, 16th over-all, in 1979 Entry Draft).

				Regular Season					Playoffs			
Season	Club	Lea	GP	G	A	TP	PIM	GP	G	A	TP	PIM
1977-78	Kingston	OHA	68	9	13	22	195	5	1	2	3	6
1978-79a	Kingston	OHA	48	6	21	27	100	11	2	7	9	29
1979-80	Binghamton	AHL	28	0	6	6	48	....	....	....	....	....
	Los Angeles	NHL	43	0	0	0	113	4	0	0	0	11
1980-81	Los Angeles	NHL	72	5	13	18	155	4	0	0	0	27
1981-82	Los Angeles	NHL	60	1	8	9	145	10	1	3	4	41
1982-83	Los Angeles	NHL	69	3	12	15	167	....	....	....	....	....
1983-84	Los Angeles	NHL	69	3	18	21	141	....	....	....	....	....
1984-85	Los Angeles	NHL	77	2	9	11	185	3	0	1	1	0
1985-86	Los Angeles	NHL	79	11	31	42	226	....	....	....	....	....
	NHL Totals		469	25	91	116	1132	21	1	4	5	79

a OHA First All-Star Team (1979)

WENAAS, JEFF
Born, Swift Current, Sask., September 1, 1967.
Center. Shoots left. 5'11", 185 lbs.
Last amateur club: Medicine Hat Tigers (WHL).
(Calgary's 3rd choice, 38th over-all, in 1985 Entry Draft).

				Regular Season					Playoffs			
Season	Club	Lea	GP	G	A	TP	PIM	GP	G	A	TP	PIM
1984-85	Medicine Hat	WHL	70	27	27	54	70	9	2	5	7	7
1985-86	Medicine Hat	WHL	65	20	26	46	57	25	7	10	17	20

WESLEY, TREVOR (BLAKE)

Born, Red Deer, Alta., July 10, 1959.
Defense. Shoots left. 6'1", 200 lbs.
Last amateur club: Portland Winter Hawks (WHL).
(Philadelphia's 2nd choice, 22nd over-all, in 1979 Entry Draft).

				Regular Season					Playoffs			
Season	Club	Lea	GP	G	A	TP	PIM	GP	G	A	TP	PIM
1976-77	Portland	WHL	63	8	25	33	111	10	0	5	5	32
1977-78	Portland	WHL	67	7	37	44	190	8	1	2	3	20
1978-79a	Portland	WHL	69	10	42	52	292	25	3	8	11	70
1979-80	**Philadelphia**	**NHL**	2	0	1	1	2	....	....	....	....	....
	Maine	AHL	62	12	22	34	76	12	2	5	7	62
1980-81	**Philadelphia**	**NHL**	50	3	7	10	107	....	....	....	....	....
	Maine	AHL	24	6	10	16	20	9	1	8	9	53
1981-82	**Hartford**	**NHL**	78	9	18	27	123	....	....	....	....	....
1982-83	**Hartford**	**NHL**	22	0	1	1	46	....	....	....	....	....
	Quebec	**NHL**	52	4	8	12	84	4	0	0	0	2
1983-84	**Quebec**	**NHL**	46	2	8	10	75	9	1	2	3	20
1984-85	**Quebec**	**NHL**	21	0	2	2	28	6	1	0	1	8
	Fredericton	AHL	25	3	4	7	80	2	1	0	1	2
1985-86	**Toronto**	**NHL**	27	0	1	1	21	....	....	....	....	....
	St. Catharines	AHL	37	3	4	7	56	13	0	3	3	41
	NHL Totals		298	18	46	64	486	19	2	2	4	30

a WHL Second All-Star Team (1979)
Traded to **Hartford** by **Philadelphia** with Rick MacLeish, Don Gillen and Philadelphia's first (Paul Lawless), second (Mark Paterson) and third-round (Kevin Dineen) choices in the 1982 Entry Draft for Ray Allison, Fred Arthur and Hartford's first (Ron Sutter), second (Peter Ihnacak) and third-round (Miroslav Dvorak) choices in the 1982 Entry Draft, July 3, 1981. Hartford's second round choice (Peter Ihnacak) was transferred to Toronto by Philadelphia on January 20, 1982. Traded to **Quebec** by **Hartford** for Pierre Lacroix, December 3, 1982. Signed as a free agent by **Toronto**, July 31, 1985.

WHEELDON, Simon

Born, Vancouver, B.C., August 30, 1966.
Center, Shoots left. 5'11", 170 lbs.
Last amateur club: Victoria Cougars (WHL).
(Edmonton's 11th choice, 231st over-all, in 1984 Entry Draft).

				Regular Season					Playoffs			
Season	Club	Lea	GP	G	A	TP	PIM	GP	G	A	TP	PIM
1983-84	Victoria	WHL	56	14	24	38	43	....	....	....	....	....
1984-85a	Victoria	WHL	67	50	76	126	78	....	....	....	....	....
	Nova Scotia	AHL	4	0	1	1	0	1	0	0	0	0
	Victoria	WHL	70	61	96	157	85					

a WHL Second All-Star Team, West Division (1985).

WHELAN, SHANE

Born, Kirkland Lake, Ont., February 15, 1967.
Center. Shoots left. 6'3", 195 lbs.
Last amateur club: Windsor Compuware Spitfires (OHL).
(Philadelphia's 4th choice, 63rd over-all, in 1985 Entry Draft).

				Regular Season					Playoffs			
Season	Club	Lea	GP	G	A	TP	PIM	GP	G	A	TP	PIM
1984-85	Oshawa	OHL	59	10	14	24	45	4	0	0	0	0
1985-86	Windsor	OHL	64	9	29	38	69	12	1	2	3	33

WHISTLE, ROB

Born, Thunder Bay, Ont., April 4, 1961.
Defense. Shoots right. 6'2", 195 lbs.
Last amateur club: Wilfred Laurier University (OUAA).

				Regular Season					Playoffs			
Season	Club	Lea	GP	G	A	TP	PIM	GP	G	A	TP	PIM
1982-83	Laurier	OUAA	24	6	14	20	12	....	....	....	....	....
1983-84	Laurier	OUAA	24	9	15	24	42	....	....	....	....	....
1984-85a	Laurier	OUAA	24	5	22	27	31	....	....	....	....	....
1985-86	New Haven	AHL	20	1	4	5	5	....	....	....	....	....
	NY Rangers	**NHL**	32	4	2	6	10	3	0	0	0	2
	NHL Totals		32	4	2	6	10	3	0	0	0	2

a Canadian University Player of the Year (1985)
Signed as a free agent by **NY Rangers**, August 13, 1985.

WHITAKER, GORD

Born, Edmonton, Alta., January 24, 1966.
Right wing. Shoots right. 6'2", 205 lbs.
Last amateur club: Colorado College Tigers (WCHA).
(Winnipeg's 8th choice, 177th over-all, in 1984 Entry Draft).

					Regular Season					Playoffs			
Season	Club	Lea	GP	G	A	TP	PIM	GP	G	A	TP	PIM
1983-84	Colorado	WCHA	25	8	10	18	38	....	....	....	....	....
1984-85	Colorado	WCHA	31	10	5	15	30	....	....	....	....	....
1985-86	Colorado	WCHA	34	14	16	30	53	....	....	....	....	....

WHITE, GEORGE

Born, Arlington, Mass., February 17, 1963.
Center. Shoots left. 6', 175 lbs.
Last Amateur Club: University of N. Hampshire Wildcats (ECAC)
(Washington's 9th choice, 173rd over-all, in 1981 Entry Draft)

				Regular Season					Playoffs			
Season	Club	Lea	GP	G	A	TP	PIM	GP	G	A	TP	PIM
1980-81	N. Hampshire	ECAC	32	16	19	35	30	....	....	....	....	....
1981-82	N. Hampshire	ECAC	31	10	15	25	45	....	....	....	....	....
1982-83	N. Hampshire	ECAC	34	15	11	26	21	....	....	....	....	....
1983-84	Colorado	CHL	36	5	12	17	28	....	....	....	....	....
	Peoria	IHL	7	2	0	2	7	....	....	....	....	....
1984-85	Moncton	AHL	58	11	5	16	40	....	....	....	....	....
1985-86	Moncton	AHL	73	16	12	28	24	9	0	0	0	6

Rights traded to **Calgary** by **Washington** with Howard Walker, Quebec's sixth round choice — Washington's property from an earlier deal — (Mats Kihlstron) in 1982 Entry Draft; Washington's third round choice (Parry Berezan) in 1983 Entry Draft; and Washington's second round choice in 1984 Entry Draft for Pat Riggin and Ken Houston, June 9, 1982.

WICKENHEISER, DOUGLAS PETER (DOUG)   (wick-en-HIGHZ-er)

Born, Regina, Sask., March 30, 1961.
Center. Shoots left. 6'1", 200 lbs.
Last amateur club: Regina Pats (WHL).
(Montreal's 1st choice and 1st over-all in 1980 Entry Draft).

				Regular Season					Playoffs			
Season	Club	Lea	GP	G	A	TP	PIM	GP	G	A	TP	PIM
1977-78	Regina	WHL	68	37	51	88	49	13	4	5	9	4
1978-79	Regina	WHL	68	32	62	94	141					
1979-80abc	Regina	WHL	71	*89	81	*170	99	18	14	*26	*40	20
1980-81	**Montreal**	**NHL**	41	7	8	15	20	....	....	....	....	....
1981-82	**Montreal**	**NHL**	56	12	23	35	43	....	....	....	....	....
1982-83	**Montreal**	**NHL**	78	25	30	55	49	....	....	....	....	....
1983-84	**Montreal**	**NHL**	27	5	5	10	6	....	....	....	....	....
	St. Louis	**NHL**	46	7	21	28	19	11	2	2	4	2
1984-85	**St. Louis**	**NHL**	68	23	20	43	36	....	....	....	....	....
1985-86	**St. Louis**	**NHL**	36	8	11	19	16	19	2	5	7	12
	NHL Totals		352	87	118	205	189	30	4	7	11	14

a WHL First All-Star Team (1980)
b WHL Most Valuable Player (1980)
c Named Canadian Major Junior Player of the Year (1980)
Traded to **St. Louis** by **Montreal** with Gilbert Delorme and Greg Paslawski for Perry Turnbull, December 21, 1983.

WIEMER, JAMES DUNCAN (JIM)   (WEE-mer)

Born, Sudbury, Ont., January 9, 1961.
Defense. Shoots left. 6'4", 200 lbs.
Last amateur club: Peterborough Petes (OHA).
(Buffalo's 5th choice, 83rd over-all, in 1980 Entry Draft).

				Regular Season					Playoffs			
Season	Club	Lea	GP	G	A	TP	PIM	GP	G	A	TP	PIM
1978-79	Peterborough	OHA	61	15	12	27	50	18	4	4	8	15
1979-80	Peterborough	OHA	53	17	32	49	63	14	6	9	15	19
1980-81	Peterborough	OHA	65	41	54	95	102	5	1	2	3	15
1981-82	Rochester	AHL	74	19	26	45	57	9	0	4	4	2
1982-83	**Buffalo**	**NHL**	....	....	....	....	....	1	0	0	0	0
	Rochester	AHL	74	15	44	59	43	15	5	15	20	22
1983-84	**Buffalo**	**NHL**	64	5	15	20	48	....	....	....	....	....
	Rochester	AHL	12	4	11	15	11	18	3	13	16	20
1984-85	**Buffalo**	**NHL**	10	3	2	5	4	....	....	....	....	....
	Rochester	AHL	13	1	9	10	24	....	....	....	....	....
	NY Rangers	**NHL**	22	4	3	7	30	1	0	0	0	0
	New Haven	AHL	33	9	27	36	39	....	....	....	....	....
1985-86	**NY Rangers**	**NHL**	7	3	0	3	2	8	1	0	1	6
ab	New Haven	AHL	73	24	49	73	108	....	....	....	....	....
	NHL Totals		103	15	20	35	84	10	1	0	1	6

a AHL First All-Star Team (1986)
b AHL Defenseman of the Year (1986)
Traded to **NY Rangers** by **Buffalo** with Steve Patrick for Dave Maloney and Chris Renaud, December 6, 1984.

WIEST, RICH

Born, Lethbridge, Alta., June 22, 1967.
Center. Shoots right. 6'0", 180 lbs.
Last amateur club: Calgary Wranglers (WHL).
(NY Islanders' 11th choice, 181st over-all, in 1985 Entry Draft).

				Regular Season					Playoffs			
Season	Club	Lea	GP	G	A	TP	PIM	GP	G	A	TP	PIM
1983-84	Lethbridge	WHL	71	17	16	33	138	5	1	2	3	19
1984-85	Lethbridge	WHL	65	18	19	37	305	....	....	....	....	....
1985-86	Calgary	WHL	56	13	16	29	187	....	....	....	....	....

WIITALA, MARTY

Born, Superior, Wisconsin, February 24, 1964.
Center. Shoots left. 6'1", 170 lbs.
Last amateur club: University of Wisconsin Badgers (WCHA).
(Minnesota's 5th choice, 101st over-all, in 1982 Entry Draft).

				Regular Season					Playoffs			
Season	Club	Lea	GP	G	A	TP	PIM	GP	G	A	TP	PIM
1981-82	Superior HS	Wisc.	24	40	43	83	32	....	....	....	....	....
1982-83	U. of Wisconsin	WCHA	26	5	2	7	0	....	....	....	....	....
1983-84	U. of Wisconsin	WCHA	33	11	19	30	4	....	....	....	....	....
1984-85	U. of Wisconsin	WCHA	42	10	16	26	4	....	....	....	....	....
1985-86a	U. of Wisconsin	WCHA	42	15	39	54	24	....	....	....	....	....

a WCHA Second All-Star Team (1986)

WILKINSON, NEIL
Born, Selkirk, Man., August 15, 1967.
Defense. Shoots right. 6'3", 190 lbs.
Last amateur club: Selkirk Settlers (MJHL).
(Minnesota's 2nd choice, 30th overall, in 1986 Entry Draft).

Season	Club	Lea	Regular Season GP	G	A	TP	PIM	Playoffs GP	G	A	TP	PIM
1985-86	Selkirk	MJHL	42	14	35	49	91	....	....	....	....	....

WILKS, BRIAN
Born, North York, Ont., February 27, 1966.
Center. Shoots right. 5'11", 175 lbs.
Last amateur club: Kitchener Rangers (OHL).
(Los Angeles' 2nd choice, 24th over-all, in 1984 Entry Draft).

Season	Club	Lea	Regular Season GP	G	A	TP	PIM	Playoffs GP	G	A	TP	PIM
1982-83	Kitchener	OHL	69	6	17	23	25	1	0	0	0	0
1983-84	Kitchener	OHL	64	21	54	75	36	16	6	14	20	9
1984-85	**Los Angeles**	**NHL**	2	0	0	0	0	....	....	....	....	....
	Kitchener	OHL	58	30	63	93	52	4	2	4	6	2
1985-86	**Los Angeles**	**NHL**	43	4	8	12	25	....	....	....	....	....
	NHL Totals		45	4	8	12	25	....	....	....	....	....

WILLIAMS, BRIAN
Born, Fargo, North Dakota, June 27, 1963.
Center. Shoots right. 5'9", 175 lbs.
Last amateur club: University of North Dakota Fighting Sioux (WCHA).
(Montreal's 14th choice, 187th over-all, in 1982 Entry Draft).

Season	Club	Lea	Regular Season GP	G	A	TP	PIM	Playoffs GP	G	A	TP	PIM
1982-83	North Dakota	WCHA	24	9	10	19	20	....	....	....	....	....
1983-84	North Dakota	WCHA	45	17	31	48	62	....	....	....	....	....
1984-85	North Dakota	WCHA	41	20	27	47	41	....	....	....	....	....
1985-86	North Dakota	WCHA	40	22	40	62	61	....	....	....	....	....

WILLIAMS, DAN
Born, Oak Park, Ill., April 15, 1966.
Defense. Shoots left. 6'2", 180 lbs.
Last amateur club: Elmira College Blue Bisons (ECAC).
(Chicago's 13th choice, 237th overall, in 1984 Entry Draft).

Season	Club	Lea	Regular Season GP	G	A	TP	PIM	Playoffs GP	G	A	TP	PIM
1984-85	Austin	USHL	47	15	24	39	44	8	2	5	7	28
1985-86	Elmira College	ECAC	20	4	16	20	24	....	....	....	....	....

WILLIAMS, DAVID JAMES (DAVE)
Born, Weyburn, Sask., February 3, 1954.
Left wing. Shoots left. 5'11", 190 lbs.
Last amateur club: Swift Current Broncos (WHL).
(Toronto's 2nd choice, 31st over-all, in 1974 Amateur Draft).

Season	Club	Lea	Regular Season GP	G	A	TP	PIM	Playoffs GP	G	A	TP	PIM
1971-72	Swift Current	WHL	68	12	22	34	278	....	....	....	....	....
1972-73	Swift Current	WHL	68	44	58	102	266	....	....	....	....	....
1973-74	Swift Current	WHL	68	52	56	108	310	12	14	10	24	23
1974-75	Oklahoma City	CHL	39	16	11	27	202	....	....	....	....	....
	Toronto	NHL	42	10	19	29	187	7	1	3	4	25
1975-76	Toronto	NHL	78	21	19	40	299	10	0	0	0	75
1976-77	Toronto	NHL	77	18	25	43	*338	9	3	6	9	29
1977-78	Toronto	NHL	78	19	31	50	351	12	1	2	3	*63
1978-79	Toronto	NHL	77	19	20	39	*298	6	0	0	0	*48
1979-80	Toronto	NHL	55	22	18	40	197	....	....	....	....	....
	Vancouver	NHL	23	8	5	13	81	3	0	0	0	20
1980-81	Vancouver	NHL	77	35	27	62	*343	3	0	0	0	20
1981-82	Vancouver	NHL	77	17	21	38	341	17	3	7	10	*116
1982-83	Vancouver	NHL	68	8	13	21	265	4	0	3	3	12
1983-84	Vancouver	NHL	67	15	16	31	294	4	1	0	1	13
1984-85	Detroit	NHL	55	3	8	11	158	....	....	....	....	....
	Adirondack	AHL	8	5	2	7	4	....	....	....	....	....
	Los Angeles	NHL	12	4	3	7	43	3	0	0	0	4
1985-86	Los Angeles	NHL	72	20	29	49	320	....	....	....	....	....
	NHL Totals		858	219	254	473	3515	78	9	21	30	425

Traded to **Vancouver** by **Toronto** with Jerry Butler for Rick Vaive and Bill Derlago, February 18, 1980. Traded to Detroit by Vancouver for Rob McClanahan, August 8, 1984. Traded to **Los Angeles** by **Detroit** for future considerations, March 12, 1985.

WILLIAMS, ROD
Born, Lethbridge, Alta., February 14, 1967.
Right wing. Shoots right. 6'2", 190 lbs.
Last amateur club: Victoria Cougars (WHL).
(Philadelphia's 11th choice, 231st overall, in 1985 Entry Draft).

Season	Club	Lea	Regular Season GP	G	A	TP	PIM	Playoffs GP	G	A	TP	PIM
1983-84	Lethbridge	WHL	2	0	0	0	0	....	....	....	....	....
1984-85	Kelowna	WHL	71	15	26	41	56	6	1	1	2	0
1985-86	Victoria	WHL	67	15	24	39	147	....	....	....	....	....

WILLISON, KEVIN
Born, Calgary, Alta., May 21, 1958.
Defense. Shoots left. 5'11", 172 lbs.
Last amateur club: Billings Bighorns (WHL).
(St. Louis' 3rd choice, 72nd over-all, in 1978 Amateur Draft).

Season	Club	Lea	Regular Season GP	G	A	TP	PIM	Playoffs GP	G	A	TP	PIM
1976-77	Calgary	WHL	55	11	32	43	161	9	4	6	10	10
1977-78	Billings	WHL	68	21	42	63	151	20	6	*23	29	35
1978-79	Port Huron	IHL	55	12	35	47	116	....	....	....	....	....
1979-80	Salt Lake	CHL	72	5	26	31	106	13	1	6	7	21
1980-81	Port Huron	IHL	20	2	7	9	33	4	0	0	0	4
	Salt Lake	CHL	....	....	....	....	....	3	0	0	0	0
1981-82	Milwaukee	IHL	73	10	40	50	107	5	0	4	4	17
1982-83	Milwaukee	IHL	81	10	41	51	63	11	2	5	7	17
1983-84	Milwaukee	IHL	82	21	52	73	73	4	0	2	2	0
1984-85	Muskegon	IHL	60	6	20	26	39	9	0	1	1	16
1985-86	Milwaukee	IHL	77	9	29	38	57	5	0	0	0	2

WILSON, BEHN BEVAN
Born, Toronto, Ont., December 19, 1958.
Defense. Shoots left. 6'3", 210 lbs.
Last amateur club: Kingston Canadians (OHA).
(Philadelphia's 1st choice, 6th over-all, in 1978 Amateur Draft).

Season	Club	Lea	Regular Season GP	G	A	TP	PIM	Playoffs GP	G	A	TP	PIM
1975-76	Ottawa	OHA	63	5	16	21	131	12	3	2	5	46
1976-77	Ottawa	OHA	31	8	29	37	115	....	....	....	....	....
	Windsor	OHA	17	4	16	20	38	....	....	....	....	....
	Kalamazoo	IHL	13	2	7	9	40	....	....	....	....	....
1977-78	Kingston	OHA	52	18	58	76	186	2	1	3	4	21
1978-79	**Philadelphia**	**NHL**	80	13	36	49	197	5	1	0	1	8
1979-80	**Philadelphia**	**NHL**	61	9	25	34	212	19	4	9	13	66
1980-81	**Philadelphia**	**NHL**	77	16	47	63	237	12	2	10	12	36
1981-82	**Philadelphia**	**NHL**	59	13	23	36	135	4	1	4	5	10
1982-83	**Philadelphia**	**NHL**	62	8	24	32	92	3	0	1	1	2
1983-84	**Chicago**	**NHL**	59	10	22	32	143	4	0	0	0	0
1984-85	**Chicago**	**NHL**	76	10	23	33	185	15	4	5	9	60
1985-86	**Chicago**	**NHL**	69	13	37	50	113	2	0	0	0	2
	NHL Totals		543	92	237	329	1314	64	12	29	41	184

Traded to **Chicago** by **Philadelphia** for Doug Crossman and Chicago's second round choice (Scott Mellanby) in 1984 Entry Draft, June 8, 1983.

WILSON, CAREY
Born, Winnipeg, Man., May 19, 1962.
Center. Shoots left. 6'2", 205 lbs.
Last Amateur Club: 1984 Canadian Olympic Team.
(Chicago's 8th choice, 67th over-all, in 1980 Entry Draft).

Season	Club	Lea	Regular Season GP	G	A	TP	PIM	Playoffs GP	G	A	TP	PIM
1979-80	Dartmouth	ECAC	31	16	22	38	20	....	....	....	....	....
1980-81	Dartmouth	ECAC	24	9	13	22	52	....	....	....	....	....
1981-82	Helsinki	Fin.	29	15	17	32	58	7	1	4	5	6
1982-83	Helsinki	Fin.	36	16	24	40	62	....	....	....	....	....
1983-84	Cdn. Olympic	...	56	19	24	43	34	....	....	....	....	....
	Calgary	**NHL**	15	2	5	7	2	6	3	1	4	2
1984-85	**Calgary**	**NHL**	74	24	48	72	27	4	0	0	0	0
1985-86	**Calgary**	**NHL**	76	29	29	58	24	9	0	2	2	4
	NHL Totals		165	55	82	137	53	19	3	3	6	4

Rights traded to **Calgary** by **Chicago** for Denis Cyr, November 8, 1982.

WILSON, DOUGLAS, JR. (DOUG)
Born, Ottawa, Ont., July 5, 1957.
Defense. Shoots left. 6'1", 185 lbs.
Last amateur club: Ottawa 67's (OHA).
(Chicago's 1st choice, 6th over-all, in 1977 Amateur Draft).

Season	Club	Lea	Regular Season GP	G	A	TP	PIM	Playoffs GP	G	A	TP	PIM
1975-76	Ottawa	OHA	58	26	62	88	142	12	5	10	15	24
1976-77a	Ottawa	OHA	43	25	54	79	85	19	4	20	24	34
1977-78	**Chicago**	**NHL**	77	14	20	34	72	4	0	0	0	0
1978-79	**Chicago**	**NHL**	56	5	21	26	37	....	....	....	....	....
1979-80	**Chicago**	**NHL**	73	12	49	61	70	7	2	8	10	6
1980-81	**Chicago**	**NHL**	76	12	39	51	80	3	0	3	3	2
1981-82bc	**Chicago**	**NHL**	76	39	46	85	54	15	3	10	13	32
1982-83	**Chicago**	**NHL**	74	18	51	69	58	13	4	11	15	12
1983-84	**Chicago**	**NHL**	66	13	45	58	64	5	0	3	3	2
1984-85d	**Chicago**	**NHL**	78	22	54	76	44	12	3	10	13	12
1985-86	**Chicago**	**NHL**	79	17	47	64	80	3	1	1	2	2
	NHL Totals		655	152	372	524	559	62	13	46	59	68

a OHA First All-Star Team (1977)
b Won James Norris Memorial Trophy (1982)
c NHL First All-Star Team (1982)
d NHL Second All-Star Team (1985)

WILSON, MITCH

Born, Kelowna, B.C., February 15, 1962.
Center. Shoots right. 5'8", 190 lbs.
Last amateur club: Seattle Breakers (WHL).

			Regular Season					Playoffs				
Season	Club	Lea	GP	G	A	TP	PIM	GP	G	A	TP	PIM
1980-81	Seattle	WHL	64	8	23	31	253	5	3	0	3	31
1981-82	Seattle	WHL	60	18	17	35	436	10	3	7	10	55
1982-83	Wichita	CHL	55	4	6	10	186	....	....	....	....	....
1983-84	Maine	AHL	71	6	8	14	349	17	3	6	9	98
1984-85	**New Jersey**	**NHL**	**9**	**0**	**2**	**2**	**21**	....	....	....	....	....
	Maine	AHL	51	6	3	9	220	2	0	0	0	32
1985-86	Maine	AHL	64	4	3	7	217	3	0	0	0	2
	NHL Totals		**9**	**0**	**2**	**2**	**21**	....	....	....	....	....

Signed as a free agent by **New Jersey**, October 12, 1982.

WILSON, RICHARD WILLIAM (RIK)

Born, Long Beach, California, June 17, 1962.
Defense. Shoots right. 6', 180 lbs.
Last amateur club: Kingston Canadians (OHL).
(St. Louis' 1st choice, 12th over-all, in 1980 Entry Draft).

			Regular Season					Playoffs				
Season	Club	Lea	GP	G	A	TP	PIM	GP	G	A	TP	PIM
1980-81a	Kingston	OHA	68	30	70	100	108	13	1	9	10	18
	Salt Lake	CHL	....	....	....	....	....	4	1	1	2	2
1981-82	Kingston	OHL	16	9	10	19	38	....	....	....	....	....
	St. Louis	**NHL**	**48**	**3**	**18**	**21**	**24**	**9**	**0**	**3**	**3**	**14**
1982-83	**St. Louis**	**NHL**	**56**	**3**	**11**	**14**	**50**	....	....	....	....	....
	Salt Lake	CHL	4	0	0	0	0	....	....	....	....	....
1983-84	Montana	CHL	6	0	3	3	2	....	....	....	....	....
	St. Louis	**NHL**	**48**	**7**	**11**	**18**	**53**	**11**	**0**	**0**	**0**	**9**
1984-85	**St. Louis**	**NHL**	**51**	**8**	**16**	**24**	**39**	**2**	**0**	**1**	**1**	**0**
	Flint	IHL	29	0	0	0	0	1	0	0	0	0
	Salt Lake	IHL	2	0	0	0	0	....	....	....	....	....
1985-86	**St. Louis**	**NHL**	**32**	**0**	**4**	**4**	**48**	....	....	....	....	....
	Calgary	**NHL**	**2**	**0**	**0**	**0**	**0**	....	....	....	....	....
	Nova Scotia	AHL	13	4	5	9	11	....	....	....	....	....
	Moncton	AHL	8	3	3	6	2	....	....	....	....	....
	NHL Totals		**237**	**21**	**60**	**81**	**214**	**22**	**0**	**4**	**4**	**23**

a OHA First All-Star Team (1981)

Traded to **Calgary** by **St. Louis** with Joe Mullen and Terry Johnson for Ed Beers, Charles Bourgeois and Gino Cavallini, February 1, 1986. Traded to **Chicago** by **Calgary** for Tom McMurchy, March 11, 1986.

WILSON, RON

Born, Windsor, Ont., May 28, 1955.
Defense. Shoots right. 5'10", 170 lbs.
Last amateur club: Providence College Friars (ECAC).

			Regular Season					Playoffs				
Season	Club	Lea	GP	G	A	TP	PIM	GP	G	A	TP	PIM
1973-74	Providence	ECAC	26	16	22	38	....	....	....	....	....	....
1974-85	Providence	ECAC	27	26	61	87	...	....	....	....	....	....
1975-76	Providence	ECAC	28	19	47	66	...	....	....	....	....	....
1976-77	Providence	ECAC	30	17	42	69	..	....	....	....	....	....
	Dallas	CHL	4	1	0	1	2	....	....	....	....	....
1977-78	Dallas	CHL	67	31	38	69	18	....	....	....	....	....
	Toronto	**NHL**	**13**	**2**	**1**	**3**	**0**	....	....	....	....	....
1978-79	New Brunswick	AHL	31	11	21	32	13	....	....	....	....	....
	Toronto	**NHL**	**46**	**5**	**12**	**17**	**4**	**3**	**0**	**1**	**1**	**0**
1979-80	New Brunswick	AHL	43	20	43	63	10	14	3	2	5	2
	Toronto	**NHL**	**5**	**0**	**2**	**2**	**2**	**3**	**1**	**2**	**3**	**2**
1980-81	Kloten	SWIZ	38	22	23	45	....	....	....	....	....	....
1981-82	Davos	SWIZ	38	24	23	47	....	....	....	....	....	....
1982-83	Davos	SWIZ	....	....	....	....	....	....	....	....	....	....
1983-84	Davos	SWIZ	....	....	....	....	....	....	....	....	..	..
1984-85	Davos	SWIZ	38	39	62	101	....	....	....	....	....	....
1985-86	Davos	SWIZ	32	35	43	78	....	....	....	....	....	....
	Minnesota	**NHL**	**11**	**1**	**3**	**4**	**8**	**5**	**2**	**4**	**6**	**4**
	NHL Totals		**75**	**8**	**18**	**26**	**14**	**8**	**0**	**5**	**7**	**6**

Signed as a free agent by **Minnesota**, March 7, 1986.

WILSON, RONALD LEE (RON)

Born, Toronto, Ont., May 13, 1956.
Left wing. Shoots left. 5'9", 170 lbs.
Last amateur club: St. Catharines Black Hawks (OHA).
(Montreal's 15th choice, 133rd over-all, in 1976 Amateur Draft).

			Regular Season					Playoffs				
Season	Club	Lea	GP	G	A	TP	PIM	GP	G	A	TP	PIM
1974-75	Toronto	OHA	16	6	12	18	6	23	9	17	26	6
1975-76	St. Catharines	OHA	64	37	62	99	44	4	1	6	7	7
1976-77	Nova Scotia	AHL	67	15	21	36	18	6	0	0	0	0
1977-78	Nova Scotia	AHL	59	15	25	40	17	11	4	4	8	9
1978-79	Nova Scotia	AHL	77	33	42	75	91	10	5	6	11	14
1979-80	**Winnipeg**	**NHL**	**79**	**21**	**36**	**57**	**28**	....	....	....	....	....
1980-81	**Winnipeg**	**NHL**	**77**	**18**	**33**	**51**	**55**	....	....	....	....	....
1981-82	**Winnipeg**	**NHL**	**39**	**3**	**13**	**16**	**49**	....	....	....	....	....
	Tulsa	CHL	41	20	38	58	22	3	1	0	1	2
1982-83	Sherbrooke	AHL	65	30	55	85	71	....	....	....	....	....
	Winnipeg	**NHL**	**12**	**6**	**3**	**9**	**4**	**3**	**2**	**2**	**4**	**2**
1983-84	**Winnipeg**	**NHL**	**51**	**3**	**12**	**15**	**12**	....	....	....	....	....
	Sherbrooke	AHL	22	10	30	40	16	....	....	....	....	....
1984-85	**Winnipeg**	**NHL**	**75**	**10**	**9**	**19**	**31**	**8**	**4**	**2**	**6**	**2**
1985-86	**Winnipeg**	**NHL**	**54**	**6**	**7**	**13**	**16**	**1**	**0**	**0**	**0**	**0**
	Sherbrooke	AHL	10	9	8	17	9	....	....	....	....	....
	NHL Totals		**387**	**67**	**113**	**180**	**195**	**12**	**6**	**4**	**10**	**2**

Sold to **Winnipeg** by **Montreal**, October 4, 1979.

WOLANIN, CRAIG

Born, Grosse Pointe, Mich., July 27, 1967.
Defense. Shoots left. 6'2", 185 lbs.
Last amateur club: Kitchener Rangers (OHL).
(New Jersey's 1st choice, 3rd over-all, in 1985 Entry Draft).

			Regular Season					Playoffs				
Season	Club	Lea	GP	G	A	TP	PIM	GP	G	A	TP	PIM
1983-84	Detroit Compu.	Midget	69	8	42	50	86	....	....	....	....	....
1984-85	Kitchener	OHL	60	5	16	21	95	4	1	1	2	2
1985-86	**New Jersey**	**NHL**	**44**	**2**	**16**	**18**	**74**	....	....	....	....	....
	NHL Totals		**44**	**2**	**16**	**18**	**74**	....	....	....	....	....

WOOD, DAN

Born, Toronto, Ont., October 30, 1962.
Right wing. Shoots right. 5'11", 190 lbs.
Last amateur club: 1984 Canadian Olympic Team.
(St. Louis' 8th choice, 188th over-all, in 1981 Entry Draft).

			Regular Season					Playoffs				
Season	Club	Lea	GP	G	A	TP	PIM	GP	G	A	TP	PIM
1980-81	Kingston	OHA	68	12	24	36	165	14	1	2	3	42
1981-82	Kingston	OHL	55	25	33	58	108	3	1	0	1	25
	Salt Lake	CHL	8	0	1	1	11	10	1	4	5	2
1982-83	Salt Lake	CHL	67	13	14	27	57	6	2	0	2	2
1983-84	Cdn. Olympic	...	41	5	4	9	38	....	....	....	....	....
	Montana	CHL	14	2	7	9	14	....	....	....	....	....
	Springfield	AHL	13	5	8	13	4	4	1	1	2	0
1984-85	Fredericton	AHL	61	10	9	19	26	4	0	0	0	0
1985-86	Peoria	IHL	33	8	10	18	24	11	1	2	3	32

Rights sold to **Quebec** by **St. Louis** with rights to Roger Hagglund and Richard Zemlak, June 22, 1984.

WOODLEY, DAN

Born, Oklahoma City, Oklahoma, December 29, 1967.
Center. Shoots right. 5'11", 185 lbs.
Last amateur club: Portland Winter Hawks (WHL).
(Vancouver's 1st choice, 7th overall, in 1986 Entry Draft).

			Regular Season					Playoffs				
Season	Club	Lea	GP	G	A	TP	PIM	GP	G	A	TP	PIM
1984-85	Portland	WHL	63	21	36	57	108	1	0	0	0	0
1985-86	Portland	WHL	62	45	47	92	100	12	0	8	8	31

WRIGHT, KORY

Born, Anchorage, AK. June 10, 1965.
Right wing. Shoots right. 5'10", 180 lbs.
Last amateur club: University of Northern Michigan Wildcats (WCHA).
(Winnipeg's 11th choice, 189th overall, in 1983 Entry Draft).

			Regular Season					Playoffs				
Season	Club	Lea	GP	G	A	TP	PIM	GP	G	A	TP	PIM
1983-84	N. Michigan	WCHA	29	7	4	11	19	....	....	....	....	....
1984-85	N. Michigan	WCHA	36	8	17	25	20	....	....	....	....	....
1985-86	N. Michigan	WCHA	36	12	7	19	16	....	....	....	....	....

WURST, MICHAEL

Born, Kalamazoo, Mich., October 5, 1964.
Left wing. Shoots left. 6'0", 185 lbs.
Last amateur club: Ohio State University Buckeyes (CCHA).
(Toronto's 10th choice, 213th overall, in 1984 Entry Draft).

			Regular Season					Playoffs				
Season	Club	Lea	GP	G	A	TP	PIM	GP	G	A	TP	PIM
1984-85	Ohio State	CCHA	28	5	13	18	32	....	....	....	....	....
1985-86	Ohio State	CCHA	15	1	3	4	16	....	....	....	....	....

YAREMCHUK, GARY (yair-em-CHUK)

Born, Edmonton, Alta., August 15, 1961.
Center. Shoots left. 6', 185 lbs.
Last amateur club: Portland Winter Hawks (WHL).
(Toronto's 2nd choice, 24th over-all, in 1981 Entry Draft).

			Regular Season					Playoffs				
Season	Club	Lea	GP	G	A	TP	PIM	GP	G	A	TP	PIM
1979-80	Portland	WHL	41	21	34	55	23	6	1	4	5	2
1980-81	Portland	WHL	72	56	79	135	121	....	....	....	....	....
1981-82	**Toronto**	**NHL**	**18**	**0**	**3**	**3**	**10**	....	....	....	....	....
	Cincinnati	CHL	53	21	35	56	101	4	0	2	2	4
1982-83	**Toronto**	**NHL**	**3**	**0**	**0**	**0**	**2**	....	....	....	....	....
	St. Catharines	AHL	61	17	28	45	72	....	....	....	....	....
1983-84	**Toronto**	**NHL**	**1**	**0**	**0**	**0**	**0**	....	....	....	....	....
	St. Catharines	AHL	73	24	37	61	84	7	5	1	6	2
1984-85	**Toronto**	**NHL**	**12**	**1**	**1**	**2**	**16**	....	....	....	....	....
	St. Catharines	AHL	66	17	47	64	75	....	....	....	....	....
1985-86	Adirondack	AHL	60	12	32	44	90	1	1	0	1	0
	NHL Totals		**34**	**1**	**4**	**5**	**28**	....	....	....	....	....

Signed as a free agent by **Detroit**, August 13, 1985.

YAREMCHUK, KEN

Born, Edmonton, Alta., January 1, 1964.
Center. Shoots right. 5'11", 185 lbs.
Last amateur club: Portland Winter Hawks (WHL).
(Chicago's 1st choice, 7th over-all, in 1982 Entry Draft).

			Regular Season					Playoffs				
Season	Club	Lea	GP	G	A	TP	PIM	GP	G	A	TP	PIM
1980-81	Portland	WHL	72	35	72	107	105	9	2	8	10	24
1981-82a	Portland	WHL	72	58	99	157	181	15	10	21	31	12
1982-83b	Portland	WHL	66	51	109	160	76	14	11	15	26	12
1983-84	Chicago	NHL	47	6	7	13	19	1	0	0	0	0
1984-85	Chicago	NHL	63	10	16	26	16	15	5	5	10	37
	Milwaukee	IHL	7	4	6	10	9	....	....	....	....	....
1985-86	Chicago	NHL	78	14	20	34	43	3	1	1	2	2
	NHL Totals		188	30	43	73	78	19	6	6	12	39

a WHL First All-Star Team (1982)
b WHL Second All-Star Team (1983)

YAWNEY, TRENT

Born, Hudson Bay, Sask., September 29, 1965.
Defense. Shoots left. 6'3", 185 lbs.
Last amateur club: Canadian Olympic Team.
(Chicago's 2nd choice, 45th over-all, in 1984 Entry Draft).

			Regular Season					Playoffs				
Season	Club	Lea	GP	G	A	TP	PIM	GP	G	A	TP	PIM
1982-83	Saskatoon	WHL	59	6	31	37	44	6	0	2	2	0
1983-84	Saskatoon	WHL	73	13	46	59	81	....	....	....	....	....
1984-85	Saskatoon	WHL	72	16	51	67	158	3	1	6	7	7
1985-86	Cdn. Olympic	...	73	6	15	21	60	....	....	....	....	....

YOUNG, SCOTT

Born, Clinton, Mass., October 1, 1967.
Right wing. Shoots right. 6'0", 185 lbs.
Last amateur club: Boston University Terriers (H.E.).
(Hartford's 1st choice, 11th overall, in 1986 Entry Draft).

			Regular Season					Playoffs				
Season	Club	Lea	GP	G	A	TP	PIM	GP	G	A	TP	PIM
1985-86a	Boston U.	H.E.	38	16	13	29	31	....	....	....	....	....

a Hockey East Rookie of the Year (1986)

YOUNG, WARREN HOWARD

Born, Toronto, Ont., January 11, 1956.
Center. Shoots left. 6'3", 195 lbs.
Last amateur club: Michigan Tech University Huskies (CCHA).
(California's 4th choice, 59th over-all, in 1975 Amateur Draft).

			Regular Season					Playoffs				
Season	Club	Lea	GP	G	A	TP	PIM	GP	G	A	TP	PIM
1977-78	Michigan Tech	CCHA	32	14	16	30	54	....	....	....	....	....
1978-79	Michigan Tech	CCHA	26	11	7	18	45	....	....	....	....	....
	Oklahoma City	CHL	4	0	1	1	2	....	....	....	....	....
1979-80	Oklahoma City	CHL	13	4	8	12	9	....	....	....	....	....
a	Baltimore	EHL	65	*53	53	106	75	....	....	....	....	....
1980-81	Oklahoma City	CHL	77	26	33	59	42	3	1	1	2	7
1981-82	Minnesota	NHL	1	0	0	0	0	....	....	....	....	....
	Nashville	CHL	60	31	28	59	154	....	....	....	....	....
1982-83	Minnesota	NHL	4	1	1	2	0	....	....	....	....	....
	Birmingham	CHL	75	26	58	84	144	13	3	3	6	57
1983-84	Pittsburgh	NHL	15	1	7	8	19	....	....	....	....	....
	Baltimore	AHL	59	25	38	63	142	10	2	6	8	18
1984-85b	Pittsburgh	NHL	80	40	32	72	174	....	....	....	....	....
1985-86	Detroit	NHL	79	22	24	46	161	....	....	....	....	....
	NHL Totals		179	64	64	128	354	....	....	....	....	....

a EHL Second All-Star Team (1980).
b Named to NHL All-Rookie Team)1985).

Signed as free agent by **Minnesota**, October 22, 1981. Signed as free agent by **Pittsburgh**, August 12, 1983. Signed as a free agent by **Detroit**, July 10, 1985.

YSEBAERT, PAUL

Born, Sarnia, Ont., May 15, 1966.
Center. Shoots left. 6'1", 170 lbs.
Last amateur club: Bowling Green State University Falcons (CCHA).
(New Jersey's 4th choice, 74th overall, in 1984 Entry Draft).

			Regular Season					Playoffs				
Season	Club	Lea	GP	G	A	TP	PIM	GP	G	A	TP	PIM
1984-85	Bowling Green	CCHA	42	23	32	55	54	....	....	....	....	....
1985-86a	Bowling Green	CCHA	42	23	45	68	50	....	....	....	....	....

a CCHA Second All-Star Team (1986)

YZERMAN, STEVE (EYE-zer-man)

Born, Cranbrook, B.C., May 9, 1965.
Center. Shoots right. 5'11", 175 lbs.
Last amateur club: Peterborough Petes (OHL)
(Detroit's 1st choice, 4th over-all, in 1983 Entry Draft).

			Regular Season					Playoffs				
Season	Club	Lea	GP	G	A	TP	PIM	GP	G	A	TP	PIM
1981-82	Peterborough	OHL	58	21	43	64	65	6	0	1	1	16
1982-83	Peterborough	OHL	56	42	49	91	33	4	1	4	5	0
1983-84a	Detroit	NHL	80	39	48	87	33	4	3	3	6	0
1984-85	Detroit	NHL	80	30	59	89	58	3	2	1	3	2
1985-86	Detroit	NHL	51	14	28	42	16	....	....	....	....	....
	NHL Totals		211	83	135	218	107	7	5	4	9	2

a Named to NHL All-Rookie Team (1984)

ZALAPSKI, ZARLEY

Born, Edmonton, Alta., April 22, 1968.
Defense. Shoots left. 6'1", 195 lbs.
Last amateur club: Canadian Olympic Team.
(Pittsburgh's 1st choice, 4th overall, in 1986 Entry Draft).

			Regular Season					Playoffs				
Season	Club	Lea	GP	G	A	TP	PIM	GP	G	A	TP	PIM
1985-86	Cdn Olympic	...	59	22	37	59	56	....	....	....	....	....

ZEMLACK, RICHARD ANDREW

Born, Wynard, Sask., March 3, 1963.
Center. Shoots right. 6'2", 190 lbs.
Last amateur club: Nanaimo Islanders (WHL).
(St. Louis' 9th choice, 209th over-all, in 1981 Entry Draft).

			Regular Season					Playoffs				
Season	Club	Lea	GP	G	A	TP	PIM	GP	G	A	TP	PIM
1980-81	Spokane	WHL	72	19	19	38	132	4	1	1	2	6
1981-82	Spokane	WHL	26	9	20	29	113	....	....	....	....	....
	Winnipeg	WHL	2	1	2	3	0	....	....	....	....	....
	Medicine Hat	WHL	41	11	20	31	70	....	....	....	....	....
	Salt Lake	CHL	6	0	0	0	2	1	0	0	0	0
1982-83	Medicine Hat	WHL	51	20	17	37	119	....	....	....	....	....
	Nanaimo	WHL	18	2	8	10	50	....	....	....	....	....
1983-84	Montana	CHL	14	2	2	4	17	....	....	....	....	....
	Toledo	IHL	45	8	19	27	101	....	....	....	....	....
1984-85	Muskegon	IHL	64	19	18	37	223	17	5	4	9	68
	Fredericton	AHL	16	3	4	7	59	....	....	....	....	....
1985-86	Fredericton	AHL	58	6	5	11	305	3	0	0	0	49
	Muskegon	IHL	3	1	2	3	36	....	....	....	....	....

Rights sold to **Quebec** by **St. Louis** with rights to Dan Wood and Roger Hagglund, June 22, 1984.

ZETTLER, ROB

Born, Sept Iles, Que., March 8, 1968.
Defense. Shoots left. 6'2", 190 lbs.
Last amateur club: Sault Ste. Marie Greyhounds (OHL).
(Minnesota's 5th choice, 55th overall, in 1986 Entry Draft).

			Regular Season					Playoffs				
Season	Club	Lea	GP	G	A	TP	PIM	GP	G	A	TP	PIM
1985-86	S.S. Marie	OHL	57	5	23	28	92	....	....	....	....	....

ZEZEL, PETER

Born, Toronto, Ont., April 22, 1965.
Center. Shoots left. 5'9", 200 lbs.
Last amateur club: Toronto Marlboros (OHL).
(Philadelphia's 1st choice, 41st over-all, in 1983 Entry Draft).

			Regular Season					Playoffs				
Season	Club	Lea	GP	G	A	TP	PIM	GP	G	A	TP	PIM
1981-82	Don Mills	Midget	40	43	51	94	36	....	....	....	....	....
1982-83	Toronto	OHL	66	35	39	74	28	4	2	4	6	0
1983-84	Toronto	OHL	68	47	86	133	31	9	7	5	12	4
1984-85	Philadelphia	NHL	65	15	46	61	26	19	1	8	9	28
1985-86	Philadelphia	NHL	79	17	37	54	76	5	3	1	4	4
	NHL Totals		144	32	83	115	102	24	4	9	13	32

ZOMBO, RICHARD (RICK)

Born, Des Plaines, Ill., May 8, 1963.
Defense. Shoots right. 6'1", 195 lbs.
Last amateur club: University of North Dakota Fighting Sioux (WCHA).
(Detroit's 6th choice, 149th over-all, in 1981 Entry Draft).

			Regular Season					Playoffs				
Season	Club	Lea	GP	G	A	TP	PIM	GP	G	A	TP	PIM
1983-84	North Dakota	WCHA	34	7	24	31	40	....	....	....	....	....
1984-85	Detroit	NHL	1	0	0	0	0	....	....	....	....	....
	Adirondack	AHL	56	3	32	35	70	....	....	....	....	....
1985-86	Detroit	NHL	14	0	1	1	16	....	....	....	....	....
	Adirondack	AHL	69	7	34	41	94	17	0	4	4	40
	NHL Totals		15	0	1	1	16	....	....	....	....	....

ZUKE, MICHAEL (MIKE) (ZOOK)

Born, Sault Ste. Marie, Ont., April 16, 1954.
Center. Shoots right. 6', 180 lbs.
Last amateur club: Michigan Tech University Huskies (CCHA).
(St. Louis' 3rd choice, 79th over-all, in 1974 Amateur Draft).

			Regular Season					Playoffs				
Season	Club	Lea	GP	G	A	TP	PIM	GP	G	A	TP	PIM
1974-75	Michigan Tech	CCHA	42	35	43	78	20	....	....	....	....	....
1975-76	Michigan Tech	CCHA	43	47	57	104	42	....	....	....	....	....
1976-77	Mohawk Valley	NAHL	48	42	29	71	33	....	....	....	....	....
	Indianapolis	WHA	15	3	4	7	2	....	....	....	....	....
1977-78	Edmonton	WHA	71	23	34	57	47	5	2	3	5	0
1978-79	Salt Lake	CHL	29	9	13	22	4	....	....	....	....	....
	St. Louis	NHL	34	9	17	26	18	....	....	....	....	....
1979-80	St. Louis	NHL	69	22	42	64	30	3	0	0	0	2
1980-81	St. Louis	NHL	74	24	44	68	57	11	4	5	9	4
1981-82	St. Louis	NHL	76	13	40	53	41	8	1	1	2	2
1982-83	Salt Lake	CHL	13	7	8	15	0	....	....	....	....	....
	St. Louis	NHL	43	8	16	24	14	4	1	0	1	4
1983-84	Hartford	NHL	75	6	23	29	36	....	....	....	....	....
1984-85	Hartford	NHL	67	4	12	16	12	....	....	....	....	....
1985-86	Hartford	NHL	17	0	2	2	12	....	....	....	....	....
	NHL Totals		421	86	196	282	220	26	6	6	12	12
	WHA Totals		86	26	38	64	49	5	2	3	5	0

Claimed by **Hartford** from **St. Louis** in NHL Waiver Draft, October 3, 1983.

ZYTYNSKY, TARAS JOHN   (ze-TIN-skee)

Born, Montreal, Que., May 10, 1962.
Defense. Shoots left. 6'1", 205 lbs.
Last amateur club: Montreal Juniors (QMJHL).
(Philadelphia's 4th choice, 84th over-all, in 1980 Entry Draft).

Season	Club	Lea	Regular Season					Playoffs				
			GP	G	A	TP	PIM	GP	G	A	TP	PIM
1979-80	Montreal	QMJHL	72	12	29	41	104	10	0	5	5	12
1980-81	Montreal	QMJHL	45	7	13	20	56	7	0	5	5	6
1981-82a	Montreal	QMJHL	64	18	39	57	82	14	1	3	4	31
1982-83	Maine	AHL	80	12	24	36	45	13	0	2	2	4
1983-84	Springfield	AHL	70	1	17	18	55	4	0	1	1	8
1984-85	Peoria	IHL	66	5	11	16	71	14	1	2	3	15
1985-86	Rochester	AHL	65	2	15	17	78	....	....	....	....	....

a QMJHL Second All-Star Team (1982)

NHL Records of Players out of Professional Hockey Since 1950-51 Season

Notes and abbreviations: Records include only players appearing in 35 or more NHL games. Total seasons are rounded off to the nearest full season. **A** – assists; **G** – goals; **GP** – games played; **PIM** – penalties in minutes; **TP** – total points. * – deceased.

			Regular Schedule					Playoffs					Last	Last
Name	NHL Teams	NHL Seasons	GP	G	A	TP	PIM	GP	G	A	TP	PIM	NHL Season	Pro Season
Abel, Sid	Det., Chi.	13	612	189	283	472	376	97	28	30	58	79	1953-54	1953-54
Affleck, Robert	ST.L., Van., NYI	7	280	14	66	80	86	8	0	0	0	0	1983-84	1983-84
Ahern, Fred	Cal., Clev., Colo.	2	146	31	30	61	130	2	0	1	1	2	1977-78	1980-81
Ahrens, Chris	Minnesota	1	52	0	3	3	84	1	0	0	0	0	1977-78	1977-78
Albright, Clint	NY Rangers	1	59	14	5	19	19	....	....	....	....	....	1948-49	1950-51
Aldcorn, Gary	Tor., Det., Bos.	4	226	41	56	97	78	6	1	2	3	4	1960-61	1960-61
Alexander, Claire	Tor., Van.	4	155	18	47	65	36	16	2	4	6	4	1977-78	1978-79
Amadio, Dave	Det., L.A.	2	125	11	16	27	163	16	1	2	3	18	1968-69	1973-74
Anderson, Earl	Det., Bos.	2	109	19	19	38	22	5	0	1	1	0	1976-77	1977-78
Anderson, Murray	Washington	1	40	0	1	1	68	....	....	....	....	....	1974-75	1976-77
Anderson, Ron	Det., L.A., St. L., Buf.	4	251	28	30	58	118	5	0	0	0	4	1971-72	1974-75
Anderson, Russ	Pit., Hfd., L.A.	10	519	22	99	121	1086	10	0	3	3	28	1984-85	1984-85
Andersson, Kent-Erik	Minn., NYR	7	456	72	103	175	78	50	4	11	15	4	1983-84	1983-84
Andrea, Paul	NYR, Pit., Cal., Buf.	3	150	31	49	80	10	....	....	....	....	....	1970-71	1973-74
Andruff, Ron	Mtl., Colo.	5	153	19	36	55	54	2	0	0	0	0	1978-79	1978-79
Angotti, Lou	NYR, Chi., Phi., Pit., St. L.	10	653	103	186	289	228	65	8	8	16	17	1973-74	1974-75
Antonovich, Mike	Minn., Hfd., N.J.	5	87	10	15	25	37	....	....	....	....	....	1983-84	1983-84
Apps, Syl	NYR, Pit., L.A.	9	727	183	423	606	311	23	5	5	10	23	1979-80	1979-80
Arbour, Al	Det., Chi., Tor., St. L.	11	626	12	58	70	617	86	1	8	9	92	1970-71	1970-71
Arbour, John	Bos., Pit., Van., St. L.	6	106	1	9	10	149	5	0	0	0	0	1971-72	1976-77
Armstrong, Bob	Boston	10	542	13	86	99	671	42	1	7	8	28	1961-62	1962-63
Armstrong, George	Toronto	20	1187	296	417	713	721	110	26	34	60	52	1970-71	1970-71
Arnason, Chuck	Mtl., Atl., Pitt., K.C., Colo., Clev., Min., Wash.	6	401	109	90	199	122	9	2	4	6	4	1978-79	1979-80
Arthur, Fred	Hfd., Phi.	3	80	1	8	9	49	4	0	0	0	2	1982-83	1982-83
*Ashbee, Barry	Bos., Phi.	5	284	15	70	85	291	17	0	4	4	22	1973-74	1973-74
*Ashby, Don	Tor., Colo., Edm.	3	188	40	56	96	40	12	1	0	1	4	1980-81	1980-81
Atanas, Walt	NY Rangers	1	49	13	8	21	40	....	....	....	....	....	1944-45	1955-56
Atkinson, Steve	Bos., Buf., Wash.	5	302	60	51	111	104	1	0	0	0	0	1974-75	1974-75
Aubin, Normand	Toronto	2	69	18	13	31	30	1	0	0	0	0	1982-83	1984-85
Awrey, Don	Bos., St. L., Mtl., Pit., NYR	15	923	30	154	184	1047	71	0	18	18	150	1977-78	1977-78
Babando, Pete	Bos., Det., Chi., NYR	6	351	86	73	159	194	17	3	3	6	6	1952-53	1956-57
Backor, Pete	Toronto	1	36	4	5	9	6	....	....	....	....	....	1944-45	1953-54
Backstrom, Ralph	Mtl., L.A., Chi.	16	1032	278	361	639	386	116	27	32	59	68	1972-73	1976-77
Bailey, Bob	Tor., Det., Chi.	4	150	15	21	36	207	15	0	4	4	22	1957-58	1962-63
Bailey, Garnet	Bos., Det., St. L., Wash.	10	568	107	171	278	633	15	2	4	6	28	1977-78	1980-81
Bailey, Reid	Phil., Tor., Hfd.	4	40	1	3	4	105	16	0	2	2	25	1983-84	1983-84
Baker, Bill	Mtl., Colo., St.L., NYR.	3	143	7	25	32	175	6	0	0	0	0	1982-83	1983-84
Balfour, Earl	Tor., Chi.	5	288	30	22	52	78	26	0	3	3	4	1960-61	1962-63
*Balfour, Murray	Mtl., Chi., Bos.	6	306	67	90	157	391	40	9	10	19	45	1964-65	1964-65
Ball, Terry	Phi., Buf.	3	74	7	19	26	26	....	....	....	....	....	1971-72	1975-76
Balon, Dave	NYR, Mtl., Min., Van.	2	775	192	222	414	607	78	14	21	35	109	1972-73	1973-74
Barber, Bill	Philadelphia	13	903	420	463	883	623	129	53	55	108	109	1984-85	1984-85
*Barilko, Bill	Toronto	5	252	26	36	62	456	47	5	7	12	104	1950-51	1950-51
Barkley, Doug	Chi., Det.	4	253	24	80	104	382	30	0	9	9	63	1965-66	1965-66
Barnes, Norm	Phi., Hfd.	5	156	6	38	44	178	12	0	0	0	8	1981-82	1981-82
Barlow, Bob	Minnesota	1	77	16	17	33	10	6	2	2	4	6	1970-71	1974-75
Barrett, Fred	Minn., L.A.	13	745	25	123	148	67	44	0	2	2	60	1983-84	1983-84
Barrie, Doug	Pit., Buf., L.A.	3	158	10	42	52	268	....	....	....	....	....	1971-72	1976-77
Bartlett, Jim	Mtl., NYR, Bos.	3	191	34	23	57	273	2	0	0	0	0	1960-61	1972-73
Bathe, Frank	Det., Phil.	9	224	3	28	31	27	1	3	4	42	0	1983-84	1983-84
Bathgate, Andy	NYR, Tor., Det., Pit.	16	1069	349	624	973	624	54	21	14	35	76	1970-71	1970-71
*Bauer, Bobby	Boston	7	327	123	137	260	36	48	11	8	19	6	1951-52	1951-52
Baun, Bobby	Tor., Oak., Det.	16	964	37	187	224	1493	96	3	12	15	171	1972-73	1972-73
Beckett, Bob	Boston	2	68	7	6	13	18	....	....	....	....	....	1963-64	1963-64
Bednarski, John	NYR, Edm.	3	100	2	18	20	114	1	0	0	0	0	1979-80	1981-82
Bell, Joe	NY Rangers	2	62	8	9	17	18	....	....	....	....	....	1946-47	1953-54
Beliveau, Jean	Montreal	18	1125	507	712	1219	1029	162	79	97	176	211	1970-71	1970-71
Bennett, Curt	St. L., NYR, St.L.	10	580	152	182	334	347	21	1	1	2	57	1979-80	1979-80
Bennett, Harvey	Pit., Wash., Phi., Min., St. L.	5	268	44	46	90	347	4	0	0	0	2	1978-79	1979-80
*Bentley, Doug	Chi., NYR	13	566	219	324	543	217	23	9	8	17	8	1953-54	1961-62
Bentley, Max	Chi., Tor., NYR	12	646	245	299	544	179	52	18	27	45	14	1953-54	1958-59
Berenson, Red	Mtl., NYR, St. L., Det.	16	987	261	397	658	305	85	23	14	37	49	1977-78	1977-78
Bergeron, Michel	Det., NYI, Wash.	5	229	80	58	138	165	....	....	....	....	....	1978-79	1979-80
Bergman, Gary	Det., Min., K.C.	12	838	68	299	367	1249	21	0	5	5	20	1975-76	1975-76
Bergman, Thommie	Detroit	6	246	21	44	65	243	7	0	2	2	2	1979-80	1979-80
Bernier, Serge	Phi., L.A., Que.	5	302	78	119	197	234	5	1	1	2	0	1980-81	1980-81
Berry, Bob	Mtl., L.A.	8	541	159	191	350	344	26	2	6	8	6	1976-77	1977-78
Berry, Doug	Colorado	2	121	10	33	43	25	....	....	....	....	....	1979-80	1981-82
Bettio, Sylvio	Boston	1	44	9	12	21	32	....	....	....	....	....	1949-50	1961-62
Beverley, Nick	Bos., Pit., NYR, Min., L.A., Colo.	11	502	18	94	112	156	7	0	1	1	0	1979-80	1979-80
Bialowas, Dwight	Atl., Min.	4	164	11	46	57	46	....	....	....	....	....	1976-77	1977-78
Bianchin, Wayne	Pit., Edm.	7	276	68	41	109	137	3	0	1	1	6	1979-80	1979-80
Bionda, Jack	Tor., Bos.	3	83	3	9	92	113	11	0	1	1	14	1958-59	1966-67
Black, Steve	Det., Chi.	2	113	11	20	31	77	13	0	0	0	13	1950-51	1953-54
Blackburn, Don	Bos., Phi., NYR, NYI, Min.	3	185	23	44	67	87	12	3	0	3	10	1972-73	1974-75
Blackburn, Bob	NYR, Pit.	2	135	8	12	20	105	6	0	0	0	4	1970-71	1971-72
Bladon, Tom	Phi., Pit., Edm., Wpg., Det.	9	610	73	197	270	392	86	8	29	37	70	1970-71	1971-72
Blight, Rick	Van., L.A.	7	326	96	125	221	170	5	0	5	5	2	1982-83	1982-83
Bloom, Mike	Wash., Det.	3	201	30	47	77	215	....	....	....	....	....	1976-77	1978-79
Boddy, Gregg	Vancouver	5	273	23	44	67	263	3	0	0	0	0	1975-76	1976-77
Bodnar, Gus	Tor., Chi., Bos.	12	667	142	254	396	207	32	4	3	7	10	1954-55	1954-55
Boileau, Marc	Detroit	1	54	5	6	11	8	....	....	....	....	....	1961-62	1969-70
Boimistruck, Fred	Toronto	2	83	4	14	18	45	....	....	....	....	....	1982-83	1983-84
Boivin, Leo	Tor., Bos., Det., Pit., Min.	18	1150	72	250	322	1192	54	3	10	13	59	1969-70	1969-70
Boldirev, Ivan	Bos., Cal., Chi., Atl., Van., Det.	15	1052	361	505	866	507	48	13	20	33	14	1984-85	1984-85
Bolduc, Danny	Det., Cgy.	3	102	22	19	41	33	1	0	0	0	0	1983-84	1984-85
Bolonchuk, Larry	Van., Wash.	1	74	3	9	12	97	....	....	....	....	....	1977-78	1979-80
Bolton, Hugh	Toronto	6	235	10	51	61	221	17	0	5	5	14	1956-57	1957-58
Bonar, Dan	Los Angeles	3	170	25	39	64	208	14	3	4	7	22	1982-83	1984-85
Bonin, Marcel	Det., Bos., Mtl.	8	454	97	175	272	336	50	11	14	25	51	1961-62	1961-62
Bordeleau, Christian	Mtl., St. L., Chi.	4	205	38	65	103	82	19	4	7	11	17	1971-72	1979-80
Bordeleau, J.P.	Chicago	9	519	97	126	223	143	48	3	6	9	12	1979-80	1981-82
Bordeleau, Paulin	Vancouver	3	183	33	56	89	47	5	2	1	3	0	1975-76	1978-79
Boucha, Henry	Det., Min., K.C., Colo.	6	247	53	49	102	157	....	....	....	....	....	1976-77	1976-77
Bouchard, Emile	Montreal	15	785	49	144	193	863	113	11	21	32	121	1955-56	1955-56
Bouchard, Pierre	Mtl., Wash.	11	595	24	82	106	233	76	3	10	13	56	1981-82	1981-82

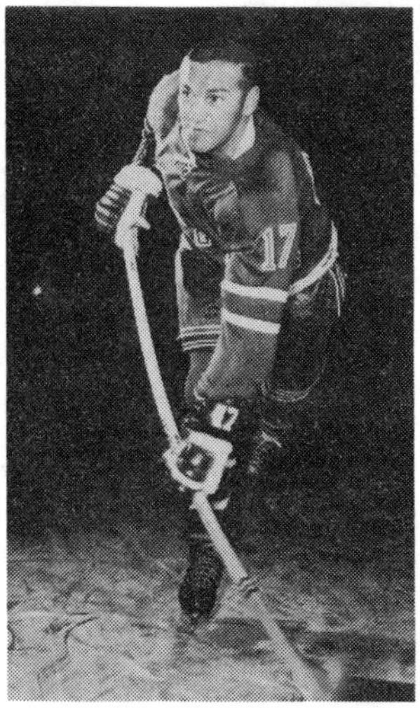
Dave Balon

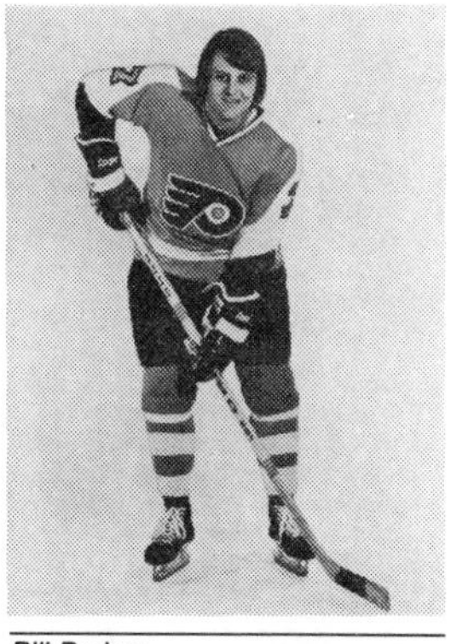
Bill Barber

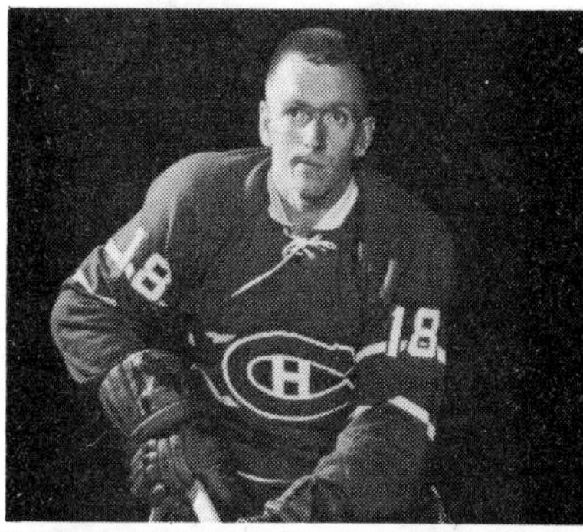
Red Berenson

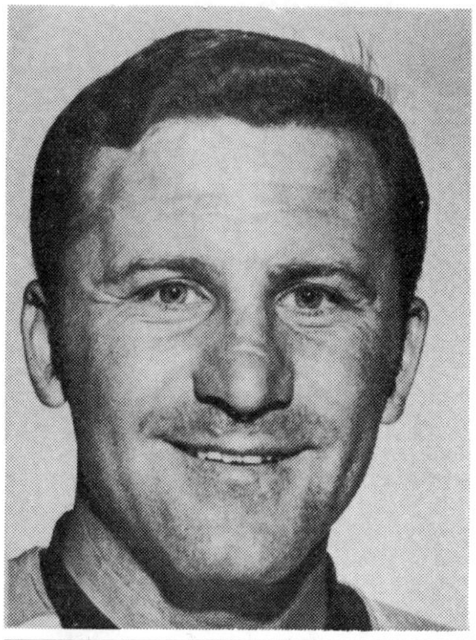
Wally Boyer

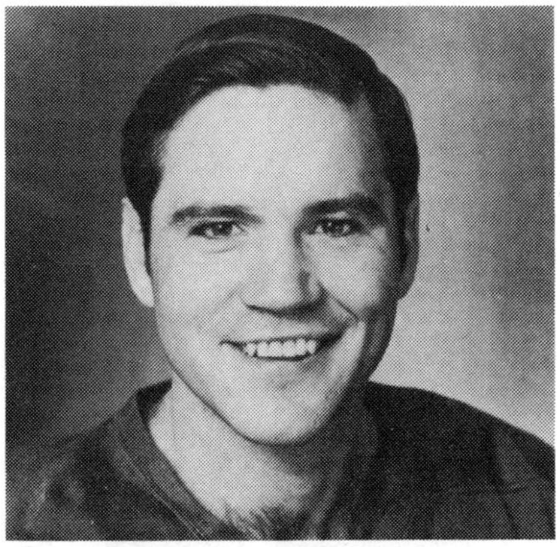

Arnie Brown

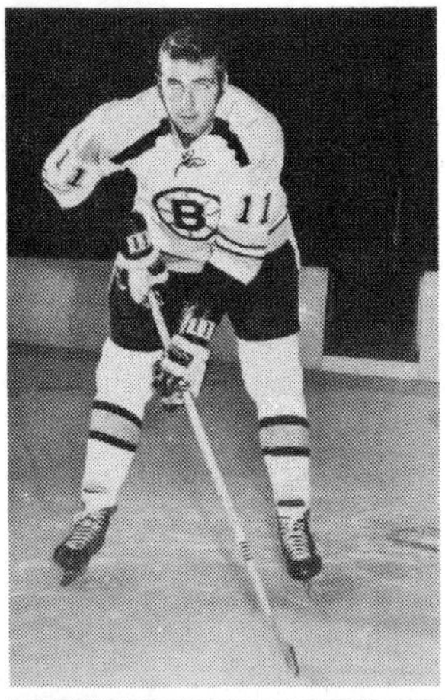

Wayne Carleton

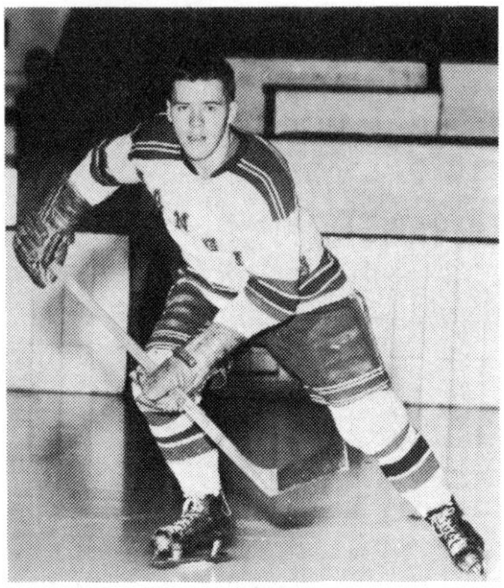

Billy Dea

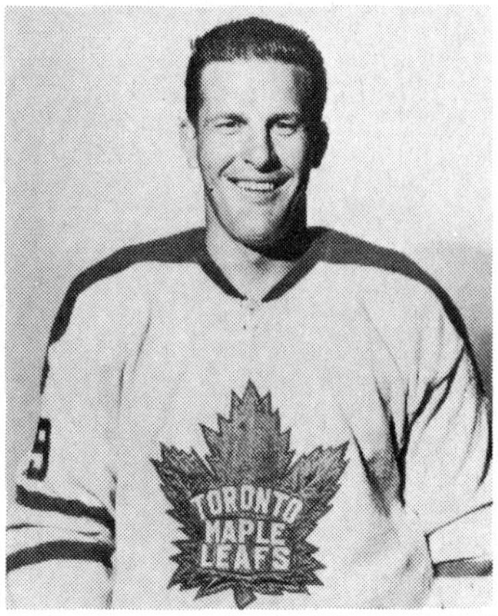

Kent Douglas

			Regular Schedule					Playoffs					Last	Last
Name	NHL Teams	NHL Seasons	GP	G	A	TP	PIM	GP	G	A	TP	PIM	NHL Season	Pro Season
Boudrias, Andre	Mtl., Min., St. L., Van.	9	662	151	340	91	218	34	6	104	16	12	1975-76	1977-78
Bourbonnais, Dan	Hartford	2	59	3	25	28	11	....	....	....	....	....	1983-84	1984-85
Bourbonnais, Rick	St. Louis	1	71	9	15	24	29	4	0	1	1	0	1977-78	1979-80
Boutette, Pat	Tor., Hfd., Pit.,	10	756	171	282	453	1354	46	10	14	24	109	1984-85	1984-85
Bowman, Kirk	Chicago	2	88	11	17	28	19	7	1	0	1	0	1978-79	1978-79
Bownass, Jack	Mtl., NYR	2	80	3	8	11	58	....	....	....	....	....	1961-62	1963-64
Bowness, Rick	Atl., Det., St. L., Wpg.	7	173	18	37	55	191	5	0	0	0	2	1981-82	1983-84
Boyer, Wally	Tor., Chi., Oak., Pit.	6	365	54	105	159	163	15	1	3	4	0	1971-72	1972-73
Brasar, Per-Olov	Min., Van.	5	348	64	142	206	33	13	1	2	3	0	1981-82	1981-82
Breitenbach, Ken	Buffalo	3	68	1	13	14	49	7	0	1	1	4	1978-79	1978-79
Brenneman, John	Chi., NYR, Tor., Det., Oak.	2	152	21	19	40	46	....	....	....	....	....	1968-69	1968-69
Brewer, Carl	Tor., Det., St. L.	12	604	25	198	223	1037	72	3	17	20	146	1979-80	1979-80
*Brière, Michel	Pittsburgh	1	76	12	32	44	20	10	5	3	8	17	1969-70	1969-70
Brooks, Gord	St. L., Wash.	1	70	7	18	25	37	....	....	....	....	....	1974-75	1980-81
Brossart, Willie	Phi., Tor., Wash.	3	129	1	14	15	88	1	0	0	0	0	1975-76	1975-76
*Brown, Adam	Det., Chi., Bos.	9	391	104	113	217	333	22	2	4	6	4	1951-52	1953-54
Brown, Arnie	Tor., NYR, Det., NYI, Atl.	10	681	44	141	185	738	22	0	6	6	23	1974-75	1974-75
Brown, Larry	NYR, Det., Phi., L.A.	9	455	7	53	60	180	35	0	4	4	10	1977-78	1979-80
Bruneteau, Ed	Detroit	4	180	40	42	82	35	26	7	6	13	0	1948-49	1953-54
Bucyk, John	Det., Bos.	23	1540	556	813	1369	497	124	41	62	103	42	1977-78	1977-78
*Buller, Hy	Det., NYR	3	188	22	58	80	215	....	....	....	....	....	1953-54	1953-54
Bulley, Ted	Chi., Wsh., Pit.	8	414	101	113	214	704	29	5	5	10	24	1983-84	1984-85
Burns, Charlie	Det., Bos., Oak., Pit., Min.	11	749	106	198	304	252	31	5	4	9	4	1972-73	1973-74
Burns, Robin	Pit., K.C.	3	190	31	38	69	139	....	....	....	....	....	1975-76	1975-76
Burrows, Dave	Pit., Tor.	10	724	29	135	164	373	29	1	5	6	25	1980-81	1980-81
Burton, Cumming	Detroit	1	43	0	2	2	21	3	0	0	0	0	1958-59	1962-63
Butler, Jerry	NYR, St. L., Tor., Van., Wpg.	11	641	99	120	219	515	48	3	3	6	79	1982-83	1982-83
Butters, Bill	Minnesota	1	72	1	4	5	77	....	....	....	....	....	1978-79	1979-80
Byers, Jerry	Min., Atl., NYR	1	43	2	5	7	15	....	....	....	....	....	1977-78	1979-80
Byers, Mike	Tor., Phi., Buf., L.A.	4	166	42	34	76	39	4	0	1	1	0	1971-72	1976-77
Caffery, Jack	Tor., Bos.	1	57	3	2	5	22	10	1	0	1	4	1957-58	1960-61
Cahan, Larry	Tor., NYR, Oak., L.A.	11	665	38	92	130	700	29	1	1	2	38	1970-71	1973-74
Callander, Drew	Phi., Van.	3	39	6	2	8	7	....	....	....	....	....	1979-80	1981-82
Callighen, Brett	Edmonton	3	160	56	89	145	132	14	4	6	10	8	1981-82	1981-82
Cameron, Al	Det., Wpg.	5	282	11	44	55	356	7	0	1	1	2	1980-81	1980-81
Cameron, Dave	Colo., N.J.	3	168	25	28	53	238	....	....	....	....	....	1983-84	1984-85
Cameron, Craig	Det., St. L., Min., NYI	8	552	87	65	152	202	27	3	1	4	17	1975-76	1976-77
Campbell, Bryan	L.A., Chi.	5	260	35	71	106	74	22	3	4	7	2	1971-72	1971-72
Campbell, Colin	Pit., Colo., Edm. Van., Det.	11	636	25	103	128	1292	45	4	10	14	181	1984-85	1984-85
Campbell, Scott	Wpg., St. L.	2	80	4	21	25	243	....	....	....	....	....	1981-82	1981-82
Cardwell, Steve	Pittsburgh	1	53	9	11	20	35	4	0	0	0	2	1972-73	1975-76
Carlson, Jack	Minn., St.L.	5	228	30	15	45	404	25	1	2	3	72	1983-84	1983-84
Carleton, Wayne	Tor., Bos., Cal.	4	278	55	73	128	172	18	2	4	6	14	1971-72	1973-74
Caron, Alain	Oak., Mtl.	2	60	9	13	22	18	....	....	....	....	....	1968-69	1971-72
Carr, Gene	St. L., NYR, L.A., Atl., Pit.	11	465	79	136	215	365	35	5	8	13	66	1978-79	1978-79
Carriere, Larry	Buf., Atl., Van., L.A., Tor.	7	416	17	83	100	517	27	0	3	3	42	1979-80	1979-80
Carveth, Joe	Det., Bos., Mtl.	10	504	150	189	339	81	69	21	16	37	28	1950-51	1951-52
Cashman, Wayne	Boston	17	1027	277	516	893	1041	145	31	57	88	250	1982-83	1982-83
Cernik, Frantisek	Detroit	1	49	5	4	9	13	....	....	....	....	....	1984-85	1984-85
Chad, John	Chicago	2	80	15	22	37	29	8	0	1	1	2	1945-46	1952-53
Chapman, Blair	Pit., St. L.	7	402	106	125	231	158	25	4	6	10	15	1982-83	1982-83
Charron, Guy	Mtl., Det., K.C., Wash.	11	734	221	309	530	146	....	....	....	....	....	1980-81	1980-81
Chartraw, Rick	Mtl., L.A., NYR, Edm.	10	420	28	64	92	399	75	7	9	16	80	1983-84	1983-84
Cherry, Dick	Bos., Phi.	2	145	12	10	22	45	4	1	0	1	4	1969-70	1970-71
Chevrefils, Real	Bos., Det.	7	387	104	97	201	185	30	5	4	9	20	1958-59	1962-63
Chipperfield, Ron	Edm., Que.	2	83	22	24	46	34	....	....	....	....	....	1980-81	1980-81
Chorney, Marc	Pit., L.A.	4	210	8	27	35	209	7	0	1	1	2	1983-84	1984-85
Chouinard, Guy	Atl., Cgy., St. L.	10	578	205	370	575	120	46	9	28	37	12	1983-84	1984-85
Christie. Mike	Cal., Clev., Colo., Van.	6	412	15	101	116	550	2	0	0	0	0	1980-81	1980-81
Christoff, Steve	Minn., Cgy., L.A.	5	248	77	64	141	108	35	16	12	28	25	1983-84	1983-84
Chrystal, Bob	NY Rangers	2	132	11	14	25	112	....	....	....	....	....	1954-55	1958-59
*Ciesla, Hank	Chi., NYR	4	269	26	51	77	87	6	0	2	2	0	1958-59	1964-65
Clackson, Kim	Pit., Que.	2	106	0	8	8	37	8	0	0	0	70	1980-81	1980-81
Clancy, Terry	Oak., Tor.	2	93	6	6	12	39	....	....	....	....	....	1972-73	1974-75
Clarke, Bobby	Philadelphia	15	1144	358	852	1210	1453	136	42	77	119	152	1983-84	1983-84
Clement, Bill	Phi., Wash., Atl., Cgy.	11	719	148	208	356	383	50	5	3	8	26	1981-82	1981-82
Cloutier, Real	Que., Buf.	6	369	283	383	566	169	48	33	30	63	31	1984-85	1984-85
Collins, Bill	Min., Mtl., Det., St. L., NYR, Phi., Wash.	11	768	157	154	311	415	18	3	5	8	12	1977-78	1977-78
Colwill, Leslie	NY Rangers	1	69	7	6	13	16	....	....	....	....	....	1958-59	1959-60
Comeau, Rey	Mtl., Atl., Colo.	8	564	98	141	239	175	9	2	1	3	8	1979-80	1980-81
Conacher, Brian	Tor., Det.	3	154	28	28	56	84	12	3	2	5	21	1971-72	1972-73
Conacher, Jim	Det., Chi., NYR	6	328	85	117	202	91	19	5	2	7	4	1952-53	1952-53
Conacher, Pete	Chi., NYR, Tor.	4	229	47	39	86	57	7	0	0	0	0	1957-58	1965-66
Conacher, Roy	Bos., Det., Chi.	10	490	226	200	426	90	42	15	15	30	14	1951-52	1952-52
Connelly, Wayne	Mtl., Bos., Min., Det., St. L., Van.	10	543	133	174	307	156	24	11	7	18	4	1971-72	1976-77
Contini, Joe	Colo., Min.	3	68	17	21	38	34	2	0	0	0	0	1980-81	1981-82
Cook, Bob	Van., Det., NYI, Min.	2	72	13	9	22	22	....	....	....	....	....	1974-75	1974-75
Cooper, Ed	Colorado	2	49	8	7	15	46	....	....	....	....	....	1981-82	1981-82
Corrigan, Mike	L.A., Van., Pit.	9	594	152	195	347	698	17	2	3	5	20	1977-78	1977-78
Cory, Ross	Winnipeg	2	51	2	10	12	41	....	....	....	....	....	1980-81	1981-82
Cossette, Jacques	Pittsburgh	2	64	8	6	14	29	3	0	1	1	4	1978-79	1979-80
Costello, Murray	Chi., Bos., Det.	3	162	13	19	32	54	5	0	0	0	2	1956-57	1956-57
Cournoyer, Yvan	Montreal	16	968	428	435	863	255	147	64	63	127	47	1978-79	1978-79
Couture, Gerry	Det., Mtl., Chi.	7	385	86	70	156	89	45	9	7	16	4	1953-54	1957-58
Cowick, Bruce	Phi., Wash., St. L.	1	70	5	6	11	43	8	0	0	0	9	1975-76	1975-76
Crashley, Bart	Det., K.C., L.A.	2	140	7	36	43	50	....	....	....	....	....	1975-76	1975-76
*Crawford, John	Boston	12	547	38	140	178	202	66	4	13	17	36	1949-50	1951-52
Creighton, Dave	Bos., Chi., Tor., NYR	10	615	140	174	314	223	51	11	13	24	20	1959-60	1968-69
Cressman, Dave	Minnesota	2	85	6	8	14	37	....	....	....	....	....	1975-76	1976-77
Crisp, Terry	Bos., St. L., NYI, Phi.	11	536	67	134	201	135	110	15	28	43	40	1976-77	1976-77
Crombeen, Mike	Clev., St. L., Hfd.	8	475	55	68	123	218	27	6	2	8	32	1984-85	1984-85
Croteau, Gary	L.A., Det., Cal., K.C., Colo.	12	684	144	175	319	143	11	3	2	5	8	1979-80	1979-80
Crowder, Bruce	Bos., Pit.	4	243	47	51	98	156	31	8	4	12	41	1984-85	1984-85
Cullen, Barry	Tor., Det.	4	219	32	52	84	111	6	0	0	0	2	1959-60	1963-64
Cullen, Brian	Tor., NYR	6	326	56	100	156	93	19	3	0	3	2	1960-61	1962-63
Cullen, Ray	NYR, Det., Min., Van.	5	313	92	123	215	120	20	3	10	13	2	1970-71	1970-71
Cummins, Barry	California	1	36	1	2	3	39	....	....	....	....	....	1973-74	1974-75
Curry, Floyd	Montreal	9	601	105	99	204	147	91	23	17	40	38	1957-58	1958-59
Curtis, Paul	Mtl., L.A., St. L.	3	185	3	34	37	151	5	0	0	0	2	1972-73	1975-76
Cushehan, Ian	Chi., Mtl., NYR, Det.	2	129	3	11	14	134	....	....	....	....	....	1963-64	1965-66
Daigle, Alain	Chicago	6	389	56	50	106	122	17	0	1	1	0	1979-80	1979-80
Dailey, Bob	Van., Phi.	9	561	94	231	325	814	63	12	34	46	106	1981-82	1981-82
David, Richard	Quebec	3	31	4	4	8	10	1	0	0	0	0	1982-83	1982-83
Davidson, Gord	NY Rangers	1	51	3	6	9	8	....	....	....	....	....	1943-44	1950-51
Davis, Kim	Pit., Tor.	3	36	5	7	12	51	....	....	....	....	....	1980-81	1981-82
Davis, Lorne	Mtl., Chi., Det., Bos.	2	95	8	12	20	20	18	3	1	4	10	1959-60	1960-61
Dea, Billy	NYR, Det., Chi., Pit.	6	397	67	54	121	44	11	2	0	2	6	1970-71	1971-72
Deadmarsh, Butch	Buf., Atl., K.C.	2	137	12	5	17	155	4	0	0	0	17	1974-75	1977-78
Dean, Barry	Colo., Phi.	3	165	25	56	81	146	....	....	....	....	....	1978-79	1981-82
Debenedet, Nelson	Det., Pit.	1	46	10	4	14	3	....	....	....	....	....	1974-75	1975-76
DeBol, Dave	Hartford	2	92	26	26	52	4	3	0	0	0	0	1980-81	1982-83
Delparte, Guy	Colorado	1	48	1	8	9	18	....	....	....	....	....	1976-77	1980-81

Name	NHL Teams	NHL Seasons	Regular Schedule GP	G	A	TP	PIM	Playoffs GP	G	A	TP	PIM	Last NHL Season	Last Pro Season
Delorme, Ron	Colo., Van.	9	524	83	83	166	667	25	1	2	3	59	1984-85	1984-85
Delvecchio, Alex	Detroit	23	1549	456	825	1281	383	121	35	69	104	29	1973-74	1973-74
DeMarco, Ab	Chi., Bos., Tor., NYR	4	209	72	93	165	53	11	3	0	3	2	1946-47	1951-52
DeMarco, Albert	NYR, St. L., Pit., Van., L.A., Bos.	13	344	44	80	124	75	25	1	2	3	17	1978-79	1978-79
Dewsbury, Al	Det., Chi.	5	347	30	78	108	365	14	1	5	6	60	1955-56	1957-58
Dickens, Ernie	Tor., Chi.	5	178	12	44	56	98	13	0	0	0	4	1950-51	1951-52
Dillabough, Bob	Det., Bos., Pit., Oak.	5	283	32	54	86	76	17	3	0	3	0	1971-72	1972-73
Dillon, Wayne	NYR, Wpg.	4	229	43	66	109	60	3	0	1	1	0	1979-80	1981-82
Dineen, Bill	Det., Chi.	5	323	51	44	95	122	37	1	1	2	18	1957-58	1970-71
Doak, Gary	Det., NYR, Van., Bos.	16	789	23	107	130	908	78	2	4	6	121	1980-81	1980-81
Dorey, Jim	Tor., NYR	5	232	25	74	99	553	11	0	2	2	40	1971-72	1978-79
Dornhoefer, Gary	Bos., Phi.	14	787	214	328	542	1291	80	17	19	36	203	1977-78	1977-78
Douglas, Jordy	Hfd., Min., Wpg.	6	268	76	62	138	160	6	0	0	0	4	1984-85	1984-85
Douglas, Kent	Tor., Oak., Det.	7	428	33	115	148	631	19	1	3	4	33	1968-69	1975-76
Driscoll, Peter	Edmonton	2	60	3	8	11	97	3	0	0	0	0	1980-81	1981-82
Drouin, Jude	Mtl., Min., NYI, Wpg.	10	666	151	305	456	346	72	27	41	68	33	1980-81	1980-81
Dube, Norm	Kansas City	1	57	8	10	18	54	....	....	....	....	....	1975-76	1979-80
Dudley, Rick	Buf., Wpg.	6	309	75	99	174	292	25	7	2	9	69	1980-81	1981-82
Duff, Dick	Tor., NYR, Mtl., L.A., Buf.	17	1030	283	289	572	743	114	30	49	79	78	1971-72	1971-72
Dumart, Woody	Boston	15	771	211	218	429	99	82	12	15	27	23	1953-54	1954-55
Dunlop, Blake	Minn., Phil., St.L., Det.	11	550	130	274	404	172	40	4	10	14	18	1983-84	1983-84
Dunn, Dave	Van., Tor.	3	184	14	41	55	313	10	1	1	2	41	1975-76	1977-78
Dupere, Denis	Tor., Wash., St. L., K.C.	7	421	80	99	179	66	16	1	0	1	0	1977-78	1977-78
Dupont, Andre	NYR., St. L., Phi., Que.	13	810	59	185	244	1986	140	14	18	32	352	1982-83	1982-83
Dupont, Norm	Mtl., Wpg., Hfd.	5	256	55	85	140	52	13	4	2	6	0	1983-84	1983-84
Durbano, Steve	St. L., Pit., K.C., Colo.	6	220	13	60	73	1127	5	0	2	2	8	1978-79	1978-79
Dvorak, Miroslav	Phi.	3	193	11	74	85	51	18	0	2	2	6	1984-85	1984-85
Dwyer, Mike	Colo., Cgy.	4	31	2	6	8	25	1	1	0	1	0	1981-82	1982-83
Dussault, Norm	Montreal	4	206	31	62	93	47	7	3	1	4	0	1950-51	1954-55
Ecclestone, Tim	St. L., Det., Tor., Atl.	11	692	126	233	359	346	48	6	11	17	76	1977-78	1977-78
Edberg, Rolf	Washington	3	184	45	58	103	24	....	....	....	....	....	1980-81	1980-81
*Eddolls, Frank	Mtl., NYR	6	317	23	43	66	114	31	0	2	2	10	1951-52	1953-54
Edestrand, Darryl	St. L., Phi., Pit., Bos., L.A.	10	455	34	90	124	404	42	3	9	12	57	1978-79	1979-80
Edmundston, Garry	Mtl., Tor.	1	43	4	6	10	49	11	0	1	1	8	1960-61	1963-64
Edur, Thomas	Colo., Pit.	2	158	17	70	87	67	....	....	....	....	....	1977-78	1977-78
Egan, Pat	NYA, Det., Bos., NYR	10	554	77	153	230	776	44	9	4	13	44	1950-51	1958-59
Egers, Jack	NYR, St. L., Wash.	4	284	64	69	133	154	32	5	6	11	32	1975-76	1975-76
Ehman, Gerry	Bos., Det., Tor., Oak.	6	429	96	118	214	100	41	10	10	21	12	1970-71	1970-71
Eldebrink, Anders	Van., Que.	2	55	3	11	14	29	14	0	0	0	0	1982-83	1982-83
Ellis, Ron	Toronto	15	1034	332	308	640	207	70	18	8	26	20	1980-81	1980-81
Eloranta, Kari	Cgy., L.A.	4	254	12	97	109	146	20	1	5	6	19	1984-85	1984-85
Erickson, Aut	Bos., Chi., Oak.	4	226	7	24	31	182	7	0	0	0	2	1969-70	1970-71
Eriksson, Bengt	Min., Van.	3	193	48	95	143	26	2	1	0	1	0	1978-79	1978-79
Esposito, Phil	Chi., Bos., NYR	18	1282	717	873	1590	910	130	61	76	137	137	1980-81	1980-81
Evans, Chris	Tor., Buf., St. L., Det. K.C.	4	241	19	42	61	143	12	1	1	2	8	1974-75	1980-81
Evans, Jack	NYR, Chi.	12	752	19	80	99	989	56	2	2	4	97	1962-63	1971-72
Evans, Paul	Phi.	3	103	14	25	39	34	1	0	0	0	0	1982-83	1984-85
Ezinicki, Bill	Tor., Bos., NYR	7	368	79	105	184	713	40	5	8	13	87	1954-55	1954-55
Fairbairn, Bill	NYR, Min., St. L.	11	658	162	261	423	173	54	13	22	35	42	1978-79	1978-79
Falkenberg, Bob	Detroit	1	54	1	5	6	26	....	....	....	....	....	1971-72	1971-72
Faubert, Mario	Pittsburgh	7	231	21	90	111	292	10	2	2	4	6	1981-82	1981-82
Faulkner, Alex	Tor., Det.	2	101	15	17	32	15	12	5	0	5	2	1963-64	1970-71
Feamster, Dave	Chicago	4	169	13	24	37	155	33	3	5	8	61	1984-85	1984-85
Featherstone, Tony	Oak., Cal., Min.	2	130	17	21	38	65	2	0	0	0	0	1973-74	1975-76
Ferguson, John	Montreal	8	500	145	158	303	1214	85	20	18	38	260	1970-71	1970-71
Ferguson, Lorne	Bos., Det., Chi.	7	422	82	80	162	193	31	6	3	9	24	1958-59	1961-62
Ferguson, Norm	Oak., Cal.	4	279	73	66	139	72	10	1	4	5	7	1971-72	1977-78
Fidler, Mike	Clev., Min., Hfd., Chi.	7	271	84	97	181	124	....	....	....	....	....	1982-83	1983-84
Field, Wilf	NYA, Mtl., Chi.	5	218	17	25	42	151	3	0	0	0	0	1944-45	1951-52
Finney, Sid	Chicago	1	59	10	7	17	4	7	0	0	0	2	1953-54	1963-64
Fisher, Dunc	NYR, Bos., Det.	5	275	45	70	115	10	221	4	4	8	14	1958-59	1959-60
Fitchner, Dave	Quebec	2	78	12	20	32	59	3	0	0	0	10	1980-81	1980-81
Flaman, Fern	Bos., Tor.	15	910	34	174	208	1370	63	4	8	12	93	1960-61	1963-64
Fleming, Reg	Mtl., Chi., Bos., NYR, Phi., Buf.	11	749	108	132	240	1468	50	3	6	9	106	1970-71	1973-74
Flett, Bill	L.A., Phi., Tor., Atl., Edm.	11	689	202	215	417	501	52	7	16	23	42	1979-80	1979-80
Flockhart, Rob	Van., Min.	5	55	2	5	7	14	1	1	0	1	2	1980-81	1984-85
Fogolin, Lee	Det., Chi.	7	427	10	48	58	575	28	0	2	2	30	1955-56	1956-57
Foley, Gerry	Tor., NYR, L.A.	2	142	9	14	23	99	9	0	1	1	2	1957-58	1968-69
Foley, Rick	Chi., Phi., Det.	1	67	11	26	37	180	4	0	1	1	4	1973-74	1975-76
Fontaine, Len	Detroit	1	46	8	11	19	10	....	....	....	....	....	1973-74	1973-74
Fonteyne, Val	Det., NYR, Pit.	13	820	75	154	229	26	59	3	10	13	8	1971-72	1973-74
Fontinato, Lou	NYR, Mtl.	9	535	26	78	104	1247	21	0	2	2	42	1962-63	1962-63
Forbes, Dave	Bos., Wash.	6	363	64	64	128	341	45	1	4	5	13	1978-79	1979-80
Fortier, Dave	Tor., NYI, Van.	4	205	8	21	29	335	20	0	2	2	33	1976-77	1977-78
Fortin, Ray	St. Louis	2	92	2	6	8	33	6	0	0	0	8	1969-70	1973-74
Fox, Greg	Atl., Chi., Pit.	8	494	14	92	106	637	44	1	9	10	67	1984-85	1984-85
Frig, Len	Chi., Cal., Clev., St. L.	6	311	13	51	64	479	14	2	1	3	0	1979-80	1980-81
Ftorek, Robbie	Det., Que., NYR,	8	334	77	150	227	262	19	9	6	15	28	1984-85	1984-85
Fusco, Mark	Hartford	2	80	3	12	15	42	....	....	....	....	....	1984-85	1984-85
Gadsby, Bill	Chi., NYR, Det.	20	1248	130	437	567	1539	67	4	23	27	92	1965-66	1965-66
Gagnon, Germain	Mtl., NYI, Chi., K.C.	4	259	40	101	141	72	19	2	3	5	2	1975-76	1975-76
Gamble, Dick	Mtl., Chi., Tor.	3	195	41	41	82	66	14	1	2	3	4	1966-67	1969-70
Gambucci, Gary	Minnesota	1	51	2	7	9	9	....	....	....	....	....	1973-74	1975-76
Gardner, Cal	NYR, Tor., Chi., Bos.	11	696	154	238	392	517	61	7	10	17	20	1956-57	1960-61
Gardner, Dave	Mtl., St. L., Cal., Clev., Phi.	7	350	75	115	190	41	....	....	....	....	....	1979-80	1979-80
Gariepy, Ray	Bos., Tor.	1	36	1	6	7	43	....	....	....	....	....	1955-56	1955-56
*Garland, Scott	Tor., L.A.	3	91	13	24	37	115	7	1	2	3	35	1978-79	1978-79
*Gassoff, Bob	St. Louis	4	245	11	47	58	866	9	0	1	1	16	1976-77	1976-77
Gassoff, Brad	Vancouver	2	122	19	17	36	163	3	0	0	0	0	1978-79	1979-80
Gauthier, Jean	Mtl., Phi., Bos.	3	166	6	29	35	150	14	1	3	4	22	1969-70	1973-74
*Gee, George	Chi., Det.	9	551	135	183	318	245	41	6	13	19	32	1953-54	1953-54
Gendron, Jean-Guy	NYR, Mtl., Bos., Phi.	13	863	182	201	383	701	42	7	4	11	47	1971-72	1973-74
Geoffrion, Bernie	Mtl., NYR	16	883	393	429	822	689	132	58	60	118	88	1967-68	1967-68
Geoffrion, Dan	Mtl., Wpg.	3	111	20	32	52	99	2	0	0	0	7	1981-82	1982-83
Gibbs, Barry	Bos., Min., Atl., St. L., L.A.	12	797	58	224	282	945	36	4	2	6	67	1979-80	1980-81
Gibson, Doug	Bos., Wash.	1	63	9	19	28	0	1	0	0	0	0	1977-78	1979-80
Gibson, John	L.A., Tor., Wpg.	3	48	0	2	2	120	....	....	....	....	....	1983-84	1983-84
Gilbert, Ed	K.C., Pit.	3	166	21	31	52	22	....	....	....	....	....	1976-77	1976-77
Gilbert, Rod	NY Rangers	16	1065	406	615	1021	508	79	34	33	67	43	1977-78	1977-78
Gilbertson, Stan	Cal., St. L., Wash., Pit.	7	428	85	89	174	148	3	1	1	2	2	1976-77	1976-77
Gillis, Mike	Colo., Bos.	6	246	33	43	76	186	27	2	5	7	10	1983-84	1983-84
Girard, Bob	Cal., Clev., Wash.	5	305	45	69	114	140	....	....	....	....	....	1979-80	1979-80
Giroux, Larry	St. L., K.C., Det., Hfd.	9	274	15	74	89	333	5	0	0	0	0	1979-80	1979-80
Gladu, Jean-Paul	Boston	1	40	6	14	20	2	....	....	....	....	....	1944-45	1955-56
Glennie, Brian	Tor., L.A.	10	572	14	100	114	621	32	0	1	1	66	1978-79	1978-79
Glover, Fred	Det., Chi.	2	92	13	11	24	62	4	0	0	0	0	1952-53	1967-68
Glover, Howie	Chi., Det., NYR, Mtl.	3	144	29	17	46	101	11	1	2	3	2	1968-69	1969-70
Godfrey, Warren	Bos., Det.	12	786	32	125	157	752	52	1	4	5	42	1967-68	1968-69
Goegan, Pete	Det., NYR, Min.	6	383	19	67	86	365	33	1	3	4	61	1967-68	1968-69
Goldham, Bob	Tor., Chi., Det.	11	650	28	143	171	400	66	3	14	17	53	1955-56	1955-56
Goldsworthy, Bill	Bos., Min., NYR	15	771	283	258	541	793	40	18	19	37	30	1977-78	1978-79
Gooden, Bill	NY Rangers	1	53	9	11	20	15	....	....	....	....	....	1943-44	1955-56

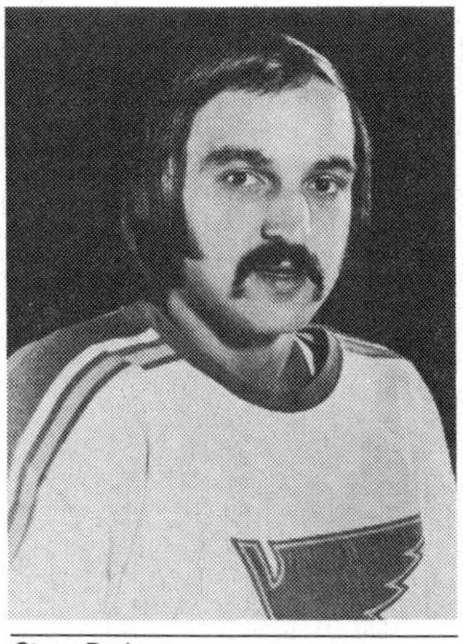

Steve Durbano

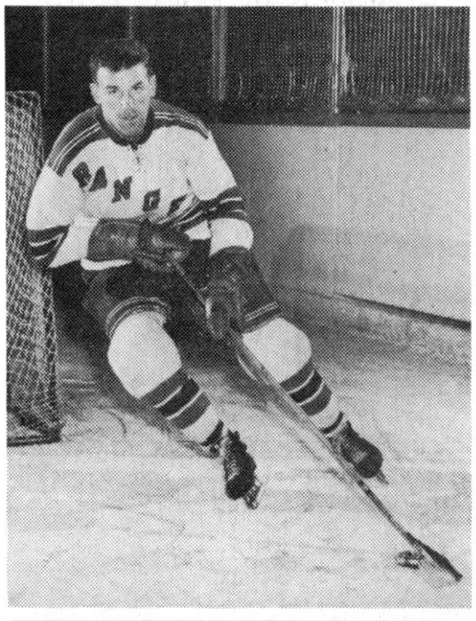

Jack Evans

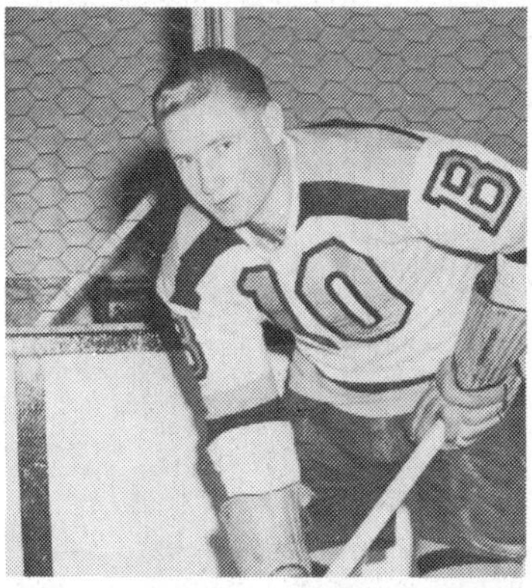

Fernie Flaman

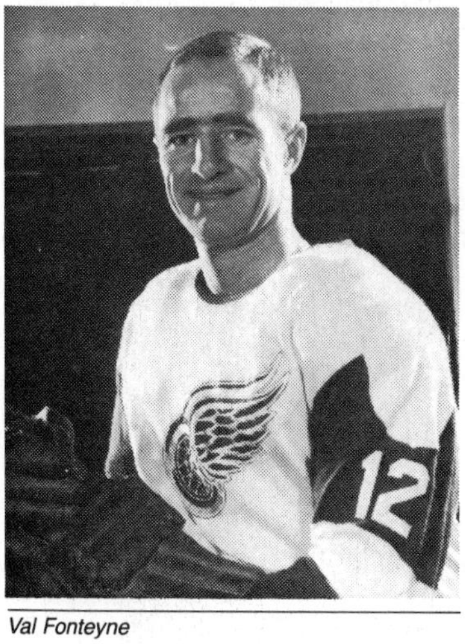

Val Fonteyne

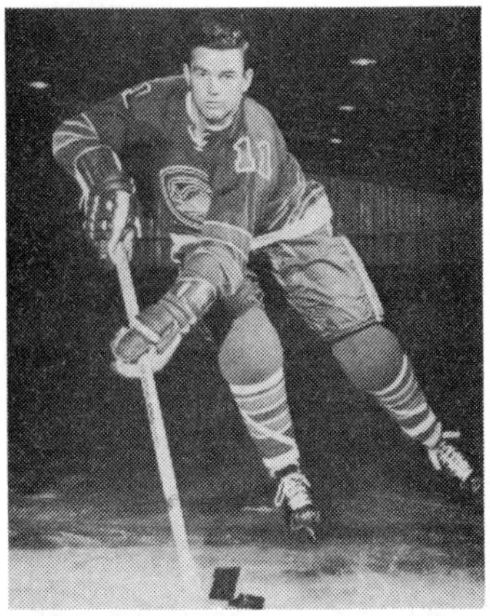
Ted Hampson

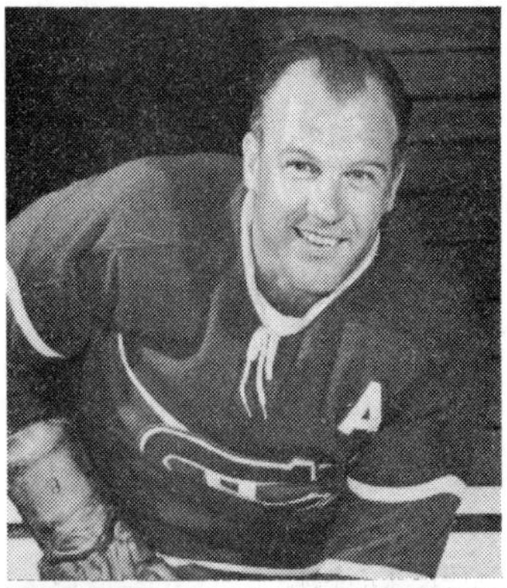
Glen Harmon

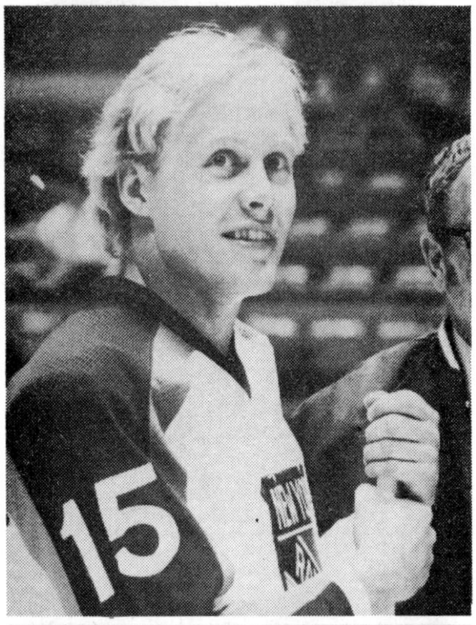
Anders Hedberg

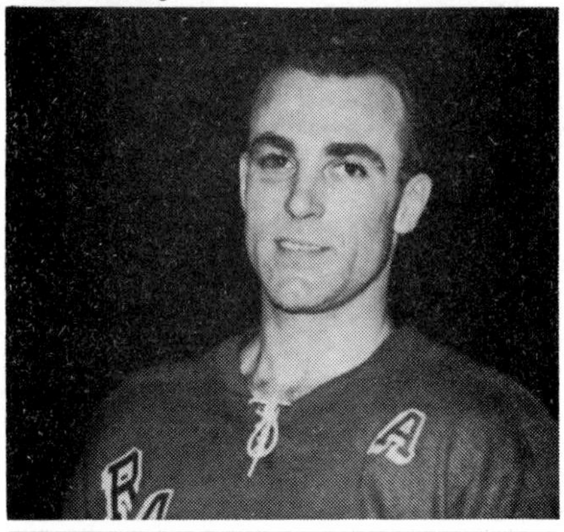
Harry Howell

			Regular Schedule					Playoffs					Last	Last
Name	NHL Teams	NHL Seasons	GP	G	A	TP	PIM	GP	G	A	TP	PIM	NHL Season	Pro Season
Goodenough, Larry	Phi., Van.	6	242	22	77	99	179	22	3	15	18	10	1979-80	1982-83
Gorence, Tom	Phi., Edm.	6	303	58	53	111	89	37	9	6	15	47	1983-84	1984-85
Goring, Butch	L.A., NYI., Bos.	16	1107	375	513	888	102	134	38	50	88	32	1984-85	1984-85
Gould, John	Buf., Van., Atl.	9	504	131	138	269	113	14	3	2	5	4	1979-80	1979-80
Goyer, Gerry	Chicago	1	40	1	2	3	4	3	0	0	0	2	1967-68	1973-74
Goyette, Phil	Mtl., NYR, St. L., Buf.	15	941	207	467	674	131	94	17	29	46	26	1971-72	1971-72
Graham, Pat	Pit., Tor.	3	103	11	17	28	136	4	0	0	0	2	1983-84	1984-85
Grant, Danny	Mtl., Det., Min., L.A.	13	736	263	273	536	239	43	10	14	24	19	1978-79	1981-82
Gratton, Norm	NYR, Atl., Buf., Min.	4	201	39	44	83	64	6	0	1	1	2	1975-76	1975-76
Gravelle, Leo	Mtl., Det.	4	223	44	34	78	42	17	4	1	5	2	1950-51	1955-56
Graves, Hilliard	Cal., Atl., Van., Wpg.	9	556	118	163	281	209	2	0	0	0	0	1979-80	1979-80
Gray, Terry	Bos., Mtl., L.A., St. L.	3	147	26	28	54	64	35	5	5	10	22	1970-71	1973-74
Green, Ted	Boston	11	620	48	206	254	1029	31	4	8	12	54	1971-72	1978-79
Grenier, Lucien	Mtl., L.A.	3	151	14	14	28	18	2	0	0	0	0	1971-72	1974-75
Grisdale, John	Tor., Van.	6	250	4	39	43	346	10	0	1	1	15	1978-79	1978-79
Gruen, Danny	Det., Colo.	3	49	9	13	22	19	....	....	....	....	....	1976-77	1978-79
Gryp, Bob	Bos., Wash.	3	74	11	13	24	33	....	....	....	....	....	1975-76	1975-76
Guevremont, Jocelyn	Van., Buf., NYR	9	571	84	223	307	319	40	4	17	21	18	1979-80	1979-80
Guidolin, Aldo	NY Rangers	3	182	9	15	24	117	....	....	....	....	....	1955-56	1968-69
Guidolin, Bep	Bos., Det., Chi.	9	519	107	171	278	606	24	5	7	12	35	1951-52	1954-55
Hadfield, Vic	NYR, Pit.	16	1002	323	389	712	1154	73	27	21	48	117	1976-77	1976-77
Hagman, Matti	Bos., Edm.	4	237	56	89	145	36	20	5	2	7	6	1981-82	1981-82
Hale, Larry	Philadelphia	4	196	5	37	42	90	8	0	0	0	12	1971-72	1978-79
Hall, Murray	Chi., Det., Min., Van.	3	164	35	48	83	46	6	0	0	0	0	1971-72	1975-76
Hamel, Jean	St.L., Det., Que., Mtl.	12	699	26	95	121	766	33	0	2	2	44	1983-84	1983-84
Hamil, Red	Bos., Chi.	7	442	128	94	222	160	13	1	2	3	12	1950-51	1950-51
Hamilton, Al	NYR, Buf., Edm.	7	257	10	78	88	258	7	0	0	0	2	1979-80	1979-80
Hamilton, Jack	Toronto	3	138	331	48	79	76	11	2	1	3	0	1945-46	1953-54
Hamilton, Jim	Pittsburgh	8	95	14	18	32	28	6	3	0	3	0	1984-85	1984-85
Hammarstrom, Inge	Tor., St. L.	6	427	116	123	239	86	13	2	3	5	4	1978-79	1978-79
Hampson, Ted	Tor., NYR, Det., Oak., Cal., Min.	12	676	108	245	353	94	35	7	10	17	2	1971-72	1979-80
Hampton, Rick	Cal., Clev., L.A.	5	337	59	113	172	147	2	0	0	0	0	1979-80	1980-81
Hangsleben, Al	Hfd., Wash., L.A.	3	185	21	48	69	396	....	....	....	....	....	1981-82	1983-84
Hanna, John	NYR, Mtl., Phi.	4	198	6	26	32	206	....	.....	....	....	....	1971-72	1972-73
*Hannigan, Gord	Toronto	3	161	29	31	60	117	9	2	0	2	8	1955-56	1957-58
Hannigan, Pat	Tor., NYR, Phi.	3	182	30	39	69	116	11	1	2	3	11	1968-69	1970-71
Harbaruk, Nick	Pit., St. L.	5	364	45	75	120	273	14	3	1	4	20	1973-74	1976-77
Hardy, Jocelyn	Oak., Cal.	2	63	9	14	23	51	4	0	0	0	0	1970-71	1977-78
Hargreaves, Jim	Vancouver	1	66	1	7	8	105	....	....	....	....	....	1972-73	1974-75
Harmon, Glen	Montreal	9	452	50	96	146	334	53	5	10	15	37	1950-51	1954-55
Harper, Terry	Mtl., L.A., Det., St. L., Colo.	18	1066	35	221	256	1362	112	4	13	17	140	1980-81	1980-81
Harris, Ted	Mtl., Min., Det. , St. L., Phi.	11	788	30	168	198	1000	100	1	22	23	230	1974-75	1974-75
Harris, Hugh	Buffalo	1	60	12	26	38	17	3	0	0	0	0	1972-73	1977-78
Harris, Ron	Det., Oak., Atl., NYR	8	476	20	91	111	484	28	4	3	7	33	1975-76	1975-76
Harris, Billy	NYI, L.A., Tor.	12	897	231	327	558	394	71	19	19	38	48	1983-84	1983-84
Harris, Billy	Tor., Det., Oak., Pit.	12	769	126	219	345	205	62	8	10	18	30	1968-69	1968-69
Harrison, Ed	Bos., NYR	3	194	27	24	51	53	9	1	0	1	2	1950-51	1953-54
Harrison, Jim	Bos., Tor., Chi., Edm.	8	324	67	86	153	435	13	1	1	2	43	1979-80	1979-80
Hart, Gerry	Det., NYI, Que., St. L.	15	730	29	150	179	1240	78	3	12	15	175	1982-83	1982-83
Harvey, Doug	Mtl., NYR, Det., St. L.	18	1113	88	452	540	1216	137	8	64	72	152	1968-69	1968-69
Harvey, Fred	Min., Atl., K.C., Det.	5	407	90	118	208	131	14	0	2	2	8	1976-77	1977-78
Hassard, Bob	Tor., Chi.	2	126	9	28	37	22	....	....	....	....	....	1954-55	1957-58
Hatoum, Ed	Det., Van.	2	47	3	6	9	25	....	....	....	....	....	1970-71	1973-74
Hay, Bill	Chicago	8	506	113	273	386	244	67	15	21	36	62	1966-67	1966-67
Hay, Jim	Detroit	2	75	1	5	6	22	9	1	0	1	2	1954-55	1970-71
Heaslip, Mark	NYR, L.A.	2	117	10	19	29	110	5	0	0	0	2	1978-79	1979-80
Hebenton, Andy	NYR, Bos.	9	630	189	202	391	83	22	6	5	11	8	1963-64	1974-75
Hedberg, Anders	NY Rangers	7	465	172	225	397	144	58	22	24	46	31	1984-85	1984-85
Hienrich, Lionel	Boston	1	35	1	1	2	33	....	....	....	....	....	1955-56	1957-58
Heiskala, Earl	Philadelphia	3	127	13	11	24	294	....	....	....	....	....	1970-71	1973-74
*Heller, Ott	NY Rangers	15	647	55	176	231	465	61	6	8	14	61	1945-46	1954-55
Henderson, Murray	Boston	7	405	24	62	86	305	41	2	3	4	23	1951-52	1955-56
Henderson, Paul	Det., Tor., Atl.	13	707	236	241	477	304	56	11	14	25	28	1979-80	1979-80
Henning, Lorne	NY Islanders	8	544	73	111	184	102	81	7	7	14	8	1980-81	1980-81
Henry, Camille	NYR, Chi., St. L.	12	727	279	249	528	88	47	6	12	18	7	1969-70	1969-70
Hergesheimer, Phil	Chi., Bos.	3	125	21	41	62	19	7	0	0	0	2	1942-43	1950-51
Hergesheimer, Wally	NYR, Chi.	6	351	114	85	199	106	5	1	0	1	0	1958-59	1961-62
Hess, Bob	St. L., Buf., Hfd.	8	329	27	95	122	178	4	1	1	2	2	1983-84	1984-85
Hextall, Bryan	NYR, Pit., Atl., Det., Min.	9	549	99	161	260	738	18	0	4	4	59	1975-76	1975-76
Hextall, Dennis	NYR, L.A., Cal., Min., Det., Wash.	13	681	153	350	503	1398	22	3	3	6	45	1979-80	1979-80
Hicke, Bill	Mtl., NYR, Oak.	12	729	168	234	402	395	42	3	10	13	41	1971-72	1972-73
Hicke, Ernie	Cal., Atl., NYI, Min., L.A.	8	520	132	140	272	407	2	1	0	1	0	1977-78	1979-80
Hickey, Pat	NYR., Colo., Tor., Que., St. L.	10	646	192	212	404	351	55	5	11	16	37	1984-85	1984-85
Hicks, Doug	Min., Chi., Edm., Wash.	9	561	37	131	168	442	....	....	....	....	....	1982-83	1983-84
Hicks, Wayne	Chi., Bos., Mtl., Phi., Pit.	2	115	13	23	36	22	2	0	1	1	2	1967-68	1973-74
Hildebrand, Ike	NYR, Chi.	2	41	7	11	18	16	....	....	....	....	....	1954-55	1955-56
Hillman, Larry	Det., Bos., Tor., Min., Mtl., Phi., L.A., Buf.	12	790	36	196	232	579	74	2	9	11	30	1972-73	1974-75
Hillman, Wayne	Chi., NYR, Min., Phi.	12	691	18	86	104	534	28	0	3	3	19	1972-73	1974-75
Hilworth, John	Detroit	2	57	1	1	2	89	....	....	....	....	....	1979-80	1980-81
Hislop, Jamie	Que., Cgy.	5	345	75	103	178	86	28	3	2	5	11	1983-84	1983-84
Hlinka, Ivan	Vancouver	2	137	42	81	123	28	16	3	10	13	8	1982-83	1982-83
Hodge, Ken	Chi., Bos., NYR	13	881	328	472	800	779	97	34	47	81	120	1977-78	1977-78
Hoekstra, Ed	Philadelphia	1	70	15	21	36	6	7	0	1	1	0	1967-68	1973-74
Hoene, Phil	Los Angeles	1	37	2	4	6	22	....	....	....	....	....	1974-75	1975-76
Hogaboam, Bill	Atl., Det., Min.	8	332	80	109	189	100	2	0	0	0	0	1979-80	1982-83
Hoganson, Dale	Mtl., L.A., Que.	8	343	13	77	90	186	11	0	3	3	12	1981-82	1981-82
Holbrook, Terry	Minnesota	2	43	3	6	9	4	6	0	0	0	0	1973-74	1976-77
Holland, Jerry	NY Rangers	1	37	8	4	12	6	....	....	....	....	....	1975-76	1978-79
*Hollingworth, Gordy	Chi., Det.	3	163	4	14	18	201	3	0	0	0	2	1957-58	1961-62
Holmgren, Paul	Phi., Min.	10	527	144	179	323	1684	82	19	32	51	195	1984-85	1984-85
Holt, Gary	Cal., Clev., St. L.	2	101	13	11	24	183	....	....	....	....	....	1977-78	1978-79
Holt, Randy	Chi., Clev., Van., L.A., Cgy., Wash., Phil.	10	395	4	37	41	1438	21	2	3	5	83	1983-84	1983-84
Hopkins, Larry	Tor., Wpg.	4	60	13	16	29	26	6	0	0	0	2	1982-83	1982-83
Horeck, Pete	Chi., Det., Bos.	8	426	106	118	224	340	34	6	8	14	43	1951-52	1951-52
Hornung, Larry	St. Louis	1	48	2	9	11	10	11	0	2	2	2	1971-72	1971-72
*Horton, Tim	Tor., NYR, Pit., Buf.	22	1446	115	403	518	1611	126	11	39	50	183	1973-74	1973-74
Horvath, Bronco	NYR, Mtl., Bos., Chi., Tor., Min.	7	434	141	185	326	319	36	12	9	21	18	1967-68	1969-70
Houde, Claude	Kansas City	2	59	3	6	9	40	....	....	....	....	....	1975-76	1976-77
Houle, Rejean	Montreal	11	635	161	247	408	395	90	14	34	48	66	1982-83	1982-83
Houston, Ken	Atl., Cgy., Wash., L.A.	9	570	161	167	328	624	35	10	9	19	66	1983-84	1983-84
Howe, Gordie	Det., Hfd.	26	1767	801	1049	1850	1685	157	68	42	160	220	1979-80	1979-80
Howe, Marty	Hfd., Bos.	6	449	67	117	184	460	75	9	14	23	85	1984-85	1984-85
Howatt, Garry	NYI, Hfd., N.J.	12	720	112	156	268	1836	87	12	14	26	289	1983-84	1983-84
Howell, Harry	NYR, Oak., L.A.	21	1411	94	324	418	1298	38	3	3	6	32	1972-73	1973-74
Hoyda, Dave	Phi., Wpg.	3	132	6	17	23	299	12	0	0	0	17	1980-81	1980-81
Hrechkosy, Dave	Cal., St. L.	2	140	42	24	66	41	3	1	0	1	2	1979-80	1979-80
Hubick, Greg	Tor., Van.	2	77	6	9	15	10	....	....	....	....	....	1979-80	1981-82
Huck, Fran	Mtl., St. L.	2	94	24	30	54	38	11	3	4	7	2	1972-73	1974-75
Hucul, Fred	Chi., St. L.	2	164	11	30	41	113	6	1	0	1	10	1967-68	1968-69

Name	NHL Teams	NHL Seasons	Regular Schedule GP	G	A	TP	PIM	Playoffs GP	G	A	TP	PIM	Last NHL Season	Last Pro Season
Hudson, Dave	NYI, K.C., Colo.	5	409	59	124	183	89	2	1	1	2	0	1977-78	1977-78
Hughes, Brent	L.A., Phi., St. L, Det., K.C.	8	435	15	117	132	440	22	1	3	4	53	1974-75	1979-80
Hughes, Howie	Los Angeles	3	168	25	32	57	30	14	2	0	2	2	1969-70	1974-75
Hughes, Jack	Colorado	2	46	2	5	7	104	....	....	....	....	....	1981-82	1981-82
Hughes, John	Van., Edm., NYR	2	70	2	14	16	211	7	0	1	1	16	1980-81	1981-82
Hull, Bobby	Chic., Wpg., Hfd.	16	1063	610	560	1170	640	119	62	67	129	102	1979-80	1979-80
Hull, Dennis	Chi., Det.	14	959	303	351	654	261	104	33	34	67	30	1977-78	1977-78
Hurst, Ron	Toronto	1	64	9	7	16	7	3	0	2	2	4	1956-57	1959-60
Huston, Ron	California	2	79	15	31	46	8	....	....	....	....	....	1974-75	1974-75
Hutchison, David	L.A., Tor., Chi., N.J.	10	584	19	97	116	1550	48	2	12	14	149	1983-84	1983-84
Ingarfield, Earl	NYR, Pit., Oak., Cal.	12	746	179	226	405	239	21	9	8	17	10	1970-71	1970-71
Ingarfield, Earl, Jr.	Atl., Cgy., Det.	2	39	4	4	8	22	2	0	1	1	0	1980-81	1982-83
Inglis, Bill	L.A., Buf.	1	36	1	3	4	4	11	1	2	3	4	1970-71	1977-78
Ingram, Ron	Chi., Det., NYR	2	114	5	15	20	81	2	0	0	0	0	1964-65	1969-70
Irvine, Ted	Bos., L.A., NYR, St. L.	11	724	154	177	331	657	83	16	24	40	115	1976-77	1976-77
Irwin, Ivan	Mtl., NYR	3	155	2	27	29	214	5	0	0	0	8	1957-58	1959-60
Jacobs, Tim	California	1	46	0	10	10	35	....	....	....	....	....	1975-76	1978-79
James, Gerry	Toronto	3	149	14	26	40	257	15	1	0	1	8	1959-60	1960-61
Jankowski, Lou	Det., Chi.	2	127	19	18	37	15	1	0	0	0	0	1954-55	1968-69
Jarrett, Doug	Chi., NYR	13	775	38	182	220	631	99	7	16	23	82	1976-77	1976-77
Jarrett, Gary	Tor., Det., Oak., Cal.	5	341	72	92	164	131	11	3	1	4	9	1971-72	1975-76
Jarry, Pierre	NYR, Tor., Det., Min.	7	344	88	117	205	142	5	0	1	1	0	1977-78	1977-78
Jeffrey, Larry	Det., Tor., NYR	6	368	39	62	101	293	38	4	10	14	42	1968-69	1968-69
Jensen, Steve	Min., L.A.	7	439	113	107	220	318	12	0	3	3	9	1981-82	1981-82
Jodzio, Rick	Colo., Clev.	1	70	2	8	10	71	....	....	....	....	....	1977-78	1979-80
Johansen, Trevor	Tor., Colo., L.A.	5	286	11	46	57	282	13	0	3	3	21	1981-82	1982-83
Johns, Don	NYR, Mtl., Min.	3	153	2	21	23	76	....	....	....	....	....	1967-68	1968-69
Johnson, Al	Mtl., Det.	2	105	21	28	49	30	11	2	2	4	6	1961-62	1968-69
Johnson, Danny	Tor., Van., Det.	2	121	18	19	37	24	....	....	....	....	....	1971-72	1974-75
Johnson, Jim	NYR, Phi., L.A.	5	302	75	111	186	73	7	0	2	2	2	1971-72	1974-75
Johnson, Norm	Bos., Chi.	2	61	5	20	25	41	14	4	0	4	6	1958-59	1970-71
Johnson, Tom	Mtl., Bos.	15	978	51	213	264	960	111	8	15	23	109	1964-65	1964-65
Johnston, Bernie	Hartford	2	57	12	24	36	44	3	0	1	1	0	1980-81	1982-83
Johnston, George	Chicago	2	58	20	12	32	2	....	....	....	....	....	1946-47	1952-53
Johnston, Joey	Min., Cal., Chi.	5	332	85	106	191	320	....	....	....	....	....	1975-76	1975-76
Johnston, Larry	L.A., Det., K.C., Colo.	7	320	9	64	73	580	....	....	....	....	....	1976-77	1976-77
Johnston, Marshall	Min., Cal.	5	251	14	52	66	58	6	0	0	0	2	1973-74	1973-74
Jonathan, Stan	Bos., Pit.	8	411	91	110	201	751	63	8	4	12	137	1982-83	1982-83
Jones, Jimmy	Toronto	2	148	13	18	31	68	19	1	5	6	11	1979-80	1980-81
Jones, Ron	Bos., Pit., Wash.	5	54	1	4	5	31	....	....	....	....	....	1975-76	1976-77
Joyal, Eddie	Det., Tor., L.A., Phi.	7	466	128	134	262	103	50	11	8	19	18	1971-72	1974-75
Juzda, Bill	NYR, Tor.	8	393	14	54	68	398	42	0	3	3	46	1951-52	1955-56
Kabel, Bob	NY Rangers	1	48	5	13	18	34	....	....	....	....	....	1960-61	1969-70
Kaiser, Vern	Montreal	1	50	7	5	12	33	2	0	0	0	0	1950-51	1953-54
Kachur, Eddie	Chicago	2	96	10	14	24	35	....	....	....	....	....	1957-58	1969-70
Kaleta, Alex	Chi., NYR	7	387	92	121	213	190	17	1	6	7	2	1950-51	1954-55
Kallur, Anders	NY Islanders	6	383	101	110	211	149	78	12	23	35	32	1984-85	1984-85
Kannegiesser, Sheldon	Pit., NYR, L.A., Van.	6	366	14	67	81	202	18	0	2	2	10	1977-78	1977-78
Karlander, Al	Detroit	4	212	36	56	92	70	4	0	1	1	0	1972-73	1976-77
Kaszycki, Mike	NYI., Wsh., Tor.	5	226	42	80	122	108	19	2	6	8	10	1982-83	1984-85
Kea, Ed	Atl., St. L.	10	583	30	145	175	508	32	2	4	6	39	1982-83	1982-83
Kearns, Dennis	Vancouver	10	677	31	290	321	386	11	1	2	3	8	1980-81	1980-81
Keenan, Larry	Tor., St. L., Buf., Phi.	5	233	38	64	102	28	46	15	16	31	12	1971-72	1973-74
Kehoe, Rick	Tor., Pit.	14	906	371	396	767	120	39	4	17	21	4	1984-85	1984-85
Kelly, Bob	St. L., Pit., Chi.	6	425	87	109	196	687	23	6	3	9	40	1978-79	1979-80
Kelly, Bob	Phi., Wash.	12	837	154	208	362	1454	101	9	14	23	172	1981-82	1981-82
Kelly, Red	Det., Tor.	20	1316	281	542	823	327	164	33	59	92	51	1966-67	1966-67
Kennedy, Forbes	Chi., Det., Bos., Phi., Tor.	10	603	70	108	178	988	12	2	4	6	64	1968-69	1969-70
Kennedy, Ted	Toronto	13	696	231	329	560	432	78	29	31	60	32	1956-57	1956-57
Keon, Dave	Tor., Hfd.	18	1296	396	590	986	117	92	32	36	68	6	1981-82	1981-82
Kerr, Reg	Clev., Chi., Edm.	6	263	66	94	160	169	7	1	0	1	7	1983-84	1983-84
Kessell, Rick	Pit., Cal.	2	135	4	24	28	6	....	....	....	....	....	1973-74	1975-76
Ketter, Kerry	Atlanta	1	41	0	2	2	58	....	....	....	....	....	1972-73	1974-75
Ketola, Veli-Pekka	Colorado	1	44	9	5	14	4	....	....	....	....	....	1981-82	1981-82
Kitchen, Mike	Colo., N.J.	8	474	12	62	74	370	2	0	0	0	2	1983-84	1984-85
Kindrachuk, Orest	Phi., Pit., Wash.	9	508	118	261	379	648	76	20	20	40	53	1981-82	1981-82
King, Wayne	California	3	73	5	18	23	34	....	....	....	....	....	1975-76	1976-77
Klassen, Ralph	Cal., Clev., Colo., St. L.	9	497	52	93	145	120	26	4	2	6	12	1983-84	1983-84
Klukay, Joe	Tor., Bos.	10	566	109	127	236	189	71	13	10	23	23	1955-56	1955-56
Knibbs, Bill	Boston	1	53	7	10	17	4	....	....	....	....	....	1964-65	1974-75
Komodoski, Neil	L.A., St. L.	8	502	16	76	92	632	23	0	2	2	4	1980-81	1980-81
Konik, George	Pittsburgh	1	52	7	8	15	26	....	....	....	....	....	1967-68	1967-68
Korab, Jerry	Chi., Van., Buf., L.A.	15	975	114	341	455	1629	93	8	18	26	201	1984-85	1984-85
Korney, Mike	Det., NYR	1	77	9	10	19	59	....	....	....	....	....	1978-79	1979-80
Koroll, Cliff	Chicago	11	814	208	254	462	376	85	19	29	48	67	1979-80	1979-80
Kozak, Don	L.A., Van.	7	437	96	86	182	480	29	7	2	9	69	1978-79	1979-80
Kraftcheck, Steve	Bos., NYR, Tor.	3	157	11	18	29	83	6	0	0	0	7	1958-59	1963-64
Krake, Skip	Bos., L.A., Buf.	4	249	23	40	73	182	10	1	0	1	17	1970-71	1975-76
Kryskow, Dave	Chi., Wash., Det., Atl.	4	231	33	56	89	174	12	2	0	2	4	1975-76	1977-78
Kryzanowski, Ed	Bos., Chi.	4	237	15	22	37	65	18	0	1	1	4	1952-53	1955-56
Kullman, Eddie	NY Rangers	6	343	56	70	126	298	6	1	0	1	2	1953-54	1954-55
Kurtenbach, Orland	NYR, Bos., Tor., Van.	11	639	119	213	232	628	19	2	4	6	70	1973-74	1973-74
Kuzyk, Ken	Cleveland	1	41	5	9	14	8	....	....	....	....	....	1977-78	1979-80
Kyle, Gus	NYR, Bos.	3	203	6	20	26	362	14	1	2	3	34	1951-52	1955-56
Labine, Leo	Bos., Det.	10	643	128	193	321	730	60	11	12	23	82	1961-62	1966-67
Labossiere, Gord	NYR, L.A., Min.	4	215	44	62	106	75	10	2	3	5	28	1971-72	1975-76
Labraaten, Dan	Det., Cgy.	4	268	71	73	144	47	5	1	0	1	4	1981-82	1981-82
Labre, Yvon	Pit., Wash.	7	371	14	87	101	788	....	....	....	....	....	1980-81	1980-81
Lach, Elmer	Montreal	13	664	215	408	623	478	76	19	45	64	36	1953-54	1953-54
Lacombe, François	Oak., Buf., Que.	1	78	2	17	19	54	3	1	0	1	0	1979-80	1979-80
Lacroix, Andre	Phi., Chi., Hfd.	6	325	79	119	198	44	16	2	5	7	0	1979-80	1979-80
Lacroix, Pierre	Que., Hfd.	4	274	24	108	132	197	8	0	2	2	10	1982-83	1982-83
Lafleur, Guy	Montreal	14	961	518	728	1246	381	124	57	76	133	67	1984-85	1984-85
Laframboise, Pete	Cal., Wash., Pit.	4	227	33	55	88	70	9	1	0	1	0	1974-75	1978-79
Lagace, Jean-Guy	Pit., Buf., K.C.	5	187	9	39	48	251	....	....	....	....	....	1975-76	1976-77
Lajeunesse, Serge	Det., Phi.	2	103	1	4	5	103	7	1	2	3	4	1974-75	1975-76
Lalande, Hec	Chi., Det.	3	151	21	39	60	120	....	....	....	....	....	1957-58	1962-63
Lalonde, Bobby	Van., Atl., Bos., Cgy.	10	641	124	210	334	298	16	4	2	6	6	1981-82	1981-82
Lalonde, Ron	Pit., Wash.	7	397	45	78	123	106	....	....	....	....	....	1978-79	1979-80
Lambert, Yvon	Mtl., Buff.	10	683	206	273	479	340	90	27	22	49	67	1981-82	1983-84
*Lamirande, Jean-P.	NYR, Mtl.	2	49	5	5	10	26	8	0	0	0	4	1954-55	1960-61
Lampman, Mike	St. L., Van., Wash.	5	96	17	20	37	34	....	....	....	....	....	1976-77	1976-77
Lane, Gord	Wsh., NYI.	10	539	19	94	113	1228	75	3	14	17	214	1984-85	1984-85
Langelle, Pete	Toronto	3	137	22	51	73	11	41	5	9	14	4	1941-42	1951-52
Langlois, Al	Mtl., NYR, Det., Bos.	8	448	21	91	112	488	53	1	5	6	60	1965-66	1966-67
Laperriere, Jacques	Montreal	11	691	40	242	282	674	88	9	22	31	101	1973-74	1973-74
Lapointe, Guy	Mtl., St. L., Bos.	15	884	171	451	622	893	123	26	44	70	138	1983-84	1983-84
Laprade, Edgar	NY Rangers	10	501	108	172	280	42	18	4	9	13	4	1954-55	1954-55
Larose, Claude	Mtl., Min., St. L.	15	943	226	257	483	887	97	14	18	32	143	1977-78	1977-78
Laughton, Mike	Oak., Cal.	4	189	39	48	87	101	11	2	4	6	0	1970-71	1974-75
Laurence, Red	Atl., St. L.	2	79	15	22	37	14	....	....	....	....	....	1979-80	1983-84
Lavender, Brian	St. L., NYI, Det., Cal.	3	184	16	26	42	174	3	0	0	0	2	1974-75	1974-75
Lawson, Danny	Det., Min., Buf.	5	219	28	29	57	61	16	0	1	1	2	1971-72	1976-77
Laycoe, Hal	NYR, Mtl., Bos.	11	531	25	77	102	292	40	2	5	7	39	1955-56	1955-56

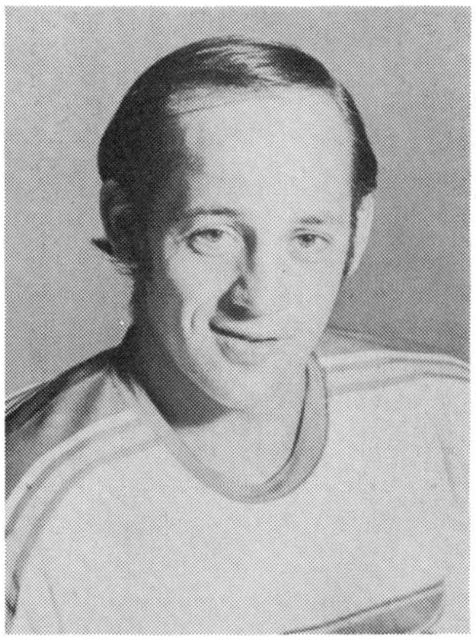

Fran Huck

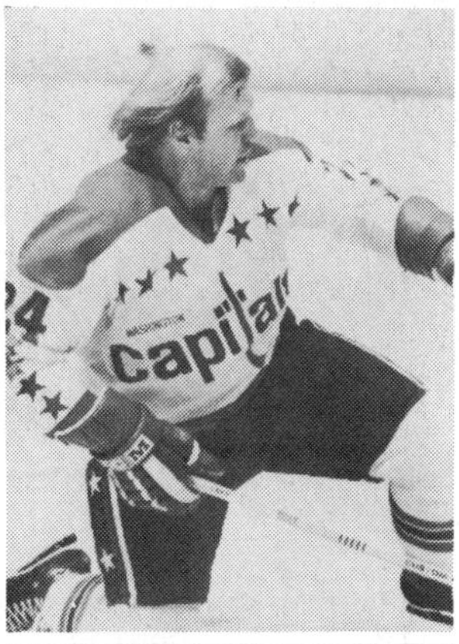

Bob Kelly

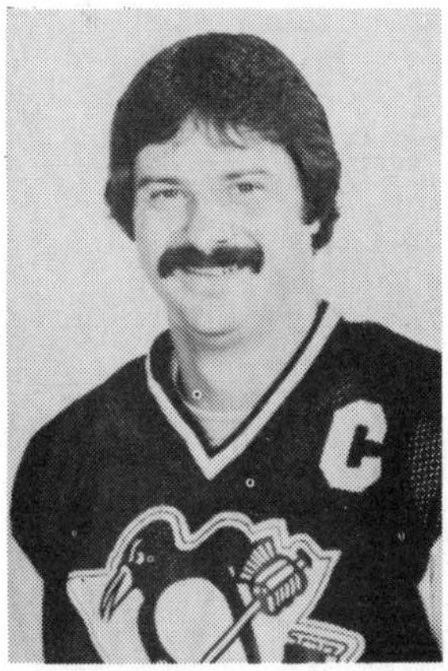

Orest Kindrachuk

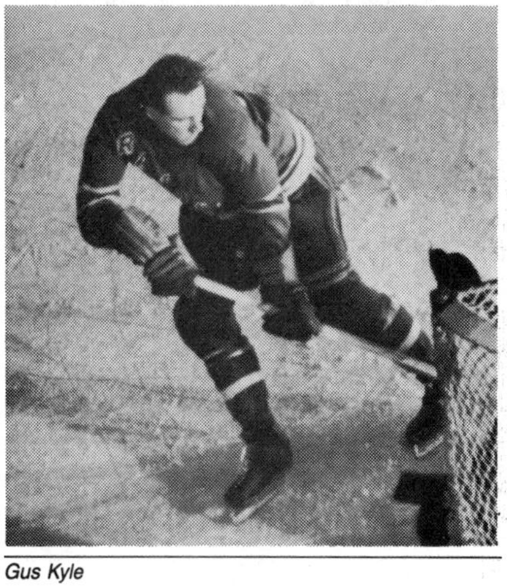

Gus Kyle

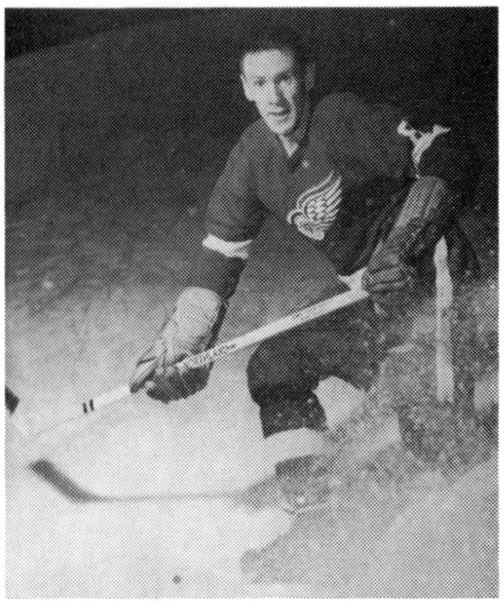
Leo Labine

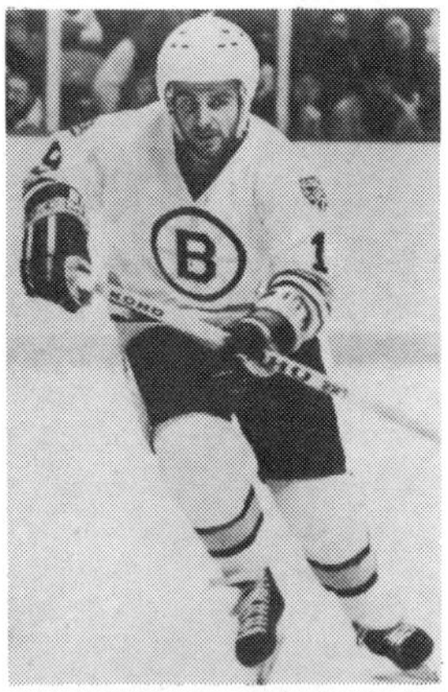
Bobby Lalonde

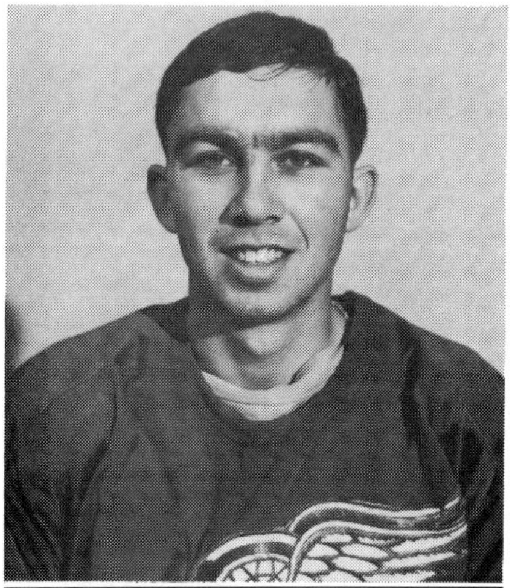
Nick Libett

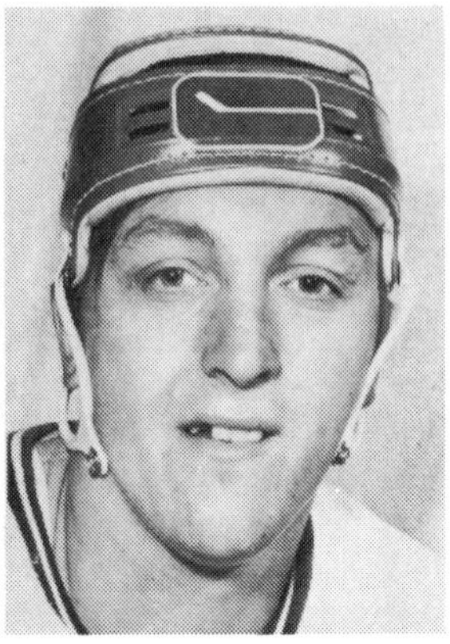
Wayne Maki

			Regular Schedule					Playoffs					Last	Last
Name	NHL Teams	NHL Seasons	GP	G	A	TP	PIM	GP	G	A	TP	PIM	NHL Season	Pro Season
Leach, Reggie	Bos., Cal., Phil., Det.	13	934	381	285	666	387	94	47	22	69	22	1982-83	1983-84
Leblanc, J.P.	Chi., Det.	3	153	14	30	44	87	2	0	0	0	0	1978-79	1980-81
Leclair, Jackie	Montreal	3	160	20	40	60	56	20	6	1	7	6	1956-57	1961-62
Leclerc, Rene	Detroit	2	87	10	11	21	105	....	....	....	....	....	1970-71	1978-79
Lecuyer, Doug	Chi., Wpg., Pit.	4	126	11	31	42	178	7	4	0	4	15	1982-83	1982-83
Leduc, Richard	Bos., Que.	3	130	28	38	66	55	5	0	0	0	9	1980-81	1980-81
Lee, Peter	Pittsburgh	6	431	114	131	245	257	19	0	8	8	4	1982-83	1982-83
Lefley, Bryan	NYI, K.C., Colo.	4	228	7	29	36	101	2	0	0	0	0	1977-78	1977-78
Lefley, Chuck	Mtl., St. L.	8	407	128	164	292	137	29	5	8	13	10	1979-80	1979-80
*Leger, Roger	NYR, Mtl.	4	187	18	53	71	71	20	0	7	7	14	1949-50	1955-56
Legge, Barry	Que., Wpg.	3	107	1	11	12	144	....	....	....	....	....	1981-82	1981-82
Lehtonen, Antero	Washington	1	65	9	12	21	14	....	....	....	....	....	1979-80	1979-80
Leinonen, Mikko	NYR., Wsh.	4	162	31	78	109	71	20	2	11	13	28	1984-85	1984-85
Leiter, Bob	Bos., Pit., Atl.	7	447	98	126	224	144	8	3	0	3	2	1975-76	1975-76
Lemaire, Jacques	Montreal	12	853	366	469	835	217	145	61	78	139	63	1978-79	1978-79
Lemelin, Roger	K.C., Colo.	1	36	1	2	3	27	....	....	....	....	....	1977-78	1978-79
Lemieux, Jean	Atl., Wash.	5	204	23	63	86	39	3	1	1	2	0	1977-78	1978-79
*Lemieux, Real	Det., L.A., NYR, Buf.	7	456	51	104	155	262	18	2	4	6	10	1973-74	1973-74
Lemieux, Richard	Van., K.C., Atl.	4	274	39	82	121	132	2	0	0	0	0	1975-76	1975-76
Leveille, Normand	Boston	2	75	17	25	42	49	....	....	....	....	....	1982-83	1982-83
Lesuk, Bill	Bos., Phi., L.A., Wash., Wpg.	8	388	44	63	107	368	9	1	0	1	12	1979-80	1979-80
Leswick, Tony	NYR, Det., Chi.	12	740	165	159	324	900	59	13	10	23	91	1957-58	1959-60
Lewicki, Danny	Tor., NYR, Chi.	8	461	105	135	240	177	28	0	4	4	8	1958-59	1962-63
Ley, Rick	Tor., Hfd.	6	310	12	72	84	528	14	0	2	2	20	1980-81	1980-81
Libett, Nick	Det., Pit.	14	92	237	268	505	472	16	6	2	8	2	1980-81	1980-81
Lindsay, Ted	Det., Chi.	17	1068	379	472	851	1808	133	47	49	96	194	1964-65	1964-65
Litzenberger, Ed	Mtl., Chi., Det., Tor.	10	618	178	238	416	283	40	5	13	18	34	1963-64	1965-66
Locas, Jacques	Montreal	1	59	7	8	15	66	....	....	....	....	....	1948-49	1959-60
Lochead, Bill	Det., Colo., NYR	6	330	69	62	131	180	7	3	0	3	6	1979-80	1979-80
Logan, Dave	Chi., Van.	6	218	5	29	34	470	12	0	0	0	10	1980-81	1982-83
Long, Barry	L.A., Det., Wpg.	5	280	11	58	79	250	5	0	1	1	18	1981-82	1981-82
Lonsberry, Ross	Bos., L.A., Phi., Pit.	13	968	256	310	566	806	100	21	25	46	87	1980-81	1980-81
Lorentz, Jim	Bos., St. L., NYR, Buf.	9	659	161	238	399	208	54	12	10	22	30	1977-78	1977-78
*Lowe, Ross	Bos., Mtl.	2	77	6	8	14	82	2	0	0	0	0	1951-52	1954-55
Luce, Don	NYR, Det., Buf., L.A., Tor.	13	894	225	329	554	364	71	17	22	39	52	1981-82	1981-82
Lukowich, Bernie	Pitt., St. L.	2	79	13	15	28	34	2	0	0	0	0	1974-75	1976-77
Lund, Pentti	Bos., NYR	5	259	44	55	99	40	18	7	5	12	0	1952-53	1952-53
Lunde, Len	Det., Chi., Min., Van.	5	321	39	83	122	75	20	3	2	5	2	1970-71	1970-71
Lundrigan, Joe	Tor., Wash.	1	52	2	8	10	22	....	....	....	....	....	1974-75	1974-75
Lundy, Pat	Det., Chi.	3	150	37	32	69	31	9	1	1	2	2	1950-51	1955-56
Lupien, Gilles	Mtl., Pit., Hfd.	4	226	5	25	30	416	25	0	0	0	21	1981-82	1981-82
Lyle, George	Det., Hfd.	4	99	24	38	62	51	....	....	....	....	....	1982-83	1982-83
Lynch, Jack	Pit., Det., Wash.	7	382	24	106	130	336	....	....	....	....	....	1978-79	1978-79
Lynn, Vic	Det., Mtl., Tor., Bos., Chi.	6	326	49	76	125	274	47	7	10	17	46	1954-55	1958-59
MacAdam, Al	Phi., Cal., Clev., Min., Van.	12	864	240	351	591	509	64	20	24	44	21	1984-85	1984-85
MacDonald, Blair	Edm., Van.	4	219	91	100	191	65	11	0	6	6	2	1982-83	1982-83
MacDonald, Lowell	Det., L.A., Pit.	8	506	180	210	390	92	30	11	11	22	12	1977-78	1977-78
MacDonald, Parker	Tor., NYR, Bos., Det., Min.	11	676	144	179	323	253	75	14	14	28	20	1968-69	1968-69
MacGregor, Bruce	Det., NYR	13	893	213	257	470	217	107	19	28	47	44	1973-74	1975-76
MacKay, Callum	Det., Mtl.	5	237	50	55	105	214	38	5	13	18	20	1954-55	1955-56
Mackell, Fleming	Tor., Bos.	11	665	149	220	369	562	80	22	41	63	75	1959-60	1962-63
MacKinnon, Paul	Wash.	5	147	5	23	28	91	....	....	....	....	....	1983-84	1983-84
MacLeish, Rick	Phil., Hfd., Pitt., Det.	14	846	349	410	759	434	114	54	53	107	38	1983-84	1983-84
MacMillan, Bob	NYR., St. L., Atl., Cgy., Colo., N.J.	11	753	228	349	577	260	31	8	11	19	16	1984-85	1984-85
MacMillan, John	Tor., Det.	2	104	5	10	15	32	12	0	1	1	2	1963-64	1970-71
MacMillan, Billy	Tor., Atl., NYI	7	446	74	77	151	184	53	6	6	12	40	1976-77	1977-78
MacNeil, Al	Tor., Mtl., Chi., NYR, Pit.	8	524	17	75	92	617	37	0	4	4	67	1967-68	1969-70
MacPherson, Bud	Montreal	5	259	5	33	38	233	29	0	3	3	21	1956-57	1960-61
MacSweyn, Ralph	Philadelphia	1	47	0	5	5	10	8	0	0	0	6	1971-72	1975-76
Maggs, Darryl	Chi., Cal., Tor.	2	135	14	19	33	54	4	0	0	0	0	1979-80	1979-80
Magnuson, Keith	Chicago	11	589	14	125	139	1442	68	3	9	12	164	1979-80	1979-80
Mahovlich, Frank	Tor., Det., Mtl.	17	1181	533	570	1103	1056	137	51	67	118	163	1973-74	1977-78
Mahovlich, Peter	Det., Mtl., Pit.	14	884	288	485	793	916	88	30	42	72	134	1980-81	1981-82
Mair, Jim	Phi., NYI, Van.	2	76	4	15	19	49	3	1	2	3	4	1974-75	1974-75
Maki, Chico	Chicago	13	841	143	292	435	345	113	17	36	53	43	1975-76	1975-76
*Maki, Wayne	Chi., St. L., Van.	4	246	57	79	136	184	2	1	0	1	2	1972-73	1972-73
Maloney, Dan	Chi., L.A., Det., Tor.	11	737	192	259	451	1489	40	4	7	11	35	1981-82	1981-82
Maloney, Dave	NYR., Buf.	11	657	71	246	317	1154	49	7	17	24	91	1984-85	1984-85
Maloney, Phil	Bos., Tor., Chi.	3	158	28	43	71	16	6	0	0	0	0	1959-60	1969-70
Manery, Kris	Clev., Min., Van., Wpg.	4	250	63	64	127	91	....	....	....	....	....	1980-81	1981-82
Manery, Randy	Det., Atl., L.A.	10	582	50	206	256	415	13	0	2	2	12	1979-80	1979-80
Manno, Bob	Van., Tor., Det.	8	371	41	131	172	274	17	2	4	6	12	1984-85	1984-85
Marcetta, Milan	Tor., Min.	2	54	7	15	22	10	17	7	7	14	4	1968-69	1972-73
Marchinko, Brian	Tor., NYI	1	47	2	6	8	0	....	....	....	....	....	1973-74	1974-75
Marcon, Lou	Detroit	2	60	0	4	4	42	....	....	....	....	....	1962-63	1967-68
Marcotte, Don	Boston	14	868	230	254	484	317	132	34	27	61	81	1981-82	1981-82
Mariucci, John	Chicago	5	223	11	34	45	308	8	0	3	3	26	1947-48	1950-51
Markell, John	Wpg., St. L., Min.	4	55	11	10	21	36	....	....	....	....	....	1984-85	1984-85
Marks, John	Chicago	10	648	112	163	275	330	57	5	9	14	60	1981-82	1981-82
Marotte, Gilles	Bos., Chi., L.A., NYR, St. L.	12	808	56	265	321	872	29	3	3	6	26	1977-78	1977-78
Marsh, Peter	Wpg., Chi.	5	279	48	71	119	224	26	1	5	6	33	1983-84	1983-84
Marshall, Bert	Det., Oak., Cal., NYR, NYI	14	868	17	181	198	296	72	4	22	26	99	1978-79	1979-80
Marshall, Don	Mtl., NYR, Buf., Tor.	17	1176	265	324	589	127	94	8	15	23	14	1971-72	1971-72
Marshall, Paul	Pit., Tor., Hfd.	5	95	15	18	33	17	1	0	0	0	0	1982-83	1982-83
Marson, Mike	Wash., L.A.	3	196	24	24	48	233	....	....	....	....	....	1979-80	1979-80
Martin, Clare	Bos., Det., Chi., NYR	5	237	12	28	40	78	22	0	2	2	6	1951-52	1951-52
Martin, Frank	Bos., Chi.	5	282	11	46	57	122	10	0	1	1	2	1957-58	1964-65
Martin, Pit	Det., Bos., Chi., Van.	17	1101	324	485	609	809	100	27	31	58	56	1978-79	1978-79
Martin, Richard	Buf., L.A.	10	685	384	317	701	477	63	24	29	53	74	1981-82	1981-82
Martineau, Don	Atl., Min., Det.	2	90	6	10	16	63	....	....	....	....	....	1976-77	1977-78
Masnick, Paul	Mtl., Chi., Tor.	6	232	18	41	59	139	33	4	5	9	27	1957-58	1960-61
*Masterton, Bill	Minnesota	1	38	4	8	12	4	....	....	....	....	....	1967-68	1967-68
Mattiussi, Dick	Pit., Oak., Cal.	3	200	8	31	39	124	8	0	1	1	6	1970-71	1975-76
Maxner, Wayne	Boston	1	62	8	9	17	48	....	....	....	....	....	1965-66	1970-71
Maxwell, Bryan	Min., St. L., Wpg., Pit.	8	331	18	77	95	745	15	1	1	2	86	1984-85	1984-85
Mazur, Eddie	Mtl., Chi.	3	107	8	20	28	120	25	4	5	9	22	1956-57	1964-65
McCaig, Doug	Det., Chi.	6	263	8	21	29	255	17	0	1	1	8	1950-51	1951-52
McCallum, Dunc	NYR, Pit.	3	187	14	35	49	230	10	1	2	3	12	1970-71	1972-73
McCann, Rick	Detroit	1	43	1	4	5	6	....	....	....	....	....	1974-75	1975-76
McCarthy, Tom	Det., Bos.	1	60	8	9	17	8	....	....	....	....	....	1960-61	1969-70
McClanahan, Rob	Buff., Hfd., NYR	5	224	38	63	101	126	34	4	12	16	31	1983-84	1983-84
McCord, Bob	Bos., Det., Min., St. L.	6	316	58	68	126	262	14	2	5	7	10	1972-73	1974-75
McCormack, John	Tor., Mtl., Chi.	6	311	25	49	74	35	22	1	1	2	0	1954-55	1955-56
McCourt, Dale	Det., Buff., Tor.	7	532	194	284	478	124	21	9	7	16	6	1983-84	1983-84
McCreary, Keith	Mtl., Pit., Atl.	8	532	131	112	243	294	16	0	4	4	6	1974-75	1974-75
McCreary, Bill	NYR, Det., Mtl., St. L.	5	309	53	62	115	108	48	6	16	22	14	1970-71	1970-71
McCutcheon, Brian	Detroit	1	37	3	1	4	7	....	....	....	....	....	1976-77	1977-78
McDonald, Ab	Mtl., Chi., Bos., Det., Pit., St. L.	12	762	182	248	430	200	84	21	29	50	42	1971-72	1973-74
McDonough, Al	L.A., Pit., Atl., Det.	4	237	73	88	161	73	8	0	1	1	2	1977-78	1977-78
McDougall, Mike	NYR, Hfd.	4	61	8	10	18	43	....	....	....	....	....	1982-83	1983-84
McElmury, Jim	Min., K.C., Colo.	3	180	14	47	61	49	....	....	....	....	....	1977-78	1977-78
McFadden, Jim	Det., Chi.	7	412	100	126	226	89	49	10	9	19	30	1953-54	1956-57

Name	NHL Teams	NHL Seasons	Regular Schedule GP	G	A	TP	PIM	Playoffs GP	G	A	TP	PIM	Last NHL Season	Last Pro Season
McGill, Jack	Boston	3	97	23	36	59	42	27	7	4	11	17	1946-47	1953-54
McIlhargey, Jack	Phi., Van., Hfd.	8	393	11	36	47	1102	27	0	3	3	68	1981-82	1981-82
McIntosh, Paul	Buffalo	2	48	0	2	2	66	2	0	0	0	7	1975-76	1978-79
McIntyre, Jack	Bos., Chi., Det.	9	499	109	102	211	173	29	7	6	13	4	1959-60	1963-64
McIntyre, Larry	Toronto	1	41	0	3	3	26	....	....	....	....	....	1972-73	1975-76
McKechnie, Walt	Minn., Cal., Bos., Det., Wash., Clev., Tor., Colo.	16	955	214	392	606	469	15	7	5	12	9	1982-83	1983-84
McKendry, Alex	NYI, Cgy.	4	46	3	6	9	21	6	2	2	4	0	1980-81	1982-83
McKenney, Don	Bos., NYR, Tor., Det., St. L.	12	798	237	345	582	211	58	18	29	47	10	1967-68	1969-70
McKenny, Jim	Tor., Min.	14	604	82	247	329	294	37	7	9	16	10	1978-79	1978-79
McKenzie, John	Chi., Det., NYR, Bos.	10	691	206	268	474	917	69	15	32	47	133	1971-72	1978-79
McLeod, Jackie	NY Rangers	3	106	14	23	37	12	7	0	0	0	0	1954-55	1959-60
McMahon, Mike	NYR, Min., Chi., Det., Pit., Buf.	8	224	15	68	83	171	14	3	7	10	4	1971-72	1976-77
McManama, Bob	Pittsburgh	2	99	11	25	36	28	8	0	1	1	6	1975-76	1975-76
McNab, Max	Detroit	2	128	16	19	35	24	25	1	0	1	4	1950-51	1958-59
McNeill, Billy	Detroit	5	257	21	46	67	142	4	1	1	2	4	1963-64	1970-71
McSheffrey, Bryan	Van., Buf.	2	90	13	7	20	44	....	....	....	....	....	1974-75	1976-77
McTaggart, Jim	Washington	2	71	3	10	13	205	....	....	....	....	....	1981-82	1983-84
Meehan, Gerry	Tor., Phi., Buf., Van., Atl., Wash.	10	670	180	243	423	111	10	0	1	1	0	1978-79	1978-79
Meeke, Brent	Cal., Clev.	2	75	9	22	31	8	....	....	....	....	....	1976-77	1976-77
Meeker, Howie	Toronto	7	346	83	102	185	329	42	6	9	15	50	1953-54	1954-55
Meger, Paul	Montreal	4	212	39	52	91	112	35	3	8	11	16	1954-55	1954-55
Meighan, Ron	Minn., Pitt.	2	48	3	7	10	18	....	....	....	....	....	1982-83	1983-84
Meissner, Dick	Bos., NYR	3	171	11	15	26	37	....	....	....	....	....	1964-65	1971-72
Melnyk, Gerry	Det., Chi., St. L.	4	269	39	77	116	34	53	7	7	12	6	1967-68	1967-68
Menard, Howie	Det., L.A., Chi., Oak.	3	151	23	42	65	87	19	3	7	10	36	1969-70	1975-76
Meredith, Greg	Calgary	2	38	6	4	10	8	5	3	1	4	4	1982-83	1983-84
Merrick, Wayne	St. L., Cal., Clev., NYI	12	774	191	265	456	303	102	19	30	49	30	1983-84	1983-84
Micheletti, Joe	St. L., Colo.	4	158	11	60	71	114	11	1	11	12	10	1981-82	1981-82
*Mickey, Larry	Chi., NYR, Tor., Mtl., L.A., Phi., Buf.	5	292	39	53	92	160	9	1	0	1	10	1974-75	1974-75
Mickoski, Nick	NYR, Chi., Det., Bos.	11	703	158	184	342	319	18	1	6	7	6	1959-60	1964-65
Migay, Rudy	Toronto	8	418	59	92	151	293	15	1	0	1	20	1959-60	1964-65
Mikita, Stan	Chicago	22	1394	541	926	1467	1270	155	59	91	150	169	1979-80	1979-80
Mikkelson, Bill	L.A., NYI, Wash.	3	147	4	18	22	105	....	....	....	....	....	1976-77	1976-77
Miller, Bob	Bos., Colo.	4	341	71	103	174	185	34	4	6	10	27	1981-82	1982-83
Miller, Robert	Bos., Colo., L.A.	6	404	75	119	294	220	36	4	7	11	27	1984-85	1984-85
Miller, Tom	Det., NYI	3	118	16	25	41	34	....	....	....	....	....	1974-75	1974-75
Miller, Warren	NYR, Hfd.	4	262	40	50	90	137	6	1	0	1	0	1982-83	1982-83
Miszuk, John	Det., Chi., Phi., Min.	4	237	7	39	46	232	19	0	3	3	19	1969-70	1976-77
Moe, Bill	NY Rangers	5	261	11	42	53	163	1	0	0	0	0	1948-49	1951-52
Moffat, Lyle	Tor., Wpg.	2	97	12	16	28	51	....	....	....	....	....	1979-80	1980-81
Mohns, Doug	Bos., Chi., Min., Atl., Wash.	22	1390	248	462	710	1250	94	14	36	50	122	1974-75	1974-75
Molin, Lars	Vancouver	3	172	33	65	98	37	19	2	9	11	7	1983-84	1983-84
Monahan, Garry	Mtl., Det., L.A., Tor., Van.	12	748	116	169	285	484	22	3	1	4	13	1978-79	1978-79
Monahan, Hartland	Cal., NYR, Wash., Pit., L.A., St. L.	6	334	61	80	141	163	6	0	0	0	4	1980-81	1980-81
Mondou, Pierre	Montreal	9	548	194	262	456	179	69	17	28	45	26	1984-85	1984-85
Monteith, Hank	Detroit	2	77	5	12	17	6	4	0	0	0	0	1970-71	1970-71
Moore, Dickie	Mtl., Tor., St. L.	14	719	261	347	608	652	135	46	64	110	122	1967-68	1967-68
Morris, Elwyn	Tor., NYR	4	135	13	29	42	58	18	4	2	6	16	1948-49	1952-53
Morrison, Dave	L.A., Vanc.	3	39	3	3	6	4	....	....	....	....	....	1984-85	1984-85
Morrison, Don	Det., Chi.	2	112	18	28	46	12	3	0	1	1	0	1950-51	1951-52
Morrison, Gary	Philadelphia	2	43	1	15	16	70	5	0	1	1	2	1981-82	1981-82
Morrison, George	St. Louis	2	115	17	21	38	13	3	0	0	0	0	1971-72	1976-77
Morrison, Jim	Bos., Tor., Det., NYR, Pit.	11	704	40	160	200	542	36	0	12	12	38	1970-71	1972-73
Morrison, Kevin	Colorado	1	41	4	11	15	23	....	....	....	....	....	1979-80	1979-80
Morrison, Lew	Phi., Atl., Wash., Pit.	8	564	39	52	91	107	17	0	0	0	2	1977-78	1977-78
Mortson, Gus	Tor., Chi., Det.	13	797	46	152	198	1380	54	5	8	13	68	1958-59	1964-65
Mosdell, Ken	Mtl., Chi.	11	693	141	168	309	475	79	16	13	29	48	1958-59	1959-60
Mosienko, Bill	Chicago	13	711	258	282	540	117	22	10	4	14	15	1954-55	1958-59
Mott, Morris	California	3	199	18	32	50	49	....	....	....	....	....	1974-75	1974-75
Moxey, Jim	Cal., Clev., L.A.	2	127	22	27	49	59	....	....	....	....	....	1976-77	1977-78
Mulhern. Richard	Atl., L.A., Tor., Wpg.	6	303	27	93	120	217	7	0	3	3	5	1980-81	1980-81
Muloin, Wayne	Det., Oak., Cal., Min.	2	147	3	21	24	93	11	0	0	0	2	1970-71	1976-77
Mulvey, Grant	Chi., N.J.	10	586	149	135	284	816	42	10	5	15	70	1983-84	1983-84
Mulvey, Paul	Wash, Pit., L.A.	4	225	30	51	81	613	....	....	....	....	....	1981-82	1982-83
Murdoch, Bob	Cal., Clev., St. L.	4	260	72	85	157	127	....	....	....	....	....	1978-79	1979-80
Murdoch, Robert	Mtl., L.A., Atl., Cgy.	11	757	60	218	278	764	69	4	18	22	92	1981-82	1981-82
Murphy, Mike	St. L., NYR, L.A.	12	831	238	318	556	514	66	13	23	36	54	1982-83	1982-83
Murphy, Ron	NYR, Chi., Det., Bos.	16	889	205	274	479	460	53	7	8	15	26	1969-70	1969-70
Murray, Ken	Tor., NYI, Det., K.C.	2	106	1	10	11	135	....	....	....	....	....	1975-76	1978-79
Murray, Bob	Atl., Van.	4	194	6	16	22	98	9	1	1	2	15	1976-77	1976-77
Murray, Terry	Cal., Phi., Det., Wash.	6	302	4	76	80	199	18	2	2	4	10	1981-82	1981-82
Nahrgang, Jim	Detroit	1	57	5	12	17	34	....	....	....	....	....	1976-77	1977-78
Nanne, Lou	Minnesota	10	635	68	157	225	356	32	4	10	14	9	1977-78	1977-78
Nantais, Richard	Minnesota	1	63	5	4	9	79	....	....	....	....	....	1976-77	1977-78
Nattrass, Ralph	Chicago	4	223	18	38	56	308	....	....	....	....	....	1949-50	1950-51
Nedomansky, Vaclav	Det., St. L., NYR	6	421	122	156	278	88	7	3	5	8	0	1982-83	1982-83
Neely, Bob	Toronto	5	283	39	59	98	266	26	5	7	12	15	1977-78	1979-80
Neilson, Jim	NYR, Cal., Clev.	16	1023	69	299	368	904	65	1	17	18	61	1977-78	1978-79
Nesterenko, Eric	Tor., Chi.	20	1219	250	324	574	1273	124	13	24	37	127	1971-72	1971-72
Nethery, Lance	NYR, Edm.	2	41	11	14	25	14	14	5	3	8	9	1981-82	1982-83
Nevin, Bob	Tor., NYR, Min., L.A.	16	1128	307	419	726	211	84	16	18	34	24	1975-76	1975-76
Newman, Dan	NYR, Mtl., Edm.	2	126	17	24	41	63	3	0	0	0	4	1979-80	1979-80
Nicolson, Graeme	Bos., Colo., NYR.	3	52	2	7	9	60	....	....	....	....	....	1982-83	1984-85
Nicholson, Neil	Oak., NYI	4	39	3	1	4	23	2	0	0	0	0	1977-78	1978-79
Nicholson, Paul	Washington	1	62	4	8	12	18	....	....	....	....	....	1976-77	1977-78
Nigro, Frank	Toronto	2	68	8	18	26	39	3	0	0	0	2	1983-84	1983-84
Nilsson, Ulf	NY Rangers	4	170	57	112	169	85	25	8	14	22	27	1982-83	1982-83
Nolet, Simon	Phi., K.C., Pit., Colo.	9	562	150	182	332	187	34	6	3	9	8	1976-77	1976-77
Noris, Joe	Pit., St. L., Buf.	1	55	2	5	7	22	....	....	....	....	....	1973-74	1977-78
Nowak, Hank	Pit., Det., Bos.	4	180	26	29	55	161	13	1	0	1	8	1976-77	1978-79
Norwich, Craig	Wpg., St. L., Colo.	2	104	17	58	75	60	....	....	....	....	....	1980-81	1981-82
Nyrop, Bill	Mtl., Min.	4	207	12	51	63	101	35	1	7	8	22	1981-82	1981-82
O'Brien, Dennis	Min., Colo., Clev., Bos.	10	592	31	91	122	1017	34	1	2	3	101	1979-80	1979-80
*O'Connor, Buddy	Mtl., NYR	10	509	140	257	397	34	53	15	21	36	6	1950-51	1951-52
Oddleifson, Chris	Bos., Van.	8	424	95	191	286	464	14	1	6	7	8	1980-81	1980-81
O'Donnell, Fred	Boston	2	115	15	11	26	98	5	0	1	1	5	1973-74	1975-76
O'Donoghue, Don	Oak., Cal.	3	125	18	17	35	35	3	0	0	0	0	1971-72	1973-74
Odrowski, Gerry	Det., Oak., St. L.	5	299	12	19	31	111	30	0	1	1	16	1971-72	1974-75
O'Flaherty, Gerry	Tor., Atl., Van.	8	438	99	95	194	168	7	2	2	4	6	1978-79	1978-79
Ogilvie, Brian	Chi., St. L.	2	90	15	21	36	29	....	....	....	....	....	1978-79	1979-80
Oliver, Murray	Det., Bos., Tor., Min.	16	1127	274	454	728	319	35	9	16	25	10	1974-75	1974-75
Olmstead, Bert	Chi., Mtl., Tor.	13	848	181	421	602	884	115	16	42	58	101	1961-62	1961-62
Orban, Bill	Chi., Min.	2	114	8	15	23	67	3	0	0	0	0	1969-70	1974-75
O'Ree, Willie	Boston	1	45	4	10	14	26	....	....	....	....	....	1960-61	1973-74
O'Reilly, Terry	Boston	14	891	204	402	606	2095	108	25	42	67	335	1984-85	1984-85
Orr, Bobby	Bos., Chi.	12	657	270	645	915	953	74	26	66	92	107	1978-79	1978-79
O'Shea, Danny	Min., Chi., St. L.	5	369	64	115	179	265	39	3	7	10	62	1972-73	1974-75
O'Shea, Kevin	Buf., St. L.	3	134	13	18	31	85	12	2	1	3	10	1972-73	1974-75
Owchar, Dennis	Pit., Colo.	6	288	30	85	115	200	10	1	1	2	8	1979-80	1981-82
Pachal, Clayton	Bos., Colo.	1	35	2	3	5	95	....	....	....	....	....	1978-79	1979-80

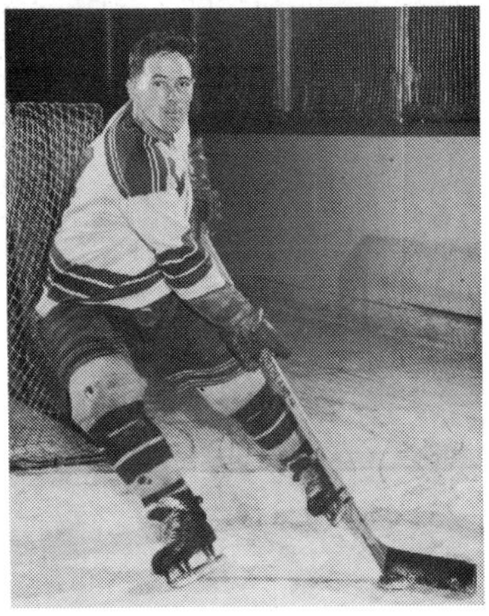
Jackie McLeod

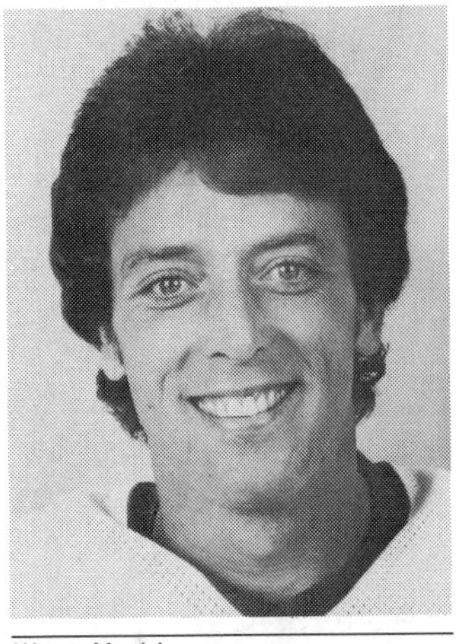
Wayne Merrick

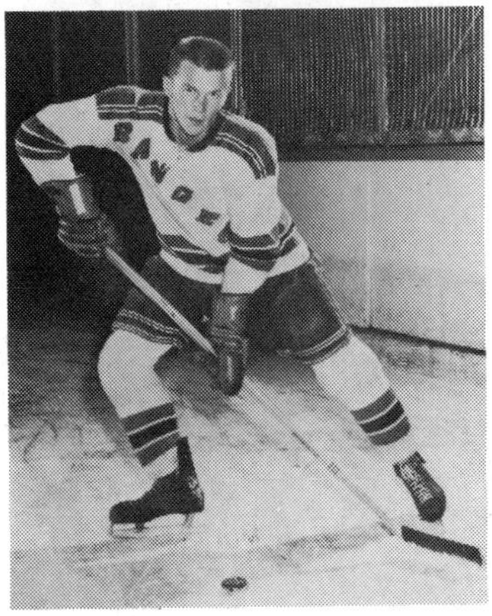
Ron Murphy

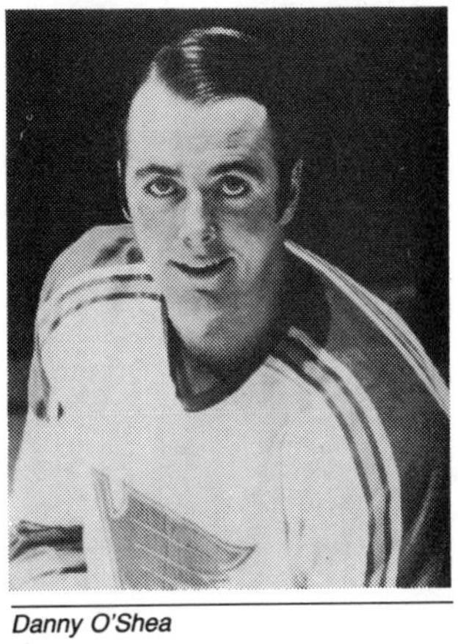
Danny O'Shea

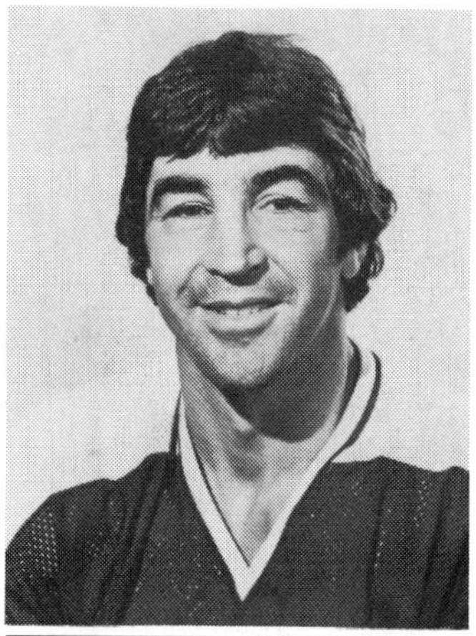

J.P. Parise

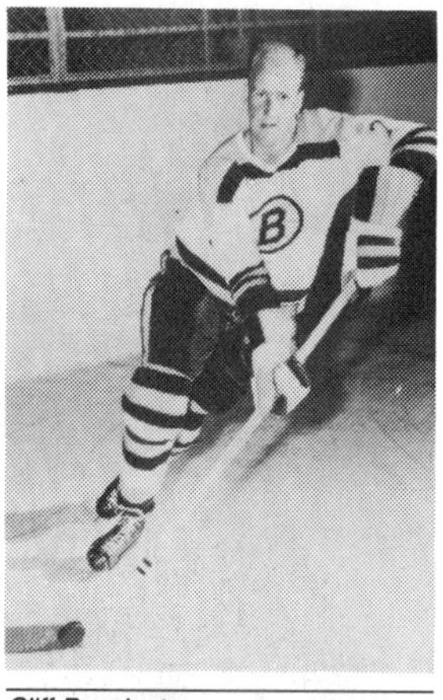

Cliff Pennington

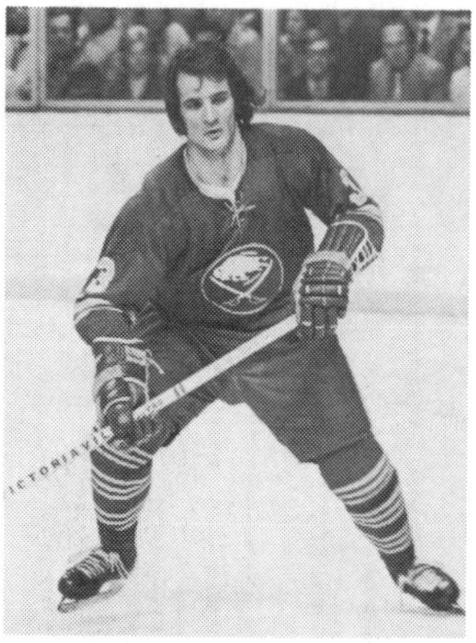

Mike Robitaille

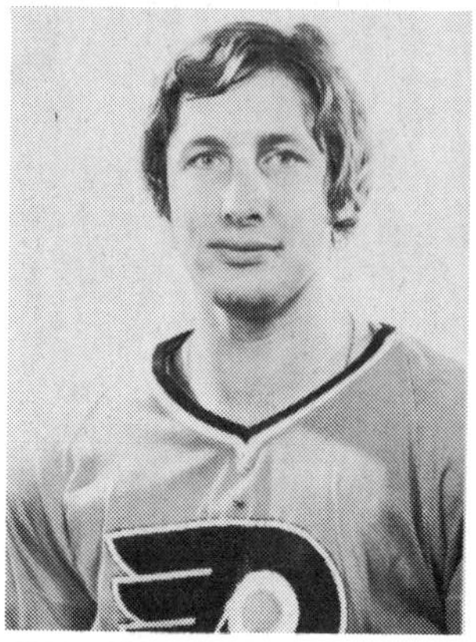

Don Saleski

			Regular Schedule					Playoffs					Last	Last
Name	NHL Teams	NHL Seasons	GP	G	A	TP	PIM	GP	G	A	TP	PIM	NHL Season	Pro Season
Paiement, Rosaire	Phi., Van.	3	190	48	52	100	343	3	3	0	3	0	1971-72	1977-78
Palazzari, Doug	St. Louis	3	108	18	20	38	23	2	0	0	0	0	1978-79	1981-82
Palmer, Brad	Minn., Bos.	3	168	32	38	70	58	29	9	5	14	16	1982-83	1983-84
Pappin, Jim	Tor., Chi., Cal., Clev.	14	767	278	295	573	667	92	33	34	67	101	1976-77	1976-77
Paradise, Bob	Min., Atl., Pit., Wash.	8	368	8	54	62	393	12	0	1	1	19	1978-79	1978-79
Parise, Jean-Paul	Bos., Tor., Min., NYI, Clev.	14	890	238	356	594	706	86	27	31	58	87	1978-79	1978-79
Parizeau, Michel	St. L., Phi.	1	58	3	14	17	18	....	....	....	....	....	1971-72	1978-79
Park, Brad	NYR., Bos., Det.	17	1113	213	683	896	1429	161	35	90	125	217	1984-85	1984-85
Patey, Larry	Cal., St. L., NYR.	12	717	153	163	316	631	40	8	10	18	57	1984-85	1984-85
Patrick, Craig	Cal., St. L., K.C., Wash.	8	401	72	91	163	61	2	0	1	1	0	1978-79	1978-79
Patrick, Glen	St. L., Cal., Clev.	1	38	2	3	5	72	....	....	....	....	....	1976-77	1977-78
Patterson, Dennis	K.C., Phi.	3	138	6	22	28	67	....	....	....	....	....	1979-80	1982-83
Pavelich, Marty	Detroit	10	634	93	159	252	454	91	13	15	28	74	1956-57	1956-57
Pearson, Mel	NYR, Pit.	2	38	2	6	8	25	....	....	....	....	....	1967-68	1972-73
Peirson, John	Boston	10	545	153	173	326	315	49	9	17	26	26	1957-58	1957-58
Pelyk, Mike	Toronto	7	441	26	88	114	566	40	0	3	3	41	1977-78	1977-78
Pennington, Cliff	Mtl., Bos.	2	101	17	42	59	6	....	....	....	....	....	1962-63	1965-66
Perry, Brian	Oak., Buf.	2	96	16	29	45	24	8	1	1	2	4	1970-71	1974-75
Pesut, George	California	2	92	3	22	25	130	....	....	....	....	....	1975-76	1976-77
Peters, Garry	Mtl., NYR, Phi., Bos.	5	331	34	34	68	261	9	2	2	4	31	1971-72	1973-74
Peters, Jim	Mtl., Bos., Det., Chi.	9	574	125	150	275	186	60	5	9	14	22	1953-54	1953-54
Peters, Jimmy Jr.	Det., L.A.	5	309	37	36	73	48	11	0	2	2	2	1974-75	1975-76
Phillipoff, Harold	Atl., Chi.	3	141	26	57	83	267	6	0	2	2	9	1979-80	1981-82
Picard, Noel	Mtl., St. L.	6	335	12	63	75	616	50	2	11	13	167	1972-73	1972-73
Pilote, Pierre	Chi., Tor.	13	890	80	418	498	1251	86	8	53	61	102	1968-69	1968-69
Pinder, Gerry	Chi., Cal.	3	223	55	69	124	135	17	0	4	4	6	1971-72	1971-72
Pirus, Alex	Min., Det.	3	159	30	28	58	94	2	0	1	1	2	1979-80	1980-81
Plager, Barclay	St. L.	9	614	44	187	231	1115	68	3	20	23	182	1976-77	1977-78
Plager, Robert	NYR, St. L.	10	644	20	126	146	800	74	2	17	19	195	1977-78	1977-78
Plager, Bill	Min., St. L., Atl.	4	263	4	34	38	292	31	0	2	2	26	1975-76	1975-76
Plamondon, Gerry	Montreal	2	74	7	13	20	10	10	5	2	7	2	1950-51	1955-56
Plante, Pierre	Phi., St. L., Chi., NYR, Que.	9	599	125	172	297	599	33	2	6	8	51	1979-80	1979-80
Pleau, Larry	Montreal	3	94	9	15	24	27	4	0	0	0	0	1971-72	1978-79
Poile, Bud	Tor., Chi., NYR, Bos.	6	311	107	122	229	91	23	4	4	8	8	1949-50	1954-55
Poile, Don	Detroit	1	66	7	9	16	12	4	0	0	0	0	1957-58	1961-62
Polich, Mike	Mtl., Min.	4	226	24	29	53	57	23	2	1	3	2	1980-81	1980-81
Polis, Greg	Pit., St. L., NYR, Wash.	10	615	174	169	343	391	7	0	2	2	6	1979-80	1979-80
Popein, Larry	NYR, Oak.	7	449	80	141	221	162	16	1	4	5	6	1967-68	1969-70
Popiel, Poul	Bos., L.A., Det., Van., Edm.	8	224	13	41	54	210	4	1	0	1	4	1979-80	1979-80
Porvari, Jukki	Colo, NJ.	2	39	3	9	12	4	....	....	....	....	....	1982-83	1982-83
Potvin, Jean	L.A., Phi., NYI, Clev., Min.	11	613	63	224	287	478	39	2	9	11	17	1980-81	1980-81
Pouzar, Jaroslav	Edmonton	3	174	32	45	77	129	24	5	3	8	14	1984-85	1984-85
Powis, Lynn	Chi., K.C.	2	130	19	33	52	25	1	0	0	0	0	1974-75	1977-78
Pratt, Babe	NYR, Tor., Bos.	13	517	83	209	292	473	63	12	17	29	90	1946-47	1951-52
Pratt, Tracy	Oak., Pit., Buf., Colo., Tor.	10	580	17	97	114	1026	25	0	1	1	62	1976-77	1976-77
Prentice, Dean	NYR, Bos., Pit., Min.	22	1378	391	469	860	484	54	13	17	30	38	1973-74	1973-74
Price, Jack	Chi.	1	57	4	6	10	24	4	0	0	0	0	1953-54	1965-66
Price, Noel	Tor., NYR, Det., Pit., L.A., Atl.	8	499	14	114	128	333	12	0	1	1	8	1975-76	1975-76
Pronovost, Andre	Mtl., Bos., Det., Min.	8	556	94	104	198	408	70	11	11	22	58	1967-68	1968-69
Pronovost, Marcel	Det., Tor.	20	1206	88	257	345	851	134	8	23	31	104	1969-70	1970-71
Pronovost, Jean	Pit., Atl., Wash.	14	998	391	383	774	413	35	11	9	20	14	1981-82	1981-82
*Provost, Claude	Mtl.	15	1005	254	335	589	469	126	25	38	63	86	1969-70	1969-70
Prystai, Metro	Chi., Det.	11	674	151	179	330	231	43	12	14	26	8	1957-58	1958-59
Pulford, Bob	Tor., L.A.	16	1079	281	362	643	792	89	25	26	51	126	1971-72	1971-72
Quackenbush, Max	Bos., Chi.	2	61	4	7	11	30	6	0	0	0	4	1951-52	1954-55
Quackenbush, Bill	Det., Bos.	13	774	62	222	284	95	79	2	19	21	8	1955-56	1955-56
Quinn, Pat	Tor., Van., Atl.	9	606	18	113	131	950	11	0	1	1	21	1976-77	1976-77
Raglan, Clare	Det., Chi.	3	100	4	9	13	52	3	0	0	0	0	1952-53	1957-58
Raleigh, Don	NYR	10	535	101	219	320	96	18	6	5	11	6	1955-56	1957-58
Ramsay, Craig	Buffalo	14	1070	252	420	672	201	89	17	31	48	27	1984-85	1984-85
Ratelle, Jean	NYR, Bos.	20	1281	491	776	1267	276	123	32	66	98	24	1980-81	1980-81
Rausse, Errol	Washington	3	31	7	3	10	0	....	....	....	....	....	1981-82	1982-83
Ravlich, Matt	Bos., Chi., Det., L.A.	7	410	12	78	90	364	24	1	5	6	16	1972-73	1973-74
Reardon, Terry	Bos., Mtl.	5	193	47	53	100	73	30	8	10	18	12	1946-47	1954-55
Reaume, Marc	Tor., Det., Mtl., Van.	6	344	8	43	51	273	21	0	2	2	8	1970-71	1970-71
Reay, Billy	Det., Mtl.	8	479	105	162	267	202	63	13	16	29	43	1952-53	1954-55
Redmond, Dick	Min., Cal., Chi., St. L., Atl., Bos.	12	771	133	312	445	504	66	9	22	31	27	1981-82	1981-82
Redmond, Mickey	Mtl., Det.	9	538	233	195	428	219	16	2	3	5	2	1975-76	1975-76
Regan, Larry	Bos., Tor.	5	280	41	95	136	71	42	7	14	21	18	1960-61	1965-66
Reibel, Earl	Det., Chi., Bos.	6	409	84	161	245	75	39	6	14	20	4	1958-59	1960-61
Reid, Tom	Chi., Min.	11	701	17	113	130	654	42	1	13	14	49	1977-78	1977-78
Reise, Leo	Chi., Det., NYR	8	494	28	81	109	399	52	8	5	13	68	1953-54	1953-54
Renaud, Mark	Hfd., Buf.	5	152	6	50	56	86	....	....	....	....	....	1983-84	1984-85
Richard, Henri	Montreal	20	1256	358	688	1046	928	180	49	80	129	181	1974-75	1974-75
Richard, Jacques	Atl., Buf., Que.	10	556	160	187	347	307	35	5	5	10	34	1982-83	1982-83
Richard, Maurice	Montreal	18	978	544	421	965	1285	133	82	44	126	188	1959-60	1959-60
Richardson, Dave	NYR, Chi., Det.	1	45	3	2	5	27	....	....	....	....	....	1967-68	1969-70
Richardson, Ken	St. Louis	1	49	8	13	21	16	....	....	....	....	....	1978-79	1979-80
Riley, Bill	Wash., Wpg.	5	139	31	30	61	320	....	....	....	....	....	1979-80	1983-84
Riopelle, Rip	Montreal	3	169	27	16	43	73	8	1	1	2	2	1949-50	1954-55
Rivers, Wayne	Det., Bos., St. L., NYR	4	108	15	30	45	94	....	....	....	....	....	1968-69	1976-77
Rizzuto, Garth	Vancouver	1	37	3	4	7	16	....	....	....	....	....	1970-71	1973-74
Robert, Rene	Tor., Pit., Buf., Colo.	11	744	284	418	702	597	50	22	19	41	73	1981-82	1981-82
Roberto, Phil	Mtl., St. L., Det., K.C., Colo., Clev.	6	385	75	106	181	464	31	9	8	17	69	1976-77	1977-78
Roberts, Doug	Det., Oak., Cal., Bos.	8	419	43	104	147	342	16	2	3	5	46	1974-75	1976-77
Roberts, Jim	Mtl., St. L.	15	1006	126	194	320	621	153	20	16	36	160	1977-78	1977-78
Roberts, Jimmy	Minnesota	2	106	17	23	40	33	2	0	0	0	0	1978-79	1979-80
Robinson, Doug	Chi., NYR, L.A.	4	239	44	67	111	34	11	4	3	7	0	1970-71	1971-72
Robitaille, Mike	NYR, Det., Buf., Van.	8	382	23	105	128	280	13	0	1	1	4	1976-77	1976-77
Rochefort, Leon	NYR, Mtl., Phi., L.A., Det., Atl., Van.	10	617	121	147	268	93	39	4	4	8	16	1975-76	1975-76
Rolfe, Dale	L.A., Det., NYR	8	509	25	125	150	556	71	5	24	29	89	1974-75	1974-75
Romanchych, Larry	Chi., Atl.	5	298	68	97	165	102	7	2	2	4	4	1976-77	1977-78
Rombough, Doug	Buf., NYI, Min.	3	150	24	27	51	80	....	....	....	....	....	1975-76	1977-78
Ronty, Paul	Bos., NYR, Mtl.	8	488	101	211	312	103	21	1	7	8	6	1954-55	1954-55
Ross, Jim	NY Rangers	2	51	2	9	11	25	....	....	....	....	....	1952-53	1954-55
Rota, Darcy	Chi., Atl., Van.	11	794	256	239	495	973	60	14	7	21	147	1983-84	1983-84
Rota, Randy	Mtl., L.A., K.C., Colo.,	4	212	38	39	77	60	5	0	1	1	0	1976-77	1977-78
Rousseau, Bobby	Mtl., Min., NYR	14	942	245	458	703	359	128	27	57	84	69	1974-75	1974-75
Rowe, Tom	Wash., Hfd., Det.	7	357	85	100	185	615	3	2	0	2	0	1982-83	1983-84
Rupp, Duane	NYR, Tor., Min., Pit.	7	374	24	93	117	220	10	2	2	4	8	1972-73	1976-77
Russell, Churchill	NY Rangers	3	90	20	16	36	12	....	....	....	....	....	1947-48	1950-51
Sabourin, Gary	St. L., Tor., Cal., Clev.	10	627	169	188	357	397	62	19	11	30	58	1976-77	1976-77
Sacharuk, Larry	NYR, St. L.	5	151	29	33	62	42	2	1	1	2	2	1976-77	1979-80
Saganiuk, Rocky	Tor., Pit.	6	259	57	65	122	201	6	1	0	1	15	1983-84	1984-85
St. Laurent, Andre	NYI., Det., L.A., Pit.	11	644	129	187	316	749	59	8	12	20	48	1983-84	1984-85
St. Laurent, Dollard	Mtl., Chi.	11	652	29	133	162	496	92	2	22	24	87	1961-62	1962-63
St. Marseille, Frank	St. L., L.A.	11	707	140	285	425	242	88	20	25	45	18	1976-77	1977-78
St. Sauveur, Claude	Atlanta	1	79	24	24	48	23	2	0	0	0	0	1975-76	1976-77
Saleski, Don	Phi., Colo.	9	543	128	125	253	629	82	13	17	30	131	1979-80	1979-80
Salovaara, Barry	Detroit	2	90	2	13	15	70	....	....	....	....	....	1975-76	1975-76

Name	NHL Teams	NHL Seasons	Regular Schedule					Playoffs					Last NHL Season	Last Pro Season
			GP	G	A	TP	PIM	GP	G	A	TP	PIM		
Sanderson, Derek	Bos., NYR, St. L., Van., Pit.	9	598	202	250	452	911	56	18	12	30	187	1977-78	1977-78
Sandford, Ed	Bos., Det., Chi.	9	502	106	145	251	355	42	13	11	24	27	1955-56	1955-56
Sargent, Gary	L.A., Min.	8	402	61	161	222	273	20	5	7	12	8	1982-83	1982-83
Sarrazin, Dick	Philadelphia	2	100	20	35	55	22	4	0	0	0	0	1971-72	1975-76
Sather, Glen	Bos., Pit., NYR, St. L., Mtl., Min.	10	658	80	113	193	724	72	1	5	6	86	1975-76	1976-77
Savard, Andre	Bos., Buf., Que.	12	790	211	271	482	411	85	13	18	31	77	1984-85	1984-85
Savard, Jean	Chi., Hfd.	2	43	7	12	19	29	....	....	....	....	....	1979-80	1980-81
Savard, Serge	Mtl., Wpg.	16	1040	106	333	439	592	130	19	49	68	88	1982-88	1982-83
Scamurra, Peter	Washington	2	132	8	25	33	59	....	....	....	....	....	1979-80	1979-80
Schella, John	Vancouver	2	115	2	18	20	224	....	....	....	....	....	1971-72	1978-79
Schinkel, Ken	NYR, Pit.	11	636	127	198	325	163	19	7	2	9	4	1972-73	1972-73
Schmautz, Bobby	Chi., Bos., Edm., Colo., Van.	12	764	271	286	557	988	73	28	33	61	92	1980-81	1980-81
Schmautz, Cliff	Buff., Phi.	1	56	13	19	32	33	....	....	....	....	....	1970-71	1972-73
Schmidt, Milt	Boston	16	776	229	346	575	466	86	24	25	49	60	1954-55	1954-55
Schock, Ron	Bos., St. L., Pit., Buf.	15	909	166	351	517	260	55	4	16	20	29	1977-78	1979-80
Schoenfeld, Jim	Buf., Det., Bos.	13	719	51	204	255	1132	75	3	13	16	151	1984-85	1984-85
Schultz, Dave	Phi., L.A., Pit., Buf.	9	535	79	121	200	2294	73	8	12	20	412	1979-80	1979-80
Sclisizzi, Enio (Jim)	Det., Chi.	2	81	12	11	23	26	13	0	0	0	6	1952-53	1958-59
Sedlbauer, Ron	Van., Chi., Tor.	7	430	143	86	229	210	19	1	3	4	27	1980-81	1981-83
Seguin, Dan	Min., Van.	2	37	2	6	8	50	....	....	....	....	....	1973-74	1976-77
Seiling, Rod	Tor., NYR, Wash., Atl., St. L.	18	979	62	269	331	603	77	4	8	12	55	1978-79	1978-79
Selby, Brit	Tor., Phi., St. L.	5	350	55	62	117	163	16	1	1	2	8	1971-72	1973-74
Selwood, Brad	Tor., L.A.	3	163	7	40	47	153	6	0	0	0	4	1979-80	1981-82
Shack, Eddie	NYR, Tor., Bos., L.A., Buf., Pit.	17	1047	239	226	465	1437	74	6	7	13	151	1974-75	1974-75
Shanahan, Sean	Mtl., Colo., Bos.	1	40	1	3	4	47	....	....	....	....	....	1977-78	1978-79
Shand, Dave	Atl., Tor., Wsh.	8	421	19	84	103	544	26	1	2	3	83	1984-85	1984-85
Sharpley, Glen	Min., Chi.	6	389	117	161	278	199	27	7	11	18	24	1981-82	1981-82
Sheehan, Bobby	Mtl., Cal., Chi., Det., NYR, Colo., L.A.	9	310	48	63	111	50	25	4	3	7	8	1981-82	1982-83
Sheppard, Gregg	Bos., Pit.	10	657	205	293	498	243	92	32	40	72	31	1981-82	1981-82
Shero, Fred	NY Rangers	3	145	6	14	20	136	13	0	2	2	8	1948-49	1957-58
Shill, Bill	Boston	2	79	21	13	34	18	7	1	2	3	2	1946-47	1951-52
Shinske, Rick	Clev., St. L.	3	63	5	16	21	10	....	....	....	....	....	1978-79	1982-83
Shires, Jim	Det., St. L., Pit.	3	56	3	6	9	32	....	....	....	....	....	1972-73	1973-74
Shmyr, Paul	Chi., Cal., Min., Hfd.	7	343	13	72	85	528	34	3	3	6	44	1981-82	1981-82
Shutt, Steve	Mtl., L.A.	13	930	424	393	817	410	99	50	48	98	65	1984-85	1984-85
Sims, Al	Bos., Hfd., L.A.	9	475	49	116	165	286	41	0	2	2	14	1981-82	1981-82
Sinclair, Reg	NYR, Det.	3	208	49	43	92	139	3	1	0	1	0	1952-53	1952-53
Sittler, Darryl	Tor., Phi., Det.	15	1096	484	637	1121	948	76	29	45	74	137	1984-85	1984-85
Sjoberg, Lars	Winnipeg	1	79	7	27	34	48	....	....	....	....	....	1979-80	1979-80
Skinner, Larry	Colorado	4	47	10	12	22	8	2	0	0	0	0	1979-80	1982-83
Skov, Glen	Det., Chi., Mtl.	10	650	106	136	242	413	53	7	7	14	48	1960-61	1960-61
Sloan, Tod	Tor., Chi.	12	745	220	262	482	781	47	9	12	21	47	1960-61	1960-61
Slowinski, Ed	NY Rangers	6	291	58	74	132	63	16	2	6	8	6	1952-53	1957-58
Sly, Darryl	Tor., Min., Van.	2	79	1	2	3	20	....	....	....	....	....	1970-71	1970-71
Smith, Barry	Bos., Colo.	3	114	7	7	14	10	....	....	....	....	....	1980-81	1980-81
Smith, Brian D.	L.A., Min.	1	61	10	10	20	33	7	0	0	0	0	1968-69	1969-70
Smith, Brian S.	Detroit	2	81	2	8	10	12	5	0	0	0	0	1960-61	1967-68
Smith, Dallas	Bos., NYR	13	890	55	252	307	959	86	3	29	32	128	1977-78	1977-78
Smith, Derek	Buff., Det.	5	335	78	116	194	60	30	9	14	23	13	1982-83	1983-84
Smith, Floyd	Bos., NYR, Det., Tor., Buf.	11	616	129	178	307	207	48	12	11	23	16	1971-72	1971-72
Smith, Gord	Wash., Wpg.	6	299	9	30	39	284	....	....	....	....	....	1979-80	1982-83
Smith, Ken	Boston	7	331	78	93	171	49	30	8	13	21	6	1950-51	1956-57
Smith, Rick	Bos., Cal., St. L., Det., Wash.	12	687	52	167	219	560	78	3	23	26	73	1980-81	1980-81
Smith, Sid	Toronto	10	601	186	183	369	94	44	17	10	27	2	1957-58	1957-58
Smith, Stuart, Gordon	Hartford	4	77	2	10	12	95	....	....	....	....	....	1982-83	1984-85
Smrke, John	St. L., Que.	3	103	11	17	28	33	....	....	....	....	....	1979-80	1981-82
Snell, Ted	Pit., K.C.,. Det.	2	104	7	18	25	22	....	....	....	....	....	1974-75	1975-76
Solinger, Bob	Tor., Det.	3	99	10	11	21	19	....	....	....	....	....	1959-60	1963-64
Songin, Tom	Boston	3	43	5	5	10	22	....	....	....	....	....	1980-81	1982-83
Speer, Bill	Pit., Bos.	3	130	5	20	25	79	8	1	0	1	4	1970-71	1973-74
Spencer, Brian	Tor., NYI, Buf., Pit.	10	553	80	143	223	634	37	1	5	6	29	1978-79	1979-80
Spencer, Irv	NYR, Bos., Det.	4	230	12	38	50	127	16	0	0	0	8	1967-68	1971-72
Spring, Don	Winnipeg	4	259	1	54	55	80	6	0	0	0	10	1983-84	1983-84
Spring, Frank	Bos., St. L., Cal., Clev.	1	61	14	20	34	12	....	....	....	....	....	1976-77	1977-78
Spruce, Andy	Van., Col.	3	172	31	42	115	111	2	0	2	2	0	1978-79	1981-82
Stackhouse, Ron	Cal., Det., Pit.	12	889	87	372	459	824	32	5	8	13	38	1981-82	1981-82
Stamler, Lorne	L.A., Tor., Wpg.	4	116	14	11	25	16	....	....	....	....	....	1979-80	1983-84
Stanfield, Fred	Chi., Bos., Min., Buf.	14	914	211	405	616	134	106	21	35	56	10	1977-78	1978-79
Stankiewicz, Myron	St. L., Phi.	1	35	0	7	7	36	1	0	0	0	0	1968-69	1968-69
Stanley, Allan	NYR, Chi., Bos., Tor., Phi.	21	1244	100	333	433	792	109	7	36	43	80	1968-69	1968-69
Stanowski, Wally	Tor., NYR	10	428	23	88	111	160	60	3	14	17	13	1950-51	1951-52
Stapleton, Pat	Bos., Chi.	10	635	43	294	337	353	65	10	39	49	38	1972-73	1977-78
Stasiuk, Vic	Chi., Det., Bos.	13	745	183	254	437	669	69	16	18	34	40	1961-62	1965-66
Steen, Anders	Winnipeg	1	42	5	11	16	22	....	....	....	....	....	1980-81	1980-81
Stemkowski, Pete	Tor., Det., NYR, L.A.	15	967	206	349	555	866	83	25	29	54	136	1977-78	1978-79
Stewart, Blair	Det., Wash., Que.	5	229	34	44	78	326	....	....	....	....	....	1979-80	1980-81
Stewart, Bob	Bos., Cal., Clev., St. L., Pit.	9	510	27	101	128	809	5	1	1	2	2	1979-80	1979-80
Stewart, Gaye	Tor., Chi., Det., NYR, Mtl.	9	502	185	159	344	274	25	2	9	11	16	1953-54	1953-54
Stewart, Jack	Det., Chi.	12	565	31	84	115	765	80	5	14	19	143	1951-52	1951-52
Stewart, John	Pit., Atl., Cal.	4	258	58	60	118	158	4	0	0	0	10	1974-75	1977-78
Stewart, Ralph	Van., NYI	7	252	57	73	130	28	19	4	4	8	2	1975-76	1978-79
Stewart, Ron	Tor., Bos., St. L., NYR, Van., NYI	21	1353	276	253	529	560	119	14	21	35	60	1972-73	1972-73
Stoddard, Jack	NY Rangers	2	80	16	15	31	31	....	....	....	....	....	1952-53	1955-56
Stoughton, Blaine	Pit., Tor., Hfd., NYR.	8	526	258	191	449	204	8	4	2	6	2	1983-84	1984-85
Strain, Neil	NY Rangers	1	52	11	13	24	12	....	....	....	....	....	1952-53	1953-54
State, Gord	Detroit	2	61	0	0	0	34	....	....	....	....	....	1958-59	1961-62
Stratton, Art	NYR, Det., Chi., Pit., Phi.	2	95	18	33	51	24	5	0	0	0	0	1967-68	1974-75
Sullivan, Bob	Hartford	1	62	18	19	37	18	....	....	....	....	....	1982-83	1983-84
Sullivan, Red	Bos., Chi., NYR	9	557	107	239	346	441	18	1	2	3	7	1960-61	1962-63
Sullivan, Peter	Winnipeg	2	126	28	54	82	40	....	....	....	....	....	1980-81	1981-82
Sutherland, Bill	Mtl., Phi., Tor., St. L., Det.	5	250	70	58	128	99	14	2	4	6	0	1971-72	1973-74
Suzor, Mark	Phi., Colo.	1	64	4	16	20	60	....	....	....	....	....	1977-78	1979-80
Svensson, Leif	Washington	2	121	6	40	46	49	....	....	....	....	....	1979-80	1979-80
Swarbrick, George	Oak., Pit., Phi.	3	132	17	25	42	173	....	....	....	....	....	1970-71	1973-74
Szura, Joe	Oakland	2	90	10	15	25	30	7	2	3	5	2	1968-69	1973-74
Talafous, Dean	Atl., Min., NYR	8	479	104	154	258	163	21	4	7	11	11	1981-82	1981-82
Talbot, Jean-Guy	Mtl., Min., Det., St. L., Buf.	16	1056	43	242	285	1006	150	4	26	30	142	1970-71	1970-71
Tallon, Dale	Van., Chi., Pit.	10	642	98	238	336	568	33	2	10	12	45	1979-80	1979-80
Tannahill, Don	Vancouver	2	111	30	33	63	25	....	....	....	....	....	1973-74	1977-78
Tardif, Marc	Mtl., Que.	8	517	194	207	401	443	62	13	15	28	75	1982-83	1982-83
Taylor, Harry	Tor., Chi.	2	66	5	10	15	30	1	0	0	0	0	1951-52	1954-55
Taylor, Ted	NYR, Det., Min., Van.	3	166	23	35	58	181	....	....	....	....	....	1971-72	1977-78
Terbenche, Paul	Chi., Buf.	3	189	5	26	31	28	12	0	0	0	0	1973-74	1979-80
Tessier, Orval	Mtl., Bos.	2	59	5	7	12	6	....	....	....	....	....	1960-61	163-64
Theberge, Greg	Wasington	5	153	15	63	78	73	4	0	1	1	0	1983-84	1983-84
Thomas, Reg	Quebec	1	39	9	7	16	6	....	....	....	....	....	1979-80	1982-83
Thompson, Errol	Tor., Det., Pit.	9	599	208	185	393	184	34	7	5	12	11	1980-81	1980-81
Thomson, Floyd	St. Louis	7	411	56	97	153	341	10	0	2	2	6	1979-80	1981-82
Thomson, Jim	Tor., Chi.	12	787	19	215	234	920	63	2	13	15	135	1957-58	1957-58
Thurier, Fred	NYA, NYR	2	80	25	27	52	18	....	....	....	....	....	1944-45	1951-52

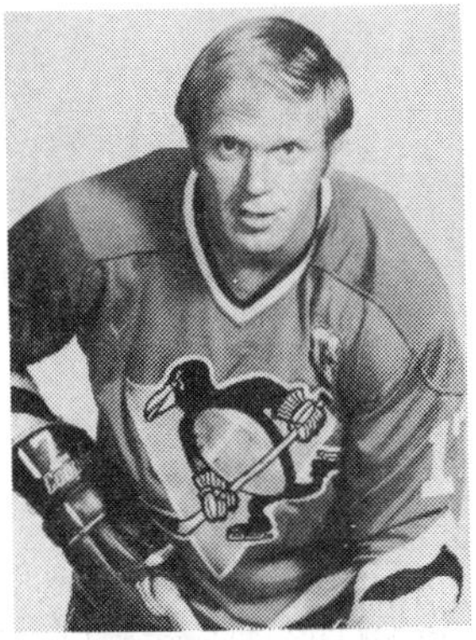
Ron Schock

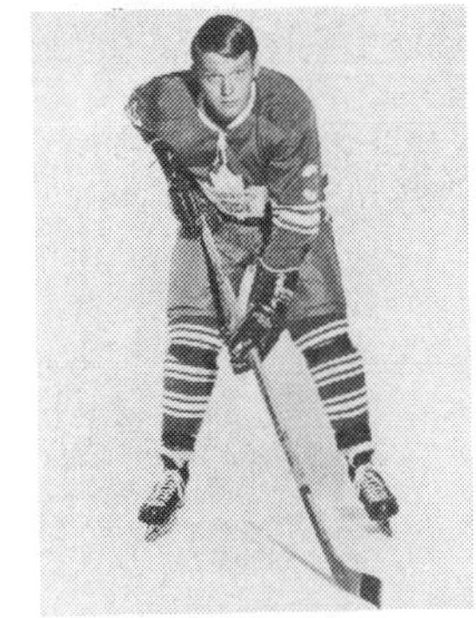
Brad Selwood

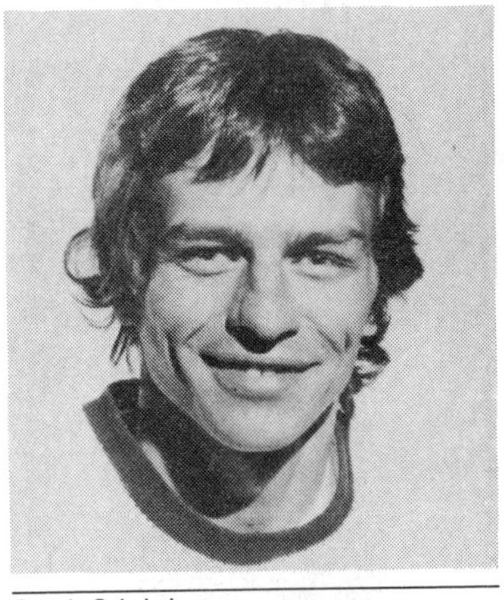
Dennis Sobchuk

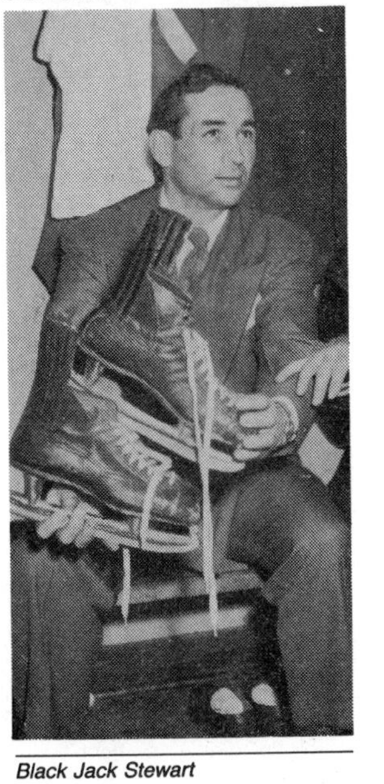
Black Jack Stewart

Jean Guy Talbot

John Wensink

Name	NHL Teams	NHL Seasons	Regular Schedule					Playoffs					Last NHL Season	Last Pro Season
			GP	G	A	TP	PIM	GP	G	A	TP	PIM		
Timgren, Ray	Tor., Chi.	5	251	14	44	58	70	30	3	9	12	6	1954-55	1955-56
Tkaczuk, Walt	NY Rangers	13	945	227	451	678	556	93	19	32	51	119	1980-81	1980-81
Toppazzini, Jerry	Bos., Chi., Det.	12	783	163	244	407	436	40	13	9	22	13	1963-64	1966-67
Toppazzini, Zellio	Bos., NYR, Chi.	3	123	21	22	43	49	2	0	0	0	0	1956-57	1963-64
Tremblay, Gilles	Montreal	9	509	168	162	330	161	48	9	14	23	4	1968-69	1968-69
Tremblay, Jean-Claude	Montreal	13	794	57	306	363	204	108	14	51	65	58	1971-72	1978-79
Trimper, Tim	Chi., Wpg., Min.	6	190	30	36	66	153	2	0	0	0	2	1984-85	1984-85
Trottier, Guy	NYR, Tor.	2	115	28	17	45	37	9	1	0	1	16	1971-72	1973-74
Turnbull, Ian	Tor., L.A., Pit.	11	628	123	317	440	753	55	13	32	45	94	1982-83	1982-83
Turner, Bob	Mtl., Chi.	8	478	19	51	70	307	68	1	4	5	44	1962-63	1963-64
Turner, Dean	NYR, Colo., L.A.	4	35	1	0	1	59	....	....	....	....	....	1982-83	1982-83
Ubriaco, Gene	Pit., Oak., Chi.	3	177	39	35	74	50	11	2	0	2	4	1969-70	1969-70
Ullman, Norm	Det., Tor.	20	1410	490	739	1229	712	106	30	53	83	67	1974-75	1976-77
Unger, Garry	Tor., Det., St. L., Atl., L.A., Edm.	16	1105	413	391	804	1075	52	12	18	30	105	1982-83	1982-83
Vadnais, Carol	Mtl., Oak., Cal., Bos., NYR, NJ	17	1087	169	418	587	1813	106	10	40	50	185	1982-83	1982-83
Valentine, Chris	Washington	3	105	43	52	95	127	2	0	0	0	4	1983-84	1983-84
Valiquette, Jack	Tor., Colo.	5	350	84	134	218	79	23	3	6	9	4	1980-81	1980-81
Van Boxmeer, John	Mtl., Colo., Buf., Que.	11	588	84	274	358	465	38	5	15	20	37	1983-84	1984-85
Van Impe, Ed	Chi., Phi., Pit.	11	700	27	126	153	1025	66	1	12	13	131	1976-77	1976-77
Vail, Eric	Atl., Cgy., Det.	9	591	216	260	476	281	20	5	6	11	6	1981-82	1982-83
Vasko, Elmer	Chi., Min.	12	786	34	166	200	719	78	2	7	9	73	1969-70	1969-70
Vautour, Yvon	NYI., Colo., N.J., Que.	6	204	26	33	59	401	....	....	....	....	....	1984-85	1984-85
Venasky, Vic	Los Angeles	7	430	61	101	162	66	21	1	5	6	12	1978-79	1979-80
Ververgaert, Dennis	Van., Phi., Wash.	8	583	176	216	392	247	8	1	2	3	6	1980-81	1980-81
Vickers, Steve	NY Rangers	10	698	246	340	586	330	68	24	25	49	58	1981-82	1981-82
Vigneault, Alain	St. Louis	2	42	2	5	7	82	4	0	1	1	26	1982-83	1983-84
Volmar, Doug	Det., L.A.	1	62	13	8	21	26	2	1	0	1	0	1972-73	1974-75
Walker, Howard	Wash., Cgy.	3	83	2	13	15	133	....	....	....	....	....	1982-83	1982-83
Walker, Kurt	Toronto	1	71	4	5	9	152	16	0	0	0	34	1977-78	1979-80
Wall, Bob	Det., L.A., St. L.	5	322	30	55	85	155	22	0	3	3	2	1971-72	1975-76
Wallin, Peter	NY Rangers	2	52	3	14	17	14	14	2	6	8	4	1981-82	1982-83
Walton, Michael	Tor., Bos., Van., Chi., St. L.	12	588	201	247	448	357	47	14	10	24	45	1978-79	1978-79
Ward, Ron	Tor., Van.	2	89	2	5	7	6	....	....	....	....	....	1970-71	1974-75
Warwick, Grant	NYR, Bos., Mtl.	9	395	147	142	289	220	16	2	4	6	6	1949-50	1951-52
Watson, Harry	NYA, Det., Tor., Chi.	14	805	236	207	443	150	62	16	9	25	27	1956-57	1957-58
Watson, Bryan	Mtl., Oak., Pit., Det., St. L., Wash.	17	878	17	135	152	2212	32	2	0	2	70	1978-79	1978-79
Watson, Jim A.	Det., Buf.	3	221	4	19	23	345	....	....	....	....	....	1971-72	1974-75
Watson, Jim	Philadelphia	9	613	38	148	186	492	101	5	34	39	89	1981-82	1981-82
Watson, Joe	Bos., Phi., Colo.	14	835	38	178	216	447	84	3	12	15	82	1977-78	1978-79
Webster, Tom	Bos., Det., Cal.	2	102	33	42	75	61	1	0	0	0	0	1979-80	1979-80
Weir, Stan	Cal., Tor., Edm., Colo., Det.	10	642	139	207	346	183	37	6	5	11	4	1982-83	1983-84
Wensink, John	Bos., Que., Colo., NJ, St. L.	8	403	70	68	138	840	43	2	6	8	86	1982-83	1982-83
Westfall, Ed	Bos., NYI	18	1227	231	394	625	544	95	22	37	59	41	1978-79	1978-79
Wharram, Ken	Chicago	12	766	252	281	533	222	80	16	27	43	38	1968-69	1968-69
White, Bill	L.A., Chi.	9	604	50	215	265	495	91	7	32	39	76	1975-76	1975-76
White, Tony	Wash., Min.	3	164	37	28	65	104	....	....	....	....	....	1979-80	1980-81
*Widing, Juha	NYR, L.A., Clev.	9	575	144	226	370	208	8	1	2	3	2	1976-77	1977-78
Wiley, Jim	Pit., Van.	2	63	4	10	14	8	....	....	....	....	....	1976-77	1979-80
Wilkins, Barry	Bos., Van., Pit.	9	418	27	125	152	663	6	0	1	1	4	1975-76	1978-79
Williams, Fred	Detroit	1	44	2	5	7	10	....	....	....	....	....	1976-77	1977-78
Williams, Tom	Bos., Min., Cal., Wash.	10	663	161	269	430	177	10	2	5	7	2	1975-76	1975-76
Williams, Butch	St. L., Cal.	3	108	14	35	49	131	....	....	....	....	....	1975-76	1976-77
Williams, Tommy	NYR, L.A.	8	397	115	138	253	73	29	8	7	15	4	1978-79	1979-80
Wilson, Bert	NYR, St. L., L.A., Cgy.	8	478	37	44	81	646	21	0	2	2	42	1980-81	1982-83
Wilson, Johnny	Det., Chi., Tor., NYR	11	688	161	171	332	190	66	14	13	27	11	1961-62	1961-62
*Wilson, Larry	Det., Chi.	3	152	21	48	69	75	4	0	0	0	0	1955-56	1967-68
Wilson, Murray	Mtl., L.A.	7	386	94	95	189	162	53	5	14	19	32	1978-79	1978-79
Wilson, Rick	Mtl., St. L., Det.	4	239	6	26	32	165	3	0	0	0	0	1976-77	1977-78
Wilson, Ron	Toronto	1	64	7	15	22	6	6	1	3	4	2	1979-80	1979-80
Wiste, Jim	Chi., Van.	1	52	1	10	11	8	....	....	....	....	....	1970-71	1974-75
Wochy, Steve	Det.	1	54	19	20	39	17	6	0	1	1	0	1946-47	1954-55
Wolt, Benny	Det., Chi.	5	334	7	26	33	170	41	2	6	8	18	1968-69	1968-69
Woods, Paul	Detroit	7	501	72	124	196	276	7	0	5	5	4	1983-84	1984-85
Woytowich, Bob	Bos., Min., Pit., L.A.	8	503	32	126	158	352	24	1	3	4	20	1971-72	1974-75
Wright, John	Van., St. L., K.C.	2	127	16	36	52	67	....	....	....	....	....	1974-75	1974-75
Wright, Larry	Phi., Cal., Det.	5	66	3	6	9	13	1	0	1	1	7	1977-78	1978-79
Wyrozub, Randy	Buffalo	2	100	8	10	18	10	....	....	....	....	....	1973-74	1974-75
Young, Howie	Det., Chi., Van.	8	336	12	62	74	851	19	2	4	6	46	1970-71	1974-75
Young, Tim	Min., Wpg., Phi.	10	620	195	341	536	438	36	7	24	31	27	1984-85	1984-85
Younghans, Tom	Min., NYR	6	429	44	41	85	373	24	2	1	3	21	1981-82	1981-82
Zaharko, Miles	Atl., Chi.	4	129	5	32	37	84	3	0	0	0	0	1981-82	1982-83
Zaine, Rod	Pit., Buf.	2	61	10	6	16	25	....	....	....	....	....	1971-72	1974-75
Zanussi, Joe	NYR, Bos., St. L.	2	87	1	13	14	46	4	0	1	1	2	1976-77	1977-78
Zanussi, Ron	Minn., Tor.	5	299	52	83	135	373	17	0	4	4	17	1981-82	1983-84
Zeidel, Larry	Det., Chi., Phi.	3	158	3	16	19	198	12	0	1	1	12	1968-69	1968-69

1986-87 Goaltender Register

Notes: The 1986-87 Goaltender Register lists every goaltender who appeared in an NHL game in the 1985-86 season, every goaltender drafted in the first two rounds of the 1985 and 1986 Entry Drafts and other goaltenders on NHL Reserve Lists.

To calculate a goaltenders' goals-against-per-game average (**Avg**), divide goals against (**GA**) by minutes played (**Mins**) and multiply this result by **60**.

Abbreviations: A list of league names can be found at the beginning of the Player Register. **Avg** – goals against per game average; **GA** – goals against; **GP** – games played; **L** – losses; **Lea** – league; **SO** – shutouts; **T** – ties; **W** – wins.

Player Register begins on page 195.

BANNERMAN, MURRAY

Born, Fort Frances, Ont., April 27, 1957.
Goaltender. Catches left. 5′11″, 185 lbs.
Last amateur club: Victoria Cougars (WHL).
(Vancouver's 5th choice, 58th over-all, in 1977 Amateur Draft).

			Regular Season								Playoffs						
Season	**Club**	**Lea**	**GP**	**W**	**L**	**T**	**Mins**	**GA**	**SO**	**Avg**	**GP**	**W**	**L**	**Mins**	**GA**	**SO**	**Avg**
1973-74	Winnipeg	WHL	6	....	....	....	258	29	0	6.74	....	....	....	....	....	....	....
1974-75	Winnipeg	WHL	28	3	12	5	1351	113	0	5.02	....	....	....	....	....	....	....
1975-76	Victoria	WHL	44	....	....	....	2450	179	1	4.36	15	....	....	878	50	0	3.42
1976-77	Victoria	WHL	67	....	....	....	3893	262	2	4.04	4	....	....	234	20	0	5.13
1977-78	**Vancouver**	**NHL**	**1**	**0**	**0**	**0**	**20**	**0**	**0**	**0.00**	....	....	....	....	....	....	....
a	Fort Wayne	IHL	44	....	....	....	2435	133	1	3.28	6	....	....	335	26	0	4.66
1978-79	New Brunswick	AHL	47	22	14	5	2557	151	0	3.54	3	1	1	122	10	0	4.92
1979-80b	New Brunswick	AHL	61	32	20	5	3361	186	*3	3.32	17	10	6	1049	51	0	2.92
1980-81	**Chicago**	**NHL**	**15**	**2**	**10**	**2**	**865**	**62**	**0**	**4.30**	....	....	....	....	....	....	....
1981-82	**Chicago**	**NHL**	**29**	**11**	**12**	**4**	**1671**	**116**	**1**	**4.17**	**10**	**5**	**4**	**555**	**35**	**0**	**3.79**
1982-83	**Chicago**	**NHL**	**41**	**24**	**12**	**5**	**2460**	**127**	**4**	**3.10**	**8**	**4**	**4**	**480**	**32**	**0**	**4.00**
1983-84	**Chicago**	**NHL**	**56**	**23**	**29**	**4**	**3335**	**188**	**2**	**3.38**	**5**	**2**	**3**	**300**	**17**	**0**	**3.40**
1984-85	**Chicago**	**NHL**	**60**	**27**	**25**	**4**	**3371**	**215**	**0**	**3.83**	**15**	**9**	**6**	**906**	**72**	**0**	**4.77**
1985-86	**Chicago**	**NHL**	**48**	**20**	**19**	**6**	**2689**	**201**	**1**	**4.48**	**2**	**0**	**1**	**81**	**9**	**0**	**4.85**
	NHL Totals		**250**	**107**	**107**	**25**	**14411**	**909**	**8**	**3.78**	**40**	**20**	**18**	**2322**	**165**	**0**	**4.26**

a IHL First All-Star Team (1978)
b AHL Second All-Star Team (1980)

Traded to **Chicago** by **Vancouver**, May 27, 1978 to complete an earlier deal when Vancouver received Pit Martin, November 4, 1977.

BARRASSO, TOM

Born, Boston, Mass., March 31, 1965.
Goaltender. Catches right. 6′3″, 200 lbs.
Last amateur club: Acton Boxboro High School (Massachusetts)
(Buffalo's 1st choice, 5th over-all, in 1983 Entry Draft).

			Regular Season								Playoffs						
Season	**Club**	**Lea**	**GP**	**W**	**L**	**T**	**Mins**	**GA**	**SO**	**Avg**	**GP**	**W**	**L**	**Mins**	**GA**	**SO**	**Avg**
1981-82	Acton-Boxboro	Mass.	23	....	....	....	1035	32	7	1.39	....	....	....	....	....	....	....
1982-83	Acton-Boxboro	Mass.	23	....	....	....	1035	17	10	0.73	....	....	....	....	....	....	....
1983-84abcd	**Buffalo**	**NHL**	**42**	**26**	**12**	**3**	**2475**	**117**	**2**	**2.84**	**3**	**0**	**2**	**139**	**8**	**0**	**3.45**
1984-85ef	**Buffalo**	**NHL**	**54**	**25**	**18**	**10**	**3248**	**144**	***5**	**2.66**	**5**	**2**	**3**	**300**	**22**	**0**	**4.40**
	Rochester	AHL	5	3	1	1	267	6	1	1.35	....	....	....	....	....	....	....
1985-86	**Buffalo**	**NHL**	**60**	**29**	**24**	**5**	**3561**	**214**	**2**	**3.61**	....	....	....	....	....	....	....
	NHL Totals		**156**	**80**	**54**	**18**	**9284**	**475**	**9**	**3.07**	**8**	**2**	**5**	**439**	**30**	**0**	**4.10**

a NHL First All-Star Team (1984)
b Won Vezina Trophy (1984)
c Won Calder Memorial Trophy (1984)
d Named to NHL All-Rookie Team (1984)
e NHL Second All-Star Team (1985)
f Shared William Jennings Trophy with Bob Sauve (1985)

BEAUPRE, DONALD WILLIAM (DON) (boh-PRAY)

Born, Waterloo, Ont., September 19, 1961.
Goaltender. Catches left. 5′8″, 150 lbs.
Last amateur club: Sudbury Wolves (OHA).
(Minnesota's 2nd choice, 37th over-all, in 1980 Entry Draft).

			Regular Season								Playoffs						
Season	**Club**	**Lea**	**GP**	**W**	**L**	**T**	**Mins**	**GA**	**SO**	**Avg**	**GP**	**W**	**L**	**Mins**	**GA**	**SO**	**Avg**
1978-79	Sudbury	OHA	54	....	....	....	3248	260	2	4.78	10	....	....	600	44	0	4.20
1979-80a	Sudbury	OHA	59	28	29	2	3447	248	0	4.32	9	5	4	552	38	0	4.13
1980-81	**Minnesota**	**NHL**	**44**	**18**	**14**	**11**	**2585**	**138**	**0**	**3.20**	**6**	**4**	**2**	**360**	**26**	**0**	**4.33**
1981-82	Nashville	CHL	5	2	3	0	299	25	0	5.02	....	....	....	....	....	....	....
	Minnesota	**NHL**	**29**	**11**	**8**	**9**	**1634**	**101**	**0**	**3.71**	**2**	**0**	**1**	**60**	**4**	**0**	**4.00**
1982-83	Birmingham	CHL	10	8	2	0	599	31	0	3.11	....	....	....	....	....	....	....
	Minnesota	**NHL**	**36**	**19**	**10**	**5**	**2011**	**120**	**0**	**3.58**	**4**	**2**	**2**	**245**	**20**	**0**	**4.90**
1983-84	Salt Lake	CHL	7	2	5	0	419	30	0	4.30	....	....	....	....	....	....	....
	Minnesota	**NHL**	**33**	**16**	**13**	**2**	**1791**	**123**	**0**	**4.12**	**13**	**6**	**7**	**782**	**40**	**1**	**3.07**
1984-85	**Minnesota**	**NHL**	**31**	**10**	**17**	**3**	**1770**	**109**	**1**	**3.69**	**4**	**1**	**1**	**184**	**12**	**0**	**3.91**
1985-86	**Minnesota**	**NHL**	**52**	**25**	**20**	**6**	**3073**	**182**	**1**	**3.55**	**5**	**2**	**3**	**300**	**17**	**0**	**3.40**
	NHL Totals		**225**	**99**	**82**	**36**	**12864**	**773**	**2**	**3.61**	**34**	**15**	**16**	**1931**	**119**	**1**	**3.70**

a OHA First All-Star Team (1980)

BEEDON, ROGER

Born, Marysville, Mich., May 30, 1967.
Goaltender. Catches left. 6′0″, 175 lbs.
Last amateur club: Ohio State University Buckeyes (CCHA).
(Montreal's 11th choice, 184th over-all, in 1985 Entry Draft).

			Regular Season								Playoffs						
Season	**Club**	**Lea**	**GP**	**W**	**L**	**T**	**Mins**	**GA**	**SO**	**Avg**	**GP**	**W**	**L**	**Mins**	**GA**	**SO**	**Avg**
1985-86	Ohio St.	CCHA	27	12	11	0	1393	115	0	4.95	....	....	....	....	....	....	....

BEHREND, MARC (BAY-rend)

Born, Madison, Wisconsin, January 11, 1961.
Goaltender. Catches left. 6′1″, 180 lbs.
Last amateur club: 1984 United States Olympic Team.
(Winnipeg's 5th choice, 85th over-all, in 1981 Entry Draft).

			Regular Season								Playoffs						
Season	**Club**	**Lea**	**GP**	**W**	**L**	**T**	**Mins**	**GA**	**SO**	**Avg**	**GP**	**W**	**L**	**Mins**	**GA**	**SO**	**Avg**
1980-81	U. of Wisconsin	WCHA	16	11	4	1	913	50	0	3.25	....	....	....	....	....	....	....
1981-82	U. of Wisconsin	WCHA	25	21	3	1	1502	65	2	2.60	....	....	....	....	....	....	....
1982-83a	U. of Wisconsin	WCHA	19	17	1	1	1315	49	2	*2.24	....	....	....	....	....	....	....
1983-84	U.S. National	....	33	....	....	....	1895	89	0	2.82	....	....	....	....	....	....	....
	U.S. Olympic	....	4	....	....	....	200	11	0	3.30	....	....	....	....	....	....	....
	Winnipeg	**NHL**	**6**	**2**	**4**	**0**	**351**	**32**	**0**	**5.47**	**2**	**0**	**2**	**121**	**9**	**0**	**4.46**
1984-85	**Winnipeg**	**NHL**	**23**	**8**	**10**	**2**	**1173**	**87**	**1**	**4.45**	**4**	**1**	**1**	**179**	**10**	**0**	**3.35**
	Sherbrooke	AHL	7	2	3	2	427	25	0	3.51	....	....	....	....	....	....	....
1985-86	**Winnipeg**	**NHL**	**9**	**2**	**5**	**0**	**422**	**41**	**0**	**5.83**	**1**	**0**	**0**	**12**	**0**	**0**	**0.0**
	Sherbrooke	AHL	35	16	5	2	2028	132	1	3.91	....	....	....	....	....	....	....
	NHL Totals		**38**	**12**	**19**	**0**	**1946**	**160**	**1**	**4.93**	**7**	**1**	**3**	**312**	**19**	**0**	**3.65**

a Named to NCAA All-Tournament Team (1983).

BERNHARDT, TIMOTHY JOHN (TIM) (burn-HEART)

Born, Sarnia, Ont., January 17, 1958.
Goaltender. Catches left. 5′9″, 160 lbs.
Last amateur club: Cornwall Royals (QMJHL).
(Atlanta's 2nd choice, 47th over-all, in 1978 Amateur Draft).

			Regular Season								Playoffs						
Season	**Club**	**Lea**	**GP**	**W**	**L**	**T**	**Mins**	**GA**	**SO**	**Avg**	**GP**	**W**	**L**	**Mins**	**GA**	**SO**	**Avg**
1976-77a	Cornwall	QJHL	44	....	....	....	2497	151	0	3.63	12	....	....	720	47	0	3.92
1977-78a	Cornwall	QJHL	54	....	....	....	3165	179	2	3.39	9	....	....	540	27	2	3.00
1978-79	Tulsa	CHL	46	....	....	....	2705	191	0	4.24	....	....	....	....	....	....	....
1979-80	Birmingham	CHL	34	15	16	1	1933	122	1	3.79	3	....	....	160	17	0	6.38
1980-81	Birmingham	CHL	29	11	13	2	1598	106	1	3.98	....	....	....	....	....	....	....
1981-82	Oklahoma City	CHL	10	1	8	0	526	45	0	5.13	....	....	....	....	....	....	....
	Rochester	AHL	29	15	10	.2	1586	95	0	3.59	9	4	3	527	29	0	3.30
1982-83	**Calgary**	**NHL**	**6**	**0**	**5**	**0**	**280**	**21**	**0**	**4.50**	....	....	....	....	....	....	....
	Colorado	CHL	34	19	11	1	1896	122	0	3.86	5	2	3	304	19	0	3.75
1983-84	St. Catharines	AHL	42	25	13	4	2461	154	0	3.75	5	2	3	288	17	0	3.54
1984-85	**Toronto**	**NHL**	**37**	**13**	**19**	**4**	**2182**	**136**	**0**	**3.74**	....	....	....	....	....	....	....
	St. Catharines	AHL	14	5	7	2	801	55	0	412	....	....	....	....	....	....	....
1985-86	**Toronto**	**NHL**	**23**	**4**	**12**	**3**	**1266**	**107**	**0**	**5.07**	....	....	....	....	....	....	....
	St.Catharines	AHL	14	6	4	2	776	38	1	2.94	3	0	3	140	12	0	5.14
	NHL Totals		**66**	**17**	**36**	**7**	**3728**	**264**	**0**	**4.25**	....	....	....	....	....	....	....

a QMJHL First All-Star Team (1977, 1978)
Signed as a free agent by **Toronto,** December 5, 1984.

BERTHIAUME, DANIEL

Born, Longueuil, Que., January 26, 1966.
Goaltender. Catches left. 5′9″, 150 lbs.
Last amateur club: Chicoutimi Sagueneens (QMJHL).
(Winnipeg's 3rd choice, 60th over-all, in 1985 Entry Draft).

			Regular Season								Playoffs						
Season	**Club**	**Lea**	**GP**	**W**	**L**	**T**	**Mins**	**GA**	**SO**	**Avg**	**GP**	**W**	**L**	**Mins**	**GA**	**SO**	**Avg**
1984-85	Chicoutimi	QMJHL	59	40	11	2	2177	149	0	4.11	14	8	6	770	51	0	3.97
1985-86	Chicoutimi	QMJHL	66	34	29	3	3718	286	1	4.62	9	4	5	580	36	0	3.72
	Winnipeg	**NHL**	....	....	....	....	....	....	....	....	**1**	**0**	**1**	**68**	**4**	**0**	**3.53**
	NHLTotals		....	....	....	....	....	....	....	....	**1**	**0**	**1**	**68**	**4**	**0**	**3.53**

BESTER, ALLAN J.

Born, Hamilton, Ont., March 26, 1964.
Goaltender. Catches left. 5′7″, 150 lbs.
Last amateur club: Brantford Alexanders (OHL).
(Toronto's 3rd choice, 48th over-all, in 1983 Entry Draft).

			Regular Season								Playoffs						
Season	**Club**	**Lea**	**GP**	**W**	**L**	**T**	**Mins**	**GA**	**SO**	**Avg**	**GP**	**W**	**L**	**Mins**	**GA**	**SO**	**Avg**
1981-82	Brantford	OHL	19	4	11	0	970	68	0	4.21	....	....	....	....	....	....	....
1982-83a	Brantford	OHL	56	29	21	3	3210	188	0	3.51	8	3	3	480	20	*1	*2.50
1983-84	**Toronto**	**NHL**	**32**	**11**	**16**	**4**	**1848**	**134**	**0**	**4.35**	....	....	....	....	....	....	....
	Brantford	OHL	23	12	9	1	1271	71	1	3.35	1	0	1	60	5	0	5.00
1984-85	**Toronto**	**NHL**	**15**	**3**	**9**	**1**	**767**	**54**	**1**	**4.22**	....	....	....	....	....	....	....
	St. Catharines	AHL	30	9	18	1	1669	133	0	4.78	....	....	....	....	....	....	....
1985-86	**Toronto**	**NHL**	**1**	**0**	**0**	**0**	**20**	**2**	**0**	**6.00**	....	....	....	....	....	....	....
	St.Catharines	AHL	50	23	23	3	2855	173	1	3.64	11	7	3	637	27	0	2.54
	NHL Totals		**48**	**14**	**25**	**5**	**2635**	**190**	**1**	**4.33**	....	....	....	....	....	....	....

a OHL First All-Star Team (1983)

BILLINGTON, CRAIG

Born, London, Ont., September 11, 1966.
Goaltender. Catches left. 5′10″, 150 lbs.
Last amateur club: Belleville Bulls (OHL).
(New Jersey's 2nd choice, 23rd over-all, in 1984 Entry Draft).

			Regular Season								Playoffs						
Season	**Club**	**Lea**	**GP**	**W**	**L**	**T**	**Mins**	**GA**	**SO**	**Avg**	**GP**	**W**	**L**	**Mins**	**GA**	**SO**	**Avg**
1982-83	London	OPJHL	23	....	....	....	1338	76	0	3.39	....	....	....	....	....	....	....
1983-84	Belleville	OHL	44	20	19	0	2335	162	1	4.16	1	0	0	30	3	0	6.00
1984-85a	Belleville	OHL	47	26	19	0	2544	180	1	4.25	14	7	5	761	47	1	3.71
1985-86	**New Jersey**	**NHL**	**18**	**4**	**9**	**1**	**902**	**77**	**0**	**5.12**	....	....	....	....	....	....	....
	Belleville	OHL	3	2	1	0	180	11	0	3.67	20	9	6	1133	68	0	3.60
	NHLTotals		**18**	**4**	**9**	**1**	**902**	**77**	**0**	**5.12**	....	....	....	....	....	....	....

a OHL First All-Star Team (1985)

BLAIR, GRANT

Born, Stoney Creek, Ont., August 15, 1964.
Goaltender. Catches left. 6'0", 150 lbs.
Last amateur club: Harvard University Crimson (ECAC)..
(Calgary's 8th choice, 111th overall, in 1983 Entry Draft).

			Regular Season								Playoffs						
Season	Club	Lea	GP	W	L	T	Mins	GA	SO	Avg	GP	W	L	Mins	GA	SO	Avg
1982-83	Harvard	ECAC	26	19	7	0	1575	72	2	2.74	....	....	....	....	....	....	....
1983-84	Harvard	ECAC	23	10	11	2	1391	71	1	3.06	....	....	....	....	....	....	....
1984-85	Harvard	ECAC	31	19	9	2	1785	86	2	2.89	....	....	....	....	....	....	....
1985-86a	Harvard	ECAC	31	24	6	1	1812	82	2	2.72	....	....	....	....	....	....	....

a NCAA East Second All-American Team (1986)

BOUCHARD, DANIEL HECTOR (BOO-shahr)

Born, Val d'Or, Que., December 12, 1950.
Goaltender. Catches left. 6', 190 lbs.
Last amateur club: London Knights (OHA).
(Boston's 5th choice, 27th over-all, in 1970 Amateur Draft).

			Regular Season								Playoffs						
Season	Club	Lea	GP	W	L	T	Mins	GA	SO	Avg	GP	W	L	Mins	GA	SO	Avg
1969-70	London	OHA	41	....	....	....	2452	159	2	3.89	....	....	....	....	....	....	....
1970-71	Hershey	AHL	36	....	....	....	2029	106	1	3.13	....	....	....	....	....	....	....
1971-72	Oklahoma City	CHL	1	....	....	....	60	3	0	3.00	....	....	....	....	....	....	....
ab	Boston	AHL	50	....	....	....	2915	122	*4	2.51	6	....	....	311	14	0	2.70
1972-73	Atlanta	NHL	34	9	15	10	1944	100	2	3.09	....	....	....	....	....	....	....
1973-74	Atlanta	NHL	46	19	18	8	2660	123	5	2.77	1	0	1	60	4	0	4.00
1974-75	Atlanta	NHL	40	20	15	5	2400	111	3	2.77	....	....	....	....	....	....	....
1975-76	Atlanta	NHL	47	19	17	8	2671	113	2	2.54	2	0	2	120	3	0	*1.50
1976-77	Atlanta	NHL	42	17	17	5	2378	139	1	3.51	1	0	1	60	5	0	5.00
1977-78	Atlanta	NHL	58	25	12	19	3340	153	2	2.75	2	0	2	120	7	0	3.50
1978-79	Atlanta	NHL	64	32	21	7	3624	201	3	3.33	2	0	2	100	9	0	5.40
1979-80	Atlanta	NHL	53	23	19	10	3076	163	2	3.18	4	1	3	241	14	0	3.49
1980-81	Calgary	NHL	14	4	5	3	760	51	0	4.02	....	....	....	....	....	....	....
	Quebec	NHL	29	19	5	5	1740	92	2	3.17	5	2	3	286	19	*1	3.99
1981-82	Quebec	NHL	60	27	22	11	3572	230	1	3.86	11	4	7	677	38	0	3.37
1982-83	Quebec	NHL	50	20	21	8	2947	197	1	4.01	4	1	3	242	11	0	2.73
1983-84	Quebec	NHL	57	29	18	8	3373	180	1	3.20	9	5	4	543	25	0	2.76
1984-85	Quebec	NHL	29	12	13	4	1738	101	0	3.49	1	0	1	60	7	0	7.00
1985-86	Winnipeg	NHL	32	11	14	2	1696	107	2	3.79	1	0	1	40	5	0	7.50
	NHL Totals		655	286	232	113	37919	2061	27	3.26	43	13	30	2549	147	1	3.46

a AHL First All-Star Team (1972)
b Shared Harry "Hap" Holmes Award (AHL's Leading Goaltenders) with Ross Brooks (1972)

Claimed by **Atlanta** from **Boston** in Expansion Draft, June 6, 1972. Traded to **Quebec** by **Calgary** for Jamie Hislop, January 30, 1981. Traded to **Winnipeg** by **Quebec** for Winnipeg's seventh round draft choice (in 1986) Mark Vermette, October 14, 1985.

BRODEUR, RICHARD (brah-DEUR)

Born, Longueuil, Que., September 15, 1952.
Goaltender. Catches left. 5'7", 160 lbs.
Last amateur club: Cornwall Royals (QJHL).
(NY Islanders' 7th choice, 97th over-all, in 1972 Amateur Draft).

			Regular Season								Playoffs						
Season	Club	Lea	GP	W	L	T	Mins	GA	SO	Avg	GP	W	L	Mins	GA	SO	Avg
1970-71	Verdun	QJHL	6	....	....	....	360	47	0	7.83	....	....	....	....	....	....	....
	Cornwall	QJHL	35	....	....	....	2102	144	0	4.11	....	....	....	....	....	....	....
1971-72	Cornwall	QJHL	58	....	....	....	3481	170	5	2.93	16	....	....	960	44	0	2.75
1972-73	Quebec	WHA	24	....	....	....	1288	102	0	4.75	....	....	....	....	....	....	....
1973-74	Quebec	WHA	30	....	....	....	1607	89	1	3.32	....	....	....	....	....	....	....
	Maine	NAHL	16	....	....	....	927	47	0	3.04	....	....	....	....	....		....
1974-75	Quebec	WHA	51	....	....	....	2938	188	0	3.84	15	....	....	906	48	1	3.18
1975-76	Quebec	WHA	69	....	....	....	3967	244	2	3.69	5	....	....	299	22	0	4.41
1976-77	Quebec	WHA	53	....	....	....	2906	167	2	3.45	17	....	....	1007	55	*1	3.28
1977-78	Quebec	WHA	36	18	15	2	1962	121	0	3.70	11	....	....	622	38	*1	3.67
1978-79	Quebec	WHA	42	....	....	....	2433	126	*3	3.11	3	....	....	114	14	0	7.37
1979-80	NY Islanders	NHL	2	1	1	0	80	6	0	4.50	....	....	....	....	....	....	....
ab	Indianapolis	CHL	46	22	19	5	2722	131	*4	*2.88	6	3	3	357	12	*1	*2.02
1980-81	Vancouver	NHL	52	17	18	16	3024	177	0	3.51	3	0	3	185	13	0	4.22
1981-82	Vancouver	NHL	52	20	18	12	3010	168	2	3.35	17	11	6	1089	49	0	2.70
1982-83	Vancouver	NHL	58	21	26	8	3291	208	0	3.79	3	0	3	193	13	0	4.04
1983-84	Vancouver	NHL	36	10	21	5	2110	141	1	4.01	4	1	3	222	12	1	3.24
1984-85	Vancouver	NHL	51	16	27	6	2930	228	0	4.67	....	....	....	....	....	....	....
	Fredericton	AHL	4	3	0	1	249	13	0	3.13	....	....	....	....	....	....	....
1985-86	Vancouver	NHL	64	19	32	8	3541	240	2	4.07	2	0	2	120	12	0	6.00
	NHL Totals		315	104	143	55	17986	1168	5	3.90	29	12	17	1809	99	1	3.28
	WHA Totals		305	....	....	....	17101	1037	8	3.64	51	....	....	2948	177	3	3.60

a CHL First All-Star Team (1980)
b Shared Terry Sawchuk Trophy (CHL's Leading Goaltenders) with Jim Park (1980)

Reclaimed by **NY Islanders** from **Quebec** prior to Expansion Draft, June 9, 1979. Traded to **Vancouver** by **NY Islanders** with NY Islanders' fifth-round choice (Moe Lemay) in 1981 Entry Draft for Vancouver's fifth-round choice (Jacques Sylvestre) in the 1981 Entry Draft, October 6, 1980.

BROWER, SCOTT

Born, Viking,Alta., September 26, 1964.
Goaltender. Catches left. 6'0", 185 lbs.
Last amateur club: University of North Dakota Fighting Sioux (WCHA).
(NY Rangers' 12th choice, 243rd over-all, in 1984 Entry Draft).

			Regular Season								Playoffs						
Season	Club	Lea	GP	W	L	T	Mins	GA	SO	Avg	GP	W	L	Mins	GA	SO	Avg
1984-85	North Dakota	WCHA	31	15	12	2	1808	99	0	3.28	....	....	....	....	....	....	....
1985-86	North Dakota	WCHA	20	11	6	0	1096	67	0	3.47	....	....	....	....	....	....	....

BRUNETTA, MARIO

Born, Quebec City, Que., January 25, 1967.
Goaltender. Catches right. 6'2", 180 lbs.
Last amateur club: Laval Titans (QMJHL).
(Quebec's 9th choice, 162nd over-all, in 1985 Entry Draft).

			Regular Season								Playoffs						
Season	Club	Lea	GP	W	L	T	Mins	GA	SO	Avg	GP	W	L	Mins	GA	SO	Avg
1984-85	Quebec	QMJHL	45	20	21	1	2255	192	0	5.11	2	0	2	120	13	0	6.50
1985-86	Laval	QMJHL	63	30	25	1	3383	279	0	4.95	14	9	5	834	60	0	4.32

BURCHILL, RICH

Born, Boston, Mass., January 3, 1967.
Goaltender. Catches right. 6'0", 180 lbs.
Last amateur club: University of New Hampshire Wildcats (H.E.).
(St. Louis' 5th choice 121st over-all, in 1985 Entry Draft).

			Regular Season								Playoffs						
Season	Club	Lea	GP	W	L	T	Mins	GA	SO	Avg	GP	W	L	Mins	GA	SO	Avg
1985-86	New Hampshire	H.E.	15	2	10	1	840	76	0	5.43	....	....	....	....	....	....	....

BURKE, SEAN

Born, Windsor, Ont., January 29, 1967.
Goaltender. Catches left. 6'3", 185 lbs.
Last amateur club: Toronto Marlboros (OHL).
(New Jersey's 2nd choice, 24th over-all, in 1985 Entry Draft).

			Regular Season								Playoffs						
Season	Club	Lea	GP	W	L	T	Mins	GA	SO	Avg	GP	W	L	Mins	GA	SO	Avg
1984-85	Toronto	OHL	49	25	21	3	2987	211	0	4.24	5	1	3	266	25	0	5.64
1985-86	Toronto	OHL	47	16	27	3	2840	233	0	4.92	4	0	4	238	24	0	6.05

CAPRICE, FRANK (ka-PREESE)

Born, Hamilton, Ont., May 2, 1962.
Goaltender. Catches left. 5'9", 150 lbs.
Last amateur club: London Knights (OHL).
(Vancouver's 8th choice, 178th over-all, in 1981 Entry Draft).

			Regular Season								Playoffs						
Season	Club	Lea	GP	W	L	T	Mins	GA	SO	Avg	GP	W	L	Mins	GA	SO	Avg
1979-80	London	OHA	18	3	7	3	919	74	1	4.84	3	1	1	94	10	0	6.38
1980-81	London	OHA	42	11	26	0	2171	190	0	5.25	....	....	....	....	....	....	....
1981-82a	London	OHL	45	24	17	2	2614	196	0	4.50	4	1	3	240	18	0	4.50
	Dallas	CHL	3	0	3	0	178	19	0	6.40	....	....	....	....	....	....	....
1982-83	Vancouver	NHL	1	0	0	0	20	3	0	9.09	....	....	....	....	....	....	....
	Fredericton	AHL	14	5	8	1	819	50	0	3.67	....	....	....	....	....	....	....
1983-84	Vancouver	NHL	19	8	2	2	1098	62	1	3.39	....	....	....	....	....	....	....
	Fredericton	AHL	18	11	5	2	1089	49	2	2.70	....	....	....	....	....	....	....
1984-85	Vancouver	NHL	28	8	14	3	1523	122	0	4.81	....	....	....	....	....	....	....
1985-86	Vancouver	NHL	7	0	3	2	308	28	0	5.46	....	....	....	....	....	....	....
	Fredericton	AHL	26	12	11	2	1526	109	0	4.29	6	2	4	333	22	0	3.96
	NHL Totals		55	16	19	7	2949	215	1	4.37	....	....	....	....	....	....	....

a OHL Third All-Star Team (1982).

CASEY, JON

Born, Grand Rapids, Minn., August 29, 1962.
Goaltender. Catches right. 5'9", 155 lbs.
Last amateur club: University of North Dakota Fighting Sioux (WCHA).

			Regular Season								Playoffs						
Season	Club	Lea	GP	W	L	T	Mins	GA	SO	Avg	GP	W	L	Mins	GA	SO	Avg
1980-81	North Dakota	WCHA	5	3	1	0	300	19	0	3.80	....	....	....	....	....	....	....
1981-82	North Dakota	WCHA	18	15	3	0	1038	48	1	2.77	....	....	....	....	....	....	....
1982-83	North Dakota	WCHA	17	9	6	2	1020	42	0	2.51	....	....	....	....	....	....	....
1983-84	North Dakota	WCHA	37	25	10	2	2180	115	2	3.13	....	....	....	....	....	....	....
	Minnesota	NHL	2	1	0	0	84	6	0	4.29	....	....	....	....	....	....	....
1984-85ab	Baltimore	AHL	46	30	11	4	2646	116	4	2.63	13	8	3	689	38	0	3.31
1985-86	Minnesota	NHL	26	11	11	1	1402	91	0	3.89	....	....	....	....	....	....	....
	Springfield	AHL	9	4	3	1	464	30	0	3.88	....	....	....	....	....	....	....
	NHL Totals		28	12	11	1	1486	97	0	3.92	....	....	....	....	....	....	....

a won Baz Bastien Trophy (1985)
b AHL First All-Star Team (1985)
Signed as a free agent by **Minnesota**, April 1, 1984.

CHEVRIER, ALAIN

Born, Cornwall Ont., April 23, 1961.
Goaltender. Catches left. 5'8", 170 lbs.
Last amateur club: University of Miami (Ohio) Redskins (CCHA).

			Regular Season								Playoffs						
Season	Club	Lea	GP	W	L	T	Mins	GA	SO	Avg	GP	W	L	Mins	GA	SO	Avg
1982-83	Miami-Ohio	CCHA	33	15	16	1	1894	125	0	3.96	....	....	....	....	....	....	....
1983-84	Miami-Ohio	CCHA	32	9	19	1	1509	123	0	4.89	....	....	....	....	....	....	....
1984-85	Fort Wayne	IHL	56	26	21	7	3219	194	0	3.62	9	5	4	556	28	0	3.02
1985-86	New Jersey	NHL	37	11	18	2	1862	143	0	4.61	....	....	....	....	....	....	....
	NHL Totals		37	11	18	2	1862	143	0	4.61	....	....	....	....	....	....	....

Signed as a free agent by **New Jersey**, May 31, 1985.

CLIFFORD, CHRIS

Born, Kingston, Ont., May 26, 1966.
Goaltender. Catches left. 5'9", 150 lbs.
Last amateur club: Kingston Canadians (OHL).
(Chicago's 6th choice, 111th over-all, in 1984 Entry Draft).

			Regular Season								Playoffs						
Season	Club	Lea	GP	W	L	T	Mins	GA	SO	Avg	GP	W	L	Mins	GA	SO	Avg
1983-84	Kingston	OHL	50	16	28	0	2808	229	2	4.89	....	....	....	....	....	....	....
1984-85	Kingston	OHL	52	15	34	0	2768	241	0	5.22	....	....	....	....	....	....	....
1985-86	Kingston	OHL	50	26	21	3	2988	178	1	3.57	10	5	5	564	31	1	3.30

CLOUTIER, JACQUES (clootz-YAY)

Born, Noranda, Que., January 3, 1960.
Goaltender. Catches left. 5'7", 155 lbs.
Last amateur club: Trois Rivières Draveurs (QMJHL).
(Buffalo's 4th choice, 55th over-all, in 1979 Entry Draft).

			Regular Season								Playoffs						
Season	Club	Lea	GP	W	L	T	Mins	GA	SO	Avg	GP	W	L	Mins	GA	SO	Avg
1977-78	Trois Rivières	QJHL	71	....	....	....	4134	240	*4	3.48	13	....	....	779	40	1	3.08
1978-79a	Trois Rivières	QJHL	72	....	....	....	4168	218	*3	*3.14	13	....	....	780	36	0	*2.77
1979-80	Trois Rivières	QJHL	55	27	20	7	3222	231	2	4.30	7	3	4	420	33	0	4.71
1980-81	Rochester	AHL	61	27	27	6	3478	209	1	3.61	....	....	....	....	....	....	....
1981-82	Rochester	AHL	23	14	7	2	1366	64	0	2.81	....	....	....	....	....	....	....
	Buffalo	**NHL**	**7**	**5**	**1**	**0**	**311**	**13**	**0**	**2.51**	....	....	....	....	....	....	....
1982-83	**Buffalo**	**NHL**	**25**	**10**	**7**	**6**	**1390**	**81**	**0**	**3.50**	....	....	....	....	....	....	....
	Rochester	AHL	13	7	3	1	634	42	0	3.97	16	12	4	992	47	0	2.84
1983-84	Rochester	AHL	51	26	22	1	2841	172	1	3.63	18	9	9	1145	68	0	3.56
1984-85	**Buffalo**	**NHL**	**1**	**0**	**0**	**1**	**65**	**4**	**0**	**3.69**	....	....	....	....	....		
	Rochester	AHL	14	10	2	1	803	36	0	2.69	....	....	....	....	....	....	....
1985-86	**Buffalo**	**NHL**	**15**	**5**	**9**	**1**	**872**	**49**	**1**	**3.37**	....	....	....	....	....	....	....
	Rochester	AHL	14	10	2	2	835	38	1	2.73	....	....	....	....	....	....	....
	NHL Totals		**48**	**20**	**17**	**8**	**2638**	**147**	**1**	**3.34**	....	....	....	....	....	....	....

a QMJHL First All-Star Team (1979)

COOPER, JEFFREY

Born, Ottawa, Ont., June 12, 1962.
Goaltender. Catches right. 5'10", 170 lbs.
Last amateur club: Colgate University Red Raiders (ECAC).

			Regular Season								Playoffs						
Season	Club	Lea	GP	W	L	T	Mins	GA	SO	Avg	GP	W	L	Mins	GA	SO	Avg
1982-83	Colgate	ECAC	26	12	10	2	1486	100	1	4.04	....	....	....	....	....	....	....
1983-84	Colgate	ECAC	32	18	12	1	1874	121	1	*3.87	....	....	....	....	....	....	....
1984-85	Colgate	ECAC	31	13	18	0	1778	110	3	3.71	....	....	....	....	....	....	....
1985-86	Baltimore	AHL	23	6	13	0	1099	77	2	4.20	....	....	....	....	....	....	....

Signed as a free agent by **Pittsburgh**, April 6, 1985.

CRAIG, MIKE

Born, Calgary, Alta., November 1, 1962.
Goaltender. Catches left. 6'0", 165 lbs.
Last amateur club: University of Calgary Dinosaurs (CWUAA).
(Buffalo's 14th choice, 205th over-all, in 1982 Entry Draft).

			Regular Season								Playoffs						
Season	Club	Lea	GP	W	L	T	Mins	GA	SO	Avg	GP	W	L	Mins	GA	SO	Avg
1984-85	Rochester	AHL	29	11	7	3	1431	88	0	3.69	4	0	3	198	17	0	5.26
1985-86	Rochester	AHL	47	16	21	5	2573	183	0	4.27	....	....	....	....	....	....	....

D'AMOUR, MARC

Born, Sudbury, Ont., April 29, 1961.
Goaltender. Catches left. 5'9", 185 lbs.
Last amateur club: Sault Ste. Marie Greyhounds (OHL).

			Regular Season								Playoffs						
Season	Club	Lea	GP	W	L	T	Mins	GA	SO	Avg	GP	W	L	Mins	GA	SO	Avg
1979-80	Sault Ste. Marie	OHA	33	16	15	0	1429	117	0	4.91	....	....	....	....	....	....	....
1980-81	Sault Ste. Marie	OHA	16	7	1	1	653	38	0	3.49	14	5	4	683	41	0	3.60
1981-82a	Sault Ste. Marie	OHL	41	28	12	1	3284	130	1	*3.27	10	3	2	504	30	0	3.57
1982-83	Colorado	CHL	42	16	21	2	2373	153	1	3.87	1	....	....	59	4	0	4.08
1983-84	Colorado	CHL	36	18	12	1	1917	131	0	4.10	1	0	0	20	0	0	0.00
1984-85	Moncton	AHL	37	18	14	2	2051	115	0	3.36	....	....	....	....	....	....	....
	Salt Lake	IHL	12	7	2	2	694	33	0	2.85	....	....	....	....	....	....	....
1985-86	**Calgary**	**NHL**	**15**	**2**	**4**	**2**	**560**	**32**	**0**	**3.43**	....	....	....	....	....	....	....
	Moncton	AHL	21	6	9	3	1129	72	0	3.83	5	1	4	296	20	0	4.05
	NHL Totals		**15**	**2**	**4**	**2**	**560**	**32**	**0**	**3.43**	....	....	....	....	....	....	....

a OHL First All-Star Team (1982)

Signed as free agent by **Calgary**, June 7, 1982.

DASKALAKIS, CLEON

Born, Boston, Mass., September 29, 1962.
Goaltender. Catches left. 5'9", 175 lbs.
Last amateur club: Boston University Terriers (H.E.).

			Regular Season								Playoffs						
Season	Club	Lea	GP	W	L	T	Mins	GA	SO	Avg	GP	W	L	Mins	GA	SO	Avg
1980-81	Boston U.	ECAC	8	4	2	0	399	24	0	3.61	....	....	....	....	....	....	....
1981-82	Boston U.	ECAC	20	9	6	3	1101	59	3	3.22	....	....	....	....	....	....	....
1982-83	Boston U.	ECAC	24	15	7	1	1398	78	1	3.35	....	....	....	....	....	....	....
1983-84	Boston U.	ECAC	35	25	10	0	1972	96	0	2.92	....	....	....	....	....	....	....
1984-85	**Boston**	**NHL**	**8**	**1**	**2**	**1**	**289**	**24**	**0**	**4.98**	....	....	....	....	....	....	....
	Hershey	AHL	30	9	13	4	1614	119	0	4.42	....	....	....	....	....	....	....
1985-86	**Boston**	**NHL**	**2**	**0**	**2**	**0**	**120**	**10**	**0**	**5.00**	....	....	....	....	....	....	....
	Moncton	AHL	41	19	14	6	2343	141	0	3.61	6	4	1	372	13	....	2.10
	NHL Totals		**10**	**1**	**4**	**1**	**409**	**34**	**0**	**4.99**	....	....	....	....	....	....	....

Signed as a free agent by **Boston**, June 1, 1984.

DOWIE, BRUCE

Born, Oakville, Ont., December 9, 1962.
Goaltender. Catches left. 5'10", 170 lbs.
Last amateur club: Toronto Marlboros (OHL).

			Regular Season								Playoffs						
Season	Club	Lea	GP	W	L	T	Mins	GA	SO	Avg	GP	W	L	Mins	GA	SO	Avg
1979-80	Toronto	OHA	60	31	24	3	3513	247	0	4.22	4	0	4	253	19	0	4.51
1980-81	Toronto	OHA	57	28	26	0	3215	253	0	4.73	5	2	2	272	23	0	5.07
1981-82	Toronto	OHL	37	16	17	0	2022	150	1	4.25	2	0	2	120	10	0	5.00
1982-83	St. Catharines	AHL	8	2	3	1	424	35	0	4.95	....	....	....	....	....	....	....
	Toronto	OHL	30	....	....	....	1830	123	0	4.03	2	....	....	120	10	0	5.00
1983-84	Muskegon	IHL	25	....	....	....	1306	100	2	4.59	....	....	....	....	....	....	....
	Toronto	**NHL**	**2**	**0**	**1**	**0**	**72**	**4**	**0**	**3.33**	....	....	....	....	....	....	....
	St. Catharines	AHL	9	2	2	1	410	41	0	6.00	....	....	....	....	....	....	....
1984-85	St. Catharines	AHL	10	2	7	1	596	55	0	5.54	....	....	....	....	....	....	....
	Toledo	IHL	5	2	1	2	310	20	0	3.87	....	....	....	....	....	....	....
1985-86	St. Catharines	AHL	5	1	1	0	139	14	0	6.04	....	....	....	....	....	....	....
	NHL Totals		**2**	**0**	**1**	**0**	**72**	**4**	**0**	**3.33**	....	....	....	....	....	....	....

Signed as a free agent by **Toronto**, May 6, 1983.

DUFOUR, MICHEL

Born, Val D'or, Que., August 31, 1962.
Goaltender. Catches right. 5'6", 160 lbs.
Last amateur club: Trois Rivières Draveurs (QMJHL).

			Regular Season								Playoffs						
Season	Club	Lea	GP	W	L	T	Mins	GA	SO	Avg	GP	W	L	Mins	GA	SO	Avg
1979-80	Sorel	QMJHL	59	13	35	4	3178	206	0	5.78	....	....	....	....	....	....	....
1980-81a	Sorel	QMJHL	54	25	14	3	2703	164	0	3.64	7	3	4	391	25	0	3.84
1981-82	Trois Rivières	QMJHL	58	....	....	....	3316	238	1	4.31	23	....	....	1345	106	2	4.73
1982-83	Fredericton	AHL	1	1	0	0	60	5	0	5.00	....	....	....	....	....	....	....
	Kalamazoo	IHL	27	....	....	....	1424	89	0	3.75	3	....	....	140	8	0	3.43
1983-84	Milwaukee	IHL	21	....	....	....	1255	79	0	3.78	....	....	....	....	....	....	....
	Fredericton	AHL	6	5	0	1	365	19	0	3.13	4	....	....	194	14	0	4.33
1984-85	Muskegon	IHL	50	24	20	3	2937	174	1	3.55	17	11	6	1036	52	0	3.01
1985-86b	Muskegon	IHL	52	29	14	0	2935	151	0	3.09	1	0	1	65	5	0	4.62

a QMJHL Second All-Star Team (1981)
b IHL Second All-Star Team (1986)

Signed as a free agent by **Quebec**, September 24, 1981.

EDMONDS, JIM

Born, St. Catharines, Ont., August 8, 1965.
Goaltender. Catches left. 5'10", 170 lbs.
Last amateur club: Cornell University Big Red (ECAC).
(Winnipeg's 12th choice, 240th over-all, in 1984 Entry Draft).

			Regular Season								Playoffs						
Season	Club	Lea	GP	W	L	T	Mins	GA	SO	Avg	GP	W	L	Mins	GA	SO	Avg
1983-84	Cornell	ECAC	17	6	8	0	920	63	0	4.04	....	....	....	....	....	....	....
1984-85	Cornell	ECAC	2	1	0	0	80	7	0	5.25	....	....	....	....	....	....	....
1985-86	Cornell	ECAC	3	0	0	0	48	8	0	10.00	....	....	....	....	....	....	....

EDWARDS, DONALD LAURIE (DON)

Born, Hamilton, Ont., September 28, 1955.
Goaltender. Catches left. 5'9", 160 lbs.
Last amateur club: Kitchener Rangers (OHA).
(Buffalo's 6th choice, 89th over-all, in 1975 Amateur Draft).

			Regular Season								Playoffs						
Season	Club	Lea	GP	W	L	T	Mins	GA	SO	Avg	GP	W	L	Mins	GA	SO	Avg
1973-74a	Kitchener	OHA	35	....	....	....	2089	95	*3	*2.73	....	....	....	....	....	....	....
1974-75a	Kitchener	OHA	55	....	....	....	3294	258	1	4.70	....	....	....	....	....	....	....
1975-76b	Hershey	AHL	39	23	12	2	2253	128	3	3.41	5	1	3	293	18	0	3.68
1976-77	Hershey	AHL	47	26	15	6	2797	136	*5	2.91	....	....	....	....	....	....	....
	Buffalo	**NHL**	**25**	**16**	**7**	**2**	**1480**	**62**	**2**	**2.51**	**5**	**2**	**3**	**300**	**15**	**0**	**3.00**
1977-78c	**Buffalo**	**NHL**	**72**	**38**	**16**	**17**	**4209**	**185**	**5**	**2.64**	**8**	**3**	**5**	**482**	**22**	**0**	**2.74**
1978-79	**Buffalo**	**NHL**	**54**	**26**	**18**	**9**	**3160**	**159**	**2**	**3.02**	....	....	....	....	....	....	....
1979-80cd	**Buffalo**	**NHL**	**49**	**27**	**9**	**12**	**2920**	**125**	**2**	**2.57**	**6**	**3**	**3**	**360**	**17**	**1**	**2.83**
1980-81	**Buffalo**	**NHL**	**45**	**23**	**10**	**12**	**2700**	**133**	***3**	**2.96**	**8**	**4**	**4**	**503**	**28**	**0**	**3.34**
1981-82	**Buffalo**	**NHL**	**62**	**26**	**23**	**12**	**3500**	**205**	**0**	**3.51**	**4**	**1**	**3**	**214**	**16**	**0**	**4.48**
1982-83	**Calgary**	**NHL**	**39**	**16**	**15**	**6**	**2209**	**148**	**1**	**4.02**	**5**	**1**	**5**	**226**	**22**	**0**	**5.84**
1983-84	**Calgary**	**NHL**	**41**	**13**	**19**	**5**	**2303**	**157**	**0**	**4.09**	**6**	**2**	**1**	**217**	**12**	**0**	**3.31**
1984-85	**Calgary**	**NHL**	**34**	**11**	**15**	**2**	**1691**	**115**	**1**	**4.08**	....	....	....	....	....	....	....
1985-86	**Toronto**	**NHL**	**38**	**12**	**23**	**0**	**2009**	**160**	**0**	**4.78**	....	....	....	....	....	....	....
	NHL Totals		**459**	**208**	**155**	**77**	**26181**	**1449**	**16**	**3.32**	**42**	**16**	**21**	**2302**	**132**	**1**	**3.44**

a OHA First All-Star Team (1974, 1975)
b AHL Second All-Star Team (1976)
c NHL Second All-Star Team (1978, 1980)
d Shared Vezina Trophy with Robert Sauve (1980)

Traded to **Calgary** by **Buffalo** with Richie Dunn and Buffalo's second round choice (Richard Kromm) in the 1982 Entry Draft for Calgary's first (Paul Cyr) and second round choices (Jens Johansson) in the 1982 Entry Draft and second round choice (John Tucker) in the 1983 Entry Draft, June 9, 1982. In addition, the two clubs exchanged first round draft choices in 1983 — Buffalo claimed Normand Lacombe and Calgary selected Dan Quinn. Traded to **Toronto** by **Calgary** for Toronto's third or fourth round choice in 1987 Entry Draft, May 29, 1985.

ELIOT, DARREN

Born, Hamilton, Ont., November 26, 1961.
Goaltender. Catches right. 6'1", 175 lbs.
Last amateur club: 1984 Canadian Olympic Team.
(Los Angeles' 8th choice, 115th over-all, in 1980 Entry Draft).

			Regular Season								Playoffs						
Season	Club	Lea	GP	W	L	T	Mins	GA	SO	Avg	GP	W	L	Mins	GA	SO	Avg
1979-80	Cornell	ECAC	26	14	8	0	1362	94	0	4.10	5	3	2	300	20	0	4.00
1980-81	Cornell	ECAC	18	8	7	0	912	52	1	3.29	3	1	1	119	7	0	2.33
1981-82	Cornell	ECAC	7	1	3	0	337	25	0	4.44	....	....	....	....	....	....	....
1982-83ab	Cornell	ECAC	26	13	10	3	1606	100	1	3.66	....	....	....	....	....	....	....
1983-84	Cdn. Olympic	...	31	....	....	....	1676	111	0	3.97	....	....	....	....	....	....	....
	New Haven	AHL	7	4	1	0	365	30	0	4.93	....	....	....	....	....	....	....
1984-85	**Los Angeles**	**NHL**	**33**	**12**	**11**	**6**	**1882**	**137**	**0**	**4.37**	....	....	....	....	....	....	....
1985-86	**Los Angeles**	**NHL**	**27**	**5**	**17**	**3**	**1481**	**121**	**0**	**4.90**	....	....	....	....	....	....	....
	New Haven	AHL	3	1	2	1	180	19	0	6.33	1	0	1	60	4	0	4.00
	NHL Totals		**60**	**17**	**28**	**9**	**3363**	**258**	**0**	**4.60**	....	....	....	....	....	....	....

a ECAC First All-Star Team (1983)
b Named to NCAA All-American Team (1983)

ESSENSA, BOB

Born, Toronto, Ont., January 14, 1965.
Goaltender. Catches left. 6', 160 lbs.
Last amateur club: Michigan State University Spartans (WCHA).
(Winnipeg's 5th choice, 71st over-all, in 1983 Entry Draft).

			Regular Season								Playoffs						
Season	Club	Lea	GP	W	L	T	Mins	GA	SO	Avg	GP	W	L	Mins	GA	SO	Avg
1983-84	Michigan State	CCHA	17	11	4	0	946	44	2	2.79	....	....	....	....	....	....	....
1984-85	Michigan State	CCHA	18	15	2	0	1059	29	2	1.64	....	....	....	....	....	....	....
1985-86a	Michigan State	CCHA	23	17	4	1	1333	74	1	3.33	....	....	....	....	....	....	....

a CCHA Second All-Star Team (1986).

FALLE, JAMES (JAMIE)

Born, Montreal, Que., August 26, 1964.
Goaltender. Catches left. 5'11", 190 lbs.
Last amateur club: Clarkson College Golden Knights (ECAC).
(Hartford's 11th choice, 149th over-all, in 1983 Entry Draft).

			Regular Season								Playoffs						
Season	Club	Lea	GP	W	L	T	Mins	GA	SO	Avg	GP	W	L	Mins	GA	SO	Avg
1982-83	Clarkson	ECAC	22	16	8	0	1220	67	0	3.30	....	....	....	....	....	....	....
1983-84	Clarkson	ECAC	27	16	7	2	1493	77	0	3.09	....	....	....	....	....	....	....
1984-85	Clarkson	ECAC	26	15	6	0	1668	81	0	2.91	....	....	....	....	....	....	....
1985-86	Clarkson	ECAC	27	15	9	3	1634	91	0	3.34	....	....	....	....	....	....	....

FORD, BRIAN

Born, Edmonton, Alta., September 22, 1961.
Goaltender. Catches left. 5'10", 170 lbs.
Last amateur club: Billings Bighorns (WHL).

			Regular Season								Playoffs						
Season	Club	Lea	GP	W	L	T	Mins	GA	SO	Avg	GP	W	L	Mins	GA	SO	Avg
1980-81	Billings	WHL	44	14	26	0	2435	204	0	5.03	3	....	....	143	15	0	4.66
1981-82	Billings	WHL	53	19	26	1	2791	256	0	5.50	5	....	....	226	26	0	5.86
1982-83	Carolina	ACHL	4	....	....	....	203	7	0	2.07	....	....	....	....	....	....	....
	Fredericton	AHL	27	14	7	2	1443	84	0	3.49	1	0	0	11	1	0	5.56
1983-84	**Quebec**	**NHL**	**3**	**1**	**1**	**0**	**123**	**13**	**0**	**6.34**	....	....	....	....	....	....	....
a	Fredericton	AHL	36	17	17	1	2132	105	2	2.96	4	1	3	223	18	0	4.84
1984-85	**Pittsburgh**	**NHL**	**8**	**2**	**6**	**0**	**457**	**48**	**0**	**6.30**	....	....	....	....	....	....	....
	Baltimore	AHL	6	3	3	0	363	21	0	3.47	....	....	....	....	....	....	....
	Muskegon	IHL	22	17	5	0	1321	59	1	2.68	....	....	....	....	....	....	....
1985-86	Baltimore	AHL	39	12	20	4	2230	136	1	3.66	....	....	....	....	....	....	....
	Muskegon	IHL	9	4	4	0	513	33	0	3.06	13	12	1	793	41	0	3.10
	NHL Totals		**11**	**3**	**7**	**0**	**580**	**61**	**0**	**6.31**	....	....	....	....	....	....	....

a Won Harry (Hap) Holmes Memorial Trophy (AHL's leading goaltender) (1984).

Signed as a free agent by **Quebec**, August 1, 1982. Traded to **Pittsburgh** by **Quebec** for Tom Thornbury, December 6, 1984.

FOSTER, NORM

Born, Vancouver, B.C., February 10, 1965.
Goaltender. Catches left. 5'9", 175 lbs.
Last amateur club: Michigan State University Spartans (CCHA).
(Boston's 11th choice, 222nd over-all, in 1983 Entry Draft).

			Regular Season								Playoffs						
Season	Club	Lea	GP	W	L	T	Mins	GA	SO	Avg	GP	W	L	Mins	GA	SO	Avg
1984-85	Michigan State	CCHA	26	22	4	0	1531	67	0	2.63	....	....	....	....	....	....	....
1985-86	Michigan State	CCHA	24	17	5	1	1414	87	0	3.69	....	....	....	....	....	....	....

FRANZOSA, JOHN

Born, Reading, Mass., March 3, 1963.
Goaltender. Catches right. 5'10", 175 lbs.
Last amateur club: Brown University Bruins (ECAC)
(Los Angeles' 10th choice, 195th over-all, in 1982 Entry Draft).

			Regular Season								Playoffs						
Season	Club	Lea	GP	W	L	T	Mins	GA	SO	Avg	GP	W	L	Mins	GA	SO	Avg
1981-82	Brown	ECAC	17	6	10	0	935	85	0	5.46	....	....	....	....	....	....	....
1982-83	Brown	ECAC	10	0	8	1	570	54	0	5.68	....	....	....	....	....	....	....
1983-84	Brown	ECAC	12	4	5	1	752	54	0	4.31	....	....	....	....	....	....	....
1984-85	Brown	ECAC	25	9	17	0	1436	89	1	3.72	....	....	....	....	....	....	....
1985-86	New Haven	AHL	3	0	3	0	180	22	0	7.33	....	....	....	....	....	....	....
	Toledo	IHL	36	13	19	0	2021	160	0	4.75	....	....	....	....	....	....	....

FRIESEN, KARL

Born, Winnipeg, Man., June 30, 1958.
Goaltender. Catches left. 6'0", 185 lbs.
Last amateur club: West German Olympic Team.

			Regular Season								Playoffs						
Season	Club	Lea	GP	W	L	T	Mins	GA	SO	Avg	GP	W	L	Mins	GA	SO	Avg
1985-86	Maine	AHL	35	16	15	5	1983	115	2	3.48	5	1	4	340	14	0	2.47

Signed as a free agent by **New Jersey**, April 24, 1985.

FROESE, ROBERT GLENN (BOB) (FROZE)

Born, St. Catharines, Ont., June 30, 1958.
Goaltender. Catches left. 5'11", 175 lbs.
Last amateur club: Niagara Falls Flyers (OHA).
(St. Louis' 11th choice, 160th over-all, in 1978 Amateur Draft).

			Regular Season								Playoffs						
Season	Club	Lea	GP	W	L	T	Mins	GA	SO	Avg	GP	W	L	Mins	GA	SO	Avg
1975-76	St. Catharines	OHA	39	....	....	....	1976	193	0	5.83	4	....	....	240	20	0	5.00
1976-77	Niagara Falls	OHA	39	....	....	....	2063	162	2	4.68	....	....	....	....	....	....	....
1977-78	Niagara Falls	OHA	52	....	....	....	3128	249	0	4.71	3	....	....	236	17	0	4.36
1978-79	Saginaw	IHL	21	....	....	....	1050	58	0	3.31	....	....	....	....	....	....	....
	Milwaukee	IHL	14	....	....	....	715	42	1	3.52	7	....	....	334	23	0	4.14
1979-80	Maine	AHL	1	0	1	0	60	5	0	5.00	....	....	....	....	....	....	....
	Saginaw	IHL	52	....	....	....	2827	178	0	3.78	4	....	....	213	13	0	3.66
1980-81	Saginaw	IHL	43	....	....	....	2298	114	3	2.98	13	....	....	806	29	*2	*2.16
1981-82	Maine	AHL	33	16	11	4	1900	104	2	3.28	....	....	....	....	....	....	....
1982-83	Maine	AHL	33	18	11	3	1966	110	2	3.36	....	....	....	....	....	....	....
	Philadelphia	**NHL**	**25**	**17**	**4**	**2**	**1407**	**59**	**4**	**2.52**	....	....	....	....	....	....	....
1983-84	**Philadelphia**	**NHL**	**48**	**28**	**13**	**7**	**2863**	**150**	**2**	**3.14**	**3**	**0**	**2**	**154**	**11**	**0**	**4.28**
1984-85	**Philadelphia**	**NHL**	**17**	**13**	**2**	**0**	**923**	**37**	**1**	**2.41**	**4**	**0**	**1**	**146**	**11**	**0**	**4.52**
	Hershey	AHL	4	1	2	1	245	15	0	3.67	....	....	....	....	....	....	....
1985-86a	**Philadelphia**	**NHL**	**51**	**31**	**10**	**3**	**2728**	**116**	**5**	**2.55**	**5**	**2**	**3**	**293**	**15**	**0**	**3.07**
	NHL Totals		**141**	**89**	**29**	**12**	**7921**	**362**	**12**	**2.74**	**12**	**2**	**6**	**593**	**37**	**0**	**3.74**

a NHL Second All-Star Team (1986).

Signed as a free agent by **Philadelphia**, June 18, 1981.

FUHR, GRANT (FYUR)

Born, Spruce Grove, Alta., September 28, 1962.
Goaltender. Catches right. 5'10", 180 lbs.
Last amateur club: Victoria Cougars (WHL).
(Edmonton's 1st choice, 8th over-all, in 1981 Entry Draft).

			Regular Season								Playoffs						
Season	Club	Lea	GP	W	L	T	Mins	GA	SO	Avg	GP	W	L	Mins	GA	SO	Avg
1979-80ab	Victoria	WHL	43	30	12	0	2488	130	2	3.14	8	5	3	465	22	0	2.84
1980-81a	Victoria	WHL	59	48	9	1	3448	160	*4	*2.78	15	12	3	899	45	*1	*3.00
1981-82c	**Edmonton**	**NHL**	**48**	**28**	**5**	**14**	**2847**	**157**	**0**	**3.31**	**5**	**2**	**3**	**309**	**26**	**0**	**5.05**
1982-83	Moncton	AHL	10	4	5	1	604	40	0	3.98	....	....	....	....	....	....	....
	Edmonton	**NHL**	**32**	**13**	**12**	**5**	**1803**	**129**	**0**	**4.29**	**1**	**0**	**0**	**11**	**0**	**0**	**0.00**
1983-84	**Edmonton**	**NHL**	**45**	**30**	**10**	**4**	**2625**	**171**	**1**	**3.91**	**16**	**11**	**4**	**883**	**44**	**1**	**2.99**
1984-85d	**Edmonton**	**NHL**	**46**	**26**	**8**	**7**	**2559**	**165**	**1**	**3.87**	**18**	**15**	**3**	**1064**	**55**	**0**	**3.10**
1985-86	**Edmonton**	**NHL**	**40**	**29**	**8**	**0**	**2184**	**143**	**0**	**3.93**	**9**	**5**	**4**	**541**	**28**	**0**	**3.11**
	NHL Totals		**211**	**126**	**43**	**30**	**12018**	**765**	**2**	**3.82**	**49**	**33**	**14**	**2808**	**153**	**1**	**3.27**

a WHL First All-Star Team (1980, 1981)
b WHL Rookie of the Year (1980)
c NHL Second All-Star Team (1982)
d Shared Shutout with Andy Moog, January 8, 1985 vs. Quebec.

GAMBLE, TROY

Born, Wetaskiwin, Alta., April 7, 1967.
Goaltender. Catches left. 5'11", 180 lbs.
Last amateur club: Medicine Hat Tigers (WHL).
(Vancouver's 2nd choice, 25th over-all, in 1985 Entry Draft).

			Regular Season								Playoffs						
Season	Club	Lea	GP	W	L	T	Mins	GA	SO	Avg	GP	W	L	Mins	GA	SO	Avg
1984-85a	Medicine Hat	WHL	37	27	6	2	2095	100	3	2.86	2	1	1	120	9	0	4.50
1985-86	Medicine Hat	WHL	45	28	11	0	2264	142	0	3.76	11	5	4	530	31	0	3.51

a WHL First All-Star Team, East Division (1985).

GARRETT, JOHN MURDOCH

Born, Trenton, Ont., June 17, 1951.
Goaltender. Catches left. 5'8", 175 lbs.
Last amateur club: Peterborough Petes (OHA).
(St. Louis' 2nd choice, 38th over-all, in 1971 Amateur Draft).

			Regular Season								Playoffs						
Season	Club	Lea	GP	W	L	T	Mins	GA	SO	Avg	GP	W	L	Mins	GA	SO	Avg
1969-70	Peterborough	OHA	48	....	....	....	2850	142	*3	2.99	....	....	....	....	....	....	....
1970-71a	Peterborough	OHA	51	....	....	....	3062	151	*5	*2.96	....	....	....	....	....	....	....
1971-72	Kansas City	CHL	35	....	....	....	2041	121	*3	3.55	....	....	....	....	....	....	....
1972-73	Portland	WHL	17	....	....	....	951	52	2	3.28	....	....	....	....	....	....	....
	Richmond	AHL	37	....	....	....	2138	117	0	3.26	3	....	....	123	17	0	8.29
1973-74	Minnesota	WHA	40	21	18	0	2290	137	1	3.59	7	4	2	372	25	0	4.04
1974-75	Minnesota	WHA	58	30	23	2	3294	180	2	3.28	12	6	6	726	41	1	3.39
1975-76	Minnesota	WHA	52	26	22	4	3179	177	2	3.34	....	....	....	....	....	....	....
	Toronto	WHA	9	3	6	0	551	33	1	3.59	....	....	....	....	....	....	....
1976-77	Birmingham	WHA	65	24	34	4	3803	224	*4	3.53	....	....	....	....	....	....	....
1977-78	Birmingham	WHA	58	24	31	1	3306	210	2	3.81	5	1	4	271	26	0	5.76
1978-79	New England	WHA	41	20	17	4	2496	149	2	3.58	8	4	3	447	32	0	4.30
1979-80	**Hartford**	**NHL**	**52**	**16**	**24**	**11**	**3046**	**202**	**0**	**3.98**	**1**	**0**	**1**	**60**	**8**	**0**	**8.00**
1980-81	**Hartford**	**NHL**	**54**	**15**	**27**	**12**	**3152**	**241**	**0**	**4.59**	....	....	....	....	....	....	....
1981-82	**Hartford**	**NHL**	**16**	**5**	**6**	**4**	**898**	**63**	**0**	**4.21**	....	....	....	....	....	....	....
	Quebec	**NHL**	**12**	**4**	**5**	**3**	**720**	**62**	**0**	**5.17**	**5**	**3**	**2**	**323**	**21**	**0**	**3.90**
1982-83	**Quebec**	**NHL**	**17**	**6**	**8**	**2**	**953**	**64**	**0**	**4.03**	....	....	....	....	....	....	....
	Vancouver	**NHL**	**17**	**7**	**6**	**3**	**934**	**48**	**1**	**3.08**	**1**	**1**	**0**	**60**	**4**	**0**	**4.00**
1983-84	**Vancouver**	**NHL**	**29**	**14**	**10**	**2**	**1653**	**113**	**0**	**4.10**	**2**	**0**	**0**	**18**	**0**	**0**	**0.00**
1984-85	**Vancouver**	**NHL**	**10**	**1**	**5**	**0**	**407**	**44**	**0**	**6.49**	....	....	....	....	....	....	....
1985-86	Fredericton	AHL	3	2	1	0	179	9	0	3.02	....	....	....	....	....	....	....
	NHL Totals		**207**	**68**	**91**	**37**	**11763**	**837**	**1**	**4.27**	**9**	**4**	**3**	**461**	**33**	**0**	**4.30**
	WHA Totals		323	148	151	15	18919	1110	14	3.52	32	15	15	1816	124	1	4.10

a OHA First All-Star Team (1971)

Rights traded to **Chicago** by **St. Louis** for Christian Bordeleau, September 19, 1972. Reclaimed by **Chicago** from **Hartford** prior to Expansion Draft, June 9, 1979. Claimed by **Hartford** as priority selection, June 9, 1979. Traded to **Quebec** by **Hartford** for Michel Plasse and a fourth round choice (Ron Chyzowski) in 1983 Entry Draft, January 12, 1982. Traded to **Vancouver** by **Quebec** for Anders Eldebrink, February 4, 1983.

GILLES, BRUCE

Born, Denver, Colo., December 14, 1961.
Goaltender. Catches left. 6'0", 200 lbs.
Last amateur club: University of New Hampshire Wildcats (H.E.)

			Regular Season								Playoffs						
Season	Club	Lea	GP	W	L	T	Mins	GA	SO	Avg	GP	W	L	Mins	GA	SO	Avg
1982-83	New Hampshire	H.E.	7	5	0	1	417	23	0	3.31	....	....	....	....	....	....	....
1983-84	New Hampshire	H.E.	34	19	15	0	1945	113	0	3.49	....	....	....	....	....	....	....
1984-85	New Hampshire	H.E.	28	11	16	1	1422	89	0	4.19	....	....	....	....	....	....	....
1985-86	Nova Scotia	AHL	1	0	1	0	60	4	0	4.00	....	....	....	....	....	....	....
	Muskegon	IHL	29	15	10	0	1501	104	0	4.16	....	....	....	....	....	....	....

Signed as a free agent by **Edmonton**, June 5, 1985.

GILMOUR, DARRYL

Born, Winnipeg, Man., February 13, 1967.
Goaltender. Shoots left. 5'11", 165 lbs.
Last amateur club: Moose Jaw Warriors (WHL).
(Philadelphia's 3rd choice, 48th over-all, in 1985 Entry Draft).

			Regular Season								Playoffs						
Season	Club	Lea	GP	W	L	T	Mins	GA	SO	Avg	GP	W	L	Mins	GA	SO	Avg
1984-85	Moose Jaw	WHL	58	15	35	0	3004	297	0	5.93	....	....	....	....	....	....	....
1985-86a	Moose Jaw	WHL	62	19	34	3	3482	276	1	4.76	9	4	4	490	48	0	5.88

a WHL First All-Star Team, East Division (1986).

GOSSELIN, MARIO

Born, Thetford Mines, Que., June 15, 1963.
Goaltender. Catches left. 5'9", 160 lbs.
Last amateur club: 1984 Canadian Olympic Team.
(Quebec's 3rd choice, 55th over-all, in 1982 Entry Draft).

| | | | | | Regular Season | | | | | Playoffs | | | | |
Season	Club	Lea	GP	W	L	T	Mins	GA	SO	Avg	GP	W	L	Mins	GA	SO	Avg
1980-81	Shawinigan	QMJHL	21	4	9	0	907	75	0	4.96	1	0	0	20	2	0	6.00
1981-82a	Shawinigan	QMJHL	60	....	....	....	344	230	0	4.05	14	....	....	788	58	0	4.42
1982-83	Shawinigan	QMJHL	46	32	9	1	2556	133	3	3.12	8	5	3	457	29	0	3.81
1983-84	Cdn. Olympic	....	36	....	....	....	2007	126	0	3.77	....	....	....	....	....	....	....
	Quebec	NHL	3	2	0	0	148	3	1	1.21	....	....	....	....	....	....	....
1984-85	Quebec	NHL	36	19	11	3	2020	111	0	3.30	17	9	8	1059	54	0	3.06
1985-86	Quebec	NHL	31	14	14	1	1726	111	2	3.86	1	0	1	40	5	0	7.50
	Fredericton	AHL	5	2	2	1	304	15	0	2.94	....	....	....	....	....	....	....
	NHL Totals		70	35	25	4	3894	225	4	3.47	18	9	9	1099	59	0	3.22

a QMJHL Second All-Star Team (1982)

GOWANS, MARK

Born, Bay City, Mich., March 26, 1967.
Goaltender. Catches left. 6'0", 160 lbs.
Last amateur club: Oshawa Generals (OHL).
(Detroit's 4th choice, 71st over-all, in 1985 Entry Draft).

| | | | | | Regular Season | | | | | Playoffs | | | | |
Season	Club	Lea	GP	W	L	T	Mins	GA	SO	Avg	GP	W	L	Mins	GA	SO	Avg
1984-85	Windsor	OHL	36	13	18	3	2112	162	0	4.60	....	....	....	....	....	....	....
1985-86	Oshawa	OHL	25	13	6	0	1187	87	0	4.25	3	1	2	159	12	0	4.52

GUENETTE, LUC

Born, St. Jerome, Que., July 22, 1964.
Goaltender. Catches left. 5'9", 158 lbs.
Last amateur club: Quebec Remparts (QMJHL).
(Quebec's 4th choice, 92nd over-all, in 1983 Entry Draft).

| | | | | | Regular Season | | | | | Playoffs | | | | |
Season	Club	Lea	GP	W	L	T	Mins	GA	SO	Avg	GP	W	L	Mins	GA	SO	Avg
1981-82	Quebec	QMJHL	38	....	....	....	1809	202	0	6.70	....	....	....	....	....	....	....
1982-83a	Quebec	QMJHL	59	23	33	4	3285	299	0	5.46	....	....	....	....	....	....	....
1983-84	Quebec	QMJHL	67	....	....	....	3729	314	0	5.05	5	....	....	299	24	0	4.82
1984-85	Muskegon	IHL	13	9	4	0	674	48	0	4.27	....	....	....	....	....	....	....
	Fort Worth	IHL	2	0	2	0	94	10	0	6.38	....	....	....	....	....	....	....
1985-86	Fredericton	AHL	20	4	12	1	1021	76	0	4.47	2	0	0	32	6	0	11.25

a QMJHL Second All-Star Team (1983).

GUENETTE, STEVE

Born, Gloucester Ont., November 13, 1965.
Goaltender. Catches right. 5'9", 170 lbs.
Last amateur club: Guelph Platers (OHL).

| | | | | | Regular Season | | | | | Playoffs | | | | |
Season	Club	Lea	GP	W	L	T	Mins	GA	SO	Avg	GP	W	L	Mins	GA	SO	Avg
1983-84	Guelph	OHL	38	9	18	2	1808	155	0	5.14	....	....	....	....	....	....	....
1984-85	Guelph	OHL	47	16	22	4	2593	200	1	4.63	....	....	....	....	....	....	....
1985-86a	Guelph	OHL	48	26	20	1	2908	165	3	3.40	20	15	3	1167	54	1	2.77

a OHL Second All-Star Team (1986).

Signed as a free agent by Pittsburgh, April 6, 1985.

HANLON, GLEN

Born, Brandon, Man., February 20, 1957.
Goaltender. Catches right. 6', 185 lbs.
Last amateur club: Brandon Wheat Kings (WHL).
(Vancouver's 3rd choice, 40th over-all, in 1977 Amateur Draft).

| | | | | | Regular Season | | | | | Playoffs | | | | |
Season	Club	Lea	GP	W	L	T	Mins	GA	SO	Avg	GP	W	L	Mins	GA	SO	Avg
1974-75	Brandon	WHL	43	....	....	....	2498	176	0	4.22	5	....	....	284	29	0	6.12
1975-76a	Brandon	WHL	64	....	....	....	3523	234	4	3.99	5	....	....	300	33	0	6.60
1976-77a	Brandon	WHL	65	....	....	....	3784	195	*4	*3.09	16	....	....	914	53	0	3.48
1977-78	Vancouver	NHL	4	1	2	1	200	9	0	2.70	....	....	....	....	....	....	....
bc	Tulsa	CHL	53	....	....	....	3123	160	*3	3.07	2	....	....	120	5	0	*2.50
1978-79	Vancouver	NHL	31	12	13	5	1821	94	3	3.10	2	0	0	60	3	0	3.00
1979-80	Vancouver	NHL	57	17	29	10	3341	193	0	3.47	....	....	....	....	....	....	....
1980-81	Vancouver	NHL	17	5	8	0	798	59	1	4.44	....	....	....	....	....	....	....
	Dallas	CHL	4	3	1	0	239	8	1	2.01	....	....	....	....	....	....	....
1981-82	Vancouver	NHL	28	8	14	5	1610	106	1	3.95	....	....	....	....	....	....	....
	St. Louis	NHL	2	0	1	0	76	8	0	6.30	3	0	2	109	9	0	4.95
1982-83	St. Louis	NHL	14	3	8	1	671	50	0	4.47	....	....	....	....	....	....	....
	NY Rangers	NHL	21	9	10	1	1173	67	0	3.43	1	0	1	60	5	0	5.00
1983-84	NY Rangers	NHL	50	28	14	4	2837	166	1	3.51	5	2	3	308	13	1	2.53
1984-85	NY Rangers	NHL	44	14	14	7	2510	175	0	4.18	3	0	3	168	14	0	5.00
1985-86	NY Rangers	NHL	23	5	12	1	1170	65	0	3.33	3	0	0	75	6	0	4.80
	Adirondack	AHL	10	5	4	1	605	33	0	3.27	....	....	....	....	....	....	....
	New Haven	AHL	5	3	2	0	279	22	0	4.73	....	....	....	....	....	....	....
	NHL Totals		291	102	131	35	16207	992	6	3.67	17	2	8	780	50	1	3.85

a WHL First All-Star Team (1976, 1977)
b CHL Rookie of the Year (1978)
c CHL First All-Star Team (1978)

Traded to St. Louis by Vancouver for Tony Currie, Jim Nill, Rick Heinz and St. Louis' fourth round choice (Shawn Kilroy) in 1982 Entry Draft, March 9, 1982. Traded to NY Rangers by St. Louis with Vaclav Nedomansky for Andre Dore, January 4, 1983.

HANSCH, RANDY

Born, Edmonton, Alta., February 8, 1966.
Goaltender. Catches right. 5'10", 165 lbs.
Last amateur club: Victoria Cougars (WHL).
(Detroit's 5th choice, 112th over-all, in 1984 Entry Draft).

| | | | | | Regular Season | | | | | Playoffs | | | | |
Season	Club	Lea	GP	W	L	T	Mins	GA	SO	Avg	GP	W	L	Mins	GA	SO	Avg
1983-84	Victoria	WHL	36	12	19	0	1894	144	0	4.56	....	....	....	....	....	....	....
1984-85a	Victoria	WHL	52	....	....	....	3021	260	0	5.16	....	....	....	....	....	....	....
1985-86	Kamloops	WHL	31	10	21	0	1821	172	0	5.67	14	11	2	820	36	1	2.63

a WHL First All-Star Team, West Division (1985).

HAYWARD, BRIAN

Born, Georgetown, Ont., June 25, 1960.
Goaltender. Catches left. 5'10", 175 lbs.
Last amateur club: Cornell University Big Red (ECAC).

| | | | | | Regular Season | | | | | Playoffs | | | | |
Season	Club	Lea	GP	W	L	T	Mins	GA	SO	Avg	GP	W	L	Mins	GA	SO	Avg
1978-79	Cornell	ECAC	25	18	6	0	1469	95	0	3.88	3	2	1	179	14	0	4.66
1979-80	Cornell	ECAC	12	2	7	0	508	52	0	6.02	....	....	....	....	....	....	....
1980-81	Cornell	ECAC	19	11	4	1	967	58	1	3.54	4	2	1	181	18	0	4.50
1981-82ab	Cornell	ECAC	22	11	10	1	1320	68	0	3.09	....	....	....	....	....	....	....
1982-83	Sherbrooke	AHL	....	....	....	....	1208	89	1	4.42	....	....	....	....	....	....	....
	Winnipeg	NHL	24	10	12	2	1440	89	0	3.71	3	0	3	160	14	0	5.24
1983-84	Winnipeg	NHL	28	7	18	2	1530	124	0	4.86	....	....	....	....	....	....	....
	Sherbrooke	AHL	15	4	8	0	781	69	0	5.30	....	....	....	....	....	....	....
1984-85	Winnipeg	NHL	61	33	17	8	3481	224	0	3.86	6	2	4	309	23	0	4.47
1985-86	Winnipeg	NHL	52	13	28	5	2721	217	0	4.79	2	0	1	68	6	0	5.29
	Sherbrooke	AHL	3	2	0	1	185	5	0	1.62	....	....	....	....	....	....	....
	NHL Totals		165	63	75	17	9172	654	1	4.28	11	2	8	537	43	0	4.80

a ECAC First All-Star Team (1982)
b Named to NCAA All-America Team (1982)

Signed as a free agent by Winnipeg, May 5, 1982.
Traded to Montreal by Winnipeg for Steve Penny and the rights to Jan Ingman, August 19, 1986.

HEALY, GLEN

Born, Pickering, Ont., August 23, 1962.
Goaltender. Catches left. 5'10", 185 lbs.
Last amateur club: Western Michigan University Broncos (CCHA).

| | | | | | Regular Season | | | | | Playoffs | | | | |
Season	Club	Lea	GP	W	L	T	Mins	GA	SO	Avg	GP	W	L	Mins	GA	SO	Avg
1981-82	W. Michigan	CCHA	27	7	19	1	1569	116	0	4.44	....	....	....	....	....	....	....
1982-83	W. Michigan	CCHA	30	8	19	2	1732	116	0	4.01	....	....	....	....	....	....	....
1983-84	W. Michigan	CCHA	38	19	16	3	2241	146	0	3.90	....	....	....	....	....	....	....
1984-85	W. Michigan	CCHA	37	21	14	2	2171	118	0	3.26	....	....	....	....	....	....	....
1985-863	New Haven	AHL	43	21	15	4	2410	160	0	3.98	2	0	2	49	11	0	5.55
	Los Angeles	NHL	1	0	0	0	51	6	0	7.06	....	....	....	....	....	....	....
	NHL Totals		1	0	0	0	51	6	0	7.06	....	....	....	....	....	....	....

Signed as a free agent by Los Angeles, June 13, 1985.

HEINZ, RICHARD (RICK)   (HIGHNZ)

Born, Essex, Ont., May 30, 1955.
Goaltender. Catches left. 5'10", 165 lbs.
Last amateur club: University of Minnesota-Duluth Bulldogs (WCHA).

| | | | | | Regular Season | | | | | Playoffs | | | | |
Season	Club	Lea	GP	W	L	T	Mins	GA	SO	Avg	GP	W	L	Mins	GA	SO	Avg
1977-78	Minn-Duluth	WCHA	33	....	....	....	1961	157	0	4.80	....	....	....	....	....	....	....
1978-79	Salt Lake	CHL	1	....	....	....	59	3	0	3.05	....	....	....	....	....	....	....
a	Port Huron	IHL	54	....	....	....	2800	157	*5	3.36	6	....	....	281	18	*1	3.84
1979-80b	Salt Lake	CHL	39	22	11	5	2353	119	0	3.03	5	1	3	324	16	0	2.96
1980-81	Salt Lake	CHL	36	19	14	3	2210	128	3	3.48	14	10	4	859	39	0	*2.72
b	St. Louis	NHL	4	2	1	1	220	8	0	2.18	....	....	....	....	....	....	....
1981-82	St. Louis	NHL	9	2	5	0	433	35	0	4.85	....	....	....	....	....	....	....
	Salt Lake	CHL	19	14	3	2	433	35	0	3.65	....	....	....	....	....	....	....
	Vancouver	NHL	3	2	1	0	180	9	1	3.00	....	....	....	....	....	....	....
1982-83	St. Louis	NHL	9	1	5	1	335	24	0	4.30	....	....	....	....	....	....	....
	Salt Lake	CHL	17	9	8	0	1031	58	1	3.38	....	....	....	....	....	....	....
1983-84	St. Louis	NHL	22	7	7	3	1118	80	0	4.29	....	....	....	....	....	....	....
1984-85	St. Louis	NHL	2	0	0	0	70	3	0	2.57	....	....	....	....	....	....	....
cd	Peoria	IHL	43	24	12	4	2443	129	0	3.17	10	6	4	607	31	1	3.06
1985-86	Binghamton	AHL	1	0	1	0	60	9	0	9.00	....	....	....	....	....	....	....
	Salt Lake	IHL	52	22	20	0	3000	185	1	3.70	5	1	4	299	26	0	5.22
	NHL Totals		49	14	19	5	2356	159	2	4.05	....	....	....	....	....	....	....

a IHL Second All-Star Team (1979)
b CHL Second All-Star Team (1980, 1981)
c won James Norris Trophy (IHL Top Goaltender) (1985)
d IHL First All-Star Team (1985)

Signed as a free agent by St. Louis, August 16, 1979. Traded to Vancouver by St. Louis with Tony Currie, Jim Nill and St. Louis' fourth round choice (Shawn Kilroy) in 1982 Entry Draft for Glen Hanlon, March 9, 1982. Rights sold to St. Louis by Vancouver, June 3, 1982.

HELMUTH, ANDY

Born, Detroit, Mich., March 18, 1967.
Goaltender. Catches right. 5'10", 172 lbs.
Last amateur club: Ottawa 67's (OHL).
(Chicago's 2nd choice, 53rd over-all, in 1985 Entry Draft).

| | | | | | Regular Season | | | | | Playoffs | | | | |
Season	Club	Lea	GP	W	L	T	Mins	GA	SO	Avg	GP	W	L	Mins	GA	SO	Avg
1984-85	Ottawa	OHL	40	16	20	2	2102	189	0	5.39	....	....	....	....	....	....	....
1985-86	Ottawa	OHL	20	4	15	0	1175	97	0	4.95	....	....	....	....	....	....	....

HERRON, DENIS (ehr-OHN, den-EE)

Born, Chambly, Que., June 18, 1952.
Goaltender. Catches left. 5'11", 165 lbs.
Last amateur club: Trois-Rivières Ducs (QJHL).
(Pittsburgh's 3rd choice, 40th over-all, in 1972 Amateur Draft).

			Regular Season								Playoffs						
Season	Club	Lea	GP	W	L	T	Mins	GA	SO	Avg	GP	W	L	Mins	GA	SO	Avg
1970-71	Trois Rivières	QJHL	33	....	....	....	1573	108	0	4.12	7	....	....	420	23	1	3.28
1971-72	Trois Rivières	QJHL	40	....	....	....	2400	160	2	4.00	4	....	....	200	19	0	5.70
1972-73	**Pittsburgh**	**NHL**	**18**	**6**	**7**	**2**	**967**	**55**	**2**	**3.41**	....	....	....	....	....	....	....
	Hershey	AHL	21	....	....	....	1185	63	0	3.19	4	....	....	240	16	0	4.00
1973-74	**Pittsburgh**	**NHL**	**5**	**1**	**3**	**0**	**260**	**18**	**0**	**4.15**	....	....	....	....	....	....	....
	Salt Lake	WHL	9	....	....	....	530	32	0	3.62	....	....	....	....	....	....	....
	Hershey	AHL	17	....	....	....	967	52	0	3.22	4	....	....	242	7	0	1.73
1974-75	Hershey	AHL	12	....	....	....	615	45	0	4.39	....	....	....	....	....	....	....
	Pittsburgh	**NHL**	**3**	**1**	**1**	**0**	**108**	**11**	**0**	**6.11**	....	....	....	....	....	....	....
	Kansas City	**NHL**	**22**	**4**	**13**	**4**	**1280**	**80**	**0**	**3.75**	....	....	....	....	....	....	....
1975-76	**Kansas City**	**NHL**	**64**	**11**	**39**	**11**	**3620**	**243**	**0**	**4.03**	....	....	....	....	....	....	....
1976-77	**Pittsburgh**	**NHL**	**34**	**15**	**11**	**5**	**1920**	**94**	**1**	**2.94**	**3**	**1**	**2**	**180**	**11**	**0**	**3.67**
1977-78	**Pittsburgh**	**NHL**	**60**	**20**	**25**	**15**	**3534**	**210**	**0**	**3.57**	....	....	....	....	....	....	....
1978-79	**Pittsburgh**	**NHL**	**56**	**22**	**19**	**12**	**3208**	**180**	**0**	**3.37**	**7**	**2**	**5**	**421**	**24**	**0**	**3.42**
1979-80	**Montreal**	**NHL**	**34**	**25**	**3**	**3**	**1909**	**80**	**0**	**2.51**	**5**	**2**	**3**	**300**	**15**	**0**	**3.00**
1980-81a	**Montreal**	**NHL**	**25**	**6**	**9**	**6**	**1147**	**67**	**1**	**3.50**	....	....	....	....	....	....	....
1981-82bc	**Montreal**	**NHL**	**27**	**12**	**6**	**8**	**1547**	**68**	***3**	***2.64**	....	....	....	....	....		
1982-83	**Pittsburgh**	**NHL**	**31**	**5**	**18**	**5**	**1707**	**151**	**1**	**5.31**	....	....	....	....	....	....	....
1983-84	**Pittsburgh**	**NHL**	**38**	**8**	**24**	**2**	**2028**	**138**	**1**	**4.08**	....	....	....	....	....	....	....
1984-85	**Pittsburgh**	**NHL**	**42**	**10**	**22**	**3**	**2193**	**170**	**1**	**4.65**	....	....	....	....	....	....	....
1985-86	**Pittsburgh**	**NHL**	**3**	**0**	**3**	**0**	**180**	**14**	**0**	**4.67**	....	....	....	....	....	....	....
	Baltimore	AHL	27	10	11	4	1510	86	0	3.42	....	....	....	....	....	....	....
	NHL Totals		462	146	203	76	25608	1579	10	3.70	15	5	10	901	50	0	3.33

a Shared Vezina Trophy with Michel Larocque and Richard Sévigny (1981)
b Shared shutout with Richard Sevigny, November 11, 1981 vs. Colorado.
c Shared William Jennings Trophy with Rick Wamsley (1982)

Traded to **Kansas City** by **Pittsburgh** with Jean-Guy Lagace for goaltender Michel Plasse, January 10, 1975. Signed by **Pittsburgh** as free agent, August 7, 1976. As compensation, **Colorado (Kansas City)** received goaltender Michel Plasse and Simon Nolet from Pittsburgh. Traded to **Montreal** by **Pittsburgh** with Pittsburgh's second round choice (Jocelyn Gauvreau) in the 1982 Entry Draft for Pat Hughes and Robbie Holland, August 30, 1979. Traded to **Pittsburgh** by **Montreal** for Pittsburgh's third round choice in the 1985 Entry Draft, September 15, 1982.

HEXTALL, RON

Born, Winnipeg, Man., May 3, 1964.
Goaltender. Catches left. 6'2", 174 lbs.
Last amateur club: Brandon Wheat Kings (WHL).
(Philadelphia's 6th choice, 119th over-all, in 1982 Entry Draft).

			Regular Season								Playoffs						
Season	Club	Lea	GP	W	L	T	Mins	GA	SO	Avg	GP	W	L	Mins	GA	SO	Avg
1981-82	Brandon	WHL	30	12	11	0	1398	133	0	5.71	3	0	2	103	16	0	9.32
1982-83	Brandon	WHL	44	13	30	0	2589	249	0	5.77	....	....	....	....	....	....	....
1983-84	Brandon	WHL	46	29	13	2	2670	190	0	4.27	10	5	5	592	37	0	3.75
1984-85	Hershey	AHL	11	4	6	0	555	34	0	3.68	....	....	....	....	....	....	....
	Kalamazoo	IHL	19	6	11	1	1103	80	0	4.35	....	....	....	....	....	....	....
1985-86	Hershey	AHL	53	30	19	2	3061	174	5	3.41	13	5	7	780	42	1	3.23

HOLDEN, MARK

Born, Weymouth, Mass., June 12, 1957.
Goaltender. Catches left. 5'10", 165 lbs.
Last amateur club: Brown University Bruins (ECAC).
(Montreal's 16th choice, 160th over-all, in 1977 Amateur Draft).

			Regular Season								Playoffs						
Season	Club	Lea	GP	W	L	T	Mins	GA	SO	Avg	GP	W	L	Mins	GA	SO	Avg
1978-79	Brown	ECAC	13	7	6	0	754	49	0	3.90	....	....	....	....	....	....	....
1979-80	Brown	ECAC	26	10	14	2	1562	93	0	3.70	....	....	....	....	....	....	....
1980-81	Nova Scotia	AHL	42	20	17	1	2223	127	2	3.43	3	0	3	159	12	0	4.53
1981-82	**Montreal**	**NHL**	**1**	**0**	**0**	**0**	**20**	**0**	**0**	**0.00**	....	....	....	....	....		
	Nova Scotia	AHL	44	19	19	5	2534	142	0	3.36	7	2	5	435	21	0	2.90
1982-83	**Montreal**	**NHL**	**2**	**0**	**1**	**1**	**87**	**6**	**0**	**4.14**	....	....	....	....	....	....	....
	Nova Scotia	AHL	41	....	....	....	2369	160	0	4.05	6	....	....	319	13	0	2.44
1983-84	**Montreal**	**NHL**	**1**	**0**	**1**	**0**	**52**	**4**	**0**	**4.60**	....	....	....	....	....	....	....
	Nova Scotia	AHL	47	19	8	7	2739	153	0	3.35	10	4	6	534	40	0	4.49
1984-85	**Winnipeg**	**NHL**	**4**	**2**	**0**	**0**	**213**	**15**	**0**	**4.23**	....	....	....	....	....	....	....
	Nova Scotia	AHL	22	8	12	1	1261	87	1	4.14	....	....	....	....	....	....	....
1985-86	**Sherbrooke**	**AHL**	**12**	**5**	**7**	**0**	**696**	**52**	**0**	**4.48**	....	....	....	....	....	....	....
	Fort Wayne	IHL	9	3	3	0	496	26	1	3.14	....	....	....	....	....	....	....
	NHL Totals		**8**	**2**	**2**	**1**	**372**	**25**	**0**	**4.03**	....	....	....	....	....	....	....

Traded to **Winnipeg** by **Montreal** for Doug Soetaert, October 9, 1984.

HRIVNAK, JIMMY (RIV-nik)

Born, Montreal, Que., May 28, 1968.
Goaltender. Catches left. 6'1", 180 lbs.
Last amateur club: Merrimack College Warriors (ECAC).
(Washington's 4th choice, 61st over-all, in 1986 Entry Draft).

			Regular Season								Playoffs						
Season	Club	Lea	GP	W	L	T	Mins	GA	SO	Avg	GP	W	L	Mins	GA	SO	Avg
1985-86	Merrimack	ECAC	21	12	8	0	1230	75	0	3.66	....	....	....	....	....	....	....

HRUDEY, KELLY STEPHEN (ROO-dee)

Born, Edmonton, Alta., January 13, 1961.
Goaltender. Catches left. 5'10", 185 lbs.
Last amateur club: Medicine Hat Tigers (WHL).
(NY Islanders' 2nd choice, 38th over-all, in 1980 Entry Draft).

			Regular Season								Playoffs						
Season	Club	Lea	GP	W	L	T	Mins	GA	SO	Avg	GP	W	L	Mins	GA	SO	Avg
1978-79	Medicine Hat	WHL	57	12	34	7	3093	318	0	6.17	....	....	....	....	....	....	....
1979-80	Medicine Hat	WHL	57	25	23	4	3049	212	1	4.17	13	6	6	638	48	0	4.51
1980-81a	Medicine Hat	WHL	55	32	19	1	3023	200	*4	3.97	4	....	....	244	17	0	4.18
	Indianapolis	CHL	....	....	....	....	....	....	....	....	2	....	....	135	8	0	3.56
1981-82bc	Indianapolis	CHL	51	27	19	4	3033	149	1	*2.95	13	11	2	842	34	*1	*2.42
1982-83bcd	Indianapolis	CHL	47	26	17	1	2744	139	2	3.04	10	7	3	637	28	0	2.64
1983-84	Indianapolis	CHL	6	3	2	1	370	21	0	3.40	....	....	....	....	....	....	....
	NY Islanders	**NHL**	**12**	**7**	**2**	**0**	**535**	**28**	**0**	**3.14**	....	....	....	....	....	....	....
1984-85	**NY Islanders**	**NHL**	**41**	**19**	**17**	**3**	**2335**	**141**	**2**	**3.62**	**5**	**1**	**3**	**281**	**8**	**0**	**1.71**
1985-86	**NY Islanders**	**NHL**	**45**	**19**	**15**	**8**	**2563**	**137**	**1**	**3.21**	**2**	**0**	**2**	**120**	**6**	**0**	**3.00**
	NHL Totals		**98**	**45**	**34**	**11**	**5433**	**306**	**3**	**3.39**	**7**	**1**	**5**	**401**	**14**	**0**	**2.09**

a WHL Second All-Star Team (1981)
b CHL First All-Star Team (1982, 1983)
c Shared Terry Sawchuk Trophy (CHL's Leading Goaltenders) with Rob Holland (1982, 1983)
d Won Tommy Ivan Trophy (CHL's Most Valuable Player) (1983)

HYDUKE, JOHN

Born, Hibbing, Minn., June 23, 1967.
Goaltender. Catches left. 5'10", 155 lbs.
Last amateur club: University of Minnesota-Duluth Bulldogs (WCHA).
(Los Angeles' 8th choice, 156th over-all, in 1985 Entry Draft).

			Regular Season								Playoffs						
Season	Club	Lea	GP	W	L	T	Mins	GA	SO	Avg	GP	W	L	Mins	GA	SO	Avg
1985-86	Minn-Duluth	WCHA	24	14	17	3	1401	84	0	3.60	....	....	....	....	....	....	....

JABLONSKI, PAT

Born, Toledo, Ohio, June 20, 1967.
Goaltender. Catches right. 6'0", 170 lbs.
Last amateur club: Windsor Compuware Spitfires (OHL).
(St. Louis' 6th choice, 138th over-all, in 1985 Entry Draft).

			Regular Season								Playoffs						
Season	Club	Lea	GP	W	L	T	Mins	GA	SO	Avg	GP	W	L	Mins	GA	SO	Avg
1985-86	Windsor	OHL	29	6	16	4	1600	119	1	4.46	6	0	3	263	20	0	4.56

JOHNSON, GARY

Born, Winnipeg, Man., February 16, 1965.
Goaltender. Catches left. 5'10", 150 lbs.
Last amateur club: Brandon Wheat Kings (WHL).

			Regular Season								Playoffs						
Season	Club	Lea	GP	W	L	T	Mins	GA	SO	Avg	GP	W	L	Mins	GA	SO	Avg
1982-83	Winnipeg	WHL	29	18	9	0	1695	117	1	4.14	2	0	2	93	8	0	5.16
1983-84	Medicine Hat	WHL	35	21	10	1	1928	129	0	4.01	12	8	4	721	45	1	3.74
1984-85	Medicine Hat	WHL	38	25	9	0	2092	114	2	3.27	8	4	4	463	27	0	3.50
1985-86	Brandon	WHL	13	4	6	0	553	44	0	4.77	....	....	....	....	....	....	....

Signed as a free agent by **NY Islanders**, June 6, 1985.

JANECYK, ROBERT (BOB)

Born, Chicago, Ill., May 18, 1957.
Goaltender. Catches left. 6'1", 180 lbs.
Last amateur club: Fort Wayne Komets (IHL)

			Regular Season								Playoffs						
Season	Club	Lea	GP	W	L	T	Mins	GA	SO	Avg	GP	W	L	Mins	GA	SO	Avg
1979-80	Flint	IHL	2	....	....	....	119	5	0	2.53	....	....	....	....	....	....	....
a	Fort Wayne	IHL	42	....	....	....	2327	133	1	3.43	3	....	....	89	4	0	2.70
1980-81	New Brunswick	AHL	34	11	18	1	1915	131	0	4.10	....	....	....	....	....	....	....
1981-82bc	New Brunswick	AHL	53	32	13	7	3224	153	2	2.85	14	11	2	818	32	*1	*2.35
1982-83b	Springfield	AHL	47	....	....	....	2754	167	3	3.64	....	....	....	....	....	....	....
1983-84	**Chicago**	**NHL**	**8**	**2**	**3**	**1**	**412**	**28**	**0**	**4.08**	....	....	....	....	....	....	....
	Springfield	AHL	30	14	11	4	1664	94	0	3.39	....	....	....	....	....	....	....
1984-85	**Los Angeles**	**NHL**	**51**	**22**	**21**	**8**	**3002**	**183**	**2**	**3.66**	**3**	**0**	**3**	**184**	**10**	**0**	**3.26**
1985-86	**Los Angeles**	**NHL**	**38**	**14**	**16**	**4**	**2083**	**162**	**0**	**4.67**	....	....	....	....	....	....	....
	NHL Totals		**97**	**38**	**40**	**13**	**5497**	**373**	**2**	**4.07**	**3**	**0**	**3**	**184**	**10**	**0**	**3.26**

a IHL Second All-Star Team (1980)
b AHL First All-Star Team (1982, 1983)
c Shared Harry "Hap" Holmes Memorial Trophy (AHL's Leading Goaltenders) with Warren Skorodenski (1982)

Signed as free agent by **Chicago**, June 3, 1980. Traded to **Los Angeles** by **Chicago** with Chicago's first round (Craig Redmond), third round (John English) and fourth round (Thomas Glavine) choices in 1984 Entry Draft for Los Angeles' first round (Ed Olczyk) and fourth round (Tommy Eriksson) choices in 1984 Entry Draft, June 9, 1984.

JENSEN, ALLAN RAYMOND (AL)

Born, Hamilton, Ont., November 27, 1958.
Goaltender. Catches left. 5′10″, 180 lbs.
Last amateur club: Hamilton Fincups (OHA).
(Detroit's 4th choice, 31st over-all, in 1978 Amateur Draft).

			Regular Season								Playoffs						
Season	Club	Lea	GP	W	L	T	Mins	GA	SO	Avg	GP	W	L	Mins	GA	SO	Avg
1976-77a	St. Catharines	OHA	48	....	....	....	2726	168	2	3.70	13	....	....	707	36	1	2.97
1977-78b	Hamilton	OHA	43	....	....	....	2582	146	3	3.35	17	....	....	967	43	1	2.54
1978-79	Kalamazoo	IHL	47	....	....	....	2596	156	2	3.61	12	....	....	718	34	0	*2.84
1979-80	Adirondack	AHL	57	27	24	5	3406	199	2	3.51	4	0	4	212	15	0	4.25
1980-81	**Detroit**	**NHL**	**1**	**0**	**1**	**0**	**60**	**7**	**0**	**7.00**	....	....	....	....	....	....	....
	Adirondack	AHL	60	27	21	3	3169	203	*3	3.84	11	7	4	626	46	0	4.41
1981-82	**Washington**	**NHL**	**26**	**8**	**8**	**4**	**1274**	**81**	**0**	**3.82**	....	....	....	....	....	....	....
	Hershey	AHL	8	4	1	1	407	24	0	3.54	3	2	1	162	9	0	3.33
1982-83	**Washington**	**NHL**	**40**	**22**	**12**	**6**	**2358**	**135**	**1**	**3.44**	**3**	**1**	**2**	**139**	**10**	**0**	**4.31**
1983-84	Hershey	AHL	3	1	.2	....	180	16	0	5.33	....	....	....	....	....	....	....
c	**Washington**	**NHL**	**43**	**25**	**13**	**3**	**2414**	**117**	***4**	**2.91**	**6**	**3**	**1**	**258**	**14**	**0**	**3.26**
1984-85	**Washington**	**NHL**	**14**	**10**	**3**	**1**	**803**	**34**	**1**	**2.54**	**3**	**1**	**2**	**201**	**8**	**0**	**2.39**
	Binghamton	AHL	3	2	1	0	180	9	0	3.00	....	....	....	....	....	....	....
1985-86	**Washington**	**NHL**	**44**	**28**	**9**	**3**	**2437**	**129**	**2**	**3.18**	....	....	....	....	....	....	....
	NHL Totals		**168**	**93**	**46**	**17**	**9346**	**503**	**8**	**3.23**	**12**	**5**	**5**	**598**	**32**	**0**	**3.21**

a OHA Second All-Star Team (1977)
b OHA First All-Star Team (1978)
c Shared William Jennings Trophy with Pat Riggin (1984)

Traded to **Washington** by **Detroit** for Mark Lofthouse, July 23, 1981.

JENSEN, DARREN AKSEL

Born, Creston, B.C., May 27, 1960.
Goaltender. Catches left. 5′9″, 165 lbs.
Last amateur club: University of North Dakota Fighting Sioux (WCHA).
(Hartford's 5th choice, 92nd over-all, in 1980 Entry Draft).

			Regular Season								Playoffs						
Season	Club	Lea	GP	W	L	T	Mins	GA	SO	Avg	GP	W	L	Mins	GA	SO	Avg
1979-80	North Dakota	WCHA	15	....	....	....	890	33	1	2.22	....	....	....	....	....	....	....
1980-81	North Dakota	WCHA	25	....	....	....	1510	110	0	4.37	....	....	....	....	....	....	....
1981-82	North Dakota	WCHA	16	....	....	....	909	45	1	2.96	....	....	....	....	....	....	....
1982-83	North Dakota	WCHA	15	....	....	....	905	45	0	2.98	....	....	....	....	....	....	....
1983-84abc	Fort Wayne	IHL	56	40	12	3	3325	162	*4	*2.92	6	2	4	358	21	0	3.52
1984-85	**Philadelphia**	**NHL**	**1**	**0**	**1**	**0**	**60**	**7**	**0**	**7.00**	....	....	....	....	....	....	....
	Hershey	AHL	39	12	20	6	2263	150	1	3.98	....	....	....	....	....	....	....
1985-86d	**Philadelphia**	**NHL**	**29**	**15**	**9**	**1**	**1436**	**88**	**2**	**3.68**	....	....	....	....	....	....	....
	Hershey	AHL	14	11	1	1	795	38	1	2.87	7	5	1	365	19	0	3.12
	NHL Totals		**30**	**15**	**10**	**1**	**1496**	**95**	**2**	**3.81**	....	....	....	....	....	....	....

a IHL First All-Star Team (1984)
b Named IHL's Most Valuable Player (1984)
c Named IHL's Rookie of the Year (1984)
d Shared William Jennings Trophy with Bob Froese (1986)

Signed as free agent by **Philadelphia**, May 1, 1984.

JOPLING, BRIAN

Born, Stoughton, Mass., June 14, 1964.
Goaltender. Catches left. 6′, 190 lbs.
Last amateur club: Rensselaer Polytechnic Institute (ECAC).
(Philadelphia's 10th choice, 230th over-all, in 1983 Entry Draft).

			Regular Season								Playoffs						
Season	Club	Lea	GP	W	L	T	Mins	GA	SO	Avg	GP	W	L	Mins	GA	SO	Avg
1984-85	RPI	ECAC	12	5	1	0	454	18	0	2.38	....	....	....	....	....	....	....
1985-86	RPI	ECAC	28	16	9	1	1471	99	2	4.04	....	....	....	....	....	....	....

KEANS, DOUGLAS FREDERICK (DOUG)

Born, Pembroke, Ont., January 7, 1958.
Goaltender. Catches left. 5′7″, 175 lbs.
Last amateur club: Oshawa Generals (OHA).
(Los Angeles' 2nd choice, 94th over-all, in 1978 Amateur Draft).

			Regular Season								Playoffs						
Season	Club	Lea	GP	W	L	T	Mins	GA	SO	Avg	GP	W	L	Mins	GA	SO	Avg
1976-77	Oshawa	OHA	48	....	....	....	2632	291	0	6.63	....	....	....	....	....	....	....
1977-78	Oshawa	OHA	42	....	....	....	2500	173	1	4.12	5	....	....	299	23	0	4.63
1978-79	Saginaw	IHL	59	....	....	....	3207	217	0	4.06	2	....	....	120	10	0	5.05
1979-80	Binghamton	AHL	7	3	3	2	429	25	0	3.50	....	....	....	....	....	....	....
	Saginaw	IHL	22	....	....	....	1070	67	1	3.76	....	....	....	....	....	....	....
	Los Angeles	**NHL**	**10**	**3**	**3**	**3**	**559**	**23**	**0**	**2.47**	**1**	**0**	**1**	**40**	**7**	**0**	**10.50**
1980-81	**Los Angeles**	**NHL**	**9**	**2**	**3**	**1**	**454**	**37**	**0**	**4.89**	....	....	....	....	....	....	....
	Houston	CHL	11	3	4	4	699	27	0	2.32	....	....	....	....	....	....	....
	Oklahoma City	CHL	9	3	5	0	492	32	1	3.90	....	....	....	....	....	....	....
1981-82	New Haven	AHL	13	5	5	1	686	33	2	2.89	....	....	....	....	....	....	....
	Los Angeles	**NHL**	**31**	**8**	**10**	**7**	**1436**	**103**	**0**	**4.30**	**2**	**0**	**1**	**32**	**1**	**0**	**1.88**
1982-83	**Los Angeles**	**NHL**	**6**	**0**	**2**	**2**	**304**	**24**	**0**	**4.73**	....	....	....	....	....	....	....
	New Haven	AHL	30	13	13	2	1724	125	0	4.35	....	....	....	....	....	....	....
1983-84	**Boston**	**NHL**	**33**	**19**	**8**	**3**	**1779**	**92**	**2**	**3.10**	....	....	....	....	....	....	....
1984-85	**Boston**	**NHL**	**25**	**16**	**6**	**3**	**1497**	**82**	**1**	**3.29**	**4**	**2**	**2**	**240**	**15**	**0**	**3.75**
1985-86	**Boston**	**NHL**	**30**	**14**	**13**	**3**	**1757**	**107**	**0**	**3.65**	....	....	....	....	....	....	....
	NHL Totals		**144**	**62**	**45**	**22**	**7786**	**468**	**3**	**3.61**	**7**	**2**	**4**	**312**	**23**	**0**	**4.42**

Claimed on waivers by **Boston** from **Los Angeles**, May 24, 1983.

KEMP, JOHN

Born, Burlington, Ont., July 31, 1963.
Goaltender. Shoots left. 6′0″, 190 lbs.
Last amateur club: Canadian Olympic Team.

			Regular Season								Playoffs						
Season	Club	Lea	GP	W	L	T	Mins	GA	SO	Avg	GP	W	L	Mins	GA	SO	Avg
1983-84	U. of Toronto	OUAA	29	24	3	2	1627	80	3	2.95	....	....	....	....	....	....	....
1984-85	U. of Toronto	OUAA	22	18	2	2	1494	68	0	2.69	....	....	....	....	....	....	....
1985-86	Cdn. Olympic	....	35	10	11	1	1368	96	0	4.21	....	....	....	....	....	....	....
	Hershey	AHL	8	2	6	0	440	40	0	5.45	....	....	....	....	....	....	....

Signed as a free agent by **Philadelphia**, January 14, 1986.

KILROY, SHAWN

Born, Ottawa, Ont., April 22, 1964.
Goaltender. Catches left. 5′11″, 175 lbs.
Last amateur club: Peterborough Petes (OHL).
(Vancouver's 3rd choice, 71st over-all, in 1983 Entry Draft).

			Regular Season								Playoffs						
Season	Club	Lea	GP	W	L	T	Mins	GA	SO	Avg	GP	W	L	Mins	GA	SO	Avg
1981-82a	Peterborough	OHL	17	8	6	2	972	48	1	2.96	5	2	3	255	21	0	4.94
1982-83	Peterborough	OHL	39	24	11	2	2137	142	0	3.99	2	0	2	90	7	0	4.67
1983-84	Peterborough	OHL	49	26	15	4	2784	193	0	4.16	8	4	4	480	33	0	4.13
1984-85	Peoria	IHL	2	0	2	0	116	12	0	6.21	....	....	....	....	....	....	....
1985-86	Mohawk Valley	ACHL	....	....	....	....	....	....	....	....	....	....	....	....	....	....	....
	Kalamazoo	IHL	2	0	1	0	77	5	0	3.90	....	....	....	....	....	....	....
	Flint	IHL	12	5	6	0	610	47	0	4.62	....	....	....	....	....	....	....

a Rookie Goaltender of the Year (OHL) (1982)

KLEISINGER, TERRY

Born, Regina, Sask., October 10, 1960.
Goaltender. Catches right. 6′0″, 190 lbs.
Last amateur club: University of Wisconsin Badgers (WCHA).

			Regular Season								Playoffs						
Season	Club	Lea	GP	W	L	T	Mins	GA	SO	Avg	GP	W	L	Mins	GA	SO	Avg
1982-83	Wisconsin	WCHA	18	11	6	1	1021	48	1	2.82	....	....	....	....	....	....	....
1983-84	Wisconsin	WCHA	24	11	11	1	1406	96	0	4.10	....	....	....	....	....	....	....
1984-85	DID NOT PLAY																
1985-86	Flint	IHL	4	0	3	0	200	25	0	7.50	....	....	....	....	....	....	....
	Toledo	IHL	14	1	10	0	786	76	0	5.80	....	....	....	....	....	....	....
	New Haven	AHL	10	2	5	2	497	34	0	4.10	....	....	....	....	....	....	....
	NY Rangers	**NHL**	**4**	**0**	**2**	**0**	**191**	**14**	**0**	**4.40**	....	....	....	....	....	....	....
	NHL Totals		**4**	**0**	**2**	**0**	**191**	**14**	**0**	**4.40**	....	....	....	....	....	....	....

Signed as a free agent by **NY Rangers**, October 8, 1985.

KNICKLE, RICHARD (RICK)

Born, Chatham, N.B., February 26, 1960.
Goaltender. Catches left. 5′10″, 155 lbs.
Last amateur club: Brandon Wheat Kings (WHL).
(Buffalo's 7th choice, 116th over-all, in 1979 Entry Draft).

			Regular Season								Playoffs						
Season	Club	Lea	GP	W	L	T	Mins	GA	SO	Avg	GP	W	L	Mins	GA	SO	Avg
1977-78	Brandon	WHL	49	34	5	7	2806	182	0	3.89	8	....	....	450	36	0	4.82
1978-79a	Brandon	WHL	38	26	3	8	2240	118	1	*3.16	16	12	3	886	41	*1	*2.78
1979-80	Brandon	WHL	33	11	14	1	1604	125	0	4.68	....	....	....	....	....	....	....
	Muskegon	IHL	16	....	....	....	829	52	0	3.76	3	....	....	156	17	0	6.54
1980-81b	Erie	EHL	43	....	....	....	2347	125	1	*3.20	8	....	....	446	14	0	*1.88
1981-82	Rochester	AHL	31	10	12	5	1753	108	1	3.70	3	0	2	125	7	0	3.37
1982-83	Flint	IHL	27	....	....	....	1638	92	2	3.37	3	....	....	193	10	0	3.11
1983-84c	Flint	IHL	60	32	21	5	3518	203	3	3.46	8	8	0	480	24	0	3.00
1984-85	Sherbrooke	AHL	14	7	6	0	780	53	0	4.08	....	....	....	....	....	....	....
	Flint	IHL	36	18	11	3	2018	115	2	3.42	7	3	4	401	27	0	4.04
1985-86	Saginaw	IHL	39	16	15	0	2235	135	2	3.62	3	2	1	193	12	0	3.73

a WHL First All-Star Team (1979)
b EHL First All-Star Team (1981)
c IHL Second All-Star Team (1984)

Signed as a free agent by **Montreal**, February 8, 1985.

KOMONOSKY, WARD

Born, Regina, Sask., December 3, 1964.
Goaltender. Catches left. 6′, 195 lbs.
Last amateur club: Prince Albert Raiders (WHL).

			Regular Season								Playoffs						
Season	Club	Lea	GP	W	L	T	Mins	GA	SO	Avg	GP	W	L	Mins	GA	SO	Avg
1982-83	Prince Albert	WHL	34	5	27	1	1748	176	0	6.04	....	....	....	....	....	....	....
1983-84	Prince Albert	WHL	45	23	16	2	2521	207	1	4.93	5	1	3	283	23	0	4.88
1984-85	Prince Albert	WHL	38	30	7	1	2287	134	0	3.52	12	....	....	687	35	0	3.06
1985-86	DID NOT PLAY																

Signed as free agent by **Minnesota**, September 19, 1983.

KOSTI, RICHARD STEPHEN (RICK)

Born, Kincaid, Sask., September 13, 1963.
Goaltender. Catches left. 5′10″, 185 lbs.
Last amateur club. University of Minnesota-Duluth Bulldogs (WCHA).

			Regular Season								Playoffs						
Season	Club	Lea	GP	W	L	T	Mins	GA	SO	Avg	GP	W	L	Mins	GA	SO	Avg
1983-84a	Minn-Duluth	WCHA	38	27	9	2	2735	146	3	3.04	....	....	....	....	....	....	....
1984-85bc	Minn-Duluth	WCHA	45	33	9	3	2347	119	1	3.20	....	....	....	....	....	....	....
1985-86	Moncton	AHL	15	5	7	1	705	44	1	3.74	....	....	....	....	....	....	....
	Salt Lake	IHL	25	9	12	0	1330	99	0	4.46	....	....	....	....	....	....	....

a WCHA Rookie of the Year (1984)
b WCHA First All-Star Team (1985)
c Named to NCAA All-American Team (1985)

Signed as a free agent by **Calgary**, May 29, 1985.

LaFOREST, MARK ANDREW

Born, Welland, Ont., July 10, 1962.
Goaltender. Catches left. 5′10″, 178 lbs.
Last amateur club: North Bay Centennials (OHL).

			Regular Season								Playoffs						
Season	Club	Lea	GP	W	L	T	Mins	GA	SO	Avg	GP	W	L	Mins	GA	SO	Avg
1981-82	Niagara Falls	OHL	24	10	13	1	1365	105	1	4.62	5	1	2	300	19	0	3.80
1982-83	North Bay	OHL	54	34	17	1	3140	195	0	3.73	8	4	4	474	31	0	3.92
1983-84	Adirondack	AHL	7	3	3	1	351	29	0	4.96	....	....	....	....	....	....	....
	Kalamazoo	IHL	13	4	5	2	718	48	1	4.01	....	....	....	....	....	....	....
1984-85	Adirondack	AHL	11	2	3	1	430	35	0	488	....	....	....	....	....	....	....
1985-86	**Detroit**	**NHL**	**28**	**4**	**21**	**0**	**1383**	**114**	**1**	**4.95**	....	....	....	....	....	....	....
	Adirondack	AHL	19	13	5	1	1142	57	0	2.99	17	12	5	1075	58	0	3.24
	NHL Totals		**28**	**4**	**21**	**0**	**1383**	**114**	**1**	**4.95**	....	....	....	....	....	....	....

Signed as free agent by **Detroit**, April 29, 1983.

LAROCHELLE, ALAIN

Born, Ponteiz, Sask., October 27, 1964.
Goaltender. Catches left. 5'9", 185 lbs.
Last amateur club: Saskatoon Blades (WHL).
(Boston's 4th choice, 84th over-all, in 1983 Entry Draft).

			Regular Season								Playoffs						
Season	Club	Lea	GP	W	L	T	Mins	GA	SO	Avg	GP	W	L	Mins	GA	SO	Avg
1981-82	Portland	WHL	23	....	....	....	1245	94	0	4.53	2	....	....	34	3	0	5.29
1982-83	Saskatoon	WHL	41	....	....	....	2295	153	2	4.00	6	....	....	33	21	0	3.78
1983-84	Saskatoon	WHL	56	27	24	0	3033	244	0	4.83	....	....	....	....	....	....	....
1984-85	Portland	WHL	53	19	29	0	2785	268	0	5.77	6	1	5	284	30	0	6.34
1985-86	Moncton	AHL	6	1	2	0	216	17	0	4.72	....	....	....	....	....	....	....
	Milwaukee	IHL	8	3	2	1	455	34	0	4.48	....	....	....	....	....	....	....

LEMELIN, REJEAN (REGGIE) (lem-E-lin)

Born, Sherbrooke, Que., November 19, 1954.
Goaltender. Catches left. 5'11", 170 lbs.
Last amateur club: Sherbrooke Beavers (QJHL).
(Philadelphia's 6th choice, 125th over-all, in 1974 Amateur Draft).

			Regular Season								Playoffs						
Season	Club	Lea	GP	W	L	T	Mins	GA	SO	Avg	GP	W	L	Mins	GA	SO	Avg
1972-73	Sherbrooke	QJHL	28	....	....	....	1681	146	0	5.21	2	....	....	120	12	0	6.00
1973-74	Sherbrooke	QJHL	35	....	....	....	2061	158	0	4.60	1	....	....	60	3	0	3.00
1974-75	Philadelphia	NAHL	43	....	....	....	2277	131	3	3.45	....	....	....	....	....	....	....
1975-76	Philadelphia	NAHL	29	....	....	....	1601	97	1	3.63	3	....	....	171	15	0	5.26
1976-77	Springfield	AHL	3	2	1	0	180	10	0	3.33	....	....	....	....	....	....	....
	Philadelphia	NAHL	51	26	19	1	2763	170	1	3.61	3	....	....	191	14	0	4.40
1977-78a	Philadelphia	AHL	60	31	21	7	3585	177	4	2.96	2	0	2	119	12	0	6.05
1978-79	Philadelphia	AHL	13	3	9	1	780	36	0	2.77	....	....	....	....	....	....	....
	Atlanta	**NHL**	**18**	**8**	**8**	**1**	**994**	**55**	**0**	**3.32**	**1**	**0**	**0**	**20**	**0**	**0**	**0.00**
1979-80	**Atlanta**	**NHL**	**3**	**0**	**2**	**0**	**150**	**15**	**0**	**6.00**	....	....	....	....	....	....	....
	Birmingham	CHL	38	13	21	2	2188	137	0	3.76	2	0	1	79	5	0	3.80
1980-81	Birmingham	CHL	13	3	8	2	757	56	0	4.44	....	....	....	....	....	....	....
	Calgary	**NHL**	**29**	**14**	**6**	**7**	**1629**	**88**	**2**	**3.24**	**6**	**3**	**3**	**366**	**22**	**0**	**3.61**
1981-82	**Calgary**	**NHL**	**34**	**10**	**5**	**6**	**1866**	**135**	**0**	**4.34**	....	....	....	....	....	....	....
1982-83	**Calgary**	**NHL**	**39**	**16**	**12**	**8**	**2211**	**133**	**0**	**3.61**	**7**	**3**	**3**	**327**	**27**	**0**	**4.95**
1983-84	**Calgary**	**NHL**	**51**	**21**	**12**	**9**	**2568**	**150**	**0**	**3.50**	**8**	**4**	**4**	**448**	**32**	**0**	**4.28**
1984-85	**Calgary**	**NHL**	**56**	**30**	**12**	**10**	**3176**	**183**	**1**	**3.46**	**4**	**1**	**3**	**248**	**15**	**1**	**3.63**
1985-86	**Calgary**	**NHL**	**60**	**29**	**24**	**4**	**3369**	**229**	**1**	**4.08**	**3**	**0**	**1**	**109**	**7**	**0**	**3.85**
	NHL Totals		**290**	**128**	**81**	**45**	**15963**	**988**	**4**	**3.71**	**29**	**11**	**14**	**1518**	**103**	**1**	**4.07**

a AHL First All-Star Team (1978)

Signed as free agent by **Atlanta**, August 17, 1978.

LIUT, MICHAEL (MIKE) (LEE-oot)

Born, Weston, Ont., January 7, 1956.
Goaltender. Catches left. 6'2", 195 lbs.
Last amateur club: Bowling Green State University Falcons (CCHA).
(St. Louis' 5th choice, 56th over-all, in 1976 Amateur Draft).

			Regular Season								Playoffs						
Season	Club	Lea	GP	W	L	T	Mins	GA	SO	Avg	GP	W	L	Mins	GA	SO	Avg
1973-74	Bowling Green	CCHA	24	10	12	0	1272	88	1	4.15	....	....	....	....	....	....	....
1974-75	Bowling Green	CCHA	20	12	6	1	1174	78	0	3.99	....	....	....	....	....	....	....
1975-76	Bowling Green	CCHA	21	13	5	0	1171	50	2	2.56	....	....	....	....	....	....	....
1976-77	Bowling Green	CCHA	24	18	4	0	1346	61	2	2.72	....	....	....	....	....	....	....
1977-78	Cincinnati	WHA	27	8	12	0	1215	86	0	4.25	....	....	....	....	....	....	....
1978-79	Cincinnati	WHA	54	23	27	4	3181	184	*3	3.47	3	1	2	179	12	0	4.02
1979-80	**St. Louis**	**NHL**	**64**	**32**	**23**	**9**	**3661**	**194**	**2**	**3.18**	**3**	**0**	**3**	**193**	**12**	**0**	**3.73**
1980-81ab	**St. Louis**	**NHL**	**61**	**33**	**14**	**13**	**3570**	**199**	**1**	**3.34**	**11**	**5**	**6**	**685**	**50**	**0**	**4.38**
1981-82	**St. Louis**	**NHL**	**64**	**28**	**28**	**7**	**3691**	**250**	**2**	**4.06**	**10**	**5**	**3**	**494**	**27**	**0**	**3.28**
1982-83	**St. Louis**	**NHL**	**68**	**21**	**27**	**13**	**3794**	**235**	**1**	**3.72**	**4**	**1**	**3**	**240**	**15**	**0**	**3.75**
1983-84	**St. Louis**	**NHL**	**58**	**25**	**29**	**4**	**3425**	**197**	**3**	**3.45**	**11**	**6**	**5**	**714**	**29**	**1**	**2.44**
1984-85	**St. Louis**	**NHL**	**32**	**12**	**12**	**6**	**1869**	**119**	**1**	**3.82**	....	....	....	....	....	....	....
	Hartford	**NHL**	**13**	**5**	**7**	**1**	**791**	**38**	**1**	**2.88**	....	....	....	....	....	....	....
1985-86	**Hartford**	**NHL**	**57**	**27**	**23**	**4**	**3282**	**198**	**2**	**3.62**	**8**	**5**	**2**	**441**	**14**	**1**	**1.90**
	NHL Totals		**417**	**183**	**163**	**57**	**24083**	**1430**	**13**	**3.56**	**47**	**22**	**22**	**2767**	**147**	**2**	**3.19**
	WHA Totals		81	31	39	4	4396	270	3	3.69	3	1	2	179	12	0	4.02

a NHL First All-Star Team (1981)
b Won Lester B. Pearson Award (1981)

Reclaimed by **St. Louis** from Cincinnati (WHA) prior to Expansion Draft, June 9, 1979. Traded to **Hartford** by **St. Louis** with Jorgen Pettersson for Mark Johnson and Greg Millen, February 21, 1985.

LOW, RONALD ALBERT (RON) (LOH)

Born, Birtle, Man., June 21, 1950.
Goaltender. Catches left. 6'1", 205 lbs.
Last amateur club: Jacksonville Rockets (EHL).
(Toronto's 8th choice, 103rd over-all, in 1970 Amateur Draft).

			Regular Season								Playoffs						
Season	Club	Lea	GP	W	L	T	Mins	GA	SO	Avg	GP	W	L	Mins	GA	SO	Avg
1970-71	Jacksonville	EHL	49	....	....	....	2940	293	1	5.98	....	....	....	....	....	....	....
	Tulsa	CHL	4	....	....	....	192	11	0	5.11	....	....	....	....	....	....	....
1971-72	Richmond	AHL	1	....	....	....	60	2	0	2.00	....	....	....	....	....	....	....
	Tulsa	CHL	43	....	....	....	2428	135	1	3.33	8	....	....	474	15	*1	*1.89
1972-73a	**Toronto**	**NHL**	**42**	**12**	**24**	**4**	**2343**	**152**	**1**	**3.89**	....	....	....	....	....	....	....
1973-74b	Tulsa	CHL	56	....	....	....	3213	169	1	3.16	....	....	....	....	....	....	....
1974-75	**Washington**	**NHL**	**48**	**8**	**36**	**2**	**2588**	**235**	**1**	**5.45**	....	....	....	....	....	....	....
1975-76	**Washington**	**NHL**	**43**	**6**	**31**	**2**	**2289**	**208**	**0**	**5.45**	....	....	....	....	....	....	....
1976-77c	**Washington**	**NHL**	**54**	**16**	**27**	**5**	**2918**	**188**	**0**	**3.87**	....	....	....	....	....	....	....
1977-78	**Detroit**	**NHL**	**32**	**9**	**12**	**9**	**1816**	**102**	**1**	**3.37**	**4**	**1**	**3**	**240**	**17**	**0**	**4.25**
1978-79de	Kansas City	CHL	63	....	....	....	3795	244	0	3.86	4	....	....	237	15	0	3.80
1979-80	Syracuse	AHL	15	5	9	1	905	70	0	4.64	....	....	....	....	....	....	....
	Quebec	**NHL**	**15**	**5**	**7**	**2**	**828**	**51**	**0**	**3.70**	....	....	....	....	....	....	....
	Edmonton	**NHL**	**11**	**8**	**2**	**1**	**650**	**37**	**0**	**3.42**	**3**	**0**	**3**	**212**	**12**	**0**	**3.40**
1980-81	**Edmonton**	**NHL**	**24**	**5**	**13**	**3**	**1260**	**93**	**0**	**4.43**	....	....	....	....	....	....	....
	Wichita	CHL	2	0	2	0	120	10	0	5.00	....	....	....	....	....	....	....
1981-82	**Edmonton**	**NHL**	**29**	**17**	**7**	**1**	**1554**	**100**	**0**	**3.86**	....	....	....	....	....	....	....
1982-83	**Edmonton**	**NHL**	**3**	**0**	**1**	**0**	**104**	**10**	**0**	**5.78**	....	....	....	....	....	....	....
	New Jersey	**NHL**	**11**	**2**	**7**	**1**	**608**	**41**	**0**	**4.05**	....	....	....	....	....	....	....
1983-84	**New Jersey**	**NHL**	**44**	**8**	**25**	**4**	**2218**	**161**	**0**	**4.35**	....	....	....	....	....	....	....
1984-85	**New Jersey**	**NHL**	**26**	**6**	**11**	**4**	**1326**	**85**	**1**	**3.85**	....	....	....	....	....	....	....
1985-86	Nova Scotia	AHL	6	1	5	0	299	24	0	4.82	....	....	....	....	....	....	....
	NHL Totals		**382**	**102**	**203**	**37**	**20502**	**1463**	**4**	**4.28**	**7**	**1**	**6**	**452**	**29**	**0**	**3.85**

a Shared shutouts with Jacques Plante, November 25, 1972 vs. California and December 29, 1972 vs. Pittsburgh.
b CHL Second All-Star Team (1974)
c Shared shutout with Roger Crozier, March 18, 1977 vs. Colorado.
d CHL First All-Star Team (1979)
e Won Tommy Ivan Trophy (CHL's Most Valuable Player) (1979)

Claimed by **Washington** from **Toronto** in Expansion Draft, June 12, 1974. Signed by **Detroit** as free agent, August 17, 1977. As compensation, **Washington** received Walt McKechnie and Detroit's third-round choice (John (Jay) Johnston) in the 1978 Amateur Draft and second-round choice (Errol Rausse) in the 1979 Entry Draft. **Detroit** also received Washington's third round choice (Boris Fistric) in the 1978 Entry Draft. Claimed by **Quebec** from **Detroit** in Expansion Draft, June 13, 1979. Traded to **Edmonton** by **Quebec** for Ron Chipperfield, March 11, 1980. Traded to **New Jersey** by **Edmonton** with Jim McTaggart for Lindsay Middlebrook and Paul Miller, February 19, 1983.

LUMBARD, TODD

Born, Brandon, Man., August 31, 1963.
Goaltender. Catches left. 6', 181 lbs.
Last amateur club: Regina Pats (WHL).
(New York Islanders' 5th choice, 84th over-all, in 1981 Entry Draft).

			Regular Season								Playoffs						
Season	Club	Lea	GP	W	L	T	Mins	GA	SO	Avg	GP	W	L	Mins	GA	SO	Avg
1980-81	Brandon	WHL	28	9	13	1	1408	106	1	4.52	5	1	4	262	27	0	6.18
1981-82	Brandon	WHL	54	22	27	1	2906	274	0	5.66	3	0	2	106	25	0	14.15
1982-83a	Regina	WHL	56	38	16	0	3194	194	2	3.64	5	1	4	298	21	0	4.23
1983-84	Toledo	IHL	11	7	4	0	664	38	0	3.43	....	....	....	....	....	....	....
	Peoria	IHL	1	0	1	0	60	7	0	7.00	....	....	....	....	....	....	....
	Indianapolis	CHL	25	12	11	1	1491	106	1	4.27	4	1	2	167	12	0	4.32
1984-85	Springfield	AHL	6	0	5	1	348	35	0	6.03	....	....	....	....	....	....	....
	Flint	IHL	2	0	2	0	120	14	0	7.00	....	....	....	....	....	....	....
	Indianapolis	IHL	16	3	11	1	932	73	0	4.70	2	1	0	61	2	0	1.97
1985-86	Erie	ACHL	....	....	....	....	....	....	....	....	....	....	....	....	....	....	....
	Milwaukee	IHL	6	2	3	0	305	23	0	4.52	....	....	....	....	....	....	....

a WHL Second All-Star Team (1983).

MacKENZIE, SHAWN KENNETH

Born, Bedford, N.S., August 22, 1962.
Goaltender. Catches left. 5'10", 175 lbs.
Last amateur club: Oshawa Generals (OHL).
(Colorado's 8th choice, 169th over-all, in 1980 Entry Draft).

			Regular Season								Playoffs						
Season	Club	Lea	GP	W	L	T	Mins	GA	SO	Avg	GP	W	L	Mins	GA	SO	Avg
1979-80	Windsor	OHA	41	17	14	1	1964	158	0	4.83	13	6	6	680	45	0	3.97
1980-81	Windsor	OHA	60	30	27	2	3540	282	1	4.78	11	3	4	622	47	0	4.53
1981-82	Windsor	OHL	17	6	11	0	1001	77	0	4.62	....	....	....	....	....	....	....
	Oshawa	OHL	32	20	12	0	1934	124	1	3.85	12	7	5	707	53	0	4.50
1982-83	**New Jersey**	**NHL**	**4**	**0**	**1**	**0**	**130**	**15**	**0**	**6.91**	....	....	....	....	....	....	....
	Wichita	CHL	36	10	23	2	2083	148	1	4.26	....	....	....	....	....	....	....
1983-84	Maine	AHL	34	14	13	5	1946	113	0	3.48	1	0	0	0	0	0	0.00
1984-85	Maine	AHL	24	8	8	3	1254	70	3	3.35	2	0	1	69	9	0	7.83
1985-86	Hershey	AHL	10	5	3	0	521	36	0	4.15	....	....	....	....	....	....	....
	Kalamazoo	IHL	6	4	2	0	362	27	0	4.40	....	....	....	....	....	....	....
	NHL Totals		**4**	**0**	**1**	**0**	**130**	**15**	**0**	**6.91**	....	....	....	....	....	....	....

Signed as a free agent by **Philadelphia**, January 15, 1986.

MALARCHUK, CLINT

Born, Grande, Alta., May 1, 1961.
Goaltender. Catches left. 5'10", 175 lbs.
Last amateur club: Portland Winter Hawks (WHL).
(Quebec's 3rd choice, 74th over-all, in 1981 Entry Draft).

			Regular Season								Playoffs						
Season	Club	Lea	GP	W	L	T	Mins	GA	SO	Avg	GP	W	L	Mins	GA	SO	Avg
1979-80	Portland	WHL	37	21	10	0	1948	147	0	4.53	1	0	0	40	3	0	4.50
1980-81	Portland	WHL	38	28	8	0	2235	142	3	3.81	4	....	....	307	21	0	4.10
1981-82	**Quebec**	**NHL**	**2**	**0**	**1**	**1**	**120**	**14**	**0**	**7.00**	....	....	....	....	....	....	....
	Fredericton	AHL	51	15	34	2	2906	247	0	5.10	....	....	....	....	....	....	....
1982-83	Fredericton	AHL	25	....	....	....	1506	78	0	3.11	....	....	....	....	....	....	....
	Quebec	**NHL**	**15**	**8**	**5**	**2**	**900**	**71**	**0**	**4.73**	....	....	....	....	....	....	....
1983-84	Fredericton	AHL	11	5	5	1	663	40	0	3.62	....	....	....	....	....	....	....
	Quebec	**NHL**	**23**	**10**	**9**	**2**	**1215**	**80**	**0**	**3.95**	**1**	**0**	**0**	**0**	**0**	**0**	**0.00**
1984-85	Fredericton	AHL	56	26	25	4	3347	198	2	3.55	6	2	4	379	20	0	3.17
1985-86	**Quebec**	**NHL**	**46**	**26**	**12**	**4**	**2657**	**142**	**4**	**3.21**	**3**	**0**	**2**	**143**	**11**	**0**	**4.62**
	NHL Totals		**86**	**44**	**27**	**9**	**4892**	**307**	**4**	**3.77**	**4**	**0**	**2**	**143**	**11**	**0**	**4.62**

MASON, BOB

Born, International Falls, MN, April 22, 1961.
Goaltender. Catches right. 6'1", 180 lbs.
Last amateur club: 1984 United States Olympic Team.

			Regular Season								Playoffs						
Season	**Club**	**Lea**	**GP**	**W**	**L**	**T**	**Mins**	**GA**	**SO**	**Avg**	**GP**	**W**	**L**	**Mins**	**GA**	**SO**	**Avg**
1981-82	Minn-Duluth	WCHA	26	....	....	....	1401	115	0	4.45	....	....	....	....	....	....	....
1982-83	Minn-Duluth	WCHA	43	....	....	....	2593	151	1	3.49	....	....	....	....	....	....	....
1983-84	U.S. National	...	33	....	....	....	1895	89	0	2.82	....	....	....	....	....	....	....
	U.S. Olympic	...	3	....	....	....	160	10	0	3.75	....	....	....	....	....	....	....
	Hershey	AHL	5	1	4	0	282	26	0	5.53	....	....	....	....	....	....	....
	Washington	**NHL**	**2**	**2**	**0**	**0**	**120**	**3**	**0**	**1.50**	....	....	....	....	....	....	....
1984-85	**Washington**	**NHL**	**12**	**8**	**2**	**1**	**661**	**31**	**1**	**2.81**	....	....	....	....	....	....	....
	Binghamton	AHL	20	10	6	1	1052	58	1	3.31	....	....	....	....	....	....	....
1985-86	**Washington**	**NHL**	**1**	**1**	**0**	**0**	**16**	**0**	**0**	**0.00**	....	....	....	....	....	....	....
	Binghamton	AHL	34	20	11	2	1940	126	0	3.90	3	1	1	124	9	0	4.35
	NHL Totals		**15**	**11**	**2**	**1**	**797**	**34**	**1**	**2.56**	....	....	....	....	....	....	....

Signed as a free agent by **Washington**, February 21, 1984.

MAY, DARRELL GERALD

Born, Edmonton, Alta., March 6, 1962.
Goaltender. Catches left. 6', 175 lbs.
Last amateur club: Portland Winter Hawks (WHL).
(Vancouver's 4th choice, 91st over-all, in 1980 Entry Draft).

			Regular Season								Playoffs						
Season	**Club**	**Lea**	**GP**	**W**	**L**	**T**	**Mins**	**GA**	**SO**	**Avg**	**GP**	**W**	**L**	**Mins**	**GA**	**SO**	**Avg**
1978-79	Portland	WHL	21	12	2	2	1113	64	0	3.45	2	1	0	80	7	0	5.25
1979-80	Portland	WHL	43	32	8	1	2416	143	1	3.55	8	3	5	439	27	0	3.69
1980-81	Portland	WHL	36	28	7	1	2128	122	3	3.44	4	....	....	243	21	0	5.19
1981-82	Portland	WHL	52	31	20	2	3097	226	0	4.38	15	....	....	851	59	0	4.16
1982-83	Fort Wayne	IHL	46	....	....	....	2584	177	0	4.11	2	....	....	120	13	0	6.50
1983-84	Erie	ACHL	43	21	16	2	2404	163	1	4.07	....	....	....	....	....	....	....
1984-85	Peoria	IHL	19	13	4	2	1133	56	1	2.97	10	6	4	609	33	0	3.25
1985-86	**St. Louis**	**NHL**	**3**	**1**	**2**	**0**	**184**	**13**	**0**	**4.23**	....	....	....	....	....	....	....
	Peoria	IHL	56	33	21	0	3321	179	1	3.23	11	6	5	634	38	1	3.60
	NHL Totals		**3**	**1**	**2**	**0**	**184**	**13**	**0**	**4.23**	....	....	....	....	....	....	....

McLEAN, KIRK

Born, Willowdale, Ont., June 26, 1966.
Goaltender. Catches right. 6', 175 lbs.
Last amateur club: Oshawa Generals (OHL).
(New Jersey's 6th choice, 107th over-all, in 1984 Entry Draft).

			Regular Season								Playoffs						
Season	**Club**	**Lea**	**GP**	**W**	**L**	**T**	**Mins**	**GA**	**SO**	**Avg**	**GP**	**W**	**L**	**Mins**	**GA**	**SO**	**Avg**
1983-84	Oshawa	OHL	17	5	9	0	940	67	0	4.28	....	....	....	....	....	....	....
1984-85	Oshawa	OHL	47	23	17	2	2581	143	1	3.32	5	1	3	271	21	0	4.65
1985-86	**New Jersey**	**NHL**	**2**	**1**	**1**	**0**	**111**	**11**	**0**	**5.95**	....	....	....	....	....	....	....
	Oshawa	OHL	51	24	21	2	2830	169	1	3.58	4	1	2	201	18	0	5.37
	NHL Totals		**2**	**1**	**1**	**0**	**111**	**11**	**0**	**5.95**	....	....	....	....	....	....	....

MELANSON, ROLAND JOSEPH (ROLLIE) (mel-AWN-son)

Born, Moncton, N.B., June 28, 1960.
Goaltender. Catches left. 5'10", 180 lbs.
Last amateur club: Oshawa Generals (OHA).
(NY Islanders' 4th choice, 59th over-all, in 1979 Entry Draft).

			Regular Season								Playoffs						
Season	**Club**	**Lea**	**GP**	**W**	**L**	**T**	**Mins**	**GA**	**SO**	**Avg**	**GP**	**W**	**L**	**Mins**	**GA**	**SO**	**Avg**
1978-79a	Windsor	OHA	58	....	....	....	3468	258	1	4.41	7	....	....	392	31	0	4.75
1979-80	Windsor	OHA	22	11	8	0	1099	90	0	4.91	....	....	....	....	....	....	....
	Oshawa	OHA	38	26	12	0	2240	136	3	3.64	7	3	4	420	32	0	4.57
1980-81bc	Indianapolis	CHL	52	31	16	3	3056	131	2	*2.57	....	....	....	....	....	....	....
	NY Islanders	**NHL**	**11**	**8**	**1**	**1**	**620**	**32**	**0**	**3.10**	**3**	**1**	**0**	**92**	**6**	**0**	**3.91**
1981-82	**NY Islanders**	**NHL**	**36**	**22**	**7**	**6**	**2115**	**114**	**0**	**3.23**	**3**	**0**	**1**	**64**	**5**	**0**	**4.67**
1982-83de	**NY Islanders**	**NHL**	**44**	**24**	**12**	**5**	**2460**	**109**	**1**	**2.66**	**5**	**2**	**2**	**238**	**10**	**0**	**2.52**
1983-84	**NY Islanders**	**NHL**	**37**	**20**	**11**	**2**	**2019**	**110**	**0**	**3.27**	**6**	**0**	**1**	**87**	**5**	**0**	**3.45**
1984-85	**NY Islanders**	**NHL**	**8**	**3**	**3**	**0**	**425**	**35**	**0**	**4.94**	....	....	....	....	....	....	....
	Minnesota	**NHL**	**20**	**5**	**10**	**3**	**1142**	**78**	**0**	**4.10**	....	....	....	....	....	....	....
1985-86	**Minnesota**	**NHL**	**6**	**2**	**1**	**2**	**325**	**24**	**0**	**4.43**	....	....	....	....	....	....	....
	Los Angeles	**NHL**	**22**	**4**	**16**	**1**	**1246**	**87**	**0**	**4.19**	....	....	....	....	....	....	....
	New Haven	AHL	3	1	2	0	179	13	0	4.36	....	....	....	....	....	....	....
	NHL Totals		**184**	**88**	**61**	**20**	**10352**	**589**	**1**	**3.41**	**17**	**3**	**4**	**481**	**26**	**0**	**3.24**

a OHA Second All-Star Team (1979)
b CHL First All-Star Team (1981)
c Won Ken McKenzie Trophy (CHL's Rookie of the Year) (1981)
d Shared William Jennings Trophy with Billy Smith (1983)
e NHL Second All-Star Team (1983)

Traded to **Minnesota** by **NY Islanders** for Minnesota's first round choice in 1985 Entry draft (Brad Dalgarno), November 19, 1984. Traded to **NY Rangers** by **Minnesota** for New York's second round draft choice in 1986 (Neil Wilkinson) and fourth round choice in 1987, December 9, 1985. Traded to **Los Angeles** by **NY Rangers** with Grant Ledyard for Brian MacLellan and Los Angeles' fourth round draft choice in 1987, December 9, 1985.

MELOCHE, GILLES (meh-LAWSH, JHIL)

Born, Montreal, Que., July 12, 1950.
Goaltender. Catches left. 5'9", 185 lbs.
Last amateur club: Verdun Maple Leafs (QJHL).
(Chicago's 5th choice, 70th over-all, in 1970 Amateur Draft).

			Regular Season								Playoffs						
Season	**Club**	**Lea**	**GP**	**W**	**L**	**T**	**Mins**	**GA**	**SO**	**Avg**	**GP**	**W**	**L**	**Mins**	**GA**	**SO**	**Avg**
1969-70	Verdun	QJHL	45	....	....	....	2679	221	1	4.95	11	....	....	660	34	0	3.09
1970-71	**Chicago**	**NHL**	**2**	**2**	**0**	**0**	**120**	**6**	**0**	**3.00**	....	....	....	....	....	....	....
	Flint	IHL	33	....	....	....	1866	104	2	3.34	3	....	....	183	1i	0	3.61
1971-72	**California**	**NHL**	**56**	**16**	**25**	**13**	**3121**	**173**	**4**	**3.33**	....	....	....	....	....	....	....
1972-73	**California**	**NHL**	**59**	**12**	**32**	**14**	**3473**	**235**	**1**	**4.06**	....	....	....	....	....	....	....
1973-74	**California**	**NHL**	**47**	**9**	**33**	**5**	**2800**	**198**	**1**	**4.24**	....	....	....	....	....	....	....
1974-75	**California**	**NHL**	**47**	**9**	**27**	**10**	**2771**	**186**	**1**	**4.03**	....	....	....	....	....	....	....
1975-76	**California**	**NHL**	**41**	**12**	**23**	**6**	**2440**	**140**	**1**	**3.44**	....	....	....	....	....	....	....
1976-77	**Cleveland**	**NHL**	**51**	**19**	**24**	**6**	**2961**	**171**	**2**	**3.47**	....	....	....	....	....	....	....
1977-78	**Cleveland**	**NHL**	**54**	**16**	**27**	**8**	**3100**	**195**	**1**	**3.77**	....	....	....	....	....	....	....
1978-79	**Minnesota**	**NHL**	**53**	**20**	**25**	**7**	**3118**	**173**	**2**	**3.33**	....	....	....	....	....	....	....
1979-80	**Minnesota**	**NHL**	**54**	**27**	**20**	**5**	**3141**	**160**	**1**	**3.06**	**11**	**5**	**4**	**564**	**34**	**1**	**3.62**
1980-81	**Minnesota**	**NHL**	**38**	**17**	**14**	**6**	**2215**	**120**	**2**	**3.25**	**13**	**8**	**5**	**802**	**47**	**0**	**3.52**
1981-82	**Minnesota**	**NHL**	**51**	**26**	**15**	**9**	**3026**	**175**	**1**	**3.47**	**4**	**1**	**2**	**184**	**8**	**0**	**2.61**
1982-83	**Minnesota**	**NHL**	**47**	**20**	**13**	**11**	**2689**	**160**	**1**	**3.57**	**5**	**2**	**3**	**319**	**18**	**0**	**3.38**
1983-84	**Minnesota**	**NHL**	**52**	**21**	**17**	**8**	**2883**	**201**	**2**	**4.18**	**4**	**1**	**2**	**200**	**11**	**0**	**3.30**
1984-85	**Minnesota**	**NHL**	**32**	**10**	**13**	**6**	**1817**	**115**	**0**	**3.80**	**8**	**4**	**3**	**395**	**25**	**1**	**3.80**
1985-86	**Pittsburgh**	**NHL**	**34**	**13**	**15**	**5**	**1989**	**119**	**0**	**3.59**	....	....	....	....	....	....	....
	NHL Totals		**718**	**249**	**323**	**119**	**41664**	**2527**	**20**	**3.64**	**45**	**21**	**19**	**2464**	**143**	**2**	**3.48**

Traded to **California** by **Chicago** with Paul Shmyr for goaltender Gerry Desjardins, October 18, 1971. Protected by **Minnesota** prior to Cleveland-Minnesota Dispersal Draft, June 15, 1978. Traded to **Edmonton** by **Minnesota** for Paul Houck, May 31, 1985. Traded to **Pittsburgh** by **Edmonton** for Tim Hrynewich and Marty McSorley, September 11, 1985.

MESZAROS, DAVE

Born, Toronto, Ont., February 16, 1964.
Goaltender. Catches left. 5'8", 180 lbs.
Last amateur club: Toronto Marlboros (OHL).
(Calgary's 4th choice, 65th over-all, in 1982 Entry Draft).

			Regular Season								Playoffs						
Season	**Club**	**Lea**	**GP**	**W**	**L**	**T**	**Mins**	**GA**	**SO**	**Avg**	**GP**	**W**	**L**	**Mins**	**GA**	**SO**	**Avg**
1981-82	Toronto	OHL	37	21	14	0	2085	139	0	4.00	9	3	3	480	38	0	4.75
1982-83	Toronto	OHL	40	17	21	2	2396	179	0	4.48	2	0	1	120	8	0	4.00
1983-84	Toronto	OHL	53	30	21	0	3106	232	1	4.48	9	4	5	517	51	0	5.92
1984-85	Moncton	AHL	14	4	6	2	715	46	0	3.86	....	....	....	....	....	....	....
	Salt Lake	IHL	25	10	11	3	1486	102	0	4.12	4	2	0	168	11	0	3.93
1985-86	Moncton	AHL	6	0	1	0	105	7	0	4.00	....	....	....	....	....	....	....

MICALEF, CORRADO (mick-AH-leff)

Born, Montreal, Que., April 20, 1961.
Goaltender. Catches right. 5'8", 170 lbs.
Last amateur club: Sherbrooke Beavers (QJHL).
(Detroit's 2nd choice, 44th over-all, in 1981 Entry Draft).

			Regular Season								Playoffs						
Season	**Club**	**Lea**	**GP**	**W**	**L**	**T**	**Mins**	**GA**	**SO**	**Avg**	**GP**	**W**	**L**	**Mins**	**GA**	**SO**	**Avg**
1979-80a	Sherbrooke	QJHL	64	37	17	7	3598	252	1	4.20	15	10	5	842	52	0	3.71
1980-81bc	Sherbrooke	QJHL	64	35	26	3	3764	280	2	4.46	14	7	7	842	46	*1	*3.28
1981-82	**Detroit**	**NHL**	**18**	**4**	**10**	**1**	**809**	**63**	**0**	**4.67**	....	....	....	....	....	....	....
	Adirondack	AHL	1	0	0	0	10	0	0	0.00	....	....	....	....	....	....	....
	Kalamazoo	IHL	20	....	....	....	1146	91	1	4.76	1	....	....	25	5	0	11.90
1982-83	**Detroit**	**NHL**	**34**	**11**	**13**	**5**	**1756**	**106**	**2**	**3.62**	....	....	....	....	....	....	....
	Adirondack	AHL	11	....	....	....	660	37	0	3.36	....	....	....	....	....	....	....
1983-84	**Detroit**	**NHL**	**14**	**5**	**8**	**1**	**808**	**52**	**0**	**3.86**	**1**	**0**	**0**	**7**	**2**	**0**	**16.67**
	Adirondack	AHL	29	14	10	5	1767	132	0	4.48	1	0	0	1	0	0	0.00
1984-85	**Detroit**	**NHL**	**36**	**5**	**19**	**7**	**1856**	**136**	**0**	**4.40**	**2**	**0**	**0**	**42**	**6**	**0**	**8.57**
	Adirondack	AHL	1	1	0	0	60	2	0	2.00	....	....	....	....	....	....	....
1985-86	**Detroit**	**NHL**	**11**	**1**	**9**	**1**	**565**	**52**	**0**	**5.52**	....	....	....	....	....	....	....
	Adirondack	AHL	25	12	9	2	1436	93	0	3.89	....	....	....	....	....	....	....
	NHL Totals		**113**	**26**	**59**	**15**	**5794**	**409**	**2**	**4.24**	....	....	....	....	....	....	....

a QMJHL Second All-Star Team (1980)
b QMJHL First All-Star Team (1981)
c Named to Memorial Cup Tournament All-Star Team (1981)

MIDDLEBROOK, LINDSAY

Born, Collingwood, Ont., September 7, 1955.
Goaltender. Catches right. 5'7", 160 lbs.
Last amateur club: St. Louis University Bilikens (CCHA).

			Regular Season								Playoffs						
Season	**Club**	**Lea**	**GP**	**W**	**L**	**T**	**Mins**	**GA**	**SO**	**Avg**	**GP**	**W**	**L**	**Mins**	**GA**	**SO**	**Avg**
1975-76	St. Louis U.	CCHA	30	....	....	....	1767	88	0	2.99	....	....	....	....	....	....	....
1976-77	St. Louis U.	CCHA	18	....	....	....	1058	54	1	3.07	....	....	....	....	....	....	....
1977-78	New Haven	AHL	17	....	....	....	968	71	0	4.40	....	....	....	....	....	....	....
	Toledo	IHL	16	....	....	....	949	45	*2	*2.85	13	....	....	739	32	0	2.60
1978-79ab	New Haven	AHL	54	29	19	5	3221	173	1	3.22	5	2	3	301	16	0	3.19
1979-80	**Winnipeg**	**NHL**	**10**	**2**	**8**	**0**	**580**	**40**	**0**	**4.14**	....	....	....	....	....	....	....
	Tulsa	CHL	37	16	15	3	2073	102	0	2.95	2	0	2	119	8	0	4.03
1980-81	**Winnipeg**	**NHL**	**14**	**0**	**9**	**3**	**653**	**65**	**0**	**5.97**	....	....	....	....	....	....	....
c	Tulsa	CHL	36	17	16	2	2115	120	2	3.63	8	4	4	479	33	0	4.13
1981-82	**Minnesota**	**NHL**	**3**	**0**	**2**	**0**	**140**	**7**	**0**	**3.00**	....	....	....	....	....	....	....
	Nashville	CHL	31	17	11	2	1868	93	*3	2.99	3	0	3	179	11	0	3.69
1982-83	**New Jersey**	**NHL**	**9**	**0**	**6**	**1**	**412**	**37**	**0**	**5.39**	....	....	....	....	....	....	....
	Wichita	CHL	13	....	....	....	779	46	0	3.54	....	....	....	....	....	....	....
	Moncton	AHL	11	....	....	....	669	42	0	3.77	....	....	....	....	....	....	....
	Edmonton	**NHL**	**1**	**1**	**0**	**0**	**60**	**3**	**0**	**3.00**	....	....	....	....	....	....	....
1983-84	Montana	CHL	36	10	22	3	2104	162	0	4.62	....	....	....	....	....	....	....
1984-85	Toledo	IHL	50	18	25	3	2791	183	0	3.93	6	2	4	339	24	0	4.25
1985-86	Milwaukee	IHL	56	33	10	0	3318	191	3	3.45	5	1	4	298	18	1	3.62
	NHL Totals		**37**	**3**	**25**	**4**	**1845**	**152**	**0**	**4.94**	....	....	....	....	....	....	....

a AHL First All-Star Team (1979)
b Won Harry "Hap" Holmes Memorial Trophy (AHL's Leading Goaltender) (1979)
c CHL Second All-Star Team (1981)

Signed as free agent by **NY Rangers**, October 12, 1977. Claimed by **Winnipeg** from **NY Rangers** in Expansion Draft, June 13, 1979. Sold to **Minnesota** by **Winnipeg**, July 31, 1981. Signed as free agent by **New Jersey**, September 25, 1982. Traded to **Edmonton** by **New Jersey** with Paul Miller for Ron Low and Jim McTaggart, February 19, 1983.

MILLEN, GREG H.

Born, Toronto, Ont., June 25, 1957.
Goaltender. Catches right. 5'9", 175 lbs.
Last amateur club: Sault Ste. Marie Greyhounds (OHA).
(Pittsburgh's 4th choice, 102nd over-all, in 1977 Amateur Draft).

			Regular Season								Playoffs						
Season	Club	Lea	GP	W	L	T	Mins	GA	SO	Avg	GP	W	L	Mins	GA	SO	Avg
1976-77	Peterborough	OHA	59	....	....	....	3457	244	0	4.23	4	....	....	240	23	0	5.75
1977-78	Kalamazoo	IHL	3	....	....	....	180	14	0	4.67	....	....	....	....	....	....	....
	Sault Ste. Marie	OHA	25	....	....	....	1449	105	1	4.29	13	....	....	774	61	0	4.73
1978-79	Pittsburgh	NHL	28	14	11	1	1532	86	2	3.37	....	....	....	....	....	....	....
1979-80	Pittsburgh	NHL	44	18	18	7	2586	157	2	3.64	5	2	3	300	21	0	4.20
1980-81	Pittsburgh	NHL	63	25	27	10	3721	258	0	4.16	5	2	3	325	19	0	3.51
1981-82	Hartford	NHL	55	11	30	12	3201	229	0	4.29	....	....	....	....	....	....	....
1982-83	Hartford	NHL	60	14	38	6	3520	282	1	4.81	....	....	....	....	....	....	....
1983-84	Hartford	NHL	60	21	30	9	3583	221	2	3.70	....	....	....	....	....	....	....
1984-85	Hartford	NHL	44	16	22	6	2659	187	1	4.22	....	....	....	....	....	....	....
	St. Louis	NHL	10	2	7	1	607	35	0	3.46	1	0	1	60	2	0	2.00
1985-86	St. Louis	NHL	36	14	16	6	2168	129	1	3.57	10	6	3	586	29	0	2.97
	NHL Totals		400	135	199	58	23577	1584	9	4.03	21	10	10	1271	71	0	3.35

Signed as free agent by **Hartford**, June 15, 1981. As compensation, **Pittsburgh** received Pat Boutette and the rights to Kevin McLelland, June 29, 1981. Traded to **St. Louis** by **Hartford** with Mark Johnson for Mike Liut and Jorgen Pettersson, February 21, 1985.

MIO, EDWARD (ED) (MEE-oh)

Born, Windsor, Ont., January 31, 1954.
Goaltender. Catches left. 5'10", 180 lbs.
Last amateur club: Colorado College Tigers (WCHA).
(Chicago's 7th choice, 124th over-all, in 1974 Amateur Draft).

			Regular Season								Playoffs						
Season	Club	Lea	GP	W	L	T	Mins	GA	SO	Avg	GP	W	L	Mins	GA	SO	Avg
1974-75	Colorado	WCHA	21	....	....	....	1260	83	0	3.95	....	....	....	....	....	....	....
1975-76	Colorado	WCHA	34	....	....	....	2038	144	0	4.24	....	....	....	....	....	....	....
1976-77	Tidewater	SHL	19	....	....	....	1123	66	1	3.53	....	....	....	....	....	....	....
	Erie	NAHL	17	....	....	....	771	42	0	3.27	2	....	....	80	8	0	6.00
1977-78	Hampton	AHL	19	....	....	....	949	53	2	3.35	....	....	....	....	....	....	....
	Indianapolis	WHA	17	6	8	0	900	64	0	4.27	....	....	....	....	....	....	....
1978-79	Dallas	CHL	7	....	....	....	424	25	0	3.54	....	....	....	....	....	....	....
	Indianapolis	WHA	5	....	....	....	242	13	1	3.22	....	....	....	....	....	....	....
	Edmonton	WHA	22	....	....	....	1068	71	1	3.99	3	....	....	90	6	0	4.00
1979-80	Edmonton	NHL	34	9	13	5	1711	120	1	4.21	....	....	....	....	....	....	....
1980-81	Edmonton	NHL	43	16	15	9	2393	155	0	3.89	....	....	....	....	....	....	....
1981-82	Wichita	CHL	11	3	8	0	657	46	0	4.20	....	....	....	....	....	....	....
	NY Rangers	NHL	25	13	6	5	1500	89	0	3.56	8	4	3	443	28	0	3.79
1982-83	NY Rangers	NHL	41	16	18	6	2365	136	2	3.45	8	5	3	480	32	0	4.00
1983-84	Adirondack	AHL	4	1	1	2	250	11	0	2.64	....	....	....	....	....	....	....
	Detroit	NHL	24	7	11	3	1295	95	1	4.40	1	0	1	63	3	0	2.86
1984-85	Detroit	NHL	7	1	3	2	376	27	0	4.31	....	....	....	....	....	....	....
	Adirondack	AHL	33	19	12	1	1871	871	2	3.75	....	....	....	....	....	....	....
1985-86	Detroit	NHL	18	2	7	0	788	83	0	6.32	....	....	....	....	....	....	....
	Adirondack	AHL	8	4	1	3	487	32	0	3.94	....	....	....	....	....	....	....
	NHL Totals		192	83	85	31	12299	822	6	4.01	17	9	7	986	63	0	3.83
	WHA Totals		44	....	....	....	2210	148	2	4.02	3	....	....	90	6	0	4.00

Rights traded to **Minnesota** by **Chicago** with a player to be named later (Pierre Plante) for Doug Hicks and Minnesota's third round choice (Marcel Frere) in the 1980 Entry Draft, March 14, 1978. Reclaimed by **Minnesota** from **Edmonton** prior to Expansion Draft, June 9, 1979. Claimed as priority selection by **Edmonton**, June 9, 1979. Traded to **NY Rangers** by **Edmonton** for Lance Nethery, December 11, 1981. Traded to **Detroit** by **NY Rangers** with Ron Duguay and Eddie Johnstone for Willie Huber, Mike Blaisdell and Mark Osborne, June 15, 1983.

MOOG, DONALD ANDREW (ANDY) (MOGUE)

Born, Penticton, B.C., February 18, 1960.
Goaltender. Catches left. 5'8", 165 lbs.
Last amateur club: Billings Bighorns (WHL).
(Edmonton's 6th choice, 132nd over-all, in 1980 Entry Draft).

			Regular Season								Playoffs						
Season	Club	Lea	GP	W	L	T	Mins	GA	SO	Avg	GP	W	L	Mins	GA	SO	Avg
1978-79	Billings	WHL	26	13	5	4	1306	90	4	4.13	5	1	3	229	21	0	5.50
1979-80a	Billings	WHL	46	23	14	1	2435	149	1	3.67	3	2	1	190	10	0	3.16
1980-81	Edmonton	NHL	7	3	3	0	313	20	0	3.83	9	5	4	526	32	0	3.65
	Wichita	CHL	29	14	13	1	1602	89	0	3.33	5	3	2	300	16	0	3.20
1981-82	Edmonton	NHL	8	3	5	0	399	32	0	4.81	....	....	....	....	....	....	....
b	Wichita	CHL	40	23	13	3	2391	119	1	2.99	7	3	4	434	23	0	3.18
1982-83	Edmonton	NHL	50	8	7	1	2833	167	1	3.54	16	11	5	949	48	0	3.03
1983-84	Edmonton	NHL	38	27	8	1	2212	139	1	3.77	7	4	0	263	12	0	2.74
1984-85c	Edmonton	NHL	39	22	9	3	2019	111	1	3.30	2	0	0	20	0	0	0.00
1985-86	Edmonton	NHL	47	27	9	7	2664	164	1	3.69	1	1	0	60	1	0	1.00
	NHL Totals		189	90	41	12	10440	633	4	3.64	35	21	9	1818	93	0	3.07

a WHL Second All-Star Team (1980)
b CHL Second All-Star Team (1982)
c Shared shutout with Grant Fuhr, January 8, 1985 vs. Quebec.

PAGEAU, PAUL (pa-JHOH)

Born, Montreal, Que., October 1, 1959.
Goaltender. Catches right. 5'9", 160 lbs.
Last amateur club: Shawinigan Cataractes (QJHL).

			Regular Season								Playoffs						
Season	Club	Lea	GP	W	L	T	Mins	GA	SO	Avg	GP	W	L	Mins	GA	SO	Avg
1978-79	Quebec	QJHL	7	....	....	....	345	28	0	4.87	....	....	....	....	....	....	....
	Shawinigan	QMJHL	43	....	....	....	2352	199	0	5.05	4	....	....	236	27	0	6.86
1979-80	Cdn. National	...	10	....	....	....	506	16	1	1.89	....	....	....	....	....	....	....
	Cdn. Olympic	...	4	....	....	....	237	11	0	2.79	....	....	....	....	....	....	....
a	Shawinigan	QMJHL	43	19	18	4	2438	175	2	4.31	7	3	4	421	34	0	4.85
1980-81	Los Angeles	NHL	1	0	1	0	60	8	0	8.00	....	....	....	....	....	....	....
	Houston	CHL	21	9	9	3	1282	64	0	3.00	....	....	....	....	....	....	....
	Oklahoma City	CHL	11	4	4	0	590	32	0	3.25	....	....	....	....	....	....	....
	Saginaw	IHL	1	....	....	....	60	4	0	4.00	....	....	....	....	....	....	....
1981-82	Saginaw	IHL	29	....	....	....	1621	140	0	5.18	4	....	....	249	18	0	4.34
1982-83	New Haven	AHL	37	....	....	....	1939	123	2	3.81	6	....	....	374	21	0	3.37
1983-84	Sherbrooke	AHL	45	12	26	3	2432	205	0	5.06	....	....	....	....	....	....	....
1984-85	Sherbrooke	AHL	20	8	11	0	1074	66	0	3.69	3	0	1	80	5	0	3.75
	Flint	IHL	6	0	5	0	3331	37	0	6.71	....	....	....	....	....	....	....
1985-86	Sherbrooke	AHL	31	9	14	6	1767	132	0	4.48	....	....	....	....	....	....	....
	NHL Totals		1	0	1	0	60	8	0	8.00	....	....	....	....	....	....	....

a QMJHL First All-Star Team (1980)

Signed as a free agent by **Los Angeles**, May 6, 1980.

PANG, DARREN

Born, Medford, Ontario Feb. 17, 1964
Goaltender. Catches left. 5'5" 155 lbs.
Last Amateur Club; Ottawa 67's (OHL)

			Regular Season								Playoffs						
Season	Club	Lea	GP	W	L	T	Mins	GA	SO	Avg	GP	W	L	Mins	GA	SO	Avg
1982-83	Belleville	OHL	12	....	....	....	570	44	0	4.63	....	....	....	....	....	....	....
	Ottawa	OHL	47	....	....	....	2729	166	1	3.65	9	5	4	510	33	0	3.88
1983-84	Ottawa	OHL	43	....	....	....	2318	117	2	3.03	....	....	....	....	....	....	....
1984-85	Milwaukee	IHL	53	19	29	3	3129	226	0	4.33	....	....	....	....	....	....	....
	Chicago	NHL	1	0	0	0	60	4	0	4.00	....	....	....	....	....	....	....
1985-86	Saginaw	IHL	44	21	21	0	2638	148	2	3.37	8	3	5	492	32	0	3.90
	NHL Totals		1	0	0	0	60	32	0	3.90	....	....	....	....	....	....	....

Signed as a free agent by **Chicago**, August 15, 1984.

PARRO, DAVID (DAVE) (PAIR-oh)

Born, Saskatoon, Sask., April 30, 1957.
Goaltender. Catches left. 5'11", 165 lbs.
Last amateur club: Saskatoon Blades (WHL).
(Boston's 2nd choice, 34th over-all, in 1977 Amateur Draft).

			Regular Season								Playoffs						
Season	Club	Lea	GP	W	L	T	Mins	GA	SO	Avg	GP	W	L	Mins	GA	SO	Avg
1974-75	Saskatoon	WHL	1	....	....	....	60	2	0	2.00	....	....	....	....	....	....	....
1975-76	Saskatoon	WHL	36	....	....	....	2100	119	1	3.40	9	....	....	414	31	0	4.49
1976-77a	Saskatoon	WHL	69	....	....	....	3956	246	1	3.73	6	....	....	360	23	0	3.83
1977-78	Rochester	AHL	46	....	....	....	2694	164	0	3.65	3	....	....	180	9	0	3.00
1978-79	Grand Rapids	IHL	7	....	....	....	419	25	0	3.58	....	....	....	....	....	....	....
	Rochester	AHL	36	....	....	....	2065	130	*2	3.78	....	....	....	....	....	....	....
1979-80	Hershey	AHL	48	....	....	....	3159	172	0	3.27	8	....	....	479	34	0	4.26
1980-81	Washington	NHL	18	4	7	2	811	49	1	3.63	....	....	....	....	....	....	....
	Hershey	AHL	14	7	6	1	834	60	0	4.32	....	....	....	....	....	....	....
1981-82	Washington	NHL	52	16	26	7	2942	206	1	4.20	....	....	....	....	....	....	....
1982-83	Washington	NHL	6	1	3	1	261	19	0	4.37	....	....	....	....	....	....	....
b	Hershey	AHL	47	....	....	....	2714	175	1	3.87	4	....	....	240	15	0	3.75
1983-84	Washington	NHL	1	0	0	0	1	0	0	0.00	....	....	....	....	....	....	....
	Hershey	AHL	42	12	21	5	2277	190	1	5.01	....	....	....	....	....	....	....
1984-85	Salt Lake	IHL	28	11	14	3	1672	102	0	3.66	....	....	....	....	....	....	....
1985-86	Flint	IHL	46	10	34	0	2527	235	0	5.30	....	....	....	....	....	....	....
	Ft. Worth	IHL	5	1	3	1	305	18	0	3.54	....	....	....	....	....	....	....
	NHL Totals		77	21	36	10	4015	274	2	4.09	....	....	....	....	....	....	....

a WHL Second All-Star Team (1977)
b AHL Second All-Star Team (1983)

Claimed by **Quebec** from **Boston** in Expansion Draft, June 13, 1979. Traded to **Washington** by **Quebec** for Nelson Burton, June 15, 1979.

PEETERS, PETER (PETE)

Born, Edmonton, Alta., August 1, 1957.
Goaltender. Catches left. 6', 170 lbs.
Last amateur club: Medicine Hat Tigers (WHL).
(Philadelphia's 9th choice, 135th over-all, in 1977 Amateur Draft).

			Regular Season								Playoffs						
Season	Club	Lea	GP	W	L	T	Mins	GA	SO	Avg	GP	W	L	Mins	GA	SO	Avg
1975-76	Medicine Hat	WHL	37	....	....	....	2074	147	0	4.25	....	....	....	....	....	....	....
1976-77	Medicine Hat	WHL	62	....	....	....	3423	232	1	4.07	4	....	....	204	17	0	5.00
1977-78	Milwaukee	IHL	32	....	....	....	1698	93	1	3.29	....	....	....	....	....	....	....
	Maine	AHL	17	....	....	....	855	40	1	2.80	11	....	....	562	25	*1	2.67
1978-79	Philadelphia	NHL	5	1	2	1	280	16	0	3.43	....	....	....	....	....	....	....
ab	Maine	AHL	35	25	6	3	2067	100	*2	*2.90	6	5	0	329	15	0	2.74
1979-80	Philadelphia	NHL	40	29	5	5	2373	108	1	2.73	13	8	5	799	37	1	2.78
1980-81	Philadelphia	NHL	40	22	12	5	2333	115	2	2.96	3	2	1	180	12	0	4.00
1981-82	Philadelphia	NHL	44	23	18	3	2591	160	0	3.71	4	1	2	220	17	0	4.63
1982-83cd	Boston	NHL	62	40	11	9	*3611	142	*8	*2.36	17	9	8	1024	61	1	3.57
1983-84	Boston	NHL	50	29	16	2	2868	151	0	3.16	3	0	3	180	10	0	3.33
1984-85	Boston	NHL	51	19	26	4	2975	172	1	347	1	0	1	60	4	0	4.00
1985-86	Boston	NHL	8	3	4	1	485	31	0	3.84	....	....	....	....	....	....	....
	Washington	NHL	34	19	11	3	2021	113	1	3.35	9	5	4	544	24	0	2.65
	NHL Totals		334	185	105	33	19537	1008	13	3.10	50	25	24	3007	165	2	3.29

a AHL Second All-Star Team (1979)
b Shared Harry "Hap" Holmes Memorial Trophy (AHL's Leading Goaltenders) with Robbie Moore (1979)
c NHL First All-Star Team (1983)
d Won Vezina Trophy (1983)

Traded to **Boston** by **Philadelphia** for Brad McCrimmon, June 9, 1982. Traded to **Washington** by **Boston** for Pat Riggin, November 14, 1985.

PENNEY, STEVE

Born, Ste-Foy, Que., February 2, 1961.
Goaltender. Catches left. 6'1", 190 lbs.
Last amateur club: Shawinigan Cataractes (QMJHL).
(Montreal's 10th choice, 165th over-all, in 1980 Entry Draft).

			Regular Season								Playoffs						
Season	Club	Lea	GP	W	L	T	Mins	GA	SO	Avg	GP	W	L	Mins	GA	SO	Avg
1978-79	Shawinigan	QJHL	36	....	....	....	1631	180	0	6.62	1	....	....	4	0	0	0.00
1979-80	Shawinigan	QJHL	31	9	14	5	1682	143	0	5.10	....	....	....	....	....	....	....
1980-81	Shawinigan	QJHL	62	30	25	4	3456	244	0	4.24	5	1	4	279	21	0	4.52
1981-82	Nova Scotia	AHL	6	....	....	....	308	22	0	4.29	....	....	....	....	....	....	....
	Flint	IHL	36	....	....	....	2040	147	1	4.32	4	....	....	222	17	0	4.59
1982-83	Flint	IHL	48	....	....	....	2552	179	0	4.21	3	....	....	111	10	0	5.40
1983-84	Nova Scotia	AHL	27	11	12	4	1571	92	0	3.51	....	....	....	....	....	....	....
	Montreal	NHL	4	0	4	0	240	19	0	4.75	15	9	6	871	32	*3	*2.20
1984-85a	Montreal	NHL	54	26	18	8	3252	167	1	3.08	12	6	6	733	40	1	3.27
1985-86	Montreal	NHL	18	6	8	2	990	72	0	4.36	....	....	....	....	....	....	....
	NHL Totals		76	32	30	10	4482	258	1	3.45	27	15	12	1604	72	4	2.69

a Named to NHL All-Rookie Team (1985)

Traded to **Winnipeg** by **Montreal** with the rights to Jan Ingman for Brian Hayward, August 19, 1986.

PERRY, ALAN

Born, Providence, R.I., August 30, 1966.
Goaltender. Catches right. 5'8", 155 lbs.
Last amateur club: Windsor Spitfires (OHL).
(St. Louis' 5th choice, 56th over-all, in 1984 Entry Draft).

			Regular Season								Playoffs						
Season	Club	Lea	GP	W	L	T	Mins	GA	SO	Avg	GP	W	L	Mins	GA	SO	Avg
1984-85	Windsor	OHL	34	15	17	0	1905	135	1	4.25	2	0	2	120	14	0	7.00
1985-86	Windsor	OHL	42	28	10	2	2424	131	3	3.24	13	8	5	697	51	0	4.39

PIETRANGELO, FRANK (Peter-AN-gelo)

Born, Port Robinson, Ont., December 17, 1964.
Goaltender. Catches left. 5'11", 190 lbs.
Last amateur club: University of Minnesota Gophers, (WCHA).
(Pittsburgh's 4th choice, 64th over-all, in 1983 Entry Draft).

			Regular Season								Playoffs						
Season	Club	Lea	GP	W	L	T	Mins	GA	SO	Avg	GP	W	L	Mins	GA	SO	Avg
1982-83	U. of Minnesota	WCHA	25	15	6	1	1348	80	1	3.55	....	....	....	....	....	....	....
1983-84	U. of Minnesota	WCHA	20	13	7	0	1141	66	0	3.47	....	....	....	....	....	....	....
1984-85	U. of Minnesota	WCHA	17	8	3	3	912	52	0	3.42	....	....	....	....	....	....	....
1985-86	U. of Minnesota	WCHA	23	15	7	0	1284	76	0	3.55	....	....	....	....	....	....	....

PROULX, MARIO

Born, Drummondville, Que., November 29, 1961.
Goaltender. Catches left. 5'11", 180 lbs.
Last amateur club: Providence College Friars (ECAC).
(New York Rangers' 10th choice, 198th over-all, in 1981 Entry Draft).

			Regular Season								Playoffs						
Season	Club	Lea	GP	W	L	T	Mins	GA	SO	Avg	GP	W	L	Mins	GA	SO	Avg
1980-81	Providence	ECAC	18	8	6	0	884	56	0	3.80	....	....	....	....	....	....	....
1981-82	Providence	ECAC	21	13	8	0	1206	72	3	3.58	....	....	....	....	....	....	....
1982-83	Providence	ECAC	35	26	9	0	2060	122	1	3.55	....	....	....	....	....	....	....
1983-84	Providence	ECAC	28	17	9	2	1672	101	1	3.62	....	....	....	....	....	....	....
1984-85	New Haven	AHL	5	0	3	0	234	19	0	4.87	....	....	....	....	....	....	....
	Salt Lake	IHL	3	1	2	0	180	18	0	6.00	....	....	....	....	....	....	....
	Toledo	IHL	9	2	7	0	518	45	0	5.21	1	0	0	20	1	0	3.00
1985-86	Toledo	IHL	22	4	13	0	1140	93	1	4.90	....	....	....	....	....	....	....

PUPPA, DARREN

Born, Kirkland Lake, Ont., March 23, 1963.
Goaltender. Catches right. 6'3", 195 lbs.
Last amateur club: Rensselaer Polytechnic Institute Engineers (ECAC).
(Buffalo's 7th choice, 76th over-all, in 1983 Entry Draft).

			Regular Season								Playoffs						
Season	Club	Lea	GP	W	L	T	Mins	GA	SO	Avg	GP	W	L	Mins	GA	SO	Avg
1983-84	RPI	ECAC	32	24	6	0	....	....	....	2.94	....	....	....	....	....	....	....
1984-85	RPI	ECAC	32	31	1	0	1830	78	0	2.56	....	....	....	....	....	....	....
1985-86	**Buffalo**	**NHL**	**7**	**3**	**4**	**0**	**401**	**21**	**1**	**3.14**	....	....	....	....	....	....	....
	Rochester	AHL	20	8	11	0	1092	79	0	4.34	....	....	....	....	....	....	....
	NHL Totals		**7**	**3**	**4**	**0**	**401**	**21**	**1**	**3.14**	....	....	....	....	....	....	....

PUSEY, CHRIS

Born, Brantford, Ont., June 30, 1965.
Goaltender. Catches left. 6', 180 lbs.
Last amateur club: Brantford Alexanders (OHL).
(Detroit's 7th choice, 160th over-all, in 1983 Entry Draft).

			Regular Season								Playoffs						
Season	Club	Lea	GP	W	L	T	Mins	GA	SO	Avg	GP	W	L	Mins	GA	SO	Avg
1982-83	Brantford	OHL	20	5	11	0	991	85	0	5.15	....	....	....	....	....	....	....
1983-84a	Brantford	OHL	50	26	18	2	2858	158	2	3.32	5	0	1	300	17	0	3.40
1984-85	Hamilton	OHL	49	17	19	2	2450	179	1	4.38	15	7	6	824	73	0	5.32
1985-86	**Detroit**	**NHL**	**1**	**0**	**0**	**0**	**40**	**3**	**0**	**4.50**	....	....	....	....	....	....	....
	Adirondack	AHL	22	7	12	1	1171	76	1	3.89	1	0	0	27	4	0	8.89
	NHL Totals		**1**	**0**	**0**	**0**	**40**	**3**	**0**	**4.50**	....	....	....	....	....	....	....

a OHL Second All-Star Team (1984).

RACINE, BRUCE

Born, Cornwall, Ont., August 9, 1966.
Goaltender. Catches left. 6'0", 160 lbs.
Last amateur club: Northeastern University Huskies (H.E.).
(Pittsburgh's 3rd choice, 58th over-all, in 1985 Entry Draft).

			Regular Season								Playoffs						
Season	Club	Lea	GP	W	L	T	Mins	GA	SO	Avg	GP	W	L	Mins	GA	SO	Avg
1984-85	Northeastern	H.E.	26	11	14	1	1615	103	1	3.83	....	....	....	....	....	....	....
1985-86	Northeastern	H.E.	32	17	14	1	1920	147	0	4.56	....	....	....	....	....	....	....

RALPH, JAMES RICHARD (JIM)

Born, Sault Ste. Marie, Ont., May 13 1962.
Goaltender. Catches right. 5'11", 165 lbs.
Last amateur club: Ottawa 67's (OHL).
(Chicago's 12th choice, 162nd over-all, in 1980 Entry Draft).

			Regular Season								Playoffs						
Season	Club	Lea	GP	W	L	T	Mins	GA	SO	Avg	GP	W	L	Mins	GA	SO	Avg
1979-80	Ottawa	OHA	45	26	12	2	2451	171	0	4.19	4	1	1	210	17	0	4.86
1980-81a	Ottawa	OHA	57	38	14	2	3266	202	*2	3.71	7	2	4	367	23	0	3.77
1981-82b	Ottawa	OHL	53	35	16	2	3211	185	1	3.45	17	8	8	999	67	0	4.02
1982-83	Springfield	AHL	26	....	....	....	1498	105	0	4.21	....	....	....	....	....	....	....
	Colorado	CHL	5	3	2	0	300	18	0	3.60	....	....	....	....	....	....	....
1983-84	Springfield	AHL	9	5	3	0	479	42	0	5.26	....	....	....	....	....	....	....
	Baltimore	AHL	25	12	10	2	1455	87	0	3.59	2	....	....	82	6	0	4.38
1984-85	Milwaukee	IHL	19	3	13	2	1072	78	0	4.37	....	....	....	....	....	....	....
1985-86	Nova Scotia	AHL	9	2	5	2	549	46	0	5.03	....	....	....	....	....	....	....
	Milwaukee	IHL	14	7	6	0	819	58	1	4.25	....	....	....	....	....	....	....

a OHA First All-Star Team (1981)
b OHL Second All-Star Team (1982)

RANFORD, BILL

Born, Brandon, Man., December 14, 1966.
Goaltender. Catches left. 5'10", 170 lbs.
Last amateur club: New Westminster Bruins (WHL).
(Boston's 2nd choice, 52nd overall, in 1985 Entry Draft).

			Regular Season								Playoffs						
Season	Club	Lea	GP	W	L	T	Mins	GA	SO	Avg	GP	W	L	Mins	GA	SO	Avg
1983-84	N. Westminster	WHL	27	10	14	0	1450	130	0	5.38	1	0	0	27	2	0	4.44
1984-85	N. Westminster	WHL	38	19	17	0	2034	142	0	4.19	7	2	3	309	26	0	5.05
1985-86	**N. Westminster**	**WHL**	**53**	**17**	**29**	**1**	**2791**	**225**	**0**	**4.84**	....	....	....	....	....	....	....
	Boston	**NHL**	**4**	**3**	**1**	**0**	**240**	**10**	**0**	**2.50**	**2**	**0**	**2**	**120**	**7**	**0**	**3.50**
	NHL Totals		**4**	**3**	**1**	**0**	**240**	**10**	**0**	**2.50**	**2**	**0**	**2**	**120**	**7**	**0**	**3.50**

RAYMOND, ALAIN

Born, Rimouski, Que., June 24, 1965.
Goaltender. Catches left. 5'10", 177 lbs.
Last amateur club: Canadian Olympic Team.
(Washington's 11th choice, 224th over-all, in 1983 Entry Draft).

			Regular Season								Playoffs						
Season	Club	Lea	GP	W	L	T	Mins	GA	SO	Avg	GP	W	L	Mins	GA	SO	Avg
1983-84	Trois Rivières	QMJHL	53	18	25	0	2725	223	3	4.91	....	....	....	....	....	....	....
1984-85a	Trois Rivères	QMJHL	58	29	26	1	3295	220	2	4.01	7	3	5	438	32	0	4.38
1985-86	Cdn. Olympic	....	46	25	18	3	2571	151	4	3.52	....	....	....	....	....	....	....

a QMJHL Second All-Star Team (1985).

REAUGH, DARYL (RAY)

Born, Prince George, B.C., February 13, 1965.
Goaltender. Catches left. 6'4", 190 lbs.
Last amateur club: Kamloops Junior Oilers (WHL).
(Edmonton's 2nd choice, 42nd over-all, in 1984 Entry Draft).

			Regular Season								Playoffs						
Season	Club	Lea	GP	W	L	T	Mins	GA	SO	Avg	GP	W	L	Mins	GA	SO	Avg
1982-83	Cowichan	BCJHL	32	....	....	....	1673	191	0	5.96	....	....	....	....	....	....	....
1983-84	Kamloops	WHL	55	....	....	....	2748	199	1	4.34	17	....	....	972	57	0	3.52
1984-85	**Edmonton**	**NHL**	**1**	**0**	**1**	**0**	**60**	**5**	**0**	**5.00**	....	....	....	....	....	....	....
a	Kamloops	WAL	49	....	....	....	2749	170	2	3.71	14	....	....	787	56	0	4.27
1985-86	Nova Scotia	AHL	38	15	18	4	2205	156	0	4.24	....	....	....	....	....	....	....
	NHL Totals		**1**	**0**	**1**	**0**	**60**	**5**	**0**	**5.00**	....	....	....	....	....	....	....

a WHL First All-Star Team, West Division (1985).

REDDICK, ELDON

Born, Halifax, N.S., October 6, 1964.
Goaltender. Catches left. 5'8", 170 lbs.
Last amateur club: Brandon Wheat Kings (WHL).

			Regular Season								Playoffs						
Season	Club	Lea	GP	W	L	T	Mins	GA	SO	Avg	GP	W	L	Mins	GA	SO	Avg
1982-83	Nanaimo	WHL	66	19	38	1	3549	383	0	6.46	....	....	....	....	....	....	....
1983-84	N. Westminster	WHL	50	24	22	2	2930	215	0	4.40	9	4	5	542	53	0	5.87
1984-85	Brandon	WHL	47	14	30	1	2585	243	0	5.64	....	....	....	....	....	....	....
1985-86	Fort Wayne	IHL	29	15	11	0	1674	86	3	3.00	....	....	....	....	....	....	....

Signed as a free agent by **Winnipeg**, September 27, 1985.

REESE, JEFF

Born, Brantford, Ont., March 24, 1966.
Goaltender. Catches right. 5'9", 150 lbs.
Last amateur club: London Knights (OHL).
(Toronto's 3rd choice, 67th over-all, in 1984 Entry Draft).

			Regular Season								Playoffs						
Season	Club	Lea	GP	W	L	T	Mins	GA	SO	Avg	GP	W	L	Mins	GA	SO	Avg
1983-84	London	OHL	43	18	19	0	2308	173		4.50	6	3	3	327	27	0	4.95
1984-85	London	OHL	50	31	15	1	2878	186	1	3.88	8	5	2	440	20	1	2.73
1985-86	London	OHL	57	25	26	3	3281	215	0	3.93	5	0	4	299	25	0	5.02

REID, JOHN

Born, Windsor, Ont., February 18, 1967.
Goaltender. Catches right. 5'11", 202 lbs.
Last amateur club: North Bay Centennials (OHL).
(Chicago's 8th choice, 158th over-all, in 1985 Entry Draft).

			Regular Season								Playoffs						
Season	Club	Lea	GP	W	L	T	Mins	GA	SO	Avg	GP	W	L	Mins	GA	SO	Avg
1984-85	Belleville	OHL	31	16	6	0	1443	92	0	3.83	2	1	0	79	4	0	3.04
1985-86	North Bay	OHL	47	28	14	2	2627	164	1	3.75	10	5	4	577	37	0	3.85

RESCH, GLENN ALLAN (CHICO) (RESH)

Born, Moose Jaw, Sask., July 10, 1948.
Goaltender. Catches left. 5′9″, 165 lbs.
Last amateur club: Muskegon Mohawks (IHL)

			Regular Season								Playoffs						
Season	Club	Lea	GP	W	L	T	Mins	GA	SO	Avg	GP	W	L	Mins	GA	SO	Avg
1969-70	Minn-Duluth	WCHA	25	....	....	....	1492	97	1	3.90	....	....	....	....	....	....	....
1970-71	Minn-Duluth	WCHA	27	....	....	....	1619	114	0	4.23	....	....	....	....	....	....	....
1971-72a	Muskegon	IHL	59	....	....	....	3488	180	*4	*3.09	11	....	....	617	29	0	2.82
1972-73	New Haven	AHL	43	....	....	....	2408	166	0	4.13	....	....	....	....	....	....	....
1973-74	**NY Islanders**	**NHL**	**2**	**1**	**1**	**0**	**120**	**6**	**0**	**3.00**	....	....	....	....	....	....	....
bc	Fort Worth	CHL	55	....	....	....	3300	175	2	3.18	5	....	....	300	21	0	3.60
1974-75	**NY Islanders**	**NHL**	**25**	**12**	**7**	**5**	**1432**	**59**	**3**	**2.47**	**12**	**8**	**4**	**692**	**25**	**1**	**2.17**
1975-76d	**NY Islanders**	**NHL**	**44**	**23**	**11**	**8**	**2546**	**88**	**7**	**2.07**	**7**	**3**	**3**	**357**	**18**	**0**	**3.03**
1976-77	**NY Islanders**	**NHL**	**46**	**26**	**13**	**6**	**2711**	**103**	**4**	**2.28**	**3**	**1**	**1**	**144**	**5**	**0**	**2.08**
1977-78	**NY Islanders**	**NHL**	**45**	**28**	**9**	**7**	**2637**	**112**	**3**	**2.55**	**7**	**3**	**4**	**388**	**15**	**0**	**2.32**
1978-79d	**NY Islanders**	**NHL**	**43**	**26**	**7**	**10**	**2539**	**106**	**2**	**2.50**	**5**	**2**	**3**	**300**	**11**	***1**	**2.20**
1979-80	**NY Islanders**	**NHL**	**45**	**23**	**14**	**6**	**2606**	**132**	**3**	**3.04**	**4**	**0**	**2**	**120**	**9**	**0**	**4.50**
1980-81	**NY Islanders**	**NHL**	**32**	**18**	**7**	**5**	**1817**	**93**	***3**	**3.07**	....	....	....	....	....	....	....
	Colorado	**NHL**	**8**	**2**	**4**	**2**	**449**	**28**	**0**	**3.74**	....	....	....	....	....	....	....
1981-82e	**Colorado**	**NHL**	**61**	**16**	**31**	**11**	**3424**	**230**	**0**	**4.03**	....	....	....	....	....	....	....
1982-83	**New Jersey**	**NHL**	**65**	**15**	**35**	**12**	**3650**	**242**	**0**	**3.98**	....	....	....	....	....	....	....
1983-84	**New Jersey**	**NHL**	**51**	**9**	**31**	**3**	**2641**	**184**	**1**	**4.18**	....	....	....	....	....	....	....
1984-85	**New Jersey**	**NHL**	**51**	**15**	**27**	**5**	**2884**	**200**	**0**	**4.16**	....	....	....	....	....	....	....
1985-86	**New Jersey**	**NHL**	**31**	**10**	**20**	**0**	**1769**	**126**	**0**	**4.27**	....	....	....	....	....	....	....
	Philadelphia	**NHL**	**5**	**1**	**2**	**0**	**187**	**10**	**0**	**3.21**	**1**	**0**	**0**	**7**	**1**	**0**	**8.57**
	NHL Totals		**554**	**225**	**219**	**80**	**31412**	**1719**	**26**	**3.28**	**39**	**17**	**17**	**2008**	**84**	**2**	**2.51**

a IHL First All-Star Team (1972)
b CHL First All-Star Team (1974)
c Won Tommy Ivan Trophy (CHL's Playoff MVP) (1974)
d NHL Second All-Star Team (1976, 1979)
e Won Bill Masterton Memorial Trophy (1982)

Sold to **NY Islanders** by **Montreal** with Denis DeJordy, Germain Gagnon, Tony Featherstone, Murray Anderson and Alex Campbell, June 26, 1972. Traded to **Colorado** by **NY Islanders** with Steve Tambellini for Mike McEwen and Jari Kaarela, March 10, 1981. Traded to **Philadelphia** by **New Jersey** for Philadelphia's third-round draft choice in 1986 (Marc Laniel), March 11, 1986.

RIENDEAU, VINCENT

Born, St. Hyacinthe, Que., April 20, 1966.
Goaltender. Catches left. 5′10″, 185 lbs.
Last amateur club: Drummondville Voltigeurs (QMJHL).

			Regular Season								Playoffs						
Season	Club	Lea	GP	W	L	T	Mins	GA	SO	Avg	GP	W	L	Mins	GA	SO	Avg
1985-86a	Drummondville	QMJHL	57	33	20	3	3336	215	2	3.87	23	10	13	1271	106	1	5.00

a QMJHL Second All-Star Team (1986)

Signed as a free agent by **Montreal**, October 9, 1985

RICHTER, MIKE

Born, Philadelphia, Penn., February 22, 1966.
Goaltender. Catches left. 5′11″, 170 lbs.
Last amateur club: University of Wisconsin Badgers (WCHA).
(NY Rangers' 2nd choice, 28th over-all, in 1985 Entry Draft.)

			Regular Season								Playoffs						
Season	Club	Lea	GP	W	L	T	Mins	GA	SO	Avg	GP	W	L	Mins	GA	SO	Avg
1985-86a	Wisconsin	WCHA	24	14	9	0	1394	92	1	3.96	....	....	....	....	....	....	....

a WCHA Rookie of the Year (1986).

RIGGIN, PATRICK MICHAEL (PAT)

Born, Kincardine, Ont., May 26, 1959.
Goaltender. Catches right. 5′9″, 170 lbs.
Last amateur club: London Knights (OHA).
(Atlanta's 3rd choice, 33rd over-all, in 1979 Entry Draft).

			Regular Season								Playoffs						
Season	Club	Lea	GP	W	L	T	Mins	GA	SO	Avg	GP	W	L	Mins	GA	SO	Avg
1976-77a	London	OHA	48	....	....	....	2809	140	2	2.95	20	....	....	1197	66	2	3.20
1977-78b	London	OHA	38	....	....	....	2266	140	0	3.65	9	....	....	536	27	0	3.03
1978-79	Birmingham	WHA	46	....	....	....	2511	158	1	3.78	....	....	....	....	....	....	....
1979-80	**Atlanta**	**NHL**	**25**	**11**	**9**	**2**	**1368**	**73**	**2**	**3.20**	....	....	....	....	....	....	....
	Birmingham	CHL	12	8	2	2	746	32	0	2.57	....	....	....	....	....	....	....
1980-81	**Calgary**	**NHL**	**42**	**21**	**16**	**4**	**2411**	**154**	**0**	**3.83**	**11**	**6**	**4**	**629**	**37**	**0**	**3.53**
1981-82	**Calgary**	**NHL**	**52**	**19**	**19**	**11**	**2934**	**207**	**2**	**4.23**	**3**	**0**	**3**	**194**	**10**	**0**	**3.10**
1982-83	**Washington**	**NHL**	**38**	**16**	**9**	**9**	**2161**	**121**	**0**	**3.36**	**3**	**0**	**1**	**101**	**8**	**0**	**4.76**
1983-84	Hershey	AHL	3	2	0	1	185	7	0	2.27	....	....	....	....	....	....	....
cd	**Washington**	**NHL**	**41**	**21**	**14**	**2**	**2299**	**102**	***4**	***2.66**	**5**	**1**	**3**	**230**	**9**	**0**	**2.35**
1984-85	**Washington**	**NHL**	**57**	**28**	**20**	**7**	**3388**	**168**	**2**	**2.98**	**2**	**1**	**1**	**122**	**5**	**0**	**2.46**
1985-86	**Washington**	**NHL**	**7**	**2**	**3**	**1**	**369**	**23**	**0**	**3.74**	....	....	....	....	....	....	....
	Boston	**NHL**	**39**	**17**	**11**	**8**	**2272**	**127**	**1**	**3.35**	**1**	**0**	**1**	**60**	**3**	**0**	**3.00**
	NHL Totals		**301**	**135**	**101**	**44**	**17202**	**975**	**11**	**3.40**	**25**	**8**	**13**	**1336**	**72**	**0**	**3.23**
	WHA Totals		46	....	....	....	2511	158	1	3.78	....	....	....	....	....	....	....

a OHA First All-Star Team (1977)
b OHA Second All-Star Team (1978)
c NHL Second All-Star Team (1984)
d Shared William Jennings Trophy with Al Jensen (1984)

Traded to **Washington** by **Calgary** with Ken Houston for Howard Walker, George White, Washington's sixth round choice (Mats Kihlstron) in 1982 Entry Draft; third round choice (Parry Berezan) in 1983 Entry Draft; and second round choice (Paul Ranheim) in 1984 Entry Draft, June 9, 1982. Traded to **Boston** by **Washington** for Pete Peeters, November 14, 1985.

ROACH, DAVE

Born, Burnaby, B.C., January 10, 1965.
Goaltender. Catches left. 5′10″, 170 lbs.
Last amateur club: Michigan Tech University Huskies (WCHA).
(Edmonton's 8th choice, 180th over-all, in 1983 Entry Draft.)

			Regular Season								Playoffs						
Season	Club	Lea	GP	W	L	T	Mins	GA	SO	Avg	GP	W	L	Mins	GA	SO	Avg
1983-84	Michigan Tech.	WCHA	24	12	12	0	1407	79	0	3.31	....	....	....	....	....	....	....
1984-85	Michigan Tech.	WCHA	19	7	11	0	1085	75	0	4.15	....	....	....	....	....	....	....
1985-86	Michigan Tech.	WCHA	20	5	12	2	1081	87	0	4.83	....	....	....	....	....	....	....

ROMANO, ROBERTO

Born, Montreal, Que., October 10, 1962.
Goaltender. Catches left. 5′6″, 170 lbs.
Last amateur club: Hull Olympiques (QMJHL).

			Regular Season								Playoffs						
Season	Club	Lea	GP	W	L	T	Mins	GA	SO	Avg	GP	W	L	Mins	GA	SO	Avg
1979-80	Quebec	QMJHL	52	21	17	3	2411	183	0	4.55	3	1	1	150	12	0	4.80
1980-81	Quebec	QMJHL	59	24	26	2	3174	233	0	4.40	4	1	2	164	18	0	6.59
1981-82a	Hull	QMJHL	56	....	....	....	3090	194	1	3.77	13	....	....	760	50	0	3.95
1982-83	**Pittsburgh**	**NHL**	**3**	**0**	**3**	**0**	**155**	**18**	**0**	**6.98**	....	....	....	....	....	....	....
	Baltimore	AHL	38	....	....	....	2163	146	0	4.05	....	....	....	....	....	....	....
1983-84	**Pittsburgh**	**NHL**	**18**	**6**	**11**	**0**	**1020**	**78**	**1**	**4.59**	....	....	....	....	....	....	....
	Baltimore	AHL	31	23	6	1	1759	106	0	3.62	9	5	3	544	36	0	3.97
1984-85	**Pittsburgh**	**NHL**	**31**	**9**	**17**	**2**	**1629**	**120**	**1**	**4.42**	....	....	....	....	....	....	....
	Baltimore	AHL	12	2	8	2	719	44	0	3.67	....	....	....	....	....	....	....
1985-86	**Pittsburgh**	**NHL**	**46**	**21**	**20**	**3**	**2684**	**159**	**2**	**3.55**	....	....	....	....	....	....	....
	NHL Totals		**98**	**36**	**51**	**5**	**5488**	**375**	**4**	**4.10**	....	....	....	....	....	....	....

a QMJHL First All-Star Team (1982)

Signed as a free agent by **Pittsburgh**, December 6, 1982.

ROY, PATRICK

Born, Quebec City, Que., October 5, 1965.
Goaltender. Catches left. 6′, 165 lbs.
Last amateur club: Granby Bisons (QMJHL).
(Montreal's 4th choice, 51st over-all, in 1984 Entry Draft).

			Regular Season								Playoffs						
Season	Club	Lea	GP	W	L	T	Mins	GA	SO	Avg	GP	W	L	Mins	GA	SO	Avg
1982-83	Granby	QMJHL	54	....	....	....	2808	293	0	6.26	....	....	....	....	....	....	....
1983-84	Granby	QMJHL	61	29	29	1	3585	265	0	4.44	4	0	4	244	22	0	5.41
1984-85	Granby	QMJHL	44	16	25	1	2463	228	0	5.55	....	....	....	....	....	....	....
	Sherbrooke	AHL	2	1	0	0	60	4	0	4.00	12	10	3	769	37	0	2.89
1985-86ab	**Montreal**	**NHL**	**47**	**23**	**19**	**3**	**2651**	**150**	**1**	**3.39**	**20**	**15**	**5**	**1218**	**39**	**1**	**1.92**
	NHL Totals		**47**	**23**	**19**	**3**	**2651**	**150**	**1**	**3.39**	**20**	**15**	**5**	**1218**	**39**	**1**	**1.92**

a Won Conn Smythe Trophy (1986).
b Named to NHL All-Rookie Team (1986).

ST. CROIX, RICK (ST. CROY)

Born, Kenora, Ont., January 3, 1955.
Goaltender. Catches left. 5′10″, 160 lbs.
Last amateur club: Oshawa Generals (OHA).
(Philadelphia's 3rd choice, 72nd over-all, in 1975 Amateur Draft).

			Regular Season								Playoffs						
Season	Club	Lea	GP	W	L	T	Mins	GA	SO	Avg	GP	W	L	Mins	GA	SO	Avg
1973-74	Oshawa	OHA	33	....	....	....	1930	130	1	4.04	....	....	....	....	....	....	....
1974-75	Oshawa	OHA	32	....	....	....	1965	131	1	4.00	1	....	....	60	9	0	9.00
1975-76	Flint	IHL	42	....	....	....	2201	118	0	3.22	....	....	....	....	....	....	....
1976-77	Springfield	AHL	1	....	....	....	60	3	0	3.00	....	....	....	....	....	....	....
	Flint	IHL	53	....	....	....	2956	179	*3	3.63	5	....	....	337	30	0	5.34
1977-78	**Philadelphia**	**NHL**	**7**	**2**	**4**	**1**	**395**	**20**	**0**	**3.04**	....	....	....	....	....	....	....
	Maine	AHL	40	....	....	....	2266	116	2	3.07	4	....	....	174	18	0	6.21
1978-79	**Philadelphia**	**NHL**	**2**	**0**	**1**	**1**	**117**	**6**	**0**	**3.08**	....	....	....	....	....	....	....
	Philadelphia	AHL	9	4	4	1	484	22	0	2.73	....	....	....	....	....	....	....
	Maine	AHL	22	10	9	3	1312	63	0	2.88	....	....	....	....	....	....	....
1979-80	**Philadelphia**	**NHL**	**1**	**1**	**0**	**0**	**60**	**2**	**0**	**2.00**	....	....	....	....	....	....	....
ab	Maine	AHL	46	25	14	7	2729	132	1	*2.90	5	1	4	311	16	0	3.09
1980-81	**Philadelphia**	**NHL**	**27**	**13**	**7**	**6**	**1567**	**65**	**2**	**2.49**	**9**	**4**	**5**	**541**	**27**	***1**	**2.99**
1981-82	**Philadelphia**	**NHL**	**29**	**13**	**9**	**6**	**1729**	**112**	**0**	**3.89**	**1**	**0**	**1**	**20**	**1**	**0**	**3.00**
1982-83	**Philadelphia**	**NHL**	**16**	**9**	**5**	**2**	**940**	**54**	**0**	**3.45**	....	....	....	....	....	....	....
	Toronto	**NHL**	**16**	**4**	**9**	**2**	**900**	**57**	**0**	**3.80**	**1**	**0**	**0**	**1**	**1**	**0**	**60.00**
1983-84	**Toronto**	**NHL**	**20**	**5**	**10**	**0**	**939**	**80**	**0**	**5.11**	....	....	....	....	....	....	....
	St. Catharines	AHL	8	7	1	0	482	29	0	3.61	3	1	1	133	10	0	4.50
1984-85	**Toronto**	**NHL**	**11**	**2**	**9**	**0**	**628**	**54**	**0**	**5.16**	....	....	....	....	....	....	....
	St. Catharines	AHL	18	6	10	1	1076	92	0	5.13	....	....	....	....	....	....	....
1985-86	Fort Wayne	IHL	42	25	13	0	2474	132	2	3.20	8	3	4	411	30	0	4.38
	NHL Totals		**129**	**49**	**54**	**18**	**7275**	**450**	**2**	**3.71**	**11**	**4**	**6**	**562**	**29**	**1**	**3.10**

a AHL First All-Star Team (1980)
b Shared Harry "Hap" Holmes Trophy (AHL's Leading Goaltenders) with Robbie Moore (1980)

Traded to **Toronto** by **Philadelphia** for Michel Larocque, January 10, 1983.

ST. LAURENT, SAM

Born, Arvida, Que., February 16, 1959.
Goaltender. Catches left. 5′10″, 190 lbs.
Last amateur club: Chicoutimi Sagueneens (QJHL).

			Regular Season								Playoffs						
Season	Club	Lea	GP	W	L	T	Mins	GA	SO	Avg	GP	W	L	Mins	GA	SO	Avg
1977-78	Chicoutimi	QJHL	60	....	....	....	3251	351	0	6.46	....	....	....	....	....	....	....
1978-79	Chicoutimi	QJHL	70	....	....	....	3806	290	0	4.57	1	....	....	47	8	0	10.21
1979-80	Maine	AHL	5	2	1	0	229	17	0	4.45	....	....	....	....	....	....	....
	Toledo	IHL	38	....	....	....	2143	138	2	3.86	4	....	....	239	24	0	6.03
1980-81	Maine	AHL	7	3	3	0	363	28	0	4.63	....	....	....	....	....	....	....
	Toledo	IHL	30	....	....	....	1614	113	1	4.20	....	....	....	....	....	....	....
1981-82	Toledo	IHL	4	....	....	....	248	11	0	2.66	....	....	....	....	....	....	....
	Maine	AHL	25	15	7	1	1396	76	0	3.27	4	1	3	240	18	0	4.50
1982-83	Maine	AHL	30	....	....	....	1739	109	0	3.76	17	....	....	1012	54	0	3.20
1983-84	Maine	AHL	38	14	18	4	2158	145	0	4.03	12	9	2	708	32	1	2.71
1984-85a	Maine	AHL	55	26	22	7	3245	168	4	3.11	10	5	5	656	45	0	4.12
1985-86	**New Jersey**	**NHL**	**4**	**2**	**1**	**0**	**188**	**13**	**1**	**4.15**	....	....	....	....	....	....	....
	Maine	AHL	50	24	20	4	2862	161	1	3.38	....	....	....	....	....	....	....
	NHL Totals		**4**	**2**	**1**	**0**	**188**	**13**	**1**	**4.15**	....	....	....	....	....	....	....

a AHL Second All-Star Team (1985)

Signed as a free agent by **Philadelphia**, October l0, l979.

Traded to **Detroit** by **New Jersey** for Steve Richmond, August 18, 1986.

SANDS, MICHAEL (MIKE)

Born, Mississauga, Ont., April 6, 1963.
Goaltender. Catches left. 5′9″, 155 lbs.
Last amateur club: Sudbury Wolves (OHL).
(Minnesota's 3rd choice, 31st over-all, in 1981 Entry Draft).

			Regular Season								Playoffs						
Season	Club	Lea	GP	W	L	T	Mins	GA	SO	Avg	GP	W	L	Mins	GA	SO	Avg
1980-81	Sudbury	OHA	50	15	28	2	2789	236	0	5.08	....	....	....	....	....	....	....
1981-82	Sudbury	OHL	53	13	33	1	2854	265	1	5.57	....	....	....	....	....	....	....
	Nashville	CHL	7	3	3	1	380	26	0	4.11	....	....	....	....	....	....	....
1982-83	Sudbury	OHL	43	11	27	0	2320	204	1	5.28	....	....	....	....	....	....	....
	Birmingham	CHL	4	0	4	0	169	14	0	4.97	....	....	....	....	....	....	....
1983-84	Salt Lake	CHL	23	7	12	1	1145	93	0	4.87	....	....	....	....	....	....	....
1984-85	**Minnesota**	**NHL**	**3**	**0**	**3**	**0**	**139**	**14**	**0**	**6.04**	**....**	**....**	**....**	**....**	**....**	**....**	**....**
	Springfield	AHL	46	23	17	3	2589	140	2	3.24	3	0	3	130	15	0	6.92
1985-86	Springfield	AHL	27	8	15	1	1490	94	0	3.79	....	....	....	....	....	....	....
	NHL Totals		**3**	**0**	**3**	**0**	**139**	**14**	**0**	**6.04**	**....**	**....**	**....**	**....**	**....**	**....**	**....**

SAUVE, ROBERT (SOH-vay)

Born, Ste. Genevieve, Que., June 17, 1955.
Goaltender. Catches left. 5′8″, 165 lbs.
Last amateur club: Laval Nationals (QJHL).
(Buffalo's 1st choice, 17th over-all, in 1975 Amateur Draft).

			Regular Season								Playoffs						
Season	Club	Lea	GP	W	L	T	Mins	GA	SO	Avg	GP	W	L	Mins	GA	SO	Avg
1973-74	Laval	QJHL	61	....	....	....	3621	341	0	5.65	5	....	....	300	19	0	3.80
1974-75	Laval	QJHL	57	....	....	....	3403	287	0	5.06	16	....	....	960	81	0	5.06
1975-76	Providence	AHL	14	....	....	....	848	44	0	3.11	....	....	....	....	....	....	....
	Charlotte	SHL	17	....	....	....	979	36	2	2.21	7	....	....	420	10	*2	*1.43
1976-77	Rhode Island	AHL	25	....	....	....	1346	94	0	4.14	....	....	....	....	....	....	....
	Buffalo	**NHL**	**4**	**1**	**2**	**0**	**184**	**11**	**0**	**3.59**	**....**	**....**	**....**	**....**	**....**	**....**	**....**
	Hershey	AHL	9	....	....	....	539	38	0	4.23	....	....	....	....	....	....	....
1977-78	**Buffalo**	**NHL**	**11**	**6**	**2**	**0**	**480**	**20**	**0**	**2.50**	**....**	**....**	**....**	**....**	**....**	**....**	**....**
	Hershey	AHL	16	....	....	....	872	59	0	4.05	....	....	....	....	....	....	....
1978-79	Hershey	AHL	5	....	....	....	278	14	0	3.02	....	....	....	....	....	....	....
	Buffalo	**NHL**	**29**	**10**	**10**	**7**	**1610**	**100**	**0**	**3.73**	**3**	**1**	**2**	**181**	**9**	**0**	**2.98**
1979-80a	**Buffalo**	**NHL**	**32**	**20**	**8**	**4**	**1880**	**74**	**4**	***2.36**	**8**	**6**	**2**	**501**	**17**	***2**	***2.04**
1980-81	**Buffalo**	**NHL**	**35**	**16**	**10**	**9**	**2100**	**111**	**2**	**3.17**	**....**	**....**	**....**	**....**	**....**	**....**	**....**
1981-82	**Buffalo**	**NHL**	**14**	**6**	**1**	**5**	**760**	**35**	**0**	**2.76**	**....**	**....**	**....**	**....**	**....**	**....**	**....**
	Detroit	**NHL**	**41**	**11**	**25**	**4**	**2365**	**165**	**0**	**4.19**	**....**	**....**	**....**	**....**	**....**	**....**	**....**
1982-83	**Buffalo**	**NHL**	**54**	**25**	**20**	**7**	**3110**	**179**	**1**	**3.45**	**10**	**6**	**4**	**545**	**28**	***2**	**3.08**
1983-84	**Buffalo**	**NHL**	**40**	**22**	**13**	**4**	**2375**	**138**	**0**	**3.49**	**2**	**0**	**1**	**41**	**5**	**0**	**7.35**
1984-85b	**Buffalo**	**NHL**	**27**	**13**	**10**	**3**	**1564**	**84**	**0**	**3.22**	**....**	**....**	**....**	**....**	**....**	**....**	**....**
1985-86	**Chicago**	**NHL**	**38**	**19**	**13**	**2**	**2099**	**138**	**0**	**3.95**	**2**	**0**	**2**	**99**	**8**	**0**	**4.85**
	NHL Totals		**325**	**149**	**114**	**49**	**18527**	**1055**	**7**	**3.42**	**25**	**13**	**11**	**1367**	**67**	**4**	**2.94**

a Shared Vezina Trophy with Don Edwards (1980)
b Shared Jennings Trophy with Tom Barrasso (1985)

Traded to **Detroit** by **Buffalo** for future considerations, December 2, 1981. Signed as free agent by **Buffalo**, June 1, 1982. Traded to **Chicago** by **Buffalo** for Chicago's third round draft choice in 1986 (Kevin Kerr), October 15, 1985.

SCOTT, RON

Born, Guelph, Ont., July 21, 1960.
Goaltender. Catches left. 5′8″, 155 lbs.
Last amateur club: Michigan State University Spartans (CCHA).

			Regular Season								Playoffs						
Season	Club	Lea	GP	W	L	T	Mins	GA	SO	Avg	GP	W	L	Mins	GA	SO	Avg
1980-81	Michigan State	WCHA	33	11	21	1	1899	123	2	3.89	....	....	....	....	....	....	....
1981-82	Michigan State	CCHA	39	24	13	1	2298	109	2	2.85	....	....	....	....	....	....	....
1982-83a	Michigan State	CCHA	40	29	9	1	2273	100	2	2.64	....	....	....	....	....	....	....
1983-84	**NY Rangers**	**NHL**	**9**	**2**	**3**	**3**	**485**	**29**	**0**	**3.59**	**....**	**....**	**....**	**....**	**....**	**....**	**....**
b	Tulsa	CHL	29	13	13	3	1717	109	0	3.81	5	....	....	280	20	0	4.28
1984-85	New Haven	AHL	36	13	18	4	2047	130	0	3.81	....	....	....	....	....	....	....
1985-86	**NY Rangers**	**NHL**	**4**	**0**	**3**	**0**	**156**	**11**	**0**	**4.23**	**....**	**....**	**....**	**....**	**....**	**....**	**....**
	New Haven	AHL	19	8	8	1	1069	66	1	3.70	2	1	1	143	8	0	3.36
	NHL Totals		**13**	**2**	**6**	**3**	**641**	**40**	**0**	**3.74**	**....**	**....**	**....**	**....**	**....**	**....**	**....**

a CCHA First All-Star Team (1983)
b Shared Terry Sawchuk Trophy (CHL's leading goaltenders) with John Vanbiesbrouck (1984)

Signed as a free agent by **NY Rangers**, May 25, 1983.

SEVIGNY, RICHARD (seh-VIN-yay)

Born, Montreal, Que., April 11, 1957.
Goaltender. Catches left. 5′8″, 175 lbs.
Last amateur club: Sherbrooke Beavers (QJHL).
(Montreal's 11th choice, 124th over-all, in 1977 Amateur Draft).

			Regular Season								Playoffs						
Season	Club	Lea	GP	W	L	T	Mins	GA	SO	Avg	GP	W	L	Mins	GA	SO	Avg
1975-76	Sherbrooke	QJHL	55	....	....	....	3058	196	2	3.85	15	....	....	797	56	0	4.22
1976-77	Sherbrooke	QJHL	65	....	....	....	3656	248	2	4.07	18	....	....	1058	60	2	3.40
1977-78a	Kalamazoo	IHL	35	....	....	....	1897	95	1	3.01	7	....	....	296	12	0	*2.43
1978-79	Springfield	AHL	22	6	12	3	1302	77	0	3.55	....	....	....	....	....	....	....
	Nova Scotia	AHL	20	12	6	1	1169	57	1	2.93	10	5	5	607	37	0	3.66
1979-80	**Montreal**	**NHL**	**11**	**5**	**4**	**2**	**632**	**31**	**0**	**2.94**	**....**	**....**	**....**	**....**	**....**	**....**	**....**
	Nova Scotia	AHL	35	17	12	4	2104	114	*3	3.25	4	1	3	239	15	0	3.77
1980-81b	**Montreal**	**NHL**	**33**	**20**	**4**	**3**	**1777**	**71**	**2**	***2.40**	**3**	**0**	**3**	**180**	**13**	**0**	**4.33**
1981-82c	**Montreal**	**NHL**	**19**	**11**	**4**	**2**	**1027**	**53**	**0**	**3.10**	**....**	**....**	**....**	**....**	**....**	**....**	**....**
1982-83	**Montreal**	**NHL**	**38**	**15**	**11**	**8**	**2130**	**122**	**1**	**3.44**	**1**	**0**	**0**	**28**	**0**	**0**	**0.00**
1983-84	**Montreal**	**NHL**	**40**	**16**	**8**	**2**	**2203**	**124**	**1**	**3.38**	**2**	**0**	**0**	**0**	**0**	**0**	**0.00**
1984-85	**Quebec**	**NHL**	**20**	**10**	**6**	**2**	**1104**	**62**	**1**	**3.37**	**....**	**....**	**....**	**....**	**....**	**....**	**....**
1985-86	**Quebec**	**NHL**	**11**	**3**	**5**	**1**	**468**	**33**	**0**	**4.23**	**....**	**....**	**....**	**....**	**....**	**....**	**....**
	Fredericton	AHL	6	3	3	0	362	21	0	3.48	....	....	....	....	....	....	....
	NHL Totals		**172**	**90**	**42**	**20**	**9341**	**496**	**5**	**3.18**	**6**	**0**	**3**	**208**	**13**	**0**	**3.75**

a IHL Second All-Star Team (1978)
b Shared Vezina Trophy with Denis Herron and Michel Larocque (1981)
c Shared shutout with Denis Herron, November 11, 1981 vs. Colorado

Signed as a free agent by **Quebec**, July 4, 1984.

SIDORKIEWICZ, PETER (suh-DORK-oh-WITZ)

Born, Dabrown Bialostocka, Poland, June 29, 1963.
Goaltender. Catches left. 5′9″, 165 lbs.
Last amateur club: Oshawa Generals (OHL).
(Washington's 5th choice, 91st over-all, in 1981 Entry Draft).

			Regular Season								Playoffs						
Season	Club	Lea	GP	W	L	T	Mins	GA	SO	Avg	GP	W	L	Mins	GA	SO	Avg
1980-81	Oshawa	OHA	7	3	3	0	308	24	0	4.68	5	2	2	266	20	0	4.52
1981-82	Oshawa	OHL	29	14	11	1	1553	123	*2	4.75	1	0	0	13	1	0	4.62
1982-83	Oshawa	OHL	60	36	20	3	3536	213	0	3.61	17	15	1	1020	60	0	3.53
1983-84a	Oshawa	OHL	52	28	21	1	2966	250	1	4.15	7	3	4	420	27	*1	3.86
1984-85	Binghamton	AHL	45	31	9	5	2691	137	3	3.05	8	4	4	481	31	0	3.87
	Fort Worth	IHL	10	4	4	2	590	43	0	4.37	....	....	....	....	....	....	....
1985-86	Binghamton	AHL	49	21	22	3	2819	150	2	3.19	4	1	3	235	12	0	3.06

a OHL Third All-Star Team (1984).

Traded to **Hartford** by **Washington** with Dean Evason for David Jensen, March 12, 1985.

SIMPSON, SHAWN

Born, Gloucester Ont., August 10, 1968.
Goaltender. Catches left. 5′11″, 180 lbs.
Last amateur club: Sault Ste. Marie Greyhounds (OHL).
(Washington's 3rd choice, 60th over-all, in 1986 Entry Draft).

			Regular Season								Playoffs						
Season	Club	Lea	GP	W	L	T	Mins	GA	SO	Avg	GP	W	L	Mins	GA	SO	Avg
1985-86	Sault Ste. Marie	OHL	42	10	26	1	2213	217	1	5.88	....	....	....	....	....	....	....

SKORODENSKI, WARREN

Born, Winnipeg, Man., March 22, 1960.
Goaltender. Catches left. 6′1″, 180 lbs.
Last amateur club: Calgary Wranglers (WHL)

			Regular Season								Playoffs						
Season	Club	Lea	GP	W	L	T	Mins	GA	SO	Avg	GP	W	L	Mins	GA	SO	Avg
1977-78	Calgary	WHL	53	8	22	10	2460	213	1	5.20	....	....	....	....	....	....	....
1978-79	Calgary	WHL	66	26	31	5	3595	309	1	5.16	15	7	8	884	61	0	4.14
1979-80	Calgary	WHL	66	39	23	2	3724	261	1	4.21	7	3	4	357	29	0	4.87
1980-81	New Brunswick	AHL	2	0	1	0	124	9	0	4.35	....	....	....	....	....	....	....
	Flint	IHL	47	....	....	....	2602	189	2	4.36	6	....	....	301	18	0	3.58
1981-82	**Chicago**	**NHL**	**1**	**0**	**1**	**0**	**60**	**5**	**0**	**5.00**	**....**	**....**	**....**	**....**	**....**	**....**	**....**
a	New Brunswick	AHL	28	16	8	4	1644	70	*3	*2.55	2	0	2	90	6	0	4.00
1982-83	Springfield	AHL	13	....	....	....	592	49	0	4.97	....	....	....	....	....	....	....
	Birmingham	CHL	25	11	11	1	1450	81	1	3.35	5	....	....	195	19	0	5.85
1983-84	Sherbrooke	AHL	19	5	10	2	1048	88	0	5.04	....	....	....	....	....	....	....
	Springfield	AHL	14	3	11	0	756	67	0	5.32	2	0	2	124	13	0	6.28
1984-85	**Chicago**	**NHL**	**27**	**11**	**9**	**3**	**1396**	**75**	**2**	**3.22**	**2**	**0**	**0**	**33**	**6**	**0**	**10.91**
1985-86	**Chicago**	**NHL**	**1**	**0**	**1**	**0**	**60**	**6**	**0**	**6.00**	**....**	**....**	**....**	**....**	**....**	**....**	**....**
	Nova Scotia	AHL	32	11	14	2	1716	109	0	3.81	....	....	....	....	....	....	....
	NHL Totals		**29**	**11**	**11**	**3**	**1516**	**86**	**2**	**3.40**	**2**	**0**	**0**	**33**	**6**	**0**	**10.91**

a Shared Harry (Hap) Holmes Memorial Trophy with Bob Janecyk (1982).

Signed as a free agent by **Chicago,** August 12, 1979.

SMITH, WILLIAM JOHN (BILL)

Born, Perth, Ont., December 12, 1950.
Goaltender. Catches left. 5′10″, 185 lbs.
Last amateur club: Cornwall Royals (QJHL).
(Los Angeles' 3rd choice, 59th over-all, in 1970 Amateur Draft).

			Regular Season								Playoffs						
Season	Club	Lea	GP	W	L	T	Mins	GA	SO	Avg	GP	W	L	Mins	GA	SO	Avg
1969-70	Cornwall	QJHL	55	....	....	....	3305	249	1	4.52	6	....	....	360	14	1	2.33
1970-71	Springfield	AHL	49	....	....	....	2728	160	2	3.51	12	....	....	682	29	1	*2.56
1971-72	**Los Angeles**	**NHL**	**5**	**1**	**3**	**1**	**300**	**23**	**0**	**4.60**	**....**	**....**	**....**	**....**	**....**	**....**	**....**
	Springfield	AHL	28	....	....	....	1649	77	*4	2.80	4	....	....	192	13	0	4.06
1972-73	**NY Islanders**	**NHL**	**37**	**7**	**24**	**3**	**2122**	**147**	**0**	**4.16**	**....**	**....**	**....**	**....**	**....**	**....**	**....**
1973-74	**NY Islanders**	**NHL**	**46**	**9**	**23**	**12**	**2615**	**134**	**0**	**3.07**	**....**	**....**	**....**	**....**	**....**	**....**	**....**
1974-75	**NY Islanders**	**NHL**	**58**	**21**	**18**	**17**	**3368**	**156**	**3**	**2.78**	**6**	**1**	**4**	**333**	**23**	**0**	**4.14**
1975-76	**NY Islanders**	**NHL**	**39**	**19**	**10**	**9**	**2254**	**98**	**3**	**2.61**	**8**	**4**	**3**	**437**	**21**	**0**	**2.88**
1976-77	**NY Islanders**	**NHL**	**36**	**21**	**8**	**6**	**2089**	**87**	**2**	**2.50**	**10**	**7**	**3**	**580**	**27**	**0**	**2.79**
1977-78a	**NY Islanders**	**NHL**	**38**	**20**	**8**	**8**	**2154**	**95**	**2**	**2.65**	**1**	**0**	**0**	**47**	**1**	**0**	**1.28**
1978-79	**NY Islanders**	**NHL**	**40**	**25**	**8**	**4**	**2261**	**108**	**1**	**2.87**	**5**	**4**	**1**	**315**	**10**	***1**	***1.90**
1979-80b	**NY Islanders**	**NHL**	**38**	**15**	**4**	**7**	**2114**	**104**	**2**	**2.95**	**20**	**15**	**4**	**1198**	**56**	**1**	**2.80**
1980-81	**NY Islanders**	**NHL**	**41**	**22**	**10**	**8**	**2363**	**129**	**2**	**3.28**	**17**	**14**	**3**	**994**	**42**	**0**	***2.54**
1981-82cd	**NY Islanders**	**NHL**	**46**	**32**	**9**	**4**	**2685**	**133**	**0**	**2.97**	**18**	**15**	**3**	**1120**	**47**	***1**	**2.52**
1982-83ef	**NY Islanders**	**NHL**	**41**	**14**	**7**	**2**	**2340**	**112**	**1**	**2.87**	**17**	**13**	**3**	**962**	**43**	***2**	***2.68**
1983-84	**NY Islanders**	**NHL**	**42**	**23**	**13**	**2**	**2279**	**130**	**2**	**3.42**	**21**	**12**	**8**	**1190**	**54**	**0**	**2.72**
1984-85	**NY Islanders**	**NHL**	**37**	**18**	**14**	**3**	**2090**	**133**	**0**	**3.82**	**6**	**3**	**3**	**342**	**19**	**0**	**3.33**
1985-86	**NY Islanders**	**NHL**	**41**	**20**	**14**	**4**	**2308**	**143**	**1**	**3.72**	**1**	**0**	**1**	**60**	**4**	**0**	**4.00**
	NHL Totals		**585**	**267**	**173**	**90**	**33342**	**1732**	**19**	**3.12**	**130**	**88**	**36**	**7578**	**347**	**5**	**2.75**

a Shared shutout with Goran Hogosta versus Atlanta, November 1, 1977.
b Credited with a goal against Colorado Rockies (November 28, 1979).
c Won Vezina Trophy (1982)
d NHL First All-Star Team (1982)
e Won Conn Smythe Trophy (1983)
f Shared William Jennings Trophy with Roland Melanson (1983)

Claimed by **NY Islanders** from **Los Angeles** in Expansion Draft, June 6, 1972.

SOETAERT, DOUGLAS HENRY (DOUG) (SOH-tart)

Born, Edmonton, Alta., April 21, 1955.
Goaltender. Catches left. 6', 180 lbs.
Last amateur club: Edmonton Oil Kings (WHL).
(NY Rangers' 2nd choice, 30th over-all, in 1975 Amateur Draft).

			Regular Season								Playoffs						
Season	Club	Lea	GP	W	L	T	Mins	GA	SO	Avg	GP	W	L	Mins	GA	SO	Avg
1971-72	Edmonton	WHL	37	....	....	....	1738	105	3	3.62	6	....	....	267	13	0	2.92
1972-73	Edmonton	WHL	43	....	....	....	2111	129	1	3.67	6	....	....	339	33	0	5.84
1973-74	Edmonton	WHL	39	....	....	....	2190	163	1	4.47	3	....	....	141	9	0	3.83
1974-75	Edmonton	WHL	65	....	....	....	3706	273	1	4.42	....	....	....	....	....	....	....
1975-76	**NY Rangers**	**NHL**	**8**	**2**	**2**	**0**	**273**	**24**	**0**	**5.27**	....	....	....	....	....	....	....
	Providence	AHL	16	....	....	....	896	65	0	4.35	1	....	....	59	6	0	6.10
1976-77	**NY Rangers**	**NHL**	**12**	**3**	**4**	**1**	**570**	**28**	**1**	**2.95**	....	....	....	....	....	....	....
	New Haven	AHL	16	....	....	....	947	61	0	3.86	....	....	....	....	....	....	....
1977-78	**NY Rangers**	**NHL**	**6**	**2**	**2**	**2**	**360**	**20**	**0**	**3.33**	....	....	....	....	....	....	....
	New Haven	AHL	38	....	....	....	2252	141	0	3.75	15	....	....	916	53	0	3.47
1978-79	New Haven	AHL	3	2	1	0	180	11	1	3.67	....	....	....	....	....	....	....
	NY Rangers	**NHL**	**17**	**5**	**7**	**3**	**900**	**57**	**0**	**3.80**	....	....	....	....	....	....	....
1979-80	**NY Rangers**	**NHL**	**8**	**5**	**2**	**0**	**435**	**33**	**0**	**4.55**	....	....	....	....	....	....	....
	New Haven	AHL	32	17	18	5	1808	108	*3	3.58	8	5	3	478	24	0	3.01
1980-81	**NY Rangers**	**NHL**	**39**	**16**	**16**	**7**	**2320**	**152**	**0**	**3.93**	....	....	....	....	....	....	....
	New Haven	AHL	12	5	5	1	668	35	2	3.14	4	0	3	220	19	0	5.18
1981-82	**Winnipeg**	**NHL**	**39**	**13**	**14**	**8**	**2157**	**155**	**2**	**4.31**	**2**	**1**	**1**	**120**	**8**	**0**	**4.00**
1982-83	**Winnipeg**	**NHL**	**44**	**19**	**19**	**6**	**2533**	**174**	**0**	**4.12**	**1**	**0**	**0**	**20**	**0**	**0**	**0.00**
1983-84	**Winnipeg**	**NHL**	**47**	**18**	**15**	**7**	**2539**	**182**	**0**	**4.30**	**1**	**0**	**1**	**20**	**5**	**0**	**15.15**
1984-85	**Montreal**	**NHL**	**28**	**14**	**9**	**4**	**1606**	**91**	**0**	**3.40**	**1**	**0**	**0**	**20**	**1**	**0**	**3.00**
1985-86	**Montreal**	**NHL**	**23**	**11**	**6**	**2**	**1215**	**56**	**3**	**2.77**	....	....	....	....	....	....	....
	NHL Totals		**271**	**108**	**96**	**42**	**14908**	**972**	**6**	**3.91**	**5**	**1**	**2**	**180**	**14**	**0**	**4.67**

Traded to **Winnipeg** by **NY Rangers** for Winnipeg's third round choice (Vesa Salo) in the 1983 Entry Draft, September 8, 1981. Traded to **Montreal** by **Winnipeg** for Mark Holden, October 9, 1984. Signed as a free agent by **NY Rangers**, July 24, 1986.

STEFAN, GREGORY STEVEN (GREG) (ste-FAN)

Born, Brantford, Ont., February 11, 1961.
Goaltender. Catches left. 5'11", 175 lbs.
Last amateur club. Oshawa Generals (OHA).
(Detroit's 5th choice, 128th over-all, in 1981 Entry Draft).

			Regular Season								Playoffs						
Season	Club	Lea	GP	W	L	T	Mins	GA	SO	Avg	GP	W	L	Mins	GA	SO	Avg
1979-80	Oshawa	OHA	17	8	6	0	897	58	0	3.88	....	....	....	....	....	....	....
1980-81	Oshawa	OHA	46	23	14	3	2407	174	0	4.34	6	2	3	298	20	0	4.02
1981-82	**Detroit**	**NHL**	**2**	**0**	**2**	**0**	**120**	**10**	**0**	**5.00**	....	....	....	....	....	....	....
	Adirondack	AHL	29	11	13	3	1571	99	2	3.78	1	0	0	20	0	0	0.00
1982-83	**Detroit**	**NHL**	**35**	**6**	**16**	**9**	**1847**	**139**	**0**	**4.52**	....	....	....	....	....	....	....
1983-84	**Detroit**	**NHL**	**50**	**19**	**22**	**2**	**2600**	**152**	**2**	**3.51**	**3**	**1**	**2**	**210**	**8**	**0**	**2.29**
1984-85	**Detroit**	**NHL**	**46**	**21**	**19**	**3**	**2635**	**190**	**0**	**4.33**	**3**	**0**	**3**	**138**	**17**	**0**	**7.39**
1985-86	**Detroit**	**NHL**	**37**	**10**	**20**	**5**	**2068**	**155**	**1**	**4.50**	....	....	....	....	....	....	....
	NHL Totals		**170**	**56**	**79**	**19**	**9270**	**646**	**3**	**4.18**	**6**	**1**	**5**	**348**	**25**	**0**	**4.31**

STROME, GREG

Born, Muenster, Sask., July 28, 1965.
Goaltender. Catches left. 5'9", 160 lbs.
Last amateur club: University of North Dakota Fighting Sioux (WCHA).
(Los Angeles' 6th choice, 108th over-all, in 1984 Entry Draft).

			Regular Season								Playoffs						
Season	Club	Lea	GP	W	L	T	Mins	GA	SO	Avg	GP	W	L	Mins	GA	SO	Avg
1983-84	North Dakota	WCHA	6	4	2	0	385	24	0	3.81	....	....	....	....	....	....	....
1984-85	North Dakota	WCHA	13	9	4	0	743	47	0	3.70	....	....	....	....	....	....	....
1985-86	North Dakota	WCHA	21	9	9	0	1189	78	0	3.90	....	....	....	....	....	....	....

TAILLEFER, TERRY

Born, Edmonton, Alta., July 23, 1965.
Goaltender. Catches left. 6'0", 162 lbs.
Last amateur club: Boston University Terriers (H.E.).
(Boston's 6th choice, 122nd over-all, in 1983 Entry Draft).

			Regular Season								Playoffs						
Season	Club	Lea	GP	W	L	T	Mins	GA	SO	Avg	GP	W	L	Mins	GA	SO	Avg
1983-84	Boston U.	ECAC	10	3	1	1	412	20	0	2.91	....	....	....	....	....	....	....
1984-85	Boston U.	H.E.	15	9	4	2	938	47	0	3.01	....	....	....	....	....	....	....
1985-86a	Boston U.	H.E.	20	11	5	2	1113	65	1	3.50	....	....	....	....	....	....	....

a Hockey East Second All-Star Team (1986).

TAKKO, KARI

Born, Kaupunski, Finland, June 23, 1963.
Goaltender. Catches left. 6'2", 180 lbs.
Last amateur club: Finnish Olympic Team
(Minnesota's 5th choice, 97th over-all, in 1984 Entry Draft).

			Regular Season								Playoffs						
Season	Club	Lea	GP	W	L	T	Mins	GA	SO	Avg	GP	W	L	Mins	GA	SO	Avg
1985-86	Springfield	AHL	43	18	19	3	2286	161	1	4.05	....	....	....	....	....	....	....
	Minnesota	**NHL**	**1**	**0**	**1**	**0**	**60**	**3**	**0**	**3.00**	....	....	....	....	....	....	....
	NHL Totals		**1**	**0**	**1**	**0**	**60**	**3**	**0**	**3.00**	....	....	....	....	....	....	....

TERRERI, CHRIS

Born, Providence, R.I., November 15, 1964.
Goaltender. Catches left. 5'9", 155 lbs.
Last amateur club: Providence College Friars (H.E.).
(New Jersey's 3rd choice, 87th over-all, in 1983 Entry Draft).

			Regular Season								Playoffs						
Season	Club	Lea	GP	W	L	T	Mins	GA	SO	Avg	GP	W	L	Mins	GA	SO	Avg
1982-83	Providence	ECAC	11	7	1	0	528	17	2	1.93	....	....	....	....	....	....	....
1983-84	Providence	ECAC	10	4	2	0	391	20	0	3.07	....	....	....	....	....	....	....
1984-85abc	Providence	H.E.	33	15	13	5	1956	116	1	3.35	....	....	....	....	....	....	....
1985-86	Providence	H.E.	22	6	16	0	1320	84	0	3.74	....	....	....	....	....	....	....

a Hockey East All-Star Team
b Hockey East Player of the Year (1985)
c Named to NCAA All-American Team (1985)

TESSIER, BRIAN

Born, Walden, Ont., May 23, 1967.
Goaltender. Catches left. 5'11", 163 lbs.
Last amateur club: Kingston Canadians (OHL).
(Edmonton's 5th choice, 125th over-all, in 1985 Entry Draft).

			Regular Season								Playoffs						
Season	Club	Lea	GP	W	L	T	Mins	GA	SO	Avg	GP	W	L	Mins	GA	SO	Avg
1984-85	North Bay	OHL	10	4	5	0	539	38	0	4.30	2	0	1	69	8	0	6.96
1985-86	Kingston	OHL	13	8	5	0	780	55	0	4.23	2	0	0	48	6	0	7.50

TITUS, STEVE

Born, St. John, N.B., February 2, 1962.
Goaltender. Catches left. 5'11", 155 lbs.
Last amateur club: Cornwall Royals (OHL).
(Pittsburgh's 7th choice, 128th over-all, in 1985 Entry Draft).

			Regular Season								Playoffs						
Season	Club	Lea	GP	W	L	T	Mins	GA	SO	Avg	GP	W	L	Mins	GA	SO	Avg
1984-85	Cornwall	OHL	47	24	17	2	2568	217	1	5.07	9	4	5	492	42	0	5.12
1985-86	Cornwall	OHL	33	13	18	1	1846	163	0	5.23	1	0	1	60	9	0	9.00

VANBIESBROUCK, JOHN (van-BEEZ-brook)

Born, Detroit, Mich., September 4, 1963.
Goaltender. Catches left. 5'7", 165 lbs.
Last amateur club: Sault Ste. Marie Greyhounds (OHL).
(NY Rangers' 5th choice, 72nd over-all, in 1981 Entry Draft).

			Regular Season								Playoffs						
Season	Club	Lea	GP	W	L	T	Mins	GA	SO	Avg	GP	W	L	Mins	GA	SO	Avg
1980-81a	S.S. Marie	OHA	56	31	16	1	2941	203	0	4.14	11	3	3	457	24	1	3.15
1981-82	**NY Rangers**	**NHL**	**1**	**1**	**0**	**0**	**60**	**1**	**0**	**1.00**	....	....	....	....	....	....	....
	S.S. Marie	OHL	31	12	12	2	1686	102	0	3.62	7	1	4	276	20	0	4.35
1982-83b	S.S. Marie	OHL	62	39	21	1	3471	209	0	3.61	16	7	6	944	56	*1	3.56
1983-84	**NY Rangers**	**NHL**	**3**	**2**	**1**	**0**	**180**	**10**	**0**	**3.33**	**1**	**0**	**0**	**1**	**0**	**0**	**0.00**
cde	Tulsa	CHL	37	20	13	2	2153	124	*3	3.46	4	4	0	240	10	0	*2.50
1984-85	**NY Rangers**	**NHL**	**42**	**12**	**24**	**3**	**2358**	**166**	**1**	**4.22**	**1**	**0**	**0**	**20**	**0**	**0**	**0.00**
1985-86fg	**NY Rangers**	**NHL**	**61**	**31**	**21**	**5**	**3326**	**184**	**3**	**3.32**	**16**	**8**	**8**	**899**	**49**	**1**	**3.27**
	NHL Totals		**107**	**46**	**46**	**8**	**5924**	**361**	**4**	**3.66**	**18**	**8**	**8**	**920**	**49**	**1**	**3.19**

a OHA Third All-Star Team (1981).
b OHL Second All-Star Team (1983).
c CHL First All-Star Team (1984)
d Shared Terry Sawchuk Trophy (CHL's leading goaltenders) with Ron Scott (1984)
e Shared Tommy Ivan Trophy (CHL's Most Valuable Player) with Bruce Affleck of Indianapolis (1984)
f Won Vezina Trophy (1986).
g NHL First All-Star Team (1986).

VERNON, MICHAEL (MIKE)

Born, Calgary, Alta., February 24, 1963.
Goaltender. Catches left. 5'9", 150 lbs.
Last amateur club: Calgary Wranglers (WHL).
(Calgary's 2nd choice, 56th over-all, in 1981 Entry Draft).

			Regular Season								Playoffs						
Season	Club	Lea	GP	W	L	T	Mins	GA	SO	Avg	GP	W	L	Mins	GA	SO	Avg
1980-81	Calgary	WHL	59	33	17	1	3154	198	1	3.77	22	....	....	271	82	1	3.87
1981-82ab	Calgary	WHL	42	22	14	2	2329	143	3	3.68	9	....	....	527	30	0	3.42
	Oklahoma City	CHL	....	....	....	....	....	....	....	....	1	0	1	70	4	0	3.43
1982-83	**Calgary**	**NHL**	**2**	**0**	**2**	**0**	**100**	**11**	**0**	**6.59**	....	....	....	....	....	....	....
ab	Calgary	WHL	50	19	18	2	2856	155	3	3.26	16	9	7	925	60	0	3.89
1983-84	**Calgary**	**NHL**	**1**	**0**	**1**	**0**	**11**	**4**	**0**	**22.22**	....	....	....	....	....	....	....
c	Colorado	CHL	46	30	13	2	2648	148	1	*3.35	6	2	4	347	21	0	3.63
1984-85	Moncton	AHL	41	10	20	4	2050	134	0	3.92	....	....	....	....	....	....	....
1985-86	**Calgary**	**NHL**	**18**	**9**	**3**	**3**	**921**	**52**	**1**	**3.39**	**21**	**12**	**9**	**1229**	**60**	**0**	**2.93**
	Moncton	AHL	6	3	1	2	374	21	0	3.37	....	....	....	....	....	....	....
	NHL Totals		**21**	**9**	**6**	**3**	**1032**	**67**	**1**	**3.89**	**21**	**12**	**9**	**1229**	**60**	**0**	**2.93**

a WHL First All-Star Team (1982, 1983)
b Named WHL's Most Valuable Player (1982, 1983)
c CHL Second All-Star Team (1984)

VOLPE, MIKE

Born, Vancouver, B.C., January 2, 1967.
Goaltender. Catches left. 5'11", 165 lbs.
Last amateur club: Kitchener Rangers (OHL).
(NY Islanders' 13th choice, 223rd over-all, in 1985 Entry Draft).

			Regular Season								Playoffs						
Season	Club	Lea	GP	W	L	T	Mins	GA	SO	Avg	GP	W	L	Mins	GA	SO	Avg
1985-86	Kitchener	OHL	36	15	15	2	1927	138	0	4.30	1	0	1	60	5	0	5.00

WAKALUK, DARCY

Born, Pincher Creek, Alta., March 14, 1966.
Goaltender. Catches left. 5'11", 180 lbs.
Last amateur club: Spokane Chiefs (WHL).
(Buffalo's 7th choice, 144th over-all, in 1984 Entry Draft).

			Regular Season								Playoffs						
Season	Club	Lea	GP	W	L	T	Mins	GA	SO	Avg	GP	W	L	Mins	GA	SO	Avg
1983-84	Kelowna	WHL	31	....	....	....	1555	163	0	6.29	....	....	....	....	....	....	....
1984-85	Kelowna	WHL	54	19	30	4	3094	244	0	4.73	5	1	4	282	22	0	4.68
1985-86	Spokane	WHL	47	21	22	1	2562	224	1	5.25	7	3	4	419	37	0	5.30

WAKELYN, MARTY

Born, Victoria, B.C., July 18, 1962.
Goaltender. Catches left. 5'11", 170 lbs.
Last amateur club: Colorado College Tigers (WCHA).

Season	Club	Lea	GP	W	L	T	Mins	GA	SO	Avg	GP	W	L	Mins	GA	SO	Avg
1982-83	Colorado	WCHA	16	3	11	0	944	74	2	2.97	....	....	....	....	....	....	....
1983-84	Colorado	WCHA	30	6	22	1	1743	140	0	4.82	....	....	....	....	....	....	....
1984-85	Colorado	WCHA	35	16	19	0	2030	154	1	4.46	....	....	....	....	....	....	....
1985-86	Colorado	WCHA	24	8	14	1	1380	100	0	4.34	....	....	....	....	....	....	....

Signed as a free agent by **NY Islanders**, June 23, 1986.

WAMSLEY, RICHARD (RICK)   (WAHMS-lee)

Born, Simcoe, Ont., May 25, 1959.
Goaltender. Catches left. 5'11", 185 lbs.
Last amateur club: Brantford Alexanders (OHA).
(Montreal's 5th choice, 58th over-all, in 1979 Entry Draft).

Season	Club	Lea	GP	W	L	T	Mins	GA	SO	Avg	GP	W	L	Mins	GA	SO	Avg
1977-78	Hamilton	OHA	25	....	....	....	1495	74	2	2.97	....	....	....	....	....	....	....
1978-79	Brantford	OHA	24	....	....	....	1444	128	0	5.32	....	....	....	....	....	....	....
1979-80	Nova Scotia	AHL	40	19	16	2	2305	125	3	3.25	3	1	1	143	12	0	5.03
1980-81	Montreal	NHL	5	3	0	1	253	8	1	1.90	....	....	....	....	....	....	....
	Nova Scotia	AHL	43	17	19	3	2372	155	0	3.92	4	2	1	199	6	*1	1.81
1981-82a	Montreal	NHL	38	23	7	7	2206	101	2	2.75	5	2	3	300	11	0	*2.20
1982-83	Montreal	NHL	46	27	12	5	2583	151	3	3.51	3	0	3	152	7	0	2.77
1983-84	Montreal	NHL	42	19	17	3	2333	144	2	3.70	1	0	1	32	0	0	0.00
1984-85	St. Louis	NHL	40	23	12	2	2319	126	0	3.26	2	0	2	120	7	0	3.50
1985-86	St. Louis	NHL	42	22	16	3	2517	144	1	3.43	10	4	6	569	29	0	3.90
NHL Totals			213	117	67	24	12211	674	6	3.31	21	6	15	1173	54	0	2.76

a Shared Williams Jennings Trophy with Denis Herron (1982)

Traded to **St. Louis** by **Montreal** with Hartford's second round choice (Brian Benning); — Montreal property via earlier deal — Montreal's second round choice (Anthony Hrkac) and third round choice (Robert Dirk), all in the 1984 Entry Draft, for St. Louis' first (Shayne Corson) and second round (Stephane Richer) choices in the 1984 Entry Draft, June 9, 1984.

WEEKS, STEPHEN (STEVE)

Born, Scarborough, Ont., June 30, 1958.
Goaltender. Catches left. 5'11", 165 lbs.
Last amateur club: Northern Michigan University Wildcats (CCHA).
(NY Rangers' 12th choice, 176th over-all, in 1978 Amateur Draft).

Season	Club	Lea	GP	W	L	T	Mins	GA	SO	Avg	GP	W	L	Mins	GA	SO	Avg
1977-78	N. Michigan	CCHA	19	....	....	....	1015	56	1	3.31	....	....	....	....	....	....	....
1978-79	N. Michigan	CCHA	25	....	....	....	1437	82	0	3.42	....	....	....	....	....	....	....
1979-80	N. Michigan	CCHA	36	29	6	1	2133	105	2	2.95	....	....	....	....	....	....	....
1980-81	New Haven	AHL	36	14	17	3	2065	142	1	4.04	....	....	....	....	....	....	....
	NY Rangers	NHL	1	0	1	0	60	2	0	2.00	1	0	0	14	1	0	4.29
1981-82	NY Rangers	NHL	49	23	16	9	2852	179	.1	3.77	4	1	2	127	9	0	4.25
1982-83	NY Rangers	NHL	18	9	5	3	1040	68	0	3.92	....	....	....	....	....	....	....
	Tulsa	CHL	19	8	10	0	1116	60	0	3.23	....	....	....	....	....	....	....
1983-84	NY Rangers	NHL	26	10	11	2	1361	90	0	3.97	....	....	....	....	....	....	....
	Tulsa	CHL	3	3	0	0	180	7	0	2.33	....	....	....	....	....	....	....
1984-85	Hartford	NHL	23	9	12	2	1397	91	2	3.91	....	....	....	....	....	....	....
	Binghamton	AHL	5	5	0	0	303	13	0	2.57	....	....	....	....	....	....	....
1985-86	Hartford	NHL	27	13	13	0	1544	99	1	3.85	3	1	2	169	8	0	2.84
NHL Totals			144	64	58	16	8254	529	4	3.84	8	2	4	310	18	0	3.48

WHITMORE, KAY

Born, Sudbury,Ont., April 10, 1967.
Goaltender. Catches left. 5'11", 165 lbs.
Last amateur club: Peterborough Petes (OHL).
(Hartford's 2nd choice, 26th over-all, in 1985 Entry Draft).

Season	Club	Lea	GP	W	L	T	Mins	GA	SO	Avg	GP	W	L	Mins	GA	SO	Avg
1983-84	Peterborough	OHL	29	17	8	0	1471	110	0	4.49	....	....	....	....	....	....	....
1984-85a	Peterborough	OHL	53	35	16	2	3077	172	3	3.35	17	10	4	1020	58	0	3.41
1985-86b	Peterborough	OHL	41	27	12	2	2467	114	3	2.77	14	8	5	837	40	0	2.87

a OHL Third All-Star Team (1985).
b OHL First All-Star Team (1986).

WREGGET, KEN

Born, Brandon, Man., March 25, 1964.
Goaltender. Catches left. 6'1", 180 lbs.
Last amateur club: Lethbridge Broncos (WHL).
(Toronto's 4th choice, 45th over-all, in 1982 Entry Draft).

Season	Club	Lea	GP	W	L	T	Mins	GA	SO	Avg	GP	W	L	Mins	GA	SO	Avg
1981-82	Lethbridge	WHL	36	19	12	0	1713	118	0	4.13	3	....	....	84	3	0	2.14
1982-83	Lethbridge	WHL	48	26	17	1	2696	157	0	3.49	20	14	5	1154	58	1	3.02
1983-84	Toronto	NHL	3	1	1	1	165	14	0	5.09	....	....	....	....	....	....	....
a	Lethbridge	WHL	53	32	20	0	3053	161	0	*3.16	4	1	3	210	18	0	5.14
1984-85	Toronto	NHL	23	2	15	3	1278	103	0	4.84	....	....	....	....	....	....	....
	St. Catharines	AHL	12	2	8	1	688	48	0	4.19	....	....	....	....	....	....	....
1985-86	Toronto	NHL	30	9	13	4	1566	113	0	4.33	10	6	4	607	32	1	3.16
	St. Catharines	AHL	18	8	9	0	1058	78	1	4.42	....	....	....	....	....	....	....
NHL Totals			56	12	29	8	3009	230	0	4.59	10	6	4	607	32	1	3.16

a WHL First All-Star Team, East Division (1984).

YOUNG, WENDELL

Born, Halifax, N.S., August 1, 1963.
Goaltender. Catches left. 5'8", 185 lbs.
Last amateur club: Kitchener Rangers (OHL).
(Vancouver's 3rd choice, 73rd over-all, in 1981 Entry Draft).

Season	Club	Lea	GP	W	L	T	Mins	GA	SO	Avg	GP	W	L	Mins	GA	SO	Avg
1980-81	Kitchener	OHA	42	19	15	0	2215	164	1	4.44	14	9	1	800	42	*1	3.15
1981-82	Kitchener	OHL	60	38	17	2	3470	195	1	3.37	15	12	1	900	35	*1	*2.33
1982-83a	Kitchener	OHL	61	41	19	0	3611	231	1	3.84	12	6	5	720	43	0	3.58
1983-84	Fredericton	AHL	11	7	3	0	569	39	1	4.11	....	....	....	....	....	....	....
	Milwaukee	IHL	6	....	....	....	339	17	0	3.01	....	....	....	....	....	....	....
	Salt Lake	CHL	20	11	6	0	1094	80	0	4.39	4	0	2	122	11	0	5.42
1984-85	Fredericton	AHL	22	7	11	3	1242	83	0	4.01	....	....	....	....	....	....	....
1985-86	Vancouver	NHL	22	4	9	3	1023	61	0	3.58	1	0	1	60	5	0	5.00
	Fredericton	AHL	24	12	8	4	1457	78	0	3.21	....	....	....	....	....	....	....
NHL Totals			22	4	9	3	1023	61	0	3.58	1	0	1	60	5	0	5.00

a OHL Third All-Star Team (1983).

ZANIER, MICHAEL (MIKE)

Born, Trail, B.C., August 22, 1962.
Goaltender. Catches left. 5'11", 183 lbs.
Last amateur club: Calgary Wranglers (WHL).

Season	Club	Lea	GP	W	L	T	Mins	GA	SO	Avg	GP	W	L	Mins	GA	SO	Avg
1980-81	N. Westminster	WHL	49	11	27	1	2494	275	0	6.62	....	....	....	....	....	....	....
1981-82	Spokane	WHL	9	1	7	0	476	55	0	6.98	....	....	....	....	....	....	....
	Billings	WHL	11	1	8	0	327	64	0	7.76	....	....	....	....	....	....	....
	Medicine Hat	WHL	13	3	8	0	620	70	0	6.77	....	....	....	....	....	....	....
	Calgary	WHL	11	5	5	0	526	28	1	3.19	1	0	0	25	1	0	2.40
1982-83	Trail	WIHL	30	....	....	....	1734	116	0	4.01	....	....	....	....	....	....	....
1983-84	Moncton	AHL	31	11	15	1	1743	96	0	3.30	....	....	....	....	....	....	....
1984-85	Edmonton	NHL	3	1	1	1	185	12	0	3.89	....	....	....	....	....	....	....
	Nova Scotia	AHL	44	20	17	5	2484	143	1	3.45	....	....	....	....	....	....	....
1985-86	Indianapolis	IHL	47	21	10	0	2727	151	0	3.32	2	1	1	120	9	0	4.50
NHL Totals			3	1	1	1	185	12	0	3.89	....	....	....	....	....	....	....

Signed as a free agent by **Edmonton**, October 4, 1983.

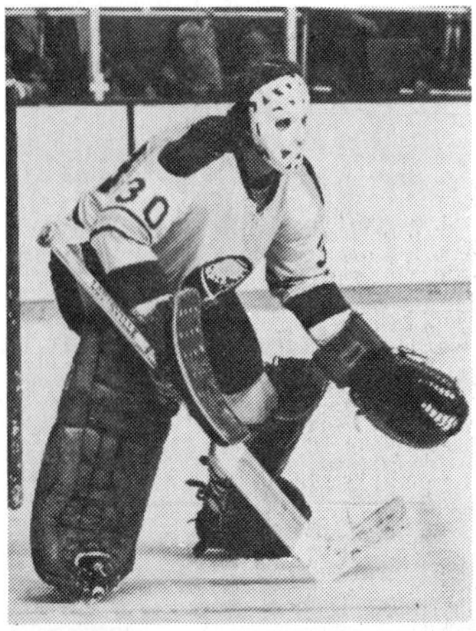

Dave Dryden

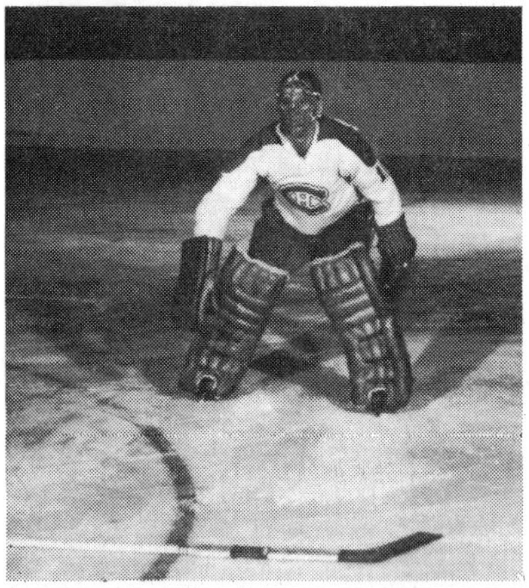

Jacques Plante

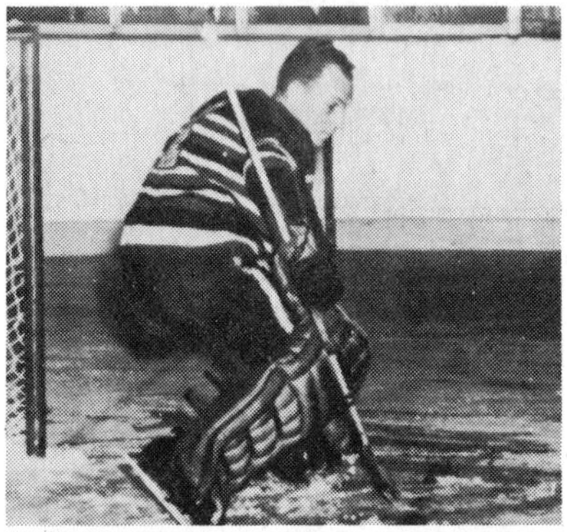

Al Rollins

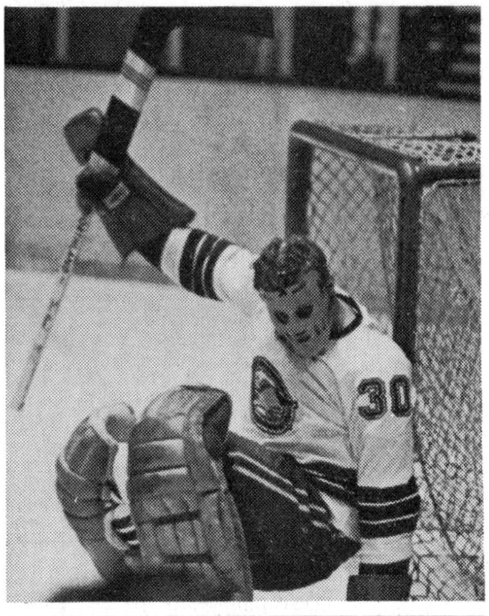

Gary Smith

NHL Records of Goaltenders out of Professional Hockey Since 1950-51 Season

Abbreviations: Avg – goals against per 60 minutes played; **GA** – goals against; **GP** – games played; **Mins** – minutes played; **SO** – shutouts.

			Regular Schedule					Playoffs						
Name	**NHL Teams**	**NHL Seasons**	**GP**	**Mins**	**GA**	**SO**	**Avg**	**GP**	**Mins**	**GA**	**SO**	**Avg**	**Last NHL Season**	**Last Pro Season**
Astrom, Hardy	NYR, Colo.	3	83	4456	277	0	3.73	....	....	....	....	....	1980-81	1981-82
Baker, Steve	NY Rangers	4	57	3081	190	3	3.70	14	826	55	0	4.00	1982-83	1983-84
Baron, Marco	Bos., L.A., Edm.	6	86	4822	292	1	3.63	1	20	3	0	9.00	1984-85	1984-85
Bassen, Hank	Chi., Det., Pit.	5	157	8829	441	5	2.99	5	274	11	0	2.41	1967-68	1967-68
Bedard, Jim	Washington	2	73	4232	278	1	3.94	....	....	....	....	....	1978-79	1979-80
Belanger, Yves	St. L., Atl., Bos.	5	78	4134	259	2	3.76	....	....	....	....	....	1979-80	1979-80
Belhumeur, Michel	Phi., Wash.	3	65	3306	254	0	4.61	1	10	1	0	6.00	1975-76	1977-78
*Bibeault, Paul	Mtl., Tor., Bos., Chi.	6	213	12780	785	10	3.69	20	1237	71	2	3.44	1946-47	1951-52
Binkley, Les	Pittsburgh	5	196	11046	575	11	3.12	7	428	15	0	2.10	1971-72	1974-75
Blake, Mike	Los Angeles	3	40	2117	150	0	4.25	....	....	....	....	....	1983-84	1984-85
Bower, Johnny	NYR, Tor.	12	552	32077	1347	37	2.52	74	4350	184	5	2.54	1969-70	1969-70
*Broda, Turk	Toronto	12	628	37680	1605	62	2.56	101	6348	211	13	1.99	1951-52	1951-52
Bromley, Gary	Buf., Van.	6	1361	7427	425	7	3.43	7	360	25	0	4.17	1980-81	1981-82
Brooks, Ross	Boston	3	54	3047	134	4	2.64	1	20	3	0	9.00	1974-75	1975-76
Brown, Andy	Det., Pit.	4	62	3373	213	1	3.79	....	....	....	....	....	1973-74	1976-77
Caron, Jacques	L.A., St. L., Van.	4	72	3846	211	2	3.29	12	639	34	0	3.19	1973-74	1977-78
Chadwick, Ed	Tor., Bos.	3	184	11040	551	14	2.99	....	....	....	....	....	1961-62	1967-68
Cheevers, Gerry	Tor., Bos.	13	418	24394	1175	26	2.89	88	5396	242	8	3.30	1979-80	1979-80
Crha, Jiri	Toronto	2	69	3942	261	0	3.97	5	186	21	0	6.77	1980-81	1981-82
Crozier, Roger	Det., Buf., Wash.	14	518	28567	1446	30	3.04	31	1789	82	1	2.75	1976-77	1976-77
Daley, Joe	Pit., Buf., Det.	4	105	5836	326	3	3.35	....	....	....	....	....	1971-72	1978-79
Davidson, John	St. L., NYR.	10	301	17109	1004	7	3.52	31	1862	77	1	2.48	1982-83	1982-83
DeJordy, Denis	Chi., L.A., Mtl., Det.	8	316	17798	929	15	3.13	18	946	55	0	3.49	1973-74	1973-74
Desjardins, Gerry	L.A., Chi., NYI, Buf.	10	331	19014	1042	12	3.29	35	1874	108	0	3.46	1977-78	1977-78
Dion, Connie	Detroit	2	38	2280	119	0	3.13	5	300	17	0	3.40	1944-45	1953-54
Dion Michel	Que., Pit., Wpg.	6	227	12695	898	2	4.24	5	304	22	0	4.34	1984-85	1984-85
Dryden, Dave	NYR, Chi., Buf., Edm.	9	203	10424	555	9	3.19	3	133	9	0	4.06	1979-80	1979-80
Dryden, Kenneth	Montreal	8	397	23352	870	46	2.24	112	6841	274	10	2.40	1978-79	1978-79
Dyck, Ed	Vancouver	2	49	2453	178	1	4.35	....	....	....	....	....	1973-74	1974-75
Edwards, Gary	St. L., L.A., Clev., Min., Edm., Pit.	12	286	16002	973	11	3.65	11	537	34	0	3.80	1981-82	1981-82
Edwards, Roy	Det., Pit.	6	236	13109	637	12	2.91	4	206	11	0	3.43	1973-74	1973-74
Edwards, Marv	Pit., Tor., Cal.	3	61	3467	218	2	3.77	....	....	....	....	....	1973-74	1973-74
Esposito, Tony	Mtl., Chi.	16	886	52585	2563	76	2.92	99	6017	308	6	3.07	1983-84	1983-84
Favell, Douglas	Phi., Tor., Colo.	12	373	20771	1096	18	3.17	21	1270	66	1	3.12	1978-79	1978-79
Francis, Emile	Chi., NYR	3	95	5700	355	1	3.74	....	....	....	....	....	1951-52	1959-60
*Gamble, Bruce	NYR, Bos., Tor., Phi.	8	327	18442	992	22	3.23	5	206	25	0	7.29	1971-72	1971-72
Gardner, George	Det., Van.	4	66	3313	207	0	3.75	....	....	....	....	....	1971-72	1973-74
Gelineau, Jack	Bos., Chi.	3	143	8580	447	7	3.12	4	260	7	1	1.62	1953-54	1954-55
Giacomin, Ed	NYR, Det.	13	610	35693	1675	54	2.82	65	3834	180	1	2.82	1977-78	1977-78
Grahame, Ron	Bos., L.A., Que.	4	114	6472	409	5	3.79	4	202	7	0	2.08	1980-81	1980-81
Grant, Doug	Det., St. L.	7	77	4199	280	2	4.00	....	....	....	....	....	1979-80	1979-80
Gratton, Gilles	St. L., NYR	2	47	2299	154	0	4.02	....	....	....	....	....	1976-77	1977-78
Hall, Glenn	Det., Chi., St. L.	16	906	53484	2239	84	2.51	115	6899	321	6	2.79	1970-71	1970-71
Hamel, Pierre	Tor., Wpg.	4	69	3766	276	0	4.40	....	....	....	....	....	1980-81	1981-82
Harrison, Paul	Min., Tor., Pit., Buf.	7	109	5806	408	2	4.22	4	157	9	0	3.44	1981-82	1982-83
Head, Don	Boston	1	38	2280	161	2	4.24	....	....	....	....	....	1961-62	1970-71
Henderson, John	Boston	1	46	2700	113	5	2.51	2	120	8	0	4.00	1955-56	1969-70
Henry, Sugar Jim	NYR, Chi., Bos.	8	404	24240	1166	28	2.88	29	1741	81	2	2.79	1954-55	1954-55
Hodge, Charlie	Mtl., Oak., Van.	8	358	20593	927	24	2.70	16	803	32	2	2.39	1970-71	1970-71
Holland, Robbie	Pittsburgh	2	44	2513	171	1	4.06	....	....	....	....	....	1980-81	1983-84
Inness, Gary	Pit., Phi., Wash.	7	162	8710	494	2	3.40	9	540	24	0	2.67	1980-81	1980-81
Johnston, Eddie	Bos., Tor., St. L., Chi.	16	592	34209	1855	32	3.25	18	1023	57	1	3.34	1977-78	1977-78
Larocque, Michel	Mtl., Tor., Phi., St.L.,	11	312	17615	978	17	3.33	14	759	37	1	2.92	1983-84	1984-85
Laskoski, Gary	Los Angeles	2	59	2942	228	0	4.65	....	....	....	....	....	1983-84	1983-84
Lessard, Mario	Los Angeles	6	240	13529	843	9	3.74	20	1136	83	0	4.38	1983-84	1983-84
*Lindbergh, Pelle	Philadelphia	4	157	9151	503	7	3.30	23	1214	63	3	3.11	1985-86	1985-86
Lockett, Ken	Vancouver	2	55	2348	131	2	3.35	1	60	6	0	6.00	1976-77	1976-77
LoPresti, Pete	Min., Edm.	6	175	9858	668	5	4.07	2	77	6	0	4.68	1980-81	1980-81
Lozinski, Larry	Detroit	1	30	1459	105	0	4.32	....	....	....	....	....	1980-81	1982-83
Lumley, Harry	NYR, Det., Chi., Tor., Bos.	13	804	48107	2210	71	2.76	76	4759	199	7	2.51	1959-60	1960-61
Maniago, Cesare	Tor., Mtl., NYR, Min., Van.	15	568	32570	1774	30	3.27	34	2125	94	3	2.65	1977-78	1977-78
Mattson, Markus	Wpg., Min., L.A.	5	92	5007	343	6	4.11	....	....	....	....	....	1983-84	1983-84
McDuffe, Peter	St. L., NYR, K.C., Det.	13	57	3207	218	0	4.08	1	60	7	0	7.00	1975-76	1976-77
McKenzie, Bill	Det., K.C., Colo.	6	91	4776	326	2	4.10	....	....	....	....	....	1979-80	1979-80
McNeil, Gerry	Montreal	5	276	16560	650	28	2.36	35	2288	72	5	1.89	1956-57	1960-61
McRae, Gord	Toronto	5	71	3799	221	1	3.49	8	454	22	0	2.91	1977-78	1977-78
Myre, Phil	Mtl., Atl., St. L., Phi., Colo., Buf.	14	439	25220	1482	14	3.53	12	747	41	1	3.29	1982-83	1983-84
Norris, Jack	Bos., Chi., L.A.	3	58	3119	202	2	3.89	....	....	....	....	....	1970-71	1974-75
Oleschuk, Bill	K.C., Colo.	4	55	2835	188	1	3.98	....	....	....	....	....	1979-80	1982-83
Paille, Marcel	NY Rangers	3	107	6342	362	2	3.42	....	....	....	....	....	1964-65	1973-74
Palmateer, Mike	Tor., Wash.	8	356	20131	1183	17	3.53	29	1765	89	2	3.03	1983-84	1983-84
Parent, Bernie	Bos., Tor., Phi.	13	608	35136	1493	55	2.55	71	4302	174	6	2.43	1978-79	1978-79
Plante, Jacques	Mtl., NYR, St. L, Tor., Bos.	17	837	49633	1965	82	2.37	112	6651	240	14	2.16	1972-73	1973-74
Plasse, Michel	Mtl., St. L., K.C., Pit., Colo., Que.	10	299	16760	1058	2	3.79	4	195	9	1	2.77	1981-82	1981-82
Rayner, Charlie	NYA, NYR	8	424	25384	1294	25	3.06	18	1134	46	1	2.43	1952-53	1953-54
Ridley, Curt	NYR, Van., Tor.	6	104	5498	355	1	387	2	120	8	0	4.00	1980-81	1981-82
Rivard, Fern	Minnesota	4	55	2865	190	2	3.98	....	....	....	....	....	1974-75	1974-75
Rollins, Al	Tor., Chi., NYR	8	430	25717	1196	28	2.79	13	755	30	0	2.38	1959-60	1961-62
Rutledge, Wayne	Los Angeles	3	82	4325	241	2	3.34	8	378	20	0	3.17	1969-70	1977-78
*Sawchuk, Terry	Det., Bos., Tor., L.A., NYR	20	971	57205	2401	103	2.52	106	6291	267	12	2.64	1969-70	1969-70
Simmons, Don	Bos., Tor., NYR	6	247	14435	705	20	2.93	24	1436	64	2	2.67	1968-69	1968-69
Simmons, Gary	Oak., L.A.	4	107	6162	366	5	3.56	1	20	1	0	3.00	1977-78	1978-79
Smith, Al	Tor., Pit., Det., Buf., Hfd., Colo.	9	233	12752	735	10	3.46	6	317	21	0	3.97	1980-81	1980-81
Smith, Gary	Tor., Oak., Cal., Chi., Van., Wash., Min., Wpg.	14	532	29619	1675	26	3.39	20	1153	62	1	3.23	1979-80	1979-80
Staniowski, Ed	St.L., Wpg., Hfd.	10	219	12075	818	2	4.06	8	428	28	0	3.92	1984-85	1984-85
Stephenson, Wayne	St. L., Phi., Wash.	9	328	18343	937	14	3.06	26	1522	79	2	3.11	1980-81	1980-81
Taylor, Bobby	Phi., Pit.	6	46	2268	155	0	4.10	....	....	....	....	....	1975-76	1975-76
Thomas, Wayne	Mtl., NYR	8	243	13768	766	10	3.34	15	849	50	1	3.53	1980-81	1980-81
Tremblay, Vincent	Tor., Pit.	5	58	2785	223	1	4.80	....	....	....	....	....	1983-84	1984-85
Vachon, Rogatien	Mtl., L.A., Det., Bos.	16	785	46298	2310	51	2.99	48	2876	133	2	2.77	1981-82	1981-82
Veisor, Mike	Chi., Hfd., Wpg.	10	139	7806	532	5	4.09	4	180	15	0	5.00	1983-84	1983-84
Villemure, Gilles	NYR., Chi.	10	205	11581	542	13	2.81	13	655	32	0	2.93	1976-77	1976-77
Wakely, Ernest	Mtl., St. L.	5	113	6344	290	8	2.79	10	509	37	1	4.36	1971-72	1978-79
Wilson, Duncan	Phil., Van., Tor., NYR., Pit.	10	287	15851	988	8	3.74	....	....	....	....	....	1978-79	1978-79
Wolfe, Bernard	Washington	4	120	6104	424	1	4.17	....	....	....	....	....	1978-79	1978-79
Worsley, Gump	NYR, Mtl., Min.	20	860	50201	2432	43	2.91	70	4080	192	5	2.82	1973-74	1973-74

* Deceased.

CELEBRATE HOCKEY with NHL publications

Notes